IMMIGRATION LAW HANDBOOK

IMMIGRATION LAW HANDBOOK

Eleventh Edition

FRANCES ALLEN

JULIA GASPARRO

JO SWANEY

MARGARET PHELAN

JAMES GILLESPIE

OXFORD
UNIVERSITY PRESS

OXFORD
UNIVERSITY PRESS

Great Clarendon Street, Oxford, OX2 6DP,
United Kingdom

Oxford University Press is a department of the University of Oxford.
It furthers the University's objective of excellence in research, scholarship,
and education by publishing worldwide. Oxford is a registered trade mark of
Oxford University Press in the UK and in certain other countries

First Edition published in 1997
Tenth Edition published in 2018
Eleventh Edition published in 2023

Published in the United States of America by Oxford University Press
198 Madison Avenue, New York, NY 10016, United States of America

British Library Cataloguing in Publication Data
Data available

Library of Congress Control Number is on file at the Library of Congress

ISBN 978–0–19–289629–2

DOI: 10.1093/oso/9780192896292.001.0001

Printed in Italy by
L.E.G.O. S.p.A. Lavis (TN)

PREFACE

This is the 11th edition of the *Immigration Law Handbook* and once again eclipses previous editions in terms of size. This edition encompasses the myriad changes to immigration law as a result of Brexit. The changes are wide-ranging, the drafting is tortuous, and the idea that somehow immigration law might have been simplified is simply wrong.

The Statutes, Statutory Instruments and European Materials sections contain new materials and omit old materials no longer in force. The changes as a result of Brexit are not straightforward,—in particular, the Immigration (European Economic Area) Regulations 2016 are subject to transitional and saving provisions set out in three Statutory Instruments which have been included in this edition: The Citizens' Rights (Application Deadline and Temporary Protection) (EU Exit) Regulations 2020; The Citizens' Rights (Restrictions of Rights of Entry and Residence) (EU Exit) Regulations 2020 and The Immigration and Social Security Co-ordination (EU Withdrawal) Act 2020 (Consequential, Saving, Transitional and Transitory Provisions) (EU Exit) Regulations 2020.

The Statutes and Statutory Instruments sections include all new legislation/instruments passed on or made up to (statutory instruments section up to date 6 August 2022) and the European and International Materials include changes made up to and including 26 July 2022.

The Immigration Rules have been subject to 29 statements of changes since the last edition, some of which are significant. The Rules are now characterised by much greater use of appendices for specific categories of leave. The last statement of changes incorporated in this edition was published on 20 July 2022 (HC 511). It is particularly important given the frequency of amendments to the Rules that users of the Handbook should have regard to both the archived Immigration Rules (https://www.gov.uk/government/collections/archive-immigration-rules) for the wording of the Rules in force as at a particular date and for any statements of changes that may have been published after this edition went to print (https://www.gov.uk/government/collections/immigration-rules-statement-of-changes).

The new Procedure Rules and Practice Directions and Statements section includes The First-tier Tribunal and Upper Tribunal Procedure Rules updated to include changes made on or up to 2 August 2022 and Practice Statement No 1 of 2022 for the First-tier Tribunal (IAC).

Any omitted material (or parts of material not directly relevant to immigration law) is publicly available online.

Frances Allen
Julia Gasparro
Jo Swaney
19 February 2023

CONTENTS

STATUTES

PROCEDURE RULES AND PRACTICE DIRECTIONS AND STATEMENTS

IMMIGRATION RULES

STATUTORY INSTRUMENTS

EUROPEAN MATERIALS

INTERNATIONAL MATERIALS

STATUTES

Immigration Act 1971
(1971, c. 77)

Arrangement of Sections

Part I. Regulation of Entry into and Stay in United Kingdom

Part 1A
Electronic travel authorisation

Part II. Appeals

. . .

Part III. Criminal Proceedings

PART 3A
MARITIME ENFORCEMENT

PART IV. SUPPLEMENTARY

SCHEDULES

An Act to amend and replace the present immigration laws, to make certain related changes in the citizenship law and enable help to be given to those wishing to return abroad, and for purposes connected therewith. [28 October 1971]

PART I
REGULATION OF ENTRY INTO AND STAY IN UNITED KINGDOM

1. General principles

(1) All those who are in this Act expressed to have the right of abode in the United Kingdom shall be free to live in and to come and go into and from, the United Kingdom without let or hindrance except such as may be required under and in accordance with this Act to enable their right to be established or as may be otherwise lawfully imposed on any person.

(2) Those not having that right may live, work and settle in the United Kingdom by permission and subject to such regulation and control of their entry into, stay in and departure from the United Kingdom as is imposed by this Act; and indefinite leave to enter or remain in the United Kingdom shall, by virtue of this provision, be treated as having been given under this Act to those in the United Kingdom at its coming into force, if they are then settled there (and not exempt under this Act from the provisions relating to leave to enter or remain).

(3) Arrival in and departure from the United Kingdom on a local journey from or to any of the Islands (that is to say, the Channel Islands and Isle of Man) or the Republic of Ireland shall not be subject to control under this Act, nor shall a person require leave to enter the United Kingdom on so arriving, except in so far as any of those places is for any purpose excluded from this subsection under the powers conferred by this Act; and in this Act the United Kingdom and those places, or such of them as are not so excluded, are collectively referred to as 'the common travel area'.

(4) The rules laid down by the Secretary of State as to the practice to be followed in the administration of this Act for regulating the entry into and stay in the United Kingdom of persons not having the right of abode shall include provision for admitting (in such cases and subject to such restrictions as may be provided by the rules, and subject or not to conditions as to length of stay or otherwise) persons coming for the purpose of taking employment, or for purposes of study, or as visitors, or as dependants of persons lawfully in or entering the United Kingdom.

(5) …

Note: Section 1(5) repealed by Immigration Act 1988, s 1.

[2. Statement of right of abode in United Kingdom

(1) A person is under this Act to have the right of abode in the United Kingdom if—

(a) he is a British citizen; or

(b) he is a Commonwealth citizen who—

(i) immediately before the commencement of the British Nationality Act 1981 was a Commonwealth citizen having the right of abode in the United Kingdom by virtue of section 2(1)(d) or section 2(2) of this Act as then in force; and

(ii) has not ceased to be a Commonwealth citizen in the meanwhile.

(2) In relation to Commonwealth citizens who have the right of abode in the United Kingdom by virtue of subsection (1)(b) above, this Act, except this section, [section 5(2) and section 25], shall apply as if they were British citizens; and in this Act (except as aforesaid) 'British citizen' shall be construed accordingly.]

Note: Section 2 substituted by British Nationality Act 1981, s 39(2). Words in square brackets in s 2(2) substituted by the Immigration Act 1988, s 3(3). Words in square brackets at section 2(2)substituted by Immigration, Nationality and Asylum (EU Exit) Regulations 2019/745 Pt 2(1), reg 4(2) (31 December 2020: shall come into force on IP completion day not exit day as specified in 2020 c. 1 s 39(1) and Sch 5 para 1(1)).

[2A. Deprivation of right of abode

(1) The Secretary of State may by order remove from a specified person a right of abode in the United Kingdom which he has under section 2(1)(b).

(2) The Secretary of State may make an order under subsection (1) in respect of a person only if the Secretary of State thinks that it would be conducive to the public good for the person to be excluded or removed from the United Kingdom.

(3) An order under subsection (1) may be revoked by order of the Secretary of State.

(4) While an order under subsection (1) has effect in relation to a person—

(a) section 2(2) shall not apply to him, and

(b) any certificate of entitlement granted to him shall have no effect.]

Note: Section 2A inserted by Immigration, Asylum and Nationality Act 2006, s 57(1) from 16 June 2006 (SI 2006/1497).

3. General provisions for regulation and control

(1) Except as otherwise provided by or under this Act, where a person is not [a British citizen]—

(a) he shall not enter the United Kingdom unless given leave to do so in accordance with [the provisions of, or made under,] this Act;

(b) he may be given leave to enter the United Kingdom (or, when already there, leave to remain in the United Kingdom) either for a limited or for an indefinite period);

[(c) if he is given limited leave to enter or remain in the United Kingdom, it may be given subject to all or any of the following conditions, namely—

(i) a condition restricting his [work]or occupation in the United Kingdom;

[(ia) a condition restricting his studies in the United Kingdom;]

(ii) a condition requiring him to maintain and accommodate himself, and any dependants of his, without recourse to public funds …

(iii) a condition requiring him to register with the police.

{(iv) a condition requiring him to report to an immigration officer or the Secretary of State; and

(v) a condition about residence.}]

(2) The Secretary of State shall from time to time (and as soon as may be) lay before Parliament statements of the rules, or of any changes in the rules, laid down by him as to the practice to be followed in the administration of this Act for regulating the entry into and stay in the United Kingdom of persons required by this Act to have leave to enter, including any rules as to the period for which leave is to be given and the conditions to be attached in different circumstances; and section 1(4) above shall not be taken to require uniform provision to be made by the rules as regards admission of persons for a purpose or in a capacity specified in section 1(4) (and in particular, for this as well as other purposes of this Act, account may be taken of citizenship or nationality).

If a statement laid before either House of Parliament under this subsection is disapproved by a resolution of that House passed within the period of forty days beginning with the date of laying (and exclusive of any period during which Parliament is dissolved or prorogued or during which both Houses are adjourned for more than four days), then the Secretary of State shall as soon as may be make such changes or further changes in the rules as appear to him to be required in the circumstances, so that the statement of those changes be laid before Parliament at latest by the end of the period of forty days beginning with the date of the resolution (but exclusive as aforesaid).

(3) In the case of a limited leave to enter or remain in the United Kingdom—

(a) a person's leave may be varied, whether by restricting, enlarging or removing the limit on its duration, or by adding, varying or revoking conditions, but if the limit on its duration is removed, any conditions attached to the leave shall cease to apply; and

(b) the limitation on and any conditions attached to a person's leave [(whether imposed originally or on a variation) shall], if not superseded, apply also to any subsequent leave he may obtain after an absence from the United Kingdom within the period limited for the duration of the earlier leave.

(4) A person's leave to enter or remain in the United Kingdom shall lapse on his going to a country or territory outside the common travel area (whether or not he lands there), unless within the period for which he had leave he returns to the United Kingdom in circumstances in which he is not required to obtain leave to enter; but, if he does so return, his previous leave (and any limitation on it or conditions attached to it) shall continue to apply.

[(5) A person who is not a British citizen is liable to deportation from the United Kingdom if—

(a) the Secretary of State deems his deportation to be conducive to the public good; or

(b) another person to whose family he belongs is or has been ordered to be deported.]

[(5A) The Secretary of State may not deem a relevant person's deportation to be conducive to the public good under subsection (5) if the person's deportation—

(a) would be in breach of the obligations of the United Kingdom under Article 20 of the EU withdrawal agreement, Article 19 of the EEA EFTA separation agreement or Article 17 or 20(3) of the Swiss citizens' rights agreement, or

(b) would be in breach of those obligations if the provision in question mentioned in paragraph (a) applied in relation to the person.]

(6) Without prejudice to the operation of subsection (5) above, a person who is not [a British citizen] shall also be liable to deportation from the United Kingdom if, after he has attained the age of seventeen, he is convicted of an offence for which he is punishable with imprisonment and on his conviction is recommended for deportation by a court empowered by this Act to do so.

[(6A) A court may not recommend under subsection (6) that a relevant person be deported if the offence for which the person was convicted consisted of or included conduct that took place before IP completion day.]

(7) Where it appears to Her Majesty proper so to do by reason of restrictions or conditions imposed on [British citizens, British Dependent Territories citizens or British Overseas citizens] when leaving or seeking to leave any country or the territory subject to the government of any country, Her Majesty may by Order in Council make provision for prohibiting persons who are nationals or citizens of that country and are not [British citizens] from embarking in the United Kingdom, or from doing so elsewhere than at a port of exit, or for imposing restrictions or conditions on them when embarking or about to embark in the United Kingdom; and Her Majesty may also make provision by Order in Council to enable those who are not [British citizens] to be, in such cases as may be prescribed by the Order, prohibited in the interests of safety from so embarking on a ship or aircraft specified or indicated in the prohibition.

Any Order in Council under this subsection shall be subject to annulment in pursuance of a resolution of either House of Parliament.

(8) When any question arises under this Act whether or not a person is [a British citizen], or is entitled to any exemption under this Act, it shall lie on the person asserting it to prove that he is.

[(9) A person seeking to enter the United Kingdom and claiming to have the right of abode there shall prove it by means of—

(a) a United Kingdom passport describing him as a British citizen,

(b) a United Kingdom passport describing him as a British subject with the right of abode in the United Kingdom, {or}

(c) …

(d) …

(e) a certificate of entitlement.]

[(10) For the purposes of this section, a person is a 'relevant person'—

(a) if the person is in the United Kingdom (whether or not they have entered within the meaning of section 11(1)) having arrived with entry clearance granted by virtue of relevant entry clearance immigration rules,

(b) if the person has leave to enter or remain in the United Kingdom granted by virtue of residence scheme immigration rules,

[[(ba) if the person is in the United Kingdom (whether or not they have entered within the meaning of section 11(1)) having arrived with entry clearance granted by virtue of Article 23 of the Swiss citizens' rights agreement,]]

(c) if the person may be granted leave to enter or remain in the United Kingdom as a person who has a right to enter the United Kingdom by virtue of—

(i) Article 32(1)(b) of the EU withdrawal agreement,

(ii) Article 31(1)(b) of the EEA EFTA separation agreement, or

(iii) Article 26a(1)(b) of the Swiss citizens' rights agreement, whether or not the person has been granted such leave, or

(d) if the person may enter the United Kingdom by virtue of regulations made under section 8 of the European Union (Withdrawal Agreement) Act 2020 (frontier workers), whether or not the person has entered by virtue of those regulations.

(11) In this section—

• 'EEA EFTA separation agreement' and 'Swiss citizens' rights agreement' have the same meanings as in the European Union (Withdrawal Agreement) Act 2020 (see section 39(1) of that Act);

• 'relevant entry clearance immigration rules' and 'residence scheme immigration rules' have the meanings given by section 17 of the European Union (Withdrawal Agreement) Act 2020.]

Note: Section 3(1)(c) substituted by Asylum and Immigration Act 1996 from 1 November 1996. Words in square brackets in s 3(6)–(8) and first square brackets in s 3(1) substituted by British Nationality Act 1981. Words in square brackets in s 3(3) substituted by Immigration Act 1988. Words in square brackets in s 3(1)(a) inserted by Immigration and Asylum Act 1999 from 14 February 2000. Section 3(5) substituted by Immigration and Asylum Act 1999 from 2 October 2000. Section 3(9) substituted by Immigration, Asylum and Nationality Act 2006, s 30 from 16 June 2006 (SI 2006/1497). Subsection (1)(c)(iv) and (v) inserted by UK Borders Act 2007, s 16 from 31 January 2008 (SI 2008/99). Subsection (1)(c)(ia) inserted by Borders, Citizenship and Immigration Act 2009, s 50(1) from 21 July 2009. Subsections (9)(c) and (d) omitted by Identity Documents Act 2010, Schedule, paragraph 1 from 21 January 2011 (s 14). Section 3 has effect in a form modified by and in circumstances specified by the Channel Tunnel (International Arrangements) Order (SI 1993/1813) as amended by SIs 1994/1405, 2000/913, 2001/178, 2001/3707, 2006/1003 and 2007/3759. Words in square brackets in s 3(1)(c)(i) substituted by Immigration Act 2016, s 34 from 12 July 2016 (SI 2016/603). Words in square brackets inserted at subsection (5A) inserted by European Union (Withdrawal Agreement) Act 2020 c. 1 Pt 3, s 10(2) (31 January 2020: insertion has effect on 31 January 2020 at 23:00 as specified in 2018 c. 16 s 20(1) subject to transitory provision specified in 2020 c. 1 Sch. 5 para 63(1)). Words in square brackets inserted subsection (6A) by European Union (Withdrawal Agreement) Act 2020 c. 1 Pt 3, s 10(3) (31 January 2020 at 23.00 as specified in 2018 c. 16 s 20(1)). Words in square brackets at subsection)(10) inserted by European Union (Withdrawal Agreement) Act 2020 c. 1 Sch. 5(3) para 63(2) (31 December 2020: insertion comes into force on IP completion day). Words in square brackets at s 3(11) added by European Union (Withdrawal Agreement) Act 2020 c. 1 Pt 3, s 10(4) (31 January 2020: insertion has effect on 31 January 2020 at 23:00 as specified in 2018 c. 16 s 20(1) and transitory provision specified in 2020 c. 1 Sch. 5 para 63(2)). Words in double square brackets inserted at s 3(10) (ba) by Citizens' Rights (Application Deadline and Temporary Protection) (EU Exit) Regulations 2020/1210 reg 3(2) (31 December 2020 at 23.00 being the time and date SI 2016/1052 is revoked).

[3ZA. Irish citizens

(1) An Irish citizen does not require leave to enter or remain in the United Kingdom, unless subsection (2), (3) or (4) applies to that citizen. (2) This subsection applies to an Irish citizen if the Irish citizen is subject to a deportation order made under section 5(1). (3) This subsection applies to an Irish citizen if—

(a) the Secretary of State has issued directions for the Irish citizen not to be given entry to the United Kingdom on the ground that the Irish citizen's exclusion is conducive to the public good,

(b) the Secretary of State has given the Irish citizen notice of the directions, and
(c) the directions have not been withdrawn.

(4) This subsection applies to an Irish citizen if the Irish citizen is an excluded person for the purposes of section 8B (persons excluded under certain instruments).

(5) Where subsection (2), (3) or (4) applies to an Irish citizen, section 1(3) does not permit the Irish citizen to enter the United Kingdom without leave on arriving in the United Kingdom on a local journey from any place in the common travel area.]

Note: Section 3ZA inserted by Immigration and Social Security Co-ordination (EU Withdrawal) Act 2020 c. 20 Pt 1, s 2(2) (31 December 2020: shall come into force immediately before IP completion day).

[3A. Further provision as to leave to enter

(1) The Secretary of State may by order make further provision with respect to the giving, refusing or varying of leave to enter the United Kingdom.

(2) An order under subsection (1) may, in particular, provide for—

(a) leave to be given or refused before the person concerned arrives in the United Kingdom;
(b) the form or manner in which leave may be given, refused or varied;
(c) the imposition of conditions;
(d) a person's leave to enter not to lapse on his leaving the common travel area.

(3) The Secretary of State may by order provide that, in such circumstances as may be prescribed—

(a) an entry visa, or
(b) such other form of entry clearance as may be prescribed, is to have effect as leave to enter the United Kingdom.

(4) An order under subsection (3) may, in particular—

(a) provide for a clearance to have effect as leave to enter—
(i) on a prescribed number of occasions during the period for which the clearance has effect;
(ii) on an unlimited number of occasions during that period;
(iii) subject to prescribed conditions; and
(b) provide for a clearance which has the effect referred to in paragraph (a)(i) or (ii) to be varied by the Secretary of State or an immigration officer so that it ceases to have that effect.

(5) Only conditions of a kind that could be imposed on leave to enter given under section 3 may be prescribed.

(6) In subsections (3), (4) and (5) 'prescribed' means prescribed in an order made under subsection (3).

(7) The Secretary of State may, in such circumstances as may be prescribed in an order made by him, give or refuse leave to enter the United Kingdom.

(8) An order under subsection (7) may provide that, in such circumstances as may be prescribed by the order, paragraphs 2, 4, 6, 7, 8, 9 and 21 of Part I of Schedule 2 to this Act are to be read, in relation to the exercise by the Secretary of State of functions which he has as a result of the order, as if references to an immigration officer included references to the Secretary of State.

(9) Subsection (8) is not to be read as affecting any power conferred by subsection (10).

(10) An order under this section may—

(a) contain such incidental, supplemental, consequential and transitional provision as the Secretary of State considers appropriate; and

(b) make different provision for different cases.

(11) This Act and any provision made under it has effect subject to any order made under this section.

(12) An order under this section must be made by statutory instrument.

(13) But no such order is to be made unless a draft of the order has been laid before Parliament and approved by a resolution of each House.]

Note: Section 3A inserted by Immigration and Asylum Act 1999 from 14 February 2000.

[3B. Further provision as to leave to remain

(1) The Secretary of State may by order make further provision with respect to the giving, refusing or varying of leave to remain in the United Kingdom.

(2) An order under subsection (1) may, in particular, provide for—

(a) the form or manner in which leave may be given, refused or varied;

(b) the imposition of conditions;

(c) a person's leave to remain in the United Kingdom not to lapse on his leaving the common travel area.

(3) An order under this section may—

(a) contain such incidental, supplemental, consequential and transitional provision as the Secretary of State considers appropriate; and

(b) make different provision for different cases.

(4) This Act and any provision made under it has effect subject to any order made under this section.

(5) An order under this section must be made by statutory instrument.

(6) But no such order is to be made unless a draft of the order has been laid before Parliament and approved by a resolution of each House.]

Note: Section 3B inserted by Immigration and Asylum Act 1999 from 14 February 2000.

[3C. Continuation of leave pending variation decision

(1) This section applies if—

(a) a person who has limited leave to enter or remain in the United Kingdom applies to the Secretary of State for variation of the leave,

(b) the application for variation is made before the leave expires, and

(c) the leave expires without the application for variation having been decided.

(2) The leave is extended by virtue of this section during any period when—

(a) the application for variation is neither decided nor withdrawn,

(b) an appeal under section 82(1) of the Nationality, Asylum and Immigration Act 2002 could be brought [while the appellant is in the United Kingdom] against the decision on the application for variation (ignoring any possibility of an appeal out of time with permission),

(c) an appeal under that section against that decision [, brought while the appellant is in the United Kingdom,] is pending (within the meaning of section 104 of that Act) [[(ca) an appeal could be brought under the Immigration (Citizens' Rights Appeals) (EU Exit) Regulations 2020 (the 2020 Regulations), while the appellant is in the United Kingdom, against the decision on the application for variation (ignoring any possibility of an appeal out of time with permission),

(cb) an appeal under the 2020 Regulations against that decision, brought while the appellant is in the United Kingdom, is pending (within the meaning of those Regulations), or]]

(d) an administrative review of the decision on the application for variation—

(i) could be sought, or

(ii) is pending]

(3) Leave extended by virtue of this section shall lapse if the applicant leaves the United Kingdom.

[(3A) Leave extended by virtue of this section may be cancelled if the applicant—

(a) has failed to comply with a condition attached to the leave, or

(b) has used or uses deception in seeking leave to remain (whether successfully or not).]

(4) A person may not make an application for variation of his leave to enter or remain in the United Kingdom while that leave is extended by virtue of this section.

(5) But subsection (4) does not prevent the variation of the application mentioned in subsection (1)(a).

[(6) The Secretary of State may make regulations determining when an application is decided for the purposes of this section; and the regulations—

(a) may make provision by reference to receipt of a notice,

(b) may provide for a notice to be treated as having been received in specified circumstances,

(c) may make different provision for different purposes or circumstances,

(d) shall be made by statutory instrument, and

(e) shall be subject to annulment in pursuance of a resolution of either House of Parliament.]

[(7) In this section—

'administrative review' means a review conducted under the immigration rules; the question of whether an administrative review is pending is to be determined in accordance with the immigration rules.]

Note: Section 3C substituted by Nationality, Immigration and Asylum Act 2002, s 118 from 1 April 2003 (SI 2003/754). Transitional provisions set out in SI 2003/754. Subsection (2)(d) and (7) inserted by Sch. 9 Immigration Act 2014 from 20 October 2014 with savings set out in articles 9–11 SI 2014/2771. Other words added to subsection (2)(b) and (c) and subsection (6) substituted by Immigration, Nationality and Asylum Act 2006, s 11 from 31 August 2006 (SI 2006/2226), applying to applications made before that date in respect of which no decision has been made, as it applies to applications made on or after that date. Words inserted in square brackets at subsection (3A) by Immigration Act 2016, s 62 from 1 December 2016 (SI 2016/1037). Words in double square brackets omitted at subsection (2)(c) and inserted at subsection (2)(ca) and (cb) by Immigration (Citizens' Rights Appeals) (EU Exit) Regulations 2020/61 Sch.4(1) para 1 (31 January 2020: shall come into on force on exit day as specified in 2018 c. 16 s 20(1) 2020 c. 1 Sch. 5 para 1(1) does not apply to these regulations).

[3D. . . .]

Note: repealed by Immigration Act 2016, s 64 from 1 December 2016 (SI 2016/1037).

4. Administration of control

(1) The power under this Act to give or refuse leave to enter the United Kingdom shall be exercised by immigration officers, and the power to give leave to remain in the United Kingdom, or to vary any leave under section 3(3)(a) (whether as regards duration or conditions [or to cancel any leave under section 3C(3A)], shall be exercised by the Secretary of State; and, unless otherwise [allowed by or under] this Act, those powers shall be exercised by notice in writing given to the person affected, except that the powers under section 3(3)(a) may be exercised generally in respect of any class of persons by order made by statutory instrument.

(2) The provisions of Schedule 2 to this Act shall have effect with respect to—

(a) the appointment and powers of immigration officers and medical inspectors for purposes of this Act;

(b) the examination of persons arriving in or leaving the United Kingdom by ship or aircraft, and the special powers exercisable in the case of those who arrive as, or with a view to becoming, members of the crews of ships and aircraft; and

(c) the exercise by immigration officers of their powers in relation to entry into the United Kingdom, and the removal from the United Kingdom of persons refused leave to enter or entering or remaining unlawfully; and

(d) the detention of persons pending examination or pending removal from the United Kingdom;

and for other purposes supplementary to the foregoing provisions of this Act.

(3) The Secretary of State may by regulations made by statutory instrument, which shall be subject to annulment in pursuance of a resolution of either House of Parliament, make provision as to the effect of a condition under this Act requiring a person to register with the police; and the regulations may include provision—

(a) as to the officers of police by whom registers are to be maintained, and as to the form and content of the registers;

(b) as to the place and manner in which anyone is to register and as to the documents and information to be furnished by him, whether on registration or on any change of circumstances;

(c) as to the issue of certificates of registration and as to the payment of fees for certificates of registration;

and the regulations may require anyone who is for the time being subject to such a condition to produce a certificate of registration to such persons and in such circumstances as may be prescribed by the regulations.

(4) The Secretary of State may by order made by statutory instrument, which shall be subject to annulment in pursuance of a resolution of either House of Parliament, make such provision as appears to him to be expedient in connection with this Act for records to be made and kept of persons staying at hotels and other premises where lodging or sleeping accommodation is provided, and for persons (whether [British citizens] or not) who stay at any such premises to supply the necessary information.

Note: Words in square brackets in s 4(4) substituted by British Nationality Act 1981, s 39(6). Words in square brackets in s 4(1) substituted by Immigration and Asylum Act 1999 from 14 February 2000. Section 4 has effect in a form modified by and in circumstances specified by the Channel Tunnel (International Arrangements) Order (SI 1993/1813) as amended by SIs 1994/1405, 2000/913, 2001/178, 2001/3707, 2006/1003 and 2007/3759. Words in square brackets are inserted at subsection (1) by Immigration Act 2016, s 62 from 1 December 2016 (SI 2016/1037).

5. Procedure for, and further provisions as to, deportation

(1) Where a person is under section 3(5) or (6) above liable to deportation, then subject to the following provisions of this Act the Secretary of State may make a deportation order against him, that is to say an order requiring him to leave and prohibiting him from entering the United Kingdom; and a deportation order against a person shall invalidate any leave to enter or remain in the United Kingdom given him before the order is made or while it is in force.

(2) A deportation order against a person may at any time be revoked by a further order of the Secretary of State, and shall cease to have effect if he becomes [a British citizen].

(3) A deportation order shall not be made against a person as belonging to the family of another person if more than eight weeks have elapsed since the other person left the United Kingdom after the making of the deportation order against him; and a deportation order made against a person on that ground shall cease to have effect if he ceases to belong to the family of the other person, or if the deportation order made against the other person ceases to have effect.

(4) For purposes of deportation the following shall be those who are regarded as belonging to another person's family—

(a) where that other person is a man, his wife [or civil partner,] and his or her children under the age of eighteen; and

[(b) where that other person is a woman, her husband [or civil partner,] and her or his children under the age of eighteen;]

and for purposes of this subsection an adopted child, whether legally adopted or not, may be treated as the child of the adopter and, if legally adopted, shall be regarded as the child only of the adopter; an illegitimate child (subject to the foregoing rule as to adoptions) shall be regarded as the child of the mother; and 'wife' includes each of two or more wives.

(5) The provisions of Schedule 3 to this Act shall have effect with respect to the removal from the United Kingdom of persons against whom deportation orders are in force and with respect to the detention or control of persons in connection with deportation.

(6) Where a person is liable to deportation under section [3(5)] or (6) above but, without a deportation order being made against him, leaves the United Kingdom to live permanently abroad, the Secretary of State may make payments of such amounts as he may determine to meet that person's expenses in so leaving the United Kingdom, including travelling expenses for members of his family or household.

Note: Words in square brackets in s 5(2) substituted by British Nationality Act 1981, s 39(6). Figures in square brackets in s 5(6) substituted by Immigration Act 1988, s 10. Section 5(4)(b) substituted by Asylum and Immigration Act 1996 from 1 October 1996. Transitional provisions set out in SI 2003/754. Words in square brackets in subsection (4) inserted by Sch. 27 Civil Partnership Act 2004 from 5 December 2005 (SI 2005/3175).

6. Recommendations by court for deportation

(1) Where under section 3(6) above a person convicted of an offence is liable to deportation on the recommendation of a court, he may be recommended for deportation by any court having power to sentence him for the offence unless the court commits him to be sentenced or further dealt with for that offence by another court:

Provided that in Scotland the power to recommend a person for deportation shall be exercisable only by the sheriff or the High Court of Justiciary, and shall not be exercisable by the latter on an appeal unless the appeal is against a conviction on indictment or against a sentence upon such a conviction.

(2) A court shall not recommend a person for deportation unless he has been given not less than seven days notice in writing stating that a person is not liable to deportation if he is [a British citizen] describing the persons who are [British citizens] and stating (so far as material) the effect of section 3(8) above and section 7 below; but the powers of adjournment conferred by [section 10(3) of the Magistrates' Courts Act 1980], [section 179 or 380 of the Criminal Procedure (Scotland) Act 1975] or any corresponding enactment for the time being in force in Northern Ireland shall include power to adjourn, after convicting an offender, for the purpose of enabling a notice to be given to him under this subsection or, if a notice was so given to him less than seven days previously, for the purpose of enabling the necessary seven days to elapse.

(3) For purposes of section 3(6) above—

(a) a person shall be deemed to have attained the age of seventeen at the time of his conviction if, on consideration of any available evidence, he appears to have done so to the court making or considering a recommendation for deportation; and

(b) the question whether an offence is one for which a person is punishable with imprisonment shall be determined without regard to any enactment restricting the imprisonment of young offenders or [persons who have not previously been sentenced to imprisonment]; and for purposes of deportation a person who on being charged with an offence is found to have committed it shall, notwithstanding any enactment to the contrary and notwithstanding that the court does not proceed to conviction, be regarded as a person convicted of the offence, and references to conviction shall be construed accordingly.

(4) Notwithstanding any rule of practice restricting the matters which ought to be taken into account in dealing with an offender who is sentenced to imprisonment, a recommendation for deportation may be made in respect of an offender who is sentenced to imprisonment for life.

(5) Where a court recommends or purports to recommend a person for deportation, the validity of the recommendation shall not be called in question except on an appeal against the recommendation or against the conviction on which it is made; but—

(a) the recommendation shall be treated as a sentence for the purpose of any enactment providing an appeal against sentence;

(b) ...

(6) A deportation order shall not be made on the recommendation of a court so long as an appeal or further appeal is pending against the recommendation or against the conviction on which it was made; and for this purpose an appeal or further appeal shall be treated as pending (where one is competent but has not been brought) until the expiration of the time for bringing that appeal or, in Scotland, until the expiration of twenty-eight days from the date of the recommendation.

(7) For the purpose of giving effect to any of the provisions of this section in its application to Scotland, the High Court of Justiciary shall have power to make rules by act of adjournal.

Note: Words in first and second square brackets in s 6(2) substituted by British Nationality Act 1981, s 39(6). Words in third square brackets in s 6(2) substituted by Magistrates' Courts Act 1980, s 154. Words in fourth square brackets in s 6(2) substituted by Criminal Procedure (Scotland) Act

1975, s 461. Words in square brackets in s 6(3)(b) substituted (E.W.) by Criminal Justice Act 1972, s 64(1). Words omitted from s 6(5) repealed by Criminal Justice (Scotland) Act 1980, s 83(3) and Criminal Justice Act 1982, ss 77, 78.

7. Exemption from deportation for certain existing residents

(1) Notwithstanding anything in section 3(5) or (6) above but subject to the provisions of this section, a Commonwealth citizen or citizen of the Republic of Ireland who was such a citizen at the coming into force of this Act and was then ordinarily resident in the United Kingdom—

(a) . . .

[(b) shall not be liable to deportation under section 3(5) if at the time of the Secretary of State's decision he had for the last five years been ordinarily resident in the United Kingdom and Islands;] and

(c) shall not on conviction of an offence be recommended for deportation under section 3(6) if at the time of the conviction he had for the last five years been ordinarily resident in the United Kingdom and Islands.

(2) A person who has at any time become ordinarily resident in the United Kingdom or in any of the Islands shall not be treated for the purposes of this section as having ceased to be so by reason only of his having remained there in breach of the immigration laws.

(3) The 'last five years' before the material time under subsection (1)(b) or (c) above is to be taken as a period amounting in total to five years exclusive of any time during which the person claiming exemption under this section was undergoing imprisonment or detention by virtue of a sentence passed for an offence on a conviction in the United Kingdom and Islands, and the period for which he was imprisoned or detained by virtue of the sentence amounted to six months or more.

(4) For purposes of subsection (3) above—

(a) 'sentence' includes any order made on conviction of an offence; and

(b) two or more sentences for consecutive (or partly consecutive) terms shall be treated as a single sentence; and

(c) a person shall be deemed to be detained by virtue of a sentence—

(i) at any time when he is liable to imprisonment or detention by virtue of the sentence, but is unlawfully at large; and

(ii) (unless the sentence is passed after the material time) during any period of custody by which under any relevant enactment the term to be served under the sentence is reduced.

In paragraph (c)(ii) above 'relevant enactment' means [section 240{, 240ZA or 240A} of the Criminal Justice Act 2003] (or, before that section operated, section 17(2) of the Criminal Justice Administration Act 1962) and any similar enactment which is for the time being or has (before or after the passing of this Act) been in force in any part of the United Kingdom and Islands.

(5) Nothing in this section shall be taken to exclude the operation of section 3(8) above in relation to an exemption under this section.

Note: Subsection (1)(a) repealed by Nationality, Immigration and Asylum Act 2002, s 75 from 10 February 2003 (SI 2003/1). Subsection (1)(b) substituted by Nationality, Immigration and Asylum Act 2003, s 75 from 10 February 2003 (SI 2003/1). Words in square brackets in subsection 4 substituted by Sch. 32 Criminal Justice Act 2003 from 4 April 2005 (SI 2005/950). Words in curly brackets in subsection 4 inserted by Legal Aid, Sentencing and Punishment of Offenders Act 2012, Sch. 13, paragraph 7, from 3 December 2012 (SI 2012/2906).

8. Exceptions for seamen, aircrews and other special cases

(1) Where a person arrives at a place in the United Kingdom as a member of the crew of a ship or aircraft under an engagement requiring him to leave on that ship as a member of the crew, or to leave within seven days on that or another aircraft as a member of its crew, then unless either—

(a) there is in force a deportation order made against him; or

(b) he has at any time been refused leave to enter the United Kingdom and has not since then been given leave to enter or remain in the United Kingdom; or

(c) an immigration officer requires him to submit to examination in accordance with Schedule 2 to this Act;

he may without leave enter the United Kingdom at that place and remain until the departure of the ship or aircraft on which he is required by his engagement to leave.

[(1A) Subsection (1) does not apply in relation to a member of the crew of a ship who is an offshore worker within the meaning of section 11A.]

(2) The Secretary of State may by order exempt any person or class of persons, either unconditionally or subject to such conditions as may be imposed by or under the order, from all or any of the provisions of this Act relating to those who are not [British citizens].

An order under this subsection, if made with respect to a class of persons, shall be made by statutory instrument, which shall be subject to annulment in pursuance of a resolution of either House of Parliament.

(3) [Subject to subsection 3A below,] the provisions of this Act relating to those who are not [British citizens] shall not apply to any person so long as he is a member of a mission (within the meaning of the Diplomatic Privileges Act 1964), a person who is a member of the family and forms part of the household of such a member, or a person otherwise entitled to the like immunity from jurisdiction as is conferred by that Act on a diplomatic agent.

[(3A) For the purposes of subsection (3), a member of a mission other than diplomatic agent (as defined by the 1964 Act) is not to count as a member of a mission unless—

(a) he was resident outside the United Kingdom, and was not in the United Kingdom, when he was offered a post as such a member; and

(b) he has not ceased to be such a member after having taken up the post.]

(4) The provisions of this Act relating to those who are not [British citizens], other than the provisions relating to deportation, shall also not apply to any person so long as either—

(a) he is subject, as a member of the home forces, to service law; or

(b) being a member of a Commonwealth force or of a force raised under the law of any . . . colony, protectorate or protected state, is undergoing or about to undergo training in the United Kingdom with any body, contingent or detachment of the home forces; or

(c) he is serving or posted for service in the United Kingdom as a member of a visiting force or of any force raised as aforesaid or as a member of an international headquarters or defence organisation designated for the time being by an Order in Council under section 1 of the International Headquarters and Defence Organisations Act 1964.

(5) Where a person having a limited leave to enter or remain in the United Kingdom becomes entitled to an exemption under this section, that leave shall continue to apply after he ceases to be entitled to the exemption, unless it has by then expired [or otherwise ceased to be in force]; and a person is not to be regarded for purposes of this Act as having

been [settled in the United Kingdom at any time when he was entitled under the former immigration laws to any exemption corresponding to any of those afforded by subsection (3) or (4)(b) or (c) above or by any order under subsection (2) above].

[(5A) An order under subsection (2) above may, as regards any person or class of persons to whom it applies, provide for that person or class to be in specified circumstances regarded (notwithstanding the order) as settled in the United Kingdom for the purposes of section 1(1) of the British Nationality Act 1981.]

(6) In this section 'the home forces' means any of Her Majesty's forces other than a Commonwealth force or a force raised under the law of any associated state, colony, protectorate or protected state; 'Commonwealth force' means a force of any country to which provisions of the Visiting Forces Act 1952 apply without an Order in Council under section 1 of the Act; and 'visiting force' means a body, contingent or detachment of the forces of a country to which any of those provisions apply, being a body, contingent or detachment for the time being present in the United Kingdom on the invitation of Her Majesty's Government in the United Kingdom.

Note: Section 8(3A) inserted by Immigration and Asylum Act 1999 from 1 March 2000. First words in square brackets in s 8(3) inserted by Immigration Act 1988. Other words in square brackets in s 8(2), (3), (4) and (5) substituted and s 8(5A) inserted by British Nationality Act 1981. Section 8(3A) substituted by Immigration and Asylum Act 1999 from 1 March 2000. Section 8 has effect in a form modified by and in circumstances specified by the Channel Tunnel (International Arrangements) Order (SI 1993/1813) as amended by SIs 1994/1405, 2000/913, 2001/178, 2001/3707, 2006/1003 and 2007/3759. Words in square brackets inserted at subsection 8(5) by Immigration Act 2016, s 76 from 12 July 2016 (SI 2016/603). Subsection (1A) inserted by Nationality and Border Act 2022 c.36 Sch.6 para 2 (date to be appointed)

[8A. Persons ceasing to be exempt

(1) A person is exempt for the purposes of this section if he is exempt from provisions of this Act as a result of section 8(2) or (3).

(2) If a person who is exempt—

(a) ceases to be exempt, and

(b) requires leave to enter or remain in the United Kingdom as a result, he is to be treated as if he had been given leave to remain in the United Kingdom for a period of 90 days beginning on the day on which he ceased to be exempt.

(3) If—

(a) a person who is exempt ceases to be exempt, and

(b) there is in force in respect of him leave for him to enter or remain in the United Kingdom which expires before the end of the period mentioned in subsection (2), his leave is to be treated as expiring at the end of that period.]

[(4) References in this section to a person who ceases to be exempt do not include a person who ceases to be exempt by virtue of section 8B(3)].

Note: Section 8A inserted by Immigration and Asylum Act 1999 from 1 March 2000. Subsection (4) inserted by Immigration Act 2016, s 76 from 12 July 2016 (SI 2016/603).

[8B. Persons excluded from the United Kingdom under [[certain instruments]]

(1) An excluded person must be refused—

(a) leave to enter the United Kingdom;

(b) leave to remain in the United Kingdom[and any leave given to a person who is an excluded person is invalid].

(2) A person's leave to enter or remain in the United Kingdom is cancelled on his becoming an excluded person.

(3) [Any exemption of a person from the provisions of this Act under section 8(1), (2) or (3) does not apply while the person is an excluded person.]

(4) [['*Excluded person*' means—

(a) a person named by or under, or of a description specified in, an instrument falling within subsection (5), or

(b) a person who under regulations under section 1 of the Sanctions and Anti-Money Laundering Act 2018 is an excluded person for the purposes of this section (see section 4 of that Act).]]

(5) [An instrument falls within this subsection] if it is a resolution of the Security Council of the United Nations or an instrument made by the Council of the European Union and it—

(a) requires that a person is not to be admitted to the United Kingdom (however that requirement is expressed); or

(b) recommends that a person should not be admitted to the United Kingdom (however that recommendation is expressed).

[(5A) Subsection (1), (2) or (3) does not apply to a person if—

(a) the application of that subsection to that person would be contrary to the United Kingdom's obligations under—

(i) the Human Rights Convention (within the meaning given by section 167(1) of the Immigration and Asylum Act 1999), or

(ii) the Refugee Convention (within the meaning given by that provision), or

(b) the person has been exempted from the application of[[the person is within subsection (4)(a) and not within subsection (4)(b) and has been exempted from the application of subsection (1), (2) or (3), as the case may be,]]]

[[(5B) In relation to any person within subsection (4)(b), subsections (1) to (3) are subject to any exception created under, or direction given by virtue of, section 15(4) of the Sanctions and Anti-Money Laundering Act 2018 (power to create exceptions etc).]]

(6) ...

(7) ...

(8) ...

Note: Section 8B inserted by Immigration and Asylum Act 1999 from 1 March 2000. Words inserted in square brackets at subsection (1)(b); words in square brackets substituted at subsection (3), (4) & (5) by Immigration Act 2016, s 76 from 12 July 2016 (SI 2016/603). Subsection (5A) inserted, and subsection (6) to (8) omitted by Immigration Act 2016, s 76 from 12 July 2016 (SI 2016/603). Words in double square brackets substituted in heading substituted by Sanctions and Anti-Money Laundering Act 2018 c. 13 Sch 1 para (1)(2); words in double brackets at subsection (4) by Sch. 1 para (1)(3); words in double brackets at subsection (5) by Sch 1 para (1)(4) and inserted at subsection (5B) by Sch. 1 para (1)(5).

9. Further provisions as to common travel area

(1) Subject to subsection (5) below, the provisions of Schedule 4 to this Act shall have effect for the purpose of taking account in the United Kingdom of the operation in any of the Islands of the immigration laws there.

(2) Persons who lawfully enter the United Kingdom on a local journey from a place in the common travel area after having either—

(a) entered any of the Islands or the Republic of Ireland on coming from a place outside the common travel area; or

(b) left the United Kingdom while having a limited leave to enter or remain which has since expired;

if they are not [British citizens] [[or Irish citizen]](and are not to be regarded under Schedule 4 to this Act as having leave to enter the United Kingdom), shall be subject in the United Kingdom to such restrictions on the period for which they may remain, and such conditions restricting their employment or occupation or requiring them to register with the police or both, as may be imposed by an order of the Secretary of State and may be applicable to them.

(3) Any provision of this Act applying to a limited leave or to conditions attached to a limited leave shall, unless otherwise provided, have effect in relation to a person subject to any restriction or condition by virtue of an order under subsection (2) above as if the provisions of the order applicable to him were terms on which he had been given leave under this Act to enter the United Kingdom.

(4) Section 1(3) above shall not be taken to affect the operation of a deportation order; and, subject to Schedule 4 to this Act, a person who is not [a British citizen] [[or an Irish citizen]] may not by virtue of section 1(3) enter the United Kingdom without leave on a local journey from a place in the common travel area if either—

(a) he is on arrival in the United Kingdom given [[..]] notice by an immigration officer stating that, the Secretary of State having issued directions for him not to be given entry to the United Kingdom on the ground that his exclusion is conducive to the public good[[..]], he is accordingly refused leave to enter the United Kingdom; or

(b) he has at any time been refused leave to enter the United Kingdom and has not since then been given leave to enter or remain in the United Kingdom.

(5) If it appears to the Secretary of State necessary so to do by reason of differences between the immigration laws of the United Kingdom and any of the Islands, he may by order exclude that island from section 1(3) above for such purposes as may be specified in the order, and references in this Act to the Islands... shall apply to an island so excluded so far only as may be provided by order of the Secretary of State.

(6) The Secretary of State shall also have power by order to exclude the Republic of Ireland from section 1(3) for such purposes as may be specified in the order.

(7) An order of the Secretary of State under this section shall be made by statutory instrument, which shall be subject to annulment in pursuance of a resolution of either House of Parliament.

Note: Words in square brackets in s 9(2) and (4) substituted by British Nationality Act 1981, s 39(6). Words omitted from s 9(5) repealed by British Nationality Act 1981, s 52(8). Words in double brackets at subsections (2)(b) and (4) inserted by Immigration and Social Security Co-ordination (EU Withdrawal) Act 2020 Pt1 s.2(3) (December 31, 2020: shall come into force immediately before IP completion day). Words in double square brackets omitted in subsection (4)(a) by Immigration and Social Security Co-ordination (EU Withdrawal) Act 2020 (Consequential, Saving, Transitional and Transitory Provisions) (EU Exit) Regulations 2020/1309 Pt2(1) reg.5(2)(b) (December 31, 2020: at the time and date 2020.c20 Sch.1 para 2(2) comes into force)

10. Entry otherwise than by sea or air

(1) Her Majesty may by Order in Council direct that any of the provisions of this Act shall have effect in relation to persons entering or seeking to enter the United Kingdom on

arrival otherwise than by ship or aircraft as they have effect in the case of a person arriving by ship or aircraft; . . .

[(1A) Her Majesty may by Order in Council direct that paragraph 27B or 27C of Schedule 2 shall have effect in relation to trains or vehicles as it has effect in relation to ships or aircraft.

(1B) Any Order in Council under this section may make—

(a) such adaptations or modifications of the provisions concerned, and

(b) such supplementary provisions,

as appear to Her Majesty to be necessary or expedient for the purposes of the Order.]

(2) The provision made by an Order in Council under [subsection (1)] may include provision for excluding the Republic of Ireland from section 1(3) of this Act either generally or for any specified purposes.

(3) No recommendation shall be made to Her Majesty to make an Order in Council under this section unless a draft of the Order has been laid before Parliament and approved by a resolution of each House of Parliament.

Note: Words omitted from s 10(1), s 10(1A), s 10(1B) and words in square brackets in s 10(2) substituted by Immigration and Asylum Act 1999, Sch 14 from 3 December 2012 (SI 2012/2906).

11. Construction of references to entry and other phrases relating to travel

(1) A person arriving in the United Kingdom by ship or aircraft shall for purposes of this Act be deemed not to enter the United Kingdom unless and until he disembarks, and on disembarkation at a port shall further be deemed not to enter the United Kingdom so long as he remains in such area (if any) at the port as may be approved for this purpose by an immigration officer; and a person who has not otherwise entered the United Kingdom shall be deemed not to do so as long as he is detained, [[]] [or section 62 of the Nationality, Immigration and Asylum Act 2002] under the powers conferred by Schedule 2 to this Act [[]] [[[or an immigration bail within the meaning of Schedule 10 to the Immigration Act 2016]]] [[]].

[(1ZA) See also section 11A (additional means by which persons arriving in United Kingdom waters for work can enter the UK).]

[1A . . .]

(2) In this Act 'disembark' means disembark from a ship or aircraft, and 'embark' means embark in a ship or aircraft; and, except in subsection (1) above,—

(a) references to disembarking in the United Kingdom do not apply to disembarking after a local journey from a place in the United Kingdom or elsewhere in the common travel area; and

(b) references to embarking in the United Kingdom do not apply to embarking for a local journey to a place in the United Kingdom or elsewhere in the common travel area.

(3) Except in so far as the context otherwise requires, references in this Act to arriving in the United Kingdom by ship shall extend to arrival by any floating structure, and 'disembark' shall be construed accordingly; but the provisions of this Act specially relating to members of the crew of a ship shall not by virtue of this provision apply in relation to any floating structure not being a ship.

(4) For purposes of this Act 'common travel area' has the meaning given by section 1(3), and a journey is, in relation to the common travel area, a local journey if but only if it begins and ends in the common travel area and is not made by a ship or aircraft which—

(a) in the case of a journey to a place in the United Kingdom, began its voyage from, or has during its voyage called at, a place not in the common travel area; or

(b) in the case of a journey from a place in the United Kingdom, is due to end its voyage in, or call in the course of its voyage at, a place not in the common travel area.

(5) A person who enters the United Kingdom lawfully by virtue of section 8(1) above, and seeks to remain beyond the time limited by section 8(1), shall be treated for purposes of this Act as seeking to enter the United Kingdom.

Note: Words in first square brackets in subsection (1) inserted by Immigration and Asylum Act 1999, Sch.14, paragraph 48 from a date to be appointed. Words in second square brackets in subsection (1) inserted by Nationality, Immigration and Asylum Act 2002, s 62 from 10 February 2003 (SI 2003/1). Words in third square brackets inserted by SI 2003/1016 from 4 April 2003. Subsection (1A) repealed from 2 August 1993 (SI 1993/1813). Section 11 has effect in a form modified by and in circumstances specified by the Channel Tunnel (International Arrangements) Order (SI 1993/1813) as amended by SIs 1994/1405, 2000/913, 2001/178, 2001/3707, 2006/1003 and 2007/3759. Subsection (1A) deleted from 5 November 1993 (SI 1993/1813). Words in double square brackets omitted and substituted in s 1 by Immigration Act 2016, Schedule 10 from January 15, 2018 subject to transitional provisions in SI 2017/1241. Subsection (1ZA) inserted by Nationality and Borders Act 2022 c.36 Sch.6 para 3 (date to be appointed)

[11A Working in United Kingdom waters

(1) An "offshore worker" is a person who arrives in United Kingdom waters—

(a) for the purpose of undertaking work in those waters, and

(b) without first entering the United Kingdom (see, in particular, section 11(1)).

But see subsection (6).

(2) An offshore worker arrives in the United Kingdom for the purposes of this Act when they arrive in United Kingdom waters as mentioned in subsection (1)(a).

(3) An offshore worker enters the United Kingdom for the purposes of this Act when they commence working in United Kingdom waters.

(4) Any reference in, or in a provision made under, the Immigration Acts to a person arriving in or entering the United Kingdom, however expressed, is to be read as including a reference to an offshore worker arriving in or entering the United Kingdom as provided for in subsection (2) or (3).

(5) References in this section to work, or to a person working, are to be read in accordance with section 24B(10).

(6) A person is not an offshore worker if they arrive in United Kingdom waters while working as a member of the crew of a ship that is—

(a) exercising the right of innocent passage through the territorial sea or the right of transit passage through straits used for international navigation, or

(b) passing through United Kingdom waters from non-UK waters to a place in the United Kingdom or vice versa.

(7) For the purposes of any provision of, or made under, the Immigration Acts, a person working in United Kingdom waters who, in connection with that work, temporarily enters non-UK waters is not to be treated by virtue of doing so as leaving, or being outside, the United Kingdom.

(8) In this section—

"non-UK waters" means the sea beyond the seaward limits of the territorial sea;

"right of innocent passage", "right of transit passage" and "straits used for international navigation" are to be read in accordance with the United Nations Convention on the Law of the Sea 1982 (Cmnd 8941) and any modifications of that Convention agreed after the passing of the Nationality and Borders Act 2022 that have entered into force in relation to the United Kingdom;

"the territorial sea" means the territorial sea adjacent to the United Kingdom;

"United Kingdom waters" means the sea and other waters within the seaward limits of the territorial sea.

Note: inserted by Nationality and Borders Act 2022 c.36 Pt3 s.43(1)(date to be appointed:2022 c.36 s.43 came into force on April 28, 2022 as specified in 2022 c.36 s.87(4)(d) for limited purpose of making (and, where required, consulting on) regulations; not yet in force otherwise)

11B Offshore workers: requirements to notify arrival and entry dates etc

(1) The Secretary of State may by regulations make provision for and in connection with requiring—

(a) an offshore worker, or

(b) if an offshore worker has one, their sponsor;

to give notice to the Secretary of State or an immigration officer of the dates on which the offshore worker arrives in, enters and leaves the United Kingdom.

(2) The regulations may make provision for the failure of an offshore worker to comply with a requirement imposed under the regulations to be a ground for—

(a) the cancellation or variation of their leave to enter or remain in the United Kingdom;

(b) refusing them leave to enter or remain in the United Kingdom.

(3) The failure of an offshore worker's sponsor to comply with a requirement imposed under the regulations may be taken into account by the Secretary of State when operating immigration skills arrangements made with the sponsor.

(4) Regulations under this section—

(a) are to be made by statutory instrument;

(b) may make different provision for different cases;

(c) may make incidental, supplementary, consequential, transitional, transitory or saving provision.

(5) A statutory instrument containing regulations under this section is subject to annulment in pursuance of a resolution of either House of Parliament.

(6) For the purposes of this section—

(a) "offshore worker" has the same meaning as in section 11A;

(b) a person is an offshore worker's "sponsor" if they have made immigration skills arrangements with the Secretary of State in relation to the offshore worker;

(c) "immigration skills arrangements" has the meaning given by section 70A(2) of the Immigration Act 2014.]

Note: inserted by Nationality and Borders Act 2022 c.36 Pt3 s.43(1)(date to be appointed:2022 c.36 s.43 came into force on April 28, 2022 as specified in 2022 c.36 s.87(4)(d) for the limited purpose of making (and, where required, consulting on) regulations; not yet in force otherwise)

PART 1A

ELECTRONIC TRAVEL AUTHORISATIONS

11C Electronic travel authorisations

(1) In this Act, "an ETA" means an authorisation in electronic form to travel to the United Kingdom.

(2) Immigration rules may require an individual of a description specified in the rules not to travel to the United Kingdom from any place (including a place in the common travel area), whether with a view to entering the United Kingdom or to passing through it without entering, unless the individual has an ETA that is valid for the individual's journey to the United Kingdom.

(3) The rules may not impose this requirement on an individual if—

(a) the individual is a British citizen, or

(b) the individual would, on arrival in the United Kingdom, be entitled to enter without leave.

(4) In relation to an individual travelling to the United Kingdom on a local journey from a place in the common travel area, subsection (3)(b) applies only if the individual would also be entitled to enter without leave if the journey were instead from a place outside the common travel area.

(5) The rules may impose the requirement mentioned in subsection (2) on an individualal who—

(a) travels to the United Kingdom on a local journey from a place in any of the Islands, and

(b) has leave to enter or remain in that island,

only if it appears to the Secretary of State necessary to do so by reason of differences between the immigration laws of the United Kingdom and that island.

(6) The rules must—

(a) provide for the form or manner in which an application for an ETA may be made, granted or refused;

(b) specify the conditions (if any) which must be met before an application for an ETA may be granted;

(c) specify the grounds on which an application for an ETA must or may be refused;

(d) specify the criteria to be applied in determining—

(i) the period for which an ETA is valid;

(ii) the number of journeys to the United Kingdom during that period for which it is valid (which may be unlimited);

(e) require an ETA to include provision setting out the matters mentioned in paragraph (d)(i) and (ii);

(f) provide for the form or manner in which an ETA may be varied or cancelled;

(g) specify the grounds on which an ETA must or may be varied or cancelled.

(7) The rules may also—

(a) provide for exceptions to the requirement described in subsection (2), and

(b) make other provision relating to ETAs.

(8) Rules made by virtue of this section may make different provision for different cases or descriptions of case.

Note: inserted by Nationality and Borders Act 2022 c.36 Pt3 s.43(1) (date to be appointed: 2022 came into force on April 28, 2022 as specified in 2022 c.36 s.87(4)(d) for the limited purpose of making (and, where required, consulting on) regulations; not yet in force otherwise)

11D Electronic travel authorisations and the Islands

(1) The Secretary of State may by regulations make provision about the effects in the United Kingdom of the grant or refusal under the law of any of the Islands of an authorisation in electronic form to travel to that island.

(2) Regulations under subsection (1) may in particular make provision about—

(a) the recognition in the United Kingdom of an authorisation granted as mentioned in subsection (1);

(b) the conditions or limitations that are to apply in the United Kingdom to such an authorisation;

(c) the effects in the United Kingdom of such an authorisation being varied or cancelled under the law of any of the Islands;

(d) the circumstances in which the Secretary of State or an immigration officer may vary or cancel such an authorisation (so far as it applies in the United Kingdom).

(3) The Secretary of State may, where requested to do so by any of the Islands, carry out functions on behalf of that island in relation to the granting of authorisations in electronic form to travel to that island.

(4) Regulations under subsection (1)—

(a) may make provision modifying the effect of any provision of, or made under, this Act or any other enactment (whenever passed or made);

(b) may make different provision for different purposes;

(c) may make transitional, transitory or saving provision;

(d) may make incidental, supplementary or consequential provision.

(5) Regulations under subsection (1) are to be made by statutory instrument.

(6) A statutory instrument containing regulations under subsection (1) is subject to annulment in pursuance of a resolution of either House of Parliament.

Note: inserted by Nationality and Borders Act 2022 c.36 Pt3 s.43(1) (date to be appointed: 2022 c.36 s.43 came into force on April 28, 2022, as specified in 2022 c.36 s.87(4)(d) for limited purpose of making (and, where required, consulting on) regulations; not yet in force otherwise)

Part II
Appeals

...

Note: Part II repealed by Immigration and Asylum Act 1999 from 2 October 2000 (SI 2000/2444). Transitional provisions set out in SI 2003/754.

Part III
Criminal Proceedings

24. Illegal entry and similar offences

[(A1) A person who knowingly enters the United Kingdom in breach of a deportation order commits an offence.

(B1) A person who—

(a) requires leave to enter the United Kingdom under this Act, and

(b) knowingly enters the United Kingdom without such leave, commits an offence.

(C1) A person who—

(a) has only a limited leave to enter or remain in the United Kingdom, and

(b) knowingly remains beyond the time limited by the leave, commits an offence.

(D1) A person who—

(a) requires entry clearance under the immigration rules, and

(b) knowingly arrives in the United Kingdom without a valid entry clearance, commits an offence.

(E1) A person who—

(a) is required under immigration rules not to travel to the United Kingdom without an ETA that is valid for the person's journey to the United Kingdom, and

(b) knowingly arrives in the United Kingdom without such an ETA, commits an offence.

(F1) A person who commits an offence under any of subsections (A1) to (E1) is liable—

(a) on summary conviction in England and Wales, to imprisonment for a term not exceeding 12 months or a fine (or both);

(b) on summary conviction in Scotland, to imprisonment for a term not exceeding 12 months or a fine not exceeding the statutory maximum (or both);

(c) on summary conviction in Northern Ireland, to imprisonment for a term not exceeding six months or a fine not exceeding the statutory maximum (or both);

(d) on conviction on indictment—

(i) for an offence under subsection (A1), to imprisonment for a term not exceeding five years or a fine (or both);

(ii) for an offence under any of subsections (B1) to (E1), to imprisonment for a term not exceeding four years or a fine (or both).

(G1) In relation to an offence committed before paragraph 24(2) of Schedule 22 to the Sentencing Act 2020 comes into force, the reference in subsection (F1)(a) to 12 months is to be read as a reference to six months.]

(1) A person who is not [a British citizen] shall be guilty of an offence punishable on summary conviction with a fine of not more than [level 5] on the standard scale or with imprisonment for not more than six months, or with both, in any of the following cases:—

(a) [. . .]

(aa) . . .

(b) if, having only a limited leave to enter or remain in the United Kingdom, he knowingly [fails to observe a condition of leave;]

(c) if, having lawfully entered the United Kingdom without leave by virtue of section 8(1) above, he remains without leave beyond the time allowed by section 8(1);

(d) if, without reasonable excuse, he fails to comply with any requirement imposed on him under Schedule 2 to this Act to report to a medical officer of health, or to attend, or submit to a test or examination, as required by such an officer;

(e) [;]

(f) if he disembarks in the United Kingdom from a ship or aircraft after being placed on board under Schedule 2 or 3 to this Act with a view to his removal from the United Kingdom;

(g) if he embarks in contravention of a restriction imposed by or under an Order in Council under section 3(7) of this Act [if the person is on immigration bail within the meaning of Schedule 10 to the Immigration Act 2016 and, without reasonable excuse, the person breaches a bail condition within the meaning of that Schedule].

[(**1A**) A person commits an offence under [[subsection (C1)]] above on the day when he first knows that the time limited by his leave has expired and continues to commit it throughout any period during which he is in the United Kingdom thereafter; but a person shall not be prosecuted under that provision more than once in respect of the same limited leave.]

(2) ...

(3) The extended time limit for prosecutions which is provided for by section [28(1)] below shall apply to offences under[[subsections (A1), (B1), (D1), (E1) and (1)(c)]] above.

[(**3A**) The extended time limit for prosecutions which is provided for by section 28(1A) below shall apply to offences under subsection (1)(h) above.]

(4) In proceedings for an offence [[under subsection (B1)]]above of entering the United Kingdom without leave,—

(a) any stamp purporting to have been imprinted on a passport or other travel document by an immigration officer on a particular date for the purpose of giving leave shall be presumed to have been duly so imprinted, unless the contrary is proved;

(b) proof that a person had leave to enter the United Kingdom shall lie on the defence[[]].

[(5) In proceedings for an offence under subsection (D1) above of arriving in the United Kingdom without a valid entry clearance—

(a) any document attached to a passport or other travel document purporting to have been issued by the Secretary of State for the purposes of providing evidence of entry clearance for a particular period is to be presumed to have been duly so issued unless the contrary is proved;

(b) proof that a person had a valid entry clearance is to lie on the defence.]

Note: Words in first square brackets in s 24(1) substituted by British Nationality Act 1981. Words in second square brackets in s 24(1) substituted by Asylum and Immigration Act 1996 from 1 October 1996. Words in first square brackets in s 24(1)(e) added by and words in square brackets in s 24(3) substituted by Immigration Act 1988. Words in second square brackets in subsection 24(1)(e) substituted by Nationality, Immigration and Asylum Act 2002, s 62, from 10 February 2003 (SI 2003/1). Section 24(1A) added by Immigration Act 1988, s 6, except in relation to persons whose leave had expired before 10 July 1988. Sections 24(1)(aa) and 24(2) omitted by Immigration and Asylum Act 1999 from 14 February 2000. Subsection (1)(d) applies in Scotland in modified form (1972 c 58, Sch 6). Section 24 has effect in a form modified by and in circumstances specified by the Channel Tunnel (International Arrangements) Order (SI 1993/1813) as amended by SIs 1994/1405, 2000/913, 2001/178, 2001/3707, 2006/1003 and 2007/3759. Words omitted at subsection (1)(e) and inserted in square brackets at (g) by Immigration Act 2016, Schedule 10 from January 15, 2018 subject to transitional provisions in SI 2017/1241. Word substituted in square brackets at subsection (3) and inserted at subsection (3A) by Immigration Act 2016, Schedule 10 from January 15, 2018 subject to transitional provisions in SI 2017/1241. Subsections (A1)- (G1) inserted by Nationality and Borders Act 2022 c.36 Pt3 s.40(2) (June 28, 2022: insertion has effect as SI 2022/590 reg.2 and Sch.1 para.20 subject to transitional and saving provisions specified in SI 2022/590 reg.3 and Sch.2 para.7) Words omitted in subsection (1)(a) and substituted in subsection (1)(b) by Nationality and Borders Act 2022 c.36 Pt 3s.40(3)(June 28, 2022): omission and substitution has effect as SI 2022/590 reg.2 and Sch.1 para 20 subject to transitional and saving provisions specified in SI 2022/590 reg.3 and Sch.2 para.7). Words substituted in double square brackets in subsection (1A) by Nationality and Borders Act 2022 c.36 Pt3 .40(3)(b) (June 28, 2022): substitution has effect as SI 2022/590 reg.2 and Sch.1 para.20 subject to transitional and saving provisions specified in SI 2022/590 reg.3 and Sch.2 para.7). Words substituted in double brackets in subsection (3) by Nationality and Borders Act 2022 c.36 Pt 3 s.40(c) (June 28, 2022): substitution has effect as SI 2022/590 reg.2 and Sch.1 para 20 subject to transitional and savings provisions specified in SI 2022/590 reg.3 and Sch.2 para.7). Words in double square brackets at subsection (4) substituted and omitted by Nationality and Borders Act 2022 c.36 s.40(3)(d)(June 28, 2022: substitution and omission has effect as SI 2022/590 reg.2 and Sch.1 para.20 subject to transitional and saving provisions specified in SI2022/590 reg.3 and Sch.2 para.7). Subsection (5) inserted by Nationality and Borders Act 2022 c.36 Pt3 s.40(3)(e) (June 28, 2022: insertion has effect as SI 2022/590 reg.2 and Sch.1 para.20 subject to transitional and saving provisions specified in SI 2022/590 reg.3 and Sch.2 para.7)

[24A. Deception

(1) A person who is not a British citizen is guilty of an offence if, by means which include deception by him—

(a) he obtains or seeks to obtain

[[(i) leave to enter or remain in the United Kingdom; or

(ii) an ETA.]]

(b) he secures or seeks to secure the avoidance, postponement or revocation of enforcement action against him.

(2) 'Enforcement action', in relation to a person, means—

(a) the giving of directions for his removal from the United Kingdom ('directions') under Schedule 2 to this Act or section 10 of the Immigration and Asylum Act 1999;

(b) the making of a deportation order against him under section 5 of this Act; or

(c) his removal from the United Kingdom in consequence of directions or a deportation order.

(3) A person guilty of an offence under this section is liable—

(a) on summary conviction, to imprisonment for a term not exceeding six months or to a fine not exceeding the statutory maximum, or to both; or

(b) on conviction on indictment, to imprisonment for a term not exceeding two years or to a fine, or to both.

(4) . . .]

Note: Section 24A inserted by Immigration and Asylum Act 1999 from 14 February 2000. Section 24A(4) repealed by Nationality, Immigration and Asylum Act 2002, s 156 from 10 February 2003 (SI 2003/1). Words inserted in double square brackets at subsection 1 by Nationality and Borders Act 2022 c.36 Pt6 s.75(3) (June 28, 2022)

[24B Illegal working

(1) A person ('P') who is subject to immigration control commits an offence if—

(a) P works at a time when P is disqualified from working by reason of P's immigration status, and

(b) at that time P knows or has reasonable cause to believe that P is disqualified from working by reason of P's immigration status.

(2) For the purposes of subsection (1) a person is disqualified from working by reason of the person's immigration status if—

(a) the person has not been granted leave to enter or remain in the United Kingdom, or

(b) the person's leave to enter or remain in the United Kingdom—

(i) is invalid,

(ii) has ceased to have effect (whether by reason of curtailment, revocation, cancellation, passage of time or otherwise), or

(iii) is subject to a condition preventing the person from doing work of that kind.

(3) A person who is guilty of an offence under subsection (1) is liable on summary conviction—

(a) in England and Wales, to imprisonment for a term not exceeding 51 weeks or a fine, or both,

(b) in Scotland or Northern Ireland, to imprisonment for a term not exceeding 6 months or a fine not exceeding level 5 on the standard scale, or both.

(4) In relation to an offence committed before section 281(5) of the Criminal Justice Act 2003 comes into force, the reference in subsection (3)(a) to 51 weeks is to be read as a reference to 6 months.

(5) If a person is convicted of an offence under subsection (1) in England and Wales, the prosecutor must consider whether to ask the court to commit the person to the Crown Court under section 70 of the Proceeds of Crime Act 2002 (committal with view to confiscation order being considered).

(6) If a person is convicted of an offence under subsection (1) in Scotland, the prosecutor must consider whether to ask the court to act under section 92 of the Proceeds of Crime Act 2002 (making of confiscation order).

(7) If a person is convicted of an offence under subsection (1) in Northern Ireland, the prosecutor must consider whether to ask the court to commit the person to the Crown Court under section 218 of the Proceeds of Crime Act 2002 (committal with view to confiscation order being considered).

(8) The reference in subsection (1) to a person who is subject to immigration control is to a person who under this Act requires leave to enter or remain in the United Kingdom.

(9) Where a person is on immigration bail within the meaning of Part 1 of Schedule 10 to the Immigration Act 2016—

(a) the person is to be treated for the purposes of subsection (2) as if the person had been granted leave to enter the United Kingdom, but

(b) any condition as to the person's work in the United Kingdom to which the person's immigration bail is subject is to be treated for those purposes as a condition of leave.

(10) The reference in subsection (1) to a person working is to that person working—

(a) under a contract of employment,

(b) under a contract of apprenticeship,

(c) under a contract personally to do work,

(d) under or for the purposes of a contract for services,

(e) for a purpose related to a contract to sell goods,

(f) as a constable,

(g) in the course of Crown employment,

(h) as a relevant member of the House of Commons staff, or

(i) as a relevant member of the House of Lords staff.

(11) In subsection (10)—

'contract to sell goods' means a contract by which a person acting in the course of a trade, business, craft or profession transfers or agrees to transfer the property in goods to another person (and for this purpose 'goods' means any tangible moveable items);

'Crown employment'—

(a) in relation to England and Wales and Scotland, has the meaning given by section 191(3) of the Employment Rights Act 1996;

(b) in relation to Northern Ireland, has the meaning given by Article 236(3) of the Employment Rights (Northern Ireland) Order 1996 (SI 1996/1919 (NI 16));

'relevant member of the House of Commons staff' has the meaning given by section 195(5) of the Employment Rights Act 1996;

'relevant member of the House of Lords staff' has the meaning given by section 194(6) of the Employment Rights Act 1996.

(12) Subsection (1) does not apply to—

(a) service as a member of the naval, military or air forces of the Crown, or

(b) employment by an association established for the purposes of Part 11 of the Reserve Forces Act 1996.

(13) In this section 'contract' means a contract whether express or implied and, if express, whether oral or in writing.]

Note: Section 24B inserted by Immigration Act 2016, s 34 from 12 July 2016 (SI 2016/603) subject to transitional provisions specified in SI 2016/712.

[24C Driving when unlawfully in the United Kingdom

(1) A person commits an offence if—

(a) the person drives a motor vehicle on a road or other public place at a time when the person is not lawfully resident in the United Kingdom, and

(b) at that time the person knows or has reasonable cause to believe that the person is not lawfully resident in the United Kingdom.

(2) A person who is guilty of an offence under subsection (1) is liable on summary conviction—

(a) in England and Wales, to imprisonment for a term not exceeding 51 weeks, to a fine or to both;

(b) in Scotland or Northern Ireland, to imprisonment for a term not exceeding 6 months, to a fine not exceeding level 5 on the standard scale or to both.

(3) In relation to an offence committed before section 281(5) of the Criminal Justice Act 2003 comes into force, the reference in subsection (2)(a) to 51 weeks is to be read as a reference to 6 months.

(4) In this section 'motor vehicle' and 'road'—

(a) in relation to England and Wales and Scotland, have the same meanings as in the Road Traffic Act 1988;

(b) in relation to Northern Ireland, have the same meanings as in the Road Traffic (Northern Ireland) Order 1995 (SI 1995/2994 (NI 18)).

(5) For the purposes of this section a person is not lawfully resident in the United Kingdom if the person requires leave to enter or remain in the United Kingdom but does not have it.]

Note: Section 24C inserted by Immigration Act 2016, s 44 from a date to be appointed.

[24D Detention of motor vehicles

(1) If a person ('P') has been arrested for an offence under section 24C committed in England and Wales or Northern Ireland, a senior officer or a constable may detain a relevant vehicle.

(2) Subject to regulations under subsection (8), a vehicle detained under subsection (1) must be released—

(a) when a decision is taken not to charge P with the offence, or

(b) if P is charged with the offence—

(i) when P is acquitted, the charge against P is dismissed or the proceedings are discontinued, or

(ii) if P is convicted, when the court decides not to order forfeiture of the vehicle.

(3) If a person ('P') has been arrested for an offence under section 24C committed in Scotland, a senior officer or a constable may detain a relevant vehicle.

(4) Subject to regulations under subsection (8) a vehicle detained under subsection (3) must be released—

(a) when a decision is taken not to institute criminal proceedings against P for the offence, or

(b) if criminal proceedings are instituted against P for the offence—

(i) when P is acquitted or, under section 147 of the Criminal Procedure (Scotland) Act 1995, liberated or the trial diet is deserted simpliciter, or

(ii) if P is convicted, when the court decides not to order forfeiture of the vehicle.

(5) For the purposes of subsection (4) criminal proceedings are instituted against a person ('P') at whichever is the earliest of P's first appearance before the sheriff or the service on P of a complaint.

(6) A power in subsection (1) or (3) may be exercised by a senior officer or constable at any place at which the senior officer or constable is lawfully present.

(7) A vehicle is a relevant vehicle in relation to P if the officer or constable concerned has reasonable grounds for believing it was used in the commission by P of an offence under section 24C.

(8) The Secretary of State may by regulations make provision about the release of a vehicle detained under subsection (1) or (3).

(9) Regulations under subsection (8) may in particular make provision—

(a) for the release of a vehicle before the time mentioned in subsection (2) or (4);

(b) about the procedure by which a person may seek to have a vehicle released before or after that time;

(c) about the persons to whom a vehicle may or must be released before or after that time;

(d) prescribing conditions to be met before a vehicle may be released before or after that time (including a condition requiring the payment of costs in relation to detention of the vehicle and any application for its release);

(e) as to the destination of payments made in compliance with such a condition;

(f) enabling a person specified in the regulations to waive compliance with such a condition;

(g) as to the disposal of a vehicle in a case where such a condition is not met;

(h) as to the destination of the proceeds arising from the disposal of a vehicle in such a case.

(10) Regulations under subsection (8)—

(a) are to be made by statutory instrument;

(b) may make different provision for different cases;

(c) may make incidental, supplementary, consequential, transitional, transitory or saving provision.

(11) A statutory instrument containing regulations under subsection (8) is subject to annulment in pursuance of a resolution of either House of Parliament.

(12) In this section 'senior officer' means an immigration officer not below the rank of chief immigration officer.]

Note: Section 24D inserted by Immigration Act 2016, s 44 from date to be appointed.

[24E Powers to enter premises to detain motor vehicle

(1) A senior officer or a constable may enter and search any premises for the purposes of detaining a vehicle under section 24D.

(2) The power in subsection (1) may be exercised—

(a) only to the extent that it is reasonably required for that purpose, and

(b) only if the senior officer or constable knows that a vehicle which may be detained under section 24D is to be found on the premises.

(3) The power in subsection (1) may be exercised—

(a) by a senior officer ('S') only if S produces identification showing that S is an immigration officer (whether or not S is asked to do so);

(b) by a constable ('C') only if C produces identification showing that C is a constable (whether or not C is asked to do so).

(4) Subsection (5) applies if, on an application by a senior officer or constable, a justice of the peace is satisfied that there are reasonable grounds for suspecting that a vehicle which may be detained under section 24D may be found on premises mentioned in subsection (6).

(5) The justice of the peace may issue a warrant authorising any senior officer or constable to enter, if need be by force, the premises for the purpose of searching for and detaining the vehicle.

(6) The premises referred to in subsection (4) are—

(a) one or more sets of premises specified in the application, or

(b) subject to subsection (10), any premises occupied or controlled by a person specified in the application, including such sets of premises as are so specified (in which case the application is for an 'all premises warrant').

(7) If the application is for an all premises warrant, the justice of the peace must also be satisfied—

(a) that there are reasonable grounds for believing that it is necessary to search premises occupied or controlled by the person in question which are not specified in the application in order to find the vehicle, and

(b) that it is not reasonably practicable to specify in the application all the premises which the person occupies or controls and which might need to be searched.

(8) Subject to subsection (10), the warrant may authorise entry to and search of premises on more than one occasion if, on the application, the justice of the peace is satisfied that it is necessary to authorise multiple entries in order to achieve the purpose for which the justice issues the warrant.

(9) If it authorises multiple entries, the number of entries authorised may be unlimited, or limited to a maximum.

(10) A justice of the peace in Scotland may not issue—

(a) an all premises warrant under this section, or

(b) a warrant under this section authorising multiple entries.

(11) In the application of this section to Scotland, references to a justice of the peace are to be read as references to the sheriff or a justice of the peace.

(12) In this section 'senior officer' means an immigration officer not below the rank of chief immigration officer.]

Note: Section 24E inserted by Immigration Act 2016, s 44 from a date to be appointed.

[24F Orders following conviction of offence under section 24C

(1) If a person is convicted of an offence under section 24C, the court may order the forfeiture of the vehicle used in the commission of the offence.

(2) Where a person who claims to have an interest in the vehicle applies to the court to make representations on the question of forfeiture, the court may not make an order under this section in respect of the vehicle

(3) For the purposes of subsection (2) the persons who have an interest in a vehicle include—

(a) a person who owns it,

(b) the person in whose name the vehicle is registered under the Vehicle Excise and Registration Act 1994, and

(c) a person who is in possession of it under a hire purchase agreement (or, in the case of a detained vehicle, was in possession of it under a hire purchase agreement immediately before its detention).

(4) The Secretary of State may by regulations make provision about—

(a) the disposal of a vehicle forfeited under this section;

(b) the destination of the proceeds arising from the disposal of such a vehicle.

(5) Regulations under subsection (4)—

(a) are to be made by statutory instrument;

(b) may make different provision for different cases;

(c) may make incidental, supplementary, consequential, transitional, transitory or saving provision.

(6) A statutory instrument containing regulations under subsection (4) is subject to annulment in pursuance of a resolution of either House of Parliament.]

Note: Section 24F inserted by the Immigration Act 2016, s 44 from a date to be appointed.

[25. Assisting unlawful immigration to member State {or the United Kingdom}

(1) A person commits an offence if he—

(a) does an act which facilitates the commission of a breach [[or attempted breach]] of immigration law by an individual who is a {a national of the United Kingdom},

(b) knows or has reasonable cause for believing that the act facilitates the commission of a breach [[or attempted breach]] of immigration law by the individual, and

(c) knows or has reasonable cause for believing that the individual is a {national of the United Kingdom}.

(2) In subsection (1) 'immigration law' means a law which has effect in a member State {or the United Kingdom} and which controls, in respect of some or all persons who {or as the case may be the United Kingdom} are not nationals of the State, entitlement to—

(a) enter [[or arrive in]]the State {or the United Kingdom},

(b) transit across the State {or the United Kingdom}, or

(c) be in the State {or the United Kingdom}.

{(2A) In subsections (1) and (2), 'national of the United Kingdom' means—

(a) a British citizen;

(b) a person who is a British subject by virtue of Part 4 of the British Nationality Act 1981(4) and who has the right of abode in the United Kingdom; or

(b) a person who is a British overseas territories citizen by virtue of a connection with Gibraltar};

(3) A document issued by the government of a member State certifying a matter of law in that State—

(a) shall be admissible in proceedings for an offence under this section, and

(b) shall be conclusive as to the matter certified.

[(4) Subsection (1) applies to things done whether inside or outside the United Kingdom.]

(5) ...

(6) A person guilty of an offence under this section shall be liable—

(a) on conviction on indictment, to imprisonment for [[life]], to a fine or to both, or

(b) on summary conviction, to imprisonment for a term not exceeding six months, to a fine not exceeding the statutory maximum or to both.

[(7) In this section—

(a) a reference to a member State includes a reference

Note: Section 25 substituted by Nationality, Immigration and Asylum Act 2002, s 143, from 10 February 2003 (SI 2003/1). Subsections (7) and (8) inserted by Asylum and Immigration Act 2004, s 1 from 1 October 2004. Subsection (4) substituted and subsection (5) deleted by UK Borders Act 2007 (s 30) from 31 January 2008 (SI 2008/99). The term 'EU' substituted from 22 April 2011 (SI 2011/1043). Section 25 has effect in a form modified by and in circumstances specified by the Channel Tunnel (International Arrangements) Order (SI 1993/1813) as amended by SIs 1994/1405, 2000/913, 2001/178, 2001/3707, 2006/1003 and 2007/3759. Words in double square brackets inserted at subsection (1)(a) and (b) by Schedule 14 to the Immigration Act 2016 on 31 May 2016 (SI 2016/603). Words in curly brackets in subsection (1)(a) & (c) substituted by Immigration and Social Security Co-ordination (EU Withdrawal) Act 2020 (Consequential, Saving, Transitional and Transitory Provisions (EU Exit) Regulations 2020/1309 Pt2(1) reg 5(3)(a) (December 31,2020 at 23.00 being the time and date 2020 c.20 Sch.1 para 2(2) comes into force). Words inserted in the heading, and at subsections (1)(a), (1)(c), (2), (2)(a), (2)(b), (2)(c) and (2A), and substituted at subsection (1)(a), (1)(c), (7)(a) and (7)(b) and omitted at subsection (8) by Immigration, Nationality and Asylum 2019 (EU Exit) Regulations 2019/745 Pt 2(1) reg 3 (31 December2020; shall come into force on IP completion day not exit day specified in 2020 c. 1 s 39(1) and Sch 5 para 1(1)). Words in double brackets inserted at subsection (2)(a) by Nationality and Borders Act 2022, c.36 Pt3 s.40(4) (June 28, 2022: insertion has effect as SI 2022/590 reg.2 and Sch.1 para.20 subject to transitional and saving provisions specified in SI 2022/590 reg.3 and Sch.2 para.7). Words substituted in double brackets in subsection (6)(a) by Nationality and Borders Act 2022 c.36 Pt3 s.41(2)(June 28, 2022: substitution has effect as SI 2022/590 reg.2 and Sch.1 para 21 subject to transitional and saving provisions specified in SI 2022/590 reg.3 and Sch.2 para.7)

25A. Helping asylum-seeker to enter United Kingdom

(1) A person commits an offence if—

(a) he knowingly {and for gain} facilitates the arrival [[or attempted arrival]] in [, or the entry [[or attempted entry]] into,] the United Kingdom of an individual, and

(b) he knows or has reasonable cause to believe that the individual is an asylum-seeker.

(2) In this section 'asylum-seeker' means a person who intends to claim that to remove him from or require him to leave the United Kingdom would be contrary to the United Kingdom's obligations under—

(a) the Refugee Convention (within the meaning given by section 167(1) of the Immigration and Asylum Act 1999 (c. 33) (interpretation)), or

(b) the Human Rights Convention (within the meaning given by that section).

(3) Subsection (1) does not apply to anything done by a person acting on behalf of an organisation which—

(a) aims to assist asylum-seekers, and

(b) does not charge for its services.

(4) [Subsections (4) and (6)] of section 25 apply for the purpose of the offence in subsection (1) of this section as they apply for the purpose of the offence in subsection (1) of that section.]

Note: Section 25A inserted by Nationality, Immigration and Asylum Act 2002, s 143 from 10 February 2003 (SI 2003/1). Words in square brackets in subsections (1)(a) and (4) inserted by UK Borders Act 2007, ss 29–30 from 31 January 2008 (SI 2008/99). Words in double square brackets at subsection (1)(a) inserted by Schedule 14 to the Immigration Act 2016 from 31 May 2016 (SI 2016/603). Words in curly brackets omitted by Nationality and Borders Act 2022 c.36 Pt3 s.41(3) (June 28, 2022: omission has effect as SI 2022/590 reg.2 and Sch.1 para.21 subject to transitional and saving provisions specified in SI 2022/590 reg.3 and para.)

25B …

Note: Omitted by Immigration and Social Security Co-Ordination (EU Withdrawal) Act 2020 (Consequential, Saving, Transitional and Transitory Provision (EU Exit) Regulations 2020 (SI 2020/1309) regs. 1(2), 5(4) (with reg.5(7)) from 31.12.2020

[25BA Facilitation offences: application to rescuers

(1) A person does not commit a facilitation offence if the act of facilitation was an act done by or on behalf of, or co-ordinated by—

(a) Her Majesty's Coastguard, or

(b) an overseas maritime search and rescue authority exercising similar functions to those of Her Majesty's Coastguard.

(2) In proceedings for a facilitation offence, it is a defence for the person charged with the offence to show that—

(a) the assisted individual had been in danger or distress at sea, and

(b) the act of facilitation was an act of providing assistance to the individual at any time between—

(i) the time when the assisted individual was first in danger or distress at sea, and

(ii) the time when the assisted individual was delivered to a place of safety on land.

(3) For the purposes of subsection (2), the following are not to be treated as an act of providing assistance—

(a) the act of delivering the assisted individual to the United Kingdom in circumstances where—

(i) the United Kingdom was not the nearest place of safety on land to which the assisted individual could have been delivered, and

(ii) the person charged with the offence did not have a good reason for delivering the assisted individual to the United Kingdom instead of to a nearer place of safety on land;

(b) the act of steering a ship in circumstances where the person charged with the offence was on the same ship as the assisted individual at the time when the individual was first in danger or distress at sea.

(4) A person is taken to have shown a fact mentioned in subsection (2) if—

(a) sufficient evidence of the fact is adduced to raise an issue with respect to it, and

(b) the contrary is not proved beyond reasonable doubt.

(5) In this section—

"act of facilitation"—

(a) in relation to an offence under section 25 (assisting unlawful immigration), means the act mentioned in subsection (1)(a) of that section;

(b) in relation to an offence under section 25A (helping asylum-seeker to enter the UK), means the act of facilitating the arrival (or attempted arrival) in, or entry (or attempted entry) into, the United Kingdom of an individual, as mentioned in subsection (1)(a) of that section;

(c) in relation to an offence under section 25B(1) (facilitating breach of deportation order), means the act mentioned in subsection (1)(a) of that section;

(d) in relation to an offence under section 25B(3) (assisting entry to UK in breach of an exclusion order), means the act mentioned in subsection (3) (a) of that section;

"assisted individual"—

(a) in relation to an offence under section 25, means the individual whose breach (or attempted breach) of immigration law is facilitated by the act of facilitation;

(b) in relation to an offence under section 25A, means the individual whose arrival (or attempted arrival) in, or entry (or attempted entry) into, the United Kingdom is facilitated by the act of facilitation;

(c) in relation to an offence under section 25B(1), means the individual whose breach (or attempted breach) of a deportation order is facilitated by the act of facilitation;

(d) in relation to an offence under section 25B(3), means the individual who is assisted to arrive in, enter or remain (or to attempt to arrive in, enter or remain) in the United Kingdom by the act of facilitation;

"facilitation offence" means—

(a) an offence under section 25 (assisting unlawful immigration),

(b) an offence under section 25A (helping asylum-seeker to enter the United Kingdom), or

(c) an offence under section 25B (assisting entry to the United Kingdom in breach of deportation or exclusion order) to the extent that the section continues to apply by virtue of regulation 5(7) of the Immigration and Social Security Co-ordination (EU Withdrawal) Act 2020 (Consequential, Saving, Transitional and Transitory Provisions) (EU Exit) Regulations 2020 (S.I. 2020/1309);

"ship" includes—

(a) every description of vessel (including a hovercraft), and

(b) any other structure (whether with or without means of propulsion) constructed or used to carry persons, goods, plant or machinery by water.]

Note: inserted by Nationality and Border Act 2022 c.36 Pt3 s.41(4)(June 28, 2022: insertion has effect as SI 2022/590 reg.2 and Sch.1 para 21 subject to transitional and saving provisions specified in SI 2022/590 reg.3 and Sch.2 para.7)

[25BB Facilitation offences: defences relating to stowaways

(1) In proceedings for a facilitation offence brought against a master of a ship, it is a defence for the master to show—

(a) that the assisted individual was a stowaway when the act of facilitation took place, and

(b) that the master, or a person acting on the master's behalf, reported the presence of the assisted individual on the ship to the Secretary of State or an immigration officer—

(i) in a case where the ship was scheduled to go to the United Kingdom, as soon as reasonably practicable after the time when the ship's next scheduled port of call became a port in the United Kingdom, or

(ii) in a case where the ship was not scheduled to go to the United Kingdom but the master of the ship decided that the ship needed to go to the United Kingdom (whether for reasons relating to the presence of the assisted individual on board or for other reasons), as soon as reasonably practicable after the master made that decision.

(2) In proceedings for a facilitation offence, it is a defence for the person charged with the offence to show—

(a) that the assisted individual was a stowaway when the act of facilitation took place,

(b) that they were acting to ensure the security, general health, welfare or safety of the assisted individual, and

(c) that they had reported the presence of the assisted individual to the master of the ship as soon as reasonably practicable.

(3) A person is taken to have shown a fact mentioned in subsection (1) or (2) if—

(a) sufficient evidence of the fact is adduced to raise an issue with respect to it, and

(b) the contrary is not proved beyond reasonable doubt.

(4) For the purposes of this section, an individual is a stowaway on a ship if—

(a) they boarded the ship without the knowledge of the master of the ship, and

(b) the master was not aware of their presence on the ship when the ship departed from the port where the individual boarded.

(5) But an individual ceases to be a stowaway if, after the master of the ship has become aware of their presence on the ship, the individual is given permission to leave the ship by the immigration authorities of a country that the ship arrives at (whether or not they do in fact leave the ship there).

(6) In this section, "act of facilitation", "assisted individual", "facilitation offence" and "ship" have the same meanings as in section 25BA.]

Note: inserted by Nationality and Borders Act 2022 c.36 Pt3 s.41(4) (June 28, 2022: insertion has effect as SI 2022/590 reg.2 and Sch.1 para.21 subject to transitional and saving provisions specified in SI 2022/590 reg.3 and Sch.2 para 7)

[25C. Forfeiture of vehicle, ship or aircraft

(1) This section applies where a person is convicted on indictment of an offence under section 25 [or] 25A.

(2) The court may order the forfeiture of a vehicle used or intended to be used in connection with the offence if the convicted person—

(a) owned the vehicle at the time the offence was committed,

(b) was at that time a director, secretary or manager of a company which owned the vehicle,

(c) was at that time in possession of the vehicle under a hire-purchase agreement,

(d) was at that time a director, secretary or manager of a company which was in possession of the vehicle under a hire-purchase agreement, or

(e) was driving the vehicle in the course of the commission of the offence.

(3) The court may order the forfeiture of a ship or aircraft used or intended to be used in connection with the offence if the convicted person—

(a) owned the ship or aircraft at the time the offence was committed,

(b) was at that time a director, secretary or manager of a company which owned the ship or aircraft,

(c) was at that time in possession of the ship or aircraft under a hire-purchase agreement,

(d) was at that time a director, secretary or manager of a company which was in possession of the ship or aircraft under a hire-purchase agreement,

(e) was at that time a charterer of the ship or aircraft, or

(f) committed the offence while acting as captain of the ship or aircraft.

(4) But in a case to which subsection (3)(a) or (b) does not apply, forfeiture may be ordered only—

(a) in the case of a ship, if subsection (5) or (6) applies;

(b) in the case of an aircraft, if subsection (5) or (7) applies.

(5) This subsection applies where—

(a) in the course of the commission of the offence, the ship or aircraft carried more than 20 illegal entrants, and

(b) a person who, at the time the offence was committed, owned the ship or aircraft or was a director, secretary or manager of a company which owned it, knew or ought to have known of the intention to use it in the course of the commission of an offence under section 25 [or] 25A.

(6) This subsection applies where a ship's gross tonnage is less than 500 tons.

(7) This subsection applies where the maximum weight at which an aircraft (which is not a hovercraft) may take off in accordance with its certificate of airworthiness is less than 5,700 kilogrammes.

(8) Where a person who claims to have an interest in a vehicle, ship or aircraft applies to a court to make representations on the question of forfeiture, the court may not make an order under this section in respect of the ship, aircraft or vehicle unless the person has been given an opportunity to make representations.

(9) In the case of an offence under section 25, the reference in subsection (5)(a) to an illegal entrant shall be taken to include a reference to—

(a) an individual who seeks to enter a member State in breach of immigration law [(for which purpose 'member State'{or the United Kingdom} and 'immigration law' have the meanings given by section 25(2) and (7))] and

(b) an individual who is [[the victim of conduct which constitutes an offence under section 2 of the Modern Slavery Act 2015 (human trafficking)]].

(10) In the case of an offence under section 25A, the reference in subsection (5)(a) to an illegal entrant shall be taken to include a reference to—

(a) an asylum-seeker (within the meaning of that section), and(b) an individual who is [[the victim of conduct which constitutes an offence under section 2 of the Modern Slavery Act 2015 (human trafficking)]].

(11) In the case of an offence under section 25B, the reference in subsection (5)(a) to an illegal entrant shall be taken to include a reference to an individual who is [[the victim of conduct which constitutes an offence under section 2 of the Modern Slavery Act (human trafficking)]].

Note: Section 25C inserted by Nationality, Immigration and Asylum Act 2002, s 143 from 10 February 2003 (SI 2003/1). Words in square brackets in subsection 9(a) substituted by Asylum and Immigration (Treatment of Claimants etc.) Act 2004, s 1 from 1 October 2004. Other words in square brackets inserted by Asylum and Immigration (Treatment of Claimants etc.) Act 2004, s 5 from 1 December 2004 (SI 2004/2999; SSI 2004/494). Words in double square brackets substituted at subsection (9)(b), (10)(b) and (11) from 31 July 2015 by Sch. 5(1) para 2 to the Modern Slavery Act 2015 (SI 2015/1476) subject to transitional provisions and savings specified in SI 2015/1476 Art 4. Word in square brackets substituted in subsection (1) and (5)(b) by The Immigration and Social Security Co-ordination (EU Withdrawal) Act 2020 (Consequential, Saving, Transitional and Transitory Provisions)(EU Exit) Regulations 2020 (SI2020/1309), reg 1(2), Sch.1 para 1(1)(a)(with Sch.1 para 1(5)). Words in curly brackets inserted at subsection (9)(a) by Immigration, Nationality and Asylum Regulations 2019/745 Pt 2(1) reg 4(4) (31 December2020: shall come into force on IP completion day not exit day as specified in 2020 c. 1 s 39(1) and Sch. 5 para 1(1)).

[25D. Detention of ship, aircraft or vehicle

(1) If a person has been arrested for an offence under section 25[, 25A or 25B], a senior officer or a constable may detain a relevant ship, aircraft or vehicle—

(a) until a decision is taken as to whether or not to charge the arrested person with that offence; or

(b) if the arrested person has been charged—

(i) until he is acquitted, the charge against him is dismissed or the proceedings are discontinued; or

(ii) if he has been convicted, until the court decides whether or not to order forfeiture of the ship, aircraft or vehicle.

(2) A ship, aircraft or vehicle is a relevant ship, aircraft or vehicle, in relation to an arrested person, if it is one which the officer or constable concerned has reasonable grounds for believing could, on conviction of the arrested person for the offence for which he was arrested, be the subject of an order for forfeiture made under [section 25C].

(3) [A person (other than the arrested person) may apply to the court for the release of a ship, aircraft or vehicle on the grounds that—

(a) he owns the ship, aircraft or vehicle,

(b) he was, immediately before the detention of the ship, aircraft or vehicle, in possession of it under a hire-purchase agreement, or

(c) he is a charterer of the ship or aircraft.]

(4) The court to which an application is made under subsection (3) may, on such security or surety being tendered as it considers satisfactory, release the ship, aircraft or vehicle on condition that it is made available to the court if—

(a) the arrested person is convicted; and

(b) an order for its forfeiture is made under [section 25C].

(5) In the application to Scotland of subsection (1), for paragraphs (a) and (b) substitute—

'(a) until a decision is taken as to whether or not to institute criminal proceedings against the arrested person for that offence; or

(b) if criminal proceedings have been instituted against the arrested person—

(i) until he is acquitted or, under section 65 or 147 of the Criminal Procedure (Scotland) Act 1995, discharged or liberated or the trial diet is deserted simpliciter;

(ii) if he has been convicted, until the court decides whether or not to order forfeiture of the ship, aircraft or vehicle, and for the purposes of this subsection, criminal proceedings are instituted against a person at whichever is the earliest of his first appearance before the sheriff on petition, or the service on him of an indictment or complaint.'

(6) 'Court' means—

(a) in England and Wales—

[(ia) if the arrested person has not been charged, or he has been charged but proceedings for the offence have not begun to be heard, a magistrates' court;]

(iii) if he has been charged and proceedings for the offence are being heard, the court hearing the proceedings;

(b) in Scotland, the sheriff; and

(c) in Northern Ireland—

(i) if the arrested person has not been charged, the magistrates' court for the county court division in which he was arrested;

(ii) if he has been charged but proceedings for the offence have not begun to be heard, the magistrates' court for the county court division in which he was charged;

(iii) if he has been charged and proceedings for the offence are being heard, the court hearing the proceedings.

(7) …

(8) 'Senior officer' means an immigration officer not below the rank of chief immigration officer.]

Note: Section 25D (previously s 25A) renumbered by Nationality, Immigration and Asylum Act 2002 from 10 February 2003 (SI 2003/1) and inserted by Immigration and Asylum Act 1999 from 2 October 2000. Words in square brackets in subsection (2) substituted by and subsection (3) substituted by Nationality, Immigration and Asylum Act 2002, s 144 from 10 February 2003 (SI 2003/1). Words in square brackets in subsection (4)(b) substituted by and subsection (7) omitted by Nationality, Immigration and Asylum Act 2002, s 144 from 10 February 2003 (SI 2003/1). Words in square brackets in subsection (6)(a)(ia) substituted for original (6)(a)(i) and (ii) by Sch. 8 Courts Act 2003 from 1 April 2005 (SI 2005/190).

26. General offences in connection with administration of Act

(1) A person shall be guilty of an offence punishable on summary conviction with a fine of not more than [level 5 on the standard scale] or with imprisonment for not more than six months, or with both, in any of the following cases—

(a) if, without reasonable excuse, he refuses or fails to submit to examination under Schedule 2 of this Act;

(b) if, without reasonable excuse, he refuses or fails to furnish or produce any information in his possession, or any documents in his possession or control, which he is on an examination under that Schedule required to furnish or produce;

(c) if on any such examination or otherwise he makes or causes to be made to an immigration officer or other person lawfully acting in the execution of [a relevant enactment] a return, statement or representation which he knows to be false or does not believe to be true;

(d) if, without lawful authority, he alters any [certificate of entitlement], entry clearance, work permit or other document issued or made under or for the purposes of this Act, or uses for the purposes of this Act, or has in his possession for such use, any passport, [certificate of entitlement], entry clearance, work permit or other document which he knows or has reasonable cause to believe to be false;

(e) if, without reasonable excuse, he fails to complete and produce a landing or embarkation card in accordance with any order under Schedule 2 of this Act;

(f) if, without reasonable excuse, he fails to comply with any requirement of regulations under section 4(3) or of an order under section 4(4) above;

(g) if, without reasonable excuse, he obstructs an immigration officer or other person lawfully acting in the execution of this Act.

[(h) if, without reasonable excuse, the person fails to comply with a direction under paragraph 1(6) of Schedule 2 (direction to move a container for the purposes of a search).]

(2) The extended time limit for prosecutions which is provided for by section 28 below shall apply to offences under subsection (1)(c) and (d) above.

[(3) 'Relevant enactment' means—

(a) this Act;

(b) the Immigration Act 1988;

(c) the Asylum and Immigration Appeals Act 1993 (apart from section 4 or 5) ...

(d) the Immigration and Asylum Act 1999 (apart from Part VI)]; [or

(e) the Nationality, Immigration and Asylum Act 2002 (apart from Part 5).]

Note: Words in first square brackets in s 26(1) substituted by virtue of Criminal Justice Act 1982and amended by Asylum and Immigration Act 1996 from 1 October 1996. Words in square brackets in s 26(1)(d) substituted by British Nationality Act 1981, s 39(6). Words in square brackets in s 26(1)(c) and subsection (3) inserted by Immigration and Asylum Act 1999 from 14 February 2000. Subsection 3(e) inserted by and words in subsection 3(c) omitted by Nationality, Immigration and Asylum Act 2002, s 151 from 10 February 2003 (SI 2003/1). Subsection (1)(h) inserted by Nationality and Borders Act 2022 c.36 s.44(4) (June 28, 2022)

[26A. Registration card

(1) In this section 'registration card' means a document which—

(a) carries information about a person (whether or not wholly or partly electronically), and

[(b) is issued by the Secretary of State to the person wholly or partly in connection with—

(i) a [[protection claim]] (whether or not made by that person) [[(ii) a claim for support under section 95A of the Immigration and Asylum Act 1999 (whether or not made by that person).]]]

(2) In subsection (1) '[[protection claim]]' has the meaning given by section 18 of the Nationality, Immigration and Asylum Act 2002.

(3) A person commits an offence if he—

(a) makes a false registration card,

(b) alters a registration card with intent to deceive or to enable another to deceive,

(c) has a false or altered registration card in his possession without reasonable excuse,

(d) uses or attempts to use a false registration card for a purpose for which a registration card is issued,

(e) uses or attempts to use an altered registration card with intent to deceive,

(f) makes an article designed to be used in making a false registration card,

(g) makes an article designed to be used in altering a registration card with intent to deceive or to enable another to deceive, or

(h) has an article within paragraph (f) or (g) in his possession without reasonable excuse.

(4) In subsection (3) 'false registration card' means a document which is designed to appear to be a registration card.

(5) A person who is guilty of an offence under subsection (3)(a), (b), (d), (e), (f) or (g) shall be liable—

(a) on conviction on indictment, to imprisonment for a term not exceeding ten years, to a fine or to both, or

(b) on summary conviction, to imprisonment for a term not exceeding six months, to a fine not exceeding the statutory maximum or to both.

(6) A person who is guilty of an offence under subsection (3)(c) or (h) shall be liable—

(a) on conviction on indictment, to imprisonment for a term not exceeding two years, to a fine or to both, or

(b) on summary conviction, to imprisonment for a term not exceeding six months, to a fine not exceeding the statutory maximum or to both.

(7) The Secretary of State may by order—

(a) amend the definition of 'registration card' in subsection (1);

(b) make consequential amendment of this section.

(8) An order under subsection (7)—

(a) must be made by statutory instrument, and

(b) may not be made unless a draft has been laid before and approved by resolution of each House of Parliament.]

Note: Section 26A inserted by Nationality, Immigration and Asylum Act 2002, s 148 from 10 February 2003 (SI 2003/1). Subsection (1)(b) substituted by The Immigration (Registration Card) Order 2008 (SI 2008/1693) from 27 June 2008. Words omitted in subsection (1)(b)(ii), inserted at subsection (1)(b)(aa), substituted in subsection (1)(b)(i) and (2) by Schedule 11 to the Immigration Act 2016 from a date to be appointed.

[26B. Possession of immigration stamp

(1) A person commits an offence if he has an immigration stamp in his possession without reasonable excuse.

(2) A person commits an offence if he has a replica immigration stamp in his possession without reasonable excuse.

(3) In this section—

(a) 'immigration stamp' means a device which is designed for the purpose of stamping documents in the exercise of an immigration function,

(b) 'replica immigration stamp' means a device which is designed for the purpose of stamping a document so that it appears to have been stamped in the exercise of an immigration function, and

(c) 'immigration function' means a function of an immigration officer or the Secretary of State under the Immigration Acts.

(4) A person who is guilty of an offence under this section shall be liable—

(a) on conviction on indictment, to imprisonment for a term not exceeding two years, to a fine or to both, or

(b) on summary conviction, to imprisonment for a term not exceeding six months, to a fine not exceeding the statutory maximum or to both.]

Note: Section 26B inserted by Nationality, Immigration and Asylum Act 2002, s 148 from 10 February 2003 (SI 2003/1).

27. Offences by persons connected with ships or aircraft or with ports

(1) A person shall be guilty of an offence punishable on summary conviction with a fine of not more than [level 5 on the standard scale] or with imprisonment for not more than six months, or with both, in any of the following cases—

(a) if, being the captain of a ship or aircraft,—

(i) he knowingly permits a person to disembark in the United Kingdom when required under Schedule 2 or 3 to this Act to prevent it, or fails without reasonable excuse to take any steps he is required by or under Schedule 2 to take in connection with the disembarkation or examination of passengers or for furnishing a passenger list or particulars of members of the crew; or

(ii) he fails, without reasonable excuse, to comply with any directions given him under Schedule 2 or 3 [or under the Immigration and Asylum Act 1999] with respect to the removal of a person from the United Kingdom;

(b) if, as owner or agent of a ship or aircraft—

(i) he arranges, or is knowingly concerned in any arrangements, for the ship or air craft to call at a port other than a port of entry contrary to any provision of Schedule 2 to this Act; or

(ii) he fails, with reasonable excuse, to take any steps required by an order under Schedule 2 for the supply to passengers of landing or embarkation cards; or

(iii) he fails, without reasonable excuse, to make arrangements for [or in connection with] the removal of a person from the United Kingdom when required to do so by directions given under Schedule 2 or 3 to this Act [or under the Immigration and Asylum Act 1999]; or

[(iiia) he fails, without reasonable excuse, to comply with a direction under paragraph 5B of Schedule 2; or]

(iv) he fails, without reasonable excuse, to comply with [[any other requirement] imposed by or under Schedule 2]

(c) if, as a person concerned in the management of a port, he fails, without reasonable excuse, to take any steps required by Schedule 2 in relation to the embarkation or disembarkation of passengers where a control area is designated.

[(ca) if as a person concerned in the management of a port he fails, without reasonable excuse, to comply with a direction under paragraph 5B of Schedule 2.]

[(2) Proceedings may not be instituted against a person under subsection (1)(a)(i) or (1)(b)(iv) for a failure to provide information or otherwise to comply with a requirement imposed under paragraph 27, 27B or 27BA of Schedule 2 where—

(a) the person has paid a penalty in respect of the same failure, or a failure to provide the same information, by virtue of regulations made under—

(i) paragraph 27BB of Schedule 2,

(ii) section 32B of the Immigration, Asylum and Nationality Act 2006, or

(iii) section 24 of the Counter-Terrorism and Security Act 2015 (penalty for breach of authority-to-carry scheme); or

(b) proceedings have been instituted against the person under section 34 of the Immigration, Asylum and Nationality Act 2006 in respect of a failure to provide the same information.]

Note: Words in first square brackets in s 27 substituted by virtue of Criminal Justice Act 1982 and amended by Asylum and Immigration Act 1996 from 1 October 1996. Words in square brackets in subsection (b)(iv) substituted and words omitted from subsection (c) by Immigration, Asylum and Nationality Act 2006, s 31 from 1 March 2008 (SI 2007/3138 as amended by SI 2007/3580). Subsections (b)(iiia) and (ca) inserted and words in first square brackets in subsection (iv) substituted by Sch 8

Immigration Act 2014 from 28 July 2014 (SI 2014/1820). Other words in square brackets inserted by Immigration and Asylum Act 1999 from 2 October 2000. Section 27 has effect in a form modified by and in circumstances specified by the Channel Tunnel (International Arrangements) Order (SI 1993/1813) as amended by SIs 1994/1405, 2000/913, 2001/178, 2001/3707, 2006/1003 and 2007/3759. Subsection () inserted from 12 February 2015 by Counter Terrorism and Security Act 2015, Schedule 5.

28. Proceedings

[(A1) Proceedings for an offence under this Part that is committed in the territorial sea adjacent to the United Kingdom may be taken, and the offence may for all incidental purposes be treated as having been committed, in any place in the United Kingdom.]

(1) Where the offence is one to which, under section [[24(3)]], […] or 26 above, an extended time limit for prosecutions is to apply, then—

(a) an information relating to the offence may in England and Wales be tried by a magistrates' court if it is laid within six months after the commission of the offence, or if it is laid within three years after the commission of the offence and not more than two months after the date certified by [an officer of police above the rank of chief superintendent] to be the date on which evidence sufficient to justify proceedings came to the notice of an officer of [the police force to which he belongs] and;

(b) summary proceedings for the offence may in Scotland be commenced within six months after the commission of the offence, or within three years after the commission of the offence and not more than two months after the date on which evidence sufficient in the opinion of the Lord Advocate to justify proceedings came to his knowledge; and

(c) a complaint charging the commission of the offence may in Northern Ireland be heard and determined by a magistrates' court if it is made within six months after the commission of the offence, or if it is made within three years after the commission of the offence and not more than two months after the date certified by an officer of police not below the rank of assistant chief constable to be the date on which evidence sufficient to justify the proceedings came to the notice of the police in Northern Ireland.

[(1A) Where the offence is one to which, under section 24(3A), an extended time limit for prosecutions is to apply, then—

(a) an information relating to the offence may in England and Wales be tried by a magistrates' court if it is laid—

(i) within the period of six months beginning with the date of the commission of the offence, or

(ii) within the period of three months beginning with the date when the person is first arrested for the offence or under paragraph 10 of Schedule 10 to the Immigration Act 2016 (arrest for breach of bail condition), if that period expires after the end of the period mentioned in sub-paragraph (i),

(b) summary proceedings for the offence may in Scotland be commenced—

(i) within the period of six months beginning with the date of the commission of the offence, or

(ii) within the period of three months beginning with the date when the person is first arrested for the offence or under paragraph 10 of Schedule 10 to the Immigration Act 2016 (arrest for breach of bail condition), if that period expires after the end of the period mentioned in sub-paragraph (i), and

(c) a complaint charging the commission of an offence under this paragraph may in Northern Ireland be heard and determined by a magistrates' court if it is made—

(i) within the period of six months beginning with the date of the commission of the offence, or

(ii) within the period of three months beginning with the date when the person is first arrested for the offence or under paragraph 10 of Schedule 10 to the Immigration Act 2016 (arrest for breach of bail condition), if that period expires after the end of the period mentioned in sub-paragraph (i).]

(2) For purposes of [[subsections(1)(b) and (1A)(b)]] above proceedings shall be deemed to be commenced on the date on which a warrant to apprehend or to cite the accused is granted, if such warrant is executed without undue delay; and a certificate of the Lord Advocate as to the date on which such evidence as is mentioned in subsection (1)(b) and (1A)(b) came to his knowledge shall be conclusive evidence.

[(2A) Section 3 of the Territorial Waters Jurisdiction Act 1878 (consent of Secretary of State for certain prosecutions) does not apply to proceedings for an offence under [[..]] {this Part}]

(3) For the purposes of the trial of a person for an offence under this Part of this Act, the offence shall be deemed to have been committed either at the place at which it actually was committed or at any place at which he may be.

(4) Any powers exercisable under this Act in the case of any person may be exercised notwithstanding that proceedings for an offence under this Part of this Act have been taken against him.

Note: Words omitted from subsection (1) by Nationality, Immigration and Asylum Act 2002, s 156 from 10 February 2003 (SI 2003/1). Words in square brackets in s 28(1)(a) substituted by Immigration Act 1988. Words in double square brackets substituted in subsection (1) and (2) by Schedule 10, para 17 to the Immigration Act 2016 from January 15, 2018 subject to transitional provisions in SI2017/1241. Subsection (1A) inserted by Schedule 10, para 17 to the Immigration Act 2016 from 15 January 2018 subject to transitional provisions in SI2017/1241. Words substituted in double square brackets by Immigration and Social Security Co-ordination (EU Withdrawal) Act 2020 (Consequential, Saving, Transitional and Transitory Provisions) (EU Exit) Regulations 2020/1309 Sch.1 para 9(a)(iv) (December 31, 2020: substitution has effect subject to saving provisions in SI 2020/1309 Sch.1 para 1((9)). Words substituted in curly brackets in subsection (2A) by Nationality and Borders Act 2022 c.36 Sch.6 para 4(b) (August 24, 2022). Subsection (A1) inserted by Nationality and Borders Act 2022 c.36 Sch.6 para 4(a) (date to be appointed).

[28A. Arrest without warrant

(1) [An] immigration officer may arrest without warrant a person—

(a) who has committed or attempted to commit an offence under section 24 or 24A; or

(b) whom he has reasonable grounds for suspecting has committed or attempted to commit such an offence.

(2) But subsection (1) does not apply in relation to an offence under section 24(1)(d).

(3) An immigration officer may arrest without warrant a person—

(a) who has committed{{or attempted to commit an offence}} an offence under section [[[24B]], {24C,} 25, 25A or 25B]; or

(b) whom he has reasonable grounds for suspecting has committed {{or attempted to commit}} that offence.

(4) . . .

(5) An immigration officer may arrest without warrant a person ('the suspect') who, or whom he has reasonable grounds for suspecting—

(a) has committed or attempted to commit an offence under section 26(1)(g); or

(b) is committing or attempting to commit that offence.

(6) The power conferred by subsection (5) is exercisable only if either the first or the second condition is satisfied.

(7) The first condition is that it appears to the officer that service of a summons (or, in Scotland, a copy complaint) is impracticable or inappropriate because—

(a) he does not know, and cannot readily discover, the suspect's name;

(b) he has reasonable grounds for doubting whether a name given by the suspect as his name is his real name;

(c) the suspect has failed to give him a satisfactory address for service; or

(d) he has reasonable grounds for doubting whether an address given by the suspect is a satisfactory address for service.

(8) The second condition is that the officer has reasonable grounds for believing that arrest is necessary to prevent the suspect—

(a) causing physical injury to himself or another person;

(b) suffering physical injury; or

(c) causing loss of or damage to property.

(9) For the purposes of subsection (7), an address is a satisfactory address for service if it appears to the officer—

(a) that the suspect will be at that address for a sufficiently long period for it to be possible to serve him with a summons (or copy complaint); or

(b) that some other person specified by the suspect will accept service of a summons (or copy complaint) for the suspect at that address.

[(9A) [An] immigration officer may arrest without warrant a person—

(a) who has committed an offence under section 26A or 26B; or

(b) who he has reasonable grounds for suspecting has committed an offence under section 26A or 26B.]

[(9B) An immigration officer may arrest without warrant a person who, or whom the immigration officer has reasonable grounds for suspecting—

(a) has committed or attempted to commit an offence under section 21(1) or (1A) of the Immigration, Asylum and Nationality Act 2006 (employment of illegal worker etc), or

(b) is committing or attempting to commit that offence].

[(9C) An immigration officer may arrest without warrant a person who, or whom the immigration officer has reasonable grounds for suspecting—

(a) has committed or attempted to commit an offence under section 33A or 33B of the Immigration Act 2014 (offences relating to residential tenancies), or

(b) is committing or attempting to commit that offence.]

(10) In relation to the exercise of the powers conferred by subsections (3)(b){, [[(5)and {(9B)]] and (9C)}, it is immaterial that no offence has been committed.

(11) In Scotland the powers conferred by subsections (3){,[[(5) and (9B)]] and (9C)} may also be exercised by a constable.]

Note: Section 28A inserted by Immigration and Asylum Act 1999 from 14 February 2000. Words in square brackets in subsection (3)(a) substituted by and subsection (4) omitted by Nationality, Immigration and Asylum Act 2002, s 144 from 10 February 2003 (SI 2003/1). Subsection (9A) inserted by Nationality, Immigration and Asylum Act 2002, s 150 from 10 February 2003 (SI

2003/1). Words omitted from subsections (10) and (11) by Nationality, Immigration and Asylum Act 2002, s 144 from 10 February 2003 (SI 2003/1). Words in square brackets in subsections (1) and (9A) substituted (England and Wales) by Serious Organised Crime and Police Act 2005, Schedule 7 paragraph 53 from 1 April 2006 (SI 2006/378). Subsection (9B) and words in double square brackets inserted and substituted at subsection (10) and (11) by Immigration Act 2016, s 34 from 12 July 2016 (SI 2016/603). Subsection (9C) and words in curly brackets at (10) and (11) inserted and substituted by Immigration Act 2016, s 39 from 1 November 2016 (SI 2016/1037). Words inserted in curly brackets in section 28A are inserted by the Immigration Act 2016, s 44 from date to be appointed. Words in double curly brackets at subsections (3)(a) and (b) inserted by Sch 14 to the Immigration Act 2016 from 31 May 2016 (SI 2016/603).

[28AA. Arrest with warrant

(1) This section applies if on an application by an immigration officer a justice of the peace is satisfied that there are reasonable grounds for suspecting that a person has committed an offence under [section 24(1)(d)].

(2) The justice of the peace may grant a warrant authorising any immigration officer to arrest the person.

(3) In the application of this section to Scotland a reference to a justice of the peace shall be treated as a reference to the sheriff or a justice of the peace.]

Note: Section 28AA inserted by Nationality, Immigration and Asylum Act 2002, s 152 from 10 February 2003 (SI 2003/1). Subsection (1)(b) substituted by UK Borders Act 2007, s 27 from 29 February 2008 (SI 2008/309). Words in square brackets substituted by Immigration Act 2016, s 35 from 12 July 2016 (SI 2016/603).

[28B. Search and arrest by warrant

(1) Subsection (2) applies if a justice of the peace is, by written information on oath, satisfied that there are reasonable grounds for suspecting that a person ('the suspect') who is liable to be arrested for a relevant offence is to be found on any premises.

(2) The justice may grant a warrant authorising any immigration officer or constable to enter, if need be by force, the premises named in the warrant for the purpose of searching for and arresting the suspect.

(3) Subsection (4) applies if in Scotland the sheriff or a justice of the peace is by evidence on oath satisfied as mentioned in subsection (1).

(4) The sheriff or justice may grant a warrant authorising any immigration officer or constable to enter, if need be by force, the premises named in the warrant for the purpose of searching for and arresting the suspect.

(5) 'Relevant offence' means an offence under section[[24(A1),(B1), (C1), (D1), (E1) or (1)(b)]], (c), (d),{{(f) or (h)}}, [24A, [[24B]],{24C}26A or 26B].]

Note: Section 28B inserted by Immigration and Asylum Act 1999 from 14 February 2000. Words in square brackets in subsection (5) substituted by Nationality, Immigration and Asylum Act 2002, ss 144, 150 from 10 February 2003 (SI 2003/1). Words in double square brackets inserted at subsection (5) by Immigration Act, s.34 from 12 July 2016 (SI 2016/603). Words in curly brackets at subsection (5) inserted by Immigration Act 2016, s 44 from a date to be appointed. Words in double curly brackets at subsection (5) substituted by Immigration Act 2016, Schedule 10, para 18 from January 15, 2018 subject to transitional provisions in SI 2017/1241. Words in double brackets substituted in subsection 5 by Nationality and Borders Act 2022 c.36 s.40(5) (June 28, 2022: substitution has effect as SI 2022/590 reg.2 and Sch.1 para.20 subject to transitional and savings provisions specified in SI 2022/590 reg.3 and Sch.2 para 7)

[28C. Search and arrest without warrant

(1) An immigration officer may enter and search any premises for the purpose of arresting a person for an offence under [section 25, 25A or 25B].

(2) The power may be exercised—

(a) only to the extent that it is reasonably required for that purpose; and

(b) only if the officer has reasonable grounds for believing that the person whom he is seeking is on the premises.

(3) In relation to premises consisting of two or more separate dwellings, the power is limited to entering and searching—

(a) any parts of the premises which the occupiers of any dwelling comprised in the premises use in common with the occupiers of any such other dwelling; and

(b) any such dwelling in which the officer has reasonable grounds for believing that the person whom he is seeking may be.

(4) The power may be exercised only if the officer produces identification showing that he is an immigration officer (whether or not he is asked to do so).]

Note: Section 28C inserted by Immigration and Asylum Act 1999 from 14 February 2000. Words in square brackets in subsection (1) substituted by Nationality, Immigration and Asylum Act 2002, s 144 from 10 February 2003 (SI 2003/1).

[28CA. Business premises: entry to arrest

(1) A constable or immigration officer may enter and search any business premises for the purpose of arresting a person—

(a) for an offence under section 24,

(b) for an offence under section 24A,

[(ba) for an offence under section 24B],

[(bb) for an offence under section 24 C, or]

(c) under paragraph 17 of Schedule 2.

(2) The power under subsection (1) may be exercised only—

(a) to the extent that it is reasonably required for a purpose specified in subsection (1),

(b) if the constable or immigration officer has reasonable grounds for believing that the person whom he is seeking is on the premises,

(c) with the authority of the Secretary of State (in the case of an immigration officer) or a Chief Superintendent (in the case of a constable), and

(d) if the constable or immigration officer produces identification showing his status.

(3) Authority for the purposes of subsection (2)(c)—

(a) may be given on behalf of the Secretary of State only by a civil servant of the rank of at least Assistant Director, and

(b) shall expire at the end of the period of seven days beginning with the day on which it is given.

(4) Subsection (2)(d) applies—

(a) whether or not a constable or immigration officer is asked to produce identification, but

(b) only where premises are occupied.

(5) Subsection (6) applies where a constable or immigration officer—

(a) enters premises in reliance on this section, and

(b) detains a person on the premises.

(6) A detainee custody officer may enter the premises for the purpose of carrying out a search.

(7) In subsection (6)—

'detainee custody officer' means a person in respect of whom a certificate of authorisation is in force under section 154 of the Immigration and Asylum Act 1999 (c. 33) (detained persons: escort and custody), and

'search' means a search under paragraph 2(1)(a) of Schedule 13 to that Act (escort arrangements: power to search detained person).]

Note: Section 28CA inserted by Nationality, Immigration and Asylum Act 2002, s 153 from 10 February 2003 (SI 2003/1). Subsection (ba) inserted by Immigration Act 2016, s 34 from 12 July 2016 (SI 2016/603). Words in curly brackets at subsection (1)(ba) are inserted by Immigration Act 2016, s 34 from 12 July 2016 (SI 2016/603). Subsection (1)(bb) inserted by the Immigration Act 2016, s 44 from a date to be appointed.

[28D. Entry and search of premises

(1) If, on an application made by an immigration officer, a justice of the peace is satisfied that there are reasonable grounds for believing that—

(a) a relevant offence has been committed,

(b) there is material on premises [[mentioned in subsection (1A)]] which is likely to be of substantial value (whether by itself or together with other material) to the investigation of the offence,

(c) the material is likely to be relevant evidence,

(d) the material does not consist of or include items subject to legal privilege, excluded material or special procedure material, and

(e) any of the conditions specified in subsection (2) applies, he may issue a warrant authorising an immigration officer to enter and search the premises [[in relation to each set of premises specified in the application]].

[(1A) The premises referred to in subsection (1)(b) above are—

(a) one or more sets of premises specified in the application, or

(b) subject to subsection (2A), any premises occupied or controlled by a person specified in the application, including such sets of premises as are so specified (in which case the application is for an 'all premises warrant').

(1B) If the application is for an all premises warrant, the justice of the peace must also be satisfied—

(a) that because of the particulars of the offence referred to in paragraph (a) of subsection (1), there are reasonable grounds for believing that it is necessary to search premises occupied or controlled by the person in question which are not specified in the application in order to find the material referred to in paragraph (b) of that subsection, and

(b) that it is not reasonably practicable to specify in the application all the premises which the person occupies or controls and which might need to be searched.

(1C) Subject to subsection (2A), the warrant may authorise entry to and search of premises on more than one occasion if, on the application, the justice of the peace is satisfied that it is necessary to authorise multiple entries in order to achieve the purpose for which the justice issues the warrant.

(1D) If it authorises multiple entries, the number of entries authorised may be unlimited, or limited to a maximum.]

(2) The conditions [[referred to in subsection (1)(e)]] are that—

(a) it is not practicable to communicate with any person entitled to grant entry to the premises;

(b) it is practicable to communicate with a person entitled to grant entry to the premises but it is not practicable to communicate with any person entitled to grant access to the evidence;

(c) entry to the premises will not be granted unless a warrant is produced;

(d) the purpose of a search may be frustrated or seriously prejudiced unless an immigration officer arriving at the premises can secure immediate entry to them.

[(2A) A justice of the peace in Scotland may not issue—

(a) an all premises warrant under this section, or

(b) a warrant under this section authorising multiple entries.]

(3) An immigration officer may seize and retain anything for which a search has been authorised under subsection (1).

(4) 'Relevant offence' means an offence under section[[24(A1), (B1), (C1), (D1), (E1) or (1)(b)]], (c), (d),{(f) or (h)}, [24A, [[24B]], {24C}, 25, 25A, 25B, 26A or 26B].

(5) In relation to England and Wales, expressions which are given a meaning by the Police and Criminal Evidence Act 1984 have the same meaning when used in this section.

(6) In relation to Northern Ireland, expressions which are given a meaning by the Police and Criminal Evidence (Northern Ireland) Order 1989 have the same meaning when used in this section.

(7) In the application of [[this section]] to Scotland—

(a) read [[references]] to a justice of the peace as [[references]] to the sheriff or a justice of the peace; and

(b) in [[subsection (1)(d)]], omit the reference to excluded material and special procedure material.]

Note: Section 28D inserted by Immigration and Asylum Act 1999 from 14 February 2000. Words in square brackets in subsection (4) substituted by Nationality, Immigration and Asylum Act 2002, ss 144, 150 from 10 February 2003 (SI 2003/1). Words in double square brackets at subsection (4) inserted by Immigration Act 2016, s 34 from 12 July 2016 (SI 2016/603).Words in curly brackets in subsection (4) inserted by the Immigration Act 2016, s 44 from a date to be appointed. Words in double curly brackets in subsection (4) inserted by the Immigration Act 2016, s 34 on 1 December 2014. Words in double square brackets substituted in subsections (1)(b) and (e), (2) and (7), (7)(1)(a) and (b) by Immigration Act 2016, Schedule 8 from 1 December 2016 (SI 2016/1037). Words inserted at subsection (1A)–(1D), and (2A) inserted by Immigration Act 2016, Schedule 8 from 1 December 2016 (SI 2016/1037). Words in double square brackets in subsection (7) by Immigration Act 2016, Schedule 8 from 1 December 2016 (SI 2016/1037). Words in double square brackets substituted at subsection (4) by Immigration Act 2016, Schedule 10, para 19 from January 15, 2018 subject to transitional provisions in SI 2017/1241. Words in double square brackets substituted by Nationality and Borders Act 2022 c.36 Pt 3 s.40(6) (June 28, 2022: substitution has effect as SI 2022/590 reg.2 and Sch.1 para.20 subject to transitional and savings provisions specified in SI 2022/590 reg.3 and Sch.2 para.7)

[28E. Entry and search of premises following arrest

(1) This section applies if a person is arrested for an offence under this Part at a place other than a police station.

(2) An immigration officer may enter and search any premises—

(a) in which the person was when arrested, or

(b) in which he was immediately before he was arrested, for evidence relating to the offence for which the arrest was made ('relevant evidence').

(3) The power may be exercised—

(a) only if the officer has reasonable grounds for believing that there is relevant evidence on the premises; and

(b) only to the extent that it is reasonably required for the purpose of discovering relevant evidence.

(4) In relation to premises consisting of two or more separate dwellings, the power is limited to entering and searching—

(a) any dwelling in which the arrest took place or in which the arrested person was immediately before his arrest; and

(b) any parts of the premises which the occupier of any such dwelling uses in common with the occupiers of any other dwellings comprised in the premises.

(5) An officer searching premises under subsection (2) may seize and retain anything he finds which he has reasonable grounds for believing is relevant evidence.

(6) Subsection (5) does not apply to items which the officer has reasonable grounds for believing are items subject to legal privilege.]

Note: Section 28E inserted by Immigration and Asylum Act 1999 from 14 February 2000.

[28F. Entry and search of premises following arrest under section 25, 25A or 25B

(1) An immigration officer may enter and search any premises occupied or controlled by a person arrested for an offence under [section 25, 25A, 25B.]

(2) The power may be exercised—

(a) only if the officer has reasonable grounds for suspecting that there is relevant evidence on the premises;

(b) only to the extent that it is reasonably required for the purpose of discovering relevant evidence; and

(c) subject to subsection (3), only if a senior officer has authorised it in writing.

(3) The power may be exercised—

(a) before taking the arrested person to a place where he is to be detained; and

(b) without obtaining an authorisation under subsection (2)(c), if the presence of that person at a place other than one where he is to be detained is necessary for the effective investigation of the offence.

(4) An officer who has relied on subsection (3) must inform a senior officer as soon as is practicable.

(5) The officer authorising a search, or who is informed of one under subsection (4), must make a record in writing of—

(a) the grounds for the search; and

(b) the nature of the evidence that was sought.

(6) An officer searching premises under this section may seize and retain anything he finds which he has reasonable grounds for suspecting is relevant evidence.

(7) 'Relevant evidence' means evidence, other than items subject to legal privilege, that relates to the offence in question.

(8) 'Senior officer' means an immigration officer not below the rank of chief immigration officer.]

Note: Section 28F inserted by Immigration and Asylum Act 1999 from 14 February 2000. Words in square brackets in subsection (1) substituted by Nationality, Immigration and Asylum Act 2002, s 144 from 10 February 2003 (SI 2003/1).

[28FA. Search for personnel records: warrant unnecessary

(1) This section applies where—

(a) a person has been arrested for an offence under section 24[[]] or 24A(1),

(b) a person has been arrested under paragraph 17 of Schedule 2,

(c) a constable or immigration officer reasonably believes that a person is liable to arrest for an offence under section 24[[]], [[24A(1) or 24B(1)]]

(d) a constable or immigration officer reasonably believes that a person is liable to arrest under paragraph 17 of Schedule 2.

(2) A constable or immigration officer may search business premises where the arrest was made or where the person liable to arrest is if the constable or immigration officer reasonably believes—

(a) that a person has committed an immigration employment offence in relation to the person arrested or liable to arrest, and

(b) that employee records, other than items subject to legal privilege, will be found on the premises and will be of substantial value (whether on their own or together with other material) in the investigation of the immigration employment offence.

(3) A constable or officer searching premises under subsection (2) may seize and retain employee records, other than items subject to legal privilege, which he reasonably suspects will be of substantial value (whether on their own or together with other material) in the investigation of—

(a) an immigration employment offence, or

(b) an offence under section 105 or 106 of the Immigration and Asylum Act 1999 (c. 33) (support for asylum-seeker: fraud).

(4) The power under subsection (2) may be exercised only—

(a) to the extent that it is reasonably required for the purpose of discovering employee records other than items subject to legal privilege,

(b) if the constable or immigration officer produces identification showing his status, and

(c) if the constable or immigration officer reasonably believes that at least one of the conditions in subsection (5) applies.

(5) Those conditions are—

(a) that it is not practicable to communicate with a person entitled to grant access to the records,

(b) that permission to search has been refused,

(c) that permission to search would be refused if requested, and

(d) that the purpose of a search may be frustrated or seriously prejudiced if it is not carried out in reliance on subsection (2).

(6) Subsection (4)(b) applies—

(a) whether or not a constable or immigration officer is asked to produce identification, but

(b) only where premises are occupied.

(7) In this section 'immigration employment offence' means [an offence under section 21 of the Immigration, Asylum and Nationality Act 2006] (employment).]

Note: Section 28FA inserted by Nationality, Immigration and Asylum Act 2002, s 154 from 10 February 2003 (SI 2003/1). Words in square brackets in subsection (7) substituted by UK Borders Act 2007, s 28 from 29 February 2008 (SI 2008/309). Words in double square brackets inserted by Immigration Act 2016, s 34 from 12 July 2016 (SI 2016/303). Word in double square brackets in subsection (1)(a) & (c) substituted by Nationality and Borders Act 2022 c.36 Pt3 s.40(7)(a) &(b) (June 28, 22: substitution has effect as SI 2022/590 reg.2 and Sch.1 para.20 subject to transitional and saving provisions specified in SI 2022/590 reg.3 and Sch.2 para.7)

[28FB. Search for personnel records: with warrant

(1) This section applies where on an application made by an immigration officer in respect of business premises [[mentioned in subsection (1A)]] a justice of the peace is satisfied that there are reasonable grounds for believing—

(a) that an employer has provided inaccurate or incomplete information under section 134 of the Nationality, Immigration and Asylum Act 2002 (compulsory disclosure by employer),

(b) that employee records, other than items subject to legal privilege, will be found on the premises and will enable deduction of some or all of the information which the employer was required to provide, and

(c) that at least one of the conditions in subsection (2) is satisfied [[in relation to each set of premises specified in the application]].

[(1A) The premises referred to in subsection (1) above are—

(a) one or more sets of premises specified in the application, or

(b) subject to subsection (3C), any premises occupied or controlled by a person specified in the application, including such sets of premises as are so specified (in which case the application is for an 'all premises warrant').

(1B) If the application is for an all premises warrant, the justice of the peace must also be satisfied—

(a) that there are reasonable grounds for believing that it is necessary to search premises occupied or controlled by the person in question which are not specified in the application in order to find the records referred to in subsection (1)(b), and

(b) that it is not reasonably practicable to specify in the application all the premises which the person occupies or controls and which might need to be searched.]

(2) [[The conditions referred to in subsection (1)(c) are]]

(a) that it is not practicable to communicate with a person entitled to grant access to the premises,

(b) that it is not practicable to communicate with a person entitled to grant access to the records,

(c) that entry to the premises or access to the records will not be granted unless a warrant is produced, and

(d) that the purpose of a search may be frustrated or seriously prejudiced unless an immigration officer arriving at the premises can secure immediate entry.

(3) The justice of the peace may issue a warrant authorising an immigration officer to enter and search the premises.

[(3A) Subject to subsection (3C), the warrant may authorise entry to and search of premises on more than one occasion if, on the application, the justice of the peace is satisfied that it is necessary to authorise multiple entries in order to achieve the purpose for which the justice issues the warrant.

(3B) If it authorises multiple entries, the number of entries authorised may be unlimited, or limited to a maximum.

(3C) A justice of the peace in Scotland may not issue—
an all premises warrant under this section, or
a warrant under this section authorising multiple entries.]

(4) Subsection (7)(a) of section 28D shall have effect for the purposes of this section as it has effect for the purposes of that section.

(5) An immigration officer searching premises under a warrant issued under this section may seize and retain employee records, other than items subject to legal privilege, which he reasonably suspects will be of substantial value (whether on their own or together with other material) in the investigation of—

(a) an offence under section 137 of the Nationality, Immigration and Asylum Act 2002 (disclosure of information: offences) in respect of a requirement under section 134 of that Act, or

(b) an offence under section 105 or 106 of the Immigration and Asylum Act 1999 (c. 33) (support for asylum-seeker: fraud).]

Note: Section 28FB inserted by Nationality, Immigration and Asylum Act 2002, s 154 from 10 February 2003 (SI 2003/1). Words in double square brackets inserted at subsections (1) and (2) by Immigration Act 2016, Schedule 8 from 1 December 2016 (SI 2016/1037). Subsections (1A)–(1B) and (3A)–(3C) inserted by Immigration Act 2016, Schedule 8 from 1 December 2016 (SI 2016/1037).

[28G. Searching arrested persons

(1) This section applies if a person is arrested for an offence under this Part at a place other than a police station.

(2) An immigration officer may search the arrested person if he has reasonable grounds for believing that the arrested person may present a danger to himself or others.

(3) The officer may search the arrested person for—

(a) anything which he might use to assist his escape from lawful custody; or

(b) anything which might be evidence relating to the offence for which he has been arrested.

(4) The power conferred by subsection (3) may be exercised—

(a) only if the officer has reasonable grounds for believing that the arrested person may have concealed on him anything of a kind mentioned in that subsection; and

(b) only to the extent that it is reasonably required for the purpose of discovering any such thing.

(5) A power conferred by this section to search a person is not to be read as authorising an officer to require a person to remove any of his clothing in public other than an outer coat, jacket or glove; but it does authorise the search of a person's mouth.

(6) An officer searching a person under subsection (2) may seize and retain anything he finds, if he has reasonable grounds for believing that that person might use it to cause physical injury to himself or to another person.

(7) An officer searching a person under subsection (3) may seize and retain anything he finds, if he has reasonable grounds for believing—

(a) that that person might use it to assist his escape from lawful custody; or

(b) that it is evidence which relates to the offence in question.

(8) Subsection (7)(b) does not apply to an item subject to legal privilege.]

Note: Section 28G inserted by Immigration and Asylum Act 1999 from 14 February 2000.

[28H. Searching persons in police custody

(1) This section applies if a person—

(a) has been arrested for an offence under this Part; and

(b) is in custody at a police station or in police detention at a place other than a police station.

(2) An immigration officer may at any time, search the arrested person in order to see whether he has with him anything—

(a) which he might use to—

(i) cause physical injury to himself or others;

(ii) damage property;

(iii) interfere with evidence; or

(iv) assist his escape; or

(b) which the officer has reasonable grounds for believing is evidence relating to the offence in question.

(3) The power may be exercised only to the extent that the custody officer concerned considers it to be necessary for the purpose of discovering anything of a kind mentioned in subsection (2).

(4) An officer searching a person under this section may seize anything he finds, if he has reasonable grounds for believing that—

(a) that person might use it for one or more of the purposes mentioned in subsection (2)(a); or

(b) it is evidence relating to the offence in question.

(5) Anything seized under subsection (4)(a) may be retained by the police.

(6) Anything seized under subsection (4)(b) may be retained by an immigration officer.

(7) The person from whom something is seized must be told the reason for the seizure unless he is—

(a) violent or appears likely to become violent; or

(b) incapable of understanding what is said to him.

(8) An intimate search may not be conducted under this section.

(9) The person carrying out a search under this section must be of the same sex as the person searched.

(10) 'Custody officer'—

(a) in relation to England and Wales, has the same meaning as in the Police and Criminal Evidence Act 1984;

(b) in relation to Scotland, means the officer in charge of a police station; and

(c) in relation to Northern Ireland, has the same meaning as in the Police and Criminal Evidence (Northern Ireland) Order 1989.

(11) 'Intimate search'—

(a) in relation to England and Wales, has the meaning given by section 65 of the Act of 1984;

(b) in relation to Scotland, means a search which consists of the physical examination of a person's body orifices other than the mouth; and

(c) in relation to Northern Ireland, has the same meaning as in the 1989 Order.

(12) 'Police detention'—

(a) in relation to England and Wales, has the meaning given by section 118(2) of the 1984 Act; and

(b) in relation to Northern Ireland, has the meaning given by Article 2 of the 1989 Order.

(13) In relation to Scotland, a person is in police detention if—

(a) he has been taken to a police station after being arrested for an offence; or

(b) he is arrested at a police station after attending voluntarily at the station, accompanying a constable to it or being detained under section 14 of the Criminal Procedure (Scotland) Act 1995, and is detained there or is detained elsewhere in the charge of a constable, but is not in police detention if he is in court after being charged.]

Note: Section 28H inserted by Immigration and Asylum Act 1999 from 14 February 2000.

[28ZI Retention of seized material

(1) This section applies to anything seized by an immigration officer under this Part for the purposes of the investigation of an offence or on the basis that it may be evidence relating to an offence.

(2) Anything seized as mentioned in subsection (1) may be retained so long as is necessary in all the circumstances and in particular—

(a) may be retained, except as provided for by subsection (3)—

(i) for use as evidence at a trial for an offence, or

(ii) for forensic examination or for investigation in connection with an offence, and

(b) may be retained in order to establish its lawful owner, where there are reasonable grounds for believing that it has been obtained in consequence of the commission of an offence.

(3) Nothing may be retained for a purpose mentioned in subsection (2)(a) if a photograph or copy would be sufficient for that purpose.]

Note: Section 28ZI inserted by Immigration Act 2016, s 50 from 12 July 2016 (SI 2016/603).

[28I. Seized material: access and copying

(1) If a person showing himself—

(a) to be the occupier of the premises on which seized material was seized, or

(b) to have had custody or control of the material immediately before it was seized,

asks the immigration officer who seized the material for a record of what he seized, the officer must provide the record to that person within a reasonable time.

(2) If a relevant person asks an immigration officer for permission to be granted access to seized material, the officer must arrange for him to have access to the material under the supervision—

(a) in the case of seized material within subsection (8)(a), of an immigration officer;

(b) in the case of seized material within subsection (8)(b), of a constable.

(3) An immigration officer may photograph or copy, or have photographed or copied, seized material.

(4) If a relevant person asks an immigration officer for a photograph or copy of seized material, the officer must arrange for—

(a) that person to have access to the material for the purpose of photographing or copying it under the supervision—

(i) in the case of seized material within subsection (8)(a), of an immigration officer;

(ii) in the case of seized material within subsection (8)(b), of a constable; or

(b) the material to be photographed or copied.

(5) A photograph or copy made under subsection (4)(b) must be supplied within a reasonable time.

(6) There is no duty under this section to arrange for access to, or the supply of a photograph or copy of, any material if there are reasonable grounds for believing that to do so would prejudice—

(a) the exercise of any functions in connection with which the material was seized; or

(b) an investigation which is being conducted under this Act, or any criminal proceedings which may be brought as a result.

(7) 'Relevant person' means—

(a) a person who had custody or control of seized material immediately before it was seized, or

(b) someone acting on behalf of such a person.

(8) 'Seized material' means anything—

(a) seized and retained by an immigration officer, or

(b) seized by an immigration officer and retained by the police, under this Part.]

Note: Section 28I inserted by Immigration and Asylum Act 1999 from 14 February 2000.

[28J. Search warrants: safeguards

(1) The entry or search of premises under a warrant is unlawful unless it complies with this section and section 28K.

(2) If an immigration officer applies for a warrant, he must—

(a) state the ground on which he makes the application and the provision of this Act under which the warrant would be issued;

[(aa) if the application is for a warrant authorising entry and search on more than one occasion, state the ground on which the officer applies for such a warrant, and whether the officer seeks a warrant authorising an unlimited number of entries, or (if not) the maximum number of entries desired];

(b) [[specify the matters set out in subsection (2A) below]]; and

(c) identify, so far as is practicable, the persons or articles to be sought.

[(2A) The matters which must be specified pursuant to subsection (2)(b) above are—

(a) if the application relates to one or more sets of premises specified in the application, each set of premises which it is desired to enter and search;

(b) if the application relates to any premises occupied or controlled by a person specified in the application—

(i) as many sets of premises which it is desired to enter and search as it is reasonably practicable to specify;

(ii) the person who is in occupation or control of those premises and any others which it is desired to enter and search;

(iii) why it is necessary to search more premises than those specified under sub-paragraph (i);

(iv) why it is not reasonably practicable to specify all the premises which it is desired to enter and search.]

(3) In Northern Ireland, an application for a warrant is to be supported by a complaint in writing and substantiated on oath.

(4) Otherwise, an application for a warrant is to be made ex parte and supported by an information in writing or, in Scotland, evidence on oath.

(5) The officer must answer on oath any question that the justice of the peace or sheriff hearing the application asks him.

(6) A warrant shall authorise an entry on one occasion only [[unless it specifies that it authorizes multiple entries]].

[(6A) If it specifies that it authorises multiple entries, it must also specify whether the number of entries authorised is unlimited, or limited to a specified maximum.]

(7) A warrant must specify—

(a) the name of the person applying for it;

(b) the date on which it is issued;

[[(c) each set of premises to be searched, or (in the case of an all premises warrant) the person who is in occupation or control of premises to be searched, together with any premises under the person's occupation or control which can be specified and which are to be searched; and]].

(d) the provision of this Act under which it is issued.

(8) A warrant must identify, so far as is practicable, the persons or articles to be sought.

(9) [[Two copies must be made of a warrant which specifies only one set of premises and does not authorise multiple entries; and as many copies as are reasonably required may be made of any other kind of warrant.]]

(10) The copies must be clearly certified as copies.

[(10A) 'All premises warrant' means a warrant issued in response to an application of the kind mentioned in section 24E(6)(b), 28D(1A)(b) or 28FB(1A)(b) or paragraph 25A(6AA)(b) of Schedule 2.

(10B) References in this section to a warrant authorising multiple entries is to a warrant of the kind mentioned in section 24E(8), 28D(1C) or 28FB(3A) or paragraph 25A(6AC) of Schedule 2.]

(11) 'Warrant' means a warrant to enter and search premises issued to an immigration officer under this Part or under paragraph 17(2) [or 25A(6A)] of Schedule 2.]

Note: Section 28J inserted by Immigration and Asylum Act 1999 from 14 February 2000. Words in square brackets in subsection (11) inserted by Immigration Act 2014, Sch. 1 from 28 July 2014 (SI 2014/1820). Subsection (2)(aa), (2)(A), (6A), (10)(A)–(b) inserted by Immigration Act 2016, Sch. 8 from 1 December 2016 (SI 2016/1037). Words in double square brackets at subsections (2)(b), (6), (7)(c) and (9) substituted by Immigration Act 2016, Sch. 8 from 1 December (SI 2016/1037).

[28K. Execution of warrants

(1) A warrant may be executed by any immigration officer.

(2) A warrant may authorise persons to accompany the officer executing it.

(2A) A person so authorised has the same powers as the officer whom the person accompanies in respect of—

(a) the execution of the warrant, and

(b) the seizure or detention of anything to which the warrant relates.

(2B) But the person may exercise those powers only in the company, and under the supervision, of an immigration officer.]

(3) Entry and search under a warrant must be—

(a) within [[three months]] from the date of its issue; and

(b) at a reasonable hour, unless it appears to the officer executing it that the purpose of a search might be frustrated.

[**(3A)** If the warrant is an all premises warrant, no premises which are not specified in it may be entered or searched unless an immigration officer of at least the rank of chief immigration officer has in writing authorised them to be entered.

(3B) No premises may be entered or searched for the second or any subsequent time under a warrant which authorises multiple entries unless an immigration officer of at least the rank of chief immigration officer has in writing authorised that entry to those premises.]

(4) If the occupier of premises which are to be entered and searched is present at the time when an immigration officer seeks to execute a warrant, the officer must—

(a) identify himself to the occupier and [[if not in uniform]] produce identification showing that he is an immigration officer;

(b) show the occupier the warrant; and

(c) supply him with a copy of it.

(5) If—

(a) the occupier is not present, but

(b) some other person who appears to the officer to be in charge of the premises is present,

subsection (4) has effect as if each reference to the occupier were a reference to that other person.

(6) If there is no person present who appears to the officer to be in charge of the premises, the officer must leave a copy of the warrant in a prominent place on the premises.

(7) A search under a warrant may only be a search to the extent required for the purpose for which the warrant was issued.

(8) An officer executing a warrant must make an endorsement on it stating—

(a) whether the persons or articles sought were found; and

(b) whether any articles, other than articles which were sought, were seized.

[**(8A)** Unless the warrant is a warrant specifying one set of premises only, the officer must comply with subsection (8) separately in respect of each set of premises entered and searched.

(8B) Subject to subsection (8C), a warrant must be returned in accordance with subsection (9)—

(a) when it has been executed, or

(b) in the case of a specific premises warrant which has not been executed, an all premises warrant or any warrant authorising multiple entries, on the expiry of the period of three months referred to in subsection (3) or sooner.

(8C) Subsection (8B) does not apply to a warrant issued by a justice of the peace in Scotland or by the sheriff if the warrant has been executed.]

(9) [[The warrant]]must be returned—

[(a) if issued by a justice of the peace in England and Wales, to the designated officer for the local justice area in which the justice was acting when he issued the warrant;]

(b) if issued by a justice of the peace in Northern Ireland, to the clerk of petty sessions for the petty sessions district in which the premises are situated;

(c) if issued by a justice of the peace in Scotland, to the clerk of the district court for the commission area for which the justice of the peace was appointed;

(d) if issued by the sheriff, to the sheriff clerk.

(10) A warrant returned under subsection (9)(a) must be retained for 12 months by the [designated officer].

(11) A warrant issued under subsection (9)(b) or (c) must be retained for 12 months by the clerk.

(12) A warrant returned under subsection (9)(d) must be retained for 12 months by the sheriff clerk.

(13) If during that 12-month period the occupier of the premises to which it relates asks to inspect it, he must be allowed to do so.

[**(13A)** In subsection (8B)—

'specific premises warrant' means a warrant which is not an all premises warrant;

'all premises warrant' means a warrant issued in response to an application of the kind mentioned in section 24E(6)(b), 28D(1A)(b) or 28FB(1A)(b) or paragraph 25A(6AA)(b) of Schedule 2.

(13B) The reference in subsection (8B) to a warrant authorising multiple entries is to a warrant of the kind mentioned in section 24E(8), 28D(1C) or 28FB(3A) or paragraph 25A(6AC) of Schedule 2.]

(14) 'Warrant' means a warrant to enter and search premises issued to an immigration officer under this Part or under paragraph 17(2) [or 25A(6A)] of Schedule 2.]

Note: Section 28K inserted by Immigration and Asylum Act 1999 from 14 February 2000. Words in square brackets in subsections (9) and (10) substituted by Sch 8 Courts Act 2003 from 1 April 2005 (SI 2005/910). Words in square brackets in subsection (14) inserted by Immigration Act 2014 Sch 1 from 28 July 2014 (SI 2014/1820). Subsection (2A), (2B),(3A), (3B), (8A),(8B), (8C), (13A) and (13B) inserted by Immigration Act 2016, Schedule 8 from 1 December 2016 (SI 2016/1037). Words in double square brackets in subsections (3), (4(a)) and (9) substituted by Immigration Act 2016, Sch 8 from 1 December 2016 (SI 2016/1037).

[28L. Interpretation of Part III

[(1)] [[Subject to subsection (1A) in]] this Part, 'premises' and 'items subject to legal privilege' have the same meaning—

(a) in relation to England and Wales, as in the Police and Criminal Evidence Act 1984;

(b) in relation to Northern Ireland, as in the Police and Criminal Evidence (Northern Ireland) Order 1989; and

(c) in relation to Scotland, as in {section 412 of the Proceeds of Crime Act 2002}.

[[(1A) in this Part "premises" also includes any artificial island, installations or structure (including one in territorial sea adjacent to the United Kingdom).]]

[(2) In this Part, 'business premises' means premises (or any part of premises) not used as a dwelling.

(3) In this Part, 'employee records' means records which show an employee's—

(a) name,

(b) date of birth,

(c) address,

(d) length of service,

(e) rate of pay, or

(f) nationality or citizenship.

(4) The Secretary of State may by order amend section 28CA(3)(a) to reflect a change in nomenclature.

(5) An order under subsection (4)—

(a) must be made by statutory instrument, and

(b) shall be subject to annulment in pursuance of a resolution of either House of Parliament.]

Note: Section 28L inserted by Immigration and Asylum Act 1999 from 14 February 2000. Words in curly brackets in subsection (1) substituted from 24 February 2003 by Proceeds of Crime Act 2002 Sch 11. Subsections (2)–(5) inserted by Nationality, Immigration and Asylum Act 2002, s 155 from 10 February 2003 (SI 2003/1). Words inserted in double square brackets in subsection (1), and subsection (1A) by Nationality and Borders Act 2022 c.36 Sch.6 para 5 (date to be appointed)

PART 3A
MARITIME ENFORCEMENT

28LA Enforcement powers in relation to ships: United Kingdom

(1) An immigration officer or an enforcement officer may exercise the powers set out in Part A1 of Schedule 4A ("Part A1 powers") in relation to any of the following in United Kingdom waters, foreign waters or international waters—

(a) a United Kingdom ship;

(b) a ship without nationality;

(c) a foreign ship;

(d) a ship registered under the law of a relevant territory.

(2) But Part A1 powers may be exercised only—

(a) for the purpose of preventing, detecting, investigating or prosecuting a relevant offence, and

(b) in accordance with the rest of this section.

(3) The authority of the Secretary of State is required before an immigration officer or an enforcement officer may exercise Part A1 powers in relation to—

(a) a United Kingdom ship in foreign waters,

(b) a ship without nationality,

(c) a foreign ship, or

(d) a ship registered under the law of a relevant territory.

Note: inserted by Nationality and Borders Act 2022 c.36 Sch.7 para 2 (June 28, 2022: insertion has effect as SI2022/590 reg.2 and Sch.1 para 22 subject to transitional and savings provision specified in SI2022/590 reg.3 and Sch.2 para 8)

[28M. Enforcement powers in relation to ships: England and Wales

(1) [[An English and Welsh constable]] may exercise the powers set out in Part 1 of Schedule 4A ('Part 1 powers') in relation to any of the following in England and Wales waters—

(a) a United Kingdom ship;

(b) a ship without nationality;

(c) a foreign ship;

(d) a ship registered under the law of a relevant territory.

(2) But Part 1 powers may be exercised only—

(a) for the purpose of preventing, detecting, investigating or prosecuting an offence under

(i) {section 24B,} 25, [[or 25A]], {or

(ii) section 21 of the Immigration, Asylum and Nationality Act 2006, and

(b) in accordance with the rest of this section.

(3) The authority of the Secretary of State is required before[[..]], an English and Welsh constable [[..]]may exercise Part 1 powers in relation to a foreign ship, or a ship registered under the law of a relevant territory, within the territorial sea adjacent to the United Kingdom.

(4) Authority for the purposes of subsection (3) may be given in relation to a foreign ship only if the Convention permits the exercise of Part 1 powers in relation to the ship.]

Note: Subsection 28M inserted by paragraph 7 of Schedule 14 to the Immigration Act 2016 from 31 May 2016(SI 2016/603). Words substituted in double square brackets by Immigration and Social Security (Co-ordination (EU Withdrawal) Act 2020 (Consequential, Saving, Transitional and Transitory Provisions) (EU Exit) Regulations 2020/1309 Sch.1 para 1(a)(vii) (December 31, 2020: substitution has effect subject to saving provisions in SI 2020/1309 Sch.1 para 1((5)). Words substituted and inserted in curly brackets at subsection (2)(a) by Nationality and Borders Act 2022 c.36 Sch.6 para 6 (date to be appointed). Words in double square brackets substituted in subsection (1) and omitted in subsection (3) by Nationality and Borders Act 2022 c.36 Sch.7 para 2(3)(a) & (b)(June 28: omission has effect as SI 2022/590/reg.2 and Sch.1 para 22 subject to transitional and saving provisions specified in SI 2022/590 reg.3 and sch.2 para 8).

[28N. Enforcement powers in relation to ships: Scotland

(1) [[A Scottish constable]] may exercise the powers set out in Part 2 of Schedule 4A ('Part 2 powers') in relation to any of the following in Scotland waters—

(a) a United Kingdom ship;

(b) a ship without nationality;

(c) a foreign ship;

(d) a ship registered under the law of a relevant territory.

(2) But Part 2 powers may be exercised only—

(a) for the purpose of preventing, detecting, investigating or prosecuting an offence under

{(i) section 24 B, section 25, [[or 25A]], or

(ii) section 21 of the Immigration, Asylum and Nationality Act 2006, and}

(b) in accordance with the rest of this section.

(3) The authority of the Secretary of State is required before[[..]], a Scottish constable [[..]]may exercise Part 2 powers in relation to a foreign ship, or a ship registered under the law of a relevant territory, within the territorial sea adjacent to the United Kingdom.

(4) Authority for the purposes of subsection (3) may be given in relation to a foreign ship only if the Convention permits the exercise of Part 2 powers in relation to the ship.]

Note: Subsection 28N inserted by paragraph 7 of Schedule 14 to the Immigration Act 2016 from 31 May 2016 (SI 2016/603). Words substituted in double square brackets at subsection (2)(a) by Immigration and Social Security (Co-ordination (EU Withdrawal) Act 2020 (Consequential, Saving, Transitional and Transitory Provisions) (EU Exit) Regulations 2020/1309 Sch.1 para 1(a)(viii) (December 31, 2020: substitution has effect subject to saving provisions in SI 2020/1309 Sch.1 para 1((5)). Words substituted in curly brackets at subsection (2)(a) by Nationality and Borders Act 2022 c.36 Sch.6 para 7 (date to be appointed). Words in double square brackets substituted in subsection (1) and omitted in subsection (3) by Nationality and Borders Act 2022 c.36 Sch.7 para 2(4)(a) & (b)(June 28: omission has effect as SI 2022/590/reg.2 and Sch.1 para 22 subject to transitional and saving provisions specified in SI 2022/590 reg.3 and sch.2 para 8).

[28O. Enforcement powers in relation to ships: Northern Ireland

(1) [[A Northern Ireland constable]] may exercise the powers set out in Part 3 of Schedule 4A ('Part 3 powers') in relation to any of the following in Northern Ireland waters—

(a) a United Kingdom ship;
(b) a ship without nationality;
(c) a foreign ship;
(d) a ship registered under the law of a relevant territory.

(2) But Part 3 powers may be exercised only—

(a) for the purpose of preventing, detecting, investigating or prosecuting an offence under

{(i) section 24B, 25, or 25A [[]], or
(ii) section 21 of the Immigration, Asylum and Nationality Act 2006, and}

(b) in accordance with the rest of this section.

(3) The authority of the Secretary of State is required before[[..]] a Northern Ireland constable [[..]]may exercise Part 3 powers in relation to a foreign ship, or a ship registered under the law of a relevant territory, within the territorial sea adjacent to the United Kingdom.

(4) Authority for the purposes of subsection (3) may be given in relation to a foreign ship only if the Convention permits the exercise of Part 3 powers in relation to the ship.]

Note: Subsection 28O inserted by paragraph 7 of Schedule 14 to the Immigration Act 2016 from 31 May 2016 (SI 2016/603). Words substituted in double square brackets at subsection (2)(a) by Immigration and Social Security (Co-ordination (EU Withdrawal) Act 2020 (Consequential, Saving, Transitional and Transitory Provisions) (EU Exit) Regulations 2020/1309 Sch.1 para 1(a)(ix) (December 31, 2020: substitution has effect subject to saving provisions in SI 2020/1309 Sch.1 para 1((5)). Words substituted in curly brackets at subsection (2)(a) by Nationality and Borders Act 2022 c.36 Sch.6 para 8 (date to be appointed). Words in double square brackets substituted in subsection (1) and omitted in subsection (3) by Nationality and Borders Act 2022 c.36 Sch.7 para 2(5)(a) & (b)(June 28: omission has effect as SI 2022/590/reg.2 and Sch.1 para 22 subject to transitional and saving provisions specified in SI 2022/590 reg.3 and sch.2 para 8).

[28P. Hot pursuit of ships in United Kingdom waters

(1) [[An English or Welsh constable]] may exercise Part 1 powers in relation to a ship in Scotland waters or in Northern Ireland waters if—

(a) the ship is pursued there,

(b) immediately before the pursuit of the ship, the ship was in England and Wales waters, and

(c) the condition in subsection (7) is met.

(2) Part 1 powers may be exercised under subsection (1) only—

(a) for the purpose mentioned in subsection (2)(a) of section 28M, and

(b) (if relevant) in accordance with subsections (3) and (4) of that section.

(3) [[A Scottish constable]] may exercise Part 2 powers in relation to a ship in England and Wales waters or in Northern Ireland waters if—

(a) the ship is pursued there,

(b) immediately before the pursuit of the ship, the ship was in Scotland waters, and

(c) the condition in subsection (7) is met.

(4) Part 2 powers may be exercised under subsection (3) only—

(a) for the purpose mentioned in subsection (2)(a) of section 28N, and

(b) (if relevant) in accordance with subsections (3) and (4) of that section.

(5) [[A Northern Ireland constable]] may exercise Part 3 powers in relation to a ship in England and Wales waters or in Scotland waters if—

(a) the ship is pursued there,

(b) immediately before the pursuit of the ship, the ship was in Northern Ireland waters, and

(c) the condition in subsection (7) is met.

(6) Part 3 powers may be exercised under subsection (5) only—

(a) for the purpose mentioned in subsection (2)(a) of section 28O, and

(b) (if relevant) in accordance with subsections (3) and (4) of that section.

(7) The condition referred to in subsection (1)(c), (3)(c) and (5)(c) is that—

(a) before the pursuit of the ship, a signal is given for it to stop, and

(b) the pursuit of the ship is not interrupted.

(8) The signal referred to in subsection (7)(a) must be given in such a way as to be audible or visible from the ship.

(9) For the purposes of subsection (7)(b), pursuit is not interrupted by reason only of the fact that—

(a) the method of carrying out the pursuit, or

(b) the identity of the ship or aircraft carrying out the pursuit, changes during the course of the pursuit.

(10) Nothing in this Part affects any other legal right of hot pursuit that a constable [[..]]may have.]

Note: Subsection 28P inserted by paragraph 7 of Schedule 14 to the Immigration Act 2016 from 31 May 2016 (SI 2016/603). Words substituted in subsections (1), (3) & (5), and omitted in subsection (10 by Nationality and Borders Act 2022 c.36 Sch.7 para 2(6) (June 28, 2022: substitution and omission has effect as SI 2022.reg.590 reg.2 and Sch.1 para 22 subject to transitional and saving provisions specified in SI 2022/590 reg.3 and Sch.2 para 8).

28PA Power to seize and dispose of ships etc.

(1) This section applies if—

(a) an immigration officer has reasonable grounds to suspect that a ship has been used in the commission of a relevant offence, and

(b) the ship is in United Kingdom waters or otherwise in the United Kingdom.

(2) Subject to subsection (3), the immigration officer may seize the ship and any property relating to the operation or use of the ship.

(3) The authority of the Secretary of State is required before an immigration officer may seize anything under this section.

(4) If an immigration officer seizes a foreign ship or a ship registered under the law of a relevant territory, the Secretary of State must notify the home state or relevant territory in question that the ship has been seized.

(5) In subsection (4) "home state", in relation to a foreign ship, means—

(a) the State in which the ship is registered, or

(b) the State whose flag the ship is otherwise entitled to fly.

(6) Where a ship without nationality, or property relating to the operation or use of a ship without nationality, is seized under this section—

(a) section 26 of the UK Borders Act 2007 (disposal of property) and any regulations made under that section do not apply in respect of that ship or other property, and

(b) subsections (7) to (12) apply instead.

(7) The Secretary of State may—

(a) return the ship or other property to the person whom the Secretary of State believes to be its owner, or

(b) after the relevant period—

(i) dispose of the ship or other property, or

(ii) determine that the ship or other property is to be retained to be used in the course of, or in connection with, a function under the Immigration Acts.

(8) On the making of a determination under subsection (7)(b)(ii), the ship or other property vests in the Secretary of State.

(9) The relevant period is the period of 31 days beginning with the date on which the ship or other property was seized.

(10) Before exercising a power under subsection (7)(b), the Secretary of State must make reasonable efforts to—

(a) ascertain the identity of the owner of the ship or other property, and

(b) subject to subsection (11), notify that person that the ship or other property has been seized.

(11) The Secretary of State is not required to notify a person under subsection (10)(b) if to do so may prejudice any criminal investigation or criminal proceedings.

(12) Disposal under this section may be in any manner the Secretary of State thinks fit, including—

(a) by sale;

(b) by dismantling;

(c) by destruction;

(d) by donation of the ship or other property to a charity or other not-for-profit body.

Note: inserted by Nationality and Borders Act c.36 Sch.7 para 7 (June 28, 2022: insertion has effect as SI 2022/590 reg.2 and Sch.1 para 22 subject to transitional and savings provisions specified I SI 2022/590 reg.3 and Sch.2 para 8)

[28Q. Interpretation of Part 3A

(1) In this Part—

'the Convention' means the United Nations Convention on the Law of the Sea 1982 (Cmnd 8941) and any modifications of that Convention agreed after the passing of this Act that have entered into force in relation to the United Kingdom;

'enforcement officer' means—

(a) a person who is a commissioned officer of any of Her Majesty's ships, or

(b) a person in command or charge of any aircraft or hovercraft of the Royal Navy, the Army or the Royal Air Force;

'England and Wales waters' means the sea and other waters within the seaward limits of the territorial sea adjacent to England and Wales;

'English and Welsh constable' means only a person who is—

(a) a member of a police force in England and Wales,

(b) a member of the British Transport Police Force, or

(c) a port constable, within the meaning of section 7 of the Marine Navigation Act 2013, or a person appointed to act as a constable under provision made by virtue of section 16 of the Harbours Act 1964;

'foreign ship' means a ship which—

(a) is registered in a State other than the United Kingdom, or

(b) is not so registered but is entitled to fly the flag of a State other than the United Kingdom;

[['foreign waters' means the sea and other waters within the seaward limits of the territorial sea adjacent toa any relevant territory or any State other than the United Kingdom';]]

[['international waters' means the waters beyond the territorial sea of the United Kingdom or any other State or relevant territory;]]

'Northern Ireland constable' means only a person who is—

(a) a member of the Police Service of Northern Ireland,

(b) a member of the Police Service of Northern Ireland Reserve, or

(c) a person appointed as a special constable in Northern Ireland by virtue of provision incorporating section 79 of the Harbours, Docks, and Piers Clauses Act 1847;

'Northern Ireland waters' means the sea and other waters within the seaward limits of the territorial sea adjacent to Northern Ireland;

[['Part A1 powers' means the powers set out in Part A1 of Schedule 4A;]]

'Part 1 powers' means the powers set out in Part 1 of Schedule 4A;

'Part 2 powers' means the powers set out in Part 2 of that Schedule;

'Part 3 powers' means the powers set out in Part 3 of that Schedule;

[['relevant offence' means—

(a) an offence under section 24(A1), (B1), (D1) or (E1), 24B, 25 or 25A,

(b) offence under section 25B to the extent that the section continues to apply by virtue of regulation 5(7) of the Immigration and Social Security Co-ordination (EU Withdrawal) Act 2020 (Consequential, Saving, Transitional and Transitory Provisions) (EU Exit) Regulations 2020 (S.I. 2020/1309),

(c) an offence under section 21 of the Immigration, Asylum and Nationality Act 2006, or

(d) an offence under section 1 of the Criminal Attempts Act 1981 or Article 3 of the Criminal Attempts and Conspiracy (Northern Ireland) Order 1983 (S.I. 1983/1120

(N.I. 13)), or in Scotland at common law, of attempting to commit an offence mentioned in paragraph (a) to (c); and]]

'relevant territory' means—

(a) the Isle of Man;

(b) any of the Channel Islands;

(c) a British overseas territory;

'Scottish constable' means only a person who is a constable, within the meaning of section 99 of the Police and Fire Reform (Scotland) Act 2012 (asp 8);

'Scotland waters' means the sea and other waters within the seaward limits of the territorial sea adjacent to Scotland;

'ship' includes [[

(a) every description of vessel (including a hovercraft), and

(b) any other structure (whether with or without means of propulsion) constructed or used to carry persons, goods, plant or machinery by water;]];

'ship without nationality' means a ship which—

(a) is not registered in, or otherwise entitled to fly the flag of, any State or relevant territory, or

(b) sails under the flags of two or more States or relevant territories, or under the flags of a State and relevant territory, using them according to convenience;

'United Kingdom ship' means a ship which—

(a) is registered under Part 2 of the Merchant Shipping Act 1995,

(b) is a Government ship within the meaning of that Act,

(c) is not registered in any State or relevant territory but is wholly owned by persons each of whom has a United Kingdom connection, or

(d) is registered under an Order in Council under section 1 of the Hovercraft Act 1968.

[[' United Kingdom ship' means a ship which—

(a) is registered under Part 2 of the Merchant Shipping Act 1995,

(b) is a Government ship within the meaning of that Act,

(c) is not registered in any State or relevant territory but is wholly owned by persons each of whom has a United Kingdom connection, or

(d) is registered under an Order in Council under section 1 of the Hovercraft Act 1968.

'United Kingdom waters' means the sea and other waters within the seaward limits of the United Kingdom territorial sea]].

(2) For the purposes of paragraph (c) of the definition of 'United Kingdom ship' in subsection (1), a person has a 'United Kingdom connection' if the person is—

(a) a British citizen, a British overseas territories citizen or a British Overseas citizen,

(b) an individual who is habitually resident in the United Kingdom, or

(c) a body corporate which is established under the law of a part of the United Kingdom and has its principal place of business in the United Kingdom.]

Note: Subsection 28Q inserted by paragraph 7 of Schedule 14 to the Immigration Act 2016 from 31 May 2016 (SI 2016/603). Words (definitions) inserted in double square brackets and substituted by Nationality and Borders Act 2022 c.36 Sch.7 para 8 (June 28, 2022: insertion and substitution has effect subject as SI 2022/590 reg.2 and Sch.1 para.22 subject to transitional and saving provisions specified in SI 2022/590 reg.3 and Sch.2 para 8)

PART IV

SUPPLEMENTARY

29. . . .

Note: Repealed by Nationality, Immigration and Asylum Act 2002, s 58 and Sch 9 from 1 April 2003 (SI 2003/754).

30. . . .

Note: Repealed by British Nationality Act 1981, s 52(8) and Mental Health (Scotland) Act 1984, s 127(2).

31. Expenses

There shall be defrayed out of moneys provided by Parliament any expenses incurred [by the Lord Chancellor under Schedule 5 to this Act or] by a Secretary of State under or by virtue of this Act—

(a) by way of administrative expenses ... or

(b) in connection with the removal of any person from the United Kingdom under Schedule 2 or 3 to this Act or the departure with him of his dependants, or his or their maintenance pending departure; or

(c) ...

(d) ...

Note: Words in square brackets in s 31 inserted and s 31(c) repealed by SI 1987/465. Words omitted from s 31(a) repealed by British Nationality Act 1981, s 52(8). Section 31(d) repealed by Nationality, Immigration and Asylum Act 2002, s 58 and Sch 9 from 1 April 2003 (SI 2003/754).

[31A..]

Note: Section 31A repealed by Immigration, Asylum and Nationality Act 2006, s 50 from 29 February 2008 (SI 2008/310).

32. General provisions as to Orders in Council, etc.

(1) Any power conferred by Part I of this Act to make an Order in Council or order (other than a deportation order) or to give any directions includes power to revoke or vary the Order in Council, order or directions.

(2) Any document purporting to be an order, notice or direction made or given by the Secretary of State for the purposes of [the Immigration Acts] and to be signed by him or on his behalf, and any document purporting to be a certificate of the Secretary of State so given and to be signed by him [or on his behalf] shall be received in evidence, and shall, until the contrary is proved, be deemed to be made or issued by him.

(3) Prima facie evidence of any such order, notice, direction or certificate as aforesaid may, in any legal proceedings or [other proceedings under the Immigration Acts], be given by the production of a document bearing a certificate purporting to be signed by or on behalf of the Secretary of State and stating that the document is a true copy of the order, notice, direction or certificate.

(4) Where an order under section 8(2) above applies to persons specified in a schedule to the order, or any directions of the Secretary of State given for the purposes of [the Immigration Acts] apply to persons specified in a schedule to the directions, prima facie evidence of the provisions of the order or directions other than the schedule and of any entry contained in the schedule may, in any legal proceedings or [other proceedings under the Immigration Acts], be given by the production of a document purporting to be signed by or on behalf of the Secretary of State and stating that the document is a true copy of the said provisions and of the relevant entry.

(5) ...

Note: Words in square brackets in subsections (2), (3) and (4) inserted by Immigration and Asylum Act 1999 from 6 December 1999. Subsection (5) substituted by Nationality, Immigration and Asylum Act 2002, s 158 from 10 February 2003 (SI 2003/1). Subsection (5) ceased to have effect by Immigration, Asylum and Nationality Act 2006, s 61 and Sch 3 from 30 March 2006 (Royal Assent).

33. Interpretation

(1) For purposes of this Act, except in so far as the context otherwise requires—

'aircraft' includes hovercraft, 'airport' includes hoverport and 'port' includes airport;

'captain' means master (of a ship) or commander (of an aircraft);

['certificate of entitlement' means a certificate under section 10 of the Nationality, Immigration and Asylum Act 2002 that a person has the right of abode in the United Kingdom];

['Convention adoption' has the same meaning as in the Adoption Act 1976 and {the Adoption and Children (Scotland) Act 2007}{or in the Adoption and Children Act 2002};]

'crew', in relation to a ship or aircraft, means all persons actually employed in the working or service of the ship or aircraft, including the captain, and 'member of the crew' shall be construed accordingly;

['entrant' means a person entering or seeking to enter the United Kingdom and 'illegal entrant' means a person—

(a) unlawfully entering or seeking to enter in breach of a deportation order or of the immigration laws, or

(b) entering or seeking to enter by means which include deception by another person, and includes also a person who has entered as mentioned in paragraph (a) or (b) above;]

'entry clearance' means a visa, entry certificate or other document which, in accordance with the immigration rules, is to be taken as evidence [or the requisite evidence] of a person's eligibility, though not [a British citizen], for entry into the United Kingdom (but does not include a work permit);

'immigration laws' means this Act and any law for purposes similar to this Act which is for the time being or has (before or after the passing of this Act) been in force in any part of the United Kingdom and Islands;

'immigration rules' means the rules for the time being laid down as mentioned in section 3(2) above;

'the Islands' means the Channel Islands and the Isle of Man, and 'the United Kingdom and Islands' means the United Kingdom and the Islands taken together;

'legally adopted' means adopted in pursuance of an order made by any court in the United Kingdom and Islands [under a Convention adoption] or by any adoption specified as an overseas adoption by order of the Secretary of State under [section 72(2) the Adoption Act 1976] {or by regulations made by the Scottish Ministers under section 67(1) of the Adoption and Children (Scotland) Act 2007};

'limited leave' and 'indefinite leave' mean respectively leave under this Act to enter or remain in the United Kingdom which is, and one which is not, limited as to duration;

'settled' shall be construed in accordance with [subsection (2A) below];

'ship' includes every description of vessel used in navigation;

['United Kingdom passport' means a current passport issued by the Government of the United Kingdom, or by the Lieutenant-Governor of any of the Islands or by the Government of any territory which is for the time being a dependent territory within the meaning of the British Nationality Act 1981;]

'work permit' means a permit indicating, in accordance with the immigration rules, that a person named in it is eligible, though not [a British citizen], for entry into the United Kingdom for the purpose of taking employment.

(1A) A reference to being the owner of a vehicle, ship or aircraft includes a reference to being any of a number of persons who jointly own it.

(2) It is hereby declared that, except as otherwise provided in this Act, a person is not to be treated for the purposes of any provision of this Act as ordinarily resident in the United Kingdom or in any of the Islands at a time when he is there in breach of the immigration laws.

(2A) Subject to section 8(5) above, references to a person being settled in the United Kingdom are references to his being ordinarily resident there without being subject under the immigration laws to any restriction on the period for which he may remain.]

(3) The ports of entry for purposes of this Act, and the ports of exit for purposes of any Order in Council under section 3(7) above, shall be such ports as may from time to time be designated for the purpose by order of the Secretary of State made by statutory instrument.

[**(4)** For the purposes of this Act, the question of whether an appeal is pending shall be determined {in accordance with section 104 of the Nationality, Immigration and Asylum Act 2002 (pending appeals)}.]

(5) This Act shall not be taken to supersede or impair any power exercisable by Her Majesty in relation to aliens by virtue of Her prerogative.

Note: Definition of certificate of entitlement in s 33(1) substituted by Nationality, Immigration and Asylum Act 2002, s 10 from 21 December 2006 (SI 2006/3144). Definition of 'Convention adoption' and amendment to definition of 'legally adopted' inserted by Adoption (Intercountry Aspects) Act 1999, Sch 2 from 1 June 2003 (SI 2003/362) and amended by Adoption and Children Act 2002 and further amended from 14 July 2011 by the Adoption and Children (Scotland) Act 2007 (Consequential Modifications) Order 2007 (SI 2011/1740). Definition of 'entrant' in s 33(1) substituted by Asylum and Immigration Act 1996 from 1 October 1996. Words in fifth square brackets in s 33(1) substituted by Adoption Act 1976. Other words in square brackets in s 33(1) substituted by British Nationality Act 1981. Subsection (1A) inserted by Nationality, Immigration and Asylum Act 2002, s 144 from 10 February 2003 (SI 2003/1). Subsection (2A) inserted by British Nationality Act 1981. Subsection (4) substituted by Immigration and Asylum Act 1999 from 2 October 2000. Words in curly brackets in subsection (4) substituted by Sch 7 Nationality, Immigration and Asylum Act 2002 from 1 April 2003 (SI 2003/754). Section 33 has effect in a form modified by and in circumstances specified by the Channel Tunnel (International Arrangements) Order (SI 1993/1813) as amended by SIs 1994/1405, 2000/913, 2001/178, 2001/3707, 2006/1003 and 2007/3759.

34. Repeal, transitional and temporary

(1) Subject to the following provisions of this section, the enactments mentioned in Schedule 6 to this Act are hereby repealed, as from the coming into force of this Act, to the extent mentioned in column 3 of the Schedule; and—

(a) this Act, as from its coming into force, shall apply in relation to entrants or others arriving in the United Kingdom at whatever date before or after it comes into force; and

(b) after this Act comes into force anything done under or for the purposes of the former immigration laws shall have effect, in so far as any corresponding action could be taken under or for the purposes of this Act, as if done by way of action so taken, and in relation to anything so done this Act shall apply accordingly.

(2) Without prejudice to the generality of subsection (1)(a) and (b) above, a person refused leave to land by virtue of the Aliens Restriction Act 1914 shall be treated as having been refused leave to enter under this Act, and a person given leave to land by virtue of that Act shall be treated as having been given leave to enter under this Act; and similarly with the Commonwealth Immigrants Acts 1962 and 1968.

(3) A person treated in accordance with subsection (2) above as having leave to enter the United Kingdom—

(a) shall be treated as having an indefinite leave, if he is not at the coming in to force of this Act subject to a condition limiting his stay in the United Kingdom; and

(b) shall be treated, if he is then subject to such a condition, as having a limited leave of such duration, and subject to such conditions (capable of being attached to leave under this Act), as correspond to the conditions to which he is then subject, but not to conditions not capable of being so attached.

This subsection shall have effect in relation to any restriction or requirement imposed by Order in Council under the Aliens Restriction Act 1914 as if it had been imposed by way of a landing condition.

(4) Notwithstanding anything in the foregoing provisions of this Act, the former immigration laws shall continue to apply, and this Act shall not apply,—

(a) in relation to the making of deportation orders and matters connected therewith in any case where a decision to make the order has been notified to the person concerned before the coming into force of this Act;

(b) in relation to removal from the United Kingdom and matters connected therewith (including detention pending removal or pending the giving of directions for removal) in any case where a person is to be removed in pursuance of a decision taken before the coming into force of this Act or in pursuance of a deportation order to the making of which paragraph (a) above applies;

(c) in relation to appeals against any decision taken or other thing done under the former immigration laws, whether taken or done before the coming into force of this Act or by virtue of this subsection.

(5) Subsection (1) above shall not be taken as empowering a court on appeal to recommend for deportation a person whom the court below could not recommend for deportation, or as affecting any right of appeal in respect of a recommendation for deportation made before this Act comes into force, or as enabling a notice given before this Act comes into force and not complying with section 6(2) to take the place of the notice required by section 6(2) to be given before a person is recommended for deportation.

(6) ...

Note: Section 34(6) repealed by Statute Law (Repeals) Act 1993, s 1.

35. Commencement, and interim provisions

(1) Except as otherwise provided by this Act, Parts I to III of this Act shall come into force on such day as the Secretary of State may appoint by order made by statutory instrument; and references to the coming into force of this Act shall be construed as references to the beginning of the day so appointed.

(2) Section 25 above, except section 25(2), and section 28 in its application to offences under section 25(1) shall come into force at the end of one month beginning with the date this Act is passed.

(3) …

(4) …

(5) …

Note: Section 35(3)–(5) repealed by Statute Law (Repeals) Act 1986.

36. Power to extend to Islands

Her Majesty may by Order in Council direct that any of the provisions of this Act shall extend, with such exceptions, adaptations and modifications, if any, as may be specified in the Order, to any of the Islands; and any Order in Council under this subsection may be varied or revoked by a further Order in Council.

Note: Part 1, Part 3 and Part 4 (except for ss 29–30, 34–36) extended to the Isle of Man with modifications: see SI 2008/680 as amended by SI 2011/1408.

37. Short title and extent

(1) This Act may be cited as the Immigration Act 1971.

(2) It is hereby declared that this Act extends to Northern Ireland, and (without prejudice to any provision of Schedule 1 to this Act as to the extent of that Schedule) where an enactment repealed by this Act extends outside the United Kingdom, the repeal shall be of like extent.

Schedules

Schedule 1

Note: Repealed by British Nationality Act 1981, s 52(8).

Schedule 2

Section 4

Administrative Provisions as to Control on Entry etc.

Part I General Provisions

Immigration officers and medical inspectors

1.—(1) Immigration officers for the purposes of this Act shall be appointed by the Secretary of State, and he may arrange with the Commissioners of Customs and Excise for the employment of officers of customs and excise as immigration officers under this Act.

(2) Medical inspectors for the purposes of this Act may be appointed by the Secretary of State or, in Northern Ireland, by the Minister of Health and Social Services or other appropriate Minister of the Government of Northern Ireland in pursuance of arrangements made between that Minister and the Secretary of State, and shall be fully qualified medical practitioners.

[(2A) The Secretary of State may direct that his function of appointing medical inspectors under sub-paragraph (2) is also to be exercisable by such persons specified in the direction who exercise functions relating to health in England or Wales.]

(3) In the exercise of their functions under this Act immigration officers shall act in accordance with such instructions (not inconsistent with the immigration rules) as may be given them by the Secretary of State, and medical inspectors shall act in accordance with such instructions as may be given them by the Secretary of State or, in Northern Ireland, as may be given in pursuance of the arrangements mentioned in sub-paragraph (2) above by the Minister making appointments of medical inspectors in Northern Ireland.

(4) An immigration officer or medical inspector may board any ship [or aircraft] for the purpose of exercising his functions under this Act.

(5) An immigration officer, for the purpose of satisfying himself whether there are persons he may wish to examine under paragraph 2 below, may search any ship [or aircraft] and anything on board it, or any vehicle [[or container]] taken off a ship or aircraft on which it has been brought to the United Kingdom.

[(6) For the purposes of searching a container under sub-paragraph (5), an immigration officer may direct any person who has control of the container to deliver the container to a place specified by the immigration officer.

(7) In this paragraph, "container" has the same meaning as in the Customs and Excise Management Act 1979 (see section 1(1) of that Act).]

Note: Words in square brackets in subparagraphs (4) and (5) substituted by SI 1993/1813. Subparagraph (2A) inserted by Health Protection Agency Act 2004, s 12(3) and Sch 3 from 22 September 2004. Paragraph 1 has effect in a form modified by and in circumstances specified by the Channel Tunnel (International Arrangements) Order (SI 1993/1813) as amended by SIs 1994/1405, 2000/913, 2001/178, 2001/3707, 2006/1003 and 2007/3759. Words in double brackets in sub-paragraph 5 inserted by Nationality and Border Act 2022 c.36 s44(2) (June 28, 2022). Sub-paragraphs (6) & (7) inserted by Nationality and Borders Act 2022 c.36 s.44(3)(June 28,2022)

Examination by immigration officers, and medical examination

2.—(1) An immigration officer may examine any persons [[within sub-paragraph (1A) by ship [or aircraft] (including transit passengers, members of the crew and others not seeking to enter the United Kingdom) for the purpose of determining—

(a) whether any of them is or is not [a British citizen]; and

(b) whether, if he is not, he may or may not enter the United Kingdom without leave; and

[(c) whether, if he may not—

(i) he has been given leave which is still in force,

(ii) he should be given leave and for what period or on what conditions (if any), or

(iii) he should be refused leave.]

[(d) whether, if he has been given leave which is still in force, his leave should be curtailed.]

(**1A**) The persons are—

(a) any person who has arrived in the United Kingdom by ship or aircraft (including transit passengers, members of the crew and others not seeking to enter the United Kingdom);

(b) any person who has arrived in United Kingdom waters by ship or aircraft who the immigration officer has reason to believe is an offshore worker.

(**1B**) In sub-paragraph (1A), "offshore worker" and "United Kingdom waters" have the same meaning as in section 11A.

(2) Any such person, if he is seeking to enter the United Kingdom, may be examined also by a medical inspector or by any qualified person carrying out a test or examination required by a medical inspector.

(3) A person, on being examined under this paragraph by an immigration officer or medical inspector, may be required in writing by him to submit to further examination; but a requirement under this sub-paragraph shall not prevent a person who arrives as a transit passenger, or as a member of the crew of a ship or aircraft, or for the purpose of joining a ship or aircraft as a member of the crew, from leaving by his intended ship or aircraft.

Note: Words in first square brackets substituted by SI 1993/1813. Words in square brackets in subparagraph (1)(a) substituted by British Nationality Act 1981, s 39(6). Subparagraph (1)(c) substituted by Immigration and Asylum Act 1999 from 14 February 2000. Paragraph 2 has effect in a form modified by and in circumstances specified by the Channel Tunnel (International Arrangements) Order (SI 1993/1813) as amended by SIs 1994/1405, 2000/913, 2001/178, 2001/3707, 2006/1003 and 2007/3759. Subparagraph (1)(d) inserted by Immigration Act 2016, s 46 from 12 July 2016 (SI 2016/603). Words substituted in double square brackets, and subsection (1A) &(1B) by Nationality and Borders Act 2022 c.36 Sch.6 para 9 (date to be appointed)

[Examination of persons who arrive with continuing leave

2A.—(1) This paragraph applies to a person who has arrived in the United Kingdom with leave to enter which is in force but which was given to him before his arrival.

(2) He may be examined by an immigration officer for the purpose of establishing—

(a) whether there has been such a change in the circumstances of his case, since that leave was given, that it should be cancelled;

(b) whether that leave was obtained as a result of false information given by him or his failure to disclose material facts; or

(c) whether there are medical grounds on which that leave should be cancelled.

[(**2A**) Where the person's leave to enter derives, by virtue of section 3A(3), from an entry clearance, he may also be examined by an immigration officer for the purpose of establishing whether the leave should be cancelled on the grounds that the person's purpose in arriving in the United Kingdom is different from the purpose specified in the entry clearance.]

[(**2B**) The detention under sub-paragraph (2) of a person to whom section 60 (limitation on detention of pregnant women) of the Immigration Act 2016 applies is subject to that section.]

(3) He may also be examined by an immigration officer for the purpose of determining whether it would be conducive to the public good for that leave to be cancelled.

(4) He may also be examined by a medical inspector or by any qualified person carrying out a test or examination required by a medical inspector.

(5) A person examined under this paragraph may be required by the officer or inspector to submit to further examination.

(6) A requirement under sub-paragraph (5) does not prevent a person who arrives—

(a) as a transit passenger,

(b) as a member of the crew of a ship or aircraft, or

(c) for the purpose of joining a ship or aircraft as a member of the crew, from leaving by his intended ship or aircraft.

(7) An immigration officer examining a person under this paragraph may by notice suspend his leave to enter until the examination is completed.

(8) An immigration officer may, on the completion of any examination of a person under this paragraph, cancel his leave to enter.

(9) {}

(10) A requirement imposed under sub-paragraph (5) and a notice given under sub-paragraph (7) must be in writing.]

Note: Paragraph 2A inserted by Immigration and Asylum Act 1999 from 14 February 2000. Words in first square brackets in paragraph 2A(9) substituted by Sch 7 Nationality, Immigration and Asylum Act 2002 from 1 April 2003 (SI 2003/754). Words in second square brackets in paragraph 2A(9) substituted by Sch 9 Immigration Act 2014 from 20 October 2014 with savings set out in articles 9–11 SI 2014/2771. Subparagraph (2A) inserted by Asylum and Immigration Act 2004, s 18 from 1 October 2004 (SI 2004/2523). Subparagraph (2B) inserted by Immigration Act 2016 (SI 2016/603). Subparagraph (9) omitted by Immigration Act 2016, s 65 from 1 December 2016 (SI 2016/1037).

3.—(1) An immigration officer [or designated person] may examine any person who is embarking or seeking to embark in the United Kingdom for the purpose of determining whether he is [a British citizen] [and, if he is not a British citizen, for the purpose of establishing—

(a) his identity;

(b) whether he entered the United Kingdom lawfully;

(c) whether he has complied with any conditions of leave to enter or remain in the United Kingdom;

(d) whether his return to the United Kingdom is prohibited or restricted.

[(1A) If a person is examined under sub-paragraph (1) (whether by an immigration officer or designated person), an immigration officer may require the person, by notice in writing, to submit to further examination by the immigration officer for a purpose specified in that sub-paragraph.]]

(2) So long as any Order in Council is in force under section 3(7) of this Act, an immigration officer may examine any person who is embarking or seeking to embark in the United Kingdom for the purpose of determining—

(a) whether any of the provisions of the Order apply to him; and

(b) whether, if so, any power conferred by the Order should be exercised in relation to him and in what way.

Note: Words in first square brackets in subparagraph (1) inserted and subparagraph (1A) substituted by Sch 8 Immigration Act 2014 from 28 July 2014 (SI 2014/1820). Words in second square brackets in subparagraph (1) substituted by British Nationality Act 1981. Other words in square brackets substituted by Immigration, Asylum and Nationality Act 2006, s 42 from 31 August 2006 (SI 2006/2226). Paragraph 3 has effect in a form modified by and in circumstances specified by the Channel Tunnel (International Arrangements) Order (SI 1993/1813) as amended by SIs 1994/1405, 2000/913, 2001/178, 2001/3707, 2006/1003 and 2007/3759.

Information and documents

4.—(1) It shall be the duty of any person examined under paragraph 2, [2A] or 3 above to furnish to the person carrying out the examination all such information in his possession as that person may require for the purpose of [that or any other person's functions] under that paragraph.

(2) A person on his examination under paragraph 2, [2A] or 3 above by an immigration officer [, or on his examination under paragraph 3 above by a designated person, shall, if so required by an immigration officer or designated person]—

(a) produce either a valid passport with photograph or some other document satisfactorily establishing his identity and nationality or citizenship; and

(b) declare whether or not he is carrying or conveying [, or has carried or conveyed] documents of any relevant description specified by [the immigration officer or designated person], and produce any documents of that description which he is carrying or conveying.

In paragraph (b), 'relevant description' means any description appearing to [the immigration officer or designated person] to be relevant for the purposes of the examination.

(3) Where under sub-paragraph (2)(b) above a person has been required to declare whether or not he is carrying or conveying [, or has carried or conveyed,] documents of any description,

[(a) he and any baggage or vehicle belonging to him or under his control; and

(b) any ship, aircraft or vehicle in which he arrived in the United Kingdom];

may be searched with a view to ascertaining whether he is doing, [or, as the case may be, has done], so by [an immigration officer or a person acting under the directions of an immigration officer]: provided that no woman or girl shall be searched except by a woman.

[(4) Where a passport or other document is [produced to or found by an immigration officer] in accordance with this paragraph [the] immigration officer may examine it and detain it—

(a) for the purpose of examining it, for a period not exceeding 7 days;

(b) for any purpose, until the person to whom the document relates is given leave to enter the United Kingdom or is about to depart or be removed following refusal of leave or until it is decided that the person does not require leave to enter;

(c) after a time described in paragraph (b), while the immigration officer thinks that the document may be required in connection with proceedings in respect of an appeal under the Immigration Acts or in respect of an offence.

[(4A) Where a passport or other document is produced to a designated person in accordance with this paragraph, the designated person—

(a) may examine it and detain it; and

(b) must deliver any detained passport or document to an immigration officer as soon as reasonably practicable.

(4B) If a passport or document is delivered to an immigration officer in accordance with sub-paragraph (4A)(b), sub-paragraph (4) applies as if the immigration officer had detained the document (and, accordingly, the immigration officer may continue to detain it in accordance with sub-paragraph (4)(a), (b) or (c)).]

(5) For the purpose of ascertaining that a passport or other document produced or found in accordance with this paragraph relates to a person examined under paragraph 2, 2A or 3 above, the person carrying out the examination may require the person being examined to provide [biometric] information (whether or not by submitting to a process by means of which information is obtained or recorded)[. . .]

[(6) 'Biometric information' has the meaning given by section 15 of the UK Borders Act 2007.]

[(7) A person ('P') who is under 16 may not be required to provide biometric information under sub-paragraph (5) unless—

(a) the decision to require P to provide the information has been confirmed by a chief immigration officer, and

(b) the information is provided in the presence of a person of full age who is—

(i) P's parent or guardian, or

(ii) a person who for the time being takes responsibility for P.

(8) The person mentioned in sub-paragraph (7)(b)(ii) may not be—

(a) a person who is entitled to require the provision of information under sub-paragraph (5) (an 'authorised person'), or

(b) an officer of the Secretary of State who is not such a person.

(9) Sub-paragraph (7) does not prevent an authorised person requiring the provision of biometric information by a person the authorised person reasonably believes to be 16 or over.]

Note: Words in first square brackets in paragraph 4(1) and first and third square brackets in paragraph 4(2) inserted by Immigration and Asylum Act 1999 from 14 February 2000. Subparagraph (2A) ceased to have effect and subparagraph 4 substituted by Immigration, Asylum and Nationality Act 2006, s 27 from 31 August 2006 (SI 2006/2226). Where, immediately before that date, a passport or other document produced or found in accordance with paragraph 4 is being examined or detained by an immigration officer under paragraph 4(2A) or paragraph 4(4), paragraph 4(4) shall apply to the examination or detention of those documents on or after 31 August 2006 as if it had been in force on the date on which the passport or other document was produced or found, and paragraph 4(2A) shall cease to have effect. Paragraph 4(5) shall apply only where the examination under paragraph 2, 2A or 3 of that Schedule begins on or after 31 August 2006. Other words in square brackets in subparagraphs (1), (2), (3) and (4) substituted and subparagraphs (4A) and (4B) inserted by Sch 8 Immigration Act 2014 from 28 July 2014 (SI 2014/1820). Word in square brackets inserted and other words omitted from subparagraph (5) and subparagraph (6) inserted by Sch 2 Immigration Act 2014 from 28 July 2014 (SI 2014/1820). Subparagraphs (7)–(9) inserted by s 13 Immigration Act 2014 from 28 July 2014 (SI 2014/1820).

5. The Secretary of State may by order made by statutory instrument make provision for [requiring (a) passengers] disembarking or embarking in the United Kingdom, or any class of such passengers, to produce to an immigration officer, if so required, landing or embarkation [cards, and (b) passengers embarking in the United Kingdom, or any class of such passengers, to produce to a designated person, if so required, embarkations cards, in such form] as the Secretary of State may direct, and for requiring the owners or agents of ships and aircraft to supply such cards to those passengers.

Note: Paragraph 5 has effect in a form modified by and in circumstances specified by the Channel Tunnel (International Arrangements) Order (SI 1993/1813) as amended by SIs 1994/1405, 2000/913, 2001/178, 2001/3707, 2006/1003 and 2007/3759. Words in square brackets substituted by Schedule 8 Immigration Act 2014 from 28 July 2014 (SI 2014/1820).

[*Designated persons*

5A.—(1) In this Schedule 'designated person' means a person designated by the Secretary of State for the purposes of this Schedule.

(2) A designation under this paragraph is subject to such limitations as may be specified in the designation.

(3) A limitation under sub-paragraph (2) may, in particular, relate to the functions that are exercisable by virtue of the designation (and, accordingly, the exercise of functions under this Schedule by a designated person is subject to any such limitations specified in the person's designation).

(4) A designation under this paragraph—

(a) may be permanent or for a specified period,

(b) may (in either case) be withdrawn, and

(c) may be varied.

(5) The power to designate, or to withdraw or vary a designation, is exercised by the Secretary of State giving notice to the person in question.

(6) The Secretary of State may designate a person under this paragraph only if the Secretary of State is satisfied that the person—

(a) is capable of effectively carrying out the functions that are exercisable by virtue of the designation,

(b) has received adequate training in respect of the exercise of those functions, and

(c) is otherwise a suitable person to exercise those functions.]

Note: Paragraph 5A inserted by Sch 8 Immigration Act 2014 from 28 July 2014 (SI 2014/1820).

[Directions to carriers and operators of ports etc

5B.—(1) The Secretary of State may direct—

(a) an owner or agent of a ship or aircraft, or

(b) a person concerned in the management of a port, to make arrangements for designated persons to exercise a specified function, or a function of a specified description, in relation to persons of a specified description.

(2) A direction under this paragraph must specify—

(a) the port where, and

(b) the date (or dates) and time (or times) when, a function is to be exercised under the arrangements.

(3) A direction under this paragraph must be in writing.

(4) A direction under this paragraph may specify a description of persons by reference, in particular, to—

(a) the destination to which persons are travelling;

(b) the route by which persons are travelling;

(c) the date and time when the persons are travelling.

(5) In this paragraph—

'function' means a function under this Schedule;

'specified' means specified in a direction under this paragraph.]

Note: Paragraph 5B inserted by Sch 8 Immigration Act 2014 from 28 July 2014 (SI 2014/1820).

Notice of leave to enter or of refusal of leave

6.—(1) Subject to sub-paragraph (3) below, where a person examined by an immigration officer under paragraph 2 above is to be given a limited leave to enter the United Kingdom or is to be refused leave, the notice giving or refusing leave shall be given not later than [twenty four] hours after the conclusion of his examination (including any further examination) in pursuance of that paragraph; and if notice giving or refusing leave is not given him before the end of those [twenty four] hours, he shall (if not [a British citizen]) be deemed to have been given [leave to enter the United Kingdom for a period of six months subject to a condition prohibiting his taking employment] and the immigration officer shall as soon as may be given him written notice of that leave.

(2) Where on a person's examination under paragraph 2 above he is given notice of leave to enter the United Kingdom, then at any time before the end of [twenty four hours] from the conclusion of the examination he may be given a further notice in writing by an immigration officer cancelling the earlier notice and refusing him leave to enter.

(3) Where in accordance with this paragraph a person is given notice refusing him leave to enter the United Kingdom, that notice may at any time be cancelled by notice in writing given him by an immigration officer; and where a person is given a notice of cancellation under this sub-paragraph, [and the immigration officer does not at the same time give him indefinite or limited leave to enter {or require him to submit to further examination}, he shall be deemed to have been given leave to enter for a period of six months subject to a condition prohibiting his taking employment and the immigration officer shall as soon as may be give him written notice of that leave.]

(4) Where an entrant is a member of a party in charge of a person appearing to the immigration officer to be a responsible person, any notice to be given in relation to that entrant in accordance with this paragraph shall be duly given if delivered to the person in charge of the party.

Note: Words in third square brackets substituted by British Nationality Act 1981, s 39(6); other words in square brackets substituted by Immigration Act 1988, s 10. Words in curly brackets in paragraph 6(3) inserted by Nationality, Immigration and Asylum Act 2002, s 119 from 8 January 2003 (SI 2002/2811).

[Power to require medical examination after entry

7.—(1) This paragraph applies if an immigration officer examining a person under paragraph 2 decides—

(a) that he may be given leave to enter the United Kingdom; but

(b) that a further medical test or examination may be required in the interests of public health.

(2) This paragraph also applies if an immigration officer examining a person under paragraph 2A decides—

(a) that his leave to enter the United Kingdom should not be cancelled; but

(b) that a further medical test or examination may be required in the interests of public health.

(3) The immigration officer may give the person concerned notice in writing requiring him—

(a) to report his arrival to such medical officer of health as may be specified in the notice; and

(b) to attend at such place and time and submit to such test or examination (if any), as that medical officer of health may require.

(4) In reaching a decision under paragraph (b) of sub-paragraph (1) or (2), the immigration officer must act on the advice of—

(a) a medical inspector; or

(b) if no medical inspector is available, a fully qualified medical practitioner.]

Note: Paragraph 7 substituted by Immigration and Asylum Act 1999 from 14 February 2000.

Removal of persons refused leave to enter and illegal entrants

8.—(1) Where a person arriving in the United Kingdom is refused leave to enter, an immigration officer may, subject to sub-paragraph (2) below—

(a) give the captain of the ship or aircraft in which he arrives directions requiring the captain to remove him from the United Kingdom in that ship or aircraft; or

(b) give the owners or agents of that ship or aircraft directions requiring them to remove him from the United Kingdom in any ship or aircraft specified or indicated in the directions, being a ship or aircraft of which they are the owners or agents; or

(c) give those owners or agents directions requiring them to make arrangements for his removal from the United Kingdom in any ship or aircraft specified or indicated in the directions to a country or territory so specified, being either—

(i) a country of which he is a national or citizen; or

(ii) a country or territory in which he has obtained a passport or other document of identity; or

(iii) a country or territory in which he embarked for the United Kingdom; or

(iv) a country or territory to which there is reason to believe that he will be admitted.

(2) No directions shall be given under this paragraph in respect of anyone after the expiration of two months beginning with the date on which he was refused leave to enter the United Kingdom [(ignoring any period during which an appeal by him under the Immigration Acts is pending)] [except that directions may be given under sub-paragraph (1)(b) or (c) after the end of that period if the immigration officer has within that period given written notice to the owners or agents in question of his intention to give directions to them in respect of that person].

Note: Words in first square brackets in subparagraph (2) inserted by Sch 7 Nationality, Immigration and Asylum Act 2002 from 1 April 2003 (SI 2003/754). Words in second square brackets in subparagraph (2) added by Immigration Act 1988, s 10. Paragraph 8 modified in relation to certain persons entering or seeking to enter through Republic of Ireland with effect from 17 July 2002: see the Immigration (Entry otherwise than by Sea or Air) Order 2002 (SI 2002/1832). Paragraph 8 has effect in a form modified by and in circumstances specified by the Channel Tunnel (International Arrangements) Order (SI 1993/1813) as amended by SIs 1994/1405, 2000/913, 2001/178, 2001/3707, 2006/1003 and 2007/3759.

9.—(1) Where an illegal entrant is not given leave to enter or remain in the United Kingdom, an immigration officer may give any such directions in respect of him as in a case within paragraph 8 above are authorised by paragraph 8(1).

[(2) Any leave to enter the United Kingdom which is obtained by deception shall be disregarded for the purposes of this paragraph.]

Note: Paragraph 9(2) added by Asylum and Immigration Act 1996 from 1 October 1996. Subparagraph (1) modified in relation to certain persons entering or seeking to enter through Republic of Ireland with effect from 17 July 2002: see the Immigration (Entry otherwise than by Sea or Air) Order 2002 (SI 2002/1832). Paragraph 9 has effect in a form modified by and in circumstances specified by the Channel Tunnel (International Arrangements) Order (SI 1993/1813) as amended by SIs 1994/1405, 2000/913, 2001/178, 2001/3707, 2006/1003 and 2007/3759.

10.—(1) Where it appears to the Secretary of State either—

(a) that directions might be given in respect of a person under paragraph 8 or 9 above, but that it is not practicable for them to be given or that, if given, they would be ineffective; or

(b) that directions might have been given in respect of a person under paragraph 8 above [but that the requirements of paragraph 8(2) have not been complied with];

then the Secretary of State may give to the owners or agents of any ship or aircraft any such directions in respect of that person as are authorised by paragraph 8(1)(c).

(2) Where the Secretary of State may give directions for a person's removal in accordance with sub-paragraph (1) above, he may instead give directions for his removal in accordance with arrangements to be made by the Secretary of State to any country or territory to which he could be removed under sub-paragraph (1).

(3) The costs of complying with any directions given under this paragraph shall be defrayed by the Secretary of State.

Note: Paragraph 10 has effect in a form modified by and in circumstances specified by the Channel Tunnel (International Arrangements) Order (SI 1993/1813) as amended by SIs 1994/1405, 2000/913, 2001/178, 2001/3707, 2006/1003 and 2007/3759.

[**10A.** Where directions are given in respect of a person under any of paragraphs 8 to 10 above, directions to the same effect may be given under that paragraph in respect of a member of the person's family].

Note: Paragraph 10A inserted by Nationality, Immigration and Asylum Act 2002 from 10 February 2003 (SI 2003/1).

11. A person in respect of whom directions are given under any of paragraphs 8 to 10 above may be placed, under the authority of an immigration officer [or the Secretary of State], on board any ship or aircraft in which he is to be removed in accordance with the directions.

Note: Paragraph 11 modified in relation to certain persons entering or seeking to enter through Republic of Ireland with effect from 17 July 2002: see the Immigration (Entry otherwise than by Sea or Air) Order 2002 (SI 2002/1832). Paragraph 11 has effect in a form modified by and in circumstances specified by the Channel Tunnel (International Arrangements) Order (SI 1993/1813) as amended by SIs 1994/1405, 2000/913, 2001/178, 2001/3707, 2006/1003 and 2007/3759. Words in square brackets inserted by Sch 9 Immigration Act 2014 from 20 October 2014 with saving set out in SI 2014/2771 articles 9–11.

Seamen and aircrews

12.—(1) If, on a person's examination by an immigration officer under paragraph 2 above, the immigration officer is satisfied that he has come to the United Kingdom for the purpose of joining a ship or aircraft as a member of the crew, then the immigration officer may limit the duration of any leave he gives that person to enter the United Kingdom by requiring him to leave the United Kingdom in a ship or aircraft specified or indicated by the notice giving leave.

(2) Where a person (not being [a British citizen]) arrives in the United Kingdom for the purpose of joining a ship or aircraft as a member of the crew and, having been given leave to enter as mentioned in sub-paragraph (1) above, remains beyond the time limited

by that leave, or is reasonably suspected by an immigration officer of intending to do so, an immigration officer may—

(a) give the captain of that ship or aircraft directions requiring the captain to remove him from the United Kingdom in that ship or aircraft; or

(b) give the owners or agents of that ship or aircraft directions requiring them to remove him from the United Kingdom in any ship or aircraft specified or indicated in the directions, being a ship or aircraft of which they are the owners or agents; or

(c) give those owners or agents directions requiring them to make arrangements for his removal from the United Kingdom in any ship or aircraft specified or indicated in the directions to a country or territory so specified, being either—

(i) a country of which he is a national or citizen; or

(ii) a country or territory in which he has obtained a passport or other document of identity; or

(iii) a country or territory in which he embarked for the United Kingdom; or

(iv) a country or territory where he was engaged as a member of the crew of the ship or aircraft which he arrived in the United Kingdom to join; or

(v) a country or territory to which there is reason to believe that he will be admitted.

Note: Words in square brackets substituted by British Nationality Act 1981, s 39(6).

13.—(1) Where a person being a member of the crew of a ship or aircraft is examined by an immigration officer under paragraph 2 above, the immigration officer may limit the duration of any leave he gives that person to enter the United Kingdom—

(a) in the manner authorised by paragraph 12(1) above; or

(b) if that person is to be allowed to enter the United Kingdom in order to receive hospital treatment, by requiring him, on completion of that treatment, to leave the United Kingdom in accordance with arrangements to be made for his repatriation; or

(c) by requiring him to leave the United Kingdom within a specified period in accordance with arrangements to be made for his repatriation.

(2) Where a person (not being [a British citizen]) arrives in the United Kingdom as a member of the crew of a ship or aircraft, and either—

(A) having lawfully entered the United Kingdom without leave by virtue of section 8(1) of this Act, he remains without leave beyond the time allowed by section 8(1), or is reasonably suspected by an immigration officer of intending to do so; or

(B) having been given leave limited as mentioned in sub-paragraph (1) above, he remains beyond the time limited by that leave, or is reasonably suspected by an immigration officer of intending to do so; an immigration officer may—

(a) give the captain of the ship or aircraft in which he arrived directions requiring the captain to remove him from the United Kingdom in that ship or aircraft; or

(b) give the owners or agents of that ship or aircraft directions requiring them to remove him from the United Kingdom in any ship or aircraft specified or indicated in the directions, being a ship or aircraft of which they are the owners or agents; or

(c) give those owners or agents directions requiring them to make arrangements for his removal from the United Kingdom in any ship or aircraft specified or indicated in the directions to a country or territory so specified, being either—

(i) a country of which he is a national or citizen; or

(ii) a country or territory in which he has obtained a passport or other document of identity; or

(iii) a country in which he embarked for the United Kingdom; or

(iv) a country or territory in which he was engaged as a member of the crew of the ship or aircraft in which he arrived in the United Kingdom; or

(v) a country or territory to which there is reason to believe that he will be admitted.

Note: Words in square brackets substituted by British Nationality Act 1981, s 39(6). Paragraph 13 has effect in a form modified by and in circumstances specified by the Channel Tunnel (International Arrangements) Order (SI 1993/1813) as amended by SIs 1994/1405, 2000/913, 2001/178, 2001/3707, 2006/1003 and 2007/3759.

14.—(1) Where it appears to the Secretary of State that directions might be given in respect of a person under paragraph 12 or 13 above, but that it is not practicable for them to be given or that, if given, they would be ineffective, then the Secretary of State may give to the owners or agents of any ship or aircraft any such directions in respect of that person as are authorised by paragraph 12(2)(c) or 13(2)(c).

(2) Where the Secretary of State may give directions for a person's removal in accordance with sub-paragraph (1) above, he may instead give directions for his removal in accordance with arrangements to be made by the Secretary of State to any country or territory to which he could be removed under sub-paragraph (1).

(3) The costs of complying with any directions given under this paragraph shall be defrayed by the Secretary of State.

15. A person in respect of whom directions are given under any of paragraphs 12 to 14 above may be placed, under the authority of an immigration officer, on board any ship or aircraft in which he is to be removed in accordance with the directions.

Note: Paragraph 15 has effect in a form modified by and in circumstances specified by the Channel Tunnel (International Arrangements) Order (SI 1993/1813) as amended by SIs 1994/1405, 2000/913, 2001/178, 2001/3707, 2006/1003 and 2007/3759.

[Search of premises in connection with removal

15A. (1) This paragraph applies if—

(a) an immigration officer is lawfully on any premises, and

(b) a person who is liable to be detained under paragraph 16(2) is on the premises.

(2) The immigration officer may search the premises for documents which—

(a) relate to the person, and

(b) may be evidence for a ground on which the person's leave to enter or remain in the United Kingdom may be curtailed.

(3) The power may be exercised—

(a) only if the immigration officer has reasonable grounds for believing there are documents within sub-paragraph (2) on the premises, and

(b) only to the extent that it is reasonably required for the purpose of discovering such documents.

(4) An immigration officer searching premises under this paragraph may seize any document the officer finds which the officer has reasonable grounds for believing is a document within sub- paragraph (2).

(5) Sub-paragraph (6) applies where—

(a) an immigration officer is searching premises under this paragraph, and

(b) any document the officer has reasonable grounds for believing is a document within sub-paragraph (2) is stored in any electronic form and is accessible from the premises.

(6) The immigration officer may require the document to be produced in a form in which it can be taken away and in which it is visible and legible or from which it can readily be produced in a visible and legible form.

(7) If a requirement under sub-paragraph (6) is not complied with or a document to which that sub-paragraph applies cannot be produced in a form of the kind mentioned in that sub-paragraph, the immigration officer may seize the device or medium on which it is stored.

(8) But sub-paragraphs (4) to (7) do not apply to a document which the immigration officer has reasonable grounds for believing is an item subject to legal privilege.

(9) An immigration officer may retain a document seized under this paragraph while—

(a) the person to whom the document relates is liable to be detained under paragraph 16(2), and

(b) the document falls within sub-paragraph (2)(b).

(10) But a document may not be retained for the purpose mentioned in sub-paragraph (9) if a photograph or copy would be sufficient for that purpose.]

Note: Paragraph 15A is inserted by Immigration Act 2016, s 46 from 12 July 2016 (SI 2016/603).

Detention of persons liable to examination or removal

16.—(1) A person who may be required to submit to examination under paragraph 2 above may be detained under the authority of an immigration officer pending his examination and pending a decision to give or refuse him leave to enter.

[(**1A**) A person whose leave to enter has been suspended under paragraph 2A may be detained under the authority of an immigration officer pending—

(a) completion of his examination under that paragraph; and

(b) a decision on whether to cancel his leave to enter.]

[(**1B**) A person who has been required to submit to further examination under paragraph 3(1A) may be detained under the authority of an immigration officer, for a period not exceeding 12 hours, pending the completion of the examination.]

[(2) If there are reasonable grounds for suspecting that a person is someone in respect of whom directions may be given under any of paragraphs [8 to 10A] or 12 to 14, that person may be detained under the authority of an immigration officer pending—

(a) a decision whether or not to give such directions;

(b) his removal in pursuance of such directions.]

[(**2A**) But the detention of an unaccompanied child under sub-paragraph (2) is subject to paragraph 18B]

[(**2B**) The detention under sub-paragraph (2) of a person to whom section 60 (limitation on detention of pregnant women) of the Immigration Act 2016 applies is subject to that section.]

(3) A person on board a ship or aircraft may, under the authority of an immigration officer, be removed from the ship or aircraft for detention under this paragraph; but if an immigration officer so requires the captain of a ship or aircraft shall prevent from disembarking in the United Kingdom any person who has arrived in the United Kingdom in

the ship or aircraft and been refused leave to enter, and the captain may for that purpose detain him in custody on board the ship or aircraft.

(4) The captain of a ship or aircraft, if so required by an immigration officer, shall prevent from disembarking in the United Kingdom or before the directions for his removal have been fulfilled any person placed on board the ship or aircraft under paragraph 11 or 15 above, and the captain may for that purpose detain him in custody on board the ship or aircraft.

Note: Subparagraph (1A) inserted by Immigration and Asylum Act 1999 from 14 February 2000, subparagraph (2) substituted by Immigration and Asylum Act 1999. Words in square brackets substituted by Nationality, Immigration and Asylum Act 2002 from 10 February 2003 (SI 2003/1). Subparagraph (1B) inserted by Immigration, Asylum and Nationality Act 2006, s 42 from 31 August 2006 (SI 2006/2226). Paragraph 16 has effect in a form modified by and in circumstances specified by the Channel Tunnel (International Arrangements) Order (SI 1993/1813) as amended by SIs 1994/1405, 2000/913, 2001/178, 2001/3707, 2006/1003 and 2007/3759. Subparagraph (2A) inserted by s 5 Immigration Act 2014 from 28 July 2014 (SI 2014/1820). Words inserted at subparagraph (2B) by Immigration Act 2016, s 60 from 12 July 2016 (SI 2016/603).

17.—(1) A person liable to be detained under paragraph 16 above may be arrested without warrant by a constable or by an immigration officer.

(2) If—

(a) a justice of the peace is by written information on oath satisfied that there is reasonable ground for suspecting that a person liable to be arrested under this paragraph is to be found on any premises; or

(b) in Scotland, a sheriff, or a… justice of the peace, having jurisdiction in the place where the premises are situated is by evidence on oath so satisfied; he may grant a warrant [authorising any immigration officer or constable to enter], [if need be by reasonable force], the premises named in the warrant for the purpose of searching for and arresting that person.

[(3) Sub-paragraph (4) applies where an immigration officer or constable—

(a) enters premises in reliance on a warrant under sub-paragraph (2), and

(b) detains a person on the premises.

(4) A detainee custody officer may enter the premises, if need be by reasonable force, for the purpose of carrying out a search.

(5) In sub-paragraph (4)—

'detainee custody officer' means a person in respect of whom a certificate of authorisation is in force under section 154 of the Immigration and Asylum Act 1999 (c. 33) (detained persons: escort and custody), and

'search' means a search under paragraph 2(1)(a) of Schedule 13 to that Act (escort arrangements: power to search detained person).]

Note: Words omitted from (2)(b) repealed by Asylum and Immigration Act 1996 from 1 October 1996; other words omitted by Police and Criminal Evidence Act 1984, s 119(2). Words in first square brackets in (2)(b) substituted by Immigration and Asylum Act 1999, s 140(2); words in second square brackets substituted by Nationality, Immigration and Asylum Act 2002 from 10 February 2003 (SI 2003/1).

18.—(1) Persons may be detained under paragraph 16 above in such places as the Secretary of State may direct (when not detained in accordance with paragraph 16 on board a ship or aircraft).

[(1A) But the detention of an unaccompanied child under paragraph 16(2) is subject to paragraph 18B].

(2) Where a person is detained [or liable to be detained] under paragraph 16, any immigration officer, constable or prison officer, or any other person authorised by the Secretary of State, may take all such steps as may be reasonably necessary for photographing, measuring or otherwise identifying him.

[(2A) The power conferred by sub-paragraph (2) includes power to take [biometric information (within the meaning given by section 15 of the UK Borders Act 2007)]].

[(2B) Paragraph 4(7) to (9) applies to sub-paragraph (2) as it applies to paragraph 4(5).]

(3) Any person detained under paragraph 16 may be taken in the custody of a constable, [an immigration officer or] any person acting under the authority of an immigration officer, to and from any place where his attendance is required for the purpose of ascertaining his citizenship or nationality or of making arrangements for his admission to a country or territory other than the United Kingdom, or where he is required to be for any other purpose connected with the operation of this Act.

(4) A person shall be deemed to be in legal custody at any time when he is detained under paragraph 16 or is being removed in pursuance of sub-paragraph (3) above.

Note: Subparagraph (2A) inserted by Immigration and Asylum Act 1999 from 11 December 1999 (SI 2000/3099). Subparagraph (1A) inserted by s 5 Immigration Act 2014, words in square brackets in subparagraph (2) inserted by s 2 that Act, words in square brackets in subparagraph (2A) substituted by Sch 2 that Act, subparagraph (2B) inserted by s 13 that Act, words in square brackets in subparagraph (3) substituted by Sch 1 of that Act from 28 July 2014 (SI 2014/1820).

[**18A.**—(1) An immigration officer or constable may search a person ('P') who is detained under paragraph 16 for anything which P might use—

(a) to cause physical injury to P or others, or

(b) to assist P's escape from legal custody.

(2) The power to search P—

(a) unless sub-paragraph (3) applies, does not include power to require P to remove any clothing other than an outer coat, jacket or glove, but

(b) includes power to require P to open P's mouth.

(3) This sub-paragraph applies if an immigration officer or constable has reasonable grounds to believe that there is concealed on P anything which P might use as mentioned in sub-paragraph (1).

(4) The power to search P may be exercised only to the extent reasonably required for the purpose of discovering anything which P might use as mentioned in sub-paragraph (1).

(5) An intimate search (as defined in section 28H(11)) may not be conducted under this paragraph.

(6) An immigration officer or constable may seize and retain anything found on a search of P if the officer or constable has reasonable grounds to believe P might use it as mentioned in sub-paragraph (1).

(7) Nothing seized under sub-paragraph (6) may be retained when P is released from detention under paragraph 16.]

Note: Paragraph 18A inserted by Schedule 1 Immigration Act 2014 from 28 July 2014 (SI 2014/1820).

[**18B.**—(1) Where a person detained under paragraph 16(2) is an unaccompanied child, the only place where the child may be detained is a short-term holding facility, except where—

(a) the child is being transferred to or from a short-term holding facility, or

(b) sub-paragraph (3) of paragraph 18 applies.

(2) An unaccompanied child may be detained under paragraph 16(2) in a short-term holding facility for a maximum period of 24 hours, and only for so long as the following two conditions are met.

(3) The first condition is that—

(a) directions are in force that require the child to be removed from the short-term holding facility within the relevant 24 hour period, or

(b) a decision on whether or not to give directions is likely to result in such directions.

(4) The second condition is that the immigration officer under whose authority the child is being detained reasonably believes that the child will be removed from the short-term holding facility within the relevant 24 hour period in accordance with those directions.

(5) An unaccompanied child detained under paragraph 16(2) who has been removed from a short-term holding facility and detained elsewhere may be detained again in a short-term holding facility but only if, and for as long as, the relevant 24 hour period has not ended.

(6) An unaccompanied child who has been released following detention under paragraph 16(2) may be detained again in a short-term holding facility in accordance with this paragraph.

(7) In this paragraph—

'relevant 24 hour period', in relation to the detention of a child in a short-term holding facility, means the period of 24 hours starting when the child was detained (or, in a case falling within sub-paragraph (5), first detained) in a short-term holding facility;

'short-term holding facility' has the same meaning as in Part 8 of the Immigration and Asylum Act 1999;

'unaccompanied child' means a person—

(a) who is under the age of 18, and

(b) who is not accompanied (whilst in detention) by his or her parent or another individual who has care of him or her.]

Note: Paragraph 18B inserted by s 5 Immigration Act 2014 from 8 July 2014 (SI 2014/1820).

19.—(1) Where a person is refused leave to enter the United Kingdom and directions are given in respect of him under paragraph 8 or 10 above, then subject to the provisions of this paragraph the owners or agents of the ship or aircraft in which he arrived shall be liable to pay the Secretary of State on demand any expenses incurred by the latter in respect of the custody, accommodation or maintenance of that person [for any period (not exceeding 14 days)] after his arrival while he was detained or liable to be detained under paragraph 16 above.

(2) Sub-paragraph (1) above shall not apply to expenses in respect of a person who, when he arrived in the United Kingdom, held a [certificate of entitlement] or a current entry clearance or was the person named in a current work permit; and for this purpose a document purporting to be a [certificate of entitlement], entry clearance or work permit is to be regarded as being one unless its falsity is reasonably apparent.

(3) If, before the directions for a person's removal under paragraph 8 or 10 above have been carried out, he is given leave to enter the United Kingdom, or if he is afterwards given that leave in consequence of the determination in his favour of an appeal under this Act (being an appeal against a refusal of leave to enter by virtue of which the directions were given), or it is determined on an appeal under this Act that he does not require leave

to enter (being an appeal occasioned by such a refusal), no sum shall be demanded under sub-paragraph (1) above for expenses incurred in respect of that person and any sum already demanded and paid shall be refunded.

(4) Sub-paragraph (1) above shall not have effect in relation to directions which in consequence of an appeal under this Act, have ceased to have effect or are for the time being of no effect; and the expenses to which that sub-paragraph applies include expenses in conveying the person in question to and from the place where he is detained or accommodated unless the journey is made for the purpose of attending an appeal by him under this Act.

Note: Words in square brackets in subparagraph (1) substituted by Asylum and Immigration Act 1996 from 1 October 1996. Words in square brackets in subparagraph (2) substituted by British Nationality Act 1981, s 39(6). Paragraph 19 has effect in a form modified by and in circumstances specified by the Channel Tunnel (International Arrangements) Order (SI 1993/1813) as amended by SIs 1994/1405, 2000/913, 2001/178, 2001/3707, 2006/1003 and 2007/3759.

20.—(1) Subject to the provisions of this paragraph, in either of the following cases, that is to say,—

(a) where directions are given in respect of an illegal entrant under paragraph 9 or 10 above; and

(b) where a person has lawfully entered the United Kingdom without leave by virtue of section 8(1) of this Act, but directions are given in respect of him under paragraph 13(2)(A) above or, in a case within paragraph 13(2)(A), under paragraph 14;

the owners or agents of the ship or aircraft in which he arrived in the United Kingdom shall be liable to pay the Secretary of State on demand any expenses incurred by the latter in respect of the custody, accommodation or maintenance of that person [for any period (not exceeding 14 days)] after his arrival while he was detained or liable to be detained under paragraph 16 above.

[(1A) Sub-paragraph (1) above shall not apply to expenses in respect of an illegal entrant if he obtained leave to enter by deception and the leave has not been cancelled under paragraph 6(2) above.]

(2) If, before the directions for a person's removal from the United Kingdom have been carried out, he is given leave to remain in the United Kingdom, no sum shall be demanded under sub-paragraph (1) above for expenses incurred in respect of that person and any sum already demanded and paid shall be refunded.

(3) Sub-paragraph (1) above shall not have effect in relation to directions which, in consequence of an appeal under this Act, are for the time being of no effect; and the expenses to which that sub-paragraph applies include expenses in conveying the person in question to and from the place where he is detained or accommodated unless the journey is made for the purpose of attending an appeal by him under this Act.

Note: Words in square brackets substituted and (1A) inserted by Asylum and Immigration Act 1996 from 1 October 1996. Paragraph 20 has effect in a form modified by and in circumstances specified by the Channel Tunnel (International Arrangements) Order (SI 1993/1813) as amended by SIs 1994/1405, 2000/913, 2001/178, 2001/3707, 2006/1003 and 2007/3759.

Temporary admission of persons liable to detention

(21) …

(22) …

(23) …

(24) ...

(25) ...

Note: Paragraphs 21–25 omitted by Immigration Act 2016, Schedule 10 from 15 January 2018 subject to transitional provisions in SI 2017/1241.

[Entry and search of premises

25A.—(1) This paragraph applies if—

(a) a person is arrested under this Schedule; or

(b) a person who was arrested [other than under this Schedule] is detained by an immigration officer under this Schedule.

(2) An immigration officer may enter and search any premises—

(a) occupied or controlled by the arrested person, or

(b) in which that person was when he was arrested, or immediately before he was arrested, for relevant documents.

(3) The power may be exercised—

(a) only if the officer has reasonable grounds for believing that there are relevant documents on the premises;

(b) only to the extent that it is reasonably required for the purpose of discovering relevant documents; and

(c) subject to sub-paragraph (4), only if a senior officer has authorised its exercise in writing.

(4) An immigration officer may conduct a search under sub-paragraph (2)—

(a) before taking the arrested person to a place where he is to be detained; and

(b) without obtaining an authorisation under sub-paragraph (3)(c), if the presence of that person at a place other than one where he is to be detained is necessary to make an effective search for any relevant documents.

(5) An officer who has conducted a search under sub-paragraph (4) must inform a senior officer as soon as is practicable.

(6) The officer authorising a search, or who is informed of one under sub-paragraph (5), must make a record in writing of—

(a) the grounds for the search; and

(b) the nature of the documents that were sought.

[(6A) If, on an application made by an immigration officer, a justice of the peace is satisfied that—

(a) there are reasonable grounds for believing that relevant documents may be found on premises not within sub-paragraph (2) which are [[in sub-paragraph (6AA)]], and

(b) any of the conditions in sub-paragraph (6B) is met [[in relation to each set of premises specified in the application]], the justice of the peace may issue a warrant authorising an immigration officer to enter and search the premises.

[(6AA) The premises referred to in sub-paragraph (6A) above are—

(a) one or more sets of premises specified in the application, or

(b) subject to sub-paragraph (6BA), any premises occupied or controlled by a person specified in the application, including such sets of premises as are so specified (in which case the application is for an 'all premises warrant').

(6AB) If the application is for an all premises warrant, the justice of the peace must also be satisfied—

(a) that there are reasonable grounds for believing that it is necessary to search premises occupied or controlled by the person in question which are not specified in the application in order to find the relevant documents, and

(b) that it is not reasonably practicable to specify in the application all the premises which the person occupies or controls and which might need to be searched.

(6AC) Subject to sub-paragraph (6BA), the warrant may authorise entry to and search of premises on more than one occasion if, on the application, the justice of the peace is satisfied that it is necessary to authorise multiple entries in order to achieve the purpose for which the justice issues the warrant.

(6AD) If it authorises multiple entries, the number of entries authorised may be unlimited, or limited to a maximum.]

(6B) The conditions [[mentioned in sub-paragraph (6A)(b)]] are that—

(a) it is not practicable to communicate with any person entitled to grant entry to the premises;

(b) it is practicable to communicate with a person entitled to grant entry to the premises but it is not practicable to communicate with any person entitled to grant access to the relevant documents;

(c) entry to the premises will not be granted unless a warrant is produced;

(d) the purpose of a search may be frustrated or seriously prejudiced unless an immigration officer arriving at the premises can secure immediate entry.

[**(6BA)** A justice of the peace in Scotland may not issue—

(a) an all premises warrant under this paragraph, or

(b) a warrant under this paragraph authorising multiple entries.]

(6C) In the application of)[[sub-paragraphs (6A) to (6BA)]]to Scotland, references to a justice of the peace are to be treated as references to the sheriff or a justice of the peace.]

(7) An officer searching premises under [this paragraph]—

(a) may seize... any documents he finds which he has reasonable grounds for believing are relevant documents;

[**7A)** Sub-paragraph (7B) applies where—

(a) an officer is searching premises under this paragraph, and

(b) any document the officer has reasonable grounds for believing is a relevant document is stored in any electronic form and is accessible from the premises.

(7B) The officer may require the document to be produced in a form in which it can be taken away and in which it is visible and legible or from which it can readily be produced in a visible and legible form.

(7C) If a requirement under sub-paragraph (7B) is not complied with or a document to which that sub-paragraph applies cannot be produced in a form of the kind mentioned in that sub-paragraph, the officer may seize the device or medium on which it is stored.]

(8) But [sub-paragraphs (7) to (7A) do] not apply to documents which the officer has reasonable grounds for believing are items subject to legal privilege.

[**(8A)** An immigration officer may retain a document seized under [{this}paragraph] while the officer has reasonable grounds for believing that—

(a) the arrested person may be liable to removal from the United Kingdom in accordance with a provision of the Immigration Acts, and

(b) retention of the document may facilitate the person's removal.]

(9) 'Relevant documents' means any documents which might—

(a) establish the arrested person's identity, nationality or citizenship; or

(b) indicate the place from which he has travelled to the United Kingdom or to which he is proposing to go.

(10) 'Senior officer' means an immigration officer not below the rank of chief immigration officer.]

Note: Paragraph 25A inserted by Immigration and Asylum Act 1999 from 14 February 2000. Subparagraphs (6A), (6B), (6C) and (8A) inserted, words in square brackets substituted and words omitted from subparagraph (7) by Sch 1 Immigration Act 2014 from 28 July 2014 (SI 2014/1820). Subparagraph (7A)–(7C) inserted by Immigration Act 2016, s 46 from 12 July 2016 (SI 2016/603). Words in square brackets at sub-paragraphs (8) and (8A) amended by the Immigration Act 2016, s 46 from 12 July 2016 (SI 2016/603). Words in double square brackets substituted at sub-paragraph (6A) and inserted at (6A)(b) by the Immigration Act 2016, Schedule 8 from 1 December 2016 (SI 2016/1037). Subparagraphs (6AA)–(6AD) and (6BA) inserted by Immigration Act 2016, Schedule 8 from 1 December 2016 (SI 2016/1037). Words in double square brackets inserted in subparagraph (6B) and substituted in (6C) by Immigration Act 2016, Schedule 8 from 1 December 2016 (SI 2016/1037).

[Searching persons arrested by immigration officers

25B.—(1) This paragraph applies if a person is arrested under this Schedule.

(2) An immigration officer may search the arrested person if he has reasonable grounds for believing that the arrested person may present a danger to himself or others.

(3) The officer may search the arrested person for—

(a) anything which he might use to assist his escape from lawful custody; or

(b) any document which might—

(i) establish his identity, nationality or citizenship; or

(ii) indicate the place from which he has travelled to the United Kingdom or to which he is proposing to go.

(4) The power conferred by sub-paragraph (3) may be exercised—

(a) only if the officer has reasonable grounds for believing that the arrested person may have concealed on him anything of a kind mentioned in that sub-paragraph; and

(b) only to the extent that it is reasonably required for the purpose of discovering any such thing.

(5) A power conferred by this paragraph to search a person is not to be read as authorising an officer to require a person to remove any of his clothing in public other than an outer coat, jacket or glove; but it does authorise the search of a person's mouth.

(6) An officer searching a person under sub-paragraph (2) may seize and retain anything he finds, if he has reasonable grounds for believing that the person searched might use it to cause physical injury to himself or to another person.

(7) An officer searching a person under sub-paragraph (3)(a) may seize and retain anything he finds, if he has reasonable grounds for believing that he might use it to assist his escape from lawful custody.

(8) An officer searching a person under sub-paragraph (3)(b) may seize and retain anything he finds, other than an item subject to legal privilege, if he has reasonable grounds for believing that it might be a document falling within that sub-paragraph.

{(8A) Sub-paragraph (8B) applies where—

(a) an officer is searching a person under this paragraph, and

(b) any document the officer has reasonable grounds for believing is a document within sub-paragraph (3)(b) is stored in any electronic form on a device or medium found on the person.

(8B) The officer may require the document to be produced in a form in which it can be taken away and in which it is visible and legible or from which it can readily be produced in a visible and legible form.

(8C) If a requirement under sub-paragraph (8B) is not complied with or a document to which that sub-paragraph applies cannot be produced in a form of the kind mentioned in that sub-paragraph, the officer may seize the device or medium on which it is stored.

(8D) Sub-paragraphs (8B) and (8C) do not apply to a document which the officer has reasonable grounds for believing is an item subject to legal privilege.}

(9) Nothing seized under sub-paragraph (6) or (7) may be retained when the person from whom it was seized—

(a) is no longer in custody, or

(b) is in the custody of a court but has been released on bail.]

Note: Paragraph 25B inserted by Immigration and Asylum Act 1999 from 14 February 2000. Sub-paragraph (8A)–(8D) inserted by Immigration Act 2016, s 46 from 12 July 2016 (SI 2016/603).

[Searching persons in police custody

25C.—(1) This paragraph applies if a person—

(a) has been arrested under this Schedule; and

(b) is in custody at a police station.

(2) An immigration officer may, at any time, search the arrested person in order to ascertain whether he has with him—

(a) anything which he might use to—

(i) cause physical injury to himself or others;

(ii) damage property;

(iii) interfere with evidence; or

(iv) assist his escape; or

(b) any document which might—

(i) establish his identity, nationality or citizenship; or

(ii) indicate the place from which he has travelled to the United Kingdom or to which he is proposing to go.

(3) The power may be exercised only to the extent that the officer considers it to be necessary for the purpose of discovering anything of a kind mentioned in sub-paragraph (2).

(4) An officer searching a person under this paragraph may seize and retain anything he finds, if he has reasonable grounds for believing that—

(a) that person might use it for one or more of the purposes mentioned in sub-paragraph (2)(a); or

(b) it might be a document falling within sub-paragraph (2)(b).

(5) But the officer may not retain anything seized under sub-paragraph (2)(a)—

(a) for longer than is necessary in view of the purpose for which the search was carried out; or

(b) when the person from whom it was seized is no longer in custody or is in the custody of a court but has been released on bail.

(6) The person from whom something is seized must be told the reason for the seizure unless he is—

(a) violent or appears likely to become violent; or

(b) incapable of understanding what is said to him.

(7) An intimate search may not be conducted under this paragraph.

(8) The person carrying out a search under this paragraph must be of the same sex as the person searched.

(9) 'Intimate search' has the same meaning as in section 28H(11).]

Note: Paragraph 25C inserted by Immigration and Asylum Act 1999 from 14 February 2000.

[Entry of premises to search for driving licence

25CA.—(1) An authorised officer may exercise the powers in this section if the officer has reasonable grounds for believing that a person—

(a) is in possession of a driving licence, and

(b) is not lawfully resident in the United Kingdom.

(2) The authorised officer may enter and search any premises—

(a) occupied or controlled by the person, or

(b) in which the person was when the person was encountered by the officer, for the driving licence.

(3) The power conferred by sub-paragraph (2) may be exercised—

(a) only if the authorised officer has reasonable grounds for believing that the driving licence is on the premises,

(b) only to the extent that it is reasonably required for the purpose of discovering the driving licence, and

(c) unless the authorised officer is a constable, only if a senior officer has authorised its exercise in writing.

(4) Sub-paragraph (3)(c) does not apply where it is not reasonably practicable for the authorised officer to obtain the authorisation of a senior officer before exercising the power.

(5) An authorised officer who has conducted a search in reliance on sub- paragraph (4) must inform a senior officer as soon as is practicable.

(6) The senior officer authorising a search, or who is informed of one under sub-paragraph (5), must make a record in writing of the grounds for the search.

(7) In this paragraph and paragraphs 25CB and 25CC—'authorised officer' means—

(a) an immigration officer,

(b) a constable, or

(c) a person of a kind authorised for the purposes of this paragraph and paragraphs 25CB and 25CC by the Secretary of State;

'driving licence'—

(a) means a licence to drive a motor vehicle granted under Part 3 of the Road Traffic Act 1988 or Part II of the Road Traffic (Northern Ireland) Order 1981 (SI 1981/154 (NI 1)), and

(b) includes a licence of that kind which has been revoked;

'senior officer' means—

(a) in relation to an authorised officer who is an immigration officer, an immigration officer not below the rank of chief immigration officer;

(b) in relation to an authorised officer other than an immigration officer, a person of a kind designated by the Secretary of State for the purposes of this paragraph in relation to an authorised officer of that kind.

(8) For the purposes of this paragraph and paragraphs 25CB and 25CC a person is not lawfully resident in the United Kingdom if the person requires leave to enter or remain in the United Kingdom but does not have it.

Searching persons for driving licences

25CB.—(1) An authorised officer may exercise the powers in this section if the officer has reasonable grounds for believing that a person—

(a) is in possession of a driving licence, and

(b) is not lawfully resident in the United Kingdom.

(2) The authorised officer may search the person for the driving licence.

(3) The power conferred by sub-paragraph (2) may be exercised—

(a) only if the authorised officer has reasonable grounds for believing that the driving licence may be concealed on the person, and

(b) only to the extent that it is reasonably required for the purpose of discovering the driving licence.

(4) An intimate search may not be carried out under sub-paragraph (2).

(5) In sub-paragraph (4) 'intimate search' has the same meaning as in section 28H(11).

Seizure and retention of driving licence

25CC.—(1) If an authorised officer who is exercising a power to search a person or premises finds a driving licence to which this sub-paragraph applies in the course of the search, the officer may seize and retain the licence.

(2) Sub-paragraph (1) applies to a driving licence if—

(a) the authorised officer finds the licence in the possession of a person who the authorised officer has reasonable grounds for believing is not lawfully resident in the United Kingdom, or

(b) the authorised officer has reasonable grounds for believing that the holder of the licence is not lawfully resident in the United Kingdom.

(3) A driving licence seized under sub-paragraph (1) must, as soon as practicable, be given to—

(a) the Secretary of State, in the case of a licence granted by the Secretary of State, or

(b) the Department for Infrastructure for Northern Ireland, in the case of a licence granted by the Department.

(4) A person who is in possession of a driving licence by virtue of sub- paragraph (3) must retain it if—

(a) it has not been revoked,

(b) it has been revoked but the time limit for an appeal against revocation of the licence has not expired, or

(c) it has been revoked, such an appeal has been brought but the appeal has not been determined.

(5) A driving licence which is required to be retained under sub-paragraph (4) must be retained—

(a) until a decision is taken not to revoke it, or

(b) if it has been or is subsequently revoked—

(i) until the time limit for an appeal against revocation of the licence expires without an appeal being brought, or

(ii) until such an appeal is determined.

(6) A driving licence which is in the possession of a person by virtue of sub-paragraph (3) but which is not required to be retained under sub-paragraphs (4) and (5) must be returned to the holder if—

(a) a decision is taken not to revoke the licence, or

(b) an appeal against revocation of the licence is determined in favour of the holder.

(7) Otherwise the driving licence may be dealt with in such manner as that person thinks fit.

(8) Neither the Secretary of State nor the Department for Infrastructure for Northern Ireland is obliged to re-issue a licence which has been seized and retained under this paragraph.

(9) References in this paragraph to an appeal against the revocation of a licence are to—

(a) an appeal under section 100 of the Road Traffic Act 1988, in the case of a licence granted by the Secretary of State, or

(b) an appeal under Article 16 of the Road Traffic (Northern Ireland) Order 1981 (SI 1981/154 (NI 1)), in the case of a licence granted by the Department for Infrastructure for Northern Ireland.

(10) References in this paragraph to the holder of a driving licence, in relation to a licence that has been revoked, include the person who was the holder of the licence before it was revoked.}

Note: Paragraph 25CA, 25CB and 25CC inserted by Immigration Act 2016, s 43 from a from 31 July 2017 for specified purposes.

[Access and copying

25D.—(1) If a person showing himself—

(a) to be the occupier of the premises on which seized material was seized, or

(b) to have had custody or control of the material immediately before it was seized, asks the immigration officer who seized the material for a record of what he seized, the officer must provide the record to that person within a reasonable time.

(2) If a relevant person asks an immigration officer for permission to be granted access to seized material, the officer must arrange for that person to have access to the material under the supervision of an immigration officer.

(3) An immigration officer may photograph or copy, or have photographed or copied, seized material.

(4) If a relevant person asks an immigration officer for a photograph or copy of seized material, the officer must arrange for—

(a) that person to have access to the material under the supervision of an immigration officer for the purpose of photographing or copying it; or

(b) the material to be photographed or copied.

(5) A photograph or copy made under sub-paragraph (4)(b) must be supplied within a reasonable time.

(6) There is no duty under this paragraph to arrange for access to, or the supply of a photograph or copy of, any material if there are reasonable grounds for believing that to do so would prejudice—

(a) the exercise of any functions in connection with which the material was seized; or

(b) an investigation which is being conducted under this Act, or any criminal proceedings which may be brought as a result.

(7) 'Relevant person' means—

(a) a person who had custody or control of seized material immediately before it was seized, or

(b) someone acting on behalf of such a person.

(8) 'Seized material' means anything which has been seized and retained under this Schedule.][[other than a driving licence seized under paragraph 25CC]].

Note: Paragraph 25D inserted by Immigration and Asylum Act 1999 from 14 February 2000. Words in double square brackets inserted by Immigration Act 2016, s 43(3) from 31 July 2017 for specified purposes.

[**25E.** Section 28L applies for the purposes of this Schedule as it applies for the purposes of Part III.]

Note: Paragraph 25E inserted by Immigration and Asylum Act 1999 from 14 February 2000.

Supplementary duties of those connected with ships or aircraft or with ports

26.—(1) The owners or agents of a ship or aircraft employed to carry passengers for reward shall not, without the approval of the Secretary of State, arrange for the ship or aircraft to call at a port in the United Kingdom other than a port of entry for the purpose of disembarking passengers, if any of the passengers on board may not enter the United Kingdom without leave, or for the purpose of embarking passengers unless the owners or agents have reasonable cause to believe all of them to be [British citizens].

[(1A) Sub-paragraph (1) does not apply in such circumstances, if any, as the Secretary of State may by order prescribe.]

(2) The Secretary of State may from time to time give written notice to the owners or agents of any ships or aircraft designating control areas for the embarkation or disembarkation of passengers in any port in the United Kingdom, and specifying the conditions and restrictions (if any) to be observed in any control area; and where by notice given to any owners or agents a control area is for the time being designated for the embarkation or disembarkation of passengers at any port, the owners or agents shall take all reasonable steps to secure that, in the case of their ships or aircraft, passengers do not embark or disembark, as the case may be, at the port outside the control area and that any conditions or restrictions notified to them are observed.

(3) The Secretary of State may also from time to time give to any persons concerned with the management of a port in the United Kingdom written notice designating control areas in the port and specifying conditions or restrictions to be observed in any control area; and any such person shall take all reasonable steps to secure that any conditions or restrictions as notified to him are observed.

[(3A) The power conferred by sub-paragraph (1A) is exercisable by statutory instrument; and any such instrument shall be subject to annulment by a resolution of either House of Parliament.]

[(4) Part 1A of this Schedule makes provision for and in connection with the imposition of a penalty for certain breaches of sub-paragraph (2) or (3)].

Note: Words in square brackets substituted by British Nationality Act 1981. Words omitted from paragraph 26(1) and paragraphs 26(1A) and 26(3A) inserted by Immigration and Asylum Act 1999 from 14 February 2000. Paragraph 26 has effect in a form modified by and in circumstances specified by the Channel Tunnel (International Arrangements) Order (SI 1993/1813) as amended by SIs 1994/1405, 2000/913, 2001/178, 2001/3707, 2006/1003 and 2007/3759. Subparagraph (4) inserted by Immigration Act 2016, s 74 from a date to be appointed.

27.—(1) The captain of a ship or aircraft arriving in the United Kingdom—

(a) shall take such steps as may be necessary to secure that persons on board do not disembark there unless either they have been examined by an immigration officer, or they disembark in accordance with arrangements approved by an immigration officer, or they are members of the crew who may lawfully enter the United Kingdom without leave by virtue of section 8(1) of this Act; and

(b) where the examination of persons on board is to be carried out on the ship or aircraft, shall take such steps as may be necessary to secure that those to be examined are presented for the purpose in an orderly manner.

[[(1A) Sub-paragraph (1) also applies to the captain of a ship or aircraft arriving in United Kingdom waters if—

(a) there are offshore workers on board, or

(b) an immigration officer has informed the captain that they wish to examine any person on board in the exercise of the power under paragraph 2.

(1B) In sub-paragraph (1A), "offshore worker" and "United Kingdom waters" have the same meaning as in section 11A.]]

[(2) The Secretary of State may by order require, or enable an immigration officer to require, a responsible person in respect of a ship or aircraft to supply—

(a) a passenger list showing the names and nationality or citizenship of passengers arriving or leaving on board the ship or aircraft;

(b) particulars of members of the crew of the ship or aircraft.

(3) An order under sub-paragraph (2) may relate—

(a) to all ships or aircraft arriving or expected to arrive in the United Kingdom;

(b) to all ships or aircraft leaving or expected to leave the United Kingdom;

(c) to ships or aircraft arriving or expected to arrive in the United Kingdom from or by way of a specified country;

(d) to ships or aircraft leaving or expected to leave the United Kingdom to travel to or by way of a specified country;

(e) to specified ships or specified aircraft.

(4) For the purposes of sub-paragraph (2) the following are responsible persons in respect of a ship or aircraft—

(a) the owner or agent, and

(b) the captain.

(5) An order under sub-paragraph (2)—

(a) may specify the time at which or period during which information is to be provided,

(b) may specify the form and manner in which information is to be provided,

[(ba) may require a responsible person to be able to receive, in a specified form and manner, communications sent by the Secretary of State or an immigration officer relating to the information,]

(c) shall be made by statutory instrument, and

(d) shall be subject to annulment in pursuance of a resolution of either House of Parliament.]

Note: Subparagraph (2) substituted (from 5 November 2007 (SI 2007/3138)) and subparagraphs (3)–(5) inserted (from 1 March 2008 (SI 2007/3138 as amended by SI 2007/3580)) by Immigration, Asylum and Nationality Act 2006, s 31. Paragraph 27 has effect in a form modified by and in circumstances specified by the Channel Tunnel (International Arrangements) Order (SI 1993/1813) as amended by SIs 1994/1405, 2000/913, 2001/178, 2001/3707, 2006/1003 and 2007/3759. Subparagraph (ba) inserted from 12 February 2015 by Counter Terrorism and Security Act 2015, Schedule 5. Subparagraphs (1A) & (1B) inserted by Nationality and Borders Act 2022 c.36 Sch.6 para 9(3) (date to be appointed)

27A. …

Note: Repealed by Channel Tunnel (International Arrangements) Order 1993/1813 Sch 6(1) para 1 (2 August 1993).

[Passenger information

27B.—(1) This paragraph applies to ships or aircraft—

(a) which have arrived, or are expected to arrive, in the United Kingdom; or

(b) which have left, or are expected to leave, the United Kingdom.

[(1A) This paragraph also applies to ships or aircraft—

(a) which have offshore workers on board, and

(b) which—

(i) have arrived, or are expected to arrive, in United Kingdom waters, or

(ii) have left, or are expected to leave, United Kingdom waters.

(2) If an immigration officer asks the owner or agent ('the carrier') of a ship or aircraft for passenger information [or service information], the carrier must provide that information to the officer.

(3) The officer may ask for passenger information [or service information] relating to—

(a) a particular ship or particular aircraft of the carrier;

(b) particular ships or aircraft (however described) of the carrier; or

(c) all of the carrier's ships or aircraft.

(4) The officer may ask for—

(a) all passenger information [or service information] in relation to the ship or aircraft concerned; or

(b) particular passenger information [or service information] in relation to that ship or aircraft.

[(4A) The officer may ask the carrier to provide a copy of all or part of a document that relates to a passenger and contains passenger information [or service information].]

(5) A request under sub-paragraph (2)—

(a) must be in writing;

(b) must state the date on which it ceases to have effect; and

(c) continues in force until that date, unless withdrawn earlier by written notice by an immigration officer.

(6) The date may not be later than six months after the request is made.

(7) The fact that a request under sub-paragraph (2) has ceased to have effect as a result of sub-paragraph (5) does not prevent the request from being renewed.

(8) The information must be provided—

(a) in such form and manner as the Secretary of State may direct; and

(b) at such time as may be stated in the request.

[(8A) The officer may require a carrier to be able to receive communications from the officer in such form and manner as the Secretary of State may direct.]

(9) 'Passenger information' [or service information] means such information relating to the passengers carried, or expected to be carried, by the ship or aircraft as may be specified.

[(9A) 'Service information' means such information relating to the voyage or flight undertaken by the ship or aircraft as may be specified.]

[[(9B) "Offshore waters" and "United Kingdom waters" have the same meaning in this paragraph as in section 11 A.]]

(10) 'Specified' means specified in an order made by statutory instrument by the Secretary of State.

(11) Such an instrument shall be subject to annulment in pursuance of a resolution of either House of Parliament.]

Note: Paragraph 27B inserted by Immigration and Asylum Act 1999 from 3 April 2000. Subparagraph 4A inserted by Asylum and Immigration (Treatment of Claimants etc.) Act 2004, s 16 from a date to be appointed. Words in square brackets and subparagraph (9A) inserted by Immigration, Asylum and Nationality Act 2006, s 31 from 5 November 2007 (SI 2007/3138). Paragraph 27(B2) modified in its extension to Guernsey by Art 6, Sch 3, SI 2011/2444. Subparagraph (8A) inserted from 12 February 2015 by Counter Terrorism and Security Act 2015, Schedule 5. Subparagraphs (1A) and (9A) inserted by Nationality and Borders Act 2022 c.36 Sch.6 para 9(4) (date to be appointed)

[**27BA.**—(1) The Secretary of State may make regulations requiring responsible persons in respect of ships or aircraft—

(a) which have arrived, or are expected to arrive, in the United Kingdom, or

(b) which have left, or are expected to leave, the United Kingdom, to supply information to the Secretary of State or an immigration officer.

[[(1A) The Secretary of State may also make regulations requiring responsible persons in respect of ships or aircraft—

(a) which have offshore workers on board, and

(b) which—

(i) have arrived, or are expected to arrive, in United Kingdom waters, or

(ii) have left, or are expected to leave, United Kingdom waters, to supply information to the Secretary of State or an immigration officer.]]

(2) The following information may be required under sub-paragraph (1)[[or (1A)—

(a) information about the persons on board;

(b) information about the voyage or flight.

...

(4) The regulations must—

(a) specify or describe the classes of ships or aircraft to which they apply;

(b) specify the information required to be supplied;

(c) specify the time by which the information must be supplied;

(d) specify the form and manner in which the information must be supplied.

(5) The regulations may require responsible persons to be able to receive, in a specified form and manner, communications sent by the Secretary of State or an immigration officer relating to the information.

[[(5A) For the purposes of this paragraph, "offshore workers" and "United Kingdom waters have the same meaning as in section 11A.]]

(6) For the purposes of this paragraph, the following are responsible persons in respect of a ship or aircraft—

(a) the owner or agent, and

(b) the captain.

(7) Regulations under this paragraph may make different provision for different purposes, and in particular may make different provision for different types of carrier, journey or person on board.

(8) The power to make regulations under this paragraph is exercisable by statutory instrument; but no regulations under this paragraph are to be made unless a draft of the regulations has been laid before Parliament and approved by a resolution of each House.

27BB.—(1) The Secretary of State may make regulations imposing penalties for failure to comply with—

(a) an order under paragraph 27(2) (order requiring passenger list or particulars of member of crew),

(b) any request or requirement under paragraph 27B (passenger and service information), or

(c) regulations under paragraph 27BA (passenger, crew and service information).

(2) Regulations under sub-paragraph (1) may in particular make provision—

(a) about how a penalty is to be calculated;

(b) about the procedure for imposing a penalty;

(c) about the enforcement of penalties;

(d) allowing for an appeal against a decision to impose a penalty;

and the regulations may make different provision for different purposes.

(3) Provision in the regulations about the procedure for imposing a penalty must provide for a person to be given an opportunity to object to a proposed penalty in the circumstances set out in the regulations.

(4) The regulations must provide that no penalty may be imposed on a person for failure to comply with an order under paragraph 27(2), a request or requirement under paragraph 27B or regulations under paragraph 27BA where—

(a) proceedings have been instituted against the person under section 27 in respect of the same failure; or

(b) the failure consists of a failure to provide information that the person has also been required to provide under section 32 or 32A of the Immigration, Asylum and Nationality Act 2006 and—

(i) a penalty has been imposed on the person in respect of a failure to provide that information by virtue of regulations made under section 32B of that Act, or

(ii) proceedings have been instituted against the person under section 34 of that Act in respect of a failure to provide that information; or

(c) the failure consists of a failure to provide information that the person has also been required to provide under an authority-to-carry scheme made under section 22 of the Counter-Terrorism and Security Act 2015 and a penalty has been imposed on the person in respect of a failure to provide that information by virtue of regulations made under section 24 of that Act.

(5) Any penalty paid by virtue of this paragraph must be paid into the Consolidated Fund.

(6) The power to make regulations under this paragraph is exercisable by statutory instrument; but no regulations under this paragraph are to be made unless a draft of the regulations has been laid before Parliament and approved by a resolution of each House.]

Note: Paragraphs 27BA and 27BB inserted from 12 February 2015 by Counter Terrorism and Security Act 2015, Schedule 5. Subsections (1A) & (5A) inserted, and words inserted in double brackets in sub- paragraph (2) by Nationality and Borders Act 2022 c.36 Sch.6 para 9(5) (date to be appointed)

[PART 1A
PENALTY FOR BREACH OF PARAGRAPH 26(2) OR (3)

28.—(1) Sub-paragraph (2) applies where the Secretary of State has given written notice under paragraph 26(2) to the owner or agent of an aircraft—

(a) designating a control area for the embarkation or disembarkation of passengers in an airport in the United Kingdom, and

(b) specifying conditions or restrictions to be observed in the control area.

(2) The Secretary of State may impose a penalty on the owner or agent if the owner or agent fails to take all reasonable steps to secure that—

(a) passengers embarking on or disembarking from the aircraft at the airport do not embark or disembark at the airport outside the control area, or

(b) the conditions or restrictions specified in the notice are observed.

(3) Sub-paragraph (4) applies where the Secretary of State has given written notice under paragraph 26(3) to a person concerned with the management of an airport in the United Kingdom—

(a) designating a control area in the airport, and

(b) specifying conditions or restrictions to be observed in the control area.

(4) The Secretary of State may impose a penalty on the person if the person fails to take all reasonable steps to secure that the conditions or restrictions specified in the notice are observed.

(5) The Secretary of State may impose a separate penalty under sub-paragraph (2) or (4) in respect of each failure of the kind mentioned in that sub-paragraph.

(6) The amount of a penalty imposed under sub-paragraph (2) or (4) may be such an amount as the Secretary of State considers appropriate; but the amount of each penalty must not exceed the prescribed maximum.

Codes of practice

28A.—(1) The Secretary of State must issue a code of practice to be followed by—

(a) agents and operators of aircraft to whom notices under paragraph 26(2) have been given, and

(b) persons concerned with the management of airports in the United Kingdom to whom notices under paragraph 26(3) have been given.

(2) The Secretary of State must have regard to the code (in addition to any other matters the Secretary of State thinks relevant)—

(a) when deciding whether to impose a penalty under paragraph 28, and

(b) when considering a notice of objection under paragraph 28C.

(3) The Secretary of State must issue a code of practice specifying matters to be considered in determining the amount of a penalty under paragraph 28.

(4) The Secretary of State must have regard to the code (in addition to any other matters the Secretary of State thinks relevant)—

(a) when imposing a penalty under paragraph 28, and

(b) when considering a notice of objection under paragraph 28C.

(5) Before issuing a code under this paragraph the Secretary of State must lay the code before Parliament.

(6) A code under this paragraph comes into force in accordance with provision made by regulations made by the Secretary of State.

(7) The Secretary of State may from time to time review a code under this paragraph and may revise and re-issue it following a review.

(8) References in sub-paragraphs (5) and (6) to a code include a revised code.

Penalty notices

28B.—(1) If the Secretary of State decides that a person is liable to a penalty under paragraph 28, the Secretary of State must notify the person of that decision.

(2) A notice under sub-paragraph (1) (a 'penalty notice') must—

(a) be in writing,

(b) state why the Secretary of State thinks the recipient is liable to the penalty,

(c) state the amount of the penalty,

(d) specify the date on which the penalty notice is given,

(e) specify the date, at least 28 days after the date specified in the notice as the date on which it is given, before which the penalty must be paid,

(f) specify how the penalty must be paid,

(g) include an explanation of the steps that the person may take if the person objects to the penalty (including specifying the manner and form in which any notice of objection must be given to the Secretary of State), and

(h) include an explanation of the steps the Secretary of State may take to recover any unpaid penalty.

Objections

28C.—(1) The recipient of a penalty notice ('the recipient') may object to the penalty notice by giving a notice of objection to the Secretary of State.

(2) A notice of objection must—

(a) be in writing,

(b) give the reasons for the objection,

(c) be given in the manner and form specified in the penalty notice, and

(d) be given before the end of the period of 28 days beginning with the date specified in the penalty notice as the date on which it is given.

(3) Where the Secretary of State receives a notice of objection, the Secretary of State must consider it and—

(a) cancel the penalty,

(b) reduce the penalty,

(c) increase the penalty, or

(d) determine not to alter the penalty.

(4) After reaching a decision as to how to proceed under sub-paragraph (3), the Secretary of State must notify the recipient of the decision in writing.

(5) A notification under sub-paragraph (4) must be given before the end of the period of 70 days beginning with the date specified in the penalty notice as the date on which it is given, or such longer period as the Secretary of State may agree with the recipient.

(6) A notification under sub-paragraph (4), other than one notifying the recipient that the Secretary of State has decided to cancel the penalty, must—

(a) state the amount of the penalty following the Secretary of State's consideration of the notice of objection,

(b) state the Secretary of State's reasons for the decision under sub-paragraph (3),

(c) specify the date, at least 28 days after the date on which the notification is given, before which the penalty must be paid,

(d) specify how the penalty must be paid,

(e) include an explanation of the recipient's rights of appeal, and

(f) include an explanation of the steps the Secretary of State may take to recover any unpaid penalty.

Appeals

28D.—(1) A person ('the appellant') may appeal to the court against a decision to require the person to pay a penalty under paragraph 28.

(2) An appeal may be brought only if the appellant has given a notice of objection and the Secretary of State has—

(a) reduced the penalty under paragraph 28C(3)(b),

(b) increased the penalty under paragraph 28C(3)(c), or

(c) determined not to alter the penalty under paragraph 28C(3)(d).

(3) An appeal must be brought within the period of 28 days beginning with the date on which the appellant is notified of the Secretary of State's decision on the notice of objection under paragraph 28C(4).

(4) On appeal, the court may—

(a) allow the appeal and cancel the penalty,

(b) allow the appeal and reduce the penalty, or

(c) dismiss the appeal.

(5) An appeal is to be a re-hearing of the Secretary of State's decision to impose a penalty and is to be determined having regard to—

(a) any code of practice under paragraph 28A(1) which had effect at the time of the events to which the penalty relates,

(b) any code of practice under paragraph 28A(3) which has effect at the time of the appeal, and

(c) any other matters which the court thinks relevant (which may include matters of which the Secretary of State was unaware).

(6) Sub-paragraph (5) has effect despite any provision of rules of court.

(7) In this paragraph 'the court' means—

(a) the county court, if the appeal relates to a penalty imposed under paragraph 28 in relation to an airport in England and Wales;

(b) the sheriff, if the appeal relates to a penalty imposed under paragraph 28 in relation to an airport in Scotland;

(c) a county court in Northern Ireland, if the appeal relates to a penalty imposed under paragraph 28 in relation to an airport in Northern Ireland.

(8) But—

(a) the county court in England and Wales, or a county court in Northern Ireland, may transfer proceedings under this paragraph to the High Court, and

(b) the sheriff may transfer proceedings under this paragraph to the Court of Session.

Enforcement

28E.—(1) This section applies where a sum is payable to the Secretary of State as a penalty under paragraph 28.

(2) In England and Wales the penalty is recoverable as if it were payable under an order of the county court in England and Wales.

(3) In Scotland the penalty may be enforced in the same manner as an extract registered decree arbitral bearing a warrant for execution issued by the sheriff court of any sheriffdom in Scotland.

(4) In Northern Ireland the penalty is recoverable as if it were payable under an order of a county court in Northern Ireland.

(5) Where action is taken under this paragraph for the recovery of a sum payable as a penalty under this Chapter, the penalty is—

(a) in relation to England and Wales, to be treated for the purposes of section 98 of the Courts Act 2003 (register of judgments and orders etc) as if it were a judgment entered in the county court;

(b) in relation to Northern Ireland, to be treated for the purposes of Article 116 of the Judgments Enforcement (Northern Ireland) Order 1981 (S.I. 1981/226 (N.I. 6)) (register of judgments) as if it were a judgment in respect of which an application has been accepted under Article 22 or 23(1) of that Order.

(6) Money paid to the Secretary of State by way of a penalty under paragraph 28 must be paid into the Consolidated Fund.

Service of documents

28F.—(1) A document which is to be issued or served on a person outside the United Kingdom for the purposes of paragraph 28B or 28C or in the course of proceedings under paragraph 28E may be issued or served—

(a) in person,

(b) by post,

(c) by facsimile transmission,

(d) by e-mail, or

(e) in any other prescribed manner.

(2) The Secretary of State may by regulations provide that a document issued or served in a manner listed in sub-paragraph (1) in accordance with the regulations is to be taken to have been received at a time specified by or determined in accordance with the regulations.

Interpretation of this Part of this Schedule

28G. In this Part of this Schedule—

'penalty notice' has the meaning given by paragraph 28B(2); 'prescribed' means prescribed by regulations made by the Secretary of State.

Regulations under this Part of this Schedule

28H.—(1) Regulations under this Part of this Schedule are to be made by statutory instrument.

(2) A statutory instrument containing (whether alone or with other provision) regulations under paragraph 28(6) may not be made unless a draft of the instrument has been laid before, and approved by a resolution of, each House of Parliament.

(3) A statutory instrument containing any other regulations under this Part of this Schedule and to which sub-paragraph (2) does not apply is subject to annulment in pursuance of a resolution of either House of Parliament.

(4) Regulations under this Part of this Schedule—

(a) may make different provision for different purposes;

(b) may make incidental, supplementary, consequential, transitional, transitory or saving provision.]

Note: Schedule 2 Part 1A inserted by Immigration Act 2016, Schedule 13 from a date to be appointed.

Part II
Effect of Appeals

Stay on directions for removal

28. ...

Note: Paragraph 28 omitted by Immigration and Asylum Act 1999 from 2 October 2000. Transitional provisions set out in SI 2003/754.

Grant of bail pending appeal

Note: Paragraphs 29–34 omitted by Immigration Act 2016, Schedule 10 from a date to be appointed.

SCHEDULE 3 Section 5

SUPPLEMENTARY PROVISIONS AS TO DEPORTATION

Removal of persons liable to deportation

1.—(1) Where a deportation order is in force against any person, the Secretary of State may give directions for his removal to a country or territory specified in the directions being either—

(a) a country of which he is a national or citizen; or

(b) a country or territory to which there is reason to believe that he will be admitted.

(2) The directions under sub-paragraph (1) above may be either—

(a) directions given to the captain of a ship or aircraft about to leave the United Kingdom requiring him to remove the person in question in that ship or aircraft; or

(b) directions given to the owners or agents of any ship or aircraft requiring them to make arrangements for his removal in a ship or aircraft specified or indicated in the directions; or

(c) directions for his removal in accordance with arrangements to be made by the Secretary of State.

(3) In relation to directions given under this paragraph, paragraphs 11 and 16(4) of Schedule 2 to this Act shall apply, with the substitution of references to the Secretary of State for references to an immigration officer, as they apply in relation to directions for removal given under paragraph 8 of that Schedule.

(4) The Secretary of State, if he thinks fit, may apply in or towards payment of the expenses of or incidental to the voyage from the United Kingdom of a person against whom a deportation order is in force, or the maintenance until departure of such a person and his dependants, if any, any money belonging to that person; and except so far as they are paid as aforesaid, those expenses shall be defrayed by the Secretary of State.

Detention or control pending deportation

2.—(1) Where a recommendation for deportation made by a court is in force in respect of any person, [and that person is not detained in pursuance of the sentence or order of any court] he shall [[be detained pending the making of a deportation order in pursuance of the recommendation, unless—

(a) the court by which the recommendation is made grants bail to the person, or

(b) the person is released on immigration bail under Schedule 10 to the Immigration Act 2016.]]

[(1A) Where—

(a) a recommendation for deportation made by a court on a conviction of a person is in force in respect of him; and

(b) he appeals against his conviction or against that recommendation, the powers that the court determining the appeal may exercise include power to [[release the person on bail without setting aside the recommendation.]]]

(2) Where notice has been given to a person in accordance with regulations under [section 105 of the Nationality, Immigration and Asylum Act 2002 (notice of decision)] of a decision to make a deportation order against him, [and he is not detained in pursuance of the sentence or order of a court], he may be detained under the authority of the Secretary of State pending the making of the deportation order.

(3) Where a deportation order is in force against any person, he may be detained under the authority of the Secretary of State pending his removal or departure from the United Kingdom (and if already detained by virtue of sub-paragraph (1) or (2) above when the order is made, shall continue to be detained [[unless he is released on immigration bail under Schedule 10 to the Immigration Act 2016]]).

(4) In relation to detention under sub-paragraph (2) or (3) above, paragraphs 17 [,[to 18A] and 25A to 25E] of Schedule 2 to this Act shall apply as they apply in relation to detention under paragraph 16 of that Schedule[; and for that purpose the reference in paragraph 17(1) to a person liable to detention includes a reference to a person who would be liable to detention upon receipt of a notice which is ready to be given to him].

[(4ZA) The detention under sub-paragraph (1), (2) or (3) of a person to whom section 60 (limitation on detention of pregnant women) of the Immigration Act 2016 applies is subject to that section.]

[(5) The provisions of Schedule 10 to the Immigration Act 2016 that apply in relation to the grant of immigration bail by the First-tier Tribunal apply in relation to the grant of bail by the court under sub-paragraph (1) or (1A).

(6) If the court grants bail to a person under sub-paragraph (1) or (1A), Schedule 10 to the Immigration Act 2016 applies in relation to that person as if the person had been granted immigration bail by the First-tier Tribunal under that Schedule.

(7) A reference in any provision of, or made under, an enactment other than this paragraph to immigration bail granted, or a condition imposed, under Schedule 10 to the Immigration Act 2016 includes bail granted by the court under sub-paragraph (1) or (1A) or (as the case may be) a condition imposed by the court on the grant of such bail.]

Note: Paragraph 1 has effect in a form modified by and in circumstances specified by the Channel Tunnel (International Arrangements) Order (SI 1993/1813) as amended by SIs 1994/1405, 2000/913, 2001/178, 2001/3707, 2006/1003 and 2007/3759. Paragraph 2: words in second square brackets in paragraph 2(1) and paragraphs 2(1A), (5) and (6) added by Criminal Justice Act 1982. Words in first square brackets in paragraph 2(2) substituted by Sch 7 Nationality, Immigration and Asylum Act 2002 from 1 April 2003 (SI 2003/754). Other words in square brackets in paragraphs 2(1) and (2) substituted by Sch 2 Asylum and Immigration (Treatment of Claimants, etc.) Act 2004 from 4 April 2005 (SI 2005/565). Other words in square brackets in paragraph 2(2) and paragraph 2(4A) inserted by Immigration and Asylum Act 1999, s 54 from 10 February 2003 (SI 2003/2). Words in first square brackets in paragraph 2(4) substituted by Sch 2 Immigration Act 2014 from 28 July 2014 (SI 2014/1820). Words in first square brackets in paragraph 2(5) added by Immigration Act 1988, s 10, other words in square brackets inserted by Asylum and Immigration Act 1996 from 1 October 1996. Words in last square brackets in paragraph 2(4) inserted by Immigration, Asylum and Nationality Act 2006 from 31 August 2006 (SI 2006/2226). Subparagraph (4ZA) inserted by Immigration Act 2016, s 60 from 12 July 2016 (SI 2016/603). Words omitted and substituted in square brackets subsection (1) by Schedule 10, para 2 of the Immigration Act 2016 on January 15, 2018 subject to transitional provisions specified in SI2017/1241. Words added in double square brackets at subsection (1A) and (3), and (4ZA) by Schedule 10. Para 2 of the Immigration Act 2016 on January 15, 2018 subject to transitional provisions specified in SI2017/1241. Subparagraphs (5)-(7) substituted for Schedule 3 subparagraphs (4A)-(6) by Immigration Act 2016 on January 15, 2018 subject to transitional provisions specified in SI2017/1241

(3) ...

(4) ...

(5) ...

(6) ...

(7) …

(8) …

(9) …

(10) …

Note: Paras (3)–(10) omitted by Schedule 10, para 21 of the Immigration Act 2016 from January 15, 2018 subject to transitional provisions within SI2017/1241.

SCHEDULE 4

Section 9

INTEGRATION WITH UNITED KINGDOM LAW OF IMMIGRATION LAW OF ISLANDS

Leave to enter

1.—(1) Where under the immigration laws of any of the Islands a person is or has been given leave to enter or remain in the island, or is or has been refused leave, this Act shall have effect in relation to him, if he is not [a British citizen], as if the leave were leave (of like duration) given under this Act to enter or remain in the United Kingdom, or, as the case may be, as if he had under this Act been refused leave to enter the United Kingdom.

(2) Where under the immigration laws of any of the Islands a person has a limited leave to enter or remain in the island subject to any such conditions as are authorised in the United Kingdom by section 3(1) of this Act (being conditions imposed by notice given to him, whether the notice of leave or a subsequent notice), then on his coming to the United Kingdom this Act shall apply, if he is not [a British citizen], as if those conditions related to his stay in the United Kingdom and had been imposed by notice under this Act.

(3) Without prejudice to the generality of sub-paragraphs (1) and (2) above, anything having effect in the United Kingdom by virtue of either of those sub-paragraphs may in relation to the United Kingdom be varied or revoked under this Act in like manner, and subject to the like appeal (if any), as if it had originated under this Act as mentioned in that sub-paragraph.

(4) Where anything having effect in the United Kingdom by virtue of sub-paragraph (1) or (2) above ceases to have effect or is altered in effect as mentioned in sub-paragraph (3) or otherwise by anything done under this Act, sub-paragraph (1) or (2) shall not thereafter apply to it or, as the case may be, shall apply to it as so altered in effect.

(5) Nothing in this paragraph shall be taken as conferring on a person a right of appeal under this Act against any decision or action taken in any of the Islands.

2. Notwithstanding section 3(4) of this Act, leave given to a person under this Act to enter or remain in the United Kingdom shall not continue to apply on his return to the United Kingdom after an absence if he has during that absence entered any of the Islands in circumstances in which he is required under the immigration laws of that island to obtain leave to enter.

Deportation

[**3.**—(1) This Act has effect in relation to a person who is subject to an Islands deportation order as if the order were a deportation order made against him under this Act.

(2) Sub-paragraph (1) does not apply if the person concerned is—

(a) a British citizen;

[(aa) an Irish citizen;]

(b)

[(ca) a relevant person (see paragraph 3A); or]

(d) a member of the family of a British citizen who is neither [a British citizen not an Irish citizen.]

(3) The Secretary of State does not, as a result of sub-paragraph (1), have power to revoke an Islands deportation order.

(4) In any particular case, the Secretary of State may direct that paragraph [[(aa), (ca)]] or (d) of sub-paragraph (2) is not to apply in relation to the Islands deportation order.

(5) Nothing in this paragraph makes it unlawful for a person in respect of whom an Islands deportation order is in force in any of the Islands to enter the United Kingdom on his way from that island to a place outside the United Kingdom.

(6) 'Islands deportation order' means an order made under the immigration laws of any of the Islands under which a person is, or has been, ordered to leave the island and forbidden to return.

(7) Subsections (10) and (12) to (14) of section 80 of the Immigration and Asylum Act 1999 apply for the purposes of this section as they apply for the purposes of that section.]

Note: words in double square brackets inserted and omitted in sub-paragraphs (2) & (4) by Immigration and Social Security (EU Withdrawal) Act 2020 (Consequential, Saving, Transitional and Transitory Provisions) (EU Exit) Regulations 2020/1309 Pt2(1) reg5(5)(a) (December 31, 2020 at 23.00 being the time and date 2020 c.20 Sch.1 para 2(2) comes into force).

[(3A) Relevant person for purposes of paragraph 3

(1) For the purposes of paragraph 3, a person is a "relevant person"—

(a) if the person is in the United Kingdom (whether or not they have entered within the meaning of section 11(1)) having arrived with entry clearance granted by virtue of relevant entry clearance immigration rules;

(b) if the person has leave to enter or remain in the United Kingdom granted by virtue of residence scheme immigration rules;

(c) if the person may be granted leave to enter or remain in the United Kingdom as a person who has a right to enter the United Kingdom by virtue of —

(i) Article 32(1)(b) of the EU withdrawal agreement;

(ii) Article 31(1)(b) of the EEA EFTA separation agreement, or

(iii) Article 26(a)(1)(b) of the Swiss citizens' rights agreement,

whether or not the person has been granted such leave, or

(d) if the person may enter the United Kingdom by virtue of regulations made under section 8 of the European Union (Withdrawal Agreement) Act 2020 (frontier workers), whether or not the person has entered by virtue of those regulations.

(2) In this paragraph—

"EEA EFTA separation agreement" and "Swiss citizens' rights agreement" have the same meanings as in the European Union (Withdrawal Agreement) Act 2020 (see section 39(1) of that Act);

"relevant entry clearance immigration rules" and "residence scheme immigration rules" have the meanings given by section 17 of the European Union (Withdrawal Agreement) Act 2020.]

Note: inserted by Immigration and Social Security Co-ordination (EU Withdrawal) Act 2020 (Consequential, Saving, Transitional and Transitory Provisions) (EU Exit) Regulations 2020/1309 Pt2 (1) reg.5(6) (December 31, 2020 at 23.00 being the time and date 2020 c.20 Sch.1 para 2(2) comes into force)

Illegal entrants

4. Notwithstanding anything in section 1(3) of this Act, it shall not be lawful for a person who is not [a British citizen] to enter the United Kingdom from any of the Islands where his presence was unlawful under the immigration laws of that island, unless he is given leave to enter.

Note: Words in square brackets substituted by British Nationality Act 1981, s 39(6). Paragraph 3 substituted by Immigration and Asylum Act 1999 from 2 October 2000.

SCHEDULE 4A — Sections 28M, 28N and 28O

ENFORCEMENT POWERS IN RELATION TO SHIPS

[Part A1 United Kingdom

A1 Introductory

A1 (1) This Part of this Schedule sets out the powers exercisable by immigration officers and enforcement officers (referred to in this Part of this Schedule as "relevant officers") under section 28LA.

(2) In this Part of this Schedule—

"items subject to legal privilege" means items in respect of which a claim to legal professional privilege (in Scotland, to confidentiality of communications) could be maintained in legal proceedings;

"the ship" means the ship in relation to which the powers set out in this Part of this Schedule are exercised.

B2 Power to stop, board, divert and detain

B1 (1) This paragraph applies if a relevant officer has reasonable grounds to suspect that—

(a) a relevant offence is being, or has been, committed on the ship, or

(b) the ship is otherwise being used in connection with the commission of a relevant offence.

(2) The relevant officer may—

(a) stop the ship;

(b) board the ship;

(c) require the ship to be taken to any place (on land or on water) in the United Kingdom or elsewhere and detained there;

(d) require the ship to leave United Kingdom waters.

(3) The relevant officer may require the master of the ship or any member of its crew to take such action as is necessary for the purposes of sub-paragraph (2).

(4) Where a ship is required to be taken to a place under sub-paragraph (2)(c), the relevant officer may require any person on board the ship to take such action as is reasonably necessary to ensure that person is taken to that place or to any other place determined by the relevant officer.

(5) Where a ship is required to leave United Kingdom waters under sub-paragraph (2)(d), the relevant officer may require any person on board the ship to take such action as is reasonably necessary to ensure that person leaves United Kingdom waters.

(6) The authority of the Secretary of State is required before a relevant officer may exercise the power under sub-paragraph (2)(c) to require the ship to be taken to any place—

(a) within a State other than the United Kingdom, or

(b) within a relevant territory.

(7) But a relevant officer acting under authority given under section 28LA(3)(c) or (d) in relation to a foreign ship or a ship registered under the law of a relevant territory may require the ship to be taken to a place mentioned in sub-paragraph (8) without authority under sub-paragraph (6).

(8) Those places are—

(a) a place in the home state or relevant territory in question, or

(b) if the home state or relevant territory requests, a place in any other State or relevant territory willing to receive the ship.

(9) A relevant officer must give notice in writing to the master of any ship detained under this paragraph.

(10) The notice must state that the ship is to be detained until the notice is withdrawn by the giving of a further notice in writing signed by a relevant officer.

(11) The requirement to give notice under sub-paragraph (9) does not apply where it is not reasonably possible to identify who is the master of the ship.

(12) In this paragraph "home state", in relation to a foreign ship, means—

(a) the State in which the ship is registered, or

(b) the State whose flag the ship is otherwise entitled to fly.

C1 Power to search and obtain information

C1 (1) This paragraph applies if a relevant officer has reasonable grounds to suspect that there is evidence on the ship (other than items subject to legal privilege) relating—

(a) to a relevant offence or,

(b) to an offence that is connected with a relevant offence.

(2) The relevant officer may search—

(a) the ship;

(b) anyone on the ship;

(c) anything on the ship (including cargo).

(3) The relevant officer may require a person on the ship to give information about themselves or about anything on the ship.

(4) The power to search conferred by sub-paragraph (2)—

(a) is only a power to search to the extent that it is reasonably required for the purpose of discovering evidence of the kind mentioned in sub-paragraph (1), and

(b) in the case of a search of a person, does not authorise a relevant officer to require the person to remove any clothing in public other than an outer coat, jacket or gloves.

(5) In exercising a power conferred by sub-paragraph (2) or (3) a relevant officer may—

(a) open any containers;

(b) require the production of documents, books or records relating to the ship or anything on it (but not including anything the relevant officer has reasonable grounds to believe is an item subject to legal privilege);

(c) make photographs or copies of anything the production of which the relevant officer has power to require.

(6) The power in sub-paragraph (5)(b) to require the production of documents, books or records includes, in relation to documents, books or records kept in electronic form, power to require the provision of the documents, books or records in a form in which they are legible and can be taken away.

(7) Sub-paragraph (5) is without prejudice to the generality of the powers conferred by sub-paragraphs (2) and (3).

(8) A power conferred by this paragraph may be exercised on the ship or elsewhere.

D1 Power of arrest and seizure

D1 (1) This paragraph applies if a relevant officer has reasonable grounds to suspect that a relevant offence has been, or is being, committed on the ship.

(2) The relevant officer may arrest without a warrant anyone whom the officer has reasonable grounds for suspecting to be guilty of the offence.

(3) The relevant officer may seize and retain anything found on the ship which appears to the officer to be evidence of the offence (but not including anything that the officer has reasonable grounds to believe to be an item subject to legal privilege).

(4) A power conferred by this paragraph may be exercised on the ship or elsewhere.

E1 Protective searches of persons

E1 (1) A relevant officer may search a person found on the ship for anything which the officer has reasonable grounds to believe the person might use to—

(a) cause physical injury,
(b) cause damage to property, or
(c) endanger the safety of any ship.

(2) The power conferred by sub-paragraph (1) may be exercised—

(a) only if the officer has reasonable grounds to believe that anything of a kind mentioned in that sub-paragraph is concealed on the person, and

(b) only to the extent that it is reasonably required for the purpose of discovering any such thing.

(3) The relevant officer may seize and retain anything which the officer has grounds to believe might—

(a) cause physical injury,

(b) cause damage to property, or

(c) endanger the safety of any ship.

(4) If the person is detained, nothing seized under sub-paragraph (3) may be retained when the person is released from detention.

(5) A power conferred by this paragraph to search a person does not authorise a relevant officer to require the person to remove any clothing in public other than an outer coat, jacket or gloves, but it does authorise the search of a person's mouth.

(6) A power conferred by this paragraph may be exercised on the ship or elsewhere.

F1 Search for nationality documents

F1 (1) A relevant officer may require a person found on the ship to produce a nationality document.

(2) The relevant officer may search a person found on the ship where the officer has reasonable grounds to believe that a nationality document is concealed on the person.

(3) The power conferred by sub-paragraph (2) may be exercised—

(a) only if the officer has reasonable grounds to believe that a nationality document is concealed on the person, and

(b) only to the extent that it is reasonably required for the purpose of discovering any such document.

(4) Subject as follows, the officer may seize and retain a nationality document for as long as the officer believes the person to whom it relates will arrive in the United Kingdom by virtue of the exercise of the power under paragraph B1.

(5) The power to retain a nationality document under sub-paragraph (4) does not affect any other power of an immigration officer to retain a document.

(6) Where a nationality document has been seized and retained by a relevant officer who is not an immigration officer, the document must be passed to an immigration officer as soon as is practicable after the ship has arrived in the United Kingdom.

(7) The power conferred by this paragraph to search a person does not authorise a relevant officer to—

(a) require the person to remove any clothing in public other than an outer coat, jacket or gloves, or

(b) seize and retain any document the officer has reasonable grounds to believe to be an item subject to legal privilege.

(8) In this paragraph a "nationality document", in relation to a person, means any document which might—

(a) establish the person's identity, nationality or citizenship, or

(b) indicate the place from which the person has travelled to the United Kingdom or to which the person is proposing to go.

(9) A power conferred by this paragraph may be exercised on the ship or elsewhere.

G1 Assistants

G1 (1) A relevant officer may—

(a) be accompanied by other persons, and

(b) take equipment or materials, to assist the officer in the exercise of powers under this Part of this Schedule.

(2) A person accompanying a relevant officer under sub-paragraph (1) may perform any of the officer's functions under this Part of this Schedule, but only under the officer's supervision.

H1 Reasonable force

H1 A relevant officer may use reasonable force, if necessary, in the performance of functions under this Part of this Schedule.

I1 Evidence of authority

I1 A relevant officer must produce evidence of the relevant officer's authority if asked to do so.

J1 Protection of relevant officers

J1 A relevant officer is not liable in any criminal or civil proceedings for anything done in the purported performance of functions under this Part of this Schedule if the court is satisfied that—

(a) the act was done in good faith, and

(b) there were reasonable grounds for doing it.

K1 Offences under the law of England and Wales

K1 (1) A person commits an offence under the law of England and Wales if the person—

(a) intentionally obstructs a relevant officer in the performance of functions under this Part of this Schedule in England and Wales, England and Wales waters, foreign waters or international waters, or

(b) fails without reasonable excuse to comply with a requirement made by a relevant officer in the performance of such functions.

(2) A person who provides information in response to a requirement made by a relevant officer in the performance of functions under this Part of this Schedule in England and Wales, England and Wales waters, foreign waters or international waters commits an offence under the law of England and Wales if—

(a) the information is false in a material particular, and the person either knows it is, or is reckless as to whether it is, or

(b) the person intentionally fails to disclose any material particular.

(3) A relevant officer may arrest without warrant anyone whom the officer has reasonable grounds for suspecting to be guilty of an offence under this paragraph.

(4) A person guilty of an offence under this paragraph is liable on summary conviction to imprisonment for a term not exceeding 51 weeks, to a fine or to both.

(5) In the application of sub-paragraph (4) in relation to an offence committed before the coming into force of section 281(5) of the Criminal Justice Act 2003 the reference to 51 weeks is to be read as a reference to 6 months.

L1 Offences under the law of Scotland

L1 (1) A person commits an offence under the law of Scotland if the person—

(a) intentionally obstructs a relevant officer in the performance of functions under this Part of this Schedule in Scotland, Scotland waters, foreign waters or international waters, or

(b) fails without reasonable excuse to comply with a requirement made by a relevant officer in the performance of such functions.

(2) A person who provides information in response to a requirement made by a relevant officer in the performance of functions under this Part of this Schedule in Scotland, Scotland waters, foreign waters or international waters commits an offence under the law of Scotland if—

(a) the information is false in a material particular, and the person either knows it is, or is reckless as to whether it is, or

(b) the person intentionally fails to disclose any material particular.

(3) A relevant officer may arrest without warrant anyone whom the officer has reasonable grounds for suspecting to be guilty of an offence under this paragraph.

(4) A person guilty of an offence under this paragraph is liable on summary conviction to imprisonment for a term not exceeding 12 months, to a fine not exceeding level 5 on the standard scale or to both.

M1 Offences under the law of Northern Ireland

M1 (1) A person commits an offence under the law of Northern Ireland if the person—

(a) intentionally obstructs a relevant officer in the performance of functions under this Part of this Schedule in Northern Ireland, Northern Ireland waters, foreign waters or I international waters, or

(b) fails without reasonable excuse to comply with a requirement made by a relevant officer in the performance of such functions.

(2) A person who provides information in response to a requirement made by a relevant officer in the performance of functions under this Part of this Schedule in Northern Ireland, Northern Ireland waters, foreign waters or international waters commits an offence under the law of Northern Ireland if—

(a) the information is false in a material particular, and the person either knows it is, or is reckless as to whether it is, or

(b) the person intentionally fails to disclose any material particular.

(3) A relevant officer may arrest without warrant anyone whom the officer has reasonable grounds for suspecting to be guilty of an offence under this paragraph.

(4) A person guilty of an offence under this paragraph is liable on summary conviction to a term not exceeding 6 months, to a fine not exceeding level 5 on the standard scale or to both.]

Note: Part A1 inserted by Nationality and Borders Act 2022 c.36 Sch.7 para 10 (June 28, 2022: insertion has effect as SI 2022/590 reg.2 & Sch.1 para 22 subject to transitional and saving provisions specified in SI 2022/590 reg. 3 & Sch.2 para 8)

Part 1 England and Wales

1.—(1) This Part of this Schedule sets out the powers exercisable by[[..]]English and Welsh constables[[..]](referred to in this Part of this Schedule as 'relevant officers') under sections 28M and 28P(1).

(2) In this Part of this Schedule—

['the 2006 Act' means the Immigration, Asylum and Nationality Act 2006;]

'items subject to legal privilege' has the same meaning as in the Police and Criminal Evidence Act 1984 (see section 10 of that Act);

'the ship' means the ship in relation to which the powers set out in this Part of this Schedule are exercised.

Note: words inserted in square brackets by Nationality and Borders Act 2022 c.36 Sch.6 para 10(2) (date to be appointed). Words omitted in double square brackets by Nationality and Borders Act 2022 c.36 Sch.7 para 11 (June 28, 2022: omission has effect as SI 2022/590 reg.2 & Sch.1 para 22 subject to transitional and saving provisions specified in SI 2022/590 reg.3 & Sch.2 para 8)

Power to stop, board, divert and detain

2.—(1) This paragraph applies if a relevant officer has reasonable grounds to suspect that—

(a) an offence under section [24B, 25, 25A or 25B of this Act or section 21 of the 2006 Act] is being, or has been, committed on the ship, or

(b) the ship is otherwise being used in connection with the commission of an offence under any of those sections.

(2) The relevant officer may—

(a) stop the ship;

(b) board the ship;

(c) require the ship to be taken to a port in the United Kingdom and detained there.

(3) The relevant officer may require the master of the ship, or any member of its crew, to take such action as is necessary for the purposes of sub-paragraph (2)(c).

(4) A relevant officer must give notice in writing to the master of any ship detained under this paragraph.

(5) The notice must state that the ship is to be detained until the notice is withdrawn by the giving of a further notice in writing signed by a relevant officer.

Note: words inserted in square brackets by Nationality and Borders Act 2022 c.36 Sch.6 para 10(3) (date to be appointed)

Power to search and obtain information

3.—(1) This paragraph applies if a relevant officer has reasonable grounds to suspect that there is evidence on the ship (other than items subject to legal privilege) relating—

(a) to an offence under section [24B, 25, 25A]or 25 B of this Act or section 21 of the 2006 Act,] or

(b) to an offence that is connected with an offence under any of those sections.

(2) The relevant officer may search—

(a) the ship;

(b) anyone on the ship;

(c) anything on the ship (including cargo).

(3) The relevant officer may require a person on the ship to give information about himself or herself or about anything on the ship.

(4) The power to search conferred by sub-paragraph (2)—

(a) is only a power to search to the extent that it is reasonably required for the purpose of discovering evidence of the kind mentioned in sub-paragraph (1), and

(b) in the case of a search of a person, does not authorise a relevant officer to require the person to remove any clothing in public other than an outer coat, jacket or gloves.

(5) In exercising a power conferred by sub-paragraph (2) or (3) a relevant officer may—

(a) open any containers;

(b) require the production of documents, books or records relating to the ship or anything on it (but not including anything the relevant officer has reasonable grounds to believe to be an item subject to legal privilege);

(c) make photographs or copies of anything the production of which the relevant officer has power to require.

(6) The power in sub-paragraph (5)(b) to require the production of documents, books or records includes, in relation to documents, books or records kept in electronic form, power to require the provision of the documents, books or records in a form in which they are legible and can be taken away.

(7) Sub-paragraph (5) is without prejudice to the generality of the powers conferred by sub-paragraphs (2) and (3).

(8) A power conferred by this paragraph may be exercised on the ship or elsewhere.

Note: words inserted in square brackets at sub-paragraph 3(1)(a) by Nationality and Borders Act 2022 c.36 para 10 (4) (date to be appointed)

Power of arrest and seizure

4.—(1) This paragraph applies if a relevant officer has reasonable grounds to suspect that an offence under section [24B, 25, 25A or 25B of this Act or section 21 of the 2006 Act] has been, or is being, committed on the ship.

(2) The relevant officer may arrest without warrant anyone whom the [[..]]officer has reasonable grounds for suspecting to be guilty of the offence.

(3) The relevant officer may seize and retain anything found on the ship which appears to the officer to be evidence of the offence (but not including anything that the [[..]]constable or officer has reasonable grounds to believe to be an item subject to legal privilege).

(4) A power conferred by this paragraph may be exercised on the ship or elsewhere.

Note: words substituted in square brackets in subparagraph (1) by Nationality and Borders Act 2022 c.36 Sch.6 para 10(5) (date to be appointed). Word in double square bracket omitted in subparagraph (2) & (3) by Nationality and Borders Act 2022 c.35 Sch.7 para 12 (June 28, 2022: omission has effect as SI/2022/590 reg.2 & Sch.1 para 22 subject to transitional and saving provisions specified in SI 2022/590 reg.3 & Sch.2 para 8)

Protective searches of persons

5.—(1) A relevant officer may search a person found on the ship for anything which the officer has reasonable grounds to believe the person might use to—

(a) cause physical injury,

(b) cause damage to property, or

(c) endanger the safety of any ship.

(2) The power conferred by sub-paragraph (1) may be exercised—

(a) only if the officer has reasonable grounds to believe that anything of a kind mentioned in that sub-paragraph is concealed on the person; and

(b) only to the extent that it is reasonably required for the purpose of discovering any such thing.

(3) The relevant officer may seize and retain anything which the officer has reasonable grounds to believe might—

(a) cause physical injury,

(b) cause damage to property, or

(c) endanger the safety of any ship.

(4) If the person is detained, nothing seized under sub-paragraph (3) may be retained when the person is released from detention.

(5) A power conferred by this paragraph to search a person does not authorise a relevant officer to require the person to remove any clothing in public other than an outer coat, jacket or gloves, but it does authorise the search of a person's mouth.

(6) A power conferred by this paragraph may be exercised on the ship or elsewhere.

Search for nationality documents

6.—(1) A relevant officer may require a person found on the ship to produce a nationality document.

(2) The relevant officer may search a person found on the ship where the officer has reasonable grounds to believe that a nationality document is concealed on the person.

(3) The power conferred by sub-paragraph (2) may be exercised—

(a) only if the officer has reasonable grounds to believe that a nationality document is concealed on the person; and

(b) only to the extent that it is reasonably required for the purpose of discovering any such document.

(4) Subject as follows, the officer may seize and retain a nationality document for as long as the officer believes the person to whom it relates will arrive in the United Kingdom by virtue of the exercise of the power in paragraph 2.

(5) …

(6) [A nationality document that has been seized and retained by a relevant officer] must be passed to an immigration officer as soon as is practicable after the ship has arrived in the United Kingdom.

(7) The power conferred by this paragraph to search a person does not authorise a relevant officer to—

(a) require the person to remove any clothing in public other than an outer coat, jacket or gloves, or

(b) seize and retain any document the officer has reasonable grounds to believe to be an item subject to legal privilege.

(8) In this paragraph a 'nationality document', in relation to a person, means any document which might—

(a) establish the person's identity, nationality or citizenship, or

(b) indicate the place from which the person has travelled to the United Kingdom or to which the person is proposing to go.

(9) A power conferred by this paragraph may be exercised on the ship or elsewhere.

Note: subparagraph (5) by Nationality and Borders Act 2022 sch.7 para 13(a) (June 28, 2022: omission has effect as SI 2022/590 reg.2 & Sch.1 para 22 subject to transitional and saving provisions specified in SI 2022/590 reg.3 & Sch.2 para 8). Word substituted in subparagraph 6 by Nationality and Borders Act 2022 c.36 para 13(b) (date to be appointed: substitution has effect as SI 2022/590 reg.2 & Sch.1 para 22 subject to transitional and saving provisions specified in SI 2022/590 reg.3 Sch.2 para 8)

Assistants

7.—(1) A relevant officer may—

(a) be accompanied by other persons, and

(b) take equipment or materials, to assist the officer in the exercise of powers under this Part of this Schedule.

(2) A person accompanying a relevant officer under sub-paragraph (1) may perform any of the officer's functions under this Part of this Schedule, but only under the officer's supervision.

Reasonable force

8. A relevant officer may use reasonable force, if necessary, in the performance of functions under this Part of this Schedule.

Evidence of authority

9. A relevant officer must produce evidence of the officer's authority if asked to do so.

Protection of relevant officers

10. A relevant officer is not liable in any criminal or civil proceedings for anything done in the purported performance of functions under this Part of this Schedule if the court is satisfied that—

(a) the act was done in good faith, and

(b) there were reasonable grounds for doing it.

Offences

11.—(1) A person commits an offence under the law of England and Wales if the person—

(a) intentionally obstructs a relevant officer in the performance of functions under this Part of this Schedule, or

(b) fails without reasonable excuse to comply with a requirement made by a relevant officer in the performance of those functions.

(2) A person who provides information in response to a requirement made by a relevant officer in the performance of functions under this Part of this Schedule commits an offence under the law of England and Wales if—

(a) the information is false in a material particular, and the person either knows it is or is reckless as to whether it is, or

(b) the person intentionally fails to disclose any material particular.

(3) A relevant officer may arrest without warrant anyone whom the officer has reasonable grounds for suspecting to be guilty of an offence under this paragraph.

(4) A person guilty of an offence under this paragraph is liable on summary conviction to imprisonment for a term not exceeding 51 weeks, to a fine or to both.

(5) In the application of sub-paragraph (4) in relation to an offence committed before the coming into force of section 281(5) of the Criminal Justice Act 2003 the reference to 51 weeks is to be read as a reference to 6 months.

Introductory

Part 2 Scotland

12.—(1) This Part of this Schedule sets out the powers exercisable by[..], Scottish constables [..](referred to in this Part of this Schedule as 'relevant officers') under sections 28N and 28P(3).

(2) In this Part of this Schedule—

["the 2006 Act" means the Immigration, Asylum and Nationality Act 2006,]

'items subject to legal privilege' has the same meaning as in Chapter 3 of Part 8 of the Proceeds of Crime Act 2002 (see section 412 of that Act);

'the ship' means the ship in relation to which the powers set out in this Part of this Schedule are exercised.

Note: words inserted in by Nationality and Borders Act 2022 c.36 Sch.6 para 10(6) (date to be appointed). Words in square brackets omitted in subparagraph 1 by Nationality and Borders Act 2022 c.36 Sch.7 para 14 (June 28, 2022: omission has effect as SI 2022/590 reg.2 & Sch.1 para 22 subject to transitional and saving provisions specified in SI 2022/590 reg.3 & Shc.2 para 8)

Power to stop, board, divert and detain

13.—(1) This paragraph applies if a relevant officer has reasonable grounds to suspect that—

(a) an offence under section [24B, 25 or 25A of this Act or section 21 of the 2006 Act] is being, or has been, committed on the ship, or

(b) the ship is otherwise being used in connection with the commission of an offence under any of those sections.

(2) The relevant officer may—

(a) stop the ship;

(b) board the ship;

(c) require the ship to be taken to a port in the United Kingdom and detained there.

(3) The relevant officer may require the master of the ship, or any member of its crew, to take such action as is necessary for the purposes of sub-paragraph (2)(c).

(4) A relevant officer must give notice in writing to the master of any ship detained under this paragraph.

(5) The notice must state that the ship is to be detained until the notice is withdrawn by the giving of a further notice in writing signed by a relevant officer.

Note: words substituted in subparagraph (1)(a) by Nationality and Borders Act 2022 c.36 para 10(7) (date to be appointed)

Power to search and obtain information

14.—(1) This paragraph applies if a relevant officer has reasonable grounds to suspect that there is evidence on the ship (other than items subject to legal privilege) relating—

(a) to an offence under section[24B, 25 or 25A of this Act or section 21 of the 2006 Act], or

(b) to an offence that is connected with an offence under any of those sections.

(2) The relevant officer may search—

(a) the ship;
(b) anyone on the ship;
(c) anything on the ship (including cargo).

(3) The relevant officer may require a person on the ship to give information about himself or herself or about anything on the ship.

(4) The power to search conferred by sub-paragraph (2)—

(a) is only a power to search to the extent that it is reasonably required for the purpose of discovering evidence of the kind mentioned in sub-paragraph (1), and

(b) in the case of a search of a person, does not authorise a relevant officer to require the person to remove any clothing in public other than an outer coat, jacket or gloves.

(5) In exercising a power conferred by sub-paragraph (2) or (3) a relevant officer may—

(a) open any containers;

(b) require the production of documents, books or records relating to the ship or anything on it (but not including anything the relevant officer has reasonable grounds to believe to be an item subject to legal privilege);

(c) make photographs or copies of anything the production of which the relevant officer has power to require.

(6) The power in sub-paragraph (5)(b) to require the production of documents, books or records includes, in relation to documents, books or records kept in electronic form, power to require the provision of the documents, books or records in a form in which they are legible and can be taken away.

(7) Sub-paragraph (5) is without prejudice to the generality of the powers conferred by sub-paragraphs (2) and (3).

(8) A power conferred by this paragraph may be exercised on the ship or elsewhere.

Note: words substituted in subparagraph (1)(a) by Nationality and Borders Act 2022 c.36 para 10(9) (date to be appointed)

Power of arrest and seizure

15.—(1) This paragraph applies if a relevant officer has reasonable grounds to suspect that an offence under section [24B, 25 or 25A of this Act or section 21 of the 2006 Act] has been, or is being, committed on the ship.

(2) The relevant officer may arrest without warrant anyone whom the officer has reasonable grounds for suspecting to be guilty of the offence.

(3) The relevant officer may seize and retain anything found on the ship which appears to the officer to be evidence of the offence (but not including anything that the officer has reasonable grounds to believe to be an item subject to legal privilege).

(4) A power conferred by this paragraph may be exercised on the ship or elsewhere.

Note: words substituted in sub-paragraph (1) by Nationality and Borders Act 2022 c.36 Sch.6 para 10(9) (date to be appointed)

Protective searches of persons

16.—(1) The relevant officer may search a person found on the ship for anything which the officer has reasonable grounds to believe the person might use to—

(a) cause physical injury,

(b) cause damage to property, or

(c) endanger the safety of any ship.

(2) The power conferred by sub-paragraph (1) may be exercised—

(a) only if the officer has reasonable grounds to believe that anything of a kind mentioned in that sub-paragraph is concealed on the person; and

(b) only to the extent that it is reasonably required for the purpose of discovering any such thing.

(3) The relevant officer may seize and retain anything which the officer has reasonable grounds to believe might—

(a) cause physical injury,

(b) cause damage to property, or

(c) endanger the safety of any ship.

(4) If the person is detained, nothing seized under sub-paragraph (3) may be retained when the person is released from detention.

(5) A power conferred by this paragraph to search a person does not authorise a relevant officer to require the person to remove any clothing in public other than an outer coat, jacket or gloves, but it does authorise the search of a person's mouth.

(6) A power conferred by this paragraph may be exercised on the ship or elsewhere.

Search for nationality documents

17.—(1) The relevant officer may require a person found on the ship to produce a nationality document.

(2) The relevant officer may search a person found on the ship where the officer has reasonable grounds to believe that a nationality document is concealed on the person.

(3) The power conferred by sub-paragraph (2) may be exercised—

(a) only if the officer has reasonable grounds to believe that a nationality document is concealed on the person; and

(b) only to the extent that it is reasonably required for the purpose of discovering any such document.

(4) Subject as follows, the officer may seize and retain a nationality document for as long as the officer believes the person to whom it relates will arrive in the United Kingdom by virtue of the exercise of the power in paragraph 13.

(5)

(6) [A nationality document that has been seized and retained by the relevant officer] must be passed to an immigration officer as soon as is practicable after the ship has arrived in the United Kingdom.

(7) The power conferred by this paragraph to search a person does not authorise a relevant officer to—

(a) require the person to remove any clothing in public other than an outer coat, jacket or gloves, or

(b) seize and retain any document the officer has reasonable grounds to believe to be an item subject to legal privilege.

(8) In this paragraph a 'nationality document', in relation to a person, means any document which might—

(a) establish the person's identity, nationality or citizenship, or

(b) indicate the place from which the person has travelled to the United Kingdom or to which the person is proposing to go.

(9) A power conferred by this paragraph may be exercised on the ship or elsewhere.

Note: subparagraph (5) omitted by Nationality and Borders Act 2022 sch.7 para 15(a) (June 28, 2022: omission has effect as SI 2022/590 reg.2 & Sch.1 para 22 subject to transitional and saving provisions specified in SI 2022/590 reg.3 & Sch.2 para 8). Word substituted in subparagraph 6 by Nationality and Borders Act 2022 c.36 para 15(b) (date to be appointed: substitution has effect as SI 2022/590 reg.2 & Sch.1 para 22 subject to transitional and saving provisions specified in SI 2022/590 reg.3 Sch.2 para 8)

Assistants

18.—(1) A relevant officer may—

(a) be accompanied by other persons, and

(b) take equipment or materials, to assist the officer in the exercise of powers under this Part of this Schedule.

(2) A person accompanying a relevant officer under sub-paragraph (1) may perform any of the officer's functions under this Part of this Schedule, but only under the officer's supervision.

Reasonable force

19. A relevant officer may use reasonable force, if necessary, in the performance of functions under this Part of this Schedule.

Evidence of authority

20. A relevant officer must produce evidence of the officer's authority if asked to do so.

Protection of relevant officers

21. A relevant officer is not liable in any criminal or civil proceedings for anything done in the purported performance of functions under this Part of this Schedule if the court is satisfied that—

(a) the act was done in good faith, and

(b) there were reasonable grounds for doing it.

Offences

22.—(1) A person commits an offence under the law of Scotland if the person—

(a) intentionally obstructs a relevant officer in the performance of functions under this Part of this Schedule, or

(b) fails without reasonable excuse to comply with a requirement made by a relevant officer in the performance of those functions.

(2) A person who provides information in response to a requirement made by a relevant officer in the performance of functions under this Part of this Schedule commits an offence under the law of Scotland if—

(a) the information is false in a material particular, and the person either knows it is or is reckless as to whether it is, or

(b) the person intentionally fails to disclose any material particular.

(3) A relevant officer may arrest without warrant anyone whom the officer has reasonable grounds for suspecting to be guilty of an offence under this paragraph.

(4) A person guilty of an offence under this paragraph is liable on summary conviction to imprisonment for a term not exceeding 12 months, to a fine not exceeding level 5 on the standard scale or to both.

INTRODUCTORY

Part 3 Northern Ireland

23.—(1) This Part of this Schedule sets out the powers exercisable by[..], Northern Ireland constables [.](referred to in this Part of this Schedule as 'relevant officers') under sections 28O and 28P(5).

(2) In this Part of this Schedule—

["the 2006 Act" means the Immigration, Asylum and Nationality Act 2006,]

'items subject to legal privilege' has the same meaning as in the Police and Criminal Evidence (Northern Ireland) Order 1989 (SI 1989/1341 (NI 12)) (see Article 12 of that Order);

'the ship' means the ship in relation to which the powers set out in this Part of this Schedule are exercised.

Note: words inserted in square brackets by Nationality and Borders Act 2022 c.36 Sch.7 para 10(10) (date to be appointed). Words omitted at subparagraph 1 by Nationality and Borders Act 2022 c.36 Sch.7 para 17(a) (June 28, 22: omission has effect as SI 2022/590 reg.2 and Sch.1 para 22 subject to transition and saving provisions specified in SI 2022/590 reg.3 & Sch.2 para 8)

Power to stop, board, divert and detain

24.—(1) This paragraph applies if a relevant officer has reasonable grounds to suspect that—

(a) an offence under section [24B, 25 or 25A of this Act or section 21 of the 2006 Act] is being, or has been, committed on the ship, or

(b) the ship is otherwise being used in connection with the commission of an offence under any of those sections.

(2) The relevant officer may—

(a) stop the ship;

(b) board the ship;

(c) require the ship to be taken to a port in the United Kingdom and detained there.

(3) The relevant officer may require the master of the ship, or any member of its crew, to take such action as is necessary for the purposes of sub-paragraph (2)(c).

(4) A relevant officer must give notice in writing to the master of any ship detained under this paragraph.

(5) The notice must state that the ship is to be detained until the notice is withdrawn by the giving of a further notice in writing signed by a relevant officer.

Note: words substituted in sub-paragraph (1)(a) by Nationality and Borders Act 2022 c.36 Sch.6 para 10(11) (date to be appointed)

Power to search and obtain information

25.—(1) This paragraph applies if a relevant officer has reasonable grounds to suspect that there is evidence on the ship (other than items subject to legal privilege) relating—

(a) to an offence under section [..][[24B, 25 or 25A of this Act or section 21 of the 2006 Act]], or

(b) to an offence that is connected with an offence under any of those sections.

(2) The relevant officer may search—

(a) the ship;

(b) anyone on the ship;

(c) anything on the ship (including cargo).

(3) The relevant officer may require a person on the ship to give information about himself or herself or about anything on the ship.

(4) The power to search conferred by sub-paragraph (2)—

(a) is only a power to search to the extent that it is reasonably required for the purpose of discovering evidence of the kind mentioned in sub-paragraph (1), and

(b) in the case of a search of a person, does not authorise a relevant officer to require the person to remove any clothing in public other than an outer coat, jacket or gloves.

(5) In exercising a power conferred by sub-paragraph (2) or (3) a relevant officer may—

(a) open any containers;

(b) require the production of documents, books or records relating to the ship or anything on it (but not including anything the officer has reasonable grounds to believe to be an item subject to legal privilege);

(c) make photographs or copies of anything the production of which the officer has power to require.

(6) The power in sub-paragraph (5)(b) to require the production of documents, books or records includes, in relation to documents, books or records kept in electronic form, power to require the provision of the documents, books or records in a form in which they are legible and can be taken away.

(7) Sub-paragraph (5) is without prejudice to the generality of the powers conferred by sub-paragraphs (2) and (3).

(8) A power conferred by this paragraph may be exercised on the ship or elsewhere.

Note: words in square brackets at sub-paragraph (1)(a) substituted by Immigration and Social Security Co-ordination (EU Withdrawal) Act 2020 (Consequential, Saving, Transitional and Transitory Provisions) (EU Exit) Regulations 2020/1309 Sch.1 para 1(a)(x) (December 31, 2020; substitution has effect subject to saving specified in SI 2020/1309 Sch.1 para 1(5))). Words substituted in double square brackets in sub-paragraph (1)(a) by Nationality and Borders Act 2022 c.36 Sch.6 para 10(12) (date to be appointed)

Power of arrest and seizure

26.—(1) This paragraph applies if a relevant officer has reasonable grounds to suspect that an offence under section [..][[24B, 25 or 25A of this Act or section 21 of the 2006 Act]] has been, or is being, committed on the ship.

(2) The relevant officer may arrest without warrant anyone whom the officer has reasonable grounds for suspecting to be guilty of the offence.

(3) The relevant officer may seize and retain anything found on the ship which appears to the officer to be evidence of the offence (but not including anything that the [..]officer has reasonable grounds to believe to be an item subject to legal privilege).

(4) A power conferred by this paragraph may be exercised on the ship or elsewhere.

Note: words in square brackets at sub-paragraph (1)(a) substituted by Immigration and Social Security Co-ordination (EU Withdrawal) Act 2020 (Consequential, Saving, Transitional and Transitory Provisions) (EU Exit) Regulations 2020/1309 Sch.1 para 1(a)(x) (December 31, 2020; substitution has effect subject to saving specified in SI 2020/1309 Sch.1 para 1(5))). Words substituted in double square brackets in sub-paragraph (1)(a) by Nationality and Borders Act 2022 c.36 Sch.6 para 10(13) (date to be appointed). Word in square bracket in subparagraph (3) omitted by Nationality and Borders Act 2022 c.36 Sch.7 para 17 (June 28,2022: omission has effect as SI 2022/590 reg.2 & Sch.1 para 22 subject to transitional and saving provision specified in SI 2022/590 reg.3 & Sch.2 para 8)

Protective searches of persons

27.—(1) The relevant officer may search a person found on the ship for anything which the officer has reasonable grounds to believe the person might use to—

(a) cause physical injury,

(b) cause damage to property, or

(c) endanger the safety of any ship.

(2) The power conferred by sub-paragraph (1) may be exercised—

(a) only if the officer has reasonable grounds to believe that anything of a kind mentioned in that sub-paragraph is concealed on the person; and

(b) only to the extent that it is reasonably required for the purpose of discovering any such thing.

(3) The relevant officer may seize and retain anything which the officer has reasonable grounds to believe might—

(a) cause physical injury,

(b) cause damage to property, or

(c) endanger the safety of any ship

(4) If the person is detained, nothing seized under sub-paragraph (3) may be retained when the person is released from detention.

(5) A power conferred by this paragraph to search a person does not authorise a relevant officer to require the person to remove any clothing in public other than an outer coat, jacket or gloves, but it does authorise the search of a person's mouth.

(6) A power conferred by this paragraph may be exercised on the ship or elsewhere.

Search for nationality documents

28.—(1) The relevant officer may require a person found on the ship to produce a nationality document.

(2) The relevant officer may search a person found on the ship where the officer has reasonable grounds to believe that a nationality document is concealed on the person.

(3) The power conferred by sub-paragraph (2) may be exercised—

(a) only if the officer has reasonable grounds to believe that a nationality document is concealed on the person; and

(b) only to the extent that it is reasonably required for the purpose of discovering any such document.

(4) Subject as follows, the officer may seize and retain a nationality document for as long as the officer believes the person to whom it relates will arrive in the United Kingdom by virtue of the exercise of the power in paragraph 24.

(5)

(6) [A nationality document that has been seized and retained by a relevant officer] must be passed to an immigration officer as soon as is practicable after the ship has arrived in the United Kingdom.

(7) The power conferred by this paragraph to search a person does not authorise a relevant officer to—

(a) require the person to remove any clothing in public other than an outer coat, jacket or gloves, or

(b) seize and retain any document the officer has reasonable grounds to believe to be an item subject to legal privilege.

(8) In this paragraph a 'nationality document', in relation to a person, means any document which might—

(a) establish the person's identity, nationality or citizenship, or

(b) indicate the place from which the person has travelled to the United Kingdom or to which the person is proposing to go.

(9) A power conferred by this paragraph may be exercised on the ship or elsewhere.

Note: subparagraph (5) omitted by Nationality and Borders Act 2022 sch.7 para 13(a) (June 28, 2022: omission has effect as SI 2022/590 reg.2 & Sch.1 para 22 subject to transitional and saving provisions specified in SI 2022/590 reg.3 & Sch.2 para 8). Word substituted in subparagraph 6 by Nationality and Borders Act 2022 c.36 para 13(b) (date to be appointed: substitution has effect as SI 2022/590 reg.2 & Sch.1 para 22 subject to transitional and saving provisions specified in SI 2022/590 reg.3 Sch.2 para 8)

Assistants

29.—(1) A relevant officer may—

(a) be accompanied by other persons, and

(b) take equipment or materials, to assist the officer in the exercise of powers under this Part of this Schedule.

(2) A person accompanying a relevant officer under sub-paragraph (1) may perform any of the officer's functions under this Part of this Schedule, but only under the officer's supervision.

Reasonable force

30. A relevant officer may use reasonable force, if necessary, in the performance of functions under this Part of this Schedule.

Evidence of authority

31. A relevant officer must produce evidence of the officer's authority if asked to do so.

Protection of relevant officers

32. A relevant officer is not liable in any criminal or civil proceedings for anything done in the purported performance of functions under this Part of this Schedule if the court is satisfied that—

(a) the act was done in good faith, and

(b) there were reasonable grounds for doing it.

Offences

33.—(1) A person commits an offence under the law of Northern Ireland if the person—

(a) intentionally obstructs a relevant officer in the performance of functions under this Part of this Schedule, or

(b) fails without reasonable excuse to comply with a requirement made by a relevant officer in the performance of those functions.

(2) A person who provides information in response to a requirement made by a relevant officer in the performance of functions under this Part of this Schedule commits an offence under the law of Northern Ireland if—

(a) the information is false in a material particular, and the person either knows it is or is reckless as to whether it is, or

(b) the person intentionally fails to disclose any material particular.

(3) A relevant officer may arrest without warrant anyone whom the officer has reasonable grounds for suspecting to be guilty of an offence under this paragraph.

(4) A person guilty of an offence under this paragraph is liable on summary conviction to imprisonment for a term not exceeding 6 months, to a fine not exceeding level 5 on the standard scale or to both.

Note: Schedule 4A inserted by Schedule 14 to the Immigration Act 2016 from 31 May 2016.

SCHEDULE 5

Note: Schedule 5 repealed by Immigration and Asylum Act 1999 from 14 February 2000.

SCHEDULE 6

Section 34

. . .

REPEALS

British Nationality Act 1981

(1981, c. 61)

Arrangement of Sections

Part I. British Citizenship

Acquisition after commencement

An Act to make fresh provision about citizenship and nationality, and to amend the Immigration Act 1971 as regards the right of abode in the United Kingdom.

[30October 1981]

PART I

BRITISH CITIZENSHIP

Acquisition after commencement

1. Acquisition by birth or adoption

(1) A person born in the United Kingdom after commencement [, or in a qualifying territory on or after the appointed day,] shall be a British citizen if at the time of the birth his father or mother is—

(a) a British citizen; or

(b) settled in the United Kingdom [or that territory].

[(1A) A person born in the United Kingdom or a qualifying territory on or after the relevant day shall be a British citizen if at the time of the birth his father or mother is a member of the armed forces.]

(2) A new-born infant who, after commencement, is found abandoned in the United Kingdom [, or on or after the appointed day is found abandoned in a qualifying territory,] shall, unless the contrary is shown, be deemed for the purposes of subsection (1)—

(a) to have been born in the United Kingdom after commencement; [or in that territory on or after the appointed day] and

(b) to have been born to a parent who at the time of the birth was a British citizen or settled in the United Kingdom [or that territory].

(3) A person born in the United Kingdom after commencement who is not a British citizen by virtue of subsection (1)[, (1A)] or (2) shall be entitled to be registered as a British citizen if, while he is a minor—

(a) his father or mother becomes a British citizen or becomes settled in the United Kingdom; and

(b) an application is made for his registration as a British citizen.

[(3A) A person born in the United Kingdom on or after the relevant day who is not a British citizen by virtue of subsection (1), (1A) or (2) shall be entitled to be registered as a British citizen if, while he is a minor—

(a) his father or mother becomes a member of the armed forces; and

(b) an application is made for his registration as a British citizen.]

(4) A person born in the United Kingdom after commencement who is not a British citizen by virtue of subsection (1) [,(1A)] or (2) shall be entitled, on an application for his registration as a British citizen made at any time after he has attained the age of ten years, to be registered as such a citizen if, as regards each of the first ten years of that person's life, the number of days on which he was absent from the United Kingdom in that year does not exceed 90.

[(5) Where—

(a) any court in the United Kingdom [or, on or after the appointed day, any court in a qualifying territory] makes an order authorising the adoption of a minor who is not a British citizen; or

(b) a minor who is not a British citizen is adopted under a Convention adoption, that minor shall, if the requirements of subsection (5A) are met, be a British citizen as from the date on which the order is made or the Convention adoption is effected, as the case may be {effected under the law of a country or territory outside the United Kingdom}.

(5A) Those requirements are that on the date on which the order is made or the Convention adoption is effected (as the case may be)—

(a) the adopter or, in the case of a joint adoption, one of the adopters is a British citizen; and

(b) in a case within subsection (5)(b), the adopter or, in the case of a joint adoption, both of the adopters are habitually resident in the United Kingdom {or in a designated territory}.]

(6) Where an order [or a Convention adoption] in consequence of which any person became a British citizen by virtue of subsection (5) ceases to have effect, whether on annulment or otherwise, the cesser shall not effect the status of that person as a British citizen.

(7) If in the special circumstances of any particular case the Secretary of State thinks fit, he may for the purposes of subsection (4) treat the person to whom the application relates as fulfilling the requirement specified in that subsection although, as regards any one or more of the first ten years of that person's life, the number of days on which he was absent from the United Kingdom in that year or each of the years in question exceeds 90.

(8) In this section and elsewhere in this Act 'settled' has the meaning given by section 50 ...

[(9) The relevant day for the purposes of subsection (1A) or (3A) is the day appointed for the commencement of section 42 of the Borders, Citizenship and Immigration Act 2009 (which inserted those subsections)].

Note: Subsection (5) substituted and words in square brackets in subsection (6) inserted by Adoption (Intercountry Aspects) Act 1999, s 7 from 1 June 2003 (SI 2003/362). Subsections (1A), (3A) and (9) and words in square brackets in subsections (3)–(4) inserted by s 42 Borders Citizenship and Immigration Act 2009 from 13 January 2010 (SI 2009/2731). Other words in square brackets inserted by Sch 1 British Overseas Territories Act 2002, from 21 May 2002 (SI 2002/1252). The reference in subsection (5)(a) to an order authorising the adoption of a minor is to be read as including a reference to a parental order in respect of a minor and the reference in subsection (5A)(a) to the adopter or, in the case of a joint adoption, one of the adopters is to be read as including a reference to one of the persons who obtained the parental order (SI 2010/985). Words in curly brackets inserted and words omitted from subsection (8) by Adoption and Children Act 2002 from 30 December 2005.

2. Acquisition by descent

(1) A person born outside the United Kingdom [and the qualifying territories] after commencement shall be a British citizen if at the time of the birth his father or mother—

(a) is a British citizen otherwise than by descent; or

(b) is a British citizen and is serving outside the United Kingdom [and the qualifying territories] in service to which this paragraph applies, his or her recruitment for that service having taken place in the United Kingdom [or a qualifying territory]; or

(c) is a British citizen and is serving outside the United Kingdom [and the qualifying territories] in service under a {EU} institution, his or her recruitment for that service having taken place in a country which at the time of the recruitment was a member of the {European Union}.

(2) Paragraph (b) of subsection (1) applies to—

(a) Crown service under the government of the United Kingdom [or of a qualifying territory]; and

(b) service of any description for the time being designated under subsection (3).

(3) For the purposes of this section the Secretary of State may by order made by statutory instrument designate any description of service which he considers to be closely associated with the activities outside the United Kingdom [and the qualifying territories] of Her Majesty's government in the United Kingdom [or in a qualifying territory].

(4) Any order made under subsection (3) shall be subject to annulment in pursuance of a resolution of either House of Parliament.

Note: Words in square brackets inserted by Sch 1 British Overseas Territories Act 2002 from 21 May 2002 (SI 2002/1252), but without effect to the operation of this section in relation to persons born before that date.

3. Acquisition by registration: minors

(1) If while a person is a minor an application is made for his registration as a British citizen, the Secretary of State may, if he thinks fit, cause him to be registered as such a citizen.

(2) A person born outside the United Kingdom [and the qualifying territories] shall be entitled, on an application for his registration as a British citizen made [while he is a minor], to be registered as such a citizen if the requirements specified in subsection (3) or, in the case of a person born stateless, the requirements specified in paragraphs (a) and (b) of that subsection, are fulfilled in the case of either that person's father or his mother ('the parent in question').

(3) The requirements referred to in subsection (2) are—

(a) that the parent in question was a British citizen by descent at the time of the birth; and

(b) that the father or mother of the parent in question—

(i) was a British citizen otherwise than by descent at the time of the birth of the parent in question; or

(ii) became a British citizen otherwise than by descent at commencement, or would have become such a citizen otherwise than by descent at commencement but for his or her death; and

(c) that, as regards some period of three years ending with a date not later than the date of the birth—

(i) the parent in question was in the United Kingdom [or a qualifying territory] at the beginning of that period; and

(ii) the number of days on which the parent in question was absent from the United Kingdom [and the qualifying territories] in that period does not exceed 270.

(4) . . .

(5) A person born outside the United Kingdom [and the qualifying territories] shall be entitled, on an application for his registration as a British citizen made while he is a minor, to be registered as such a citizen if the following requirements are satisfied, namely—

(a) that at the time of that person's birth his father or mother was a British citizen by descent; and

(b) subject to subsection (6), that that person and his father and mother were in the United Kingdom [or a qualifying territory] at the beginning of the period of three years ending with the date of the application and that, in the case of each of them, the number of days on which the person in question was absent from the United Kingdom [and the qualifying territories] in that period does not exceed 270; and

(c) subject to subsection (6), that the consent of his father and mother to the registration has been signified in the prescribed manner.

(6) In the case of an application under subsection (5) for the registration of a person as a British citizen—

(a) if his father or mother died, or their marriage [or civil partnership] was terminated, on or before the date of the application, or his father and mother were legally separated on that date, the references to his father and mother in paragraph (b) of that subsection shall be read either as references to his father or as references to his mother; [and]

(b) if his father or mother died on or before that date, the reference to his father and mother in paragraph (c) of that subsection shall be read as a reference to either of them; [. . .]

(c) [. . .]

Note: Last word in square brackets in subsection (6)(a) inserted and words deleted from subsections (6)(b) and (c) by, Nationality, Immigration and Asylum Act 2002, s 9 from 7 November 2002, with effect in relation to children born on or after a date to be appointed. Other words in square brackets inserted by Sch 1 British Overseas Territories Act 2002, from 21 May 2002 (SI 2002/1252) but without effect to the operation of this section in relation to persons born before that date. Words in first square brackets in subsection (6)(a) inserted by Sch 27 Civil Partnership Act 2004 from 5 December 2005 (SI 2005/3175). Words in second square brackets in subsection (2) substituted and subsection (4) revoked by s 43 Borders, Citizenship and Immigration Act 2009 from 13 January 2010 (SI 2009/2731).

4. Acquisition by registration: [British overseas territories] citizens etc.

(1) This section applies to any person who is a [British overseas territories] citizen, [a British National (Overseas)] a British Overseas citizen, a British subject under this Act or a British protected person.

(2) A person to whom this section applies shall be entitled, on an application for his registration as a British citizen, to be registered as such a citizen if the following requirements are satisfied in the case of that person, namely—

(a) subject to subsection (3), that he was in the United Kingdom at the beginning of the period of five years ending with the date of the application and that the number of days on which he was absent from the United Kingdom in that period does not exceed 450; and

(b) that the number of days on which he was absent from the United Kingdom in the period of twelve months so ending does not exceed 90; and

(c) that he was not at any time in the period of twelve months so ending subject under the immigration law to any restriction on the period for which he might remain in the United Kingdom; and

(d) that he was not at any time in the period of five years so ending in the United Kingdom in breach of the immigration laws.

(3) So much of subsection (2)(a) as requires the person in question to have been in the United Kingdom at the beginning of the period there mentioned shall not apply in relation to a person who was settled in the United Kingdom immediately before commencement.

(4) If in the special circumstances of any particular case the Secretary of State thinks fit, he may for the purposes of subsection (2) do all or any of the following things, namely—

[(za) treat the person to whom the application relates as fulfilling the first requirement specified in subsection (2)(a) although the person was not in the United Kingdom at the beginning of the period there mentioned;]

(a) treat the person to whom the application relates as fulfilling the [second requirement specified in subsection (2)(a) or the requirement specified in] subsection (2)(b), or both, although the number of days on which he was absent from the United Kingdom in the period there mentioned exceeds the number there mentioned;

(b) disregard any such restriction as is mentioned in subsection (2)(c), not being a restriction to which that person was subject on the date of the application;

(c) treat that person as fulfilling the requirement specified in subsection (2)(d) although he was in the United Kingdom in breach of the immigration laws in the period there mentioned.

(4A) Subsection (4B) applies where, on an application for registration as a British citizen made by a person to whom this section applies, the applicant has indefinite leave to enter or remain in the United Kingdom.

(4B) The Secretary of State may for the purposes of subsection (2) treat the applicant as fulfilling the requirement specified in subsection (2)(d), without enquiring into whether or not the applicant was in the United Kingdom in breach of the immigration laws in the period there mentioned.

(4C) The reference in subsection (4A) to having indefinite leave to enter or remain is to be construed in accordance with the Immigration Act 1971.]

(5) If, on an application for registration as a British citizen made by a person to whom this section applies, the Secretary of State is satisfied that the applicant has at any time served in service to which this subsection applies, he may, if he thinks fit in the special circumstances of the applicant's case, cause him to be registered as such a citizen.

(6) Subsection (5) applies to—

(a) Crown service under the government of a [British overseas territory]; and

(b) paid or unpaid service (not falling within paragraph (a)) as a member of any body established by law in a [British overseas territory] members of which are appointed by or on behalf of the Crown.

Note: Words in second square brackets in s 4(1) inserted by SI 1986/948. Dependent territories became British overseas territories from 26 February 2002, British Overseas Territories Act 2002, s 1. Words inserted at subsection (4)(za) by Nationality and Borders Act 2022 c.36 Sch.1 para 2(a) (June 28, 2022: insertion has effect as SI 2022/590 reg.2 and Sch.1 para.8 subject to transitional and saving provisions specified in SI 2022/590 reg.3 and Sch.2 para.3). Words substituted in square brackets at subsection (4)(a) by Nationality and Borders Act 2022 c. 36 Sch.1 para.2(2)(b) (June 28, 2022: substitution has effect as SI 2022/590 reg.2 and Sch.1 para.8 subject to transitional and saving provisions specified in SI 2022/590 reg.3 and Sch.2 para.3). Subsections (4A)-(4C) inserted by Nationality and Borders Act 2022 c. 36 Sch.1 para.2(3) (June 28, 2022: insertion has effect as SI 2022/590 reg.2 and Sch.1 para.8 subject to transitional and saving provisions specified in SI 2022/590 reg.3 and Sch.2 para.3)

[4A. Acquisition by registration: further provision for British overseas territories citizens

(1) If an application is made to register as a British citizen a person who is a British overseas territories citizen, the Secretary of State may if he thinks fit cause the person to be so registered.

(2) Subsection (1) does not apply in the case of a British overseas territories citizen who—

(a) is such a citizen by virtue only of a connection with the Sovereign Base Areas of Akrotiri and Dhekelia; or

(b) has ceased to be a British citizen as a result of a declaration of renunciation.]

Note: Section 4A inserted by British Overseas Territories Act, s 4 from 21 May 2002 (SI 2002/1252).

[4B. Acquisition by registration: certain persons without other citizenship

(1) This section applies to a person who has the status of—

(a) British Overseas citizen,

(b) British subject under this Act, . . .

(c) British protected person [, or

(d) British National (Overseas).]

(2) A person to whom this section applies shall be entitled to be registered as a British citizen if—

(a) he applies for registration under this section,

(b) the Secretary of State is satisfied that the person does not have, apart from the status mentioned in subsection (1), any citizenship or nationality, and

(c) the Secretary of State is satisfied that the person has not after [the relevant day] renounced, voluntarily relinquished or lost through action or inaction any citizenship or nationality.]

[(3) For the purposes of subsection (2)(c), the 'relevant day' means—

(a) in the case of a person to whom this section applies by virtue of subsection (1)(d) only, 19 March 2009, and

(b) in any other case, 4 July 2002.]

Note: Section 4B inserted by Nationality, Immigration and Asylum Act 2002, s 12 from 30 April 2003 (SI 2003/754). Subsections (1)(d) and (3) inserted and words in square brackets in subsection (2)(c) substituted by s 44 Borders, Citizenship and Immigration Act 2009 from 13 January 2010 (SI 2009/2731).

[4C. Acquisition by registration: certain persons born between 1961 and 1983

(1) A person is entitled to be registered as a British citizen if—

(a) he applies for registration under this section, and

(b) he satisfies each of the following conditions.

(2) The first condition is that the applicant was born [. . .] before 1 January 1983.

[(3) The second condition is that the applicant would at some time before 1 January 1983 have become a citizen of the United Kingdom and Colonies—

(a) under section 5 of, or paragraph 3 of Schedule 3 to, the 1948 Act if assumption A had applied,

(b) under section 12(3), (4) or (5) of that Act if assumption B had applied and as a result of its application the applicant would have been a British subject immediately before 1st January 1949, or

(c) under section 12(2) of that Act if one or both of the following had applied—

(i) assumption A had applied;

(ii) assumption B had applied and as a result of its application the applicant would have been a British subject immediately before 1st January 1949.

(3A) Assumption A is that—

(a) section 5 or 12(2) of, or paragraph 3 of Schedule 3 to, the 1948 Act (as the case may be) provided for citizenship by descent from a mother in the same terms as it provided for citizenship by descent from a father, and

(b) references in that provision to a father were references to the applicant's mother.

(3B) Assumption B is that—

(a) a provision of the law at some time before 1st January 1949 which provided for a nationality status to be acquired by descent from a father provided in the same terms for its acquisition by descent from a mother, and

(b) references in that provision to a father were references to the applicant's mother.

(3C) For the purposes of subsection (3B), a nationality status is acquired by a person ('P') by descent where its acquisition—

(a) depends, amongst other things, on the nationality status of one or both of P's parents, and

(b) does not depend upon an application being made for P's registration as a person who has the status in question.

[[(3D) In determining for the purposes of subsection (3) whether a person would have been a citizen of the United Kingdom and Colonies, the requirement that a person's birth was registered at a United Kingdom consulate, as set out in section 5(1)(b) of the British Nationality Act 1948, is to be ignored.]]

(4) The third condition is that immediately before 1st January 1983 the applicant would have had the right of abode in the United Kingdom by virtue of section 2 of the Immigration Act 1971 (c. 77) had he become a citizen of the United Kingdom and Colonies as described in subsection (3) above.

[(5) For the purposes of the interpretation of section 5 of the 1948 Act in its application in the case of assumption A to a case of descent from a mother, the reference in the proviso to subsection (1) of that section to 'a citizen of the United Kingdom and Colonies by descent only' includes a reference to a female person who became a citizen of the United Kingdom and Colonies by virtue of—

(a) section 12(2), (4) or (6) only of the 1948 Act,

(b) section 13(2) of that Act,

(c) paragraph 3 of Schedule 3 to that Act, or

(d) section 1(1)(a) or (c) of the British Nationality (No. 2) Act 1964.]

Note: Section 4C inserted by Nationality, Immigration and Asylum Act 2002, s 13 from 30 April 2003 (SI 2003/754). Words omitted in subsections (2), subsections (3) substituted and subsections (5) inserted by s 45 Borders, Citizenship and Immigration Act 2009 from 13 January 2010 (SI 2009/2731). Words substituted in double brackets in subsection (3D) by Nationality and Borders Act 2022 c. 36 Pt 1 s.6(2) (June 28, 2022: substitution has effect as SI 2022/590 reg.2 and Sch.1 para.5 subject to transitional and saving provision specified in reg.3 and Sch.2 para.2)

[4D. Acquisition by registration: children of members of the armed forces

(1) A person ('P') born outside the United Kingdom and the qualifying territories on or after the relevant day is entitled to be registered as a British citizen if—

(a) an application is made for P's registration under this section; and

(b) each of the following conditions is satisfied.

(2) The first condition is that, at the time of P's birth, P's father or mother was—
(a) a member of the armed forces; and
(b) serving outside the United Kingdom and the qualifying territories.

(3) The second condition is that, if P is a minor on the date of the application, the consent of P's father and mother to P's registration as a British citizen has been signified in the prescribed manner.

(4) But if P's father or mother has died on or before the date of the application, the reference in subsection (3) to P's father and mother is to be read as a reference to either of them.

(5) The Secretary of State may, in the special circumstances of a particular case, waive the need for the second condition to be satisfied.

(6) The relevant day for the purposes of this section is the day appointed for the commencement of section 46 of the Borders, Citizenship and Immigration Act 2009 (which inserted this section).]

Note: Section 4D inserted by s 46 Borders, Citizenship and Immigration Act 2009 from 13 January 2010 (SI 2009/2731).

[4E. The general conditions

For the purposes of sections 4F to 4I, a person ('P') meets the general conditions if—
(a) …[[;]]
(b) at the time of P's birth, P's mother—
(i) was not married, or
(ii) was married to a person other than P's natural father;

(c) no person is treated as the father of P under section 28 of the Human Fertilisation and Embryology Act 1990 [[or under section 35 or 36 of the Human Fertilisation and Embryology Act 2008]]; and

[[(ca) no person is treated as a parent of P under section 42 or 43 of the Human Fertilisation and Embryology Act 2008;]]
(d) P has never been a British citizen.]

Note: inserted by s 65 Immigration Act 2014 from April 6. 2015. Words in double brackets omitted in subsection (4E)(a) by Nationality and Borders Act 2022 c. 36 Pt 1 s.7(2)(a) (June 28, 2022). Words inserted in double brackets in subsection (4E)(b) & (ca) by Nationality and Borders Act 2022 c. 36 Pt 1 s.7(2)(c) (June 28, 2022)

[4F. Person unable to be registered under other provisions of this Act

(1) A person ('P') is entitled to be registered as a British citizen on an application made under this section if—
(a) P meets the general conditions; and
(b) P would be entitled to be registered as a British citizen under—
(i) section 1(3),
(ii) section 3(2),
(iii) section 3(5),
[[(iiia) section 4D,]]

(iv) paragraph 4 of Schedule 2, or
(v) paragraph 5 of Schedule 2,

had P's mother been married to P's natural father at the time of P's birth.

(2) In the following provisions of this section 'relevant registration provision' means the provision under which P would be entitled to be registered as a British citizen (as mentioned in subsection (1)(b)).

(3) If the relevant registration provision is section 3(2), a person who is registered as a British citizen under this section is a British citizen by descent.

(4) If the relevant registration provision is section 3(5), the Secretary of State may, in the special circumstances of the particular case, waive the need for any or all of the parental consents to be given.

(5) For that purpose, the 'parental consents' are—

(a) the consent of P's natural father, and
(b) the consent of P's mother,

insofar as they would be required by section 3(5)(c) (as read with section 3(6)(b)), had P's mother been married to P's natural father at the time of P's birth.]

Note: inserted by s 65 Immigration Act 2014 6 April 2015..Words inserted in double brackets at subsection (1)(b)(iiia) by Nationality and Borders Act 2022 c. 36 Pt 1 s.7(3) (June 28, 2022)

[4G. Person unable to become citizen automatically after commencement

(1) A person P is entitled to be registered as a British citizen on an application made under this section if—

(a) P meets the general conditions; and

(b) at any time in the period after commencement, P would have automatically become a British citizen at birth by the operation of any provision of this Act or the British Nationality (Falkland Islands) Act 1983, had P's mother been married to P's natural father at the time of P's birth.

(2) A person who is registered as a British citizen under this section is a British citizen by descent if the British citizenship which the person would have acquired at birth (as mentioned in subsection (1)(b)) would (by virtue of section 14) have been British citizenship by descent.

(3) If P is under the age of 18, no application may be made unless the consent of P's natural father and mother to the registration has been signified in the prescribed manner.

(4) But if P's natural father or mother has died on or before the date of the application, the reference in subsection (3) to P's natural father and mother is to be read as a reference to either of them.

(5) The Secretary of State may, in the special circumstances of a particular case, waive the need for any or all of the consents required by subsection (3) (as read with subsection (4)) to be given.

(6) The reference in this section to the period after commencement does not include the time of commencement (and, accordingly, this section does not apply to any case in which a person was unable to become a British citizen at commencement).]

Note: inserted by s 65 Immigration Act 2014 from 6 April 2015.

[4H. Citizen of UK and colonies unable to become citizen at commencement

(1) A person 'P is entitled to be registered as a British citizen on an application made under this section if—

(a) P meets the general conditions;

(b) P was a citizen of the United Kingdom and Colonies immediately before commencement; and

(c) P would have automatically become a British citizen at commencement, by the operation of any provision of this Act, had P's mother been married to P's natural father at the time of P's birth.

(2) A person who is registered as a British citizen under this section is a British citizen by descent if the British citizenship which the person would have acquired at commencement (as mentioned in subsection (1)(c)) would (by virtue of section 14) have been British citizenship by descent.]

Note: inserted by s 65 Immigration Act 2014 from 6 April 2015.

[4I. Other person unable to become citizen at commencement

(1) A person P is entitled to be registered as a British citizen on an application made under this section if—

(a) P meets the general conditions;

(b) P is either—

(i) an eligible former British national, or

(ii) an eligible non-British national; and

(c) had P's mother been married to P's natural father at the time of P's birth, P—

(i) would have been a citizen of the United Kingdom and Colonies immediately before commencement, and

(ii) would have automatically become a British citizen at commencement by the operation of any provision of this Act.

[[(1A) In determining for the purposes of subsection (1)(c)(i) whether a person would have been a citizen of the United Kingdom and Colonies, the requirement that a person's birth was registered at a United Kingdom consulate, as set out in section 5(1)(b) of the British Nationality Act 1948, is to be ignored.]]

(2) P is an eligible former British national if P was not a citizen of the United Kingdom and Colonies immediately before commencement and either—

(a) P ceased to be a British subject or a citizen of the United Kingdom and Colonies by virtue of the commencement of any independence legislation, but would not have done so had P's mother been married to P's natural father at the time of P's birth, or

(b) P was a British subject who did not automatically become a citizen of the United Kingdom and Colonies at commencement of the British Nationality Act 1948 by the operation of any provision of it, but would have done so had P's mother been married to P's natural father at the time of P's birth.

(3) P is an eligible non-British national if—

(a) P was never a British subject or citizen of the United Kingdom and Colonies; and

(b) had P's mother been married to P's natural father at the time of P's birth, P would have automatically become a British subject or citizen of the United Kingdom and Colonies—

(i) at birth, or

(ii) by virtue of paragraph 3 of Schedule 3 to the British Nationality Act 1948 (child of male British subject to become citizen of the United Kingdom and Colonies if the father becomes such a citizen).

(4) A person who is registered as a British citizen under this section is a British citizen by descent if the British citizenship which the person would have acquired at commencement (as mentioned in subsection (1)(c)(ii)) would (by virtue of section 14) have been British citizenship by descent.

(5) In determining for the purposes of subsection (1)(c)(i) whether P would have been a citizen of the United Kingdom and Colonies immediately before commencement, it must be assumed that P would not have—

(a) renounced or been deprived of any notional British nationality, or

(b) lost any notional British nationality by virtue of P acquiring the nationality of a country or territory outside the United Kingdom.

(6) A 'notional British nationality is—

(a) in a case where P is an eligible former British national, any status as a British subject or a citizen of the United Kingdom and Colonies which P would have held at any time after P's nationality loss (had that loss not occurred and had P's mother had been married to P's natural father at the time of P's birth);

(b) in a case where P is an eligible non-British national—

(i) P's status as a British subject or citizen of the United Kingdom and Colonies mentioned in subsection (3)(b), and

(ii) any other status as a British subject or citizen of the United Kingdom and Colonies which P would have held at any time afterwards (had P's mother been married to P's natural father at the time of P's birth).

(7) In this section—

'British subject has any meaning which it had for the purposes of the British Nationality and Status of Aliens Act 1914;

independence legislation means an Act of Parliament or any subordinate legislation (within the meaning of the Interpretation Act 1978) forming part of the law in the United Kingdom (whenever passed or made, and whether or not still in force)—

(a) providing for a country or territory to become independent from the United Kingdom, or

(b) dealing with nationality, or any other ancillary matters, in connection with a country or territory becoming independent from the United Kingdom;

P's nationality loss means P's—

(a) ceasing to be a British subject or citizen of the United Kingdom and Colonies (as mentioned in subsection (2)(a)), or

(b) not becoming a citizen of the United Kingdom and Colonies (as mentioned in subsection (2)(b)).]

Note: inserted by s 65 Immigration Act 2014 6 April 2014.. Words in double brackets at subsection (1A) inserted by Nationality and Borders Act 2022 c. 36 Pt 1 s.6(3) (June 28, 2022: substitution has effect as SI 2022/590 reg.2 and Sch.1 para.5 subject to transitional and saving provision specified in reg.3 and Sch.2 para.2)

[4J. Sections 4E to 4I: supplementary provision

(1) In sections 4E to 4I and this section, a person's 'natural father' is a person who satisfies the requirements as to proof of paternity that are prescribed in regulations under section 50(9B).

(2) The power under section 50(9B) to make different provision for different circumstances includes power to make provision for the purposes of any provision of sections 4E to 4I which is different from other provision made under section 50(9B).

(3) The following provisions apply for the purposes of sections 4E to 4I.

(4) A reference to a person automatically becoming a British citizen, or a citizen of the United Kingdom and Colonies, is a reference to the person becoming such a citizen without the need for—

(a) the person to be registered as such a citizen by the Secretary of State or any other minister of the Crown;

(b) the birth of the person to be registered by a diplomatic or consular representative of the United Kingdom; or

(c) the person to be naturalised as such a citizen.

(5) If the mother of a person could not actually have been married to the person's natural father at the time of the person's birth (for whatever reason), that fact does not prevent an assumption being made that the couple were married at the time of the birth.]

Note: inserted by s 65 Immigration Act 2014 from 6 April 6, 2015.

[4K Acquisition by registration: certain British overseas territories citizens

(1) A person is entitled to be registered as a British citizen on an application made under this section if—

(a) they are entitled to be registered as a British overseas territories citizen under section 17A, 17C, 17D, 17E, 17F or 17H, or

(b) they would be entitled to be registered as a British overseas territories citizen under any of those sections but for the fact that they have already become a British overseas territories citizen under a different provision.

(2) Subsection (1) does not apply in the case of a person—

(a) who is or would be entitled to be registered as a British overseas territories citizen by virtue only of a connection with the Sovereign Base Areas of Akrotiri and Dhekelia, or

(b) who has previously been a British citizen.

(3) The Secretary of State may not register a person as a British citizen on an application under subsection (1)(a) unless the person is also registered as a British overseas territories citizen.]

Note: inserted by Nationality and Borders Act 2022 c. 36 Pt 1 s.4(2) (June 28, 2022 except for the purpose specified in reg.2, Sch.1 para.3; not yet in force otherwise)

[4L Acquisition by registration: special circumstances

(1) If an application is made for a person of full age and capacity ("P") to be registered as a British citizen, the Secretary of State may cause P to be registered as such a citizen if, in the Secretary of State's opinion, P would have been, or would have been able to become, a British citizen but for—

(a) historical legislative unfairness,

(b) an act or omission of a public authority, or

(c) exceptional circumstances relating to P.

(2) For the purposes of subsection (1)(a), "historical legislative unfairness" includes circumstances where P would have become, or would not have ceased to be, a British subject,

a citizen of the United Kingdom and Colonies or a British citizen, if an Act of Parliament or subordinate legislation (within the meaning of the Interpretation Act 1978) had, for the purposes of determining a person's nationality status—

(a) treated males and females equally,

(b) treated children of unmarried couples in the same way as children of married couples, or

(c) treated children of couples where the mother was married to someone other than the natural father in the same way as children of couples where the mother was married to the natural father.

(3) In subsection (1)(b), "public authority" means any public authority within the meaning of section 6 of the Human Rights Act 1998, other than a court or tribunal.

(4) In considering whether to grant an application under this section, the Secretary of State may take into account whether the applicant is of good character.]

Note: inserted by Nationality and Borders Act 2022 c. 36 Pt 1 s.8(2) (June 28, 2022)

5 Acquisition by registration: [British overseas territories citizens having connection with Gibraltar

A person who is a British overseas territories citizen by virtue of a connection with Gibraltar is entitled to be registered as a British citizen if an application is made for their registration as such a citizen.]

Note: British dependent territories became British overseas territories from 26 February 2002, British Overseas Territories Act 2002, s 1. Section 5 substituted by Immigration, Nationality and Asylum (EU Exit) Regulations 2019/745 Pt 2(1) reg7 (December 31, 2020: substitution has effect subject to saving and transitional provisions specified in SI 2019/745 Sch 2 Pt 2 para.2). .

6. Acquisition by naturalisation

(1) If, on an application for naturalisation as a British citizen made by a person of full age and capacity, the Secretary of State is satisfied that the applicant fulfils the requirements of Schedule 1 for naturalisation as such a citizen under this subsection, he may, if he thinks fit, grant to him a certificate of naturalisation as such a citizen.

(2) If, on an application for naturalisation as a British citizen made by a person of full age and capacity who on the date of the application [has a relevant family association], the Secretary of State is satisfied that the applicant fulfils the requirements of Schedule 1 for naturalisation as such a citizen under this subsection, he may, if he thinks fit, grant to him a certificate of naturalisation as such a citizen.

[(3) For the purposes of this section and Schedule 1, a person ('A') has a relevant family association if A has a connection of a prescribed description to a person of a prescribed description.

(4) If in the special circumstances of any particular case the Secretary of State thinks fit, the Secretary of State may for the purposes of subsection (3) treat A as having a relevant family association on the date of the application although the relevant family association ceased to exist before that date.]

Note: Words in square brackets substituted and subsections (3)–(4) inserted by s 40 Borders, Citizenship and Immigration Act 2009 from a date to be appointed.

Acquisition after commencement: special cases

7. . . .

Note: Section 7 repealed by Sch 2 of Nationality, Immigration and Asylum Act 2002 from 1 April 2003 (SI 2003/754).

8. . . .

Note: Section 8 repealed by Sch 2 of Nationality, Immigration and Asylum Act 2002 from 1 April 2003 (SI 2003/754).

9. . . .

Note: Section 9 repealed by Sch 2 of Nationality, Immigration and Asylum Act 2002 from 1 April 2003 (SI 2003/754).

10. Registration following renunciation of citizenship of UK and Colonies

(1) Subject to subsection (3), a person shall be entitled, on an application for his registration as a British citizen, to be registered as such a citizen if immediately before commencement he would (had he applied for it) have been entitled under section 1(1) of the British Nationality Act 1964 (resumption of citizenship) to be registered as a citizen of the United Kingdom and Colonies by virtue of having an appropriate qualifying connection with the United Kingdom or, [. . .] by virtue of having been married before commencement to a person who has, or would if living have, such a connection.

(2) On an application for his registration as a British citizen made by a person of full capacity who had before commencement ceased to be a citizen of the United Kingdom and Colonies as a result of a declaration of renunciation, the Secretary of State may, if he thinks fit, cause that person to be registered as a British citizen if that person—

(a) has an appropriate qualifying connection with the United Kingdom; or

(b) [. . .] has been married to [, or has been the civil partner of,] a person who has, or would if living have, such a connection.

(3) A person shall not be entitled to registration under subsection (1) on more than one occasion.

(4) For the purposes of this section a person shall be taken to have an appropriate qualifying connection with the United Kingdom if he, his father or his father's father—

(a) was born in the United Kingdom; or

(b) is or was a person naturalised in the United Kingdom; or

(c) was registered as a citizen of the United Kingdom and Colonies in the United Kingdom or in a country which at the time was mentioned in section 1(3) of the 1948 Act.

Note: The words deleted from subsections (1) and (2) repealed by Nationality, Immigration and Asylum Act 2002, s 5 from 7 November 2002 in relation to applications made after that date or not yet decided before that date (s 162(3)). Words in square brackets in subsection (2) inserted by Sch 27 Civil Partnership Act 2004 from 5 December 2005 (SI 2005/3175).

[10A. Acquisition in connection with immigration rules Appendix EU

(1) This section applies to a person born in the United Kingdom(2) on or after 1st July 2021 who is not a British citizen on the relevant date by virtue of any other provision of this Act.

(2) A person to whom this section applies ("C") is a British citizen as from the relevant date if conditions 1 to 3 are satisfied in the case of either C's father or mother ("P").

(3) Condition 1 is that, on or after 1st July 2021, P is granted—

(a) UK related indefinite leave under paragraph EU2 of Appendix EU to the UK immigration rules(3);

(b) Isle of Man related indefinite leave under paragraph EU2 of Appendix EU to the Isle of Man immigration rules(4),

and the date of grant of such leave is referred to in this section as "the relevant date".

(4) Condition 2 is that—

(a) P is granted the leave described in subsection (3)(a) or (b) pursuant to an application made before 1st July 2021, or

(b) immediately before 1st July 2021, P would have met the eligibility requirements for—

(i) UK related indefinite leave within paragraph EU11 or EU12 of Appendix EU to the UK immigration rules, or

(ii) Isle of Man related indefinite leave within paragraph EU11 or EU12 of Appendix EU to the Isle of Man immigration rules,

if an application had been made at that time.

(5) Condition 3 is that P is ordinarily resident in the United Kingdom on the relevant date.

(6) In determining whether subsection (4)(b) applies, it is to be assumed that P was not entitled to any exemption under section 8 of the Immigration Act 1971(5) immediately before 1st July 2021.

(7) Any subsequent change to the immigration status of P does not affect the status of C as a British citizen.

(8) In this section—

"Isle of Man immigration rules" means the rules laid down under section 3(2) of the Immigration Act 1971(6) as that section extends to the Isle of Man(7);

"Isle of Man related indefinite leave" means indefinite leave as defined in section 33(1) of the Immigration Act 1971 as that section extends to the Isle of Man(8);

"the relevant date" has the meaning given in subsection (3);

"UK immigration rules" means the rules laid down under section 3(2) of the Immigration Act 1971;

"UK related indefinite leave" means indefinite leave as defined in section 33(1) of the Immigration Act 1971.]

Note: inserted by British Nationality Act 1981 (Immigration Rules Appendix EU)(Amendment) Regulations 2021/743 reg.2 Amendment of the British Nationality Act 1981 (July 1, 2021)

Acquisition at commencement

11. Citizens of UK and Colonies who are to become British citizens at commencement

(1) Subject to subsection (2), a person who immediately before commencement—

(a) was a citizen of the United Kingdom and Colonies; and

(b) had the right of abode in the United Kingdom under the Immigration Act 1971 as then in force, shall at commencement become a British citizen.

(2) A person who was registered as a citizen of the United Kingdom and Colonies under section 1 of the British Nationality (No. 2) Act 1964 (stateless persons) on the ground mentioned in subsection (1)(a) of that section (namely that his mother was a citizen of the United Kingdom and Colonies at the time when he was born) shall not become a British citizen under subsection (1) unless—

(a) his mother becomes a British citizen under subsection (1) or would have done so but for her death; or

(b) immediately before commencement he had the right of abode in the United Kingdom by virtue of section 2(1)(c) of the Immigration Act 1971 as then in force (settlement in United Kingdom, combined with five or more years' ordinary residence there as a citizen of the United Kingdom and Colonies).

(3) A person who—

(a) immediately before commencement was a citizen of the United Kingdom and Colonies by virtue of having been registered under subsection (6) of section 12 of the 1948 Act (British subjects before commencement of 1948 Act becoming citizens of United Kingdom and Colonies) under arrangements made by virtue of subsection (7) of that section (registration in independent Commonwealth country by United Kingdom High Commissioner); and

(b) was so registered on an application under the said subsection (6) based on the applicant's descent in the male line from a person ('the relevant person') possessing one of the qualifications specified in subsection (1)(a) and (b) of that section (birth or naturalisation in the United Kingdom and Colonies), shall at commencement become a British citizen if the relevant person was born or naturalised in the United Kingdom.

Renunciation and resumption

12. Renunciation

(1) If any British citizen of full age and capacity makes in the prescribed manner a declaration of renunciation of British citizenship, then, subject to subsections (3) and (4), the Secretary of State shall cause the declaration to be registered.

(2) On the registration of a declaration made in pursuance of this section the person who made it shall cease to be a British citizen.

(3) A declaration made by a person in pursuance of this section shall not be registered unless the Secretary of State is satisfied that the person who made it will after the registration have or acquire some citizenship or nationality other than British citizenship; and if that person does not have any such citizenship or nationality on the date of registration and does not acquire some such citizenship or nationality within six months from that date, he shall be, and be deemed to have remained, a British citizen notwithstanding the registration.

(4) The Secretary of State may withhold registration of any declaration made in pursuance of this section if it is made during any war in which Her Majesty may be engaged in right of Her Majesty's government in the United Kingdom.

(5) For the purposes of this section any person who has been married [or has formed a civil partnership] shall be deemed to be of full age.

Note: Words in square brackets in subsection (5) inserted by Sch 27 Civil Partnership Act 2004 from 5 December 2005 (SI 2005/3175).

13. Resumption

(1) Subject to subsection (2), a person who has ceased to be a British citizen as a result of a declaration of renunciation shall be entitled, on an application for his registration as a British citizen, to be registered as such a citizen if—

(a) he is of full capacity; and

(b) his renunciation of British citizenship was necessary to enable him to retain or acquire some other citizenship or nationality.

(2) A person shall not be entitled to registration under subsection (1) on more than one occasion.

(3) If a person of full capacity who has ceased to be a British citizen as a result of a declaration of renunciation (for whatever reason made) makes an application for his registration as such a citizen, the Secretary of State may, if he thinks fit, cause him to be registered as such a citizen.

Supplementary

14. Meaning of British citizen 'by descent'

(1) For the purposes of this Act a British citizen is a British citizen 'by descent' if and only if—

(a) he is a person born outside the United Kingdom after commencement who is a British citizen by virtue of section 2(1)(a) only or by virtue of registration under section 3(2) or 9; or

(b) subject to subsection (2), he is a person born outside the United Kingdom before commencement who became a British citizen at commencement and immediately before commencement—

(i) was a citizen of the United Kingdom and Colonies by virtue of section 5 of the 1948 Act (citizenship by descent); or

(ii) was a person who, under any provision of the British Nationality Acts 1948 to 1965, was deemed for the purposes of the proviso to section 5(1) of the 1948 Act to be a citizen of the United Kingdom and Colonies by descent only, or would have been so deemed if male; or

(iii) had the right of abode in the United Kingdom by virtue only of paragraph (b) of subsection (1) of section 2 of the Immigration Act 1971 as then in force (connection with United Kingdom through parent or grandparent), or by virtue only of that paragraph and paragraph (c) of that subsection (settlement in United Kingdom with five years' ordinary residence there), or by virtue only of being or having been the wife of a person who immediately before commencement had that right by virtue only of the said paragraph (b) or the said paragraphs (b) and (c); or

(iv) being a woman, was a citizen of the United Kingdom and Colonies as a result of her registration as such a citizen under section 6(2) of the 1948 Act by virtue of having been married to a man who at commencement became a British citizen by descent or would have done so but for his having died or ceased to be a citizen of the United Kingdom and Colonies as a result of a declaration of renunciation; or

(c) he is a British citizen by virtue of registration under section 3(1) and either—

(i) his father or mother was a British citizen at the time of the birth; or

(ii) his father or mother was a citizen of the United Kingdom and Colonies at that time and became a British citizen at commencement, or would have done so but for his or her death; or

(d) he is a British citizen by virtue of registration under [section 4B [4C] or 5]; or

[(da) the person is a British citizen by descent by virtue of section 4F(3), 4G(2), 4H(2) or 4I(4); or]

[(db) the person is a British citizen by virtue of registration under section 4K and is—

(i) a British overseas territories citizen by virtue of registration under section 17A, or

(ii) a British overseas territories citizen by descent by virtue of section 17C(3), 17D(2), 17E(2) or 17F(5); or]

(e) subject to subsection (2), being a woman born outside the United Kingdom before commencement, she is a British citizen as a result of her registration as such a citizen under section 8 by virtue of being or having been married to a man who at commencement became a British citizen by descent or would have done so but for his having died or ceased to be a citizen of the United Kingdom and Colonies as a result of a declaration of renunciation; or

(f) he is a British citizen by virtue of registration under section 10 who, having before commencement ceased to be a citizen of the United Kingdom and Colonies as a result of a declaration of renunciation, would, if he had not so ceased, have at commencement become a British citizen by descent by virtue of paragraph (b); or

(g) he is a British citizen by virtue of registration under section 13 who, immediately before he ceased to be a British citizen as a result of a declaration of renunciation, was such a citizen by descent; or

(h) he is a person born in a [British overseas territory] after commencement who is a British citizen by virtue of paragraph 2 of Schedule 2.

(2) A person born outside the United Kingdom before commencement is not a British citizen 'by descent' by virtue of subsection (1)(b) or (e) if his father was at the time of his birth serving outside the United Kingdom—

(a) in service of a description mentioned in subsection (3), his recruitment for the service in question having taken place in the United Kingdom; or

(b) in service under a [EU] institution, his recruitment for that service having taken place in a country which at the time of the recruitment was a member of the [European Union].

(3) The descriptions of service referred to in subsection (2) are—

(a) Crown service under the government of the United Kingdom; and

(b) service of any description at any time designated under section 2(3).

Note: First words in square brackets in subsection (1)(d) substituted by Nationality, Immigration and Asylum Act 2002, s 12 from 30 April 2003 (SI 2003/754). Second words in square brackets in subsection (1)(d) inserted by Nationality, Immigration and Asylum Act 2002, s 13 from 30 April 2003 (SI 2003/754). Subsection (1)(da) inserted by Sch 9 Immigration Act 2014 from April 4, 2015. British dependent territories became British overseas territories from 26 February 2002, British Overseas Territories Act 2002, s 1. Subsection (1)(db) inserted by Nationality and Borders Act 2022 c. 36 Pt 1 s.4(3) (June 28, 2022)

Part II
[British Overseas Territories] Citizenship

Acquisition after commencement

15. Acquisition by birth or adoption

(1) A person born in a [British overseas territory] after commencement shall be a [British overseas territories] citizen if at the time of the birth his father or mother is—

(a) a [British overseas territories] citizen; or

(b) settled in a [British overseas territory].

(2) A new-born infant who, after commencement, is found abandoned in a [British overseas territory] shall, unless the contrary is shown, be deemed for the purposes of subsection (1)—

(a) to have been born in that territory after commencement; and

(b) to have been born to a parent who at the time of the birth was a [British over-seas territories] citizen or settled in a [British overseas territory].

(3) A person born in a [British overseas territory] after commencement who is not a [British overseas territories] citizen by virtue of subsection (1) or (2) shall be entitled to be registered as such a citizen if, while he is a minor—

(a) his father or mother becomes such a citizen or becomes settled in a [British overseas territory]; and

(b) an application is made for his registration as such a citizen.

(4) A person born in a [British overseas territory] after commencement who is not a [British overseas territories] citizen by virtue of subsection (1) or (2) shall be entitled, on an application for his registration as a [British overseas territories] citizen made at any time after he has attained the age of ten years, to be registered as such a citizen if, as regards each of the first ten years of that person's life, the number of days on which he was absent from that territory in that year does not exceed 90.

(5) Where after commencement an order authorising the adoption of a minor who is not a [British overseas territories] citizen is made by a court in any [British overseas territory], he shall be a [British overseas territories] citizen as from the date on which the order is made if the adopter or, in the case of a joint adoption, one of the adopters, is a [British overseas territories] citizen on that date.

[(5A) Where—

(a) a minor who is not a British overseas territories citizen is adopted under a Convention adoption,

(b) on the date on which the adoption is effected—

(i) the adopter or, in the case of a joint adoption, one of the adopters is a British overseas territories citizen, and

(ii) the adopter or, in the case of a joint adoption, both of the adopters are habitually resident in a designated territory, and

(c) the Convention adoption is effected under the law of a country or territory outside the designated territory,

the minor shall be a British overseas territories citizen as from that date.]

(6) Where an order [or a Convention adoption] in consequence of which any person became a [British overseas territories] citizen by virtue of subsection (5) ceases to have

effect, whether on annulment or otherwise, the cesser shall not affect the status of that person as such a citizen.

(7) If in the special circumstances of any particular case the Secretary of State thinks fit, he may for the purposes of subsection (4) treat the person to whom the application relates as fulfilling the requirements specified in that subsection although, as regards any one or more of the first ten years of that person's life, the number of days on which he was absent from the [British overseas territory] there mentioned in that year or each of the years in question exceeds 90.

Note: British dependent territories became British overseas territories from 26 February 2002, British Overseas Territories Act 2002, s 1. Subsection (5A) and words in subsection (6) inserted from 30 December 2005 by Adoption and Children Act 2002.

16. Acquisition by descent

(1) A person born outside the [British overseas territories] after commencement shall be a [British overseas territories] citizen if at the time of the birth his father or mother—

(a) is such a citizen otherwise than by descent; or

(b) is such a citizen and is serving outside the [British overseas territories] in service to which this paragraph applies, his or her recruitment for that service having taken place in a [British overseas territory].

(2) Paragraph (b) of subsection (1) applies to—

(a) Crown service under the government of a [British overseas territory]; and

(b) service of any description for the time being designated under subsection (3).

(3) For the purposes of this section the Secretary of State may by order made by statutory instrument designate any description of service which he considers to be closely associated with the activities outside the [British overseas territories] of the government of any [British overseas territory].

(4) Any order made under subsection (3) shall be subject to annulment in pursuance of a resolution of either House of Parliament.

Note: British dependent territories became British overseas territories from 26 February 2002, British Overseas Territories Act 2002, s 1.

17. Acquisition by registration: minors

(1) If while a person is a minor an application is made for his registration as a [British overseas territories] citizen the Secretary of State may, if he thinks fit, cause him to be registered as such a citizen.

(2) A person born outside the [British overseas territories] shall be entitled, on an application for his registration as a [British overseas territories] citizen[[while the person is a minor]], to be registered as such a citizen if the requirements specified in subsection (3) or, in the case of a person born stateless, the requirements specified in paragraphs (a) and (b) of that subsection, are fulfilled in the case of either that person's father or his mother ('the parent in question').

(3) The requirements referred to in subsection (2) are—

(a) that the parent in question was a [British overseas territories] citizen by descent at the time of the birth; and

(b) that the father or mother of the parent in question—

(i) was a [British overseas territories] citizen otherwise than by descent at the time of the birth of the parent in question; or

(ii) became a [British overseas territories] citizen otherwise than by descent at commencement, or would have become such a citizen otherwise than by descent at commencement but for his or her death; and

(c) that, as regards some period of three years ending with a date not later than the date of the birth—

(i) the parent in question was in a [British overseas territory] at the beginning of that period; and

(ii) the number of days on which the parent in question was absent from that territory in that period does not exceed 270.

(4 …

(5) A person born outside the [British overseas territories] shall be entitled, on an application for his registration as a [British overseas territories citizen] made while he is a minor, to be registered as such a citizen if the following requirements are satisfied, namely—

(a) that at the time of that person's birth his father or mother was a [British overseas territories] citizen by descent; and

(b) subject to subsection (6), that that person and his father and mother were in one and the same [British overseas territory] (no matter which) at the beginning of the period of three years ending with the date of the application and that, in the case of each of them, the number of days on which the person in question was absent from the last-mentioned territory in that period does not exceed 270; and

(c) subject to subsection (6), that the consent of his father and mother to the registration has been signified in the prescribed manner.

(6) In the case of an application under subsection (5) for the registration of a person as a [British overseas territories] citizen—

(a) if his father or mother died, or their marriage [or civil partnership] was terminated, on or before the date of the application, or his father and mother were legally separated on that date, the references to his father and mother in paragraph (b) of that subsection shall be read either as references to his father or as references to his mother; [and]

(b) if his father or mother died on or before that date, the reference to his father and mother in paragraph (c) of that subsection shall be read as a reference to either of them; […

(c) …]

Note: Last word in square brackets in subsection (6)(a) inserted, and words deleted from subsections (6)(b) and (c) by Nationality, Immigration and Asylum Act 2002, s 9 from 7 November 2002, in relation to children born on or after a date to be appointed. British dependent territories became British overseas territories from 26 February 2002, British Overseas Territories Act 2002, s 1. Words in first square brackets in subsection (6)(a) inserted by Sch 27 Civil Partnership Act 2004 from 5 December 2005 (SI 2005/3175). Words in double square brackets in subsection (2) substituted by Nationality and Borders Act 2022 c. 36 Pt 1 s.5(1)(a) (June 28, 2022: substitution has effect as SI 2022/590 reg.2 and Sch.1 para.4 subject to transitional and saving provision specified in reg.3 and Sch.2 para.1.Subsection (4) omitted by Nationality and Borders Act 2022 c. 36 Pt 1 s.5(1)(b) (June 28, 2022: substitution has effect as SI 2022/590 reg.2 and Sch.1 para.4 subject to transitional and saving provision specified in reg.3 and Sch.2 para.1)

[17A Registration: remedying inability of mothers to transmit citizenship

(1) On an application for registration under this section, a person ("P") is entitled to be registered as a British overseas territories citizen if the following three conditions are met.

(2) The first condition is that—

(a) P would have become a citizen of the United Kingdom and Colonies under any of the following provisions of the British Nationality Act 1948—

(i) section 5 (person born on or after 1 January 1949: citizenship by descent);

(ii) section 12(2) (person born before 1 January 1949: citizenship by descent);

(iii) section 12(3) (person born before 1 January 1949 in British protectorate etc);

(iv) section 12(4) (person born before January 1949 not becoming citizen of other country);

(v) section 12(5) (woman married before 1 January 1949 to a man who became or would have become a citizen of the United Kingdom and Colonies);

(vi) paragraph 3 of Schedule 3 (person born on or after 1 January 1949 to a British subject without citizenship);

had P's parents been treated equally, by that Act or by any relevant previous provision, for the purposes of determining P's nationality status; or

(b) P would have been a citizen of the United Kingdom and Colonies immediately before commencement had P's parents been treated equally, for the purposes of determining P's nationality status, by any independence legislation that caused P to lose that citizenship.

(3) In subsection (2)—

"relevant previous provision" means a provision of the law that was in force at some time before 1 January 1949 which provided for a nationality status to be transmitted from a parent to a child without the need for an application to be made for the child to be registered as a person with that nationality status;

"independence legislation" means an Act of Parliament or any subordinate legislation (within the meaning of the Interpretation Act 1978) forming part of the law in the United Kingdom (whenever passed or made, and whether or not still in force)—

(a) providing for a country or territory to become independent from the United Kingdom, or

(b) dealing with nationality, or any other ancillary matters, in connection with a country or territory becoming independent from the United Kingdom.

(4) In determining for the purposes of subsection (2) whether a person would have become a citizen of the United Kingdom and Colonies under section 5 of the British Nationality Act 1948, the requirement that a person's birth was registered at a United Kingdom consulate, as set out in subsection (1)(b) of that section, is to be ignored.

(5) The second condition is that, if P had become or been a citizen of the United Kingdom and Colonies as mentioned in subsection (2), P would at commencement have become a British Dependent Territories citizen under section 23(1)(b) or (c).

(6) The third condition is that, if P had become a British Dependent Territories citizen as mentioned in subsection (5), P would have become a British overseas territories citizen on the commencement of section 2 of the British Overseas Territories Act 2002.

Note: Section 17 A inserted by Nationality and Borders Act 2022 c.36. Pt1s.1(2) (June 28, 2022)

17B Registration: unmarried fathers; the general conditions

For the purposes of sections 17C to 17F, a person ("P") meets the general conditions if—

(a) at the time of P's birth, P's mother—

(i) was not married, or

(ii) was married to a person other than P's natural father;

(b) no person is treated as the father of P under—

(i) section 28 of the Human Fertilisation and Embryology Act 1990, or

(ii) section 35 or 36 of the Human Fertilisation and Embryology Act 2008;

(c) no person is treated as a parent of P under section 42 or 43 of the Human Fertilisation and Embryology Act 2008; and

(d) P has never been a British overseas territories citizen or a British Dependent Territories citizen.

Note: inserted by Nationality and Borders Act 2022 c.36, Pt1s.2(2) June 28, 2022

17C Person unable to be registered under other provisions of this Act

(1) A person ("P") is entitled to be registered as a British overseas territories citizen on an application made under this section if—

(a) P meets the general conditions; and

(b) P would be entitled to be registered as a British overseas territories citizen under—

(i) section 15(3),

(ii) section 17(2),

(iii) section 17(5),

(iv) paragraph 4 of Schedule 2, or

(v) paragraph 5 of Schedule 2,

had P's mother been married to P's natural father at the time of P's birth.

(2) In the following provisions of this section, "relevant registration provision" means the provision under which P would be entitled to be registered as a British overseas territories citizen (as mentioned in subsection (1)(b)).

(3) If the relevant registration provision is section 17(2), a person who is registered as a British overseas territories citizen under this section is a British overseas territories citizen by descent.

(4) If the relevant registration provision is section 17(5), the Secretary of State may, in the special circumstances of the particular case, waive the need for any or all of the parental consents to be given.

(5) For that purpose, the "parental consents" are—

(a) the consent of P's natural father, and

(b) the consent of P's mother,

insofar as they would be required by section 17(5)(c) (as read with section 17(6)(b)), had P's mother been married to P's natural father at the time of P's birth.

Note: inserted by Nationality and Borders Act 2022 c.36 Pt1 s.2(2) (June 28, 2022).

17D Person unable to become citizen automatically after commencement

(1) A person ("P") is entitled to be registered as a British overseas territories citizen on an application made under this section if—

(a) P meets the general conditions;

(b) at any time in the period after commencement, P would have automatically become a British Dependent Territories citizen or a British overseas territories citizen at birth by the operation of—

(i) section 15(1),

(ii) section 16, or

(iii) paragraph 1 of Schedule 2,

had P's mother been married to P's natural father at the time of P's birth; and

(c) in a case where P would have become a British Dependent Territories citizen as mentioned in paragraph (b), P would then have automatically become a British overseas territories citizen by the operation of section 2 of the British Overseas Territories Act 2002.

(2) A person who is registered as a British overseas territories citizen under this section is a British overseas territories citizen by descent if the citizenship which the person would have acquired at birth (as mentioned in subsection (1)(b)) would (by virtue of section 25) have been citizenship by descent.

(3) If P is under the age of 18, no application may be made unless the consent of P's natural father and mother to the registration has been signified in the prescribed manner.

(4) But if P's natural father or mother has died on or before the date of the application, the reference in subsection (3) to P's natural father and mother is to be read as a reference to either of them.

(5) The Secretary of State may, in the special circumstances of a particular case, waive the need for any or all of the consents required by subsection (3) (as read with subsection (4)) to be given.

(6) The reference in this section to the period after commencement does not include the time of commencement (and, accordingly, this section does not apply to any case in which a person was unable to become a British Dependent Territories citizen at commencement).

Note: inserted by Nationality and Borders Act 2022 c.36 Pt 1 s.2(2) (June 28, 2022)

17E Citizen of UK and Colonies unable to become citizen at commencement

(1) A person ("P") is entitled to be registered as a British overseas territories citizen on an application made under this section if—

(a) P meets the general conditions;

(b) P—

(i) was a citizen of the United Kingdom and Colonies immediately before commencement, or

(ii) would have become such a citizen as mentioned in section 17A(2)(a), or

(iii) would have been such a citizen immediately before commencement as mentioned in section 17A(2)(b);

(c) P would then have automatically become a British Dependent Territories citizen at commencement by the operation of section 23, had P's mother been married to P's natural father at the time of P's birth; and

(d) P would then have automatically become a British overseas territories citizen by the operation of section 2 of the British Overseas Territories Act 2002.

(2) A person who is registered as a British overseas territories citizen under this section is a British overseas territories citizen by descent if the citizenship which the person would

have acquired at commencement (as mentioned in subsection (1)(c)) would (by virtue of section 25) have been citizenship by descent.

Note: inserted by Nationality and Borders Act 2022 c.36 Pt1 s2(2) (June 2028, 2022)

[17F Other person unable to become citizen at commencement

(1) A person ("P") is entitled to be registered as a British overseas territories citizen on an application made under this section if—

(a) P meets the general conditions;

(b) P is either—

(i) an eligible former British national, or

(ii) an eligible non-British national; and

(c) had P's mother been married to P's natural father at the time of P's birth, P—

(i) would have been a citizen of the United Kingdom and Colonies immediately before commencement,

(ii) would have automatically become a British Dependent Territories citizen at commencement by the operation of section 23, and

(iii) would have automatically become a British overseas territories citizen by the operation of section 2 of the British Overseas Territories Act 2002.

(2) In determining for the purposes of subsection (1)(c)(i) whether a person would have been a citizen of the United Kingdom and Colonies, the requirement that a person's birth was registered at a United Kingdom consulate, as set out in section 5(1)(b) of the British Nationality Act 1948, is to be ignored.

(3) P is an "eligible former British national" if P was not a citizen of the United Kingdom and Colonies immediately before commencement and either—

(a) P ceased to be a British subject or a citizen of the United Kingdom and Colonies by virtue of the commencement of any independence legislation, but would not have done so had P's mother been married to P's natural father at the time of P's birth, or

(b) P was a British subject who did not automatically become a citizen of the United Kingdom and Colonies at commencement of the British Nationality Act 1948 by the operation of any provision of it, but would have done so had P's mother been married to P's natural father at the time of P's birth.

(4) P is an "eligible non-British national" if—

(a) P was never a British subject or citizen of the United Kingdom and Colonies; and

(b) had P's mother been married to P's natural father at the time of P's birth, P would have automatically become a British subject or citizen of the United Kingdom and Colonies—

(i) at birth, or

(ii) by virtue of paragraph 3 of Schedule 3 to the British Nationality Act 1948 (child of male British subject to become citizen of the United Kingdom and Colonies if father becomes such a citizen).

(5) A person who is registered as a British overseas territories citizen under this section is a British overseas territories citizen by descent if the citizenship which the person would have acquired at commencement (as mentioned in subsection (1)(c)(ii)) would (by virtue of section 25) have been citizenship by descent.

(6) In determining for the purposes of subsection (1)(c)(i) whether P would have been a citizen of the United Kingdom and Colonies immediately before commencement, it must be assumed that P would not have—

(a) renounced or been deprived of any notional British nationality, or

(b) lost any notional British nationality by virtue of P acquiring the nationality of a country or territory outside the United Kingdom.

(7) A "notional British nationality" is—

(a) in a case where P is an eligible former British national, any status as a British subject or a citizen of the United Kingdom and Colonies which P would have held at any time after P's nationality loss (had that loss not occurred and had P's mother been married to P's natural father at the time of P's birth);

(b) in a case where P is an eligible non-British national—

(i) P's status as a British subject or citizen of the United Kingdom and Colonies as mentioned in subsection (4)(b), and

(ii) any other status as a British subject or citizen of the United Kingdom and Colonies which P would have held at any time afterwards (had P's mother been married to P's natural father at the time of P's birth).

(8) In this section—

"British subject" has any meaning which it had for the purposes of the British Nationality and Status of Aliens Act 1914;

"independence legislation" means an Act of Parliament or any subordinate legislation (within the meaning of the Interpretation Act 1978) forming part of the law in the United Kingdom (whenever passed or made, and whether or not still in force)—

(a) providing for a country or territory to become independent from the United Kingdom, or

(b) dealing with nationality, or any other ancillary matters, in connection with a country or territory becoming independent from the United Kingdom;

"P's nationality loss" means P's—

(a) ceasing to be a British subject or citizen of the United Kingdom and Colonies (as mentioned in subsection (3)(a)), or

(b) not becoming a citizen of the United Kingdom and Colonies (as mentioned in subsection (3)(b)).]

Note: inserted by Nationality and Borders Act 2022 c.36 Pt1 s2(2) (June 28, 2022)

[17G Sections 17B to 17F: supplementary provision

(1) In sections 17B to 17F and this section, a person's "natural father" is a person who satisfies the requirements as to proof of paternity that are prescribed in regulations under section 50(9B).

(2) The power under section 50(9B) to make different provision for different circumstances includes power to make provision for the purposes of any provision of sections 17B to 17F which is different from other provision made under section 50(9B).

(3) The following provisions apply for the purposes of sections 17B to 17F.

(4) A reference to a person automatically becoming a citizen of a certain type is a reference to the person becoming a citizen of that type without the need for—

(a) the person to be registered as such a citizen by the Secretary of State or any other minister of the Crown;

(b) the birth of the person to be registered by a diplomatic or consular representative of the United Kingdom; or

(c) the person to be naturalised as such a citizen.

(5) If the mother of a person could not actually have been married to the person's natural father at the time of the person's birth (for whatever reason), that fact does not prevent an assumption being made that the couple were married at the time of the birth.]

Note: inserted by Nationality and Borders Act 2022 c,36 Pt1 s.2(2) (June 28, 2022)

[17H Acquisition by registration: descendants of those born in British Indian Ocean Territory

(1) A person is entitled to be registered as a British overseas territories citizen on an application made under this section if—

(a) they are a direct descendant of a person ("P") who was a citizen of the United Kingdom and Colonies by virtue of P's birth in the British Indian Ocean Territory or, prior to 8 November 1965, in those islands designated as the British Indian Ocean Territory on that date, and

(b) they have never been a British overseas territories citizen or a British Dependent Territories citizen.

(2) An application under this section must be made—

(a) in the case of a person aged 18 years or over on the commencement date, before the end of the period of five years beginning with the commencement date;

(b) in the case of a person aged under 18 on the commencement date, or a person who is born before the end of the period of five years beginning with the commencement date, before they reach the age of 23 years.

(3) In subsection (2), "the commencement date" means the date on which this section comes into force.]

Note: inserted by Nationality and Borders Act 2022 c.36 Pt 1 s.3 (date to be appointed)

[17I Acquisition by registration: special circumstances

(1) If an application is made for a person of full age and capacity ("P") to be registered as a British overseas territories citizen, the Secretary of State may cause P to be registered as such a citizen if, in the Secretary of State's opinion, P would have been, or would have been able to become, a British overseas territories citizen but for—

(a) historical legislative unfairness,

(b) an act or omission of a public authority, or

(c) exceptional circumstances relating to P.

(2) For the purposes of subsection (1)(a), "historical legislative unfairness" includes circumstances where P would have become, or would not have ceased to be, a British subject, a citizen of the United Kingdom and Colonies, a British Dependent Territories Citizen or a British overseas territories citizen, if an Act of Parliament or subordinate legislation (within the meaning of the Interpretation Act 1978) had, for the purposes of determining a person's nationality status—

(a) treated males and females equally,

(b) treated children of unmarried couples in the same way as children of married couples, or

(c) treated children of couples where the mother was married to someone other than the natural father in the same way as children of couples where the mother was married to the natural father.

(3) In subsection (1)(b), "public authority" means any public authority within the meaning of section 6 of the Human Rights Act 1998, other than a court or tribunal.

(4) In considering whether to grant an application under this section, the Secretary of State may take into account whether the applicant is of good character.]

Note: inserted by Nationality and Borders Act 2022 c. 36 Pt 1 s.8(3) (June 28, 2022)

18. Acquisition by naturalisation

(1) If, on an application for naturalisation as a [British overseas territories] citizen made by a person of full age and capacity, the Secretary of State is satisfied that the applicant fulfils the requirements of Schedule 1 for naturalisation as such a citizen under this subsection, he may, if he thinks fit, grant to him a certificate of naturalisation as such a citizen.

(2) If, on an application for naturalisation as a [British overseas territories] citizen made by a person of full age and capacity who on the date of the application is married to such a citizen [or is the civil partner of such a citizen] the Secretary of State is satisfied that the applicant fulfils the requirements of Schedule 1 for naturalisation as such a citizen under this subsection, he may, if he thinks fit, grant to him a certificate of naturalisation as such a citizen.

(3) Every application under this section shall specify the [British overseas territory] which is to be treated as the relevant territory for the purposes of that application; and, in relation to any such application, references in Schedule 1 to the relevant territory shall be construed accordingly.

Note: British dependent territories became British overseas territories from 26 February 2002, British Overseas Territories Act 2002, s 1. Words in square brackets in subsection (2) inserted by Sch 27 Civil Partnership Act 2004 from 5 December 2005 (SI 2005/3175).

Acquisition after commencement: special cases

19. …

Note: Section 19 repealed by Sch 2 Nationality, Immigration and Asylum Act 2002 from 1 April 2003 (SI 2003/754).

20. …

Note: Section 20 repealed by Sch 2 Nationality, Immigration and Asylum Act 2002 from 1 April 2003 (SI 2003/754).

21. …

Note: Section 21 repealed by Sch 2 Nationality, Immigration and Asylum Act 2002 from 1 April 2003 (SI 2003/754).

22. Right to registration replacing right to resume citizenship of UK and Colonies

(1) Subject to subsection (3), a person shall be entitled, on an application for his registration as a [British overseas territories] citizen, to be registered as such a citizen if

immediately before commencement he would (had he applied for it) have been entitled under section 1(1) of the British Nationality Act 1964 (resumption of citizenship) to be registered as a citizen of the United Kingdom and Colonies by virtue of having an appropriate qualifying connection with a [British overseas territory] or, [. . . ,] by virtue of having been married before commencement to a person who has, or would if living have, such a connection.

(2) On an application for his registration as a [British overseas territories] citizen made by a person of full capacity who had before commencement ceased to be a citizen of the United Kingdom and Colonies as a result of a declaration of renunciation, the Secretary of State may, if he thinks fit, cause that person to be registered as a [British overseas territories] citizen if that person—

(a) has an appropriate qualifying connection with a [British overseas territory]; or

(b) [. . .] has been married to [or has been the civil partner of,] a person who has, or would if living have, such a connection.

(3) A person shall not be entitled to registration under subsection (1) on more than one occasion.

(4) For the purposes of this section a person shall be taken to have an appropriate qualifying connection with a [British overseas territory] if he, his father or his father's father—

(a) was born in that territory; or

(b) is or was a person naturalised in that territory; or

(c) was registered as a citizen of the United Kingdom and Colonies in that territory; or

(d) became a British subject by reason of the annexation of any territory included in that territory.

Note: The words deleted from subsections (1) and (2) cease to have effect with regard to applications made after 7 November 2002, or applications not determined before that date: Nationality, Immigration and Asylum Act 2002, s 5. British dependent territories became British overseas territories from 26 February 2002, British Overseas Territories Act 2002, s 1. Words in square brackets in subsection (2)(b) inserted by Sch 27 Civil Partnership Act 2004 from 5 December 2005 (SI 2005/3175).

Acquisition at commencement

23. Citizens of UK and Colonies who are to become [British overseas territories] citizens at commencement

(1) A person shall at commencement become a [British overseas territories] citizen if—

(a) immediately before commencement he was a citizen of the United Kingdom and Colonies who had that citizenship by his birth, naturalisation or registration in a [British overseas territory]; or

(b) he was immediately before commencement a citizen of the United Kingdom and Colonies, and was born to a parent—

(i) who at the time of the birth ('the material time') was a citizen of the United Kingdom and Colonies; and

(ii) who either had that citizenship at the material time by his birth, naturalisation or registration in a [British overseas territory] or was himself born to a parent who at the time of that birth so had that citizenship; or

(c) being a woman, she was immediately before commencement a citizen of the United Kingdom and Colonies and either was then, or had at any time been, the wife of a man who under paragraph (a) or (b) becomes a [British overseas territories] citizen at commencement or would have done so but for his death.

(2) A person shall at commencement become a [British overseas territories] citizen if—

(a) immediately before commencement he was a citizen of the United Kingdom and Colonies by virtue of registration under section 7 of the 1948 Act (minor children) or section 1 of the British Nationality (No. 2) Act 1964 (stateless persons); and

(b) he was so registered otherwise than in a [British overseas territory]; and

(c) his father or mother (in the case of a person registered under the said section 7) or his mother (in the case of a person registered under the said section 1)—

(i) was a citizen of the United Kingdom and Colonies at the time of the registration or would have been such a citizen at that time but for his or her death; and

(ii) becomes a [British overseas territories] citizen at commencement or would have done so but for his or her death.

(3) A person who—

(a) immediately before commencement was a citizen of the United Kingdom and Colonies by virtue of having been registered under subsection (6) of section 12 of the 1948 Act (British subjects before commencement of 1948 Act becoming citizens of United Kingdom and Colonies) otherwise than in a [British overseas territory]; and

(b) was so registered on an application under that subsection based on the applicant's descent in the male line from a person ('the relevant person') possessing one of the qualifications specified in subsection (1) of that section (birth or naturalisation in the United Kingdom and Colonies, or acquisition of the status of British subject by reason of annexation of territory),

shall at commencement become a [British overseas territories] citizen if the relevant person—

(i) was born or naturalised in a [British overseas territory]; or

(ii) became a British subject by reason of the annexation of any territory included in a [British overseas territory].

(4) A person who—

(a) immediately before commencement was a citizen of the United Kingdom and Colonies by virtue of registration under section 1 of the British Nationality Act 1964 (resumption of citizenship); and

(b) was so registered otherwise than in a [British overseas territory]; and

(c) was so registered by virtue of having an appropriate qualifying connection with a [British overseas territory] or, if a woman, by virtue of having been married to a person who at the time of the registration had or would, if then living, have had such a connection,

shall at commencement become a [British overseas territories] citizen.

(5) For the purposes of subsection (4) a person shall be taken to have an appropriate qualifying connection with a [British overseas territory] if he, his father or his father's father—

(a) was born in a [British overseas territory]; or

(b) is or was a person naturalised in a [British overseas territory]; or

(c) was registered as a citizen of the United Kingdom and Colonies in a [British overseas territory]; or

(d) became a British subject by reason of the annexation of any territory included in a [British overseas territory].

(6) For the purposes of subsection (1)(b) references to citizenship of the United Kingdom and Colonies shall, in relation to a time before the year 1949, be construed as references to British nationality.

Note: British dependent territories became British overseas territories from 26 February 2002, British Overseas Territories Act 2002, s 1.

Renunciation and resumption

24. Renunciation and resumption

The provisions of sections 12 and 13 shall apply in relation to [British overseas territories] citizens and [British Overseas Territories] citizenship as they apply in relation to British citizens and British citizenship.

Note: British dependent territories became British overseas territories from 26 February 2002, British Overseas Territories Act 2002, s 1.

Supplementary

25. Meaning of [British overseas territories] citizen 'by descent'

(1) For the purposes of this Act a [British overseas territories] citizen is such a citizen 'by descent' if and only if—

(a) he is a person born outside the [British overseas territories] after commencement who is a [British overseas territories] citizen by virtue of section 16(1)(a) only or by virtue of registration under section 17(2) or 21; or

(b) subject to subsection (2), he is a person born outside the [British overseas territories] before commencement who became a [British overseas territories] citizen at commencement and immediately before commencement—

(i) was a citizen of the United Kingdom and Colonies by virtue of section 5 of the 1948 Act (citizenship by descent); or

(ii) was a person who, under any provision of the British Nationality Acts 1948 to 1965, was deemed for the purposes of the proviso to section 5(1) of the 1948 Act to be a citizen of the United Kingdom and Colonies by descent only, or would have been so deemed if male; or

(c) he is a [British overseas territories] citizen by virtue of registration under section 17(1) and either—

(i) his father or mother was a [British overseas territories] citizen at the time of the birth; or

(ii) his father or mother was a citizen of the United Kingdom and Colonies at that time and became a [British overseas territories] citizen at commencement, or would have done so but for his or her death; or

[(ca) the person is a British overseas territories citizen by virtue of registration under section 17A; or

(cb) the person is a British overseas territories citizen by descent by virtue of section 17C(3), 17D(2), 17E(2) or 17F(5); or

(d) subject to subsection (2), he is a person born outside the [British overseas territories] before commencement who became a [British overseas territories] citizen at commencement under section 23(1)(b) only; or

(e) subject to subsection (2), being a woman, she became a [British overseas territories] citizen at commencement under section 23(1)(c) only, and did so only by virtue of having been, immediately before commencement or earlier, the wife of a man who immediately after commencement was, or would but for his death have been, a [British overseas territories] citizen by descent by virtue of paragraph (b) or (d) of this subsection; or

(f) subject to subsection (2), being a woman born outside the [British overseas territories] before commencement, she is a [British overseas territories] citizen as a result of her registration as such a citizen under section 20 by virtue of being or having been married to a man who at commencement became such a citizen by descent or would have done so but for his having died or ceased to be a citizen of the United Kingdom and Colonies as a result of a declaration of renunciation; or

(g) he is a [British overseas territories] citizen by virtue of registration under section 22 who, having before commencement ceased to be a citizen of the United Kingdom and Colonies as a result of a declaration of renunciation, would, if he had not so ceased, have at commencement become a [British overseas territories] citizen by descent by virtue of paragraph (b), (d) or (e);

(h) he is a [British overseas territories] citizen by virtue of registration under section 13 (as applied by section 24) who, immediately before he ceased to be a [British overseas territories] citizen as a result of a declaration of renunciation, was such a citizen by descent; or

(i) he is a person born in the United Kingdom after commencement who is a [British overseas territories] citizen by virtue of paragraph 1 of Schedule 2.

(2) A person born outside the [British overseas territories] before commencement is not a [British overseas territories] citizen 'by descent' by virtue of subsection (1)(b), (d), (e) or (f) if his father was at the time of his birth serving outside the [British overseas territories] in service of a description mentioned in subsection (3), his recruitment for the service in question having taken place in a [British overseas territory].

(3) The descriptions of service referred to in subsection (2) are—

(a) Crown service under the government of a [British overseas territory]; and

(b) service of any description at any time designated under section 16(3).

Note: British dependent territories became British overseas territories from 26 February 2002, British Overseas Territories Act 2002, s 1. Subsection (1)(ca) inserted by Nationality and Borders Act 2022 c.36 Pt1 s.1(3) (June 28, 2022). Subsection (1)(cb) inserted by Nationality and Borders Act 2022 c.36 Pt 1 s.2(3) 9June 28, 2022).

Part III
British Overseas Citizenship

26. Citizens of UK and Colonies who are to become British Overseas citizens at commencement

Any person who was a citizen of the United Kingdom and Colonies immediately before commencement and who does not at commencement become either a British citizen or a [British overseas territories] citizen shall at commencement become a British Overseas citizen.

Note: British dependent territories became British overseas territories from 26 February 2002, British Overseas Territories Act 2002, s 1.

27. Registration of minors

(1) If while a person is a minor an application is made for his registration as a British Overseas citizen, the Secretary of State may, if he thinks fit, cause him to be registered as such a citizen.

(2) . . .

Note: Section 27(2) repealed by Sch 2 Nationality, Immigration and Asylum Act 2002 from 1 April 2003 (SI 2003/754).

28. . . .

Note: Section 28 repealed by Sch 2 Nationality, Immigration and Asylum Act 2002 from 1 April 2003 (SI 2003/754).

29. Renunciation

The provisions of section 12 shall apply in relation to British Overseas citizens and British Overseas citizenship as they apply in relation to British citizens and British citizenship.

Part IV
British Subjects

30. Continuance as British subjects of existing British subjects of certain descriptions

A person who immediately before commencement was—

(a) a British subject without citizenship by virtue of section 13 or 16 of the 1948 Act; or

(b) a British subject by virtue of section 1 of the British Nationality Act 1965 (registration of alien women who have been married to British subjects of certain descriptions), shall as from commencement be a British subject by virtue of this section.

31. Continuance as British subjects of certain former citizens of Eire

(1) A person is within this subsection if immediately before 1st January 1949 he was both a citizen of Eire and a British subject.

(2) A person within subsections (1) who immediately before commencement was a British subject by virtue of section 2 of the 1948 Act (continuance of certain citizens of Eire as British subjects) shall as from commencement be a British subject by virtue of this subsection.

(3) If at any time after commencement a citizen of the Republic of Ireland who is within subsection (1) but is not a British subject by virtue of subsection (2) gives notice in writing to the Secretary of State claiming to remain a British subject on either or both of the following grounds, namely—

(a) that he is or has been in Crown Service under the government of the United Kingdom; and

(b) that he has associations by way of descent, residence or otherwise with the United Kingdom or with any [British overseas territory], he shall as from that time be a British subject by virtue of this subsection.

(4) A person who is a British subject by virtue of subsection (2) or (3) shall be deemed to have remained a British subject from 1 January 1949 to the time when (whether already a British subject by virtue of the said section 2 or not) he became a British subject by virtue of that subsection.

Note: British dependent territories became British overseas territories from 26 February 2002, British Overseas Territories Act 2002, s 1.

32. Registration of minors

If while a person is a minor an application is made for his registration as a British subject, the Secretary of State may, if he thinks fit, cause him to be registered as a British subject.

33. …

Note: Section 33 repealed by Sch 2 Nationality, Immigration and Asylum Act 2002 from 1 April 2003 (SI 2003/754).

34. Renunciation

The provisions of section 12 shall apply in relation to British subjects and the status of a British subject as they apply in relation to British citizens and British citizenship.

35. Circumstances in which British subjects are to lose that status

A person who under this Act is a British subject otherwise than by virtue of section 31 shall cease to be such a subject if, in whatever circumstances and whether under this Act or otherwise, he acquires any other citizenship or nationality whatever.

Part V

Miscellaneous and Supplementary

36. Provisions for reducing statelessness

The provisions of Schedule 2 shall have effect for the purpose of reducing statelessness.

37. Commonwealth citizenship

(1) Every person who—

(a) under [the British Nationality Acts 1981 and 1983] [or the British Overseas Territories Act 2002] is a British citizen, a [British overseas territories] citizen, [a British National (Overseas),] a British Overseas citizen or a British subject; or

(b) under any enactment for the time being in force in any country mentioned in Schedule 3 is a citizen of that country, shall have the status of a Commonwealth citizen.

(2) Her Majesty may by Order in Council amend Schedule 3 by the alteration of any entry, the removal of any entry, or the insertion of any additional entry.

(3) Any Order in Council made under this section shall be subject to annulment in pursuance of a resolution of either House of Parliament.

(4) After commencement no person shall have the status of a Commonwealth citizen or the status of a British subject otherwise than under this Act.

Note: Words in first square brackets in subsection (1) substituted by British Nationality (Falkland Islands) Act 1983. Words in second square brackets inserted by Sch 1 British Overseas Territories Act 2002 from 21 May 2002 (SI 2002/1252). Words in fourth square brackets in subsection (1) inserted by SI 1986/948. British dependent territories became British overseas territories from 26 February 2002, British Overseas Territories Act 2002, s 1.

38. British protected persons

(1) Her Majesty may by Order in Council made in relation to any territory which was at any time before commencement—

(a) a protectorate or protected state for the purposes of the 1948 Act; or

(b) a United Kingdom trust territory within the meaning of that Act,

declare to be British protected persons for the purposes of this Act any class of persons who are connected with that territory and are not citizens of any country mentioned in Schedule 3 which consists of or includes that territory.

(2) Any Order in Council made under this section shall be subject to annulment in pursuance of a resolution of either House of Parliament.

39. Amendment of Immigration Act 1971

(1) ...

(2) ...

(3) ...

(4) ...

(5) ...

(6) ...

(7) ...

(8) A certificate of patriality issued under the Immigration Act 1971 and in force immediately before commencement shall have effect after commencement as if it were a certificate of entitlement issued under that Act [as in force after commencement] unless at commencement the holder ceases to have the right of abode in the United Kingdom.

Note: Section 39(1), (2), (4), (6) amend Immigration Act 1971. Section 39(3), (5) repealed, and words in square brackets in subsection (8) substituted by Immigration Act 1988, s 3. Section 39(7) amended Mental Health Act 1959, Mental Health (Scotland) Act 1960.

[40. Deprivation of citizenship

(1) In this section a reference to a person's 'citizenship status' is a reference to his status as—

(a) a British citizen,

(b) a British overseas territories citizen,
(c) a British Overseas citizen,
(d) a British National (Overseas),
(e) a British protected person, or
(f) a British subject.

[(2) The Secretary of State may by order deprive a person of a citizenship status if the Secretary of State is satisfied that deprivation is conducive to the public good.]

(3) The Secretary of State may by order deprive a person of a citizenship status which results from his registration or naturalisation if the Secretary of State is satisfied that the registration or naturalisation was obtained by means of—
(a) fraud,
(b) false representation, or
(c) concealment of a material fact.

(4) The Secretary of State may not make an order under subsection (2) if he is satisfied that the order would make a person stateless.

[(4A) But that does not prevent the Secretary of State from making an order under subsection (2) to deprive a person of a citizenship status if—
(a) the citizenship status results from the person's naturalisation,
(b) the Secretary of State is satisfied that the deprivation is conducive to the public good because the person, while having that citizenship status, has conducted him or herself in a manner which is seriously prejudicial to the vital interests of the United Kingdom, any of the Islands, or any British overseas territory, and
(c) the Secretary of State has reasonable grounds for believing that the person is able, under the law of a country or territory outside the United Kingdom, to become a national of such a country or territory.]

(5) Before making an order under this section in respect of a person the Secretary of State must give the person written notice specifying—
(a) that the Secretary of State has decided to make an order,
(b) the reasons for the order, and
(c) the person's right of appeal under section 40A(1) or under section 2B of the Special Immigration Appeals Commission Act 1997 (c. 68).

[(5A) Subsection (5) does not apply if—
(a) the Secretary of State does not have the information needed to be able to give notice under that subsection,
(b) the Secretary of State reasonably considers it necessary, in the interests of—
(i) national security,
(ii) the investigation or prosecution of organised or serious crime,
(iii) preventing or reducing a risk to the safety of any person, or
(iv) the relationship between the United Kingdom and another country,
that notice under that subsection should not be given.

(5B) In subsection (5A), references to giving notice under subsection (5) are to giving that notice in accordance with such regulations under section 41(1)(e) as for the time being apply.

(5C) Subsection (5D) applies where—
(a) the Secretary of State has made an order under subsection (2) and, in reliance on subsection (5A), has not given the notice required by subsection (5), and
(b) the person in respect of whom the order was made makes contact with the Secretary of State for the Home Department.

(5D) The Secretary of State must, as soon as is reasonably practicable, give the person written notice specifying—

(a) that the Secretary of State has made the order,

(b) the reasons for the order, and

(c) the person's right of appeal under section 40A(1) or under section 2B of the Special Immigration Appeals Commission Act 1997.

(5E) Schedule 4A makes provision for the Special Immigration Appeals Commission to consider a decision of the Secretary of State—

(a) not to give notice to a person before depriving them of a citizenship status on the grounds mentioned in subsection (2) (deprivation conducive to the public good), or

(b) not to give late notice to a person who has been deprived of a citizenship status on those grounds without having been given prior notice.]

(6) Where a person acquired a citizenship status by the operation of a law which applied to him because of his registration or naturalisation under an enactment having effect before commencement, the Secretary of State may by order deprive the person of the citizenship status if the Secretary of State is satisfied that the registration or naturalisation was obtained by means of—

(a) fraud,

(b) false representation, or

(c) concealment of a material fact.]

Note: Section 40 substituted by Nationality, Immigration and Asylum Act 2002, s 4 from 1 April 2003 (SI 2003/754). Subsection (2) substituted by Immigration, Asylum and Nationality Act 2006, s 56 from 16 June 2006 (SI 2006/1498). Subsection (4A) inserted by s 66 Immigration Act 2014 from 28 July 2014 (SI 2014/1820). Subsections (5A)-(5E) inserted by Nationality and Borders Act 2022 c. 36 Pt 1 s.10(2) (date to be appointed)

[40A. Deprivation of citizenship: appeal

[[(1) A person—

(a) who is given notice under section 40(5) of a decision to make an order in respect of the person under section 40, or

(b) in respect of whom an order under section 40 is made without the person having been given notice under section 40(5) of the decision to make the order,

may appeal against the decision to the First-tier Tribunal.]]

(2) Subsection (1) shall not apply to a decision if the Secretary of State certifies that it was taken wholly or partly in reliance on information which in his opinion should not be made public—

(a) in the interests of national security,

(b) in the interests of the relationship between the United Kingdom and another country, or

(c) otherwise in the public interest.

[[(2A) In the case of an order made as described in subsection (1)(b), for the purposes of any rule or other provision limiting the time within which an appeal under this section may be brought, time does not start to run unless and until the person is given notice of the fact that the order has been made (see section 40(5D) and Schedule 4A).]]

[(3) The following provisions of the Nationality, Immigration and Asylum Act 2002 (c. 41) shall apply in relation to an appeal under this section as they apply in relation to an appeal under section 82 [. . .] of that Act—

(a) . . .
(b) section 106 (rules),
(c) section 107 (practice directions)] [, and
(d) section 108 (forged document: proceedings in private).]
(6) . . .
(7) . . .
(8) . . .]

Note: Section 40A inserted by Nationality, Immigration and Asylum Act 2002, s 4 from 1 April 2003 (SI 2003/754). Words in first square brackets substituted and subsections (3)(b) revoked from 15 February 2010 (SI 2010/21). Words in other square brackets substituted by and subsections (6)–(8) omitted by Sch 2 Asylum and Immigration (Treatment of Claimants etc.) Act 2004 from 4 April 2005 (SI 2005/565). Words in square brackets in subsection (3) and subsection (3)(e) inserted by Immigration, Asylum and Nationality Act 2006, s 56 from 16 June 2006 (SI 2006/1498). Numbers in subsection (3) and subsection (3)(a) omitted by Sch 9 Immigration Act 2014 from 20 October 2014 with savings set out in SI 2014/2771 articles 9-11. Words substituted in double square brackets at subsection (1) by Nationality and Borders Act 2022 c. 36 Pt 1 s.10(3)(a) (date to be appointed) Words inserted in double square brackets in subsection (2A) by Nationality and Borders Act 2022 c. 36 Pt 1 s.10(3)(b) (date to be appointed)

[40B. Review of power under section 40(4A)

(1) The Secretary of State must arrange for a review of the operation of the relevant deprivation power to be carried out in relation to each of the following periods—
(a) the initial one year period;
(b) each subsequent three year period.

(2) The 'relevant deprivation power' is the power to make orders under section 40(2) to deprive persons of a citizenship status in the circumstances set out in section 40(4A).

(3) A review must be completed as soon as practicable after the end of the period to which the review relates.

(4) As soon as practicable after a person has carried out a review in relation to a particular period, the person must—
(a) produce a report of the outcome of the review, and
(b) send a copy of the report to the Secretary of State.

(5) The Secretary of State must lay before each House of Parliament a copy of each report sent under subsection (4)(b).

(6) The Secretary of State may, after consultation with the person who produced the report, exclude a part of the report from the copy laid before Parliament if the Secretary of State is of the opinion that it would be contrary to the public interest or prejudicial to national security for that part of the report to be made public.

(7) The Secretary of State may—

(a) make such payments as the Secretary of State thinks appropriate in connection with the carrying out of a review, and

(b) make such other arrangements as the Secretary of State thinks appropriate in connection with the carrying out of a review (including arrangements for the provision of staff, other resources and facilities).

(8) In this section—

'initial one year period' means the period of one year beginning with the day when section 40(4A) comes into force;

'subsequent three year period' means a period of three years beginning with the first day after the most recent of—

(a) the initial one year period, or

(b) the most recent subsequent three year period.]

Note: Section 40B inserted by s 66 Immigration Act 2014 from 28 July 2014 (SI 2014/1820).

41. Regulations and Orders in Council

(1) The Secretary of State may by regulations make provision generally for carrying into effect the purposes of this Act, and in particular provision—

(a) for prescribing anything which under this Act is to be prescribed;

(b) for prescribing the manner in which, and the persons to and by whom, applications for registration or naturalisation under any provision of this Act may or must be made;

[(bza) requiring an application for registration or naturalisation of a person as a British citizen to be accompanied by biometric information, or enabling an authorised person to require an individual to whom such an application relates to provide biometric information;]

[(ba) for determining whether a person has sufficient knowledge of a language for the purpose of an application for naturalisation;

(bb) for determining whether a person has sufficient knowledge about life in the United Kingdom for the purpose of an application for naturalisation;]

[(bc) for amending paragraph 4B(3)(a) or (b) or (4)(a) or (b) of Schedule 1 to substitute a different number for the number for the time being specified there;

(bd) for determining whether a person has, for the purposes of an application for naturalisation under section 6, participated in activities prescribed for the purposes of paragraph 4B(5)(a) of Schedule 1;

(be) for determining whether a person is to be treated for the purposes of such an application as having so participated;]

(c) for the registration of anything required or authorised by or under this Act to be registered;

[(d) for the time within which an obligation to make a citizenship oath and pledge at a citizenship ceremony must be satisfied;

(da) for the time within which an obligation to make a citizenship oath or pledge must be satisfied;

(db) for the content and conduct of a citizenship ceremony;

(dc) for the administration and making of a citizenship oath or pledge;

(dd) for the registration and certification of the making of a citizenship oath or pledge;

(de) for the completion and grant of a certificate of registration or naturalisation;]

(e) for the giving of any notice required or authorised to be given to any person under this Act;

(f) for the cancellation of the registration of, and the cancellation and amendment of certificates of naturalisation relating to, persons deprived of citizenship [or of the status of a British National (overseas)] under this Act, and for requiring such certificates to be delivered up for those purposes;

(g) for the births and deaths of persons of any class or description born or dying in a country mentioned in Schedule 3 to be registered there by the High Commissioner for Her Majesty's government in the United Kingdom or by members of his official staff;

(h) for the births and deaths of persons of any class or description born or dying in a foreign country to be registered there by consular officers or other officers in the service of Her Majesty's government in the United Kingdom;

(i) for enabling the births and deaths of British citizens, [British overseas territories citizens], [British Nationals (Overseas),] British Overseas citizens, British subjects and British protected persons born or dying in any country in which Her Majesty's government in the United Kingdom has for the time being no diplomatic or consular representatives to be registered—

(i) by persons serving in the diplomatic, consular or other foreign service of any country which, by arrangement with Her Majesty's government in the United Kingdom, has undertaken to represent that government's interest in that country, or

(ii) by a person authorised in that behalf by the Secretary of State.

[(j) as to the consequences of failure to comply with provision made under any of paragraphs (a) to (i).]

[**(1ZA)** In subsection (1)(bza) 'authorised person' and 'biometric information' have the same meaning as in section 126 of the Nationality, Immigration and Asylum Act 2002.

(1ZB) Section 126(4) to (7) of that Act applies to regulations under subsection (1) (bza) as it applies to regulations under section 126(1) of that Act.

(1ZC) Section 8 of the UK Borders Act 2007 (power to make regulations about use and retention of biometric information) applies to biometric information provided in accordance with regulations under subsection (1)(bza) as it applies to biometric information provided in accordance with regulations under section 5(1) of that Act.

(1ZD) But (despite section 8(5)(b) of that Act) regulations made by virtue of subsection (1ZC) may provide for photographs of a person who is registered or naturalised as a British citizen to be retained until the person is issued with a United Kingdom passport describing the person as a British citizen.]

[**(1A)** Regulations under subsection (1)(ba) or (bb) may, in particular—

(a) make provision by reference to possession of a specified qualification;

(b) make provision by reference to possession of a qualification of a specified kind;

(c) make provision by reference to attendance on a specified course;

(d) make provision by reference to attendance on a course of a specified kind;

(e) make provision by reference to a specified level of achievement;

(f) enable a person designated by the Secretary of State to determine sufficiency of knowledge in specified circumstances;

(g) enable the Secretary of State to accept a qualification of a specified kind as evidence of sufficient knowledge of a language].

[**(1B)** Regulations under subsection (1)(bc) may make provision so that—

(a) the number specified in sub-paragraph (3)(a) of paragraph 4B of Schedule 1 is the same as the number specified in sub-paragraph (4)(a) of that paragraph;

(b) the number specified in sub-paragraph (3)(b) of that paragraph is the same as the number specified in sub-paragraph (4)(b) of that paragraph.

(1C) Regulations under subsection (1)(bd) or (be)—

(a) may make provision that applies in relation to time before the commencement of section 41 of the Borders, Citizenship and Immigration Act 2009;

(b) may enable the Secretary of State to make arrangements for such persons as the Secretary of State thinks appropriate to determine whether, in accordance with those regulations, a person has, or (as the case may be) is to be treated as having, participated in an activity.]

(2) ...

(3) Regulations under subsection (1) ... may make different provision for different circumstances; and—

(a) regulations under subsection (1) may provide for the extension of any time-limit for the [making of oaths and pledges of citizenship]; and

...

[(3A) Regulations under subsection (1)(d) to (de) may, in particular—

(a) enable the Secretary of State to designate or authorise a person to exercise a function (which may include a discretion) in connection with a citizenship ceremony or a citizenship oath or pledge;

(b) require, or enable the Secretary of State to require, a local authority to provide specified facilities and to make specified arrangements in connection with citizenship ceremonies;

(c) impose, or enable the Secretary of State to impose, a function (which may include a discretion) on a local authority or on a registrar.

[(3B) In subsection (3A)—

'local authority' means—

(a) in relation to England and Wales, a county council, a county borough council, a metropolitan district council, a London Borough Council and the Common Council of the City of London, and

(b) in relation to Scotland, a council constituted under section 2 of the Local Government etc. (Scotland) Act 1994 (c. 39), and

'registrar' means—

(a) in relation to England and Wales, a superintendent registrar of births, deaths and marriages (or, in accordance with section 8 of the Registration Service Act 1953 (c. 37), a deputy superintendent registrar), and

(b) in relation to Scotland, a district registrar within the meaning of section 7(12) of the Registration of Births, Deaths and Marriages (Scotland) Act 1965 (c. 49).]

(4) Her Majesty may by Order in Council provide for any Act or Northern Ireland legislation to which this subsection applies to apply, with such adaptations and modifications as appear to Her necessary, to births and deaths registered—

(a) in accordance with regulations made in pursuance of subsection (1)(g) to (i) of this section or subsection (1)(f) and (g) of section 29 of the 1948 Act; or

(b) at a consulate of Her Majesty in accordance with regulations made under the British Nationality and Status of Aliens Acts 1914 to 1943 or in accordance with instructions of the Secretary of State; or

(c) by a High Commissioner for Her Majesty's government in the United Kingdom or members of his official staff in accordance with instructions of the Secretary of State; and an Order in Council under this subsection may exclude, in relation to births and deaths so registered, any of the provisions of section 45.

(5) Subsection (4) applies to—

(a) the Births and Deaths Registration Act 1953, the Registration Service Act 1953 and the Registration of Births, Deaths and Marriages (Scotland) Act 1965; and

(b) so much of any Northern Ireland legislation for the time being in force (whether passed or made before or after commencement) as relates to the registration of births and deaths.

(6) The power to make regulations under subsection (1) or (2) shall be exercisable by statutory instrument.

(7) Any regulations or Order in Council made under this section [(other than regulations referred to in subsection (8))] shall be subject to annulment in pursuance of a resolution of either House of Parliament.

[(8) Any regulations (whether alone or with other provision)—

(a) under subsection (1)(a) for prescribing activities for the purposes of paragraph 4B(5)(a) of Schedule 1; or

(b) under subsection [(1)(bza), (bc)], (bd) or (be), may not be made unless a draft has been laid before and approved by a resolution of each House of Parliament.]

Note: Words in square brackets in subsections (1)(f), (1)(i), inserted by SI 1986/948. Subsections (1)(ba), (bb) inserted by Nationality, Immigration and Asylum Act 2002, s 1 from 6 July 2004 (SI 2004/1707) and s 1A inserted by s 1 of that Act from 1 November 2005 (SI 2005/2782). Section 41(1)(d) substituted by paragraph 4, Sch 1 Nationality, Immigration and Asylum Act 2002 from 1 January 2004 (SI 2003/3156). Words in square brackets in subsections (3)(a) substituted by paragraph 5, Sch 1 of the Nationality, Immigration and Asylum Act 2002 from 1 January 2004 (SI 2003/3156). Subsections (3A) and (3B) inserted by paragraph 7, Sch 1, Nationality, Immigration and Asylum Act 2002 from 1 January 2004 (SI 2003/3156). British dependent territories became British overseas territories from 26 February 2002, British Overseas Territories Act 2002, s 1. Subsection (1)(j) inserted and subsections (2), (3)(b) and words in (3)(a) omitted by Sch 2 Immigration, Asylum and Nationality Act 2006 from 1 April 2003 (SI 2003/754). Subsections (1) (bc)–(be), (1B)–(1C),(8) and words in square brackets in subsection (7) inserted by s 41 Borders, Citizenship and Immigration Act 2009 from a date to be appointed. Words omitted from subsections (1)(g), (h) and (i) and words substituted in subsection (4) by SI 2014/542 from a date to be appointed. Subsections (1)(bza) inserted by s 10(2) of Immigration Act 2014, from 28 July 2014 (SI 2014/1820). Sections (1ZA)–(1ZD) inserted by s10(3) by Immigration Act 2014 from 28 July 2014 (SI1014/1820). Words in square brackets in subsection (8)(b) substituted by s 10(4)of Immigration Act 2014 (SI 2014/ 1820), it is provided that in s 41(8) (b) the words "(1)(bza), (bc)" be substituted for "(1)(bc)" (28.7.2014) despite s 41(8) not being inserted until 27.10.2014 and the words "(bc), (bd) or (be)" in s 41(8)(b) being excluded from the commencement of that insertion.

[41A.Registration: requirement to be of good character

(1) An application for registration of an adult or young person as a British citizen under section 1(3), (3A) or (4), 3(1), (2) or (5), 4(2) or (5), 4A, [], 4D, [], 5, 10(1) or (2) or 13(1) or (3) must not be granted unless the Secretary of State is satisfied that the adult or young person is of good character.

[[(1A) An application for registration of an adult or young person as a British citizen under section 4F, so far as the relevant registration provision (as defined in section 4F(2)) is section 1(3), 3(2)[[,3(5)or 4D]], must not be granted unless the Secretary of State is satisfied that the adult or young person is of good character.]]

(2) An application for registration of an adult or young person as a British overseas territories citizen under section 15(3) or (4), 17(1),[[(2)]] or (5), 22(1) or (2) or 24 must not be granted unless the Secretary of State is satisfied that the adult or young person is of good character.

[[2A) An application for registration of an adult or young person as a British overseas territories citizen under section 17C, so far as the relevant registration provision (as defined in section 17C(2)) is section 15(3), 17(2) or 17(5), must not be granted unless the Secretary of State is satisfied that the adult or young person is of good character.]]

(2B) Subsection (2C) applies to an application for registration of an adult or young person as a British citizen under section 4K who is, or would have been, entitled to be registered as a British overseas territories citizen under section 17C, so far as the relevant registration provision (as defined in section 17C(2)) is section 15(3), 17(2) or 17(5).

(2C) The application must not be granted unless the Secretary of State is satisfied that the adult or young person is of good character.]]

(3) An application for registration of an adult or young person as a British Overseas citizen under section 27(1) must not be granted unless the Secretary of State is satisfied that the adult or young person is of good character.

(4) An application for registration of an adult or young person as a British subject under section 32 must not be granted unless the Secretary of State is satisfied that the adult or young person is of good character.

(5) In this section, 'adult or young person' means a person who has attained the age of 10 years at the time when the application is made.]

Note: Section 41A inserted by s 47 Borders, Citizenship and Immigration Act 2009 from 13 January 2010 (SI 2001/2731). Words in square brackets in subs-s (1) substituted by Sch 9 Immigration Act 2014 from a date to be appointed. Words in square brackets in subsection (1) omitted by British Nationality Act 1981 (Remedial) Order 2019/1164 art.2(2) from 25 July 2019. Subsection (1A) inserted by British Nationality Act 1981 (Remedial) Order 2019/1165 art.2(2) from 25 July 2019. Subsection (2A) inserted by Nationality And Borders Act 2022 c.36 Pt1 s.2(4) (June 28, 2022) Subsection (2B) & (2C) inserted by Nationality and Borders Act 2022 c.36 Pt1 s.4(4) (June 28, 2022). Word in double square brackets in subsection (2A) –(2C) inserted by Nationality and Borders Act 2022 c. 36 Pt 1 s.5(2) (June 28, 2022: insertion has effect as SI 2022/590 reg.2 and Sch.1 para.4 subject to transitional and saving provision specified in reg.3 and Sch.2 para.1) Words inserted in double brackets in subsection (1A) by Nationality and Borders Act 2022 c. 36 Pt 1 s.7(3) (June 28, 2022)

[42. Registration and naturalisation: citizenship ceremony, oath and pledge

(1) A person of full age shall not be registered under this Act as a British citizen unless he has made the relevant citizenship oath and pledge specified in Schedule 5 at a citizenship ceremony.

(2) A certificate of naturalisation as a British citizen shall not be granted under this Act to a person of full age unless he has made the relevant citizenship oath and pledge specified in Schedule 5 at a citizenship ceremony.

(3) A person of full age shall not be registered under this Act as a British overseas territories citizen unless he has made the relevant citizenship oath and pledge specified in Schedule 5.

(4) A certificate of naturalisation as a British overseas territories citizen shall not be granted under this Act to a person of full age unless he has made the relevant citizenship oath and pledge specified in Schedule 5.

(5) A person of full age shall not be registered under this Act as a British Overseas citizen or a British subject unless he has made the relevant citizenship oath specified in Schedule 5.

(6) Where the Secretary of State thinks it appropriate because of the special circumstances of a case he may—

(a) disapply any of subsections (1) to (5), or

(b) modify the effect of any of those subsections.

(7) Sections 5 and 6 of the Oaths Act 1978 (c. 19) (affirmation) apply to a citizenship oath; and a reference in this Act to a citizenship oath includes a reference to a citizenship affirmation.]

Note: Section 42 substituted by paragraph 1, Sch 1 Nationality, Immigration and Asylum Act 2002 from 1 January 2004 (SI 2003/3156).

[42A. …]

Note: Section 42A inserted by paragraph 1, Sch 1 Nationality, Immigration and Asylum Act 2002 from 1 January 2004 (SI 2003/3156). Ceases to have effect from 2 April 2007, Sch 3 Immigration, Asylum and Nationality Act 2006 (SI 2007/1109).

[42B. Registration and naturalisation: timing

(1) A person who is registered under this Act as a citizen of any description or as a British subject shall be treated as having become a citizen or subject—

(a) immediately on making the required citizenship oath and pledge in accordance with section 42, or

(b) where the requirement for an oath and pledge is disapplied, immediately on registration.

(2) A person granted a certificate of naturalisation under this Act as a citizen of any description shall be treated as having become a citizen—

(a) immediately on making the required citizenship oath and pledge in accordance with section 42, or

(b) where the requirement for an oath and pledge is disapplied, immediately on the grant of the certificate.

(3) In the application of subsection (1) to registration as a British Overseas citizen or as a British subject the reference to the citizenship oath and pledge shall be taken as a reference to the citizenship oath.]

Note: Section 42B inserted by paragraph 1, Sch 1 Nationality, Immigration and Asylum Act 2002 from January 2004 (SI 2003/3156).

43. Exercise of functions of Secretary of State by Governors and others

(1) Subject to subsection (3), the Secretary of State may in the case of any of his functions under this Act with respect to any of the matters mentioned in subsection (2), make arrangements for that function to be exercised—

(a) in any of the Islands, by the Lieutenant-Governor in cases concerning British citizens or British citizenship;

(b) in any [British overseas territory] […], by the Governor in cases concerning [British overseas territories] citizens or [British overseas territories] citizenship [and in cases concerning British National (Overseas) or the status of a British National (Overseas)];

(2) The said matters are—

(a) registration and naturalisation; and

(b) renunciation, resumption and deprivation of British citizenship or [British overseas territories] citizenship.

[(c) renunciation and deprivation of the status of a British National (Overseas).]

(3) Nothing in this section applies in the case of any power to make regulations or rules conferred on the Secretary of State by this Act.

(4) Arrangements under subsection (1) may provide for any such function as is there mentioned to be exercisable only with the approval of the Secretary of State.

Note: Words in fifth square brackets in subsection (1)(b) and subsection (2)(c) added by SI 1986/948. British dependent territories became British overseas territories from 26 February 2002, British Overseas Territories Act 2002, s 1.

44. Decisions involving exercise of discretion

(1) Any discretion vested by or under this Act in the Secretary of State, a Governor or a Lieutenant-Governor shall be exercised without regard to the race, colour or religion of any person who may be affected by its exercise.

(2) …

(3) …

Note: Subsections (2) and (3) cease to have effect from 7 November 2002, Nationality, Immigration and Asylum Act 2002, s 7.

[44A. Waiver of requirement for full capacity

Where a provision of this Act requires an applicant to be of full capacity, the Secretary of State may waive the requirement in respect of a specified applicant if he thinks it in the applicant's best interests.]

Note: Section 44A inserted by Immigration, Asylum and Nationality Act 2006, s 49 from 31 August 2006 (SI 2006/2226, which contains transitional provisions).

45. Evidence

(1) Every document purporting to be a notice, certificate, order or declaration, or an entry in a register, or a subscription of an oath of allegiance, given, granted or made under this Act or any of the former nationality Acts shall be received in evidence and shall, unless the contrary is proved, be deemed to have been given, granted or made by or on behalf of the person by whom or on whose behalf it purports to have been given, granted or made.

(2) Prima facie evidence of any such document may be given by the production of a document purporting to be certified as a true copy of it by such person and in such manner as may be prescribed.

(3) Any entry in a register made under this Act or any of the former nationality Acts shall be received as evidence (and in Scotland as sufficient evidence) of the matters stated in the entry.

(4) A certificate given by or on behalf of the Secretary of State that a person was at any time in Crown service under the government of the United Kingdom or that a person's recruitment for such service took place in the United Kingdom shall, for the purposes of this Act, be conclusive evidence of that fact.

46. Offences and proceedings

(1) Any person who for the purpose of procuring anything to be done or not to be done under this Act—

(a) makes any statement which he knows to be false in a material particular; or

(b) recklessly makes any statement which is false in a material particular, shall be liable on summary conviction in the United Kingdom to imprisonment for a term not exceeding three months or to a fine not exceeding [level 5 on the standard scale], or both.

(2) Any person who without reasonable excuse fails to comply with any requirement imposed on him by regulations made under this Act with respect to the delivering up of

certificates of naturalisation shall be liable on summary conviction in the United Kingdom to a fine not exceeding [level 4 on the standard scale].

(3) In the case of an offence under subsection (1)—

(a) any information relating to the offence may in England and Wales be tried by a magistrates' court if it is laid within six months after the commission of the offence, or if it is laid within three years after the commission of the offence and not more than two months after the date certified by a chief officer of police to be the date on which evidence sufficient to justify proceedings came to the notice of an officer of his police force; and

(b) summary proceedings for the offence may in Scotland be commenced within six months after the commission of the offence, or within three years after the commission of the offence and not more than two months after the date on which evidence sufficient in the opinion of the Lord Advocate to justify proceedings came to his knowledge; and

(c) a complaint charging the commission of the offence may in Northern Ireland be heard and determined by a magistrates' court if it is made within six months after the commission of the offence, or if it is made within three years after the commission of the offence and not more than two months after the date certified by an officer of police not below the rank of assistant chief constable to be the date on which evidence sufficient to justify the proceedings came to the notice of the police in Northern Ireland.

(4) For the purposes of subsection (3)(b) proceedings shall be deemed to be commenced on the date on which a warrant to apprehend or to cite the accused is granted, if such warrant is executed without undue delay; and a certificate of the Lord Advocate as to the date on which such evidence as is mentioned in subsection (3)(b) came to his knowledge shall be conclusive evidence.

(5) For the purposes of the trial of a person for an offence under subsection (1) or (2), the offence shall be deemed to have been committed either at the place at which it actually was committed or at any place at which he may be.

(6) In their application to the Bailiwick of Jersey subsections (1) and (2) shall have effect with the omission of the words 'on summary conviction'.

Note: Words in square brackets in s 46(1), (2), substituted by virtue of Criminal Justice Act 1982, s 46.

47. . . .

Note: Section 47 ceases to have effect in relation to a child born on or after 1 July 2006, Nationality, Immigration and Asylum Act 2002, s 9(SI 2006/1498).

48. Posthumous children

Any reference in this Act to the status of description of the father or mother of a person at the time of that person's birth shall, in relation to a person born after the death of his father or mother, be construed as a reference to the status or description of the parent in question at the time of that parent's death; and where that death occurred before, and the birth occurs after, commencement, the status or description which would have been applicable to the father or mother had he or she died after commencement shall be deemed to be the status or description applicable to him or her at the time of his or her death.

49. Registration and naturalisation under British Nationality Acts 1948 to 1965

...

Note: Section 49 repealed by s 52(8) and Sch 9 of this Act.

50. Interpretation

(1) In this Act, unless the context otherwise requires—

'the 1948 Act' means the British Nationality Act 1948;

'alien' means a person who is neither a Commonwealth citizen nor a British protected person nor a citizen of the Republic of Ireland;

['appointed day' means the day appointed by the Secretary of State under section 8 of the British Overseas Territories Act 2002 for the commencement of Schedule 1 to that Act;]

'association' means an unincorporated body of persons;

['British National (Overseas)' means a person who is a British National (Overseas) under the Hong Kong (British Nationality) Order 1986, and 'status of a British National (Overseas)' shall be construed accordingly;

'British Overseas citizen' includes a person who is a British Overseas citizen under the Hong Kong (British Nationality) Order 1986.]

['British overseas territory' means a territory mentioned in Schedule 6;

'British protected person' means a person who is a member of any class of persons declared to be British protected persons by an Order in Council for the time being in force under section 38 or is a British protected person by virtue of the Solomon Islands Act 1978;

'commencement', without more, means the commencement of this Act;

'Commonwealth citizen' means a person who has the status of a Commonwealth citizen under this Act;

'company' means a body corporate;

['Convention adoption' means an adoption effected under the law of a country or territory in which the Convention is in force, and certified in pursuance of Article 23(1) of the Convention;]

'Crown service' means the service of the Crown, whether within Her Majesty's dominions or elsewhere;

'Crown service under the government of the United Kingdom' means Crown service under Her Majesty's government in the United Kingdom or under Her Majesty's government in Northern Ireland [or under the Scottish Administration] [or under the Welsh Assembly Government];

['designated territory' means a qualifying territory, or the Sovereign Base Areas of Akrotiri and Dhekelia, which is designated by Her Majesty by Order in Council under subsection (14)]

[...]

'enactment' includes an enactment comprised in Northern Ireland legislation;

'foreign country' means a country other than the United Kingdom, a [British overseas territory], a country mentioned in Schedule 3 and the Republic of Ireland;

'the former nationality Acts' means—

(a) the British Nationality Acts 1948 to 1965;

(b) the British Nationality and Status of Aliens Acts 1914 to 1943; and

(c) any Act repealed by the said Acts of 1914 to 1943 or by the Naturalization Act 1870;

'Governor', in relation to a [British overseas territory], includes the officer for the time being administering the government of that territory;

'High Commissioner' includes an acting High Commissioner;

'immigration laws'—

(a) in relation to the United Kingdom, means the Immigration Act 1971 and any law for purposes similar to that Act which is for the time being or has at any time been in force in any part of the United Kingdom;

(b) in relation to a [British overseas territory], means any law for purposes similar to the Immigration Act 1971 which is for the time being or has at any time been in force in that territory;

'the Islands' means the Channel Islands and the Isle of Man;

'minor' means a person who has not attained the age of eighteen years;

'prescribed' means prescribed by regulations made under section 41;

['qualifying territory' means a British overseas territory other than the Sovereign Base Areas of Akrotiri and Dhekelia;]

'settled' shall be construed in accordance with subsections (2) to (4);

'ship' includes a hovercraft;

'statutory provision' means any enactment or any provision contained in—

(a) subordinate legislation (as defined in section 21(1) of the Interpretation Act 1978); or

(b) any instrument of a legislative character made under any Northern Ireland legislation;

'the United Kingdom' means Great Britain, Northern Ireland and the Islands, taken together;

'United Kingdom consulate' means the office of a consular officer of Her Majesty's government in the United Kingdom where a register of births is kept or, where there is no such office, such office as may be prescribed.

[**(1A)** Subject to subsection (1B), references in this Act to being a member of the armed forces are references to being—

(a) a member of the regular forces within the meaning of the Armed Forces Act 2006, or

(b) a member of the reserve forces within the meaning of that Act subject to service law by virtue of paragraph (a), (b) or (c) of section 367(2) of that Act.

(1B) A person is not to be regarded as a member of the armed forces by virtue of subsection (1A) if the person is treated as a member of a regular or reserve force by virtue of—

(a) section 369 of the Armed Forces Act 2006, or

(b) section 4(3) of the Visiting Forces (British Commonwealth) Act 1933.]

(2) Subject to subsection (3), references in this Act to a person being settled in the United Kingdom or in a [British overseas territory] are references to his being ordinarily resident in the United Kingdom or, as the case may be, in that territory without being subject under the immigration laws to any restriction on the period for which he may remain.

(3) Subject to subsection (4), a person is not to be regarded for the purposes of this Act—

(a) as having been settled in the United Kingdom at any time when he was entitled to an exception under section 8(3) or (4)(b) or (c) of the Immigration Act 1971 or, unless the order under section 8(2) of that Act conferring the exemption in question provides otherwise, to an exemption under the said section 8(2), or to any corresponding exemption under the former immigration laws; or

(b) as having been settled in a [British overseas territory] at any time when he was under the immigration laws entitled to any exemption corresponding to any such exemption as is mentioned in paragraph (a) (that paragraph being for the purposes of this paragraph read as if the words from 'unless' to 'otherwise' were omitted).

(4) A person to whom a child is born in the United Kingdom after commencement is to be regarded for the purposes of section 1(1) as being settled in the United Kingdom at the time of the birth if—

(a) he would fall to be so regarded but for his being at that time entitled to an exemption under section 8(3) of the Immigration Act 1971; and

(b) immediately before he became entitled to that exemption he was settled in the United Kingdom; and

(c) he was ordinarily resident in the United Kingdom from the time when he became entitled to that exemption to the time of the birth;

but this subsection shall not apply if at the time of the birth the child's father or mother is a person on whom any immunity from jurisdiction is conferred by or under the Diplomatic Privileges Act 1964.

(5) It is hereby declared that a person is not to be treated for the purpose of any provision of this Act as ordinarily resident in the United Kingdom or in a [British overseas territory] at a time when he is in the United Kingdom or, as the case may be, in that territory in breach of the immigration laws.

(6) For the purposes of this Act—

(a) a person shall be taken to have been naturalised in the United Kingdom if, but only if, he is—

(i) a person to whom a certificate of naturalisation was granted under any of the former nationality Acts by the Secretary of State or, in any of the Islands, by the Lieutenant-Governor; or

(ii) a person who by virtue of section 27(2) of the British Nationality and Status of Aliens Act 1914 was deemed to be a person to whom a certificate of naturalisation was granted, if the certificate of naturalisation in which his name was included was granted by the Secretary of State; or

(iii) a person who by virtue of section 10(5) of the Naturalisation Act 1870 was deemed to be a naturalised British subject by reason of his residence with his father or mother;

(b) a person shall be taken to have been naturalised in a [British overseas territory] if, but only if, he is—

(i) a person to whom a certificate of naturalisation was granted under any of the former nationality Acts by the Governor of that territory or by a person for the time being specified in a direction given in relation to that territory under paragraph 4 of Schedule 3 to the West Indies Act 1967 or for the time being holding an office so specified; or

(ii) a person who by virtue of the said section 27(2) was deemed to be a person to whom a certificate of naturalisation was granted, if the certificate of naturalisation in which his name was included was granted by the Governor of that territory; or

(iii) a person who by the law in force in that territory enjoyed the privileges of naturalisation within that territory only;

and references in this Act to naturalisation in the United Kingdom or in a [British overseas territory] shall be construed accordingly.

(7) For the purposes of this Act a person born outside the United Kingdom aboard a ship or aircraft—

(a) shall be deemed to have been born in the United Kingdom if—

(i) at the time of the birth his father or mother was a British citizen; or

(ii) he would, but for this subsection, have been born stateless,

and (in either case) at the time of the birth the ship or aircraft was registered in the United Kingdom or was an unregistered ship or aircraft of the government of the United Kingdom; but

(b) subject to paragraph (a), is to be regarded as born outside the United Kingdom, whoever was the owner of the ship or aircraft at that time, and irrespective of whether or where it was then registered.

[(7A) For the purposes of this Act a person born outside a qualifying territory aboard a ship or aircraft—

(a) shall be deemed to have been born in that territory if—

(i) at the time of the birth his father or mother was a British citizen or a British overseas territories citizen; or

(ii) he would, but for this subsection, have been born stateless,

and (in either case) at the time of the birth the ship or aircraft was registered in that territory or was an unregistered ship or aircraft of the government of that territory; but

(b) subject to paragraph (a), is to be regarded as born outside that territory, whoever was the owner of the ship or aircraft at the time, and irrespective of whether or where it was then registered.

(7B) For the purposes of this Act a person born outside a British overseas territory, other than a qualifying territory, aboard a ship or aircraft—

(a) shall be deemed to have been born in that territory if—

(i) at the time of the birth his father or mother was a British overseas territories citizen; or

(ii) he would, but for this subsection, have been born stateless,

and (in either case) at the time of the birth the ship or aircraft was registered in that territory or was an unregistered ship or aircraft of the government of that territory; but

(b) subject to paragraph (a), is to be regarded as born outside that territory, whoever was the owner of the ship or aircraft at the time, and irrespective of whether or where it was then registered.]

(8) For the purposes of this Act an application under any provision thereof shall be taken to have been made at the time of its receipt by a person authorised to receive it on behalf of the person to whom it is made; and references in this Act to the date of such an application are references to the date of its receipt by a person so authorised.

[(9) For the purposes of this Act a child's mother is the woman who gives birth to the child.

(9A) For the purposes of this Act a child's father is—

(a) the husband, [[or male civil partner]]at the time of the child's birth, of the woman who gives birth to the child, or

[(b) where a person is treated as the father of the child under section 28 of the Human Fertilisation and Embryology Act 1990 or section 35 or 36 of the Human Fertilisation and Embryology Act 2008, that person, or

(ba) where a person is treated as a parent of the child under section 42 or 43 of the Human Fertilisation and Embryology Act 2008, that person, or

(c) where none of paragraphs (a) to (ba) applies, a person who satisfies prescribed requirements as to proof of paternity.]

(b) where a person is treated as the father of the child under section 28 of the Human Fertilisation and Embryology Act 1990 (c. 37) (father), that person, or

(c) where neither paragraph (a) nor paragraph (b) applies, any person who satisfies prescribed requirements as to proof of paternity.

(9B) In subsection (9A)(c) 'prescribed' means prescribed by regulations of the Secretary of State; and the regulations—

(a) may confer a function (which may be a discretionary function) on the Secretary of State or another person,

(b) may make provision which applies generally or only in specified circumstances,

(c) may make different provision for different circumstances,

(d) must be made by statutory instrument, and

(e) shall be subject to annulment in pursuance of a resolution of either House of Parliament.

(9C) The expressions 'parent', 'child' and 'descended' shall be construed in accordance with subsections (9) and (9A).]

(10) For the purposes of this Act—

(a) a period 'from' or 'to' a specified date includes that date; and

(b) any reference to a day on which a person was absent from the United Kingdom or from a [British overseas territory] or from the [British overseas] territories is a reference to a day for the whole of which he was so absent.

(11) For the purposes of this Act—

(a) a person is of full age if he has attained the age of eighteen years, and of full capacity if he is not of unsound mind; and

(b) a person attains any particular age at the beginning of the relevant anniversary of the date of his birth.

(12) References in this Act to any country mentioned in Schedule 3 include references to the dependencies of that country.

(13) Her Majesty may by Order in Council subject to annulment in pursuance of a resolution of either House of Parliament amend Schedule 6 in any of the following circumstances, namely—

(a) where the name of any territory mentioned in it is altered; or

(b) where any territory mentioned in it is divided into two or more territories.

(14) For the purposes of the definition of 'designated territory' in subsection (1), an Order in Council may—

(a) designate any qualifying territory, or the Sovereign Base Areas of Akrotiri and Dhekelia, if the Convention is in force there, and

(b) make different designations for the purposes of section 1 and section 15; and, for the purposes of this subsection and the definition of 'Convention adoption' in subsection (1), 'the Convention' means the Convention on the Protection of Children and Co-operation in respect of Intercountry Adoption, concluded at the Hague on 29th May 1993.

An Order in Council under this subsection shall be subject to annulment in pursuance of a resolution of either House of Parliament.]

Note: Words in second square brackets in s 50(1) inserted by SI 1986/948. 'Scottish Administration' inserted from 6 May 1999 (SI 1999/1042). 'Welsh Assembly' inserted from 6 November 2009 (SI

2009/2958). Other words in square brackets inserted in subsection 1 and subsections (7A) and (7B) substituted by Sch 1 British Overseas Territories Act from 21 May 2002 (SI 2002/1252). Subsection (9) substituted by Nationality, Immigration and Asylum Act 2002, s 9, from 7 November 2002, with effect in relation to children born on or after 1 July 2006 (SI 2006/1498). British dependent territories became British overseas territories from 26 February 2002, British Overseas Territories Act 2002, s 1. Definitions of 'Convention adoption' and 'designated territory inserted and subsection (14) inserted by Adoption and Children Act 2002, s 137 and Schedule 4 from 30 December 2005 (SI 2005/2213). Subsection (1A)–(1B) inserted by s 59 Borders, Citizenship and Immigration Act 2009 from 13 January 2010 (SI 2009/2731). Subsections 9A(b)–(c) substituted by Sch 6 Human Fertilisation and Embryology Act 2008 from 6 April 2010 (SI 2010/987). Words in double square brackets at subsection (9A) inserted by Civil Partnership (Opposite-sex Couples) Regulations 2019/1458 Pt 4 reg 22 from 2 December 2019.

[50A. Meaning of references to being in breach of immigration laws

(1) This section applies for the construction of a reference to being in the United Kingdom in breach of the immigration laws in—

(a) section 4(2) or (4);

(b) section 50(5); or

(c) Schedule 1.

(2) It applies only for the purpose of determining on or after the relevant day—

(a) whether a person born on or after the relevant day is a British citizen under section 1(1),

(b) whether, on an application under section 1(3) or 4(2) made on or after the relevant day, a person is entitled to be registered as a British citizen, or

(c) whether, on an application under section 6(1) or (2) made on or after the relevant day, the applicant fulfils the requirements of Schedule 1 for naturalisation as a British citizen under section 6(1) or (2).

(3) But that is subject to section 48(3)(d) and (4) of the Borders, Citizenship and Immigration Act 2009 (saving in relation to section 11 of the Nationality, Immigration and Asylum Act 2002).

(4) A person is in the United Kingdom in breach of the immigration laws if (and only if) the person—

(a) is in the United Kingdom;

(b) does not have the right of abode in the United Kingdom within the meaning of section 2 of the Immigration Act 1971;

[[(ba)is not an Irish citizen who does not require leave to enter or remain in the United Kingdom (see section 3ZA of the Immigration Act 1971);]]

(c) does not have leave to enter or remain in the United Kingdom (whether or not the person previously had leave);

(d)

(e)

(f) is not entitled to enter and remain in the United Kingdom by virtue of section 8(1) of the Immigration Act 1971 (crew) (whether or not the person was previously entitled); and

(g) does not have the benefit of an exemption under section 8(2) to (4) of that Act (diplomats, soldiers and other special cases) (whether or not the person previously had the benefit of an exemption).

(5) . . .

(6) Section 11(1) of the Immigration Act 1971 (person deemed not to be in the United Kingdom before disembarkation, while in controlled area or while under immigration control) applies for the purposes of this section as it applies for the purposes of that Act.

(7) This section is without prejudice to the generality of—

(a) a reference to being in a place outside the United Kingdom in breach of immigration laws, and

(b) a reference in a provision other than one specified in subsection (1) to being in the United Kingdom in breach of immigration laws.

(8) The relevant day for the purposes of subsection (2) is the day appointed for the commencement of section 48 of the Borders, Citizenship and Immigration Act 2009 (which inserted this section).]

Note: Section 50A inserted by s 48 Borders, Citizenship and Immigration Act 2009 from 13 January 2010 (SI 2009/2731). Words in double square brackets inserted at subsection (4)(ba) and subsections (4)(d) & (e) omitted by Immigration and Social Security Co-ordination (EU Withdrawal) Act 2020 (Consequential, Saving, Transitional and Transitory Provisions)(EU Exit) Regulations 2020/1309 Pt 4(1) reg 78(2)(a) (December 31, 2020 at 23.00 being the time and date 2020 c.20 Sch 1 para 2(2) comes into force). Subsection (5) omitted by reg 78(2)(b) of these regulations as of December 31, 2020 at 23.00).

51. Meaning of certain expressions relating to nationality to other Acts and instruments

(1) Without prejudice to subsection (3)(c), in any enactment or instrument whatever passed or made before commencement 'British subject' and 'Commonwealth citizen' have the same meaning, that is—

(a) in relation to any time before commencement—

(i) a person who under the 1948 Act was at that time a citizen of the United Kingdom and Colonies or who, under any enactment then in force in a country mentioned in section 1(3) of that Act as then in force, was at that time a citizen of that country; and

(ii) any other person who had at that time the status of a British subject under that Act or any other enactment then in force;

(b) in relation to any time after commencement, a person who has the status of a Commonwealth citizen under this Act.

(2) In any enactment or instrument whatever passed or made after commencement—

'British subject' means a person who has the status of a British subject under this Act;

'Commonwealth citizen' means a person who has the status of a Commonwealth citizen under this Act.

(3) In any enactment or instrument whatever passed or made before commencement—

(a) 'citizen of the United Kingdom and Colonies'—

(i) in relation to any time before commencement, means a person who under the 1948 Act was at that time a citizen of the United Kingdom and Colonies;

(ii) in relation to any time after commencement, means a person who under [the British Nationality Acts 1981 and 1983] [or the British Overseas Territories Act 2002] is a British citizen, a [British overseas territories] citizen or a British Overseas citizen [or who under the Hong Kong (British Nationality) Order 1986 is a British National (Overseas)];

(b) any reference to ceasing to be a citizen of the United Kingdom and Colonies shall, in relation to any time after commencement, be construed as a reference to becoming a person who is neither a British citizen nor a [British overseas territories] citizen [nor a British National (Overseas)] nor a British Overseas citizen;

(c) any reference to a person who is a British subject (or a British subject without citizenship) by virtue of section 2, 13, or 16 of the 1948 Act or by virtue of, or of section 1 of, the British Nationality Act 1965 shall, in relation to any time after commencement, be construed as a reference to a person who under this Act is a British subject.

(4) In any statutory provision, whether passed or made before or after commencement, and in any other instrument whatever made after commencement 'alien', in relation to any time after commencement, means a person who is neither a Commonwealth citizen nor a British protected person nor a citizen of the Republic of Ireland.

(5) The preceding provisions of this section—

(a) shall not apply in cases where the context otherwise requires; and

(b) shall not apply to this Act or to any instrument made under this Act.

Note: Words in first square brackets in s 51(3) substituted by British Nationality (Falkland Islands) Act 1983. Words in second square brackets inserted by Sch 1 British Overseas Territories Act 2002 from 21 May 2002 (SI 2002/1252). Words at end of subsection (3)(a)(ii) and in second square brackets in subsection (3)(b) inserted by SI 1986/948. British dependent territories became British overseas territories from 26 February 2002, British Overseas Territories Act 2002, s 1.

52. Consequential amendments, transitional provisions, repeals and savings

(1) In any enactment or instrument whatever passed or made before commencement, for any reference to section 1(3) of the 1948 Act (list of countries whose citizens are Commonwealth citizens under that Act) there shall be substituted a reference to Schedule 3 to this Act, unless the context makes that substitution inappropriate.

(2) Subject to subsection (3), Her Majesty may by Order in Council make such consequential modifications of—

(a) any enactment of the Parliament of the United Kingdom passed before commencement;

(b) any provision contained in any Northern Ireland legislation passed or made before commencement; or

(c) any instrument made before commencement under any such enactment or provision, as appear to Her necessary or expedient for preserving after commencement the substantive effect of that enactment, provision or instrument.

(3) Subsection (2) shall not apply in relation to—

(a) the Immigration Act 1971; or

(b) any provision of this Act not contained in Schedule 7.

(4) Any Order in Council made under subsection (2) shall be subject to annulment in pursuance of a resolution of either House of Parliament.

(5) Any provision made by Order in Council under subsection (2) after commencement may be made with retrospective effect as from commencement or any later date.

(6) The enactments specified in Schedule 7 shall have effect subject to the amendments there specified, being amendments consequential on the provisions of this Act.

(7) This Act shall have effect subject to the transitional provisions contained in Schedule 8.

(8) The enactments mentioned in Schedule 9 are hereby repealed to the extent specified in the third column of that Schedule.

(9) Without prejudice to section 51, nothing in this Act affects the operation, in relation to any time before commencement, of any statutory provision passed or made before commencement.

(10) Nothing in this Act shall be taken as prejudicing the operation of sections 16 and 17 of the Interpretation Act 1978 (which relate to the effect of repeals).

(11) In this section 'modifications' includes additions, omissions and alterations.

53. Citation, commencement and extent

(1) This Act may be cited as the British Nationality Act 1981.

(2) This Act, except the provisions mentioned in subsection (3), shall come into force on such day as the Secretary of State may by order made by statutory instrument appoint; and references to the commencement of this Act shall be construed as references to the beginning of that day.

(3) Section 49 and this section shall come into force on the passing of this Act.

(4) This Act extends to Northern Ireland.

(5) The provisions of this Act, except those mentioned in subsection (7), extend to the Islands and all [British overseas territories]; and section 36 of the Immigration Act 1971 (power to extend provisions of that Act to Islands) shall apply to the said excepted provisions as if they were provisions of that Act.

(6) . . .

(7) The provisions referred to in subsections (5) . . . are—

(a) section 39 and Schedule 4;

(b) section 52(7) and Schedule 8 so far as they relate to the Immigration Act 1971; and

(c) section 52(8) and Schedule 9 so far as they relate to provisions of the Immigration Act 1971 other than Schedule 1.

Note: Subsection (6) and words in subsection 7 repealed by Statute Law Repeals Act 1995 Schedule 1, Pt. II. British dependent territories became British overseas territories from 26 February 2002, British Overseas Territories Act 2002, s 1.

SCHEDULES

SCHEDULE 1 — Sections 6 and 18

REQUIREMENTS FOR NATURALISATION

Naturalisation as a British citizen under section 6(1)

1.—(1) Subject to paragraph 2, the requirements for naturalisation as a British citizen under section 6(1) are, in the case of any person who applies for it—

(a) the requirements specified in sub-paragraph (2) of this paragraph, [. . .]; and

(b) that he is of good character; and

(c) that he has a sufficient knowledge of the English, Welsh or Scottish Gaelic language; and

[(ca) that he has sufficient knowledge about life in the United Kingdom; and]

(d) that either—

(i) his intentions are such that, in the event of a certificate of naturalisation as a British citizen being granted to him, his home or (if he has more than one) his principal home will be in the United Kingdom; or

(ii) he intends, in the event of such a certificate being granted to him, to enter into, or continue in, Crown service under the government of the United Kingdom, or service under an international organisation of which the United Kingdom or Her Majesty's government therein is a member, or service in the employment of a company or association established in the United Kingdom.

[(2) The requirements referred to in sub-paragraph (1)(a) of this paragraph are—

(a) that the applicant ('A') was in the United Kingdom at the beginning of the qualifying period;

(b) that the number of days on which A was absent from the United Kingdom in each year of the qualifying period does not exceed 90;

(c) that A had a qualifying immigration status for the whole of the qualifying period;

(d) that on the date of the application A has probationary citizenship leave, permanent residence leave, a qualifying CTA entitlement, a Commonwealth right of abode or a permanent EEA entitlement;

(e) that, where on the date of the application A has probationary citizenship leave granted for the purpose of taking employment in the United Kingdom, A has been in continuous employment since the date of the grant of that leave; and

(f) that A was not at any time in the qualifying period in the United Kingdom in breach of the immigration laws.]

(3) . . .

Note: Words omitted from subparagraph (1)(a), subparagraph (2) substituted and subparagraph (3) revoked by s 39 Borders, Citizenship and Immigration Act 2009 from a date to be appointed. Subparagraph (1)(ca) inserted by s 1 Nationality, Immigration and Asylum Act 2002, from 1 November 2005 (SI 2005/2782).

2.—[(1)] If in the special circumstances of any particular case the Secretary of State thinks fit, he may for the purposes of paragraph 1 do all or any of the following things, namely—

[[(za) treat the applicant as fulfilling the first requirement specified in paragraph 1(2)(a) although the applicant was not in the United Kingdom at the beginning of the period there mentioned;]]

[(a) treat the applicant as fulfilling the [[second requirement specified in paragraph 1(2)(a) or the requirement specified in paragraph 1(2)(b)]] although the number of days on which the applicant was absent from the United Kingdom in a year of the qualifying period exceeds 90;]

(b) treat the applicant as having been in the United Kingdom for the whole or any part of any period during which he would otherwise fall to be treated under paragraph 9(1) as having been absent;

[(ba) treat the applicant as fulfilling the requirement specified in paragraph 1(2)(c) where the applicant has had a qualifying immigration status for only part of the qualifying period;

(bb) treat the applicant as fulfilling the requirement specified in paragraph 1(2)(d) where the applicant has had probationary citizenship leave but it expired in the qualifying period;]

(c) . . .

[(ca) treat the applicant as fulfilling the requirement specified in paragraph 1(2)(e) although the applicant has not been in continuous employment since the date of the grant mentioned there;]

(d) treat the applicant as fulfilling the requirement specified in paragraph [1(2)(f)] although he was in the United Kingdom in breach of the immigration laws in the [qualifying period] there mentioned;

(e) waive the need to fulfil [either or both of the requirements specified in paragraph 1(1)(c) and (ca)] if he considers that because of the applicant's age or physical or mental condition it would be unreasonable to [expect him to fulfil that requirement or those requirements].

(1A) Sub-paragraph (1B) applies where the applicant has indefinite leave to enter or remain in the United Kingdom.

(1B) The Secretary of State may for the purposes of paragraph 1 treat the applicant as fulfilling the requirement specified in paragraph 1(2)(d), without enquiring into whether or not the applicant was in the United Kingdom in breach of the immigration laws in the period there mentioned.

(1C) The reference in sub-paragraph (1A) to having indefinite leave to enter or remain is to be construed in accordance with the Immigration Act 1971

[(2) . . .

(3) . . .

(4) An exceptional Crown service case is a case where—

(a) the applicant is, on the date of the application, serving outside the United Kingdom in Crown service under the government of the United Kingdom; and

(b) the Secretary of State considers the applicant's performance in the service to be exceptional.]

[(5) In paragraph 1(2)(e) and sub-paragraph (1)(ca) of this paragraph, 'employment' includes self-employment.]

[(2) Sub-paragraph (3) applies in a case where, on the date of the application, the applicant is or has been a member of the armed forces.

(3) If in the special circumstances of the particular case the Secretary of State thinks fit, he may for the purposes of paragraph 1 treat the applicant as fulfilling the requirement specified in paragraph 1(2)(a) although the applicant was not in the United Kingdom at the beginning of the period there mentioned.]

Note: Subparagraph (1)(a) and words in square brackets in subparagraph (1)(d) substituted, subparagraph (1)(c) revoked and subparagraphs (1)(ba)–(bb), (ca), (2)–(5) inserted by s 39 Borders, Citizenship and Immigration Act 2009 from a date to be appointed. Words in square brackets in paragraph 2(e) substituted by s 1 Nationality, Immigration and Asylum Act 2002, from 1 November 2005 (SI 2005/2782). Para 2 becomes para 2(1) and subparagraphs (2) and (3) inserted by s 1 Citizenship (Armed Forces) Act 2014 from 13 May 2014. Words inserted at subparagraph (1)(za) by Nationality and Borders Act 2022 c. 36 Sch.1 para.3(2)(a) (June 28, 2022: insertion has effect as SI 2022/590 reg.2 and Sch.1 para.8 subject to transitional and saving provisions specified in SI 2022/590 reg.3 and Sch.2 para.3). Words in double square brackets substituted at subparagraph ((1)(a) by Nationality and Borders Act 2022 c. 36 Sch.1 para.3(2)(b) (June 28, 2022: substitution has effect as SI 2022/590 reg.2 and Sch.1 para.8 subject to transitional and saving provisions specified in SI 2022/590 reg.3 and Sch.2 para.3). Words inserted at subparagraphs (1A)-(1C) by Nationality and Borders Act 2022 c. 36 Sch.1 para.3(2)(b) (June 28, 2022: substitution has effect as SI 2022/590 reg.2 and Sch.1 para.8 subject to transitional and saving provisions specified in SI

2022/590 reg.3 and Sch.2 para.3). Words omitted at subparagraph (3) & (4) by Nationality and Borders Act 2022 c. 36 Sch.1 para.3(2)(d) (June 28, 2022: repeal has effect as SI 2022/590 reg.2 and Sch.1 para.8 subject to transitional and saving provisions specified in SI 2022/590 reg.3 and Sch.2 para.3)

[**2A.**—(1) A person has a qualifying immigration status for the purposes of paragraph 1(2) if the person has—

(a) qualifying temporary residence leave;

(b) probationary citizenship leave;

(c) permanent residence leave;

(d) a qualifying CTA entitlement;

(e) a Commonwealth right of abode; or

(f) a temporary or permanent EEA entitlement.

(2) A person who is required for those purposes to have a qualifying immigration status for the whole of the qualifying period need not have the same qualifying immigration status for the whole of that period.]

Note: Paragraph 2A inserted by s 39 Borders, Citizenship and Immigration Act 2009 from a date to be appointed.

Naturalisation as a British citizen under section 6(2)

[**3**(1) Subject to paragraph 4, the requirements for naturalisation as a British citizen under section 6(2) are, in the case of any person ('A') who applies for it—

(a) the requirements specified in sub-paragraph (2) of this paragraph;

(b) the requirement specified in sub-paragraph (3) of this paragraph;

(c) that A is of good character;

(d) that A has a sufficient knowledge of the English, Welsh or Scottish Gaelic language; and

(e) that A has sufficient knowledge about life in the United Kingdom.

(2) The requirements referred to in sub-paragraph (1)(a) are—

(a) that A was in the United Kingdom at the beginning of the qualifying period;

(b) that the number of days on which A was absent from the United Kingdom in each year of the qualifying period does not exceed 90;

(c) that, subject to sub-paragraph (5)—

(i) A had a relevant family association for the whole of the qualifying period, and

(ii) A had a qualifying immigration status for the whole of that period;

(d) that on the date of the application—

(i) A has probationary citizenship leave, or permanent residence leave, based on A's having the relevant family association referred to in section 6(2), or

(ii) A has a qualifying CTA entitlement or a Commonwealth right of abode; and

(e) that A was not at any time in the qualifying period in the United Kingdom in breach of the immigration laws.

(3) The requirement referred to in sub-paragraph (1)(b) is—

(a) that A's intentions are such that, in the event of a certificate of naturalisation as a British citizen being granted to A, A's home or (if A has more than one) A's principal home will be in the United Kingdom;

(b) that A intends, in the event of such a certificate being granted to A, to enter into, or continue in, service of a description mentioned in sub-paragraph (4); or

(c) that, in the event of such a certificate being granted to A—

(i) the person with whom A has the relevant family association referred to in section 6(2) ('B') intends to enter into, or continue in, service of a description mentioned in sub-paragraph (4); and

(ii) A intends to reside with B for the period during which B is in the service in question.

(4) The descriptions of service referred to in sub-paragraph (3) are—

(a) Crown service under the government of the United Kingdom;

(b) service under an international organisation of which the United Kingdom, or Her Majesty's government in the United Kingdom, is a member; or

(c) service in the employment of a company or association established in the United Kingdom.

(5) Where the relevant family association referred to in section 6(2) is (in accordance with regulations under section 41(1)(a)) that A is the partner of a person who is a British citizen or who has permanent residence leave—

(a) the requirement specified in sub-paragraph (2)(c)(i) is fulfilled only if A was that person's partner for the whole of the qualifying period, and

(b) for the purposes of sub-paragraph (2)(c)(ii), A can rely upon having a qualifying immigration status falling within paragraph 4A(1)(a), (b) or (c) only if that partnership is the relevant family association upon which the leave to which the status relates is based.

(6) For the purposes of sub-paragraph (5), A is a person's partner if—

(a) that person is A's spouse or civil partner or is in a relationship with A that is of a description that the regulations referred to in that sub-paragraph specify, and

(b) the marriage, civil partnership or other relationship satisfies the conditions (if any) that those regulations specify.

(7) For the purposes of sub-paragraph (5), the relationship by reference to which A and the other person are partners need not be of the same description for the whole of the qualifying period.]

Note: Paragraph 3 substituted by s 40 Borders, Citizenship and Immigration Act 2009 from a date to be appointed.

[**4.** Paragraph 2 shall apply in relation to paragraph 3 with the following modifications, namely—

(a) [the references] to the purposes of paragraph shall be read as [references] to the purposes of paragraph 3;

(b) the references to paragraphs 1(2)(a), 1(2)(b) and 1(2)(d) shall be read as references to paragraphs 3(a), 3(b) and 3(d) respectively;

(c) paragraph 2(c) [..] shall be omitted; and

(d) after paragraph (e) there shall be added—

(f) waive the need to fulfil all or any of the requirements specified in paragraph 3(a) and (b) if on the date of the application the person to whom the applicant is married [, or of whom the applicant is the civil partner,] is serving in service to which section 2(1)(b) applies, that person's recruitment for that service having taken place in the United Kingdom.

Note: Words in square brackets in sub-paragraph (c) omitted by Nationality, Immigration and Asylum Act 2002 Pt1 s.2(1)(b) (July 28, 2002). Words in square brackets inserted at sub-paragraph (f) by Civil Partnership Act 2002 c.33 Sch.27 para 78(2) (December 5, 2005). Words in square brackets substituted in sub-paragraph (a) by Nationality and Borders Act 2022 c.36 Sch.1 para 3(3) (date to be appointed)

[**4A.**—(1) Subject to paragraph 3(5), a person has a qualifying immigration status for the purposes of paragraph 3 if the person has—

(a) qualifying temporary residence leave based on a relevant family association;

(b) probationary citizenship leave based on a relevant family association;
(c) permanent residence leave based on a relevant family association;
(d) a qualifying CTA entitlement; or
(e) a Commonwealth right of abode.

(2) For the purposes of paragraph 3 and this paragraph, the leave mentioned in sub-paragraph (1)(a), (b) or (c) is based on a relevant family association if it was granted on the basis of the person having a relevant family association.

(3) A person who is required for the purposes of paragraph 3 to have, for the whole of the qualifying period, a qualifying immigration status and a relevant family association need not, for the whole of that period—

(a) have the same qualifying immigration status; or
(b) (subject to paragraph 3(5)) have the same relevant family association.

(4) Where, by virtue of sub-paragraph (3)(a), a person relies upon having more than one qualifying immigration status falling within sub-paragraph (1)(a), (b) or (c)—

(a) subject to paragraph 3(5), it is not necessary that the leave to which each status relates is based on the same relevant family association, and

(b) in a case where paragraph 3(5) applies, the relationship by reference to which the persons referred to in paragraph 3(5) are partners need not be of the same description in respect of each grant of leave.]

Note: Paragraph 4A inserted by s 40 Borders, Citizenship and Immigration Act 2009 from a date to be appointed.

[The qualifying period for naturalisation as a British citizen under section 6

4B.—(1) The qualifying period for the purposes of paragraph 1 or 3 is a period of years which ends with the date of the application in question.

(2) The length of the period is determined in accordance with the following provisions of this paragraph.

(3) In the case of an applicant who does not meet the activity condition, the number of years in the period is—

(a) 8, in a case within paragraph 1;
(b) 5, in a case within paragraph 3.

(4) In the case of an applicant who meets the activity condition, the number of years in the period is—

(a) 6, in a case within paragraph 1;
(b) 3, in a case within paragraph 3.

(5) The applicant meets the activity condition if the Secretary of State is satisfied that the applicant—

(a) has participated otherwise than for payment in prescribed activities; or
(b) is to be treated as having so participated.]

Note: Paragraph 4B inserted by s 41 Borders, Citizenship and Immigration Act 2009 from a date to be appointed.

Naturalisation as a [British overseas territories] citizen under section 18(1)

5.—(1) Subject to paragraph 6, the requirements for naturalisation as a [British overseas territories] citizen under section 18(1) are, in the case of any person who applies for it—

(a) the requirements specified in sub-paragraph (2) of this paragraph, or the alternative requirement specified in sub-paragraph (3) of this paragraph; and

(b) that he is of good character; and

(c) that he has a sufficient knowledge of the English language or any other language recognised for official purposes in the relevant territory; and

(d) that either—

(i) his intentions are such that, in the event of a certificate of naturalisation as a [British overseas territories] citizen being granted to him, his home or (if he has more than one) his principal home will be in the relevant territory; or

(ii) he intends, in the event of such a certificate being granted to him, to enter into, or continue in, Crown service under the government of that territory, or service under an international organisation of which that territory or the government of that territory is a member, or service in the employment of a company or association established in that territory.

(2) The requirements referred to in sub-paragraph (1)(a) of this paragraph are—

(a) that he was in the relevant territory at the beginning of the period of five years ending with the date of the application, and that the number of days on which he was absent from that territory in that period does not exceed 450; and

(b) that the number of days on which he was absent from that territory in the period of twelve months so ending does not exceed 90; and

(c) that he was not at any time in the period of twelve months so ending subject under the immigration laws to any restriction on the period for which he might remain in that territory; and

(d) that he was not at any time in the period of five years so ending in that territory in breach of the immigration laws.

(3) The alternative requirement referred to in sub-paragraph (1)(a) of this paragraph is that on the date of the application he is serving outside the relevant territory in Crown service under the government of that territory.

Note: Words in square brackets substituted by s 2 British Overseas Territories Act 2002 from 26 February 2002.

Naturalisation as a British overseas territories citizen under section 18(1): waiver of requirements in special circumstances

6(1) If in the special circumstances of any particular case the Secretary of State thinks fit, he may for the purposes of paragraph 5 do all or any of the following things, namely—

[(za) treat the applicant as fulfilling the first requirement specified in paragraph 5(2)(a) although the applicant was not in the relevant territory at the beginning of the period there mentioned;]

(a) treat the applicant as fulfilling the [second requirement specified in paragraph 5(2)(a)]or paragraph 5(2)(b), or both, although the number of days on which he was absent from the relevant territory in the period there mentioned exceeds the number there mentioned;

(b) treat the applicant as having been in the relevant territory for the whole or any part of any period during which he would otherwise fall to be treated under paragraph 9(2) as having been absent;

(c) disregard any such restriction as is mentioned in paragraph 5(2)(c), not being a restriction to which the applicant was subject on the date of the application;

(d) treat the applicant as fulfilling the requirement specified in paragraph 5(2)(d) although he was in the relevant territory in breach of the immigration laws in the period there mentioned;

(e) waive the need to fulfil the requirement specified in paragraph 5(1)(c) if he considers that because of the applicant's age or physical or mental condition it would be unreasonable to expect him to fulfil it.

[(2) Sub-paragraph (3) applies where the applicant has indefinite leave to enter or remain in the relevant territory.

(3) The Secretary of State may for the purposes of paragraph 5 treat the applicant as fulfilling the requirement specified in paragraph 5(2)(d), without enquiring into whether or not the applicant was in the relevant territory in breach of the immigration laws in the period there mentioned.

(4) The reference in sub-paragraph (2) to having indefinite leave to enter or remain is to be construed as a reference to any status formally granted under the immigration laws in force in the relevant territory which is broadly equivalent to the status of having indefinite leave to enter or remain under the Immigration Act 1971.]

Note: Existing Sch.1 para.6 renumbered as Sch.1 para.6(1), words substituted and Sch.1 para.6(1) (za) inserted by Nationality and Borders Act 2022 c. 36 Sch.1 para.3(4) (June 28, 2022: substitution has effect as SI 2022/590 reg.2 and Sch.1 para.8 subject to transitional and saving provisions specified in SI 2022/590 reg.3 and Sch.2 para.3). Sub-paragraphs (2)-(4) inserted by Nationality and Borders Act 2022 c. 36 Sch.1 para.3(4)(d) (date to be appointed)

Naturalisation as a [British overseas territories] citizen under section 18(2)

7. Subject to paragraph 8, the requirements for naturalisation as a [British overseas territories] citizen under section 18(2) are, in the case of any person who applies for it—

(a) that he was in the relevant territory at the beginning of the period of three years ending with the date of the application, and that the number of days on which he was absent from that territory in that period does not exceed 270; and

(b) that the number of days on which he was absent from that territory in the period of twelve months so ending does not exceed 90; and

(c) that on the date of the application he was not subject under the immigration laws to any restriction on the period for which he might remain in that territory; and

(d) that he was not at any time in the period of three years ending with the date of the application in that territory in breach of the immigration laws; and

(e) the [requirements specified in paragraph 5(1)(b) and (c)].

Note: Words in square brackets in subparagraph (e) substituted by s 2 of Nationality, Immigration and Asylum Act 2002, from 1 November 2005 (SI 2005/2782).

8. Paragraph 6 shall apply in relation to paragraph 7 with the following modifications, namely—

(a) the [references]to the purposes of paragraph 5 shall be read as [references]to the purposes of paragraph 7;

(b) the references to paragraphs 5(2)(a), 5(2)(b) and 5(2)(d) shall be read as references to paragraphs 7(a), 7(b) and 7(d) respectively;

(c) paragraph 6(c) [...] shall be omitted; and

(d) after paragraph (e) there shall be added—

'(f) waive the need to fulfil all or any of the requirements specified in paragraph 7(a) and (b) if on the date of the application the person to whom the applicant is married [, or of whom the applicant is the civil partner,] is serving in service to which section 16(1)(b) applies, that person's recruitment for that service having taken place in a [British overseas territory]'.

Note: Words in square brackets in paragraph 8(c) omitted by Nationality, Immigration and Asylum Act 2002, s 2 from 1 November 2005 (SI 2005/2782). Words in square brackets in subparagraph 8(d) inserted by Sch 27 Civil Partnerships Act 2004 from 5 December 2005 (SI 2005/3175). Words substituted in paragraph (a) by Nationality and Borders Act 2022 c. 36 Sch.1 para.3(5)(a)-(b) (June 28, 2022: substitution has effect as SI 2022/590 reg.2 and Sch.1 para.8 subject to transitional and saving provisions specified in SI 2022/590 reg.3 and Sch.2 para.3)

Periods to be treated as periods of absence from UK or a [British overseas territory]

9.—(1) For the purposes of this Schedule a person shall (subject to [paragraph 2(1)(b) or 4(b)]) be treated as having been absent from the United Kingdom during any of the following periods, that is to say—

(a) any period when he was in the United Kingdom and either was entitled to an exemption under section 8(3) or (4) of the Immigration Act 1971 (exemptions for diplomatic agents etc. and members of the forces) or was a member of the family and formed part of the household of a person so entitled;

(b) any period when he was detained—

(i) in any place of detention in the United Kingdom in pursuance of a sentence passed on him by a court in the United Kingdom or elsewhere for any offence;

(ii) in any hospital in the United Kingdom under a hospital order made under [Part III of the Mental Health Act 1983] or section 175 or 376 of the Criminal Procedure (Scotland) Act 1975 or Part III of the Mental Health [(Northern Ireland) Order 1986], being an order made in connection with his conviction of an offence; or

(iii) under any power of detention conferred by the immigration laws of the United Kingdom;

(c) any period when, being liable to be detained as mentioned in paragraph (b)(i) or (ii) of this sub-paragraph, he was unlawfully at large or absent without leave and for that reason liable to be arrested or taken into custody;

(d) any period when, his actual detention under any such power as is mentioned in paragraph (b)(iii) of this sub-paragraph being required or specifically authorised, he was unlawfully at large and for that reason liable to be arrested.

(2) For the purposes of this Schedule a person shall (subject to paragraph 6(b)) be treated as having been absent from any particular [British overseas territory] during any of the following periods, that is to say—

(a) any period when he was in that territory and either was entitled to an exemption under the immigration laws of that territory corresponding to any such exemption as is mentioned in sub-paragraph (1)(a) or was a member of the family and formed part of the household of a person so entitled;

(b) any period when he was detained—

(i) in any place of detention in the relevant territory in pursuance of a sentence passed on him by a court in that territory or elsewhere for any offence;

(ii) in any hospital in that territory under a direction (however described) made under any law for purposes similar to [Part III of the Mental Health Act 1983] which was for the time being in force in that territory, being a direction made in connection with his conviction of an offence and corresponding to a hospital order under that Part; or

(iii) under any power of detention conferred by the immigration laws of that territory;

(c) any period when, being liable to be detained as mentioned in paragraph (b)(i) or (ii) of this sub-paragraph, he was unlawfully at large or absent without leave and for that reason liable to be arrested or taken into custody;

(d) any period when, his actual detention under any such power as is mentioned in paragraph (b)(iii) of this sub-paragraph being required or specifically authorised, he was unlawfully at large and for that reason liable to be arrested.

Note: Words in first square brackets in subparagraphs (1)(b) and 9(2)(b) substituted by Mental Health Act 1983, s 148. Words in second square brackets in subparagraph (1)(b) substituted by SI 1956/596. Words in first square brackets in paragraph 9 substituted by s 49 Borders, Citizenship and Immigration Act 2009 from 13 January 2010 (SI 2009/2731).

Interpretation

10. In this Schedule 'the relevant territory' has the meaning given by section 18(3).

[**11.**—(1) This paragraph applies for the purposes of this Schedule.

(2) A person has qualifying temporary residence leave if—

(a) the person has limited leave to enter or remain in the United Kingdom, and

(b) the leave is granted for a purpose by reference to which a grant of probationary citizenship leave may be made.

(3) A person has probationary citizenship leave if—

(a) the person has limited leave to enter or remain in the United Kingdom, and

(b) the leave is of a description identified in rules under section 3 of the Immigration Act 1971 as 'probationary citizenship leave', and the reference in sub-paragraph (2) to a grant of probationary citizenship leave is to be construed accordingly.

(4) A person has permanent residence leave if the person has indefinite leave to enter or remain in the United Kingdom.

(5) A person has a qualifying CTA entitlement if the person—

(a) is a citizen of the Republic of Ireland,

(b) last arrived in the United Kingdom on a local journey (within the meaning of the Immigration Act 1971) from the Republic of Ireland, and

(c) on that arrival, was a citizen of the Republic of Ireland and was entitled to enter without leave by virtue of section 1(3) of the Immigration Act 1971 (entry from the common travel area).

(6) A person has a Commonwealth right of abode if the person has the right of abode in the United Kingdom by virtue of section 2(1)(b) of the Immigration Act 1971.

(7) A person has a permanent EEA entitlement if the person is entitled to reside in the United Kingdom permanently by virtue of any provision made under section 2(2) of the European Communities Act 1972.

(8) A person has a temporary EEA entitlement if the person does not have a permanent EEA entitlement but is entitled to reside in the United Kingdom by virtue of any provision made under section 2(2) of the European Communities Act 1972.

(9) A reference in this paragraph to having leave to enter or remain in the United Kingdom is to be construed in accordance with the Immigration Act 1971.]

Note: Paragraph 11 inserted by s 49 Borders, Citizenship and Immigration Act 2009 from 13 January 2010 (SI 2009/2731).

Section 36

Schedule 2

Provisions For Reducing Statelessness

Persons born in the United Kingdom after commencement

1.—(1) Where a person born in the United Kingdom after commencement would, but for this paragraph, be born stateless, then, subject to sub-paragraph (3)—

(a) if at the time of the birth his father or mother is a citizen or subject of a description mentioned in sub-paragraph (2), he shall be a citizen or subject of that description; and accordingly

(b) [...] at the time of the birth each of his parents is a citizen or subject of a different description so mentioned, he shall be a citizen or subject of the same description so mentioned as each of them is respectively at that time.

(2) The descriptions referred to in sub-paragraph (1) are a [British overseas territories] citizen, a British Overseas citizen and a British subject under this Act.

(3) A person shall not be a British subject by virtue of this paragraph if by virtue of it he is a citizen of a description mentioned in sub-paragraph (2).

Note: British dependent territories became British overseas territories from 26 February 2002, British Overseas Territories Act 2002, s 1. Words deleted from paragraphs 1(1)(b) cease to have effect in relation to children born on or after 1 July 2006 (SI 2006/1498).

Persons born in a [British overseas territory] after commencement

2.—(1) Where a person born in a [British overseas territory] after commencement would, but for this paragraph, be born stateless, then, subject to sub-paragraph (3)—

(a) if at the time of the birth his father or mother is a citizen or subject of a description mentioned in sub-paragraph (2), he shall be a citizen or subject of that description; and accordingly

(b) [...] at the time of the birth each of his parents is a citizen or subject of a different description so mentioned, he shall be a citizen or subject of the same description so mentioned as each of them is respectively at that time.

(2) The descriptions referred to in sub-paragraph (1) are a British citizen, a British Overseas citizen and a British subject under this Act.

(3) A person shall not be a British subject by virtue of this paragraph if by virtue of it he is a citizen of a description mentioned in sub-paragraph (2).

Note: British dependent territories became British overseas territories from 26 February 2002, British Overseas Territories Act 2002, s 1. Words deleted from paragraph 2(1)(b) cease to have effect in relation to children born on or after 1 July 2006 (SI 2006/1498).

Persons [aged 18–22] born in the United Kingdom or a [British overseas territory] after commencement

3.—(1) A person born in the United Kingdom or a [British overseas territory] after commencement shall be entitled, on an application for his registration under this paragraph, to be so registered if the following requirements are satisfied in his case, namely—

(a) that he is and always has been stateless; and

(b) that on the date of the application he [...] [[had attained the age of eighteen but]]was under the age of twenty-two; and

(c) that he was in the United Kingdom or a [British overseas territory] (no matter which) at the beginning of the period of five years ending with that date and that (subject to paragraph 6) the number of days on which he was absent from both the United Kingdom and the [British overseas territories] in that period does not exceed 450.

(2) A person entitled to registration under this paragraph—

(a) shall be registered under it as a British citizen if, in the period of five years mentioned in sub-paragraph (1), the number of days wholly or partly spent by him in the United Kingdom exceeds the number of days wholly or partly spent by him in the [British overseas territories];

(b) in any other case, shall be registered under it as a [British overseas territories] citizen.

Note: British dependent territories became British overseas territories from 26 February 2002, British Overseas Territories Act 2002, s 1. Words deleted from paragraph 3(1)(b) cease to have effect in relation to an application made on or after 1 April 2003 or an application not determined by that date, Nationality, Immigration and Asylum Act 2002, s 8 and SI 2003/754. Words in square brackets in heading inserted by Nationality and Borders Act 2022 c. 36 Pt 1 s.11(3) (June 28, 2022)

[Minors aged 5 to 17 born in the United Kingdom or a British overseas territory after commencement

3A (1) A person born in the United Kingdom or a British overseas territory after commencement is entitled, on an application for the person to be registered under this paragraph, to be so registered if—

(a) the person is and always has been stateless,

(b) on the date of the application, the person was a minor,

(c) the person was in the United Kingdom or a British overseas territory (no matter which) at the beginning of the period of five years ending with that date and (subject to paragraph 6) the number of days on which the person was absent from both the United Kingdom and the British overseas territories in that period does not exceed 450, and

(d) the Secretary of State is satisfied that the person is unable to acquire another nationality in accordance with sub-paragraph (2).

(2) A person is able to acquire a nationality in accordance with this sub-paragraph if—

(a) the nationality is the same as that of one of the person's parents,

(b) the person has been entitled to acquire the nationality since birth, and

(c) in all the circumstances, it is reasonable to expect the person (or someone acting on their behalf) to take the steps which would enable the person to acquire the nationality in question.

(3) For the purposes of sub-paragraph (2)(b), a person is not entitled to acquire a nationality if its acquisition is conditional on the exercise of a discretion on the part of the country or territory in question.

(4) A person entitled to registration under this paragraph—

(a) is to be registered as a British citizen if, in the period of five years mentioned in sub-paragraph (1), the number of days wholly or partly spent by the person in the United Kingdom exceeds the number of days wholly or partly spent by the person in the British overseas territory;

(b) in any other case, is to be registered as a British overseas territories citizen.]

Note: inserted by Nationality and Borders Act 2022 c. 36 Pt 1 s.11(4) (June 28, 2022)

Persons born outside the United Kingdom and the [British Overseas Territories] after commencement

4.—(1) A person born outside the United Kingdom and the [British overseas territories] after commencement shall be entitled, on an application for his registration under this paragraph, to be so registered if the following requirements are satisfied, namely—

(a) that that person is and always has been stateless; and

(b) that at the time of that person's birth his father or mother was a citizen or subject of a description mentioned in sub-paragraph (4); and

(c) that that person was in the United Kingdom or a [British overseas territory] (no matter which) at the beginning of the period of three years ending with the date of the application and that (subject to paragraph 6) the number of days on which he was absent from both the United Kingdom and the [British overseas territories] in that period does not exceed 270.

(2) A person entitled to registration under this paragraph—

(a) shall be registered under it as a citizen or subject of a description available to him in accordance with sub-paragraph (3); and

(b) if more than one description is so available to him, shall be registered under this paragraph as a citizen of whichever one or more of the descriptions so available to him is or are stated in the application under this paragraph to be wanted.

(3) For the purposes of this paragraph the descriptions of citizen or subject available to a person entitled to registration under this paragraph are—

(a) in the case of a person whose father or mother was at the time of that person's birth a citizen of a description mentioned in sub-paragraph (4), any description of citizen so mentioned which applied to his father or mother at that time;

(b) in any case, a British subject under this Act.

(4) The description referred to in sub-paragraphs (1) to (3) are a British citizen, a [British overseas territories] citizen, a British Overseas citizen and a British subject under this Act.

Note: British dependent territories became British overseas territories from 26 February 2002, British Overseas Territories Act 2002, s 1.

Persons born stateless before commencement

5.—(1) A person born before commencement shall be entitled, on an application for his registration under this paragraph, to be so registered if the circumstances are such that, if—

(a) this Act had not been passed, and the enactments repealed or amended by this Act had continued in force accordingly; and

(b) an application for the registration of that person under section 1 of the British Nationality (No. 2) Act 1964 (stateless persons) as a citizen of the United Kingdom and Colonies had been made on the date of the application under this paragraph, that person would have been entitled under that section to be registered as such a citizen.

(2) A person entitled to registration under this paragraph shall be registered under it as such a citizen as he would have become at commencement if, immediately before commencement, he had been registered as a citizen of the United Kingdom and Colonies under section 1 of the British Nationality (No. 2) Act 1964 on whichever of the grounds mentioned in subsection (1)(a) to (c) of that section he would have been entitled to be

so registered on in the circumstances described in sub-paragraph (1)(a) and (b) of this paragraph.

Supplementary

6. If in the special circumstances of any particular case the Secretary of State thinks fit, he may for the purposes of paragraph 3, [3A] or 4 treat the person who is the subject of the application as fulfilling the requirement specified in sub-paragraph (1)(c) of that paragraph although the number of days on which he was absent from both the United Kingdom and the [British overseas territories] in the period there mentioned exceeds the number there mentioned.

Note: British dependent territories became British overseas territories from 26 February 2002, British Overseas Territories Act 2002, s 1. Wors inserted in square brackets by Nationality and Borders Act 2022 c. 36 Pt 1 s.11(5) (June 28, 2022)

SCHEDULE 3 — Section 37

COUNTRIES WHOSE CITIZENS ARE COMMONWEALTH CITIZENS

Antigua and Barbuda
Australia
The Bahamas
Bangladesh
Barbados
Belize
Botswana
[Brunei]
[Cameroon]
Canada
Kenya
Kiribati
Lesotho
Malawi
Malaysia
[]
Malta
Mauritius
[Mozambique]
Nauru
New Zealand
Nigeria
[Pakistan]
[Rwanda]
Uganda
Vanuatu
Western Samoa
Papua New Guinea
[Saint Christopher and Nevis]
Saint Lucia
Saint Vincent and the Grenadines
Republic of Cyprus
Dominica
Fiji
[[[The Gambia]]
Ghana
Grenada
Guyana
India
Jamaica
Seychelles
Sierra Leone
Singapore
Solomon Islands
Sri Lanka
Swaziland
Tanzania
Tonga
Trinidad and Tobago
Tuvalu
Zambia
Zimbabwe

[Namibia]

Note: 'Brunei' inserted by SI 1983/1699; 'Maldives' inserted by Brunei and Maldives Act 1985; 'Pakistan' inserted by SI 1989/1331; 'Saint Christopher and Nevis' inserted by SI 1983/882; 'Namibia' inserted by SI 1990/1502. 'Cameroon' and 'Mozambique' inserted by SI 1998/3161 from 25 January 1999. 'Rwanda' inserted from 10 March 2010 (SI 2010/246). The Gambia omitted by SI2015/1771. Maldives omitted by SI2017/568. The Gambia inserted by SI 2018/620.

Schedule 4

Note: Schedule 4 amends Immigration Act 1971, ss 3–6, 8, 9, 13, 14, 22, 24–26, 29, 33, Schs 2, 4.

...

[Schedule 4A — Section 40(5E)

Deprivation of Citizenship without notice: judicial oversight

1 Deprivation without notice: application to Special Immigration Appeals Commission

1 (1) If the Secretary of State proposes to make a conducive grounds deprivation order without notice, the Secretary of State may apply to the Special Immigration Appeals Commission under this paragraph.

(2) If the Secretary of State makes a conducive grounds deprivation order without notice, the Secretary of State must apply to the Special Immigration Appeals Commission under this paragraph within the period of seven days beginning with the day on which the order is made (unless an application has already been made under sub-paragraph (1)).

(3) The function of the Commission on an application under this paragraph is to determine whether, in respect of each condition in section 40(5A) on which the Secretary of State relies, the Secretary of State's view is obviously flawed.

(4) In determining that question, the Commission must apply the principles that would be applicable on an application for judicial review.

(5) If the Commission determines that the Secretary of State's view is obviously flawed in respect of each condition in section 40(5A) on which the Secretary of State relies—

(a) if the order in question has not been made, section 40(5) applies in relation to the order (notwithstanding section 40(5A));

(b) if the order has been made, the Secretary of State must, within the period of 14 days beginning with the day on which the Commission made the determination—

(i) give late notice in respect of the order,

(ii) revoke the order, or

(iii) make an application under sub-paragraph (6).

(6) The Secretary of State may (at any time) make an application to the Special Immigration Appeals Commission for fresh consideration of a decision the Secretary of State has made under section 40(5A) where—

(a) in the opinion of the Secretary of State, circumstances have changed materially since the determination mentioned in sub-paragraph (5), or

(b) the Secretary of State wishes to provide further evidence to the Commission.

Sub-paragraphs (3) to (5) apply to an application under this sub-paragraph.

2 Deprivation of citizenship without notice: review

2 (1) Sub-paragraphs (2) to (5) apply if—

(a) the Secretary of State makes a conducive grounds deprivation order without notice, and

(b) the Special Immigration Appeals Commission has not made the determination mentioned in paragraph 1(5) (Secretary of State's decision obviously flawed).

(2) The Secretary of State must, at least once in every review period, review the circumstances of the person in respect of whom the order was made (so far as known) and decide whether to give late notice in respect of the order.

(3) On such a review, the Secretary of State must decide to give late notice to the person unless it appears to the Secretary of State that any of the conditions in section 40(5A) is met (reading any reference in those provisions to notice under section 40(5) as a reference to late notice).

(4) If the Secretary of State decides at any point to give late notice in respect of the order—

(a) the Secretary of State must give the notice as soon as reasonably practicable, and

(b) once the notice is given, sub-paragraph (2) ceases to apply in relation to the person.

(5) If on the expiry of the final review period the Secretary of State has not given, or has not decided to give, late notice in respect of the order, the Secretary of State must make an application to the Special Immigration Appeals Commission within the period of seven days beginning with the day after the final day of that review period.

(6) Sub-paragraphs (3) to (6) of paragraph 1 (except sub-paragraph (5)(a)) apply for the purposes of an application under sub-paragraph (5) as they apply for the purposes of an application under that paragraph.

(7) For the purposes of this paragraph, each of the following is a "review period"—

(a) the period of four months beginning with the day after the day on which the Special Immigration Appeals Commission first determined an application in relation to the order under paragraph 1, and

(b) each of the next five successive periods of four months.

3 Interpretation

3 (1) In this Schedule, references to making a conducive grounds deprivation order without notice are to making an order under section 40(2) without giving notice under subsection (5) of that section (in reliance on subsection (5A) of that section).

(2) In this Schedule, "late notice", in respect of an order under section 40(5), means written notice to the person in respect of whom the order was made specifying—

(a) that the Secretary of State has made the order,

(b) the reasons for the order, and

(c) the person's right of appeal under section 40A(1) or under section 2B of the Special Immigration Appeals Commission Act 1997.]

Note: inserted by Nationality and Borders Act 2022 c. 36 Sch.2 para.1 (date to be appointed)

Schedule 5 — Section 42(1)

Citizenship Oath and Pledge

1. The form of citizenship oath and pledge is as follows for registration of or naturalisation as a British citizen—

OATH

'I, [name], swear by Almighty God that, on becoming a British citizen, I will be faithful and bear true allegiance to Her Majesty Queen Elizabeth the Second, Her Heirs and Successors according to law.'

PLEDGE

'I will give my loyalty to the United Kingdom and respect its rights and freedoms. I will uphold its democratic values. I will observe its laws faithfully and fulfil my duties and obligations as a British citizen.'

2. The form of citizenship oath and pledge is as follows for registration of or naturalisation as a British overseas territories citizen—

OATH

'I, [name], swear by Almighty God that, on becoming a British overseas territories citizen, I will be faithful and bear true allegiance to Her Majesty Queen Elizabeth the Second, Her Heirs and Successors according to law.'

PLEDGE

'I will give my loyalty to [name of territory] and respect its rights and freedoms. I will uphold its democratic values. I will observe its laws faithfully and fulfil my duties and obligations as a British overseas territories citizen.'

3. The form of citizenship oath is as follows for registration of a British Overseas citizen—

'I, [name], swear by Almighty God that, on becoming a British Overseas citizen, I will be faithful and bear true allegiance to Her Majesty Queen Elizabeth the Second, Her Heirs and Successors according to law.'

4. The form of citizenship oath is as follows for registration of a British subject—

'I, [name], swear by Almighty God that, on becoming a British subject, I will be faithful and bear true allegiance to Her Majesty Queen Elizabeth the Second, Her Heirs and Successors according to law.']

Note: Schedule 5 substituted by Nationality, Immigration and Asylum Act 2002, Sch 1, paragraph 2, from 1 January 2004 (SI 2003/3156).

SCHEDULE 6 **Section 50(1)**

[BRITISH OVERSEAS TERRITORIES]

Anguilla
Bermuda
British Antarctic Territory
British Indian Ocean Territory
Cayman Islands
Falkland Islands [...]
Gibraltar
...
Montserrat
Pitcairn, Henderson, Ducie and Oeno Islands
...
[St Helena, Ascension and Tristan da Cunha]
[South Georgia and the South Sandwich Islands]
The Sovereign Base Areas of Akrotiri and Dhekelia (that is to say the areas mentioned in section 2(1) of the Cyprus Act 1960)
Turks and Caicos Islands
Virgin Islands

Note: British dependent territories became British overseas territories from 26 February 2002, British Overseas Territories Act 2002, s 1. First words omitted in Sch 6 repealed by SI 2002/3497. Second words omitted repealed by SI 1986/948. Third words omitted repealed by SI 1983/893. Words in first square brackets substituted from 14 November 2009 (SI 2009/2744), words in second square brackets inserted by SI 2001/3497 from 4 December 2001.

Senior Courts Act 1981

(1981, c. 54)

Note: Citation of Act altered to Senior Courts Act (formerly Supreme Court Act) by Constitutional Reform Act 2005 Schedule 11 from 1 October 2009 (SI 2009/1604).

31A. Transfer of judicial review applications to Upper Tribunal

(1) This section applies where an application is made to the High Court—

(a) for judicial review, or

(b) for permission to apply for judicial review.

(2) If Conditions 1, 2 and 3 are met, the High Court must by order transfer the application to the Upper Tribunal.

[(2A) ...]

(3) If Conditions 1 [and 2] are met, but Condition 3 is not, the High Court may by order transfer the application to the Upper Tribunal if it appears to the High Court to be just and convenient to do so.

(4) Condition 1 is that the application does not seek anything other than—

(a) relief under section 31(1)(a) and (b);

(b) permission to apply for relief under section 31(1)(a) and (b);

(c) an award under section 31(4);

(d) interest;

(e) costs.

(5) Condition 2 is that the application does not call into question anything done by the Crown Court.

(6) Condition 3 is that the application falls within a class specified under section 18(6) of the Tribunals, Courts and Enforcement Act 2007.

(7) ...

[(8) ...]

Note: Section 31A inserted by Tribunal, Courts and Enforcement Act 2007, s 19 from 3 November 2008 (SI 2008/2696). Subsections (2A) and (8) inserted by Borders, Citizenship and Immigration Act 2009, s 53 from 8 August 2011 (SI 2011/1741). Subsections (2A), (7) and (8) omitted and numbers in square brackets in subsection (2)–(3) substituted from 1 November 2013 by section 22 Crime and Courts Act 2013.

Immigration Act 1988
(1988, c. 14)

An Act to make further provision for the regulation of immigration into the United Kingdom; and for connected purposes. [10 May 1988]

1. Termination of saving in respect of Commonwealth citizens settled before 1973

...

Note: Section 1 repeals Immigration Act 1971, s 1(5).

2. Restriction on exercise of right of abode in cases of polygamy

(1) this section applies to any woman who—

(a) has the right of abode in the United Kingdom under section 2(1)(b) of the principal Act as, or as having been, the wife of a man ('the husband')—

(i) to whom she is or was polygamously married; and

(ii) who is or was such a citizen of the United Kingdom and Colonies, Commonwealth citizen or British subject as is mentioned in section 2(2)(a) or (b) of that Act as in force immediately before the commencement of the British Nationality Act 1981; and

(b) has not before the coming into force of this section and since her marriage to the husband been in the United Kingdom.

(2) A woman to whom this section applies shall not be entitled to enter the United Kingdom in the exercise of the right of abode mentioned in subsection (1)(a) above or to be granted a certificate of entitlement in respect of that right if there is another woman living (whether or not one to whom this section applies) who is the wife or widow of the husband and who—

(a) is, or at any time since her marriage to the husband has been, in the United Kingdom; or

(b) has been granted a certificate of entitlement in respect of the right of abode mentioned in subsection (1)(a) above or an entry clearance to enter the United Kingdom as the wife of the husband.

(3) So long as a woman is precluded by subsection (2) above from entering the United Kingdom in the exercise of her right of abode or being granted a certificate of entitlement in respect of that right the principal Act shall apply to her as it applies to a person not having a right of abode.

(4) Subsection (2) above shall not preclude a woman from re-entering the United Kingdom if since her marriage to the husband she has at any time previously been in the United Kingdom and there was at that time no such other woman living as is mentioned in that subsection.

(5) Where a woman claims that this section does not apply to her because she had been in the United Kingdom before the coming into force of this section and since her marriage to the husband it shall be for her to prove that fact.

(6) For the purposes of this section a marriage may be polygamous although at its inception neither party has any spouse additional to the other.

(7) For the purposes of subsection (1)(b), (2)(a), (4) and (5) above there shall be disregarded presence in the United Kingdom as a visitor or an illegal entrant and presence in circumstances in which a person is deemed by section 11(1) of the principal Act not to have entered the United Kingdom.

(8) In subsection (2)(b) above the reference to a certificate of entitlement includes a reference to a certificate treated as such a certificate by virtue of section 39(8) of the British Nationality Act 1981.

(9) No application by a woman for a certificate of entitlement in respect of such a right of abode as is mentioned in subsection (1)(a) above or for an entry clearance shall be granted if another application for such a certificate or clearance is pending and that application is made by a woman as the wife or widow of the same husband.

(10) For the purposes of subsection (9) above an application shall be regarded as pending so long as it and any appeal proceedings relating to it have not been finally determined.

3. Proof of right of abode

...

Note: Amends Immigration Act 1971, ss 3(9), 13(3), 2(2); British Nationality Act 1981, s 39.

4. Members of diplomatic missions

...

Note: Amends Immigration Act 1971, s 8.

5. ...

Note: Section 5 repealed by Immigration and Asylum Act 1999 from 2 October 2000, transitional provisions set out in SI 2003/754.

6. Knowingly overstaying limited leave

(1) ...

(2) ...

(3) These amendments do not apply in relation to a person whose leave has expired before the coming into force of this section.

Note: Section 6(1) and (2) amend Immigration Act 1971, s 24.

7.

Note: Omitted by Immigration and Social Security Co-ordination (EU Withdrawal) Act 2020 c.20 Sch1(1) para 1 (December 31, 2020: repeal as effect subject to savings specified in SI202/1309 reg 83 and Sch 4 paras 5–7).

8. …

Note: Section 8 repealed by Sch 14 Immigration and Asylum Act 1999 from a date to be notified.

9. …

Note: Section 9 repealed by Sch 14 Immigration and Asylum Act 1999 from 30 June 2003 (SI 2003/1469).

10. Miscellaneous minor amendments

The principal Act shall have effect with the amendments specified in the Schedule to this Act.

11. Expenses and receipts

(1) There shall be paid out of money provided by Parliament any expenses incurred by the Secretary of State in consequences of this Act.

(2) Any sums received by the Secretary of State by virtue of this Act shall be paid into the Consolidated Fund.

12. Short title, interpretation, commencement and extent

(1) This Act may be cited as the Immigration Act 1988.

(2) In this Act 'the principal Act' means the Immigration Act 1971 and any expression which is also used in that Act has the same meaning as in that Act.

(3) Except as provided in subsection (4) below this Act shall come into force at the end of the period of two months beginning with the day on which it is passed.

(4) Sections 1, 2, 3, 4, 5 and 7(1) and paragraph 1 of the Schedule shall come into force on such day as may be appointed by the Secretary of State by an order made by statutory instrument; and such an order may appoint different days for different provisions and contain such transitional provisions and savings as the Secretary of State thinks necessary or expedient in connection with any provision brought into force.

(5) This Act extends to Northern Ireland and section 36 of the principal Act (power to extend any of its provisions to the Channel Islands or the Isle of Man) shall apply also to the provisions of this Act.

Section 10

SCHEDULE

MINOR AMENDMENTS

…

Asylum and Immigration Appeals Act 1993

(1993, c. 23)

Asylum and Immigration Appeals Act 1993An Act to make provision about persons who claim asylum in the United Kingdom and their dependants; to amend the law with respect to certain rights of appeal under the Immigration Act 1971; and to extend the provisions of the Immigration (Carriers' Liability) Act 1987 to transit passengers. [1 July 1993]

Introductory

1. Interpretation

In this Act—

'the 1971 Act' means the Immigration Act 1971;

'claim for asylum' means a claim made by a person (whether before or after the coming into force of this section) that it would be contrary to the United Kingdom's obligations under the Convention for him to be removed from, or required to leave, the United Kingdom; and

'the Convention' means the Convention relating to the Status of Refugees done at Geneva on 28 July 1951 and the Protocol to that Convention.

2. Primacy of Convention

Nothing in the immigration rules (within the meaning of the 1971 Act) shall lay down any practice which would be contrary to the Convention.

Treatment of Persons who Claim Asylum

3. …

Note: Section 3 repealed by Immigration and Asylum Act 1999 from 11 December 2000.

4. …

Note: Section 4 repealed by Immigration and Asylum Act 1999 from 3 April 2000.

5. …

Note: Section 5 repealed by Immigration and Asylum Act 1999 from 3 April 2000.

6. . . .

Note: Section 6 repealed by Immigration and Asylum Act 1999 from 11 November 1999, with effect from 26 July 1993.

7. . . .

Note: Section 7 repealed by Immigration and Asylum Act 1999 from 2 October 2000.

8. . . .

Note: Section 8 repealed by Immigration and Asylum Act 1999 from 2 October 2000, transitional provisions set out in SI 2003/754.

9. . . .

Note: Section 9 repealed by Immigration and Asylum Act 1999 from 2 October 2000.

[9A. . . .

Note: Section 9A repealed by Sch 2 Asylum and Immigration Act 2004 from 4 April 2005 (SI 2005/565).

10. Visitors, short-term and prospective students and their dependants

. . .

Note: Section 10 repealed by Immigration and Asylum Act 1999 from 2 October 2000.

11. Refusals which are mandatory under immigration rules

. . .

Note: Section 11 repealed by Immigration and Asylum Act 1999 from 2 October 2000.

12. . . .

Note: Section 12 repealed by Immigration and Asylum Act 1999.

Supplementary

13. Financial provision

(1) There shall be paid out of money provided by Parliament—

(a) any expenditure incurred by the Secretary of State under this Act; and

(b) any increase attributable to this Act in the sums payable out of such money under any other enactment.

(2) Any sums received by the Secretary of State by virtue of this Act shall be paid into the Consolidated Fund.

14. Commencement

(1) Sections 4 to 11 above (and section 1 above so far as it relates to those sections) shall not come into force until such day as the Secretary of State may by order appoint, and different days may be appointed for provisions or for different purposes.

(2) An order under subsection (1) above—

(a) shall be made by statutory instrument; and

(b) may contain such transitional and supplemental provisions as the Secretary of State thinks necessary or expedient.

(3) Without prejudice to the generality of subsections (1) and (2) above, with respect to any provision of section 4 above an order under subsection (1) above may appoint different days in relation to different descriptions of asylum-seekers and dependants of asylum-seekers; and any such descriptions may be framed by reference to nationality, citizenship, origin or other connection with any particular country or territory, but not by reference to race, colour or religion.

15. Extent

(1) Her Majesty may by Order in Council direct that any of the provisions of this Act shall extend, with such modifications as appear to Her Majesty to be appropriate, to any of the Channel Islands or the Isle of Man.

(2) This Act extends to Northern Ireland.

16. Short title

This Act may be cited as the Asylum and Immigration Appeals Act 1993.

SCHEDULES

SCHEDULE 1

...

Note: Schedule 1 repealed by Immigration and Asylum Act 1999 from 3 April 2000.

Section 8(6)

SCHEDULE 2

SCHEDULE 2

Note: Schedule 2 repealed by Immigration and Asylum Act 1999 from 2 October 2000.

Special Immigration Appeals Commission Act 1997

(1997, c. 68)

Special Immigration Appeals Commission Act 1997An Act to establish the Special Immigration Appeals Commission; to make provision with respect to its jurisdiction; and for connected purposes [17 December 1997]

1. Establishment of the commission

(1) There shall be a commission, known as the Special Immigration Appeals Commission, for the purpose of exercising the jurisdiction conferred by this Act.

(2) Schedule 1 to this Act shall have effect in relation to the Commission.

[(3) The Commission shall be a superior court of record.

(4) A decision of the Commission shall be questioned in legal proceedings only in accordance with—

(a) section 7, [[and section 7B-7D]] or

(b) ...]

Note: Words in square brackets inserted by Anti-terrorism, Crime and Security Act 2001, s 35 from 13 December 2001. Subsection 4(b) repealed by Prevention of Terrorism Act 2005, s 16 from 14 March 2005. Words in double square brackets inserted at subsection (4)(a) by Criminal Justice and Courts Act 2015 c.2 Pt 3 s 66(3) (June 28, 2018: insertion has effect on June 28, 2018 as SI 2018/732 art.2 subject to transitional provision as specified in SI2018/732 art.3).

[2. Jurisdiction: appeals

(1) A person may appeal to the Special Immigration Appeals Commission against a decision if—

(a) he would be able to appeal against the decision under section 82(1) [...] of the Nationality, Immigration and Asylum Act 2002 but for a certificate of the Secretary of State under section 97 of that Act (national security &c.), or

(b) an appeal against the decision under section 82(1) [...] of that Act lapsed under section 99 of that Act by virtue of a certificate of the Secretary of State under section 97 of that Act.

(2) The following provisions shall apply, with any necessary modifications, in relation to an appeal against an immigration decision under this section as they apply in relation to an appeal under section 82(1) of the Nationality, Immigration and Asylum Act 2002—

(a) section 3C of the Immigration Act 1971 (c. 77) [continuation of leave],

(b) section 78 of the Nationality, Immigration and Asylum Act 2002 (no removal while appeal pending),

(c) section 79 of that Act (deportation order: appeal),

[(ca) section 78A of that Act (restriction on removal of children and their parents),]

(d) ...

(e) section 84 of that Act (grounds of appeal),

(f) section 85 of that Act (matters to be considered),

(g) section 86 of that Act (determination of appeal),
(h) ...
(i) section 96 of that Act (earlier right of appeal),
(j) section 104 of that Act (pending appeal),
(k) section 105 of that Act (notice of immigration decision), and
(l) ...

(3) ...

(4) ...

(5) A person may bring or continue an appeal [...] under this section while he is in the United Kingdom only if he would be able to bring or continue the appeal while he was in the United Kingdom if it were an appeal under section 82(1) of that Act.

(6) ...

[2A. ...]

Note: Section 2 substituted and s 2A ceased to have effect by Sch 7 Nationality, Immigration and Asylum Act 2002 from 1 April 2003 (SI 2003/754). Words in square brackets in s 2 inserted or substituted by Sch 1 Immigration, Asylum and Nationality Act 2006 from 31 August 2006 (SI 2006/2226). Subsections (2)(d), (h), (l), (3), (4) and (6) omitted and words omitted from subsection (1) and (5) by Sch 9 Immigration Act 2014 from a date to be appointed. Subsection (2)(ca) inserted by Sch 9 Immigration Act 2014 from 28 July 2014 (SI 2014/1820). Words omitted from s 2(2)(a) by Immigration Act 2016, s 64 from 1 December 2016 (SI 2016/1037).

[2B. A person may appeal to the Special Immigration Appeals Commission against a decision to make an order under section 40 of the British Nationality Act 1981 (c. 61) (deprivation of citizenship) if he is not entitled to appeal under section 40A(1) of that Act because of a certificate under section 40A(2)] [...]

Note: Section 2B inserted by Nationality, Immigration and Asylum Act 2002, s 4 from 1 April 2003 (SI 2003/754). Transitional provisions set out in SI 2003/754. Words in second square brackets in s 2B inserted by Sch 2 Asylum and Immigration Act 2004 from 4 April 2004 (SI 2005/565) and omitted by Sch 9 Immigration Act 2014 from a date to be appointed.

[2C. Jurisdiction: review of certain exclusion decisions

(1) Subsection (2) applies in relation to any direction about the exclusion of a {person} from the United Kingdom which—

(a) is made by the Secretary of State wholly or partly on the ground that the exclusion from the United Kingdom of the {person} is conducive to the public good,

(b) is not subject to a right of appeal, and

(c) is certified by the Secretary of State as a direction that was made wholly or partly in reliance on information which, in the opinion of the Secretary of State, should not be made public—

(i) in the interests of national security,

(ii) in the interests of the relationship between the United Kingdom and another country, or

(iii) otherwise in the public interest.

(2) The add {person} to whom the direction relates may apply to the Special Immigration Appeals Commission to set aside the direction.

(3) In determining whether the direction should be set aside, the Commission must apply the principles which would be applied in judicial review proceedings.

(4) If the Commission decides that the direction should be set aside, it may make any such order, or give any such relief, as may be made or given in judicial review proceedings.

(5) [[]]]References in this section to the Secretary of State are to the Secretary of State acting in person.]

Note: Section 2C inserted by s 15 Justice and Security Act 2013 from 25 April 2013. Words in curly brackets at subsection (1), (1)(a) & (2) substituted by Immigration and Social Security Co-ordination (EU Withdrawal) Act 2020 (Consequential, Saving, Transitional and Transitory Provisions) (EU Exit) Regulations 2020/1309 Pt 2 (1) reg.11(2)(a) (December 31, 2020 at 23.00 being the time and date 2020 c.20 Sch1 para 2(2) comes into force). Words in double brackets at subsection 5 omitted by Immigration and Social Security Co-ordination (EU Withdrawal) Act 2020 (Consequential, Saving, Transitional and Transitory Provisions)(EU Exit) Regulations 2020/1309 1309 Pt 2 (1) reg.11(2)(a) (December 31, 2020 at 23.00 being the time and date 2020 c.20 Sch1 para 2(2) comes into force).

[2D. Jurisdiction: review of certain naturalisation and citizenship decisions

(1) Subsection (2) applies in relation to any decision of the Secretary of State which—

(a) is either—

(i) a refusal to issue a certificate of naturalisation under section 6 of the British Nationality Act 1981 to an applicant under that section, or

(ii) a refusal to grant an application of the kind mentioned in section 41A of that Act (applications to register an adult or young person as a British citizen etc.), and

(b) is certified by the Secretary of State as a decision that was made wholly or partly in reliance on information which, in the opinion of the Secretary of State, should not be made public—

(i) in the interests of national security,

(ii) in the interests of the relationship between the United Kingdom and another country, or

(iii) otherwise in the public interest.

(2) The applicant to whom the decision relates may apply to the Special Immigration Appeals Commission to set aside the decision.

(3) In determining whether the decision should be set aside, the Commission must apply the principles which would be applied in judicial review proceedings.

(4) If the Commission decides that the decision should be set aside, it may make any such order, or give any such relief, as may be made or given in judicial review proceedings.]

Note: Section 2D inserted by s 15 Justice and Security Act 2013 from 25 April 2013.

[2E. Jurisdiction: review of certain deportation decisions

(1) Subsection (2) applies in relation to a relevant deportation decision which has been certified under section 97 or 97A(1) of the Nationality, Immigration and Asylum Act 2002 (certification on grounds of national security etc).

(2) The person to whom the decision relates may apply to the Special Immigration Appeals Commission to set aside the decision.

(3) In determining whether the decision should be set aside, the Commission must apply the principles which would be applied in judicial review proceedings.

(4) If the Commission decides that the decision should be set aside, it may make any such order, or give any such relief, as may be made or given in judicial review proceedings.

(5) In this section 'relevant deportation decision' means a decision of the Secretary of State about the deportation of a person from the United Kingdom, if and to the extent that—

(a) the decision is not subject to a right of appeal, or

(b) the decision (being subject to a right of appeal) gives rise to issues which may not be raised on such an appeal.]

Note: Section 2E inserted by s 18 Immigration Act 2014 from April 6, 2015.

[2F Jurisdiction: review of certain immigration decisions

(1) Subsection (2) applies in relation to any decision of the Secretary of State which—

(a) relates to a person's entitlement to enter, reside in or remain in the United Kingdom, or to a person's removal from the United Kingdom,

(b) is not subject—

(i) to a right of appeal, or

(ii) to a right under a provision other than subsection (2) to apply to the Special Immigration Appeals Commission for the decision to be set aside, and

(c) is certified by the Secretary of State acting in person as a decision that was made wholly or partly in reliance on information which, in the opinion of the Secretary of State, should not be made public—

(i) in the interests of national security,

(ii) in the interests of the relationship between the United Kingdom and another country, or

(iii) otherwise in the public interest.

(2) The person to whom the decision relates may apply to the Special Immigration Appeals Commission to set aside the decision.

(3) In determining whether the decision should be set aside, the Commission must apply the principles which would be applied in judicial review proceedings.

(4) If the Commission decides that the decision should be set aside, it may make any such order, or give any such relief, as may be made or given in judicial review proceedings.]

Note: inserted by Nationality and Borders Act 2022 c.36 Pt 6 s.77 (June 28, 2022)

3. Jurisdiction: bail

(1) In the case of a person to whom subsection (2) below applies, the provisions of [Schedule 10 to the Immigration Act 2016] specified in Schedule 3 to this Act shall have effect with the modifications set out there.

(2) This subsection applies to a person who is detained under the Immigration Act 1971 [or the Nationality, Immigration and Asylum Act 2002] if—

(a) the Secretary of State certifies that his detention is necessary in the interests of national security,

(b) he is detained following a decision to refuse him leave to enter the United Kingdom on the ground that his exclusion is in the interests of national security, or

(c) he is detained following a decision to make a deportation order against him on the ground that his deportation is in the interests of national security.

Note: Words in square brackets inserted from 4 April 2003 (SI 2003/1016). Words in square brackets substituted by Schedule 10, para 23 to the Immigration Act 2016 from January 15, 2018 subject to transitional provisions in SI2017/1241.

4. …

Note: Section 4 ceased to have effect from 1 April 2003 (SI 2003/754), Sch 7 Nationality, Immigration and Asylum Act 2002. Transitional provisions set out in SI 2003/754.

5. Procedure in relation to jurisdiction under sections 2 and 3

(1) The Lord Chancellor may make rules—

(a) for regulating the exercise of the rights of appeal conferred by section 2 [or 2B]… above,

(b) for prescribing the practice and procedure to be followed on or in connection with appeals under [section 2 [or 2B] …] above, including the mode and burden of proof and admissibility of evidence on such appeals, and

(c) for other matters preliminary or incidental to or arising out of such appeals, including proof of the decisions of the Special Immigration Appeals Commission.

(2) Rules under this section shall provide that an appellant has the right to be legally represented in any proceedings before the Commission on an appeal under section 2 [or 2B] […] above, subject to any power conferred on the Commission by such rules.

[(2A) Rules under this section may, in particular, do anything which may be done by [Tribunal Procedure Rules].

(3) Rules under this section may, in particular—

(a) make provision enabling proceedings before the Commission to take place without the appellant being given full particulars of the reasons for the decision which is the subject of the appeal,

(b) make provision enabling the Commission to hold proceedings in the absence of any person, including the appellant and any legal representative appointed by him,

(c) make provision about the functions in proceedings before the Commission of persons appointed under section 6 below, and

(d) make provision enabling the Commission to give the appellant a summary of any evidence taken in his absence.

(4) Rules under this section may also include provision—

(a) enabling any functions of the Commission which relate to matters preliminary or incidental to an appeal, or which are conferred by [Schedule 10 to the Immigration Act 2016], to be performed by a single member of the Commission, or

(b) conferring on the Commission such ancillary powers as the Lord Chancellor thinks necessary for the purposes of the exercise of its functions.

(5) The power to make rules under this section shall include power to make rules with respect to applications to the Commission under [Schedule 10 to the Immigration Act 2016] and matters arising out of such applications.

[(5A) Rules under this section must secure that, where the Commission has decided not to release a person [on immigration bail under Schedule 10 to the Immigration Act 2016], the Commission is required to dismiss any further application by the person for release on [immigration bail] that is made during the period of 28 days starting with the date of the Commission's decision, unless there has been a material change in circumstances.]

(6) In making rules under this section, the Lord Chancellor shall have regard, in particular, to—

(a) the need to secure that decisions which are the subject of appeals are properly reviewed, and

(b) the need to secure that information is not disclosed contrary to the public interest.

(7) …

(8) The power to make rules under this section shall be exercisable by statutory instrument.

(9) No rules shall be made under this section unless a draft of them has been laid before and approved by resolution of each House of Parliament.

Note: Subsection (7) omitted by Sch 5 Regulation of Investigatory Powers Act 2000 from 2 October 2002 (SI 2000/2543). Words deleted from and words in square brackets in subsections 5(1) and 5(2), and subsection 5(2A) inserted by Sch 7 Nationality, Immigration and Asylum Act 2002 from 1 April 2003 (SI 2003/754, which sets out transitional provisions). Words in square brackets in subsection (2A) substituted from 15 February 2010 (SI 2010/21). Subsection (5A) inserted by Sch 9 Immigration Act 2014 from 20 October 2014 with savings, SI 2014/2771 articles 9–11. Words in square brackets substituted by Sch 10 to the Immigration Act 2016 from 15 January 2018 subject to transitional provisions specified in SI 2017/1241.

6. Appointment of person to represent the appellant's interests

(1) The relevant law officer may appoint a person to represent the interests of an appellant in any proceedings before the Special Immigration Appeals Commission from which the appellant and any legal representative of his are excluded.

(2) For the purposes of subsection (1) above, the relevant law officer is—

(a) in relation to proceedings before the Commission in England and Wales, the Attorney General,

(b) in relation to proceedings before the Commission in Scotland, the Lord Advocate, and

(c) in relation to proceedings before the Commission in Northern Ireland, the Attorney General for Northern Ireland.

(3) A person appointed under subsection (1) above—

(a) if appointed for the purposes of proceedings in England and Wales, shall have a general qualification for the purposes of section 71 of the Courts and Legal Services Act 1990,

(b) if appointed for the purposes of proceedings in Scotland, shall be—

(i) an advocate, or

(ii) a solicitor who has by virtue of section 25A of the Solicitors (Scotland) Act 1980 rights of audience in the Court of Session and the High Court of Justiciary, and

(c) if appointed for the purposes of proceedings in Northern Ireland, shall be a member of the Bar of Northern Ireland.

(4) A person appointed under subsection (1) above shall not be responsible to the person whose interests he is appointed to represent.

[6A. Procedure in relation to jurisdiction under sections 2C [to [[2F]]

(1) Sections 5 and 6 apply in relation to reviews under section 2C [, 2D [[,2E or 2F]]] as they apply in relation to appeals under section 2 or 2B.

(2) Accordingly—

(a) references to appeals are to be read as references to reviews (and references to appeals under section 2 or 2B are to be read as references to reviews under section 2C [, 2D[[,2E or 2F]]]), and

(b) references to an appellant are to be read as references to an applicant under section 2C(2) [, 2D(2)[[.], 2E(2) or (as the case may be) 2F(2)]]]

Note: Section 6A inserted by Sch 2 Justice and Security Act 2013 from 26 June 2013 (SI 2013/1482). Words in square brackets substituted by Sch 9 Immigration Act 2014 from 20 October 2014 with savings set out in articles 9–11 SI 2014/2771. Words substituted in double square brackets in heading, subsection (1), & (2)(a) & (b) by Nationality and Borders Act 2022 c.36 s.77(a)(b)(c) & (d) (June 208, 2022).

7. Appeals from the Commission

(1) Where the Special Immigration Appeals Commission has made a final determination of an appeal, any party to the appeal may bring a further appeal to the appropriate appeal court on any question of law material to that determination.

[(1A) Where the Commission has made a final determination of a review under section 2C [[, 2D {,2E or 2F}]], any party to the review may bring an appeal against that determination to the appropriate appeal court.]

(2) An appeal under this section may be brought only with the leave of the Commission or, if such leave is refused, with the leave of the appropriate appeal court.

(3) In this section [[and sections 7B-7D]]'the appropriate appeal court' means—

(a) in relation to a determination made by the Commission in England and Wales, the Court of Appeal,

(b) in relation to a determination made by the Commission in Scotland, the Court of Session, and

(c) in relation to a determination made by the Commission in Northern Ireland, the Court of Appeal in Northern Ireland.

(4) . . .

Note: Section 7(4) omitted by Immigration and Asylum Act 1999 from 2 October 2000. Subsection (1A) inserted by Sch 2 Justice and Security Act 2013 from 26 June 2013 (SI 2013/1482). Words in double square brackets in subsection (1A) substituted by Sch 9 Immigration Act 2014 from a date to be appointed. Words in square brackets inserted at subsection (3) by Criminal Justice and Courts Act 2015 c.2 Pt 3 s 66(4) (June 28, 2018: insertion has effect on June 28, 2018 as SI 2018/732 art.2 subject to transitional provision as specified in SI 2018/732 art.3). Words substituted in curly brackets in subsection (1A) by Nationality and Borders Act 2022 c.36 Pt 6 s.77(4) (June 28, 2022: commenced by an amendment)

[7A. . . .]

Note: section 7A inserted by Immigration and Asylum Act 1999 from 2 October 2000. Omitted from 1 April 2003 (SI 2003/754), Sch 7 Nationality, Immigration and Asylum Act 2002. SI 2003/754 sets out transitional provisions.

[7B. Appeals to Supreme Court: grant of certificate by Commission

(1) If the Special Immigration Appeals Commission is satisfied that—

(a) the conditions in subsection (4) or (5) are fulfilled in relation to a final determination to which section 7(1) or (1A) applies, and

(b) in respect of that final determination, a sufficient case for an appeal to the Supreme Court has been made out to justify an application under section 7C,

the Commission may grant a certificate to that effect.

(2) The Commission may grant a certificate under this section only on an application made by a party to the appeal or review to which the final determination relates.

(3) The Commission may not grant a certificate under this section if the final determination is made by the Commission in Scotland.

(4) The conditions in this subsection are that a point of law of general public importance is involved in the final determination and that point of law is—

(a) a point of law that—

(i) relates wholly or mainly to the construction of an enactment or statutory instrument, and

(ii) has been fully argued in the proceedings on the appeal or review to which the final determination relates and fully considered in the judgment of the Commission, or

(b) a point of law—

(i) in respect of which the Commission is bound by a decision of the appropriate appeal court or the Supreme Court in previous proceedings, and

(ii) that was fully considered in the judgments given by the appropriate appeal court or, as the case may be, the Supreme Court in those previous proceedings.

(5) The conditions in this subsection are that a point of law of general public importance is involved in the final determination and that—

(a) the proceedings entail a decision relating to a matter of national importance or consideration of such a matter,

(b) the result of the proceedings is so significant (whether considered on its own or together with other proceedings or likely proceedings) that, in the opinion of the Commission, a hearing by the Supreme Court is justified, or

(c) the Commission is satisfied that the benefits of earlier consideration by the Supreme Court outweigh the benefits of consideration by the Court of Appeal.

(6) No appeal lies against the grant or refusal of a certificate under subsection (1).

Note: Inserted by Criminal Justice and Courts Act 2015 c.2 Pt 3 s 66(2) (June 28, 2018 as SI 2018/732 art.2 subject to transitional provision as specified in SI 2018/732 art.3).

7C. Appeals to Supreme Court: permission to appeal

(1) If the Special Immigration Appeals Commission grants a certificate under section 7B in relation to a final determination, a party to the appeal or review to which the final

determination relates may apply to the Supreme Court for permission to appeal directly to the Supreme Court.

(2) An application under subsection (1) must be made—

(a) within one month from the date on which that certificate is granted, or

(b) within such time as the Supreme Court may allow in a particular case.

(3) If on such an application it appears to the Supreme Court to be expedient to do so, the Supreme Court may grant permission for such an appeal.

(4) If permission is granted under this section—

(a) no appeal from the final determination to which the certificate relates lies to the appropriate appeal court, but

(b) an appeal lies from that determination to the Supreme Court.

(5) An application under subsection (1) is to be determined without a hearing.

(6) Subject to subsection (4), no appeal lies to the appropriate appeal court from a final determination of the Commission in respect of which a certificate is granted under section 7B until—

(a) the time within which an application can be made under subsection (1) has expired, and

(b) where such an application is made, that application has been determined in accordance with this section.

Note: Inserted by Criminal Justice and Courts Act 2015 c.2 Pt 3 s 66 (2) (June 28, 2018 as SI 2018/732 art.2 subject to transitional provision as specified in SI 2018/732 art.3).

7D. Appeals to Supreme Court: exclusions

(1) No certificate may be granted under section 7B in respect of a final determination of the Special Immigration Appeals Commission where, by virtue of any enactment (other than sections 7B and 7C), no appeal would lie from that decision of the Commission to the appropriate appeal court, with or without the leave or permission of the Commission or the appropriate appeal court.

(2) No certificate may be granted under section 7B in respect of a final determination of the Commission where, by virtue of any enactment, no appeal would lie from a decision of the appropriate appeal court on that determination of the Commission to the Supreme Court, with or without the permission or leave of the appropriate appeal court or the Supreme Court.

(3) Where no appeal would lie to the appropriate appeal court from a final determination of the Commission except with the leave or permission of the Commission or the appropriate appeal court, no certificate may be granted under section 7B in respect of a final determination unless it appears to the Commission that it would be a proper case for granting leave to appeal to the appropriate appeal court.

(4) No certificate may be granted under section 7B in respect of a decision or order of the Commission made by it in the exercise of its jurisdiction to punish for contempt.

Note: Inserted by Criminal Justice and Courts Act 2015 c.2 Pt 3 s66(2) (June 28, 2018 as SI 2018/732 art.2 subject to transitional provision as specified in SI 2018/732 art.3).

8. Procedure on applications to the Commission for leave to appeal [etc]

(1) The Lord Chancellor may make rules regulating, and prescribing the procedure to be followed on, applications to the Special Immigration Appeals Commission for leave to appeal under section 7 above [or for the grant of a certificate under section 7B.]

(2) Rules under this section may include provision enabling an application []to be heard by a single member of the Commission.

(3) The power to make rules under this section shall be exercisable by statutory instrument.

(4) No rules shall be made under this section unless a draft of them has been laid before and approved by resolution of each House of Parliament.

Note: Words inserted at heading and subsection (1) and omitted in subsection (2) by Criminal Justice and Courts Act 2015 c.2 Pt 3 s 66 (June 28, 2018: insertion has effect on June 28, 2018 as SI 2018/732 art.2 subject to transitional provision as specified in SI 2018/732 art.3).

9. Short title, commencement and extent

(1) This Act may be cited as the Special Immigration Appeals Commission Act 1997.

(2) This Act, except for this section, shall come into force on such day as the Secretary of State may by order made by statutory instrument appoint; and different days may be so appointed for different purposes.

(3) Her Majesty may by Order in Council direct that any of the provisions of this Act shall extend, with such modifications as appear to Her Majesty to be appropriate, to any of the Channel Islands or the Isle of Man.

(4) This Act extends to Northern Ireland.

Note: Commencement: s 9 on 17 December 1997, ss 5 and 8 on 11 June 1998, remainder of Act on 3 August 1998.

SCHEDULES

Section 1

SCHEDULE 1 *SCHEDULE 3*

THE COMMISSION

Members

1.—(1) The Special Immigration Appeals Commission shall consist of such number of members appointed by the Lord Chancellor as he may determine.

(2) A member of the Commission shall hold and vacate office in accordance with the terms of his appointment and shall, on ceasing to hold office, be eligible for reappointment.

(3) A member of the Commission may resign his office at any time by notice in writing to the Lord Chancellor.

Chairman

2. The Lord Chancellor shall appoint one of the members of the Commission to be its chairman.

Payments to members

3.—(1) The Lord Chancellor may pay to the members of the Commission such remuneration and allowances as he may determine.

(2) The Lord Chancellor may, if he thinks fit in the case of any member of the Commission, pay such pension, allowance or gratuity to or in respect of the member, or such sums towards the provision of such pension, allowance or gratuity, as he may determine.

(3) If a person ceases to be a member of the Commission and it appears to the Lord Chancellor that there are special circumstances which make it right that the person should receive compensation, he may pay to that person a sum of such amount as he may determine.

Proceedings

4. The Commission shall sit at such times and in such places as the Lord Chancellor may direct and may sit in two or more divisions.

5. The Commission shall be deemed to be duly constituted if it consists of three members of whom—

(a) at least one holds or has held high judicial office (within the meaning of [Part 3 of the Constitutional Reform Act 2005) or is or has been a member of the Judicial Committee of the Privy Council]), and

[(b) at least one is or has been [a judge of the First-tier Tribunal, or of the Upper Tribunal, who is assigned to a chamber with responsibility for immigration and asylum matters].

Note: Paragraph 5(b) substituted by Sch 2 Asylum and Immigration Act 2004 from 4 April 2005 (SI 2005/565). Words in first square brackets substituted from 1 October 2009 by Sch 17 Constitutional Reform Act 2005. Words in second square brackets substituted from 15 February 2010 (SI 2010/21).

6. The chairman or, in his absence, such other member of the Commission as he may nominate, shall preside at sittings of the Commission and report its decisions.

Staff

7. The Lord Chancellor may appoint such officers and servants for the Commission as he thinks fit.

Expenses

8. The Lord Chancellor shall defray the remuneration of persons appointed under paragraph 7 above and such expenses of the Commission as he thinks fit.

Section 2

SCHEDULE 2

APPEALS: SUPPLEMENTARY

...

Note: Schedule 2 ceased to have effect from 1 April 2003 (SI 2003/754), Sch 7 Nationality, Immigration and Asylum Act 2002. SI 2003/754 sets out transitional provisions.

[Section 3

SCHEDULE 3

BAIL: MODIFICATIONS OF SCHEDULE 10 TO THE IMMIGRATION ACT 2016

1. Paragraph 1(3) (power to grant bail) has effect as if—

(a) for 'The First-tier Tribunal' there were substituted 'The Special Immigration Appeals Commission', and

(b) for 'the Tribunal' there were substituted 'the Commission'.

2. Paragraph 2 (conditions of immigration bail) has effect as if—

(a) in sub-paragraphs (1)(a), (7) and (8) for 'the First-tier Tribunal' there were substituted 'the Special Immigration Appeals Commission', and

(b) in sub-paragraph (7) for 'the Tribunal' there were substituted 'the Commission'.

3. Paragraph 3 (exercise of power to grant immigration bail) has effect as if—

(a) in sub-paragraphs (1), (2)(f), (3), (4), (5) and (6) for 'the First-tier Tribunal' there were substituted 'the Special Immigration Appeals Commission', and

(b) in sub-paragraph (5) for 'the Tribunal' there were substituted 'the Commission'.

4. Paragraph 4(2)(d) (arrangements under electronic monitoring condition) has effect as if for 'the First-tier Tribunal' there were substituted 'the Special Immigration Appeals Commission'.

5. Paragraph 5(5) (payment of sum under financial condition) has effect as if for 'the First-tier Tribunal' there were substituted 'the Special Immigration Appeals Commission'.

6. Paragraph 6 (power to vary bail conditions) has effect as if—

(a) in sub-paragraphs (3), (4), (6) and (7) for 'the First-tier Tribunal' there were substituted 'the Special Immigration Appeals Commission',

(b) in sub-paragraph (5) for 'The First-tier Tribunal' there were substituted 'The Special Immigration Appeals Commission,', and

(c) in sub-paragraphs (3), (4) and (6) for 'the Tribunal' there were substituted 'the Commission'.

7. Paragraph 7(1)(a)(ii) (removal etc of electronic monitoring condition: bail managed by Secretary of State) has effect as if—

(a) for 'the First-tier Tribunal' there were substituted 'the Special Immigration Appeals Commission', and

(b) for 'the Tribunal' there were substituted 'the Commission'.

8. Paragraph 8 (amendment etc of electronic monitoring condition: bail managed by First-tier Tribunal) has effect as if—

(a) in sub-paragraphs (1)(a), (2), (3), (4) and (5) for 'the First-tier Tribunal' there were substituted 'the Special Immigration Appeals Commission', and

(b) in sub-paragraph (1)(a) for 'the Tribunal' there were substituted 'the Commission'.

9. Paragraph 10(10) (meaning of 'relevant authority') has effect as if for 'the First-tier Tribunal' in both places there were substituted 'the Special Immigration Appeals Commission'.']

Note: Schedule 3 substituted by Schedule 10 to the Immigration Act 2016 from 15 January 2018 (SI 2017/1241).

Crime (Sentences) Act 1997

(1997, c. 43)

32A. Removal of prisoners liable to removal from United Kingdom

(1) Where P—

(a) is a life prisoner in respect of whom a minimum term order has been made, and

(b) is liable to removal from the United Kingdom,

the Secretary of State may remove P from prison under this section at any time after P has served the relevant part of the sentence (whether or not the Parole Board has directed P's release under section 28).

(2) But if P is serving two or more life sentences—

(a) this section does not apply to P unless a minimum term order has been made in respect of each of those sentences; and

(b) the Secretary of State may not remove P from prison under this section until P has served the relevant part of each of them.

(3) If P is removed from prison under this section—

(a) P is so removed only for the purpose of enabling the Secretary of State to remove P from the United Kingdom under powers conferred by—

(i) Schedule 2 or 3 to the Immigration Act 1971, or

(ii) section 10 of the Immigration and Asylum Act 1999, and

(b) so long as remaining in the United Kingdom, P remains liable to be detained in pursuance of the sentence.

(4) So long as P, having been removed from prison under this section, remains in the United Kingdom but has not been returned to prison, any duty or power of the Secretary of State under section 28 or 30 is exercisable in relation to P as if P were in prison.

(5) In this section—

'liable to removal from the United Kingdom' has the meaning given by section 259 of the Criminal Justice Act 2003;

'the relevant part' has the meaning given by section 28.

Note: Sections 32A and 32B inserted from 1 May 2012 by the Legal Aid, Sentencing and Punishment of Offenders Act 2012, s 119.

32B. Re-entry into United Kingdom of offender removed from prison

(1) This section applies if P, having been removed from prison under section 32A, is removed from the United Kingdom.

(2) If P enters the United Kingdom—

(a) P is liable to be detained in pursuance of the sentence from the time of P's entry into the United Kingdom;

(b) if no direction was given by the Parole Board under subsection (5) of section 28 before P's removal from prison, that section applies to P;

(c) if such a direction was given before that removal, P is to be treated as if P had been recalled to prison under section 32.

(3) A person who is liable to be detained by virtue of subsection (2)(a) is, if at large, to be taken for the purposes of section 49 of the Prison Act 1952 (persons unlawfully at large) to be unlawfully at large.

(4) Subsection (2)(a) does not prevent P's further removal from the United Kingdom.

Note: Sections 32A and 32B inserted from 1 May 2012 by the Legal Aid, Sentencing and Punishment of Offenders Act 2012, s 119.

Human Rights Act 1998

(1998, c. 42)

Arrangement of Sections

Introduction

Schedules

An Act to give further effect to rights and freedoms guaranteed under the European Convention on Human Rights; to make provision with respect to holders of certain judicial offices who become judges of the European Court of Human Rights; and for connected purposes. [9 November 1998]

Introduction

1. The Convention Rights

(1) In this Act 'the Convention rights' means the rights and fundamental freedoms set out in—

(a) Articles 2 to 12 and 14 of the Convention,

(b) Articles 1 to 3 of the First Protocol, and

(c) [Article 1 of the Thirteenth Protocol] as read with Articles 16 to 18 of the Convention.

(2) Those Articles are to have effect for the purposes of this Act subject to any designated derogation or reservation (as to which see sections 14 and 15).

(3) The Articles are set out in Schedule 1.

(4) The [Secretary of State] may by order make such amendments to this Act as he considers appropriate to reflect the effect, in relation to the United Kingdom, of a protocol.

(5) In subsection (4) 'protocol' means a protocol to the Convention—

(a) which the United Kingdom has ratified; or

(b) which the United Kingdom has signed with a view to ratification.

(6) No amendment may be made by an order under subsection (4) so as to come into force before the protocol concerned is in force in relation to the United Kingdom.

Note: Commencement 2 October 2000. Words in square brackets in subsection (1)(c) substituted from 22 June 2004 (SI 2004/1574). Words in square brackets in subsection (4) substituted from 19 August 2003 (SI 2003/1887).

2. Interpretation of Convention Rights

(1) A court or tribunal determining a question which has arisen in connection with a Convention right must take into account any—

(a) judgment, decision, declaration or advisory opinion of the European Court of Human Rights,

(b) opinion of the Commission given in a report adopted under Article 31 of the Convention,

(c) decision of the Commission in connection with Article 26 or 27(2) of the Convention, or

(d) decision of the Committee of Ministers taken under Article 46 of the Convention, whenever made or given, so far as, in the opinion of the court or tribunal, it is relevant to the proceedings in which that question has arisen.

(2) Evidence of any judgment, decision, declaration or opinion of which account may have to be taken under this section is to be given in proceedings before any court or tribunal in such manner as may be provided by rules.

(3) In this section 'rules' means rules of court or, in the case of proceedings before a tribunal, rules made for the purposes of this section—

(a) by [the Lord Chancellor or] the Secretary of State, in relation to any proceedings outside Scotland;

(b) by the Secretary of State, in relation to proceedings in Scotland; or

(c) by a Northern Ireland department, in relation to proceedings before a tribunal in Northern Ireland—

(i) which deals with transferred matters; and

(ii) for which no rules made under paragraph (a) are in force.

Note: Commencement 2 October 2000. Words in square brackets in subsection (3)(a) omitted from 19 August 2003 (SI 2003/1887), re-inserted from 12 January 2006 (SI 2005/3429).

Legislation

3. Interpretation of legislation

(1) So far as it is possible to do so, primary legislation and subordinate legislation must be read and given effect in a way which is compatible with the Convention rights.

(2) This section—

(a) applies to primary legislation and subordinate legislation whenever enacted;

(b) does not affect the validity, continuing operation or enforcement of any incompatible primary legislation; and

(c) does not affect the validity, continuing operation or enforcement of any incompatible subordinate legislation if (disregarding any possibility of revocation) primary legislation prevents removal of the incompatibility.

Note: Commencement 2 October 2000.

4. Declaration of incompatibility

(1) Subsection (2) applies in any proceedings in which a court determines whether a provision of primary legislation is compatible with a Convention right.

(2) If the court is satisfied that the provision is incompatible with a Convention right, it may make a declaration of that incompatibility.

(3) Subsection (4) applies in any proceedings in which a court determines whether a provision of subordinate legislation, made in the exercise of a power conferred by primary legislation, is compatible with a Convention right.

(4) If the court is satisfied—

(a) that the provision is incompatible with a Convention right, and

(b) that (disregarding any possibility of revocation) the primary legislation concerned prevents removal of the incompatibility, it may make a declaration of that incompatibility.

(5) In this section 'court' means—

[(a) the Supreme Court;]

(b) the Judicial Committee of the Privy Council;

(c) the [Court Martial Appeal Court];

(d) in Scotland, the High Court of Justiciary sitting otherwise than as a trial court or the Court of Session;

(e) in England and Wales or Northern Ireland, the High Court or the Court of Appeal.

[(f) the Court of Protection, in any matter being dealt with by the President of the Family Division, the Vice-Chancellor or a puisne judge of the High Court.]

(6) A declaration under this section ('a declaration of incompatibility')—

(a) does not affect the validity, continuing operation or enforcement of the provision in respect of which it is given; and

(b) is not binding on the parties to the proceedings in which it is made.

Note: Commencement 2 October 2000. Subsection (5)(a) substituted by the Constitutional Reform Act 2005 Sch 9 from 1 October 2009 (SI 2009/1604). Words substituted in subsection (5)(c) by Armed Forces Act 2006 Sch 16 from 28 March 2009 (for certain purposes) (SI 2009/812) and from 31 October 2009 otherwise (SI 2009/1167). Subsection (5)(f) inserted by Mental Capacity Act 2005 Sch 6 from 1 October 2007 (SI 2007/1897).

5. Right of Crown to intervene

(1) Where a court is considering whether to make a declaration of incompatibility, the Crown is entitled to notice in accordance with rules of court.

(2) In any case to which subsection (1) applies—

(a) a Minister of the Crown (or a person nominated by him),

(b) a member of the Scottish Executive,

(c) a Northern Ireland Minister,

(d) a Northern Ireland department, is entitled, on giving notice in accordance with rules of court, to be joined as a party to the proceedings.

(3) Notice under subsection (2) may be given at any time during the proceedings.

(4) A person who has been made a party to criminal proceedings (other than in Scotland) as the result of a notice under subsection (2) may, with leave, appeal to [the Supreme Court] against any declaration of incompatibility made in the proceedings.

(5) In subsection (4)—

'criminal proceedings' includes all proceedings before the [Court-Martial Appeal Court]; and

'leave' means leave granted by the court making the declaration of incompatibility or by [the Supreme Court].

Note: Commencement 2 October 2000. Words 'the Supreme Court' substituted by the Constitutional Reform Act 2005 Sch 9 from 1 October 2009 (SI 2009/1604). Words 'Court Martial Appeal Court' substituted by Armed Forces Act 2006 Sch 16 from 28 March 2009 (for certain purposes) (SI 2009/812) and from 31 October 2009 otherwise (SI 2009/1167).

Public authorities

6. Acts of public authorities

(1) It is unlawful for a public authority to act in a way which is incompatible with a Convention right.

(2) Subsection (1) does not apply to an act if—

(a) as the result of one or more provisions of primary legislation, the authority could not have acted differently; or

(b) in the case of one or more provisions of, or made under, primary legislation which cannot be read or given effect in a way which is compatible with the Convention rights, the authority was acting so as to give effect to or enforce those provisions.

(3) In this section 'public authority' includes—

(a) a court or tribunal, and

(b) any person certain of whose functions are functions of a public nature, but does not include either House of Parliament or a person exercising functions in connection with proceedings in Parliament.

(4) …

(5) In relation to a particular act, a person is not a public authority by virtue only of subsection (3)(b) if the nature of the act is private.

(6) 'An act' includes a failure to act but does not include a failure to—

(a) introduce in, or lay before, Parliament a proposal for legislation; or

(b) make any primary legislation or remedial order.

Note: Commencement 2 October 2000. Subsection (4) deleted by the Constitutional Reform Act 2005 Sch 9 from 1 October 2009 (SI 2009/1604).

7. Proceedings

(1) A person who claims that a public authority has acted (or proposes to act) in a way which is made unlawful by section 6(1) may—

(a) bring proceedings against the authority under this Act in the appropriate court or tribunal, or

(b) rely on the Convention right or rights concerned in any legal proceedings, but only if he is (or would be) a victim of the unlawful act.

(2) In subsection (1)(a) 'appropriate court or tribunal' means such court or tribunal as may be determined in accordance with rules; and proceedings against an authority include a counterclaim or similar proceeding.

(3) If the proceedings are brought on an application for judicial review, the applicant is to be taken to have a sufficient interest in relation to the unlawful act only if he is, or would be, a victim of that act.

(4) If the proceedings are made by way of a petition for judicial review in Scotland, the applicant shall be taken to have title and interest to sue in relation to the unlawful act only if he is, or would be, a victim of that act.

(5) Proceedings under subsection (1)(a) must be brought before the end of—

(a) the period of one year beginning with the date on which the act complained of took place; or

(b) such longer period as the court or tribunal considers equitable having regard to all the circumstances, but that is subject to any rule imposing a stricter time limit in relation to the procedure in question.

(6) In subsection (1)(b) 'legal proceedings' includes—

(a) proceedings brought by or at the instigation of a public authority; and

(b) an appeal against the decision of a court or tribunal.

(7) For the purposes of this section, a person is a victim of an unlawful act only if he would be a victim for the purposes of Article 34 of the Convention if proceedings were brought in the European Court of Human Rights in respect of that act.

(8) Nothing in this Act creates a criminal offence.

(9) In this section 'rules' means—

(a) in relation to proceedings before a court or tribunal outside Scotland, rules made by [the Lord Chancellor or] the Secretary of State for the purposes of this section or rules of court,

(b) in relation to proceedings before a court or tribunal in Scotland, rules made by the Secretary of State for those purposes,

(c) in relation to proceedings before a tribunal in Northern Ireland—

(i) which deals with transferred matters; and

(ii) for which no rules made under paragraph (a) are in force, rules made by a Northern Ireland department for those purposes, and includes provision made by order under section 1 of the Courts and Legal Services Act 1990.

(10) In making rules, regard must be had to section 9.

(11) The Minister who has power to make rules in relation to a particular tribunal may, to the extent he considers it necessary to ensure that the tribunal can provide an appropriate remedy in relation to an act (or proposed act) of a public authority which is (or would be) unlawful as a result of section 6(1), by order add to—

(a) the relief or remedies which the tribunal may grant; or

(b) the grounds on which it may grant any of them.

(12) An order made under subsection (11) may contain such incidental, supplemental, consequential or transitional provision as the Minister making it considers appropriate.

(13) 'The Minister' includes the Northern Ireland department concerned.

Note: Commencement 2 October 2000. Words in square brackets in subsection (9)(a) omitted from 19 August 2003 (SI 2003/1887), re-inserted from 12 January 2006 (SI 2005/3429).

7A Limitation: overseas armed forces proceedings

(1) A court or tribunal exercising its discretion under section 7(5)(b) in respect of overseas armed forces proceedings must do so—

(a) in accordance with subsection (2), and

(b) subject to the rule in subsection (4).

(2) The court or tribunal must have particular regard to—

(a) the effect of the delay in bringing proceedings on the cogency of evidence adduced or likely to be adduced by the parties, with particular reference to—

(i) the likely impact of the operational context on the ability of individuals who are (or, at the time of the events to which the proceedings relate, were) members of Her Majesty's forces to remember relevant events or actions fully or accurately, and

(ii) the extent of dependence on the memories of such individuals, taking into account the effect of the operational context on the ability of such individuals to record, or to retain records of, relevant events or actions;

(b) the likely impact of the proceedings on the mental health of any witness or potential witness who is (or, at the time of the events to which the proceedings relate, was) a member of Her Majesty's forces.

(3) In subsection (2) references to "the operational context" are to the fact that the events to which the proceedings relate took place in the context of overseas operations, and include references to the exceptional demands and stresses to which members of Her Majesty's forces are subject.

(4) The rule referred to in subsection (1)(b) is that overseas armed forces proceedings must be brought before the later of—

(a) the end of the period of 6 years beginning with the date on which the act complained of took place;

(b) the end of the period of 12 months beginning with the date of knowledge.

(5) In subsection (4), the "date of knowledge" means the date on which the person bringing the proceedings first knew, or first ought to have known, both—

(a) of the act complained of, and

(b) that it was an act of the Ministry of Defence or the Secretary of State for Defence.

(6) "Overseas armed forces proceedings" means proceedings—

(a) against the Ministry of Defence or the Secretary of State for Defence, and

(b) in connection with overseas operations.

(7) "Overseas operations" means any operations outside the British Islands, including peacekeeping operations and operations for dealing with terrorism, civil unrest or serious public disorder, in the course of which members of Her Majesty's forces come under attack or face the threat of attack or violent resistance.

(8) In this section the reference to the British Islands includes the territorial sea adjacent to the United Kingdom and the territorial sea adjacent to any of the Channel Islands or the Isle of Man.

(9) In this section "Her Majesty's forces" has the same meaning as in the Armed Forces Act 2006 (see section 374 of that Act).

Note: inserted by Overseas Operations (Service Personal and Veterans) Act 2021 c.23 Pt2 s.11(2) (June 30, 2021)

8. Judicial remedies

(1) In relation to any act (or proposed act) of a public authority which the court finds is (or would be) unlawful, it may grant such relief or remedy, or make such order, within its powers as it considers just and appropriate.

(2) But damages may be awarded only by a court which has power to award damages, or to order the payment of compensation, in civil proceedings.

(3) No award of damages is to be made unless, taking account of all the circumstances of the case, including—

(a) any other relief or remedy granted, or order made, in relation to the act in question (by that or any other court), and

(b) the consequences of any decision (of that or any other court) in respect of that act, the court is satisfied that the award is necessary to afford just satisfaction to the person in whose favour it is made.

(4) In determining—

(a) whether to award damages, or

(b) the amount of an award, the court must take into account the principles applied by the European Court of Human Rights in relation to the award of compensation under Article 41 of the Convention.

(5) A public authority against which damages are awarded is to be treated—

(a) in Scotland, for the purposes of section 3 of the Law Reform (Miscellaneous Provisions) (Scotland) Act 1940 as if the award were made in an action of damages in which the authority has been found liable in respect of loss or damage to the person to whom the award is made;

(b) for the purposes of the Civil Liability (Contribution) Act 1978 as liable in respect of damage suffered by the person to whom the award is made.

(6) In this section—

'court' includes a tribunal;

'damages' means damages for an unlawful act of a public authority; and

'unlawful' means unlawful under section 6(1).

Note: Commencement 2 October 2000.

9. Judicial acts

(1) Proceedings under section 7(1)(a) in respect of a judicial act may be brought only—

(a) by exercising a right of appeal;

(b) on an application (in Scotland a petition) for judicial review; or

(c) in such other forum as may be prescribed by rules.

(2) That does not affect any rule of law which prevents a court from being the subject of judicial review.

(3) In proceedings under this Act in respect of a judicial act done in good faith, damages may not be awarded otherwise than—

(a) to compensate a person to the extent required by Article 5(5) of the Convention, or

(b) to compensate a person for a judicial act that is incompatible with Article 6 of the Convention in circumstances where the person is detained and, but for the incompatibility, the person would not have been detained or would not have been detained for so long.

(4) An award of damages permitted by subsection (3) is to be made against the Crown; but no award may be made unless the appropriate person, if not a party to the proceedings, is joined.

(5) In this section—

'appropriate person' means the Minister responsible for the court concerned, or a person or government department nominated by him;

'court' includes a tribunal;

'judge' includes a member of a tribunal, a justice of the peace [(or, in Northern Ireland, a lay magistrate)] and a clerk or other officer entitled to exercise the jurisdiction of a court;

'judicial act' means a judicial act of a court and includes an act done on the instructions, or on behalf, of a judge; and 'rules' has the same meaning as in section 7(9).

Note: Commencement 2 October 2000. Words in square brackets in subsection (5) inserted (NI) by Justice (Northern Ireland) Act 2002 Sch 4 from 1 April 2005 (SR 2005/109). Words substituted at subsection 3 by art.2(1) of Human Rights Act (Remedial) Order 2020 from 21 October 2020.

Remedial action

10. Power to take remedial action

(1) This section applies if—

(a) a provision of legislation has been declared under section 4 to be incompatible with a Convention right and, if an appeal lies—

(i) all persons who may appeal have stated in writing that they do not intend to do so;

(ii) the time for bringing an appeal has expired and no appeal has been brought within that time; or

(iii) an appeal brought within that time has been determined or abandoned; or

(b) it appears to a Minister of the Crown or Her Majesty in Council that, having regard to a finding of the European Court of Human Rights made after the coming into force of this section in proceedings against the United Kingdom, a provision of legislation is incompatible with an obligation of the United Kingdom arising from the Convention.

(2) If a Minister of the Crown considers that there are compelling reasons for proceeding under this section, he may by order make such amendments to the legislation as he considers necessary to remove the incompatibility.

(3) If, in the case of subordinate legislation, a Minister of the Crown considers—

(a) that it is necessary to amend the primary legislation under which the subordinate legislation in question was made, in order to enable the incompatibility to be removed, and

(b) that there are compelling reasons for proceeding under this section, he may by order make such amendments to the primary legislation as he considers necessary.

(4) This section also applies where the provision in question is in subordinate legislation and has been quashed, or declared invalid, by reason of incompatibility with a Convention right and the Minister proposes to proceed under paragraph 2(b) of Schedule 2.

(5) If the legislation is an Order in Council, the power conferred by subsection (2) or (3) is exercisable by Her Majesty in Council.

(6) In this section 'legislation' does not include a Measure of the Church Assembly or of the General Synod of the Church of England.

(7) Schedule 2 makes further provision about remedial orders.

Note: Commencement 2 October 2000.

Other rights and proceedings

11. Safeguard for existing human rights

A person's reliance on a Convention right does not restrict—

(a) any other right or freedom conferred on him by or under any law having effect in any part of the United Kingdom; or

(b) his right to make any claim or bring any proceedings which he could make or bring apart from sections 7 to 9.

Note: Commencement 2 October 2000.

12. Freedom of expression

(1) This section applies if a court is considering whether to grant any relief which, if granted, might affect the exercise of the Convention right to freedom of expression.

(2) If the person against whom the application for relief is made ('the respondent') is neither present nor represented, no such relief is to be granted unless the court is satisfied—

(a) that the applicant has taken all practicable steps to notify the respondent; or

(b) that there are compelling reasons why the respondent should not be notified.

(3) No such relief is to be granted so as to restrain publication before trial unless the court is satisfied that the applicant is likely to establish that publication should not be allowed.

(4) The court must have particular regard to the importance of the Convention right to freedom of expression and, where the proceedings relate to material which the respondent claims, or which appears to the court, to be journalistic, literary or artistic material (or to conduct connected with such material), to—

(a) the extent to which—

(i) the material has, or is about to, become available to the public; or

(ii) it is, or would be, in the public interest for the material to be published;

(b) any relevant privacy code.

(5) In this section—

'court' includes a tribunal; and

'relief' includes any remedy or order (other than in criminal proceedings).

Note: Commencement 2 October 2000.

13. Freedom of thought, conscience and religion

(1) If a court's determination of any question arising under this Act might affect the exercise by a religious organisation (itself or its members collectively) of the Convention right to freedom of thought, conscience and religion, it must have particular regard to the importance of that right.

(2) In this section 'court' includes a tribunal.

Note: Commencement 2 October 2000.

Derogations and reservations

14. *Derogations*

(1) In this Act 'designated derogation' means [...] any derogation by the United Kingdom from an Article of the Convention, or of any protocol to the Convention, which is designated for the purposes of this Act in an order made by the [Secretary of State].

(2) ...

(3) If a designated derogation is amended or replaced it ceases to be a designated derogation.

(4) But subsection (3) does not prevent the Secretary of State from exercising his power under subsection (1)[...] to make a fresh designation order in respect of the Article concerned.

(5) The Secretary of State must by order make such amendments to Schedule 3 as he considers appropriate to reflect—

(a) any designation order; or

(b) the effect of subsection (3).

(6) A designation order may be made in anticipation of the making by the United Kingdom of a proposed derogation.

Note: Commencement 2 October 2000. Words omitted from 1 April 2001 (SI 2001/1216). Words in square brackets in subsection (4) substituted from 19 August 2003 (SI 2003/1887).

15. Reservations

(1) In this Act 'designated reservation' means—

(a) the United Kingdom's reservation to Article 2 of the First Protocol to the Convention; and

(b) any other reservation by the United Kingdom to an Article of the Convention, or of any protocol to the Convention, which is designated for the purposes of this Act in an order made by the [Secretary of State].

(2) The text of the reservation referred to in subsection (1)(a) is set out in Part II of Schedule 3.

(3) If a designated reservation is withdrawn wholly or in part it ceases to be a designated reservation.

(4) But subsection (3) does not prevent the [Secretary of State] from exercising his power under subsection (1)(b) to make a fresh designation order in respect of the Article concerned.

(5) The [Secretary of State] must by order make such amendments to this Act as he considers appropriate to reflect—

(a) any designation order; or

(b) the effect of subsection (3).

Note: Commencement 2 October 2000. Words in square brackets substituted from 19 August 2003 (SI 2003/1887).

16. Period for which designated derogations have effect

(1) If it has not already been withdrawn by the United Kingdom, a designated derogation ceases to have effect for the purposes of this Act—

[. . .] at the end of the period of five years beginning with the date on which the order designation was made.

(2) At any time before the period—

(a) fixed by subsection (1)... or

(b) extended by an order under this subsection, comes to an end, the [Secretary of State] may by order extend it by a further period of five years.

(3) An order under section 14(1)... ceases to have effect at the end of the period for consideration, unless a resolution has been passed by each House approving the order.

(4) Subsection (3) does not affect—

(a) anything done in reliance on the order; or

(b) the power to make a fresh order under section 14(1)[...].

(5) In subsection (3) 'period for consideration' means the period of forty days beginning with the day on which the order was made.

(6) In calculating the period for consideration, no account is to be taken of any time during which—

(a) Parliament is dissolved or prorogued; or

(b) both Houses are adjourned for more than four days.

(7) If a designated derogation is withdrawn by the United Kingdom, the [Secretary of State] must by order make such amendments to this Act as he considers are required to reflect that withdrawal.

Note: Commencement 2 October 2000. Words omitted from 1 April 2001 (SI 2001/1216). Words in square brackets substituted from 19 August 2003 (SI 2003/1887).

17. Periodic review of designated reservations

(1) The appropriate Minister must review the designated reservation referred to in section 15(1)(a)—

(a) before the end of the period of five years beginning with the date on which section 1(2) came into force; and

(b) if that designation is still in force, before the end of the period of five years beginning with the date on which the last report relating to it was laid under subsection (3).

(2) The appropriate Minister must review each of the other designated reservations (if any)—

(a) before the end of the period of five years beginning with the date on which the order designating the reservation first came into force; and

(b) if the designation is still in force, before the end of the period of five years beginning with the date on which the last report relating to it was laid under subsection (3).

(3) The Minister conducting a review under this section must prepare a report on the result of the review and lay a copy of it before each House of Parliament.

Note: Commencement 2 October 2000.

Judges of the European Court of Human Rights

18. Appointment to European Court of Human Rights

(1) In this section 'judicial office' means the office of—

(a) Lord Justice of Appeal, Justice of the High Court or Circuit judge, in England and Wales;

(b) judge of the Court of Session or sheriff, in Scotland;

(c) Lord Justice of Appeal, judge of the High Court or county court judge, in Northern Ireland.

(2) The holder of a judicial office may become a judge of the European Court of Human Rights ('the Court') without being required to relinquish his office.

(3) But he is not required to perform the duties of his judicial office while he is a judge of the Court.

(4) In respect of any period during which he is a judge of the Court—

(a) a Lord Justice of Appeal or Justice of the High Court is not to count as a judge of the relevant court for the purposes of section 2(1) or 4(1) of the [the Senior Courts Act 1981] (maximum number of judges) nor as a judge of the [Senior Courts] for the purposes of section 12(1) to (6) of that Act (salaries etc.);

(b) a judge of the Court of Session is not to count as a judge of that court for the purposes of section 1(1) of the Court of Session Act 1988 (maximum number of judges) or of section 9(1)(c) of the Administration of Justice Act 1973 ('the 1973 Act') (salaries etc.);

(c) a Lord Justice of Appeal or judge of the High Court in Northern Ireland is not to count as a judge of the relevant court for the purposes of section 2(1) or 3(1) of the Judicature (Northern Ireland) Act 1978 (maximum number of judges) nor as a judge of the [Court of Judicature] of Northern Ireland for the purposes of section 9(1)(d) of the 1973 Act (salaries etc.);

(d) a Circuit judge is not to count as such for the purposes of section 18 of the Court Act 1971 (salaries etc.);

(e) a sheriff is not to count as such for the purposes of section 14 of the Sheriff Courts (Scotland) Act 1907 (salaries etc.);

(f) a county court judge of Northern Ireland is not to count as such for the purposes of section 106 of the County Courts Act (Northern Ireland) 1959 (salaries etc.).

(5) If a sheriff principal is appointed a judge of the Court, section 11(1) of the Sheriff Courts (Scotland) Act 1971 (temporary appointment of sheriff principal) applies, while he holds that appointment, as if his office is vacant.

(6) Schedule 4 makes provision about judicial pensions in relation to the holder of a judicial office who serves as a judge of the Court.

(7) The Lord Chancellor or the Secretary of State may by order make such transitional provision (including, in particular, provision for a temporary increase in the maximum number of judges) as he considers appropriate in relation to any holder of a judicial office who has completed his service as a judge of the Court.

[(7A) The following paragraphs apply to the making of an order under subsection (7) in relation to any holder of a judicial office listed in subsection (1)(a)—

(a) before deciding what transitional provision it is appropriate to make, the person making the order must consult the Lord Chief Justice of England and Wales;

(b) before making the order, that person must consult the Lord Chief Justice of England and Wales.

(7B) The following paragraphs apply to the making of an order under subsection (7) in relation to any holder of a judicial office listed in subsection (1)(c)—

(a) before deciding what transitional provision it is appropriate to make, the person making the order must consult the Lord Chief Justice of Northern Ireland;

(b) before making the order, that person must consult the Lord Chief Justice of Northern Ireland.

(7C) The Lord Chief Justice of England and Wales may nominate a judicial office holder (within the meaning of section 109(4) of the Constitutional Reform Act 2005) to exercise his functions under this section.

(7D) The Lord Chief Justice of Northern Ireland may nominate any of the following to exercise his functions under this section—

(a) the holder of one of the offices listed in Schedule 1 to the Justice (Northern Ireland) Act 2002;

(b) a Lord Justice of Appeal (as defined in section 88 of that Act).]

Note: Commencement 9 November 1998. Subsections (7A)–(7D) inserted by Sch 4 Constitutional Reform Act from 3 April 2006 (SI 2006/1014). Words in subsection (4) substituted by Constitutional Reform Act 2005 Sch 11 from 1 October 2009 (SI 2009/1604).

Parliamentary procedure

19. Statements of compatibility

(1) A Minister of the Crown in charge of a Bill in either House of Parliament must, before Second Reading of the Bill—

(a) make a statement to the effect that in his view the provisions of the Bill are compatible with the Convention rights ('a statement of compatibility'); or

(b) make a statement to the effect that although he is unable to make a statement of compatibility the government nevertheless wishes the House to proceed with the Bill.

(2) The statement must be in writing and be published in such manner as the Minister making it considers appropriate.

Note: Commencement 24 November 1998.

Supplemental

20. Orders etc. under this Act

(1) Any power of a Minister of the Crown to make an order under this Act is exercisable by statutory instrument.

(2) The power of [the Lord Chancellor or] the Secretary of State to make rules (other than rules of court) under section 2(3) or 7(9) is exercisable by statutory instrument.

(3) Any statutory instrument made under section 14, 15 or 16(7) must be laid before Parliament.

(4) No order may be made by [the Lord Chancellor or] the Secretary of State under section 1(4), 7(11) or 16(2) unless a draft of the order has been laid before, and approved by, each House of Parliament.

(5) Any statutory instrument made under section 18(7) or Schedule 4, or to which subsection (2) applies, shall be subject to annulment in pursuance of a resolution of either House of Parliament.

(6) The power of a Northern Ireland department to make—

(a) rules under section 2(3)(c) or 7(9)(c), or

(b) an order under section 7(11), is exercisable by statutory rule for the purposes of the Statutory Rules (Northern Ireland) Order 1979.

(7) Any rules made under section 2(3)(c) or 7(9)(c) shall be subject to negative resolution; and section 41(6) of the Interpretation Act (Northern Ireland) 1954 (meaning of 'subject to negative resolution') shall apply as if the power to make the rules were conferred by an Act of the Northern Ireland Assembly.

(8) No order may be made by a Northern Ireland department under section 7(11) unless a draft of the order has been laid before, and approved by, the Northern Ireland Assembly.

Note: Commencement 9 November 1998. Words in square brackets omitted from 19 August 2003 (SI 2003/1887), re-inserted from 12 January 2006 (SI 2005/3429).

21. Interpretation, etc.

(1) In this Act—

'amend' includes repeal and apply (with or without modifications);

'the appropriate Minister' means the Minister of the Crown having charge of the appropriate authorised government department (within the meaning of the Crown Proceedings Act 1947);

'the Commission' means the European Commission of Human Rights;

'the Convention' means the Convention for the Protection of Human Rights and Fundamental Freedoms, agreed by the Council of Europe at Rome on 4 November 1950 as it has effect for the time being in relation to the United Kingdom;

'declaration of incompatibility' means a declaration under section 4;

'Minister of the Crown' has the same meaning as in the Ministers of the Crown Act 1975;

'Northern Ireland Minister' includes the First Minister and the deputy First Minister in Northern Ireland;

'primary legislation' means any—

(a) public general Act;
(b) local and personal Act;
(c) private Act;
(d) Measure of the Church Assembly;
(e) Measure of the General Synod of the Church of England;
(f) Order in Council—
(i) made in exercise of Her Majesty's Royal Prerogative;
(ii) made under section 38(1)(a) of the Northern Ireland Constitution Act 1973 or the corresponding provision of the Northern Ireland Act 1998; or
(iii) amending an Act of a kind mentioned in paragraph (a), (b) or (c);

and includes an order or other instrument made under primary legislation (otherwise than by the [Welsh Ministers, the First Minister for Wales, the Counsel General to the Welsh Assembly Government,] a member of the Scottish Executive, a Northern Ireland Minister or a Northern Ireland department) to the extent to which it operates to bring one or more provisions of that legislation into force or amends any primary legislation;

'the First Protocol' means the protocol to the Convention agreed at Paris on 20 March 1952;

. . .

'the Eleventh Protocol' means the protocol to the Convention (restructuring the control machinery established by the Convention) agreed at Strasbourg on 11 May 1994;

['the Thirteenth Protocol' means the protocol to the Convention (concerning the abolition of the death penalty in all circumstances) agreed at Vilnius on 3 May 2002;]

'remedial order' means an order under section 10;

'subordinate legislation' means any—

(a) Order in Council other than one—

(i) made in exercise of Her Majesty's Royal Prerogative;

(ii) made under section 38(1)(a) of the Northern Ireland Constitution Act 1973 or the corresponding provision of the Northern Ireland Act 1998; or

(iii) amending an Act of a kind mentioned in the definition of primary legislation;

(b) Act of the Scottish Parliament;

[(ba) Measure of the National Assembly for Wales;

(bb) Act of the National Assembly for Wales;]

(c) Act of the Parliament of Northern Ireland;

(d) Measure of the Assembly established under section 1 of the Northern Ireland Assembly Act 1973;

(e) Act of the Northern Ireland Assembly;

(f) order, rules, regulations, scheme, warrant, byelaw or other instrument made under primary legislation (except to the extent to which it operates to bring one or more provisions of that legislation into force or amends any primary legislation);

(g) order, rules, regulations, scheme, warrant, byelaw or other instrument made under legislation mentioned in paragraph (b), (c), (d) or (e) or made under an Order in Council applying only to Northern Ireland;

(h) order, rules, regulations, scheme, warrant, byelaw or other instrument made by a member of the Scottish Executive, [Welsh Ministers, the First Minister for Wales, the Counsel General to the Welsh Assembly Government,] a Northern Ireland Minister or a Northern Ireland department in exercise of prerogative or other executive functions of Her Majesty which are exercisable by such a person on behalf of Her Majesty;

'transferred matters' has the same meaning as in the Northern Ireland Act 1998; and

'tribunal' means any tribunal in which legal proceedings may be brought.

(2) The references in paragraphs (b) and (c) of section 2(1) to Articles are to Articles of the Convention as they had effect immediately before the coming into force of the Eleventh Protocol.

(3) The reference in paragraph (d) of section 2(1) to Article 46 includes a reference to Articles 32 and 54 of the Convention as they had effect immediately before the coming into force of the Eleventh Protocol.

(4) The references in section 2(1) to a report or decision of the Commission or a decision of the Committee of Ministers include references to a report or decision made as provided by paragraphs 3, 4 and 6 of Article 5 of the Eleventh Protocol (transitional provisions).

(5) ...

Note: Commencement of s 21(5) on 9 November 1998, remainder of s 21 on 2 October 2000. Words omitted and second words in square brackets in subsection (1) substituted by SI 2004/1574 from 22 June 2004. Other words in square brackets substituted from 4 May 2007, Government of Wales Act 2006, s 160. Subsection (5) omitted from 31 October 2009 by Sch 17 Armed Forces Act 2006.

22. Short title, commencement, application and extent

(1) This Act may be cited as the Human Rights Act 1998.

(2) Sections 18, 20 and 21(5) and this section come into force on the passing of this Act.

(3) The other provisions of this Act come into force on such day as the Secretary of State may by order appoint; and different days may be appointed for different purposes.

(4) Paragraph (b) of subsection (1) of section 7 applies to proceedings brought by or at the instigation of a public authority whenever the act in question took place; but otherwise that subsection does not apply to an act taking place before the coming into force of that section.

(4A) Section 7A (limitation: overseas armed forces proceedings) applies to proceedings brought under section 7(1)(a) on or after the date on which section 7A comes into force, whenever the act in question took place.

(5) This Act binds the Crown.

(6) This Act extends to Northern Ireland.

(7) …

Note: Commencement 9 November 1998. Subsection (7) deleted by Armed Forces Act 2006 Sch 17 from 28 March 2009 (for certain purposes) (SI 2009/812) and from 31 October 2009 otherwise (SI 2009/1167). Subsection (4A) inserted by Overseas Operations (Service Personnel and Veterans) Act 2021 c.23 Pt2 s.11(3) (June 30, 2021)

Schedules

Section 1(3)

Schedule 1

The Articles

Part I

The Convention

Rights and Freedoms

Article 2 *Right to life*

1. Everyone's right to life shall be protected by law. No one shall be deprived of his life intentionally save in the execution of a sentence of a court following his conviction of a crime for which this penalty is provided by law.

2. Deprivation of life shall not be regarded as inflicted in contravention of this Article when it results from the use of force which is no more than absolutely necessary:

(a) in defence of any person from unlawful violence;

(b) in order to effect a lawful arrest or to prevent the escape of a person lawfully detained;

(c) in action lawfully taken for the purpose of quelling a riot or insurrection.

Article 3 *Prohibition of torture*

No one shall be subjected to torture or to inhuman or degrading treatment or punishment.

Article 4 *Prohibition of slavery and forced labour*

1. No one shall be held in slavery or servitude.

2. No one shall be required to perform forced or compulsory labour.

3. For the purpose of this Article the term 'forced or compulsory labour' shall not include:

(a) any work required to be done in the ordinary course of detention imposed according to the provisions of Article 5 of this Convention or during conditional release from such detention;

(b) any service of a military character or, in case of conscientious objectors in countries where they are recognised, service exacted instead of compulsory military service;

(c) any service exacted in case of an emergency or calamity threatening the life or well-being of the community;

(d) any work or service which forms part of normal civic obligations.

Article 5 *Right to liberty and security*

1. Everyone has the right to liberty and security of person. No one shall be deprived of his liberty save in the following cases and in accordance with a procedure prescribed by law:

(a) the lawful detention of a person after conviction by a competent court;

(b) the lawful arrest or detention of a person for non-compliance with the lawful order of a court or in order to secure the fulfilment of any obligation prescribed by law;

(c) the lawful arrest or detention of a person effected for the purpose of bringing him before the competent legal authority on reasonable suspicion of having committed an offence or when it is reasonably considered necessary to prevent his committing an offence or fleeing after having done so;

(d) the detention of a minor by lawful order for the purpose of educational supervision or his lawful detention for the purpose of bringing him before the competent legal authority;

(e) the lawful detention of persons for the prevention of the spreading of infectious diseases, of persons of unsound mind, alcoholics or drug addicts or vagrants;

(f) the lawful arrest or detention of a person to prevent his effecting an unauthorised entry into the country or of a person against whom action is being taken with a view to deportation or extradition.

2. Everyone who is arrested shall be informed promptly, in a language which he understands, of the reasons for his arrest and of any charge against him.

3. Everyone arrested or detained in accordance with the provisions of paragraph 1(c) of this Article shall be brought promptly before a judge or other officer authorised by law to exercise judicial power and shall be entitled to trial within a reasonable time or to release pending trial. Release may be conditioned by guarantees to appear for trial.

4. Everyone who is deprived of his liberty by arrest or detention shall be entitled to take proceedings by which the lawfulness of his detention shall be decided speedily by a court and his release ordered if the detention is not lawful.

5. Everyone who has been the victim of arrest or detention in contravention of the provisions of this Article shall have an enforceable right to compensation.

Article 6 *Right to a fair trial*

1. In the determination of his civil rights and obligations or of any criminal charge against him, everyone is entitled to a fair and public hearing within a reasonable time by an independent and impartial tribunal established by law. Judgment shall be pronounced publicly but the press and public may be excluded from all or part of the trial in the interest of morals, public order or national security in a democratic society, where the interests of juveniles or the protection of the private life of the parties so require, or to the extent strictly necessary in the opinion of the court in special circumstances where publicity would prejudice the interests of justice.

2. Everyone charged with a criminal offence shall be presumed innocent until proved guilty according to law.

3. Everyone charged with a criminal offence has the following minimum rights:

(a) to be informed promptly, in a language which he understands and in detail, of the nature and cause of the accusation against him;

(b) to have adequate time and facilities for the preparation of his defence;

(c) to defend himself in person or through legal assistance of his own choosing or, if he has not sufficient means to pay for legal assistance, to be given it free when the interests of justice so require;

(d) to examine or have examined witnesses against him and to obtain the attendance and examination of witnesses on his behalf under the same conditions as witnesses against him;

(e) to have the free assistance of an interpreter if he cannot understand or speak the language used in court.

Article 7 *No punishment without law*

1. No one shall be held guilty of any criminal offence on account of any act or omission which did not constitute a criminal offence under national or international law at the time when it was committed. Nor shall a heavier penalty be imposed than the one that was applicable at the time the criminal offence was committed.

2. This Article shall not prejudice the trial and punishment of any person for any act or omission which, at the time when it was committed, was criminal according to the general principles of law recognised by civilised nations.

Article 8 *Right to respect for private and family life*

1. Everyone has the right to respect for his private and family life, his home and his correspondence.

2. There shall be no interference by a public authority with the exercise of this right except such as is in accordance with the law and is necessary in a democratic society in the interests of national security, public safety or the economic well being of the country, for the prevention of disorder or crime, for the protection of health or morals, or for the protection of the rights and freedoms of others.

Article 9 *Freedom of thought, conscience and religion*

1. Everyone has the right to freedom of thought, conscience and religion; this right includes freedom to change his religion or belief and freedom, either alone or in community with others and in public or private, to manifest his religion or belief, in worship, teaching, practice and observance.

2. Freedom to manifest one's religion or beliefs shall be subject only to such limitations as are prescribed by law and are necessary in a democratic society in the interests of public safety, for the protection of public order, health or morals, or for the protection of the rights and freedoms of others.

Article 10 — *Freedom of expression*

1. Everyone has the right to freedom of expression. This right shall include freedom to hold opinions and to receive and impart information and ideas without interference by public authority and regardless of frontiers. This Article shall not prevent States from requiring the licensing of broadcasting, television or cinema enterprises.

2. The exercise of these freedoms, since it carries with it duties and responsibilities, may be subject to such formalities, conditions, restrictions or penalties as are prescribed by law and are necessary in a democratic society, in the interests of national security, territorial integrity or public safety, for the prevention of disorder or crime, for the protection of health or morals, for the protection of the reputation or rights of others, for preventing the disclosure of information received in confidence, or for maintaining the authority and impartiality of the judiciary.

Article 11 — *Freedom of assembly and association*

1. Everyone has the right to freedom of peaceful assembly and to freedom of association with others, including the right to form and to join trade unions for the protection of his interests.

2. No restrictions shall be placed on the exercise of these rights other than such as are prescribed by law and are necessary in a democratic society in the interests of national security or public safety, for the prevention of disorder or crime, for the protection of health or morals or for the protection of the rights and freedoms of others. This Article shall not prevent the imposition of lawful restrictions on the exercise of these rights by members of the armed forces, of the police or of the administration of the State.

Article 12 — *Right to marry*

Men and women of marriageable age have the right to marry and to found a family, according to the national laws governing the exercise of this right.

Article 14 — *Prohibition of discrimination*

The enjoyment of the rights and freedoms set forth in this Convention shall be secured without discrimination on any ground such as sex, race, colour, language, religion, political or other opinion, national or social origin, association with a national minority, property, birth or other status.

Article 16 — *Restrictions on political activity of aliens*

Nothing in Articles 10, 11 and 14 shall be regarded as preventing the High Contracting Parties from imposing restrictions on the political activity of aliens.

Article 17 *Prohibition of abuse of rights*

Nothing in this Convention may be interpreted as implying for any State, group or person any right to engage in any activity or perform any act aimed at the destruction of any of the rights and freedoms set forth herein or at their limitation to a greater extent than is provided for in the Convention.

Article 18 *Limitation on use of restrictions on rights*

The restrictions permitted under this Convention to the said rights and freedoms shall not be applied for any purpose other than those for which they have been prescribed.

PART II
THE FIRST PROTOCOL

Article 1 ***Protection of property***

Every natural or legal person is entitled to the peaceful enjoyment of his possessions. No one shall be deprived of his possessions except in the public interest and subject to the conditions provided for by law and by the general principles of international law.

The preceding provisions shall not, however, in any way impair the right of a State to enforce such laws as it deems necessary to control the use of property in accordance with the general interest or to secure the payment of taxes or other contributions or penalties.

Article 2 ***Right to education***

No person shall be denied the right to education. In the exercise of any functions which it assumes in relation to education and to teaching, the State shall respect the right of parents to ensure such education and teaching in conformity with their own religious and philosophical convictions.

Article 3 ***Right to free elections***

The High Contracting Parties undertake to hold free elections at reasonable intervals by secret ballot, under conditions which will ensure the free expression of the opinion of the people in the choice of the legislature.

[PART III
ARTICLE 1 OF THE THIRTEENTH PROTOCOL

Abolition of the death penalty

The death penalty shall be abolished. No one shall be condemned to such penalty or executed.]

Note: Part 3 substituted from 22 June 2004 (SI 2004/1574).

Section 10

SCHEDULE 2

REMEDIAL ORDERS

Orders

1.—(1) A remedial order may—

(a) contain such incidental, supplemental, consequential or transitional provision as the person making it considers appropriate;

(b) be made so as to have effect from a date earlier than that on which it is made;

(c) make provision for the delegation of specific functions;

(d) make different provision for different cases.

(2) The power conferred by sub-paragraph (1)(a) includes—

(a) power to amend primary legislation (including primary legislation other than that which contains the incompatible provision); and

(b) power to amend or revoke subordinate legislation (including subordinate legislation other than that which contains the incompatible provision).

(3) A remedial order may be made so as to have the same extent as the legislation which it affects.

(4) No person is to be guilty of an offence solely as a result of the retrospective effect of a remedial order.

Procedure

2. No remedial order may be made unless—

(a) a draft of the order has been approved by a resolution of each House of Parliament made after the end of the period of 60 days beginning with the day on which the draft was laid; or

(b) it is declared in the order that it appears to the person making it that, because of the urgency of the matter, it is necessary to make the order without a draft being so approved.

Orders laid in draft

3.—(1) No draft may be laid under paragraph 2(a) unless—

(a) the person proposing to make the order has laid before Parliament a document which contains a draft of the proposed order and the required information; and

(b) the period of 60 days, beginning with the day on which the document required by this sub-paragraph was laid, has ended.

(2) If representations have been made during that period, the draft laid under paragraph 2(a) must be accompanied by a statement containing—

(a) a summary of the representations; and

(b) if, as a result of the representations, the proposed order has been changed, details of the changes.

Urgent cases

4.—(1) If a remedial order ('the original order') is made without being approved in draft, the person making it must lay it before Parliament, accompanied by the required information, after it is made.

(2) If representations have been made during the period of 60 days beginning with the day on which the original order was made, the person making it must (after the end of that period) lay before Parliament a statement containing—

(a) a summary of the representations; and

(b) if, as a result of the representations, he considers it appropriate to make changes to the original order, details of the changes.

(3) If sub-paragraph (2)(b) applies, the person making the statement must—

(a) make a further remedial order replacing the original order; and

(b) lay the replacement order before Parliament.

(4) If, at the end of the period of 120 days beginning with the day on which the original order was made, a resolution has not been passed by each House approving the original or replacement order, the order ceases to have effect (but without that affecting anything previously done under either order or the power to make a fresh remedial order).

Definitions

5. In this Schedule—

'representations' means representations about a remedial order (or proposed remedial order) made to the person making (or proposing to make) it and includes any relevant Parliamentary report or resolution; and

'required information' means—

(a) an explanation of the incompatibility which the order (or proposed order) seeks to remove, including particulars of the relevant declaration, finding or order; and

(b) a statement of the reasons for proceeding under section 10 and for making an order in those terms.

Calculating periods

6. In calculating any period for the purposes of this Schedule, no account is to be taken of any time during which—

(a) Parliament is dissolved or prorogued; or

(b) both Houses are adjourned for more than four days.

[7.—(1) This paragraph applies in relation to–

(a) any remedial order made, and any draft of such an order proposed to be made,

(i) by the Scottish Ministers; or

(ii) within devolved competence (within the meaning of the Scotland Act 1998) by Her Majesty in Council; and

(b) any document or statement to be laid in connection with such an order (or proposed order).

(2) This Schedule has effect in relation to any such order (or proposed order), document or statement subject to the following modifications.

(3) Any reference to Parliament, each House of Parliament or both Houses of Parliament shall be construed as a reference to the Scottish Parliament.

(4) Paragraph 6 does not apply and instead, in calculating any period for the purposes of this Schedule, no account is to be taken of any time during which the Scottish Parliament is dissolved or is in recess for more than four days.]

Note: Paragraph (7) inserted from 27 July 2000 (SI 2000/2040).

Section 14 and 15

SCHEDULE 3
DEROGATION AND RESERVATION

PART II
Reservation

At the time of signing the present (First) Protocol, I declare that, in view of certain provisions of the Education Acts in the United Kingdom, the principle affirmed in the second sentence of Article 2 is accepted by the United Kingdom only so far as it is compatible with the provision of efficient instruction and training, and the avoidance of unreasonable public expenditure.

Dated 20 March 1952. Made by the United Kingdom Permanent Representative to the Council of Europe.

Note: Part 1 repealed from 1 April 2001 (SI 2001/1216), new Part 1 inserted from 20 December 2001 (SI 2001/4032) and repealed from 8 April 2005 (SI 2005/1071).

Section 18(6)

SCHEDULE 4
JUDICIAL PENSIONS

. . .

Immigration and Asylum Act 1999
(1999, c. 33)

Arrangement of Sections

Part I. Immigration: General

Leave to enter, or remain in, the United Kingdom

Provision of support

Support and Assistance by local authorities

Appeals

Offences

Expenditure

Exclusions

An Act to make provision about immigration and asylum; provision about procedures in connection with marriage on superintendent registrar's certificate; and for connected purposes. 11 November 1999]

PART I
IMMIGRATION: GENERAL

Leave to enter, or remain in, the United Kingdom

1. . . .

Note: Amends Immigration Act 1971, s 3A.

2. ...

Note: Amends Immigration Act 1971, s 3B.

3. ...

Note: Amends Immigration Act 1971, s 3C.

4. ...

Note: Repealed by Schedule 11 to Immigration Act 2016 from 15 January 2018 (SI 2017/1241) subject to savings and transitional provisions.

5. ...

Note: Ceased to have effect from 2 April 2007, Sch 2 Immigration, Asylum and Nationality Act 2006 (SI 2007/1109).

Exemption from immigration control

6. ...

Note: Amends Immigration Act 1971, s 8.

7. ...

Note: Amends Immigration Act 1971, s 8.

8. ...

Note: Amends Immigration Act 1971, s 8.

Removal from the United Kingdom

9. Treatment of certain overstayers

(1) During the regularisation period overstayers may apply, in the prescribed manner, for leave to remain in the United Kingdom.

(2) The regularisation period begins on the day prescribed for the purposes of this subsection and is not to be less than three months.

(3) The regularisation period ends—
(a) on the day prescribed for the purposes of this subsection; or
(b) if later, on the day before that on which section 65 comes into force.

(4) Section 10 and paragraph 12 of Schedule 15 come into force on the day after that on which the regularisation period ends.

(5) The Secretary of State must publicise the effect of this section in the way appearing to him to be best calculated to bring it to the attention of those affected.

(6) 'Overstayer' means a person who, having only limited leave to enter or remain in the United Kingdom, remains beyond the time limited by the leave.

Note: Commencement 11 November 1999, s 170.

[10 Removal of certain persons unlawfully in the United Kingdom

(1) A person [[is liable to removal]]from the United Kingdom [[]] if the person requires leave to enter or remain in the United Kingdom but does not have it.

(2) [[Where are a person is liable to removal, or has been removed, from the United Kingdom under this section, a member of P's family who meets the following three conditions is also liable to removal from the United Kingdom, provided that the Secretary of State or an immigration officer has given the family member written notice of the fact that they are liable to removal.]]

(3) The first condition is that the family member is—

(a) P's partner,

(b) P's child, or a child living in the same household as P in circumstances where P has care of the child,

(c) in a case where P is a child, P's parent, or

(d) an adult dependent relative of P.

(4) The second condition is that—

(a) in a case where the family member has leave to enter or remain in the United Kingdom, that leave was granted on the basis of his or her family life with P;

(b) in a case where the family member does not have leave to enter or remain in the United Kingdom, in the opinion of the Secretary of State or immigration officer the family member—

(i) would not, on making an application for such leave, be granted leave in his or her own right, but

(ii) would be granted leave on the basis of his or her family life with P, if P had leave to enter or remain.

(5) The third condition is that the family member [[is none of the following

(a) a British citizen,

(b) an Irish citizen,

(c) a person who has leave to enter or remain in the United Kingdom which was granted by virtue of residence scheme immigration rules]].

(6) A notice given to a family member under subsection (2) invalidates any leave to enter or remain in the United Kingdom previously given to the family member.

[[(6A) A person who is liable to removal from the United Kingdom under this section may be removed only under the authority of the Secretary of State or an immigration officer and in accordance with sections 10A to 10 E.]]

(7) For the purposes of removing a person from the United Kingdom under [[this section]], the Secretary of State or an immigration officer may give any such direction for the removal of the person as may be given under paragraphs 8 to 10 of Schedule 2 to the 1971 Act.

(8) But subsection (7) does not apply where a deportation order is in force against a person (and any directions for such a person's removal must be given under Schedule 3 to the 1971 Act).

(9) The following paragraphs of Schedule 2 to the 1971 Act apply in relation to directions under subsection (7) (and the persons subject to those directions) as they apply in relation to directions under paragraphs 8 to 10 of Schedule 2 (and the persons subject to those directions)—

(a) paragraph 11 (placing of person on board ship or aircraft);

(b) paragraph 16(2) to (4) (detention of person where reasonable grounds for suspecting removal directions may be given or pending removal in pursuance of directions);

(c) paragraph 17 (arrest of person liable to be detained and search of premises for person liable to arrest);

(d) paragraph 18 (supplementary provisions on detention);

(e) paragraph 18A (search of detained person);

(f) paragraph 18B (detention of unaccompanied children);

(g) paragraphs 19 and 20 (payment of expenses of custody etc.);

(h) ...

(i) ...

(j) paragraphs 25A to 25E (searches etc.).

(10) The Secretary of State may by regulations make further provision about—

(a) the time period during which a family member may be removed under [[this section]];

(b) the service of a notice under subsection (2) [[or sections 10A to 10 E]].

(11) In this section 'child' means a person who is under the age of 18.]

Note: Section 10 substituted by s 1 Immigration Act 2014 from 20 October 2014 with savings set out in articles 9–11, 14–15 of SI 2014/2771, and transitional provisions in SI 2014/1820. Paragraphs (h) & (i) of section 10(9) omitted by Sch 10 to Immigration Act 2016 from 15 January 2018 subject to transitional provisions specified in SI 2017/1241. Words in double square brackets substituted in subsection (10)(5) by Immigration and Social Security Co-ordination (EU Withdrawal) Act 2020 (Consequential, Saving, Transitional and Transitory Provisions) (EU Exit) Regulations 2020/1309 Pt 2(1) reg 12(2) (31 December 2020 at 23.00 being the time and date 2020 c. Sch 1 para 2(2) comes into force). Words substituted and omitted in double square brackets by Nationality and Borders Act 2022 c.36 Pt3 s46(2)(a) &(b) (date to be appointed). Words substituted in subsection (2) by Nationality and Borders Act 2022 c.36 Pt3 s.46(3) (date to be appointed). Subsection (6A) inserted by Nationality and Borders Act 2022 c.36 Pt3 s.46(4)(date to be appointed). Words substituted in subsection (7) by Nationality and Borders Act 2022 c.36 Pt3 s.46(5)(date to be appointed). Words substituted and inserted at subsection 10 by Nationality and Borders Act 2022 c.36 Pt3 s.46(6).

[10A Removal: general notice requirements

(1) This section applies to a person who is liable to removal under section 10; but see sections 10C to 10E for the circumstances in which such a person may be removed otherwise than in accordance with this section.

(2) The person may be removed if—

(a) the Secretary of State or an immigration officer has given the person—

(i) a notice of intention to remove (see subsection (3)), and

(ii) a notice of departure details (see subsection (4)), and

(b) any notice period has expired.

(3) A notice of intention to remove is a written notice which—

(a) states that the person is to be removed,

(b) sets out the notice period, (see subsection (7)), and

(c) states the destination to which the person is to be removed.

(4) A notice of departure details under this section is a written notice which—

(a) states the date on which the person is to be removed,

(b) states the destination to which the person is to be removed and any stops that are expected to be made on the way to that destination, and

(c) if subsection (6) applies, sets out the notice period (see subsection (7)).

(5) The notice of intention to remove and the notice of departure details may be combined.

(6) This subsection applies if the notice of departure details states, under subsection (4)(b)—

(a) a destination which is different to the destination stated under subsection (3)(c) in the notice of intention to remove, or

(b) any stops that were not stated in the notice of intention to remove, other than a stop in—

(i) the United Kingdom, or

(ii) a country that is for the time being specified in Part 2 of Schedule 3 to the Asylum and Immigration (Treatment of Claimants, etc) Act 2004.

(7) The notice period must be no shorter than the period of five working days beginning with the day after the day on which the person is given the notice.

(8) At any time before the person is removed, the Secretary of State or an immigration officer may replace a notice of departure details under this section.

(9) This section is subject to section 10B (failed removals).

(10) In this section "working day" means a day other than a Saturday, a Sunday, Christmas Day, Good Friday or a bank holiday under the Banking and Financial Dealings Act 1971 in the part of the United Kingdom where the person is when they are given the notice.]

Note: inserted by Nationality and Borders Act 2022 c.36 Pt3 s.46(7) (date to be appointed)

[10B Failed removals

(1) This section applies where as a result of matters reasonably beyond the control of the Secretary of State, such as—

(a) adverse weather conditions,

(b) technical faults or other issues causing delays to transport, or

(c) disruption by the person to be removed or others,

a person is not removed from the United Kingdom on the date stated in a notice of departure details under section 10A ("the original notice").

(2) The person may be removed from the United Kingdom if—

(a) the Secretary of State or an immigration officer has given the person a notice of departure details (see subsection (3)), and

(b) they are removed before the end of the period of 21 days beginning with the date stated in the original notice.

(3) A notice of departure details under this section is a written notice which—

(a) states the date on which the person is to be removed, and

(b) states the destination to which the person is to be removed and any stops that are expected to be made on the way to that destination.

(4) But this section does not apply if the notice under subsection (3) states, under subsection (3)(b)—

(a) a destination which is different to the destination stated in the original notice, or

(b) any stops that were not stated in the original notice, other than a stop in—

(i) the United Kingdom, or

(ii) a country that is for the time being specified in Part 2 of Schedule 3 to the Asylum and Immigration (Treatment of Claimants, etc) Act 2004.

(5) At any time before the person is removed, the Secretary of State or an immigration officer may replace a notice of departure details under this section.]

Note: inserted by Nationality and Borders Act 2022 c.36 s.46(7) (date to be appointed)

[10C Removal: notice requirements in port cases

(1) This section applies to a person who is liable to removal under section 10 if the person was refused leave to enter upon their arrival in the United Kingdom.

(2) The person may be removed if—

(a) the Secretary of State or an immigration officer has given the person a notice of departure details under this section which—

(i) states the date on which the person is to be removed, and

(ii) states the destination to which the person is to be removed and any stops that are expected to be made on the way to that destination, and

(b) the date stated under paragraph (a)(i) is a date before the end of the period of seven days beginning with the day after the day on which the person was refused leave to enter.

(3) At any time before the person is removed, the Secretary of State or an immigration officer may replace a notice of departure details under this section.]

Note: inserted by Nationality and Borders Act 2022 c.36 Pt3 s.46(7) (date to be appointed)

[10D Removal: PRN recipients

(1) This section applies to a person who is liable to removal under section 10 and is a PRN recipient.

(2) If the person does not make a protection claim or a human rights claim before the PRN cut-off date, the person may be removed from the United Kingdom if—

(a) the Secretary of State or an immigration officer has given the person a notice of departure details (see subsection (4)), and

(b) they are removed before the end of the period of 21 days beginning with the day after the PRN cut-off date.

(3) If the PRN recipient makes a protection claim or a human rights claim, the person may be removed from the United Kingdom if—

(a) the Secretary of State or an immigration officer has given the person a notice of departure details (see subsection (4)),

(b) their appeal rights are exhausted, and

(c) they are removed before the end of the period of 21 days beginning with the day after the date on which their appeal rights are exhausted;

and for the purposes of this subsection, whether a PRN recipient's appeal rights are exhausted is to be determined in accordance with section 20(3) of the Nationality and Borders Act 2022 (and see, in particular, section 82A of the Nationality, Immigration and Asylum Act 2002).

(4) A notice of departure details under this section is a written notice which—

(a) states the date on which the person is to be removed,

(b) states the destination to which the person is to be removed and any stops that are expected to be made on the way to that destination.

(5) But this section does not apply unless the priority removal notice stated—

(a) a destination to which the person is to be removed which is the same as the destination stated in the notice of departure details under subsection (4)(b), and

(b) stops, other than stops falling within subsection (6), that are expected to be made on the way to that destination which are the same as those stated in the notice of departure details under subsection (4)(b).

(6) A stop falls within this subsection if it is a stop in—

(a) the United Kingdom, or

(b) a country that is for the time being specified in Part 2 of Schedule 3 to the Asylum and Immigration (Treatment of Claimants, etc) Act 2004.

(7) At any time before the person is removed, the Secretary of State or an immigration officer may replace a notice of departure details under this section.

(8) For the purposes of this section and section 10E—

"priority removal notice", "PRN cut-off date" and "PRN recipient" have the same meaning as in section 20 of the Nationality and Borders Act 2022;

"protection claim" and "human rights claim" have the same meaning as in Part 5 of the Nationality, Immigration and Asylum Act 2002.]

Note: inserted by Nationality and Borders Act 2022 c.36 Pt 3 s.46(7) (date to be appointed)

[10E Removal: judicial review

(1) This section applies to a person (whether or not they are a PRN recipient) who is liable to removal under section 10 where—

(a) the person has made an application for judicial review or (in Scotland) an application to the supervisory jurisdiction of the Court of Session, relating to their removal, and

(b) a court or tribunal has made a decision the effect of which is that the person may be removed from the United Kingdom.

(2) The person may be removed from the United Kingdom if—

(a) the Secretary of State or an immigration officer has given the person a notice of departure details (see subsection (3)), and

(b) they are removed before the end of the period of 21 days beginning with the day after the day on which the court or tribunal made the decision mentioned in subsection (1)(b).

(3) A notice of departure details under this section is a written notice which—

(a) states the date on which the person is to be removed,

(b) states the destination to which the person is to be removed and any stops that are expected to be made on the way to that destination.

(4) But this section does not apply unless the person has received a priority removal notice or a notice of intention to remove under section 10A(3) which stated—

(a) a destination to which the person is to be removed which is the same as the destination stated in the notice of departure details under subsection (3)(b), and

(b) stops, other than stops falling within subsection (5), that are expected to be made on the way to that destination which are the same as those stated in the notice of departure details under subsection (3)(b).

(5) A stop falls within this subsection if it is a stop in—

(a) the United Kingdom, or

(b) a country that is for the time being specified in Part 2 of Schedule 3 to the Asylum and Immigration (Treatment of Claimants, etc) Act 2004.

(6) At any time before the person is removed, the Secretary of State or an immigration officer may replace a notice of departure details under this section.]

Note: inserted by Nationality and Borders Act 2022 c.36 s.46(7) (date to be appointed)

11. …

Note: Section 11 ceased to have effect from 1 October 2004: Asylum and Immigration Act 2004, s 33 (SI 2004/2523).

12. …

Note: Section 12 ceased to have effect from 1 October 2004: Asylum and Immigration Act 2004, s 33 (SI 2004/2523).

13. Proof of identity of persons to be removed or deported

(1) This section applies if a person—

(a) is to be removed from the United Kingdom to a country of which he is a national or citizen; but

(b) does not have a valid passport or other document establishing his identity and nationality or citizenship and permitting him to travel.

(2) If the country to which the person is to be removed indicates that he will not be admitted to it unless identification data relating to him are provided by the Secretary of State, he may provide them with such data.

(3) In providing identification data, the Secretary of State must not disclose whether the person concerned has made a claim for asylum.

[(4) For the purposes of Article 49(1)(d) of the [[UK GDPR]], the provision under this section of identification data is a transfer of personal data which is necessary for important reasons of public interest.]

[(4A) 'The UK GDPR' has the same meaning as in Parts 5 to 7 of the Data Protection Act 2018 (see section 3(10) and (14) of that Act).]

(5) 'Identification data' means—

(a) fingerprints taken under section 141; or

(b) data collected in accordance with regulations made under section 144.

(6) 'Removed' means removed as a result of directions given under section 10 or under Schedule 2 or 3 to the 1971 Act.

Note: Commenced 11 December 2000, SI 2000/3099. Subsection (4) substituted and subsection (4A) inserted by Data Protection Act 2018, SI 2018/625, Sch.19, para.47 (2) from 25 May 2018 as specified in 2018 c. 12 s 212(2)(f) for the limited purpose of the power to make regulations or Tribunal Procedure Rules or is otherwise necessary for enabling the exercise of such a power on or after 23 May 2018; 25 May 2018 as SI 2018/625 reg 2(g) otherwise. Words in double square brackets at subsection (4) and square brackets at subsection (4A) substituted by Data Protection, Privacy and Electronic Communications (Amendments etc.) (EU Exit) Regulations 2019/419, Sch. 3(2) para 19(2) & (3) (31 December 2020: shall come into force on IP completion day not exit day as specified in 2020 c. 1 s 39(1) and Sch .5 para.1).

14. Escorts for persons removed from the United Kingdom under directions

(1) Directions for, or requiring arrangements to be made for, the removal of a person from the United Kingdom may include or be amended to include provision for the person who is to be removed to be accompanied by an escort consisting of one or more persons specified in the directions.

(2) The Secretary of State may by regulations make further provision supplementing subsection (1).

(3) The regulations may, in particular, include provision—

(a) requiring the person to whom the directions are given to provide for the return of the escort to the United Kingdom;

(b) requiring him to bear such costs in connection with the escort (including, in particular, remuneration) as may be prescribed;

(c) as to the cases in which the Secretary of State is to bear those costs;

(d) prescribing the kinds of expenditure which are to count in calculating the costs incurred in connection with escorts.

Note: Commencement 1 March 2000 (SI 2000/168).

15. …

Note: Section 15 repealed by Nationality, Immigration and Asylum Act 2002, s 77 from 1 April 2003 (SI 2003/754).

Provision of financial security

16. Security on grant of entry clearance

(1) In such circumstances as may be specified, the Secretary of State may require security to be given, with respect to a person applying for entry clearance, before clearance is given.

(2) In such circumstances as may be specified—

(a) the Secretary of State may accept security with respect to a person who is applying for entry clearance but for whom security is not required; and

(b) in determining whether to give clearance, account may be taken of any security so provided.

(3) 'Security' means—

(a) the deposit of a sum of money by the applicant, his agent or any other person, or

(b) the provision by the applicant, his agent or any other person of a financial guarantee of a specified kind, with a view to securing that the applicant will, if given leave to enter the United Kingdom for a limited period, leave the United Kingdom at the end of that period.

(4) Immigration rules must make provision as to the circumstances in which a security provided under this section—

(a) is to be repaid, released or otherwise cancelled; or

(b) is to be forfeited or otherwise realised by the Secretary of State.

(5) No security provided under this section may be forfeited or otherwise realised unless the person providing it has been given an opportunity, in accordance with immigration rules, to make representations to the Secretary of State.

(6) Immigration rules may, in particular—

(a) fix the maximum amount that may be required, or accepted, by way of security provided under this section;

(b) specify the form and manner in which such a security is to be given or may be accepted;

(c) make provision, where such a security has been forfeited or otherwise realised, for the person providing it to be reimbursed in such circumstances as may be specified;

(d) make different provision for different cases or descriptions of case.

(7) 'Specified' means specified by immigration rules.

(8) Any security forfeited or otherwise realised by the Secretary of State under this section must be paid into the Consolidated Fund.

Note: Commencement on a date to be appointed.

17. Provision of further security on extension of leave

(1) This section applies if security has been provided under section 16(1) or (2) with respect to a person who, having entered the United Kingdom (with leave to do so), applies—

(a) to extend his leave to enter the United Kingdom; or

(b) for leave to remain in the United Kingdom for a limited period.

(2) The Secretary of State may refuse the application if security of such kind as the Secretary of State considers appropriate is not provided, or continued, with respect to the applicant.

(3) Immigration rules must make provision as to the circumstances in which a security provided under this section—

(a) is to be repaid, released or otherwise cancelled; or

(b) is to be forfeited or otherwise realised by the Secretary of State.

(4) No security provided under this section may be forfeited or otherwise realised unless the person providing it has been given an opportunity, in accordance with immigration rules, to make representations to the Secretary of State.

(5) Subsection (7) of section 16 applies in relation to this section as it applies in relation to that section.

(6) Any security forfeited or otherwise realised by the Secretary of State under this section must be paid into the Consolidated Fund.

Note: Commencement on a date to be appointed.

Information

18. . . .

Note: Amends paragraph 27B, Sch 2 Immigration Act 1971.

19. . . .

Note: Amends paragraph 27C, Sch 2 Immigration Act 1971. Omitted from 12 February 2015 by Counter Terrorism and Security Act 2015, Schedule 5.

20. Power to supply information etc. to Secretary of State

(1) This section applies to information held by—

(a) [[a public authority, or

[(b) any specified person, for the purposes specified in relation to that person.]]

[(1A) This section also applies to a document or article which—

(a) comes into the possession of [[a public authority or someone acting on behalf of a public authority]] or

(b) is discovered by a [[public authority or someone acting on behalf of a public authority.]]

[(1B) This section does not apply to—

(a) information which is held by the Crown Prosecution Service, or

(b) a document or article which comes into the possession of, or is discovered by, the Crown Prosecution Service, or someone acting on behalf of the Crown Prosecution Service, if section 40 of the UK Borders Act 2007 applies to the information, document or article.]

(2) The information [, document or article] may be supplied to the Secretary of State for use for immigration purposes.

[(2A) The Secretary of State may—

(a) retain for immigration purposes a document or article supplied to him under subsection (2), and

(b) dispose of a document or article supplied to him under subsection (2) in such manner as he thinks appropriate (and the reference to use in subsection (2) includes a reference to disposal).]

[(2B) Subsection (2A)(a) does not affect any other power of the Secretary of State to retain a document or article.]

(3) 'Immigration purposes' means any of the following—

(a) the administration of immigration control under the Immigration Acts;

(b) the prevention, detection, investigation or prosecution of criminal offences under those Acts;

(c) the imposition of penalties or charges under Part II;

(d) the provision of support for asylum-seekers and their dependants under Part VI;

[(da) anything else that is done in connection with the exercise of a function under any of the Immigration Acts;]

(e) such other purposes as may be specified.

[(**3A**) 'Public authority' means a person with functions of a public nature but does not include—

(a) Her Majesty's Revenue and Customs,

(b) either House of Parliament or a person exercising functions in connection with proceedings in Parliament,

(c) the Scottish Parliament or a person exercising functions in connection with proceedings in the Scottish Parliament,

(d) the National Assembly for Wales or a person exercising functions in connection with proceedings in that Assembly, or

(e) the Northern Ireland Assembly or a person exercising functions in connection with proceedings in that Assembly.]

(**4**) ...

(**5**) 'Specified' means specified in an order made by the Secretary of State.

(**6**) This section does not limit the circumstances in which information [, documents or articles] may be supplied apart from this section.

[(7) Nothing in this section authorises information, a document or an article to be supplied if to do so would contravene a restriction on the disclosure of information (however imposed).]

Note: Commencement 1 January 2000 (SI 1999/3190). Subsection (1)(b) substituted by Sch 4 Serious Organised Crime and Police Act 2005 from 1 April 2006 (SI 2006/378), and words in square brackets in subs-s (1)(b) substituted by Crime and Courts Act 2013 Sch 8 from 7 October 2013 (SI 2013/1682). Subsection (1)(d) omitted from 31 January 2008 (Schedule, UK Borders Act 2007). Subsection (1A) and subsection (2A) inserted by s 132 Nationality, Immigration and Asylum Act 2002 from 10 February 2003 (SI 2003/1). Words in square brackets in subsections (2) and (6) inserted by s 132 Nationality, Immigration and Asylum Act 2002 from 10 February 2003 (SI 2003/1). Subsection (2)(b) substituted by Sch 8 Crime and Courts Act 2013 from 7 October 2013 (SI 2013/1682). Words in double square brackets at subsection (1)(a) and (b) substituted by Immigration Act 2016, s 55 from 12 July 2016 (SI 2016/603). Words in double square brackets at subsection (2)(a) and (b) substituted by Immigration Act 2016, s 55 from 12 July 2016 (SI 2016/603). Subsections (1B), (2A), (3)(da), (3A) and (7) inserted, and subsection (4) omitted by Immigration Act 2016, s 55 from 12 July 2016 (SI 2016/603).

[20A. Duty to supply nationality documents to Secretary of State

20A.(**1**) This section applies to a nationality document which the Secretary of State has reasonable grounds for believing is lawfully in the possession of a person listed in Schedule A1.

(**2**) The Secretary of State may direct the person to supply the document to the Secretary of State if the Secretary of State suspects that—

(a) a person to whom the document relates may be liable to removal from the United Kingdom in accordance with a provision of the Immigration Acts, and

(b) the document may facilitate the removal.

(3) A person to whom a direction is given must, as soon as is practicable, supply the document to the Secretary of State.

(4) If the document was originally created in hard copy form and the person possesses the original document, it must be supplied to the Secretary of State unless it is required by the person for the performance of any of the person's functions.

(5) If the original document is required by the person for the performance of any of the person's functions—

(a) the person must, as soon as is practicable, supply a copy of the document to the Secretary of State, and

(b) if subsequently the person no longer requires the original document, the person must supply it to the Secretary of State as soon as is practicable after it is no longer required.

(6) Subsection (5)(b) does not apply if the Secretary of State notifies the person that the original document is no longer required.

(7) If subsection (5) applies the person may make a copy of the original document before supplying it to the Secretary of State.

(8) The Secretary of State may retain a nationality document supplied under this section while the Secretary of State suspects that—

(a) a person to whom the document relates may be liable to removal from the United Kingdom in accordance with a provision of the Immigration Acts, and

(b) retention of the document may facilitate the removal.

(9) Subsection (8) does not affect any other power of the Secretary of State to retain a document.

(10) The Secretary of State may dispose of a nationality document supplied under this section in such manner as the Secretary of State thinks appropriate.

(11) Nothing in this section authorises or requires a document to be supplied if to do so would contravene a restriction on the disclosure of information (however imposed).

(12) The Secretary of State may by regulations amend Schedule A1 so as to add, modify or remove a reference to a person or description of person.

(13) Regulations under subsection (12) may not amend Schedule A1 so as to apply this section to—

(a) either House of Parliament or a person exercising functions in connection with proceedings in Parliament,

(b) the Scottish Parliament or a person exercising functions in connection with proceedings in the Scottish Parliament,

(c) the National Assembly for Wales or a person exercising functions in connection with proceedings in that Assembly, or

(d) the Northern Ireland Assembly or a person exercising functions in connection with proceedings in that Assembly.

(14) In this section 'nationality document' means a document which might—

(a) establish a person's identity, nationality or citizenship, or indicate the place from which a person has travelled to the United Kingdom or to which a person is proposing to go.}

Note: Section 20A inserted by Immigration Act 2016, s 55 from 12 July 2016 (SI 2016/603).

21. Supply of information by Secretary of State

(1) This section applies to information held by the Secretary of State in connection with the exercise of functions under any of the Immigration Acts.

(2) The information may be supplied to—

(a) a chief officer of police, for use for police purposes;

[(b) the National Crime Agency, for use in connection with the discharge of any function of that Agency;]

(c) …

(d) the Commissioners of Customs and Excise, or a person providing services to them, for use for customs purposes; or

(e) any specified person, for use for purposes specified in relation to that person.

(3) 'Police purposes' means any of the following—

(a) the prevention, detection, investigation or prosecution of criminal offences;

(b) safeguarding national security;

(c) such other purposes as may be specified.

[(4) …

(6) 'Customs purposes' means any of the Commissioners' functions in relation to—

(a) the prevention, detection, investigation or prosecution of criminal offences;

(b) the prevention, detection or investigation of conduct in respect of which penalties which are not criminal penalties are provided for by or under any enactment;

(c) the assessment or determination of penalties which are not criminal penalties;

(d) checking the accuracy of information relating to, or provided for purposes connected with, any matter under the care and management of the Commissioners or any assigned matter (as defined by section 1(1) of the Customs and Excise Management Act 1979);

(e) amending or supplementing any such information (where appropriate);

(f) legal or other proceedings relating to anything mentioned in paragraphs (a) to (e);

(g) safeguarding national security; and

(h) such other purposes as may be specified.

(7) 'Chief officer of police' and 'specified' have the same meaning as in section 20.

(8) This section does not limit the circumstances in which information may be supplied apart from this section.

Note: Commencement 1 January 2000 (SI 1999/3190). Subsection (2)(b) substituted and subsection (4) omitted by Sch 8 Crime and Courts Act 2013 from 7 October 2013 (SI 2013/1682).

Employment: code of practice

22. …

Note: Amends Asylum and Immigration Act 1996, s 8A.

Monitoring entry clearance

23.…

Note: Repealed by Sch 9 Immigration Act 2014 from 20 October 2014 with savings set out in articles 9–11, SI 2014/2771.

Reporting suspicious marriages

24. Duty to report suspicious marriages

(1) Subsection (3) applies if—

(a) a superintendent registrar to whom a notice of marriage has been given under section 27 of the Marriage Act 1949,

[(aa) a superintendent registrar, or registrar of births, deaths and marriages, who receives information in advance of a person giving such a notice,]

(b) any other person who, under section 28(2) of that Act, has attested a declaration accompanying such a notice,

(c) a district registrar to whom a marriage notice or an approved certificate has been submitted under section 3 of the Marriage (Scotland) Act 1977, [. . .]

[(ca) a district registrar who receives information in advance of a person submitting such a notice or certificate,]

(d) a registrar or deputy registrar to whom notice has been given under section 13 of the Marriages (Ireland) Act 1844 or section 4 of the Marriage Law (Ireland) Amendment Act 1863,

[(da) a registrar or deputy registrar who receives information in advance of a person giving such a notice,] has reasonable grounds for suspecting that the marriage will be a sham marriage.]

(2) Subsection (3) also applies if—

(a) a marriage is solemnized in the presence of a registrar of marriages or, in relation to Scotland, an authorised registrar (within the meaning of the Act of 1977); and

(b) before, during or immediately after solemnization of the marriage, the registrar has reasonable grounds for suspecting that the marriage will be, or is, a sham marriage.

(3) The person concerned must report his suspicion to the Secretary of State without delay and in such form and manner as may be prescribed by regulations.

(4) The regulations are to be made—

(a) in relation to England and Wales, by the Registrar General for England and Wales with the approval of [the Secretary of State];

(b) in relation to Scotland, by the Secretary of State after consulting the Registrar General of Births, Deaths and Marriages for Scotland;

(c) in relation to Northern Ireland, by the Secretary of State after consulting the Registrar General in Northern Ireland.

[(5) A marriage (whether or not it is void) is a 'sham marriage' if—

(a) either, or both, of the parties to the marriage is not a relevant national,

(b) there is no genuine relationship between the parties to the marriage, and

(c) either, or both, of the parties to the marriage enter into the marriage for one or more of these purposes—

(i) avoiding the effect of one or more provisions of United Kingdom immigration law or the immigration rules;

(ii) enabling a party to the marriage to obtain a right conferred by that law or those rules to reside in the United Kingdom.

(6) In subsection (5)—

'relevant national' means—

(a) a British citizen,

[[(aa) an Irish citizen, or

(ab) a person who is not an Irish citizen and who—

(i) has leave to enter or remain in the United Kingdom which was granted by virtue of residence scheme immigration rules, or

(ii) is an applicant for the purposes of regulation 4 of the Citizens' Rights (Application Deadline and Temporary Protection) (EU Exit) Regulations 2020 (applications which have not been finally determined by the deadline) where the relevant period within the meaning of that regulation has not expired;]]

(b)

(c)

[[...]]

Note: Commencement 1 January 2001 (SI 2000/2698). Words in square brackets in subsection (4)(a) substituted by SI 2008/678 from 3 April 2008. Subsections (1)(aa), (ca) and (da) inserted by s 56 Immigration Act 2014 from 14 July 2014 (SI 2014/1820). Subsection (5) and (6) substituted by s 55 Immigration Act 2014 from 1 March 2015. Definition in double square brackets omitted by Immigration, Nationality and Asylum (EU Exit) Regulations 2019/745 Pt 2(1) reg 11(3)(b) (31 December 2020: shall come into force on IP completion date not exit day as specified in 2020 c.1 s 39(1) and Sch. 5 para 1(1)). Words in double brackets at subsection (6)(aa) & (ab) inserted by Immigration and Social Security Co-ordination (EU Withdrawal) Act 2020 (Consequential, Saving, Transitional and Transitory Provisions) (EU Exit) Regulations 2020/1309 Pt 2(1) reg 12(3)(a) (1 July 2021). Subsections (6)(b) & (c) omitted by Immigration and Social Security Co-ordination (EU Withdrawal) Act 2020 (Consequential, Saving, Transitional and Transitory Provisions) (EU Exit) Regulations 2020/1309 Pt 2(1) reg 12(3)(b)(1 July 2021).

[24A. Duty to report suspicious civil partnerships

(1) Subsection (3) applies if—

(a) a registration authority to whom a notice of proposed civil partnership has been given under section 8 of the Civil Partnership Act 2004,

[(aa) a registration authority that receives information in advance of a person giving such a notice,]

(b) any person who, under section 8 of the 2004 Act, has attested a declaration accompanying such a notice,

(c) a district registrar to whom a notice of proposed civil partnership has been given under section 88 of the 2004 Act,

[(ca) a district registrar who receives information in advance of a person giving such a notice,]

(d) a registrar to whom a civil partnership notice has been given under section 139 of the 2004 Act, [or

[(da) a registrar who receives information in advance of a person giving such a notice,] has reasonable grounds for suspecting that the civil partnership will be a sham civil partnership.

(2) Subsection (3) also applies if—

(a) two people register as civil partners of each other under Part 2, 3 or 4 of the 2004 Act in the presence of the registrar, and

(b) before, during or immediately after they do so, the registrar has reasonable grounds for suspecting that the civil partnership will be, or is, a sham civil partnership.

(3) The person concerned must report his suspicion to the Secretary of State without delay and in such form and manner as may be prescribed by regulations.

(4) The regulations are to be made—

(a) in relation to England and Wales, by the Registrar General for England and Wales with the approval of [the Secretary of State];

(b) in relation to Scotland, by the Secretary of State after consulting the Registrar General of Births, Deaths and Marriages for Scotland;

(c) in relation to Northern Ireland, by the Secretary of State after consulting the Registrar General in Northern Ireland.

[(5) A civil partnership (whether or not it is void) is a 'sham civil partnership' if—

(a) either, or both, of the parties to the civil partnership is not a relevant national,

(b) there is no genuine relationship between the parties to the civil partnership, and

(c) either, or both, of the parties to the civil partnership enter into the civil partnership for one or more of these purposes—

(i) avoiding the effect of one or more provisions of United Kingdom immigration law or the immigration rules;

(ii) enabling a party to the civil partnership to obtain a right conferred by that law or those rules to reside in the United Kingdom.

(5A) In subsection (5)—

'relevant national' means—

(a) a British citizen,

[[(aa) an Irish citizen; or

(ab) a person who is not an Irish citizen and who—

(i) has leave to enter or remain in the United Kingdom which was granted by virtue of residence scheme immigration rules, or

(ii) is an applicant for the purposes of regulation 4 of the Citizens' Rights (Application Deadline and Temporary Protection) (EU Exit) Regulations 2020 (applications which have not been finally determined by the deadline) where the relevant period within the meaning of that regulation has not expired.]]

(b) [[..]]

(c) [[. . .]]

[]

(6) 'The registrar' means—

(a) in relation to England and Wales, the civil partnership registrar acting under Part 2 of the 2004 Act;

(b) in relation to Scotland, the authorised registrar acting under Part 3 of the 2004 Act;

(c) in relation to Northern Ireland, the registrar acting under Part 4 of the 2004 Act.]

Note: Section 24A inserted by Sch 27 Civil Partnership Act 2004 from 15 April 2004 for the purposes of making regulations (SI 2005/1112), remainder 5 December 2005 (SI 2005/3175). Words in square brackets in subsection (4)(a) substituted by SI 2008/678 from 3 April 2008. Subsections (1)(aa),(ca) and (da) inserted by s 56 Immigration Act 2014 from 14 July 2014 (SI 2014/1820). Subsection (5) substituted by s 55 Immigration Act 2014 from a date to be appointed. Words omitted in square brackets below subsection (5A)by Immigration, Nationality and Asylum Regulations 2019/745 Pt 2(1) reg 11(4)(b) (31 December 2020: shall come into force on IP completion day not exit day as specified in 2020 c. 1, s 39(1) and Sch 5 para 1(1)). Words in double square brackets at subsection (5A) (aa) & (ab) inserted by Immigration and Social Security Co-ordination (EU Withdrawal) Act 2020 (Consequential, Saving, Transitional and Transitory Provisions)(EU Exit) Regulations 2020/1309 Pt 2(1) reg 12(4)(a) (1 July 2021). Words omitted in subsection (5A)(b) & (c) by Immigration and Social Security Co-ordination (EU Withdrawal) Act 2020 (Consequential, Saving, Transitional and Transitory Provisions) (EU Exit) Regulations 2020/1309 Pt 2(1) reg 12(4)(b)(1 July 2021).

Immigration control: facilities and charges

25. Provision of facilities for immigration control at ports

(1) The person responsible for the management of a control port ('the manager') must provide the Secretary of State free of charge with such facilities at the port as the Secretary of State may direct as being reasonably necessary for, or in connection with, the operation of immigration control there.

(2) Before giving such a direction, the Secretary of State must consult such persons likely to be affected by it as he considers appropriate.

(3) If the Secretary of State gives such a direction, he must send a copy of it to the person appearing to him to be the manager.

(4) If the manager persistently fails to comply with the direction (or part of it), the Secretary of State may—

(a) in the case of a control port which is not a port of entry, revoke any approval in relation to the port given under paragraph 26(1) of Schedule 2 to the 1971 Act;

(b) in the case of a control port which is a port of entry, by order revoke its designation as a port of entry.

(5) A direction under this section is enforceable, on the application of the Secretary of State—

(a) by injunction granted [in England and Wales by the county court or in Northern Ireland] by a county court; or

(b) in Scotland, by an order under section 45 of the Court of Session Act 1988.

(6) 'Control port' means a port in which a control area is designated under paragraph 26(3) of Schedule 2 to the 1971 Act.

(7) 'Facilities' means accommodation, facilities, equipment and services of a class or description specified in an order made by the Secretary of State.

Note: Commenced on 17 February 2003 for the purpose of enabling the Secretary of State to exercise power to make subordinate legislation; otherwise commenced on 1 April 2003 (SI 2003/2). Words inserted in subsection (5)(a) by Sch 9 Crime and Courts Act 2013 from 22 April 2014; insertion has effect as SI2014/954 subject to savings transitional provisions specified in 2013.

26. Charges: immigration control

(1) The Secretary of State may, at the request of any person and in consideration of such charges as he may determine, make arrangements—

(a) for the provision at any control port of immigration officers or facilities in addition to those (if any) needed to provide a basic service at the port;

(b) for the provision of immigration officers or facilities for dealing with passengers of a particular description or in particular circumstances.

(2) 'Control port' has the same meaning as in section 25.

(3) 'Facilities' includes equipment.

(4) 'Basic service' has such meaning as may be prescribed.

Note: Commenced on 5 June 2003 for purpose of enabling Secretary of State to make subordinate legislation; remainder commenced on 30 June 2003 (SI 2003/1469).

Charges: travel documents

27. …

Note: Repealed 2 April 2007 Sch 2 Immigration, Asylum and Nationality Act 2006 (SI 2007/1109).

Offences

28. …

Note: Amends Immigration Act 1971, s 24A.

29. …

Note: Repealed by Sch 9 Nationality, Immigration and Asylum Act 2002 from 1 April 2003 (SI 2003/754).

30. …

Note: Amends Immigration Act 1971, s 26.

31. Defences based on Article 31(1) of the Refugee Convention

(1) It is a defence for a refugee charged with an offence to which this section applies to show that, having come to the United Kingdom directly from a country where his life or freedom was threatened (within the meaning of the Refugee Convention), he—

(a) presented himself to the authorities in the United Kingdom without delay;

(b) showed good cause for his illegal entry or presence; and

(c) made a claim for asylum as soon as was reasonably practicable after his arrival in the United Kingdom.

(2) If, in coming from the country where his life or freedom was threatened, the refugee stopped in another country outside the United Kingdom, subsection (1) applies only if he shows that he could not reasonably [be expected to have sought] protection under the Refugee Convention in that other country.

(3) In England and Wales and Northern Ireland the offences to which this section applies are any offence, and any attempt to commit an offence, under—

(a) Part I of the Forgery and Counterfeiting Act 1981 (forgery and connected offences);

[(aa) section 4 or 6 of the Identity Documents Act 2010;]

(b) section 24A of the 1971 Act (deception); or

(c) section 26(1)(d) of the 1971 Act (falsification of documents).

(4) In Scotland, the offences to which this section applies are those—

(a) of fraud,

(b) of uttering a forged document,

[(ba) under section 4 or 6 of the Identity Documents Act 2010;]

(c) under section 24A of the 1971 Act (deception), or

(d) under section 26(1)(d) of the 1971 Act (falsification of documents), and any attempt to commit any of those offences.

[(**4A**) But this section does not apply to an offence committed by a refugee in the course of an attempt to leave the United Kingdom.]

(5) A refugee who has made a claim for asylum is not entitled to the defence provided by subsection (1) in relation to any offence committed by him after making that claim.

(6) 'Refugee' has the same meaning as it has for the purposes of the Refugee Convention.

(7) If the Secretary of State has refused to grant a claim for asylum made by a person who claims that he has a defence under subsection (1), that person is to be taken not to be a refugee unless he shows that he is.

(8) A person who—

(a) was convicted in England and Wales or Northern Ireland of an offence to which this section applies before the commencement of this section, but

(b) at no time during the proceedings for that offence argued that he had a defence based on Article 31(1), may apply to the Criminal Cases Review Commission with a view to his case being referred to the Court of Appeal by the Commission on the ground that he would have had a defence under this section had it been in force at the material time.

(9) A person who—

(a) was convicted in Scotland of an offence to which this section applies before the commencement of this section, but

(b) at no time during the proceedings for that offence argued that he had a defence based on Article 31(1), may apply to the Scottish Criminal Cases Review Commission with a view to his case being referred to the High Court of Justiciary by the Commission on the ground that he would have had a defence under this section had it been in force at the material time.

(10) The Secretary of State may by order amend—

(a) subsection (3), or

(b) subsection (4), by adding offences to those for the time being listed there.

(11) Before making an order under subsection (10)(b), the Secretary of State must consult the Scottish Ministers.

Note: Commencement 11 November 1999, s 170. Subsections (3)(aa) and (4)(ba) substituted by Identity Documents Act 2010, Schedule, paragraph 10 from 21 January 2011 (s 14). Words substituted in square brackets in subsection (2) and inserted in subsection (4A) by Nationality and Borders Act 2022 c.36 Pt2 s.37(5)(a) & (b) (June 28, 2022: substitution and insertion has effect as SI 2022/590 reg.2 and Sch.1 para 19 subject to transitional and saving provision specified in SI2022/590 reg.3 and Sch.2 para 6)

Part II
Carriers' Liability

[Penalties for failure to secure goods vehicles and for carrying clandestine entrants]

31A Penalty for failure to secure goods vehicle etc

(1) The Secretary of State may impose a penalty on a person responsible for a goods vehicle which has arrived at a place mentioned in subsection (2) if—

(a) on its arrival at that place, the vehicle is not adequately secured against unauthorised access (see subsection (4)(a)), and

(b) the person has not taken the actions specified in regulations under subsection (4)(b) as actions to be taken by that person in relation to the securing of the vehicle against unauthorised access before or during its journey to that place.

(2) Those places are—

(a) a place where immigration control is operated, and

(b) in a case where the vehicle previously arrived at a place outside the United Kingdom where immigration control is operated and then journeyed to a place in the United Kingdom, that place in the United Kingdom.

(3) A penalty may be imposed under subsection (1) regardless of whether any person has obtained unauthorised access to the vehicle during its journey to the place mentioned in subsection (2).

(4) The Secretary of State must specify in regulations for the purposes of subsection (1)—

(a) what is meant by a goods vehicle being adequately secured against unauthorised access, and

(b) the actions to be taken by each person responsible for a goods vehicle in relation to the securing of the vehicle against unauthorised access.

(5) The actions that may be specified in regulations under subsection (4)(b) include, in particular—

(a) actions in relation to checking a person has not gained unauthorised access to the vehicle,

(b) actions in relation to the reporting of any unauthorised access to the vehicle, and

(c) actions in relation to the keeping of records to establish that other actions specified in the regulations have been taken.

(6) Before making regulations under subsection (4), the Secretary of State must consult such persons as the Secretary of State considers appropriate.

(7) In imposing a penalty under subsection (1), the Secretary of State—

(a) must specify an amount which does not exceed the maximum prescribed for the purpose of this paragraph,

(b) may impose separate penalties on more than one of the persons responsible for a goods vehicle, and

(c) may not impose penalties which amount in aggregate to more than the maximum prescribed for the purpose of this paragraph.

(8) A penalty imposed under subsection (1) must be paid to the Secretary of State before the end of the prescribed period.

(9) A person is not liable to the imposition of a penalty under subsection (1) if that person's failure to take the actions specified in regulations under subsection (4)(b) was as a result of duress.

(10) If a penalty is imposed under subsection (1) in relation to the arrival of a goods vehicle in a place outside the United Kingdom where immigration control is operated, a penalty may not be imposed in relation to the vehicle's arrival in the United Kingdom as part of the same journey.

(11) A penalty may not be imposed on a person under subsection (1) if a penalty is imposed on that person under section 32(2) in respect of the same circumstances.

(12) Where a penalty is imposed under subsection (1) on a person who is the driver of a goods vehicle pursuant to a contract (whether or not a contract of employment) with a person ("P") who is the vehicle's owner or hirer—

(a) the driver and P are jointly and severally liable for the penalty imposed on the driver (whether or not a penalty is also imposed on P), and

(b) a provision of this Part about notification, objection or appeal has effect as if the penalty imposed on the driver were also imposed on P (whether or not a penalty is also imposed on P in P's capacity as the owner or hirer of the vehicle).

(13) In the case of a detached trailer, subsection (12) has effect as if a reference to the driver were a reference to the operator.

(14) For the purposes of this section the persons responsible for a goods vehicle are—

(a) if the goods vehicle is a detached trailer, the owner, hirer and operator of the trailer, and

(b) if it is not, the owner, hirer and driver of the vehicle.

(15) Where by virtue of subsection (14) a person is responsible for a goods vehicle in more than one capacity, a separate penalty may be imposed on the person under subsection (1) in respect of each capacity.

(16) In this section "immigration control" means United Kingdom immigration control and includes any United Kingdom immigration control operated in a prescribed control zone outside the United Kingdom.

Note: inserted by Nationality and Borders Act 2022 c.36 Sch.5 para 3(date to be appointed: 2022 c.36 Sch.5 para.3 came into force on April 28, 2022 as specified in 2022 c.36 s.87(4)(c) for the limited purpose of making (and, where required, consulting on) regulations; not yet in force otherwise)

32. Penalty for carrying clandestine entrants

(1) A person is a clandestine entrant if—

(a) he arrives in the United Kingdom concealed in a vehicle, ship or aircraft,

[(aa) he arrives in the United Kingdom concealed in a rail freight wagon,]

(b) he passes, or attempts to pass, through immigration control concealed in a vehicle, or

(c) he arrives in the United Kingdom on a ship or aircraft, having embarked—

(i) concealed in a vehicle; and

(ii) at a time when the ship or aircraft was outside the United Kingdom,

and claims, or indicates that he intends to seek, asylum in the United Kingdom or evades, or attempts to evade, immigration control.

[(2) The Secretary of State may require a person who is responsible for a clandestine entrant to pay—

(a) a penalty in respect of the clandestine entrant;

(b) a penalty in respect of any person who was concealed with the clandestine entrant in the same transporter.]

[(2A) In imposing a penalty under subsection (2) the Secretary of State—

(a) must specify an amount which does not exceed the maximum prescribed for the purpose of this paragraph,

(b) may, in respect of a clandestine entrant or a concealed person, impose separate penalties on more than one of the persons responsible for the clandestine entrant, and

(c) may not impose penalties in respect of a clandestine entrant or a concealed person which amount in aggregate to more than the maximum prescribed for the purpose of this paragraph.]

[(**2B**) The Secretary of State may reduce the amount of a penalty under this section if the responsible person can show that they took the actions specified in regulations under subsection (2C) in relation to the securing of the transporter against unauthorised access.

(**2C**) The Secretary of State must specify in regulations the actions that a responsible person must have taken in order to be eligible for a reduction in the amount of a penalty.

(**2D**) The actions that may be specified in regulations under subsection (2C) include, in particular—

(a) actions in relation to checking a person has not gained unauthorised access to the transporter,

(b) actions in relation to the reporting of any unauthorised access to the transporter, and

(c) actions in relation to the keeping of records to establish that other actions specified in the regulations have been taken.

(**2E**) Before making regulations under subsection (2C), the Secretary of State must consult such persons as the Secretary of State considers appropriate.]]

(**3**) A penalty imposed under this section must be paid to the Secretary of State before the end of the prescribed period.

[(**4**) Where a penalty is imposed under subsection (2) on a person who is the driver of a vehicle pursuant to a contract (whether or not a contract of employment) with a person ("P") who is the vehicle's owner or hirer—

(a) the driver and P are jointly and severally liable for the penalty imposed on the driver (whether or not a penalty is also imposed on P), and

(b) a provision of this Part about notification, objection or appeal has effect as if the penalty imposed on the driver were also imposed on P (whether or not a penalty is also imposed on P in P's capacity as the owner or hirer of the vehicle).]

[(**4A**) In the case of a detached trailer, subsection (4) shall have effect as if a reference to the driver were a reference to the operator.]

(**5**) In the case of a clandestine entrant to whom subsection (1)(a) applies, each of the following is a responsible person—

(a) if the transporter is a ship or aircraft, the owner [and] captain;

(b) if it is a vehicle (but not a detached trailer), the owner, hirer [and] driver of the vehicle;

(c) if it is a detached trailer, the owner, hirer [and] operator of the trailer.

[(**5A**) In the case of a clandestine entrant to whom subsection (1)(aa) applies, the responsible person is—

(a) where the entrant arrived concealed in a freight train, the train operator who, at the train's last scheduled stop before arrival in the United Kingdom, was responsible for certifying it as fit to travel to the United Kingdom, or

(b) where the entrant arrived concealed in a freight shuttle wagon, the operator of the shuttle-train of which the wagon formed part.]

(**6**) In the case of a clandestine entrant to whom subsection (1)(b) or (c) applies, each of the following is a responsible person—

(a) if the transporter is a detached trailer, the owner, hirer [and] operator of the trailer;

(b) if it is not, the owner, hirer [and] driver of the vehicle.

[(**6A**) Where a person falls within the definition of responsible person in more than one capacity, a separate penalty may be imposed on him under subsection (2) in respect of each capacity.]

[[(6B) A penalty may not be imposed on a person under subsection (2) if a penalty is imposed on that person under section 31(A) in respect of the same circumstances.]]

(7) Subject to any defence provided by section 34, it is immaterial whether a responsible person knew or suspected—

(a) that the clandestine entrant was concealed in the transporter; or

(b) that there were one or more other persons concealed with the clandestine entrant in the same transporter.

(8) Subsection (9) applies if a transporter ('the carried transporter') is itself being carried in or on another transporter.

(9) If a person is concealed in the carried transporter, the question whether any other person is concealed with that person in the same transporter is to be determined by reference to the carried transporter and not by reference to the transporter in or on which it is carried.

(**10**) 'Immigration control' means United Kingdom immigration control and includes any United Kingdom immigration control operated in a prescribed control zone outside the United Kingdom.

Note: Sections 32(2)(a), 32(3) and 32(10) commenced 6 December 1999 (SI 1999/3190), remainder on 3 April 2000 (SI 2000/464). Subsections (1)(aa), (2A), (4A), (5A) and (6A) inserted and subsections (2) and (4) substituted by and words in square brackets in subsections (5) and (6) inserted by Sch 8 Nationality, Immigration and Asylum Act 2002 from 8 December 2002 (SI 2002/2811) for certain purposes; from 11 May 2012 for other purposes (SI 2012/1263). Subsections (2B)-(2E) & (6B) inserted by Nationality and Borders Act 2022 c.36 Sch.5 para 4(2) & (4)(came into force on April 28, 2022 as specified in 2022 c.36 s.87(4)(c) for the limited purpose of making (and, where required, consulting on) regulations; otherwise not yet in force). Subsection 4 substituted by Nationality and Borders Act 2022 c.36 Sch.5 para 4(3) (April 28, 2022 as specified in 2022 c.36 s.97(4)(c) for the limited purpose of making (and, where required, consulting on) regulations; otherwise not yet in force)

[32A. Level of penalty: code of practice

[(**A1**) The Secretary of State must issue a code of practice specifying matters to be considered in determining the amount of a penalty under section 31A.

(**B1**) The Secretary of State must have regard to the code (in addition to any other matters the Secretary of State thinks relevant)—

(a) when imposing a penalty under section 31A, and

(b) when considering a notice of objection under section 35(4) in relation to a penalty under section 31A.]

(1) The Secretary of State shall issue a code of practice specifying matters to be considered in determining the amount of a penalty under section 32.

(2) The Secretary of State shall have regard to the code (in addition to any other matters he thinks relevant)—

(a) when imposing a penalty under section 32, and

(b) when considering a notice of objection under section 35(4)[[in relation to a penalty under section 32.]].

(3) Before issuing [[a code under this section]] the Secretary of State shall lay a draft before Parliament.

(4) After laying [[a draft code]]before Parliament the Secretary of State may bring the code into operation by order.

(5) The Secretary of State may from time to time revise the whole or any part of [[a code under this section]] and issue the code as revised.

(6) Subsections (3) and (4) also apply to a revision or proposed revision of [[a code]].]

Note: Section 32A inserted by Sch 8 Nationality, Immigration and Asylum Act 2002 from 14 November 2002 for the purpose of enabling the Secretary of State to exercise the power under s 32A(1), (3) and (4); otherwise takes effect from 8 December 2002 (SI 2002/2811) for certain purposes and from 11 May 2012 for other purposes (SI 2012/1263). Subsections (A1) & (B1) inserted by Nationality and Borders Act 2022 c.36 Sch.5 para 5(2) (April 28, 2022 as specified by 2022 c.36 s87(4)(c) for the limited purposes of making (and, where required, consulting on) regulations, not yet in force otherwise). Words in double square brackets substituted in subsections (2)(b), (3), (4), (5) & (6) by Nationality and Borders Act 2022 c.36 Sch.5 para 5(3)(4)(5)(6) & (7) (April 28, 2022 as specified by 2022 c.36 s.87(4)(c) for the limited purposes of making (and, where required, consulting on) regulations; not yet in force otherwise)

33. [Prevention of clandestine entrants: code of practice]

Note: Commenced 6 December 1999 (SI 1999/3190). Heading substituted and words omitted from subsection (2)(b) by Sch 8 Nationality, Immigration and Asylum Act 2002 from 8 December 2002 (SI 2002/2811) for certain purposes and for other purposes from 11 May 2012 (SI 2012/1263). Omitted by Nationality and Borders Act 2022 c.36 Sch.5 para 6 (April 28, 2022 as specified in 2022 c.36 s87(4)(c) for the limited purpose of making (and, where required, consulting on) regulations; not yet in force otherwise)

34. Defences to claim that penalty is due under section 32

[(1) A person ('the carrier') shall not be liable to the imposition of a penalty under section 32(2) if he has a defence under this section.]

(2) It is a defence for the carrier to show that he, or an employee of his who was directly responsible for allowing the clandestine entrant to be concealed, was acting under duress.

(3)

[(3A) It is also a defence for the carrier to show that—

(a) he knew or suspected that a clandestine entrant was or might be concealed in a rail freight wagon, having boarded after the wagon began its journey to the United Kingdom;

(b) he could not stop the train or shuttle-train of which the wagon formed part without endangering safety; [[and,

(c) the carrier had taken the actions specified in regulations under subsection (3B) in relation to the securing of the wagon against unauthorised access]].

(d) ...]

[[(3B)The Secretary of State must specify in regulations the actions to be taken for the purposes of subsection (3A)(c) in relation to the securing of a rail freight wagon against unauthorised access.

(3C) The actions that may be specified in regulations under subsection (3B) include, in particular—

(a) actions in relation to checking a person has not gained unauthorised access to the wagon,

(b) actions in relation to the reporting of any unauthorised access to the wagon, and

(c) actions in relation to the keeping of records to establish that other actions specified in the regulations have been taken.

(3D) Before making regulations under subsection (3B), the Secretary of State must consult such persons as the Secretary of State considers appropriate.]]

(4) …

(5) …

[(6) Where a person has a defence under subsection (2) in respect of a clandestine entrant, every other responsible person in respect of the clandestine entrant is also entitled to the benefit of the defence.]

Note: Commencement 3 April 2000 (SI 2000/464). Subsections (1) and (6) substituted by and subsection (3A) inserted by and words in subsection (3)(c) omitted by and subsection (5) omitted by Sch 8 Nationality, Immigration and Asylum Act 2002 from 8 December 2002 (SI 2002/2811) for certain purposes and from 11 May 2012 for other purposes (SI 2012/1263). Words at subparagraphs (3) & (4) omitted by Nationality and Borders Act 2022 c.36 Sch.5 para 7(2) & (5) (date to be appointed: 2022 c.36 Sch.5 para 7 came into force April 28, 2022 as specified in 2022 c.36 s.87(4)(c) for the limited purpose of making (and, where required, consulting on) regulations; not yet in force otherwise). Words substituted in double square brackets at subsection (3A) and omitted at (3A)(d) by Nationality and Borders Act 2022 c.36 Sch.5 para 7(3) (date to be appointed: 2022 c.36 Sch.5 para 7(3) came into force April 28, 2022 as specified in 2022 c.36 s.87(4)(c) for the limited purpose of making (and, where required, consulting on) regulations; not yet in force otherwise). Subsection (3B) & (3C) inserted by Nationality and Border Act 2022 (date to be appointed: 2022 c.36 Sch.5 para 7 came into force April 28, 2022 as specified in 2022 c.36 s.87(4)(c) of the limited purpose of making (and, where required, consulting on) relations; otherwise not yet in force)

35. Procedure

(1) If the Secretary of State decides that a person ('P') is liable to one or more penalties under section [section 31A or]32, he must notify P of his decision.

(2) A notice under subsection (1) (a 'penalty notice') must—

(a) state the Secretary of State's reasons for deciding that P is liable to the penalty (or penalties);

(b) state the amount of the penalty (or penalties) to which P is liable;

(c) specify the date before which, and the manner in which, the penalty (or penalties) must be paid; []

(d) include an explanation of the steps—

(i) that P [may] take if he objects to the penalty;

(ii) that the Secretary of State may take under this Part to recover any unpaid penalty and

(e) be issued before the end of such period as may be prescribed].

[(3)

(4) The person may give a notice of objection to the Secretary of State.

(5) A notice of objection must—
(a) be in writing,
(b) give the objector's reasons, and
(c) be given before the end of such period as may be prescribed.

(6) Where the Secretary of State receives a notice of objection to a penalty in accordance with this section he shall consider it and—
(a) cancel the penalty,
(b) reduce the penalty,
(c) increase the penalty, or
(d) determine to take no action under paragraphs (a) to (c).

(7) Where the Secretary of State considers a notice of objection under subsection (6) he shall—
(a) inform the objector of his decision before the end of such period as may be prescribed or such longer period as he may agree with the objector,
(b) if he increases the penalty, issue a new penalty notice under subsection (1), and
(c) if he reduces the penalty, notify the objector of the reduced amount.]

(8) …

(9) The Secretary of State may by regulations provide, in relation to detached trailers, for a penalty notice which is [issued] in such manner as may be prescribed to have effect as a penalty notice properly [issued to] the responsible person or persons concerned under this section.

(10) Any sum payable to the Secretary of State as a penalty under section [31A or]32 may be recovered by the Secretary of State as a debt due to him.

[(11) In proceedings for enforcement of a penalty under subsection (10) no question may be raised as to—
(a) liability to the imposition of the penalty, or
(b) its amount.

(12) A document which is to be issued to or served on a person outside the United Kingdom for the purpose of subsection (1) or (7) or in the course of proceedings under subsection (10) may be issued or served—
(a) in person,
(b) by post,
(c) by facsimile transmission, []
[(ca) by electronic mail, or]
(d) in another prescribed manner.

(13) The Secretary of State may by regulations provide that a document issued or served in a manner listed in subsection (12) in accordance with the regulations is to be taken to have been received at a time specified by or determined in accordance with the regulations.]

Note: Section 35(7)–(9) commenced 6 December 1999 (SI 1999/3190), remainder 3 April 2000 (SI 2000/464). Subsections (3)–(7) substituted by and subsection (8) omitted by and subsections (11)–(13) inserted by and words in square brackets in subsection (2) and (9) substituted by Sch. 8 Nationality, Immigration and Asylum Act 2002 from 8 December 2002 (SI 2002/2811) for certain purposes and from 11 May 2012 for other purposes (SI 2012/1263). Words omitted at subsection (3) and inserted in subsection (2), (10) and (12) by Nationality and Borders Act 2022 c.36 Sch.5 para 8 (date to be appointed: 2022 c.36 Sch.5 para 8 came into force on April 28, 2022 by s.87(4) (c) for limited purpose of making (and, where required, consulting on) regulations; not yet in force otherwise)

[35A. Appeal

(1) A person may appeal to the court against a penalty imposed on him under section [31A or]32 on the ground that—

(a) he is not liable to the imposition of a penalty, or

(b) the amount of the penalty is too high.

(2) On an appeal under this section the court may—

(a) allow the appeal and cancel the penalty,

(b) allow the appeal and reduce the penalty, or

(c) dismiss the appeal.

(3) An appeal under this section shall be a re-hearing of the Secretary of State's decision to impose a penalty and shall be determined having regard to—

(a) any code of practice under section 32A which has effect at the time of the appeal, [and]

(b)

(c) any other matters which the court thinks relevant (which may include matters of which the Secretary of State was unaware).

(4) Subsection (3) has effect despite any provision of Civil Procedure Rules.

(5) An appeal may be brought by a person under this section against a penalty whether or not—

(a) he has given notice of objection under section 35(4);

(b) the penalty has been increased or reduced under section 35(6).]

Note: Section 35A inserted by Sch. 8 Nationality, Immigration and Asylum Act 2002 from 8 December 2002 (SI 2002/2811) for certain purposes and from 11 May 2012 for other purposes (SI 2012/1263). Words inserted at subsection (1) and subsection (3)(a) and omitted at subsection (3)(d) by Nationality and Borders Act 2022 c.36 (date to be appointed: 2022 c.36 Sch.5 para 9 came into force on April 28, 2022 as specified by 2022 c.36 s.87(4)(c) for the limited purpose of making (and, where required, consulting on) regulations; otherwise not yet in force)

36. Power to detain vehicles etc. in connection with penalties under section [section 31 A or]32

(1) If a penalty notice has been [issued] under section 35, a senior officer may detain any relevant—

(a) vehicle,

(b) small ship, . . .

(c) small aircraft,. . . [or

(d) rail freight wagon,] until all penalties to which the notice relates, and any expenses reasonably incurred by the Secretary of State in connection with the detention, have been paid.

(2) That power—

(a) may be exercised only if, in the opinion of the senior officer concerned, there is a significant risk that the penalty (or one or more of the penalties) will not be paid before the end of the prescribed period if the transporter is not detained; and

(b) may not be exercised if alternative security which the Secretary of State considers is satisfactory, has been given.

[(2A) A vehicle may be detained under subsection (1) only if—

(a) the driver of the vehicle [[drives the vehicle pursuant to a contract (whether or not a contract of employment) with the owner of hirer of the vehicle]],

(b) the driver of the vehicle is its owner or hirer, or
(c) a penalty notice is issued to the owner or hirer of the vehicle.

[[2AA) In the case of a detached trailer, subsection (2A) has effect as if
(a) a reference to the driver where a reference to the operator, and
(b) the reference to driving the vehicle were a reference to operating it.]]

(2B) A senior officer may detain a relevant vehicle, small ship, small aircraft or rail freight wagon pending—
(a) a decision whether to issue a penalty notice,
(b) the issue of a penalty notice, or
(c) a decision whether to detain under subsection (1).

(2C) That power may not be exercised in any case—
(a) for longer than is necessary in the circumstances of the case, or
(b) after the expiry of the period of 24 hours beginning with the conclusion of the first search of the vehicle, ship, aircraft or wagon by an immigration officer after it arrived in the United Kingdom.]

(3) If a transporter is detained under this section, the owner, consignor or any other person who has an interest in any freight or other thing carried in or on the transporter may remove it, or arrange for it to be removed, at such time and in such way as is reasonable.

(4) The detention of a transporter under this section is lawful even though it is subsequently established that the penalty notice on which the detention was based was ill-founded in respect of all or any of the penalties to which it related.

(5) But subsection (4) does not apply if the Secretary of State was acting unreasonably in issuing the penalty notice.

(6) A document which is to be issued to or served on a person outside the United Kingdom for the purposes of this section may be issued or served—
(a) in person,
(b) by post,
(c) by facsimile transmission,
(d) by electronic mail, or
(e) in another prescribed manner.

(7) The Secretary of State may by regulations provide that a document issued or served in a manner listed in subsection (6) in accordance with the regulations is to be taken to have been received at a time specified by or determined in accordance with the regulations.

Note: Section 36(2)(a) commenced 6 December 1999 (SI 1999/3190), remainder 3 April 2000 (SI 2000/464). Subsections (2A), (2B) and (2C) inserted by and words in square brackets in subsection (1) substituted by Sch 8 Nationality Immigration and Asylum Act 2002 from 8 December 2002 (SI 2002/2811) for certain purposes and from 11 May 2012 for other purposes (SI 2012/1263). Words inserted in heading, substituted in double square brackets, and inserted at subsection (2AA), (6) & (7) by Nationality and Borders Act 2022 c.33 Sch.5 para 10 (date to be appointed: 2022 c.36 Sch.5 para 10 came in to force on April 28, 2022 as specified by 2022 c.36 s.87(4)(c) for the limited purpose of making (and, where required, consulting on) regulations; otherwise not yet in force)

[36A. Detention in default of payment

(1) This section applies where a person to whom a penalty notice has been issued under section 35 fails to pay the penalty before the date specified in accordance with section 35(2)(c).

(2) The Secretary of State may make arrangements for the detention of any vehicle, small ship, small aircraft or rail freight wagon which the person to whom the penalty notice was issued uses in the course of a business.

(3) A vehicle, ship, aircraft or wagon may be detained under subsection (2) whether or not the person to whom the penalty notice was issued owns it.

(4) But a vehicle may be detained under subsection (2) only if the person to whom the penalty notice was issued—

(a) is the owner or hirer of the vehicle, or

(b) [[drove the vehicle pursuant to a contract (whether or not a contract of employment) with]] the owner or hirer of the vehicle when the penalty notice was issued.

[(4A) In the case of a detached trailer, subsection (4)(b) has effect as if the reference to driving the vehicle were a reference to operating it.]

(5) The power under subsection (2) may not be exercised while an appeal against the penalty under section 35A is pending or could be brought (ignoring the possibility of an appeal out of time with permission).

(6) The Secretary of State shall arrange for the release of a vehicle, ship, aircraft or wagon detained under this section if the person to whom the penalty notice was issued pays—

(a) the penalty, and

(b) expenses reasonably incurred in connection with the detention.]

(7) If a transporter is detained under this section, the owner, consignor or any other person who has an interest in any freight or other thing carried in or on the transporter may remove it, or arrange for it to be removed, at such time and in such way as is reasonable.

(8) The detention of a transporter under this section is lawful even though it is subsequently established that the penalty notice on which the detention was based was ill-founded in respect of all or any of the penalties to which it related.

(9) But subsection (8) does not apply if the Secretary of State was acting unreasonably in issuing the penalty notice.

(10) A document which is to be issued to or served on a person outside the United Kingdom for the purposes of this section may be issued or served—

(a) in person,

(b) by post,

(c) by facsimile transmission,

(d) by electronic mail, or

(e) in another prescribed manner.

(11) The Secretary of State may by regulations provide that a document issued or served in a manner listed in subsection (10) in accordance with the regulations is to be taken to have been received at a time specified by or determined in accordance with the regulations.

Note: Section 36A inserted by Sch. 8 Nationality, Immigration and Asylum Act 2002 from 8 December 2002 (SI 2002/2811) for certain purposes and from 11 May 2012 for other purposes (SI 2012/1263). Words substituted in double square brackets in subsection (4)(b) and subsection (4A), (7)-(11) by Nationality and Borders Act 2022 c.36 Sch.5 para 11 (date to be appointed: 2022 c.36 Sch.5 para 11 came in to force on April 28, 2022 as specified by 2022 c.36 s.87(4)(c) for the limited purpose of making (and, where required, consulting on) regulations; otherwise not yet in force)

37. Effect of detention

(1) This section applies if a transporter is detained under [section 36(1)].

(2) The person to whom the penalty notice was addressed, or the owner or any other person [whose interests may be affected by detention of the transporter], may apply to the court for the transporter to be released.

(3) The court may release the transporter if it considers that—

(a) satisfactory security has been tendered in place of the transporter for the payment of the penalty alleged to be due and connected expenses;

(b) there is no significant risk that the penalty (or one or more of the penalties) and any connected expenses will not be paid; or

(c) there is a significant doubt as to whether the penalty is payable.

[(3A) The court may also release the transporter on the application of the owner of the transporter under subsection (2) if—

(a) a penalty notice was not issued to the owner or an employee of his, and

(b) the court considers it right to release the transporter.

(3B) In determining whether to release a transporter under subsection (3A) the court shall consider—

(a) the extent of any hardship caused by detention,

(b) the extent (if any) to which the owner is responsible for the matters in respect of which the penalty notice was issued, and

(c) any other matter which appears to the court to be relevant (whether specific to the circumstances of the case or of a general nature).]

(4) If the court has not ordered the release of the transporter, the Secretary of State may sell it if the penalty in question and connected expenses are not paid before the end of the period of 84 days beginning with the date on which the detention began.

(5) 'Connected expenses' means expenses reasonably incurred by the Secretary of State in connection with the detention.

[(5A) The power of sale under subsection (4) may be exercised only when no appeal against the imposition of the penalty is pending or can be brought (ignoring the possibility of an appeal out of time with permission).

(5B) The power of sale under subsection (4) shall lapse if not exercised within a prescribed period.]

(6) Schedule 1 applies to the sale of transporters under this section.

[(7) This section applies to a transporter detained under section 36A as it applies to a transporter detained under section 36(1); but for that purpose—

(a) the court may release the transporter only if the court considers that the detention was unlawful or under subsection (3A) (and subsection (3) shall not apply), and

(b) the reference in subsection (4) to the period of 84 days shall be taken as a reference to a period prescribed for the purpose of this paragraph.]

Note: Section 37(6) commenced 6 December 1999 (SI 1999/3190), remainder 3 April 2000 (SI 2000/464). Subsections (3A)–(3B), (5A)–(5B) and (7) inserted by Sch 8 Nationality, Immigration and Asylum Act 2002 from 8 December 2002 (SI 2002/2811). Words in square brackets in subsections (1) and (2) and words in subsection (3)(c) omitted by Sch 8 Nationality, Immigration and Asylum Act 2002 from 8 December 2002 (SI 2002/2811) for certain purposes and from 11 May 2012 for other purposes (SI 2012/1263).

38. Assisting illegal entry and harbouring

...

Note: Inserts s 25A of Immigration Act 1971 from 3 April 2000. Subsections (1) and (3) repealed by Sch 9 Nationality, Immigration and Asylum Act 2002 from a date to be appointed.

39....

Note: Section 39 repealed by Sch 8 Nationality, Immigration and Asylum Act 2002 from 8 December 2002 (SI 2002/2811).

[Individuals without proper documentation or authorisation]

[40. [[Charge in respect of individual without proper documents or authorisation]]

[[(1) The Secretary of State may charge the owner of a ship or aircraft the sum of £2,000 where—

(a) an individual who would not, on arrival in the United Kingdom, be entitled to enter without leave arrives by travelling on the ship or aircraft, and

(b) at least one of the Cases set out in subsections (1A) to (1C) applies.]]

[[(1A) Case 1 is where, on being required to do so by an immigration officer, the individual fails to produce an immigration document which is valid and which satisfactorily establishes the individual's identity and the individual's nationality or citizenship.

(1B) Case 2 is where—

(a) the individual requires an entry clearance,

(b) an entry clearance in electronic form of the required kind has not been granted, and

(c) if required to do so by an immigration officer, the individual fails to produce an entry clearance in documentary form of the required kind.

(1C) Case 3 is where—

(a) the individual was required not to travel to the United Kingdom unless the individual had an authorisation in electronic form ("an ETA") under immigration rules made by virtue of section 11C of the Immigration Act 1971 that was valid for the individual's journey to the United Kingdom, and

(b) the individual did not have such an ETA.]]

(2) ...

(3) The charge shall be payable to the Secretary of State on demand.

(4) [No charge will be payable on the basis that Case 1 applies in respect of any individual if the owner provides evidence that the individual produced an immigration document of the kind mentioned in subsection)(1A)] to the owner or his employee or agent when embarking on the ship or aircraft for the voyage or flight to the United Kingdom.

(4A) No charge shall be payable on the basis that Case 2 applies in respect of any individual if the owner provides evidence that—

(a) the individual produced an entry clearance in documentary form of the required kind to the owner or an employee or agent of the owner when embarking on the ship or aircraft for the voyage or flight to the United Kingdom,

(b) the owner or an employee or agent of the owner reasonably believed, on the basis of information provided by the Secretary of State in respect of the individual, that the individual did not require an entry clearance of the kind in question,

(c) the owner or an employee or agent of the owner reasonably believed, on the basis of information provided by the Secretary of State, that an entry clearance in electronic form of the required kind had been granted, or

(d) the owner or an employee or agent of the owner was unable to establish whether an entry clearance in electronic form of the required kind had been granted in respect of the individual and had a reasonable excuse for being unable to do so.

(4B) No charge shall be payable on the basis that Case 3 applies in respect of any individual if the owner provides evidence that the owner or an employee or agent of the owner—

(a) reasonably believed, on the basis of information provided by the Secretary of State in respect of the individual, that the individual was not required to have an ETA that was valid for the individual's journey to the United Kingdom,

(b) reasonably believed, on the basis of information provided by the Secretary of State, that the individual had such an ETA, or

(c) was unable to establish whether the individual had such an ETA and had a reasonable excuse for being unable to do so.

(5) For the purpose of subsection [[(4) or (4A)(a)]] an owner shall be entitled to regard a document as—

(a) being what it purports to be unless its falsity is reasonably apparent, and

(b) relating to the individual producing it unless it is reasonably apparent that it does not relate to him.

(6) For the purposes of this section an individual requires [an entry clearance]]if—

(a) under the immigration rules he requires [an entry clearance]] for entry into the United Kingdom, or

(b) as a result of section 41 he requires a visa for passing through the United Kingdom.

(7) The Secretary of State may by order amend this section for the purpose of applying it in relation to an individual who—

(a) requires leave to enter the United Kingdom, and

(b) arrives in the United Kingdom by train.

(8) An order under subsection (7) may provide for the application of this section—

(a) except in cases of a specified kind;

(b) subject to a specified defence.

(9) In this section 'immigration document' means—

(a) a passport, and

(b) a document which relates to a national of a country other than the United Kingdom and which is designed to serve the same purpose as a passport.

(10) The Secretary of State may by order substitute a sum for the sum in subsection [[(1)]]]

Note: Section 40 substituted by Sch 8 Nationality, Immigration and Asylum Act 2002 from 8 December 2002 (SI 2003/2811). Italic heading before and hearing at section 40 substituted by Nationality and Borders Act 2022 c.36 Pt6 s.76(9)(a) & (b) (date to be appointed). Words in double square brackets in subsection (40)(1)-(1C) by Nationality and Borders Act 2022 c.36 Pt6 s.76(2)(date to be appointed). Words omitted at subsection (2) by Nationality and Borders Act 2022 c.36 s.76(3)(date to be appointed). Words substituted in double brackets at subsection (4) by Nationality and Borders Act 2022 c.36 s.76(4) (date to be appointed). Subsections (4A) & (4B) by Nationality and Borders Act 2022 c.36 s.76(5) (date to be appointed). Words substituted in double square brackets at subsection (5),(6) &(10) by Nationality and Borders Act 2022 c.36 s.76(6)(7) &(8) (date to be appointed).

[40A. Notification and objection

(1) If the Secretary of State decides to charge a person under section 40, the Secretary of State must notify the person of his decision.

(2) A notice under subsection (1) (a 'charge notice') must—

(a) state the Secretary of State's reasons for deciding to charge the person,

(b) state the amount of the charge,

(c) specify the date before which, and the manner in which, the charge must be paid,

(d) include an explanation of the steps that the person may take if he objects to the charge, and

(e) include an explanation of the steps that the Secretary of State may take under this Part to recover any unpaid charge.

(3) Where a person on whom a charge notice is served objects to the imposition of the charge on him, he may give a notice of objection to the Secretary of State.

(4) A notice of objection must—

(a) be in writing,

(b) give the objector's reasons, and

(c) be given before the end of such period as may be prescribed.

(5) Where the Secretary of State receives a notice of objection to a charge in accordance with this section, he shall—

(a) consider it, and

(b) determine whether or not to cancel the charge.

(6) Where the Secretary of State considers a notice of objection, he shall inform the objector of his decision before the end of—

(a) such period as may be prescribed, or

(b) such longer period as he may agree with the objector.

(7) Any sum payable to the Secretary of State as a charge under section 40 may be recovered by the Secretary of State as a debt due to him.

(8) In proceedings for enforcement of a charge under subsection (7) no question may be raised as to the validity of the charge.

(9) Subsections (12) and (13) of section 35 shall have effect for the purpose of this section as they have effect for the purpose of section 35(1), (7) and (10).]

Note: Section 40A inserted by Sch 8 Nationality, Immigration and Asylum Act 2002 from 8 December 2002 (SI 2002/2811).

[40B. Appeal

(1) A person may appeal to the court against a decision to charge him under section 40.

(2) On an appeal under this section the court may—

(a) allow the appeal and cancel the charge, or

(b) dismiss the appeal.

(3) An appeal under this section—

(a) shall be a re-hearing of the Secretary of State's decision to impose a charge, and

(b) may be determined having regard to matters of which the Secretary of State was unaware.

(4) Subsection (3)(a) has effect despite any provision of Civil Procedure Rules.

(5) An appeal may be brought by a person under this section against a decision to charge him whether or not he has given notice of objection under section 40A(3).]

Note: Section 40B inserted by Sch 8 Nationality, Immigration and Asylum Act 2002 from 8 December 2002 (SI 2002/2811).

41. Visas for transit passengers

(1) The Secretary of State may by order require transit passengers to hold a transit visa.

(2) 'Transit passengers' means persons of any description specified in the order who on arrival in the United Kingdom pass through to another country without entering the United Kingdom; and 'transit visa' means a visa for that purpose.

(3) The order—

(a) may specify a description of persons by reference to nationality, citizenship, origin or other connection with any particular country but not by reference to race, colour or religion;

(b) may not provide for the requirement imposed by the order to apply to any person who under the 1971 Act has the right of abode in the United Kingdom;

(c) may provide for any category of persons of a description specified in the order to be exempt from the requirement imposed by the order;

(d) may make provision about the method of application for visas required by the order.

Note: Commenced 8 December 2002 (SI 2002/2815).

42. . . .

Note: Section 42 repealed by Sch 8 Nationality, Immigration and Asylum Act from 8 December 2002 (SI 2002/2811).

Interpretation

43. Interpretation of Part II

[(1)] In this Part—

'aircraft' includes hovercraft;

'captain' means the master of a ship or commander of an aircraft;

'concealed' includes being concealed in any freight, stores or other thing carried in or on the vehicle, ship [, aircraft or rail freight wagon] concerned;

. . .

'detached trailer' means a trailer, semi-trailer, caravan or any other thing which is designed or adapted for towing by a vehicle but which has been detached for transport—

(a) in or on the vehicle concerned; or

(b) in the ship or aircraft concerned (whether separately or in or on a vehicle);

'equipment', in relation to an aircraft, includes—

(a) any certificate of registration, maintenance or airworthiness of the aircraft;

(b) any log book relating to the use of the aircraft; and
(c) any similar document;
['freight shuttle wagon' means a wagon which—
(a) forms part of a shuttle-train, and
(b) is designed to carry commercial goods vehicles;
'freight train' means any train other than—
(a) a train engaged on a service for the carriage of passengers, or
(b) a shuttle-train;]
['goods vehicle' means
(a) a mechanically propelled vehicle which-
(i) is designed or adapted solely or principally to be used for the carriage or haulage of good, and
(ii) at the time in question, is being used for a commercial purpose. Or
(b) any trailer, semi-trailer or other thing which-
(i) is designed or adapted to be towed by a vehicle within paragraph (a) (i), and
(ii) at the time in question, is being used for commercial purpose', and]

'hirer', in relation to a vehicle, means any person who has hired the vehicle from another person;

'operating weight', in relation to an aircraft, means the maximum total weight of the aircraft and its contents at which the aircraft may take off anywhere in the world, in the most favourable circumstances, in accordance with the certificate of airworthiness in force in respect of the aircraft;

'owner' includes—
(a) in relation to a ship or aircraft, the agent or operator of the ship or aircraft;
...
(b) ... and in relation to a transporter which is the subject of a hire-purchase agreement, includes the person in possession of it under that agreement;

'penalty notice' has the meaning given in section 35(2);

['rail freight wagon' means—
(a) any rolling stock, other than a locomotive, which forms part of a freight train, or
(b) a freight shuttle wagon, and for the purpose of this definition, 'rolling stock' and 'locomotive' have the meanings given by section 83 of the Railways Act 1993 (c. 43);]

'senior officer' means an immigration officer not below the rank of chief immigration officer;

'ship' includes every description of vessel used in navigation;

['shuttle-train' has the meaning given by section 1(9) of the Channel Tunnel Act 1987 (c. 53);]

'small aircraft' means an aircraft which has an operating weight of less than 5,700 kilogrammes;

'small ship' means a ship which has a gross tonnage of less than 500 tonnes;

'train' means a train which—
(a) is engaged on an international service as defined by section 13(6) of the Channel Tunnel Act 1987; but
(b) is not a shuttle train as defined by section 1(9) of that Act;

'train operator', in relation to a person arriving in the United Kingdom on a train, means the operator of trains who embarked that person on that train for the journey to the United Kingdom;

'transporter' means a vehicle, ship, [aircraft or rail freight wagon] together with—

(a) its equipment; and

(b) any stores for use in connection with its operation;

'vehicle' includes a trailer, semi-trailer, caravan or other thing which is designed or adapted to be towed by another vehicle [(including a goods vehicle)].

[(**1A**) References in this Part to the securing of a goods vehicle against unauthorised access include references to the securing of any container which is being carried by a goods vehicle against unauthorised access.

(**1B**) In subsection (1A) "container" means any container or other thing which is designed or adapted to be carried by a goods vehicle.]

[(**2**) A reference in this Part to 'the court' is a reference—

(a) in England and Wales, to [the county court],

(b) in Scotland, to the sheriff, and

(c) in Northern Ireland, to a county court.

(**3**) But—

(a) a county court [in Northern Ireland, or the county court in England and Wales,] may transfer proceedings under this Part to the High Court, and

(b) the sheriff may transfer proceedings under this Part to the Court of Session.]

Note: Commenced 6 December 1999 (SI 1999/3190). Subsections (2) and (3) and words in square brackets in subsection (1) inserted by and words in subsection (1) omitted by Sch. 8 Nationality, Immigration and Asylum Act from 8 December 2002 (SI 2002/2811). Words in square brackets in subsection (2)(a) substituted and in square brackets in subsection (3)(a) inserted by Sch. 9 Crime and Courts Act 2013 from 22 April 2014 subject to savings and transitional provisions specified in 2013. Words in square brackets inserted in subsection (1), and subsection (1A) & (1B) by Nationality and Borders Act 2022 c.36 Sch.5 para 12 (date to be appointed: 2022 c.36 Sch.5 para 12 came into force on April 28, 2022 as specified in 2022 c.36 s87(4)(c) for the limited purpose of making (and, where required, consulting on) regulations; not yet in force otherwise)

Part III

Bail

Routine bail hearings

...

44–52. ...

Note: Sections 44 to 52 repealed by the Nationality, Immigration and Asylum Act 2002, s 68 from 10 February 2003 (SI 2003/1).

Bail hearings under other enactments

53. Applications for bail in immigration cases

(**1**) The Secretary of State may by regulations make new provision in relation to applications for bail by persons detained under the 1971 Act [or under section 62 of the Nationality, Immigration and Asylum Act 2002].

(2) The regulations may confer a right to be released on bail in prescribed circumstances.

(3) The regulations may, in particular, make provision—

(a) creating or transferring jurisdiction to hear an application for bail by a person detained under the 1971 Act [or under section 62 of the Nationality, Immigration and Asylum Act 2002];

(b) as to the places in which such an application may be held;

(c) as to the procedure to be followed on, or in connection with, such an application;

(d) as to circumstances in which, and conditions (including financial conditions) on which, an applicant may be released on bail;

(e) amending or repealing any enactment so far as it relates to such an application.

(4) ...

(5) ...

(6) Regulations under this section require the approval of the Lord Chancellor.

[(6A) In so far as regulations under this section relate to England and Wales, the Lord Chancellor must consult the Lord Chief Justice of England and Wales before giving his approval.

(6B) In so far as regulations under this section relate to Northern Ireland, the Lord Chancellor must consult the Lord Chief Justice of Northern Ireland before giving his approval.]

(7) In so far as regulations under this section relate to the sheriff or the Court of Session, the Lord Chancellor must obtain the consent of the Scottish Ministers before giving his approval.

[(8) The Lord Chief Justice of England and Wales may nominate a judicial office holder (as defined in section 109(4) of the Constitutional Reform Act 2005) to exercise his functions under this section.

(9) The Lord Chief Justice of Northern Ireland may nominate any of the following to exercise his functions under this section—

(a) the holder of one of the offices listed in Schedule 1 to the Justice (Northern Ireland) Act 2002;

(b) a Lord Justice of Appeal (as defined in section 88 of that Act).]

Note: Section 53 commenced 10 February 2003 (SI 2003/2). Words in square brackets in subsections (1) and (3) inserted by and subsection (5) omitted by Nationality, Immigration and Asylum Act 2002, ss 62, 68 from 10 February 2003 (SI 2003/1). Words in square brackets in subsection (4) substituted by Sch 7 Nationality, Immigration and Asylum Act 2002 from 1 April 2003 (SI 2003/754). Subsections (6A), (8)–(9) inserted by Sch 4 Constitutional Reform Act 2005 from 3 April 2006 (SI 2006/1014). Any function of the Lord Chancellor under subsection (6) to become a protected function from a date to be appointed, Sch 7 Constitutional Reform Act 2005. Subsection 4 omitted by Schedule 10 to the Immigration Act 2016 from 15 January 2018 subject to transitional provisions specified in SI 2017/1241 (as amended by SI2018/31).

54. Extension of right to apply for bail in deportation cases

Note: Amends paragraph 2, Sch 3 Immigration Act 1971.

Grants

55. ...

Note: Section 55 ceased to have effect from 10 February 2003, Nationality, Immigration and Asylum Act 2002, s 68.

Part IV

Appeals

...

Note: Part IV repealed by the Nationality, Immigration and Asylum Act 2002, s 114 and Sch 9 from 1 April 2003 (SI 2003/754, which sets out transitional provisions).

Part V

Immigration Advisers and Immigration Service Providers

Interpretation

82. Interpretation of Part V

(1) In this Part—

'claim for asylum' means a claim that it would be contrary to the United Kingdom's obligations under—

(a) the Refugee Convention, or

(b) Article 3 of the Human Rights Convention, for the claimant to be removed from, or required to leave, the United Kingdom;

'the Commissioner' means the Immigration Services Commissioner;

'the complaints scheme' means the scheme established under paragraph 5(1) of Schedule 5;

'designated judge' has the same meaning as in section 119(1) of the Courts and Legal Services Act 1990;

'designated professional body' has the meaning given by section 86;

['designated qualifying regulator' has the meaning given by section 86A;]

'immigration advice' means advice which—

(a) relates to a particular individual;

(b) is given in connection with one or more relevant matters;

(c) is given by a person who knows that he is giving it in relation to a particular individual and in connection with one or more relevant matters; and

(d) is not given in connection with representing an individual before a court in criminal proceedings or matters ancillary to criminal proceedings;

'immigration services' means the making of representations on behalf of a particular individual—

(a) in civil proceedings before a court, tribunal or adjudicator in the United Kingdom, or

(b) in correspondence with a Minister of the Crown or government department, in connection with one or more relevant matters;

'Minister of the Crown' has the same meaning as in the Ministers of the Crown Act 1975;

'qualified person' means a person who is qualified for the purposes of section 84;

'registered person' means a person who is registered with the Commissioner under section 85;

'relevant matters' means any of the following—

(a) a claim for asylum;

[[(aa) an application for an ETA (within the meaning of section 11C of the Immigration Act 1971 (electronic travel authorisations));]]

(b) an application for, or for the variation of, entry clearance or leave to enter or remain in the United Kingdom;

[(ba) an application for an immigration employment document;]

(c) unlawful entry into the United Kingdom;

(d) nationality and citizenship under the law of the United Kingdom;

(e) [[

(f)

(g)

]]

(h) removal or deportation from the United Kingdom;

(i) an application for bail under the Immigration Acts or under the Special Immigration Appeals Commission Act 1997;

(j) an appeal against, or an application for judicial review in relation to, any decision taken in connection with a matter referred to in paragraphs (a) to (i).

[. . .]

(2) In this Part, references to the provision of immigration advice or immigration services are to the provision of such advice or services by a person—

(a) in the United Kingdom (regardless of whether the persons to whom they are provided are in the United Kingdom or elsewhere); and

(b) in the course of a business carried on (whether or not for profit) by him or by another person.

[(3) In the definition of 'relevant matters' in subsection (1) 'immigration employment document' means—

(a) a work permit (within the meaning of section 33(1) of the Immigration Act 1971 (interpretation)), and

(b) any other document which relates to employment and is issued for a purpose of immigration rules or in connection with leave to enter or remain in the United Kingdom.]

Note: Commenced 22 May 2000 (SI 2000/1282). First words in square brackets in subsection (1) inserted Sch 18 Legal Services Act 2007 from 1 April 2011 (SI 2011/720). Second words in square brackets in subsection (1) and subsection (3) inserted by Nationality, Immigration and Asylum Act 2002, s 123 from 1 April 2004 (SI 2003/2993). Words omitted from subsection (1) from 18 January 2010 (SI 2010/22). Words in double square brackets omitted in subsection (1) by Immigration and Social Security Co-ordination (EU Withdrawal) Act 2020 (Consequential, Saving, Transitional and Transitory Provisions)(EU Exit) Regulations 2020/1309 Pt 2(1) reg 12(5)(31 December 2020 at 23.00 being the time and date 2020 c. 20 Sch 1 para 2(2) comes into force). Words in double square brackets inserted at paragraph (aa) by Nationality and Borders Act 2022 c.36 s.75(5) (June 28, 2022)

The Immigration Services Commissioner

83. The Commissioner

(1) There is to be an Immigration Services Commissioner (referred to in this Part as 'the Commissioner').

(2) The Commissioner is to be appointed by the Secretary of State after consulting the Lord Chancellor and the Scottish Ministers.

(3) It is to be the general duty of the Commissioner to promote good practice by those who provide immigration advice or immigration services.

(4) In addition to any other functions conferred on him by this Part, the Commissioner is to have the regulatory functions set out in Part I of Schedule 5.

(5) The Commissioner must exercise his functions so as to secure, so far as is reasonably practicable, that those who provide immigration advice or immigration services—

(a) are fit and competent to do so;

(b) act in the best interests of their clients;

(c) do not knowingly mislead any court, tribunal or adjudicator in the United Kingdom;

(d) do not seek to abuse any procedure operating in the United Kingdom in connection with immigration or asylum (including any appellate or other judicial procedure);

(e) do not advise any person to do something which would amount to such an abuse.

(6) The Commissioner—

(a) must arrange for the publication, in such form and manner and to such extent as he considers appropriate, of information about his functions and about matters falling within the scope of his functions; and

(b) may give advice about his functions and about such matters.

[(6A) The duties imposed on the Commissioner by subsections (3) and (5) apply in relation to persons within section 84(2)(ba) only to the extent that those duties have effect in relation to the Commissioner's functions under section 92 or 92A.]

(7) Part II of Schedule 5 makes further provision with respect to the Commissioner.

Note: Section 83(4) and (5) commenced 22 May 2000 for the purposes of Sch 5, and 30 October 2000 (SI 2000/1985). Subsection (6A) inserted by Sch 18 Legal Services Act 2007 from 1 April 2011 (SI 2011/720).

The general prohibition

84. Provision of immigration services

(1) No person may provide immigration advice or immigration services unless he is a qualified person.

[(2) A person is a qualified person if he is—

(a) a registered person,

(b) authorised by a designated professional body to practise as a member of the profession whose members the body regulates,

[(ba) a person authorised to provide immigration advice or immigration services by a designated qualifying regulator,]

(c) [[...

(d) ...]]or

(e) acting on behalf of, and under the supervision of, a person within any of paragraphs (a) to[[ba]](whether or not under a contract of employment).

(3) Subsection (2)(a) and (e) are subject to

[(a)] any limitation on the effect of a person's registration imposed under paragraph 2(2) of Schedule 6.]

[(b) paragraph 4B(5) of that Schedule (effect of suspension of registration).]

[(3A) A person's entitlement to provide immigration advice or immigration services by virtue of subsection (2)(ba)—

(a) is subject to any limitation on that person's authorisation imposed by the regulatory arrangements of the designated qualifying regulator in question, and

(b) does not extend to the provision of such advice or services by the person other than in England and Wales (regardless of whether the persons to whom they are provided are in England and Wales or elsewhere).

(3B) In subsection (3A) 'regulatory arrangements' has the same meaning as in the Legal Services Act 2007 (see section 21 of that Act).]

(4) Subsection (1) does not apply to a person who—

(a) …

(b) …

(c) …

(d) … falls within a category of person specified in an order made by the Secretary of State for the purposes of this subsection.

(5) …

(6) Subsection (1) does not apply to a person—

(a) holding an office under the Crown, when acting in that capacity;

(b) employed by, or for the purposes of, a government department, when acting in that capacity;

(c) acting under the control of a government department; or

(d) otherwise exercising functions on behalf of the Crown.

(7) …

Note: Subsections (4)(a) and (d), (5) and (7) commenced 30 October 2000 (SI 2000/1985), remainder on 30 April 2001 (SI 2001/1394). Subsections (2) and (3) substituted by Asylum and Immigration (Treatment of Claimants etc.) Act 2004, s 37 from 1 October 2004 (SI 2004/2523). Subsections (2)(ba), (3A) and (3B) and words in square brackets in subsection (2)(c)(ii) inserted by Sch 18 Legal Services Act 2007 from 1 April 2011 (SI 2011/720). Words omitted from subs-s (4) and subs-ss (5) and (7) omitted; subs-s (3)(b) inserted by Sch 7 Immigration Act 2014 from 17 November 2014 (SI 2014/2771). Words in double square brackets omitted in subsections (2)(c) & (d) and substituted at subsection (2)(e) by Immigration, Nationality and Asylum (EU Exit) Regulations 2019/745, reg 11(6)(a) & (b) (31 December 2020: shall come into force on IP completion day and not exit day as specified in 2020 c. 1 s 39(1) and Sch 5 para 1(1)).

85. Registration and exemption by the Commissioner

(1) The Commissioner must prepare and maintain a register for the purposes of section 84(2)(a) …

(2) …

(3) Schedule 6 makes further provision with respect to registration.

Note: Subsection (3) commenced 1 August 2000, remainder 30 October 2000 (SI 2000/1985). Words omitted from subsection (1) by Asylum and Immigration (Treatment of Claimants etc.) Act 2004, s 37 from 1 October 2004 (SI 2004/2523). Subsection (2) omitted by Sch 7 Immigration Act 2014 from 17 November 2014 (SI 2014/2771).

86. Designated professional bodies

(1) 'Designated professional body' means—

(a) The Law Society;

(b) The Law Society of Scotland;

(c) The Law Society of Northern Ireland;

(d) ...

(e) ...

(f) The Faculty of Advocates; or

(g) The General Council of the Bar of Northern Ireland.

[(2) The Secretary of State may by order remove a body from the list in subsection (1) if he considers that the body—

(a) has failed to provide effective regulation of its members in their provision of immigration advice or immigration services, or

(b) has failed to comply with a request of the Commissioner for the provision of information (whether general or in relation to a particular case or matter).]

(3) If a designated professional body asks the Secretary of State to amend subsection (1) so as to remove its name, the Secretary of State may by order do so.

(4) If the Secretary of State is proposing to act under subsection (2) he must, before doing so—

(a) consult the Commissioner;

(b) ...

(c) consult the [Scottish Legal Complaints Commission], if the proposed order would affect a designated professional body in Scotland;

(d) consult the[Legal Services Oversight Commissioner for Northern Ireland], if the proposed order would affect a designated professional body in Northern Ireland;

(e) notify the body concerned of his proposal and give it a reasonable period within which to make representations; and

(f) consider any representations so made.

(5) An order under subsection (2) requires the approval of—

(a) the Lord Chancellor, if it affects a designated professional body in... Northern Ireland;

(b) the Scottish Ministers, if it affects a designated professional body in Scotland.

(6) Before deciding whether or not to give his approval under subsection (5)(a), the Lord Chancellor must consult—

(a) ...

(b) the Lord Chief Justice of Northern Ireland, if [the order] affects a designated professional body in Northern Ireland.

(7) Before deciding whether or not to give their approval under subsection (5)(b), the Scottish Ministers must consult the Lord President of the Court of Session.

(8) If the Secretary of State considers that a body [(other than a body in England and Wales)] which—

(a) is concerned (whether wholly or in part) with regulating the legal profession, or a branch of it, in [[Scotland or Northern Ireland]],

(b) is not a designated professional body, and

(c) is capable of providing effective regulation of its members in their provision of immigration advice or immigration services, ought to be designated, he may by order amend subsection (1) to include the name of that body.

(9) The Commissioner must—

(a) keep under review the list of designated professional bodies set out in subsection (1); and

[(b) report to the Secretary of State if the Commissioner considers that a designated professional body—

(i) is failing to provide effective regulation of its members in their provision of immigration advice or immigration services, or

(ii) has failed to comply with a request of the Commissioner for the provision of information (whether general or in relation to a particular case or matter).]

[(**9A**) A designated professional body shall comply with a request of the Commissioner for the provision of information (whether general or in relation to a specified case or matter).]

(**10**) For the purpose of meeting the costs incurred by the Commissioner in discharging his functions under this Part, each designated professional body must pay to the Commissioner, in each year and on such date as may be specified, such fee as may be specified.

(**11**) Any unpaid fee for which a designated professional body is liable under subsection (10) may be recovered from that body as a debt due to the Commissioner.

(**12**) 'Specified' means specified by an order made by the Secretary of State.

Note: Subsections (1)–(9) commenced 22 May 2000 (SI 2000/1282), remainder 30 October 2000 (SI 2000/1985). Words in square brackets substituted by Asylum and Immigration (Treatment of Claimants etc.) Act 2004, s 41 from 1 October 2004 (SI 2004/2523). Words in square brackets in subsection (4)(c) substituted by s 196 Legal Services Act 2007 from 1 October 2008 (SI 2008/1436). Subsections (1)(a), (d) and (e), (4)(b) and (6)(a) omitted and words in subsection (5)(a) omitted and words in subsection (6)(b) substituted by Schs 18 and 23 Legal Services Act 2007 from 1 April 2011 (SI 2011/720). Words in square brackets at subsection (4)(d) substituted by Legal Complaints and Regulation Act (Northern Ireland) 2016, Sch 4 para 5 from a date to be appointed. Word in double square brackets in subsection (8) substituted by Immigration, Nationality and Asylum (EU Exit) Regulations 2019 /745 Pt 2(1) reg 11(7) (31 December 2020: shall come into force on IP completion day not exit day as specified in 2020 c. 1 s 39(1) and Sch 5 para 1(1)).

[86A. Designated qualifying regulators

(**1**) 'Designated qualifying regulator' means a body which is a qualifying regulator and is listed in subsection (2).

(**2**) The listed bodies are—

(a) the Law Society;

(b) the Institute of Legal Executives;

(c) the General Council of the Bar.

(**3**) The Secretary of State may by order remove a body from the list in subsection (2) if the Secretary of State considers that the body has failed to provide effective regulation of relevant authorised persons in their provision of immigration advice or immigration services.

(**4**) If a designated qualifying regulator asks the Secretary of State to amend subsection (2) so as to remove its name, the Secretary of State may by order do so.

(**5**) Where, at a time when a body is listed in subsection (2), the body ceases to be a qualifying regulator by virtue of paragraph 8(1)(a) of Schedule 18 to the Legal Services Act 2007 (loss of approved regulator status), the Secretary of State must, by order, remove it from the list.

(**6**) If the Secretary of State considers that a body which—

(a) is a qualifying regulator,

(b) is not a designated qualifying regulator, and

(c) is capable of providing effective regulation of relevant authorised persons in their provision of immigration advice or immigration services, ought to be designated, the Secretary of State may, by order, amend the list in subsection (2) to include the name of that body.

(7) If the Secretary of State is proposing to act under subsection (3) or (6), the Secretary of State must, before doing so, consult the Commissioner.

(8) If the Secretary of State is proposing to act under subsection (3), the Secretary of State must, before doing so, also—

(a) notify the body concerned of the proposal and give it a reasonable period within which to make representations, and

(b) consider any representations duly made.

(9) An order under subsection (3) or (6) requires the approval of the Lord Chancellor.

(10) If the Legal Services Board considers that a designated qualifying regulator is failing to provide effective regulation of relevant authorised persons in their provision of immigration advice or immigration services, the Legal Services Board must make a report to this effect to—

(a) the Secretary of State, and

(b) the Lord Chancellor.

(11) In this section—

'qualifying regulator' means a body which is a qualifying regulator for the purposes of this Part of this Act by virtue of Part 1 of Schedule 18 to the Legal Services Act 2007 (approved regulators approved by the Legal Services Board in relation to immigration matters);

'relevant authorised persons', in relation to a designated qualifying regulator, means persons who are authorised by the designated qualifying regulator to provide immigration advice or immigration services.]

Note: Section 86A inserted by Sch 18 Legal Services Act 2007 from 1 April 2011 (SI 2011/720).

87. [Appeals to the First-tier Tribunal]

(1) ...

(2) Any person aggrieved by a relevant decision of the Commissioner may appeal to the [First-tier Tribunal] against the decision.

(3) 'Relevant decision' means a decision—

(a) to refuse an application for registration made under paragraph 1 of Schedule 6;

(b) ...

(c) under paragraph 2(2) of that Schedule to register with limited effect;

(d) to refuse an application for continued registration made under paragraph 3 of that Schedule;

(e) to vary a registration on an application under paragraph 3 of that Schedule;

[(ea) to vary a registration under paragraph 3A of that Schedule;] or

[(eb) to cancel a registration under paragraph 4A(e) of that Schedule.]

(f) ...

[(3A) A relevant decision of the Commissioner is not to have effect while the period within which an appeal may be brought against the decision is running.

(3B) In the case of an appeal under this section, Tribunal Procedure Rules may include provision permitting the First-tier Tribunal to direct that while the appeal is being dealt with—

(a) no effect is to be given to the decision appealed against; or

(b) only such limited effect is to be given to it as may be specified in the direction.

(3C) If provision is made in Tribunal Procedure Rules by virtue of subsection (3B), the rules must also include provision requiring the First-tier Tribunal to consider applications by the Commissioner for the cancellation or variation of directions given by virtue of that subsection;]

[(4) For [further functions] of the First-tier Tribunal under this Part, see paragraph 9(1)(e) of Schedule 5 (disciplinary charges laid by the Commissioner) [and paragraph 4B of Schedule 6 (suspension of registration by First-tier Tribunal)].]

(5) . . .

Note: Subsection (5) commenced 1 August 2000, remainder 30 October 2000 (SI 2000/1985). Words in square brackets inserted by Nationality, Immigration and Asylum Act 2002, s 140 from 8 January 2003 (SI 2003/1). Heading, words in square brackets in subsection (2) and subsection (4) substituted; subsections (3A)–(3C) inserted and subsections (1) and (5) revoked from 18 January 2010 (SI 2010/22). Subsection (3)(b) omitted and (3)(eb) inserted; by Sch 7 Immigration Act 2014 from 17 November 2014 (SI 2014/2771). First words in square brackets in subsection (4) substituted and last words inserted by Sch 7 Immigration Act 2014 from 17 November 2014 (SI 2014/2771).

88. Appeal upheld by the [First-tier Tribunal]

(1) This section applies if the [First-tier Tribunal] allows an appeal under section 87.

(2) If the [First-tier Tribunal] considers it appropriate, it may direct the Commissioner—

(a) to register the applicant or to continue the applicant's registration;

(b) to make or vary the applicant's registration so as to have limited effect in any of the ways mentioned in paragraph 2(2) of Schedule 6;

(c) . . . or

(d) to quash a decision recorded under paragraph 9(1)(a) of Schedule 5 and the record of that decision.

Note: Commenced 30 October 2000 (SI 2000/1985). Words in square brackets substituted from 18 January 2010 (SI 2010/22). Subsection (2)(c) omitted by Sch 7 Immigration Act 2014 from 17 November 2014 (SI 2014/2771).

89. Disciplinary charge upheld by the [First-tier Tribunal]

(1) This section applies if the [First-tier Tribunal] upholds a disciplinary charge laid by the Commissioner under paragraph 9(1)(e) of Schedule 5 against a person ('the person charged').

[(2) Subsections (2A) and (2B) apply if the person charged was, at the time to which the charge relates, a registered person or a person acting on behalf of a registered person.

(2A) If the registered person mentioned in subsection (2) is still registered, the First-tier Tribunal may direct the Commissioner—

(a) to record the charge and the First-tier Tribunal's decision on it for consideration in connection with that person's next application for continued registration;

(b) to cancel that person's registration.

(2B) If the registered person mentioned in subsection (2) is no longer registered, the First-tier Tribunal may direct the Commissioner to record the charge and the First-tier Tribunal's decision on it for consideration in connection with any application by that person for registration.]

(4) …

(5) If the person charged is found to have charged unreasonable fees for immigration advice or immigration services, the [First-tier Tribunal] may direct him to repay to the clients concerned such portion of those fees as it may determine.

(6) The [First-tier Tribunal] may direct the person charged to pay a penalty to the Commissioner of such sum as it considers appropriate.

(7) A direction given by the [First-tier Tribunal] under subsection (5) (or under subsection (6) may be enforced by the clients concerned (or by the Commissioner)—

(a) as if it were an order of a county court [in Northern Ireland or the county court in England and Wales]; or

(b) in Scotland, as if it were an extract registered decree arbitral bearing a warrant for execution issued by the sheriff court of any sheriffdom in Scotland.

(8) The [First-tier Tribunal] may direct that the person charged or any person [acting on his behalf or] under his supervision is to be—

(a) subject to such restrictions on the provision of immigration advice or immigration services as the [First-tier Tribunal] considers appropriate;

(b) suspended from providing immigration advice or immigration services for such period as the [First-tier Tribunal] may determine; or

(c) prohibited from providing immigration advice or immigration services indefinitely.

(9) The Commissioner must keep a record of the persons against whom there is in force a direction given by the [First-tier Tribunal] under subsection (8).

Note: Commenced 30 October 2000 (SI 2000/1985). 'First-tier Tribunal' substituted from 18 January 2010 (SI 2010/22). Subsection (2) substituted and subsection (4) omitted by Sch 7 Immigration Act 2014 from 17 November 2014 (SI 2014/2771). Words in square brackets in subsection (7)(a) inserted by Sch 9 Crime and Courts Act 2013 from 22 April 2014 (SI 2014/954).

90. Orders by disciplinary bodies

(1) A disciplinary body may make an order directing that a person subject to its jurisdiction is to be—

(a) subject to such restrictions on the provision of immigration advice or immigration services as the body considers appropriate;

(b) suspended from providing immigration advice or immigration services for such period as the body may determine; or

(c) prohibited from providing immigration advice or immigration services indefinitely.

(2) 'Disciplinary body' means any body—

[(a) appearing to the Secretary of State to be established for the purpose of hearing disciplinary charges against—

(i) members of a designated professional body, or

(ii) persons regulated by designated qualifying regulators; and]

(b) specified in an order made by the Secretary of State.

(3) The Secretary of State must consult the designated professional body [or designated qualifying regulator] concerned before making an order under subsection (2)(b).

(4) For the purposes of this section, a person is subject to the jurisdiction of a disciplinary body if he is an authorised person or [acting on his behalf or] an authorised person.

(5) 'Authorised person' means [—

(a)], a person who is authorised by the designated professional body concerned to practise as a member of the profession whose members are regulated by that body [, or

(b) a person who is authorised by the designated qualifying regulator concerned to provide immigration advice or immigration services.]

Note: Commenced 1 August 2000 (SI 2000/1985). Words in square brackets in subsection (4) substituted by Asylum and Immigration (Treatment of Claimants etc.) Act 2004, s 37 from 1 October 2004 (SI 2004/2523). Other words in square brackets inserted and substituted by Sch 18 Legal Services Act 2007 from 1 April 2011 (SI 2011/720).

Enforcement

91. Offences

(1) A person who provides immigration advice or immigration services in contravention of section 84 or of a restraining order is guilty of an offence and liable—

(a) on summary conviction, to imprisonment for a term not exceeding six months or to a fine not exceeding the statutory maximum, or to both; or

(b) on conviction on indictment, to imprisonment for a term not exceeding two years or to a fine, or to both.

(2) 'Restraining order' means—

(a) a direction given by the [First-tier Tribunal] under section 89(8) or paragraph 9(3) of Schedule 5; or

(b) an order made by a disciplinary body under section 90(1).

(3) If an offence under this section committed by a body corporate is proved—

(a) to have been committed with the consent or connivance of an officer, or

(b) to be attributable to neglect on his part, the officer as well as the body corporate is guilty of the offence and liable to be proceeded against and punished accordingly.

(4) 'Officer', in relation to a body corporate, means a director, manager, secretary or other similar officer of the body, or a person purporting to act in such a capacity.

(5) If the affairs of a body corporate are managed by its members, subsection (3) applies in relation to the acts and defaults of a member in connection with his functions of management as if he were a director of the body corporate.

(6) If an offence under this section committed by a partnership in Scotland is proved—

(a) to have been committed with the consent or connivance of a partner, or

(b) to be attributable to neglect on his part, the partner as well as the partnership is guilty of the offence and liable to be proceeded against and punished accordingly.

(7) 'Partner' includes a person purporting to act as a partner.

Note: Commenced 30 April 2001 (SI 2001/1394). Words in square brackets in subsection (2) substituted from 18 January 2010 (SI 2010/22).

92. Enforcement

(1) If it appears to the Commissioner that a person—

(a) is providing immigration advice or immigration services in contravention of section 84 or of a restraining order, and

(b) is likely to continue to do so unless restrained, the Commissioner may apply to a county court [in Northern Ireland or the county court in England and Wales] for an injunction, or to the sheriff for an interdict, restraining him from doing so.

(2) If the court is satisfied that the application is well-founded, it may grant the injunction or interdict in the terms applied for or in more limited terms.

(3) 'Restraining order' has the meaning given by section 91.

Note: Commenced 30 April 2001 (SI 2001/1394). Words in square brackets in subsection (1)(b) inserted by Sch 9 Crime and Courts Act 2013 from 22 April 2014 (SI 2014/954).

[92A. Investigation of offence: power of entry

(1) On an application made by the Commissioner a justice of the peace may issue a warrant authorising the Commissioner to enter and search premises.

(2) A justice of the peace may issue a warrant in respect of premises only if satisfied that there are reasonable grounds for believing that—

(a) an offence under section 91 has been committed,

(b) there is material on the premises which is likely to be of substantial value (whether by itself or together with other material) to the investigation of the offence, and

(c) any of the conditions specified in subsection (3) is satisfied.

(3) Those conditions are—

(a) that it is not practicable to communicate with a person entitled to grant entry to the premises,

(b) that it is not practicable to communicate with a person entitled to grant access to the evidence,

(c) that entry to the premises will be prevented unless a warrant is produced, and

(d) that the purpose of a search may be frustrated or seriously prejudiced unless the Commissioner can secure immediate entry on arrival at the premises.

(4) The Commissioner may seize and retain anything for which a search is authorised under this section.

(5) A person commits an offence if without reasonable excuse he obstructs the Commissioner in the exercise of a power by virtue of this section.

(6) A person guilty of an offence under subsection (5) shall be liable on summary conviction to—

(a) imprisonment for a term not exceeding six months,

(b) a fine not exceeding level 5 on the standard scale, or

(c) both.

(7) In this section—

(a) a reference to the Commissioner includes a reference to a member of his staff authorised in writing by him,

(b) a reference to premises includes a reference to premises used wholly or partly as a dwelling, and

(c) a reference to material—

(i) includes material subject to legal privilege within the meaning of the Police and Criminal Evidence Act 1984 (c. 60),

(ii) does not include excluded material or special procedure material,

(iii) includes material whether or not it would be admissible in evidence at a trial.

(8) In the application of this section to Scotland—

(a) a reference to a justice of the peace shall be taken as a reference to the sheriff,

(b) for sub-paragraph (i) of subsection (7)(c) there is substituted—

'(i) includes material comprising items subject to legal privilege (as defined by section 412 of the Proceeds of Crime Act 2002 (c. 29))', and

(c) sub-paragraph (ii) of subsection (7)(c) shall be ignored.

(9) In the application of this section to Northern Ireland the reference to the Police and Criminal Evidence Act 1984 shall be taken as a reference to the Police and Criminal Evidence (Northern Ireland) Order 1989 (SI1989/1341 (NI 12)).]

Note: Section 92A inserted by Asylum and Immigration (Treatment of Claimants etc.) Act 2004, s 38 from 1 October 2004 (SI 2004/2523).

[92B. Advertising

(1) A person commits an offence if—

(a) he offers to provide immigration advice or immigration services, and

(b) provision by him of the advice or services would constitute an offence under section 91.

(2) For the purpose of subsection (1) a person offers to provide advice or services if he—

(a) makes an offer to a particular person or class of person,

(b) makes arrangements for an advertisement in which he offers to provide advice or services, or

(c) makes arrangements for an advertisement in which he is described or presented as competent to provide advice or services.

(3) A person guilty of an offence under this section shall be liable on summary conviction to a fine not exceeding level 4 on the standard scale.

(4) Subsections (3) to (7) of section 91 shall have effect for the purposes of this section as they have effect for the purposes of that section.

(5) An information relating to an offence under this section may in England and Wales be tried by a magistrates' court if—

(a) it is laid within the period of six months beginning with the date (or first date) on which the offence is alleged to have been committed, or

(b) it is laid—

(i) within the period of two years beginning with that date, and

(ii) within the period of six months beginning with a date certified by the Immigration Services Commissioner as the date on which the commission of the offence came to his notice.

(6) In Scotland, proceedings for an offence under this section may be commenced—

(a) at any time within the period of six months beginning with the date (or first date) on which the offence is alleged to have been committed, or

(b) at any time within both—

(i) the period of two years beginning with that date, and

(ii) the period of six months beginning with a date specified, in a certificate signed by or on behalf of the procurator fiscal, as the date on which evidence sufficient in his opinion to warrant such proceedings came to his knowledge, any such certificate purporting to be so signed shall be deemed so signed unless the contrary is proved and be conclusive as to the facts stated in it.

(7) Subsection (3) of section 136 of the Criminal Procedure (Scotland) Act 1995 (c. 46) (date on which proceedings are deemed commenced) has effect to the purposes of subsection (6) as it has effect for the purposes of that section.

(8) A complaint charging the commission of an offence under this section may in Northern Ireland be heard and determined by a magistrates' court if—

(a) it is made within the period of six months beginning with the date (or first date) on which the offence is alleged to have been committed, or

(b) it is made—

(i) within the period of two years beginning with that date, and

(ii) within the period of six months beginning with a date certified by the Immigration Services Commissioner as the date on which the commission of the offence came to his notice.]

Note: Section 92B inserted by Asylum and Immigration (Treatment of Claimants etc.) Act 2004, s 39 from 1 October 2004 (SI 2004/2523).

Miscellaneous

93. Information

(1) No enactment or rule of law prohibiting or restricting the disclosure of information prevents a person from—

(a) giving the Commissioner information which is necessary for the discharge of his functions; or

(b) giving the [First-tier Tribunal] information which is necessary for the discharge of its functions.

(2) No relevant person may at any time disclose information which—

(a) has been obtained by, or given to, the Commissioner under or for purposes of this Act,

(b) relates to an identified or identifiable individual or business, and

(c) is not at that time, and has not previously been, available to the public from other sources,

unless the disclosure is made with lawful authority.

(3) For the purposes of subsection (2), a disclosure is made with lawful authority only if, and to the extent that—

(a) it is made with the consent of the individual or of the person for the time being carrying on the business;

(b) it is made for the purposes of, and is necessary for, the discharge of any of the Commissioner's functions under this Act[];

(c) it is made for the purposes of any civil or criminal proceedings arising under or by virtue of this Part, or otherwise; or

(d) having regard to the rights and freedoms or legitimate interests of any person, the disclosure is necessary in the public interest.

(4) A person who knowingly or recklessly discloses information in contravention of subsection (2) is guilty of an offence and liable—

(a) on summary conviction, to a fine not exceeding the statutory maximum; or

(b) on conviction on indictment, to a fine.

(5) 'Relevant person' means a person who is or has been—

(a) the Commissioner;

(b) a member of the Commissioner's staff; or

(c) an agent of the Commissioner.

Note: Commenced 22 May 2000 (SI 2000/1282). Words in square brackets in subsection (1)(b) substituted from 18 January 2010 (SI 2010/22). The term 'EU' substituted from 22 April 2011 (SI 2011/1043). Words in square brackets omitted in subsection (3)(b) by Immigration, Nationality and Asylum (EU Exit) Regulations 2019 /745 Pt 2(1) reg11(8) (31 December 2020: shall come into force from IP completion day and not exit day as specified in 2020 c.1 s.39(1) and Sch.5 para 1(1)).

Part VI

Support for Asylum-Seekers

Interpretation

94. Interpretation of Part VI

(1) In this Part—

[. . .];

[[['asylum seeker' means a person falling within subsection (2A) or (2B) but also see subsection (3C)]]—

(a) who is at least 18 years old,

(b) who is in the United Kingdom,

(c) who has made a [protection claim] at a place designated by the Secretary of State,

(d) whose claim has been recorded by the Secretary of State, and

(e) whose claim has not been determined;]

'{}the Department' means the Department of Health and Social Services for Northern Ireland;

['dependant' in relation to an asylum-seeker[[, a failed asylum seeker]] or a supported person means a person who—

(a) is in the United Kingdom, and

(b) is within a prescribed class;]

'the Executive' means the Northern Ireland Housing Executive;

[['failed asylum seeker' has the meaning given by section (2D)]]

[['further qualifying submissions' has the meaning given by subsection (2C);]]

'housing accommodation' includes flats, lodging houses and hostels;

'local authority' means—

(a) in England and Wales, a county council, a county borough council, a district council, a London borough council, the Common Council of the City of London or the Council of the Isles of Scilly;

(b) in Scotland, a council constituted under section 2 of the Local Government etc. (Scotland) Act 1994;

['Northern Ireland authority' has the meaning given by section 110(9).];

[[protection claim' has the meaning given by s 82(2) of the Nationality, Immigration and Asylum Act 2002;]]

'supported person' means—

(a) in relation to support under section 95, an asylum-seeker, or a dependant of an asylum-seeker, who has applied for support and for whom support is provided under that section, and

(b) in relation to support under section 95A, a failed asylum-seeker, or a dependant of a failed asylum-seeker, who has applied for support and for whom support is provided under that section.'

(2) References in this Part to support provided under section 95[[or 95A]] include references to support which is provided under arrangements made by the Secretary of State under that section.

[(2A) A person is an asylum-seeker for the purposes of this Part if—

(a) the person is at least 18 years old,

(b) the person has made a protection claim, and

(c) the person's claim—

(i) has been recorded by the Secretary of State, but

(ii) has not been determined.

(2B) A person is also an asylum-seeker for the purposes of this Part if—

(a) the person is at least 18 years old,

(b) the person has made further qualifying submissions (see subsection (2C)), and

(c) the person's submissions—

(i) have been recorded by the Secretary of State, but

(ii) have not been determined before the end of such period as may be prescribed.

(2C) A person makes 'further qualifying submissions' if—

(a) the person makes submissions to the Secretary of State that the person's removal from the United Kingdom would breach any of the obligations mentioned in section 82(2)(a)(i) or (ii) of the Nationality, Immigration and Asylum Act 2002 (protection claims), and

(b) the submissions fall to be considered by the Secretary of State under paragraph 353 of the immigration rules.]

[(2D) A person is a failed asylum-seeker for the purposes of this Part if—

(b) the person is at least 18 years old,

(c) the person—

(i) was an asylum-seeker, or

(ii) would have been an asylum-seeker at any time if the person had been at least 18 years old at that time,

(d) the person's protection claim has been rejected, and

(e) the person is not an asylum-seeker.]

[(3) [[For the purposes of this part,]] a [[protection claim]] [[is]]determined[[]]at the end of such period [[]]beginning [[]]—

(a) the date on which the Secretary of State notifies the claimant of his decision on the claim, or

(b) if the claimant [[has appealed]] against the Secretary of State's decision, the date on which the appeal is disposed of [[as may be proscribed]].

[(3A) For the purposes of this Part, further qualifying submissions made by a person are determined—

(d) at the end of a prescribed period beginning with the relevant day (see subsection (3B)), or

(e) in a case where no period is prescribed for the purposes of paragraph (a), at the end of the relevant day.

(3B) In subsection (3A) 'the relevant day' means the day on which the Secretary of State notifies the person that the submissions made by the person are to be—

(a) accepted,

(b) rejected without being treated as a fresh protection claim, or

(c) treated as a fresh protection claim.

(3C) If—

(a) further qualifying submissions made by a person are rejected without being treated as a fresh protection claim, and

(b) the person is granted permission to apply for judicial review of that rejection,

the person is to be treated as an asylum-seeker for the purposes of this Part during the review period (see subsection (3D)).

(3D) In subsection (3C) 'the review period' means the period—

(a) beginning with the day on which permission to apply for judicial review is granted, and

(b) ending with—

(i) a prescribed period beginning with the day on which the judicial review is disposed of, or

(ii) in a case where no period is prescribed for the purposes of sub-paragraph (i), that day.]

(4) An appeal is disposed of when it is no longer pending for the purposes of the Immigration Acts or the Special Immigration Appeals Commission Act 1997.

(5) . . .

(6) . . .

(7) For the purposes of this Part, the Secretary of State may inquire into, and decide, the age of any person.

(8) A notice under subsection (3)[or (3B)] must be given in writing.

(9) If such a notice is sent by the Secretary of State by first class post, addressed—

(a) to the asylum-seeker's representative, or

(b) to the asylum-seeker's last known address,

it is to be taken to have been received by the asylum-seeker on the second day after the day on which it was posted.

Note: Commenced 11 November 1999, s 170. Words in third square brackets in subsection (1) inserted by the same Act, s 60 from 10 February 2003 (SI 2003/1). Definition of 'asylum-seeker' modified in relation to ss 110 and 111 from 11 November 2002 so as not to exclude persons under 18 (Nationality, Immigration and Asylum Act 2002, s 48). Words omitted in subsection (1) from 3 November 2008 (SI 2008/2833). Definition of 'asylum seeker', 'dependant', and 'executive' modified; 'claim for asylum' omitted; 'supported person' substituted, and 'further qualifying submissions' and 'protection claim' inserted by Schedule 11 to the Immigration Act 2016 from a date to be appointed. Subsections (2A)–(2C) and (3A)–(3D) inserted, and words in double square brackets substituted in subsection (2), (3), and inserted in subsection (8) by Sc 11 to the Immigration Act 2016 from a date to be appointed. Subsections (5) and (6) omitted by Sch 11 to the Immigration Act 2016 from a date to be appointed. Words in double square brackets omitted and inserted by Sch 11 to the Immigration Act 2016 from a date to be appointed. Paragraph 41 of Sch 11 repeals s 44 of the Nationality, Immigration and Asylum Act 2002 which amended this section but was never brought into force.

Provision of support

95. {Support for asylum seekers, etc.}

(1) The Secretary of State may provide, or arrange for the provision of, support for—

(a) asylum-seekers, or

(b) dependants of asylum-seekers, who appear to the Secretary of State to be destitute or to be likely to become destitute within such period as may be prescribed.

[(2) In prescribed circumstances, a person who would otherwise fall within subsection (1) is excluded.

(3) For the purposes of this section, a person is destitute if—

(a) he does not have adequate accommodation or any means of obtaining it (whether or not his other essential living needs are met); or

(b) he has adequate accommodation or the means of obtaining it, but cannot meet his other essential living needs.

(4) If a person has dependants, subsection (3) is to be read as if the references to him were references to him and his dependants taken together.

(5) In determining, for the purposes of this section, whether a person's accommodation is adequate, the Secretary of State—

(a) must have regard to such matters as may be prescribed for the purposes of this paragraph; but

(b) may not have regard to such matters as may be prescribed for the purposes of this paragraph or to any of the matters mentioned in subsection (6).

(6) Those matters are—

(a) the fact that the person concerned has no enforceable right to occupy the accommodation;

(b) the fact that he shares the accommodation, or any part of the accommodation, with one or more other persons;

(c) the fact that the accommodation is temporary;

(d) the location of the accommodation.

(7) In determining, for the purposes of this section, whether a person's other essential living needs are met, the Secretary of State—

(a) must have regard to such matters as may be prescribed for the purposes of this paragraph; but

(b) may not have regard to such matters as may be prescribed for the purposes of this paragraph.

(8) The Secretary of State may by regulations provide that items or expenses of such a description as may be prescribed are, or are not, to be treated as being an essential living need of a person for the purposes of this Part.]

(9) Support may be provided subject to conditions.

[(9A) A condition imposed under subsection (9) may, in particular, relate to—

(a) any matter relating to the use of the support provided, or

(b) compliance with a [[condition imposed under Schedule 10 to the Immigration Act 2016 (immigration bail).]]]

(10) The conditions must be set out in writing.

(11) A copy of the conditions must be given to the supported person.

(12) Schedule 8 gives the Secretary of State power to make regulations supplementing this section.

(13) Schedule 9 makes temporary provision for support in the period before the coming into force of this section.

Note: Commenced in part 11 November 1999 and 6 December 1999, remainder 1 January 2000 (SI 1999/3190). Subsection 9A inserted by Nationality, Immigration and Asylum Act 2002, s 50 from 7 November 2002. Words in double square brackets substituted in subsection (9A) by Schedule 10 to the Immigration Act 2016 from January 15, 2018 subject to transitional provisions in SI 2017/1241. Title substituted by Sch11 to the Immigration Act 2016 from 15 January 2018 (SI 2017/1241). Sch 11 of this Act repeals section 44 of the Nationality, Immigration and Asylum Act 2002 which was not brought into force.

[95A Support for failed asylum-seekers, etc. who are unable to leave UK

(1) The Secretary of State may provide, or arrange for the provision of, support for a person, for such period or periods as may be prescribed, if—

(a) the person is a failed asylum-seeker, or a dependant of a failed asylum-seeker,

(b) an application for support under this section is made in respect of the person which meets such requirements as may be prescribed,

(c) it appears to the Secretary of State that the person is destitute, or is likely to become destitute within such period as may be prescribed, and

(d) the person faces a genuine obstacle to leaving the United Kingdom.

(2) Subsections (3) to (8) of section 95 (meaning of 'destitute') apply for the purposes of this section as they apply for the purposes of that section.

(3) Regulations made by the Secretary of State may make provision for determining what is, or is not, to be regarded as a genuine obstacle to leaving the United Kingdom for the purposes of this section.

(4) The Secretary of State may make regulations prescribing other criteria to be used in determining—

(a) whether or not to provide support, or arrange for the provision of support, for a person under this section;

(b) whether or not to continue to provide support, or arrange for the provision of support, for a person under this section.

(5) Regulations under subsection (4) may, in particular—

(a) provide for the provision of support (or the continuation of the provision of support) to be subject to conditions;

(b) provide for the provision of support (or the continuation of the provision of support) to be a matter for the Secretary of State's discretion to a prescribed extent or in cases of a prescribed description.

(6) A condition imposed by regulations under subsection (5)(a) may, in particular, relate to any of the following—

(a) any matter relating to the use of the support provided;

(b) compliance with a condition imposed under Schedule 10 to the Immigration Act 2016 (immigration bail);

(c) the person's performance of, or participation in, community activities in accordance with arrangements made by the Secretary of State.

(7) A copy of any conditions imposed by regulations under subsection (5)(a) must be given to the supported person.

(8) For the purposes of subsection (6)(c)—

(a) 'community activities' means activities that appear to the Secretary of State to be beneficial to the public or a section of the public, and

(b) the Secretary of State may, in particular—

(i) appoint one person to supervise or manage the performance of, or participation in, activities by another person;

(ii) enter into a contract (with a local authority or any other person) for the provision of services by way of making arrangements for community activities in accordance with this section;

(iii) pay, or arrange for the payment of, allowances to a person performing or participating in community activities in accordance with arrangements under this section.

(9) Regulations by virtue of subsection (6)(c) may, in particular, provide for a condition requiring the performance of, or participation in, community activities to apply to a person only if—

(a) accommodation is to be, or is being, provided for the person under this section, and

(b) the Secretary of State has made arrangements for community activities in an area that includes the place where the accommodation is to be, or is being, provided.

(10) A local authority or other person may undertake to manage or participate in arrangements for community activities in accordance with this section.

(11) The powers conferred by Schedule 8 (supplementary regulation-making powers) are exercisable with respect to the powers conferred by this section as they are exercisable with respect to the powers conferred by section 95, but with the modification in subsection (12).

(12) Paragraph 9 of Schedule 8 (notice to quit) has effect with respect to the powers conferred by this section as if sub-paragraph (2)(b) were omitted.]

Note: Section 95(A) inserted by Schedule 11 to the Immigration Act 2016, s 66 from a date to be appointed.

96. Ways in which support may be provided

(1) Support may be provided under section 95 [or 95A]—

(a) by providing accommodation appearing to the Secretary of State to be adequate for the needs of the supported person and his dependants (if any);

[(b) by providing the supported person and his dependants (if any) with food or other essential items;]

(c) to enable the supported person (if he is [an asylum-seeker) to meet what appear to the Secretary of State to be expenses (other than legal expenses or other expenses of a prescribed description) incurred in connection with his claim [protection claim];

(d) to enable [an] asylum-seeker and his dependants[or a failed asylum-seeker and his dependants] to attend bail proceedings in connection with his detention under any provision of the Immigration Acts; or

(e) to enable [an] asylum-seeker and his dependants to attend bail proceedings in connection with the detention of a dependant [or a failed asylum-seeker and his dependants] of his under any such provision.

[(1A) Support under section 95A may, in particular, be provided in the form of vouchers which may be exchanged for goods or services (as well as in the form of cash).]

(2) If the Secretary of State considers that the circumstances of a particular case are exceptional, he may provide support under section 95 [or 95A] in such other ways as he considers necessary to enable the supported person and his dependants (if any) to be supported.

(3) …

(4) …

(5) …

(6) …

Note: Commenced 3 April 2000 (SI 2000/464). Subsection 1(b) substituted by Nationality, Immigration and Asylum Act 2002, s 45 from a date to be appointed. Subsection (3) repealed from 8 April 2002 (SI 2002/782). Subsections (4)–(6) repealed by the same Act, s 61 from 7 November 2002. Words substituted in square brackets at subsection (1), (1)(c)(d) & (e) and (2)inserted at (1A) by Sch 11 to the Immigration Act 2016 from a date to be appointed.

97. Supplemental

(1) When exercising his power under section 95 [or 95A] to provide accommodation, the Secretary of State must have regard to [the following]—

(a) [in the case of the provision of accommodation under section 95] the fact that the accommodation is to be temporary pending determination of the asylum-seeker's claim;

(b) the desirability, in general, of providing accommodation in areas in which there is a ready supply of accommodation; and

(c) such other matters (if any) as may be prescribed.

(2) But he may not have regard to—

(a) any preference that the supported person or his dependants (if any) may have as to the locality in which the accommodation is to be provided; or

(b) such other matters (if any) as may be prescribed.

(3) The Secretary of State may by order repeal all or any of the following—

(a) subsection (1)(a);

(b) subsection (1)(b);

(c) subsection (2)(a).

[(3A) When exercising the power under section 95 (support for asylum seekers) or [[section 95A (support for failed asylum seeker]] to provide or arrange for the provision of accommodation, the Secretary of State may decide to provide or arrange for the provision of different types of accommodation to [[supported persons]] on the basis of either or both of the following matters—

(a) the stage that their [[protection claim]] has reached, including whether they have been notified that their claim is being considered for a declaration of inadmissibility (see sections 80A and 80B of the Nationality, Immigration and Asylum Act 2002);

(b) their previous compliance with any conditions imposed on them under any of the following—

(i) section 95(9) (conditions for support under section 95);

(ii) Schedule 10 to the Immigration Act 2016 (conditions of immigration bail);

(iii) [[regulations made under section 95A(5) (conditions for support under section 95A);]]]

[[(iv) regulations under section 30 of the Nationality, Immigration and Asylum Act 2002 (conditions of residence in accommodation centre).]]

(4) When exercising his power under section 95 [or 95A] to provide, the Secretary of State—

(a) must have regard to such matters as may be prescribed for the purposes of this paragraph; but

(b) may not have regard to such other matters as may be prescribed for the purposes of this paragraph.

(5) In addition, when exercising his power under section 95 [or 95A] to provide, the Secretary of State may limit the overall amount of the expenditure which he incurs in connection with a particular supported person—

[(za) to such portion of the maximum amount of an award of universal credit under section 8(1) of the Welfare Reform Act 2012, or]

(a) ...

(b) to such portion of any components [or elements] of that amount, as he considers appropriate having regard to the temporary nature of the support that he is providing.

(6) For the purposes of subsection (5), any support of a kind falling within section 96(1)(c) is to be treated as if it were the provision of essential [items].

(7) In determining how to provide, or arrange for the provision of, support under section 95 [or 95A], the Secretary of State may disregard any preference which the supported person or his dependants (if any) may have as to the way in which the support is to be given.

[(8) A tenancy is not a Scottish secure tenancy (within the meaning of the Housing (Scotland) Act 2001 (asp 10)) if it is granted in order to provide accommodation under section 95A.

(9) A tenancy which would be a Scottish secure tenancy but for subsection (8) becomes a Scottish secure tenancy if the landlord notifies the tenant that it is to be regarded as such.]

Note: Commenced for the purposes of enabling subordinate legislation 1 January 2000 (SI 1999/3190), remainder 3 April 2000 (SI 2000/464). Subsection (5)(za) and words in square brackets in s (5)(b) inserted by Sch 2 Welfare Reform Act from 29 April 2013 (SI 2013/983). Subsection (5)(a) omitted by Sch 14 Welfare Reform Act 2012 from a date to be appointed. Words in square brackets inserted in subsections (1), (1)(a), (4), (5), (7) and sections (8) and (9) by Sch 11 to the Immigration Act 2016 from a date to be appointed. Sch 11 of this Act repeals s 45 which was not brought into force. Words in square brackets inserted at subsection 3A by Nationality and Borders act 2022 c.36 Pt2 s.13(1) (June 28,22). Words inserted in double brackets in subsection (3A) in double brackets by Nationality and Borders Act 2022 c.36 Pt2 s.13(2)(a)(i)(date to be appointed). Words inserted in double brackets at subsection (3A) para (a) by Nationality and Borders act 2022 c.36 Pt s.13(2)(b) (date to be appointed). Words substituted in double brackets in subsection (3A) para (b(i)) by Nationality and Borders Act 2022 c.36 Pt2 (2)(c)(i)(date to be appointed). Words substituted in square brackets in subsection (3A) para (b)(ii) by Nationality and Borders Act 2022 c.36 s.13(2)(c)(ii) (date to be appointed).

98. Temporary support for asylum seekers, etc.

(1) The Secretary of State may provide, or arrange for the provision of, support for—

(a) asylum-seekers, or

(b) dependants of asylum-seekers, who it appears to the Secretary of State may be destitute.

(2) Support may be provided under this section only until the Secretary of State is able to determine whether support may be provided under section 95.

(3) Subsections (2) to (11) of section 95 apply for the purposes of this section as they apply for the purposes of that section.

Note: Subsection (3) commenced for the purposes of enabling subordinate legislation 1 March 2000, remainder 3 April 2000 (SI 2000/464). Title amended by Sch 11 to the Immigration Act 2016 from a date to be appointed.

[98A Temporary support for failed asylum-seekers, etc.

(1) The Secretary of State may provide, or arrange for the provision of, support for persons within subsection (2) who it appears to the Secretary of State—

(a) may be destitute, and

(b) may face a genuine obstacle to leaving the United Kingdom.

(2) The persons referred to in subsection (1) are—

(a) failed asylum-seekers, and

(b) dependants of failed asylum-seekers.

(3) Support may be provided under this section only until the Secretary of State is able to determine whether support may be provided under section 95A.

(4) Subsections (3) to (12) of section 95A apply for the purposes of this section as they apply for the purposes of that section.]

Note: Section 98A inserted by Sch 11 to the Immigration Act 2016 from a date to be appointed.

Support and assistance by local authorities etc.

99. Provision of support by local authorities

(1) A local authority [or Northern Ireland authority] may provide support for [persons] in accordance with arrangements made by the Secretary of State under section [[]] 95 [[, 95A, 98 or 98A]].

(2) Support may be provided by an authority in accordance with arrangements made with the authority or with another person.

(3) Support may be provided by an authority in accordance with arrangements made under section 95[[or 95A]] only in one or more of the ways mentioned in [[section 96(1) to (2)]].

(4) [An authority] may incur reasonable expenditure in connection with the preparation of proposals for entering into arrangements under section [[]] 95 [[95A, 98 or 98A]].

(5) The powers conferred on [an authority] by this section include power to—

(a) provide services outside their area;

(b) provide services jointly with one or more [other bodies];

(c) form a company for the purpose of providing services;

(d) tender for contracts (whether alone or with any other person).

Note: Subsections (1)–(3) commenced 3 April 2000 (SI 2000/464). Subsections (4) and (5) commenced 11 November 1999, s 170. Words in second and third square brackets in subsection (1) and second square brackets in subsection (4) substituted by Immigration, Nationality and Asylum Act 2006, s 43 from 16 June 2006 (SI 2006/1497). Subsections (2) and (3) substituted by and other words in square brackets substituted by Nationality, Immigration and Asylum Act 2002, s 56 from 7 November 2002. Words in double square brackets omitted, substituted or inserted by Sch 11 Immigration Act 2016 from a date to be appointed. In section 99(4) repeal has effect subject to savings and transitional provisions specified in Immigration Act 2016, Sch 11, para 46.

100. Local authority and other assistance for Secretary of State

(1) This section applies if the Secretary of State asks—

(a) a local authority,

[(aa) a private registered provider of social housing,]

(b) a registered social landlord,

(c) a registered housing association in Scotland or Northern Ireland, or

(d) the Executive, to assist him to exercise his power under section 95[[or 95A]] to provide accommodation.

(2) The person to whom the request is made must cooperate in giving the Secretary of State such assistance in the exercise of that power as is reasonable in the circumstances.

(3) Subsection (2) does not require [a private registered provider of social housing, or] a registered social landlord to act beyond its powers.

(4) A local authority must supply to the Secretary of State such information about their housing accommodation (whether or not occupied) as he may from time to time request.

(5) The information must be provided in such form and manner as the Secretary of State may direct.

(6) 'Registered social landlord' has the same meaning as in Part I of the Housing Act 1996.

(7) 'Registered housing association' has the same meaning—

(a) in relation to Scotland, as in the Housing Associations Act 1985; and

(b) in relation to Northern Ireland, as in Part II of the Housing (Northern Ireland) Order 1992.

Note: Commenced 3 April 2000 (SI 2000/464). Words in square brackets inserted by SI 2010/866 from 1 April 2010. Words inserted at in double square brackets subsection (1) by Sch 11 to the Immigration Act 2016 from a date to be appointed.

101. Reception zones

(1) The Secretary of State may by order designate as reception zones—

(a) areas in England and Wales consisting of the areas of one or more local authorities;

(b) areas in Scotland consisting of the areas of one or more local authorities;

(c) Northern Ireland.

(2) Subsection (3) applies if the Secretary of State considers that—

(a) a local authority whose area is within a reception zone has suitable housing accommodation within that zone; or

(b) the Executive has suitable housing accommodation.

(3) The Secretary of State may direct the local authority or the Executive to make available such of the accommodation as may be specified in the direction for a period so specified—

(a) to him for the purpose of providing support under section 95 [[or 95A]]; or

(b) to a person with whom the Secretary of State has made arrangements under section 95 [[or 95A]].

(4) A period specified in a direction under subsection (3)—

(a) begins on a date so specified; and

(b) must not exceed five years.

(5) A direction under subsection (3) is enforceable, on an application made on behalf of the Secretary of State, by injunction or in Scotland an order under section 45(b) of the Court of Session Act 1988.

(6) The Secretary of State's power to give a direction under subsection (3) in respect of a particular reception zone must be exercised by reference to criteria specified for the purposes of this subsection in the order designating that zone.

(7) The Secretary of State may not give a direction under subsection (3) in respect of a local authority in Scotland unless the Scottish Ministers have confirmed to him that the criteria specified in the designation order concerned are in their opinion met in relation to that authority.

(8) Housing accommodation is suitable for the purposes of subsection (2) if it—

(a) is unoccupied;

(b) would be likely to remain unoccupied for the foreseeable future if not made available; and

(c) is appropriate for the accommodation of persons supported under this Part or capable of being made so with minor work.

(9) If housing accommodation for which a direction under this section is, for the time being, in force—

(a) is not appropriate for the accommodation of persons supported under this Part, but

(b) is capable of being made so with minor work, the direction may require the body to whom it is given to secure that that work is done without delay.

(10) The Secretary of State must make regulations with respect to the general management of any housing accommodation for which a direction under subsection (3) is, for the time being, in force.

(11) Regulations under subsection (10) must include provision—

(a) as to the method to be used in determining the amount of rent or other charges to be payable in relation to the accommodation;

(b) as to the times at which payments of rent or other charges are to be made;

(c) as to the responsibility for maintenance of, and repairs to, the accommodation;

(d) enabling the accommodation to be inspected, in such circumstances as may be prescribed, by the body to which the direction was given;

(e) with respect to the condition in which the accommodation is to be returned when the direction ceases to have effect.

(12) Regulations under subsection (10) may, in particular, include provision—

(a) for the cost, or part of the cost, of minor work required by a direction under this section to be met by the Secretary of State in prescribed circumstances;

(b) as to the maximum amount of expenditure which a body may be required to incur as a result of a direction under this section.

(13) The Secretary of State must by regulations make provision ('the dispute resolution procedure') for resolving disputes arising in connection with the operation of any regulations made under subsection (10).

(14) Regulations under subsection (13) must include provision—

(a) requiring a dispute to be resolved in accordance with the dispute resolution procedure;

(b) requiring the parties to a dispute to comply with obligations imposed on them by the procedure; and

(c) for the decision of the person resolving a dispute in accordance with the procedure to be final and binding on the parties.

(15) Before—

(a) designating a reception zone in Great Britain,

(b) determining the criteria to be included in the order designating the zone, or

(c) making regulations under subsection (13), the Secretary of State must consult such local authorities, local authority associations and other persons as he thinks appropriate.

(16) Before—

(a) designating Northern Ireland as a reception zone, or

(b) determining the criteria to be included in the order designating Northern Ireland, the Secretary of State must consult the Executive and such other persons as he thinks appropriate.

(17) Before making regulations under subsection (10) which extend only to Northern Ireland, the Secretary of State must consult the Executive and such other persons as he thinks appropriate.

(18) Before making any other regulations under subsection (10), the Secretary of State must consult—

(a) such local authorities, local authority associations and other persons as he thinks appropriate; and

(b) if the regulations extend to Northern Ireland, the Executive.

Note: Commenced 3 April 2000 (SI 2000/464). Words inserted at [[]] subsection (3) by Sch 11 to the Immigration Act 2016 from a date to be appointed.

Appeals

102. …

Note: Commenced 3 April 2000 (SI 2000/464). Revoked from 3 November 2008 (SI 2008/2833).

[103. Appeals.

(1) If, on an application for support under section 95, the Secretary of State decides that the applicant does not qualify for support under that section, the applicant may appeal to [the First-tier Tribunal].

(2) If the Secretary of State decides to stop providing support for a person under section 95 before that support would otherwise have come to an end, that person may appeal to [the First-tier Tribunal]

(2A) ...

(3) On an appeal under this section, the [First-tier Tribunal] may—

(a) require the Secretary of State to reconsider the matter;

(b) substitute [its] decision for the decision appealed against; or

(c) dismiss the appeal.

[...]

(5) The decision of the [First-tier Tribunal] is final.

(6) If an appeal is dismissed, no further application by the appellant for support under [section [[....]]95] is to be entertained unless the Secretary of State is satisfied that there has been a material change in the circumstances.

(7) The Secretary of State may by regulations provide for decisions as to where support provided under [section [[...]] 95] is to be provided to be appealable to [the First-tier Tribunal] under this Part.

(8) Regulations under subsection (7) may provide for any provision of this section to have effect, in relation to an appeal brought by virtue of the regulations, subject to such modifications as may be prescribed.

(9) The Secretary of State may pay any reasonable travelling expenses incurred by an appellant in connection with attendance at any place for the purposes of an appeal under this section.

Note: Section 103 substituted by Nationality, Immigration and Asylum Act 2002, s 53 from a date to be appointed. Subsection (1) and words in square brackets in subsection (7) substituted by Asylum and Immigration (Treatment of Claimants etc.) Act 2004, s 10 from 31 March 2005 (SI 2005/372). Other words in square brackets substituted from 3 November 2008 (SI 2008/2833). Subsection (2A) and words in double square brackets substituted and omitted by Sch 11 to Immigration Act 2016 from a date to be appointed: repeal has effect subject to savings and transitional provisions specified in Immigration Act 2016, Sch 11, para 46.

(104. ...

Note: Commenced 1 January 2000 (SI 1999/3190). Revoked from 3 November 2008 (SI 2008/2833).

Offences

105. False representations

(1) A person is guilty of an offence if, with a view to obtaining support for himself or any other person under any provision made by or under this Part, he—

(a) makes a statement or representation which he knows is false in a material particular;

(b) produces or gives to a person exercising functions under this Part, or knowingly causes or allows to be produced or given to such a person, any document or information which he knows is false in a material particular;

(c) fails, without reasonable excuse, to notify a change of circumstances when required to do so in accordance with any provision made by or under this Part; or

(d) without reasonable excuse, knowingly causes another person to fail to notify a change of circumstances which that other person was required to notify in accordance with any provision made by or under this Part.

(2) A person guilty of an offence under this section is liable on summary conviction to imprisonment for a term not exceeding [51 weeks] or to a fine not exceeding level 5 on the standard scale, or to both.

Note: Commenced 11 November 1999, s 170. Words in square brackets in subsection (2) substituted by Sch 26 Criminal Justice Act 2003, from a date to be appointed.

106. Dishonest representations

(1) A person is guilty of an offence if, with a view to obtaining any benefit or other payment or advantage under this Part for himself or any other person, he dishonestly—

(a) makes a statement or representation which is false in a material particular;

(b) produces or gives to a person exercising functions under this Part, or causes or allows to be produced or given to such a person, any document or information which is false in a material particular;

(c) fails to notify a change of circumstances when required to do so in accordance with any provision made by or under this Part; or

(d) causes another person to fail to notify a change of circumstances which that other person was required to notify in accordance with any provision made by or under this Part.

(2) A person guilty of an offence under this section is liable—

(a) on summary conviction, to imprisonment for a term not exceeding six months or to a fine not exceeding the statutory maximum, or to both; or

(b) on conviction on indictment, to imprisonment for a term not exceeding seven years or to a fine, or to both.

(3) In the application of this section to Scotland, in subsection (1) for 'dishonestly' substitute 'knowingly'.

Note: Commenced 11 November 1999, s 170.

107. Delay or obstruction

(1) A person is guilty of an offence if, without reasonable excuse, he—

(a) intentionally delays or obstructs a person exercising functions conferred by or under this Part; or

(b) refuses or neglects to answer a question, give any information or produce a document when required to do so in accordance with any provision made by or under this Part.

(2) A person guilty of an offence under subsection (1) is liable on summary conviction to a fine not exceeding level 3 on the standard scale.

Note: Commenced 11 November 1999, s 170.

108. Failure of sponsor to maintain

(1) A person is guilty of an offence if, during any period in respect of which he has given a written undertaking in pursuance of the immigration rules to be responsible for the maintenance and accommodation of another person—

(a) he persistently refuses or neglects, without reasonable excuse, to maintain that person in accordance with the undertaking; and

(b) in consequence of his refusal or neglect, support under any provision made by or under this Part is provided for or in respect of that person.

(2) A person guilty of an offence under this section is liable on summary conviction to imprisonment for a term not exceeding [51 weeks] or to a fine not exceeding level 4 on the standard scale, or to both.

(3) For the purposes of this section, a person is not to be taken to have refused or neglected to maintain another person by reason only of anything done or omitted in furtherance of a trade dispute.

Note: Commenced 11 November 1999, s 170. Words in square brackets in subsection (2) substituted by Sch 26 Criminal Justice Act 2003, from a date to be appointed.

109. Supplemental

(1) If an offence under section 105, 106, 107 or 108 committed by a body corporate is proved—

(a) to have been committed with the consent or connivance of an officer, or

(b) to be attributable to neglect on his part,

the officer as well as the body corporate is guilty of the offence and liable to be proceeded against and punished accordingly.

(2) 'Officer', in relation to a body corporate, means a director, manager, secretary or other similar officer of the body, or a person purporting to act in such a capacity.

(3) If the affairs of a body corporate are managed by its members, subsection (1) applies in relation to the acts and defaults of a member in connection with his functions of management as if he were a director of the body corporate.

(4) If an offence under section 105, 106, 107 or 108 committed by a partnership in Scotland is proved—

(a) to have been committed with the consent or connivance of a partner, or

(b) to be attributable to neglect on his part,

the partner as well as the partnership is guilty of the offence and liable to be proceeded against and punished accordingly.

(5) 'Partner' includes a person purporting to act as a partner.

Note: Commenced 11 November 1999, s 170.

[109A. Arrest

An immigration officer may arrest without warrant a person whom the immigration officer reasonably suspects has committed an offence under section 105 or 106.]

Note: Section 109A inserted from 31 January 2008 (SI 2008/99).

[109B. Entry, search and seizure

(1) An offence under section 105 or 106 shall be treated as—

(a) a relevant offence for the purposes of sections 28B and 28D of the Immigration Act 1971, and

(b) an offence under Part 3 of that Act (criminal proceedings) for the purposes of sections 28(4), 28E, 28G and 28H (search after arrest, &c.) of that Act.

(2) The following provisions of the Immigration Act 1971 (c. 77) shall have effect in connection with an offence under section 105 or 106 of this Act as they have effect in connection with an offence under that Act—

(a) section 28I (seized material: access and copying),

(b) section 28J (search warrants: safeguards),

(c) section 28K (execution of warrants), and

(d) section 28L(1) (interpretation).]

Note: Section 109B inserted from 31 January 2008 (SI 2008/99).

Expenditure

110. Payments to local authorities

(1) The Secretary of State may from time to time pay to any local authority or Northern Ireland authority such sums as he considers appropriate in respect of expenditure incurred, or to be incurred, by the authority in connection with—

(a) persons who are, or have been, asylum-seekers; and

(b) their dependants.

(2) The Secretary of State may from time to time pay to any—

(a) local authority,

(b) local authority association, or

(c) Northern Ireland authority,

such sums as he considers appropriate in respect of services provided by the authority or association in connection with the discharge of functions under this Part.

(3) The Secretary of State may make payments to any local authority towards the discharge of any liability of supported persons or their dependants in respect of council tax payable to that authority.

(4) The Secretary of State must pay to a body to which a direction under section 101(3) is given such sums as he considers represent the reasonable costs to that body of complying with the direction.

(5) The Secretary of State must pay to a directed body sums determined to be payable in relation to accommodation made available by that body under section 101(3)(a).

(6) The Secretary of State may pay to a directed body sums determined to be payable in relation to accommodation made available by that body under section 101(3)(b).

(7) In subsections (5) and (6)—

'determined' means determined in accordance with regulations made by virtue of subsection (11)(a) of section 101, and

'directed body' means a body to which a direction under subsection (3) of section 101 is given.

(8) Payments under subsection (1), (2) or (3) may be made on such terms, and subject to such conditions, as the Secretary of State may determine.

(9) 'Northern Ireland authority' means—

(a) the Executive; or

(b) a Health and Social Services Board established under Article 16 of the Health and Personal Social Services (Northern Ireland) Order 1972 [; or

(c) a Health and Social Services trust established under the Health and Personal Social Services (Northern Ireland) Order 1991 (S.I. 1991/194 (N.I. 1).]

Note: Subsections (1), (2) and (8) commenced 11 November 1999, s 170, subsection (9) 6 December 1999 (SI 1999/3190), remainder 3 April 2000 (SI 2000/464). Subsection (9)(c) inserted by Nationality, Immigration and Asylum Act 2002, s 60 from 7 November 2002.

111. Grants to voluntary organisations

(1) The Secretary of State may make grants of such amounts as he thinks appropriate to voluntary organisations in connection with—

(a) the provision by them of support (of whatever nature) to persons who are, or have been, asylum-seekers and to their dependants; and

(b) connected matters.

(2) Grants may be made on such terms, and subject to such conditions, as the Secretary of State may determine.

Note: Commenced 11 November 1999, s 170.

112. Recovery of expenditure on support: misrepresentation etc.

(1) This section applies if, on an application made by the Secretary of State, the court determines that—

(a) a person ('A') has misrepresented or failed to disclose a material fact (whether fraudulently or otherwise); and

(b) as a consequence of the misrepresentation or failure, support has been provided under [section 95, 95A, 98 or 98A] (whether or not to A).

(2) If the support was provided by the Secretary of State, the court may order A to pay to the Secretary of State an amount representing the monetary value of the support which would not have been provided but for A's misrepresentation or failure.

(3) If the support was provided by another person ('B') in accordance with arrangements made with the Secretary of State under [section 95, 95A, 98 or 98A)], the court may order A to pay to the Secretary of State an amount representing the payment to B which would not have been made but for A's misrepresentation or failure.

(4) 'Court' means a county court [in Northern Ireland or the county court in England and Wales], or, in Scotland, the sheriff.

Note: Commenced 3 April 2000 (SI 2000/464). Words inserted in subsection (4) by Sch 9 Crime and Courts Act 2013 from a date to be appointed. Words substituted in subsections (1)(b) and (3) by Schedule 11 to the Immigration Act 2016 from a date to be appointed.

113. Recovery of expenditure on support from sponsor

(1) This section applies if—

(a) a person ('the sponsor') has given a written undertaking in pursuance of the immigration rules to be responsible for the maintenance and accommodation of another person; and

(b) during any period in relation to which the undertaking applies, support under section 95 [or 95A] is provided to or in respect of that other person.

(2) The Secretary of State may make a complaint against the sponsor to a magistrates' court for an order under this section.

(3) The court—

(a) must have regard to all the circumstances (and in particular to the sponsor's income); and

(b) may order him to pay to the Secretary of State such sum (weekly or otherwise) as it considers appropriate.

(4) But such a sum is not to include any amount attributable otherwise than to support provided under section 95 [or 95A].

(5) In determining—

(a) whether to order any payments to be made in respect of support provided under section 95 [or 95A] for any period before the complaint was made, or

(b) the amount of any such payments, the court must disregard any amount by which the sponsor's current income exceeds his income during that period.

(6) An order under this section is enforceable as a magistrates' court maintenance order within the meaning of section 150(1) of the Magistrates' Courts Act 1980.

(7) In the application of this section to Scotland—

(a) omit subsection (6);

(b) for references to a complaint substitute references to an application; and

(c) for references to a magistrates' court substitute references to the sheriff.

(8) In the application of this section to Northern Ireland, for references to a magistrates' court substitute references to a court of summary jurisdiction and for subsection (6) substitute—

'(6) An order under this section is an order to which Article 98(11) of the Magistrates' Courts (Northern Ireland) Order 1981 applies.'

Note: Commenced 3 April 2000 (SI 2000/464). Words inserted at subsections (1)(b), (4) and (5)(a) by Schedule 11 to the Immigration Act 2016 from a date to be appointed.

114. Overpayments

(1) Subsection (2) applies if, as a result of an error on the part of the Secretary of State, support has been provided to a person under [section 95, 95A, 98 or 98A].

(2) The Secretary of State may recover from a person who is, or has been, a supported person an amount representing the monetary value of support provided to him as a result of the error.

(3) An amount recoverable under subsection (2) may be recovered as if it were a debt due to the Secretary of State.

(4) The Secretary of State may by regulations make provision for other methods of recovery, including deductions from support provided under [section 95, 95A, 98 or 98A].

Note: Commenced 1 January 2000 for the purposes of enabling subordinate legislation (SI 1999/3190), otherwise commenced on 3 April 2000 (SI 2000/464). Words substituted in subsections (1) and (4) by Schedule 11 to the Immigration Act 2016 from a date to be appointed.

Exclusions

115. Exclusion from benefits

(1) No person is entitled [to universal credit under Part 1 of the Welfare Reform Act 2012 or] to income-based jobseeker's allowance under the Jobseekers Act 1995 or [… to state pension credit under the State Pension Credit Act 2002]… [or to personal independence payment] or to

(a) attendance allowance,
(b) severe disablement allowance,
(c) [carer's allowance],
(d) …
(e) …
(f) …
(g) …
(h) a social fund payment,
[(ha) health in pregnancy grant,] [or]
(i) child benefit,
(j) …
(j) …
(k) …

under the Social Security Contributions and Benefits Act 1992 while he is a person to whom this section applies.

(2) No person in Northern Ireland is entitled to [state pension credit under the State Pension Credit Act (Northern Ireland) 2002, or to]—

(a) income-based jobseeker's allowance under the Jobseekers (Northern Ireland) Order 1995, or

(b) [disability living allowance or] any of the benefits mentioned in paragraphs [(a) to (i)] of subsection (1), under the Social Security Contributions and Benefits (Northern Ireland) Act 1992 while he is a person to whom this section applies.

(3) This section applies to a person subject to immigration control unless he falls within such category or description, or satisfies such conditions, as may be prescribed.

(4) Regulations under subsection (3) may provide for a person to be treated for prescribed purposes only as not being a person to whom this section applies.

(5) In relation to [health in pregnancy grant or] [child benefit], 'prescribed' means prescribed by regulations made by the Treasury.

(6) In relation to the matters mentioned in subsection (2) (except so far as it relates to [health in pregnancy grant or] [child benefit]), 'prescribed' means prescribed by regulations made by the Department.

(7) Section 175(3) to (5) of the Social Security Contributions and Benefits Act 1992 (supplemental powers in relation to regulations) applies to regulations made by the Secretary of State or the Treasury under subsection (3) as it applies to regulations made under that Act.

(8) Sections 133(2), 171(2) and 172(4) of the Social Security Contributions and Benefits (Northern Ireland) Act 1992 apply to regulations made by the Department under subsection (3) as they apply to regulations made by the Department under that Act.

(9) 'A person subject to immigration control' means a person []who—

(a) requires leave to enter or remain in the United Kingdom but does not have it;

(b) has leave to enter or remain in the United Kingdom which is subject to a condition that he does not have recourse to public funds;

(c) has leave to enter or remain in the United Kingdom given as a result of a maintenance undertaking; or

(d) has leave to enter or remain in the United Kingdom only as a result of paragraph 17 of Schedule 4.

(10) 'Maintenance undertaking', in relation to any person, means a written undertaking given by another person in pursuance of the immigration rules to be responsible for that person's maintenance and accommodation.

Note: Commenced for the purposes of enabling subordinate legislation 1 January 2000 (SI 1999/3190), remainder 3 April 2000 (SI 2000/464). First words in square brackets in subsection (1) inserted by s 4 State Pension Credit Act 2002, from 6 October 2003 (SI 2003/1766). Second words in square brackets in subsection (1) inserted by Sch 3 Welfare Reform Act 2007 from 27 October 2008 (SI 2008/787). Subsection (1)(c) substituted from 1 April 2003 (SI 2002/1457). Words in square brackets in subsection (2) substituted by s 4 State Pension Credit Act (Northern Ireland) 2002 from 2 December 2002 (SI 2002/366). Subsection (1)(ha) inserted and words in first square brackets in subsections (5) and (6) substituted by s 138 Health and Social Care Act 2008 from 1 January 2009 (SI 2009/2994). Words in second square brackets in subsections (5) and (6) substituted by Sch 4 Tax Credits Act 2002 from 7 April 2003 (SI 2003/392). Subsection (1)(e) revoked by Sch 7 Welfare Reform Act 2009 from a date to be appointed. Words in first square brackets in subsection (1) inserted by Sch 2 Welfare Reform Act 2012 from 29 April 2013 (SI 2013/983). Word inserted in subsection (1)(ha) and substituted in second square brackets in subsection (2)(b) by Sch 3 Welfare Reform Act 2012 from a date to be appointed. Words in third square brackets in subsection (1) and first square brackets in subsection (2)(b) inserted by Sch 9 Welfare Reform Act 2012 from 10 June 2013 (SI 2013/1250). Words deleted from subsection (1) and subsections (1)(d), (e), (j) and (k) repealed by Sch 14 Welfare Reform Act 2012 from a date to be appointed. Words in square brackets at subsection (9) omitted by Immigration and Social Security Co-ordination (EU Withdrawal) Act 2020 (Consequential, Saving, Transitional and Transitory Provisions) (EU Exit) Regulations 2020/1309 Pt 2(1) reg 12(6) (31 December 2020 at 23.00 being the time and date 2020 c. 20 Sch 1 comes into force).

116. . . .

Note: Amends National Assistance Act 1948, s 21.

117. . . .

Note: Amends Health Services and Public Health Act 1968, s 4; Sch 8 National Health Service Act 1977; and Housing Act 1996, ss 161, 185–187.

118. Housing authority accommodation

(1) Each housing authority must secure that, so far as practicable, a tenancy of, or licence to occupy, housing accommodation provided under the accommodation provisions is not granted to a person subject to immigration control unless—

(a) he is of a class specified in an order made by the Secretary of State; or

(b) the tenancy of, or licence to occupy, such accommodation is granted in accordance with arrangements made under section [[[]] 95[[95A, 98 or 98A]].

(2) 'Housing authority' means—

(a) in relation to England and Wales, a local housing authority within the meaning of the Housing Act 1985;

(b) in relation to Scotland, a local authority within the meaning of the Housing (Scotland) Act 1987; and

(c) in relation to Northern Ireland, the Executive.

(3) 'Accommodation provisions' means—

(a) in relation to England and Wales, Part II of the Housing Act 1985;

(b) in relation to Scotland, Part I of the Housing (Scotland) Act 1987;

(c) in relation to Northern Ireland, Part II of the Housing (Northern Ireland) Order 1981.

(4) 'Licence to occupy', in relation to Scotland, means a permission or right to occupy.

(5) 'Tenancy', in relation to England and Wales, has the same meaning as in the Housing Act 1985.

(6) 'Person subject to immigration control' means a person who under the 1971 Act requires leave to enter or remain in the United Kingdom (whether or not such leave has been given).

(7) This section does not apply in relation to any allocation of housing to which Part VI of the Housing Act 1996 (allocation of housing accommodation) applies.

Note: Commenced 1 January 2000 for purposes of enabling subordinate legislation (SI 1999/3190), remainder 1 March 2000 (SI 2000/464). Words in square brackets in subsection (1)(b) substituted by Immigration, Nationality and Asylum Act 2006, s 43 from 16 June 2006 (SI 2006/1497). Words in double square brackets omitted and inserted at subsection (1)(b) by Schedule 11 to the Immigration Act 2016 from a date to be appointed. Repeal at section 118(1)(b) has effect subject to savings and transitional provisions specified in Immigration Act 2016, Sch 11, para 46.

119. Homelessness: Scotland and Northern Ireland

(1) A person subject to immigration control—

(a) is not eligible for accommodation or assistance under the homelessness provisions, and

(b) is to be disregarded in determining for the purposes of those provisions, whether [a person falling within subsection (1A)]—

(i) is homeless or is threatened with homelessness, or

(ii) has a priority need for accommodation, unless he is of a class specified in an order made by the Secretary of State.

[(1A) A person falls within this subsection if the person—

(a) falls within a class specified in an order under subsection (1); but

(b) [[is not a person who, immediately before IP completion day, was—
(i) a national of an EEA State or Switzerland, and
(ii) within a class specified in an order under subsection (1) which had effect at that time.]]
]

(2) An order under subsection (1) may not be made so as to include in a specified class any person to whom section 115 applies.

(3) 'The homelessness provisions' means—
(a) in relation to Scotland, Part II of the Housing (Scotland) Act 1987; and
(b) in relation to Northern Ireland, Part II of the Housing (Northern Ireland) Order 1988.

(4) 'Person subject to immigration control' has the same meaning as in section 118.

Note: Commenced 1 January 2000 for purposes of enabling subordinate legislation, remainder 1 March 2000 (SI 2000/464). Words in square brackets substituted and s 1A inserted by Sch 15 Housing and Regeneration Act 2008 from 2 March 2009 in relation to applications (a) for accommodation or assistance in obtaining accommodation under Part I (provision of housing) or Part II (homeless persons) of the Housing (Scotland) Act 1987, or (b) for housing assistance under Part II (housing the homeless) of the Housing (Northern Ireland) Order 1988, made on or after 2 March 2009 (SI 2009/415). Words in double square brackets at subsection (1A)(b) substituted by Immigration and Social Security Co-ordination (EU Withdrawal) Act 2020 (Consequential, Saving, Transitional and Transitory Provisions) (EU Exit) Regulations 2020/1390 Pt 2(1) reg 12(7) (31 December 2020 at 23.00 being the time and date 2020 c. 20 Sch 1 para 2(2) comes into force.

120. …

Note: Amends Social Work (Scotland) Act 1968, ss 2 and 13, Mental Health (Scotland) Act 1984, ss 7–8 and Asylum and Immigration Appeals Act 1993, ss 4–5 and Sch 1.

121. …

Note: Amends Health and Personal Social Services (Northern Ireland) Order 1972.

122.— Support for children.

(1) In this section 'eligible person' means a person who appears to the Secretary of State to be a person for whom support may be provided under section 95 [or 95A].

(2) Subsections (3) and (4) apply if an application for support under section 95 [(or as the case may be) 95A] has been made by an eligible person whose household includes a dependant under the age of 18 ('the child').

(3) If it appears to the Secretary of State that adequate accommodation is not being provided for the child, he must exercise his powers under section 95 [or 95A] by offering, and if his offer is accepted by providing or arranging for the provision of, adequate accommodation for the child as part of the eligible person's household.

(4) If it appears to the Secretary of State that essential living needs of the child are not being met, he must exercise his powers under section 95 [or 95A] by offering, and if his

offer is accepted by providing or arranging for the provision of, essential living needs for the child as part of the eligible person's household.

(5) No local authority may provide assistance under any of the child welfare provisions in respect of a dependant under the age of 18, or any member of his family, at any time when—

(a) the Secretary of State is complying with this section in relation to him; or

(b) there are reasonable grounds for believing that—

(i) the person concerned is a person for whom support may be provided under section 95 [or by 95A]; and

(ii) the Secretary of State would be required to comply with this section if that person had made an application under section 95 [(or as the case may be) 95A].

(6) 'Assistance' means the provision of accommodation or of any essential living needs.

(7) 'The child welfare provisions' means—

(a) section 17 of the Children Act 1989 (local authority support for children and their families);

(b) section 22 of the Children (Scotland) Act 1995 (equivalent provision for Scotland); and

(c) Article 18 of the Children (Northern Ireland) Order 1995 (equivalent provision for Northern Ireland).

(8) Subsection (9) applies if accommodation provided in the discharge of the duty imposed by subsection (3) has been withdrawn.

(9) Only the relevant authority may provide assistance under any of the child welfare provisions in respect of the child concerned.

(10) 'Relevant authority' means—

(a) in relation to Northern Ireland, the authority within whose area the withdrawn accommodation was provided;

(b) in any other case, the local authority within whose area the withdrawn accommodation was provided.

(11) In such circumstances as may be prescribed, subsection (5) does not apply.

Note: Commencement from 1 March 2000, (SI 2000/464). Words in square brackets inserted by Schedule 11 to Immigration Act 2016 from a date to be appointed.

123. Back-dating of benefits where person recorded as refugee

...

Note: Section 123 ceased to have effect from 30 April 2003 Asylum and Immigration Act 2004, s 12.

Miscellaneous

124. Secretary of State to be corporation sole for purposes of Part VI

(1) For the purpose of exercising his functions under this Part, the Secretary of State is a corporation sole.

(2) Any instrument in connection with the acquisition, management or disposal of property, real or personal, heritable or moveable, by the Secretary of State under this Part may be executed on his behalf by a person authorised by him for that purpose.

(3) Any instrument purporting to have been so executed on behalf of the Secretary of State is to be treated, until the contrary is proved, to have been so executed on his behalf.

Note: Commenced 11 November 1999, s 170.

125. Entry of premises

(1) This section applies in relation to premises in which accommodation has been provided under [section 95, 95A, 98 or 98A] for a supported person.

(2) If, on an application made by a person authorised in writing by the Secretary of State, a justice of the peace is satisfied that there is reason to believe that—

(a) the supported person or any dependants of his for whom the accommodation is provided is not resident in it,

(b) [in the case of accommodation provided under section 95 or 98,] the accommodation is being used for any purpose other than the accommodation of the asylum-seeker or any dependant of his, [..]

[(ba) in the case of accommodation provided under section 95A or 98A, the accommodation is being used for any purpose other than the accommodation of the failed asylum-seeker or any dependant of his,]

(c) any person other than the supported person and his dependants (if any) is residing in the accommodation, he may grant a warrant to enter the premises to the person making the application.

(3) A warrant granted under subsection (2) may be executed—

(a) at any reasonable time;

(b) using reasonable force.

(4) In the application of subsection (2) to Scotland, read the reference to a justice of the peace as a reference to the sheriff or a justice of the peace.

Note: Commenced 3 April 2000 (SI 2000/464). Words in square brackets in subsection (1) and (2)(b) substituted, and subsection (ba) inserted by Schedule 11 to the Immigration Act 2016 from a date to be appointed.

126. Information from property owners

(1) The power conferred by this section is to be exercised with a view to obtaining information about premises in which accommodation is or has been provided for supported persons.

(2) The Secretary of State may require any person appearing to him—

(a) to have any interest in, or

(b) to be involved in any way in the management or control of,

such premises, or any building which includes such premises, to provide him with such information with respect to the premises and the persons occupying them as he may specify.

(3) A person who is required to provide information under this section must do so in accordance with such requirements as may be prescribed.

(4) Information provided to the Secretary of State under this section may be used by him only in the exercise of his functions under this Part.

Note: Commenced 3 April 2000 (SI 2000/464).

127. Requirement to supply information about redirection of post

(1) The Secretary of State may require any person conveying postal packets to supply redirection information to the Secretary of State—

(a) for use in the prevention, detection, investigation or prosecution of criminal offences under this Part;

(b) for use in checking the accuracy of information relating to support provided under this Part; or

(c) for any other purpose relating to the provision of support to asylum-seekers[or failed asylum seekers].

(2) The information must be supplied in such manner and form, and in accordance with such requirements, as may be prescribed.

(3) The Secretary of State must make payments of such amount as he considers reasonable in respect of the supply of information under this section.

(4) 'Postal packet' has the same meaning as in the [Postal Services Act 2000].

(5) 'Redirection information' means information relating to arrangements made with any person conveying postal packets for the delivery of postal packets to addresses other than those indicated by senders on the packets.

Note: Commenced 3 April 2000 (SI 2000/464). Words in square brackets in subsection (4) substituted from 26 March 2001 (SI 2001/1149). Words inserted at in square brackets subsection (1)(c) by Schedule 11 to the Immigration Act 2016 from a date to be appointed.

Part VII

Power to Arrest, Search and Fingerprint

Power to arrest

128. ...

Note: Amends Immigration Act 1971, s 28.

Power to search and arrest

129. ...

Note: Amends Immigration Act 1971, s 28.

130. ...

Note: Amends Immigration Act 1971, s 28.

Power to enter and search premises

131. ...

Note: Amends Immigration Act 1971, s 28.

132. …

Note: Amends Immigration Act 1971, s 28 and Sch 2, paragraph 25.

133. …

Note: Amends Immigration Act 1971, s 28.

Power to search persons

134. …

Note: Amends Immigration Act 1971, s 28 and Sch 2, paragraph 25.

135. …

Note: Amends Immigration Act 1971, s 28 and Sch 2, paragraph 25.

Seized material: access and copying

136. …

Note: Amends Immigration Act 1971, s 28 and Sch 2, paragraph 25.

Search warrants

137. …

Note: Amends Immigration Act 1971, s 28.

138. …

Note: Amends Immigration Act 1971, s 28.

139. …

Note: Amends Immigration Act 1971, s 28 and Sch 2, paragraph 25.

Detention

140. …

Note: Amends Immigration Act 1971, Sch 2, paragraphs 16–17.

Fingerprinting

141. Fingerprinting

(1) Fingerprints may be taken by an authorised person from a person to whom this section applies.

(2) Fingerprints may be taken under this section only during the relevant period.

(3) Fingerprints may not be taken under this section from a person under the age of sixteen ('the child') except in the presence of a person of full age who is—

(a) the child's parent or guardian; or

(b) a person who for the time being takes responsibility for the child.

(4) The person mentioned in subsection (3)(b) may not be—

(a) an officer of the Secretary of State who is not an authorised person;

(b) an authorised person.

(5) 'Authorised person' means—

(a) a constable;

(b) an immigration officer;

(c) a prison officer;

(d) an officer of the Secretary of State authorised for the purpose; or

(e) a person who is employed by a contractor in connection with the discharge of the contractor's duties under a [removal centre] contract.

(6) In subsection (5)(e) 'contractor' and '[removal centre] contract' have the same meaning as in Part VIII.

(7) This section applies to—

(a) any person ('A') who, on being required to do so by an immigration officer on his arrival in the United Kingdom, fails to produce a valid passport with photograph or some other document satisfactorily establishing his identity and nationality or citizenship;

(b) any person ('B') who has been refused leave to enter the United Kingdom but has been {granted immigration bail under Schedule 10 to the Immigration Act 2016} [[subject to a condition mentioned in paragraph 2(1)(c) or (d) of that Schedule if an immigration officer reasonably suspects that B might break the condition]];

[(c) any person ('C') in respect of whom the Secretary of State has decided—

(i) to make a deportation order, or

(ii) that section 32(5) of the UK Borders Act 2007 (automatic deportation of foreign criminals) applies;

(ca) any person ('CA') who requires leave to enter or remain in the United Kingdom but does not have it;]

(d) any person ('D') who has been [detained under paragraph 16 of Schedule 2 to the 1971 Act or arrested under paragraph 17 of that Schedule;]

(e) any person ('E') who has made a [[protection claim]];

[(f) any person ('F') who is—

(i) a member of the family of a person within any of paragraphs (a), (b) or (ca) to (e), or

(ii) a dependant of a person within paragraph (c)(i).]

(8) 'The relevant period' begins—

(a) for A, on his failure to produce the passport or other document;

(b) for B, on the decision to {grant him bail};

[(c) for C, when he is notified of the decision mentioned in subsection (7)(c);

(ca) for CA, when he becomes a person to whom this section applies,]

(d) for D, on his [detention or arrest;]

(e) for E, on the making of his [[protection claim]]; and

(f) for F, at the same time as for the person [of whose family he is a member of or whose dependent he is.]

(9) 'The relevant period' ends on the earliest of the following—

(a) the grant of leave to enter or remain in the United Kingdom;

(b) for A, B, C [, CA] or D, his removal or deportation from the United Kingdom;

[(c) for C—

(i) the time when the [decision mentioned in subsection (7)(c)] ceases to have effect, whether as a result of an appeal or otherwise, or

(ii) if a deportation order has been made against him, its revocation or its otherwise ceasing to have effect;]

[(ca) for CA, when he no longer requires leave to enter or remain in the United Kingdom;]

(d) for D, his release if he is no longer liable to be detained under paragraph 16 of Schedule 2 to the 1971 Act;

(e) for E, the final determination or abandonment of his [[protection claim]]; and

(f) for F, at the same time as for the person [of whose family he is a member of or whose dependant he is].

(10) No fingerprints may be taken from A if the immigration officer considers that A has a reasonable excuse for the failure concerned.

(11) No fingerprints may be taken from B unless the decision to take them has been confirmed by a chief immigration officer.

(12) An authorised person may not take fingerprints from a person under the age of sixteen unless his decision to take them has been confirmed—

(a) if he is a constable, by a person designated for the purpose by the chief constable of his police force;

(b) if he is a person mentioned in subsection (5)(b) or (e), by a chief immigration officer;

(c) if he is a prison officer, by a person designated for the purpose by the governor of the prison;

(d) if he is an officer of the Secretary of State, by a person designated for the purpose by the Secretary of State.

(13) Neither subsection (3) nor subsection (12) prevents an authorised person from taking fingerprints if he reasonably believes that the person from whom they are to be taken is aged sixteen or over.

[(13A) For the purposes of subsection (7)(f)(i), a person is a member of the family of another person ('P') if—

(a) the person is—

(i) P's partner,

(ii) P's child, or a child living in the same household as P in circumstances where P has care of the child,

(iii) in a case where P is a child, P's parent, or

(iv) an adult dependant relative of P, and

(b) the person does not have a right of abode in the United Kingdom or indefinite leave to enter or remain in the United Kingdom.

(13B) In subsection (13A) 'child' means a person who is under the age of 18.]

(14) For the purposes of subsection (7)(f)[(ii)], a person is a dependant of another person if—

(a) he is that person's spouse or child under the age of eighteen; and

(b) he does not have a right of abode in the United Kingdom or indefinite leave to enter or remain in the United Kingdom.

(15) [['Protection claim']]has the same meaning as in Part VI.

[**(16)** ...]

[**(17)** Section 157(1) applies to this section (in so far as it relates to removal centres by virtue of subsection (5)(e)) as it applies to Part VIII.]

Note: Commenced 11 December 2000 (SI 2000/3099). Words in first and second square brackets substituted by Nationality, Immigration and Asylum Act 2002, s 66 from 10 February 2003 (SI 2003/1). Words in square brackets in subsections (7)(c), (8)(c) and (9)(c) substituted and subsection (16) added by Asylum and Immigration (Treatment of Claimants etc.) Act 2004, s 15 from 1 October 2004 (SI 2004/2523), subsection (16) deleted by Sch 9 Immigration Act 2014 from 20 October 2014 with savings in articles 9–11 SI 2014/2771. Words in square brackets in subsections (7)(d) and (8)(d) substituted and subsection (17) added by Immigration, Asylum and Nationality Act 2006, s 28 from 31 August 2006 (SI 2006/2226). Words in square brackets in subsections (7)(f) inserted by s 51 Borders, Citizenship and Immigration Act 2009 from 15 November 2009 (SI 2009/2731). Subsections (7)(c), (8)(c) and words in second square brackets in (7)(f) and (9)(c)(i) substituted; letters in subsection (9)(b) and subsection (9)(ca) inserted by Sch 9 Immigration Act 2014 from 20 October 2014 with savings set out in articles 9–11 SI 2014/2771. Words in square brackets substituted at subsection (7), and inserted at subsection (8)(f) and (9)(f) by Immigration Act 2016, s 57 from 12 July 2016 (SI 2016/603). Subsection (13A) and (13B) inserted by Immigration Act 2016, s 57 on 12 July 2016 (SI 2016/603). Words in square brackets substituted at subsection 14 by Immigration Act 2016, s 57 from 12 July 2016 (SI 2016/603). Words in curly brackets at subsection (7)(b) and (8)(b) are substituted by Schedule 10 to the Immigration Act 2016 from 15 January 2018 subject to transitional provisions in SI 2017/1241. Words in double square brackets at subsection (7)(b) are substituted by Immigration Act 2016) (Consequential Amendments)(Biometrics and Legal Aid) Regulations from January 2018 being the day on which 2016 c.19 Sch10 para 1 comes into force. Words in double square brackets substituted at subsection (7)(e), (8)(e), (9)(e) and (15) by Sch 11 to the Immigration Act 2016 from a date to be appointed.

142. Attendance for fingerprinting

(1) The Secretary of State may, by notice in writing, require a person to whom section 141 applies to attend at a specified place for fingerprinting.

[**(2)** In the case of a notice given to a person of a kind specified in section 141(7)(a) to (d) or (f) (in so far as it applies to a [member of the family of, or a dependant of,] a person of a kind specified in section 141(7)(a) to (d)), the notice—

(a) must require him to attend during a specified period of at least seven days beginning with a day not less than seven days after the date given in the notice as its date of issue, and

(b) may require him to attend at a specified time of day or during specified hours.

(2A) In the case of a notice given to a person of a kind specified in section 141(7)(e) or (f) (in so far as it applies to a [member of the family of, or a dependant of], a person of a kind specified in section 141(7)(e)), the notice—

(a) may require him to attend during a specified period beginning with a day not less than three days after the date given in the notice as its date of issue,

(b) may require him to attend on a specified day not less than three days after the date given in the notice as its date of issue, and

(c) may require him to attend at a specified time of day or during specified hours.]

(3) A constable or immigration officer may arrest without warrant a person who has failed to comply with a requirement imposed on him under this section (unless the requirement has ceased to have effect).

(4) Before a person arrested under subsection (3) is released—

(a) he may be removed to a place where his fingerprints may conveniently be taken; and

(b) his fingerprints may be taken (whether or not he is so removed).

(5) A requirement imposed under subsection (1) ceases to have effect at the end of the relevant period (as defined by section 141).

Note: Commenced 11 December 2000 (SI 2000/3099). Subsection (2) substituted and subsection 2A inserted by Immigration, Asylum and Nationality Act 2006, s 29 from 31 August 2006 (SI 2006/2226). Words in square brackets at subsections (2) and (2A) inserted by Immigration Act 2016, s 57 from 12 July 2016 (SI 2016/603).

143. …

Note: Repealed by Sch 9 Immigration Act 2014 from a date to be appointed.

144. Other methods of collecting data about physical characteristics

[(1)] The Secretary of State may make regulations containing provisions equivalent to sections 141, [and 142] in relation to such other methods of collecting [biometric information] as may be prescribed.

[(2) 'Biometric information' has the meaning given by section 15 of the UK Borders Act 2007.]

Note: Commenced 11 December 2000 (SI 2000/3099). Subsection (2) inserted by Nationality, Immigration and Asylum Act 2002, s 128 from 10 February 2003 (SI 2003/1). Words in first square brackets in subsection (1) substituted by Sch 9 Immigration Act 2014 from a date to be appointed. Words in second square brackets in subsection (1) and subsection (2) substituted by Sch 2 Immigration Act 2014 from 28 July 2014 (SI 2014/1820).

[144A. Use and retention of fingerprints etc.

(1) Section 8 of the UK Borders Act 2007 (power to make regulations about use and retention of biometric information) applies to—

(a) fingerprints taken by virtue of section 141, and

(b) biometric information taken by virtue of regulations under section 144, as it applies to biometric information provided in accordance with regulations under section 5(1) of that Act.

(2) Regulations made by virtue of subsection (1)(a) must require fingerprints taken from a person ('F') by virtue of section 141(7)(f) to be destroyed when fingerprints taken from the person [of whose family F is a member of or] whose dependant F is are destroyed.

(3) Regulations made by virtue of subsection (1)(b) must make equivalent provision in relation to biometric information taken by virtue of any provision of regulations under section 144 which is equivalent to section 141(7)(f).]

Note: Section 144A inserted by s 14 Immigration Act 2014 from 28 July 2014 (SI 2014/1820). Words in square brackets at subsection (2) inserted by Immigration Act 2016, s 57 from 12 July 2016 (SI 2016/603).

Codes of practice

145. Codes of practice

(1) An immigration officer exercising any specified power to—

(a) arrest, question, search or take fingerprints from a person,

(b) enter and search premises, or

(c) seize property found on persons or premises,

must have regard to such provisions of a code as may be specified.

(2) Subsection (1) also applies to an authorised person exercising the power to take fingerprints conferred by section 141.

[(2A) A person exercising a power under regulations made by virtue of section 144 must have regard to such provisions of a code as may be specified.]

(3) Any specified provision of a code may have effect for the purposes of this section subject to such modifications as may be specified.

(4) 'Specified' means specified in a direction given by the Secretary of State.

(5) 'Authorised person' has the same meaning as in section 141.

(6) 'Code' means—

(a) in relation to England and Wales, any code of practice for the time being in force under the Police and Criminal Evidence Act 1984;

(b) in relation to Northern Ireland, any code of practice for the time being in force under the Police and Criminal Evidence (Northern Ireland) Order 1989.

(7) This section does not apply to any person exercising powers in Scotland.

Note: Commenced 11 November 1999, s 170. Subsection (2A) inserted by Nationality, Immigration and Asylum Act 2002, s 128 from 10 February 2003 (SI 2003/1).

Use of force

146. Use of force

(1) An immigration officer exercising any power conferred on him by [the Immigration Acts] may, if necessary, use reasonable force.

[(2) A person exercising a power under any of the following may if necessary use reasonable force—

[(za) section 24E(1) (powers to enter premises to detain motor vehicle) of the 1971 Act]

(a) section 28CA, 28FA or 28FB of the 1971 Act (business premises: entry to arrest or search),

[(aa) paragraph 25CA, 25CB or 25CC of Schedule 2 to the 1971 Act (powers to search for and seize driving licences),]

(b) section 141 or 142 of this Act, and

(c) regulations under section 144 of this Act.]

Note: Commenced 1 November 1999, s 170 (Royal Assent). Words in square brackets in subsection (1) substituted by Sch 1 Immigration Act 2014 from 28 July 2014 (SI 2014/1820). Subsection (2) substituted by Nationality, Immigration and Asylum Act 2002, s 153 from 8 January 2003 (SI 2003/1). Subsection (2)(aa) inserted by Immigration Act 2016, s 43 from July 31, 2017 in relation to areas of Kent and West Yorkshire, not yet in force otherwise. Subsection (2)(za) inserted by Immigration Act 2016, s 44 from a date to be appointed.

Part VIII
[Removal Centres] and Detained Persons

Interpretation

147. Interpretation of Part VIII

In this Part—

'certificate of authorisation' means a certificate issued by the Secretary of State under section 154;

'certified prisoner custody officer' means a prisoner custody officer certified under section 89 of the Criminal Justice Act 1991, or section 114 of the Criminal Justice and Public Order Act 1994, to perform custodial duties;

'contract monitor' means a person appointed by the Secretary of State under section 149(4);

'contracted out [removal centre]' means a [removal centre] in relation to which a [removal centre] contract is in force;

'contractor', in relation to a [removal centre] which is being run in accordance with a [removal centre] contract, means the person who has contracted to run it;

'custodial functions' means custodial functions at a [removal centre];

['detained children' means detained persons who are under the age of 18;]

'detained persons' means persons detained or required to be detained under the 1971 Act [or under section 62 of the Nationality, Immigration and Asylum Act 2002 (detention by Secretary of State);]

'detainee custody officer' means a person in respect of whom a certificate of authorisation is in force;

. . .

'[removal centre] contract' means a contract entered into by the Secretary of State under section 149;

'[removal] centre rules' means rules made by the Secretary of State under section 153;

'directly managed [removal centre]' means a [removal centre] which is not a contracted out [removal centre];

'escort arrangements' means arrangements made by the Secretary of State under section 156;

'escort functions' means functions under escort arrangements;

'escort monitor' means a person appointed under paragraph 1 of Schedule 13;

['pre-departure accommodation' means a place used solely for the detention of detained children and their families for a period of—

(a) not more than 72 hours, or

(b) not more than seven days in cases where the longer period of detention is authorised personally by a Minister of the Crown (within the meaning of the Ministers of the Crown Act 1975);]

'prisoner custody officer'—

(a) in relation to England and Wales, has the same meaning as in the Criminal Justice Act 1991;

(b) in relation to Scotland, has the meaning given in section 114(1) of the Criminal Justice and Public Order Act 1994;

(c) in relation to Northern Ireland, has the meaning given in section 122(1) of that Act of 1994;

['removal centre' means a place which is used solely for the detention of detained persons but which is not a short-term holding [pre-departure accommodation,] facility, a prison or part of a prison;]

'short-term holding facility' means a place used

[–(a) solely for the detention of detained persons for a period of not more than seven days or for such other period as may be prescribed [, or

(b) for the detention of—

(i) detained persons for a period of not more than seven days or for such other period as may be prescribed, and

(ii) persons other than detained persons for any period] [but which is not pre-departure accommodation].

Note: Commenced 1 August 2000 (SI 2000/1985). Definition of removal centre inserted by Nationality, Immigration and Asylum Act 2002, s 66 from 10 February 2003 (SI 2003/1). Definition of detained persons amended by Nationality, Immigration and Asylum Act 2002, s 62 from 10 February 2003 (SI 2003/1). Definition of 'short term holding facility' amended by s 25 Borders, Citizenship and Immigration Act 2009 from 21 July 2009 (s 57). Definitions of 'detained children', 'pre-departure accommodation' and words in square brackets in definition of removal centre and words in last square brackets inserted by s 6 Immigration Act 2014 from 28 July 2014 (SI 2014/1820). Other words in square brackets inserted by Nationality, Immigration and Asylum Act 2002, s 66 from 10 February 2003 (SI 2003/1).

[Removal centres]

148. Management of [removal centres]

(1) A manager must be appointed for every [removal centre].

(2) In the case of a contracted out [removal centre], the person appointed as manager must be a detainee custody officer whose appointment is approved by the Secretary of State.

(3) The manager of a [removal centre] is to have such functions as are conferred on him by [removal centre] rules.

(4) The manager of a contracted out [removal centre] may not—

(a) enquire into a disciplinary charge laid against a detained person;

(b) conduct the hearing of such a charge; or

(c) make, remit or mitigate an award in respect of such a charge.

(5) The manager of a contracted out [removal centre] may not, except in cases of urgency, order—

(a) the removal of a detained person from association with other detained persons;

(b) the temporary confinement of a detained person in special accommodation; or

(c) the application to a detained person of any other special control or restraint (other than handcuffs).

Note: Subsection (3) commenced 1 August 2000 (SI 2000/1985). Remainder commenced 2 April 2001 (SI 2001/239). Words in square brackets substituted by Nationality, Immigration and Asylum Act 2002, s 66 from 10 February 2003 (SI 2003/1).

149. Contracting out of certain [removal centres]

(1) The Secretary of State may enter into a contract with another person for the provision or running (or the provision and running) by him, or (if the contract so provides) for the running by sub-contractors of his, of any [removal centre] or part of a [removal centre].

(2) While a [removal centre] contract for the running of a [removal centre] or part of a [removal centre] is in force—

(a) the [removal centre] or part is to be run subject to and in accordance with the provisions of or made under this Part; and

(b) in the case of a part, that part and the remaining part are to be treated for the purposes of those provisions as if they were separate [removal centres].

(3) If the Secretary of State grants a lease or tenancy of land for the purposes of a detention centre contract, none of the following enactments applies to the lease or tenancy—

(a) Part II of the Landlord and Tenant Act 1954 (security of tenure);

(b) section 146 of the Law of Property Act 1925 (restrictions on and relief against forfeiture);

(c) section 19(1), (2) and (3) of the Landlord and Tenant Act 1927 and the Landlord and Tenant Act 1988 (covenants not to assign etc.);

(d) the Agricultural Holdings Act 1986;

(e) sections 4 to 7 of the Law Reform (Miscellaneous Provisions) (Scotland) Act 1985 (irritancy clauses);

(f) the Agricultural Holdings (Scotland) Act 1991 [and the Agricultural Holdings (Scotland) Act 2003 (asp 11)];

(g) section 14 of the Conveyancing Act 1881;

(h) the Conveyancing and Law of Property Act 1892;

(i) the Business Tenancies (Northern Ireland) Order 1996.

(4) The Secretary of State must appoint a contract monitor for every contracted out [removal centre].

(5) A person may be appointed as the contract monitor for more than one [removal centre].

(6) The contract monitor is to have—

(a) such functions as may be conferred on him by [removal centre] rules;

(b) the status of a Crown servant.

(7) The contract monitor must—

(a) keep under review, and report to the Secretary of State on, the running of a [removal centre] for which he is appointed; and

(b) investigate, and report to the Secretary of State on, any allegations made against any person performing custodial functions at that centre.

(8) The contractor, and any sub-contractor of his, must do all that he reasonably can (whether by giving directions to the officers of the [removal centre] or otherwise) to facilitate the exercise by the contract monitor of his functions.

(9) 'Lease or tenancy' includes an underlease, sublease or sub-tenancy.

(10) In relation to a [removal centre] contract entered into by the Secretary of State before the commencement of this section, this section is to be treated as having been in force at that time.

Note: Subsections (1), (3), (6)(a) and (9) commenced 1 August 2000 (SI 2000/1985). Remainder commenced 2 April 2001, s 66 (SI 2001/239). Words in square brackets substituted by Nationality, Immigration and Asylum Act 2002, s 66 from 10 February 2003 (SI 2003/1). Words in square brackets in subsection (3)(f) inserted by Agricultural Holdings (Scotland) Act 2003 Schedule paragraph 52 from 27 November 2003 (SI 2003/511).

150. Contracted out functions at directly managed [removal centres]

(1) The Secretary of State may enter into a contract with another person—

(a) for functions at, or connected with, a directly managed [removal centre] to be performed by detainee custody officers provided by that person; or

(b) for such functions to be performed by certified prisoner custody officers who are provided by that person.

(2) For the purposes of this section '[removal centre]' includes a short-term holding facility.

Note: Commenced 2 April 2001 (SI 2001/239). Words in square brackets substituted by Nationality, Immigration and Asylum Act 2002, s 66 from 10 February 2003 (SI 2003/1).

151. Intervention by Secretary of State

(1) The Secretary of State may exercise the powers conferred by this section if it appears to him that—

(a) the manager of a contracted out [removal centre] has lost, or is likely to lose, effective control of the centre or of any part of it; or

(b) it is necessary to do so in the interests of preserving the safety of any person, or of preventing serious damage to any property.

(2) The Secretary of State may appoint a person (to be known as the Controller) to act as manager of the [removal centre] for the period—

(a) beginning with the time specified in the appointment; and

(b) ending with the time specified in the notice of termination under subsection (5).

(3) During that period—

(a) all the functions which would otherwise be exercisable by the manager or the contract monitor are to be exercisable by the Controller;

(b) the contractor and any sub-contractor of his must do all that he reasonably can to facilitate the exercise by the Controller of his functions; and

(c) the staff of the detention centre must comply with any directions given by the Controller in the exercise of his functions.

(4) The Controller is to have the status of a Crown servant.

(5) If the Secretary of State is satisfied that a Controller is no longer needed for a particular detention centre, he must (by giving notice to the Controller) terminate his appointment at a time specified in the notice.

(6) As soon as practicable after making an appointment under this section, the Secretary of State must give notice of the appointment to those entitled to notice.

(7) As soon as practicable after terminating an appointment under this section, the Secretary of State must give a copy of the notice of termination to those entitled to notice.

(8) Those entitled to notice are the contractor, the manager, the contract monitor and the Controller.

Note: Commenced 2 April 2001 (SI 2001/239). Words in square brackets substituted by Nationality, Immigration and Asylum Act 2002, s 66 from 10 February 2003 (SI 2003/1).

152. Visiting Committees and inspections

(1) The Secretary of State must appoint a committee (to be known as the Visiting Committee) for each detention centre.

(2) The functions of the Visiting Committee for a [removal centre] are to be such as may be prescribed by the [removal centre] rules.

(3) Those rules must include provision—

(a) as to the making of visits to the centre by members of the Visiting Committee;

(b) for the hearing of complaints made by persons detained in the centre;

(c) requiring the making of reports by the Visiting Committee to the Secretary of State.

(4) Every member of the Visiting Committee for a [removal centre] may at any time enter the centre and have free access to every part of it and to every person detained there.

(5) . . .

Note: Subsections (2) and (3) commenced for the purposes of enabling subordinate legislation 1 August 2000 (SI 2000/1985). Otherwise commenced 2 April 2001 (SI 2001/239). Subsection (5) amends the Prison Act 1952, s 5A. Words in square brackets substituted by Nationality, Immigration and Asylum Act 2002, s 66 from 10 February 2003 (SI 2003/1).

153. [Removal centre] rules

(1) The Secretary of State must make rules for the regulation and management of [removal centres].

(2) [Removal centre] rules may, among other things, make provision with respect to the safety, care, activities, discipline and control of detained persons.

Note: Commenced for the purposes of enabling subordinate legislation 1 August 2000 (SI 2000/1985). Otherwise commenced 2 April 2001 (SI 2001/239). Words in square brackets substituted by Nationality, Immigration and Asylum Act 2002, s 66 from 10 February 2003 (SI 2003/1).

[153A. Detained persons: national minimum wage

A detained person does not qualify for the national minimum wage in respect of work which he does in pursuance of removal centre rules.]

Note: Inserted by Immigration, Asylum and Nationality Act 2006, s 59 from 31 August 2006 (SI 2006/2226).

Custody and movement of detained persons

154. Detainee custody officers

(1) On an application made to him under this section, the Secretary of State may certify that the applicant—

(a) is authorised to perform escort functions; or

(b) is authorised to perform both escort functions and custodial functions.

(2) The Secretary of State may not issue a certificate of authorisation unless he is satisfied that the applicant—

(a) is a fit and proper person to perform the functions to be authorised; and

(b) has received training to such standard as the Secretary of State considers appropriate for the performance of those functions.

(3) A certificate of authorisation continues in force until such date, or the occurrence of such event, as may be specified in the certificate but may be suspended or revoked under paragraph 7 of Schedule 11.

(4) A certificate which authorises the performance of both escort functions and custodial functions may specify one date or event for one of those functions and a different date or event for the other.

[(5) The Secretary of State may confer functions of detainee custody officers on prison officers or prisoner custody officers.]

(6) A prison officer acting under arrangements made under subsection (5) has all the powers, authority, protection and privileges of a constable.

(7) Schedule 11 makes further provision about detainee custody officers.

Note: Commenced 2 April 2001 (SI 2001/239). Subsection (5) substituted by Nationality, Immigration and Asylum Act 2002, s 65 from 10 February 2003 (SI 2003/1).

155. Custodial functions and discipline etc. at [removal centres]

(1) Custodial functions may be discharged at a [removal centre] only by—

(a) a detainee custody officer authorised, in accordance with section 154(1), to perform such functions; or

(b) a prison officer, or a certified prisoner custody officer, exercising functions in relation to the [removal centre]—

(i) in accordance with arrangements made under section 154(5); or

(ii) as a result of a contract entered into under section 150(1)(b).

(2) Schedule 12 makes provision with respect to discipline and other matters at [removal centres] and short-term holding facilities [and in pre-departure accommodation.]

Note: Subsection (2) commenced 1 August 2000 (SI 2000/1985). Remainder commenced 2 April 2001 (SI 2001/239). Words in last square brackets in subsection (2) inserted by s 6 Immigration Act 2014 from 28 July 2014 (SI 2014/1820). Other words in square brackets substituted by Nationality, Immigration and Asylum Act 2002, s 66 from 10 February 2003 (SI 2003/1).

156. Arrangements for the provision of escorts and custody

(1) The Secretary of State may make arrangements for—

(a) the delivery of detained persons to premises in which they may lawfully be detained;

(b) the delivery of persons from any such premises for the purposes of their removal from the United Kingdom in accordance with directions given under the 1971 Act or this Act;

(c) the custody of detained persons who are temporarily outside such premises;

(d) the custody of detained persons held on the premises of any court.

(2) Escort arrangements may provide for functions under the arrangements to be performed, in such cases as may be determined by or under the arrangements, by detainee custody officers.

(3) 'Court' includes—

[(a) the First-tier Tribunal;

(b) the Upper Tribunal; and]

(c) the Commission.

(4) Escort arrangements may include entering into contracts with other persons for the provision by them of—

(a) detainee custody officers; or

(b) prisoner custody officers who are certified under section 89 of the Criminal Justice Act 1991, or section 114 or 122 of the Criminal Justice and Public Order Act 1994, to perform escort functions.

(5) Schedule 13 makes further provision about escort arrangements.

(6) A person responsible for performing a function of a kind mentioned in subsection (1), in accordance with a transfer direction, complies with the direction if he does all that he reasonably can to secure that the function is performed by a person acting in accordance with escort arrangements.

(7) 'Transfer direction' means a transfer direction given under—

(a) section 48 of the Mental Health Act 1983 or section 71 of the Mental Health (Scotland) Act 1984 (removal to hospital of, among others, persons detained under the 1971 Act); or

(b) in Northern Ireland, article 54 of the Mental Health (Northern Ireland) Order 1986 (provision corresponding to section 48 of the 1983 Act).

Note: Subsection (5) commenced 1 August 2000 (SI 2000/1985). Remainder commenced 2 April 2001 (SI 2001/239). Words in square brackets substituted from 15 February 2010 (SI 2010/21).

157. Short-term holding facilities

(1) The Secretary of State may by regulations extend any provision made by or under this Part in relation to [removal centres] (other than one mentioned in subsection (2)) to short-term holding facilities.

(2) Subsection (1) does not apply to section 150.

(3) The Secretary of State may make rules for the regulation and management of short-term holding facilities.

Note: Commenced for the purposes of enabling subordinate legislation 1 August 2000 (SI 2000/1985). Otherwise commenced 2 April 2001 (SI 2001/239). Words in square brackets substituted by Nationality, Immigration and Asylum Act 2002, s 66 from 10 February 2003 (SI 2003/1).

[157A. Pre-departure accommodation

(1) The following provisions of this Part apply to pre-departure accommodation as they apply to removal centres—

(a) section 149 (contracting out of certain removal centres);

(b) section 150 (contracting out functions at directly managed removal centres);

(c) section 151 (intervention by Secretary of State).

(2) In the application of those provisions to pre-departure accommodation—

(a) references to a removal centre contract are to be read as a contract made under section 149(1) for the provision or running of pre-departure accommodation;

(b) references to a contracted out removal centre are to be read as references to pre-departure accommodation in relation to which a contract under section 149(1) is in force;

(c) references to a directly managed removal centre are to be read as references to pre-departure accommodation in relation to which there is no contract under section 149(1) in force;

(d) references to removal centre rules are to be read as references to rules made under subsection (4).

(3) The Secretary of State may by regulations extend to pre-departure accommodation any other provision made by or under this Part in relation to removal centres.

(4) The Secretary of State may make rules for the regulation and management of pre-departure accommodation.]

Note: Section 157A inserted by s 6 Immigration Act 2014 from 28 July 2014 (SI 2014/1820).

Miscellaneous

158. Wrongful disclosure of information

(1) A person who is or has been employed (whether as a detainee custody officer, prisoner custody officer or otherwise)—

(a) in accordance with escort arrangements,

(b) at a contracted out [removal centre], or

(c) to perform contracted out functions at a directly managed detention centre, is guilty of an offence if he discloses, otherwise than in the course of his duty or as authorised by the Secretary of State, any information which he acquired in the course of his employment and which relates to a particular detained person.

(2) A person guilty of such an offence is liable—

(a) on conviction on indictment, to imprisonment for a term not exceeding two years or to a fine or to both;

(b) on summary conviction, to imprisonment for a term not exceeding six months or to a fine not exceeding the statutory maximum or to both.

(3) 'Contracted out functions' means functions which, as the result of a contract entered into under section 150, fall to be performed by detainee custody officers or certified prisoner custody officers.

Note: Commenced 2 April 2001 (SI 2001/239). Words in square brackets substituted by Nationality, Immigration and Asylum Act 2002, s 66 from 10 February 2003 (SI 2003/1).

159. Power of constable to act outside his jurisdiction

(1) For the purpose of taking a person to or from a [removal centre] under the order of any authority competent to give the order, a constable may act outside the area of his jurisdiction.

(2) When acting under this section, the constable concerned retains all the powers, authority, protection and privileges of his office.

Note: Commenced 2 April 2001 (SI 2001/239). Words in square brackets substituted by Nationality, Immigration and Asylum Act 2002, s 66 from 10 February 2003 (SI 2003/1).

Part IX
Registrar's Certificates: Procedure

160. …

Note: Amends Marriage Act 1949, ss 26–7, 31.

161. …

Note: Amends the Marriage Act 1949, ss 26–7 and the Marriage Law (Ireland) Amendment Act 1863, s 2.

162. …

Note: Amends the Marriage Act 1949, s 28 and the Marriage Law (Ireland) Amendment Act 1863 s 3.

163. …

Note: Amends the Marriage Act 1949, s 31 and the Marriages (Ireland) Act 1844, s 16.

Part X
Miscellaneous and Supplemental

164. …

Note: Amends the Prosecution of Offences Act 1985, s 3.

165. …

Note: Amends Immigration Act 1971, s 31.

166. Regulations and orders

(1) Any power to make rules, regulations or orders conferred by this Act is exercisable by statutory instrument.

(2) But subsection (1) does not apply in relation to [orders made under section 90(1),] rules made under paragraph 1 of Schedule 5 or immigration rules.

(3) Any statutory instrument made as a result of subsection (1) may—

(a) contain such incidental, supplemental, consequential and transitional provision as the person making it considers appropriate;

(b) make different provision for different cases or descriptions of case; and

(c) make different provision for different areas.

(4) No order is to be made under—

(a) section 20,

(b) section 21,

(c) section 31(10),

[(da) section 86A(3)]

(d) section 86(2),

(e) …

(f) section 97(3),

(g) …; or

(h) paragraph 4 of Schedule 5,

unless a draft of the order has been laid before Parliament and approved by a resolution of each House.

(5) No regulations are to be made under—

(za) …

(a) section 9,

(b) section 46(8),

(c) section 53,

[(ca) section 95A, or]

(d) section 144,

unless a draft of the regulations has been laid before Parliament and approved by a resolution of each House.

[(5A) No regulations under section 20A(12) which amend Schedule A1 so as to—

(a) add a reference to a person or description of person, or

(b) modify a reference to a person or description of person otherwise than in consequence of a change of name or transfer of functions,

are to be made unless a draft of the regulations has been laid before Parliament and approved by a resolution of each House.]

[(5A) No regulations under paragraph 1 of Schedule 8 which make provision with respect to the powers conferred by section 95A are to be made unless a draft of the regulations has been laid before Parliament and approved by a resolution of each House.

(5B) Subsection (5A) does not apply to regulations under paragraph 1 of that Schedule which make provision of the kind mentioned in paragraph 3(a) of that Schedule.]

(6) Any statutory instrument made under this Act, apart from one made—

(a) under any of the provisions mentioned in subsection (4) or (5),

[[(aa) under the provision mentioned in subsection 5A and containing regulations to which that subsection applies, or]]

[(ab) under section 20A(12) and which falls within subsection(5A)],

(b) under section 24(3) [, 24A(3)] or 170(4) or (7), shall be subject to annulment by a resolution of either House of Parliament.

Note: Commencement 11 November 1999, s 170. Subsection (4)(e) omitted by Nationality, Immigration and Asylum Act 2002, s 61 from 7 November 2002. Words in square brackets in subsection (2) inserted by Asylum and Immigration Act 2004, s 41 from 1 October 2004 (SI 2004/2523). Subsection (4)(da) inserted by Sch 18 Legal Services Act from 1 April 2011 (SI 2011/720). Subsection (5)(za) inserted by Asylum and Immigration Act 2004, s 10 from 1 December 2004 (SI 2004/2999). Words in square brackets in subsection 6(b) inserted by Civil Partnership Act 2004 Schedule 27 from 15 April 2005 SI 2005/1112). Subsection (4)(g) omitted by Sch 9 Immigration Act 2014 from a date to be appointed. Sections (5A) and 6(ab) are inserted by Immigration Act 2016, s 55 on 12 July 2016 (SI 2016/603). Subsection (5)(za) omitted by Schedule 11 to the Immigration Act 2016 from a date to be appointed: repeal has effect subject to savings and transitional provisions specified in 2016 c.19 Sch11 para 46. Words in double square brackets at subsection (6)(aa) inserted by Sch 11 to Immigration Act 2016 from a date to be appointed. Subsection (5)(ca) and (5A) (as it appears the second time) and (5B) inserted by Sch 11 to the Immigration Act 2016 from a date to be appointed: repeal has effect subject to savings and transitional provisions specified in Immigration Act 2016, Sch 11, para 46.

167. Interpretation

(1) In this Act—

'the 1971 Act' means the Immigration Act 1971;

'adjudicator' (except in Part VI) means an adjudicator appointed under section 57;

'Chief Adjudicator' means the person appointed as Chief Adjudicator under section 57(2);

'claim for asylum' ([Part 5]) means a claim that it would be contrary to the United Kingdom's obligations under the Refugee Convention for the claimant to be removed from, or required to leave, the United Kingdom;

'the Commission' means the Special Immigration Appeals Commission;

'country' includes any territory;

'EEA State' means a State which is a Contracting Party to the Agreement on the European Economic Area signed at Oporto on 2nd May 1992 as it has effect for the time being;

'the Human Rights Convention' means the Convention for the Protection of Human Rights and Fundamental Freedoms, agreed by the Council of Europe at Rome on 4 November 1950 as it has effect for the time being in relation to the United Kingdom;

. . .

'prescribed' means prescribed by regulations made by the Secretary of State;

'the Refugee Convention' means the Convention relating to the Status of Refugees done at Geneva on 28 July 1951 and the Protocol to the Convention;

[['residence scheme immigration rules' has the meaning given by section 17 of the European Union (Withdrawal Agreement) Act 2020;]]

'voluntary organisations' means bodies (other than public or local authorities) whose activities are not carried on for profit.

(2) The following expressions have the same meaning as in the 1971 Act—

'certificate of entitlement';

'entry clearance';

'illegal entrant';

'immigration officer';

'immigration rules';

'port';

'United Kingdom passport';

'work permit'.

Note: Commencement 11 November 1999, s 170. Words omitted ceased to have effect from 30 March 2006, s 64 Immigration, Asylum and Nationality Act 2006 (Royal Assent). Words in square brackets in subsection (1) substituted by Schedule 11 to the Immigration Act 2016 from a date to be appointed. Words in double brackets inserted by Immigration and Social Security Co-ordination (EU Withdrawal) Act 2020 (Consequential, Savings, Transitional and Transitory Provisions) (EU Exit) Regulations 2020/1309 Pt 2(1) reg 12(8) (31 December 2020 at 23.00 being the time and date 2020 c. 20 Sch 1 para 2(2) comes into force).

168. Expenditure and receipts

(1) There is to be paid out of money provided by Parliament—

(a) any expenditure incurred by the Secretary of State or the Lord Chancellor in consequence of this Act; and

(b) any increase attributable to this Act in the sums so payable by virtue of any other Act.

(2) Sums received by the Secretary of State under section 5, 32, 40, 112 or 113 or by the Lord Chancellor under section 48(4) or 49(4) must be paid into the Consolidated Fund.

Note: Commencement 11 November 1999, s 170.

169. Minor and consequential amendments, transitional provisions and repeals

(1) Schedule 14 makes minor and consequential amendments.

(2) Schedule 15 contains transitional provisions and savings.

(3) The enactments set out in Schedule 16 are repealed.

170. Short title, commencement and extent

(1) This Act may be cited as the Immigration and Asylum Act 1999.

(2) Subsections (1) and (2) of section 115 come into force on the day on which the first regulations made under Schedule 8 come into force.

(3) The following provisions come into force on the passing of this Act—

(a) section 4;

(b) section 9;

(c) section 15;
(d) section 27;
(e) section 31;
(f) section 94;
(g) section 95(13);
(h) section 99(4) and (5);
(i) sections 105 to 109;
(j) section 110(1), (2) and (8) (so far as relating to subsections (1) and (2));
(k) section 111;
(l) section 124;
(m) section 140;
(n) section 145;
(o) section 146(1);
(p) sections 166 to 168;
(q) this section;
(r) Schedule 9;
(s) paragraphs 62(2), 73, 78, 79, 81, 82, 87, 88 and 102 of Schedule 14;
(t) paragraph 2 and 13 of Schedule 15.

(4) The other provisions of this Act, except section 10 and paragraph 12 of Schedule 15 (which come into force in accordance with section 9), come into force on such day as the Secretary of State may by order appoint.

(5) Different days may be appointed for different purposes.

(6) This Act extends to Northern Ireland.

(7) Her Majesty may by Order in Council direct that any of the provisions of this Act are to extend, with such modifications (if any) as appear to Her Majesty to be appropriate, to any of the Channel Islands or the Isle of Man.

Note: Commenced 11 November 1999.

SCHEDULE A1 *SCHEDULE A1* Section 20A

PERSONS TO WHOM SECTION 20A APPLIES

Law enforcement

1 The chief officer of police for a police area in England and Wales.

2 The chief constable of the Police Service of Scotland.

3 The Chief Constable of the Police Service of Northern Ireland.

4 The Chief Constable of the British Transport Police Force.

5 A Port Police Force established under an order made under section 14 of the Harbours Act 1964.

6 The Port Police Force established under Part 10 of the Port of London Act 1968.

7 A Port Police Force established under section 79 of the Harbours, Docks and Piers Clauses Act 1847.

8 The National Crime Agency.

Local government

9 A county council or district council in England.

10 A London borough council.

11 The Greater London Authority.

12 The Common Council of the City of London in its capacity as a local authority.

13 The Council of the Isles of Scilly.

14 A county council or a county borough council in Wales.

15 A council constituted under section 2 of the Local Government etc. (Scotland) Act 1994.

16 A district council in Northern Ireland.

Regulatory bodies

17 The Gangmasters and Labour Abuse Authority.

18 The Security Industry Authority.

Health bodies

19 An NHS trust established under section 25 of the National Health Service Act 2006 or under section 18 of the National Health Service (Wales) Act 2006.

20 An NHS foundation trust within the meaning given by section 30 of the National Health Service Act 2006.

21 A Local Health Board established under section 11 of the National Health Service (Wales) Act 2006.

22 A National Health Service Trust established under section 12A of the National Health Service (Scotland) Act 1978.

23 A Health and Social Care trust established under Article 10 of the Health and Personal Social Services (Northern Ireland) Order 1991 (SI 1991/194 (NI 1)).

Education bodies

24 The proprietor of a school or 16 to 19 Academy within the meaning of the Education Act 1996 (see sections 4 and 579(1) of that Act).

25 The governing body of an institution within the further education sector within the meaning of the Further and Higher Education Act 1992 (see sections 90 and 91 of that Act).

26 The governing body of a qualifying institution within the meaning of Part 2 of the Higher Education Act 2004 (see sections 11 and 21 of that Act).

27 The proprietor or governing body of a school within the meaning of the Education (Scotland) Act 1980 (see section 135(1) of that Act).

28 The proprietor or governing body of a post-16 education body within the meaning of the Further and Higher Education (Scotland) Act 2005 (see section 35 of that Act).

29 The proprietor of a school within the meaning of the Education and Libraries (Northern Ireland) Order 1986 (SI 1986/594 (NI 3)) (see Article 2(2) of that Order).

30 The governing body of an institution of further education within the meaning of the Further Education (Northern Ireland) Order 1997 (SI 1997/1772 (NI 15)) (see Article 2(2) of that Order).

31 The governing body of a higher education institution as defined by Article 30(3) of the Education and Libraries (Northern Ireland) Order 1993 (SI 1993/2810 (NI 12)).

Registration officials

32 The Registrar General for England and Wales.

33 A superintendent registrar of births, deaths and marriages.

34 A registrar of births, deaths and marriages.

35 A civil partnership registrar within the meaning of Chapter 1 of Part 2 of the Civil Partnership Act 2004 (see section 29 of that Act).

36 The Registrar General for Scotland.

37 A district registrar within the meaning of section 7 of the Registration of Births, Deaths and Marriages (Scotland) Act 1965.

38 A senior registrar within the meaning of that section.

39 An assistant registrar within the meaning of that section.

40 The Registrar General for Northern Ireland.

41 A person appointed under Article 31(1) or (3) of the Marriage (Northern Ireland) Order 2003 (SI 2003/413 (NI 3)).

42 A person appointed under section 152(1) or (3) of the Civil Partnership Act 2004.

Other bodies: Northern Ireland

43 The Northern Ireland Housing Executive.

Schedule 1

Sections 37(6) and 42(8)

Sale of Transporters

…

Schedule 2

Section 56(2)

The Immigration Appeal Tribunal

…

Note: Schedule 2 repealed by Sch 9 Nationality, Immigration and Asylum Act 2002 from 1 April 2003 (SI 2003/754, which sets out transitional provisions).

SCHEDULE 3

ADJUDICATORS

. . .

Note: Schedule 3 repealed by Sch 9 Nationality, Immigration and Asylum Act 2002 from 1 April 2003 (SI 2003/754, which sets out transitional provisions).

SCHEDULE 4

APPEALS

. . .

Note: Schedule 4 repealed by Sch 9 Nationality, Immigration and Asylum Act 2002 from 1 April 2003 (SI 2003/754, which sets out transitional provisions).

SCHEDULE 5 — Section 83

THE IMMIGRATION SERVICES COMMISSIONER

PART I

Regulatory Functions

The Commissioner's rules

1.—(1) The Commissioner may make rules regulating any aspect of the professional practice, conduct or discipline of—

(a) registered persons, and

[(b) those acting on behalf of registered persons.]

(2) Before making or altering any rules, the Commissioner must consult such persons appearing to him to represent the views of persons engaged in the provision of immigration advice or immigration services as he considers appropriate.

(3) In determining whether a registered person is competent or otherwise fit to provide immigration advice or immigration services, the Commissioner may take into account any breach of the rules by—

(a) that person; and

[(b) any person acting on behalf of that person.]

(4) The rules may, among other things, make provision requiring the keeping of accounts or the obtaining of indemnity insurance.

Note: Sub-paragraphs (1)(b) and (3)(b) substituted by s 37 Asylum and Immigration (Treatment of Claimants) Act 2004 from 1 October 2004 (SI 2004/2523).

2.—(1) The Commissioner's rules must be made or altered by an instrument in writing.

(2) Such an instrument must specify that it is made under this Schedule.

(3) Immediately after such an instrument is made, it must be printed and made available to the public.

(4) The Commissioner may charge a reasonable fee for providing a person with a copy of the instrument.

(5) A person is not to be taken to have contravened a rule made by the Commissioner if he shows that at the time of the alleged contravention the instrument containing the rule had not been made available in accordance with this paragraph.

(6) The production of a printed copy of an instrument purporting to be made by the Commissioner on which is endorsed a certificate signed by an officer of the Commissioner authorised by him for that purpose and stating—

(a) that the instrument was made by the Commissioner,

(b) that the copy is a true copy of the instrument, and

(c) that on a specified date the instrument was made available to the public in accordance with this paragraph, is evidence (or in Scotland sufficient evidence) of the facts stated in the certificate.

(7) A certificate purporting to be signed as mentioned in sub-paragraph (6) is to be treated as having been properly signed unless the contrary is shown.

(8) A person who wishes in any legal proceedings to rely on an instrument containing the Commissioner's rules may require him to endorse a copy of the instrument with a certificate of the kind mentioned in sub-paragraph (6).

Code of Standards

3.—(1) The Commissioner must prepare and issue a code setting standards of conduct which those to whom the code applies are expected to meet.

(2) The code is to be known as the Code of Standards but is referred to in this Schedule as 'the Code'.

(3) The Code is to apply to any person providing immigration advice or immigration services other than—

(a) a person who is authorised by a designated professional body to practise as a member of the profession whose members are regulated by that body;

[(aa) a person who is authorised by a designated qualifying regulator to provide immigration advice or immigration services;]

[(b) a person who is acting on behalf of a person who is within paragraph (a), [or (aa)]];

(4) It is the duty of any person to whom the Code applies to comply with its provisions in providing immigration advice or immigration services.

(5) If the Commissioner alters the Code, he must re-issue it.

(6) Before issuing the Code or altering it, the Commissioner must consult—

(a) each of the designated professional bodies;

[(aa) each of the designated qualifying regulators;]

(b) ...

(c) the Lord President of the Court of Session;

(d) the Lord Chief Justice of Northern Ireland; and

(e) such other persons appearing to him to represent the views of persons engaged in the provision of immigration advice or immigration services as he considers appropriate.

(7) The Commissioner must publish the Code in such form and manner as the Secretary of State may direct.

Note: Subparagraphs (3)(aa), (6)(aa) and first words in square brackets in subparagraph (3)(b) inserted by Sch 18 Legal Services Act 2007 from 1 April 2011 (SI 2011/720). Subparagraph (3)(b) substituted by s 37 Asylum and Immigration (Treatment of Claimants) Act 2004 from 1 October 2004 (SI 2004/2523).

Extension of scope of the Code

4.—(1) The Secretary of State may by order provide for the provisions of the Code, or such provisions of the Code as may be specified by the order, to apply to—

(a) persons authorised by any designated professional body to practise as a member of the profession whose members are regulated by that body; and

[(b) persons acting on behalf of persons who are within paragraph (a)].

(2) If the Secretary of State is proposing to act under sub-paragraph (1) he must, before doing so, consult—

(a) the Commissioner;

(b) ...

(c) the [Scottish Legal Complaints Commission], if the proposed order would affect a designated professional body in Scotland;

(d) the lay observers appointed under Article 42 of the Solicitors (Northern Ireland) Order 1976, if the proposed order would affect a designated professional body in Northern Ireland.

(3) An order under sub-paragraph (1) requires the approval of—

(a) the Lord Chancellor, if it affects a designated professional body in... Northern Ireland;

(b) the Scottish Ministers, if it affects a designated professional body in Scotland.

(4) Before deciding whether or not to give his approval under sub-paragraph (3)(a), the Lord Chancellor must consult—

(a) ...

(b) the Lord Chief Justice of Northern Ireland, if it affects a designated professional body in Northern Ireland.

(5) Before deciding whether or not to give their approval under sub-paragraph (3)(b), the Scottish Ministers must consult the Lord President of the Court of Session.

Note: Subparagraph (1)(b) substituted by s 37 Asylum and Immigration (Treatment of Claimants) Act 2004 from 1 October 2004 (SI 2004/2523). Subparagraphs (2)(b), (4)(a), and words in (3)(a) omitted, words in square brackets in (2)(c) substituted by Sch 18 Legal Services Act 2007 from 1 April 2011 (SI 2011/720).

[Inspections

4A. The Commissioner may carry out inspections of the activities and businesses of registered persons.]

Note: Paragraph 4A inserted by Sch 7 Immigration Act 2014 from 28 July 2014 (SI 2014/1820).

Investigation of complaints

5.—(1) The Commissioner must establish a scheme ('the complaints scheme') for the investigation by him of relevant complaints made to him in accordance with the provisions of the scheme.

(2) Before establishing the scheme or altering it, the Commissioner must consult—

(a) each of the designated professional bodies; and

(b) such other persons appearing to him to represent the views of persons engaged in the provision of immigration advice or immigration services as he considers appropriate.

(3) A complaint is a relevant complaint if it relates to—

[(za) the competence or fitness to provide immigration advice or immigration services of a person who, at the time to which the complaint relates, was a registered person,]

(a) the competence or fitness of [any other person] to provide immigration advice or immigration services,

[(aa) the competence or fitness of a person who, at the time to which the complaint relates, was acting on behalf of a registered person,]

(b) the competence or fitness of [any other person] [acting on behalf of] a person providing immigration advice or immigration services,

(c) an alleged breach of the Code,

(d) an alleged breach of one or more of the Commissioner's rules by [a person who, at the time to which the complaint relates, was a registered person or a person acting on behalf of a registered person], or

[(e) an alleged breach of a rule of a relevant regulatory body]

[butnot if the complaint is excluded by sub-paragraph (3A).]

[(3A) A complaint is excluded if—

(a) it relates to a person who is excluded from the application of subsection (1) of section 84 by subsection (6) of that section, or

(b) it relates to a person within section 84(2)(ba).]

(4) The Commissioner may, on his own initiative, investigate any matter which he would have power to investigate on a complaint made under the complaints scheme.

(5) In investigating any such matter on his own initiative, the Commissioner must proceed as if his investigation were being conducted in response to a complaint made under the scheme.

Note: Subparagraphs (3)(za), (3)(aa) inserted, words in first square brackets in (3)(b) and square brackets in (3)(a) and (3)(d) substituted by Sch 7 Immigration Act 2014 from 17 November 2014 (SI 2014/2771). Words in second square brackets in subparagraph (3)(b) and subparagraph (3)(e) substituted by s 37 Asylum and Immigration (Treatment of Claimants) Act 2004 from 1 October 2004 (SI 2004/2523). Other words in square brackets in subparagraph (3) and (3A) inserted by Sch 18 Legal Services Act 2007 from 1 April 2011 (SI 2011/720).

6.—(1) The complaints scheme must provide for a person who is the subject of an investigation under the scheme to be given a reasonable opportunity to make representations to the Commissioner.

(2) Any person who is the subject of an investigation under the scheme must—

(a) take such steps as are reasonably required to assist the Commissioner in his investigation; and

(b) comply with any reasonable requirement imposed on him by the Commissioner.

(3) If a person fails to comply with sub-paragraph (2)(a) or with a requirement imposed under sub-paragraph (2)(b) the Commissioner may—

(a) in the ease of a registered person, cancel his registration;

(b) ... or

[(c) in any other case, refer the matter to any relevant regulatory body.]

Note: Subparagraph (3)(c) substituted by s 37 Asylum and Immigration (Treatment of Claimants) Act 2004 from 1 October 2004 (SI 2004/2523). Subparagraph (3)(b) omitted by Sch 7 Immigration Act 2014 from 17 November 2014 (SI 2014/2771).

7. …

Note: Paragraph 7 and heading omitted by Sch 7 Immigration Act 2014 from 17 November 2014 (SI 2014/2771).

Determination of complaints

8.—(1) On determining a complaint under the complaints scheme, the Commissioner must give his decision in a written statement.

(2) The statement must include the Commissioner's reasons for his decision.

(3) A copy of the statement must be given by the Commissioner to—

(a) the person who made the complaint; and

(b) the person who is the subject of the complaint.

9.—(1) On determining a complaint under the complaints scheme, the Commissioner may—

[(a) if the person to whom the complaint relates was at the time to which the complaint relates—

(i) a registered person, or

(ii) a person acting on behalf of a registered person, record the complaint and the decision on it to be considered in connection with the next relevant application;]

(b) …

[(c) refer the complaint and his decision on it to a relevant regulatory body;]

(d) …

(e) lay before the [First-tier Tribunal] a disciplinary charge against a relevant person.

[(1A) In sub-paragraph (1)(a) 'relevant application' means—

(a) if the registered person referred to in that sub-paragraph is still registered, an application by that person for continued registration, and

(b) otherwise, an application by that person for registration.]

[(1B) Sub-paragraph (1)(a) is subject to paragraph 4A(e) of Schedule 6 (duty of Commissioner to cancel registration of a person who is no longer competent or is otherwise unfit).]

(2) Sub-paragraph (3) applies if—

(a) the [First-tier Tribunal] is considering a disciplinary charge against a relevant person; and

(b) the Commissioner asks it to exercise its powers under that subparagraph.

(3) The [First-tier Tribunal] may give directions (which are to have effect while it is dealing with the charge)—

[(a) imposing restrictions on the provision of immigration advice or immigration services by the relevant person or by a person acting on his behalf or under his supervision;

(b) prohibiting the provision of immigration advice or immigration services by the relevant person or a person acting on his behalf or under his supervision.]

[(4) 'Relevant person' means—

(a) a person who, at the time to which the charge relates, was providing immigration advice or immigration services and was—

(i) a registered person, or

(ii) a person acting on behalf of a registered person;

[(b) a person providing immigration advice or immigration services who is—
(i) a person to who section 84(4)(d) applies, or
(ii) a person employed by, or working under the supervision of, such a person.]

Note: Words in first and second square brackets substituted by s 37 Asylum and Immigration (Treatment of Claimants) Act 2004 from 1 October 2004 (SI 2004/2523). Other words in square brackets substituted from 6 April 2010 (SI 2010/22). Subparagraphs (1)(a) and (4) substituted, (1)(b) and (1)(d) omitted and (1A) and (1B) inserted by Sch 7 Immigration Act 2014 from 17 November 2014 (SI 2014/2771).

Complaints referred to designated professional bodies

10.—(1) This paragraph applies if the Commissioner refers a complaint to a designated professional body under paragraph 9(1)(c).

(2) The Commissioner may give directions setting a timetable to be followed by the designated professional body—

(a) in considering the complaint; and

(b) if appropriate, in taking disciplinary proceedings in connection with the complaint.

(3) In making his annual report to the Secretary of State under paragraph 21, the Commissioner must take into account any failure of a designated professional body to comply (whether wholly or in part) with directions given to it under this paragraph.

(4) Sub-paragraph (5) applies if the Commissioner or the Secretary of State considers that a designated professional body has persistently failed to comply with directions given to it under this paragraph.

(5) The Commissioner must take the failure into account in determining whether to make a report under section 86(9)(b) and the Secretary of State must take it into account in determining whether to make an order under section 86(2).

[Power of entry and inspection

10A.—(1) On an application made by the Commissioner a justice of the peace (or in Scotland, the sheriff) may issue a warrant authorising the Commissioner to enter premises.

(2) A justice of the peace or sheriff may issue a warrant in respect of premises if satisfied that there are reasonable grounds for believing that—

(a) the premises are being used, or have been used, in connection with the provision of immigration advice or immigration services by a registered person,

(b) entry to the premises is reasonably required for the exercise of any of the Commissioner's functions, and

(c) entry to the premises may be prevented or delayed unless a warrant is produced.

(3) The Commissioner may enter premises by virtue of this paragraph only at a reasonable hour.

(4) Where the Commissioner enters premises by virtue of this paragraph the Commissioner may—

(a) take onto the premises any equipment that appears to the Commissioner to be necessary;

(b) require any person on the premises to produce any relevant document and, if the document is produced, to provide any explanation of it;

(c) require any person on the premises to state, to the best of the person's knowledge and belief, where any relevant document is to be found;

(d) take copies of, or extracts from, any relevant document on the premises which is produced;

(e) require any relevant information which is held in a computer and is accessible from the premises to be produced in a form—

(i) in which it can be taken away; and

(ii) in which it is visible and legible.

(5) For the purposes of sub-paragraph (4), a document or information is 'relevant' if the document or information relates to any matter connected with the provision of immigration advice or immigration services.

(6) The powers conferred on the Commissioner by sub-paragraphs (1) to (5) may also be exercised by—

(a) a member of the Commissioner's staff authorised by the Commissioner in writing, and

(b) if the Commissioner so determines, a person appointed by the Commissioner to make a report on the provision of immigration advice or immigration services from the premises in question.

(7) If a registered person fails without reasonable excuse to allow access under this paragraph to any premises under the person's occupation or control, the Commissioner may cancel the person's registration.

(8) The Commissioner may also cancel the registration of a registered person who—

(a) without reasonable excuse fails to comply with a requirement imposed under sub-paragraph (4);

(b) intentionally delays or obstructs any person exercising functions under this paragraph; or

(c) fails to take reasonable steps to prevent an employee of the registered person from obstructing any person exercising such functions.

(9) In this paragraph 'premises' includes premises used wholly or partly as a dwelling.]

Note: Paragraph 10A inserted by Sch 7 Immigration Act 2014 from 17 November 2014 (SI 2014/2771).

Part II

Commissioner's Status, Remuneration and Staff etc.

...

Schedule 6

Section 85(3)

Registration

Applications for registration

1.—(1) An application for registration under section 84(2)(a)... must—

(a) be made to the Commissioner in such form and manner, and

(b) be accompanied by such information and supporting evidence, as the Commissioner may from time to time determine.

(2) When considering an application for registration, the Commissioner may require the applicant to provide him with such further information or supporting evidence as the Commissioner may reasonably require.

Registration

2.—(1) If the Commissioner considers that an applicant for registration is competent and otherwise fit to provide immigration advice and immigration services, he must register the applicant.

(2) Registration may be made so as to have effect—

(a) only in relation to a specified field of advice or services;

(b) only in relation to the provision of advice or services to a specified category of person;

(c) only in relation to the provision of advice or services to a member of a specified category of person; or

(d) only in specified circumstances.

Review of qualifications

3.—(1) At such intervals as the Commissioner may determine, each registered person must submit an application for his registration to be continued.

(2) Different intervals may be fixed by the Commissioner in relation to different registered persons or descriptions of registered person.

(3) An application for continued registration must—

(a) be made to the Commissioner in such form and manner, and

(b) be accompanied by such information and supporting evidence, as the Commissioner may from time to time determine.

(4) When considering an application for continued registration, the Commissioner may require the applicant to provide him with such further information or supporting evidence as the Commissioner may reasonably require.

(5) . . .

(6) [Unless the Commissioner is required by paragraph 4A to cancel the applicant's registration], the Commissioner must continue the applicant's registration but may, in doing so, vary the registration—

(a) so as to make it have limited effect in any of the ways mentioned in paragraph 2(2); or

(b) so as to make it have full effect.

(7) If a registered person fails, without reasonable excuse—

(a) to make an application for continued registration as required by subparagraph (1). . . or

(b) to provide further information or evidence under sub-paragraph (4), the Commissioner may cancel the person's registration as from such date as he may determine.

Note: Amended by Sch 7 Immigration Act 2014 from 17 November 2014 (SI 2014/2771).

[Variation of registration

3A. The Commissioner may vary a person's registration—

(a) so as to make it have limited effect in any of the ways mentioned in paragraph 2(2); or

(b) so as to make it have full effect.]

Disqualification of certain persons

4. A person convicted of an offence under section 25 or 26(1)(d) or (g) of the 1971 Act is disqualified for registration under paragraph 2 or for continued registration under paragraph 3.

[**4A.** The Commissioner must cancel a person's registration if—

(a) the person asks for it to be cancelled;

(b) the person dies (in a case where the person is an individual) or is dissolved or wound up (in any other case);

(c) the person is convicted of an offence under section 25 or 26(1)(d) or (g) of the 1971 Act;

(d) under section 89(2A)(b) the First-tier Tribunal directs the Commissioner to cancel the person's registration; or

(e) the Commissioner considers that the person is no longer competent or is otherwise unfit to provide immigration advice or immigration services.]

Note: Paragraph 4A inserted by Sch 7 Immigration Act 2014 from 17 October 2014 (SI 2014/2771).

[Suspension of registration

[**4B.**—(1) The First-tier Tribunal may, on an application made to it by the Commissioner, suspend a person's registration if the person is for the time being charged with—

(a) an offence involving dishonesty or deception;

(b) an indictable offence; or

(c) an offence under section 25 or 26(1)(d) or (g) of the 1971 Act.

(2) The suspension of the person's registration ceases to have effect if one of these occurs—

(a) the person is acquitted of the offence;

(b) the charge is withdrawn;

(c) proceedings in respect of the charge are discontinued;

(d) an order is made for the charge to lie on the file, or in relation to Scotland, the diet is deserted *pro loco et tempore*.

(3) If the person is convicted of an offence under section 25 or 26(1)(d) or (g) of the 1971 Act, the suspension of the person's registration continues to have effect until the Commissioner cancels the person's registration (as required by paragraph 4A(c)).

(4) If the person is convicted of any other offence within sub-paragraph (1)—

(a) the Commissioner must as soon as reasonably practicable consider whether the person is no longer competent or is otherwise unfit to provide immigration advice or immigration services (so that the person's registration must be cancelled under paragraph 4A(e));

(b) the suspension of the person's registration continues to have effect until the Commissioner either cancels the person's registration, or decides that the person is competent and otherwise fit to provide immigration advice and immigration services.

(5) A person whose registration is suspended is not to be treated as a registered person for the purposes of section 84 (but is to be treated as a registered person for the purposes of the other provisions of this Part).

(6) Where a person's registration is suspended the Commissioner must as soon as reasonably practicable record the suspension in the register.

(7) Where a suspension ceases to have effect (and the person's registration is not cancelled) the Commissioner must as soon as reasonably practicable remove the record of the suspension from the register.]

Note: Paragraph 4B inserted by Sch 7 Immigration Act 2014 from 17 November 2014 (SI 2014/2771).

Fees

5.—(1) The Secretary of State may by order

[a] specify fees for the registration or continued registration of persons on the register.

[(b) make provision for, and in connection with, requiring or authorising the Commissioner to waive all or part of the specified fee in particular cases.]

(2) No application under paragraph 1 or 3 is to be entertained by the Commissioner unless it is accompanied by the specified fee [(but this is subject to any waiver in accordance with provision under sub-paragraph (1)(b))].

Note: Amended by Sch 7 Immigration Act 2014 from 17 November 2014 (SI 2014/2771).

Open registers

6.—(1) The register must be made available for inspection by members of the public in a legible form at reasonable hours.

(2) A copy of the register or of any entry in the register must be provided—

(a) on payment of a reasonable fee;

(b) in written or electronic form; and

(c) in a legible form.

(3) Sub-paragraphs (1) and (2) also apply to—

(a) ...

(b) the record kept by the Commissioner of the persons against whom there is in force a direction given by the [First-tier Tribunal] under section 89(8).

Note: Words omitted from subparagraph (1), by s 37 Asylum and Immigration (Treatment of Claimants) Act 2004 from 1 October 2004 (SI 2004/2523). Words in second square brackets in subparagraph (3)(7) substituted by s 37 Asylum and Immigration (Treatment of Claimants) Act 2004 from 1 October 2004 (SI 2004/2523). Paragraph 3A inserted by Nationality, Immigration and Asylum Act 2002, s 140 from 8 January 2003 (SI 2003/1). Other words in square brackets substituted from 6 April 2010 (SI 2010/22). Subparagraph (3)(a) omitted by Sch 7 Immigration Act 2014 from 17 November 2014 (SI 2014/2771).

SCHEDULE 7 — Section 87(5)

…

Note: Revoked from 6 April 2010 (SI 2010/22).

SCHEDULE 8 — Section 95(12)

PROVISION OF SUPPORT: REGULATIONS

SCHEDULE 9 — Section 95(13)

ASYLUM SUPPORT: INTERIM PROVISIONS

…

SCHEDULE 10 — Section 102(3)

ASYLUM SUPPORT ADJUDICATORS

…

Note: Revoked from 3 November 2008 (SI 2008/2833).

SCHEDULE 11 — Section 154(7)

DETAINEE CUSTODY OFFICERS

…

SCHEDULE 12 — Section 155(2)

DISCIPLINE ETC. AT [REMOVAL CENTRES]

…

SCHEDULE 13 — Section 156(5)

ESCORT ARRANGEMENTS

…

SCHEDULE 14 — Section 169(1)

CONSEQUENTIAL AMENDMENTS

…

SCHEDULE 15 Section 169(2)

TRANSITIONAL PROVISIONS AND SAVINGS

Leave to enter or remain

1.—(1) An order made under section 3A of the 1971 Act may make provision with respect to leave given before the commencement of section 1.

(2) An order made under section 3B of the 1971 Act may make provision with respect to leave given before the commencement of section 2.

Section 2 of the Asylum and Immigration Act 1996

2.—(1) This paragraph applies in relation to any time before the commencement of the repeal by this Act of section 2 of the Asylum and Immigration Act 1996.

(2) That section has effect, and is to be deemed always to have had effect, as if the reference to section 6 of the Asylum and Immigration Appeals Act 1993 were a reference to section 15, and any certificate issued under that section is to be read accordingly.

Adjudicators and the Tribunal

3. …

References to justices' chief executive

4. …

Duties under National Assistance Act 1948

5. …

Duties under Health Services and Public Health Act 1968

6. …

Duties under Social Work (Scotland) Act 1968

7. …

Duties under Health and Personal Social Services (Northern Ireland) Order 1972

8. …

Duties under National Health Service Act 1977

9. …

Duties under Mental Health (Scotland) Act 1984

10. ...

Appeals relating to deportation orders

11. Section 15 of the 1971 Act, section 5 of the Immigration Act 1988 and the Immigration (Restricted Right of Appeal against Deportation) (Exemption) Order 1993 are to continue to have effect in relation to any person on whom the Secretary of State has, before the commencement of the repeal of those sections, served a notice of his decision to make a deportation order.

12.—(1) Sub-paragraph (2) applies if, on the coming into force of section 10, sections 15 of the 1971 Act and 5 of the Immigration Act 1988 have been repealed by this Act.

(2) Those sections are to continue to have effect in relation to any person—

(a) who applied during the regularisation period fixed by section 9, in accordance with the regulations made under that section, for leave to remain in the United Kingdom, and

(b) on whom the Secretary of State has since served a notice of his decision to make a deportation order.

Assistance under Part VII of the Housing Act 1996

13. ...

Provision of support

14. ...

SCHEDULE 16 **Section 169(3)**

REPEALS

...

British Overseas Territories Act 2002
(2002, c. 8)

An Act to make provision about the name 'British overseas territories' and British citizen ship so far as relating to the British overseas territories. [26 February 2002]

Change of names

1. British overseas territories

(1) As the territories mentioned in Schedule 6 to the British Nationality Act 1981 (c. 61) are now known as 'British overseas territories'—

(a) ...
(b) ...
(c) ...

(2) In any other enactment passed or made before the commencement of this section (including an enactment comprised in subordinate legislation), any reference to a dependent territory within the meaning of the British Nationality Act 1981 shall be read as a reference to a British overseas territory.

(3) ...

Note: Subsection (1)(a)–(c) amends British Nationality Act 1981, subsection (3) amends Sch 1 Interpretation Act 1978. Commenced 26 February 2002.

2. British overseas territories citizenship

(1) Pursuant to section 1, British Dependent Territories citizenship is renamed 'British overseas territories citizenship'; and a person having that citizenship is a 'British overseas territories citizen'.

(2) ...

(3) In any other enactment passed or made before the commencement of this section (including an enactment comprised in subordinate legislation), any reference to British Dependent Territories citizenship, or a British Dependent Territories citizen, shall be read as a reference to British overseas territories citizenship, or a British overseas territories citizen.

Note: Subsection (2) amends British Nationality Act 1981. Commenced 26 February 2002.

British citizenship

3. Conferral on British overseas territories citizens

(1) Any person who, immediately before the commencement of this section, is a British overseas territories citizen shall, on the commencement of this section, become a British citizen.

(2) Subsection (1) does not apply to a person who is a British overseas territories citizen by virtue only of a connection with the Sovereign Base Areas of Akrotiri and Dhekelia.

(3) A person who is a British citizen by virtue of this section is a British citizen by descent for the purposes of the British Nationality Act 1981 if, and only if—

(a) he was a British overseas territories citizen by descent immediately before the commencement of this section, and

(b) if at that time he was a British citizen as well as a British overseas territories citizen, he was a British citizen by descent.

Note: Commenced 21 May 2002 (SI 2002/1252).

4. Acquisition by British overseas territories citizens by registration

...

Note: Amends British Nationality Act 1981, s 4.

5. Acquisition by reference to the British overseas territories

Schedule 1 (which makes provision about the acquisition of British citizenship by reference to the British overseas territories) has effect.

Note: Commenced 21 May 2002 (SI 2002/1252).

Supplementary

6. The Ilois: citizenship

(1) A person shall become a British citizen on the commencement of this section if—

(a) he was born on or after 26 April 1969 and before 1 January 1983,

(b) he was born to a woman who at the time was a citizen of the United Kingdom and Colonies by virtue of her birth in the British Indian Ocean Territory, and

(c) immediately before the commencement of this section he was neither a British citizen nor a British overseas territories citizen.

(2) A person who is a British citizen by virtue of subsection (1) is a British citizen by descent for the purposes of the British Nationality Act 1981 (c. 61).

(3) A person shall become a British overseas territories citizen on the commencement of this section if—

(a) subsection (1)(a) and (b) apply in relation to him, and

(b) immediately before the commencement of this section he was not a British overseas territories citizen.

(4) A person who is a British overseas territories citizen by virtue of subsection (3) is such a citizen by descent for the purposes of the British Nationality Act 1981.

Note: Commenced 21 May 2002 (SI 2002/1252).

7. Repeals

The enactments mentioned in Schedule 2 (which include some which are spent or effectively superseded) are repealed to the extent specified there.

Note: Commenced 26 February 2002, save in relation to the British Nationality (Falkland Islands) Act 1983, where commencement was 21 May 2002 (SI 2002/1252).

8. Short title, commencement and extent

(1) This Act may be cited as the British Overseas Territories Act 2002.

(2) The following provisions of this Act are to come into force on such day as the Secretary of State may by order made by statutory instrument appoint—

(a) sections 3 to 5 and Schedule 1,

(b) section 6, and

(c) section 7 and Schedule 2, so far as relating to the British Nationality (Falkland Islands) Act 1983 (c. 6).

(3) An order under subsection (2) may—

(a) appoint different days for different purposes, and

(b) include such transitional provision as the Secretary of State considers expedient.

(4) This Act extends to—

(a) the United Kingdom,

(b) the Channel Islands and the Isle of Man, and

(c) the British overseas territories.

Schedules

Schedule 1

British Citizenship and The British Overseas Territories

Birth or adoption

1. …

Descent

2. …

Registration of minors

3. …

Commonwealth citizens

4. …

Interpretation

5. …

6. …

Note: Amends British Nationality Act 1981, ss 1, 2, 3, 37(1)(a), 50 and 51(3)(a) from 21 May 2002 (SI 2002/1252).

SCHEDULE 2
REPEALS

…

Note: Commencement 26 February 2002.

Nationality, Immigration and Asylum Act 2002

(2002, c. 41)

Arrangement of Sections

Part I. Nationality

Part II. Accommodation Centres

Establishment

Use of centres

Operation of centres

General

PART III. OTHER SUPPORT AND ASSISTANCE

PART IV. DETENTION AND REMOVAL

Detention

Temporary release

Removal

PART INADMISSIBLE ASYLUM CLAIMS

PART V. APPEALS IN RESPECT OF PROTECTION AND HUMAN RIGHTS CLAIMS

Appeal t1o Tribunal

Exceptions and limitations

Appeal from adjudicator

Procedure

General

PART VA. ARTICLE 8 OF THE ECHR; PUBLIC INTEREST CONSIDERATIONS

Country information

142. . . .

PART VII. OFFENCES

Substance

143. . . .
144. . . .
145. Traffic in prostitution
146. Section 145: supplementary
147. . . .
148. . . .
149. . . .
150. . . .
151. . . .

Procedure

152.–156. . . .

PART VIII. GENERAL

157. Consequential and incidental provision
158. Interpretation: 'the Immigration Acts'
159. Applied provision
160. Money
161. Repeals
162. Commencement
163. Extent
164. Short title

SCHEDULES

Schedule 1— Citizenship Ceremony, Oath and Pledge
Schedule 2— Nationality: Repeal of Spent Provisions
Schedule 3— Withholding and Withdrawal of Support
Schedule 4— The Asylum and Immigration Tribunal
Schedule 5— . . .
Schedule 6— Immigration and Asylum Appeals: Transitional Provision
Schedule 7— . . .
Schedule 8— . . .
Schedule 9— . . .

An Act to make provision about nationality, immigration and asylum; to create offences in connection with international traffic in prostitution; to make provision about international projects connected with migration; and for connected purposes. [7 November 2002]

Part I
Nationality

1. Naturalisation: knowledge of language and society

. . .

Note: Amends British Nationality Act 1981, s 41 and Sch 1.

2. Naturalisation: spouse of citizen

. . .

Note: Amends Sch 1 British Nationality Act 1981.

3. Citizenship ceremony, oath and pledge

Schedule 1 (which makes provision about citizenship ceremonies, oaths and pledges) shall have effect.

Note: Commencement 1 January 2004 (SI 2003/3516).

4. Deprivation of citizenship

(1) . . .

Note: Amends British Nationality Act 1981, s 40.

(2) . . .

Note: Amends Special Immigration Appeals Commission Act 1997, s 2.

(3) . . .

Note: Amends Special Immigration Appeals Commission Act 1997, s 5.

(4) In exercising a power under section 40 of the British Nationality Act 1981 after the commencement of subsection (1) above the Secretary of State may have regard to anything which—

(a) occurred before commencement, and

(b) he could have relied on (whether on its own or with other matters) in making an order under section 40 before commencement.

Note: Commencement from 1 April 2003 (SI 2003/754).

5. Resumption of citizenship

. . .

Note: Amends British Nationality Act 1981, ss 10, 22.

6. Nationality decision: discrimination

. . .

Note: Amends Race Relations Act 1976, ss 19 and 71. Subsections (1)–(4) omitted from 4 April 2011 (SI 2011/1060).

7. Nationality decision: reasons and review

(1) . . .

Note: Amends British Nationality Act 1981, s 44.

(2) . . .

Note: Amends British Nationality (Hong Kong) Act 1990, s 1.

8. Citizenship: registration

. . .

Note: Amends paragraph 3, Sch 2 British Nationality Act 1981.

9. Legitimacy of child

(1) . . .

Note: Amends British Nationality Act 1981, s 50(9).

(2) . . .

Note: Amends British Nationality Act 1981, s 3(6).

(3) . . .

Note: Amends British Nationality Act 1981, s 17(6).

(4) . . .

Note: Amends British Nationality Act 1981, s 47.

(5) . . .

Note: Amends paragraphs 1, 2, Sch 2 British Nationality Act 1981.

10. Right of abode: certificate of entitlement

(1) The Secretary of State may by regulations make provision for the issue to a person of a certificate that he has the right of abode in the United Kingdom.

(2) The regulations may, in particular—

(a) specify to whom an application must be made;

(b) specify the place (which may be outside the United Kingdom) to which an application must be sent;

(c) provide that an application must be [accompanied by specified information;]

(d) provide that an application must be accompanied by specified documents;

(e) . . .

(f) specify the consequences of failure to comply with a requirement under any of paragraphs [(a) to (d)] above;

(g) provide for a certificate to cease to have effect after a period of time specified in or determined in accordance with the regulations;

(h) make provision about the revocation of a certificate.

(3) The regulations may—

(a) make provision which applies generally or only in specified cases or circumstances;

(b) make different provision for different purposes;

(c) include consequential, incidental or transitional provision.

(4) The regulations—

(a) must be made by statutory instrument, and

(b) shall be subject to annulment in pursuance of a resolution of either House of Parliament.

(5) . . .

(6) Regulations under this section may, in particular, include provision saving, with or without modification, the effect of a certificate which—

(a) is issued before the regulations come into force, and

(b) is a certificate of entitlement for the purposes of sections 3(9) and 33(1) of the Immigration Act 1971 as those sections have effect before the commencement of subsection (5) above.

Note: Subsection (5) amends Immigration Act 1971, ss 3, 33. Subsections (1)–(4) and (6) commenced on 7 November 2002, s 162. Subsection (2)(e) deleted by Immigration, Asylum and Nationality Act 2006, s 52 and Sch 2 from 2 April 2007 (SI 2007/182). Words in square brackets in subsection (2) substituted by Immigration, Asylum and Nationality Act 2006, s 50 from 5 November 2007 (SI 2007/3138).

11. Unlawful presence in United Kingdom

. . .

Note: Commenced 7 November 2002, s 162. Revoked by s 48 Borders, Citizenship and Immigration Act 2009 from 13 January 2010 (SI 2009/2731), with transitional provisions.

12. British citizenship: registration of certain persons without other citizenship

Note: Amends British Nationality Act 1981, ss 4, 14.

13. British citizenship: registration of certain persons born between 1961 and 1983

Note: Amends British Nationality Act 1981, ss 4, 14.

14. Hong Kong

A person may not be registered as a British overseas territories citizen under a provision of the British Nationality Act 1981 (c. 61) by virtue of a connection with Hong Kong.

Note: Commencement from 1 January 2004 (SI 2003/3156).

15. Repeal of spent provisions

Schedule 2 (which repeals spent provisions) shall have effect.

Note: Commencement 7 November 2002, s 162.

PART II

ACCOMMODATION CENTRES

Establishment

16. Establishment of centres

(1) The Secretary of State may arrange for the provision of premises for the accommodation of persons in accordance with this Part.

(2) A set of premises provided under this section is referred to in this Act as an 'accommodation centre'.

(3) The Secretary of State may arrange for—

(a) the provision of facilities at or near an accommodation centre for sittings of adjudicators appointed for the purpose of Part 5 in accordance with a determination . . . under paragraph 2 of Schedule 4;

(b) the provision of facilities at an accommodation centre for the taking of steps in connection with the determination of [protection claims] (within the meaning of section 18(3)).

Note: Commencement 7 November 2002, s 162. Words deleted by Sch 18 Constitutional Reform Act 2005 from 3 April 2006 (SI 2006/1014). Words substituted in subsection (3)(b) by Schedule 11 to the Immigration Act 2016 from a date to be appointed.

Use of centres

17. Support for destitute asylum-seeker

(1) The Secretary of State may arrange for the provision of accommodation for a person in an accommodation centre if—

(a) the person is an asylum-seeker or the dependant of an asylum-seeker, and

(b) the Secretary of State thinks that the person is destitute or is likely to become destitute within a prescribed period.

[See also section 97(3A) of the Immigration and Asylum Act 1999 (decision on type of accommodation for asylum-seekers etc).

(2) The Secretary of State may make regulations about procedure to be followed in respect of the provision of accommodation under this section.

(3) The regulations may, in particular, make provision—

(a) specifying procedure to be followed in applying for accommodation in an accommodation centre;

(b) providing for an application to be combined with an application under or in respect of another enactment;

(c) requiring an applicant to provide information;

(d) specifying circumstances in which an application may not be considered (which provision may, in particular, provide for an application not to be considered where the Secretary of State is not satisfied that the information provided is complete or accurate or that the applicant is co-operating with enquiries under paragraph (e));

(e) about the making of enquiries by the Secretary of State;

(f) requiring a person to notify the Secretary of State of a change in circumstances.

(4) Sections 18 to 20 define the following expressions for the purpose of this Part—

(a) asylum-seeker,

(b) dependant, and

(c) destitute.

Note: Commencement from a date to be appointed. Words inserted in square brackets in subsection (1) by Nationality and Borders Act 2022 c.36 Pt 2 s.13(5) (date to be appointed).

18. Asylum-seeker: definition

[(1) For the purposes of this Part a person is an 'asylum-seeker' if—

(a) he n is at least 18 years old,

(b) he is in the United Kingdom, the person has made a protection claim, and

(c) a claim for asylum has been made by him[[..]]

(d) the Secretary of State has recorded the claim; and

(e) the claim has not been determined.

[(1ZA) For the purposes of subsection (1), the circumstances in which a claim is determined include where the claim is declared inadmissible under section 80A or 80B.

(1ZB) But if a claim is—

(a) declared inadmissible under section 80B, and

(b) nevertheless considered by the Secretary of State in accordance subsection (7) of that section, the claim ceases to be treated as determined from the time of the decision to consider the claim.]

(2) A person shall continue to be treated as an asylum seeker despite subsection (1)(e) while—

(a) his household includes a dependent child who is under 18, and

(b) he does not have leave to enter or remain in the United Kingdom.

(3) A claim for asylum is a claim by a person that to remove him from or require him to leave the United Kingdom would be contrary to the United Kingdom's obligations under—

(a) the Convention relating to the Status of Refugees done at Geneva on 28th July 1951 and its Protocol, or

(b) Article 3 of the Convention for the Protection of Human Rights and Fundamental Freedoms agreed by the Council of Europe at Rome on 4th November 1950.

. . .

(3) [Protection claim' has the meaning given by section 82(2).]

Note: Commenced for the purposes of ss 55(9), 70(3) and paragraph 17(1)(b) of Sch 3 on 8 January 2003 (SI 2003/1). For the purposes of Immigration Act 1971, s 26A(2) and this Act, s 71(5), 10 February 2003 (SI 2003/01). Subsection (1) and (3) substituted, and subsection (2) omitted by Schedule 11 to the Immigration Act 2016 from a date to be appointed. Subsection (1ZA & 1ZB) inserted by Nationality and Borders Act 2022 c.36 Pt 2s.17(5) (June 28, 2022). Words in double square brackets at s.1(c) by Nationality and Borders Act 2022 c.36 Pt2 s.14(4) (date to be appointed: 2002 c14(5) came into force on April 28, 2022 for the limited purpose of making (and, where required, consulting on); not yet in force, otherwise)

19. Destitution: definition

(1) Where a person has dependants, he and his dependants are destitute for the purpose of this Part if they do not have and cannot obtain both—

(a) adequate accommodation, and

(b) food and other essential items.

(2) Where a person does not have dependants, he is destitute for the purpose of this Part if he does not have and cannot obtain both—

(a) adequate accommodation, and

(b) food and other essential items.

(3) In determining whether accommodation is adequate for the purposes of subsection (1) or (2) the Secretary of State must have regard to any matter prescribed for the purposes of this subsection.

(4) In determining whether accommodation is adequate for the purposes of subsection (1) or (2) the Secretary of State may not have regard to—

(a) whether a person has an enforceable right to occupy accommodation,

(b) whether a person shares all or part of accommodation,

(c) whether accommodation is temporary or permanent,

(d) the location of accommodation, or

(e) any other matter prescribed for the purposes of this subsection.

(5) The Secretary of State may by regulations specify items which are or are not to be treated as essential items for the purposes of subsections (1) and (2).

(6) The Secretary of State may by regulations—

(a) provide that a person is not to be treated as destitute for the purposes of this Part in specified circumstances;

(b) enable or require the Secretary of State in deciding whether a person is destitute to have regard to income which he or a dependant of his might reasonably be expected to have;

(c) enable or require the Secretary of State in deciding whether a person is destitute to have regard to support which is or might reasonably be expected to be available to the person or a dependant of his;

(d) enable or require the Secretary of State in deciding whether a person is destitute to have regard to assets of a prescribed kind which he or a dependant of his has or might reasonably be expected to have;

(e) make provision as to the valuation of assets.

Note: Commencement at a date to be appointed.

20. Dependant: definition

For the purposes of this Part a person is a 'dependant' of an asylum-seeker if (and only if) that person—

(a) is in the United Kingdom, and

(b) is within a prescribed class.

Note: Commencement at a date to be appointed.

21. Sections 17 to 20: supplementary

(1) This section applies for the purposes of sections 17 to 20.

(2) The Secretary of State may inquire into and decide a person's age.

(3) A [protection claim] shall be treated as determined at the end of such period as may be prescribed beginning with—

(a) the date on which the Secretary of State notifies the claimant of his decision on the claim, or [[9as the case may be) of the declaration of the inadmissibility under section 80A or 80B]], or

(b) if the claimant appeals against the Secretary of State's decision, the date on which the appeal is disposed of.

(4) A notice under subsection (3)(a)—

(a) must be in writing, and

(b) if sent by first class post to the claimant's last known address or to the claimant's representative, shall be treated as being received by the claimant on the second day after the day of posting.

(5) An appeal is disposed of when it is no longer pending for the purpose of—

(a) Part 5 of this Act, or

(b) the Special Immigration Appeals Commission Act 1997 (c. 68).

Note: Commencement at a date to be appointed. Words substituted at subsection (3) by Schedule 11 to the Immigration Act 2016 from a date to be appointed. Words in double square brackets at subsection (3)(a) by Nationality and Borders Act 2022 c.36 Pt2 s.17(6) (date to be appointed): substitution came into force on June 28, 2022 but cannot take effect until the commencement of 2002 c.41 s21(3)(a)

22. Immigration and Asylum Act 1999, s 95 [&98]

The Secretary of State may provide support under section 95 [or 98] of the Immigration and Asylum Act 1999 (c. 33) [(support and temporary support for asylum-seekers)] by arranging for the provision of accommodation in an accommodation centre.

Note: Commencement at a date to be appointed. Words substituted in square brackets by Nationality and Borders Act 2022, c.36 Pt 2 s.13(6) (date to be appointed)

[22A Immigration and Asylum Act 1999, sections 95A and 98A

The Secretary of State may provide support under section 95A or 98A of the Immigration and Asylum Act 1999 (support and temporary support for failed asylum-seekers) by arranging for the provision of accommodation in an accommodation centre.]

Note: inserted by Nationality and Borders Act 2022 c.36 Pt 2 s.13(7) (date to be appointed)

23. Person subject to United Kingdom entrance control

(1) A residence [condition] may include a requirement to reside at an accommodation centre.

(2) [In subsection (1) 'residence condition' means a condition imposed under Schedule 10 to the Immigration Act 2016]—

(a) paragraph 21 of Schedule 2 to the Immigration Act 1971 (c. 77) (temporary admission or release from detention), or

(b) paragraph 2(5) of Schedule 3 to that Act (control pending deportation).

(3) Where a person is required to reside in an accommodation centre by virtue of subsection (1) the Secretary of State must arrange for the provision of accommodation for the person in an accommodation centre.

(4) But if the person is required to leave an accommodation centre by virtue of section 26 or 30 he shall be treated as having broken the residence [condition] referred to in subsection (1).

(5) . . .

Note: Commencement at a date to be appointed. Words in square brackets substituted by Schedule 10 to the Immigration Act 2016 from 15 January 2018 (SI 2017/1241). Subsection (5) omitted by Schedule 11 to the Immigration Act 2016 from a date to be appointed: repeal has effect subject to savings and transitional provisions specified in Immigration Act 2016, Sch 11, para 46.

24. Provisional assistance

(1) If the Secretary of State thinks that a person may be eligible for the provision of accommodation in an accommodation centre under section 17, he may arrange for the provision for the person, pending a decision about eligibility, of—

(a) accommodation in an accommodation centre, or

(b) other support or assistance (of any kind).

(2) Section 99 of the Immigration and Asylum Act 1999 (c. 33) (provision of support by local authority) shall have effect in relation to the provision of support for persons under subsection (1) above as it has effect in relation to the provision of support for asylum-seekers under sections 95 and 98 of that Act.

[See also section 98(4) of the Immigration and Asylum Act 1999 (decision on type of accommodation for asylum-seekers etc)]

Note: Commencement at a date to be appointed. Words in square brackets inserted by Nationality and Borders Act 2022 c.36 Pt2 s.13(8) (date to be appointed)

25. Length of stay

(1) The Secretary of State may not arrange for the provision of accommodation for a person in an accommodation centre if he has been a resident of an accommodation centre for a continuous period of six months.

(2) But—

(a) subsection (1) may be disapplied in respect of a person, generally or to a specified extent, by agreement between the Secretary of State and the person, and

(b) if the Secretary of State thinks it appropriate in relation to a person because of the circumstances of his case, the Secretary of State may direct that subsection (1) shall have effect in relation to the person as if the period specified in that subsection were the period of nine months.

(3) Section 51 is subject to this section.

(4) The Secretary of State may by order amend subsection (1) or (2)(b) so as to substitute a [different] period for a period specified.

Note: Commencement at a date to be appointed. Word in square bracket at subsection (4) substituted by Nationality and Borders Act 2022 Pt2 s.13(9) (date to be appointed)

26. Withdrawal of support

(1) The Secretary of State may stop providing support for a person under section 17 or 24 if—

(a) the Secretary of State suspects that the person or a dependant of his has committed an offence by virtue of section 35, or

(b) the person or a dependant of his has failed to comply with directions of the Secretary of State as to the time or manner of travel to accommodation provided under section 17 or 24.

(2) The Secretary of State may by regulations specify other circumstances in which he may stop providing support for a person under section 17 or 24.

(3) In determining whether or not to provide a person with support or assistance under section 17 or 24 of this Act or section[] [, 95, 95A, 98 or 98A] of the Immigration and Asylum Act 1999 [] the Secretary of State may take into account the fact that—

(a) he has withdrawn support from the person by virtue of this section or section 30(4) or (5), or

(b) circumstances exist which would have enabled the Secretary of State to withdraw support from the person by virtue of this section had he been receiving support.

(4) This section is without prejudice to section 103 of the Immigration and Asylum Act 1999 (c. 33) (appeal against refusal to support).

Note: Commencement at a date to be appointed. Words in square brackets omitted or substituted by Schedule 11 to the Immigration Act 2016 from a date to be appointed. Word repealed in s 26(3) has effect subject to savings and transitional provisions specified in Immigration Act 2016, Sch 11, para 46.

Operation of centres

27. Resident of centre

A reference in this Part to a resident of an accommodation centre is a reference to a person for whom accommodation in the centre is provided—

(a) under section 17,

(b) by virtue of section 22,

[(ba) by virtue of section 22A],

(c) by virtue of section 23, or

(d) under section 24.

Note: Commencement at a date to be appointed. Subsection (ba) inserted by Nationality and Borders Act 2022, c.36 Pt2 s.13(10) (date to be appointed)

28. Manager of centre

A reference in this Part to the manager of an accommodation centre is a reference to a person who agrees with the Secretary of State to be wholly or partly responsible for the management of the centre.

Note: Commencement at a date to be appointed.

29. Facilities

(1) The Secretary of State may arrange for the following to be provided to a resident of an accommodation centre—

(a) food and other essential items;

(b) money;

(c) assistance with transport for the purpose of proceedings under the Immigration Acts or in connection with a [protection claim];

(d) transport to and from the centre;

(e) assistance with expenses incurred in connection with carrying out voluntary work or other activities;

(f) education and training;

(g) facilities relating to health;

(h) facilities for religious observance;

(i) anything which the Secretary of State thinks ought to be provided for the purpose of providing a resident with proper occupation and for the purpose of maintaining good order;

(j) anything which the Secretary of State thinks ought to be provided for a person because of his exceptional circumstances.

(2) The Secretary of State may make regulations specifying the amount or maximum amount of money to be provided under subsection (1)(b).

(3) The Secretary of State may arrange for the provision of facilities in an accommodation centre for the use of a person in providing legal advice to a resident of the centre.

(4) The Secretary of State shall take reasonable steps to ensure that a resident of an accommodation centre has an opportunity to obtain legal advice before any appointment made by an immigration officer or an official of the Secretary of State for the purpose of obtaining information from the resident to be used in determining his claim for asylum.

(5) The Secretary of State may by order amend subsection (1) so as to add a reference to facilities which may be provided.

Note: Commencement at a date to be appointed. Words substituted at subsection (1)(c) by Schedule 11 to the Immigration Act 2016 from a date to be appointed.

30. Conditions of residence

(1) The Secretary of State may make regulations about conditions to be observed by residents of an accommodation centre.

(2) Regulations under subsection (1) may, in particular, enable a condition to be imposed in accordance with the regulations by—

(a) the Secretary of State, or

(b) the manager of an accommodation centre.

(3) A condition imposed by virtue of this section may, in particular—

(a) require a person not to be absent from the centre during specified hours without the permission of the Secretary of State or the manager;

(b) require a person to report to an immigration officer or the Secretary of State.

(4) If a resident of an accommodation centre breaches a condition imposed by virtue of this section, the Secretary of State may—

(a) require the resident and any dependant of his to leave the centre;

(b) authorise the manager of the centre to require the resident and any dependant of his to leave the centre.

(5) If a dependant of a resident of an accommodation centre breaches a condition imposed by virtue of this section, the Secretary of State may—

(a) require the resident and any dependant of his to leave the centre;

(b) authorise the manager of the centre to require the resident and any dependant of his to leave the centre.

(6) Regulations under this section must include provision for ensuring that a person subject to a condition is notified of the condition in writing.

(7) A condition imposed by virtue of this section is in addition to any [condition imposed under Schedule 10 to the Immigration Act 2016].

(8) A reference in this Part to a condition of residence is a reference to a condition imposed by virtue of this section.

Note: Commencement at a date to be appointed. Words in square brackets are substituted by Schedule 10 to the Immigration Act 2016 from 15 January 2018 (SI 2017/1241).

31. Financial contribution by resident

(1) A condition of residence may, in particular, require a resident of an accommodation centre to make payments to—

(a) the Secretary of State, or

(b) the manager of the centre.

(2) The Secretary of State may make regulations enabling him to recover sums representing the whole or part of the value of accommodation and other facilities provided to a resident of an accommodation centre if—

(a) accommodation is provided for the resident in response to an application by him for support,

(b) when the application was made the applicant had assets which were not capable of being realised, and

(c) the assets have become realisable.

(3) In subsection (2) 'assets' includes assets outside the United Kingdom.

(4) An amount recoverable by virtue of regulations made under subsection (2) may be recovered—

(a) as a debt due to the Secretary of State;

(b) by another prescribed method (which may include the imposition or variation of a residence condition).

Note: Commencement at a date to be appointed.

32. Tenure

(1) A resident of an accommodation centre shall not be treated as acquiring a tenancy of or other interest in any part of the centre (whether by virtue of an agreement between the resident and another person or otherwise).

(2) Subsection (3) applies where—

(a) the Secretary of State decides to stop arranging for the provision of accommodation in an accommodation centre for a resident of the centre, or

(b) a resident of an accommodation centre is required to leave the centre in accordance with section 30.

(3) Where this subsection applies—

(a) the Secretary of State or the manager of the centre may recover possession of the premises occupied by the resident, and

(b) the right under paragraph (a) shall be enforceable in accordance with procedure prescribed by regulations made by the Secretary of State.

(4) Any licence which a resident of an accommodation centre has to occupy premises in the centre shall be an excluded licence for the purposes of the Protection from Eviction Act 1977 (c. 43).

(5) . . .

(6) . . .

(7) In this section a reference to an accommodation centre includes a reference to premises in which accommodation is provided under section 24(1)(b).

Note: Subsection (5) amends Protection from Eviction Act 1977, s 3A(7A), subsection (6) amends Rent (Scotland) Act 1984, s 23A(5A). Commencement at a date to be appointed.

33. Advisory Groups

(1) The Secretary of State shall appoint a group (to be known as an Accommodation Centre Advisory Group) for each accommodation centre.

(2) The Secretary of State may by regulations—

(a) confer functions on Advisory Groups;

(b) make provision about the constitution and proceedings of Advisory Groups.

(3) Regulations under subsection (2)(a) must, in particular, provide for members of an accommodation centre's Advisory Group—

(a) to visit the centre;

(b) to hear complaints made by residents of the centre;

(c) to report to the Secretary of State.

(4) The manager of an accommodation centre must permit a member of the centre's Advisory Group on request—

(a) to visit the centre at any time;

(b) to visit any resident of the centre at any time, provided that the resident consents.

(5) A member of an Advisory Group shall hold and vacate office in accordance with the terms of his appointment (which may include provision about retirement, resignation or dismissal).

(6) The Secretary of State may—

(a) defray expenses of members of an Advisory Group;
(b) make facilities available to members of an Advisory Group.

Note: Commencement at a date to be appointed.

General

34. . . .

Note: Section 34 deleted by UK Borders Act 2007 s 54 from 1 April 2008 (SI 2008/309).

35. Ancillary provisions

(1) The following provisions of the Immigration and Asylum Act 1999 (c. 33) shall apply for the purposes of this Part as they apply for the purposes of Part VI of that Act (support for asylum-seeker)—
(a) section 105 (false representation),
(b) section 106 (dishonest representation),
(c) section 107 (delay or obstruction),
(d) section 108 (failure of sponsor to maintain),
(e) section 109 (offence committed by body),
(f) section 112 (recovery of expenditure),
(g) section 113 (recovery of expenditure from sponsor),
(h) section 124 (corporation sole), and
(i) section 127 (redirection of post).

(2) In the application of section 112 a reference to something done under [section 95, 95A, 98 or 98A] of that Act shall be treated as a reference to something done under section 17 or 24 of this Act.

(3) In the application of section 113 a reference to section 95 [or 95A] of that Act shall be treated as a reference to section 17 of this Act.

Note: Subsection (1)(h) commenced on 7 November 2002, s 162. Remainder to commence on a date to be appointed. Words substituted in subsection (2) and inserted in subsection (3) by Schedule 11 of the Immigration Act 2016 from a date to be appointed.

36. Education: general

(1) For the purposes of section 13 of the Education Act 1996 (c. 56) (general responsibility of [local authority]) a resident of an accommodation centre shall not be treated as part of the population of a [local authority's] area.

(2) A child who is a resident of an accommodation centre may not be admitted to a maintained school or a maintained nursery (subject to section 37).

(3) But subsection (2) does not prevent a child's admission to a school which is—
(a) a community special school or a foundation special school, and
(b) named in [an EHC plan maintained for the child under section 37 of the Children and Families Act 2014 or] a statement in respect of the child under section 324 of the Education Act 1996 (c. 56) (special educational needs).

(4) In subsections (2) and (3)—

(a) 'maintained school' means a maintained school within the meaning of section 20(7) of the School Standards and Framework Act 1998 (c. 31) (definition), and

(b) 'maintained nursery' means a facility for nursery education, within the meaning of section 117 of that Act, provided by a [local authority].

(5) The following shall not apply in relation to a child who is a resident of an accommodation centre (subject to section 37)—

(a) section 86(1) and (2) of the School Standards and Framework Act 1998 (parental preference),

(b) section 94 of that Act (appeal),

(c) section 19 of the Education Act 1996 (education out of school),

(d) section 316(2) and (3) of that Act (child with special educational needs to be educated in mainstream school),

(e) paragraphs 3 and 8 of Schedule 27 to that Act (special education needs: making of statement: parental preference).

[(f) sections 33 and 34 of the Children and Families Act 2014 (mainstream education for children with special educational needs), and

(g) sections 38 and 39 of that Act (EHC plan: request of parent for named school etc)].

[(5A) The powers of the First-tier Tribunal on determining an appeal under section 51(2)(c) of the Children and Families Act 2014 (appeals against certain aspects of content of EHC plan) are subject to subsection (2) above.]

(6) The power of [the Special Educational Needs Tribunal for Wales] under section 326(3) of the Education Act 1996 (appeal against content of statement) is subject to subsection (2) above.

(7) A person exercising a function under this Act [, Part 3 of the Children and Families Act 2014] or the Education Act 1996 shall (subject to section 37) secure that a child who is a resident of an accommodation centre and who has special educational needs shall be educated by way of facilities provided under section 29(1)(f) of this Act unless that is incompatible with—

(a) his receiving the special educational provision [called for by his special educational needs or] which his learning difficulty calls for,

(b) the provision of efficient education for other children who are residents of the centre, or

(c) the efficient use of resources.

(8) A person may rely on subsection (7)(b) only where there is no action—

(a) which could reasonably be taken by that person or by another person who exercises functions, or could exercise functions, in respect of the accommodation centre concerned, and

(b) as a result of which subsection (7)(b) would not apply.

(9) An accommodation centre is not a school within the meaning of section 4 of the Education Act 1996 (definition); but—

(a) [Part 1 of the Education Act 2005 (school inspections)] shall apply to educational facilities provided at an accommodation centre as if the centre were a school (for which purpose a reference to the appropriate authority shall be taken as a reference to the person (or persons) responsible for the provision of education at the accommodation centre), [(aa) section 36 of the Children and Families Act 2014 (assessment of education, health and care needs: England) shall have effect as if an accommodation centre were a school,]

(b) section 329A of the Education Act 1996 (review or assessment of educational needs at request of responsible body) shall have effect as if—

(i) an accommodation centre were a relevant school for the purposes of that section,

(ii) a child for whom education is provided at an accommodation centre under section 29(1)(f) were a registered pupil at the centre, and

(iii) a reference in section 329A to the responsible body in relation to an accommodation centre were a reference to any person providing education at the centre under section 29(1)(f), and

(c) section 140 of the Learning and Skills Act 2000 (c. 21) (learning difficulties: assessment of post-16 needs) shall have effect as if an accommodation centre were a school.

(10) Subsections (1), (2) and (5) shall not apply in relation to an accommodation centre if education is not provided for children who are residents of the centre under section 29(1)(f).

(11) An expression used in this section and in the Education Act 1996 (c. 56) shall have the same meaning in this section as in that Act.

Note: Commencement at a date to be appointed. Words in square brackets in subsection (9) substituted by Education Act 2005, s 61 and Sch 9 from 1 September 2005 (SI 2005/2034) and from 1 September 2006 (W) (SI 2006/1338). Words in square brackets in subsection (6) substituted from 3 November 2008 (SI 2008/2833). Term 'local authority' substituted from 5 April 2010 (SI 2010/1158). Other amendments made by Schedule 3 Children and Families Act 2014 from 1 September 2014 (SI 2014/899).

37. Education: special cases

(1) This section applies to a child if a person who provides education to residents of an accommodation centre recommends in writing to the [local authority] for the area in which the centre is that this section should apply to the child on the grounds that his special circumstances call for provision that can only or best be arranged by the authority.

(2) A [local authority] may—

(a) arrange for the provision of education for a child to whom this section applies;

(b) disapply a provision of section 36 in respect of a child to whom this section applies.

(3) In determining whether to exercise a power under subsection (2) in respect of a child a [local authority] shall have regard to any relevant guidance issued by the Secretary of State.

(4) The governing body of a maintained school shall comply with a requirement of the [local authority] to admit to the school a child to whom this section applies.

(5) Subsection (4) shall not apply where compliance with a requirement would prejudice measures taken for the purpose of complying with a duty arising under section 1(6) of the School Standards and Framework Act 1998 (c. 31) (limit on infant class size).

(6) A [local authority] may not impose a requirement under subsection (4) in respect of a school unless the authority has consulted the school in accordance with regulations made by the Secretary of State.

(7) In the case of a maintained school for which the [local authority] are the admission authority, the authority may not arrange for the admission of a child to whom this section applies unless the authority has notified the school in accordance with regulations made by the Secretary of State.

(8) In this section—

(a) 'maintained school' means a maintained school within the meaning of section 20(7) of the School Standards and Framework Act 1998 (definition), and

(b) an expression which is also used in the Education Act 1996 (c. 56) shall have the same meaning as it has in that Act.

Note: Commencement at a date to be appointed. Term 'local authority' substituted from 5 April 2010 (SI 2010/1158).

38. Local authority

(1) A local authority may in accordance with arrangements made by the Secretary of State—

(a) assist in arranging for the provision of an accommodation centre;

(b) make premises available for an accommodation centre;

(c) provide services in connection with an accommodation centre.

(2) In particular, a local authority may—

(a) incur reasonable expenditure;

(b) provide services outside its area;

(c) provide services jointly with another body;

(d) form a company;

(e) tender for or enter into a contract;

(f) do anything (including anything listed in paragraphs (a) to (e)) for a preparatory purpose.

(3) In this section 'local authority' means—

(a) a local authority within the meaning of section 94 of the Immigration and Asylum Act 1999 (c. 33), and

(b) a Northern Ireland authority within the meaning of section 110 of that Act and an Education and Library Board established under Article 3 of the Education and Libraries (Northern Ireland) Order 1986 (SI 1986/594 (N.I. 3)).

Note: Commenced 7 November 2002, s 162.

39. 'Prescribed': orders and regulations

(1) In this Part 'prescribed' means prescribed by the Secretary of State by order or regulations.

(2) An order or regulations under this Part may—

(a) make provision which applies generally or only in specified cases or circumstances (which may be determined wholly or partly by reference to location);

(b) make different provision for different cases or circumstances;
(c) include consequential, transitional or incidental provision.

(3) An order or regulations under this Part must be made by statutory instrument.

(4) An order or regulations under any of the following provisions of this Part shall be subject to annulment in pursuance of a resolution of either House of Parliament—

(a) section 17,
(b) section 19,
(c) section 20,
(d) section 21,
(e) section 26,
(f) section 29,
(g) section 31,
(h) section 32,
(i) section 33,
(j) section 37,
(k) section 40, and
(l) section 41.

(5) An order under section 25 or regulations under section 30 may not be made unless a draft has been laid before and approved by resolution of each House of Parliament.

Note: Commencement at a date to be appointed.

40. Scotland

(1) The Secretary of State may not make arrangements under section 16 for the provision of premises in Scotland unless he has consulted the Scottish Ministers.

(2) The Secretary of State may by order make provision in relation to the education of residents of accommodation centres in Scotland.

(3) An order under subsection (2) may, in particular—

(a) apply, disapply or modify the effect of an enactment (which may include a provision made by or under an Act of the Scottish Parliament);

(b) make provision having an effect similar to the effect of a provision of section 36 or 37.

Note: Subsection (1) commenced on 7 November 2002, s 162. Remainder at a date to be appointed.

41. Northern Ireland

(1) The Secretary of State may not make arrangements under section 16 for the provision of premises in Northern Ireland unless he has consulted the First Minister and the deputy First Minister.

(2) The Secretary of State may by order make provision in relation to the education of residents of accommodation centres in Northern Ireland.

(3) An order under subsection (2) may, in particular—

(a) apply, disapply or modify the effect of an enactment (which may include a provision made by or under Northern Ireland legislation);

(b) make provision having an effect similar to the effect of a provision of section 36 or 37.

Note: Subsection (1) commenced on 7 November 2002, s 162. Remainder at a date to be appointed.

42. Wales

The Secretary of State may not make arrangements under section 16 for the provision of premises in Wales unless he has consulted the National Assembly for Wales.

Note: Commenced 7 November 2002, s 162.

Part III

Other Support and Assistance

43. Form of support under Part 6 of the Immigration and Asylum Act 1999

(1) The Secretary of State may make an order restricting the application of section 96(1)(b) of the Immigration and Asylum Act 1999 (c. 33) (support for [asylum seekers and failed asylum seekers, etc] essential living needs)—

(a) in all circumstances, to cases in which support is being provided under section 96(1)(a) (accommodation), or

(b) in specified circumstances only, to cases in which support is being provided under section 96(1)(a).

(2) An order under subsection (1)(b) may, in particular, make provision by reference to—

(a) location;

(b) the date of an application.

(3) An order under subsection (1) may include transitional provision.

(4) An order under subsection (1)—

(a) must be made by statutory instrument, and

(b) may not be made unless a draft has been laid before and approved by resolution of each House of Parliament.

Note: Commenced 7 November 2002, s 162. Title amended and words in square brackets substituted by Schedule 11 to the Immigration Act 2016 from a date to be appointed.

44. Destitute asylum-seeker

Note: Amends Immigration and Asylum Act 1999, ss 94, 95 (c. 33). Repealed by Schedule 11 to the Immigration Act 2016, having not being brought into force, from a date to be appointed.

45. Section 44: supplemental

(1) . . .

Note: Amends Immigration and Asylum Act 1999, s 96.

(2) . . .

Note: Amends Immigration and Asylum Act 1999, s 97.

(3) . . .

Note: Amends Immigration and Asylum Act 1999, Sch 8, paragraphs 2, 6.

(4) . . .

Note: Amends paragraph 3, Sch 9 Immigration and Asylum Act 1999.

(5) . . .

Note: Amends National Assistance Act 1948, s 21(1B) (c. 29).

(6) . . .

Note: Amends Health Services and Public Health Act 1968, s 45(4B).

(7) . . .

Note: Amends paragraph 2(2B), Sch 8 National Health Service Act 1977.

Note: Repealed by Schedule 11 to the Immigration Act 2016, having not been brought into force, from a date to be appointed.

46. Section 44: supplemental: Scotland and Northern Ireland

(1–3). . .

Note: Amends the Social Work (Scotland) Act 1968.

(4–5). . .

Note: Amends the Mental Health (Scotland) Act 1984.

(6–7). . .

Note: Amends the Health and Personal Social Services (Northern Ireland) Order 1972 (SI 1972/1265 (NI 14)).

Note: Repealed by Schedule 11 to the Immigration Act 2016, having not being brought into force, from a date to be appointed.

47. Asylum-seeker: family with children

Note: Amends Immigration and Asylum Act 1999, s 122. Repealed by Schedule 11 to the Immigration Act 2016, having not been brought into force, from a date to be appointed.

48. Young asylum-seeker

The following provisions of the Immigration and Asylum Act 1999 (c. 33) shall have effect as if the definition of asylum-seeker in section 94(1) of that Act did not exclude persons who are under 18—

(a) section 110 (local authority expenditure on asylum-seekers), and

(b) section 111 (grants to voluntary organisations).

Note: Commenced on 7 November 2002, s 162.

49. Failed asylum seeker

Note: Omitted by Schedule 11 of the Immigration Act 2016, having not been brought into force, from a date to be appointed: repeal has effect subject to savings and transitional provisions specified in Immigration Act 2016, Sch 11, para 46.

50. Conditions of support

Note: Amends Immigration and Asylum Act 1999, s 95 and Sch 9.

51. Choice of form of support

(1) The Secretary of State may refuse to provide support for a person under a provision specified in subsection (2) on the grounds that an offer has been made to the person of support under another provision specified in that subsection.

(2) The provisions are—

(a) sections 17 and 24 of this Act,

(b) . . .

(c) sections 95 and 98 of that Act (support for destitute asylum-seeker)[and

(d) a claim for support under section 95A of the Immigration and Asylum Act 1999 (whether or not made by that person)].

(3) In deciding under which of the provisions listed in subsection (2) to offer support to a person the Secretary of State may—

(a) have regard to administrative or other matters which do not concern the person's personal circumstances;

(b) regard one of those matters as conclusive;

(c) apply different criteria to different persons for administrative reasons (which may include the importance of testing the operation of a particular provision).

Note: Commencement at a date to be appointed. Subsection (2)(b) omitted by Schedule 11 to the Immigration Act 2016: repeal to have effect subject to savings and transitional provisions specified in Immigration Act 2016, Sch 11, para 46. Subsection (2)(d) inserted by Schedule 11 to the Immigration Act 2016 from a date to be appointed.

52. Back-dating of benefit for refugee

Note: Amends Immigration and Asylum Act 1999, s 123.

53. Asylum-seeker: appeal against refusal to support

Note: Amends Immigration and Asylum Act 1999, s 103. Repealed by Schedule 11 to the Immigration Act 2016 from a date to be appointed.

54. Withholding and withdrawal of support

Schedule 3 (which makes provision for support to be withheld or withdrawn in certain circumstances) shall have effect.

Note: Commenced for the purpose of making subordinate legislation 8 December 2002. Remainder commenced 8 January 2003 (SI 2002/2811).

55. Late protection claim: refusal of support

(1) The Secretary of State may not provide or arrange for the provision of support to a person under a provision mentioned in subsection (2) if—

(a) the person makes a [protection claim] which is recorded by the Secretary of State, and

(b) the Secretary of State is not satisfied that the claim was made as soon as reasonably practicable after the person's arrival in the United Kingdom.

(2) The provisions are—

(a) sections []95 and 98 of the Immigration and Asylum Act 1999 (c. 33) (support for asylum-seeker, &c.), and

[(aa) sections 95A and 98A of that Act (support for failed asylum- seeker, &c)],

(b) sections 17 and 24 of this Act (accommodation centre).

(3) An authority may not provide or arrange for the provision of support to a person under a provision mentioned in subsection (4) if—

(a) the person has made a [protection claim], and

(b) the Secretary of State is not satisfied that the claim was made as soon as reasonably practicable after the person's arrival in the United Kingdom.

(4) The provisions are—

(a) section 29(1)(b) of the Housing (Scotland) Act 1987 (c. 26) (accommodation pending review),

(b) section 188(3) or 204(4) of the Housing Act 1996 (c. 52) (accommodation pending review or appeal), and

(c) section 2 of the Local Government Act 2000 (c. 22) (promotion of well-being) [and.

[(d) section 1 of the Localism Act 2011 (local authority's general power of competence)].

(5) This section shall not prevent—

(a) the exercise of a power by the Secretary of State to the extent necessary for the purpose of avoiding a breach of a person's Convention rights (within the meaning of the Human Rights Act 1998 (c. 42)),

(b) the provision of support under section 95 of the Immigration and Asylum Act 1999 (c. 33) or section 17 of this Act in accordance with section 122 of that Act (children), or

(c) the provision of support under section 98 of the Immigration and Asylum Act 1999 or section 24 of this Act (provisional support) to a person under the age of 18 and the household of which he forms part.

(6) An authority which proposes to provide or arrange for the provision of support to a person under a provision mentioned in subsection (4)—

(a) must inform the Secretary of State if the authority believes that the person has made a [protection claim],

(b) must act in accordance with any guidance issued by the Secretary of State to determine whether subsection (3) applies, and

(c) shall not be prohibited from providing or arranging for the provision of support if the authority has complied with paragraph (a) and (b) and concluded that subsection (3) does not apply.

(7) The Secretary of State may by order—

(a) add, remove or amend an entry in the list in subsection (4);

(b) provide for subsection (3) not to have effect in specified cases or circumstances.

(8) An order under subsection (7)—

(a) may include transitional, consequential or incidental provision,

(b) must be made by statutory instrument, and

(c) may not be made unless a draft has been laid before and approved by resolution of each House of Parliament.

(9) For the purposes of this section ['protection claim'] has the same meaning as in section 18.

(10) A decision of the Secretary of State that this section prevents him from providing or arranging for the provision of support to a person is not a decision that the person does not qualify for support for the purpose of section 103 of the Immigration and Asylum Act 1999 (appeals).

(11) This section does not prevent a person's compliance with a residence restriction imposed in reliance on section 70 (induction).

Note: Commenced 8 January 2003 (SI 2002/2811). Subsection (4)(d) inserted from 28 March 2012 (SI 2012/961). Words omitted in subsection (2)(a) by Schedule 11 to Immigration Act 2016: repeal has effect subject to savings and transitional provisions specified in Immigration Act 2016, Sch 11, para 46. Words inserted in subsection (2)(aa), and substituted in subsections (1)(a), (3)(a), (6)(a) and (9) by Schedule 11 to the Immigration Act 2016 from a date to be appointed.

56. Provision of support by local authority

...

Note: Amends Immigration and Asylum Act 1999, s 99.

57. Application for support: false or incomplete information

...

Note: Amends paragraph 12, Sch 8 Immigration and Asylum Act 1999.

58. Voluntary departure from United Kingdom

(1) A person is a 'voluntary leaver' for the purposes of this section if—

(a) he is not a British citizen[],

(b) he leaves the United Kingdom for a place where he hopes to take up permanent residence (his 'new place of residence'), and

(c) the Secretary of State thinks that it is in the person's interest to leave the United Kingdom and that the person wishes to leave.

(2) The Secretary of State may make arrangements to—

(a) assist voluntary leavers;

(b) assist individuals to decide whether to become voluntary leavers.

(3) The Secretary of State may, in particular, make payments (whether to voluntary leavers or to organisations providing services for them) which relate to—

(a) travelling and other expenses incurred by or on behalf of a voluntary leaver, or a member of his family or household, in leaving the United Kingdom;

(b) expenses incurred by or on behalf of a voluntary leaver, or a member of his family or household, on or shortly after arrival in his new place of residence;

(c) the provision of services designed to assist a voluntary leaver, or a member of his family or household, to settle in his new place of residence;

(d) expenses in connection with a journey undertaken by a person (with or without his family or household) to prepare for, or to assess the possibility of, his becoming a voluntary leaver.

(4) [].

(5) . . .

Note: Subsection (5) repeals Immigration Act 1971, ss 29 and 31(d). Commenced 7 November 2002, s 162. Words in square brackets omitted at subsection (1)(a) and (4) by Immigration and Social Security Co-ordination (EU Withdrawal) Act 2020 (Consequential, Saving, Transitional and Transitory Provisions) (EU Exit) Regulations 2020/1309, reg13(1)(a) & (b).

59. International projects

(1) The Secretary of State may participate in a project which is designed to—

(a) reduce migration,

(b) assist or ensure the return of migrants,

(c) facilitate co-operation between States in matters relating to migration,

(d) conduct or consider research about migration, or

(e) arrange or assist the settlement of migrants (whether in the United Kingdom or elsewhere).

(2) In particular, the Secretary of State may—

(a) provide financial support to an international organisation which arranges or participates in a project of a kind described in subsection (1);

(b) provide financial support to an organisation in the United Kingdom or another country which arranges or participates in a project of that kind;

(c) provide or arrange for the provision of financial or other assistance to a migrant who participates in a project of that kind;

(d) participate in financial or other arrangements which are agreed between Her Majesty's Government and the government of one or more other countries and which are or form part of a project of that kind.

(3) In this section—

(a) 'migrant' means a person who leaves the country where he lives hoping to settle in another country (whether or not he is a refugee within the meaning of any international Convention), and

(b) 'migration' shall be construed accordingly.

(4) Subsection (1) does not—

(a) confer a power to remove a person from the United Kingdom, or

(b) affect a person's right to enter or remain in the United Kingdom.

Note: Commenced 7 November 2002, s 162.

60. Northern Ireland authorities

. . .

Note: Amends Immigration and Asylum Act 1999, ss 94 and 110.

61. Repeal of spent provisions

. . .

Note: Repeals Immigration and Asylum Act 1999, ss 96(4)–(6), 166(4)(e).

PART IV

DETENTION AND REMOVAL

Detention

62. Detention by Secretary of State

(1) A person may be detained under the authority of the Secretary of State pending—

(a) a decision by the Secretary of State whether to give directions in respect of the person under [section 10 of the Immigration and Asylum Act 1999 (removal of persons unlawfully in the United Kingdom) or] paragraph 10, 10A or 14 of Schedule 2 to the Immigration Act 1971 (c. 77) (control of entry: removal), or

(b) removal of the person from the United Kingdom in pursuance of directions given by the Secretary of State under any of those [provisions].

(2) Where the Secretary of State is empowered under section 3A of [the Immigration Act 1971] (powers of Secretary of State) to examine a person or to give or refuse a person leave to enter the United Kingdom, the person may be detained under the authority of the Secretary of State pending—

(a) the person's examination by the Secretary of State,

(b) the Secretary of State's decision to give or refuse the person leave to enter,

(c) a decision by the Secretary of State whether to give directions in respect of the person under paragraph 8 or 9 of Schedule 2 to that Act (removal), or

(d) removal of the person in pursuance of directions given by the Secretary of State under either of those paragraphs.

(3) A provision of Schedule 2 to that Act about a person who is detained or liable to detention under that Schedule shall apply to a person who is detained or liable to detention under this section: and for that purpose—

(a) a reference to paragraph 16 of that Schedule shall be taken to include a reference to this section,

[(aa) a reference in paragraph 18B of that Schedule to an immigration officer shall be read as a reference to the Secretary of State,]

(b) and

(c) a reference to detention under that Schedule or under a provision or Part of that Schedule shall be taken to include a reference to detention under this section.

(4) . . .

(5) . . .

(6) . . .

(7) A power under this section which is exercisable pending a decision of a particular kind by the Secretary of State is exercisable where the Secretary of State has reasonable grounds to suspect that he may make a decision of that kind.

[(7A) The detention under this section of a person to whom section 60 (limitation on detention of pregnant women) of the Immigration Act 2016 applies is subject to that section.]

(8–16) . . .

Note: Subsections 8–16 amend Immigration Act 1971, ss 11, 24, Mental Health Act 1983, ss 48, 53, Mental Health (Scotland) Act 1984, ss 71, 74, Mental Health (Northern Ireland) Order 1986, Arts 54, 59, Immigration and Asylum Act 1999, ss 53, 147, Anti-terrorism, Crime and Security Act 2001, ss 23, 24; with a commencement date of 10 February 2003 (SI 2003/1). Subsections (15)–(16) repealed by Prevention of Terrorism Act 2005, section 16(2) from 14 March 2005. Words in square brackets in subsection (1)(a) and subsection (3)(aa) inserted, words in square brackets in subsections (1)(b) and (2) substituted, and subsections (5) and (6) omitted by Sch 9 Immigration Act 2014 from 20 October 2014 with savings set out in SI 2014/2771 articles 9–11. Subsection (7A) inserted by Immigration Act 2016, s 60 from 12 July 2016 (SI 2016/603]. Subsections (3)(b) and (4) omitted by Schedule 10 to the Immigration Act 2016 from 15 January 2018 subject to transitional provisions specified in SI 2017/1241.

63. Control of entry to United Kingdom, &c.: use of force

. . .

Note: Amends paragraph 17(2), Sch 2 Immigration Act 1971.

64. Escorts

. . .

Note: Amends paragraph 17, Sch 2 Immigration Act 1971.

65. Detention centres: custodial functions

...

Note: Amends Immigration and Asylum Act 1999, s 154 and Sch 11.

66. Detention centres: change of name

(1) –(3) ...

(4) A reference in an enactment or instrument to a detention centre within the meaning of Part VIII of the Immigration and Asylum Act 1999 (c. 33) shall be construed as a reference to a removal centre within the meaning of that Part.

Note: Subsections (1)–(3) amend Immigration and Asylum Act 1999, ss 141, 147–53, 155, 157–9 and Schs 11–13 and Prison Act 1952, s 5A and Sch 4A Water Industry Act 1991. Commenced 10 February 2003 (SI 2003/01).

67. Construction of reference to person liable to detention

(1) This section applies to the construction of a provision which—

(a) does not confer power to detain a person, but

(b) refers (in any terms) to a person who is liable to detention under a provision of the Immigration Acts.

(2) The reference shall be taken to include a person if the only reason why he cannot not be detained under the provision is that—

(a) he cannot presently be removed from the United Kingdom, because of a legal impediment connected with the United Kingdom's obligations under an international agreement,

(b) practical difficulties are impeding or delaying the making of arrangements for his removal from the United Kingdom, or

(c) practical difficulties, or demands on administrative resources, are impeding or delaying the taking of a decision in respect of him.

(3) This section shall be treated as always having had effect.

Note: Commenced 7 November 2002, s 162.

Temporary release

68.

Note: omitted by Schedule 10 to the Immigration Act 2016 from 15 January 2018 subject to transitional provisions specified in SI 2017/1241.

69.

Note: omitted by Schedule 10 to the Immigration Act 2016 from 15 January 2018 subject to transitional provisions specified in SI 2017/1241.

70. Induction

(1) A residence [condition] may be imposed on an asylum-seeker or a dependant of an asylum-seeker without regard to his personal circumstances if—

(a) it requires him to reside at a specified location for a period not exceeding 14 days, and

(b) the person imposing the residence [condition] believes that a programme of induction will be made available to the asylum-seeker at or near the specified location.

(2) In subsection (1) 'residence [condition]' means a [condition] imposed under [Schedule 10 to the Immigration Act 2016].

(3) In this section—

'asylum-seeker' has the meaning given by section 18 of this Act but disregarding section 18(1)(a) [of this Act and section 94(2B) of the Immigration and Asylum Act 1999],

'dependant of an asylum-seeker' means a person who appears to the Secretary of State to be making a claim or application in respect of residence in the United Kingdom by virtue of being a dependant of an asylum-seeker, and

'programme of induction' means education about the nature of the asylum process.

(4) Regulations under subsection (3)—

(a) may make different provision for different circumstances,

(b) must be made by statutory instrument, and

(c) shall be subject to annulment in pursuance of a resolution of either House of Parliament.

(5) Subsection (6) applies where the Secretary of State arranges for the provision of a programme of induction (whether or not he also provides other facilities to persons attending the programme and whether or not all the persons attending the programme are subject to residence [conditions]).

(6) A local authority may arrange for or participate in the provision of the programme or other facilities.

(7) In particular, a local authority may—

(a) incur reasonable expenditure;

(b) provide services outside its area;

(c) provide services jointly with another body;

(d) form a company;

(e) tender for or enter into a contract;

(f) do anything (including anything listed in paragraphs (a) to (e)) for a preparatory purpose.

(8) In this section 'local authority' means—

(a) a local authority within the meaning of section 94 of the Immigration and Asylum Act 1999 (c. 33), and

(b) a Northern Ireland authority within the meaning of section 110 of that Act.

Note: Commenced 7 November 2002, s 162. Words in square brackets at subsection (1),(1)(b), (2) and (5) substituted by Schedule 10 to the Immigration Act 2016 from 15 January 2018 subject to transitional provisions specified in SI 2017/1241. Words in square brackets in subsection (3) inserted by Schedule 11 to the Immigration Act 2016 from a date to be appointed.

71. Asylum-seeker: residence, &c. restriction

(1) This section applies to—

(a) a person who makes a [protection claim] at a time when he has leave to enter or remain in the United Kingdom, and

(b) a dependant of a person within paragraph (a).

(2) The Secretary of State or an immigration officer may impose on a person to whom this section applies any [condition which may be imposed under Schedule 10 to the Immigration Act 2016] on a person liable to detention under paragraph 16 of [Schedule 2 to the Immigration Act 1971].

(3) Where a [condition]is imposed on a person under subsection (2)—

(a) the [condition] shall be treated for all purposes as a [condition] imposed under [Schedule 10 to the Immigration Act 2016], and

(b) if the person fails to comply with the restriction he shall be liable to detention under paragraph 16 of [Schedule 2 to the Immigration Act 1971].

(4) A [condition] imposed on a person under this section shall cease to have effect if he ceases to be an asylum-seeker or the dependant of an asylum-seeker.

(5) In this section—

'asylum-seeker' has the same meaning as in section 70,

'[protection claim]' has the same meaning as in section 18, and

'dependant' means a person who appears to the Secretary of State to be making a claim or application in respect of residence in the United Kingdom by virtue of being a dependant of another person.

(6) Regulations under subsection (5)—

(a) may make different provision for different circumstances,

(b) must be made by statutory instrument, and

(c) shall be subject to annulment in pursuance of a resolution of either House of Parliament.

Note: Commenced 10 February 2003 (SI 2003/1). Words in square brackets at subsections (2), (3) and (4) substituted by Schedule 10 to the Immigration Act 2016 from 15 January 2018 subject to transitional provisions specified in SI 2017/1241. Words in square brackets at subsection (1)(a) and (5) substituted by Schedule 11 to the Immigration Act 2016 from a date to be appointed.

Removal

72. Serious criminal

(1) This section applies for the purpose of the construction and application of Article 33(2) of the Refugee Convention (exclusion from [[prohibition of expulsion or return]]).

(2) A person[[is]] convicted by a final judgment of a particularly serious crime [[..]] if he is—

(a) convicted in the United Kingdom of an offence, and

(b) sentenced to a period of imprisonment of at least [[12 months]].

(3) A person[[is]]convicted by a final judgment of a particularly serious crime [[..]] if—

(a) he is convicted outside the United Kingdom of an offence,

(b) he is sentenced to a period of imprisonment of at least [[12 months]], and

(c) he could have been sentenced to a period of imprisonment of at least [[12 months]] had his conviction been a conviction in the United Kingdom of a similar offence.

(4) A person [[is]]convicted by a final judgment of a particularly serious crime [[..]] if—

(a) he is convicted of an offence specified by order of the Secretary of State, or

(b) he is convicted outside the United Kingdom of an offence and the Secretary of State certifies that in his opinion the offence is similar to an offence specified by order under paragraph (a).

(5) An order under subsection (4)—

(a) must be made by statutory instrument, and

(b) shall be subject to annulment in pursuance of a resolution of either House of Parliament.

[[(5A) A person convicted by a final judgment of a particularly serious crime (whether within or outside the United Kingdom) is to be presumed to constitute a danger to the community of the United Kingdom.]]

(6) A presumption under subsection [[5A]] that a person constitutes a danger to the community is rebuttable by that person.

(7) A presumption under subsection [[5A]] does not apply while an appeal against conviction or sentence—

(a) is pending, or

(b) could be brought (disregarding the possibility of appeal out of time with leave).

(8) Section 34(1) of the Anti-terrorism, Crime and Security Act 2001 (c. 24) (no need to consider gravity of fear or threat of persecution) applies for the purpose of considering whether a presumption [[under subsection (5A)]] has been rebutted as it applies for the purpose of considering whether Article 33(2) of the Refugee Convention applies.

(9) Subsection (10) applies where—

(a) a person appeals under section 82,. . . of this Act or under section 2 of the Special Immigration Appeals Commission Act 1997 (c. 68) wholly or partly on the ground [mentioned in section 84(1)(a) or (3)(a) of this Act (breach of the United Kingdom's obligations under the Refugee Convention), and]

(b) the Secretary of State issues a certificate that [[presumption under subsection (5A) applies]]to the person (subject to rebuttal).

(10) The [. . .] Tribunal or Commission hearing the appeal—

(a) must begin substantive deliberation on the appeal by considering the certificate, and

(b) if in agreement that [[presumption under subsection (5A) applies]](having given the appellant an opportunity for rebuttal) must dismiss the appeal in so far as it relies on the ground specified in subsection (9)(a).

[(10A) Subsection (10) also applies in relation to the Upper Tribunal when it acts under section 12(2)(b)(ii) of the Tribunals, Courts and Enforcement Act 2007.]

(11) For the purposes of this section—

(a) 'the Refugee Convention' means the Convention relating to the Status of Refugees done at Geneva on 28 July 1951 and its Protocol, and

(b) a reference to a person who is sentenced to a period of imprisonment of at [[12 months]]—

(i) does not include a reference to a person who receives a suspended sentence [(unless a court subsequently orders that the sentence or any part of it is to take effect)],

[(ia) does not include a reference to a person who is sentenced to a period of imprisonment of at least [[12 months]] only by virtue of being sentenced to consecutive sentences which amount in aggregate to more than [[12 months]],]

(ii) includes a reference to a person who is sentenced to detention, or ordered or directed to be detained, in an institution other than a prison (including, in particular, a hospital or an institution for young offenders), and

(iii) includes a reference to a person who is sentenced to imprisonment or detention, or ordered or directed to be detained, for an indeterminate period (provided that it may last for [[12 months]]).

Note: Subsections (1)–(8) and (11) commenced 10 February 2003 (SI 2003/1), remainder on 1 April 2003 (SI 2003/754). Word in subsection (10) omitted by Sch 2 Asylum and Immigration (Treatment of Claimants etc.) Act 2004 from 4 April 2005 (SI 2005/565). Serious offences for the purposes of subsection (4)(a) set out in SI 2004/1910. Words in square brackets in subsection (9) omitted and substituted by Sch 9 Immigration Act 2014 from 20 October 2014 with savings set out in articles 9–11 SI 2014/2771. Words in subsection (11)(b)(i) substituted and subsection (11)(b)(ia) inserted by UK Borders Act 2007, s 39 from 1 August 2008 (SI 2008/1818). Subsection (10A) inserted from 15 February 2010 (SI 2010/21). S 72 applied (with modifications) (31.1.2020) by The Immigration (Citizens Rights Appeals) (EU Exit) Regulations 2020 (SI 2020/61), reg. 1(2), Sch. 2 paras. 1–3. Words in double square brackets inserted at subsection (5A), and substituted and omitted in other sub-subsections by Nationality and Borders Act c.36 Pt 2 s38 (June 28, 2022: insertion, substitution or omission has effect only in relation to a person convicted on or after the date on which 2022 c.36 s.38 comes into force)

73. Family

. . .

Note: Amends Sch 2 Immigration Act 1971 (c. 77); Immigration and Asylum Act 1999, s 10.

74. Deception

. . .

Note: Amends Immigration and Asylum Act 1999, s 10(1).

75. Exemption from deportation

. . .

Note: Amends Immigration Act 1971, s 7; Immigration and Asylum Act 1999, s 10.

76. Revocation of leave to enter or remain

(1) The Secretary of State may revoke a person's indefinite leave to enter or remain in the United Kingdom if the person—

(a) is liable to deportation, but

(b) cannot be deported for legal reasons.

(2) The Secretary of State may revoke a person's indefinite leave to enter or remain in the United Kingdom if—

(a) the leave was obtained by deception,

(b) . . .

(c) . . .

(3) The Secretary of State may revoke a person's indefinite leave to enter or remain in the United Kingdom if the person, or someone of whom he is a dependant, ceases to be a refugee as a result of—

(a) voluntarily availing himself of the protection of his country of nationality,

(b) voluntarily re-acquiring a lost nationality,

(c) acquiring the nationality of a country other than the United Kingdom and availing himself of its protection, or

(d) voluntarily establishing himself in a country in respect of which he was a refugee.

(4) In this section—

'indefinite leave' has the meaning given by section 33(1) of the Immigration Act 1971 (c. 77) (interpretation),

'liable to deportation' has the meaning given by section 3(5) and (6) of that Act (deportation),

'refugee' has the meaning given by the Convention relating to the Status of Refugees done at Geneva on 28 July 1951 and its Protocol, and

. . .

(5) A power under subsection (1) or (2) to revoke leave may be exercised—

(a) in respect of leave granted before this section comes into force;

(b) in reliance on anything done before this section comes into force.

(6) A power under subsection (3) to revoke leave may be exercised—

(a) in respect of leave granted before this section comes into force, but

(b) only in reliance on action taken after this section comes into force.

(7) . . .

Note: Subsection (7) amends Immigration and Asylum Act 1999, s 10(1). Commencement 10 February 2003 (SI 2003/1). Subsections (2)(b)–(c) and definition of 'removed' omitted by Sch 9 Immigration Act from 20 October 2014 with savings set out in articles 9–11 SI 2014/2771.

77. No removal while claim for asylum pending

(1) While a person's claim for asylum is pending he may not be—

(a) removed from the United Kingdom in accordance with a provision of the Immigration Acts, or

(b) required to leave the United Kingdom in accordance with a provision of the Immigration Acts.

(2) In this section—

(a) 'claim for asylum' means a claim by a person that it would be contrary to the United Kingdom's obligations under the Refugee Convention to remove him from or require him to leave the United Kingdom, and

(b) a person's claim is pending until he is given notice of the Secretary of State's decision on it.

[(2A) This section does not prevent a person being removed to, or being required to leave to go to, a State falling within subsection (2B).

(2B) A State falls within this subsection if—

(a) it is a place where a person's life and liberty are not threatened by reason of the person's race, religion, nationality, membership of a particular social group or political opinion,

(b) it is a place from which a person will not be removed elsewhere other than in accordance with the Refugee Convention,

(c) it is a place—

(i) to which a person can be removed without their Convention rights under Article 3 (no torture or inhuman or degrading treatment or punishment) being contravened, and

(ii) from which a person will not be sent to another State in contravention of the person's Convention rights, and

(d) the person is not a national or citizen of the State.

(2C) For the purposes of this section—

(a) any State to which Part 2 or 3 of Schedule 3 to the Asylum and Immigration (Treatment of Claimants, etc) Act 2004 for the time being applies—

(i) is to be presumed to be a State falling within subsection (2B) (a) and (b), and

(ii) is, unless the contrary is shown by a person to be the case in their particular circumstances, to be presumed to be a State falling within subsection (2B) (c) (i) and (ii);

(b) any State to which Part 4 of that Schedule for the time being applies is to be presumed to be a State falling within subsection (2B) (a) and (b);

(c) a reference to anything being done in accordance with the Refugee Convention is a reference to the thing being done in accordance with the principles of the Convention, whether or not by a signatory to it;

(d) "State" includes any territory outside of the United Kingdom.]

(3) In [this section, "Convention Rights" means the rights identified as Convention rights by section 1 of the Human Rights Act 1998 (whether or not in relation to a State that is a party to the Convention); and]'the Refugee Convention' means the Convention relating to the Status of Refugees done at Geneva on 28 July 1951 and its Protocol.

(4) Nothing in this section shall prevent any of the following while a claim for asylum is pending—

(a) the giving of a direction for the claimant's removal from the United Kingdom,

(b) the making of a deportation order in respect of the claimant, or

(c) the taking of any other interim or preparatory action.

(5) . . .

Note: Subsection (5) repeals Immigration and Asylum Act 1999, s 15. Commencement 1 April 2003 (SI 2003/754). Has effect in relation to a claim for asylum pending on 31 March 2003 as it has effect in relation to claims pending under the 2002 Act (SI 2003/754). Subsections (2A)-(2C) inserted by Nationality and Borders Act 2022 c.36 Sch.4 para 1(June 28, 2022: insertion has effect as SI 2022/590 reg.2 and Sch.1 para.17 subject to transitional and saving provisions specified in SI 2022/590 reg.3 and Sch.2 para.4(4)). Words substituted in square brackets at subsection (3) by Nationality and Borders Act 2022 c.36 Sch.3 para 2 (June 28, 2022: substitution has effect as SI 2022/590 reg.2 and Sch.1 para.17 subject to transitional and saving provisions specified in SI 2022/590 reg.3 and Sch.2 para.4(4))

78. No removal while appeal pending

(1) While a person's appeal under section 82(1) is pending he may not be—

(a) removed from the United Kingdom in accordance with a provision of the Immigration Acts, or

(b) required to leave the United Kingdom in accordance with a provision of the Immigration Acts.

(2) In this section 'pending' has the meaning given by section 104.

(3) Nothing in this section shall prevent any of the following while an appeal is pending—

(a) the giving of a direction for the appellant's removal from the United Kingdom,

(b) the making of a deportation order in respect of the appellant (subject to section 79), or

(c) the taking of any other interim or preparatory action.

(4) This section applies only to an appeal brought while the appellant is in the United Kingdom in accordance with section 92.

Note: Commencement 1 April 2003 (SI 2003/754). Has effect in relation to appeals pending under the old appeal provisions as it has effect in relation to an appeal pending under s 82(1) of the 2002 Act. S 78 applied (with modifications) (31.1.2020) by The Immigration (Citizens Rights Appeals) (EU Exit) Regulations 2020 (SI 2020/61), reg. 1(2), Sch. 2 paras. 1–3

[78A. Restriction on removal of children and their parents etc.

(1) This section applies in a case where—

(a) a child is to be removed from or required to leave the United Kingdom, and

(b) an individual who—

(i) is a parent of the child or has care of the child, and

(ii) is living in a household in the United Kingdom with the child, is also to be removed from or required to leave the United Kingdom (a 'relevant parent or carer').

(2) During the period of 28 days beginning with the day on which the relevant appeal rights are exhausted—

(a) the child may not be removed from or required to leave the United Kingdom; and

(b) a relevant parent or carer may not be removed from or required to leave the United Kingdom if, as a result, no relevant parent or carer would remain in the United Kingdom.

(3) The relevant appeal rights are exhausted at the time when—

(a) neither the child, nor any relevant parent or carer, could bring an appeal under section 82 (ignoring any possibility of an appeal out of time with permission), and

(b) no appeal brought by the child, or by any relevant parent or carer, is pending within the meaning of section 104.

(4) Nothing in this section prevents any of the following during the period of 28 days mentioned in subsection (2)—

(a) the giving of a direction for the removal of a person from the United Kingdom,

(b) the making of a deportation order in respect of a person, or

(c) the taking of any other interim or preparatory action.

(5) In this section—

'child' means a person who is aged under 18;

references to a person being removed from or required to leave the United Kingdom are to the person being removed or required to leave in accordance with a provision of the Immigration Acts.]

Note: Section 78A inserted by s 2 Immigration Act 2014 from 28 July 2014 (SI 2014/1820). Ss 78–79 applied (with modifications) (31.1.2020) by The Immigration (Citizens Rights Appeals) (EU Exit) Regulations 2020 (SI 2020/61), reg. 1(2), Sch. 2 paras. 1–3

79. Deportation order: appeal

(1) A deportation order may not be made in respect of a person while an appeal under section 82(1) [that may be brought or continued from within the United Kingdom relating to] the decision to make the order—

(a) could be brought (ignoring any possibility of an appeal out of time with permission), or

(b) is pending.

(2) In this section 'pending' has the meaning given by section 104.

[(3) This section does not apply to a deportation order which states that it is made in accordance with section 32(5) of the UK Borders Act 2007.]

[(4) But a deportation order made in reliance on subsection (3) does not invalidate leave to enter or remain, in accordance with section 5(1) of the Immigration Act 1971, if and for so long as section 78 above applies.]

Note: Commencement 1 April 2003 (SI 2003/754). Has effect in relation to an appeal pending under the old appeals provisions as it has effect in relation to an appeal pending under s 82(1) of the 2002 Act. Subsections (3) and (4) inserted by UK Borders Act 2007, s 35 from 1 August 2008 (SI 2008/1818). Words in square brackets in subsection (1) substituted by Sch 9 Immigration Act 2014 from 28 July 2014 (SI 2014/1820). Ss 78–79 applied (with modifications) (31.1.2020) by The Immigration (Citizens Rights Appeals) (EU Exit) Regulations 2020 (SI 2020/61), reg. 1(2), Sch. 2 paras. 1–3

80. Removal of asylum-seeker to third country

. . .

Note: Amends Immigration and Asylum Act 1999, s 11.

Part 4A
Inadmissible Asylum Claims

80A Asylum claims by EU nationals

(1) The Secretary of State must declare an asylum claim made by a person who is a national of a member State inadmissible.

(2) An asylum claim declared inadmissible under subsection (1) cannot be considered under the immigration rules.

(3) A declaration under subsection (1) that an asylum claim is inadmissible is not a decision to refuse the claim and, accordingly, no right of appeal under section 82(1)(a) (appeal against refusal of protection claim) arises.

(4) Subsection (1) does not apply if there are exceptional circumstances as a result of which the Secretary of State considers that the claim ought to be considered.

(5) For the purposes of subsection (4) exceptional circumstances include where the member State of which the claimant is a national—

(a) is derogating from any of its obligations under the Human Rights Convention, in accordance with Article 15 of the Convention;

(b) is the subject of a proposal initiated in accordance with the procedure referred to in Article 7(1) of the Treaty on European Union and—

(i) the proposal has yet to be determined by the Council of the European Union or (as the case may be) the European Council,

(ii) the Council of the European Union has determined, in accordance with Article 7(1), that there is a clear risk of a serious breach by the member State of the values referred to in
Article 2 of the Treaty, or

(iii) the European Council has determined, in accordance with Article 7(2), the existence of a serious and persistent breach by the member State of the values referred to in Article 2 of the Treaty.

(6) In this section—

"asylum claim", "the Human Rights Convention" and "the Refugee Convention" have the meanings given by section 113;

"immigration rules" means rules under section 3(2) of the Immigration Act 1971;

"the Treaty on European Union" means the Treaty on European Union signed at Maastricht on 7 February 1992 as it had effect immediately before IP completion day.]

Note: inserted by Nationality and Borders Act 2022 c.36 s 15 (1) (June 28, 2022: insertion has effect as SI 2022/590 reg.2 and Sch.1 para.14 subject to transitional and saving provisions specified in 2022/590 reg.3 and Sch.2 para 4(3))

80B Asylum claims by persons with connection to safe third State

(1) The Secretary of State may declare an asylum claim made by a person (a "claimant") who has a connection to a safe third State inadmissible.

(2) Subject to subsection (7), an asylum claim declared inadmissible under subsection (1) cannot be considered under the immigration rules.

(3) A declaration under subsection (1) that an asylum claim is inadmissible is not a decision to refuse the claim and, accordingly, no right of appeal under section 82(1)(a) (appeal against refusal of protection claim) arises.

(4) For the purposes of this section, a State is a "safe third State" in relation to a claimant if—

(a) the claimant's life and liberty are not threatened in that State by reason of their race, religion, nationality, membership of a particular social group or political opinion,

(b) the State is one from which a person will not be sent to another State—

(i) otherwise than in accordance with the Refugee Convention, or

(ii) in contravention of their rights under Article 3 of the Human Rights Convention (freedom from torture or inhuman or degrading treatment), and

(c) a person may apply to be recognised as a refugee and (if so recognised) receive protection in accordance with the Refugee Convention, in that State.

(5) For the purposes of this section, a claimant has "a connection" to a safe third State if they meet any of conditions 1 to 5 set out in section 80C in relation to the State.

(6) The fact that an asylum claim has been declared inadmissible under subsection (1) by virtue of the claimant's connection to a particular safe third State does not prevent the Secretary of State from removing the claimant to any other safe third State.

(7) An asylum claim that has been declared inadmissible under subsection (1) may nevertheless be considered under the immigration rules—

(a) if the Secretary of State determines that there are exceptional circumstances in the particular case that mean the claim should be considered, or

(b) in such other cases as may be provided for in the immigration rules.

(8) In this section and section 80C—

(a) "asylum claim", "Human Rights Convention", "immigration rules" and "the Refugee Convention" have the same meanings as in section 80A;

(b) a reference to anything being done in accordance with the Refugee Convention is a reference to the thing being done in accordance with the principles of the Convention, whether or not by a signatory to it.

Note: inserted by Nationality and Border Act 2022 c.36 Pt 2 s.16 (June 28, 2022: insertion has effect as SI 2022/590 reg.2 an Sch.1 para 15 subject to transitional provisions and saving provisions specified in SI 2022/590 reg.3 and Sch.2 para 4(3))

80C Meaning of "connection" to a safe third State

(1) Condition 1 is that the claimant—

(a) has been recognised as a refugee in the safe third State, and

(b) remains able to access protection in accordance with the Refugee Convention in that State.

(2) Condition 2 is that the claimant—

(a) has otherwise been granted protection in a safe third State as a result of which the claimant would not be sent from the safe third State to another State—

(i) otherwise than in accordance with the Refugee Convention, or

(ii) in contravention of their rights under Article 3 of the Human Rights Convention, and

(b) remains able to access that protection in that State.

(3) Condition 3 is that the claimant has made a relevant claim to the safe third State and the claim—

(a) has not yet been determined, or

(b) has been refused.

(4) Condition 4 is that—

(a) the claimant was previously present in, and eligible to make a relevant claim to, the safe third State,

(b) it would have been reasonable to expect them to make such a claim, and

(c) they failed to do so.

(5) Condition 5 is that, in the claimant's particular circumstances, it would have been reasonable to expect them to have made a relevant claim to the safe third State (instead of making a claim in the United Kingdom).

(6) For the purposes of this section, a "relevant claim" to a safe third State is a claim—

(a) to be recognised as a refugee in the State for the purposes of the Refugee Convention, or

(b) for protection in the State of the kind mentioned in subsection (2)(a).

(7) For the purposes of this section "claimant" and "safe third State" have the same meanings as in section 80B; and see subsection (8) of that section.]

Note: inserted by Nationality and Border Act 2022 c.36 Pt 2 s.16 (June 28, 2022: insertion has effect as SI 2022/590 reg.2 an Sch.1 para 15 subject to transitional provisions and saving provisions specified in SI 2022/590 reg.3 and Sch.2 para 4(3))

Part V

[Appeals in respect of Protection and Human Rights Claims]

Note: Heading substituted by Sch 9 Immigration Act 2014 from 20 October 2014 SI 2014/2771, with savings set out in articles 9–11.

[Appeal to Tribunal

[Meaning of 'the Tribunal'

81.

. . .

In this Part 'the Tribunal' means the First-tier Tribunal.]

Note: Section 81 substituted from 15 February 2010 (SI 2010/21).

[82. Right of appeal to the Tribunal

(1) A person ('P') may appeal to the Tribunal where—

(a) the Secretary of State has decided to refuse a protection claim made by P,

(b) the Secretary of State has decided to refuse a human rights claim made by P, or

(c) the Secretary of State has decided to revoke P's protection status.

(2) For the purposes of this Part—

(a) a 'protection claim' is a claim made by a person ('P') that removal of P from the United Kingdom—

(i) would breach the United Kingdom's obligations under the Refugee Convention, or

(ii) would breach the United Kingdom's obligations in relation to persons eligible for a grant of humanitarian protection;

(b) P's protection claim is refused if the Secretary of State makes one or more of the following decisions—

(i) that removal of P from the United Kingdom would not breach the United Kingdom's obligations under the Refugee Convention;

(ii) that removal of P from the United Kingdom would not breach the United Kingdom's obligations in relation to persons eligible for a grant of humanitarian protection;

(c) a person has 'protection status' if the person has been granted leave to enter or remain in the United Kingdom as a refugee or as a person eligible for a grant of humanitarian protection;

(d) 'humanitarian protection' is to be construed in accordance with the immigration rules;

(e) 'refugee' has the same meaning as in the Refugee Convention.

(3) The right of appeal under subsection (1) is subject to the exceptions and limitations specified in this Part.]

Note: Section 82 substituted by s 15 Immigration Act 2014 from 20 October 2014 with savings set out in SI 2014/2771, articles 9–11.

82A Expedited appeal to Upper Tribunal in certain cases

(1) This section applies where —

(a) a person ("P") has been served with a priority removal notice,

(b) P has made a protection claim or a human rights claim on or after the PRN cut-off date but while the priority removal notice is still in force, and

(c) P has a right under section 82(1) to bring an appeal from within the United Kingdom (see section 92) in relation to the claim.

(2) The Secretary of State must certify P's right of appeal under this section, unless satisfied that there were good reasons for P making the claim on or after the PRN cut-off date (and P's right of appeal may not be certified if the Secretary of State is satisfied that there were good reasons).

(3) If certified under this section, P's right of appeal under section 82(1) is to the Upper Tribunal instead of the First-tier Tribunal (and any appeal brought pursuant to such a right is referred to in this section as an "expedited appeal").

(4) Tribunal Procedure Rules must make provision with a view to securing that expedited appeals are brought and determined more quickly than an appeal under section 82(1) would, in the normal course of events, be brought and determined by the First-tier Tribunal.

(5) Tribunal Procedure Rules must secure that the Upper Tribunal may, if it is satisfied that it is the only way to secure that justice is done in the case of a particular expedited appeal, order that the appeal is to be continued as an appeal to the First-tier Tribunal and accordingly is to be transferred to that Tribunal.

(6) In this section, "priority removal notice" and "PRN cut-off date" have the same meanings as in section 20 of the Nationality and Borders Act 2022.

Note: inserted by Nationality and Borders Act 2022 c.36 Pt2 s.23(1) (date to be appointed)

83. . . . ..

Note: Repealed by s 15 Immigration Act 2014 from 20 October 2014 with savings set out in SI 2014/2771, articles 9–11).

[83A.

Note: Repealed by s 15 Immigration Act 2014 from 20 October 2014 with savings set out in SI 2014/2771, articles 9–11.

[84 Grounds of appeal

(1) An appeal under section 82(1)(a) (refusal of protection claim) must be brought on one or more of the following grounds—

(a) that removal of the appellant from the United Kingdom would breach the United Kingdom's obligations under the Refugee Convention;

(b) that removal of the appellant from the United Kingdom would breach the United Kingdom's obligations in relation to persons eligible for a grant of humanitarian protection;

(c) that removal of the appellant from the United Kingdom would be unlawful under section 6 of the Human Rights Act 1998 (public authority not to act contrary to Human Rights Convention).

(2) An appeal under section 82(1)(b) (refusal of human rights claim) must be brought on the ground that the decision is unlawful under section 6 of the Human Rights Act 1998.

(3) An appeal under section 82(1)(c) (revocation of protection status) must be brought on one or more of the following grounds—

(a) that the decision to revoke the appellant's protection status breaches the United Kingdom's obligations under the Refugee Convention;

(b) that the decision to revoke the appellant's protection status breaches the United Kingdom's obligations in relation to persons eligible for a grant of humanitarian protection.]

Note: Section 84 substituted by s 15 Immigration Act 2014 from 20 October 2014 with savings set out in SI 2014/2771 articles 9–11.

85. Matters to be considered

(1) An appeal under section 82(1) against a decision shall be treated by [the Tribunal] [[or the Upper Tribunal]] as including an appeal against any decision in respect of which the appellant has a right of appeal under section 82(1).

(2) If an appellant under section 82(1) makes a statement under section 120, [the Tribunal] [[or the Upper Tribunal]] shall consider any matter raised in the statement which constitutes a ground of appeal of a kind listed in section [84] against the decision appealed against.

(3) Subsection (2) applies to a statement made under section 120 whether the statement was made before or after the appeal was commenced.

(4) On an appeal under section 82(1). . . against a decision [the Tribunal] [[or the Upper Tribunal]] may consider. . . any matter which [it] thinks relevant to the substance of the decision, including. . . a matter arising after the date of the decision.

[(5) But the Tribunal [[or the Upper Tribunal]] must not consider a new matter unless the Secretary of State has given [[the tribunal concerned]] consent to do so.

(6) A matter is a 'new matter' if—
(a) it constitutes a ground of appeal of a kind listed in section 84, and
(b) the Secretary of State has not previously considered the matter in the context of—
(i) the decision mentioned in section 82(1), or
(ii) a statement made by the appellant under section 120.]

Note: Commencement from 1 April 2003 (SI 2003/754, which sets out transitional provisions). Number in square brackets in subsection (2) substituted and words omitted from subsection (4) by Sch 9 Immigration Act 2014 from 20 October 2014, savings in articles 9–11 SI 2014/2771. Other words in square brackets substituted by Sch 2 Asylum and Immigration (Treatment of Claimants, etc.) Act 2004 from 4 April 2005 (SI 2005/565). Subsection (5) substituted by s 15 Immigration Act 2014 from 20 October 2014 with savings set out in SI 2014/2771. Words inserted in double square brackets at subsections (1),(2),(4) & (5) by Nationality and Borders Act 2022 c.36 Sch.3 para 2(a) & (b) (date to be appointed)

[85A . . .

Note: Section 85A repealed by Sch 9 Immigration Act 2014 from 20 October 2014 with savings set out in articles 9–11 SI 2014/2771.

86. Determination of appeal

(1) This section applies on an appeal under section 82(1). . .
(2) [the Tribunal][[or the Upper Tribunal]] must determine—
(a) any matter raised as a ground of appeal. . . and
(b) any matter which section 85 requires [it] to consider.
(3) . . .
(4) . . .
(5) . . .
(6) . . .

Note: Commencement from 1 April 2003 (SI 2003/754, which sets out transitional provisions). Words in square brackets in subsection (2) substituted by Sch 2 Asylum and Immigration (Treatment of Claimants, etc.) Act 2004 from 4 April 2005 (SI 2005/565). Words omitted from subsection (1) and (2) and subsections (3)–(6) omitted by Sch 9 Immigration Act 2014 from 20 October 2014, with savings in articles 9–11 of SI 2014/2771. Words inserted in double square brackets at subsection (2) by Nationality and Borders Act 2022 c.36 Sch.3 para 3 (date to be appointed)

87. . . ..

Note: Section 87 repealed by Sch 9 Immigration Act 2014 from 20 October 2014 with savings SI 2014/2771 articles 9–11.

Exceptions and limitations

88.

Note: Section 88 repealed by Sch 9 Immigration Act 2014 from 20 October 2014 with savings set out in articles 9–11 SI 2014/2771.

[88A].

Note: Section 88A repealed by Sch 9 Immigration Act 2014 from 20 October 2014 with savings set out in articles 9–11 SI 2014/2771.

[89].

Note: Section 89 repealed by Sch 9 Immigration Act 2014 from 20 October 2014 with savings in articles 9–11 SI 2014/2771.

90. . . ..

Note: Section 90 repealed by Sch 9 Immigration Act 2014 from 20 October 2014 with savings set out in articles 9–11 SI 2014/2771.

91. . . ..

Note: Section 91 repealed by Sch 9 Immigration Act 2014 from 20 October 2014 with savings set out in articles 9–11 SI 2014/2771.

[92. Place from which an appeal may be brought or continued

(1) This section applies to determine the place from which an appeal under section 82(1) may be brought or continued.

(2) In the case of an appeal under section 82(1)(a) (protection claim appeal), the appeal must be brought from outside the United Kingdom if—

(a) the claim to which the appeal relates has been certified under section [[94(7) (removal to a safe third country]]) [[]]

Otherwise, the appeal must be brought from within the United Kingdom.

(3) In the case of an appeal under section 82(1)(b) (human rights claim appeal) where the claim to which the appeal relates was made while the appellant was in the United Kingdom, the appeal must be brought from outside the United Kingdom if—

(a) the claim to which the appeal relates has been certified under section [[94(7) (removal to a safe country)]] or section 94B (certification of human rights claims[]), [[]]

Otherwise, the appeal must be brought from within the United Kingdom.

(4) In the case of an appeal under section 82(1)(b) (human rights claim appeal) where the claim to which the appeal relates was made while the appellant was outside the United Kingdom, the appeal must be brought from outside the United Kingdom.

(5) In the case of an appeal under section 82(1)(c) (revocation of protection status)—

(a) the appeal must be brought from within the United Kingdom if the decision to which the appeal relates was made while the appellant was in the United Kingdom;

(b) the appeal must be brought from outside the United Kingdom if the decision to which the appeal relates was made while the appellant was outside the United Kingdom.

(6) If, after an appeal under section 82(1)(a) or (b) has been brought from within the United Kingdom, the Secretary of State certifies the claim to which the appeal relates

under section [94(7)] or section 94B, the appeal must be continued from outside the United Kingdom.

(7) Where a person brings or continues an appeal under section 82(1)(a) (refusal of protection claim) from outside the United Kingdom, for the purposes of considering whether the grounds of appeal are satisfied, the appeal is to be treated as if the person were not outside the United Kingdom.

(8) Where an appellant brings an appeal from within the United Kingdom but leaves the United Kingdom before the appeal is finally determined, the appeal is to be treated as abandoned unless the claim to which the appeal relates has been certified under [section 94(7)or section 94B.]

Note: Section 92 substituted by s 17 Immigration Act 2014 from 20 October 2014 with savings set out in SI 2014/2771 articles 9–11, and transitional provisions in art 4 SI 2014/1820. Words omitted in square brackets by at subsection (3)(a) Immigration Act 2016, s 63 from 1 December 2016 (SI 2016/1037). Words in double square brackets substituted in subsections (2)(a), (3)(a), (6) & (8) by Nationality and Borders Act 2022 c.36 Pt2 s.28(2)(a) (June 28, 2022: substitution does not apply in relation to a protection claim or human rights claim that was certified by the Secretary of State under 2002 c.41 s.94(1) before the coming into force of 2022 c.36 s.28). Subsections (2)(b) & (3)(b) omitted by Nationality and Borders Act 2022 c.36 Sch.4 para 18 (June 28, 2022).

93. Appeal from within United Kingdom: 'third country' removal

. . .

Note: Section 93 ceased to have effect from 1 October 2004, Asylum and Immigration Act 2004, s 33 (SI 2004/2523).

94. [Certification of human rights or protection claims as unfounded or removal to safe country]

[(1) The Secretary of State may certify a protection claim or human rights claim as clearly unfounded.]

(3) If the Secretary of State is satisfied that [a] claimant is entitled to reside in a State listed in subsection (4) he shall certify the claim under subsection [(1)] unless satisfied that it is not clearly unfounded.

(4) Those States are—

(a) –(j). . .

[(k) the Republic of Albania,

(l) . . .

(m) . . .

(n) Jamaica,

(o) Macedonia,

(p) the Republic of Moldova, and

(q) . . .]

[(r) . . .

(s) Bolivia,

(t) Brazil,

(u) Ecuador,

(v) . . .
(w) South Africa, and
(x) Ukraine.]
(y) India,
[(z) Mongolia,
(aa) Ghana (in respect of men),
(bb) Nigeria (in respect of men).]
[(cc) Bosnia-Herzegovina,
(dd) Gambia (in respect of men),
(ee) Kenya (in respect of men),
(ff) Liberia (in respect of men),
(gg) Malawi (in respect of men),
(hh) Mali (in respect of men),
(ii) Mauritius,
(jj) Montenegro,
(kk) Peru,
(ll) Serbia,
(mm) Sierra Leone (in respect of men)]
[(nn) Kosovo,
(oo) South Korea]

(5) The Secretary of State may by order add a State, or part of a State, to the list in subsection (4) if satisfied that—

(a) there is in general in that State or part no serious risk of persecution of persons entitled to reside in that State or part, and

(b) removal to that State or part of persons entitled to reside there will not in general contravene the United Kingdom's obligations under the Human Rights Convention.

[(5A) If the Secretary of State is satisfied that the statements in subsection (5)(a) and (b) are true of a State or part of a State in relation to a description of person, an order under subsection (5) may add the State or part to the list in subsection (4) in respect of that description of person.

(5B) Where a State or part of a State is added to the list in subsection (4) in respect of a description of person, subsection (3) shall have effect in relation to a claimant only if the Secretary of State is satisfied that he is within that description (as well as being satisfied that he is entitled to reside in the State or part).

(5C) A description for the purposes of subsection (5A) may refer to—
(a) gender,
(b) language,
(c) race,
(d) religion,
(e) nationality,
(f) membership of a social or other group,
(g) political opinion, or
(h) any other attribute or circumstance that the Secretary of State thinks appropriate.]

[(5D) In deciding whether the statements in subsection (5)(a) and (b) are true of a State or part of a State, the Secretary of State—

(a) shall have regard to all the circumstances of the State or part (including its laws and how they are applied), and

(b) shall have regard to information from any appropriate source (including [[]] member States and international organisations).]

[(**6**) The Secretary of State may by order amend the list in subsection (4) so as to omit a State or part added under subsection (5); and the omission may be—

(a) general, or

(b) effected so that the State or part remains listed in respect of a description of person.]

[(**6A**) Subsection (3) shall not apply in relation to [a] claimant who—

(a) is the subject of a certificate under section 2 or 70 of the Extradition Act 2003 (c. 41),

(b) is in custody pursuant to arrest under section 5 of that Act,

(c) is the subject of a provisional warrant under section 73 of that Act,

[[(ca) is the subject of a certificate under section 74B of that Act]],

(d) is the subject of an authority to proceed under section 7 of the Extradition Act 1989 (c. 33) or an order under paragraph 4(2) of Schedule 1 to that Act, or

(e) is the subject of a provisional warrant under section 8 of that Act or of a warrant under paragraph 5(1)(b) of Schedule 1 to that Act.]

[(**6B**) A certificate under subsection (1A) or (2) may not be issued (and subsection (3) shall not apply) in relation to an appeal under section 82(2)(d) or (e) against a decision relating to leave to enter or remain in the United Kingdom, where the leave was given in circumstances specified for the purposes of this subsection by order of the Secretary of State.]

(7) [The Secretary of State may certify a protection claim or human rights claim made by a person if]—

(a) it is proposed to remove the person to a country of which he is not a national or citizen, and

(b) there is no reason to believe that the person's rights under the Human Rights Convention will be breached in that country.

(8) In determining whether a person in relation to whom a certificate has been issued under subsection (7) may be removed from the United Kingdom, the country specified in the certificate is to be regarded as—

(a) a place where a person's life and liberty is not threatened by reason of his race, religion, nationality, membership of a particular social group, or political opinion, and

(b) a place from which a person will not be sent to another country otherwise than in accordance with the Refugee Convention [or with the United Kingdom's obligations in relation to persons eligible for a grant of humanitarian protection].

(9) . . .

Note: Subsection (5) commenced 10 February 2003 for the purposes of enabling subordinate legislation (SI 2003/249), remainder from 1 April 2003 (SI 2003/754, which sets out transitional provisions). Subsection (6B) inserted by Immigration, Asylum and Nationality Act 2006, s 13 from a date to be appointed. Subsection 4: words in first square brackets added by SI 2003/970 from 1 April 2003, words in second square brackets added by SI 2003/1919 from 23 July 2003, Bangladesh omitted and last words in square brackets inserted from December 2005 (SI 2005/3306). First words omitted and other words in square brackets substituted or added by Asylum and Immigration (Treatment of Claimants etc.) Act 2004, s 27 from 1 October 2004 (SI 2004/2523). Other words in subsection (4) omitted from 22 April 2005 (SI 2005/1016). Subsection (5D) inserted by SI 2007/3187 from 1 December 2007. India inserted from 15 February 2005 (SI 2005/330). Serbia and Montenegro omitted from subsection (4) and (cc)–(mm) inserted from 27 July 2007 (SI 2007/2221). Sri Lanka omitted from subsection (4) from 13 December 2006 (SI 2006/3275). Bulgaria and Romania omitted from subsection (4) from 1 January 2007 (SI 2006/3215). Kosovo and South Korea inserted from 3 March 2010, but without effect to asylum claims made before that date, (SI 2010/561). Subsections (1)–(2) and words in square brackets in the heading, subsections (3), (6A), (7) substituted, words in square brackets in subsection (8)(b) inserted and subsection (9) omitted by Sch 9 Immigration Act 2014 from 20 October 2014 with savings set out in articles 9–11 SI 2014/2771. Words in double square brackets omitted in subsection (5D)(b) by Immigration, Nationality and Asylum (EU Exit) Regulations 2019/745 Pt 3(1) reg50(2) (December 31,2020: shall come into force on not exit day as specified in 2020 c.1 s 39(1) and Sch5 para 1(1)). Words in double square brackets inserted at subsection (6A)(ca) by Extradition (Provisional Arrest) Act 2020 c. 18 Sch. 1 para 9 (December 31, 2020: shall come into force on IP completion day). Heading substituted by Nationality and Borders Act 2022 c.36 s28(3)(c) (June 28, 202)

[94A] . . .

Note: Section 94A omitted by Immigration, Nationality and Asylum (EU Exit) Regulations 2019/745 Pt 3 (1) reg 50(3) (December 31 2020, shall come into force on IP completion day not exit day as specified in 2020 c1.s39 (1) and Sch. 5 para.1(1)).

[94B Appeal from within the United Kingdom: certification of human rights claims

(1) This section applies where a human rights claim has been made by a person ('P'). [[]]

(2) The Secretary of State may certify the claim if the Secretary of State considers that, despite the appeals process not having been begun or not having been exhausted, [[refusing P entry to, removing P from or requiring P to leave the United Kingdom]], pending the outcome of an appeal in relation to P's claim, would not be unlawful under section 6 of the Human Rights Act 1998 (public authority not to act contrary to Human Rights Convention).

(3) The grounds upon which the Secretary of State may certify a claim under subsection (2) include (in particular) that P would not, before the appeals process is exhausted, face a real risk of serious irreversible harm if [[[refused entry to, removed from or required to leave the United Kingdom]].]

Note: Section 94B inserted by s 17 Immigration Act 2014 from 28 July 2014 (SI 2014/1820). Words omitted in subsection (1) and words in double square brackets in subsection (2) and (3) are substituted by Immigration Act 2016, s 63 from 1 December 2016 (SI 2016/1037).

95. . . .

Note: Section 95 repealed by Sch 9 Immigration Act 2014 from 20 October 2014 with savings set out in articles 9–11 SI 2014/2771.

96. Earlier right of appeal

[(1) [A person may not bring an appeal under section 82 against a decision ('the new decision')] if the Secretary of State or an immigration officer certifies—

(a) that the person was notified of a right of appeal under that section against another. . . decision ('the old decision') (whether or not an appeal was brought and whether or not any appeal brought has been determined),

(b) that the claim or application to which the new decision relates relies on a [ground] that could have been raised in an appeal against the old decision, and

(c) that, in the opinion of the Secretary of State or the immigration officer, there is no satisfactory reason for that [ground] not having been raised in an appeal against the old decision.

[(2) A person may not bring an appeal under section 82 if the Secretary of State or an immigration officer certifies—

(a) that the person has received a notice under section 120(2),

(b) that the appeal relies on a ground that should have been, but has not been, raised in a statement made under section 120(2) or (5), and

(c) that, in the opinion of the Secretary of State or the immigration officer, there is no satisfactory reason for that ground not having been raised in a statement under section 120(2) or (5).]

(4) In subsection (1) 'notified' means notified in accordance with regulations under section 105.

(5) [Subsections (1) and (2) apply to prevent] a person's right of appeal whether or not he has been outside the United Kingdom since an earlier right of appeal arose or since a requirement under section 120 was imposed.

(6) In this section a reference to an appeal under section 82(1) includes a reference to an appeal under section 2 of the Special Immigration Appeals Commission Act 1997 (c. 68) which is or could be brought by reference to an appeal under section 82(1).

[(7) A certificate under subsection (1) or (2) shall have no effect in relation to an appeal instituted before the certificate is issued.]

Note: Commencement from 1 April 2003 (SI 2003/754, which sets out transitional provisions). Word omitted from subsection (1)(a), words in square brackets in subsection (1) and subsection (2) substituted by Sch 9 Immigration Act 2014 from 20 October 2014, savings set out in articles 9–11 SI 2014/2771. Words in other square brackets substituted and subsection (7) added by Asylum and Immigration (Treatment of Claimants, etc.) Act 2004, s 30 from 1 October 2004 (SI 2004/2523).

97. National security, &c.

(1) An appeal under section 82(1). . . against a decision in respect of a person may not be brought or continued if the Secretary of State certifies that the decision is or was taken—

(a) by the Secretary of State wholly or partly on a ground listed in subsection (2), or

(b) in accordance with a direction of the Secretary of State which identifies the person to whom the decision relates and which is given wholly or partly on a ground listed in subsection (2).

(2) The grounds mentioned in subsection (1) are that the person's exclusion or removal from the United Kingdom is—

(a) in the interests of national security, or

(b) in the interests of the relationship between the United Kingdom and another country.

(3) An appeal under section 82(1). . . against a decision may not be brought or continued if the Secretary of State certifies that the decision is or was taken wholly or partly in reliance on information which in his opinion should not be made public—

(a) in the interests of national security,

(b) in the interests of the relationship between the United Kingdom and another country, or

(c) otherwise in the public interest.

(4) In subsections (1)(a) and (b) and (3) a reference to the Secretary of State is to the Secretary of State acting in person.

Note: Commencement from 1 April 2003 (SI 2003/754, which sets out transitional provisions). Words in square brackets in subsections (1) and (3) omitted by Sch 9 Immigration Act 2014 from 20 October 2014 with savings set out in articles 9–11 SI 2014/2771.

[97A. National security: deportation

(1) This section applies where the Secretary of State certifies that the decision to make a deportation order in respect of a person was taken on the grounds that his removal from the United Kingdom would be in the interests of national security.

[(1A) This section also applies where the Secretary of State certifies, in the case of a person in respect of whom a deportation order has been made which states that it is made in accordance with section 32(5) of the UK Borders Act 2007, that the person's removal from the United Kingdom would be in the interests of national security.]

(2) Where this section applies—

(a) section 79 shall not apply,

(b) the Secretary of State shall be taken to have certified the decision to make the deportation order under section 97, and

[(c) section 2(5) of the Special Immigration Appeals Commission Act 1997 (whether appeals brought against decisions certified under section 97 may be brought from within the United Kingdom) does not apply, but see instead the following provisions of this section.]

[(2A) The person while in the United Kingdom may not bring or continue an appeal under section 2 of the Special Immigration Appeals Commission Act 1997—

(a) against the decision to make the deportation order, or

(b) against any refusal to revoke the deportation order,

unless the person has made a human rights claim while in the United Kingdom.

(2B) Subsection (2A) does not allow the person while in the United Kingdom to bring or continue an appeal if the Secretary of State certifies that removal of the person—

(a) to the country or territory to which the person is proposed to be removed, and

(b) despite the appeals process not having been begun or not having been exhausted, would not [be unlawful under section 6 of the Human Rights Act 1998 (public authority not to act contrary to Human Rights Convention)].

(2C) The grounds upon which a certificate may be given under subsection (2B) include (in particular)—

(a) that the person would not, before the appeals process is exhausted, face a real risk of serious irreversible harm if removed to the country or territory to which the person is proposed to be removed;

(b) that the whole or part of any human rights claim made by the person is clearly unfounded.

(2D) . . .

(2E) . . .

(2F) If a certificate in respect of a person is given under subsection (2B), the person may apply to the Special Immigration Appeals Commission to set aside the certificate.

(2G) If a person makes an application under subsection (2F) then the Commission, in determining whether the certificate should be set aside, must apply the principles that would be applied in judicial review proceedings.

(2H) The Commission's determination of a review under subsection (2F) is final.

(2J) The Commission may direct that a person who has made and not withdrawn an application under subsection (2F) is not to be removed from the United Kingdom at a time when the review has not been finally determined by the Commission.

(2K) Sections 5 and 6 of the Special Immigration Appeals Commission Act 1997 apply in relation to reviews under subsection (2F) (and to applicants for such reviews) as they apply in relation to appeals under section 2 or 2B of that Act (and to persons bringing such appeals).

(2L) Any exercise of power to make rules under section 5 of that Act in relation to reviews under subsection (2F) is to be with a view to securing that proceedings on such reviews are handled expeditiously.]

(3) . . .

(4) The Secretary of State may repeal this section by order.]

Note: Section 97A inserted by Immigration, Asylum and Nationality Act 2006, s 7 from 31 August 2006 (SI 2006/2226). Subsection (1A), (2A)–(2L) inserted, subsection (2)(c) substituted by s 54 Crime and Courts Act 2013 from 25 June 2013 (SI 2013/1042). Words in square brackets in subsection (2B) substituted and subsections (2D), (2E) and (3) omitted by Sch 9 Immigration Act 2014 from 20 October 2014 with savings set out in articles 9–11 SI 2014/2771. S 97A excluded (31.1.2020) by The Immigration (Citizens Rights Appeals) (EU Exit) Regulations 2020 (SI 2020/61), regs. 1(2), 15(2)

[97B . . .

Note: Section 97B inserted by s 53 Crime and Courts Act 2013 from 25 June 2013 (SI 2013/1042), repealed by Sch 9 Immigration Act 2014 from 20 October 2014 with savings set out in articles 9–11 SI 2014/2771.

98. . . ..

Note: Section 98 repealed by Schedule 9 Immigration Act 2014 from 20 October 2014 with savings set out in articles 9–11 SI 2014/2771.

99. [Section 97]: appeal in progress

(1) This section applies where a certificate is issued under section . . . [97] . . . in respect of a pending appeal.

(2) The appeal shall lapse.

Note: Commencement from 1 April 2003 (SI 2003/754, which sets out transitional provisions). Words in square brackets in title substituted and words omitted from subsection (1) by Sch 9 Immigration Act 2014 from 20 October 2014 with savings set out in articles 9–11 SI 2014/2771.

Appeal from adjudicator

100. Immigration Appeal Tribunal

. . .

Note: Section 100 ceased to have effect, Asylum and Immigration (Treatment of Claimants, etc.) Act 2004, s 26 from 4 April 2005 (SI 2005/565).

101. Appeal to Tribunal

. . .

Note: Section 101 ceased to have effect, Asylum and Immigration (Treatment of Claimants, etc.) Act 2004, s 26 from 4 April 2005 (SI 2005/565).

102. Decision

. . .

Note: Section 102 ceased to have effect from 4 April 2005 (SI 2005/565), Asylum and Immigration (Treatment of Claimants, etc.) Act 2004, s 26.

103. Appeal from Tribunal

. . .

Note: Section 103 ceased to have effect from 4 April 2005 (SI 2005/565), Asylum and Immigration (Treatment of Claimants, etc.) Act 2004, s 26.

[103A.–103E.]

Note: Sections 103A–E inserted by Asylum and Immigration (Treatment of Claimants, etc.) Act 2004, s 26 from 4 April 2005 (SI 2005/565). Revoked from 15 February 2010 (SI 2010/21).

Procedure

104. Pending appeal

(1) An appeal under section 82(1) is pending during the period—

(a) beginning when it is instituted, and

(b) ending when it is finally determined, withdrawn or abandoned (or when it lapses under section 99).

[(2) An appeal under section 82(1) is not finally determined for the purpose of subsection (1)(b) while—

(a) an application for permission to appeal under section 11 or 13 of the Tribunals, Courts and Enforcement Act 2007 could be made or is awaiting determination,

(b) permission to appeal under either of those sections has been granted and the appeal is awaiting determination, or

(c) an appeal has been remitted under section 12 or 14 of that Act and is awaiting determination.]

(3) . . .

[(4) . . .

(4A) An appeal under section 82(1) brought by a person while he is in the United Kingdom shall be treated as abandoned if the appellant is granted leave to enter or remain in the United Kingdom (subject to [subsection (4B)]).

(4B) Subsection (4A) shall not apply to an appeal in so far as it is brought on [a ground specified in section 84(1)(a) or (b) or 84(3) (asylum or humanitarian protection)] where the appellant—

(a) . . .

(b) gives notice, in accordance with [Tribunal Procedure Rules], that he wishes to pursue the appeal in so far as it is brought on that ground.

(4C). . .

(5) . . .

Note: Commencement from 1 April 2003 (SI 2003/754). Subsection (3) omitted by Sch 2 Asylum and Immigration (Treatment of Claimants, etc.) Act 2004 from 4 April 2005 (SI 2005/565). Subsection (4) substituted and subsections (4A)–(4C) inserted by Immigration, Asylum and Nationality Act 2006, s 9 from 13 November 2006 (SI 2006/2838). Subsection (2) and words in square brackets in subsections (4B)(b) substituted from 15 February 2010 (SI 2010/21). Words in square brackets in subsection (4B) substituted and subsections (4), (4B)(a), (4C) and (5) omitted by Sch 9 Immigration Act 2014 from 20 October 2014 with savings set out in articles 9–11 SI 2014/2771.

105. Notice of immigration decision

(1) The Secretary of State may make regulations requiring a person to be given written notice where an [appealable] decision is taken in respect of him.

(2) The regulations may, in particular, provide that a notice under subsection (1) of [an appealable decision] must state—

(a) that there is a right of appeal under [section 82], and

(b) how and when that right may be exercised.

(3) The regulations may make provision (which may include presumptions) about service.

[(4) In this section 'appealable decision' means a decision mentioned in section 82(1).]

Note: Commencement from 1 April 2003 (SI 2003/754). Words in square brackets substituted and subsection (4) inserted by Sch 9 Immigration Act 2014 from 20 October 2014 with savings set out in articles 9–11 SI 2014/2771. S 105 applied (with modifications) (31.1.2020) by The Immigration (Citizens Rights Appeals) (EU Exit) Regulations 2020 (SI 2020/61), reg. 1(2), Sch. 2 paras. 1–3

106. Rules

(1) . . .

[(1A) . . .

(2) . . .

[(3) In the case of an appeal under section 82 . . . [[]] Tribunal Procedure Rules may enable the Tribunal {or the Upper Tribunal} to certify that the appeal had no merit (and shall make provision for the consequences of the issue of a certificate).]

(4) A person commits an offence if without reasonable excuse he fails to comply with a requirement imposed in accordance with [Tribunal Procedure Rules in connection with proceedings under section 82.[[]] to attend before . . . the Tribunal {or the Upper Tribunal}—

(a) to give evidence, or

(b) to produce a document.

(5) A person who is guilty of an offence under subsection (4) shall be liable on summary conviction to a fine not exceeding level 3 on the standard scale.

Note: Commencement from 1 April 2003 (SI 2003/754). Subsections (1), (1A) and (2) revoked, subsection (3) and words in square brackets in subsection (4) substituted from 15 February 2010 (SI 2010/21). Words omitted from subsection (3)–(4) by Schedule 9 Immigration Act 2014 from 20 October 2014 with savings set out in articles 9–11 SI 2014/2771. S 106 applied (with modifications) (31.1.2020) by The Immigration (Citizens Rights Appeals) (EU Exit) Regulations 2020 (SI 2020/61), reg. 1(2), Sch. 2 paras. 1–3. Words in double square brackets omitted in subsection (3) & (4) by Immigration and Social Security Co-ordination (EU Withdrawal) Act 2020 c.20 Sch.1(1) para 2(3)(a) (December 31, 2020: shall come into force on IP completion day). Words inserted in curly brackets at subsections (3) & (4) by Nationality and Borders Act 2022 c.36 Sch.3 para 4 (date to be appointed)

107. Practice directions

(1) . . .

[(1A) . . .]

(2) . . .

{(2A) Subsection (3) applies to—

(a) proceedings under section 82 in the Tribunal or proceedings in the Upper Tribunal arising out of such proceedings;

(b) proceedings under section 82 in the Upper Tribunal (see section 82A and section 24 of the Nationality and Borders Act 2022).}

[(3) In the case of proceedings{to which this section applies}, practice directions under section 23 of the Tribunals, Courts and Enforcement Act 2007—

(a) may require the Tribunal to treat a specified decision of the Tribunal or Upper Tribunal as authoritative in respect of a particular matter; and

(b) may require the Upper Tribunal to treat a specified decision of the Tribunal or Upper Tribunal as authoritative in respect of a particular matter.]

[(3A) In subsection (3) the reference to a decision of the Tribunal includes—

(a) a decision of the Asylum and Immigration Tribunal, and

(b) a decision of the Immigration Appeal Tribunal.]

(4) . . .

(5) . . .

(6) . . .

(7) . . .

Note: Commencement from 1 April 2003 (SI 2003/754). Subsections (1), (1A) and (4)—(7) revoked and subsection (3) substituted and (3A) inserted from 15 February 2010 (SI 2010/21). Words omitted from subsection (3) by Sch 9 Immigration Act 2014 from 20 October 2014 with savings set out in articles 9–11 SI 2014/2771. S 107 applied (with modifications) (31.1.2020) by The Immigration (Citizens Rights Appeals) (EU Exit) Regulations 2020 (SI 2020/61), reg. 1(2), Sch. 2 paras. 1–3. Words in double square brackets at subsection 3 omitted by Immigration and Social Security (EU Withdrawal) Act 2020 c.20 Sch.1(1) para.2(3)(b) (December 31,2020: shall come into force on IP completion day). Subsection (2A) and words substituted in subsection (3) by Nationality and Borders Act 2022 c.36 Sch.3 para 5(a) &(b) (date to be appointed)

108. Forged document: proceedings in private

(1) This section applies where it is alleged—

(a) that a document relied on by a party to an appeal under section 82 . . . is a forgery, and

(b) that disclosure to that party of a matter relating to the detection of the forgery would be contrary to the public interest.

(2) [The Tribunal] [[or the Upper Tribunal]]

(a) must investigate the allegation in private, and

(b) may proceed in private so far as necessary to prevent disclosure of the matter referred to in subsection (1)(b).

Note: Commencement from 1 April 2003 (SI 2003/754). Amended by Sch 2 Asylum and Immigration (Treatment of Claimants, etc.) Act 2004, from 4 April 2005 (SI 2005/565). Words in square brackets in subsection (1)(a) substituted by Sch 1 Immigration, Asylum and Nationality Act 2006 from 31 August 2006 (SI 2006/2226) and omitted by Sch 9 Immigration Act 2014 from 20 October 2014 with savings set out in articles 9–11 SI 2014/2771. S 108 applied (with modifications) (31.1.2020) by The Immigration (Citizens Rights Appeals) (EU Exit) Regulations 2020 (SI 2020/61), reg. 1(2), Sch. 2 paras. 1–3. Words inserted in double square brackets at subsection (2) by Nationality and Borders Act 2022 c.36 Sch.3 para 6(date to be appointed)

General

109.

Omitted by Immigration and Social Security Co-ordination (EU Withdrawal) Act 2020 c.20 Sch.1(1) para,2(1) (December 31, 2020: repeal has effect subject to savings specified in SI2020/1309 reg.82 and Sch.3para.7).

110. Grants

Note: Commencement from 1 April 2003 (SI 2003/754). Ceased to have effect from 16 June 2006, Immigration, Asylum and Nationality Act 2006, s 10 (SI 2006/1497).

111. . . ..

Note: Section 111 deleted by UK Borders Act 2007 s 54(c) from 1 April 2008 (SI 2008/309).

112. Regulations, &c.

(1) Regulations under this Part shall be made by the Secretary of State.

(2) Regulations. . . under this Part. . .—

(a) must be made by statutory instrument, and

(b) shall be subject to annulment in pursuance of a resolution of either House of Parliament.

(3) Regulations. . . under this Part—

(a) may make provision which applies generally or only in a specified case or in specified circumstances,

(b) may make different provision for different cases or circumstances,

(c) may include consequential, transitional or incidental provision, and

(d) may include savings.

(3A) . . .

(4) An order under section 94(5) . . .—

(a) must be made by statutory instrument,

(b) may not be made unless a draft has been laid before and approved by resolution of each House of Parliament, and

(c) may include transitional provision.

(5) An order under section [94(6) or (6B)] . . .—

(a) must be made by statutory instrument,

(b) shall be subject to annulment in pursuance of a resolution of either House of Parliament, and

(c) may include transitional provision.

[(5A) If an instrument makes provision under section 94(5) and 94(6)—

(a) subsection (4)(b) above shall apply, and

(b) subsection (5)(b) above shall not apply.]

[(5B) An order under section 97A(4)—

(a) must be made by statutory instrument,

(b) shall be subject to annulment in pursuance of a resolution of either House of Parliament, and

(c) may include transitional provision.]

[(6) . . .

(7) . . .]

Note: Commenced 10 February 2003 (SI 2003/249). Subsection (3A) and (5A) inserted by Asylum and Immigration (Treatment of Claimants, etc.) Act 2004, ss 29 and 27 respectively from 1 October 2004 (SI 2004/2523). Words in square brackets in subsection (5) substituted and subsection (5B) inserted by Immigration, Asylum and Nationality Act 2006, ss 7, 14, 62 and Sch 1 from 31 August 2006 (SI 2006/2226). Words omitted from subsections (2) and (3) and subsections (6)–(7) revoked from 15 February 2010 (SI 2010/21, which contains savings). Subsection (3A) and words omitted from subsections (4) and (5) by Sch 9 Immigration Act 2014 from 20 October 2014 with savings set out in articles 9–11 SI 2014/2771. S 112 applied (with modifications) (31.1.2020) by The Immigration (Citizens Rights Appeals) (EU Exit) Regulations 2020 (SI 2020/61), reg. 1(2), Sch. 2 paras. 1–3

113. Interpretation

(1) In this Part, unless a contrary intention appears—

['asylum claim'—

(a) means a claim made by a person that to remove him from or require him to leave the United Kingdom would breach the United Kingdom's obligations under the Refugee Convention, but

(b) does not include a claim which, having regard to a former claim, falls to be disregarded for the purposes of this Part in accordance with immigration rules,]

. . .

['human rights claim'—

(a) means a claim made by a person that to remove him from or require him to leave the United Kingdom [or to refuse him entry into the United Kingdom] would be unlawful under section 6 of the Human Rights Act 1998 (c. 42) (public authority not to act contrary to Convention) . . . but

(b) does not include a claim which, having regard to a former claim, falls to be disregarded for the purposes of this Part in accordance with immigration rules,]

['humanitarian protection' has the meaning given in section 82(2);]

'the Human Rights Convention' has the same meaning as 'the Convention' in the Human Rights Act 1998 and 'Convention rights' shall be construed in accordance with section 1 of that Act,

. . .

'immigration rules' means rules under section 1(4) of that Act (general immigration rules),

. . .

['protection claim' has the meaning given in section 82(2)]

['protection status' has the meaning given in section 82(2)]

'the Refugee Convention' means the Convention relating to the Status of Refugees done at Geneva on 28 July 1951 and its Protocol,

. . .

. . .

(2) . . .

Note: Commenced 10 February 2003 (SI 2003/249). Definitions of asylum claim and human rights claim substituted by Immigration, Asylum and Nationality Act 2006, s 12 from a date to be appointed. Further amendments made in subsection (1) and omissions from subsection (2) by Sch 9 Immigration Act 2014 from 20 October 2014 with savings set out in articles 9–11 SI 2014/2771.

114. Repeal

(1) . . .

(2) Schedule 6 (which makes transitional provision in connection with the repeal of Part IV of that Act and its replacement by this Part) shall have effect.

(3) Schedule 7 (consequential amendments) shall have effect.

Note: Subsection (1) repeals Part IV of the Immigration and Asylum Act 1999. Subsection (3) Commenced 10 February 2003 (SI 2003/1). Remainder from 1 April 2003 (SI 2003/754).

115. . . ..

Note: Section 115 repealed by Sch 9 Immigration Act 2014 from 20 October 2014 with savings set out in articles 9–11 SI 2014/2771.

116. Special Immigration Appeals Commission: Community Legal Service

. . .

Note: Amends paragraph 2(1), Sch 2 Access to Justice Act 1999. Repealed by Legal Aid, Sentencing and Punishment of Offenders Act 2012, Sch 5, Part 2 from a date to be appointed.

117. Northern Ireland appeals: legal aid

. . .

Note: Amends Part 1, Sch 1 Legal Aid, Advice and Assistance (Northern Ireland) Order 1981.

[PART VA
ARTICLE 8 OF THE ECHR; PUBLIC INTEREST CONSIDERATIONS

Note: Part 5A inserted by s 19 Immigration Act 2014 from 28 July 2014 (SI 2014/1820).

117A. Application of this Part

(1) This Part applies where a court or tribunal is required to determine whether a decision made under the Immigration Acts—

(a) breaches a person's right to respect for private and family life under Article 8, and

(b) as a result would be unlawful under section 6 of the Human Rights Act 1998.

(2) In considering the public interest question, the court or tribunal must (in particular) have regard—

(a) in all cases, to the considerations listed in section 117B, and

(b) in cases concerning the deportation of foreign criminals, to the considerations listed in section 117C.

(3) In subsection (2), 'the public interest question' means the question of whether an interference with a person's right to respect for private and family life is justified under Article 8(2).

Note: Section 117A inserted by s 19 Immigration Act 2014 from 28 July 2014 (SI 2014/1820).

117B. Article 8: public interest considerations applicable in all cases

(1) The maintenance of effective immigration controls is in the public interest.

(2) It is in the public interest, and in particular in the interests of the economic well-being of the United Kingdom, that persons who seek to enter or remain in the United Kingdom are able to speak English, because persons who can speak English—

(a) are less of a burden on taxpayers, and

(b) are better able to integrate into society.

(3) It is in the public interest, and in particular in the interests of the economic well-being of the United Kingdom, that persons who seek to enter or remain in the United Kingdom are financially independent, because such persons—

(a) are not a burden on taxpayers, and
(b) are better able to integrate into society.

(4) Little weight should be given to—
(a) a private life, or
(b) a relationship formed with a qualifying partner, that is established by a person at a time when the person is in the United Kingdom unlawfully.

(5) Little weight should be given to a private life established by a person at a time when the person's immigration status is precarious.

(6) In the case of a person who is not liable to deportation, the public interest does not require the person's removal where—
(a) the person has a genuine and subsisting parental relationship with a qualifying child, and
(b) it would not be reasonable to expect the child to leave the United Kingdom.

Note: Section 117B inserted by s 19 Immigration Act 2014 from 28 July 2014 (SI 2014/1820).

117C. Article 8: additional considerations in cases involving foreign criminals

(1) The deportation of foreign criminals is in the public interest.

(2) The more serious the offence committed by a foreign criminal, the greater is the public interest in deportation of the criminal.

(3) In the case of a foreign criminal ('C') who has not been sentenced to a period of imprisonment of four years or more, the public interest requires C's deportation unless Exception 1 or Exception 2 applies.

(4) Exception 1 applies where—
(a) C has been lawfully resident in the United Kingdom for most of C's life,
(b) C is socially and culturally integrated in the United Kingdom, and
(c) there would be very significant obstacles to C's integration into the country to which C is proposed to be deported.

(5) Exception 2 applies where C has a genuine and subsisting relationship with a qualifying partner, or a genuine and subsisting parental relationship with a qualifying child, and the effect of C's deportation on the partner or child would be unduly harsh.

(6) In the case of a foreign criminal who has been sentenced to a period of imprisonment of at least four years, the public interest requires deportation unless there are very compelling circumstances, over and above those described in Exceptions 1 and 2.

(7) The considerations in subsections (1) to (6) are to be taken into account where a court or tribunal is considering a decision to deport a foreign criminal only to the extent that the reason for the decision was the offence or offences for which the criminal has been convicted.

Note: Section 117C inserted by s 19 Immigration Act 2014 from 28 July 2014 (SI 2014/1820).

117D. Interpretation of this Part

(1) In this Part—
'Article 8' means Article 8 of the European Convention on Human Rights;

'qualifying child' means a person who is under the age of 18 and who—

(a) is a British citizen, or

(b) has lived in the United Kingdom for a continuous period of seven years or more;

'qualifying partner' means a partner who—

(a) is a British citizen, or

(b) who is settled in the United Kingdom (within the meaning of the Immigration Act 1971—see section 33(2A) of that Act).

(2) In this Part, 'foreign criminal' means a person—

(a) who is not a British citizen,

(b) who has been convicted in the United Kingdom of an offence, and

(c) who—

(i) has been sentenced to a period of imprisonment of at least 12 months,

(ii) has been convicted of an offence that has caused serious harm, or

(iii) is a persistent offender.

(3) For the purposes of subsection (2)(b), a person subject to an order under—

(a) section 5 of the Criminal Procedure (Insanity) Act 1964 (insanity etc),

(b) section 57 of the Criminal Procedure (Scotland) Act 1995 (insanity etc.), or

(c) Article 50A of the Mental Health (Northern Ireland) Order 1986 (insanity etc.),

has not been convicted of an offence.

(4) In this Part, references to a person who has been sentenced to a period of imprisonment of a certain length of time—

(a) do not include a person who has received a suspended sentence (unless a court subsequently orders that the sentence or any part of it (of whatever length) is to take effect);

(b) do not include a person who has been sentenced to a period of imprisonment of that length of time only by virtue of being sentenced to consecutive sentences amounting in aggregate to that length of time;

(c) include a person who is sentenced to detention, or ordered or directed to be detained, in an institution other than a prison (including, in particular, a hospital or an institution for young offenders) for that length of time; and

(d) include a person who is sentenced to imprisonment or detention, or ordered or directed to be detained, for an indeterminate period, provided that it may last for at least that length of time.

(5) If any question arises for the purposes of this Part as to whether a person is a British citizen, it is for the person asserting that fact to prove it.]

Note: Section 117D inserted by s 19 Immigration Act 2014 from 28 July 2014 (SI 2014/1820).

Part VI
Immigration Procedure

Applications

118. Leave pending decision on variation application

. . .

Note: Amends Immigration Act 1971, s 3C.

119. Deemed leave on cancellation of notice

. . .

Note: Amends paragraph 6(3), Sch 2 Immigration Act 1971.

[120. Requirement to state additional grounds for application etc.

(1) Subsection (2) applies to a person ('P') if—

(a) P has made a protection claim or a human rights claim,

(b) P has made an application to enter or remain in the United Kingdom, or

(c) a decision to deport or remove P has been or may be taken.

(2) The Secretary of State or an immigration officer may serve a notice on P requiring P to provide a statement setting out—

(a) P's reasons for wishing to enter or remain in the United Kingdom,

(b) any grounds on which P should be permitted to enter or remain in the United Kingdom, and

(c) any grounds on which P should not be removed from or required to leave the United Kingdom.

(3) A statement under subsection (2) need not repeat reasons or grounds set out in—

(a) P's protection or human rights claim,

(b) the application mentioned in subsection (1)(b), or

(c) an application to which the decision mentioned in subsection (1)(c) relates.

(4) Subsection (5) applies to a person ('P') if P has previously been served with a notice under subsection (2) and—

(a) P requires leave to enter or remain in the United Kingdom but does not have it, or

(b) P has leave to enter or remain in the United Kingdom only by virtue of section 3C [] of the Immigration Act 1971 (continuation of leave pending decision or appeal).

(5) Where P's circumstances have changed since the Secretary of State or an immigration officer was last made aware of them (whether in the application or claim mentioned in subsection (1) or in a statement under subsection (2) or this subsection) so that P has—

(a) additional reasons for wishing to enter or remain in the United Kingdom,

(b) additional grounds on which P should be permitted to enter or remain in the United Kingdom, or

(c) additional grounds on which P should not be removed from or required to leave the United Kingdom, P must, as soon as reasonably practicable, provide a supplementary statement to the Secretary of State or an immigration officer setting out the new circumstances and the additional reasons or grounds.

(6) In this section—

'human rights claim' and 'protection claim' have the same meanings as in Part 5;

references to 'grounds' are to grounds on which an appeal under Part 5 may be brought (see section 84).]

Note: Commencement from 1 April 2003 (SI 2003/754). Substituted by Sch 9 Immigration Act 2014 from 20 October 2014 with savings set out in articles 9–11 SI 2014/2771. Words omitted at section 120(4)(b) by Immigration Act 2016, s 64 from 1 December 2016 (SI 2016/1037). S. 120 applied (1.2.2017 for specified purposes) by The Immigration (European Economic Area) Regulations 2016 (S.I. 2016/1052), reg. 1(2)(b), Sch. 2 para. 2(2) S. 120 applied (with modifications) (31.1.2020) by The Immigration (Citizens Rights Appeals) (EU Exit) Regulations 2020 (SI 2020/61), reg. 1(2), Sch. 2 paras. 1–3

121. Compliance with procedure

. . .

Note: Amends Immigration Act 1971, s 31A.

Work permit

122.

. . .

Note: Commenced 10 February 2003 (SI 2003/1). Ceased to have effect by Sch 2 Immigration, Asylum and Nationality Act 2006 from 2 April 2007 (SI 2007/1109).

123. Advice about work permit, &c.

. . .

Note: Amends Immigration and Asylum Act 1999, s 82.

Authority-to-carry scheme

124. Authority to carry

(1) Regulations made by the Secretary of State may authorise him to require a person (a 'carrier') to pay a penalty if the carrier brings a passenger to the United Kingdom and—

(a) the carrier was required by an authority-to-carry scheme to seek authority under the scheme to carry the passenger, and

(b) the carrier did not seek authority before the journey to the United Kingdom commenced or was refused authority under the scheme.

(2) An 'authority-to-carry scheme' is a scheme operated by the Secretary of State which requires carriers to seek authority to bring passengers to the United Kingdom.

(3) An authority-to-carry scheme must specify—

(a) the class of carrier to which it applies (which may be defined by reference to a method of transport or otherwise), and

(b) the class of passenger to which it applies (which may be defined by reference to nationality, the possession of specified documents or otherwise).

(4) The Secretary of State may operate different authority-to-carry schemes for different purposes.

(5) Where the Secretary of State makes regulations under subsection (1) he must—

(a) identify in the regulations the authority-to-carry scheme to which they refer, and

(b) lay the authority-to-carry scheme before Parliament.

(6) Regulations under subsection (1) may, in particular—

(a) apply or make provision similar to a provision of sections 40 to 43 of and Schedule 1 to the Immigration and Asylum Act 1999 (c. 33) (charge for passenger without document);

(b) do anything which may be done under a provision of any of those sections;

(c) amend any of those sections.

(7) Regulations by virtue of subsection (6)(a) may, in particular—

(a) apply a provision with modification;

(b) apply a provision which confers power to make legislation.

(8) The grant or refusal of authority under an authority-to-carry scheme shall not be taken to determine whether a person is entitled or permitted to enter the United Kingdom.

(9) Regulations under this section—

(a) must be made by statutory instrument, and

(b) may not be made unless a draft has been laid before and approved by resolution of each House of Parliament.

Note: Commencement at a date to be appointed.

Evasion of procedure

125. Carriers' liability

Schedule 8 (which amends Part II of the Immigration and Asylum Act 1999 (carriers' liability) shall have effect.

Note: Commencement 14 November 2002 for the purpose of enabling subordinate legislation; 8 December 2002 for certain purposes (SI 2002/2811) and 11 May 2012 for certain other purposes (2012/1263).

Provision of information by traveller

126. Physical data: compulsory provision

(1) The Secretary of State may by regulations—

(a) require an immigration application to be accompanied by specified [biometric information] of the applicant;

(b) enable an authorised person to require an individual who makes an immigration application to provide [biometric information];

(c) enable an authorised person to require an entrant to provide [biometric information].

(2) In subsection (1) 'immigration application' means an application for—

[(za) an ETA (within the meaning of section 11C of the Immigration Act 1971 (electronic travel authorisations))],

(a) entry clearance,

(b) leave to enter or remain in the United Kingdom,. . .

(c) variation of leave to enter or remain in the United Kingdom[[or]]

[(d) a transit visa (within the meaning of section 41 of the Immigration and Asylum Act 1999), [[]

(e).]]

(3) Regulations under subsection (1) may not—

(a) impose a requirement in respect of a person to whom section 141 of the Immigration and Asylum Act 1999 (c. 33) (fingerprinting) applies, during the relevant period within the meaning of that section, or

(b) enable a requirement to be imposed in respect of a person to whom that section applies, during the relevant period within the meaning of that section.

(4) Regulations under subsection (1) may, in particular—

(a) require, or enable an authorised person to require, the provision of [biometric] information in a specified form;

(b) require an individual to submit, or enable an authorised person to require an individual to submit, to a specified process by means of which [biometric] information is obtained or recorded;

(c) make provision about the effect of failure to provide [biometric] information or to submit to a process (which may, in particular, include provision for an application to be disregarded or dismissed if a requirement is not satisfied);

(d) confer a function (which may include the exercise of a discretion) on an authorised person;

(e) require an authorised person to have regard to a code (with or without modification);

(f) require an authorised person to have regard to such provisions of a code (with or without modification) as may be specified by direction of the Secretary of State;

[(fa) provide for biometric information to be recorded on any document issued as a result of the application in relation to which the information was provided;]

(g) . . .

(h) make provision which applies generally or only in specified cases or circumstances;

(i) make different provision for different cases or circumstances.

(5) . . .

(6) In so far as regulations under subsection (1) require an individual under the age of 16 to submit to a process, the regulations must make provision similar to section 141(3) to (5) and (13) of the Immigration and Asylum Act 1999 (fingerprints: children).

(7) In so far as regulations under subsection (1) enable an authorised person to require an individual under the age of 16 to submit to a process, the regulations must make provision similar to section 141(3) to (5), (12) and (13) of that Act (fingerprints: children).

(8) Regulations under subsection (1)—

(a) must be made by statutory instrument, and

(b) shall not be made unless a draft of the regulations has been laid before and approved by resolution of each House of Parliament.

[(8A) Section 8 of the UK Borders Act 2007 (power to make regulations about use and retention of biometric information) applies to biometric information provided in accordance with regulations under subsection (1) as it applies to biometric information provided in accordance with regulations under section 5(1) of that Act.]

(9) In this section—

'authorised person' has the meaning given by section 141(5) of the Immigration and Asylum Act 1999 (authority to take fingerprints),

['biometric information' has the meaning given by section 15 of the UK Borders Act 2007,]

'code' has the meaning given by section 145(6) of that Act (code of practice),

['document' includes a card or sticker and any other method of recording information (whether in writing or by the use of electronic or other technology or by a combination of methods),]

'entrant' has the meaning given by section 33(1) of the Immigration Act 1971 (c. 77) (interpretation),

'entry clearance' has the meaning given by section 33(1) of that Act.

Note: Commencement from 1 April 2003 (SI 2003/754). Subsections (2)(d)–(e), (4)(fa) and definition of 'document' inserted by s 8 Immigration Act 2014, subsection (8A) inserted by s 14 of that Act and words in other square brackets substituted or inserted by Sch 2 of that Act from 28 July 2014 (SI 2014/1820). Subsections (4)(g) and (5) omitted by Sch 9 Immigration Act 2014 from March 1 2015.. Words in square brackets at subsection (2)(e) and inserted at subsection (2A) by Immigration, Nationality and Asylum (EU Exit) Regulations 2019/745 Pt.2(1)reg12(3) (December 31.2020: substitution in and insertion has effect subject to saving and transitional provisions specified in SI 2019/745 Sch.2 Pt.2 para 4). Words in double square brackets inserted at subsection (2)(c) and omitted at (2)(e) by Immigration and Social Security Co-Ordination (EU Withdrawal) Act 2020 (Consequential, Savings, Transitional and Transitory Provisions) (EU Exit) Regulations 2020/1309 (December 31, 2020: repeal has effect subject to saving specified in SI 2020/1309 reg.13(5)). Words inserted in double square brackets at subsection (2)(za) by Nationality and Borders Act 2022 c.36 s75(6) (June 28,2022)

127. Physical data: voluntary provision

(1) The Secretary of State may operate a scheme under which an individual may supply, or submit to the obtaining or recording of, [biometric information] to be used (wholly or partly) in connection with entry to the United Kingdom.

(2) In particular, the Secretary of State may—

(a) require an authorised person to use [biometric] information supplied under a scheme;

(b) make provision about the collection, use and retention of [biometric] information supplied under a scheme (which may include provision requiring an authorised person to have regard to a code);

(c) charge for participation in a scheme.

(3) In this section the following expressions have the same meaning as in section 126—

(a) 'authorised person',

[(aa) 'biometric information' and]

(b) 'code',

(c) . . .

Note: Commencement from 10 December 2004 (SI 2004/2998). Amended by Sch 2 Immigration Act 2014 from 28 July 2014 (SI 2014/1820).

128. Data collection under Immigration and Asylum Act 1999

Note: Amends Immigration and Asylum Act 1999, ss 144, 145.

Disclosure of information by public authority

129. Local authority

(1) The Secretary of State may require a local authority to supply information for the purpose of establishing where a person is if the Secretary of State reasonably suspects that—

(a) the person has committed an offence under section [24(A1), (B1), (C1), (D1), (E1) or (1)(b)(c)or (f), 24A(1) or 26(1)(c) or (d) of the Immigration Act 1971 (c. 77) (illegal entry, deception, &c.), and

(b) the person is or has been resident in the local authority's area.

(2) A local authority shall comply with a requirement under this section.

(3) In the application of this section to England and Wales 'local authority' means—

(a) a county council,

(b) a county borough council,

(c) a district council,

(d) a London borough council,

(e) the Common Council of the City of London, and

(f) the Council of the Isles of Scilly.

(4) In the application of this section to Scotland 'local authority' means a council constituted under section 2 of the Local Government etc. (Scotland) Act 1994 (c. 39).

(5) In the application of this section to Northern Ireland—

(a) a reference to a local authority shall be taken as a reference to the Northern Ireland Housing Executive, and

(b) the reference to a local authority's area shall be taken as a reference to Northern Ireland.

Note: Commencement from 30 July 2003 (SI 2003/1747). Words substituted in square brackets by Nationality and Borders Act 2022 c.36 Pt3 s.40(8)(a) (June 28, 2022: substitution has effect as SI 2022/590 reg.2 and Sch.1 para.20 subject to transitional and saving provisions specified in SI 2022/590 reg.3 and Sch.2 para.7)

130. . . .

Note: Section 130 deleted by UK Borders Act 2007, ss 40(6)(b), 58 and Schedule from 31 January 2008 (SI 2008/99).

131. Police, &c.

Information may be supplied under section 20 of the Immigration and Asylum Act 1999 (c. 33) (supply of information to Secretary of State) for use for the purpose of—

[(a) determining whether an applicant for naturalisation under the British Nationality Act 1981 is of good character;

[(b) determining whether, for the purposes of an application referred to in section 41A of the British Nationality Act 1981, the person for whose registration the application is made is of good character;

(ba) determining whether, for the purposes of an application under section 1 of the Hong Kong (War Wives and Widows) Act 1996, the woman for whose registration the application is made is of good character;

(bb) determining whether, for the purposes of an application under section 1 of the British Nationality (Hong Kong) Act 1997 for the registration of an adult or young person within the meaning of subsection (5A) of that section, the person is of good character;]

(c) determining whether to make an order in respect of a person under section 40 of the British Nationality Act 1981.]

Note: Commencement 10 February 2003 (SI 2001/1). Words in square brackets substituted by UK Borders Act 2007, s 43 from 31 January 2008 (SI 2008/99). Subsections (b)–(bb) substituted by s 47 Borders, Citizenship and Immigration Act 2009 from 13 January 2010 (SI 2009/2731).

132. Supply of document, &c. to Secretary of State

. . .

Note: Amends Immigration and Asylum Act 1999, s 20.

133. Medical inspectors

(1) This section applies to a person if an immigration officer acting under Schedule 2 to the Immigration Act 1971 (c. 77) (control on entry, &c.) has brought the person to the attention of—

(a) a medical inspector appointed under paragraph 1(2) of that Schedule, or

(b) a person working under the direction of a medical inspector appointed under that paragraph.

(2) A medical inspector may disclose to a health service body—

(a) the name of a person to whom this section applies,

(b) his place of residence in the United Kingdom,

(c) his age,

(d) the language which he speaks,

(e) the nature of any disease with which the inspector thinks the person may be infected,

(f) relevant details of the person's medical history,

(g) the grounds for an opinion mentioned in paragraph (e) (including the result of any test or examination which has been carried out), and

(h) the inspector's opinion about action which the health service body should take.

(3) A disclosure may be made under subsection (2) only if the medical inspector thinks it necessary for the purpose of—

(a) preventative medicine,

(b) medical diagnosis,

(c) the provision of care or treatment, or

(d) the management of health care services.

(4) For the purposes of this section 'health service body' in relation to a person means a body which carries out functions in an area which includes his place of residence and which is—

(a) in relation to England—

[(ai) the Secretary of State,]

(i) . . .

[(ia) the National Health Service Commissioning Board,

(ib) a clinical commissioning group established under section 14D of the National Health Service Act 2006,

(ic) a local authority in relation to the exercise of functions under section 2B or 111 of, or any of paragraphs 1 to 7B or 13 of Schedule 1 to, the National Health Service Act 2006,]

(ii) a National Health Service Trust established under [. . . section 18 of the National Health Service (Wales) Act 2006], {(iia) an NHS foundation trust,}

(iii) . . . [or]

(iv) a Special Health Authority established under [section 28 of that Act or section 22 of the National Health Service (Wales) Act 2006], or

(v) . . .

(vi) . . .

(b) in relation to Wales—

[(i) a Local Health Board established under section 11 of the National Health Service (Wales) Act 2006], [or]

(ii) a National Health Service Trust established under [section 18 of the National Health Service (Wales) Act 2006], or

(iii) . . .

(iv) . . .

(c) in relation to Scotland—

[(ai) the Secretary of State,]

(i) a Health Board, Special Health Board or National Health Service Trust established under section 2 or 12A of the National Health Service (Scotland) Act 1978 (c. 29), . . .

(ii) the Common Services Agency for the Scottish Health Service established under section 10 of that Act, or

[(iia) Healthcare Improvement Scotland established under section 10A of the 1978 Act, or]

[(iii) . . .

(d) in relation to Northern Ireland—

(i) a Health and Social Services Board established under the Health and Personal Social Services (Northern Ireland) Order 1972 (S.I. 1972/1265 (N.I. 14)),

(ii) a Health and Social Services Trust established under the Health and Personal Social Services (Northern Ireland) Order 1991 (S.I. 1991/194 (N.I. 1)),

[(iia) the Regional Agency for Public Health and Social Well-being established under section 12 of the Health and Social Care (Reform) Act (Northern Ireland) 2009, or].

(iii) the Department of Health, Social Services and Public Safety,

(iv) . . .

Note: Commencement 10 February 2003 (SI 2003/1). Words in square brackets inserted and words omitted by Sch 3 Health Protection Agency Act 2004 from 1 April 2005 (SI 2005/121). Words in square brackets in subsections (4)(a)(i)–(iv) and (4)(b)(i) and (ii) substituted by National Health Service (Consequential Provisions) Act Sch 1, paragraph 228 from 1 March 2007. Subsection (4)(a)(iia) inserted by Sch 4 Health and Social Care (Community Health and Standards) Act 2003 from 1 April 2004 (SI 2004/759). Subsection (4)(c)(iia) inserted from 28 October 2011 (SI 2011/2581). Words omitted from subsections (4)(a)(ii) and 4(b)(ii) by Sch 14 Health and Social Care Act 2012 from a date to be appointed. Further amendments to subsection (4) by Schs 5, 7 Health and Social Care Act 2012 from 1 April 2013 (SI 2013/160).

Disclosure of information by private person

134. Employer

(1) The Secretary of State may require an employer to supply information about an employee whom the Secretary of State reasonably suspects of having committed an offence under—

(a) section 24(1)(a), (b), (c), (e) or (f), 24A(1) or 26(1)(c) or (d) of the Immigration Act 1971 (c. 77) (illegal entry, deception, &c.),

(b) section 105(1)(a), (b) or (c) of the Immigration and Asylum Act 1999 (c. 33) (support for asylum-seeker: fraud), or

(c) section 106(1)(a), (b) or (c) of that Act (support for asylum-seeker: fraud).

(2) The power under subsection (1) may be exercised to require information about an employee only if the information—

(a) is required for the purpose of establishing where the employee is, or

(b) relates to the employee's earnings or to the history of his employment.

(3) In this section a reference to an employer or employee—

(a) includes a reference to a former employer or employee, and

(b) shall be construed in accordance with section 8(8) of the Asylum and Immigration Act 1996 (c. 49) (restrictions on employment).

(4) Where—

(a) a business (the 'employment agency') arranges for one person (the 'worker') to provide services to another (the 'client'), and

(b) the worker is not employed by the employment agency or the client, this section shall apply as if the employment agency were the worker's employer while he provides services to the client.

Note: Commencement from 30 July 2003 (SI 2003/1747).

135. Financial institution

(1) The Secretary of State may require a financial institution to supply information about a person if the Secretary of State reasonably suspects that—

(a) the person has committed an offence under section 105(1)(a), (b) or (c) or 106(1)(a), (b) or (c) of the Immigration and Asylum Act 1999 (c. 33) (support for asylum-seeker: fraud),

(b) the information is relevant to the offence, and

(c) the institution has the information.

(2) In this section 'financial institution' means—

(a) a person who has permission under [Part 4A] of the Financial Services and Markets Act 2000 (c. 8) to accept deposits, and

(b) a building society (within the meaning given by the Building Societies Act 1986 (c. 53)).

Note: Commencement from 30 July 2003 (SI 2003/1747). Words in square brackets in subsection (2)(a) substituted by Sch 18 Financial Services Act 2012 from 1 April 2013 (SI 2013/423).

136. Notice

(1) A requirement to provide information under section 134 or 135 must be imposed by notice in writing specifying—

(a) the information,

(b) the manner in which it is to be provided, and

(c) the period of time within which it is to be provided.

(2) A period of time specified in a notice under subsection (1) (c)—

(a) must begin with the date of receipt of the notice, and

(b) must not be less than ten working days.

(3) A person on whom a notice is served under subsection (1) must provide the Secretary of State with the information specified in the notice.

(4) Information provided under subsection (3) must be provided—

(a) in the manner specified under subsection (1) (b), and

(b) within the time specified under subsection (1) (c).

(5) In this section 'working day' means a day which is not—

(a) Saturday,

(b) Sunday,

(c) Christmas Day,

(d) Good Friday, or

(e) a day which is a bank holiday under the Banking and Financial Dealings Act 1971 (c. 80) in any part of the United Kingdom.

Note: Commencement from 30 July 2003 (SI 2003/1747).

137. Disclosure of information: offences

(1) A person commits an offence if without reasonable excuse he fails to comply with section 136(3).

(2) A person who is guilty of an offence under subsection (1) shall be liable on summary conviction to—

(a) imprisonment for a term not exceeding 51 weeks,

(b) a fine not exceeding level 5 on the standard scale, or

(c) both.

Note: Commencement from 30 July 2003 (SI 2003/1747).

138. Offence by body

(1) Subsection (2) applies where an offence under section 137 is committed by a body corporate and it is proved that the offence—

(a) was committed with the consent or connivance of an officer of the body, or

(b) was attributable to neglect on the part of an officer of the body.

(2) The officer, as well as the body, shall be guilty of the offence.

(3) In this section a reference to an officer of a body corporate includes a reference to—

(a) a director, manager or secretary,

(b) a person purporting to act as a director, manager or secretary, and

(c) if the affairs of the body are managed by its members, a member.

(4) Where an offence under section 137 is committed by a partnership (other than a limited partnership), each partner shall be guilty of the offence.

(5) Subsection (1) shall have effect in relation to a limited partnership as if—

(a) a reference to a body corporate were a reference to a limited partnership, and

(b) a reference to an officer of the body were a reference to a partner.

Note: Commencement from 30 July 2003 (SI 2003/1747).

139. Privilege against self-incrimination

(1) Information provided by a person pursuant to a requirement under section 134 or 135 shall not be admissible in evidence in criminal proceedings against that person.

(2) This section shall not apply to proceedings for an offence under section 137.

Note: Commencement from 30 July 2003 (SI 2003/1747).

Immigration services

140. Immigration Services Commissioner

. . .

Note: Amends Immigration and Asylum Act 1999 s 87(3), Sch 5, paragraph 7 and Sch 6, paragraph 3.

Immigration control

141. EEA ports: juxtaposed controls

(1) The Secretary of State may by order make provision for the purpose of giving effect to an international agreement which concerns immigration control [at a United Kingdom port or] at an EEA port (whether or not it also concerns other aspects of frontier control at the port).

(2) An order under this section may make any provision which appears to the Secretary of State—

(a) likely to facilitate implementation of the international agreement (including those aspects of the agreement which relate to frontier control other than immigration control), or

(b) appropriate as a consequence of provision made for the purpose of facilitating implementation of the agreement.

(3) In particular, an order under this section may—

(a) provide for a law of England and Wales to have effect, with or without modification, in relation to a person in a specified area or anything done in a specified area;

(b) provide for a law of England and Wales not to have effect in relation to a person in a specified area or anything done in a specified area;

(c) provide for a law of England and Wales to be modified in its effect in relation to a person in a specified area or anything done in a specified area;

(d) disapply or modify an enactment in relation to a person who has undergone a process in a specified area;

(e) disapply or modify an enactment otherwise than under paragraph (b), (c) or (d);

(f) make provision conferring a function (which may include—

(i) provision conferring a discretionary function;

(ii) provision conferring a function on a servant or agent of the government of a State other than the United Kingdom);

(g) create or extend the application of an offence;

(h) impose or permit the imposition of a penalty;

(i) require the payment of, or enable a person to require the payment of, a charge or fee;

(j) make provision about enforcement (which may include—

(i) provision conferring a power of arrest, detention or removal from or to any place;

(ii) provision for the purpose of enforcing the law of a State other than the United Kingdom);

(k) confer jurisdiction on a court or tribunal;

(l) confer immunity or provide for indemnity;

(m) make provision about compensation;

(n) impose a requirement, or enable a requirement to be imposed, for a person to cooperate with or to provide facilities for the use of another person who is performing a function under the order or under the international agreement (which may include a requirement to provide facilities without charge);

(o) make provision about the disclosure of information.

(4) An order under this section may—

(a) make provision which applies generally or only in specified circumstances;

(b) make different provision for different circumstances;

(c) amend an enactment.

(5) An order under this section—

(a) must be made by statutory instrument,

(b) may not be made unless the Secretary of State has consulted with such persons as appear to him to be appropriate, and

(c) may not be made unless a draft has been laid before and approved by resolution of each House of Parliament.

(6) In this section—

'EEA port' means a port in an EEA State from which passengers are commonly carried by sea to []the United Kingdom,

'EEA State' means a State which is a contracting party to the Agreement on the European Economic Area signed at Oporto on 2 May 1992 (as it has effect from time to time),

'frontier control' means the enforcement of law which relates to, or in so far as it relates to, the movement of persons or goods into or out of the United Kingdom or another State,

'immigration control' means arrangements made in connection with the movement of persons into or out of the United Kingdom or another State,

'international agreement' means an agreement made between Her Majesty's Government and the government of another State, and

'specified area' means an area (whether of the United Kingdom or of another State) specified in an international agreement.

[United Kingdom port' means a port in the United Kingdom from which passengers are commonly carried by sea to an EEA State.]

Note: Commenced 8 January 2003 (SI 2002/2811). Words in square brackets inserted at subsection (1) and omitted at subsection (6) by Immigration, Nationality and Asylum (EU Exit) Regulations 2019/745 Pt.2(1) reg 12(4) (December 31 2020:shall come into force on IP completion day not exit day as specified in 2020 c.1 s39(1) and Sch.5 para 1(1)). Definition in [..] inserted by Immigration, Nationality and Asylum (EU Exit) Regulations 2019/745 Pt2(1) reg.12(4)(b)(ii) (December 31, 2020: shall come into force on IP completion day not exit day as specified in 2020 c.1s.39(1) and Sch.5 para.1(1)).

Country information

142. . . .

Note: Section 142 deleted by UK Borders Act 2007, s 54 from 1 April 2008 (SI 2008/309).

PART VII

OFFENCES

Substance

143. Assisting unlawful immigration, &c.

. . .

Note: Amends Immigration Act 1971, s 25.

144. Section 143: consequential amendments

. . .

Note: Amends Immigration Act 1971, ss 25A, 28A, 28B, 28C, 28D, 28F and 33.

145. . . .

Note: Commenced 10 February 2003 (SI 2003/1). Repealed by Sch 6 Sexual Offences Act 2003 from 1 May 2004 (SI 2004/874).

146. . . .

Note: Subsection (4) amends paragraph 2, Sch 4 Criminal Justice and Court Services Act 2000. Commenced 10 February 2003 (SI 2003/1). Repealed by Sexual Offences Act 2003, Sch 6 from 1 May 2004 (SI 2004/874).

147. Employment

. . .

Note: Amends Asylum and Immigration Act 1996, s 8.

148. Registration card

. . .

Note: Amends Immigration Act 1971, s 26.

149. Immigration stamp

. . .

Note: Inserts s 26B into the Immigration Act 1971.

150. Sections 148 and 149: consequential amendments

. . .

Note: Amends Immigration Act 1971, ss 28A, 28B and 28D.

151. False information

. . .

Note: Amends Immigration Act 1971, s 26(3).

Procedure

152. Arrest by immigration officer

. . .

Note: Inserts s 28AA into the Immigration Act 1971.

153. Power of entry

. . .

Note: Inserts s 28CA into the Immigration Act 1971; amends Immigration and Asylum Act 1999, s 146.

154. Power to search for evidence

. . .

Note: Inserts ss 28FA, 28FB into the Immigration Act 1971.

155. Sections 153 and 154: supplemental

. . .

Note: Amends Immigration Act 1971, s 28L.

156. Time limit on prosecution

. . .

Note: Amends Immigration Act 1971, ss 24A, 28(1).

Part VIII
General

157. Consequential and incidental provision

(1) The Secretary of State may by order make consequential or incidental provision in connection with a provision of this Act.

(2) An order under this section may, in particular—
(a) amend an enactment;
(b) modify the effect of an enactment.

(3) An order under this section must be made by statutory instrument.

(4) An order under this section which amends an enactment shall not be made unless a draft has been laid before and approved by resolution of each House of Parliament.

(5) Any other order under this section shall be subject to annulment pursuant to a resolution of either House of Parliament.

Note: Commenced 7 November 2002, s 162.

158. Interpretation: 'the Immigration Acts'

Note: Ceased to have effect by Immigration, Asylum and Nationality Act 2006, s 64 from 30 March 2006 (Royal Assent).

159. Applied provision

(1) Subsection (2) applies where this Act amends or refers to a provision which is applied by, under or for purposes of—
(a) another provision of the Act which contains the provision, or
(b) another Act.

(2) The amendment or reference shall have effect in relation to the provision as applied.

(3) Where this Act applies a provision of another Act, a reference to that provision in any enactment includes a reference to the provision as applied by this Act.

Note: Commenced 10 February 2003 (SI 2003/1).

160. Money

(1) Expenditure of the Secretary of State or the Lord Chancellor in connection with a provision of this Act shall be paid out of money provided by Parliament.

(2) An increase attributable to this Act in the amount payable out of money provided by Parliament under another enactment shall be paid out of money provided by Parliament.

(3) A sum received by the Secretary of State or the Lord Chancellor in connection with a provision of this Act shall be paid into the Consolidated Fund.

Note: Commenced 7 November 2002, s 162.

161. Repeals

The provisions listed in Schedule 9 are hereby repealed to the extent specified.

Note: Commenced 8 December 2002 (SI 2002/2811) and 10 February 2003 (SI 2003/1).

162. Commencement

(1) Subject to subsections (2) to (5), the preceding provisions of this Act shall come into force in accordance with provision made by the Secretary of State by order.

(2) The following provisions shall come into force on the passing of this Act—

(a) section 6,
(b) section 7,
(c) section 10(1) to (4) and (6),
(d) section 11,
(e) section 15 (and Schedule 2),
(f) section 16,
(g) section 35(1)(h),
(h) section 38,
(i) section 40(1),
(j) section 41(1),
(k) section 42,
(l) section 43,
(m) section 48,
(n) section 49,
(o) section 50,
(p) section 56,
(q) section 58,
(r) section 59,
(s) section 61,
(t) section 67,
(u) section 69,
(v) section 70,
(w) section 115 and paragraph 29 of Schedule 7 (and the relevant entry in Schedule 9),
(x) section 157, and
(y) section 160.

(3) Section 5 shall have effect in relation to—

(a) an application made after the passing of this Act, and
(b) an application made, but not determined, before the passing of this Act.

(4) Section 8 shall have effect in relation to—

(a) an application made on or after a date appointed by the Secretary of State by order, and
(b) an application made, but not determined, before that date.

(5) Section 9 shall have effect in relation to a child born on or after a date appointed by the Secretary of State by order.

(6) An order under subsection (1) may—

(a) make provision generally or for a specified purpose only (which may include the purpose of the application of a provision to or in relation to a particular place or area);
(b) make different provision for different purposes;
(c) include transitional provision;
(d) include savings;
(e) include consequential provision;
(f) include incidental provision.

(7) An order under this section must be made by statutory instrument.

Note: Commenced 7 November 2002 (Royal Assent). The date appointed for the purpose of subsection (5) is 1 July 2006 (SI 2006/1498).

163. Extent

(1) A provision of this Act which amends or repeals a provision of another Act or inserts a provision into another Act has the same extent as the provision amended or repealed or as the Act into which the insertion is made (ignoring, in any case, extent by virtue of an Order in Council).

(2) Sections 145 and 146 extend only to—

(a) England and Wales, and

(b) Northern Ireland.

(3) A provision of this Act to which neither subsection (1) nor subsection (2) applies extends to—

(a) England and Wales,

(b) Scotland, and

(c) Northern Ireland.

(4) Her Majesty may by Order in Council direct that a provision of this Act is to extend, with or without modification or adaptation, to—

(a) any of the Channel Islands;

(b) the Isle of Man.

(5) Subsection (4) does not apply in relation to the extension to a place of a provision which extends there by virtue of subsection (1).

164. Short title

This Act may be cited as the Nationality, Immigration and Asylum Act 2002.

SCHEDULES

SCHEDULE 1 — Section 3

CITIZENSHIP CEREMONY, OATH AND PLEDGE

1.—7. . . .

8. The Secretary of State may make a payment to a local authority in respect of anything done by the authority in accordance with regulations made by virtue of section 41(3A) of the British Nationality Act 1981 (c. 61).

9.—(1) A local authority must—

(a) comply with a requirement imposed on it by regulations made by virtue of that section, and

(b) carry out a function imposed on it by regulations made by virtue of that section.

(2) A local authority on which a requirement or function is imposed by regulations made by virtue of that section—

(a) may provide facilities or make arrangements in addition to those which it is required to provide or make, and

(b) may make a charge for the provision of facilities or the making of arrangements under paragraph (a) which does not exceed the cost of providing the facilities or making the arrangements.

Note: Paragraphs 1–7 amend the British Nationality Act 1981. Commencement 1 January 2004 (SI 2003/3156).

SCHEDULE 2 — Section 15

NATIONALITY: REPEAL OF SPENT PROVISIONS

1. . . .

2 Nothing in this Schedule has any effect in relation to a registration made under a provision before its repeal.

Note: Paragraph 1 repeals parts of British Nationality Act 1981. Commencement from 1 January 2004 (SI 2003/3156).

SCHEDULE 3 — Section 54

WITHHOLDING AND WITHDRAWAL OF SUPPORT

Ineligibility for support

1.—(1) A person to whom this paragraph applies shall not be eligible for support or assistance under—

(a) section 21 or 29 of the National Assistance Act 1948 (c. 29) (local authority: accommodation and welfare),

(b) section 45 of the Health Services and Public Health Act 1968 (c. 46) (local authority: welfare of elderly),

(c) section 12 or 13A of the Social Work (Scotland) Act 1968 (c. 49) (social welfare services),

(d) Article 7 or 15 of the Health and Personal Social Services (Northern Ireland) Order 1972 (S.I. 1972/1265 (N.I. 14)) (prevention of illness, social welfare, &c.),

[(e) section 254 of, and Schedule 20 to, the National Health Service Act 2006, or section 192 of, and Schedule 15 to, the National Health Service (Wales) Act 2006 (social services),]

(f) section 29(1)(b) of the Housing (Scotland) Act 1987 (c. 26) (interim duty to accommodate in case of apparent priority need where review of a local authority decision has been requested),

(g) section 17, 23C, [[23CZB]], [23CA,] 24A or 24B of the Children Act 1989 (c. 41) (welfare and other powers which can be exercised in relation to adults), [(ga) in relation only to a person in England to whom this paragraph applies by virtue of paragraph 4, 5 or 7B—

(i) section 23CZA of that Act (arrangements for certain former relevant children to continue to live with former foster parents), or

(ii) regulations under section 23D of that Act (personal advisers)].

(h) Article 18, 35 or [35A or 35B] of the Children (Northern Ireland) Order 1995 (SI 1995/755 (N.I. 2)) (welfare and other powers which can be exercised in relation to adults),

(i) sections 22, 29 and 30 of the Children (Scotland) Act 1995 (c. 36) (provisions analogous to those mentioned in paragraph (g)),

(j) section 188(3) or 204(4) of the Housing Act 1996 (c. 52) (accommodation pending review or appeal),

(k) section 2 of the Local Government Act 2000 (c. 22) (promotion of well-being),

[(ka) section 1 of the Localism Act 2011 (local authority's general power of competence),]

(l) a provision of the Immigration and Asylum Act 1999 (c. 33), or

(m) a provision of this Act.

(2) The duty in section 23C(4)(b) or 23CA(4) of that Act and the power in section 24B(2)(b) of that Act may not be exercised or performed in respect of a person to whom this paragraph applies so as to make a grant to enable the person to meet all or part of the person's tuition fees.

[(2A) In the case of the provisions referred to in subparagraph (1)(ga), subparagraph (2) applies only in relation to a person in England to whom this paragraph applies by virtue of paragraph 4, 5 or 7B.]

Note: words inserted in square brackets and subparagraph 1(ga) and 1(2A) by Schedule 12 to the Immigration Act 2016 from a date to be appointed. Words in double square brackets at para 1(1)(g) inserted by Children and Social Work Act 2017, Sch.2 para.5 by SI2018/346 reg 4 (a) on 1 April 2018.

1A (1) A person to whom this paragraph applies is not eligible for assistance under section 23C(4)(b), 23CA(4) or 24B(2)(b) of the Children Act 1989 (grants to meet expenses connected with education or training) which consists of a grant to enable the person to meet all or part of the person's tuition fees.

(2) The duty in section 23C(4)(b) or 23CA(4) of that Act and the power in section 24B(2)(b) of that Act may not be exercised or performed in respect of a person to whom this paragraph applies so as to make a grant to enable the person to meet all or part of the person's tuition fees.

(3) This paragraph applies to a person in England who is aged 18 or over and who—

(a) has leave to enter or remain in the United Kingdom which has been granted for a limited period,

(b) is an asylum-seeker, or

(c) has made an application for leave to enter or remain in the United Kingdom which has not been withdrawn or determined.

(4) In this paragraph 'tuition fees' means fees payable for a course of a description mentioned in Schedule 6 to the Education Reform Act 1988.]

Note: paragraph 1A inserted by Schedule 12 to the Immigration Act 2016 from a date to be appointed,

(2) A power or duty under a provision referred to in subparagraph (1) may not be exercised or performed in respect of a person to whom this paragraph applies (whether or not the person has previously been in receipt of support or assistance under the provision).

(3) An approval or directions given under or in relation to a provision referred to in subparagraph (1) shall be taken to be subject to subparagraph (2).

Exceptions

2.—(1) Paragraph 1 does not prevent the provision of support or assistance—

(a) to a British citizen, or

(b) to a child, or

(c) under or by virtue of regulations made under paragraph 8, 9 [10, 10A, or 10B] below, or

(ca) under section 95A or 98A of the Immigration and Asylum Act 1999 (support for failed asylum-seekers etc), or.

(d) in a case in respect of which, and to the extent to which, regulations made by the Secretary of State disapply paragraph 1, or

(e) in circumstances in respect of which, and to the extent to which, regulations made by the Secretary of State disapply paragraph 1.

(2) Regulations under subparagraph (1)(d) may confer a discretion on the Secretary of State.

(3) Regulations under subparagraph (1)(e) may, in particular, disapply paragraph 1 to the provision of support or assistance by a local authority to a person where the authority—

(a) has taken steps in accordance with guidance issued by the Secretary of State to determine whether paragraph 1 would (but for the regulations) apply to the person, and

(b) has concluded on the basis of those steps that there is no reason to believe that paragraph 1 would apply.

(4) Regulations under subparagraph (1)(d) or (e) may confer a discretion on an authority.

(5) A local authority which is considering whether to give support or assistance to a person under a provision listed in paragraph 1(1) shall act in accordance with any relevant guidance issued by the Secretary of State under subparagraph (3)(a).

(6) A reference in this Schedule to a person to whom paragraph 1 applies includes a reference to a person in respect of whom that paragraph is disapplied to a limited extent by regulations under subparagraph (1)(d) or (e), except in a case for which the regulations provide otherwise.

Note: words in square brackets and subparagraph 1(ca) inserted by Schedule 12 of the Immigration Act 2016 from a date to be appointed.

[**2A** (1) Paragraph 1(1)(g) or (ga) does not prevent the provision of support or assistance under a relevant provision to a person to whom paragraph 1 would otherwise apply by virtue of paragraph 7B if—

(a) conditions A and B are satisfied in relation to that person, and

(b) condition C, D or E is satisfied in relation to that person.

(2) In subparagraph (1) 'relevant provision' means—
(a) section 23C, 23CZA or 23CA of the Children Act 1989,
(b) regulations under section 23D of that Act, or
(c) section 24A or 24B of that Act.
(3) Condition A is that—
(a) the person has made an application for leave to enter or remain in the United Kingdom, and
(b) where regulations made by the Secretary of State require that the application must be of a kind specified in the regulations for this condition to be satisfied, the application is of that kind.
(4) Condition B is that—
(a) the application is the first application for leave to enter or remain in the United Kingdom that the person has made, or
(b) where regulations under subparagraph (3) (b) require that the application must be of a kind specified in the regulations for condition A to be satisfied, the application is the first application of that kind that the person has made.
(5) Condition C is that the application has not been determined or withdrawn.
(6) Condition D is that—
(a) the application has been refused,
(b) the person could bring an appeal under section 82(1) against the refusal (ignoring any possibility of an appeal out of time with permission), and
(c) if the person brought such an appeal, it would not be one that, by virtue of section 92(6), would have to be continued from outside the United Kingdom.
(7) Condition E is that—
(a) the application has been refused,
(b) the person has appealed under section 82(1) against the refusal,
(c) the appeal is not one that, by virtue of section 92(6), must be continued from outside the United Kingdom, and
(d) the appeal is pending within the meaning of section 104.
(8) For the purposes of subparagraph (3) the Secretary of State may by regulations provide for circumstances in which—
(a) a person is to be treated as having made an application for leave to enter or remain in the United Kingdom (despite not having made one), or
(b) a person is to be treated as not having made such an application where the Secretary of State is satisfied that the application made is vexatious or wholly without merit.]

Note: Paragraph 2A inserted by Schedule 12 to the Immigration Act 2016 from a date to be appointed.

3. Paragraph 1 does not prevent the exercise of a power or the performance of a duty if, and to the extent that, its exercise or performance is necessary for the purpose of avoiding a breach of—

(a) a person's Convention rights, [
(b)]

Note: Words in square brackets omitted by Immigration and Social Security Co-ordination (EU Withdrawal) Act 2020 (Consequential, Savings, Transitional and Transitory Provisions) (EU Exit) Regulations 2020/1309 Pt 2(1), reg.13(4) (a) (December 31, 2020: repeal has effect subject to saving specified in SI 2020/1309 reg.13(5))

3A Notwithstanding paragraph 3, paragraph 1(1)(g) prevents a local authority in England from providing support or assistance under section 17 of the Children Act 1989 to a person in respect of a child if—

(c) the support or assistance is of a type that could be provided to the person by virtue of paragraph 10A (see paragraph 10A(11)), and

(d) support is being provided to the person by virtue of paragraph 10A or there are reasonable grounds for believing that support will be provided to the person by virtue of that paragraph.

3B Notwithstanding paragraph 3, paragraph 1(1)(g) prevents a local authority in England from providing support or assistance under section 23C, 23CA, 24A or 24B of the Children Act 1989 to a person if—

(a) support is being provided to the person by virtue of paragraph 10B or section 95A of the Immigration and Asylum Act 1999, or

(b) there are reasonable grounds for believing that support will be provided to the person by virtue of that paragraph or section.

3C Notwithstanding paragraph 3, paragraph 1(1)(ga) prevents a local authority in England from providing support or assistance under a provision mentioned in paragraph (ga) to a person if—

(a) support is being provided to the person by virtue of paragraph 10B or section 95A of the Immigration and Asylum Act 1999, or

(b) there are reasonable grounds for believing that support will be provided to the person by virtue of that paragraph or section.]

Note: Paragraph 3A inserted by Schedule 12 to the Immigration Act 2016 from a date to be appointed.

First class of ineligible person: refugee status abroad

4.—(1) Paragraph 1 applies to a person if he—

(a) has refugee status abroad, or

(b) is the dependant of a person who is in the United Kingdom and who has refugee status abroad.

(2) For the purposes of this paragraph a person has refugee status abroad if—

(a) he does not have the nationality of an EEA State [and is not a British citizen], and

(b) the government of an EEA State [] has determined that he is entitled to protection as a refugee under the Refugee Convention.

Note: Words in square brackets inserted at para (2)(a) and omitted at para (20)(b) by Immigration, Nationality and Asylum (EU Exit) Regulations 2019/745 Pt 2(1) reg.12(5)(b)(i) (December 31 2020: shall come into force on IP completion day not exit day as specified in 2020 c.1s39(1) and Sch5 para 1(1)).

5.

Note: Omitted by Immigration and Social Security Co-ordination (EU Withdrawal) Act 2020 (Consequential, Savings, Transitionary and Transitional Provisions) (EU Exit) Regulations 2020/1309 Pt.1 reg.13(4)(b) from a date to be appointed.

Third class of ineligible person: failed asylum-seeker

6.—(1) Paragraph 1 applies to a person [in Wales, Scotland or Northern Ireland] if—

(a) he was (but is no longer) an asylum-seeker, and

(b) he fails to cooperate with removal directions issued in respect of him.

(2) Paragraph 1 also applies to a dependant of a person to whom that paragraph applies by virtue of subparagraph (1).

Note: Words in square brackets inserted by paragraph 12 of the Immigration Act 2016 from a date to be appointed.

Fourth class of ineligible person: person unlawfully in United Kingdom

7. Paragraph 1 applies to a person [in Wales, Scotland or Northern Ireland] if—

(a) he is in the United Kingdom in breach of the immigration laws within the meaning of [section 50A of the British Nationality Act 1981], and

(b) he is not an asylum-seeker.

Note: Words in square brackets inserted by Schedule 12 to the Immigration Act 2016 from a date to be appointed.

Fifth class of ineligible person: person unlawfully in United Kingdom

7A [. . .]

Note: Omitted by Schedule 11 to the Immigration Act 2016 from a date to be appointed.

Sixth class of ineligible person: person in England without leave to enter or remain

7B (1) Paragraph 1 applies to a person in England if—

(a) under the Immigration Act 1971, he requires leave to enter or remain in the United Kingdom but does not have it, and

(b) he is not an asylum-seeker.

(2) Paragraph 1 also applies to a dependant of a person to whom that paragraph applies by virtue of subparagraph (1).

Note: Inserted by Schedule 12 to the Immigration Act 2016 from a date to be appointed.

[Seventh class of ineligible person: primary carer without leave to enter or remain

7C (1) Paragraph 1 applies to a person in England ('P') if—

(a) P is a primary carer of a British citizen ('the relevant British citizen'),

(b) the relevant British citizen is residing in the United Kingdom,

(c) the relevant British citizen would be unable to reside in the United Kingdom or in [an] EEA state if P were required to leave the United Kingdom,

(d) if circumstances were not as mentioned in paragraphs (a)–(c), under the Immigration Act 1971 P would require leave to enter or remain in the United Kingdom but would not have such leave, and

(e) P is not an asylum seeker.

(2) Paragraph 1 also applies to the dependent of a person to whom that paragraph applies by virtue of subparagraph (1).

(3) In making for the purposes of this Schedule or regulations made under it a determination as to whether subparagraph (1)(c) applies in relation to P, a person may rely on-

(a) a document of a kind specified in regulations made by the Secretary of State, or

(b) information or guidance provided by the Secretary of State for the purposes of such a determination.]

Note: Inserted by Schedule 12 to the Immigration Act 2016 from a date to be appointed. Note: Words in square brackets in para 7C(1)(c) omitted by Immigration, Nationality and Asylum (EU Exit) Regulations 2019/745 Pt 2(1) reg.12(5)(d) (December 31 2020, shall come into force on IP completion day not exit day as specified in 2020 c.1s.39 (1) and Sch.5 para.1(1)).

[Eighth class of ineligible person: transitional cases

7D (1) Paragraph 1 applies to a person if—

(a) the person is a transitionally-supported person (see subparagraph (3)),

(b) the Secretary of State has certified that, in the Secretary of State's opinion, the person has failed without reasonable excuse to take reasonable steps—

(i) to leave the United Kingdom voluntarily, or

(ii) to place himself in a position in which he is able to leave the United Kingdom voluntarily,

(c) the person has received a copy of the Secretary of State's certificate, and

(d) the period of 14 days, beginning with the date on which the person receives the copy of the certificate, has elapsed.

(2) Paragraph 1 also applies to a dependant of a person to whom that paragraph applies by virtue of subparagraph (1).

(3) A person is a 'transitionally-supported person' if—

(a) accommodation is provided for the person by virtue of section 4 of the Immigration and Asylum Act 1999 as that section has effect by virtue of paragraph 46 of Schedule 11 to the Immigration Act 2016, or

(b) support is provided for the person under section 95 of the Immigration and Asylum Act 1999 by virtue of section 94(5) of that Act, as that provision has effect by virtue of paragraph 47 of that Schedule.

(4) For the purpose of subparagraph (1)(d), if the Secretary of State sends a copy of a certificate by first class post to a person's last known address, the person is treated as receiving the copy on the second day after the day on which it was posted.

(5) The Secretary of State may by regulations vary the period specified in subparagraph (1)(d).]

Note: Inserted by Schedule 11 to the Immigration Act 2016 from a date to be appointed.

Travel assistance

8. The Secretary of State may make regulations providing for arrangements to be made enabling a person to whom paragraph 1 applies by virtue of paragraph 4 []to leave the United Kingdom.

Note: words in square brackets omitted by Immigration and Social Security Co-ordination (EU Withdrawal) (Consequential, Savings, Transitional and Transitory Provisions) (EU Exit) Regulations 2020/1309 Pt. 1 reg.13(4)(c) (December 31, 2020: repeal has effect subject to saving specified in SI 2020/1309 reg.13(5))

Temporary accommodation

9.—(1) The Secretary of State may make regulations providing for arrangements to be made for the accommodation of a person to whom paragraph 1 applies pending the implementation of arrangements made by virtue of paragraph 8.

(2) Arrangements for a person by virtue of this paragraph—

(a) may be made only if the person has with him a dependent child, and

(b) may include arrangements for a dependent child.

10.—(1) The Secretary of State may make regulations providing for arrangements to be made for the accommodation of a person if—

(a) paragraph 1 applies to him by virtue of paragraph 7, and

(b) he has not failed to cooperate with removal directions issued in respect of him.

(2) Arrangements for a person by virtue of this paragraph—

(a) may be made only if the person has with him a dependent child, and

(b) may include arrangements for a dependent child.

[Accommodation and subsistence etc: England

10A (1) The Secretary of State may make regulations providing for arrangements to be made for support to be provided to a person to whom paragraph 1 applies by virtue of paragraph 7B(1) or 7C(1) and—

(e) who is destitute,

(f) who has with him a dependent child,

(g) who is not a relevant failed asylum seeker, and

(h) in relation to whom condition A, B, C, D or E is satisfied.

(2) A person is a 'relevant failed asylum seeker' for the purposes of subparagraph (1)(c) if the person is a failed asylum seeker within the meaning of Part 6 of the Immigration and Asylum Act 1999 and—

(a) the person is receiving support under section 95A of that Act,

(b) the person has made an application for such support which has not been refused, or

(c) there are reasonable grounds for believing such support would be provided to the person if an application by the person for such support were made.

(3) Condition A is that—

(a) the person has made an application for leave to enter or remain in the United Kingdom and has not withdrawn the application,

(b) where regulations under this paragraph require that the application must be of a kind specified in the regulations for this condition to be satisfied, the application is of that kind, and

(c) the application has not been determined.

(4) Condition B is that—

(a) the person could bring an appeal under section 82(1) (ignoring any possibility of an appeal out of time with permission), and

(b) if the person brought such an appeal, it would not be one that, by virtue of section 92(6), would have to be continued from outside the United Kingdom.

(5) Condition C is that—

(a) the person has appealed under section 82(1),

(b) the appeal is not one that, by virtue of section 92(6), must be continued from outside the United Kingdom, and

(c) the appeal is pending within the meaning of section 104.

(6) Condition D is that—

(a) the person's appeal rights are exhausted, and

(b) he has not failed to cooperate with arrangements that would enable him to leave the United Kingdom.

(7) Condition E is that a person specified in regulations under this paragraph is satisfied that the provision of support is necessary to safeguard and promote the welfare of a dependent child.

(8) Regulations under this paragraph may specify—

(a) factors which a person specified by virtue of subparagraph (7) may or must take into account in making a determination under that subparagraph;

(b) factors which such a person must not take into account in making such a determination.

(9) The Secretary of State may make regulations providing for arrangements to be made for support to be provided to a person ('P')—

(a) to whom paragraph 1 applies by virtue of paragraph 7B(1) or 7C(1), and

(b) who it appears to a person specified in the regulations may be destitute, until a person by whom support may be provided under arrangements by virtue of subparagraph (1) is able to determine whether such support should be provided to P.

(10) Arrangements for a person by virtue of this paragraph may include arrangements for a dependant.

(11) The support that may be provided under arrangements by virtue of this paragraph may take the form of—

(a) accommodation;

(b) subsistence in kind, or cash or vouchers to pay for subsistence.

(12) Subsections (3) to (8) of section 95 of the Immigration and Asylum Act 1999 (meaning of 'destitute') apply for the purposes of this paragraph as they apply for the purposes of that section.

(13) For the purposes of subparagraph (3) regulations under this paragraph may provide for circumstances in which—

(a) a person is to be treated as having made an application for leave to enter or remain in the United Kingdom (despite not having made one);

(b) a person is to be treated as not having made such an application where the Secretary of State is satisfied that the application made is vexatious or wholly without merit.

(14) For the purposes of subparagraph (6) a person's appeal rights are exhausted at the time when—

(a) he could not bring an appeal under section 82 (ignoring any possibility of an appeal out of time with permission), and

(b) no appeal brought by him is pending within the meaning of section 104.

10B (1) The Secretary of State may make regulations providing for arrangements to be made for support to be provided to a person to whom paragraph 1 applies by virtue of paragraph 7B(1) and—

(a) who would otherwise be eligible for support or assistance under section 23C, 23CZA or 23CA of the Children Act 1989, under regulations under section 23D of that Act or under section 24A or 24B of that Act, and

(b) in relation to whom condition A, B, C or D is satisfied.

(2) Condition A is that—

(a) the person is destitute,

(b) the person has made an application for leave to enter or remain in the United Kingdom and has not withdrawn the application,

(c) where regulations under this paragraph require that the application must be of a kind specified in the regulations for this condition to be satisfied, the application is of that kind, and

(d) the application has not been determined.

(3) Condition B is that—

(a) the person is destitute,

(b) the person could bring an appeal under section 82(1) (ignoring any possibility of an appeal out of time with permission), and

(c) if the person brought an appeal under section 82(1), it would not be one that, by virtue of section 92(6), would have to be continued from outside the United Kingdom.

(4) Condition C is that—

(a) the person is destitute,

(b) the person has appealed under section 82(1),

(c) the appeal is not one that, by virtue of section 92(6), must be continued from outside the United Kingdom, and

(d) the appeal is pending within the meaning of section 104.

(5) Condition D is that—

(a) the person's appeal rights are exhausted, and

(b) a person specified in regulations under this paragraph is satisfied that support needs to be provided to the person.

(6) Regulations under this paragraph may specify—

(a) factors which a person specified by virtue of paragraph (b) of subparagraph (5) may or must take into account in making a determination under that paragraph;

(b) factors which such a person must not take into account in making such a determination.

(7) The Secretary of State may make regulations providing for arrangements to be made for support to be provided to a person ('P')—

(a) to whom paragraph 1 applies by virtue of paragraph 7B(1), and

(b) who it appears to a person specified in the regulations may be destitute, until a person by whom support may be provided under arrangements by virtue of subparagraph (1) is able to determine whether such support should be provided to P.

(8) The support that may be provided under arrangements by virtue of this paragraph may, in particular, take the form of—

(a) accommodation;

(b) subsistence in kind, or cash or vouchers to pay for subsistence.

(9) Subsections (3) to (8) of section 95 of the Immigration and Asylum Act 1999 (meaning of 'destitute') apply for the purposes of this paragraph as they apply for the purposes of that section.

(10) For the purposes of subparagraph (2) regulations under this paragraph may provide for circumstances in which—

(a) a person is to be treated as having made an application for leave to enter or remain in the United Kingdom (despite not having made one);

(b) a person is to be treated as not having made such an application where the Secretary of State is satisfied that the application made is vexatious or wholly without merit.

(11) For the purposes of subparagraph (5) a person's appeal rights are exhausted at the time when—

(a) he could not bring an appeal under section 82 (ignoring any possibility of an appeal out of time with permission), and

(b) no appeal brought by him is pending within the meaning of section 104.]

Note: Paragraphs 10A and 10B inserted by Schedule 12 to the Immigration Act 2016 from a date to be appointed.

Assistance and accommodation: general

11. Regulations under paragraph 8, 9 or 10[, 10A, or 10B] may—

(a) provide for the making of arrangements under a provision referred to in paragraph 1(1) or otherwise;

(b) confer a function (which may include the exercise of a discretion) on the Secretary of State, a local authority or another person;

(c) provide that arrangements must be made in a specified manner or in accordance with specified principles;

(d) provide that arrangements may not be made in a specified manner;

(e) require a local authority or another person to have regard to guidance issued by the Secretary of State in making arrangements;

(f) require a local authority or another person to comply with a direction of the Secretary of State in making arrangements.

Note: Words in square brackets substituted by Schedule 12 to the Immigration Act 2016 from a date to be appointed.

12.—(1) Regulations may, in particular, provide that if a person refuses an offer of arrangements under paragraph 8 or fails to implement or cooperate with arrangements made for him under that paragraph—

(a) new arrangements may not be made for him under paragraph 8, but

(b) new arrangements may not be made for him under paragraph 9.

(2) Regulations by virtue of this paragraph may include exceptions in the case of a person who—

(a) has a reason of a kind specified in the regulations for failing to implement or cooperate with arrangements made under paragraph 8, and

(b) satisfies any requirements of the regulations for proof of the reason.

Offences

13.—(1) A person who leaves the United Kingdom in accordance with arrangements made under paragraph 8 commits an offence if he—

(a) returns to the United Kingdom, and

(b) requests that arrangements be made for him by virtue of paragraph 8, 9 or 10[, 10A or 10B].

(2) A person commits an offence if he—

(a) requests that arrangements be made for him by virtue of paragraph 8, 9 or 10[, 10A or 10B], and

(b) fails to mention a previous request by him for the making of arrangements under any of those paragraphs.

(3) A person who is guilty of an offence under this paragraph shall be liable on summary conviction to imprisonment for a term not exceeding six months.

Note: Words in square brackets substituted by Schedule 12 to the Immigration Act 2016 from a date to be appointed.

Information

14.—(1) If it appears to a local authority that paragraph 1 applies or may apply to a person in the authority's area by virtue of [paragraph 6[][[, 7, 7B or 7C]]and 7D}], the authority must inform the Secretary of State.

(2) A local authority shall act in accordance with any relevant guidance issued by the Secretary of State for the purpose of determining whether paragraph 1 applies or may apply to a person in the authority's area by virtue of [paragraph 6[][[7, 7B or 7C]] and 7D}].

Note: Words in square brackets substituted by Schedule 12 to the Immigration Act 2016 from a date to be appointed.

Power to amend Schedule

15. The Secretary of State may by order amend this Schedule so as—

(a) to provide for paragraph 1 to apply or not to apply to a class of person;

[(aa) to modify any of the classes of person to whom paragraph 1 applies;]

(b) to add or remove a provision to or from the list in paragraph 1(1);

(c) to add, amend or [modify the application of] a limitation of or exception to paragraph 1;

[(d) to enable regulations to be made by the Secretary of State providing for arrangements to be made for support to be provided to a class of person to whom paragraph 1 applies;

(e) to apply paragraph 1A in relation to Wales;

(f) to make provision which has a similar effect to paragraph 1A and which applies in relation to Scotland or Northern Ireland.]

Note: Word in square brackets at subparagraph (c) substituted by, and subparagraphs (aa), (d) (e) and (f) inserted by Schedule 12 to the Immigration Act 2016 from a date to be appointed.

Orders and regulations

16.—(1) An order or regulations under this Schedule must be made by statutory instrument.

(2) An order or regulations under this Schedule may—

(a) make provision which applies generally or only in specified cases or circumstances or only for specified purposes;

(b) make different provision for different cases, circumstances or purposes;

(c) make transitional provision;

(d) make consequential provision (which may include provision amending, [repealing or revoking] a provision made by or under this or another Act).

(3) An order under this Schedule, regulations under paragraph 2(1)(d) or (e), [2A(3)(b), 10A or 10B] or other regulations which include consequential provision amending an enactment shall not be made unless a draft has been laid before and approved by resolution of each House of Parliament.

(4) Regulations under this Schedule to which subparagraph (3) does not apply shall be subject to annulment in pursuance of a resolution of either House of Parliament.

Note: Words in square brackets inserted by Schedule 12 of the Immigration Act 2016 from a date to be appointed.

Interpretation

17.—(1) In this Schedule—

'asylum-seeker [has the meaning given by section 18]

'child' means a person under the age of eighteen,

'dependant' and 'dependent' shall have such meanings as may be prescribed by regulations made by the Secretary of State,

'EEA State' means a State which is a contracting party to the Agreement on the European Economic Area signed at Oporto on 2 May 1992 (as it has effect from time to time),

'local authority'—

(a) in relation to England and Wales, has the same meaning as in section 129(3),

(b) in relation to Scotland, has the same meaning as in section 129(4), and

(c) in relation to Northern Ireland, means a health service body within the meaning of section 133(4)(d) and the Northern Ireland Housing Executive (for which purpose a reference to the authority's area shall be taken as a reference to Northern Ireland),

'the Refugee Convention' means the Convention relating to the status of Refugees done at Geneva on 28 July 1951 and its Protocol, and

'removal directions' means directions under Schedule 2 to the Immigration Act 1971 (c. 77) (control of entry, &c.), under Schedule 3 to that Act (deportation) or under section 10 of the Immigration and Asylum Act 1999 (c. 33) (removal of person unlawfully in United Kingdom).

(2) For the purpose of the definition of 'asylum-seeker' in subparagraph (1) a claim is determined if—

(a) the Secretary of State has notified the claimant of his decision,

(b) no appeal against the decision can be brought (disregarding the possibility of an appeal out of time with permission), and

(c) any appeal which has already been brought has been disposed of.

(3) For the purpose of subparagraph (2)(c) an appeal is disposed of when it is no longer pending for the purpose of—

(a) Part 5 of this Act, or

(b) the Special Immigration Appeals Commission Act 1997 (c. 68).

(4) The giving of directions in respect of a person under a provision of the Immigration Acts is not the provision of assistance to him for the purposes of this Schedule.

Note: Paragraphs 2, 8, 9, 10, 11, 12, 15 and 16 commenced on 8 December 2002 for the purpose of enabling subordinate legislation. Remainder of Schedule commenced 8 January 2003 (SI 2002/2811). Paragraph (7A) inserted and words in square brackets in paragraph 14 substituted by Asylum and Immigration Act 2004, s 9 from 1 December 2004 (SI 2004/2999). Words in square brackets in paragraph 7(a) substituted by Borders Citizenship and Immigration Act 2009, s 48 from 13 January 2010 (SI 2009/2731). Words in square brackets in paragraph 1(1)(g) inserted by Children and Young Persons Act 2008 s 22 from 1 April 2011 (SI 2010/2981). Paragraph (1)(1)(e) substituted by National Health Service Consequential Provisions Act 2006 Sch 1 from 1 March 2007. Paragraph 1 (ka) inserted from 28 March 2012 (SI 2012/961). Letters in square brackets in paragraph 3(b) substituted by SI 2011/1043, from 22 April 2011. Paragraph 7A omitted, and words in curly brackets substituted at paragraphs 14(1) and (2) by Schedule 11 to the Immigration Act 2016 at a date to be appointed. Words in subparagraph (1) substituted by Schedule 11 to the Immigration Act 2016 from a date to be appointed. Subparagraph 7D inserted by Schedule 11 to the Immigration Act 2016 at a date to be appointed. Paragraphs 1A, 2A, 3A, 7B, 7C, 10A and 10B, and subparagraph (1)(ga), (2)(ca), 15(aa), (d),(e) and (f) are inserted by Schedule 12 to the Immigration Act 2016 at a date to be appointed. Words in square brackets substituted at paragraph 1, subparagraph (1)(h, paragraph 2, subparagraph (c) by Schedule 12 to the Immigration Act 2016 at a date to be appointed. Words inserted at paragraphs 7 and 8 by Schedule 12 to the Immigration Act 2016 at a date to be appointed. Words in square brackets substituted at paragraphs 11, and in double square brackets at 12 and 13, inserted at subparagraph 15(3), 16(2)(d) and (3) by Schedule 12 of the Immigration Act 2016 at a date to be appointed. Words in double square brackets paragraph 1 (1)(g) inserted by Children and Social Workers Act 2017 (SI 2016/413).

[SCHEDULE 4 . . .] Section 81

Note: Schedule 4 revoked from 15 February 2010 (SI 2010/21).

SCHEDULE 5 Section 100

THE IMMIGRATION APPEAL TRIBUNAL

. . .

Note: Schedule 5 ceased to have effect from 4 April 2005, subject to savings (SI 2005/565), Asylum and Immigration Act 2004, s 26.

SCHEDULE 6 — Section 114

IMMIGRATION AND ASYLUM APPEALS: TRANSITIONAL PROVISION

'Commencement'

1. In this Schedule 'commencement' means the coming into force of Part 5 this Act.

Adjudicator

2. Where a person is an adjudicator under section 57 of the Immigration and Asylum Act 1999 (c. 33) immediately before commencement his appointment shall have effect after commencement as if made under section 81 of this Act.

Tribunal

3.—(1) Where a person is a member of the Immigration Appeal Tribunal immediately before commencement his appointment shall have effect after commencement as if made under Schedule 5.

(2) Where a person is a member of staff of the Immigration Appeal Tribunal immediately before commencement his appointment shall have effect after commencement as if made under Schedule 5.

Earlier appeal

4. In the application of section 96—

(a) a reference to an appeal or right of appeal under a provision of this Act includes a reference to an appeal or right of appeal under the Immigration and Asylum Act 1999,

(b) a reference to a requirement imposed under this Act includes a reference to a requirement of a similar nature imposed under that Act,

(c) a reference to a statement made in pursuance of a requirement imposed under a provision of this Act includes a reference to anything done in compliance with a requirement of a similar nature under that Act, and

(d) a reference to notification by virtue of this Act includes a reference to notification by virtue of any other enactment.

Saving

5.—(1) This Schedule is without prejudice to the power to include transitional provision in an order under section 162.

(2) An order under that section may, in particular, provide for a reference to a provision of Part 5 of this Act to be treated as being or including a reference (with or without modification) to a provision of the Immigration and Asylum Act 1999 (c. 33).

Note: Commencement from 1 April 2003 (SI 2003/754).

SCHEDULE 7 — Section 114

IMMIGRATION AND ASYLUM APPEALS: CONSEQUENTIAL AMENDMENTS

. . .

SCHEDULE 8 — Section 125

CARRIERS' LIABILITY

. . .

Note: Amends the Immigration and Asylum Act 1999.

SCHEDULE 9 — Section 161

REPEALS

. . .

Asylum and Immigration (Treatment of Claimants, etc.) Act 2004

(2004, c. 19)

Arrangement of Sections

An Act to make provision about asylum and immigration.
[22 July 2004]

Offences

1. Assisting unlawful immigration

. . .

Note: Amends Immigration Act 1971, ss 25 and 25C.

2. Entering United Kingdom without passport, &c.

(1) A person commits an offence if at a leave or asylum interview he does not have with him an immigration document which—

(a) is in force, and

(b) satisfactorily establishes his identity and nationality or citizenship.

(2) A person commits an offence if at a leave or asylum interview he does not have with him, in respect of any dependent child with whom he claims to be travelling or living, an immigration document which—

(a) is in force, and

(b) satisfactorily establishes the child's identity and nationality or citizenship.

(3) But a person does not commit an offence under subsection (1) or (2) if—

(a) the interview referred to in that subsection takes place after the person has entered the United Kingdom, and

(b) within the period of three days beginning with the date of the interview the person provides to an immigration officer or to the Secretary of State a document of the kind referred to in that subsection.

(4) It is a defence for a person charged with an offence under subsection (1)—

(a) [to prove that he is —

(i) an Irish citizen,

(ii) has leave to enter or remain in the United Kingdom which was granted by virtue of residence scheme immigration rules, or

(iii) is a frontier worker within the meaning of regulation 3 of the Citizens' Rights (Frontier Workers) (EU Exit) Regulations 2020]

(b) []

(c) to prove that he has a reasonable excuse for not being in possession of a document of the kind specified in subsection (1),

(d) to produce a false immigration document and to prove that he used that document as an immigration document for all purposes in connection with his journey to the United Kingdom, or

(e) to prove that he travelled to the United Kingdom without, at any stage since he set out on the journey, having possession of an immigration document.

(5) It is a defence for a person charged with an offence under subsection (2) in respect of a child—

(a) [to prove that the child is—

(i) an Irish citizen,

(ii) has leave to enter or remain in the United Kingdom which was granted by virtue of residence scheme immigration rules, or

(iii) is a frontier worker within the meaning of regulation 3 of the Citizens' Rights (Frontier Workers) (EU Exit) Regulations 2020,]

(b) []

(c) to prove that the person has a reasonable excuse for not being in possession of a document of the kind specified in subsection (2),

(d) to produce a false immigration document and to prove that it was used as an immigration document for all purposes in connection with the child's journey to the United Kingdom, or

(e) to prove that he travelled to the United Kingdom with the child without, at any stage since he set out on the journey, having possession of an immigration document in respect of the child.

(6) Where the charge for an offence under subsection (1) or (2) relates to an interview which takes place after the defendant has entered the United Kingdom—

(a) subsections (4)(c) and (5)(c) shall not apply, but

(b) it is a defence for the defendant to prove that he has a reasonable excuse for not providing a document in accordance with subsection (3).

(7) For the purposes of subsections (4) to (6)—

(a) the fact that a document was deliberately destroyed or disposed of is not a reasonable excuse for not being in possession of it or for not providing it in accordance with subsection (3), unless it is shown that the destruction or disposal was—

(i) for a reasonable cause, or

(ii) beyond the control of the person charged with the offence, and

(b) in paragraph (a)(i) 'reasonable cause' does not include the purpose of—

(i) delaying the handling or resolution of a claim or application or the taking of a decision,

(ii) increasing the chances of success of a claim or application, or

(iii) complying with instructions or advice given by a person who offers advice about, or facilitates, immigration into the United Kingdom, unless in the circumstances of the case it is unreasonable to expect non-compliance with the instructions or advice.

(8) A person shall be presumed for the purposes of this section not to have a document with him if he fails to produce it to an immigration officer or official of the Secretary of State on request.

(9) A person guilty of an offence under this section shall be liable—

(a) on conviction on indictment, to imprisonment for a term not exceeding two years, to a fine or to both, or

(b) on summary conviction, to imprisonment for a term not exceeding twelve months, to a fine not exceeding the statutory maximum or to both.

(10) If [an] immigration officer reasonably suspects that a person has committed an offence under this section he may arrest the person without warrant.

(11) An offence under this section shall be treated as—

(a) a relevant offence for the purposes of sections 28B and 28D of the Immigration Act 1971 (c. 77) (search, entry and arrest), and

(b) an offence under Part III of that Act (criminal proceedings) for the purposes of sections 28(4), 28E, 28G and 28H (search after arrest, &c.) of that Act.

(12) In this section—

[]

'immigration document' means—

(a) a passport, and

(b) a document which relates to a national of a State other than the United Kingdom and which is designed to serve the same purpose as a passport, []

'leave or asylum interview' means an interview with an immigration officer or an official of the Secretary of State at which a person—

(a) seeks leave to enter or remain in the United Kingdom, or

(b) claims that to remove him from or require him to leave the United Kingdom would breach the United Kingdom's obligations under the Refugee Convention or would be unlawful under section 6 of the Human Rights Act 1998 (c. 42) as being incompatible with his Convention rights [and 'residence scheme immigration rules' has the meaning given by section 17 of the European Union (Withdrawal Agreement) Act 2020.']

(13) For the purposes of this section—

(a) a document which purports to be, or is designed to look like, an immigration document, is a false immigration document, and

(b) an immigration document is a false immigration document if and in so far as it is used—

(i) outside the period for which it is expressed to be valid,

(ii) contrary to provision for its use made by the person issuing it, or

(iii) by or in respect of a person other than the person to or for whom it was issued.

(14) Section 11 of the Immigration Act 1971 (c. 77) shall have effect for the purpose of the construction of a reference in this section to entering the United Kingdom.

(15) In so far as this section extends to England and Wales, subsection (9)(b) shall, until the commencement of[paragraph 24 of Schedule 22 to the Sentencing Act 2020], have effect as if the reference to twelve months were a reference to six months.

(16) In so far as this section extends to Scotland, subsection (9)(b) shall have effect as if the reference to twelve months were a reference to six months.

(17) In so far as this section extends to Northern Ireland, subsection (9)(b) shall have effect as if the reference to twelve months were a reference to six months.

Note: Commenced 22 September 2004, s 48. Word in square brackets in subsection (10) substituted by Sch 7 Serious Organised Crime and Police Act 2005 from 1 January 2006 (SI 2005/3495). Words in square brackets in subsection (4)(b) and (5)(b) substituted by 2011/1043 from 22 April 2011. Words in square brackets in subsection (4)(b) & (5)(b) substituted by Immigration, Nationality and Asylum (EU Exit) Regulations 2019/745 Pt 2(1) reg 14 (December 31 2020: shall come into force on IP completion day not exit day as specified in 2020 c.1 s39(1) and Sch.5 para 1(1)). Words in square brackets substituted at subsection (4)(a) and omitted at (4)(b) by Immigration and Social Security Co-ordination (EU Withdrawal) Act 2020 (Consequential, Savings, Transitional and Transitory Provisions)(EU Exit) Regulations 2020/1309 Pt2(1) reg.15(2)(a)(i) & (ii)(December 31, 2020 at 23.00 being the time and date c.20 Sch.1 para.2(2) comes into force). Words in square brackets substituted at subsection (4)(a) and omitted at (4)(b) by Immigration and Social Security Co-ordination (EU Withdrawal) Act 2020 (Consequential, Savings, Transitional and Transitory Provisions) (EU Exit) Regulations 2020/1309 Pt2(1) reg.15(2)(b)(i) & (ii)(December 31, 2020 at 23.00 being the time and date c.20 Sch.1 para.2(2) comes into force). Words omitted in subsection (2)(12) by Immigration and Social Security Co-ordination (EU Withdrawal) Act 202 (Consequential, Savings, Transitional and Transitory Provisions) (EU Exit) Regulations 2020/1309 Pt2(1) reg.15(2)(c)(i) & (ii)(December 31, 2020 at 23.00 being the time and date c.20 Sch.1 para.2(2) comes into force). Definition in square brackets inserted by Immigration and Social Security Co-ordination (EU Withdrawal) Act 202 (Consequential, Savings, Transitional and Transitory Provisions)(EU Exit) Regulations 2020/1309 Pt2(1) reg.15(2)(c)(iii)(December 31, 2020 at 23.00 being the time and date c.20 Sch.1 para.2(2) comes into force). Words in square brackets at subsection 15 substituted by paragraph 24 of the Sentencing Act 2020 by SI2020/1236 reg,2 from 1 December 2020.

3. Immigration documents: forgery

...

Note: Section 3 repealed from 7 June 2006, Identity Cards Act 2006, s 44 and Sch 2.4.

5. Section 4: supplemental

[(1) . . .

(2) . . .

(8) . . .

Note: Amends paragraph 4, Sch 4 Proceeds of Crime Act 2002.

(9) . . .

Note: Amends paragraph 4, Sch 5 Proceeds of Crime Act 2002.

(10) . . .

Note: Amends paragraph 2(1), Sch Protection of Children and Vulnerable Adults (Northern Ireland) Order 2003.

(12) . . .

(13) . . .

Note: Commenced 1 December 2004 (SI 2004/2999). Subsection (1) omitted, and subsections (12)–(13) repealed by Protection of Freedoms Act 2012, ss 110, 115, Sch 9 from 6 April 2013 (SI 2013/470). Amended in relation to Scotland by the Criminal Justice and Licensing (Scotland) Act 2010 (asp). Subsections (3) to (7) and (11) omitted from 31 July 2015 by Schedule 5 to Modern Slavery Act 2015 [SI2015/1476].

6. Employment

. . .

Note: Amends Asylum and Immigration Act 1996, s 8.

7. Advice of Director of Public Prosecutions

. . .

Note: Amends Prosecution of Offences Act 1985, s 3(2).

Treatment of claimants

8. Claimant's credibility

(1) In determining whether to believe a statement made by or on behalf of a person who makes an asylum claim or a human rights claim, a deciding authority shall take account, as damaging the claimant's credibility, of any behaviour to which this section applies.

[(1A) Tribunal Procedure Rules must secure that, where the deciding authority is the First-tier Tribunal, it must include, as part of its reasons for a decision that disposes of proceedings, a statement explaining—

(a) whether it considers that the claimant has engaged in behaviour to which this section applies, and

(b) if it considers that the claimant has engaged in such behaviour, how it has taken account of the behaviour in making its decision.

(1B) Rules under section 5 of the Special Immigration Appeals Commission Act 1997 (SIAC procedure rules) must secure that, where the deciding authority is the Special Immigration Appeals Commission, it must include, as part of its reasons for a decision that determines proceedings, a statement explaining the matters mentioned in subsection (1A) (a) and (b).]

(2) This section applies to any behaviour by the claimant that the deciding authority thinks—

(a) is designed or likely to conceal information,

(b) is designed or likely to mislead, or

(c) is designed or likely to obstruct or delay the handling or resolution of the claim or the taking of a decision in relation to the claimant.

(3) Without prejudice to the generality of subsection (2) the following kinds of behaviour shall be treated as designed or likely to conceal information or to mislead—

(a) failure without reasonable explanation to produce a passport on request to an immigration officer or to the Secretary of State,

(b) the production of a document which is not a valid passport as if it were,

(c) the destruction, alteration or disposal, in each case without reasonable explanation, of a passport,

(d) the destruction, alteration or disposal, in each case without reasonable explanation, of a ticket or other document connected with travel, and

(e) failure without reasonable explanation to answer a question asked by a deciding authority.

[**(3A)** This section also applies to any relevant behaviour by the claimant that the deciding authority thinks is not in good faith.

(3B) In subsection (3A) "relevant behaviour" means behaviour—

(a) in connection with the asylum claim or human rights claim in question or (in the case of an appeal relating to such a claim) the appeal in question,

(b) in any dealings with a person exercising immigration and nationality functions, or

(c) in connection with—

(i) a claim made, or civil proceedings brought, under any provision of immigration legislation, or

(ii) judicial review proceedings, or (in Scotland) an application to the supervisory jurisdiction of the Court of Session, relating to a decision taken by a person in exercise of immigration and nationality functions.]

(4) This section also applies to failure by the claimant to take advantage of a reasonable opportunity to make an asylum claim or human rights claim while in a safe country.

(5) This section also applies to failure by the claimant to make an asylum claim or human rights claim before being notified of an immigration decision, unless the claim relies wholly on matters arising after the notification.

(6) This section also applies to failure by the claimant to make an asylum claim or human rights claim before being arrested under an immigration provision, unless—

(a) he had no reasonable opportunity to make the claim before the arrest, or

(b) the claim relies wholly on matters arising after the arrest.

(6A) This section also applies to the late provision by the claimant of evidence in relation to the asylum claim or human rights claim in question, unless there are good reasons why the evidence was provided late.

(6B) For the purposes of subsection (6A), evidence is provided "late" by the claimant if—

(a) it is provided pursuant to an evidence notice served on the claimant under section 18(1) of the Nationality and Borders Act 2022, and

(b) it is provided on or after the date specified in the notice.

(7) In this section—

'asylum claim' has the meaning given by section 113(1) of the Nationality, Immigration and Asylum Act 2002 (c. 41) (subject to subsection (9) below),

'deciding authority' means—

(a) an immigration officer,

(b) the Secretary of State,

(c) [the First-tier Tribunal] or

(d) the Special Immigration Appeals Commission,

'human rights claim' has the meaning given by section 113(1) of the Nationality, Immigration and Asylum Act 2002 (subject to subsection (9) below),

'immigration and nationality functions' means functions exercisable by virtue of—

(a) the Immigration Acts (but see subsection (9B)), or

(b) the Nationality Acts;

(c) rules under section 3(2) of the Immigration Act 1971 (general immigration rules);

'immigration decision' means—

(a) refusal of leave to enter the United Kingdom,

(b) refusal to vary a person's leave to enter or remain in the United Kingdom,

(c) grant of leave to enter or remain in the United Kingdom,

(d) a decision that a person is to be removed from the United Kingdom by way of directions under section 10 . . . of the Immigration and Asylum Act 1999 (c. 33) (removal of persons unlawfully in United Kingdom),

(e) a decision that a person is to be removed from the United Kingdom by way of directions under paragraphs 8 to 12 of Schedule 2 to the Immigration Act 1971 (c. 77) (control of entry: removal),

(f) a decision to make a deportation order under section 5(1) of that Act, and

(g) a decision to take action in relation to a person in connection with extradition from the United Kingdom,

'immigration legislation' means—

(a) the Immigration Acts,

(b) the Nationality Acts, and

(c) rules under section 3(2) of the Immigration Act 1971 (general immigration rules);

'immigration provision' means—

(a) sections 28A, 28AA, 28B, 28C and 28CA of the Immigration Act 1971 (immigration offences: enforcement),

(b) paragraph 17 of Schedule 2 to that Act (control of entry),

(c) section 14 of this Act, and

(d) a provision of the Extradition Act 1989 (c. 33) or 2003 (c. 41),

['Nationality Acts' means—

(a) the British Nationality Act 1981,

(b) the Hong Kong Act 1985,

(c) the Hong Kong (War Wives and Widows) Act 1996, and

(d) the British Nationality (Hong Kong) Act 1997;]

'notified' means notified in such manner as may be specified by regulations made by the Secretary of State,

'passport' includes a document which relates to a national of a country other than the United Kingdom and which is designed to serve the same purpose as a passport, and

'safe country' means a country to which Part 2 of Schedule 3 applies.

(8) A passport produced by or on behalf of a person is valid for the purposes of subsection (3)(b) if it—

(a) relates to the person by whom or on whose behalf it is produced,

(b) has not been altered otherwise than by or with the permission of the authority who issued it, and

(c) was not obtained by deception.

(9) In subsection (4) a reference to an asylum claim or human rights claim shall be treated as including a reference to a claim of entitlement to remain in a country other than the United Kingdom made by reference to the rights that a person invokes in making an asylum claim or a human rights claim in the United Kingdom.

[(9A) [[In this section a]] the reference to the First-tier Tribunal includes a reference to the Upper Tribunal when acting

[[(a)]] under section 12(2)(b)(ii) of the Tribunals, Courts and Enforcement Act 2007.] [[,or

(b) in relation to

(i) an expedited appeal within the meaning of section 82A of the Nationality, Immigration and Asylum Act 2002, or

(ii) an expedited appeal within the meaning of section 24 of the Nationality and Borders Act 2022 that involves an asylum claim or human rights claim.]]

[9B) In paragraph (a) of the definition of "immigration and nationality functions" in subsection (7), the reference to the Immigration Acts does not include a reference to—

(a) sections 28A to 28K of the Immigration Act 1971 (powers of arrest, entry and search, etc), or

(b) section 14 of this Act (power of arrest).]

(10) Regulations under subsection (7) specifying a manner of notification may, in particular—

(a) apply or refer to regulations under section 105 of the Nationality, Immigration and Asylum Act 2002 (c. 41) (notice of immigration decisions);

(b) make provision similar to provision that is or could be made by regulations under that section;

(c) modify a provision of regulations under that section in its effect for the purpose of regulations under this section;

(d) provide for notice to be treated as received at a specified time if sent to a specified class of place in a specified manner.

(11) Regulations under subsection (7) specifying a manner of notification—

(a) may make incidental, consequential or transitional provision,

(b) shall be made by statutory instrument, and

(c) shall be subject to annulment in pursuance of a resolution of either House of Parliament.

(12) This section shall not prevent a deciding authority from determining not to believe a statement on the grounds of behaviour to which this section does not apply.

(13) . . .

Note: Commencement 1 January 2005 (SI 2004/3398). Words in square brackets in subsection (7)(c) substituted, subsection (9A) inserted and subsection (13) revoked from 15 February 2010 (SI 2010/21). Numbers omitted from subsection (7) by Sch 9 Immigration Act 2014 from 20 October 2014 with savings set out in SI 2014/2771 articles 9-11. Subsections (1A),(1B), (3A), (3B),(6A) (6B) & (9A) inserted by Nationality and Borders Act 2022 c.36 Pt2 s.19(2)(3)(4) & (6) (date to be appointed). Words inserted in square brackets in subsection (7) by Nationality and Borders Act 2022 c.36 Pt2s.19(5)(date to be appointed). Words inserted in double square brackets in subsection (9A) by Nationality and Borders Act 2022 c.36 Sch.3 para 7 (date to be appointed)

9. Failed asylum seekers: withdrawal of support

(1) [..].

(2)

(3) No appeal may be brought under section 103 of the Immigration and Asylum Act 1999 (asylum support appeal) against a decision—

(a) that by virtue of a provision of Schedule 3 to the Nationality, Immigration and Asylum Act 2002 (c. 41) a person is not qualified to receive support, or

(b) on the grounds of the application of a provision of that Schedule to stop providing support to a person.

(4) . . .

(5) An order under section 48 providing for this section to come into force may, in particular, provide for this section to have effect with specified modifications before the coming into force of a provision of the Nationality, Immigration and Asylum Act 2002.

Note: Commencement 1 December 2004 (SI 2004/2999). Subsections (1) & (2) amend Sch.3 of Nationality, Immigration and Asylum Act 2002. Words in square brackets in subsection (4) substituted from 3 November 2008 (SI 2008/2833). Words in subsection (1) and (4) omitted and words in square brackets omitted in subsection 3(a) &(b) by Schedule 11 to the Immigration Act 2016 from a date to be appointed.

10.

Note: omitted by Schedule 11 to the Immigration Act 2016 from a date to be appointed: repeal had effect subject to savings and transitional provisions specified in 2016 c.19 Sch 11 Para.46.

11. Accommodation for asylum seekers: local connection

(1) . . .

Note: Amends Housing Act 1996, s 199.

(2) Subsection (3) applies where—

(a) a local housing authority would (but for subsection (3)) be obliged to secure that accommodation is available for occupation by a person under section 193 of the Housing Act 1996 (homeless persons),

(b) the person was (at any time) provided with accommodation in a place in Scotland under section 95 of the Immigration and Asylum Act 1999 (support for asylum seekers),

(c) the accommodation was not provided in an accommodation centre by virtue of section 22 of the Nationality, Immigration and Asylum Act 2002 (use of accommodation centres for section 95 support), and

(d) the person has neither—

(i) a local connection with the district of a local housing authority (in England or Wales) within the meaning of section 199 of the Housing Act 1996 as amended by subsection (1) above, nor

(ii) a local connection with a district (in Scotland) within the meaning of section 27 of the Housing (Scotland) Act 1987 (c. 26).

(3) Where this subsection applies—

(a) the duty of the local housing authority under section 193 of the Housing Act 1996 in relation to the person shall not apply, but

(b) the local housing authority—

(i) may secure that accommodation is available for occupation by the person for a period giving him a reasonable opportunity of securing accommodation for his occupation, and

(ii) may provide the person (or secure that he is provided with) advice and assistance in any attempts he may make to secure that accommodation becomes available for his occupation.

Note: Commenced 4 January 2005 (SI 2004/2999).

12. Refugee: back-dating of benefits

(1) . . .

Note: Repeals Immigration and Asylum Act 1999, s 123.

(2) . . .

Note: Amends SI 1987/1967, SR 1987/459, SI 1987/1968, SR 1987/465, SI 1987/1971, SR 1987/461, SI 1992/1814.

(3) . . .

Note: Amends SI 2000/636.

(4) . . .

Note: Amends SR 2000/71.

(5) An order under section 48 bringing this section into force may, in particular, provide for this section to have effect in relation to persons recorded as refugees after a specified date (irrespective of when the process resulting in the record was begun).

Note: Commencement 14 June 2007, but not with effect to a person recorded as a refugee on or before that date (SI 2007/1602), which sets out transitional provision.

13. [Integration loans for refugees]

(1) The Secretary of State may make regulations enabling him to make loans [—

(a) to refugees, and

(b) to such other classes of person, or to persons other than refugees in such circumstances, as the regulations may prescribe.]

(2) A person is a refugee for the purpose of subsection (1) if the Secretary of State has—

(a) recorded him as a refugee within the meaning of the Convention relating to the Status of Refugees done at Geneva on 28 July 1951, and

(b) [granted him leave to enter or remain] in the United Kingdom (within the meaning of section 33(1) of the Immigration Act 1971 (c. 77)).

(3) Regulations under subsection (1)—

(a) shall specify matters which the Secretary of State shall, in addition to other matters appearing to him to be relevant, take into account in determining whether or not to make a loan (and those matters may, in particular, relate to—

(i) a person's income or assets,

(ii) a person's likely ability to repay a loan, or

(iii) the length of time since a person was recorded as a refugee [or since some other event)],

(b) shall enable the Secretary of State to specify (and vary from time to time) a minimum and a maximum amount of a loan,

(c) shall prevent a person from receiving a loan if—

(i) he is under the age of 18,

(ii) he is insolvent, within a meaning given by the regulations, or

(iii) he has received a loan under the regulations,

(d) shall make provision about repayment of a loan (and may, in particular, make provision—

(i) about interest;

(ii) for repayment by deduction from a social security benefit or similar payment due to the person to whom the loan is made),

(e) shall enable the Secretary of State to attach conditions to a loan (which may include conditions about the use of the loan),

(f) shall make provision about—

(i) the making of an application for a loan, and

(ii) the information, which may include information about the intended use of a loan, to be provided in or with an application,

(g) may make provision about steps to be taken by the Secretary of State in establishing an applicant's likely ability to repay a loan,

(h) may make provision for a loan to be made jointly to more than one refugee, and

(i) may confer a discretion on the Secretary of State.

(4) Regulations under this section—

(a) shall be made by statutory instrument, and

(b) may not be made unless a draft has been laid before and approved by resolution of each House of Parliament.

Note: Commencement 29 June 2006 (SI 2006/1517). Words in square brackets substituted from 30 June 2006, Immigration, Nationality and Asylum Act 2006, s 45 (SI 2006/1497).

Enforcement powers

14. Immigration officer: power of arrest

(1) Where an immigration officer in the course of exercising a function under the Immigration Acts forms a reasonable suspicion that a person has committed or attempted to commit an offence listed in subsection (2), he may arrest the person without warrant.

(2) Those offences are—

(a) the offence of conspiracy at common law (in relation to conspiracy to defraud),

(b) at common law in Scotland, any of the following offences—

(i) fraud,

(ii) conspiracy to defraud,

(iii) uttering and fraud,

(iv) bigamy,

(v) theft, and

(vi) reset,

(c) an offence under section 57 of the Offences against the Person Act 1861 (c. 100) (bigamy),

(d) an offence under section 3 or 4 of the Perjury Act 1911 (c. 6) (false statements),

(e) an offence under section 7 of that Act (aiding, abetting &c.) if it relates to an offence under section 3 or 4 of that Act,

(f) an offence under section 53 of the Registration of Births, Deaths and Marriages (Scotland) Act 1965 (c. 49) (knowingly giving false information to district registrar, &c.),

(g) an offence under any of the following provisions of the Theft Act 1968 (c. 60)—

(i) . . . section 1 (theft),

(ii) . . .

(iii) . . .

(iv) section 17 (false accounting), and

(v) section 22 (handling stolen goods),

(h) an offence under section 1, . . . 17 or 21 of the Theft Act (Northern Ireland) 1969 (c. 16) (N.I.),

[(ha) an offence under either of the following provisions of the Fraud Act 2006—

(i) section 1 (fraud);

(ii) section 11 (obtaining services dishonestly),]

(i) . . .

(j) . . .

(k) an offence under Article 8 or 9 of the Perjury (Northern Ireland) Order 1979 (S.I. 1979/1714 (N.I. 19)),

(l) an offence under Article 12 of that Order if it relates to an offence under Article 8 or 9 of that Order,

(m) an offence under any of the following provisions of the Forgery and Counterfeiting Act 1981 (c. 45)—

(i) section 1 (forgery),

(ii) section 2 (copying false instrument),

(iii) section 3 (using false instrument),

(iv) section 4 (using copy of false instrument), and

(v) section 5(1) and (3) (false documents),

(n) . . .

(o)

(p) . . . .

[(q) an offence under any of sections 4 to 6 of the Identity Documents Act 2010];

[(r) an offence under section 2 of the Modern Slavery Act 2015]..

(3) The following provisions of the Immigration Act 1971 (c. 77) shall have effect for the purpose of making, or in connection with, an arrest under this section as they have effect for the purpose of making, or in connection with, arrests for offences under that Act—

(a) section 28C (entry and search before arrest),

(b) sections 28E and 28F (entry and search after arrest),

(c) sections 28G and 28H (search of arrested person), and

(d) section 28I (seized material).

(4) . . .

Note: Commencement 1 December 2004 (SI 2004/2999). Subsection (4) amends Race Relations Act 1976, s 19D. Words in subsection 14(2)(o) omitted from 7 June 2006, Identity Cards Act 2006, s 30 and Sch 2, (SI 2006/1439). Subsections (2)(g), (ii)-(iii), (2)(i)-(j) omitted and words omitted in subsection (2)(h), subsection (2)(ha) inserted by Sch 1 Fraud Act 2006 from 15 January 2007 (SI 2006/3200). Subsection (2)(q) substituted by Identity Documents Act 2010, Schedule, paragraph 18 from 21 January 2011. Number in square brackets in subsection (2)(n) substituted by Protection of Freedoms Act 2012 Sch 9 from 6 April 2013 (SI 2013/470). Subsection (2)(n) &(q) omitted by Modern Day Slavery Act 2015 c.30 Sch.5 para.6(4)(a) (July 31, 2015, repeal as effect subject to transitional provisions and saving specified in SI2015/1476 art.3). Subsection (2)(n) omitted by Human Trafficking and Exploitation (Scotland) Act 2015 (Consequential Provisions and Modifications) Order 2026/1031 Sch.1para.2(b) (December 17, 2016: repeal has effect subject to transitional provisions specified in SI2016/1031 Art.4). Subsection (2)(r) inserted by Schedule 5 to the Modern Slavery Act 2015 from 31 July 2015.

15. Fingerprinting

. . .

Note: Amends Immigration and Asylum Act 1999, s 141.

16. Information about passengers

. . .

Note: Amends paragraph 27B, Sch 2 Immigration Act 1971.

17. Retention of documents

Where a document comes into the possession of the Secretary of State or an immigration officer in the course of the exercise of an immigration function, the Secretary of State or an immigration officer may retain the document while he suspects that—

(a) a person to whom the document relates may be liable to removal from the United Kingdom in accordance with a provision of the Immigration Acts, and

(b) retention of the document may facilitate the removal.

Note: Commencement 1 December 2004 (SI 2004/2999).

18. Control of entry

. . .

Note: Amends paragraph 2A, Sch 2 Immigration Act 1971.

Procedure for marriage

19. England and Wales

[(1) This section applies to a marriage that is to be solemnised on the authority of certificates issued by a superintendent registrar under Part 3 of the Marriage Act 1949 (the '1949 Act') unless each party to the marriage falls within exception A or exception B.

(1A) A party to the marriage falls within exception A if the person is a relevant national.

(1B) A party to the marriage falls within exception B if—

(a) the person is exempt from immigration control, and

(b) the notice of marriage is accompanied by the specified evidence required by section 28C(2) of the 1949 Act that the person is exempt from immigration control.]

(2) In relation to a marriage to which this section applies, the notices under section 27 of the Marriage Act 1949—

(a) shall be given to the superintendent registrar of a registration district [which is] specified for the purpose of this paragraph by regulations made by the Secretary of State [and is the appropriate registration district],

(b) shall be delivered to the superintendent registrar in person by the two parties to the marriage,

(c) may be given only if each party to the marriage has been resident in a registration district for the period of seven days immediately before the giving of his or her notice (but the district need not be that in which the notice is given and the parties need not have resided in the same district), and

(d) shall state, in relation to each party, the registration district by reference to which paragraph (c) is satisfied.

(2A) For the purposes of subsection (2) 'the appropriate registration district' means—

(a) if the parties have resided in the same specified registration district for the period of seven days immediately before the giving of the notice ('the 7 day period'), that specified registration district,

(b) if one or both of the parties have resided in a specified registration district (but not the same specified registration district) for the 7 day period, the specified registration district in which one of them has resided for that period, or

(c) if neither of the parties has resided in a specified registration district for the 7 day period, any specified registration district.

(2B) In subsection (2A), 'specified registration district' means a registration district specified for the purposes of subsection (2)(a) by regulations made under that provision.

(3) . . .

[(4) In this section—

(a) a reference to a person being a relevant national, or being exempt from immigration control, has the same meaning as in section 49 of the Immigration Act 2014;

(b) 'notice of marriage' means a notice of marriage given under section 27 of the 1949 Act.]

Note: Commencement 1 February 2005 (SI 2004/3398). Subsections (3) and (4)(c) and (d) repealed from 9 May 2011 (SI 2011/1158). Subsections (1)-(1B) and (4) substituted by s 58 Immigration Act 2014 from March 1 2015 (SI2015/171). Words in square brackets at subsection (2)(a) and subsection (2A) & (2B) inserted by Immigration and Social Security Co-ordination (EU Withdrawal) Act 2020 (Consequential, Saving, Transitional and Transitory Provisions) (EU Exit) Regulations 2020/1309, Part 2(1) reg.3(a)(i)(ii) & (b) from July 31, 2021.

20. England and Wales: supplemental

(1) The Marriage Act 1949 (c. 76) shall have effect in relation to a marriage to which section 19 applies—

(a) subject to that section, and

(b) with any necessary consequential modification.

(2) In particular—

(a) section 28(1)(b) of that Act (declaration: residence) shall have effect as if it required a declaration that—

(i) the notice of marriage is given in compliance with section 19(2) above, . . .

(b) section 48 of that Act (proof of certain matters not essential to validity of marriage) shall have effect as if the list of matters in section 48(1)(a) to (e) included compliance with section 19 above.

(3) [Regulations under section 19(2(a)—

(a) may make transitional provision,

(b) shall be made by statutory instrument, and

(c) shall be subject to annulment in pursuance of a resolution of either House of Parliament.

(4) Before making regulations under section 19(2)(a) the Secretary of State shall consult the Registrar General.

(5) An expression used in section 19 or this section and in Part III of the Marriage Act 1949 (c. 76) has the same meaning in section 19 or this section as in that Part.

(6) . . .

Note: Commenced 1 February 2005 (SI 2004/3398). Subsection (6) repealed from 8 January 2007, ss 30, 33 Legislative and Regulatory Reform Act 2006. Words omitted from subsection (2) and words substituted in subsection (3) from 9 May 2011 (SI 2011/1158).

21. Scotland

(1) This section applies to a marriage—

(a) which is intended to be solemnised in Scotland, and

(b) a party to which is subject to immigration control.

(2) In relation to a marriage to which this section applies, notice under section 3 of the Marriage (Scotland) Act 1977 (c. 15)—

(a) may be submitted to the district registrar of a registration district prescribed for the purposes of this section, and

(b) may not be submitted to the district registrar of any other registration district.

(3) . . .

(4) Where the district registrar to whom notice is submitted by virtue of subsection (2) (here the 'notified registrar') is not the district registrar for the registration district in which the marriage is to be solemnised (here the 'second registrar')—

(a) the notified registrar shall . . . send the notices and any fee, certificate or declaration [submitted in pursuance of section 3 of the Marriage (Scotland) Act 1977 (c. 15) in relation to the marriage], to the second registrar, and

(b) the second registrar shall be treated as having received the notices from the parties to the marriage on the dates on which the notified registrar received them.

(5) Subsection (4) of section 19 applies for the purposes of this section as it applies for the purposes of that section.

Note: Commenced 1 February 2005 (SI 2004/3398). Words in square brackets in subsection (4)(a) substituted by s 59 Local Electoral Administration and Registration Services (Scotland) Act 2006 (asp) from 1 January 2007 (SSI 2006/469). Subsection (3) repealed and words omitted from subsections (4) and (5) from 9 May 2011 (SI 2011/1158).

22. Scotland: supplemental

(1) The Marriage (Scotland) Act 1977 shall have effect in relation to a marriage to which section 21 applies—

(a) subject to that section, and

(b) with any necessary consequential modification.

(2) In subsection (2)(a) of that section 'prescribed' means prescribed by regulations made by the Secretary of State after consultation with the Registrar General for Scotland; and other expressions used in subsections (1) to (4) of that section and in the Marriage (Scotland) Act 1977 have the same meaning in those subsections as in that Act.

(3) Regulations made by the Secretary of State under subsection (2)(a) of that section—

(a) may make transitional provision,

(b) shall be made by statutory instrument, and

(c) shall be subject to annulment in pursuance of a resolution of either House of Parliament.

Note: Commenced 1 February 2005 (SI 2004/3398). Words omitted from subsection (3) from 9 May 2011 (SI 2011/1158).

23. Northern Ireland

(1) This section applies to a marriage—

(a) which is intended to be solemnised in Northern Ireland, and

(b) a party to which is subject to immigration control.

(2) In relation to a marriage to which this section applies, the marriage notices—

(a) shall be given only to a prescribed registrar, and

(b) shall, in prescribed cases, be given by both parties together in person at a prescribed register office.

(3) . . .

(4) . . . if the prescribed registrar is not the registrar for the purposes of Article 4 of that Order, the prescribed registrar shall send him the marriage notices and he shall be

treated as having received them from the parties to the marriage on the dates on which the prescribed registrar received them.

(5) . . .

(6) For the purposes of this section—

(a) a person is subject to immigration control if—

(i) he is not an EEA national, and

(ii) under the Immigration Act 1971 (c. 77) he requires leave to enter or remain in the United Kingdom (whether or not leave has been given),

(b) 'EEA national' means a national of a State which is a contracting party to the Agreement on the European Economic Area signed at Oporto on 2 May 1992 (as it has effect from time to time),

(c) . . .

(d) . . .

Note: Commenced 1 February 2005 (SI 2004/3398). Subsections (3), (5) and (6)(c) and (d) repealed and words omitted from subsection (4) from 9 May 2011 (SI 2011/1158).

24. Northern Ireland: supplemental

(1) The Marriage (Northern Ireland) Order 2003 (SI 2003/413 (N.I. 3)) shall have effect in relation to a marriage to which section 23 applies—

(a) subject to section 23, and

(b) with any necessary consequential modification.

(2) In section 23 'prescribed' means prescribed for the purposes of that section by regulations made by the Secretary of State after consulting the Registrar General for Northern Ireland and other expressions used in that section or this section and the Marriage (Northern Ireland) Order 2003 have the same meaning in section 23 or this section as in that Order.

(3) Section 18(3) of the Interpretation Act (Northern Ireland) 1954 (c.33 (N.I.)) (provisions as to holders of offices) shall apply to section 23 as if that section were an enactment within the meaning of that Act.

(4) Regulations of the Secretary of State under section 23—

(a) may make transitional provision,

(b) shall be made by statutory instrument, and

(c) shall be subject to annulment in pursuance of a resolution of either House of Parliament.

Note: Commenced 1 February 2005 (SI 2004/3398).

25. Application for permission under section 19(3)(b), 21(3)(b) or 23(3)(b)

Note: Repealed by s 50 Immigration, Asylum and Nationality Act 2006 from 30 April 2007 subject to savings (SI 2007/1109) and repealed for all remaining purposes from 9 May 2011 (SI 2011/1158).

Appeals

26. Unification of appeal system

(1) . . .

Note: Amends Nationality, Immigration and Asylum Act 2002, s 81.

(2) . . .

Note: Amends Nationality, Immigration and Asylum Act 2002, s 82(1).

(3) . . .

Note: Amends Nationality, Immigration and Asylum Act 2002, s 83(2).

(4) . . .

(5) . . .

Note: Amends Nationality, Immigration and Asylum Act 2002, ss 100–103 and Sch 5.

(6) . . .

(7) Schedule 2 (which makes amendments consequential on this section, and transitional provision) shall have effect.

(8) . . .

(9) . . .

(10) . . .

Note: Commenced 4 April 2005 (SI 2005/565). Subsections (4), (6), (8)–(10) revoked from 15 February 2010 (SI 2010/21). Subsections (2)–(3) repealed by Sch 9 (4) para.60 of the Immigration Act 2014 from October 20, 2014 subject to savings and transitional provisions as specified in SI2014/2771 arts.9-11.

27. Unfounded human rights or asylum claim

. . .

Note: Amends Nationality, Immigration and Asylum Act 2002, ss 94 and 112 from 1 October 2004 (SI 2004/2523). Subsections (2)–(3) repealed by Sch 9 (4) para.60 of Immigration Act 2014 from October 20, 2014 subject to savings and transitional provisions as specified in SI2014/2771 arts 9-11.

28.

. . .

Note: Amends Nationality, Immigration and Asylum Act 2002, s 92(3) from 1 October 2004 (SI 2004/2523). Repealed by Sch 9 (4) para.60 of Immigration Act 2014 c.22 from October 20, 2014 subject to savings and transitional provisions as specified in SI 2014/2771 arts 9-11).

29.

. . .

Note: Amends Nationality, Immigration and Asylum Act 2002, ss 88 and 112 from 1 October 2004 (SI 2004/2523). Repealed by Sch 9 (4) para 60 of Immigration Act 2014 from October 20, 2014 subject to savings and transitional provisions as specified in SI 2014/2771 arts 9-11).

30. Earlier right of appeal

. . .

Note: Amends Nationality, Immigration and Asylum Act 2002, s 96 from 1 October 2004 (SI 2004/2523).

31.

. . .

Note: Amends Nationality, Immigration and Asylum Act 2002, s 82 from 1 October 2004 (SI 2004/2523) Repealed by Sch 9(4) para.60 of Immigration Act 2014 from October 20, 2014 subject to savings and transitional provisions as specified in SI 2014/2771 arts 9-11.

32.

. . .

Note: Section 32 repealed from 14 March 2005, Prevention of Terrorism Act 2005, s 16(2).

Removal and detention

33. Removing asylum seeker to safe country

(1) Schedule 3 (which concerns the removal of persons claiming asylum to countries known to protect refugees and to respect human rights) shall have effect.

(2) . . .

Note: Repeals Immigration and Asylum Act 1999, ss 11 and 12.

(3) . . .

Note: Repeals Nationality, Immigration and Asylum Act 2002, ss 80 and 93. Commencement 1 October 2004 (SI 2004/2523).

34. Detention pending deportation

. . .

Note: Amends paragraph 2, Sch 3 Immigration Act 1971 from 1 October 2004 (SI 2004/2523).

35. Deportation or removal: cooperation

(1) The Secretary of State may require a person to take specified action if the Secretary of State thinks that—

(a) the action will or may enable a travel document to be obtained by or for the person, and

(b) possession of the travel document will facilitate the person's deportation or removal from the United Kingdom.

(2) In particular, the Secretary of State may require a person to—

(a) provide information or documents to the Secretary of State or to any other person;

(b) obtain information or documents;

[(c) provide biometric information (within the meaning of section 15 of the UK Borders Act 2007), or submit to a process by means of which such information is obtained or recorded];

(d) make, or consent to or cooperate with the making of, an application to a person acting for the government of a State other than the United Kingdom;

(e) cooperate with a process designed to enable determination of an application;

(f) complete a form accurately and completely;

(g) attend an interview and answer questions accurately and completely;

(h) make an appointment.

(3) A person commits an offence if he fails without reasonable excuse to comply with a requirement of the Secretary of State under subsection (1).

(4) A person guilty of an offence under subsection (3) shall be liable—

(a) on conviction on indictment, to imprisonment for a term not exceeding two years, to a fine or to both, or

(b) on summary conviction, to imprisonment for a term not exceeding twelve months, to a fine not exceeding the statutory maximum or to both.

(5) If [an] immigration officer reasonably suspects that a person has committed an offence under subsection (3) he may arrest the person without warrant.

(6) An offence under subsection (3) shall be treated as—

(a) a relevant offence for the purposes of sections 28B and 28D of the Immigration Act 1971 (c. 77) (search, entry and arrest), and

(b) an offence under Part III of that Act (criminal proceedings) for the purposes of sections 28(4), 28E, 28G and 28H (search after arrest, &c.) of that Act.

(7) In subsection (1)—

'travel document' means a passport or other document which is issued by or for Her Majesty's Government or the government of another State and which enables or facilitates travel from the United Kingdom to another State, and

'removal from the United Kingdom' means removal under—

(a) Schedule 2 to the Immigration Act 1971 (control on entry) (including a provision of that Schedule as applied by another provision of the Immigration Acts),

(b) section 10 of the Immigration and Asylum Act 1999 (c. 33) (removal of person unlawfully in United Kingdom), or

(c) Schedule 3 to this Act.

(8) While sections 11 and 12 of the Immigration and Asylum Act 1999 continue to have effect, the reference in subsection (7)(c) above to Schedule 3 to this Act shall be treated as including a reference to those sections.

(9) In so far as subsection (3) extends to England and Wales, subsection (4)(b) shall, until the commencement [paragraph 24 of Schedule 22 to the Sentencing Act 2020] (increased limit on magistrates' power of imprisonment), have effect as if the reference to twelve months were a reference to six months.

(10) In so far as subsection (3) extends to Scotland, subsection (4)(b) shall have effect as if the reference to twelve months were a reference to six months.

(11) In so far as subsection (3) extends to Northern Ireland, subsection (4)(b) shall have effect as if the reference to twelve months were a reference to six months.

Note: Commencement 1 October 2004 (s 48). Word in square bracket in subsection (5) substituted by Sch 7 Serious Organised Crime and Police Act 2005 from 1 January 2006 (SI 2005/3495) and from 1 March 2007 (NI) (SI 2007/288 NI 2). Subsection (2)(c) substituted by Schedule 2 Immigration Act 2014 from 28 July 2014 (SI 2014/1820). Words substituted in subsection 9 by Sentencing Act 2020 c.17 Sch.24(6) para.445 (December 1, 2020: substitution has effect on December 1, 2020 as amended by SI2020 reg.4(5)(a) subject to savings and transitional provisions specified in 2020 c.17 s.410 and Sch.24 Part 7).

36 . . .

Note: Omitted by Sch. 10(2) para.38 to the Immigration Act 2016 (January 15. 2018 subject to transitional provisions specified in SI 2017/1241 reg.3 and Sch.1).

Immigration services

37. Provision of immigration services

Note: Amends Immigration and Asylum Act 1999, ss 84, 85, 89, 90 and Sch 5 and 6.

38. Immigration Services Commissioner: power of entry

. . .

Note: Amends Immigration and Asylum Act 1999, s 92 and Sch 5, paragraph 7.

39. Offence of advertising services

. . .

Note: Amends Immigration and Asylum Act 1999, s 92.

40. Appeal to Immigration Services Tribunal

. . .

Note: Repeals Immigration and Asylum Act 1999, s 87(3)(f).

41. Professional bodies

. . .

Note: Amends Immigration and Asylum Act 1999, ss 86, 166 and Sch 5, paragraph 21.

Fees

42. Amount of fees

(1) . . .

[(2) . . .

[(2A) . . .

(3) An Order in Council under section 1 of the Consular Fees Act 1980 (c. 23) (fees) which prescribes a fee in relation to an application for the issue of a certificate under section 10 of the Nationality, Immigration and Asylum Act 2002 (right of abode: certificate of entitlement) may prescribe an amount which is intended to—

(a) exceed the administrative costs of determining the application, and

(b) reflect benefits that in the opinion of Her Majesty in Council are likely to accrue to the applicant if the application is successful.

[(3A) The amount of a fee under section 1 of the Consular Fees Act 1980 in respect of a matter specified in subsection (3B) may be set so as to reflect costs referable to the exercise of any function in respect of which the Secretary of State has made an order under section 68 of the Immigration Act 2014.

(3B) The matters are—

(a) the determination of applications for entry clearances (within the meaning given by section 33(1) of the Immigration Act 1971),

(b) the determination of applications for transit visas under section 41 of the Immigration and Asylum Act 1999, or

(c) the determination of applications for certificates of entitlement to the right of abode in the United Kingdom under section 10 of the Nationality, Immigration and Asylum Act 2002.]

(4) Where an instrument prescribes a fee in reliance on this section it may include provision for the refund, where an application is unsuccessful or a process is not completed, of that part of the fee which is intended to reflect the matters specified in subsection .(3) (b).

(5) Provision included by virtue of subsection (4)—

(a) may determine, or provide for the determination of, the amount to be refunded;

(b) may confer a discretion on the Secretary of State or another person (whether in relation to determining the amount of a refund or in relation to determining whether a refund should be made).

(6) An instrument may not be made in reliance on this section unless the Secretary of State has consulted with such persons as appear to him to be appropriate.

(7) An instrument may not be made in reliance on this section unless a draft has been laid before and approved by resolution of each House of Parliament . . .

(8) This section is without prejudice to the power to make an order under section 102 of the Finance (No. 2) Act 1987 (c. 51) (government fees and charges) in relation to a power under a provision specified in this section.

Note: Commencement 1 October 2004 (SI 2004/2523). Subsections (2)(da), (2A) and (3A) inserted by s 20 UK Borders Act 2007 from 31 January 2008 (SI 2008/99). Subsections (1)–(2A) and words in subsections (4) and (7) omitted, subsection (3A) substituted by Sch 9 Immigration Act 2014 from 15 December 2014 (SI 2014/2771).

43. Transfer of leave stamps

. . .

Note: Amends Immigration and Asylum Act 1999, s 5.

General

44.

. . .

Note: Section 44 repealed by Immigration, Asylum and Nationality Act 2006, s 64(3) from 30 March 2006 (Royal Assent).

45. Interpretation: immigration officer

In this Act 'immigration officer' means a person appointed by the Secretary of State as an immigration officer under paragraph 1 of Schedule 2 to the Immigration Act 1971.

Note: Commencement 1 October 2004 (SI 2004/2523).

46. Money

There shall be paid out of money provided by Parliament—

(a) any expenditure incurred by a Minister of the Crown in connection with this Act, and

(b) any increase attributable to this Act in the sums payable under any other enactment out of money provided by Parliament.

Note: Commencement 1 October 2004 (SI 2004/2523).

47. Repeals

. . .

48. Commencement

(1) Sections 2, 32(2) and 35 shall come into force at the end of the period of two months beginning with the date on which this Act is passed.

(2) Section 32(1) shall have effect in relation to determinations of the Special Immigration Appeals Commission made after the end of the period of two months beginning with the date on which this Act is passed.

(3) The other preceding provisions of this Act shall come into force in accordance with provision made—

(a) in the case of section 26 or Schedule 1 or 2, by order of the Lord Chancellor,

(b) in the case of sections 4 and 5 in so far as they extend to Scotland, by order of the Scottish Ministers, and

(c) in any other case, by order of the Secretary of State.

(4) An order under subsection (3)—

(a) may make transitional or incidental provision,

(b) may make different provision for different purposes, and

(c) shall be made by statutory instrument.

(5) Transitional provision under subsection (4)(a) in relation to the commencement of section 26 may, in particular, make provision in relation to proceedings which, immediately before commencement—

(a) are awaiting determination by an adjudicator appointed, or treated as if appointed, under section 81 of the Nationality, Immigration and Asylum Act 2002 (c. 41),

(b) are awaiting determination by the Immigration Appeal Tribunal,

(c) having been determined by an adjudicator could be brought before the Immigration Appeal Tribunal,

(d) are awaiting the determination of a further appeal brought in accordance with section 103 of that Act,

(e) having been determined by the Immigration Appeal Tribunal could be brought before another court by way of further appeal under that section,

(f) are or could be made the subject of an application under section 101 of that Act (review of decision on permission to appeal to Tribunal), or

(g) are or could be made the subject of another kind of application to the High Court or the Court of Session.

(6) Provision made under subsection (5) may, in particular—

(a) provide for the institution or continuance of an appeal of a kind not generally available after the commencement of section 26,

(b) provide for the termination of proceedings, or

(c) make any other provision that the Lord Chancellor thinks appropriate.

49. Extent

(1) This Act extends (subject to subsection (2)) to—

(a) England and Wales,

(b) Scotland, and

(c) Northern Ireland.

(2) An amendment effected by this Act has the same extent as the enactment, or as the relevant part of the enactment, amended (ignoring extent by virtue of an Order in Council).

(3) Her Majesty may by Order in Council direct that a provision of this Act is to extend, with or without modification or adaptation, to—

(a) any of the Channel Islands;

(b) the Isle of Man.

50. Short title

This Act may be cited as the Asylum and Immigration (Treatment of Claimants, etc.) Act 2004.

Schedules

Schedule 1

. . .

Note: Schedule 1 amends Nationality, Immigration and Asylum Act 2002.

Schedule 2

Section 26

Asylum and Immigration Tribunal:

Part 1
Consequential Amendments

. . .

Part 2
Transitional Provision

26. In this Part 'commencement' means the coming into force of section 26.

27. A person who immediately before commencement is, or is to be treated as, an adjudicator appointed under section 81 of the Nationality, Immigration and Asylum Act 2002 (c. 41) (appeals) (as it has effect before commencement) shall be treated as having been appointed as a member of the Asylum and Immigration Tribunal under paragraph 1 of Schedule 4 to that Act (as it has effect after commencement) immediately after commencement.

28. Where immediately before commencement a person is a member of the Immigration Appeal Tribunal—

(a) he shall be treated as having been appointed as a member of the Asylum and Immigration Tribunal under paragraph 1 of Schedule 4 to that Act immediately after commencement, and

(b) if he was a legally qualified member of the Immigration Appeal Tribunal (within the meaning of Schedule 5 to that Act) he shall be treated as having been appointed as a legally qualified member of the Asylum and Immigration Tribunal.

29. A person who immediately before commencement is a member of staff of adjudicators appointed or treated as appointed under section 81 of the Nationality, Immigration and Asylum Act 2002 (c. 41) or of the Immigration Appeal Tribunal shall be treated as having been appointed as a member of the staff of the Asylum and Immigration Tribunal under paragraph 9 of Schedule 4 to the Nationality, Immigration and Asylum Act 2002 immediately after commencement.

30. . . .

Note: Commencement 4 April 2005 (SI 2005/565). Paragraph 30 revoked from 15 February 2010 (SI 2010/21).

Section 33

SCHEDULE 3

REMOVAL OF ASYLUM SEEKER TO SAFE COUNTRY

PART 1

INTRODUCTORY

1.—(1) In this Schedule—

'asylum claim' means a claim by a person that to remove him from or require him to leave the United Kingdom would breach the United Kingdom's obligations under the Refugee Convention,

'Convention rights' means the rights identified as Convention rights by section 1 of the Human Rights Act 1998 (c. 42) (whether or not in relation to a State that is a party to the Convention),

'human rights claim' means a claim by a person that to remove him from or require him to leave the United Kingdom would be unlawful under section 6 of the Human Rights Act 1998 (public authority not to act contrary to Convention) as being incompatible with his Convention rights,

'immigration appeal' means an appeal under section 82(1) of the Nationality, Immigration and Asylum Act 2002 (c. 41) (appeal against immigration decision), and

'the Refugee Convention' means the Convention relating to the Status of Refugees done at Geneva on 28 July 1951 and its Protocol.

[["State" includes any territory outside the United Kingdom.]]

(2) In this Schedule a reference to anything being done in accordance with the Refugee Convention is a reference to the thing being done in accordance with the principles of the Convention, whether or not by a signatory to it.

[(3) Section 92 of the Nationality, Immigration and Asylum Act 2002 makes further provision about the place from which an appeal relating to an asylum or human rights claim may be brought or continued.]

Note: Subparagraph (3) inserted by Sch 9 Immigration Act 2014 from 20 October 2014 with savings set out in articles 9-11 SI 2014/2771. Words in double square brackets inserted by Nationality and Borders Act 2022 c.36 Sch.4 para 7 (June 28, 2022)

PART 2

FIRST LIST OF SAFE COUNTRIES
(REFUGEE CONVENTION AND HUMAN RIGHTS (1))

2. This Part applies to—

(a) Austria,
(b) Belgium,
[(ba) Bulgaria,]
[[(bb) Republic of Croatia]],
(c) Republic of Cyprus,
(d) Czech Republic,
(e) Denmark,
(f) Estonia,
(g) Finland,
(h) France,
(i) Germany,

(j) Greece,
(k) Hungary,
(l) Iceland,
(m) Ireland,
(n) Italy,
(o) Latvia,
[[(oa) Principality of Liechtenstein]],
(p) Lithuania,
(q) Luxembourg,
(r) Malta,
(s) Netherlands,
(t) Norway,
(u) Poland,
(v) Portugal,
[(va) Romania,]
(w) Slovak Republic,
(x) Slovenia,
(y) Spain, . . .
(z) Sweden.
{(z1) Switzerland}

Note: Words in square brackets inserted from 1 January 2007 (SI 2006/3393). Switzerland added from 20 November 2010 (SI 2010/2802); the amendment adding Switzerland (a) applies in relation to asylum and human rights claims made before 20 November 2010 (as well as those made after), but (b) does not apply in relation to an asylum or human rights claim if, before 20 November 2010, a decision is made to refuse the claimant leave to enter the United Kingdom or to remove the claimant from the United Kingdom: see Art 1(3) SI 2010/2802. Words in double square brackets at sub-para (bb) & (oa) inserted by Nationality and Borders Act 2022, c.36 Sch.4 para 8(a) & (b) (June 28, 2022)

3.—(1) This paragraph applies for the purposes of the determination by any person, tribunal or court whether a person who has made an asylum claim or a human rights claim [(the "claimant")] may be removed—

(a) from the United Kingdom, and

(b) to a State of which he is not a national or citizen.

[(1A) Unless the contrary is shown by the claimant to be the case in their particular circumstances, a State to which this Part applies is to be treated, in so far as relevant to the question mentioned in sub-paragraph (1), as a place—

(a) to which a person can be removed without their Convention rights under Article 3 (no torture or inhuman or degrading treatment or punishment) being contravened, and

(b) from which a person will not be sent to another State in contravention of their Convention rights.

(2) A State to which this Part applies shall be treated, in so far as relevant to the question mentioned in sub-paragraph (1), as a place—

(a) where a person's life and liberty are not threatened by reason of his race, religion, nationality, membership of a particular social group or political opinion,

(b) [] and

(c) from which a person will not be sent to another State otherwise than in accordance with the Refugee Convention.

Note: Words in square brackets inserted at sub-para (1) & (2) by Nationality and Borders Act 2022 c.36 Sch.4 para 5(2) & (4) (June 28, 2022). Sub-para (1A) inserted by Nationality and Borders Act 2022 c.36 Sch.4 para 3 (June 28, 2022).

4. …

Note: omitted by Nationality and Borders Act 2022 c. 36 Sch.4 para.4 (June 28, 2022: repeal has effect as SI 2022/590 reg.2 and Sch.1 para.17 subject to transitional and saving provisions specified in SI 2022/590 reg.3 and Sch.2 para.4(4))

5.—(1) This paragraph applies where the Secretary of State certifies that—

(a) it is proposed to remove a person to a State to which this Part applies, and

(b) in the Secretary of State's opinion the person is not a national or citizen of the State.

(2) . . .

(3) The person may not bring an immigration appeal [[..]] in reliance on—

(a) an asylum claim which asserts that to remove the person to a specified State to which this Part applies would breach the United Kingdom's obligations under the Refugee Convention, []

(b) …

(4) The person may not bring an immigration appeal [[..]]in reliance on a human rights claim []if the Secretary of State certifies that the claim is clearly unfounded; and the Secretary of State shall certify a human rights claim []unless satisfied that the claim is not clearly unfounded.

(5) …

Note: Subparagraph (2) omitted and words in square brackets in subparagraphs (3) and (4) substituted by Sch 9 Immigration Act 2014 from 20 October 2014 with savings set out in articles 9-11 SI 2014/2771. Sub-para (3)(b)(4)&(5) omitted by Nationality and Borders Act 2022 c.36 Sch.4 para 6 (June 28, 2022: repeal has effect subject to transitional provision specified in 2002 c.36 Sch.4 para 19(1)). Words in double square brackets omitted in sub-paras (3) & (4) by Nationality and Borders Act 2022 c.36 para 11(June 28, 2022: repeal subject to transitional provision in 2022 c.36 Sch.4 para 19(2))

6.

Note: omitted by Nationality and Borders Act 2022 c.36 Sch.4 para 12 (June 28, 22)

Part 3

Second List of Safe Countries (Refugee Convention and Human Rights (2))

7.—(1) This Part applies to such States as the Secretary of State may by order specify.

(2) An order under this paragraph—

(a) shall be made by statutory instrument, and

(b) shall not be made unless a draft has been laid before and approved by resolution of each House of Parliament.

8.—(1) This paragraph applies for the purposes of the determination by any person, tribunal or court whether a person who has made an asylum claim may be removed—

(a) from the United Kingdom, and

(b) to a State of which he is not a national or citizen.

(2) A State to which this Part applies shall be treated, in so far as relevant to the question mentioned in sub-paragraph (1), as a place—

(a) where a person's life and liberty are not threatened by reason of his race, religion, nationality, membership of a particular social group or political opinion, and

(b) from which a person will not be sent to another State otherwise than in accordance with the Refugee Convention.

9. . . .

Note: omitted by Nationality and Borders Act 2022 c. 36 Sch.4 para.4 (June 28, 2022: repeal has effect as SI 2022/590 reg.2 and Sch.1 para.17 subject to transitional and saving provisions specified in SI 2022/590 reg.3 and Sch.2 para.4(4))

10.—(1) This paragraph applies where the Secretary of State certifies that—

(a) it is proposed to remove a person to a State to which this Part applies, and

(b) in the Secretary of State's opinion the person is not a national or citizen of the State.

(2) . . .

(3) The person may not bring an immigration appeal [[..]] in reliance on an asylum claim which asserts that to remove the person to a specified State to which this Part applies would breach the United Kingdom's obligations under the Refugee Convention.

(4) The person may not bring an immigration appeal [[]] in reliance on a human rights claim if the Secretary of State certifies that the claim is clearly unfounded; and the Secretary of State shall certify a human rights claim where this paragraph applies unless satisfied that the claim is not clearly unfounded.

Note: Subparagraph (2) omitted and words in square brackets in subparagraphs (3) and (4) substituted by Sch 9(4) para.56 of Immigration Act 2014 from October 20, 2014 subject to savings and transitional provisions as specified in SI2014/2771 arts 9-11. Words omitted in sub-paras (3) & (4) by Nationality and Borders Act 2022 c.36 Sch.4 para 10 (June 28, 2022: repeal has effect subject to transitional provision in 2022 c.36 Sch.4 para 19(2))

11. . . .

Note: omitted by Nationality and Borders Act 2022 c.36 Sch.4 para 14 (June 28, 2022)

Part 4

Third List of Safe Countries (Refugee Convention Only)

12.—(1) This Part applies to such States as the Secretary of State may by order specify.

(2) An order under this paragraph—

(a) shall be made by statutory instrument, and

(b) shall not be made unless a draft has been laid before and approved by resolution of each House of Parliament.

13.—(1) This paragraph applies for the purposes of the determination by any person, tribunal or court whether a person who has made an asylum claim may be removed—

(a) from the United Kingdom, and

(b) to a State of which he is not a national or citizen.

(2) A State to which this Part applies shall be treated, in so far as relevant to the question mentioned in sub-paragraph (1), as a place—

(a) where a person's life and liberty are not threatened by reason of his race, religion, nationality, membership of a particular social group or political opinion, and

(b) from which a person will not be sent to another State otherwise than in accordance with the Refugee Convention.

14. . . .

Note: omitted by Nationality and Borders Act 2022 c. 36 Sch.4 para.4 (June 28, 2022: repeal has effect as SI 2022/590 reg.2 and Sch.1 para.17 subject to transitional and saving provisions specified in SI 2022/590 reg.3 and Sch.2 para.4(4))

15.—(1) This paragraph applies where the Secretary of State certifies that—

(a) it is proposed to remove a person to a State to which this Part applies, and

(b) in the Secretary of State's opinion the person is not a national or citizen of the State.

(2) . . .

(3) The person may not bring an immigration appeal[[..]] in reliance on an asylum claim which asserts that to remove the person to a specified State to which this Part applies would breach the United Kingdom's obligations under the Refugee Convention.

(4) The person may not bring an immigration appeal [[..]] in reliance on a human rights claim if the Secretary of State certifies that the claim is clearly unfounded.

Note: Subparagraph (2) omitted and words in square brackets in subparagraphs (3) and (4) substituted by Sch. 9 Immigration Act 2014 from 20 October 2014 with savings set out in articles 9-11 SI 2014/2771. Words in double square brackets omitted by Nationality and Borders Act 2022 c.36 Sch.4 para 15 (June 28, 2022: repeal has effect subject to transitional provision in 2022 c.36 Sch4 para 19(2))

16. . . .

Note: omitted by Nationality and Borders Act 2022 c.36 Sch.4 para 16 (June 28, 2022)

Part 5

Countries Certified as Safe for Individuals

17. This Part applies to a person who has made an asylum claim if the Secretary of State certifies that—

(a) it is proposed to remove the person to a specified State,

(b) in the Secretary of State's opinion the person is not a national or citizen of the specified State, and

(c) in the Secretary of State's opinion the specified State is a place—

(i) where the person's life and liberty will not be threatened by reason of his race, religion, nationality, membership of a particular social group or political opinion, and

(ii) from which the person will not be sent to another State otherwise than in accordance with the Refugee Convention.

18. . . .

Note: omitted by Nationality and Borders Act 2022 c. 36 Sch.4 para.4 (June 28, 2022: repeal has effect as SI 2022/590 reg.2 and Sch.1 para.17 subject to transitional and saving provisions specified in SI 2022/590 reg.3 and Sch.2 para.4(4))

19. Where this Part applies to a person—

(a) . . .

(b) he may not bring an immigration appeal [[]] in reliance on an asylum claim which asserts that to remove the person to the State specified under paragraph 17 would breach the United Kingdom's obligations under the Refugee Convention,

(c) he may not bring an immigration appeal [[]] in reliance on a human rights claim if the Secretary of State certifies that the claim is clearly unfounded, and

(d)

Note: Subparagraph (a) omitted and words in square brackets in subparagraphs (b) and (c) substituted by Sch. 9 Immigration Act 2014 from 20 October 2014 with savings set out in articles 9-11 SI 2014/2771. Paras. (4)(9)(14) & (18) omitted by Nationality and Borders Act 2022 c.36 Words omitted in double square brackets in sub-paras (b) & (c), and sub-para (d) by Nationality and Borders Act 2022 c.36 Sch.4 para 17 (June 28, 2022: repeal has effect subject to transitional provision in 2022 c.36 Sch.4 para 19(2))

Part 6

Amendment of Lists

20.—(1) The Secretary of State may by order

[(a) add a State to the list specified in paragraph 2, or.

(b) remove a state from that list.]

(2) The Secretary of State may by order—

(a) add a State to a list specified under paragraph 7 or 12, or

(b) remove a State from a list specified under paragraph 7 or 12.

Note: words within square brackets added by Nationality and Borders Act 2022 c.36 Sch.4 para 9 (June 28, 2022)

21.—(1) An order under paragraph 20(1)[(a)] or (2)(a)—

(a) shall be made by statutory instrument,

(b) shall not be made unless a draft has been laid before and approved by resolution of each House of Parliament, and

(c) may include transitional provision.

(2) An order under paragraph[20(1)(b) or (2)(b)—

(a) shall be made by statutory instrument,

(b) shall be subject to annulment in pursuance of a resolution of either House of Parliament, and

(c) may include transitional provision.

Note: Commencement 1 October 2004 (SI 2004/2523). Words substituted in square brackets by Nationality and Borders Act 2022 c.36 Sch.4 para 10 (June 28, 2022)

Schedule 4

Section 47

Repeals

. . .

Immigration, Asylum and Nationality Act 2006

(2006, c. 13)

Contents

Appeals

Employment

Information

An Act to make provision about immigration, asylum and nationality; and for connected purposes. [30 March 2006]

Appeals

1. Variation of leave to enter or remain

. . .

Note: Amends Nationality, Immigration and Asylum Act 2002, s 83. Repealed by Sch 9 Immigration Act 2014 from 20 October 2014 with savings set out in articles 9–11 SI 2014/2771.

2. Removal

. . .

Note: Amends Nationality, Immigration and Asylum Act 2002, s 82(2). Repealed by Sch 9 Immigration Act 2014 from 20 October 2014 with savings set out in articles 9–11 SI 2014/2771.

3. Grounds of appeal

. . .

Note: Amends Nationality, Immigration and Asylum Act 2002, s 84(3). Repealed by Sch 9 Immigration Act 2014 from 20 October 2014 with savings set out in articles 9–11 SI 2014/2771.

4. Entry clearance

. . .

Note: Repealed by Sch 9 Immigration Act 2014 from 20 October 2014 with savings set out in articles 9–11 SI 2014/2771.

5. Failure to provide documents

. . .

Note: Amends Nationality, Immigration and Asylum Act 2002, s 88(2). Repealed by Sch 9 Immigration Act 2014 from 20 October 2014 with savings set out in articles 9–11 SI 2014/2771.

6. Refusal of leave to enter

. . .

Note: Amends Nationality, Immigration and Asylum Act 2002, s 89. Repealed by Sch 9 Immigration Act 2014 from 20 October 2014 with savings set out in articles 9–11 SI 2014/2771.

7. Deportation

. . .

Note: Amends Nationality, Immigration and Asylum Act 2002, ss 97, 112.

8. Legal aid

. . .

Note: Amends Nationality, Immigration and Asylum Act 2002, s 103D.

9. Abandonment of appeal

. . .

Note: Amends Nationality, Immigration and Asylum Act 2002, s 104(4).

10. Grants

. . .

Note: Amends Nationality, Immigration and Asylum Act 2002, s 110.

11. Continuation of leave

. . .

Note: Amends Immigration Act 1971, s 3C and Nationality, Immigration and Asylum Act 2002, s 82(3).

12. Asylum and human rights claims: definition

. . .

Note: Amends Nationality, Immigration and Asylum Act 2002, s 113.

13. Appeal from within United Kingdom: certification of unfounded claim

. . .

Note: Amends Nationality, Immigration and Asylum Act 2002, s 94.

14. Consequential amendments

Schedule 1 (which makes amendments consequential on the preceding provisions of this Act) shall have effect.

Note: Commencement 31 August 2006 (SI 2006/2226).

Employment

15. Penalty

(1) It is contrary to this section to employ an adult subject to immigration control if—

(a) he has not been granted leave to enter or remain in the United Kingdom, or

(b) his leave to enter or remain in the United Kingdom—
(i) is invalid,
(ii) has ceased to have effect (whether by reason of curtailment, revocation, cancellation, passage of time or otherwise), or
(iii) is subject to a condition preventing him from accepting the employment.

(2) The Secretary of State may give an employer who acts contrary to this section a notice requiring him to pay a penalty of a specified amount not exceeding the prescribed maximum.

(3) An employer is excused from paying a penalty if he shows that he complied with any prescribed requirements in relation to the employment.

(4) But the excuse in subsection (3) shall not apply to an employer who knew, at any time during the period of the employment, that it was contrary to this section.

(5) The Secretary of State may give a penalty notice without having established whether subsection (3) applies.

(6) A penalty notice must—
(a) state why the Secretary of State thinks the employer is liable to the penalty,
(b) state the amount of the penalty,
(c) specify a date, at least 28 days after the date specified in the notice as the date on which it is given, before which the penalty must be paid,
(d) specify how the penalty must be paid,
(e) explain how the employer may object to the penalty [or make an appeal against it], and
(f) explain how the Secretary of State may enforce the penalty.

(7) An order prescribing requirements for the purposes of subsection (3) may, in particular—
(a) require the production to an employer of a document of a specified description;
(b) require the production to an employer of one document of each of a number of specified descriptions;
(c) require an employer to take specified steps to verify, retain, copy or record the content of a document produced to him in accordance with the order;
(d) require action to be taken before employment begins;
(e) require action to be taken at specified intervals or on specified occasions during the course of employment.

Note: Commencement for the purposes of making an order under subsections (2), (3) and (7) is 5 November 2007 (SI 2007/3138), remainder 29 February 2008, but without effect on employment which commenced before that date (SI 2008/310, which sets out transitional provisions). Words in square brackets in subsection (6)(e) inserted by Sch 9 Immigration Act 2014 from 28 July 2014 (SI 2014/1820).

16. Objection

(1) This section applies where an employer to whom a penalty notice is given objects on the ground that—
(a) he is not liable to the imposition of a penalty,
(b) he is excused payment by virtue of section 15(3), or
(c) the amount of the penalty is too high.

(2) The employer may give a notice of objection to the Secretary of State.

(3) A notice of objection must—

(a) be in writing,

(b) give the objector's reasons,

(c) be given in the prescribed manner, and

(d) be given before the end of the prescribed period.

(4) Where the Secretary of State receives a notice of objection to a penalty he shall consider it and—

(a) cancel the penalty,

(b) reduce the penalty,

(c) increase the penalty, or

(d) determine to take no action.

(5) Where the Secretary of State considers a notice of objection he shall—

(a) have regard to the code of practice under section 19 (in so far as the objection relates to the amount of the penalty),

(b) inform the objector of his decision before the end of the prescribed period or such longer period as he may agree with the objector,

(c) if he increases the penalty, issue a new penalty notice under section 15, and

(d) if he reduces the penalty, notify the objector of the reduced amount.

Note: Commencement for the purposes of making an order under subsections (3) and (5) is 5 November 2007 (SI 2007/3138), remainder 29 February 2008, but without effect on employment which commenced before that date (SI 2008/310, which sets out transitional provisions).

17. Appeal

(1) An employer to whom a penalty notice is given may appeal to the court on the ground that—

(a) he is not liable to the imposition of a penalty,

(b) he is excused payment by virtue of section 15(3), or

(c) the amount of the penalty is too high.

(2) The court may—

(a) allow the appeal and cancel the penalty,

(b) allow the appeal and reduce the penalty, or

(c) dismiss the appeal.

(3) An appeal shall be a re-hearing of the Secretary of State's decision to impose a penalty and shall be determined having regard to—

(a) the code of practice under section 19 that has effect at the time of the appeal (in so far as the appeal relates to the amount of the penalty),

and

(b) any other matters which the court thinks relevant (which may include matters of which the Secretary of State was unaware);

and this subsection has effect despite any provision of rules of court.

[(4A) An appeal may be brought only if the employer has given a notice of objection under section 16 and the Secretary of State—

(a) has determined the objection by issuing to the employer the penalty notice (as a result of increasing the penalty under section 16(4)(c)),

(b) has determined the objection by—

(i) reducing the penalty under section 16(4)(b), or

(ii) taking no action under section 16(4)(d), or

(c) has not informed the employer of a decision before the end of the period that applies for the purposes of section 16(5)(b).

(4B) An appeal must be brought within the period of 28 days beginning with the relevant date.

(4C) Where the appeal is brought under subsection (4A)(a), the relevant date is the date specified in the penalty notice issued in accordance with section 16(5)(c) as the date on which it is given.

(4D) Where the appeal is brought under subsection (4A)(b), the relevant date is the date specified in the notice informing the employer of the decision for the purposes of section 16(5)(b) as the date on which it is given.

(4E) Where the appeal is brought under subsection (4A)(c), the relevant date is the date on which the period that applies for the purposes of section 16(5)(b) ends.]

(6) In this section 'the court' means—

(a) where the employer has his principal place in England and Wales, [the county court],

(b) where the employer has his principal place of business in Scotland, the sheriff, and

(c) where the employer has his principal place of business in Northern Ireland, a county court.

Note: Commencement 29 February 2008, but without effect on employment which commenced before that date (SI 2008/310, which sets out transitional provisions). Subsections (4)–(5) substituted by s 44 Immigration Act 2014 from 28 July 2014 (SI 2014/1820).

18. Enforcement

[**(1)** This section applies where a sum is payable to the Secretary of State as a penalty under section 15.

(1A) In England and Wales the penalty is recoverable as if it were payable under an order of the county court.

(1B) In Scotland, the penalty may be enforced in the same manner as an extract registered decree arbitral bearing a warrant for execution issued by the sheriff court of any sheriffdom in Scotland.

(1C) In Northern Ireland the penalty is recoverable as if it were payable under an order of a county court in Northern Ireland.

(1D) Where action is taken under this section for the recovery of a sum payable as a penalty under section 15, the penalty is—

(a) in relation to England and Wales, to be treated for the purposes of section 98 of the Courts Act 2003 (register of judgments and orders etc) as if it were a judgment entered in the county court;

(b) in relation to Northern Ireland, to be treated for the purposes of Article 116 of the Judgments Enforcement (Northern Ireland) Order 1981 (S.I. 1981/226 (N.I. 6)) (register of judgments) as if it were a judgment in respect of which an application has been accepted under Article 22 or 23(1) of that Order.]

(3) Money paid to the Secretary of State by way of penalty shall be paid into the Consolidated Fund.

Note: Commencement 29 February 2008, but without effect on employment which commenced before that date (SI 2008/310, which sets out transitional provisions). Subsections (1)–(2) substituted by s 45 Immigration Act 2014 from 28 July 2014 (SI 2014/1820).

19. Code of practice

(1) The Secretary of State shall issue a code of practice specifying factors to be considered by him in determining the amount of a penalty imposed under section 15.

(2) The code—

(a) shall not be issued unless a draft has been laid before Parliament, and

(b) shall come into force in accordance with provision made by order of the Secretary of State.

(3) The Secretary of State shall from time to time review the code and may revise and re-issue it following a review; and a reference in this section to the code includes a reference to the code as revised.

Note: Commencement 31 August 2006 (SI 2006/2226).

20. Orders

(1) An order of the Secretary of State under section 15, 16 or 19—

(a) may make provision which applies generally or only in specified circumstances,

(b) may make different provision for different circumstances,

(c) may include transitional or incidental provision, and

(d) shall be made by statutory instrument.

(2) An order under section 15(2) may not be made unless a draft has been laid before and approved by resolution of each House of Parliament.

(3) Any other order shall be subject to annulment in pursuance of a resolution of either House of Parliament.

Note: Commencement 5 November 2007 (SI 2007/3138).

21. Offence

(1) A person commits an offence if he employs another ('the employee') knowing that the employee is[disqualified from employment by reason of the employee's immigration status].

[(**1A**) A person commits an offence if the person—

(c) employs another person ('the employee') who is disqualified from employment by reason of the employee's immigration status, and

(d) has reasonable cause to believe that the employee is disqualified from employment by reason of the employee's immigration status.

(**1B**) For the purposes of subsections (1) and (1A) a person is disqualified from employment by reason of the person's immigration status if the person is an adult subject to immigration control and—

(a) the person has not been granted leave to enter or remain in the United Kingdom, or

(b) the person's leave to enter or remain in the United Kingdom—

(i) is invalid,

(ii) has ceased to have effect (whether by reason of curtailment, revocation, cancellation, passage of time or otherwise), or

(iii) is subject to a condition preventing the person from accepting the employment.]

(2) A person guilty of an offence under this section shall be liable—

(a) on conviction on indictment—

(i) to imprisonment for a term not exceeding [five] years,

(ii) to a fine, or

(iii) to both, or

(b) on summary conviction—

(i) to imprisonment for a term not exceeding 12 months in England and Wales or 6 months in Scotland or Northern Ireland,

(ii) to a fine not exceeding the statutory maximum, or

(iii) to both.

(3) An offence under this section shall be treated as—

(a) a relevant offence for the purpose of sections 28B and 28D of the Immigration Act 1971 (c. 77) (search, entry and arrest), and

(b) an offence under Part III of that Act (criminal proceedings) for the purposes of sections 28E, 28G and 28H (search after arrest).

(3A) Proceedings for an offence under this section that is committed in the territorial sea adjacent to the United Kingdom may be taken, and the offence may for all incidental purposes be treated as having been committed, in any place in the United Kingdom.

(3B) Section 3 of the Territorial Waters Jurisdiction Act 1878 (consent of Secretary of State for certain prosecutions) does not apply to proceedings for an offence under this section.

(4) In relation to a conviction occurring before the commencement of [paragraph 24(2) of Schedule 22 to the Sentencing Act 2020] (general limit on magistrates' powers to imprison) the reference to 12 months in subsection (2)(b)(i) shall be taken as a reference to 6 months.

Note: Commencement 29 February 2008, but without effect on employment which commenced before that date (SI 2008/310, which sets out transitional provisions). Words in square brackets substituted and inserted by Immigration Act 2016, s 35 on 12 July 2016 (SI 2016/603). Words in square brackets in subsection (4) substituted by Sentencing Act 2020 c.17 Sch.24(6) para.443 (1) (December 1, 2020: substitution has effect subject to savings and transitional provisions specified in 2020 c.17 s.410 and Sch.24 Part (7). Subsections (3A) & (3B) inserted by Nationality and Borders Act 2022 c.36 Sch.6 para 10(13) (date to be appointed)

22. Offence: bodies corporate, &c.

(1) For the purposes of section 21(1) a body (whether corporate or not) shall be treated as knowing a fact about an employee if a person who has responsibility within the body for an aspect of the employment knows the fact.

[(1A) For the purposes of section 21(1A) a body (whether corporate or not) shall be treated as having reasonable cause to believe a fact about an employee if a person who has responsibility within the body for an aspect of the employment has reasonable cause to believe that fact.]

(2) If an offence under section 21(1) [or (1A)]is committed by a body corporate with the consent or connivance of an officer of the body, the officer, as well as the body, shall be treated as having committed the offence.

(3) In subsection (2) a reference to an officer of a body includes a reference to—

(a) a director, manager or secretary,

(b) a person purporting to act as a director, manager or secretary, and

(c) if the affairs of the body are managed by its members, a member.

(4) Where an offence under section 21(1) [or (1A)] is committed by a partnership (whether or not a limited partnership) subsection (2) above shall have effect, but as if a reference to an officer of the body were a reference to—

(a) a partner, and

(b) a person purporting to act as a partner.

Note: Commencement 29 February 2008, but without effect on employment which commenced before that date (SI 2008/310, which sets out transitional provisions). Subsection (1A) inserted by Immigration Act 2016, s 35 on 12 July 2016 (SI 2016/603).

23. Discrimination: code of practice

(1) The Secretary of State shall issue a code of practice specifying what an employer should or should not do in order to ensure that, while avoiding liability to a penalty under section 15 and while avoiding the commission of an offence under section 21, he also avoids contravening—

(a) [the Equality Act 2010, so far as relating to race], or

(b) the Race Relations (Northern Ireland) Order 1997 (S.I. 869 (N.I. 6)).

(2) Before issuing the code the Secretary of State shall—

(a) consult—

(i) the Commission for Equality and Human Rights,

(ii) the Equality Commission for Northern Ireland,

(iii) such bodies representing employers as he thinks appropriate, and

(iv) such bodies representing workers as he thinks appropriate,

(b) publish a draft code (after that consultation),

(c) consider any representations made about the published draft, and

(d) lay a draft code before Parliament (after considering representations under paragraph (c) and with or without modifications to reflect the representations).

(3) The code shall come into force in accordance with provision made by order of the Secretary of State; and an order—

(a) may include transitional provision,

(b) shall be made by statutory instrument, and

(c) shall be subject to annulment in pursuance of a resolution of either House of Parliament.

(4) A breach of the code—

(a) shall not make a person liable to civil or criminal proceedings, but

(b) may be taken into account by a court or tribunal.

(5) The Secretary of State shall from time to time review the code and may revise and re-issue it following a review; and a reference in this section to the code includes a reference to the code as revised.

(6) Until the dissolution of the Commission for Racial Equality, the reference in subsection (2)(a)(i) to the Commission for Equality and Human Rights shall be treated as a reference to the Commission for Racial Equality.

Note: Commencement 31 August 2006 (SI 2006/2226). Words substituted in subsection (1)(a) from 1 October 2010 by the Equality Act 2010, Sch 26, paragraph 86 as inserted by SI 2010/2279.

24. Immigration bail

Where a person is at large in the United Kingdom by virtue of [[a grant of immigration bail to the person under Schedule 10 to the Immigration Act 2016]]—

(a) he shall be treated for the purposes of sections 15(1) and [21(1B)] as if he had been granted leave to enter the United Kingdom, and

(b) any restriction as to employment imposed under [[that Schedule as a condition of that person's immigration bail]] shall be treated for those purposes as a condition of leave.

Note: Commencement 29 February 2008, but without effect on employment which commenced before that date (SI 2008/310, which sets out transitional provisions). Words in square brackets substituted by Immigration Act 2016, s 35 on 12 July 2016 (SI2016/603). Words in double square brackets substituted by Schedule 10 to the Immigration Act 2016 from January 15, 2018 subject to transitional provisions in SI 2017/1241.

25. Interpretation

In sections 15 to 24—

(a) 'adult' means a person who has attained the age of 16,

(b) a reference to employment is to employment under a contract of service or apprenticeship, whether express or implied and whether oral or written,

(c) a person is subject to immigration control if under the Immigration Act 1971 he requires leave to enter or remain in the United Kingdom, and

(d) 'prescribed' means prescribed by order of the Secretary of State.

Note: Commencement 5 November 2007 (SI 2007/3138), but without effect on employment which commenced before 29 February 2008 (SI 2008/310), which sets out transitional provisions).

26. Repeal

. . .

Note: Repeals Asylum and Immigration Act 1996, ss 8 and 8A, but without effect on employment which commenced before 29 February 2008 (SI 2008/310, which sets out transitional provisions).

Information

27. Documents produced or found

. . .

Note: Amends paragraph 4, Sch 2 Immigration Act 1971.

28. Fingerprinting

. . .

Note: Amends Immigration and Asylum Act 1999, s 141.

29. Attendance for fingerprinting

. . .

Note: Amends Immigration and Asylum Act 1999, s 142(2).

30. Proof of right of abode

. . .

Note: Amends Immigration Act 1971, s 3(9).

31. Provision of information to immigration officers

. . .

Note: Subsections (1)–(3) amend paragraph 27, Sch 2 Immigration Act 1971; subsection (4) amends s 27 of that Act.

32. Passenger and crew information: police powers

(1) This section applies to ships and aircraft which are—

[(a) arriving, or expected to arrive, at any place in the United Kingdom (whether from a place in the United Kingdom or from outside the United Kingdom), or

(b) leaving, or expected to leave, from any place in the United Kingdom (whether for a place in the United Kingdom or for outside the United Kingdom).]

(2) The owner or agent of a ship or aircraft shall comply with any requirement imposed by a constable of the rank of superintendent or above to provide passenger or service information.

(3) A passenger or member of crew shall provide to the owner or agent of a ship or aircraft any information that he requires for the purpose of complying with a requirement imposed by virtue of subsection (2).

(4) A constable may impose a requirement under subsection (2) only if he thinks it necessary—

(a) in the case of a constable in England, Wales or Northern Ireland, for police purposes, or

(b) in the case of a constable in Scotland, for police purposes which are or relate to reserved matters.

(5) In this section—

(a) 'passenger or service information' means information which is of a kind specified by order of the Secretary of State and which relates to—

(i) passengers,

(ii) members of crew, or

(iii) a voyage or flight,

(b) 'police purposes' has the meaning given by section 21(3) of the Immigration and Asylum Act 1999 (c. 33) (disclosure by Secretary of State),. . .

(c) 'reserved matters' has the same meaning as in the Scotland Act 1998 (c. 46)[, and

(d) 'ship' includes—

(i) every description of vessel used in navigation, and

(ii) hovercraft.]

(6) A requirement imposed under subsection (2)—

(a) must be in writing,

(b) may apply generally or only to one or more specified ships or aircraft,

(c) must specify a period, not exceeding six months and beginning with the date on which it is imposed, during which it has effect,

(d) must state—

(i) the information required, and

(ii) the date or time by which it is to be provided,

[(e) may include a requirement for the owner or agent of a ship or aircraft to be able to receive, in a specified form and manner, communications relating to the information.]

(7) The Secretary of State may make an order specifying a kind of information under subsection (5)(a) only if satisfied that the nature of the information is such that there are likely to be circumstances in which it can be required under subsection (2) without breaching Convention rights (within the meaning of the Human Rights Act 1998 (c. 42)).

(8) An order under subsection (5)(a)—

(a) may apply generally or only to specified cases or circumstances,

(b) may make different provision for different cases or circumstances,

(c) may specify the form and manner in which information is to be provided,

(d) shall be made by statutory instrument, and

(e) shall be subject to annulment in pursuance of a resolution of either House of Parliament.

Note: Commencement for the purposes of making an order under subsection (5)(a), 5 November 2007 (SI 2007/3138), remainder 1 March 2008 (SI 2007/3580). Subsection (1)(a) and (b) substituted and subsection (5)(d) inserted and word omitted from subsection (5)(c) by Police and Justice Act 2006, s 14, Schedule 15 from a date to be appointed. Section 32 has effect in a form modified by and in circumstances specified by the Channel Tunnel (International Arrangements) Order (SI 1993/1813) as amended by SIs 1994/1405, 2000/913, 2001/178, 2001/3707, 2006/1003 and 2007/3759. Subsection (6)(e) inserted from 12 February 2015 by Counter Terrorism and Security Act 2015, Schedule 5.

[32A Regulations requiring information to be provided to police

(1) The Secretary of State may make regulations requiring responsible persons in relation to ships or aircraft—

(a) which have arrived, or are expected to arrive, in the United Kingdom, or

(b) which have left, or are expected to leave, the United Kingdom, to provide information to the police.

(2) The following information may be required under subsection (1)—

(a) information about the persons on board;

(b) information about the voyage or flight.

(3) Regulations may impose a requirement to provide the information only if the Secretary of State thinks it necessary—

(a) in the case of a requirement to provide information to the police in England and Wales, for police purposes;

(b) in the case of a requirement to provide information to the police in Scotland, for police purposes which are or relate to reserved matters (within the meaning of the Scotland Act 1998);

(c) in the case of a requirement to provide information to the police in Northern Ireland, for police purposes which are or relate to excepted or reserved matters (within the meaning of the Northern Ireland Act 1998).

In this subsection 'police purposes' has the same meaning as in section 32.

(4) The regulations must—

(a) specify or describe the classes of ships or aircraft to which they apply;
(b) specify the information required to be provided;
(c) specify the time by which the information must be provided;
(d) specify the form and manner in which the information must be provided.

(5) The regulations may require responsible persons to be able to receive, in a specified form and manner, communications sent by the police, the Secretary of State or an immigration officer relating to the information.

(6) Regulations under this section—

(a) may apply generally or only to specified cases or circumstances,
(b) may make different provision for different cases or circumstances,
(c) shall be made by statutory instrument, and
(d) may not be made unless a draft has been laid before and approved by resolution of each House of Parliament.

(7) For the purposes of this section, the following are responsible persons in respect of a ship or aircraft—

(a) the owner or agent, and
(b) the captain.

32B Penalty for breach of section 32 or 32A

(1) The Secretary of State may make regulations imposing penalties for failure to comply with a requirement imposed—

(a) under section 32(2) (provision of passenger, crew or service information), or

(b) by regulations made under section 32A (regulations requiring information to be provided to police).

(2) Regulations under subsection (1) may in particular make provision—

(a) about how a penalty is to be calculated;
(b) about the procedure for imposing a penalty;
(c) about the enforcement of penalties;
(d) allowing for an appeal against a decision to impose a penalty;

and the regulations may make different provision for different purposes.

(3) Provision in the regulations about the procedure for imposing a penalty must provide for a person to be given an opportunity to object to a proposed penalty in the circumstances set out in the regulations.

(4) The regulations must provide that no penalty may be imposed on a person for failure to comply with a requirement imposed under section 32(2) or by regulations made under section 32A where—

(a) proceedings have been instituted against the person under section 34 in respect of the same failure, or

(b) the failure consists of a failure to provide information that the person has also been required to provide under paragraph 27, 27B or 27BA of Schedule 2 to the Immigration Act 1971 and—

(i) a penalty has been imposed on the person in respect of a failure to provide that information by virtue of regulations made under paragraph 27BB of that Schedule, or

(ii) proceedings have been instituted against the person under section 27 of that Act in respect of a failure to provide that information, or

(c) the failure consists of a failure to provide information that the person has also been required to provide under an authority to-carry scheme made under section 22 of the Counter-Terrorism and Security Act 2015 and a penalty has been imposed on the person in respect of a failure to provide that information by virtue of regulations made under section 24 of that Act.

(5) Any penalty paid by virtue of this section must be paid into the Consolidated Fund.

(6) Regulations under this section—

(a) must be made by statutory instrument, and

(b) may not be made unless a draft has been laid before and approved by resolution of each House of Parliament.]

Note: Sections 32(A) and (B) inserted from 12 February 2015 by Counter Terrorism and Security Act 2015, Schedule 5.

33. Freight information: police powers

(1) This section applies to ships, aircraft and vehicles which are—

(a) arriving, or expected to arrive, in the United Kingdom, or

(b) leaving, or expected to leave, the United Kingdom.

(2) If a constable of the rank of superintendent or above requires a person specified in subsection (3) to provide freight information he shall comply with the requirement.

(3) The persons referred to in subsection (2) are—

(a) in the case of a ship or aircraft, the owner or agent,

(b) in the case of a vehicle, the owner or hirer, and

(c) in any case, persons responsible for the import or export of the freight into or from the United Kingdom.

(4) A constable may impose a requirement under subsection (2) only if he thinks it necessary—

(a) in the case of a constable in England, Wales or Northern Ireland, for police purposes, or

(b) in the case of a constable in Scotland, for police purposes which are or relate to reserved matters.

(5) In this section—

(a) 'freight information' means information which is of a kind specified by order of the Secretary of State and which relates to freight carried,

(b) 'police purposes' has the meaning given by section 21(3) of the Immigration and Asylum Act 1999 (c. 33) (disclosure by Secretary of State), and

(c) 'reserved matters' has the same meaning as in the Scotland Act 1998 [, and

(d) 'ship' includes—

(i) every description of vessel used in navigation, and

(ii) hovercraft.]

(6) A requirement imposed under subsection (2)—

(a) must be in writing,

(b) may apply generally or only to one or more specified ships, aircraft or vehicles,

(c) must specify a period, not exceeding six months and beginning with the date on which it is imposed, during which it has effect, and

(d) must state—

(i) the information required, and

(ii) the date or time by which it is to be provided.

(7) The Secretary of State may make an order specifying a kind of information under subsection (5) (a) only if satisfied that the nature of the information is such that there are likely to be circumstances in which it can be required under subsection (2) without breaching Convention rights (within the meaning of the Human Rights Act 1998 (c. 42)).

(8) An order under subsection (5) (a)—

(a) may apply generally or only to specified cases or circumstances,

(b) may make different provision for different cases or circumstances,

(c) may specify the form and manner in which the information is to be provided,

(d) shall be made by statutory instrument, and

(e) shall be subject to annulment in pursuance of a resolution of either House of Parliament.

Note: Commencement for the purposes of making an order under subsection (5) (a) 1 April 2008 (SI 2008/310). Subsection (5) (d) inserted and word omitted from subsection (5) (c) by Police and Justice Act 2006 s 14, Schedule 15 from a date to be appointed.

34. Offence

(1) A person commits an offence if without reasonable excuse he fails to comply with a requirement [imposed—

(a) under section 32(2) or (3) or 33(2), or

(b) by regulations made under section 32A].

[(1A) Proceedings may not be instituted against a person under subsection (1) for a failure to comply with a requirement imposed under section 32(2) or by regulations made under section 32A where—

(a) the person has paid a penalty in respect of the same failure, or a failure to provide the same information, by virtue of regulations made under—

(i) section 32B,

(ii) paragraph 27BB of Schedule 2 to the Immigration Act 1971, or

(iii) section 24 of the Counter-Terrorism and Security Act 2015 (penalty for breach of authority-to-carry scheme); or

(b) proceedings have been instituted against the person under section 27 of the Immigration Act 1971 in respect of a failure to provide the same information.'

(3) In subsection (2), at the end insert ', and

(c) where a person fails without reasonable excuse to comply with a requirement imposed by regulations made under section 32A to provide information to the police in England and Wales—

(i) if the required information does not relate to a reserved matter (within the meaning of the Scotland Act 1998), the person shall not be treated as having committed the offence in Scotland (but has committed the offence in England and Wales);

(ii) if the required information does not relate to an excepted or reserved matter (within the meaning of the Northern Ireland Act 1998), the person shall not be treated as having committed the offence in Northern Ireland (but has committed the offence in England and Wales).]

(2) But—

(a) a person who fails without reasonable excuse to comply with a requirement imposed under section 32(2) or 33(2) by a constable in England and Wales or Northern Ireland otherwise than in relation to a reserved matter (within the meaning of the Scotland Act 1998 (c. 46)) shall not be treated as having committed the offence in Scotland (but has committed the offence in England and Wales or Northern Ireland), and

(b) a person who fails without reasonable excuse to comply with a requirement which is imposed under section 32(3) for the purpose of complying with a requirement to which paragraph (a) applies—

(i) shall not be treated as having committed the offence in Scotland, but

(ii) shall be treated as having committed the offence in England and Wales or Northern Ireland.

(3) A person who is guilty of an offence under subsection (1) shall be liable on summary conviction to—

(a) imprisonment for a term not exceeding 51 weeks in England and Wales or 6 months in Scotland or Northern Ireland,

(b) a fine not exceeding level 4 on the standard scale, or

(c) both.

(4) In relation to a conviction occurring before the commencement of section 281(5) of the Criminal Justice Act 2003 (c. 44) (51 week maximum term of sentences) the reference to 51 weeks in subsection (2)(a) shall be taken as a reference to three months.

Note: Commencement 1 March 2008 (SI 2007/3580). Section 34 has effect in a form modified by and in circumstances specified by the Channel Tunnel (International Arrangements) Order (SI 1993/1813) as amended by SIs 1994/1405, 2000/913, 2001/178, 2001/3707, 2006/1003 and 2007/3759. Words in square brackets substituted in subsection (1) and inserted in subsection (1A) by Counter Terrorism and Security Act 2015, Schedule 5.

35. Power of Revenue and Customs to obtain information

...

Note: Amends Customs and Excise Management Act 1979, s 35.

36. Duty to share information

(1) This section applies to—

[(a) designated customs officials,

(aa) immigration officers,

(ab) the Secretary of State in so far as the Secretary of State has general customs functions,

(ac) the Secretary of State in so far as the Secretary of State has functions relating to immigration, asylum or nationality,

(ad) the Director of Border Revenue and any person exercising functions of the Director,]

(b) a chief officer of police, and

(c) Her Majesty's Revenue and Customs.

(2) The persons specified in subsection (1) shall share information to which subsection (4) applies and which is obtained or held by them in the course of their functions to the extent that the information is likely to be of use for—

(a) immigration purposes,

(b) police purposes, or

(c) Revenue and Customs purposes.

(3) But a chief officer of police in Scotland shall share information under subsection (2) only to the extent that it is likely to be of use for—

(a) immigration purposes,

(b) police purposes, in so far as they are or relate to reserved matters within the meaning of the Scotland Act 1998, or

(c) Revenue and Customs purposes other than the prosecution of crime.

(4) This subsection applies to information which—

(a) is obtained or held in the exercise of a power specified by the Secretary of State and the Treasury jointly by order and relates to—

(i) passengers on a ship or aircraft,

(ii) crew of a ship or aircraft,

(iii) freight on a ship or aircraft, or

(iv) flights or voyages, or

(b) relates to such other matters in respect of travel or freight as the Secretary of State and the Treasury may jointly specify by order.

(5) The Secretary of State and the Treasury may make an order under subsection (4) which has the effect of requiring information to be shared only if satisfied that—

(a) the sharing is likely to be of use for—

(i) immigration purposes,

(ii) police purposes, or

(iii) Revenue and Customs purposes, and

(b) the nature of the information is such that there are likely to be circumstances in which it can be shared under subsection (2) without breaching Convention rights (within the meaning of the Human Rights Act 1998 (c. 42)).

(6) Information shared in accordance with subsection (2)—

(a) shall be made available to each of the persons [or descriptions of persons] specified in subsection (1), and

(b) may be used for immigration purposes, police purposes or Revenue and Customs purposes (regardless of its source).

(7) An order under subsection (4) may not specify—

(a) a power of Her Majesty's Revenue and Customs if or in so far as it relates to a matter to which section 7 of the Commissioners for Revenue and Customs Act 2005 (c. 11) (former Inland Revenue matters) applies, or

(b) a matter to which that section applies.

(8) An order under subsection (4)—

(a) shall be made by statutory instrument, and

(b) may not be made unless a draft has been laid before and approved by resolution of each House of Parliament.

(9) In this section—

'chief officer of police' means—

(a) in England and Wales, the chief officer of police for a police area specified in section 1 of the Police Act 1996 (c. 16),

(b) in Scotland, the chief constable of a police force maintained under the Police (Scotland) Act 1967 (c. 77), and

(c) in Northern Ireland, the chief constable of the Police Service of Northern Ireland,

['designated customs official' and 'general customs function' have the meanings given by Part 1 of the Borders, Citizenship and Immigration Act 2009,]

'immigration purposes' has the meaning given by section 20(3) of the Immigration and Asylum Act 1999 (c. 33) (disclosure to Secretary of State),

'police purposes' has the meaning given by section 21(3) of that Act (disclosure by Secretary of State), and

'Revenue and Customs purposes' means those functions of Her Majesty's Revenue and Customs specified in section 21(6) of that Act.

(10) This section has effect despite any restriction on the purposes for which information may be disclosed or used.

Note: Commencement for the purposes of making an order under subsection (4), (5) from November 2007 (SI 2007/3138), remainder 1 March 2008 (SI 2007/3580). Subsection (1)(a) substituted and words in square brackets in subsections (6) and (9) inserted by s 21 Borders, Citizenship and Immigration Act 21 July 2009, s 58(1). There is a prospective insertion of a definition, the definition of 'ship': see Police and Justice Act 2006 s 14(4). Section 36 has effect in a form modified by and in circumstances specified by the Channel Tunnel (International Arrangements) Order (SI 1993/1813) as amended by SIs 1994/1405, 2000/913, 2001/178, 2001/3707, 2006/1003 and 2007/3759.

37. Information sharing: code of practice

(1) The Secretary of State and the Treasury shall jointly issue one or more codes of practice about—

(a) the use of information shared in accordance with section 36(2), and

(b) the extent to which, or form or manner in which, shared information is to be made available in accordance with section 36(6).

(2) A code—

(a) shall not be issued unless a draft has been laid before Parliament, and

(b) shall come into force in accordance with provision made by order of the Secretary of State and the Treasury jointly.

(3) The Secretary of State and the Treasury shall jointly from time to time review a code and may revise and re-issue it following a review; and subsection (2) shall apply to a revised code.

(4) An order under subsection (2)—

(a) shall be made by statutory instrument, and

(b) shall be subject to annulment in pursuance of a resolution of either House of Parliament.

Note: Commencement for the purposes of laying a draft code before Parliament and making an order under subsection (2) is 5 November 2007 (SI 2007/3138), remainder 1 March 2008 (SI 2007/3580). Section 37 has effect in a form modified by and in circumstances specified by the Channel Tunnel (International Arrangements) Order (SI 1993/1813) as amended by SIs 1994/1405, 2000/913, 2001/178, 2001/3707, 2006/1003 and 2007/3759.

38. . . .

Note: Commencement for the purposes of making an order under subsection (4) is 5 November 2007 (SI 2007/3138), remainder 1 March 2008 (SI 2007/3580). Revoked by Sch 1 Counter-Terrorism Act 2008 from 24 December 2008, SI 2008/3296.

39. Disclosure to law enforcement agencies

(1) A chief officer of police may disclose information obtained in accordance with section 32 or 33 to—

(a) the States of Jersey police force;
(b) the salaried police force of the Island of Guernsey;
(c) the Isle of Man constabulary;
(d) any other foreign law enforcement agency.

(2) In subsection (1) 'foreign law enforcement agency' means a person outside the United Kingdom with functions similar to functions of—

(a) a police force in the United Kingdom, or
(b) the [National Crime Agency]

(3) In subsection (1) 'chief officer of police' means—

(a) in England and Wales, the chief officer of police for a police area specified in section 1 of the Police Act 1996,

(b) in Scotland, the chief constable of [the Police Service of Scotland], a police force maintained under the Police (Scotland) Act 1967, and

(c) in Northern Ireland, the chief constable of the Police Service of Northern Ireland.

Note: Commencement 1 March 2008 (SI 2007/3580). Section 39 has effect in a form modified by and in circumstances specified by the Channel Tunnel (International Arrangements) Order (SI 1993/1813) as amended by SIs 1994/1405, 2000/913, 2001/178, 2001/3707, 2006/1003 and 2007/3759. Words in square brackets in subsection (2)(b) substituted by Crime and Courts Act 2013 Sch 8 from 7 October 2013 (SI 2013/1682). Words in square brackets in subsection (3)(b) substituted from 1 April 2013 (SI 2013/602).

40. Searches: contracting out

(1) An authorised person may, in accordance with arrangements made under this section, search a searchable ship, aircraft, vehicle or other thing for the purpose of satisfying himself whether there are individuals whom an immigration officer might wish to examine under paragraph 2 of Schedule 2 to the Immigration Act 1971 (c. 77) (control of entry: administrative provisions).

(2) For the purposes of subsection (1)—

(a) 'authorised' means authorised for the purpose of this section by the Secretary of State, and

(b) a ship, aircraft, vehicle or other thing is 'searchable' if an immigration officer could search it under paragraph 1(5) of that Schedule.

(3) The Secretary of State may authorise a specified class of constable for the purpose of this section.

(4) The Secretary of State may, with the consent of the Commissioners for Her Majesty's Revenue and Customs, authorise a specified class of officers of Revenue and Customs for the purpose of this section.

(5) The Secretary of State may authorise a person other than a constable or officer of Revenue and Customs for the purpose of this section only if—

(a) the person applies to be authorised, and

(b) the Secretary of State thinks that the person is—

(i) fit and proper for the purpose, and

(ii) suitably trained.

(6) The Secretary of State—

(a) may make arrangements for the exercise by authorised constables of the powers under subsection (1),

(b) may make arrangements with the Commissioners for Her Majesty's Revenue and Customs for the exercise by authorised officers of Revenue and Customs of the powers under subsection (1), and

(c) may make arrangements with one or more persons for the exercise by authorised persons other than constables and officers of Revenue and Customs of the power under subsection (1).

(7) Where in the course of a search under this section an authorised person discovers an individual whom he thinks an immigration officer might wish to examine under paragraph 2 of that Schedule, the authorised person may—

(a) search the individual for the purpose of discovering whether he has with him anything of a kind that might be used—

(i) by him to cause physical harm to himself or another,

(ii) by him to assist his escape from detention, or

(iii) to establish information about his identity, nationality or citizenship or about his journey;

(b) retain, and as soon as is reasonably practicable deliver to an immigration officer, anything of a kind described in paragraph (a) found on a search under that paragraph;

(c) detain the individual, for a period which is as short as is reasonably necessary and which does not exceed three hours, pending the arrival of an immigration officer to whom the individual is to be delivered;

(d) take the individual, as speedily as is reasonably practicable, to a place for the purpose of delivering him to an immigration officer there;

(e) use reasonable force for the purpose of doing anything under paragraphs (a) to (d).

(8) Despite the generality of subsection (7)—

(a) an individual searched under that subsection may not be required to remove clothing other than an outer coat, a jacket or a glove (but he may be required to open his mouth), and

(b) an item may not be retained under subsection (7)(b) if it is subject to legal privilege—

(i) in relation to a search carried out in England and Wales, within the meaning of the Police and Criminal Evidence Act 1984 (c. 60),

(ii) in relation to a search carried out in Scotland, within the meaning of section 412 of the Proceeds of Crime Act 2002 (c. 29), and

(iii) in relation to a search carried out in Northern Ireland, within the meaning of the Police and Criminal Evidence (Northern Ireland) Order 1989 (SI 1989/1341 (N.I. 12)).

Note: Commencement 31 August 2006 (SI 2006/2226).

41. Section 40: supplemental

(1) Arrangements under section 40(6)(c) must include provision for the appointment of a Crown servant to—

(a) monitor the exercise of powers under that section by authorised persons (other than constables or officers of Revenue and Customs),

(b) inspect from time to time the way in which the powers are being exercised by authorised persons (other than constables or officers of Revenue and Customs), and

(c) investigate and report to the Secretary of State about any allegation made against an authorised person (other than a constable or officer of Revenue and Customs) in respect of anything done or not done in the purported exercise of a power under that section.

(2) The authorisation for the purpose of section 40 of a constable or officer of Revenue and Customs or of a class of constable or officer of Revenue and Customs—

(a) may be revoked, and

(b) shall have effect, unless revoked, for such period as shall be specified (whether by reference to dates or otherwise) in the authorisation.

(3) The authorisation of a person other than a constable or officer of Revenue and Customs for the purpose of section 40—

(a) may be subject to conditions,

(b) may be suspended or revoked by the Secretary of State by notice in writing to the authorised person, and

(c) shall have effect, unless suspended or revoked, for such period as shall be specified (whether by reference to dates or otherwise) in the authorisation.

(4) A class may be specified for the purposes of section 40(3) or (4) by reference to—

(a) named individuals,

(b) the functions being exercised by a person,

(c) the location or circumstances in which a person is exercising functions, or

(d) any other matter.

(5) An individual or article delivered to an immigration officer under section 40 shall be treated as if discovered by the immigration officer on a search under Schedule 2 to the Immigration Act 1971 (c. 77).

(6) A person commits an offence if he—

(a) absconds from detention under section 40(7)(c),

(b) absconds while being taken to a place under section 40(7)(d) or having been taken to a place in accordance with that paragraph but before being delivered to an immigration officer,

(c) obstructs an authorised person in the exercise of a power under section 40, or

(d) assaults an authorised person who is exercising a power under section 40.

(7) But a person does not commit an offence under subsection (6) by doing or failing to do anything in respect of an authorised person who is not readily identifiable—

(a) as a constable or officer of Revenue and Customs, or

(b) as an authorised person (whether by means of a uniform or badge or otherwise).

(8) A person guilty of an offence under subsection (6) shall be liable on summary conviction to—

(a) imprisonment for a term not exceeding 51 weeks, in the case of a conviction in England and Wales, or six months, in the case of a conviction in Scotland or Northern Ireland,

(b) a fine not exceeding level 5 on the standard scale, or

(c) both.

(9) In relation to a conviction occurring before the commencement of section 281(5) of the Criminal Justice Act 2003 (c. 44) (51 week maximum term of sentences) the reference in subsection (8)(a) to 51 weeks shall be treated as a reference to six months.

Note: Commencement 31 August 2006 (SI 2006/2226).

42. Information: embarking passengers

. . .

Note: Amends Sch 2 Immigration Act 1971 (c. 77).

Claimants and applicants

43. Accommodation

Note: Subsections (1) and (2) amend Immigration and Asylum Act 1999, s 99. Subsection (3) amends s 118 and subsection 7 amends s 4 of that Act. Subsection (4) amends Protection from Eviction Act 1977, s 3A; paragraph 3A, Sch 2 Housing (Northern Ireland Order 1983 (SI 1983/1118, NI 15); Rent (Scotland) Act 1984, s 23A; paragraph 4A, Sch 1 Housing Act 1985; paragraph 1B, Sch 4 Housing (Scotland) Act 1988; paragraph 12A, Sch 1 Housing Act 1988. Commenced 16 June 2006 (SI 2006/1497). Subsection (1)(b), (2), (5), (6) and (7) omitted by Schedule 11 to the Immigration Act 2016 from a date to be appointed: repeal has effect subject to savings and transitional provisions specified in Immigration Act 2016, Sch 11, para 46.

44. . . .

Note: Omitted by Schedule 11 to the Immigration Act 2016 from a date to be appointed.

45. Integration loans

. . .

Note: Amends Asylum and Immigration (Treatment of Claimants, etc.) Act 2004, s 13.

46. Inspection of detention facilities

. . .

Note: Amends Prison Act 1952, ss 5 and 5A.

47. Removal: persons with statutorily extended leave

Note: Subsection (6) amends Nationality, Immigration and Asylum Act 2002, s 82, subsection (7) amends s 92 and subsection (8) amends s 94(1A) of that Act. Commenced 1 April 2008 (SI 2008/310). Repealed by Sch 9 Immigration Act 2014 from 20 October 2014 with savings set out in articles 9–11 SI 2014/2771.

48. Removal: cancellation of leave

. . .

Note: Amends Immigration and Asylum Act 1999, s 10(8). Repealed by Sch 9 Immigration Act 2014 from 20 October 2014 with savings set out in SI 2014/2771 articles 9–11.

49. Capacity to make nationality application

. . .

Note: Amends British Nationality Act 1981, s 44.

50. Procedure

(1) Rules under section 3 of the Immigration Act 1971 (c. 77)—

(a) may require a specified procedure to be followed in making or pursuing an application or claim (whether or not under those rules or any other enactment),

(b) may, in particular, require the use of a specified form and the submission of specified information or documents,

(c) may make provision about the manner in which a fee is to be paid, and

(d) may make provision for the consequences of failure to comply with a requirement under paragraph (a), (b) or (c).

(2) In respect of any application or claim in connection with immigration (whether or not under the rules referred to in subsection (1) or any other enactment) the Secretary of State—

(a) may require the use of a specified form,

(b) may require the submission of specified information or documents, and

(c) may direct the manner in which a fee is to be paid; and the rules referred to in subsection (1) may provide for the consequences of failure to comply with a requirement under paragraph (a), (b) or (c).

(3) . . .

(4) . . .

(5) . . .

(6) . . .

Note: Subsection (3) repeals Immigration Act 1971, s 31A and Asylum and Immigration (Treatment of Claimants etc) Act 2004, s 25. Subsection (4) amends British Nationality Act 1981, s 41. Subsection (5) amends Nationality, Immigration and Asylum Act 2002, s 10. Subsection (6) repeals paragraph 2(3), Sch 23 Civil Partnership Act 2004. Commencement 31 January 2007 (SI 2007/182).

51. Fees

Note: Commencement 31 January 2007 (SI 2007/182). Repealed by Sch 9 Immigration Act 2014 from 15 December 2014 (SI 2014/2771).

52. Fees: supplemental

Note: Subsections (1)–(6) commenced 31 January 2007, (SI 2007/182), remainder 2 April 2007 (SI 2007/1109). Repealed by Sch 9 Immigration Act 2014 from 15 December 2014 (SI 2014/2771).

Miscellaneous

53. Arrest pending deportation

. . .

Note: Amends paragraph 2(4), Sch 3 Immigration Act 1971.

54. Refugee Convention: construction

(1) In the construction and application of Article 1(F) (c) of the Refugee Convention the reference to acts contrary to the purposes and principles of the United Nations shall be taken as including, in particular—

(a) acts of committing, preparing or instigating terrorism (whether or not the acts amount to an actual or inchoate offence), and

(b) acts of encouraging or inducing others to commit, prepare or instigate terrorism (whether or not the acts amount to an actual or inchoate offence).

(2) In this section—

'the Refugee Convention' means the Convention relating to the Status of Refugees done at Geneva on 28 July 1951, and

'terrorism' has the meaning given by section 1 of the Terrorism Act 2000 (c. 11).

Note: Commencement 31 August 2006 (SI 2006/2226).

55. Refugee Convention: certification

(1) This section applies to an asylum appeal where the Secretary of State issues a certificate that the appellant is not entitled to the protection of Article 33(1) of the Refugee Convention because—

(a) Article 1(F) applies to him (whether or not he would otherwise be entitled to protection), or

(b) Article 33(2) applies to him on grounds of national security (whether or not he would otherwise be entitled to protection).

(2) In this section—

(a) 'asylum appeal' means an appeal—

(i) which is brought under section 82. . . of the Nationality, Immigration and Asylum Act 2002 (c. 41) or section 2 of the Special Immigration Appeals Commission Act 1997 (c. 68), and

[(ii) which is brought on the ground mentioned in section 84(1) (a) or (3) (a) of that Act (breach of United Kingdom's obligations under the Refugee Convention);]

(b) 'the Refugee Convention' means the Convention relating to the Status of Refugees done at Geneva on 28 July 1951.

(3) The [First-tier Tribunal] or the Special Immigration Appeals Commission must begin substantive deliberations on the asylum appeal by considering the statements in the Secretary of State's certificate.

(4) If the Tribunal or Commission agrees with those statements it must dismiss such part of the asylum appeal as amounts to an asylum claim (before considering any other aspect of the case).

(5) Section 72(10) (a) of the Nationality, Immigration and Asylum Act 2002 (serious criminal: Tribunal or Commission to begin by considering certificate) shall have effect subject to subsection (3) above.

[(5A) Subsections (3) and (4) also apply in relation to the Upper Tribunal when it acts under section 12(2) (b) (ii) of the Tribunals, Courts and Enforcement Act 2007.]

(6) . . .

Note: Subsection (6) repeals Anti-terrorism, Crime and Security Act 2001, s 33. Commencement 31 August 2006 (SI 2006/2226). Words in square brackets in subsection (3) substituted and subsection (5A) inserted from 15 February 2010 (SI 2010/21). In subsection (2) words omitted and (2) (a) (ii) substituted by Sch 9 Immigration Act 2014 from 20 October 2014 with savings set out in articles 9–11 SI 2014/2771.

56. Deprivation of citizenship

(1) . . .

(2) . . .

Note: Subsection (1) amends the British Nationality Act 1981, s 42(2) subsection (2) amends s 40A of that Act.

57. Deprivation of right of abode

(1) . . .

(2) . . .

Note: Subsection (1) amends Immigration Act 1971, s 2 subsection (2) amends Nationality, Immigration and Asylum Act 2002, s 82, repealed by Sch 9 Immigration Act 2014 from 20 October 2014 with savings set out in articles 9–11 SI 2014/2771.

58. . . .

Note: Commencement from 4 December 2006, but without effect in relation to any application under the provisions listed in subsection (2) which was made before that date (SI 2006/2838). Section 50(8) of the British Nationality Act 1981 applies for the purpose of this section. Revoked by Schedule Borders, Citizenship and Immigration Act 2009 from 13 January 2010 (SI 2009/2731).

59. Detained persons: national minimum wage

(1) . . .

(2) . . .

Note: Subsection (1) amends Immigration and Asylum Act 1999, s 153. Subsection (2) amends National Minimum Wage Act 1998, s 45A.

General

60. Money

There shall be paid out of money provided by Parliament—

(a) any expenditure of the Secretary of State in connection with this Act, and

(b) any increase attributable to this Act in sums payable under another enactment out of money provided by Parliament.

Note: Commenced 16 June 2006 (SI 2006/1497).

61. Repeals

Schedule 3 (repeals) shall have effect.

Note: Commenced with regard to British Nationality Act 1981, s 40A(3) 16 June 2006 (SI 2006/1497). Remainder from 31 August 2006 (SI 2006/2226).

62. Commencement

(1) The preceding provisions of this Act shall come into force in accordance with provision made by order of the Secretary of State.

(2) An order under subsection (1)—

(a) may make provision generally or only for specified purposes,
(b) may make different provision for different purposes,
(c) may include transitional or incidental provision or savings, and
(d) shall be made by statutory instrument.

63. Extent

(1) This Act extends to—
(a) England and Wales,
(b) Scotland, and
(c) Northern Ireland.

(2) But—

(a) an amendment by this Act of another Act has the same extent as that Act or as the relevant part of that Act (ignoring extent by virtue of an Order in Council), and

(b) a provision of this Act shall, so far as it relates to nationality, have the same extent as the British Nationality Act 1981 (c. 61) (disregarding excepted provisions under section 53(7) of that Act).

(3) Her Majesty may by Order in Council direct that a provision of this Act is to extend, with or without modification or adaptation, to—
(a) any of the Channel Islands;
(b) the Isle of Man.

[(3A) In subsection (3), the reference to this Act includes—

(a) a reference to this Act as it has effect with the amendments and repeals made in it by the Police and Justice Act 2006, and

(b) a reference to this Act as it has effect without those amendments and repeals.]

(4) Subsection (3) does not apply in relation to the extension to a place of a provision which extends there by virtue of subsection (2)(b).

Note: Commencement 30 March 2006, s 62 (Royal Assent). Subsection (3A) inserted by Police and Justice Act 2006 s 54 from 8 November 2006 (Royal Assent).

64. Citation

(1) This Act may be cited as the Immigration, Asylum and Nationality Act 2006.

(2) . . .

(3) . . .

(4) . . .

Note: Subsection (2) repealed from 30 October 2007 (s 61 UK Borders Act 2007). Subsection (3) repeals the definition of the Immigration Acts in Immigration Act 1971, s 32(5) Immigration and Asylum Act 1999, s 167(1) Nationality, Immigration and Asylum Act 2002, s 158 and Asylum and Immigration (Treatment of Claimants, etc) Act 2004, s 44. Subsection (4) amends Sch. 1 Interpretation Act 1978. Commencement 30 March 2006, s 62 (Royal Assent).

SCHEDULES

SCHEDULE 1

Section 14

IMMIGRATION AND ASYLUM APPEALS: CONSEQUENTIAL AMENDMENTS

. . .

Section 52

SCHEDULE 2

FEES: CONSEQUENTIAL AMENDMENTS

. . .

Section 61

SCHEDULE 3

REPEALS

. . .

UK Borders Act 2007

(2007, c. 30)

Contents

Deportation of criminals

Information

Border and Immigration Inspectorate

General

Schedule—Repeals

An Act to make provision about immigration and asylum; and for connected purposes. [30 October 2007]

Detention at ports

1. Designated immigration officers

(1) The Secretary of State may designate immigration officers for the purposes of section 2.

(2) The Secretary of State may designate only officers who the Secretary of State thinks are—

(a) fit and proper for the purpose, and

(b) suitably trained.

(3) A designation—

(a) may be permanent or for a specified period, and

(b) may (in either case) be revoked.

Note: Commencement 31 January 2008 (SI 2008/99).

2. Detention

(1) A designated immigration officer at a port [] may detain an individual if the immigration officer thinks that the individual—

(a) may be liable to arrest by a constable under section [24(1), (2) or (3) of the Police and Criminal Evidence Act 1984, or Article 26(1), (2) or (3) of the Police and Criminal Evidence (Northern Ireland) Order 1989 (S.I 1989/1241 (N.I(12))],

(aa) is the subject of a certificate under section 74B of the Extradition Act 2003, or

(b) is subject to a warrant for arrest.

(1A) A designated immigration office at a port in Scotland may detain an individual if the immigration officer thinks that [the individual—

(a) may be liable to be [[arrested by a constable under section 1 of the Criminal Justice (Scotland) Act 2016]] in respect of an offence under section 10(1) of the Counter-Terrorism and Security Act 2015,

(aa) is the subject of a certificate under section 74B of the Extradition Act 2003, or

(b) is subject to a warrant for arrest.]

(2) A designated immigration officer who detains an individual—

(a) must arrange for a constable [, an officer belonging to the French Republic or an officer belonging to the Kingdom of Belgium] to attend as soon as is reasonably practicable,

(b) may search the individual for, and retain, anything that might be used to assist escape or to cause physical injury to the individual or another person,

(c) must retain anything found on a search which the immigration officer thinks may be evidence of the commission of an offence, and

(d) must, when the constable [, the officer belonging to the French Republic or an officer of the Kingdom of Belgium] arrives, deliver to the constable [, the officer to the French Republic or the officer belonging to the Kingdom of Belgium] the individual and anything retained on a search.

(3) An individual may not be detained under this section for longer than three hours.

(4) A designated immigration officer may use reasonable force for the purpose of exercising a power under this section.

(5) . . .

(6) Detention under this section shall be treated as detention under the Immigration Act 1971 for the purposes of Part 8 of the Immigration and Asylum Act 1999 (detained persons).

Note: Commencement 31 January 2008 (SI 2008/99). Subsection (1A) inserted by s 52 Borders, Citizenship and Immigration Act 2009 October 27, 2014. Words in square brackets omitted in subsection (1),(1A) and (5), and inserted at (1)(a),(2)(a) and (d) by The Channel Tunnel (International Arrangments) and Channel Tunnel (Miscellaneous Provisions (Amendment) Order (SI2015/856) from April 2015. Words in square brackets substituted at subsection (1A) by Counter Terrorism and Security Act 2015 c.6 Pt 1 c.2 s.10(8) from February 12, 2015. Words in double square brackets substituted in subsection (1A) by Criminal Justice (Scotland) Act 2016 (Consequential Provisions) Order 2018/46 art.20(1) from January 25, 2018: substitution does not apply in relation to a case in which a person is detained before SI 2018/46 art 20 comes into force being January 25, 2018 the day on which 1995 c.46 s.14 is repealed). Subsection (1)(aa) & (1A)(aa) inserted by Extradition Act (Provisional Arrest) Act 2020 c.18 Sch 1(2)para.28

3. Enforcement

(1) An offence is committed by a person who—

(a) absconds from detention under section 2,

(b) assaults an immigration officer exercising a power under section 2, or

(c) obstructs an immigration officer in the exercise of a power under section 2.

(2) A person guilty of an offence under subsection (1)(a) or (b) shall be liable on summary conviction to—

(a) imprisonment for a term not exceeding 51 weeks,

(b) a fine not exceeding level 5 on the standard scale,

(c) both.

(3) A person guilty of an offence under subsection (1)(c) shall be liable on summary conviction to—

(a) imprisonment for a term not exceeding 51 weeks,

(b) a fine not exceeding level 3 on the standard scale, or

(c) both.

(4) In the application of this section to Northern Ireland—

(a) the reference in subsection (2)(a) to 51 weeks shall be treated as a reference to six months, and

(b) the reference in subsection (3)(a) to 51 weeks shall be treated as a reference to one month.

[(4A) In the application of this section to Scotland, the references in subsections (2)(a) and (3)(a) to 51 weeks shall be treated as references to 12 months.]

(5) In relation to an offence committed before the commencement of section 281(5) of the Criminal Justice Act 2003 (51 week maximum term of sentences)—

(a) the reference in subsection (2)(a) to 51 weeks shall be treated as a reference to six months, and

(b) the reference in subsection (3)(a) to 51 weeks shall be treated as a reference to one month.

Note: Commencement 31 January 2008 (SI 2008/99). Subsection (4A) inserted by s 52 Borders, Citizenship and Immigration Act 2009 from 27 October 2014 (SI 2014/2634).

4. Interpretation: 'port'

(1) [In section 2 'port' means a terminal control point or an international station.]

(2) A place shall be treated for the purposes of that section as a port in relation to an individual if a designated immigration officer believes that the individual—

(a) has gone there for the purpose of embarking on a [train], or

(b) has arrived there on disembarking from a [train].

Note: Commencement 31 January 2008 (SI 2008/99). Words in square brackets at subsection (1) and (2)(a) and (b) substituted by The Channel Tunnel (International Arrangements) and Channel Tunnel (Miscellaneous Provisions)(Amendment) Order 2015 (SI 2015/856) from 16 April 2015.

Biometric registration

5. Registration regulations

(1) The Secretary of State may make regulations—

(a) requiring a person subject to immigration control to apply for the issue of a document recording biometric information (a 'biometric immigration document');

(b) requiring a biometric immigration document to be used—

(i) for specified immigration purposes,

(ii) in connection with specified immigration procedures, or

(iii) in specified circumstances, where a question arises about a person's status in relation to nationality or immigration;

(c) requiring a person who produces a biometric immigration document by virtue of paragraph (b) to provide information for comparison with information provided in connection with the application for the document.

(2) Regulations under subsection (1)(a) may, in particular—

(a) apply generally or only to a specified class of persons subject to immigration control (for example, persons making or seeking to make a specified kind of application for immigration purposes);

(b) specify the period within which an application for a biometric immigration document must be made;

(c) make provision about the issue of biometric immigration documents;

(d) make provision about the content of biometric immigration documents (which may include non-biometric information);

(e) make provision permitting a biometric immigration document to be combined with another document;

(f) make provision for biometric immigration documents to begin to have effect, and cease to have effect, in accordance with the regulations;

(g) require a person who acquires a biometric immigration document, without the consent of the person to whom it relates or of the Secretary of State, to surrender it to the Secretary of State as soon as is reasonably practicable;

(h) permit the Secretary of State to require the surrender of a biometric immigration document in other specified circumstances;

(i) permit the Secretary of State on issuing a biometric immigration document to require the surrender of other documents connected with immigration or nationality.

(3) Regulations under subsection (1)(a) may permit the Secretary of State to cancel a biometric immigration document—

(a) if the Secretary of State thinks that information provided in connection with the document was or has become false, misleading or incomplete,

(b) if the Secretary of State thinks that the document has been lost or stolen,

(c) if the Secretary of State thinks that the document (including any information recorded in it) has been altered, damaged or destroyed (whether deliberately or not),

(d) if the Secretary of State thinks that an attempt has been made (whether successfully or not) to copy the document or to do anything to enable it to be copied,

(e) if the Secretary of State thinks that a person has failed to surrender the document in accordance with subsection (2)(g) or (h),

(f) if the Secretary of State thinks that the document should be re-issued (whether because the information recorded in it requires alteration or for any other reason),

(g) if the Secretary of State thinks that the holder is to be given leave to enter or remain in the United Kingdom,

(h) if the Secretary of State thinks that the holder's leave to enter or remain in the United Kingdom is to be varied, cancelled or invalidated or to lapse,

(i) if the Secretary of State thinks that the holder has died,

(j) if the Secretary of State thinks that the holder has been removed from the United Kingdom (whether by deportation or otherwise),

(k) if the Secretary of State thinks that the holder has left the United Kingdom without retaining leave to enter or remain, and

(l) in such other circumstances as the regulations may specify.

(4) Regulations under subsection (1)(a) may require notification to be given to the Secretary of State by the holder of a biometric immigration document—

(a) who knows or suspects that the document has been lost or stolen,

(b) who knows or suspects that the document has been altered or damaged (whether deliberately or not),

(c) who knows or suspects that information provided in connection with the document was or has become false, misleading or incomplete,

(d) who was given leave to enter or remain in the United Kingdom in accordance with a provision of rules under section 3 of the Immigration Act 1971 (immigration rules) and knows or suspects that owing to a change of the holder's circumstances the holder would no longer qualify for leave under that provision, or

(e) in such other circumstances as the regulations may specify.

(5) Regulations under subsection (1)(a) may require a person applying for the issue of a biometric immigration document to provide information (which may include biographical or other non-biometric information) to be recorded in it or retained by the Secretary of State; and, in particular, the regulations may—

(a) require, or permit an authorised person to require, the provision of information in a specified form;

(b) require an individual to submit, or permit an authorised person to require an individual to submit, to a specified process by means of which biometric information is obtained or recorded;

(c) confer a function (which may include the exercise of a discretion) on an authorised person;

(d) permit the Secretary of State, instead of requiring the provision of information, to use or retain information which is (for whatever reason) already in the Secretary of State's possession.

(6) Regulations under subsection (1)(b) may, in particular, require the production or other use of a biometric immigration document that is combined with another document. . .

(7) Regulations under subsection (1)(b) may not make provision the effect of which would be to require a person to carry a biometric immigration document at all times.

(8) Regulations under subsection (1)(c) may, in particular, make provision of a kind specified in subsection (5)(a) or (b).

(9) Rules under section 3 of the Immigration Act 1971 may require a person applying for the issue of a biometric immigration document to provide non-biometric information to be recorded in it or retained by the Secretary of State.

(10) Subsections (5) to (9) are without prejudice to the generality of section 50 of the Immigration, Asylum and Nationality Act 2006 (procedure).

Note: Commencement 31 January 2008 (SI 2008/99). Words omitted from subsection (6) by the Identity Documents Act 2010, Schedule, paragraph 19 from 21 January 2011 (s 14(2)).

6. Regulations: supplemental

(1) This section applies to regulations under section 5(1).

(2) Regulations amending or replacing earlier regulations may require a person who holds a biometric immigration document issued under the earlier regulations to apply under the new regulations.

(3) In so far as regulations require an individual under the age of 16 to submit to a process for the recording of biometric information, or permit an authorised person to require an individual under the age of 16 to submit to a process of that kind, the regulations must make provision similar to section 141(3) to (5) and (13) of the Immigration and Asylum Act 1999 (fingerprints: children).

(4) Rules under section 3 of the Immigration Act 1971 (immigration rules) may make provision by reference to compliance or non-compliance with regulations.

(5) Information in the Secretary of State's possession which is used or retained in accordance with regulations under section 5(5)(d) shall be treated, for the purpose of requirements about treatment and destruction, as having been provided in accordance with the regulations at the time at which it is used or retained in accordance with them.

(6) Regulations—

(a) may make provision having effect generally or only in specified cases or circumstances,

(b) may make different provision for different cases or circumstances,

(c) may include incidental, consequential or transitional provision,

(d) shall be made by statutory instrument, and

(e) may not be made unless a draft has been laid before and approved by resolution of each House of Parliament.

Note: Commencement 31 January 2008 (SI 2008/99).

7. Effect of non-compliance

(1) Regulations under section 5(1) must include provision about the effect of failure to comply with a requirement of the regulations.

(2) In particular, the regulations may—

(a) require or permit an application for a biometric immigration document to be refused;

(b) require or permit an application or claim in connection with immigration to be disregarded or refused;

(c) require or permit the cancellation or variation of leave to enter or remain in the United Kingdom;

(d) require the Secretary of State to consider giving a notice under section 9;

(e) provide for the consequence of a failure to be at the discretion of the Secretary of State.

[(2A) If the regulations require a biometric immigration document to be used in connection with an application or claim, they may require or permit the application or claim to be disregarded or refused if that requirement is not complied with.]

(3) The regulations may also permit the Secretary of State to designate an adult as the person responsible for ensuring that a child complies with requirements of the regulations; and for that purpose—

(a) 'adult' means an individual who has attained the age of 18,

(b) 'child' means an individual who has not attained the age of 18, and

(c) sections 9 to 13 shall apply (with any necessary modifications) to a designated adult's failure to ensure compliance by a child with a requirement of regulations as they apply to a person's own failure to comply with a requirement.

Note: Commencement 31 January 2008 (SI 2008/99). Subsection (2A) inserted by s 11 Immigration Act 2014 from 28 July 2014 (SI 2014/1820).

[8 Use and retention of biometric information

(1) The Secretary of State must by regulations make provision about the use and retention by the Secretary of State of biometric information provided in accordance with regulations under section 5(1).

(2) The regulations must provide that biometric information may be retained only if the Secretary of State thinks that it is necessary to retain it for use in connection with—

(a) the exercise of a function by virtue of the Immigration Acts, or

(b) the exercise of a function in relation to nationality.

(3) The regulations may include provision permitting biometric information retained by virtue of subsection (2) also to be used—

(a) in connection with the prevention, investigation or prosecution of an offence,

(b) for a purpose which appears to the Secretary of State to be required in order to protect national security,

(c) in connection with identifying persons who have died, or are suffering from illness or injury,

(d) for the purpose of ascertaining whether a person has acted unlawfully, or has obtained or sought anything to which the person is not legally entitled, and

(e) for such other purposes (whether in accordance with functions under an enactment or otherwise) as the regulations may specify.

(4) The regulations must include provision about the destruction of biometric information.

(5) In particular the regulations must require the Secretary of State to take all reasonable steps to ensure that biometric information is destroyed if the Secretary of State—

(a) no longer thinks that it is necessary to retain the information for use as mentioned in subsection (2), or

(b) is satisfied that the person to whom the information relates is a British citizen, or a Commonwealth citizen who has a right of abode in the United Kingdom as a result of section 2(1)(b) of the Immigration Act 1971.

(6) The regulations must also—

(a) require that any requirement to destroy biometric information by virtue of the regulations also applies to copies of the information, and

(b) require the Secretary of State to take all reasonable steps to ensure—

(i) that data held in electronic form which relates to biometric information which has to be destroyed by virtue of the regulations is destroyed or erased, or

(ii) that access to such data is blocked.

(7) But a requirement to destroy biometric information or data is not to apply if and in so far as the information or data is retained in accordance with and for the purposes of another power.

(8) The regulations must include provision—

(a) entitling a person whose biometric information has to be destroyed by virtue of the regulations, on request, to a certificate issued by the Secretary of State to the effect that the Secretary of State has taken the steps required by virtue of subsection (6)(b), and

(b) requiring such a certificate to be issued within the period of 3 months beginning with the date on which the request for it is received by the Secretary of State.

(9) Section 6(6) applies to regulations under this section as it applies to regulations under section 5(1).]

Note: Commencement 31 January 2008 (SI 2008/99). Section 8 substituted by s 14 Immigration Act 2014 from 28 July 2014 (SI 2014/1820).

9. Penalty

(1) The Secretary of State may by notice require a person to pay a penalty for failing to comply with a requirement of regulations under section 5(1).

(2) The notice must—

(a) specify the amount of the penalty,

(b) specify a date before which the penalty must be paid to the Secretary of State,

(c) specify methods by which the penalty may be paid,

(d) explain the grounds on which the Secretary of State thinks the person has failed to comply with a requirement of the regulations, and

(e) explain the effect of sections 10 to 12.

(3) The amount specified under subsection (2)(a) may not exceed £1,000.

(4) The date specified under subsection (2)(b) must be not less than 14 days after the date on which the notice is given.

(5) A person who has been given a notice under subsection (1) for failing to comply with regulations may be given further notices in the case of continued failure; but a person may not be given a new notice—

(a) during the time available for objection or appeal against an earlier notice, or

(b) while an objection or appeal against an earlier notice has been instituted and is neither withdrawn nor determined.

(6) The Secretary of State may by order amend subsection (3) to reflect a change in the value of money.

Note: Commencement 25 November 2009 (SI 2008/2822).

10. Penalty: objection

(1) A person ('P') who is given a penalty notice under section 9(1) may by notice to the Secretary of State object on the grounds—

(a) that P has not failed to comply with a requirement of regulations under section 5(1),

(b) that it is unreasonable to require P to pay a penalty, or

(c) that the amount of the penalty is excessive.

(2) A notice of objection must—

(a) specify the grounds of objection and P's reasons,

(b) comply with any prescribed requirements as to form and content, and

(c) be given within the prescribed period.

(3) The Secretary of State shall consider a notice of objection and—

(a) cancel the penalty notice,

(b) reduce the penalty by varying the penalty notice,

(c) increase the penalty by issuing a new penalty notice, or

(d) confirm the penalty notice.

(4) The Secretary of State shall act under subsection (3) and notify P—

(a) in accordance with any prescribed requirements, and

(b) within the prescribed period or such longer period as the Secretary of State and P may agree.

Note: Commencement for the purposes of making an order under subsections (2) and (4) 31 January 2008 (SI 2008/99), remainder 25 November 2008 (SI 2008/2822).

11. Penalty: appeal

(1) A person ('P') who is given a penalty notice under section 9(1) may appeal to—

(a) [the county court in England and Wales or a county court in] Northern Ireland, or

(b) the sheriff, in Scotland.

(2) An appeal may be brought on the grounds—

(a) that P has not failed to comply with a requirement of regulations under section 5(1),

(b) that it is unreasonable to require P to pay a penalty, or

(c) that the amount of the penalty is excessive.

(3) The court or sheriff may—

(a) cancel the penalty notice,

(b) reduce the penalty by varying the penalty notice,

(c) increase the penalty by varying the penalty notice (whether because the court or sheriff thinks the original amount insufficient or because the court or sheriff thinks that the appeal should not have been brought), or

(d) confirm the penalty notice.

(4) An appeal may be brought—

(a) whether or not P has given a notice of objection, and

(b) irrespective of the Secretary of State's decision on any notice of objection.

(5) The court or sheriff may consider matters of which the Secretary of State was not and could not have been aware before giving the penalty notice.

(6) Rules of court may make provision about the timing of an appeal under this section.

Note: Commencement for the purposes of making rules under subsection (6) 31 January 2008 (SI 2008/99), remainder 25 November 2008 (SI 2008/2822). Words in square brackets in subsection (1)(a) substituted by Sch 9 Crime and Courts Act 2013 from 22 April 2014 (SI 2014/954).

12. Penalty: enforcement

(1) Where a penalty has not been paid before the date specified in the penalty notice in accordance with section 9(2)(b), it may be recovered as a debt due to the Secretary of State.

(2) Where a notice of objection is given in respect of a penalty notice, the Secretary of State may not take steps to enforce the penalty notice before—

(a) deciding what to do in response to the notice of objection, and

(b) informing the objector.

(3) The Secretary of State may not take steps to enforce a penalty notice while an appeal under section 11—

(a) could be brought (disregarding any possibility of an appeal out of time with permission), or

(b) has been brought and has not been determined or abandoned.

(4) In proceedings for the recovery of a penalty no question may be raised as to the matters specified in sections 10 and 11 as grounds for objection or appeal.

(5) Money received by the Secretary of State in respect of a penalty shall be paid into the Consolidated Fund.

Note: Commencement 25 November 2008 (SI 2008/2822).

13. Penalty: code of practice

(1) The Secretary of State shall issue a code of practice setting out the matters to be considered in determining—

(a) whether to give a penalty notice under section 9(1), and

(b) the amount of a penalty.

(2) The code may, in particular, require the Secretary of State to consider any decision taken by virtue of section 7.

(3) A court or the sheriff shall, when considering an appeal under section 11, have regard to the code.

(4) The Secretary of State may revise and re-issue the code.

(5) Before issuing or re-issuing the code the Secretary of State must—

(a) publish proposals,

(b) consult members of the public, and

(c) lay a draft before Parliament.

(6) The code (or re-issued code) shall come into force at the prescribed time.

Note: Commencement for the purposes of issuing a code of practice under subsection (1) and making an order under subsection (6) is 31 January 2008 (SI 2008/99), remainder 25 November 2008 (SI 2008/2822).

14. Penalty: prescribed matters

(1) In sections 10 to 13 'prescribed' means prescribed by the Secretary of State by order.

(2) An order under subsection (1) or under section 9(6)—

(a) may make provision generally or only for specified purposes,

(b) may make different provision for different purposes,

(c) shall be made by statutory instrument, and

(d) shall be subject to annulment in pursuance of a resolution of either House of Parliament.

(3) But the first order under section 13(6) shall not be made unless a draft has been laid before and approved by resolution of each House of Parliament (and shall not be subject to annulment).

Note: Commencement 31 January 2008 (SI 2008/99).

15. Interpretation

(1) For the purposes of section 5—

(a) 'person subject to immigration control' means a person who under the Immigration Act 1971 requires leave to enter or remain in the United Kingdom (whether or not such leave has been given),

(b) . . .

(c) . . .

(d) 'document' includes a card or sticker and any other method of recording information (whether in writing or by the use of electronic or other technology or by a combination of methods),

(e) 'authorised person' has the meaning given by section 141(5) of the Immigration and Asylum Act 1999 (authority to take fingerprints),

(f) 'immigration' includes asylum, and

(g) regulations permitting something to be done by the Secretary of State may (but need not) permit it to be done only where the Secretary of State is of a specified opinion.

[(**1A**) For the purposes of section 5 'biometric information' means—

(a) information about a person's external physical characteristics (including in particular fingerprints and features of the iris), and

(b) any other information about a person's physical characteristics specified in an order made by the Secretary of State.

(**1B**) An order under subsection (1A)(b)—

(a) may specify only information that can be obtained or recorded by an external examination of a person;

(b) must not specify information about a person's DNA.

(**1C**) Section 6(6) applies to an order under subsection (1A)(b) as it applies to regulations under section 5(1).]

(**2**) An application for a biometric immigration document is an application in connection with immigration for the purposes of—

(a) section 50(1) and (2) of the Immigration, Asylum and Nationality Act 2006 (procedure), and

[(b) section 68 of the Immigration Act 2014 (fees);]

and in the application of either of those sections to an application for a biometric immigration document, the prescribed consequences of non-compliance may include any of the consequences specified in section 7(2) above.

Note: Commencement 31 January 2008 (SI 2008/99). Subsections (1)(b)–(c) omitted, (1A), (1B) and (1C) inserted by s 12 Immigration Act 2014 from 28 July 2014 (SI 2014/1820). Subsection (2)(b) substituted by Sch 9 of that Act from 15 December 2014 (SI 2014/2771).

Treatment of claimants

16. Conditional leave to enter or remain

Note: Amends s 3(1)(c) Immigration Act 1971.

17. Support for failed asylum-seekers

(**1**) This section applies for the purposes of—

(a) Part 6 [] of the Immigration and Asylum Act 1999 (support and accommodation for asylum-seekers),

(b) Part 2 of the Nationality, Immigration and Asylum Act 2002 (accommodation centres), and

(c) Schedule 3 to that Act (withholding and withdrawal of support).

(**2**) A person (A-S) remains (or again becomes) an asylum-seeker, despite the fact that the claim for asylum made by A-S has been determined, during any period when—

(a) A-S can bring an in-country appeal. . . under section 82 of the 2002 Act or section 2 of the Special Immigration Appeals Commission Act 1997, or

(b) an in-country appeal, brought by A-S under either of those sections . . . is pending (within the meaning of section 104 of the 2002 Act).

(3) For the purposes of subsection (2)—

(a) 'in-country' appeal means an appeal brought while the appellant is in the United Kingdom, and

(b) the possibility of an appeal out of time with permission shall be ignored.

(4) For the purposes of the provisions mentioned in subsection (1)(a) and (b), a person's status as an asylum-seeker by virtue of subsection (2)(b) continues for a prescribed period after the appeal ceases to be pending.

(5) In subsection (4) 'prescribed' means prescribed by regulations made by the Secretary of State; and the regulations—

(a) may contain incidental or transitional provision,

(b) may make different provision for different classes of case,

(c) shall be made by statutory instrument, and

(d) shall be subject to annulment in pursuance of a resolution of either House of Parliament.

(6) This section shall be treated as always having had effect.

Note: The prescribed period for the purposes of subsection (4) is 28 days where an appeal has been disposed of by being allowed, and 21 days in all other cases (SI 2007/3102). Commencement 30 October 2007, s 59 (Royal Assent). Words omitted from subsection (2) by Sch 9 Immigration Act 2014 from 20 October 2014 with savings set out in articles 9–11 SI 2014/2771. Words omitted from subsection (1)(a) by Schedule 11 to the Immigration Act 2016 from a date to be appointed: repeal has effect subject to savings and transitional provisions specified in Immigration Act 2016, Sch 11, para 46.

18. Support for asylum-seekers: enforcement

Note: Amends s 109 Immigration and Asylum Act 1999.

19. Points-based applications: no new evidence on appeal

Note: Amends ss 85 and 106 of the Nationality, Immigration and Asylum Act 2002. Repealed by Sch 9 Immigration Act 2014 from 20 October 2014 with savings set out in articles 9–11 SI 2014/2771.

20. Fees

Note: Amends s 42 of the Asylum and Immigration (Treatment of Claimants, etc.) Act 2004. Repealed by Sch 9 Immigration Act 2014 from 15 December 2014 (SI 2014/2771).

21. Children

. . .

Note: Revoked by s 55 Borders, Citizenship and Immigration Act 2009 from 2 November 2009 (SI 2009/2731).

Enforcement

22. Assaulting an immigration officer: offence

(1) A person who assaults an immigration officer commits an offence.

(2) A person guilty of an offence under this section shall be liable on summary conviction to—

(a) imprisonment for a period not exceeding 51 weeks,
(b) a fine not exceeding level 5 on the standard scale, or
(c) both.

(3) In the application of this section to Northern Ireland the reference in subsection (2)(a) to 51 weeks shall be treated as a reference to 6 months.

(4) In the application of this section to Scotland the reference in subsection (2)(a) to 51 weeks shall be treated as a reference to 12 months.

(5) In relation to an offence committed before the commencement of section 281(5) of the Criminal Justice Act 2003 (51 week maximum term of sentences) the reference in subsection (2)(a) to 51 weeks shall be treated as a reference to 6 months.

Note: Commencement 31 January 2008 (SI 2008/99).

23. Assaulting an immigration officer: powers of arrest, &c.

(1) An immigration officer may arrest a person without warrant if the officer reasonably suspects that the person has committed or is about to commit an offence under section 22.

(2) An offence under section 22 shall be treated as—

(a) a relevant offence for the purposes of sections 28B and 28D of the Immigration Act 1971 (search, entry and arrest), and

(b) an offence under Part 3 of that Act (criminal proceedings) for the purposes of sections 28(4), 28E, 28G and 28H (search after arrest, &c.) of that Act.

(3) The following provisions of the Immigration Act 1971 shall have effect in connection with an offence under section 22 of this Act as they have effect in connection with an offence under that Act—

(a) section 28I (seized material: access and copying),
(b) section 28J (search warrants: safeguards),
(c) section 28K (execution of warrants), and
(d) section 28L(1) (interpretation).

Note: Commencement 31 January 2008 (SI 2008/99).

24. Exercise of civil recovery powers by immigration officers

(1) [Chapters 3 to 3B of Part 5 of the Proceeds of Crime Act 2002 (civil recovery) apply in relation to a constable].

(2) For that purpose—

[(a) 'unlawful conduct', in or in relation to [[sections 239 and 303C and Chapter 3B]], means conduct which—

(i) relates to the entitlement of one or more persons who are not nationals of the United Kingdom to enter, transit across, or be in, the United Kingdom (including conduct which relates to conditions or other controls on any such entitlement), or

(ii) is undertaken for the purposes of, or otherwise in relation to, a relevant nationality enactment, and (in either case) constitutes an offence,]

(c) 'senior officer' in [sections 290 [[, 297A and 303E and in Chapter 3B (see section 303Z2(4)]]] means an official of the Secretary of State who is a civil servant [at or above the grade which is designated by the Secretary of State as being equivalent to the rank of police inspector],

(d) in [[sections 292 and 303G]] the words '(in relation to England and Wales. . .' shall be disregarded,

(e) [sections 293 [[, 393A, 303H and 303I]]] shall not apply,

(f) an application for an order under section 295(2) [[or 303L]] must be made—

(i) in relation to England and Wales or Northern Ireland, by an immigration officer, and

(ii) in relation to Scotland, by the Scottish Ministers in connection with their functions under section 298 [[or as the case may be) 303O]] or by a procurator fiscal,

(g) an application for forfeiture under section 298 [[303O or 303Z14]] must be made—

(i) in relation to England and Wales or Northern Ireland, by an immigration officer, and

(ii) in relation to Scotland, by the Scottish Ministers, and

(h) any compensation under section 302 [[, 303W or 303Z18]] shall be paid by the Secretary of State.

[(2A) In subsection (2) (a) (ii) 'relevant nationality enactment' means any enactment in—

(a) the British Nationality Act 1981,

(b) the Hong Kong Act 1985,

(c) the Hong Kong (War Wives and Widows) Act 1996,

(d) the British Nationality (Hong Kong) Act 1997,

(e) the British Overseas Territories Act 2002, or

(f) an instrument made under any of those Acts.]

(3) The Secretary of State may by order amend subsection (2) (c) to reflect a change in nomenclature; and an order—

(a) shall be made by statutory instrument, and

(b) shall be subject to annulment in pursuance of a resolution of either House of Parliament.

Note: Commencement 1 April 2010 (SI 2010/606). Words in square brackets in subsection (2) (c) substituted by paragraph 113 Sch 7 Policing and Crime Act 2009 from a date to be appointed. Subsections (2) (a)–(b), words in square brackets in subsection (2) (c) substituted and (2A) inserted by Crime and Courts Act 2013, s 55, Sch 21 from 25 June 2013 (SI 2013/1042). Words omitted from subsection (2) (d) and substituted in (2) (e) by SI 2012/2595 from 18 October 2012. Title amended, subsection (1) substituted, and words in double square brackets at (2) (a), (b), (c), (d), (e), (f), (f) (ii), (g) and (h) by Criminal Finances Act 2017, s 21 from 27 April 2017 for the limited purpose of the exercise of any power to make provision by subordinate legislation; 31 January 2018 otherwise.

25. Forfeiture of detained property

(1) A court making a forfeiture order about property may order that the property be taken into the possession of the Secretary of State (and not of the police).

(2) An order may be made under subsection (1) only if the court thinks that the offence in connection with which the order is made—

(a) related to immigration or asylum, or

(b) was committed for a purpose connected with immigration or asylum.

(3)

(a)

(b)

Note: Commencement 31 March 2008 (SI 2008/309). Subsection (3)(a) omitted by Sentencing Act 2020 c.17 Sch.28 para.1 (December 1, 2020: repeal has effect on December 1, 2020 as amended by SI2020/1236 reg.4(5)(a) subject to savings and transitional provisions specified in 2020 c.17 s.412(7) and Sch.27 paras 1,2 & 5). Subsection (3)(b) omitted by Sentencing Act 2020 c.17 Sch.29 para.1 (December 1,2020: repeal has effect as subject to savings and transitional provisions specified in 2020 c.17s.412, s.416(7) & Sch.27 paras 1,2 &5).

26. Disposal of property

(1) In this section 'property' means property which—

(a) has come into the possession of an immigration officer, or

(b) has come into the possession of the Secretary of State in the course of, or in connection with, a function under the Immigration Acts.

(2) A magistrates' court may, on the application of the Secretary of State or a claimant of property—

(a) order the delivery of property to the person appearing to the court to be its owner, or

(b) if its owner cannot be ascertained, make any other order about property.

(3) An order shall not affect the right of any person to take legal proceedings for the recovery of the property, provided that the proceedings are instituted within the period of six months beginning with the date of the order.

(4) An order may be made in respect of property forfeited under section 25, or under section 25C of the Immigration Act 1971 (vehicles, &c.), only if—

(a) the application under subsection (2) above is made within the period of six months beginning with the date of the forfeiture order, and

(b) the applicant (if not the Secretary of State) satisfies the court—

(i) that the applicant did not consent to the offender's possession of the property, or

(ii) that the applicant did not know and had no reason to suspect that the property was likely to be used, or was intended to be used, in connection with an offence.

(5) The Secretary of State may make regulations for the disposal of property—

(a) where the owner has not been ascertained,

(b) where an order under subsection (2) cannot be made because of subsection (4)(a), or

(c) where a court has declined to make an order under subsection (2) on the grounds that the court is not satisfied of the matters specified in subsection (4)(b).

(6) The regulations may make provision that is the same as or similar to provision that may be made by regulations under section 2 of the Police (Property) Act 1897 (or any similar enactment applying in relation to Scotland or Northern Ireland); and the regulations—

(a) may apply, with or without modifications, regulations under that Act,

(b) may, in particular, provide for property to vest in the Secretary of State,

(c) may make provision about the timing of disposal (which, in particular, may differ from provision made by or under the Police (Property) Act 1897),

(d) shall have effect only in so far as not inconsistent with an order of a court (whether or not under subsection (2) above),

(e) shall be made by statutory instrument, and

(f) shall be subject to annulment in pursuance of a resolution of either House of Parliament.

(7) For the purposes of subsection (1) it is immaterial whether property is acquired as a result of forfeiture or seizure or in any other way.

(8) In the application of this section to Scotland a reference to a magistrates' court is a reference to the sheriff.

Note: Commencement for the purposes of making regulations under subsection (5) 31 January 2008 (SI 2008/99). Remainder from 1 April 2008 (SI 2008/309) which sets out transitional provisions.

27. Employment: arrest

Note: Amends s 28AA of the Immigration Act 1971.

28. Employment: search for personnel records

Note: Amends s 28FA(7) of the Immigration Act 1971.

29. Facilitation: arrival and entry

Note: Amends s 25A(1)(a) of the Immigration Act 1971.

30. Facilitation: territorial application

Note: Amends ss 25, 25A and 25B of the Immigration Act 1971.

31. People trafficking

Note: Amends ss 4 and 5 of the Asylum and Immigration (Treatment of Claimants, etc.) Act 2004, ss 57 and 60 of the Sexual Offences Act 2003.

Deportation of criminals

32. Automatic deportation

(1) In this section 'foreign criminal' means a person—

(a) who is not a British citizen [or an Irish citizen]

(b) who is convicted in the United Kingdom of an offence, and

(c) to whom Condition 1 or 2 applies.

(2) Condition 1 is that the person is sentenced to a period of imprisonment of at least 12 months.

(3) Condition 2 is that—

(a) the offence is specified by order of the Secretary of State under section 72(4)(a) of the Nationality, Immigration and Asylum Act 2002 (serious criminal), and

(b) the person is sentenced to a period of imprisonment.

(4) For the purpose of section 3(5)(a) of the Immigration Act 1971 (c. 77), the deportation of a foreign criminal is conducive to the public good.

(5) The Secretary of State must make a deportation order in respect of a foreign criminal (subject to section 33).

(6) The Secretary of State may not revoke a deportation order made in accordance with subsection (5) unless—

(a) he thinks that an exception under section 33 applies,

(b) the application for revocation is made while the foreign criminal is outside the United Kingdom, or

(c) section 34(4) applies.

(7) Subsection (5) does not create a private right of action in respect of consequences of non-compliance by the Secretary of State.

Note: Commencement in respect of a person for whom condition 1 applies, if the person has not been served with a notice of intention to make a deportation order before 1 August 2008, is in custody on, or has a suspended sentence at 1 August 2008 (SI 2008/1818), which sets out transitional provisions. Words in square brackets at subsection (1)(a) inserted by Immigration, Nationality and Asylum (EU Exit) Regulations 2019/745 Pt2(1) reg17(2) (December 31, 2020; shall come into force on IP completion day not exit day as specified in 2020 c.1.s39(1) and Sch.5 para 1(1)).

33. Exceptions

(1) Section 32(4) and (5)—

(a) do not apply where an exception in this section applies (subject to subsection (7) below), and

(b) are subject to sections 7 and 8 of the Immigration Act 1971 (Commonwealth citizens, Irish citizens, crew and other exemptions).

(2) Exception 1 is where removal of the foreign criminal in pursuance of the deportation order would breach—

(a) a person's Convention rights, or

(b) the United Kingdom's obligations under the Refugee Convention.

(3) Exception 2 is where the Secretary of State thinks that the foreign criminal was under the age of 18 on the date of conviction.

(4) ...

(5) Exception 4 is where the foreign criminal—

(a) is the subject of a certificate under section 2 or 70 of the Extradition Act 2003,

(b) is in custody pursuant to arrest under section 5 of that Act,

(c) is the subject of a provisional warrant under section 73 of that Act,

(ca) is the subject of a certificate under section 74B of that Act,

(d) is the subject of an authority to proceed under section 7 of the Extradition Act 1989 or an order under paragraph 4(2) of Schedule 1 to that Act, or

(e) is the subject of a provisional warrant under section 8 of that Act or of a warrant under paragraph 5(1)(b) of Schedule 1 to that Act.

(6) Exception 5 is where any of the following has effect in respect of the foreign criminal—

(a) a hospital order or guardianship order under section 37 of the Mental Health Act 1983,

(b) a hospital direction under section 45A of that Act,

(c) a transfer direction under section 47 of that Act,

(d) a compulsion order under section 57A of the Criminal Procedure (Scotland) Act 1995,

(e) a guardianship order under section 58 of that Act,

(f) a hospital direction under section 59A of that Act,

(g) a transfer for treatment direction under section 136 of the Mental Health (Care and Treatment) (Scotland) Act 2003, or

(h) an order or direction under a provision which corresponds to a provision specified in paragraphs (a) to (g) and which has effect in relation to Northern Ireland.

[(6A) Exception 6 is where the Secretary of State thinks that the application of section 32(4) and (5) would contravene the United Kingdom's obligations under the Council of Europe Convention on Action against Trafficking in Human Beings (done at Warsaw on 16 May 2005).]

[(6B) Exception 7 is where—

(a) the foreign criminal is a relevant person, and

(b) the offence for which the foreign criminal was convicted as mentioned in section 32(1)(b) consisted of or included conduct that took place before IP completion day.

(6C) For the purposes of subsection (6B), a foreign criminal is a 'relevant person'—

(a) if the foreign criminal is in the United Kingdom (whether or not they have entered within the meaning of section 11(1) of the Immigration Act 1971) having arrived with entry clearance granted by virtue of relevant entry clearance immigration rules,

(b) if the foreign criminal has leave to enter or remain in the United Kingdom granted by virtue of residence scheme immigration rules,

[[(ba) if the person is in the United Kingdom (whether or not they have entered within the meaning of s11(1) of the Immigration Act) having arrived with entry clearance granted by virtue of Article 23 of the Swiss citizens' rights agreement,]

(c) if the foreign criminal may be granted leave to enter or remain in the United Kingdom as a person who has a right to enter the United Kingdom by virtue of—

(i) Article 32(1)(b) of the EU withdrawal agreement,

(ii) Article 31(1)(b) of the EEA EFTA separation agreement, or

(iii) Article 26a(1)(b) of the Swiss citizens' rights agreement, whether or not the foreign criminal has been granted such leave, or

(d) if the foreign criminal may enter the United Kingdom by virtue of regulations made under section 8 of the European Union (Withdrawal Agreement) Act 2020 (frontier workers), whether or not the foreign criminal has entered by virtue of those regulations.

(6D) In this section—

• 'EEA EFTA separation agreement' and 'Swiss citizens' rights agreement' have the same meanings as in the European Union (Withdrawal Agreement) Act 2020 (see section 39(1) of that Act);

• 'relevant entry clearance immigration rules' and 'residence scheme immigration rules' have the meanings given by section 17 of the European Union (Withdrawal Agreement) Act 2020.]

(7) The application of an exception—

(a) does not prevent the making of a deportation order;

(b) results in it being assumed neither that deportation of the person concerned is conducive to the public good nor that it is not conducive to the public good; but section 32(4) applies despite the application of Exception 1 or 4.

Note: Commencement in respect of a person for whom condition 1 of s 32 applies, 1 August 2008 (SI 2008/1818), which sets out transitional provisions. Subsection (6A) inserted by s 146 Criminal Justice and Immigration Act 2008 from 1 April 2009 (SI 2009/860). Term 'EU' substituted from 22 April 2011 (SI 2011/1043). Subsection 4 omitted by Immigration and Social Security Co-ordination (EU Withdrawal) Act 2020 (Consequential, Saving, Transitional and Transitory Provisions) (EU Exit) Regulations 2020/1309 Pt 2(1) reg 17(2) (December 31, 2020 at 23.00 being the time and date 2020 c.20 Sch 1 para 2(2) comes into force). Subsection (5)(ca) inserted by Extradition (Provisional Arrest) Act 2020 c.18 Sch 1(2) para 29 (December 31, 2020: shall come into force on IP completion day). Subsections (6B)–(6D) inserted by European Union (Withdrawal Agreement) Act 2020 c.1 Pt 3 s 10(5) (January 31, 2020: insertion has effect on January 31, 2020 at 23.00 as specified in 2018 c.16 s 20(1) subject to 2020 c.1 s 10(6) and transitory provision specified in 2020 c.1 Sch 5 para 63(3). Subsection (6A)(ba) inserted by Citizens Rights (Restrictions of Rights of Entry and Residence) (EU Exit) Regulations 2020/1210 reg 4(2) (December 31, 2020 at 23.00 being the time and date SI 2016/1052 is revoked). Subsection (6A)(ba) omitted by European Union (Withdrawal Agreement) Act 2020 c.1 Sch 5(3) para 63(3) (January 31, 2020 at 23.00 as specified in 2018 c.16 s 20(1) until IP completion day)

34. Timing

(1) Section 32(5) requires a deportation order to be made at a time chosen by the Secretary of State.

(2) A deportation order may not be made under section 32(5) while an appeal or further appeal against the conviction or sentence by reference to which the order is to be made—

(a) has been instituted and neither withdrawn nor determined, or

(b) could be brought.

(3) For the purpose of subsection (2)(b)—

(a) the possibility of an appeal out of time with permission shall be disregarded, and

(b) a person who has informed the Secretary of State in writing that the person does not intend to appeal shall be treated as being no longer able to appeal.

(4) The Secretary of State may withdraw a decision that section 32(5) applies, or revoke a deportation order made in accordance with section 32(5), for the purpose of—

(a) taking action under the Immigration Acts or rules made under section 3 of the Immigration Act 1971 (immigration rules), and

(b) subsequently taking a new decision that section 32(5) applies and making a deportation order in accordance with section 32(5).

Note: Commencement in respect of a person for whom condition 1 of s 32 applies, 1 August 2008 (SI 2008/1818) which sets out transitional provisions.

35. Appeal

Note: Amends ss 79 and 82 of the Nationality, Immigration and Asylum Act 2002.

36. Detention

(1) A person who has served a period of imprisonment may be detained under the authority of the Secretary of State—

(a) while the Secretary of State considers whether section 32(5) applies, and

(b) where the Secretary of State thinks that section 32(5) applies, pending the making of the deportation order.

(2) Where a deportation order is made in accordance with section 32(5) the Secretary of State shall exercise the power of detention under paragraph 2(3) of Schedule 3 to the Immigration Act 1971 (detention pending removal) [unless the person is granted immigration bail under Schedule 10 to the Immigration Act 2016].

(2A) The detention under subsection (1) of a person to whom section 60 (limitation on detention of pregnant women) of the Immigration Act 2016 applies is subject to that section.

(3) A court determining an appeal against conviction or sentence may [release a person on bail] from detention under subsection (1) or (2).

[(3A) The provisions of Schedule 10 to the Immigration Act 2016 that apply in relation to the grant of immigration bail by the First-tier Tribunal apply in relation to the grant of bail by the court under subsection (3).

(3B) If the court grants bail to a person under subsection (3), Schedule 10 to the Immigration Act 2016 applies in relation to that person as if the person had been granted immigration bail by the First-tier Tribunal under that Schedule.

(3C) A reference in any provision of, or made under, an enactment other than this section to immigration bail granted, or a condition imposed, under Schedule 10 to the Immigration Act 2016 includes bail granted by the court under subsection (3) or (as the case may be) a condition imposed by the court on the grant of such bail.]

(4) Provisions of the Immigration Act 1971 which apply to detention under paragraph 2(3) of Schedule 3 to that Act shall apply to detention under subsection (1).

(5) . . .

Note: Commencement in respect of a person for whom condition 1 of s 32 applies, 1 August 2008 (SI 2008/1818) which sets out transitional provisions. Section (2A) inserted by Immigration Act 2016, s 60 from 12 July 2016 (SI 2016/603). Words in square brackets at subsection (2) and (3) substituted by Schedule 10 to the Immigration Act 2016 from January 15, 2018 subject to transitional provisions specified in SI 2017/1241. Subsections (3A) –(3C) inserted and subsection (5) omitted by Schedule 10 to the Immigration Act 2016 from January 15, 2018 subject to transitional provisions specified in SI 2017/1241.

37. Family

(1) Where a deportation order against a foreign criminal states that it is made in accordance with section 32(5) ('the automatic deportation order') this section shall have effect in place of the words from 'A deportation order' to 'after the making of the deportation order against him' in section 5(3) of the Immigration Act 1971 (period during which family members may also be deported).

(2) A deportation order may not be made against a person as belonging to the family of the foreign criminal after the end of the relevant period of 8 weeks.

(3) In the case of a foreign criminal who has not appealed in respect of the automatic deportation order, the relevant period begins when an appeal can no longer be brought (ignoring any possibility of an appeal out of time with permission).

(4) In the case of a foreign criminal who has appealed in respect of the automatic deportation order, the relevant period begins when the appeal is no longer pending (within the meaning of section 104 of the Nationality, Immigration and Asylum Act 2002).

Note: Commencement in respect of a person for whom condition 1 of s 32 applies, 1 August 2008 (SI 2008/1818) which sets out transitional provisions.

38. Interpretation

(1) In section 32(2) the reference to a person who is sentenced to a period of imprisonment of at least 12 months—

(a) does not include a reference to a person who receives a suspended sentence (unless a court subsequently orders that the sentence or any part of it (of whatever length) is to take effect),

(b) does not include a reference to a person who is sentenced to a period of imprisonment of at least 12 months only by virtue of being sentenced to consecutive sentences amounting in aggregate to more than 12 months,

(c) includes a reference to a person who is sentenced to detention, or ordered or directed to be detained, in an institution other than a prison (including, in particular, a hospital or an institution for young offenders) for at least 12 months, and

(d) includes a reference to a person who is sentenced to imprisonment or detention, or ordered or directed to be detained, for an indeterminate period (provided that it may last for 12 months).

(2) In section 32(3)(b) the reference to a person who is sentenced to a period of imprisonment—

(a) does not include a reference to a person who receives a suspended sentence (unless a court subsequently orders that the sentence or any part of it is to take effect), and

(b) includes a reference to a person who is sentenced to detention, or ordered or directed to be detained, in an institution other than a prison (including, in particular, a hospital or an institution for young offenders).

(3) For the purposes of section 32 a person subject to an order under section 5 of the Criminal Procedure (Insanity) Act 1964 (insanity, &c.) has not been convicted of an offence.

(4) In sections 32 and 33—

(a) 'British citizen' has the same meaning as in section 3(5) of the Immigration Act 1971 (and section 3(8) (burden of proof) shall apply),

(b) 'Convention rights' has the same meaning as in the Human Rights Act 1998,

(c) 'deportation order' means an order under section 5, and by virtue of section 3(5), of the Immigration Act 1971, and

(d) 'the Refugee Convention' means the Convention relating to the Status of Refugees done at Geneva on 28 July 1951 and its Protocol.

Note: Commencement in respect of a person for whom condition 1 of s 32 applies, 1 August 2008 (SI 2008/1818) which sets out transitional provisions.

39. Consequential amendments

Note: Amends s 72(11) of the Nationality, Immigration and Asylum Act 2002.

Information

40. Supply of Revenue and Customs information

(1) Her Majesty's Revenue and Customs (HMRC) and the Revenue and Customs Prosecutions Office (the RCPO) may each supply the Secretary of State with information for use for the purpose of—

(a) administering immigration control under the Immigration Acts;

(b) preventing, detecting, investigating or prosecuting offences under those Acts;

(c) determining whether to impose, or imposing, penalties or charges under Part 2 of the Immigration and Asylum Act 1999 (carriers' liability);

(d) determining whether to impose, or imposing, penalties under section 15 of the Immigration, Asylum and Nationality Act 2006 (restrictions on employment);

(e)

(f) providing support under Part 6 of that Act;

(g) determining whether an applicant for naturalisation under the British Nationality Act 1981 is of good character;

[(h) determining whether, for the purposes of an application referred to in section 41A of the British Nationality Act 1981, the person for whose registration the application is made is of good character;

(ha) determining whether, for the purposes of an application under section 1 of the Hong Kong (War Wives and Widows) Act 1996, the woman for whose registration the application is made is of good character;

(hb) determining whether, for the purposes of an application under section 1 of the British Nationality (Hong Kong) Act 1997 for the registration of an adult or young person within the meaning of subsection (5A) of that section, the person is of good character;]

(i) determining whether to make an order in respect of a person under section 40 of the British Nationality Act 1981 (deprivation of citizenship);

(j) doing anything else in connection with the exercise of immigration and nationality functions.

(2) This section applies to a document or article which comes into the possession of, or is discovered by, HMRC or the RCPO, or a person acting on behalf of HMRC or the RCPO, as it applies to information.

(3) The Secretary of State—

(a) may retain for a purpose within subsection (1) a document or article supplied by virtue of subsection (2);

(b) may dispose of a document or article supplied by virtue of subsection (2).

(4) In subsection (1) 'immigration and nationality functions' means functions exercisable by virtue of—

(a) the Immigration Acts,

(b) the British Nationality Act 1981,

(c) the Hong Kong Act 1985,

(d) the Hong Kong (War Wives and Widows) Act 1996, or

(e) the British Nationality (Hong Kong) Act 1997.

(5) A power conferred by this section on HMRC or the RCPO may be exercised on behalf of HMRC or the RCPO by a person who is authorised (generally or specifically) for the purpose.

(6) . . .

Note: Subsection (6) amends s 20(1)(d) of the Immigration and Asylum Act 1999, s 130 of the Nationality, Immigration and Asylum Act 2002 and paragraphs 17 and 20 of Sch 2 to the Commissioners for Revenue and Customs Act 2005. Commencement 31 January 2008 (SI 2008/99). Subsections (1)(h)–(hb) substituted by s 47 Borders, Citizenship and Immigration Act 2009 from 13 January 2010 (SI 2009/2731). Subsection (1)(e) omitted and words in double square brackets substituted in subsection (1)(f) by Schedule 11 to the Immigration Act 2016 from a date to be appointed. Repeal has effect subject to savings and transitional provisions specified in Immigration Act 2016, Sch 11 para 46.

41. Confidentiality

(1) A person to whom relevant information is supplied (whether before or after the commencement of this section) may not disclose that information.

(2) Information is relevant information if it is supplied by or on behalf of HMRC or the RCPO under—

(a) section 20 of the Immigration and Asylum Act 1999,

(b) section 130 of the Nationality, Immigration and Asylum Act 2002,

(c) section 36 of the Immigration, Asylum and Nationality Act 2006 (except in so far as that section relates to information supplied to a chief officer of police), or

(d) section 40 of this Act.

(3) But subsection (1) does not apply to a disclosure—

(a) which is made for a purpose within section 40(1),

(b) which is made for the purposes of civil proceedings (whether or not within the United Kingdom) relating to an immigration or nationality matter,

(c) which is made for the purposes of a criminal investigation or criminal proceedings (whether or not within the United Kingdom) relating to an immigration or nationality matter,

(d) which is made in pursuance of an order of a court,

(e) which is made with the consent (which may be general or specific) of HMRC or the RCPO, depending on by whom or on whose behalf the information was supplied, or

(f) which is made with the consent of each person to whom the information relates.

(4) Subsection (1) is subject to any other enactment permitting disclosure.

(5) The reference in subsection (1) to a person to whom relevant information is supplied includes a reference to a person who is or was acting on behalf of that person.

(6) The reference in subsection (2) to information supplied under section 40 of this Act includes a reference to documents or articles supplied by virtue of subsection (2) of that section.

(7) In subsection (3) 'immigration or nationality matter' means a matter in respect of which the Secretary of State has immigration and nationality functions (within the meaning given in section 40(4)).

(8) In subsection (4) 'enactment' does not include—

(a) an Act of the Scottish Parliament,

(b) an Act of the Northern Ireland Assembly, or

(c) an instrument made under an Act within paragraph (a) or (b).

Note: Commencement 31 January 2008 (SI 2008/1999).

[41A. Supply of information to UK Border Agency

(1) HMRC and the RCPO may each supply a person to whom this section applies with information for use for the purpose of the customs functions exercisable by that person.

(2) This section applies to—

(a) a designated customs official,

(b) the Secretary of State by whom general customs functions are exercisable,

(c) the Director of Border Revenue, and

(d) a person acting on behalf of a person mentioned in paragraphs (a) to (c).

(3) This section applies to a document or article which comes into the possession of, or is discovered by, HMRC or the RCPO, or a person acting on behalf of HMRC or the RCPO, as it applies to information.

(4) A person to whom this section applies—

(a) may retain for a purpose within subsection (1) a document or article supplied by virtue of subsection (3);

(b) may dispose of a document or article supplied by virtue of subsection (3).

(5) A power conferred by this section on HMRC or the RCPO may be exercised on behalf of HMRC or the RCPO by a person who is authorised (generally or specifically) for the purpose.

(6) In this section and section 41B 'customs function' and 'general customs function' have the meanings given by Part 1 of the Borders, Citizenship and Immigration Act 2009.

41B. UK Border Agency: onward disclosure

(1) A person to whom information is supplied under section 41A may not disclose that information.

(2) But subsection (1) does not apply to a disclosure—

(a) which is made for the purpose of a customs function, where the disclosure does not contravene any restriction imposed by the Commissioners for Her Majesty's Revenue and Customs;

(b) which is made for the purposes of civil proceedings (whether or not within the United Kingdom) relating to a customs function;

(c) which is made for the purpose of a criminal investigation or criminal proceedings (whether or not within the United Kingdom);

(d) which is made in pursuance of an order of a court;

(e) which is made with the consent (which may be general or specific) of HMRC or the RCPO, depending on by whom or on whose behalf the information was supplied;

(f) which is made with the consent of each person to whom the information relates.

(3) Subsection (1) is subject to any other enactment permitting disclosure.

(4) The reference in subsection (1) to information supplied under section 41A includes a reference to documents or articles supplied by virtue of subsection (3) of that section.

(5) The reference in that subsection to a person to whom information is supplied includes a reference to a person who is or was acting on behalf of that person.

(6) In subsection (3) 'enactment' does not include—

(a) an Act of the Scottish Parliament,

(b) an Act of the Northern Ireland Assembly, or

(c) an instrument made under an Act within paragraph (a) or (b).]

Note: Sections 41A and 41B inserted by s 20 Borders, Citizenship and Immigration Act 2009 from 21 July 2009 (s 58).

42. Wrongful disclosure

(1) An offence is committed by a person who contravenes section 41 [or 41B] by disclosing information relating to a person whose identity—

(a) is specified in the disclosure, or

(b) can be deduced from it.

(2) Subsection (1) does not apply to the disclosure of information about internal administrative arrangements of HMRC or the RCPO (whether relating to Commissioners, officers, members of the RCPO or others).

(3) It is a defence for a person ('P') charged with an offence under this section of disclosing information to prove that P reasonably believed—

(a) that the disclosure was lawful, or

(b) that the information had already and lawfully been made available to the public.

(4) A person guilty of an offence under this section shall be liable—

(a) on conviction on indictment, to imprisonment for a term not exceeding two years, to a fine or to both, or

(b) on summary conviction, to imprisonment for a term not exceeding 12 months, to a fine not exceeding the statutory maximum or to both.

(5) The reference in subsection (4)(b) to 12 months shall be treated as a reference to six months—

(a) in the application of this section to Northern Ireland;

(b) in the application of this section to England and Wales, in relation to an offence under this section committed before the commencement of section 282 of the Criminal Justice Act 2003 (imprisonment on summary conviction for certain offences in England and Wales);

(c) in the application of this section to Scotland, until the commencement of section 45(1) of the Criminal Proceedings etc. (Reform) (Scotland) Act 2007 (corresponding provision in Scotland).

(6) A prosecution for an offence under this section may be instituted—

(a) in England and Wales, only with the consent of the Director of Public Prosecutions;

(b) in Northern Ireland, only with the consent of the Director of Public Prosecutions for Northern Ireland.

Note: Commencement 31 January 2008 (SI 2008/1999). Words in square brackets in subsection (1) inserted by s 20 Borders, Citizenship and Immigration Act 2009 from 21 July 2009 (s 58).

43. Supply of police information, etc.

. . .

Note: Amends s 131 of the Nationality, Immigration and Asylum Act 2002.

[43A Requirement to state nationality

(1) An individual who is arrested for an offence must state his or her nationality if required to do so by an immigration officer or a constable in accordance with this section.

(2) A requirement may be imposed on an individual under subsection (1) only if the immigration officer or constable suspects that the individual may not be a British citizen.

(3) When imposing a requirement under subsection (1) the immigration officer or constable must inform the individual that an offence may be committed if the individual fails to comply with a requirement imposed under this section.

(4) The immigration officer or constable must make a written record of the imposition of a requirement under subsection (1) as soon as practicable.

(5) The written record is to be made in the presence of the individual where this is practicable.]

Note: Inserted by s 159 of Policing and Crime Act 2017, from date to be appointed.

43B Offence of not giving nationality

(1) A person commits an offence if, without reasonable excuse, the person fails to comply with a requirement imposed in accordance with section 43A, whether by providing false or incomplete information or by providing no information.

(2) Information provided by a person in response to a requirement imposed in accordance with section 43A is not admissible in evidence in criminal proceedings against that person other than proceedings for an offence under this section.

(3) A person who is guilty of an offence under subsection (1) is liable—

(a) on summary conviction in England and Wales, to either or both of the following—

(i) imprisonment for a term not exceeding 51 weeks (or 6 months if the offence was committed before the commencement of section 281(5) of the Criminal Justice Act 2003);

(ii) a fine;

(b) on summary conviction in Northern Ireland, to either or both of the following—

(i) imprisonment for a term not exceeding 6 months;

(ii) a fine not exceeding level 5 on the standard scale.

Note: Inserted by s 159 of the Policing and Crime Act 2017 from 31 January 2017 for specified purposes.

44. Search for evidence of nationality

(1) This section applies where an individual has been arrested on suspicion of the commission of an offence and an immigration officer or a constable suspects—

(a) that the individual may not be a British citizen, and

(b) that nationality documents relating to the individual may be found on—

(i) premises occupied or controlled by the individual,

(ii) premises on which the individual was arrested, or

(iii) premises on which the individual was, immediately before being arrested.

(2) The immigration officer or constable may enter and search the premises for the purpose of finding those documents.

(3) The power of search may be exercised only with the written authority of a senior officer; and for that purpose—

(a) 'senior officer' means—

(i) in relation to an immigration officer, an immigration officer of at least the rank of chief immigration officer, and

(ii) in relation to a constable, a constable of at least the rank of inspector, and

(b) a senior officer who gives authority must arrange for a written record to be made of—

(i) the grounds for the suspicions in reliance on which the power of search is to be exercised, and

(ii) the nature of the documents sought.

(4) The power of search may not be exercised where the individual has been released without being charged with an offence.

(5) In relation to an individual 'nationality document' means a document showing—

(a) the individual's identity, nationality or citizenship,

(b) the place from which the individual travelled to the United Kingdom, or

(c) a place to which the individual is proposing to go from the United Kingdom.

Note: Commencement 29 February 2008 (SI 2008/309) which sets out transitional provisions.

45. Search for evidence of nationality: other premises

(1) This section applies where an individual—

(a) has been arrested on suspicion of the commission of an offence, and

(b) has not been released without being charged with an offence.

(2) If, on an application made by an immigration officer or a constable, a justice of the peace is satisfied that there are reasonable grounds for believing that—

(a) the individual may not be a British citizen,

(b) nationality documents relating to the individual may be found on premises [[mentioned in subsection (2A)]],

(c) the documents would not be exempt from seizure under section 46(2), and

(d) any of the conditions in subsection (3) below applies [[in relation to each set of premises specified in the application]], the justice of the peace may issue a warrant authorising an immigration officer or constable to enter and search the premises.

[(2A) The premises referred to in subsection (2)(b) above are—

(a) one or more sets of premises specified in the application, or

(b) subject to subsection (3A), any premises occupied or controlled by a person specified in the application, including such sets of premises as are so specified (in which case the application is for an 'all premises warrant').

(2B) If the application is for an all premises warrant, the justice of the peace must also be satisfied—

(a) that there are reasonable grounds for believing that it is necessary to search premises occupied or controlled by the person in question which are not specified in the application in order to find the nationality documents, and

(b) that it is not reasonably practicable to specify in the application all the premises which the person occupies or controls and which might need to be searched.

(2C) Subject to subsection (3A), the warrant may authorise entry to and search of premises on more than one occasion if, on the application, the justice of the peace is satisfied that it is necessary to authorise multiple entries in order to achieve the purpose for which the justice issues the warrant.

(2D) If it authorises multiple entries, the number of entries authorised may be unlimited, or limited to a maximum.]

(3) The conditions [[mentioned in subsection (2)(d)]] are that—

(a) it is not practicable to communicate with any person entitled to grant entry to the premises;

(b) it is practicable to communicate with a person entitled to grant entry to the premises but it is not practicable to communicate with any person entitled to grant access to the nationality documents;

(c) entry to the premises will not be granted unless a warrant is produced;

(d) the purpose of a search may be frustrated or seriously prejudiced unless an immigration officer or constable arriving at the premises can secure immediate entry.

[(3A) A justice of the peace in Scotland may not issue—

(a) an all premises warrant under this section, or

(b) a warrant under this section authorising multiple entries.]

(4) Sections 28J and 28K of the Immigration Act 1971 (warrants: application and execution) apply, with any necessary modifications, to warrants under this section.

(5) In the application of this section to Scotland a reference to a justice of the peace shall be treated as a reference to the sheriff or a justice of the peace.

[(6) In the application of this section to Northern Ireland a reference to a justice of the peace is to be treated as a refence to a lay magistrate.]

Note: Commencement 29 February 2008 (SI 2008/309), which sets out transitional provisions. Words in double square brackets substituted in subsection (2)(b) and inserted at subsection (2)(d) and (3) by Immigration Act 2016, Schedule 8 from 1 December 2016 (SI 2016/1037). Subsection (2A)–(2D) and (3A) inserted by Immigration Act 2016, Schedule 8 from 1 December 2016 (SI 2016/1037). Subsection (6) inserted by Nationality and Borders Act 2022 c.36 Pt6 s.79(3) (June 28, 2022)

46. Seizure of nationality documents

(1) An immigration officer or constable searching premises under section 44 or 45 may seize a document which the officer or constable thinks is a nationality document in relation to the arrested individual.

(2) Subsection (1) does not apply to a document which—

(a) in relation to England and Wales or Northern Ireland, is subject to legal professional privilege, or

(b) in relation to Scotland, is an item subject to legal privilege within the meaning of section 412 of the Proceeds of Crime Act 2002.

(3) An immigration officer or constable may retain a document seized under subsection (1) while the officer or constable suspects that—

(a) the individual to whom the document relates may be liable to removal from the United Kingdom in accordance with a provision of the Immigration Acts, and

(b) retention of the document may facilitate the individual's removal.

(4) Section 28I of the Immigration Act 1971 (seized material: access and copying) shall have effect in relation to a document seized and retained by an immigration officer.

(5) Section 21 of the Police and Criminal Evidence Act 1984 or Article 23 of the Police and Criminal Evidence (Northern Ireland) Order 1989 (S.I. 1989/1341 (N.I. 12)) (seized material: access and copying) shall have effect in relation to a document seized and retained by a constable in England and Wales or Northern Ireland.

Note: Commencement 29 February 2008 (SI 2008/309), which sets out transitional provisions.

[46A Requirement to produce nationality document

(1) This section applies where—

(a) an individual has been arrested on suspicion of the commission of an offence, and

(b) the individual is to be released after arrest (whether or not on bail)—

(i) before a decision is taken on whether the individual should be charged with an offence, or

(ii) after being charged with an offence.

(2) Before the individual is released an immigration officer or a constable may give the individual a notice requiring the production of a nationality document not later than 72 hours after the individual is released.

(3) A notice may be given under subsection (2) only if the immigration officer or constable giving it suspects that the individual may not be a British citizen.

(4) A notice under subsection (2) must be given in writing.

(5) The notice must include statements that—

(a) the individual to whom it is given must produce the nationality document not later than 72 hours after the individual is released, and

(b) an offence may be committed if an individual fails to comply with a notice given under this section.

(6) The notice must also set out—

(a) the person to whom the document must be produced, and

(b) the means by which the document must be produced.

(7) In this section, and in sections 46B and 46C—

'nationality document' means a passport relating to the individual or, if there is no passport relating to the individual, one or more documents that enable the individual's nationality or citizenship to be established;

'passport' means—

(a) a United Kingdom passport (within the meaning of the Immigration Act 1971),

(b) a passport issued by or on behalf of the authorities of a country or territory outside the United Kingdom, or by or on behalf of an international organisation, or

(c) a document that can be used (in some or all circumstances) instead of a passport.]

Note: Inserted by s 160 of the Policing and Crime Act 2017 from 31 January 2017 for specified purposes.

[46B Retention of nationality document etc

(1) An immigration officer or constable may retain a nationality document produced in response to a notice under section 46A(2) while the immigration officer or constable suspects that—

(a) the individual to whom the document relates may be liable to removal from the United Kingdom in accordance with a provision of the Immigration Acts, and

(b) retention of the document may facilitate the individual's removal.

(2) Section 28I of the Immigration Act 1971 (seized material: access and copying) has effect in relation to a nationality document produced by an individual in response to a notice under section 46A(2) and retained by an immigration officer as if the nationality document had been seized when the individual had custody or control of it.

(3) Section 21 of the Police and Criminal Evidence Act 1984 or Article 23 of the Police and Criminal Evidence (Northern Ireland) Order 1989 (S.I. 1989/1341 (N.I. 12)) (seized material: access and copying) has effect in relation to a nationality document produced by an individual in response to a notice under section 46A(2) and retained by a constable in England and Wales or Northern Ireland as if the nationality document had been seized when the individual had custody or control of it.]

Note: Inserted by s 160 of the Policing and Crime Act 2017 on a date to be appointed.

[46C Offence of failing to produce nationality document

(1) A person commits an offence if, without reasonable excuse, the person fails to comply with a notice given in accordance with section 46A.

(2) The fact that a person deliberately destroyed or disposed of a nationality document is not a reasonable excuse for the purposes of subsection (1) unless the destruction or disposal was—

(a) for a reasonable cause, or

(b) beyond the control of the person charged with the offence.

(3) In subsection (2)(a) 'reasonable cause' does not include the purpose of—

(a) delaying the handling or resolution of a claim or application or the taking of a decision,

(b) increasing the chances of success of a claim or application, or

(c) complying with instructions given by a person who offers advice about, or facilitates, immigration into the United Kingdom, unless in the circumstances of the case it is unreasonable to expect non-compliance with the instructions or advice.

(4) A person who is guilty of an offence under subsection (1) is liable—

(a) on summary conviction in England and Wales, to either or both of the following—

(i) imprisonment for a term not exceeding 51 weeks (or 6 months if the offence was committed before the commencement of section 281(5) of the Criminal Justice Act 2003);

(ii) a fine;

(b) on summary conviction in Scotland, to either or both of the following—
(i) imprisonment for a term not exceeding 12 months;
(ii) a fine not exceeding level 5 on the standard scale;
(c) on summary conviction in Northern Ireland, to either or both of the following—
(i) imprisonment for a term not exceeding 6 months;
(ii) a fine not exceeding level 5 on the standard scale.]

Note: Inserted by s 160 of the Policing and Crime Act 2017 from 31 January 2017 for specified purposes.

47. Police civilians

. . .

Note: Amends Schedule 4 to the Police Reform Act 2002.

Border and Immigration Inspectorate

48. Establishment

(1) The Secretary of State shall appoint a person as Chief Inspector of [the UK Border Agency].

[(1A) The Chief Inspector shall monitor and report on the efficiency and effectiveness of the performance of functions by the following—

(a) designated customs officials, and officials of the Secretary of State exercising customs functions;

(b) immigration officers, and officials of the Secretary of State exercising functions relating to immigration, asylum or nationality;

(c) the Secretary of State in so far as the Secretary of State has general customs functions;

(d) the Secretary of State in so far as the Secretary of State has functions relating to immigration, asylum or nationality;

(e) the Director of Border Revenue and any person exercising functions of the Director.

(1B) The Chief Inspector shall monitor and report on the efficiency and effectiveness of the services provided by a person acting pursuant to arrangements relating to the discharge of a function within subsection (1A).]

(2) . . . in particular, the Chief Inspector shall consider and make recommendations about—

(a) consistency of approach [among the persons listed in subsections (1A) and (1B) (the 'listed persons')],

(b) the practice and performance of [the listed persons] compared to other persons doing similar things,

(c) practice and procedure in making decisions,

(d) the treatment of claimants and applicants,

(e) certification under section 94 of the Nationality, Immigration and Asylum Act 2002 (unfounded claim),

(f) compliance with law about discrimination in the exercise of functions, including reliance on [paragraph 17 of Schedule 3 of the Equality Act 2010] (exception for immigration functions),

(g) practice and procedure in relation to the exercise of enforcement powers (including powers of arrest, entry, search and seizure),

[(ga) practice and procedure in relation to the prevention, detection and investigation of offences,

(gb) practice and procedure in relation to the conduct of criminal proceedings,

(gc) whether customs functions have been appropriately exercised by the Secretary of State and the Director of Border Revenue,]

(h) the provision of information,

(i) the handling of complaints, and

(j) the content of information about conditions in countries outside the United Kingdom which the Secretary of State compiles and makes available, for purposes connected with immigration and asylum, to immigration officers and other officials.

[(**2A**) Unless directed to do so by the Secretary of State, the Chief Inspector shall not monitor and report on the exercise by the listed persons of—

(a) functions at removal centres and short term holding facilities [and in pre-departure accommodation], and under escort arrangements, in so far as Her Majesty's Chief Inspector of Prisons has functions under section 5A of the Prison Act 1952 in relation to such functions, and

(b) functions at detention facilities, in so far as Her Majesty's Inspectors of Constabulary, the Scottish inspectors or the Northern Ireland inspectors have functions by virtue of section 29 of the Borders, Citizenship and Immigration Act 2009 in relation to such functions.]

(3) . . .

[(**3A**) In this section 'customs function', 'designated customs official' and 'general customs function' have the meanings given by Part 1 of the Borders, Citizenship and Immigration Act 2009.]

(4) The Chief Inspector shall not aim to investigate individual cases (although this subsection does not prevent the Chief Inspector from considering or drawing conclusions about an individual case for the purpose of, or in the context of, considering a general issue).

Note: Commencement 1 April 2008 (SI 2008/309). Words in square brackets in subsection (1)–(2), subsections (1A), (1B), (2)(ga)–(gc), (2A) and (3A) inserted and words in subsection (2) and (3) omitted by s 28 Borders, Citizenship and Immigration Act 2009 from 21 July 2009 (s 58). Words substituted in subsection (2)(f) from 1 October 2010 by the Equality Act 2010, Sch 26, paragraph 86 as inserted by SI 2010/2279. Words in square brackets in subsection (2A)(a) inserted by Sch 9 Immigration Act 2014 from 28 July 2014 (SI 2014/1820).

49. Chief Inspector: supplemental

(1) The Secretary of State shall pay remuneration and allowances to the Chief Inspector.

(2) The Secretary of State—

(a) shall before the beginning of each financial year specify a maximum sum which the Chief Inspector may spend on functions for that year,

(b) may permit that to be exceeded for a specified purpose, and

(c) shall defray the Chief Inspector's expenditure for each financial year subject to paragraphs (a) and (b).

(3) The Chief Inspector shall hold and vacate office in accordance with terms of appointment (which may include provision about retirement, resignation or dismissal).

(4) The Chief Inspector may appoint staff.

(5) A person who is employed by or in any of the following may not be appointed as Chief Inspector—

(a) a government department,

(b) the Scottish Administration,

(c) the National Assembly for Wales, and

(d) a department in Northern Ireland.

Note: Commencement 1 April 2008 (SI 2008/309).

50. Reports

(1) The Chief Inspector shall report in writing to the Secretary of State—

(a) once each calendar year, in relation to the performance of the functions under section 48 generally, and

(b) at other times as requested by the Secretary of State in relation to specified matters.

(2) The Secretary of State shall lay before Parliament a copy of any report received under subsection (1).

(3) But a copy may omit material if the Secretary of State thinks that its publication—

(a) is undesirable for reasons of national security, or

(b) might jeopardise an individual's safety.

Note: Commencement 1 April 2008 (SI 2008/309).

51. Plans

(1) The Chief Inspector shall prepare plans describing the objectives and terms of reference of proposed inspections.

(2) Plans shall be prepared—

(a) at prescribed times and in respect of prescribed periods, and

(b) at such other times, and in respect of such other periods, as the Chief Inspector thinks appropriate.

(3) A plan must—

(a) be in the prescribed form, and

(b) contain the prescribed information.

(4) In preparing a plan the Chief Inspector shall consult—

(a) the Secretary of State, and

(b) prescribed persons.

(5) As soon as is reasonably practicable after preparing a plan the Chief Inspector shall send a copy to—

(a) the Secretary of State, and

(b) each prescribed person.

(6) The Chief Inspector and a prescribed person may by agreement disapply a requirement—

(a) to consult the person, or

(b) to send a copy of a plan to the person.

(7) Nothing in this section prevents the Chief Inspector from doing anything not mentioned in a plan.

Note: Commencement for the purposes of making an order under subsections (2)–(6) 1 April 2008 (SI 2008/309).

52. Relationship with other bodies: general

(1) The Chief Inspector shall cooperate with prescribed persons in so far as the Chief Inspector thinks it consistent with the efficient and effective performance of the functions under section 48.

(2) The Chief Inspector may act jointly with prescribed persons where the Chief Inspector thinks it in the interests of the efficient and effective performance of the functions under section 48.

(3) The Chief Inspector may assist a prescribed person.

(4) The Chief Inspector may delegate a specified aspect of the functions under section 48 to a prescribed person.

Note: Commencement for the purposes of making an order under these provisions 1 April 2008 (SI 2008/309).

53. Relationship with other bodies: non-interference notices

(1) Subsection (2) applies if the Chief Inspector believes that—

(a) a prescribed person proposes to inspect any aspect of the work of [a person listed in section 48(1A) or (1B)], and

(b) the inspection may impose an unreasonable burden on [such a person].

(2) The Chief Inspector may give the prescribed person a notice prohibiting a specified inspection.

(3) The prescribed person shall comply with the notice, unless the Secretary of State cancels it on the grounds that the inspection would not impose an unreasonable burden on [a person listed in section 48(1A) or (1B)].

(4) A notice must—

(a) be in the prescribed form, and

(b) contain the prescribed information.

(5) The Secretary of State may by order make provision about—

(a) the timing of notices;

(b) the publication of notices;

(c) the revision or withdrawal of notices.

Note: Commencement for the purposes of making an order under these provisions 1 April 2008 (SI 2008/309). Words in square brackets in subsections (1) and (3) substituted by s 28 Borders, Citizenship and Immigration Act 2009 from 21 July 2009 (s 58).

54. Abolition of other bodies

Note: Amends s 19E of the Race Relations Act 1976, ss 34, 111, 142 of the Nationality, Immigration and Asylum Act 2002.

55. Prescribed matters

(1) In sections 48 to 53 'prescribed' means prescribed by order of the Secretary of State.

(2) An order under any of those sections—

(a) may make provision generally or only for specified purposes,

(b) may make different provision for different purposes, and

(c) may include incidental or transitional provision.

(3) An order under any of those sections prescribing a person may specify—

(a) one or more persons, or

(b) a class of person.

(4) An order under any of those sections—

(a) shall be made by statutory instrument, and

(b) shall be subject to annulment in pursuance of a resolution of either House of Parliament.

Note: Commencement 1 April 2008 (SI 2008/309).

56. Senior President of Tribunals

(1) . . .

(2) In exercising the function under section 43 of the Tribunals, Courts and Enforcement Act 2007 the Senior President of Tribunals shall have regard to—

(a) the functions of the Chief Inspector of [the UK Border Agency], and

(b) in particular, the Secretary of State's power to request the Chief Inspector to report about specified matters.

Note: Subsection (1) amends s 43(3) of the Tribunals, Courts and Enforcement Act 2007. Commencement 1 April 2008 (SI 2008/309). Words in square brackets substituted by s 28 Borders, Citizenship and Immigration Act 2009 from 21 July 2009 (s 58).

General

56A. No rehabilitation for certain immigration or nationality purposes

(1) Section 4(1), (2) and (3) of the Rehabilitation of Offenders Act 1974 (effect of rehabilitation) do not apply—

(a) in relation to any proceedings in respect of a relevant immigration decision or a relevant nationality decision, or

(b) otherwise for the purposes of, or in connection with, any such decision.

(2) In this section—

'immigration officer' means a person appointed by the Secretary of State as an immigration officer under paragraph 1 of Schedule 2 to the Immigration Act 1971, 'relevant immigration decision' means any decision, or proposed decision, of the Secretary of State or an immigration officer under or by virtue of the Immigration Acts, or rules made under section 3 of the Immigration Act 1971 (immigration rules), in relation to the entitlement of a person to enter or remain in the United Kingdom (including, in particular, the removal of a person from the United Kingdom, whether by deportation or otherwise),

'relevant nationality decision' means any decision, or proposed decision, of the Secretary of State under or by virtue of—

(a) the British Nationality Act 1981,

(b) the British Nationality (Hong Kong) Act 1990, or

(c) the Hong Kong (War Wives and Widows) Act 1996,

in relation to the good character of a person.

(3). . .

Note: Section 56A inserted from 1 October 2012 by the Legal Aid, Sentencing and Punishment of Offenders Act 2012, s 140, subject to transitional and consequential provisions set out in s 141(7)–(9) of that Act. Subsection 3 omitted by Immigration and Social Security Co-ordination (EU Withdrawal) Act 2020 (Consequential, Savings, Transitional and Transitory Provisions)(EU Exit) Regulations 2020/1309 Pt 2(1) reg. 17(3).

57. Money

The following shall be paid out of money provided by Parliament—

(a) any expenditure of a Minister of the Crown in consequence of this Act, and

(b) any increase attributable to this Act in sums payable out of money provided by Parliament under another enactment.

Note: Commencement at a date to be appointed.

58. Repeals

. . .

59. Commencement

(1) Section 17 comes into force on the day on which this Act is passed.

(2) The other preceding provisions of this Act shall come into force in accordance with provision made by the Secretary of State by order.

(3) An order—

(a) may make provision generally or only for specified purposes,

(b) may make different provision for different purposes, and

(c) may include incidental, consequential or transitional provision.

(4) In particular, transitional provision—

(a) in the case of an order commencing section 16, may permit the adding of a condition to leave given before the passing of this Act;

(b) in the case of an order commencing section 25, may permit an order to be made in proceedings instituted before the passing of this Act;

(c) in the case of an order commencing section 26, may permit an order or regulations to have effect in relation to property which came into the possession of an immigration officer or the Secretary of State before the passing of this Act;

(d) in the case of an order commencing section 32—

(i) may provide for the section to apply to persons convicted before the passing of this Act who are in custody at the time of commencement or whose sentences are suspended at the time of commencement;

(ii) may modify the application of the section in relation to those persons so as to disapply, or apply only to a specified extent, Condition 2.

(5) An order shall be made by statutory instrument.

Note: Commencement 30 October 2007 (s 59, Royal Assent).

60. Extent

(1) Sections. . . 25 and 31(1) and (2) extend to—

(a) England and Wales, and

(b) Northern Ireland.

(2) Other provisions of this Act extend (subject to subsection (3)) to—

(a) England and Wales,

(b) Scotland, and

(c) Northern Ireland.

(3) A provision of this Act which amends another Act shall (subject to subsection (1)) have the same extent as the relevant part of the amended Act (ignoring extent by virtue of an Order in Council).

(4) Her Majesty may by Order in Council direct that a provision of this Act is to extend, with or without modification or adaptation, to—

(a) any of the Channel Islands;

(b) the Isle of Man.

Note: Commencement 30 October 2007 (s 59, Royal Assent). Numbers in subsection (1) omitted by s 52 Borders, Citizenship and Immigration Act 2009 from 27 October 2014 (SI 2014/2634).

61. Citation

(1) This Act may be cited as the UK Borders Act 2007.

(2) A reference (in any enactment, including one passed or made before this Act) to 'the Immigration Acts' is to—

(a) the Immigration Act 1971,

(b) the Immigration Act 1988,

(c) the Asylum and Immigration Appeals Act 1993,

(d) the Asylum and Immigration Act 1996,

(e) the Immigration and Asylum Act 1999,

(f) the Nationality, Immigration and Asylum Act 2002,

(g) the Asylum and Immigration (Treatment of Claimants, etc.) Act 2004,

(h) the Immigration, Asylum and Nationality Act 2006,. . .

(i) this Act[, and

(j) the Immigration Act 2014,][[

(k) the Immigration Act 2016]]{{{,and}}(l) Part 1 of the Immigration and Social Security Co-ordination (EU Withdrawal) Act 2020 (and Part 3 so far as relating to that Part).}[and

(m) the Nationality and Borders Act 2022.]

(3) . . . Section 64(2) (meaning of 'Immigration Acts') shall cease to have effect.

(4) . . .

Note: Subsection (3) repeals s 64(2) of the Immigration, Asylum and Nationality Act 2006. Subsection (4) amends Sch 1 of the Interpretation Act 1978. Commencement 30 October 2007, (s 59 Royal Assent). Subsection (2)(j) inserted by s 73 Immigration Act 2014 from 14 May 2014, s 75. Words in double brackets inserted at ss (2)(k) by Immigration Act 2016 c. 19 Pt 9 s 92(5)(b) (May 12, 2016). Words in curly brackets inserted at ss by (2)(l) and omitted at ss (2)(j) by s(4)(1)(b) of the Immigration and Social Security (Co-ordination) Act 2020 c.20 s 4(1)(b) (December 31, 2020). Words omitted in double curly brackets in subsection (2)(k) and inserted at (2)(l) & (m) by Nationality and Borders Act 2022 c.36 s.84(7)(a) &(b) (April 28, 2022)

Schedule

Repeals

Tribunals, Courts and Enforcement Act 2007
(2007, c. 15)

Chapter 2 First-tier Tribunal and Upper Tribunal

Establishment

3. The First-tier Tribunal and the Upper Tribunal

(1) There is to be a tribunal, known as the First-tier Tribunal, for the purpose of exercising the functions conferred on it under or by virtue of this Act or any other Act.

(2) There is to be a tribunal, known as the Upper Tribunal, for the purpose of exercising the functions conferred on it under or by virtue of this Act or any other Act.

(3) Each of the First-tier Tribunal, and the Upper Tribunal, is to consist of its judges and other members.

(4) The Senior President of Tribunals is to preside over both of the First-tier Tribunal and the Upper Tribunal.

(5) The Upper Tribunal is to be a superior court of record.

Note: Commenced 3 November 2008 (SI 2008/2696).

Members and composition of tribunals

4. Judges and other members of the First-tier Tribunal

(1) A person is a judge of the First-tier Tribunal if the person—

(a) is a judge of the First-tier Tribunal by virtue of appointment under paragraph 1(1) of Schedule 2,

(b) is a transferred-in judge of the First-tier Tribunal (see section 31(2)),

(c) is a judge of the Upper Tribunal,

[(ca) is within section 6A,]

(d) . . . or

(e) is a member of a panel of [Employment Judges].

(2) A person is also a judge of the First-tier Tribunal, but only as regards functions of the tribunal in relation to appeals such as are mentioned in subsection (1) of section 5 of the Criminal Injuries Compensation Act 1995 (c. 53), if the person is an adjudicator appointed under that section by the Scottish Ministers.

(3) A person is one of the other members of the First-tier Tribunal if the person—

(a) is a member of the First-tier Tribunal by virtue of appointment under paragraph 2(1) of Schedule 2,

(b) is a transferred-in other member of the First-tier Tribunal (see section 31(2)),

(c) is one of the other members of the Upper Tribunal, or

(d) is a member of a panel of members of employment tribunals that is not a panel of [Employment Judges].

(4) Schedule 2—

contains provision for the appointment of persons to be judges or other members of the First-tier Tribunal, and makes further provision in connection with judges and other members of the First-tier Tribunal.

Note: Commenced 3 November 2008 (SI 2008/2696). Subsection (1)(d) omitted from 15 February 2010 (SI 2010/21). Subsection (1)(ca) inserted and words in square brackets in subsections (1)(e) and (3)(d) substituted by Crime and Courts Act 2013, Sch 14 from 1 October 2013 (SI 2013/2200).

5. Judges and other members of the Upper Tribunal

(1) A person is a judge of the Upper Tribunal if the person—

(a) is the Senior President of Tribunals,

(b) is a judge of the Upper Tribunal by virtue of appointment under paragraph 1(1) of Schedule 3, [or]

(c) is a transferred-in judge of the Upper Tribunal (see section 31(2)),

(d) . . .

(f) is a Social Security Commissioner appointed under section 50(2) of that Act (deputy Commissioners),

(g) is within section 6(1),

(h) is a deputy judge of the Upper Tribunal (whether under paragraph 7 of Schedule 3 or under section 31(2)), or

(i) is a Chamber President or a Deputy Chamber President, whether of a chamber of the Upper Tribunal or of a chamber of the First-tier Tribunal, and does not fall within any of paragraphs (a) to (h).

(2) A person is one of the other members of the Upper Tribunal if the person—

(a) is a member of the Upper Tribunal by virtue of appointment under paragraph 2(1) of Schedule 3,

(b) is a transferred-in other member of the Upper Tribunal (see section 31(2)), [or]

(c) is a member of the Employment Appeal Tribunal appointed under section 22(1)(c) of the Employment Tribunals Act 1996 (c. 17), . . .

(d) . . .

(3) Schedule 3—

contains provision for the appointment of persons to be judges (including deputy judges), or other members, of the Upper Tribunal, and

makes further provision in connection with judges and other members of the Upper Tribunal.

Note: Commenced 3 November 2008 (SI 2008/2696). Subsections (1)(d) and 2(d) omitted from 15 February 2010 (SI 2010/21).

6. Certain judges who are also judges of First-tier Tribunal and Upper Tribunal

(1) A person is within this subsection (and so, by virtue of sections 4(1)(c) and 5(1)(g), is a judge of the First-tier Tribunal and of the Upper Tribunal) if the person—

[(za) is the Lord Chief Justice of England and Wales,

(zb) is the Master of the Rolls,

(zc) is the President of the Queen's Bench Division of the High Court in England and Wales,

(zd) is the President of the Family Division of the High Court in England and Wales, (ze) is the Chancellor of the High Court in England and Wales,]

(a) is an ordinary judge of the Court of Appeal in England and Wales (including the vice-president, if any, of either division of that Court),

(b) is a Lord Justice of Appeal in Northern Ireland,

(c) is a judge of the Court of Session,

(d) is a puisne judge of the High Court in England and Wales or Northern Ireland,

[(da) is a deputy judge of the High Court in England and Wales,

(db) is the Judge Advocate General,]

(e) is a circuit judge,

[(ea) is a Recorder,]

(f) is a sheriff in Scotland,

(g) is a county court judge in Northern Ireland,

(h) is a district judge in England and Wales or Northern Ireland, []

(i) is a District Judge (Magistrates' Courts).

[(j)is the President of Employment Tribunals (England and Wales),

(k) is the President of Employment Tribunals (Scotland),

(l) is the Vice President of Employment Tribunals (Scotland), or

(m) is a Regional Employment Judge.]

(2) References in subsection (1)(c) to (i) to office-holders do not include deputies or temporary office-holders.

Note: Commenced 3 November 2008 (SI 2008/2696). Subsections (za)–(ze) and (da)–(db) inserted by Crime and Courts Act 2013, Sch 14 from 1 October 2013 (SI 2013/2200). Words inserted in square brackets at subsections (1)(ea),(j),(k),(l) and (m) and omitted at (1)(h) by Courts and Tribunals (Judiciary and Function of Staff) Act 2018 c.33, s1(2) from 20 February 2019.

[6A Certain judges who are also judges of the First-tier Tribunal

A person is within this section (and so, by virtue of section 4(1)(ca), is a judge of the First-tier Tribunal) if the person—

(a) is a deputy Circuit judge,

(b) []

(c) is a person who holds an office listed—

(i) in the first column of the table in section 89(3C) of the Senior Courts Act 1981 (senior High Court Masters etc), or

(ii) in column 1 of Part 2 of Schedule 2 to that Act (High Court Masters etc),

(d) is a deputy district judge appointed under section 102 of that Act or section 8 of the County Courts Act 1984,

(e) is a Deputy District Judge (Magistrates' Courts), or

(f) is a person appointed under section 30(1)(a) or (b) of the Courts-Martial (Appeals) Act 1951 (assistants to the Judge Advocate General).]

Note: Section 6A inserted by Crime and Courts Act 2013, Sch 14 from 1 October 2013 (SI 2013/2200). Words in square brackets omitted in subsection (b) by Courts and Tribunals (Judiciary and Functions of Staff) Act 2018 c.33 s1(3) from 20 February 2019.

7. Chambers: jurisdiction and Presidents

(1) The Lord Chancellor may, with the concurrence of the Senior President of Tribunals, by order make provision for the organisation of each of the First-tier Tribunal and the Upper Tribunal into a number of chambers.

(2) There is—

(a) for each chamber of the First-tier Tribunal, and

(b) for each chamber of the Upper Tribunal,

to be a person, or two persons, to preside over that chamber.

(3) [A person may at a particular time—

(a) preside over more than one chamber of the First-tier Tribunal;

(b) preside over more than one chamber of the Upper Tribunal;

(c) preside over—

(i) one or more chambers of the First-tier Tribunal, and

(ii) one or more chambers of the Upper Tribunal.]

(4) A person appointed under this section to preside over a chamber is to be known as a Chamber President.

(5) Where two persons are appointed under this section to preside over the same chamber, any reference in an enactment to the Chamber President of the chamber is a reference to a person appointed under this section to preside over the chamber.

(6) [The Senior President of Tribunals may (consistently with [subsection (2)]) appoint a person who is the Chamber President of a chamber to preside instead, or to preside also, over another chamber.

(7) The [Senior President of Tribunals] may (consistently with [subsection (2)]) appoint a person who is not a Chamber President to preside over a chamber].

(8) Schedule 4 (eligibility for appointment under subsection (7), appointment of Deputy Chamber Presidents and Acting Chamber Presidents, assignment of judges and other members of the First-tier Tribunal and Upper Tribunal, and further provision about Chamber Presidents and chambers) has effect.

(9) Each of the Lord Chancellor and the Senior President of Tribunals may, with the concurrence of the other, by order—

(a) make provision for the allocation of the First-tier Tribunal's functions between its chambers;

(b) make provision for the allocation of the Upper Tribunal's functions between its chambers;

(c) amend or revoke any order made under this subsection.

Note: Subsections (1) and (9) in force from 19 September 2007 (SI 2007/2709). Remainder in force from 3 November 2008 (SI 2008/2696). Words in square brackets in subsection (7) substituted by Sch 13 Crime and Courts Act 2013 from 1 October 2013 (SI 2013/2200). Words in square brackets at subsection (3) (6) & (7) substituted by Courts and Tribunals (Judiciary and Functions of Staff) 2018 c.33 s.1(4) from February 20, 2019.

8. Senior President of Tribunals: power to delegate

(1) The Senior President of Tribunals may delegate any function he has in his capacity as Senior President of Tribunals—

(a) to any judge, or other member, of the Upper Tribunal or First-tier Tribunal;
(b) to staff appointed under section 40(1).

[(**1A**) A function under paragraph 1(1) or 2(1) of Schedule 2 may be delegated under subsection (1) only to a Chamber President of a chamber of the Upper Tribunal.]

(2) Subsection (1) does not apply to functions of the Senior President of Tribunals [under any of the following—

section 7(7);
section 7(9);
[[section 29B;
section 29D]];
paragraph 2(1) of Schedule 3;
paragraph 7(1) of Schedule 3;
paragraph 2 of Schedule 4;
paragraph 5(1) and (3) of Schedule 4;
paragraph 5(5) to (8) of Schedule 4;
paragraph 5A(2)(a) of Schedule 4;
paragraph 5A(3)(a) of Schedule 4.]
[[paragraph 3 of Schedule 5]].

(3) A delegation under subsection (1) is not revoked by the delegator's becoming incapacitated.

(4) Any delegation under subsection (1) that is in force immediately before a person ceases to be Senior President of Tribunals continues in force until varied or revoked by a subsequent holder of the office of Senior President of Tribunals.

(5) The delegation under this section of a function shall not prevent the exercise of the function by the Senior President of Tribunals.

Note: Commenced 3 November 2008 (SI 2008/2696). Subsection (1A) inserted and words in square brackets in subsection (2) substituted by Crime and Courts Act 2013 from 1 October 2013 (SI 2013/2200). Words in double square brackets in subsection (2) inserted by Courts and Tribunals (Judiciary and Function of Staff) Act 2018 c.33 Sch.1(2) para 40 from April 6, 2020.

Review of decisions and appeals

9. Review of decision of First-tier Tribunal

(1) The First-tier Tribunal may review a decision made by it on a matter in a case, other than a decision that is an excluded decision for the purposes of section 11(1) (but see subsection (9)).

(2) The First-tier Tribunal's power under subsection (1) in relation to a decision is exercisable—

(a) of its own initiative, or

(b) on application by a person who for the purposes of section 11(2) has a right of appeal in respect of the decision.

(3) Tribunal Procedure Rules may—

(a) provide that the First-tier Tribunal may not under subsection (1) review (whether of its own initiative or on application under subsection (2)(b)) a decision of a description specified for the purposes of this paragraph in Tribunal Procedure Rules;

(b) provide that the First-tier Tribunal's power under subsection (1) to review a decision of a description specified for the purposes of this paragraph in Tribunal Procedure Rules is exercisable only of the tribunal's own initiative;

(c) provide that an application under subsection (2)(b) that is of a description specified for the purposes of this paragraph in Tribunal Procedure Rules may be made only on grounds specified for the purposes of this paragraph in Tribunal Procedure Rules;

(d) provide, in relation to a decision of a description specified for the purposes of this paragraph in Tribunal Procedure Rules, that the First-tier Tribunal's power under subsection (1) to review the decision of its own initiative is exercisable only on grounds specified for the purposes of this paragraph in Tribunal Procedure Rules.

(4) Where the First-tier Tribunal has under subsection (1) reviewed a decision, the First-tier Tribunal may in the light of the review do any of the following—

(a) correct accidental errors in the decision or in a record of the decision;
(b) amend reasons given for the decision;
(c) set the decision aside.

(5) Where under subsection (4)(c) the First-tier Tribunal sets a decision aside, the First-tier Tribunal must either—

(a) re-decide the matter concerned, or
(b) refer that matter to the Upper Tribunal.

(6) Where a matter is referred to the Upper Tribunal under subsection (5)(b), the Upper Tribunal must re-decide the matter.

(7) Where the Upper Tribunal is under subsection (6) re-deciding a matter, it may make any decision which the First-tier Tribunal could make if the First-tier Tribunal were re-deciding the matter.

(8) Where a tribunal is acting under subsection (5)(a) or (6), it may make such findings of fact as it considers appropriate.

(9) This section has effect as if a decision under subsection (4)(c) to set aside an earlier decision were not an excluded decision for the purposes of section 11(1), but the First-tier Tribunal's only power in the light of a review under subsection (1) of a decision under subsection (4)(c) is the power under subsection (4)(a).

(10) A decision of the First-tier Tribunal may not be reviewed under subsection (1) more than once, and once the First-tier Tribunal has decided that an earlier decision should not be reviewed under subsection (1) it may not then decide to review that earlier decision under that subsection.

(11) Where under this section a decision is set aside and the matter concerned is then re-decided, the decision set aside and the decision made in re-deciding the matter are for the purposes of subsection (10) to be taken to be different decisions.

Note: Subsection (3) in force from 19 September 2007 (SI 2007/2709). Remainder in force from 3 November 2008 (SI 2008/2696).

10. Review of decision of Upper Tribunal

(1) The Upper Tribunal may review a decision made by it on a matter in a case, other than a decision that is an excluded decision for the purposes of section 13(1) (but see subsection (7)).

(2) The Upper Tribunal's power under subsection (1) in relation to a decision is exercisable—

(a) of its own initiative, or

(b) on application by a person who for the purposes of section 13(2) has a right of appeal in respect of the decision.

(3) Tribunal Procedure Rules may—

(a) provide that the Upper Tribunal may not under subsection (1) review (whether of its own initiative or on application under subsection (2)(b)) a decision of a description specified for the purposes of this paragraph in Tribunal Procedure Rules;

(b) provide that the Upper Tribunal's power under subsection (1) to review a decision of a description specified for the purposes of this paragraph in Tribunal Procedure Rules is exercisable only of the tribunal's own initiative;

(c) provide that an application under subsection (2)(b) that is of a description specified for the purposes of this paragraph in Tribunal Procedure Rules may be made only on grounds specified for the purposes of this paragraph in Tribunal Procedure Rules;

(d) provide, in relation to a decision of a description specified for the purposes of this paragraph in Tribunal Procedure Rules, that the Upper Tribunal's power under subsection (1) to review the decision of its own initiative is exercisable only on grounds specified for the purposes of this paragraph in Tribunal Procedure Rules.

(4) Where the Upper Tribunal has under subsection (1) reviewed a decision, the Upper Tribunal may in the light of the review do any of the following—

(a) correct accidental errors in the decision or in a record of the decision;

(b) amend reasons given for the decision;

(c) set the decision aside.

(5) Where under subsection (4)(c) the Upper Tribunal sets a decision aside, the Upper Tribunal must re-decide the matter concerned.

(6) Where the Upper Tribunal is acting under subsection (5), it may make such findings of fact as it considers appropriate.

(7) This section has effect as if a decision under subsection (4)(c) to set aside an earlier decision were not an excluded decision for the purposes of section 13(1), but the Upper Tribunal's only power in the light of a review under subsection (1) of a decision under subsection (4)(c) is the power under subsection (4)(a).

(8) A decision of the Upper Tribunal may not be reviewed under subsection (1) more than once, and once the Upper Tribunal has decided that an earlier decision should not be reviewed under subsection (1) it may not then decide to review that earlier decision under that subsection.

(9) Where under this section a decision is set aside and the matter concerned is then re-decided, the decision set aside and the decision made in re-deciding the matter are for the purposes of subsection (8) to be taken to be different decisions.

Note: Subsection (3) in force from 19 September 2007 (SI 2007/2709). Remainder in force from 3 November 2008 (SI 2008/2696).

11. Right to appeal to Upper Tribunal

(1) For the purposes of subsection (2), the reference to a right of appeal is to a right to appeal to the Upper Tribunal on any point of law arising from a decision made by the First-tier Tribunal other than an excluded decision.

(2) Any party to a case has a right of appeal, subject to subsection (8).

(3) That right may be exercised only with permission (or, in Northern Ireland, leave).

(4) Permission (or leave) may be given by—

(a) the First-tier Tribunal, or

(b) the Upper Tribunal, on an application by the party.

(5) For the purposes of subsection (1), an 'excluded decision' is—

(a) any decision of the First-tier Tribunal on an appeal made in exercise of a right conferred by the Criminal Injuries Compensation Scheme in compliance with section 5(1)(a) of the Criminal Injuries Compensation Act 1995 (c. 53) (appeals against decisions on reviews),

[(aa) any decision of the First-tier Tribunal on an appeal made in exercise of a right conferred by the Victims of Overseas Terrorism Compensation Scheme in compliance with section 52(3) of the Crime and Security Act 2010,]

(b) any decision of the First-tier Tribunal on an appeal under [section 27(3) or (5), 79(5) or (7) or 111(3) or (5) of the Data Protection Act 2018].

(c) any decision of the First-tier Tribunal on an appeal under section 60(1) or (4) of the Freedom of Information Act 2000 (c. 36) (appeals against national security certificate),

[(ca) any decision of the First-tier Tribunal under section 88, 89(3) or 92(3) of the Tax Collection and Management (Wales) Acct 2016 (anaw 6) (approval for the Welsh Revenue Authority to issue certain information notices),

(cb) any decision of the First-tier Tribunal under section 108 of that Act (approval for Welsh Revenue Authority to inspect premises),]

(d) a decision of the First-tier Tribunal under section 9—

(i) to review, or not to review, an earlier decision of the tribunal,

(ii) to take no action, or not to take any particular action, in the light of a review of an earlier decision of the tribunal,

(iii) to set aside an earlier decision of the tribunal, or

(iv) to refer, or not to refer, a matter to the Upper Tribunal,

(e) a decision of the First-tier Tribunal that is set aside under section 9 (including a decision set aside after proceedings on an appeal under this section have been begun), or

(f) any decision of the First-tier Tribunal that is of a description specified in an order made by the Lord Chancellor.

(6) A description may be specified under subsection (5)(f) only if—

(a) in the case of a decision of that description, there is a right to appeal to a court, the Upper Tribunal or any other tribunal from the decision and that right is, or includes, something other than a right (however expressed) to appeal on any point of law arising from the decision, or

(b) decisions of that description are made in carrying out a function transferred under section 30 and prior to the transfer of the function under section 30(1) there was no right to appeal from decisions of that description.

(7) Where—

(a) an order under subsection (5)(f) specifies a description of decisions, and

(b) decisions of that description are made in carrying out a function transferred under section 30, the order must be framed so as to come into force no later than the time when the transfer under section 30 of the function takes effect (but power to revoke the order continues to be exercisable after that time, and power to amend the order continues to be exercisable after that time for the purpose of narrowing the description for the time being specified).

(8) The Lord Chancellor may by order make provision for a person to be treated as being, or to be treated as not being, a party to a case for the purposes of subsection (2).

Note: Subsection (5)(f) and (6)–(8) in force from 19 September 2007 (SI 2007/2709). Remainder in force from 3 November 2008 (SI 2008/2696). Application of s 11 modified by SI 2010/22 Sch 5, paragraph 5(a) from 18 January 2010. Subsection (5)(aa) inserted from 8 April 2010 by Crime and Security Act 2010. There are other modifications/exclusions not relevant to immigration law. Words in square brackets inserted at section 11(5)(ca) and (cb) by s116 of the Tax Collection and Management (Wales) Act 2016. Words in square brackets inserted at subsection (5)(b) by Data Protection Act 2018 c.12 Sch. 19 para 131, from May 25, 2018.

[11A Finality of decisions by Upper Tribunal about permission to appeal

(1) Subsections (2) and (3) apply in relation to a decision by the Upper Tribunal to refuse permission (or leave) to appeal further to an application under section 11(4)(b).

(2) The decision is final, and not liable to be questioned or set aside in any other court.

(3) In particular–

(a) the Upper Tribunal is not to be regarded as having exceeded its powers by reason of any error made in reaching the decision;

(b) the supervisory jurisdiction does not extend to, and no application or petition for judicial review may be made or brought in relation to, the decision.

(4) Subsections (2) and (3) do not apply so far as the decision involves or gives rise to any question as to whether—

(a) the Upper Tribunal has or had a valid application before it under section 11(4)(b),

(b) the Upper Tribunal is or was properly constituted for the purpose of dealing with the application, or

(c) the Upper Tribunal is acting or has acted—

(i) in bad faith, or

(ii) in such a procedurally defective way as amounts to a fundamental breach of the principles of natural justice.

(5) Subsections (2) and (3) do not apply so far as provision giving the First-tier Tribunal jurisdiction to make the first-instance decision could (if the Tribunal did not already have that jurisdiction) be made by—

(a) an Act of the Scottish Parliament, or

(b) an Act of the Northern Ireland Assembly the Bill for which would not require the consent of the Secretary of State.

(6) The court of supervisory jurisdiction is not to entertain any application or petition for judicial review in respect of a decision of the First-tier Tribunal that it would not entertain (whether as a matter of law or discretion) in the absence of this section.

(7) In this section—

"decision" includes any purported decision;

"first-instance decision" means the decision in relation to which permission (or leave) to appeal is being sought under section 11(4)(b);

"the supervisory jurisdiction" means the supervisory jurisdiction of—

(a) the High Court, in England and Wales or Northern Ireland, or

(b) the Court of Session, in Scotland, and "the court of supervisory jurisdiction" is to be read accordingly.]

Note: inserted by Judicial Review and Courts Act 2022 c.35 Pt1 s.2(1) (July 14, 2022: insertion does not apply in relation to a decision (including any purported decision) of the Upper Tribunal made before July 14, 2022 being the day on which 2022 c.35 s.2 comes into force

12. Proceedings on appeal to Upper Tribunal

(1) Subsection (2) applies if the Upper Tribunal, in deciding an appeal under section 11, finds that the making of the decision concerned involved the making of an error on a point of law.

(2) The Upper Tribunal—

(a) may (but need not) set aside the decision of the First-tier Tribunal, and

(b) if it does, must either—

(i) remit the case to the First-tier Tribunal with directions for its reconsideration, or

(ii) re-make the decision.

(3) In acting under subsection (2)(b)(i), the Upper Tribunal may also—

(a) direct that the members of the First-tier Tribunal who are chosen to reconsider the case are not to be the same as those who made the decision that has been set aside;

(b) give procedural directions in connection with the reconsideration of the case by the First-tier Tribunal.

(4) In acting under subsection (2)(b)(ii), the Upper Tribunal—

(a) may make any decision which the First-tier Tribunal could make if the First-tier Tribunal were re-making the decision, and

(b) may make such findings of fact as it considers appropriate.

Note: Commenced 3 November 2008 (SI 2008/2696).

13. Right to appeal to Court of Appeal etc.

(1) For the purposes of subsection (2), the reference to a right of appeal is to a right to appeal to the relevant appellate court on any point of law arising from a decision made by the Upper Tribunal other than an excluded decision.

(2) Any party to a case has a right of appeal, subject to subsection (14).

(3) That right may be exercised only with permission (or, in Northern Ireland, leave).

(4) Permission (or leave) may be given by—

(a) the Upper Tribunal, or

(b) the relevant appellate court, on an application by the party.

(5) An application may be made under subsection (4) to the relevant appellate court only if permission (or leave) has been refused by the Upper Tribunal.

(6) The Lord Chancellor may, as respects an application under subsection (4) that falls within subsection (7) and for which the relevant appellate court is the Court of Appeal in England and Wales or the Court of Appeal in Northern Ireland, by order make provision for permission (or leave) not to be granted on the application unless the Upper Tribunal or (as the case may be) the relevant appellate court considers—

(a) that the proposed appeal would raise some important point of principle or practice, or

(b) that there is some other compelling reason for the relevant appellate court to hear the appeal.

[(6A) Rules of court may make provision for permission not to be granted on an application under subsection (4) to the Court of Session that falls within subsection (7) unless the court considers—

(a) that the proposed appeal would raise some important point of principle [or practice], or

(b) that there is some other compelling reason for the court to hear the appeal.]

(7) An application falls within this subsection if the application is for permission (or leave) to appeal from any decision of the Upper Tribunal on an appeal under section 11.

(8) For the purposes of subsection (1), an 'excluded decision' is—

(a) any decision of the Upper Tribunal on an appeal under [section 27(3) or (5), 79(5) or (7) or 111(3) or (5) of the Data Protection Act 2018], (appeals against national security certificate),

(b) any decision of the Upper Tribunal on an appeal under section 60(1) or (4) of the Freedom of Information Act 2000 (c. 36) (appeals against national security certificate),

[(bza) any decision of the Upper Tribunal on an expedited appeal within the meaning given by section 82A(3) of the Nationality, Immigration and Asylum Act 2002 (expedited appeal against refusal of protection claim or human rights claim),

(bzb) any decision of the Upper Tribunal on an expedited related appeal within the meaning given by section 24 of the Nationality and Borders Act 2022 (expedited appeals against refusal of protection claim or human rights claim: joining of related appeals),]

[(ba) any decision of the Upper Tribunal under section 88, 89(3) or 92(3) of the Tax Collection and Management (Wales) Act 2016 (anaw 6) (approval for Welsh Revenue Authority to issue certain information notices),]

[(bb) any decision of the Upper Tribunal under section 108 of that Act (approval for Welsh Revenue Authority to inspect premises),]

[(bc)any decision of the Upper Tribunal under section 181E or 181F of that Act (appeals relating to postponement requests),

(c) any decision of the Upper Tribunal on an application under section 11(4)(b) (application for permission or leave to appeal),

(d) a decision of the Upper Tribunal under section 10—

(i) to review, or not to review, an earlier decision of the tribunal,

(ii) to take no action, or not to take any particular action, in the light of a review of an earlier decision of the tribunal, or

(iii) to set aside an earlier decision of the tribunal,

(e) a decision of the Upper Tribunal that is set aside under section 10 (including a decision set aside after proceedings on an appeal under this section have been begun), or

(f) any decision of the Upper Tribunal that is of a description specified in an order made by the Lord Chancellor.

(9) A description may be specified under subsection (8)(f) only if—

(a) in the case of a decision of that description, there is a right to appeal to a court from the decision and that right is, or includes, something other than a right (however expressed) to appeal on any point of law arising from the decision, or

(b) decisions of that description are made in carrying out a function transferred under section 30 and prior to the transfer of the function under section 30(1) there was no right to appeal from decisions of that description.

(10) Where—

(a) an order under subsection (8)(f) specifies a description of decisions, and

(b) decisions of that description are made in carrying out a function transferred under section 30, the order must be framed so as to come into force no later than the time when the transfer under section 30 of the function takes effect (but power to revoke the order continues to be exercisable after that time, and power to amend the order continues to be exercisable after that time for the purpose of narrowing the description for the time being specified).

(11) Before the Upper Tribunal decides an application made to it under subsection (4), the Upper Tribunal must specify the court that is to be the relevant appellate court as respects the proposed appeal.

(12) The court to be specified under subsection (11) in relation to a proposed appeal is whichever of the following courts appears to the Upper Tribunal to be the most appropriate—

(a) the Court of Appeal in England and Wales;

(b) the Court of Session;

(c) the Court of Appeal in Northern Ireland.

(13) In this section except subsection (11), 'the relevant appellate court', as respects an appeal, means the court specified as respects that appeal by the Upper Tribunal under subsection (11).

(14) The Lord Chancellor may by order make provision for a person to be treated as being, or to be treated as not being, a party to a case for the purposes of subsection (2).

(15) Rules of court may make provision as to the time within which an application under subsection (4) to the relevant appellate court must be made.

Note: Subsections (6), (8)(f), (9), (10), (14) and (15) in force from 19 September 2007 (SI 2007/2709). Remainder in force from 3 November 2008 (SI 2008/2696). Application of s 11 modified by SI 2010/22 Sch 5, paragraph 5(a) from 18 January 2010. Subsection (6A) inserted by s 23 Crime and Courts Act 2013 from 15 July 2013. Words inserted in square brackets at subsection (6A)(a) inserted by s83 of the Criminal Justice and Courts Act 2015 from 13 April 2015 [SI2015/778]. Words in square brackets in subsection (8)(a) substituted by Data Protection Act 2018 c.12 Sch 19(1) para 13 (May 25,2018c.12 s211 and Sch.19 came into force on May 23, 2018 as specified in 2018 c.12 s212(2)for the limited purpose of the power to make regulations or Tribunal Procedure Rules or is otherwise necessary for enabling the exercise of such a power on or after May 23, 2018; May 25, 2018 as SI2018/625 reg.2(g) otherwise). Subsections (8)(ba) &(bb) inserted by Tax Collection and Management (Wales) Act 2016 anaw.6, Pt.4c.7 s.116(2)(January 25, 2018). Subsection (8)(bc) inserted by Tax Collection and Management (Wales) Act 2016 anaw.6 Pt.8 c.3As.181(2) (April 1, 2018 commenced by an amendment). Subsection (8)(bza) inserted by Nationality and Borders Act 2022 c.36 Pt2 s.23(2)(date to be appointed). Subsection (8)(bzb) inserted by Nationality and Borders Act 2022 c.36 s.24(9) date to be appointed)

14. Proceedings on appeal to Court of Appeal etc.

(1) Subsection (2) applies if the relevant appellate court, in deciding an appeal under section 13, finds that the making of the decision concerned involved the making of an error on a point of law.

(2) The relevant appellate court—

(a) may (but need not) set aside the decision of the Upper Tribunal, and

(b) if it does, must either—

(i) remit the case to the Upper Tribunal or, where the decision of the Upper Tribunal was on an appeal or reference from another tribunal or some other person, to the Upper Tribunal or that other tribunal or person, with directions for its reconsideration, or

(ii) re-make the decision.

(3) In acting under subsection (2)(b)(i), the relevant appellate court may also—

(a) direct that the persons who are chosen to reconsider the case are not to be the same as those who—

(i) where the case is remitted to the Upper Tribunal, made the decision of the Upper Tribunal that has been set aside, or

(ii) where the case is remitted to another tribunal or person, made the decision in respect of which the appeal or reference to the Upper Tribunal was made;

(b) give procedural directions in connection with the reconsideration of the case by the Upper Tribunal or other tribunal or person.

(4) In acting under subsection (2)(b)(ii), the relevant appellate court—

(a) may make any decision which the Upper Tribunal could make if the Upper Tribunal were re-making the decision or (as the case may be) which the other tribunal or person could make if that other tribunal or person were re-making the decision, and

(b) may make such findings of fact as it considers appropriate.

(5) Where—

(a) under subsection (2)(b)(i) the relevant appellate court remits a case to the Upper Tribunal, and

(b) the decision set aside under subsection (2)(a) was made by the Upper Tribunal on an appeal or reference from another tribunal or some other person, the Upper Tribunal may (instead of reconsidering the case itself) remit the case to that other tribunal or person, with the directions given by the relevant appellate court for its reconsideration.

(6) In acting under subsection (5), the Upper Tribunal may also—

(a) direct that the persons who are chosen to reconsider the case are not to be the same as those who made the decision in respect of which the appeal or reference to the Upper Tribunal was made;

(b) give procedural directions in connection with the reconsideration of the case by the other tribunal or person.

(7) In this section 'the relevant appellate court', as respects an appeal under section 13, means the court specified as respects that appeal by the Upper Tribunal under section 13(11).

Note: Commenced 3 November 2008 (SI 2008/2696).

[14A Appeal to Supreme Court: grant of certificate by Upper Tribunal

(1) If the Upper Tribunal is satisfied that—

(a) the conditions in subsection (4) or (5) are fulfilled in relation to the Upper Tribunal's decision in any proceedings, and

(b) as regards that decision, a sufficient case for an appeal to the Supreme Court has been made out to justify an application under section 14B,

the Upper Tribunal may grant a certificate to that effect.

(2) The Upper Tribunal may grant a certificate under this section only on an application made by a party to the proceedings.

(3) The Upper Tribunal may grant a certificate under this section only if the relevant appellate court as regards the proceedings is—

(a) the Court of Appeal in England and Wales, or (b) the Court of Appeal in Northern Ireland.

(4) The conditions in this subsection are that a point of law of general public importance is involved in the decision of the Upper Tribunal and that point of law is—

(a) a point of law that—

(i) relates wholly or mainly to the construction of an enactment or statutory instrument, and

(ii) has been fully argued in the proceedings and fully considered in the judgment of the Upper Tribunal in the proceedings, or

(b) a point of law—

(i) in respect of which the Upper Tribunal is bound by a decision of the relevant appellate court or the Supreme Court in previous proceedings, and

(ii) that was fully considered in the judgments given by the relevant appellate court or, as the case may be, the Supreme Court in those previous proceedings.

(5) The conditions in this subsection are that a point of law of general public importance is involved in the decision of the Upper Tribunal and that—

(a) the proceedings entail a decision relating to a matter of national importance or consideration of such a matter,

(b) the result of the proceedings is so significant (whether considered on its own or together with other proceedings or likely proceedings) that, in the opinion of the Upper Tribunal, a hearing by the Supreme Court is justified, or

(c) the Upper Tribunal is satisfied that the benefits of earlier consideration by the Supreme Court outweigh the benefits of consideration by the Court of Appeal.

(6) Before the Upper Tribunal decides an application made to it under this section, the Upper Tribunal must specify the court that would be the relevant appellate court if the application were an application for permission (or leave) under section 13.

(7) In this section except subsection (6) and in sections 14B and 14C, 'the relevant appellate court', as respects an application, means the court specified as respects that application by the Upper Tribunal under subsection (6).

(8) No appeal lies against the grant or refusal of a certificate under subsection (1).

14B Appeal to Supreme Court: permission to appeal

(2) If the Upper Tribunal grants a certificate under section 14A in relation to any proceedings, a party to those proceedings may apply to the Supreme Court for permission to appeal directly to the Supreme Court.

(3) An application under subsection (1) must be made—

(a) within one month from the date on which that certificate is granted, or

(b) within such time as the Supreme Court may allow in a particular case.

(4) If on such an application it appears to the Supreme Court to be expedient to do so, the Supreme Court may grant permission for such an appeal.

(5) If permission is granted under this section—

(a) no appeal from the decision to which the certificate relates lies to the relevant appellate court, but

(b) an appeal lies from that decision to the Supreme Court.

(6) An application under subsection (1) is to be determined without a hearing.

(7) Subject to subsection (4), no appeal lies to the relevant appellate court from a decision of the Upper Tribunal in respect of which a certificate is granted under section 14A until—

(a) the time within which an application can be made under subsection (1) has expired, and

(b) where such an application is made, that application has been determined in accordance with this section.

14C Appeal to Supreme Court: exclusions

(1) No certificate may be granted under section 14A in respect of a decision of the Upper Tribunal in any proceedings where, by virtue of any enactment (other than sections 14A and 14B), no appeal would lie from that decision of the Upper Tribunal to the relevant appellate court, with or without the permission (or leave) of the Upper Tribunal or the relevant appellate court.

(2) No certificate may be granted under section 14A in respect of a decision of the Upper Tribunal in any proceedings where, by virtue of any enactment, no appeal would lie from a decision of the relevant appellate court on that decision of the Upper Tribunal to the Supreme Court, with or without the permission (or leave) of the relevant appellate court or the Supreme Court.

(3) Where no appeal would lie to the relevant appellate court from the decision of the Upper Tribunal except with the permission (or leave) of the Upper Tribunal or the relevant appellate court, no certificate may be granted under section 14A in respect of a decision of the Upper Tribunal unless it appears to the Upper Tribunal that it would be a proper case for giving permission (or leave) to appeal to the relevant appellate court.

(4) No certificate may be granted under section 14A in respect of a decision or order of the Upper Tribunal made by it in the exercise of its jurisdiction to punish for contempt.]

Note: sections (14A)–(14C) inserted by s64 of the Criminal Justice and Courts Act 2015 from 8 August 2016[SI2016/717].

Judicial review

15. Upper Tribunal's 'judicial review' jurisdiction

(1) The Upper Tribunal has power, in cases arising under the law of England and Wales or under the law of Northern Ireland, to grant the following kinds of relief—

(a) a mandatory order;
(b) a prohibiting order;
(c) a quashing order;
(d) a declaration;
(e) an injunction.

(2) The power under subsection (1) may be exercised by the Upper Tribunal if—

(a) certain conditions are met (see section 18), or

(b) the tribunal is authorised to proceed even though not all of those conditions are met (see section 19(3) and (4)).

(3) Relief under subsection (1) granted by the Upper Tribunal—

(a) has the same effect as the corresponding relief granted by the High Court on an application for judicial review, and

(b) is enforceable as if it were relief granted by the High Court on an application for judicial review.

(4) In deciding whether to grant relief under subsection (1)(a), (b) or (c), the Upper Tribunal must apply the principles that the High Court would apply in deciding whether to grant that relief on an application for judicial review.

(5) In deciding whether to grant relief under subsection (1)(d) or (e), the Upper Tribunal must—

(a) in cases arising under the law of England and Wales apply the principles that the High Court would apply in deciding whether to grant that relief under section 31(2) of the [Senior Courts Act 1981] (c. 54) on an application for judicial review, and

(b) in cases arising under the law of Northern Ireland apply the principles that the High Court would apply in deciding whether to grant that relief on an application for judicial review.[

[(5A) In cases arising under the law of England and Wales, subsections (2A) and (2B) of section 31 of the Senior Courts Act 1981 apply to the Upper Tribunal when deciding whether to grant relief under subsection (1) as they apply to the High Court when deciding whether to grant relief on an application for judicial review.

(5B) If the tribunal grants relief in reliance on section 31(2B) of the Senior Courts Act 1981 as applied by subsection (5A), the tribunal must certify that the condition in section 31(2B) as so applied is satisfied.]

(6) For the purposes of the application of subsection (3)(a) in relation to cases arising under the law of Northern Ireland—

(a) a mandatory order under subsection (1)(a) shall be taken to correspond to an order of mandamus,

(b) a prohibiting order under subsection (1)(b) shall be taken to correspond to an order of prohibition, and

(c) a quashing order under subsection (1)(c) shall be taken to correspond to an order of certiorari.

Note: Commenced 3 November 2008 (SI 2008/2696). Words in square brackets is subsection (5)(a) substituted by Sch 11 Constitutional Reform Act 2005 from 1 October 2009 (SI 2009/1604). Section (5A) and (5B) inserted by s84 of the Criminal Justice and Courts Act 2015 from 8 August 2016 [SI2016/717].

16. Application for relief under section 15(1)

(1) This section applies in relation to an application to the Upper Tribunal for relief under section 15(1).

(2) The application may be made only if permission (or, in a case arising under the law of Northern Ireland, leave) to make it has been obtained from the tribunal.

(3) The tribunal may not grant permission (or leave) to make the application unless

[(a)] it considers that the applicant has a sufficient interest in the matter to which the application relates, [and

(b) in cases arising under the law of England and Wales, the applicant has provided the tribunal with any information about the financing of the application that is specified in the Tribunal Procedural Rules for the purposes of this paragraph].

[**(3A)** The information that may be specified for the purposes of subsection (3)(b) includes—

(a) information about the source, nature and extent of financial resources available, or likely to be available, to the applicant to meet liabilities arising in connection with the application, and

(b) if the applicant is a body corporate that is unable to demonstrate that it is likely to have financial resources available to meet such liabilities, information about its members and about their ability to provide financial support for the purposes of the application.

(3B) Tribunal Procedure Rules under subsection (3)(b) that specify information identifying those who are, or are likely to be, sources of financial support must provide that only a person whose financial support (whether direct or indirect) exceeds, or is likely to exceed, a level set out in the rules has to be identified.

This subsection does not apply to rules that specify information described in subsection (3A)(b).]

[**(3C)** In cases arising under the law of England and Wales, when considering whether to grant permission to make the application, the tribunal—

(a) may of its own initiative consider whether the outcome for the applicant would have been substantially different if the conduct complained of had not occurred, and

(b) must consider that question if the respondent asks it to do so.

(3D) In subsection (3C) 'the conduct complained of' means the conduct (or alleged conduct) of the respondent that the applicant claims justifies the tribunal in granting relief.

(3E) If, on considering the question mentioned in subsection (3C)(a) and (b), it appears to the tribunal to be highly likely that the outcome for the applicant would not have been substantially different, the tribunal must refuse to grant permission.

(3F) The tribunal may disregard the requirement in subsection (3E) if it considers that it is appropriate to do so for reasons of exceptional public interest.

(3G) If the tribunal grants permission in reliance on subsection (3F), the tribunal must certify that the condition in subsection (3F) is satisfied.]

(4) Subsection (5) applies where the tribunal considers—

(a) that there has been undue delay in making the application, and

(b) that granting the relief sought on the application would be likely to cause substantial hardship to, or substantially prejudice the rights of, any person or would be detrimental to good administration.

(5) The tribunal may—

(a) refuse to grant permission (or leave) for the making of the application;

(b) refuse to grant any relief sought on the application.

(6) The tribunal may award to the applicant damages, restitution or the recovery of a sum due if—

(a) the application includes a claim for such an award arising from any matter to which the application relates, and

(b) the tribunal is satisfied that such an award would have been made by the High Court if the claim had been made in an action begun in the High Court by the applicant at the time of making the application.

[(**6A**) In cases arising under the law of England and Wales, subsections (2A) and (2B) of section 31 of the Senior Courts Act 1981 apply to the Upper Tribunal as regards the making of an award under subsection (6) as they apply to the High Court as regards the making of an award under section 31(4) of the Senior Courts Act 1981.

(**6B**) If the tribunal makes an award in reliance on section 31(2B) of the Senior Courts Act 1981 as applied by subsection (6A), the tribunal must certify that the condition in section 31(2B) as so applied is satisfied.]

(7) An award under subsection (6) may be enforced as if it were an award of the High Court.

(8) Where—

(a) the tribunal refuses to grant permission (or leave) to apply for relief under section 15(1),

(b) the applicant appeals against that refusal, and

(c) the Court of Appeal grants the permission (or leave),

the Court of Appeal may go on to decide the application for relief under section 15(1).

(9) Subsections (4) and (5) do not prevent Tribunal Procedure Rules from limiting the time within which applications may be made.

Note: Commenced 3 November 2008 (SI 2008/2696). Words inserted in square brackets at subsection (3), (3A) and (3B) by s85 of the Criminal Justice and Courts Act 2015 from a date to be appointed. Words in square brackets at subsection (3A)-(3G) and (6A)-(6B) inserted by s.84 of the Criminal Justice and Courts Act 2015, from 8 August 2016 [SI2016/717].

17. Quashing orders under section 15(1): supplementary provision

[(A1)In cases arising under the law of England and Wales, section 29A of the Senior Courts Act 1981 applies in relation to a quashing order under section 15(1)© of this Act as it applies in relation to a quashing order under section 29 of that Act.]

(1) If the Upper Tribunal makes a quashing order under section 15(1)(c) in respect of a decision, it may in addition—

(a) remit the matter concerned to the court, tribunal or authority that made the decision, with a direction to reconsider the matter and reach a decision in accordance with the findings of the Upper Tribunal, or

(b) substitute its own decision for the decision in question.

(2) The power conferred by subsection (1)(b) is exercisable only if—

(a) the decision in question was made by a court or tribunal,

(b) the decision is quashed on the ground that there has been an error of law, and

(c) without the error, there would have been only one decision that the court or tribunal could have reached.

(3) Unless the Upper Tribunal otherwise directs, a decision substituted by it under subsection (1)(b) has effect as if it were a decision of the relevant court or tribunal.

Note: Commenced 3 November 2008 (SI 2008/2696). Subsection (A1) inserted and words in square brackets substituted at subsection (2)(b) by Judicial Review and Courts Act 2022 c.35 Pt1 s.1(3)

(July 14, 2022: insertion and substitution has effect only in relation to proceedings commenced on or after July 14, 2022 being the day on which 2022 c.35 s.1 comes into force)

18. Limits of jurisdiction under section 15(1)

(1) This section applies where an application made to the Upper Tribunal seeks (whether or not alone)—

(a) relief under section 15(1), or

(b) permission (or, in a case arising under the law of Northern Ireland, leave) to apply for relief under section 15(1).

(2) If Conditions 1 to 4 are met, the tribunal has the function of deciding the application.

(3) If the tribunal does not have the function of deciding the application, it must by order transfer the application to the High Court.

(4) Condition 1 is that the application does not seek anything other than—

(a) relief under section 15(1);

(b) permission (or, in a case arising under the law of Northern Ireland, leave) to apply for relief under section 15(1);

(c) an award under section 16(6);

(d) interest;

(e) costs.

(5) Condition 2 is that the application does not call into question anything done by the Crown Court.

(6) Condition 3 is that the application falls within a class specified for the purposes of this subsection in a direction given in accordance with Part 1 of Schedule 2 to the Constitutional Reform Act 2005 (c. 4).

(7) The power to give directions under subsection (6) includes—

(a) power to vary or revoke directions made in exercise of the power, and

(b) power to make different provision for different purposes.

(8) Condition 4 is that the judge presiding at the hearing of the application is either—

(a) a judge of the High Court or the Court of Appeal in England and Wales or Northern Ireland, or a judge of the Court of Session, or

(b) such other persons as may be agreed from time to time between the Lord Chief Justice, the Lord President, or the Lord Chief Justice of Northern Ireland, as the case may be, and the Senior President of Tribunals.

(9) Where the application is transferred to the High Court under subsection (3)—

(a) the application is to be treated for all purposes as if it—

(i) had been made to the High Court, and

(ii) sought things corresponding to those sought from the tribunal, and

(b) any steps taken, permission (or leave) given or orders made by the tribunal in relation to the application are to be treated as taken, given or made by the High Court.

(10) Rules of court may make provision for the purpose of supplementing subsection (9).

(11) The provision that may be made by Tribunal Procedure Rules about amendment of an application for relief under section 15(1) includes, in particular, provision about amendments that would cause the application to become transferrable under subsection (3).

(12) For the purposes of subsection (9)(a)(ii), in relation to an application transferred to the High Court in Northern Ireland—

(a) an order of mandamus shall be taken to correspond to a mandatory order under section 15(1)(a),

(b) an order of prohibition shall be taken to correspond to a prohibiting order under section 15(1)(b), and

(c) an order of certiorari shall be taken to correspond to a quashing order under section 15(1)(c).

Note: Subsections (10) and (11) in force from 19 September 2007 (SI 2007/2709). Remainder in force from 3 November 2008 (SI 2008/2696).

19. Transfer of judicial review applications from High Court

(1) . . .

(2) . . .

(3) Where an application is transferred to the Upper Tribunal under 31A of the [Senior Courts Act 1981] or section 25A of the Judicature (Northern Ireland) Act 1978 (transfer from the High Court of judicial review applications)—

(a) the application is to be treated for all purposes as if it—

(i) had been made to the tribunal, and

(ii) sought things corresponding to those sought from the High Court,

(b) the tribunal has the function of deciding the application, even if it does not fall within a class specified under section 18(6), and

(c) any steps taken, permission given, leave given or orders made by the High Court in relation to the application are to be treated as taken, given or made by the tribunal.

(4) Where—

(a) an application for permission is transferred to the Upper Tribunal under section 31A of the [Senior Courts Act 1981] and the tribunal grants permission, or

(b) an application for leave is transferred to the Upper Tribunal under section 25A of the Judicature (Northern Ireland) Act 1978 (c. 23) and the tribunal grants leave, the tribunal has the function of deciding any subsequent application brought under the permission or leave, even if the subsequent application does not fall within a class specified under section 18(6).

(5) Tribunal Procedure Rules may make further provision for the purposes of supplementing subsections (3) and (4).

(6) For the purposes of subsection (3)(a)(ii), in relation to an application transferred to the Upper Tribunal under section 25A of the Judicature (Northern Ireland) Act 1978—

(a) a mandatory order under section 15(1)(a) shall be taken to correspond to an order of mandamus,

(b) a prohibiting order under section 15(1)(b) shall be taken to correspond to an order of prohibition, and

(c) a quashing order under section 15(1)(c) shall be taken to correspond to an order of certiorari.

Note: Commenced 3 November 2008 (SI 2008/2696). Subsection (1) amends the Supreme Court Act 1981. Subsection (2) amends the Judicature (Northern Ireland) Act 1978. Words in square brackets in subsections (3) and (4) substituted by Sch 11 Constitutional Reform Act 2005 from 1 October 2009 (SI 2009/1064).

20. Transfer of judicial review applications from the Court of Session

(1) Where an application is made to the supervisory jurisdiction of the Court of Session, the Court—

(a) must, if Conditions 1 [and 2 are met, and]

[aa . . .]

(b) may, if Conditions 1 [and 3] are met, but Condition 2 is not, by order transfer the application to the Upper Tribunal.

(2) Condition 1 is that the application does not seek anything other than an exercise of the supervisory jurisdiction of the Court of Session.

(3) Condition 2 is that the application falls within a class specified for the purposes of this subsection by act of sederunt made with the consent of the Lord Chancellor.

(4) Condition 3 is that the subject matter of the application is not a devolved Scottish matter.

(5) . . .

[(5A) . . .]

(6) There may not be specified under subsection (3) any class of application which includes an application the subject matter of which is a devolved Scottish matter.

(7) For the purposes of this section, the subject matter of an application is a devolved Scottish matter if it—

(a) concerns the exercise of functions in or as regards Scotland, and

(b) does not relate to a reserved matter within the meaning of the Scotland Act 1998 (c. 46).

(8) In subsection (2), the reference to the exercise of the supervisory jurisdiction of the Court of Session includes a reference to the making of any order in connection with or in consequence of the exercise of that jurisdiction.

Note: Subsections (3), (6) and (7) in force from 19 September 2007 (SI 2007/2709). Remainder in force from 3 November 2008 (SI 2008/2696). Subsections (1)(aa) and (5A) inserted by the UK Borders Act 8 November 2009 (SI 2011/1741) and omitted by s 22 Crime and Courts Act 2013 from 1 November 2013 (SI 2013/2200). Words in square brackets in subsection (1) substituted and subsection (5) omitted from 1 November 2013 (SI 2013/2200).

[20A. Procedural steps where application transferred

(1) This section applies where the Court of Session transfers an application under section 20(1)(a).

(2) It is for the Upper Tribunal to determine—

(a) whether the application has been made timeously, and

(b) whether to grant permission for the application to proceed under section 27B of the Court of Session Act 1988 ('the 1988 Act') (requirement for permission).

(3) Accordingly—

(a) the Upper Tribunal has the same powers in relation to the application as the Court of Session would have had in relation to it under sections 27A to 27C of the 1988 Act(b),

(b) sections 27C and 27D of that Act apply in relation to a decision of the Upper Tribunal under section 27B(1) of that Act as they apply in relation to such a decision of the Court of Session.

(4) The references in section 27C(3) and (4) of the 1988 Act (oral hearings where permission refused) to a different Lord Ordinary from the one who granted or refused permission are to be read as references to different members of the Tribunal from those of whom it was composed when it refused or granted permission.].

Note: section (20A) inserted by s7 of the Court Reform (Scotland) Act 2014 (Consequential Provisions and Modifications) Order 2015 from 22 September 2015 [SI2015/700].

21. Upper Tribunal's 'judicial review' jurisdiction: Scotland

(1) The Upper Tribunal has the function of deciding applications transferred to it from the Court of Session under section 20(1).

(2) The powers of review of the Upper Tribunal in relation to such applications are the same as the powers of review of the Court of Session in an application to the supervisory jurisdiction of that Court.

(3) In deciding an application by virtue of subsection (1), the Upper Tribunal must apply principles that the Court of Session would apply in deciding an application to the supervisory jurisdiction of that Court.

(4) An order of the Upper Tribunal by virtue of subsection (1)—

(a) has the same effect as the corresponding order granted by the Court of Session on an application to the supervisory jurisdiction of that Court, and

(b) is enforceable as if it were an order so granted by that Court.

(5) Where an application is transferred to the Upper Tribunal by virtue of section 20(1), any steps taken or orders made by the Court of Session in relation to the application (other than the order to transfer the application under section 20(1)) are to be treated as taken or made by the tribunal.

(6) Tribunal Procedure Rules may make further provision for the purposes of supplementing subsection (5).

Note: Subsection (6) in force from 19 September 2007 (SI 2007/2709). Remainder in force from 3 November 2008 (SI 2008/2696).

Miscellaneous

22. Tribunal Procedure Rules

(1) There are to be rules, to be called 'Tribunal Procedure Rules', governing—

(a) the practice and procedure to be followed in the First-tier Tribunal, and

(b) the practice and procedure to be followed in the Upper Tribunal.

(2) Tribunal Procedure Rules are to be made by the Tribunal Procedure Committee.

(3) In Schedule 5—

Part 1 makes further provision about the content of Tribunal Procedure Rules,

Part 2 makes provision about the membership of the Tribunal Procedure Committee,

Part 3 makes provision about the making of Tribunal Procedure Rules by the Committee, and

Part 4 confers power to amend legislation in connection with Tribunal Procedure Rules.

(4) Power to make Tribunal Procedure Rules is to be exercised with a view to securing—

(a) that, in proceedings before the First-tier Tribunal and Upper Tribunal, justice is done,

(b) that the tribunal system is accessible and fair,

(c) that proceedings before the First-tier Tribunal or Upper Tribunal are handled quickly and efficiently,

(d) that the rules are both simple and simply expressed, and

(e) that the rules where appropriate confer on members of the First-tier Tribunal, or Upper Tribunal, responsibility for ensuring that proceedings before the tribunal are handled quickly and efficiently.

(5) In subsection (4)(b) 'the tribunal system' means the system for deciding matters within the jurisdiction of the First-tier Tribunal or the Upper Tribunal.

[(6) Tribunal Procedure Rules must be framed so as not to apply to proceedings that are governed by Online Procedure Rules except to such extent as may be provided by—

(a) Online Procedure Rules,

(b) directions under paragraph 5 of Schedule 3 to the Judicial Review and Courts Act 2022, or

(c) regulations under section 21(1)(b) of that Act.]

Note: Commenced 19 September 2007 (SI 2007/2709). Subsection (6) inserted by Judicial Review and Courts Act 2022 c.35 Sch.4 para 4(2) (date to be appointed)

23. Practice directions

(1) The Senior President of Tribunals may give directions—

(a) as to the practice and procedure of the First-tier Tribunal;

(b) as to the practice and procedure of the Upper Tribunal.

(2) A Chamber President may give directions as to the practice and procedure of the chamber over which he presides.

(3) A power under this section to give directions includes—

(a) power to vary or revoke directions made in exercise of the power, and

(b) power to make different provision for different purposes (including different provision for different areas).

(4) Directions under subsection (1) may not be given without the approval of the Lord Chancellor.

(5) Directions under subsection (2) may not be given without the approval of—

(a) the Senior President of Tribunals, and

(b) the Lord Chancellor.

(6) Subsections (4) and (5)(b) do not apply to directions to the extent that they consist of guidance about any of the following—

(a) the application or interpretation of the law;

(b) the making of decisions by members of the First-tier Tribunal or Upper Tribunal.

(7) Subsections (4) and (5)(b) do not apply to directions to the extent that they consist of criteria for determining which members of the First-tier Tribunal or Upper Tribunal may be chosen to decide particular categories of matter; but the directions may, to that extent, be given only after consulting the Lord Chancellor.

[(8) Directions under this section do not apply to proceedings that are governed by Online Procedure Rules except—

(a) to such extent as may be provided by—

(i) Online Procedure Rules, or

(ii) directions under paragraph 5 of Schedule 3 to the Judicial Review and Courts Act 2022, or

(b) to such extent as Tribunal Procedure Rules apply to the proceedings by virtue of regulations under section 21(1)(b) of that Act.]

Note: Commenced 3 November 2008 (SI 2008/2696). Subsection 8 inserted by Judicial Review and Courts Act 2022 c.35 Sch.4 para 4(3) (date to be appointed)

24. Mediation

(1) A person exercising power to make Tribunal Procedure Rules or give practice directions must, when making provision in relation to mediation, have regard to the following principles—

(a) mediation of matters in dispute between parties to proceedings is to take place only by agreement between those parties;

(b) where parties to proceedings fail to mediate, or where mediation between parties to proceedings fails to resolve disputed matters, the failure is not to affect the outcome of the proceedings.

(2) Practice directions may provide for members to act as mediators in relation to disputed matters in a case that is the subject of proceedings.

(3) The provision that may be made by virtue of subsection (2) includes provision for a member to act as a mediator in relation to disputed matters in a case even though the member has been chosen to decide matters in the case.

(4) Once a member has begun to act as a mediator in relation to a disputed matter in a case that is the subject of proceedings, the member may decide matters in the case only with the consent of the parties.

(5) Staff appointed under section 40(1) may, subject to their terms of appointment, act as mediators in relation to disputed matters in a case that is the subject of proceedings.

(6) In this section—

'member' means a judge or other member of the First-tier Tribunal or a judge or other member of the Upper Tribunal;

'practice direction' means a direction under section 23(1) or (2);

'proceedings' means proceedings before the First-tier Tribunal or proceedings before the Upper Tribunal.

Note: Commenced 3 November 2008 (SI 2008/2696).

25. Supplementary powers of Upper Tribunal

(1) In relation to the matters mentioned in subsection (2), the Upper Tribunal—

(a) has, in England and Wales or in Northern Ireland, the same powers, rights, privileges and authority as the High Court, and

(b) has, in Scotland, the same powers, rights, privileges and authority as the Court of Session.

(2) The matters are—

(a) the attendance and examination of witnesses,

(b) the production and inspection of documents, and

(c) all other matters incidental to the Upper Tribunal's functions.

(3) Subsection (1) shall not be taken—

(a) to limit any power to make Tribunal Procedure Rules;

(b) to be limited by anything in Tribunal Procedure Rules other than an express limitation.

(4) A power, right, privilege or authority conferred in a territory by subsection (1) is available for purposes of proceedings in the Upper Tribunal that take place outside that territory (as well as for purposes of proceedings in the tribunal that take place within that territory).

Note: Commenced 3 November 2008 (SI 2008/2696).

[25A First-tier Tribunal and Upper Tribunal: charging power in respect of wasted resources

(1) If, in respect of proceedings before the First-tier Tribunal or Upper Tribunal, the Tribunal considers that—

(a) a relevant participant has acted improperly, unreasonably or negligently, and

(b) as a result, the Tribunal's resources have been wasted,

it may charge the participant an amount under this section.

(2) Subsection (1) is subject to Tribunal Procedure Rules.

(3) For the purposes of this section "relevant participant", in respect of proceedings, means—

(a) any person exercising a right of audience or right to conduct the proceedings on behalf of a party to proceedings,

(b) any employee of such a person, or

(c) where the Secretary of State is a party to proceedings and has not instructed a person mentioned in paragraph (a) to act on their behalf in the proceedings, the Secretary of State.

(4) A person may be found to have acted improperly, unreasonably or negligently for the purposes of subsection (1) by reason of having failed to act in a particular way.

(5) The proceeds of amounts charged under this section must be paid into the Consolidated Fund.]

Note: inserted by Nationality and Borders Act 2022 c.36 Pt6 s.80(1) (date to be appointed)

26. First-tier Tribunal and Upper Tribunal: sitting places

Each of the First-tier Tribunal and the Upper Tribunal may decide a case—

(a) in England and Wales,

(b) in Scotland, or

(c) in Northern Ireland, even though the case arises under the law of a territory other than the one in which the case is decided.

Note: Commenced 3 November 2008 (SI 2008/2696).

27. Enforcement

(1) A sum payable in pursuance of a decision of the First-tier Tribunal or Upper Tribunal made in England and Wales—

(a) shall be recoverable as if it were payable under an order of [the county court] in England and Wales;

(b) shall be recoverable as if it were payable under an order of the High Court in England and Wales.

(2) An order for the payment of a sum payable in pursuance of a decision of the First-tier Tribunal or Upper Tribunal made in Scotland (or a copy of such an order certified in accordance with Tribunal Procedure Rules) may be enforced as if it were an extract registered decree arbitral bearing a warrant for execution issued by the sheriff court of any sheriffdom in Scotland.

(3) A sum payable in pursuance of a decision of the First-tier Tribunal or Upper Tribunal made in Northern Ireland—

(a) shall be recoverable as if it were payable under an order of a county court in Northern Ireland;

(b) shall be recoverable as if it were payable under an order of the High Court in Northern Ireland.

(4) This section does not apply to a sum payable in pursuance of—

(a) an award under section 16(6), or

(b) an order by virtue of section 21(1).

(5) The Lord Chancellor may by order make provision for subsection (1) or (3) to apply in relation to a sum of a description specified in the order with the omission of one (but not both) of paragraphs (a) and (b).

(6) Tribunal Procedure Rules—

(a) may make provision as to where, for purposes of this section, a decision is to be taken to be made;

(b) may provide for all or any of subsections (1) to (3) to apply only, or not to apply except, in relation to sums of a description specified in Tribunal Procedure Rules. Tribunals, Courts and Enforcement Act 2007 (c. 15).

Note: Subsections (5) and (6) in force from 19 September 2007 (SI 2007/2709). Remainder in force from 3 November 2008 (SI 2008/2696). Words in square brackets substituted by Schedule 9 Crime and Courts Act 2013 from 22 April 2014 (SI 2014/954).

28. Assessors

(1) If it appears to the First-tier Tribunal or the Upper Tribunal that a matter before it requires special expertise not otherwise available to it, it may direct that in dealing with that matter it shall have the assistance of a person or persons appearing to it to have relevant knowledge or experience.

(2) The remuneration of a person who gives assistance to either tribunal as mentioned in subsection (1) shall be determined and paid by the Lord Chancellor.

(3) The Lord Chancellor may—

(a) establish panels of persons from which either tribunal may (but need not) select persons to give it assistance as mentioned in subsection (1);

(b) under paragraph (a) establish different panels for different purposes;

(c) after carrying out such consultation as he considers appropriate, appoint persons to a panel established under paragraph (a);

(d) remove a person from such a panel.

Note: Commenced 3 November 2008 (SI 2008/2696).

29. Costs or expenses

(1) The costs of and incidental to—

(a) all proceedings in the First-tier Tribunal, and

(b) all proceedings in the Upper Tribunal, shall be in the discretion of the Tribunal in which the proceedings take place.

(2) The relevant Tribunal shall have full power to determine by whom and to what extent the costs are to be paid.

(3) Subsections (1) and (2) have effect subject to Tribunal Procedure Rules.

[(3A)The relevant Tribunal may, in particular, make an order in respect of costs in any proceedings mentioned in subsection (1), if it considers that a party or its legal or other representative has acted unreasonably in bringing, defending or conducting the proceedings.]

(4) In any proceedings mentioned in subsection (1), the relevant Tribunal may—

(a) disallow, or

(b) (as the case may be) order the legal or other representative concerned to meet, the whole of any wasted costs or such part of them as may be determined in accordance with Tribunal Procedure Rules.

(5) In subsection (4) 'wasted costs' means any costs incurred by a party—

(a) as a result of any improper, unreasonable or negligent act or omission on the part of any legal or other representative or any employee of such a representative, or

(b) which, in the light of any such act or omission occurring after they were incurred, the relevant Tribunal considers it is unreasonable to expect that party to pay.

(6) In this section 'legal or other representative', in relation to a party to proceedings, means any person exercising a right of audience or right to conduct the proceedings on his behalf.

(7) In the application of this section in relation to Scotland, any reference in this section to costs is to be read as a reference to expenses.

Note: Commenced 3 November 2008 (SI 2008/2696). Subsection (3A) inserted by Nationality and Borders Act 2022 c.36 Pt6 s.81(6) (date to be appointed)

[Use of live video or audio links: public participation & offences of recording etc

29ZA Enabling the public to see and hear proceedings

29ZB Offences of recording or transmission in relation to broadcasting

29ZC Offences of Recording or transmission in relation to broadcasting

29ZD Interpretation

Note: sections 29ZA-D inserted by Coronavirus Act 2020, Sch 25, para 2 from March 25, 2020. Omitted by Coronavirus Act 2020 Sch.25 para 2 (Jun3 28, 2022)

[CHAPTER 2A

EXERCISE OF TRIBUNAL FUNCTIONS BY AUTHORISED PERSONS

29A [Interpretation of Chapter]

In this Chapter—

'authorised person' means a person authorised under [a relevant Procedural Rule]to exercise functions of[a tribunal];

'judicial office holder' [means

(a) a judicial office holder within] the meaning given by section 109(4) of the Constitutional Reform Act 2005;[or

(b) the President of the Employment Tribunals (Scotland).

'relevant Procedural Rule' means

(a) A Tribunal Procedure Rule of a kind mentioned in paragraph 3 of Schedule 5 tot his Act, or

(b) An Employment Procedure Rule of a kind mentioned in paragraph 2 of Schedule A1 to the Employment Tribunals Act 1996;

'tribunal' means the First-Tier Tribunal, the Upper Tribunal, an employment tribunal or the Employment Appeals Tribunal.]

Note: words substituted in heading, and in square brackets by Judicial Review and Courts Act 2022 c.35 Pt2 c.3 s.37 (date to be appointed)

29B Directions and independence: authorised persons

(1) The Senior President of Tribunals may give directions to an authorised person.

(2) Apart from such directions, an authorised person exercising a function by virtue of [a relevant Procedural Rule] is not subject to the direction of the Lord Chancellor or any other person when exercising the function.

(3) The Senior President of Tribunals may delegate to one or more of the following the Senior President of Tribunals' functions under subsection (1)—

(a) a judicial office holder;

(b) a person appointed under section 2(1) of the Courts Act 2003 or section 40(1) of this Act.

(4)A person to whom functions of the Senior President of Tribunals are delegated under subsection (3)(b) is not subject to the direction of any person other than—

(a) the Senior President of Tribunals, or

(b) a judicial office holder nominated by the Senior President of Tribunals,

when exercising the functions.

(5) Subsections (3) to (5) of section 8 apply to—

(a) a delegation under subsection (3) of this section, and

(b) a nomination under subsection (4) of this section,

as they apply to a delegation under subsection (1) of that section.

Note: words in square brackets in subsection (2) substituted by Judicial Review and Courts Act 2022 Act 2022 c.35 Pt2 c.3 s.37(3)(a) (date to be appointed)

29C Protection of authorised persons

(1) No action lies against an authorised person in respect of what the person does or omits to do—

(a) in the execution of the person's duty as an authorised person exercising, by virtue of[a relevant Procedural Rule], functions of a tribunal, and

(b) in relation to a matter within the person's jurisdiction.

(2) An action lies against an authorised person in respect of what the person does or omits to do—

(a) in the purported execution of the person's duty as an authorised person exercising, by virtue of paragraph 3 of Schedule 5, functions of a tribunal, but

(b) in relation to a matter not within the person's jurisdiction,

if, but only if, it is proved that the person acted in bad faith.

(3) If an action is brought in a court in Scotland in circumstances in which subsection (1) or (2) provides that no action lies, the court in which the action is brought—

(a) may, on the application of the defender, dismiss the action, and

(b) if it does so, may find the person bringing the action liable in expenses.

(4) If an action is brought in any other court in circumstances in which subsection (1) or (2) provides that no action lies, the court in which the action is brought—

(a) may, on the application of the defendant, strike out the proceedings in the action, and

(b) if it does so, may if it thinks fit order the person bringing the action to pay costs.

Note: words substituted in square brackets in subsection (1)(a) by Judicial Review and Courts Act 2022 c.35 Pt2 c.3 s.37(3)(b) (date to be appointed)

29D Costs or expenses in legal proceedings: authorised persons

(1) A court may not order an authorised person to pay costs in any proceedings in respect of what the person does or omits to do in the execution (or purported execution) of the person's duty as an authorised person exercising, by virtue of[a relevant Procedural Rule], a function of a tribunal.

(2) But subsection (1) does not apply in relation to any proceedings in which an authorised person—

(a) is being tried for an offence or is appealing against a conviction, or

(b) is proved to have acted in bad faith in respect of the matters giving rise to the proceedings.

(3) A court which is prevented by subsection (1) from ordering an authorised person to pay costs in any proceedings may instead order the Lord Chancellor to make a payment in respect of the costs of a person in the proceedings.

(4) The Lord Chancellor may, after consulting the Senior President of Tribunals, make regulations specifying—

(a) circumstances in which a court must or must not exercise the power conferred on it by subsection (3), and

(b) how the amount of any payment ordered under subsection (3) is to be determined.

(5) The power to make regulations under subsection (4) includes power to make—

(a) any supplementary, incidental or consequential provision, and

(b) any transitory, transitional or saving provision,

which the Lord Chancellor considers necessary or expedient.

(6) The Senior President of Tribunals may delegate the Senior President of Tribunals' functions under subsection (4) to a person who is a judicial office holder.

(7) Subsections (3) to (5) of section 8 apply to a delegation under subsection (6) of this section as they apply to a delegation under subsection (1) of that section.

(8) In the application of this section to Scotland—

(a) references to a court ordering an authorised person to pay costs are to be read as references to a court finding an authorised person liable in expenses, and

(b) the second reference to costs in subsection (3) is to be read as a reference to expenses.

Note: words substituted in square brackets in subsection (1) by Judicial Review and Courts Act 2022 c.36 Pt2 c.3 s37 (3) (c) (date to be appointed)

29E Indemnification of authorised persons

(1) 'Indemnifiable amounts', in relation to an authorised person, means—

(a) costs which the person reasonably incurs in or in connection with proceedings in respect of anything done or omitted to be done in the exercise (or purported exercise) of the person's duty as an authorised person,

(b) costs which the person reasonably incurs in taking steps to dispute a claim which might be made in such proceedings,

(c) damages awarded against the person or costs ordered to be paid by the person in such proceedings, or

(d) sums payable by the person in connection with a reasonable settlement of such proceedings or such a claim.

(2) The Lord Chancellor must indemnify an authorised person in respect of indemnifiable amounts if, in respect of the matters giving rise to the proceedings or claim, the person acted reasonably and in good faith.

(3) The Lord Chancellor may indemnify an authorised person in respect of other indemnifiable amounts unless it is proved, in respect of the matters giving rise to the proceedings or claim, that the person acted in bad faith.

(4) Any question whether, or to what extent, an authorised person is to be indemnified under this section is to be determined by the Lord Chancellor.

(5) The Lord Chancellor may, if an authorised person claiming to be indemnified so requests, make a determination for the purposes of this section with respect to—

(a) costs such as are mentioned in subsection (1)(a) or (b), or

(b) sums such as are mentioned in subsection (1)(d),

before the costs are incurred or the settlement in connection with which the sums are payable is made.

(6) But a determination under subsection (5) before costs are incurred—

(a) is subject to such limitations (if any) as the Lord Chancellor thinks proper and to the subsequent determination of the costs reasonably incurred, and

(b) does not affect any other determination which may fall to be made in connection with the proceedings or claim in question.

(7) In the application of this section to Scotland, references to costs are to be read as references to expenses.]

Note: Sections (29A) –(29D) inserted by Courts and Tribunals (Judiciary and Functions of Staff) Act 2018, Sch.1(2) para 41 from January 10, 2020 for specified purposes by SI2020/24, reg 2(b\(iv).

Criminal Justice and Immigration Act 2008
(2008, c. 4)

Part 10. Special Immigration Status

---

130. Designation

(1) The Secretary of State may designate a person who satisfies Condition 1 or 2 (subject to subsections (4) and (5)).

(2) Condition 1 is that the person

(a) is a foreign criminal within the meaning of section 131, and

(b) is liable to deportation, but cannot be removed from the United Kingdom because of section 6 of the Human Rights Act 1998 (c. 42) (public authority not to act contrary to Convention).

(3) Condition 2 is that the person is a member of the family of a person who satisfies Condition 1.

(4) A person who has the right of abode in the United Kingdom may not be designated.

(5) The Secretary of State may not designate a person if the Secretary of State thinks that an effect of designation would breach—

(a) the United Kingdom's obligations under the Refugee Convention, [[

(b) [[]]

Note: Commencement at a date to be appointed. Words in square brackets in subsection (5)(b) substituted by Immigration, Nationality and Asylum (EU Exit) Regulations 2019/745 reg 18(2). Words at subsection (5)(b) omitted by The Immigration and Social Security Co-ordination (EU Withdrawal) Act 2020 (Consquential, Saving, Transitional and Transitory Provisions)(EU Exit) Regulations 2020 SI 2020/1309)

131. 'Foreign criminal'

(1) For the purposes of section 130 'foreign criminal' means a person who—

(a) is not a British citizen, and

(b) satisfies any of the following Conditions.

(2) Condition 1 is that section 72(2)(a) and (b) or (3)(a) to (c) of the Nationality, Immigration and Asylum Act 2002 (c. 41) applies to the person (Article 33(2) of the Refugee Convention: imprisonment for at least two years).

(3) Condition 2 is that—

(a) section 72(4)(a) or (b) of that Act applies to the person (person convicted of specified offence), and

(b) the person has been sentenced to a period of imprisonment.

(4) Condition 3 is that Article 1F of the Refugee Convention applies to the person (exclusions for criminals etc.).

(5) Section 72(6) of that Act (rebuttal of presumption under section 72(2) to (4)) has no effect in relation to Condition 1 or 2.

(6) Section 72(7) of that Act (non-application pending appeal) has no effect in relation to Condition 1 or 2.

Note: Commencement at a date to be appointed.

132. Effect of designation

(1) A designated person does not have leave to enter or remain in the United Kingdom.

(2) For the purposes of a provision of the Immigration Acts and any other enactment which concerns or refers to immigration or nationality (including any provision which applies or refers to a provision of the Immigration Acts or any other enactment about immigration or nationality) a designated person—

(a) is a person subject to immigration control,

(b) is not to be treated as an asylum-seeker or a former asylum-seeker, and

(c) is not in the United Kingdom in breach of the immigration laws.

(3) Despite subsection (2)(c), time spent in the United Kingdom as a designated person may not be relied on by a person for the purpose of an enactment about nationality.

(4) A designated person—

(a) shall not be deemed to have been given leave in accordance with paragraph 6 of Schedule 2 to the Immigration Act 1971 (c. 77) (notice of leave or refusal), and

(b) may not be granted [immigration bail under Schedule 10 to the Immigration Act 2016].

(5) Sections 134 and 135 make provision about support for designated persons and their dependants.

Note: Commencement at a date to be appointed. Words in square brackets in subsection (4)(b) substituted by Schedule 10 to the Immigration Act 2016 from a date to be appointed.

133. Conditions

(1) The Secretary of State or an immigration officer may by notice in writing impose a condition on a designated person.

(2) A condition may relate to—

(a) residence,

(b) employment or occupation, or

(c) reporting to the police, the Secretary of State or an immigration officer.

[(3) If a condition is imposed under this section on a designated person, the person imposing the condition may also impose an electronic monitoring condition within the meaning of Schedule 10 to the Immigration Act 2016 on the designated person.

(3A) Paragraph 4 (electronic monitoring conditions) of that Schedule applies in relation to a condition imposed under subsection (3) as it applies to an electronic monitoring condition imposed under that Schedule.

(4) Paragraph 9(4) and (5) (bail conditions: travelling expenses) of that Schedule applies in relation to conditions imposed under subsection (2)(c) as it applies to conditions imposed under that Schedule.]

(5) A person who without reasonable excuse fails to comply with a condition imposed under this section commits an offence.

(6) A person who is guilty of an offence under subsection (5) shall be liable on summary conviction to—

(a) a fine not exceeding level 5 on the standard scale,
(b) imprisonment for a period not exceeding 51 weeks, or
(c) both.

(7) A provision of the Immigration Act 1971 (c. 77) which applies in relation to an offence under [section 24]of that Act (illegal entry etc.) shall also apply in relation to the offence under subsection (5) above.

(8) In the application of this section to Scotland or Northern Ireland the reference in subsection (6)(b) to 51 weeks shall be treated as a reference to six months.

Note: Commencement at a date to be appointed. In the application of this section in England and Wales to offences committed before the commencement of s 281(5) of the Criminal Justice Act 2003, the maximum term of sentence in subsection (6)(b) shall be read as 6 months, Sch 27 paragraph 36. Paragraph (3), (3A) and (4) substituted by Schedule 10 to the Immigration Act 2016 from a date to be appointed. Words in square brackets in subsection (7) substituted by Nationality and Borders Act 2022 c.36 Pt3 s.40(9) (date to be appointed): substitution has effect as SI 2022/590 reg.2 and Sch.1 para 20 subject to transitional and saving provisions specified in SI 2022/590 reg.3 and Sch.2 para 7: substitution came into force on June 28, 2022 but cannot take effect until the commencement of 2008 c.4 s.133(7)

134. Support

(1) Part VI of the Immigration and Asylum Act 1999 (c. 33) (support for asylum seekers) shall apply in relation to designated persons and their dependants as it applies in relation to asylum-seekers and their dependants.

(2) But the following provisions of that Part shall not apply—

(a) section 96 (kinds of support),
(b) section 97(1)(b) (desirability of providing accommodation in well-supplied area),
(c) section 100 (duty to cooperate in providing accommodation),
(d) section 101 (reception zones),
(e) section 108 (failure of sponsor to maintain),
(f) section 111 (grants to voluntary organisations), and
(g) section 113 (recovery of expenditure from sponsor).

(3) Support may be provided under section 95 of the 1999 Act as applied by this section—

(a) by providing accommodation appearing to the Secretary of State to be adequate for a person's needs;

(b) by providing what appear to the Secretary of State to be essential living needs;

(c) in other ways which the Secretary of State thinks necessary to reflect exceptional circumstances of a particular case.

(4) Support by virtue of subsection (3) may not be provided wholly or mainly by way of cash unless the Secretary of State thinks it appropriate because of exceptional circumstances.

(5) . . .

(6) . . .

Note: Commencement at a date to be appointed. Subsection (6) repealed by Housing and Regeneration Act 2008 Sch 15 paragraph 24 from 2 March 2009 (SI 2009/415). Subsection 5 omitted by Schedule 11 to the Immigration Act 2016 from a date to be appointed.

135. Support: supplemental

(1) A reference in an enactment to Part VI of the 1999 Act or to a provision of that Part includes a reference to that Part or provision as applied by section 134 above; and for that purpose—

(a) a reference to section 96 shall be treated as including a reference to section 134(3) above,

(b) a reference to a provision of section 96 shall be treated as including a reference to the corresponding provision of section 134(3), and

(c) a reference to asylum-seekers shall be treated as including a reference to designated persons.

(2) A provision of Part VI of the 1999 Act which requires or permits the Secretary of State to have regard to the temporary nature of support shall be treated, in the application of Part VI by virtue of section 134 above, as requiring the Secretary of State to have regard to the nature and circumstances of support by virtue of that section.

(3) . . .

(4) Any . . . instrument under Part VI of the 1999 Act—

(a) may make provision in respect of that Part as it applies by virtue of section 134 above, as it applies otherwise than by virtue of that section, or both, and

(b) may make different provision for that Part as it applies by virtue of section 134 above and as it applies otherwise than by virtue of that section.

(5) In the application of paragraph 9 of Schedule 8 to the 1999 Act (regulations: notice to quit accommodation) the reference in paragraph (2)(b) to the determination of a [protection claim] shall be treated as a reference to ceasing to be a designated person.

(6) The Secretary of State may by order repeal, modify or disapply (to any extent) section 134(4).

(7) . . .

Note: Commencement at a date to be appointed. Subsection (3) omitted, and words omitted from subsection (4) by The Transfer of Tribunal Functions (Lands Tribunal and Miscellaneous

Amendments) Order 2009 Sch 1 paragraph 288(a) from 1 June 2009 (SI 2009/1307). Subsection (7) repealed by Housing and Regeneration Act 2008 Sch 15 paragraph 25 from 2 March 2009 (SI 2009/415). Words in square brackets at subsection (5) substituted by Schedule 11 to the Immigration Act 2016 from a date to be appointed.

136. End of designation

(1) Designation lapses if the designated person—

(a) is granted leave to enter or remain in the United Kingdom,

(b) [

(c) leaves the United Kingdom, or

(d) is made the subject of a deportation order under section 5 of the Immigration Act 1971 (c. 77).

(2) After designation lapses support may not be provided by virtue of section 134, subject to the following exceptions.

(3) Exception 1 is that, if designation lapses under subsection (1)(a) [], support may be provided in respect of a period which—

(a) begins when the designation lapses, and

(b) ends on a date determined in accordance with an order of the Secretary of State.

(4) Exception 2 is that, if designation lapses under subsection (1)(d), support may be provided in respect of—

(a) any period during which an appeal against the deportation order may be brought (ignoring any possibility of an appeal out of time with permission),

(b) any period during which an appeal against the deportation order is pending, and

(c) after an appeal ceases to be pending, such period as the Secretary of State may specify by order.

Note: Commencement at a date to be appointed. Words in square brackets in subsection (1)(b) by Immigration, Nationality and Asylum (EU Exit) Regulations 2019/745 reg 18(3). Words in square brackets omitted in subsection (3) by Immigration and Social Security Co-ordination (EU Withdrawal) Act 2020 (Consequential, Saving, Transitional and Transitory Provisions) (EU Exit) Regs 2020 reg 18 (3)(b). Subsection (1)(b) and word in square bracket omitted at subsection (3)(b) by Exiting the European Union Immigration and Asylum and Nationality SI 2020/1309.

137 Interpretation: general

(1) This section applies to sections 130 to 136.

(2) A reference to a designated person is a reference to a person designated under section 130.

(3) 'Family' shall be construed in accordance with section 5(4) of the Immigration Act 1971 (c. 77) (deportation: definition of 'family').

(4) 'Right of abode in the United Kingdom' has the meaning given by section 2 of that Act.

(5) 'The Refugee Convention' means the Convention relating to the Status of Refugees done at Geneva on 28 July 1951 and its Protocol.

(6) 'Period of imprisonment' shall be construed in accordance with section 72(11)(b)(i) and (ii) of the Nationality, Immigration and Asylum Act 2002 (c. 41).

(7) A voucher is not cash.

(8) A reference to a pending appeal has the meaning given by section 104(1) of that Act.

(9) A reference in an enactment to the Immigration Acts includes a reference to sections 130 to 136.

Note: Commencement at a date to be appointed.

Borders, Citizenship and Immigration Act 2009

(2009, c. 11)

Contents

An Act to provide for customs functions to be exercisable by the Secretary of State, the Director of Border Revenue and officials designated by them; to make provision about the use and disclosure of customs information; to make provision for and in connection with the exercise of customs functions and functions relating to immigration, asylum or nationality; to make provision about citizenship and other nationality matters; to make further provision about immigration and asylum; and for connected purposes. [21 July 2009] BE IT ENACTED by the Queen's Most Excellent Majesty, by and with the advice and consent of the Lords Spiritual and Temporal, and Commons, in this present Parliament assembled, and by the authority of the same, as follows:—

PART 1
BORDER FUNCTIONS

Note: Part 1 makes provision relating to the exercise of customs functions and related matters and only the sections below are reproduced. Sections are also identified that amend or repeal statutory provisions that appear elsewhere in this book.

20. Supply of Revenue and Customs information

Note: Inserts sections 41A and 41B and amends section 42(1) of the UK Borders Act 2007.

21. Duty to share information

Note: Amends section 36 of the Immigration Asylum and Nationality Act 2006.

25. Short-term holding facilities

Note: Amends section 147 of the Immigration and Asylum Act 1999.

Inspection and oversight

28. Inspections by the Chief Inspector of the UK Border Agency

(1)–(6) . . .

(7)–(8) . . .

(9) . . .

(10) The person holding the office of the Chief Inspector of the Border and Immigration Agency immediately before the day on which this section comes into force is to be treated, on and after that day, as if appointed as the Chief Inspector of the UK Border Agency under section 48(1) of the UK Borders Act 2007 (c. 30).

Note: Commenced 21 July 2009 (s 58). Subsections (1)–(6) amend section 48 of the UK Borders Act 2007. Subsections (7)–(8) amend section 53 of the UK Borders Act 2007. Subsection (9) amends section 56(2)(a) of the UK Borders Act 2007.

34. Children

. . .

. . .

Note: Commenced 21 July 2009 (s 58). Subsections (1)–(5) amend section 21 of the UK Borders Act 2007. Ceased to have effect 2 November 2009 (s 34(6)).

PART 2
CITIZENSHIP

Acquisition of British citizenship by naturalisation

39. Application requirements: general

. . .

Note: Amends paragraphs 1 and 2 and inserts paragraph 2A of Schedule 1 of the British Nationality Act 1981.

40. Application requirements: family members etc.

(1)–(2) . . .

(3)–(5) . . .

Note: Subsections (1)–(2) amend section 6 of the British Nationality Act 1981. Subsections (3)–(5) amend paragraph 3 and 4 and insert paragraph 4A of Schedule 1 of the British Nationality Act 1981.

41. The qualifying period

(1) . . .

(2)–(5) . . .

Note: Subsection (1) inserts paragraph 4B of Schedule 1 to the British Nationality Act 1981. Subsections (2)–(5) amend section 41 of the British Nationality Act 1981.

Acquisition of British citizenship by birth

42. Children born in UK etc. to members of the armed forces

Note: Amends section 1 of the British Nationality Act 1981.

Acquisition of British citizenship etc. by registration

43. Minors

Note: Amends section 3 of the British Nationality Act 1981.

44. British Nationals (Overseas) without other citizenship

Note: Amends section 4B of the British Nationality Act 1981.

45. Descent through the female line

Note: Amends section 4C of the British Nationality Act 1981.

46. Children born outside UK etc. to members of the armed forces

Note: Inserts section 4D of the British Nationality Act 1981.

47. Good character requirement

(1) . . .

(2) . . .

(3) . . .

(4) . . .

(5) . . .

Note: Subsection (1) inserts section 41A of the British Nationality Act 1981. Subsection (2) amends section 1 of the Hong Kong (War Wives and Widows) Act 1996. Subsection (3) amends section 1 of the British Nationality (Hong Kong) Act 1997. Subsection (4) amends section 131 of the Nationality, Immigration and Asylum Act 2002. Subsection (5) amends section 40 of the UK Borders Act 2007.

Interpretation etc.

48. Meaning of references to being in breach of immigration laws

(1) . . .

(2) . . .

(3) Notwithstanding its repeal, section 11 of the 2002 Act is to continue to have effect for the purpose of determining on or after the relevant day—

(a) whether a person born before the relevant day is a British citizen under section 1(1) of the British Nationality Act 1981 (c. 61),

(b) whether, on an application under section 1(3) or 4(2) of that Act made but not determined before the relevant day, a person is entitled to be registered as a British citizen,

(c) whether, on an application under section 6(1) or (2) of that Act made but not determined before the relevant day, the applicant fulfils the requirements of Schedule 1 for naturalisation as a British citizen under section 6(1) or (2) of that Act, or

(d) whether, in relation to an application under section 1(3) or 6(1) or (2) of that Act made on or after the relevant day, a person was in the United Kingdom 'in breach of the immigration laws' at a time before 7 November 2002 (the date of commencement of section 11 of the 2002 Act).

(4) Where section 11 of the 2002 Act continues to have effect by virtue of paragraph (d) of subsection (3) for the purpose of determining on or after the relevant day the matter mentioned in that paragraph, section 50A of the British Nationality Act 1981 is not to apply for the purpose of determining that matter.

(5) The relevant day for the purposes of subsection (3) is the day appointed for the commencement of this section.

(6) . . .

Note: Commenced 13 January 2010 (SI 2009/2731). Subsection (1) inserts section 50A of the British Nationality Act 1981. Subsection (2) repeals section 11 of the Nationality, Immigration and Asylum Act 2002, subject to subsection (3). Subsection (6) amends paragraph 7(a) of Schedule 3 to the Nationality, Immigration and Asylum Act 2002.

49. Other interpretation etc.

(1) . . .

(2) . . .

(3) . . .

Note: Subsection (1) commenced 13 January 2010 (SI 2009/2731), remainder on a date to be appointed. Subsection (1) amends section 50 of the British Nationality Act 1981. Subsection (2) amends Schedule 1 to the British Nationality Act 1981. Subsection (3) inserts paragraph 11 of Schedule 1 to the British Nationality Act 1981.

PART 3

IMMIGRATION

Studies

50. Restriction on studies

(1) . . .

(2) A condition under section 3(1)(c)(ia) of that Act may be added as a condition to leave given before the passing of this Act (as well as to leave given on or after its passing).

Note: Commenced 21 July 2009 (s 58). Subsection (1) amends section 3(1)(c) of the Immigration Act 1971.

Fingerprinting

51. Fingerprinting of foreign criminals liable to automatic deportation

. . .

Note: Amends section 141 of the Immigration and Asylum Act 1999.

Detention at ports in Scotland

52. Extension of sections 1 to 4 of the UK Borders Act 2007 to Scotland

(1)–(2) . . .

(3) . . .

Note: Subsections (1) and (2) amend sections 2 and 3 of the UK Borders Act 2007. Subsection (3) amends section 60(1) of the UK Borders Act 2007 repealed by para 60 of Schedule 9 to Immigration Act 2014, SI2014/2771 as amended (2 March 2015 and 6 April 2015) by SI 2015/371.

PART 4

MISCELLANEOUS AND GENERAL

Judicial review

53. Transfer of certain immigration judicial review applications

(1) . . .

(2) . . .

(3) . . .

Note: Subsection (1) amends section 31A of the Supreme Court Act 1981. Subsection (2) amends section 25A of the Judicature (Northern Ireland) Act 1978. Subsection (3) amends section 20 of the Tribunals, Courts and Enforcement Act 2007.

Trafficking people for exploitation

54. Trafficking people for exploitation

Note: Amends section 4(4) of the Asylum and Immigration (Treatment of Claimants, etc.) Act 2004.

Children

[54A. Independent Family Returns Panel

(1) The Independent Family Returns Panel is established.

(2) The Secretary of State must consult the Independent Family Returns Panel—

(a) in each family returns case, on how best to safeguard and promote the welfare of the children of the family, and

(b) in each case where the Secretary of State proposes to detain a family in pre-departure accommodation, on the suitability of so doing, having particular regard to the need to safeguard and promote the welfare of the children of the family.

(3) A family returns case is a case where—

(a) a child who is living in the United Kingdom is to be removed from or required to leave the United Kingdom, and

(b) an individual who—

(i) is a parent of the child or has care of the child, and

(ii) is living in a household in the United Kingdom with the child, is also to be removed from or required to leave the United Kingdom.

(4) The Secretary of State may by regulations make provision about—

(a) additional functions of the Independent Family Returns Panel,

(b) its status and constitution,

(c) the appointment of its members,

(d) the payment of remuneration and allowances to its members, and

(e) any other matters in connection with its establishment and operation.

(5) Regulations under this section must be made by statutory instrument.

(6) An instrument containing regulations under this section is subject to annulment in pursuance of a resolution of either House of Parliament.

(7) In this section—

'child' means a person who is under the age of 18;

'pre-departure accommodation' has the same meaning as in Part 8 of the Immigration and Asylum Act 1999;

references to a person being removed from or required to leave the United Kingdom are to the person being removed or required to leave in accordance with a provision of the Immigration Acts.]

Note: Section 54A inserted by s 3 Immigration Act 2014 from 28 July 2014 (SI 2014/1820).

55. Duty regarding the welfare of children

(1) The Secretary of State must make arrangements for ensuring that—

(a) the functions mentioned in subsection (2) are discharged having regard to the need to safeguard and promote the welfare of children who are in the United Kingdom; and

(b) any services provided by another person pursuant to arrangements which are made by the Secretary of State and relate to the discharge of a function mentioned in subsection (2) are provided having regard to that need.

(2) The functions referred to in subsection (1) are—

(a) any function of the Secretary of State in relation to immigration, asylum or nationality;

(b) any function conferred by or by virtue of the Immigration Acts on an immigration officer;

(c) any general customs function of the Secretary of State; and

(d) any customs function conferred on a designated customs official.

(3) A person exercising any of those functions must, in exercising the function, have regard to any guidance given to the person by the Secretary of State for the purpose of subsection (1).

(4) The Director of Border Revenue must make arrangements for ensuring that—

(a) the Director's functions are discharged having regard to the need to safeguard and promote the welfare of children who are in the United Kingdom; and

(b) any services provided by another person pursuant to arrangements made by the Director in the discharge of such a function are provided having regard to that need.

(5) A person exercising a function of the Director of Border Revenue must, in exercising the function, have regard to any guidance given to the person by the Secretary of State for the purpose of subsection (4).

(6) In this section—

'children' means persons who are under the age of 18;

'customs function', 'designated customs official' and 'general customs function' have the meanings given by Part 1.

(7) A reference in an enactment (other than this Act) to the Immigration Acts includes a reference to this section.

(8) . . .

Note: Commenced 2 November 2009 (SI 2009/2731). Subsection (8) repeals section 21 of the UK Borders Act 2007.

General

56. Repeals

The Schedule contains repeals.

Note: Commenced 2 November 2009 (SI 2009/2731).

57. Extent

(1) Subject to the following provisions of this section, this Act extends to—

(a) England and Wales,

(b) Scotland, and

(c) Northern Ireland.

(2) Sections 22 (application of the PACE orders) and 23 (investigations and detention: England and Wales and Northern Ireland) extend to England and Wales and Northern Ireland only.

(3) An amendment, modification or repeal by this Act has the same extent as the enactment or relevant part of the enactment to which it relates (ignoring extent by virtue of an Order in Council under any of the Immigration Acts).

(4) Subsection (3) does not apply to—

(a) the amendments made by section 52 (detention at ports in Scotland);

(b) the amendment made by section 54 (trafficking people for exploitation), which extends to England and Wales and Northern Ireland only.

(5) Her Majesty may by Order in Council provide for any of the provisions of this Act, other than any provision of Part 1 (border functions) or section 53 (transfer of certain immigration judicial review applications), to extend, with or without modifications, to any of the Channel Islands or the Isle of Man.

(6) Subsection (5) does not apply in relation to the extension to a place of a provision which extends there by virtue of subsection (3).

Note: Commenced 21 July 2009 (s 58).

58. Commencement

(1) Part 1 (border functions) comes into force on the day this Act is passed.

(2) The provisions of Part 2 (citizenship) come into force on such day as the Secretary of State may by order appoint.

(3) In Part 3 (immigration)—

(a) section 50 (restriction on studies) comes into force on the day this Act is passed;

(b) sections 51 (fingerprinting of foreign criminals) and 52 (detention at ports in Scotland) come into force on such day as the Secretary of State may by order appoint.

(4) In this Part—

(a) section 53 (transfer of certain immigration judicial review applications) comes into force on such day as the Lord Chancellor may by order appoint;

(b) sections 54 (trafficking people for exploitation) and 55 (duty regarding the welfare of children) come into force on such day as the Secretary of State may by order appoint.

(5) Any repeal in the Schedule (and section 56 so far as relating to the repeal) comes into force in the same way as the provisions of this Act to which the repeal relates.

(6) The other provisions of this Part come into force on the day this Act is passed.

(7) An order under this section must be made by statutory instrument.

(8) An order under this section—

(a) may appoint different days for different purposes;
(b) may include transitional or incidental provision or savings.

(9) An order commencing sections 39 to 41 (acquisition of British citizenship by naturalisation) must include provision that the amendments made by those sections do not have effect in relation to an application for naturalisation as a British citizen if—

(a) the date of the application is before the date on which those sections come into force in accordance with the order ('the date of commencement'), or

(b) the date of the application is before the end of the period of 24 months beginning with the date of commencement and the application is made by a person who falls within subsection (10) or (11).

(10) A person falls within this subsection if on the date of commencement the person has indefinite leave to remain in the United Kingdom.

(11) A person falls within this subsection if the person is given indefinite leave to remain in the United Kingdom on an application—

(a) the date of which is before the date of commencement, and
(b) which is decided after the date of commencement.

(12) The reference in subsection (9) to an order commencing sections 39 to 41 does not include an order commencing those sections for the purpose only of enabling regulations to be made under the British Nationality Act 1981 (c. 61).

(13) In the case of an order commencing sections 39 to 41, transitional provision may, in particular—

(a) provide that the qualifying period for the purposes of paragraph 1 or 3 of Schedule 1 to the British Nationality Act 1981 includes time before that commencement;

(b) provide for leave to enter or remain in the United Kingdom granted before that commencement to be treated as qualifying temporary residence leave or probationary citizenship leave for the purposes of that Schedule.

(14) In the case of an order commencing section 45 (acquisition of British citizenship through the female line), transitional provision may, in particular, provide that section 45 is to apply to an application made, but not determined, under section 4C of the British Nationality Act 1981 before that commencement.

(15) No order may be made commencing section 52 (detention at ports in Scotland) unless the Secretary of State has consulted the Scottish Ministers.

(16) No order may be made commencing section 53 (transfer of certain immigration judicial review applications) unless the functions of the Asylum and Immigration Tribunal in relation to appeals under Part 5 of the Nationality, Immigration and Asylum Act 2002 (c. 41) have been transferred under section 30(1) of the Tribunals, Courts and Enforcement Act 2007 (c. 15).

Note: Commenced 21 July 2009 (s 58).

59. Short title

This Act may be cited as the Borders, Citizenship and Immigration Act 2009.

Note: Commenced 21 July 2009 (s 58).

Schedule — Section 56

Note: The Schedule sets out repeals of provisions of the UK Borders Act 2007, British Nationality Act 1981, Hong Kong (War Wives and Widows) Act 1996, Nationality, Asylum and Immigration Act 2002, and the Immigration, Asylum and Nationality Act 2006.

Immigration Act 2014

(2014, c. 22)

Contents

Schedule 1

Enforcement Powers

Schedule 2

Meaning of Biometric Information

Schedule 3

Excluded Residential Tenancy Agreements

Schedule 4

Referral of Proposed Marriages and Civil Partnerships in England and Wales

Part 1—Marriage
Part 2—Civil partnership

Schedule 5

Sham Marriage and Civil Partnership: Administrative Regulations

Schedule 6

Information

Part 1—Disclosure of information etc. where proposed marriage or civil partnership referred to Secretary of State
Part 2—Disclosure of information etc. for immigration purposes etc.
Part 3—Disclosure of information etc. for prevention of crime etc.
Part 4—General provisions

Schedule 7

Immigration Advisers and Immigration Service Providers

Schedule 8

Embarkation Checks

Part 1—Functions exercisable by designated persons
Part 2—Other provision

Schedule 9

Transitional and Consequential Provision

Part 1—Provision relating to removal
Part 2—Provision relating to detention and bail
Part 3—Provision relating to biometrics
Part 4—Provision relating to appeals

An Act to make provision about immigration law; to limit, or otherwise make provision about, access to services, facilities and employment by reference to immigration status; to make provision about marriage and civil partnership involving certain foreign nationals; to make provision about the acquisition of citizenship by persons unable to acquire it because their fathers and mothers were not married to each other and provision about the removal of citizenship from persons whose conduct is seriously prejudicial to the United Kingdom's vital interests; and for connected purposes. [14th May 2014]

PART 1
REMOVAL AND OTHER POWERS

Removal

1. Removal of persons unlawfully in the United Kingdom

. . .

Note: Amends s 10 of the Immigration and Asylum Act 1999 from 20 October 2014 (SI 2014/2771) partially.

2. Restriction on removal of children and their parents etc.

. . .

Note: Inserts s 78A of the Nationality, Immigration and Asylum Act 2002 from 28 July 2014 (SI 2014/1820).

3. Independent Family Returns Panel

Note: Inserts s 54A of the Borders, Citizenship and Immigration Act 2009 from 28 July 2014 (SI 2014/1820).

Powers of immigration officers

4. Enforcement powers

Schedule 1 (enforcement powers) has effect.

Note: Commenced 28 July 2014 (SI 2014/1820).

Detention and bail

5. Restrictions on detention of unaccompanied children

. . .

Note: Amends Sch 2 to the Immigration Act 1971 from 28 July 2014 (SI 2014/1820).

6. Pre-departure accommodation for families

. . .

Note: Amends Part 8 of the Immigration and Asylum Act 1999 (removal centres and detained persons) from 28 July 2014 (SI 2014/1820).

7. Immigration bail: repeat applications and effect of removal directions

. . .

Note: Amends Sch 2 to the Immigration Act 1971. Subsection(1), (2), and (5) commenced from 28 July 2014 (SI 2014/1820]. Sections 7(4)–(7) from October 20, 2014 (SI 2014/2771).

Biometrics

8. Provision of biometric information with immigration applications

. . .

Note: Amends s 126 of the Nationality, Immigration and Asylum Act 2002 from 28 July 2014 (SI 2014/1820).

9. Identifying persons liable to detention

. . .

Note: Amends paragraph 18(2) of Sch 2 to the Immigration Act 1971 from 28 July 2014 (SI 2014/1820).

10. Provision of biometric information with citizenship applications

. . .

Note: Amends s 41 of the British Nationality Act 1981 from 28 July 2014 (SI 2014/1820).

11. Biometric immigration documents

. . .

Note: Amends s 7 of the UK Borders Act 2007 from 28 July 2014 (SI 2014/1820).

12. Meaning of 'biometric information'

. . .

Note: Amends s 15 of the UK Borders Act 2007 from 28 July 2014 (SI 2014/1820).

13. Safeguards for children

. . .

Note: Amends Sch 2 to the Immigration Act 1971 from 28 July 2014 (SI 2014/1820).

14. Use and retention of biometric information

(1) . . .

(2) . . .

(3) . . .

Note: Subsection (1) substitutes s 8 of the UK Borders Act 2007; subsection (2) inserts 144A of the Immigration and Asylum Act 1999; subsection (3) amends s 126 of the Nationality, Immigration and Asylum Act 2002 from 28 July 2014 (SI 2014/1820).

Part 2
Appeals etc

15. Right of appeal to First-tier Tribunal

. . .

Note: Amends Part 5 of the Nationality, Immigration and Asylum Act 2002 (immigration and asylum appeals) from 20 October 2014 (SI 2014/2771).

16. Report by Chief Inspector on administrative review

(1) Before the end of the period of 12 months beginning on the day on which section 15 comes into force, the Secretary of State must commission from the Chief Inspector a report that addresses the following matters—

(a) the effectiveness of administrative review in identifying case working errors;

(b) the effectiveness of administrative review in correcting case working errors;

(c) the independence of persons conducting administrative review (in terms of their separation from the original decision-maker).

(2) On completion of the report, the Chief Inspector must send it to the Secretary of State.

(3) The Secretary of State must lay before Parliament a copy of the report received under subsection (2).

(4) In this section—

'administrative review' means review conducted under the immigration rules;

'case working error' has the meaning given in the immigration rules;

the 'Chief Inspector' means the Chief Inspector established under section 48 of the UK Borders Act 2007;

'immigration rules' has the same meaning as in the Immigration Act 1971.

Note: Commencement from 20 October 2014 (SI 2014/2771).

17. Place from which appeal may be brought or continued

. . .

Note: Amends Part 5 of the Nationality, Immigration and Asylum Act 2002 (immigration and asylum appeals). Subsections (1) and (3) commenced from 28 July 2014 (SI 2014/1820). Subsection (2)) from 20 October 2014 (SI 2014/2771).

18. Review of certain deportation decisions by Special Immigration Appeals Commission

. . .

Note: Inserts s 2E into the Special Immigration Appeals Commission Act 1997. Commenced 6 April 2015 (SI 2015/371).

19. Article 8 of the ECHR: public interest considerations

. . .

Note: Inserts Part 5A of the Nationality, Immigration and Asylum Act 2002 from 28 July 2014 (SI 2014/1820).

Part 3
Access to Services etc

Chapter 1
Residential Tenancies

Key interpretation

20. Residential tenancy agreement

(1) This section applies for the purposes of this Chapter.

(2) 'Residential tenancy agreement' means a tenancy which—

(a) grants a right of occupation of premises for residential use,

(b) provides for payment of rent (whether or not a market rent), and

(c) is not an excluded agreement.

(3) In subsection (2), 'tenancy' includes—

(a) any lease, licence, sub-lease or sub-tenancy, and

(b) an agreement for any of those things, and in this Chapter references to 'landlord' and 'tenant', and references to premises being 'leased', are to be read accordingly.

(4) For the purposes of subsection (2)(a), an agreement grants a right of occupation of premises 'for residential use' if, under the agreement, one or more adults have the right to occupy the premises as their only or main residence (whether or not the premises may also be used for other purposes).

(5) In subsection (2)(b) 'rent' includes any sum paid in the nature of rent.

(6) In subsection (2)(c) 'excluded agreement' means any agreement of a description for the time being specified in Schedule 3.

(7) The Secretary of State may by order amend Schedule 3 so as to—

(a) add a new description of excluded agreement,

(b) remove any description, or

(c) amend any description.

Note: Commencement from 1 December 2014 for premises in local authorities set out in article 6 SI 2014/2771. 1 February 2016 in respect of all remaining premises located in England; not yet in force otherwise.

21. Persons disqualified by immigration status or with limited right to rent

(1) For the purposes of this Chapter, a person ('P') is disqualified as a result of their immigration status from occupying premises under a residential tenancy agreement if—

(a) P is not a relevant national, and

(b) P does not have a right to rent in relation to the premises.

(2) P does not have a 'right to rent' in relation to premises if—

(a) P requires leave to enter or remain in the United Kingdom but does not have it, or

(b) P's leave to enter or remain in the United Kingdom is subject to a condition preventing P from occupying the premises.

(3) But P is to be treated as having a right to rent in relation to premises (in spite of subsection (2)) if the Secretary of State has granted P permission for the purposes of this Chapter to occupy premises under a residential tenancy agreement.

(4) References in this Chapter to a person with a 'limited right to rent' are references to—

(a) a person who has been granted leave to enter or remain in the United Kingdom for a limited period, or

(b) a person who—

(i) is not a relevant national,

(ii) . . .

(5) In this section 'relevant national' means—

(a) a British citizen,

(aa) an Irish citizen, or

(ab) a person who is not an Irish citizen and who has leave to enter or remain in the United Kingdom which was granted by virtue of residence scheme immigration rules within the meaning given by section 17 of the European Union (Withdrawal Agreement) Act 2020.

(b) . . .

(c) . . .

Note: Commencement from 1 December 2014 for premises in local authorities set out in article 6 SI 2014/2771. 1 February 2016 in respect of all remaining premises located in England; not yet in force otherwise. Words in subsection (4)(b)(ii) in square brackets substituted and inserted, subsection (4A) inserted, and omitted in subsection (5)(b) by Immigration, Nationality and Asylum (EU Exit) Regulations 2019/745 Pt 2(1) reg.21(2)(a)(b) & (c) (December 31, 2020: shall come into force on IP completion day not exit day as specified in 2020 c.1 s.39(1) and Sch.5 para.1(1)) Subsection (4)(b)(ii) omitted, and subsection (5)(aa) & (ab) inserted and subsection (5)(b) & (c) omitted by Immigration and Social Security Co-ordination (EU Withdrawal) Acct 2020 (Consequential, Savings, Transitionary and Transitory Provisions) (EU Exit) Regulations 2020/1309 Pt 2(1) reg. 20(a), (b)(i) & (ii) from a date to be appointed.

Penalty notices

22. Persons disqualified by immigration status not to be leased premises

(1) A landlord must not authorise an adult to occupy premises under a residential tenancy agreement if the adult is disqualified as a result of their immigration status.

(2) A landlord is to be taken to 'authorise' an adult to occupy premises in the circumstances mentioned in subsection (1) if (and only if) there is a contravention of this section.

(3) There is a contravention of this section in either of the following cases.

(4) The first case is where a residential tenancy agreement is entered into that, at the time of entry, grants a right to occupy premises to—

(a) a tenant who is disqualified as a result of their immigration status,

(b) another adult named in the agreement who is disqualified as a result of their immigration status, or

(c) another adult not named in the agreement who is disqualified as a result of their immigration status (subject to subsection (6)).

(5) The second case is where—

(a) a residential tenancy agreement is entered into that grants a right to occupy premises on an adult with a limited right to rent,

(b) the adult later becomes a person disqualified as a result of their immigration status, and

(c) the adult continues to occupy the premises after becoming disqualified.

(6) There is a contravention as a result of subsection (4)(c) only if—

(a) reasonable enquiries were not made of the tenant before entering into the agreement as to the relevant occupiers, or

(b) reasonable enquiries were so made and it was, or should have been, apparent from the enquiries that the adult in question was likely to be a relevant occupier.

(7) Any term of a residential tenancy agreement that prohibits occupation of premises by a person disqualified by their immigration status is to be ignored for the purposes of determining whether there has been a contravention of this section if—

(a) the landlord knew when entering into the agreement that the term would be breached, or

(b) the prescribed requirements were not complied with before entering into the agreement.

(8) It does not matter for the purposes of this section whether or not—

(a) a right of occupation is exercisable on entering into an agreement or from a later date;

(b) a right of occupation is granted unconditionally or on satisfaction of a condition.

(9) A contravention of this section does not affect the validity or enforceability of any provision of a residential tenancy agreement by virtue of any rule of law relating to the validity or enforceability of contracts in circumstances involving illegality.

(10) In this Chapter—

'post-grant contravention' means a contravention in the second case mentioned in subsection (5);

'pre-grant contravention' means a contravention in the first case mentioned in subsection (4);

'relevant occupier', in relation to a residential tenancy agreement, means any adult who occupies premises under the agreement (whether or not named in the agreement).

Note: Commencement from 1 December 2014 for premises in local authorities set out in article 6 SI 2014/2771. 1 February 2016 in respect of all remaining premises located in England; not yet in force otherwise.

23. Penalty notices: landlords

(1) If there is a contravention of section 22, the Secretary of State may give the responsible landlord a notice requiring the payment of a penalty.

(2) The amount of the penalty is such an amount as the Secretary of State considers appropriate, but the amount must not exceed £3,000.

(3) 'Responsible landlord' means—

(a) in relation to a pre-grant contravention, the landlord who entered into the residential tenancy agreement;

(b) in relation to a post-grant contravention, the person who is the landlord under the agreement at the time of the contravention.

(4) But if there is a superior landlord in relation to the residential tenancy agreement who is responsible for the purposes of this section, the 'responsible landlord' means that superior landlord (and references to the landlord in the following provisions of this Chapter are to be read accordingly).

(5) A superior landlord is 'responsible for the purposes of this section' if arrangements in writing have been made in relation to the residential tenancy agreement between the landlord and the superior landlord under which the superior landlord accepts responsibility for—

(a) contraventions of section 22 generally, or

(b) contraventions of a particular description and the contravention in question is of that description.

(6) The Secretary of State may by order amend the amount for the time being specified in subsection (2).

Note: Commencement from 1 December 2014 for premises in local authorities set out in article 6 SI 2014/2771. 1 February 2016 in respect of all remaining premises located in England; not yet in force otherwise.

24. Excuses available to landlords

(1) This section applies where a landlord is given a notice under section 23 requiring payment of a penalty.

(2) Where the notice is given for a pre-grant contravention, the landlord is excused from paying the penalty if the landlord shows that—

(a) the prescribed requirements were complied with before the residential tenancy agreement was entered into, or

(b) a person acting as the landlord's agent is responsible for the contravention (see section 25(2)).

(3) The prescribed requirements may be complied with for the purposes of subsection (2)(a) at any time before the residential tenancy agreement is entered into.

[(4) But where compliance with the prescribed requirements discloses that a relevant occupier is a person with a limited right to rent, the landlord is excused under subsection (2)(a) only if—

(a) in respect of an original occupier who had a right of occupation under a previous residential tenancy agreement, the requirements are complied with in relation to that occupier within such period as may be prescribed in relation to the entering into of that previous residential tenancy agreement, and

(b) in respect of a new occupier, the requirements are complied with in relation to that occupier within such period as may be prescribed in relation to the entering into of the varied tenancy, tenant assigned tenancy or new joint tenancy agreement.].

(5) The excuse under subsection (2)(a) or (b) is not available if the landlord knew that entering into the agreement would contravene section 22.

(6) Where the notice is given for a post-grant contravention, the landlord is excused from paying the penalty if any of the following applies—

(a) the landlord has notified the Secretary of State of the contravention as soon as reasonably practicable;

(b) a person acting as the landlord's agent is responsible for the contravention;

(c) the eligibility period in relation to the limited right occupier whose occupation caused the contravention has not expired.

(7) For the purposes of subsection (6)(a), the landlord is to be taken to have notified the Secretary of State of the contravention 'as soon as reasonably practicable' if the landlord—

(a) complied with the prescribed requirements in relation to each limited right occupier at the end of the eligibility period, and

(b) notified the Secretary of State of the contravention without delay on it first becoming apparent that the contravention had occurred.

(8) Notification under subsection (6)(a) must be in the prescribed form and manner.

(9) In this Chapter 'limited right occupier', in relation to a residential tenancy agreement, means a relevant occupier who had a limited right to rent at the time when the occupier was first granted a right to occupy the premises under the agreement.

Note: Commencement from 1 December 2014 for premises in local authorities set out in article 6 SI 2014/2771. 1 February 2016 in respect of all remaining premises located in England; not yet in force otherwise.

25. Penalty notices: agents

(1) Subsection (3) applies where—

(a) a landlord contravenes section 22, and

(b) a person acting as the landlord's agent ('the agent') is responsible for the contravention.

(2) For the purposes of this Chapter, an agent is responsible for a landlord's contravention of section 22 if (and only if)—

(a) the agent acts in the course of a business, and

(b) under arrangements made with the landlord in writing, the agent was under an obligation for the purposes of this Chapter to comply with the prescribed requirements on behalf of the landlord.

(3) The Secretary of State may give the agent a notice requiring the agent to pay a penalty.

(4) The amount of the penalty is such an amount as the Secretary of State considers appropriate, but the amount must not exceed £3,000.

(5) The Secretary of State may by order amend the amount for the time being specified in subsection (4).

Note: Commencement from 1 December 2014 for premises in local authorities set out in article 6 SI 2014/2771. 1 February 2016 in respect of all remaining premises located in England; not yet in force otherwise.

26. Excuses available to agents

(1) This section applies where an agent is given a notice under section 25 requiring payment of a penalty.

(2) Where the notice is given for a pre-grant contravention, the agent is excused from paying the penalty if the agent shows that the prescribed requirements were complied with before the residential tenancy agreement was entered into.

(3) The prescribed requirements may be complied with for the purposes of subsection (2) at any time before the residential tenancy agreement is entered into.

(4) But where compliance with the prescribed requirements discloses that a relevant occupier is a person with a limited right to rent, the agent is excused under subsection (2) only if—

(a) in respect of an original occupier who had a right of occupation under a previous residential tenancy agreement, the requirements are complied with in relation to that occupier within such period as may be prescribed in relation to the entering into of that previous residential tenancy agreement, and

(b) in respect of a new occupier, the requirements are complied with in relation to that occupier within such period as may be prescribed in relation to the entering into of the varied tenancy, tenant assigned tenancy or new joint tenancy agreement.

(5) The excuse under subsection (2) is not available if the agent—

(a) knew that the landlord would contravene section 22 by entering into the agreement,

(b) had sufficient opportunity to notify the landlord of that fact before the landlord entered into the agreement, but

(c) did not do so.

(6) Where the notice is given for a post-grant contravention, the agent is excused from paying the penalty if either of the following applies—

(a) the agent has notified the Secretary of State and the landlord of the contravention as soon as reasonably practicable;

(b) the eligibility period in relation to the limited right occupier whose occupation caused the contravention has not expired.

(7) For the purposes of subsection (6)(a), the agent is to be taken to have notified the Secretary of State and the landlord of the contravention 'as soon as reasonably practicable' if the agent—

(a) complied with the prescribed requirements in relation to each limited right occupier at the end of the eligibility period, and

(b) notified the Secretary of State and the landlord of the contravention without delay on it first becoming apparent that the contravention had occurred.

(8) Notification under subsection (6)(a) must be in the prescribed form and manner.

Note: Commencement from 1 December 2014 for premises in local authorities set out in article 6 SI 2014/2771. 1 February 2016 in respect of all remaining premises located in England; not yet in force otherwise.

27. Eligibility period

(1) An eligibility period in relation to a limited right occupier is established if the prescribed requirements are complied with in relation to the occupier.

(2) An eligibility period established under subsection (1) may be renewed (on one or more occasions) by complying with the prescribed requirements again.

(3) But an eligibility period in relation to a limited right occupier is only established or renewed under this section at any time if it reasonably appears from the information obtained in complying with the prescribed requirements at that time that the occupier is a person with a limited right to rent.

(4) The length of an eligibility period established or renewed under this section in relation to a limited right occupier is the longest of the following periods—

(a) the period of one year beginning with the time when the prescribed requirements were last complied with in relation to the occupier;

(b) so much of any leave period as remains at that time;

(c) so much of any validity period as remains at that time.

(5) In subsection (4)—

'leave period' means a period for which the limited right occupier was granted leave to enter or remain in the United Kingdom;

'validity period' means the period for which an immigration document issued to the limited right occupier by or on behalf of the Secretary of State is valid.

(6) In subsection (5) 'immigration document' means a document of a prescribed description which—

(a)

(b) grants to the holder a right to enter or remain in the United Kingdom for such period as the document may authorise.

[(7) 'Retained enforceable EU right' means a right that—

(a) was created or arose by or under the EU Treaties before the coming into force of this subsection, and

(b) forms part of retained EU law by virtue of section 3 or 4 of the European Union (Withdrawal) Act 2018,

as that right is modified from time to time.].

Note: Commencement from 1 December 2014 for premises in local authorities set out in article 6 SI 2014/2771. 1 February 2016 in respect of all remaining premises located in England; not yet in force otherwise. Words in square brackets in subsection (6)(a) substituted and subsection (7) inserted by Immigration, Nationality and Asylum (EU Exit) Regulations 2019/745 Pt 2(1) reg.21(3) ((December 31, 2020: shall come into force on IP completion day not exit day as specified in 2020 c.1 s.39(1) and Sch.5 para.1(1)). Subsection (6)(a) omitted by Immigration and Social Security Co-ordination (EU Withdrawal) Act 2020(Consequential, Savings, Transitional and Transitory Provisions) (EU Exit) Regulations 2020/1309 Pt 2(1) reg.3 (December 31, 2020: repeal has effect subject to saving specified in SI 2020/1309 reg.20(8)).

28. Penalty notices: general

(1) The Secretary of State may give a penalty notice—

(a) to a landlord under section 23 without having established whether the landlord is excused from paying the penalty under section 24;

(b) to an agent under section 25 without having established whether the agent is excused from paying the penalty under section 26.

(2) A penalty notice must—

(a) be in writing,

(b) state why the Secretary of State thinks the recipient is liable to the penalty,

(c) state the amount of the penalty,

(d) specify a date, at least 28 days after the date specified in the notice as the date on which it is given, before which the penalty must be paid,

(e) specify how a penalty must be paid,

(f) explain how the recipient may object to the penalty or make an appeal against it, and

(g) explain how the Secretary of State may enforce the penalty.

(3) A separate penalty notice may be given in respect of each adult disqualified by their immigration status in relation to whom there is a contravention of section 22.

(4) Where a penalty notice is given to two or more persons who jointly constitute the landlord or agent in relation to a residential tenancy agreement, those persons are jointly and severally liable for any sum payable to the Secretary of State as a penalty imposed by the notice.

(5) A penalty notice may not be given in respect of any adult if—

(a) the adult has ceased to occupy the premises concerned, and

(b) a period of 12 months or more has passed since the time when the adult last occupied the premises, but this subsection is not to be taken as affecting the validity of a penalty notice given before the end of that period.

(6) Subsection (5) does not apply to a penalty notice given after the end of the 12 month period mentioned in that subsection if—

(a) it is a new penalty notice given by virtue of section 29(6)(b) on the determination of an objection to another penalty notice, and

(b) that other penalty notice was given before the end of the period.

Note: Commencement from 1 December 2014 for premises in local authorities set out in article 6 SI 2014/2771. 1 February 2016 in respect of all other premises located in England; not yet in force otherwise.

Objections, appeals and enforcement

29. Objection

(1) The recipient of a penalty notice ('the recipient') may object on the ground that—

(a) the recipient is not liable to the imposition of the penalty,

(b) the recipient is excused by virtue of section 24 or 26, or

(c) the amount of the penalty is too high.

(2) An objection must be made by giving a notice of objection to the Secretary of State.

(3) A notice of objection must—

(a) be in writing,

(b) give the reasons for the objection,

(c) be given in the prescribed manner, and

(d) be given before the end of the prescribed period.

(4) In considering a notice of objection to a penalty the Secretary of State must have regard to the code of practice under section 32.

(5) On considering a notice of objection the Secretary of State may—

(a) cancel the penalty,

(b) reduce the penalty,

(c) increase the penalty, or

(d) determine to take no action.

(6) After reaching a decision as to how to proceed under subsection (5) the Secretary of State must—

(a) notify the recipient of the decision (including the amount of any increased or reduced penalty) before the end of the prescribed period or such longer period as the Secretary of State may agree with the recipient, and

(b) if the penalty is increased, issue a new penalty notice under section 23 or (as the case may be) section 25.

Note: Commencement from 1 December 2014 for premises in local authorities set out in article 6 SI 2014/2771. 1 February 2016 in respect of all other premises located in England; not yet in force otherwise.

30. Appeals

(1) The recipient may appeal to the court on the ground that—

(a) the recipient is not liable to the imposition of a penalty,

(b) the recipient is excused payment as a result of section 24 or 26, or

(c) the amount of the penalty is too high.

(2) The court may

(a) allow the appeal and cancel the penalty,

(b) allow the appeal and reduce the penalty, or

(c) dismiss the appeal.

(3) An appeal is to be a re-hearing of the Secretary of State's decision to impose a penalty and is to be determined having regard to—

(a) the code of practice under section 32 that has effect at the time of the appeal, and

(b) any other matters which the court thinks relevant (which may include matters of which the Secretary of State was unaware).

(4) Subsection (3) has effect despite any provisions of rules of court.

(5) An appeal may be brought only if the recipient has given a notice of objection under section 29 and the Secretary of State—

(a) has determined the objection by issuing to the recipient the penalty notice (as a result of increasing the penalty under section 29(5)(c)),

(b) has determined the objection by—

(i) reducing the penalty under section 29(5)(b), or

(ii) taking no action under section 29(5)(d), or

(c) has not informed the recipient of a decision before the end of the period that applies for the purposes of section 29(6)(a).

(6) An appeal must be brought within the period of 28 days beginning with the relevant date.

(7) Where the appeal is brought under subsection (5)(a), the relevant date is the date specified in the penalty notice issued in accordance with section 29(6)(b) as the date on which it is given.

(8) Where the appeal is brought under subsection (5)(b), the relevant date is the date specified in the notice informing the recipient of the decision for the purposes of section 29(6)(a) as the date on which it is given.

(9) Where the appeal is brought under subsection (5)(c), the relevant date is the date on which the period that applies for the purposes of section 29(6)(a) ends.

(10) In this section 'the court' means—

(a) the county court, if the appeal relates to a residential tenancy agreement in relation to premises in England and Wales;

(b) the sheriff, if the appeal relates to a residential tenancy agreement in relation to premises in Scotland;

(c) a county court in Northern Ireland, if the appeal relates to a residential tenancy agreement in relation to premises in Northern Ireland.

Note: Commencement from 1 December 2014 for premises in local authorities set out in article 6 SI 2014/2771. 1 February 2016 in respect of all other premises located in England; not yet in force otherwise.

31. Enforcement

(1) This section applies where a sum is payable to the Secretary of State as a penalty under this Chapter.

(2) In England and Wales the penalty is recoverable as if it were payable under an order of the county court in England and Wales.

(3) In Scotland the penalty may be enforced in the same manner as an extract registered decree arbitral bearing a warrant for execution issued by the sheriff court of any sheriffdom in Scotland.

(4) In Northern Ireland the penalty is recoverable as if it were payable under an order of a county court in Northern Ireland.

(5) Where action is taken under this section for the recovery of a sum payable as a penalty under this Chapter, the penalty is—

(a) in relation to England and Wales, to be treated for the purposes of section 98 of the Courts Act 2003 (register of judgments and orders etc) as if it were a judgment entered in the county court;

(b) in relation to Northern Ireland, to be treated for the purposes of Article 116 of the Judgments Enforcement (Northern Ireland) Order 1981 (S.I. 1981/226 (N.I. 6)) (register of judgments) as if it were a judgment in respect of which an application has been accepted under Article 22 or 23(1) of that Order.

(6) Money paid to the Secretary of State by way of a penalty must be paid into the Consolidated Fund.

Note: Commencement from 1 December 2014 for premises in local authorities set out in article 6 SI 2014/2771. 1 February 2016 in respect of all other premises located in England; not yet in force otherwise.

Codes of practice

32. General matters

(1) The Secretary of State must issue a code of practice for the purposes of this Chapter.

(2) The code must specify factors that the Secretary of State will consider when determining the amount of a penalty imposed under this Chapter.

(3) The code may contain guidance about—

(a) factors that the Secretary of State will consider when determining whether—

(i) a residential tenancy agreement grants a right of occupation of premises for residential use, or

(ii) a person is occupying premises as an only or main residence;

(b) the reasonable enquiries that a landlord should make to determine the identity of relevant occupiers in relation to a residential tenancy agreement (so far as they are not named in the agreement);

(c) any other matters in connection with this Chapter that the Secretary of State considers appropriate.

(4) Guidance under subsection (3)(a) may in particular relate to the treatment for the purposes of this Chapter of arrangements that are made in connection with holiday lettings or lettings for purposes connected with business travel.

(5) The Secretary of State must from time to time review the code and may revise and re-issue it following a review.

(6) The code (or revised code)—

(a) may not be issued unless a draft has been laid before Parliament, and

(b) comes into force in accordance with provision made by order of the Secretary of State.

Note: Commencement from 1 December 2014 (SI 2014/2771).

33. Discrimination

(1) The Secretary of State must issue a code of practice specifying what a landlord or agent should or should not do to ensure that, while avoiding liability to pay a penalty under this Chapter, the landlord or agent also avoids contravening—

(a) the Equality Act 2010, so far as relating to race, or
(b) the Race Relations (Northern Ireland) Order 1997 (S.I. 1997/869 (N.I. 6)).

(2) The Secretary of State must from time to time review the code and may revise and re-issue it following a review.

(3) Before issuing the code (or a revised code) the Secretary of State must consult—
(a) the Commission for Equality and Human Rights,
(b) the Equality Commission for Northern Ireland, and
(c) such persons representing the interests of landlords and tenants as the Secretary of State considers appropriate.

(4) After consulting under subsection (3) the Secretary of State must—
(a) publish a draft code, and
(b) consider any representations made about the published draft.

(5) The code (or revised code)—
(a) may not be issued unless a draft has been laid before Parliament (prepared after considering representations under subsection (4)(b) and with or without modifications to reflect the representations), and
(b) comes into force in accordance with provision made by order of the Secretary of State.

(6) A breach of the code—
(a) does not make a person liable to civil or criminal proceedings, but
(b) may be taken into account by a court or tribunal.

Note: Commencement from 1 December 2014 (SI 2014/2771).

[33A Offences: landlords

(1) The landlord under a residential tenancy agreement which relates to premises in England commits an offence if the first and second conditions are met.

(2) The first condition is that the premises are occupied by an adult who is disqualified as a result of their immigration status from occupying premises under a residential tenancy agreement.

(3) The second condition is that the landlord knows or has reasonable cause to believe that the premises are occupied by an adult who is disqualified as a result of their immigration status from occupying premises under a residential tenancy agreement.

(4) But unless subsection (5) applies the landlord does not commit an offence under subsection (1) if—
(a) the premises are located in an area in relation to which section 22 is in force,
(b) the adult mentioned in subsections (2) and (3) is a limited right occupier, and
(c) the eligibility period in relation to that occupier has not expired.

(5) This subsection applies if the Secretary of State has given a notice in writing to the landlord which—
(a) identifies the adult mentioned in subsections (2) and (3), and
(b) states that the adult is disqualified as a result of their immigration status from occupying premises under a residential tenancy agreement.

(6) It is a defence for a person charged with an offence under subsection (1) to prove that—

(a) the person has taken reasonable steps to terminate the residential tenancy agreement, and

(b) the person has taken such steps within a reasonable period beginning with the time when the person first knew or had reasonable cause to believe that the premises were occupied by the adult mentioned in subsections (2) and (3).

(7) In determining whether subsection (6)(a) or (b) applies to a person, the court must have regard to any guidance which, at the time in question, had been issued by the Secretary of State for the purposes of that subsection and was in force at that time.

(8) Guidance issued for the purposes of subsection (6)—

(a) must be laid before Parliament in draft before being issued, and

(b) comes into force in accordance with regulations made by the Secretary of State.

(9) Section 22(9) applies for the purposes of subsection (1) as it applies for the purposes of that section.

(10) A person commits an offence if—

(a) there has been a post-grant contravention in relation to a residential tenancy agreement which relates to premises in England,

(b) the person is the responsible landlord in relation to the post-grant contravention,

(c) the person knows or has reasonable cause to believe that there has been a post-grant contravention in relation to the agreement, and

(d) none of paragraphs (a), (b) and (c) of section 24(6) applies in relation to the post-grant contravention.

(11) Subsection (10) applies whether or not the landlord is given a notice under section 23 in respect of the contravention.]

Note: Inserted with effect from 1 November 2016 for the purposes of making subordinate legislation only; December 1,2016 otherwise by Immigration Act 2016, s 39 (SI 2016/1037).

33B Offences: agents

(1) Subsection (2) applies to an agent who is responsible for a landlord's contravention of section 22 in relation to premises in England.

(2) The agent commits an offence if the agent—

(a) knew or had reasonable cause to believe that the landlord would contravene section 22 by entering into the residential tenancy agreement in question,

(b) had sufficient opportunity to notify the landlord of that fact before the landlord entered into the agreement, but

(c) did not do so.

(3) Subsection (4) applies where—

(a) a landlord contravenes section 22 in relation to a residential tenancy agreement relating to premises in England,

(b) the contravention is a post-grant contravention, and

(c) a person acting as the landlord's agent ('the agent') is responsible for the post-grant contravention.

(4) The agent commits an offence if—

(a) the agent knows or has reasonable cause to believe that there has been a post-grant contravention in relation to the agreement, and

(b) neither of paragraphs (a) and (b) of section 26(6) applies in relation to the post-grant contravention.

(5) Subsection (4) applies whether or not the agent is given a notice under section 25 in respect of the contravention.]

Note: Inserted with effect from November 1, 2016 for the purposes of making subordinate legislation only; December 1, 2016 otherwise by Immigration Act 2016, s 39 (SI 2016/1037).

[33C Offences: penalties etc

(1) A person who is guilty of an offence under section 33A or 33B is liable—

(a) on conviction on indictment, to imprisonment for a term not exceeding five years, to a fine or to both;

(b) on summary conviction, to imprisonment for a term not exceeding 12 months, to a fine or to both.

(2) In the application of this section in relation to an offence committed before the coming into force of [paragraph 24(2) of Schedule 22 to the Sentencing Act 2020] the reference in subsection (1)(b) to 12 months is to be read as a reference to 6 months.

(3) If an offence under section 33A or 33B is committed by a body corporate with the consent or connivance of an officer of the body, the officer, as well as the body, is to be treated as having committed the offence.

(4) In subsection (3) a reference to an officer of a body includes a reference to—

(a) a director, manager or secretary,

(b) a person purporting to act as a director, manager or secretary, and

(c) if the affairs of the body are managed by its members, a member.

(5) Where an offence under section 33A or 33B is committed by a partnership (whether or not a limited partnership) subsection (3) has effect, but as if a reference to an officer of the body were a reference to—

(a) a partner, and

(b) a person purporting to act as a partner.

(6) An offence under section 33A or 33B is to be treated as—

(a) a relevant offence for the purposes of sections 28B and 28D of the Immigration Act 1971 (search, entry and arrest), and

(b) an offence under Part 3 of that Act (criminal proceedings) for the purposes of sections 28E, 28G and 28H of that Act (search after arrest).]

Note: Inserted with effect from 1 November 2016 for the purposes of making subordinate legislation only; December 1, 2016 otherwise by the Immigration Act 2016, s 39 (SI 2016/1073). Words in square brackets at subsection (2) substituted by Sentencing Act 2020 c.17 Sch 24(6) para 443(1). (December 1, 2020: substitution has effect subject to savings and transitional provisions specified in c.17 s.410 and Sch.24 Part 7).

[Eviction

33D Termination of agreement where all occupiers disqualified

(1) The landlord under a residential tenancy agreement relating to premises in England may terminate the agreement in accordance with this section if the condition in subsection (2) is met.

(2) The condition is that the Secretary of State has given one or more notices in writing to the landlord which, taken together,—

(a) identify the occupier of the premises or (if there is more than one occupier) all of them, and

(b) state that the occupier or occupiers are disqualified as a result of their immigration status from occupying premises under a residential tenancy agreement.

(3) The landlord may terminate the residential tenancy agreement by giving notice in writing and in the prescribed form to the tenant or, in the case of a joint tenancy, all of the tenants specifying the date on which the agreement comes to an end.

(4) That date must not be earlier than the end of the period of 28 days beginning with the day specified in the notice as the day on which it is given.

(5) The notice may be given—

(a) by delivering it to the tenant or tenants,

(b) by leaving it at the premises,

(c) by sending it by post to the tenant or tenants at the address of the premises, or

(d) in any other prescribed manner.

(6) The notice is to be treated as a notice to quit in a case where a notice to quit would otherwise be required to bring the residential tenancy agreement to an end.

(7) The notice is enforceable as if it were an order of the High Court.

(8) In this section 'occupier', in relation to premises to which a residential tenancy agreement applies, means—

(a) a tenant,

(b) a person who, under the agreement, otherwise has the right to occupy the premises and is named in the agreement, and

(c) any other person who the landlord knows is occupying the premises.]

Note: Inserted with effect from 1 November 2016 for the purposes of making subordinate legislation only; 1 December 2016 otherwise by Immigration Act 2016, s 40 (SI 2016/1037).

33E Other procedures for ending agreement

(1) It is an implied term of a residential tenancy agreement to which this subsection applies that the landlord may terminate the tenancy if the premises to which it relates are occupied by an adult who is disqualified as a result of their immigration status from occupying premises under a residential tenancy agreement.

(2) Subsection (1) applies to a residential tenancy agreement relating to premises in England if—

(a) it is a tenancy or sub-tenancy or an agreement for a tenancy or sub-tenancy, but

(b) it is not a protected or statutory tenancy within the meaning of the Rent Act 1977 or an assured tenancy within the meaning of the Housing Act 1988.

(3) For provision relating to a residential tenancy agreement which is a protected or statutory tenancy where a tenant or occupier is disqualified as a result of their immigration status from occupying premises under a residential tenancy agreement, see Case 10A in Part 1 of Schedule 15 to the Rent Act 1977.

(4) For provision relating to a residential tenancy agreement which is an assured tenancy where a tenant or occupier is disqualified as a result of their immigration status from

occupying premises under a residential tenancy agreement, see Ground 7B in Part 1 of Schedule 2 to the Housing Act 1988.]

Note: Inserted with effect from 1 November 2016 for the purposes of making subordinate legislation only; 1 December 2016 otherwise by Immigration Act 2016, s 40 (SI 2016/1037).

General

34. Orders

(1) An order prescribing requirements for the purposes of this Chapter may, in particular, require a landlord or agent to—

(a) obtain a document of a prescribed description from relevant occupiers before or during the course of a residential tenancy agreement;

(b) obtain one document of each of a number of prescribed descriptions from relevant occupiers before or during the course of a residential tenancy agreement;

(c) take steps to verify, retain, copy or record the content of a document obtained in accordance with the order;

(d) take such other steps before or during the course of a residential tenancy agreement as the order may specify.

(2) If the draft of an instrument containing an order under or in connection with this Chapter would, apart from this subsection, be a hybrid instrument for the purposes of the standing orders of either House of Parliament, it is to proceed in that House as if it were not a hybrid instrument.

Note: Commencement from 1 December 2014 (SI 2014/2771).

35. Transitional provision

(1) This Chapter does not apply in relation to a residential tenancy agreement entered into before the commencement day.

(2) This Chapter does not apply in relation to a residential tenancy agreement entered into on or after the commencement day ('the renewed agreement') if—

(a) another residential tenancy agreement was entered into before the commencement day between the same parties ('the original agreement'), and

(b) the tenant has always had a right of occupation of the premises leased under the renewed agreement since entering into the original agreement.

(3) In this section 'the commencement day' means such day as the Secretary of State may by order appoint; and different days may be appointed for different purposes or areas.

[(4) References in this section to this Chapter do not include sections 33A to 33E (offences and eviction).

(5) Sections 33A to 33C apply in relation to a residential tenancy agreement entered into before or after the coming into force of section 39 of the Immigration Act 2016 (which inserted those sections into this Act).

(6) But sections 33A(10) and (11) and 33B apply only in relation to a contravention of section 22 which occurs after the coming into force of section 39 of the Immigration Act 2016].

[(7) Sections 33D and 33E apply in relation to a residential tenancy agreement entered into before or after the coming into force of section 40 of the Immigration Act 2016 (which inserted these provisions into this Act.]

Note: Commencement from 1 December 2014 (SI 2014/2771). Subsections (4)–(6) inserted by the Immigration Act 2016, s 39 from 1 December 2016 (SI 2016/1037). Subsection (7) inserted by the Immigration Act 2016, s 40 from 1 December 2016 (SI 2016/1037).

36. Crown application

This Chapter binds the Crown, except where the Crown is the responsible landlord for the purposes of section 23 [or the landlord for the purposes of section 33A].

Note: Commencement from 1 December 2014 (SI 2014/2771). Words in square brackets inserted by the Immigration Act 2016, s 39 from 1 November 2016.

37. Interpretation

(1) In this Chapter—

'adult' means a person who has attained the age of 18;
'agreement' includes an agreement in any form (whether or not in writing);
'eligibility period', in relation to a limited right occupier, is to be read in accordance with section 27;
'limited right occupier' has the meaning given in section 24(9);
'occupy' means occupy as an only or main residence;
'penalty notice' means a penalty notice given under this Chapter;
'person with a limited right to rent' has the meaning given in section 21(4);
'post-grant contravention' has the meaning given in section 22(10);
'pre-grant contravention' has the meaning given in section 22(10);
'premises' includes land, buildings, moveable structures, vehicles and vessels;
'prescribed' means prescribed in an order made by the Secretary of State;
'recipient' means the recipient of a penalty notice;
'relevant occupier' has the meaning given in section 22(10);

(2) For the purposes of this Chapter a residential tenancy agreement grants a person a right to occupy premises if—

(a) the agreement expressly grants that person the right (whether or not by naming the person), or

(b) the person is permitted to occupy the premises by virtue of an express grant given to another person, and references to a person occupying premises under an agreement are to be read accordingly.

(3) A reference in this Chapter to the 'prescribed requirements', in connection with compliance with the requirements at a particular time, is a reference only to such of the requirements as are capable of being complied with at that time.

(4) Where two or more persons jointly constitute the landlord in relation to a residential tenancy agreement—

(a) the references to the landlord in—

(i) section 22(7)(a),
(ii) section 24(5), (6)(a) and (7),[]

(iii) section 26(6)(a) and (7)(b), are to be taken as references to any of those persons;

[(iv) section 33A,]

[[(v) section 33D, and

(vi) section 33E,]]

(b) any other references to the landlord in this Chapter are to be taken as references to all of those persons.

(5) Where two or more persons jointly constitute the agent in relation to a residential tenancy agreement—

(a) the references to the agent in section 26(5), (6)(a) and (7) are to be taken as references to any of those persons;

(b) any other references to the agent in this Chapter are to be taken as references to all of those persons.

(6) The Secretary of State may by order prescribe cases in which—

(a) a residential tenancy agreement is, or is not, to be treated as being entered into for the purposes of this Chapter;

(b) a person is, or is not, to be treated as occupying premises as an only or main residence for the purposes of this Chapter.

(7) An order under subsection (6) prescribing a case may modify the application of this Chapter in relation to that case.

(8) The cases mentioned in subsection (6)(a) include, in particular, cases where—

(a) an option to renew an agreement is exercised;

(b) rights of occupation under an agreement are varied;

(c) an agreement is assigned (whether by the landlord or the tenant);

(d) a periodic tenancy arises at the end of a fixed term;

(e) an agreement grants a right of occupation on satisfaction of a condition;

(f) there is a change in the persons in occupation of the premises leased under an agreement or in the circumstances of any such person.

Note: Commencement from 1 December 2014 (SI 2014/2771). Words in square brackets omitted and inserted from 1 December 2016 by the Immigration Act 2016, s 39 (SI, 2016/1037). Words in double square brackets inserted from 1 December 2016 by Immigration Act 2016. s 40 (SI 2016/1037).

Chapter 2

Other Services etc

National Health Service

38. Immigration health charge

(1) The Secretary of State may by order provide for a charge to be imposed on—

(a) persons who apply for immigration permission, or

(b) any description of such persons.

(2) 'Immigration permission' means—

(a) leave to enter or remain in the United Kingdom for a limited period,

(b) entry clearance which, by virtue of provision made under section 3A(3) of the Immigration Act 1971, has effect as leave to enter the United Kingdom for a limited period, or

(c) any other entry clearance which may be taken as evidence of a person's eligibility for entry into the United Kingdom for a limited period.

(3) An order under this section may in particular—

(a) impose a separate charge on a person in respect of each application made by that person;

(b) specify the amount of any charge (and different amounts may be specified for different purposes);

(c) make provision about when or how a charge may or must be paid to the Secretary of State;

(d) make provision about the consequences of a person failing to pay a charge (including provision for the person's application to be refused);

(e) provide for exemptions from a charge;

(f) provide for the reduction, waiver or refund of part or all of a charge (whether by conferring a discretion or otherwise).

(4) In specifying the amount of a charge under subsection (3)(b) the Secretary of State must (among other matters) have regard to the range of health services that are likely to be available free of charge to persons who have been given immigration permission.

(5) Sums paid by virtue of an order under this section must—

(a) be paid into the Consolidated Fund, or

(b) be applied in such other way as the order may specify.

(6) In this section—

'entry clearance' has the meaning given by section 33(1) of the Immigration Act 1971;

'health services' means services provided as part of the health service in England, Wales, Scotland and Northern Ireland;

and the references to applying for leave to enter or remain for a limited period include references to applying for a variation of leave to enter or remain which would result in leave to enter or remain for a limited period.

Note: Commencement from 20 October 2014 (SI 2014/2771).

39. Related provision: charges for health services

(1) A reference in the NHS charging provisions to persons not ordinarily resident in Great Britain or persons not ordinarily resident in Northern Ireland includes (without prejudice to the generality of that reference) a reference to—

(a) persons who require leave to enter or remain in the United Kingdom but do not have it, and

(b) persons who have leave to enter or remain in the United Kingdom for a limited period [unless that leave was granted by virtue of residence scheme immigration rules.]

(2) The 'NHS charging provisions' are—

(a) section 175 of the National Health Service Act 2006 (charges in respect of persons not ordinarily resident in Great Britain);

(b) section 124 of the National Health Service (Wales) Act 2006 (charges in respect of persons not ordinarily resident in Great Britain);

(c) section 98 of the National Health Service (Scotland) Act 1978 (charges in respect of persons not ordinarily resident in Great Britain);

(d) Article 42 of the Health and Personal Social Services (Northern Ireland) Order 1972 (S.I. 1972/1265 (N.I. 14)) (provision of services to persons not ordinarily resident in Northern Ireland).

[(3) For the purposes of subsection (1) 'residence scheme immigration rules' has the meaning given by section 17 of the European Union (Withdrawal Agreement) Act 2020.]

Note: Commencement from 6 April 2015 (SI 2015/874). Words inserted in square brackets at subsection (1)(b) and (3) by Immigration and Social Security Co-ordination (EU Withdrawal) Act 2020 (Consequential, Savings, Transitionary and Transitional Provisions) (EU Exit) Regulations 2020/1309 Pt2(1) Reg.20 (4) (a) & (b).

Bank accounts

40. Prohibition on opening current accounts for disqualified persons

(1) A bank or building society ('B') must not open a current account for a person ('P') who is within subsection (2) unless—

(a) B has carried out a status check which indicates that P is not a disqualified person, or

(b) at the time when the account is opened B is unable, because of circumstances that cannot reasonably be regarded as within its control, to carry out a status check in relation to P.

(2) A person is within this subsection if he or she—

(a) is in the United Kingdom, and

(b) requires leave to enter or remain in the United Kingdom but does not have it.

(3) For the purposes of this section—

(a) carrying out a 'status check' in relation to P means checking with a specified anti-fraud organisation or a specified data-matching authority whether, according to information supplied to that organisation or authority by the Secretary of State, P is a disqualified person;

(b) a 'disqualified person' is a person within subsection (2) for whom the Secretary of State considers that a current account should not be opened by a bank or building society;

(c) opening an account for P includes—

(i) opening a joint account for P and others;

(ii) opening an account in relation to which P is a signatory or is identified as a beneficiary;

(iii) adding P as an account holder or as a signatory or identified beneficiary in relation to an account.

(4) In subsection (3)(a)—

'anti-fraud organisation' has the same meaning as in section 68 of the Serious Crime Act 2007;

'data-matching authority' means a person or body conducting data matching exercises, within the meaning of Schedule 9 to the Local Audit and Accountability Act 2014, under or by virtue of that or any other Act;

'specified' means specified by an order made by the Secretary of State for the purposes of this section.

(5) Subsection (1)(b) does not apply where—

(a) a bank or building society is required to pay a reasonable fee for carrying out status checks, and

(b) its inability to carry out a status check is due to its failure to pay the fee.

(6) A bank or building society that refuses to open a current account for someone on the ground that he or she is a disqualified person must tell the person, if it may lawfully do so, that that is the reason for its refusal.

[(7) The prohibition in subsection (1) does not apply in the case of an account to be operated (or an account that is operated) by or for a person or body of a description specified in an order made by the Treasury.]

Note: Commenced from 12 December 2014 (SI 2014/1943). Subsection (7) inserted from 12 December 2014 by Immigration Act 2014 (Bank Accounts)(Amendments) Order 2014 (SI 2014/3074).

[40A Requirement to carry out immigration checks in relation to current accounts

(1) A bank or building society must, at such times or with such frequency as is specified in regulations made by the Treasury, carry out an immigration check in relation to each current account held with it that is not an excluded account.

(2) For the purposes of this section carrying out an 'immigration check' in relation to a current account means checking whether, according to information supplied by the Secretary of State to a specified anti-fraud organisation or a specified data-matching authority, the account is operated by or for a disqualified person.

(3) A 'disqualified person' is a person—

(a) who is in the United Kingdom,

(b) who requires leave to enter or remain in the United Kingdom but does not have it, and

(c) for whom the Secretary of State considers that a current account should not be provided by a bank or building society.

(4) A current account is an excluded account for the purposes of subsection (1) if the account is operated by or for a person or body of a description specified in regulations made by the Treasury.

(5) An account is operated by or for a person or body if the person or body is an account holder or a signatory or identified as a beneficiary in relation to the account.

(6) A bank or building society must—

(a) make arrangements with a specified anti-fraud organisation or a specified data-matching authority for the purpose of enabling the bank or building society to carry out immigration checks in relation to current accounts, and

(b) pay any reasonable fee required to be paid under those arrangements.

(7) In this section 'specified anti-fraud organisation' and 'specified data-matching authority' have the same meaning as in section 40(3)(a).]

Note: Inserted by Schedule 7, para 2 to the Immigration Act 2016 and commenced on November 1, 2016 for the purposes of making subordinate legislation only; October 30, 2017 otherwise.

[40B Requirement to notify existence of current accounts for disqualified persons

(1) This section applies where, as a result of an immigration check carried out under section 40A, a bank or building society identifies a current account that is operated by or for a person who the bank or building society believes to be a disqualified person.

(2) Where this section applies, the bank or building society (as the case may be) must as soon as reasonably practicable—

(a) notify the Secretary of State that a current account held with it is operated by or for a person who it believes to be a disqualified person, and

(b) provide the Secretary of State with such other information as may be prescribed.

(3) A notification made, or information provided, under subsection (2) must be made or provided in the prescribed form and manner.

(4) In subsections (2) and (3) 'prescribed' means prescribed in regulations made by the Treasury.

(5) Regulations under subsection (2) may (in particular) require the provision of information relating to any accounts held with the bank or building society that are operated by or for the person who is believed to be a disqualified person.]

Note: Inserted by Schedule 7, para 2 to Immigration Act 2016 and commenced on November 1, 2016 for the purposes of making subordinate legislation only; October 30, 2017 otherwise.

[40C Action to be taken by Secretary of State following section 40B notification

(1) Where the Secretary of State receives a notification from a bank or building society under section 40B(2) in relation to a person, the Secretary of State must check whether the person is a disqualified person.

(2) If the Secretary of State determines that the person is a disqualified person, the Secretary of State may apply under section 40D for a freezing order in respect of one or more of the accounts held with the bank or building society that are operated by or for the disqualified person.

(3) If the Secretary of State decides not to apply for a freezing order under subsection (2), or decides to apply for a freezing order in respect of one or more but not all of the accounts held with the bank or building society that are operated by or for the disqualified person, the Secretary of State must notify the bank or building society that it is subject to the duty in section 40G(2) in relation to the disqualified person.

(4) A notification made under subsection (3) must contain the prescribed information and be made in the prescribed form and manner.

(5) In subsection (4) 'prescribed' means prescribed in regulations made by the Treasury.

(6) If the Secretary of State determines that the person is not a disqualified person, the Secretary of State must notify the bank or building society accordingly.]

Note: Inserted by Schedule 7, para 2 to the Immigration Act 2016 and commenced on November 1, 2016 for the purposes of making subordinate legislation only; October 30, 2017 otherwise.

[40D Freezing orders

(1) On an application by the Secretary of State under section 40C(2), the court may make a freezing order in respect of any account specified in the application.

(2) A freezing order in respect of an account is an order that prohibits each person and body by or for whom the account is operated from making withdrawals or payments from the account.

(3) A freezing order may be made subject to exceptions.

(4) An exception may (in particular)—

(a) make provision for the disqualified person to meet his or her reasonable living expenses and reasonable legal expenses;

(b) allow another person or body by or for whom the account is operated to make withdrawals or payments from the account.

(5) An application for a freezing order may be made without notice.

(6) The court may vary or discharge a freezing order made in respect of an account (whether made under this section or on an appeal under section 40E) on an application made by—

(a) the Secretary of State, or

(b) a person or body by or for whom the account is operated.

(7) If the Secretary of State applies for a freezing order in respect of an account and the order is not made, or the order is made but subsequently discharged, the Secretary of State must notify the bank or building society that it is subject to the duty in section 40G(2) in relation to the disqualified person.

(8) A notification made under subsection (7) must contain the information and be in the form and manner prescribed in regulations made under subsection (4) of section 40C for the purposes of subsection (3) of that section.

(9) In this section—

'the court' means—

(a) in England and Wales, a magistrates' court;

(b) in Scotland, the sheriff;

(c) in Northern Ireland, a court of summary jurisdiction; 'the disqualified person' means the person who, following a check under section 40C(1), was determined to be a disqualified person, resulting in the application for the freezing order.]

Note: Inserted by Schedule 7, para 2 to the Immigration Act 2016 and commenced on November 1, 2016 for the purposes of making subordinate legislation only; October 30, 2017 otherwise.

[40E Freezing orders: appeals

(1) An appeal may be made to the relevant appeal court against a decision of a court under section 40D.

(2) The right of appeal under subsection (1) is exercisable by—

(a) the Secretary of State, and

(b) if the decision relates to a freezing order that is in force in respect of an account, a person or body by or for whom the account is operated.

(3) On an appeal under this section the relevant appeal court may make—

(a) whatever orders are necessary to give effect to its determination of the appeal;

(b) whatever incidental or consequential orders appear to it to be just.

(4) In this section 'the relevant appeal court' means—

(a) the Crown Court, where the decision appealed against is a decision of a magistrates' court;

(b) the Sheriff Appeal Court, where the decision appealed against is a decision of the sheriff;

(c) a county court, where the decision appealed against is a decision of a court of summary jurisdiction.]

Note: Inserted by Schedule 7, para 2 to the Immigration Act 2016 and commenced on November 1, 2016 for the making of subordinate legislation only; October 30, 2017 otherwise.

[40F Freezing orders: code of practice

(1) The Secretary of State must issue a code of practice—

(a) specifying the factors that the Secretary of State will consider when deciding whether to apply for a freezing order under section 40C(2),

(b) outlining the arrangements for keeping a freezing order under review for the purpose of deciding whether to apply under section 40D(6) for its variation or discharge, and

(c) specifying the factors that the Secretary of State will consider when deciding whether to make such an application.

(2) The Secretary of State must from time to time review the code and may revise and re-issue it following a review.

(3) The code (or revised code)—

(a) may not be issued unless a draft has been laid before Parliament, and

(b) comes into force in accordance with provision contained in regulations made by the Secretary of State.]

Note: Inserted by Schedule 7, para 2 to the Immigration Act 2016 and commenced on November 1, 2016 for the making of subordinate legislation only; October 2017 otherwise.

[40G Closure of accounts not subject to freezing order

(1) This section applies where—

(a) a bank or building society makes a notification under section 40B(2) in relation to a person,

(b) the person is determined by the Secretary of State (following a check under section 40C(1)) to be a disqualified person, and

(c) the bank or building society receives a notification under section 40C(3) or 40D(7) in relation to the disqualified person.

(2) Where this section applies the bank or building society must as soon as reasonably practicable close each account held with it that—

(a) in the case of a notification under section 40C(3), is operated by or for the disqualified person and is not the subject of an application for a freezing order;

(b) in the case of a notification under section 40D(7), is operated by or for the disqualified person and in respect of which a freezing order is not in force.

(3) The bank or building society may delay closing an account which it would otherwise be required to close under subsection (2) if at the time at which it would otherwise be required to close it—

(a) the account is overdrawn, or

(b) where the account is operated by or for the disqualified person and one or more bodies or other persons, the bank or building society considers that closing the account would significantly adversely affect the interests of any of those other bodies or persons.

(4) Where subsection (3) applies, closure of the account may be delayed for such period as is reasonable (but not indefinitely).

(5) If an account falling within subsection (2) is operated by or for the disqualified person and one or more bodies or other persons, the bank or building society is to be treated as having complied with that subsection in relation to that account if, as soon as reasonably practicable, it takes all such steps as are necessary to prevent the account from being operated by or for the disqualified person (instead of closing the account).

(6) Where the bank or building society closes an account in compliance with this section, it must tell each person or body by or for whom the account is operated, if it may lawfully do so, why it has closed the account.

(7) Where the bank or building society prevents an account from being operated by or for the disqualified person by virtue of subsection (5), it must tell each person or body by or for whom the account is operated, if it may lawfully do so, why it has prevented the account from being operated by or for the disqualified person.

(8) The bank or building society must provide the Secretary of State with information about the steps that it has taken to comply with this section.

(9) Information provided under subsection (8) must be provided in the prescribed form and manner and at the prescribed times or with the prescribed frequency.

(10) In subsection (9) 'prescribed' means prescribed in regulations made by the Treasury.]

Note: Inserted by Schedule 7, para 2 to the Immigration Act 2016 and commenced from November 1, 2016 for the purposes of making subordinate legislation only; October 30, 2017 otherwise.

[40H Sections 40A to 40G: interpretation

(1) This section applies for the purposes of sections 40A to 40G.

(2) 'Account' includes a financial product by means of which a payment may be made.

(3) 'Freezing order' has the meaning given by section 40D(2).

(4) 'Disqualified person' has the meaning given by section 40A(3).

(5) References to an account being operated by or for a person or body are to be read in accordance with section 40A(5).]

Note: Inserted by Schedule 7, para 2 of Immigration Act 2016 from 1 November 2016 for the purpose of making subordinate legislation only (SI 2016/1037); October 30, 2017 otherwise.

41. Regulation by Financial Conduct Authority

(1) The Treasury may make regulations to enable the Financial Conduct Authority to make arrangements for monitoring and enforcing compliance with the prohibition imposed on banks and building societies by section 40 [and the requirements imposed on them by sections 40A, 40B and 40G]

(2) The regulations may (in particular)—

(a) provide for the Financial Conduct Authority to be given free access to the information to which banks and building societies are given access when carrying out status checks under section 40 [or immigration checks under section 40A];

(b) apply, or make provision corresponding to, any of the provisions of the Financial Services and Markets Act 2000, including in particular those mentioned in subsection (3), with or without modification.

(3) The provisions are—

(a) provisions about investigations, including powers of entry and search and criminal offences;

(b) provisions for the grant of an injunction (or, in Scotland, an interdict) in relation to a contravention or anticipated contravention;

(c) provisions giving the Financial Conduct Authority powers to impose disciplinary measures (including financial penalties) or to give directions;

(d) provisions giving a Minister of the Crown (within the meaning of the Ministers of the Crown Act 1975) or the Financial Conduct Authority powers to make subordinate legislation;

(e) provisions for the Financial Conduct Authority to charge fees.

Note: Words in square brackets inserted by Schedule 7 to the Immigration Act 2016. Commenced on November 1, 2016 for the purpose of making subordinate legislation only; October 30, 2017 otherwise.

42. 'Bank' and 'building society'

(1) In sections 40 [to 41] 'bank' means an authorised deposit-taker that has its head office or a branch in the United Kingdom. This is subject to subsection (4).

(2) In subsection (1) 'authorised deposit-taker' means—

(a) a person who under Part 4A of the Financial Services and Markets Act 2000 has permission to accept deposits;

(b) [..].

(3) A reference in subsection (2) to a person [] with permission to accept deposits does not include a person [] with permission to do so only for the purposes of, or in the course of, an activity other than accepting deposits.

(4) 'Bank' does not include—

(a) a building society;

(b) a person who is specified, or is within a class of persons specified, by an order under section 38 of the Financial Services and Markets Act 2000 (exemption orders);

(c) a credit union within the meaning given by section 31(1) of the Credit Unions Act 1979 or by Article 2(2) of the Credit Unions (Northern Ireland) Order 1985;

(d) a friendly society within the meaning given by section 116 of the Friendly Societies Act 1992.

(5) In sections 40 [to 41], and in subsection (4), 'building society' means a building society incorporated (or deemed to be incorporated) under the Building Societies Act 1986.

Note: Commencement at 14 July 2014 (SI 2014/1820). Words in square brackets inserted by Schedule 7 to the Immigration Act 2016, para 4 from November 1, 2016 for the purposes of making subordinate legislation only; October 30, 2017 otherwise. Words in square brackets omitted in subsection (2)(b) & (3) by Immigration, Nationality and Asylum (EU Exit) Regulations 2019/745 Pt 2(1) reg.21(4)(a) & (b) (December 31, 2020: shall come into force on IP completion day not exit day as specified in 2020 c.1 s.39(1) and Sch.5 para.1(1))

43. Power to amend

(1) The Treasury may by order amend any of sections 40 to 42 so as—

(a) to alter the categories of financial institution to which those sections apply;

(b) to alter the categories of account to which the prohibition in section 40(1) [or the requirement in section 40A(1)] applies;

(c) to include provision defining a category of account specified in [section 40 to 40A];

(d) to provide for the prohibition in section 40(1) not to apply in the case of an account to be operated (or an account that is operated) by or for a person or body of a specified description.

(2) An order under subsection (1) may amend a section so that it provides for a matter to be specified in a further order to be made by the Treasury.

(3) In subsection (1) 'account' includes a financial product by means of which a payment may be made.

Note: Commencement from 14 July 2014 (SI 2014/1820). Words in square brackets inserted by Schedule 7, para 5 to the Immigration Act 2016 from November 1, 2016 for the purposes of making subordinate legislation only; October 30, 2017 otherwise.

Work

44. Appeals against penalty notices

. . .

Note: Amends s 17 of the Immigration, Asylum and Nationality Act 2006 from 28 July 2014 (SI 2014/1820).

45. Recovery of sums payable under penalty notices

. . .

Note: Amends s 18 of the Immigration, Asylum and Nationality Act 2006 from 28 July 2014 (SI 2014/1820).

Driving licences

46. Grant of driving licences: residence requirement

. . .

Note: Amends s 97 of the Road Traffic Act 1988, Road Traffic (Northern Ireland) Order 1981 (SI 1981/154 (NI 1)) from 14 July 2014 (SI 2014/1820).

47. Revocation of driving licences on grounds of immigration status

. . .

Note: Amends ss 99–100 of the Road Traffic Act 1988, Road Traffic (Northern Ireland) Order 1981 (SI 1981/154 (NI 1)), from 14 July 2014 (SI 2014/1820).

PART 4
MARRIAGE AND CIVIL PARTNERSHIP

CHAPTER 1

REFERRAL AND INVESTIGATION OF PROPOSED MARRIAGES AND CIVIL PARTNERSHIPS

Investigation

48. Decision whether to investigate

(1) This section applies if—

(a) a superintendent registrar refers a proposed marriage to the Secretary of State under section 28H of the Marriage Act 1949, or

(b) a registration authority refers a proposed civil partnership to the Secretary of State under section 12A of the Civil Partnership Act 2004.

[(**1A**) This section also applies if—

(a) a registrar refers a proposed marriage to the Secretary of State under Article 3E of the Marriage (Northern Ireland) Order 2003, or

(b) a registrar refers a proposed civil partnership to the Secretary of State under section 139E of the Civil Partnership Act 2004.]

[(**1B**) This section also applies if—

(a) a district registrar refers a proposed marriage to the Secretary of State under section 3F of the Marriage (Scotland) Act 1977, or

(b) a district registrar refers a proposed civil partnership to the Secretary of State under section 88F of the Civil Partnership Act 2004.]

(**2**) The Secretary of State must decide whether to investigate whether the proposed marriage or civil partnership is a sham.

(**3**) The Secretary of State may not decide to conduct such an investigation unless conditions A and B are met.

(**4**) Condition A is met if the Secretary of State is satisfied that—

(a) only one of the parties to the proposed marriage or civil partnership is an exempt person, or

(b) neither of the parties are exempt persons.

(**5**) Condition B is met if the Secretary of State has reasonable grounds for suspecting that the proposed marriage or civil partnership is a sham.

(**6**) In making the decision whether to investigate, regard must be had to any guidance published by the Secretary of State for this purpose.

(**7**) In the case of a proposed marriage [referred to the Secretary of State as mentioned in subsection (1)(a)], the Secretary of State must give notice of the decision made under this section to—

(a) both of the parties to the proposed marriage, and

(b) the superintendent registrar who referred the proposed marriage to the Secretary of State.

(**8**) In the case of a proposed civil partnership [referred to the Secretary of State as mentioned in subsection (1)(b)], the Secretary of State must give notice of the decision made under this section to—

(a) both of the parties to the proposed civil partnership,

(b) the registration authority who referred the proposed civil partnership to the Secretary of State, and

(c) if different, the registration authority responsible for issuing the civil partnership schedule under section 14(1) of the Civil Partnership Act 2004 in relation to the proposed civil partnership.

[(**8A**) In the case of a proposed marriage referred to the Secretary of State as mentioned in subsection (1A)(a), the Secretary of State must give notice of the decision made under this section to—

(a) both of the parties to the proposed marriage, and

(b) the registrar who referred the proposed marriage to the Secretary of State.

(8B) In the case of a proposed civil partnership referred to the Secretary of State as mentioned in subsection (1A)(b), the Secretary of State must give notice of the decision made under this section to—

(a) both of the parties to the proposed civil partnership, and

(b) the registrar who referred the proposed civil partnership to the Secretary of State.]

[(8C) In the case of a proposed marriage referred to the Secretary of State as mentioned in subsection (1B)(a), the Secretary of State must give notice of the decision made under this section to—

(a) both of the parties to the proposed marriage, and

(b) the district registrar who referred the proposed marriage to the Secretary of State.

(8D) In the case of a proposed civil partnership referred to the Secretary of State as mentioned in subsection (1B)(b), the Secretary of State must give the notice of the decision made under this section to—

(a) both of the parties to the proposed civil partnership, and

(b) the district registrar who referred the proposed civil partnership to the Secretary of State.]

(9) The Secretary of State must make the decision, and give the notice, required by this section within the relevant statutory period.

Note: Commenced from 1 March 2015 (SI 2015/371). Subsection (1A) inserted by Proposed Marriages and Civil Partnerships (Northern Ireland and Miscellaneous Provisions) Order 2015 (SI 2015/395). Subsection (1B) inserted by Referral and Investigation of Proposed Marriages and Civil Partnership Orders (Scotland) Order 2015 (SI 2015/396). Words in square brackets inserted in subsection (7) and (8) by SI 2015/395 above. Subsection (8A) inserted by SI 2015/395 above. Subsection (8B) inserted by SI 2015/396 above.

49. Exempt persons

(1) A person who is a party to a proposed marriage or civil partnership is an exempt person if the person—

(a) is a relevant national;

(b) has the appropriate immigration status; or

(c) holds a relevant visa in respect of the proposed marriage or civil partnership.

(2) A person has the appropriate immigration status if the person—

(a)

(b) is exempt from immigration control; or

(c) is settled in the United Kingdom (within the meaning of the Immigration Act 1971—see section 33(2A) of that Act).

[(2A) Retained enforceable EU right means a right that—

(a) was created or arose by or under the EU Treaties before the coming into force of this subsection, and

(b) forms part of retained EU law by virtue of section 3 or 4 of the European Union (Withdrawal) Act 2018,

as that right is modified from time to time.].

(3) The question of whether a person is exempt from immigration control is to be determined in accordance with regulations made for this purpose by the Secretary of State.

(4) A person holds a relevant visa if the person holds a visa or other authorisation that is of a kind specified for this purpose in regulations made by the Secretary of State.

(5) The Secretary of State may not specify a visa or other authorisation under subsection (4) unless the Secretary of State considers that the purpose of issuing that kind of visa or authorisation is, or includes, enabling a person to enter or remain in the United Kingdom to marry or form a civil partnership.

Note: Commencement from 20 October 2014 for the purpose of making regulations (SI 2014/2771). Commencement from 1 March 2015 (SI 2015/371) for all remaining purposes. Words in subsection (2)(a) omitted by Immigration and Social Security Co-ordination (EU Withdrawal) Act 2020 (Consequential Saving, Transitional and Transitory Provisions) (EU Exit) Regulations (SI 2020/1309) regs.1(2)(2) from July 1, 2020. Subsection (2A) inserted by Immigration, Nationality and Asylum (EU Exit) Regulations 2019/745 Pt 2(1) reg.21(5)(a) & (b) (December 31, 2020: shall come into force on IP completion day not exit day as specified in 2020 c.1 s.39(1) and Sch.5 para.1(1)).

50. Conduct of investigation

(1) An investigation must be conducted in accordance with any regulations made by the Secretary of State for this purpose.

(2) In conducting an investigation, regard must also be had to any guidance published by the Secretary of State for this purpose.

(3) A relevant party must comply with a requirement specified in regulations made under section 51(4) if—

(a) the section 48 notice given to the relevant party states that he or she must do so, or

(b) the Secretary of State subsequently notifies the relevant party (orally or in writing) that he or she must do so; and the relevant party must comply with that requirement in the manner stated in the section 48 notice or in the Secretary of State's notification (if such a manner is stated there).

(4) As part of an investigation, the Secretary of State must decide whether or not each of the relevant parties has complied with the investigation (the 'compliance question').

(5) The compliance question must be decided in accordance with any regulations made by the Secretary of State for this purpose.

(6) In deciding the compliance question, regard must also be had to any guidance published by the Secretary of State for this purpose.

(7) Within the 70 day period, the Secretary of State must—

(a) decide the compliance question; and

(b) give notice of that decision to the persons to whom the Secretary of State gave the section 48 notice relating to the proposed marriage or civil partnership.

(8) If the Secretary of State's decision is that one or both of the relevant parties have not complied with the investigation, the notice under subsection (7) must include a statement of the Secretary of State's reasons for reaching that decision.

(9) Regulations made under this section may, in particular, make provision about—

(a) the circumstances in which a relevant party is to be taken to have failed to comply with a relevant requirement;

(b) the consequences of a relevant party's failure to comply with a relevant requirement.

(10) The provision that may be made under subsection (9)(b) includes provision for the compliance question to be decided (in whole or in part) by reference to a relevant party's compliance or non-compliance with one or more relevant requirements.

(11) In this section—

'70 day period' means the period of 70 days beginning with the day on which the relevant statutory period begins;

'investigation' means an investigation, conducted following a decision by the Secretary of State under section 48, whether a proposed marriage or civil partnership is a sham;

'relevant party' means a person who is a party to a proposed marriage or civil partnership that is the subject of an investigation;

'relevant requirement' [in relation to a proposed marriage or civil partnership under the law of England and Wales] means any requirement imposed by law, including a requirement imposed by or in accordance with—

(a) subsection (3);

(b) section 27E, 28B or 28C of the Marriage Act 1949;

(c) regulations under section 28D of that Act;

(d) section 8A, or any of sections 9 to 9B, of the Civil Partnership Act 2004];

'relevant requirement' in relation to a proposed marriage or civil partnership under the law of Northern Ireland, means any requirement imposed by law, including a requirement imposed by or in accordance with—

(a) subsection (3);

(b) regulations under paragraph 4 of Schedule 5;

(c) Article 3A or 3B of the Marriage (Northern Ireland) Order 2003;

(d) Article 5 of the Marriage (Northern Ireland) Order 2003 so far as that requirement relates to nationality;

(e) section 139A or 139B of the Civil Partnership Act 2004;

(f) section 141 of the Civil Partnership Act 2004 so far as that requirement relates to nationality.]

[['relevant requirement' in relation to a proposed marriage or civil partnership under the law of Scotland, means any requirement imposed by law including a requirement imposed by or in accordance with—

(a) subsection (3);

(b) regulations under paragraph 4 of Schedule 5;

(c) section 3(4A)(4), 3A or 3B of the Marriage (Scotland) Act 1977;

(d) section 88 (8)(5), 88A or 88B of the Civil Partnership Act 2004.]]

Note: Commencement from 20 October 2014 for the purpose of making regulations (SI 2014/2771). Commencement from 1 March 2015 (SI 2015/371) for all remaining purposes. Words in square brackets inserted by Referral and Investigation of Proposed Marriages and Civil Partnerships (Northern Ireland and Miscellaneous Provisions) Order 2015 (SI 2015/395). Words in double square brackets inserted by Referral and Investigation of Proposed Marriages and Civil Partnerships (Scotland) Order 2015 (SI 2015/396).

51. Investigations: supplementary

(1) A section 48 notice which states that the Secretary of State has decided to investigate whether a proposed marriage or civil partnership is a sham must include—

(a) notice that the compliance question must be decided within the period of 70 days mentioned in section 50(7);

(b) notice of the date on which that period will end;

(c) notice that a relevant party may be required to comply with one or more requirements imposed by the Secretary of State subsequently in accordance with section 50(3); and

(d) prescribed information about the investigation.

(2) The section 48 notice may also include such other information as the Secretary of State considers appropriate.

(3) For the purposes of subsection (1)(d) 'prescribed information' means information prescribed by the Secretary of State by regulations; and the information that may be prescribed includes information about—

(a) the conduct of the investigation;

(b) requirements with which the relevant parties must comply in relation to the investigation;

(c) the consequence of a failure to comply with those or any other requirements;

(d) the possible outcomes of the investigation;

(e) the consequences of those outcomes.

(4) The Secretary of State may, by regulations, specify requirements relating to the conduct of investigations which may be imposed on a relevant party by the section 48 notice or by the Secretary of State subsequently in accordance with section 50(3).

(5) Regulations made under subsection (4) may, in particular, specify any of the following requirements—

(a) a requirement to make contact with a particular person or description of persons in a particular way (including by telephoning a particular number) within a particular time period;

(b) a requirement to be present at a particular place at a particular time;

(c) a requirement to be visited at home;

(d) a requirement to be interviewed;

(e) a requirement to provide information (whether orally or in writing);

(f) a requirement to provide photographs;

(g) a requirement to provide evidence.

(6) The provisions of this Part, and any investigation or other steps taken under those provisions (including the decision of the compliance question), do not limit the powers of the Secretary of State in relation to marriages or civil partnerships that are, or are suspected to be, a sham (including any powers to investigate such marriages or civil partnerships).

(7) In this section 'investigation', 'relevant party' and 'compliance question' have the same meanings as in section 50.

Note: Commencement from 20 October 2014 for the purpose of making regulations (SI 2014/2771). Commencement from 1 March 2015 (SI 2015/371) for all remaining purposes.

Referral

52. Referral of proposed marriages and civil partnerships in England and Wales

Schedule 4 (referral of proposed marriages and civil partnerships in England and Wales) has effect.

Note: Commencement from 20 October 2014 for the purpose of making regulations for part of Schedule 4 (article 3 SI 2014/2771). Commencement from 1 March 2015 (SI 2015/371) for all remaining purposes.

Scotland and Northern Ireland

53. Extension of scheme to Scotland and Northern Ireland

(1) The Secretary of State may, by order, make such provision as the Secretary of State considers appropriate for extending the referral and investigation scheme to any of the following—

(a) proposed marriages under the law of Scotland;

(b) proposed civil partnerships under the law of Scotland;

(c) proposed marriages under the law of Northern Ireland;

(d) proposed civil partnerships under the law of Northern Ireland.

(2) An order under this section may—

(a) make provision having a similar effect to the provision made by section 58, Schedule 4, or Parts 1, 2 and 4 of Schedule 6;

(b) confer functions on any person;

(c) amend, repeal or revoke any enactment (including an enactment contained in this Act).

(3) The power under subsection (2)(b) to confer functions includes power to impose a duty of referral on persons exercising functions in Scotland or Northern Ireland in relation to marriage or civil partnership.

(4) But an order under this section may not impose that or any other duty, or otherwise confer functions, on—

(a) the Scottish Ministers,

(b) the First Minister and deputy First Minister in Northern Ireland,

(c) a Northern Ireland Minister, or

(d) a Northern Ireland department.

(5) In this section—

'duty of referral' means a duty to refer a proposed marriage or proposed civil partnership to the Secretary of State in a case where—

(a) one of the parties is not an exempt person, or

(b) both of the parties are not exempt persons;

'enactment' includes—

(a) an enactment contained in subordinate legislation within the meaning of the Interpretation Act 1978;

(b) an enactment contained in, or in an instrument made under, an Act of the Scottish Parliament;

(c) an enactment contained in, or in an instrument made under, Northern Ireland legislation;

'referral and investigation scheme' means the provision made by sections 48 to 51.

Note: Commencement from 20 October 2014 for the purpose of making orders (SI 2014/2771). Commencement from 1 March 2015 (SI 2015/371) for all remaining purposes.

54. Supplementary provision

(1) This section applies if the referral and investigation scheme is extended by an order under section 53 (an 'extension order').

(2) The Secretary of State may make administrative regulations in connection with the application of the scheme—

(a) to proposed marriages or civil partnerships under the law of Scotland (insofar as the scheme is extended to them), and

(b) to proposed marriages or civil partnerships under the law of Northern Ireland (insofar as the scheme is extended to them).

(3) For that purpose 'administrative regulations' means regulations of any kind set out in Schedule 5 (sham marriage and civil partnership: administrative regulations).

(4) The Secretary of State may by order make provision about—

(a) the information that must or may be given, or

(b) the matters in respect of which evidence must or may be given, in relation to proposed marriages or civil partnerships under the law of Scotland or Northern Ireland in cases where one or both of the parties is not a relevant national.

(5) An order under subsection (4) may amend, repeal or revoke any enactment (including an enactment contained in this Act or in provision made by an extension order or an order under subsection (4)).

(6) If an extension order makes provision ('information disclosure provision') having similar effect to the provision made by paragraph 2 of Schedule 6 about the disclosure of information for immigration purposes, the Secretary of State may by order specify other immigration purposes (in addition to those specified in provision made by an extension order or in any provision made under this subsection) for which information may be disclosed under the information disclosure provision.

(7) The Secretary of State must consult—

(a) the Registrar General for Scotland before making administrative regulations, or an order under subsection (4), in relation to proposed marriages or civil partnerships under the law of Scotland;

(b) the Registrar General for Northern Ireland before making administrative regulations, or an order under subsection (4), in relation to proposed marriages or civil partnerships under the law of Northern Ireland.

(8) Expressions used in this section or Schedule 5 that are also used in section 53 have the same meanings in this section or Schedule 5 as in section 53.

Note: Gives power to make regulations in connection with the scheme where s 53 Order made from 20 October 2014 for the purpose of making regulations (SI 2014/2771). Subsection (1) and (8) (provision supplementing section 53) from 1 March 2015 (SI 2015/371) for all remaining purposes.

Chapter 2

Sham Marriage and Civil Partnership

55. Meaning of 'sham marriage' and 'sham civil partnership'

. . .

Note: Amends the Immigration and Asylum Act 1999 from 1 March 2015 (SI 2015/371).

56. Duty to report suspicious marriages and civil partnerships

. . .

Note: Amends the Immigration and Asylum Act 1999 from 14 July 2014 (s 75).

CHAPTER 3

OTHER PROVISIONS

Persons not relevant nationals etc.: marriage on superintendent registrar's certificates

57. Solemnization of marriage according to rites of Church of England

Note: commenced 2 March 2015 subject to transitional provisions (SI 2015/371).

58. Requirement as to giving of notice of marriage or civil partnership

Note: Subsections (2)–(3) amend s 19 of the Asylum and Immigration (Treatment of Claimants, etc.) Act 2004 and subsections (5)–(9) amend Sch 23 to the Civil Partnership Act 2004 from 1 March 2015 (SI 2015/371).

Information

59. Information

Schedule 6 (information) has effect.

Note: Commencement from 14 July 2014 (s 75).

Miscellaneous

60. Regulations about evidence

(1) The Secretary of State may make regulations about evidence relevant to the determination of any of the following questions for a purpose of this Part—

(a) whether a person is a relevant national;

(b) whether a person has the appropriate immigration status;

(c) whether a person has a relevant visa.

(2) The regulations may, in particular, make provision about—

(a) the kind of evidence which is to be supplied;

(b) the form in which evidence is to be supplied;

(c) the manner in which evidence is to be supplied;

(d) the period within which evidence is to be supplied;

(e) the supply of further evidence;

(f) the sufficiency of evidence supplied;

(g) the consequences of failing to supply sufficient evidence in accordance with the regulations (including provision to secure that, in such a case, a particular decision is made or is to be treated as having been made);

(h) the retention or copying of evidence supplied.

(3) The Secretary of State must consult the Registrar General before making regulations under this section.

(4) In this section 'evidence' includes a photograph or other image.

Note: Commencement from 20 October 2014 (SI 2014/2771).

61. Notices

(1) The Secretary of State may, by regulations, make provision about the giving of—

(a) notices under any provision of this Part;

(b) notices relating to the referral of proposed marriages under section 28H of the Marriage Act 1949 which are given under any provision of that Act;

(c) notices relating to the referral of proposed civil partnerships under section 12A of the Civil Partnership Act 2004 which are given under any provision of that Act.

(2) The regulations may, in particular, make provision that a notice given in accordance with the regulations is to be presumed to have been received by the person to whom it is given.

(3) The Secretary of State must consult the Registrar General before making regulations under this section.

Note: Appointment from 20 October 2014 (SI 2014/2771).

62. Interpretation of this Part

(1) These expressions have the meanings given—

'exempt person' has the meaning given in section 49;

'registrar' means a registrar of births, deaths and marriages;

'Registrar General' means—

(a) in relation to regulations that apply to proposed marriages or civil partnerships under the law of England and Wales, the Registrar General for England and Wales;

(b) in relation to regulations that apply to proposed marriages or civil partnerships under the law of Northern Ireland, the Registrar General for Northern Ireland];

[[(c) in relation to regulations that apply to proposed marriages or civil partnerships under the law of Scotland, the Registrar General for Scotland]];

'registration authority' has the same meaning as in the Civil Partnership Act 2004 (see section 28 of that Act);

'relevant national' means—

(a) a British citizen,

{{(aa) an Irish citizen;

(ab) a person who is not an Irish citizen who—

(i) has leave to enter or remain in the United Kingdom which was granted by virtue of residence scheme immigration rules within the meaning given by section 17 of the European Union (Withdrawal Agreement) Act 2020, or

(ii) is an applicant for the purposes of regulation 4 of the Citizens' Rights (Application Deadline and Temporary Protection) (EU Exit) Regulations 2020 (applications which have not been finally determined by the deadline) where the relevant period within the meaning of that regulation has not expired;}}

(b) {{

(c) ;}}

'relevant statutory period' means—

(a) in relation to a proposed marriage under the law of England and Wales, the period—

(i) beginning the day after notice of the proposed marriage is entered in the marriage book in accordance with Part 3 of the Marriage Act 1949, or is entered in an approved electronic form by virtue of section 27(4A) of that Act, and

(ii) ending at the end of the period of 28 days beginning with that day;

(aa) in relation to a proposed marriage under the law of Northern Ireland, the period—

(i) beginning the day on which the record of the proposed marriage is made in the marriage notice book in accordance with Article 4 of the Marriage (Northern Ireland) Order 2003; and

(ii) ending at the end of the period of 28 days beginning with that day;]

[[(ab) in relation to a proposed marriage under the law of Scotland, the period—

(i) beginning the day after the receipt by the district registrar of the marriage notice (as entered by the district registrar in the marriage notice book in accordance with s 4(1) of the Marriage (Scotland) Act 1977, and

(ii) ending at the end of the period of 28 days beginning with that day;]]

(b) in relation to a proposed civil partnership under the law of England and Wales, the period—

(i) beginning the day after notice of the proposed civil partnership is recorded in the register in accordance with Chapter 1 of Part 2 of the Civil Partnership Act 2004, and

(ii) ending at the end of the period of 28 days beginning with that day;

(ba) in relation to a proposed civil partnership under the law of Northern Ireland, the period—

(i) beginning the day on which the record of the proposed civil partnership is made in the civil partnership notice book in accordance with section 140(1) of the Civil Partnership Act 2004, and

(ii) ending at the end of the period of 28 days beginning with that day;]

[[(bb) in relation to a proposed civil partnership under the law of Scotland, the period—

(i) beginning the day after the particulars of the proposed civil partnership are entered in the civil partnership book in accordance with section 89(1) of the Civil Partnership Act 2004, and

(ii) ending at the end of the period of 28 days beginning with that day;]]

'section 48 notice' [means—

(a) in relation to a proposed marriage or civil partnership under the law of England and Wales, a notice given under section 48(7) or (8),

(b) in relation to a proposed marriage or civil partnership under the law of Northern Ireland, a notice given under section 48(8A) or (8B);

[[(c) in relation to a proposed marriage or civil partnership under the law of Scotland, a notice given under section 48(8C) or (8D)]].

(2) A reference to a person being a party to a proposed marriage or civil partnership is a reference to a person who would be a party to the marriage or civil partnership if it took place as proposed.

(3) A reference to a proposed marriage or civil partnership being a sham is a reference to a marriage or civil partnership which would (if it took place as proposed) be a sham marriage or sham civil partnership (within the meaning of the Immigration and Asylum Act 1999—see section 24 or 24A of that Act).

(4) For provision about the interpretation of the following expressions, see section 49—

(a) the appropriate immigration status;

(b) a relevant visa.

(5) This section, and the provision mentioned in subsection (4), apply for the purposes of this Part.

Note: Commencement 15 July 2014 (s 75). Words in square brackets inserted and substituted from 1 March 2015 by Referral and Investigation of Proposed Marriages and Civil Partnerships (Northern Ireland and Miscellaneous Provisions) Order 2015 (SI 2015/395). Words in double square brackets inserted from 1 March 2015 by Referral and Investigation of Proposed Marriages and Civil Partnerships (Scotland) Order 2015 (SI 2015/396). Words in curly brackets in subsection (1) in double curly brackets substituted and omitted in in subsection (1)(b) & (c) by Immigration and Social Security Co-ordination (EU Withdrawal) Act 2020 (Consequential, Savings, Transitionary and Transitional Provisions) (EU Exit) Regulations 2020/1309 Pt 2(1) reg.20(6) (July 1 2021; insertion and appeal has effect subject to saving specified in SI 2020/1309 reg.20(8))

PART 5

OVERSIGHT

Office of the Immigration Services Commissioner

63. Immigration advisers and immigration service providers

Schedule 7 (immigration advisers and immigration service providers) has effect.

Note: Commencement so far as it is necessary for the purposes of the provisions of subparagraph (aa) from 28 July 2014 (SI 2014/1820). Commencement from 20 October 2014 for paragraphs 1 and 3, 17 November 2014 for the remainder of Schedule 7 (SI 2014/2771).

Police Ombudsman for Northern Ireland

64. Police Ombudsman for Northern Ireland

. . .

Note: Amends the Police (Northern Ireland) Act 1998 from 28 July 2014 (SI 2014/1820).

PART 6

MISCELLANEOUS

Citizenship

65. Persons unable to acquire citizenship: natural father not married to mother

. . .

Note: Inserts ss 4E–4J of the British Nationality Act 1981 from 6 April 2015 (SI 2015/371).

66. Deprivation if conduct seriously prejudicial to vital interests of the UK

(1) . . .

(2) In deciding whether to make an order under subsection (2) of section 40 of the British Nationality Act 1981 in a case which falls within subsection (4A) of that Act, the Secretary of State may take account of the manner in which a person conducted him or herself before this section came into force.

(3) . . .

Note: Subsection (1) amends s 40 of the British Nationality Act 1981, subsection (3) inserts s 40B of the same Act from 28 July 2014 (SI/2014/1820).

Embarkation checks

67. Embarkation checks

Schedule 8 (embarkation checks) has effect.

Note: Commencement from 28 July 2014 (SI 2014/1820).

Fees

68. Fees

(1) The Secretary of State may provide, in accordance with this section, for fees to be charged in respect of the exercise of functions in connection with immigration or nationality.

(2) The functions in respect of which fees are to be charged are to be specified by the Secretary of State by order ('a fees order').

(3) A fees order—

(a) must specify how the fee in respect of the exercise of each specified function is to be calculated, and

(b) may not provide for a fee to be charged in respect of the exercise of a function otherwise than in connection with an application or claim, or on request.

(4) For any specified fee, a fees order must provide for it to comprise one or more amounts each of which is—

(a) a fixed amount, or

(b) an amount calculated by reference to an hourly rate or other factor.

(5) Where a fees order provides for a fee (or part of a fee) to be a fixed amount, it—

(a) must specify a maximum amount for the fee (or part), and

(b) may specify a minimum amount.

(6) Where a fees order provides for a fee (or part of a fee) to be calculated as mentioned in subsection (4)(b), it—

(a) must specify—

(i) how the fee (or part) is to be calculated, and

(ii) a maximum rate or other factor, and

(b) may specify a minimum rate or other factor.

(7) For any specified fee, the following are to be set by the Secretary of State by regulations ('fees regulations')—

(a) if the fee (or any part of it) is to be a fixed amount, that amount;

(b) if the fee (or any part of it) is to be calculated as mentioned in subsection (4)(b), the hourly rate or other factor by reference to which it (or that part) is to be calculated.

(8) An amount, or rate or other factor, set by fees regulations for a fee in respect of the exercise of a specified function—

(a) must not—

(i) exceed the maximum specified for that amount, or rate or other factor;

(ii) be less than the minimum, if any, so specified;

(b) subject to that, may be intended to exceed, or result in a fee which exceeds, the costs of exercising the function.

(9) In setting the amount of any fee, or rate or other factor, in fees regulations, the Secretary of State may have regard only to—

(a) the costs of exercising the function;

(b) benefits that the Secretary of State thinks are likely to accrue to any person in connection with the exercise of the function;

(c) the costs of exercising any other function in connection with immigration or nationality;

(d) the promotion of economic growth;

(e) fees charged by or on behalf of governments of other countries in respect of comparable functions;

(f) any international agreement. This is subject to section 69(5).

(10) In respect of any fee provided for under this section, fees regulations may—

(a) provide for exceptions;

(b) provide for the reduction, waiver or refund of part or all of a fee (whether by conferring a discretion or otherwise);

(c) make provision about—

(i) the consequences of failure to pay a fee;

(ii) enforcement;

(iii) when a fee may or must be paid.

(11) Any provision that may be made by fees regulations by virtue of subsection (10) may be included instead in a fees order (and any provision so included may be amended or revoked by fees regulations).

(12) In this section and sections 69 and 70—

'costs' includes—

(a) the costs of the Secretary of State, and

(b) the costs of any other person (whether or not funded from public money);

'fees order' has the meaning given by subsection (2);

'fees regulations' has the meaning given by subsection (7);

'function' includes a power or a duty;

'function in connection with immigration or nationality' includes a function in connection with an enactment (including an enactment of a jurisdiction outside the United Kingdom) that relates wholly or partly to immigration or nationality;

'specified' means specified in a fees order.

(13) Any reference in this section or section 70 to the exercise of a function includes a reference to its exercise in particular circumstances, including its exercise—

(a) at particular times or in a particular place;

(b) under particular arrangements;

(c) otherwise in particular ways,

and, for this purpose, 'arrangements' includes arrangements for the convenience of applicants, claimants or persons making requests for the exercise of a function.

Note: Commencement from 15 December 2014 (SI 2014/2771).

69. Fees orders and fees regulations: supplemental

(1) A fees order or fees regulations may be made only with the consent of the Treasury.

(2) A fee under section 68 may relate to something done outside the United Kingdom.

(3) Fees payable by virtue of section 68 may be recovered as a debt due to the Secretary of State.

(4) Fees paid to the Secretary of State by virtue of section 68 must—

(a) be paid into the Consolidated Fund, or

(b) be applied in such other way as the relevant order may specify.

(5) Section 68 is without prejudice to—

(a) section 1 of the Consular Fees Act 1980 (fees for consular acts etc);

(b) section 102 of the Finance (No. 2) Act 1987 (government fees and charges), or

(c) any other power to charge a fee.

Note: Commencement from 15 December 2014 (SI 2014/2771).

70. Power to charge fees for attendance services in particular cases

(1) This section applies where a person exercises a function in connection with immigration or nationality in respect of which a fee is chargeable by virtue of a fees order (a 'chargeable function') in a particular case and—

(a) in doing so attends at a place outside the United Kingdom, and time, agreed with a person ('the client'), and

(b) does so at the request of the client. It is immaterial whether or not the client is a person in respect of whom the chargeable function is exercised.

(2) In this section 'attendance service' means the service described in subsection (1) except so far as it consists of the exercise of a chargeable function.

(3) The following are to be disregarded in determining whether a fee is chargeable in respect of a function by virtue of a fees order—

(a) any exception provided for by a fees order or fees regulations;

(b) any power so provided to waive or refund a fee.

(4) The person exercising the chargeable function may charge the client such fee for the purposes of recovering the costs of providing the attendance service as the person may determine.

(5) Fees paid to the Secretary of State by virtue of this section must be paid into the Consolidated Fund.

(6) A fee payable by virtue of this section may be recovered as a debt due to the Secretary of State.

(7) This section is without prejudice to—

(a) section 68;

(b) section 1 of the Consular Fees Act 1980 (fees for consular acts etc);

(c) section 102 of the Finance (No. 2) Act 1987 (government fees and charges), or

(d) any other power to charge a fee.

Note: Commencement from 28 July 2014 (SI 2014/1820).

[70A Immigration skills charge

(1) The Secretary of State may by regulations provide for a charge to be imposed on—

(a) persons who make immigration skills arrangements, or

(b) any description of such persons.

(2) 'Immigration skills arrangements' are arrangements made by a person ('the sponsor') with the Secretary of State with a view to securing that an individual who is not

exempt for the purposes of this section is granted entry clearance or leave to remain in the United Kingdom to enable the individual to work for the sponsor in the United Kingdom.

(3) Regulations under this section may in particular—

(a) impose a separate charge on a sponsor in respect of each individual in relation to whom the sponsor makes immigration skills arrangements;

(b) specify the amount of any charge (and different amounts may be specified for different purposes);

(c) make provision about when or how a charge may or must be paid to the Secretary of State;

(d) make provision about the consequences of a sponsor failing to pay a charge;

(e) provide for exemptions from a charge;

(f) provide for the reduction, waiver or refund of part or all of a charge (whether by conferring a discretion or otherwise).

(4) Sums paid by virtue of regulations under this section must—

(a) be paid into the Consolidated Fund, or

(b) be applied in such other way as the regulations may specify.

(5) Regulations under this section may be made only with the consent of the Treasury.

(6) An individual is exempt for the purposes of this section if he or she is—

(a) a British citizen;

[[(aa) an Irish citizen;]]

(b) [[a person who has leave to enter or remain in the United Kingdom granted by virtue of residence scheme immigration rules.]]

(c) [[

(d)]]

[(6A) 'Retained enforceable EU right' means a right that—

(a) was created or arose by or under the EU Treaties before the coming into force of this subsection, and

(b) forms part of retained EU law by virtue of section 3 or 4 of the European Union (Withdrawal) Act 2018,

as that right is modified from time to time.]

(7) In this section 'entry clearance' has the meaning given by section 33(1) of the Immigration Act 1971 and [[residence scheme immigration rules.]]

Note: Commencement from 21 July 2016. Words in square brackets in subsection (6)(d) substituted and in subsection (6A) inserted by Immigration, Nationality and Asylum (EU Exit) Regulations 2019/745 Pt 2(1) reg.21(7) (December 31, 2020: shall come into force on IP completion day not exit day as specified in 2020 c.1 s.39(1) and Sch.5 para.1(1)) Words in double square brackets inserted at subsection (6)(aa), substituted at subsection (6)(b), omitted at subsection (6)(c) &(d), and inserted at subsection (7) by Immigration and Social Security Co-ordination (EU Withdrawal) Act 2020 (Consequential, Savings, Transitional and Transitory)(EU Exit) Regulations 2020/1309 P t2(1) reg 20 (7) (a) & (b) (December 1, 2020: insertion has effect subject to saving specified in SI 2020/1309 reg.20(8)).

Welfare of children

71. Duty regarding the welfare of children

For the avoidance of doubt, this Act does not limit any duty imposed on the Secretary of State or any other person by section 55 of the Borders, Citizenship and Immigration Act 2009 (duty regarding the welfare of children).

Note: Commencement from 28 July 2014 (SI 2014/1820).

PART 7
FINAL PROVISIONS

72. Financial provision

The following are to be paid out of money provided by Parliament—

(a) expenditure incurred under or by virtue of this Act by the Secretary of State, and

(b) any increase attributable to this Act in the sums payable under any other Act out of money so provided.

Note: Commencement from 14 May 2013 (s 75).

73. Transitional and consequential provision

(1) The Secretary of State may, by order, make such transitional, transitory or saving provision as the Secretary of State considers appropriate in connection with the coming into force of any provision of this Act.

(2) The Secretary of State may, by order, make such provision as the Secretary of State considers appropriate in consequence of this Act.

(3) The provision that may be made by an order under subsection (2) includes provision amending, repealing or revoking any enactment.

(4) 'Enactment' includes—

(a) an enactment contained in subordinate legislation within the meaning of the Interpretation Act 1978;

(b) an enactment contained in, or in an instrument made under, an Act of the Scottish Parliament;

(c) an enactment contained in, or in an instrument made under, a Measure or Act of the National Assembly for Wales;

(d) an enactment contained in, or in an instrument made under, Northern Ireland legislation.

(5) . . .

(6) Schedule 9 (transitional and consequential provision) has effect.

Note: Subsection (5) amends s 61 of the UK Borders Act 2007. Subsection (6) commences from 20 October 2014 and 17 November 2014 with saving provisions, (SI 2014/2771), remainder 14 May 2014 (s 75). Subsection (6) in so far as it necessary for the purposes of provisions listed in subparagraph (g) form 14 July 2014, and subparagraph (cc) from 28 July 2014 (SI 2014/1820). Subsection (6) commenced on 1 March 2015 so far as necessary for the purpose of the provision of sub-paragraph (1) and (b) (SI 2015/371). Subsection (6) commenced on 6 April 2015 so far as necessary for the purpose of the provision of subparagraph (c) (SI 2015/874).

74. Orders and regulations

(1) Any power of the Secretary of State or Treasury to make an order or regulations under this Act is exercisable by statutory instrument.

(2) A statutory instrument containing any of the following orders or regulations may not be made unless a draft of the instrument has been laid before each House of Parliament and approved by a resolution of each House of Parliament—

(a) an order under section 20(7), 23(6) or 25(5);

(b) an order under section 38;

[(ba) regulations under section 40A(4);
(bb) regulations under section 40B;]
(c) regulations under section 41;
(d) an order under section 43, or under a section amended by such an order;
(e) the first regulations under section 50(1);
(f) the first regulations under section 50(5);
(g) the first regulations under section 51(3);
(h) the first regulations under section 51(4);
(i) an order under section 53 or 54(4) or (6);
(j) a fees order (within the meaning of section 68);
[(ja) regulations under section 70A;]
(k) an order under section 73(2) which amends or repeals primary legislation;
(l) an order under paragraph 2(3)(e) of Schedule 6.

(3) 'Primary legislation' means any of the following—
(a) a public general Act;
(b) an Act of the Scottish Parliament;
(c) a Measure or Act of the National Assembly for Wales;
(d) Northern Ireland legislation.

(4) A statutory instrument containing any other order or regulations made by the Secretary of State or Treasury under this Act is subject to annulment in pursuance of a resolution of either House of Parliament.

(5) But subsection (4) does not apply to a statutory instrument containing an order under any of sections 35(3), 73(1) and 75(3) (subject to subsection (7)).

(6) Subsection (7) applies if an order under section 75(3) is made which—
(a) brings into force a provision of Chapter 1 of Part 3,
(b) brings that provision into force only in relation to a particular area or areas within England and Wales, Scotland or Northern Ireland, and
(c) is the first order to be made bringing into force a provision of that Chapter only in relation to an area or areas within England and Wales, Scotland or Northern Ireland.

(7) A statutory instrument containing any subsequent order under section 75(3) (after the order mentioned in subsection (6)) that brings into force a provision of Chapter 1 of Part 3 for anywhere other than the area or areas mentioned in paragraph (b) of that subsection is subject to annulment in pursuance of a resolution of either House of Parliament.

(8) An order or regulations made by the Secretary of State or Treasury under this Act may—
(a) make different provision for different purposes or areas,
(b) make provision which applies generally or only for particular purposes or areas,
(c) make transitional, transitory or saving provision, or
(d) make incidental, supplementary or consequential provision.

Note: Commencement from 14 May 2014, s 75. Words in square brackets inserted at section 74(2)(ja) by Immigration Act 2016, s 85 from 12 July 2016. Words in square brackets inserted at subsection (2)(ba) and (bc) by Immigration Act 2016, Sch.7 para 6 November 1,2016 for the purpose of making legislation only; October 30, 2017 otherwise).

75. Commencement

(1) This Part, other than section 73(6) and Schedule 9, comes into force on the day on which this Act is passed.

(2) Section 56, section 59 and Schedule 6, and section 62 come into force at the end of the period of two months beginning with the day on which this Act is passed.

(3) Subject to subsections (1) and (2), this Act comes into force on such day as the Secretary of State may by order appoint; and different days may be appointed for different purposes or areas.

Note: Commencement from 14 May 2014.

76. Extent

(1) This Act extends to England and Wales, Scotland and Northern Ireland.

(2) Subsection (1) is subject to subsection (3).

(3) Section 59 and Schedule 6 extend to England and Wales only.

(4) Subsections (1) to (3) do not apply to an amendment, repeal or revocation made by this Act.

(5) An amendment, repeal or revocation made by this Act has the same extent as the provision amended, repealed or revoked (ignoring extent by virtue of an Order in Council).

(6) Her Majesty may by Order in Council provide for any of the provisions of this Act to extend, with or without modifications, to any of the Channel Islands or the Isle of Man.

(7) Subsection (6) does not apply in relation to the extension to a place of a provision which extends there by virtue of subsection (5).

Note: Commencement from 14 May 2014, s 75.

77. Short title

This Act may be cited as the Immigration Act 2014.

Note: Commencement from 14 May 2014, s 75.

SCHEDULES

SCHEDULE 1

ENFORCEMENT POWERS — Section 4

Note: Commencement from 28 July 2014 (SI 2014/1820).

SCHEDULE 2

MEANING OF BIOMETRIC INFORMATION — Section 12

. . .

Note: Commencement from 28 July 2014 (SI 2014/1820).

SCHEDULE 3

EXCLUDED RESIDENTIAL TENANCY AGREEMENTS

Section 20

Social housing

1.—(1) An agreement that grants a right of occupation in social housing.

(2) 'Social housing' means accommodation provided to a person by virtue of a relevant provision.

(3) 'Relevant provision' means a provision of—

(a) —

(i) Part 2 of the Housing Act 1985, or

(ii) Part 6 or 7 of the Housing Act 1996;

(b) in relation to Scotland, Part 1 or 2 of the Housing (Scotland) Act 1987;

(c) in relation to Northern Ireland—

(i) Chapter 4 of Part 2 of the Housing (Northern Ireland) Order 1981 (S.I. 1981/156 (N.I. 3)), or

(ii) Part 2 of the Housing (Northern Ireland) Order 1988 (S.I. 1988/1990 (N.I. 23)).

(4) Accommodation provided to a person by virtue of a relevant provision includes accommodation provided in pursuance of arrangements made under any such provision.

2.—(1) This paragraph applies for the purposes of paragraph 1.

(2) An allocation of housing accommodation by a local housing authority in England to a person who is already—

(a) a secure or introductory tenant, or

(b) an assured tenant of housing accommodation held by a private registered provider of social housing or a registered social landlord, is to be treated as an allocation of housing accommodation by virtue of Part 6 of the Housing Act 1996 (and accordingly section 159(4A) of that Act is to be ignored).

(3) An allocation of housing accommodation that falls within a case specified in, or prescribed under, section 160 of the Housing Act 1996 (cases where provisions about allocation under Part 6 of that Act do not apply) is to be treated as an allocation of housing accommodation by virtue of Part 6 of that Act (and accordingly that section is to be ignored).

(4) An allocation of housing accommodation by virtue of Part 1 of the Housing (Scotland) Act 1987 is to be treated as provided by virtue of a relevant provision only if it is provided by a local authority within the meaning of that Act (or in pursuance of arrangements made under or for the purposes of that Part with a local authority).

(5) Accommodation provided to a person in Northern Ireland by a registered housing association is to be treated as provided to the person by virtue of a relevant provision.

(6) Terms used in sub-paragraphs (2) and (3) have the same meanings as in Part 6 of the Housing Act 1996.

(7) In sub-paragraph (5) 'registered housing association' means a housing association, within the meaning of Part 2 of the Housing (Northern Ireland) Order 1992 (S.I. 1992/1725 (N.I. 15)), that is registered in the register of housing associations maintained under Article 14 of that Order.

Care homes

3.—(1) An agreement that grants a right of occupation in a care home.

(2) 'Care home' means—

(a) [], an establishment [in England] that is a care home for the purposes of the Care Standards Act 2000;

[(aa) premises in Wales at which a care home service within the meaning of Part 1 of the Regulation and Inspection of Social Care (Wales) Act 2016 (anaw 2) is provided wholly or mainly to persons aged 18 or over;].

(b) in relation to Scotland, accommodation that is provided as a care 2010;

(c) in relation to Northern Ireland, an establishment that is a residential care home, or a nursing home, for the purposes of the Health and Personal Social Services (Quality, Improvement and Regulation) (Northern Ireland) Order 2003 (S.I. 2003/431 (N.I. 9)).

Note: words in square brackets omitted and inserted in sub para (2)(a) and inserted at (2)(aa) by Regulations and Inspection of Social Care (Wales) Act 2016 (Consequential Amendments) Regulations 2018/195 (W.44)

Hospitals and hospices

4.—(1) An agreement that grants a right of occupation of accommodation in a hospital or hospice.

(2) 'Hospital'—

(a) in relation to England, has the meaning given in section 275 of the National Health Service Act 2006;

(b) in relation to Wales, has the meaning given in section 206 of the National Health Service (Wales) Act 2006;

(c) in relation to Scotland, has the meaning given in section 108 of the National Health Service (Scotland) Act 1978;

(d) in relation to Northern Ireland, has the meaning given in Article 2(2) of the Health and Personal Social Services (Northern Ireland) Order 1972 (S.I. 1972/1265 (N.I. 14)).

(3) 'Hospice' means an establishment other than a hospital whose primary function is the provision of palliative care to persons resident there who are suffering from a progressive disease in its final stages.

Other accommodation relating to healthcare provision

5.—(1) An agreement—

(a) under which accommodation is provided to a person as a result of a duty imposed on a relevant NHS body by an enactment, and

(b) which is not excluded by another provision of this Schedule.

(2) 'Relevant NHS body' means—

(a) in relation to England—

(i) [an integrated care board] or

(ii) the National Health Service Commissioning Board;

(b) in relation to Wales, a local health board;

(c) in relation to Scotland, a health board constituted by order made under section 2 of the National Health Service (Scotland) Act 1978;

(d) in relation to Northern Ireland, a Health and Social Services trust.

Note: words substituted in square brackets in sub-paragraph (2)(a)(i) by Health and Care Act 2022 c.31 Sch.4 para 208 (July 1, 2022)

Hostels and refuges

6.—(1) An agreement that grants a right of occupation of accommodation in a hostel or refuge.

(2) 'Hostel' means a building which satisfies the following two conditions.

(3) The first condition is that the building is used for providing to persons generally, or to a class of persons—

(a) residential accommodation otherwise than in separate and self contained premises, and

(b) board or facilities for the preparation of food adequate to the needs of those persons (or both).

(4) The second condition is that any of the following applies in relation to the building—

(a) it is managed by a registered housing association;

(b) it is not operated on a commercial basis and its costs of operation are provided wholly or in part by a government department or agency, or by a local authority;

(c) it is managed by a voluntary organisation or charity.

(5) 'Refuge' means a building which satisfies the second condition in subparagraph (4) and is used wholly or mainly for providing accommodation to persons who have been subject to any incident, or pattern of incidents, of—

(a) controlling, coercive or threatening behaviour,

(b) physical violence,

(c) abuse of any other description (whether physical or mental in nature), or

(d) threats of any such violence or abuse.

(6) In this paragraph—

'government department' includes—

(a) any part of the Scottish Administration;

(b) a Northern Ireland department;

(c) the Welsh Assembly Government;

(d) any body or authority exercising statutory functions on behalf of the Crown;

'registered housing association' means—

(a) a private registered provider of social housing;

(b) a registered social landlord within the meaning of Part 1 of the Housing Act 1996 or section 165 of the Housing (Scotland) Act 2010;

(c) a housing association which is registered in a register maintained under Article 14 of the Housing (Northern Ireland) Order 1992 (S.I. 1992/1725 (N.I. 15));

'voluntary organisation' means a body, other than a public or local authority, whose activities are not carried on for profit.

Accommodation from or involving local authorities

7.—(1) An agreement—

(a) under which accommodation is provided to a person as a result of a duty or relevant power that is imposed or conferred on a local authority by an enactment (whether or not provided by the local authority), and

(b) which is not excluded by another provision of this Schedule.

Accommodation provided by virtue of immigration provisions

8. An agreement that is provided to an individual by virtue of any of the following provisions of the Immigration and Asylum Act 1999—

(a) . . .

(b) section 95[or 95A] (provision of support to asylum seekers etc.);

(c) section 98[or 98A] (provision of temporary support to asylum seekers etc.).

Note: Paragraph (a) omitted, and words in square brackets inserted at paragraphs(b) and (c) by Schedule 11(1)to the Immigration Act 2016 from a date to be appointed.

[8A An agreement under which accommodation is provided to a person under arrangements made by virtue of paragraph 10A or 10B of Schedule 3 to the Nationality, Immigration and Asylum Act 2002 (support for certain persons who are otherwise ineligible for support by virtue of that Schedule).]

Note: paragraph 8A inserted by Schedule 12 para.16 to the Immigration Act 2016 from a date to be appointed

Mobile homes

9. An agreement to which the Mobile Homes Act 1983 applies.

Tied accommodation

10.—(1) An agreement that grants a right of occupation of tied accommodation.

(2) 'Tied accommodation' means accommodation that is provided—

(a) by an employer to an employee in connection with a contract of employment, or

(b) by a body providing training in a trade, profession or vocation to an individual in connection with that training.

(3) In this paragraph 'employer' and 'employee' have the same meanings as in the Employment Rights Act 1996 (see section 230 of that Act).

Student accommodation

11.—(1) An agreement that grants a right of occupation in a building which—

(a) is used wholly or mainly for the accommodation of students, and

(b) satisfies either of the following conditions.

(2) The first condition is that the building is owned or managed by any of the following—

(a) an institution within the meaning of paragraph 5 of Schedule 1 to the Local Government Finance Act 1992;

(b) a body that is specified in regulations made under Article 42(2A) of the Rates (Northern Ireland) Order 1977 (SI 1977/2157 (NI 28));

(c) a body established for charitable purposes only.

(3) The second condition is that the building is a hall of residence.

(4) In this paragraph and paragraph 12 'student'—

(a) in relation to England and Wales or Scotland, has the same meaning as in paragraph 4 of Schedule 1 to the Local Government Finance Act 1992;

(b) in relation to Northern Ireland, means a person who satisfies such conditions as to education or training as may be specified in regulations made under Article 42(2A) of the Rates (Northern Ireland) Order 1977 (SI 1977/2157 (NI 28)).

12. An agreement under which accommodation is provided to a student who has been nominated to occupy it by an institution or body of the kind mentioned in paragraph 11(2).

Long leases

13.—(1) An agreement that—

(a) is, or is for, a long lease, or

(b) grants a right of occupation for a term of 7 years or more.

(2) 'Long lease' means—

(a) in relation to England and Wales, a lease which is a long lease for the purposes of Chapter 1 of Part 1 of the Leasehold Reform, Housing and Urban Development Act 1993 or which, in the case of a shared ownership lease (within the meaning given by section 7(7) of that Act), would be such a lease if the tenant's total share (within the meaning given by that section) were 100 per cent;

(b) in relation to Scotland, has the meaning given by section 9(2) of the Land Registration (Scotland) Act 2012.

(3) An agreement does not grant a right of occupation for a term of 7 years or more if the agreement can be terminated at the option of a party before the end of 7 years from the commencement of the term.

Interpretation

14.—(1) This paragraph applies for the purposes of this Schedule.

(2) 'Building' includes a part of a building.

(3) 'Enactment' includes—

(a) an enactment contained in subordinate legislation within the meaning of the Interpretation Act 1978;

(b) an enactment contained in, or in an instrument made under, an Act of the Scottish Parliament;

(c) an enactment contained in, or in an instrument made under, a Measure or Act of the National Assembly for Wales;

(d) an enactment contained in, or in an instrument made under, Northern Ireland legislation.

(4) 'Local authority' means—

(a) in relation to England—

(i) a county, district or parish council in England,

(ii) a London borough council,

(iii) the Common Council of the City of London in its capacity as a local authority, or

(iv) the Council of the Isles of Scilly;

(b) in relation to Wales, any county, county borough or community council in Wales;

(c) in relation to Scotland, a council constituted under section 2 of the Local Government etc. (Scotland) Act 1994;

(d) in relation to Northern Ireland, a district council constituted under section 1 of the Local Government Act (Northern Ireland) 1972 (c. 9 (N.I.)).

Note: Commencement from 1 December 2014 for premises in local authorities set out in article 6 SI 2014/2771. 1 February 2016 in respect of all other premises located in England; not yet in force otherwise.

SCHEDULE 4

REFERRAL OF PROPOSED MARRIAGES AND CIVIL PARTNERSHIPS IN ENGLAND AND WALES — Section 52

. . .

Note: Commencement from 1 March 2015 (SI 2015/371).

SCHEDULE 5

Sham Marriage and Civil Partnership: ADMINISTRATIVE REGULATIONS — Section 54

Note: This Schedule sets out the kinds of regulations which may be made by the Secretary of State under s 54(2). Commencement from 20 October 2014 (SI 2014/2771).

SCHEDULE 6

INFORMATION — Section 59

PART 1

DISCLOSURE OF INFORMATION ETC. WHERE PROPOSED MARRIAGE OR CIVIL PARTNERSHIP REFERRED TO SECRETARY OF STATE

1.—(1) This paragraph applies if—

(a) a superintendent registrar refers a proposed marriage to the Secretary of State under section 28H of the Marriage Act 1949, or

(b) a registration authority refers a proposed civil partnership to the Secretary of State under section 12A of the Civil Partnership Act 2004.

(2) The Secretary of State may—

(a) disclose relevant information to a registration official, or

(b) supply a document containing relevant information to a registration official.

(3) In this paragraph 'relevant information' means any of the following information—

(a) the fact that the proposed marriage or civil partnership has been referred to the Secretary of State;

(b) the names of the parties to the proposed marriage or civil partnership;

(c) in the case of a proposed marriage—

(i) any information included with the referral in accordance with regulations under section 28H of the Marriage Act 1949;

(ii) any address of a party to the proposed marriage notified to the Secretary of State in accordance with such regulations or regulations under section 28D of the Marriage Act 1949;

(d) in the case of a proposed civil partnership—

(i) any information included with the referral in accordance with regulations under section 12A of the Civil Partnership Act 2004;

(ii) any address of a party to the proposed civil partnership notified to the Secretary of State in accordance with such regulations or regulations under section 9B of the Civil Partnership Act 2004;

(e) details of any immigration enforcement action taken by the Secretary of State in respect of a party to the proposed marriage or civil partnership (including any action taken after solemnization of the marriage or formation of the civil partnership);

(f) details of any immigration decision taken wholly or partly by reference to the marriage or civil partnership (whether while it was proposed or after it was solemnized or formed).

Part 2

Disclosure of Information etc. for Immigration Purposes etc.

Disclosures by registration officials

2.—(1) A registration official may—

(a) disclose any information held by the registration official, or

(b) supply any document held by the registration official,

to the Secretary of State, or to another registration official, for use for either of the following purposes.

(2) Those purposes are—

(a) immigration purposes;

(b) purposes connected with the exercise of functions relating to—

(i) the referral of proposed marriages to the Secretary of State under section 28H of the Marriage Act 1949, or

(ii) the referral of proposed civil partnerships to the Secretary of State under section 12A of the Civil Partnership Act 2004.

(3) In this paragraph 'immigration purposes' means—

(a) the administration of immigration control under the Immigration Acts;

(b) the prevention, detection, investigation or prosecution of criminal offences relating to immigration;

(c) the imposition of penalties or charges under Part 3 of the Immigration and Asylum Act 1999;

(d) the provision of support for asylum-seekers and their dependants under Part 6 of that Act;

(e) such other purposes as may be specified by the Secretary of State by order.

3. A registration official may disclose to another registration official—

(a) the fact that a suspicion about a marriage or civil partnership has been reported to the Secretary of State under section 24 or 24A of the Immigration and Asylum Act 1999, and

(b) the content of any such report,

(whether or not the suspicion was reported by the registration official making the disclosure).

Disclosures by the Secretary of State

4.—(1) The Secretary of State may—

(a) disclose any information held by the Secretary of State, or

(b) supply any document held by the Secretary of State, to a registration official for use for verification purposes.

(2) In this paragraph 'verification purposes' means—

(a) assisting in the verification of information provided to a relevant official by a person giving—

(i) notice of marriage under section 27 of the Marriage Act 1949, or

(ii) notice under section 8 of the Civil Partnership Act 2004;

(b) assisting in the verification of the immigration status of a person who contacts a relevant official in connection with the exercise of a function by a registration official;

(c) assisting in the verification of whether a person who contacts a relevant official in connection with the exercise of a function by a registration official—

(i) is suspected of involvement in crime relating to immigration, or

(ii) has been convicted of an offence relating to immigration.

(3) In this paragraph 'relevant official' means—

(a) a registration official, or

(b) any other person employed to assist the exercise of functions by registration officials.

Part 3
Disclosure of Information etc. for Prevention of Crime etc.

5.—(1) A registration official may—

(a) disclose any information held by the registration official, or

(b) supply any document held by the registration official,

to an eligible person, or to another registration official in England and Wales, for use for crime-fighting purposes.

(2) Information is disclosed, or a document is supplied, for use for crimefighting purposes if condition A and condition B are met.

(3) Condition A is met if the registration official disclosing the information or supplying the document has reasonable grounds for suspecting that a criminal offence has been, is being, or is going to be committed.

(4) Condition B is met if the registration official discloses the information or supplies the document for use for one or both of these purposes—

(a) assisting in the verification of information supplied to that or any other registration official;

(b) assisting in the prevention, detection, investigation or prosecution of a criminal offence.

(5) In this section 'eligible person' means—

(a) the Secretary of State;

(b) the Commissioners for Her Majesty's Revenue and Customs;

(c) a member of a police force operating in England and Wales or any part of it;

(d) a county council, a district council or a county borough council;

(e) the Greater London Authority, a London borough council or the Common Council of the City of London.

PART 4

GENERAL PROVISIONS

Limitations on powers

6. [(1)] This Schedule does not authorise—

(a) a disclosure, in contravention of any provisions of [the data protection legislation], of personal data which [is] not exempt from those provisions, or

(b) a disclosure which is prohibited by [any of Parts 1 to 7 or Chapter 1 of Part 9 of the Investigatory Powers Act 2016].

[(2)] In this paragraph, 'the data protection legislation' has the same meaning as in the Data Protection Act 2018 (see section 3 of that Act).]

Note: Words in square brackets substituted by Schedule 10 of the Investigatory Powers Act 2016. Words in square at sub para (1)(a) and inserted at (2) by Data Protection Act 2018, Sch 19 para 186 from May 25, 2018.

No breach of confidentiality etc.

7. A disclosure of information which is authorised by this Schedule does not breach—

(a) an obligation of confidence owed by the person making the disclosure, or

(b) any other restriction on the disclosure of information (however imposed).

Retention, copying and disposal of documents

8. A person to whom a document is supplied under any provision of this Schedule may—

(a) retain the document;

(b) copy the document;

(c) dispose of the document in such manner as the person thinks appropriate.

Saving for existing powers

9. This Schedule does not limit any other power under which—
(a) information may be disclosed, or
(b) documents may be supplied.

Meaning of 'registration official'

10. A 'registration official' is any of the following—
(a) the Registrar General;
(b) a superintendent registrar;
(c) a registrar;
(d) a registration authority or a person exercising the functions of a registration authority;
(e) a civil partnership registrar (within the meaning of Chapter 1 of Part 2 of the Civil Partnership Act 2004—see section 29 of that Act).

Note: Commencement from 14 July 2014 (s 75).

SCHEDULE 7

IMMIGRATION ADVISERS AND IMMIGRATION SERVICE PROVIDERS — Section 63

. . .

Note: Amends Part 5 of the Immigration and Asylum Act 1999 from a date to be appointed.

SCHEDULE 8

EMBARKATION CHECKS — Section 67

. . .

Note: Amends Sch 2 and s 27 to the Immigration Act 1971. Paragraphs (2), (8), (10(1) and (3), (11)–(16) and (32), and Parts 5 and 10 commenced 28 July 2014 (SI 2014/1820).

SCHEDULE 9

TRANSITIONAL AND CONSEQUENTIAL PROVISION — Section 73

Modern Slavery Act 2015

(2015 c.30)

Part 5
Protection of Victims

45 Defence for slavery or trafficking victims who commit an offence

(1) A person is not guilty of an offence if—

(a) the person is aged 18 or over when the person does the act which constitutes the offence,

(b) the person does that act because the person is compelled to do it,

(c) the compulsion is attributable to slavery or to relevant exploitation, and

(d) a reasonable person in the same situation as the person and having the person's relevant characteristics would have no realistic alternative to doing that act.

(2) A person may be compelled to do something by another person or by the person's circumstances.

(3) Compulsion is attributable to slavery or to relevant exploitation only if—

(a) it is, or is part of, conduct which constitutes an offence under section 1 or conduct which constitutes relevant exploitation, or

(b) it is a direct consequence of a person being, or having been, a victim of slavery or a victim of relevant exploitation.

(4) A person is not guilty of an offence if—

(a) the person is under the age of 18 when the person does the act which constitutes the offence,

(b) the person does that act as a direct consequence of the person being, or having been, a victim of slavery or a victim of relevant exploitation, and

(c) a reasonable person in the same situation as the person and having the person's relevant characteristics would do that act.

(5) For the purposes of this section—

'relevant characteristics' means age, sex and any physical or mental illness or disability;

'relevant exploitation' is exploitation (within the meaning of section 3) that is attributable to the exploited person being, or having been, a victim of human trafficking.

(6) In this section references to an act include an omission.

(7) Subsections (1) and (4) do not apply to an offence listed in Schedule 4.

(8) The Secretary of State may by regulations amend Schedule 4.

Note: Commenced from 31 July 2015 (SI 2015/1690).

46 Special measures for witnesses in criminal proceedings

(1) The Youth Justice and Criminal Evidence Act 1999 is amended as follows.

(2) In section 17(4) (witnesses eligible for assistance on grounds of fear or distress about testifying) for 'section 4 of the Asylum and Immigration (Treatment of Claimants, etc.) Act 2004' substitute 'section 1 or 2 of the Modern Slavery Act 2015'.

(3) In section 25(4)(a) (offences where court may direct evidence to be given in private) for 'section 4 of the Asylum and Immigration (Treatment of Claimants, etc.) Act 2004' substitute 'section 1 or 2 of the Modern Slavery Act 2015'.

(4) In section 33(6)(d) (offences where certain witnesses presumed to be under 18) for 'section 4 of the Asylum and Immigration (Treatment of Claimants, etc.) Act 2004' substitute 'section 1 or 2 of the Modern Slavery Act 2015'.

Note: Commenced from 31 July 2015 (SI 2015/1690).

47 Civil legal aid for victims of slavery

(1) Schedule 1 to the Legal Aid, Sentencing and Punishment of Offenders Act 2012 (availability of civil legal services) is amended as follows.

(2) In Part 1 (services), after paragraph 32 insert—

Victims of slavery, servitude or forced or compulsory labour

32A (1) Civil legal services provided to an individual in relation to an application by the individual for leave to enter, or to remain in, the United Kingdom where—

(a) there has been a conclusive determination that the individual is a victim of slavery, servitude or forced or compulsory labour, or

(b) there are reasonable grounds to believe that the individual is such a victim and there has not been a conclusive determination that the individual is not such a victim.

(2) Civil legal services provided in relation to a claim under employment law arising in connection with the conduct by virtue of which an individual who is a victim of slavery, servitude or forced or compulsory labour is such a victim, but only where—

(a) the services are provided to the individual, or

(b) the individual has died and the services are provided to the individual's personal representative.

(3) Civil legal services provided in relation to a claim for damages arising in connection with the conduct by virtue of which an individual who is a victim of slavery, servitude or forced or compulsory labour is such a victim, but only where—

(a) the services are provided to the individual, or

(b) the individual has died and the services are provided to the individual's personal representative.

Exclusions

(4) Sub-paragraph (1) is subject to the exclusions in Parts 2 and 3 of this Schedule.

(5) Sub-paragraphs (2) and (3) are subject to—

(a) the exclusions in Part 2 of this Schedule, with the exception of paragraphs 1, 2, 3, 4, 5, 6 and 8 of that Part, and (b) the exclusion in Part 3 of this Schedule.

Definitions

(6) For the purposes of sub-paragraph (1)(b) there are reasonable grounds to believe that an individual is a victim of slavery, servitude or forced or compulsory labour if a competent authority has determined that there are such grounds.

(7) For the purposes of sub-paragraph (1) there is a conclusive determination that an individual is or is not a victim of slavery, servitude or forced or compulsory labour when a competent authority concludes that the individual is or is not such a victim.

(8) For the purposes of this paragraph 'slavery', 'servitude' and 'forced or compulsory labour' have the same meaning as they have for the purposes of article 4 of the Human Rights Convention.

(9) The 'Human Rights Convention' means the Convention for the Protection of Human Rights and Fundamental Freedoms, agreed by the Council of Europe at Rome on 4 November 1950, as it has effect for the time being in relation to the United Kingdom.

(10) The definitions of 'competent authority', 'employment', 'employment law' and 'personal representative' in paragraph 32(8) also apply for the purposes of this paragraph.'

(3) In Part 3 (advocacy: exclusion and exceptions), in paragraph 13 for 'or 32(1)' substitute ', 32(1) or 32A(1)'.

Note: Commenced from 31 July 2015 (SI 2015/1476).

48 Independent child trafficking advocates

(1) The Secretary of State must make such arrangements as the Secretary of State considers reasonable to enable persons ('independent child trafficking advocates') to be available to represent and support children who there are reasonable grounds to believe may be victims of human trafficking.

(2) In making arrangements under subsection (1) the Secretary of State must have regard to the principle that, so far as practicable, a child should be represented and supported by someone who is independent of any person who will be responsible for making decisions about the child.

(3) The arrangements may include provision for payments to be made to, or in relation to, persons carrying out functions in accordance with the arrangements.

(4) A person appointed as an independent child trafficking advocate for a child must promote the child's well-being and act in the child's best interests.

(5) The advocate may (where appropriate) assist the child to obtain legal or other advice, assistance and representation, including (where necessary) by appointing and instructing legal representatives to act on the child's behalf.

(6) The Secretary of State must make regulations about independent child trafficking advocates, and the regulations must in particular make provision—

(a) about the circumstances in which, and any conditions subject to which, a person may act as an independent child trafficking advocate;

(b) for the appointment of a person as an independent child trafficking advocate to be subject to approval in accordance with the regulations;

(c) requiring an independent child trafficking advocate to be appointed for a child as soon as reasonably practicable, where there are reasonable grounds to believe a child may be a victim of human trafficking;

(d) about the functions of independent child trafficking advocates;

(e) requiring public authorities which provide services or take decisions in relation to a child for whom an independent child trafficking advocate has been appointed to—

(i) recognise, and pay due regard to, the advocate's functions, and

(ii) provide the advocate with access to such information relating to the child as will enable the advocate to carry out those functions effectively (so far as the authority may do so without contravening a restriction on disclosure of the information).

(7) The Secretary of State must, no later than 9 months after the day on which this Act is passed, lay before Parliament a report on the steps the Secretary of State proposes to take in relation to the powers conferred by this section.

Note: Section 48(7) commenced from 26 May 2015. Other subsections to be commenced from a date to be appointed.

49 Guidance about identifying and supporting victims

(1) The Secretary of State must issue guidance to such public authorities and other persons as the Secretary of State considers appropriate about—

(a) the sorts of things which indicate that a person may be a victim of slavery or human trafficking;

(b) arrangements for providing assistance and support to persons who there are reasonable grounds to believe[are] victims of slavery or human trafficking [or who are such victims];

(c) arrangements for determining whether there are reasonable grounds to believe that a person [is] a victim of slavery or human trafficking;

(d) arrangements for determining whether a person is a victim of slavery or human trafficking].

[(1A) Guidance issued under subsection (1) must, in particular. Provide that the determination mentioned in paragraph (d) is to be made on the balance of probabilities].

(2) The Secretary of State may, from time to time, revise the guidance issued under subsection (1).

(3) The Secretary of State must arrange for any guidance issued or revised under this section to be published in a way the Secretary of State considers appropriate.

(4) If the Secretary of State makes regulations under section 50, the references in subsection (1) to 'arrangements' include arrangements under the regulations.

Note: Commenced 15 October 2015 (SI 2015/1690). Words in square brackets in subsections (1)(b) (c) & (d) substituted and subsection (1A) inserted by Nationality and Borders Act 2022 c.36 Pt5 s.60 ((date to be appointed).

50 Regulations about identifying and supporting victims

(1) The Secretary of State may make regulations providing for assistance and support to be provided to persons—

(a) who there are reasonable grounds to believe [are] victims of slavery or human trafficking;

(b) who are victims of slavery or human trafficking.

(2) The Secretary of State may make regulations providing for public authorities to determine (for the purposes of regulations under subsection (1) or other purposes specified in the regulations) whether—

(a) there are reasonable grounds to believe that a person [is] a victim of slavery or human trafficking;

(b) a person is a victim of slavery or human trafficking.

(3) Regulations under subsection (2) may in particular make provision about the public authorities who may make such determinations, and the criteria and procedure for doing so.

[(4) If regulations under subsection (2) make provision for determining whether a person is a victim of slavery or human trafficking (as mentioned in paragraph (b) of that subsection), they must provide that the determination is to be made on the balance of probabilities.]

Note: To be commenced from a date to be appointed. Words substituted at subsection (1)(a) & (2)(a) and inserted at subsection (4) by Nationality and Borders Act 2022 c.36 Pt5 s.60(5) (date to be appointed)

51 Presumption about age

(1) This section applies where—

(a) a public authority with functions under relevant arrangements has reasonable grounds to believe that a person [is]a victim of human trafficking, and

(b) the authority is not certain of the person's age but has reasonable grounds to believe that the person may be under 18.

(2) Until an assessment of the person's age is carried out by a local authority or the person's age is otherwise determined, the public authority must assume for the purposes of its functions under relevant arrangements that the person is under 18.

(3) 'Relevant arrangements' means arrangements for providing assistance and support to persons who are, or who there are reasonable grounds to believe [are], victims of human trafficking, as set out in—

(a) guidance issued under section 49(1)(b); (b) any regulations made under section 50(1).

(4) 'Local authority' has the same meaning as in the Children Act 1989 (see section 105 of that Act).

Note: Commenced from 15 October 2015 (SI 2015/1690). Words in square brackets substituted in subsection (2) & (3) by Nationality and Borders Act 2022 c.36 Pt 5 S.60(6) (date to be appointed)

52 Duty to notify Secretary of State about suspected victims of slavery or human trafficking

(1) If a public authority to which this section applies has reasonable grounds to believe that a person may be a victim of slavery or human trafficking it must notify—

(a) the Secretary of State, or

(b) if regulations made by the Secretary of State require it to notify a public authority other than the Secretary of State, that public authority.

(2) The Secretary of State may by regulations make provision about the information to be included in a notification.

(3) Regulations under subsection (2) must provide that a notification relating to a person aged 18 or over may not include information that—

(a) identifies the person, or

(b) enables the person to be identified (either by itself or in combination with other information), unless the person consents to the inclusion of the information.

(4) Regulations under subsection (2)—

(a) may provide that a public authority which includes information in a notification in accordance with the regulations does not breach any obligation of confidence owed by the public authority in relation to that information;

(b) may not require or authorise the inclusion of information which contravenes any other restriction on the disclosure of information (however imposed).

(5) This section applies to—

(a) a chief officer of police for a police area,

(b) the chief constable of the British Transport Police Force,

(c) the National Crime Agency,

(d) a county council,

(e) a county borough council,

(f) a district council,

(g) a London borough council,

(h) the Greater London Authority,

(i) the Common Council of the City of London,

(j) the Council of the Isles of Scilly,

(k) [Gangmasters and Labour Abuse Authority].

(6) The Secretary of State may by regulations amend subsection (5) so as to—

(a) add or remove a public authority;

(b) amend the entry for a public authority.

Note: Commenced from 1 November 2015 (SI 2015/1690). Words in square brackets substituted by Schedule 3 to the Immigration Act 2016 from 12 July 2016 (SI 2016/603).

53 Overseas domestic workers

(1) Immigration rules must make provision for leave to remain in the United Kingdom to be granted to an overseas domestic worker—

(a) who has been determined to be a victim of slavery or human trafficking, and

(b) in relation to whom such other requirements are met as may be provided for by the rules.

(2) Immigration rules must make provision as to the conditions on which such leave is to be granted, and must in particular provide—

(a) that the leave is to be for the purpose of working as a domestic worker in a private household;

(b) for a person who has such leave to be able to change employer (subject to paragraph (a)).

(3) Immigration rules may specify a maximum period for which a person may have leave to remain in the United Kingdom by virtue of subsection (1). If they do so, the specified maximum period must not be less than 6 months.

(4) For the purposes of this section an overseas domestic worker has been determined to be a victim of slavery or human trafficking if a public authority has determined that he or she is such a victim—

(a) under regulations made under section 50(2)(b), or

(b) where no such regulations apply, under arrangements identified in the immigration rules.

(5) The Secretary of State must issue guidance to persons having functions under the Immigration Acts about the exercise of those functions in relation to an overseas domestic worker who may be a victim of slavery or human trafficking.

(6) The guidance must provide for a period during which no enforcement action should be taken against such an overseas domestic worker in respect of his or her—

(a) remaining in the United Kingdom beyond the time limited by his or her leave to enter or remain, or

(b) breaching a condition of that leave relating to his or her employment, if he or she did so because of the matters relied on as slavery or human trafficking.

(7) In this section—

'enforcement action' has the meaning given by section 24A of the Immigration Act 1971;

'immigration rules' has the same meaning as in that Act;

'overseas domestic worker' means a person who, under the immigration rules, has (or last had) leave to enter or remain in the United Kingdom as—

(a) a domestic worker in a private household, or

(b) a private servant in a diplomatic household.

Note: Commenced 15 October 2015 (SI 2015/1690).

Immigration Act 2016

Chapter 19

Contents

Part 1

Labour Market and Illegal Working

Chapter 1

Labour Market

Director of Labour Market Enforcement

Gangmasters and Labour Abuse Authority

Labour market enforcement undertakings

Labour market enforcement orders

Part 6

Border Security

Part 7

Language Requirements for Public Sector Workers

Part 8

Fees and Charges

Immigration

Passports and civil registration

Part 9

Miscellaneous and General

Welfare of children

Final provisions

An Act to make provision about the law on immigration and asylum; to make provision about access to services, facilities, licences and work by reference to immigration status; to make provision about the enforcement of certain legislation relating to the labour market; to make provision about language requirements for public sector workers; to make provision about fees for passports and civil registration; and for connected purposes. [12th May 2016] BE IT ENACTED by the Queen's most Excellent Majesty, by and with the advice and consent of the Lords Spiritual and Temporal, and Commons, in this present Parliament assembled, and by the authority of the same, as follows:—

PART 1

LABOUR MARKET AND ILLEGAL WORKING

CHAPTER 1

LABOUR MARKET

Director of Labour Market Enforcement

1 Director of Labour Market Enforcement

Note: Commenced 12 July 2016 (SI 2016/603).

2 Labour market enforcement strategy

Note: Commenced 12 July 2016 (SI 2016/603).

3 Non-compliance in the labour market etc: interpretation

Note: Commenced 12 July 2016 (SI 2016/603).

4 Annual and other reports

Note: Commenced 12 July 2016 (SI 2016/603).

5 Publication of strategy and reports

Note: Commenced 12 July 2016 (SI 2016/603).

6 Information gateways

Note: Commenced 12 July 2016 (SI 2016/603).

7 Information gateways: supplementary

Note: Commenced 12 July 2016 (SI 2016/603).

8 Information hub

Note: Commenced 12 July 2016 (SI 2016/603).

9 Restriction on exercising functions in relation to individual cases

Note: Commenced 12 July 2016 (SI 2016/603).

Gangmasters and Labour Abuse Authority

10 Renaming of Gangmasters Licensing Authority

Note: Commenced 12 July 2016 (SI 2016/603).

11 Functions in relation to labour market

Note: Commenced 12 July 2016 (SI 2016/603).

12 PACE powers in England and Wales for labour abuse prevention officers

Note: Commenced 12 July 2016 (SI 2016/603).

13 Relationship with other agencies: requests for assistance

Note: Commenced 12 July 2016 (SI 2016/603).

Labour market enforcement undertakings

14 Power to request LME undertaking

Note: Commenced 25 November 2016 (SI 2016/1037).

15 Measures in LME undertakings

Note: Commenced 25 November 2016 (SI 2016/1037).

16 Duration

Note: Commenced 25 November 2016 (SI 2016/1037).

17 Further provision about giving notice under section 14

Note: Commenced 25 November 2016 (SI 2016/1037).

Labour market enforcement orders

18 Power to make LME order on application

Note: Commenced 25 November 2016 (SI 2016/1037).

19 Applications

Note: Commenced 25 November 2016 (SI 2016/1037).

20 Power to make LME order on conviction

Note: Commenced 25 November 2016 (SI 2016/1037).

21 Measures in LME orders

Note: Commenced 25 November 2016 (SI 2016/1037).

22 Further provision about LME orders

Note: Commenced 25 November 2016 (SI 2016/1037).

23 Variation and discharge

Note: Commenced 25 November 2016 (SI 2016/1037).

24 Appeals

Note: Commenced 25 November 2016 (SI 2016/1037).

LME undertakings and orders: supplementary

25 Code of practice

Note: Commenced 12 July 2016 (SI 2016/603).

26 Investigative functions

Note: Commenced 25 November 2016 (SI 2016/1037).

27 Offence

Note: Commenced 25 November 2016 (SI 2016/1037).

28 Offences by bodies corporate

Note: Commenced 25 November 2016 (SI 2016/1037).

29 Application to unincorporated associations

Note: Commenced 25 November 2016 (SI 2016/1037).

30 Application to partnerships

Note: Commenced 25 November 2016 (SI 2016/1037).

Supplementary provision

31 Consequential and related amendments

Note: Commenced 12 July 2016 (SI 2016/603).

32 Regulations under Chapter 1

Note: Commenced 12 July 2016 (SI 2016/603).

33 Interpretation of Chapter 1

Note: Commenced 12 July 2016 (SI 2016/603).

Chapter 2
Illegal Working
Offences

34 Offence of illegal working

Note: Commenced 12 July 2016 (SI 2016/603). This section amends the Immigration Act 1971 as follows: subsection (2) amends section 3(1)(c)(i); subsection (3) inserts 24B; subsection (4) amends section 28A(3)(a); subsection (5) amends section 28B(5); subsection (6) amends section 28CA(1); subsection (7) amends section 28D(4); and subsection (8) amends section 28FA(1)(a) of that Act.

35 Offence of employing illegal worker

Note: Commenced 12 July 2016 (SI 2016/603). This section amends the Immigration, Asylum and Nationality Act 2006 and the Immigration Act 1971. Subsections (2)–(4) amend section 21 of that Act; subsections (5)–(7) amend section 22; subsection (8) amends section 24 of the Immigration, Asylum and Nationality Act 2006. Subsection (9) amends section 28A, and subsection (10) amends section 28AA(1) of the Immigration Act 1971.

Illegal working in licensed premises

36 Licensing Act 2003: amendments relating to illegal working

(1) Schedule 4 (Licensing Act 2003: amendments relating to illegal working) has effect.

(2) The Secretary of State may by regulations make provision which—
 (a) has a similar effect to the amendments made by Schedule 4, and
 (b) applies in relation to Scotland or Northern Ireland.

(3) Regulations under subsection (2) may—
 (a) amend, repeal or revoke any enactment;
 (b) confer functions on any person.

(4) Regulations under subsection (2) may not confer functions on—
 (a) the Scottish Ministers,
 (b) the First Minister and deputy First Minister in Northern Ireland,
 (c) a Northern Ireland Minister, or
 (d) a Northern Ireland department.

(5) In this section 'enactment' includes—

(a) an enactment contained in subordinate legislation within the meaning of the Interpretation Act 1978;

(b) an enactment contained in, or in an instrument made under, an Act of the Scottish Parliament;

(c) an enactment contained in, or in an instrument made under, Northern Ireland legislation.

Note: Commenced 6 April 2017 (SI 2017/380).

Illegal working in relation to private hire vehicles etc

37 Private hire vehicles etc

Schedule 5 (private hire vehicles etc) has effect.

Note: Commenced 1 December 2016 (SI 2016/1037).

Illegal working notices and orders

38 Illegal working closure notices and illegal working compliance orders

Schedule 6 (illegal working closure notices and illegal working compliance orders) has effect.

Note: Commenced 1 December 2016 (SI 2016/1037).

Part 2

Access to Services

Residential tenancies

39 Offence of leasing premises

Note: Commenced from 1 December 2016 (SI 2016/1037). Subsection (2) inserts section 33A, 33B and 33C in the Immigration Act 2014. Subsections (3), (4) and (5) amend the Immigration Act 2014. Subsection (6) inserts subsection (9C) in the Immigration Act 1971 and amends subsection (10) and (11) of this Act.

40 Eviction

Note: Inserts section 33D and 33E in the Immigration Act 2014 from 1 December 2016 (SI 2016/1037). Subsection (3) inserts section 35(7) and subsection (4) inserts section 37(4)(a)(v) and (vi) in the Immigration Act 2014 from 1 December 2014 (SI 2016/1037). Subsection (5)–(7) amend other acts not relevant to immigration law.

41 Order for possession of dwelling-house

Note: Amends the Housing Act 1988 from 1 December 2016 (SI 2016/1037).

42 Extension to Wales, Scotland and Northern Ireland

Note: Commencement from a date to be appointed.

Driving

43 Powers to carry out searches relating to driving licences

(1) . . .

(2) . . .

(3) . . .

(4) . . .

(5) In the period (if any) between the coming into force of subsection (2) and the coming into force of the Departments Act (Northern Ireland) 2016, references to the Department for Infrastructure for Northern Ireland in paragraph 25CC(3)(b), (8) and (9)(b) of Schedule 2 to the Immigration Act 1971 (as inserted by subsection (2)) are to be read as references to the Department of the Environment for Northern Ireland.

Note: Inserts paragraphs 25CA, 25CB and 25CC in Schedule 2 to the Immigration Act 1971; subsection 3 amends paragraph 25D(8) of Schedule 2 to the Immigration Act 1971; subsection (4) amends section 146(2) of the Immigration and Asylum Act 1999 on a date to be appointed. Comes into force on 31 July 2017 in the police areas of Kent and West Yorkshire (SI 2017/799).

44 Offence of driving when unlawfully in the United Kingdom

Note: Subsection (2) inserts 24C, 24D, 24E, 24F in the Immigration Act 1971 on date to be appointed. Subsections (3)–(6) amend the Immigration Act 1971 on date to be appointed. Subsection (7) amends section 16(2A)(b) of the Police and Criminal Evidence Act 1984 on date to be appointed. Subsection (8) amends Article 18(2A(b) of the Police and Criminal Evidence (Northern Ireland) Order 1989 (SI 1989/1341 (NI 12)) on date to be appointed. Subsection (9) amends 146(2) of the Immigration and Asylum Act 1999 on a date to be appointed.

Bank accounts

45 Bank accounts

(1) Schedule 7 (bank accounts) has effect.

(2) Before the end of the period mentioned in subsection (3), the Secretary of State must—

(a) review the operation of sections 40A to 40G of the Immigration Act 2014 (inserted by Schedule 7),

(b) prepare a report of the review, and

(c) lay a copy of the report before Parliament.

(3) The period referred to in subsection (2) is the period of 5 years beginning with the day on which Schedule 7 comes fully into force.

Note: Commenced from 30 October 2017 (SI 2017/929).

PART 3
ENFORCEMENT

Powers of immigration officers etc

46 Powers in connection with examination, detention and removal—

Note: Subsection (2) inserts paragraph 2(1)(d) to Schedule 2 of the Immigration Act 1971. Subsection (3) inserts 15A to Schedule 2 of the Immigration Act 1971. Subsection (4) inserts paragraph 25A(7A) to Schedule 2 to the Immigration Act 1971, and amends subparagraph (8) and (9) of the same. Subsection (5) inserts sub-paragraph 8 to Schedule 2 to the Immigration Act 1971. Commenced 12 July 2016 (SI 2016/603).

47 Search of premises in connection with imposition of civil penalty

(1) This section applies if an immigration officer is lawfully on any premises.

(2) The immigration officer may search the premises for documents which might be of assistance in determining whether a person is liable to the imposition of a penalty under—

(a) section 15 of the Immigration, Asylum and Nationality Act 2006 (penalty for employing illegal worker etc), or

(b) section 23 or 25 of the Immigration Act 2014 (penalty for leasing premises to disqualified person etc).

(3) The power may be exercised—

(a) only if the immigration officer has reasonable grounds for believing there are documents within subsection (2) on the premises, and

(b) only to the extent that it is reasonably required for the purpose of discovering such documents.

(4) An immigration officer searching premises under this section may seize any document the officer finds which the officer has reasonable grounds for believing is a document within subsection (2).

(5) Subsection (6) applies where—

(a) an immigration officer is searching premises under this section, and

(b) any document the officer has reasonable grounds for believing is a document within subsection (2) is stored in any electronic form and is accessible from the premises.

(6) The immigration officer may require the document to be produced in a form in which it can be taken away and in which it is visible and legible or from which it can readily be produced in a visible and legible form.

(7) If a requirement under subsection (6) is not complied with or a document to which that subsection applies cannot be produced in a form of the kind mentioned in that subsection, the immigration officer may seize the device or medium on which it is stored.

(8) But subsections (4) to (7) do not apply to a document or item which the immigration officer has reasonable grounds for believing is an item subject to legal privilege.

(9) An immigration officer may retain a document or item seized under this section while the officer has reasonable grounds for believing that the document may be required—

(a) for the purposes of determining whether a person is liable to the imposition of a penalty under a provision mentioned in subsection (2),

(b) for the purposes of any objection relating to the imposition of such a penalty, or

(c) for the purposes of any appeal or other legal proceedings relating to the imposition of such a penalty.

(10) But a document or item may not be retained for a purpose mentioned in subsection (9) if a photograph or copy would be sufficient for that purpose.

(11) Section 28I of the Immigration Act 1971 (seized material: access and copying) applies to a document seized and retained under this section as it applies to anything seized and retained under Part 3 of that Act.

Note: Commenced 12 July 2016 (SI 2016/603).

48 Seizure and retention in relation to offences

(1) This section applies if an immigration officer is lawfully on any premises.

(2) The immigration officer may seize anything which the officer finds in the course of exercising a function under the Immigration Acts if the officer has reasonable grounds for believing—

(a) that it has been obtained in consequence of the commission of an offence, and

(b) that it is necessary to seize it in order to prevent it being concealed, lost, damaged, altered or destroyed.

(3) The immigration officer may seize anything which the officer finds in the course of exercising a function under the Immigration Acts if the officer has reasonable grounds for believing—

(a) that it is evidence in relation to an offence, and

(b) that it is necessary to seize it in order to prevent the evidence being concealed, lost, altered or destroyed.

(4) The immigration officer may require any information which is stored in any electronic form and is accessible from the premises to be produced if the officer has reasonable grounds for believing—

(a) that—

(i) it is evidence in relation to an offence, or

(ii) it has been obtained in consequence of the commission of an offence, and

(b) that it is necessary to seize it in order to prevent it being concealed, lost, tampered with or destroyed.

(5) The reference in subsection (4) to information which is stored in any electronic form being produced is to such information being produced in a form—

(a) in which it can be taken away, and

(b) in which it is visible and legible or from which it can readily be produced in a visible and legible form.

(6) This section does not authorise an immigration officer to seize an item which the officer has reasonable grounds for believing is an item subject to legal privilege.

(7) Anything seized by an immigration officer under this section which relates to an immigration offence may be retained so long as is necessary in all the circumstances and in particular—

(a) may be retained, except as provided for by subsection (8)—

(i) for use as evidence at a trial for an offence, or

(ii) for forensic examination or for investigation in connection with an offence, and

(b) may be retained in order to establish its lawful owner, where there are reasonable grounds for believing that it has been obtained in consequence of the commission of an offence.

(8) Nothing may be retained for a purpose mentioned in subsection (7)(a) if a photograph or copy would be sufficient for that purpose.

(9) Section 28I of the Immigration Act 1971 (seized material: access and copying) applies to anything seized and retained under this section which relates to an immigration offence as it applies to anything seized and retained by an immigration officer under Part 3 of that Act.

(10) This section does not apply in relation to anything which may be seized by an immigration officer under—

(a) section 19 of the Police and Criminal Evidence Act 1984 as applied by an order under section 23 of the Borders, Citizenship and Immigration Act 2009, or

(b) Article 21 of the Police and Criminal Evidence (Northern Ireland) Order 1989 (SI 1989/1341 (NI 12) as applied by that section.

(11) In this section and section 49 'immigration offence' means an offence which relates to an immigration or nationality matter.

Note: Commenced 12 July 2016 (SI 2016/603).

49 Duty to pass on items seized under section 48

(1) This section applies if an immigration officer exercises—

(a) the power under section 48 to seize or take away an item on the basis that the item or information contained in it has been obtained in consequence of the commission of, or is evidence in relation to, an offence other than an immigration offence (a 'relevant offence'), or

(b) a power to that effect in Part 3 of the Immigration Act 1971 as applied by section 14(3) of the Asylum and Immigration (Treatment of Claimants etc) Act 2004.

(2) Subject to subsection (3), the immigration officer must, as soon as is reasonably practicable after the power is exercised, notify a person who the immigration officer thinks has functions in relation to the investigation of the relevant offence.

(3) If the immigration officer has reasonable grounds for believing that the item referred to in subsection (1) has also been obtained in consequence of the commission of, or is evidence in relation to, an immigration offence, the immigration officer may notify a person who the immigration officer thinks has functions in relation to the investigation of the relevant offence.

(4) A person notified under this section of the exercise of a power mentioned in subsection (1) in relation to an item must, as soon as is reasonably practicable after being so notified, inform the immigration officer whether the person will accept the item.

(5) The person may inform the immigration officer that the person will not accept the item only if—

(a) the person does not think the item or information contained in it has been obtained in consequence of the commission of, or is evidence in relation to, an offence,

(b) the person does not have functions in relation to the investigation of the relevant offence, or

(c) the person thinks that it would be more appropriate for the relevant offence to be investigated by another person with such functions.

(6) If the person informs the immigration officer that the person will accept the item, the immigration officer must give it to the person as soon as is reasonably practicable.

(7) Once the item has been given as mentioned in subsection (6), any provision of an enactment which applies to items seized or taken away by the person applies to the item as if it had been seized or taken away by the person for the purposes of the investigation of the relevant offence.

(8) If the person informs the immigration officer that the person will not accept the item because subsection (5)(a) applies, the immigration officer must, as soon as is reasonably practicable, return the item in accordance with subsection (10).

(9) If the person informs the immigration officer that the person will not accept the item because subsection (5)(b) or (c) applies, the immigration officer must, as soon as is reasonably practicable—

(a) notify the exercise of a power mentioned in subsection (1) in relation to the item to another person (if any) who the immigration officer thinks has functions in relation to the investigation of the relevant offence, or

(b) if there is no such person, return the item in accordance with subsection (10).

(10) An item which must be returned in accordance with this subsection must be returned—

(a) to the person from whom it was seized, or

(b) if there is no such person, to the place from which it was seized or taken away.

(11) Where an item to which this section applies or information contained in such an item has been obtained in consequence of the commission of, or is evidence in relation to, more than one offence, references in this section to the relevant offence are to any of those offences.

(12) A function conferred or imposed by this section on an immigration officer may be exercised by any other immigration officer.

(13) In this section 'enactment' includes—

(a) an enactment contained in subordinate legislation within the meaning of the Interpretation Act 1978,

(b) an enactment contained in, or in an instrument made under, an Act of the Scottish Parliament,

(c) an enactment contained in, or in an instrument made under, a Measure or Act of the National Assembly for Wales, and

(d) an enactment contained in, or in an instrument made under, Northern Ireland legislation.

Note: Commenced 12 July 2016 (SI 2016/603).

50 Retention of things seized under Part 3 of the Immigration Act 1971

Note: Inserts section 28ZI of the Immigration Act 1971 from 12 July 2016 (SI 2016/603).

51 Search for nationality documents by detainee custody officers etc

(1) The Secretary of State may direct a detainee custody officer, prison officer or prisoner custody officer to exercise any of the powers in subsection (6) in relation to—

(a) a detained person who is detained in a removal centre, prison or young offender institution, or

(b) a person who is detained in a short-term holding facility.

(2) The Secretary of State may direct a prison officer or prisoner custody officer to exercise any of the powers in subsection (6) in relation to a person detained in a prison or young offender institution—

(a) who has been recommended for deportation by a court under section 3(6) of the Immigration Act 1971,

(b) in respect of whom the Secretary of State has made a deportation order under section 5(1) of that Act,

(c) to whom a notice has been given in accordance with regulations under section 105 of the Nationality, Immigration and Asylum Act 2002 (notice of decision) of a decision to make a deportation order against that person, or

(d) in respect of whom the Secretary of State must make, or has made, a deportation order under section 32(5) of the UK Borders Act 2007.

(3) In this section and section 52 'relevant officer' means a detainee custody officer, prison officer or prisoner custody officer.

(4) The Secretary of State may give a direction in relation to a person detained as mentioned in subsection (1) or (2) only if the Secretary of State has reasonable grounds to believe a relevant nationality document will be found if a power in subsection (6) is exercised in relation to the person.

(5) A relevant officer to whom a direction is given under subsection (1) or (2) must (if able to do so) comply with it.

(6) The powers referred to in subsections (1), (2) and (4) are—

(a) to require the person to hand over to the relevant officer all relevant nationality documents in his or her possession,

(b) to search for such documents and to take possession of any that the relevant officer finds,

(c) to inspect any relevant nationality documents obtained in the course of the exercise of a power in paragraph (a) or (b), and

(d) to seize and retain any such documents so obtained.

(7) The power in subsection (6)(b) is a power to search any of the following—

(a) the person;

(b) anything the person has with him or her;

(c) the person's accommodation in the removal centre, short-term holding facility, prison or young offender institution;

(d) any item of the person's property in the removal centre, short-term holding facility, prison or young offender institution.

(8) A full search may be carried out under subsection (7)(a); but such a search may not be carried out in the presence of—

(a) another person detained as mentioned in subsection (1) or (2), or

(b) a person of the opposite sex.

(9) An intimate search may not be carried out under subsection (7)(a).

(10) A relevant officer may if necessary use reasonable force for the purposes of exercising a power in subsection (6)(a) or (b).

(11) A relevant officer must pass a relevant nationality document seized and retained under subsection (6)(d) to the Secretary of State as soon as is reasonably practicable.

(12) The Secretary of State may retain a relevant nationality document which comes into the Secretary of State's possession under subsection (11) while the Secretary of State suspects that—

(a) a person to whom the document relates may be liable to removal from the United Kingdom in accordance with a provision of the Immigration Acts, and

(b) retention of the document may facilitate the removal.

(13) If subsection (12) does not apply to a document which comes into the Secretary of State's possession under this section, the Secretary of State may—

(a) arrange for the document to be returned in accordance with subsection (14), or

(b) if the Secretary of State thinks that it would not be appropriate to return the document, dispose of the document in such manner as the Secretary of State thinks appropriate.

(14) A document which is required to be returned in accordance with this subsection must be returned to—

(a) the person who was previously in possession of it, or

(b) if it was not found in the possession of a person, the location in which it was found.

(15) In this section and section 52—

'full search' means a search which involves the removal of an item of clothing which—

(a) is being worn wholly or partly on the trunk, and

(b) is being so worn either next to the skin or next to an article of underwear;

'intimate search' means a search which consists of a physical examination of a person's body orifices other than the mouth;

'nationality document' means a document which might—

(a) establish a person's identity, nationality or citizenship, or

(b) indicate the place from which a person has travelled to the United Kingdom or to which a person is proposing to go.

(16) For the purposes of this section and section 52 a nationality document is 'relevant' if it relates to a person who is liable to removal from the United Kingdom in accordance with a provision of the Immigration Acts.

(17) In this section the following expressions have the same meaning as in Part 8 of the Immigration and Asylum Act 1999 (see section 147)—

'detained person'; 'detainee custody officer'; 'prisoner custody officer'; 'removal centre'; 'short-term holding facility'.

Note: Commenced 12 July 2016 (SI 2016/603).

52 Seizure of nationality documents by detainee custody officers etc

(1) A relevant officer may seize a nationality document which the relevant officer finds in the course of the exercise of a power to search other than one conferred by section 51.

(2) Where a relevant officer seizes a nationality document under subsection (1), the relevant officer—

(a) must seek the consent of the Secretary of State to retain the document, and

(b) if the relevant officer obtains the Secretary of State's consent, must pass the document to the Secretary of State as soon as is practicable.

(3) The Secretary of State may give consent under subsection (2) only if the Secretary of State has reasonable grounds to believe that—

(a) the document is a relevant nationality document, and

(b) the document may facilitate the removal of the person to whom it relates from the United Kingdom in accordance with a provision of the Immigration Acts.

(4) If the Secretary of State does not give consent under subsection (2), the Secretary of State must—

(a) direct the relevant officer to return the document as mentioned in subsection (5), or

(b) if the Secretary of State thinks that it would not be appropriate to return the document, direct the relevant officer to dispose of the document in such manner as the Secretary of State may direct.

(5) A document which is required to be returned in accordance with this subsection must be returned to—

(a) the person who was previously in possession of it, or

(b) if it was not found in the possession of a person, the location in which it was found.

(6) The Secretary of State may retain a relevant nationality document which comes into the Secretary of State's possession under this section while the Secretary of State suspects that—

(a) a person to whom the document relates may be liable to removal from the United Kingdom in accordance with a provision of the Immigration Acts, and

(b) retention of the document may facilitate the removal.

(7) If subsection (6) does not apply to a document which comes into the Secretary of State's possession under this section, the Secretary of State may—

(a) arrange for the document to be returned in accordance with subsection (5), or

(b) if the Secretary of State thinks that it would not be appropriate to return the document, dispose of the document in such manner as the Secretary of State thinks appropriate.

Note: Commenced 12 July 2016 (SI 2016/603).

53 Amendments relating to sections 51 and 52

Note: Commenced 12 July 2016 (SI 2016/603).

54 Amendments to search warrant provisions

Schedule 8 (amendments to search warrant provisions) has effect.

Note: Commenced 1 December 2016 (SI 2016/1037).

55 Supply of information to Secretary of State

Note: Subsections (1)–(10) amend section 20 of the Immigration and Asylum Act 1999 from 12 July 2016. Subsection (5) inserts subsection (1A), subsection (6) inserts subsection (2B), subsection (7) inserts subsection (3)(da), subsection (8) inserts subsection (3A) to section 20 of the Immigration and Asylum Act 1999 from 12 July 2016. Subsection (9) omits subsection (4) of the section 20 of the Immigration and Asylum Act 1999. Subsection (10) inserts subsection (7) to section 20 of the Immigration and Asylum Act 1999. Subsection (11) inserts section 20A to the Immigration and Asylum Act 1999. Subsection (12) inserts subsection (5A) at section 166 of the Immigration and Asylum Act 1999. Section 13 inserts Schedule 9 of this Act at Schedule A1 to the Immigration and Asylum Act 1999. Commenced 12 July 2016 (SI 2016/603).

56 Detention etc. by immigration officers in Scotland

Note: Amends the Criminal Law (Consolidation) (Scotland) Act 1995. Commenced 12 July 2016 (SI 2016/603).

57 Powers to take fingerprints etc. from dependants

Note: Subsections (1)–(6) amend section 141 of the Immigration and Asylum Act 1999. Subsections (7)–(9) amend section 142 of the Immigration and Asylum Act 1999. Subsection (11) amends section 144A of the Immigration and Asylum Act 1999. Commenced on 12 July 2016 (SI 2016/603).

58 Interpretation of Part

(1) In this Part 'immigration officer' means a person appointed by the Secretary of State as an immigration officer under paragraph 1 of Schedule 2 to the Immigration Act 1971.

(2) In this Part 'premises' and 'item subject to legal privilege' have the same meaning—

(a) in relation to England and Wales, as in the Police and Criminal Evidence Act 1984;

(b) in relation to Northern Ireland, as in the Police and Criminal Evidence (Northern Ireland) Order 1989 (SI 1989/1341 (NI 12));

(c) in relation to Scotland, as in section 412 of the Proceeds of Crime Act 2002.

Note: Commenced from 12 July 2016 (SI 2016/603).

Detention and bail

59 Guidance on detention of vulnerable persons

(1) The Secretary of State must issue guidance specifying matters to be taken into account by a person to whom the guidance is addressed in determining—

(a) whether a person ('P') would be particularly vulnerable to harm if P were to be detained or to remain in detention, and

(b) if P is identified as being particularly vulnerable to harm in those circumstances, whether P should be detained or remain in detention.

(2) In subsection (1) 'detained' means detained under—

(a) the Immigration Act 1971,

(b) section 62 of the Nationality, Immigration and Asylum Act 2002, or

(c) section 36 of the UK Borders Act 2007, and 'detention' is to be construed accordingly.

(3) A person to whom guidance under this section is addressed must take the guidance into account.

(4) Before issuing guidance under this section the Secretary of State must lay a draft of the guidance before Parliament.

(5) Guidance under this section comes into force in accordance with regulations made by the Secretary of State.

(6) The Secretary of State may from time to time review guidance under this section and may revise and re-issue it.

(7) References in this section to guidance under this section include revised guidance.

Note: Commenced from 12 July 2016 (SI 2016/603).

60 Limitation on detention of pregnant women

(1) This section applies to a woman if the Secretary of State is satisfied that the woman is pregnant.

(2) A woman to whom this section applies may not be detained under a relevant detention power unless the Secretary of State is satisfied that—

(a) the woman will shortly be removed from the United Kingdom, or

(b) there are exceptional circumstances which justify the detention.

(3) In determining whether to authorise the detention under a relevant detention power of a woman to whom this section applies, a person who, apart from this section, has power to authorise the detention must have regard to the woman's welfare.

(4) A woman to whom this section applies may not be detained under a relevant detention power for a period of—

(a) more than 72 hours from the relevant time, or

(b) more than seven days from the relevant time, in a case where the longer period of detention is authorised personally by a Minister of the Crown (within the meaning of the Ministers of the Crown Act 1975).

(5) In subsection (4) 'the relevant time' means the later of—

(a) the time at which the Secretary of State is first satisfied that the woman is pregnant, and

(b) the time at which the detention begins.

(6) A woman to whom this section applies who has been released following detention under a relevant detention power may be detained again under such a power in accordance with this section.

(7) This section does not apply to the detention under paragraph 16(2) of Schedule 2 to the Immigration Act 1971 of an unaccompanied child to whom paragraph 18B of that Schedule applies.

(8) In this section—

'relevant detention power' means a power to detain under—

(a) paragraph 16(2) of Schedule 2 to the Immigration Act 1971 (detention of persons liable to examination or removal),

(b) paragraph 2(1), (2) or (3) of Schedule 3 to that Act (detention pending deportation),

(c) section 62 of the Nationality, Immigration and Asylum Act 2002 (detention of persons liable to examination or removal), or

(d) section 36(1) of the UK Borders Act 2007 (detention pending deportation);

'woman' means a female of any age.

. . .

(9) . . .

Note: Commenced from 12 July 2016 (SI 2016/603). Subsection (10) inserts subsection (2B) in paragraph 16 of Schedule 2 of Immigration Act 1971; subsection (11) inserts subparagraph (4ZA) in paragraph 2 of Schedule 3 of Immigration Act 1971; subsection (12) inserts subsection (7A) in section 62 of the Nationality, Immigration and Asylum Act 2002, and subsection (13) inserts subsection (2A) in section 36 of UK Borders Act 2007.

61 Immigration bail

(1) Schedule 10 (immigration bail) has effect.

(2) In that Schedule—

(a) Part 1 contains the main provisions about immigration bail, and

(b) Part 2 contains amendments to other Acts.

(3) A person may be released and remain on bail under paragraph 22 or 29 of Schedule 2 to the Immigration Act 1971 even if the person can no longer be detained under a provision of the Immigration Acts to which that paragraph applies, if the person is liable to detention under such a provision.

(4) The reference in subsection (3) to paragraph 22 or 29 of Schedule 2 to the Immigration Act 1971 includes that paragraph as applied by any other provision of the Immigration Acts.

(5) Subsections (3) and (4) are to be treated as always having had effect.

(6) Subsections (3) to (5) are repealed on the coming into force of the repeal of paragraphs 22 and 29 of Schedule 2 to the Immigration Act 1971 by paragraph 20 of Schedule 10.

Note: Subsections (1) and (2) commenced 15 January 2018 except insofar as it relates to the provisions of Schedule 10 listed in subparagraphs (i) to (iv) of paragraph c. Subsections (3)–(6) commenced from 12 May 2016.

Power to cancel leave

62 Power to cancel leave extended under section 3C of the Immigration Act 1971

Note: Subsection (1) amends section 3C, and subsection (2) amends section 4(1) of Immigration Act from 1 December 2016 (SI 2016/1037).

Part 4

Appeals

63 Appeals within the United Kingdom: certification of human rights claims

Note: Subsections (1)–(5) amend section 94B of the Nationality, Immigration and Asylum Act 2002 and subsection (6) amends section 92(3) of Nationality, Immigration and Asylum Act 2002 from 1 December 2016 (SI 2016/1037).

64 Continuation of leave: repeals

(1) The repeals made by this section do not apply in relation to a person ('P') where—

(a) P's leave was extended by virtue of section 3D of the Immigration Act 1971 immediately before 6 April 2015, and

(b) immediately before the coming into force of this section an appeal by P against the variation or revocation of P's leave to enter or remain in the United Kingdom was pending within the meaning of section 104 of the Nationality, Immigration and Asylum Act 2002.

(2)–(5) . . .

Note: Commenced 1 December 2016 (SI 2016/103). Subsection (1) omits section 3D of Immigration Act 1971. Subsection (2) amends section 2(2)(a) of the Special Immigration Appeals Commission Act 199. Subsection (3) amends section 120(4)(b) of the Nationality, Immigration and Asylum Act 2002.

65 Deemed refusal of leave to enter: repeals

(1) . . .

(2) . . .

(3) The repeals made by this section do not apply in relation to a person if, immediately before the coming into force of this section, the person's appeal by virtue of paragraph 2A(9) of Schedule 2 to the Immigration Act 1971 against the cancellation of the person's leave to enter under paragraph 2A(8) of that Schedule was pending within the meaning of section 104 of the Nationality, Immigration and Asylum Act 2002.

Note: Commenced from the 1 December 2016 (SI 2016/1037). Subsection (1) omits paragraph 2A (9) of Schedule 2 to Immigration Act 1971. Subsection (2) repeals paragraph 23 of Schedule 9 to Immigration Act 2014.

Part 5

Support etc for Certain Categories of Migrant

Support

66 Support for certain categories of migrant

Schedule 11 (support for certain categories of migrant) has effect.

Note: Commencement from 15 January 2018 to the extent necessary to bring into force paragraph 1 of Schedule 11 to the extent that it repeals section 49(1) of the Immigration Act 1999, and paragraph 46 so far as it relates to the repeal of section 19(1) of the Immigration Act 1999 (SI 2017/1241).

67 Unaccompanied refugee children: relocation and support

(1) The Secretary of State must, as soon as possible after the passing of this Act, make arrangements to relocate to the United Kingdom and support a specified number of unaccompanied refugee children from other countries in Europe.

(2) The number of children to be resettled under subsection (1) shall be determined by the Government in consultation with local authorities.

(3) The relocation of children under subsection (1) shall be in addition to the resettlement of children under the Vulnerable Persons Relocation Scheme.

Note: Commencement from 31 May 2016 (SI 2016/603).

68 Availability of local authority support

Schedule 12 (availability of local authority support) has effect.

Note: Commencement from a date to be appointed.

Transfer of responsibility for relevant children

69 Transfer of responsibility for relevant children

(1) This section applies in relation to a local authority []('the first authority') if—

(a) the authority has functions under any of the [relevant provisions in relation to a relevant child, or

(b) functions under any of the relevant provisions may be conferred on the authority in relation to a relevant child.

(2) The first authority may make arrangements with another local authority in [the same part of the United Kingdom]('the second authority') under which—

(a) if this section applies to the authority by virtue of paragraph (a) of subsection (1), the functions mentioned in that paragraph become functions of the second authority in relation to the relevant child, and

(b) if this section applies to the authority by virtue of paragraph (b) of subsection (1), the functions mentioned in that paragraph become functions that may be conferred on the second authority in relation to the relevant child.

(3) The effect of arrangements under [subsection (2)] is that, from the time at which the arrangements have effect in accordance with their terms—

(a) functions under the relevant provisions cease to be functions of, and may not be conferred on, the first authority in relation to the relevant child ('C'),

(b) any of the relevant provisions which immediately before that time applied in relation to C as a result of C's connection with the first authority or the area of the first authority have effect as if C had that connection with the second authority or the area of the second authority (if that would not otherwise be the case), and

(c) C is to be treated for the purposes of the relevant provisions as if C were not and had never been ordinarily resident in the area of the first authority (if that would otherwise be the case).

[(3A) The first authority may make arrangements with another local authority in a different part of the United Kingdom ('the second authority') having the effects mentioned in subsection (3B).

(3B) The effects are that, from the time at which the arrangements have effect in accordance with their terms—

(a) the first authority ceases to have any functions in relation to the relevant child ('C') under the relevant provisions and functions under those provisions may not be conferred on the first authority in relation to C,

(b) C is to be treated as having a like connection with the second authority, or the area of the second authority, as C had immediately before that time with the first authority or the area of the first authority, and

(c) C is to be treated for the purposes of the relevant provisions in relation to both the first authority and the second authority as if the first authority had never had any functions in relation to C.

(3C) Where a statutory provision would, but for this subsection, require the approval of a court or of any other person for arrangements under subsection (3A), that statutory provision does not apply in relation to such arrangements.]

(4) [Subsections (3)(b) and (3B)(b)]subject to any change in C's circumstances after the time at which the arrangements have effect.

(5) Nothing in subsection (3) [or (3B)] affects any liability of the first authority in relation to C for any act or omission of the first authority before the time at which the arrangements have effect.

(6) The Secretary of State may by regulations make further provision about the effect of arrangements under this section.

(7) Arrangements under this section may not be brought to an end by the first or second authority once they have come into effect.

[(8) In this section 'local authority'—

(a) in relation to England and Wales has the same meaning as in the Children Act 1989 (see section 105(1) of that Act)(1),

(b) in relation to Scotland means a council constituted under section 2 of the Local Government etc. (Scotland) Act 1994(2), and

(c) in relation to Northern Ireland means a Health and Social Care trust established under Article 10 of the Health and Personal Services (Northern Ireland) Order 1991(3).

(8A) In this section 'the relevant provisions'—

(a) in relation to a local authority in England, means the provisions of or made under Part 3, 4 or 5 of the Children Act 1989 (support for children and families and care, supervision and protection of children), and

(b) in relation to a local authority in Wales, Scotland or Northern Ireland, means any statutory provision which confers functions on, or which are exercisable by, such an authority which correspond, or are similar, to the functions conferred on a local authority in England by or under any of those Parts of that Act.]

(9) In this section 'relevant child' means—

(a) a person under the age of 18 who is unaccompanied and has made a protection claim which has not been determined,

(b) a person under the age of 18 who is unaccompanied and who—

(i) requires leave to enter or remain in the United Kingdom but does not have it, and

(ii) is a person of a kind specified in regulations made by the Secretary of State, or

(c) a person under the age of 18 who is unaccompanied and who—

(i) has leave to enter or remain in the United Kingdom, and

(ii) is a person of a kind specified in regulations made by the Secretary of State.

(10) The Secretary of State may by regulations make provision about the meaning of 'unaccompanied' for the purposes of subsection (9).

(11) In subsection (9)—

(a) 'protection claim' has the meaning given by section 82(2) of the Nationality, Immigration and Asylum Act 2002, and

(b) the reference to a protection claim having been determined is to be construed in accordance with section 94(3) of the Immigration and Asylum Act 1999.

(12) In this section 'statutory provision' means a provision made by or under—

(a) an Act,

(b) an Act of the Scottish Parliament,

(c) a Measure or Act of the National Assembly for Wales, or

(d) an Act of the Northern Ireland Assembly.

(13) In this section a reference to a part of the United Kingdom is a reference to England, Wales, Scotland or Northern Ireland.

Note: Commencement from 31 May 2016 (SI 2016/603). Words in square brackets omitted at subsection 1, substituted at ss 1(a), 2 and 3, inserted at subsections (3A)–(3C), substituted at subsection (4), inserted at subsection (5), substituted at subsection (8), and inserted at subsections (12) & (13) by the Transfer of Responsibility for Relevant Children (Extension to Wales, Scotland and Northern Ireland) Regulations 2018/153 Reg 3.

70 Duty to provide information for the purposes of transfers of responsibility

(1) The Secretary of State may direct a local authority []to provide information of the kind specified in subsection (2) to the Secretary of State for the purposes of enabling—

(a) arrangements to be made under section 69, or

(b) the Secretary of State to exercise functions under section 72.

(2) The information mentioned in subsection (1) is—

(a) information about the support or accommodation provided to children who are looked after by the local authority within the meaning of the [relevant provisions];

(b) such other information as may be specified in regulations made by the Secretary of State.

(3) A local authority which is directed to provide information under this section must provide it—

(a) in such form and manner as the Secretary of State may direct, and

(b) before such time or before the end of such period as the Secretary of State may direct.

(4) In this section 'local authority' [and 'relevant provisions' have the same meanings] has the same meaning as in section 69.

Note: Commencement from 31 May 2016 (SI 2016/603). Words in square brackets omitted at subsection (1), substituted at subsection (2) and inserted at subsection (4) by Transfer of Responsibility for Relevant Children (Extension to Wales, Scotland and Northern Ireland) Regulations 2018/153 reg 4 (7 February 2018).

71 Request for transfer of responsibility for relevant children

(1) Subsection (2) applies if—

(a) a local authority []('the first authority') requests another local authority [] ('the second authority') to enter into arrangements under section 69, and

(b) the second authority does not comply with the first authority's request.

(2) The Secretary of State may direct the second authority to provide the first authority and the Secretary of State with written reasons for its failure to comply with the request.

(3) In this section 'local authority' has the same meaning as in section 69.

Note: Commencement from 31 May 2016 (SI 2016/603). Words omitted in subsection (1)(a) by Transfer of Responsibility for Relevant Children (Extension to Wales, Scotland and Northern Ireland) Regulations 2018/153 reg 5 (7 February 2018).

72 Scheme for transfer of responsibility for relevant children

(1) The Secretary of State may prepare a scheme for functions of, or which may be conferred on, a local authority []('the transferring authority') to become functions of, or functions which may be conferred on, one or more other local authorities [the same part of the United Kingdom](a 'receiving authority') in accordance with arrangements under section [69(2)].

(1A) The Secretary of State may prepare a scheme in relation to a local authority to which section 69 applies ('the transferring authority') and one or more other local authorities in one or more other parts of the United Kingdom ('a receiving authority') having the effects mentioned in section 69(3B).

(2) A scheme under this section—

(a) must specify the local authorities to which it relates, and

(b) unless it relates to all relevant children who may be the subject of arrangements under section 69 between the transferring authority and each receiving authority, must specify the relevant child or children, or descriptions of relevant children, to which it relates.

(3) The Secretary of State may direct the transferring authority and each receiving authority under a scheme under this section to comply with the scheme.

(4) A direction may not be given under subsection (3) unless the Secretary of State is satisfied that compliance with the direction will not unduly prejudice the discharge by each receiving authority of any of its functions.

(5) Before giving a direction under subsection (3) to a local authority, the Secretary of State must give the authority notice in writing of the proposed direction.

(6) The Secretary of State may not give a direction to a local authority before the end of the period of 14 days beginning with the day on which notice under subsection (5) was given to it.

(7) The local authority may make written representations to the Secretary of State about the proposed direction within that period.

(8) The Secretary of State may modify or withdraw a direction under subsection (3) by notice in writing to the local authorities to which it was given.

(9) A modification or withdrawal of a direction does not affect any arrangements made under section 69 pursuant to the direction before it was modified or withdrawn.

(10) Subsections (5) to (7) apply to the modification or withdrawal of a direction as they apply to the giving of a direction, but as if—

(a) the reference to the proposed direction were to the proposed modification or proposal to withdraw the direction, and

(b) subsection (6) permitted the Secretary of State to withdraw the direction before the end of the 14 day period with the agreement of the local authorities to which it applies.

(11) In this section 'local authority' [,' relevant child' and 'part of the United Kingdom'] have the same meanings as in section 69.

Note: Commencement from 31 May 2016 (SI 2016/603). Words in square brackets omitted and substituted in subsection (1), inserted at ss (1A) and substituted at subsection (11) by Transfer of Responsibility for Relevant Children (Extension to Wales, Scotland and Northern Ireland) Regulations 2018/153 reg 6 (7 February 2018).

73 Extension to Wales, Scotland and Northern Ireland

(1) The Secretary of State may by regulations make such provision as the Secretary of State considers appropriate for enabling any of the provisions of sections 69 to 72 to apply in relation to Wales, Scotland or Northern Ireland.

(2) The Secretary of State may by regulations make provision which—

(a) has a similar effect to—

(i) any of the provisions mentioned in subsection (1), or

(ii) provision which may be made under section 69(6) or (10), and

(b) applies in relation to Wales, Scotland or Northern Ireland.

(3) Regulations under subsection (1) may amend, repeal or revoke any enactment (including an enactment contained in this Act).

(4) Regulations under subsection (1) or (2) may not confer functions on—

(a) the Welsh Ministers,

(b) the Scottish Ministers,

(c) the First Minister and deputy First Minister in Northern Ireland,

(d) a Northern Ireland Minister, or

(e) a Northern Ireland department.

(5) In this section 'enactment' includes—

(a) an enactment contained in subordinate legislation within the meaning of the Interpretation Act 1978;

(b) an enactment contained in, or in an instrument made under, an Act or Measure of the National Assembly for Wales;

(c) an enactment contained in, or in an instrument made under, an Act of the Scottish Parliament;

(d) an enactment contained in, or in an instrument made under, Northern Ireland legislation.

Note: Commencement from 1 January 2018 (SI 2017/1210).

Part 6

Border Security

74 Penalties relating to airport control areas

Note: Commencement at a date to be appointed. Subsection (1) amends paragraph 26 of Schedule 2 to the Immigration Act 1971. Subsection 2 inserts Schedule 13 of this Act at Part 1A in Schedule 2 to Immigration Act 1971.

75 Maritime enforcement

Schedule 14 (maritime enforcement) has effect.

Note: Commencement from 31 May 2016 (SI 2016/603).

76 Persons excluded from the United Kingdom under international obligations

Note: Commenced on 12 July 2016 (SI 2016/603). Subsection (1) amends section 8; subsection (2) inserts subsection 8A(4); subsections (3),(4), (5), (6) and (7) amend section 8B; subsection (8) inserts subsection(5A), in section 8B and subsection (9) omits sections (6)–(8) in section 8B, of Immigration Act 1971.

Part 7

Language Requirements for Public Sector Workers

77 English language requirements for public sector workers

Note: Commencement from 21 November 2016 (SI 2016/1037).

78 Meaning of 'public authority'

Note: Commenced 21 November 2016 (SI 2016/1037).

79 Power to expand meaning of person working for public authority

Note: Commenced 21 November 2016 (SI 2016/1037).

80 Duty to issue codes of practice

Note: Commenced 21 November 2016 (SI 2016/1037).

81 Procedure for codes of practice

Note: Commenced 21 November 2016 (SI2016/1037).

82 Application of Part to Wales

Note: Commenced 21 November 2016 (SI 2016/1037).

83 Interpretation of Part

Note: Commenced 21 November 2016 (SI 2016/1037).

84 Crown application

Note: Commenced 21 November 2016 (SI 2016/1037).

PART 8

FEES AND CHARGES

Immigration

85 Immigration skills charge

Note: Commenced 12 July 2016. Subsection (1) and (2) insert section 70A in the Immigration Act 2014. Subsection (3) inserts section 74(2)(ja) in Immigration Act 2014.

Passports and civil registration

86 Power to make passport fees regulations

Note: Commenced 12 July 2016 (SI 2016/603).

87 Passport fees regulations: supplemental

Note: Commenced 12 July 2016 (SI 2016/603).

88 Power to charge for passport validation services

Note: Commenced 12 July 2016 (SI 2016/603).

89 Civil registration fees

Note: Commenced 12 July 2016 (SI 2016/603).

PART 9
MISCELLANEOUS AND GENERAL

Welfare of children

90 Duty regarding the welfare of children

For the avoidance of doubt, this Act does not limit any duty imposed on the Secretary of State or any person by section 55 of the Borders, Citizenship and Immigration Act 2009 (duty regarding welfare of children).

Note: Commenced 12 May 2016.

Final provisions

91 Financial provisions

The following are to be paid out of money provided by Parliament—

(a) any expenditure incurred under or by virtue of this Act by a Minister of the Crown, a person holding office under Her Majesty or a government department, and

(b) any increase attributable to the Act in the sums payable under any other Act out of money so provided.

Note: Commenced 12 May 2016.

92 Transitional and consequential provision

(1) The Secretary of State may by regulations make such transitional, transitory or saving provision as the Secretary of State considers appropriate in connection with the coming into force of any provision of this Act.

(2) The Secretary of State may by regulations make such provision as the Secretary of State considers appropriate in consequence of this Act.

(3) The provision that may be made by regulations under subsection (2) includes provision amending, repealing or revoking any enactment.

(4) 'Enactment' includes—

(a) an enactment contained in subordinate legislation within the meaning of the Interpretation Act 1978;

(b) an enactment contained in, or in an instrument made under, an Act of the Scottish Parliament;

(c) an enactment contained in, or in an instrument made under, a Measure or Act of the National Assembly for Wales;

(d) an enactment contained in, or in an instrument made under, Northern Ireland legislation.

(5) In section 61(2) of the UK Borders Act 2007 (meaning of 'the Immigration Acts')—

(a) omit the 'and' at the end of paragraph (i), and

(b) at the end of paragraph (j) insert ', and (k) the Immigration Act 2016.'

Note: Commenced 12 May 2016.

93 Regulations

(1) Regulations made by the Secretary of State or the Chancellor of the Duchy of Lancaster under this Act are to be made by statutory instrument.

(2) A statutory instrument containing (whether alone or with other provision) any of the following regulations may not be made unless a draft of the instrument has been laid before, and approved by a resolution of, each House of Parliament—

(a) regulations under section 3 which amend or repeal primary legislation,

(b) regulations under section 6,

(c) regulations under section 11 which amend or repeal primary legislation,

(d) regulations under section 14, 15 or 21,

(e) regulations under section 36(2),

(f) regulations under section 42(1) or (2),

[(fa) regulations under section 69(6) or (10),

(fb) regulations under section 70(2)(b),]

(g) regulations under section 73(1) or (2),

(h) regulations under section 78(9),

(i) regulations under section 79(1),

(j) passport fees regulations within the meaning of section 86 which include provision specifying functions as mentioned in subsection (1) of that section,

(k) regulations under section 92(2) which amend or repeal primary legislation,

(l) regulations under paragraph 1(13) of Schedule 6, and

(m) regulations under paragraph 2(7) of that Schedule.

(3) Primary legislation means any of the following—

(a) an Act of Parliament;

(b) an Act of the Scottish Parliament;

(c) a Measure or Act of the National Assembly for Wales;

(d) Northern Ireland legislation.

(4) A statutory instrument—

(a) containing any other regulations made by the Secretary of State or the Chancellor of the Duchy of Lancaster under this Act, and

(b) to which subsection (2) does not apply, is subject to annulment in pursuance of a resolution of either House of Parliament.

(5) Subsection (4) does not apply to regulations under section 92(1) or 94(1).

(6) Regulations made by the Secretary of State or the Chancellor of the Duchy of Lancaster under this Act—

(a) may make different provision for different purposes or areas,
(b) may make provision which applies generally or for particular purposes or areas,
(c) may make transitional, transitory or saving provision, or
(d) may make incidental, supplementary or consequential provision.

Note: Commenced 12 May 2016. Subsections (2)(fa) & (fb) inserted by Transfer of Responsibility for Relevant Children (Extension to Wales, Scotland and Northern Ireland) Regulations 2018/153 reg 7 (7 February 2018).

Part 9—Miscellaneous and general

94 Commencement

(1) Subject to subsections (3) to (5) this Act comes into force on such day as the Secretary of State appoints by regulations.

(2) Regulations under subsection (1) may appoint different days for different purposes or areas.

(3) Subsections (3) to (5) of section 61 come into force on the day on which this Act is passed.

(4) Section 85 comes into force at the end of the period of two months beginning with the day on which this Act is passed.

(5) This Part comes into force on the day on which this Act is passed.

Note: Commenced 12 May 2016.

95 Extent

(1) This Act extends to England and Wales, Scotland and Northern Ireland, subject as follows.

(2) . . .

(3) Any amendment, repeal or revocation made by this Act has the same extent within the United Kingdom as the provision to which it relates.

(4) But subsection (3) does not apply to the amendments made to the Modern Slavery Act 2015 by paragraphs 30 and 35 of Schedule 3 (for the extent of which, see the amendments to section 60 of that Act made by paragraph 33 of that Schedule).

(5) Her Majesty may by Order in Council provide for any of the provisions of this Act to extend, with or without modifications, to any of the Channel Islands or the Isle of Man.

(6) A power under any provision listed in subsection (7) may be exercised so as to extend (with or without modifications) to any of the Channel Islands or the Isle of Man any amendment or repeal made by or under this Act of any part of an Act to which the provision listed in subsection (7) relates.

(7) Those provisions are—

(a) section 36 of the Immigration Act 1971,
(b) section 52(2) of the Civil Jurisdiction and Judgments Act 1982,

(c) section 9(3) of the Special Immigration Appeals Commission Act 1997,
(d) section 170(7) of the Immigration and Asylum Act 1999,
(e) section 163(4) of the Nationality, Immigration and Asylum Act 2002,
(f) section 49(3) of the Asylum and Immigration (Treatment of Claimants, etc) Act 2004,
(g) section 63(3) of the Immigration, Asylum and Nationality Act 2006,
(h) section 60(4) of the UK Borders Act 2007,
(i) section 76(6) of the Immigration Act 2014, and
(j) section 60(6) of the Modern Slavery Act 2015.

Note: Commenced 12 May 2016. Subsection (2) omitted by Transfer of Responsibility for Relevant Children (Extension to Wales, Scotland and Northern Ireland) Regulations 2018.153 reg 7(2) (7 February 2018).

96 Short title

This Act may be cited as the Immigration Act 2016.

Note: Commenced 12 May 2016.

SCHEDULES

SCHEDULE 1

PERSONS TO WHOM DIRECTOR ETC MAY DISCLOSE INFORMATION — **Section 6**

SCHEDULE 2

FUNCTIONS IN RELATION TO LABOUR MARKET — **Section 11**

SCHEDULE 3

CONSEQUENTIAL AND RELATED AMENDMENTS — **Section 31**

SCHEDULE 4

LICENSING ACT 2003: AMENDMENTS RELATING TO ILLEGAL WORKING — **Section 36**

Part 1: Entitlement to Work in the United Kingdom

Part 2: Premises Licences

Part 3: Personal Licences

Part 4: Rights of Entry

Part 5: Appeals

Part 6: General

Part 7: Transitional Provisions

SCHEDULE 5

PRIVATE HIRE VEHICLES ETC — Section 37

SCHEDULE 6

ILLEGAL WORKING CLOSURE NOTICES AND ILLEGAL WORKING COMPLIANCE ORDERS — Section 38

SCHEDULE 7

BANK ACCOUNTS — Section 45

Note: Sections 40A–H inserted in Immigration Act 2014 from 1 November 2016.

SCHEDULE 8

AMENDMENTS TO SEARCH WARRANT PROVISIONS — SECTION 54

Note: Amends section 28D inserts section 28(1A)–(1D) and (2A); amends section 28FB and inserts section 28FB(1A)–(1B), (3A)–(3C); amends section 28J and inserts subsection (2)(aa), (2A), (6A), (7)(c) and (10A)–(10B); amends section 28K and inserts (2A)–(2B), (3A)–(3B), (8A)–(8C) of the Immigration Act 1971 from a date to be appointed. Amends and inserts sub-paragraph (6AA)–(6AD) and (6B) at paragraph 25A of Schedule 2 to Immigration Act 1971 from a date to be appointed. Amends section 45 of UK Borders Act 2007 from 1 December 2016. Inserts subsection (2A) to (2D), and (3A) of UK Borders Act 2007 from 1 December 2016.

SCHEDULE 9

DUTY TO SUPPLY NATIONALITY DOCUMENTS TO SECRETARY OF STATE: PERSONS TO WHOM DUTY APPLIES — Section 55

Note: Inserts Schedule A1 to the Immigration and Asylum Act 1999 referred to in section 55.

SCHEDULE 10
IMMIGRATION BAIL SECTION

PART 1
MAIN PROVISIONS

Power to grant immigration bail

1 (1) The Secretary of State may grant a person bail if—

(a) the person is being detained under paragraph 16(1), (1A) or (2) of Schedule 2 to the Immigration Act 1971 (detention of persons liable to examination or removal),

(b) the person is being detained under paragraph 2(1), (2) or (3) of Schedule 3 to that Act (detention pending deportation),

(c) the person is being detained under section 62 of the Nationality, Immigration and Asylum Act 2002 (detention of persons liable to examination or removal), or

(d) the person is being detained under section 36(1) of the UK Borders Act 2007 (detention pending deportation).

(2) The Secretary of State may grant a person bail if the person is liable to detention under a provision mentioned in sub-paragraph (1).

(3) The First-tier Tribunal may, on an application made to the Tribunal for the grant of bail to a person, grant that person bail if—

(a) the person is being detained under paragraph 16(1), (1A) or (2) of Schedule 2 to the Immigration Act 1971,

(b) the person is being detained under paragraph 2(1), (2) or (3) of Schedule 3 to that Act,

(c) the person is being detained under section 62 of the Nationality, Immigration and Asylum Act 2002, or

(d) the person is being detained under section 36(1) of the UK Borders Act 2007.

(4) In this Schedule references to the grant of immigration bail, in relation to a person, are to the grant of bail to that person under any of sub-paragraphs (1) to (3) or under paragraph 10(12) or (13) (release following arrest for breach of bail conditions).

(5) A person may be granted and remain on immigration bail even if the person can no longer be detained, if—

(a) the person is liable to detention under a provision mentioned in sub-paragraph (1), or

(b) the Secretary of State is considering whether to make a deportation order against the person under section 5(1) of the Immigration Act 1971.

(6) A grant of immigration bail to a person does not prevent the person's subsequent detention under a provision mentioned in sub-paragraph (1).

(7) For the purposes of this Schedule a person is on immigration bail from when a grant of immigration bail to the person commences to when it ends.

(8) A grant of immigration bail to a person ends when—

(a) in a case where sub-paragraph (5) applied to the person, that sub- paragraph no longer applies to the person,

(b) the person is granted leave to enter or remain in the United Kingdom,

(c) the person is detained under a provision mentioned in sub- paragraph (1), or

(d) the person is removed from or otherwise leaves the United Kingdom.

(9) This paragraph is subject to paragraph 3 (exercise of power to grant immigration bail).

Note: Commenced from 15 January 2018 (SI 2017/1241).

Conditions of immigration bail

2 (1) Subject to sub-paragraph (2), if immigration bail is granted to a person, it must be granted subject to one or more of the following conditions—

(a) a condition requiring the person to appear before the Secretary of State or the First-tier Tribunal at a specified time and place;

(b) a condition restricting the person's work, occupation or studies in the United Kingdom;

(c) a condition about the person's residence;

(d) a condition requiring the person to report to the Secretary of State or such other person as may be specified;

(e) an electronic monitoring condition (see paragraph 4);

(f) such other conditions as the person granting the immigration bail thinks fit.

(2) Sub-paragraph (3) applies in place of sub-paragraph (1) in relation to a person who is being detained under a provision mentioned in paragraph 1(1)(b) or (d) or who is liable to detention under such a provision.

(3) If immigration bail is granted to such a person—

(a) subject to sub-paragraphs (5) to (9), it must be granted subject to an electronic monitoring condition,

(b) if, by virtue of sub-paragraph (5) or (7), it is not granted subject to an electronic monitoring condition, it must be granted subject to one or more of the other conditions mentioned in sub-paragraph (1), and

(c) if it is granted subject to an electronic monitoring condition, it may be granted subject to one or more of those other conditions.

(4) Immigration bail granted in accordance with sub-paragraph (1) or (3) may also be granted subject to a financial condition (see paragraph 5).

(5) Sub-paragraph (3)(a) does not apply to a person who is granted immigration bail by the Secretary of State if the Secretary of State considers that to impose an electronic monitoring condition on the person would be—

(a) impractical, or

(b) contrary to the person's Convention rights.

(6) Where sub-paragraph (5) applies, the Secretary of State must not grant immigration bail to the person subject to an electronic monitoring condition.

(7) Sub-paragraph (3)(a) does not apply to a person who is granted immigration bail by the First-tier Tribunal if the Secretary of State informs the Tribunal that the Secretary of State considers that to impose an electronic monitoring condition on the person would be—

(a) impractical, or

(b) contrary to the person's Convention rights.

(8) Where sub-paragraph (7) applies, the First-tier Tribunal must not grant immigration bail to the person subject to an electronic monitoring condition.

(9) In considering for the purposes of this Schedule whether it would be impractical to impose an electronic monitoring condition on a person, or would be impractical for a person to continue to be subject to such a condition, the Secretary of State may in particular have regard to—

(a) any obstacles to making arrangements of the kind mentioned in paragraph 4 in relation to the person,

(b) the resources that are available for imposing electronic monitoring conditions on persons to whom sub-paragraph (2) applies and for managing the operation of such conditions in relation to such persons,

(c) the need to give priority to the use of those resources in relation to particular categories of persons to whom that sub-paragraph applies, and

(d) the matters listed in paragraph 3(2) as they apply to the person.

(10) In this Schedule 'Convention rights' is to be construed in accordance with section 1 of the Human Rights Act 1998.

(11) In this Schedule 'bail condition', in relation to a person on immigration bail, means a condition to which the person's bail is subject.

Note: Commenced from 15 January 2018 (SI 2017/1241) save for subparagraphs (2), (3) and (5)-(10).

Exercise of power to grant immigration bail

3 (1) The Secretary of State or the First-tier Tribunal must have regard to the matters listed in sub-paragraph (2) in determining—

(a) whether to grant immigration bail to a person, and
(b) the conditions to which a person's immigration bail is to be subject.

(2) Those matters are—

(a) the likelihood of the person failing to comply with a bail condition,

(b) whether the person has been convicted of an offence (whether in or outside the United Kingdom or before or after the coming into force of this paragraph),

(c) the likelihood of a person committing an offence while on immigration bail,

(d) the likelihood of the person's presence in the United Kingdom, while on immigration bail, causing a danger to public health or being a threat to the maintenance of public order,

(e) whether the person's detention is necessary in that person's interests or for the protection of any other person,

(ea) whether the person has failed without reasonable excuse to cooperate with any process—

(i) for determining whether the person requires or should be granted leave to enter or remain in the United Kingdom,

(ii) for determining the period for which the person should be granted such leave and any conditions to which it should be subject,

(iii) for determining whether the person's leave to enter or remain in the United Kingdom should be varied, curtailed, suspended or cancelled,

(iv) for determining whether the person should be removed from the United Kingdom, or

(v) for removing the person from the United Kingdom, and

(f) such other matters as the Secretary of State or the First-tier Tribunal thinks relevant.

(3) A person who is being detained under paragraph 16(1) of Schedule 2 to the Immigration Act 1971 must not be granted immigration bail by the First-tier Tribunal until after the end of the period of 8 days beginning with the date of the person's arrival in the United Kingdom.

(4) A person must not be granted immigration bail by the First-tier Tribunal without the consent of the Secretary of State if—

(a) directions for the removal of the person from the United Kingdom are for the time being in force, and

(b) the directions require the person to be removed from the United Kingdom within the period of [21] days beginning with the date of the decision on whether the person should be granted immigration bail.

(5) If the Secretary of State or the First-tier Tribunal decides to grant, or to refuse to grant, immigration bail to a person, the Secretary of State or the Tribunal must give the person notice of the decision.

(6) Where the First-tier Tribunal is required under sub-paragraph (5) to a give a person notice of a decision, it must also give the Secretary of State notice of the decision.

(7) Where the decision is to grant immigration bail, a notice under sub-paragraph (5) or (6) must state—

(a) when the grant of immigration bail commences, and

(b) the bail conditions.

(8) The commencement of a grant of immigration bail may be specified to be conditional on arrangements specified in the notice being in place to ensure that the person is able to comply with the bail conditions.

Note: Commenced from 15 January 2018 (SI 2017/1241). Word in square brackets in sub-paragraph (4)(b) substituted by Nationality and Borders Act 2022 c.36 s48(6) (date to be appointed). Sub-paragraph (2)(ea) inserted by Nationality and Borders Act 2022 c.36 s.48 (June 28. 2022)

Electronic monitoring condition

4 (1) In this Schedule an 'electronic monitoring condition' means a condition requiring the person on whom it is imposed ('P') to co-operate with such arrangements as the Secretary of State may specify for detecting and recording by electronic means one or more of the following—

(a) P's location at specified times, during specified periods of time or while the arrangements are in place;

(b) P's presence in a location at specified times, during specified periods of time or while the arrangements are in place;

(c) P's absence from a location at specified times, during specified periods of time or while the arrangements are in place.

(2) The arrangements may in particular—

(a) require P to wear a device;

(b) require P to make specified use of a device;

(c) require P to communicate in a specified manner and at specified times or during specified periods;

(d) involve the exercise of functions by persons other than the Secretary of State or the First-tier Tribunal.

(3) If the arrangements require P to wear, or make specified use of, a device they must—

(a) prohibit P from causing or permitting damage to, or interference with the device, and

(b) prohibit P from taking or permitting action that would or might prevent the effective operation of the device.

(4) In this paragraph 'specified' means specified in the arrangements.

(5) An electronic monitoring condition may not be imposed on a person unless the person is at least 18 years old.

Note: Commenced from 15 January 2018 (SI 2017/1241).

Financial condition

5 (1) In this Schedule a 'financial condition' means a condition requiring the payment of a sum of money by the person to whom immigration bail is granted ('P') or another person, in a case where P fails to comply with another condition to which P's immigration bail is subject.

(2) A financial condition may be imposed on P only if the person imposing the condition thinks that it would be appropriate to do so with a view to ensuring that P complies with the other bail conditions.

(3) The financial condition must specify—

(a) the sum of money required to be paid,

(b) when it is to be paid, and

(c) the form and manner in which it is to be paid.

(4) A sum to be paid under a financial condition is to be paid to the person who granted the immigration bail, subject to sub-paragraph (5).

(5) If the First-tier Tribunal has directed that the power in paragraph 6(1) (power to vary bail conditions) is to be exercisable by the Secretary of State in relation to P, the sum is to be paid to the Secretary of State.

(6) No sum is required to be paid under a financial condition unless the person who is liable to make a payment under it has been given an opportunity to make representations to the person to whom it is to be paid.

(7) In England and Wales a sum payable under a financial condition is recoverable as if it were payable under an order of the county court in England and Wales.

(8) In Scotland a sum payable under a financial condition may be enforced in the same manner as an extract registered decree arbitral bearing a warrant for execution issued by the sheriff court of any sheriffdom in Scotland.

(9) In Northern Ireland a sum payable under a financial condition is recoverable as if it were payable under an order of a county court in Northern Ireland.

(10) Where action is taken under this paragraph for the recovery of a sum payable under a financial condition, the requirement to pay the sum is—

(a) in relation to England and Wales, to be treated for the purposes of section 98 of the Courts Act 2003 (register of judgments and orders etc) as if it were a judgment entered in the county court;

(b) in relation to Northern Ireland, to be treated for the purposes of Article 116 of the Judgments Enforcement (Northern Ireland) Order 1981 (S.I. 1981/226 (N.I. 6)) (register of judgments) as if it were a judgment in respect of which an application has been accepted under Article 22 or 23(1) of that Order.

Note: Commenced from 15 January 2018 (SI 2017/1241).

Power to vary bail conditions

6 (1) Subject to this paragraph and to paragraphs 7 and 8, where a person is on immigration bail—

(a) any of the conditions to which it is subject may be amended or removed, or

(b) one or more new conditions of the kind mentioned in paragraph 2(1) or (4) may be imposed on the person.

(2) The power in sub-paragraph (1) is exercisable by the person who granted the immigration bail, subject to sub-paragraphs (3) and (4).

(3) The Secretary of State may exercise the power in sub-paragraph (1) in relation to a person to whom immigration bail was granted by the First-tier Tribunal if the Tribunal so directs.

(4) If the First-tier Tribunal gives a direction under sub-paragraph (3), the Tribunal may not exercise the power in sub-paragraph (1) in relation to the person.

(5) The First-tier Tribunal may not exercise the power in sub-paragraph (1)(a) so as to amend an electronic monitoring condition.

(6) If the Secretary of State or the First-tier Tribunal exercises, or refuses to exercise, the power in sub-paragraph (1), the Secretary of State or the Tribunal must give notice to the person who is on immigration bail.

(7) Where the First-tier Tribunal is required under sub-paragraph (6) to give notice to a person, it must also give notice to the Secretary of State.

Note: Commenced from 15 January 2018 (SI 2017/1241).

Removal etc of electronic monitoring condition: bail managed by Secretary of State

7 (1) This paragraph applies to a person who—

(a) is on immigration bail—

(i) pursuant to a grant by the Secretary of State, or

(ii) pursuant to a grant by the First-tier Tribunal in a case where the Tribunal has directed that the power in paragraph 6(1) is exercisable by the Secretary of State, and

(b) before the grant of immigration bail, was detained or liable to detention under a provision mentioned in paragraph 1(1)(b) or (d).

(2) Where the person is subject to an electronic monitoring condition, the Secretary of State—

(a) must not exercise the power in paragraph 6(1) so as to remove the condition unless sub-paragraph (3) applies, but

(b) if that sub-paragraph applies, must exercise that power so as to remove the condition.

(3) This sub-paragraph applies if the Secretary of State considers that—

(a) it would be impractical for the person to continue to be subject to the condition, or

(b) it would be contrary to that person's Convention rights for the person to continue to be subject to the condition.

(4) If, by virtue of paragraph 2(5) or (7) or this paragraph, the person is not subject to an electronic monitoring condition, the Secretary of State—

(a) must not exercise the power in paragraph 6(1) so as to impose such a condition on the person unless sub-paragraph (5) applies, but

(b) if that sub-paragraph applies, must exercise that power so as to impose such a condition on the person.

(5) This sub-paragraph applies if, having considered whether it would be impractical or contrary to the person's Convention rights to impose such a condition on the person, the Secretary of State—

(a) does not consider that it would be impractical to do so, and

(b) does not consider that it would be contrary to the person's Convention rights to do so.

Note: Commencement from a date to be appointed.

Amendment etc of electronic monitoring condition: bail managed by First-tier Tribunal

8 (1) This paragraph applies to a person who—

(a) is on immigration bail pursuant to a grant by the First-tier Tribunal in a case where the Tribunal has not directed that the power in paragraph 6(1) is exercisable by the Secretary of State, and

(b) before the person was granted immigration bail, was detained or liable to detention under a provision mentioned in paragraph 1(1)(b) or (d).

(2) Where the person is subject to an electronic monitoring condition, the First- tier Tribunal—

(a) must not exercise the power in paragraph 6(1) so as to remove the condition unless sub-paragraph (3) applies, but

(b) if that sub-paragraph applies, must exercise that power so as to remove the condition.

(3) This sub-paragraph applies if the Secretary of State notifies the First-tier Tribunal that the Secretary of State considers that—

(a) it would be impractical for the person to continue to be subject to the condition, or

(b) it would be contrary to that person's Convention rights for the person to continue to be subject to the condition.

(4) If, by virtue of paragraph 2(7) or this paragraph, the person is not subject to an electronic monitoring condition, the First-tier Tribunal—

(a) must not exercise the power in paragraph 6(1) so as to impose such a condition on the person unless sub-paragraph (5) applies, but

(b) if that sub-paragraph applies, must exercise that power so as to impose such a condition on the person.

(5) This sub-paragraph applies if the Secretary of State notifies the First-tier Tribunal that the Secretary of State—

(a) does not consider that it would be impractical to impose such a condition on the person, and

(b) does not consider that it would be contrary to the person's Convention rights to impose such a condition on the person.

Note: Commencement from a date to be appointed.

Powers of Secretary of State to enable person to meet bail conditions

9 (1) Sub-paragraph (2) applies where—

(a) a person is on immigration bail subject to a condition requiring the person to reside at an address specified in the condition, and

(b) the person would not be able to support himself or herself at the address unless the power in sub-paragraph (2) were exercised.

(2) The Secretary of State may provide, or arrange for the provision of, facilities for the accommodation of that person at that address.

(3) But the power in sub-paragraph (2) applies only to the extent that the Secretary of State thinks that there are exceptional circumstances which justify the exercise of the power.

(4) The Secretary of State may make a payment to a person on immigration bail in respect of travelling expenses which the person has incurred or will incur for the purpose of complying with a bail condition.

(5) But the power in sub-paragraph (4) applies only to the extent that the Secretary of State thinks that there are exceptional circumstances which justify the making of the payment.

Arrest for breach of immigration bail

10 (1) An immigration officer or a constable may arrest without warrant a person on immigration bail if the immigration officer or constable—

(a) has reasonable grounds for believing that the person is likely to fail to comply with a bail condition, or

(b) has reasonable grounds for suspecting that the person is failing, or has failed, to comply with a bail condition.

(2) Sub-paragraph (3) applies if an appropriate judicial officer is satisfied that there are reasonable grounds for believing that a person liable to be arrested under this paragraph is to be found on any premises.

(3) The appropriate judicial officer may issue a warrant authorising any immigration officer or constable to enter, by reasonable force if necessary, the premises named in the warrant for the purposes of searching for and arresting that person.

(4) Sections 28J and 28K of the Immigration Act 1971 (warrants: application and execution) apply, with any necessary modifications, to warrants under sub-paragraph (3).

(5) Sub-paragraph (6) applies where—

(a) a warrant under this paragraph is issued for the purposes of the arrest of a person under this paragraph, and

(b) an immigration officer or a constable enters premises in reliance on the warrant and detains a person on the premises.

(6) A detainee custody officer may enter the premises, if need be by reasonable force, for the purpose of carrying out a search.

(7) In sub-paragraph (6)—

'detainee custody officer' means a person in respect of whom a certificate of authorisation is in force under section 154 of the Immigration and Asylum Act 1999 (detained persons: escort and custody), and

'search' means a search under paragraph 2(1)(a) of Schedule 13 to that Act (escort arrangements: power to search detained person).

(8) Paragraphs 25A to 25C of Schedule 2 to the Immigration Act 1971 (entry and search of persons and premises) apply in relation to a person arrested under this paragraph as they apply in relation to a person arrested under that Schedule.

(9) A person arrested under this paragraph—

(a) must, as soon as is practicable after the person's arrest, be brought before the relevant authority, and

(b) may be detained under the authority of the Secretary of State in the meantime.

(10) The relevant authority is—

(a) the Secretary of State, if the Secretary of State granted immigration bail to the arrested person or the First-tier Tribunal has directed that the power in paragraph 6(1) is exercisable by the Secretary of State in relation to that person, or

(b) otherwise, the First-tier Tribunal.

(11) Where an arrested person is brought before the relevant authority, the relevant authority must decide whether the arrested person has broken or is likely to break any of the bail conditions.

(12) If the relevant authority decides the arrested person has broken or is likely to break any of the bail conditions, the relevant authority must—

(a) direct that the person is to be detained under the provision mentioned in paragraph 1(1) under which the person is liable to be detained, or

(b) grant the person bail subject to the same or different conditions, subject to sub-paragraph (14).

(13) If the relevant authority decides the person has not broken and is not likely to break any of the bail conditions, the relevant authority must grant the person bail subject to the same conditions (but this is subject to sub-paragraph (14), and does not prevent the subsequent exercise of the powers in paragraph 6).

(14) The power in sub-paragraph (12) to grant bail subject to the same conditions and the duty in sub-paragraph (13) to do so do not affect the requirement for the grant of bail to comply with paragraph 2.

(15) In this paragraph—

'appropriate judicial officer' means—

(a) in relation to England and Wales, a justice of the peace;

(b) in relation to Scotland, the sheriff or a justice of the peace;

(c) in relation to Northern Ireland, a lay magistrate;

'premises'—

(a) in relation to England and Wales, has the same meaning as in the Police and Criminal Evidence Act 1984;

(b) in relation to Scotland, has the same meaning as in section 412 of the Proceeds of Crime Act 2002;

(c) in relation to Northern Ireland, has the same meaning as in the Police and Criminal Evidence (Northern Ireland) Order 1989 (SI 1989/1341 (NI 12)).

Duty to arrange consideration of bail

11 (1) Subject as follows, the Secretary of State must arrange a reference to the First-tier Tribunal for the Tribunal to decide whether to grant bail to a person if—

(a) the person is being detained under a provision mentioned in paragraph 1(1)(a) or (c), and

(b) the period of four months beginning with the relevant date has elapsed.

(2) In sub-paragraph (1)(b) 'the relevant date' means—

(a) the date on which the person's detention began, or

(b) if a relevant event has occurred in relation to the person since that date, the last date on which such an event has occurred in relation to the person.

(3) The following are relevant events in relation to a person for the purposes of sub-paragraph (2)(b)—

(a) consideration by the First-tier Tribunal of whether to grant immigration bail to the person;

(b) withdrawal by the person of an application for immigration bail treated as made by the person as the result of a reference under this paragraph;

(c) withdrawal by the person of a notice given under sub-paragraph (6)(b).

(4) The reference in sub-paragraph (3)(a) to consideration of whether to grant immigration bail to a person—

(a) includes such consideration regardless of whether there is a hearing or the First-tier Tribunal makes a determination in the case in question;

(b) includes the dismissal of an application by virtue of provision made under paragraph 12(2).

(5) The reference in sub-paragraph (3)(a) to consideration of whether to grant immigration bail to a person does not include such consideration in a case where—

(a) the person has made an application for bail, other than one treated as made by the person as the result of a reference under this paragraph, and

(b) the First-tier Tribunal is prevented from granting bail to the person by paragraph 3(4) (requirement for Secretary of State's consent to bail).

(6) The duty in sub-paragraph (1) to arrange a reference does not apply if—

(a) section 3(2) of the Special Immigration Appeals Commission Act 1997 (persons detained in interests of national security etc) applies to the person, or

(b) the person has given to the Secretary of State, and has not withdrawn, written notice that the person does not wish the person's case to be referred to the First-tier Tribunal under this paragraph.

(7) A reference to the First-tier Tribunal under this paragraph in relation to a person is to be treated for all purposes as an application by that person for the grant of bail under paragraph 1(3).

Tribunal Procedure Rules

12 (1) Tribunal Procedure Rules must make provision with respect to applications to the First-tier Tribunal under this Schedule and matters arising out of such applications.

(2) Tribunal Procedure Rules must secure that, where the First-tier Tribunal has decided not to grant a person immigration bail, the Tribunal must dismiss without a hearing any further application for the person to be granted immigration bail which—

(a) is an application to which sub-paragraph (3) applies, but

(b) is not an application to which sub-paragraph (4) applies.

(3) This sub-paragraph applies to an application made during the period of 28 days beginning with the date of the decision mentioned in sub-paragraph (2).

(4) This sub-paragraph applies to an application on which the person demonstrates there has been a material change in the person's circumstances.

Transitional provision

13 (1) Regulations under section 92(1) may, in particular, provide for a person to whom this sub-paragraph applies to be treated, for such purposes as may be specified, as having been granted immigration bail in such circumstances and subject to such conditions as may be specified.

(2) Sub-paragraph (1) applies to a person who, at the specified time, was not in detention on the basis that—

(a) the person had been temporarily admitted to the United Kingdom under paragraph 21 of Schedule 2 to the Immigration Act 1971,

(b) the person had been released from detention under that paragraph,

(c) the person was liable to be detained under paragraph 2(1) of Schedule 3 to the Immigration Act 1971 but, by virtue of a direction of the Secretary of State or the court, was not so detained,

(d) the person was liable to be detained under paragraph 2(2) or (3) of that Schedule but was not so detained,

(e) the person had been released from detention under section 36(3) of the UK Borders Act 2007, or

(f) the person had been released on bail from detention under any provision of the Immigration Acts.

(3) Regulations under section 92(1) may, in particular—

(a) make provision about the circumstances in which the power in paragraph 6(1) may or must be exercised so as to impose an electronic monitoring condition on a person to whom this sub-paragraph applies;

(b) enable the Secretary of State to exercise a discretion in determining whether an electronic monitoring condition should be imposed on such a person,

and may, in particular, do so by providing for paragraph 7 or 8 to have effect with modifications in relation to such a person.

(4) Sub-paragraph (3) applies to a person who—

(a) by virtue of regulations under section 92(1) is treated as having been granted immigration bail as a result of falling within—

(i) sub-paragraph (2)(c), (d) or (e), or

(ii) sub-paragraph (2)(f) on the basis that the person had been released on bail from detention under paragraph 2 of Schedule 3 to the Immigration Act 1971,

(b) is not treated as being subject to an electronic monitoring condition, and

(c) is not otherwise subject to an electronic monitoring condition.

(5) Sub-paragraph (3) applies to a person who—

(a) is on immigration bail pursuant to a grant before the coming into force of paragraph 2(2) and (3), or the coming into force of those provisions in relation to grants of that kind,

(b) before the grant of immigration bail, was detained or liable to detention under a provision mentioned in paragraph 1(1)(b) or (d), and

(c) is not subject to an electronic monitoring condition.

(6) In this paragraph 'specified' means specified in regulations under section 92(1).

Part 2

Amendments to Other Acts

Note: Amends s 11, 24, 28, 28B, 28D and Schedule 2 and 3 of Immigration Act 1971. Amends section sections 3 and 5 of the Special Immigration Appeals Commission Act 1997 and substitutes Schedule 3 to that Act from 15 January 2018 (SI 2017/1241). Amends sections 10(9), 53, 95(9A) and 141 of the Immigration and Asylum Act 1999 from 15 January 2018 (SI 2017/1241). Amends sections 23, 30, 62, 70 and 71 of the Nationality, Immigration and Asylum Act 2002 and omits sections 68 and 69 of that Act from 15 January 2018 (SI 2017/1241). Omits section 36 of Asylum and Immigration (Treatment of Claimants, etc) Act 2004 from 15 January 2018 subject to transitional provisions specified in SI 2017/1241. Amends section 24 of the Immigration, Asylum and Nationality Act 2006 from 15 January 2018 (SI 2017/1241). Amends section 132(4) and substitutes subsections (3)(3A) and (4) of the Criminal Justice and Immigration Act 2008 from 15 January 2018 (SI 2017/1241).

Schedule 11

Support for Certain Categories of Migrant Section 66

Part 1

Amendments of the Immigration Acts

Note: Repeals section 4 of the Immigration and Asylum Act 1999. Modifies definition of 'asylum seeker'; omits definition of 'claim for asylum' and inserts definition for 'further qualifying submissions' and 'protection claim'. Inserts subsections (2A)–(2C) and (3A)–(3D) in section 94, and amends subsection (3) and (8) of section 94 of Immigration and Asylum Act 1999 from a date to be appointed. Amends sections 96, 141, 167 of the Immigration and Asylum Act 1999. Amends paragraph 2(b) of Schedule 8 to the Immigration and Asylum Act 1999, Amends section 135 of the Criminal Justice and Immigration Act 2008. Inserts section 95A and amends title and section 96 of the Immigration and Asylum Act 1999.

Part 2

Transitional and Saving Provision

46 (1) The repeals made by paragraphs 1 and 2 do not apply in relation to—

(a) any person for whom accommodation is being provided under section 4 of the Immigration and Asylum Act 1999 immediately before the day on which those paragraphs come into force,

(b) any person who has made an application before that day for accommodation to be provided under that section and whose application has not been determined or withdrawn before that day,

(c) any person who has appealed before that day against a decision not to provide accommodation for the person under that section, or a decision not to continue to provide accommodation for the person under that section, and whose appeal has not been determined or withdrawn before that day, and

(d) any dependant of a person within paragraph (a), (b) or (c). This is subject to sub-paragraph (2).

(2) The repeals made by paragraph 2(d) (which remove the right to appeal against a decision not to continue to provide accommodation for a person under section 4 of the Immigration and Asylum Act 1999) apply in relation to any decision not to continue to provide accommodation under that section for any person within sub-paragraph (1) which is made on or after the day on which paragraph 2(d) comes into force.

(3) On and after the day on which paragraphs 1 and 2 come into force, section 4 of the Immigration and Asylum Act 1999 has effect in relation to persons within sub-paragraph (1) as if in subsection (11)(b) the word 'not' were omitted.

(4) In this paragraph 'dependant' has the same meaning as in Part 6 of the Immigration and Asylum Act 1999 (see section 94 of that Act).

47 (1) The repeal made by paragraph 7(5) does not apply in relation to—

(a) any person for whom support is being provided under section 95 of the Immigration and Asylum Act 1999 by virtue of section 94(5) of that Act immediately before the day on which paragraph 7(5) comes into force,

(b) any person who has made an application before that day for support to be provided under section 95 of that Act and whose application has not been determined or withdrawn before that day,

(c) any person who has appealed before that day against a decision not to provide support for the person under that section, or a decision not to continue to provide support for the person under that section, and whose appeal has not been determined or withdrawn before that day, and

(d) any dependant of a person within paragraph (a), (b) or (c).

(2) Where by virtue of sub-paragraph (1) a person is provided with support under section 95 of the Immigration and Asylum Act 1999 by virtue of section 94(5) of that Act on or after the day on which paragraph 7(5) comes into force, section 103 of that Act (appeals) does not apply in relation to any decision not to continue to provide that support for that person which is made on or after that day.

(3) In this paragraph 'dependant' has the same meaning as in Part 6 of the Immigration and Asylum Act 1999 (see section 94 of that Act).

Schedule 12

Availability of Local Authority Support — Section 68

Note: Amends Schedule 3 to the Nationality, Immigration and Asylum Act 2002.

Schedule 13

Penalties Relating to Airport Control Areas — Section 74

Note: Inserted at Part 1A of Schedule 2 to Immigration Act 1971, referred to in section 74(2), from a date to be appointed.

Schedule 14

Maritime Enforcement

Section 75

Note: Amends section 25, 25A, 25B, 28, 28A and 28M to 28O and Schedule 4A of the Immigration Act 1971 is amended as follows.

Schedule 15

Civil Registration Fees

Section 89

Part 1

Powers to Make Regulations for the Charging of Fees

Immigration and Social Security Co-ordination (EU Withdrawal) Act 2020

2020 CHAPTER 20

Immigration and Social Security Co-ordination (EU Withdrawal) Act 2020
An Act to make provision to end rights to free movement of persons under retained EU law and to repeal other retained EU law relating to immigration; to confer power to modify retained direct EU legislation relating to social security co-ordination; and for connected purposes. [11th November 2020]

BE IT ENACTED by the Queen's most Excellent Majesty, by and with the advice and consent of the Lords Spiritual and Temporal, and Commons, in this present Parliament assembled, and by the authority of the same, as follows:—

PART 1

MEASURES RELATING TO ENDING FREE MOVEMENT

1. Repeal of the main retained EU law relating to free movement etc.

Schedule 1 makes provision to—

(a) end rights to free movement of persons under retained EU law, including by repealing the main provisions of retained EU law relating to free movement, and

(b) end other EU-derived rights, and repeal other retained EU law, relating to immigration.

2. Irish citizens: entitlement to enter or remain without leave

Note: inserts section 3ZA into the Immigration Act 1971.

3. Protection claimants: legal routes from the EU and family reunion

(1) The Secretary of State must review, or arrange for a review of, the ways in which protection claimants who are in a member State are able to enter the United Kingdom lawfully.

(2) For the purposes of this section a 'protection claimant' is a person who—

(a) has made an application for international protection to a member State, or

(b) is not a national of a member State and is seeking to come to the United Kingdom from a member State for the purpose of making a protection claim.

(3) The review under subsection (1) must, in particular—

(a) consider the position of unaccompanied children in member States who are protection claimants and are seeking to come to the United Kingdom to join relatives there, and

(b) include a public consultation on that aspect of the review.

(4) The Secretary of State must, within the period of three months beginning with the day on which this Act is passed, lay before Parliament a statement providing further details about the review under subsection (1) and, in particular, about the aspect of the review described in subsection (3).

(5) After the review, the Secretary of State must—

(a) prepare a report on the outcome of the review or arrange for such a report to be prepared, and

(b) publish the report and lay it before Parliament.

(6) In this section—

application for international protection' has the meaning given by Article 2(h) of Directive 2011/95/EU of the European Parliament and of the Council on standards for the qualification of third-country nationals or stateless persons as beneficiaries of international protection, for a uniform status for refugees or for persons eligible for subsidiary protection, and for the content of the protection granted;

'protection claim' has the same meaning as in Part 5 of the Nationality, Immigration and Asylum Act 2002 (see section 82(2) of that Act);

'relative', in relation to an unaccompanied child, means a parent, grandparent, uncle, aunt, brother or sister of the child;

'unaccompanied child' means a person under the age of 18 ('the child') who is not in the care of a person who—

(a) is aged 18 or over, and

(b) by law or custom of the country or territory in which the child is present, has responsibility for caring for the child.

Note: S. 3(4) in force from January 11, 2021. S 3(2)(6) in force for specified purposes at 11.1.2021

4. Meaning of 'the Immigration Acts' etc.

Note: amends s 61 of the UK Borders Act 2007.

5. Consequential etc. provision

(1) The Secretary of State may by regulations made by statutory instrument make such provision as the Secretary of State considers appropriate in consequence of, or in connection with, any provision of this Part.

(2) The power to make regulations under subsection (1) may (among other things) be exercised by modifying—

(a) any provision made by or under primary legislation passed before, or in the same Session as, this Act;

(b) retained direct EU legislation.

(3) The power to make regulations under subsection (1) includes power—

(a) to make supplementary, incidental, transitional, transitory or saving provision;

(b) to make different provision for different purposes.

(4) Regulations under subsection (1) may (among other things) make provision applying to persons who, immediately before the coming into force of the repeal of section 7(1) of the Immigration Act 1988 by paragraph 1 of Schedule 1, were not entitled by virtue of section 7(1) of that Act to enter or remain in the United Kingdom without leave.

(5) Regulations under subsection (1) may (among other things) modify provision relating to the imposition of fees or charges which is made by or under primary legislation passed before, or in the same Session as, this Act.

(6) The first statutory instrument containing regulations under subsection (1)—

(a) must be laid before Parliament after being made, and

(b) ceases to have effect at the end of the period of 40 days beginning with the day on which the instrument is made unless, during that period, the instrument is approved by a resolution of each House of Parliament.

(7) Any other statutory instrument containing regulations under subsection (1) that amend or repeal any provision of primary legislation (whether alone or with other provision) is not to be made unless a draft of the instrument has been laid before, and approved by a resolution of, each House of Parliament.

(8) A statutory instrument containing regulations under subsection (1), other than a statutory instrument to which subsection (6) or (7) applies, is subject to annulment in pursuance of a resolution of either House of Parliament.

(9) In calculating the period of 40 days for the purposes of subsection (6), no account is to be taken of any time during which—

(a) Parliament is dissolved or prorogued, or

(b) either House of Parliament is adjourned for more than 4 days.

(10) If regulations cease to have effect as a result of subsection (6), that—

(a) does not affect the validity of anything previously done under the regulations, and

(b) does not prevent the making of new regulations.

Note: commenced from November 11, 2020 by S.I. 2020/1279, reg. 2(a)

Part 2

Social security co-ordination

6. Power to modify retained direct EU legislation relating to social security co-ordination

'Note::commenced from November 14, 2020 by S.I. 2020/1279, reg. 2(b)

Part 3

General

7. Interpretation

In this Act—

• 'domestic law' means the law of England and Wales, Scotland or Northern Ireland;

• 'Minister of the Crown' has the same meaning as in the Ministers of the Crown Act 1975 and also includes the Commissioners for Her Majesty's Revenue and Customs;

• 'modify' includes amend, repeal or revoke (and related expressions are to be read accordingly);

'primary legislation' means—a) an Act of Parliament;

(b) an Act of the Scottish Parliament;

(c) an Act or Measure of Senedd Cymru;

(d) Northern Ireland legislation.

8. Extent

(1) Subject to subsections (2) to (5), this Act extends to England and Wales, Scotland and Northern Ireland.

(2) Her Majesty may by Order in Council provide for any of the provisions of Part 1 of this Act, and of sections 7 and 10 (so far as relating to that Part), to extend, with or without modifications, to—

(a) any of the Channel Islands;
(b) the Isle of Man;
(c) any of the British overseas territories.

(3) A power listed in subsection (4) may be exercised so as to extend, with or without modifications, to any of the Channel Islands or the Isle of Man any repeal or other amendment, made by Part 1, of legislation to which the power relates.

(4) The powers are the powers under any of the following provisions—

(a) section 36 of the Immigration Act 1971;
(b) section 163(4) of the Nationality, Immigration and Asylum Act 2002;
(c) section 60(4) of the UK Borders Act 2007.

(5) Regulations under section 5 may provide that an amendment, repeal or revocation made by those regulations has the same extent as the provision amended, repealed or revoked (ignoring extent by virtue of an Order in Council under any of the Immigration Acts).

9. Commencement

(1) Subject to subsection (2), Part 1 comes into force on such day as the Secretary of State may by regulations made by statutory instrument appoint.

(2) The following provisions of section 3 come into force at the end of the period of two months beginning with the day on which this Act is passed—

(a) subsection (4);
(b) subsections (2) and (6) so far as relating to subsection (4).

(3) Regulations under subsection (1) may make different provision for different purposes.

(4) Part 2 comes into force on such day as the Secretary of State or the Treasury may by regulations made by statutory instrument appoint.

(5) Regulations under subsection (4) may make different provision for different purposes or areas.

(6) This Part comes into force on the day on which this Act is passed.

(7) The power of the Secretary of State or the Treasury to appoint a day under subsection (1) or (4) includes a power to appoint a time on a day if the Secretary of State or, as the case may be, the Treasury considers it appropriate to do so.

10. Short title

This Act may be cited as the Immigration and Social Security Co-ordination (EU Withdrawal) Act 2020.

Schedules

Section 1

Schedule 1

Repeal of the main retained EU law relating to free movement etc.

Part 1

EU-derived domestic legislation

1 ...

2(1) ...

(2) ...

(3) ...

3 ...

Note: para 1 omits section 7 of the Immigration Act 1988; para 2(1) omits section 109 of Nationality, Immigration and Asylum Act 2002; para 2(2) revokes Immigration (European Economic Area) Regulations 2016(SI2016/1052); para 2(3)(i) &(ii) amend sections 106(3) & (4) of the 2002 Act, and para 3 inserts para (2A) into the Provision of Services 2009 (SI2009/2999).

Part 2

Retained direct EU legislation

4 (1) Article 1 of the Workers Regulation is omitted.

(2) Articles 2 to 10 of the Workers Regulation cease to apply so far as—

(a) they are inconsistent with any provision made by or under the Immigration Acts (including, and as amended by, this Act), or

(b) they are otherwise capable of affecting the interpretation, application or operation of any such provision.

(3) In this paragraph, 'the Workers Regulation' means Regulation (EU) No 492/2011 of the European Parliament and of the Council of 5 April 2011 on freedom of movement for workers within the Union.

Part 3

EU-derived rights etc.

5 (1) Any rights, powers, liabilities, obligations, restrictions, remedies and procedures which—

(a) continue to be recognised and available in domestic law by virtue of section 4 of the European Union (Withdrawal) Act 2018, and

(b) are derived from Articles 1, 2, 3(1) to (4), 4, 6, 7, 12, 13, 17(b), 20, 23 or 24 of Annex 1 of the Swiss free movement agreement (or, so far as relating to any of those Articles of that Annex, Articles 3 to 6 of the agreement), cease to be recognised and available in domestic law.

(2) In sub-paragraph (1), 'the Swiss free movement agreement' means the Agreement between the European Community and its Member States, of the one part, and the Swiss Confederation, of the other, on the free movement of persons (done at Luxembourg on 21 June 1999).

6 (1) Any other EU-derived rights, powers, liabilities, obligations, restrictions, remedies and procedures cease to be recognised and available in domestic law so far as—

(a) they are inconsistent with, or are otherwise capable of affecting the interpretation, application or operation of, any provision made by or under the Immigration Acts (including, and as amended by, this Act), or

(b) they are otherwise capable of affecting the exercise of functions in connection with immigration.

(2) The reference in sub-paragraph (1) to any other EU-derived rights, powers, liabilities, obligations, restrictions, remedies and procedures is a reference to any rights, powers, liabilities, obligations, restrictions, remedies and procedures which—

(a) continue to be recognised and available in domestic law by virtue of section 4 of the European Union (Withdrawal) Act 2018 (including as they are modified by domestic law from time to time), and

(b) are not those described in paragraph 5 of this Schedule.

(3) The reference in sub-paragraph (1) to provision made by or under the Immigration Acts includes provision made after that sub-paragraph comes into force.

SCHEDULE 2 Section 6(8)

FURTHER PROVISION ABOUT THE SCOPE OF THE POWER UNDER SECTION 6

SCHEDULE 3 Section 6(9)

REGULATIONS UNDER SECTION 6

Part 3
Citizens' Rights

Rights in relation to entry and residence

7 Rights related to residence: application deadline and temporary protection

(1) A Minister of the Crown may by regulations make such provision as the Minister considers appropriate for any of the following purposes—

(a) specifying the deadline that applies for the purposes of—

(i) the first sub-paragraph of Article 18(1)(b) of the withdrawal agreement (deadline for the submission of applications for the new residence status described in Article 18(1));

(ii) the first sub-paragraph of Article 17(1)(b) of the EEA EFTA separation agreement (deadline for the submission of applications for the new residence status described in Article 17(1));

(iii) the first sentence of Article 16(1)(b) of the Swiss citizens' rights agreement (deadline for the submission of applications for the new residence status described in Article 16(1));

(b) implementing Article 18(2) of the withdrawal agreement (protection for Union citizens etc. in the period prior to the deadline for the submission of applications for the new residence status described in Article 18(1));

(c) implementing Article 17(2) of the EEA EFTA separation agreement (protection for EEA EFTA nationals etc. in the period prior to the deadline for the submission of applications for the new residence status described in Article 17(1));

(d) implementing Article 16(2) of the Swiss citizens' rights agreement (protection for Swiss nationals etc. in the period prior to the deadline for the submission of applications for the new residence status described in Article 16(1));

(e) implementing Article 18(3) of the withdrawal agreement (protection for Union citizens etc. pending a final decision on an application for the new residence status described in Article 18(1));

(f) implementing Article 17(3) of the EEA EFTA separation agreement (protection for EEA EFTA nationals etc. pending a final decision on an application for the new residence status described in Article 17(1));

(g) implementing Article 16(3) of the Swiss citizens' rights agreement (protection for Swiss nationals etc. pending a final decision on an application for the new residence status described in Article 16(1)).

(2) If the Minister considers it appropriate, regulations under subsection (1) relating to the implementation of a provision mentioned in subsection (1)(b), (c) or (d) may be made so as to apply both to—

(a) persons to whom the provision in question applies, and

(b) persons to whom that provision does not apply but who may be granted leave to enter or remain in the United Kingdom by virtue of residence scheme immigration rules (see section 17) and who do not have such leave.

(3) If the Minister considers it appropriate, regulations under subsection (1) relating to the implementation of a provision mentioned in subsection (1)(e), (f) or (g) may be made so as to apply both to—

(a) persons to whom the provision in question applies, and

(b) persons to whom that provision does not apply but who make an application for leave to enter or remain in the United Kingdom by virtue of residence scheme immigration rules.

(4) The power to make regulations under subsection (1) may (among other things) be exercised by modifying any provision made by or under an enactment.

8 Frontier workers

(1) A Minister of the Crown may by regulations make such provision as the Minister considers appropriate for the purpose of implementing any of the following—

(a) Articles 24(3) and 25(3) of the withdrawal agreement (rights of employed and self-employed frontier workers) other than as regards rights enjoyed as workers (see section 14(1));

(b) Articles 23(3) and 24(3) of the EEA EFTA separation agreement (rights of employed and self-employed frontier workers) other than as regards rights enjoyed as workers (see section 14(2));

(c) Article 20(2) of the Swiss citizens' rights agreement (rights of frontier workers to enter and exit).

(2) A Minister of the Crown may by regulations make such provision as the Minister considers appropriate for the purpose of implementing any of the following—

(a) Article 26 of the withdrawal agreement (issue of documents);

(b) Article 25 of the EEA EFTA separation agreement (issue of documents);

(c) Article 21(1)(a) and (2) of the Swiss citizens' rights agreement (issue of documents).

(3) The power to make regulations under subsection (1) or (2) may (among other things) be exercised by modifying any provision made by or under the Immigration Acts.

9 Restrictions of rights of entry and residence

(1) A Minister of the Crown may by regulations make such provision as the Minister considers appropriate for the purpose of implementing any of the following—

(a) Article 20(1), (3) and (4) of the withdrawal agreement (restrictions of the rights of entry and residence);

(b) Article 19(1), (3) and (4) of the EEA EFTA separation agreement (restrictions of the rights of entry and residence);

(c) Articles 17(1) and (3) and 20(3) of the Swiss citizens' rights agreement (restrictions of the rights of entry and residence).

(2) If the Minister considers it appropriate, regulations under subsection (1) relating to the implementation of a provision mentioned in subsection (1)(a), (b) or (c) may be made so as to apply both to—

(a) persons to whom the provision in question applies, and
(b) persons to whom that provision does not apply but who—

(i) have entry clearance granted by virtue of relevant entry clearance immigration rules (see section 17),

(ii) have leave to enter or remain in the United Kingdom granted by virtue of residence scheme immigration rules (see section 17), or

(iii) otherwise have leave to enter granted after arriving with entry clearance granted by virtue of relevant entry clearance immigration rules.

(3) In subsection (2)(b), references to a person who has entry clearance or leave to enter or remain include references to a person who would have had entry clearance or leave to enter or remain but for—

(a) the making of a deportation order under section 5(1) of the Immigration Act 1971, or

(b) the making of any other decision made in connection with restricting the right of the person to enter the United Kingdom.

(4) The power to make regulations under subsection (1) may (among other things) be exercised by modifying any provision made—

(a) by or under the Immigration Acts, or (b) under other primary legislation.

10 Retention of existing grounds for deportation

(1) ...

(2) ...

(3) ...

(4) ...

(5) ...

Note: subsections (1)-(4) amend section 3 of the Immigration Act 1971.

Note: subsection 5 amends section 33 of the UK Borders Act 2007 (exceptions to automatic deportation.

(6) In section 3(10) of the Immigration Act 1971 and section 33(6C) of the UK Borders Act 2007 (for which see subsections (4) and (5) above), references to having leave to enter or remain in the United Kingdom granted by virtue of residence scheme immigration rules include references to having such leave granted by virtue of those rules before section 17 comes into force.

11 Appeals etc. against citizens' rights immigration decisions

(1) A Minister of the Crown may by regulations make provision for, or in connection with, appeals against citizens' rights immigration decisions of a kind described in the regulations.

(2) For the purposes of this section, each of the following is a "citizens' rights immigration decision"—

(a) a decision made in connection with entry clearance by virtue of relevant entry clearance immigration rules (see section 17);

(b) a decision made in connection with leave to enter or remain in the United Kingdom by virtue of residence scheme immigration rules (see section 17);

(c) a decision made in connection with entry clearance for the purposes of acquiring leave to enter or remain in relation to a healthcare right of entry;

(d) a decision made in connection with leave to enter or remain in the United Kingdom in relation to a healthcare right of entry;

(e) a decision made in connection with a right to enter or remain in the United Kingdom by virtue of regulations made under section 8 (frontier workers);

(f) a decision to make, or a refusal to revoke, a deportation order under section 5(1) of the Immigration Act 1971 in relation to a relevant person;

(g) any other decision made in connection with restricting the right of a relevant person to enter the United Kingdom.

(3) A Minister of the Crown may also by regulations make provision for, or in connection with, reviews (including judicial reviews) of decisions within subsection (2)(g).

(4) The power to make regulations under subsection (1) or (3) may (among other things) be exercised by modifying any provision made by or under an enactment.

(5) Such regulations may, for example, apply with or without modifications any enactment which applies in relation to appeals under section 82 of the Nationality, Immigration and Asylum Act 2002 or section 2 of the Special Immigration Appeals Commission Act 1997.

(6) For the purposes of subsection (2), a "healthcare right of entry" is a right to enter the United Kingdom that a person has by virtue of—

(a) Article 32(1)(b) of the withdrawal agreement,

(b) Article 31(1)(b) of the EEA EFTA separation agreement, or (c) Article 26a(1)(b) of the Swiss citizens' rights agreement.

(7) For the purposes of subsection (2)(f) and (g), a person is a "relevant person" if—

(a) Article 20 of the withdrawal agreement, Article 19 of the EEA EFTA separation agreement or (as the case may be) Articles 17 or 20(3) of the Swiss citizens' rights agreement (restrictions of the rights of entry and residence) applies to the person, or

(b) the person is not within paragraph (a) but—

(i) has entry clearance granted by virtue of relevant entry clearance immigration rules,

(ii) has leave to enter or remain in the United Kingdom granted by virtue of residence scheme immigration rules, or

(iii) otherwise has leave to enter granted after arriving with entry clearance granted by virtue of relevant entry clearance immigration rules.

(8) In subsection (7)(b), references to a person who has entry clearance or leave to enter or remain include references to a person who would have had entry clearance or leave to enter or remain but for—

(a) the making of a deportation order under section 5(1) of the Immigration Act 1971, or

(b) the making of any other decision made in connection with restricting the right of the person to enter the United Kingdom.

Professional qualifications

12 Recognition of professional qualifications

Co-ordination of social security systems

13 Co-ordination of social security systems

Equal treatment etc.

14 Non-discrimination, equal treatment and rights of workers etc.

Independent Monitoring Authority

15 Independent Monitoring Authority for the Citizens' Rights Agreements

General

16 Regulations: supplementary

17 Interpretation: Part 3

(1) In this Part, "residence scheme immigration rules" means—

(a) Appendix EU to the immigration rules except those rules, or changes to that Appendix, which are identified in the immigration rules as not having effect in connection with the residence scheme that operates in connection with the withdrawal of the United Kingdom from the EU, and

(b) any other immigration rules which are identified in the immigration rules as having effect in connection with the withdrawal of the United Kingdom from the EU.

(2) In this Part, "relevant entry clearance immigration rules" means any immigration rules which are identified in the immigration rules as having effect in connection with the granting of entry clearance for the purposes of acquiring leave to enter or remain in the United Kingdom by virtue of residence scheme immigration rules.

(3) In this Part, references to having leave to enter or remain in the United Kingdom granted by virtue of residence scheme immigration rules include references to having such leave granted by virtue of those rules before this section comes into force.

(4) In this Part, a reference to a Chapter, Title, Part or other provision of the withdrawal agreement, EEA EFTA separation agreement or Swiss citizens' rights agreement includes a reference to—

(a) any other provision of the agreement in question so far as relating to that Chapter, Title, Part or other provision, and

(b) any provision of EU law which is applied by, or referred to in, that Chapter, Title, Part or other provision (to the extent of the application or reference).

(5) In this Part—

"entry clearance" has the meaning given by section 33(1) of the Immigration Act 1971 (interpretation);

"immigration rules" has the same meaning as in the Immigration Act 1971.

Schedule 4

Regulations Under This Act

Part 1

procedure

Rights in relation to entry and residence

1 (1) A statutory instrument containing—

(a) the first regulations under section 7(1)(b), (c), (d), (e), (f) or (g), 8(1) or 9, or

(b) regulations under section 7, 8 or 9 which amend, repeal or revoke primary legislation or retained direct principal EU legislation, may not be made unless a draft of the instrument has been laid before, and approved by a resolution of, each House of Parliament.

(2) Any other statutory instrument containing regulations under section 7, 8 or 9 is subject to annulment in pursuance of a resolution of either House of Parliament.

2 (1) A statutory instrument containing the first regulations under section 11—

(a) must be laid before Parliament after being made, and

(b) ceases to have effect at the end of the period of 40 days beginning with the day on which the instrument is made unless, during that period, the instrument is approved by a resolution of each House of Parliament.

(2) Any other statutory instrument containing regulations under section 11 which amend, repeal or revoke—

(a) primary legislation, or

(b) retained direct principal EU legislation, may not be made unless a draft of the instrument has been laid before, and approved by a resolution of, each House of Parliament.

(3) A statutory instrument containing regulations under section 11, other than a statutory instrument to which sub-paragraph (1) or (2) applies, is subject to annulment in pursuance of a resolution of either House of Parliament.

(4) In calculating the period of 40 days for the purposes of sub-paragraph (1) no account is to be taken of any time during which— (a) Parliament is dissolved or prorogued, or

(b) either House of Parliament is adjourned for more than four days.

(5) If regulations cease to have effect as a result of sub-paragraph (1) that—

(a) does not affect the validity of anything previously done under the regulations, and

(b) does not prevent the making of new regulations.

Powers under sections 12, 13 and 14: sole exercise

3 …

Powers under sections 12, 13 and 14: joint exercise

4 …

Power to amend definition of "IP completion day"

5 A statutory instrument containing regulations under section 39(4) is subject to annulment in pursuance of a resolution of either House of Parliament.

Consequential provision

6 …

The IMA

7 …

Power under paragraph 1(3) of Schedule 5: sole exercise

8 …

Power under paragraph 1(3) of Schedule 5: joint exercise

9 …

Power under paragraph 3(2) of Schedule 5

10 …

Combinations of instruments

11 …

Nationality and Borders Act 2022

Contents

Part 1
Nationality

British overseas territories citizenship

British citizenship

Powers of the Secretary of State relating to citizenship etc

Registration of stateless minors

Part 2
Asylum

Treatment of refugees; support for asylum-seekers

Place of claim

Inadmissibility

Supporting evidence

Priority removal notices

Late evidence

Appeals

Interpretation of Refugee Convention

Interpretation

PART 3
IMMIGRATION CONTROL

Immigration offences and penalties

Working in United Kingdom waters: arrival and entry

Enforcement

NATIONALITY AND BORDERS ACT 2022

2022 CHAPTER 36

An Act to make provision about nationality, asylum and immigration; to make provision about victims of slavery or human trafficking; to provide a power for Tribunals to charge participants where their behaviour has wasted the Tribunal's resources; and for connected purposes. [28th April 2022]

BE IT ENACTED by the Queen's most Excellent Majesty, by and with the advice and consent of the Lords Spiritual and Temporal, and Commons, in this present Parliament assembled, and by the authority of the same, as follows:—

PART 1

NATIONALITY

British overseas territories citizenship

1 Historical inability of mothers to transmit citizenship

Note: inserts 17A & s.25(1)(a) of British Nationality Act 1981 from June 28, 2022 (SI 2022/590).

2 Historical inability of unmarried fathers to transmit citizenship

Note: inserts 17B-17B British Nationality Act 1981 from June 28, 2022 (SI 2022/590). Inserts s.25(1)(cb) & s41(2A) of 1981 c.61 from June 28, 2022 (SI 2022/590)

3 Provision for Chagos Islanders to acquire British Nationality

Note: inserts 17H of British Nationality Act 1981 (date to be appointed)

4 Sections 1 to 3: related British citizenship

Note: inserts 4K of the British Nationality Act 1981 (SI 2022/590). Inserts s.14(1)(db) & s.41(2B) & (2C) of 1981 c. 61 (SI2022/590)

5 Period for registration of person born outside the British overseas territories

Note: Amends s17 & 41 of British Nationality Act 1981 from June 28, 2022 (SI 2022/590)

British citizenship

6 Disapplication of historical registration requirements

Note: inserts s.4C(3D) & s.41(1A) of British Nationality Act 1981 from June 28, 2022 (SI 2022/590)

7 Citizenship where mother married to someone other than natural father

Note: amends s.4E, s.4F & s.41A of British Nationality Act 1981 from June 28, 2022 (SI 2022/590)

Powers of the Secretary of State relating to citizenship etc

8 Citizenship: registration in special cases

Note: inserts 4L & 17I of British Nationality Act 1981 from June 28, 2022 (SI 2022/590)

9 Requirements for naturalisation etc

Note: Omits s.39, 40, 41(1)–(3), & 49(2)-(3), and amends of Borders, Citizenship and Immigration Act 2009 from June 28, 2022 (SI 2022/590)

10 Notice of decision to deprive a person of citizenship

Note: inserts s.40(5A)-(5E) and s.40A(1), (2A) and Schedule 4A of British and Nationality Act 2022 (date to be appointed)

Registration of stateless minors

11 Citizenship: stateless minors

Note: inserts paragraph 3A and amends Schedule 2 of British Nationality Act 1982 from June 28, 2022 (SI 2022/590)

Part 2

Asylum

Treatment of refugees; support for asylum-seekers

12 Differential treatment of refugees

(1) For the purposes of this section—

(a) a refugee is a Group 1 refugee if they have complied with both of the requirements set out in subsection (2) and, where applicable, the additional requirement in subsection (3);

(b) otherwise, a refugee is a Group 2 refugee.

(2) The requirements in this subsection are that—

(a) they have come to the United Kingdom directly from a country or territory where their life or freedom was threatened (in the sense of Article 1 of the Refugee Convention), and

(b) they have presented themselves without delay to the authorities. Subsections (1) to (3) of section 37 apply in relation to the interpretation of paragraphs (a) and (b) as they apply in relation to the interpretation of those requirements in Article 31(1) of the Refugee Convention.

(3) Where a refugee has entered or is present in the United Kingdom unlawfully, the additional requirement is that they can show good cause for their unlawful entry or presence.

(4) For the purposes of subsection (3), a person's entry into or presence in the United Kingdom is unlawful if they require leave to enter or remain and do not have it.

(5) The Secretary of State or an immigration officer may treat Group 1 and Group 2 refugees differently, for example in respect of—

(a) the length of any period of limited leave to enter or remain which is given to the refugee;

(b) the requirements that the refugee must meet in order to be given indefinite leave to remain;

(c) whether a condition under section 3(1)(c)(ii) of the Immigration Act 1971 (no recourse to public funds) is attached to any period of limited leave to enter or remain that is given to the refugee;

(d) whether leave to enter or remain is given to members of the refugee's family.

(6) The Secretary of State or an immigration officer may also treat the family members of Group 1 and Group 2 refugees differently, for example in respect of—

(a) whether to give the person leave to enter or remain;

(b) the length of any period of limited leave to enter or remain which is given to the person;

(c) the requirements that the person must meet in order to be given indefinite leave to remain;

(d) whether a condition under section 3(1)(c)(ii) of the Immigration Act 1971 (no recourse to public funds) is attached to any period of limited leave to enter or remain that is given to the person.

(7) But subsection (6) does not apply to family members who are refugees themselves.

(8) Immigration rules may include provision for the differential treatment allowed for by subsections (5) and (6).

(9) In this section—

"limited leave" and "indefinite leave" have the same meaning as in the Immigration Act 1971 (see section 33 of that Act);

"refugee" has the same meaning as in the Refugee Convention.

13 Accommodation for asylum-seekers etc

Note: inserts s.97(3A), 98(4) & 98A(5) and amends s.97(3A) of Immigration and Asylum Act 1999. Amends s,17, s.22 and inserts s.22A of Nationality, Immigration and Asylum Act 2002. S.13(1) & (3) only commenced from June 28, 2022 (SI 2022/590)

Place of claim

14 Requirement to make asylum claim at "designated place"

(1) An asylum claim must be made in person at a designated place.

(2) A "designated place" means any of the following places in the United Kingdom—

(a) a place identified in a notice published by the Secretary of State as an asylum intake unit;

(b) a removal centre (within the meaning of section 147 of the Immigration and Asylum Act 1999);

(c) a port (within the meaning of section 33 of the Immigration Act 1971);

(d) a place where there is a person present who, for the purposes of the immigration rules, is authorised to accept an asylum claim on behalf of the Secretary of State;

(e) a place to which the claimant has been directed by the Secretary of State or an immigration officer to make the claim;

(f) such other place, or a place of such other description, as the Secretary of State may by regulations designate.

(3) …

(4) …

(5) …

(6) In this section "asylum claim" means a claim made in accordance with the immigration rules by a person to the Secretary of State that to remove the person from, or require the person to leave, the United Kingdom would breach the United Kingdom's obligations under the Refugee Convention.

(7) The reference to the United Kingdom in subsection (2), so far as it has effect for the purposes of paragraph (d) of that subsection, does not include a reference to the territorial sea of the United Kingdom.

(8) Regulations under subsection (2)(f) are subject to negative resolution procedure.

Note: subsections (3) –(5) amend s.18 & s.21 of Nationality, Immigration and Asylum Act 2002. Subsections (1), (2), (6) and (7)(remainder) commenced from June 28, 2022 (SI 2022/590)

Inadmissibility

15 Asylum claims by EU nationals: inadmissibility

Note: inserts s.80A to Nationality, Immigration and Asylum Act 2022 from June 28, 2022 (SI 2022/590)

16 Asylum claims by persons with connection to safe third State: inadmissibility

Note: inserts s.80B & 80C to Nationality, Immigration and Asylum Act 2002 from June 28, 2022

17 Clarification of basis for support where asylum claim inadmissible

Note: inserts s.94(4A)-(4C) of Immigration and Asylum Act 1999 from June 28, 2022 (SI 2022/590). Inserts s.18(1ZA)& (1ZB) and amends s.31 and para 17 of Sch.3 of Nationality, Immigration and Asylum Act 2022 from June 28, 2022 (SI 2022/590)

Supporting evidence

18 Provision of evidence in support of protection or human rights claim

(1) The Secretary of State or an immigration officer may serve an evidence notice on a person who has made a protection claim or a human rights claim.

(2) An "evidence notice" is a notice requiring the recipient to provide, before the specified date, any evidence in support of the claim.

(3) Subsection (5) applies if the recipient of an evidence notice provides the Secretary of State or an immigration officer with evidence in support of the claim on or after the specified date.

(4) Subsection (5) also applies if the recipient of an evidence notice provides the First-tier Tribunal, the Upper Tribunal (when acting in the circumstances mentioned in section 22(9)) or the Special Immigration Appeals Commission with evidence in support of the claim where the evidence—

(a) should have been provided in response to the evidence notice but was not, and
(b) is provided on or after the specified date.

(5) The recipient must also provide a statement setting out their reasons for not providing the evidence before the specified date (and see section 26 of this Act and section 8 of the Asylum and Immigration (Treatment of Claimants, etc) Act 2004).

(6) In this section, "specified date" means the date specified in an evidence notice.

Note: commences on date to be appointed

19 Asylum or human rights claim: damage to claimant's credibility

Note: inserts s.1(1A), s.1(3A) &(3B), s.1(6A) & (6B) and s1(9B) and amends s.1(7) of Asylum and Immigration (Treatment of Claimants, etc) Act 2004 from a date to be appointed

Priority removal notices

20 Priority removal notices

(1) The Secretary of State or an immigration officer may serve a person who is liable to removal or deportation from the United Kingdom with a priority removal notice.

(2) A person who receives such a notice is referred to in this section as the "PRN recipient".

(3) A priority removal notice is a notice—

(a) requiring the PRN recipient to provide to the Secretary of State (and any other competent authority specified in the notice)—

(i) a statement setting out the matters described in section 120(2)(a) to (c) of the Nationality, Immigration and Asylum Act 2002 (reasons and grounds for application etc),

(ii) any relevant status information (within the meaning given by section 58(3)), and

(iii) any evidence in support of the matters mentioned in sub- paragraphs (i) and (ii), and

(b) setting out the date (the "PRN cut-off date") before which the PRN recipient must comply with that requirement.

(4) The requirement in subsection (3)(a) does not apply in relation to anything that the PRN recipient has previously provided to the Secretary of State or any other competent authority.

(5) Subsection (7) applies if the PRN recipient provides the Secretary of State or any other competent authority with any statement, information or evidence mentioned in subsection (3)(a) on or after the PRN cut-off date.

(6) Subsection (7) also applies if the PRN recipient provides the First-tier Tribunal, the Upper Tribunal (when acting in the circumstances mentioned in section 22(9)) or the Special Immigration Appeals Commission with any statement, information or evidence mentioned in subsection (3)(a) that—

(a) should have been provided in response to the priority removal notice but was not, and

(b) is provided on or after the PRN cut-off date.

(7) The PRN recipient must also provide a statement setting out their reasons for not providing the statement, information or evidence before the PRN cut-off date (and see sections 22 and 26).

(8) For the purposes of this section, a person is "liable to removal or deportation from the United Kingdom" if they are liable to—

(a) removal under section 10 of the Immigration and Asylum Act 1999 (removal of persons unlawfully in the United Kingdom), or

(b) deportation under section 3(5) or (6) of the Immigration Act 1971 (deportation of foreign nationals where conducive to the public good or on conviction of offence punishable with imprisonment etc).

(9) In this section "competent authority" has the same meaning as in Part 5 (see section 69).

Note: commences from date to be appointed

21. Priority removal notices: supplementary

(1) A priority removal notice remains in force until the end of the period of 12 months beginning with—

(a) the PRN cut-off date, or

(b) if later, the day on which any appeal rights of the PRN recipient in respect of a relevant claim are exhausted.

See section 82A of the Nationality, Immigration and Asylum Act 2002 (the "2002 Act") for the consequences of a priority removal notice being in force.

(2) In subsection (1) "relevant claim" means a protection claim or a human rights claim brought by the PRN recipient while the priority removal notice is in force.

(3) For the purposes of subsection (1), the PRN recipient's appeal rights in respect of a claim are exhausted at the time when—

(a) the PRN recipient's claim has been determined,

(b) the PRN recipient could not bring an appeal in respect of the claim under section 82 of the 2002 Act (ignoring any possibility of an appeal out of time with permission), and

(c) no appeal brought by the PRN recipient is pending within the meaning of section 104 of that Act.

(4) A priority removal notice remains in force until the end of the period mentioned in subsection (1) even if the PRN recipient ceases to be liable to removal or deportation from the United Kingdom during that period.

(5) A priority removal notice may not be served on a person in relation to whom such a notice is already in force (but this does not prevent a further notice from being served once the previous notice ceases to be in force as mentioned in subsection (1)).

(6) Subsection (7) applies if the PRN recipient has previously been served with—

(a) an evidence notice under section 18,

(b) a slavery or trafficking information notice under section 58, or

(c) a notice under section 120 of the 2002 Act (requirement to provide reasons and grounds).

(7) The previous notice ceases to have effect on the service of the priority removal notice.

(8) Expressions used in this section that are defined for the purposes of section 20 have the same meaning in this section as in that section.

Note: commences from date to be appointed

22. Late compliance with priority removal notice: damage to credibility

(1) This section applies where—

(a) a PRN recipient provided material in response to the priority removal notice served on them,

(b) the material was provided late, and

(c) a relevant decision is being made.

(2) This section also applies where—

(a) a PRN recipient provided material to the First-tier Tribunal, the Upper Tribunal (when acting in the circumstances mentioned in subsection (9)) or the Special Immigration Appeals Commission,

(b) the material should have been provided in response to the priority removal notice served on the PRN recipient but was not,

(c) the material was provided late, and

(d) a relevant decision is being made.

(3) A "relevant decision" is being made if—

(a) a protection claim or a human rights claim made by the PRN recipient is being considered, or

(b) a competent authority is making a reasonable grounds decision or a conclusive grounds decision in relation to the PRN recipient (decisions concerning status as victim of slavery or human trafficking).

(4) In determining whether to believe a statement made by or on behalf of the PRN recipient, a deciding authority must take account, as damaging the PRN recipient's

credibility, of the late provision of the material, unless there are good reasons why it was provided late.

(5) Tribunal Procedure Rules must secure that, where the First-tier Tribunal or the Upper Tribunal (when acting in the circumstances mentioned in subsection (9)) is making a decision that disposes of proceedings, it must include, as part of its reasons for the decision, a statement explaining—

(a) whether it considers that this section applies, and

(b) if it considers that this section does apply, how, in making its decision, it has taken account of the fact that the PRN recipient provided the material late.

(6) Rules under section 5 of the Special Immigration Appeals Commission Act 1997 (SIAC procedure rules) must secure that, where the Special Immigration Appeals Commission is making a decision that determines proceedings, it must include, as part of its reasons for the decision, a statement explaining the matters mentioned in subsection (5)(a) and (b).

(7) For the purposes of this section, material is provided "late" by the PRN recipient if it is provided on or after the PRN cut-off date.

(8) In subsection (4) "deciding authority"—

(a) in relation to a decision mentioned in subsection (3)(a) means—

(i) the Secretary of State,

(ii) an immigration officer,

(iii) the First-tier Tribunal,

(iv) the Upper Tribunal in the circumstances described in subsection (9), or

(v) the Special Immigration Appeals Commission;

(b) in relation to a decision mentioned in subsection (3)(b), means the competent authority.

(9) The circumstances are when the Upper Tribunal is acting—

(a) under section 12(2)(b)(ii) of the Tribunals, Courts and Enforcement Act 2007 (Upper Tribunal re-making First-tier Tribunal decision on finding of error of law), or

(b) in relation to—

(i) an expedited appeal within the meaning of section 82A of the Nationality, Immigration and Asylum Act 2002, or

(ii) an expedited related appeal within the meaning of section 24 that involves a protection claim or a human rights claim.

(10) In this section—

"competent authority", "conclusive grounds decision" and "reasonable grounds decision" have the same meanings as in Part 5;

"priority removal notice", "PRN cut-off date", "PRN recipient" and "relevant status information" have the same meanings as in section 20.

(11) Section 26 makes further provision about the effect of a PRN recipient providing evidence late.

Note: commences from date to be appointed

23. Priority removal notices: expedited appeals

Note: inserts s82A of Nationality, Immigration and Asylum Act 2002 from date to be appointed. Amends s.13(8) of Tribunals, Courts and Enforcement Act 2007 from date to be appointed

24. Expedited appeals: joining of related appeals

(1) For the purposes of this section, an "expedited section 82 appeal" is an expedited appeal within the meaning of section 82A of the Nationality, Immigration and Asylum Act 2002 (expedited appeals for claims brought on or after PRN cut-off date).

(2) For the purposes of this section, a "related appeal" is an appeal under any of the following—

(a) section 82(1) of the Nationality, Immigration and Asylum Act 2002 (appeals in respect of protection and human rights claims), other than one which is an expedited section 82 appeal;

(b) section 40A of the British Nationality Act 1981 (appeal against deprivation of citizenship);

(c) the Immigration (Citizens' Rights Appeals) (EU Exit) Regulations 2020 (S.I. 2020/61) (appeal rights in respect of EU citizens' rights immigration decisions etc);

(d) regulation 36 of the Immigration (European Economic Area) Regulations 2016 (S.I. 2016/1052) (appeals against EEA decisions) as it continues to have effect following its revocation.

(3) If a person brings an expedited section 82 appeal at a time when a related appeal brought by that person is pending before the First-tier Tribunal, the related appeal is, from that time, to be continued as an appeal to the Upper Tribunal and accordingly is to be transferred to the Upper Tribunal.

(4) If an expedited section 82 appeal brought by a person is pending, any right that the person would otherwise have to bring a related appeal to the First-tier Tribunal is instead a right to bring it to the Upper Tribunal.

(5) A related appeal within subsection (3) or brought to the Upper Tribunal as mentioned in (4) is referred to in this section as an "expedited related appeal".

(6) Tribunal Procedure Rules must make provision with a view to securing that the Upper Tribunal consolidates an expedited related appeal and the expedited section 82 appeal concerned or hears them together (and see section 82A(4) of the Nationality, Immigration and Asylum Act 2002).

(7) Tribunal Procedure Rules must secure that the Upper Tribunal may, if it is satisfied that it is the only way to secure that justice is done in the case of a particular expedited related appeal, order that the appeal is to be continued as an appeal to the First-tier Tribunal and accordingly is to be transferred to that Tribunal.

(8) For the purposes of this section, an appeal is "pending"—

(a) in the case of an appeal under section 82 of the Nationality, Immigration and Asylum Act 2002 (including an expedited section 82 appeal), if it is pending within the meaning of section 104 of that Act;

(b) in the case of an appeal under section 40A of the British Nationality Act 1981, during the period—

(i) beginning when it is instituted, and

(ii) ending when it is finally determined or withdrawn;

(c) in the case of an appeal under the Immigration (Citizens' Rights Appeals) (EU Exit) Regulations 2020, if it is pending within the meaning of regulation 13 of those Regulations;

(d) in the case of an appeal under the regulation 36 of the Immigration (European Economic Area) Regulations 2016, if it is pending within the meaning of Part 6 of those Regulations (see regulation 35).

Note: commences on date to be appointed. S.9 inserts s.13(8)(bzb) of Tribunals, Courts and Enforcement Act 2007 from a date to be appointed

25. Civil legal services for recipients of priority removal notices

Note: amends Legal Aid, Sentencing and Punishment of Offenders Act 2012, Civil Legal Aid (Merits Criteria) Regulations 2013 (SI 2013/104) and Civil Legal Aid (Financial Resources and Payment for Services) Regulations 2013 (SI 2013/480)

Late evidence

26. Late provision of evidence in asylum or human rights claim: weight

(1) This section applies where—

(a) evidence is provided late by a claimant in relation to an asylum claim or a human rights claim, and

(b) the evidence falls to be considered by a deciding authority for the purpose of determining—

(i) the claim, or

(ii) where a decision in respect of the claim is the subject of a relevant appeal, the appeal.

(2) Unless there are good reasons why the evidence was provided late, the deciding authority must, in considering it, have regard to the principle that minimal weight should be given to the evidence.

(3) For the purposes of subsection (1)(a), evidence is provided "late" by a claimant if it is within subsection (4) or (5).

(4) Evidence is within this subsection if—

(a) it is provided pursuant to an evidence notice served on the claimant under section 18(1), and

(b) it is provided on or after the date specified in the notice.

(5) Evidence is within this subsection if—

(a) it is provided pursuant to a priority removal notice served on the claimant under section 20 in support of the matters mentioned in subsection (3)(a)(i) of that section (reasons and grounds for application), and

(b) it is provided on or after the PRN cut-off date.

(6) The reference in subsection (1)(b)(i) to determining a claim includes a reference to determining—

(a) whether to certify the claim under section 94(1) of the 2002 Act (unfounded claims);

(b) whether to accept or reject further submissions made by the claimant for the purposes of the immigration rules.

(7) In this section—

"the 2002 Act" means the Nationality, Immigration and Asylum Act 2002; "asylum claim" has the meaning given by section 113(1) of the 2002 Act; "deciding authority" means—

(a) an immigration officer,

(b) the Secretary of State,

(c) the First-tier Tribunal,

(d) the Upper Tribunal in the circumstances described in subsection (8), or

(e) the Special Immigration Appeals Commission; "PRN cut-off date" has the same meaning as in section 20; "relevant appeal" means an appeal under—

(a) section 82 of the 2002 Act, or

(b) section 2 of the Special Immigration Appeals Commission Act 1997.

(8) The circumstances are when the Upper Tribunal is acting—

(a) under section 12(2)(b)(ii) of the Tribunals, Courts and Enforcement Act 2007 (Upper Tribunal re-making First-tier Tribunal decision on finding of error of law), or

(b) in relation to—

(i) an expedited appeal within the meaning of section 82A of the Nationality, Immigration and Asylum Act 2002, or

(ii) an expedited related appeal within the meaning of section 24 that involves an asylum claim or a human rights claim.

Note: commences from a date to be appointed

Appeals

27. Accelerated detained appeals

(1) In this section "accelerated detained appeal" means a relevant appeal (see subsection (6)) brought—

(a) by a person who—

(i) was detained under a relevant detention provision (see subsection (7)) at the time at which they were given notice of the decision which is the subject of the appeal, and

(ii) remains in detention under a relevant detention provision, and

(b) against a decision that—

(i) is of a description prescribed by regulations made by the Secretary of State, and

(ii) when made, was certified by the Secretary of State under this section.

(2) The Secretary of State may only certify a decision under this section if the Secretary of State considers that any relevant appeal brought in relation to the decision would likely be disposed of expeditiously.

(3) Tribunal Procedure Rules must secure that the following time limits apply in relation to an accelerated detained appeal—

(a) any notice of appeal must be given to the First-tier Tribunal not later than 5 working days after the date on which the appellant was given notice of the decision against which the appeal is brought;

(b) the First-tier Tribunal must make a decision on the appeal, and give notice of that decision to the parties, not later than 25 working days after the date on which the appellant gave notice of appeal to the tribunal;

(c) any application (whether to the First-tier Tribunal or the Upper Tribunal) for permission to appeal to the Upper Tribunal must be determined by the tribunal concerned not later than 20 working days after the date on which the applicant was given notice of the First-tier Tribunal's decision.

(4) A relevant appeal ceases to be an accelerated detained appeal on the appellant being released from detention under any relevant detention provision.

(5) Tribunal Procedure Rules must secure that the First-tier Tribunal or (as the case may be) the Upper Tribunal may, if it is satisfied that it is the only way to secure that justice is done in a particular case, order that a relevant appeal is to cease to be an accelerated detained appeal.

(6) For the purposes of this section, a "relevant appeal" is an appeal to the First-tier Tribunal under any of the following—

(a) section 82(1) of the Nationality, Immigration and Asylum Act 2002 (appeals in respect of protection and human rights claims);

(b) section 40A of the British Nationality Act 1981 (appeal against deprivation of citizenship);

(c) the Immigration (Citizens' Rights Appeals) (EU Exit) Regulations 2020 (S.I. 2020/61) (appeal rights in respect of EU citizens' rights immigration decisions etc);

(d) regulation 36 of the Immigration (European Economic Area) Regulations 2016 (S.I. 2016/1052) (appeals against EEA decisions) as it continues to have effect following its revocation.

(7) For the purposes of this section, a "relevant detention provision" is any of the following—

(a) paragraph 16(1), (1A) or (2) of Schedule 2 to the Immigration Act 1971 (detention of persons liable to examination or removal);

(b) paragraph 2(1), (2) or (3) of Schedule 3 to that Act (detention pending deportation);

(c) section 62 of the Nationality, Immigration and Asylum Act 2002 (detention of persons liable to examination or removal);

(d) section 36(1) of the UK Borders Act 2007 (detention pending deportation).

(8) In this section "working day" means any day except—

(a) a Saturday or Sunday, Christmas Day, Good Friday or 26 to 31 December, and

(b) any day that is a bank holiday under section 1 of the Banking and Financial Dealings Act 1971 in the part of the United Kingdom where the appellant concerned is detained.

(9) Regulations under this section are subject to negative resolution procedure.

Note: commences from date to be appointed

28. Claims certified as clearly unfounded: removal of right of appeal

Note: amends s.92 and s.94, and inserts s.94(3A) of Nationality, Immigration and Asylum Act 2002 from a date to be appointed

Removal to safe third country

29. Removal of asylum seeker to safe country

Note: amends s.77 to Nationality, Immigration and Asylum Act 2002 (no removal while claim for asylum pending), and Sch. 3 to Asylum and Immigration (Treatment of Claimants, etc) Act 2004 (removal of asylum seeker to safe country) from June 28 2022 for specified purposes

Interpretation of Refugee Convention

30. Refugee Convention: general

(1) The following sections apply for the purposes of the determination by any person, court or tribunal whether a person (referred to in those sections as an "asylum seeker") is a refugee within the meaning of Article 1(A)(2) of the Refugee Convention—

(a) section 31 (persecution);

(b) section 32 (well-founded fear);

(c) section 33 (reasons for persecution);

(d) section 34 (protection from persecution);

(e) section 35 (internal relocation).

(2) Section 36 applies for the purposes of the determination by any person, court or tribunal whether the provisions of the Refugee Convention do not apply to a person as a result of Article 1(F) of that Convention (disapplication of Convention to serious criminals etc).

(3) Section 37 applies for the purposes of the determination by any person, court or tribunal whether Article 31(1) of the Refugee Convention (immunity from certain penalties) applies in relation to a person who is a refugee within the meaning of Article 1(A)(2) of the Refugee Convention.

(4) The Refugee or Person in Need of International Protection (Qualification) Regulations 2006 (S.I. 2006/2525) are revoked.

(5) Subsections (1) and (2), and sections 31 to 36, apply only in relation to a determination relating to a claim for asylum where the claim was made on or after the day on which this section comes into force.

(6) For the purposes of subsection (5), a claim for asylum includes a claim, in any form or to any person, which falls to be determined as mentioned in subsection (1).

Note: commenced from June 28, 2022 (SI 2022/590) save subsection (4) from June 28, 2022 (subject to transitional and saving provisions specified in SI 2022/590 reg.3 and Sch.2

31. Article 1(A)(2): persecution

(1) For the purposes of Article 1(A)(2) of the Refugee Convention, persecution can be committed by any of the following (referred to in this Part as "actors of persecution")—

(a) the State,

(b) any party or organisation controlling the State or a substantial part of the territory of the State, or

(c) any non-State actor, if it can be demonstrated that the actors mentioned in paragraphs (a) and (b), including any international organisation, are unable or unwilling to provide reasonable protection against persecution.

(2) For the purposes of that Article, the persecution must be—

(a) sufficiently serious by its nature or repetition as to constitute a severe violation of a basic human right, in particular a right from which derogation cannot be made under Article 15 of the Human Rights Convention, or

(b) an accumulation of various measures, including a violation of a human right, which is sufficiently severe as to affect an individual in a similar manner as specified in paragraph (a).

(3) The persecution may, for example, take the form of—

(a) an act of physical or mental violence, including an act of sexual violence;

(b) a legal, administrative, police or judicial measure which in itself is discriminatory or which is implemented in a discriminatory manner;

(c) prosecution or punishment which is disproportionate or discriminatory;

(d) denial of judicial redress resulting in a disproportionate or discriminatory punishment;

(e) prosecution or punishment for refusal to perform military service in a conflict, where performing military service would include crimes or acts as described in Article 1(F) of the Refugee Convention (on which, see section 36).

Note: commenced June 28, 2022

32. Article 1(A)(2): well-founded fear

(1) In deciding for the purposes of Article 1(A)(2) of the Refugee Convention whether an asylum seeker's fear of persecution is well-founded, the following approach is to be taken.

(2) The decision-maker must first determine, on the balance of probabilities—

(a) whether the asylum seeker has a characteristic which could cause them to fear persecution for reasons of race, religion, nationality, membership of a particular social group or political opinion (or has such a characteristic attributed to them by an actor of persecution), and

(b) whether the asylum seeker does in fact fear such persecution in their country of nationality (or in a case where they do not have a nationality, the country of their former habitual residence) as a result of that characteristic.

(See also section 8 of the Asylum and Immigration (Treatment of Claimants, etc) Act 2004 (asylum claims etc: behaviour damaging to claimant's credibility).)

(3) Subsection (4) applies if the decision-maker finds that—

(a) the asylum seeker has a characteristic mentioned in subsection (2)(a) (or has such a characteristic attributed to them), and

(b) the asylum seeker fears persecution as mentioned in subsection (2)(b).

(4) The decision-maker must determine whether there is a reasonable likelihood that, if the asylum seeker were returned to their country of nationality (or in a case where they do not have a nationality, the country of their former habitual residence)—

(a) they would be persecuted as a result of the characteristic mentioned in subsection (2)(a), and

(b) they would not be protected as mentioned in section 34.

(5) The determination under subsection (4) must also include a consideration of the matter mentioned in section 35 (internal relocation).

Note: commenced June 28, 2022

33. Article 1(A)(2): reasons for persecution

(1) For the purposes of Article 1(A)(2) of the Refugee Convention—

(a) the concept of race may include consideration of matters such as a person's colour, descent or membership of a particular ethnic group;

(b) the concept of religion may include consideration of matters such as—

(i) the holding of theistic, non-theistic or atheistic beliefs,

(ii) the participation in formal worship in private or public, either alone or in community with others, or the abstention from such worship,

(iii) other religious acts or expressions of view, or

(iv) forms of personal or communal conduct based on or mandated by any religious belief;

(c) the concept of nationality is not confined to citizenship (or lack of citizenship) but may include consideration of matters such as membership of a group determined by its cultural, ethnic or linguistic identity, common geographical or political origins or its relationship with the population of another State;

(d) the concept of political opinion includes the holding of an opinion, thought or belief on a matter related to a potential actor of persecution and to its policies or methods, whether or not the person holding that opinion, thought or belief has acted upon it.

(2) A group forms a particular social group for the purposes of Article 1(A)(2) of the Refugee Convention only if it meets both of the following conditions.

(3) The first condition is that members of the group share—

(a) an innate characteristic,

(b) a common background that cannot be changed, or

(c) a characteristic or belief that is so fundamental to identity or conscience that a person should not be forced to renounce it.

(4) The second condition is that the group has a distinct identity in the relevant country because it is perceived as being different by the surrounding society.

(5) A particular social group may include a group based on a common characteristic of sexual orientation, but for these purposes sexual orientation does not include acts that are criminal in any part of the United Kingdom.

Note: commenced June 28, 2022

34. Article 1(A)(2): protection from persecution

(1) For the purposes of Article 1(A)(2) of the Refugee Convention, protection from persecution can be provided by—

(a) the State, or

(b) any party or organisation, including any international organisation, controlling the State or a substantial part of the territory of the State.

(2) An asylum seeker is to be taken to be able to avail themselves of protection from persecution if—

(a) the State, party or organisation mentioned in subsection (1) takes reasonable steps to prevent the persecution by operating an effective legal system for the detection, prosecution and punishment of acts constituting persecution, and

(b) the asylum seeker is able to access the protection.

Note: commenced June 28, 2022

35. Article 1(A)(2): internal relocation

(1) An asylum seeker is not to be taken to be a refugee for the purposes of Article 1(A)(2) of the Refugee Convention if—

(a) they would not have a well-founded fear of being persecuted in a part of their country of nationality (or in a case where they do not have a nationality, the country of their former habitual residence), and

(b) they can reasonably be expected to travel to and remain in that part of the country.

(2) In considering whether an asylum seeker can reasonably be expected to travel to and remain in a part of a country, a decision-maker—

(a) must have regard to—

(i) the general circumstances prevailing in that part of the country, and

(ii) the personal circumstances of the asylum seeker;

(b) must disregard any technical obstacles relating to travel to that part of that country.

Note: commenced June 28, 2022

36. Article 1(F): disapplication of Convention in case of serious crime etc

(1) A person has committed a crime for the purposes of Article 1(F)(a) or (b) of the Refugee Convention if they have instigated or otherwise participated in the commission of the crimes specified in those provisions.

(2) In Article 1(F)(b), the reference to a serious non-political crime includes a particularly cruel action, even if it is committed with an allegedly political objective.

(3) In that Article, the reference to a crime being committed by a person outside the country of refuge prior to their admission to that country as a refugee includes a crime committed by that person at any time up to and including the day on which they are issued with a relevant biometric immigration document by the Secretary of State.

(4) For the purposes of subsection (3), a relevant biometric immigration document is a document that—

(a) records biometric information (as defined in section 15(1A) of the UK Borders Act 2007), and

(b) is evidence of leave to remain in the United Kingdom granted to a person as a result of their refugee status.

Note: commenced June 28, 2022

37. Article 31(1): immunity from penalties

(1) A refugee is not to be taken to have come to the United Kingdom directly from a country where their life or freedom was threatened if, in coming from that country, they stopped in another country outside the United Kingdom, unless they can show that they could not reasonably be expected to have sought protection under the Refugee Convention in that country.

(2) A refugee is not to be taken to have presented themselves without delay to the authorities unless—

(a) in the case of a person who became a refugee while they were outside the United Kingdom, they made a claim for asylum as soon as reasonably practicable after their arrival in the United Kingdom;

(b) in the case of a person who became a refugee while they were in the United Kingdom—

(i) if their presence in the United Kingdom was lawful at that time, they made a claim for asylum before the time when their presence in the United Kingdom became unlawful;

(ii) if their presence in the United Kingdom was unlawful at that time, they made a claim for asylum as soon as reasonably practicable after they became aware of their need for protection under the Refugee Convention.

(3) For the purposes of subsection (2)(b), a person's presence in the United Kingdom is unlawful if they require leave to enter or remain and do not have it.

(4) A penalty is not to be taken as having been imposed on account of a refugee's illegal entry or presence in the United Kingdom where the penalty relates to anything done by the refugee in the course of an attempt to leave the United Kingdom.

(5) In section 31 of the Immigration and Asylum Act 1999 (defences based on Art.31(1) of the Refugee Convention)—

(a) in subsection (2), for "have expected to be given" substitute "be expected to have sought";

(b) after subsection (4) insert—

"(4A) But this section does not apply to an offence committed by a refugee in the course of an attempt to leave the United Kingdom."

(6) In this section—

"claim for asylum" means a claim that it would be contrary to the United Kingdom's obligations under the Refugee Convention for the claimant to be removed from, or required to leave, the United Kingdom;

"country" includes any territory;

"refugee" has the same meaning as in the Refugee Convention.

Note: commenced June 28, 2022

38. Article 33(2): particularly serious crime

(1) Section 72 of the Nationality, Immigration and Asylum Act 2002 (serious criminal) is amended as follows.

(2) In subsection (1), for "protection" substitute "prohibition of expulsion or return".

(3) In subsection (2)—

(a) in the words before paragraph (a)—

(i) for "shall be presumed to have been" substitute "is";

(ii) omit "and to constitute a danger to the community of the United Kingdom";

(b) in paragraph (b), for "two years" substitute "12 months".

(4) In subsection (3)—

(a) in the words before paragraph (a)—

(i) for "shall be presumed to have been" substitute "is";

(ii) omit "and to constitute a danger to the community of the United Kingdom";

(b) in paragraph (b), for "two years" substitute "12 months";

(c) in paragraph (c), for "two years" substitute "12 months".

(5) In subsection (4), in the words before paragraph (a)—

(a) for "shall be presumed to have been" substitute "is";

(b) omit "and to constitute a danger to the community of the United Kingdom".

(6) After subsection (5) insert—

"(5A) A person convicted by a final judgment of a particularly serious crime (whether within or outside the United Kingdom) is to be presumed to constitute a danger to the community of the United Kingdom."

(7) In subsection (6), for "(2), (3) or (4)" substitute "(5A)".

(8) In subsection (7), for "(2), (3) or (4)" substitute "(5A)".

(9) In subsection (8), for "mentioned in subsection (6)" substitute "under subsection (5A)".

(10) In subsection (9)(b), for "presumptions under subsection (2), (3) or (4) apply" substitute "a presumption under subsection (5A) applies".

(11) In subsection (10)(b), for "presumptions under subsections (2), (3) or (4) apply" substitute "a presumption under subsection (5A) applies".

(12) In subsection (11)(b)—

(a) in the opening words, for "two years" substitute "12 months";

(b) in sub-paragraph (ia), for "two years", in both places it occurs, substitute "12 months";

(c) in sub-paragraph (iii), for "two years" substitute "12 months".

(13) The amendments made by this section apply only in relation to a person convicted on or after the date on which this section comes into force.

Note: commenced June 28, 2022

Interpretation

39. Interpretation of Part 2

In this Part—

"human rights claim" has the meaning given by section 113 of the Nationality, Immigration and Asylum Act 2002;

the "Human Rights Convention" means the Convention for the Protection of Human Rights and Fundamental Freedoms agreed by the Council of Europe at Rome on 4 November 1950 as it has effect for the time being in relation to the United Kingdom;

"immigration officer" means a person appointed by the Secretary of State as an immigration officer under paragraph 1 of Schedule 2 to the Immigration Act 1971;

"immigration rules" means rules under section 3(2) of the Immigration Act 1971;

the "Refugee Convention" means the Convention relating to the Status of Refugees done at Geneva on 28 July 1951 and its Protocol;

"protection claim" has the meaning given by section 82(2) of the Nationality, Immigration and Asylum Act 2002.

Part 3
Immigration Control

Immigration offences and penalties

40. Illegal entry and similar offences

Note: inserts.24(A1)-(G1) and amends s24, 25, 28B & 28FA of Immigration Act 1971 from June 28, 2022 (except for the purpose specified in SI 202/590 Sch.1 para 20; not yet in force otherwise)

41. Assisting unlawful immigration or asylum seeker

Note: amends s.25 & s.25A and inserts s.25BA-BB to Immigration Act 1971 from June 28, 2022

42. Penalty for failure to secure goods vehicle

Schedule 5 amends the Immigration and Asylum Act 1999 to make provision for the imposition of a penalty for failure adequately to secure a goods vehicle against unauthorised access and other related matters.

Note: commences from April 28, 2022 (for the purposes of making (and, where required, consulting on) regulations, not yet in force otherwise)

Working in United Kingdom waters: arrival and entry

43. Working in United Kingdom waters: arrival and entry

Note: inserts s.11A-B to Immigration Act 1971 from April 28, 2022 for the purposes of making (and, where required, consulting on) regulations; not yet in force otherwise

Enforcement

44. Power to search container unloaded from ship or aircraft

Note: inserts paragraph 1(6) & (7) to Schedule 2, and s.26(1)(h) of Immigration Act 1971 from June 28, 2022

Removals

45. Maritime Enforcement

Note: commences June 28, 2022 (SI 2022/590)

46. Removals: notice requirements

Note: amends s.10 and inserts s.10A-E of the Immigration and Asylum Act 1999 from date to be appointed save s.46(6)-(6)(b) from June 28, 2022 (SI 2022/590)

47. Prisoners liable to removal from the United Kingdom

Note: amends the Criminal Justice Act 2003 from June 28, 2002

Immigration bail

48. Matters relevant to decisions relating to immigration bail

Note: inserts paragraph 3(2)(ea) to Sch.10 of Immigration Act 2016 from June 28, 2022

PART 4

AGE ASSESSMENTS

49. Interpretation of Part etc

(1) In this Part, "age-disputed person" means a person—

(a) who requires leave to enter or remain in the United Kingdom (whether or not such leave has been given), and

(b) in relation to whom—

(i) a local authority,

(ii) a public authority specified in regulations under section 50(1)(b), or

(iii) the Secretary of State,

has insufficient evidence to be sure of their age.

(2) In this Part—

"decision-maker" means a person who conducts an age assessment under section 50 or 51;

"designated person" means an official of the Secretary of State who is designated by the Secretary of State to conduct age assessments under section 50 or 51;

"immigration functions" means functions exercisable by virtue of the Immigration Acts;

"immigration officer" means a person appointed by the Secretary of State as an immigration officer under paragraph 1 of Schedule 2 to the Immigration Act 1971;

"local authority"—

(a) in relation to England and Wales, means a local authority within the meaning of the Children Act 1989 (see section 105(1) of that Act),

(b) in relation to Scotland, means a council constituted under section 2 of the Local Government etc (Scotland) Act 1994, and

(c) in relation to Northern Ireland, means a Health and Social Care trust established under Article 10 of the Health and Personal Social Services (Northern Ireland) Order 1991 (S.I. 1991/194 (N.I. 1));

"public authority" means a public authority within the meaning of section 6 of the Human Rights Act 1998, other than a court or tribunal;

"specified scientific method" means a method used for assessing a person's age which is specified in regulations under section 52(1).

(3) In this Part, "relevant children's legislation" means—

(a) in relation to a local authority in England, any provision of or made under Part 3, 4 or 5 of the Children Act 1989 (support for children and families; care and supervision; protection of children);

(b) in relation to a local authority in Wales, Scotland or Northern Ireland, any statutory provision (including a provision passed or made after the coming into force of this Part) that confers a corresponding function on such an authority.

(4) In subsection (3)—

"corresponding function" means a function that corresponds to a function conferred on a local authority in England by or under Part 3, 4 or 5 of the Children Act 1989;

"statutory provision" means a provision made by or under—

(a) an Act,

(b) an Act of the Scottish Parliament,

(c) an Act or Measure of Senedd Cymru, or

(d) Northern Ireland legislation.

(5) ..

Note: commences June 28, 2022 save for subsection (5) from at date to be appointed. Subsection (5) amends s.94 of the Immigration and Asylum Act 1999

50. Persons subject to immigration control: referral or assessment by local authority etc

(1) The following authorities may refer an age-disputed person to a designated person for an age assessment under this section—

(a) a local authority;

(b) a public authority specified in regulations made by the Secretary of State.

(2) Subsections (3) and (4) apply where—

(a) a local authority needs to know the age of an age-disputed person for the purposes of deciding whether or how to exercise any of its functions under relevant children's legislation in relation to the person, or

(b) the Secretary of State notifies a local authority in writing that the Secretary of State doubts that an age-disputed person in relation to whom the local authority has exercised or may exercise functions under relevant children's legislation is the age that they claim (or are claimed) to be.

(3) The local authority must—

(a) refer the age-disputed person to a designated person for an age assessment under this section,

(b) conduct an age assessment on the age-disputed person itself and inform the Secretary of State in writing of the result of its assessment, or

(c) inform the Secretary of State in writing that it is satisfied that the person is the age they claim (or are claimed) to be, without the need for an age assessment.

(4) Where a local authority—

(a) conducts an age assessment itself, or

(b) informs the Secretary of State that it is satisfied that an age-disputed person is the age they claim (or are claimed) to be,

it must, on request from the Secretary of State, provide the Secretary of State with such evidence as the Secretary of State reasonably requires for the Secretary of State to consider the local authority's decision under subsection (3)(b) or (c).

(5) Where a local authority refers an age-disputed person to a designated person for an age assessment under subsection (1) or (3)(a), the local authority must provide any assistance that the designated person reasonably requires from the authority for the purposes of conducting that assessment.

(6) The standard of proof for an age assessment under this section is the balance of probabilities.

(7) An age assessment of an age-disputed person conducted by a designated person following a referral from a local authority under subsection (1) or (3)(a) is binding—

(a) on the Secretary of State and immigration officers when exercising immigration functions, and

(b) on a local authority that—

(i) has exercised or may exercise functions under relevant children's legislation in relation to the age-disputed person, and

(ii) is aware of the age assessment conducted by the designated person.

But this is subject to section 54(5) (decision of Tribunal to be binding on Secretary of State and local authorities) and section 56 (new information following age assessment or appeal).

(8) Regulations under subsection (1)(b) are subject to negative resolution procedure.

Note: commences April 28, 2022 (for the purposes of making (and, where required, consulting on) regulations; not yet in force otherwise)

51. Persons subject to immigration control: assessment for immigration purposes

(1) A designated person may conduct an age assessment on an age-disputed person for the purposes of deciding whether or how the Secretary of State or an immigration officer should exercise any immigration functions in relation to the person.

(2) An assessment under subsection (1) may be conducted—

(a) in a case where subsections (3) and (4) of section 50 do not apply, or

(b) in a case where those subsections do apply—

(i) at any time before a local authority has referred the age- disputed person to a designated person under section 50(3)(a) or has informed the Secretary of State as mentioned in subsection (3)(b) or (c) of that section, or

(ii) if the Secretary of State has reason to doubt a local authority's decision under subsection (3)(b) or (c) of that section.

(3) An age assessment under this section is binding on the Secretary of State and immigration officers when exercising immigration functions.

But this is subject to section 54(5) (decision of Tribunal to be binding on Secretary of State and local authorities) and section 56 (new information following age assessment or appeal).

(4) The standard of proof for an age assessment under this section is the balance of probabilities.

Note: commences from a date to be appointed

52. Use of scientific methods in age assessments

(1) The Secretary of State may make regulations specifying scientific methods that may be used for the purposes of age assessments under section 50 or 51.

(2) The types of scientific method that may be specified include methods involving—

(a) examining or measuring parts of a person's body, including by the use of imaging technology;

(b) the analysis of saliva, cell or other samples taken from a person (including the analysis of DNA in the samples).

(3) A method may not be specified in regulations under subsection (1) unless the Secretary of State determines, after having sought scientific advice, that the method is appropriate for assessing a person's age.

(4) A specified scientific method may be used for the purposes of an age assessment under section 50 or 51 only if the appropriate consent is given.

(5) The appropriate consent is—

(a) where the age-disputed person has the capacity to consent to the use of the scientific method in question, their consent;

(b) where the age-disputed person does not have the capacity to consent to the use of the scientific method in question, the consent of—

(i) the person's parent or guardian, or

(ii) another person, of a description specified in regulations made by the Secretary of State, who is able to give consent on behalf of the age-disputed person.

(6) Subsection (7) applies where—

(a) the age-disputed person or, in a case where the age-disputed person lacks capacity, a person mentioned in subsection (5)(b), decides not to consent to the use of a specified scientific method, and

(b) there are no reasonable grounds for that decision.

(7) In deciding whether to believe any statement made by or on behalf of the age- disputed person that is relevant to the assessment of their age, the decision- maker must take into account, as damaging the age-disputed person's credibility (or the credibility of a person who has made a statement on their behalf), the decision not to consent to the use of the specified scientific method.

(8) Regulations under this section are subject to affirmative resolution procedure.

(9) This section does not prevent the use of a scientific method that is not a specified scientific method for the purposes of an age assessment under section 50 or 51 if the decision-maker considers it appropriate to do so and, where necessary, the appropriate consent is given.

Note: April 28, 2022 (for the purposes of making (and, where required, consulting on) regulations; not yet in force otherwise)

53. Regulations about age assessments

(1) The Secretary of State may make regulations about age assessments under section 50 or 51, which may in particular include provision about—

(a) the processes to be followed, including—

(i) the information and evidence that must be considered and the weight to be given to it,

(ii) the circumstances in which an abbreviated age assessment may be appropriate,

(iii) protections or safeguarding measures for the age-disputed person, and

(iv) where consent is required for the use of a specified scientific method, the processes for assessing a person's capacity to consent, for seeking consent and for recording the decision on consent;

(b) the qualifications or experience necessary for a person to conduct an age assessment;

(c) where an age assessment includes use of specified scientific methods—

(i) the qualifications or experience necessary for a person to conduct tests in accordance with those methods, and

(ii) the settings in which such tests must be carried out;

(d) the content and distribution of reports on age assessments;

(e) the communication of decisions to the age-disputed person and any other person affected by the decision, and notification of appeal rights (see section 54); and

(f) the consequences of a lack of co-operation with the assessment by the age-disputed person, which may include damage to the person's credibility.

(2) The regulations may also include provision about—

(a) referrals under section 50(1) or (3)(a), including the process for making such a referral and about the withdrawal of a referral;

(b) how and when a local authority must inform the Secretary of State as mentioned in section 50(3)(b) and (c);

(c) evidence that the Secretary of State may require as mentioned in section 50(4).

(3) Regulations under this section are subject to affirmative resolution procedure.

Note: April 28, 2022 (for the purpose of making (and, where required, consulting on) regulations; not yet in force otherwise)

54. Appeals relating to age assessments

(1) This section applies if—

(a) an age assessment is conducted on an age-disputed person ("P") under section 50 or 51, and

(b) the decision-maker decides that P is an age other than the age that P claims (or is claimed) to be.

(2) P may appeal to the First-tier Tribunal against the decision-maker's decision.

(3) On the appeal, the Tribunal must—

(a) determine P's age on the balance of probabilities, and

(b) assign a date of birth to P.

(4) In making the determination, the Tribunal may consider any matter which it thinks relevant, including—

(a) any matter of which the decision-maker was unaware, and

(b) any matter arising after the date of the decision appealed against.

(5) A determination on an appeal under subsection (2) is binding—

(a) on the Secretary of State and immigration officers when exercising immigration functions in relation to P, and

(b) on a local authority that has exercised or may exercise functions under relevant children's legislation in relation to P.

(6) This section is subject to—

(a) section 55 (appeals relating to age assessments: supplementary), and

(b) section 56 (new information following age assessment or appeal).

Note: commences from date to be appointed

55. Appeals relating to age assessments: supplementary

(1) This section applies to an appeal under section 54(2).

(2) The appeal must be brought from within the United Kingdom.

(3) If the person who brings the appeal leaves the United Kingdom before the appeal is finally determined, the appeal is to be treated as abandoned.

(4) The person who brings the appeal may make an application to the First-tier Tribunal for an order that, until the appeal is finally determined, withdrawn or abandoned, the local authority must exercise its functions under relevant children's legislation in relation to the person on the basis that they are the age that they claim (or are claimed) to be.

(5) Subsection (6) applies if it is alleged—

(a) that a document relied on by a party to an appeal is a forgery, and

(b) that disclosure to that party of a matter relating to the detection of the forgery would be contrary to the public interest.

(6) The First-tier Tribunal—

(a) must investigate the allegation in private, and

(b) may proceed in private so far as necessary to prevent disclosure of the matter referred to in subsection (5)(b).

(7) Subsection (8) applies in relation to—

(a) proceedings on an appeal, and

(b) proceedings in the Upper Tribunal arising out of proceedings within paragraph (a).

(8) Practice directions under section 23 of the Tribunals, Courts and Enforcement Act 2007 may require the First-tier Tribunal or the Upper Tribunal to treat a specified decision of the First-tier Tribunal or the Upper Tribunal as authoritative in respect of a particular matter.

(9) For the purposes of this Part an appeal is not finally determined if—

(a) an application for permission to appeal under section 11, 13 or 14B of the Tribunals, Courts and Enforcement Act 2007 could be made (ignoring any possibility of an application out of time) or is awaiting determination,

(b) an application for permission to appeal to the Supreme Court from—

(i) the Court of Appeal in England and Wales,

(ii) the Court of Session, or

(iii) the Court of Appeal in Northern Ireland,

could be made (ignoring any possibility of an application out of time) or is awaiting determination,

(c) permission to appeal of the kind mentioned in paragraph (a) or (b) has been granted and the appeal is awaiting determination, or

(d) an appeal has been remitted under section 12 or 14 of the Tribunals, Courts and Enforcement Act 2007, or by the Supreme Court, and is awaiting determination.

Note: commences from a date to be appointed

56. New information following age assessment or appeal

(1) This section applies where—

(a) an age assessment has been conducted on an age-disputed person ("P") under section 50 or 51,

(b) an appeal under section 54(2) could no longer be brought (ignoring any possibility of an appeal out of time) or has been finally determined, and

(c) the decision-maker becomes aware of new information relating to P's age.

(2) In this section, the age assessment referred to in subsection (1)(a) is referred to as the "first age assessment".

(3) In a case where the first age assessment was conducted by a designated person, they must—

(a) decide whether the new information is significant new evidence, and

(b) if they decide that it is, conduct a further age assessment on P.

(4) In a case where the first age assessment was conducted by a local authority, it must—

(a) decide whether the new information is significant new evidence or refer the new information to a designated person for a decision on that matter, and

(b) if it is decided that the new information is significant new evidence—

(i) conduct a further age assessment on P, or

(ii) refer P to a designated person for a further age assessment.

(5) For the purposes of subsections (3) and (4), new information is "significant new evidence" if there is a realistic prospect that, if a further age assessment were to be conducted on P, taking into account the new information, P's age would be assessed as different from the age determined in the first age assessment or in the appeal proceedings.

(6) A further age assessment conducted by a designated person under subsection (3) or (4)(b)(ii) is to be treated—

(a) in a case where the first age assessment was conducted under section 50, as an age assessment conducted by the designated person following a referral under subsection (3)(a) of that section;

(b) in a case where the first age assessment was conducted under section 51, as an age assessment conducted under that section.

(7) A further age assessment conducted by a local authority under subsection (4)(b)(i) is to be treated as an age assessment conducted by a local authority under section 50(3)(b).

(8) A person conducting a further age assessment under this section does not need to revisit matters that were considered in the first age assessment if they do not think it is necessary to do so.

Note: commences from a date to be appointed

57. Civil legal services relating to age assessments

Note: amends the Legal Aid, Sentencing and Punishment of Offenders Act 2012, from date to be appointed

PART 5

MODERN SLAVERY

58. Provision of information relating to being a victim of slavery or human trafficking

(1) The Secretary of State may serve a slavery or trafficking information notice on a person who has made a protection claim or a human rights claim.

(2) A "slavery or trafficking information notice" is a notice requiring the recipient to provide the Secretary of State (and any other competent authority specified in the notice), before the specified date, with any relevant status information the recipient has.

(3) "Relevant status information" is information that may be relevant for the purpose of making a reasonable grounds decision or a conclusive grounds decision in relation to the recipient.

(4) Subsection (5) applies if the recipient of a slavery or trafficking information notice provides the Secretary of State or competent authority with relevant status information on or after the specified date.

(5) The recipient must also provide a statement setting out their reasons for not providing the relevant status information before the specified date (and see section 59).

(6) In this section—

"protection claim" and "human rights claim" have the same meanings as in Part 2;

"specified date" means the date specified in the slavery or trafficking information notice.

Note: commences from date to be appointed

59. Late compliance with slavery or trafficking information notice: damage to credibility

(1) This section applies where—

(a) a person aged 18 or over has been served with a slavery or trafficking information notice under section 58,

(b) the person provided relevant status information late, and

(c) a competent authority is making a reasonable grounds decision or a conclusive grounds decision in relation to the person.

(2) In determining whether to believe a statement made by or on behalf of the person, the competent authority must take account, as damaging the person's credibility, of the late provision of the relevant status information, unless there are good reasons why the information was provided late.

(3) For the purposes of this section, relevant status information is provided "late" by the person if it is provided on or after the date specified in the slavery or trafficking information notice.

(4) In this section, "relevant status information" has the same meaning as in section 58 (see subsection (3) of that section).

Note: commences from date to be appointed

60. Identification of potential victims of slavery or human trafficking

Note: Amends s.49-56 of Modern Slavery Act 2015 from date to be appointed.

61. Identified potential victims of slavery or human trafficking: recovery period

(1) This section applies to a person (an "identified potential victim") if—

(a) a decision is made by a competent authority that there are reasonable grounds to believe that the person is a victim of slavery or human trafficking (a "positive reasonable grounds decision"), and

(b) that decision is not a further RG decision (as to which, see section 62).

(2) Subject to section 63(2), the identified potential victim may not be removed from, or required to leave, the United Kingdom during the recovery period.

(3) The "recovery period", in relation to an identified potential victim, is the period—

(a) beginning with the day on which the positive reasonable grounds decision is made, and

(b) ending with whichever of the following is the later—

(i) the day on which the conclusive grounds decision is made in relation to the identified potential victim;

(ii) the end of the period of 30 days beginning with the day mentioned in paragraph (a).

Note: commences from date to be appointed

62. No entitlement to additional recovery period etc

(1) This section applies where—

(a) a competent authority has previously made a positive reasonable grounds decision in relation to a person (the "first RG decision"), and

(b) a further positive reasonable grounds decision is made in relation to the person, in a case where the reasonable grounds for believing that the person is a victim of slavery or human trafficking arise from things done wholly before the first RG decision was made (the "further RG decision").

(2) If the competent authority considers it appropriate in the circumstances of a particular case, the authority may determine that the person may not be removed from, or required to leave, the United Kingdom during the period—

(a) beginning with the day on which the further RG decision is made, and

(b) ending with whichever of the following is the later—

(i) the day on which the conclusive grounds decision is made in relation to the further RG decision;

(ii) the end of the period of 30 days beginning with the day mentioned in paragraph (a).

This is subject to section 63(2).

Note: commences from date to be appointed

63. Identified potential victims etc: disqualification from protection

(1) A competent authority may determine that subsection (2) is to apply to a person in relation to whom a positive reasonable grounds decision has been made if the authority is satisfied that the person—

(a) is a threat to public order, or

(b) has claimed to be a victim of slavery or human trafficking in bad faith.

(2) Where this subsection applies to a person the following cease to apply—

(a) any prohibition on removing the person from, or requiring them to leave, the United Kingdom arising under section 61 or 62, and

(b) any requirement under section 65 to grant the person limited leave to remain in the United Kingdom.

(3) For the purposes of this section, the circumstances in which a person is a threat to public order include, in particular, where—

(a) the person has been convicted of a terrorist offence;

(b) the person has been convicted of any other offence listed in Schedule 4 to the Modern Slavery Act 2015 anywhere in the United Kingdom, or of a corresponding offence;

(c) the person is subject to a TPIM notice (within the meaning given by section 2 of the Terrorism Prevention and Investigation Measures Act 2011);

(d) there are reasonable grounds to suspect that the person is or has been involved in terrorism-related activity within the meaning given by section 4 of that Act (whether or not the terrorism-related activity is attributable to the person being, or having been, a victim of slavery or human trafficking);

(e) the person is subject to a temporary exclusion order imposed under section 2 of the Counter-Terrorism and Security Act 2015;

(f) the person is a foreign criminal within the meaning given by section 32(1) of the UK Borders Act 2007 (automatic deportation for foreign criminals);

(g) the Secretary of State has made an order in relation to the person under section 40(2) of the British Nationality Act 1981 (order depriving person of citizenship status where to do so is conducive to the public good);

(h) the Refugee Convention does not apply to the person by virtue of Article 1(F) of that Convention (serious criminals etc);

(i) the person otherwise poses a risk to the national security of the United Kingdom.

(4) In subsection (3)(a), "terrorist offence" means any of the following (whenever committed)—

(a) an offence listed in—

(i) Schedule A1 to the Sentencing Code (terrorism offences: England and Wales), or

(ii) Schedule 1A to the Counter-Terrorism Act 2008 (terrorism offences: Scotland and Northern Ireland);

(b) an offence that was determined to have a terrorist connection under—

(i) section 69 of the Sentencing Code (in the case of an offender sentenced in England and Wales), or

(ii) section 30 of the Counter-Terrorism Act 2008 (in the case of an offender sentenced in Northern Ireland, or an offender sentenced in England and Wales before the Sentencing Code applied);

(c) an offence that has been proved to have been aggravated by reason of having a terrorist connection under section 31 of the Counter-Terrorism Act 2008 (in the case of an offender sentenced in Scotland);

(d) an act constituting an offence under the law in force in a country outside the United Kingdom that—

(i) would have constituted an offence within paragraph (a) if it had been committed in any part of the United Kingdom, or

(ii) was, or took place in the course of, an act of terrorism or was done for the purposes of terrorism.

(5) In subsection (3)(b) "corresponding offence" means—

(a) an offence under the law of Scotland or of Northern Ireland which corresponds to an offence listed in Schedule 4 to the Modern Slavery Act 2015;

(b) an act constituting an offence under the law in force in a country outside the United Kingdom that would have constituted an offence listed in that Schedule if it had been committed in England or Wales.

(6) For the purposes of this section an act punishable under the law in force in a country outside the United Kingdom is regarded as constituting an offence under that law however it is described in that law.

(7) In this section—

"act" includes an omission;

"the Refugee Convention" means the Convention relating to the Status of Refugees done at Geneva on 28 July 1951 and its Protocol;

"terrorism" has the same meaning as in the Terrorism Act 2000 (see section 1 of that Act).

Note: commences from date to be appointed

64. Identified potential victims etc in England and Wales: assistance and support

Note: inserts s.50A to Modern Slavery Act 2015 from date to be appointed

65. Leave to remain for victims of slavery or human trafficking

(1) This section applies if a positive conclusive grounds decision is made in respect of a person—

(a) who is not a British citizen, and

(b) who does not have leave to remain in the United Kingdom.

(2) The Secretary of State must grant the person limited leave to remain in the United Kingdom if the Secretary of State considers it is necessary for the purpose of—

(a) assisting the person in their recovery from any physical or psychological harm arising from the relevant exploitation,

(b) enabling the person to seek compensation in respect of the relevant exploitation, or

(c) enabling the person to co-operate with a public authority in connection with an investigation or criminal proceedings in respect of the relevant exploitation.

(3) Subsection (2) is subject to section 63(2).

(4) Leave is not necessary for the purpose mentioned in—

(a) subsection (2)(a) if the Secretary of State considers that the person's need for assistance is capable of being met in a country or territory within paragraph (a) or (b) of subsection (5) (or both);

(b) subsection (2)(b) if the Secretary of State considers that—

(i) the person is capable of seeking compensation from outside the United Kingdom, and

(ii) it would be reasonable for the person to do so in the circumstances.

(5) A country or territory is within this subsection if—

(a) it is a country of which the person is a national or citizen;

(b) it is one to which the person may be removed in accordance with an agreement between that country or territory and the United Kingdom (which may be, but does not need to be, an agreement contemplated by Article 40(2) of the Trafficking Convention).

(6) Subsection (7) applies if the Secretary of State is satisfied that—

(a) the person is a threat to public order, or

(b) the person has claimed to be a victim of slavery or human trafficking in bad faith.

(7) Where this subsection applies—

(a) the Secretary of State is not required to grant the person leave under subsection (2), and

(b) if such leave has already been granted to the person, it may be revoked.

(8) Leave granted to a person under subsection (2) may be revoked in such other circumstances as may be prescribed in immigration rules.

(9) Subsections (3) to (7) of section 63 apply for the purposes of this section as they apply for the purposes of that section.

(10) In this section—

"positive conclusive grounds decision" means a decision made by a competent authority that a person is a victim of slavery or human trafficking;

"public authority" means any public authority within the meaning of section 6 of the Human Rights Act 1998;

"the relevant exploitation" means the conduct resulting in the positive conclusive grounds decision.

(11) This section is to be treated for the purposes of section 3 of the Immigration Act 1971 as if it were provision made by that Act.

Note: commences from date to be appointed

66. Civil legal services under section 9 of LASPO: add-on services in relation to the national referral mechanism

Note: amends Sch.1 of Legal Aid, Sentencing and Punishment of Offenders Act 2012 from date to be appointed

67. Civil legal services under section 10 of LASPO: add-on services in relation to national referral mechanism

Note: amends s.10 of the Legal Aid, Sentencing and Punishment of Offenders Act 2012 from date to be appointed

68. Disapplication of retained EU law deriving from Trafficking Directive

(1) Section 4 of the European Union (Withdrawal) Act 2018 (saving for rights etc under section 2(1) of the European Communities Act 1972) ceases to apply to rights, powers, liabilities, obligations, restrictions, remedies and procedures derived from the Trafficking Directive so far as their continued existence would otherwise be incompatible with provision made by or under this Act.

(2) "The Trafficking Directive" means Council Directive 2011/36/EU of the European Parliament and of the Council of 5 April 2011 on preventing and combating trafficking in human beings and protecting its victims.

Note: commences from a date to be appointed

69. Part 5: interpretation

(1) In this Part—

"competent authority" means a person who is a competent authority of the United Kingdom for the purposes of the Trafficking Convention; "conclusive grounds decision" means a decision by a competent authority

as to whether a person is a victim of slavery or human trafficking;

"positive reasonable grounds decision" has the meaning given by section 61(1);

"reasonable grounds decision" means a decision by a competent authority as to whether there are reasonable grounds to believe that a person is a victim of slavery or human trafficking;

the "Trafficking Convention" means the Council of Europe Convention on Action against Trafficking in Human Beings (done at Warsaw on 16 May 2005);

"victim of slavery" and "victim of human trafficking" have the meanings given in regulations made by the Secretary of State.

(2) Regulations under subsection (1) are subject to affirmative resolution procedure.

Note: commences from a date to be appointed

Part 6

Miscellaneous

70. Visa penalty provision: general

(1) The immigration rules may make such visa penalty provision as the Secretary of State considers appropriate in relation to a country specified under section 71 or 72.

(2) "Visa penalty provision" is provision that does one or more of the following in relation to applications for entry clearance made by persons as nationals or citizens of a specified country—

(a) requires that entry clearance must not be granted pursuant to such an application before the end of a specified period;

(b) suspends the power to grant entry clearance pursuant to such an application;

(c) requires such an application to be treated as invalid for the purposes of the immigration rules;

(d) requires the applicant to pay £190 in connection with the making of such an application, in addition to any fee or other amount payable pursuant to any other enactment.

(3) The Secretary of State may by regulations substitute a different amount for the amount for the time being mentioned in subsection (2)(d).

(4) Before making visa penalty provision in relation to a specified country, the Secretary of State must give the government of that country reasonable notice of the proposal to do so.

(5) The immigration rules must secure that visa penalty provision does not apply in relation to an application made before the day on which the provision comes into force.

(6) Visa penalty provision may—

(a) make different provision for different purposes;

(b) provide for exceptions or exemptions, whether by conferring a discretion or otherwise;

(c) include incidental, supplementary, transitional, transitory or saving provision.

(7) Regulations under subsection (3)—

(a) are subject to affirmative resolution procedure if they increase the amount for the time being specified in subsection (2)(d);

(b) are subject to negative resolution procedure if they decrease that amount.

(8) Sums received by virtue of subsection (2)(d) must be paid into the Consolidated Fund.

(9) In this section—

"country" includes any territory outside the United Kingdom;

"entry clearance" has the same meaning as in the Immigration Act 1971 (see section 33(1) of that Act);

"immigration rules" means rules under section 3(2) of the Immigration Act 1971;

"specified" means specified in the immigration rules.

Note: commences from April 28, 2022

71. Visa penalties for countries posing risk to international peace and security etc

(1) A country may be specified under this section if, in the opinion of the Secretary of State, the government of the country has taken action that—

(a) gives, or is likely to give, rise to a threat to international peace and security,

(b) results, or is likely to result, in armed conflict, or

(c) gives, or is likely to give, rise to a breach of international humanitarian law.

(2) In deciding whether to specify a country for the purposes of this section, the Secretary of State must take the following into account—

(a) the extent of the action taken;

(b) the likelihood of further action falling within subsection (1) being taken;

(c) the reasons for the action being taken;

(d) such other matters as the Secretary of State considers appropriate.

(3) In this section—

"action" includes a failure to act;

"country" and "specified" have the same meanings as in section 70.

Note: commences from April 28, 2022

72. Removals from the UK: visa penalties for uncooperative countries

(1) A country may be specified under this section if, in the opinion of the Secretary of State—

(a) the government of the country is not cooperating in relation to the return to the country from the United Kingdom of any of its nationals or citizens who require leave to enter or remain in the United Kingdom but do not have it, and

(b) as a result, there are nationals or citizens of the country that the Secretary of State has been unable to return to the country, whether or not others have been returned.

(2) In forming an opinion as to whether a country is cooperating in relation to returns, the Secretary of State must take the following into account—

(a) any arrangements (whether formal or informal) entered into by the government of the country with the United Kingdom government or the Secretary of State with a view to facilitating returns;

(b) the extent to which the government of the country is—

(i) taking the steps that are in practice necessary or expedient in relation to facilitating returns, and

(ii) doing so promptly;

(c) such other matters as the Secretary of State considers appropriate.

(3) In determining whether to specify a country for the purposes of this section, the Secretary of State must take the following into account—

(a) the length of time for which the government of the country has not been cooperating in relation to returns;

(b) the extent of the lack of cooperation;

(c) the reasons for the lack of cooperation;

(d) such other matters as the Secretary of State considers appropriate.

(4) In this section—

"cooperating in relation to returns" means cooperating as mentioned in subsection (1)(a);

"country" and "specified" have the same meanings as in section 70; "facilitating returns" means facilitating the return of nationals or citizens to a country as mentioned in subsection (1)(a).

Note: commences from June 28, 2022

73. Visa penalties under section 71: review and revocation

(1) This section applies where any visa penalty provision made pursuant to section 71 is in force in relation to a country.

(2) The Secretary of State must, before the end of each relevant period—

(a) review the extent to which the country's government is continuing to act in a way that, in the opinion of Secretary of State, has or is likely to have any of the consequences mentioned in section 71(1), and

(b) in light of that review, determine whether it is appropriate to amend the visa penalty provision.

(3) If, at any time, the Secretary of State forms the opinion that, despite the fact that the country's government has taken or is taking action as mentioned in section 71(1), the visa penalty provision is not necessary or expedient in connection with—

(a) the promotion of international peace and security,

(b) the resolution or prevention of armed conflict, or

(c) the promotion of compliance with international humanitarian law,

the Secretary of State must as soon as practicable revoke the visa penalty provision.

(4) Each of the following is a relevant period—

(a) the period of 2 months beginning with the day on which the visa penalty provision came into force;

(b) each subsequent period of 2 months.

(5) In this section, "visa penalty provision" has the same meaning as in section 70.

Note: commences from April 28, 2022

74. Visa penalties under section 72: review and revocation

(1) This section applies where any visa penalty provision made pursuant to section 72 is in force in relation to a country.

(2) The Secretary of State must, before the end of each relevant period—

(a) review the extent to which the country's cooperation in relation to returns has improved, and

(b) in light of that review, determine whether it is appropriate to amend the visa penalty provision.

(3) If at any time the Secretary of State is no longer of the opinion mentioned in section 72(1), the Secretary of State must as soon as practicable revoke the visa penalty provision.

(4) Each of the following is a relevant period—

(a) the period of 2 months beginning with the day on which the visa penalty provision came into force;

(b) each subsequent period of 2 months.

(5) In this section—

(a) "visa penalty provision" has the same meaning as in section 70;

(b) "cooperation in relation to returns" means cooperation as mentioned in section 72(1)(a).

Note: commences from June 28, 2022

75. Electronic travel authorisations

Note: inserts s.11C & 11CD and amends s.24A & s.33 Immigration Act 1971, s.82 of Immigration and Asylum Act 1999, and s.126 of Nationality, Immigration and Act 2002 from June 28, 2022 (SI 2022/590)

76. Liability of Carriers

Note: amends s.40 of Immigration and Asylum Act 1999 from a date to be appointed

77. Special Immigration Appeals Commission

Note: amends the Special Appeals Commission Act 1997 and s.115(8) of the Equality Act 2010 from June 28, 2022 (SI 2022/590)

78. Counter-terrorism questioning of detained entrants away from place of arrival

Note: amends Sch.7 of the Terrorism Act 2000 from June 28, 2022

79. References to justices of the peace in relation to Northern Ireland

Note: amends s.33(1) of Immigration Act 1971, s.167(1) of Immigration and Asylum Act 1999 and s.45 of the UK Borders Act 2007 commences from June 28, 2022 (SI 2022/590)

80. Tribunal charging power in respect of wasted resources

Note: inserts s.25 A and paragraph 11A to Sch.5 to Tribunals, Courts and Enforcement Act 2007 from a date to be appointed

81. Tribunal Procedure Rules to be made in respect of costs orders etc

(1) Tribunal Procedure Rules governing proceedings before the Tribunal (see subsection (4)) must prescribe conduct that, in the absence of evidence to the contrary, is to be treated as—

(a) improper, unreasonable or negligent for the purposes of—

(i) section 25A(1) of the Tribunals, Courts and Enforcement Act 2007 (charge in respect of wasted resources);

(ii) section 29(4) of that Act (wasted costs);

(b) an unreasonable act for the purposes of section 29(3A) of that Act (unreasonable costs orders).

(2) Tribunal Procedure Rules must make provision to the effect that the Tribunal, if satisfied that conduct prescribed under subsection (1) has taken place, must consider whether to impose a charge or make an order in accordance with the provisions mentioned in that subsection.

(3) Nothing in Tribunal Procedure Rules may compel the Tribunal to impose a charge, or make an order, mentioned in subsection (1) in relation to conduct (whether or not that conduct is prescribed under that subsection).

(4) In this section "the Tribunal" means the Immigration and Asylum Chamber of the First-Tier Tribunal and of the Upper Tribunal (see Articles 2 and 9 of The First-tier Tribunal and Upper Tribunal (Chambers) Order 2010 (S.I. 2010/ 2655)).

(5) In this section "conduct" includes acts and omissions.

(6) ...

Note: subsection 6 inserts s.29(3A) to Tribunals, Courts and Enforcement Act 2007 from date to be appointed.

82. Pre-consolidation amendments of immigration legislation

(1) The Secretary of State may by regulations make such amendments and modifications of the Acts relating to immigration as in the Secretary of State's opinion facilitate, or are otherwise desirable in connection with, the consolidation of the whole or a substantial part of the Acts relating to immigration.

(2) The Acts relating to immigration are—

(a) the Immigration Act 1971;

(b) the Immigration Act 1988;

(c) the Asylum and Immigration Appeals Act 1993;

(d) the Asylum and Immigration Act 1996;

(e) the Special Immigration Appeals Commission Act 1997;
(f) the Immigration and Asylum Act 1999;
(g) the Nationality, Immigration and Asylum Act 2002;
(h) the Asylum and Immigration (Treatment of Claimants, etc) Act 2004;
(i) the Immigration, Asylum and Nationality Act 2006;
(j) the UK Borders Act 2007;
(k) Parts 10 and 12 of the Criminal Justice and Immigration Act 2008;
(l) the Borders, Citizenship and Immigration Act 2009;
(m) section 147 of and Schedule 8 to the Anti-Social Behaviour, Crime and Policing Act 2014;
(n) the Immigration Act 2014;
(o) the Immigration Act 2016;
(p) Parts 1 and 3 of the Immigration and Social Security Co-ordination (EU Withdrawal) Act 2020;
(q) this Act, other than Part 1;
(r) any other provision of an Act relating to immigration, whenever passed.

(3) For the purposes of this section, "amend" includes repeal (and similar terms are to be read accordingly).

(4) Regulations made under this section do not come into force unless an Act is passed consolidating the whole or a substantial part of the Acts relating to immigration.

(5) If such an Act is passed, any regulations made under this section come into force immediately before the Act comes into force.

(6) Regulations under this section are subject to affirmative resolution procedure.

Note: from April 28, 2022 (for the purpose of making (and, where required, consulting on, regulations); June 28 2022 otherwise.)

PART 7

GENERAL

83. Financial provision

The following are to be paid out of money provided by Parliament—

a. expenditure incurred under or by virtue of this Act by a Minister of the Crown, and

b. any increase attributable to this Act in the sums payable under any other Act out of money so provided.

Note: from April 28, 2022

84. Transitional and consequential provision

(1) The Secretary of State may by regulations make such transitional, transitory or saving provision as the Secretary of State considers appropriate in connection with the coming into force of any provision of this Act.

(2) The Secretary of State may by regulations make such provision as the Secretary of State considers appropriate in consequence of this Act.

(3) The provision that may be made by regulations under subsection (2) includes provision amending, repealing or revoking any enactment.

(4) "Enactment" includes—

(a) an enactment contained in subordinate legislation within the meaning of the Interpretation Act 1978;

(b) an enactment contained in, or in an instrument made under, an Act of the Scottish Parliament;

(c) an enactment contained in, or in an instrument made under, a Measure or Act of Senedd Cymru;

(d) an enactment contained in, or in an instrument made under, Northern Ireland legislation.

(5) Regulations under subsection (2) that amend—

(a) an Act of Parliament,

(b) retained direct principal EU legislation,

(c) an Act of the Scottish Parliament,

(d) a Measure or Act of Senedd Cymru, or

(e) Northern Ireland legislation,

are subject to affirmative resolution procedure.

(6) Otherwise, regulations under subsection (2) are subject to negative resolution procedure.

(7) …

Note: subsection 6 amends s.61(2) of UK Borders Act 2007 from April 28, 2022.

85. Regulations

(1) A power to make regulations under this Act is exercisable by statutory instrument.

(2) Regulations under this Act—

(a) may make different provision for different purposes;

(b) may make transitional, transitory or saving provision;

(c) may make incidental, supplementary or consequential provision.

(3) Where regulations under this Act are subject to "negative resolution procedure" the statutory instrument containing the regulations is subject to annulment in pursuance of a resolution of either House of Parliament.

(4) Where regulations under this Act are subject to "affirmative resolution procedure" the regulations may not be made unless a draft of the instrument containing them has been laid before and approved by a resolution of each House of Parliament.

(5) Any provision that may be made by regulations under this Act subject to negative resolution procedure may instead be made by regulations under this Act subject to affirmative resolution procedure.

(6) Any provision that may be made by regulations under this Act for which no Parliamentary procedure is prescribed may instead be made by regulations subject to negative or affirmative resolution procedure.

Note: commenced from April 28, 2022

86. Extent

(1) This Act extends to England and Wales, Scotland and Northern Ireland, subject as follows.

(2) Any amendment, repeal or revocation made by this Act has the same extent within the United Kingdom as the provision to which it relates.

(3) Part 1 (nationality) also extends to the Channel Islands and the Isle of Man and the British overseas territories within the meaning of the British Nationality Act 1981 (see section 50(1) of that Act).

(4) Her Majesty may by Order in Council provide for any of the provisions of this Act to extend, with or without modifications, to any of the Channel Islands or the Isle of Man.

(5) A power under any provision listed in subsection (6) may be exercised so as to extend (with or without modification) to any of the Channel Islands or the Isle of Man any amendment or repeal made by or under this Act of any part of an Act to which the provision listed in subsection (6) relates.

(6) Those provisions are—

(a) section 36 of the Immigration Act 1971,

(b) section 15(1) of the Asylum and Immigration Appeals Act 1993,

(c) section 13(5) of the Asylum and Immigration Act 1996,

(d) section 9(3) of the Special Immigration Appeals Commission Act 1997,

(e) section 170(7) of the Immigration and Asylum Act 1999,

(f) section 163(4) of the Nationality, Immigration and Asylum Act 2002,

(g) section 338 of the Criminal Justice Act 2003,

(h) section 49(3) of the Asylum and Immigration (Treatment of Claimants, etc) Act 2004,

(i) section 63(3) of the Immigration, Asylum and Nationality Act 2006,

(j) section 60(4) of the UK Borders Act 2007,

(k) section 57(5) of the Borders, Citizenship and Immigration Act 2009,

(l) section 76(6) of the Immigration Act 2014,

(m) section 60(6) of the Modern Slavery Act 2015,

(n) section 95(5) of the Immigration Act 2016, and

(o) section 8(2) of the Immigration and Social Security (EU Withdrawal) Act 2020.

Note: commences from April 28, 2022

87. Commencement

(1) Subject to subsections (3) to (5), this Act comes into force on such day as the Secretary of State appoints by regulations.

(2) Regulations under subsection (1) may appoint different days for different purposes or areas.

(3) The following provisions come into force on the day on which this Act is passed—

(a) section 10(1) and (6) to (8) (effect of failure to give notice of pre- commencement decision to deprive a person of citizenship);

(b) sections 70, 71 and 73 (visa penalties in relation to countries posing a risk to international peace and security etc);

(c) this Part.

(4) The following provisions come into force on the day on which this Act is passed for the purposes of making (and, where required, consulting on) regulations—

(a) section 14 (requirement to make asylum claim at "designated place");

(b) section 27 (accelerated detained appeals);

(c) section 42 and Schedule 5 (penalty for failure to secure goods vehicle etc);

(d) section 43 (working in United Kingdom waters: arrival and entry);

(e) section 50 (persons subject to immigration control: referral or age assessment by local authority);

(f) section 52 (use of scientific methods in age assessments);

(g) section 53 (regulations about age assessments);

(h) section 69 (interpretation of Part 5);

(i) section 82 (pre-consolidation amendments of immigration legislation).

(5) The following provisions come into force at the end of the period of two months beginning with the day on which this Act is passed—

(a) section 28 (claims certified as clearly unfounded: removal of right of appeal);

(b) paragraphs 5 to 19 of Schedule 4, and section 29 so far as it relates to those paragraphs (removal of asylum seeker to safe third country);

(c) section 30(1), (2) and (4) to (6) (Refugee Convention: general);

(d) sections 31 to 36 and 38 (interpretation of Refugee Convention);

(e) section 39 (interpretation of Part 2);

(f) section 44 (power to search container);

(g) section 49(1) to (4) (interpretation of Part 4);

(h) sections 72 and 74 (visa penalties in relation to uncooperative countries);

(i) section 78 (counter-terrorism questioning of detained entrants away from place of arrival).

Note: commences from April 28, 2022

88. Short title

This Act may be cited as the Nationality and Borders Act 2022.

SCHEDULES

SCHEDULE 1 — Section 9

WAIVER OF REQUIREMENT OF PRESENCE IN UK ETC

Note: British Nationality Act 1981 and s.1 of the Citizenship (Armed Forces) Act 2014 from June 28, 2022 (subject to transitional and saving provisions specified in SI 2022/590)

SCHEDULE 2 — Section 10(4)

DEPRIVATION OF CITIZENSHIP WITHOUT NOTICE: JUDICIAL OVERSIGHT

Note: inserts Sch.4A to British Nationality Act 1981 from date to be appointed

SCHEDULE 3 — Section 23

EXPEDITED APPEALS WHERE PRIORITY REMOVAL NOTICE SERVED: CONSEQUENTIAL AMENDMENTS

Note: amends Nationality, Immigration and Asylum Act 2002 and s.8 of the Asylum and Immigration (Treatment of Claimants, etc) Act 2004 from a date to be appointed

SCHEDULE 4 **Section 29**

REMOVAL OF ASYLUM SEEKER TO SAFE COUNTRY

Note: amends s. 77 of the Nationality, Immigration and Asylum Act 2002 and Sch. 3 to the Asylum and Immigration (Treatment of Claimants, etc) Act 2004 from June 28, 2022 (subject to transitional and provisions specified in SI 2022/590 reg.3 and Sch.2 para 4(4))

SCHEDULE 5 **Section 42**

PENALTY FOR FAILURE TO SECURE GOODS VEHICLE ETC

Note: amends Part 2 of the Immigration and Asylum Act 1999 from April 28, 2022 (for the purposes of making (and, where required, consulting on) regulations; not yet in force otherwise)

SCHEDULE 6 **Section 43(2)**

WORKING IN UNITED KINGDOM WATERS: CONSEQUENTIAL AND RELATED AMENDMENTS

Note: amends the Immigration Act 1971 and Immigration, Asylum and Nationality Act 2006.

SCHEDULE 7 **Section 45**

MARITIME ENFORCEMENT

Note: amends Part 3A and inserts A1-M1 to Sch. 4A of Immigration Act 1971 from June 28, 2022 (subject to transitional and saving provisions specified in SI 2022/590 reg.3 and Sch.2 para 8)

SCHEDULE 8 **Section 47(11)**

PRISONERS RETURNING TO THE UK: MODIFICATIONS OF CRIMINAL JUSTICE ACT 2003

Note: inserts Sch.19B to Criminal Justice Act 2003 from Jude 28, 2022 (subject to transitional and saving provisions specified in SI 2022/590 reg.3 an Sch.2 para 9)

PROCEDURE RULES AND PRACTICE DIRECTIONS AND STATEMENTS

The Tribunal Procedure (First-tier Tribunal) (Immigration and Asylum Chamber) Rules 2014
(SI 2014, No. 2604)

Contents

SCHEDULE—THE FAST TRACK RULES

Having consulted in accordance with paragraph 28(1) of Schedule 5 to the Tribunals, Courts and Enforcement Act 2007, the Tribunal Procedure Committee has made the following Rules in exercise of the powers conferred by—

(a) sections 9, 22, 29(3) and (4) of and Schedule 5 to the Tribunals, Courts and Enforcement Act 2007,
(b) paragraph 25 of Schedule 2 to the Immigration Act 1971,
(c) section 106(3) of the Nationality, Immigration and Asylum Act 2002,
(d) section 40A(3) of the British Nationality Act 1981, and
(e) Schedule 1 to the Immigration (European Economic Area) Regulations 2006.

The Lord Chancellor has allowed the Rules in accordance with paragraph 28(3) of Schedule 5 to the Tribunals, Courts and Enforcement Act 2007.

PART 1

INTRODUCTION

Citation, commencement, application and interpretation

1.—(1) These Rules may be cited as the Tribunal Procedure (First-tier Tribunal) (Immigration and Asylum Chamber) Rules 2014 and come into force on 20th October 2014.

(2) They apply to proceedings before the Immigration and Asylum Chamber of the First-tier Tribunal.

(3) [. . .]

(4) In these Rules—

'the 1999 Act' means the Immigration and Asylum Act 1999;

'the 2002 Act' means the Nationality, Immigration and Asylum Act 2002;

'the 2004 Act' means the Asylum and Immigration (Treatment of Claimants, etc.) Act 2004;

'[. . .];

'the 2007 Act' means the Tribunals, Courts and Enforcement Act 2007;

['the 2020 Regulations' means the Immigration (Citizens' Rights Appeals) (EU Exit) Regulations 2020;]

'appealable decision' means a decision from which there is a right of appeal to the Immigration and Asylum Chamber of the First-tier Tribunal;

'appellant' means a person who has provided a notice of appeal to the Tribunal against an appealable decision in accordance with these Rules;

['appointment' means (except in rule 10(5)), a case management meeting conducted by a member of the Tribunal's staff authorised to carry out functions of a judicial nature pursuant to rule 3(2), held for the purpose of carrying out any of those functions;]

'asylum claim' has the meaning given in section 113(1) of the 2002 Act;

'certificate of fee satisfaction' means a certificate of fee satisfaction issued by the Lord Chancellor under article 8 of the Fees Order;

'decision maker' means the maker of a decision against which an appeal is brought;

'dispose of proceedings' includes, unless indicated otherwise, disposing of a part of the proceedings;

'document' means anything in which information is recorded in any form, and an obligation under these Rules to provide or allow access to a document or a copy of a document for any purpose means, unless the Tribunal directs otherwise, an obligation to provide or allow access to such document or copy in a legible form or in a form which can be readily made into a legible form;

[. . .]

'the Fees Order' means the First-tier Tribunal (Immigration and Asylum Chamber) Fees Order 2011;

'hearing' means an oral hearing and includes a hearing conducted in whole or in part by video link, telephone or other means of instantaneous two-way electronic communication;

'the Immigration Acts' means the Acts referred to in section 61 of the UK Borders Act 2007;

'party' means—

(a) an appellant or respondent to proceedings;

(b) a party to a bail application as provided for in rule 37(3) and 37(4); and

(c) the UNHCR where notice has been given to the Tribunal in accordance with rule 8(3);

'practice direction' means a direction given under section 23 of the 2007 Act;

'qualified representative' means a person who is a qualified person in accordance with section 84(2) of the 1999 Act;

'respondent' means—

(a) the decision maker specified in the notice of decision against which a notice of appeal has been provided; and

(b) a person substituted or added as a respondent in accordance with rule 8.

'Tribunal' means the First-tier Tribunal;

'the UNHCR' means the United Kingdom Representative of the United Nations High Commissioner for Refugees; and

'working day' means any day except—

(a) a Saturday or Sunday, Christmas Day, Good Friday or a bank holiday under section 1 of the Banking and Financial Dealings Act 1971; and

(b) 27th to 31st December inclusive.

(5) A rule or Part referred to by number alone, means a rule in, or Part of, these Rules.

Note: definition of 'the 2020 Regulations' inserted from 31 January 2020 (SI 2020/61). Paragraph (3) and definition of 'Fast Track Rules' in paragraph (4) omitted from 21 July 2020 (SI 2020/651). Definition of 'the 2006 Regulations' omitted from 23.00 on 31 December 2020 (SI 2020/1309) but this amendment does not apply where:

(5)(a) any appeal which has been brought under the Immigration (European Economic Area) Regulations 2006 and has not been finally determined before commencement day;

(b) any appeal which has been brought under the Immigration (European Economic Area) Regulations 2016 (whether taken before or after commencement day), and has yet to be finally determined;

(c) any EEA decision under the Immigration (European Economic Area) Regulations 2016 (whether taken before or after commencement day), in respect of which an appeal has not been brought.

(6) For the purposes of paragraph (5)—

(a) references to the Immigration (European Economic Area) Regulations 2016 are to those Regulations as they continue to have effect by virtue of these Regulations, the Citizens' Rights (Application Deadline and Temporary Protection) (EU Exit) Regulations 2020 or the Citizens' Rights (Restrictions of Rights of Entry and Residence) (EU Exit) Regulations 2020;

(b) an appeal is not to be treated as finally determined while a further appeal may be brought, and, if such a further appeal is brought, the original appeal is not to be treated as finally determined until the further appeal is determined, withdrawn or abandoned (reg 5-6 of SI/1309).

Definition of 'appointment' inserted 6 April 2022 (SI 2022/312).

Overriding objective and parties' obligation to cooperate with the Tribunal

2.—(1) The overriding objective of these Rules is to enable the Tribunal to deal with cases fairly and justly.

(2) Dealing with a case fairly and justly includes—

(a) dealing with the case in ways which are proportionate to the importance of the case, the complexity of the issues, the anticipated costs and the resources of the parties and of the Tribunal;

(b) avoiding unnecessary formality and seeking flexibility in the proceedings;

(c) ensuring, so far as practicable, that the parties are able to participate fully in the proceedings;

(d) using any special expertise of the Tribunal effectively; and

(e) avoiding delay, so far as compatible with proper consideration of the issues.

(3) The Tribunal must seek to give effect to the overriding objective when it—

(a) exercises any power under these Rules; or

(b) interprets any rule or practice direction.

(4) Parties must—

(a) help the Tribunal to further the overriding objective; and

(b) cooperate with the Tribunal generally.

PART 2

GENERAL POWERS AND PROVISIONS

Delegation to staff

3.—(1) Anything of a formal or administrative nature which is required or permitted to be done by the Tribunal under these Rules may be done by a member of the Tribunal's staff.

(2) Staff appointed [under section 40(1) of the 2007 Act (tribunal staff and services) or section 2(1) of the Courts Act 2003 (court officers, staff and services)] may, [if authorized by] the Senior President of Tribunals {under paragraph 3(3) of Schedule 5 to the 2007 Act}, carry out functions of a judicial nature permitted or required to be done by the Tribunal.

(3) [. . .]

(4) Within 14 days after the date on which the Tribunal sends notice of a decision made by a member of staff under paragraph (2) to a party, that party may apply in writing to the Tribunal for that decision to be considered afresh by a judge.

Note: Words in square brackets in paragraph (2) substituted and words in curly brackets in paragraph (2) inserted and paragraph (3) omitted from 21 July 2020 (SI 2020/651).

Case management powers

4.—(1) Subject to the provisions of the 2007 Act and any other enactment, the Tribunal may regulate its own procedure.

(2) The Tribunal may give a direction in relation to the conduct or disposal of proceedings at any time, including a direction amending, suspending or setting aside an earlier direction.

(3) In particular, and without restricting the general powers in paragraphs (1) and (2), the Tribunal may—

(a) extend or shorten the time for complying with any rule, practice direction or direction;

(b) consolidate or hear together two or more sets of proceedings or parts of proceedings raising common issues;

(c) permit or require a party to amend a document;

(d) permit or require a party or another person to provide documents, information, evidence or submissions to the Tribunal or a party;

(e) provide for a particular matter to be dealt with as a preliminary issue;

(f) hold a hearing [or appointment] to consider any matter, including a case management issue;

(g) decide the form of any hearing [or appointment];

(h) adjourn or postpone a hearing [or appointment];

(i) require a party to produce a bundle for a hearing [or appointment];

(j) stay (or, in Scotland, sist) proceedings;

(k) transfer proceedings to another court or tribunal if that other court or tribunal has jurisdiction in relation to the proceedings and—

(i) because of a change of circumstances since the proceedings were started, the Tribunal no longer has jurisdiction in relation to the proceedings; or

(ii) the Tribunal considers that the other court or tribunal is a more appropriate forum for the determination of the case; or

(l) suspend the effect of its own decision pending the determination by the Tribunal or the Upper Tribunal of an application for permission to appeal against, and any appeal or review of, that decision.

Note: Words inserted in paragraphs (4)(3) (f),(g),(h) and (i) from 6 April 2022 (SI 2022/312).

[Coronavirus temporary rule (decisions without a hearing)

4A. . . .]

Note: Rule 4A inserted from 10 April 2020 (SI 2020/416) and deleted from 25 March 2022 (Rule 1(2) of SI 2020/416).

Procedure for applying for and giving directions

5.—(1) The Tribunal may give a direction on the application of one or more of the parties or on its own initiative.

(2) An application for a direction may be made—

(a) by sending or delivering a written application to the Tribunal; or

(b) orally during the course of a hearing.

(3) An application for a direction must include the reason for making that application.

(4) Unless the Tribunal considers that there is good reason not to do so, the Tribunal must send written notice of any direction to every party and to any other person affected by the direction.

(5) If a party or any other person sent notice of the direction under paragraph (4) wishes to challenge the direction which the Tribunal has given, they may do so by applying for another direction which amends, suspends or sets aside the first direction.

Failure to comply with rules etc.

6.—(1) An irregularity resulting from a failure to comply with any requirement in these Rules, a practice direction or a direction does not of itself render void the proceedings or any step taken in the proceedings.

(2) If a party has failed to comply with a requirement in these Rules, a practice direction or a direction, the Tribunal may take such action as it considers just, which may include—

(a) waiving the requirement;

(b) requiring the failure to be remedied; or

(c) exercising its power under paragraph (3).

(3) The Tribunal may refer to the Upper Tribunal, and ask the Upper Tribunal to exercise its power under section 25 (supplementary powers of Upper Tribunal) of the 2007 Act in relation to, any failure by a person to comply with a requirement imposed by the Tribunal—

(a) to attend at any place for the purpose of giving evidence;

(b) otherwise to make themselves available to give evidence;

(c) to swear an oath in connection with the giving of evidence;

(d) to give evidence as a witness;

(e) to produce a document; or

(f) to facilitate the inspection of a document or any other thing (including any premises).

Striking out of an appeal for non-payment of fee and reinstatement

7.—(1) Where the Tribunal is notified by the Lord Chancellor that a certificate of fee satisfaction has been revoked, the appeal shall automatically be struck out without order of the Tribunal and the Tribunal must notify each party that the appeal has been struck out.

(2) Where an appeal has been struck out in accordance with paragraph (1), the appeal may be reinstated if—

(a) the appellant applies to have the appeal reinstated; and

(b) the Lord Chancellor has issued a new certificate of fee satisfaction.

(3) An application made under paragraph (2)(a) must be made in writing and received by the Tribunal within 14 days, or if the appellant is outside the United Kingdom within 28 days, of the date on which the Tribunal sent notification of the striking out to the appellant.

Substitution and addition of parties

8.—(1) The Tribunal may give a direction substituting a [party] if—

(a) the wrong person has been named as a [party]; or

(b) the substitution has become necessary because of a change in circumstances since the start of proceedings.

(2) The Tribunal may give a direction adding a person to the proceedings as a respondent.

(3) The UNHCR may give notice to the Tribunal that they wish to participate in any proceedings where the appellant has made an asylum claim and on giving such notice becomes a party to the proceedings.

(4) If—

(a) the Tribunal gives a direction under paragraph (1) or (2); or

(b) the UNHCR gives notice to the Tribunal under paragraph (3),

the Tribunal may give such consequential directions as it considers appropriate.

Note: Words in paragraph (1) substituted from 6 April 2022 (SI 2022/312).

Orders for payment of costs and interest on costs (or, in Scotland, expenses)

9.—(1) If the Tribunal allows an appeal, it may order a respondent to pay by way of costs to the appellant an amount no greater than—

(a) any fee paid under the Fees Order that has not been refunded; and

(b) any fee which the appellant is or may be liable to pay under that Order.

(2) The Tribunal may otherwise make an order in respect of costs only—

(a) under section 29(4) of the 2007 Act (wasted costs) and costs incurred in applying for such costs; or

(b) if a person has acted unreasonably in bringing, defending or conducting proceedings.

(3) The Tribunal may make an order under this rule on an application or on its own initiative.

(4) A person making an application for an order for costs—

(a) must, unless the application is made orally at a hearing, send or deliver an application to the Tribunal and to the person against whom the order is sought to be made; and

(b) may send or deliver together with the application a schedule of the costs claimed in sufficient detail to allow summary assessment of such costs by the Tribunal.

(5) An application for an order for costs may be made at any time during the proceedings but must be made within 28 days after the date on which the Tribunal sends—

(a) a notice of decision recording the decision which disposes of the proceedings; or

(b) notice that a withdrawal has taken effect under rule 17 (withdrawal).

(6) The Tribunal may not make an order for costs against a person (in this rule called the 'paying person') without first giving that person an opportunity to make representations.

(7) The amount of costs to be paid under an order under this rule may be determined by—

(a) summary assessment by the Tribunal;

(b) agreement of a specified sum by the paying person and the person entitled to receive the costs (in this rule called the 'receiving person');

(c) detailed assessment of the whole or a specified part of the costs (including the costs of the assessment) incurred by the receiving person, if not agreed.

(8) Except in relation to paragraph (9), in the application of this rule in relation to Scotland, any reference to costs is to be read as a reference to expenses.

(9) Following an order for detailed assessment made by the Tribunal under paragraph (7)(c) the paying person or the receiving person may apply—

(a) in England and Wales, to the county court for a detailed assessment of the costs on the standard basis or, if specified in the order, on the indemnity basis; and the Civil Procedure Rules 1998, section 74 (interest on judgment debts, etc.) of the County Courts Act 1984 and the County Court (Interest on Judgment Debts) Order 1991 shall apply, with necessary modifications, to that application and assessment as if the proceedings in the Tribunal had been proceedings in a court to which the Civil Procedure Rules 1998 apply;

(b) in Scotland, to the Auditor of the Sheriff Court or the Court of Session (as specified in the order) for the taxation of the expenses according to the fees payable in that court; or

(c) in Northern Ireland, to the Taxing Office of the High Court of Northern Ireland for taxation on the standard basis or, if specified in the order, on the indemnity basis.

Representatives

10.—(1) A party may be represented by any person not prohibited from representing by section 84 of the 1999 Act.

(2) Where a party is or has been represented by a person prohibited from representing by section 84 of the 1999 Act, that does not of itself render void the proceedings or any step taken in the proceedings.

(3) If a party appoints a representative, that party (or the representative if the representative is a qualified representative) must send or deliver to the Tribunal written notice of the representative's name and address, which may be done at a hearing.

(4) Anything permitted or required to be done by a party under these Rules, a practice direction or a direction may be done by the representative of that party, except signing a witness statement.

(5) A person who receives notice of the appointment of a representative—

(a) must provide to the representative any document which is required to be provided to the represented party, and need not provide that document to the represented party; and

(b) may assume that the representative is and remains authorised as such until they receive written notification that this is not so from the representative or the represented party.

(6) As from the date on which a person has notified the Tribunal that they are acting as the representative of an appellant and has given an address for service, if any document is

provided to the appellant a copy must also at the same time be provided to the appellant's representative.

Calculating time

11.—(1) An act required or permitted to be done on or by a particular day by these Rules, a practice direction or a direction must, unless otherwise directed, be done by midnight on that day.

(2) Subject to the Tribunal directing that this paragraph does not apply, if the time specified by these Rules, a practice direction or a direction for doing any act ends on a day other than a working day, the act is done in time if it is done on the next working day.

Sending, delivery and language of documents

12.—(1) Any document to be provided to the Tribunal or any person under these Rules, a practice direction or a direction must be—

(a) delivered, or sent by post, to an address;
(b) sent via a document exchange to a document exchange number or address;
(c) [. . .]
(d) sent by e-mail to an e-mail address; [
(da) uploaded to the Tribunal's secure portal in a compatible file format; or]
(e) sent or delivered by any other method,

identified for that purpose by the Tribunal or person to whom the document is directed.

(2) A document to be provided to an individual may be provided by leaving it with that individual.

(3) If the respondent believes that the address specified under paragraph (1) for the provision of documents to the appellant is not appropriate for that purpose, the respondent must notify the Tribunal in writing of that fact and, if aware of it, an address which would be appropriate.

(4) If any document is provided to a person who has notified the Tribunal that they are acting as the representative of a party, it shall be deemed to have been provided to that party.

(5) Subject to paragraph (6)—

(a) any notice of appeal or application notice provided to the Tribunal must be completed in English; and

(b) if a document provided to the Tribunal is not written in English, it must be accompanied by an English translation.

(6) In proceedings that are in Wales or have a connection with Wales, a document or translation may be provided to the Tribunal in Welsh.

Note: Paragraph (1)(c) omitted and paragraph (1)(da) inserted from 6 April 2022 (SI 2022/312).

[Providing contact details

12A. —(1) An appellant must provide the Tribunal with—

(a) the postal address at which they are living, if they have one; and
(b) their email address, if they have one.

(2) The Tribunal must be notified of any change to the details provided under paragraph (1) as soon as reasonably practicable.

(3) If the appellant has a representative, the representative shall take all reasonable steps to ensure that the appellant complies with paragraphs (1) and (2).

(4) If the respondent decides to remove or deport an appellant from the United Kingdom whilst proceedings before the Tribunal, including any application for permission to appeal, are pending the respondent must inform the Tribunal of that fact and take all reasonable steps before any removal or deportation—

(a) to obtain from the appellant an email address and postal address in the country to which it is intended to remove or deport the appellant to which correspondence may be sent to the appellant; and

(b) to provide that information to the Tribunal and to the appellant's representative, if they have one, as soon as reasonably practicable and in any event before removal or deportation.]

Note: Rule 12A inserted from 6 April 2022 (SI 2022/312).

Use of documents and information

13.—(1) The Tribunal may make an order prohibiting the disclosure or publication of—

(a) specified documents or information relating to the proceedings; or

(b) any matter likely to lead members of the public to identify any person whom the Tribunal considers should not be identified.

(2) The Tribunal may give a direction prohibiting the disclosure of a document or information to a person if—

(a) the Tribunal is satisfied that such disclosure would be likely to cause that person or some other person serious harm; and

(b) the Tribunal is satisfied, having regard to the interests of justice, that it is proportionate to give such a direction.

(3) If a party ('the first party') considers that the Tribunal should give a direction under paragraph (2) prohibiting the disclosure of a document or information to another party ('the second party'), the first party must—

(a) exclude the relevant document or information from any documents to be provided to the second party; and

(b) provide to the Tribunal the excluded document or information, and the reason for its exclusion, so that the Tribunal may decide whether the document or information should be disclosed to the second party or should be the subject of a direction under paragraph (2).

(4) The Tribunal must conduct proceedings as appropriate in order to give effect to a direction given under paragraph (2).

(5) If the Tribunal gives a direction under paragraph (2) which prevents disclosure to a party who has appointed a representative, the Tribunal may give a direction that the documents or information be disclosed to that representative if the Tribunal is satisfied that—

(a) disclosure to the representative would be in the interests of the party; and

(b) the representative will act in accordance with paragraph (6).

(6) Documents or information disclosed to a representative in accordance with a direction under paragraph (5) must not be disclosed either directly or indirectly to any other person without the Tribunal's consent.

(7) The Tribunal may, on the application of a party or on its own initiative, give a direction that certain documents or information must or may be disclosed to the Tribunal on the basis that the Tribunal will not disclose such documents or information to other persons, or specified other persons.

(8) A party making an application for a direction under paragraph (7) may withhold the relevant documents or information from other parties until the Tribunal has granted or refused the application.

(9) In a case involving matters relating to national security, the Tribunal must ensure that information is not disclosed contrary to the interests of national security.

(10) The Tribunal must conduct proceedings and record its decision and reasons appropriately so as not to undermine the effect of an order made under paragraph (1), a direction given under paragraph (2), (5) or (7) or the duty imposed by paragraph (9).

Evidence and submissions

14.—(1) Without restriction on the general powers in rule 4 (case management powers), the Tribunal may give directions as to—

(a) issues on which it requires evidence or submissions;

(b) the nature of the evidence or submissions it requires;

(c) whether the parties are permitted or required to provide expert evidence;

(d) any limit on the number of witnesses whose evidence a party may put forward, whether in relation to a particular issue or generally;

(e) the manner in which any evidence or submissions are to be provided, which may include a direction for them to be given—

(i) orally at a hearing; or

(ii) by witness statement or written submissions; and

(f) the time at which any evidence or submissions are to be provided.

(2) The Tribunal may admit evidence whether or not—

(a) the evidence would be admissible in a civil trial in the United Kingdom; or

(b) subject to section 85A(4) of the 2002 Act, the evidence was available to the decision maker.

(3) The Tribunal may consent to a witness giving, or require any witness to give, evidence on oath or affirmation, and may administer an oath or affirmation for that purpose.

Summoning or citation of witnesses and orders to answer questions or produce documents

15.—(1) On the application of a party or on its own initiative, the Tribunal may—

(a) by summons (or, in Scotland, citation) require any person to attend as a witness at a hearing at the time and place specified in the summons or citation; or

(b) order any person to answer any questions or produce any documents in that person's possession or control which relate to any issue in the proceedings.

(2) A summons or citation under paragraph (1)(a) must—

(a) give the person required to attend 14 days' notice of the hearing or such shorter period as the Tribunal may direct; and

(b) where the person is not a party, make provision for the person's necessary expenses of attendance to be paid, and state who is to pay them.

(3) No person may be compelled to give any evidence or produce any document that the person could not be compelled to give or produce on a trial of an action in a court of law in the part of the United Kingdom where the proceedings are to be determined.

(4) A summons, citation or order under this rule must—

(a) state that the person on whom the requirement is imposed may apply to the Tribunal to vary or set aside the summons, citation or order, if they have not had an opportunity to object to it; and

(b) state the consequences of failure to comply with the summons, citation or order.

Appeal treated as abandoned [. . .]

16.—(1) A party must notify the Tribunal if they are aware that—

(a) the appellant has left the United Kingdom;

(b) the appellant has been granted leave to enter or remain in the United Kingdom;[or]

(c) a deportation order has been made against the appellant;

[. . .].

[(**1A**) A party to an appeal under the 2020 Regulations must also notify the Tribunal if they are aware that the appeal is to be treated as abandoned under regulation 13 of those Regulations.]

(2) Where an appeal is treated as abandoned pursuant to section {92(8) or 104(4A)} of the 2002 Act [[. . .]] [or regulation 13(3) of the 2020 Regulations], the Tribunal must send the parties a notice informing them that the appeal is being treated as abandoned [. . .].

(3) Where an appeal would otherwise fall to be treated as abandoned pursuant to section 104(4A) of the 2002 Act [or regulation 13(3) of the 2020 Regulations], but the appellant wishes to pursue their appeal, the appellant must provide a notice, which must comply with any relevant practice direction, to the Tribunal and each other party so that it is received within 28 days of the date on which the appellant was sent notice of the grant of leave to enter or remain in the United Kingdom [[. . .]].

Note: Paragraph (1A) and words in square brackets in paragraphs (2) and (3) inserted from 31 January 2020 (SI 2020/61). Words in heading and at the end of paragraph (2) omitted and words in curly brackets in paragraph (2) inserted from 21 July 2020 (SI 2020/651). Word 'or' inserted at the end of paragraph 1(b), paragraph 1(d) and words in double square brackets in paragraphs (2) and (3) omitted from 23.00 on 31 December 2020 (SI 2020/1309) but these amendments do not take affect where:

(5) (a) any appeal which has been brought under the Immigration (European Economic Area) Regulations 2006 and has not been finally determined before commencement day;

(b) any appeal which has been brought under the Immigration (European Economic Area) Regulations 2016 (whether taken before or after commencement day), and has yet to be finally determined;

(c) any EEA decision under the Immigration (European Economic Area) Regulations 2016 (whether taken before or after commencement day), in respect of which an appeal has not been brought.

(6) For the purposes of paragraph (5)—

(a) references to the Immigration (European Economic Area) Regulations 2016 are to those Regulations as they continue to have effect by virtue of these Regulations, the Citizens' Rights (Application Deadline and Temporary Protection) (EU Exit) Regulations 2020 or the Citizens' Rights (Restrictions of Rights of Entry and Residence) (EU Exit) Regulations 2020;

(b) an appeal is not to be treated as finally determined while a further appeal may be brought, and, if such a further appeal is brought, the original appeal is not to be treated as finally determined until the further appeal is determined, withdrawn or abandoned (reg 5-6 of SI/1309).

Withdrawal

17.—(1) A party may give notice of the withdrawal of their appeal—

(a) by providing to the Tribunal a written notice of withdrawal of the appeal; or

(b) orally at a hearing,

and in either case must specify the reasons for that withdrawal.

(2) The Tribunal must (save for good reason) treat an appeal as withdrawn if the respondent notifies the Tribunal and each other party that the decision (or, where the appeal relates to more than one decision, all of the decisions) to which the appeal relates has been withdrawn and specifies the reasons for the withdrawal of the decision.

(3) The Tribunal must notify each party in writing that a withdrawal has taken effect under this rule and that the proceedings are no longer regarded by the Tribunal as pending.

Certification of pending appeal

18.—(1) The Secretary of State must, upon issuing a certificate under section 97 or 98 of the 2002 Act which relates to a pending appeal, provide notice of the certification to the Tribunal.

(2) Where a notice of certification is provided under paragraph (1), the Tribunal must—

(a) notify the parties; and

(b) take no further action in relation to the appeal.

PART 3

PROCEEDINGS BEFORE THE TRIBUNAL

CHAPTER 1

Before the Hearing

Notice of appeal

19.—(1) An appellant must start proceedings by providing a notice of appeal to the Tribunal.

(2) If the person is in the United Kingdom, the notice of appeal must be received not later than 14 days after they are sent the notice of the decision against which the appeal is brought.

(3) If the person is outside the United Kingdom, the notice of appeal must be received—

(a) not later than 28 days after their departure from the United Kingdom if the person—

(i) was in the United Kingdom when the decision against which they are appealing was made, and

(ii) may not appeal while they are in the United Kingdom by reason of a provision of the 2002 Act; or

(b) in any other case, not later than 28 days after they receive the notice of the decision.

[(3A) But paragraphs (2) and (3) do not apply in relation to the bringing of an appeal against a citizens' rights immigration decision.

'A citizens' rights immigration decision' is a decision which can be appealed against under the 2020 Regulations.

(3B) The notice of appeal in relation to an appeal against a citizens' rights immigration decision must be received—

(a) if the person is in the United Kingdom, not later than 14 days after the appellant is sent the notice of the decision;

(b) if the person is outside the United Kingdom, not later than 28 days after the appellant receives the notice of the decision.

But this paragraph is subject to paragraph (3D).

(3C) Paragraph (3D) applies where—

(a) a person ('P') applies for an administrative review of a citizens' rights immigration decision ('the original decision') under the relevant rules, and

(b) P had not, before P receives notice of the decision on administrative review, started proceedings in relation to the original decision.

(3D) Where this paragraph applies, the notice of appeal against the original decision must be received—

(a) if P is in the United Kingdom, not later than 14 days after P is sent the notice of the decision on administrative review;

(b) if P is outside the United Kingdom, not later than 28 days after P receives the notice of the decision on administrative review.

[(3E) In this rule, 'the relevant rules' means—

{(a) Appendix AR(EU) and Appendix AR (administrative review) to the immigration rules}, or

(b) the Citizens' Rights (Frontier Workers) (EU Exit) Regulations 2020 (see regulations 21 to 23 of those Regulations).]]

(4) The notice of appeal must—

(a) [identify which of the available statutory grounds of appeal are relied upon;];

(b) be signed and dated by the appellant or their representative;

(c) if the notice of appeal is signed by the appellant's representative, the representative must certify in the notice of appeal that it has been completed in accordance with the appellant's instructions;

[...]

(5) The appellant must provide with the notice of appeal—

(a) the notice of decision against which the appellant is appealing or if it is not practicable to include the notice of decision, the reasons why it is not practicable;

(b) any statement of reasons for that decision;

(c) any documents in support of the appellant's case which have not been supplied to the respondent;

(d) an application for the Lord Chancellor to issue a certificate of fee satisfaction;

(e) any further information or documents required by an applicable practice direction.

(6) The Tribunal must send a copy of the notice of appeal and the accompanying documents or information provided by the appellant to the respondent.

(7) An appellant may, with the permission of the Tribunal, vary the grounds on which they rely in the notice of appeal.

[(8) A practice direction may require that, in a specified category of case, the notice of appeal must also set out the grounds of appeal.]

Note: Paragraphs (3A) to (3E) inserted from 31 January 2020 (SI 2020/61), paragraph (3E) substituted from 4 November 2020 (SI 2020/1213) and paragraph (3E)(a) substituted from 31 December 2020 (SI 2020/1372). Words in paragraph (4)(a) substituted, paragraphs (4)(d) to (f) deleted and paragraph (8) inserted from 6 April 2022 (SI 2022/312).

Late notice of appeal

20.—(1) Where a notice of appeal is provided outside the time limit in rule 19, including any extension of time directed under rule 4(3)(a) (power to extend time), the notice of appeal must include an application for such an extension of time and the reason why the notice of appeal was not provided in time.

(2) If, upon receipt of a notice of appeal, the notice appears to the Tribunal to have been provided outside the time limit but does not include an application for an extension of time, the Tribunal must (unless it extends time of its own initiative) notify the person in writing that it proposes to treat the notice of appeal as being out of time.

(3) Where the Tribunal gives notification under paragraph (2), the person may by written notice to the Tribunal contend that—

(a) the notice of appeal was given in time; or

(b) time for providing the notice of appeal should be extended,

and, if so, that person may provide the Tribunal with written evidence in support of that contention.

(4) The Tribunal must decide any issue under this rule as to whether a notice of appeal was given in time, or whether to extend the time for appealing, as a preliminary issue, and may do so without a hearing.

(5) Where the Tribunal makes a decision under this rule it must provide to the parties written notice of its decision, including its reasons.

Special provision for imminent removal cases (late notice of appeal)

21.—(1) This rule applies in any case to which rule 20 applies, where the respondent notifies the Tribunal that directions have been given for the removal of that person from the United Kingdom on a date within 5 days of the date on which the notice of appeal was received.

(2) The Tribunal must, if reasonably practicable, make any decision under rule 20 before the date and time proposed for the removal.

(3) Rule 20 shall apply, subject to the modifications that the Tribunal may—

(a) give notification under rule 20(2) orally, which may include giving it by telephone,

(b) direct a time for providing evidence under rule 20(3), and

(c) direct that evidence in support of a contention under rule 20(3) is to be given orally, which may include requiring the evidence to be given by telephone, and hold a hearing for the purpose of receiving such evidence.

Circumstances in which the Tribunal may not accept a notice of appeal

22.—(1) Where a person has provided a notice of appeal to the Tribunal and any of the circumstances in paragraph (2) apply, the Tribunal may not accept the notice of appeal.

(2) The circumstances referred to in paragraph (1) are that—

(a) there is no appealable decision; or

(b) the Lord Chancellor has refused to issue a certificate of fee satisfaction.

(3) Where the Tribunal does not accept a notice of appeal, it must—

(a) notify the person providing the notice of appeal and the respondent; and

(b) take no further action on that notice of appeal.

Response: entry clearance cases

23.—(1) This rule applies to an appeal against a refusal of entry clearance [. . .].

(2) When a respondent is provided with a copy of a notice of appeal from a refusal of entry clearance [. . .], the respondent must provide the Tribunal with—

(a) the notice of the decision to which the notice of appeal relates and any other document the respondent provided to the appellant giving reasons for that decision;

(b) [. . .]

(c) any statement of evidence or application form completed by the appellant;

(d) any record of an interview with the appellant in relation to the decision being appealed;

(e) any other unpublished document which is referred to in a document mentioned in sub-paragraph (a) or relied upon by the respondent;

(f) the notice of any other appealable decision made in relation to the appellant [;and

(g)any documents provided to the respondent in support of the original application.]

(3) The respondent must send to the Tribunal and the other parties the documents listed in paragraph (2) within 28 days of the date on which the respondent received from the Tribunal a copy of the notice of appeal and any accompanying documents or information provided under rule 19(6).

Note: Words in paragraphs (1) and (2) omitted from 23.00 on 31 December 2020 (SI 2020/1309) but these amendments do not take affect where:

(5) (a) any appeal which has been brought under the Immigration (European Economic Area) Regulations 2006 and has not been finally determined before commencement day;

(b) any appeal which has been brought under the Immigration (European Economic Area) Regulations 2016 (whether taken before or after commencement day), and has yet to be finally determined;

(c) any EEA decision under the Immigration (European Economic Area) Regulations 2016 (whether taken before or after commencement day), in respect of which an appeal has not been brought.

(6) For the purposes of paragraph (5)—

(a) references to the Immigration (European Economic Area) Regulations 2016 are to those Regulations as they continue to have effect by virtue of these Regulations, the Citizens' Rights (Application Deadline and Temporary Protection) (EU Exit) Regulations 2020 or the Citizens' Rights (Restrictions of Rights of Entry and Residence) (EU Exit) Regulations 2020;
(b) an appeal is not to be treated as finally determined while a further appeal may be brought, and, if such a further appeal is brought, the original appeal is not to be treated as finally determined until the further appeal is determined, withdrawn or abandoned (reg 5-6 of SI 2020/1309).

Paragraph (2)(b) omitted and paragraph (2)(g) inserted from 6 April 2022 (SI 2022/312).

Response: other cases

24.—(1) Except in appeals to which rule 23 applies, when a respondent is provided with a copy of a notice of appeal, the respondent must provide the Tribunal with—

(a) the notice of the decision to which the notice of appeal relates and any other document the respondent provided to the appellant giving reasons for that decision;

(b) any statement of evidence or application form completed by the appellant;

(c) any record of an interview with the appellant in relation to the decision being appealed;

(d) any other unpublished document which is referred to in a document mentioned in sub-paragraph (a) or relied upon by the respondent;

(e) the notice of any other appealable decision made in relation to the appellant [;and

(f)any documents provided to the respondent in support of the original application.]

(2) [...]

(3) The documents listed in paragraph (1) [...] must be provided in writing within 28 days of the date on which the Tribunal sent to the respondent a copy of the notice of appeal and any accompanying documents or information provided under rule 19(6).

Note: Paragraph (1)(f) inserted, paragraph (2) and words in paragraph (3) omitted from 6 April 2022 (SI 2022/312).

[Further Steps

24A.—(1) If the appellant is represented, upon the respondent complying with rule 23(2) or rule 24(1), as the case may be, the appellant must provide the Tribunal with—

(a) an appeal skeleton argument which complies with any relevant practice direction; and

(b) copies of the evidence relied upon in the appeal skeleton argument, insofar as that evidence is not already contained in the documents provided by the respondent under rule 23(2) or rule 24(1).

(2) The documents in paragraph (1) are to be provided to the Tribunal within 28 days after the respondent complies with rule 23(2) or rule 24(1), as the case may be, or within 42 days after the notice of appeal is provided to the Tribunal, whichever is later.

(3) The respondent must no later than 14 days after compliance with paragraph (1) provide to the Tribunal and the appellant a written statement which complies with any relevant practice direction, of whether the respondent opposes all or part of the appellant's case and if so the grounds for such opposition.

(4) A practice direction may disapply the requirement in paragraph (1) in a specified category of case.]

Note: Rule 24A inserted from 6 April 2022 (SI 2022/312).

CHAPTER 2
Hearings

Consideration of decision with or without a hearing

25.—(1) The Tribunal must hold a hearing before making a decision which disposes of proceedings except where—

(a) each party has consented to, or has not objected to, the matter being decided without a hearing;

(b) the appellant has not consented to the appeal being determined without a hearing but the Lord Chancellor has refused to issue a certificate of fee satisfaction for the fee payable for a hearing;

(c) the appellant is outside the United Kingdom and does not have a representative who has an address for service in the United Kingdom;

(d) it is impracticable to give the appellant notice of the hearing;

(e) a party has failed to comply with a provision of these Rules, a practice direction or a direction and the Tribunal is satisfied that in all the circumstances, including the extent of the failure and any reasons for it, it is appropriate to determine the appeal without a hearing;

(f) the appeal is one to which rule 16(2) or 18(2) applies; or

(g) subject to paragraph (2), the Tribunal considers that it can justly determine the matter without a hearing.

(2) Where paragraph (1)(g) applies, the Tribunal must not make the decision without a hearing without first giving the parties notice of its intention to do so, and an opportunity to make written representations as to whether there should be a hearing.

(3) This rule does not apply to decisions under Part 4 or Part 5.

Notice of hearings

26. The Tribunal must give each party entitled to attend a hearing reasonable notice of the time and place of the hearing (including any adjourned or postponed hearing) and any changes to the time and place of the hearing.

Public and private hearings

27.—(1) Subject to the following paragraphs and to section 108 of the 2002 Act, all hearings must be held in public.

(2) The Tribunal may give a direction that a hearing, or part of it, is to be held in private.

[(2A) . . .]

(3) Where a hearing, or part of it, is to be held in private, the Tribunal may determine who is permitted to attend the hearing or part of it.

(4) The Tribunal may give a direction excluding from any hearing, or part of it—

(a) any person whose conduct the Tribunal considers is disrupting or is likely to disrupt the hearing;

(b) any person whose presence the Tribunal considers is likely to prevent another person from giving evidence or making submissions freely;

(c) any person who the Tribunal considers should be excluded in order to give effect to a direction under rule 13(2) (withholding a document or information likely to cause serious harm); or

(d) any person where the purpose of the hearing would be defeated by the attendance of that person.

(5) The Tribunal may give a direction excluding a witness from a hearing until that witness gives evidence.

Note: Paragraph (2A) inserted from 10 April 2020 (SI 2020/416) and omitted from 6 April 2022 (Rule 1(2) of 2020/416).

[Coronavirus temporary rule (recording of remote hearings)

27A. . . .]

Note: Rule 27A inserted from 10 April 2020 (SI 2020/416) and omitted from 25 March 2022 (Rule 1(2) of SI 2020/416). Paragraph (4) inserted from 21 July 2020 (SI 2020/651) and omitted from 22 March 2022 (Rule 1(2) of SI 2020/651).

Hearing in a party's absence

28. If a party fails to attend a hearing the Tribunal may proceed with the hearing if the Tribunal—

(a) is satisfied that the party has been notified of the hearing or that reasonable steps have been taken to notify the party of the hearing; and

(b) considers that it is in the interests of justice to proceed with the hearing.

CHAPTER 3
Decisions

Decisions and notice of decisions

29.—(1) The Tribunal may give a decision orally at a hearing.

(2) Subject to rule 13(2) (withholding information likely to cause serious harm), the Tribunal must provide to each party as soon as reasonably practicable after making a decision (other than a decision under Part 4) which disposes of the proceedings—

(a) a notice of decision stating the Tribunal's decision; and

(b) notification of any right of appeal against the decision and the time within which, and the manner in which, such right of appeal may be exercised.

(3) Where the decision of the Tribunal relates to—

(a) an asylum claim or a humanitarian protection claim, the Tribunal must provide, with the notice of decision in paragraph (2)(a), written reasons for its decision;

(b) any other matter, the Tribunal may provide written reasons for its decision but, if it does not do so, must notify the parties of the right to apply for a written statement of reasons.

(4) Unless the Tribunal has already provided a written statement of reasons, a party may make a written application to the Tribunal for such statement following a decision which disposes of the proceedings.

(5) An application under paragraph (4) must be received within 28 days of the date on which the Tribunal sent or otherwise provided to the party a notice of decision relating to the decision which disposes of the proceedings.

(6) If a party makes an application in accordance with paragraphs (4) and (5) the Tribunal must, subject to rule 13(2) (withholding a document or information likely to cause serious harm), send a written statement of reasons to each party as soon as reasonably practicable.

Part 4

Correcting, Setting Aside, Reviewing and Appealing Tribunal Decisions

Interpretation

30. In this Part—

'appeal' means the exercise of a right of appeal on a point of law under section 11 of the 2007 Act;

'review' means the review of a decision by the Tribunal under section 9 of the 2007 Act.

Clerical mistakes and accidental slips or omissions

31. The Tribunal may at any time correct any clerical mistake or other accidental slip or omission in a decision, direction or any document produced by it, by—

(a) providing notification of the amended decision or direction, or a copy of the amended document, to all parties; and

(b) making any necessary amendment to any information published in relation to the decision, direction or document.

Setting aside a decision which disposes of proceedings

32.—(1) The Tribunal may set aside a decision which disposes of proceedings, or part of such a decision, and re-make the decision, or the relevant part of it, if—

(a) the Tribunal considers that it is in the interests of justice to do so; and

(b) one or more of the conditions in paragraph (2) are satisfied.

(2) The conditions are—

(a) a document relating to the proceedings was not provided to, or was not received at an appropriate time by, a party or a party's representative;

(b) a document relating to the proceedings was not provided to the Tribunal at an appropriate time;

(c) a party, or a party's representative, was not present at a hearing related to the proceedings; or

(d) there has been some other procedural irregularity in the proceedings.

(3) An application for a decision, or part of a decision, to be set aside under paragraph (1) must be made—

(a) if the appellant is outside the United Kingdom, within 28 days; or

(b) in any other case, within 14 days, of the date on which the party was sent the notice of decision.

Application for permission to appeal to the Upper Tribunal

33.—(1) A party seeking permission to appeal to the Upper Tribunal must make a written application to the Tribunal for permission to appeal.

(2) Subject to paragraph (3), an application under paragraph (1) must be [sent] to the Tribunal so that it is received no later than 14 days after the date on which the party making the application was [sent the] written reasons for the decision.

(3) Where an appellant is outside the United Kingdom, an application to the Tribunal under paragraph (1) must be [sent] to the Tribunal so that it is received no later than 28 days after the date on which the party making the application was [sent the] written reasons for the decision.

(4) The time within which a party may apply for permission to appeal against an amended notice of decision runs from the date on which the party is sent the amended notice of decision.

(5) An application under paragraph (1) must—

(a) identify the decision of the Tribunal to which it relates;

(b) identify the alleged error or errors of law in the decision; and

(c) state the result the party making the application is seeking and include any application for an extension of time and the reasons why such an extension should be given.

(6) If a person makes an application under paragraph (1) when the Tribunal has not given a written statement of reasons for its decision—

(a) the Tribunal must, if no application for a written statement of reasons has been made, treat the application for permission as such an application; and

(b) may—

(i) direct under rule 36 that the application is not to be treated as an application for permission to appeal; or

(ii) determine the application for permission to appeal.

(7) If an application for a written statement of reasons has been, or is, refused because the application was received out of time [or the application for permission was received out of time], the Tribunal must only admit the application for permission if the Tribunal considers that it is in the interests of justice to do so.

Note: Words in paragraphs (2) and (3) substituted from 14 May 2018 (SI 2018/511). Words in paragraph (7) inserted from 6 April 2022 (SI 2022/312).

Tribunal's consideration of an application for permission to appeal to the Upper Tribunal

34.—(1) On receiving an application for permission to appeal the Tribunal must first consider whether to review the decision in accordance with rule 35.

(2) If the Tribunal decides not to review the decision, or reviews the decision and decides to take no action in relation to the decision, or part of it, the Tribunal must consider whether to give permission to appeal in relation to the decision or that part of it.

(3) The Tribunal must send a record of its decision to the parties as soon as practicable.

(4) If the Tribunal refuses permission to appeal it must send with the record of its decision—

(a) a statement of its reasons for such refusal; and

(b) notification of the right to make an application to the Upper Tribunal for permission to appeal and the time within which, and the manner in which, such application must be made.

(5) The Tribunal may give permission to appeal on limited grounds, but must comply with paragraph (4) in relation to any grounds on which it has refused permission.

Review of a decision

35.—(1) The Tribunal may only undertake a review of a decision—

(a) pursuant to rule 34 (review on an application for permission to appeal); and

(b) if it is satisfied that there was an error of law in the decision.

(2) The Tribunal must notify the parties in writing of the outcome of any review, and of any right of appeal in relation to the outcome.

(3) If the Tribunal takes any action in relation to a decision following a review without first giving every party an opportunity to make representations—

(a) the notice under paragraph (2) must state that any party that did not have an opportunity to make representations may apply for such action to be set aside; and

(b) the Tribunal may regard the review as incomplete and act accordingly.

Power to treat an application as a different type of application

36. The Tribunal may treat an application for a decision to be corrected, set aside or reviewed, or for permission to appeal against a decision, as an application for any other one of those things.

Part 5

Bail

Scope of this Part and interpretation

37.—(1) This Part applies to bail proceedings, meaning bail applications and any matter relating to bail which the Tribunal is considering on its own initiative.

[(2) In this Part—

'the 2016 Act' means the Immigration Act 2016;

'bail application' includes a reference to the Tribunal under paragraph 11 of Schedule 10 to the 2016 Act;

'bail party' means—

(a) a person released on bail or applying to the Tribunal to be released on bail; or

(b) a person in respect of whom a reference has been made to the Tribunal under paragraph 11 of Schedule 10 to the 2016 Act; and

'financial condition' has the meaning given in paragraph 5 of Schedule 10 to the 2016 Act.]

(3) Except where paragraph (4) applies, the parties to bail proceedings are the bail party and the Secretary of State.

[(4) Where the proceedings concern payment of a sum under a financial condition, the parties are the Secretary of State, the bail party and any other person who is liable to make payment under the financial condition.]

Note: Paragraphs 2 and 4 substituted from 15 January 2018 (SI 2017/1168) being the day that the provisions of the Immigration Act 2016 c.19 specified in rule 2 of SI 2017/1168 come into force.

Bail applications

38.—(1) A bail application must be made by sending or delivering to the Tribunal an application notice containing the information specified below.

(2) A bail application must specify whether it is for—

(a) the bail party to be released on bail;

(b) variation of bail conditions;

(c) [. . .]

[(d) payment of a sum under a financial condition; or

(e) a reference for consideration under paragraph 11 of Schedule 10 to the 2016 Act.]

(3) Subject to [paragraphs (4) and (4A)], a bail application must contain the following details—

(a) the bail party's—

(i) full name;

(ii) date of birth; and

(iii) date of their most recent arrival in the United Kingdom;

(b) the address of any place where the bail party is detained;

(c) the address where the bail party will reside if the bail application is granted, or, if unable to give such an address, the reason why an address is not given;

[(d) the terms of the financial condition to which the bail party is, or is proposed to be, subject;]

(e) whether the bail party has a pending appeal to the Tribunal or any pending application for further appeal relating to such an appeal;

[(f) the full name, address, date of birth and any occupation of any person other than the bail party who is, or is proposed to be, subject to a financial condition];

(g) where the bail party is aged 18 or over, whether the bail party will, if required, agree [to co-operate with an electronic monitoring condition under paragraph 2 of Schedule 10 to the 2016 Act];

(h) the grounds on which the application is made and, where a previous application has been refused, when it was refused and [,where the previous refusal took place less than 28 days before the application,] details of any material change in circumstances since the refusal; and

(i) whether an interpreter will be required at the hearing, and in respect of what language and dialect.

(4) Where the application is for [payment of a sum under a financial condition], paragraph (3) applies except for sub-paragraphs (a)(iii), (b), (c), (e) and (g) of that paragraph.

[(4A) Where the application is a reference under paragraph 11 of Schedule 10 to the 2016 Act—

(a) paragraph (3) applies except for sub-paragraph (h); and

(b) the application must also contain—

(i) details of the provision or provisions under which the bail party is detained;

(ii) a copy of any previous Secretary of State decision on whether to grant bail; and

(iii) any documents relevant to (i) or (ii).]

(5) An application made by the bail party must be signed by the bail party or their representative.

[(6) On receipt of a bail application, the Tribunal must record the date on which it was received and provide a copy of the application as soon as reasonably practicable to—

(a) the Secretary of State, the bail party and any other person subject to a financial condition, in the case of an application to vary a financial condition;

(b) the bail party, in the case of a reference under paragraph 11 of Schedule 10 to the 2016 Act; and

(c) the Secretary of State, in the case of other bail applications.]

Note: Paragraph (2)(c) omitted, and paragraphs (2)(e) and (4A) inserted, paragraphs 2(d), (3)(d), (3)(f) and (6) substituted and words in square brackets in opening to paragraph 3, 3(g) and (4) substituted from 15 January 2018 (SI 2017/1168) being the day that the provisions of the Immigration Act 2016 c.19 specified in rule 2 of SI 2017/1168 come into force. Words in paragraph (3)(h) inserted from 6 April 2022 (SI 2022/312).

Bail hearings

39.—(1) Subject to paragraph (3), where a bail application is for the bail party to be released on bail [or is a reference under paragraph 11 of Schedule 10], the Tribunal must, as soon as reasonably practicable, hold a hearing of the application.

(2) In all other bail proceedings, the Tribunal may determine the matter without a hearing if it considers it can justly do so.

(3) Where an application for release on bail is received by the Tribunal within 28 days after a Tribunal decision made at a hearing under paragraph (1) not to release the bail party on bail, the Tribunal—

(a) must determine whether the bail party has demonstrated that there has been a material change in circumstances since the decision;

(b) if the Tribunal so determines, must apply paragraph (1);

(c) otherwise, must dismiss the application without a hearing.

(4) [. . .]

Note: Words in square brackets in paragraph (1) inserted and paragraph (4) omitted from 15 January 2018 (SI 2017/1168) being the day that the provisions of the Immigration Act 2016 c.19 specified in rule 2 of SI 2017/1168 come into force.

Response to a bail application

40.—(1) If the Secretary of State opposes a bail application, the Secretary of State must provide the Tribunal and the bail party with a written statement of the reasons for doing so—

(a) not later than 2.00 pm on the working day before the hearing; or

(b) if the Secretary of State was provided with notice of the hearing less than 24 hours before that time, as soon as reasonably practicable.

(2) Where the Secretary of State's reasons for opposition include that directions are in force for the removal of the bail party from the United Kingdom, the Secretary of State must provide a copy of the notice of those directions.

[(3) If the bail party intends to respond to a reference under paragraph 11 of Schedule 10 to the 2016 Act, the bail party must provide the Tribunal and the Secretary of State with a written statement—

(a) not later than 2.00 pm on the working day before the hearing; or

(b) if the bail party was provided with notice of the hearing less than 24 hours before that time, as soon as reasonably practicable.]

Note: Paragraph (3) inserted from 15 January 2018 (SI 2017/1168) being the day that the provisions of the Immigration Act 2016 c.19 specified in rule 2 of SI 2017/1168 come into force.

Decision in bail proceedings

41.—(1) The Tribunal must provide written notice of its decision to—

(a) the parties; and

(b) if the bail application is for the bail party to be released on bail, the person having custody of the bail party.

[(2) Where bail is granted or varied, the notice must state—

(a) when the grant of bail commences;

(b) any bail conditions, including any amounts payable under a financial condition; and

(c) the information required under rule 42.]

(3) Where bail is refused or where the Tribunal orders [payment of a sum under a financial condition], the notice must include reasons for the decision.

(4) [. . .]

(5) Paragraph (6) applies where the Tribunal determines that directions for the removal of the bail party from the United Kingdom are for the time being in force and the directions require the bail party to be removed from the United Kingdom within 14 days of the date of the decision to release the bail party on bail [. . .].

(6) The notice provided under paragraph (1) must state—

(a) the determination of the Tribunal under paragraph (5);

(b) whether the Secretary of State has consented to the release of the bail party;

(c) where the Secretary of State has not consented to that release, that the bail party must therefore not be released on bail.

Note: Paragraph (2) and words in square brackets in paragraph (3) substituted and paragraph (4) omitted from 15 January 2018 (SI 2017/1168) being the day that the provisions of the Immigration Act 2016 c.19 specified in rule 2 of SI 2017/1168 come into force. Words omitted from paragraph (5) from 30 October 2018 (SI 2018/1053).

[Power to vary bail conditions

41A.—(1) Subject to paragraph (2), where bail is granted by the Tribunal, the Tribunal may direct that the Secretary of State has the power to amend or remove bail conditions or impose new bail conditions.

(2) The Tribunal may not give a direction under paragraph (1) without first giving the bail party and any other person subject to a financial condition an opportunity to make representations.

(3) Where the Tribunal has made a direction under paragraph (1), it may not amend or remove bail conditions or impose new bail conditions in relation to the bail party.]

Note: Rule 41A inserted from 15 January 2018 (SI 2017/1168) being the day that the provisions of the Immigration Act 2016 c.19 specified in rule 2 of SI 2017/1168 come into force.

[Financial conditions

42.—(1) Any financial condition must be in writing and must state—

(a) the bail conditions, including the sum of money to be paid under the financial condition;

(b) when it is to be paid;

(c) the form and manner in which it is to be paid; and

(d) that the bail party, and any other person who is liable to make payment under it, understand the bail conditions and that, if the bail party fails to comply with those conditions, they may be liable to make payment under it.

(2) The financial condition must be signed by the bail party and any other person who is liable to make payment under it and provided to the Tribunal, and a copy provided to—

(a) the parties, and

(b) any person having custody of the bail party.]

Note: Rule 42 substituted from 15 January 2018 (SI 2017/1168) being the day that the provisions of the Immigration Act 2016 c.19 specified in rule 2 of SI 2017/1168 come into force.

Release of bail party

43. The person having custody of the bail party must release the bail party upon—

(a) being provided with a notice of decision to grant bail; or

(b) being provided with a notice of decision fixing the amount and conditions of the bail,

[. . .]

Note: Paragraph (b)(ii) omitted from 15 January 2018 (SI 2017/1168) being the day that the provisions of the Immigration Act 2016 c.19 specified in rule 2 of SI 2017/1168 come into force.

[Application of this Part to Scotland

44. . . .]

Note: Rule 44 omitted from 15 January 2018 (SI 2017/1168) being the day that the provisions of the Immigration Act 2016 c.19 specified in rule 2 of SI 2017/1168 come into force.

PART 6

FINAL

Revocations

45. The statutory instruments listed in the left hand column of Table 1 below are revoked to the extent specified in the right hand column.

Table 1 Revocations

Statutory Instrument	*Extent of revocation*
The Asylum and Immigration Tribunal (Procedure) Rules 2005 (S.I. 2005/230)	The entire Rules
The Asylum and Immigration Tribunal (Procedure) (Amendment) Rules 2006 (S.I. 2006/2788)	The entire Rules
The Asylum and Immigration Tribunal (Procedure) Rules 2007 (S.I. 2007/835)	The entire Rules
The Asylum and Immigration Tribunal (Procedure) (Amendment No. 2) Rules 2007 (S.I. 2007/3170)	The entire Rules
The Asylum and Immigration Tribunal (Procedure) (Amendment) Rules 2008 (S.I. 2008/1088)	The entire Rules
The Tribunal Procedure (Amendment No. 2) Rules 2010 (S.I. 2010/44)	Rules 23 to 28 inclusive
The Tribunal Procedure (Amendment No. 3) Rules 2010 (S.I. 2010/2653)	Rule 4
The Tribunal Procedure (Amendment) (No. 2) Rules 2011 (S.I. 2011/2840)	The entire Rules
The Asylum and Immigration Tribunal (Fast Track Procedure) Rules 2005 (S.I. 2005/560)	The entire Rules
The Asylum and Immigration Tribunal (Fast Track Procedure) (Amendment) Rules 2006 (S.I. 2006/2789)	The entire Rules
The Asylum and Immigration Tribunal (Fast Track Procedure) (Amendment) Rules 2008 (S.I. 2008/1089)	The entire Rules

Transitional provisions

46.—(1) The Tribunal may give any direction to ensure that proceedings are dealt with fairly and, in particular, may—

(a) apply any provision of the Asylum and Immigration Tribunal (Procedure) Rules 2005 or the Asylum and Immigration Tribunal (Fast Track Procedure) Rules 2005 which applied to the proceedings immediately before the date these Rules came into force; or

(b) disapply provisions of these Rules (including the Fast Track Rules).

(2) A time period which has started to run before the date on which these Rules come into force and which has not expired shall continue to apply.

SCHEDULE

RULE 1(3)

THE FAST TRACK RULES

PART 1
INTRODUCTION AND SCOPE

Interpretation and relationship with the Principal Rules

1.—(1) The rules in this Schedule are the Fast Track Rules.

(2) A rule or Part referred to in this Schedule by number alone means a rule in, or Part of, the Fast Track Rules.

(3) In these Rules, the 'Principal Rules' means rules 1 to 46 of the Tribunal Procedure (First-tier Tribunal) (Immigration and Asylum Chamber) Rules 2014.

(4) The Principal Rules, except for those provisions referred to in Table 2 below apply for the purposes of and the interpretation of the Fast Track Rules.

(5) Where the Fast Track Rules cease to apply to an appeal or application because—

(a) the condition referred to in rule 2(1)(b) ceases to apply; or

(b) the Tribunal makes an order under rule 14, the Principal Rules shall apply to the appeal or application.

(6) Where—

(a) a period of time for taking a step has started to run under a provision of the Fast Track Rules, and

(b) that provision ceases to apply in the circumstances to which paragraph (5) refers,

if the Principal Rules contain a time limit for taking such step, the time limit in the Principal Rules shall apply, and the relevant period of time shall be treated as running from the date on which the period of time under the Fast Track Rules started to run.

Table 2 Principal Rules which do not apply in the fast track

Rule numbers refer to the Principal Rules	*Notes*
Rule 3(2) – (4) (delegation to staff)	
Rule 4(3)(a) (case management powers: reducing or extending time)	Rule 5(2) – (6) of the Fast Track Rules (time limits) applies
Rule 4(3)(h) (case management powers: adjourning or postponing hearing)	Rule 12 of the Fast Track Rules (adjournment) applies
Rule 4(3)(j) (case management powers: stay or sist proceedings)	
Rule 4(3)(k) (case management powers: transfer of proceedings)	
Rule 4(3)(l) (suspending effect of decision pending onward appeal etc.)	
Rule 7 (striking out of appeal for non-payment of fee and reinstatement)	
Rule 9(1) (costs orders for payment of Tribunal fees)	
Rule 19 (notice of appeal)	Rules 3 to 6 of the Fast Track Rules apply
Rules 20 and 21 (late notice of appeal; special provision for imminent removal cases)	Rule 5 of the Fast Track Rules (time limits) applies
Rule 22, except for the purposes of paragraph (2)(a) (no appealable decision)	
Rules 23 – 24 (response: entry clearance and other cases)	Rule 7 of the Fast Track Rules (filing of documents by respondent) applies
Rule 29(2) to (6) (provision of written statement of reasons for Tribunal's decision)	Rule 10 of the Fast Track Rules (decisions and notice of decisions) applies
Rule 33(2) and (3) (time limit for applying to the Tribunal for permission to appeal to the Upper Tribunal)	Rule 11 of the Fast Track Rules (time limit for making an application for permission to appeal) applies
Rule 34(1) (Tribunal to consider first whether to review decision)	

Scope of Fast Track Rules

2.—(1) The Fast Track Rules apply to an appeal to the Tribunal or an application for permission to appeal to the Upper Tribunal where the appellant—

(a) was detained under the Immigration Acts at a place specified in paragraph (3) when provided with notice of the appealable decision against which the appellant is appealing; and

(b) has been continuously detained under the Immigration Acts at a place or places specified in paragraph (3) since that notice was served on the appellant.

(2) An appellant does not, for the purposes of this rule, cease to satisfy the condition in paragraph (1)(b) by reason only of—

(a) being transported from one place of detention specified in paragraph (3) to another place which is so specified; or

(b) leaving and returning to such a place of detention for any purpose between the hours of 6 am and 10 pm.

(3) The places specified for the purposes of this rule are—

(a) Colnbrook House Immigration Removal Centre, Harmondsworth, Middlesex;

(b) Harmondsworth Immigration Removal Centre, Harmondsworth, Middlesex;

(c) Yarl's Wood Immigration Removal Centre, Clapham, Bedfordshire.

PART 2

APPEALS TO THE TRIBUNAL

Notice of appeal

3.—(1) An appellant must start proceedings by providing a notice of appeal to the Tribunal.

(2) The notice of appeal must—

(a) set out the grounds of appeal;

(b) be signed and dated by the appellant or their representative;

(c) if a notice of appeal is signed by the appellant's representative, the representative must certify in the notice of appeal that it has been completed in accordance with the appellant's instructions;

(d) state whether the appellant requires an interpreter at any hearing and if so for which language and dialect;

(e) state whether the appellant intends to attend at any hearing; and

(f) state whether the appellant will be represented at any hearing.

(3) The appellant must provide with the notice of appeal—

(a) the notice of decision against which the appellant is appealing or if it is not practicable to include the notice of decision, the reasons why it is not practicable;

(b) any statement of reasons for that decision;

(c) any documents in support of the appellant's case which have not been supplied to the respondent;

(d) an application for the Lord Chancellor to issue a certificate of fee satisfaction;

(e) any further information or documents required by an applicable practice direction.

(4) An appellant may, with the permission of the Tribunal, vary the grounds on which they rely in the notice of appeal.

Providing notice of appeal

4.—(1) An appellant may provide a notice of appeal to the Tribunal either—

(a) by providing it to the Tribunal; or

(b) by providing it to the person having custody of the appellant.

(2) Where a notice of appeal is provided under paragraph (1)(b), the person having custody of the appellant must—

(a) endorse on the notice the date that it is provided to the person having custody of the appellant; and

(b) provide it to the Tribunal immediately.

Time limits

5.—(1) The notice of appeal must be provided not later than 2 working days after the day on which the appellant was provided with notice of the decision against which the appeal is brought.

(2) Where a notice of appeal is provided outside the time limit in paragraph (1), the Tribunal must not extend the time for appealing unless it considers that it is in the interests of justice to do so.

(3) Subject to paragraph (5), the Tribunal must consider any issue as to—

(a) whether a notice of appeal was given outside the time limit in paragraph (1); and

(b) whether to extend the time for appealing,

at the hearing fixed for the hearing of the appeal under the Fast Track Rules under rule 8, and rules 9, 12 and 14 apply to the consideration and decision of such an issue as they apply to the consideration and decision of an appeal.

(4) Where a notice of appeal is provided outside the time limit in paragraph (1) and the respondent notifies the Tribunal that directions have been given for the removal of that person from the United Kingdom on a date within 5 working days of the date on which the notice of appeal was received, the Tribunal must, if reasonably practicable, make any decision on an issue referred to in paragraph (3) before the date and time proposed for the removal, and may do so as a preliminary issue.

(5) Where the Tribunal decides that the notice of appeal was provided outside the time limit and does not extend the time for appealing, the Tribunal must provide to the parties notice of its decision, including its reasons, not later than 1 working day after the date on which that decision was made, after which it shall take no further action in relation to the notice of appeal.

(6) In a case to which paragraph (5) applies, the notice of decision may be given orally at a hearing.

Service of notice of appeal etc. on respondent

6. When the Tribunal receives a notice of appeal and any further documents or information from the appellant under rule 4, it must immediately provide a copy to the respondent.

Filing of documents by respondent

7. The respondent must, not later than 2 working days after the day on which the Tribunal provides the respondent with the notice of appeal, provide the following documents to the Tribunal—

(a) the notice of the decision to which the notice of appeal relates, and any other document the respondent provided to the appellant giving reasons for that decision;

(b) any statement of evidence or application form completed by the appellant;

(c) any record of an interview with the appellant, in relation to the decision being appealed;

(d) any other unpublished document which is referred to in a document mentioned in sub-paragraph (a) or relied upon by the respondent; and

(e) the notice of any other appealable decision made in relation to the appellant.

Fixing date of appeal hearing

8.—(1) The Tribunal must fix a date for the hearing of the appeal which is—

(a) not later than 3 working days after the day on which the respondent provides the documents under rule 7; or

(b) if the Tribunal is unable to arrange a hearing within that time, as soon as practicable.

(2) The Tribunal must provide notice of the date, time and place of the hearing to every party as soon as practicable and in any event not later than noon on the working day before the hearing.

(3) A practice direction may provide that, as regards—

(a) all appellants detained at one of the places specified in rule 2(3); or

(b) a class or category of appellants detained in any of those specified places,

a period of 6 working days shall apply instead of the period of 3 working days provided for in paragraph (1).

Consideration with or without a hearing

9.—(1) The Tribunal must conclude the hearing of the appeal on the date fixed under the Fast Track Rules.

(2) Where—

(a) the appeal—

(i) lapses pursuant to section 99 of the 2002 Act;

(ii) is treated as abandoned pursuant to section 104(4A) of the 2002 Act; or

(iii) is withdrawn by the appellant or treated as withdrawn in accordance with rule 17 of the Principal Rules;

(b) the Tribunal postpones or adjourns the hearing under rule 12 or 14(2)(a); or

(c) all of the parties to the appeal consent to the Tribunal deciding the appeal without a hearing;

the requirement referred to in paragraph (1) ceases.

Decisions and notice of decisions

10.—(1) Where the Tribunal decides an appeal, it must provide to each party—

(a) a notice of decision and the reasons for it;

(b) notification of any right of appeal against the decision and the time within which, and the manner in which, such right of appeal may be exercised.

(2) The Tribunal must provide the notice and the notification—

(a) where rule 9(1) applies, not later than 2 working days after the day on which the hearing of the appeal was concluded; or

(b) in any other case, not later than 2 working days after the day on which the appeal was decided.

Part 3

Appeals to the Upper Tribunal

Time limit for making an application for permission to appeal

11. An application for permission to appeal to the Upper Tribunal must be provided to the Tribunal so that it is received no later than 3 working days after the date on which the party making the application was provided with the notice of decision.

Part 4

General Provisions

Adjournment

12. Unless the Tribunal makes an order under rule 14, the Tribunal may postpone or adjourn the hearing of the appeal only where the Tribunal is satisfied that—

(a) the appeal could not justly be decided if the hearing were to be concluded on the date fixed under the Fast Track Rules; and

(b) there is an identifiable future date, not more than 10 working days after the date so fixed, upon which the Tribunal can conclude the hearing and justly decide the appeal within the timescales provided for in the Fast Track Rules.

Correction of errors and determinations

13. Where a notice of decision is amended under the Principal Rules, the Tribunal must, not later than one working day after making the amendment, provide an amended version to every party to whom it provided the original.

Part 5

Transfer out of fast track

Transfer out of fast track

14.—(1) Where the Fast Track Rules apply to an appeal or application, the Tribunal must order that the Fast Track Rules shall cease to apply—

(a) if all the parties consent; or

(b) if the Tribunal is satisfied that the case cannot justly be decided within the timescales provided for in the Fast Track Rules.

(2) When making an order under paragraph (1), the Tribunal may, notwithstanding rule 1(5) or (6) of the Fast Track Rules or the application of the Principal Rules—

(a) postpone or adjourn any hearing of the appeal or application; and

(b) give directions in relation to the conduct of the proceedings.

The Tribunal Procedure (Upper Tribunal) Rules 2008
(SI 2008, No. 2698)

Contents

Schedules

. . .

Part 1

Introduction

Citation, commencement, application and interpretation

1.—(1) These Rules may be cited as the Tribunal Procedure (Upper Tribunal) Rules 2008 and came into force on 3rd November 2008.

(2) These Rules apply to proceedings before the Upper Tribunal [except proceedings in the Lands Chamber].

(3) In these Rules—

'the 2007 Act' means the Tribunals, Courts and Enforcement Act 2007;

['appellant' means—

(a) a person who makes an appeal, or applies for permission to appeal, to the Upper Tribunal;

(b) in proceedings transferred or referred to the Upper Tribunal from the First-tier Tribunal, a person who started the proceedings in the First-tier Tribunal; or

(c) a person substituted as an appellant under rule 9(1) (substitution and addition of parties);]

['applicant' means—

(a) a person who applies for permission to bring, or does bring, judicial review proceedings before the Upper Tribunal and, in judicial review proceedings transferred to the Upper Tribunal from a court, includes a person who was a claimant or petitioner in the proceedings immediately before they were transferred; or

(b) a person who refers a financial services [or a wholesale energy case] case to the Upper Tribunal;]

['appropriate national authority' means, in relation to an appeal, the Secretary of State, the Scottish Ministers [, the Department of the Environment in Northern Ireland] or the Welsh Ministers, as the case may be;]

['asylum case' means proceedings before the Upper Tribunal on appeal against a decision in proceedings under section 82, 83 or 83A of the Nationality, Immigration and Asylum Act 2002 in which a person claims that removal from, or a requirement to leave, the United Kingdom would breach the United Kingdom's obligations under the Convention relating to the Status of Refugees done at Geneva on 28 July 1951 and the Protocol to the Convention;]

['authorised person' means—

(a) an examiner appointed by the Secretary of State under section 66A of the Road Traffic Act 1988;

(b) an examiner appointed by the Department of the Environment in Northern Ireland under Article 74 of the Road Traffic (Northern Ireland) Order 1995; or

(c) any person authorised in writing by the Department of the Environment in Northern Ireland for the purposes of the Goods Vehicles (Licensing of Operators) Act (Northern Ireland) 2010;

and includes a person acting under the direction of such an examiner or other authorised person, who has detained the vehicle to which an appeal relates;]

['disability discrimination in schools case' means proceedings concerning discrimination in the education of a child or young person or related matters;]

[. . .]

'dispose of proceedings' includes, unless indicated otherwise, disposing of a part of the proceedings;

'document' means anything in which information is recorded in any form, and an obligation under these Rules or any practice direction or direction to provide or allow access to a document or a copy of a document for any purpose means, unless the Upper Tribunal directs otherwise, an obligation to provide or allow access to such document or copy in a legible form or in a form which can be readily made into a legible form;

[. . .]

['financial sanctions case' means an appeal to the Upper Tribunal under section 147(6) of the Policing and Crime Act 2017.]

['financial services case' means a reference to the Upper Tribunal in respect of—

[(a) a decision of the Financial Conduct Authority;

(aa) a decision of the Prudential Regulation Authority;]

(b) a decision of the Bank of England;

(c) a decision of the Pensions Regulator;

(d) a decision of a person relating to the assessment of any compensation or consideration under the Banking (Special Provisions) Act 2008 or the Banking Act 2009;] or

[(e) any determination, calculation or dispute which may be referred to the Upper Tribunal under the Financial Services and Markets Act 2000 (Contribution to Costs of Special Resolution Regime) Regulations 2010 (and in these Rules a decision in respect of which a reference has been made to the Upper Tribunal in a financial services case includes any such determination, calculation or, except for the purposes of rule 5(5), dispute relating to the making of payments under the Regulations);]

[. . .]

'hearing' means an oral hearing and includes a hearing conducted in whole or in part by video link, telephone or other means of instantaneous two-way electronic communication;

['immigration case' means proceedings before the Upper Tribunal on appeal against a decision in proceedings under section 40A of the British Nationality Act 1981, section 82 of the Nationality, Immigration and Asylum Act 2002 [. . .] {or the Immigration (Citizens' Rights Appeals) (EU Exit) Regulations 2020} that are not an asylum case [. . .];]

['immigration judicial review proceedings' means judicial review proceedings which are designated as an immigration matter—

(a) In a direction made in accordance with Part 1 of Schedule 2 to the Constitutional Reform Act 2005 specifying a class of case for the purposes of section 18(6) of the 2007 Act; or

(b) in an order of the High Court in England and Wales made under section 31A(3) of the Senior Courts Act 1981, transferring to the Upper Tribunal an application of a kind described in section 31A(1) of that Act;]

'interested party' means—

(a) a person who is directly affected by the outcome sought in judicial review proceedings, and has been named as an interested party under rule 28 or 29 (judicial review), or has been substituted or added as an interested party under rule 9 [(addition, substitution and removal of parties)];

(b) in judicial review proceedings transferred to the Upper Tribunal under section 25A(2) or (3) of the Judicature (Northern Ireland) Act 1978 or section 31A(2) or (3) of the Supreme Court Act 1981, a person who was an interested party in the proceedings immediately before they were transferred to the Upper Tribunal;

[{. . .}

(c) in a financial services case [or a wholesale energy case], any person other than the applicant who could have referred the case to the Upper Tribunal and who has been added or substituted as an interested party under rule 9 (addition, substitution and removal of parties);]

[(d) in a financial sanctions case, any person other than the appellant upon whom the Treasury has imposed a monetary penalty under Part 8 of the Policing and Crime Act 2017 in connection with the same matters as led to the decision that is the subject of the appeal and who has been added or substituted as an interested party under rule 9 (addition, substitution and removal of parties).] [and

(e) in a trade remedies case, any person other than the appellant who could have appealed to the Upper Tribunal and who has been added or substituted as an interested party under rule 9 (addition, substitution and removal of parties);]

'judicial review proceedings' means proceedings within the jurisdiction of the Upper Tribunal pursuant to section 15 or 21 of the 2007 Act, whether such proceedings are started in the Upper Tribunal or transferred to the Upper Tribunal;

[. . .]

'mental health case' means proceedings before the Upper Tribunal on appeal against a decision in proceedings under the Mental Health Act 1983 or paragraph 5(2) of the Schedule to the Repatriation of Prisoners Act 1984;

['national security certificate appeal' means an appeal under section 28 of the Data Protection Act 1998 {, sections 27, 79 or 111 of the Data Protection Act 2018} or section 60 of the Freedom of Information Act 2000 (including that section as applied and modified by regulation 18 of the Environmental Information Regulations 2004);]

'party' means a person who is an appellant, an applicant, a respondent or an interested party in proceedings before the Upper Tribunal, a person who has referred a question [or matter] to the Upper Tribunal or, if the proceedings have been concluded, a person who was an appellant, an applicant, a respondent or an interested party when the [Upper] Tribunal finally disposed of all issues in the proceedings;

'permission' includes leave in cases arising under the law of Northern Ireland;

'practice direction' means a direction given under section 23 of the 2007 Act;

['QCS Board' means a Board constituted under Part 2 of the Transport Act 2000);

'quality contracts scheme' has the meaning provided for in section 124(3) (quality contracts scheme) of the Transport Act 2000;

'quality contracts scheme case' means proceedings in the Upper Tribunal under Part 2 of the Transport Act 2000;]

['reference', in a financial services case, includes an appeal;]

['relevant minister' means the Minister or designated person responsible for the signing of the certificate to which a national security certificate appeal relates;]

'respondent' means—

(a) in an appeal, or application for permission to appeal, against a decision of another tribunal, any person other than the appellant who—

(i) was a party before that other tribunal;

(ii) . . .

(iii) otherwise has a right of appeal against the decision of the other tribunal and has given notice to the Upper Tribunal that they wish to be a party to the appeal;

[(b)in any other any other application for permission to appeal, or any other appeal except a road transport case, the person who made the decision that has been challenged;]

(c) in judicial review proceedings—

(i) in proceedings started in the Upper Tribunal, the person named by the applicant as the respondent;

(ii) in proceedings transferred to the Upper Tribunal under section 25A(2) or (3) of the Judicature (Northern Ireland) Act 1978 or section 31A(2) or (3) of the Supreme Court Act 1981, a person who was a defendant in the proceedings immediately before they were transferred;

(iii) in proceedings transferred to the Upper Tribunal under section 20(1) of the 2007 Act, a person to whom intimation of the petition was made before the proceedings were transferred, or to whom the Upper Tribunal has required intimation to be made.

[(ca) in proceedings transferred or referred to the Upper Tribunal from the First-tier Tribunal, a person who was a respondent in the proceedings in the First-tier Tribunal;]

(d) in a reference under the Forfeiture Act 1982, the person whose eligibility for a benefit or advantage is in issue;

[(da) in a financial services case—

(i) where the case is a multiple regulator case, both the primary and secondary regulator as defined in Schedule 3 to these rules (but subject to the operation of paragraph 4A(3) of that Schedule);

(ii) where the case is a single regulator case, the maker of the decision in respect of which a reference has been made;]

[(db) in a wholesale energy case, in relation to Great Britain, the Gas and Electricity Markets Authority or, in relation to Northern Ireland, the Northern Ireland Authority for Utility Regulation; or]

(e) a person substituted or added as a respondent under rule 9 (substitution and addition of parties);

[road transport case' means an appeal against a decision of—

(a) a traffic commissioner, other than an appeal pursuant to—

(i) section 6F of the Transport Act 1985, or

(ii) section 123T of the Transport Act 2000, or

(b) the Department of the Environment in Northern Ireland;]

['special educational needs case' means proceedings concerning the education of a child or young person who has or may have special educational needs, including proceedings relating to—

(a) an EHC needs assessment within the meaning of section 36(2) of the Children and Families Act 2014; [. . .

(aa) a detained person's EHC needs assessment within the meaning of section 70(5) of the Children and Families Act 2014; or]

(b) an EHC plan within the meaning of section 37(2) of that Act,

of such a child or young person;]

['TRA' means the Trade Remedies Authority;

'trade remedies case' means an appeal pursuant to the Trade Remedies (Reconsideration and Appeals) (EU Exit) Regulations (2019) against a decision made by the TRA or a determination of the Secretary of State;]

['tribunal' does not include a traffic commissioner;]

['wholesale energy case' means a reference to the Upper Tribunal in respect of a decision of—

(a) in relation to Great Britain, the Gas and Electricity Markets Authority under the Electricity and Gas (Market Integrity and Transparency) (Enforcement etc.) Regulations 2013; or

(b) in relation to Northern Ireland, the Northern Ireland Authority for Utility Regulation under the Electricity and Gas (Market Integrity and Transparency) (Enforcement etc.) Regulations (Northern Ireland) 2013;]

. . .

'working day' means any day except a Saturday or Sunday, Christmas Day, Good Friday or a bank holiday under section 1 of the Banking and Financial Dealings Act 1971;

['young person' means, in relation to a special educational needs case or a disability discrimination in schools case, a person over compulsory school age but under 25.]

Note: Words in square brackets in paragraph (2) and definitions of 'appropriate national authority', 'authorised person' and 'tribunal' inserted from 1 September 2009 (SI 2009/1975). Definition of appellant substituted, definition of 'legal representative' omitted and in definition of respondent subparagraph (a)(ii) omitted and (ca) inserted from 1 April 2009 (SI 2009/274). Definitions of 'national security certificate appeal' and 'relevant minister' inserted from 18 January 2010 (SI 2010/43). Definitions of 'asylum case', 'immigration case' and 'fast-track case' inserted from 15 February 2010 (SI 2010/44) and definition of 'fast-track case' omitted from 21 July 2020 (SI 2020/651). Definition of 'applicant' and words in square brackets in subparagraph (a) of definition of 'interested party' substituted; definitions of 'financial services case' and 'reference', subparagraph (c) of definition of 'interested party' and words in square brackets in definition of 'party' and subparagraph (da) in definition of respondent inserted from 6 April 2010 (SI 2010/747). Subparagraph (e) in definition of 'financial services case' inserted from 1 April 2011 (SI 2011/651). Definition of 'fresh claim proceedings' inserted from 17 October 2011 (SI 2011/2343) and omitted from 1 November 2013 (SI 2013/2067). Words inserted in the definition of 'appropriate national authority', definition of 'authorised person' substituted, definition of 'respondent' further amended and definition of 'road transport case' inserted from 1 July 2012 (SI 2012/1363). Definition of 'road transport case' substituted from 3 June 2019 (SI 2019/925). Definition of 'immigration review proceedings' and word in square brackets in definition of 'party' inserted by SI 2013/2067 from 1 November 2013. Subparagraphs (a)–(aa) of 'financial services case' substituted by SI 2013/606 from 1 April 2013. Subparagraph (db) of 'respondent', definition of 'wholesale energy case' and words in subparagraphs (b) of 'applicant' and (c) of 'interested party' inserted and word omitted from subparagraph (c) of 'financial services case' from 6 April 2014 (SI 2014/514). Definitions of 'disability discrimination in a school case', 'special educational needs case' and 'young person' inserted from 1 September 2014 (SI 2014/2128). Definitions of 'QCS Board', 'quality contracts scheme' and 'quality contracts scheme case' inserted and definition of 'special educational needs case' amended from 21 August 2015 (SI 2015/1510). Definition of 'financial sanctions case' and subparagraph (d) in the definition of 'interested party' inserted from 27 July 2017 (SI 2017/723). Subparagraph (e) in the definition of 'interested party' inserted from 3 June 2019 (SI 2019/925). Definition of 'TRA' and 'Trade Remedies Case' inserted from 3 June 2019 (SI 2019/925) subject to transitional provision in rule 6(a) of SI 2019/925). Words in curly brackets inserted in definition of 'national security certificate appeal' and sub-paragraph (b) in the definition of respondent substituted from 30 October 2018 (SI 2018/1053). Words inserted at the end of the definition of 'immigration case' from 31 January 2020 (SI 2020/61) and omitted from 21 July 2020 (SI 2020/651) and words in curly brackets inserted from 21 July 2020 (SI 2020/651). Words omitted from definition of 'immigration case' from 23.00 on 31 December 2020 (SI 2020/1309) subject to saving provision in reg 33(4) of SI 2020/1309.

Overriding objective and parties' obligation to cooperate with the Upper Tribunal

2.—(1) The overriding objective of these Rules is to enable the Upper Tribunal to deal with cases fairly and justly.

(2) Dealing with a case fairly and justly includes—

(a) dealing with the case in ways which are proportionate to the importance of the case, the complexity of the issues, the anticipated costs and the resources of the parties;

(b) avoiding unnecessary formality and seeking flexibility in the proceedings;

(c) ensuring, so far as practicable, that the parties are able to participate fully in the proceedings;

(d) using any special expertise of the Upper Tribunal effectively; and

(e) avoiding delay, so far as compatible with proper consideration of the issues.

(3) The Upper Tribunal must seek to give effect to the overriding objective when it—

(a) exercises any power under these Rules; or

(b) interprets any rule or practice direction.

(4) Parties must—

(a) help the Upper Tribunal to further the overriding objective; and

(b) cooperate with the Upper Tribunal generally.

Alternative dispute resolution and arbitration

3.—(1) The Upper Tribunal should seek, where appropriate—

(a) to bring to the attention of the parties the availability of any appropriate alternative procedure for the resolution of the dispute; and

(b) if the parties wish and provided that it is compatible with the overriding objective, to facilitate the use of the procedure.

(2) Part 1 of the Arbitration Act 1996 does not apply to proceedings before the Upper Tribunal.

Part 2

General Powers and Provisions

Delegation to staff

4.—(1) Staff appointed under section 40(1) of the 2007 Act (tribunal staff and services) [or section 2(1) of the Courts Act 2003 (court officers, staff and services)] may, {if authorized by} the Senior President of Tribunals [under paragraph 3(3) of Schedule 5 to the 2007 Act], carry out functions of a judicial nature permitted or required to be done by the Upper Tribunal.

(2) [. . .]

(3) Within 14 days after the date on which the Upper Tribunal sends notice of a decision made by a member of staff under paragraph (1) to a party, that party may apply in writing to the Upper Tribunal for that decision to be considered afresh by a judge.

Note: In paragraph (1) words in square brackets inserted and words in curly brackets substituted and paragraph (2) omitted from 21 July 2020 (SI 2020/651).

Case management powers

5.—(1) Subject to the provisions of the 2007 Act and any other enactment, the Upper Tribunal may regulate its own procedure.

(2) The Upper Tribunal may give a direction in relation to the conduct or disposal of proceedings at any time, including a direction amending, suspending or setting aside an earlier direction.

(3) In particular, and without restricting the general powers in paragraphs (1) and (2), the Upper Tribunal may—

(a) extend or shorten the time for complying with any rule, practice direction or direction;

(b) consolidate or hear together two or more sets of proceedings or parts of proceedings raising common issues, or treat a case as a lead case;

(c) permit or require a party to amend a document;

(d) permit or require a party or another person to provide documents, information, evidence or submissions to the Upper Tribunal or a party;

(e) deal with an issue in the proceedings as a preliminary issue;

(f) hold a hearing to consider any matter, including a case management issue;

(g) decide the form of any hearing;

(h) adjourn or postpone a hearing;

(i) require a party to produce a bundle for a hearing;

(j) stay (or, in Scotland, sist) proceedings;

(k) transfer proceedings to another court or tribunal if that other court or tribunal has jurisdiction in relation to the proceedings; and—

(i) because of a change of circumstances since the proceedings were started, the Upper Tribunal no longer has jurisdiction in relation to the proceedings; or

(ii) the Upper Tribunal considers that the other court or tribunal is a more appropriate forum for the determination of the case;

(l) suspend the effect of its own decision pending an appeal or review of that decision;

(m) in an appeal, or an application for permission to appeal, against the decision of another tribunal, suspend the effect of that decision pending the determination of the application for permission to appeal, and any appeal;

[(n) require any person, body or other tribunal whose decision is the subject of proceedings before the Upper Tribunal to provide reasons for the decision, or other information or documents in relation to the decision or any proceedings before that person, body or tribunal.]

(4) [. . .]

[(5) In a financial services case, the Upper Tribunal may direct that the effect of the decision in respect of which the reference has been made is to be suspended pending the determination of the reference, if it is satisfied that to do so would not prejudice—

(a) the interests of any persons (whether consumers, investors or otherwise) intended to be protected by that notice; [. . .]

(b) the smooth operation or integrity of any market intended to be protected by that notice [; or

(c) the stability of the financial system of the United Kingdom.]

[(5A) In a financial sanctions case, the Upper Tribunal may direct that the payment of a monetary penalty that is the subject of an appeal be suspended pending the determination of the appeal or its withdrawal.]

(6) Paragraph (5) does not apply in the case of a reference in respect of a decision of the Pensions Regulator.

[(7) In a wholesale energy case, the Upper Tribunal may direct that the effect of the decision in respect of which the reference has been made is to be suspended pending the determination of the reference.]

Note: Paragraph (3)(n) substituted from 1 September 2009 (SI 2009/1975). Paragraph (4) inserted from 15 February 2010 (SI 2010/44) and omitted from 21 July 2020 (2020/651). Paragraph (5) inserted from 6 April 2010 (SI 2010/747). Word omitted at end of subparagraph (5)(a) and subparagraph (5)(c) inserted by SI 2013/606 from 1 April 2013 and subparagraph (7) inserted by SI 2014/514 from 6 April 2014. Paragraph (5A) inserted from 27 July 2017 (SI 2017/723).

[Coronavirus temporary rule (decisions without a hearing)

5A . . .]

Note: Rule 5A inserted from 10 April 2020 (SI 2020/416) and omitted from 25 March 2022 (Rule 1(2) of SI 2020/416).

Procedure for applying for and giving directions

6.—(1) The Upper Tribunal may give a direction on the application of one or more of the parties or on its own initiative.

(2) An application for a direction may be made—

(a) by sending or delivering a written application to the Upper Tribunal; or

(b) orally during the course of a hearing.

(3) An application for a direction must include the reason for making that application.

(4) Unless the Upper Tribunal considers that there is good reason not to do so, the Upper Tribunal must send written notice of any direction to every party and to any other person affected by the direction.

(5) If a party or any other person sent notice of the direction under paragraph (4) wishes to challenge a direction which the Upper Tribunal has given, they may do so by applying for another direction which amends, suspends or sets aside the first direction.

Failure to comply with rules etc.

7.—(1) An irregularity resulting from a failure to comply with any requirement in these Rules, a practice direction or a direction, does not of itself render void the proceedings or any step taken in the proceedings.

(2) If a party has failed to comply with a requirement in these Rules, a practice direction or a direction, the Upper Tribunal may take such action as it considers just, which may include—

(a) waiving the requirement;

(b) requiring the failure to be remedied;

(c) exercising its power under rule 8 (striking out a party's case); or

(d) except in [a mental health case, an asylum case or an immigration case], restricting a party's participation in the proceedings.

(3) Paragraph (4) applies where the First-tier Tribunal has referred to the Upper Tribunal a failure by a person to comply with a requirement imposed by the First-tier Tribunal—

(a) to attend at any place for the purpose of giving evidence;
(b) otherwise to make themselves available to give evidence;
(c) to swear an oath in connection with the giving of evidence;
(d) to give evidence as a witness;
(e) to produce a document; or
(f) to facilitate the inspection of a document or any other thing (including any premises).

(4) The Upper Tribunal may exercise its power under section 25 of the 2007 Act (supplementary powers of the Upper Tribunal) in relation to such non-compliance as if the requirement had been imposed by the Upper Tribunal.

Note: Words in square brackets in paragraph (2)(d) substituted from 15 February 2010 (SI 2010/44).

Striking out a party's case

8.—[(1A) Except for paragraph (2), this rule does not apply to an asylum case or an immigration case.]

[(1) The proceedings, or the appropriate part of them, will automatically be struck out—

(a) if the appellant or applicant has failed to comply with a direction that stated that failure by the appellant or applicant to comply with the direction would lead to the striking out of the proceedings or part of them; or

[(b) in immigration judicial review proceedings, when a fee has not been paid, as required, in respect of an application under rule 30(4) or upon the grant of permission.]]

(2) The Upper Tribunal must strike out the whole or a part of the proceedings if the Upper Tribunal—

(a) does not have jurisdiction in relation to the proceedings or that part of them; and

(b) does not exercise its power under rule 5(3)(k)(i) (transfer to another court or tribunal) in relation to the proceedings or that part of them.

(3) The Upper Tribunal may strike out the whole or a part of the proceedings if—

(a) the appellant or applicant has failed to comply with a direction which stated that failure by the appellant or applicant to comply with the direction could lead to the striking out of the proceedings or part of them;

(b) the appellant or applicant has failed to cooperate with the Upper Tribunal to such an extent that the Upper Tribunal cannot deal with the proceedings fairly and justly; or

(c) in proceedings which are not an appeal from the decision of another tribunal or judicial review proceedings, the Upper Tribunal considers there is no reasonable prospect of the appellant's or the applicant's case, or part of it, succeeding.

(4) The Upper Tribunal may not strike out the whole or a part of the proceedings under paragraph (2) or (3)(b) or (c) without first giving the appellant or applicant an opportunity to make representations in relation to the proposed striking out.

(5) If the proceedings have been struck out under paragraph (1) or (3)(a), the appellant or applicant may apply for the proceedings, or part of them, to be reinstated.

(6) An application under paragraph (5) must be made in writing and received by the Upper Tribunal within 1 month after the date on which the Upper Tribunal sent notification of the striking out to the appellant or applicant.

(7) This rule applies to a respondent [or an interested party] as it applies to an appellant or applicant except that—

(a) a reference to the striking out of the proceedings is to be read as a reference to the barring of the respondent [or interested party] from taking further part in the proceedings; and

(b) a reference to an application for the reinstatement of proceedings which have been struck out is to be read as a reference to an application for the lifting of the bar on the respondent [or interested party] [. . .] taking further part in the proceedings.

(8) If a respondent [or an interested party] has been barred from taking further part in proceedings under this rule and that bar has not been lifted, the Upper Tribunal need not consider any response or other submission made by that respondent [or interested party, and may summarily determine any or all issues against that respondent or interested party].

Note: Paragraph (1A) inserted from 15 February 2010 (SI 2010/44). Words in paragraph (7)(b) omitted and words in square brackets in paragraphs (7)–(8) inserted from 1 April 2009 (SI 2009/274). Paragraph 1 substituted from 17 October 2011 (SI 2011/2343). Subparagraph (1)(b) substituted by SI 2013/2067 from 1 November 2013.

[Addition, substitution and removal of parties

9.—(1) The Upper Tribunal may give a direction adding, substituting or removing a party as an appellant, a respondent or an interested party.

(2) If the Upper Tribunal gives a direction under paragraph (1) it may give such consequential directions as it considers appropriate.

(3) A person who is not a party may apply to the Upper Tribunal to be added or substituted as a party.

(4) If a person who is entitled to be a party to proceedings by virtue of another enactment applies to be added as a party, and any conditions applicable to that entitlement have been satisfied, the Upper Tribunal must give a direction adding that person as a respondent or, if appropriate, as an appellant.]

[(5) In an asylum case, the United Kingdom Representative of the United Nations High Commissioner for Refugees ('the United Kingdom Representative') may give notice to the Upper Tribunal that the United Kingdom Representative wishes to participate in the proceedings.

(6) If the United Kingdom Representative gives notice under paragraph (5)—

(i) the United Kingdom Representative is entitled to participate in any hearing; and

(ii) all documents which are required to be sent or delivered to parties must be sent or delivered to the United Kingdom Representative.]

Note: Rule 9 substituted from 1 September 2009 (SI 2009/1975). Paragraphs (5) and (6) inserted from 15 February 2010 (SI 2010/44).

[Orders for costs

10.—(1) The Upper Tribunal may not make an order in respect of costs (or, in Scotland, expenses) in proceedings [transferred or referred by, or on appeal from,] another tribunal except—

[(aa) in a national security certificate appeal, to the extent permitted by paragraph (1A);]

(a) in proceedings [transferred by, or on appeal from,] the Tax Chamber of the First-tier Tribunal; or

(b) to the extent and in the circumstances that the other tribunal had the power to make an order in respect of costs (or, in Scotland, expenses).

[(1A) In a national security certificate appeal—

(a) the Upper Tribunal may make an order in respect of costs or expenses in the circumstances described at paragraph (3)(c) and (d);

(b) if the appeal is against a certificate, the Upper Tribunal may make an order in respect of costs or expenses against the relevant Minister and in favour of the appellant if the Upper Tribunal allows the appeal and quashes the certificate to any extent or the Minister withdraws the certificate;

(c) if the appeal is against the application of a certificate, the Upper Tribunal may make an order in respect of costs or expenses—

(i) against the appellant and in favour of any other party if the Upper Tribunal dismisses the appeal to any extent; or

(ii) in favour of the appellant and against any other party if the Upper Tribunal allows the appeal to any extent.]

(2) The Upper Tribunal may not make an order in respect of costs or expenses under section 4 of the Forfeiture Act 1982.

(3) In other proceedings, the Upper Tribunal may not make an order in respect of costs or expenses except—

(a) in judicial review proceedings;

(b) [. . .]

(c) under section 29(4) of the 2007 Act (wasted costs) [and costs incurred in applying for such costs];

(d) if the Upper Tribunal considers that a party or its representative has acted unreasonably in bringing, defending or conducting the proceedings [;

(e) if, in a financial services case [or a wholesale energy case], the Upper Tribunal considers that the decision in respect of which the reference was made was unreasonable] [; or

(f) if, in a financial sanctions case, the Upper Tribunal considers that the decision to impose or uphold a monetary penalty in respect of which the appeal was made was unreasonable.]

(4) The Upper Tribunal may make an order for costs (or, in Scotland, expenses) on an application or on its own initiative.

(5) A person making an application for an order for costs or expenses must—

(a) send or deliver a written application to the Upper Tribunal and to the person against whom it is proposed that the order be made; and

(b) send or deliver with the application a schedule of the costs or expenses claimed sufficient to allow summary assessment of such costs or expenses by the Upper Tribunal.

(6) An application for an order for costs or expenses may be made at any time during the proceedings but may not be made later than 1 month after the date on which the Upper Tribunal sends—

(a) a decision notice recording the decision which finally disposes of all issues in the proceedings; or

[(b) notice under rule 17(5) that a withdrawal which ends the proceedings has taken effect.]

(7) The Upper Tribunal may not make an order for costs or expenses against a person (the 'paying person') without first—

(a) giving that person an opportunity to make representations; and

(b) if the paying person is an individual and the order is to be made under paragraph (3)(a), (b) or (d), considering that person's financial means.

(8) The amount of costs or expenses to be paid under an order under this rule may be ascertained by—

(a) summary assessment by the Upper Tribunal;

(b) agreement of a specified sum by the paying person and the person entitled to receive the costs or expenses ('the receiving person'); or

(c) assessment of the whole or a specified part of the costs or expenses [, including the costs or expenses of the assessment,] incurred by the receiving person, if not agreed.

(9) Following an order for assessment under paragraph (8)(c), the paying person or the receiving person may apply—

(a) in England and Wales, to the High Court or the Costs Office of the Supreme Court (as specified in the order) for a detailed assessment of the costs on the standard basis or, if specified in the order, on the indemnity basis; and the Civil Procedure Rules 1998 shall apply, with necessary modifications, to that application and assessment as if the proceedings in the tribunal had been proceedings in a court to which the Civil Procedure Rules 1998 apply;

(b) in Scotland, to the Auditor of the Court of Session for the taxation of the expenses according to the fees payable in that court; or

(c) in Northern Ireland, to the Taxing Office of the High Court of Northern Ireland for taxation on the standard basis or, if specified in the order, on the indemnity basis.

[(10) Upon making an order for the assessment of costs, the [Upper] Tribunal may order an amount to be paid on account before the costs or expenses are assessed.]

Note: Rule 10 substituted from 1 April 2009 (SI 2009/274). Words in square brackets in paragraph (1) and (1)(a) substituted and paragraph (3)(b) omitted from 1 September 2009 (SI 2009/1975). Paragraph(1)(aa) and (1A) inserted from 18 January 2010 (SI 2010/43). Paragraph (3)(e) inserted from 6 April 2010 (SI 2010/747). Paragraph (6)(b) substituted, paragraph (10) and words in square brackets in paragraph (8)(c) and (3)(c) inserted by SI 2013/477 from 1 April 2013. Word in square brackets in (10) inserted by SI 2013/2067 from 1 November 2013. Words in square brackets in (3)(e) inserted by SI 2014/514 from 6 April 2014. Paragraph (3)(f) inserted from 27 July 2017 (SI 2017/723).

Representatives

11.—(1) [Subject to paragraph 5A, a] party may appoint a representative (whether a legal representative or not) to represent that party in the proceedings [save that a party in an asylum or immigration case may not be represented by any person prohibited from representing by section 84 of the Immigration and Asylum Act 1999].

(2) If a party appoints a representative, that party (or the representative if the representative is a legal representative) must send or deliver to the Upper Tribunal [. . .] written notice of the representative's name and address.

[(2A) If the Upper Tribunal receives notice that a party has appointed a representative under paragraph (2), it must send a copy of that notice to each other party.]

(3) Anything permitted or required to be done by a party under these Rules, a practice direction or a direction may be done by the representative of that party, except signing a witness statement.

(4) A person who receives due notice of the appointment of a representative—

(a) must provide to the representative any document which is required to be provided to the represented party, and need not provide that document to the represented party; and

(b) may assume that the representative is and remains authorised as such until they receive written notification that this is not so from the representative or the represented party.

(5) [Subject to paragraph (5B), at] a hearing a party may be accompanied by another person whose name and address has not been notified under paragraph (2) but who, subject to paragraph (8) and with the permission of the Upper Tribunal, may act as a representative or otherwise assist in presenting the party's case at the hearing.

[(5A) In [immigration judicial review] proceedings, a party may appoint as a representative only a person authorised under the Legal Services Act 2007 to undertake the conduct of litigation in the High Court.]

[(5B) At a hearing of [immigration judicial review] proceedings, rights of audience before the Upper Tribunal are restricted to persons authorised to exercise those rights in the High Court under the Legal Services Act 2007.]

(6) Paragraphs (2) to (4) do not apply to a person who accompanies a party under paragraph (5).

(7) In a mental health case if the patient has not appointed a representative the Upper Tribunal may appoint a legal representative for the patient where—

(a) the patient has stated that they do not wish to conduct their own case or that they wish to be represented; or

(b) the patient lacks the capacity to appoint a representative but the Upper Tribunal believes that it is in the patient's best interests for the patient to be represented.

(8) In a mental health case a party may not appoint as a representative, or be represented or assisted at a hearing by—

(a) a person liable to be detained or subject to guardianship or after-care under supervision, or who is a community patient, under the Mental Health Act 1983; or

(b) a person receiving treatment for mental disorder at the same hospital [or] home as the patient.

[(9) In this rule 'legal representative' means [a person who, for the purposes of the Legal Services Act 2007, is an authorised person in relation to an activity which constitutes the exercise of a right of audience or the conduct of litigation within the meaning of that Act], [a qualified person as defined in section 84(2) of the Immigration and Asylum Act 1999,] an advocate or solicitor in Scotland or a barrister or solicitor in Northern Ireland.]

[(10) In an asylum case or an immigration case, an appellant's representative before the First-tier Tribunal will be treated as that party's representative before the Upper Tribunal, unless the Upper Tribunal receives notice—

(a) of a new representative under paragraph (2) of this rule; or

(b) from the appellant stating that they are no longer represented.]

Note: Words omitted from paragraph (2), paragraphs (2A) and (9) inserted from 1 April 2009 (SI 2009/274). Word in square brackets in paragraph (8)(b) inserted from 1 September 2009 (SI 2009/275). Words in first square brackets in paragraph (9) substituted from 18 January 2010 (SI 2010/43). Paragraph (10), words in square brackets in paragraph (1) and second square brackets in paragraph (9) inserted from 15 February 2010 (SI 2010/44). Words inserted in paragraphs (1) and (5) and paragraphs (5A) and (5B) inserted from 17 October 2011 (SI 2011/2343). Words in square brackets in paragraphs (5A) and (5B) substituted by 2013/2067 from 1 November 2013.

Calculating time

12.—(1) An act required by these Rules, a practice direction or a direction to be done on or by a particular day must be done by 5pm on that day.

(2) If the time specified by these Rules, a practice direction or a direction for doing any act ends on a day other than a working day, the act is done in time if it is done on the next working day.

(3) In a special educational needs case or a disability discrimination in schools case, the following days must not be counted when calculating the time by which an act must be done—

(a) 25th December to 1st January inclusive; and

(b) any day in August.

[(3A) In an asylum case or an immigration case, when calculating the time by which an act must be done, in addition to the days specified in the definition of 'working days' in rule 1 (interpretation), the following days must also not be counted as working days—

(a) 27th to 31st December inclusive; [. . .

(b) . . .]

(4) Paragraph (3) [or (3A)] does not apply where the Upper Tribunal directs that an act must be done by or on a specified date.

(5) [. . .]

Note: Paragraph (5) inserted from 1 April 2009 (SI 2009/274) and omitted from 1 September 2014 by SI 2014/2128. Paragraph (3A) and words in square brackets in paragraph (4) inserted from 15 February 2010 (SI 2010/44). Subparagraph (3A)(b) omitted from 20 October 2014 by SI 2014/2128.

Sending and delivery of documents

13.—(1) Any document to be provided to the Upper Tribunal under these Rules, a practice direction or a direction must be—

(a) sent by pre-paid post or [by document exchange, or delivered by hand,] to the address specified for the proceedings;

(b) sent by fax to the number specified for the proceedings; or

(c) sent or delivered by such other method as the Upper Tribunal may permit or direct.

(2) Subject to paragraph (3), if a party provides a fax number, email address or other details for the electronic transmission of documents to them, that party must accept delivery of documents by that method.

(3) If a party informs the Upper Tribunal and all other parties that a particular form of communication, other than pre-paid post or delivery by hand, should not be used to provide documents to that party, that form of communication must not be so used.

(4) If the Upper Tribunal or a party sends a document to a party or the Upper Tribunal by email or any other electronic means of communication, the recipient may request that the sender provide a hard copy of the document to the recipient. The recipient must make such a request as soon as reasonably practicable after receiving the document electronically.

(5) The Upper Tribunal and each party may assume that the address provided by a party or its representative is and remains the address to which documents should be sent or delivered until receiving written notification to the contrary.

[(6) Subject to paragraph (7), if a document submitted to the Upper Tribunal is not written in English, it must be accompanied by an English translation.

(7) In proceedings that are in Wales or have a connection with Wales, a document or translation may be submitted to the [Upper] Tribunal in Welsh.]

[(8) In judicial review proceedings, unless the contrary is proved, a document sent by first class post will be deemed to be provided or received on the second working day after it was posted.]

Note: Words in square brackets in paragraph (1)(a) substituted from 1 April 2009 (SI 2009/274). Paragraphs (6) and (7) inserted from 15 February 2010 (SI 2010/44). Word in square brackets in paragraph (7) inserted by SI 2013/2067 from 1 November 2013. Paragraph (8) inserted from 6 April 2022 (SI 2022/312).

Use of documents and information

14.—(1) The Upper Tribunal may make an order prohibiting the disclosure or publication of—

(a) specified documents or information relating to the proceedings; or

(b) any matter likely to lead members of the public to identify any person whom the Upper Tribunal considers should not be identified.

(2) The Upper Tribunal may give a direction prohibiting the disclosure of a document or information to a person if—

(a) the Upper Tribunal is satisfied that such disclosure would be likely to cause that person or some other person serious harm; and

(b) the Upper Tribunal is satisfied, having regard to the interests of justice, that it is proportionate to give such a direction.

(3) If a party ('the first party') considers that the Upper Tribunal should give a direction under paragraph (2) prohibiting the disclosure of a document or information to another party ('the second party'), the first party must—

(a) exclude the relevant document or information from any documents that will be provided to the second party; and

(b) provide to the Upper Tribunal the excluded document or information, and the reason for its exclusion, so that the Upper Tribunal may decide whether the document or information should be disclosed to the second party or should be the subject of a direction under paragraph (2).

(4) [. . .]

(5) If the Upper Tribunal gives a direction under paragraph (2) which prevents disclosure to a party who has appointed a representative, the Upper Tribunal may give a direction that the documents or information be disclosed to that representative if the Upper Tribunal is satisfied that—

(a) disclosure to the representative would be in the interests of the party; and

(b) the representative will act in accordance with paragraph (6).

(6) Documents or information disclosed to a representative in accordance with a direction under paragraph (5) must not be disclosed either directly or indirectly to any other person without the Upper Tribunal's consent.

(7) Unless the Upper Tribunal gives a direction to the contrary, information about mental health cases and the names of any persons concerned in such cases must not be made public.

[(8) The Upper Tribunal may, on its own initiative or on the application of a party, give a direction that certain documents or information must or may be disclosed to the Upper Tribunal on the basis that the Upper Tribunal will not disclose such documents or information to other persons, or specified other persons.

[[(8A) In a trade remedies case, the Upper Tribunal may give a direction under paragraph (8) if the Upper Tribunal is satisfied that—

(a) where such documents or information have been supplied to the TRA, the TRA is treating such documents or information as confidential in accordance with—

(i) regulation 45 of the Trade Remedies (Dumping and Subsidisation) (EU Exit) Regulations 2019;

(ii) regulation 16 of the Trade Remedies (Increase in Imports Causing Serious Injury to UK Producers) (EU Exit) Regulations 2019; or

(iii) regulation 5 of the Trade Remedies (Reconsideration and Appeals) (EU Exit) Regulations 2019; or

(b) where such documents or information have not been supplied to the TRA, if such documents or information were to be supplied to the TRA in accordance with regulation 5 of the Trade Remedies (Reconsideration and Appeals) (EU Exit) Regulations 2019, the TRA would be entitled to treat such documents or information as confidential in accordance with that regulation,

and the Upper Tribunal is not precluded from considering such documents or information in making its decision in the case.]]

(9) A party making an application for a direction under paragraph (8) may withhold the relevant documents or information from other parties until the Upper Tribunal has granted or refused the application.

(10) In a case involving matters relating to national security, the Upper Tribunal must ensure that information is not disclosed contrary to the interests of national security.

(11) The Upper Tribunal must conduct proceedings and record its decision and reasons appropriately so as not to undermine the effect of an order made under paragraph (1), a direction given under paragraph (2) or (8) or the duty imposed by paragraph (10).]

Note: Paragraph (4) omitted and paragraphs (8)–(11) inserted from 1 September 2009 (SI 2009/1975) and paragraph (8A) inserted from 3 June 2019 (SI 2019/925) subject to transitional provisions in rule 6(b) of SI 2019/925.

Evidence and submissions

15.—(1) Without restriction on the general powers in rule 5(1) and (2) (case management powers), the Upper Tribunal may give directions as to—

(a) issues on which it requires evidence or submissions;

(b) the nature of the evidence or submissions it requires;

(c) whether the parties are permitted or required to provide expert evidence, and if so whether the parties must jointly appoint a single expert to provide such evidence;

(d) any limit on the number of witnesses whose evidence a party may put forward, whether in relation to a particular issue or generally;

(e) the manner in which any evidence or submissions are to be provided, which may include a direction for them to be given—

(i) orally at a hearing; or

(ii) by written submissions or witness statement; and

(f) the time at which any evidence or submissions are to be provided.

(2) The Upper Tribunal may—

(a) admit evidence whether or not—

(i) the evidence would be admissible in a civil trial in the United Kingdom; or

(ii) the evidence was available to a previous decision maker; or

(b) exclude evidence that would otherwise be admissible where—

(i) the evidence was not provided within the time allowed by a direction or a practice direction;

(ii) the evidence was otherwise provided in a manner that did not comply with a direction or a practice direction; or

(iii) it would otherwise be unfair to admit the evidence.

[(2A) In an asylum case or an immigration case—

(a) if a party wishes the Upper Tribunal to consider evidence that was not before the First-tier Tribunal, that party must send or deliver a notice to the Upper Tribunal and any other party—

(i) indicating the nature of the evidence; and

(ii) explaining why it was not submitted to the First-tier Tribunal; and

(b) when considering whether to admit evidence that was not before the First-tier Tribunal, the Upper Tribunal must have regard to whether there has been unreasonable delay in producing that evidence.]

(3) The Upper Tribunal may consent to a witness giving, or require any witness to give, evidence on oath, and may administer an oath for that purpose.

Note: Paragraph 2A inserted from 15 February 2010 (SI 2010/44).

Summoning or citation of witnesses and orders to answer questions or produce documents

16.—(1) On the application of a party or on its own initiative, the Upper Tribunal may—

(a) by summons (or, in Scotland, citation) require any person to attend as a witness at a hearing at the time and place specified in the summons or citation; or

(b) order any person to answer any questions or produce any documents in that person's possession or control which relate to any issue in the proceedings.

(2) A summons or citation under paragraph (1)(a) must—

(a) give the person required to attend 14 days' notice of the hearing or such shorter period as the Upper Tribunal may direct; and

(b) where the person is not a party, make provision for the person's necessary expenses of attendance to be paid, and state who is to pay them.

(3) No person may be compelled to give any evidence or produce any document that the person could not be compelled to give or produce on a trial of an action in a court of law in the part of the United Kingdom where the proceedings are due to be determined.

[(4) A person who receives a summons, citation or order may apply to the Upper Tribunal for it to be varied or set aside if they did not have an opportunity to object to it before it was made or issued.

(5) A person making an application under paragraph (4) must do so as soon as reasonably practicable after receiving notice of the summons, citation or order.

(6) A summons, citation or order under this rule must—

(a) state that the person on whom the requirement is imposed may apply to the Upper Tribunal to vary or set aside the summons, citation or order, if they did not have an opportunity to object to it before it was made or issued; and

(b) state the consequences of failure to comply with the summons, citation or order.]

Note: Paragraph (4) substituted from 1 April 2009 (SI 2009/274).

Withdrawal

17.—(1) Subject to paragraph (2), a party may give notice of the withdrawal of its case, or any part of it—

(a) [. . .] by sending or delivering to the Upper Tribunal a written notice of withdrawal; or

(b) orally at a hearing.

(2) Notice of withdrawal will not take effect unless the Upper Tribunal consents to the withdrawal except in relation to an application for permission to appeal.

(3) A party which has withdrawn its case may apply to the Upper Tribunal for the case to be reinstated.

(4) An application under paragraph (3) must be made in writing and be received by the Upper Tribunal within 1 month after—

(a) the date on which the Upper Tribunal received the notice under paragraph (1)(a); or

(b) the date of the hearing at which the case was withdrawn orally under paragraph (1)(b).

(5) The Upper Tribunal must notify each party in writing [that a withdrawal has taken effect] under this rule.

[(6) Paragraph (3) does not apply to a financial services case other than a reference against a penalty.]

Note: Paragraph (6) inserted from 6 April 2010 (SI 2010/747). Words omitted from (1)(a) and substituted in (5) from 1 April 2013 (SI 2013/477).

[Appeal treated as abandoned or finally determined in an asylum case or an immigration case

17A.—(1) A party to an asylum case or an immigration case before the Upper Tribunal must notify the [Upper] Tribunal if they are aware that—

(a) the appellant has left the United Kingdom;

(b) the appellant has been granted leave to enter or remain in the United Kingdom; [or]

(c) a deportation order has been made against the appellant; [

(d) . . .]

[(1A) A party to an appeal under the Immigration (Citizens' Rights Appeals) (EU Exit) Regulations 2020 ('the 2020 Regulations') before the Upper Tribunal must also notify the Upper Tribunal if they are aware that the appeal is to be treated as abandoned under regulation [13] of those Regulations.]

(2) Where an appeal is treated as abandoned pursuant to section {92(8),}104(4) or (4A) of the Nationality, Immigration and Asylum Act 2002 [. . .] [or regulation 13(3) of the 2020 Regulations], or as finally determined pursuant to section 104(5) of the Nationality, Immigration and Asylum Act 2002, the Upper Tribunal must send the parties a notice informing them that the appeal is being treated as abandoned or finally determined.

(3) Where an appeal would otherwise fall to be treated as abandoned pursuant to section 104(4A) of the Nationality, Immigration and Asylum Act 2002 [or regulation 13(3) of the 2020 Regulations], but the appellant wishes to pursue their appeal, the appellant must send or deliver a notice, which must comply with any relevant practice directions, to the Upper Tribunal and the respondent so that it is received within thirty days of the date on which the notice of the grant of leave to enter or remain in the United Kingdom was sent to the appellant.

(4) Where a notice of grant of leave to enter or remain is sent electronically or delivered personally, the time limit in paragraph (3) is twenty eight days.

(5) Notwithstanding rule 5(3)(a) (case management powers) and rule 7(2) (failure to comply with rules etc.), the Upper Tribunal must not extend the time limits in paragraph (3) and (4).]

Note: Rule 17A inserted from 15 February 2010 (SI 2010/44). Word inserted in paragraph (1) by SI 2013/2067 from 1 November 2013. Paragraph (1A) and words in square brackets in paragraphs (2) and (3) inserted from 31 January 2020 (SI 2020/61). Words in curly brackets in paragraph (2) inserted from 21 July 2020 (SI 2020/651). Word at end of paragraph (1)(b) inserted and paragraph (1)(d) and words in paragraph (2) omitted from 2300 on 31 December 2020 (SI 2020/1309) subject to saving provision in reg 33(4) of SI 2020/1309. Word substituted in paragraph (1A) from immediately after 2300 on 31 December 2020 (SI 2020/1372).

Notice of funding of legal services

18. If a party is granted funding of legal services at any time, that party must as soon as practicable—

(a) (i) if [civil legal services (within the meaning of section 8 of the Legal Aid, Sentencing and Punishment of Offenders Act 2012) are provided under arrangements made for the purposes of Part 1 of that Act or by] the Northern Ireland Legal Services Commission, send a copy of the [certificate or] funding notice to the Upper Tribunal; or

(ii) if funding is granted by the Scottish Legal Aid Board, send a copy of the legal aid certificate to the Upper Tribunal; and

(b) notify every other party in writing that funding has been granted.

Note: Words in first square brackets substituted and words in second square brackets inserted by SI 2013/477 from 1 April 2013.

[Confidentiality in social security and child support cases

19.—(1) Paragraph (4) applies to an appeal against a decision of the First-tier Tribunal—

(a) in proceedings under the Child Support Act 1991 in the circumstances described in paragraph (2), other than an appeal against a reduced benefit decision (as defined in section 46(10)(b) of the Child Support Act 1991, as that section had effect prior to the commencement of section 15(b) of the Child Maintenance and Other Payments Act 2008); or

(b) in proceedings where the parties to the appeal include former joint claimants who are no longer living together in the circumstances described in paragraph (3).

(2) The circumstances referred to in paragraph (1)(a) are that—

(a) in the proceedings in the First-tier Tribunal in respect of which the appeal has been brought, there was an obligation to keep a person's address confidential; or

(b) an absent parent, non-resident parent or person with care would like their address or the address of the child to be kept confidential and has given notice to that effect to the Upper Tribunal—

(i) in an application for permission to appeal or notice of appeal;

(ii) within 1 month after an enquiry by the Upper Tribunal; or

(iii) when notifying any subsequent change of address after proceedings have been started.

(3) The circumstances referred to in paragraph (1)(b) are that—

(a) in the proceedings in the First-tier Tribunal in respect of which the appeal has been brought, there was an obligation to keep a person's address confidential; or

(b) one of the former joint claimants would like their address to be kept confidential and has given notice to that effect to the Upper Tribunal—

(i) in an application for permission to appeal or notice of appeal;

(ii) within 1 month after an enquiry by the Upper Tribunal; or

(iii) when notifying any subsequent change of address after proceedings have been started.

(4) Where this paragraph applies, the Secretary of State or other decision maker and the Upper Tribunal must take appropriate steps to secure the confidentiality of the address and of any information which could reasonably be expected to enable a person to identify the address, to the extent that the address or that information is not already known to each other party.

(5) In this rule—

'absent parent', 'non-resident parent' and 'person with care' have the meanings set out in section 3 of the Child Support Act 1991;

'joint claimants' means the persons who made a joint claim for a jobseeker's allowance under the Jobseekers Act 1995, a tax credit under the Tax Credits Act 2002 or in relation to whom an award of universal credit is made under Part 1 of the Welfare Reform Act 2012.]

Note: Rule 19 substituted by SI 2014/2128 from 20 October 2014.

Power to pay expenses and allowances

20.—(1) In proceedings brought under section 4 of the Safeguarding Vulnerable Groups Act 2006 [. . .], the Secretary of State may pay such allowances for the purpose of or in connection with the attendance of persons at hearings as the Secretary of State may, with the consent of the Treasury, determine.

(2) Paragraph (3) applies to proceedings on appeal from a decision of—

(a) the First-tier Tribunal in proceedings under the Child Support Act 1991, section 12 of the Social Security Act 1998 or paragraph 6 of Schedule 7 to the Child Support, Pensions and Social Security Act 2000;

(b) the First-tier Tribunal in a war pensions and armed forces case (as defined in the Tribunal Procedure (First-tier Tribunal) (War Pensions and Armed Forces Compensation Chamber) Rules 2008; or

(c) a Pensions Appeal Tribunal for Scotland or Northern Ireland.

(3) The Lord Chancellor (or, in Scotland, the Secretary of State) may pay to any person who attends any hearing such travelling and other allowances, including compensation for loss of remunerative time, as the Lord Chancellor (or, in Scotland, the Secretary of State) may determine.

Note: Words omitted from paragraph (1) from 1 April 2009 (SI 2009/274).

[Procedure for applying for a stay of a decision pending an appeal

20A.—(1) This rule applies where another enactment provides in any terms for the Upper Tribunal to stay or suspend, or to lift a stay or suspension of, a decision which is or may be the subject of an appeal to the Upper Tribunal ('the substantive decision') pending such appeal.

(2) A person who wishes the Upper Tribunal to decide whether the substantive decision should be stayed or suspended must make a written application to the Upper Tribunal which must include—

(a) the name and address of the person making the application;

(b) the name and address of any representative of that person;

(c) the address to which documents for that person should be sent or delivered;

(d) the name and address of any person who will be a respondent to the appeal;

(e) details of the substantive decision and any decision as to when that decision is to take effect, and copies of any written record of, or reasons for, those decisions; and

(f) the grounds on which the person making the application relies.

(3) In the case of an application under paragraph (2) [in a road transport case]—

(a) the person making the application must notify the [decision maker] when making the application;

(b) within 7 days of receiving notification of the application the [decision maker] must send or deliver written reasons for refusing or withdrawing the stay—

(i) to the Upper Tribunal; and

(ii) to the person making the application, if the [decision maker] has not already done so.

(4) If the Upper Tribunal grants a stay or suspension following an application under this rule—

(a) the Upper Tribunal may give directions as to the conduct of the appeal of the substantive decision; and

(b) the Upper Tribunal may, where appropriate, grant the stay or suspension subject to conditions.

(5) Unless the Upper Tribunal considers that there is good reason not to do so, the Upper Tribunal must send written notice of any decision made under this rule to each party.]

Note: Rule 20A inserted from 1 September 2009 (SI 2009/1975). Paragraph (3) amended from 1 July 2012 (SI 2012/1363).

PART 3
[PROCEDURE FOR CASES IN] THE UPPER TRIBUNAL

Application to the Upper Tribunal for permission to appeal

21.—(1) [. . .]

[**1A**) This rule does not apply to an application for permission to appeal to the Upper Tribunal if such application is made under rule 24 (response to notice of appeal).]

(2) A person may apply to the Upper Tribunal for permission to appeal to the Upper Tribunal against a decision of another tribunal only if—

(a) they have made an application for permission to appeal to the tribunal which made the decision challenged; and

(b) that application has been refused or has not been admitted [or has been granted only on limited grounds].

(3) An application for permission to appeal must be made in writing and received by the Upper Tribunal no later than—

(a) in the case of an application under section 4 of the Safeguarding Vulnerable Groups Act 2006, 3 months after the date on which written notice of the decision being challenged was sent to the appellant;

[(aa) in an asylum case or an immigration case where the appellant is in the United Kingdom at the time that the application is made, 14 days after the date on which notice of the First-tier Tribunal's refusal of permission was sent to the appellant;]

(ab) [. . .]

(b) otherwise, a month after the date on which the tribunal that made the decision under challenge sent notice of its refusal of permission to appeal, or refusal to admit the application for permission to appeal, to the appellant.

(3A) [. . .]

(4) The application must state—

(a) the name and address of the appellant;

(b) the name and address of the representative (if any) of the appellant;

(c) an address where documents for the appellant may be sent or delivered;

(d) details (including the full reference) of the decision challenged;

(e) the grounds on which the appellant relies; and

(f) whether the appellant wants the application to be dealt with at a hearing.

(5) The appellant must provide with the application a copy of—

(a) any written record of the decision being challenged;

(b) any separate written statement of reasons for that decision; and

(c) if the application is for permission to appeal against a decision of another tribunal, the notice of refusal of permission to appeal, or notice of refusal to admit the application for permission to appeal, from that other tribunal.

(6) If the appellant provides the application to the Upper Tribunal later than the time required by paragraph (3) or by an extension of time allowed under rule 5(3)(a) (power to extend time)—

(a) the application must include a request for an extension of time and the reason why the application was not provided in time; and

(b) unless the Upper Tribunal extends time for the application under rule 5(3)(a) (power to extend time) the Upper Tribunal must not admit the application.

(7) If the appellant makes an application to the Upper Tribunal for permission to appeal against the decision of another tribunal, and that other tribunal refused to admit the appellant's application for permission to appeal because the application for permission or for a written statement of reasons was not made in time—

(a) the application to the Upper Tribunal for permission to appeal must include the reason why the application to the other tribunal for permission to appeal or for a written statement of reasons, as the case may be, was not made in time; and

(b) the Upper Tribunal must only admit the application if the Upper Tribunal considers that it is in the interests of justice for it to do so.

[(8) In this rule, a reference to notice of a refusal of permission to appeal is to be taken to include a reference to notice of a grant of permission to appeal on limited grounds.]

Note: Paragraph (1) omitted from 1 September 2009 (SI 2009/1975). Paragraphs (3)(aa)–(ab) and (3A) inserted from 15 February 2010 (SI 2010/44) and paragraphs 3(ab) and (3A) omitted by SI 2014/2128 from 20 October 2014. Paragraph (3)(aa) substituted from 21 July 2020 (SI 2020/651). Paragraph (8) and words in para (2)(b) inserted from 6 April 2014 (SI 2014/514). Paragraph (1A) inserted from 6 April 2022 (SI 2022/312).

Decision in relation to permission to appeal

22.—(1) [Except where rule 22A (special procedure for providing notice of a refusal of permission to appeal in an asylum case) applies], if the Upper Tribunal refuses permission to appeal [or refuses to admit a late application for permission], it must send written notice of the refusal and of the reasons for the refusal to the appellant.

(2) If the Upper Tribunal gives permission to appeal—

(a) the Upper Tribunal must send written notice of the permission, and of the reasons for any limitations or conditions on such permission, to each party;

(b) subject to any direction by the Upper Tribunal, the application for permission to appeal stands as the notice of appeal and the Upper Tribunal must send to each respondent a copy of the application for permission to appeal and any documents provided with it by the appellant; and

(c) the Upper Tribunal may, with the consent of the appellant and each respondent, determine the appeal without obtaining any further response.

[(3) Paragraph (4) applies where the Upper Tribunal, without a hearing, determines an application for permission to appeal—

(a) against a decision of—

(i) the Tax Chamber of the First-tier Tribunal;

(ii) the Health, Education and Social Care Chamber of the First-tier Tribunal;

[(iia) the General Regulatory Chamber of the First-tier Tribunal;]
(iib) [. . .]
(iii) the Mental Health Review Tribunal for Wales; or
(iv) the Special Educational Needs Tribunal for Wales; or
(b) under section 4 of the Safeguarding Vulnerable Groups Act 2006.]

(4) [Subject to paragraph (4A),] In the circumstances set out at paragraph (3) the appellant may apply for the decision to be reconsidered at a hearing if the Upper Tribunal—

(a) refuses permission to appeal [or refuses to admit a late application for permission]; or

(b) gives permission to appeal on limited grounds or subject to conditions.

[(4A) Where the Upper Tribunal considers the whole or part of an application to be totally without merit, it shall record that fact in its decision notice and, in those circumstances, the person seeking permission may not request the decision or part of the decision (as the case may be) to be reconsidered at a hearing.]

(5) An application under paragraph (4) must be made in writing and received by the Upper Tribunal within 14 days after the date on which the Upper Tribunal sent written notice of its decision regarding the application to the appellant.

Note: Paragraph (3) substituted from 1 April 2009 (SI 2009/274). Paragraph (3)(a)(iia) inserted from 1 September 2009 (SI 2009/1975). Words in first square brackets in paragraph (1) substituted by SI 2014/2128 from 20 October 2014. Words in other square brackets in (1) and (4)(a) inserted from 6 April 2014 (SI 2014/514) and paragraph (3)(a)(iib) omitted from 14 May 2018 (SI 2018/511). Words at the beginning of paragraph (4) and paragraph (4A) inserted from 6 April 2022 (SI 2022/312).

[Special procedure for providing notice of a refusal of permission to appeal in an asylum case

22A.—(1) This rule applies to a decision in an asylum case to refuse permission to appeal or to refuse to admit a late application for permission to appeal, where—

(a) the appellant is not the Secretary of State [and];

(b) at the time the application is made the appellant is in the United Kingdom.

(c) [. . .]

(2) The Upper Tribunal must provide written notice of the refusal and of the reasons for the refusal ('the notice') to the Secretary of State as soon as reasonably practicable.

(3) The Secretary of State must—

(a) send the notice to the appellant not later than 30 days after the Upper Tribunal provided it to the Secretary of State; and

(b) as soon as practicable after doing so, inform the Upper Tribunal of the date on which, and the means by which, it was sent.

(4) If the Secretary of State does not give the Upper Tribunal the information required by paragraph (3)(b) within 31 days after the notice was provided to the Secretary of State, the Upper Tribunal must send the notice to the appellant as soon as reasonably practicable.]

Note: Rule 22A inserted by SI 2014/2128 from 20 October 2014. Word inserted at end of paragraph (1)(a) and paragraph (1)(c) omitted from 21 July 2020 (SI 2020/651).

Notice of appeal

23.—[(1) This rule applies—

(a) to proceedings on appeal to the Upper Tribunal for which permission to appeal is not required, except proceedings to which rule 26A[, 26B or 26C] applies;

(b) if another tribunal has given permission for a party to appeal to the Upper Tribunal; or

(c) subject to any other direction by the Upper Tribunal, if the Upper Tribunal has given permission to appeal and has given a direction that the application for permission to appeal does not stand as the notice of appeal.

[(1A) In an asylum case or an immigration case in which the First-tier Tribunal has given permission to appeal, subject to any direction of the First-tier Tribunal or the Upper Tribunal, the application for permission to appeal sent or delivered to the First-tier Tribunal stands as the notice of appeal and accordingly paragraphs (2) to (6) of this rule do not apply.]

(2) The appellant must provide a notice of appeal to the Upper Tribunal so that it is received within 1 month after—

(a) the date that the tribunal that gave permission to appeal sent notice of such permission to the appellant; or

[(b) if permission to appeal is not required, the date on which notice of decision to which the appeal relates—

(i) was sent to the appellant;[. . .]

(ii) in a quality contracts scheme case, if the notice was not sent to the appellant, the date on which the notice was published in a newspaper in accordance with the requirement of section 125 (notice and consultation requirements) of the Transport Act 2000[,or]]

[(iii) in a trade remedies case—

(aa) where the appeal is against a decision made by the TRA and notice is required to be published in accordance with the Trade Remedies (Reconsideration and Appeals) (EU Exit) Regulations 2019, the date of such publication or (if later) when the notice comes into effect;

(bb) where the appeal is against a decision made by the TRA and no notice is required to be published in accordance with the Trade Remedies (Reconsideration and Appeals) (EU Exit) Regulations 2019, the date on which the appellant is notified of the decision, or

(cc) where the appeal is against a determination of the Secretary of State under the Taxation (Cross-border Trade) Act 2018, the Trade Remedies (Dumping and Subsidisation) (EU Exit) Regulations 2019, the Trade Remedies (Increase in Imports Causing Serious Injury to UK Producers) (EU Exit) Regulations 2019 or the Trade Remedies (Reconsideration and Appeals) (EU Exit) Regulations 2019 (as the case may be), the date on which the notice is published in accordance with the relevant provision or (if later) when the notice comes into effect;]

(3) The notice of appeal must include the information listed in rule 21(4)(a) to (e) (content of the application for permission to appeal) and, where the Upper Tribunal has given permission to appeal, the Upper Tribunal's case reference.

(4) If another tribunal has granted permission to appeal, the appellant must provide with the notice of appeal a copy of—

(a) any written record of the decision being challenged;

(b) any separate written statement of reasons for that decision; and
(c) the notice of permission to appeal.

(5) If the appellant provides the notice of appeal to the Upper Tribunal later than the time required by paragraph (2) or by an extension of time allowed under rule 5(3)(a) (power to extend time)—

(a) the notice of appeal must include a request for an extension of time and the reason why the notice was not provided in time; and

(b) unless the Upper Tribunal extends time for the notice of appeal under rule 5(3)(a) (power to extend time) the Upper Tribunal must not admit the notice of appeal.

[(6) When the Upper Tribunal receives the notice of appeal it must send a copy of the notice and any accompanying documents—

(a) to each respondent; [. . .]
[(b) in a road transport case, to—
(i) the decision maker;
(ii) the appropriate national authority; and
(iii) in a case relating to the detention of a vehicle, the authorised person.][; or

(c) in an appeal against a decision of a traffic commissioner pursuant to section 6F of the Transport Act 1985 or section 123T of the Transport Act 2000, to—
(i) the respondent, and
(ii) the traffic commissioner who was the decision maker.

(6A) In a case to which paragraph (6)(c) applies, the Upper Tribunal must at the same time require such commissioner to—

(a) send or deliver to the Upper Tribunal (within such time as the Upper Tribunal may specify)—

(i) a copy of any written record of the decision under challenge, and any statement of reasons for that decision, and

(ii) copies of all documents relevant to the case in such commissioner's possession, and

(b) provide copies of such documents to each other party at the same time as they are provided to the Upper Tribunal.]

[(7) Paragraph (6)(a) does not apply in a quality contracts scheme case, in respect of which Schedule A1 makes alternative and further provision.]

Note: Paragraphs (1), (2) and (6) substituted from 1 September 2009 (SI 2009/1975). Paragraph (1A) inserted from 15 February 2010 (SI 2010/44). Words in paragraph (1)(a) substituted from 27 July 2017 (SI 2017/723). Paragraph 6(b) substituted from 1 July 2012 (SI 2012/1363). Paragraph (2)(b) substituted and paragraph (7) inserted from 21 August 2015 (SI 2015/1510). Paragraph (2)(b) (iii) inserted from 3 June 2019 (SI 2019/925) subject to transitional provision in rule 6(c) of SI 2019/925. Word at end of paragraph 6(a) omitted and paragraphs (6)(c) and (6A) inserted from 3 June 2019 (SI 2019/925).

Response to the notice of appeal

24.—[(1) This rule and rule 25 do not apply to—

(a) a road transport case, in respect of which Schedule 1 makes alternative provision; or

(b) a financial sanctions case in respect of which Schedule 4 makes alternative provision.]

(1A) Subject to any direction given by the Upper Tribunal, a respondent may [,and if paragraph (1B) applies must,] provide a response to a notice of appeal.

[(1B) In the case of an appeal against the decision of another tribunal, a respondent must provide a response to a notice of appeal if the respondent—

(a wishes the Upper Tribunal to uphold the decision for reasons other than those given by the tribunal; or

(b) relies on any grounds on which the respondent was unsuccessful in the proceedings which are the subject of the appeal.

(1C) If paragraph (1B) applies, to the extent that the respondent needs any permission, including permission to appeal to the Upper Tribunal, the response must include an application to the Upper Tribunal for such permission.]

(2) Any response provided under paragraph [(1A)] must be in writing and must be sent or delivered to the Upper Tribunal so that it is received—

[(a) if an application for permission to appeal stands as the notice of appeal, no later than one month after the date on which the respondent was sent notice that permission to appeal had been granted;]

(aa) [. . .]

[(ab) in a quality contracts scheme case, no later than 1 month after the date on which a copy of the notice of appeal is sent to the respondent;] [or]

(b) in any other case, no later than 1 month after the date on which the Upper Tribunal sent a copy of the notice of appeal to the respondent.

(3) The response must state—

(a) the name and address of the respondent;

(b) the name and address of the representative (if any) of the respondent;

(c) an address where documents for the respondent may be sent or delivered;

(d) whether the respondent opposes the appeal;

(e) the grounds [

(i) to uphold the decision for reasons other than those given by the tribunal; or

(ii) on which the respondent was unsuccessful in the proceedings which are the subject of the appeal;]

[(ea) the reasons why any permission applied for under paragraph (1C) should be given; and]

(f) whether the respondent wants the case to be dealt with at a hearing.

(4) If the respondent provides the response to the Upper Tribunal later than the time required by paragraph (2) or by an extension of time allowed under rule 5(3)(a) (power to extend time), the response must include a request for an extension of time and the reason why the [response] was not provided in time.

(5) When the Upper Tribunal receives the response it must send a copy of the response and any accompanying documents to the appellant and each other party.

[(6) Paragraph (5) does not apply in a quality contracts scheme case, in respect of which Schedule A1 makes alternative and further provision.]

Note: Paragraph (2)(a) substituted from 15 February 2010 (SI 2010/44). Word in paragraph (2) substituted from 18 January 2010 (SI 2010/43). Word in square bracket in paragraph (4) substituted from 1 April 2009 (SI 2009/274). Paragraph (6) inserted from 21 August 2015 (SI 2015/1510). Paragraph (1) substituted from 27 July 2017 (SI 2017/723). Paragraph (2)(aa) omitted and word inserted at the end of paragraph (2)(ab) from 21 July 2020 (SI 2020/651). Words inserted in paragraph (1A) and paragraphs (1B) and (1C) inserted from 6 April 2022 (SI 2022/312). Words in paragraph 3(e) substituted and paragraph 3(ea) inserted from 6 April 2022 (SI 2022/312).

Appellant's reply

25.—(1) Subject to any direction given by the Upper Tribunal, the appellant may provide a reply to any response provided under rule 24 (response to the notice of appeal).

(2) [Subject to paragraph (2A), any] reply provided under paragraph (1) must be in writing and must be sent or delivered to the Upper Tribunal so that it is received within one month after the date on which the Upper Tribunal sent a copy of the response to the appellant.

[(2A) In an asylum case or an immigration case, the time limit in paragraph (2) is one month after the date on which the Upper Tribunal sent a copy of the response to the appellant, or five days before the hearing of the appeal, whichever is the earlier.]

[(2B) In a quality contracts scheme case, the time limit in paragraph (2) is 1 month from the date on which the respondent sent a copy of the response to the appellant.]

(3) When the Upper Tribunal receives the reply it must send a copy of the reply and any accompanying documents to each respondent.

[(4) Paragraph (3) does not apply in a quality contracts scheme case, in respect of which Schedule A1 makes alternative and further provision.]

Note: Words in square brackets in paragraph (2) substituted from 15 February 2010 (SI 2010/44). Paragraphs (2B) and (4) inserted from 21 August 2015 (SI 2015/1510). Paragraph (2A) substituted from 21 July 2020 (SI 2020/651).

References under the Forfeiture Act 1982

26.—(1) If a question arises which is required to be determined by the Upper Tribunal under section 4 of the Forfeiture Act 1982, the person to whom the application for the relevant benefit or advantage has been made must refer the question to the Upper Tribunal.

(2) The reference must be in writing and must include—

(a) a statement of the question for determination;

(b) a statement of the relevant facts;

(c) the grounds upon which the reference is made; and

(d) an address for sending documents to the person making the reference and each respondent.

(3) When the Upper Tribunal receives the reference it must send a copy of the reference and any accompanying documents to each respondent.

(4) Rules 24 (response to the notice of appeal) and 25 (appellant's reply) apply to a reference made under this rule as if it were a notice of appeal.

[Cases transferred or referred to the Upper Tribunal, applications made directly to the Upper Tribunal {, cases where an offence has been certified}and proceedings without notice to a respondent

26A.—[(1) Paragraphs (2) and (3) apply to—

(a) a case transferred or referred to the Upper Tribunal from the First-tier Tribunal; [. . .]

(b) a case, other than an appeal or a case to which rule 26 (references under the Forfeiture Act 1982) applies, which is started by an application made directly to the Upper Tribunal [;or

(c) a case where an offence has been certified to the Upper Tribunal.]

(2) In a case to which this paragraph applies—

(a) the Upper Tribunal must give directions as to the procedure to be followed in the consideration and disposal of the proceedings;

[(aa) in a reference under Schedule 1D of the Charities Act 1993, the Upper Tribunal may give directions providing for an application to join the proceedings as a party and the time within which it may be made; and]

(b) the preceding rules in this Part will only apply to the proceedings to the extent provided for by such directions.

(3) If a case or matter to which this paragraph applies is to be determined without notice to or the involvement of a respondent—

(a) any provision in these Rules requiring a document to be provided by or to a respondent; and

(b) any other provision in these Rules permitting a respondent to participate in the proceedings does not apply to that case or matter.]

[(4) Schedule 2 makes further provision for national security certificate appeals transferred to the Upper Tribunal.]

Note: Rule 26A inserted from 1 April 2009 (SI 2009/274). Paragraph (1) substituted from 1 September 2009 (SI 2009/1975). Word 'or' omitted from end of paragraph (1)(a) and paragraph (1)(c) inserted from 3 June 2019 (SI 2019/925). Paragraph (4) inserted from 18 January 2010 (SI 2010/43). Subparagraph (2)(aa) inserted from 6 April 2012 (SI 2012/500). Words in curly brackets inserted in heading from 3 June 2019 (SI 2019/925).

[Financial services cases [and wholesale energy cases]

26B. Schedule 3 makes provision for financial services cases [and wholesale energy cases].]

Note: Rule 26B inserted from 6 April 2010 (SI 2010/747). Words inserted from 6 April 2014 (SI 2014/514).

[Financial sanctions cases

26C. Schedule 4 makes provision for financial sanctions cases.]

Note: Rule 26C inserted from 27 July 2017 (SI 2017/723).

PART 4

JUDICIAL REVIEW PROCEEDINGS IN THE UPPER TRIBUNAL

Application of this Part to judicial review proceedings transferred to the Upper Tribunal

27.—(1) When a court transfers judicial review proceedings to the Upper Tribunal, the Upper Tribunal—

(a) must notify each party in writing that the proceedings have been transferred to the Upper Tribunal; and

(b) must give directions as to the future conduct of the proceedings.

(2) The directions given under paragraph (1)(b) may modify or disapply for the purposes of the proceedings any of the provisions of the following rules in this Part.

(3) In proceedings transferred from the Court of Session under section 20(1) of the 2007 Act, the directions given under paragraph (1)(b) must—

(a) if the Court of Session did not make a first order specifying the required intimation, service and advertisement of the petition, state the Upper Tribunal's requirements in relation to those matters;

(b) state whether the Upper Tribunal will consider summary dismissal of the proceedings; and

(c) where necessary, modify or disapply provisions relating to permission in the following rules in this Part.

Applications for permission to bring judicial review proceedings

28.—(1) A person seeking permission to bring judicial review proceedings before the Upper Tribunal under section 16 of the 2007 Act must make a written application to the Upper Tribunal for such permission.

(2) Subject to paragraph (3), an application under paragraph (1) must be made promptly and, unless any other enactment specifies a shorter time limit, must be sent or delivered to the Upper Tribunal so that it is received no later than 3 months after the date of the decision[, action or omission] to which the application relates.

(3) An application for permission to bring judicial review proceedings challenging a decision of the First-tier Tribunal may be made later than the time required by paragraph (2) if it is made within 1 month after the date on which the First-tier Tribunal sent—

(a) written reasons for the decision; or

(b) notification that an application for the decision to be set aside has been unsuccessful, provided that that application was made in time.

(4) The application must state—

(a) the name and address of the applicant, the respondent and any other person whom the applicant considers to be an interested party;

(b) the name and address of the applicant's representative (if any);

(c) an address where documents for the applicant may be sent or delivered;

(d) details of the decision challenged (including the date, the full reference and the identity of the decision maker);

(e) that the application is for permission to bring judicial review proceedings;

(f) the outcome that the applicant is seeking; and

(g) the facts and grounds on which the applicant relies.

(5) If the application relates to proceedings in a court or tribunal, the application must name as an interested party each party to those proceedings who is not the applicant or a respondent.

(6) The applicant must send with the application—

(a) a copy of any written record of the decision in the applicant's possession or control; and

(b) copies of any other documents in the applicant's possession or control on which the applicant intends to rely.

(7) If the applicant provides the application to the Upper Tribunal later than the time required by paragraph (2) or (3) or by an extension of time allowed under rule 5(3)(a) (power to extend time)—

(a) the application must include a request for an extension of time and the reason why the application was not provided in time; and

(b) unless the Upper Tribunal extends time for the application under rule 5(3)(a) (power to extend time) the Upper Tribunal must not admit the application.

(8) [Except where rule 28A(2)(a) (special provisions for [immigration judicial review] proceedings) applies,] when the Upper Tribunal receives the application it must send a copy of the application and any accompanying documents to each person named in the application as a respondent or interested party.

Note: Words in square brackets in paragraph (2) inserted from 1 April 2009 (SI 2009/274). Words inserted in paragraph (8) from 17 October 2011 (SI 2011/2343). Words in second square brackets in paragraph (8) substituted from 1 November 2013 (SI 2013/2067).

[Special provisions for [immigration judicial review] proceedings

28A.—(1) The Upper Tribunal must not accept an application for permission to bring [immigration judicial review] proceedings unless it is either accompanied by any required fee or the Upper Tribunal accepts an undertaking that the fee will be paid.

(2) Within 9 days of making an application referred to in paragraph (1), an applicant must provide—

(a) a copy of the application and any accompanying documents to each person named in the application as a respondent or an interested party; and

(b) the Upper Tribunal with a written statement of when and how this was done.]

Note: Rule 28A inserted from 17 October 2011 (SI 2011/2343). Words in square brackets substituted from 1 November 2013 (SI 2013/2067).

Acknowledgment of service

29.—(1) A person who is sent [or provided with] a copy of an application for permission under rule 28(8) (application for permission to bring judicial review proceedings) [or rule 28A(2)(a) (special provisions for {immigration judicial review} proceedings)] and wishes to take part in the proceedings must [provide] to the Upper Tribunal an acknowledgment of service so that it is received no later than 21 days after the date on which the Upper Tribunal sent, [or in {immigration judicial review} proceedings the applicant provided,] a copy of the application to that person.

(2) An acknowledgment of service under paragraph (1) must be in writing and state—

(a) whether the person intends to [support or] oppose the application for permission;

(b) their grounds for any [support or] opposition under sub-paragraph (a), or any other submission or information which they consider may assist the Upper Tribunal; and

(c) the name and address of any other person not named in the application as a respondent or interested party whom the person providing the acknowledgment considers to be an interested party.

[(2A) In {immigration judicial review} proceedings, a person who provides an acknowledgement of service under paragraph (1) must also provide a copy to—

(a) the applicant; and

(b) any other person named in the application under rule 28(4)(a) or acknowledgement of service under paragraph (2)(c) no later than the time specified in paragraph (1).]

(3) A person who is {provided with} a copy of an application for permission under rule 28(8) [or 28A(2)(a)] but does not provide an acknowledgment of service [to the Upper Tribunal] may not take part in the application for permission {unless allowed to do so by the Upper Tribunal}, but may take part in the subsequent proceedings if the application is successful.

Note: Word in square brackets in paragraph (2) inserted from 1 April 2009 (SI 2009/274). Words in curly brackets in paragraph (3) inserted from 1 April 2011 (SI 2011/651). Words inserted/substituted in paragraph (1), paragraph (2A) inserted and words in square brackets in paragraph (3) inserted/substituted from 17 October 2011 (SI 2011/2343). Words in curly brackets in (1) and (2A) substituted from 1 November 2013 (SI 2013/2067).

Decision on permission or summary dismissal, and reconsideration of permission or summary dismissal at a hearing

30.—(1) The Upper Tribunal must send to the applicant, each respondent and any other person who provided an acknowledgment of service to the Upper Tribunal, and may send to any other person who may have an interest in the proceedings, written notice of—

(a) its decision in relation to the application for permission; and

[(b) the reasons for any—

(i) refusal of the application or refusal to admit the late application, or

(ii) limitations or conditions on permission.]

(2) In proceedings transferred from the Court of Session under section 20(1) of the 2007 Act, where the Upper Tribunal has considered whether summarily to dismiss of the proceedings, the Upper Tribunal must send to the applicant and each respondent, and may send to any other person who may have an interest in the proceedings, written notice of—

(a) its decision in relation to the summary dismissal of proceedings; and

(b) the reasons for any decision summarily to dismiss part or all of the proceedings, or any limitations or conditions on the continuation of such proceedings.

(3) Paragraph (4) applies where the Upper Tribunal, without a hearing—

[(a) determines an application for permission to bring judicial review proceedings by—

(i) refusing permission or refusing to admit the late application, or

(ii) giving permission on limited grounds or subject to conditions;] or

(b) in proceedings transferred from the Court of Session, summarily dismisses part or all of the proceedings, or imposes any limitations or conditions on the continuation of such proceedings.

(4) [Subject to paragraph (4A), in] the circumstances specified in paragraph (3) the applicant may apply for the decision to be reconsidered at a hearing.

[(4A) Where the Upper Tribunal refuses permission to bring immigration judicial review proceedings [or refuses to admit a late application for permission to bring such proceedings] and considers the application to be totally without merit, it shall record that fact in its decision notice and, in those circumstances, the applicant may not request the decision to be reconsidered at a hearing.]

(5) An application under paragraph (4) must be made in writing and must be sent or delivered to the Upper Tribunal so that it is received within 14 days, [or in [[immigration judicial review]] proceedings 9 days,] after the date on which the Upper Tribunal sent written notice of its decision regarding the application to the applicant.

Note: Words inserted in paragraph (5) from 17 October 2011 (SI 2011/2343). Paragraph (4A) inserted and words in square brackets in (4) and in double square brackets in (5) substituted from 1 November 2013 (SI 2013/2067). Paragraphs (1)(b) and 3(a) substituted and words in square brackets in (4A) inserted from 6 April 2014 (SI 2014/514).

Responses

31.—(1) Any person to whom the Upper Tribunal has sent notice of the grant of permission under rule 30(1) (notification of decision on permission), and who wishes to contest the application or support it on additional grounds, must provide detailed grounds for contesting or supporting the application to the Upper Tribunal.

(2) Any detailed grounds must be provided in writing and must be sent or delivered to the Upper Tribunal so that they are received not more than 35 days after the Upper Tribunal sent notice of the grant of permission under rule 30(1).

Applicant seeking to rely on additional grounds

32. The applicant may not rely on any grounds, other than those grounds on which the applicant obtained permission for the judicial review proceedings, without the consent of the Upper Tribunal.

Right to make representations

33. Each party and, with the permission of the Upper Tribunal, any other person, may—

(a) submit evidence, except at the hearing of an application for permission;

(b) make representations at any hearing which they are entitled to attend; and

(c) make written representations in relation to a decision to be made without a hearing.

[Amendments and additional grounds resulting in transfer of proceedings to the High Court in England and Wales

33A.—(1) This rule applies only to judicial review proceedings arising under the law of England and Wales.

(2) In relation to such proceedings—

(a) the powers of the Upper Tribunal to permit or require amendments under rule 5(3)(c) extend to amendments which would, once in place, give rise to an obligation or power to transfer the proceedings to the High Court in England and Wales under section 18(3) of the 2007 Act or paragraph (3);

(b) except with the permission of the Upper Tribunal, additional grounds may not be advanced, whether by an applicant or otherwise, if they would give rise to an obligation or power to transfer the proceedings to the High Court in England and Wales under section 18(3) of the 2007 Act or paragraph (3).

(3) Where the High Court in England and Wales has transferred judicial review proceedings to the Upper Tribunal under any power or duty and subsequently the proceedings are amended or any party advances additional grounds—

(a) if the proceedings in their present form could not have been transferred to the Upper Tribunal under the relevant power or duty had they been in that form at the time of the transfer, the Upper Tribunal must transfer the proceedings back to the High Court in England and Wales;

(b) subject to sub-paragraph (a), where the proceedings were transferred to the Upper Tribunal under section 31A(3) of the Senior Courts Act 1981 (power to transfer judicial review proceedings to the Upper Tribunal), the Upper Tribunal may transfer proceedings back to the High Court in England and Wales if it appears just and convenient to do so.]

Note: Rule 33A inserted from 17 October 2011 (SI 2011/2343).

PART 5
HEARINGS

Decision with or without a hearing

34.—(1) Subject to [paragraphs (2) and (3)], the Upper Tribunal may make any decision without a hearing.

(2) The Upper Tribunal must have regard to any view expressed by a party when deciding whether to hold a hearing to consider any matter, and the form of any such hearing.

[(3) In immigration judicial review proceedings, the Upper Tribunal must hold a hearing before making a decision which disposes of proceedings.

(4) Paragraph (3) does not affect the power of the Upper Tribunal to—

(a) strike out a party's case, pursuant to rule 8(1)(b) or 8(2);

(b) consent to withdrawal, pursuant to rule 17;

(c) determine an application for permission to bring judicial review proceedings, pursuant to rule 30; or

(d) make a consent order disposing of proceedings, pursuant to rule 39, without a hearing.]

Note: Words substituted in (1) and paragraphs (3)–(4) inserted from 1 November 2013 (SI 2013/2067).

Entitlement to attend a hearing

35.—(1) Subject to rule 37(4) (exclusion of a person from a hearing), each party is entitled to attend a hearing.

[(2) In a national security certificate appeal the relevant Minister is entitled to attend any hearing.]

Note: Paragraph (2) inserted from 18 January 2010 (SI 2010/43).

Notice of hearings

36.—(1) The Upper Tribunal must give each party entitled to attend a hearing reasonable notice of the time and place of the hearing (including any adjourned or postponed hearing) and any change to the time and place of the hearing.

(2) The period of notice under paragraph (1) must be at least 14 days except that—

(a) in applications for permission to bring judicial review proceedings, the period of notice must be at least 2 working days; [and]

(aa) [. . .]

(b) [. . .] the Upper Tribunal may give shorter notice—

(i) with the parties' consent; or

(ii) in urgent or exceptional cases.

Note: Paragraph (2)(aa) and words at the beginning of paragraph (2) (b) omitted from 21 July 2020 (SI 2020/651). Word inserted at the end of paragraph (2)(a) from 21 July 2020 (SI 2020/651).

[Special time limits for hearing an appeal in a fast-track case

36A. . . .]

Note: Rule 36A inserted from 15 February 2010 (SI 2010/44) and omitted from 6 April 2021 (SI 2021/322).

Public and private hearings

37.—(1) Subject to the following paragraphs, all hearings must be held in public.

(2) The Upper Tribunal may give a direction that a hearing, or part of it, is to be held in private.

[(2ZA) Without prejudice to paragraph (2), the Upper Tribunal may direct that a hearing, or part of it, is to be held in private if—

(a) the Upper Tribunal directs that the proceedings are to be conducted wholly or partly as video proceedings or audio proceedings;

(b) it is not reasonably practicable for such a hearing, or such part, to be accessed in a court or tribunal venue by persons who are not parties entitled to participate in the hearing;

(c) a media representative is not able to access the proceedings remotely while they are taking place; and

(d) such a direction is necessary to secure the proper administration of justice.]

[(2A) In a national security certificate appeal, the Upper Tribunal must have regard to its duty under rule 14(10) (no disclosure of information contrary to the interests of national security) when considering whether to give a direction that a hearing, or part of it, is to be held in private.]

(3) Where a hearing, or part of it, is to be held in private, the Upper Tribunal may determine who is entitled to attend the hearing or part of it.

(4) The Upper Tribunal may give a direction excluding from any hearing, or part of it—

(a) any person whose conduct the Upper Tribunal considers is disrupting or is likely to disrupt the hearing;

(b) any person whose presence the Upper Tribunal considers is likely to prevent another person from giving evidence or making submissions freely;

(c) any person who the Upper Tribunal considers should be excluded in order to give effect to [the requirement at rule 14(11) (prevention of disclosure or publication of documents and information)];

(d) any person where the purpose of the hearing would be defeated by the attendance of that person[; or

(e) a person under [18, other than a young person who is a party in a special educational needs case or a disability discrimination in schools case]].

(5) The Upper Tribunal may give a direction excluding a witness from a hearing until that witness gives evidence.

Note: Paragraph (2A) inserted from 18 January 2010 (SI 2010/43) and Rule (2ZA) inserted from 10 April 2020 (SI 2020/416) and shall cease to have effect on the same day that, and immediately after, section 55(b) (public participation in proceedings conducted by video or audio) of the Coronavirus Act 2020(1) expires for all purposes (Rule 1(2) of SI 2020/416). Words in square brackets in paragraph (4)(c) substituted from 1 September 2009 (SI 2009/1975). Paragraph (4)(e) inserted from 1 April 2009 (SI 2009/274). Words in square brackets in para(4)(e) substituted from 1 September 2014 (SI 2014/2128).

[Coronavirus temporary rule (recording of remote hearings)

37A. . . .]

Note: Rule 37A inserted from 10 April 2020 (SI 2020/416) and omitted from 25 March 2022 (Rule 1(2) of SI 2020/416). Paragraph (4) inserted from 21 July 2020 and omitted from 22 March 2022 (Rule 1(2) of SI 2020/651).

Hearings in a party's absence

38. If a party fails to attend a hearing, the Upper Tribunal may proceed with the hearing if the Upper Tribunal—

(a) is satisfied that the party has been notified of the hearing or that reasonable steps have been taken to notify the party of the hearing; and

(b) considers that it is in the interests of justice to proceed with the hearing.

PART 6

DECISIONS

Consent orders

39.—(1) The Upper Tribunal may, at the request of the parties but only if it considers it appropriate, make a consent order disposing of the proceedings and making such other appropriate provision as the parties have agreed.

(2) Notwithstanding any other provision of these Rules, the [Upper] Tribunal need not hold a hearing before making an order under paragraph (1) [. . .]

Note: Words omitted from paragraph (2) from 1 April 2009 (SI 2009/274). Word inserted in (2) from 1 November 2013 (SI 2013/2067).

Decisions

40.—(1) The Upper Tribunal may give a decision orally at a hearing.

[(**1A**) Subject to paragraph (1B), in immigration judicial review proceedings, a decision which disposes of proceedings shall be given at a hearing.

(**1B**) Paragraph (1A) does not affect the power of the Upper Tribunal to—

(a) strike out a party's case, pursuant to rule 8(1)(b) or 8(2);

(b) consent to withdrawal, pursuant to rule 17;

(c) determine an application for permission to bring judicial review proceedings, pursuant to rule 30; or

(d) make a consent order disposing of proceedings, pursuant to rule 39, without a hearing.]

(2) [Except where [rule 22 (decision in relation to permission to appeal) or rule 22A (special procedure for providing notice of a refusal of permission to appeal in an asylum case)] applies,] the Upper Tribunal must provide to each party as soon as reasonably practicable after making [a decision (other than a decision under Part 7) which finally disposes of all issues in the proceedings or of a preliminary issue dealt with following a direction under rule 5(3)(e)] —

(a) a decision notice stating the [Upper] Tribunal's decision; and

(b) notification of any rights of review or appeal against the decision and the time and manner in which such rights of review or appeal may be exercised.

(3) [Subject to rule [14(11) (prevention of disclosure or publication of documents and information)],] the Upper Tribunal must provide written reasons for its decision with a decision notice provided under paragraph (2)(a) unless—

(a) the decision was made with the consent of the parties; or

(b) the parties have consented to the Upper Tribunal not giving written reasons.

(4) The [Upper] Tribunal may provide written reasons for any decision to which paragraph (2) does not apply.

[(5) In a national security certificate appeal, when the Upper Tribunal provides a notice or reasons to the parties under this rule, it must also provide the notice or reasons to the relevant Minister and the Information Commissioner, if they are not parties.]

Note: Words in square brackets in paragraphs (3) substituted and in (4) inserted from 1 September 2009 (SI 2009/1975). Paragraph (5) inserted from 18 January 2010 (SI 2010/43). Paragraphs (1A)–(1B) inserted from 1 November 2013 (SI 2013/2067). Words in first and third square brackets in (2) substituted and word in second square brackets in (2)(a) inserted from 1 April 2013 (SI 2013/477). Words in second square brackets in paragraph (2) substituted from 20 October 2014 (SI 2014/2128).

[Special procedure for providing notice of a decision relating to an asylum case

40A. . . .]

Note: Rule 40A omitted from 20 October 2014 (SI 2014/2128).

Part 7

Correcting, Setting Aside, Reviewing and Appealing Decisions of the Upper Tribunal

Interpretation

41. In this Part—

'appeal' [, except in rule 44(2) (application for permission to appeal),] means the exercise of a right of appeal under section 13 of the 2007 Act; and

'review' means the review of a decision by the Upper Tribunal under section 10 of the 2007 Act.

Note: Words in square brackets inserted from 1 April 2009 (SI 2009/274).

Clerical mistakes and accidental slips or omissions

42. The Upper Tribunal may at any time correct any clerical mistake or other accidental slip or omission in a decision or record of a decision by—

(a) sending notification of the amended decision, or a copy of the amended record, to all parties; and

(b) making any necessary amendment to any information published in relation to the decision or record.

Setting aside a decision which disposes of proceedings

43.—(1) The Upper Tribunal may set aside a decision which disposes of proceedings, or part of such a decision, and re-make the decision or the relevant part of it, if—

(a) the Upper Tribunal considers that it is in the interests of justice to do so; and

(b) one or more of the conditions in paragraph (2) are satisfied.

(2) The conditions are—

(a) a document relating to the proceedings was not sent to, or was not received at an appropriate time by, a party or a party's representative;

(b) a document relating to the proceedings was not sent to the Upper Tribunal at an appropriate time;

(c) a party, or a party's representative, was not present at a hearing related to the proceedings; or

(d) there has been some other procedural irregularity in the proceedings.

(3) [Except where paragraph (4) applies,] a party applying for a decision, or part of a decision, to be set aside under paragraph (1) must make a written application to the Upper Tribunal so that it is received no later than 1 month after the date on which the [Upper] Tribunal sent notice of the decision to the party.

[(4) In an asylum case or an immigration case, the written application referred to in paragraph (3) must be sent or delivered so that it is received by the Upper Tribunal—

(a) where the person who appealed to the First-tier Tribunal is in the United Kingdom at the time that the application is made, no later than twelve days after the date on which the Upper Tribunal or, as the case may be in an asylum case, the Secretary of State for the Home Department, sent notice of the decision to the party making the application; or

(b) where the person who appealed to the First-tier Tribunal is outside the United Kingdom at the time that the application is made, no later than thirty eight days after the date on which the Upper Tribunal sent notice of the decision to the party making the application.

(5) Where a notice of decision is sent electronically or delivered personally, the time limits in paragraph (4) are ten working days.]

Note: Paragraph (4) and words in square brackets in paragraph (3) inserted from 15 February 2010 (SI 2010/44). Word in second square brackets in (3) inserted from 1 November 2013 (SI 2013/2067).

Application for permission to appeal

44.—(1) [Subject to [paragraphs (4A) and (4B)],] a person seeking permission to appeal must make a written application to the Upper Tribunal for permission to appeal.

(2) Paragraph (3) applies to an application under paragraph (1) in respect of a decision—

(a) on an appeal against a decision in a social security and child support case (as defined in the Tribunal Procedure (First-tier Tribunal) (Social Entitlement Chamber) Rules 2008);

(b) on an appeal against a decision in proceedings in the War Pensions and Armed Forces Compensation Chamber of the First-tier Tribunal;

[(ba) on an appeal against a decision of a Pensions Appeal Tribunal for Scotland or Northern Ireland; or]

(c) in proceedings under the Forfeiture Act 1982.

(3) Where this paragraph applies, the application must be sent or delivered to the Upper Tribunal so that it is received within 3 months after the date on which the Upper Tribunal sent to the person making the application—

(a) written notice of the decision;

(b) notification of amended reasons for, or correction of, the decision following a review; or

(c) notification that an application for the decision to be set aside has been unsuccessful.

[(3A) An application under paragraph (1) in respect of a decision in an asylum case or an immigration case must be sent or delivered to the Upper Tribunal so that it is received within the appropriate period after the Upper Tribunal or, as the case may be in an asylum case, the Secretary of State for the Home Department, sent any of the documents in paragraph (3) to the party making the application.

(3B) The appropriate period referred to in paragraph (3A) is as follows—

(a) where the person who appealed to the First-tier Tribunal is in the United Kingdom at the time that the application is made—

(i) [twelve working days]; or

(ii) if the party making the application is in detention under the Immigration Acts, seven working days; and

(b) where the person who appealed to the First-tier Tribunal is outside the United Kingdom at the time that the application is made, thirty-eight days.

(3C) Where a notice of decision is sent electronically or delivered personally, the time limits in paragraph (3B) are—

(a) in sub-paragraph (a)(i), ten working days;

(b) in sub-paragraph (a)(ii), five working days; and

(c) in sub-paragraph (b), ten working days.]

[(3D) An application under paragraph (1) in respect of a decision in a financial services case must be sent or delivered to the Upper Tribunal so that it is received within 14 days after the date on which the Upper Tribunal sent to the person making the application—

(a) written notice of the decision;

(b) notification of amended reasons for, or correction of, the decision following a review; or

(c) notification that an application for the decision to be set aside has been unsuccessful.]

(4) Where paragraph (3)[, (3A)[, (3D) or (4C)]] does not apply, an application under paragraph (1) must be sent or delivered to the Upper Tribunal so that it is received within 1 month after the latest of the dates on which the Upper Tribunal sent to the person making the application—

(a) written reasons for the decision;

(b) notification of amended reasons for, or correction of, the decision following a review; or

(c) notification that an application for the decision to be set aside has been unsuccessful.

[(4A) Where a decision that disposes of immigration judicial review proceedings is given at a hearing, a party may apply at that hearing for permission to appeal, and the Upper Tribunal must consider at the hearing whether to give or refuse permission to appeal.

(4B) Where a decision that disposes of immigration judicial review proceedings is given at a hearing and no application for permission to appeal is made at that hearing—

(a) the Upper Tribunal must nonetheless consider at the hearing whether to give or refuse permission to appeal; and

(b) if permission to appeal is given to a party, it shall be deemed for the purposes of section 13(4) of the 2007 Act to be given on application by that party.

(4C) Where a decision that disposes of immigration judicial review proceedings is given pursuant to rule 30 and the Upper Tribunal records under rule 30(4A) that the application is totally without merit, an application under paragraph (1) must be sent or delivered to the Upper Tribunal so that it is received within 7 days after the later of the dates on which the Upper Tribunal sent to the applicant—

(a) written reasons for the decision; or

(b) notification of amended reasons for, or correction of, the decision following a review.]

(5) The date in paragraph (3)(c) or (4)(c) applies only if the application for the decision to be set aside was made within the time stipulated in rule 43 (setting aside a decision which disposes of proceedings) or any extension of that time granted by the Upper Tribunal.

(6) If the person seeking permission to appeal provides the application to the Upper Tribunal later than the time required by paragraph (3), [3A]{, 3D} or (4), or by any extension of time under rule 5(3)(a) (power to extend time)—

(a) the application must include a request for an extension of time and the reason why the application notice was not provided in time; and

(b) unless the Upper Tribunal extends time for the application under rule 5(3)(a) (power to extend time) the Upper Tribunal must refuse the application.

(7) An application under paragraph (1) [or (4A)] must—

(a) identify the decision of the [Upper] Tribunal to which it relates;

(b) identify the alleged error or errors of law in the decision; and

(c) state the result the party making the application is seeking.

Note: Paragraph (2)(ba) inserted from 1 April 2009 (SI 2009/274). Paragraphs (3A)–(3C) and numbers in square brackets in paragraph (6) inserted from 15 February 2010 (SI 2010/44). Paragraph (3D) and numbers in curly brackets in paragraph (6) inserted and numbers in square brackets in paragraph (4) substituted from 6 April 2010 (SI 2010/747). Subparagraph (3B)(a)(i) amended from 1 April 2011 (SI 2011/651). Paragraph (4A) and words in first square brackets in paragraphs (1) and (7) inserted from 11 December 2012 (SI 2012/2890). Paragraph (4A), words in second square brackets in (1) and (4) substituted from 1 November 2013 (SI 2013/2067). Word in first square brackets in (7) inserted from 11 December 2012 (SI 2012/2890), word in second square brackets in (7) inserted from 1 November 2013 (SI 2013/2067).

Upper Tribunal's consideration of application for permission to appeal

45.—(1) On receiving an application for permission to appeal the Upper Tribunal may review the decision in accordance with rule 46 (review of a decision), but may only do so if—

(a) when making the decision the Upper Tribunal overlooked a legislative provision or binding authority which could have had a material effect on the decision; or

(b) since the Upper Tribunal's decision, a court has made a decision which is binding on the Upper Tribunal and which, had it been made before the Upper Tribunal's decision, could have had a material effect on the decision.

(2) If the Upper Tribunal decides not to review the decision, or reviews the decision and decides to take no action in relation to the decision or part of it, the Upper Tribunal must consider whether to give permission to appeal in relation to the decision or that part of it.

(3) The Upper Tribunal must [provide] a record of its decision to the parties as soon as practicable.

(4) If the Upper Tribunal refuses permission to appeal it must [provide] with the record of its decision—

(a) a statement of its reasons for such refusal; and

(b) notification of the right to make an application to the relevant appellate court for permission to appeal and the time within which, and the method by which, such application must be made.

(5) The Upper Tribunal may give permission to appeal on limited grounds, but must comply with paragraph (4) in relation to any grounds on which it has refused permission.

Note: Word in square brackets in paragraphs (3) and (4) substituted from 1 November 2013 (SI 2013/2067).

Review of a decision

46.—[(1) The Upper Tribunal may only undertake a review of a decision pursuant to rule 45(1) (review on an application for permission to appeal).]

(2) The Upper Tribunal must notify the parties in writing of the outcome of any review and of any rights of review or appeal in relation to the outcome.

(3) If the Upper Tribunal decides to take any action in relation to a decision following a review without first giving every party an opportunity to make representations, the notice under paragraph (2) must state that any party that did not have an opportunity to make representations may apply for such action to be set aside and for the decision to be reviewed again.

Note: Paragraph (1) substituted from 17 October 2011 (SI 2011/2343).

[Setting aside] a decision in proceedings under the Forfeiture Act 1982

47.—(1) A person who referred a question to the Upper Tribunal under rule 26 (references under the Forfeiture Act 1982) must refer the Upper Tribunal's previous decision in relation to the question to the Upper Tribunal if they—

(a) consider that the decision should be [set aside and re-made under this rule]; or

(b) have received a written application for the decision to be [set aside and re-made under this rule] from the person to whom the decision related.

(2) The Upper Tribunal may [set aside the decision, either in whole or in part, and re-make it] if—

(a) [. . .]

(b) the decision was made in ignorance of, or was based on a mistake as to, some material fact; or

(c) there has been a relevant change in circumstances since the decision was made.

[(3) Rule 26(2) to (4), Parts 5 and 6 and this Part apply to a reference under this rule as they apply to a reference under rule 26(1).]

(4) [. . .]

(5) [. . .]

Note: Words inserted/substituted in heading, paragraphs (1) and (2), subparagraph 2(a) omitted, paragraph (3) substituted and paragraphs (4) and (5) omitted from 17 October 2011 (SI 2011/2343).

[Power to treat an application as a different type of application

48. The [Upper] Tribunal may treat an application for a decision to be corrected, set aside or reviewed, or for permission to appeal against a decision, as an application for any other one of those things.]

Note: Rule 48 inserted from 29 November 2010 (SI 2010/2653). Word in square brackets inserted from 1 November 2013 (SI 2013/2067).

SCHEDULE A1

RULE 23

Procedure in Quality Contracts Scheme Cases

. . .

Schedule 1

Rule 24(1)

Procedure after the notice of appeal in [road transport cases]

. . .

Schedule 2

Rule 26A(4)

Additional procedure in national security certificate cases

. . .

Schedule 3

Rule 26B

Procedure in Financial Services Cases [and Wholesale Energy Cases]

. . .

Schedule 4

Rule 26C

Procedure in financial sanctions cases

. . .

Practice Statement No.1 of 2022, of the First-tier Tribunal (Immigration and Asylum Chamber) on or after 13 May 2022

Tribunals Judiciary

JUDGE MICHAEL CLEMENTS

PRESIDENT OF THE FIRST-TIER TRIBUNAL IMMIGRATION AND ASYLUM CHAMBER

Practice Statement No 1 of 2022

Contents

Annex C — where an appeal is brought by a person without representation by a qualified person within the meaning of s.84 of the Immigration and Asylum Act 1999 (where the appellant appeals online not using MyHMCTS)
Annex D — Child, vulnerable adult and sensitive appellants guidance

Part 1
Preliminary

1. Background

1.1 This Practice Statement replaces all previous Practice Statements issued by the President insofar as they relate to the First-tier Tribunal (Immigration and Asylum Chamber).

2. Interpretation, etc.

2.2 In this Practice Statement:

"AEC" means Appellant's Explanation of Case "ASA" means Appeal Skeleton Argument

"the 2008 Order" means the First-tier Tribunal and Upper Tribunal (Composition of Tribunal) Order 2008 (as amended by the First-tier Tribunal and Upper Tribunal (Composition of Tribunal) (Amendment) Order 2018);

"President" means the President of the First-tier Tribunal (Immigration and Asylum Chamber);

"CMA" means a case management appointment before a Legal Officer; "CMR" means a case management review hearing before a Judge; "decision" includes any decision of the Tribunal;

"rule", followed by a number, means the rule bearing that number in the Tribunal Procedure (First-tier Tribunal) (Immigration and Asylum Chamber) Rules 2014;

"final hearing" means the hearing at which a Judge or panel decide the substantive issues in the appeal such that the appeal is either allowed, dismissed or brought to an end in some other way;

"record of proceedings" means the audio record of any hearing or CMA made by a judge or Legal Officer, or, in the absence of an audio record any notes, made in writing or digitally, howsoever stored or any written record made in its stead;

"Legal Officer" means a person approved by the President to carry out specified functions in the Tribunal.

Part 2

3. Where the Tribunal may not accept a notice of appeal (rule 22)

3.1 The Tribunal will scrutinise a notice of appeal as soon as practicable after it has been lodged. Rule 22 makes no provision for any issue arising under this rule to be determined by means of a hearing or by reference to any representations of the parties.

3.2 The fact that a hearing date may have been given to the parties does not mean that the appeal must be permitted to proceed. Accordingly, if at a hearing it transpires that the notice of appeal does not relate to a decision against which there is, in the circumstances, an exercisable right of appeal, the Tribunal must so find; but it will do so in the form of a decision and reasons, rather than by means of a notice under rule 22.

3.3 If an appellant appeals online a Legal Officer may only decide an issue under rule 22 if they have been authorised by the President and, in any event, may not do so after an ASA or AEC, as the case may be, has been uploaded.

3.4 If an appellant appeals offline a Legal Officer may only decide an issue under rule 22 if they have been authorised by the President and the appeal has not yet been listed for final hearing.

3.5 Judges and Legal Officers should not normally accept that it is impractical to start an appeal online by reason of temporary difficulties, such as those involved in registering with MyHMCTS or other problems of a technical nature, even where such problems may result in non-compliance with the time limits prescribed by rule 19. To prevent any disadvantage or unfairness that may otherwise result from such temporary difficulties, the following procedure should normally be followed in such circumstances –

(i) Where an appeal against an appealable decision is started offline and the Tribunal concludes that it would be reasonably practicable to start that appeal online, the appellant shall be notified that the appeal has been stayed for a period of three months under rule 4(3)(j) in the expectation that the appeal will be recommenced online.

(ii) Where the Tribunal accepts an online appeal that is substantially the same as an earlier offline appeal, those appeals should normally be consolidated under rule 4(3)(b).

(iii) Where an offline appeal against an appealable decision is brought within the relevant time limit prescribed by rule 19 and is stayed under (i) above, the Tribunal should normally grant an application to extend the time for starting an online appeal provided that (a) the online appeal is substantially the same as the earlier offline appeal, and (b) the online appeal was started within 14 days of being sent notice of the stay of the offline appeal. For the avoidance of doubt, all other applications for an extension of time to start an appeal (whether offline or online) should be determined upon their individual merits.

(iv) Where the stay of an offline appeal under (i) above ends without an online appeal being brought under (iii) above, the offline appeal shall be decided without a hearing under rule 25(1).

4. Circumstances in which it shall be deemed not reasonably practicable to commence an appeal by using MyHMCTS (pursuant to paragraph 2.4 of the Practice Direction)

4.1 Examples of circumstances in which it shall be deemed not to be reasonably practicable to commence an appeal using MyHMCTS will be published on the First- tier Tribunal website.

5. Review of decision of Legal Officer

5.1 Where a Legal Officer makes any decision then, in accordance with rule 3(4), the decision must include the following:

"The decision to issue this Notice was taken by a Legal Officer in exercise of a specified power granted by the Senior President of Tribunals under rule 3(2) of the Tribunal Procedure (First-tier Tribunal) (Immigration and Asylum Chamber) Rules 2014. You may within 14 days of the date of this notice apply to the Tribunal in writing for the matter to be considered afresh by a judge under rule 3(4) of the Tribunal Procedure Rules 2014."

6. Record of proceedings

6.1 Any application for access to the audio record or other written document made in its stead shall be made in writing to the President.

6.2. The application must include:

(a) the appeal reference number;

(b) the date or dates of the hearing or CMA in respect of which the application is made;

(c) the purpose for which access is sought;

(d) whether an anonymity order is in place with respect to that appeal;

(e) an undertaking that the record of proceedings will be used:

(i) only for the purpose or purposes stated in the application; and

(ii) that any conditions imposed will be adhered to;

(f) a statement as follows: *"I understand that a breach of the undertaking which I have given may result in contempt proceedings being brought against me."*;

(g) if a fee is required proof of payment of that fee.

Part 3

7. Presiding Judge

7.1 Where more than one member of the Tribunal is to decide a matter, the presiding judge for the purposes of article 7 of the 2008 Order and this Practice Statement is to be decided by the panel in advance of the hearing.

8. Transfer of proceedings

8.1 Where: —

(a) the Tribunal has started to hear an appeal but has not completed the hearing or given its decision; and

(b) the President or their nominee decides that it is not practicable for the original tribunal to complete the hearing or give its decision without undue delay, the President or their nominee may direct the appeal to be transferred to a differently constituted tribunal.

8.2 Where an appeal has been transferred under paragraph 8.1: -

(a) any documents sent to or given by the Tribunal shall be deemed to have been sent to the differently constituted tribunal; and

(b) the differently constituted tribunal will deal with the appeal as if it had been commenced before it.

9. Format of decisions

9.1 In order to ensure consistency in the formatting of decisions and statements of reasons, every decision of the Tribunal must: -

(a) state in the heading whether the appeal is being decided following a hearing or without a hearing and the hearing centre to which it relates;

(b) state, on each page, the reference number of the case;

(c) have a copyright symbol and year at the foot of the first page;

(d) state whether or not an anonymity order or direction has been made;

(e) state whether a fee award has been made and if so the amount, including, if appropriate, brief reasons for any reduction in the full award;

(f) state whether all the persons participating in the appeal were present in person and if not the means by which they participated;

(g) be set out in sequentially numbered paragraphs; and

(i) be signed and dated at its end or employ such electronic or other methods as the President may approve for signifying that the decision is finalised.

9.2 Where there is a panel comprising more than one judge the resulting decision will not express any dissenting view or indicate that it is that of a majority.

Part 4

10. Where an appeal is brought online using "MyHMCTS"

10.1 Model Directions appear at Annex A and will usually apply in all online appeals using MyHMCTS where an appellant is represented.

11. Where an appeal is brought, or case managed online, not using "MyHMCTS"

11.1 Model Directions appear at Annex B and will usually apply in all online appeals not using MyHMCTS. They should ordinarily be used where the Tribunal accepts that it is not reasonably practicable for the appeal to proceed using MyHMCTS.

12. Where an appeal is brought by a person without representation

12.1 Model Directions appear at Annex C will usually apply in appeals where the appellant is unrepresented and appeals online not using MyHMCTS.

12.2 Directions made by the Tribunal will take into account the means by which the appellant will communicate with the Tribunal, for example by ordinary post, other offline means or online.

13 Where an appeal is brought in any other circumstances.

13.1 Where the appellant appeals offline, by ordinary post or any other means and the Tribunal determines that it is in the interests of justice for the appeal to continue in that way, the Tribunal will make directions on a case by case basis using the directions above as the starting point but make such modifications as required having regard to the overriding objective.

PART 5

14. Child, vulnerable adult and sensitive appellants

14.1 In the case of a child, vulnerable adult and/or sensitive appellant, regard is to be had in the first instance to the latest version of the Equal Treatment Bench Book. Where it appears to the Tribunal that a Litigation Friend (in Scotland, Curator ad Litem), an Intermediary or a ground rules hearing may be required the matter shall be referred to the Resident Judge.

15. Anonymity directions and orders

15.1 When considering if an anonymity direction should be made, guidance issued by the President should be followed.

16 Granting of bail

16.1 When considering an application for bail, guidance issued by the President should be followed.
Michael Clements President FtTIAC
13 May 2022

PART 6

ANNEX A

Provision of documents in the online procedure

A.1 These Directions refer throughout to material being 'provided'. Material is provided only when it is uploaded on to the online system, whereupon an email notification will be sent to the parties that the new material has been provided. Time starts to run from when the material is provided.

Online Procedure

A.2 Grounds of appeal are not required when a Notice of Appeal is provided to the Tribunal in the online procedure.

A.3 *Respondent's Bundle.* Not later than 28 days after the Notice of Appeal is provided, the respondent must provide a bundle compliant with rule 24(1) of the Tribunal Procedure (First- tier Tribunal) (Immigration and Asylum Chamber) Rules 2014. This bundle must include the refusal decision and any material submitted in support of the application.

A.4 *Appeal Skeleton Argument.* Not later than 28 days after the respondent's bundle is provided, or 42 days after the Notice of Appeal, whichever is the later, the appellant must provide an Appeal Skeleton Argument ("ASA").

A.5 The ASA must contain three sections: (1) a brief summary of the appellant's factual case; (2) a schedule of issues; (3) the appellant's brief submissions on those issues which should state why the appellant disagrees with the respondent's decision with sufficient detail to enable the reasons for the challenge to be understood. A template is available online.

A.6 The ASA must:

(a) be concise;

(b) be set out in numbered paragraphs;

(c) engage with the decision letter under challenge;

(d) not include extensive quotations from documents or authorities;

(e) identify but not quote from any evidence or principle of law that will enable the basis of challenge to be understood.

A.7 *Appellant's Bundle.* Where the ASA refers to material which is not included in the respondent's bundle, that material must be provided in an indexed and paginated bundle at the same time.

A.8 *Respondent's Response.* Within fourteen days of the ASA being provided the respondent must undertake a meaningful review of the appellant's case, taking into account the ASA and appellant's bundle, providing the result of that review and particularising the grounds of refusal relied upon.

A.9 Pro-forma or standardised responses will be rejected by the Tribunal. The Review must engage with the submissions made and the evidence provided to the Tribunal.

A.10 The appeal will be actively case managed.

A.11 Any requirement set out above may be varied but in the absence of any such variation, the procedure set out above is to be followed.

A.12

Timetable

Period within which step is to be taken	*Action*
Day 1	Notice of appeal provided to Tribunal by MyHMCTS
Not later than 14 days after notice of appeal	Respondent's bundle ("RB") must be provided
28 days after provision of RB or 42 days after notice of appeal, whichever is later	Appellant must provide: (i) ASA (ii) Bundle of evidence in support
14 days after provision of appellant's ASA and evidence	Respondent must provide: Review with counter-schedule

Late Material

A.13 Any material provided outside the time limits may not be relied upon without leave.

A.14 Where any material is provided after 5 working days prior to the hearing, including on the day of the hearing, the Judge must deal with the admissibility of that material at the hearing as a preliminary matter.

A.15 A party may not rely on material which has not been provided.

A.16 If an application is made to admit material and

(a) the material is ruled inadmissible the material shall not be uploaded, though the Judge must give reasons in the Decision and Reasons for the exclusion of that material and identify the material excluded, and

(b) the material is admitted the Judge must stand the appeal down and cause the material to be uploaded as soon as reasonably practicable and will not proceed with the appeal until the material has been uploaded. The original material uploaded shall be returned to the party who provided it unless there is a good reason for not doing so.

A.17 A party may apply to adduce material after the hearing has concluded but only in exceptional circumstances. Such material will only be admissible upon application unless the Judge has directed the provision of that material. The application must be made using the online procedure, unless it is made orally at the hearing. Any material ruled admissible **must** be uploaded.

A.18 The Tribunal may not accept any material after the Decision and Reasons has been promulgated. This direction does not apply to any application for permission to appeal to the Upper Tribunal.

Change of Representation

A.19 In the event of the appellant either changing representation or becoming unrepresented the Tribunal must be notified as soon as reasonably practicable. The Tribunal will then make further directions.

ANNEX B
Provision of Information by the Parties

B.1 Within 5 working days of the date of this Notice parties must provide a direct contact number and dedicated email address to the Tribunal and to the other party to enable the Tribunal and the parties to communicate online and to take part in such remote hearings as are required.

Provision of Documents

B.2 These Directions refer throughout to material being 'provided'. Material must be provided by email to the email address which appears at the foot of this Notice and to the other party or made available in such remote hearings as are required.

Provision of Information by Respondent

B.3 Not later than 14 days after the date of this Notice, unless already provided, the respondent must provide a bundle compliant with rule 24(1) of the Tribunal Procedure (First-tier Tribunal) (Immigration and Asylum Chamber) Rules 2014. This bundle must include the refusal decision and any material which was submitted in support of the application.

Appeal Skeleton Argument

B.4 Not later than 28 days after the respondent's bundle is provided, or 42 days after the Notice of Appeal, whichever is the later the appellant must provide an Appeal Skeleton Argument ("ASA").

B.5 The ASA must contain three sections:

(a) a brief summary of the appellant's factual case;

(b) a schedule of issues;

(c) the appellant's brief submissions on those issues which should state why the appellant disagrees with the respondent' s decision with sufficient detail to enable the reasons for the challenge to be understood.

B.6 The ASA must:

(a) be concise;

(b) be set out in numbered paragraphs;

(c) engage with the decision letter under challenge;

(d) not include extensive quotations from documents or authorities;

(e) Identify but not quote from any evidence or principle of law that will enable the basis of challenge to be understood.

Appellant's Bundle

B.7 Where the ASA refers to material, which is not included in the respondent's bundle, that material must be provided in an indexed and paginated bundle at the same time.

Respondent's Response

B.8 Within fourteen days of the ASA being provided the respondent must undertake a meaningful review of the appellant's case, taking into account the ASA and appellant's bundle and provide the result of that review and particularise any additional grounds of refusal.

B.9 Pro-forma or standardised responses will be rejected by the Tribunal. The Review must engage with the submissions made and the evidence provided.

B.10 The appeal will be actively case managed.

B.11

Summary Timetable

Period within which step is to be taken	*Action*
Not later than 14 days after the date of this Notice	Respondent's bundle ("RB") must be provided
28 days after provision of RB or 42 days after notice of appeal, whichever is later	Appellant must provide: (i) ASA (ii) Bundle of evidence in support
14 days after provision of appellant's ASA and evidence	Respondent must provide: Review with counter-schedule

Late Material

B.12 Any material provided to the Tribunal outside the time limits provided for in paragraph 8 may not be relied upon without leave.

B.13 Where any material is provided after 5 working days prior to the hearing, including on the day of the hearing, the Judge must deal with the admissibility of that material at the hearing of the appeal as a preliminary matter.

Case Management and Listing

B.14 At each stage the appeal shall be considered by a Legal Officer or Judge who will decide on a case by case basis what additional directions, if any, are to be made in respect of that appeal and whether the appeal would benefit from a Case Management Appointment.

B.15 A party may apply at any time for a variation of these directions.

B.16 A party may apply at any time for a Case Management Appointment.

ANNEX C

Provision of Information by the Parties

C.1 Within 5 working days of the date of this Notice parties must provide a direct contact number and dedicated email address to the Tribunal and to the other party to enable the Tribunal and the parties to communicate online and to take part in such remote hearings as are required.

Provision of Documents

C.2 These Directions refer throughout to material being 'provided'. Material must be provided by email to the email address which appears at the foot of this Notice and to the other party or made available in such remote hearings as are required.

Provision of Information by Respondent

C.3 Not later than 14 days after the date of this Notice, unless already provided, the respondent must provide a bundle compliant with rule 24(1) of the Tribunal Procedure (First-tier Tribunal) (Immigration and Asylum Chamber) Rules 2014. This bundle must include the refusal decision and any material which was submitted in support of the application.

Appellant's Explanation of Case (AEC)

C.4 Not later than 28 days after the respondent's bundle is provided, or 42 days after the Notice of Appeal, whichever is the later, the appellant must provide an explanation of their case. This should contain reasons why the appellant believes the decision giving rise to the appeal is wrong. This is to enable the respondent to review the decision. (Upon receipt of the AEC a Tribunal Case Worker will consider, before the document is sent to the Respondent, whether there should be a Case Management Appointment to enable the appellant to identify the issues in the appeal).

Appellant's Bundle

C.5 Where the AEC refers to material, which is not included in the respondent's bundle, that material must be provided in a paginated bundle at the same time.

Respondent's Response

C.6 Within fourteen days of the AEC being provided the respondent must undertake a meaningful review of the appellant's case, taking into account the AEC and appellant's bundle, and provide the result of that review and particularise any additional grounds of refusal.

C.7 Pro-forma or standardised responses will be rejected by the Tribunal. The Review must engage with the submissions made and the evidence provided.

C.8 The appeal will be actively case managed.

C.9

Summary Timetable

Period within which step is to be taken	Action
Not later than 14 days after the date of this Notice	Respondent's bundle ("RB") must be provided
28 days after provision of RB or 42 days after notice of appeal, whichever is later	Appellant must provide: Appellant's Explanation of Case Bundle of evidence in support
14 days after provision of appellant's AEC and evidence	Respondent must provide: Review with counter-schedule

Late Material

C.10 Any material provided to the Tribunal outside the time limits provided for in directions may not be relied upon without permission from the Tribunal.

C.11 Where any material is provided after 5 working days prior to the hearing, including on the day of the hearing, the Judge must deal with the admissibility of that material at the hearing of the appeal as a preliminary matter.

Case Management and Listing

C.12 At each stage the appeal shall be considered by a Legal Officer or Judge who will decide on a case by case basis what additional directions, if any, are to be made in respect of that appeal and whether the appeal would benefit from a Case Management Appointment.

C.13 A party may apply at any time for a variation of these directions.

C.14 A party may apply at any time for a Case Management Appointment.

Change of Representation

C.15 In the event of the appellant becoming represented the Tribunal must be notified as soon as reasonably practicable. The Tribunal will then make further directions.

Practice Direction of the Immigration and Asylum Chamber of the First-tier Tribunal on or after 13 May 2022

Contents

PART 1

PRELIMINARY

1. Interpretation, etc.

1.1. In this Practice Direction:

"the 2007 Act" means the Tribunals, Courts and Enforcement Act 2007; "AIT" means the Asylum and Immigration Tribunal;

"audio recording" includes a digital or analogue recording, as well as a video recording which includes an audio recording;

"ASA" means an Appeal Skeleton Argument, which must contain three sections:

(1) a brief summary of the appellant's factual case;

(2) a schedule of issues;

(3) the appellant's brief submissions on those issues, which should state why the appellant disagrees with the respondent's decision with sufficient detail to enable the reasons for the challenge to be understood;

and must:

(a) be concise;

(b) be set out in numbered paragraphs;

(c) engage with the decision letter under challenge;

(d) not include extensive quotations from documents or authorities; and

(e) identify but not quote from any evidence or principle of law that will enable the basis of challenge to be understood;

"child" means a person who has not attained the age of 18;

"CMA" means a Case Management Appointment before a Legal Officer; "CMR" means a Case Management Review hearing before a Judge;

"final hearing" means a hearing at which the appeal is expected to be allowed, dismissed or brought to an end in some other way;

"IAT" means the Immigration Appeal Tribunal;

"Legal Officer" means a member of staff appointed under section 40(1) of the 2007 Act or section 2(1) of the Courts Act 2003 and designated as a Legal Officer by the President;

"linked appeal" means an appeal where the appeal of one or more appellants raise common issues;

"offline appeal" means an appeal that is started by means other than using the MyHMCTS platform;

"online appeal" means an appeal that is started using the MyHMCTS platform; "Practice Statement" means a statement of guidance by the Immigration and Asylum Chamber President of the First-tier Tribunal made under paragraph 7 of Schedule 4 to the 2007 Act.

"rule", followed by a number, means the rule bearing that number in the Tribunal Procedure (First-tier Tribunal) (Immigration and Asylum Chamber) Rules 2014;

"sensitive witness" means an adult witness where the quality of evidence given by the witness is likely to be diminished by reason of fear or distress on the part of the witness in connection with giving evidence in the appeal;

"the President" means the President of the Immigration and Asylum Chamber of the First- tier Tribunal;

"the Tribunal" means the Immigration and Asylum Chamber of the First-tier Tribunal;

"vulnerable adult" has the same meaning as in the Safeguarding Vulnerable Groups Act 2006.

1.2. Except where expressly stated to the contrary, any reference in this Practice Direction to an enactment is a reference to that enactment as amended by or under any other enactment.

1.3. Other expressions in this Practice Direction have the same meanings as in the 2007 Act.

1.4. Unless the contrary expressly appears this Practice Direction replaces all previous Practice Directions relating to the Tribunal. Where any previous Practice Directions which this Practice Direction replaces made provision in part or in whole to the Upper Tribunal, this Practice Direction relates only to the First-tier Tribunal. Any such previous Practice Directions therefore are to be read as if they do not apply to the First-tier Tribunal.

PART 2

2. Starting an appeal in the Tribunal

2.1 All appeals to the Tribunal must be started using the online procedure (accessed through MyHMCTS) unless it is not reasonably practicable to do so.

2.2 Where it is not reasonably practicable to start an appeal by using MyHMCTS, the notice of appeal must be in the appropriate form as displayed on the Gov.uk website at the time when the notice is given, or that form with any variations that circumstances may require.

2.3 Where an appellant asserts that it is not reasonably practicable to start an appeal by using MyHMCTS, the appellant must at the same time state why it is not reasonably practicable to do so. If the Tribunal agrees, the appellant may proceed without using MyHMCTS. In such a case, the notice of appeal must set out the grounds of appeal relied upon.

2.4 The President may issue Practice Statements to judges and Legal Officers as to those circumstances in which the Tribunal will or is likely to accept that it is not reasonably practicable to start an online appeal.

2.5 Where the Tribunal does not accept an offline appeal, the appellant must provide the Tribunal with the following information when making any consequential application to extend the time for bringing an online appeal:

(i) the date when the offline appeal was provided and its appeal number;

(ii) the date when the Tribunal declined to accept it.

2.6 In linked appeals the appellant must provide to the Tribunal the notice of appeal together with the reference number or numbers of any linked appeals if known. If an appeal becomes linked after the bringing of an appeal the appellant must provide to the Tribunal the reference number or numbers of any linked appeals as soon as reasonably practicable.

2.7 The President may issue Practice Statements setting out directions which shall ordinarily apply:

(a) where an appeal is brought online using "MyHMCTS";

(b) where an appeal is brought not using "MyHMCTS";

(c) where an appeal is brought by a person without representation; and

(d) where an appeal is brought in any other circumstances.

2.8 An appellant without representation, or an appellant in an offline appeal, does not need to provide an ASA.

2.9 Subject to the above, the form of notice approved for the purpose of:

(a) rule 19 (notice of appeal); and

(b) rule 33 (application for permission to appeal);

as the case may be, is the appropriate form as displayed on the Tribunal's website at the time when the notice is given, or that form with any variations that circumstances may require.

3. Case Management

3.1 Upon receipt of a notice of appeal the Tribunal will take steps in the order in which they appear below:

(a) decide whether there is a right of appeal against the decision to which it relates;

(b) decide whether the appeal has been brought in time, and if not whether to allow an extension of time;

(c) issue any directions.

3.2 The Tribunal will hold a CMA or CMR whenever it considers it necessary to do so in order to further the overriding objective of dealing with cases fairly and justly under rule 2. This will include (but will not be limited to) holding a CMA or CMR for the purpose of –

(a) identifying and/or narrowing the issues, and consequentially the evidence necessary to decide the appeal;

(b) dealing with preliminary issues;

(c) deciding any applications made by either party;

(d) giving case management directions;

(e) deciding the mode of hearing;

(f) fixing a date for the final hearing.

3.3 It is important that the parties and their representatives understand that a CMR is a hearing in the appeal and that the appeal may be decided if a party does not appear and is not represented at that hearing.

3.4 In addition to the directions referred to above, at the end of a CMA or CMR the Tribunal will also give to the parties written confirmation of:

(a) any issues that have been agreed at a CMA or CMR as being relevant to the appeal; and

(b) any concessions made by a party.

4. Adjournments

4.1. An application for the adjournment of an appeal must be made no later than 16:00 one clear working day before the date of the hearing.

4.2. For the avoidance of doubt, where a case is listed for hearing on, for example, a Monday, the application must be received by 16:00 on the previous Thursday.

4.3. An application for an adjournment must be supported by full reasons.

4.4. Any application made later than the end of the period mentioned in paragraph 4.1 must be made at the hearing and will, save in exceptional circumstances, require the attendance of the party or the representative of the party seeking the adjournment.

4.5. Parties must not assume that an application will be successful even if made in accordance with paragraph 4.1.

4.6 If an adjournment is not granted and the party fails to attend the hearing, the Tribunal may proceed with the hearing in that party's absence.

5. Evidence Generally

5.1 A witness statement should be capable of standing as the totality of the evidence in chief of the person giving that statement.

5.2 A witness statement may be added to by the provision of a supplementary statement provided that the supplementary statement is filed and served in accordance with any directions given in the appeal.

5.3 Only in exceptional circumstances and with the leave of the Tribunal, will a witness be permitted to provide additional evidence in chief.

5.4 Where a hearing is adjourned because of the introduction of late evidence the Tribunal will consider whether to exercise its costs powers.

Body of witness statement

5.5 The witness statement must, if practicable, be in the intended witness's own words and must in any event be drafted in a language they understand. The statement should be expressed in the first person and should also state:

(a) the full name of the witness,

(b) their place of residence or, if they are making the statement in their professional, business or other occupational capacity, the address at which they work, the position they hold and the name of their firm or employer,

(c) their occupation, if they have one,

(d) the fact that they are a party to the proceedings or are the employee of such a party if it be the case, and

(e) the process by which it has been prepared, for example, face-to-face, over the telephone, and/or through an interpreter.

5.6 A witness statement must indicate:

(a) which of the statements in it are made from the witness's own knowledge and which are matters of information or belief, and

(b) the source for any matters of information or belief.

5.7 An exhibit used in conjunction with a witness statement should be verified and identified by the witness and remain separate from the witness statement.

5.8 Where a witness refers to an exhibit or exhibits, they should state 'I refer to the (description of exhibit) marked ... ''.

5.9 Where a witness makes more than one witness statement to which there are exhibits, in the same proceedings, the numbering of the exhibits should run consecutively throughout and not start again with each witness statement.

Statement of Truth

5.10 A witness statement is the equivalent of the oral evidence which that witness would, if called, give in evidence. It must include a statement by the intended witness in their own language that they believe the facts in it are true.

5.11 To verify a witness statement the statement of truth is as follows:

> 'I believe that the facts stated in this witness statement are true. I understand that proceedings for contempt of court may be brought against anyone who makes, or causes to be made, a false statement in a document verified by a statement of truth without an honest belief in its truth.'

5.12 Where a witness statement is in a language other than English—

(a) the party wishing to rely on it must—

(i) have it translated; and

(ii) file the translation and the foreign language witness statement with the tribunal; and

(b) the translator must sign the original statement and must certify that the translation is accurate.

6. Expert evidence

6.1 An expert's report should be addressed to the Tribunal and not to the party from whom the expert has received instructions.

6.2. An expert's report must:

(a) give details of the expert's qualifications;

(b) give details of any literature or other material which the expert has relied on in making the report;

(c) contain a statement setting out the substance of all facts and instructions given to the expert which are material to the opinions expressed in the report or upon which those opinions are based;

(d) make clear which of the facts stated in the report are within the expert's own knowledge;

(e) say who carried out any examination, measurement or other procedure which the expert has used for the report, give the qualifications of that person, and say whether or not the procedure has been carried out under the expert's supervision;

(f) where there is a range of opinion on the matters dealt with in the report:

(i) summarise the range of opinion, so far as reasonably practicable, and

(ii) give reasons for the expert's own opinion;

(g) contain a summary of the conclusions reached;

(h) if the expert is not able to give an opinion without qualification, state the qualification; and

(i) contain a statement that the expert understands his or her duty to the Tribunal and has complied and will continue to comply with that duty.

6.3 An expert's report must be verified by a statement of truth as well as containing the statements required in paragraph 6.2(h) and (i).

6.4 The form of the statement of truth is as follows: *"I confirm that insofar as the facts stated in my report are within my own knowledge I have made clear which they are and I believe them to be true, and that the opinions I have expressed represent my true and complete professional opinion"*.

7. Circumstances under which a child, vulnerable adult or sensitive witness may give evidence

7.1 Regard is to be had to the latest version of the Equal Treatment Bench Book produced by the Judicial College. Without prejudice to the forgoing regard is to be had to the following considerations.

7.2 A child, vulnerable adult or sensitive witness will only be required to attend as a witness and give evidence at a hearing where the Tribunal determines that the evidence is necessary to enable the fair hearing of the appeal and their welfare would not be prejudiced by doing so.

7.3 In determining whether it is necessary for a child, vulnerable adult or sensitive witness to give evidence to enable the fair hearing of an appeal the Tribunal should have regard to all the available evidence and any representations made by the parties.

7.4 In determining whether the welfare of the child, vulnerable adult or sensitive witness would be prejudiced it may be appropriate for the Tribunal to invite submissions from interested persons, such as a child's parents.

7.5. The Tribunal may decline to issue a witness summons under the Tribunal Procedure Rules or to permit a child, vulnerable adult or sensitive witness to give evidence where it is satisfied that the evidence is not necessary to enable the fair hearing of the appeal and must decline to do so where the witness's welfare would be prejudiced by them giving evidence.

Manner in which evidence is given

7.6 The Tribunal must consider how to facilitate the giving of any evidence by a child, vulnerable adult or sensitive witness.

7.7 It may be appropriate for the Tribunal to direct that the evidence should be given by telephone, video link or other means directed by the Tribunal, or to direct that a person be appointed as an intermediary, or where appropriate Litigation Friend (in Scotland, Curator ad Litem).

8. Citation of unreported decisions

8.1 A decision or judgment of any court or tribunal which has not been reported may not be cited in proceedings unless:

(a) the person who is or was the appellant before the Tribunal, or a member of that person's family, was a party to the proceedings in which the previous decision was issued; or

(b) the Tribunal gives permission.

8.2. An application for permission to cite an unreported decision or judgment must:

(a) include a full transcript of the decision or judgment;

(b) identify the proposition for which the decision or judgment is to be cited; and

(c) certify that the proposition is not to be found in any reported decision or judgment.

9. Starred and Country Guidance decisions

9.1 Reported decisions of the Upper Tribunal, the AIT, and the IAT, which are "starred" shall be treated by the Tribunal as authoritative in respect of the matter to which the "starring" relates, unless inconsistent with other authority that is binding on the Tribunal.

9.2 A reported decision of the Upper Tribunal, the AIT, or IAT, bearing the letters "CG" shall be treated as an authoritative finding on the country guidance issue identified in the decision, based upon the evidence before the members of the Upper Tribunal, the AIT, and the IAT that decided the appeal. As a result, unless it has been expressly superseded or replaced by any later "CG" decision, or is inconsistent with other authority that is binding on the Tribunal, such a country guidance case is authoritative in any subsequent appeal, so far as that appeal:

(a) relates to the country guidance issue in question; and

(b) depends upon the same or similar evidence.

9.3 A list of current CG cases will be maintained on the Upper Tribunal's website. Any representative of a party to an appeal concerning a particular country will be expected to be familiar with the current CG decisions relating to that country.

9.4 Because of the principle that like cases should be treated in like manner, any failure to follow a clear, apparently applicable CG case or to show why it does not apply to the case in question is likely to be regarded as a ground for appeal on a point of law.

10. Bail applications

10.1 The form for application for bail approved for the purpose of rule 38 is the appropriate form as displayed on the Gov.uk website at the time when the application is made, or that form with any variations that circumstances may require. Subject to rule 39(3), an application for bail must, if practicable, be listed for hearing within six working days of receipt by the Tribunal of the notice of application.

10.2 Any such notice which is received by the Tribunal after 15:30 on a particular day will be treated for the purposes of this paragraph as if it were received on the next business day.

10.3 An Upper Tribunal judge may exercise bail jurisdiction by reason of being also a First- tier Tribunal Judge.

11. Assignment of judicial functions in the First-tier Tribunal

11.1 Any case management function that has been delegated by the Senior President of Tribunals to a Legal Officer, in respect of which the President has also given their authorisation, will normally be exercised by a Legal Officer, subject to the right of a party to apply for any decision made by a Legal Officer to be considered afresh by a judge under rule 3(4).

11.2 Legal Officers will only be permitted to conduct a CMA where they have demonstrated their competence to the satisfaction of the President in accordance with the Practice Statement made under this Direction.

12. Record of proceedings

12.1 The Tribunal will keep a record of the proceedings of every hearing.

12.2 The record of proceedings referred to in paragraph 12.1 will normally be an audio recording rather than a written record. Accordingly, any written record of the proceedings taken by the Tribunal will only be disclosed to the parties if an audio recording was not made or has become unavailable.

12.3 Any application made to the Tribunal for disclosure of the record of proceedings shall be considered by the President.

12.4 If an anonymity direction or order has been made in relation to an appeal or any linked appeal then the President shall consider whether redaction or gisting of part or parts of the record of proceedings would permit disclosure of the record of proceedings.

12.5 If a case file is stored digitally then it will be sufficient to make provision (such as a hyperlink) within the digital file to access the record of proceedings.

12.6 The President may issue a Practice Statement to provide for, subject to any fee which may be payable, the manner and circumstances in which access to the record of proceedings may be made available as well as the use to which it may be put.

12.7 A breach of any conditions imposed by the President attaching to the disclosure of any record of proceedings may result in proceedings for contempt of court.

13 Practice Statements by President

13.1 In addition to those matters set out at paragraphs 2.4, 2.7, 11.2 and 12.6, the President may issue Practice Statements.

14 Judicial Titles and Forms of Address

14.1 In formal documents, judges' titles will be set out as follows:-

i) Upper Tribunal Judges sitting in the First-tier Tribunal will be identified in their written judicial decisions as "Upper Tribunal Judge X sitting in the First-tier Tribunal".

ii) Deputy Judges of the Upper Tribunal, whether or not they are also Judges of the First-tier Tribunal, will when sitting in the Upper Tribunal, but only when sitting in that capacity, be identified in their written judicial decisions as "Deputy Upper Tribunal Judge X".

iii) Resident Judges when sitting in the First-tier Tribunal will be identified in their written judicial decisions as "Resident Judge X of the First-tier Tribunal".

iv) Designated Judges when sitting in the First-tier Tribunal will be identified in their written judicial decisions as "Designated Judge X of the First-tier Tribunal".

v) Assistant Resident Judges and all other Judges of the First-tier Tribunal sitting in the First-tier Tribunal will be identified in their written decisions as "Judge X of the First-tier Tribunal".

vi) The decision will be signed indicating the capacity in which the judge is sitting: i.e. a Judge of the Upper Tribunal or a Judge of the First-tier Tribunal.

14.2 All judges are to be addressed as "Judge" or "Sir" or "Madam" as the case may be.

This Practice Direction is made by the Senior President of Tribunals with the agreement of the Lord Chancellor under section 23 of the 2007 Act.

13 May 2022
Sir Keith Lindblom
Senior President of Tribunals

Practice Directions
Immigration Judicial Review in the Immigration and Asylum Chamber of the Upper Tribunal

Contents

Part 1
Preliminary

1. Interpretation

1.1 In these Practice Directions:

'applicant' has the same meaning as in the UT Rules;

'the application' means the written application under rule 28 for permission to bring judicial review proceedings;

'immigration judicial review proceedings' has the same meaning as in the UT Rules;

'party' has the same meaning as in the UT Rules;

'respondent' has the same meaning as in the UT Rules;

'the Tribunal' means the Immigration and Asylum Chamber of the Upper Tribunal;

'UKBA' means the UK Border Agency of the Home Office;

'UT Rules' means the Tribunal Procedure (Upper Tribunal) Rules 2008 and 'rule', followed by a number, means the rule bearing that number in the UT Rules.

Part 2
Scope

2. Scope

2.1 Parts 3 and 4 of these Practice Directions apply to immigration judicial review proceedings.

2.2 Part 5 of these Practice Directions applies to proceedings to which Part 3 applies, where:

(a) a person has been served with a copy of directions for that person's removal from the United Kingdom by UKBA and notified that Part 5 applies; and

(b) that person makes an application to the Tribunal or a court for permission to bring judicial review proceedings or to apply for judicial review, before the removal takes effect.

2.3 In the case of proceedings transferred to the Tribunal by a court, the Tribunal will expect the applicant to have complied with all relevant Practice Directions of that court that applied up to the point of transfer. In the event of non-compliance, the Tribunal will make such directions pursuant to rule 27(1)(b) as are necessary and which may, in particular, include applying provisions of these Practice Directions.

Part 3
General Provisions

The application to bring judicial review proceedings

3. Form of application

3.1 The application must be made using the form displayed on the Upper Tribunal's website at the time the application is made.

4. Additional materials to be filed with the application

4.1 Without prejudice to rule 28, the application must be accompanied by:

(a) any written evidence on which it is intended to rely (but see paragraph 4.2 below);

(b) copies of any relevant statutory material; and

(c) a list of essential documents for advance reading by the Tribunal (with page references to the passages relied on).

4.2 The applicant may rely on the matters set out in the application as evidence under this Practice Direction if the application is verified by a statement of truth.

5. Bundle of documents to be sent etc. with the application

5.1 The applicant must file two copies of a paginated and indexed bundle containing all the documents required by rule 28 and these Practice Directions to be sent or delivered with the application.

6. Permission without a hearing

6.1 The Tribunal will generally, in the first instance, consider the question of permission without a hearing.

The substantive hearing

7. Additional grounds at the substantive hearing

7.1 Where an applicant who has been given permission to bring judicial review proceedings intends to apply under rule 32 to rely on additional grounds at the substantive hearing, the applicant must give written notice to the Tribunal and to any other person served with the application, not later than 7 working days before that hearing.

8. Skeleton arguments for the substantive hearing

8.1 The applicant must serve a skeleton argument on the Tribunal and on any other person served with the application, not later than 21 days before the substantive hearing.

8.2 The respondent and any other party wishing to make representations at the hearing must serve a skeleton argument on the Tribunal and on the applicant, not later than 14 days before the hearing.

8.3 Skeleton arguments must contain:

(a) a time estimate for the complete hearing, including the giving of the decision by the Tribunal;

(b) a list of issues;

(c) a list of the legal points to be taken (together with any relevant authorities with page references to the passages relied on);

(d) a chronology of events (with page references to the bundle of documents (see Practice Direction 9 below);

(e) a list of essential documents for the advance reading of the Tribunal (with page references to the passages relied on) (if different from that served with the application) and a time estimate for that reading; and

(f) a list of persons referred to.

9. Bundle of documents for the substantive hearing

9.1 The applicant must serve on the Tribunal and any other person served with the application a paginated and indexed bundle of all relevant documents required for the substantive hearing, when the applicant's skeleton argument is served.

9.2 The bundle must also include those documents required by the respondent and any other person who is expected to make representations at the hearing.

10. Agreed final order

10.1 If the parties agree about the final order to be made, the applicant must file at the Tribunal a document (with 2 copies) signed by all the parties setting out the terms of the proposed agreed order, together with a short statement of the matters relied on as justifying the proposed agreed order and copies of any authorities or statutory provisions relied on.

10.2 The Tribunal will consider the documents referred to in paragraph 10.1 above and will make the order if satisfied that the order should be made.

10.3 If the Tribunal is not satisfied that the order should be made, a hearing date will be set.

Part 4

Urgent Applications For Permission To Bring Judicial Review Proceedings

11. Request for Urgent Consideration

11.1 Where it is intended to request the Tribunal to deal urgently with the application or where an interim injunction is sought, the applicant must serve with the application a written 'Request for Urgent Consideration', in the form displayed on the Upper Tribunal's website at the time the application is made, which states:

(a) the need for urgency;

(b) the timescale sought for the consideration of the application (e.g. within 72 hours or sooner if necessary); and

(c) the date by which the substantive hearing should take place.

11.2 Where an interim injunction is sought, the applicant must, in addition, provide:

(a) the draft order; and

(b) the grounds for the injunction.

12. Notifying the other parties

12.1 The applicant must serve (by fax and post) the application form and the Request for Urgent Consideration on the respondent and interested parties, advising them of the application and that they may make representations.

12.2 Where an interim injunction is sought, the applicant must serve (by fax and post) the draft order and grounds for the injunction on the respondent and interested parties, advising them of the application and that they may make representations.

13. Consideration by Tribunal

13.1 The Tribunal will consider the application within the time requested and may make such order as it considers appropriate.

13.2 If the Tribunal specifies that a hearing shall take place within a specified time, the representatives of the parties must liaise with the Tribunal and each other to fix a hearing of the application within that time.

Part 5

Applications Which Challenge Removal

14. General

14.1 The requirements contained in this Part are additional to those contained in Part 3 and (where applicable) Part 4 of these Practice Directions.

14.2 Nothing in these Practice Directions prevents a person from making the application after that person has been removed from the United Kingdom.

15. Special requirements regarding the application

15.1 Without prejudice to rule 28, the application must:

(a) indicate on its face that this Part of these Practice Directions applies; and

(b) be accompanied by:

(i) a copy of the removal directions and the decisions to which the application relates; and

(ii) any document served with the removal directions including any document which contains UKBA's factual summary of the case; and

(c) contain or be accompanied by the detailed statement of the applicant's grounds for making the application.

15.2 If the applicant is unable to comply with paragraph 15.1(b) or (c) above, the application must contain or be accompanied by a statement of the reasons why.

15.3 Notwithstanding rule 28A, immediately upon issue of the application, the applicant must send copies of the issued application form and accompanying documents to the address specified by the United Kingdom Border Agency.

16. Referral in case of non-compliance

16.1 Where the applicant has not complied with Practice Direction 15.1(b) or (c) above and has provided reasons for not complying, and the Tribunal has issued the application form, the Tribunal's staff will:

(a) refer the matter to a Judge for consideration as soon as practicable; and
(b) notify the parties that they have done so.

17. Application clearly without merit

17.1 If, upon a refusal to grant permission to bring judicial review proceedings, the Tribunal considers that the application is totally without merit, that fact will be included in the decision notice.

These Practice Directions are made by the Senior President of Tribunals with the agreement of the Lord Chancellor. They are made in the exercise of powers conferred by the Tribunals, Courts and Enforcement Act 2007.

LORD JUSTICE CARNWATH
SENIOR PRESIDENT OF TRIBUNALS
17 October 2011

Amended By
SIR JEREMY SULLIVAN
SENIOR PRESIDENT OF TRIBUNALS
01 November 2013

Practice Statement
Immigration Judicial Reviews in the Immigration and Asylum Chamber of the Upper Tribunal on or After 1 November 2013

1. Introduction

1.1 This Practice Statement supplements the Senior President's Practice Direction (PD) in respect of applications for judicial review, where the application and the proceedings to which it relates are designated as an immigration matter, either in a direction made by the Lord Chief Justice in accordance with Part 1 of Schedule 2 to the Constitutional Reform Act 2005, or in an order made under section 31A(3) of the Senior Courts Act 1981, transferring a specific application from the High Court to the Upper Tribunal (hereafter the proceedings).[1]

1.2 The direction and the PD are available on the Senior President's web site at: http://www.judiciary.gov.uk/publications-and-reports/practice--directions/tribunals/tribunals-pd

1.3 References in this statement to the Upper Tribunal are references to the Immigration and Asylum Chamber of the Upper Tribunal; and references to Rules are to the Tribunal Procedure (Upper Tribunal) Rules 2008 as amended, available at the same location.

1.4 This Practice Statement replaces the Practice Statement: Fresh Claim Judicial reviews in the Immigration and Asylum Chamber of the Upper Tribunal on or after 29 April 2013.

2. Permission applications

Lodging

2.1 An application for permission to bring the proceedings may be made direct to the Upper Tribunal, where the application is designated as an immigration matter in the Lord Chief Justice's direction. That application may be filed at Field House, London[2] or at one of the regional centres of that Tribunal[3]. An application made to the High Court which falls within the Lord Chief Justice's direction will be transferred to Upper Tribunal, to be dealt with by that Tribunal. So too will any application that the High Court decides in the exercise of its discretion under section 31A(3) to transfer to the Upper Tribunal as an immigration matter. The relevant forms for an application to the Upper Tribunal may be found at http://www.justice.gov.uk/forms/hmcts/upper where there is also some guidance on their completion and submission.

[1] For the content of the application see UT rule 28(4).

[2] Field House, 15–25 Breams Buildings, London, EC4A 1DZ.

[3] Birmingham, Civil Justice Centre, Priory Courts, 5th Floor, 33 Bull Street, Birmingham, B4 6DS; Cardiff Civil Justice Centre, 2 Park Street, Cardiff, CF10 1ET; Leeds Combined Court, 1 Oxford Row, Leeds, LS1 3BG; Manchester Civil Justice Centre, 1 Bridge Street West, Manchester, M60 9DJ.

Considering permission

2.2 The application for permission will not be considered before the time for lodging an Acknowledgment of Service (AOS) has expired[4] unless:

i. the Respondent has indicated that no AOS will be lodged or has asked for urgent consideration of the application;

ii. an application for urgent relief to prevent removal has been refused and the judge considers it is appropriate to refuse the application for permission at the same time.

2.3 An application for an extension of time to lodge the application will be determined at the same time as the application for permission and permission will not be granted unless extension of time is allowed[5].

Extension of time

2.4 An application for an extension of time will be refused unless:

i. Satisfactory written reasons are given why the application was not made promptly and in any event within three months of the decision under challenge. In deciding what is 'prompt' regard may be had to any relevant time limits for statutory appeals[6].

ii. Any factual assertion made in the explanation is supported by evidence or an explanation of why such evidence has not been lodged.

No jurisdiction

A judge considering an application for permission made to the Upper Tribunal must transfer the application to the Administrative Court if the application is not within the Lord Chief Justice's direction. In such a case, the High Court may, nevertheless decide that the application should be transferred to the Tribunal on a discretionary basis (see paragraphs 1.1 and 2.1 above).

Permission decisions

2.6 Where the Upper Tribunal is entitled to grant the relief sought, the Upper Tribunal judge may, on considering the permission application:

i. Grant the application.

ii. Grant the application on some grounds and refuse it on others.

iii. Adjourn the application for permission to an oral hearing.

iv. Refuse the application.

2.7 Where the application is refused the judge may also:

i. Make any order for costs of the Acknowledgement of Service as is appropriate in all the circumstances.

ii. Curtail the period for renewal of the application from the 9 days permitted under the Upper Tribunal Rules[7]. The Upper Tribunal judge will normally curtail time for renewal to 7 days and may curtail time further where there is a compelling case for

[4] 21 days after sending see UT rule 29(1).
[5] UT rule 28(7).
[6] See also UT rule 28(3) (I month time limit for challenges of First-tier Tribunal decisions).
[7] UT rule 30(5).

expedition. The judge may also state that renewal of the application shall not operate as a bar on removal.

iii. Record that the application is considered to be totally without merit; and if so that any renewal of the application shall not operate as a bar on removal.

2.8 The judge must give brief written reasons for refusing the application or any part of it[8] and may give reasons for the other decisions made if considered appropriate to identify the issues or otherwise assist the preparation for the next hearing.

Renewed applications

2.9 Where a judge refuses the application on some or all grounds without a hearing, the applicant may apply by notice in writing for that decision to be reconsidered at a hearing. However, where the application has been refused and the decision records that the application is considered to be totally without merit, the applicant may not request the decision to be reconsidered at a hearing.[9]

2.10 Such notice must explain:

i. The grounds on which permission is being renewed;

ii. The basis on which the application is renewed; and

iii. The response the applicant makes to any reasons given by the judge in refusing permission.

2.11 A renewed application for permission will be listed promptly in a permission list at Field House, London. Save with the parties' consent or in urgent or exceptional cases, at least two days notice of such a hearing will be given to the applicant and any party that has served an AOS[10].

2.12 Legal representatives based outside London who wish to be heard by video link shall notify the Upper Tribunal in good time, giving details of the proposed arrangements. The Upper Tribunal will have regard to the guidance to be found in CPR 32PD32 (see in particular paragraphs 8–14 of Annex 3).

2.13 A renewed permission application shall be assigned a time estimate of 45 minutes, unless either party has previously applied to the Upper Tribunal explaining:-

i. why a longer hearing is necessary;

ii. what steps have or will be taken to keep the extension of time to the minimum necessary; and

iii. giving a realistic revised time estimate.

Decisions on renewed application

2.14 If permission is refused at a hearing[11], at the conclusion of that hearing the judge shall:

i. deliver a judgment giving the decision and explaining in summary terms why the application or any part of it has been refused[12];

[8] UT rule 30(1) (b).
[9] UT rule 30(4A); paragraph 2.7iii above.
[10] UT rule 36 (a) and (b).
[11] See UT rules 34 and 40.
[12] UT rule 40(1).

ii. consider an application made at that hearing for permission to appeal to the Court of Appeal. If no such application is made, the judge must nonetheless consider at the hearing whether to give or refuse permission to appeal[13]. If the judge considers that the circumstances warrant it, the hearing may, however, be adjourned for a short time, in order to give the party concerned more time to make his or her own application for permission to appeal.

iii. arrange for service of a written notice of the decision on the application and of the decision granting or refusing permission[14];

iv. consider any costs orders to be made arising from the application;

v. consider any application for a stay on removal pending an application made to the Court of Appeal for permission to appeal.

2.15 The Tribunal's permission is required if an applicant seeks to rely on grounds other than those for which the applicant has been given permission to proceed.

2.16 When a written notice is served refusing permission on all grounds at the oral hearing the decision is a decision of the Upper Tribunal which disposes of proceedings.

3. Urgent applications

3.1 An application for urgent consideration (an 'urgent application') under 11.1 of the Senior President's PD, can only be considered by a judge of the Upper Tribunal on the papers where the judicial review proceedings have been issued. Applications for urgent relief made before an application for judicial review has been made should accordingly be made to the Administrative Court.

3.2 An application for a stay on removal or an injunction must be accompanied by statement from the applicant's legal representative (i) explaining why the application is made urgently: (ii) stating when the decision under challenge came to the claimant's notice and justifying any delay since that date; and (iii) certifying that there is nothing in the application that the legal representative does not consider to be properly arguable. Such applications must be served on the respondent together with the application for permission.

3.3 An urgent application lodged after 9.30am and before 4.15pm on a working day will be considered by a judge of the Upper Tribunal that day. An urgent application lodged outside these times will be referred to a duty judge of the Queen Bench Division to consider, acting as a judge of the Upper Tribunal.

3.4 Special arrangements have been made for applications lodged at centres outside London for urgent applications made before permission is granted to be considered by judges at those centres before the case is transferred to Field House.

3.5 An urgent application for a stay on removal will be considered on the papers by a judge of the Upper Tribunal, unless the judge adjourns the application for an oral hearing at which both sides can makes submissions.

3.6 An application for an injunction requiring the respondent to return a person who has been previously removed from the United Kingdom may only be made after an oral hearing of which the respondent has notice.

[13] UT rule 44(4A) and (4B).

[14] UT rule 40(2).

3.7 Where a judge considers an urgent application on the papers, and concludes that further information is needed from the respondent, the judge may telephone the UKBA and seek the further information. A note shall be kept of any information supplied.

3.8 Where an urgent application is granted, the judge shall forthwith draw up an order and give short reasons for it that shall be sent to both parties.

3.9 Where an urgent application is refused, the judge shall give short written reasons for the decision and shall append to those reasons any material information obtained from UKBA.

3.10 An urgent application that is refused on the papers may be renewed orally to a judge of the Upper Tribunal upon application being made promptly to the Tribunal and notice given to the respondent. The Tribunal will list such application as soon as practicable in all the circumstances of the case.

3.11 A refusal of an oral urgent application is final.

3.12 The provisions of paragraphs 2.14 to 2.18 of this Guidance Note shall, so far as relevant, apply to urgent applications.

4. Costs

4.1 Where a judge of the Upper Tribunal makes an order that the applicant is to pay a sum to the respondent in respect of the acknowledgment of service or the costs of resisting an urgent application, pursuant to rule 10(3)(a) of the Upper Tribunal Rules and there has been no prior opportunity on the paying party to make representations or to have an inquiry into that party's means, the order takes effect as a provisional order subject to representations to be made in writing within 10 working days of the order.

4.2 Where no representations have been received within the time specified in the order, the order for costs shall become absolute. In other cases, the representations shall be referred promptly to the judge making the order or such other judge as is available for determination.

Sir Jeremy Sullivan
Senior President of Tribunals
01 November 2013

IMMIGRATION RULES

Immigration Rules
(HC 395)

Note: The version of the Immigration Rules set out below includes all amendments to the Rules published up to 20 July 2022. The annotations identify the amendments made since the last edition of this work, that is to say, the changes resulting from the 28 *Statements of Changes to the Immigration Rules* published between 7 December 2017 and (HC 309) and 20 July 2022 (HC 511). There is one further statement of changes published on 18 October 2022 which is not included in this edition. Amendments made prior to that are incorporated in the text but not identified in the annotations. Where amendments are subject to savings or transitional provisions (normally for applications for entry clearance or leave to remain made before a specified date) this is indicated in the annotations. There have been 29 statements of changes to the Rules since December 2017 and there are many provisions which have been amended multiple times. In such cases users may need to consult previous versions of the Rules: these are archived on the gov.uk website and can be accessed at www.gov.uk/government/collections/archive-immigration-rules. In addition, users of this work should be aware of the importance of checking what further amendments have been made after HC 511. All *Statements of Changes to the Immigration Rules* are published on the gov.uk website and can be accessed at www.gov.uk/government/collections/immigration-rules-statement-of-changes.

Laid before Parliament on 23 May 1994 under section 3(2) of the Immigration Act 1971.

INDEX

Appendices 2, A, AR, AR(EU), Armed Forces, B, C, E, ECAA: Extension of stay, ECAA: Settlement, EU, EU(Family Permit), F, FM, FM-SE, KoLL, SN, Settlement Protection, T, V: Visitor, Visitor: permitted activities, Visitor: Visa national list, Visitor: Permit Free Festival List, Visitor: Transit Without Visa Scheme, S2 Healthcare Visitor, Student, Short-term Student (English language), Child Student, Parent of a Child Student, Graduate, Skilled Worker, Skilled Occupations, Shortage Occupation List, Global Business Mobility Routes, T2 Minister of Religion, Representative of an Overseas Business, UK Ancestry, Global Talent, Global Talent: Prestigious Prizes, High Potential Individual, Scale-up, Start-up, Innovator, International Sportsperson, Sports Governing Bodies, Overseas Domestic Worker, Domestic Worker in a Private Household, Domestic Worker who is a Victim of Modern Slavery, Domestic Worker Statement, Temporary Work: Seasonal Worker, Youth Mobility Scheme, Youth Mobility Scheme: eligible nationals, Temporary Work: Creative Worker, Temporary Work: Religious Worker, Temporary Work: Charity Worker, Temporary Work: International Agreement, Temporary Work: Government Authorised Exchange, Government Authorised Exchange Schemes, Creative Worker Codes of Practice, Service Providers from Switzerland, Hong Kong British National (Overseas), Ukraine Scheme, Private Life, Settlement Family Life, ATAS: Academic Technology Approval Scheme (ATAS), English Language, KOL UK, Finance, Continuous Residence, and Relationship with Partner

---

Introduction

1. The Home Secretary has made changes in the Rules laid down by him as to the practice to be followed in the administration of the Immigration Acts for regulating entry into and the stay of persons in the United Kingdom and contained in the statement laid before Parliament on 23 March 1990 (HC 251) (as amended). This statement contains the Rules as changed and replaces the provisions of HC 251 (as amended).

2. Immigration Officers, Entry Clearance Officers and all staff of the Home Office will carry out their duties without regard to the race, colour or religion of persons seeking to enter or remain in the United Kingdom.

3. In these Rules words importing the masculine gender include the feminine unless the contrary intention appears.

Implementation and transitional provisions

4. These Rules come into effect on 1 October 1994 and will apply to all decisions taken on or after that date save that any application made before 1 October 1994 for entry clearance, leave to enter or remain or variation of leave to enter or remain other than an application for leave by a person seeking asylum shall be decided under the provisions of HC 251, as amended, as if these Rules had not been made.

[Provision for Irish citizens]

Note: Heading substituted from 23:00 on 31 December 2020 subject to savings for applications made before that time (HC 813).

5. [DELETED]

Note: Amendments from 1 October 2019 (HC 2631). Paragraph deleted from 23:00 on 31 December 2020 subject to savings for applications made before that time (HC 813).

5A. [DELETED]

Note: Paragraph inserted from 09:00 on 5 October 2020 subject to savings for applications made before that time (HC 707). Paragraph deleted from 23:00 on 31 December 2020 subject to savings for applications made before that time (HC 813).

5B. [DELETED]

Note: Paragraph inserted from 09:00 on 5 October 2020 subject to savings for applications made before that time (HC 707). Paragraph deleted from 23:00 on 31 December 2020 subject to savings for applications made before that time (HC 813).

[**5C.** Save where expressly indicated throughout these rules, these rules do not apply to an Irish citizen who as a result of section 3ZA of the Immigration Act 1971 does not require leave to enter or remain, but an Irish citizen who does require leave to enter or remain is covered by these rules.]

Note: Paragraph inserted from 23:00 on 31 December 2020 subject to savings for applications made before that time (HC 813).

[**5D.** Paragraph 5C does not apply to paragraph 11, Appendix EU, Appendix S2 Healthcare Visitor, Appendix Service Providers from Switzerland, Appendix EU (Family Permit), Appendix AR (EU), Part 11 (asylum) or Part 13 (deportation).]

Note: Paragraph inserted from 23:00 on 31 December 2020 subject to savings for applications made before that time (HC 813).

[**5E.** An Irish citizen who as a result of section 3ZA of the Immigration Act 1971 does not require leave to enter or remain is considered settled for the purposes of these rules.]

Note: Paragraph inserted from 23:00 on 31 December 2020 subject to savings for applications made before that time (HC 813).

Interpretation

6. [DELETED]

Note: Amendments from 11 January 2018 subject to savings for applications made before that date (HC 309). Amendments from 6 July 2018 subject to savings for applications made before that date (HC 1154). Amendments from 10 January 2019 subject to savings for applications made before that date; amendments from 1 August 2019 (HC 1779). Amendments from 29 March 2019 subject to savings for applications made before that date; amendments from 30 March 2019 subject to savings for applications made before that date (HC 1919). Amendments from 1 October 2019 (HC 2631). Amendments from 20 February 2020 subject to savings for applications made before that date (HC 56). Amendments from 09:00 on 5 October 2020 subject to savings for applications made before that time (HC 707). Paragraph deleted from 09:00 on 1 December 2020 subject to savings for applications made before that time (HC 813)

[**6.1.** In these rules, unless the contrary intention appears, references to paragraphs are to paragraphs of the Immigration Rules (HC 395 as amended) made under section 3(2) of the Immigration Act 1971, and references to Appendices are to Appendices to those rules.]

Note: Paragraph inserted from 09:00 on 1 December 2020 subject to savings for applications made before that time (HC 813).

[6.2. In these rules:

(a) references to primary and secondary legislation refers to that legislation as amended from time to time; and

(b) unless the contrary intention appears, the following definitions apply:

'Accompanying Person' in Appendix S2 Healthcare Visitor is a person with a healthcare right of entry and who is accompanying a patient (P) to the UK at the same time as P's entry into the UK, or who is joining P in the UK on a date after P's entry into the UK, for the purpose of providing P with care or support during their course of planned healthcare treatment.

'Accredited Institution' means an institution which is:

(a) the holder of a student sponsor licence; or

(b) the holder of valid accreditation from Accreditation UK, the Accreditation Body for Language Services (ABLS), the British Accreditation Council (BAC), or the Accreditation Service for International Colleges (ASIC); or

(c) the holder of a valid and satisfactory full institutional inspection, review or audit by Estyn, Education Scotland, the Independent Schools Inspectorate, Office for Standards in Education, the Office for Students, the Quality Assurance Agency for Higher Education or the Education and Training Inspectorate Northern Ireland; or

(d) an overseas higher education institution offering only part of its programmes in the UK.

'Adequate' and **'adequately'** in relation to a maintenance and accommodation requirement means that, after income tax, national insurance contributions and housing costs have been deducted, there must be available to the person or family the level of income or funds that would be available to them if the person or family was in receipt of income support.

'Administrative review' means a review conducted in accordance with Appendix AR, or where applicable Appendix AR (EU).

'Adoption' includes a de facto adoption in accordance with the requirements of paragraph 309A, and 'adopted' and 'adoptive parent' shall be construed accordingly.

'Agreement on the Free Movement of Persons' in Appendix Service Providers from Switzerland means the agreement between the Swiss Confederation and the European Union and its member states, which was signed in 1999 and came into force in 2002.

'Amateur' means a person who engages in a sport or creative activity solely for personal enjoyment and who is not seeking to derive a living from the activity.

'Applicant' means a person who is making an application for entry clearance, permission to enter or permission to stay (and a person seeking entry at the UK Border is to be regarded as making an application for permission to enter).

'Application for asylum' has the meaning given in paragraph 327 of these rules.

'Application for leave to remain' and **'application for permission to stay'** includes an application for variation of leave to enter or remain of a person in the UK.

'Application Centre' in the context of an application for entry clearance, means a commercial partner, a British Diplomatic Mission or Consular Post overseas, or designated government office overseas, authorised by the Secretary of State to take biometrics and receive documents from applicants for entry clearance.

'Approved Destination Status Agreement with China' means the Memorandum of Understanding on visa and related issues concerning tourist groups from the People's Republic of China to the United Kingdom as an approved destination, signed on 21 January 2005.

'Approved qualification' means a qualification which meets the Approved qualification requirements in Appendix Student.

'Approved sponsor' means a sponsor which is listed in the register of licensed sponsors: workers or register of licensed sponsors: students on the gov.uk website as being licensed for the relevant route of these rules and found at: https://www.gov.uk/government/publications/register-of-licensed-sponsors-workers https://www.gov.uk/government/publications/register-of-licensed-sponsors-students.

[**'Approved sponsor'** under the **Homes for Ukraine Sponsorship Scheme'** means a sponsor who meets eligibility and suitability requirements under the Homes for Ukraine sponsor guidance, published by the Department for Levelling Up, Housing and Communities at https://www.gov.uk/guidance/homes-for-ukraine-sponsor-guidance. Or, in the case of a child who is not applying with or to join their parent or legal guardian in the UK, a sponsor who is approved as a sponsor for that applicant under the Homes for Ukraine Scheme under the guidance: 'Homes for Ukraine - Applications to Homes for Ukraine for children who are not travelling or reuniting with their parent or legal guardian: Guidance for Councils'.]

Note: Definition inserted from 30 March 2022 (HC 1220). Definition substituted from 10 August 2022 (HC 511).

[**'Aunt'** in Appendix Ukraine Scheme means the sister, or step-sister, of either of the UK-based sponsor's parents, or the female partner of the UK-based sponsor's uncle or aunt.]

Note: Definition inserted from 30 March 2022 (HC 1220).

'Biometrics' has the same meaning as 'biometric information' in section 15 of the UK Borders Act 2007 and means, in particular, a record of a person's fingerprints and a photograph of a person's face.

'Biometric immigration document' means a document recording biometric information issued in accordance with regulations made under section 5 of the UK Borders Act 2007.

'Bona fide private education institution' is a private education institution which:

(a) maintains satisfactory records of enrolment and attendance of students, and supplies these to the Home Office when requested; and

(b) provides courses which involve a minimum of 15 hours' organised daytime study per week; and

(c) ensures a suitably qualified tutor is present during the hours of study to offer teaching and instruction to the students; and

(d) offers courses leading to qualifications recognised by the appropriate accreditation bodies; and

(e) employs suitably qualified staff to provide teaching, guidance and support to the students; and

(f) provides adequate accommodation, facilities, staffing levels and equipment to support the numbers of students enrolled at the institution; and

(g) if it offers tuition support to external students at degree level, ensures that such students are registered with the UK degree awarding body.

'Born in the UK or Islands' in Appendix UK Ancestry means born:

(a) in the UK; or

(b) in the Channel Islands (Bailiwick of Guernsey, Bailiwick of Jersey); or

(c) in the Isle of Man; or

(d) before 31 March 1922, in Ireland; or

(e) on a British-owned or registered ship or aircraft if the requirements of either section 50(7)(a) of the British Nationality Act 1981, or section 32(5) of the British Nationality Act 1948, as applicable, are met.

'BN(O) Adult Dependent Relative' means a person granted permission as a BN(O) Adult Dependent Relative under Appendix Hong Kong British National (Overseas).

'BN(O) Household Child' means a person falling within HK 15.1. and who is granted permission as a BN(O) Household Child under Appendix Hong Kong British National (Overseas).

'BN(O) Household Member' means a person granted permission as a BN(O) Household Member under Appendix Hong Kong British National (Overseas).

'BN(O) Status Holder' means a person granted permission as a BN(O) Status Holder under Appendix Hong Kong British National (Overseas).

'Breach of immigration laws' - a person is in breach of immigration laws for the purpose of these rules where the person is an overstayer; is an illegal entrant; is in breach of a condition of their permission; or used deception in relation to their most recent application for entry clearance or permission; and **'previously breached immigration laws'**—a person previously breached immigration laws if they overstayed or used deception in relation to a previous application for entry clearance or permission.

'Business day' means any day other than Saturday or Sunday, a day which is a bank holiday under the Banking and Financial Dealings Act 1971 in the part of the UK to which the notice is sent, Christmas Day or Good Friday.

[**'Cabotage operations'** in Appendix Visitor: Permitted Activities means

(a) in relation to goods, national carriage for hire or reward carried out on a temporary basis in the UK; or

(b) in relation to passengers either:

i. national road passenger services for hire and reward carried out on a temporary basis by a carrier in the UK, or

ii. the picking up and setting down of passengers within the UK, in the course of a regular international service, provided that it is not the principal purpose of the service.]

Note: Definition inserted from 23:00 on 31 December 2020 for decisions made on or after that time (HC 1043).

'Calendar year' means a year beginning on 1 January and ending on 31 December.

'Cancellation' in Part 9, Appendix S2 Healthcare Visitor and Appendix Service Providers from Switzerland means cancellation, variation in duration, or curtailment, of entry clearance or permission, which can take effect immediately or at a specified future date and whether the person is in the UK or overseas.

[**'Certificate of Sponsorship'** means either:

(a) an electronic document with a unique reference number issued by a sponsor via the Sponsor Management System, or

(b) confirmation of sponsorship, issued by a sponsor using the successor to the Sponsorship Management System, that confirms the details of the job for which the sponsor is sponsoring the applicant.]

Note: Definition substituted from 6 April 2022 (HC 1118).

['**Charity Worker**' means a person who has, or had, permission under any of the following:

(i) Appendix Temporary Work – Charity Worker; or

(ii) Appendix T5 (Temporary Worker) Charity Worker under the rules in force between 1 December 2020 and 10 October 2021 (inclusive); or

(iii) as a Tier 5 (Temporary Worker) migrant in the Charity Worker sub-category under part 6A of the rules in force before 1 December 2020.]

Note: Definition substituted from 09:00 on 11 October 2021 subject to savings for applications made before that time (HC 617)

'**Child**' means a person who is aged under 18 years.

'**Child Student**' means a person who has, or had, permission under Appendix Child Student, Appendix CS: Child Student under the rules in force before 1 December 2020, or as a Tier 4 (Child) Student under the rules in force before 5 October 2020.

'**Civil partnership**' means a civil partnership under or by virtue of the Civil Partnership Act 2004.

'**Close relative**' means a grandparent, brother, sister, step-parent, uncle (brother or half-brother of a child's parent) or aunt (sister or half-sister of a child's parent) who is aged 18 or over.

'**Common Travel Area**' is as defined in section 1(3) of the Immigration Act 1971.

['**Commonwealth citizen**' means:

(a) a British Overseas Territories citizen, a British National (Overseas), a British Overseas citizen or a British subject; or

(b) a citizen of a country listed in Schedule 3 to the British Nationality Act 1981]

Note: Definition substituted from 6 April 2021 subject to savings for applications made before that date (HC 1248).

'**Condition**' means a condition of leave to enter or leave to remain under section 3(1)(c) of the Immigration Act 1971, such as a prohibition on employment or study.

'**Confirmation of Acceptance for Studies reference number**' means a number which links to a single Confirmation of Acceptance for Studies that was assigned to a Student or Child Student by their student sponsor.

['**Consecutive engagements**' means where:

(a) the applicant is being sponsored for more than one engagement in the UK as a [Creative Worker] regardless of whether the applicant has engagements outside the UK that take place between those engagements in the UK; and

(b) the applicant will be sponsored by more than one sponsor for those engagements,

(c) each sponsor has issued a Certificate of Sponsorship on the [Creative Worker] route for the relevant engagement, or engagements; and

(d) there is no more than 14 days between each individual engagement in the UK, and for the purposes of calculating that 14-day period, time spent by the applicant outside the UK (including the dates of their departure from and return to the UK) will not be counted towards this period.]

Note: Definition substituted from 6 April 2021 (HC 1248). Words in (a) and (c) substituted from 6 April 2022 (HC 1118).

'**Contact point meeting**' means for the purpose of Appendix Start-up and Appendix Innovator a meeting between the applicant and their Endorsing body to assess progress against the applicant's business plan. For Start-up contact point meetings must be held at least after 6 months and 12 months from the date the application was granted. For Innovator contact point meetings must be held at least after 6 months, 12 months and 24 months from the date the application was granted.

'Control Zone' is as defined by article 2(1) of, and Schedule 1 to, the Channel Tunnel (International Arrangements) Order 1993 (SI 1993/1813) and article 2 of the Nationality, Immigration and Asylum Act 2002 (Juxtaposed Controls) Order 2003 (SI 2003/2818) (as amended from time to time).

[**'Course of study'** means the course for which a Confirmation of Acceptance for Studies was assigned, or a new course with the person's current student sponsor which they were permitted to study without applying for further permission on the Student route.]

Note: Definition substituted from 6 April 2021 subject to savings for applications made before that date (HC 1248).

'Confirmation of Acceptance for Studies' means an electronic document with a unique reference number electronically issued by a student sponsor via the Sponsor Management System, to a person who the student sponsor has agreed to sponsor, for use in an application as a Student or Child Student, in accordance with these rules.

'Conviction' means conviction for a criminal offence in the UK or any other country.

[**'Cousin'** in Appendix Ukraine Scheme means the biological, adopted or step-child of the UK-based sponsor's uncle or aunt.]

Note: Definition inserted from 30 March 2022 (HC 1220).

[**'Creative Worker'** means a person who has, or had, permission under any of the following:

(i) Appendix Temporary Work – Creative Worker; or

(ii) Appendix T5 (Temporary Worker) Creative or Sporting Worker, working in the creative sector under the rules in force between 1 December 2020 and 10 October 2021 (inclusive); or

(iii) as a Tier 5 (Temporary Worker) migrant in the Creative and Sporting sub-category working in the creative sector under part 6A of the rules in force before 1 December 2020 (inclusive).]

Note: Definition substituted from 09:00 on 11 October 2021 subject to savings for applications made before that time (HC 617).

'Crew member' has the same meaning as in the Immigration Act 1971.

'Curtailment', in relation to the curtailment of a person's leave to enter or leave to remain, means cancelling or curtailing their leave such that they will have a shorter period of, or no, leave remaining.

'Custodial sentence' means a period of imprisonment, not including a suspended sentence.

'Customs breach' means a breach of any provision of the Customs and Excise Acts or any other breach relating to an assigned matter (which is any matter in relation to which the Commissioners or officers of Her Majesty's Revenue and Customs have a power or duty which the Home Office may exercise at the border).

'Date of application' means:

If applying for entry clearance either:

(a) the date of payment of the relevant fee; or

(b) where a fee is not required, the date on which the application is submitted online; or

(c) where a fee is not required and an online application is not available, the date on which the paper application form is received by the Home Office.

If applying for permission to enter, the date the person seeks entry.

If applying for permission to stay:

(a) where the paper application form is sent by post by Royal Mail, whether or not accompanied by a fee waiver request form, the date of posting as shown on the tracking information provided by Royal Mail or, if not tracked, by the postmark date on the envelope; or

(b) where the paper application form is sent by courier, or other postal services provider, the date on which it is delivered to the Home Office; or

(c) where the application is made via the online application process, and there is no request for a fee waiver, the date on which the online application is submitted, and the relevant fee is paid; or

(d) where the application is made via the online application process, and includes a request for a fee waiver, the date on which the online request for a fee waiver is submitted, as long as the completed application is submitted within 10 days of the receipt of the decision on the request for a fee waiver.

'Decision maker' means an entry clearance officer, immigration officer or the Secretary of State, as the case may be.

'Deemed sponsorship status' [DELETED]

Note: Definition substituted from 09:00 on 11 October 2021 subject to savings for applications made before that time (HC 617). Definition deleted from 6 April 2022 (HC 1118).

'Degree level study' means a course which leads to a recognised UK bachelor's degree, or an equivalent qualification at level 6 of the Regulated Qualifications Framework, or at level 9 or 10 of the Scottish Credit and Qualifications Framework.

'Deportation order' means an order made under section 5(1) of the Immigration Act 1971.

[**'Distance learning course'** means a course being undertaken at a UK Accredited Institution by a person who is overseas, and which does not require the person to be physically present in the UK for the majority of the course.]

Note: Definition inserted from 6 October 2021 subject to savings for applications made before that date (HC 617).

'Doctorate extension scheme' means a sponsored scheme which enables successful applicants to remain in the UK for 12 months from the expected end date of a course leading to the award of a PhD as in Appendix Student, or under the rules in force before 1 December 2020.

[**'Domestic Worker in a Private Household'** means a person who has, or had, permission under Appendix Domestic Worker in a Private Household, or as a domestic worker in a private household under paragraph 159EA of the rules in force before 6 May 2021.]

Note: Definition inserted from 6 May 2021 subject to savings for applications (including for administrative review) made before that date (HC 1248).

[**'Domestic Worker who is a Victim of Modern Slavery'** means a person who has, or had, permission under Appendix Domestic Worker Victim of Modern Slavery, or as a domestic worker who is a victim of slavery or human trafficking under paragraph 159J of the rules in force before 6 May 2021.]

Note: Definition inserted from 6 May 2021 subject to savings for applications (including for administrative review) made before that date (HC 1248).

'ECAA route' means Appendix ECAA Extension of Stay or under the ECAA rules in force on 30 December 2020.

[**'Ecctis'** is a service which provides information, advice and opinion on academic, vocational and professional qualifications and skills from all over the world, set out at https://ecctis.com/.]

Note: Definition inserted from 6 October 2021 subject to savings for applications made before that date (HC 617).

'EEA citizen' and **'EEA national'** means a person who is a national of: Austria, Belgium, Bulgaria, Croatia, Republic of Cyprus, Czech Republic, Denmark, Estonia, Finland, France, Germany, Greece, Hungary, Iceland, Ireland, Italy, Latvia, Liechtenstein, Lithuania, Luxembourg, Malta, Netherlands, Norway, Poland, Portugal, Romania, Slovakia, Slovenia, Spain, Sweden or Switzerland; and who is not also a British citizen.

'EEA EFTA separation agreement' means (as modified from time to time in accordance with any provision of it) the Agreement on arrangements between Iceland, the Principality of Liechtenstein, the Kingdom of Norway and the United Kingdom of Great Britain and Northern Ireland following the withdrawal of the United Kingdom from the European Union, the EEA Agreement and other agreements applicable between the United Kingdom and the EEA EFTA States by virtue of the United Kingdom's membership of the European Union.

'EEA Regulations' means:

(a) (where relevant to something done before 11pm on 31 December 2020) the Immigration (European Economic Area) Regulations 2016 (as they have effect immediately before that date or, in the case of an application made under these rules where the date of decision is before 11pm on 31 December 2020, as they have effect at the date of application); or

(b) (where relevant to something done after 11pm on 31 December 2020) the Immigration (European Economic Area) Regulations 2016 (as, despite the revocation of those Regulations, they continue to have effect, with specified modifications, by virtue of regulations made under section 7, 9 or 11 of the European Union (Withdrawal Agreement) Act 2020).

'Employment' includes paid and unpaid employment, paid and unpaid work placements undertaken as part of a course or period of study, self-employment and engaging in business or any professional activity.

'Employment as a doctor or dentist in training' means employment in a medical post or training programme which has been approved by the General Medical Council, or employment in a postgraduate training programme in dentistry.

'Endorsed funder' means an organisation accepted by UKRI, and on a list published by them, as prestigious funders of research and innovation who have an excellent track record of awarding funding to researchers with critical skills, following a rigorous peer review process.

'Endorsing body' means an organisation which has been approved by the Home Office to endorse an application under one or more of the following routes:

(a) Start-up;

(b) Innovator;

(c) Global Talent.

'Endorsement letter' means an official letter issued by an endorsing body, confirming that the endorsing body has endorsed the applicant in the relevant category.

'English language course' means a course that solely consists of English language study.

'EU National' [DELETED]

Note: Definition of 'EU National' inserted from 23:00 on 31 December 2020 for decisions made on or after that time (CP 361). Definition deleted from 09:00 on 11 October 2021 subject to savings for applications made before that time (HC617).

'Evidence of P's permission to enter or remain' under Appendix S2 Healthcare Visitor means:

(a) a valid document which is either a biometric immigration document, stamp or endorsement in a passport (whether or not the passport has expired), or other document or electronic document issued by the Home Office, confirming that the patient (P) has permission to enter or remain in the UK as an S2 Healthcare Visitor, which has not been cancelled; or

(b) the decision maker is otherwise satisfied from the information available that P has permission as an S2 Healthcare Visitor, which has not been cancelled.

'Exclusion decision' means a decision made personally by the Secretary of State that a person be excluded from the UK.

'Exclusion order' means an order made under regulation 23(5) of the EEA Regulations that the exclusion of an EEA national or the family member of an EEA national is justified on the grounds of public policy, public security or public health.

'Expected end date of a course leading to the award of a PhD' means the date the PhD is expected to be formally confirmed, by the student sponsor, as completed to the standard required for the award of a PhD and recorded on the Confirmation of Acceptance for Studies which applies to the application on the doctorate extension scheme.

'External student' means a student studying for a degree from a UK degree awarding body without any requirement to attend the UK degree awarding body's premises or a UK listed body's premises for lectures and tutorials.

'False document' includes:

(a) a document which has been altered or tampered with; and

(b) a counterfeit document; and

(c) a document which is being used by an imposter; and

(d) a document which has been fraudulently obtained or issued; and

(e) a document which contains a falsified or counterfeit entry clearance, visa or endorsement.

'Fee' means the amount the applicant must pay to the Secretary of State as specified in regulations made in exercise of the powers in sections 68, 69 and 74 of the Immigration Act 2014.

[**'Fee Waiver'** means a decision by the Secretary of State that the usual fee in relation to an immigration function need not be paid or need only be paid in specified part (whether a fee waiver can be requested for an application or service is set out in the Immigration and Nationality (Fees) Regulations).]

Note: Definition inserted from 6 April 2022 (HC 1118).

'Foundation degree' means a programme of study which leads to a qualification awarded by an English higher education provider with degree awarding powers which is at a minimum of level 5 on the Regulated Qualifications Framework, or awarded on a directly equivalent basis in the devolved administrations.

'Full-time course' means a course which is:

(a) a full-time course of course of study at UK bachelor's degree level or above; or

(b) an overseas higher education course that a Student is studying in the UK and leads to a qualification from an overseas higher education institution that is recognised as being equivalent to a UK higher education qualification; or

(c) a course of study below UK degree level that involves a minimum of 15 hours a week of classroom-based, daytime study (08:00–18:00, Monday to Friday), but scheduled breaks do not count towards the 15 hours.

[**'Global Business Mobility routes'** means any of the following:

(a) Appendix Global Business Mobility – Graduate Trainee; or
(b) Appendix Global Business Mobility – Secondment Worker; or
(c) Appendix Global Business Mobility – Senior or Specialist Worker; or
(d) Appendix Global Business Mobility – Service Supplier; or
(e) Appendix Global Business Mobility – UK Expansion Worker.]

Note: Definition inserted from 09:00 on 11 April 2022 subject to savings for applications made before that time (HC 1118).

'Global Talent' means the route, or a person with permission as a lead applicant on the route, under Appendix Global Talent or as a Global Talent migrant under Appendix W of the rules in force before 1 December 2020, or as a Tier 1 (Exceptional Talent) Migrant.

[**'Global Universities List'** means the list of universities published by the Home Office on the Gov.uk website, which is compiled on an annual basis and consists of all non-UK institutions that are ranked in the top 50 of at least two of the following ranking systems:

(a) Times Higher Education World University Rankings; and
(b) Quacquarelli Symonds World University Rankings; and
(c) The Academic Ranking of World Universities.]

Note: Definition inserted from 09:00 on 30 May 2022 subject to savings for applications made before that time (HC 1118).

'Government Authorised Exchange Scheme' means a scheme under the T5 (Temporary Worker) Government Authorised Exchange Worker route which is endorsed by a Government Department in support of Government objectives and provides temporary work in an occupation which appears in Table 1 or Table 2 of Appendix Skilled Occupations and where the migrant will be supernumerary.

[**'Government Authorised Exchange route'** means any of the following:

(i) the route in Appendix Temporary Work – Government Authorised Exchange; or

(ii) the route in Appendix T5 (Temporary Worker) Government Authorised Exchange Worker, under the rules in force between 1 December 2020 and 10 October 2021 (inclusive); or

(iii) the Government Authorised Exchange sub-category in the Tier 5 (Temporary Worker) route under part 6A of the rules in force before 1 December 2020.]

Note: Definition substituted (previously 'Government Authorised Exchange Worker') from 09:00 on 11 October 2021 subject to savings for applications made before that time (HC 617).

[**'Graduate'** means a person who has, or had, permission as a Graduate under Appendix Graduate of these Rules.]

Note: Definition inserted from 6 April 2021 subject to savings for applications made before that date (HC 1248).

[**'Graduate Trainee'** means a person who has, or had, permission under any of the following:

(a) Appendix Global Business Mobility – Graduate Trainee; or

(b) the Intra-Company Graduate Trainee route of Appendix Intra-Company Routes under the rules in force before 11 April 2022; or

(c) as a Tier 2 (Intra-Company Transfer) migrant in the Graduate Trainee sub-category under the rules in force before 0900 on 1 December 2020.]

Note: Definition inserted from 09:00 on 11 April 2022 subject to savings for applications made before that time (HC 1118).

[**'Grandchild'** in Appendix Ukraine Scheme means a biological grandchild, step-grandchild or grandchild by reason of an adoption recognised by the laws of the UK relating to adoption.]

Note: Definition inserted from 30 March 2022 (HC 1220).

[**'Grandparent'** in Appendix UK Ancestry and Appendix Ukraine Scheme means a biological grandparent or grandparent by reason of an adoption recognised by the laws of the UK relating to adoption.]

Note: Definition substituted from 30 March 2022 (HC 1220).

[**'High earner'** means a person on the Global Business Mobility – Senior or Specialist Worker route or Global Business Mobility – UK Expansion Worker route who is sponsored in a job with a gross annual salary of £73,900 or more (based on working a maximum of 48 hours per week) as confirmed by their sponsor.]

Note: Definition substituted from 09:00 on 11 April 2022 subject to savings for applications made before that time (HC 1118).

'Higher education provider' means a student sponsor which:

(a) in England, is an institution that is required to register with the Office for Students, because it is an 'English Higher Education Provider', as defined in the Office for Students Regulations and section 83 of the Higher Education and Research Act 2017; or

(b) in Northern Ireland, is a higher education institution as set out in the Education and Libraries (Northern Ireland) Order 1993, or a body that provides higher education, and is recognised under the Further Education (Northern Ireland) Order 1997, with 'in developmental' or 'established provider' status; or

(c) in Scotland, is an institution that provides higher education within the meaning of section 38 of the Further and Higher Education (Scotland) Act 1992 and which is a post-16 education body within the meaning of section 35(1) of the Further and Higher Education (Scotland) Act 2005; or

(d) in Wales, is an institution that offers higher education provision and is a 'regulated institution', as defined in the Higher Education (Wales) Act 2015 (for the purpose of the 2015 Act, higher education is defined as education provided by means of a course of any description mentioned in Schedule 6 to the Education Reform Act 1988).

[**'High Potential Individual'** means a person who has, or had, permission as a High Potential Individual under Appendix High Potential Individual.]

Note: Definition inserted from 09:00 on 30 May 2022 subject to savings for applications made before that time (HC 1118).

[**'High Potential Individual route'** means the route under Appendix High Potential Individual.]

Note: Definition inserted from 09:00 on 30 May 2022 subject to savings for applications made before that time (HC 1118).

'Human Rights Convention' means the Convention for the Protection of Human Rights and Fundamental Freedoms, agreed by the Council of Europe at Rome on 4th November 1950, as it has effect for the time being in relation to the UK.

[**'Humanitarian protection'** means status granted under paragraph 339C and which has not been revoked under paragraphs 339G to 339H.]

Note: Definition substituted from 28 June 2022 subject to savings for applications made before that date (HC 17).

'Illegal entrant' has the same meaning as in section 33(1) of the Immigration Act 1971.

'Immigration Acts' has the same meaning as in section 61(2) of the UK Borders Act 2007.

'Immigration employment document' means a work permit or any other document which relates to employment and is issued for the purpose of these rules or in connection with leave to enter or remain in the UK.

'Immigration Health Charge' means a charge under section 38 of the Immigration Act 2014 and the Immigration (Health Charge) Order 2015.

'Immigration Officer' includes a Customs Officer acting as an Immigration Officer.

'Immigration Skills Charge' means a charge payable under regulations made under section 70A of the Immigration Act 2014.

'Independent School' means:

(a) a school in England or Wales (which is not an Academy, a school maintained by a local authority, or a non-maintained special school), at which full-time education is provided for:

(i) five or more pupils of compulsory school age (whether or not such education is also provided at it for pupils under or over that age); or

(ii) for at least one pupil of compulsory school age (whether or not such education is also provided at it for pupils under or over that age) for whom an education, health and care (EHC) plan or a statement of special educational needs is maintained, or who is looked after by a local authority (within the meaning of section 22 of the Children Act 1989); or

(b) a school in Scotland (which is not a public school or a grant-aided school), at which full-time education is provided for pupils of school age (whether or not such education is also provided for pupils under or over that age); or

(c) a school in Northern Ireland (which is not grant-aided), which has been registered with the Department of Education.

'Innovator' means a person who has, or had, permission as an Innovator under Appendix Innovator or as an Innovator migrant under Appendix W of the rules in force before 1 December 2020.

'Intention to live permanently with the other in the UK' or **'intend to live together permanently in the UK'** means an intention to live together, evidenced by a clear commitment from both parties that they will live together permanently in the UK immediately following the outcome of the application in question or as soon as circumstances permit thereafter. However, where an application is made under Appendix Armed Forces the words 'in the UK' in this definition do not apply. Where an application is made under Appendix FM and the sponsor is a permanent member of HM Diplomatic Service, or a comparable UK-based staff member of the British Council, the Foreign, Commonwealth and Development Office or the Home Office on a tour of duty outside the UK, the words 'in the UK' in this definition do not apply.

[**'International Agreement route'** means any of the following:

(i) the route in Appendix Temporary Work – International Agreement; or

(ii) the route in Appendix T5 (Temporary Worker) International Agreement Worker under the rules in force between 1 December 2020 and 10 October 2021 (inclusive); or

(iii) the International Agreement sub-category in the Tier 5 (Temporary Worker) route under part 6A of the rules in force before 1 December 2020.]

Note: Definition substituted (previously 'International Agreement Worker') from 09:00 on 11 October 2021 subject to savings for applications made before that time (HC 617).

[**'International Operator Licence'** in Appendix Visitor: Permitted Activities means:

(a) a licence issued by the competent authority of a country other than the United Kingdom authorising an operator to undertake international carriage of goods or passengers by road in accordance with an international agreement to which the United Kingdom is a party; or

(b) a community licence issued by a Member State of the Union in accordance with Regulation (EC) No 1072/2009 or Regulation (EC) No 1073/2009.]

Note: Definition inserted from 23:00 on 31 December 2020 for decisions made on or after that time (HC 1043).

'International scholarship agency' means an international institution or organisation which provides funding to students studying in the UK.

[**'International Sportsperson'** means a person who has, or had, permission under any of the following:

(i) Appendix International Sportsperson; or

(ii) Appendix T2 Sportsperson under the rules in force between 1 December 2020 and 10 October 2021 (inclusive); or

(iii) as a sporting worker under Appendix T5 (Temporary Worker) Creative or Sporting Worker under the rules in force between 1 December 2020 and 10 October 2021 (inclusive); or

(iv) as a Tier 5 (Temporary Worker) migrant in the Creative and Sporting subcategory as a sporting worker under part 6A of the rules in force before 1 December 2020, and/or (v) as a Tier 2 (Sportsperson) Migrant under part 6A of the rules in force before 1 December 2020.]

Note: Definition inserted from 09:00 on 11 October 2021 subject to savings for applications made before that time (HC 617).

'Intra-Company Graduate Trainee' [DELETED]

Note: Definition deleted from 09:00 on 11 April 2022 subject to savings for applications made before that time (HC 1118).

'Intra-Company Transfer' [DELETED]

Note: Definition deleted from 09:00 on 11 April 2022 subject to savings for applications made before that time (HC 1118).

['**Intra-Company routes**' means any of the following:

(a) Appendix Global Business Mobility – Senior or Specialist Worker; or

(b) Appendix Global Business Mobility – Graduate Trainee; or

(c) Appendix Intra-Company routes under the rules in force before 11 April 2022; or

(d) the Tier 2 (Intra-Company Transfer) route under the rules in force before 0900 on 1 December 2020.]

Note: Definition substituted from 09:00 on 11 April 2022 subject to savings for applications made before that time (HC 1118).

'**Islands**' means any of the Channel Islands or the Isle of Man.

'**Lead applicant**', under Appendix KOLL, Appendix KOL UK and Appendix English Language, means the applicant on whose status, or previous status, a dependent partner or dependent child is relying as the basis of their application.

'**Legal guardian**' is a person appointed according to local laws to take care of a child.

'**Letter of authority**' means a written authorisation from a person that they wish to appoint or change their immigration adviser (who must be a qualified person as required by section 84 of the Immigration and Asylum Act 1999 or regulated by the Office of the Immigration Services Commissioner).

['**Marriage/Civil Partnership visitor**'] means a person who has, or had, entry clearance under Appendix V: Visitor to marry or form a civil partnership, or give notice of marriage or civil partnership, in the UK.

Note: Words substituted from 6 October 2021 subject to savings for applications made before that date (HC 617).

'**Media representative**' means a person who has, or had, permission on the Representative of an Overseas Business route having met the requirement at ROB 4.4.(b) of Appendix Representative of an Overseas Business, or as a Representative of an Overseas Business having met the requirement of paragraph 144(ii)(b) of Part 5 of the rules in force before 1 December 2020.

'**Medical inspector**' means a medical inspector appointed under Schedule 2 to the Immigration Act 1971.

'**Must not be leading an independent life**' or '**is not leading an independent life**' means that the person:

(a) does not have a partner; and

(b) is living with their parent (except where they are at boarding school, college or university as part of their full-time education); and

(c) is not in full-time employment (unless aged 18 or over); and

(d) is wholly or mainly dependent upon their parent for financial support (unless aged 18 or over); and

(e) is wholly or mainly dependent upon their parent for emotional support.

Where under these rules a relative other than a parent may act as the sponsor or carer of the person, references in this definition to 'parent' shall be read as applying to that other relative.

'**National minimum wage**' means as defined in the National Minimum Wage Act 1998.

'**National Referral Mechanism**' means the arrangements administered by the Competent Authorities as set out in the guidance found at: https://www.gov.uk/government/publications/victims-of-trafficking-guidance-for-competent-bodies.

['Niece' in Appendix Ukraine Scheme means the female biological, adopted or step-child of the UK-based sponsor's brother or sister.]

Note: Definition inserted from 30 March 2022 (HC 1220).

['Nephew' in Appendix Ukraine Scheme means the male biological, adopted or step-child of the UK-based sponsor's brother or sister.]

Note: Definition inserted from 30 March 2022 (HC 1220).

'Notice of liability for removal' means a notice given that a person is or will be liable for removal under section 10 of the Immigration and Asylum Act 1999, and for notices that pre-date the Immigration Act 2014 coming into force, refers to a decision to remove in accordance with section 10 of the Immigration and Asylum Act 1999, a decision to remove an illegal entrant by way of directions under paragraphs 8 to 10 of Schedule 2 to the Immigration Act 1971, or a decision to remove in accordance with section 47 of the Immigration, Asylum and Nationality Act 2006.

'Occupation code' means the relevant 4-digit code in the Standard Occupational Classification (SOC) 2010 system, published by the Office for National Statistics at: https://www.ons.gov.uk/methodology/classificationsandstandards/standardoccupationalclassificationsoc/soc2010.

'Occupy exclusively' in relation to accommodation means that part of the accommodation must be for the exclusive use of the person or family.

'Overcrowded' means overcrowded within the meaning of the Housing Act 1985, the Housing (Scotland) Act 1987 or the Housing (Northern Ireland) Order 1988 (as appropriate).

'Overseas Business' is a business which has it main place of operation outside of the UK.

[**'Overseas Domestic Worker'** means a person who has, or had, permission under Appendix Overseas Domestic Worker, or as a domestic worker in a private household under paragraph 159A of the rules in force before 6 May 2021.]

Note: Definition inserted from 6 May 2021 subject to savings for applications (including for administrative review) made before that date (HC 1248).

'Overseas Government Language Programme' means an overseas Government sponsored professional language development programme under the Government Authorised Exchange Scheme where the person concerned delivers language training and participates in a cultural exchange programme that is fully or partially paid for by the overseas government or an organisation affiliated to an overseas government.

'Overseas higher education institution' means an institution which holds overseas accreditation confirmed by [Ecctis] as offering degree programmes which are equivalent to UK degree level qualifications, and which teaches no more than half of a degree programme in the UK as a study abroad programme.

Note: Words substituted from 6 October 2021 subject to savings for applications made before that date (HC 617).

[**Overseas service provider'** means a business based outside the UK with no commercial presence in the UK, that is one of the following:

(a) a natural or legal person that has a contract to provide services to a UK business, where that UK business is on the register of licensed sponsors maintained by the Home Office; or

(b) a natural or legal person that is subcontracted to provide services to a UK business by a natural or legal person coming within paragraph (a)]

Note: Definition inserted 09:00 on 11 April 2022 subject to savings for applications made before that time (HC 1118).

'Overstayed' or **'overstaying'** means the person has stayed in the UK beyond the latest of:

(a) the time limit attached to the last permission granted; or

(b) the period that the permission was extended under section 3C or 3D of the Immigration Act 1971.

[**'Own Account'** in Appendix Visitor: Permitted Activities means the transport of goods by a business where the following conditions are fulfilled:

(a) the goods carried are the property of the business or have been sold, bought, let out on hire or hired, produced, extracted, processed or repaired by the business; and

(b) the purpose of the journey is to carry the goods to or from the premises of the business or to move them, either inside or outside the business for its own requirements; and

(c) the vehicles used for such transport are driven by personnel employed by, or put at the disposal of, the business under a contractual obligation; and

(d) the vehicles carrying the goods are owned by the business, have been bought by it on deferred terms or have been hired; and

(e) such transport is no more than ancillary to the overall activities of the business.]

Note: Definition inserted from 23:00 on 31 December 2020 for decisions made on or after that time (HC 1043).

'Parent' includes:

(a) the stepfather of a child whose father is dead, and reference to stepfather includes a relationship arising through civil partnership; and

(b) the stepmother of a child whose mother is dead, and reference to stepmother includes a relationship arising through civil partnership; and

(c) the father, as well as the mother, of an illegitimate child where the person is proved to be the father; and

(d) an adoptive parent, where a child was adopted in accordance with a decision taken by the competent administrative authority or court in a country whose adoption orders are recognised by the UK or where a child is the subject of a de facto adoption in accordance with the requirements of paragraph 309A (except that an adopted child or a child who is the subject of a de facto adoption may not make an application for leave to enter or remain in order to accompany, join or remain with an adoptive parent under paragraphs 297 to 303); and

(e) in the case of a child born in the UK who is not a British citizen, a person to whom there has been a genuine transfer of parental responsibility on the ground of the original parents' inability to care for [the child; and]

[(f) in Appendix Ukraine Scheme a parent also includes a step-father or step-mother, whether or not the biological parent is dead.]

Note: Words in (e) substituted and (f) inserted from 30 March 2022 (HC 1220).

'Parent of a Child Student' means a person who has, or had, permission under Appendix Parent of a Child Student or as a Parent of a Tier 4 (Child) Student under the rules in force before 5 October 2020.

'Partner' means a person's:

(a) spouse; or

(b) civil partner; or

(c) unmarried partner, where the couple have been living together in a relationship similar to marriage or a civil partnership for at least two years.

'Partner Institution' means an institution which has a partnership agreement with a student sponsor, which has been approved by the Home Office in accordance with the requirements set out in the student sponsor guidance published on the gov.uk website. Teaching partnerships allow a student sponsor's students to undertake study of a specified type at a partner institution's site.

'Passport' means a document which:

(a) is issued by or on behalf of the government of any country recognised by the UK, or dealt with as a government by the UK, and which complies with international passport practice; and

(b) shows both the identity and nationality of the holder; and

(c) gives the holder the right to enter the country of the government which issued the document; and

(d) is authentic and not unofficially altered or tampered with; and

(e) is not damaged in a way that compromises the integrity of the document; and

(f) is used by the rightful holder; and

(g) has not expired.

'Pathway Course' means a course which prepares a student for progression to another course at a specific UK recognised body or a body in receipt of public funding as a higher education institution from the Department for the Economy in Northern Ireland, the Office for Students, the Higher Education Funding Council for Wales, the Scottish Funding Council or any other provider registered with the Office for Students. It does not include a pre-sessional course.

'Patient', in Appendix S2 Healthcare Visitor, means a person who is undergoing or plans to undergo a course of planned healthcare treatment in the UK.

'PAYE' means HM Revenue and Customs' Pay As You Earn system for collecting Income Tax and National Insurance from employee earnings.

'Peer reviewed research fellowship or award' means a specific fellowship or award which appears on the list of peer reviewed research fellowships or awards published by The Royal Society, The Royal Academy of Engineering or The British Academy.

'Pending appeal' has the same meaning as in section 104 of the Nationality, Immigration and Asylum Act 2002.

'Period of imprisonment' has the same meaning as in section 38(2) of the UK Borders Act 2007.

'Permission to enter' has the same meaning as leave to enter under the Immigration Act 1971.

'Permission to stay' has the same meaning as leave to remain under the Immigration Act 1971 (and includes a variation of leave to enter or remain and an extension of leave to enter or remain).

And references in these rules to a person having, having had or being granted **'Permission'** means either permission to enter or permission to stay.

[**'Permitted Paid Engagement Visitor'**] means a person who has, or had, permission under Appendix V: Visitor to undertake specific paid engagements for up to one month.

Note: Words substituted from 6 October 2021 subject to savings for applications made before that date (HC 617).

'Postgraduate doctor or dentist' in Appendix Student means a student undertaking a recognised Foundation Programme with Health Education England following completion of a recognised degree in medicine or dentistry in the UK.

'Postgraduate level study' means a course at level 7 or above of the Regulated Qualifications Framework, or level 11 or above of the Scottish Credit and Qualifications Framework, which leads to a recognised UK postgraduate degree at master's level or above, or an equivalent qualification at the same level.

'Premium Sponsor' means a sponsor which is recorded as holding Premium status on the register of licensed sponsors maintained by the Home Office.

[**'Present and settled'** means that the person concerned is settled in the UK and, at the date of application, is physically present in the UK.

Where the person concerned is a British Citizen or settled in the UK and is:

(a) a member of HM Forces serving overseas; or

(b) an employee of the UK Government, a Northern Ireland department, the Scottish Administration or the Welsh Government, or a permanent member of the British Council on a tour of duty outside the UK, and the applicant has provided the evidence specified in paragraph 26A of Appendix FM-SE, then for the purposes of Appendix FM and Appendix Settlement Family Life, where the applicant is applying for settlement the person is to be regarded as present and settled in the UK, and in paragraphs R-LTRP.1.1.(a) and RILRP.1.1.(a) of Appendix FM the requirement "and their partner must be in the UK" is to be disregarded.]

Note: Definition substituted from 20 June 2022 subject to savings for applications made before that date (HC 1118).

'Primary degree' means a qualification obtained from a course of degree level study, which did not feature as an entry requirement a previous qualification obtained from degree level study, for example an undergraduate degree is a primary degree, but a master's degree that has a bachelor's degree as an entry requirement is not a primary degree.

'Private foster care arrangement' means an arrangement in which a child aged under 16, or aged under 18 if disabled, is cared for, on a full-time basis for a period of 28 days or more, by a person aged 18 or over who is not the child's parent or a close relative.

'Private medical insurance' means insurance to cover treatment provided by a private health provider, or a reciprocal arrangement in place with another country by which certain nationals may receive NHS treatment.

'Private medical treatment' means treatment provided by a private health provider, or by the NHS where there is a reciprocal arrangement in place with another country by which certain nationals may receive NHS treatment.

'Probationary Sponsor' means a student sponsor which is recorded as having 'Probationary Sponsor status' on the register of licensed student sponsors maintained by the Home Office.

'Professional Sportsperson' means a person who is one or more of the following:

(a) currently providing services as a sportsperson, or is playing or coaching in any capacity, at a professional or semi-professional level of sport (whether paid or unpaid); or

(b) currently receiving payment, including payment in kind, for playing or coaching, and that payment covers all, or the majority of, their costs for travelling to, and living in, the UK, or has received such payment within the previous 4 years; or

(c) currently registered to a professional or semi-professional sports team or has been so registered within the previous 4 years (this includes all academy and development team age groups); or

(d) has represented their nation or national team within the previous two years, including all youth and development age groups from under 17s upwards; or

(e) has represented their state or regional team within the previous two years, including all youth and development age groups from under 17s upwards; or

(f) has an established international reputation in their chosen field of sport; or

(g) engages an agent or representative, with the aim of finding opportunities as a sportsperson, and/or developing a current or future career as a sportsperson, or has engaged such an agent in the last 12 months; or

(h) is providing services as a sportsperson or coach, unless they are doing so as an 'Amateur' in a charity event; or

(i) is providing services as a sportsperson or coach, unless they are doing so as a Student who is studying a course at degree level or above at a higher education provider and playing or coaching sport as an Amateur or as part of a work placement that is undertaken as an integral and assessed part of their course.

'Prohibited degree of relationship' has the same meaning as in the Marriage Act 1949, the Marriage (Prohibited Degrees of Relationship) Act 1986 and the Civil Partnership Act 2004.

'Protection claim' has the same meaning as in section 82(2)(a) of the Nationality, Immigration and Asylum Act 2002.

[**'Provisional rating'** means a sponsor which is recorded as having a rating of "Provisional" on the register of licensed sponsors: workers on the gov.uk website at: www.gov.uk/government/publications/register-of-licensed-sponsors-workers.]

Note: Definition inserted from 09:00 on 11 April 2022 subject to savings for applications made before that time (HC 1118).

'Public funds' means:

(a) housing under Part VI or VII of the Housing Act 1996 and under Part II of the Housing Act 1985, Part I or II of the Housing (Scotland) Act 1987, Part II of the Housing (Northern Ireland) Order 1981 or Part II of the Housing (Northern Ireland) Order 1988; and

(b) attendance allowance, severe disablement allowance, carer's allowance and disability living allowance under Part III of the Social Security Contribution and Benefits Act 1992; income support, council tax benefit and housing benefit under Part VII of that Act; a social fund payment under Part VIII of that Act; child benefit under Part IX of that Act; income based jobseeker's allowance under the Jobseekers Act 1995, income related allowance under Part 1 of the Welfare Reform Act 2007 (employment and support allowance) state pension credit under the State Pension Credit Act 2002; or child tax credit and working tax credit under Part 1 of the Tax Credits Act 2002; and

(c) attendance allowance, severe disablement allowance, carer's allowance and disability living allowance under Part III of the Social Security Contribution and Benefits (Northern Ireland) Act 1992; income support, council tax benefit and, housing benefit under Part VII of that Act; a social fund payment under Part VIII of that Act; child benefit under Part IX of that Act; income based jobseeker's allowance under the Jobseekers (Northern Ireland) Order 1995 or income related allowance under Part 1 of the Welfare Reform Act (Northern Ireland) 2007; and

(d) Universal Credit under Part 1 of the Welfare Reform Act 2012 or Personal Independence Payment under Part 4 of that Act; and

(e) Universal Credit, Personal Independence Payment or any domestic rate relief under the Welfare Reform (Northern Ireland) Order 2015; and

(f) a council tax reduction under a council tax reduction scheme made under section 13A of the Local Government Finance Act 1992 in relation to England or Wales or a council tax reduction pursuant to the Council Tax Reduction (Scotland) Regulations 2012 or the Council Tax Reduction (State Pension Credit) (Scotland) Regulations 2012; and

(g) a payment made from a welfare fund under the Welfare Funds (Scotland) Act 2015; and

(h) a discretionary support payment made in accordance with any regulations made under article 135 of the Welfare Reform (Northern Ireland) Order 2015; and

[(i) a discretionary payment made by a local authority under section 1 of the Localism Act 2011, not including any payment made under the Energy Rebate Scheme 2022]

For the purpose of these rules,

(i) a person (P) is not to be regarded as having (or potentially having) recourse to public funds merely because P is (or will be) reliant in whole or in part on public funds provided to P's family sponsor unless, as a result of P's presence in the UK, the family sponsor is (or would be) entitled to increased or additional public funds (save where such entitlement to increased or additional public funds is by virtue of P and the family sponsor's joint entitlement to benefits under the regulations referred to in subparagraph (ii) below; and

(ii) subject to subparagraph (iii) below, a person (P) shall not be regarded as having recourse to public funds if P is entitled to benefits specified under section 115 of the Immigration and Asylum Act 1999 by virtue of regulations made under sub-sections (3) and (4) of that section or section 42 of the Tax Credits Act 2002; and

(iii) a person (P) making an application from outside the UK will be regarded as having recourse to public funds where P relies upon the future entitlement to any public funds that would be payable to P or to P's family sponsor as a result of P's presence in the UK (including those benefits to which P or the family sponsor would be entitled as a result of P's presence in the UK under the regulations referred to in subparagraph (ii) above).

Note: Sub-paragraph (i) substituted from 30 March 2022 (HC 1220).

'Recreational Course' means a course undertaken purely for leisure purposes[, other than English Language training,] that does not lead to a formal qualification, for example, a leisure course in pottery or horse riding.

Note: Words inserted from 09:00 on 1 July 2021 subject to savings for applications (including for administrative review) made before that time (HC 1248).

[**'Refugee'** has the same meaning as in Article 1 of the 1951 Refugee Convention.]

Note: Definition substituted from 28 June 2022 subject to savings for applications made before that date (HC 17).

'Refugee Convention' means the 1951 United Nations Convention and its 1967 Protocol relating to the Status of Refugees.

[**'Refugee permission to stay'** means permission to stay granted to a refugee under paragraph 339QA of these rules which has not been revoked under paragraph 339QD.]

Note: Definition inserted from 28 June 2022 subject to savings for applications made before that date (HC 17).

'Refugee status' means status granted under paragraph 334 of these rules which has not been revoked under paragraphs 339A to 339B.]

Note: Definition substituted from 28 June 2022 subject to savings for applications made before that date (HC 17).

'Refugee leave' [DELETED]

Note: Definition deleted from 28 June 2022 subject to savings for applications made before that date (HC 17).

'Relevant NHS body' in Part 9, and in paragraphs S-EC.2.3., S-LTR.2.3. and S-ILR.2.3. of Appendix FM, means:

(a) in relation to England-

(i) a National Health Service Trust established under section 25 of the National Health Service Act 2006; or

(ii) a National Health Service foundation trust; and

(b) in relation to Wales-

(i) a Local Health Board established under section 11 of the National Health Service (Wales) Act 2006; or

(ii) a National Health Service Trust established under section 18 of the National Health Service (Wales) Act 2006; or

(iii) a Special Health Authority established under 22 of the National Health Service (Wales) Act 2006; and

(c) in relation to Scotland-

(i) a Health Board or Special Health Board established under section 2 of the National Health Service (Scotland) Act 1978 (c. 29); or

(ii) the Common Services Agency for the Scottish Health Service established under section 10 of that Act; or

(iii) Healthcare Improvement Scotland established under section 10A of that Act; and

(d) in relation to Northern Ireland-

(i) the Regional Health and Social Care Board established under the Health and Social Care (Reform) Act (Northern Ireland) 2009; or

(ii) a Health and Social Care trust established under the Health and Personal Social Services (Northern Ireland) Order 1991 (S.I. 1991/194 (N.I. 1)) and renamed under the Health and Social Care (Reform) Act (Northern Ireland) 2009.

'Relevant NHS regulations' means:

(a) in Wales, the National Health Service (Charges to Overseas Visitors) Regulations 1989 (1989 No 306); and

(b) in Scotland, the National Health Service (Charges to Overseas Visitors) (Scotland) Regulations 1989 as amended (1989 No 364); and

(c) in Northern Ireland, the Provision of Health Services to Persons Not Ordinarily Resident Regulations (Northern Ireland) 2015 (2015 No 227); and

(d) in England, the National Health Service (Charges to Overseas Visitors) Regulations 2015 (2015 No 238).

[**'Religious Worker'** means a person who has, or had, permission under any of the following:

(i) Appendix Temporary Work – Religious Worker; or

(ii) Appendix T5 (Temporary Worker) Religious Worker under the rules in force between 1 December 2020 and 10 October 2021 (inclusive); or

(iii) as a Tier 5 (Temporary Worker) migrant in the Religious Worker sub-category under part 6A of the rules in force before 1 December 2020.]

Note: Definition substituted from 09:00 on 11 October 2021 subject to savings for applications made before that time (HC 617).

'Representative of an Overseas Business' means a person who has, or had, permission under Appendix Representative of an Overseas Business or as a Representative of an Overseas Business under Part 5 of the rules in force before 1 December 2020.

'Research Programme' means research programmes and fellowships under a Government Authorised Exchange Scheme where the person is working on a scientific, academic, medical, or government research project at either a UK higher education institution or another research institution operating under the authority and/or financial sponsorship of a relevant Government Department.

'Rough sleeping' means sleeping, or bedding down, in the open air (for example on the street or in doorways) or in buildings or other places not designed for habitation (for example sheds, car parks or stations).

'S2 certificate of entitlement to scheduled treatment' has the same meaning as a portable document S2 issued under Regulation (EC) No 883/2004.

'S2 Healthcare Visitor' means a patient (P) or an accompanying person (AP) who meets the requirements of Appendix S2 Healthcare Visitor.

[**'Scale-up route'** means the route under Appendix Scale-up.]

Note: Definition inserted from 22 August 2022 subject to savings for applications made before that date (HC 1118).

[**'Scale-up Worker'** means a person who has, or had, permission as Scale-up Worker under Appendix Scale-up.]

Note: Definition inserted from 22 August 2022 subject to savings for applications made before that date (HC 1118).

'Seasonal work' is work which fluctuates or is restricted according to the season or time of the year.

[**'Seasonal Worker** means a person who has, or had, permission under any of the following:

(i) Appendix Temporary Work – Seasonal Worker; or

(ii) Appendix T5 (Temporary Worker) Seasonal Worker under the rules in force between 1 December 2020 and 10 October 2021 (inclusive); or

(iii) as a Tier 5 (Temporary Worker) migrant in the Seasonal Worker sub-category under part 6A of the rules in force before 1 December 2020.]

Note: Definition substituted from 09:00 on 11 October 2021 subject to savings for applications made before that time (HC 617).

'Seeking entry' refers to a person applying for entry clearance or permission to enter the UK.

'Self-employed' means a person who is registered as self-employed with HM Revenue & Customs, or an overseas equivalent, or is employed by a company of which the person is a controlling shareholder.

'Self-employed Lawyer' means a person granted permission outside the rules under the concession for self-employed lawyers that formerly appeared in Chapter 6, Section 1 Annex D of the Immigration Directorate Instructions.

['**Secondment Worker**' means a person who has, or last had, permission as a Secondment Worker under Appendix Global Business Mobility – Secondment Worker.]

Note: Definition inserted from 09:00 on 11 April 2022 subject to savings for applications made before that time (HC 1118).

['**Senior or Specialist Worker**' means a person who has, or last had, permission under any of the following routes:

(a) Appendix Global Business Mobility – Senior or Specialist Worker; or

(b) the Intra-Company Transfer route under the rules in force before 11 April 2022; or

(c) as a Tier 2 (Intra-Company Transfer) migrant in the Long-Term Staff sub-category under the rules in force before 0900 on 1 December 2020.]

Note: Definition inserted from 09:00 on 11 April 2022 subject to savings for applications made before that time (HC 1118).

'**Series of events**' in relation to sport is two or more linked events, such as a tour, or rounds of a competition, which do not add up to a league or a season.

['**Service Supplier**' means a person who has, or last had, permission under Appendix Global Business Mobility – Service Suppliers, or as a contractual service supplier or independent professional under any of the following routes:

(a) Appendix Temporary Work – International Agreement under the rules in force before 11 April 2022; or

(b) Appendix T5 (Temporary Worker) International Agreement Worker under the rules in force between 0900 1 December 2020 and 10 October 2021 (inclusive); or

(c) the International Agreement sub-category in the Tier 5 (Temporary Worker) route under part 6A of the rules in force before 0900 on 1 December 2020.]

Note: Definition inserted from 09:00 on 11 April 2022 subject to savings for applications made before that time (HC 1118).

'**Settled**' has the same meaning as in section 33(1) of the Immigration Act 1971.

'**Settled worker**' means:

(a) a British citizen; or

(b) a person who is resident in the UK in accordance with the EEA Regulations or who holds a permanent right of residence in the UK in accordance with regulation 15 of the EEA Regulations; or

(c) a person with leave to remain or indefinite leave to remain granted under Appendix EU; or

(d) a British Overseas Territories citizen, except those from the Sovereign Base Areas in Cyprus; or

(e) a Commonwealth citizen who has been granted permission on the UK Ancestry route on the basis that they have a grandparent born in the UK and Islands; or

(f) a person who is otherwise settled within the meaning of section 33(2A) of the Immigration Act 1971.

'**Settlement**' means indefinite leave to enter or remain.

'**Sham marriage**' and '**sham civil partnership**' has the same meaning as in section 62 of the Immigration Act 2014 and '**involvement in a sham marriage or sham civil partnership**' means a person who is a party to a sham marriage or sham civil partnership, or who has enabled the marriage or civil partnership to take place.

'Short-term Student' means a person who has, or had, permission under Appendix Short Term Student, or paragraph A57E of the rules in force before 1 December 2020.

[**'Sibling'** in Appendix Ukraine Scheme means the UK-based sponsor or their partner's biological, adopted or step-brothers and step-sisters.]

Note: Definition inserted from 30 March 2022 (HC 1220).

'Skilled Worker' means a person who has, or had, permission under Appendix Skilled Worker, or as a Tier 2 (General) migrant under the rules in force before 1 December 2020.

'Sole Representative' means a person who has, or had, permission on the Representative of an Overseas Business route having met the requirement at ROB 4.4.(a) of Appendix Representative of an Overseas Business, or as a Representative of an Overseas Business having met the requirement of paragraph 144(ii)(a) of Part 5 of the rules in force before 1 December 2020.

'Sponsor' and **'family sponsor'**, in relation to a family member, means the person in relation to whom an applicant is seeking leave to enter or remain as their spouse, fiancé(e), civil partner, proposed civil partner, unmarried partner, same-sex partner or dependent relative, as the case may be, under paragraphs 277 to 295O or 317 to 319 or the person in relation to whom an applicant is seeking entry clearance or leave as their partner or dependent relative under Appendix FM.

'Sponsor', in relation to study or work, means the person or organisation licensed by the Home Office that the Certificate of Sponsorship or Confirmation of Acceptance for Studies records as being the sponsor for a person.

[**'Sponsor group'**, under the Global Business Mobility routes, means the sponsor and any business or organisation that is linked to the sponsor by common ownership or control, or by a joint venture on which the applicant is sponsored to work.]

Note: Definition inserted from 09:00 on 11 April 2022 subject to savings for applications made before that time (HC 1118).

'Sponsor group', under Appendix Intra-Company routes, means the sponsor and any business or organisation that is linked to the sponsor by common ownership or control, or by a joint venture on which the applicant is sponsored to work.

'Sponsor licence' means a licence granted by the Home Office to a person who, by virtue of such a grant, is licensed as a sponsor in relation to applications to study or work in the UK.

[**'Standard Visitor'**] means a person who has, or had, permission under Appendix V: Visitor to undertake the activities of a standard visitor set out in Appendix Visitor: Permitted Activities.

Note: Words substituted from 6 October 2021 subject to savings for applications made before that date (HC 617).

'Start-up route' means Appendix Start-up, and also includes a person who has, or had, permission as a Start-Up migrant under Appendix W of the rules in force before 1 December 2020.

'State-funded school or academy' means:

(a) in England, an 'Academy' as defined by and established under the Academies Act 2010, including academy schools, 16-19 academies and alternative provision academies; and

(b) in England and Wales, a 'school maintained by a local authority' being an institution defined in the School Standards and Framework Act 1998 or the Education Act 1996, including community schools, foundation schools, voluntary aided schools, voluntary controlled schools, community special schools, foundation special schools, pupil referral units and maintained nursery schools; and

(c) in Northern Ireland, a 'grant-aided school' being a school to which grants are paid under the Education Orders as defined in the Education and Libraries (Northern Ireland) Order 1986, including controlled, maintained, grant-maintained integrated schools and voluntary grammar schools; and

(d) in Scotland, a 'public school' and a 'grant-aided school', defined in section 135 of the Education (Scotland) Act 1980 (for the avoidance of doubt, these definitions include any such nursery schools and special schools) and 'Special school' has the meaning given in section 29(1) of the Education (Additional Support for Learning) (Scotland) Act 2004.

'Student' means a person who has, or had, permission under Appendix Student, or Appendix ST: Student of the rules in force immediately before 1 December 2020, or as a Tier 4 (General) Student under the rules in force before 5 October 2020.

'Student sponsor' means a sponsor which listed on the register of licensed sponsors maintained by the Home Office: https://www.gov.uk/government/publications/register-of-licensed-sponsors-students.

'Student Union Sabbatical Officer' means a person who has, or had, permission under Appendix Student, Appendix ST: Student of the rules in force immediately before 1 December 2020, or under paragraph 245ZV or paragraph 245ZX of the rules in force before 5 October 2020, and has been elected to a full-time, salaried, executive union position in the student union of the person's sponsor institution or with the National Union of Students of the UK.

'Studying in London' means the applicant's Confirmation of Acceptance for Studies confirms they will be studying at an institution wholly within the Greater London Area. If the applicant will be studying at more than one site, one or more of which is in Greater London Area and one or more outside, then the applicant will be considered to be studying in London if the applicant's Confirmation of Acceptance for Studies states that the applicant will be spending the majority of time studying at a site or sites situated within the Greater London Area.

'Studying outside London' means the applicant's Confirmation of Acceptance for Studies confirms they will be studying in the UK but the site of study does not meet the definition of Studying in London.

[**'Successfully completed'** means the Student or Child Student has completed their course and been assessed by their sponsor, and has been or will be awarded, a qualification that is:

(a) for the course of study for which their Confirmation of Acceptance for Studies was assigned; or

(b) a degree at either UK Bachelor's degree level or UK postgraduate degree level, as part of an integrated programme for which their Confirmation of Acceptance for Studies was assigned; or

(c) for the course of study with their student sponsor to which they were allowed to change without applying for further permission on the Student route.]

Note: Definition substituted from 09:00 on 1 July 2021 subject to savings for applications (including for administrative review) made before that time (HC 1248).

'Supplementary employment' means employment in a job (other than the job for which the person is being sponsored) which appears on the Shortage Occupation Lists in Appendix Shortage Occupation Lists, or in the same profession and at the same professional level as the job for which the person is being sponsored, provided that:

(a) the person remains working for the sponsor in the job for which the Certificate of Sponsorship records the person is being sponsored; and

(b) the other employment does not exceed 20 hours per week and takes place outside of the hours when the person is contracted to work for the sponsor in the job for which the person is being sponsored.

'Swiss citizens' rights agreement' means (as modified from time to time in accordance with any provision of it) the Agreement signed at Bern on 25 February 2019 between the United Kingdom of Great Britain and Northern Ireland and the Swiss Confederation on citizens' rights following the withdrawal of the United Kingdom from:

(a) the European Union; and

(b) the Agreement on the Free Movement of Persons.

[**'Temporary refugee permission to stay'** means permission to stay granted to a refugee under paragraph 339QB of these rules which has not been revoked under paragraph 339QD.]

Note: Definition inserted from 28 June 2022 subject to savings for applications made before that date (CH 17).

[**'Temporary humanitarian permission to stay'** means permission to stay granted to an individual with humanitarian protection under paragraph 339QC of these rules which has not been revoked under paragraph 339QD.]

Note: Definition inserted from 28 June 2022 subject to savings for applications made before that date (CH 17).

'Tier 1 (Entrepreneur) Migrant' means a person who has, or had leave under paragraphs 245D to 245DF.

'Tier 1 (Exceptional Talent) Migrant' means a person who was granted leave under paragraphs 245B to 245BF of the rules in force before 1 December 2020.

'Tier 1 (General) Migrant' means a person who was granted leave under paragraphs 245C to 245CE of the rules in force before 6 April 2018.

'Tier 1 (Graduate Entrepreneur) Migrant' means a person who was granted leave under paragraphs 245F to 245FB of the rules in force on or after 6 April 2012 and before 29 March 2019.

'Tier 1 (Investor) Migrant' means a person who has, or had, leave under paragraphs 245E to 245EF.

'Tier 1 (Post-Study Work) Migrant' [DELETED]

Note: Definition of 'Tier 1 (Post-Study Work) Migrant' deleted from 6 April 2021 subject to savings for applications made before that date (HC 1248).

'Tier 2 (General) Migrant' means a person granted leave under paragraphs 245H to 245HF and who obtained points under paragraphs 76 to 84A of Appendix A of the rules in force before 1 December 2020.

'Tier 2 (Intra-Company Transfer) Migrant' means a person granted leave under paragraphs 245G to 245GF of the rules in force before 1 December 2020.

'Tier 2 Migrant' means a person granted leave as a Tier 2 (Intra-Company Transfer) Migrant, a Tier 2 (General) Migrant, a Tier 2 (Minister of Religion) Migrant or a Tier 2 (Sportsperson) Migrant under the rules in force before 1 December 2020.

'Tier 2 (Minister of Religion) Migrant' means a person granted leave under the Tier 2 Minister of Religion route as a missionary or a member of a religious order under paragraphs 245H to 245HF of the rules in force before 1 December 2020.

'T2 Minister of Religion' means a person who has, or had, permission under Appendix T2 Minister of Religion, or as a Tier 2 (Minister of Religion) migrant under the rules in force before 1 December 2020.

'Tier 2 (Sportsperson) Migrant' means a person granted leave under paragraphs 245H to 245HF (and who obtained points under paragraphs 93 to 100 of Appendix A) of the rules in force before 1 December 2020.

'Tier 2 Sportsperson' [DELETED]

Note: Definition of 'Tier 2 Sportsperson' deleted from 09:00 on 11 October 2021 subject to savings for applications made before that time (HC 617).

'Tier 4 (Child) Student' means a person granted leave under paragraphs 245ZZ to 245ZZD of the rules in force before 5 October 2020.

'Tier 4 (General) Student' means a person granted leave under paragraphs 245ZT to 245ZY of the rules in force before 5 October 2020.

'Tier 4 Migrant' means a Tier 4 (General) Student or a Tier 4 (Child) Student.

'Tier 5 Migrant' means a person granted leave as either a Tier 5 (Temporary Worker) Migrant or a Tier 5 (Youth Mobility Scheme) Temporary Migrant under the rules in force before 1 December 2020.

[**'Temporary Worker'** means a person who has, or had, permission as a Charity Worker, Creative Worker, Religious Worker, Seasonal Worker, on the International Agreement route, Youth Mobility Scheme or Government Authorised Exchange route.]

Note: definition substituted (previously T5 (Temporary Worker) from 09:00 on 11 October 2021 subject to savings for applications made before that time (HC 617).

'Tier 5 (Temporary Worker) Migrant' means a person granted leave under paragraphs 245ZM to 245ZS of the rules in force before 1 December 2020.

'Track record of compliance' means a 4-year track record of immigration compliance and Educational Oversight, established by a student sponsor in accordance with the requirements set out in the student sponsor guidance which is published on the visa and immigration pages of the gov.uk website.

'Training Programme' means a training programme under a Government Authorised Exchange Scheme where the person concerned either receives formal, practical training in the fields of science and / or medicine or will be trained by HM Forces or by UK emergency services.

[**'Transit Visitor'** means a person who has, or had, permission under Appendix V: Visitor, or Appendix Visitor: Transit Without Visa Scheme, to transit the UK on route to another country outside the Common Travel Area.]

Note: Definition inserted from 6 October 2021 subject to savings for applications made before that date (HC 617).

'UK' means the United Kingdom.

'UK Ancestry route' means the route in Appendix UK Ancestry, or paragraphs 186 to 199B in Part 5 of the Rules in force before 1 December 2020, and **'person with UK Ancestry'** means a person applying for, or granted, permission on the basis that they have a grandparent born in the UK and Islands and meet the requirements in Appendix UK Ancestry, or under paragraphs 186 to 193 in Part 5 of the Rules in force before 1 December 2020.

'UK bachelor's degree' means:

(a) a programme of study or research which leads to the award by or on behalf of a university, college or other body which is authorised by Royal Charter, an Act of Parliament, the Privy Council or the Office for Students to grant degrees, of a qualification designated by the awarding institution to be of bachelor's degree level; or

(b) a programme of study or research, which leads to a recognised award for the purposes of section 214(2)(c) of the Education Reform Act 1988, of a qualification designated by the awarding institution to be of bachelor's degree level.

'UK Border' means immigration control at a UK port and a control zone in France or Belgium or a supplementary control zone in France as defined by Article 2(1) and Schedule 1 to the Channel Tunnel (International Arrangements) Order 1993 (SI 1993/1813) and Article 2 of the Nationality, Immigration and Asylum Act 2002 (Juxtaposed Controls) Order 2003 (SI 2003/2818).

[**'UK Expansion Worker'** means a person who has, or last had, permission as a UK Expansion Worker under Appendix Global Business Mobility – UK Expansion Worker.]

Note: Definition inserted from 09:00 on 11 April 2022 subject to savings for applications made before that time (HC 1118).

'UK listed body' is an institution which is not a UK recognised body but which provides full courses that lead to the award of a degree by a UK recognised body.

'UK NARIC' [DELETED]

Note: Definition of 'UK NARIC' deleted from 6 October 2021 subject to savings for applications made before that date (HC 617).

[**'UK postgraduate degree'** means:

(a) a programme of study or research which leads to an award, by or on behalf of a university, college or another body which is authorised by a Royal Charter, an Act of Parliament, the Privy Council or the Office for Students to grant degrees, of a qualification designated by the awarding institution to be of master's degree level or above; or

(b) a programme of study or research, which leads to a recognised award for the purposes of section 214(2)(c) of the Education Reform Act 1988, of a qualification designated by the awarding institution to be of master's degree level or above.]

Note: Definition inserted from 6 April 2021 subject to savings for applications made before that date (HC 1248).

[**'Ukraine Scheme'** means the routes set out in Appendix Ukraine Scheme: the Ukraine Family Scheme, Homes for Ukraine Sponsorship Scheme, and Ukraine Extension Scheme.]

Note: Definition inserted from 30 March 2022 (HC 1220).

'UK recognised body' means a higher learning institution that has been granted degree awarding powers by Royal Charter, an Act of Parliament, the Privy Council or the Office for Students, and for the purposes of these rules, Health Education South London and Health Education England are equivalent to UK recognised bodies, as set out at: https://www.gov.uk/check-a-university-is-officially-recognised.

[**'UK Regulated Profession'** means a profession regulated by UK law which is listed at: https://cpq.ecctis.com/Individuals/Inbound/Regulated%20Professions.]

Note: Definition substituted from 6 October 2021 subject to savings for applications made before that date (HC 617).

'UK Regulated Profession' means a profession regulated by UK law under Directive 2005/36/EC, modified by Directive 2013/55/EU, as listed at:

http://cpq.naric.org.uk/Professions/Regulated%20professions/Default.

'UKRI' means UK Research and Innovation.

[**'Uncle'** in Appendix Ukraine Scheme, means the brother, or step-brother, of either of the UK-based sponsor's parents, or the male partner of the UK-based sponsor's uncle or aunt.]

Note: Definition inserted from 30 March 2022 (HC 1220).

'United Kingdom passport' has the same meaning as in the Immigration Act 1971.

'Unmarried partner', under Appendix ECAA Extension of Stay or Appendix ECAA Settlement, means a person who is:

(a) resident with the ECAA worker or ECAA business person unless applying for entry clearance; and

(b) intends to live, or continue living, with the ECAA worker or ECAA business person; and

(c) is in a relationship with the ECAA worker or ECAA business person that is genuine and subsisting.

'Valid application' means an application made in accordance with the requirements of Part 1, or the validity requirements of the route in question, whichever is applicable.

'Visa nationals' means persons specified in Appendix Visitor: Visa National list as needing a visa, or entry clearance, for the UK for a visit or for any other purposes where seeking entry for 6 months or less and **'Non-visa nationals'** are persons who are not so specified in that Appendix.

'Visitor' means a person granted permission under paragraphs 40-56Z, 75A-M or 82-87 of the rules in force before 24 April 2015 or Appendix V on or after 24 April 2015 or Appendix V: Visitor after 9am on 1 December 2020.

'Voluntary fieldwork' means activities which would not normally be offered at a waged or salaried rate and which contribute directly to the achievement or advancement of the sponsor's charitable purpose. It does not include work ancillary to the sponsor's charitable purpose including, for example, routine back office administrative roles, retail or other sales roles, fund-raising roles and roles involved in the maintenance of the sponsor's offices and other assets.

'Voluntary work' has the same meaning as applies to a voluntary worker in the National Minimum Wage Act 1998.

'Week' means a period of 7 days beginning with a Monday.

'Withdrawal Agreement' means the agreement between the United Kingdom and the EU under Article 50(2) of the Treaty on European Union which sets out the arrangements for the United Kingdom's withdrawal from the EU (as that agreement is modified from time to time in accordance with any provision of it).

'Work' has the same meaning as **'Employment'**, except that work does not include being party to an employment contract but not working.

'Work Experience Programme' means work experience including volunteering and job-shadowing, internships and work exchange programmes under a Government Authorised Exchange Scheme.

'Work placement' means a placement that forms an integral and assessed part of the course of study which meets the requirements in Appendix Student or Appendix Child Student.

'Working day' means a business day in the part of the UK in which the applicant resides or (as the case may be) is detained.

'Working illegally' means working in breach of a condition of leave or working in the UK without valid leave where such leave is required.

[**'Youth Mobility Scheme'** means a person who has, or had, permission under any of the following:

(i) Appendix Youth Mobility Scheme; or

(ii) Appendix T5 (Temporary Worker) Youth Mobility Scheme under the rules in force between 1 December 2020 and 10 October 2021(inclusive); or

(iii) as a Tier 5 Youth Mobility Scheme migrant under part 6A of the rules in force before 1 December 2020.]

Note: Definition substituted (previously 'Youth Mobility Scheme route') from 09:00 on 11 October 2021 subject to savings for applications made before that time (HC 617).

Paragraph inserted from 09:00 on 1 December 2020 subject to savings for applications made before that time (HC 813).

6A. For the purpose of these Rules, a person ('P') is not to be regarded as having (or potentially having) recourse to public funds merely because P is (or will be) reliant in whole or in part on public funds provided to P's sponsor unless, as a result of P's presence in the United Kingdom, the sponsor is (or would be) entitled to increased or additional public funds (save where such entitlement to increased or additional public funds is by virtue of P and the sponsor's joint entitlement to benefits under the regulations referred to in paragraph 6B).

6B. Subject to paragraph 6C, a person (P) shall not be regarded as having recourse to public funds if P is entitled to benefits specified under section 115 of the Immigration and Asylum Act 1999 by virtue of regulations made under sub-sections (3) and (4) of that section or section 42 of the Tax Credits Act 2002.

6C. A person (P) making an application from outside the United Kingdom will be regarded as having recourse to public funds where P relies upon the future entitlement to any public funds that would be payable to P or to P's sponsor as a result of P's presence in the United Kingdom, (including those benefits to which P or the sponsor would be entitled as a result of P's presence in the United Kingdom under the regulations referred to in paragraph 6B).

Part I

General Provisions Regarding Leave to Enter or Remain in the United Kingdom

Leave to enter the United Kingdom

7. A person who is neither a British citizen nor a Commonwealth citizen with the right of abode nor a person who is entitled to enter or remain in the United Kingdom by virtue of [section 3ZA of the Immigration Act 1971] requires leave to enter the United Kingdom.

Note: Words substituted from 09:00 on 1 December 2020 subject to savings for applications made before that time (HC 813).

8. Under Sections 3 and 4 of the Immigration Act 1971 an Immigration Officer when admitting to the United Kingdom a person subject to immigration control under that Act may give leave to enter for a limited period and, if he does, may impose all or any of the following conditions:

(i) a condition restricting employment or occupation in the United Kingdom;

(ii) a condition requiring the person to maintain and accommodate himself, and any dependants of his, without recourse to public funds;

(iii) a condition requiring the person to register with the police; and

(iv) a condition restricting his studies in the United Kingdom.

He may also require him to report to the appropriate Medical Officer of Environmental Health. Under Section 24 of the 1971 Act it is an offence knowingly to remain beyond the time limit or fail to comply with such a condition or requirement.

9. The time limit and any conditions attached will be made known to the person concerned either:

(i) by written notice given to him or endorsed by the Immigration Officer in his passport or travel document; or

(ii) in any other manner permitted by the Immigration (Leave to Enter and Remain) Order 2000.

Exercise of the power to refuse leave to enter the United Kingdom or to cancel leave to enter or remain which is in force

10. The power to refuse leave to enter the United Kingdom or to cancel leave to enter or remain which is already in force is not to be exercised by an Immigration Officer acting on his own. The authority of a Chief Immigration Officer or of an Immigration Inspector must always be obtained.

Suspension of leave to enter or remain in the United Kingdom

10A. Where a person has arrived in the United Kingdom with leave to enter or remain which is in force but which was given to him before his arrival he may be examined by an Immigration Officer under paragraph 2A of Schedule 2 to the Immigration Act 1971. An Immigration Officer examining a person under paragraph 2A may suspend that person's leave to enter or remain in the United Kingdom until the examination is completed.

Cancellation of leave to enter or remain in the United Kingdom

10B. Where a person arrives in the United Kingdom with leave to enter or remain in the United Kingdom which is already in force, an Immigration Officer may cancel that leave.

Requirement for persons arriving in the United Kingdom or seeking entry through the Channel Tunnel to produce evidence of identity and nationality

11. A person must, on arrival in the United Kingdom or when seeking entry through the Channel Tunnel, produce on request by [an immigration officer]:

(i) a valid national passport or[, subject to paragraph 11A,] other document satisfactorily establishing [their] identity and nationality; and

(ii) such information as may be required to establish whether [they require] leave to enter the United Kingdom and, if so, whether and on what terms leave to enter should be given.

Note: Words in introduction substituted, words in (i) and (ii) substituted from 1 October 2021 (HC 617).

[**11A.** A national identity card is not valid for the purposes of paragraph 11(i), except where the holder is one of the following:

(a) a British citizen of Gibraltar; or

(b) a national of Switzerland with a valid entry clearance granted under Appendix Service Providers from Switzerland to these Rules; or

(c) a national of one of the countries listed in paragraph 11B with valid indefinite or limited leave to enter or remain granted under Appendix EU to these Rules, or who has made a valid application under that Appendix (other than as a joining family member of a relevant sponsor, as defined in Annex 1 to that Appendix) which has not yet been finally determined; or

(d) a national of one of the countries listed at paragraph 11B with a valid entry clearance in the form of an EU Settlement Scheme Family Permit; or

(e) a national of one of the countries listed at paragraph 11B with a frontier worker permit; or

(f) a national of one of the countries listed at paragraph 11B seeking to come to the UK as an S2 Healthcare Visitor; or

(g) a national of one of the countries listed at paragraph 11B who has been granted immigration permission equivalent to that set out in sub-paragraphs (b) to (f) above by the Islands, or who has made a valid application under the equivalent in the Islands of Appendix EU to these rules (other than as the equivalent of a joining family member of a relevant sponsor, as defined in Annex 1 to that Appendix) which has not yet been finally determined.]

Note: Paragraph inserted from 1 October 2021 (HC 617).

[**11B.** For the purposes of subparagraphs (c) to (g) of paragraph 11A, the holder must be a national of one of the following countries:

Austria
Belgium
Bulgaria
Croatia
Cyprus
Czech Republic
Denmark
Estonia
Finland
France
Germany
Greece
Hungary
Iceland
Italy
Latvia
Liechtenstein
Lithuania
Luxembourg
Malta
Netherlands
Norway
Poland
Portugal
Romania
Slovakia
Slovenia
Spain
Sweden
Switzerland.]

Note: Paragraph inserted from 1 October 2021 (HC 617).

Requirement for a person not requiring leave to enter the United Kingdom to prove that he has the right of abode

12. A person claiming to be a British citizen must prove that he has the right of abode in the United Kingdom by producing either:

(i) a United Kingdom passport describing him as a British citizen or as a citizen of the United Kingdom and Colonies having the right of abode in the United Kingdom; or

(ii) a certificate of entitlement duly issued by or on behalf of the Government of the United Kingdom certifying that he has the right of abode.

13. A person claiming to be a Commonwealth citizen with the right of abode in the United Kingdom must prove that he has the right of abode by producing a certificate of entitlement duly issued to him by or on behalf of the Government of the United Kingdom certifying that he has the right of abode.

14. A Commonwealth citizen who has been given limited leave to enter the United Kingdom may later claim to have the right of abode. The time limit on his stay may be removed if he is able to establish a claim to the right of abode, for example by showing that:

(i) immediately before the commencement of the British Nationality Act 1981 he was a Commonwealth citizen born to or legally adopted by a parent who at the time of the birth had citizenship of the United Kingdom and Colonies by his birth in the United Kingdom or any of the Islands; and

(ii) he has not ceased to be a Commonwealth citizen in the meanwhile.

Common travel area

15. The United Kingdom, the Channel Islands, the Isle of Man and the Republic of Ireland collectively form a common travel area. A person who has been examined for the purpose of immigration control at the point at which he entered the area does not normally require leave to enter any other part of it. However certain persons subject to the Immigration (Control of Entry through the Republic of Ireland) Order 1972 (as amended) who enter the United Kingdom through the Republic of Ireland do require leave to enter. This includes:

(i) those who merely passed through the Republic of Ireland;

(ii) persons requiring visas;

(iii) persons who entered the Republic of Ireland unlawfully;

(iv) persons who are subject to directions given by the Secretary of State for their exclusion from the United Kingdom on the ground that their exclusion is conducive to the public good;

(v) persons who entered the Republic from the United Kingdom and Islands after entering there unlawfully or overstaying their leave.

Admission of certain British passport holders

16. A person in any of the following categories may be admitted freely to the United Kingdom on production of a United Kingdom passport issued in the United Kingdom and Islands or the Republic of Ireland prior to 1 January 1973, unless his passport has been endorsed to show that he was subject to immigration control:

(i) a British Dependent Territories citizen;

(ii) a British National (Overseas);

(iii) a British Overseas citizen;

(iv) a British protected person;

(v) a British subject by virtue of Section 30(a) of the British Nationality Act 1981, (who, immediately before the commencement of the 1981 Act would have been a British subject not possessing citizenship of the United Kingdom and Colonies or the citizenship of any other Commonwealth country or territory).

17. British Overseas citizens who hold United Kingdom passports wherever issued and who satisfy the Immigration Officer that they have, since 1 March 1968, been given indefinite leave to enter or remain in the United Kingdom may be given indefinite leave to enter.

Persons outside the United Kingdom

17A. Where a person is outside the United Kingdom but wishes to travel to the United Kingdom an Immigration Officer may give or refuse him leave to enter. An Immigration Officer may exercise these powers whether or not he is, himself, in the United Kingdom. However, an Immigration Officer is not obliged to consider an application for leave to enter from a person outside the United Kingdom.

17B. Where a person having left the common travel area, has leave to enter the United Kingdom which remains in force under article 13 of the Immigration (Leave to Enter and Remain) Order 2000, an Immigration Officer may cancel that leave. An Immigration Officer may exercise these powers whether or not he is, himself, in the United Kingdom. If a person outside the United Kingdom has leave to remain in the United Kingdom which is in force in this way, the Secretary of State may cancel that leave.

Returning residents

18. A person [...] may [resume their residence in the UK] [. . .] provided the Immigration Officer is satisfied that the person concerned:

(i) had indefinite leave to enter or remain in the United Kingdom when he last left; and

(ii) has not been away from the United Kingdom for more than 2 years; and

(iii) did not receive assistance from public funds towards the cost of leaving the United Kingdom; and

(iv) now seeks admission for the purpose of settlement.

Note: Words deleted; words inserted from 6 July 2018 subject to savings for applications made before that date (HC 1154).

18A. Those who qualify [to resume their residence] [. . .]in accordance with paragraph 18 do not need a visa to enter the UK.

Note: Words inserted; words deleted from 6 July 2018 subject to savings for applications made before that date (HC 1154).

19. A person who does not benefit from the preceding paragraph by reason only of having been [absent from the United Kingdom for more than two consecutive years, must have applied for, and been granted indefinite leave to enter by way of entry clearance] [. . .] if [he can demonstrate he has strong ties to the United Kingdom and intends to make the United Kingdom his permanent home.] [. . .].

Note: Words substituted; words deleted from 6 July 2018 subject to savings for applications made before that date (HC 1154).

19A. Sub paragraphs (ii) and (iii) of paragraph 18 shall not apply where a person who has indefinite leave to enter or remain in the United Kingdom accompanies on an overseas posting, [a partner, parent] a spouse, civil partner, unmarried partner or same-sex partner who is:

(a) a member of HM Forces serving overseas; or
(b) a British citizen or is settled in the UK and
(i) a permanent member of HM Diplomatic Service;
(ii) a comparable United Kingdom based [permanent] staff member of the British Council;
(iii) a [permanent] staff member of the Department for International Development; or
(iv) a [permanent] Home Office employee.

Note: Words inserted from 6 July 2018 subject to savings for applications made before that date (HC 1154).

20. The leave of a person whose stay in the United Kingdom is subject to a time limit lapses on his going to a country or territory outside the common travel area if the leave was given for a period of six months or less or conferred by a visit visa. In other cases, leave lapses on the holder remaining outside the United Kingdom for a continuous period of more than two years. A person whose leave has lapsed and who returns after a temporary absence abroad within the period of this earlier leave has no claim to admission as a returning resident. His application to re-enter the United Kingdom should be considered in the light of all the relevant circumstances. The same time limit and any conditions attached will normally be reimposed if he meets the requirements of these Rules, unless he is seeking admission in a different capacity from the one in which he was last given leave to enter or remain.

Non-lapsing leave

20A. Leave to enter or remain in the United Kingdom will usually lapse on the holder going to a country or territory outside the common travel area. However, under article 13 of the Immigration (Leave to Enter and Remain) Order 2000 such leave will not lapse where it was given for a period exceeding six months or where it was conferred by means of an entry clearance (other than a visit visa).

20B. Those who seek leave to enter the United Kingdom within the period of their earlier leave and for the same purpose as that for which that leave was granted, unless it
(i) was for a period of six months or less; or
(ii) was extended by statutory instrument or by section 3C of the Immigration Act 1971 (inserted by section 3 of the Immigration and Asylum Act 1999); do not need a visa to enter the UK.

Holders of restricted travel documents and passports

21. The leave to enter or remain in the United Kingdom of the holder of a passport or travel document whose permission to enter another country has to be exercised before a given date may be restricted so as to terminate at least 2 months before that date.

22. If his passport or travel document is endorsed with a restriction on the period for which he may remain outside his country of normal residence, his leave to enter or remain in the United Kingdom may be limited so as not to extend beyond the period of authorised absence.

23. The holder of a travel document issued by the Home Office should not be given leave to enter or remain for a period extending beyond the validity of that document. This paragraph and paragraphs 21–22 do not apply to a person who is eligible for admission for settlement or to a spouse or civil partner who is eligible for admission under paragraph 282 or to a person who qualifies for the removal of the time limit on his stay.

Leave to enter granted on arrival in the United Kingdom

23A. A person who is not a visa national and who is seeking leave to enter on arrival in the United Kingdom for a period not exceeding 6 months for a purpose for which prior entry clearance is not required under these Rules may be granted such leave, for a period not exceeding 6 months. This paragraph does not apply where the person is a British National (Overseas), a British overseas territories citizen, a British Overseas citizen, a British protected person, or a person who under the British Nationality Act 1981 is a British subject.

23B. A person who is a British National (Overseas), a British overseas territories citizen, a British Overseas citizen, a British protected person, or a person who under the British Nationality Act 1981 is a British subject, and who is seeking leave to enter on arrival in the United Kingdom for a purpose for which prior entry clearance is not required under these Rules may be granted such leave, irrespective of the period of time for which he seeks entry, for a period not exceeding 6 months.

Entry clearance

[**24.** The following:

(i) a visa national;

(ii) a non visa national [. . .] not a British national and is seeking entry for a period exceeding six months, or for [a] purpose for which prior entry clearance is required under these Rules;

(iii) a British national without the right of abode who is seeking entry for a purpose for [which] prior entry clearance is required under these Rules, must either:

(i) produce to the Immigration Officer a valid passport or other identity document endorsed with a United Kingdom entry clearance, issued to him for the purpose for which he seeks entry, which is still in force, or:

(ii) where he has been granted a United Kingdom entry clearance which was issued to him in electronic form for the purpose for which he seeks entry and which is still in force, produce to the Immigration Officer a valid passport or other identity document. Such a person will be refused leave to enter if he has no such current entry clearance. Any other person who wishes to ascertain in advance whether he is eligible for admission to the United Kingdom may apply for the issue of an entry clearance.]

Note: Paragraph 24 substituted from 11 January 2018 subject to savings for applications made before that date (HC 309). Words in sub-paragraphs (ii) and (iii) deleted and inserted from 6 July 2018 subject to savings for applications made before that date (HC 1154).

25. Entry clearance takes the form of a visa (for visa nationals) or an entry certificate (for non visa nationals). [A visa or an entry certificate may be issued in electronic form.] These documents are to be taken as evidence of the holder's eligibility for entry into the United Kingdom, and accordingly accepted as 'entry clearances' within the meaning of the Immigration Act 1971.

Note: Words inserted from 11 January 2018 subject to savings for applications made before that date (HC 309).

25A. An entry clearance which satisfies the requirements set out in article 3 of the Immigration (Leave to Enter and Remain) Order 2000 will have effect as leave to enter the United Kingdom. The requirements are that the entry clearance must specify the purpose for which the holder wishes to enter the United Kingdom and should be endorsed with the conditions to which it is subject or with a statement that it has effect as indefinite leave to enter the United Kingdom. The holder of such an entry clearance will not require leave to enter on arrival in the United Kingdom and, for the purposes of these Rules, will be treated as a person who has arrived in the United Kingdom with leave to enter the United Kingdom which is in force but which was given to him before his arrival.

26. An application for entry clearance will be considered in accordance with the provisions in these Rules governing the grant or refusal of leave to enter. Where appropriate, the term 'Entry Clearance Officer' should be substituted for 'Immigration Officer'.

27. An application for entry clearance is to be decided in the light of the circumstances existing at the time of the decision, except that an applicant will not be refused an entry clearance where entry is sought in one of the categories contained in paragraphs 296–316 or paragraph EC-C of Appendix FM solely on account of his attaining the age of 18 years between receipt of his application and the date of the decision on it.

28. An applicant for an entry clearance must be outside the United Kingdom and Islands at the time of the application. An application for an entry clearance as a visitor or as a short-term student [or under Appendix Ukraine Scheme] must be made to any post designated by the Secretary of State to accept such applications. Subject to paragraph 28A, any other application must be made to a post in the country or territory where the applicant is living which has been designated by the Secretary of State to accept applications for entry clearance for that purpose and from that category of applicant. Where there is no such post the applicant must apply to the appropriate designated post outside the country or territory where he is living.

Note: Words inserted from 30 March 2022 (HC 1220).

28A.

(a) An application for entry clearance [under {Appendix Temporary Work – Creative Worker}] may also be made at the post in the country or territory where the applicant is situated at the time of the application, provided that:

(i) the post has been designated by the Secretary of State to accept applications for entry clearance for that purpose and from that category of applicant,

(ii) the applicant is in that country or territory for a similar purpose to the activity he proposes to undertake in the UK, and

(iii) the applicant is able to demonstrate to the Entry Clearance Officer that he has authority to be living in that country or territory in accordance with its immigration laws. Those applicants who are known to the authorities of that country or territory but who have not been given permission to live in that country or territory will not be eligible to make an application.

(b) An application for entry clearance [as a Global Talent migrant] or {under Appendix Youth Mobility Scheme} may also be made at the post in the country or territory where the applicant is situated at the time of the application, provided that:

(i) the post has been designated by the Secretary of State to accept applications for entry clearance for that purpose and from that category of applicant, and

(ii) the applicant is able to demonstrate to the Entry Clearance Officer that he has authority to be living in that country or territory in accordance with its immigration laws and that when he was given authority to live in that country or territory he was given authority to live in that country or territory for a period of more than 6 months. Those applicants who are known to the authorities of that country or territory but who have not been given permission to live in that country or territory will not be eligible to make an application.

Note: Words in square brackets in (b) substituted from 20 February 2020 subject to savings for applications made before that date (HC 56). Words in (a), substituted, amendment to (b) from 09:00 on 1 December 2020 subject to savings for applications made before that date (HC 813). **NB:** HC 813 refers to sub-paragraphs 28(a) and (b) which do not exist, so it is clear the amendments are intended to apply to paragraph 28A. Words in curly brackets in (a) and (b) substituted from 6 April 2022 (HC 1118).

29. For the purposes of paragraph 28 'post' means a British Diplomatic Mission, British Consular post or the office of any person outside the United Kingdom and Islands who has been authorised by the Secretary of State to accept applications for entry clearance. A list of designated posts is published by the Foreign and Commonwealth Office.

30. An application for an entry clearance is not made until any fee required to be paid under the regulations made under sections 68 and 69 of the Immigration Act 2014 has been paid.

30A. [DELETED]

Note: Amendments from 07:00 on 30 March 2019 (HC 1919). Amendments from 09:00 on 1 December 2020 subject to savings for applications made before that time (HC 813). Paragraph deleted from 6 April 2021 (HC 1248).

30B. An entry clearance shall cease to have effect where the entry clearance has effect as leave to enter and an Immigration Officer cancels that leave in accordance with paragraph 2A(8) of Schedule 2 to the Immigration Act 1971.

30C. An Immigration Officer may cancel an entry clearance which is capable of having effect as leave to enter if the holder arrives in the United Kingdom before the day on which the entry clearance becomes effective or if the holder seeks to enter the United Kingdom for a purpose other than the purpose specified in the entry clearance.

Variation of leave to enter or remain in the United Kingdom

31. [DELETED]

Note: Paragraph deleted from 6 April 2022 (HC 1118).

31A. [DELETED]

Note: Paragraph deleted from 6 April 2022 (HC 1118).

32. DELETED

33. DELETED

33A. Where a person having left the common travel area, has leave to enter or remain in the United Kingdom which remains in force under article 13 of the Immigration (Leave to Enter and Remain) Order 2000, his leave may be varied (including any condition to which it is subject in such form and manner as permitted for the giving of leave to enter. However, the Secretary of State is not obliged to consider an application for variation of leave to enter or remain from a person outside the United Kingdom.

33B–33G. DELETED

Specified forms and procedures for applications or claims in connection with immigration
[How to make a valid application for permission to stay in the UK]

Note: Heading inserted from 09:00 on 1 December 2020 subject to savings for applications made before that time (HC 813). Heading substituted from 6 April 2022 (HC 1118).

[A34. Paragraphs 34 and 34A do not apply to an application made under the following:

[[Appendix Settlement Protection: settlement for people on a protection route]]
Appendix V: Visitor
Appendix S2 Healthcare Visitor
Appendix Student
Appendix Short-term Student
[[Appendix Graduate]]
Appendix Child Student
Appendix Parent of a Child Student
Appendix Skilled Worker
{{Appendix Global Business Mobility – Senior or Specialist Worker
Appendix Global Business Mobility – Graduate Trainee
Appendix Global Business Mobility – UK Expansion Worker
Appendix Global Business Mobility – Service Supplier
Appendix Global Business Mobility – Secondment Worker
Appendix ECAA: Extension of Stay
Appendix Settlement Protection
Appendix Graduate
Appendix Overseas Domestic Worker
Appendix Domestic Worker who is a Victim of Modern Slavery
Appendix Domestic Workers in a Private Household}}
[. . .]
Appendix T2 Minister of Religion
{Appendix International Sportsperson}
Appendix Representative of an Overseas Business
Appendix UK Ancestry
Appendix Global Talent
Appendix Start-up
Appendix Innovator
{Appendix Temporary Worker – Seasonal Worker}
{Appendix Youth Mobility Scheme}
{Appendix Temporary Work – Creative Worker}
{Appendix Temporary Work – Religious Worker}
{Appendix Temporary Work – Charity Worker}
{Appendix Temporary Worker – International Agreement}
{Appendix Temporary Work – Government Authorised Exchange}
Appendix Service Providers from Switzerland
Appendix Hong Kong British National (Overseas)
[[[Appendix Settlement Family Life
Appendix Private Life]]]
Appendix EU.]
[{[Appendix Ukraine Scheme]}]

Note: Paragraph inserted from 09:00 on 1 December 2020 subject to savings for applications made before that time (HC 813). Words in double square brackets inserted from 6 October 2021 subject to savings for applications made before that date; words in curly brackets substituted from 09:00 on 11 October 2021 subject to savings for applications made before that time (HC 617). Words deleted, words in double curly brackets inserted from 09:00 on 11 April 2022 subject to savings for applications made before that time; words in triple square brackets inserted from 20 June 2022 subject to savings for applications made before that date (HC 1118). Words in square curly square brackets inserted from 30 March 2022 (HC 1220).

[**34.** […]An application for [permission to stay] must be made in accordance with subparagraphs (1) to (9) below.

(1) (a) Subject to paragraph 34(1)(c), the application must be made on an application form which is specified for the immigration category under which the applicant is applying on the date on which the application is made.

(b) An application form is specified when it is posted on the visa and immigration pages of the GOV.UK website.

(c) An application can be made on a previous version of a specified paper application form (and shall be treated as made on a specified form) as long as it is no more than 21 days out of date.

(2) All mandatory sections of the application form must be completed.

(3) Where the applicant is required to pay a fee, this fee must be paid in full in accordance with the process set out in the application form [unless the applicant has made an application for a fee waiver which has been granted in whole or in part.]

(4) Where the applicant is required to pay the Immigration Health Surcharge, this must be paid in accordance with the process set out on the visa and immigration pages of the GOV.UK website.

(5) (a) Subject to paragraph 34(5)(c), the applicant must provide proof of identity as described in 34(5)(b) below and in accordance with the process set out in the application form.

(b) Proof of identity for the purpose of this paragraph means:

(i) a valid passport or, if an applicant (except a PBS applicant) does not have a valid passport, a valid national identity card; or

(ii) if the applicant does not have a valid passport or national identity card, their most recent passport or (except a PBS applicant) their most recent national identity card; or

(iii) if the applicant does not have any of the above, a valid travel document.

(c) Proof of identity need not be provided where:

(i) the applicant's passport, national identity card or travel document is held by the Home Office at the date of application; or

(ii) the applicant's passport, nationality identity card or travel document has been permanently lost or stolen and there is no functioning national government to issue a replacement; or

(iii) the applicant's passport, nationality identity card or travel document has been retained by an employer or other person in circumstances which have led to the applicant being the subject of a positive conclusive grounds decision made by a competent authority under the National Referral Mechanism; or

(iv) the application is for limited leave to enable access to public funds pending an application under paragraph 289A of, or under Part 6 of Appendix Armed Forces or section DVILR of Appendix FM to these Rules; or

(v) the application is made under Part 14 of these Rules for leave as a stateless person or as the family member of a stateless person; or

(vi) the application was made by a person in the UK with refugee leave or humanitarian protection; or

(vii) the applicant provides a good reason beyond their control why they cannot provide proof of their identity.

(6) Where any of paragraph 34(5)(c)(ii)-(vii) applies, the Secretary of State may ask the applicant to provide alternative satisfactory evidence of their identity and nationality.

(7) Where the main applicant is under the age of eighteen, their parent or legal guardian must provide written consent to the application.

(8) Where the application is made on a paper application form, it must be sent by prepaid post or courier to the address on the application form.

(9) An applicant must comply with the application process set out on the visa and immigration pages on GOV.UK and in the invitation to enrol biometrics which is provided as part of the application process in relation to –

(a) making an appointment to provide biometrics, and

(b) providing any evidence requested by the Secretary of State in support of their application.]

Note: Paragraph 34 substituted from 1 November 2018 for applications made on or after that date (HC 1534). Amendments from 09:00 on 5 October 2020 subject to savings for applications made before that time (HC 707). Words in introduction deleted from 09:00 on 1 December 2020 subject to savings for applications made before that time (HC 813). Words in introduction substituted, words in (3) inserted from 6 April 2022 (HC 1118).

[Invalid applications

34A. Subject to paragraph 34B, where an application for [[permission to stay]] does not meet the requirements of paragraph 34, it is invalid and will not be considered.]

Note: Heading and paragraph substituted from 1 November 2018 for applications made on or after that date (HC 1534). Words in double square brackets substituted from 6 April 2022 (HC 1118).

[**34B.** [(**1**) Where an application for *permission to stay* does not meet the requirements of paragraph 34(1) to(9), or the validity requirements [[for the route under which they are applying]], the Secretary of State may notify the applicant and give them one opportunity to correct the error(s) or omission(s) identified by the Secretary of State within the timescale specified in the notification.]

[(2) Where an applicant does not comply with the notification in paragraph 34B(1), or with the requirements in paragraph 34G(4), the application is invalid and will not be considered unless the Secretary of State exercises discretion to treat an invalid application as valid and the requirements of paragraph 34(3) and (5), [[or a requirement to pay a fee and provide biometrics has been met]].]

(3) Notice of invalidity will be given in writing and served in accordance with Appendix SN of these Rules.]

Note: Paragraph 34B and heading substituted from 1 November 2018 for applications made on or after that date (HC 1534). Sub-paragraphs (1) and (2) substituted from 09:00 on 5 October 2020 subject to savings for applications made before that time (HC 707). Words in double square brackets in (1) and (2) substituted from 09:00 on 1 December 2020 subject to savings for applications made before that time (HC 813).

[Variation of an application]

Note: Heading substituted from 6 April 2022 (HC 1118).

[**34BB.** Except where one or more applications have been made under Appendix EU (see paragraph EU10 of Appendix EU):

(1) Where an applicant has an outstanding application for entry clearance or permission to stay which has not been decided ("the previous application"), any further application for entry clearance or permission to stay will be treated as an application to vary the previous application and only the most recent application will be considered.

(2) An application to vary a previous application must comply with the requirements of paragraph 34, or the validity requirements for the route applied for or, subject to paragraph 34B, the application to vary will be invalid and will not be considered.

(3) Any valid application to vary a previous application will be decided in accordance with the immigration rules in force at the date the application to vary is made.

(4) Where an application to vary a previous application has been made, the Secretary of State will contact the applicant to notify them that the application is being treated as an application to vary and that any previous application will have been varied.

(5) Where more than one application to vary has been made, or where it is not clear which is the most recent application, the Secretary of State will request that the applicant confirm which application they want to be considered.

(6) If the applicant does not provide confirmation within 14 days of the request, the most recent application will be considered and any other applications will be treated as varied, unless it is not clear which is the most recent application, in which case all applications will be treated as invalid.

(7) Where a human rights claim is made as part of an application and a subsequent application is made which varies that application under paragraph 34BB(1), if the applicant is then granted entry clearance or permission to stay, any outstanding human rights claim will be treated as withdrawn, but where any subsequent application is refused, the human rights claim, if not already decided, remains outstanding and will be considered at a time decided by the Secretary of State.]

Note: Paragraph 34BB substituted from 1 November 2018 for applications made on or after that date (HC 1534). Paragraph substituted from 6 April 2022 (HC 1118).

[Applications made by dependants]

Note: Heading substituted from 6 April 2022 (HC 1118).

[**34C.** A dependent applicant can be included on a main applicant's application form where the application form allows the dependant to be included. [[Otherwise, a dependent must make a separate application.]]]

Note: Paragraph 34C substituted from 1 November 2018 for applications made on or after that date (HC 1534). Words in double square brackets inserted from 6 October 2021 subject to savings for applications made before that date (HC 617).

[**34DA.** An applicant applying as a dependent partner or dependent child must be applying as the partner or child of a person (P) where:

(i) P has made a valid application for entry clearance, permission to enter, permission to stay or settlement on the same route as the applicant and that application has not been decided; or

(ii) P has entry clearance, permission to enter, or permission to stay, on the same route as the route on which the applicant is applying; or

(iii) P is settled or a British citizen, providing P had permission on the route on which the applicant is applying when they settled, and the applicant had permission as their partner or child at that time.]

Note: Paragraph inserted from 6 April 2022 (HC 1118).

34D. [DELETED]

Note: Paragraph 34D deleted from 1 November 2018 (HC 1534).

[. . .]

34E. [DELETED]

Note: Paragraph 34E and heading substituted from 1 November 2018 for applications made on or after that date (HC 1534). Paragraph substituted again from 09:00 on 5 October 2020 subject to savings for applications made before that time (HC 707). Amendments from 09:00 on 1 December 2020 subject to savings for applications made before that time (HC 813). Paragraph 34E and heading substituted from 6 October 2021 subject to savings for applications made before that date (HC 617). Paragraph and heading deleted from 6 April 2022 (HC 1118).

34F. [DELETED]

Note: Paragraph 34F substituted from 1 November 2018 for applications made on or after that date (HC 1534). Paragraph substituted from 6 October 2021 subject to savings for applications made before that date (HC 617). Paragraph deleted from 6 April 2022 (HC 1118).

[Date of application (or variation of application) for permission to stay]

[**34G.** For the purposes of these rules, and subject to paragraph 34GB, the date on which an application is made is:

(1) where the paper application form is sent by post by Royal Mail, whether or not accompanied by a fee waiver request form, the date of posting as shown on the tracking information provided by Royal Mail or, if not tracked, by the postmark date on the envelope; or

(2) where the paper application form is sent by courier, or other postal services provider, the date on which it is delivered to the Home Office; or

(3) where the application is made via the online application process, and there is no request for a fee waiver, the date on which the online application is submitted; or

(4) where the online application includes a request for a fee waiver, the date on which the online request for a fee waiver is submitted, as long as the completed application for

permission to stay is submitted within 10 days of the receipt of the decision on the fee waiver application.]

Note: Paragraph 34G substituted from 1 November 2018 for applications made on or after that date (HC 1534). Paragraph substituted from 6 October 2021 subject to savings for applications made before that date (HC 617).

[34GA. Where an application is rejected as invalid that decision will be served in accordance with Appendix SN.]

Note: Paragraph inserted from 6 October 2021 subject to savings for applications made before that date (HC 617).

[34GB. Where a variation application is made in accordance with paragraph 34BB, the date the variation application (the new application) is made is deemed to be the date the previous application was made prior to it being varied (the old application).]

Note: Paragraph inserted from 6 October 2021 subject to savings for applications made before that date (HC 617). Paragraph substituted from 6 April 2022 (HC 1118).

34GC. Where a partner, child or other dependent is included in the variation application (the new application) and was not included in the application which has been varied (the old application) the date of application for the dependant's application is the date the variation application (the new application) was made.

Note: Paragraph inserted from 6 October 2021 subject to savings for applications made before that date (HC 617).

[Withdrawal of an application for entry clearance, permission to enter and permission to stay in the United Kingdom]

[34H. An applicant may ask to withdraw their application for entry clearance, permission to enter or permission to stay at any time before a decision is made on the application by making a request in writing or by completing the withdrawal process at www.gov.uk/cancel-visa. If the request to withdraw the application is accepted the date of withdrawal is the date on which the request was received by the Home Office.]

Note: Paragraph 34H deleted from 1 November 2018 (HC 1534). Paragraph and heading re-inserted from 6 October 2021 subject to savings for applications made before that date.

34I. There is no requirement to agree to the withdrawal of an application for entry clearance, permission to enter or permission to stay and the decision maker may instead decide the application.

Note: Paragraph 34I deleted from 1 November 2018 (HC 1534). Paragraph re-inserted from 6 October 2021 subject to savings for applications made before that date (HC 617).

[...]

[34J. The proof of identity provided under paragraph 34(5), or any other application for permission to stay, will be returned to the applicant whilst their application is being considered, unless the Secretary of State considers it necessary to retain it.]

Note: Paragraph 34J and heading substituted from 1 November 2018 for applications made on or after that date (HC 1534). Paragraph substituted from 09:00 on 5 October 2020 subject to savings for applications made before that date (HC 707). Amendments from 09:00 on 1 December 2020 subject to savings for applications made before that time (HC 813). Heading deleted and paragraph substituted from 6 October 2021 subject to savings for applications made before that date (HC 617).

[**34K.** Where a decision on an application for permission to stay has not been made and the applicant travels outside the common travel area their application will be treated as withdrawn on the date the applicant left the common travel area.]

Note: Paragraph substituted from 1 November 2018 for applications made on or after that date (HC 1534). Paragraph substituted from 09:00 on 5 October 2020 subject to savings for applications made before that date (HC 707). Amendments from 09:00 on 1 December 2020 subject to savings for applications made before that time (HC 813). Paragraph substituted from 6 October 2021 subject to savings for applications made before that date (HC 617).

Specified forms and procedures in connection with applications for administrative review

Notice of an eligible decision

34L. (1) Unless sub-paragraph (2) applies, written notice must be given to a person of any eligible decision. The notice given must:

(a) include or be accompanied by a statement of reasons for the decision to which it relates, and

(b) include information on how to apply for an administrative review and the time limit for making an application.

(2) Sub-paragraph (1) does not apply where the eligible decision is a grant of leave to remain.

Making an application

34M. An application for administrative review must be made in accordance with the requirements set out in paragraphs 34N to 34S. If it is not it will be invalid and will not be considered.

34N. (1) Unless sub-paragraph (2) [or (2A)] applies only one valid application for administrative review may be made in respect of an eligible decision.

(2) A further application for administrative review in respect of an eligible decision [as set out in Appendix AR] may be made where the outcome of the administrative review is as set out in paragraph AR2.2(d) of Appendix AR of these Rules.

[(2A) A further application for administrative review in respect of an eligible decision under Appendix AR (EU) may be made where a decision is withdrawn and a new decision made in accordance with paragraph AR(EU)2.2. of Appendix AR (EU).]

(3) An application for administrative review of an eligible decision [under Appendix AR] may not be made if the applicant has previously signed an administrative review waiver form in respect of the eligible decision, in accordance with paragraph AR2.10 of Appendix AR of these Rules.

(4) If, after receiving notice of the eligible decision, an application for entry clearance, leave to enter or leave to remain is made during the time within which an application

for administrative review [under Appendix AR] may be brought within paragraph 34R (including any possibility of an administrative review out-of-time under paragraph 34R(3)), an application for administrative review of the eligible decision may not be made [under Appendix AR].

Note: Words in sub-paragraphs (1), (2), (3) and (4), sub-paragraph (2A) inserted from 1 November 2018 for applications made on or after that date (HC 1534).

[**34O.** An application for administrative review under Appendix AR or Appendix AR (EU) must be made online in accordance with paragraph 34U, unless the eligible decision relates to an application that was a valid paper application, in which case it can be made:

(a) in accordance with paragraph 34U;

(b) in relation to a leave to enter or remain application, in accordance with paragraph 34V; or

(c) in relation to an entry clearance application, in accordance with paragraph 34VA.]

Note: Amendments from 1 November 2018 for applications made on or after that date (HC 1534). Paragraph substituted from 1 October 2019 (HC 2631).

34P. The application must be made in relation to an eligible decision.

34Q. [An application under Appendix AR must be made]:

(a) when the administrative review is in relation to an eligible decision on an in country application, as defined in paragraph AR3.2 of Appendix AR, while the applicant is in the UK;

(b) when the administrative review is in relation to an eligible decision made on arrival at the United Kingdom, as defined in paragraph AR4.2 of Appendix AR, while the applicant is in the UK, unless the eligible decision is made in the *Control Zone* (as defined in Appendix AR of these Rules), in which case administrative review may not be applied for and will not be considered until after the applicant has left or been removed from the *Control Zone*;

(c) when the administrative review is in relation to an eligible decision on an application for entry clearance, as defined in paragraph AR5.2 of Appendix AR, while the applicant is outside the UK.

Note: Words in introduction substituted from 1 November 2018 for applications made on or after that date (HC1534).

[**34QA.** An application under Appendix AR (EU) of these Rules may be made from either inside or outside the UK.]

Note: Paragraph inserted from 1 November 2018 for applications made on or after that date (HC1534). Paragraph substituted from 21 January 2019 save that applications made under Appendix EU on or after 1 November 2018 and before 22 December 2018 will be decided in accordance with the Rules in force on 21 December 2018 (HC 1849). Paragraph substituted from 07:00 on 30 March 2019 subject to savings for applications made before that time (HC 1919).

34R. (1) [An application under Appendix AR must be made]:

(a) where the applicant is in the UK and not detained, no more than 14 calendar days after receipt by the applicant of the notice of the eligible decision;

(b) where the applicant is in detention in the UK under the Immigration Acts, no more than 7 calendar days after receipt by the applicant of the notice of the eligible decision;

(c) where the applicant is overseas, no more than 28 calendar days after receipt by the applicant of the notice of the eligible decision; or

(d) where the eligible decision is a grant of leave to remain, no more than 14 calendar days after receipt by the applicant of the biometric immigration document which states the length and conditions of leave granted.

[(1A) An application under Appendix AR (EU) must be made:

(a) where the applicant is in the UK and not detained, no more than 28 calendar days after receipt by the applicant of the notice of the eligible decision;

(b) where the applicant is in detention in the UK under the Immigration Acts, no more than 7 calendar days after receipt by the applicant of the notice of the eligible decision;

(c) where the applicant is overseas, no more than 28 calendar days after receipt by the applicant of the notice of the eligible decision.]

(2) An application which is permitted under paragraph 34N(2) [or 34N(2A)] of these Rules must be made within the relevant time limit stated in paragraph 34R(1) as if it was an initial application, and the notice of the outcome of the previous administrative review will be treated as the notice of the eligible decision.

(3) But the application may be accepted out of time if the Secretary of State is satisfied that it would be unjust not to waive the time limit and that the application was made as soon as reasonably practicable.

(5) For provision about when an application is made see paragraph 34W.

Note: Words in sub-paragraph (1) substituted, sub-paragraph 34R(1A), words in sub-paragraph (2) inserted from 1 November 2018 for applications made on or after that date (HC 1534). Sub-paragraph (1A) substituted from 1 October 2019 subject to savings where notice of an eligible decision under Appendix AR (EU) is received between 3 September 2019 and 30 September 2019 (HC 2631).

34S. An applicant may only include an application on behalf of a dependant of the applicant if that dependant:

(a) was a dependant on the application which resulted in the eligible decision; or

(b) was previously granted leave to enter or remain as a dependant of the applicant and that leave is being cancelled at the same time as that of the applicant.

Notice of invalidity

34T. A notice of invalidity will be given in writing and served in accordance with Appendix SN of these Rules.

Online applications for administrative review

34U. (1) In this paragraph:

'the relevant online application process' means the application process accessible via the gov.uk website and identified there as relevant for applications for administrative review; and

'specified' in relation to the relevant online application process means specified in the online guidance accompanying that process.

(2) An application may be made online by completing the relevant online application process.

(3) Where an application is made online:

(a) any specified fee in connection with the application must be paid in accordance with the method specified;

(b) any section of the online application which is designated as mandatory must be completed as specified; and

(c) documents specified as mandatory on the online application or in the related guidance must be submitted either electronically with the online application and in the specified manner, where this is permitted, or received by post and in the specified manner no more than [seven] working days after the day on which the online application is submitted.

Note: Word in sub-paragraph (3)(c) substituted from 1 November 2018 for applications made on or after that date (HC 1534).

Postal applications for administrative review

34V. [(1) Subject to paragraph 34O, an application may be made by post or courier in accordance with this paragraph.]

(2) Where an application is made by post or courier:

(a) it must be made on the application form as specified within the meaning of paragraph 34 (but see paragraph 34Y);

(b) any specified fee in connection with the application must be paid in accordance with the method specified in the application form, separate payment form or related guidance notes (as applicable);

(c) any section of the application form which is designated as mandatory in the form itself or related guidance notes must be completed;

(d) the form must be signed by the applicant or their representative;

(e) the application must be accompanied by any documents specified as mandatory in the application form or related guidance notes; and

(f) the application must be sent to the address specified on the form.

Note: Sub-paragraph (1) substituted from 1 October 2019 (HC 2631).

Applications for administrative review of entry clearance decisions

34VA. [(1) Subject to paragraph 34O, an application may be made by post, courier, hand, fax or email in accordance with this paragraph.]

(2) Where an application is made by post, courier, hand, fax or email:

(a) it must be made on the application form as specified within the meaning of paragraph 34 (but see paragraph 34Y);

(b) any section of the application form which is designated as mandatory in the form itself or related guidance notes must be completed;

(c) the form must be signed by the applicant or their representative;

(d) the application must be accompanied by any documents specified as mandatory in the application form or related guidance notes; [. . .]

(e) the application must be delivered to the postal address, email address or fax number specified on the form[; and] [(f) any specified fee in connection with the application must be paid in accordance with the method specified in the application form, separate payment form or related guidance notes (as applicable).]

Note: Sub-paragraph (1) substituted from 1 October 2019 (HC 2631). Words in (d) deleted; words in (e) substituted, sub-paragraph (f) inserted from 6 April 2021 subject to savings for applications made before that date (HC 1248).

Determining the date of an application

34W. (1) An application for administrative review is made:

(a) where it is made by post in accordance with paragraph 34V, on the marked date of posting;

(b) where it is made by courier in accordance with paragraph 34V, on the date on which it is delivered; and

(c) where it is made online in accordance with paragraph 34U, on the date on which it is submitted.

(2) Accepting an application has been made does not mean that it is accepted as being valid.

Withdrawal of applications

34X. (1) An application which may only be brought from within the UK and has not been determined will be treated as withdrawn if the applicant requests the return of their passport for the purpose of travel outside the UK.

(2) An application which may only be brought from within the UK and which has not been determined will be treated as withdrawn if the applicant leaves the UK.

(3) The application for administrative review may be withdrawn by the applicant. A request to withdraw an application must be made in writing to the Home Office at the address provided for that purpose on the visas and immigration pages of the gov.uk website. The application will be treated as withdrawn on the date on which the request is received.

(4) An application for administrative review which has not been determined will be treated as withdrawn if the applicant makes an application for entry clearance, leave to enter or leave to remain.

[(5) Subparagraphs (1), (2) and (4) above do not apply to an application for administrative review made under:

(a) Appendix AR (EU); or

(b) Appendix AR where the decision being reviewed is a decision to do one of the following:

(i) cancel leave to enter or remain which is in force under paragraph A3.2(b) of Annex 3 to Appendix EU or paragraph A3.4(b) of Annex 3 to Appendix EU (Family Permit); or

(ii) cancel permission to enter or permission to stay which is in force under paragraph HV 11.1(c) of Appendix S2 Healthcare Visitor; or

(iii) cancel permission to enter which is in force under paragraph SPS 9.1(c) of Appendix Service Providers from Switzerland.]

Note: Sub-paragraph (5) inserted from 1 November 2018 for applications made on or after that date (HC 1534). Sub-paragraph (5) substituted from 6 April 2022 (HC 1118).

Transitional arrangements for specified forms used in postal and courier applications

34Y. Where an application is made no more than 21 days after the date on which a form is specified (within the meaning of paragraph 34 [or the validity requirements for the route applied for]) and on a form that was specified immediately prior to the date of the new specification, the application is deemed to have been made on the specified form (and is therefore not to be treated as invalid by reason only of being made on the 'wrong' form).

Note: Words inserted from 09:00 on 1 December 2020 subject to savings for applications made before that time (HC 813).

Undertakings

35. A sponsor of a person seeking leave to enter or remain in the United Kingdom may be asked to give an undertaking in writing to be responsible for that person's maintenance, accommodation and (as appropriate) personal care for the period of any leave granted, including any further variation or for a period of 5 years from date of grant where indefinite leave to enter or remain is granted. Under the Social Security Administration Act 1992 and the Social Security Administration (Northern Ireland) Act 1992, the Department of Social Security or, as the case may be, the Department of Health and Social Services in Northern Ireland, may seek to recover from the person giving such an undertaking any income support paid to meet the needs of the person in respect of whom the undertaking has been given. Under the Immigration and Asylum Act 1999 the Home Office may seek to recover from the person giving such an undertaking amounts attributable to any support provided under section 95 of the Immigration and Asylum Act 1999 (support for asylum seekers) to, or in respect of, the person in respect of whom the undertaking has been given. Failure by the sponsor to maintain that person in accordance with the undertaking, may also be an offence under section 105 of the Social Security Administration Act 1992 and/or under section 108 of the Immigration and Asylum Act 1999 if, as a consequence, asylum support and/or income support is provided to, or in respect of, that person.

Medical

36. A person who intends to remain in the United Kingdom for more than 6 months should normally be referred to the Medical Inspector for examination. If he produces a medical certificate he should be advised to hand it to the Medical Inspector. Any person seeking entry who mentions health or medical treatment as a reason for his visit, or who appears not to be in good mental or physical health, should also be referred to the Medical Inspector; and the Immigration Officer has discretion, which should be exercised sparingly, to refer for examination in any other case.

37. Where the Medical Inspector advises that a person seeking entry is suffering from a specified disease or condition which may interfere with his ability to support himself or his dependants, the Immigration Officer should take account of this, in conjunction with other factors, in deciding whether to admit that person. The Immigration Officer should also take account of the Medical Inspector's assessment of the likely course of treatment in deciding whether a person seeking entry for private medical treatment has sufficient means at his disposal.

38. A returning resident should not be refused leave to enter or have existing leave to enter or remain cancelled on medical grounds. But where a person would be refused leave to enter or have existing leave to enter or remain cancelled on medical grounds if he were not a returning resident or in any case where it is decided on compassionate grounds not to exercise the power to refuse leave to enter or to cancel existing leave to enter or remain, or in any other case where the Medical Inspector so recommends, the Immigration Officer should give the person concerned a notice requiring him to report to the Medical Officer of Environmental Health designated by the Medical Inspector with a view to further examination and any necessary treatment.

A39. Any person making an application for entry clearance to come to the UK for more than six months[, except for applications made under Appendix Ukraine Scheme,] or as a fiancé(e) or proposed civil partner applying for leave to enter under Section EC-P: Entry clearance as a partner under Appendix FM, having been present in a country listed in Appendix T for more than six months immediately prior to their application, must present, at the time of application, a valid medical certificate issued by a medical practitioner approved by the Secretary of State for these purposes, as listed on the Gov.uk website, confirming that they have undergone screening for active pulmonary tuberculosis and that this tuberculosis is not present in the applicant.

Note: Words inserted from 30 March 2022 (HC 1220).

B39. Applicants seeking leave to enter as a returning resident under paragraph 19 of these rules, having been absent from the United Kingdom for more than two years are also subject to the requirements in paragraph A39.

C39. Where a person has lawfully been present in a country not mentioned in Appendix T for more than six months and they are applying for entry clearance as in A39 in a country in Appendix T but have not been in that country or any other country mentioned in Appendix T for more than six months immediately before making their application, they will not be required to produce a medical certificate showing they are free from active pulmonary TB. This does not alter the discretionary powers as in paragraph 39 below.

39. The Entry Clearance Officer has the same discretion as an Immigration Officer to refer applicants for entry clearance for medical examination and the same principles will apply to the decision whether or not to issue an entry clearance.

39A. [DELETED]

Note: Paragraph deleted from 09:00 on 5 October 2020 subject to savings for applications made before that date (HC 707).

Specified documents

39B.

(a) Where these Rules state that specified documents must be provided, that means documents specified in these Rules as being specified documents for the route under which the applicant is applying. If the specified documents are not provided, the applicant will not meet the requirement for which the specified documents are required as evidence.

(b) Where these Rules specify documents that are to be provided, those documents are considered to be specified documents, whether or not they are named as such, and as such are subject to the requirements in (c) to (f) below.

(c) If the Entry Clearance Officer or Secretary of State has reasonable cause to doubt the genuineness of any document submitted by an applicant which is, or which purports to be, a specified document under these Rules, and having taken reasonable steps to verify the document is unable to verify that it is genuine, the document will be discounted for the purposes of this application.

(d) Specified documents [may be originals or copies], except where stated otherwise.

(e) Specified documents must contain, or the applicant must provide, full contact details to allow each document to be verified.

(f) Where any specified documents provided are not in English or Welsh, the applicant must provide [the version in the original language] and a full translation that can be independently verified by the Entry Clearance Officer, Immigration Officer or the Secretary of State.

The translation must be dated and include:

(i) confirmation that it is an accurate translation of the original document;

(ii) the full name and [. . .] signature of the translator or an authorised official of the translation company;

(iii) the translator or translation company's contact details; and

(iv) if the applicant is applying for leave to remain or indefinite leave to remain, certification by a qualified translator and details of the translator or translation company's credentials.

Note: Words in sub-paragraphs (d) and (f) substituted; word in sub-paragraph (f)(ii) deleted from 1 November 2018 for applications made on or after that date (HC 1534).

Indefinite leave to enter or remain

39C. (a) An applicant for indefinite leave to enter or remain must, unless the applicant provides a reasonable explanation, comply with any request made by the Secretary of State to attend an interview.

(b) If the decision-maker has reasonable cause to doubt (on examination or interview or on any other basis) that any evidence submitted by or on behalf of an applicant for the purposes of satisfying the requirements of Appendix KoLL of these Rules was genuinely obtained, that evidence may be discounted for the purposes of the application.

(c) Where sub-paragraph (b) applies, the decision-maker may give the applicant a further opportunity to demonstrate sufficient knowledge of the English language and about life in the United Kingdom in accordance with paragraph 3.2 or 3.3 of Appendix KoLL.

(d) A decision-maker may decide not to give the applicant a further opportunity under sub-paragraph (c) where the decision-maker does not anticipate that the supply of further evidence will lead to a grant of leave to enter or remain in the United Kingdom because the application may be refused for other reasons.

Power to interview a person with limited leave to enter or remain

[**39D.** For the purpose of assessing whether any of the grounds of cancellation of entry clearance or permission under Part 9 apply the Secretary of State may request a person to:

(a) provide additional information to the Home Office at the address specified in the request within 28 calendar days of the date the request is sent; and

(b) attend an interview.]

Note: Paragraph substituted from 09:00 on 1 December 2020 subject to savings for applications made before that time (HC 813).

Exceptions for overstayers

[39E. This paragraph applies where:

(1) the application was made within 14 days of the applicant's leave expiring and the Secretary of State considers that there was a good reason beyond the control of the applicant or their representative, provided in or with the application, why the application could not be made in-time; or

(2) the application was made:

(a) following the refusal of a previous application for leave which was made in-time; and

(b) within 14 days of:

(i) the refusal of the previous application for leave; or

(ii) the expiry of any leave extended by section 3C of the Immigration Act 1971; or

(iii) the expiry of the time-limit for making an in-time application for administrative review or appeal (where applicable); or

(iv) any administrative review or appeal being concluded, withdrawn, abandoned or lapsing; or

(3) the period of overstaying was between 24 January and 31 August 2020; or

(4) where the applicant has, or had, permission on the Hong Kong BN(O) route, and the period of overstaying was between 1 July 2020 and 31 January 2021.]

Note: Amendments from 6 July 2018 subject to savings for applications made before that date (HC 1154). Amendments from 09:00 on 1 December 2020 subject to savings for applications made before that time (HC 813). Amendments from 6 April 2021 subject to savings for applications made before that date (HC 1248). Paragraph substituted from 6 October 2021 subject to savings for applications made before that date (HC 617).

Part 2

Persons seeking to enter or remain in the United Kingdom for visits

Visitors

40.–56Z. DELETED

Transitional provisions Part 2 and Appendix V: Immigration Rules for Visitors

1. [DELETED]
2. [DELETED]
3. [DELETED]
4. [DELETED]

Note: Paragraphs 1 to 4 deleted from 09:00 on 1 December 2020 subject to savings for applications made before that time (HC 813).

Part 3

Persons seeking to enter or remain in the United Kingdom for studies

Persons seeking to enter the UK for short-term study

Introduction

A57A. [DELETED]

Note: Amendments from 11 January 2018 subject to savings for applications made before that date (HC 309). Paragraph deleted from 09:00 on 1 December 2020 subject to savings for applications made before that time (HC 813).

A57B. [DELETED]

Note: Amendments from 11 January 2018 subject to savings for applications made before that date (HC 309). Amendments from 6 July 2018 subject to savings for applications made before that date (HC 1154). Amendments from 6 April 2020 subject to savings for applications made before that date (HC 120). Amendments from 09:00 on 5 October 2020 subject to savings for applications made before that time (HC 707). Paragraph deleted from 09:00 on 1 December 2020 subject to savings for applications made before that time (HC 813).

Requirements for entry clearance or leave to enter—Short-Term Student

A57C. [DELETED]

Note: Amendments from 11 January 2018 subject to savings for applications made before that date (HC 309). Paragraph deleted from 09:00 on 1 December 2020 subject to savings for applications made before that time (HC 813).

A57D. [DELETED]

Note: Amendments from 11 January 2018 subject to savings for applications made before that date (HC 309). Amendments from 6 July 2018 subject to savings for applications made before that date (HC 1154). Amendments from 1 August 2019 (HC 1779). Paragraph deleted from 09:00 on 1 December 2020 subject to savings for applications made before that time (HC 813).

A57E. [DELETED]

Note: Amendments from 11 January 2018 subject to savings for applications made before that date (HC 309). Amendments from 6 July 2018 subject to savings for applications made before that date (HC 1154). Paragraph deleted from 09:00 on 1 December 2020 subject to savings for applications made before that time (HC 813).

Period and conditions of grant of entry clearance or leave to enter for short-term students

A57F. [DELETED]

Note: Amendments from 6 July 2018 subject to savings for applications made before that date (HC 1154). Paragraph deleted from 09:00 on 1 December 2020 subject to savings for applications made before that time (HC 813).

Requirements for entry clearance or leave to enter —Short-term student (child)

A57G. [DELETED]

Note: Amendments from 11 January 2018 subject to savings for applications made before that date (HC309). Paragraph deleted from 09:00 on 1 December 2020 subject to savings for applications made before that time (HC 813).

Period and conditions of grant of entry clearance or leave to enter as a short-term student (child)

A57H. [DELETED]

Note: Paragraph deleted from 09:00 on 1 December 2020 subject to savings for applications made before that time (HC 813).

76. to 81. [DELETED]

Note: Paragraphs 76 to 81 deleted from 11 January 2018 subject to savings for applications made before that date (HC 309).

Prospective Students

A82. DELETED

82. DELETED

83. DELETED

84. DELETED

85. DELETED

86. DELETED

87. DELETED

Students' Union sabbatical officers

87A.-87F. DELETED

PART 4
PERSONS SEEKING TO ENTER OR REMAIN IN THE UNITED KINGDOM IN AN 'AU PAIR' PLACEMENT, AS A WORKING HOLIDAYMAKER OR FOR TRAINING OR WORK EXPERIENCE

'Au pair' placements

88.-94. DELETED

Working holidaymakers

95.-100. DELETED

Children of working holidaymakers

101.-103. DELETED

Seasonal agricultural workers

104.-109. DELETED

Teachers and language assistants coming to the United Kingdom under approved exchange schemes

110.-115. DELETED

Home Office approved training or work experience

116.-121. DELETED

Spouses of persons with limited leave to enter or remain under paragraphs 110–121

Requirements for leave to enter or remain as the spouse or civil partners of a person with limited leave to enter or remain in the United Kingdom under paragraphs 110–121

122. [DELETED]

Note: Paragraph deleted from 09:00 on 1 December 2020 subject to savings for applications made before that time (HC 813).

Leave to enter or remain as the spouse of a person with limited leave to enter or remain in the United Kingdom under paragraphs 110–121

123. [DELETED]

Note: Amendments from 11 January 2018 subject to savings for applications before that date (HC 309). Amendments from 6 July 2018 subject to savings for applications before that date (HC 1154). Paragraph deleted from 09:00 on 1 December 2020 subject to savings for applications made before that time (HC 813).

Refusal of leave to enter or remain as the spouse of a person with limited leave to enter or remain in the United Kingdom under paragraphs 110–121

124. [DELETED]

Note: Amendments from 11 January 2018 subject to savings for applications before that date (HC 309). Paragraph deleted from 09:00 on 1 December 2020 subject to savings for applications made before that time (HC 813).

Children of persons with limited leave to enter or remain under paragraphs 110–121

Requirements for leave to enter or remain as the child of a person with limited leave to enter or remain in the United Kingdom under paragraphs 110–121

125. [DELETED]

Note: Paragraph deleted from 09:00 on 1 December 2020 subject to savings for applications made before that date (HC 813).

Leave to enter or remain as the child of a person with limited leave to enter or remain in the United Kingdom under paragraphs 110–121

126. [DELETED]

Note: Amendments from 11 January 2018 subject to savings for applications before that date (HC 309). Amendments from 6 July 2018 subject to savings for applications before that date (HC 1154). Paragraph deleted from 09:00 on 1 December 2020 subject to savings for applications made before that date (HC 813).

Refusal of leave to enter or remain as the child of a person with limited leave to enter or remain in the United Kingdom under paragraphs 110–121

127. [DELETED]

Note: Amendments from 11 January 2018 subject to savings for applications before that date (HC 309). Paragraph deleted from 09:00 on 1 December 2020 subject to savings for applications made before that date (HC 813).

Part 5
Persons seeking to enter or remain in the United Kingdom for employment

Work permit employment

General requirements for indefinite leave to remain

128A. [DELETED]

Note: Amendments from 11 January 2018 subject to savings for applications made before that date (HC 309). Amendments from 6 July 2018 subject to savings for applications made before that date (HC 1154). Amendments from 29 March 2019 subject to savings for applications made before that date (HC 1919). Paragraph deleted from 09:00 on 1 December 2020 subject to savings for applications made before that time (HC 813).

Requirements for leave to enter the United Kingdom for work permit employment

128. [DELETED]

Note: Paragraph deleted from 09:00 on 1 December 2020 subject to savings for applications made before that time (HC 813).

Indefinite leave to remain for a work permit holder

134. [DELETED]

Note: Paragraph deleted from 09:00 on 1 December 2020 subject to savings for applications made before that time (HC 813).

134-SD. [DELETED]

Note: Amendments from 5 November 2018 (HC 1534). Paragraph deleted from 09:00 on 1 December 2020 subject to savings for applications made before that date (HC 813).

Refusal of indefinite leave to remain for a work permit holder

135. [DELETED]

Note: Paragraph deleted from 09:00 on 1 December 2020 subject to savings for applications made before that time (HC 813).

Highly skilled migrants

Requirements for indefinite leave to remain as a highly skilled migrant

135G. [DELETED]

Note: Amendments from 29 March 2019 subject to savings for applications made before that date (HC 1919). Paragraph deleted from 09:00 on 1 December 2020 subject to savings for applications made before that time (HC 813).

Indefinite leave to remain as a highly skilled migrant

135GA. [DELETED]

Note: Paragraph deleted from 09:00 on 1 December 2020 subject to savings for applications made before that time (HC 813).

Refusal of indefinite leave to remain as a highly skilled migrant

135H. [DELETED]

Note: Paragraph deleted from 09:00 on 1 December 2020 subject to savings for applications made before that time (HC 813).

Additional grounds for refusal for highly skilled migrants

135HA. [DELETED]

Note: Paragraph deleted from 09:00 on 1 December 2020 subject to savings for applications made before that time (HC 813).

Representatives of overseas newspapers, news agencies and broadcasting organisations

Requirements for leave to enter as a representative of an overseas newspaper, news agency or broadcasting organisation

136. [DELETED]

Note: Paragraph deleted from 27 November 2008 by HC 1113 except insofar as relevant to paragraphs 142 and 143. Paragraph deleted from 09:00 on 1 December 2020 subject to savings for applications made before that time (HC 813).

137–141. [DELETED]

Note: Paragraphs deleted from 27 November 2008 by HC1113 except insofar as relevant to paragraphs 142 and 143.

Indefinite leave to remain for a representative of an overseas newspaper, news agency or broadcasting organisation

142. [DELETED]

Note: Paragraph deleted from 09:00 on 1 December 2020 subject to savings for applications made before that time (HC 813).

142-SD. [DELETED]

Note: Amendments from 5 November 2018 (HC 1534). Paragraph deleted from 09:00 on 1 December 2020 subject to savings for applications made before that time (HC 813).

Refusal of indefinite leave to remain for a representative of an overseas newspaper, news agency or broadcasting organisation.

143. [DELETED]

Note: Paragraph deleted from 09:00 on 1 December 2020 subject to savings for applications made before that time (HC 813).

Representatives of overseas businesses

Requirements for leave to enter as a representative of an overseas business

144. [DELETED]

Note: Amendments from 6 April 2020 (HC 120). Amendments from 4 June 2020 subject to savings for applications made before that date and where an application is supported by a Certificate of Sponsorship or endorsement assigned before that date (CP 232). Paragraph deleted from 09:00 on 1 December 2020 subject to savings for applications made before that time (HC 813).

144-SD. [DELETED]

Note: Amendments from 5 November 2018 (HC 1534). Paragraph deleted from 09:00 on 1 December 2020 subject to savings for applications made before that time (HC 813).

Leave to enter as a representative of an overseas business

145. [DELETED]

Note: Amendments from 11 January 2018 subject to savings for applications made before that date (HC 309). Amendments from 6 July 2018 subject to savings for applications made before that date (HC 1154). Amendments from 09:00 on 5 October 2020 subject to savings for applications made before that time. Where consequential changes relating to the need for an ATAS certificate have been made, they take effect for all applications made or granted on or after 5 October 2020 at 09:00 (HC 707). Paragraph deleted from 09:00 on 1 December 2020 subject to savings for applications made before that time (HC 813).

Refusal of leave to enter as a representative of an overseas business

146. [DELETED]

Note: Amendments from 11 January 2018 subject to savings for applications made before that date (HC 309). Paragraph deleted from 09:00 on 1 December 2020 subject to savings for applications made before that time (HC 813).

Requirements for an extension of stay as a representative of an overseas business

147. [DELETED]

Note: Amendments from 4 June 2020 subject to savings for applications made before that date and where an application is supported by a Certificate of Sponsorship or endorsement assigned before that date (CP 232). Paragraph deleted from 09:00 on 1 December 2020 subject to savings for applications made before that time (HC 813).

Extension of stay as a representative of an overseas business

148. [DELETED]

Note: Amendments from 09:00 on 5 October 2020 subject to savings for applications made before that time. Where consequential changes relating to the need for an ATAS certificate have been made, they take effect for all applications made or granted on or after 5 October 2020 at 09:00 (HC 707). Paragraph deleted from 09:00 on 1 December 2020 subject to savings for applications made before that time (HC 813).

Refusal of extension of stay as a representative of an overseas business

149. [DELETED]

Note: Paragraph deleted from 09:00 on 1 December 2020 subject to savings for applications made before that time (HC 813).

Indefinite leave to remain for a representative of an overseas business

150. [DELETED]

Note: Paragraph deleted from 09:00 on 1 December 2020 subject to savings for applications made before that time (HC 813).

150-SD. [DELETED]

Note: Amendments from 5 November 2018 (HC 1534). Paragraph deleted from 09:00 on 1 December 2020 subject to savings for applications made before that time (HC 813).

Refusal of indefinite leave to remain for a sole representative of an overseas business

151. [DELETED]

Note: Paragraph deleted from 09:00 on 1 December 2020 subject to savings for applications made before that time (HC 813).

Private servants in diplomatic households

Requirements for leave to enter as a private servant in a diplomatic household

152. Deleted on 27 November 2008 by paragraph 39 of Statement of Changes HC 1113 except insofar as relevant to paragraph 158 and 159.

Indefinite leave to remain for a servant in a diplomatic household

158. Indefinite leave to remain may be granted, on application, to a private servant in a diplomatic household provided the applicant:

(i) has spent a continuous period of 5 years lawfully in the United Kingdom in this capacity; and

(ii) has met the requirements of paragraph 155 throughout the 5 year period; and

(iii) is still required for the employment in question, as certified by the employer; and

(iv) has demonstrated sufficient knowledge of the English language and sufficient knowledge about life in the United Kingdom, in accordance with Appendix KoLL; and

(v) does not fall for refusal under the general grounds for refusal; and

(vi) is not in the UK in breach of immigration laws except that, where paragraph 39E of these Rules applies, any current period of overstaying will be disregarded; and

(vii) provides the specified documents in paragraph 158-SD to evidence the reason for the absences set out in paragraph 128A.

158-SD. Specified documents

The specified documents referred to in paragraph 158(vii) are:

(a) A letter from the employer detailing the purpose and period of absences in connection with the employment, including periods of annual leave.

(b) Where the absence was due to a serious or compelling reason, a personal letter from the applicant which includes full details of the reason for the absences and all [. . .] supporting documents in relation to those reasons—e.g. medical certificates, birth/death certificates, information about the reasons which led to the absence from the UK.

Note: Word in sub-paragraph (b) deleted from 5 November 2018 (HC 1534).

Refusal of indefinite leave to remain for a servant in a diplomatic household

159. [DELETED]

Note: Paragraph deleted from 6 May 2021 subject to savings for applications (including for administrative review) made before that date (HC 1248).

Domestic workers in private households

Requirements for leave to enter as a domestic worker in a private household

159A. [DELETED]

Note: Amendments from 11 January 2018 subject to savings for applications made before that date (HC 309). Amendments from 09:00 on 1 December 2020 subject to savings for applications made before that time (HC 813). Paragraph deleted from 09:00 on 11 October 2021 subject to savings for applications made before that time (HC 617).

Leave to enter as a domestic worker in a private household

159B. [DELETED]

Note: Amendments from 11 January 2018 subject to savings for applications made before that date (HC 309). Amendments from 6 July 2018 subject to savings for applications made before that date (HC 1154). Paragraph deleted from 09:00 on 11 October 2021 subject to savings for applications made before that time (HC 617).

Refusal of leave to enter as a domestic worker in a private household

159C. [DELETED]

Note: Amendments from 11 January 2018 subject to savings for applications made before that date (HC 309). Paragraph deleted from 09:00 on 11 October 2021 subject to savings for applications made before that time (HC 617).

Requirements for extension of stay as a domestic worker in a private household

159D. [DELETED]

Note: Paragraph deleted from 09:00 on 11 October 2021 subject to savings for applications made before that time (HC 617).

Extension of stay as a domestic worker in a private household

159E. [DELETED]

Note: Paragraph deleted from 09:00 on 11 October 2021 subject to savings for applications made before that time (HC 617).

Requirements for extension of stay as a domestic worker in a private household for applicants who entered the United Kingdom under the Rules in place before 6 April 2012

159EA. [DELETED]

Note: Paragraph deleted from 09:00 on 11 October 2021 subject to savings for applications made before that time (HC 617).

Extension of stay as a domestic worker in a private household for applicants who entered the United Kingdom under the Rules in place before 6 April 2012

159EB. [DELETED]

Note: Paragraph deleted from 09:00 on 11 October 2021 subject to savings for applications made before that time (HC 617).

Refusal of extension of stay as a domestic worker in a private household

159F. [DELETED]

Note: Paragraph deleted from 09:00 on 11 October 2021 subject to savings for applications made before that time (HC 617).

Indefinite leave to remain for a domestic worker in a private household

159G. [DELETED]

Note: Paragraph deleted from 09:00 on 11 October 2021 subject to savings for applications made before that time (HC 617).

159G-SD. [DELETED]

Note: Amendments from 5 November 2018 (HC 1534). Paragraph deleted from 09:00 on 11 October 2021 subject to savings for applications made before that time (HC 617).

Refusal of indefinite leave to remain for a domestic worker in a private household

159H. [DELETED]

Note: Paragraph deleted from 09:00 on 11 October 2021 subject to savings for applications made before that time (HC 617).

Domestic workers who are the victim of slavery or human trafficking

Requirements for leave to remain as a domestic worker who is the victim of slavery or human trafficking

159I. [DELETED]

Note: Paragraph deleted from 09:00 on 11 October 2021 subject to savings for applications made before that time (HC 617).

Leave to remain as a domestic worker who is the victim of slavery or human trafficking

159J. [DELETED]

Note: Paragraph deleted from 09:00 on 11 October 2021 subject to savings for applications made before that time (HC 617).

159JA. [DELETED]

Note: Paragraph deleted from 09:00 on 11 October 2021 subject to savings for applications made before that time (HC 617).

Refusal of leave to remain as a domestic worker who is the victim of slavery or human trafficking

159K. [DELETED]

Note: Paragraph deleted from 09:00 on 11 October 2021 subject to savings for applications made before that time (HC 617).

Overseas government employees

Requirements for leave to enter as an overseas government employee

160–166. Deleted from 27 November 2008 by HC 1113 except insofar as relevant to paragraphs 167 and 168.

Indefinite leave to remain for an overseas government employee

167. Indefinite leave to remain may be granted, on application, to an overseas government employee provided the applicant:

(i) has spent a continuous period of 5 years lawfully in the United Kingdom in this capacity; and

(ii) has met the requirements of paragraph 164 throughout the 5 year period; and

(iii) is still required for the employment in question, as certified by the employer; and

(iv) has demonstrated sufficient knowledge of the English language and sufficient knowledge about life in the United Kingdom, in accordance with Appendix KoLL; and

(v) does not fall for refusal under the general grounds for refusal; and

(vi) is not in the UK in breach of immigration laws except that, where paragraph 39E of these Rules applies, any current period of overstaying will be disregarded; and

(vii) provides the specified documents in paragraph 167-SD to evidence the reason for the absences set out in paragraph 128A.

167-SD. Specified documents

The specified documents referred to in paragraph 167(vii) are:

(a) A letter from the employer detailing the purpose and period of absences in connection with the employment, including periods of annual leave.

(b) Where the absence was due to a serious or compelling reason, a personal letter from the applicant which includes full details of the reason for the absences and all [. . .] supporting documents in relation to those reasons—e.g. medical certificates, birth/death certificates, information about the reasons which led to the absence from the UK.

Note: Word in sub-paragraph (b) deleted from 5 November 2018 (HC 1534).

Refusal of indefinite leave to remain for an overseas government employee

168. Indefinite leave to remain in the United Kingdom for an overseas government employee is to be refused if the Secretary of State is not satisfied that each of the requirements of paragraph 167 is met.

Ministers of religion, missionaries and members of religious orders

169. [DELETED]

Note: Paragraph deleted from 09:00 on 1 December 2020 subject to savings for applications made before that time (HC 813).

Requirements for leave to enter as a minister of religion, missionary, or member of a religious order

170. [DELETED]

Note: Paragraph deleted from 09:00 on 1 December 2020 subject to savings for applications made before that time (HC 813).

Refusal of extension of stay as a minister of religion, missionary or member of a religious order

175. [DELETED]

Note: Paragraph deleted from 09:00 on 1 December 2020 subject to savings for applications made before that time (HC 813).

Indefinite leave to remain for a minister of religion, missionary or member of a religious order

176. [DELETED]

Note: Paragraph deleted from 09:00 on 1 December 2020 subject to savings for applications made before that time (HC 813).

176-SD. [DELETED]

Note: Amendments from 5 November 2018 (HC 1534). Paragraph deleted from 09:00 on 1 December 2020 subject to savings for applications made before that time (HC 813).

Refusal of indefinite leave to remain for a minister of religion, missionary or member of a religious order

177. [DELETED]

Note: Paragraph deleted from 09:00 on 1 December 2020 subject to savings for applications made before that time (HC 813).

Airport-based operational ground staff of overseas-owned airlines

Requirements for leave to enter the United Kingdom as a member of the operational ground staff of an overseas-owned airline

178–183. [DELETED]

Note: Paragraphs deleted from 27 November 2008 by HC 1113 except insofar as relevant to paragraphs 184 and 185.

Indefinite leave to remain for a member of the operational ground staff of an overseas owned airline

184. Indefinite leave to remain may be granted, on application, to a member of the operational ground staff of an overseas-owned airline provided the applicant:

(i) has spent a continuous period of 5 years lawfully in the United Kingdom in this capacity; and

(ii) has met the requirements of paragraph 181 throughout the 5 year period; and

(iii) is still required for the employment in question as certified by the employer; and

(iv) has demonstrated sufficient knowledge of the English language and sufficient knowledge about life in the United Kingdom, in accordance with Appendix KoLL; and

(v) does not fall for refusal under the general grounds for refusal; and

(vi) is not in the UK in breach of immigration laws except that, where paragraph 39E of these Rules applies, any current period of overstaying will be disregarded; and

(vii) provides the specified documents in paragraph 184-SD to evidence the reason for the absences set out in paragraph 128A.

184-SD. Specified documents

The specified documents referred to in paragraph 184(vii) are:

(a) A letter from the employer detailing the purpose and period of absences in connection with the employment, including periods of annual leave.

(b) Where the absence was due to a serious or compelling reason, a personal letter from the applicant which includes full details of the reason for the absences and all [. . .] supporting documents in relation to those reasons—e.g. medical certificates, birth/death certificates, information about the reasons which led to the absence from the UK.

Note: Word in sub-paragraph (b) deleted from 5 November 2018 (HC 1534).

Refusal of indefinite leave to remain for a member of the operational ground staff of an overseas owned airline

185. Indefinite leave to remain in the United Kingdom for a member of the operational ground staff of an overseas owned airline is to be refused if the Secretary of State is not satisfied that each of the requirements of paragraph 184 is met.

Persons with United Kingdom ancestry

Requirements for leave to enter on the grounds of United Kingdom ancestry

186. [DELETED]

Note: Paragraph deleted from 09:00 on 1 December 2020 subject to savings for applications made before that time (HC 813).

Leave to enter the United Kingdom on the grounds of United Kingdom ancestry

187. [DELETED]

Note: Amendments from 11 January 2018 subject to savings for applications made before that date (HC 309). Amendments from 6 July 2018 subject to savings for applications made before that date (HC 1154). Amendments from 09:00 on 5 October 2020 subject to savings for applications made before that time. Where consequential changes relating to the need for an ATAS certificate have been made, they take effect for all applications made or granted on or after 5 October 2020 at 09:00 (HC 707). Paragraph deleted from 09:00 on 1 December 2020 subject to savings for applications made before that time (HC 813).

Refusal of leave to enter on the grounds of United Kingdom ancestry

188. [DELETED]

Note: Amendments from 11 January 2018 subject to savings for applications made before that date (HC 309). Paragraph deleted from 09:00 on 1 December 2020 subject to savings for applications made before that time (HC 813).

Requirements for an extension of stay on the grounds of United Kingdom ancestry

189. [DELETED]

Note: Paragraph deleted from 09:00 on 1 December 2020 subject to savings for applications made before that time (HC 813).

Extension of stay on the grounds of United Kingdom ancestry

190. [DELETED]

Note: Amendments from 09:00 on 5 October 2020 subject to savings for applications made before that time. Where consequential changes relating to the need for an ATAS certificate have been made, they take effect for all applications made or granted on or after 5 October 2020 at 09:00 (HC 707). Paragraph deleted from 09:00 on 1 December 2020 subject to savings for applications made before that time (HC 813).

Refusal of extension of stay on the grounds of United Kingdom ancestry

191. [DELETED]

Note: Paragraph deleted from 09:00 on 1 December 2020 subject to savings for applications made before that time (HC 813).

Indefinite leave to remain on the grounds of United Kingdom ancestry

192. [DELETED]

Note: Amendments from 10 January 2019 subject to savings for applications made before that date (HC 1779). Paragraph deleted from 09:00 on 1 December 2020 subject to savings for applications made before that time (HC 813).

192-SD. [DELETED]

Note: Amendments from 5 November 2018 (HC 1534). Paragraph deleted from 10 January 2019 subject to savings for applications made before that date (HC 1779).

Refusal of indefinite leave to remain on the grounds of United Kingdom ancestry

193. [DELETED]

Note: Paragraph deleted from 09:00 on 1 December 2020 subject to savings for applications made before that time (HC 813).

Partners of persons who have or have had leave to enter or remain under paragraphs 128–193 (but not paragraphs 135I–135K)

193A. Nothing in paragraphs 194–196F is to be construed as allowing a person to be granted entry clearance, leave to enter, leave to remain or variation of leave as a partner of a person granted entry clearance or leave to enter under Paragraph 159A where that entry clearance or leave to enter was granted under 159A on or after 6 April 2012.

Requirements for leave to enter as the partner of a person with limited leave to enter or remain in the United Kingdom under paragraphs 128–193 (but not paragraphs 135I–135K)

194. The requirements to be met by a person seeking leave to enter the United Kingdom as the partner of a person with limited leave to enter or remain in the United Kingdom under paragraphs 128–193 (but not paragraphs 135I–135K) are that:

(i) the applicant is the spouse, civil partner, unmarried or same-sex partner of a person with limited leave to enter or remain in the United Kingdom under paragraphs 128–193 (but not paragraphs 135I–135K); and

(ii) if an unmarried or same-sex partner:

(1) any previous marriage or civil partnership (or similar relationship) by either partner has permanently broken down; and

(2) the parties are not involved in a consanguineous relationship with one another; and

(3) the parties have been living together in a relationship akin to marriage or civil partnership which has subsisted for 2 years or more; and

(iii) each of the parties intends to live with the other as his or her partner during the applicant's stay and the relationship is [genuine and] subsisting; and

(iv) there will be adequate accommodation for the parties and any dependants without recourse to public funds in accommodation which they own or occupy exclusively; and

(v) the parties will be able to maintain themselves and any dependants adequately without recourse to public funds; and

(vi) the applicant does not intend to stay in the United Kingdom beyond any period of leave granted to his partner; and

(vii) the applicant does not fall for refusal under the general grounds for refusal; and

(viii) the applicant holds a valid United Kingdom entry clearance for entry in this capacity.[; and]

[(ix) where the applicant is accompanying or joining a person granted entry clearance or leave to enter or limited leave to remain as the sole representative of an overseas business within the meaning of paragraph 144(ii)(a), the applicant does not have a majority stake in, or otherwise own or control, that overseas business, whether that ownership or control is by means of a shareholding, partnership agreement, sole proprietorship or any other arrangement]

Note: Words in sub-paragraph (iii) inserted from 11 January 2018 subject to savings for applications made before that date (HC 309). Punctuation and word at end of (viii) and (xi) inserted from 4 June 2020 subject to savings for applications made before that date and where an application is supported by a Certificate of Sponsorship or endorsement assigned before that date (CP 232).

Leave to enter as the partner of a person with limited leave to enter or remain in the United Kingdom under paragraphs 128–193 (but not paragraphs 135I–135K)

195. A person seeking leave to enter the United Kingdom as the partner of a person with limited leave to enter or remain in the United Kingdom under paragraphs 128–193 (but not paragraphs 135I–135K) may be given leave to enter for a period not in excess of that granted to the person with limited leave to enter or remain under paragraphs 128–193 (but not paragraphs 135I–135K), subject to a condition on study as set out in [Appendix ATAS] of these Rules, provided the Immigration Officer is satisfied that each of the requirements of paragraph 194 is met. [. . .]

Note: Words substituted from 09:00 on 5 October 2020 subject to savings for applications made before that time. Where consequential changes relating to the need for an ATAS certificate have been made, they take effect for all applications made or granted on or after 5 October 2020 at 09:00 (HC 707). Words deleted from 09:00 on 1 December 2020 subject to savings for applications made before that time (HC 813).

Refusal of leave to enter as the partner of a person with limited leave to enter or remain in the United Kingdom under paragraphs 128–193 (but not paragraphs 135I–135K)

196. Leave to enter the United Kingdom as the partner of a person with limited leave to enter or remain in the United Kingdom under paragraphs 128–193 (but not paragraphs 135I–135K) is to be refused if the Immigration Officer is not satisfied that each of the requirements of paragraph 194 is met.

Requirements for extension of stay as the partner of a person who has or has had leave to enter or remain in the United Kingdom under paragraphs 128–193 (but not paragraphs 135I–135K)

196A. The requirements to be met by a person seeking an extension of stay in the United Kingdom as the partner of a person who has or has had leave to enter or remain in the United Kingdom under paragraphs 128–193 (but not paragraphs 135I–135K) are that the applicant:

(i) is the spouse, civil partner, unmarried or same sex partner of a person who:

(1) has limited leave to enter or remain in the United Kingdom under paragraphs 128–193 (but not paragraphs 135I–135K); or

(2) has indefinite leave to remain in the United Kingdom or has become a British citizen, and who had limited leave to enter or remain in the United Kingdom under paragraphs 128–193 (but not paragraphs 135I–135K) immediately before being granted indefinite leave to remain; and

(ii) meets the requirements of paragraph 194(ii)–(vii); and

[(iii) was not last granted:

(1) entry clearance or leave to enter as a visitor, short-term student [[or]] short-term student (child),

(2) temporary admission,

(3) temporary release, or

(4) after the date on which paragraph 1 of Schedule 10 to the Immigration Act 2016 is commenced, immigration bail in circumstances in which temporary admission or temporary release would previously have been granted; and]

(iv) must not be in the UK in breach of immigration laws except that, where paragraph 39E of these Rules applies, any current period of overstaying will be disregarded.

Note: Sub-paragraph (iii) substituted from the date of commencement of Schedule 10 to the Immigration Act 2016 (HC 309). Word in double square brackets in sub-paragraph (iii)(1) substituted from 6 July 2018 subject to savings for applications made before that date HC 1154).

Extension of stay as the partner of a person who has or has had leave to enter or remain in the United Kingdom under paragraphs 128–193 (but not paragraphs 135I–135K)

196B. An extension of stay in the United Kingdom as:

(i) the partner of a person who has limited leave to enter or remain under paragraphs 128–193 (but not paragraphs 135I–135K) may be granted, subject to a condition on study as set out in [Appendix ATAS] of these Rules, for a period not in excess of that granted to the person with limited leave to enter or remain; or

(ii) the partner of a person who is being admitted at the same time for settlement, or the partner of a person who has indefinite leave to remain or has become a British citizen, may be granted for a period not exceeding 2 years, subject to a condition on study as set out in [Appendix ATAS] of these Rules in both instances, provided the Secretary of State is satisfied that each of the requirements of paragraph 196A is met.

[. . .]

Note: Words substituted from 09:00 on 5 October 2020 subject to savings for applications made before that time. Where consequential changes relating to the need for an ATAS certificate have been made, they take effect for all applications made or granted on or after 5 October 2020 at 09:00 (HC 707). Words deleted from 09:00 on 1 December 2020 subject to savings for applications made before that time (HC 813).

Refusal of extension of stay as the partner of a person who has or has had leave to enter or remain in the United Kingdom under paragraphs 128–193 (but not paragraphs 135I–135K)

196C. An extension of stay in the United Kingdom as the partner of a person who has or has had leave to enter or remain in the United Kingdom under paragraphs 128–193 (but not paragraphs 135I–135K) is to be refused if the Secretary of State is not satisfied that each of the requirements of paragraph 196A is met.

Requirements for indefinite leave to remain for the partner of a person who has or has had leave to enter or remain in the United Kingdom under paragraphs 128–193 (but not paragraphs 135I–135K)

196D. The requirements to be met by a person seeking indefinite leave to remain in the United Kingdom as the partner of a person who has or has had leave to enter or remain in the United Kingdom under paragraphs 128–193 (but not paragraphs 135I–135K) are that the applicant:

(i) is the spouse, civil partner, unmarried or same-sex partner of a person who:

(1) has limited leave to enter or remain in the United Kingdom under paragraphs 128–193 (but not paragraphs 135I–135K) and who is being granted indefinite leave to remain at the same time; or

(2) is the spouse, civil partner, unmarried or same-sex partner of a person who has indefinite leave to remain in the United Kingdom or has become a British citizen, and who had limited leave to enter or remain in the United Kingdom under paragraphs

128–193 (but not paragraphs 135I–135K) immediately before being granted indefinite leave to remain; and

(ii) meets the requirements of paragraph 194(ii)–(vii); and

(iii) has demonstrated sufficient knowledge of the English language and sufficient knowledge about life in the United Kingdom, in accordance with Appendix KoLL; and

[(iv) was not last granted:

(1) entry clearance or leave to enter as a visitor, short-term student [[or]] short-term student (child),

(2) temporary admission,

(3) temporary release, or

(4) after the date on which paragraph 1 of Schedule 10 to the Immigration Act 2016 is commenced, immigration bail in circumstances in which temporary admission or temporary release would previously have been granted; and]

(iv) was not last granted:

(1) entry clearance or leave as a visitor, [short-term student or short-term student (child)],

(2) temporary admission, or

(3) temporary release; and

(v) must not be in the UK in breach of immigration laws except that, where paragraph 39E of these Rules applies, any current period of overstaying will be disregarded.

Note: Sub-paragraph (iv) substituted from the date of commencement of Schedule 10 to the Immigration Act 2016 (HC 309). Word in double square brackets in sub-paragraph (iv)(1) substituted from 6 July 2018 subject to savings for applications made before that date (HC 1154).

Indefinite leave to remain as the partner of a person who has or has had leave to enter or remain in the United Kingdom under paragraphs 128–193 (but not paragraphs 135I–135K)

196E. Indefinite leave to remain in the United Kingdom as the partner of a person who has or has had leave to enter or remain in the United Kingdom under paragraphs 128–193 (but not paragraphs 135I–135K) may be granted provided the Secretary of State is satisfied that each of the requirements of paragraph 196D is met.

Refusal of indefinite leave to remain as the partner of a person who has or has had leave to enter or remain in the United Kingdom under paragraphs 128–193 (but not paragraphs 135I–135K)

196F. Indefinite leave to remain in the United Kingdom as the partner of a person who has or has had limited leave to enter or remain in the United Kingdom under paragraphs 128–193 (but not paragraphs 135I–135K) is to be refused if the Secretary of State is not satisfied that each of the requirements of paragraph 196D is met.

Children of persons with limited leave to enter or remain in the United Kingdom under paragraphs 128–193 (but not paragraphs 135I–135K)

196G. Nothing in paragraphs 197–199 is to be construed as allowing a person to be granted entry clearance, leave to enter, leave to remain or variation of leave as the child of a person granted entry clearance or leave to enter under Paragraph 159A where that entry clearance or leave to enter was granted under 159A on or after 6 April 2012.

Requirements for leave to enter or remain as the child of a person with limited leave to enter or remain in the United Kingdom under paragraphs 128–193 (but not paragraphs 135I–135K)

197. The requirements to be met by a person seeking leave to enter or remain in the United Kingdom as a child of a person with limited leave to enter or remain in the United Kingdom under paragraphs 128–193 (but not paragraphs 135I–135K) are that:

(i) he is the child of a parent with limited leave to enter or remain in the United Kingdom under paragraphs 128–193 (but not paragraphs 135I–135K) or, in respect of applications for leave to remain only, of a parent who has indefinite leave to remain in the UK but who immediately before that grant had limited leave to enter or remain under those paragraphs; and

(ii) he is under the age of 18 or has current leave to enter or remain in this capacity; and

(iii) he is unmarried and is not a civil partner, has not formed an independent family unit and is not leading an independent life; and

(iv) he can and will be maintained and accommodated adequately without recourse to public funds in accommodation which his parent(s) own or occupy exclusively; and

(v) he will not stay in the United Kingdom beyond any period of leave granted to his parent(s); and

(vi) both parents are being or have been admitted to or allowed to remain in the United Kingdom save where:

(a) the parent he is accompanying or joining is his sole surviving parent; or

(b) the parent he is accompanying or joining has had sole responsibility for his upbringing;

or

(c) there are serious and compelling family or other considerations which make exclusion from the United Kingdom undesirable and suitable arrangements have been made for his care; and

[(vii) if seeking leave to enter, he holds a valid United Kingdom entry clearance for entry in this capacity or, if seeking leave to remain, he was not last granted:

(1) entry clearance or leave to enter as a visitor, short-term student [[or]] short-term student (child),

(2) temporary admission,

(3) temporary release, or

(4) after the date on which paragraph 1 of Schedule 10 to the Immigration Act 2016 is commenced, immigration bail in circumstances in which temporary admission or temporary release would previously have been granted; and]

Note: Sub-paragraph (vii) substituted from the date of commencement of Schedule 10 to the Immigration Act 2016 (HC 309). Word in double square brackets substituted from 6 July 2018 subject to savings for applications made before that date (HC 1154).

Leave to enter or remain as the child of a person with limited leave to enter or remain in the United Kingdom under paragraphs 128–193 (but not paragraphs 135I–135K)

198. (a) A person seeking leave to enter or remain in the United Kingdom as the child of a person with limited leave to enter or remain in the United Kingdom under paragraphs 128–193 (but not paragraphs 135I–135K) may be given leave to enter or remain in the United Kingdom for a period of leave not in excess of that granted to the person with limited leave to enter or remain under paragraphs 128–193 (but not paragraphs 135I–135K), subject to a condition on study as set out in {Appendix ATAS} of these Rules where the applicant is 18 years of age or over at the time their leave is granted, or will be aged 18 before their period of limited leave expires, provided that:

(i) in relation to an application for leave to enter, he is able to produce to the Immigration Officer, on arrival, [a valid passport or other identity document and [[has]] entry clearance for entry in this capacity;] or

[(ii) in the case of an application for limited leave to remain, he was not last granted:

(1) entry clearance or leave as a visitor, short-term student or shortterm student (child),

(2) temporary admission,

(3) temporary release, or

(4) after the date on which paragraph 1 of Schedule 10 to the Immigration Act 2016 is commenced, immigration bail in circumstances in which temporary release or temporary admission would previously been granted, and is able to satisfy the Secretary of State that each of the requirements of paragraph 197 (i)-(vi) and (viii) is met.]

(b) A person seeking leave to remain as the child of a parent who has indefinite leave to remain in the UK and who had limited leave under paragraphs 128–193 (but not paragraphs 135l–135K) immediately before being granted indefinite leave may be given leave to remain in the UK for a period of 30 months, subject to a condition on study as set out in {Appendix ATAS} of these Rules where the applicant is 18 years of age or over at the time their leave is granted, or will be aged 18 before their period of limited leave expires, provided he is in the UK with valid leave under paragraph 198 and is able to satisfy the Secretary of State that each of the requirements of paragraph 197(i) and 197(ii)–(vi) and (viii) is met.

Note: Words in square brackets in sub-paragraph (a)(i) substituted from 11 January 2018 subject to savings for applications made before that date (HC 309). Word in double square brackets in sub-paragraph (a)(i), sub-paragraph (a)(ii) substituted from 6 July 2018 subject to savings for applications made before that date (HC 1154). Words in curly brackets substituted from 09:00 on 5 October 2020 subject to savings for applications made before that time. Where consequential changes relating to the need for an ATAS certificate have been made, they take effect for all applications made or granted on or after 5 October 2020 at 09:00 (HC 707).

Refusal of leave to enter or remain as the child of a person with limited leave to enter or remain in the United Kingdom under paragraphs 128–193 (but not paragraphs 135I–135K)

198A. Leave to enter or remain in the United Kingdom as the child of a person with limited leave to enter or remain in the United Kingdom under paragraphs 128–193 (but not paragraphs 135I–135K) is to be refused if:

(i) in relation to an application for leave to enter, [a valid passport or other identity document is not produced to the Immigration Officer on arrival and the applicant does not have entry clearance for entry in this capacity;] or

[(ii) in the case of an application for limited leave to remain, if the applicant was last granted:

(1) entry clearance or leave to enter as a visitor, short-term student [[or]] short-term student (child),

(2) temporary admission,

(3) temporary release, or

(4) after the date on which paragraph 1 of Schedule 10 to the Immigration Act 2016 is commenced, immigration bail in circumstances in which temporary release or temporary admission would previously been granted,]

Note: Words in sub-paragraph (i) substituted from 11 January 2018 subject to savings for applications made before that date; sub-paragraph (ii) substituted from the date of commencement of Schedule 10 to the Immigration Act 2016 (HC 309). Word in double square brackets in sub-paragraph (ii)(1) substituted from 6 July 2018 subject to savings for applications made before that date (HC 1154).

Requirements for indefinite leave to remain as the child of a person who has or has had leave to enter or remain in the United Kingdom under paragraphs 128–193 (but not paragraphs 135I–135K)

199. The requirements to be met by a person seeking indefinite leave to remain in the United Kingdom as the child of a person who has or has had leave to enter or remain in the United Kingdom under paragraphs 128–193 (but not paragraphs 135I–135K) are that the applicant:

(i) is the child of a person who:

(1) has limited leave to enter or remain in the United Kingdom under paragraphs 128–193 (but not paragraphs 135I–135K) and who is being granted indefinite leave to remain at the same time; or

(2) has indefinite leave to remain in the United Kingdom and who had limited leave to enter or remain in the United Kingdom under paragraphs 128–193 (but not paragraphs 135I–135K) immediately before being granted indefinite leave to remain; and

(ii) meets the requirements of paragraph 197(i)–(vi) and (viii); and

[(iii) was not last granted:

(1) entry clearance or leave to enter as a visitor, short-term student [[or]] short-term student (child),

(2) temporary admission,

(3) temporary release, or

(4) after the date on which paragraph 1 of Schedule 10 to the Immigration Act 2016 is commenced, immigration bail in circumstances in which temporary release or temporary admission would previously been granted; and]

(iv) does not fall for refusal under the general grounds for refusal; and

(v) must not be in the UK in breach of immigration laws except that, where paragraph 39E of these Rules applies, any current period of overstaying will be disregarded; and

(vi) has demonstrated sufficient knowledge of the English language and sufficient knowledge about life in the United Kingdom, in accordance with Appendix KoLL, unless he is under the age of 18 at the date on which the application is made.

Note: Sub-paragraph (iii) substituted from the date of commencement of Schedule 10 to the Immigration Act 2016 (HC 309). Word in sub-paragraph (iii)(1) substituted from 6 July 2018 subject to savings for applications made before that date (HC 1154).

Indefinite leave to remain as the child of a person who has or has had leave to enter or remain in the United Kingdom under paragraphs 128–193 (but not paragraphs 135I–135K)

199A. Indefinite leave to remain in the United Kingdom as the child of a person who has or has had leave to enter or remain in the United Kingdom under paragraphs 128–193 (but not paragraphs 135I–135K) may be granted provided the Secretary of State is satisfied that each of the requirements of paragraph 199 is met.

Refusal of indefinite leave to remain as the child of a person who has or has had leave to enter or remain in the United Kingdom under paragraphs 128–193 (but not paragraphs 135I–135K)

199B. Indefinite leave to remain in the United Kingdom as the child of a person who has or has had limited leave to enter or remain in the United Kingdom under paragraphs 128–193 (but not paragraphs 135I–135K) is to be refused if the Secretary of State is not satisfied that each of the requirements of paragraph 199 is met.

PART 6

PERSONS SEEKING TO ENTER OR REMAIN IN THE UNITED KINGDOM AS A BUSINESSMAN, SELF-EMPLOYED PERSON, INVESTOR, WRITER OR COMPOSER OR ARTIST

200A. DELETED

Person intending to establish themselves in business

Requirements for leave to enter the United Kingdom as a person intending to establish himself in business

200.–208. [DELETED]

Note: Paragraphs deleted from 30 June 2008 by HC 607 except insofar as relevant to paragraph 209. See Appendix F for the wording of these Rules in a case in which they are relevant. Paragraphs deleted from 09:00 on 1 December 2020 subject to savings for applications made before that time (HC 813).

Innovators

Requirements for leave to enter the United Kingdom as an innovator

210A.–210F. [DELETED]

Note: Paragraphs deleted from 30 June 2008 by HC 607 except insofar as relevant to paragraph 210G. See Appendix F for the wording of these Rules in a case in which they are relevant. Paragraphs deleted from 09:00 on 1 December 2020 subject to savings for applications made before that time (HC 813).

Persons intending to establish themselves in business under provisions of EC Association Agreements

Requirements for leave to enter the United Kingdom as a person intending to establish himself in business under the provisions of an EC Association Agreement

Investors

224.–229. Deleted from 30 June 2008 by HC 607 except insofar as relevant to paragraph 230. See Appendix F for the wording of these Rules in a case in which they are relevant.

Writers, composers and artists

Requirements for leave to enter the United Kingdom as a writer, composer or artist

232.–237. Deleted from 30 June 2008 by HC 607 except insofar as relevant to paragraph 238. See Appendix F for the wording of these Rules in a case in which they are relevant.

Part 6A

Points-Based System

245AAA. General requirements for indefinite leave to remain

[The following rules apply to all requirements for indefinite leave to remain in Part 6A and Appendix A:]

[(za) References to "PhD level occupation" refer to the following occupation codes:
2111 Chemical scientists
2112 Biological scientists and biochemists
2113 Physical scientists
2114 Social and humanities scientists
2119 Natural and social science professionals not elsewhere classified [Note: For immigration purposes this code includes researchers in research organisations other than universities.]
2150 Research and development managers
2311 Higher education teaching professionals.]

[(a) References to a 'continuous period' 'lawfully in the UK' means, subject to paragraph (e), residence in the UK for an unbroken period with valid leave, and for these purposes a period shall be considered unbroken where:]

[(i) the applicant has not been absent from the UK for more than 180 days during any 12 month period in the continuous period, except that:

(1) any absence from the UK for the purpose of assisting with a national or international humanitarian or environmental crisis overseas shall not count towards the 180 days, if the applicant provides evidence that this was the purpose of the absence(s) and that their Sponsor, if there was one, agreed to the absence(s) for that purpose; and

(2) for any absences from the UK during periods of leave granted under the Rules in place before 11 January 2018, the applicant must not have been absent from the UK for more than 180 days during each consecutive 12 month period, ending on the same date of the year as the date of the application for indefinite leave to remain[, and]]

[(3) for any applicant who has or has had leave as a Tier 2 (General) migrant, where the Certificate of Sponsorship Checking Service entry shows that they were sponsored to work in any [[PhD level occupation listed in (za)]] when the absence occurred, any absence from the UK for the purpose of research activities overseas shall not count towards the 180 days, if the applicant provides evidence from their sponsor showing that:

(a) research was the purpose of the absence(s); and

(b) the sponsor, agreed to the absence(s) for that purpose; and

(c) the absence(s) directly related to their Tier 2 employment in the UK] {, and}

[(4) for any applicant who has or has had leave as a Tier 1 (Exceptional Talent) Migrant, where they were endorsed by the Royal Society, the British Academy or the Royal Academy of Engineering, any absence from the UK for the purpose of research activities overseas shall not count towards the 180 days, if it occurred while they held this leave.]

[(ii) the applicant has existing limited leave to enter or remain upon their departure and return, except that:

(1) where that leave expired no more than 28 days prior to a further application for entry clearance which was made before 24 November 2016 and subsequently granted,

(2) where, on or after 24 November 2016, the applicant makes a further application for entry clearance during the currency of continuing limited leave which is subsequently granted, or

(3) where, on or after 24 November 2016, the applicant makes a further application for entry clearance within 14 days of the applicant's leave expiring and the Secretary of State considers that there was a good reason beyond the control of the applicant or their representative, provided in or with the application for indefinite leave to remain, why the application could not be made during the currency of continuing limited leave, or

(4) where a successful application for entry clearance is made following the refusal of a previous application to which (2) or (3) otherwise applies, and the application was made within 14 days of that refusal (or the expiry of the time-limit for making an in-time application for administrative review, or any administrative review or appeal being concluded, withdrawn or abandoned or lapsing),

that period spent without existing leave, pending the applicant's re-entry into the United Kingdom, shall be disregarded; and]

(iii) the applicant has any current period of overstaying disregarded where paragraph 39E of these Rules applies; and

(iv) the applicant has any previous period of overstaying between periods of leave disregarded where: the further application was made before 24 November 2016 and within 28 days of the expiry of leave; or the further application was made on or after 24 November 2016 and paragraph 39E of these Rules applied.

[. . .]

(c) Except for periods where the applicant had leave as a Tier 1 (Investor) Migrant, a Tier 1 (Entrepreneur) Migrant, a Tier 1 (Exceptional Talent) Migrant or a highly skilled migrant, any absences from the UK during [the relevant qualifying period] must have been for a purpose that is consistent with the applicant's basis of stay here, including paid annual leave, or for serious or compelling reasons.

[(d) The continuous period will be considered as ending on whichever of the following dates is most beneficial to the applicant:

(i) the date of application;

(ii) the date of decision; or

(iii) any date up to 28 days after the date of application

(e) References to a continuous period spent with valid leave in the UK include time spent with valid leave in the Bailiwick of Guernsey, the Bailiwick of Jersey or the Isle of Man, where that leave was granted for an equivalent purpose to one of the categories stated in the relevant paragraph, provided that the most recent period prior to the date of application was spent in the UK with valid leave in the relevant category.]

Note: Words in introduction, (a), (a)(i), (c) substituted; (b) deleted; (d) and (e) inserted from 11 January 2018 subject to savings for applications made before that date (HC 309). Sub-paragraphs (a)(i), (ii) substituted from 6 July 2018 subject to savings for applications made before that date (HC 1154). Word in (a)(i)(2) substituted, (a)(i)(3) inserted from 1 October 2019 subject to savings for applications made before that date (HC 2631). Word in curly brackets in (a)(i)(3) and sub-paragraph (a)(i)(4) inserted from 20 February 2020 subject to savings for applications made before that date

(HC 56). Sub-paragraph (za) inserted, words in double square brackets in (a)(i)(3) substituted from 6 April 2022 (HC 1118).

245AA. Documents not submitted with applications

(a) Subject to sub-paragraph (b), and where otherwise indicated where Part 6A or any appendices referred to in Part 6A state that specified documents must be provided, the decision maker (that is the Entry Clearance Officer, Immigration Officer or the Secretary of State) will only consider documents received by the Home Office before the date on which the application is considered.

(b) If the applicant has submitted the specified documents and:

(i) [specified evidence is missing from the documents; or]

(ii) a document is in the wrong format (for example, if a letter is not on letterhead paper as specified); or

[...]

(iv) a document does not contain all of the specified information;

the decision maker may contact the applicant or his representative in writing, and request the correct documents. [The] requested documents must be received at the address specified in the request within 10 working days of the date of the request.

[(c) Documents will not be requested where the decision maker does not think that the submission of missing or correct documents will lead to a grant because the application will be refused for other reasons.]

[(d) If the applicant has omitted to provide specified evidence, or submitted it in the wrong format, but the missing information is verifiable from other documents provided with the application or elsewhere, the decision maker may grant the application despite the error or omission, if they are satisfied that the applicant meets all the other requirements of the Rules.]

the decision maker may request the correct document under sub-paragraph (b), or may grant the application despite the error or omission, if satisfied that the specified documents are genuine and the applicant meets all the other requirements of the Rules.

Note: Words in (b)(i) and (iv), (c) and (d) substituted; (b)(iii) deleted from 5 November 2018 (HC 1534).

245A. Specified documents for students previously sponsored by an overseas government or international scholarship agency

Where Part 6A of these Rules state that specified documents must be provided to show that a sponsoring government or international scholarship agency has provided its unconditional written consent to the application, the specified documents are [...] letters, on the official letter-headed paper or stationery of the organisation(s), bearing the official stamp of that organisation and issued by an authorised official of that organisation. The documents must confirm that the organisation gives the applicant unconditional consent to remain in or re-enter the UK for an unlimited time.

Note: Word deleted from 5 November 2018 (HC 1534).

Tier 1 (Exceptional Talent) Migrants

245B. DELETED]

Note: Paragraph substituted from 20 February 2020 subject to savings for applications made before that date (HC 56). Paragraph deleted from 09:00 on 1 December 2020 subject to savings for applications made before that time (HC 813).

245BA. [DELETED]

Note: Paragraph deleted from 20 February 2020 subject to savings for applications made before that date (HC 56).

245BB [DELETED]

Note: Paragraph deleted from 20 February 2020 subject to savings for applications made before that date (HC 56).

245BC. [DELETED]

Note: Amendments from 10 January 2019 subject to savings for applications made before that date (HC 1179). Paragraph deleted from 20 February 2020 subject to savings for applications made before that date (HC 56).

245BD. [DELETED]

Note: Amendments from 30 March 2019 subject to savings for applications made before that date (HC 1919). Paragraph deleted from 20 February 2020 subject to savings for applications made before that date (HC 56).

245BE. [DELETED]

Note: Paragraph deleted from 20 February 2020 subject to savings for applications made before that date (HC 56).

245BF. [DELETED]

Note: Amendments from 11 January 2018 subject to savings for applications made before that date (HC 309). Amendments from 30 March 2019 subject to savings for applications made before that date (HC 1919). Paragraph substituted from 20 February 2020 subject to savings for applications made before that date (HC 56). Paragraph deleted from 09:00 on 1 December 2020 subject to savings for applications made before that time (HC 813).

Tier 1 (General) Migrants

245C. [DELETED]

Note: Paragraph deleted from 6 July 2018 subject to savings for applications made before that date (HC 1154).

245CA. [DELETED]

Note: Paragraph deleted from 6 July 2018 subject to savings for applications made before that date (HC 1154).

245CB. [DELETED]

Note: Paragraph deleted from 6 July 2018 subject to savings for applications made before that date (HC 1154).

245CD. [DELETED]

Note: Amendments from 11 January 2018 subject to savings for applications made before that date (HC 309). Amendment from 29 March 2019 subject to savings for applications made before that date (HC 1919). Paragraph deleted from 6 July 2018 subject to savings for applications made before that date (HC 1154).

245CD-SD. [DELETED]

Note: Paragraph deleted from 6 July 2018 subject to savings for applications made before that date (HC 1154).

Tier 1 (Entrepreneur) Migrants

245D. Purpose of this route and meaning of business

[(a)(i) This category is now closed to new applicants.

(ii) Individuals who have entry clearance, leave to enter or leave to remain as:

(1) a Tier 1 (Entrepreneur) Migrant

(2) a Tier 1 (Graduate Entrepreneur) Migrant, or

(3) a Start-up migrant, having previously held leave as a Tier 1 (Graduate Entrepreneur) Migrant, or have had such leave in the 12 months immediately before the date of application, may apply under these rules to extend their stay or for indefinite leave to remain.

(iii) Other migrants who wish to establish[…] one or more businesses in the UK may apply under the rules for the Start-up or Innovator categories, which are set out in Appendix W.]

(b) For the purpose of paragraphs 245D to 245DF and paragraphs 35 to 53 of Appendix A 'business' means an enterprise as:

(i) a sole trader,

(ii) a partnership, or

(iii) a company registered in the UK.

(c) Where paragraphs 245D to 245DF and paragraphs 35 to 53 of Appendix A,

(i) 'Available' means that the funds are:

(1) in the applicant's own possession,

[(2) in the financial accounts of the UK business(es) which they are relying on to claim points, or]

(3) available from the third party or parties named in the application under the terms of the declaration(s) referred to in paragraph [41(a)(vi)] of Appendix A.

(ii) 'Invested' means that the funds have been invested into a business or businesses which the applicant is running as self-employed or as a director or member of a partnership. 'Invested' or 'spent' excludes spending on:

(1) the applicant's own remuneration,

(2) [buying any business] from a previous owner, where the money ultimately goes to that previous owner (irrespective of whether it is received or held directly or indirectly by that previous owner) rather than into the business being purchased (This applies regardless of whether the money is channeled through the business en route to the previous owner, for example by means of the applicant or business purchasing 'goodwill' or other assets which were previously part of the business.),

(3) investing in businesses, other than those which the applicant is running as self-employed or as a director, and

(4) any spending which is not directly for the purpose of establishing or running the applicant's own business or businesses.

Note: Sub-paragraph (c)(i)(2), words in (c)(i)(3) and (c)(ii)(2) substituted from 11 January 2018 subject to savings for applications made before that date (HC 309). Sub-paragraph (a) substituted from 29 March 2019 subject to savings for applications made before that date (HC 1919). Words in (a)(iii) deleted from 1 October 2019 subject to savings for applications made before that date (HC 2631).

245DA. Entry to the UK

All migrants arriving in the UK and wishing to enter as a Tier 1 (Entrepreneur) Migrant must have a valid entry clearance for entry under this route. If they do not have a valid entry clearance, entry will be refused.

245DB. Requirements for entry clearance

To qualify for entry clearance as a Tier 1 (Entrepreneur) Migrant, an applicant must meet the requirements listed below. If the applicant meets those requirements, entry clearance will be granted. If the applicant does not meet these requirements, the application will be refused.

Requirements:

(a) The applicant must not fall for refusal under the general grounds for refusal.

(b) The applicant must have a minimum of 75 points under paragraphs 35 to 53 of Appendix A.

(c) The applicant must have a minimum of 10 points under paragraphs 1 to 15 of Appendix B.

(d) The applicant must have a minimum of 10 points under paragraphs 1 to 2 of Appendix C.

[(e) The applicant must have entry clearance, leave to enter or leave to remain as:

(i) a Tier 1 (Entrepreneur) Migrant

(ii) a Tier 1 (Graduate Entrepreneur) Migrant, or

(iii) a Start-up migrant, having previously held leave as a Tier 1 (Graduate Entrepreneur) Migrant,

or have had such leave in the 12 months immediately before the date of application.]

[...]

(g) The applicant must provide a business plan, setting out his proposed business activities in the UK and how he expects to make his business succeed.

[...]

(i) Where the applicant [has entry clearance, leave to enter or leave to remain as a Tier 1 (Entrepreneur) Migrant, or has had such leave in the 12 months immediately before the application], and is being assessed under Table 5 of Appendix A, the Entry Clearance Officer must be satisfied that:

(i) the applicant has established, taken over or become a director of one or more genuine businesses in the UK, and has genuinely operated that business or businesses while he had leave as a Tier 1 (Entrepreneur) Migrant; and

(ii) the applicant has genuinely invested the money referred to in Table 5 of Appendix A into one or more genuine businesses in the UK to be spent for the purpose of that business or businesses; and

(iii) the applicant genuinely intends to continue operating one or more businesses in the UK; and

(iv) the applicant does not intend to take employment in the United Kingdom other than under the terms of paragraph 245DE.

(j) In making the assessment in (i), the Entry Clearance Officer will assess the balance of probabilities. The Entry Clearance Officer may take into account the following factors:

(i) the evidence the applicant has submitted;

(ii) the viability and credibility of the source of the money referred to in Table 5 of Appendix A;

(iii) the credibility of the financial accounts of the business or businesses;

(iv) the credibility of the applicant's business activity in the UK, including when he had leave as a Tier 1 (Entrepreneur) Migrant;

(v) the credibility of the job creation for which the applicant is claiming points in Table 5 of Appendix A;

(vii) if the nature of the business requires mandatory accreditation, registration and/or insurance, whether that accreditation, registration and/or insurance has been obtained; and

(viii) any other relevant information.

(k) The Entry Clearance Officer reserves the right to request additional information and evidence to support [the assessment in (i)], and to refuse the application if the information or evidence is not provided. Any requested documents must be received by the Entry Clearance Officer at the address specified in the request within 28 calendar days of the date of the request.

(l) If the Entry Clearance Officer is not satisfied with the genuineness of the application in relation to a points-scoring requirement in Appendix A, those points will not be awarded.

(m) The Entry Clearance Officer may decide not to carry out [the assessment in (i)] if the application already falls for refusal on other grounds, but reserves the right to carry out this assessment in any reconsideration of the decision.

(n) The applicant must, unless he provides a reasonable explanation, comply with any request made by the Entry Clearance Officer to attend for interview.

(o) The applicant must be at least 16 years old.

(p) Where the applicant is under 18 years of age, the application must be supported by the applicant's parents or legal guardian or by one parent if that parent has sole legal responsibility for the child.

(q) Where the applicant is under 18 years of age, the applicant's parents or legal guardian, or one parent if that parent has sole legal responsibility for the child, must confirm that they consent to the arrangements for the applicant's care in the UK.

(r) Where the applicant is 18 years of age or older, the applicant must provide [. . .] a criminal record certificate from the relevant authority in any country in which they have been [present] for 12 months or more (whether continuously or in total) in the past 10 years, while aged 18 or over. This requirement does not need to be met where the Secretary of State is satisfied, by way of an explanation provided in or with the application, that it is not reasonably practicable for the applicant to obtain a certificate from the relevant authority.

(s) If the applicant has failed to provide a criminal record certificate or an explanation in accordance with sub-paragraph (r), the decision maker may contact the applicant or his representative in writing, and request the certificate(s) or explanation. The requested certificate(s) or explanation must be received at the address specified in the request within 28 calendar days of the date of the request.

[(t) The application must have been made:

(i) before 6 July 2021, if the applicant has ever previously had leave as a Tier 1 (Graduate Entrepreneur) Migrant and is claiming points for an initial application under Table 4 of Appendix A; or

(ii) before 6 July 2025, if the applicant has ever previously had leave as a Tier 1 (Graduate Entrepreneur) Migrant and is claiming points for an extension application under Table 5 of Appendix A; or

(iii) before 6 April 2023, in all other cases.]

Note: Words in (i), word in (r) substituted from 11 January 2018 subject to savings for applications made before that date (HC 309). Words in (r) deleted from 5 November 2018 (HC 1534). Sub-paragraph (e), words in (k) and (m) substituted; (f) and (h) deleted; (t) inserted from 29 March 2019 subject to savings for applications made before that date (HC 1919).

245DC. Period and conditions of grant

[(a) Entry clearance will be granted:

(i) for a period of 2 years, to an applicant who has, or has had, leave as a Tier 1 (Entrepreneur) Migrant in the 12 months immediately before the date of application,

(ii) for a period of 3 years and four months, to an applicant who has, or has had, leave as a Tier 1 (Graduate Entrepreneur) Migrant or a Start-up migrant in the 12 months immediately before the date of application.

(b) Entry clearance will be subject to the following conditions:]

(i) no recourse to public funds,

(ii) registration with the police, if this is required by paragraph 326 of these Rules, and

(iii) no employment other than working for the business(es) the applicant has established, joined or taken over, but working for such business(es) does not include anything undertaken by the applicant pursuant to a contract of service or apprenticeship, whether express or implied and whether or written, with another business,

(iv) no employment as a professional sportsperson (including as a sports coach), and

(v) study subject to the condition set out in [Appendix ATAS] of these Rules where the applicant is 18 years of age or over at the time their leave is granted, or will be aged 18 before their period of limited leave expires.

Note: Sub-paragraph (a) and introduction in (b) substituted from 29 March 2019 subject to savings for applications made before that date (HC 1919). Words in (b)(v) substituted from 09:00 on 5 October 2020 subject to savings for applications made before that time. Where consequential changes relating to the need for an ATAS certificate have been made, they take effect for all applications made or granted on or after 5 October 2020 at 09:00 (HC 707).

245DD. Requirements for leave to remain

To qualify for leave to remain as a Tier 1 (Entrepreneur) Migrant under this rule, an applicant must meet the requirements listed below. If the applicant meets these requirements, leave to remain will be granted. If the applicant does not meet these requirements, the application will be refused.

Requirements:

(a) The applicant must not fall for refusal under the general grounds for refusal, except that paragraph 322(10) shall not apply, and must not be an illegal entrant.

(b) The applicant must have a minimum of 75 points under paragraphs 35 to 53 of Appendix A.

(c) The applicant must have a minimum of 10 points under paragraphs 1 to 15 of Appendix B.

(d) The applicant must have a minimum of 10 points under paragraphs 1 to 2 of Appendix C.

[(e) The applicant who is applying for leave to remain must have, or have last been granted, entry clearance, leave to enter or remain as:

(i) a Tier 1 (Entrepreneur) Migrant,

(ii) a Tier 1 (Graduate Entrepreneur) Migrant, or

(iii) a Start-up migrant, having previously held leave as a Tier 1 (Graduate Entrepreneur) Migrant.]

[...]

(g) The applicant must not be in the UK in breach of immigration laws except that, where paragraph 39E of these Rules applies, any current period of overstaying will be disregarded.

[...]

(i) The applicant must provide a business plan, setting out his proposed business activities in the UK and how he expects to make his business succeed.

[...]

(k) Where the applicant has, or was last granted, leave as a Tier 1 (Entrepreneur) Migrant, and is being assessed under Table 5 of Appendix A, the Secretary of State must be satisfied that:

(i) the applicant has established, taken over or become a director of one or more genuine businesses in the UK, and has genuinely operated that business or businesses while he had leave as a Tier 1 (Entrepreneur) Migrant; and

(ii) the applicant has genuinely invested the money referred to in Table 5 of Appendix A into one or more genuine businesses in the UK to be spent for the purpose of that business or businesses; and

(iii) the applicant genuinely intends to continue operating one or more businesses in the UK; and

(iv) the applicant does not intend to take employment in the United Kingdom other than under the terms of paragraph 245DE.

(l) In making the assessment in (k), the Secretary of State will assess the balance of probabilities. The Secretary of State may take into account the following factors:

(i) the evidence the applicant has submitted;

(ii) the viability and credibility of the source of the money referred to in Table 5 of Appendix A;

(iii) the credibility of the financial accounts of the business or businesses;

(iv) the credibility of the applicant's business activity in the UK, including when he had leave as a Tier 1 (Entrepreneur) Migrant;

(v) the credibility of the job creation for which the applicant is claiming points in Table 5 of Appendix A;

(vii) if the nature of the business requires mandatory accreditation, registration and/or insurance, whether that accreditation, registration and/or insurance has been obtained; and

(viii) any other relevant information.

(m) The Secretary of State reserves the right to request additional information and evidence to support [the assessment in (k)], and to refuse the application if the information or evidence is not provided. Any requested documents must be received by the Secretary of State at the address specified in the request within 28 calendar days of the date of the request.

(n) If the Secretary of State is not satisfied with the genuineness of the application in relation to a points-scoring requirement in Appendix A, those points will not be awarded.

(o) The Secretary of State may decide not to carry out [the assessment in (k)] if the application already falls for refusal on other grounds, but reserves the right to carry out this assessment in any reconsideration of the decision.

(p) The applicant must, unless he provides a reasonable explanation, comply with any request made by the Secretary of State to attend for interview.

(q) The applicant must be at least 16 years old.

(r) Where the applicant is under 18 years of age, the application must be supported by the applicant's parents or legal guardian or by one parent if that parent has sole legal responsibility for the child.

(s) Where the applicant is under 18 years of age, the applicant's parents or legal guardian, or one parent if that parent has sole legal responsibility for the child, must confirm that they consent to the arrangements for the applicant's care in the UK.

[(t) The application must have been made:

(i) before 6 July 2021, if the applicant has, or was last granted, entry clearance, leave to enter or remain as a Tier 1 (Graduate Entrepreneur) Migrant or a Start-up migrant; or

(ii) before 6 July 2025, if the applicant has ever previously had leave as a Tier 1 (Graduate Entrepreneur) Migrant and is claiming points for an extension application under Table 5 of Appendix A; or (iii) before 6 April 2023, in all other cases.]

Note: Amendments to (e) from 11 January 2018 subject to savings for applications made before that date (HC 309). Amendments to (e) from 6 July 2018 subject to savings for applications made before that date (HC 1154). Amendments to (e) from 1 August 2019 (HC 1779). Sub-paragraph (e) substituted, words in (m) and (o); (f), (h) and (j) deleted; (t) inserted from 29 March 2019 subject to savings for applications made before that date (HC 1919).

245DE. Period, conditions and curtailment of grant

(a) Leave to remain will be granted:

(i) for a period of 2 years, to an applicant who has, or was last granted, leave as a Tier 1 (Entrepreneur) Migrant,

(ii) for a period of 3 years, [to an applicant who has, or was last granted, leave as a Tier 1 (Graduate Entrepreneur) Migrant or a Start-up migrant].

(b) Leave to remain under this route will be subject to the following conditions:

(i) no recourse to public funds,

(ii) registration with the police, if this is required by paragraph 326 of these Rules, and

(iii) no employment, other than working for the business or businesses which he has established, joined or taken over, but working for such business(es) does not include anything undertaken by the applicant pursuant to a contract of service or apprenticeship, whether express or implied and whether oral or written, with another business, and

(iv) no employment as a professional sportsperson (including as a sports coach), and

(v) study subject to the condition set out in [Appendix ATAS] of these Rules where the applicant is 18 years of age or over at the time their leave is granted, or will be aged 18 before their period of limited leave expires.

(c) Without prejudice to the grounds for curtailment in paragraph 323 of these Rules, leave to enter or remain granted to a Tier 1 (Entrepreneur) Migrant may be curtailed if:

(i) within 6 months of the date specified in paragraph (d), the applicant has not done one or more of the following things:

(1) registered with HM Revenue and Customs as self-employed,

(2) registered a new company or partnership in which he is a director or member, or

(3) registered as a director or member of an existing business or partnership, or

(ii) the funds referred to in the relevant sections of Appendix A cease to be available to him, except where they have been spent for the purposes of his business or businesses.

(d) The date referred to in paragraph (c) is:

(i) the date of the applicant's entry to the UK, in the case of an applicant granted entry clearance as a Tier 1 (Entrepreneur) Migrant where there is evidence to establish the applicant's date of entry to the UK,

(ii) the date of the grant of entry clearance to the applicant, in the case of an applicant granted entry clearance as a Tier 1 (Entrepreneur) Migrant where there is no evidence to establish the applicant's date of entry to the UK, or

(iii) the date of the grant of leave to remain to the applicant, in any other case.

Note: Words in (a)(ii) substituted from 29 March 2019 subject to savings for applications made before that date (HC 1919). Words in (b)(v) substituted from 09:00 on 5 October 2020 subject to savings for applications made before that time. Where consequential changes relating to the need for an ATAS certificate have been made, they take effect for all applications made or granted on or after 5 October 2020 at 09:00 (HC 707).

245DF. Requirements for indefinite leave to remain

To qualify for indefinite leave to remain as a Tier 1 (Entrepreneur) Migrant, an applicant must meet the requirements listed below. If the applicant meets these requirements, indefinite leave to remain will be granted. If the applicant does not meet these requirements, the application will be refused.

Requirements:

(a) DELETED

(b) The applicant must not fall for refusal under the general grounds for refusal, and must not be an illegal entrant.

(c) The applicant must have a minimum of 75 points under paragraphs 35 to 53 of Appendix A.

(d) The applicant must have demonstrated sufficient knowledge of the English language and sufficient knowledge about life in the United Kingdom, in accordance with Appendix KoLL.

(e) The applicant must not be in the UK in breach of immigration laws except that, where paragraph 39E of these Rules applies, any current period of overstaying will be disregarded.

(f) The Secretary of State must be satisfied that:

(i) the applicant has established, taken over or become a director of one or more genuine businesses in the UK, and has genuinely operated that business or businesses while he had leave as a Tier 1 (Entrepreneur) Migrant; and

(ii) the applicant has genuinely invested the money referred to in Table 6 of Appendix A into one or more businesses in the UK to be spent for the purpose of that business or businesses; and

(iii) the applicant genuinely intends to continue operating one or more businesses in the UK.

(g) In making the assessment in (f), the Secretary of State will assess the balance of probabilities. The Secretary of State may take into account the following factors:

(i) the evidence the applicant has submitted;

(ii) the viability and credibility of the source of the money referred to in Table 6 of Appendix A;

(iii) the credibility of the financial accounts of the business or businesses;

(iv) the credibility of the applicant's business activity in the UK, including when he had leave as a Tier 1 (Entrepreneur) Migrant;

(v) the credibility of the job creation for which the applicant is claiming points in Table 6 of Appendix A;

(vii) if the nature of the business requires mandatory accreditation, registration and/or insurance, whether that accreditation, registration and/or insurance has been obtained; and

(viii) any other relevant information.

(h) The Secretary of State reserves the right to request additional information and evidence to support the assessment in (f), and to refuse the application if the information or evidence is not provided. Any requested documents must be received by the Secretary of State at the address specified in the request within 28 calendar days of the date of the request.

(i) If the Secretary of State is not satisfied with the genuineness of the application in relation to a points-scoring requirement in Appendix A, those points will not be awarded.

(j) The Secretary of State may decide not to carry out the assessment in (f) if the application already falls for refusal on other grounds, but reserves the right to carry out this assessment in any reconsideration of the decision.

(k) The applicant must, unless he provides a reasonable explanation, comply with any request made by the Secretary of State to attend for interview.

[(l) The application for indefinite leave to remain must have been made:

(i) before 6 July 2027, if the applicant has ever previously had leave as a Tier 1 (Graduate Entrepreneur) Migrant; or

(ii) before 6 April 2025, in all other cases.]

Note: Sub-paragraph (l) inserted from 29 March 2019 subject to savings for applications made before that date (HC 1919).

Tier 1 (Investor) Migrants

245E. Purpose

This route is for high net worth individuals making a substantial financial investment to the UK. [This route is now closed to new applicants. Individuals who already have entry clearance, leave to enter or remain as a Tier 1 (Investor) Migrant may apply under these rules to extend their stay or for indefinite leave to remain.]

Note: Words inserted from 16:00 on 17 February 2022 subject to savings for applications made before that time (CP 632).

245EA. Entry to the UK

All migrants arriving in the UK and wishing to enter as a Tier 1 (Investor) Migrant must have a valid entry clearance for entry under this route. If they do not have a valid entry clearance, entry will be refused.

245EB. Requirements for entry clearance

To qualify for entry clearance [. . .]as a Tier 1 (Investor) Migrant, an applicant must meet the requirements listed below. If the applicant meets these requirements, entry clearance will be granted. If the applicant does not meet these requirements, the application will be refused.

Requirements:

[(aa) The applicant must have leave as a Tier 1 (Investor) Migrant on, or must have had such leave within the last 12 months immediately before, the date of application.]

(a) The applicant must not fall for refusal under the general grounds for refusal.

(b) The applicant must have a minimum of 75 points under paragraphs 54 to 65-SD of Appendix A.

[...]

(d) The applicant must be at least 18 years old and the assets and investment he is claiming points for must be wholly under his control.

(e) The Entry Clearance Officer must not have reasonable grounds to believe that:

[(i) notwithstanding that the applicant has provided the relevant specified documents required under Appendix A or (where relevant) was awarded points in a previous application as a Tier 1 (Investor) Migrant, the applicant is or was not in control of and at liberty to freely invest the money specified in their application for the purposes of meeting the requirements of Appendix A to these Rules; or]

(ii) any of the money specified in the application for the purposes of meeting the requirements [...] of Appendix A to these Rules held by:

(1) the applicant; or

(2) where any of the specified money has been made available to the applicant by another party, that party, has been acquired by means of conduct which is unlawful in the UK, or would constitute unlawful conduct if it occurred in the UK[, or has been or will be transferred internationally by means which are unlawful in any of the countries involved]; or

(iii) where any of the money specified in the application for the purposes of meeting the requirements [...] of Appendix A to these Rules has been made available by another party, the character, conduct or associations of that party are such that approval of the application would not be conducive to the public good, and where the Entry Clearance Officer does have reasonable grounds to believe one or more of the above applies, no points from [Appendix A].

(f) Where the applicant is 18 years of age or older, the applicant must provide [...] a criminal record certificate from the relevant authority in any country in which they have been [present] for 12 months or more (whether continuously or in total) in the past 10 years, while aged 18 or over. This requirement does not need to be met where the Secretary of State is satisfied, by way of an explanation provided in or with the application, that it is not reasonably practicable for the applicant to obtain a certificate from the relevant authority.

(g) If the applicant has failed to provide a criminal record certificate or an explanation in accordance with sub-paragraph (f), the decision maker may contact the applicant or his representative in writing, and request the certificate(s) or explanation. The requested certificate(s) or explanation must be received at the address specified in the request within 28 calendar days of the date of the request.

[(h) The application must be made before 17th February 2026.]

Note: Word in (f) substituted from 11 January 2018 subject to savings for applications made before that date (HC 309). Words in (f) deleted from 5 November 2018 (HC 1534). Sub-paragraph (e)(i), words at end of (e) substituted; words in (e)(ii) and (iii) deleted; words in (e)(ii) inserted from 29 March 2019 subject to savings for applications made before that date (HC 1919). Amendment to (c) from 09:00 on 5 October 2020 subject to savings for applications made before that time. Where consequential changes relating to the need for an ATAS certificate have been made, they take effect for all applications made or granted on or after 5 October 2020 at 09:00 (HC 707). Words in introduction, sub-paragraph (c) deleted; sub-paragraphs (aa) and (h) inserted from 16:00 on 17 February 2022 subject to savings for applications made before that time (CP 632).

245EC. Period and conditions of grant

[(a) Entry clearance will be granted for a period of 2 years.]

(b) [Entry clearance will be subject to the following conditions:]

(i) no recourse to public funds,

(ii) registration with the police, if this is required by paragraph 326 of these Rules,

(iii) no Employment as a Doctor or Dentist in Training, unless the applicant has obtained a primary degree in medicine or dentistry at bachelor's level or above from a UK institution that is a UK recognised or listed body, or which holds a [*student sponsor* licence under the Points Based System], and

(iv) no employment as a professional sportsperson (including as a sports coach), and

(v) study subject to the condition set out in [Appendix ATAS] of these Rules.

Note: Sub-paragraph (a) and introduction in (b) substituted from 29 March 2019 subject to savings for applications made before that date (HC 1919). Words in (b)(iii) and (v) substituted from 09:00 on 5 October 2020 subject to savings for applications made before that time. Where consequential changes relating to the need for an ATAS certificate have been made, they take effect for all applications made or granted on or after 5 October 2020 at 09:00 (HC 707). Sub-paragraph (a) substituted from 16:00 on 17 February 2022 subject to savings for applications made before that time (CP 632).

245ED. Requirements for leave to remain

To qualify for leave to remain as a Tier 1 (Investor) Migrant, an applicant must meet the requirements listed below. If the applicant meets these requirements, leave to remain will be granted. If the applicant does not meet these requirements, the application will be refused.

Requirements:

(a) The applicant must not fall for refusal under the general grounds for refusal, and must not be an illegal entrant.

(b) The applicant must have a minimum of 75 points under paragraphs 54 to 65-SD of Appendix A.

[(c) The applicant must have, or have last been granted, entry clearance, leave to enter or remain as a Tier 1 (Investor) Migrant.]

[…]

(e) The applicant must be at least 18 years old and the assets and investment he is claiming points for must be wholly under his control.

(f) The applicant must not be in the UK in breach of immigration laws except that, where paragraph 39E of these Rules applies, any current period of overstaying will be disregarded.

(g) The Secretary of State must not have reasonable grounds to believe that:

[(i) notwithstanding that the applicant has provided the relevant specified documents required under Appendix A or (where relevant) was awarded points in a previous application as a Tier 1 (Investor) Migrant, the applicant is not or was not in control of and at liberty to freely invest the money specified in their application for the purposes of meeting the requirements of Appendix A to these Rules; or]

(ii) any of the money specified in the application for the purposes of meeting the requirements […] of Appendix A to these Rules held by:

(1) the applicant; or

(2) where any of the specified money has been made available to the applicant by another party, that party,

has been acquired by means of conduct which is unlawful in the UK[, or has been or will be transferred internationally by means which are unlawful in any of the countries involved], or would constitute unlawful conduct if it occurred in the UK; or

(iii) where any of the money specified in the application for the purposes of meeting the requirements […] of Appendix A to these Rules has been made available by another party, the character, conduct or associations of that party are such that approval of the application would not be conducive to the public good,

and where the Secretary of State does have reasonable grounds to believe one or more of the above applies, no points from [Appendix A] will be awarded.

[(h) The application must be made before 17th February 2026.]

Note: Words in (c)(xvi)(1) substituted (subsequently amended further, see HC 2631 below); (c)(v) deleted from 11 January 2018 subject to savings for applications made before that date (HC 309). Words in double square brackets in (c)(xvi)(1) substituted (subsequently amended further, see HC 2631 below) from 6 July 2018 subject to savings for applications made before that date (HC 1154). Sub-paragraph (g)(i) substituted; words in (g)(ii) and (iii) deleted; words in (g)(ii), words at end of (g) inserted from 29 March 2019 subject to savings for applications made before that date (HC 1919). Amendment to (c) from 1 October 2019 (HC 2631). Amendments to (c) and (d) from 09:00 on 5 October 2020 subject to savings for applications made before that time. Where consequential changes relating to the need for an ATAS certificate have been made, they take effect for all applications made or granted on or after 5 October 2020 at 09:00 (HC 707). Amendment to (c) from 09:00 on 1 December 2020 subject to savings for applications made before that time (HC 813). Sub-paragraph (c) substituted, sub-paragraph (d) deleted, sub-paragraph (h) inserted from 16:00 on 17 February 2022 subject to savings for applications made before that time (CP 632).

245EE. Period, conditions and curtailment of grant

[(a) Leave to remain will be granted for a period of 2 years.]

(b) Leave to remain under this route will be subject to the following conditions:

(i) no recourse to public funds,

(ii) registration with the police, if this is required by paragraph 326 of these Rules,

(iii) no Employment as a Doctor or Dentist in Training, unless the applicant:

(1) has obtained a primary degree in medicine or dentistry at bachelor's level or above from a UK institution that is a UK recognised or listed body, or which holds a [*student sponsor* licence under the Points Based System], and provides evidence of this degree; or

(2) has, or has last been granted, entry clearance, leave to enter or leave to remain that was not subject to any condition restricting him from taking employment as a Doctor in Training, has been employed during that leave as a Doctor in Training, and provides a letter from the Postgraduate Deanery or NHS Trust employing them which confirms that they have been working in a post or programme that has been approved by the General Medical Council as a training programme or post; or

(3) has, or has last been granted, entry clearance, leave to enter or leave to remain that was not subject to any condition restricting him from taking employment as a Dentist in Training, has been employed during that leave as a Dentist in Training, and provides a letter from the Postgraduate Deanery or NHS Trust employing them which confirms that they have been working in a post or programme that has been approved by the Joint Committee for Postgraduate Training in Dentistry as a training programme or post, and

(iv) no employment as a professional sportsperson (including as a sports coach), and

(v) study subject to the condition set out in [Appendix ATAS] of these Rules.

(c) Without prejudice to the grounds for curtailment in paragraph 323 of these Rules, leave to enter or remain as a Tier 1 (Investor) Migrant may be curtailed if:

(i) within 3 months of the date specified in paragraph (d), the applicant has not invested, or had invested on his behalf, at least the amount of capital specified in paragraph (e) in the UK by way of UK Government bonds [(where the applicant's initial grant of leave as a Tier 1 (Investor) Migrant was granted under the Rules in place before 29 March 2019 and the date of application is before 6 April 2023)], share capital or loan capital in active and trading UK registered companies other than those principally engaged in property investment, or

(ii) the applicant does not maintain at least the level of investment in (i) throughout the remaining period of his leave.

(d) The date referred to in paragraph (c) is:

(i) the date of the applicant's entry to the UK, in the case of an applicant granted entry clearance as a Tier 1 (Investor) Migrant where there is evidence to establish the applicant's date of entry to the UK,

(ii) the date of the grant of entry clearance to the applicant, in the case of an applicant granted entry clearance as a Tier 1 (Investor) Migrant where there is no evidence to establish the applicant's date of entry to the UK, or

(iii) the date of the grant of leave to remain to the applicant, in any other case.

(e) The amount of capital referred to in paragraph (c) is:

(i) at least £2 million if the applicant was last granted leave under the Rules in place from 6 November 2014 and was awarded points as set out in Table 7 or Table 8A of Appendix A to these Rules in that last grant, or

(ii) at least £750,000 if the applicant was last granted leave under the Rules in place before 6 November 2014 or was awarded points as set out in Table 8B of Appendix A to these Rules in his last grant.

(f) Paragraph 245EE(c) does not apply where the applicant's two most recent grants of leave were as a Tier 1 (Investor) Migrant.

Note: Words in (c)(i) inserted from 29 March 2019 subject to savings for applications made before that date (HC 1919). Words in (b)(iii)(1) and (b)(v) substituted from 09:00 on 5 October 2020 subject to savings for applications made before that time. Where consequential changes relating to the need for an ATAS certificate have been made, they take effect for all applications made or granted on or after 5 October 2020 at 09:00 (HC 707). Sub-paragraph (a) substituted from 16:00 on 17 February 2022 subject to savings for applications made before that time (CP 632).

245EF. Requirements for indefinite leave to remain

To qualify for indefinite leave to remain, a Tier 1 (Investor) Migrant must meet the requirements listed below. if the applicant meets these requirements, indefinite leave to remain will be granted. if the applicant does not meet these requirements, the application will be refused.

Requirements:

(a) DELETED

(b) The applicant must not fall for refusal under the general grounds for refusal, and must not be an illegal entrant.

(c) The applicant must have a minimum of 75 points under paragraphs 54 to 65-SD of Appendix A.

(d) The applicant must have demonstrated sufficient knowledge of the English language and sufficient knowledge about life in the United Kingdom, in accordance with Appendix KoLL.

(e) The applicant must not be in the UK in breach of immigration laws except that, where paragraph 39E of these Rules applies, any current period of overstaying will be disregarded.

[(f) The Secretary of State must not have reasonable grounds to believe that:

(i) notwithstanding that the applicant was awarded points in a previous application as a Tier 1 (Investor) Migrant, the applicant is or was not in control of and at liberty to freely invest the money specified in their application for the purposes of meeting the requirements of Appendix A to these Rules; or

(ii) any of the money specified in the application for the purposes of meeting the requirements of Appendix A to these Rules held by:

(1) the applicant; or

(2) where any of the specified money has been made available to the applicant by another party, that party, has been acquired by means of conduct which is unlawful in the UK, or would constitute unlawful conduct if it occurred in the UK, or has been transferred internationally by means which are unlawful in any of the countries involved; or

(iii) where any of the money specified in the application for the purposes of meeting the requirements of Appendix A to these Rules has been made available by another party, the character, conduct or associations of that party are such that approval of the application would not be conducive to the public good, and where the Secretary of State does have reasonable grounds to believe one or more of the above applies, no points from Appendix A will be awarded.]

[(g) The application must be made before 17th February 2028.]

Note: Sub-paragraph (f) inserted from 29 March 2019 subject to savings for applications made before that date (HC 1919). Sub-paragraph (g) inserted from 16:00 on 17 February 2022 subject to savings for applications made before that time (CP 632).

[Tier 1 (Graduate Entrepreneur) Migrants]

[**245F.** This category is now closed and has been replaced with the Start-up category in Appendix W.]

Note: Amendments from 1 August 2019 (HC 1779). Paragraph substituted from 6 July 2019 subject to savings for applications made before that date (HC 1919).

245FA. [DELETED]

Note: Paragraph deleted from 6 July 2019 subject to savings for applications made before that date (HC 1919).

245FB. [DELETED]

Note: Amendments from 1 August 2019 (HC 1779). Paragraph deleted from 6 July 2019 subject to savings for applications made before that date (HC 1919).

245FC. [DELETED]

Note: Paragraph deleted from 6 July 2019 subject to savings for applications made before that date (HC 1919).

Tier 2 Migrants

Tier 2 (Intra-Company Transfer) Migrants

245G. [DELETED]

Note: Amendment from 11 January 2018 subject to savings for applications made before that date (HC 309). Paragraph deleted from 09:00 on 1 December 2020 subject to savings for applications made before that time (HC 813).

245GA. [DELETED]

Note: Paragraph deleted from 09:00 on 1 December 2020 subject to savings for applications made before that time (HC 813).

245GB. [DELETED]

Note: Amendment from 11 January 2018 subject to savings for applications made before that time (HC 309). Amendment from 09:00 on 5 October 2020 subject to savings for applications made before that time. Where consequential changes relating to the need for an ATAS certificate have been made, they take effect for all applications made or granted on or after 5 October 2020 at 09:00 (HC 707). Paragraph deleted from 09:00 on 1 December 2020 subject to savings for applications made before that time (HC 813).

245GC. [DELETED]

Note: Amendment from 09:00 on 5 October 2020 subject to savings for applications made before that time. Where consequential changes relating to the need for an ATAS certificate have been made, they take effect for all applications made or granted on or after 5 October 2020 at 09:00 (HC 707). Paragraph deleted from 09:00 on 1 December 2020 subject to savings for applications made before that time (HC 813).

245GD. [DELETED]

Note: Paragraph deleted from 09:00 on 1 December 2020 subject to savings for applications made before that time (HC 813).

245GE. [DELETED]

Note: Amendments from 10 January 2019 subject to savings for applications made before that date (HC 1779). Amendment from 09:00 on 5 October 2020 subject to savings for applications made before that time. Where consequential changes relating to the need for an ATAS certificate have been made, they take effect for all applications made or granted on or after 5 October 2020 at 09:00 (HC 707). Paragraph deleted from 09:00 on 1 December 2020 subject to savings for applications made before that time (HC 813).

245GF. [DELETED]

Note: Amendment from 11 January 2018 subject to savings for applications made before that date (HC 309). Amendment from 5 November 2018 (HC 1534). Amendment from 1 October 2019 subject to savings for applications made before that date (HC 2631). Paragraph deleted from 4 June 2020 subject to savings for applications made before that date and where an application is supported by a Certificate of Sponsorship or endorsement assigned before that date (CP 232).

245GF-SD. [DELETED]

Note: Amendments from 6 July 2018 subject to savings for applications made before that date (HC 1154). Amendments from 5 November 2018 (HC 1534). Amendment from 1 October 2019 (HC

2631). Paragraph deleted from 4 June 2020 subject to savings for applications made before that date and where an application is supported by a Certificate of Sponsorship or endorsement assigned before that date (CP 232).

Tier 2 (General) Migrants, Tier 2 (Minister of Religion) Migrants and Tier 2 (Sportsperson) Migrants

245H. [DELETED]

Note: Paragraph deleted from 09:00 on 1 December 2020 subject to savings for applications made before that time (HC 813).

245HA. [DELETED]

Note: Paragraph deleted from 09:00 on 1 December 2020 subject to savings for applications made before that time (HC 813).

245HB. [DELETED]

Note: Amendment from 11 January 2018 subject to savings for applications made before that time (HC 309). Amendment from 6 July 2018 subject to savings for applications made before that date (HC 1154). Amendments from 5 November 2018 (HC 1534). Amendment from 1 October 2019 subject to savings for applications made before that date (HC 2631). Amendment from 09:00 on 5 October 2020 subject to savings for applications made before that time. Where consequential changes relating to the need for an ATAS certificate have been made, they take effect for all applications made or granted on or after 5 October 2020 at 09:00 (HC 707). Paragraph deleted from 09:00 on 1 December 2020 subject to savings for applications made before that date (HC 813).

245HC. [DELETED]

Note: Amendment from 09:00 on 5 October 2020 subject to savings for applications made before that time. Where consequential changes relating to the need for an ATAS certificate have been made, they take effect for all applications made or granted on or after 5 October 2020 at 09:00 (HC 707). Paragraph deleted from 09:00 on 1 December 2020 subject to savings for applications made before that time (HC 813).

245HD. [DELETED]

Note: Amendments from 11 January 2018 subject to savings for applications made using a Certificate of Sponsorship assigned before that date (HC 309). Amendment from 6 July 2018 subject to savings for applications made before that date (HC 1154). Amendments from 5 November 2018 (HC 1534). Amendment from 1 August 2019 (HC 1779). Amendments from 30 March 2019 subject to savings for applications made before that date (HC 1919). Amendments from 20 February 2020 subject to savings for applications made before that date (HC 56). Amendments from 09:00 on 5 October 2020 subject to savings for applications made before that time. Where consequential changes relating to the need for an ATAS certificate have been made, they take effect for all applications made or granted on or after 5 October 2020 at 09:00 (HC 707). Paragraph deleted from 09:00 on 1 December 2020 subject to savings for applications made before that time (HC 813).

245HE. [DELETED]

Note: Amendments from 30 March 2019 subject to savings for applications made before that date (HC 1919). Amendment from 09:00 on 5 October 2020 subject to savings for applications made before that time. Where consequential changes relating to the need for an ATAS certificate have been made, they take effect for all applications made or granted on or after 5 October 2020 at 09:00 (HC 707). Paragraph deleted from 09:00 on 1 December 2020 subject to savings for applications made before that time (HC 813).

245HF. [DELETED]

Note: Amendment from 11 January 2018 subject to savings for applications made before that date (HC 309). Amendments from 30 March 2019 subject to savings for applications made before that date (HC 1919). Amendments from 1 October 2019 with and without savings (HC 2631). Amendments from 20 February 2020 subject to savings for applications made before that date (HC 56). Amendments from 6 April 2020 (HC 120). Paragraph deleted 09:00 on 1 December 2020 subject to savings for applications made before that time (HC 813).

245HG. [DELETED]

Note: Amendments from 11 January 2018 subject to savings for applications made before that date (HC 309). Amendments from 30 March 2019 subject to savings for applications made before that date (HC 1919). Amendments from 20 February 2020 subject to savings for applications made before that date (HC 56). Paragraph deleted from 09:00 on 1 December 2020 subject to savings for applications made before that time (HC 813).

245HH. [DELETED]

Note: Amendments from 5 November 2018 (HC 1534). Amendments from 1 October 2019 (HC 2631). Paragraph deleted from 09:00 on 1 December 2020 subject to savings for applications made before that time (HC 813).

Tier 5 (Youth Mobility Scheme) Temporary Migrants

245ZI. [DELETED]

Note: Paragraph deleted from 09:00 on 1 December 2020 subject to savings for applications made before that time (HC 813).

245ZJ. [DELETED]

Note: Paragraph deleted from 09:00 on 1 December 2020 subject to savings for applications made before that time (HC 813).

245ZK. [DELETED]

Note: Paragraph deleted from 09:00 on 1 December 2020 subject to savings for applications made before that time (HC 813).

245ZL. **[DELETED]**

Note: Amendments from 09:00 on 5 October 2020 subject to savings for applications made before that time. Where consequential changes relating to the need for an ATAS certificate have been made, they take effect for all applications made or granted on or after 5 October 2020 at 09:00 (HC 707). Paragraph deleted from 09:00 on 1 December 2020 subject to savings for applications made before that time (HC 813).

Tier 5 (Temporary Worker) Migrants

245ZM. [DELETED]

Note: Amendment from 10 January 2019 subject to savings for applications made before that date (HC 1779). Paragraph deleted from 09:00 on 1 December 2020 subject to savings for applications made before that time (HC 813).

245ZN. [DELETED]

Note: Paragraph deleted from 09:00 on 1 December 2020 subject to savings for applications made before that time (HC 813).

245ZO. [DELETED]

Note: Amendments from 11 January 2018 subject to savings for applications made before that date (HC 309). Amendment from 10 January 2019 subject to savings for applications made before that date (HC 1779). Paragraph deleted from 09:00 on 1 December 2020 subject to savings for applications made before that time (HC 813).

245ZP. [DELETED]

Note: Amendment from 10 January 2019 subject to savings for applications made before that date (HC 1779). Amendment from 09:00 on 5 October 2020 subject to savings for applications made before that time. Where consequential changes relating to the need for an ATAS certificate have been made, they take effect for all applications made or granted on or after 5 October 2020 at 09:00 (HC 707). Paragraph deleted from 09:00 on 1 December 2020 subject to savings for applications made before that time (HC 813).

245ZQ. [DELETED]

Note: Amendment from 10 January 2019 subject to savings for applications made before that date; amendment from 1 August 2019 (HC 1779). Amendments from 09:00 on 5 October 2020 subject to savings for applications made before that time. Where consequential changes relating to the need for an ATAS certificate have been made, they take effect for all applications made or granted on or after 5 October 2020 at 09:00 (HC 707). Paragraph deleted from 09:00 on 1 December 2020 subject to savings for applications made before that time (HC 813).

245ZR. [DELETED]

Note: Amendment from 09:00 on 5 October 2020 subject to savings for applications made before that time. Where consequential changes relating to the need for an ATAS certificate have been made, they take effect for all applications made or granted on or after 5 October 2020 at 09:00 (HC 707). Paragraph deleted from 09:00 on 1 December 2020 subject to savings for applications made before that time (HC 813).

245ZS. [DELETED]

Note: Amendments from 5 November 2018 (HC 1534). Paragraph deleted from 09:00 on 1 December 2020 subject to savings for applications made before that time (HC 813).

Tier 4 (General) Student

245ZT. [DELETED]

Notes: Amendment from 6 July 2018 subject to savings for applications made before that date (HC 1154). Paragraph deleted from 09:00 on 5 October 2020 subject to savings for applications made before that time (HC 707).

245ZU. [DELETED]

Note: Paragraph deleted from 09:00 on 5 October 2020 subject to savings for applications made before that time (HC 707).

245ZV. [DELETED]

Note: Amendment from 11 January 2018 subject to savings for applications made before that date (HC 309). Amendment from 6 July 2018 subject to savings for applications made before that date (HC 1154). Amendments from 5 November 2018 (HC 1534). Amendments from 1 August 2019 (HC 1779). Amendments from 6 April 2019 subject to savings for applications made before that date (HC 1919). Paragraph deleted from 09:00 on 5 October 2020 subject to savings for applications made before that time (HC 707).

245ZW. [DELETED]

Note: Amendments from 11 January 2018 subject to savings for applications made before that date (HC 309). Amendments from 6 July 2018 subject to savings for applications made before that date (HC 1154). Amendments from 1 August 2019 (HC 1779). Amendments from 1 October 2019 with and without savings (HC 2631). Paragraph deleted from 09:00 on 5 October 2020 subject to savings for applications made before that time (HC 707).

245ZX. [DELETED]

Note: Amendment from 11 January 2018 subject to savings for applications made before that date (HC 309). Amendment from 6 July 2018 subject to savings for applications made before that date (HC 1154). Amendments from 5 November 2018 (HC 1534). Amendments from 10 January 2019 subject to savings for applications made before that date; amendments from 1 August 2019 (HC 1779). Amendments from 6 April 2019 subject to savings for applications made before that date (HC 1919). Amendment from 1 October 2019 (2631). Paragraph deleted from 09:00 on 5 October 2020 subject to savings for applications made before that time (HC 707).

245ZY. [DELETED]

Note: Amendments from 11 January 2018 subject to savings for applications made before that date (HC 309). Amendments from 6 July 2018 subject to savings for applications made before that date (HC 1154). Amendments from 1 August 2019 (HC 1779). Amendments from 1 October 2019 with and without savings (HC 2631). Paragraph deleted from 09:00 on 5 October 2020 subject to savings for applications made before that date (HC 707).

Tier 4 (Child) Student

245ZZ. [DELETED]

Note: Amendment from 11 January 2018 subject to savings for applications made before that date (HC 309). Amendment from 6 July 2018 subject to savings for applications made before that date (HC 1154). Paragraph deleted from 09:00 on 5 October 2020 subject to savings for applications made before that time (HC 707).

245ZZA. [DELETED]

Note: Amendments from 5 November 2018 (HC 1534). Paragraph deleted from 09:00 on 5 October 2020 subject to savings for applications made before that time (HC 707).

245ZZB. [DELETED]

Note: Amendments from 6 July 2018 subject to savings for applications made before that date (HC 1154). Amendments from 1 August 2019 (HC 1779). Paragraph deleted from 09:00 on 5 October 2020 subject to savings for applications made before that time (HC 707).

245ZZC. [DELETED]

Note: Amendments from 5 November 2018 (HC 1534). Paragraph deleted from 09:00 on 5 October 2020 subject to savings for applications made before that time (HC 707).

245ZZD. [DELETED]

Note: Amendments from 6 July 2018 subject to savings for applications made before that date (HC 1154). Amendments from 1 August 2019 (HC 1779). Paragraph deleted from 09:00 on 5 October 2020 subject to savings for applications made before that time (HC 707).

245ZZE. [DELETED]

Note: Paragraph deleted from 09:00 on 5 October 2020 subject to savings for applications made before that time (HC 707).

Part 7

Other Categories

Persons exercising rights of access to a child resident in the United Kingdom

Requirements for leave to enter the United Kingdom as a person exercising rights of access to a child resident in the United Kingdom

A246. Paragraphs 246 to 248F apply only to a person who has made an application before 9 July 2012 for leave to enter or remain or indefinite leave to remain as a person exercising rights of access to a child resident in the UK, or who before 9 July 2012 has been granted leave to enter or remain as a person exercising rights of access to a child resident in the UK.

AB246. Where an application for leave to enter or remain is made on or after 9 July 2012 as a person exercising rights of access to a child resident in the UK Appendix FM will apply.

246. The requirements to be met by a person seeking leave to enter the United Kingdom to exercise access rights to a child resident in the United Kingdom are that:

(i) the applicant is the parent of a child who is resident in the United Kingdom; and

(ii) the parent or carer with whom the child permanently resides is resident in the United Kingdom; and

(iii) the applicant produces evidence that he has access rights to the child in the form of:

(a) a Residence Order or a Contact Order granted by a Court in the United Kingdom; or

(b) a certificate issued by a district judge confirming the applicant's intention to maintain contact with the child; and

(iv) the applicant intends to take an active role in the child's upbringing; and

(v) the child is under the age of 18; and

(vi) there will be adequate accommodation for the applicant and any dependants without recourse to public funds in accommodation which the applicant owns or occupies exclusively; and

(vii) the applicant will be able to maintain himself and any dependants adequately without recourse to public funds; and

(viii) the applicant holds a valid United Kingdom entry clearance for entry in this capacity.

Leave to enter the United Kingdom as a person exercising rights of access to a child resident in the United Kingdom

247. Leave to enter as a person exercising access rights to a child resident in the United Kingdom may be granted for 12 months in the first instance, [provided that on arrival a valid passport or other identity document is produced to the Immigration Officer and the applicant has entry clearance for entry in this capacity.]

Note: Words substituted from 11 January 2018 subject to savings for applications made before that date (HC 309).

Refusal of leave to enter the United Kingdom as a person exercising rights of access to a child resident in the United Kingdom

248. Leave to enter as a person exercising rights of access to a child resident in the United Kingdom is to be refused if [on arrival, a valid passport or other identity document is not produced to the Immigration Officer and the applicant does not have entry clearance for entry in this capacity.]

Note: Words substituted from 11 January 2018 subject to savings for applications made before that date (HC 309).

Requirements for leave to remain in the United Kingdom as a person exercising rights of access to a child resident in the United Kingdom

248A. The requirements to be met by a person seeking leave to remain in the United Kingdom to exercise access rights to a child resident in the United Kingdom are that:

(i) the applicant is the parent of a child who is resident in the United Kingdom; and

(ii) the parent or carer with whom the child permanently resides is resident in the United Kingdom; and

(iii) the applicant produces evidence that he has access rights to the child in the form of:

(a) a Residence Order or a Contact Order granted by a Court in the United Kingdom; or

(b) a certificate issued by a district judge confirming the applicant's intention to maintain contact with the child; or

(c) a statement from the child's other parent (or, if contact is supervised, from the supervisor) that the applicant is maintaining contact with the child; and

(iv) the applicant takes and intends to continue to take an active role in the child's upbringing; and

(v) the child visits or stays with the applicant on a frequent and regular basis and the applicant intends this to continue; and

(vi) the child is under the age of 18; and

(vii) the applicant has limited leave to remain in the United Kingdom as the spouse, civil partner, unmarried partner or same-sex partner of a person present and settled in the United Kingdom who is the other parent of the child; and

(viii) the applicant has not remained in breach of the immigration laws; and

(ix) there will be adequate accommodation for the applicant and any dependants without recourse to public funds in accommodation which the applicant owns or occupies exclusively; and

(x) the applicant will be able to maintain himself and any dependants adequately without recourse to public funds.

Leave to remain in the United Kingdom as a person exercising rights of access to a child resident in the United Kingdom

248B. Leave to remain as a person exercising access rights to a child resident in the United Kingdom may be granted for 12 months in the first instance, provided the Secretary of State is satisfied that each of the requirements of paragraph 248A is met.

Refusal of leave to remain in the United Kingdom as a person exercising rights of access to a child resident in the United Kingdom

248C. Leave to remain as a person exercising rights of access to a child resident in the United Kingdom is to be refused if the Secretary of State is not satisfied that each of the requirements of paragraph 248A is met.

Indefinite leave to remain in the United Kingdom as a person exercising rights of access to a child resident in the United Kingdom

248D. The requirements for indefinite leave to remain in the United Kingdom as a person exercising rights of access to a child resident in the United Kingdom are that:

(i) the applicant was admitted to the United Kingdom or granted leave to remain in the United Kingdom for a period of 12 months as a person exercising rights of access to a child and has completed a period of 12 months as a person exercising rights of access to a child; and

(ii) the applicant takes and intends to continue to take an active role in the child's upbringing; and

(iii) the child visits or stays with the applicant on a frequent and regular basis and the applicant intends this to continue; and

(iv) there will be adequate accommodation for the applicant and any dependants without recourse to public funds in accommodation which the applicant owns or occupies exclusively; and

(v) the applicant will be able to maintain himself and any dependants adequately without recourse to public funds; and

(vi) the child is under 18 years of age; and

(vii) the applicant must have demonstrated sufficient knowledge of the English language and sufficient knowledge about life in the United Kingdom, in accordance with Appendix KoLL; and

(viii) the applicant does not fall for refusal under the general grounds for refusal.

Indefinite leave to remain as a person exercising rights of access to a child resident in the United Kingdom

248E. Indefinite leave to remain as a person exercising rights of access to a child may be granted provided the Secretary of State is satisfied that each of the requirements of paragraph 248D is met.

Refusal of indefinite leave to remain in the United Kingdom as a person exercising rights of access to a child resident in the United Kingdom

248F. Indefinite leave to remain as a person exercising rights of access to a child is to be refused if the Secretary of State is not satisfied that each of the requirements of paragraph 248D is met.

Holders of special vouchers

Requirements for indefinite leave to enter as the holder of a special voucher

249. DELETED

Indefinite leave to enter as the holder of a special voucher

250. DELETED

Refusal of indefinite leave to enter as the holder of a special voucher

251. DELETED

Requirements for indefinite leave to enter as the spouse or child of a special voucher holder

252. DELETED

Indefinite leave to enter as the spouse or child of a special voucher holder

253. DELETED

Refusal of indefinite leave to enter as the spouse or child of a special voucher holder

254. DELETED

EEA Nationals and their families

Settlement

255–255B. DELETED

256. DELETED

257–257B. DELETED

257C–257E. DELETED

The EEA family permit

258–262. DELETED

Retired persons of independent means

263–265. DELETED

Requirements for an extension of stay as a retired person of independent means

266. The requirements for an extension of stay as a retired person of independent means are that the applicant:

(i) entered the United Kingdom with a valid United Kingdom entry clearance as a retired person of independent means; and

(ii) meets the following requirements:

(a) has under his control and disposable in the United Kingdom an income of his own of not less than £25,000 per annum; and

(b) is able and willing to maintain and accommodate himself and any dependants indefinitely in the United Kingdom from his own resources with no assistance from any other person and without taking employment or having recourse to public funds; and

(c) can demonstrate a close connection with the United Kingdom; and

(iii) has made the United Kingdom his main home; and

(iv) must not be in the UK in breach of immigration laws, except that, where paragraph 39E of these Rules applies, any current period of overstaying will be disregarded.

Extension of stay as a retired person of independent means

266A–266E. DELETED

267. An extension of stay as a retired person of independent means, with a prohibition on the taking of employment and a condition on study as set out in Part 15 of these Rules, may be granted so as to bring the person's stay in this category up to a maximum of 5 years in aggregate, provided the Secretary of State is satisfied that each of the requirements of paragraph 266 is met.

Refusal of extension of stay as a retired person of independent means

268. An extension of stay as a retired person of independent means is to be refused if the Secretary of State is not satisfied that each of the requirements of paragraph 266 is met.

Indefinite leave to remain for a retired person of independent means

269. Indefinite leave to remain may be granted, on application, to a person admitted as a retired person of independent means provided the applicant:

(i) has spent a continuous period of 5 years lawfully in the United Kingdom in this capacity; and

(ii) has met the requirements of paragraph 266 throughout the 5 year period and continues to do so; and

(iii) does not fall for refusal under the general grounds for refusal; and

(iv) must not be in the UK in breach of immigration laws, except that, where paragraph 39E of these Rules applies, any current period of overstaying will be disregarded; and

(v) in the case of absences for serious or compelling reasons, submits a personal letter which includes full details of the reason for the absences and all [...] supporting documents in relation to those reasons—e.g. medical certificates, birth/death certificates, information about the reasons which led to the absence from the UK 'continuous period of 5 years lawfully in the UK' means residence in the United Kingdom for an unbroken period with valid leave, and for these purposes a period shall not be considered to have been broken where:

(i) the applicant has been absent from the UK for a period of 180 days or less in any of the five consecutive 12 calendar month periods preceding the date of the application for indefinite leavę to remain; and

(ii) the applicant has existing limited leave to enter or remain upon their departure and return, except that:

(1) where that leave expired no more than 28 days prior to a further application for entry clearance which was made before 24 November 2016 and subsequently granted, that period and any period pending the applicant's re-entry into the United Kingdom shall be disregarded; and

(2) where, on or after 24 November 2016, the applicant makes a further application for entry clearance during the currency of continuing limited leave which is subsequently granted, the period spent outside the UK with continuing leave and any period pending the applicant's re-entry into the United Kingdom shall be disregarded; and

(iii) the applicant has any current period of overstaying disregarded where paragraph 39E of these Rules applies; and

(iv) the applicant has any previous period of overstaying between periods of leave disregarded where: the further application was made before 24 November 2016 and within 28 days of the expiry of leave; or the further application was made on or after 24 November 2016 and paragraph 39E of these Rules applied.

Note: Word in (v) deleted from 5 November 2018 (HC 1534).

Refusal of indefinite leave to remain for a retired person of independent means

270. Indefinite leave to remain in the United Kingdom for a retired person of independent means is to be refused if the Secretary of State is not satisfied that each of the requirements of paragraph 269 is met.

Partners of persons with limited leave to enter or remain in the United Kingdom as retired persons of independent means

Requirements for leave to enter or remain as the partners of a person with limited leave to enter or remain in the United Kingdom as a retired person of independent means

271. The requirements to be met by a person seeking leave to enter the United Kingdom as the partner of a person with limited leave to enter or remain in the United Kingdom as a retired person of independent means are that:

(i) the applicant is the spouse, civil partner, unmarried or same-sex partner of a person with limited leave to enter or remain in the United Kingdom as a retired person of independent means; and

(ii) if an unmarried or same-sex partner:

(1) any previous marriage or civil partnership (or similar relationship) by either partner has permanently broken down; and

(2) the parties are not involved in a consanguineous relationship with one another; and

(3) the parties have been living together in a relationship akin to marriage or civil partnership which has subsisted for 2 years or more; and

(iii) each of the parties intends to live with the other as his or her partner during the applicant's stay and the relationship is subsisting; and

(iv) there will be adequate accommodation for the parties and any dependants without recourse to public funds in accommodation which they own or occupy exclusively; and

(v) the parties will be able to maintain themselves and any dependants adequately without recourse to public funds; and

(vi) the applicant does not intend to stay in the United Kingdom beyond any period of leave granted to his partner; and

(vii) the applicant does not fall for refusal under the general grounds for refusal; and

(viii) the applicant holds a valid United Kingdom entry clearance for entry in this capacity.

Leave to enter as the partner of a person with limited leave to enter or remain in the United Kingdom as a retired person of independent means

272. A person seeking leave to enter the United Kingdom as the partner of a person with limited leave to enter or remain in the United Kingdom as a retired person of independent means may be given leave to enter for a period not in excess of that granted to the person with limited leave to enter or remain as a retired person of independent means subject to a condition on study as set out in Part 15 of these Rules, provided the Immigration Officer is satisfied that each of the requirements of paragraph 271 is met.

Refusal of leave to enter as the partner of a person with limited leave to enter or remain in the United Kingdom as a retired person of independent means

273. Leave to enter as the partner of a person with limited leave to enter or remain in the United Kingdom as a retired person of independent means is to be refused if the Immigration Officer is not satisfied that each of the requirements of paragraph 271 is met.

Requirements for extension of stay as the partner of a person who has or has had leave to enter or remain in the United Kingdom as a retired person of independent means

273A. The requirements to be met by a person seeking an extension of stay in the United Kingdom as the partner of a person who has or has had leave to enter or remain in the United Kingdom as a retired person of independent means are that the applicant:

(i) is the spouse, civil partner, unmarried or same sex partner of a person who:

(1) has limited leave to enter or remain in the United Kingdom as a retired person of independent means; or

(2) has indefinite leave to remain in the United Kingdom or has become a British citizen, and who had limited leave to enter or remain in the United Kingdom as a retired person of independent means immediately before being granted indefinite leave to remain; and

(ii) meets the requirements of paragraph 271(ii)–(vii); and

[(iii) was not last granted:

(1) entry clearance or leave to enter as a visitor, short-term student ot short-term student (child),

(2) temporary admission,

(3) temporary release, or

(4) after the date on which paragraph 1 of Schedule 10 to the Immigration Act 2016 is commenced, immigration bail in circumstances in which temporary release or temporary admission would previously been granted; and]

(iv) must not be in the UK in breach of immigration laws except that, where paragraph 39E of these Rules applies, any current period of overstaying will be disregarded.]

Note: Sub-paragraph (iii) substituted from the date of commencement of Schedule 10 to the Immigration Act 2016 (HC 309).

Extension of stay as the partner of a person who has or has had leave to enter or remain in the United Kingdom as a retired person of independent means

273B. An extension of stay in the United Kingdom as:

(i) the partner of a person who has limited leave to enter or remain as a retired person of independent means may be granted for a period not in excess of that granted to the person with limited leave to enter or remain, subject to a condition on study as set out in Part 15 of these Rules; or

(ii) the partner of a person who is being admitted at the same time for settlement or the partner of a person who has indefinite leave to remain or has become a British citizen may be granted for a period not exceeding 2 years, subject to a condition on study as set out in Part 15 of these Rules, in both instances, provided the Secretary of State is satisfied that each of the requirements of paragraph 273A is met.

Refusal of extension of stay as the partner of a person who has or has had leave to enter or remain in the United Kingdom as a retired person of independent means

273C. An extension of stay in the United Kingdom as the partner of a person who has or has had leave to enter or remain in the United Kingdom as a retired person of independent means is to be refused if the Secretary of State is not satisfied that each of the requirements of paragraph 273A is met.

Requirements for indefinite leave to remain for the partner of a person who has or has had leave to enter or remain in the United Kingdom as a retired person of independent means

273D. The requirements to be met by a person seeking indefinite leave to remain in the United Kingdom as the partner of a person who has or has had leave to enter or remain in the United Kingdom as a retired person of independent means are that the applicant:

(i) is the spouse, civil partner, unmarried or same-sex partner of a person who:

(1) has limited leave to enter or remain in the United Kingdom as a retired person of independent means and who is being granted indefinite leave to remain at the same time; or

(2) is the spouse, civil partner, unmarried or same-sex partner of a person who has indefinite leave to remain in the United Kingdom or has become a British citizen, and

who had limited leave to enter or remain in the United Kingdom as a retired person of independent means immediately before being granted indefinite leave to remain; and

(ii) meets the requirements of paragraph 271(ii)–(vii); and

(iii) has demonstrated sufficient knowledge of the English language and sufficient knowledge about life in the United Kingdom, in accordance with Appendix KoLL; and

[(iv) was not last granted:

(1) entry clearance or leave to enter as a visitor, short-term student ot short-term student (child),

(2) temporary admission,

(3) temporary release, or

(4) after the date on which paragraph 1 of Schedule 10 to the Immigration Act 2016 is commenced, immigration bail in circumstances in which temporary release or temporary admission would previously been granted; and]

(v) must not be in the UK in breach of immigration laws except that, where paragraph 39E of these Rules applies, any current period of overstaying will be disregarded.

Note: Sub-paragraph (iv) substituted from the date of commencement of Schedule 10 to the Immigration Act 2016 (HC 309).

Indefinite leave to remain as the partner of a person who has or has had leave to enter or remain in the United Kingdom as a retired person of independent means

273E. Indefinite leave to remain in the United Kingdom as the partner of a person who has or has had leave to enter or remain in the United Kingdom as a retired person of independent means may be granted provided the Secretary of State is satisfied that each of the requirements of paragraph 273D is met.

Refusal of indefinite leave to remain as the partner of a person who has or has had leave to enter or remain in the United Kingdom as a retired person of independent means

273F. Indefinite leave to remain in the United Kingdom as the partner of a person who has or has had leave to enter or remain in the United Kingdom as a retired person of independent means is to be refused if the Secretary of State is not satisfied that each of the requirements of paragraph 273D is met.

Children of persons with limited leave to enter or remain in the United Kingdom as retired persons of independent means

Requirements for leave to enter or remain as the child of a person with limited leave to enter or remain in the United Kingdom as a retired person of independent means

274. The requirements to be met by a person seeking leave to enter or remain in the United Kingdom as the child of a person with limited leave to enter or remain in the United Kingdom as a retired person of independent means are that:

(i) he is the child of a parent who has been admitted to or allowed to remain in the United Kingdom as a retired person of independent means or, for applications for leave to remain, of a parent with indefinite leave to remain in the UK and who had limited leave as a retired person of independent means immediately before being granted indefinite leave; and

(ii) he is under the age of 18 or has current leave to enter or remain in this capacity; and

(iii) he is unmarried and is not a civil partner, has not formed an independent family unit and is not leading an independent life; and

(iv) he can, and will, be maintained and accommodated adequately without recourse to public funds in accommodation which his parent(s) own or occupy exclusively; and

(v) he will not stay in the United Kingdom beyond any period of leave granted to his parent(s); and

(vi) both parents are being or have been admitted to or allowed to remain in the United Kingdom save where:

(a) the parent he is accompanying or joining is his sole surviving parent; or

(b) the parent he is accompanying or joining has had sole responsibility for his upbringing; or

(c) there are serious and compelling family or other considerations which make exclusion from the United Kingdom undesirable and suitable arrangements have been made for his care; and

[(vii) if seeking leave to enter, he holds a valid United Kingdom entry clearance for entry in this capacity or, if seeking leave to remain, he was not last granted:

(1) entry clearance or leave to enter as a visitor, short-term student or short-term student (child),

(2) temporary admission,

(3) temporary release, or

(4) after the date on which paragraph 1 of Schedule 10 to the Immigration Act 2016 is commenced, immigration bail in circumstances in which temporary release or temporary admission would previously been granted; and]

(viii) if seeking leave to remain, must not be in the UK in breach of immigration laws except that, where paragraph 39E of these Rules applies, any current period of overstaying will be disregarded.

Note: Sub-paragraph (vii) substituted from the date of commencement of Schedule 10 to the Immigration Act 2016 (HC 309).

Leave to enter or remain as the child of a person with limited leave to enter or remain in the United Kingdom as a retired person of independent means

275. (a) A person seeking leave to enter or remain in the United Kingdom as the child of a person with limited leave to enter or remain in the United Kingdom as a retired person of independent means, subject to a condition on study as set out in Part 15 of these Rules, may be given leave to enter or remain in the United Kingdom for a period of leave not in excess of that granted to the person with limited leave to enter or remain as a retired person of independent means if:

(i) in relation to an application for leave to enter, [[…] on arrival, a valid passport or other identity document is produced to the Immigration Officer and the applicant has entry clearance for entry in this capacity;] or

[(ii) in the case of an application for limited leave to remain, he was not last granted:

(1) entry clearance or leave to enter as a visitor, short-term student ot short-term student (child),

(2) temporary admission,

(3) temporary release, or

(4) after the date on which paragraph 1 of Schedule 10 to the Immigration Act 2016 is commenced, immigration bail in circumstances in which temporary release or temporary admission would previously been granted;

and is able to satisfy the Secretary of State that each of the requirements of paragraph 274(i)-(vi) and (viii) is met.]

(b) A person seeking limited leave to remain as the child of a parent who has indefinite leave to remain in the UK and who had limited leave as a retired person of independent means immediately before being granted indefinite leave may be given leave to remain in the UK for a period of 30 months, subject to a condition on study as set out in Part 15 of these Rules, provided he is in the UK with valid leave under paragraph 275 and is able to satisfy the Secretary of State that each of the requirements of paragraph 274(i) to (vi) and (viii) are satisfied.

Note: Words in (a)(i) substituted from 11 January 2018 subject to savings for applications made before that date; sub-paragraph (a)(ii) substituted from the date of commencement of Schedule 10 to the Immigration Act 2016 (HC 309). Word in (a)(i) deleted from 6 July 2018 subject to savings for applications made before that date (HC 1154).

275A. An application for indefinite leave to remain in this category may be granted provided the applicant meets the requirements listed below. If the applicant meets these requirements, indefinite leave to remain will be granted. If the applicant does not meet these requirements, the application will be refused.

Requirements

(i) he is the child of a parent with limited leave to enter or remain in the United Kingdom as a retired person of independent means who is, at the same time, being granted indefinite leave to remain, or he is the child of a parent who has indefinite leave to remain in the United Kingdom and who had limited leave under paragraphs 263–269 immediately before being granted indefinite leave; and

(ii) he is under the age of 18 or has current leave to enter or remain in this capacity; and

(iii) he is unmarried and is not a civil partner, has not formed an independent family unit and is not leading an independent life; and

(iv) he can and will be maintained and accommodated adequately without recourse to public funds in accommodation which his parent(s) own or occupy exclusively; and

(v) he will not stay in the United Kingdom beyond any period of leave granted to his parent(s); and

(vi) both parents are being or have been admitted to or allowed to remain in the United Kingdom save where:

(a) the parent he is accompanying or joining is his sole surviving parent; or

(b) the parent he is accompanying or joining has had sole responsibility for his upbringing; or

(c) there are serious and compelling family or other considerations which make exclusion from the United Kingdom undesirable and suitable arrangements have been made for his care;

(vii) he must not be in the UK in breach of immigration laws except that, where paragraph 39E of these Rules applies, any current period of overstaying will be disregarded;

(viii) if aged 18 or over, he has sufficient knowledge of the English language and sufficient knowledge about life in the United Kingdom in accordance with Appendix KoLL of these Rules;

(ix) indefinite leave to remain is, at the same time, being granted to the person with limited leave as a retired person of independent means unless, at the time when indefinite leave to remain was granted to that person, the applicant was aged 18 or over and unable to satisfy paragraph 275A(viii) and the applicant has continued to be in the United Kingdom with leave to remain as a child of that person.

Refusal of leave to enter or remain as the child of a person with limited leave to enter or remain in the United Kingdom as a retired person of independent means

276. Leave to enter or remain in the United Kingdom as the child of a person with limited leave to enter or remain in the United Kingdom as a retired person of independent means is to be refused if, in relation to an application for leave to enter, [on arrival, a valid passport or other identity document is not produced to the Immigration Officer and the applicant does not have entry clearance for entry in this capacity,] or in the case of an application for limited leave to remain, if the applicant was not admitted with a valid United Kingdom entry clearance for entry in this capacity or is unable to satisfy the Secretary of State that each of the requirements of paragraph 274(i)–(vi) and (viii) is met. An application for indefinite leave to remain in this category is to be refused if the applicant was not admitted with a valid United Kingdom entry clearance for entry in this capacity or is unable to satisfy the Secretary of State that each of the requirements of paragraph 275 is met.

Note: Words substituted from 11 January 2018 subject to savings for applications made before that date (HC 309).

Long residence

Long residence in the United Kingdom

276A. For the purposes of paragraphs 276B to 276D [. . .]

(a) 'continuous residence' means residence in the United Kingdom for an unbroken period, and for these purposes a period shall not be considered to have been broken where an applicant is absent from the United Kingdom for a period of 6 months or less at any one time, provided that the applicant in question has existing limited leave to enter or remain upon their departure and return, but shall be considered to have been broken if the applicant:

(i) has been removed under Schedule 2 of the 1971 Act, section 10 of the 1999 Act, has been deported or has left the United Kingdom having been refused leave to enter or remain here; or

(ii) has left the United Kingdom and, on doing so, evidenced a clear intention not to return; or

(iii) left the United Kingdom in circumstances in which he could have had no reasonable expectation at the time of leaving that he would lawfully be able to return; or

(iv) has been convicted of an offence and was sentenced to a period of imprisonment or was directed to be detained in an institution other than a prison (including, in particular, a hospital or an institution for young offenders), provided that the sentence in question was not a suspended sentence; or

(v) has spent a total of more than 18 months absent from the United Kingdom during the period in question.

(b) 'lawful residence' means residence which is continuous residence pursuant to:

(i) existing leave to enter or remain; or

(ii) temporary admission within section 11 of the 1971 Act (as previously in force), or immigration bail within section 11 of the 1971 Act, where leave to enter or remain is subsequently granted; or

(iii) an exemption from immigration control, including where an exemption ceases to apply if it is immediately followed by a grant of leave to enter or remain.

[. . .]

Note: Words in introduction, sub-paragraph (c), sub-paragraph (2) deleted from 20 June 2022 subject to savings for applications made before that date (HC 1118).

276A0. [DELETED]

Note: Paragraph deleted from 20 June 2022 subject to savings for applications made before that date (HC 1118).

276A00. [DELETED]

Note: Paragraph deleted from 20 June 2022 subject to savings for applications made before that date (HC 1118).

[276A01. [. . .]

(2) Where leave to enter is granted in accordance with paragraph 276A01(1), paragraph 276BE(1) shall apply to an application for leave to remain on the grounds of private life in the UK as if for 'leave to remain under this sub-paragraph' there were substituted 'leave to enter in accordance with paragraph 276A01(1).]

Note: Paragraph 276A01 inserted from 6 April 2015 for applications decided on or after that date (HC 1025). Words in (1) substituted from the date on which Schedule 10 to the Immigration Act 2016 comes into force (HC 667). Sub-paragraph (1) deleted from 20 June 2022 subject to savings for applications made before that date (HC 1118).

276A02. [DELETED]

Note: Paragraph deleted from 20 June 2022 subject to savings for applications made before that date (HC 1118).

[276A03. Where a person aged 18 or over is granted limited leave to remain under this Part (on the basis of long residence or outside the rules on Article 8 grounds), or where a person granted such limited leave to enter or remain will be aged 18 before that period of limited leave expires, the leave will, in addition to any other conditions which may apply, be granted subject to the condition in Appendix ATAS of these rules.]

Note: Amendments from 09:00 on 5 October 2020 subject to savings for applications made before that time. Where consequential changes relating to the need for an ATAS certificate have been made, they take effect for all applications made or granted on or after 5 October 2020 at 09:00 (HC 707). Paragraph substituted from 20 June 2022 subject to savings for applications made before that date (HC 1118).

[276A04. Where a person who has made an application for indefinite leave to remain under this Part does not meet the requirements for indefinite leave to remain, but the Secretary of State believes the person may qualify for limited leave to remain under this

Part (on the basis of long residence, Appendix Private Life or outside the rules on Article 8 grounds):

(a) the Secretary of State will instead treat the application for indefinite leave to remain as an application for limited leave to remain; and

(b) the Secretary of State will notify the applicant in writing of any requirement to pay an immigration health charge under the Immigration (Health Charge) Order 2015 in relation to the application for leave to remain; and

(c) if any required immigration health charge is not paid, the application for limited leave to remain will be invalid and will not be considered and the Secretary of State will not refund any fee paid in respect of the application for indefinite leave to remain.]

Note: Paragraph substituted from 20 June 2022 subject to savings for applications made before that date (HC 1118).

Requirements for an extension of stay on the ground of long residence in the United Kingdom

276A1. The requirement to be met by a person seeking an extension of stay on the ground of long residence in the United Kingdom is that the applicant meets each of the requirements in paragraph 276B(i)–(ii) and (v).

Extension of stay on the ground of long residence in the United Kingdom

276A2. An extension of stay on the ground of long residence in the United Kingdom may be granted for a period not exceeding 2 years provided that the Secretary of State is satisfied that the requirement in paragraph 276A1 is met (but see paragraph 276A04), and a person granted such an extension of stay following an application made before 9 July 2012 will remain subject to the rules in force on 8 July 2012.

Conditions to be attached to extension of stay on the ground of long residence in the United Kingdom

276A3. Where an extension of stay is granted under paragraph 276A2:

(i) if the applicant has spent less than 20 years in the UK, the grant of leave should be subject to the same conditions attached to his last period of lawful leave, or

(ii) if the applicant has spent 20 years or more in the UK, the grant of leave should not contain any restriction on employment.

Refusal of extension of stay on the ground of long residence in the United Kingdom

276A4. An extension of stay on the ground of long residence in the United Kingdom is to be refused if the Secretary of State is not satisfied that the requirement in paragraph 276A1 is met.

Requirements for indefinite leave to remain on the ground of long residence in the United Kingdom

276B. The requirements to be met by an applicant for indefinite leave to remain on the ground of long residence in the United Kingdom are that:

(i) (a) he has had at least 10 years continuous lawful residence in the United Kingdom.

(ii) having regard to the public interest there are no reasons why it would be undesirable for him to be given indefinite leave to remain on the ground of long residence, taking into account his:

(a) age; and

(b) strength of connections in the United Kingdom; and

(c) personal history, including character, conduct, associations and employment record; and

(d) domestic circumstances; and

(e) compassionate circumstances; and

(f) any representations received on the person's behalf; and

(iii) the applicant does not fall for refusal under the general grounds for refusal.

(iv) the applicant has demonstrated sufficient knowledge of the English language and sufficient knowledge about life in the United Kingdom, in accordance with Appendix KoLL.

(v) the applicant must not be in the UK in breach of immigration laws, except that, where paragraph 39E of these Rules applies, any current period of overstaying will be disregarded. Any previous period of overstaying between periods of leave will also be disregarded where –

(a) the further application was made before 24 November 2016 and within 28 days of the expiry of leave; or

(b) the further application was made on or after 24 November 2016 and paragraph 39E of these Rules applied.

Indefinite leave to remain on the ground of long residence in the United Kingdom

276C. Indefinite leave to remain on the ground of long residence in the United Kingdom may be granted provided that the Secretary of State is satisfied that each of the requirements of paragraph 276B is met.

Refusal of indefinite leave to remain on the ground of long residence in the United Kingdom

276D. Indefinite leave to remain on the ground of long residence in the United Kingdom is to be refused if the Secretary of State is not satisfied that each of the requirements of paragraph 276B is met.

Private life

Requirements to be met by an applicant for leave to remain on the grounds of private life

276ADE(1). [DELETED]

Note: Amendments from 6 July 2018 for all decisions made on or after that date (HC 1154). Paragraph deleted from 20 June 2022 subject to savings for applications made before that date (HC 1118).

276ADE(2). [DELETED]

Note: Paragraph deleted from 20 June 2022 subject to savings for applications made before that date (HC 1118).

Leave to remain on the grounds of private life in the UK

276BE(1). [DELETED]

Note: Amendment from 6 April 2019 (HC 1919). Paragraph deleted from 20 June 2022 subject to savings for applications made before that date (HC 1118).

276BE(2). [DELETED]

Note: Paragraph deleted from 20 June 2022 subject to savings for applications made before that date (HC 1118).

276BE(3). [DELETED]

Note: Paragraph deleted from 20 June 2022 subject to savings for applications made before that date (HC 1118).

Refusal of limited leave to remain on the grounds of private life in the UK

276CE. [DELETED]

Note: Paragraph deleted from 20 June 2022 subject to savings for applications made before that date (HC 1118).

Requirements for indefinite leave to remain on the grounds of private life in the UK

276DE. [DELETED]

Note: Amendments from 6 April 2015 for applications decided on or after that date (HC 1025). Amendments from 24 November 2016 for applications made on or after that date (HC 667). Paragraph deleted from 20 June 2022 subject to savings for applications made before that date (HC 1118).

Indefinite leave to remain on the grounds of private life in the UK

276DF. [DELETED]

Note: Paragraph deleted from 20 June 2022 subject to savings for applications made before that date (HC 1118).

276DG. [DELETED]

Note: Paragraph deleted from 20 June 2022 subject to savings for applications made before that date (HC 1118).

Refusal of indefinite leave to remain on the grounds of private life in the UK

276DH. [DELETED]

Note: Paragraph deleted from 20 June 2022 subject to savings for applications made before that date (HC 1118).

HM Forces

Transitional provisions and interaction between paragraphs 276E to 276AI of Part 7 and Appendix Armed Forces

276DI. From 1 December 2013, Appendix Armed Forces will apply to all applications to which paragraphs 276E to 276AI of this Part applied on or before 30 November 2013, except where the provisions of 276E to 276AI are preserved and continue to apply in accordance with paragraph 276DL.

276DJ. The requirements to be met under paragraphs 276E to 276AI from 1 December 2013 may be modified or supplemented by the requirements in Appendix Armed Forces or Appendix FM-SE.

276DK. The requirements in paragraphs 8 and 9 of Appendix Armed Forces apply to applications made under paragraphs 276E to 276AI where the decision is made on or after 1 December 2013 (and irrespective of the date of the application).

276DL. Paragraphs 276E–276AI also continue to apply to applications:

(i) made before 1 December 2013 under paragraphs 276E to 276AI but which have not been decided before that date; and

(ii) by persons who have been granted entry clearance or limited leave to enter or remain under paragraphs 276E to 276AI before 1 December 2013 or in accordance with sub-paragraph (i) above and, where it is a requirement of Part 7, that leave to enter or remain is extant.

Definition of Gurkha

276E. For the purposes of these Rules the term 'Gurkha' means a citizen or national of Nepal who has served in the Brigade of Gurkhas of the British Army under the Brigade of Gurkhas' terms and conditions of service.

Leave to enter or remain in the United Kingdom as a Gurkha discharged from the British Army

Requirements for indefinite leave to enter the United Kingdom as a Gurkha discharged from the British Army

276F. The requirements for indefinite leave to enter the United Kingdom as a Gurkha discharged from the British Army are that:

(i) the applicant has completed at least four years' service as a Gurkha with the British Army; and

(ii) was discharged from the British Army in Nepal on completion of engagement on or after 1 July 1997; and

(iii) was not discharged from the British Army more than 2 years prior to the date on which the application is made; and

(iv) holds a valid United Kingdom entry clearance for entry in this capacity; and

(v) does not fall for refusal under the general grounds for refusal.

Indefinite leave to enter the United Kingdom as a Gurkha discharged from the British Army

276G. A person seeking indefinite leave to enter the United Kingdom as a Gurkha discharged from the British Army may be granted indefinite leave to enter [provided that, on arrival, a valid passport or other identity document is produced to the Immigration Officer and the applicant has entry clearance for entry in this capacity.]

Note: Words substituted from 11 January 2018 subject to savings for applications made before that date (HC 309).

Refusal of indefinite leave to enter the United Kingdom as a Gurkha discharged from the British Army

276H. Indefinite leave to enter the United Kingdom as a Gurkha discharged from the British Army is to be refused if [on arrival, a valid passport or other identity document is not produced to the Immigration Officer and the applicant does not have entry clearance in this capacity].

Note: Words substituted from 11 January 2018 subject to savings for applications made before that date (HC 309).

Requirements for indefinite leave to remain in the United Kingdom as a Gurkha discharged from the British Army

276I. The requirements for indefinite leave to remain in the United Kingdom as a Gurkha discharged from the British Army are that the applicant:

(i) has completed at least four years' service as a Gurkha with the British Army; and

(ii) was discharged from the British Army in Nepal on completion of engagement on or after 1 July 1997; and

(iii) was not discharged from the British Army more than 2 years prior to the date on which the application is made unless they are applying following a grant of limited leave to remain under paragraph 276KA; and

(iv) is not in the UK in breach of immigration laws except that, where paragraph 39E of these Rules applies, any current period of overstaying will be disregarded; and

(v) does not fall for refusal under the general grounds for refusal.

Indefinite leave to remain in the United Kingdom as a Gurkha discharged from the British Army

276J. A person seeking indefinite leave to remain in the United Kingdom as a Gurkha discharged from the British Army may be granted indefinite leave to remain provided the Secretary of State is satisfied that each of the requirements of paragraph 276I is met.

Refusal of indefinite leave to remain in the United Kingdom as a Gurkha discharged from the British Army

276K. Indefinite leave to remain in the United Kingdom as a Gurkha discharged from the British Army is to be refused if the Secretary of State is not satisfied that each of the requirements of paragraph 276I is met.

Leave to remain in the United Kingdom as a Gurkha discharged from the British Army

276KA. If a Gurkha discharged from the British Army does not meet the requirements for indefinite leave to remain only because paragraph 322(1C)(iii) or 322(1C)(iv) applies, the applicant may be granted limited leave to remain for a period not exceeding 30 months.

Leave to enter or remain in the United Kingdom as a foreign or Commonwealth citizen discharged from HM Forces

Requirements for indefinite leave to enter the United Kingdom as a foreign or Commonwealth citizen discharged from HM Forces

276L. The requirements for indefinite leave to enter the United Kingdom as a foreign or Commonwealth citizen discharged from HM Forces are that the applicant:

(i) has completed at least four years' service with HM Forces; and

(ii) was discharged from HM Forces on completion of engagement; and

(iii) was not discharged from HM Forces more than 2 years prior to the date on which the application is made; and

(iv) holds a valid United Kingdom entry clearance for entry in this capacity; and

(v) does not fall for refusal under the general grounds for refusal.

Indefinite leave to enter the United Kingdom as a foreign or Commonwealth citizen discharged from HM Forces

276M. A person seeking indefinite leave to enter the United Kingdom as a foreign or Commonwealth citizen discharged from HM Forces may be granted indefinite leave to enter [provided that, on arrival, a valid passport or other identity document is produced to the Immigration Officer and the applicant has entry clearance for entry in this capacity].

Note: Words substituted from 11 January 2018 subject to savings for applications made before that date (HC 309).

Refusal of indefinite leave to enter the United Kingdom as a foreign or Commonwealth citizen discharged from HM Forces

276N. Indefinite leave to enter the United Kingdom as a foreign or Commonwealth citizen discharged from HM Forces is to be refused if [on arrival, a valid passport or other identity document is not produced to the Immigration Officer and the applicant does not have entry clearance in this capacity].

Note: Words substituted from 11 January 2018 subject to savings for applications made before that date (HC 309).

Requirements for indefinite leave to remain in the United Kingdom as a foreign or Commonwealth citizen discharged from HM Forces

276O. The requirements for indefinite leave to remain in the United Kingdom as a foreign or Commonwealth citizen discharged from HM Forces are that the applicant:

(i) has completed at least four years' service with HM Forces; and

(ii) was discharged from HM Forces on completion of engagement; and

(iii) was not discharged from HM Forces more than 2 years prior to the date on which the application is made unless they are applying following a grant of limited leave to remain under paragraph 276QA; and

(iv) is not in the UK in breach of immigration laws except that, where paragraph 39E of these Rules applies, any current period of overstaying will be disregarded; and

(v) does not fall for refusal under the general grounds for refusal.

Indefinite leave to remain in the United Kingdom as a foreign or Commonwealth citizen discharged from HM Forces

276P. A person seeking indefinite leave to remain in the United Kingdom as a foreign or Commonwealth citizen discharged from HM Forces may be granted indefinite leave to remain provided the Secretary of State is satisfied that each of the requirements of paragraph 276O is met.

Refusal of indefinite leave to remain in the United Kingdom as a foreign or Commonwealth citizen discharged from HM Forces

276Q. Indefinite leave to remain in the United Kingdom as a foreign or Commonwealth citizen discharged from HM Forces is to be refused if the Secretary of State is not satisfied that each of the requirements of paragraph 276O is met.

Leave to remain in the United Kingdom as a foreign or Commonwealth citizen discharged from HM Forces

276QA. If a foreign or Commonwealth citizen discharged from HM Forces does not meet the requirements for indefinite leave to remain only because paragraph 322(1C)(iii) or 322(1C)(iv) applies, the applicant may be granted limited leave to remain for a period not exceeding 30 months.

Spouses, civil partners, unmarried or same-sex partners of persons settled or seeking settlement in the United Kingdom in accordance with paragraphs 276E to 276Q (HM Forces rules) or of members of HM Forces who are exempt from immigration control under section 8(4)(a) of the Immigration Act 1971 and have at least 5 years' continuous service

Leave to enter or remain in the UK as the spouse, civil partner, unmarried or same-sex partner of a person present and settled in the United Kingdom or being granted settlement on the same occasion in accordance with paragraphs 276E to 276Q or of a member of HM Forces who is exempt from immigration control under section 8(4)(a) of the Immigration Act 1971 and has at least 5 years' continuous service.

Requirements for indefinite leave to enter the United Kingdom as the spouse, civil partner, unmarried or same-sex partner of a person present and settled in the United Kingdom or being admitted on the same occasion for settlement under paragraphs 276E to 276Q or of a member of HM Forces who is exempt from immigration control under section 8(4)(a) of the Immigration Act 1971 and has at least 5 years' continuous service

276R. The requirements to be met by a person seeking indefinite leave to enter the United Kingdom as the spouse, civil partner, unmarried or same-sex partner of a person present and settled in the United Kingdom or being admitted on the same occasion for settlement in accordance with paragraphs 276E to 276Q or of a member of HM Forces who is exempt from immigration control under section 8(4)(a) of the Immigration Act 1971 and has at least 5 years' continuous service are that:

(i) the applicant is married to, or the civil partner, unmarried or same-sex partner of, a person present and settled in the United Kingdom or who is being admitted on the same occasion for settlement in accordance with paragraphs 276E to 276Q or of a member of HM Forces who is exempt from immigration control under section 8(4)(a) of the Immigration Act 1971 and has at least 5 years' continuous service; and

(ii) the parties to the marriage, or civil partnership or relationship akin to marriage or civil partnership have met; and

(iii) the parties were married or formed a civil partnership or a relationship akin to marriage or civil partnership at least 2 years ago; and

(iv) each of the parties intends to live permanently with the other as his or her spouse, civil partner, unmarried or same-sex partner; and

(v) the marriage, civil partnership or relationship akin to marriage or civil partnership is subsisting; and

(vi) the applicant holds a valid United Kingdom entry clearance for entry in this capacity; and

(vii) the applicant does not fall for refusal under the general grounds for refusal.

Indefinite leave to enter the United Kingdom as the spouse, civil partner, unmarried or same-sex partner of a person present and settled in the United Kingdom or being admitted on the same occasion for settlement in accordance with paragraphs 276E to 276Q or of a member of HM Forces who is exempt from immigration control under section 8(4)(a) of the Immigration Act 1971 and has at least 5 years' continuous service

276S. A person seeking leave to enter the United Kingdom as the spouse, civil partner, unmarried or same-sex partner of a person present and settled in the United Kingdom or being admitted on the same occasion for settlement in accordance with paragraphs 276E to 276Q or of a member of HM Forces who is exempt from immigration control under section 8(4)(a) of the Immigration Act 1971 and has at least 5 years' continuous service may be granted indefinite leave to enter [provided, on arrival, that a valid passport or other identity document is produced to the Immigration Officer and the applicant has entry clearance for entry in this capacity].[. . .]

Note: Words substituted from 11 January 2018 subject to savings for applications made before that date (HC 309). Additional punctuation deleted from 6 July 2018 subject to savings for applications made before that date (HC 1154).

Refusal of indefinite leave to enter the United Kingdom as the spouse, civil partner, unmarried or same-sex partner of a person present and settled in the UK or being admitted on the same occasion for settlement in accordance with paragraphs 276E to 276Q or of a member of HM Forces who is exempt from immigration control under section 8(4)(a) of the Immigration Act 1971 and has at least 5 years' continuous service

276T. Leave to enter the United Kingdom as the spouse, civil partner, unmarried or same-sex partner of a person present and settled in the United Kingdom or being admitted on the same occasion for settlement in accordance with paragraphs 276E to 276Q or of a member of HM Forces who is exempt from immigration control under section 8(4)(a) of the Immigration Act 1971 and has at least 5 years' continuous service is to be refused if [on arrival, a valid passport or other identity document is not produced to the Immigration Officer he does not have entry clearance for entry in this capacity].

Note: Words substituted from 11 January 2018 subject to savings for applications made before that date (HC 309).

Requirement for indefinite leave to remain in the United Kingdom as the spouse, civil partner, unmarried or same-sex partner of a person present and settled in the United Kingdom under paragraphs 276E to 276Q or being granted settlement on the same occasion in accordance with paragraphs 276E to 276Q or of a member of HM Forces who is exempt from immigration control under section 8(4)(a) of the Immigration Act 1971 and has at least 5 years' continuous service

276U. The requirements to be met by a person seeking indefinite leave to remain in the United Kingdom as the spouse, civil partner, unmarried or same-sex partner of a person present and settled in the United Kingdom or being granted settlement on the same occasion in accordance with paragraphs 276E to 276Q or of a member of HM Forces who is exempt from immigration control under section 8(4)(a) of the Immigration Act 1971 and has at least 5 years' continuous service are that:

(i) the applicant is married to or the civil partner or unmarried or same-sex partner of a person present and settled in the United Kingdom or being granted settlement on the same occasion in accordance with paragraphs 276E to 276Q or of a member of HM Forces who is exempt from immigration control under section 8(4)(a) of the Immigration Act 1971 and has at least 5 years' continuous service; and

(ii) the parties to the marriage, civil partnership or relationship akin to marriage or civil partnership have met; and

(iii) the parties were married or formed a civil partnership or relationship akin to marriage or civil partnership at least 2 years ago; and

(iv) each of the parties intends to live permanently with the other as his or her spouse, civil partner, unmarried or same-sex partner; and

(v) the marriage, civil partnership or relationship akin to marriage or civil partnership is subsisting; and

(vi) has, or has last been granted, leave to enter or remain in the United Kingdom as the spouse, civil partner, unmarried or same-sex partner; and

(vii) the applicant does not fall for refusal under the general grounds for refusal.

Indefinite leave to remain in the United Kingdom as the spouse, civil partner, unmarried or same-sex partner of a person present and settled in the United Kingdom or being granted settlement on the same occasion in accordance with paragraphs 276E to 276Q or of a member of HM Forces who is exempt from immigration control under section 8(4)(a) of the Immigration Act 1971 and has at least 5 years' continuous service

276V. Indefinite leave to remain in the United Kingdom as the spouse, civil partner, unmarried or same-sex partner of a person present and settled in the United Kingdom or being granted settlement on the same occasion in accordance with paragraphs 276E to 276Q or of a member of HM Forces who is exempt from immigration control under section 8(4)(a) of the Immigration Act 1971 and has at least 5 years' continuous service may be granted provided the Secretary of State is satisfied that each of the requirements of paragraph 276U is met.

Refusal of indefinite leave to remain in the United Kingdom as the spouse, civil partner, unmarried or same-sex partner of a person present and settled in the United Kingdom or being granted settlement on the same occasion in accordance with paragraphs 276E to 276Q or of a member of HM Forces who is exempt from immigration control under section 8(4)(a) of the Immigration Act 1971 and has at least 5 years' continuous service

276W. Indefinite leave to remain in the United Kingdom as the spouse, civil partner, unmarried or same-sex partner of a person present and settled in the United Kingdom or being granted settlement on the same occasion in accordance with paragraphs 276E to 276Q or of a member of HM Forces who is exempt from immigration control under section 8(4)(a) of the Immigration Act 1971 and has at least 5 years' continuous service is to be refused if the Secretary of State is not satisfied that each of the requirements of paragraph 276U is met.

Children of a parent, parents or a relative settled or seeking settlement in the United Kingdom under paragraphs 276E to 276Q (HM Forces rules) or of members of HM Forces who are exempt from immigration control under section 8(4)(a) of the Immigration Act 1971 and have at least 5 years' continuous service

Leave to enter or remain in the United Kingdom as the child of a parent, parents or a relative present and settled in the United Kingdom or being granted settlement on the same occasion in accordance with paragraphs 276E to 276Q or of a member of HM Forces who is exempt from immigration control under section 8(4)(a) of the Immigration Act 1971 and has at least 5 years' continuous service

Requirements for indefinite leave to enter the United Kingdom as the child of a parent, parents or a relative present and settled in the United Kingdom or being admitted for settlement on the same occasion in accordance with paragraphs 276E to 276Q or of a member of HM Forces who is exempt from immigration control under section 8(4)(a) of the Immigration Act 1971 and has at least 5 years' continuous service

276X. The requirements to be met by a person seeking indefinite leave to enter the United Kingdom as the child of a parent, parents or a relative present and settled in the United Kingdom or being admitted for settlement on the same occasion in accordance with paragraphs 276E to 276Q or of a member of HM Forces who is exempt from immigration control under section 8(4)(a) of the Immigration Act 1971 and has at least 5 years' continuous service are that:

(i) the applicant is seeking indefinite leave to enter to accompany or join a parent, parents or a relative in one of the following circumstances:

(a) both parents are present and settled in the United Kingdom; or

(b) both parents are being admitted on the same occasion for settlement; or

(c) one parent is present and settled in the United Kingdom or is a member of HM Forces who is exempt from immigration control under section 8(4)(a) of the Immigration Act 1971 and has at least 5 years' continuous service and the other is being admitted on the same occasion for settlement or is a member of HM Forces who is exempt from immigration control under section 8(4)(a) of the Immigration Act 1971 and has at least 5 years' continuous service; or

(d) one parent is present and settled in the United Kingdom or being admitted on the same occasion for settlement or is a member of HM Forces who is exempt from immigration control under section 8(4)(a) of the Immigration Act 1971 and has at least 5 years' continuous service and the other parent is dead; or

(e) one parent is present and settled in the United Kingdom or being admitted on the same occasion for settlement or is a member of HM Forces who is exempt from immigration control under section 8(4)(a) of the Immigration Act 1971 and has at least 5 years' continuous service and has had sole responsibility for the child's upbringing; or

(f) one parent or a relative is present and settled in the United Kingdom or being admitted on the same occasion for settlement or is a member of HM Forces who is exempt from immigration control under section 8(4)(a) of the Immigration Act 1971 and has at least 5 years' continuous service and there are serious and compelling family or other considerations which make exclusion of the child undesirable and suitable arrangements have been made for the child's care; and

(ii) is under the age of 18; and

(iii) is not leading an independent life, is unmarried and is not a civil partner, and has not formed an independent family unit; and

(iv) holds a valid United Kingdom entry clearance for entry in this capacity; and

(v) the applicant does not fall for refusal under the general grounds for refusal.

Indefinite leave to enter the United Kingdom as the child of a parent, parents or a relative present and settled in the United Kingdom or being admitted for settlement on the same occasion in accordance with paragraphs 276E to 276Q or of a member of HM Forces who is exempt from immigration control under section 8(4)(a) of the Immigration Act 1971 and has at least 5 years' continuous service

276Y. Indefinite leave to enter the United Kingdom as the child of a parent, parents or a relative present and settled in the United Kingdom or being admitted for settlement on the same occasion in accordance with paragraphs 276E to 276Q or of a member of HM Forces who is exempt from immigration control under section 8(4)(a) of the Immigration Act 1971 and has at least 5 years' continuous service may be granted [provided that, on arrival, a valid passport or other identity document is produced to the Immigration Officer and the applicant has entry clearance in this capacity.]

Note: Words substituted from 11 January 2018 subject to savings for applications made before that date (HC 309).

Refusal of indefinite leave to enter the United Kingdom as the child of a parent, parents or a relative present and settled in the United Kingdom or being admitted for settlement on the same occasion in accordance with paragraphs 276E to 276Q or of a member of HM Forces who is exempt from immigration control under section 8(4)(a) of the Immigration Act 1971 and has at least 5 years' continuous service

276Z. Indefinite leave to enter the United Kingdom as the child of a parent, parents, or a relative present and settled in the United Kingdom or being admitted for settlement on the same occasion in accordance with paragraphs 276E to 276Q or of a member of HM Forces who is exempt from immigration control under section 8(4)(a) of the Immigration Act 1971 and has at least 5 years' continuous service is to be refused if a [on arrival, a valid passport or other identity document is not produced to the Immigration Officer and the applicant does not have entry clearance for entry in this capacity].

Note: Words substituted from 11 January 2018 subject to savings for applications made before that date (HC 309).

Requirements for indefinite leave to remain in the United Kingdom as the child of a parent, parents or a relative present and settled in the United Kingdom or being granted settlement on the same occasion in accordance with paragraphs 276E to 276Q or of a member of HM Forces who is exempt from immigration control under section 8(4)(a) of the Immigration Act 1971 and has at least 5 years' continuous service

276AA. The requirements to be met by a person seeking indefinite leave to remain in the United Kingdom as the child of a parent, parents or a relative present and settled in the United Kingdom or being granted settlement on the same occasion in accordance with paragraphs 276E to 276Q or of a member of HM Forces who is exempt from immigration control under section 8(4)(a) of the Immigration Act 1971 and has at least 5 years' continuous service are that:

(i) the applicant is seeking indefinite leave to remain with a parent, parents or a relative in one of the following circumstances:

(a) both parents are present and settled in the United Kingdom or being granted settlement on the same occasion; or

(ab) one parent is present and settled in the United Kingdom or is a member of HM Forces who is exempt from immigration control under section 8(4)(a) of the Immigration Act 1971 and has at least 5 years' continuous service and the other is being granted settlement on the same occasion or is a member of HM Forces who is exempt from immigration control under section 8(4)(a) of the Immigration Act 1971 and has at least 5 years' continuous service; or

(b) one parent is present and settled in the United Kingdom or being granted settlement on the same occasion or is a member of HM Forces who is exempt from immigration control under section 8(4)(a) of the Immigration Act 1971 and has at least 5 years' continuous service and the other parent is dead; or

(c) one parent is present and settled in the United Kingdom or being granted settlement on the same occasion or is a member of HM Forces who is exempt from immigration control under section 8(4)(a) of the Immigration Act 1971 and has at least 5 years' continuous service and has had sole responsibility for the child's upbringing; or

(d) one parent or a relative is present and settled in the United Kingdom or being granted settlement on the same occasion or is a member of HM Forces who is exempt from immigration control under section 8(4)(a) of the Immigration Act 1971 and has at least 5 years' continuous service and there are serious and compelling family or other considerations which make exclusion of the child undesirable and suitable arrangements have been made for the child's care; and

(ii) is under the age of 18; and

(iii) is not leading an independent life, is unmarried and is not a civil partner, and has not formed an independent family unit; and

(iv) is not in the UK in breach of immigration laws except that, where paragraph 39E of these Rules applies, any current period of overstaying will be disregarded; and

(v) the applicant does not fall for refusal under the general grounds for refusal.

Indefinite leave to remain in the United Kingdom as the child of a parent, parents or a relative present and settled in the United Kingdom or being granted settlement on the same occasion in accordance with paragraphs 276E to 276Q or of a member of HM Forces who is exempt from immigration control under section 8(4)(a) of the Immigration Act 1971 and has at least 5 years' continuous service

276AB. Indefinite leave to remain in the United Kingdom as the child of a parent, parents or a relative present and settled in the United Kingdom or being granted settlement on the same occasion in accordance with paragraphs 276E to 276Q or of a member of HM Forces who is exempt from immigration control under section 8(4)(a) of the Immigration Act 1971 and has at least 5 years' continuous service may be granted if the Secretary of State is satisfied that each of the requirements of paragraph 276AA is met.

Refusal of indefinite leave to remain in the United Kingdom as the child of a parent, parents or a relative present and settled in the United Kingdom or being granted settlement on the same occasion in accordance with paragraphs 276E to 276Q or of a member of HM Forces who is exempt from immigration control under section 8(4)(a) of the Immigration Act 1971 and has at least 5 years' continuous service

276AC. Indefinite leave to remain in the United Kingdom as the child of a parent, parents or a relative present and settled in the United Kingdom or being granted settlement on the same occasion in accordance with paragraphs 276E to 276Q or of a member of HM Forces who is exempt from immigration control under section 8(4)(a) of the Immigration Act 1971 and has at least 5 years' continuous service is to be refused if the Secretary of State is not satisfied that each of the requirements of paragraph 276AA is met.

Spouses, civil partners, unmarried or same-sex partners of armed forces members who are exempt from immigration control under section 8(4) of the Immigration Act 1971

Requirements for leave to enter or remain as the spouse, civil partner, unmarried or same-sex partner of an armed forces member who is exempt from immigration control under section 8(4) of the Immigration Act 1971

276AD. The requirements to be met by a person seeking leave to enter or remain in the United Kingdom as the spouse, civil partner, unmarried or same-sex partner of an armed forces member who is exempt from immigration control under section 8(4) of the Immigration Act 1971 are that:

(i) the applicant is married to or the civil partner, unmarried or same-sex partner of an armed forces member who is exempt from immigration control under section 8(4) of the Immigration Act 1971; and

(ii) each of the parties intends to live with the other as his or her spouse or civil partner, unmarried or same-sex partner during the applicant's stay and the marriage, civil partnership, or relationship akin to a marriage or civil partnership is subsisting; and

(iii) there will be adequate accommodation for the parties and any dependants without recourse to public funds in accommodation which they own or occupy exclusively; and

(iv) the parties will be able to maintain themselves and any dependants adequately without recourse to public funds;

(v) the applicant does not intend to stay in the United Kingdom beyond his or her spouse's, civil partner's, unmarried or same-sex partner's enlistment in the home forces, or period of posting or training in the United Kingdom; and

(vi) where the applicant is the unmarried or same-sex partner of an armed forces member who is exempt from immigration control under section 8(4) of the Immigration Act 1971, the following requirements are also met:

(a) any previous marriage or civil partnership or relationship akin to a marriage by the applicant or the exempt armed forces member must have permanently broken down,

(b) the applicant and the exempt armed forces member must not be so closely related that they would be prohibited from marrying each other in the UK, and

(c) the applicant and the exempt armed forces member must have been living together in a relationship akin to marriage or civil partnership for a period of at least 2 years.

Leave to enter or remain as the spouse, civil partner, unmarried or same-sex partner of an armed forces member who is exempt from immigration control under section 8(4) of the Immigration Act 1971

276AE. A person seeking leave to enter or remain in the United Kingdom as the spouse, civil partner, unmarried or same-sex partner of an armed forces member who is exempt from immigration control under section 8(4) of the Immigration Act 1971 may be given leave to enter or remain in the United Kingdom for a period not exceeding 4 years or the expected duration of the enlistment, posting or training of his or her spouse, civil partner, unmarried or same-sex partner, whichever is shorter, provided that the Immigration Officer, or in the case of an application for leave to remain, the Secretary of State, is satisfied that each of the requirements of paragraph 276AD (i)–(vi) is met. Study will be subject to a condition as set out in Part 15 of these Rules.

Refusal of leave to enter or remain as the spouse, civil partner, unmarried or same-sex partner of an armed forces member who is exempt from immigration control under section 8(4) of the Immigration Act 1971

276AF. Leave to enter or remain in the United Kingdom as the spouse, civil partner, unmarried or same-sex partner of an armed forces member who is exempt from immigration control under section 8(4) of the Immigration Act 1971 is to be refused if the Immigration Officer, or in the case of an application for leave to remain, the Secretary of State, is not satisfied that each of the requirements of paragraph 276AD(i)–(vi) is met.

Children of armed forces members who are exempt from immigration control under section 8(4) of the Immigration Act 1971

Requirements for leave to enter or remain as the child of an armed forces member exempt from immigration control under section 8(4) of the Immigration Act 1971

276AG. The requirements to be met by a person seeking leave to enter or remain in the United Kingdom as the child of an armed forces member exempt from immigration control under section 8(4) of the Immigration Act 1971 are that:

(i) he is the child of a parent who is an armed forces member exempt from immigration control under section 8(4) of the Immigration Act 1971; and

(ii) he is under the age of 18 or has current leave to enter or remain in this capacity; and

(iii) he is unmarried and is not a civil partner, has not formed an independent family unit and is not leading an independent life; and

(iv) he can and will be maintained and accommodated adequately without recourse to public funds in accommodation which his parent(s) own or occupy exclusively; and

(v) he will not stay in the United Kingdom beyond the period of his parent's enlistment in the home forces, or posting or training in the United Kingdom; and

(vi) his other parent is being or has been admitted to or allowed to remain in the United Kingdom save where:

(a) the parent he is accompanying or joining is his sole surviving parent; or

(b) the parent he is accompanying or joining has had sole responsibility for his upbringing; or

(c) there are serious and compelling family or other considerations which make exclusion from the United Kingdom undesirable and suitable arrangements have been made for his care.

Leave to enter or remain as the child of an armed forces member exempt from immigration control under section 8(4) of the Immigration Act 1971

276AH. A person seeking leave to enter or remain in the United Kingdom as the child of an armed forces member exempt from immigration control under section 8(4) of the Immigration Act 1971 may be given leave to enter or remain in the United Kingdom for a period not exceeding 4 years or the duration of the enlistment, posting or training of his parent, whichever is the shorter, provided that the Immigration Officer, or in the case of an application for leave to remain, the Secretary of State, is satisfied that each of the requirements of 276AG (i)–(vi) is met. Study will be subject to a condition set out in Part 15 of these Rules where the applicant is 18 years of age or over at the time their leave is granted, or will be aged 18 before their period of limited leave expires.

Refusal of leave to enter or remain as the child of an armed forces member exempt from immigration control under section 8(4) of the Immigration Act 1971

276AI. Leave to enter or remain in the United Kingdom as the child of an armed forces member exempt from immigration control under section 8(4) of the Immigration Act 1971 is to be refused if the Immigration Officer, or in the case of an application for leave to remain, the Secretary of State, is not satisfied that each of the requirements of paragraph 276AG (i)–(vi) is met.

[Entry clearance to come to the United Kingdom as a relevant Afghan Citizen]

[276BA1. A person seeking to come to the UK as a relevant Afghan citizen must apply for and obtain entry clearance as a relevant Afghan citizen before they arrive in the UK.]

Note: Paragraph and heading substituted from 6 October 2021 (HC 617).

[276BA2. Where the requirements for entry clearance as a relevant Afghan citizen are met, they will be granted entry clearance, which will have effect on arrival in the UK as indefinite leave to enter, unless the application falls for refusal under paragraph 276BC1

Note: Paragraph and heading substituted from 6 October 2021 (HC 617).

[Definition of a 'relevant Afghan citizen']

[276BB1. A relevant Afghan citizen is a person who: (i) is an Afghan citizen; and (ii) is aged 18 years or over; and (iii) falls within this paragraph under: (a) the Afghan Relocations and Assistance Policy (see paragraphs 276BB2 to 276BB5); or (b) the Afghanistan Locally Employed Staff Ex-Gratia Scheme (see paragraph 276BB6).]

Note: Amendments from 6 July 2018 subject to savings for applications made before that date (HC 1154). Paragraph substituted from 09:00 on 1 December 2020 subject to savings for applications made before that time (HC 813). Amendment from 23:00 on 31 December 2020 for decisions made on or after that time (CP 361). Amendment from 1 April 2021 subject to savings for applications made before that date (HC 1248). Paragraph and heading substituted from 6 October 2021 (HC 617). Paragraph substituted from 16:00 on 14 December 2021 (HC 913).

[276BB2. A person falls within paragraph 276BB1 under the Afghan Relocations and Assistance Policy if the person:

(i) submits an application on or after 1 April 2021; and

(ii) falls within at least one of:

(a) paragraph 276BB3 (high and imminent risk of threat to life);

(b) paragraph 276BB4 (former employees eligible for relocation); and

(c) paragraph 276BB5 (special cases)[[; and]]]

[(iii) where directly employed by, or contracted to, a UK Government Department or Unit, was not dismissed from their job (except in circumstances where the Secretary of State considers that the person was dismissed for a minor reason).]

Note: Paragraph inserted from 16:00 on 14 December 2021 (HC 913). Words in double square brackets in (c)(ii) substituted, (iii) inserted from 6 April 2022 (HC 1118).

[276BB3. A person falls within this paragraph if: (i) the person was at any time on or after 1 October 2001 directly employed in Afghanistan by a UK government department; and (ii) because of that employment, there is a high and imminent risk of a threat to the person's life.]

Note: Paragraph inserted from 16:00 on 14 December 2021 (HC 913).

[276BB4. A person falls within this paragraph if:

(i) at any time on or after 1 October 2001, the person:

(a) was directly employed in Afghanistan by a UK government department; or

(b) provided linguistic services to or for the benefit of members of the UK's armed forces in Afghanistan under contract to a UK government department (whether as, or on behalf of, a party to the contract); and

(ii) the nature of the role in which the person was employed was such that the UK's operations in Afghanistan would have been materially less efficient or materially less successful if a role or roles of that nature had not been performed; and

(iii) the nature of the role exposed the person to being publicly recognised as having performed that role; and

(iv) as a result of that public recognition, the person's safety is at risk.]

Note: Paragraph inserted from 16:00 on 14 December 2021 (HC 913).

[276BB5. A person falls within this paragraph if the person meets conditions 1 and 2 and one or both of conditions 3 and 4. For the purposes of this paragraph:

(i) condition 1 is that at any time on or after 1 October 2001, the person:

(a) was directly employed in Afghanistan by a UK government department; or

(b) provided goods or services in Afghanistan under contract to a UK government department (whether as, or on behalf of, a party to the contract); or

(c) worked in Afghanistan alongside a UK government department, in partnership with or closely supporting and assisting that department;

(ii) condition 2 is that the person, in the course of that employment or work or the provision of those services, made a substantive and positive contribution towards the achievement of:

(a) the UK government's military objectives with respect to Afghanistan; or

(b) the UK government's national security objectives with respect to Afghanistan (and for these purposes, the UK government's national security objectives include counter-terrorism, counter-narcotics and anti-corruption objectives);

(iii) condition 3 is that because of that employment, that work or those services, the person:

(a) is or was at an elevated risk of targeted attacks; and

(b) is or was at high risk of death or serious injury;

(iv) condition 4 is that the person holds information the disclosure of which would give rise to or aggravate a specific threat to the UK government or its interests.]

Note: Paragraph inserted from 16:00 on 14 December 2021 (HC 913).

[276BB6. A person falls within paragraph 276BB1 under the Afghanistan Locally Employed Staff Ex-Gratia Scheme if:

(i) the person was directly employed in Afghanistan by a UK government department; and

(ii) the person was made redundant or resigned on or after 1 May 2006; and

(iii) the person served for a minimum of 12 months prior to either redundancy or resignation and served on frontline duties in an exposed role; and

(iv) the person submits an application for consideration not later than 30 November 2022; and

(v) a UK government department has determined that the person should qualify for relocation under the ex-gratia redundancy or resignation package including confirmation that they served on frontline duties in an exposed role.]

Note: Paragraph inserted from 16:00 on 14 December 2021 (HC 913).

[Refusal of entry clearance as a relevant Afghan citizen]

[276BC1. An applicant will be refused entry clearance as a relevant Afghan citizen if their application falls for refusal under the grounds of refusal contained in Part 9 of these Rules.]

Note: Paragraph and heading substituted from 6 October 2021 (HC 617).

[Cancellation of entry clearance, leave to enter or remain or indefinite leave to enter or remain in the United Kingdom as a relevant Afghan citizen]

[**276BD1.** Entry clearance, leave to enter or remain or indefinite leave to enter or remain in the UK as a relevant Afghan citizen may be cancelled in accordance with Part 9 of these Rules, to the extent permitted by the Immigration Acts.]

Note: Paragraph and heading substituted from 6 October 2021 (HC 617).

[Dependants of a relevant Afghan citizen]

[**276BE1.** A partner of a relevant Afghan citizen and a minor dependent child of a relevant Afghan citizen or of a partner of a relevant Afghan citizen may apply for entry clearance or indefinite leave to remain as their dependants.]

Note: Amendment from 6 April 2019 (HC 1919). Paragraph and heading substituted from 6 October 2021 (HC 617). Paragraph substituted from 16:00 on 14 December 2021 (HC 913).

276BF1. [DELETED]

Note: Paragraph substituted from 6 October 2021 (HC 617). Paragraph deleted from 16:00 on 14 December 2021 (HC 913)

[**276BG1.** The relevant Afghan citizen [[who is the principal applicant]] must include details of all dependants seeking relocation in their application at the time their application is made, including any dependants who intend to relocate to the UK after the relevant Afghan citizen.]

Note: Paragraph substituted from 6 April 2019 (HC 1919). Paragraph substituted from 6 October 2021 (HC 617). Words in double square brackets inserted from 16:00 on 14 December 2021 (HC 913).

276BH1. [DELETED]

Note: Paragraph deleted from 6 April 2019 (HC 1919).

[**276BI1.** If the relevant Afghan citizen [[has more than one partner (as defined in paragraph 276BK1)]], only one partner can apply to come to, or remain in the UK.]

Note: Paragraph substituted from 6 October 2021 (HC 617). Words in double square brackets substituted from 16:00 on 14 December 2021 (HC 913).

[Entry clearance to come to the United Kingdom as the partner of a relevant Afghan citizen]

[**276BJ1.** A person seeking to come to the UK [[under paragraph 276BE1)]] as the partner of a relevant Afghan citizen must apply for and obtain entry clearance as the partner of a relevant Afghan citizen before they arrive in the UK.]

Note: Paragraph and heading substituted from 6 October 2021 (HC 617). Words in double square brackets inserted from 16:00 on 14 December 2021 (HC 913).

[**276BJ2.** Where the partner of a relevant Afghan citizen meets the requirements for entry clearance and:

(i) the relationship requirements under paragraph 276BL1 are met; and

(ii) the application does not fall for refusal under paragraph 276BM1, they will be granted entry clearance to enter the UK, which will have effect on arrival in the UK as indefinite leave to enter.]

Note: Paragraph substituted from 6 October 2021 (HC 617).

[Definition of 'partner' of a relevant Afghan citizen]

[276BK1. [[For the purposes of rules 276BA1-276BS5]] a partner of a relevant Afghan citizen, including where the relevant Afghan citizen has already been granted entry clearance, leave to enter or remain or indefinite leave to enter or remain, is a person who:

(i) is the relevant Afghan citizen's spouse; or

(ii) is the relevant Afghan citizen's civil partner; or

(iii) has been living together with the relevant Afghan citizen in a relationship akin to a marriage or civil partnership for at least two years prior to the date of application.]

Note: Amendment from 6 April 2019 (HC 1919). Paragraph and heading substituted from 6 October 2021 (HC 617). Words in double square brackets substituted from 16:00 on 14 December 2021 (HC 913).

276BK2. [DELETED]

Note: Paragraph inserted from 6 April 2019 (HC 1919). Paragraph deleted from 6 October 2021 (HC 617).

[Relationship requirements for a partner of a relevant Afghan citizen]

[276BL1. The relationship requirements for a partner of a relevant Afghan citizen are that:

(i) the applicant is the partner (as defined in paragraph 276BK1) of the principal applicant, who must have been granted entry clearance under paragraph 276BA2, or who must be being granted entry clearance under that paragraph at the same time, or who must otherwise hold leave to enter or remain in the United Kingdom as a relevant Afghan citizen.

(ii) they are aged 18 or over at the date of application; and

(iii) they are in a relationship with the principal applicant that is not within the prohibited degree of relationship; and

(iv) they have met the principal applicant in person; and

(v) they are in a genuine and subsisting relationship with the principal applicant; and

(vi) if the principal applicant and partner are married or in a civil partnership, they must be in a valid marriage or civil partnership and must provide reasonable evidence to the equivalent of a marriage certificate or civil partnership certificate issued in the UK and valid under the law in force in the relevant country; and

(vii) any previous relationship of the relevant Afghan citizen or their partner must have broken down permanently, unless it is a relationship which falls with paragraph 278(i) of these rules; and

(vii) they must intend to live together permanently in the UK with the principal applicant.]

Note: Paragraph and heading substituted from 6 October 2021 (HC 617). Paragraph substituted from 16:00 on 14 December 2021 (HC 913).

[Refusal of entry clearance as the partner of a relevant Afghan citizen]

[276BM1. A partner of a relevant Afghan citizen will be refused entry clearance to the UK where the requirements of these Rules are not met, or if their application falls for refusal under the grounds of refusal contained in Part 9 of these Rules.]

Note: Paragraph and heading substituted from 6 October 2021 (HC 617).

[Cancellation of entry clearance, leave to enter or remain or indefinite leave to enter or remain the United Kingdom as the partner of a relevant Afghan citizen]

[276BN1. Entry clearance, leave to enter or remain or indefinite leave to enter or remain in the UK as the partner of a relevant Afghan citizen may be cancelled in accordance with Part 9 of these rules, to the extent permitted by the Immigration Acts.]

Note: Paragraph and heading substituted from 6 October 2021 (HC 617).

[Entry clearance to come to the United Kingdom as the minor dependent child of a relevant Afghan citizen or of their partner]

[276BO1. A person seeking to come to the UK as a minor dependent child of a relevant Afghan citizen or of their partner must apply for and obtain entry clearance as a minor dependent child of a relevant Afghan citizen or of their partner before they arrive in the UK] [[under paragraph 276BE1.]]

Note: Paragraph and heading substituted from 6 October 2021 (HC 617). Words in double square brackets inserted from 16:00 on 14 December 2021 (HC 913).

[276BO2. Where the minor dependent child of a relevant Afghan citizen or of their partner meets the requirements for entry clearance and:

(i) the relationship requirements under paragraph 276BQ1 are met; and

(ii) the application does not fall for refusal under paragraph 276BR1, they will be granted indefinite leave to enter the UK, which will have effect on arrival in the UK as indefinite leave to enter.]

Note: Paragraph substituted from 6 October 2021 (HC 617).

[Definition of 'minor dependent child' of a relevant Afghan citizen or of their partner]

[276BP1. For the purposes of [[paragraphs 276BA1-276BS5]] a minor dependent child of a relevant Afghan citizen or of their partner is a person who:

(i) is the child of the relevant Afghan citizen or of their partner subject to paragraph 276BQ1; and who

(ii) is under the age of 18 at time of application;

(iii) is not married or in a civil partnership;

(iv) has not formed an independent family unit; and

(v) is not leading an independent life.]

Note: Amendments from 6 April 2019 (HC 1919). Paragraph and heading substituted from 6 October 2021 (HC 617). Words in double square brackets substituted from 16:00 on 14 December 2021 (HC 913).

[Relationship requirements for a minor dependent child of a relevant Afghan citizen or of their partner]

[**276BQ1.** The relationship requirements for a minor dependent child of a relevant Afghan citizen or of their partner are that the applicant satisfies sub-paragraph (i) below and also satisfies one of sub-paragraphs (ii) to (vi) below, namely that the applicant:

(i) is the child of

(a) the principal applicant, who must have been granted entry clearance under paragraph 276BA2, or who must be being granted entry clearance under that paragraph at the same time, or who must otherwise hold leave to enter or remain in the United Kingdom as a relevant Afghan citizen; or

(b) the principal applicant's partner (as defined in paragraph 276BK1), who must have been granted entry clearance under paragraph 276BJ2, or who must be being granted entry clearance under that paragraph at the same time;

(ii) is the child of the principal applicant and the child's other parent is the principal applicant's partner;

(iii) is the child of the principal applicant; and

(a) the child's other parent is dead; or

(b) the principal applicant has sole responsibility for the child's upbringing;

(iv) is the child of the principal applicant's partner; and

(a) the child's other parent is dead; or

(b) the principal applicant's partner has sole responsibility for the child's upbringing;

(v) is the adopted child of the principal applicant as defined at paragraphs 309A or 309B of these Rules and where the requirements at paragraph 310 (vi) - (xi) of these Rules are fulfilled;

(vi) is the adopted child of the principal applicant's partner and as defined at paragraphs 309A or 309B of these Rules and where the requirements at paragraph 310 (vi) - (xi) of these Rules are fulfilled.]

Note: Amendments from 6 April 2019 (HC 1919). Paragraph and heading substituted from 6 October 2021 (HC 617). Paragraph substituted from 16:00 on 14 December 2021 (HC 913).

[Refusal of entry clearance the United Kingdom as the minor dependent child of a relevant Afghan citizen or of their partner]

[**276BR1.** A minor dependent child of a relevant Afghan citizen or of their partner will be refused entry clearance where the requirements of these Rules are not met, or if their application falls for refusal under the grounds of refusal contained in Part 9 of these Rules.]

Note: Amendments from 6 April 2019 (HC 1919). Paragraph and heading substituted from 6 October 2021 (HC 617).

[Cancellation of entry clearance, leave to enter or remain or indefinite leave to enter or remain in the United Kingdom as the minor dependent child of a relevant Afghan citizen or of their partner]

[**276BS1.** Entry clearance, leave to enter or remain or indefinite leave to enter or remain in the UK as the minor dependent child of a relevant Afghan citizen or of their partner may be cancelled in accordance with Part 9 of these rules, to the extent permitted by the Immigration Acts.]

Note: Amendments from 6 April 2019 (HC 1919). Paragraph and heading substituted from 6 October 2021 (HC 617).

[Grant or refusal of indefinite leave to remain as a relevant Afghan citizen or their dependant]

[276BS2. Indefinite leave to remain will be granted to

(i) a relevant Afghan citizen;

(ii) their partner within the meaning of 276BK1;

(iii) their minor dependant child within the meaning of 276BP1 unless that person falls for refusal under Part 9 of these Rules, in which case that person will be refused indefinite leave to remain.]

Note: Paragraph and heading inserted from 6 July 2018 subject to savings for applications made before that date (HC 1154). Paragraph and heading substituted from 6 October 2021 (HC 617). Paragraph substituted from 16:00 on 14 December 2021 (HC 913).

276BS3. [DELETED]

Note: Paragraph inserted from 6 July 2018 subject to savings for applications made before that date (HC 1154). Paragraph substituted from 6 October 2021 (HC 617). Paragraph deleted from 16:00 on 14 December 2021 (HC 913).

276BS4. [DELETED]

Note: Paragraph inserted from 6 July 2018 subject to savings for applications made before that date (HC 1154). Paragraph and heading substituted from 6 October 2021 (HC 617). Paragraph and heading deleted from 16:00 on 14 December 2021 (HC 913).

276BS5. [DELETED]

Note: Paragraph inserted from 6 October 2021 (HC 617). Paragraph and heading deleted from 16:00 on 14 December 2021 (HC 913).

Parent of a [Child Student]

Requirements for leave to enter or remain as the parent of a [*Child Student*]

276BT1. [DELETED]

Note: Amendments from 09:00 on 5 October 2020 subject to savings for applications made before that time (HC 707). Paragraph deleted from 09:00 on 12 December 2020 subject to savings for applications made before that time (HC 813).

Leave to enter or remain as the parent of a [*Child Student*]

276BU1. [DELETED]

Note: Amendments from 09:00 on 5 October 2020 subject to savings for applications made before that time (HC 707). Paragraph deleted from 09:00 on 1 December 2020 subject to savings for applications made before that time (HC 813).

Refusal of leave to enter or remain as the parent of a [*Child Student*]

276BV1. [DELETED]

Note: Amendments from 09:00 on 5 October 2020 subject to savings for applications made before that time (HC 707). Paragraph deleted from 09:00 on 1 December 2020 subject to savings for applications made before that time (HC 813).

PART 8

FAMILY MEMBERS

Transitional provisions and interaction between Part 8, Appendix FM and Appendix FM-SE

A277. From 9 July 2012 Appendix FM will apply to all applications to which Part 8 of these rules applied on or before 8 July 2012 except where the provisions of Part 8 are preserved and continue to apply, as set out in paragraphs A280 to A280B.

A277A. Where the Secretary of State is considering an application for limited leave to remain or indefinite leave to remain to which Part 8 of these rules continues to apply (excluding an application from a family member of a Relevant Points Based System Migrant [or Appendix W Worker]), and where the applicant:

(a) does not meet the requirements of Part 8 for indefinite leave to remain (where the application is for indefinite leave to remain), and

(b) meets or continues to meet the requirements for limited leave to remain under Part 8 in force at the date of decision,

subject to compliance with any requirement notified under paragraph A277D(b) further limited leave to remain under Part 8 may be granted of such a period and subject to such conditions as the Secretary of State deems appropriate. For the purposes of this subparagraph an applicant last granted limited leave to enter under Part 8 will be considered as if they had last been granted limited leave to remain under Part 8; or

(c) if the applicant does not meet the requirements of Part 8 for indefinite leave to remain as a bereaved partner (where the application is for indefinite leave to remain as a bereaved partner) only because paragraph 322(1C)(iii) or 322(1C)(iv) of these rules applies, the applicant will (subject to compliance with any requirement notified under paragraph A277D(b)) be granted limited leave to remain under Part 8 for a period not exceeding 30 months and subject to such conditions as the Secretary of State deems appropriate.

Note: Words in introduction inserted from 29 March 2019 subject to savings for applications made before that date (HC 1919).

A277B. Where the Secretary of State is considering an application for limited leave to remain or indefinite leave to remain to which Part 8 of these rules continues to apply (excluding an application from a family member of a Relevant Points Based System Migrant [or Appendix W Worker], from a victim of domestic violence or from a bereaved spouse, civil partner, unmarried partner or same sex partner) and where the application does not meet the requirements for indefinite leave to remain (where the application is for indefinite leave to remain) or limited leave to remain under Part 8 in force at the date of decision:

(a) the application will also be considered under paragraphs R-LTRP.1.1.(a), (b) and (d), R-LTRC.1.1.(a), (b) and (d), R-LTRPT.1.1.(a), (b) and (d) [. . .] of Appendix FM (family life) and [Appendix Private Life] of these rules;

(b) if the applicant meets the requirements for leave under those paragraphs of Appendix FM or [Appendix Private Life] (except the requirement for a valid application under that route), the applicant will (subject to compliance with any requirement notified under paragraph A277D(b)) be granted leave under those provisions; and

(c) if the applicant is granted leave under those provisions, the period of the applicant's continuous leave under Part 8 at the date of application will be counted towards the period of continuous leave which must be completed before the applicant can apply for indefinite leave to remain under paragraph 276B.

Note: Words in (a) deleted from 6 July 2018 for decisions made on or after that date (HC 1154). Words in introduction inserted from 29 March 2019 subject to savings for applications made before that date (HC 1919). Words in (a) and (b) substituted from 20 June 2022 subject to savings for applications made before that date (HC 1118).

[**A277C.** Subject to paragraphs A277 to A280B and paragraph GEN.1.9. of Appendix FM, the Secretary of State may consider any application to which the provisions of Appendix FM (family life) and Appendix Private life of these rules do not apply, under paragraphs R-LTRP.1.1.(a), (b) and (d), R-LTRPT.1.1.(a), (b) and (d), R-LTRC.1.1.(a), (b) and (d) of Appendix FM (family life) and Appendix Private life of these rules. If the applicant meets the requirements for leave under those provisions (except the requirement for a valid application), the applicant will be granted leave under paragraph D-LTRP.1.2., D-LTRPT.1.2. or D-LTRC.1.1. of Appendix FM or under Appendix Private Life.]

Note: Amendments from 6 July 2018 for decisions made on or after that date (HC 1154). Paragraph substituted from 20 June 2022 subject to savings for applications made before that date (HC 1118).

A277D. Where, pursuant to paragraphs A277A to A277C, a person who has made an application for indefinite leave to remain to which Part 8 of these rules continues to apply does not meet the requirements for indefinite leave to remain but falls to be granted limited leave to remain under Part 8, [Appendix Private Life] or Appendix FM, or outside the rules on Article 8 grounds:

(a) The Secretary of State will treat that application for indefinite leave to remain as an application for limited leave to remain;

(b) The Secretary of State will notify the applicant in writing of any requirement to pay an immigration health charge under the Immigration (Health Charge) Order 2015; and

(c) If there is such a requirement and that requirement is not met, the application for limited leave to remain will be invalid and the Secretary of State will not refund any application fee paid in respect of the application for indefinite leave to remain.

Note: Words substituted from 20 June 2022 subject to savings for applications made before that date (HC 1118).

A278. The requirements to be met under Part 8 after 9 July 2012 may be modified or supplemented by the requirements in Appendix FM and Appendix FM-SE.

A279. Paragraphs A398-399D apply to all immigration decisions made further to applications under Part 8 and paragraphs 276A–276D where a decision is made on or after 28 July 2014, irrespective of the date the application was made.

A280. The following provisions of Part 8 apply in the manner and circumstances specified:

(a) The following paragraphs apply in respect of all applications made under Part 8 and Appendix FM, irrespective of the date of application or decision:

277–280
289AA
295AA
296

(b) The following paragraphs of Part 8 continue to apply to all applications made on or after 9 July 2012. The paragraphs apply in their current form unless an additional requirement by reference to Appendix FM is specified:

Paragraph number	Additional requirement
295J	None
297–300	Where the applicant falls under paragraph 297, the applicant must not fall for refusal under paragraph S-EC.1.9. of Appendix FM in respect of a parent of the applicant. For these purposes, 'a parent of the applicant' is to be construed as including 'a relative of the applicant' under paragraph 297.
304–309	Where the applicant falls under paragraph 305, the applicant must not fall for refusal under paragraph S-EC.1.9. of Appendix FM in respect of a parent of the applicant.
309A–316F	Where: (1) the applicant: • falls under paragraph 314(i)(a); or • falls under paragraph 316A(i)(d) or (e); and • is applying on or after 9 July 2012; and (2) the 'other parent' mentioned in paragraph 314(i)(a), or one of the prospective parents mentioned in paragraph 316A(i)(d) or (e), has or is applying for entry clearance or limited leave to remain as a partner under Appendix FM, the application must also meet the requirements of paragraphs E-ECC 2.1–2.3 (entry clearance applications) or E-LTRC 2.1–2.3 (leave to remain applications) of Appendix FM. Where the applicant: • falls under paragraph 314(i)(d); • is applying on or after 9 July 2012; and • has two parents or prospective parents and one of the applicant's parents or prospective parents does not have right of abode, indefinite leave to enter or remain, is not present and settled in the UK or being admitted for settlement on the same occasion as the applicant is seeking admission, but otherwise has or is applying for entry clearance or limited leave to remain as a partner under Appendix FM, the application must also meet the requirements of paragraphs E-ECC 2.1–2.3 (entry clearance applications) or E-LTRC 2.1–2.3 (leave to remain applications) of Appendix FM.
319X	None

(c) The following provisions of Part 8 continue to apply on or after 9 July 2012, and are not subject to any additional requirement listed in (b) above:

(i) to persons who have made an application before 9 July 2012 under Part 8 which was not decided as at 9 July 2012; and

(ii) to applications made by persons in the UK who have been granted entry clearance or limited leave to enter or remain under Part 8 before 9 July 2012 and, where this is a requirement of Part 8, this leave to enter or limited leave to remain is extant:

281–289
289A–289C
290–295
295A–295O
297–316F
317–319
319L–319U
319V–319Y

(d) (i) The following provisions of Part 8 continue to apply to applications made in the period beginning with 9 July 2012 and ending on 30 November 2013, including those that have not been decided before 1 December 2013, and are not subject to any additional requirement listed in (b) above, by persons who have made an application for entry clearance, leave to enter or remain as the fiancé(e), proposed civil partner, spouse, civil partner, unmarried partner, same sex partner, or child or other dependant relative of a British citizen or settled person who is a full-time member of HM Forces:

281–289
289A–289C
290–295
295A–295O
297–316F
317–319

(ii) Subject to the following provisions, from 1 December 2013, Appendix Armed Forces applies to all applications for entry clearance, leave to enter or remain as the fiancé(e), proposed civil partner, spouse, civil partner, unmarried partner, same sex partner or child of a British citizen or settled person who is a full-time member of HM Forces.

(iii) Except, from 1 December 2013, the provisions in paragraph A280(d)(i) continue to apply to persons who were granted entry clearance, limited leave to enter or remain under Part 8 before 1 December 2013, and where it is a requirement of Part 8, that leave to enter or remain is extant.

(iv) Applications may continue to be made under paragraphs 297 to 316F of Part 8 by the child of a British citizen or settled person who is a full-time member of HM Forces regardless of the date of application and paragraph A280(b) continues to apply to these applications as appropriate.

(v) A new application by a dependent relative of a British citizen or settled person who is a full time member of HM Forces may no longer be made under paragraphs 317–319 on or after 1 December 2013. Those applications must meet the requirements of Appendix FM unless an application was submitted on or before 30 November 2013. An application made by a dependent relative of a British citizen or settled person who is a full time member of HM Forces on or before 30 November 2013 will be considered under the relevant paragraphs 317–319 which apply.

(vi) For the avoidance of doubt, paragraph A280(e) will continue to apply to the spouse, civil partner, unmarried partner or same sex partner of a British citizen or settled person who is a full-time member of HM Forces when the spouse, civil partner, unmarried partner or same sex partner was admitted to the UK under paragraph 282(c) or 295B(c) where the applicant has not yet applied for indefinite leave to remain, including where an application relying on paragraph A280(e) is made on or after 1 December 2013.

(vii) The requirements in paragraphs 8 and 9 of Appendix Armed Forces apply to applications for entry clearance, leave to enter or remain as the fiancé(e), proposed civil partner, spouse, civil partner, unmarried partner, same sex partner, or child or other dependent relative of a British citizen or settled person who is a full-time member of HM Forces making an application under Part 8 (where paragraph A280 (d) has permitted such an application) where the decision is made on or after 1 December 2013 (and irrespective of the date of the application).

(e) The following provisions of Part 8 shall continue to apply to applications made on or after 9 July 2012, and are not subject to any additional requirement listed in (b) above, by a spouse, civil partner, unmarried partner or same sex partner who was admitted to the UK before 9 July 2012 further to paragraph 282(c) or 295B(c) of these Rules who has not yet applied for indefinite leave to remain:

284–286
287(a)(i)(c)
287(a)(ii)–(vii)
287(b)
288–289
289A–289C
295D–295F
295G(i)(c)
295G(ii)–(vii)
295H–295I

(f) Paragraphs 301–303F continue to apply to applications made under this route on or after 9 July 2012, and are not subject to any additional requirement listed in (b) above, by a child of a person to whom those paragraphs relate who has been granted limited leave to enter or remain or an extension of stay following an application made before 9 July 2012.

(g) For the avoidance of doubt, notwithstanding the introduction of Appendix FM, paragraphs 319AA–319J of Part 8 continue to apply, and are not subject to any additional requirement listed in paragraph (b) above, to applications for entry clearance or leave to enter or remain as the spouse, civil partner, unmarried partner, same sex partner, or child of a Relevant Points Based System Migrant [or Appendix W Worker].

Note: Words in (g) inserted from 29 March 2019 subject to savings for applications made before that date (HC 1919).

A280A. The sponsor of an applicant under Part 8 for limited or indefinite leave to remain as a spouse, civil partner, unmarried partner or same sex partner must be the same person as the sponsor of the applicant's last grant of leave in that category.

A280AA. Where a person aged 18 or over is granted limited leave to enter or remain under Part 8 of these rules, or where a person granted such limited leave to enter or remain will be aged 18 before that period of limited leave expires, the leave will, in addition to any other conditions which may apply, be granted subject to the condition in Part 15 of these rules.

A280B. An applicant aged 18 or over may not rely on paragraph A280 where, since their last grant of limited leave to enter or remain under Part 8, they have been granted or refused leave under Appendix FM, Appendix Armed Forces or [Appendix Private Life] of these rules, or been granted limited leave to enter or remain in a category outside their original route to settlement.

Note: Words substituted from 20 June 2022 subject to savings for applications made before that date (HC 1118).

A281. In Part 8 'specified' means specified in Appendix FM-SE, unless otherwise stated, and 'English language test provider approved by the Secretary of State' means a provider specified in Appendix O.

[**A282.** From 1 December 2020, all references to 'refusal under General Grounds for Refusal' in Part 8 are to be read as 'refusal under Part 9: grounds for refusal'.]

Note: Paragraph inserted from 09:00 on 1 December 2020 subject to savings for applications made before that time (HC 813).

Spouses and civil partners

277. Nothing in these Rules shall be construed as permitting a person to be granted entry clearance, leave to enter, leave to remain or variation of leave as a spouse or civil partner of another if either the applicant or the sponsor will be aged under 18 on the date of arrival in the United Kingdom or (as the case may be) on the date on which the leave to remain or variation of leave would be granted. In these rules the term 'sponsor' includes 'partner' as defined in GEN 1.2 of Appendix FM.

278. Nothing in these Rules shall be construed as allowing a person to be granted entry clearance, leave to enter, leave to remain or variation of leave as the spouse and civil partner of a man or woman (the sponsor) if:

(i) his or her marriage or civil partnership to the sponsor is polygamous; and

(ii) there is another person living who is the husband or wife of the sponsor and who:

(a) is, or at any time since his or her marriage or civil partnership to the sponsor has been, in the United Kingdom; or

(b) has been granted a certificate of entitlement in respect of the right of abode mentioned in Section 2(1)(a) of the Immigration Act 1988 or an entry clearance to enter the United Kingdom as the husband or wife of the sponsor.

For the purpose of this paragraph a marriage or civil partnership may be polygamous although at its inception neither party had any other spouse or civil partner.

279. Paragraph 278 does not apply to any person who seeks entry clearance, leave to enter, leave to remain or variation of leave where:

(i) he or she has been in the United Kingdom before 1 August 1988 having been admitted for the purpose of settlement as the husband or wife of the sponsor; or

(ii) he or she has, since their marriage or civil partnership to the sponsor, been in the United Kingdom at any time when there was no such other spouse or civil partner living as is mentioned in paragraph 278(ii).

But where a person claims that paragraph 278 does not apply to them because they have been in the United Kingdom in circumstances which cause them to fall within sub paragraphs (i) or (ii) of that paragraph it shall be for them to prove that fact.

280. For the purposes of paragraphs 278 and 279 the presence of any wife or husband in the United Kingdom in any of the following circumstances shall be disregarded:

(i) as a visitor; or

(ii) an illegal entrant; or

(iii) in circumstances whereby a person is deemed by Section 11(1) of the Immigration Act 1971 not to have entered the United Kingdom.

Spouses or civil partners of persons present and settled in the United Kingdom or being admitted on the same occasion for settlement

Requirements for leave to enter the United Kingdom with a view to settlement as the spouse or civil partner of a person present and settled in the United Kingdom or being admitted on the same occasion for settlement

281. The requirements to be met by a person seeking leave to enter the United Kingdom with a view to settlement as the spouse or civil partner of a person present and settled in the United Kingdom or who is on the same occasion being admitted for settlement are that:

(i) (a) (i) the applicant is married to or the civil partner of a person present and settled in the United Kingdom or who is on the same occasion being admitted for settlement; and

(ii) the applicant provides an original English language test certificate in speaking and listening from an English language test provider approved by the Secretary of State for these purposes, which clearly shows the applicant's name and the qualification obtained (which must meet or exceed level A1 of the Common European Framework of Reference) unless:

(a) the applicant is aged 65 or over at the time he makes his application; or

(b) the applicant has a physical or mental condition that would prevent him from meeting the requirement; or;

(c) there are exceptional compassionate circumstances that would prevent the applicant from meeting the requirement; or

(iii) the applicant is a national of one of the following countries: Antigua and Barbuda; Australia; The Bahamas; Barbados; Belize; Canada; Dominica; Grenada; Guyana; Jamaica; New Zealand; St Kitts and Nevis; St Lucia; St Vincent and the Grenadines; Trinidad and Tobago; United States of America; or

(iv) the applicant has obtained an academic qualification (not a professional or vocational qualification), which is deemed by [Ecctis] to meet the recognised standard of a Bachelor's or Master's degree or PhD in the UK, from an educational establishment in one of the following countries: Antigua and Barbuda; Australia; The Bahamas; Barbados; Belize; Dominica; Grenada; Guyana; Ireland; Jamaica; New Zealand; St Kitts and Nevis; St Lucia; St Vincent and The Grenadines; Trinidad and Tobago; the UK; the USA; and provides the specified documents; or

(v) the applicant has obtained an academic qualification (not a professional or vocational qualification) which is deemed by [Ecctis] to meet the recognised standard of a Bachelor's or Master's degree or PhD in the UK, and

(1) provides the specified evidence to show he has the qualification, and

(2) [Ecctis] has confirmed that the qualification was taught or researched in English, or

(vi) has obtained an academic qualification (not a professional or vocational qualification) which is deemed by [Ecctis] to meet the recognised standard of a Bachelor's or Master's degree or PhD in the UK, and provides the specified evidence to show:

(1) he has the qualification, and

(2) that the qualification was taught or researched in English.

or

(b) (i) the applicant is married to or the civil partner of a person who has a right of abode in the United Kingdom or indefinite leave to enter or remain in the United Kingdom and is on the same occasion seeking admission to the United Kingdom for the purposes of settlement and the parties were married or formed a civil partnership at least 4 years ago, since which time they have been living together outside the United Kingdom; and

(b) (ii) the applicant has demonstrated sufficient knowledge of the English language and sufficient knowledge about life in the United Kingdom, in accordance with Appendix KoLL; and

(b) (iii) DELETED

(ii) the parties to the marriage or civil partnership have met; and

(iii) each of the parties intends to live permanently with the other as his or her spouse or civil partner and the marriage or civil partnership is subsisting; and

(iv) there will be adequate accommodation for the parties and any dependants without recourse to public funds in accommodation which they own or occupy exclusively; and

(v) the parties will be able to maintain themselves and any dependants adequately without recourse to public funds; and

(vi) the applicant holds a valid United Kingdom entry clearance for entry in this capacity; and

(vii) the applicant does not fall for refusal under the general grounds for refusal. For the purposes of this paragraph and paragraphs 282–289 a member of HM Forces serving overseas, or a permanent member of HM Diplomatic Service or a comparable UK-based staff member of the British Council on a tour of duty abroad, or a staff member of the Department for International Development who is a British Citizen or is settled in the United Kingdom, is to be regarded as present and settled in the United Kingdom.

Note: Words substituted from 6 October 2021 subject to savings for applications made before that date (HC 617)

Leave to enter as the spouse or civil partner of a person present and settled in the United Kingdom or being admitted for settlement on the same occasion

282. A person seeking leave to enter the United Kingdom as the spouse or civil partner of a person present and settled in the United Kingdom or who is on the same occasion being admitted for settlement may:

(a) in the case of a person who meets the requirements of paragraph 281(i)(a)(i) and one of the requirements of paragraph 281(i)(a)(ii)–(vi) be admitted for an initial period not exceeding 27 months, or

(b) in the case of a person who meets all of the requirements in paragraph 281(i)(b), be granted indefinite leave to enter, or

(c) in the case of a person who meets the requirement in paragraph 281(i)(b)(i), but not the requirement in paragraph 281(i)(b)(ii) to have sufficient knowledge of the English language and about life in the United Kingdom, be admitted for an initial period not exceeding 27 months, in all cases provided the Immigration Officer is satisfied that each of the relevant requirements of paragraph 281 is met.

Refusal of leave to enter as the spouse or civil partner of a person present and settled in the United Kingdom or being admitted on the same occasion for settlement

283. Leave to enter the United Kingdom as the spouse or civil partner of a person present and settled in the United Kingdom or who is on the same occasion being admitted for settlement is to be refused if the Immigration Officer is not satisfied that each of the requirements of paragraph 281 is met.

Requirements for an extension of stay as the spouse or civil partner of a person present and settled in the United Kingdom

284. The requirements for an extension of stay as the spouse or civil partner of a person present and settled in the United Kingdom are that:

(i) the applicant has or was last granted limited leave to enter or remain in the United Kingdom which meets the following requirements:

(a) The leave was given in accordance with any of the provisions of these Rules; and

(b) The leave was granted for a period of 6 months or more, unless it was granted as a fiancé(e) or proposed civil partner; and

(c) The leave was not as the spouse, civil partner, unmarried or same-sex partner of a Relevant Points-Based System Migrant; and

(ii) the applicant is married to or the civil partner of a person present and settled in the United Kingdom; and

(iii) the parties to the marriage or civil partnership have met; and

(iv) the applicant must not be in the UK in breach of immigration laws (except that, where paragraph 39E of these Rules applies, any current period of overstaying will be disregarded); and

(v) the marriage or civil partnership has not taken place after a decision has been made to deport the applicant or he has been recommended for deportation or been given notice under Section 6(2) of the Immigration Act 1971 or been given directions for his removal under section 10 of the Immigration and Asylum Act 1999; and

(vi) each of the parties intends to live permanently with the other as his or her spouse or civil partner and the marriage or civil partnership is subsisting; and

(vii) there will be adequate accommodation for the parties and any dependants without recourse to public funds in accommodation which they own or occupy exclusively; and

(viii) the parties will be able to maintain themselves and any dependants adequately without recourse to public funds; and

(ix) (a) the applicant provides an [...] English language test certificate in speaking and listening from an English language test provider approved by the Secretary of State for these purposes, which clearly shows the applicant's name and the qualification obtained (which must meet or exceed level A1 of the Common European Framework of Reference) unless:

(i) the applicant is aged 65 or over at the time he makes his application; or

(ii) the applicant has a physical or mental condition that would prevent him from meeting the requirement; or

(iii) there are exceptional compassionate circumstances that would prevent the applicant from meeting the requirement; or

(b) the applicant is a national of one of the following countries: Antigua and Barbuda; Australia; The Bahamas; Barbados; Belize; Canada; Dominica; Grenada;

Guyana; Jamaica; New Zealand; St Kitts and Nevis; St Lucia; St Vincent and the Grenadines; Trinidad and Tobago; United States of America; or

(c) the applicant has obtained an academic qualification, which is deemed by [[Ecctis]] to meet the recognised standard of a Bachelor's or Master's degree or PhD in the UK, from an educational establishment in one of the following countries: Antigua and Barbuda; Australia; The Bahamas; Barbados; Belize; Dominica; Grenada; Guyana; Ireland; Jamaica; New Zealand; St Kitts and Nevis; St Lucia; St Vincent and The Grenadines; Trinidad and Tobago; the UK; the USA; and provides the specified documents; or

(d) the applicant has obtained an academic qualification which is deemed by [[Ecctis]] to meet the recognised standard of a Bachelor's or Master's degree or PhD in the UK, and

(1) provides the specified evidence to show he has the qualification, and

(2) [[Ecctis]] has confirmed that the qualification was taught or researched in English, or

(e) has obtained an academic qualification which is deemed by [[Ecctis]] to meet the recognised standard of a Bachelor's or Master's degree or PhD in the UK, and provides the specified evidence to show:

(1) he has the qualification, and

(2) that the qualification was taught or researched in English.

Note: Word in (ix)(a) deleted from 5 November 2018 (HC 1534). Words in double square brackets substituted from 6 October 2021 subject to savings for applications made before that date (HC 617).

Extension of stay as the spouse or civil partner of a person present and settled in the United Kingdom

285. An extension of stay as the spouse or civil partner of a person present and settled in the United Kingdom may be granted for a period of 2 years in the first instance, provided the Secretary of State is satisfied that each of the requirements of paragraph 284 is met.

Refusal of extension of stay as the spouse or civil partner of a person present and settled in the United Kingdom

286. An extension of stay as the spouse or civil partner of a person present and settled in the United Kingdom is to be refused if the Secretary of State is not satisfied that each of the requirements of paragraph 284 is met.

Requirements for indefinite leave to remain for the spouse or civil partner of a person present and settled in the United Kingdom

287. (a) The requirements for indefinite leave to remain for the spouse or civil partner of a person present and settled in the United Kingdom are that:

(i) (a) the applicant was admitted to the United Kingdom for a period not exceeding 27 months or given an extension of stay for a period of 2 years in accordance with paragraphs 281 to 286 of these Rules and has completed a period of 2 years as the spouse or civil partner of a person present and settled in the United Kingdom; or

(b) the applicant was admitted to the United Kingdom for a period not exceeding 27 months or given an extension of stay for a period of 2 years in accordance with paragraphs 295AA to 295F of these Rules and during that period married or formed a civil partnership with the person whom he or she was admitted or granted an extension of stay to join and has completed a period of 2 years as the unmarried or same-sex partner and then the spouse or civil partner of a person present and settled in the United Kingdom; or

(c) was admitted to the United Kingdom in accordance with leave granted under paragraph 282(c) of these rules; or

(d) the applicant was admitted to the UK or given an extension of stay as the spouse or civil partner of a Relevant Points Based System Migrant [or an Appendix W Worker]; and then obtained an extension of stay under paragraphs 281 to 286 of these Rules and has completed a period of 2 years as the spouse or civil partner of the person who is now present and settled here; or

(e) the applicant was admitted to the UK or given an extension of stay as the unmarried or same-sex partner of a Relevant Points Based System Migrant [or Appendix W Worker]; and during that period married or formed a civil partnership with the person whom he or she was admitted or granted an extension of stay to join and has completed a period of 2 years as the unmarried or same-sex partner and then the spouse or civil partner of the person who is now present and settled in the UK; or

(f) the applicant was admitted into the UK in accordance with paragraph 319L and has completed a period of 2 years limited leave as the spouse or civil partner of a refugee or beneficiary of humanitarian protection who is now present and settled in the UK or as the spouse or civil partner of a former refugee or beneficiary of humanitarian protection who is now a British Citizen.

(ii) the applicant is still the spouse or civil partner of the person he or she was admitted or granted an extension of stay to join and the marriage or civil partnership is subsisting; and

(iii) each of the parties intends to live permanently with the other as his or her spouse or civil partner; and

(iv) there will be adequate accommodation for the parties and any dependants without recourse to public funds in accommodation which they own or occupy exclusively; and

(v) the parties will be able to maintain themselves and any dependants adequately without recourse to public funds; and

(vi) the applicant has demonstrated sufficient knowledge of the English language and sufficient knowledge about life in the United Kingdom, in accordance with Appendix KoLL; and

(vii) the applicant does not fall for refusal under the general grounds for refusal.

(b) The requirements for indefinite leave to remain for the bereaved spouse or civil partner of a person who was present and settled in the United Kingdom are that:

(i) (a) the applicant was admitted to the United Kingdom for a period not exceeding 27 months or given an extension of stay for a period of 2 years as the spouse or civil partner of a person present and settled in the United Kingdom in accordance with paragraphs 281 to 286 of these Rules; or

(b) the applicant was admitted to the United Kingdom for a period not exceeding 27 months or given an extension of stay for a period of 2 years as the unmarried or same-sex partner of a person present and settled in the United Kingdom in accordance with paragraphs 295AA to 295F of these Rules and during that period married or formed a civil partnership with the person whom he or she was admitted or granted an extension of stay to join; and

(ii) the person whom the applicant was admitted or granted an extension of stay to join died during that period; and

(iii) the applicant was still the spouse or civil partner of the person he or she was admitted or granted an extension of stay to join at the time of the death; and

(iv) each of the parties intended to live permanently with the other as his or her spouse or civil partner and the marriage or civil partnership was subsisting at the time of the death; and

(v) the applicant does not fall for refusal under the general grounds for refusal.

Note: Words in (a)(i)(d) and (e) inserted from 29 March 2019 subject to savings for applications made before that date (HC 1919).

Indefinite leave to remain for the spouse or civil partner of a person present and settled in the United Kingdom

288. Indefinite leave to remain for the spouse or civil partner of a person present and settled in the United Kingdom may be granted provided the Secretary of State is satisfied that each of the requirements of paragraph 287 is met.

Refusal of indefinite leave to remain for the spouse or civil partner of a person present and settled in the United Kingdom

289. Indefinite leave to remain for the spouse or civil partner of a person present and settled in the United Kingdom is to be refused if the Secretary of State is not satisfied that each of the requirements of paragraph 287 is met.

Victims of domestic violence

Requirements for indefinite leave to remain in the United Kingdom as the victim of domestic violence

289A. The requirements to be met by a person who is the victim of domestic violence and who is seeking indefinite leave to remain in the United Kingdom are that the applicant:

(i) (a) the applicant was last admitted to the UK for a period not exceeding 27 months in accordance with sub-paragraph 282(a), 282(c), 295B(a) or 295B(c) of these Rules; or

(b) the applicant was last granted leave to remain as the spouse or civil partner or unmarried partner or same-sex partner of a person present and settled in the UK in accordance with paragraph 285 or 295E of these Rules, except where that leave extends leave originally granted to the applicant as the partner of a Relevant Points Based System Migrant [or Appendix W Worker]; or

(c) the applicant was last granted leave to enable access to public funds pending an application under paragraph 289A and the preceding grant of leave was given in accordance with paragraph 282(a), 282(c), 285, 295B(a), 295B(c) or 295E of these Rules, except where that leave extends leave originally granted to the applicant as the partner of a Relevant Points Based System Migrant [or Appendix W Worker]; and

(ii) the relationship with their spouse or civil partner or unmarried partner or same-sex partner, as appropriate, was subsisting at the beginning of the last period of leave granted in accordance with paragraph 282(a), 282(c), 285, 295B(a), 295B(c) or 295E of these Rules; and

(iii) is able to produce evidence to establish that the relationship was caused to permanently break down before the end of that period as a result of domestic violence;

Note: Words in (i)(b) and (c) inserted from 29 March 2019 subject to savings for applications made before that date (HC 1919).

Indefinite leave to remain as the victim of domestic violence

289B. Indefinite leave to remain as the victim of domestic violence may be granted provided the Secretary of State is satisfied that each of the requirements of paragraph 289A is met.

Refusal of indefinite leave to remain as the victim of domestic violence

289C. Indefinite leave to remain as the victim of domestic violence is to be refused if the Secretary of State is not satisfied that each of the requirements of paragraph 289A is met.

289D. If the applicant does not meet the requirements for indefinite leave to remain as a victim of domestic violence only because paragraph 322(1C)(iii) or 322(1C)(iv) applies, they may be granted further limited leave to remain for a period not exceeding 30 months and subject to such conditions as the Secretary of State deems appropriate.

Fiance(e)s and proposed civil partners

289AA. Nothing in these Rules shall be construed as permitting a person to be granted entry clearance, leave to enter or variation of leave as a fiance(e) or proposed civil partner if either the applicant or the sponsor will be aged under 18 on the date of arrival of the applicant in the United Kingdom or (as the case may be) on the date on which the leave to enter or variation of leave would be granted.

Requirements for leave to enter the United Kingdom as a fiance(e) or proposed civil partner (i.e. with a view to marriage or civil partnership and permanent settlement in the United Kingdom)

290. The requirements to be met by a person seeking leave to enter the United Kingdom as a fiance(e) or proposed civil partner are that:

(i) the applicant is seeking leave to enter the United Kingdom for marriage or civil partnership to a person present and settled in the United Kingdom or who is on the same occasion being admitted for settlement; and

(ii) the parties to the proposed marriage or civil partnership have met; and

(iii) each of the parties intends to live permanently with the other as his or her spouse or civil partner after the marriage or civil partnership; and

(iv) adequate maintenance and accommodation without recourse to public funds will be available for the applicant until the date of the marriage or civil partnership; and

(v) there will, after the marriage or civil partnership, be adequate accommodation for the parties and any dependants without recourse to public funds in accommodation which they own or occupy exclusively; and

(vi) the parties will be able after the marriage or civil partnership to maintain themselves and any dependants adequately without recourse to public funds; and

(vii) (a) the applicant provides an original English language test certificate in speaking and listening from an English language test provider approved by the Secretary of State for these purposes, which clearly shows the applicant's name and the qualification obtained (which must meet or exceed level A1 of the Common European Framework of Reference) unless:

(i) the applicant is aged 65 or over at the time he makes his application; or

(ii) the applicant has a physical or mental condition that would prevent him from meeting the requirement; or;

(iii) there are exceptional compassionate circumstances that would prevent the applicant from meeting the requirement; or

(vii) (b) the applicant is a national of one of the following countries: Antigua and Barbuda; Australia; The Bahamas; Barbados; Belize; Canada; Dominica; Grenada; Guyana; Jamaica; New Zealand; St Kitts and Nevis; St Lucia; St Vincent and the Grenadines; Trinidad and Tobago; United States of America; or

(vii) (c) the applicant has obtained an academic qualification which is deemed by [Ecctis] to meet the recognised standard of a Bachelor's or Master's degree or PhD in the UK, from an educational establishment in one of the following countries: Antigua and Barbuda; Australia; The Bahamas; Barbados; Belize; Dominica; Grenada; Guyana; Ireland; Jamaica; New Zealand; St Kitts and Nevis; St Lucia; St Vincent and The Grenadines; Trinidad and Tobago; the UK; the USA; and provides the specified documents; or

(vii) (d) the applicant has obtained an academic qualification which is deemed by [Ecctis] to meet the recognised standard of a Bachelor's or Master's degree or PhD in the UK, and

(1) provides the specified evidence to show he has the qualification, and

(2) [Ecctis] has confirmed that the qualification was taught or researched in English, or

(vii) (e) has obtained an academic qualification which is deemed by [Ecctis] to meet the recognised standard of a Bachelor's or Master's degree or PhD in the UK, and provides the specified evidence to show:

(1) he has the qualification, and

(2) that the qualification was taught or researched in English.

and

(viii) the applicant holds a valid United Kingdom entry clearance for entry in this capacity.

Note: Words substituted from 6 October 2021 subject to savings for applications made before that date (HC 617).

290A. DELETED

Leave to enter as a fiance(e) or proposed civil partner

291. A person seeking leave to enter the United Kingdom as a fiance(e) or proposed civil partner may be admitted, with a prohibition on employment, for a period not exceeding 6 months to enable the marriage or civil partnership to take place [provided that, on arrival, a valid passport or other identity document is produced to the Immigration Officer and the applicant has entry clearance for entry in this capacity].

Note: Words substituted from 11 January 2018 subject to savings for applications made before that date (HC 309).

Refusal of leave to enter as a fiance(e) or proposed civil partner

292. Leave to enter the United Kingdom as a fiance(e) or proposed civil partner is to be refused if[, on arrival, a valid passport or other identity document is not produced to the Immigration Officer and the applicant does not have entry clearance for entry in this capacity.]

Note: Words substituted from 11 January 2018 subject to savings for applications made before that date (HC 309).

Requirements for an extension of stay as a fiance(e) or proposed civil partner

293. The requirements for an extension of stay as a fiance(e) or proposed civil partner are that:

(i) the applicant was admitted to the United Kingdom with a valid United Kingdom entry clearance as a fiance(e) or proposed civil partner; and

(ii) good cause is shown why the marriage or civil partnership did not take place within the initial period of leave granted under paragraph 291; and

(iii) there is satisfactory evidence that the marriage or civil partnership will take place at an early date; and

(iv) the requirements of paragraph 290 (ii)–(vii) are met.

Extension of stay as a fiance(e) or proposed civil partner

294. An extension of stay as a fiance(e) or proposed civil partner may be granted for an appropriate period with a prohibition on employment to enable the marriage or civil partnership to take place provided the Secretary of State is satisfied that each of the requirements of paragraph 293 is met.

Refusal of extension of stay as a fiance(e) or proposed civil partner

295. An extension of stay is to be refused if the Secretary of State is not satisfied that each of the requirements of paragraph 293 is met.

Unmarried and same-sex partners

Leave to enter as the unmarried or same-sex partner of a person present and settled in the United Kingdom or being admitted on the same occasion for settlement

295AA. Nothing in these Rules shall be construed as permitting a person to be granted entry clearance, leave to enter or variation of leave as an unmarried or same-sex partner if either the applicant or the sponsor will be aged under 18 on the date of arrival of the applicant in the United Kingdom or (as the case may be) on the date on which the leave to enter or variation of leave would be granted.

Requirements for leave to enter the United Kingdom with a view to settlement as the unmarried or same-sex partner of a person present and settled in the United Kingdom or being admitted on the same occasion for settlement

295A. The requirements to be met by a person seeking leave to enter the United Kingdom with a view to settlement as the unmarried or same-sex partner of a person present and settled in the United Kingdom or being admitted on the same occasion for settlement, are that:

(i) (a) (i) the applicant is the unmarried or same-sex partner of a person present and settled in the United Kingdom or who is on the same occasion being admitted for settlement and the parties have been living together in a relationship akin to marriage or civil partnership which has subsisted for two years or more; and

(ii) the applicant provides an original English language test certificate in speaking and listening from an English language test provider approved by the Secretary of State for these purposes, which clearly shows the applicant's name and the qualification obtained (which must meet or exceed level A1 of the Common European Framework of Reference) unless:

(a) the applicant is aged 65 or over at the time he makes his application; or

(b) the applicant has a physical or mental condition that would prevent him from meeting the requirement; or

(c) there are exceptional compassionate circumstances that would prevent the applicant from meeting the requirement; or

(iii) the applicant is a national of one of the following countries: Antigua and Barbuda; Australia; The Bahamas; Barbados; Belize; Canada; Dominica; Grenada; Guyana; Jamaica; New Zealand; St Kitts and Nevis; St Lucia; St Vincent and the Grenadines; Trinidad and Tobago; United States of America; or

(iv) the applicant has obtained an academic qualification (not a professional or vocational qualification), which is deemed by [Ecctis] to meet the recognised standard of a Bachelor's or Master's degree or PhD in the UK, from an educational establishment in one of the following countries: Antigua and Barbuda; Australia; The Bahamas; Barbados; Belize; Dominica; Grenada; Guyana; Ireland; Jamaica; New Zealand; St Kitts and Nevis; St Lucia; St Vincent and The Grenadines; Trinidad and Tobago; the UK; the USA; and provides the specified documents; or

(v) the applicant has obtained an academic qualification (not a professional or vocational qualification) which is deemed by [Ecctis] to meet the recognised standard of a Bachelor's or Master's degree or PhD in the UK, and

(1) provides the specified evidence to show he has the qualification, and

(2) [Ecctis] has confirmed that the qualification was taught or researched in English, or

(vi) has obtained an academic qualification (not a professional or vocational qualification) which is deemed by [Ecctis] to meet the recognised standard of a Bachelor's or Master's degree or PhD in the UK, and provides the specified evidence to show:

(1) he has the qualification, and

(2) that the qualification was taught or researched in English.

or

(b) (i) the applicant is the unmarried or same-sex partner of a person who has a right of abode in the United Kingdom or indefinite leave to enter or remain in the United Kingdom and is on the same occasion seeking admission to the United Kingdom for the purposes of settlement and the parties have been living together outside the United Kingdom in a relationship akin to marriage or civil partnership which has subsisted for 4 years or more; and

(b) (ii) the applicant has demonstrated sufficient knowledge of the English language and sufficient knowledge about life in the United Kingdom, in accordance with Appendix KoLL; and

(b) (iii) DELETED

(ii) any previous marriage or civil partnership (or similar relationship) by either partner has permanently broken down; and

(iii) the parties are not involved in a consanguineous relationship with one another; and

(iv) DELETED

(v) there will be adequate accommodation for the parties and any dependants without recourse to public funds in accommodation which they own or occupy exclusively; and

(vi) the parties will be able to maintain themselves and any dependants adequately without recourse to public funds; and

(vii) the parties intend to live together permanently; and

(viii) the applicant holds a valid United Kingdom entry clearance for entry in this capacity; and

(ix) the applicant does not fall for refusal under the general grounds for refusal.

For the purposes of this paragraph and paragraphs 295B–295I, a member of HM Forces serving overseas, or a permanent member of HM Diplomatic Service or a comparable UK-based staff member of the British Council on a tour of duty abroad, or a staff member of the Department for International Development who is a British Citizen or is settled in the United Kingdom, is to be regarded as present and settled in the United Kingdom.

Note: Words substituted from 6 October 2021 subject to savings for applications made before that date (HC 617).

Leave to enter the United Kingdom with a view to settlement as the unmarried or same-sex partner of a person present and settled in the United Kingdom or being admitted on the same occasion for settlement

295B. A person seeking leave to enter the United Kingdom as the unmarried or same-sex partner of a person present and settled in the United Kingdom or who is on the same occasion being admitted for settlement may:

(a) in the case of a person who meets the requirements of paragraph 295A(i)(a)(i), and one of the requirements of paragraph 295A(i)(a)(ii)–(vi) be admitted for an initial period not exceeding 27 months, or

(b) in the case of a person who meets all of the requirements in paragraph 295A(i)(b), be granted indefinite leave to enter, or

(c) in the case of a person who meets the requirement in paragraph 295A(i)(b)(i), but not the requirement in paragraph 295A(i)(b)(ii) to have sufficient knowledge of the English language and about life in the United Kingdom, be admitted for an initial period not exceeding 27 months, in all cases provided the Immigration Officer is satisfied that each of the relevant requirements of paragraph 295A is met.

Refusal of leave to enter the United Kingdom with a view to settlement as the unmarried or same-sex partner of a person present and settled in the United Kingdom or being admitted on the same occasion for settlement

295C. Leave to enter the United Kingdom with a view to settlement as the unmarried or same-sex partner of a person present and settled in the United Kingdom or being admitted on the same occasion for settlement, is to be refused if the Immigration Officer is not satisfied that each of the requirements of paragraph 295A is met.

Leave to remain as the unmarried or same-sex partner of a person present and settled in the United Kingdom

Requirements for leave to remain as the unmarried or same-sex partner of a person present and settled in the United Kingdom

295D. The requirements to be met by a person seeking leave to remain as the unmarried or same-sex partner of a person present and settled in the United Kingdom are that:

(i) the applicant has or was last granted limited leave to enter or remain in the United Kingdom which was given in accordance with any of the provisions of these Rules, unless:

(a) as a result of that leave he would not have been in the United Kingdom beyond 6 months from the date on which he was admitted to the United Kingdom; or

(b) the leave was granted as the unmarried or same-sex partner of a Relevant Points Based System Migrant [or Appendix W Worker]; and

(ii) any previous marriage or civil partnership (or similar relationship) by either partner has permanently broken down; and

(iii) the applicant is the unmarried or same-sex partner of a person who is present and settled in the United Kingdom; and

(iv) the applicant must not be in the UK in breach of immigration laws (except that, where paragraph 39E of these Rules applies, any current period of overstaying will be disregarded); and

(v) the parties are not involved in a consanguineous relationship with one another; and

(vi) the parties have been living together in a relationship akin to marriage or civil partnership which has subsisted for two years or more; and

(vii) the parties' relationship pre-dates any decision to deport the applicant, recommend him for deportation, give him notice under Section 6(2) of the Immigration Act 1971, or give directions for his removal under section 10 of the Immigration and Asylum Act 1999; and

(viii) there will be adequate accommodation for the parties and any dependants without recourse to public funds in accommodation which they own or occupy exclusively; and

(ix) the parties will be able to maintain themselves and any dependants adequately without recourse to public funds; and

(x) the parties intend to live together permanently; and

(xi) (a) the applicant provides an [...] English language test certificate in speaking and listening from an English language test provider approved by the Secretary of State for these purposes, which clearly shows the applicant's name and the qualification obtained (which must meet or exceed level A1 of the Common European Framework of Reference) unless:

(i) the applicant is aged 65 or over at the time he makes his application; or

(ii) the applicant has a physical or mental condition that would prevent him from meeting the requirement; or

(iii) there are exceptional compassionate circumstances that would prevent the applicant from meeting the requirement; or

(b) the applicant is a national of one of the following countries: Antigua and Barbuda; Australia; The Bahamas; Barbados; Belize; Canada; Dominica; Grenada; Guyana; Jamaica; New Zealand; St Kitts and Nevis; St Lucia; St Vincent and the Grenadines; Trinidad and Tobago; United States of America; or

(c) the applicant has obtained an academic qualification, which is deemed by [[Ecctis]] to meet the recognised standard of a Bachelor's or Master's degree or PhD in the UK, from an educational establishment in one of the following countries: Antigua and Barbuda; Australia; The Bahamas; Barbados; Belize; Dominica; Grenada; Guyana; Ireland; Jamaica; New Zealand; St Kitts and Nevis; St Lucia; St Vincent and The Grenadines; Trinidad and Tobago; the UK; the USA; and provides the specified documents; or

(d) the applicant has obtained an academic qualification which is deemed by [[Ecctis]] to meet the recognised standard of a Bachelor's or Master's degree or PhD in the UK, and

(1) provides the specified evidence to show he has the qualification, and

(2) [[Ecctis]] has confirmed that the qualification was taught or researched in English, or

(e) has obtained an academic qualification which is deemed by [[Ecctis]] to meet the recognised standard of a Bachelor's or Master's degree or PhD in the UK, and provides the specified evidence to show:

(1) he has the qualification, and

(2) that the qualification was taught or researched in English.

Note: Word in (xi)(a) deleted from 5 November 2018 (HC 1534). Words in (i)(b) inserted from 29 March 2019 subject to savings for applications made before that date (HC 1919). Words in double square brackets substituted from 6 October 2021 subject to savings for applications made before that date (HC 617).

Leave to remain as the unmarried or same-sex partner of a person present and settled in the United Kingdom

295E. Leave to remain as the unmarried or same-sex partner of a person present and settled in the United Kingdom may be granted for a period of 2 years in the first instance provided that the Secretary of State is satisfied that each of the requirements of paragraph 295D are met.

Refusal of leave to remain as the unmarried or same-sex partner of a person present and settled in the United Kingdom

295F. Leave to remain as the unmarried or same-sex partner of a person present and settled in the United Kingdom is to be refused if the Secretary of State is not satisfied that each of the requirements of paragraph 295D is met.

Indefinite leave to remain as the unmarried or same-sex partner of a person present and settled in the United Kingdom

Requirements for indefinite leave to remain as the unmarried or same-sex partner of a person present and settled in the United Kingdom

295G. The requirements to be met by a person seeking indefinite leave to remain as the unmarried partner of a person present and settled in the United Kingdom are that:

(i) (a) the applicant was admitted to the United Kingdom for a period not exceeding 27 months or given an extension of stay for a period of 2 years in accordance with paragraphs 295AA to 295F of these Rules and has completed a period of 2 years as the unmarried or same-sex partner of a person present and settled here; or

(b) the applicant was admitted to the UK or given an extension of stay as the unmarried or same-sex partner of a Relevant Points Based System Migrant [or Appendix W Worker]; and then obtained an extension of stay under paragraphs 295AA to 295F of these Rules; and the person has completed a period of 2 years as the unmarried or same-sex partner of the person who is now present and settled here; or

(c) the applicant was admitted to the United Kingdom in accordance with leave granted under paragraph 295B(c) of these rules; or

(d) the applicant was admitted into the UK in accordance with paragraph 319O and has completed a period of 2 years limited leave as the unmarried or same-sex partner of a refugee or beneficiary of humanitarian protection who is now present and settled in the UK or as the unmarried or same-sex partner of a former refugee or beneficiary of humanitarian protection who is now a British Citizen.

(ii) the applicant is still the unmarried or same-sex partner of the person he was admitted or granted an extension of stay to join and the relationship is still subsisting; and

(iii) each of the parties intends to live permanently with the other as his partner; and

(iv) there will be adequate accommodation for the parties and any dependants without recourse to public funds in accommodation which they own or occupy exclusively; and

(v) the parties will be able to maintain themselves and any dependants adequately without recourse to public funds; and

(vi) the applicant has demonstrated sufficient knowledge of the English language and sufficient knowledge about life in the United Kingdom, in accordance with Appendix KoLL; and

(vii) the applicant does not fall for refusal under the general grounds for refusal.

Note: Words in (i)(b) inserted from 29 March 2019 subject to savings for applications made before that date (HC 1919).

Indefinite leave to remain as the unmarried or same-sex partner of a person present and settled in the United Kingdom

295H. Indefinite leave to remain as the unmarried or same-sex partner of a person present and settled in the United Kingdom may be granted provided that the Secretary of State is satisfied that each of the requirements of paragraph 295G is met.

Refusal of indefinite leave to remain as the unmarried or same-sex partner of a person present and settled in the United Kingdom

295I. Indefinite leave to remain as the unmarried or same-sex partner of a person present and settled in the United Kingdom is to be refused if the Secretary of State is not satisfied that each of the requirements of paragraph 295G is met.

Leave to enter or remain as the unmarried or same-sex partner of a person with limited leave to enter or remain in the United Kingdom under paragraphs 128–193; 200–239; or 263–270

Requirements for leave to enter or remain as the unmarried or same-sex partner of a person with limited leave to enter or remain in the United Kingdom under paragraphs 128–193; 200–239; or 263–270

295J–295L. DELETED

Indefinite leave to remain for the bereaved unmarried or same-sex partner of a person present and settled in the United Kingdom

Requirements for indefinite leave to remain for the bereaved unmarried or same-sex partner of a person present and settled in the United Kingdom

295M. The requirements to be met by a person seeking indefinite leave to remain as the bereaved unmarried or same-sex partner of a person present and settled in the United Kingdom, are that:

(i) the applicant was admitted to the United Kingdom for a period not exceeding 27 months; or given an extension of stay for a period of 2 years in accordance with paragraphs 295AA to 295F of these Rules as the unmarried partner of a person present and settled in the United Kingdom; and

(ii) the person whom the applicant was admitted or granted an extension of stay to join died during that period of leave; and

(iii) the applicant was still the unmarried or same-sex partner of the person he was admitted or granted an extension of stay to join at the time of the death; and

(iv) each of the parties intended to live permanently with the other as his partner and the relationship was subsisting at the time of the death; and

(v) the applicant does not fall for refusal under the general grounds for refusal.

Indefinite leave to remain for the bereaved unmarried or same-sex partner of a person present and settled in the United Kingdom

295N. Indefinite leave to remain for the bereaved unmarried partner of a person present and settled in the United Kingdom, may be granted provided that the Secretary of State is satisfied that each of the requirements of paragraph 295M is met.

Refusal of indefinite leave to remain for the bereaved unmarried or same-sex partner of a person present and settled in the United Kingdom

295O. Indefinite leave to remain for the bereaved unmarried or same-sex partner of a person present and settled in the United Kingdom, is to be refused if the Secretary of State is not satisfied that each of the requirements of paragraph 295M is met.

Children

296. Nothing in these Rules shall be construed as permitting a child to be granted entry clearance, leave to enter or remain, or variation of leave where his parent is party to a polygamous marriage or civil partnership and any application by that parent for admission or leave to remain for settlement or with a view to settlement would be refused pursuant to paragraphs 278 or 278A.

Leave to enter or remain in the United Kingdom as the child of a parent, parents or a relative present and settled or being admitted for settlement in the United Kingdom

Requirements for indefinite leave to enter the United Kingdom as the child of a parent, parents or a relative present and settled or being admitted for settlement in the United Kingdom

297. The requirements to be met by a person seeking indefinite leave to enter the United Kingdom as the child of a parent, parents or a relative present and settled or being admitted for settlement in the United Kingdom are that he:

(i) is seeking leave to enter to accompany or join a parent, parents or a relative in one of the following circumstances:

(a) both parents are present and settled in the United Kingdom; or

(b) both parents are being admitted on the same occasion for settlement; or

(c) one parent is present and settled in the United Kingdom and the other is being admitted on the same occasion for settlement; or

(d) one parent is present and settled in the United Kingdom or being admitted on the same occasion for settlement and the other parent is dead; or

(e) one parent is present and settled in the United Kingdom or being admitted on the same occasion for settlement and has had sole responsibility for the child's upbringing; or

(f) one parent or a relative is present and settled in the United Kingdom or being admitted on the same occasion for settlement and there are serious and compelling family or other considerations which make exclusion of the child undesirable and suitable arrangements have been made for the child's care; and

(ii) is under the age of 18; and

(iii) is not leading an independent life, is unmarried and is not a civil partner, and has not formed an independent family unit; and

(iv) can, and will, be accommodated adequately by the parent, parents or relative the child is seeking to join without recourse to public funds in accommodation which the parent, parents or relative the child is seeking to join, own or occupy exclusively; and

(v) can, and will, be maintained adequately by the parent, parents, or relative the child is seeking to join, without recourse to public funds; and

(vi) holds a valid United Kingdom entry clearance for entry in this capacity; and

(vii) does not fall for refusal under the general grounds for refusal.

Requirements for indefinite leave to remain in the United Kingdom as the child of a parent, parents or a relative present and settled or being admitted for settlement in the United Kingdom

298. The requirements to be met by a person seeking indefinite leave to remain in the United Kingdom as the child of a parent, parents or a relative present and settled in the United Kingdom are that he:

(i) is seeking to remain with a parent, parents or a relative in one of the following circumstances:

(a) both parents are present and settled in the United Kingdom; or

(b) one parent is present and settled in the United Kingdom and the other parent is dead; or

(c) one parent is present and settled in the United Kingdom and has had sole responsibility for the child's upbringing or the child normally lives with this parent and not their other parent; or

(d) one parent or a relative is present and settled in the United Kingdom and there are serious and compelling family or other considerations which make exclusion of the child undesirable and suitable arrangements have been made for the child's care; and

(ii) has or has had limited leave to enter or remain in the United Kingdom, and

(a) is under the age of 18; or

(b) was given leave to enter or remain with a view to settlement under paragraph 302 or Appendix FM; or

(c) was admitted into the UK in accordance with paragraph 319R and has completed a period of 2 years limited leave as the child of a refugee or beneficiary of humanitarian protection who is now present and settled in the UK or as the child of a former refugee or beneficiary of humanitarian protection who is now a British Citizen, or

(d) the applicant has limited leave to enter or remain in the United Kingdom in accordance with paragraph 319X, as the child of a relative with limited leave to remain as a refugee or beneficiary of humanitarian protection in the United Kingdom and who is now present and settled here; or

(e) was last given limited leave to remain under paragraph 298A; and

(iii) is not leading an independent life, is unmarried, and has not formed an independent family unit; and

(iv) can, and will, be accommodated adequately by the parent, parents or relative the child was admitted to join, without recourse to public funds in accommodation which the parent, parents or relative the child was admitted to join, own or occupy exclusively; and

(v) can, and will, be maintained adequately by the parent, parents or relative the child was admitted to join, without recourse to public funds; and

(vi) does not fall for refusal under the general grounds for refusal, and

(vii) if aged 18 or over, was admitted to the United Kingdom under paragraph 302, or Appendix FM, or 319R or 319X and has demonstrated sufficient knowledge of the English language and sufficient knowledge about life in the United Kingdom in accordance with Appendix KoLL.

298A. If an applicant does not meet the requirements of paragraph 298 only because:

(a) the applicant does not meet the requirement in paragraph 298(vi) by reason of a sentence or disposal of a type mentioned in paragraph [9.4.3. of Part 9 of these Rules]; or

(b) an applicant aged 18 or over does not meet the requirement in paragraph 298(vii); or

(c) the applicant would otherwise be refused indefinite leave to remain under paragraph [9.4.3. of Part 9 of these Rules],

the applicant may be granted limited leave to remain for a period not exceeding 30 months and subject to a condition of no recourse to public funds.

Note: Words substituted from 6 April 2021 subject to savings for applications made before that date (HC 1248).

Indefinite leave to enter or remain in the United Kingdom as the child of a parent, parents or a relative present and settled or being admitted for settlement in the United Kingdom

299. Indefinite leave to enter the United Kingdom as the child of a parent, parents or a relative present and settled or being admitted for settlement in the United Kingdom may be granted provided [provided that, on arrival, a valid passport or other identity document is produced to the Immigration Officer and the applicant has entry clearance for entry in this capacity.] Indefinite leave to remain in the United Kingdom as the child of a parent, parents or a relative present and settled in the United Kingdom may be granted provided the Secretary of State is satisfied that each of the requirements of paragraph 298 is met.

Note: Words substituted from 11 January 2018 subject to savings for applications made before that date (HC 309).

Refusal of indefinite leave to enter or remain in the United Kingdom as the child of a parent, parents or a relative present and settled or being admitted for settlement in the United Kingdom

300. Indefinite leave to enter the United Kingdom as the child of a parent, parents or a relative present and settled or being admitted for settlement in the United Kingdom is to be refused if [on arrival, a valid passport or other identity document is not produced to the Immigration Officer and the applicant does not have entry clearance for entry in this capacity.] Indefinite leave to remain in the United Kingdom as the child of a parent, parents or a relative present and settled in the United Kingdom is to be refused if the Secretary of State is not satisfied that each of the requirements of paragraph 298 is met.

Note: Words substituted from 11 January 2018 subject to savings for applications made before that date (HC 309).

Requirements for limited leave to enter or remain in the United Kingdom with a view to settlement as the child of a parent or parents given limited leave to enter or remain in the United Kingdom with a view to settlement

301. The requirements to be met by a person seeking limited leave to enter or remain in the United Kingdom with a view to settlement as the child of a parent or parents given limited leave to enter or remain in the United Kingdom with a view to settlement are that he:

(i) is seeking leave to enter to accompany or join or remain with a parent or parents in one of the following circumstances:

(a) one parent is present and settled in the United Kingdom or being admitted on the same occasion for settlement and the other parent is being or has been given limited leave to enter or remain in the United Kingdom with a view to settlement; or

(b) one parent is being or has been given limited leave to enter or remain in the United Kingdom with a view to settlement and has had sole responsibility for the child's upbringing; or

(c) one parent is being or has been given limited leave to enter or remain in the United Kingdom with a view to settlement and there are serious and compelling family or other considerations which make exclusion of the child undesirable and suitable arrangements have been made for the child's care; and

(ii) is under the age of 18; and

(iii) is not leading an independent life, is unmarried and is not a civil partner, and has not formed an independent family unit; and

(iv) can, and will, be accommodated adequately without recourse to public funds, in accommodation which the parent or parents own or occupy exclusively; and

(iva) can, and will, be maintained adequately by the parent or parents without recourse to public funds; and

(ivb) does not qualify for limited leave to enter as a child of a parent or parents given limited leave to enter or remain as a refugee or beneficiary of humanitarian protection under paragraph 319R; and

(v) (where an application is made for limited leave to remain with a view to settlement) has limited leave to enter or remain in the United Kingdom; and

(vi) if seeking leave to enter, holds a valid United Kingdom entry clearance for entry in this capacity.

Limited leave to enter or remain in the United Kingdom with a view to settlement as the child of a parent or parents given limited leave to enter or remain in the United Kingdom with a view to settlement

302. A person seeking limited leave to enter the United Kingdom with a view to settlement as the child of a parent or parents given limited leave to enter or remain in the United Kingdom with a view to settlement may be admitted for a period not exceeding 27 months provided he is able, on arrival, to produce to the Immigration Officer [a valid passport or other identity document and the applicant has entry clearance in this capacity.] A person seeking limited leave to remain in the United Kingdom with a view to settlement as the child of a parent or parents given limited leave to enter or remain in the United Kingdom with a view to settlement may be given limited leave to remain for a period not exceeding 27 months provided the Secretary of State is satisfied that each of the requirements of paragraph 301 (i)–(v) is met.

Note: Words substituted from 11 January 2018 subject to savings for applications made before that date (HC 309).

Refusal of limited leave to enter or remain in the United Kingdom with a view to settlement as the child of a parent or parents given limited leave to enter or remain in the United Kingdom with a view to settlement

303. Limited leave to enter the United Kingdom with a view to settlement as the child of a parent or parents given limited leave to enter or remain in the United Kingdom with a view to settlement is to be refused if[, on arrival, a valid passport or other identity document is not produced to the Immigration Officer and the applicant does not have entry clearance for entry in this capacity.] Limited leave to remain in the United Kingdom with a view to settlement as the child of a parent or parents given limited leave to enter or remain in the United Kingdom with a view to settlement is to be refused if the Secretary of State is not satisfied that each of the requirements of paragraph 301 (i)–(v) is met.

Note: Words substituted from 11 January 2018 subject to savings for applications made before that date (HC 309).

Leave to enter and extension of stay in the United Kingdom as the child of a parent who is being, or has been admitted to the United Kingdom as a fiancé(e) or proposed civil partner

Requirements for limited leave to enter the United Kingdom as the child of a fiancé(e) or proposed civil partner

303A. The requirements to be met by a person seeking limited leave to enter the United Kingdom as the child of a fiancé(e) or proposed civil partner, are that:

(i) he is seeking to accompany or join a parent who is, on the same occasion that the child seeks admission, being admitted as a fiancé(e) or proposed civil partner, or who has been admitted as a fiancé(e) or proposed civil partner; and

(ii) he is under the age of 18; and

(iii) he is not leading an independent life, is unmarried and is not a civil partner, and has not formed an independent family unit; and

(iv) he can and will be maintained and accommodated adequately without recourse to public funds with the parent admitted or being admitted as a fiancé(e) or proposed civil partner; and

(v) there are serious and compelling family or other considerations which make the child's exclusion undesirable, that suitable arrangements have been made for his care in the United Kingdom, and there is no other person outside the United Kingdom who could reasonably be expected to care for him; and

(vi) he holds a valid United Kingdom entry clearance for entry in this capacity.

Limited leave to enter the United Kingdom as the child of a parent who is being, or has been admitted to the United Kingdom as a fiancé(e) or proposed civil partner

303B. A person seeking limited leave to enter the United Kingdom as the child of a fiancé(e) or proposed civil partner, may be granted limited leave to enter the United Kingdom for a period not in excess of that granted to the fiancé(e) or proposed civil partner, provided that [on arrival a valid passport or other identity document is produced to the Immigration Officer and the applicant has entry clearance for entry in this capacity.] Where the period of limited leave granted to a fiancé(e) will expire in more than 6 months, a person seeking limited leave to enter as the child of the fiancé(e) or proposed civil partner should be granted leave for a period not exceeding six months.

Note: Words substituted from 11 January 2018 subject to savings for applications made before that date (HC 309).

Refusal of limited leave to enter the United Kingdom as the child of a parent who is being, or has been admitted to the United Kingdom as a fiancé(e) or proposed civil partner

303C. Limited leave to enter the United Kingdom as the child of a fiancé(e) or proposed civil partner, is to be refused if [on arrival, a valid passport or other identity document is not produced to the Immigration Officer and the applicant does not have entry clearance for entry in this capacity.]

Note: Words substituted from 11 January 2018 subject to savings for applications made before that date (HC 309).

Requirements for an extension of stay in the United Kingdom as the child of a fiancé(e) or proposed civil partner

303D. The requirements to be met by a person seeking an extension of stay in the United Kingdom as the child of a fiancé(e) or proposed civil partner are that:

(i) the applicant was admitted with a valid United Kingdom entry clearance as the child of a fiancé(e) or proposed civil partner; and

(ii) the applicant is the child of a parent who has been granted limited leave to enter, or an extension of stay, as a fiancé(e) or proposed civil partner; and

(iii) the requirements of paragraph 303A (ii)–(v) are met.

Extension of stay in the United Kingdom as the child of a fiancé(e) or proposed civil partner

303E. An extension of stay as the child of a fiance(e) or proposed civil partner may be granted provided that the Secretary of State is satisfied that each of the requirements of paragraph 303D is met.

Refusal of an extension of stay in the United Kingdom as the child of a fiancé(e) or proposed civil partner

303F. An extension of stay as the child of a fiancé(e) or proposed civil partner is to be refused if the Secretary of State is not satisfied that each of the requirements of paragraph 303D is met.

Children born in the United Kingdom who are not British citizens

304. This paragraph and paragraphs 305–309 apply only to dependent children under 18 years of age who are unmarried and are not civil partners and who were born in the United Kingdom on or after 1 January 1983 (when the British Nationality Act 1981 came into force) but who, because neither of their parents was a British Citizen or settled in the United Kingdom at the time of their birth, are not British Citizens and are therefore subject to immigration control. Such a child requires leave to enter where admission to the United Kingdom is sought, and leave to remain where permission is sought for the child to be allowed to stay in the United Kingdom. If he qualifies for entry clearance, leave to enter or leave to remain under any other part of these Rules, a child who was born in the United Kingdom but is not a British Citizen may be granted entry clearance, leave to enter or leave to remain in accordance with the provisions of that other part.

Requirements for leave to enter or remain in the United Kingdom as the child of a parent or parents given leave to enter or remain in the United Kingdom

305. The requirements to be met by a child born in the United Kingdom who is not a British Citizen who seeks leave to enter or remain in the United Kingdom as the child of a parent or parents given leave to enter or remain in the United Kingdom are that he:

(i) (a) is accompanying or seeking to join or remain with a parent or parents who have, or are given, leave to enter or remain in the United Kingdom; or

(b) is accompanying or seeking to join or remain with a parent or parents one of whom is a British Citizen or has the right of abode in the United Kingdom; or

(c) is a child in respect of whom the parental rights and duties are vested solely in a local authority; and

(ii) is under the age of 18; and

(iii) was born in the United Kingdom; and

(iv) is not leading an independent life, is unmarried and is not a civil partner, and has not formed an independent family unit; and

(v) (where an application is made for leave to enter) has not been away from the United Kingdom for more than 2 years.

Leave to enter or remain in the United Kingdom

306. A child born in the United Kingdom who is not a British Citizen and who requires leave to enter or remain in the circumstances set out in paragraph 304 may be given leave to enter for the same period as his parent or parents where paragraph 305(i)(a) applies, provided the Immigration Officer is satisfied that each of the requirements of paragraph 305(ii)–(v) is met. Where leave to remain is sought, the child may be granted leave to remain for the same period as his parent or parents where paragraph 305(i)(a) applies, provided the Secretary of State is satisfied that each of the requirements of paragraph 305(ii)–(iv) is met. Where the parent or parents have or are given periods of leave of different duration, the child may be given leave to whichever period is longer except that if the parents are living apart the child should be given leave for the same period as the parent who has day to day responsibility for him.

307. If a child does not qualify for leave to enter or remain because neither of his parents has a current leave, (and neither of them is a British Citizen or has the right of abode), he will normally be refused leave to enter or remain, even if each of the requirements of paragraph 305(ii)–(v) has been satisfied. However, he may be granted leave to enter or remain for a period not exceeding 3 months if both of his parents are in the United Kingdom and it appears unlikely that they will be removed in the immediate future, and there is no other person outside the United Kingdom who could reasonably be expected to care for him.

308. A child born in the United Kingdom who is not a British Citizen and who requires leave to enter or remain in the United Kingdom in the circumstances set out in paragraph 304 may be given indefinite leave to enter where paragraph 305(i)(b) or (i)(c) applies provided the Immigration Officer is satisfied that each of the requirements of paragraph 305(ii)–(v) is met. Where an application is for leave to remain, such a child may be granted indefinite leave to remain where paragraph 305(i)(b) or (i)(c) applies, provided the Secretary of State is satisfied that each of the requirements of paragraph 305(ii)–(iv) is met.

Refusal of leave to enter or remain in the United Kingdom

309. Leave to enter the United Kingdom where the circumstances set out in paragraph 304 apply is to be refused if the Immigration Officer is not satisfied that each of the requirements of paragraph 305 is met. Leave to remain for such a child is to be refused if the Secretary of State is not satisfied that each of the requirements of paragraph 305(i)–(iv) is met.

Adopted children

309A. For the purposes of adoption under paragraphs 310–316C a de facto adoption shall be regarded as having taken place if:

(a) at the time immediately preceding the making of the application for entry clearance under these Rules the adoptive parent or parents have been living abroad (in applications involving two parents both must have lived abroad together) for at least a period of time equal to the first period mentioned in sub-paragraph (b)(i) and must have cared for the child for at least a period of time equal to the second period material in that sub-paragraph; and

(b) during their time abroad, the adoptive parent or parents have:

(i) lived together for a minimum period of 18 months, of which the 12 months immediately preceding the application for entry clearance must have been spent living together with the child; and

(ii) have assumed the role of the child's parents, since the beginning of the 18 month period, so that there has been a genuine transfer of parental responsibility.

309B. Inter-country adoptions may be subject to section 83 of the Adoption and Children Act 2002 or the equivalent legislation in Scotland or Northern Ireland if the adopter's habitual residence is there. Where this is the case, a letter obtained from the Department for Education (England and Wales habitual residents) or the equivalent from the relevant central authority (Scotland or Northern Ireland habitual residents) confirming the issue of a Certificate of Eligibility must be provided with any entry clearance adoption application under paragraphs 310–316C.

Requirements for indefinite leave to enter the United Kingdom as the adopted child of a parent or parents present and settled or being admitted for settlement in the United Kingdom

310. The requirements to be met in the case of a child seeking indefinite leave to enter the United Kingdom as the adopted child of a parent or parents present and settled or being admitted for settlement in the United Kingdom are that he:

(i) is seeking leave to enter to accompany or join an adoptive parent or parents in one of the following circumstances;

(a) both parents are present and settled in the United Kingdom; or

(b) both parents are being admitted on the same occasion for settlement; or

(c) one parent is present and settled in the United Kingdom and the other is being admitted on the same occasion for settlement; or

(d) one parent is present and settled in the United Kingdom or being admitted on the same occasion for settlement and the other parent is dead; or

(e) one parent is present and settled in the United Kingdom or being admitted on the same occasion for settlement and has had sole responsibility for the child's upbringing; or

(f) one parent is present and settled in the United Kingdom or being admitted on the same occasion for settlement and there are serious and compelling family or other considerations which make exclusion of the child undesirable and suitable arrangements have been made for the child's care; or

(g) in the case of a de facto adoption one parent has a right of abode in the United Kingdom or indefinite leave to enter or remain in the United Kingdom and is seeking admission to the United Kingdom on the same occasion for the purposes of settlement; and

(ii) is under the age of 18; and

(iii) is not leading an independent life, is unmarried and is not a civil partner, and has not formed an independent family unit; and

(iv) can, and will, be accommodated and maintained adequately without recourse to public funds in accommodation which the adoptive parent or parents own or occupy exclusively; and

(v) DELETED

(vi) (a) was adopted in accordance with a decision taken by the competent administrative authority or court in his country of origin or the country in which he is resident, being a country whose adoption orders are recognised by the United Kingdom; or

(b) is the subject of a de facto adoption; and

(vii) was adopted at a time when:

(a) both adoptive parents were resident together abroad; or

(b) either or both adoptive parents were settled in the United Kingdom; and

(viii) has the same rights and obligations as any other child of the adoptive parent's or parents' family; and

(ix) was adopted due to the inability of the original parent(s) or current carer(s) to care for him and there has been a genuine transfer of parental responsibility to the adoptive parents; and

(x) has lost or broken his ties with his family of origin; and

(xi) was adopted, but the adoption is not one of convenience arranged to facilitate his admission to or remaining in the United Kingdom; and

(xii) holds a valid United Kingdom entry clearance for entry in this capacity; and

(xiii) does not fall for refusal under the general grounds for refusal.

Requirements for indefinite leave to remain in the United Kingdom as the adopted child of a parent or parents present and settled in the United Kingdom

311. The requirements to be met in the case of a child seeking indefinite leave to remain in the United Kingdom as the adopted child of a parent or parents present and settled in the United Kingdom are that he:

(i) is seeking to remain with adoptive parent or parents in one of the following circumstances:

(a) both parents are present and settled in the United Kingdom; or

(b) one parent is present and settled in the United Kingdom and the other parent is dead; or

(c) one parent is present and settled in the United Kingdom and has had sole responsibility for the child's upbringing; or

(d) one parent is present and settled in the United Kingdom and there are serious and compelling family or other considerations which make exclusion of the child undesirable and suitable arrangements have been made for the child's care; or

(e) in the case of a de facto adoption one parent has a right of abode in the United Kingdom or indefinite leave to enter or remain in the United Kingdom and is seeking admission to the United Kingdom on the same occasion for the purpose of settlement; and

(ii) has limited leave to enter or remain in the United Kingdom, and

(a) is under the age of 18; or

[(b) if aged 18 or over, was given leave to enter or remain with a view to settlement under paragraph 315 or paragraph 316B and has demonstrated sufficient knowledge of the English language and sufficient knowledge about life in the United Kingdom in accordance with Appendix KoLL; and]

(iii) is not leading an independent life, is unmarried and is not a civil partner, and has not formed an independent family unit; and

(iv) can, and will, be accommodated and maintained adequately without recourse to public funds in accommodation which the adoptive parent or parents own or occupy exclusively; and

(v) DELETED

(vi) (a) was adopted in accordance with a decision taken by the competent administrative authority or court in his country of origin or the country in which he is resident, being a country whose adoption orders are recognised by the United Kingdom; or

(b) is the subject of a de facto adoption; and

(vii) was adopted at a time when:
(a) both adoptive parents were resident together abroad; or
(b) either or both adoptive parents were settled in the United Kingdom; and

(viii) has the same rights and obligations as any other child of the adoptive parent's or parents' family; and

(ix) was adopted due to the inability of the original parent(s) or current carer(s) to care for him and there has been a genuine transfer of parental responsibility to the adoptive parents; and

(x) has lost or broken his ties with his family of origin; and

(xi) was adopted, but the adoption is not one of convenience arranged to facilitate his admission to or remaining in the United Kingdom; and

(xii) does not fall for refusal under the general grounds for refusal.

Note: Sub-paragraph (ii)(b) substituted from 6 July 2018 subject to savings for applications made before that date (HC 1154).

Indefinite leave to enter or remain in the United Kingdom as the adopted child of a parent or parents present and settled or being admitted for settlement in the United Kingdom

312. Indefinite leave to enter the United Kingdom as the adopted child of a parent or parents present and settled or being admitted for settlement in the United Kingdom may be granted provided[, on arrival a valid passport or other identity document is produced to the Immigration Officer and the applicant has entry clearance for entry in this capacity.] Indefinite leave to remain in the United Kingdom as the adopted child of a parent or parents present and settled in the United Kingdom may be granted provided the Secretary of State is satisfied that each of the requirements of paragraph 311 is met.

Note: Words substituted from 11 January 2018 subject to savings for applications made before that date (HC 309).

Refusal of indefinite leave to enter or remain in the United Kingdom as the adopted child of a parent or parents present and settled or being admitted for settlement in the United Kingdom

313. Indefinite leave to enter the United Kingdom as the adopted child of a parent or parents present and settled or being admitted for settlement in the United Kingdom is to be refused if[, on arrival, a valid passport or other identity document is not produced to the Immigration Officer and the applicant does not have entry clearance for entry in this capacity.] Indefinite leave to remain in the United Kingdom as the adopted child of a parent or parents present and settled in the United Kingdom is to be refused if the Secretary of State is not satisfied that each of the requirements of paragraph 311 is met. [[If an applicant aged 18 or over does not meet the requirements of paragraph 311 only because the applicant does not meet the requirement in paragraph 311(ii)(b) to have demonstrated sufficient knowledge of the English language and sufficient knowledge about life in the United Kingdom in accordance with Appendix KoLL, the applicant may be granted limited leave to remain for a period not exceeding 30 months and subject to a condition of no recourse to public funds.]]

Note: Words in square brackets substituted from 11 January 2018 subject to savings for applications made before that date (HC 309). Words in double square brackets inserted from 6 July 2018 subject to savings for applications made before that date (HC 1154).

Requirements for limited leave to enter or remain in the United Kingdom with a view to settlement as the adopted child of a parent or parents given limited leave to enter or remain in the United Kingdom with a view to settlement

314. The requirements to be met in the case of a child seeking limited leave to enter or remain in the United Kingdom with a view to settlement as the adopted child of a parent or parents given limited leave to enter or remain in the United Kingdom with a view to settlement are that he:

(i) is seeking leave to enter to accompany or join or remain with a parent or parents in one of the following circumstances:

(a) one parent is present and settled in the United Kingdom or being admitted on the same occasion for settlement and the other parent is being or has been given limited leave to enter or remain in the United Kingdom with a view to settlement; or

(b) one parent is being or has been given limited leave to enter or remain in the United Kingdom with a view to settlement and has had sole responsibility for the child's upbringing; or

(c) one parent is being or has been given limited leave to enter or remain in the United Kingdom with a view to settlement and there are serious and compelling family or other considerations which make exclusion of the child undesirable and suitable arrangements have been made for the child's care; or

(d) in the case of a de facto adoption one parent has a right of abode in the United Kingdom or indefinite leave to enter or remain in the United Kingdom and is seeking admission to the United Kingdom on the same occasion for the purpose of settlement; and

(ii) is under the age of 18; and

(iii) is not leading an independent life, is unmarried and is not a civil partner, and has not formed an independent family unit; and

(iv) can, and will, be accommodated and maintained adequately without recourse to public funds in accommodation which the adoptive parent or parents own or occupy exclusively; and

(v) (a) was adopted in accordance with a decision taken by the competent administrative authority or court in his country of origin or the country in which he is resident, being a country whose adoption orders are recognised by the United Kingdom; or

(b) is the subject of a de facto adoption; and

(vi) was adopted at a time when:

(a) both adoptive parents were resident together abroad; or

(b) either or both adoptive parents were settled in the United Kingdom; and

(vii) has the same rights and obligations as any other child of the adoptive parent's or parents' family; and

(viii) was adopted due to the inability of the original parent(s) or current carer(s) to care for him and there has been a genuine transfer of parental responsibility to the adoptive parents; and

(ix) has lost or broken his ties with his family of origin; and

(x) was adopted, but the adoption is not one of convenience arranged to facilitate his admission to the United Kingdom; and

(xi) (where an application is made for limited leave to remain with a view to settlement) has limited leave to enter or remain in the United Kingdom; and

(xii) if seeking leave to enter, holds a valid United Kingdom entry clearance for entry in this capacity.

Limited leave to enter or remain in the United Kingdom with a view to settlement as the adopted child of a parent or parents given limited leave to enter or remain in the United Kingdom with a view to settlement

315. A person seeking limited leave to enter the United Kingdom with a view to settlement as the adopted child of a parent or parents given limited leave to enter or remain in the United Kingdom with a view to settlement may be admitted for a period not exceeding 12 months provided he is able, on arrival, to produce to the Immigration Officer [a valid passport or other identity document and has entry clearance for entry in this capacity.] A person seeking limited leave to remain in the United Kingdom with a view to settlement as the adopted child of a parent or parents given limited leave to enter or remain in the United Kingdom with a view to settlement may be granted limited leave for a period not exceeding 12 months provided the Secretary of State is satisfied that each of the requirements of paragraph 314(i)–(xi) is met.

Note: Words substituted from 11 January 2018 subject to savings for applications made before that date (HC 309).

Refusal of limited leave to enter or remain in the United Kingdom with a view to settlement as the adopted child of a parent or parents given limited leave to enter or remain in the United Kingdom with a view to settlement

316. Limited leave to enter the United Kingdom with a view to settlement as the adopted child of a parent or parents given limited leave to enter or remain in the United Kingdom with a view to settlement is to be refused if[, on arrival, a valid passport or other identity document is not produced to the Immigration Officer and the applicant does not have entry clearance in this capacity.] Limited leave to remain in the United Kingdom with a view to settlement as the adopted child of a parent or parents given limited leave to enter or remain in the United Kingdom with a view to settlement is to be refused if the Secretary of State is not satisfied that each of the requirements of paragraph 314(i)–(xi) is met.

Note: Words substituted from 11 January 2018 subject to savings for applications made before that date (HC 309).

Requirements for limited leave to enter the United Kingdom with a view to settlement as a child for adoption

316A. The requirements to be satisfied in the case of a child seeking limited leave to enter the United Kingdom for the purpose of being adopted (which, for the avoidance of doubt, does not include a de facto adoption) in the United Kingdom are that he:

(i) is seeking limited leave to enter to accompany or join a person or persons who wish to adopt him in the United Kingdom (the 'prospective parent(s)'), in one of the following circumstances:

(a) both prospective parents are present and settled in the United Kingdom; or

(b) both prospective parents are being admitted for settlement on the same occasion that the child is seeking admission; or

(c) one prospective parent is present and settled in the United Kingdom and the other is being admitted for settlement on the same occasion that the child is seeking admission; or

(d) one prospective parent is present and settled in the United Kingdom and the other is being given limited leave to enter or remain in the United Kingdom with a view to settlement on the same occasion that the child is seeking admission, or has previously been given such leave; or

(e) one prospective parent is being admitted for settlement on the same occasion that the other is being granted limited leave to enter with a view to settlement, which is also on the same occasion that the child is seeking admission; or

(f) one prospective parent is present and settled in the United Kingdom or is being admitted for settlement on the same occasion that the child is seeking admission, and has had sole responsibility for the child's upbringing; or

(g) one prospective parent is present and settled in the United Kingdom or is being admitted for settlement on the same occasion that the child is seeking admission, and there are serious and compelling family or other considerations which would make the child's exclusion undesirable, and suitable arrangements have been made for the child's care; and

(ii) is under the age of 18; and

(iii) is not leading an independent life, is unmarried and is not a civil partner, and has not formed an independent family unit; and

(iv) can, and will, be maintained and accommodated adequately without recourse to public funds in accommodation which the prospective parent or parents own or occupy exclusively; and

(v) will have the same rights and obligations as any other child of the marriage or civil partnership; and

(vi) is being adopted due to the inability of the original parent(s) or current carer(s) (or those looking after him immediately prior to him being physically transferred to his prospective parent or parents) to care for him, and there has been a genuine transfer of parental responsibility to the prospective parent or parents; and

(vii) has lost or broken or intends to lose or break his ties with his family of origin; and

(viii) will be adopted in the United Kingdom by his prospective parent or parents in accordance with the law relating to adoption in the United Kingdom, but the proposed adoption is not one of convenience arranged to facilitate his admission to the United Kingdom.

Limited leave to enter the United Kingdom with a view to settlement as a child for adoption

316B. A person seeking limited leave to enter the United Kingdom with a view to settlement as a child for adoption may be admitted for a period not exceeding 24 months provided he is able, on arrival, to produce to the Immigration Officer [a valid passport or other identity document and has entry clearance for entry in this capacity.]

Note: Words substituted from 11 January 2018 subject to savings for applications made before that date (HC 309).

Refusal of limited leave to enter the United Kingdom with a view to settlement as a child for adoption

316C. Limited leave to enter the United Kingdom with a view to settlement as a child for adoption is to be refused if[, on arrival, a valid passport or other identity document is not produced to the Immigration Officer and the applicant does not have entry clearance for entry in this capacity.]

Note: Words substituted from 11 January 2018 subject to savings for applications made before that date (HC 309).

Requirements for limited leave to enter the United Kingdom with a view to settlement as a child for adoption under the Hague Convention

316D. The requirements to be satisfied in the case of a child seeking limited leave to enter the United Kingdom for the purpose of being adopted in the United Kingdom under the Hague Convention are that he:

(i) is seeking limited leave to enter to accompany one or two people each of whom are habitually resident in the United Kingdom and who wish to adopt him under the Hague Convention ('the prospective parents');

(ii) is the subject of an agreement made under Article 17(c) of the Hague Convention; and

(iii) has been entrusted to the prospective parents by the competent administrative authority of the country from which he is coming to the United Kingdom for adoption under the Hague Convention; and

(iv) is under the age of 18; and

(v) can, and will, be maintained and accommodated adequately without recourse to public funds in accommodation which the prospective parent or parents own or occupy exclusively; and

(vi) holds a valid United Kingdom entry clearance for entry in this capacity.

Limited leave to enter the United Kingdom with a view to settlement as a child for adoption under the Hague Convention

316E. A person seeking limited leave to enter the United Kingdom with a view to settlement as a child for adoption under the Hague Convention may be admitted for a period not exceeding 24 months provided he is able, on arrival, to produce to the Immigration Officer [[a]] [valid passport or other identity document and has entry clearance for entry in this capacity.]

Note: Words in square brackets substituted from 11 January 2018 subject to savings for applications made before that date (HC 309). Word in double brackets inserted from 6 July 2018 subject to savings for applications made before that date (HC 1154).

Refusal of limited leave to enter the United Kingdom with a view to settlement as a child for adoption under the Hague Convention

316F. Limited leave to enter the United Kingdom with a view to settlement as a child for adoption under the Hague Convention is to be refused if[, on arrival, a valid passport or other identity document is not produced to the Immigration Officer and the applicant does not have entry clearance for entry in this capacity.]

Note: Words substituted from 11 January 2018 subject to savings for applications made before that date (HC 309).

Parents, grandparents and other dependent relatives of persons present and settled in the United Kingdom

Requirements for indefinite leave to enter or remain in the United Kingdom as the parent, grandparent or other dependent relative of a person present and settled in the United Kingdom

317. The requirements to be met by a person seeking indefinite leave to enter or remain in the United Kingdom as the parent, grandparent or other dependent relative of a person present and settled in the United Kingdom are that the person:

(i) is related to a person present and settled in the United Kingdom in one of the following ways:

(a) parent or grandparent who is divorced, widowed, single or separated aged 65 years or over; or

(b) parents or grandparents travelling together of whom at least one is aged 65 or over; or

(c) a parent or grandparent aged 65 or over who has entered into a second relationship of marriage or civil partnership but cannot look to the spouse, civil partner or children of that second relationship for financial support; and where the person settled in the United Kingdom is able and willing to maintain the parent or grandparent and any spouse or civil partner or child of the second relationship who would be admissible as a dependant; or

(d) parent or grandparent under the age of 65 if living alone outside the United Kingdom in the most exceptional compassionate circumstances; or

(e) parents or grandparents travelling together who are both under the age of 65 if living in the most exceptional compassionate circumstances; or

(f) the son, daughter, sister, brother, uncle or aunt over the age of 18 if living alone outside the United Kingdom in the most exceptional compassionate circumstances; and

(ii) is joining or accompanying a person who is present and settled in the United Kingdom or who is on the same occasion being admitted for settlement; and

(iii) is financially wholly or mainly dependent on the relative present and settled in the United Kingdom; and

(iv) can, and will, be accommodated adequately, together with any dependants, without recourse to public funds, in accommodation which the sponsor owns or occupies exclusively; and

(iva) can, and will, be maintained adequately, together with any dependants, without recourse to public funds; and

(v) has no other close relatives in his own country to whom he could turn for financial support; and

(vi) if seeking leave to enter, holds a valid United Kingdom entry clearance for entry in this capacity; and

(vii) does not fall for refusal under the general grounds for refusal.

Indefinite leave to enter or remain as the parent, grandparent or other dependent relative of a person present and settled in the United Kingdom

318. Indefinite leave to enter the United Kingdom as the parent, grandparent or other dependent relative of a person present and settled in the United Kingdom may be granted provided[, on arrival, a valid passport or other identity document is produced to the Immigration Officer and the applicant has entry clearance for entry in this capacity.] Indefinite leave to remain in the United Kingdom as the parent, grandparent or other dependent relative of a person present and settled in the United Kingdom may be granted provided the Secretary of State is satisfied that each of the requirements of paragraph 317(i)–(v) is met.

Note: Words substituted from 11 January 2018 subject to savings for applications made before that date (HC 309).

Refusal of indefinite leave to enter or remain in the United Kingdom as the parent, grandparent or other dependent relative of a person present and settled in the United Kingdom

319. Indefinite leave to enter the United Kingdom as the parent, grandparent or other dependent relative of a person settled in the United Kingdom is to be refused if[, on arrival, a valid passport or other identity document is not produced to the Immigration Officer and the applicant does not have entry clearance for entry in this capacity.] Indefinite leave to remain in the United Kingdom as the parent, grandparent or other dependent relative of a person present and settled in the United Kingdom is to be refused if the Secretary of State is not satisfied that each of the requirements of paragraph 317(i)–(v) is met.

Note: Words substituted from 11 January 2018 subject to savings for applications made before that date (HC 309).

[Family members of relevant points-based system migrants and Appendix W Workers]

[Partners of Relevant Points Based System Migrants and Appendix W Workers]

[**319AA.** In paragraphs A277A to 319K, Appendix C and Appendix E:

[(a) Relevant Points Based System migrant means a T1 (Entrepreneur) or T1 (Investor).]

[. . .]

Note: Paragraph substituted from 10 January 2019 subject to savings for applications made before that date (HC 1779). Paragraph (including headings) substituted again from 29 March 2019 subject to savings for applications made before that date (HC 1919). Amendment from 09:00 on 5 October 2020 subject to savings for applications made before that time. Where consequential changes relating to the need for an ATAS certificate have been made, they take effect for all applications made or granted on or after 5 October 2020 at 09:00 (HC 707). Sub-paragraph (a) substituted; (b) deleted from 09:00 on 1 December 2020 subject to savings for applications made before that time (HC 813).

319A. Purpose

This route is for the spouse, civil partner, unmarried or same-sex partner of a Relevant Points Based System Migrant [or Appendix W Worker] (Partner of a Relevant Points

Based System Migrant [or Appendix W Worker]). Paragraphs 277 to 280 of these Rules apply to spouses or civil partners of Relevant Points Based System Migrant [or Appendix W Worker]; paragraph 277 of these Rules applies to civil partners of Relevant Points Based System Migrant [or Appendix W Worker]; and paragraph 295AA of these Rules applies to unmarried and same-sex partners of Relevant Points Based System Migrants [or Appendix W Workers].

Note: Words inserted from 29 March 2019 subject to savings for applications made before that date (HC 1919).

319B. Entry to the UK

[(a) any person wishing to enter as the Partner of a relevant Points Based System Migrant Worker must on arrival in the UK have a valid entry clearance for entry under this route.]

[. . .]

Note: Amendment to (a) from 29 March 2019 subject to savings for applications made before that date (HC 1919). Amendment to (a) and (b) from 09:00 on 1 December 2020 subject to savings for applications made before that time (HC 813). Sub-paragraph (a) substituted, (b) deleted from 6 April 2021 subject to savings for applications made before that date (HC 1248).

319C. Requirements for entry clearance or leave to remain

To qualify for entry clearance or leave to remain as the Partner of a Relevant Points Based System Migrant [or Appendix W Worker], an applicant must meet the requirements listed below. If the applicant meets these requirements, entry clearance or leave to remain will be granted. If the applicant does not meet these requirements, the application will be refused.

Requirements:

(a) The applicant must not fall for refusal under the general grounds for refusal, and if applying for leave to remain, must not be an illegal entrant.

(b) The applicant must be the spouse or civil partner, unmarried or same-sex partner of a person who:

(i) has valid leave to enter or remain as a Relevant Points Based System Migrant [or Appendix W Worker],

or

(ii) is, at the same time, being granted entry clearance or leave to remain as a Relevant Points Based System Migrant [or Appendix W Worker], or

(iii) has indefinite leave to remain as a Relevant Points Based System Migrant [or Appendix W Worker], or is at the same time being granted indefinite leave to remain as a Relevant Points Based System Migrant [or Appendix W Worker], where the applicant is applying for further leave to remain, or has been refused indefinite leave to remain solely because the applicant has not met the requirements of paragraph 319E(g), and was last granted leave:

(1) as the partner of that same Relevant Points Based System Migrant [or Appendix W Worker]: or

(2) as the spouse or civil partner, unmarried or same-sex partner of that person at a time when that person had leave under another category of these Rules; or

(iv) has become a British Citizen where prior to that they held indefinite leave to Remain as a Relevant Points Based System Migrant [or Appendix W Worker] and where the applicant is applying for further leave to remain, or has been refused indefinite leave to remain solely because the applicant has not met the requirements of paragraph 319E(g), and was last granted leave:

(1) as the partner of that same Relevant Points Based System Migrant [or Appendix W Worker], or

(2) as the spouse or civil partner, unmarried or same-sex partner of that person at a time when that person had leave under another category of these Rules.

(c) An applicant who is the unmarried or same-sex partner of a Relevant Points Based System Migrant [or Appendix W Worker] must also meet the following requirements:

(i) any previous marriage or civil partnership or similar relationship by the applicant or the Relevant Points Based System Migrant [or Appendix W Worker] with another person must have permanently broken down,

(ii) the applicant and the Relevant Points Based System Migrant [or Appendix W Worker] must not be so closely related that they would be prohibited from marrying each other in the UK, and

(iii) the applicant and the Relevant Points Based System Migrant [or Appendix W Worker] must have been living together in a relationship similar to marriage or civil partnership for a period of at least 2 years.

(d) The marriage or civil partnership, or relationship similar to marriage or civil partnership, must be [genuine and] subsisting at the time the application is made.

(e) The applicant and the Relevant Points Based System Migrant [or Appendix W Worker] must intend to live with the other as their spouse or civil partner, unmarried or same-sex partner throughout the applicants stay in the UK.

(f) The applicant must not intend to stay in the UK beyond any period of leave granted to the Relevant Points Based System Migrant [or Appendix W Worker].

(g) Unless [the applicant is applying as the Partner of a Relevant Points Based System Migrant who] is a Tier 1 (Investor) Migrant { ... }, { ... } there must be a sufficient level of funds available to the applicant, as set out in Appendix E.

(h) An applicant who is applying for leave to remain must not have last been granted:

(i) entry clearance or leave as a:

(a) visitor, including where they entered the United Kingdom from the Republic of Ireland to stay under the terms of articles 3A and 4 of the Immigration (Control of Entry through the Republic of Ireland) Order 1972 (as amended by the Immigration (Control of Entry through Republic of Ireland) (Amendment) Order 2014) on the basis of a visa issued by the Republic of Ireland authorities endorsed with the letters 'BIVS' for the purpose of travelling and staying in the Republic for a period of 90 days or fewer; or

(b) short-term student or short term student (child); or

[...]

unless [the applicant is applying as the Partner of a Relevant Points Based System Migrant who] has, or is being granted, leave to remain as a Tier 5 (Temporary Worker) Migrant in the creative and sporting subcategory on the basis of having met the requirement at paragraph 245ZQ(b)(ii);

[(ii) temporary admission;]

[(iii) temporary release; or]

[(iv) after the date on which paragraph 1 of Schedule 10 to the Immigration Act 2016 is commenced, a grant of immigration bail in circumstances in which temporary admission or temporary release would previously have been granted.]

[...]

(j) The applicant must not be in the UK in breach of immigration laws except that, where paragraph 39E of these Rules applies, any current period of overstaying will be disregarded.

(k) Where the applicant is 18 years of age or older and seeking entry clearance as the partner of a person specified below, the applicant must provide [...] a criminal record certificate from the relevant authority in any country in which they have been [present] for 12 months (whether continuously or in total) or more in the past 10 years, while Secretary of State is satisfied, by way of an explanation provided in or with the application, that it is not reasonably practicable for the applicant to obtain a certificate from the relevant authority.

(l) For the purposes of sub-paragraph (k), a specified person is a person who is seeking, or has been granted, entry clearance or leave to remain as a:

(a) Tier 1 (Entrepreneur) Migrant,

(b) Tier 1 (Investor) Migrant,

[...]

(m) If the applicant has failed to provide a criminal record certificate or an explanation in accordance with sub-paragraph (k), the decision maker may contact the applicant or his representative in writing, and request the certificate(s) or explanation. The requested certificate(s) or explanation must be received at the address specified in the request within 28 calendar days of the date of the request.

Note: Words in (d), amendments to (i)(i), (i)(ii)(1), (i)(iv)(1), (i)(iv)(1)(a), (i)(iv)(1)(b), (i)(iv)(2)(a) and (i)(iv)(2)(b), and words in (k) substituted from 11 January 2018 subject to savings for applications made before that date. Sub-paragraphs (h)(ii) and (iii) substituted and (h)(iv) inserted from the date of commencement of Schedule 10 to the Immigration Act 2016. (HC 309). Amendments to (i)(ii)(1), (i)(ii)(2)(b), and (i)(ii)(2)(b) (c), (d) and (e) from 6 July 2018 subject to savings for applications made before that date (HC 1154). Words in (k) deleted from 5 November 2018 (HC 1534). Amendment to (i)(ii)(2) from 1 August 2019 (HC 1779). Words in (b)(i), (ii) and (iii), (b)(iii)(1), (b)(iv), (b)(iv)(1), (c), (c)(i), (ii) and (iii), (e), (f), (g), (h)(i)(c) inserted; amendment to (i) from 29 March 2019 subject to savings for applications made before that date (HC 1919). Amendment to (g) (subsequently deleted, see HC 813 below) from 20 February 2020 subject to savings for applications made before that date (HC 56). Sub-paragraphs (h)(i)(c) and (i) deleted from 09:00 on 5 October 2020 subject to savings for applications made before that time. Where consequential changes relating to the need for an ATAS certificate have been made, they take effect for all applications made or granted on or after 5 October 2020 at 09:00 (HC 707). Words in curly brackets in (g), (k)(1)(c) deleted from 09:00 on 1 December 2020 subject to savings for applications made before that time (HC 813).

319D Period and conditions of grant

(a) (i) Entry clearance or limited leave to remain will be granted for a period which expires on the same day as the leave granted to the Relevant Points Based System Migrant [or Appendix W Worker], or

(ii) If the Relevant Points-Based System Migrant [or Appendix W Worker] has indefinite leave to remain as a Relevant Points Based System Migrant [or Appendix W Worker], or is, at the same time being granted indefinite leave to remain as a Relevant Points Based System Migrant [or Appendix W Worker], or where the Relevant Points-Based System Migrant [or Appendix W Worker] has since become a British Citizen, leave to remain will be granted to the applicant for a period of 3 years.

(b) Entry clearance and leave to remain under this route will be subject to the following conditions:

(i) no recourse to public funds,

(ii) registration with the police, if this is required under paragraph 326 of these Rules,

[...]

[...]

(v) no employment as a professional sportsperson (including as a sports coach),

(vi) study subject to the condition set out in Part 15 of these Rules where the applicant is 18 years of age or over at the time their leave is granted, or will be aged 18 before their period of limited leave expires.

Note: Amendments to (b)(iv)(1) from 11 January 2018 subject to savings for applications made before that date (HC 309). Amendments to (b)(iv)(1) from 6 July 2018 subject to savings for applications made before that date (HC 1154). Words in (a)(i) and (ii) inserted; amendments to (b)(iv) from 29 March 2019 subject to savings for applications made before that date (HC 1919). Amendments to (b)(iii)(1); (b)(iv) deleted from 09:00 on 5 October 2020 subject to savings for applications made before that time. Where consequential changes relating to the need for an ATAS certificate have been made, they take effect for all applications made or granted on or after 5 October 2020 at 09:00 (HC 707). Sub-paragraph (b)(iii) deleted from 09:00 on 1 December 2020 subject to savings for applications made before that time (HC 813).

319E. Requirements for indefinite leave to remain

To qualify for indefinite leave to remain as the Partner of a Relevant Points Based System Migrant [or Appendix W Worker], an applicant must meet the requirements listed below. If the applicant meets these requirements, indefinite leave to remain will be granted. If the applicant does not meet these requirements, the application will be refused.

Requirements:

(a) The applicant must not fall for refusal under the general grounds for refusal, and must not be an illegal entrant.

(b) The applicant must be the spouse or civil partner, unmarried or same-sex partner of a person who:

(i) has indefinite leave to remain as a Relevant Points Based System Migrant [or Appendix W Worker]; or

(ii) is, at the same time being granted indefinite leave to remain as a Relevant Points Based System Migrant [or Appendix W Worker], or

(iii) has become a British Citizen where prior to that they held indefinite leave to remain as a Relevant Points Based System Migrant [or Appendix W Worker].

(c) The applicant must have, or have last been granted, leave as the partner of the Relevant Points Based System Migrant [or Appendix W Worker] who:

(i) has indefinite leave to remain as a Relevant Points Based System Migrant [or Appendix W Worker]; or

(ii) is, at the same time being granted indefinite leave to remain as a Relevant Points Based System Migrant [or Appendix W Worker], or

(iii) has become a British Citizen where prior to that they held indefinite leave to remain as a Relevant Points Based System Migrant [or Appendix W Worker].

(d) The applicant and the Relevant Points Based System Migrant [[or Appendix W Worker]] must have been living together in the UK in a marriage or civil partnership, or in a relationship similar to marriage or civil partnership, for {at least a continuous period of 5 years, during which the applicant must:}

(a) have been in a relationship with the same Relevant Points Based System Migrant (or Appendix W Worker] for this entire period,

(b) have spent the most recent part of the 5 year period with leave as the Partner of that Relevant Points Based System Migrant [or Appendix W Worker], and during that part of the period have met all of the requirements of paragraph 319C(a) to (e), [. . .]

(c) have spent the remainder of the 5 year period, where applicable, with leave as the spouse or civil partner, unmarried or same-sex partner of that person at a time when that person had leave under another category of these Rules[, and] [(d) not have been absent from the UK for more than 180 days during any 12 month period in the continuous period, except that:

(1) any absence from the UK for the purpose of assisting with a national or international humanitarian or environmental crisis overseas shall not count towards the 180 days, if the applicant provides evidence that this was the purpose of the absence(s), and

(2) any absence from the UK during periods of leave granted under the Rules in place before 11 January 2018 shall not count towards the 180 days][; and]

[(3) for any applicant who has or has had leave as the dependant partner of a Tier 2 (General) migrant, where the Tier 2 migrant's Certificate of Sponsorship Checking Service entry shows that they were sponsored to work in any [[PhD level occupation listed in paragraph 245AAA(za) of these rules]] when the absence occurred, any absence of the applicant from the UK to accompany their partner while the partner carried out research activities overseas shall not count towards the 180 days, if the applicant provides evidence from their partner's sponsor showing that:

(a) research was the purpose of the partner's absence(s); and

(b) the partner's sponsor agreed to the partner's absence(s) for that purpose; and

(c) the absence(s) were directly related to the Tier 2 employment in the UK.

(4) for any applicant who has leave as a PBS partner of a settled migrant who, at the point they applied for settlement, held leave as a Tier 2 (General) migrant, where the Certificate of Sponsorship Checking Service entry showed that they were sponsored to work in any [[PhD level occupation listed in paragraph 245AAA(za) of these rules]], any absence from the UK to accompany the settled migrant for the purpose of their research activities overseas shall not count towards the 180 days, if the applicant provides evidence from their settled partner's employer showing that:

(a) the settled partner remained working in [[a Phd level occupation listed in paragraph 245AAA(za) of these rules]] during the period of absence(s);

(b) research was the purpose of the partner's absence(s); and

(c) the settled partner's employer agreed to the absence(s) for that purpose; and

(d) the absence(s) directly related to the settled partner's employment in the UK.]

[(5) for any applicant who has or has had leave as the Partner of a Tier 1 (Exceptional Talent) Migrant, or Partner of a Global Talent migrant, where the Tier 1 or Global Talent migrant was endorsed by The Royal Society, The British Academy, The Royal Academy of Engineering, or UK Research and Innovation, any absence from the UK for the purpose of research activities overseas shall not count towards the 180 days if it occurred while the applicant held this leave.

(6) for any applicant who has leave as the Points Based System Partner or Appendix W Partner of a settled migrant who, at the point they applied for settlement, held leave as a Tier 1 (Exceptional Talent) Migrant or Global Talent migrant, where they were endorsed by The Royal Society, The British Academy, The Royal Academy of Engineering, UK Research and Innovation, any absence from the UK for the purpose of research activities overseas shall not count towards the 180 days.]

{{ ... }}Any time spent lawfully in the Bailiwick of Guernsey, Bailiwick of Jersey or the Isle of Man shall be deemed to be time spent in the UK.

(e) The marriage or civil partnership, or relationship similar to marriage or civil partnership, must be [genuine and] subsisting at the time the application is made.

(f) The applicant and the Relevant Points Based System Migrant [or Appendix W Worker] must intend to live permanently with the other as their spouse or civil partner, unmarried or same-sex partner.

(g) The applicant has demonstrated sufficient knowledge of the English language and sufficient knowledge about life in the United Kingdom, in accordance with Appendix KoLL.

(h) DELETED

(i) The applicant must not be in the UK in breach of immigration laws except that, where paragraph 39E of these Rules applies, any current period of overstaying will be disregarded.

Note: Words in (b)(iv)(1), (d)(ii)(c) and (e), sub-paragraphs (d)(ii)(d), (d)(iii) inserted; words in introduction of (d) substituted; word in (d)(ii)(b) deleted from 11 January 2018 subject to savings for applications made before that date (HC 309). Amendments to (d) from 1 October 2019 subject to savings for applications made before that date (HC 2631). Words in double square brackets in sub-paragraph (d); words in (b)(i), (ii) and (iii), (c), (c)(i), (ii) and (iii) inserted, amendments to (d) (subsequently amended further by HC 813, see below) from 29 March 2019 subject to savings for applications made before that date (HC 1919). Sub-paragraphs (d)(d)(4) and (5) inserted from 20 February 2020 subject to savings for applications made before that date (HC 56). Words in curly brackets in (d) substituted; (d)(i) and (d) (ii), numbering in double curly brackets deleted from 09:00 on 1 December 2020 subject to savings for applications made before that time (HC 813). Words in double square brackets in (d)(d)(3), (d)(d)(4), and (d)(d)(4)(a) substituted from 6 April 2022 (HC 1118).

Children of relevant points-based system migrants

319F. Purpose

This route is for the children of a Relevant Points Based System Migrant [or Appendix W Worker] who are under the age of 18 when they apply to enter under this route. Paragraph 296 of these Rules applies to children of a Relevant Points Based System Migrants [or Appendix W Workers].

Note: Words inserted from 29 March 2019 subject to savings for applications made before that date (HC 1919).

319G. Entry to the UK

(a) Subject to paragraph (b), all migrants wishing to enter as the child of a relevant Points Based System Migrant [or Appendix W Worker] must have a valid entry clearance for entry under this route. If they do not have a valid entry clearance, entry will be refused.

[...]

Note: Words inserted from 29 March 2019 subject to savings for applications made before that date (HC 1919). Sub-paragraph (b) deleted from 09:00 on 1 December 2020 subject to savings for applications made before that time (HC 813).

319H. Requirements for entry clearance or leave to remain

To qualify for entry clearance or leave to remain under this route, an applicant must meet the requirements listed below. If the applicant meets these requirements, entry clearance or leave to remain will be granted. If the applicant does not meet these requirements, the application will be refused.

Requirements:

(a) The applicant must not fall for refusal under the general grounds for refusal, and if applying for leave to remain, must not be an illegal entrant.

(b) The applicant must be the child of a parent who has, or is at the same time being granted, valid entry clearance, leave to enter or remain, or indefinite leave to remain, as:

(i) a Relevant Points Based System Migrant [or Appendix W Worker], or

(ii) the partner of a Relevant Points Based System Migrant [or Appendix W Worker].

or who has obtained British citizenship having previously held indefinite leave to remain as above.

(c) The applicant must be under the age of 18 on the date the application is made, or if over 18 and applying for leave to remain, must have, or have last been granted, leave as the child of a Relevant Points Based System Migrant [or Appendix W Worker] or as the child of the parent who had leave under another category of these Rules and who has since been granted, or, is at the same time being granted, leave to remain as a Relevant Points Based System Migrant [or Appendix W Worker].

(d) The applicant must not be married or in a civil partnership, must not have formed an independent family unit, and must not be leading an independent life, and, if he is over the age of 16 on the date the application is made, he must provide the specified documents and information in paragraph 319H-SD to show that this requirement is met.

(e) The applicant must not intend to stay in the UK beyond any period of leave granted to the Relevant Points Based System Migrant [or Appendix W Worker] parent.

(f) Both of the applicant's parents must either be lawfully present (other than as a visitor) in the UK, or being granted entry clearance or leave to remain (other than as a visitor) at the same time as the applicant or one parent must be lawfully present (other than as a visitor) in the UK and the other is being granted entry clearance or leave to remain (other than as a visitor) at the same time as the applicant, unless:

(i) The Relevant Points Based System Migrant [or Appendix W Worker] is the applicant's sole surviving parent, or

(ii) The Relevant Points Based System Migrant [or Appendix W Worker] parent has and has had sole responsibility for the applicant's upbringing, or

(iii) there are serious or compelling family or other considerations which would make it desirable not to refuse the application and suitable arrangements have been made in the UK for the applicant's care.

(g) Unless [the applicant is applying as the Child of a Relevant Points Based System Migrant who] is a Tier 1 (Investor) Migrant { . . . } { . . . }, there must be a sufficient level of funds available to the applicant, as set out in Appendix E.

(h) An applicant who is applying for leave to remain must not have last been granted:

(i) entry clearance or leave as a:

(a) visitor, including where they entered the United Kingdom from the Republic of Ireland to stay under the terms of articles 3A and 4 of the Immigration (Control of Entry through the Republic of Ireland) Order 1972 (as amended by the Immigration (Control of Entry through Republic of Ireland) (Amendment) Order 2014) on the basis of a visa issued by the Republic of Ireland authorities endorsed with the letters 'BIVS' for the purpose of travelling and staying in the Republic for a period of 90 days or fewer; or

(b) short-term student (child) [[. . .]];

[(ii) temporary admission;]

[(iii) temporary release; or]

[(iv) after the date on which paragraph 1 of Schedule 10 to the Immigration Act 2016 is commenced, a grant of immigration bail in circumstances in which temporary admission or temporary release would previously have been granted.]

[. . .]

[…]

(k) If the applicant is a child born in the UK to a Relevant Points Based System Migrant [or Appendix W Worker] and their partner, the applicant must provide a full UK birth certificate showing the names of both parents.

(l) All arrangements for the child's care and accommodation in the UK must comply with relevant UK legislation and regulations.

(m) The applicant must not be in the UK in breach of immigration laws except that, where paragraph 39E of these Rules applies, any current period of overstaying will be disregarded.

Note: Sub-paragraphs (h)(ii) and (iii) substituted; (h)(iv) inserted from date of commencement of Schedule 10 to the Immigration Act 2016. Amendments to (i)(i), (i)(ii)(1), (i)(iv)(1), (i)(iv)(1)(a), (i)(iv)(1)(b), (i)(iv)(2)(a), (i)(iv)(2)(b), (j)(1) and (j)(2) from 11 January 2018 subject to savings for applications made before that date (HC 309). Amendments to (i)(ii)(1), (i)(ii)(2)(b), (c), (d) and (e) from 6 July 2018 subject to savings for applications made before that date (HC 1154). Amendment to (i)(ii)(2) from 1 August 2019 (HC 1779). Words in (b)(i) and (ii), (c), (e), (f)(i) and (ii) and (k) inserted; Words in (g), (h)(i)(b) substituted from 29 March 2019 subject to savings for applications made before that date (HC 1919). Amendment to (g) (subsequently deleted, see HC 813 below) from 20 February 2020 subject to savings for applications made before that date (HC 56). Sub-paragraphs (i) and (j) deleted from 09:00 on 5 October 2020 subject to savings for applications made before that time. Where consequential changes relating to the need for an ATAS certificate have been made, they take effect for all applications made or granted on or after 5 October 2020 at 09:00 (HC 707). Words in curly brackets in (g), words in double square brackets in (h)(i)(b) deleted from 09:00 on 1 December 2020 subject to applications made before that time (HC 813).

319H-SD. Specified documents and information

Applicants who are over the age of 16 on the date the application is made must provide the following specified documents and information:

(a) The applicant must provide two items from the list below confirming his residential address:

(i) bank statements,

(ii) credit card bills,

(iii) driving licence,

(iv) NHS Registration document,

(v) letter from his current school, college or university, on official headed paper and bearing the official stamp of that organisation, and issued by an authorised official of that organisation.

(b) The documents submitted must be from two separate sources and dated no more than one calendar month before the date of the application.

(c) If the applicant pays rent or board, he must provide details of how much this amounts to each calendar month.

(d) If the applicant is residing separately from the Relevant Points Based System Migrant [or Appendix W Worker], he must provide:

(i) reasons for residing away from the family home. Where this is due to academic endeavours he must provide confirmation from his university or college confirming his enrolment and attendance on the specific course, on official headed paper and bearing the official stamp of that organisation, and issued by an authorised official of that organisation,

(ii) the following evidence that he has been supported financially by his parents whilst residing away from the family home:

(1) bank statements for the applicant covering the three months before the date of the application clearly showing the origin of the deposits; and

(2) bank statements for the applicant's parent covering the three months before the date of the application also showing corroborating payments out of their account.

Note: Words in (d) inserted from 29 March 2019 subject to savings for applications made before that date (HC 1919).

319I. Period and conditions of grant

(a) Entry clearance and leave to remain will be granted for:

(i) a period which expires on the same day as the leave granted to the parent whose leave expires first, or

(ii) Where both parents have, or are at the same time being granted, indefinite leave to remain, or have since become British citizens, leave to remain will be granted to the applicant for a period of 3 years.

(b) Entry clearance and leave to remain under this route will be subject to the following conditions:

(i) no recourse to public funds,

(ii) registration with the police, if this is required under paragraph 326 of these Rules, and

[...]

(iv) no employment as a professional sportsperson (including a sports coach).

Note: Amendments to (b)(iii)(1) from 11 January 2018 subject to savings for applications made before that date (HC 309). Amendments to (b)(iii)(1) from 6 July 2018 subject to savings for applications made before that date (HC 1154). Amendment to (b)(iii) from 29 March 2019 subject to savings for applications made before that date (HC 1919). Sub-paragraph (b)(iii) deleted from 09:00 on 5 October 2020 subject to savings for applications made before that time. Where consequential changes relating to the need for an ATAS certificate have been made, they take effect for all applications made or granted on or after 5 October 2020 at 09:00 (HC 707).

319J. Requirements for indefinite leave to remain

To qualify for indefinite leave to remain under this route, an applicant must meet the requirements listed below. If the applicant meets these requirements, indefinite leave to remain will be granted. If the applicant does not meet these requirements, the application will be refused.

Requirements:

(a) The applicant must not fall for refusal under the general grounds for refusal, and must not be an illegal entrant.

(b) The applicant must be the child of a parent who has, or is at the same time being granted, indefinite leave to remain as:

(i) a Relevant Points Based System Migrant [or Appendix W Worker], or

(ii) the partner of a Relevant Points Based System Migrant [or Appendix W Worker].

(c) The applicant must have, or have last been granted, leave as the child of or have been born in the United Kingdom to, the [Relevant Points Based System Migrant or Appendix W Worker], or the partner of a [Relevant Points Based System migrant or Appendix W Worker] who is being granted indefinite leave to remain.

(d) The applicant must not be married or in a civil partnership, must not have formed an independent family unit, and must not be leading an independent life, and if he is over the age of 16 on the date the application is made, he must provide the specified documents and information in paragraph 319H-SD to show that this requirement is met.

(e) Both of an applicant's parents must either be lawfully settled in the UK, or being granted indefinite leave to remain at the same time as the applicant, unless:

(i) [The Relevant Points Based System Migrant or Appendix W Worker] is the applicant's sole surviving parent, or

(ii) [The Relevant Points Based System Migrant or Appendix W Worker] parent has and has had sole responsibility for the applicant's upbringing, or

(iii) there are serious and compelling family or other considerations which would make it desirable not to refuse the application and suitable arrangements have been made for the applicant's care, or

(iv) One parent is, at the same time, being granted indefinite leave to remain as a Relevant Points Based System Migrant, the other parent is lawfully present in the UK or being granted leave at the same time as the applicant, and the applicant was granted leave as the child of a Relevant Points Based System Migrant under the Rules in place before 9 July 2012.

(f) The applicant has demonstrated sufficient knowledge of the English language and sufficient knowledge about life in the United Kingdom, in accordance with Appendix KoLL, unless he is under the age of 18 at the date on which the application is made.

(g) If the applicant is a child born in the UK to a Relevant Points Based System migrant [or Appendix W Worker] and their partner, the applicant must provide a full UK birth certificate showing the names of both parents.

(h) All arrangements for the child's care and accommodation in the UK must comply with relevant UK legislation and regulations.

(i) The applicant must not be in the UK in breach of immigration laws except that, where paragraph 39E of these Rules applies, any current period of overstaying will be disregarded.

Note: Words in (b)(i) and (ii), (e)(i), (ii) and (g) inserted; words in (c), (c)(i)(and (ii) substituted from 29 March 2019 subject to savings for applications made before that date (HC 1919).

Other family members of persons with limited leave to enter or remain in the United Kingdom as a refugee or beneficiary of humanitarian protection

Requirements for leave to enter the United Kingdom as the spouse or civil partner of a person with limited leave to enter or remain in the United Kingdom as a refugee or beneficiary of humanitarian protection

319L. The requirements to be met by a person seeking leave to enter the United Kingdom as the spouse or civil partner of a person with limited leave to enter or remain in the United Kingdom as a refugee or beneficiary of humanitarian protection, are that:

(i) (a) the applicant is married to or the civil partner of a person who has limited leave to enter or remain in the United Kingdom as a refugee or beneficiary of humanitarian protection granted such status under the immigration rules and the parties are married or have formed a civil partnership after the person granted asylum or humanitarian protection left the country of his former habitual residence in order to seek asylum or humanitarian protection; and

(b) the applicant provides an original English language test certificate in speaking and listening from an English language test provider approved by the Secretary of

State for these purposes, which clearly shows the applicant's name and the qualification obtained (which must meet or exceed level A1 of the Common European Framework of Reference) unless:

(i) the applicant is aged 65 or over at the date he makes his application; or

(ii) the Secretary of State or Entry Clearance Officer considers that the applicant has a physical or mental condition that would prevent him from meeting the requirement; or

(iii) the Secretary of State or entry Clearance officer considers there are exceptional compassionate circumstances that would prevent the applicant from meeting the requirement; or

(iv) the applicant is a national of one of the following countries: Antigua and Barbuda; Australia; The Bahamas; Barbados; Belize; Canada; Dominica; Grenada; Guyana; Jamaica; New Zealand; St Kitts and Nevis; St Lucia; St Vincent and the Grenadines; Trinidad and Tobago; USA; [Malta;] or

(v) the applicant has obtained an academic qualification (not a professional or vocational qualification), which is deemed by [[Ecctis]] to meet the recognised standard of a Bachelor's or Masters degree or PhD in the UK, from an educational establishment in one of the following countries: Antigua and Barbuda; Australia; The Bahamas; Barbados; Belize; Dominica; Grenada; Guyana; Ireland; Jamaica; New Zealand; St Kitts and Nevis; St Lucia; St Vincent and The Grenadines; Trinidad and Tobago; the UK; the USA; [Malta;] and provides the specified documents; or

(vi) the applicant has obtained an academic qualification (not a professional or vocational qualification) which is deemed by [[Ecctis]] to meet the recognised standard of a Bachelor's or Masters degree or PhD in the UK, and

(1) provides the specified evidence to show he has the qualification, and

(2) [[Ecctis]] has confirmed that the degree was taught or researched in English, or

(vii) has obtained an academic qualification (not a professional or vocational qualification) which is deemed by [[Ecctis]] to meet the recognised standard of a Bachelor's or Masters degree or PhD in the UK, and provides the specified evidence to show:

(1) he has the qualification, and

(2) that the qualification was taught or researched in English; and

(ii) the parties to the marriage or civil partnership have met; and

(iii) each of the parties intends to live permanently with the other as his or her spouse or civil partner and the marriage or civil partnership is subsisting; and

(iv) there will be adequate accommodation for the parties and any dependants without recourse to public funds in accommodation which they own or occupy exclusively; and

(v) the parties will be able to maintain themselves and any dependants adequately without recourse to public funds; and

(vi) the applicant holds a valid United Kingdom entry clearance for entry in this capacity.

Note: Words in (i)(b)(iv) and (v) inserted from 09:00 on 1 December 2020 subject to savings for applications made before that time (HC 813). Words in double square brackets substituted from 6 October 2021 subject to savings for applications made before that date (HC 617).

319M. Leave to enter the United Kingdom as the spouse or civil partner of a refugee or beneficiary of humanitarian protection may be granted for 63 months provided the Immigration Officer is satisfied that each of the requirements of paragraph 319L(i)–(vi) are met.

319N. Leave to enter the United Kingdom as the spouse or civil partner of a refugee or beneficiary of humanitarian protection is to be refused if the Immigration Officer is not satisfied that each of the requirements of paragraph 319L(i)–(vi) are met.

Requirements for leave to enter the United Kingdom as the unmarried or same-sex partner of a person with limited leave to enter or remain in the United Kingdom as a refugee or beneficiary of humanitarian protection.

319O. The requirements to be met by a person seeking leave to enter the United Kingdom as the unmarried or same-sex partner of a person with limited leave to enter or remain in the United Kingdom as a refugee or beneficiary of humanitarian protection, are that:

(i) (a) the applicant is the unmarried or same-sex partner of a person who has limited leave to enter or remain in the United Kingdom as a refugee or beneficiary of humanitarian protection granted such status under the immigration rules, and the parties have been living together in a relationship akin to either a marriage or civil partnership subsisting for two years or more after the person granted asylum or humanitarian protection left the country of his former habitual residence in order to seek asylum or humanitarian protection; and

(b) the applicant provides an […] English language test certificate in speaking and listening from an English language test provider approved by the Secretary of State for these purposes, which clearly shows the applicant's name and the qualification obtained (which must meet or exceed level A1 of the Common European Framework of Reference) unless:

(i) the applicant is aged 65 or over at the time he makes his application;

(ii) the Secretary of State or entry Clearance officer considers that the applicant has a physical or mental condition that would prevent him from meeting the requirement;

(iii) the Secretary of State or Entry Clearance Officer considers there are exceptional compassionate circumstances that would prevent the applicant from meeting the requirement;

(iv) the applicant is a national of one of the following countries: Antigua and Barbuda; Australia; The Bahamas; Barbados; Belize; Canada; Dominica; Grenada; Guyana; Jamaica; New Zealand; St Kitts and Nevis; St Lucia; St Vincent and the Grenadines; Trinidad and Tobago; the USA; [Malta;]

(v) the applicant has obtained an academic qualification (not a professional or vocational qualification), which is deemed by [[Ecctis]] to meet the recognised standard of a Bachelor's or Masters degree or PhD in the UK, from an educational establishment in one of the following countries: Antigua and Barbuda; Australia; The Bahamas; Barbados; Belize; Dominica; Grenada; Guyana; Ireland; Jamaica; New Zealand; St Kitts and Nevis; St Lucia; St Vincent and The Grenadines; Trinidad and Tobago; the UK; the USA; [Malta;] and provides the specified documents; or

(vi) the applicant has obtained an academic qualification (not a professional or vocational qualification) which is deemed by [[Ecctis]] to meet the recognised standard of a Bachelor's or Masters degree or PhD in the UK, and

(1) provides the specified evidence to show he has the qualification, and

(2) [[Ecctis]] has confirmed that the degree was taught or researched in English, or

(vii) has obtained an academic qualification (not a professional or vocational qualification) which is deemed by [[Ecctis]] to meet the recognised standard of a Bachelor's or Masters degree or PhD in the UK, and provides the specified evidence to show:

(1) he has the qualification, and

(2) that the qualification was taught or researched in English; and

(ii) any previous marriage or civil partnership (or similar relationship) by either partner has permanently broken down; and

(iii) the parties are not involved in a consanguineous relationship with one another; and

(iv) there will be adequate accommodation for the parties and any dependants without recourse to public funds in accommodation which they own or occupy exclusively; and

(v) the parties will be able to maintain themselves and any dependants adequately without recourse to public funds; and

(vi) the parties intend to live together permanently; and

(vii) the applicant holds a valid United Kingdom entry clearance for entry in this capacity.

Note: Word in (i)(b) deleted from 5 November 2018 (HC 1534). Words in (i)(b)(iv) and (v) inserted from 09:00 on 1 December 2020 subject to savings for applications made before that time (HC 813). Words in double square brackets substituted from 6 October 2021 subject to savings for applications made before that date (HC 617).

319P. Leave to enter the United Kingdom as the unmarried or same-sex partner of a refugee or beneficiary of humanitarian protection may be granted for 63 months provided the Immigration Officer is satisfied that each of the requirements of paragraph 319O (i)–(vii) are met.

319Q. Leave to enter the United Kingdom as the unmarried or same-sex partner of a refugee or beneficiary of humanitatrian protection is to be refused if the Immigration Officer is not satisfied that each of the requirements of paragraph 319O (i)–(vii) are met.

Requirements for leave to enter the United Kingdom as the child of a parent or parents given limited leave to enter or remain in the United Kingdom as a refugee or beneficiary of humanitarian protection

319R. The requirements to be met by a person seeking leave to enter the United Kingdom as the child of a parent or parents given limited leave to enter or remain in the United Kingdom as a refugee or beneficiary of humanitarian protection, are that the applicant:

(i) is the child of a parent or parents granted limited leave to enter or remain as a refugee or beneficiary of humanitarian protection granted as such under the immigration rules; and

(ii) is under the age of 18, and

(iii) is not leading an independent life, is unmarried, is not in a civil partnership, and has not formed an independent family unit; and

(iv) was conceived after the person granted asylum or humanitarian protection left the country of his habitual residence in order to seek asylum in the UK; and

(v) can, and will, be accommodated adequately by the parent or parents the child is seeking to join without recourse to public funds in accommodation which the parent or parents the child is seeking to join, own or occupy exclusively; and

(vi) can, and will, be maintained adequately by the parent or parents the child is seeking to join, without recourse to public funds; and

(vii) if seeking leave to enter, holds a valid United Kingdom entry clearance for entry in this capacity.

319S. Limited leave to enter the United Kingdom as the child of a refugee or beneficiary of humanitarian protection may be granted for 63 months provided the Immigration Officer is satisfied that each of the requirements in paragraph 319R(i)–(vii) are met.

319T. Limited leave to enter the United Kingdom as the child of a refugee or beneficiary humanitarian protection is to be refused if the Immigration Officer is not satisfied that each of the requirements in paragraph 319R(i)–(vii) are met.

Requirements for indefinite leave to remain in the United Kingdom as the spouse or civil partner, unmarried or same-sex partner or child of a refugee or beneficiary of humanitatrian protection present and settled in the United Kingdom

319U. To qualify for indefinite leave to remain in the UK, an applicant must meet the requirements set out in paragraph 287 if the applicant is a spouse or civil partner, paragraph 295G if they are an unmarried or same-sex partner, or 298 if the applicant is a child and the sponsor must be present and settled in the United Kingdom at the time the application is made. If an applicant meets the requirements as set out in the relevant paragraphs, indefinite leave to remain will be granted. If the applicant does not meet these requirements, the application will be refused.

Parents, grandparents and other dependent relatives of persons with limited leave to enter or remain in the United Kingdom as a refugee or beneficiary of humanitarian protection

Requirements for leave to enter or remain in the United Kingdom as the parent, grandparent or other dependent relative of a person with limited leave to enter or remain in the United Kingdom as a refugee or beneficiary of humanitarian protection

319V. The requirements to be met by a person seeking leave to enter or remain in the United Kingdom as the parent, grandparent or other dependent relative of a person with limited leave to enter or remain in the United Kingdom as a refugee or beneficiary of humanitarian protection are that the person:

(i) is related to a refugee or beneficiary of humanitarian protection with limited leave to enter or remain in the United Kingdom in one of the following ways:

(a) parent or grandparent who is divorced, widowed, single or separated aged 65 years or over; or

(b) parents or grandparents travelling together of whom at least one is aged 65 or over; or

(c) a parent or grandparent aged 65 or over who has entered into a second relationship of marriage or civil partnership but cannot look to the spouse, civil partner or children of that second relationship for financial support; and where the person with limited leave to enter or remain in the United Kingdom is able and willing to maintain the parent or grandparent and any spouse or civil partner or child of the second relationship who would be admissible as a dependant; or

(d) a parent or grandparent under the age of 65 if living alone outside the United Kingdom in the most exceptional compassionate circumstances; or

(e) parents or grandparents travelling together who are both under the age of 65 if living in the most exceptional compassionate circumstances; or

(f) the son, daughter, sister, brother, uncle or aunt over the age of 18 if living alone outside the United Kingdom in the most exceptional compassionate circumstances; and

(ii) is joining a refugee or beneficiary of humanitarian protection with limited leave to enter or remain in the United Kingdom; and

(iii) is financially wholly or mainly dependent on the relative who has limited leave to enter or remain as a refugee or beneficiary of humanitarian protection in the United Kingdom; and

(iv) can, and will, be accommodated adequately, together with any dependants, without recourse to public funds, in accommodation which the sponsor owns or occupies exclusively; and

(v) can, and will, be maintained adequately, together with any dependants, without recourse to public funds; and

(vi) has no other close relatives in his own country to whom he could turn for financial support; and

(vii) if seeking leave to enter, holds a valid United Kingdom entry clearance for entry in this capacity, or, if seeking leave to remain, holds valid leave to remain in another capacity.

319VA. Limited leave to enter the United Kingdom as the parent, grandparent or other dependent relative of a refugee or beneficiary of humanitarian protection with limited leave to enter or remain in the United Kingdom may be granted for 5 years provided [on arrival, a valid passport or other identity document is produced to the Immigration Officer and the applicant has entry clearance for entry in this capacity.] Limited leave to remain in the United Kingdom as the parent, grandparent or other dependent relative of a refugee or beneficiary of humanitarian protection with limited leave to enter or remain in the United Kingdom may be granted provided the Secretary of State is satisfied that each of the requirements of paragraph 319V(i)–(vii) is met.

Note: Words substituted from 11 January 2018 subject to savings for applications made before that date (HC 309).

319VB. Limited leave to enter the United Kingdom as the parent, grandparent or other dependent relative of a refugee or beneficiary of humanitarian protection with limited leave to enter or remain in the United Kingdom is to be refused if[, on arrival, a valid passport or other identity document is not produced to the Immigration Officer and the applicant does not have entry clearance for entry in this capacity.] Limited leave to remain in the United Kingdom as the parent, grandparent or other dependent relative of a refugee or beneficiary of humanitarian protection with limited leave to enter or remain in the United Kingdom is to be refused if the Secretary of State is not satisfied that each of the requirements of paragraph 319V(i)–(vii) is met.

Note: Words substituted from 11 January 2018 subject to savings for applications made before that date (HC 309).

Requirements for indefinite leave to remain in the United Kingdom as the parent, grandparent or other dependent relative of a refugee or beneficiary of humanitarian protection who is present and settled in the United Kingdom or of a former refugee or beneficiary humanitarian protection, who is now a British Citizen.

319W. The requirements for indefinite leave to remain in the United Kingdom as the parent, grandparent or other dependent relative of a refugee or beneficiary of humanitarian protection who is now present and settled in the United Kingdom or who is now a British Citizen are that:

(i) the applicant has limited leave to enter or remain in the United Kingdom in accordance with paragraph 319V as a dependent relative of a refugee or beneficiary of humanitarian protection with limited leave to enter or remain in the United Kingdom; and

(ii) the sponsor the applicant was admitted to join is now present and settled in the United Kingdom, or is now a British Citizen; and

(iii) the applicant is financially wholly or mainly dependent on the relative who is present and settled in the United Kingdom; and

(iv) the applicant can, and will, be accommodated adequately, together with any dependants, without recourse to public funds, in accommodation which the sponsor owns or occupies exclusively; and

(v) the applicant can, and will, be maintained adequately, together with any dependants, without recourse to public funds; and

(vi) the applicant has no other close relatives in their country of former habitual residence to whom he could turn for financial support; and

(vii) does not fall for refusal under the general grounds for refusal.

319WA. Indefinite leave to remain in the United Kingdom as the parent, grandparent or other dependent relative of a refugee or beneficiary of humanitarian protection who is present and settled in the United Kingdom, or who is now a British Citizen may be granted provided the Secretary of State is satisfied that each of the requirements of paragraph 319W(i)–(vii) is met.

319WB. Indefinite leave to remain in the United Kingdom as the parent, grandparent or other dependent relative of a person present and settled in the United Kingdom is to be refused if the Secretary of State is not satisfied that each of the requirements of paragraph 319W(i)–(vii) is met.

Requirements for leave to enter or remain in the United Kingdom as the child of a relative with limited leave to enter or remain in the United Kingdom as a refugee or beneficiary of humanitarian protection.

319X. The requirements to be met by a person seeking leave to enter or remain in the United Kingdom as the child of a relative with limited leave to remain as a refugee or beneficiary of humanitarian protection in the United Kingdom are that:

(i) the applicant is seeking leave to enter or remain to join a relative with limited leave to enter or remain as a refugee or person with humanitarian protection; and

(ii) the relative has limited leave in the United Kingdom as a refugee or beneficiary of humanitarian protection and there are serious and compelling family or other considerations which make exclusion of the child undesirable and suitable arrangements have been made for the child's care; and

(iii) the relative is not the parent of the child who is seeking leave to enter or remain in the United Kingdom; and

(iv) the applicant is under the age of 18; and

(v) the applicant is not leading an independent life, is unmarried and is not a civil partner, and has not formed an independent family unit; and

[(vi) (a) the applicant can, and will, be accommodated adequately by the relative the child is seeking to join in the UK without recourse to public funds and in accommodation which the relative in the UK owns or occupies exclusively; or

(b) there are exceptional circumstances (as defined in paragraph 319XAA); and]

[(vii) (a) the applicant can, and will, be maintained adequately by the relative in the UK without recourse to public funds; or

(b) there are exceptional circumstances (as defined in paragraph 319XAA); and]

(viii) if seeking leave to enter, the applicant holds a valid United Kingdom entry clearance for entry in this capacity or, if seeking leave to remain, holds valid leave to remain in this or another capacity.

Note: Sub-paragraphs (vi) and (vii) substituted from 28 June 2022 subject to savings for applications made before that date (HC 17).

319XA. Limited leave to enter the United Kingdom as the child of a relative with limited leave to enter or remain as a refugee or beneficiary of humanitarian protection in the United Kingdom may be granted for {the same duration as their sponsor in the UK ('leave in line') provided} 5 years provided [on arrival, a valid passport or other identity document is produced to the Immigration Officer and the applicant has [[entry]] clearance for entry in this capacity.] Limited leave to remain in the United Kingdom as the child of a relative with limited leave to enter or remain as a refugee or beneficiary of humanitarian protection in the United Kingdom may be granted provided the Secretary of State is satisfied that each of the requirements of paragraph 319X(i)–(viii) is met.

Note: Words in square brackets substituted from 11 January 2018 subject to savings for applications made before that date (HC 309). Word in double square brackets inserted from 6 July 2018 subject to savings for applications made before that date (HC 1154). Words in curly brackets inserted from 28 June 2022 subject to savings for applications made before that date (HC 17).

[Granting leave to enter or remain where there are exceptional circumstances]

Note: Heading inserted from 28 June 2022 subject to savings for applications made before that date (HC 17).

[**319XAA.** Where the requirements of paragraph 319X (vi)(b) or (vii)(b) apply, the decision-maker must consider, on the basis of the information provided by the applicant, whether there are exceptional circumstances which may justify a grant of leave to enter or remain, for the same duration as the sponsor ("leave in line").

Where the applicant is a child under the age of 18 years who is seeking to join a relative with refugee status or who is a beneficiary of humanitarian protection in the UK, relevant factors when considering whether there are exceptional circumstances include:

(a) they have no parent with them; and

(b) they have no family other than in the UK that could reasonably be expected to support them; and

(c) there is an existing, genuine family relationship between them and the UK based relative; and

(d) they are dependent on the UK based relative.

In the event of a refusal of leave to enter or remain, if the decision maker is not satisfied there are exceptional circumstances, consideration will also be given to whether refusal of the application would be a breach of Article 8 ECHR.]

Note: Paragraph inserted from 28 June 2022 subject to savings for applications made before that date (HC 17).

319XB. Limited leave to enter the United Kingdom as the child of a relative with limited leave to enter or remain as a refugee or beneficiary of humanitarian protection in the United Kingdom is to be refused if [on arrival, a valid passport or other identity document is not produced to the Immigration Officer and the applicant does not have entry clearance for entry in this capacity.] Limited leave to remain in the United Kingdom as the child of a relative with limited leave to enter or remain as a refugee or beneficiary of humanitarian protection in the United Kingdom is to be refused if the Secretary of State is not satisfied that each of the requirements of paragraph 319X(i)–(viii) is met.

Note: Words substituted from 11 January 2018 subject to savings for applications made before that date (HC 309).

Requirements for indefinite leave to remain in the United Kingdom as the child of a relative who is present and settled in the United Kingdom or as a former refugee or beneficiary of humanitarian protection who is now a British Citizen

319Y. To qualify for indefinite leave to remain as the child of a relative who is present and settled in the United Kingdom, an applicant must meet the requirements set out in paragraph 298.

[Part 9
Grounds for refusal

Suitability requirements apply to all routes and must be met in addition to validity and eligibility requirements.
Where this Part applies a person will not meet the suitability requirements if they fall for refusal under this Part.
A person may also have their entry clearance or permission cancelled on suitability grounds.
More than one grounds for refusal or cancellation may apply, for example, the presence of a foreign criminal in the UK may not be conducive to the public good.
The Immigration Act 1971, section 76 of the Nationality, Immigration and Asylum Act 2002 (revocation of indefinite leave), the Immigration (Leave to Enter and Remain) Order 2000 and Schedule 2 of the Immigration Act 1971 set out the powers to cancel entry clearance or permission. These rules set out how those powers are to be exercised.
Decisions on suitability are either mandatory (must) or discretionary (may) and must be compatible with the UK obligations under the Refugee Convention and the European Convention on Human Rights, which are mainly provided for under other provisions in these Rules.
Some routes have their own, or additional, suitability requirements.
This Part is in 5 sections.

1. *Application of this Part;*
2. *Grounds for refusal, or cancellation of, entry clearance, permission to enter and permission to stay;*
3. *Additional grounds for refusal of entry, or cancellation of entry clearance or permission, on arrival in the UK;*
4. *Additional grounds for refusal, or cancellation, of permission to stay;*
5. *Additional grounds for cancellation of entry clearance, permission to enter and permission to stay which apply to specified routes.*

Section 1: Application of this Part

9.1.1. Part 9 does not apply to the following:

(a) Appendix FM, except paragraphs 9.2.2, 9.3.2, 9.4.5, 9.9.2, 9.15.1, 9.15.2, 9.15.3, 9.16.2, 9.19.2, 9.20.1, 9.23.1 and 9.24.1. apply, and paragraph 9.7.3 applies to permission to stay; and paragraph 9.8.2 (a) and (c). applies where the application is for entry clearance; and

[(b) an application on grounds of private life under Appendix Private Life, except paragraphs 9.6.1. and 9.6.2.; and]

(c) Appendix Armed Forces, except paragraphs 9.2.2, 9.3.2, 9.4.5, 9.7.3, 9.8.1. to 9.8.8, 9.9.2, 9.15.1. to 9.15.3, 9.16.2, 9.19.2, 9.20.1, 9.23.1. and 9.24.1. apply; and paragraph 9.10.2. applies where the application is under Part 9, 9A or 10 of Appendix Armed Forces; and

(d) Appendix EU; and

(e) Appendix EU (Family Permit); and

[(f) Paragraph DWMS 2.1, except paragraphs 9.2.1(c), 9.2.2, 9.3.1, 9.3.2, 9.4.1(b), 9.4.1(c), 9.4.2, 9.4.5, 9.7.1, 9.7.2, 9.7.3, 9.9.1, 9.9.2. 9.16.2, 9.20.1, 9.23.1, 9.24.1; and]

(g) Part 11 (Asylum), except Part 9 does apply to paragraphs 352ZH to 352ZS, and 352I to 352X; [and 352A to 352FJ] and

(h) applications for entry clearance or permission to stay granted by virtue of the ECAA Association Agreement, except that in relation to permission granted under the Agreement paragraphs 9.2.2, 9.3.2, 9.4.2, 9.4.5, 9.6.2, 9.7.3 and 9.21.2 apply where the criminal offence or adverse conduct occurred after 11pm on 31 December 2020; and

(i) applications for permission to stay under Appendix ECAA Extension of Stay, except paragraphs 9.2.1, 9.3.1, 9.4.1, 9.4.3, 9.6.1, 9.7.1, 9.7.2, 9.11.1, 9.12.1 and 9.21.1, and in relation to such permission paragraphs 9.2.2, 9.3.2, 9.4.2, 9.4.5, 9.6.2, 9.7.3 and 9.21.2 apply where the criminal offence or adverse conduct occurred after 11pm on 31 December 2020; and

(j) Appendix S2 Healthcare Visitor; and

(k) Appendix Service Providers from Switzerland.

[(l) Appendix Ukraine Scheme, except paragraphs 9.2.1 to 9.7.3, 9.10.1 to 9.10.2, 9.14.1 to 9.20.2, 9.23.1 and 9.24.1.]

[(m) Appendix Settlement Protection; and]

[(n) Appendix Settlement Family Life, except paragraphs 9.6.1. and 9.6.2.]

Note: Words in (g) inserted from 23:00 on 31 December 2020 for decisions made on or after that time (CP 361). Subparagraph (f) substituted from 09:00 on 11 October 2021 subject to savings for applications made before that time (HC 617). Sub-paragraph (b) substituted, (m) and (n) inserted from 20 June 2022 subject to savings for applications made before that date (HC 1118). Sub-paragraph (l) inserted from 30 March 2022 (HC 1220).

Section 2: Grounds for refusal, or cancellation, of entry clearance, permission to enter and permission to stay

Exclusion or deportation order grounds

9.2.1. An application for entry clearance, permission to enter or permission to stay must be refused where:

(a) the Secretary of State has personally directed that the applicant be excluded from the UK; or

(b) the applicant is the subject of an exclusion order; or.

(c) the applicant is the subject of a deportation order, or a decision to make a deportation order.

9.2.2. Entry clearance or permission held by a person must be cancelled where the Secretary of State has personally directed that the person be excluded from the UK.

Non-conducive grounds

9.3.1. An application for entry clearance, permission to enter or permission to stay must be refused where the applicant's presence in the UK is not conducive to the public good because of their conduct, character, associations or other reasons (including convictions which do not fall within the criminality grounds).

9.3.2. Entry clearance or permission held by a person must be cancelled where the person's presence in the UK is not conducive to the public good.

Criminality grounds

9.4.1. An application for entry clearance, permission to enter or permission to stay must be refused where the applicant:

(a) has been convicted of a criminal offence in the UK or overseas for which they have received a custodial sentence of 12 months or more; or

(b) is a persistent offender who shows a particular disregard for the law; or

(c) has committed a criminal offence, or offences, which caused serious harm.

9.4.2. Entry clearance or permission held by a person must be cancelled where the person:

(a) has been convicted of a criminal offence in the UK or overseas for which they have received a custodial sentence of 12 months or more; or

(b) is a persistent offender who shows a particular disregard for the law; or

(c) has committed a criminal offence, or offences, which caused serious harm.

9.4.3. An application for entry clearance, permission to enter or permission to stay may be refused (where paragraph 9.4.2. and 9.4.4. do not apply) where the applicant:

(a) has been convicted of a criminal offence in the UK or overseas for which they have received a custodial sentence of less than 12 months; or

(b) has been convicted of a criminal offence in the UK or overseas for which they have received a non-custodial sentence, or received an out-of-court disposal that is recorded on their criminal record.

9.4.4. An application for entry clearance or permission to enter under Appendix V: Visitor, or where a person is seeking entry on arrival in the UK for a stay for less than 6 months, must be refused where the applicant:

(a) has been convicted of a criminal offence in the UK or overseas for which they have received a custodial sentence of less than 12 months, unless more than 12 months have passed since the end of the custodial sentence; or

(b) has been convicted of a criminal offence in the UK or overseas for which they have received a non-custodial sentence, or received an out-of-court disposal that is recorded on their criminal record, unless more than 12 months have passed since the date of conviction.

9.4.5. Entry clearance or permission held by a person may be cancelled (where paragraph 9.4.2. does not apply) where the person:

(a) has been convicted of a criminal offence in the UK or overseas for which they have received a custodial sentence of less than 12 months; or

(b) has been convicted of a criminal offence in the UK or overseas for which they have received a non-custodial sentence, or received an out-of-court disposal that is recorded on their criminal record.

Exclusion from asylum or humanitarian protection grounds

9.5.1. An application for entry clearance, permission to enter or permission to stay may be refused where the Secretary of State:

(a) has at any time decided that paragraph 339AA (exclusion from Refugee Convention), 339AC (danger to the UK), 339D (exclusion from a grant of humanitarian protection) or 339GB (revocation of humanitarian protection on grounds of exclusion) of these rules applies to the applicant; or

(b) has decided that paragraph 339AA, 339AC, 339D or 339GB of these rules would apply, but for the fact that the person has not made a protection claim in the UK, or that the person has made a protection claim which was finally determined without reference to any of the relevant matters described in paragraphs 339AA, 339AC, 339D or 339GB.

9.5.2. Entry clearance or permission held by a person may be cancelled where the Secretary of State:

(a) has at any time decided that paragraph 339AA (exclusion from Refugee Convention), 339AC (danger to the UK), 339D (exclusion from a grant of humanitarian protection) or 339GB (revocation of humanitarian protection on grounds of exclusion) of these rules applies to the applicant; or

(b) has decided that paragraph 339AA, 339AC, 339D or 339GB of these rules would apply, but for the fact that the person has not made a protection claim in the UK, or that the person has made a protection claim which was finally determined without reference to any of the relevant matters described in paragraphs 339AA, 339AC, 339D or 339GB.

Involvement in a sham marriage or sham civil partnership grounds

9.6.1. An application for entry clearance, permission to enter or permission to stay may be refused where the decision maker is satisfied that it is more likely than not that the applicant is, or has been, involved in a sham marriage or sham civil partnership.

9.6.2. Entry clearance or permission held by a person may be cancelled where the decision maker is satisfied that it is more likely than not the person is, or has been, involved in a sham marriage or sham civil partnership.

False representations, etc. grounds

9.7.1. An application for entry clearance, permission to enter or permission to stay may be refused where, in relation to the application, or in order to obtain documents from the Secretary of State or a third party provided in support of the application:

(a) false representations are made, or false documents or false information submitted (whether or not relevant to the application, and whether or not to the applicant's knowledge); or

(b) relevant facts are not disclosed.

9.7.2. An application for entry clearance, permission to enter or permission to stay must be refused where the decision maker can prove that it is more likely than not the applicant used deception in the application.

[**9.7.3.** Entry clearance or permission held by a person may be cancelled where, in relation to an application, or in order to obtain documents from the Secretary of State or a third party provided in support of the application:

(a) false representations were made, or false documents or false information submitted (whether or not relevant to the application, and whether or not to the applicant's knowledge); or

(b) relevant facts were not disclosed.]

Note: Paragraph substituted from 6 October 2021 subject to savings for applications made before that date (HC 617).

9.7.4. Permission extended under section 3C of the Immigration Act 1971 may be cancelled where the decision maker can prove that it is more likely than not the applicant used deception in the application for permission to stay.

Previous breach of immigration laws grounds

9.8.1. An application for entry clearance or permission to enter must be refused if:

(a) the applicant has previously breached immigration laws; and

(b) the application is for entry clearance or permission to enter and it was made within the relevant time period in paragraph 9.8.7.

9.8.2. An application for entry clearance or permission to enter may be refused where:

(a) the applicant has previously breached immigration laws; and

(b) the application was made outside the relevant time period in paragraph 9.8.7; and

(c) the applicant has previously contrived in a significant way to frustrate the intention of the rules, or there are other aggravating circumstances (in addition to the immigration breach), such as a failure to cooperate with the redocumentation process, such as using a false identity, or a failure to comply with enforcement processes, such as failing to report, or absconding.

9.8.3. An application for permission to stay may be refused where a person has previously failed to comply with the conditions of their permission, unless permission has been granted in the knowledge of the previous breach.

[**9.8.3A.** An application for entry clearance, permission to enter, or permission to stay may be refused where a person used deception in relation to a previous application (whether or not successfully).]

Note: Paragraph inserted from 6 October 2021 subject to savings for applications made before that date (HC 617). Paragraph substituted from 6 April 2022 (HC 1118).

9.8.4. In paragraphs 9.8.1. and 9.8.2, a person will only be treated as having previously breached immigration laws if, when they were aged 18 or over, they:

(a) overstayed their permission and neither paragraph 9.8.5. nor paragraph 9.8.6. apply; or

(b) breached a condition attached to their permission and entry clearance or further permission was not subsequently granted in the knowledge of the breach; or

(c) were (or still are) an illegal entrant; or

(d) used deception in relation to an application (whether or not successfully).

9.8.5. A period of overstaying will be disregarded for the purpose of paragraph 9.8.4. (a) where the person left the UK voluntarily, not at the expense (directly or indirectly) of the Secretary of State, and:

(a) the person overstayed for 90 days or less, where the overstaying began before 6 April 2017; or

(b) the person overstayed for 30 days or less, where the overstaying began on or after 6 April 2017; or

(c) paragraph 39E applied to the period of overstaying.

9.8.6. A period of overstaying will be disregarded for the purpose of paragraph 9.8.4.(a) where the overstaying arose from a decision to refuse an application, or cancellation of permission, which was subsequently withdrawn, or quashed, or reconsidered by direction of a court or tribunal, unless the legal challenge which led to the reconsideration was brought more than 3 months after the date of the decision to refuse or cancel.

9.8.7. The relevant time period under paragraphs 9.8.1. and 9.8.2. is as set out in the following table (and where the person previously breached more than one immigration law, only the breach which leads to the longest period of absence from the UK will be taken into account):

[Time from date the person left the UK (or date of refusal of the application under row (f))]	This applies where the applicant	And the applicant left the UK	And the applicant left the UK
(a) 12 months	left voluntarily	at their own expense	N/A
(b) 2 years	left voluntarily	at public expense	Within 6 months of being given notice of liability for removal or when they no longer had a pending appeal or administrative review, whichever is later.
(c) 5 years	left voluntarily	at public expense	more than 6 months after being given notice of liability for removal or when they no longer had a pending appeal or administrative review, whichever is later.
(d) 5 years	left or was removed from the UK	as a condition of a caution issued in accordance with section 22 of the Criminal Justice Act 2003 (and providing that any condition prohibiting their return to the UK has itself expired)	-

[Time from date the person left the UK (or date of refusal of the application under row (f))]	This applies where the applicant	And the applicant left the UK	And the applicant left the UK
(e) 10 years	was deported or removed from the UK	at public expense	–
(f) 10 years	Used deception [in an application (for visits this applies to applications for entry clearance only)]	–	–

Note: Words in heading and in row (f) in table substituted from 23:00 on 31 December 2020 for decisions made on or after that time (CP 361).

9.8.8. Permission (including permission extended under section 3C of the Immigration Act 1971) may be cancelled where the person has failed to comply with the conditions of their permission.

Failure to provide required information, etc grounds

9.9.1. An application for entry clearance, permission to enter or permission to stay may be refused where a person fails without reasonable excuse to comply with a reasonable requirement to:

(a) attend an interview; or
(b) provide information; or
(c) provide biometrics (whether or not requested as part of an application); or
(d) undergo a medical examination; or
(e) provide a medical report.

9.9.2. Any entry clearance or permission held by a person may be cancelled where the person fails without reasonable excuse to comply with a reasonable requirement to:

(a) attend an interview; or
(b) provide information; or
(c) provide biometrics; or
(d) undergo a medical examination; or
(e) provide a medical report.

Admissibility to the Common Travel Area or other countries grounds

9.10.1. An application for entry clearance or permission to enter must be refused where a person is seeking entry to the UK with the intention of entering another part of the

Common Travel Area and fails to satisfy the decision maker that they are acceptable to the immigration authorities there.

9.10.2. An application for entry clearance, permission to enter or permission to stay may be refused where a person seeking entry fails to satisfy the decision maker that they will be admitted to another country after a stay in the UK.

Debt to the NHS grounds

9.11.1. An application for entry clearance, permission to enter or permission to stay may be refused where a relevant NHS body has notified the Secretary of State that the applicant has failed to pay charges under relevant NHS regulations on charges to overseas visitors and the outstanding charges have a total value of at least £500.

Unpaid litigation costs grounds

9.12.1. An application for entry clearance, permission to enter or permission to stay may be refused where a person has failed to pay litigation costs awarded to the Home Office.

Purpose not covered by the Immigration Rules grounds

9.13.1. An application for entry clearance, permission to enter or permission to stay may be refused where a person is seeking to come to or stay in the UK for a purpose not covered by these rules.

Section 3: Additional grounds for refusal of entry on arrival in the UK

No entry clearance grounds

9.14.1. Permission to enter must be refused if the person seeking entry is required under these rules to hold on arrival entry clearance for the purpose for which entry is sought, or the person is a visa national, and the person does not hold the required entry clearance.

Failure to produce recognised passport or travel document grounds

9.15.1. Permission to enter must be refused if the person seeking entry fails to produce a passport or other travel document that satisfies the decision maker as to their identity and nationality, unless the person holds a travel document issued by the national authority of a state of which the person is not a national and the person's statelessness or other status prevents the person from obtaining a document satisfactorily establishing their identity and nationality.

9.15.2. Permission to enter may be refused if the person seeking entry produces a passport or other travel document which:

(a) was issued by a territorial entity or authority which is not recognised by Her Majesty's Government as a state, or is not dealt with as a government by them; or

(b) was issued by a territorial entity or authority which does not accept valid UK passports for the purpose of its own immigration controls; or

(c) does not comply with international passport practice.

9.15.3. Entry clearance or permission held by a person may be cancelled where on arrival a person fails to produce a passport or other travel document that meets the requirements in paragraph 9.15.1. or 9.15.2.

Medical grounds

9.16.1. Permission to enter must be refused where a medical inspector advises that for medical reasons it is undesirable to grant entry to the person, unless the decision maker is satisfied that there are strong compassionate reasons justifying admission.

9.16.2. Entry clearance or permission held by a person may be cancelled where a medical inspector advises that for medical reasons it is undesirable to grant entry to the person.

Consent for a child to travel grounds

9.17.1. A child may be refused permission to enter if they are not travelling with their parent or legal guardian and, if required to do so, the child's parent or legal guardian fails to provide the decision maker with written consent to the child seeking entry to the UK.

Returning residents grounds

9.18.1. A person seeking entry as a returning resident under paragraph 18 of these rules may be refused permission to enter if they fail to satisfy the decision maker that they meet the requirements of that paragraph, or that they are seeking entry for the same purpose as that for which their previous permission was granted.

Customs breaches grounds

9.19.1. Permission to enter may be refused where the decision maker is satisfied that a person has committed a customs breach, whether or not a criminal prosecution is pursued.

9.19.2. Where the decision maker is satisfied that a person has committed a customs breach, whether or not a criminal prosecution is pursued, any entry clearance or permission held by the person may be cancelled.

Change of circumstances or purpose grounds

9.20.1. Entry clearance or permission held by a person may be cancelled where there has been such a change in circumstances since the entry clearance or permission was granted that it should be cancelled.

9.20.2. Entry clearance or permission to enter held by a person on arrival in the UK may be cancelled where the person's purpose in seeking entry is different from the purpose specified in their entry clearance.

Section 4: Additional grounds for refusal of permission to stay

Rough sleeping in the UK

[**9.21.1.** Permission to stay may be refused where the decision maker is satisfied that a person has been rough sleeping in the UK and has repeatedly refused offers of suitable support and has engaged in persistent anti-social behaviour.]

Note: Paragraph substituted from 6 April 2021 subject to savings for applications made before that date (HC 1248).

[**9.21.2.** Where the decision maker is satisfied that a person has been rough sleeping in the UK and has repeatedly refused offers of suitable support, and has engaged in persistent anti-social behaviour, any permission held by the person may be cancelled.]

Note: Paragraph substituted from 6 April 2021 subject to savings for applications made before that date (HC 1248).

Crew members

9.22.1. Where a person has permission to enter as a crew member an application for permission to stay may be refused, unless permission to stay is granted to fulfil the purpose for which the person has permission to enter.

Section 5: Additional grounds for cancellation of entry clearance, permission to enter and permission to stay

Ceasing to meet requirement of rules

9.23.1. A person's entry clearance or permission may be cancelled if they cease to meet the requirements of the rules under which the entry clearance or permission was granted.

Dependent grounds

9.24.1. A person's entry clearance or permission may be cancelled where they are the dependent of another person whose permission is, or has been, cancelled.

Withdrawal of sponsorship or endorsement grounds

9.25.1. A person's entry clearance or permission may be cancelled where their sponsorship or endorsement has been withdrawn and they have entry clearance or permission on one of the following routes:

(a) Student; or
(b) Child Student; or
(c) Skilled Worker; or
(d) Intra-Company Transfer; or
(e) Intra-Company Graduate Trainee; or
(f) Representative of an Overseas Business; or
(g) T2 Minister of Religion; or
[(h) International Sportsperson; or]
[(i) Temporary Worker; or]
(j) Start-up; or
(k) Innovator; or
(l) Global Talent[; or]
[(m) Global Business Mobility routes; or]
[(n) Scale-up (subject to paragraph 9.33.1.).]

Note: Subparagraphs (h) and (i) substituted from 09:00 on 11 October 2021 subject to savings for applications made before that time (HC 617). Words in (l) substituted, sub-paragraph (m) inserted from 09:00 on 11 April 2022 subject to savings for applications made before that time; sub-paragraph (n) inserted from 22 August 2022 subject to savings for applications made before that date (HC 1118).

9.25.2. A Student's permission may be cancelled where the sponsor withdraws their sponsorship of the Student because, having completed a pre- sessional course, the student does not have a knowledge of English equivalent to level B2 or above of the Council of Europe's Common European Framework for Language Learning in all four components (reading, writing, speaking and listening).

[**9.25.3.** Entry clearance or permission held under the Global Talent route may be cancelled where the prize named in Appendix Global Talent: Prestigious Prizes which they used to qualify, has been withdrawn.]

Note: Paragraph inserted from 5 May 2021 (HC 1248).

Student does not start course or ceases to study

9.26.1. The entry clearance or permission of a Student or Child Student may be cancelled if:

(a) they do not start their studies with their sponsor; or

(b) they or their sponsor confirm that their course of study has ceased, or will cease before the end date recorded on the Certificate of Acceptance for Studies; or

(c) the start date for the course is delayed for more than 28 days; or

(d) they cease to study with their sponsor.

Worker does not start work or ceases their employment

9.27.1. [A person's entry clearance or permission on the Skilled Worker, Intra-Company, Global Business Mobility, Representative of an Overseas Business, [[Scale-up Worker (subject to paragraph 9.33.1.),]] T2 Minister of Religion, International Sportsperson or Temporary Worker routes, may be cancelled if:]

(a) they do not start working for their sponsor; or

(b) they or their sponsor confirm that their employment, volunteering, training or job shadowing has ceased or will cease before the end date recorded on the Certificate of Sponsorship; or

(c) the start date for the job, as recorded in the Certificate of Sponsorship, is delayed by more than 28 days; or

(d) they cease to work for their sponsor.

Note: Amendments to introduction from 09:00 on 11 October 2021 subject to savings for applications made before that time (HC 617). Introduction substituted from 09:00 on 11 April 2022 subject to savings for applications made before that time; words in double square brackets in introduction inserted from 22 August 2022 subject to savings for applications made before that date (HC 1118).

Sponsor loses licence or transfers business

9.28.1. [A person on the Student, Child Student, Skilled Worker, Intra-Company, Global Business Mobility, [[Scale-up Worker (subject to paragraph 9.33.1.),]] T2 Minister of Religion, International Sportsperson or Temporary Worker routes, may have their entry clearance or permission cancelled if:]

(a) their sponsor does not have a sponsor licence; or

(b) their sponsor transfers the business for which the person works, or at which they study, to another business or institution, and that business or institution:

(i) fails to apply for a sponsor licence; or

(ii) fails to apply for a sponsor licence within 28 days of the date of a transfer of their business or institution; or

(iii) applies for a sponsor licence but is refused; or

(iv) makes a successful application for a sponsor licence, but the sponsor licence granted is not in a category that would allow the sponsor to issue a Certificate of Sponsorship or Confirmation of Acceptance for Studies to the person.

Note: Amendments to introduction from 09:00 on 11 October 2021 subject to savings for applications made before that time (HC 617). Introduction substituted from 09:00 on 11 April 2022 subject to savings for applications made before that time; words in double square brackets inserted from 22 August 2022 subject to savings for applications made before that date (HC 1118).

Change of employer

9.29.1. [A person on the Skilled Worker, Intra-Company, Global Business Mobility, [[Scale-up Worker (subject to paragraph 9.33.1.),]] T2 Minister of Religion, International Sportsperson or Temporary Worker routes, may have their permission cancelled where they have changed their employer, unless any of the following exceptions apply:]

[(a) they are a person on the Government Authorised Exchange route or a Seasonal Worker and the change of employer is authorised by the sponsor; or]

(b) they are working for a different sponsor unless the change of sponsor does not result in a change of employer, or the change in employer is covered by the Transfer of Undertakings (Protection of Employment) Regulations 2006, equivalent statutory transfer schemes, or the Cabinet Office Statement of Practice on Staff Transfers in the Public Sector; or

(c) they have permission as a [an International Sportsperson], and all of the following apply:

(i) they are sponsored by a sports club; and

(ii) they are sponsored as a player and are being temporarily loaned to another sports club; and

(iii) player loans are specifically permitted in rules set down by the relevant sports governing body; and

(iv) their sponsor has made arrangements with the loan club to enable to the sponsor to continue to meet its sponsor duties; and

(v) the player will return to working for the sponsor at the end of the loan.

Note: Amendments to introduction; subparagraph (a); words in (c) substituted from 09:00 on 11 October 2021 subject to savings for applications made before that time (HC 617). Introduction substituted from 09:00 on 11 April 2022 subject to savings for applications made before that time; words in double square brackets inserted from 22 August 2022 subject to savings for applications made before that date (HC 1118).

Absence from employment

9.30.1. A person on the Skilled Worker, Intra-Company, Representative of an Overseas Business, {Scale-up (subject to paragraph 9.33.1.),} [[Global Business Mobility]] T2 Minister of Religion, [International Sportsperson or Temporary Worker] routes who has been absent from work without pay, or on reduced pay, for more than 4 weeks during any calendar year may have their permission cancelled unless the reason for absence is one of the following:

[(a) statutory maternity leave, paternity leave, parental leave, or shared parental leave; or]

(b) statutory adoption leave; or

(c) sick leave; or

(d) assisting with a national or international humanitarian or environmental crisis, providing their sponsor agreed to the absence for that purpose; or

(e) taking part in legally organised industrial action.

Note: Words in square brackets in introduction substituted from 09:00 on 11 October 2021 subject to savings for applications made before that time; subparagraph (a) substituted from 6 October 2021 (HC 617). Words in double square brackets inserted from 09:00 on 11 April 2022 subject to savings for applications made before that time; words in curly brackets inserted from 22 August 2022 subject to savings for applications made before that date (HC 1118).

Change of job or lower salary rate

9.31.1. A person on the Skilled Worker, Intra-Company, Representative of an Overseas Business, {Scale-up (subject to paragraph 9.33.1.)} [[Global Business Mobility,]] T2 Minister of Religion or [Temporary Worker] routes may have their permission cancelled where they have changed jobs or they receive a lower salary rate (unless any of paragraphs 9.31.2. to 9.31.3. apply) if:

[(a) they are a person on the Intra-Company, Global Business Mobility, or Skilled Worker {or a Scale-up Worker} routes and have changed to a different job in the same occupation code but the salary rate for the new job is lower than the salary rate for the old job as set out in Appendix Skilled Occupations.]

(b) they are a Skilled Worker and scored points for a job in a Shortage Occupation and the new job does not appear in Appendix Shortage Occupation List.

(c) they have changed jobs and the new job has a different occupation code to that recorded by the Certificate of Sponsorship (unless paragraph 9.31.2. applies); or

(d) the person no longer meets the salary requirement or going rate requirement for the job.

Note: Words in square brackets in introduction substituted from 09:00 on 11 October 2021 subject to savings for applications made before that time (HC 617). Words in double square brackets inserted, sub-paragraph (a) substituted from 09:00 on 11 April 2022 subject to savings for applications made before that time; words in curly brackets inserted from 22 August 2022 subject to savings for applications made before that date (HC 1118).

9.31.2. The following exception applies to paragraph 9.31.1.(c):

[(a) the person is a Graduate Trainee on a graduate training programme covering multiple roles within the sponsor group; and]

(b) the person is on an Intra-Company route and a reduction in salary coincides with working for the sponsor group while the person is not physically present in the UK; or

(c) their sponsor has notified the Home Office of the change of job and any change in salary.

Note: Sub-paragraph (a) substituted from 09:00 on 11 April 2022 subject to savings for applications made before that time (HC 1118).

9.31.3. The following exceptions apply to reduction in salary under paragraph 9.31.1:

(a) a reduction in salary coincides with an absence from employment permitted under paragraph 9.30.1; or

[(b) the person is on the Intra-Company or Global Business Mobility routes and a reduction in salary coincides with working for the sponsor group while the person is not physically present in the UK; or]

[(c) the person is a Skilled Worker and:

(i) if the person has permission under Appendix Skilled Worker, they would, after the change to the job, score 20 tradeable points in either the same option in the table in paragraph SW 4.2, or under paragraph SW 14.5(b), whichever they had scored points under when obtaining their most recent grant of permission; or

(ii) if the person has permission as a Tier 2 (General) Migrant, they would, after the change to the job, score 20 tradeable points under option A or F in the table in paragraph SW 4.2, or under paragraph SW 14.5(b), if they were to apply under Appendix Skilled Worker; or

(iii) if the person has permission as a Tier 2 (General) Migrant who was considered a new entrant in their application for that Tier 2 (General) permission, they would, after the change to the job, score 20 tradeable points under option E in the table in paragraph SW 4.2, if they were to apply under Appendix Skilled Worker.]

Note: Sub-paragraph (c) substituted from 6 April 2021 subject to savings for applications made before that date (HC 1248). Sub-paragraph (c) substituted from 6 October 2021 subject to savings for applications made before that date (HC 617). Sub-paragraph (b) substituted from 09:00 on 11 April 2022 subject to savings for applications made before that time (HC 1118).

[Endorsing body no longer approved]

[**9.32.1.** Where a person has entry clearance or permission on the Global Talent, Start-up or Innovator route their entry clearance or permission may be cancelled if their endorsing body ceases to hold that status for the route in which they were endorsed.]

Note: Heading and paragraph inserted from 09:00 on 1 December 2020 subject to savings for applications made before that time (HC 813).

[Exception for Scale-up Workers]

[**9.33.1** Paragraphs 9.25.1. and 9.27.1. to 9.31.1. only apply to a Scale-up Worker during the 6-month period that the Scale-up Worker is required to work for a Sponsor under Appendix Scale-up.]

Note: Heading and paragraph inserted from 22 August 2022 subject to savings for applications made before that date (HC 1118).

Part 9 substituted from 09:00 on 1 December 2020 subject to savings for applications made before that date (HC 813). Amendments to previous version of Part 9 pursuant to HC 309, CM 9765, HC 1779, HC 1849, HC 1919, HC 2099, HC 2631, HC 170, HC 56, HC 120, HC 707).

Part 10

Registration with the police

325. For the purposes of paragraph 326, a 'relevant foreign national' is a person aged 16 or over who is:

(i) a national or citizen of a country or territory listed in Appendix 2 to these Rules;
(ii) a stateless person; or
(iii) a person holding a non-national travel document.

326. (1) Subject to sub-paragraph (2) below, a condition requiring registration with the police should normally be imposed on any relevant foreign national who is:

(i) given limited leave to enter the United Kingdom for longer than six months; or

(ii) given limited leave to remain which has the effect of allowing him to remain in the United Kingdom for longer than six months, reckoned from the date of his arrival (whether or not such a condition was imposed when he arrived).

(2) Such a condition should not normally be imposed where the leave is given:

(i) as a [Seasonal Worker];

(ii) as a [Temporary Worker], provided the Certificate of Sponsorship Checking System reference for which points were awarded records that the applicant is being sponsored as an overseas government employee or a private servant is a diplomatic household;

(iii) as a [T2 Minister of Religion];

(iv) on the basis of marriage to or civil partnership with a person settled in the United Kingdom or as the unmarried or same-sex partner of a person settled in the United Kingdom;

(v) as a person exercising access rights to a child resident in the United Kingdom;

(vi) as the [Parent of a *Child Student*]; or

(vii) following the grant of asylum.

(3) Such a condition should also be imposed on any foreign national given limited leave to enter the United Kingdom where, exceptionally, the Immigration Officer considers it necessary to ensure that he complies with the terms of the leave.

Note: Words in (2)(vi) substituted from 09:00 on 5 October 2020 subject to savings for applications made before that time. Where consequential changes relating to the need for an ATAS certificate have been made, they take effect for all applications made or granted on or after 5 October 2020 at 09:00 (HC 707). Words in (2)(i),(ii), and (iii) substituted from 6 April 2022 (HC 1118).

Part 11

Asylum

Procedure

326A. The procedures set out in these Rules shall apply to [protection claims].

Note: Words substituted from 28 June 2022 subject to savings for applications made before that date (HC 17).

326B. Where the Secretary of State is considering [an application for asylum and/or a claim for] humanitarian protection under this Part, she will consider any Article 8 elements of that claim in line with the provisions of Appendix FM (family life) and[, for applications made before 20 June 2022, in line with paragraphs 276ADE(1) to 276DH (private life) or, for applications made on or after 20 June 2022, Appendix Private Life] of these Rules which are relevant to those elements unless the person is someone to whom Part 13 of these Rules applies.

Note: Words substituted from 28 June 2022 subject to savings for applications made before that date (HC 17).

Definition of EU asylum applicant

326C. [DELETED]

Note: Paragraph deleted from 28 June 2022 subject to savings for applications made before that date (HC 17).

326D. [DELETED]

Note: Paragraph deleted from 28 June 2022 subject to savings for applications made before that date (HC 17).

Inadmissibility of EU asylum applications

326E. [DELETED]

Note: Paragraph deleted from 28 June 2022 subject to savings for applications made before that date (HC 17).

326F. [DELETED]

Note: Paragraph deleted from 28 June 2022 subject to savings for applications made before that date (HC 17).

Definition of asylum applicant

[**327.** Under this Part:

(i) An "application for asylum" (or an "asylum application") is a claim by a person to be recognised as a refugee under the Refugee Convention on the basis that it would be contrary to the United Kingdom's obligations under the Refugee Convention for them to be removed from or required to leave the United Kingdom, and which is recorded as valid or a claim deemed to be an application for asylum in accordance with paragraph 327EC.

(ii) An "asylum applicant" is someone who makes a claim under paragraph 327(i) or who is deemed to have made such a claim in accordance with paragraph 327EC.]

Note: Amendments from 23:00 on 31 December 2020 subject to savings for applications for asylum made before that time (HC 1043). Paragraph substituted from 28 June 2022 subject to savings for applications made before that date (HC 17).

327A. [DELETED]

Note: Paragraph deleted from 28 June 2022 subject to savings for applications made before that date (HC 17).

[**327AB.** An application for asylum will only be recorded as valid if:

(i) it is made at a designated place as defined in section 14 of the Nationality and Borders Act 2022 unless subsequently or otherwise accepted by the Secretary of State; and

(ii) it is made in person; and

(iii) it is made by a person who is not a British Citizen; and

(iv) it is particularised (if the applicant is 18 or over); and

(v) it does not fall for consideration under paragraph 353 of the Immigration Rules, unless and until it has been accepted as a fresh claim under paragraph 353 of the Immigration Rules.]

Note: Paragraph inserted from 28 June 2022 subject to savings for applications made before that date (HC 17).

[**327AC.** If a claim does not meet these requirements, it will not be recorded as a valid asylum application.]

Note: Paragraph inserted from 28 June 2022 subject to savings for applications made before that date (HC 17).

327B. [DELETED]

Note: Paragraph inserted from 23:00 on 31 December 2020 subject to savings for applications for asylum made before that time (HC 1043). Paragraph deleted from 28 June 2022 subject to savings for applications made before that date (HC 17).

327C. [DELETED]

Note: Paragraph inserted from 23:00 on 31 December 2020 subject to savings for applications for asylum made before that time (HC 1043). Paragraph deleted from 28 June 2022 subject to savings for applications made before that date (HC 17).

327D. [DELETED]

Note: Paragraph inserted from 23:00 on 31 December 2020 subject to savings for applications for asylum made before that time (HC 1043). Paragraph deleted from 28 June 2022 subject to savings for applications made before that date (HC 17).

[Definition of a claim for humanitarian protection]

Note: Heading inserted from 28 June 2022 subject to savings for applications made before that date (HC 17).

[**327EA.** Under this Part, a claim for humanitarian protection is a request by a person for international protection due to a claim that if they are removed from or required to leave the UK, they would face a real risk of suffering serious harm (as defined in paragraph 339CA) in their country of origin, and they are unable, or owing to such risk, unwilling to avail themselves of the protection of that country.]

Note: Paragraph inserted from 28 June 2022 subject to savings for applications made before that date (HC 17).

[**327EB.** A claim for humanitarian protection must meet the requirements of paragraphs 327AB(i) to (iv) otherwise it will not be recorded as a valid claim for humanitarian protection.]

Note: Paragraph inserted from 28 June 2022 subject to savings for applications made before that date (HC 17).

[**327EC.** If someone makes a claim for humanitarian protection, they will be deemed to be an asylum applicant and to have made an application for asylum for the purposes of these Rules. The claim will be recorded, subject to meeting the requirements of Rule 327AB(i) to (iv), as an application for asylum and will be assessed under paragraph 334 for refugee status in the first instance. If the application for refugee status is refused, then the Secretary of State will go on to consider the claim as a claim for humanitarian protection.]

Note: Paragraph inserted from 28 June 2022 subject to savings for applications made before that date (HC 17).

[Inadmissibility of a claim for Humanitarian Protection]

Note: Heading inserted from 28 June 2022 subject to savings for applications made before that date (HC 17).

[**327F.** If an application for asylum is declared inadmissible under section 80A or 80B of the Nationality Immigration and Asylum Act 2002 then any associated claim for humanitarian protection (meaning a claim made on the same facts) will also be inadmissible. Such an outcome is not a decision to refuse the claim and, accordingly, no right of appeal under section 82(1)(a) of the Nationality, Immigration and Asylum Act 2002 (appeal against refusal of protection claim) arises.]

Note: Paragraph inserted from 28 June 2022 subject to savings for applications made before that date (HC 17).

Applications for asylum

328. All asylum applications will be determined by the Secretary of State in accordance with the Refugee Convention [and the Immigration Rules]. Every asylum application made by a person at a port or airport in the United Kingdom will be referred by the Immigration Officer for determination by the Secretary of State in accordance with these Rules.

Note: Words inserted from 28 June 2022 subject to savings for applications made before that date (HC 17).

328A. [DELETED]

Note: Paragraph deleted from 28 June 2022 subject to savings for applications made before that date (HC 17).

[**329.** For so long as an asylum applicant cannot be removed from or required to leave the UK because section 77 of the Nationality, Immigration and Asylum Act 2002 applies, any dependants who meet the definition under paragraph 349 must also not be removed from or required to leave the UK.]

Note: Paragraph substituted from 28 June 2022 subject to savings for applications made before that date (HC 17).

330. If the Secretary of State decides to grant refugee status [or humanitarian protection] and the person has not yet been given leave to enter, the Immigration Officer will grant limited leave to enter.

Note: Words inserted from 28 June 2022 subject to savings for applications made before that date (HC 17).

331. If a person seeking leave to enter is refused asylum or their application for asylum is withdrawn or treated as withdrawn under paragraph 333C of these Rules, the Immigration Officer will consider whether or not they are in a position to decide to give or refuse leave to enter without interviewing the person further. If the Immigration Officer decides that a further interview is not required they may serve the notice giving or refusing leave to enter by post. If the Immigration Officer decides that a further interview is required, they will then resume their examination to determine whether or not to grant the person leave to enter under any other provision of these Rules. If the person fails at any time to comply with a requirement to report to an Immigration Officer for examination, the Immigration Officer may direct that the person's examination shall be treated as concluded at that time. The Immigration Officer will then consider any outstanding applications for entry on the basis of any evidence before them.

332. If a person who has been refused leave to enter makes an application for asylum and that application is refused or withdrawn or treated as withdrawn under paragraph 333C of these Rules, leave to enter will again be refused unless the applicant qualifies for admission under any other provision of these Rules.

333. Written notice of decisions on applications for asylum shall be given [to the asylum applicant]. Where the applicant is legally represented, notice may instead be given to the representative. Where the applicant has no legal representative and free legal assistance is not available, they shall be informed of the decision on the application for asylum and, if the application is [refused], how to challenge the decision, in a language that they may reasonably be supposed to understand.

Note: Words in substituted from 28 June 2022 subject to savings for applications made before that date (HC 17).

[**333A.** The Secretary of State shall ensure that a decision is taken on each application for asylum as soon as possible, without prejudice to an adequate and complete examination.

Where a decision on an application for asylum has not been taken within:

(a) six months of the date it was recorded; or

(b) within any revised timeframe notified to an applicant during or after the initial six-month period in accordance with this paragraph, and

(c) where the applicant has made a specific written request for an update, the Secretary of State shall inform the applicant of the delay and provide information on the timeframe within which the decision on their application is to be expected. The provision of such information shall not oblige the Secretary of State to take a decision within the expected timeframe.]

Note: Paragraph substituted from 28 June 2022 subject to savings for applications made before that date (HC 17).

333B. Applicants for asylum shall be allowed an effective opportunity to consult, at their own expense or at public expense in accordance with provision made for this by the Legal Aid Agency or otherwise, a person who is authorised under Part V of the Immigration and Asylum Act 1999 to give immigration advice. This paragraph shall also apply where the Secretary of State is considering revoking a person's refugee status in accordance with these Rules.

Withdrawal of applications

333C. If an application for asylum is withdrawn either explicitly or implicitly, consideration of it may be discontinued. An application will be treated as explicitly withdrawn if the applicant signs the relevant form provided by the Secretary of State. An application may be treated as [implicitly] withdrawn if an applicant fails to attend the personal interview as provided in paragraph 339NA of these Rules unless the applicant demonstrates within a reasonable time that that failure was due to circumstances beyond their control. The Secretary of State will indicate on the applicant's asylum file that the application for asylum has been withdrawn and consideration of it has been discontinued.

Note: Words substituted from 28 June 2022 subject to savings for applications made before that date (HC 17).

Grant of refugee status

[334. An asylum applicant will be granted refugee status in the United Kingdom following a claim if the Secretary of State is satisfied that:

(i) they are in the United Kingdom or have arrived at a port of entry in the United Kingdom; and

(ii) they are a refugee, as defined in Article 1 of the 1951 Refugee Convention; and

(iii) there are no reasonable grounds for regarding them as a danger to the security of the United Kingdom in accordance with Article 33(2) of the Refugee Convention; and

(iv) having been convicted by a final judgment of a particularly serious crime, they do not constitute a danger to the community of the United Kingdom in accordance with Article 33(2) of the Refugee Convention as defined in Section 72 of the Nationality Immigration and Asylum Act 2002; and

(v) refusing their application would result in them being required to go (whether immediately or after the time limited by any existing leave to enter or remain in the UK) in breach of the Refugee Convention, to a country in which they would be persecuted on account of their race, religion, nationality, political opinion or membership of a particular social group.]

Note: Paragraph substituted from 28 June 2022 subject to savings for applications made before that date (HC 17).

335. If the Secretary of State decides to grant refugee status to a person who has been given leave to enter (whether or not the leave has expired) or to a person who has previously entered without leave, the Secretary of State will vary the existing leave or grant limited leave to remain. [Where a person has an existing grant of indefinite leave to remain, their leave to remain will not be varied.]

Note: Words inserted from 28 June 2022 subject to savings for applications made before that date (HC 17).

Refusal of asylum

336. An application which does not meet the criteria set out in paragraph 334 will be refused. Where an application for asylum is refused, the reasons in fact and law shall be stated in the decision and information provided in writing on how to challenge the decision.

337. DELETED

338. DELETED

339. DELETED

Revocation [. . .]

Note: Words in heading deleted from 28 June 2022 subject to savings for applications made before that date (HC 17).

[338A. A person's grant of refugee status under paragraph 334 must be revoked if any of paragraphs 339A, 339AA, 339AB or 339AC apply.]

Note: Paragraph substituted from 28 June 2022 subject to savings for applications made before that date (HC 17).

Refugee Convention ceases to apply (cessation)

[339A. This paragraph applies where the Secretary of State is satisfied that the person should have been, or is, excluded from being a refugee in accordance with Article 1D and 1E of the 1951 Refugee Convention and Article 1F of the Refugee Convention, as defined in section 36 of the Nationality and Borders Act 2022.]

Note: Paragraph substituted from 28 June 2022 subject to savings for applications made before that date (HC 17).

Exclusion from the Refugee Convention

[339AA. This paragraph applies where the Secretary of State is satisfied that the person should have been, or is, excluded from being a refugee in accordance with Article 1D and 1E of the 1951 Refugee Convention and Article 1F of the Refugee Convention, as defined in section 36 of the Nationality and Borders Act 2022.]

Note: Paragraph substituted from 28 June 2022 subject to savings for applications made before that date (HC 17).

Misrepresentation

339AB. This paragraph applies where the Secretary of State is satisfied that the person's misrepresentation or omission of facts, including the use of false documents, were decisive for the grant of refugee status[, and the person does not otherwise qualify for refugee status under paragraph 334].

Note: Words inserted from 28 June 2022 subject to savings for applications made before that date (HC 17).

Danger to the United Kingdom

339AC. This paragraph applies where the Secretary of State is satisfied that: [Article 33(2) of the Refugee Convention applies in that:]

(i) there are reasonable grounds for regarding the person as a danger to the security of the United Kingdom; or

(ii) having been convicted by a final judgment of a particularly serious crime, the person constitutes a danger to the community of the United Kingdom [(see section 72 of the Nationality Immigration and Asylum Act 2002)].

Note: Words inserted from 28 June 2022 subject to savings for applications made before that date (HC 17).

339B. When a person's grant of refugee status is revoked or not renewed any limited or indefinite leave which they have may be curtailed or cancelled.

339BA. Where the Secretary of State is considering revoking refugee status [or humanitarian protection] in accordance with these Rules, the following procedure will apply. The person concerned shall be informed in writing that the Secretary of State is reconsidering their qualification for refugee status [or humanitarian protection]and the reasons for the reconsideration. That person shall be given the opportunity to submit, in a personal interview or in a written statement, reasons as to why their refugee status [or humanitarian protection] should not be revoked. If there is a personal interview, it shall be subject to the safeguards set out in these Rules.

Note: Words inserted from 28 June 2022 subject to savings for applications made before that date (HC 17).

[**339BB.** The procedure in paragraph 339BA does not need to be followed where the person:

(i) acquires British citizenship; or

(ii) has unequivocally renounced their refugee status or humanitarian protection.]

Note: Paragraph substituted from 28 June 2022 subject to savings for applications made before that date (HC 17).

339BC. If the [asylum applicant] leaves the United Kingdom, the procedure set out in paragraph 339BA may be initiated, and completed, while the [asylum applicant] is outside the United Kingdom.

Note: Words inserted from 28 June 2022 subject to savings for applications made before that date (HC 17).

Grant of humanitarian protection

339C. A person will be granted humanitarian protection in the United Kingdom if the Secretary of State is satisfied that:

(i) they are in the United Kingdom or have arrived at a port of entry in the United Kingdom;

[(ii) they are not a refugee within the meaning of Article 1 of the 1951 Refugee Convention;]

(iii) substantial grounds have been shown for believing that the person concerned, if returned to the [country of origin], would face a real risk of suffering serious harm and is unable, or, owing to such risk, unwilling to avail themselves of the protection of that country; and

(iv) they are not excluded from a grant of humanitarian protection.

Note: Sub-paragraph (ii) substituted from 28 June 2022 subject to savings for applications made before that date; words in (iii) substituted from 16:00 on 11 May 2022 subject to savings for applications made before that time (HC 17).

339CA. For the purposes of paragraph 339C, serious harm consists of:

(i) the death penalty or execution;

(ii) unlawful killing;

(iii) torture or inhuman or degrading treatment or punishment of a person in the [country of origin]; or

(iv) serious and individual threat to a civilian's life or person by reason of indiscriminate violence in situations of international or internal armed conflict.

Note: Words in (iii) substituted from 16:00 on 11 May 2022 subject to savings for applications made before that time (HC 17).

Exclusion from humanitarian protection

[**339D.** An asylum applicant is excluded from a grant of humanitarian protection for the purposes of paragraph 339C(iv) where the Secretary of State is satisfied that there are serious reasons for considering that the asylum applicant:

(i) has committed, instigated or otherwise participated in the commission of a crime against peace, a war crime, a crime against humanity, as defined in the international instruments drawn up to make provision in respect of such crimes; or

(ii) has committed, instigated or otherwise participated in the commission of a serious non-political crime outside the UK prior to their admission to the UK as a person granted humanitarian protection; or

(iii) has been guilty of acts contrary to the purposes and principles of the United Nations; or

(iv) having been convicted by a final judgement of a particularly serious crime (as defined in Section 72 of the Nationality, Immigration and Asylum Act 2002), constitutes a danger to the community of the UK; or

(v) is a danger to the security of the UK.]

Note: Paragraph substituted from 28 June 2022 subject to savings for applications made before that date (HC 17).

[**339DA.** In 339D(ii):

(i) the reference to a serious non-political crime includes a particularly cruel action, even if it is committed with an allegedly political objective; and

(ii) the reference to a crime being committed by a person outside the UK prior to their admission to the UK as a person granted humanitarian protection includes a crime committed by that person at any time up to and including the day on which they are issued with a relevant biometric immigration document by the Secretary of State.]

Note: Paragraph inserted from 28 June 2022 subject to savings for applications made before that date (HC 17).

[**339DB.** For the purposes of 339DA(ii), a relevant biometric immigration document is a document that:

(i) records biometric information (as defined in section 15(1A) of the UK Borders Act 2007); and

(ii) is evidence of leave to remain in the United Kingdom granted to a person as a result of being granted humanitarian protection.]

Note: Paragraph inserted from 28 June 2022 subject to savings for applications made before that date (HC 17).

339E. If the Secretary of State decides to grant humanitarian protection and the person has not yet been given leave to enter, the Secretary of State or an Immigration Officer will grant limited leave to enter [or remain]. If the Secretary of State decides to grant humanitarian protection to a person who has been given limited leave to enter (whether or not that leave has expired) or a person who has entered without leave, the Secretary of State will vary the existing leave or grant limited leave to remain.

Note: Words inserted from 28 June 2022 subject to savings for applications made before that date (HC 17).

Refusal of humanitarian protection

339F. Where the criteria set out in paragraph 339C is not met humanitarian protection will be refused.

Revocation of[…] humanitarian protection

Note: Words in heading deleted from 28 June 2022 subject to savings for applications made before that date (HC 17).

[**339G.** A person's humanitarian protection granted under paragraph 339C must be revoked if any of paragraphs 339GA, 339GB or 339GD apply.]

Note: Paragraph substituted from 28 June 2022 subject to savings for applications made before that date (HC 17).

Humanitarian protection ceases to apply

339GA. This paragraph applies where the Secretary of State is satisfied that the circumstances which led to the grant of humanitarian protection have ceased to exist or have changed to such a degree that such protection is no longer required. In applying this paragraph the Secretary of State shall have regard to whether the change of circumstances is of such a significant and non-temporary nature that the person no longer faces a real risk of serious harm.

Revocation of humanitarian protection on the ground of exclusion

[**339GB.** This paragraph applies where the Secretary of State is satisfied that the person granted humanitarian protection should have been or is excluded from humanitarian protection under paragraph 339D of these rules.]

Note: Paragraph substituted from 28 June 2022 subject to savings for applications made before that date (HC 17).

339GC. DELETED

Revocation of humanitarian protection on the basis of misrepresentation

339GD. This paragraph shall apply where the Secretary of State is satisfied that the person granted humanitarian protection misrepresented or omitted facts, including the use of false documents, which were decisive to the grant of humanitarian protection [and the person does not otherwise qualify for humanitarian protection under paragraph 339C].

Note: Words inserted from 28 June 2022 subject to savings for applications made before that date (HC 17).

339H. When a person's humanitarian protection is revoked [. . .] any limited or indefinite leave which they have may be curtailed or cancelled.

Note: Words deleted from 28 June 2022 subject to savings for applications made before that date (HC 17).

Consideration of applications

339HA. The Secretary of State shall ensure that the personnel examining applications for asylum and taking decisions on the Secretary of State's behalf have the knowledge with respect to relevant standards applicable in the field of asylum and refugee law.

[**339I.** When the Secretary of State considers an applicant's protection claim, or human rights claim it is the duty of the person to submit to the Secretary of State as soon as possible all material factors needed to substantiate the protection claim or substantiate the human rights claim, which the Secretary of State shall assess in cooperation with the person.

The material factors include:

(i) the person's statement on the reasons for making protection claim or for making a human rights claim; and

(ii) all documentation at the person's disposal regarding the person's age, background (including background details of relevant relatives), identity, nationality(ies), country(ies) and place(s) of previous residence, previous asylum applications, travel routes; and

(iii) identity and travel documents.]

Note: Paragraph substituted from 28 June 2022 subject to savings for applications made before that date (HC 17).

339IA. For the purposes of examining individual applications for asylum

(i) information provided in support of an application and the fact that an application has been made shall not be disclosed to the alleged actor(s) of persecution of the applicant, and

(ii) information shall not be obtained from the alleged actor(s) of persecution that would result in their being directly informed that an application for asylum has been made by the applicant in question and would jeopardise the physical integrity of the applicant and their dependants, or the liberty and security of their family members still living in the country of origin.

This paragraph shall also apply where the Secretary of State is considering revoking a person's refugee status [or humanitarian protection] in accordance with these Rules.

Note: Words inserted from 28 June 2022 subject to savings for applications made before that date (HC 17).

339J. The assessment by the Secretary of State of [a protection claim] or a human rights claim will be carried out on an individual, objective and impartial basis. This will include taking into account in particular:

(i) all relevant facts as they relate to the country of origin or country of return at the time of taking a decision on the grant; including laws and regulations of the country of origin [...]and the manner in which they are applied;

(ii) relevant statements and documentation presented by the person including information on whether the person has been or may be subject to persecution or serious harm;

(iii) the individual position and personal circumstances of the person, including factors such as background, gender and age, so as to assess whether, on the basis of the person's personal circumstances, the acts to which the person has been or could be exposed would amount to persecution or serious harm;

(iv) whether the person's activities since leaving the country of origin [...]were engaged in for the sole or main purpose of creating the necessary conditions for making [a protection claim] or a human rights claim, so as to assess whether these activities will expose the person to persecution or serious harm if returned to that country; and

(v) whether the person could reasonably be expected to avail themselves of the protection of another country where they could assert citizenship.

Note: Words in introduction and (iv) substituted from 28 June 2022 subject to savings for applications made before that date; words in (i) and (iv) deleted from 16:00 on 11 May 2022 subject to savings for applications made before that time (HC 17).

339JA. Reliable and up-to-date information shall be obtained from various sources as to the general situation prevailing in the countries of origin of applicants for asylum and, where necessary, in countries through which they have transited. Such information shall be made available to the personnel responsible for examining applications and taking decisions and may be provided to them in the form of a consolidated country information report.

This paragraph shall also apply where the Secretary of State is considering revoking a person's refugee status [or humanitarian protection] in accordance with these Rules.

Note: Words inserted from 28 June 2022 subject to savings for applications made before that date (HC 17).

339K. The fact that a person has already been subject to persecution or serious harm, or to direct threats of such persecution or such harm, will be regarded as a serious indication of the person's well-founded fear of persecution or real risk of suffering serious harm, unless there are good reasons to consider that such persecution or serious harm will not be repeated.

339L. It is the duty of the person to substantiate the [protection claim] or substantiate their human rights claim. Where aspects of the person's statements are not supported by documentary or other evidence, those aspects will not need confirmation when all of the following conditions are met:

(i) the person has made a genuine effort to substantiate their [protection claim] or substantiate his human rights claim;

(ii) all material factors at the person's disposal have been submitted, and a satisfactory explanation regarding any lack of other relevant material has been given;

(iii) the person's statements are found to be coherent and plausible and do not run counter to available specific and general information relevant to the person's case;

(iv) the person has made an [protection claim] or made [an] human rights claim at the earliest possible time, unless the person can demonstrate good reason for not having done so; and

(v) the general credibility of the person has been established.

Note: Words in introduction, (i) and (iv) substituted from 28 June 2022 subject to savings for applications made before that date (HC 17).

339M. The Secretary of State may consider that a person has not substantiated their [protection claim] or substantiated his human rights claim, and thereby [refuse] their application for asylum, determine that they are not eligible for humanitarian protection or [refuse] their human rights claim, if they fail, without reasonable explanation, to make a prompt and full disclosure of material facts, either orally or in writing, or otherwise to assist the Secretary of State in establishing the facts of the case; this includes, for example, failure to report to a designated place to be fingerprinted, failure to complete an asylum questionnaire or failure to comply with a requirement to report to an immigration officer for examination.

Note: Words substituted from 28 June 2022 subject to savings for applications made before that date (HC 17).

339MA. Applications for asylum shall be neither rejected nor excluded from examination on the sole ground that they have not been made as soon as possible.

339N. In determining whether the general credibility of the person has been established the Secretary of State will apply the provisions in s 8 of the Asylum and Immigration (Treatment of Claimants, etc.) Act 2004.

Personal interview

339NA. Before a decision is taken on the application for asylum, the applicant shall be given the opportunity of a personal interview on their application for asylum with a representative of the Secretary of State who is legally competent to conduct such an interview.

The personal interview may be omitted where:

(i) the Secretary of State is able to take a positive decision [(a grant of refugee status or humanitarian protection)] on the basis of evidence available;

(ii) the Secretary of State has already had a meeting with the applicant for the purpose of assisting them with completing their application and submitting the essential information regarding the application;

(iii) the applicant, in submitting their application and presenting the facts, has only raised issues that are not relevant or of minimal relevance to the examination of whether they are a refugee, as defined in [Article 1 of the Refugee Convention and/or has only raised issues that are not relevant or of minimal relevance to the examination of whether they are eligible for humanitarian protection];

(iv) the applicant has made inconsistent, contradictory, improbable or insufficient representations which make their claim clearly unconvincing in relation to having been the object of persecution [or serious harm];

(v) the applicant has submitted a subsequent application which does not raise any relevant new elements with respect to their particular circumstances or to the situation in their country of origin;

(vi) the applicant is making an application merely in order to delay or frustrate the enforcement of an earlier or imminent decision which would result in their removal;

(vii) it is not reasonably practicable, in particular where the Secretary of State is of the opinion that the applicant is unfit or unable to be interviewed owing to enduring circumstances beyond their control; or

(viii) the applicant is an EU national whose claim the Secretary of State has nevertheless decided to consider substantively in accordance with [section 80A(4) of the Nationality, Immigration and Asylum Act 2002].

The omission of a personal interview shall not prevent the Secretary of State from taking a decision on the application.

Where the personal interview is omitted, the applicant and dependants shall be given a reasonable opportunity to submit further information.

Note: Words in (i) and (iv) inserted, words in (iii) and (viii) substituted from 28 June 2022 subject to savings for applications made before that date (HC 17).

339NB.

(i) The personal interview mentioned in paragraph 339NA above shall normally take place without the presence of the applicant's family members unless the Secretary of State considers it necessary for an appropriate examination to have other family members present.

(ii) The personal interview shall take place under conditions which ensure appropriate confidentiality.

339NC.

(i) A written report shall be made of every personal interview containing at least the essential information regarding the asylum application as presented by the applicant in accordance with paragraph 339I of these Rules.

(ii) The Secretary of State shall ensure that the applicant has timely access to the report of the personal interview and that access is possible as soon as necessary for allowing an appeal to be prepared and lodged in due time.

339ND. The Secretary of State shall provide at public expense an interpreter for the purpose of allowing the applicant to submit their case, wherever necessary. The Secretary of State shall select an interpreter who can ensure appropriate communication between the applicant and the representative of the Secretary of State who conducts the interview.

339NE. The Secretary of State may require an audio recording to be made of the personal interview referred to in paragraph 339NA. Where an audio recording is considered necessary for the processing of [an application for] asylum, the Secretary of State shall inform the applicant in advance that the interview will be recorded.

Note: Words substituted from 28 June 2022 subject to savings for applications made before that date (HC 17).

Internal relocation

[**339O.** (i) The Secretary of State will not:

(a) grant refugee status if section 35 of the Nationality and Borders Act 2022 applies; or

(b) grant humanitarian protection if in part of the country of origin a person would not face a real risk of serious harm, and the person can reasonably be expected to stay in that part of the country.

(ii) Any assessment under paragraph 339O(i)(b) must:

(a) have regard to the general circumstances prevailing in that part of the country, and

(b) have regard to the personal circumstances of the person; and
(c) disregard any technical obstacles relating to travel to that part of that country.]

Note: Paragraph substituted from 16:00 on 11 May 2022 subject to savings for applications made before that time; paragraph substituted again from 28 June 2022 subject to savings for applications made before that date (HC 17).

Sur place claims

339P. A person may have a well-founded fear of being persecuted or a real risk of suffering serious harm based on events which have taken place since the person left the [country of origin] and/or activities which have been engaged in by a person since they left the country of origin or country of return, in particular where it is established that the activities relied upon constitute the expression and continuation of convictions or orientations held in the [country of origin].

Note: Words substituted from 16:00 on 11 May 2022 subject to savings for applications made before that time (HC 17).

[...]

Note: Heading deleted from 28 June 2022 subject to savings for applications made before that date (HC 17).

[339Q. DELETED]

Note: Paragraph deleted from 28 June 2022 subject to savings for applications made before that date (HC 17).

[Permission to stay on a protection route]

Note: Heading inserted from 28 June 2022 subject to savings for applications made before that date (HC 17).

[339QA. Where the Secretary of State has granted an asylum applicant refugee status under paragraph 334, the asylum applicant may be granted permission to stay on a protection route at the same time as or as soon as possible after the grant of refugee status. Group 1 refugees and Group 2 refugees, as defined in section 12 of the Nationality and Borders Act 2022, may be granted different periods of permission to stay and subject to different conditions:

(i) where the asylum applicant is a Group 1 refugee, they will be granted refugee permission to stay for a minimum period of 5 years; and

(ii) where the asylum applicant is a Group 2 refugee, they will be granted temporary refugee permission to stay for a minimum period of 30 months, unless exceptional circumstances apply.

Permission to stay will be renewable upon application where the person still has and remains eligible for refugee status. Applications for further permission to stay under this Part should be made within the last 28 days of the applicant's permission to stay.]

Note: Paragraph inserted from 28 June 2022 subject to savings for applications made before that date (HC 17).

[339QB. Where the Secretary of State has granted an asylum applicant humanitarian protection under paragraph 339C, the asylum applicant will be granted temporary humanitarian permission to stay at the same time as or as soon as possible after the grant of humanitarian protection. Permission to stay will be valid for a minimum period of 30 months. Permission to stay will be renewable upon application where the person still has and remains eligible for humanitarian protection. Applications for further permission to stay under this Part should be made within the last 28 days of the applicant's permission to stay.]

Note: Paragraph inserted from 28 June 2022 subject to savings for applications made before that date (HC 17).

[339QC. Where the Secretary of State has granted an asylum applicant refugee status or humanitarian protection, any dependant of the asylum applicant who meets the requirements of paragraph 349 may be granted permission to stay. Permission to stay will not be granted to dependants where they would, if they were an asylum applicant, be excluded under Article 1(F) of the 1951 Refugee Convention (as defined in Section 36 of the Nationality and Borders Act 2022), be refused refugee status under paragraph 334(iii) or paragraph 334(iv), or be excluded from humanitarian protection under paragraph 339D. Permission to stay will be granted with the same expiry date and with the same conditions as that which is granted to the asylum applicant. Permission to stay will be renewable upon application where the dependant still meets the requirements of the Rules under which they were granted, and the asylum applicant who was granted refugee status or humanitarian protection is being granted further permission to stay at the same time or already has further permission to stay. An adult who was last granted permission to stay as a dependent child of a parent who has or had at the time that permission to stay as a dependant was granted, permission to stay on a protection route, may still qualify for further permission to stay as a dependant where they meet the other requirements of the Rules under which they were granted permission to stay. Applications for further permission to stay should be made at the same time as the asylum applicant's application and within the last 28 days of the applicant's permission to stay.]

Note: Paragraph inserted from 28 June 2022 subject to savings for applications made before that date (HC 17).

[339QD. The Secretary of State may curtail, revoke or refuse to grant further permission to stay under paragraphs 339QA or 339QB where a person's refugee status or humanitarian protection is revoked.]

Note: Paragraph inserted from 28 June 2022 subject to savings for applications made before that date (HC 17).

[339QE. The Secretary of State may curtail, revoke or refuse to grant further permission to stay to a dependant granted permission to stay under paragraph 339QC where the refugee status or humanitarian protection of the applicant on whom they are a dependant is revoked, or where they no longer meet the requirements of the Rules under which they were granted.]

Note: Paragraph inserted from 28 June 2022 subject to savings for applications made before that date (HC 17).

Requirements for indefinite leave to remain for persons granted refugee status or humanitarian protection

339R. [DELETED]

Note: Paragraph deleted from 6 October 2021 subject to savings for applications made before that date (HC 617).

Indefinite leave to remain for a person granted refugee status or humanitarian protection

339S. [DELETED]

Note: Paragraph deleted from 6 October 2021 subject to savings for applications made before that date (HC 617).

Refusal of indefinite leave to remain for a person granted refugee status or humanitarian protection

339T. [DELETED]

Note: Paragraph deleted from 6 October 2021 subject to savings for applications made before that date (HC 617).

Consideration of asylum applications and human rights claims

340. DELETED
341. DELETED
342. DELETED
343. DELETED
344. DELETED

Travel documents

344A. [(i). After having received a complete application for a travel document, the Secretary of State will issue to a person in the United Kingdom who meets the definition of a refugee in Article 1 of the Refugee Convention and their dependants travel documents, in the form set out in the Schedule to the Refugee Convention, for the purpose of travel outside the United Kingdom, unless compelling reasons of national security or public order otherwise require.]

(ii) After having received a complete application for a travel document, the Secretary of State will issue to a person granted humanitarian protection in the United Kingdom and their [dependants] a travel document, where that person is unable to obtain a national passport or other identity documents which enable that person to travel, unless compelling reasons of national security or public order otherwise require.

(iii) Where the person referred to in (ii) can obtain a national passport or identity documents but has not done so, the Secretary of State will issue that person with a travel document where that person can show they have made reasonable attempts to obtain a national passport or identity document and there are serious humanitarian reasons for travel.

(iv) For the purposes of paragraph 344A, a ['dependant'] refers only to a person who has been treated as a dependant under paragraph 349 of these Rules or a person who has been granted leave to remain in accordance with paragraphs 352A-352FJ of these Rules.

Note: Sub-paragraph (i). words in (ii) and (iv) substituted from 28 June 2022 subject to savings for applications made before that date (HC 17).

Access to Employment

344B. The Secretary of State will not impose conditions restricting the employment or occupation in the United Kingdom of a person granted refugee status or humanitarian protection.

Information

344C. A person who is granted refugee status or humanitarian protection will be provided with access to information in a language that they may reasonably be supposed to understand which sets out the rights and obligations relating to that status. The Secretary of State will provide the information as soon as possible after the grant of refugee status or humanitarian protection.

Inadmissibility of non-EU applications for asylum

345A. [DELETED]

Note: Amendment from 6 April 2018 for decisions made on or after that date (HC 895). Paragraph substituted from 1 October 2019 (HC 2631). Paragraph substituted from 23:00 on 31 December 2020 for decisions made on or after that time (HC 1043). Paragraph deleted from 28 June 2022 subject to savings for applications made before that date (HC 17).

345AA. [DELETED]

Note: Paragraph inserted from 1 October 2019 (HC 2631). Paragraph deleted from 23:00 on 31 December 2020 subject to savings for applications for asylum made before that time (HC 1043).

345AB. [DELETED]

Note: Paragraph inserted from 1 October 2019 (HC 2631). Paragraph deleted from 23:00 on 31 December 2020 subject to savings for applications for asylum made before that time (HC 1043).

345AC. [DELETED]

Note: Paragraph inserted from 1 October 2019 (HC 2631). Paragraph deleted from 23:00 on 31 December 2020 subject to savings for applications for asylum made before that time (HC 1043).

[Safe Third Country of Asylum]

Note: Heading inserted from 23:00 on 31 December 2020 for decisions made on or after that time (HC 1043).

345B. [DELETED]

Note: Paragraph substituted from 1 October 2019 (HC 2631). Paragraph substituted from 23:00 on 31 December 2020 for decisions made on or after that time (HC 1043). Paragraph deleted from 28 June 2022 subject to savings for applications made before that date (HC 17).

345C. [DELETED]

Note: Paragraph substituted from 23:00 on 31 December 2020 for decisions made on or after that time (HC 1043). Paragraph deleted from 28 June 2022 subject to savings for applications made before that date (HC 17).

[Exceptions for admission of inadmissible claims to UK asylum process made under section 80B(7)(b) of the Nationality, Immigration Act 2002 (as amended)]

Note: Heading inserted from 23:00 on 31 December 2020 for decisions made on or after that time (HC 1043). Heading substituted from 28 June 2022 subject to savings for applications made before that date (HC 17).

[345D. When an application has been treated as inadmissible and the Secretary of State believes removal to a safe third country within a reasonable period of time is unlikely, the applicant will be admitted for consideration of the claim in the UK]

Note: Paragraph substituted from 23:00 on 31 December 2020 for decisions made on or after that time (HC 1043). Paragraph substituted from 28 June 2022 subject to savings for applications made before that date (HC 17).

[Dublin Transfers]

345E. [DELETED]

Note: Paragraph and heading substituted from 1 October 2019 (HC 2631). Paragraph deleted from 23:00 on 31 December 2020 for decisions made on or after that time (HC 1043).

Previously rejected applications

346. DELETED

347. DELETED

Rights of appeal

348. DELETED

Dependants

349. A spouse, civil partner, unmarried or same sex partner, or minor child accompanying a principal applicant may be included in the application for asylum as a dependant, provided, in the case of an adult dependant with legal capacity, the dependant consents to being treated as such at the time the application is lodged. A spouse, civil partner, unmarried or same sex partner or minor child may also claim asylum in their own right. If the principal applicant is granted refugee status or humanitarian protection and leave to enter or remain any spouse, civil partner, unmarried or same sex partner or minor child will be granted leave to enter or remain for the same duration. The case of any dependant who claims asylum in their own right will be also considered individually in accordance with paragraph 334 above. An applicant under this paragraph, including an accompanied child, may be interviewed where they make a [protection] claim as a dependant or in their own right.

If the spouse, civil partner, unmarried or same sex partner, or minor child in question has a [protection] claim in their own right, that claim should be made at the earliest opportunity. Any failure to do so will be taken into account and may damage credibility if no reasonable explanation for it is given. Where an asylum or humanitarian protection application is unsuccessful, at the same time that asylum or humanitarian protection is refused the applicant may be notified of removal directions or served with a notice of the Secretary of State's intention to deport them, as appropriate. In this paragraph and paragraphs 350–352 a child means a person who is under 18 years of age or who, in the absence of documentary evidence establishing age, appears to be under that age. An unmarried or same sex partner for the purposes of this paragraph, is a person who has been living together with the principal applicant in a subsisting relationship akin to marriage or a civil partnership for two years or more.

Note: Words inserted from 28 June 2022 subject to savings for applications made before that date (HC 17).

Unaccompanied children

350. Unaccompanied children may also [make a protection claim] and, in view of their potential vulnerability, particular priority and care is to be given to the handling of their cases.

Note: Words substituted from 28 June 2022 subject to savings for applications made before that date (HC 17).

351. A person of any age may qualify for refugee status under the Convention and the criteria in paragraph 334 apply to all cases. However, account should be taken of the applicant's maturity and in assessing the [protection] claim of a child more weight should be given to objective indications of risk than to the child's state of mind and understanding of their situation. An asylum application made on behalf of a child should not be refused solely because the child is too young to understand their situation or to have formed a well founded fear of persecution. Close attention should be given to the welfare of the child at all times.

Note: Word inserted from 28 June 2022 subject to savings for applications made before that date (HC 17).

352. Any child over the age of 12 who has claimed asylum in their own right shall be interviewed about the substance of their [protection] claim unless the child is unfit or unable to be interviewed[, or one of the exceptions in paragraph 339NA applies]. When an interview takes place it shall be conducted in the presence of a parent, guardian, representative or another adult independent of the Secretary of State who has responsibility for the child. The interviewer shall have specialist training in the interviewing of children and have particular regard to the possibility that a child will feel inhibited or alarmed. The child shall be allowed to express themselves in their own way and at their own speed. If they appear tired or distressed, the interview will be suspended. The interviewer should then consider whether it would be appropriate for the interview to be resumed the same day or on another day.

Note: Word inserted from 28 June 2022 subject to savings for applications made before that date (HC 17).

352ZA. The Secretary of State shall as soon as possible after an unaccompanied child makes an application for asylum take measures to ensure that a representative represents and/or assists the unaccompanied child with respect to the examination of the application and ensure that the representative is given the opportunity to inform the unaccompanied child about the meaning and possible consequences of the interview and, where appropriate, how to prepare themselves for the interview. The representative shall have the right to be present at the interview and ask questions and make comments in the interview, within the framework set by the interviewer.

352ZB. The decision on the application for asylum shall be taken by a person who is trained to deal with [protection claims] from children.

Note: Words substituted from 28 June 2022 subject to savings for applications made before that date (HC 17).

Requirements for limited leave to remain as an unaccompanied asylum seeking child.

352ZC. The requirements to be met in order for a grant of limited leave to remain to be made in relation to an unaccompanied asylum seeking child under paragraph 352ZE are:

(a) the applicant is an unaccompanied asylum seeking child under the age of 17½ years throughout the duration of leave to be granted in this capacity;

(b) the applicant must have applied for asylum and been granted neither refugee status nor Humanitarian Protection;

(c) there are no adequate reception arrangements in the country to which they would be returned if leave to remain was not granted;

(d) the applicant must not be excluded from being a refugee under [Article 1D and 1E of the 1951 Refugee Convention and Article 1F of the Refugee Convention, as defined in section 36 of the Nationality and Borders Act 2022] or excluded from a grant of Humanitarian Protection under paragraph 339D or both;

(e) there are no reasonable grounds for regarding the applicant as a danger to the security of the United Kingdom;

(f) the applicant [does not constitute a danger to the community in the United Kingdom as a result of having been] convicted by a final judgment of a particularly serious crime, [(as defined in section 72 of the Nationality, Immigration and Asylum Act 2002)]; and

(g) the applicant is not, at the date of their application, the subject of a deportation order or a decision to make a deportation order.

Note: Words in (d) and (f) substituted from 28 June 2022 subject to savings for applications made before that date (HC 17).

352ZD An unaccompanied asylum seeking child is a person who:

a) is under 18 years of age when the asylum application is submitted;

b) is applying for asylum in their own right; and

c) is separated from both parents and is not being cared for by an adult who in law or by custom has responsibility to do so.

352ZE. Limited leave to remain should be granted for a period of 30 months or until the child is 17½ years of age whichever is shorter, provided that the Secretary of State is satisfied that the requirements in paragraph 352ZC are met.

352ZF. Limited leave granted under this provision will cease if

(a) any one or more of the requirements listed in paragraph 352ZC cease to be met, or

(b) a misrepresentation or omission of facts, including the use of false documents, were decisive for the grant of leave under 352ZE.

[Section 67 of the Immigration Act 2016 leave]

[**352ZG.** Paragraphs 352ZH to 352ZS only apply where a person has been transferred to the United Kingdom under Section 67 of the Immigration Act 2016.]

Note: Paragraph 352ZG and heading inserted from 6 July 2018 for decisions made on or after that date (HC 1154).

[Grant of Section 67 of the Immigration Act 2016 leave]

[**352ZH.** The person described in paragraph 352ZG will be granted Section 67 of the Immigration Act 2016 leave to remain in the United Kingdom ('Section 67 leave') if the Secretary of State is satisfied that:

(i) the person is not excluded from being a refugee under [Article 1D and 1E of the 1951 Refugee Convention and Article 1F of the Refugee Convention, as defined in section 36 of the Nationality and Borders Act 2022] or excluded from a grant of humanitarian protection under paragraph 339D of these Rules;

[(ii) where the person has made an application for refugee status or humanitarian protection, that application has been refused;]

(iii) there are no reasonable grounds for regarding the person as a danger to the security of the United Kingdom;

[(iv) the applicant does not constitute a danger to the community in the United Kingdom as a result of having been convicted by a final judgment of a particularly serious crime (as defined in section 72 of the Nationality, Immigration and Asylum Act 2002); and]

(v) [[must not fall for refusal under paragraphs 9.2.1 (c), 9.3.1, 9.4.1, 9.4.3, 9.5.1, 9.7.1, 9.7.2, 9.8.1. to 9.8.4, 9.9.1, 9.11.1, 9.12.1 or 9.13.1 of Part 9 Grounds for refusal.]]]

Note: Paragraph and heading inserted from 6 July 2018 for decisions made on or after that date (HC 1154). Sub-paragraph (ii) substituted from 1 October 2019 (HC 2631). Words in double square brackets in (v) substituted from 09:00 on 1 December 2020 subject to savings for applications made before that time (HC 813). Words in (i), sub-paragraph (iv) substituted from 28 June 2022 subject to savings for applications made before that date (HC 17).

[**352ZHA.** For persons arriving in the United Kingdom after 1 October 2019, the grant of Section 67 leave will be made upon their arrival in the United Kingdom.]

Note: Paragraph inserted from 1 October 2019 (HC 2631).

[Residence Permits]

[**352ZI.** The Secretary of State will issue to a person granted Section 67 leave a residence permit as soon as possible after the grant of Section 67 leave. The residence permit will be valid for five years.]

Note: Paragraph and heading inserted from 6 July 2018 for decisions made on or after that date (HC 1154).

[**352ZJ.** The Secretary of State will issue a residence permit to a dependant of a person granted Section 67 leave in accordance with paragraph 352ZO.]

Note: Paragraph inserted from 6 July 2018 for decisions made on or after that date (HC 1154).

[**352ZK.** The Secretary of State may revoke a person's residence permit where their grant of Section 67 leave is revoked under the provisions in these Rules.]

Note: Paragraph inserted from 6 July 2018 for decisions made on or after that date (HC 1154).

[Requirements for indefinite leave to remain for a person granted Section 67 leave]

[**352ZL.** A person may apply for indefinite leave to remain under paragraph 352ZN where:

(i) they have been granted Section 67 leave; or

(ii) they transferred to the UK under Section 67 of the Immigration Act 2016 and, having been granted refugee status or humanitarian protection, that person has had their status ended or refused under either paragraph 339A or paragraph 339G of the Immigration Rules following a review.]

Note: Paragraph and heading inserted from 6 July 2018 for decisions made on or after that date (HC 1154).

[**352ZM.** The requirements for indefinite leave to remain for a person described in paragraph 352ZL are that:

(i) each of the requirements of paragraph 352ZH continue to be met;

(ii) the person has held a residence permit issued under paragraph 352ZI, 352ZJ[, 339QA or 339QB] for a continuous period of five years in the UK;

(iii) the person's residence permit has not been revoked; and

(iv) the person has not in the view of the Secretary of State, at the date on which the application has been decided, demonstrated the undesirability of granting settlement in the United Kingdom in light of his or her conduct (including convictions which do not fall within paragraphs 339R(iii)(a-e)), character or associations or the fact that he or she represents a threat to national security.]

Note: Paragraph inserted from 6 July 2018 for decisions made on or after that date (HC 1154). Words in (ii) substituted from 28 June 2022 subject to savings for applications made before that date (HC 17).

[Indefinite leave to remain for a person granted Section 67 leave]

[**352ZN.** Indefinite leave to remain will, on application, be granted to a person described in paragraph 352ZL where each of the requirements in paragraph 352ZM is met.]

Note: Paragraph and heading inserted from 6 July 2018 for decisions made on or after that date (HC 1154).

[Dependants of a person transferred to the UK under Section 67 of the Immigration Act 2016]

[**352ZO.** The dependent child of a person granted leave to remain under paragraph 352ZH or 352ZN, will be granted leave to enter or remain for the same duration as that person ('leave in line') provided that the requirements of paragraph 352ZH (except for (ii)); and 352ZM (iv) are met. For the purposes of this paragraph, a dependent child means a child who is under 18 years of age and for whom the person has parental responsibility.]

Note: Paragraph and heading inserted from 6 July 2018 for decisions made on or after that date (HC 1154).

[Curtailment and Revocation of Section 67 leave]

[**352ZP.** A person's grant of leave under paragraph 352ZH or 352ZN may be curtailed or revoked if any of the grounds in paragraph [[9.3.2, 9.4.2 (b), 9.4.2(c), 9.4.5, 9.7.3, 9.8.8 and 9.9.2 of Part 9 Grounds for refusal apply.]]]

Note: Paragraph and heading inserted from 6 July 2018 for decisions made on or after that date (HC 1154). Words in double square brackets substituted from 09:00 on 1 December 2020 subject to savings for applications made before that time (HC 813).

[**352ZQ.** Any curtailment or revocation of a person's leave under paragraph 352ZP shall also apply to any leave in line granted to a dependent child of that person.]

Note: Paragraph inserted from 6 July 2018 for decisions made on or after that date (HC 1154).

[Travel documents]

[**352ZR.** Following receipt of a completed application for a travel document, the Secretary of State will issue to a person granted Section 67 leave, unless compelling reasons of national security or public order otherwise require, a travel document if that person can demonstrate they are unable to obtain a national passport or other identity documents which enable that person to travel.]

Note: Paragraph and heading inserted from 6 July 2018 for decisions made on or after that date (HC 1154).

[**352ZS.** Where the person referred to in paragraph 352ZR can obtain a national passport or identity documents but has not done so, the Secretary of State will issue that person with a travel document if that person can show that they have made reasonable attempts to obtain a national passport or identity document and there are compelling reasons for travel.]

Note: Paragraph inserted from 6 July 2018 for decisions made on or after that date (HC 1154).

Family Reunion Requirements for leave to enter or remain as the partner of a refugee

352A. The requirements to be met by a person seeking leave to enter or remain in the United Kingdom as the of a person granted [refugee permission to stay] are that:

(i) the applicant is the partner of a person who currently has refugee status granted under the Immigration Rules in the United Kingdom; and

(ii) the marriage or civil partnership did not take place after the person granted refugee status left the country of their former habitual residence in order to seek asylum or the parties have been living together in a relationship akin to marriage or a civil partnership which has subsisted for two years or more before the person granted refugee status left the country of their former habitual residence in order to seek asylum; and

(iii) the relationship existed before the person granted refugee status left the country of their former habitual residence in order to seek asylum; and

(iv) the applicant would not be excluded from protection by virtue of paragraph 334(iii) or (iv) of these Rules or Article 1F of the Refugee Convention [(as defined in Section 36 of the Nationality and Borders Act 2022)] if they were to seek asylum in their own right; and

[(v) each of the parties intends to live permanently with the other as their partner and the relationship is genuine and subsisting]

(vi) if seeking leave to enter, the applicant holds a valid United Kingdom entry clearance for entry in this capacity.

Note: Sub-paragraph (v) substituted from 11 January 2018 subject to savings for applications made before that date (HC 309). Words in introduction substituted, words in (iv) inserted from 28 June 2022 subject to savings for applications made before that date (HC 17).

352AA. DELETED

[**352AB.** The requirements to be met by a person seeking leave to enter or remain in the United Kingdom as the partner of a person granted refugee status and temporary refugee permission are that paragraph 352A (i) to (vii) has been met and there are insurmountable obstacles to the couple living together anywhere other than in the UK, and a refusal of their application would breach the UK's obligations under Article 8 of the ECHR.]

Note: Paragraph inserted from 28 June 2022 subject to savings for applications made before that date (HC 17).

Granting family reunion to the partner of a refugee

352B. Limited leave to enter the United Kingdom as the partner of a person who currently has refugee status may be granted provided [on arrival, a valid passport or other identity document is produced to the Immigration officer and the applicant has entry clearance for entry in this capacity.] Limited leave to remain in the United Kingdom as the partner of a person who currently has refugee status may be granted provided the Secretary of State is satisfied that each of the requirements of paragraph 352A (i) to (vi) [[or 352AB]] are met.

Note: Words in square brackets substituted from 11 January 2018 subject to savings for applications made before that date (HC 309). Words in double square brackets inserted from 28 June 2022 subject to savings for applications made before that date (HC 17).

352BA. Limited leave to enter the United Kingdom as the unmarried or same sex partner of a person who currently has refugee status may be granted provided [on arrival, a valid passport or other identity document is produced to the Immigration Officer and the applicant has entry clearance for entry in this capacity.] Limited leave to remain in the United Kingdom as the unmarried or same sex partner of a person who currently has refugee status may be granted provided the Secretary of State is satisfied that each of the requirements of paragraph 352AA (i) - (vii) [[or 352AB]] are met.

Note: Words in square brackets substituted from 11 January 2018 subject to savings for applications made before that date (HC 309). Words in double square brackets inserted from 28 June 2022 subject to savings for applications made before that date (HC 17).

Refusing family reunion to the partner of a refugee

352C. Limited leave to enter the United Kingdom as the partner of a person who currently has refugee status is to be refused if, [on arrival, a valid passport or other identity document is not produced to the Immigration Officer and the applicant does not have entry clearance for entry in this capacity.] Limited leave to remain as the partner of a person who currently has refugee status is to be refused if the Secretary of State is not satisfied that each of the requirements of paragraph 352A (i) to (vi) [[or 352AB]] are met.

Note: Words in square brackets substituted from 11 January 2018 subject to savings for applications made before that date (HC 309). Words in double square brackets inserted from 28 June 2022 subject to savings for applications made before that date (HC 17).

352CA. DELETED

Requirements for leave to enter or remain as the child of a refugee

352D. The requirements to be met by a person seeking leave to enter or remain in the United Kingdom in order to join or remain with the parent who currently has refugee status [and refugee permission] are that the applicant:

(i) is the child of a parent who currently has refugee status [and refugee permission] granted under the immigration rules in the United Kingdom; and

[(ii) (a) is under the age of 18; or

(b) is over 18 and there are exceptional circumstances (within the meaning of paragraph 352DB);]

(iii) is not leading an independent life, is unmarried and is not a civil partner, and has not formed an independent family unit; and

(iv) was part of the family unit of the person granted asylum at the time that the person granted asylum left the country of their habitual residence in order to seek asylum; and

(v) the applicant would not be excluded from protection by virtue of paragraph 334(iii) or (iv) of these Rules or Article 1F of the Refugee Convention [(as defined in section 36 of the Nationality and Borders Act 2022)] if they were to seek asylum in their own right; and

(vi) if seeking leave to enter, holds a valid United Kingdom entry clearance for entry in this capacity.

Note: Words in introduction, (i) and (v) inserted, sub-paragraph (ii) substituted from 28 June 2022 subject to savings for applications made before that date (HC 17).

[352DA. he requirements to be met by a person seeking leave to enter or remain in the United Kingdom in order to join or remain with a parent who currently has refugee status and temporary refugee permission are that paragraph 352D(i) to (vi) has been met and:

(a) there are insurmountable obstacles to the child and parent living together anywhere other than in the UK; and

(b) a refusal of the application would breach the UK's obligations under Article 8 of the ECHR.]

Note: Paragraph inserted from 28 June 2022 subject to savings for applications made before that date (HC 17).

[Granting leave to enter or remain under exceptional circumstances]

Note: Heading inserted from 28 June 2022 subject to savings for applications made before that date (HC 17).

[352DB. Where the requirements of paragraph 352D(ii)(b) apply, the decision-maker must consider, on the basis of the information provided by the applicant, whether there are exceptional circumstances which may justify a grant of leave to enter or remain, for the same duration as the sponsor ("leave in line").

In the case of an adult child seeking to join a parent with refugee status and refugee permission or temporary refugee permission, or is a beneficiary of humanitarian protection in the UK, criteria which may amount to exceptional circumstances include:

(i) they are dependent on the financial and emotional support of one or both or their parents in the country of origin or in the UK; and

(ii) the parent or parents they depend on is either in the UK, or qualifies for family reunion or resettlement and intends to travel to the UK, or has already travelled to the UK; and

(iii) (a) the applicant is not leading an independent life; and

(b) they have no other relatives to provide means of support; and

(c) they could not access support or employment in the country in which they are living and would therefore likely become destitute if left on their own.

In the event of a refusal of leave to enter or remain on the basis the decision maker is not satisfied there are exceptional circumstances, consideration will also be given to whether refusal of the application would be a breach of Article 8 ECHR.]

Note: Paragraph inserted from 28 June 2022 subject to savings for applications made before that date (HC 17).

Granting family reunion to the child of a refugee

352E. Limited leave to enter the United Kingdom as the child of a person who currently has refugee status may be granted provided[, on arrival, a valid passport or other identity document is produced to the Immigration Officer and the applicant has entry clearance for entry in this capacity.] Limited leave to remain in the United Kingdom as the child of a person who currently has refugee status may be granted provided the Secretary of State is satisfied that each of the requirements of paragraph 352D (i) to (v) [[or 352DA]] are met.

Note: Words in square brackets substituted from 11 January 2018 subject to savings for applications made before that date (HC 309). Words in double square brackets substituted from 28 June 2022 subject to savings for applications made before that date (HC 17).

Refusing family reunion to the child of a refugee

352F. Limited leave to enter the United Kingdom as the child of a person who currently has refugee status is to be refused if, [on arrival, a valid passport or other identity document is not produced to the Immigration Officer and the applicant does not have entry clearance for entry in this capacity.] Limited leave to remain as the child of a person who currently has refugee status is to be refused if the Secretary of State is not satisfied that each of the requirements of paragraph 352D (i) to (v) [[or 352DA]] are met.

Note: Words in square brackets substituted from 11 January 2018 subject to savings for applications made before that date (HC 309). Words in double square brackets substituted from 28 June 2022 subject to savings for applications made before that date (HC 17).

Requirements for leave to enter or remain as the partner of a person with humanitarian protection

352FA. The requirements to be met by a person seeking leave to enter or remain in the United Kingdom as the partner of a person who currently has humanitarian protection and was granted that status on or after 30 August 2005 are that:

(i) the applicant is the civil partner of a person who currently has humanitarian protection granted under the Immigration Rules in the United Kingdom and was granted that status on or after 30 August 2005; and

(ii) the marriage or civil partnership did not take place after the person granted humanitarian protection left the country of their former habitual residence in order to seek asylum in the United Kingdom or the parties have been living together in a relationship akin to marriage or a civil partnership which has subsisted for two years or more before the person granted humanitarian protection left the country of their former habitual residence in order to seek asylum; and

(iii) the relationship existed before the person granted humanitarian protection left the country of their former habitual residence in order to seek asylum; and

(iv) the applicant would not be excluded from a grant of humanitarian protection for any of the reasons in paragraph 339D; and

[(v) each of the parties intends to live permanently with the other as their partner and the relationship is genuine and subsisting]

(vi) the applicant and their partner must not be within the prohibited degree of relationship; and

(vii) if seeking leave to enter, the applicant holds a valid United Kingdom entry clearance for entry in this capacity[; and]

[(xii) there are insurmountable obstacles to the couple living anywhere other than the UK and a refusal of leave would breach the UK's obligations under Article 8 ECHR.]

Note: Sub-paragraph (v) substituted from 11 January 2018 subject to savings for applications made before that date (HC 309). Words in (vii) substituted, sub-paragraph (xii) inserted from 28 June 2022 subject to savings for applications made before that date (HC 17).

Granting family reunion to the partner of a person with humanitarian protection

352FB. Limited leave to enter the United Kingdom as the partner of a person who currently has humanitarian protection may be granted provided[, on arrival, a valid passport or other identity document is produced to the Immigration Officer and the applicant has entry clearance for entry in this capacity.] Limited leave to remain in the United Kingdom as the partner of a person who currently has humanitarian protection may be granted provided the Secretary of State is satisfied that each of the requirements in sub paragraphs 352FA(i) to [[(viii)]] are met.

Note: Words in square brackets substituted from 11 January 2018 subject to savings for applications made before that date (HC 309). Words in double square brackets substituted from 28 June 2022 subject to savings for applications made before that date (HC 17).

Refusing family reunion to the partner of a person with humanitarian protection

352FC. Limited leave to enter the United Kingdom as the partner of a person who currently has humanitarian protection is to be refused if [on arrival, a valid passport or other identity document is not produced to the Immigration Officer and the applicant does not have entry clearance for entry in this capacity.] Limited leave to remain as the partner of a person who currently has humanitarian protection is to be refused if the Secretary of State is not satisfied that each of the requirements in sub paragraphs 352FA (i) to [[(viii)]] are met.

Note: Words in square brackets substituted from 11 January 2018 subject to savings for applications made before that date (HC 309). Words in double square brackets substituted from 28 June 2022 subject to savings for applications made before that date (HC 17).

352FD. DELETED

52FE. DELETED

352FF. DELETED

Requirements for leave to enter or remain as the child of a person with humanitarian protection

352FG. The requirements to be met by a person seeking leave to enter or remain in the United Kingdom in order to join or remain with their parent who currently has humanitarian protection and was granted that status on or after 30 August 2005 are that the applicant:

(i) is the child of a parent who currently has humanitarian protection and was granted that status on or after 30 August 2005 under the Immigration Rules in the United Kingdom; and

[(ii) (a) is under the age of 18; or

(b) is over 18 and there are exceptional circumstances (within the meaning of paragraph 352FGA);]

(iii) is not leading an independent life, is unmarried or is not in a civil partnership, and has not formed an independent family unit; and

(iv) was part of the family unit of the person granted humanitarian protection at the time that the person granted humanitarian protection left the country of their habitual residence in order to seek asylum in the United Kingdom; and

(v) would not be excluded from a grant of humanitarian protection for any of the reasons in paragraph 339D; and

(vi) if seeking leave to enter, holds a valid United Kingdom entry clearance for entry in this capacity[; and]

[(vii) there are insurmountable obstacles to family life continuing elsewhere; and]

[(viii) the Secretary of State is satisfied that family reunion in the UK is in the child's best interests]

Note: Sub-paragraph (ii) and words in (vi) substituted, sub-paragraphs (vii) and (viii) inserted from 28 June 2022 subject to savings for applications made before that date (HC 17).

[Granting leave to enter or remain under exceptional circumstances]

Note: Heading inserted from 28 June 2022 subject to savings for applications made before that date (HC 17).

[**352FGA.** Where the requirements of paragraph 352FG(ii)(b) apply, the decision-maker must consider, on the basis of the information provided by the applicant, whether there are exceptional circumstances which may justify a grant of leave to enter or remain, for the same duration as the sponsor ("leave in line").

In the case of an adult child seeking to join a parent with humanitarian protection and who was granted that status on or after 30 August 2005, relevant factors include:

(i) they are dependent on the financial and emotional support of one or both of their parents in the country of origin or in the UK; and

(ii) the parent or parents they depend on is either in the UK, or qualifies for family reunion or resettlement and intend to travel to the UK, or have already travelled to the UK; and

(iii) (a) the applicant is not leading an independent life; and

(b) they have no other relatives to provide means of support; and

(c) they could not access support or employment in the country in which they are living and would therefore likely become destitute if left on their own.

In the event of a refusal of leave to enter or remain on the basis the decision maker is not satisfied there are exceptional circumstances, consideration will also be given to whether refusal of the application would be a breach of Article 8 ECHR.]

Note: Paragraph inserted from 28 June 2022 subject to savings for applications made before that date (HC 17).

Granting family reunion to the child of a person with humanitarian protection

352FH. Limited leave to enter the United Kingdom as the child of a person who currently has humanitarian protection may be granted provided [on arrival, a valid passport or other identity document is produced to the Immigration Officer and the applicant has entry clearance for entry in this capacity.] Limited leave to remain in the United Kingdom as the child of a person who currently has humanitarian protection may be granted provided the Secretary of State is satisfied that each of the requirements in sub paragraphs 352FG (i) to [[(viii)]] are met.

Note: Words in square brackets substituted from 11 January 2018 subject to savings for applications made before that date (HC 309). Words in double square brackets substituted from 28 June 2022 subject to savings for applications made before that date (HC 17).

Refusing family reunion to the child of a person with humanitarian protection

352FI. Limited leave to enter the United Kingdom as the child of a person who currently has humanitarian protection is to be refused if [on arrival, a valid passport or other identity document is not produced to the Immigration Officer and the applicant does not have entry clearance for entry in this capacity.] Limited leave to remain as the child of a person who currently has humanitarian protection is to be refused if the Secretary of State is not satisfied that each of the requirements in subparagraphs 352FG (i) to [(viii)] are met.

Note: Words in square brackets substituted from 11 January 2018 subject to savings for applications made before that date (HC 309). Words in double square brackets substituted from 28 June 2022 subject to savings for applications made before that date (HC 17).

Refusing family reunion where the sponsor is a British Citizen

352FJ. Nothing in paragraphs 352A to 352FI shall allow a person to be granted leave to enter or remain in the United Kingdom as the partner or child of a person who has been granted refugee status, or granted humanitarian protection under the immigration rules in the United Kingdom on or after 30 August 2005, if the person granted refugee status or granted humanitarian protection, is a British Citizen.

Interpretation

352G. For the purposes of this Part:

[. . .]

(c) 'Country of origin' means the country or countries of nationality or, for a stateless person, or [the country of] former habitual residence.

(d) 'Partner' means the applicant's spouse, civil partner, or a person who has been living together with the applicant in a relationship akin to a marriage or civil partnership for at least two years prior to the date of application;

[. . .]

[(f) 'Refugee permission to stay' means permission to stay granted to refugees under paragraph 339QA of these rules which has not been revoked under paragraph 339QD;]

[(g) 'Temporary refugee permission to stay' means permission to stay granted to refugees under paragraph 339QB of these rules which has not been revoked under paragraph 339QD;]

[(h) 'Temporary humanitarian permission to stay' means permission to stay granted to individuals with humanitarian protection under paragraph 339QC of these rules which has not been revoked under paragraph 339QD.]

Note: Sub-paragraph (b) deleted from 16:00 on 11 May 2022 subject to savings for applications made before that time; sub-paragraph (e) deleted, words in (c), new sub-paragraphs (f), (g) and (h) inserted from 28 June 2022 subject to savings for applications made before that date (HC 17).

Restriction on study

352H. Where a person is granted leave in accordance with the provisions set out in Part 11 of the Immigration Rules that leave will, in addition to any other conditions which may apply, be granted subject to the conditions in [Appendix ATAS] of these Rules.

Note: Words substituted from 09:00 on 5 October 2020 subject to savings for applications made before that time. Where consequential changes relating to the need for an ATAS certificate have been made, they take effect for all applications made or granted on or after 5 October 2020 at 09:00 (HC 707).

[Calais leave to remain in the United Kingdom

352I. Paragraphs 352I to 352X only apply to a person who was transferred to the United Kingdom:

(i) from 17 October 2016 to 13 July 2017 inclusive; and

(ii) in connection with the clearing of the Calais migrant camp; and

(iii) for the purpose of being reunited with family in the United Kingdom, and either:

(a) as part of the expedited process operated by the Secretary of State;

(b) pursuant to an order of the Tribunal; or

(c) under the Dublin III Regulation.]

Note: Paragraph and heading inserted from 5 November 2018 (HC 1534).

[Grant of Calais leave

352J. The person described in paragraph 325I will be granted Calais leave to remain in the United Kingdom ('Calais leave') for a period of five years if the Secretary of State is satisfied that:

(i) the person is not excluded from being a refugee under [Article 1F of the 1951 Refugee Convention (as defined in section 36 of the Nationality and Borders Act 2022)] or excluded from a grant of humanitarian protection under paragraph 339D of these Rules;

(ii) the person's application for refugee status or humanitarian protection has been refused;

(iii) there are no reasonable grounds for regarding the person as a danger to the security of the United Kingdom;

[(iv) the applicant does not constitute a danger to the community in the United Kingdom as a result of having been convicted by a final judgment of a particularly serious crime (as defined in section 72 of the Nationality, Immigration and Asylum Act 2002); and]

[(v) must not fall for refusal under paragraphs 9.2.1 (c), 9.3.1, 9.4.1, 9.4.3, 9.5.1, 9.7.1, 9.7.2, 9.8.1 to 9.8.4, 9.9.1, 9.11.1, 9.12.1 or 9.13.1 of Part 9: grounds for refusal.]

Note: Paragraph and heading inserted from 5 November 2018 (HC 1534). Amendments to (v) from 09:00 on 1 December 2020 subject to savings for applications made before that time (HC 813). Sub-paragraph (v) substituted from 23:00 on 31 December 2020 for decisions made on or after that time (CP 361). Words in (i), sub-paragraph (iv) substituted from 28 June 2022 subject to savings for applications made before that date (HC 17).

[352K. At the end of the five-year period, if each of the requirements of paragraph 352J continue to be met, the person will be granted Calais leave for a further period of five years.]

Note: Paragraph inserted from 5 November 2018 (HC 1534).

[Persons previously granted a form of protection

352L. Where a person was transferred to the UK in accordance with paragraph 352I and, having been granted refugee status or humanitarian protection, that person has had their status ended or refused under either paragraph 339A or paragraph 339G of the Immigration Rules following a review, that person will be entitled to a grant of Calais leave providing that the requirements of paragraph 352J (except sub-paragraph (ii)) are met.]

Note: Paragraph and heading inserted from 5 November 2018 (HC 1534).

[Residence Permits

352M. The Secretary of State will issue to a person granted Calais leave a residence permit as soon as possible after the grant of Calais leave. The residence permit will be valid for five years.]

Note: Paragraph and heading inserted from 5 November 2018 (HC 1534).

[**352N.** The Secretary of State will issue a residence permit to a dependant of a person granted Calais leave in accordance with paragraph 352T.]

Note: Paragraph inserted from 5 November 2018 (HC 1534).

[**352O.** The Secretary of State may revoke or refuse to renew a person's residence permit where their grant of Calais leave is revoked under the provisions in these Rules.]

Note: Paragraph inserted from 5 November 2018 (HC 1534).

[**352P.** At the end of the five-year period, if the person's Calais leave has been renewed, they will be issued with another residence permit, valid for a further period of five years.

Note: Paragraph inserted from 5 November 2018 (HC 1534).

[Requirements for indefinite leave to remain for a person granted Calais leave

[**352Q.** A person may apply for indefinite leave to remain under paragraph 352S where:

(i) they have been granted Calais leave for a continuous period of ten years; or

(ii) having been granted Calais leave under paragraph 352L, they have been granted leave to remain in the UK for a continuous period of ten years.]

Note: Paragraph and heading inserted from 5 November 2018 (HC 1534).

[**352R.** The requirements for indefinite leave to remain for a person described in paragraph 352Q are that:

(i) each of the requirements of paragraph 352J continue to be met;

(ii) the person has held residence permits issued under paragraph 352M, 352N or 352P, and, in the case of a person to whom paragraph 352L applies, paragraph [339QA or 339QB], for a continuous period of ten years in the UK;

(iii) the person's residence permit has not been revoked; and

(iv) the person has not in the view of the Secretary of State, at the date on which the application has been decided, demonstrated the undesirability of granting settlement in the United Kingdom in light of his or her conduct (including convictions which do not fall within paragraphs 339R(iii)(a-e)), character or associations or the fact that he or she represents a threat to national security.]

Note: Paragraph inserted from 5 November 2018 (HC 1534). Words in (ii) substituted from 28 June 2022 subject to savings for applications made before that date (HC 17).

[Indefinite leave to remain for a person granted Calais leave

352S. Indefinite leave to remain will, on application, be granted to a person described in paragraph 352Q where each of the requirements in paragraph 352R is met.]

Note: Paragraph and heading inserted from 5 November 2018 (HC 1534).

[Dependants of a person granted Calais leave

352T. The dependent child of a person granted leave to remain under paragraph 352J or 352S, will be granted leave to enter or remain for the same duration as that person ('leave in line') provided that the requirements of paragraph 352J (except for (ii)); and

352R (iv) are met. For the purposes of this paragraph, a dependent child means a child who is under 18 years of age and for whom the person has parental responsibility.]

Note: Paragraph and heading inserted from 5 November 2018 (HC 1534).

[Curtailment and Revocation of Calais leave

352U. A person's grant of leave under paragraph 352J or 352S may be curtailed or revoked if any of the grounds in paragraph [[9.3.2, 9.4.2 (b), 9.4.2(c), 9.4.5, 9.7.3, 9.8.8. and 9.9.2. of Part 9 Grounds for refusal apply.]]]

Note: Paragraph and heading inserted from 5 November 2018 (HC 1534). Words in double square brackets substituted from 09:00 on 1 December 2020 subject to savings for applications made before that time (HC 813).

[352V. Any curtailment or revocation of a person's leave under paragraph 352U shall also apply to any leave in line granted to a dependent child of that person.]

Note: Paragraph inserted from 5 November 2018 (HC 1534).

[Travel documents]

[352W. Following receipt of a completed application for a travel document, the Secretary of State will issue to a person granted Calais leave, unless compelling reasons of national security or public order otherwise require, a travel document if that person can demonstrate they are unable to obtain a national passport or other identity documents which enable that person to travel.]

Note: Paragraph and heading inserted from 5 November 2018 (HC 1534).

[352X. Where the person referred to in paragraph 352W can obtain a national passport or identity documents but has not done so, the Secretary of State will issue that person with a travel document if that person can show that they have made reasonable attempts to obtain a national passport or identity document and there are compelling reasons for travel.]

Note: Paragraph inserted from 5 November 2018 (HC 1534).

Part 11A

Temporary Protection

Definition of Temporary Protection Directive

354. For the purposes of paragraphs 355 to 356B, 'Temporary Protection Directive' means Council Directive 2001/55/EC of 20 July 2001 regarding the giving of temporary protection by Member States in the event of a mass influx of displaced persons.

Grant of temporary protection

355. An applicant for temporary protection will be granted temporary protection if the Secretary of State is satisfied that:

(i) the applicant is in the United Kingdom or has arrived at a port of entry in the United Kingdom; and

(ii) the applicant is a person entitled to temporary protection as defined by, and in accordance with, the Temporary Protection Directive; and

(iii) the applicant does not hold an extant grant of temporary protection entitling him to reside in another Member State of the European Union. This requirement is subject to the provisions relating to dependants set out in paragraphs 356 to 356B and to any agreement to the contrary with the Member State in question; and

(iv) the applicant is not excluded from temporary protection under the provisions in paragraph 355A.

355A. An applicant or a dependant may be excluded from temporary protection if:

(i) there are serious reasons for considering that:

(a) he has committed a crime against peace, a war crime, or a crime against humanity, as defined in the international instruments drawn up to make provision in respect of such crimes; or

(b) he has committed a serious non-political crime outside the United Kingdom prior to his application for temporary protection; or

(c) he has committed acts contrary to the purposes and principles of the United Nations, or

(ii) there are reasonable grounds for regarding the applicant as a danger to the security of the United Kingdom or, having been convicted by a final judgment of a particularly serious crime, to be a danger to the community of the United Kingdom.

Consideration under this paragraph shall be based solely on the personal conduct of the applicant concerned. Exclusion decisions or measures shall be based on the principle of proportionality.

355B. If temporary protection is granted to a person who has been given leave to enter or remain (whether or not the leave has expired) or to a person who has entered without leave, the Secretary of State will vary the existing leave or grant limited leave to remain.

355C. A person to whom temporary protection is granted will be granted limited leave to enter or remain, which is not to be subject to a condition prohibiting employment, for a period not exceeding 12 months. On the expiry of this period, he will be entitled to apply for an extension of this limited leave for successive periods of 6 months thereafter.

355D. A person to whom temporary protection is granted will be permitted to return to the United Kingdom from another Member State of the European Union during the period of a mass influx of displaced persons as established by the Council of the European Union pursuant to Article 5 of the Temporary Protection Directive.

355E. A person to whom temporary protection is granted will be provided with a document in a language likely to be understood by him in which the provisions relating to temporary protection and which are relevant to him are set out. A person with temporary protection will also be provided with a document setting out his temporary protection status.

355F. The Secretary of State will establish and maintain a register of those granted temporary protection. The register will record the name, nationality, date and place of birth and marital status of those granted temporary protection and their family relationship to any other person who has been granted temporary protection.

355G. If a person who makes an asylum application is also eligible for temporary protection, the Secretary of State may decide not to consider the asylum application until the applicant ceases to be entitled to temporary protection.

Dependants

356. In this part:

'dependant' means a family member or a close relative.

'family member' means:

(i) the spouse or civil partner of an applicant for, or a person who has been granted, temporary protection; or

(ii) the unmarried or same-sex partner of an applicant for, or a person who has been granted, temporary protection where the parties have been living together in a relationship akin to marriage which has subsisted for 2 years or more; or

(iii) the minor child (who is unmarried and not a civil partner); of an applicant for, or a person who has been granted, temporary protection or his spouse, who lived with the principal applicant as part of the family unit in the country of origin immediately prior to the mass influx.

'close relative' means:

(i) the adult child (who is unmarried and not a civil partner), parent or grandparent of an applicant for, or person who has been granted, temporary protection; or

(ii) sibling (who is unmarried and not a civil partner or the uncle or aunt of an applicant for, or person who has been granted, temporary protection, who lived with the principal applicant as part of the family unit in the country of origin immediately prior to the mass influx and was wholly or mainly dependent upon the principal applicant at that time, and would face extreme hardship if reunification with the principal applicant did not take place.

356A. A dependant may apply for temporary protection. Where the dependant falls within paragraph 356 and does not fall to be excluded under paragraph 355A, he will be granted temporary protection for the same duration and under the same conditions as the principal applicant.

356B. When considering any application by a dependant child, the Secretary of State shall take into consideration the best interests of that child.

Part 11B

Asylum

Reception Conditions for non-EU asylum applicants

357. Part 11B only applies to asylum applicants (within the meaning of these Rules) who are not nationals of a member State.

Information to be provided to asylum applicants

357A. The Secretary of State shall inform asylum applicants in a language they may reasonably be supposed to understand and within a reasonable time after their claim for asylum has been recorded of the procedure to be followed, their rights and obligations during the procedure, and the possible consequences of non-compliance and non-cooperation. They shall be informed of the likely timeframe for consideration of the application and the means at their disposal for submitting all relevant information.

358. The Secretary of State shall inform asylum applicants within a reasonable time not exceeding fifteen days after their claim for asylum has been recorded of the benefits and services that they may be eligible to receive and of the rules and procedures with which they must comply relating to them. The Secretary of State shall also provide information on non-governmental organisations and persons that provide legal assistance to asylum applicants and which may be able to help asylum applicants or provide information on available benefits and services.

358A. The Secretary of State shall ensure that the information referred to in paragraph 358 is available in writing and, to the extent possible, will provide the information in a language that asylum applicants may reasonably be supposed to understand. Where appropriate, the Secretary of State may also arrange for this information to be supplied orally.

Information to be provided by asylum applicants

358B. An asylum applicant must notify the Secretary of State of his current address and of any change to his address or residential status. If not notified beforehand, any change must be notified to the Secretary of State without delay after it occurs.

The United Nations High Commissioner for Refugees

358C. A representative of the United Nations High Commissioner for Refugees (UNHCR) or an organisation working in the United Kingdom on behalf of the UNHCR pursuant to an agreement with the government shall:

(a) have access to applicants for asylum, including those in detention;

(b) have access to information on individual applications for asylum, on the course of the procedure and on the decisions taken on applications for asylum, provided that the applicant for asylum agrees thereto;

(c) be entitled to present his views, in the exercise of his supervisory responsibilities under Article 35 of the Geneva Convention, to the Secretary of State regarding individual applications for asylum at any stage of the procedure.

This paragraph shall also apply where the Secretary of State is considering revoking a person's refugee status in accordance with these Rules.

Documentation

359. The Secretary of State shall ensure that, within three working days of recording an asylum application, a document is made available to that asylum applicant, issued in his own name, certifying his status as an asylum applicant or testifying that he is allowed to remain in the United Kingdom while his asylum application is pending. For the avoidance of doubt, in cases where the Secretary of State declines to examine an application it will no longer be pending for the purposes of this rule.

359A. The obligation in paragraph 359 above shall not apply where the asylum applicant is detained under the Immigration Acts, the Immigration and Asylum Act 1999 or the Nationality, Immigration and Asylum Act 2002.

359B. A document issued to an asylum applicant under paragraph 359 does not constitute evidence of the asylum applicant's identity.

359C. In specific cases the Secretary of State or an Immigration Officer may provide an asylum applicant with evidence equivalent to that provided under rule 359. This might be, for example, in circumstances in which it is only possible or desirable to issue a time-limited document.

Right to request permission to take up employment

360. An asylum applicant may apply to the Secretary of State for permission to take up employment if a decision at first instance has not been taken on the applicant's asylum application within one year of the date on which it was recorded. The Secretary of State shall only consider such an application if, in the Secretary of State's opinion, any delay in reaching a decision at first instance cannot be attributed to the applicant.

360A. If permission to take up employment is granted under paragraph 360, that permission will be subject to the following restrictions:

(i) employment may only be taken up in a post which is, at the time an offer of employment is accepted, included on the list of shortage occupations published by the United Kingdom Border Agency (as that list is amended from time to time);

(ii) no work in a self-employed capacity; and

(iii) no engagement in setting up a business.

360B. If an asylum applicant is granted permission to take up employment under paragraph 360 this shall only be until such time as his asylum application has been finally determined.

360C. Where an individual makes further submissions which raise asylum grounds and which fall to be considered under paragraph 353 of these Rules, that individual may apply to the Secretary of State for permission to take up employment if a decision pursuant to paragraph 353 of these Rules has not been taken on the further submissions within one year of the date on which they were recorded. The Secretary of State shall only consider such an application if, in the Secretary of State's opinion, any delay in reaching a decision pursuant to paragraph 353 of these Rules cannot be attributed to the individual.

360D. If permission to take up employment is granted under paragraph 360C, that permission will be subject to the following restrictions:

(i) employment may only be taken up in a post which is, at the time an offer of employment is accepted, included on the list of shortage occupations published by the United Kingdom Border Agency (as that list is amended from time to time);

(ii) no work in a self-employed capacity; and

(iii) no engagement in setting up a business.

360E. Where permission to take up employment is granted pursuant to paragraph 360C, this shall only be until such time as:

(i) a decision has been taken pursuant to paragraph 353 that the further submissions do not amount to a fresh claim; or

(ii) where the further submissions are considered to amount to a fresh claim for asylum pursuant to paragraph 353, all rights of appeal from the immigration decision made in consequence of the rejection of the further submissions have been exhausted.

Interpretation

361. For the purposes of this Part—

(a) 'working day' means any day other than a Saturday or Sunday, a bank holiday, Christmas day or Good Friday;

(b) 'member State' has the same meaning as in Schedule 1 to the European Communities Act 1972.

PART 12

PROCEDURE AND RIGHTS OF APPEAL

Fresh Claims

353. When a human rights or protection claim has been refused or withdrawn or treated as withdrawn under paragraph 333C of these Rules and any appeal relating to that claim is no longer pending, the decision maker will consider any further submissions and, if rejected, will then determine whether they amount to a fresh claim. The submissions will amount to a fresh claim if they are significantly different from the material that has previously been considered. The submissions will only be significantly different if the content:

(i) had not already been considered; and

(ii) taken together with the previously considered material, created a realistic prospect of success, notwithstanding its rejection.

This paragraph does not apply to claims made overseas.

353A. Consideration of further submissions shall be subject to the procedures set out in these Rules. An applicant who has made further submissions shall not be removed before the Secretary of State has considered the submissions under paragraph 353 or otherwise.

Exceptional Circumstances

353B. Where further submissions have been made and the decision maker has established whether or not they amount to a fresh claim under paragraph 353 of these Rules, or in cases with no outstanding further submissions whose appeal rights have been exhausted and which are subject to a review, the decision maker will also have regard to the migrant's:

(i) character, conduct and associations including any criminal record and the nature of any offence of which the migrant concerned has been convicted;

(ii) compliance with any conditions attached to any previous grant of leave to enter or remain and compliance with any conditions of temporary admission or immigration bail where applicable;

(iii) length of time spent in the United Kingdom spent for reasons beyond the migrant's control after the human rights or asylum claim has been submitted or refused;

in deciding whether there are exceptional circumstances which mean that removal from the United Kingdom is no longer appropriate.

This paragraph does not apply to submissions made overseas.

This paragraph does not apply where the person is liable to deportation.

PART 13

DEPORTATION

A deportation order

A362. Where Article 8 is raised in the context of deportation under Part 13 of these Rules, the claim under Article 8 will only succeed where the requirements of these rules as at 28 July 2014 are met, regardless of when the notice of intention to deport or the deportation order, as appropriate, was served.

362. A deportation order requires the subject to leave the United Kingdom and authorises his detention until he is removed. It also prohibits him from re-entering the country for as long as it is in force and invalidates any leave to enter or remain in the United Kingdom given him before the Order is made or while it is in force.

363. The circumstances in which a person is liable to deportation include:

(i) where the Secretary of State deems the person's deportation to be conducive to the public good;

(ii) where the person is the spouse or civil partner or child under 18 of a person ordered to be deported; and

(iii) where a court recommends deportation in the case of a person over the age of 17 who has been convicted of an offence punishable with imprisonment.

363A. Prior to 2 October 2000, a person would have been liable to deportation in certain circumstances in which he is now liable to administrative removal. However, such a person remains liable to deportation, rather than administrative removal where:

(i) a decision to make a deportation order against him was taken before 2 October 2000; or

(ii) the person has made a valid application under the Immigration (Regularisation Period for Overstayers) Regulations 2000.

Deportation of family members

364. DELETED

364A. DELETED

365. The Secretary of State will not normally decide to deport the spouse or civil partner of a deportee under section 5 of the Immigration Act 1971 where:

(i) he has qualified for settlement in his own right; or

(ii) he has been living apart from the deportee.

366. The Secretary of State will not normally decide to deport the child of a deportee under section 5 of the Immigration Act 1971 where:

(i) he and his mother or father are living apart from the deportee; or

(ii) he has left home and established himself on an independent basis; or

(iii) he married or formed a civil partnership before deportation came into prospect.

367. DELETED

368. DELETED

Right of appeal against destination

369. DELETED

Restricted right of appeal against deportation in cases of breach of limited leave

370. DELETED

Exemption to the restricted right of appeal

371. DELETED

372. DELETED

A deportation order made on the recommendation of a Court

373. DELETED

Where deportation is deemed to be conducive to the public good

374. DELETED

375. DELETED

Hearing of appeals

376. DELETED

377. DELETED

378. DELETED

Persons who have claimed asylum

379. DELETED

379A. DELETED

380. DELETED

Procedure

381. When a decision to make a deportation order has been taken (otherwise than on the recommendation of a court) a notice will be given to the person concerned informing him of the decision.

382. Following the issue of such a notice the Secretary of State may authorise detention or make an order restricting a person as to residence, employment or occupation and requiring him to report to the police, pending the making of a deportation order.

383. DELETED

384. DELETED

Arrangements for removal

385. A person against whom a deportation order has been made will normally be removed from the United Kingdom. The power is to be exercised so as to secure the person's return to the country of which he is a national, or which has most recently provided him with a travel document, unless he can show that another country will receive him. In considering any departure from the normal arrangements, regard will be had to the public interest generally, and to any additional expense that may fall on public funds.

386. DELETED

Supervised departure

387. DELETED

Returned deportees

388. Where a person returns to this country when a deportation order is in force against him, he may be deported under the original order. The Secretary of State will consider every such case in the light of all the relevant circumstances before deciding whether to enforce the order.

Returned family members

389. Persons deported in the circumstances set out in paragraphs 365-368 above (deportation of family members) may be able to seek re-admission to the United Kingdom under the Immigration Rules where:

(i) a child reaches 18 (when he ceases to be subject to the deportation order); or

(ii) in the case of a spouse or civil partner, the marriage or civil partnership comes to an end.

Revocation of deportation order

390. An application for revocation of a deportation order will be considered in the light of all the circumstances including the following:

(i) the grounds on which the order was made;

(ii) any representations made in support of revocation;

(iii) the interests of the community, including the maintenance of an effective immigration control;

(iv) the interests of the applicant, including any compassionate circumstances.

390A. Where paragraph 398 applies the Secretary of State will consider whether paragraph 399 or 399A applies and, if it does not, it will only be in exceptional circumstances that the public interest in maintaining the deportation order will be outweighed by other factors.

391. In the case of a person who has been deported following conviction for a criminal offence, the continuation of a deportation order against that person will be the proper course:

(a) in the case of a conviction for an offence for which the person was sentenced to a period of imprisonment of less than 4 years, unless 10 years have elapsed since the making of the deportation order when, if an application for revocation is received, consideration will be given on a case by case basis to whether the deportation order should be maintained, or

(b) in the case of a conviction for an offence for which the person was sentenced to a period of imprisonment of at least 4 years, at any time,

Unless, in either case, the continuation would be contrary to the Human Rights Convention or the Convention and Protocol Relating to the Status of Refugees, or there are other exceptional circumstances that mean the continuation is outweighed by compelling factors.

391A. In other cases, revocation of the order will not normally be authorised unless the situation has been materially altered, either by a change of circumstances since the order was made, or by fresh information coming to light which was not before the appellate authorities or the Secretary of State. The passage of time since the person was deported may also in itself amount to such a change of circumstances as to warrant revocation of the order.

392. Revocation of a deportation order does not entitle the person concerned to re-enter the United Kingdom; it renders him eligible to apply for admission under the Immigration Rules. Application for revocation of the order may be made to the Entry Clearance Officer or direct to the Home Office.

Rights of appeal in relation to a decision not to revoke a deportation order

393. DELETED

394. DELETED

395. DELETED

396. Where a person is liable to deportation the presumption shall be that the public interest requires deportation. It is in the public interest to deport where the Secretary of State must make a deportation order in accordance with section 32 of the UK Borders Act 2007.

397. A deportation order will not be made if the person's removal pursuant to the order would be contrary to the UK's obligations under the Refugee Convention or the Human Rights Convention. Where deportation would not be contrary to these obligations, it will only be in exceptional circumstances that the public interest in deportation is outweighed.

Deportation and Article 8

A398. These rules apply where:

(a) a foreign criminal liable to deportation claims that his deportation would be contrary to the United Kingdom's obligations under Article 8 of the Human Rights Convention;

(b) a foreign criminal applies for a deportation order made against him to be revoked.

398. Where a person claims that their deportation would be contrary to the UK's obligations under Article 8 of the Human Rights Convention, and

(a) the deportation of the person from the UK is conducive to the public good and in the public interest because they have been convicted of an offence for which they have been sentenced to a period of imprisonment of at least 4 years;

(b) the deportation of the person from the UK is conducive to the public good and in the public interest because they have been convicted of an offence for which they have been sentenced to a period of imprisonment of less than 4 years but at least 12 months; or

(c) the deportation of the person from the UK is conducive to the public good and in the public interest because, in the view of the Secretary of State, their offending has caused serious harm or they are a persistent offender who shows a particular disregard for the law,

the Secretary of State in assessing that claim will consider whether paragraph 399 or 399A applies and, if it does not, the public interest in deportation will only be outweighed by other factors where there are very compelling circumstances over and above those described in paragraphs 399 and 399A.

399. This paragraph applies where paragraph 398(b) or (c) applies if –

(a) the person has a genuine and subsisting parental relationship with a child under the age of 18 years who is in the UK, and

(i) the child is a British Citizen; or

(ii) the child has lived in the UK continuously for at least the 7 years immediately preceding the date of the immigration decision; and in either case

(a) it would be unduly harsh for the child to live in the country to which the person is to be deported; and

(b) it would be unduly harsh for the child to remain in the UK without the person who is to be deported; or

(b) the person has a genuine and subsisting relationship with a partner who is in the UK and is a British citizen or settled in the UK, and

(i) the relationship was formed at a time when the person (deportee) was in the UK lawfully and their immigration status was not precarious; and

(ii) it would be unduly harsh for that partner to live in the country to which the person is to be deported, because of compelling circumstances over and above those described in paragraph EX.2. of Appendix FM; and

(iii) it would be unduly harsh for that partner to remain in the UK without the person who is to be deported.

399A. This paragraph applies where paragraph 398(b) or (c) applies if—

(a) the person has been lawfully resident in the UK for most of his life; and

(b) he is socially and culturally integrated in the UK; and

(c) there would be very significant obstacles to his integration into the country to which it is proposed he is deported.

399B. Where an Article 8 claim from a foreign criminal is successful:

(a) in the case of a person who is in the UK unlawfully or whose leave to enter or remain has been cancelled by a deportation order, limited leave may be granted for periods not exceeding 30 months and subject to such conditions as the Secretary of State considers appropriate;

(b) in the case of a person who has not been served with a deportation order, any limited leave to enter or remain may be curtailed to a period not exceeding 30 months and conditions may be varied to such conditions as the Secretary of State considers appropriate;

(c) indefinite leave to enter or remain may be revoked under section 76 of the 2002 Act and limited leave to enter or remain granted for a period not exceeding 30 months subject to such conditions as the Secretary of State considers appropriate;

(d) revocation of a deportation order does not confer entry clearance or leave to enter or remain or re-instate any previous leave.

399C. DELETED

399D. Where a foreign criminal has been deported and enters the United Kingdom in breach of a deportation order enforcement of the deportation order is in the public interest and will be implemented unless there are very exceptional circumstances.

[**400.** Where a person claims that their removal under paragraphs 8 to 10 of Schedule 2 to the Immigration Act 1971, section 10 of the Immigration and Asylum Act 1999 or section 47 of the Immigration, Asylum and Nationality Act 2006 would be contrary to the UK's obligations under Article 8 of the Human Rights Convention, the Secretary of State may require an application under Appendix Private Life or under paragraphs R-LTRP.1.1.(a), (b) and (d), R-LTRPT.1.1.(a), (b) and (d) and EX.1. of Appendix FM (family life as a partner or parent) of these rules. Where an application is not required, in assessing that claim the Secretary of State or an immigration officer will, subject to paragraph 353, consider that claim against the requirements to be met (except the requirement to make a valid application) under Appendix Private Life or paragraphs R-LTRP.1.1.(a), (b) and (d),

R-LTRPT.1.1.(a), (b) and (d) and EX.1. of Appendix FM (family life as a partner or parent) of these rules as appropriate and if appropriate, the removal decision will be cancelled.]

Note: Paragraph substituted from 20 June 2022 subject to savings for applications made before that date (HC 1118).

Part 14

Stateless persons

Definition of a stateless person

401. For the purposes of this Part a stateless person is a person who:

(a) satisfies the requirements of Article 1(1) of the 1954 United Nations Convention relating to the Status of Stateless Persons, as a person who is not considered as a national by any State under the operation of its law;

(b) is in the United Kingdom; and

(c) is not excluded from recognition as a Stateless person under paragraph 402.

Exclusion from recognition as a stateless person

402. A person is excluded from recognition as a stateless person if there are serious reasons for considering that they:

(a) are at present receiving from organs or agencies of the United Nations, other than the United Nations High Commissioner for Refugees, protection or assistance, so long as they are receiving such protection or assistance;

(b) are recognised by the competent authorities of the country of their former habitual residence as having the rights and obligations which are attached to the possession of the nationality of that country;

(c) have committed a crime against peace, a war crime, or a crime against humanity, as defined in the international instruments drawn up to make provisions in respect of such crimes;

(d) have committed a serious non-political crime outside the UK prior to their arrival in the UK;

(e) have been guilty of acts contrary to the purposes and principles of the United Nations.

Requirements for limited leave to remain as a stateless person

403. The requirements for leave to remain in the United Kingdom as a stateless person are that the applicant:

(a) has made a valid application to the Secretary of State for limited leave to remain as a stateless person;

(b) is recognised as a stateless person by the Secretary of State in accordance with paragraph 401;

[(c) has taken reasonable steps to facilitate admission to their country of former habitual residence or any other country but has been unable to secure the right of admission;]

(d) has obtained and submitted all reasonably available evidence to enable the Secretary of State to determine whether they are stateless [or whether they are admissible to another country under the meaning of paragraph 403(c)].

[(e) has sought and failed to obtain or re-establish their nationality with the appropriate authorities of the relevant country; and

(f) if, in the case of a child born in the UK, has provided evidence that they have attempted to register their birth with the relevant authorities but have been refused.]

Note: Sub-paragraph (c) substituted; words in (d), sub-paragraphs (e) and (f) inserted from 6 April 2019 subject to savings for applications made before that date (HC 1919).

Refusal of limited leave to remain as a stateless person

404. An applicant will be refused leave to remain in the United Kingdom as a stateless person if:

(a) they do not meet the requirements of paragraph 403;
(b) there are reasonable grounds for considering that they are:
(i) a danger to the security of the United Kingdom;
(ii) a danger to the public order of the United Kingdom; or
(c) their application would fall to be refused under any of the grounds set out in [Part 9] of these Rules.

Note: Words in (c) substituted from 09:00 on 1 December 2020 subject to savings for applications made before that time (HC 813).

Grant of limited leave to remain to a stateless person

405. Where an applicant meets the requirements of paragraph 403 they may be granted limited leave to remain in the United Kingdom for a period not exceeding [five years].

Note: Words substituted from 6 April 2019 subject to savings for applications made before that date (HC 1919).

Curtailment of limited leave to remain as a stateless person

406. Limited leave to remain as a stateless person under paragraph 405 may be curtailed where the stateless person is a danger to the security or public order of the United Kingdom or where leave would be [cancelled under Part 9] of these Rules.

Note: Words substituted from 09:00 on 1 December 2020 subject to savings for applications made before that time (HC 813).

Requirements for indefinite leave to remain as a stateless person

407. The requirements for indefinite leave to remain as a stateless person are that the applicant:

(a) has made a valid application to the Secretary of State for indefinite leave to remain as a stateless person;

(b) was last granted limited leave to remain as a stateless person in accordance with paragraph 405;

(c) has spent a continuous period of five years in the United Kingdom with [stateless leave granted under Rule 405], except that, where paragraph 39E of these Rules applies, any current period of overstaying will be disregarded. Any previous period of overstaying between periods of leave will also be disregarded where: the further application was made before 24 November 2016 and within 28 days of the expiry of leave; or the further application was made on or after 24 November 2016 and paragraph 39E of these Rules applied;

(d) continues to meet the requirements of paragraph 403.

Note: Words in (c) substituted from 6 April 2019 subject to savings for applications made before that date (HC 1919).

Grant of indefinite leave remain as a stateless person

408. Where an applicant meets the requirements of paragraph 407 they may be granted indefinite leave to remain.

Refusal of indefinite leave to remain as a stateless person

409. An applicant will be refused indefinite leave to remain if:

(a) the applicant does not meet the requirements of paragraph 407;

(b) there are reasonable grounds for considering that the applicant is:

(i) a danger to the security of the United Kingdom;

(ii) a danger to the public order of the United Kingdom; or

(c) the application would fall to be refused under [Part 9] of these Rules.

Note: Words in (c) substituted from 09:00 on 1 December 2020 subject to savings for applications made before that time (HC 813).

Requirements for limited leave to enter or remain as the family member of a stateless person

410. For the purposes of this Part a family member of a stateless person means their:

(a) spouse;

(b) civil partner;

(c) unmarried [. . .] partner with whom they have lived together in a subsisting relationship akin to marriage or a civil partnership for two years or more;

(d) child under 18 years of age who:

(i) is not leading an independent life;

[(ii) is not married, in a civil partnership or has an unmarried partner with whom they have lived together in a subsisting relationship akin to marriage or a civil partnership for two years or more; and]

(iii) has not formed an independent family unit.

Note: Words in (c) deleted; (d)(ii) substituted from 6 April 2019 subject to savings for applications made before that date (HC 1919).

411. The requirements for leave to enter or remain in the United Kingdom as the family member of a stateless person are that the applicant:

(a) has made a valid application to the Secretary of State for leave to enter or remain as the family member of a stateless person;

(b) is the family member of a person granted leave to remain under paragraphs 405 or 408;

(c) if seeking leave to enter, holds a valid United Kingdom entry clearance for entry in this capacity.

Refusal of leave to enter or remain as the family member of a stateless person

412. A family member will be refused leave to enter or remain if:

(a) they do not meet the requirements of paragraph 411;

(b) there are reasonable grounds for considering that:

(i) they are a danger to the security of the United Kingdom;

(ii) they are a danger to the public order of the United Kingdom; or

(c) their application would fall to be refused under [Part 9] of these Rules.

Note: Words in (c) substituted from 09:00 on 1 December 2020 subject to savings for applications made before that time (HC 813).

Grant of leave to enter or remain as the family member of a stateless person

413. A person who meets the requirements of paragraph 411 may be granted leave to enter or remain for a period not exceeding [five years].

Note: Words substituted from 6 April 2019 subject to savings for applications made before that date (HC 1919).

Curtailment of limited leave to enter or remain as the family member of a stateless person

414. Limited leave to remain as the family member of a stateless person under paragraph 413 may be curtailed where the family member is a danger to the security or public order of the United Kingdom or where leave would be [cancelled under Part 9] of these Rules.

Note: Words in (c) substituted from 09:00 on 1 December 2020 subject to savings for applications made before that time (HC 813).

Requirements for indefinite leave to remain as the family member of a stateless person

415. The requirements for indefinite leave to remain as the family member of a stateless person are that the applicant:

(a) has made a valid application to the Secretary of State for indefinite leave to remain as the family member of a stateless person;

(b) was last granted limited leave to remain as a family member of a stateless person in accordance with paragraph 413; and

(i) is still a family member of a stateless person; or

(ii) is over 18 and was last granted leave as the family member of a stateless person; and

(a) is not leading an independent life;

(b) is not married or a civil partner;

(c) has not formed an independent family unit; and

(c) has spent a continuous period of five years with [stateless leave granted under Rule 413] leave in the United Kingdom, except that, where paragraph 39E of these Rules applies, any current period of overstaying will be disregarded. Any previous period of overstaying between periods of leave will also be disregarded where: the further application was made before 24 November 2016 and within 28 days of the expiry of leave; or the further application was made on or after 24 November 2016 and paragraph 39E of these Rules applied.

Note: Words in (c) substituted from 6 April 2019 subject to savings for applications made before that date (HC 1919).

Refusal of indefinite leave to remain as the family member of a stateless person

416. An applicant will be refused indefinite leave to remain as a family member of a stateless person if:

(a) they do not meet the requirements of paragraph 415;

(b) there are reasonable grounds for considering that:

(i) they are a danger to the security of the United Kingdom;

(ii) they are a danger to the public order of the United Kingdom; or

(c) the application would fall to be refused [under Part 9] of these Rules.

Note: Words in (c) substituted from 09:00 on 1 December 2020 subject to savings for applications made before that time (HC 813).

Part 15 [DELETED]

Note: Amendments from 6 July 2018 subject to savings for applications made before that date (HC 1154). Amendments from 1 August 2019 (HC 1779). Part deleted from 09:00 on 5 October 2020 subject to savings for applications made before that time (HC 707).

Appendix 2

Countries or Territories Whose Nationals or Citizens are Relevant Foreign Nationals for the Purposes of Part 10 of These Rules (Registration with the Police)

Afghanistan
Algeria
Argentina
Armenia
Azerbaijan
Bahrain
Belarus
Bolivia
Brazil
China
Colombia
Cuba
Egypt
Georgia
Iran
Iraq
Israel
Jordan
Kazakhstan
Kuwait
Kyrgyzstan
Lebanon
Libya
Moldova
Morocco
North Korea
Oman
Palestine
Peru
Qatar
Russia
Saudi Arabia
Sudan
Syria
Tajikistan
Tunisia
Turkey
Turkmenistan
United Arab Emirates
Ukraine
Uzbekistan
Yemen

[Appendix 6—DELETED]

Note: Appendix substituted from 1 January 2019 for decisions made on or after that date where an applicant is required to provide a certificate in accordance with Appendix 6 and has submitted with their application a certificate which they requested from the Foreign and Commonwealth Office (FCO) before 1 January 2019 (the date on which the Joint Academic Coding System (JACS) codes change to Common Aggregation Hierarchy (CAH) codes and the FCO updates the list of courses which require a certificate), the old course codes in force on 31 December 2018 will be treated as valid on the certificate (HC 1534). Appendix deleted from 09:00 on 5 October 2020 subject to savings for applications made before that time (HC 707).

[Appendix 7–DELETED]

Note: Amendments from 5 November 2018 (HC 1534). Appendix deleted from 09:00 on 11 October 2021 subject to savings for applications made before that time (HC 617)

Appendix A

Attributes

Attributes for Tier 1 (Exceptional Talent) Migrants

1. [DELETED]

Note: Amendments from 20 February 2020 subject to savings for applications made before that date (HC 56). Paragraph deleted from 09:00 on 1 December 2020 subject to savings for applications made before that time (HC 813).

2. [DELETED]

Note: Paragraph deleted from 09:00 on 1 December 2020 subject to savings for applications made before that time (HC 813).

3. [DELETED]

Note: Table 1 substituted from 20 February 2020 subject to savings for applications made before that date (HC 56). Paragraph and Table 1 deleted from 09:00 on 1 December 2020 subject to savings for applications made before that time (HC 813).

4. [DELETED]

Note: Amendments from 11 January 2018 subject to savings for applications made before that date (HC 309). Amendments from 6 July 2018 subject to savings for applications made before that date (HC 1154). Paragraph deleted from 20 February 2020 subject to savings for applications made before that date (HC 56).

5. [DELETED]

Note: Amendments from 11 January 2018 subject to savings for applications made before that date (HC 309). Amendments from 6 July 2018 subject to savings for applications made before that date (HC 1154). Paragraph deleted from 20 February 2020 subject to savings for applications made before that date (HC 56).

6. [DELETED]

Note: Paragraph deleted from 20 February 2020 subject to savings for applications made before that date (HC 56).

Money earned in the UK

6A. [DELETED]

Note: Amendments from 5 November 2018 (HC 1534). Amendments from 20 February 2020 subject to savings for applications made before that date (HC 56). Paragraph deleted from 09:00 on 1 December 2020 subject to savings for applications made before that time (HC 813).

Attributes for Tier 1 (General) Migrants

7. DELETED
8. DELETED
9. DELETED
10. DELETED
11. DELETED
12. DELETED

Qualifications: notes

13. DELETED
14. DELETED

14-SD. DELETED

15. DELETED
16. DELETED
17. DELETED
18. DELETED
19. DELETED
19-SD. DELETED

Period for assessment

20. DELETED
21. DELETED
21-SD. DELETED
22. DELETED

Earnings

23. DELETED
24. DELETED
25. DELETED
26. DELETED

Converting foreign currencies

27. DELETED
28. DELETED
29. DELETED
30. DELETED
31. DELETED
32. DELETED

Age: notes

33. DELETED
34. DELETED
34-SD. DELETED

Note: Paragraphs 7 to 34-SD deleted from 6 July 2018 subject to savings for applications made before that date (HC 1154).

[Attributes for Tier 1 (Entrepreneur) Migrants

35. An applicant applying for entry clearance, leave to remain or indefinite leave to remain as a Tier 1 (Entrepreneur) Migrant must score 75 points for attributes.]

Note: Paragraph and heading substituted from 11 January 2018 subject to savings for applications made before that date (HC 309).

[**36.** Available points are shown in Table 4 for initial applications for applicants who have entry clearance, leave to enter or leave to remain as a Tier 1 (Graduate Entrepreneur) Migrant or a Start-up migrant, or have had such leave in the 12 months immediately before the date of application.]

Note: Paragraph substituted from 11 January 2018 subject to savings for applications made before that date (HC 309). Paragraph substituted from 29 March 2019 subject to savings for applications made before that date (HC 1919).

[**37.** Available points are shown in Table 5 for extension applications for applicants who have entry clearance, leave to enter or leave to remain as a Tier 1 (Entrepreneur) Migrant, or have had such leave in the 12 months immediately before the date of application.]

Note: Paragraph substituted from 11 January 2018 subject to savings for applications made before that date (HC 309).

[**38.** Available points for applications for indefinite leave to remain are shown in Table 6.]

Note: Paragraph substituted from 11 January 2018 subject to savings for applications made before that date (HC 309).

[Notes

39. (a) In all cases, an applicant cannot score points from any of the following:

(i) the same money being used to score points for maintenance funds for themselves or their dependants under Appendices C or E,

(ii) money made available from a third party, where the third party is another Tier 1 (Entrepreneur) Migrant, or that migrant's business or close family member,

(iii) money invested in their business more than 12 months (or 24 months if the applicant was previously granted leave as a Tier 1 (Graduate Entrepreneur) Migrant) before the date of the application which led to their first grant of leave as a Tier 1 (Entrepreneur) Migrant,

(iv) money invested in the form of a director's loan unless it is unsecured and subordinated to other creditors' loans to the business, or

(v) investment in any residential accommodation, property development or property management, meaning:

(1) any development of property owned by the applicant or their business to increase the value of the property with a view to earning a return either through rent or a future sale or both, or

(2) management of property (whether or not it is owned by the applicant or their business) for the purposes of renting it out or resale.

For the avoidance of doubt, (v) requires that the business income is generated from the supply of goods and/or services, and not derived from the increased value of property or any income generated from property, such as rent.

(b) Points will only be awarded for an applicant's business if it is a UK business.

(c) A business will be considered to be a UK business if the applicant provides the specified evidence in this Appendix to show that:

(i) it is trading within the UK economy,

(ii) it has its registered office in the UK, or, in the case of multinational companies with no UK registered office, its head office in the UK, except where the applicant is registered with HM Revenue & Customs as self-employed and does not have a business office,

(iii) it has a UK bank account, and
(iv) it is subject to UK taxation.

(d) Points will not be awarded for being the director of a UK business or member of a UK partnership if the applicant is on Companies House's list of disqualified directors.

(e) Where evidence from an accountant is required, it will only be accepted if the accountant:

(i) is not the applicant,
(ii) has prepared and signed off the accounts in accordance with all relevant statutory requirements,
(iii) has a valid licence to practice or practising certificate, and
(iv) is a member of at least one of the following:
(1) the Institute of Chartered Accountants in England and Wales,
(2) the Institute of Chartered Accountants in Scotland,
(3) the Institute of Chartered Accountants in Ireland,
(4) the Association of Chartered Certified Accountants,
(5) the Association of Authorised Public Accountants,
(6) the Chartered Institute of Public Finance and Accountancy,
(7) the Institute of Financial Accountants,
(8) the Chartered Institute of Management Accountants,
(9) the Association of International Accountants, or
(10) the Association of Accounting Technicians.

(f) Where personal or business bank statements are required:

(i) The bank or building society must be based in the UK and regulated by the Financial Conduct Authority (FCA) and the Prudential Regulation Authority (PRA).

(ii) Each statement must be on the institution's official stationery showing the institution's name and logo, and confirm the applicant's name (and, where relevant, the applicant's entrepreneurial team partner's name), the account number and the date of the statement.

(iii) Each statement must have been issued by an authorised official of that institution.

(iv) If the statements are printouts of electronic statements, they must either be accompanied by a supporting letter from the institution, on its headed paper, confirming the authenticity of the statements, or bear the official stamp of the institution on each page of the statement.

(g) Further notes to accompany Table 4 appear below Table 4.
(h) Further notes to accompany Tables 5 and 6 appear below Table 6.]

Table 4: Initial applications as referred to in paragraph 36

Row	Investment and business activity	Points
[1]	[At least £50,000 is available to the applicant or their business, or has been invested in their business due to their activity.]	[25]
2	The money is held in one or more financial institutions, which are regulated by the appropriate regulatory body for the country in which they operate.	25
3	The money is disposable in the UK. If the applicant is applying for leave to remain, the money must be held in the UK.	25

Note: Heading, paragraph and table substituted from 11 January 2018 subject to savings for applications made before that date (HC 309). Row 1 in table substituted from 29 March 2019 subject to savings for applications made before that date (HC 1919).

[Available money: notes]

[**40.** (a) Available money must be cash, not Individual Savings Accounts or other assets such as stocks and shares.

(b) Where multiple documents are provided, they must show the total amount required is available on the same date.

(c) The money must either be held in a UK regulated financial institution or be transferable to the UK and convertible to sterling.

(d) If the money is available to the applicant's business, rather than to the applicant themselves, the business must be a company or partnership and the applicant must be registered as a director, in the case of a company, or member, in the case of a partnership.

(e) The money must remain available to the applicant or their business until it is spent for the purposes of the applicant's business(es). The Secretary of State reserves the right to request further evidence or otherwise verify that the money will remain available, and to refuse the application if this evidence is not provided or cannot be satisfactorily verified.

[. . .]

(g) Money is disposable in the UK if all of the money is held in a UK based financial institution and free from sanctions or if the money is freely transferable to the UK and convertible to sterling. Funds in a foreign currency will be converted to pounds sterling (£) using the spot exchange rate which appeared on www.oanda.com on the date of application.

(h) [No points will be awarded unless the money is held in a financial institution permitted under Appendix Finance.]

Note: Paragraph and heading substituted from 11 January 2018 subject to savings for applications made before that date (HC 309). Sub-paragraph (f) deleted from 29 March 2019 subject to savings for applications made before that date (HC 1919). Words in (h) substituted from 09:00 on 1 December 2020 subject to savings for applications made before that time (HC 813).

[Available money: specified documents]

[**41.** (a) If all or part of the money has not yet been invested in the applicant's business, the applicant must provide all of the specified documents set out in the relevant row of Table 4A below. If the applicant is claiming points for available money from more than one source, the applicant must provide the specified documents for each row which applies.

Table 4A: Specified documents showing available money

Row	Available money	Specified documents (see descriptions below table)
1	Money available from a seed funding competition or a UK or Devolved Government Department, as set out in Table 4	(i)
[2]	Money available from a third party, other than those in [row 1 above], where the money is still held by the third party	All of (vi)-(viii)

Row	Available money	Specified documents (see descriptions below table)
[3]	Money held by the applicant for less than 90 consecutive days, ending no earlier than 31 days before the date of application, where the source of that money is other than those in row 1 above.	(vi)and (vii), and either (ix) or (x) as appropriate
[4]	Money held by the applicant for at least 90 consecutive days, ending no earlier than 31 days before the date of application	Either (ix) or (x) as appropriate

Note: Table substituted from 11 January 2018 subject to savings for applications made before that date (HC 309). Row 2 deleted, subsequent rows renumbered; words in new row 2 substituted from 29 March 2019 subject to savings for applications made before that date (HC 1919).

Specified documents:

(i) A letter confirming the amount of money available to the applicant, the entrepreneurial team or the applicant's business from the seed funding competition or a UK or Devolved Government Department. The letter must be from an authorised official of that organisation or, in the case of a UK or Devolved Government Department, a letter from an authorised official of an intermediary public body providing it confirms that it has been authorised to award funds from that Department for the specific purpose of establishing or expanding UK businesses.

[...]

[...]

[...]

[...]

(vi) [A] written declaration from each third party that they have made the money available to invest in the applicant's business in the UK, containing:

(1) the names of the third party and the applicant (and their entrepreneurial team partner's name where relevant), or the name of the applicant's business,

(2) the date of the declaration,

(3) the applicant's signature and the signature of the third party (and the signature of the applicant's entrepreneurial team partner where relevant),

(4) the amount of money available in pounds sterling,

(5) the relationship(s) of the third party to the applicant,

(6) if the third party is another business in which the applicant is self-employed or a director, evidence of the applicant's status within that business and that the applicant is the sole controller of that business's finances, or, where the applicant is not the sole controller, the letter must be signed by another authorised official of that business who is not the applicant, and

(7) confirmation that the money will remain available until such time as it is transferred to the applicant, the entrepreneurial team or the applicant's business.

(vii) A letter (or letters) from one or more legal representatives, who are not the applicant or the third party, which confirm(s) that [all letters and declarations in (ii)-(vi) and (viii) (where required)] contain the genuine signatures of the required signatories. The letter(s) must clearly show the registration or authority of the legal representative to practise legally in the country where the third party or the money is.

(viii) A letter from each financial institution holding the funds, issued by an authorised official of that institution, confirming in each case the amount of money that the third party intends to make available, and that the institution is not aware of the third party having promised to make that money available to any other person available.

(ix) For money held outside the UK, a letter from each financial institution holding the funds, issued by an authorised official of that institution, confirming the minimum balance available from the applicant's own funds held in that institution on the date of the letter and, in the case as described in [row 4 of Table 4A], during a consecutive 90-day period of time ending on the date of the letter.

(x) For money held in the UK, recent [...] personal bank or building society statements, with the most recent statement being dated no earlier than 31 days before the date of application, which taken altogether show that the relevant required sum of available money is held in the account(s) on the date of the most recent statement(s). In the case described in [row 4 of Table 4A], the statements must show the sum has been held for a consecutive 90 day period of time immediately before the date of the statement.

(b) Each letter referred to in [(a)(i)] and (vii)-(ix) above must:

[...]

(2) be on the organisation's official headed paper,

(3) be dated no earlier than three months [(in the case of (i) and (vii)], or 31 days (in the case of (viii) and (ix)), immediately before the date of application,

(4) state the applicant's name, and their entrepreneurial team partner's name where relevant, or the name of the applicant's business,

(5) include the contact details of the person or (where relevant) an official of the organisation issuing the letter

(6) include (where relevant) the name of the third party providing the money, including their full address, postal code, telephone contact number and any email address,

(7) in the case of (vii), include the number of the third party or their authorised representative's identity document (such as a passport or national identity card), the place of issue and dates of issue and expiry[...].

(8) in the case of (viii)-(ix), show the account number,

(9) in the case of (viii)-(ix), confirm that the financial institution is regulated by the appropriate body and, if not regulated by the Financial Conduct Authority (FCA) and the Prudential Regulation Authority (PRA), that the money can be transferred into the UK.]

Note: Paragraph and heading substituted from 11 January 2018 subject to savings for applications made before that date (HC 309). Words in (a)(vii) substituted from 6 July 2018 subject to savings for applications made before that date (HC 1154). Word in (a)(vi) substituted; words in (a)(x), (b)(1) deleted from 5 November 2018 (HC 1534). Sub-paragraphs (a)(ii) to (v), words in (b)(7) deleted; words in (b) and (b)(3) substituted from 29 March 2019 subject to savings for applications made before that date (HC 1919). Words in (a)(ix) and (x) substituted from 1 October 2019 subject to savings for applications made before that date (HC 2631).

[**42.** If the money is available to the applicant's business, rather than to the applicant themselves, the applicant must also provide a Companies House document showing the address of the business's registered office in the UK, or head office in the UK if it has no registered office in the UK, and that the applicant is a director, in the case of a company, or member, in the case of a partnership.]

Note: Paragraph substituted from 11 January 2018 subject to savings for applications made before that date (HC 309).

[**43.** If all or part of the money has been invested in the applicant's business, the applicant must provide:

(a) all of the specified documents required in paragraph 45 to show the amount of money invested, and

(b) all of the specified documents required in paragraph 48 to show that the applicant has established a new UK business or joined or taken over an existing UK business, in which the money was invested.]

Note: Paragraph substituted from 11 January 2018 subject to savings for applications made before that date (HC 309).

[...]

44. [DELETED]

Note: Amendments from 11 January 2018 subject to savings for applications made before that date (HC 309). Amendments from 5 November 2018 (HC 1534). Paragraph and heading deleted from 29 March 2019 subject to savings for applications made before that date (HC 1919).

Table 5: Extension applications as referred to in paragraph 37

Row	Investment, business activity and job creation	Points
1	The applicant has invested or has caused investment to be made by one or more third parties, totalling at least £200,000 (or £50,000 if they were awarded points for £50,000 funding or investment in their last grant of leave) in cash directly into one or more UK businesses. The applicant does not need to provide evidence of this investment if they were awarded points under Table 5 in their last grant of entry clearance or leave to remain as a Tier 1 (Entrepreneur) Migrant.	20
2	The applicant has: – registered with HM Revenue & Customs as self-employed, or – registered with Companies House as a director of a UK company, or member of a UK partnership. The applicant must have registered as above within 6 months of entering the UK (if they were most recently granted entry clearance and there is evidence to establish their date of entry) or, in any other case, within 6 months of the date on which the most recent leave was granted.	20
3	Within the three months before the date of application, the applicant was: (a) registered with HM Revenue & Customs as self-employed, or (b) registered with Companies House as a director of a UK company or member of a UK partnership.	15
4	The applicant has: (a) established a new business or businesses that has or have created the equivalent of at least 2 new full time jobs for settled workers, or	20

Row	Investment, business activity and job creation	Points
	(b) taken over or invested in an existing business or businesses and their services or investment have resulted in a net increase in the employment provided by the business or businesses for settled workers by creating the equivalent of at least 2 new full time jobs for settled workers. The jobs must have existed for at least 12 months during the applicant's most recent grant of leave as a Tier 1 (Entrepreneur) Migrant or, where that leave was granted less than 12 months ago, for at least the 12 months immediately before the date of application.	

Note: Table substituted from 11 January 2018 subject to savings for applications made before that date (HC 309).

Table 6: Applications for indefinite leave to remain as referred to in paragraph 38

Row	Investment, business activity and job creation	Points
1	The applicant has invested or has caused investment to be made by one or more third parties, totalling at least £200,000 (or £50,000 if they were awarded points for £50,000 funding or investment in their last grant of leave) in cash directly into one or more UK businesses. The applicant does not need to provide evidence of this investment if they were last granted entry clearance or leave to remain as a Tier 1 (Entrepreneur) Migrant, having been awarded points under Table 5.	20
2	The applicant was: (a) registered with HM Revenue & Customs as self-employed, or registered with Companies House as a director of a UK company or member of a UK partnership. The above requirement must have been met: (i) within 6 months of entering the UK (if they were most recently granted entry clearance and there is evidence to establish their date of entry) or, in any other case, within 6 months from the date the most recent leave was granted, and (ii) within the three months before the date of application. The applicant does not need to provide evidence of (i) if they were last granted entry clearance or leave to remain as a Tier 1 (Entrepreneur) Migrant, having been awarded points under Table 5.	20

Row	Investment, business activity and job creation	Points
3	The applicant has: (a) established a new business or businesses that has or have created the equivalent of at least 2 new full time jobs for settled workers, or (b) taken over or invested in an existing business or businesses and their services or investment have resulted in a net increase in the employment provided by the business or businesses for settled workers by creating the equivalent of at least 2 new full time jobs for settled workers. The jobs must have existed for at least 12 months during the applicant's most recent grant of leave or, where that leave was granted less than 12 months ago, for at least the 12 months immediately before the date of application. [In respect of an applicant who was granted a COVID-19 related extension of leave, the applicant must have: (i) created two jobs meeting the criteria in (a) or (b) for at least the 12-month period referred to above; and (ii) created at least a further two jobs meeting the criteria in (a) or (b) that have been in existence for at least 12 months by the date of application (these jobs can be the same as (i) providing they meet the requirement of existing for at least a further 12 months).]	20
4	(a) The applicant has spent a continuous period of 5 years lawfully in the UK with leave as a Tier 1 (Entrepreneur) Migrant, or (b) The applicant has spent a continuous period of 3 years lawfully in the UK as a Tier 1 (Entrepreneur) Migrant, and has: (i) created the equivalent of at least 10 (including the [. . .] jobs already relied upon to score points under row 3) new full time jobs which meet the requirements in row 3 above, or (ii) established a new UK business or businesses that has or have had a gross income from business activity of at least £5 million during the 3 year continuous period, or (iii) taken over or invested in an existing UK business or businesses and the applicant's services or investment have resulted in a net increase in gross income from business activity of £5 million during the 3 year continuous period, when compared to the 3 year period immediately before the date the applicant became involved with the business.	15

Note: Table substituted from 11 January 2018 subject to savings for applications made before that date (HC 309). Words in Row 3 substituted; word in Row 4 deleted from 6 October 2021 (HC 617).

[Investment: specified documents

45. The applicant must provide their business accounts and accompanying evidence of their investment, which must meet the following requirements:

(a) if the applicant's business is legally required to produce audited accounts, the audited accounts must be provided;

(b) if the applicant's business is not legally required to produce audited accounts, unaudited accounts and an accounts compilation report must be provided from an accountant;

(c) the audited or unaudited accounts must show the investment in money made directly in the business by:

(i) the applicant, in their own name,

(ii) one or more seed funding competitions or UK or Devolved Government Departments, as set out in Table 4, and the accounts must be accompanied by a letter from the source, confirming that the investment was made on the applicant's behalf, or

[(iii) a third party other than those in (ii), and the accounts must either:

(1) confirm that the investment was made as a result of the applicant's activity, or

(2) be accompanied by a letter from the Department for International Trade, confirming that the investment was made as a result of the applicant's activity;]

(d) if the applicant has made the investment in the form of a director's loan:

(i) it must be shown in the relevant set of accounts provided,

(ii) [[unless the investment was made on or before 19 November 2015]] [and the date of application is before 19 November 2021], the investment must be shown through readily identifiable transactions in the applicant's business bank statements, which must clearly show the transfer of this money from the applicant to their business, and

(iii) the applicant must provide a legal agreement, between the applicant (in the name that appears on their application) and the business, showing:

(1) the terms of the loan,

(2) any interest that is payable,

(3) the period of the loan, and

(4) that the loan is unsecured and subordinated to other creditors' loans to the business;

(e) if the applicant has made the investment in the form of share capital, the accounts must show the shareholders, the amount and value of the shares (on the date of purchase) in the applicant's name as it appears on their application. If the value of the applicant's share capital is not shown in the accounts, then a printout of the company's register of members from Companies House must be provided;

(f) the accounts must clearly show the name of the accountant, the date the accounts were produced, and how much the applicant has invested in the business;

(g) if the applicant is claiming points for investment from a venture capital firm, they must also provide [a], dated letter from the venture capital firm, on its headed paper, confirming:

(i) the applicant's name,

(ii) the date(s) the money was transferred to the applicant or invested in their business, [. . .]

(iii) that the venture capital firm was registered with the Financial Conduct Authority on the date(s) in (ii) above[, and]

[(iv) confirmation that the venture capital firm will verify the contents of the letter to the Home Office on request.]

[(h) if the applicant is claiming points for investing £50,000 from one of the following sources, and has not been awarded points for those funds in a previous application, they must also provide the following documents:

(i) if the source is a seed funding competition or a UK or devolved government department, the applicant must provide the specified evidence in Table 4A above as evidence of the source of the funds (except that the letter referred to in paragraph 41(a)(i) does not need to be dated within the three months immediately before the date of the application);

(ii) if the source is a venture capital firm, the applicant must provide:

(1) A letter from a director, partner or fund manager of the venture capital firm, which includes:

(a) confirmation of the amount of money that was made available to the applicant, the entrepreneurial team or the applicant's business from the organisation,

(b) a statement providing detailed information on the strategy, structure and financial exposure of the fund,

(c) a statement detailing the rationale for the investment, providing specific information about the circumstances which led to the investment decision,

(d) a statement confirming that the business/proposed business is a genuine and credible proposition, and

(e) confirmation that the venture capital firm was, at the time the investment was made, registered with the Financial Conduct Authority (FCA) and its entry in the register included a permission to arrange, deal in or manage investments, or to manage alternative investment funds.

(2) A copy of the completed term sheet for the investment, signed by all parties to the transaction, which must include details of the company valuation, company structure, founder and investor rights, the structure of funding and the type of security being taken.

(3) A breakdown of the technical, legal, commercial and financial due diligence conducted by the venture capital firm in support of the investment.

(4) A letter from an accountant, validating the financial condition of the fund.

(5) A letter from a legal representative, who is not the applicant, which confirms that the letters and declarations in (1)-(4) contain the genuine signatures of the required signatories. The letter must clearly show the registration or authority of the legal representative to practise legally in the UK.]

Note: Paragraph and heading substituted from 11 January 2018 subject to savings for applications made before that date (HC 309). Sub-paragraph (c)(iii) substituted from 6 July 2018 subject to savings for applications made before that date (HC 1154). Words in (g), punctuation in (g)(iii) substituted; word in (g)(ii) deleted; (g)(iv) inserted from 5 November 2018 (HC 1534). Words in square brackets in (d)(ii) inserted; (h) substituted from 29 March 2019 subject to savings for applications made before that date (HC 1919). Words in double square brackets in (d)(ii) substituted from 1 October 2019 subject to savings for applications made before that date (HC 2631).

[Business activity: notes

46. A business will only be considered to be a 'new' business for the purposes of paragraph 43 and Tables 5 and 6 if it was established by the applicant no earlier than 12 months (or 24 months if the applicant was previously granted leave as a Tier 1 (Graduate Entrepreneur) Migrant) before the date of the application which led to the applicant's first grant of leave as a Tier 1 (Entrepreneur) Migrant.]

Note: Paragraph and heading substituted from 11 January 2018 subject to savings for applications made before that date (HC 309).

[Business activity: specified documents

47. The applicant must provide the following specified documents, showing that they obtained the necessary business registration within the 6 month period referred to in Table 5 or 6:

(a) if the applicant was self-employed, evidence of their registration with HM Revenue & Customs;

(b) if the applicant was a director of a UK company or member of a UK partnership, a printout from Companies House of the company's filing history page and of the applicant's personal appointments history, showing the date of their appointment as a director or member.]

Note: Paragraph and heading substituted from 11 January 2018 subject to savings for applications made before that date (HC 309).

[**48.** The applicant must provide the following specified documents to show that they have established a new UK business or joined or taken over an existing business, and that they are engaged in business in the UK when they make their application:

(a) if the applicant is self-employed, they must provide:

(i) evidence of their registration with HM Revenue & Customs to show that their business is based in the UK, and such evidence is dated no earlier than three months before the date of application,

(ii) HM Revenue & Customs evidence that the applicant is making tax returns within the self-assessment tax system, and

(iii) a personal bank statement showing transactions for their business, or a business bank statement, or a letter from a UK regulated financial institution, on the institution's headed paper, confirming that the applicant has a business and acts through that bank for the purposes of that business;

(b) if the applicant is a director of a UK company or member of a UK partnership, they must provide:

(i) printouts of Companies House documents, dated no earlier than three months before the date of the application, showing all of the following:

(1) the address of the registered office in the UK, or head office in the UK if it has no registered office,

(2) the applicant's name, as a director or member,

(3) the date of the applicant's appointment as a director or member, and

(4) that the business is actively trading (not dormant, struck-off, dissolved or in liquidation),

(ii) evidence from HM Revenue & Customs confirming that the company is registered for corporation tax (if the applicant is a director of a company) or that the applicant is making tax returns within the self-assessment tax system (if the applicant is self-employed), and

(iii) a business bank statement from a UK account which shows business transactions, or a letter from the UK bank in question, on its headed paper, confirming that the company or partnership has a bank account, that the applicant is a signatory of that account, and that the company or partnership uses that account for the purposes of their business.]

[(c) regardless of whether the applicant is self-employed, a director or member, they must also provide:

(i) an overview of the business's activity, including an explanation of the goods or services it provides to its customers or clients; and

(ii) the applicant's job title and job description, setting out their role within the company, how they are implementing their business plan and what their main tasks and responsibilities are in running the business on a day-to-day basis.]

Note: Paragraph substituted from 11 January 2018 subject to savings for applications made before that date (HC 309). Sub-paragraph (c) inserted from 29 March 2019 subject to savings for applications made before that date (HC 1919).

[Job creation: notes

49. (a) A full time job is one involving at least 30 hours of paid work per week.

(b) 'The equivalent of' a full time job means two or more part time jobs that add up to 30 hours per week, if each of the jobs exist for at least 12 months. However, one full time job of more than 30 hours of work per week will not count as more than one full time job.

(c) A job may count even if it does not last 12 consecutive months (for example it lasts for 6 months in one year and 6 months the following year) provided that it is the same job.

(d) The jobs need not exist on the date of application, provided that they existed for at least 12 months as specified in Table 5 (row 4) and Table 6 (row 3).

(e) Different jobs that have existed for less than 12 months cannot be combined together to make up a 12 month job. [. . .].

(f) If jobs are being combined the employees being relied upon must be clearly identified by the applicant in their application.

(g) The jobs must comply with all relevant UK legislation including, but not limited to, the National Minimum Wage Regulations in effect at the time and the Working Time Regulations 1998.]

[(h) A job will be considered one for settled worker if the worker met the definition of settled worker in the Immigration Rules in force at the time they started the job, and they remained employed for the whole claimed 12 month period, even if they ceased to be a settled worker at a later date.]

Note: Paragraph and heading substituted from 11 January 2018 subject to savings for applications made before that date (HC 309). Words in (e) deleted from 6 April 2019 subject to savings for applications made before that date (HC 1919). Sub-paragraph (h) inserted from 09:00 on 1 December 2020 subject to savings for applications made before that time (HC 813).

[Job creation: specified documents

50. If the applicant is required to score points for job creation in Table 5 or Table 6, they must provide all of the following specified documents:

(a) printouts of Real Time Full Payment Submissions showing that the applicant complied with Pay As You Earn (PAYE) reporting requirements to HM Revenue & Customs in respect of each relevant settled worker as legally required, and has done so for the full period of employment used to claim points. These must show every payment made to each settled worker as well as any deductions;

(b) duplicate payslips or wage slips for each settled worker used to claim points, covering the full period(s) of the employment for which points are being claimed;

(c) confirmation of the employment start date, [job title, job description,] hours paid per pay period and the hourly rate for each settled worker relied upon, including any changes to the same and the dates of those changes;

(d) copies of any of the following documents which demonstrate that each employee has settled status in the UK:

(i) the biometric data page of a British or EEA passport, showing the photograph and personal details of the employee,

(ii) a birth certificate, showing the employee was born in the UK and Colonies before 1 January 1983,

(iii) if the employee was born in the UK on or after 1 January 1983, a birth certificate, together with documentation, such as a passport or naturalisation certificate, which confirms one of their parents had settled status in the UK when the employee was born, and additionally, if the parent is the employee's father, a marriage certificate to the mother,

(iv) if the employee is an EEA national, a UK registration certificate/permanent residence document,

(v) if the employee is the spouse of an EEA national, the biometric data page of their passport, showing their photograph and personal details, or a residence card, and any of the documents in (i) or (iv) above which relate to the EEA national, together with their marriage certificate to the EEA national, or

(vi) if the worker is an overseas national with settled status in the UK, the biometric data page of their passport containing their photograph and personal details, and the pages where a UK Government stamp or an endorsement appear, or a biometrics residence permit, or official documentation from the Home Office which confirms their settled status in the UK;

(e) if the applicant was self-employed at the time a settled worker was employed by their business, the specified documents in paragraph 48(a) above showing the dates that the applicant became registered with HMRC as self-employed, with the bank statements referred to in 48(a)(iii) showing all the payments made to the settled worker in the full period of employment used to claim points, and the address of the business;

(f) if the applicant was a director of a UK company or member of a UK partnership at the time the settled worker was employed by their business, a printout from Companies House of the company's filing history page and of the applicant's personal appointments history, showing this;

(g) if the applicant took over or joined a business, they must provide [a] signed and dated letter from an accountant, showing:

(i) the name and contact details of the business,

(ii) the applicant's status in the business,

(iii) the number of jobs created in the business and the hours paid in each of the jobs,

(iv) the start dates and end dates (where applicable) of the jobs relied upon,

(v) the registration or permission of the accountant to operate in the UK,

(vi) confirmation that the business did not employ any workers before the applicant took over or joined it, if relevant and

(vii) confirmation that the accountant will verify the contents of the letter to the Home Office on request;

This applies regardless of how long the business existed for before the applicant took over or joined it;

(h) if the business referred to in (g) employed workers before the applicant took over or joined it, they must also provide the following documents for the year immediately before the applicant joined the business and the years that the jobs were created, showing the net increase in employment and signed and dated by the applicant:

(i) duplicate Real Time Full Payment Submissions sent to HM Revenue & Customs, or

(ii) if the business started employing settled workers for whom points are being claimed, before reporting under Real Time, a form P35.]

Note: Paragraph and heading substituted from 11 January 2018 subject to savings for applications made before that date (HC 309). Word in (g) substituted from 5 November 2018 (HC 1534). Words in (c) inserted from 29 March 2019 subject to savings for applications made before that date (HC 1919).

[Settlement on the basis of £5 million business activity: specified documents

51. (a) Where Table 6 applies and the applicant is relying on the business activity of a new UK business or businesses, they must provide audited (if the business is legally required to produce audited accounts) or unaudited accounts which show the gross income resulting from the business' activities and that this reached at least £5 million.

(b) Where Table 6 applies and the applicant is relying on business activity from an existing UK business which they have taken over or invested in, they must provide both of the following:

(i) audited accounts (if the business is legally required to produce audited accounts) or unaudited accounts clearly showing:

(1) the name of the accountant,

(2) the date the accounts were produced,

(3) the gross income from business activity for the 3 year period immediately before the date on which the applicant became involved with the business, and

(4) a net increase of at least £5 million in gross income from business activity during the three year for which the applicant is claiming points under Table 6, row 4;

(ii) [a] signed and dated accountant's letter, confirming:

(1) the name and contact details of the business,

(2) an explanation of the applicant's status in the business,

(3) the net increase in business activity,

(4) the registration or permission of the accountant to operate in the United Kingdom, and,

(5) that the accountant will verify the content of the letter to the Home Office on request.]

Note: Paragraph and heading substituted from 11 January 2018 subject to savings for applications made before that date (HC 309). Word in (b)(ii) substituted from 5 November 2018 (HC 1534).

[Entrepreneurial teams: notes

52. Two applicants, but no more than two applicants, may claim points for the same investment, available funds, jobs created and business activity in Tables 4, 5 or 6 provided all of the following requirements are met:

(a) The applicants have equal level of control over the funds and (where relevant) equal status as owners, directors and/or members of the business or businesses in question.

(b) The applicants are both shown by name, passport number and (where relevant) Points-Based System reference number in each other's applications and in the specified evidence required in the relevant table.

(c) Neither applicant has previously been granted leave as a Tier 1 (Entrepreneur) Migrant on the basis of investment and/or business activity linked in this way with any applicant other than each other, if the same funds were relied on in a previous application.]

Note: Paragraph and heading substituted from 11 January 2018 subject to savings for applications made before that date (HC 309).

[**53.** (a) No points will be awarded for money that is made available to any individual other than the applicant, except:

(i) under the terms of paragraph 52 above; or

(ii) where the money is held in a joint account with the applicant's spouse, civil partner or partner (defined as a person who has been living together with the applicant in a relationship akin to a marriage or civil partnership for at least two years prior to the date of application), and that spouse or partner is not (and is not applying to be) another Tier 1 (Entrepreneur) Migrant.

(b) No points will be awarded for investment, job creation and business activity shared with another Tier 1 (Entrepreneur) applicant, except under the terms of paragraph 52 above.

(c) If the applicant is not the sole member or director in their business, they must provide confirmation of:

(i) the names of the other members or directors,

(ii) whether any of the other members or directors are also Tier 1 (Entrepreneur) Migrants, and

(iii) if so:

(1) the dates they became members or directors,

(2) whether they are applying under the provisions in paragraph 52 above, and

(3) if they have made (or are making at the same time) an application in which they claimed points for creating jobs, the names of the jobholders in question.]

Note: Paragraph substituted from 11 January 2018 subject to savings for applications made before that date (HC 309).

Attributes for Tier 1 (Investor) Migrants

54. An applicant applying for entry clearance, leave to remain or indefinite leave to remain as a Tier 1 (Investor) Migrant must score 75 points for attributes.

55. [DELETED]

Note: Paragraph deleted from 16:00 on 17 February 2022 subject to savings for applications made before that time (CP 632).

[**56.** (a) Available points for entry clearance or leave to remain are shown in Table 8A for an applicant who has had entry clearance, leave to enter or leave to remain as a Tier 1 (Investor) Migrant in the 12 months immediately before the date of application, unless Table 8B applies.

(b) Available points for entry clearance or leave to remain are shown in Table 8B where **all** of the following apply:

(i) The applicant has had entry clearance, leave to enter or leave to remain as a Tier 1 (Investor) Migrant, in the 12 months immediately before the date of application.

(ii) The applicant's initial grant of entry clearance or leave to remain as a Tier 1 (Investor) Migrant was under the Rules in place before 6 November 2014.

(iii) The date of application is before 6 April 2020.]

Note: Amendments from 29 March 2019 subject to savings for applications made before that date (HC 1919). Paragraph substituted from 1 October 2019 subject to savings for applications made before that date (HC 2631).

57. [(a) Available points for applications for indefinite leave to remain are shown in Table 9A for an applicant who was last granted as a Tier 1 (Investor) Migrant, unless Table 9B applies.]

(b) Available points for applications for indefinite leave to remain are shown in Table 9B [where the date of application is before 6 April 2022 and the applicant] was last granted as a Tier 1 (Investor) Migrant under the Rules in place before 6 November 2014, or was awarded points as set out in Table 8B of Appendix A in his last grant.

Note: Words in (b) substituted from 29 March 2019 subject to savings for applications made before that date (HC 1919). Sub-paragraph (a) substituted from 1 October 2019 subject to savings for applications made before that date (HC 2631).

[**58.** Notes to accompany Tables 8A to Table 9B appear below Table 9B.]

Note: Paragraph substituted from 16:00 on 17 February 2022 subject to savings for applications made before that time (CP 632).

Table 7 [DELETED]

Note: Table deleted from 16:00 on 17 February 2022 subject to savings for applications made before that time (CP 632).

Table 8A: Applications for entry clearance or leave to remain referred to in paragraph 56(a)]

Money and investment	Points
The applicant has invested not less than £2 million [of his own under his control] in the UK by way of UK Government bonds, share capital or loan capital in active and trading UK registered companies, subject to the restrictions set out in paragraph 65 below. [[Where the applicant's initial grant of leave as a Tier 1 (Investor) Migrant was granted under the Rules in place from 29 March 2019, no points will be awarded for investments in UK government bonds. Where the applicant's initial grant of leave as a Tier 1 (Investor) Migrant was granted under the Rules in place before 29 March 2019 and the date of application is on or after 6 April 2023, no points will be awarded for investments that were held in UK Government bonds on or after 6 April 2023.]] The investment referred to above was made: (1) within 3 months of the applicant's entry to the UK, if he was granted entry clearance as a Tier 1 (Investor) Migrant and there is evidence to establish his date of entry to the UK, unless there are exceptionally compelling reasons for the delay in investing, or (2) where there is no evidence to establish his date of entry in the UK or where the applicant was granted entry clearance in a category other than Tier 1 (Investor) Migrant, within 3 months of the date of the grant of entry clearance or leave to remain as a Tier 1 (Investor) Migrant, unless there are exceptionally compelling reasons for the delay in investing, or	75

Money and investment	Points
(3) where the investment was made prior to the application which led to the first grant of leave as a Tier 1 (Investor) Migrant, no earlier than 12 months before the date of such application[.] [Where the applicant was awarded points as set out in Table 8B in their last grant as a Tier 1 (Investor) Migrant, at least £1 million of the above investment must have been made within the timescales in (1) to (3) above. The remaining balance of the £2 million investment must have been made before the date of application and be shown in the most recent portfolio report referred to in paragraph 65-SD(a) below.	
In each case, the level of investment must have been at least maintained for the whole of the remaining period of that leave.]	
'Compelling reasons for the delay in investing' must be unforeseeable and outside of the applicant's control. Delays caused by the applicant failing to take timely action will not be accepted. Where possible, the applicant must have taken reasonable steps to mitigate such delay.	

Note: Amendments to first paragraph from 29 March 2019 subject to savings for applications made before that date (HC 1919). Title, words in double square brackets in first paragraph, punctuation in (3), words in square brackets in (3) substituted from 1 October 2019 subject to savings for applications made before that date (HC 2631).

Table 8B: Applications for entry clearance or leave to remain from applicants who initially applied to enter the category before 6 November 2014 as referred to in paragraph 56(b)

Money and investment	Points
The applicant:	30
(a) has money of his own under his control in the UK amounting to not less than £1 million, or	
(b) (i) owns personal assets which, taking into account any liabilities to which they are subject, have a value of not less than £2 million; and	
(ii) has money under his control and disposable in the UK amounting to not less than £1 million which has been loaned to him by a UK regulated financial institution.	
The applicant has invested not less than £750,000 of his capital in the UK by way of UK Government bonds, share capital or loan capital in active and trading UK registered companies, subject to the restrictions set out in paragraph 65 below and has invested the remaining balance of £1,000,000 in the UK by the purchase of assets or by maintaining the money on deposit in a UK regulated financial institution.	30
(i) The investment referred to above was made:	15
(1) within 3 months of the applicant's entry to the UK, if he was granted entry clearance as a Tier 1 (Investor) Migrant and there is evidence to establish his date of entry to the UK, unless there are exceptionally compelling reasons for the delay in investing; or	

Money and investment	Points
(2) where there is no evidence to establish his date of entry in the UK or where the applicant was granted entry clearance in a category other than Tier 1 (Investor) Migrant, within 3 months of the date of the grant of entry clearance or leave to remain as a Tier 1 (Investor) Migrant, unless there are exceptionally compelling reasons for the delay in investing; or (3) where the investment was made prior to the application which led to the first grant of leave as a Tier 1 (Investor) Migrant, no earlier than 12 months before the date of such application, and in each case the level of investment has been at least maintained for the whole of the remaining period of that leave. 'Compelling reasons for the delay in investing' must be unforeseeable and outside of the applicant's control. Delays caused by the applicant failing to take timely action will not be accepted. Where possible, the applicant must have taken reasonable steps to mitigate such delay.	

Table 9A: Applications for indefinite leave to remain referred to in paragraph 57(a)]

Row	Money and investment	Points
1	The applicant has invested money of his own under his control amounting to at least: (a) £10 million; or (b) £5 million; or (c) £2 million in the UK by way of UK Government bonds, share capital or loan capital in active and trading UK registered companies, subject to the restrictions set out in paragraph 65 below. [Where the applicant's initial grant of leave as a Tier 1 (Investor) Migrant was granted under the Rules in place from 29 March 2019, no points will be awarded for investments in UK Government bonds. Where the applicant's initial grant of leave as a Tier 1 (Investor) Migrant was granted under the Rules in place before 29 March 2019 and the date of application is on or after 6 April 2025, no points will be awarded for investments that were held in UK Government bonds on or after 6 April 2025.]	40
2	The applicant has spent the specified continuous period lawfully in the UK, with absences from the UK of no more than 180 days in any 12 calendar months during that period. The specified continuous period must have been spent with leave as a Tier 1 (Investor) Migrant. The specified continuous period is:	20

Row	Money and investment	Points
	(a) 2 years if the applicant scores points from row 1(a) above; (b) 3 years if the applicant scores points from row 1(b) above; or (c) 5 years if the applicant scores points from row 1(c) above. [...]	
3	The investment referred to above was made no earlier than 12 months before the date of the application which led to the first grant of leave as a Tier 1 (Investor) Migrant. The level of investment has been at least maintained throughout the relevant specified continuous period referred to in row 2, other than in the first 3 months of that period, and the applicant has provided the specified documents to show that this requirement has been met. When calculating the specified continuous period, the first day of that period will be taken to be the later of: (a) the date the applicant first entered the UK as a Tier 1 (Investor) Migrant, (or the date entry clearance was granted as a Tier 1 (Investor) Migrant) or the date the applicant first entered the Bailiwick of Guernsey, the Bailiwick of Jersey or the Isle of Man with leave in a category equivalent to Tier 1 (Investor) if this is earlier; or (b) the date 3 months before the full specified amount was invested in the UK, or before the full required amount in an equivalent category was invested in the Bailiwick of Guernsey, the Bailiwick of Jersey or the Isle of Man.	15

Note: Words in Row 2 deleted from 11 January 2018 subject to savings for applications made before that date (HC 309). Amendment to Row 1 inserted from 29 March 2019 subject to savings for applications made before that date (HC 1919). Title, words in square brackets in Row 1 substituted from 1 October 2019 subject to savings for applications made before that date (HC 2631).

Table 9B: Applications for indefinite leave to remain from applicants who initially applied to enter the category before 6 November 2014 as referred to in paragraph 57(b)

Row	Money and investment	Points
1	The applicant: (a) (i) has money of his own under his control in the UK amounting to not less than £10 million; or (ii) (1) owns personal assets which, taking into account any liabilities to which they are subject, have a value of not less than £20 million; and (2) has money under his control and disposable in the UK amounting to not less than £10 million which has been loaned to him by a UK regulated financial institution, or (b) (i) has money of his own under his control in the UK amounting to not less than £5 million; or	20

Row	Money and investment	Points
	(ii) (1) owns personal assets which, taking into account any liabilities to which they are subject, have a value of not less than £10 million; and (2) has money under his control and disposable in the UK amounting to not less than £5 million which has been loaned to him by a UK regulated financial institution; or (c) (i) has money of his own under his control in the UK amounting to not less than £1 million; or (ii) (1) owns personal assets which, taking into account any liabilities to which they are subject, have a value of not less than £2 million; and (2) has money under his control and disposable in the UK amounting to not less than £1 million which has been loaned to him by a UK regulated financial institution.	
2	The applicant has invested not less than 75% of the specified invested amount of his capital in the UK by way of UK Government bonds, share capital or loan capital in active and trading UK registered companies, subject to the restrictions set out in paragraph 65 below, and has invested the remaining balance of the specified invested amount in the UK by the purchase of assets or by maintaining the money on deposit in a UK regulated financial institution. The specified invested amount is: (a) £10,000,000 if the applicant scores points from row 1(a) above, (b) £5,000,000 if the applicant scores points from row 1(b) above, or (c) £1,000,000 if the applicant scores points from row 1(c) above.	20
3	The applicant has spent the specified continuous period lawfully in the UK, with absences from the UK of no more than 180 days in any 12 calendar months during that period. The specified continuous period must have been spent with leave as a Tier 1 (Investor) Migrant. The specified continuous period is: (a) 2 years if the applicant scores points from row 1(a) above, (b) 3 years if the applicant scores points from row 1(b) above, or (c) 5 years if the applicant scores points from row 1(c) above. [...]	20
4	The investment referred to above was made no earlier than 12 months before the date of the application which led to the first grant of leave as a Tier 1 (Investor) Migrant. The level of investment has been at least maintained throughout the time spent with leave as a Tier 1 (Investor) Migrant in the UK in the relevant specified continuous period referred to in row 3, other than in the first 3 months of that period.	15

Row	Money and investment	Points
	In relation to time spent with leave as a Tier 1 (Investor) Migrant in the UK, the applicant has provided the specified documents to show that this requirement has been met. When calculating the specified continuous period, the first day of that period will be taken to be the later of: (a) the date the applicant first entered the UK as a Tier 1 (Investor) Migrant (or the date entry clearance was granted as a Tier 1 (Investor) Migrant), or the date the applicant first entered the Bailiwick of Guernsey, the Bailiwick of Jersey or the Isle of Man with leave in a category equivalent to Tier 1 (Investor) if this is earlier, or (b) the date 3 months before the full specified amount was invested in the UK, or before the full required amount in an equivalent category was invested in the Bailiwick of Guernsey, the Bailiwick of Jersey or the Isle of Man.	

Note: Words in Row 3 deleted from 11 January 2018 subject to savings for applications made before that date (HC 309).

UK bank account: notes

59. [DELETED]

Note: Amendments from 5 November 2018 (HC 1534). Amendments from 29 March 2019 subject to savings for applications made before that date (HC 1919). Paragraph deleted from 16:00 on 17 February 2022 subject to savings for applications made before that time (CP 632).

Money and assets: notes

60. Money is disposable in the UK if all of the money is held in a UK based financial institution or if the money is freely transferable to the UK and convertible to sterling. Funds in a foreign currency will be converted to pounds sterling (£) using the spot exchange rate which appeared on www.oanda.com* on the date on which the application was made.

61. 'Money of his own', 'personal assets' and 'his capital' include money or assets belonging to the applicant's spouse, civil partner or unmarried or same-sex partner, provided that:

(a) the applicant's spouse, civil partner or unmarried or same-sex partner meets the requirements of paragraphs 319C(c) and (d) of these rules, and the specified documents in paragraph 61-SD are provided, and

(b) specified documents in paragraph 61-SD are provided to show that the money or assets are under the applicant's control and that he is free to invest them.

61A. [[In Tables 8A to 9B]], 'money of his own under his control' and 'money under his control' exclude money that a loan has been secured against, where another party would have a claim on the money if loan repayments were not met, except where:

(i) the applicant made an application before 13 December 2012 [...]which led to a grant of entry clearance or leave to remain as a Tier 1 (Investor) migrant,

(ii) the applicant has not been granted entry clearance, leave to enter or leave to remain in any other category since the grant referred to in (i)[...]

(iii) the money is under the applicant's control, except for the fact that the loan referred to in paragraph (b) in Table 8B or row 1 in Table 9B has been secured against it[, and]

[(iv) the date of application is before 6 April 2020.]

Note: Words in (i), (ii) deleted; word in (iii), (iv) inserted from 29 March 2019 subject to savings for applications made before that date (HC 1919). Words in double square brackets substituted from 16:00 on 17 February 2022 subject to savings for applications made before that time (CP 632).

61-SD. The specified documents in paragraph 61, as evidence of the relationship and to show that the money or assets are under the applicant's control and that he is free to invest them, are as follows:

(a) The applicant must provide:

(i) The [...] certificate of marriage or civil partnership, to confirm the relationship, which includes the name of the applicant and the husband, wife or civil partner, or

(ii) At least three of the following types of specified documents to demonstrate a relationship similar in nature to marriage or civil partnership, including unmarried and same-sex relationships, covering a full two-year period immediately before the date of the application:

(1) a bank statement or letter from a bank confirming a joint bank account held in both names,

(2) an official document such as a mortgage agreement showing a joint mortgage,

(3) official documents such as deeds of ownership or a mortgage agreement showing a joint investment, such as in property or business,

(4) a joint rent (tenancy) agreement,

(5) any other official correspondence linking both partners to the same address, such as example bills for council tax or utilities,

(6) a life insurance policy naming the other partner as beneficiary,

(7) birth certificates of any children of the relationship, showing both partners as parents, or

(8) any other evidence that adequately demonstrates the couple's long-term commitment to one another.

(b) The applicant must provide [a] declaration from the applicant's husband, wife, civil partner, or unmarried or same-sex partner that he will permit all joint or personal money used to claim points for the application to be under the control of the applicant in the UK, known as a gift of beneficial ownership of the money while retaining the legal title, which clearly shows:

(1) the names of husband, wife, civil partner, or unmarried or same-sex partner and the applicant,

(2) the date of the declaration,

(3) the signatures of the husband, wife, civil partner, or unmarried or same-sex partner and applicant,

(4) the amount of money available, and

(5) a statement that the husband, wife, civil partner, or unmarried or same-sex partner agrees that the applicant has sole control over the money.

(c) The applicant must provide a letter, from a legal adviser who is permitted to practise in the country where the declaration was made, confirming that the declaration is valid and which clearly shows:

(1) the name of the legal adviser confirming that the declaration is valid,

(2) the registration or authority of the legal adviser to practise legally in the country in which the document was drawn up,

(3) the date of the confirmation of the declaration,

(4) the names of the applicant and husband, wife, civil partner, or unmarried or same-sex partner, and

(5) that the declaration is signed and valid according to the laws of the country in which it was made.

Note: Word in (a)(i) deleted; word in (b) substituted from 5 November 2018 (HC 1534).

[**62.** A regulated financial institution is one which is regulated by the appropriate regulatory body for the country in which the financial institution operates.]

Note: Paragraph substituted from 1 October 2019 subject to savings for applications made before that date (HC 2631).

62A. DELETED

63. [DELETED]

Note: Paragraph deleted from 16:00 on 17 February 2022 subject to savings for applications made before that time (CP 632).

Source of money: notes

64. [DELETED]

Note: Amendment from 29 March 2019 subject to savings for applications made before that date (HC 1919). Paragraph deleted from 16:00 on 17 February 2022 subject to savings for applications made before that time (CP 632).

64-SD. [The specified document requirements in paragraph 64B-SD(a)(ii) are as follows:]

(a) The applicant must provide:

(i) A portfolio report produced by a UK regulated financial institution, or a breakdown of investments in [a] letter produced by a UK regulated financial institution, on the official letter-headed paper of the institution, issued by an authorised official of that institution. The portfolio report or letter must cover a consecutive [[2-year]] period of time, ending no earlier than one calendar month before the date of application. The portfolio report or letter must confirm all the following:

(1) the amount of the money held in the investments,

(2) the beneficial owner of the funds,

(3) the date of the investment period covered,

(4) that the institution is a UK regulated financial institution, with the details of the registration shown on the documentation, and

(5) that the money can be transferred into the UK should the application be successful, if it is held abroad, or that the money has already been invested in the UK in the form of [. . .] share capital or loan capital in active and trading UK registered companies, and the dates of these investments;

(ii) If the applicant manages his own investments, or has a portfolio manager who does not operate in the UK and is not therefore regulated by the Financial Conduct Authority (FCA) (and the Prudential Regulation Authority (PRA) where applicable), he must provide one or more of the documents from the list below, as relevant to their type of investments, covering a consecutive [[2-year]] period of time, ending no earlier than one calendar month before the date of application:

(1) certified copies of bond documents showing the value of the bonds, the date of purchase and the owner;

(2) share documents showing the value of the shares, the date of purchase and the owner,

(3) the latest audited annual accounts of the organisation in which the investment has been made, clearly showing the amount of money held in the investments, the name of the applicant (or applicant and/or husband, wife, civil partner, or unmarried or same-sex partner), and the date of investment, or, if no accounts have been produced, a certificate from an accountant showing the amount of money held in the investments, and

(4) [. . .]trust fund documents from a legal adviser showing the amount of money in the fund, the date that the money is available and the beneficial owner, and including the name and contact details of the legal adviser and at least one of the trustees;

(iii) [Personal] bank statements on the official bank stationery from a bank that is regulated by the official regulatory body for the country in which the institution operates and the funds are located, showing the account number and the amount of money available in the name of the applicant (or applicant and/or husband, wife, civil partner, or unmarried or same-sex partner), covering a consecutive [[2-year]] period of time, ending no earlier than one calendar month before the date of application. The most recent statement must be no more than one calendar month old at the date of application. Electronic bank statements must be accompanied by a supporting letter from the bank on the institution's official headed paper, issued by an authorising official of that institution, confirming the content and that the document is genuine;

(iv) If the applicant cannot provide bank statements, [a] letter from a bank that is regulated by the official regulatory body for the country in which the institution operates and the funds are located. The letter must be on the institution's official headed paper, issued by an authorised official of that institution, and dated no more than one calendar month before the date of application. The letter must confirm:

(1) the name of the applicant (or applicant and/or husband, wife, civil partner, or unmarried or same-sex partner), and that the money is available in their name(s),

(2) the account number,

(3) that the bank is regulated by the official regulatory body for the country in which the institution operates and the funds are located,

(4) the dates of the period covered, including both the day the letter was produced and three full consecutive months immediately before the date of the letter, and

(5) the balance of the account to cover the required amount of money as a minimum credit balance on the date of the letter and throughout the three full consecutive months before the date of the letter;

(b) If the funds are not held in the UK, the applicant must also provide [a] letter from a bank or financial institution that is regulated by the official regulatory body for the country in which the institution operates and the funds are located, on the institution's official headed paper, issued by an authorised official of that institution, which confirms:

(1) the name of the beneficial owner, which should be the applicant (or applicant and/or husband, wife, civil partner, or unmarried or same-sex partner),

(2) the account number,

(3) the date of the letter,

(4) the amount of money to be transferred,

(5) that the money can be transferred to the UK if the application is successful, and

(6) that the institution will confirm the content of the letter to the Home Office on request.

If the applicant is providing the letter in (a)(iv) above, this information may be contained in the same letter.

(c) If specified documents are provided from accountants, the accountant must have a valid licence to practice or practising certificate and must:

(i) if based in the UK, be a member of the Institute of Chartered Accountants in England and Wales, the Institute of Chartered Accountants in Scotland, the Institute of Chartered Accountants in Ireland, the Association of Chartered Certified Accountants, the Association of Authorised Public Accountants, the Chartered Institute of Public Finance and Accountancy, the Institute of Financial Accountants, the Chartered Institute of Management Accountants, or the Association of International Accountants, or

(ii) if not based in the UK, be a member of an equivalent, appropriate supervisory or regulatory body in the country in which they operate.

Note: Words in (a)(i), (iii), (iv) and (b) substituted; word in (a)(ii)(4) deleted from 5 November 2018 (HC 1534). Words in double square brackets substituted; words in (a)(i)(5) deleted from 29 March 2019 subject to savings for applications made before that date (HC 1919). Words in introduction substituted from 16:00 on 17 February 2022 subject to savings for applications made before that time (CP 632).

64A-SD. [For the purposes of paragraph 64B-SD(b),] the applicant must provide all the specified documents from the following list, with contact details that enable verification:

(a) [Documents] in the form of:

(i) Money given to the applicant (or applicant and/or husband, wife, civil partner, or unmarried or same-sex partner) within the [2 years] immediately before the application must be shown in an irrevocable memorandum of gift, which clearly shows:

(1) the name and signature of the person receiving the gift,

(2) the name and signature of the person giving the gift,

(3) the date of the memorandum,

(4) the relationship between the person giving the gift and the person receiving it,

(5) the amount of money being given,

(6) a statement that the legal ownership of the gift is transferred and that the document is the memorandum of transfer,

(7) a clear description of the gift, and

(8) a statement that the gift is irrevocable;

(ii) If a memorandum of gift in (i) is provided, it must be accompanied by [a] confirmation letter from a legal adviser permitted to practise in the country where the gift was made, which clearly shows:

(1) the name of the legal adviser who is confirming the details,

(2) the registration or authority of the legal adviser to practise legally in the country in which the gift was made,

(3) the date of the confirmation of the memorandum,

(4) the names of the person giving the gift and the person receiving it,

(5) the relationship between the person giving the gift and the person receiving it,

(6) the amount of money given,

(7) the date that the money was transferred to the applicant, or to the husband, wife, civil partner, or unmarried partner or same-sex partner of the applicant,

(8) that the memorandum is signed and valid,

(9) that the gift is irrevocable, and

(10) that the memorandum is binding according to the laws of the country in which it was made;

(iii) Deeds of sale of assets such as business or property, if the applicant has generated these funds within the [2 years] immediately before the date of application, which meet the relevant legal requirements of the country of sale and clearly show:

(1) the name of the applicant (or applicant and/or husband, wife, civil partner, or unmarried or same-sex partner),

(2) the amount of money raised, and

(3) the date of the sale;

(iv) If a deed of sale in (iii) is provided, it must be accompanied by [a] confirmation letter from a legal adviser permitted to practise in the country where the sale was made, which clearly shows:

(1) the name of the legal adviser confirming the details,

(2) the registration or authority of the legal adviser to practise legally in the country in which the sale was made,

(3) the date of the sale,

(4) the date of production of the letter confirming the sale,

(5) the details of what was sold and the amount of money received from the sale,

(6) the name of the person receiving the money from the sale,

(7) the date that the money was transferred, and

(8) that the sale was valid according to the laws of the country in which it was made;

(v) If the funds are currently held in the applicant's business (or the business of the applicant and/or the applicant's husband, wife, civil partner, or unmarried or same-sex partner), the applicant must provide business accounts, which:

(1) are profit and loss accounts (or income and expenditure accounts if the organisation is not trading for profit),

(2) are prepared and signed off in accordance with statutory requirements, and

(3) clearly show the amount of money available for investment;

(vi) If business accounts in (v) are provided, they must be accompanied by [a] letter from a legal adviser who is permitted to practise in the country where business was operating, confirming that the applicant (or applicant and/or husband, wife, civil partner, or unmarried or same-sex partner) can lawfully extract the money from the business, which clearly shows:

(1) the name of the legal adviser who is confirming the details,

(2) the registration or authority of the legal adviser to practise legally in the country in which the business is operating,

(3) the date on which the details are confirmed, and

(4) that the applicant (or applicant and/or husband, wife, civil partner, or unmarried or same-sex partner) can lawfully extract the money from the business in question;

(vii) If the applicant (or applicant and/or husband, wife, civil partner, or unmarried or same sex partner) has been the beneficiary of a will within the [2 years] before making the application, and has received money as a result, the applicant must provide a notarised copy of the will. If the applicant (or applicant and/or husband, wife, civil partner, or unmarried or same-sex partner) has received possessions or assets, rather than money, then the applicant (or applicant and/or husband, wife, civil partner, or unmarried or same-sex partner) may not use estimates of the value of the items as evidence of funds for investment. The notarised copy of the will must clearly show:

(1) the date of the will,

(2) the beneficiary of the will (this should be the applicant or applicant and/or husband, wife, civil partner, or unmarried or same-sex partner),

(3) the amount of money that the applicant (or applicant and/or husband, wife, civil partner, or unmarried or same-sex partner) has inherited, and

(4) the names of any executors, plus any codicils (additions) to the will that affect the amount of money that was received;

(viii) If a notarised copy of a will in (vii) is provided, it must be accompanied by [a] confirmation letter from a legal adviser who is permitted to practise in the country where the will was made, confirming the validity of the will, which clearly shows:

(1) the name of the legal adviser confirming the details,

(2) the registration or authority of the legal adviser to practise legally in the country in which the will was made,

(3) the date of the document produced by the legal adviser confirming the will,

(4) the date that the applicant received the money as a result of the settlement of the will,

(5) the names of the person making the will and the beneficiary,

(6) the relationship between the person making the will and the beneficiary,

(7) confirmation of the amount of money received by the applicant (or applicant and/or husband, wife, civil partner, or unmarried or same-sex partner).

(8) that the will is signed and valid, and

(9) that the will is valid according to the laws of the country in which it was made;

(ix) If the applicant (or applicant and/or husband, wife, civil partner, or unmarried or same-sex partner) has obtained money as a result of a divorce settlement within the [2 years] immediately before the date of application, the applicant must provide a notarised copy of a financial agreement following a divorce. If the applicant (or applicant and/or husband, wife, civil partner, or unmarried or same-sex partner) has received possessions or assets, rather than money, estimates of the value of the items will not be accepted as evidence of money for investment.

(x) If a divorce settlement in (ix) is provided, it must be accompanied by [a] confirmation letter from a legal adviser who is permitted to practise in the country where the divorce took place, which clearly shows:

(1) the name of the legal adviser confirming the details,

(2) the registration or authority of the legal adviser to practise legally in the country in which the divorce took place,

(3) the date of the document produced by the legal adviser confirming the divorce settlement,

(4) the date that the applicant received the money as a result of the settlement,

(5) the names of the persons who are divorced,

(6) confirmation of the amount of money received by the applicant (or applicant and/or husband, wife, civil partner, or unmarried or same-sex partner),

(7) that the divorce settlement is complete and valid, and

(8) that the divorce settlement is valid according to the laws of the country in which it was made;

(xi) If the applicant is relying on a financial award or winnings as a source of funds, he must provide [a] letter from the organisation issuing the financial award or winnings, which clearly shows:

(1) the name of the applicant (or applicant and/or husband, wife, civil partner, or unmarried or same-sex partner),

(2) the date of the award,

(3) the amount of money won,

(4) the winnings are genuine, and

(5) the contact details for the organisation issuing the award or winnings;

(xii) If a letter showing a financial award or winnings in (xi) is provided, it must be accompanied by [a] confirmation letter from a legal adviser who is permitted to practise in the country where the award was made, which clearly shows:

(1) the name of the legal adviser confirming the details,

(2) the registration or authority of the legal adviser to practise legally in the country in which the award was made,

(3) the date of the letter of confirmation,

(4) the date of the award,

(5) the name of the recipient of the award,

(6) the amount of the winnings,

(7) the source of the winnings, and

(8) the date that the money was transferred to the applicant, or husband, wife, civil partner, or unmarried or same-sex partner;

(xiii) If the applicant (or applicant and/or husband, wife, civil partner, or unmarried or same-sex partner) has received money from a source not listed above, the applicant must provide relevant […] documentation as evidence of the source of the money, together with independent supporting evidence, which both clearly confirm:

(1) the amount of money received,

(2) the date that the money was received,

(3) the source of the money, and

(4) that the applicant (or applicant and/or husband, wife, civil partner, or unmarried or same-sex partner) was the legal recipient of the money.

Note: Words in (a), (a)(ii), (iv), (vi), (viii), (x), (xi), and (xii) substituted; word in (a)(xiii) deleted from 5 November 2018 (HC 1534). Words in (a)(i), (a)(iii), (vii) and (ix) substituted from 1 October 2019 subject to savings for applications made before that date (HC 2631). Words in introduction substituted from 16:00 on 17 February 2022 subject to savings for applications made before that time (CP 632).

64B-SD. In the case of an application where Table 9A, row 1 (a) or (b), or Table 9B, row 1 (a)(i) or (b)(i) applies, points will only be awarded if the applicant:

(a) (i) has had the additional money (or the additional assets in respect of an application to which either row 1 (a)(i) or (b)(i) of Table 9B applies) that he was not awarded points for in [their previous grant for a consecutive 2-year period of time (or a consecutive 90-day period of time if their initial leave as a Tier 1 (Investor) Migrant was granted under the Rules in place before 29 March 2019 and the date of application is before 6 April 2025], ending on the date(s) this additional capital was invested (as set out in row 1 of Table 9A or row 2 of Table 9B), and

[(ii) provides the specified documents in paragraph 64-SD (or the additional assets in respect of an application to which either row 1 (a)(i) or (b)(i) of Table 9B applies), with the following differences:

(1) References to 'date of application' in paragraph 64-SD are taken to read 'date of investment';

(2) The evidence in paragraph 64-SD(a)(i)(5) may also include evidence that the money has already been invested in the UK in the form of UK Government bonds, if the applicant's initial leave as a Tier 1 (Investor) Migrant was granted under the Rules in place before 29 March 2019 and the date of application is before 6 April 2025; or]

(b) provides the additional specified documents in paragraph 64A-SD of the source of the additional money (with the difference that references to 'date of application' in that paragraph are taken to read 'date of investment').

Note: Words in (a)(i), (a)(ii) substituted from 29 March 2019 subject to savings for applications made before that date (HC 1919).

64C-SD. In the case of an application where Table 9B, row 1 (a)(ii) or (b)(ii) applies, points will only be awarded if the applicant provides [a] letter of confirmation from each UK regulated financial institution the applicant has taken out a loan with to obtain the additional funds that he was not awarded points for in his previous grant of leave. The letter must have been issued by an authorised official, on the official letter-headed paper of the institution(s), and confirm:

(i) the amount of money that the institution(s) has loaned to the applicant,

(ii) the date(s) the loan(s) was taken out by the applicant, which must be no later than the date(s) this additional capital was invested (as set out in Table 9B, row 2),

(iii) that the institution is a UK regulated financial institution for the purpose of granting loans,

(iv) that the applicant has personal assets with a net value of at least £2 million, £10 million or £20 million (as appropriate), and that the institution(s) will confirm the content of the letter to the Home Office on request.

Note: Word substituted from 5 November 2018 (HC 1534).

Qualifying investments (Table 8A to Table 9B): notes

65. Investment excludes investment by the applicant by way of:

[(a) an offshore company or trust, or investments that are held in offshore custody except that investments held in offshore custody will not be excluded where:

(i) the applicant made an application before 13 December 2012 which led to a grant of entry clearance or leave to remain as a Tier 1 (Investor) migrant,

(ii) the applicant has not since been granted entry clearance, leave to enter or leave to remain in any other category, and

(iii) the date of application is before 6 April 2020.]

(b) Open-ended investment companies, investment trust companies, investment syndicate companies or pooled investment vehicles, [except that investment via pooled investment vehicles is permitted if such vehicles receive funding from a UK or devolved government department or one if its agencies, and the applicant provides a letter from a financial institution regulated by the Financial Conduct Authority to confirm this.]

(c) Companies mainly engaged in property investment, property management or property development (meaning in this context any investment or development of property to increase the value of the property with a view to earning a return either through rent or a future sale or both, or management of property for the purposes of renting it out or resale. The principle is that business income must be generated from the supply of goods and/or services and not derived from the increased value of property or any income generated through property, such as rent.),

(d) Deposits with a bank, building society or other enterprise whose normal course of business includes the acceptance of deposits,

(e) ISAs, premium bonds and saving certificates issued by the [National Savings and Investment (NS&I)], for an applicant who has, or last had leave as a Tier 1 (Investor) Migrant, [. . .]

(f) Leveraged investment funds, except where the leverage in question is the security against the loan referred to in [paragraph (b) in Table 8B or row 1 of Table 9B] (as appropriate), and paragraph 61A(i)-(iii) apply[[, or]]

[(g) UK government bonds, if:

(i) the applicant's initial grant of leave as a Tier 1 (Investor) Migrant was granted under the Rules in place from 29 March 2019, or

(ii) [[the investments were held in UK Government bonds on or after 6 April 2023 and]] the date of application is on or after:

(1) 6 April 2023, if the application is for entry clearance or leave to remain;

(2) 6 April 2025, if the application is for indefinite leave to remain.]

Note: Words in (e) substituted from 11 January 2018 subject to savings for applications made before that date (HC 309). Words in (f) substituted from 6 July 2018 subject to savings for applications made before that date (HC 1154). Sub-paragraph (a) substituted; words in (b), words in double square brackets in (f), sub-paragraph (g) inserted; word in (e) deleted from 29 March 2019 subject to savings for applications made before that date (HC 1919). Words in double square brackets in (g)(ii) inserted from 1 October 2019 subject to savings for applications made before that date (HC 2631).

[**65AA.** If an applicant invests in an entity which acts as an intermediary vehicle to invest or otherwise channel the funds elsewhere (including to another intermediary vehicle):

(a) Their investment will be considered to be where the funds are finally invested, not in the intermediary vehicle(s) (except in the case of a government-funded pooled investment vehicle permitted under paragraph 65(b) above, where the investment will be considered to be in that vehicle);

(b) The investment in the final destination must itself be a qualifying investment, as set out in these Rules;

(c) Any intermediary vehicle(s) involved must not fall within the exclusions in paragraph 65(a), (b) or (f) above;

(d) Any intermediary vehicle(s) involved must be based in the UK and regulated by the Financial Conduct Authority, if:

(i) the applicant's initial grant of leave as a Tier 1 (Investor) Migrant was granted under the Rules in place from 29 March 2019, or

(ii) the date of application is on or after:

(1) 6 April 2023, if the application is for entry clearance or leave to remain;

(2) 6 April 2025, if the application is for indefinite leave to remain;

(e) The applicant must provide the specified evidence in paragraph 65-SD in relation to the transfer of their funds to and between any intermediary vehicle(s), and from the intermediary vehicle to the final investment destination. This applies regardless of how long any chain of intermediary vehicles is.]

Note: Paragraph inserted from 29 March 2019 subject to savings for applications made before that date (HC 1919).

[**65A.** (a) 'Active and trading UK registered companies' must meet the definition set out in (b) if:

(i) the applicant's initial grant of leave as a Tier 1 (Investor) Migrant was granted under the Rules in place from 29 March 2019, or

(ii) the date of application is on or after:

(1) 6 April 2023, if the application is for entry clearance or leave to remain;

(2) 6 April 2025, if the application is for indefinite leave to remain.

(b) In the applications set out in (a), 'active and trading UK registered companies' means companies which:

(i) are registered with Companies House in the UK;

(ii) are registered with HM Revenue and Customs for corporation tax and PAYE;

(iii) have accounts and a UK business bank account, both showing regular trading of its own goods or services;

(iv) have at least two UK-based employees who are not its directors.

(c) 'Active and trading UK registered companies' must meet the definition set out in (d) if:

(i) the applicant's initial grant of leave as a Tier 1 (Investor) Migrant was granted under the Rules in place before 29 March 2019, and

(ii) the date of application is before:

(1) 6 April 2023, if the application is for entry clearance or leave to remain;

(2) 6 April 2025, if the application is for indefinite leave to remain.

(d) In the applications set out in (c), 'active and trading UK registered companies' means companies which:

(i) have a registered office or head office in the UK;

(ii) have a UK bank account showing current business transactions; and

(iii) are subject to UK taxation.]

Note: Paragraph substituted from 29 March 2019 subject to savings for applications made before that date (HC 1919).

65B. [No points will be awarded where the specified documents show that the funds are held in a financial institution which is not permitted under Appendix Finance.]

Note: Words substituted from 09:00 on 1 December 2020 subject to savings for applications made before that time (HC 813).

65C. (a) In the case of an application where Table 8A or Table 9A applies, points for maintaining the level of investment for the specified continuous period of leave will only be awarded:

(i) if the applicant has purchased a portfolio of qualifying investments for a price of at least £2 million (or £5 million or £10 million, as appropriate); and

(ii) where any part of the qualifying investments in the portfolio is sold (whether at a gain or at a loss) during the specified continuous period of leave, their gross proceeds are re-invested in qualifying investments before the end of the next reporting period, or within six months of the date of completion of the sale, whichever is sooner.

(b) In the case of an application where Table 8B or Table 9B applies, points for maintaining the level of investment for the relevant period of leave will only be awarded if:

(i) the applicant has maintained a portfolio of qualifying investments with a market value of at least £750,000 (or £3,750,000 or £7,500,000 as appropriate);

(ii) any fall in the market value of the portfolio below the amount in (i) is corrected before the end of the next reporting period, or within six months of the date of completion of the sale, whichever is sooner by the purchase of further qualifying investments with a market value equal to the amount of any such fall; and

(iii) the applicant has maintained a total level of investment (including the qualifying investments at (i) and (ii) above) of £1,000,000.

(c) In the case of an application where one of Tables 8A, 8B, 9A or 9B applies:

[(i) The applicant may withdraw interest accrued and dividends declared after the date on which the applicant purchased the qualifying investments in the portfolio;]

(ii) Fees, for example those charged by institutions for managing the portfolio, and transaction costs and tax incurred through buying and selling investments cannot be paid for from the investment funds for which the applicant scores points; and

(iii) If the applicant has invested more than the required level in qualifying investments, the fees, transaction costs and tax referred to in (ii) above may be paid from the surplus investment, providing the surplus investment was made at the same time or before the fees, transaction costs and tax were incurred (for example, if the applicant scores points for investing £2 million in qualifying investments, but has actually invested £2.1 million in qualifying investments, up to £100,000 in fees, transaction costs and tax may be paid for from the investment funds. The applicant must have invested £2.1 million at or by the time he pays these costs; he cannot pay out of a £2 million investment and invest a further £100,000 at a later date to compensate).

Note: Sub-paragraph (c)(i) substituted from 6 July 2018 subject to savings for applications made before that date (HC 1154).

65-SD. The following specified documents must be provided as evidence of investment:

(a) The applicant must provide a series of investment portfolio reports, certified as correct by a UK regulated financial institution, which must:

(i) cover the required period, beginning no later than the end of the 3 month timescale specified in the relevant table;

(ii) continue to the last reporting date of the most recent reporting period directly before the date of the application;

[(iii) include the price the applicant paid for the investments, which must total at least the amount for which points are being claimed throughout the required period;]

(iv) certify that the total investment was maintained as required by paragraph 65C as applicable;

(v) show the dates that the investments were made;

(vi) show the destination of the investments;

(vii) for investments made as loan funds to companies, be accompanied by audited accounts or unaudited accounts with an accounts compilation report for the investments made, giving the full details of the applicant's investment. The accountant must have a valid licence to practice or practising certificate and must be a member of the Institute of Chartered Accountants in England and Wales, the Institute of Chartered Accountants in Scotland, the Institute of Chartered Accountants in Ireland, the Association of Chartered Certified Accountants, the Association of Authorised Public Accountants, the Chartered Institute of Public Finance and Accountancy, the Institute of Financial Accountants, the Chartered Institute of Management Accountants, or the Association of International Accountants;

(viii) include the name and contact details of the financial institution that has certified the portfolio as [correct and, except for National Savings and Investment (NS&I) portfolio reports, confirmation that] this institution is regulated by the Financial Conduct Authority (FCA) (and the Prudential Regulation Authority (PRA) where applicable);

(ix) confirm that the investments were made in the applicant's name and/or that of his spouse, civil partner, unmarried or same-sex partner and not in the name of an offshore company or trust even if this is wholly owned by the applicant;

(x) include the date that each portfolio report was certified by the financial institution; [...]

(xi) state that the institution will confirm the content of the reports to the Home Office on request[; and]

[(xii) confirmation that the portfolio is unencumbered and has no loans secured against it; and

(xiii) confirmation that none of the investments being relied on are prohibited by paragraph 65(a) to (f).]

(c) Where the applicant is applying under Table 8B or Table 9B and has invested at least 75% of the specified investment amount but less than 100%, he must provide one or more of the following specified documents as evidence of the balance of the funds required to bring his total investment in the UK up to the specified investment amount:

(i) Documents confirming the purchase of assets in the UK, showing the assets purchased, the value of these assets and the dates of purchase. When using property, [only the unmortgaged portion of the applicant's own main home, excluding any share owned by any other person in the case of a tenancy in common, will count towards the balance of funds. The valuation of the portion of the property that the applicant may rely on, must be provided in a report issued by a surveyor (who is a member of the Royal Institution of Chartered Surveyors), which is dated not earlier than six months prior to the date of application. The property must be:

(1) wholly owned by the applicant or

(2) co-owned by the applicant and their spouse, civil partner, or partner, or

(3) co-owned by the applicant with one or more persons as tenants in common;]

(ii) If the applicant maintained money on deposit in the UK, a statement or statements of account on the official stationery of the institution that holds the funds. These statements must be in the name of the applicant (or applicant and/or the husband, wife, civil partner, or unmarried or same-sex partner of the applicant) and confirm the dates and amount of money held. The applicant must ensure that the institution will confirm the content of the statement to the Home Office on request;

(iii) [A] letter from the financial institution that holds the cash on deposit, on the institution's official headed paper, issued by an authorised official of that institution, which confirms the dates and amount of money held and that the institution will confirm the content of the letter to the Home Office on request.

(d) If the applicant wishes the start of the 3 month timescale specified in Table 8A Table 8B, Table 9A or Table 9B to be taken as the date he entered the UK, he must provide evidence which proves this date, such as a stamp in the applicant's passport, or an aircraft boarding card.

(e) Evidence of the investment having been maintained, from the date that the funds were invested for the full period of remaining leave, will be determined using the portfolio reports provided in (a).

Note: Words in (a)(viii), (c)(i) substituted from 11 January 2018 subject to savings for applications made before that date (HC 309). Word in (a)(x) deleted; word in (a)(xi substituted; (a)(xii) and (xiii) inserted from 6 July 2018 subject to savings for applications made before that date (HC 1154). Word in (c)(iii) substituted from 5 November 2018 (HC 1534). Sub-paragraph (a)(iii) substituted from 29 March 2019 subject to savings for applications made before that date (HC 1919).

[Attributes for Tier 1 (Graduate Entrepreneur) Migrants]

66. The attributes for this category have been deleted as the category is now closed and has been replaced by the Start-up category in Appendix W.]

Note: Paragraph and heading substituted from 6 July 2019 subject to savings for applications made before that date (HC 1919).

67.-72. [DELETED.]

Note: Amendments to various paragraphs from 5 November 2018 (HC 1534). Paragraphs deleted from 6 July 2019 subject to savings for applications made before that date (HC 1919). **NB:** HC 1779 refers to amendments to Table 10 and paragraphs 69 and 71 from 1 August 2019, however they were deleted from 6 July 2019 pursuant to HC 1919).

Attributes for Tier 2 (Intra-Company Transfer) Migrants

73.-112. [DELETED]

Note: Amendments to various paragraphs from 11 January 2018 subject to savings for applications made using a Certificate of Sponsorship assigned before that date (HC 309). Amendments to various paragraphs from 6 July 2018 with and without savings (HC 1154). Amendments to various paragraphs from 5 November 2018 (HC 1534). Amendments to various paragraphs from 10 January 2019 subject to savings for applications made before that date and from 1 August 2019 without savings (HC 1779). Amendments to various paragraphs from 30 March 2019 subject to savings for applications made before that date (HC 1919). Amendments to various paragraphs from 1 October 2019 with and without savings, and from 6 October 2019 subject to savings for applications made before that date (HC 2631). Paragraphs deleted from 09:00 on 1 December 2020 subject to savings for applications made before that time (HC 813).

Attributes for Tier 4 (General) Students

113. [DELETED]

Note: Paragraph deleted from 09:00 on 5 October 2020 subject to savings for applications made before that time (HC 707).

114. [DELETED]

Note: Paragraph deleted from 09:00 on 5 October 2020 subject to savings for applications made before that time (HC 707).

115. [DELETED]

Note: Paragraph deleted from 09:00 on 5 October 2020 subject to savings for applications made before that time (HC 707).

115A. [DELETED]

Note: Paragraph deleted from 09:00 on 5 October 2020 subject to savings for applications made before that time (HC 707).

115B.-115I. [DELETED]

116. [DELETED]

Note: Amendments from 11 January 2018 subject to savings for applications made before that date (HC 309). Amendments from 1 August 2019 (HC 1779). Paragraph deleted from 09:00 on 5 October 2020 subject to savings for applications made before that time (HC 707).

117. [DELETED]

Note: Paragraph deleted from 09:00 on 5 October 2020 subject to savings for applications made before that time (HC 707).

118. [DELETED]

Note: Amendments from 1 November 2018 subject to savings for applications made before that date (HC 1534). Amendments from 1 August 2019 (HC 1779). Amendments from 1 October 2019 subject to savings for applications made before that date (HC 2631). Paragraph deleted from 09:00 on 5 October 2020 subject to savings for applications made before that time (HC 707).

119. [DELETED]

Note: Paragraph deleted from 09:00 on 5 October 2020 subject to savings for applications made before that time (HC 707).

120. [DELETED]

Note: Amendments from 11 January 2018 subject to savings for applications made before that date (HC 309). Amendments from 6 July 2018 subject to savings for applications made before that date (HC 1154). Amendments from 1 August 2019 (HC 1779). Paragraph deleted from 09:00 on 5 October 2020 subject to savings for applications made before that time (HC 707).

120-SD. [DELETED]

Note: Amendments from 6 July 2018 subject to savings for applications made before that date (HC 1154). Amendments from 5 November 2018 (HC 1534). Paragraph deleted from 09:00 on 5 October 2020 subject to savings for applications made before that time (HC 707).

120A. [DELETED]

Note: Amendments from 11 January 2018 subject to savings for applications made before that date (HC 309). Amendments from 1 August 2019 (HC 1779). Amendments from 1 October 2019 subject to savings for applications made before that date (HC 2631). Paragraph deleted from 09:00 on 5 October 2020 subject to savings for applications made before that time (HC 707).

121. [DELETED]

Note: Paragraph deleted from 09:00 on 5 October 2020 subject to savings for applications made before that time (HC 707).

122. [DELETED]

Note: Paragraph deleted from 09:00 on 5 October 2020 subject to savings for applications made before that time (HC 707).

123. [DELETED]

Note: Paragraph deleted from 09:00 on 5 October 2020 subject to savings for applications made before that time (HC 707).

123A. [DELETED]

Note: Paragraph deleted from 09:00 on 5 October 2020 subject to savings for applications made before that time (HC 707).

124. [DELETED]

Note: Paragraph deleted from 09:00 on 5 October 2020 subject to savings for applications made before that time (HC 707).

125. [DELETED]

Note: Paragraph deleted from 09:00 on 5 October 2020 subject to savings for applications made before that time (HC 707).

125A. [DELETED]

Note: Amendment from 1 November 2018 subject to savings for applications made before that date (HC 1534). Paragraph deleted from 09:00 on 5 October 2020 subject to savings for applications made before that time (HC 707).

125-SD. [DELETED]

Note: Paragraph substituted from 6 July 2018 subject to savings for applications made before that date (HC 1154). Amendments from 5 November 2018 (HC 1534). Paragraph deleted from 09:00 on 5 October 2020 subject to savings for applications made before that time (HC 707).

126. [DELETED]

Note: Amendments from 1 August 2019 (HC 1779). Paragraph deleted from 09:00 on 1 December 2020 subject to savings for applications made before that time (HC 813).

Appendix AR
Administrative Review

Introduction

Administrative review is available where an eligible decision has been made. Decisions eligible for administrative review are listed in paragraph AR3.2, AR4.2 or AR5.2 of this Appendix.

Administrative review will consider whether an eligible decision is wrong because of a case working error and, if it is considered to be wrong, the decision will be withdrawn or amended as set out in paragraph AR2.2 of this Appendix.

Rules about how to make a valid application for administrative review are set out at paragraphs 34M to 34Y of these Rules.

Definitions

AR1.1 For the purpose of this Appendix the following definitions apply:

Applicant	the individual applying for administrative review.
Case working error	an error in decision-making listed in paragraph AR2.11.has the
Control Zone	meaning given collectively by Schedule 1 to the (International Arrangements Order 1994 and regulation 2 of the Nationality, Immigration and Asylum Act 2002 (Juxtaposed Controls) Order 2003. In these Rules it also includes a 'supplementary control zone' as defined by Schedule 1 to the Channel Tunnel (International Arrangements) Order 1993.
Valid application	an application for administrative review made in accordance with paragraphs 34M to 34Y of these Rules.
Pending	as defined in paragraph AR2.9.
Reviewer	the Home Office case worker or Immigration Officer or Entry Clearance Officer conducting the administrative review.
Original decision maker	the Home Office case worker or Immigration Officer or Entry Clearance Officer who made the eligible decision.

General Principles

What is Administrative Review?

AR2.1 Administrative review is the review of an *eligible decision* to decide whether the decision is wrong due to a *case working error.*

Outcome of Administrative Review

AR2.2 The outcome of an administrative review will be:

(a) Administrative review succeeds and the *eligible decision* is withdrawn; or

(b) Administrative review does not succeed and the *eligible decision* remains in force and all of the reasons given for the decision are maintained; or

(c) Administrative review does not succeed and the *eligible decision* remains in force but one or more of the reasons given for the decision are withdrawn; or

(d) Administrative review does not succeed and the *eligible decision* remains in force but with different or additional reasons to those specified in the decision under review.

What will be Considered on Administrative Review?

AR2.3 The *eligible decision* will be reviewed to establish whether there is a *case working error*, either as identified in the application for administrative review, or identified by the *Reviewer* in the course of conducting the administrative review.

AR2.4 The *Reviewer* will not consider any evidence that was not before the *original decision maker* except where:

(a) evidence that was not before the *original decision maker* is submitted to demonstrate that a *case working error* as defined in paragraph AR2.11(a), (b) or (c) has been made; or

(b) the evidence is submitted to demonstrate that the refusal of an [application for permission to stay under paragraphs 9.7.1, 9.7.2 or 9.7.3 of Part 9] of these Rules was a *case working error* and the *applicant* has not previously been served with a decision to:

(i) refuse an application for entry clearance, leave to enter or leave to remain;

(ii) revoke entry clearance, leave to enter or leave to remain;

(iii) cancel leave to enter or leave to remain;

(iv) curtail leave to enter or leave to remain; or

(v) remove a person from the UK, with the effect of invalidating leave to enter or leave to remain, which relied on the same findings of facts.

Note: Words in (b) substituted from 09:00 on 1 December 2020 subject to savings for applications made before that time (HC 813).

AR2.5 If the *applicant* has identified a *case working error* as defined in paragraph AR2.11(a), (b) or (c), the *Reviewer* may contact the applicant or his representative in writing, and request relevant evidence. The requested evidence must be received at the address specified in the request within 7 working days of the date of the request.

AR2.6 The *Reviewer* will not consider whether the applicant is entitled to leave to remain on some other basis and nothing in these rules shall be taken to mean that the *applicant* may make an application for leave or vary an existing application for leave, or make a protection or human rights claim, by seeking administrative review.

Applying for Administrative Review

AR2.7 The rules setting out the process to be followed for making an application for administrative review are at 34M to 34Y of these Rules.

Effect of Pending Administrative Review on Liability for Removal

AR2.8 Where administrative review is pending the Home Office will not seek to remove the *applicant* from the United Kingdom.

When is Administrative Review Pending?

AR2.9 Administrative review is pending for the purposes of paragraph AR2.8 of this Appendix and sections 3C(2)(d) and 3D(2)(c) of the Immigration Act 1971:

(a) While an application for administrative review can be made in accordance with 34M to 34Y of these Rules, ignoring any possibility of an administrative review out-of-time under paragraph 34R(3);

(b) While a further application for administrative review can be made in accordance with paragraph 34M(2) of these Rules following a notice of outcome at AR2.2(d) served in accordance with Appendix SN of these Rules;

(c) When an application for administrative review has been made until:

(i) the application for administrative review is rejected as invalid because it does not meet the requirements of paragraph 34N to 34S of these Rules;

(ii) the application for administrative review is withdrawn in accordance with paragraph 34X; or

(iii) the notice of outcome at AR2.2(a), (b) or (c) is served in accordance with Appendix SN of these Rules.

AR2.10 Administrative review is not *pending* when:

(a) an administrative review waiver form has been signed by an individual in respect of whom an *eligible decision* has been made. An administrative review waiver form is a form where the person can declare that although they can make an application in accordance with paragraphs 34M to 34Y of these Rules, they will not do so.

(b) administrative review has previously been *pending* and the individual in respect of whom the *eligible decision* has been made submits a fresh application for entry clearance, leave to enter or leave to remain. In this case the day prior to the day on which the fresh application is submitted is the last day on which the administrative review is *pending*.

What is a case working error?

[**AR2.11.** (a) Where the original decision maker's decision to:

(i) refuse an application on the basis of paragraph 9.7.1, 9.7.2, 9.8.1 or 9.8.2 of Part 9 of these Rules; or

(ii) cancel entry clearance or permission which is in force under paragraph 9.7.3 of Part 9 of these Rules; or

(iii) refuse an application of the type specified in paragraph AR3.2(d) of these Rules on grounds of deception; or

(iv) cancel leave to enter or remain which is in force under paragraph A3.2(b) of Annex 3 to Appendix EU or paragraph A3.4(b) of Annex 3 to Appendix EU (Family Permit) of these Rules; or

(v) cancel permission to enter or stay which is in force under paragraph HV11.1(c) of Appendix S2 Healthcare Visitor; or

(vi) cancel permission to enter which is in force under paragraph SPS9.1(c) of Appendix Service Providers from Switzerland; is incorrect;]

[(b) Where the original decision maker's decision to refuse an application on the basis that the date of application was beyond any time limit in these Rules was incorrect;

(c) Where the original decision maker's decision not to request specified documents under paragraph 245AA of these Rules was incorrect;

(d) Where the original decision maker otherwise applied the Immigration Rules incorrectly; or

(e) Where the original decision maker failed to apply the Secretary of State's relevant published policy and guidance in relation to the application.]

Note: Amendment to (a) from 6 April 2020 subject to savings for applications for Administrative Review made before that date (HC 120). Amendments from 09:00 on 1 December 2020 subject to savings for applications made before that time (HC 813). Amendments from 23:00 on 31 December 2020 for decisions made on or after that time (CP 361). Amendments from 6 April 2021 (HC 1248). Paragraph substituted from 6 October 2021 (HC 617). Sub-paragraphs (b) to (e) inserted from 16:00 on 1 November 2021 (HC 803).

AR2.12 Additionally, where the eligible decision is one specified in paragraph AR3.2, a *case working error* is also where there has been an error in calculating the correct period or conditions of immigration leave either held or to be granted.

Administrative Review in the UK

Decisions Eligible for Administrative Review in the United Kingdom

AR3.1 Administrative review is only available where an *eligible decision* has been made.

AR3.2 An *eligible decision* is:

(a) A decision on an application where the application was made on or after 20th October 2014 for leave to remain as:

(i) a Tier 4 Migrant under the Points Based System; or

(ii) the partner of a Tier 4 Migrant under paragraph 319C of the Immigration Rules; or

(iii) the child of a Tier 4 Migrant under paragraph 319H of the Immigration Rules.

[(aa) A decision on an application where the application was made on or after 5 October 2020 at 0900 for *permission to stay* as:

(i) a *Student* under Appendix ST: Student; or

(ii) a *Child Student* under Appendix CS: Child Student; or

(iii) the dependant partner of a *Student* under Appendix ST: Student; or

(iv) the dependant child of a *Student* under Appendix ST: Student; or

(v) the Parent of a *Child Student* under Part 7.]

(b) A decision on an application where the application was made on or after 2nd March 2015 for leave to remain, as:

(i) a Tier 1, 2 or 5 Migrant under the Points Based System; or

(ii) the partner of a Tier 1, 2 or 5 Migrant under paragraphs 319C or 319E of the Immigration Rules; or

(iii) the child of a Tier 1, 2 or 5 Migrant under paragraphs 319H or 319J of the Immigration Rules.

(c) A decision made on or after 6th April 2015 on an application for leave to remain made under these Rules unless it is an application as a visitor, [or an application under Appendix Ukraine Scheme,] or where an application or human rights claim is made under:

(i) Paragraph 276B (Long residence);

(ii) Paragraphs 276ADE(1) or 276DE (private life);

(iii) Paragraphs 276U and 276AA (partner or child of a member of HM Forces);

(iv) Paragraphs 276AD and 276AG (partner or child of a member of HM Forces and has at least 4 years' reckonable service in HM Forces at the date of application;

(v) Part 8 of these Rules (family members) where the sponsor is present and settled in the UK (unless the application is made under paragraphs 319AA to 319J of these Rules, or under paragraph 284, 287, 295D or 295G where the sponsor was granted settlement as a Points Based System Migrant) or has refugee or humanitarian protection status in the UK;

(vi) Part 11 of these Rules (asylum);

(vii) Part 4 or Part 7 of Appendix Armed Forces (partner or child of a member of HM Forces) where the sponsor is a British citizen or has at least 4 years' reckonable service in HM Forces at the date of application;

(viii) Appendix FM (family members), but not where an application is made under section BPILR (bereavement) or section DVILR (domestic violence)[;]

[(ix) Appendix Private Life;]

[(x) Appendix Settlement Family Life;]

[(xi) Appendix Settlement Protection.]

[. . .]

(d) A decision made on or after 6th April 2015 on an application … for leave to remain made by a Turkish national or their family member pursuant to the UK's obligations under Article 41 of the Additional Protocol to the European Community Association Agreement (ECAA) with Turkey, and under Article 6(1) of Decision 1/80 of the Association Council established by that agreement.

[(e) A decision on an application where the application was made on or after 1 December 2020 for permission to stay as:

(i) a Student under Appendix Student; or

(ii) a Child Student under Appendix Child Student; or

(iii) the Parent of a Child Student under Appendix Parent of a Child Student; or

(iv) a Skilled Worker under Appendix Skilled Worker; or

(v) an Intra-company routes worker under Appendix Intra-Company Routes; or

(vi) a Minister of Religion under Appendix T2 Minister of Religion; or

(vii) a Sportsperson under Appendix T2 Sportsperson; or

(viii) a Representative of an Overseas Business under Appendix Representative of an Overseas Business; or

(ix) a person with UK Ancestry under Appendix UK Ancestry; or

(x) a person on the Global Talent route under Appendix Global Talent; or

(xi) a person on the Start-up route under Appendix Start-up; or

(xii) an Innovator under Appendix Innovator; or

(xiii) a Seasonal Worker under Appendix T5 (Temporary Worker) Seasonal Worker; or

(xiv) a Youth Mobility Worker under Appendix T5 (Temporary Worker) Youth Mobility Scheme; or

(xv) a Religious Worker under Appendix T5 (Temporary Worker) Religious Worker; or

(xvi) a Charity Worker under Appendix T5 (Temporary Worker) Charity Worker; or

(xvii) a Creative or Sporting Worker under Appendix T5 (Temporary Worker) Creative or Sporting Worker; or

(xviii) an International Agreement Worker under Appendix T5 (Temporary Worker) International Agreement Worker; or

(xix) a Government Authorised Exchange Worker under Appendix T5 (Temporary Worker) Government Authorised Exchange Worker route.]

[(f) A decision on an application where the application was made on or after 1 December 2020 for permission to stay as the dependent partner or dependent child of:

(i) a Student under Appendix Student; or

(ii) a Skilled Worker under Appendix Skilled Worker; or

(iii) an Intra-company routes worker under Appendix Intra-Company Routes; or

(iv) a Minister of Religion under Appendix T2 Minister of Religion; or

(v) a Sportsperson under Appendix T2 Sportsperson; or

(vi) a Representative of an Overseas Business under Appendix Representative of an Overseas Business; or

(vii) a person with UK Ancestry under Appendix UK Ancestry; or

(viii) a person on the Global Talent route under Appendix Global Talent; or

(ix) a person on the Start-up route under Appendix Start-up; or

(x) an Innovator under Appendix Innovator; or

(xi) a Religious Worker under Appendix T5 (Temporary Worker) Religious Worker; or

(xii) a Charity Worker under Appendix T5 (Temporary Worker) Charity Worker; or

(xiii) a Creative or Sporting Worker under Appendix T5 (Temporary Worker) Creative or Sporting Worker; or

(xiv) an International Agreement Worker under Appendix T5 (Temporary Worker) International Agreement Worker; or

(xv) a Government Authorised Exchange Worker under Appendix T5 (Temporary Worker) Government Authorised Exchange Worker route.]

[(g) A decision on an application where the application was made on or after 31 January 2021 for permission to stay as:

(i) a Hong Kong British National (Overseas) under Appendix Hong Kong British National (Overseas); or

(ii) the dependent partner, BN(O) Household Child, BN(O) Household Member, or Adult Dependent Relative of a Hong Kong British National (Overseas) under Appendix Hong Kong British National (Overseas).]

[(h) A decision on an application where the application was made on or after 6 May 2021 for permission to stay as:

(i) a Domestic Worker in a Private Household under Appendix Domestic Worker in a Private Household; or

(ii) the dependant partner or dependant child of a Domestic Worker in a Private Household under Appendix Domestic Worker in a Private Household; or

(iii) a Domestic Worker Victim of Modern Slavery under Appendix Domestic Worker Victim of Modern Slavery.]

[(i) A decision on an application where the application was made on or after 0900 on 1 July 2021 for permission to stay as either:

(i) a Graduate under Appendix Graduate; or

(ii) the dependant partner or dependant child of a Graduate under Appendix Graduate.]

[(j) A decision on an application where the application was made on or after 0900 on 11 October 2021 for permission to stay as:

(i) an International Sportsperson under Appendix International Sportsperson; or

(ii) a Seasonal Worker under Appendix Temporary Work - Seasonal Worker; or

(iii) a person on the Youth Mobility Scheme route under Appendix Youth Mobility Scheme; or

(iv) a Religious Worker under Appendix Temporary Work - Religious Worker; or

(v) a Charity Worker under Appendix Temporary Work - Charity Worker; or

(vi) a Creative Worker under Appendix Temporary Work - Creative Worker; or

(vii) a person on the International Agreement route under Appendix Temporary Work - International Agreement; or

(viii) a person on the Government Authorised Exchange route under Appendix Temporary Work - Government Authorised Exchange.]

[(k) A decision on an application where the application was made on or after 0900 on 11 October 2021 for permission to stay as the dependent partner or dependent child of:

(i) an International Sportsperson under Appendix International Sportsperson; or

(ii) a Religious Worker under Appendix Temporary Work - Religious Worker; or

(iii) a Charity Worker under Appendix Temporary Work - Charity Worker; or

(iv) a Creative Worker under Appendix Temporary Work - Creative Worker; or

(v) a person on the International Agreement route under Appendix Temporary Work – International Agreement; or

(vi) a person on the Government Authorised Exchange route under Appendix Temporary Work - Government Authorised Exchange.]

[(l) A decision on an application where the application was made for permission to stay as:

(i) a Scale-up Worker under Appendix Scale-up; or

(ii) the partner or child of a Scale-up Worker under Appendix Scale-up.]

[(m) A decision on an application where the application was made for permission to stay as:

(i) a High Potential Individual under Appendix High Potential Individual; or

(ii) the partner or child of a High Potential Individual under Appendix High Potential Individual.]

[(n) A decision on an application where the application was made for permission to stay as:

(i) a Senior or Specialist Worker under Appendix Global Business Mobility – Senior or Specialist Worker; or

(ii) a Graduate Trainee under Appendix Global Business Mobility – Graduate Trainee; or

(iii) an Expansion Worker under Appendix Global Business Mobility – UK Expansion Worker; or

(iv) a Secondment Worker under Appendix Global Business Mobility – Secondment Worker; or

(v) a Service Supplier under Appendix Global Business Mobility – Service Supplier.]

[(o) A decision on an application where the application was made for permission to stay as the partner or child of:

(i) a Senior or Specialist Worker under Appendix Global Business Mobility – Senior or Specialist Worker; or

(ii) a Graduate Trainee under Appendix Global Business Mobility – Graduate Trainee; or

(iii) an Expansion Worker under Appendix Global Business Mobility – UK Expansion Worker; or

(iv) a Secondment Worker under Appendix Global Business Mobility – Secondment Worker; or

(v) a Service Supplier under Appendix Global Business Mobility – Service Supplier.]

Note: Sub-paragraph (aa) inserted from 09:00 on 5 October 2020 subject to savings for applications made before that time. Where consequential changes relating to the need for an ATAS certificate have been made, they take effect for all applications made or granted on or after 5 October 2020 at 09:00 (HC 707). Sub-paragraphs (e), (f) and (g) inserted from 09:00 on 1 December 2020 subject to savings for applications made before that time (HC 813). Sub-paragraph (h) inserted from 6 May 2021 subject to savings for applications (including for administrative review) made before that date; sub-paragraph (i) inserted from 09:00 on 1 July 2021 subject to savings for applications (including for administrative review) made before that date (HC 1248). Sub-paragraphs (j) and (k) inserted from 09:00 on 11 October 2021 subject to savings for applications made before that time (HC 617). Punctuation in (c)(viii) substituted, (c)(ix), (x) and (xi) inserted, words in (c) deleted, sub-paragraphs (l), (m), (n), and (o) inserted from 6 April 2022 subject to savings for applications made before that date (HC 1118). Words in (c) inserted from 30 March 2022 (HC 1220).

AR3.3. An *eligible decision* in paragraph AR3.2 is either a decision to refuse an application for leave to remain or a decision to grant leave to remain where a review is requested of the period or conditions of leave granted.

AR3.4 DELETED

Administrative Review on arrival in the UK

Decisions eligible for administrative review on arrival in the United Kingdom

AR4.1 Administrative review is only available where an *eligible decision* has been made.

AR4.2 An *eligible decision* is a decision made on or after 6th April 2015 to cancel leave to enter or remain with the result that the applicant has no leave to enter or remain, where the reason for cancellation is:

(a) there has been such a change of circumstances in the applicant's case since that leave was given that it should be cancelled;

(b) the leave was obtained as a result of false information given by the applicant or the applicant's failure to disclose material facts.

AR4.3 Where the *eligible decision* is made in the *Control Zone*, administrative review may not be applied for and will not be considered until after the applicant has left or been removed from the *Control Zone.*

Administrative Review overseas

Decisions eligible for administrative review overseas

AR5.1 Administrative review is only available where an *eligible decision* has been made.

AR5.2 (a) An *eligible decision* is a refusal of an application for entry clearance made on or after 6th April 2015 under the Rules unless it is an application under Part 3 of these Rules (short-term students)[, under Appendix EU (Family Permit)][[, under Appendix Ukraine Scheme,]] or as a visitor, or where an application or human rights claims is made under:

(i) Paragraphs 276R and 276X (partner or child or a member of HM Forces);

(ii) Paragraphs 276AD and 276AG (partner or child of a member of HM Forces) where the sponsor is a foreign or Commonwealth member of HM Forces and has at least 4 years' reckonable service at the date of application;

(iii) Part 8 of these Rules (family members) where the sponsor is present and settled in the UK (unless the application is made under paragraphs 319AA to 319J of these Rules) or has refugee or humanitarian protection status in the UK;

(iv) Part 4 or Part 7 of Appendix Armed Forces (partner or child of a member of HM Armed Forces) where the sponsor is a British citizen or has at least 4 years' reckonable service in HM Forces as at the date of application;

(v) Appendix FM (family members), in which case the appropriate remedy is an appeal under section 82 of the Nationality, Immigration and Asylum Act 2002 rather than an application for administrative review.

[(aa) An eligible decision is also a refusal of an application for entry clearance made on or after 5 October 2020 as:

(i) a Student; or

(ii) a Child Student; or

(iii) the Parent of a Child Student; or
(iv) the dependent partner or dependent child of a Student.]

(b) An *eligible decision* is also a refusal of an application for entry clearance made on or after 6th April 2015 by a Turkish national or their family member pursuant to the UK's obligations under Article 41 of the Additional Protocol to the European Community Association Agreement (ECAA) with Turkey.

[(c) An eligible decision is also a refusal of an application for entry clearance made on or after 1 December 2020 as:

(i) a Short-term Student under Appendix Short-term Student (English language); or
(ii) a Skilled Worker under Appendix Skilled Worker; or
(iii) an Intra-company Transfer route worker under Appendix Intra-Company Routes; or
(iv) a Minister of Religion under Appendix T2 Minister of Religion; or
(v) a Sportsperson under Appendix T2 Sportsperson; or
(vi) a Representative of an Overseas Business under Appendix Representative of an Overseas Business; or
(vii) a person with UK Ancestry under Appendix UK Ancestry; or
(viii) a person on the Global Talent route under Appendix Global Talent; or
(ix) a person on the Start-up route under Appendix Start-up; or
(x) an Innovator under Appendix Innovator; or
(xi) a Seasonal Worker under Appendix T5 (Temporary Worker) Seasonal Worker; or
(xii) a Youth Mobility Worker under Appendix T5 (Temporary Worker) Youth Mobility Scheme; or
(xiii) a Religious Worker under Appendix T5 (Temporary Worker) Religious Worker; or
(xiv) a Charity Worker under Appendix T5 (Temporary Worker) Charity Worker; or
(xv) a Creative or Sporting Worker under Appendix T5 (Temporary Worker) Creative or Sporting Worker; or
(xvi) an International Agreement Worker under Appendix T5 (Temporary Worker) International Agreement Worker; or
(xvii) a Government Authorised Exchange Worker under Appendix T5 (Temporary Worker) Government Authorised Exchange Worker route.]

[(d) An eligible decision is also a refusal of an application for entry clearance made on or after 1 December 2020 as the dependent partner or dependent child of:

(i) a Skilled Worker under Appendix Skilled Worker; or
(ii) an Intra-company routes worker under Appendix Intra-Company Routes; or
(iii) a Minister of Religion under Appendix T2 Minister of Religion; or
(iv) a Sportsperson under Appendix T2 Sportsperson; or
(v) a Representative of an Overseas Business under Appendix Representative of an Overseas Business; or
(vi) a person with UK Ancestry under Appendix UK Ancestry; or
(vii) a person on the Global Talent route under Appendix Global Talent; or
(viii) a person on the Start-up route under Appendix Start-up; or
(ix) an Innovator under Appendix Innovator; or
(x) a Religious Worker under Appendix T5 (Temporary Worker) Religious Worker; or

(xi) a Charity Worker under Appendix T5 (Temporary Worker) Charity Worker; or

(xii) a Creative or Sporting Worker under Appendix T5 (Temporary Worker) Creative or Sporting Worker; or

(xiii) an International Agreement Worker under Appendix T5 (Temporary Worker) International Agreement Worker; or

(xiv) a Government Authorised Exchange Worker under Appendix T5 (Temporary Worker) Government Authorised Exchange Worker route.]

[(e) An eligible decision is also a refusal of an application for entry clearance made on or after 31 January 2021 as:

(i) a Hong Kong British National (Overseas) under Appendix Hong Kong British National (Overseas); or

(ii) the dependent partner, BN(O) Household Child, BN(O) Household Member, or Adult Dependent Relative of a Hong Kong British National (Overseas) under Appendix Hong Kong British National (Overseas).]

[(f) An eligible decision is also a refusal of an application for entry clearance made on or after 6 May 2021 as:

(i) an Overseas Domestic Worker under Appendix Overseas Domestic Worker.]

[(g) An eligible decision is also a refusal of an application for entry clearance made on or after 0900 on 11 October 2021 as:

(i) an International Sportsperson under Appendix International Sportsperson; or

(ii) a Seasonal Worker under Appendix Temporary Work - Seasonal Worker; or

(iii) a person on the Youth Mobility Scheme route under Appendix Youth Mobility Scheme; or

(iv) a Religious Worker under Appendix Temporary Work - Religious Worker; or

(v) a Charity Worker under Appendix Temporary Work - Charity Worker; or

(vi) a Creative Worker under Appendix Temporary Work - Creative Worker; or

(vii) a person on the International Agreement route under Appendix Temporary Work - International Agreement; or

(viii) a person on the Government Authorised Exchange route under Appendix Temporary Work - Government Authorised Exchange.]

[(h) An eligible decision is also a refusal of an application for entry clearance made on or after 0900 on 11 October 2021as the dependent partner or dependent child of:

(i) an International Sportsperson under Appendix International Sportsperson; or

(ii) a Religious Worker under Appendix Temporary Work - Religious Worker; or

(iii) a Charity Worker under Appendix Temporary Work - Charity Worker; or

(iv) a Creative Worker under Appendix Temporary Work - Creative Worker; or

(v) a person on the International Agreement route under Appendix Temporary Work - International Agreement; or

(vi) a person on the Government Authorised Exchange route under Appendix Temporary Work - Government Authorised Exchange.]

[(i) An eligible decision is also a refusal of an application for entry clearance as:

(i) a Scale-up Worker under Appendix Scale-up; or

(ii) the partner or child of a Scale-up Worker under Appendix Scale-up.]

[(j) An eligible decision is also a refusal of an application for entry clearance as:

(i) a High Potential Individual under Appendix High Potential Individual; or

(ii) the partner or child of a High Potential Individual under Appendix High Potential Individual.]

[(k) An eligible decision is also a refusal of an application for entry clearance as:

(i) a Senior or Specialist Worker under Appendix Global Business Mobility – Senior or Specialist Worker; or

(ii) a Graduate Trainee under Appendix Global Business Mobility – Graduate Trainee; or

(iii) an Expansion Worker under Appendix Global Business Mobility – UK Expansion Worker; or

(iv) a Secondment Worker under Appendix Global Business Mobility – Secondment Worker; or

(v) a Service Supplier under Appendix Global Business Mobility – Service Supplier.]

[(l) An eligible decision is also a refusal of an application for entry clearance as the partner or child of:

(i) a Senior or Specialist Worker under Appendix Global Business Mobility – Senior or Specialist Worker; or

(ii) a Graduate Trainee under Appendix Global Business Mobility – Graduate Trainee; or

(iii) an Expansion Worker under Appendix Global Business Mobility – UK Expansion Worker; or

(iv) a Secondment Worker under Appendix Global Business Mobility – Secondment Worker; or

(v) a Service Supplier under Appendix Global Business Mobility – Service Supplier.]

Note: Words in square brackets in (a) inserted from 22 April 2019 (HC 2099). Sub-paragraphs (aa), (c), (d) and (e) inserted from 09:00 on 1 December 2020 subject to savings for applications made before that time (HC 813). Sub-paragraph (f) inserted from 6 May 2021 subject to savings for applications (including for administrative review) made before that date (HC 1248). Sub-paragraphs (g) and (h) inserted from 09:00 on 11 October 2021 subject to savings for applications made before that time (HC 617). Sub-paragraphs (i), (j), (k), and (l) inserted from 6 April 2022 subject to savings for applications made before that date (HC 1118). Words in double square brackets in (a) inserted from 30 March 2022 (HC 1220).

[Appendix AR (EU)

Eligible decisions

[AR(EU)A1. An application for administrative review of an eligible decision made under Appendix EU, Appendix EU (Family Permit), Appendix S2 Healthcare Visitor or Appendix Service Providers from Switzerland may only be made in accordance with this Appendix. Appendix AR does not apply to such applications.]

Note: Paragraph inserted from 1 October 2019 (HC 2631). Amendment from 23:00 on 31 December 2020 subject to savings for applications made before that time (HC 813). Paragraph substituted from 6 April 2021 subject to savings for applications made before that date (HC 1248).

[AR(EU)1.1. An applicant may only apply for an administrative review where an eligible decision has been made. An eligible decision is a decision to:

(a) Refuse an application under paragraph EU6 of Appendix EU because the applicant does not meet the eligibility requirements for indefinite leave to enter or remain under paragraph EU11, EU11A or EU12 or for limited leave to enter or remain under paragraph EU14 or EU14A; or

(b) Grant limited leave to enter or remain under paragraph EU3 of Appendix EU and not indefinite leave to enter or remain under paragraph EU2; or

(c) Grant limited leave to enter or remain under paragraph EU3A of Appendix EU and not indefinite leave to enter or remain under paragraph EU2A; or

(d) Cancel leave granted under Appendix EU on the grounds that the person ceases to meet the requirements of that Appendix for that leave; or

(e) Cancel leave to enter granted by virtue of having arrived in the UK with an entry clearance that was granted under Appendix EU (Family Permit) where since the entry clearance was granted, there has been a change in circumstances that is, or would have been, relevant to that person's eligibility for that entry clearance, such that their leave to enter ought to be cancelled; or

(f) Refuse an application under paragraph HV9.1 of Appendix S2 Healthcare Visitor because the applicant does not meet the eligibility requirements for permission to enter or remain as an S2 Healthcare Visitor; or

(g) [Cancel] permission to enter to a person who holds entry clearance under Appendix S2 Healthcare Visitor, where, since the entry clearance was granted, there has been a change in circumstances which means the person no longer meets the eligibility requirements for permission to enter; or

(h) Refuse permission to enter to a non-visa national seeking to come to the UK as an S2 Healthcare Visitor for 6 months or less, because they do not meet the eligibility requirements of Appendix S2 Healthcare Visitor; or

(i) Refuse an application for entry clearance under paragraph SPS7.1 of Appendix Service Providers from Switzerland because the applicant does not meet the eligibility requirements of that Appendix; or

(j) [Cancel] permission to enter to a person who holds an entry clearance under Appendix Service Providers from Switzerland, where, since the entry clearance was granted, there has been a change in circumstances which means the person no longer meets the eligibility requirements for permission to enter.]

Note: Amendments in (a) and (b) from 22 April 2019 (HC 2099). Paragraph substituted from 4 December 2019 for applications made under Appendix EU on or after that date (HC 170). Paragraph substituted from 6 April 2020 (HC 120). Paragraph substituted from 23:00 on 31 December 2020 subject to savings for applications made before that time (HC 813). Words in (g) and (j) substituted from 6 October 2021 (HC 617).

AR(EU)1.1A. [DELETED]

Note: Paragraph inserted from 1 October 2019 (HC 2631). Paragraph substituted from 6 April 2020 (HC 120). Paragraph deleted from 23:00 on 31 December 2020 subject to savings for applications made before that time (HC 813).

[AR(EU)1.2. An applicant may not apply for an administrative review where a decision has been made to:

(a) Refuse an application under paragraph EU6 of Appendix EU on suitability grounds as set out in paragraph EU15 or EU16; or

(b) Refuse an application under paragraph HV9.1 of Appendix S2 Healthcare Visitor where the suitability requirements are not met; or

(c) Refuse permission to enter to a person who holds entry clearance under Appendix S2 Healthcare Visitor, where, since the entry clearance was granted, there has been a change in circumstances which means the person no longer meets the suitability requirements for permission to enter; or

(d) Refuse an application for entry clearance under paragraph SPS 7.1 of Appendix Service Providers from Switzerland because the applicant does not meet the suitability requirements of that Appendix; or

(e) Refuse permission to enter to a person who holds an entry clearance under Appendix Service Providers from Switzerland, where, since the entry clearance was granted, there has been a change in circumstances which means the person no longer meets the suitability requirements for permission to enter.]

Note: Paragraph substituted from 4 December 2019 for applications made under Appendix EU on or after that date (HC 170). Paragraph substituted from 6 April 2020 (HC 120). Paragraph substituted from 23:00 on 31 December 2020 subject to savings for applications made before that time (HC 813).

[**AR(EU)1.3.** An applicant may not apply for an administrative review where their application has been rejected as invalid under paragraph EU10(1) of Appendix EU, paragraph HV1.7. of Appendix S2 Healthcare Visitor or paragraph SPS 1.4. of Appendix Service Providers from Switzerland.]

Note: Paragraph substituted from 4 December 2019 for applications made under Appendix EU on or after that date (HC 170). Paragraph substituted from 6 April 2020 (HC 120). Paragraph substituted from 23:00 on 31 December 2020 subject to savings for applications made before that time (HC 813).

Consideration

[**AR(EU)2.1.** The person considering the administrative review on behalf of the Secretary of State ('the reviewer') will decide whether the decision is incorrect because:

(a) The decision maker failed to apply, or incorrectly applied, the relevant Immigration Rules;

(b) The decision maker failed to apply, or incorrectly applied, the published guidance in relation to the application; or

(c) Information or evidence that was not before the decision maker has been provided to the reviewer which shows that the applicant qualifies for:

(i) a grant, or a different grant, of leave under Appendix EU; or

(ii) permission to enter or stay in the UK under Appendix S2 Healthcare Visitor; or

(iii) entry clearance or permission to enter under Appendix Service Providers from Switzerland.]

Note: Amendments from 4 December 2019 for applications made under Appendix EU on or after that date (HC 170). Amendments from 6 April 2020 (HC 120). Paragraph substituted from 23:00 on 31 December 2020 subject to savings for applications made before that time (HC 813).

AR(EU)2.2. Where the reviewer considers that the decision is incorrect in accordance with paragraph AR(EU)2.1., the decision will be withdrawn and a new decision made. Otherwise, the decision will be maintained.

AR(EU)2.3. The reviewer will consider any information and evidence submitted with the application for administrative review, including information and evidence that was not before the original decision-maker.

AR(EU)2.4. The reviewer may contact the applicant or their representative to request further information or evidence, to be provided within a reasonable timeframe specified in the request.

AR(EU)2.5. The reviewer will notify the applicant of the outcome of the administrative review by notice under Appendix SN.

Applications for administrative review

AR(EU)3.1. A valid application for administrative review under this Appendix must be made in accordance with paragraphs 34M to 34Y of these Rules.

AR(EU)3.2. An application for administrative review under this Appendix is decided when:

(a) It is rejected as invalid because it does not meet the requirements of paragraph 34N to 34S of these Rules;

(b) It is withdrawn in accordance with paragraph 34X of these Rules; or

(c) The notice of outcome is served in accordance with Appendix SN.]

[Effect of a pending administrative review on liability for removal]

[**AR(EU)4.1.** Where an administrative review under this Appendix is pending the Home Office will not seek to remove the applicant from the United Kingdom.]

Note: Paragraph and heading inserted from 23:00 on 31 December 2020 subject to savings for applications made before that time (HC 813).

[**AR(EU)4.2.** For the purposes of paragraph AR(EU)4.1., an administrative review is pending where:

(a) An application for administrative review can be made in accordance with 34M to 34Y of these Rules, ignoring any possibility of an administrative review out-of-time under paragraph 34R(3);

(b) A further application for administrative review can be made in accordance with paragraph 34M(2A) of these Rules; or

(c) An application for administrative review has been made and has not yet been decided.]

Note: Paragraph inserted from 23:00 on 31 December 2020 subject to savings for applications made before that time (HC 813).

[**AR(EU)4.3.** However, an administrative review is not pending where the applicant has waived their right to apply for an administrative review of an eligible decision by signing an administrative review waiver form.]

Note: Paragraph inserted from 23:00 on 31 December 2020 subject to savings for applications made before that time (HC 813).

Appendix inserted from 1 November 2018 in respect of applications made under Appendix EU on or after that date (HC 1534).

Appendix Armed Forces

Part 1 General

Who these rules apply to

1. The rules contained in this Appendix apply to those seeking to enter or remain in the United Kingdom as:

(a) a foreign or Commonwealth member of HM Forces (on discharge);

(b) a partner, child or other dependant of a member of HM Forces;

(c) a partner or child of a member of non-HM Forces who is exempt from immigration control by virtue of section 8(4)(b) or (c) of the Immigration Act 1971;

(d) a member of non-HM Forces who is not exempt from immigration control;

(e) a partner or child of a member of non-HM Forces who is not exempt from immigration control;

(f) a Relevant Civilian Employee as defined in paragraph 2(j)(a); and

(g) a partner, child or other dependant of a Relevant Civilian Employee.

Interpretation and general provisions

2. In this Appendix (including as it applies to applications under Part 7 or 8 of these Rules):

(a) an application for leave to enter or remain includes an application for variation of leave to enter or remain;

(b) a reference to a British Citizen in the United Kingdom includes:

(i) a British Citizen who is coming to the United Kingdom with the applicant as the applicant's partner or parent; and

(ii) a British Citizen who has naturalised having accrued 5 years' reckonable service in HM Forces;

(ba) a reference to a civilian employee of a NATO force includes an employee of the American National Red Cross working with US Forces in the United Kingdom;

(c) 'Gurkha' means a member of HM Forces who is serving or has served in the Brigade of Gurkhas of the British Army under the Brigade of Gurkhas' terms and conditions of service;

(d) 'a member of HM Forces' is a person who, subject to sub-paragraphs (e) and (f), is a member of the regular forces within the meaning of the Armed Forces Act 2006;

(e) a person is not to be regarded as a member of HM Forces if the person is treated as a member of a regular force by virtue of:

(i) section 369 of the Armed Forces Act 2006, or

(ii) section 4(3) of the Visiting Forces (British Commonwealth) Act 1933;

(f) a reference to a member of HM Forces includes a person who was a member of HM Forces but was discharged within the period of 2 years prior to the date of the application under these Rules made in relation to that member (unless a different meaning applies elsewhere in this Appendix);

(g) 'a member of non-HM Forces' means a member of other armed forces who is:

(i) exempt from immigration control under section 8(4)(b) or (c) of the Immigration Act 1971, or

(ii) not exempt from immigration control;

(ga) 'other dependant' means an applicant under Part 10 of this Appendix, other than a partner or child under the age of 18, who is named on the original movement or posting order;

(h) 'partner' means (unless a different meaning of partner applies elsewhere in this Appendix):

(i) the applicant's spouse;

(ii) the applicant's civil partner;

(iii) the applicant's fiancé(e) or proposed civil partner; or

(iv) a person who has been living together with the applicant in a relationship akin to a marriage or civil partnership for at least 2 years prior to the date of the application;

(j) 'reckonable service' is the service which counts towards pension, which starts from the first day of paid service in HM Forces;

(ja) a reference to a Relevant Civilian Employee means a civilian who is being employed to work in the United Kingdom by:

(i) a NATO force

(ii) a company under contract to a NATO force; or

(iii) the Australian Department of Defence;

(k) 'specified' means specified in Appendix FM-SE and Appendix O to these Rules;

(l) where a financial or maintenance requirement applies in this Appendix, paragraphs A. to 21 of Appendix FM-SE to these Rules shall apply as appropriate.

3. If an Entry Clearance Officer, or the Secretary of State, has reasonable cause to doubt the genuineness of any document submitted in support of an application, and having taken reasonable steps to verify the document, is unable to verify that it is genuine, the document will be discounted for the purposes of the application.

4. A reference to an application being considered under this Appendix includes, where relevant, an application considered under Part 7 or 8 of these Rules which requires compliance with this Appendix.

5. Paragraphs 277–280, 289AA, 295AA and 296 of Part 8 of these Rules apply to applications made under this Appendix.

5A. Where a person aged 18 or over is granted entry clearance or limited leave to enter or remain under this Appendix, or where a person granted such entry clearance or limited leave to enter or remain will be aged 18 before that period of limited leave expires, the entry clearance or leave will, in addition to any other conditions which may apply, be granted subject to the conditions in [Appendix ATAS] of these Rules.

Note: Words substituted from 09:00 on 5 October 2020 subject to savings for applications made before that time. Where consequential changes relating to the need for an ATAS certificate have been made, they take effect for all applications made or granted on or after 5 October 2020 at 09:00 (HC 707).

Leave to enter

6. The requirements to be met by a person seeking leave to enter the United Kingdom under this Appendix are that the person:

(a) must have a valid entry clearance for entry in a route under this Appendix;, unless they are: (i) a non-visa national; (ii) not seeking entry for a period exceeding 6 months; and (iii) applying for leave to enter under paragraphs 56, 61B or 64 of this Appendix; and

(b) must produce to the Immigration Officer on arrival a valid national passport or other document satisfactorily establishing their identity and nationality.

7. If a person does not meet the requirements of paragraph 6, entry will be refused.

Part 2 Suitability requirements

8. An application under this Appendix will be refused on the grounds of suitability if any of the provisions in this paragraph apply:

(a) in respect of applications for entry clearance or leave to enter, the Secretary of State has personally directed that the exclusion of the applicant from the United Kingdom is conducive to the public good;

(b) the applicant is currently the subject of a deportation order;

(c) subject to sub-paragraph (d), permitting the applicant to enter, or remain in, the United Kingdom is not conducive to the public good because he or she has been convicted of an offence for which he or she has been sentenced to a period of imprisonment of:

(i) at least 4 years; or

(ii) at least 12 months, but less than 4 years, unless:

(aa) in respect of applications for entry clearance or leave to enter: a period of 10 years has passed since the end of the sentence; or

(bb) in respect of applications for indefinite leave to remain: a period of 15 years has passed since the end of the sentence; or

(iii) in respect of applications for entry clearance or leave to enter or indefinite leave to remain, less than 12 months, unless:

(aa) in respect of applications for entry clearance or leave to enter: a period of 5 years has passed since the end of the sentence; or

(bb) in respect of applications for indefinite leave to remain: a period of 7 years has passed since the end of the sentence;

(ca) in respect of applications for limited or indefinite leave to remain, where:

(i) the Secretary of State has made a decision under Article 1F of the Refugee Convention to exclude the person from the Refugee Convention or under paragraph 339D of these Rules to exclude them from humanitarian protection; or

(ii) the Secretary of State has previously made a decision that they are a person to whom Article 33(2) of the Refugee Convention applies because there are reasonable grounds for regarding them as a danger to the security of the United Kingdom; or

(iii) the Secretary of State considers that they are a person to whom sub-paragraph (i) or (ii) would apply except that (a) the person has not made a protection claim, or (b) the person made a protection claim which has already been finally determined without reference to Article 1F of the Refugee Convention or paragraph 339D of these Rules; or

(iv) the Secretary of State has previously made a decision that they are a person to whom Article 33(2) of the Refugee Convention applies because, having been convicted by a final judgment of a particularly serious crime, they constitute a danger to the community of the United Kingdom.

[...]

(e) in respect of applications for limited leave to remain or indefinite leave to remain, in the view of the Secretary of State,

(i) the applicant's offending has caused serious harm; or

(ii) the applicant is a persistent offender who shows a particular disregard for the law;

(f) in respect of applications for indefinite leave to remain, the applicant has, within the 24 months prior to the date on which the application is decided, been convicted of or admitted an offence for which they received a non-custodial sentence or other out of court disposal that is recorded on their criminal record;

(g) permitting the applicant to enter, or remain in, the UK is not conducive to the public good because, for example, their conduct (including convictions which do not fall within sub-paragraph (c) or (f) as appropriate, character, associations, or other reasons, make it undesirable to grant them entry clearance or allow them to remain in the UK;

(h) in respect of applications for entry clearance or leave to enter, the applicant left or was removed from the United Kingdom pursuant to a condition attached to a conditional caution given under section 22 of the Criminal Justice Act 2003 less than 5 years before the date on which the application is decided;

(i) the applicant has failed without reasonable excuse to comply with a requirement to:

(i) attend an interview;

(ii) provide information;

(iii) provide physical data; or

(iv) undergo a medical examination or provide a medical report; or

(j) it is undesirable to grant entry clearance or leave to enter to the applicant for medical reasons.

Note: Sub-paragraph (d) deleted from the date of commencement of Schedule 10 to the Immigration Act 2016 (HC 309).

9. An application under this Appendix will normally be refused on the grounds of suitability if any of the provisions in this paragraph apply:

(a) whether or not to the applicant's knowledge:

(i) false information, representations or documents have been submitted in relation to the application (including false information submitted to any person to obtain a document used in support of the application); or

(ii) there has been a failure to disclose material facts in relation to the application;

(b) one or more relevant NHS bodies (within the meaning of paragraph 6 of these Rules) has notified the Secretary of State that:

(c) a maintenance and accommodation undertaking has been requested or required under this Appendix or paragraph 35 of these Rules or otherwise and has not been provided;

(d) in respect of applications for entry clearance or leave to enter, the exclusion of the applicant from the United Kingdom is conducive to the public good because:

(i) within the 12 months prior to the date on which the application is decided, the person has been convicted of or admitted an offence for which they received a non-custodial sentence or other out of court disposal that is recorded on their criminal record; or

(ii) in the view of the Secretary of State: (aa) the person's offending has caused serious harm; or (bb) the person is a persistent offender who shows a particular disregard for the law.

10. In respect of applications for limited leave to remain or indefinite leave to remain, when considering whether the presence of the applicant in the UK is not conducive to the public good any legal or practical reasons why the applicant cannot presently be removed from the United Kingdom must be ignored.

10A. The applicant may be refused on grounds of suitability if the applicant has failed to pay litigation costs awarded to the Home Office.

10B. An application under this Appendix may be refused on the grounds of suitability if one or more relevant NHS bodies has notified the Secretary of State that the applicant has failed to pay charges in accordance with the relevant NHS regulations on charges to overseas visitors and the outstanding charges have a total value of at least £500.

Part 3 Discharged members of HM Forces

General eligibility requirements

11. The general eligibility requirements to be met as a discharged member of HM Forces are that:

(a) the applicant:

(i) has completed at least 4 years' reckonable service in HM Forces; or

(ii) meets the medical discharge criteria in paragraph 12; and

(b) on the date on which the application is made:

(i) the applicant has been discharged from HM Forces for a period of less than 2 years; or

(ii) in the case of an applicant who was medically discharged more than 2 years before, new information regarding his or her prognosis is being considered by the Secretary of State; or

(iii) the applicant has been granted his or her most recent period of limited leave:

(aa) under paragraph 15 or 19 of this Appendix as a foreign or Commonwealth citizen who has been discharged from HM Forces; or

(bb) under paragraph 276KA or 276QA of these Rules; or

(cc) under the concession which existed outside these Rules, whereby the Secretary of State exercised her discretion to grant leave to enter or remain to members of HM Forces who have been medically discharged; and

(c) in relation to an application made by a Gurkha, the Gurkha is a citizen or national of Nepal.

Medical discharge

12. The medical discharge criteria are satisfied where the applicant was medically discharged from HM Forces:

(a) where the cause was attributable to service in HM Forces and it came about owing to deployment in an operational theatre; or

(b) where the cause was attributable to service in HM Forces, it did not come about owing to deployment in an operational theatre but it is appropriate to grant leave to enter or remain in the United Kingdom following an assessment of the following factors:

(i) the seriousness of the illness or injury;

(ii) the need for further medical treatment in relation to the illness or injury and the availability of such medical treatment in the applicant's country of origin;

(iii) the prognosis for recovery, including whether the injury or illness will affect the applicant's ability to support themselves in their country of origin; and

(iv) the length of reckonable service in HM Forces at the time of the applicant's discharge.

Indefinite leave to enter

13. Entry clearance and indefinite leave to enter as a foreign or Commonwealth citizen discharged from HM Forces will be granted to an applicant who:

(a) is outside the United Kingdom;

(b) has made a valid application for entry clearance and indefinite leave to enter as a foreign or Commonwealth citizen discharged from HM Forces;

(c) does not fall to be refused on the grounds of suitability under paragraph 8 or 9; and

(d) meets the general eligibility requirements in paragraph 11.

Leave to remain

14. Limited leave to remain as a foreign or Commonwealth citizen discharged from HM Forces will be granted to an applicant who:

(a) is in the United Kingdom;

(b) is not in breach of immigration laws, except that, where paragraph 39E of these Rules applies, any current period of overstaying will be disregarded;

(c) has made a valid application for limited leave to remain as a foreign or Commonwealth citizen discharged from HM Forces;

(d) does not fall to be refused on the grounds of suitability under paragraph 8 or 9; and

(e) meets the general eligibility requirements in paragraph 11.

15. Limited leave to remain granted under paragraph 14 will normally be granted for a period not exceeding 30 months and will be subject to such conditions as the Secretary of State considers appropriate.

Indefinite leave to remain

16. Indefinite leave to remain as a foreign or Commonwealth citizen discharged from HM Forces will be granted to an applicant who:

(a) is in the United Kingdom;

(b) is not in breach of immigration laws, except that, where paragraph 39E of these Rules applies, any current period of overstaying will be disregarded;

(c) has made a valid application for indefinite leave to remain as a foreign or Commonwealth citizen discharged from HM Forces;

(d) does not fall to be refused on the grounds of suitability under paragraph 8 or 9; and

(e) meets the general eligibility requirements in paragraph 11.

Circumstances in which limited leave to remain may be granted to applicants for indefinite leave to remain under Paragraph 16

17. Limited leave to remain as a foreign or Commonwealth citizen discharged from HM Forces may be granted to a person who fails to meet the requirements for indefinite leave to remain in paragraph 16 of this Appendix by reason only of failing to meet the suitability requirements in paragraph 8 or 9 in respect of a grant of indefinite leave to remain (but not a grant of limited leave to remain).

18. Limited leave to remain as a foreign or Commonwealth citizen discharged from HM Forces may be granted to a person ('P') who fails to meet the requirements for indefinite leave to remain in paragraph 16 of this Appendix by reason only of being unable to meet the medical discharge criteria in paragraph 12, provided that the following conditions are met:

(a) P has been medically discharged from HM Forces;

(b) the cause of P's discharge was attributable to service in HM Forces; and

(c) before P can return to P's country of origin it is appropriate to grant limited leave to remain to facilitate:

(i) further medical treatment for P; or

(ii) a period of recovery for P.

19. Limited leave to remain granted under paragraph 17 or 18 will normally be granted for a period not exceeding 30 months and will be subject to such conditions as the Secretary of State considers appropriate.

Part 4 Partners of members of HM Forces

General eligibility requirements

20. The general eligibility requirements to be met by the partner ('P') of a member of HM Forces are that on the date the application is made:

(a) P's sponsor is a member of HM Forces (as defined in paragraph 2(d) of this Appendix) who:

(i) is exempt from immigration control; or

(ii) has leave to enter or remain under paragraphs 13–19 of this Appendix or paragraphs 276E–QA of these Rules or under the concession which existed outside these Rules whereby the Secretary of State exercised her discretion to grant leave to enter or remain to a member of HM Forces who has been medically discharged; or

(iii) is being granted leave to enter or remain under paragraphs 13–19 of this Appendix or paragraphs 276E–QA of these Rules at the same time as P; or

(iv) is a British Citizen;

(b) P and P's sponsor:

(i) are both aged 18 or over;

(ii) must not be within a prohibited degree of relationship;

(iii) must intend to live together permanently; and

(iv) must have met in person;

(c) the relationship between P and P's sponsor is genuine and subsisting; and

(d) any previous relationship of P or P's sponsor must have broken down permanently, unless it is a relationship which falls within paragraph 278(i) of these Rules.

20A. For this Part, a reference to a member of HM Forces includes a former member of HM Forces who was discharged more than 2 years ago if that member of HM Forces:

(a)

(i) is a British citizen; or

(ii) was granted leave under this Appendix; and

(b) the applicant had leave under these Rules as the partner or child of a member of HM Forces prior to their sponsor's discharge.

21. If P and P's sponsor are married or in a civil partnership, it must be a valid marriage or civil partnership as specified in Appendix FM-SE.

22. If P is the fiancé(e) or proposed civil partner of P's sponsor, P must be seeking entry to the UK to enable their marriage or civil partnership to take place.

Leave to enter

23. Entry clearance and leave to enter as the partner of a member of HM Forces will be granted to an applicant who:

(a) is outside the United Kingdom;

(b) has made a valid application for entry clearance and leave to enter as the partner of a member of HM Forces;

(c) does not fall to be refused on the grounds of suitability under paragraph 8 or 9;

(d) meets the general eligibility requirements in paragraph 20;

(e) meets the English language requirement in Part 11 of this Appendix; and

(f) meets the financial requirements in Part 12 of this Appendix.

24. Entry clearance and leave to enter granted under paragraph 23 will normally be:

(a) for whichever is the shortest period of:

(i) 5 years;

(ii) the remaining duration of the applicant's partner's enlistment;

(iii) the remaining duration of the applicant's partner's extant leave under paragraph 276KA or 276QA of these Rules or paragraph 15 or 19 of this Appendix or under the concession which existed outside these Rules whereby the Secretary of State exercised her discretion to grant leave to enter or remain to a member of HM Forces who has been medically discharged; or

(iv) in the case of a fiancé(e) or proposed civil partner, a period not exceeding 6 months; and

(b) subject to the following conditions:

(i) no recourse to public funds; and

(ii) in the case of a fiancé(e) or proposed civil partner, a prohibition on employment.

Indefinite leave to enter

25. Entry clearance and indefinite leave to enter as the partner of a member of HM Forces will be granted to an applicant who:

(a) is outside the United Kingdom;

(b) has made a valid application for entry clearance and indefinite leave to enter as the partner of a member of HM Forces;

(c) has a partner who:

(i) is a foreign or Commonwealth citizen who is a member of HM Forces with at least 5 years' reckonable service in HM Forces; or

(ii) has been granted indefinite leave to enter or remain under paragraph 13 or 16 of this Appendix or paragraphs 276E–Q of these Rules and is in the United Kingdom; or

(iii) is a British Citizen;

(d) does not fall to be refused on the grounds of suitability under paragraph 8 or 9;

(e) meets the general eligibility requirements in paragraph 20;

(f) can demonstrate sufficient knowledge of the English language and sufficient knowledge about life in the UK in accordance with the requirements of Appendix KoLL to these Rules;

(g) meets the financial requirements in Part 12 of this Appendix; and

(h) has completed a continuous period of 60 months with leave under this Appendix as the partner of the same member of HM Forces, excluding any period of entry clearance or limited leave as a fiancé(e) or proposed civil partner.

26. Entry clearance and limited leave to enter as a partner (excluding as a fiancé(e) or proposed civil partner) of a member of HM Forces for a period of 30 months may be granted:

(a) where an applicant fails to meet the requirements of paragraph 25 by reason only of failing to meet the requirements of paragraph 25(c)(i) or (ii), provided that the applicant's sponsor has been granted leave to enter or remain under paragraph 15 or 19 of this Appendix; or

(b) where an applicant fails to meet the requirements of paragraph 25 by reason only of failing to meet the requirements of paragraph 25(f).

27. Entry clearance and limited leave to enter granted under paragraph 26 will be subject to a condition of no recourse to public funds.

Leave to remain

28. Limited leave to remain as the partner of a member of HM Forces will be granted to an applicant who:

[(a) is in the United Kingdom, but not:

(i) as a visitor;

(ii) with valid leave that was granted for a period of 6 months or less, unless that leave:

(aa) is as a fiancé(e) or proposed civil partner; or

(bb) was granted pending the outcome of family court or divorce proceedings;

(iii) on temporary admission or temporary release; or

(iv) after the date on which paragraph 1 of Schedule 10 to the Immigration Act 2016 is commenced, a grant of immigration bail in circumstances in which temporary admission or temporary release would previously have been granted;]

(b) is not in breach of immigration laws, except that, where paragraph 39E of these Rules applies, any current period of overstaying will be disregarded;

(c) has made a valid application for limited leave to remain as the partner of a member of HM Forces;

(d) does not fall to be refused on the grounds of suitability under paragraph 8 or 9;

(e) meets the general eligibility requirements in paragraph 20;

(f) is not a fiancé(e) or proposed civil partner of the member of HM Forces, unless:

(i) the applicant is in the United Kingdom with leave as a fiancé(e) or proposed civil partner under paragraph 23 (and that earlier leave was granted in respect of the current sponsor);

(ii) there is good reason why the marriage or civil partnership has not taken place during that period of leave; and

(iii) there is evidence that the marriage or civil partnership will take place within the next 6 months;

(g) meets the English language requirement in Part 11 of this Appendix; and

(h) meets the financial requirements in Part 12 of this Appendix.

Note: Sub-paragraph (a) substituted from the date of commencement of Schedule 10 to the Immigration Act 2016 (HC 309).

29. Limited leave to remain granted under paragraph 28 will normally be granted:

(a) for whichever is the shortest period of:

(i) 5 years;

(ii) the remaining duration of the applicant's partner's enlistment; or

(iii) the remaining duration of the applicant's partner's extant leave under paragraph 276KA or 276QA of these Rules or paragraph 15 or 19 of this Appendix or under the concession which existed outside these Rules whereby the Secretary of State exercised her discretion to grant leave to enter or remain to a member of HM Forces who has been medically discharged; or

(iv) in the case of a fiancé(e) or proposed civil partner, a period not exceeding 6 months; and

(b) subject to the following conditions:

(i) no recourse to public funds; and

(ii) in the case of a fiancé(e) or proposed civil partner, a prohibition on employment.

30. An applicant granted limited leave to remain under paragraph 29 will be eligible to apply for settlement after a continuous period of 60 months with such leave under this Appendix as the partner of the same member of HM Forces, excluding any period of entry clearance or limited leave as a fiancé(e) or proposed civil partner.

Indefinite leave to remain

31. Indefinite leave to remain as the partner of a member of HM Forces will be granted to an applicant who:

(a) is in the United Kingdom;

(b) is not in breach of immigration laws, except that, where paragraph 39E of these Rules applies, any current period of overstaying will be disregarded;

(c) has a partner who:

(i) is a foreign or Commonwealth citizen who is a member of HM Forces with at least 5 years' reckonable service in HM Forces; or

(ii) has been granted, or is being granted at the same time as the applicant, indefinite leave to enter or remain under paragraph 13 or 16 of this Appendix or paragraphs 276E–Q of these Rules; or

(iii) is a British Citizen;

(d) does not fall to be refused on the grounds of suitability under paragraph 8 or 9;

(e) meets the general eligibility requirements in paragraph 20;

(f) can demonstrate sufficient knowledge of the English language and sufficient knowledge about life in the UK in accordance with the requirements of Appendix KoLL to these Rules;

(g) meets the financial requirements in Part 12 of this Appendix; and

(h) has completed a continuous period of 60 months with leave under this Appendix as the partner of the same member of HM Forces, excluding any period of entry clearance or limited leave as a fiancé(e) or proposed civil partner.

32. Limited leave to remain as the partner (excluding as a fiancé(e) or proposed civil partner) of a member of HM Forces for a period of 30 months may be granted where the applicant fails to meet the requirements for indefinite leave to remain in paragraph 31:

(a) by reason only of failing to satisfy the suitability requirements in paragraph 8 or 9 in respect of a grant of indefinite leave to remain (but not a grant of limited leave to remain); or

(b) by reason only of failing to meet the requirements of paragraph 31(c)(i) or (ii), provided that the applicant's sponsor has been granted leave to enter or remain under paragraph 15 or 19 of this Appendix; or

(c) by reason only of failing to meet the requirements of paragraph 31(f).

33. Limited leave to remain granted under paragraph 32 will be subject to a condition of no recourse to public funds.

Part 5 Bereaved partners of members of HM Forces

General eligibility requirements

34. The general eligibility requirements to be met by a bereaved partner of a member of HM Forces are that:

(a) the applicant's partner at the time of the applicant's last grant of leave as a partner (other than as a fiancé(e) or proposed civil partner) was:

(i) a foreign or Commonwealth citizen who was a serving member of HM Forces; or

(ii) a discharged member of HM Forces who had been granted, or was seeking at the same time as the applicant, leave to enter or remain under paragraphs 13–19 of this Appendix or paragraphs 276E–QA of these Rules; or

(iii) a British Citizen in HM Forces;

(b) the applicant's partner has died;

(c) at the time of the applicant's partner's death the applicant and the partner:

(i) were both aged 18 or over;

(ii) were not within a prohibited degree of relationship; and

(iii) had met in person; and

(d) at the time of the applicant's partner's death the relationship between the applicant and the partner was genuine and subsisting and each of the parties intended to live together permanently.

34A. For this Part, a reference to a member of HM Forces includes a former member of HM Forces who was discharged more than 2 years ago if that member of HM Forces:

(a)

(i) is a British citizen; or

(ii) was granted leave under this Appendix; and

(b) the applicant had leave under these Rules as the partner or child of a member of HM Forces prior to their sponsor's discharge.

Indefinite leave to enter

35. Entry clearance and indefinite leave to enter as a bereaved partner of a member of HM Forces will be granted to an applicant who:

(a) is outside the United Kingdom as a result of accompanying their sponsor on an overseas posting;

(b) has made a valid application for entry clearance and indefinite leave to enter as the bereaved partner of a member of HM Forces;

(c) does not fall to be refused on the grounds of suitability under paragraph 8 or 9; and

(d) meets the general eligibility requirements in paragraph 34.

Indefinite leave to remain

36. Indefinite leave to remain as a bereaved partner of a member of HM Forces will be granted to an applicant who:

(a) is in the United Kingdom;

(b) has made a valid application for indefinite leave to remain as the bereaved partner of a member of HM Forces;

(c) does not fall to be refused on the grounds of suitability under paragraph 8 or 9; and

(d) meets the general eligibility requirements in paragraph 34.

37. Limited leave to remain as a bereaved partner of a member of HM Forces for a period of 30 months may be granted to a person who fails to meet the requirements for indefinite leave to remain in paragraph 36 by reason only of failing to meet the suitability requirements in paragraph 8 or 9 in respect of a grant of indefinite leave to remain (but not a grant of limited leave to remain).

38. Limited leave to remain granted under paragraph 37 will be subject to a condition of no recourse to public funds.

Part 6 Partners of members of HM Forces who are the victim of domestic violence

General eligibility requirements

39. The general eligibility requirements to be met by the partner of a member of HM Forces who is a victim of domestic violence are that:

(a) the applicant is in the UK and was:

(i) last admitted to the UK under paragraph 276AD of these Rules or paragraph 23, 26, 28 or 32 of this Appendix; or

(ii) last granted leave to enable access to public funds pending an application under this paragraph and the preceding grant of leave was given in accordance with paragraph 276AD of these Rules or paragraph 23, 26, 28 or 32 of this Appendix;

(b) the leave referred to in sub-paragraph (a) (i) or, where applicable, the preceding grant of leave referred to in sub paragraph (a)(ii) was as the partner (other than a fiancé(e) or proposed civil partner) of a member of HM Forces who is:

(i) a British Citizen; or

(ii) a foreign or Commonwealth citizen with at least 4 years' reckonable service in HM Forces at the date of application under this paragraph;

(c) the applicant does not fall to be refused on grounds of suitability under paragraph 8 or 9;

(d) the applicant has made a valid application for indefinite leave to remain as a victim of domestic violence; and

(e) the applicant must provide evidence that during the last period of limited leave as a partner the applicant's relationship with their partner broke down permanently as a result of domestic violence.

Indefinite leave to remain

40. Indefinite leave to remain as the partner of a member of HM Forces who is a victim of domestic violence will be granted to an applicant who meets the general eligibility requirements in paragraph 39.

41. Limited leave to remain for a period of 30 months may be granted to a partner of a member of HM Forces who is a victim of domestic violence who fails to meet the requirements for indefinite leave to remain in paragraph 40 by reason only of failing to meet the suitability requirements in paragraph 8 or 9 in respect of a grant of indefinite leave to remain (but not a grant of limited leave to remain). This will be subject to such conditions as the Secretary of State considers appropriate.

Part 7 Children of members of HM Forces

General eligibility requirements

42. The general eligibility requirements to be met by the child of a member of HM Forces are that:

(a) the applicant is the child of a parent who is:

(i) a foreign or Commonwealth citizen who is a serving member of HM Forces; or

(ii) a discharged member of HM Forces who has been granted, or who is being granted at the same time as the applicant, leave to enter or remain under paragraphs 13–19 of this Appendix or paragraphs 276E–QA of these Rules or under the concession which existed outside these Rules whereby the Secretary of State exercised her discretion to grant leave to enter or remain to a member of HM Forces who has been medically discharged; or

(iii) a member of HM Forces who is a British Citizen; and

(b) the applicant meets one of the following criteria:

(i) the applicant's other parent must:

(aa) also come within paragraph 42(a); or

(bb) have been granted leave to enter or remain under paragraphs 23–33 of this Appendix or paragraph 276S, 276V or 276AE of these Rules; or

(cc) be being granted leave to enter or remain under paragraphs 23–33 of this Appendix or paragraph 276S, 276V or 276AE of these Rules at the same time as the applicant; or

(dd) have died; or

(ii) the parent under paragraph 42(a) has sole responsibility for the applicant's upbringing; or

(iii) there are serious and compelling family or other considerations which make the applicant's exclusion from the United Kingdom undesirable and suitable arrangements have been made for their care.

Leave to enter

43. Entry clearance and leave to enter as the child of a member of HM Forces will be granted to an applicant who:

(a) was either:

(i) under 18 years of age at the date of application; or

(ii) aged 18 or over at the date of application; and was last granted leave to enter or remain under paragraph 43 or 47 of this Appendix or paragraph 276AH of these Rules;

(b) is outside the United Kingdom;

(c) is not married or in a civil partnership;

(d) has not formed an independent family unit;

(e) is not leading an independent life;

(f) has made a valid application for entry clearance and leave to enter as the child of a member of HM Forces;

(g) does not fall to be refused on the grounds of suitability under paragraph 8 or 9;

(h) meets the general eligibility requirements in paragraph 42;

(i) either:

(i) meets the financial requirement in Part 12 of this Appendix; or

(ii) in a case in which sub-paragraph (b)(i)(aa), (b)(i)(dd) or (b)(ii) of paragraph 42 applies will be:

(aa) accommodated adequately by the parent or parents the applicant will be joining without recourse to public funds in accommodation which the parent or parents own or occupy exclusively; and

(bb) maintained adequately by the parent or those parents without recourse to public funds; and

(j) has not applied and does not qualify for indefinite leave to enter under paragraph 45.

44. Entry clearance and leave to enter granted under paragraph 43 will be granted:

(a) for whichever is the shortest period of:

(i) 5 years; or

(ii) the remaining duration of the applicant's parent's enlistment; or

(iii) the remaining duration of the applicant's parent's leave; and

(b) subject to a condition of no recourse to public funds.

Indefinite leave to enter

45. Entry clearance and indefinite leave to enter as the child of a member of HM Forces will be granted to an applicant who:

(a) was either:

(i) under 18 years of age at the date of application; or

(ii) aged 18 or over at the date of application and was last granted leave to enter or remain under paragraph 43 or 47 of this Appendix or paragraph 276AH of these Rules;

(b) is outside the United Kingdom;

(c) is not married or in a civil partnership;

(d) has not formed an independent family unit;

(e) is not leading an independent life;

(f) has made a valid application for entry clearance and indefinite leave to enter as the child of a member of HM Forces;

(g) is the child of:

(i) a foreign or Commonwealth citizen who is a serving member of HM Forces who has completed at least 5 years' reckonable service; or

(ii) a person who has been granted indefinite leave to enter or remain under paragraph 13 or 16 of this Appendix or paragraphs 276E–Q of these Rules and is in the UK; or

(iii) a member of HM Forces who is a British Citizen;

(h) meets one of the following criteria:

(i) the applicant's other parent must:

(aa) come within paragraph 45(g); or

(bb) have been granted indefinite leave to enter or remain under paragraph 25 or 31 of this Appendix or paragraph 276S or 276V of these Rules; or

(cc) be being granted indefinite leave to enter or remain under paragraph 25 or 31 of this Appendix or paragraph 276S or 276V of these Rules at the same time as the applicant; or

(dd) have died; or

(ii) the parent under paragraph 45(g) has sole responsibility for the applicant's upbringing; or

(iii) there are serious and compelling family or other considerations which make the applicant's exclusion from the United Kingdom undesirable and suitable arrangements have been made for their care;

(i) does not fall to be refused on the grounds of suitability under paragraph 8 or 9;

(j) meets the general eligibility requirements in paragraph 42;

(k) where the applicant is aged 18 or over, can demonstrate sufficient knowledge of the English language and about life in the United Kingdom, in accordance with the requirements of Appendix KoLL to these Rules;

(l) will be accommodated adequately by the parent or parents the applicant is seeking to join without recourse to public funds in accommodation which the parent or parents the applicant is seeking to join, own or occupy exclusively; and

(m) will be maintained adequately by the parent or parents the applicant is seeking to join, without recourse to public funds.

46. Entry clearance and limited leave to enter as a child of a member of HM Forces for a period of 30 months may be granted subject to a condition of no recourse to public funds where:

(a) an applicant fails to meet the requirements for indefinite leave to enter in paragraph 45 by reason solely of failing to meet the requirements of paragraph 45(k); or

(b) an applicant fails to meet the requirements of paragraph 45 by reason only of failing to meet the requirements of paragraph 45(g)(i) or (ii), provided that the applicant's sponsor has been granted leave to enter or remain under paragraph 15 or 19 of this Appendix.

Leave to remain

47. Limited leave to remain as the child of a member of HM Forces will be granted to an applicant who:

(a) was either:

(i) under 18 years of age at the date of application; or

(ii) aged 18 or over at the date of application and who was last granted leave under paragraph 43 or 47 of this Appendix or paragraph 276AH of these Rules;

(b) is not married or in a civil partnership;

(c) has not formed an independent family unit;

(d) is not leading an independent life;

(e) is not in breach of immigration laws, except that, where paragraph 39E of these Rules applies, any current period of overstaying will be disregarded;

(f) is in the United Kingdom;

(g) has made a valid application for leave to remain as the child of a member of HM Forces;

(h) does not fall to be refused on the grounds of suitability under paragraph 8 or 9;

(i) meets:

(i) the general eligibility requirements in paragraph 42; or

(ii) those general eligibility requirements, except that subparagraph (b)(ii) does not apply but the parent of the applicant falls under paragraph 49(h) and the applicant normally lives with this parent and not their other parent; and

(j) either:

(i) meets the financial requirement in Part 12 of this Appendix; or

(ii) in a case in which sub-paragraph (b)(i)(aa), (b)(i)(dd) or (b)(ii) of paragraph 42 applies (and including the application of sub-paragraph (b)(i) as modified by paragraph (i) above) will be:

(aa) accommodated adequately by the parent or parents the applicant will be joining without recourse to public funds in accommodation which the parent or parents own or occupy exclusively; and (bb) maintained adequately by the parent or those parents without recourse to public funds; and

48. Leave to remain granted under paragraph 47 will be:

(a) for whichever is the shortest period of:

(i) 5 years; or

(ii) the remaining duration of the applicant's parent's enlistment; or

(iii) the remaining duration of the applicant's parent's leave; and

(b) subject to a condition of no recourse to public funds.

Indefinite leave to remain

49. Indefinite leave to remain as the child of a member of HM Forces will be granted to an applicant who has or has had leave to enter or remain under paragraph 43 or 47 of this Appendix or paragraph 276AH of these Rules and who:

(a) was either:

(i) under 18 years of age at the date of application; or

(ii) aged 18 or over at the date of application and who was last granted leave under paragraph 43 or 47 of this Appendix or paragraph 276AH of these Rules;

(b) is not married or in a civil partnership;

(c) has not formed an independent family unit;

(d) is not leading an independent life;

(e) is in the United Kingdom;

(f) has made a valid application for indefinite leave to remain as the child of a member of HM Forces;

(g) is not in breach of immigration laws, except that, where paragraph 39E of these Rules applies, any current period of overstaying will be disregarded;

(h) is the child of:

(i) a foreign or Commonwealth citizen who is a serving member of HM Forces who has completed at least 5 years' reckonable service; or

(ii) a person who has been granted, or is being granted at the same time as the applicant, indefinite leave to enter or remain under paragraph 13 or 16 of this Appendix or paragraphs 276E–Q of these Rules; or

(iii) a member of HM Forces who is a British Citizen;

(i) meets one of the following criteria:

(i) the applicant's other parent must:

(aa) also come within paragraph 49(h); or

(bb) have been granted indefinite leave to enter or remain under paragraph 25 or 31 of this Appendix or paragraph 276S or 276V of these Rules; or

(cc) be being granted indefinite leave to enter or remain under paragraph 25 or 31 of this Appendix or paragraph 276S or 276V of these Rules at the same time as the applicant; or

(dd) have died; or

(ii) the parent under paragraph 49(h) has sole responsibility for the applicant's upbringing or the applicant normally lives with this parent and not their other parent; or

(iii) there are serious and compelling family or other considerations which make the applicant's exclusion from the United Kingdom undesirable and suitable arrangements have been made for their care;

(j) does not fall to be refused on the grounds of suitability under paragraph 8 or 9;

(k) meets the general eligibility requirements in paragraph 42;

(l) where the applicant is aged 18 or over, can demonstrate sufficient knowledge of the English language and about life in the United Kingdom, in accordance with the requirements of Appendix KoLL to these Rules;

(m) will be accommodated adequately by the parent or parents the applicant is seeking to remain with without recourse to public funds in accommodation which the parent or parents the applicant is seeking to join own or occupy exclusively; and

(n) will be maintained adequately by the parent or parents the applicant is seeking to join, without recourse to public funds.

50. Limited leave to remain as a child of a member of HM Forces for a period of 30 months and subject to a condition of no recourse to public funds will be granted:

(a) where an applicant fails to meet the requirements for indefinite leave to remain in paragraph 49 by reason only of failing to satisfy the suitability requirements in paragraph 8 or 9 in respect of a grant of indefinite leave to remain (but not a grant of limited leave to remain); or

(b) where an applicant fails to meet the requirements for indefinite leave to remain by reason only of failing to meet the requirements in paragraph 49(l); or

(c) by reason only of failing to meet the requirements of paragraph 49(h)(i) or (ii), provided that the applicant's sponsor has been granted leave to enter or remain under paragraph 15 or 19 of this Appendix.

Part 8 Bereaved children of members of HM Forces

General eligibility requirements

51. The general eligibility requirements to be met by a bereaved child of a member of HM Forces are that:

(a) one of their parents has died and at the time of their death was:

(i) a foreign or Commonwealth citizen who was a serving member of HM Forces; or

(ii) a discharged member of HM Forces who had been granted, or was seeking at the same time as the applicant, leave to enter or remain under paragraphs 13–19 of this Appendix or paragraphs 276E–QA of these Rules; or

(iii) a British Citizen who was a member of HM Forces; and

(b) they meet one of the following criteria:

(i) their other parent must:

(aa) also come within sub-paragraph 51(a); or

(bb) have been granted, or be being granted at the same time as the applicant, leave to enter or remain under paragraphs 23–33 or 35–37 of this Appendix, under paragraph 276S, 276V or 276AE of these Rules or under any concession that existed outside these Rules whereby the Secretary of State exercised her discretion to grant leave to enter or remain to bereaved partners of foreign or Commonwealth members of HM Forces; or

(cc) have died; or

(ii) the parent referred to in sub-paragraph (a) had sole responsibility for their upbringing; or

(iii) there are serious and compelling family or other considerations which make exclusion of the applicant from the United Kingdom undesirable and suitable arrangements have been made for their care.

Indefinite leave to enter

52. Entry clearance and indefinite leave to enter as a bereaved child of a member of HM Forces will be granted to an applicant who:

(a) was either:

(i) under 18 years of age at the date of application; or

(ii) aged 18 or over at the date of application and was last granted leave to enter or remain under paragraph 43 or 47 of this Appendix or paragraph 276AH of these Rules;

(b) is outside the United Kingdom;

(c) is not married or in a civil partnership;

(d) has not formed an independent family unit;

(e) is not leading an independent life;

(f) has made a valid application for entry clearance and indefinite leave to enter as the bereaved child of a member of HM Forces;

(g) does not fall to be refused on the grounds of suitability under paragraph 8 or 9; and

(h) meets the general eligibility requirements in paragraph 51.

Indefinite leave to remain

53. Indefinite leave to remain as a bereaved child of a member of HM Forces will be granted to an applicant who:

(a) is in the United Kingdom;

(b) was either:

(i) under 18 years of age at the date of application; or

(ii) aged 18 or over at the date of application and was last granted leave to enter or remain under paragraph 43 or 47 of this Appendix or paragraph 276AH of these Rules; and

(c) is not married or in a civil partnership;

(d) has not formed an independent family unit;

(e) is not leading an independent life;

(f) has made a valid application for indefinite leave to remain as the bereaved child of a member of HM Forces;

(g) does not fall to be refused on the grounds of suitability under paragraph 8 or 9; and

(h) meets the general eligibility requirements in paragraph 51.

54. Limited leave to remain as a bereaved child of a member of HM Forces for a period of 30 months will be granted subject to a condition of no recourse to public funds to an applicant who fails to meet the requirements for indefinite leave to remain in paragraph 53 by reason solely of failing to meet the suitability requirements in paragraph 8 or 9 in respect of a grant of indefinite leave (but not a grant of limited leave to remain).

Part 9 Members of Armed Forces who are not exempt from immigration control

General eligibility requirements

55. The general eligibility requirements for members of armed forces who are not exempt from immigration control are that they:

(a) are a member of a foreign armed force;

(b) have been invited by:

(i) HM Forces to undergo training in the United Kingdom which HM Forces will provide; or

(ii) the Ministry of Defence to study, or become familiarised with military equipment being supplied by a firm in the United Kingdom;

(c) will leave the United Kingdom after the period of training, study or familiarisation;

(d) can provide evidence that they are able to maintain themselves and any dependants adequately in the United Kingdom without recourse to public funds;

(e) can provide evidence that there will be adequate accommodation, without recourse to public funds, for themselves and any dependants in the United Kingdom, including any other dependants who are not included in the application but who will live in the same household in the United Kingdom, which the applicant and their dependants own or occupy exclusively: accommodation will not be regarded as adequate if:

(i) it is, or will be, overcrowded; or

(ii) it contravenes public health regulations.

Leave to enter

56. Entry clearance (where required under paragraph 6(a)) or leave to enter as a member of an armed force not exempt from immigration control will be granted to an applicant who:

(a) is outside the United Kingdom;

(b) has made a valid application for entry clearance or leave to enter as a member of an armed force not exempt from immigration control;

(c) does not fall to be refused on the grounds of suitability under paragraph 8 or 9; and

(d) meets the general eligibility requirements in paragraph 55.

57. Entry clearance or leave to enter granted under paragraph 56 will be granted:

(a) for whichever is the shorter period of:

(i) 4 years; and

(ii) the duration of the training, study or familiarisation; and

(b) subject to the following conditions:

(i) no recourse to public funds; and

(ii) a prohibition on employment other than that for the purposes for which the applicant was granted leave to enter.

58. Entry clearance or leave to enter granted under paragraph 56 may be granted subject to the conditions in paragraph 57(b) for an additional period of 3 months beyond the end of the training, study or familiarisation where:

(a) such leave is required in order to enable the applicant to meet third country transit regulations which require passengers to have 3 months' extant leave in the United Kingdom;

(b) travel to the third country forms part of the training, study or familiarisation; and

(c) the total period of leave granted does not exceed 4 years.

Leave to remain

59. Limited leave to remain as a member of an armed force not exempt from immigration control will be granted to an applicant who:

(a) is in the United Kingdom;

(b) was last granted leave to enter or remain under paragraph 56 or 59 of this Appendix or under the concession which existed outside these Rules whereby the Secretary of State exercised her discretion to grant leave to enter or remain to members of armed forces who are not exempt from immigration control;

(c) is not in breach of immigration laws, except that, where paragraph 39E of these Rules applies, any current period of overstaying will be disregarded;

(d) has made a valid application for leave to remain as a member of an armed force not exempt from immigration control;

(e) does not fall to be refused on the grounds of suitability under paragraph 8 or 9; and

(f) meets the general eligibility requirements in paragraph 55.

60. Limited leave to remain granted under paragraph 59 will be granted:

(a) for whichever is the shorter period of:

(i) 4 years; or

(ii) the duration of the training, study or familiarisation; and provided the total period of leave granted (including any leave granted under paragraph 57 or 59) does not exceed 4 years; and

(b) subject to the following conditions:

(i) no recourse to public funds; and

(ii) a prohibition on employment other than that for the purposes for which the applicant was granted leave to remain.

61. Limited leave to remain granted under paragraph 59 may be granted subject to the conditions in paragraph 60(b) for an additional 3 months beyond the end of the training, study or familiarisation where:

(a) such leave is required in order to enable the applicant to meet third country transit regulations which require passengers to have 3 months' extant leave in the United Kingdom;

(b) travel to the third country forms part of the training, study or familiarisation; and

(c) the total period of leave granted (including any leave granted under paragraph 57 or 59 or the concession which existed outside these Rules) whereby the Secretary of State exercised her discretion to grant leave to enter or remain to members of armed forces who are not exempt from immigration control does not exceed 4 years.

Part 9A Relevant Civilian Employees

General Eligibility Requirements

61A. The general eligibility requirements for Relevant Civilian Employees are that the applicant:

(a) is a Relevant Civilian Employee;

(b) will leave the United Kingdom at the end of their period of employment;

(c) can provide evidence that they are able to maintain themselves and any dependants adequately in the United Kingdom without recourse to public funds; and

(d) can provide evidence that there will be adequate accommodation, without recourse to public funds, for themselves and any dependants in the United Kingdom, including any other dependants who are not included in the application but who will live in the same household in the United Kingdom, which the applicant and their dependants own or occupy exclusively: accommodation will not be regarded as adequate if:

(i) it is, or will be, overcrowded; or

(ii) it contravenes public health regulations.

Leave to enter

61B. Entry clearance (where required under paragraph 6(a)) or leave to enter as a Relevant Civilian Employee will be granted to an applicant who:

(a) is outside the United Kingdom;

(b) has made a valid application for entry clearance or leave to enter as a Relevant Civilian Employee;

(c) does not fall to be refused on the grounds of suitability under paragraph 8 or 9; and

(d) meets the general eligibility requirements in paragraph 61A.

61C. Entry clearance or leave to enter granted under paragraph 61B will be granted:

(a) for

(i) in respect of an application from a civilian employee of a NATO force or the Australian Department of Defence:

(aa) 6 months, where the duration of their period of employment in the United Kingdom does not exceed 6 months; or

(bb) five years, where the duration of their period of employment in the United Kingdom exceeds 6 months; or

(ii) in respect of a civilian employee of a company under contract to a NATO force, the duration of their period of employment in the United Kingdom or, if the shorter period, 4 years; and

(b) subject to the following conditions:

(i) no recourse to public funds; and

(ii) a prohibition on employment other than for the purposes for which the applicant was last granted leave to enter.

Leave to remain

61D. Leave to remain as a Relevant Civilian Employee will be granted to an applicant who:

(a) is in the United Kingdom;

(b) was last:

(i) granted leave to enter or remain under paragraph 61C or 61E of this Appendix or under the concessions which existed outside these Rules whereby the Secretary of State exercised her discretion to grant leave to enter or remain to Relevant Civilian Employees; or

(ii) exempt from control under section 8(4)(b) of the Immigration Act 1971 and has been offered employment as a Relevant Civilian Employee;

(c) is not in breach of any immigration laws, except that, where paragraph 39E of these Rules applies, any current period of overstaying will be disregarded

(d) has made a valid application for leave to remain as a Relevant Civilian Employee;

(e) does not fall to be refused on the grounds of suitability under paragraph 8 or 9; and

(f) meets the general eligibility requirements set out in paragraph 61A.

61E. Leave to remain granted under paragraph 61D will be granted:

(a) for:

(i) in respect of an application from a civilian employee of a NATO force or the Australian Department of Defence, five years; or

(ii) in respect of an application from a civilian employee of a company under contract to NATO, the duration of their period of employment in the United Kingdom, or, if the shorter period, four years; and

(b) subject to the following conditions:

(i) no recourse to public funds; and

(ii) a prohibition on employment other than for the purposes for which the applicant was last granted leave to enter or remain.

Part 10 Dependants of non-HM Forces and of Relevant Civilian Employees

General eligibility requirements

62. The general eligibility requirements to be met by dependants of a member of non-HM Forces or of a Relevant Civilian Employee are that:

(a) the applicant is sponsored by:

(i) a serving armed forces member who is exempt from immigration control under section 8(4)(b) or (c) of the Immigration Act 1971; or

(ii) a serving armed forces member who: (aa) has leave to enter or remain under paragraph 56 or 59 of this Appendix or under any concession that existed outside these Rules whereby the Secretary of State exercised her discretion to grant leave to enter or remain to members of armed forces who are not exempt from immigration control; or (bb) is being granted leave to enter or remain under paragraph 56 or 59 of this Appendix at the same time as the applicant; or

(iii) a Relevant Civilian Employee who: (aa) has been granted leave to enter or remain under paragraph 61B or 61D or under the concession which existed outside these Rules whereby the Secretary of State exercised her discretion to grant leave to enter or remain to a Relevant Civilian Employee; or (bb) is being granted leave to enter or remain under paragraph 61B or 61D at the same time as the applicant;

(b) the applicant's sponsor is:

(i) the applicant's partner (except a fiancé(e) or proposed civil partner) where: (aa) both parties are aged 18 or over; (bb) both parties intend to live with the other during their stay in the United Kingdom; and (cc) the relationship is genuine and subsisting; or

(ii) the applicant's parent and the applicant:

(aa) is under 18 years of age at the date of application;

(bb) is not married or in a civil partnership;

(cc) has not formed an independent family unit; and

(dd) is not living an independent life; or

(iii) a serving armed forces member who is exempt from immigration control under section 8(4)(b) or (c) of the Immigration Act 1971 or a civilian employed to work in the UK by a NATO force or the Australian Department of Defence and the applicant:

(aa) is a dependant other than a partner within the meaning of section 12(4)(b) of the Visiting Forces Act 1952 or Article I(c) of the NATO Status of Forces Agreement; and

(bb) is listed as a dependant of the sponsor on the sponsor's military movement orders or equivalent civilian posting letter;

(c) the applicant must provide evidence that their sponsor is able to maintain and accommodate themselves, the applicant and any dependants adequately in the United Kingdom without recourse to public funds;

(d) the applicant must provide evidence that there will be adequate accommodation, without recourse to public funds, for the applicant, the applicant's sponsor and any other family members of the applicant, including other family members who are not included in the application but who will live in the same household, which the applicant, the applicant's sponsor and the other family members own or occupy exclusively: accommodation will not be regarded as adequate if—

(i) it is, or will be, overcrowded; or

(ii) it contravenes public health regulations; and

(e) the applicant intends to leave the United Kingdom at the end of their sponsor's period of posting, employment, training, study or familiarisation in the United Kingdom.

63. Where the sponsor is the applicant's parent, the applicant must meet one of the following criteria:

(a) their other parent must:

(i) also meet the criteria set out in paragraph 62(a)(i), (ii) or (iii); or

(ii) either: (aa) have been granted leave to enter or remain as a partner in relation to that member of non-HM Forces or Relevant Civilian Employee under paragraph 64 or 66 of this Appendix or paragraph 276AE of these Rules or under any concession that existed outside these Rules whereby the Secretary of State exercised her discretion to grant leave to enter or remain to partners of non-exempt members of armed forces or Relevant Civilian Employees; or (bb) be being granted leave to enter or remain under paragraph 64 or 66 at the same time as the applicant; or

(iii) have died; or

(iv) be exempt from immigration control; or

(b) the parent they are joining in paragraph 62(a) has sole responsibility for their upbringing; or

(c) there are serious and compelling family or other considerations which make the applicant's exclusion from the United Kingdom undesirable and suitable arrangements have been made for their care.

Leave to enter

64. Entry clearance (where required under paragraph 6(a)) or leave to enter as the dependant of a member of non-HM Forces or of a Relevant Civilian Employee will be granted to an applicant who:

(a) is outside the United Kingdom;

(b) has made a valid application for entry clearance or leave to enter as the dependant of a member of non-HM Forces or of a Relevant Civilian Employee;

(c) does not fall to be refused on the grounds of suitability under paragraph 8 or 9; and

(d) meets the general eligibility requirements in paragraph 62 and where relevant one of the criteria in paragraph 63.

65. Entry clearance or leave to enter granted under paragraph 64 will be granted:

(a) for

(i) in respect of an application from the dependant of an armed forces member who is not exempt from immigration control or of a civilian employee of a company under contract to a NATO force, the duration of the sponsor's period of posting, employment, training, study or familiarisation in the United Kingdom or, if the shorter period, 4 years; or

(ii) in respect of an application from the dependant of an armed forces member who is exempt from immigration control under section 8(4)(b) or (c) of the Immigration Act 1971 or of a civilian employee of a NATO force or the Australian Department of Defence:

(aa) 6 months, where the duration of the sponsor's period of posting, employment, training, study or familiarisation in the United Kingdom does not exceed 6 months; or (bb) a maximum of 5 years, where the duration of the sponsor's period of posting, employment, training, study or familiarisation in the United Kingdom exceeds 6 months; and

(iii) the duration of the sponsor's period of posting, employment, training, study or familiarisation in the United Kingdom; and

(b) subject to the following conditions:

(i) no recourse to public funds; and

(ii) in respect of applications from dependants of Relevant Civilian Employees or of armed forces members who are not exempt from immigration control and are being granted leave to enter for less than 6 months, a prohibition on employment.

Leave to remain

66. Leave to remain as the dependant of a member of non-HM Forces or of Relevant Civilian Employees will be granted to an applicant who:

(a) is in the United Kingdom;

(b) in relation to an application to which sub-paragraph 62(a)(ii) applies, was last granted leave to enter or remain under paragraph 64 or 66 of this Appendix or under the concession which existed outside these Rules whereby the Secretary of State exercised her discretion to grant leave to enter or remain to the dependant of a member of the armed forces who is not exempt from immigration control;

(c) is not in breach of immigration laws, except that, where paragraph 39E of these Rules applies, any current period of overstaying will be disregarded;

(d) has made a valid application for leave to remain as the dependant of a member of non-HM Forces or of a Relevant Civilian Employee;

(e) does not fall to be refused on the grounds of suitability under paragraph 8 or 9; and

(f) meets the general eligibility criteria in paragraph 62 and, where the sponsor is the applicant's parent, one of the criteria in paragraph 63, except that the applicant does not need to be under 18 years of age at the date of application where:

(i) paragraph 66(b) applies; or

(ii) sub-paragraph 62(a)(iii) applies and the applicant was last granted leave to enter or remain under paragraph 64 or 66 of this Appendix or under the concession which existed outside these Rules whereby the Secretary of State exercised her discretion to grant leave to enter or remain to the dependant of an employee of a company under contract to a NATO force; or

(iii) paragraph 62(b)(iii) applies.

67. Leave to remain granted under paragraph 66 will be granted:

(a) (i) in respect of an application from the dependant of an armed forces member who is not exempt from immigration control or of a civilian employee of a company under contract to a NATO force, the duration of the sponsor's period of posting, employment, training, study or familiarisation in the United Kingdom, or, if the shorter period, 4 years; or

(ii) in respect of an application from the dependant of an armed forces member who is exempt from immigration control under section 8(4)(b) or (c) of the Immigration Act 1971 or of a civilian employee of a NATO force or the Australian Department of Defence, a maximum of 5 years; and

(b) subject to the following conditions:

(i) no recourse to public funds; and

(ii) in respect of applications from dependants of Relevant Civilian Employees or of armed forces members who are not exempt from immigration control and are being granted leave to remain for less than 6 months, a prohibition on employment.

Part 11 English language requirements

Meeting the English language requirement in applications for leave to enter or remain

68. Where an English language requirement applies to an application for leave to enter or remain made by a partner under this Appendix, and if the applicant has not met the requirement in a previous application for leave as a partner, the applicant must provide specified evidence set out in Appendix FM-SE and Appendix O that they:

(a) are a national of a majority English speaking country listed in paragraph 70 of this Part;

[(b) have passed and English language test in speaking and listening at a minimum level of A1 of the Common European Framework of Reference for Languages with a provider approved by the Secretary of State for these purposes and at an approved Secure English Language Test centre. Details of the approved tests and Secure English Language Test centres are published on the UK Visas and Immigration pages of Gov.uk:

Where two or more components (reading, writing, speaking and listening) of an English language test are examined and awarded together, for example a combined exam and certificate for reading and writing skills, the specified evidence submitted by the applicant must show that he achieved the required scores in all the relevant components during a single sitting of that examination, unless exempted from sitting a component on the basis of his disability;]

(c) have an academic qualification recognised by [[Ecctis]] to be equivalent to the standard of a Bachelor's or Master's degree or PhD in the UK, which was taught in English; or

(d) are exempt from the English language requirement under paragraph 69 of this Part.

Note: Sub-paragraph (b) substituted from 1 October 2019 subject to savings for applications made before that date (HC 2631). Words in double square brackets substituted from 6 October 2021 subject to savings for applications made before that date (HC 617).

Exemptions from the English language requirement

69. The applicant is exempt from the English language requirement if at the date of application:

(a) the applicant is aged 65 or over;

(b) the applicant has a disability (physical or mental condition) which prevents the applicant from meeting the requirement; or

(c) there are exceptional circumstances which prevent the applicant from being able to meet the requirement, which for an application for entry clearance is prior to entry to the UK.

Majority English speaking countries

70. For the purposes of paragraph 68(a) of this Part the applicant must be a national of:

Antigua and Barbuda, Australia, the Bahamas, Barbados, Belize, Canada, Dominica, Grenada, Guyana, Jamaica, New Zealand, St Kitts and Nevis, St Lucia, St Vincent and the Grenadines, Trinidad and Tobago, or the United States of America.

70A. For the avoidance of doubt paragraphs 27–32D of Appendix FM-SE apply to applications for entry clearance and limited leave to enter or remain made under Part 4 of this Appendix where English language requirements apply, regardless of the date of application.

Part 12 Financial requirements

This Part applies where the financial requirements in Part 12 must be met in an application for leave to enter or remain or for indefinite leave to enter or remain made under this Appendix by a partner or child of a member of HM Forces. Paragraphs A to 21 of Appendix FM-SE to these Rules apply to applications to which this Part applies. References in this Part to the applicant's parent or the applicant's parent's partner relate only to applications made by a child under this Appendix. References in this Part to a partner or to the applicant's partner do not refer to the partner of a child making an application under this Appendix.

Financial requirements for applications for leave to enter

71. The applicant must provide specified evidence, from the sources listed in paragraph 73, of:

(a) a specified gross annual income of at least:

(i) £18,600;

(ii) an additional £3,800 for the first child; and

(iii) an additional £2,400 for each additional child; alone or in combination with

(b) specified savings of:

(i) £16,000; and

(ii) additional savings of an amount equivalent to the difference—multiplied by the length in years of the period of limited leave for which the applicant has applied (or by the part-year equivalent if the applicant has applied for less than 12 months' limited leave)—between the gross annual income from the sources listed in paragraph 73(a)–(f) and the total amount required under paragraph 71(a); or

(c) the requirements in paragraph 74 are met.

72. In paragraph 71 'child' means a dependent child of the applicant or of the applicant's parent who is:

(a) under the age of 18 years, or who was under the age of 18 years when they were first granted entry under this route;

(b) applying for entry clearance or has limited leave to enter or remain in the United Kingdom under this Appendix;

(c) not a British Citizen or settled in the United Kingdom; and

(d) not an EEA national with a right to be admitted under the Immigration (EEA) Regulations 2006.

73. When determining whether the financial requirements in paragraph 71 are met only the following sources will be taken into account:

(a) income of the applicant's partner or the applicant's parent's partner from specified employment or self-employment, which, in respect of a partner (or applicant's parent's partner) returning to the United Kingdom with the applicant, can include specified employment or self-employment overseas and in the United Kingdom;

(b) income of the applicant's parent from specified employment or self-employment if they are in the United Kingdom unless they are working illegally;

(c) specified pension income of the applicant and their partner or of the applicant's parent and that parent's partner;

(d) any specified maternity allowance or bereavement benefit in the UK, or any specified benefit relating to service in HM Forces, received by the applicant and their partner or by the applicant's parent and that parent's partner;

(e) other specified income of the applicant and their partner or of the applicant's parent and that parent's partner; and

(f) income from the sources at sub-paragraphs (b), (d) and (e) of a dependent child of the applicant or the applicant's parent under paragraph 72 who is aged 18 or over; and

(g) specified savings of the applicant and their partner; or of the applicant's parent and that parent's partner; or of a dependent child of the applicant or the applicant's parent under paragraph 72 who is aged 18 or over.

74. The requirements to be met under this paragraph are:

(a) the applicant's partner or the applicant's parent's partner must be receiving one or more of the following:

(i) Disability Living Allowance;

(ii) Severe Disablement Allowance;

(iii) Industrial Injury Disablement Benefit;

(iv) Attendance Allowance;

(v) Carer's Allowance;

(vi) Personal Independence Payment;

(vii) Armed Forces Independence Payment or Guaranteed Income Payment under the Armed Forces Compensation Scheme; or

(viii) Constant Attendance Allowance, Mobility Supplement or War Disablement Pension under the War Pensions Scheme; and

(b) the applicant must provide evidence that their partner (or their parent's partner) is able to maintain and accommodate themselves, the applicant (and their parent) and any dependants adequately in the UK without recourse to public funds.

75. The applicant must provide evidence that there will be adequate accommodation, without recourse to public funds, for the family, including other family members who are not included in the application but who live in the same household, which the family own or occupy exclusively: accommodation will not be regarded as adequate if:

(a) it is, or will be, overcrowded; or

(b) it contravenes public health regulations.

Financial requirements for applications for leave to remain

76. The applicant must provide specified evidence, from the sources listed in paragraph 78, of:

(a) a specified gross annual income of at least:

(i) £18,600;

(ii) an additional £3,800 for the first child; and

(iii) an additional £2,400 for each additional child; alone or in combination with

(b) specified savings of:

(i) £16,000; and

(ii) additional savings of an amount equivalent to the difference—multiplied by the length in years of any period of limited leave for which the applicant has applied (or by the part-year equivalent if the applicant has applied for less than 12 months' limited leave)—between the gross annual income from the sources listed in paragraph 78(a)–(f) and the total amount required under paragraph 76(a); or

(c) the requirements in paragraph 79 are met.

77. In paragraph 76, 'child' means a dependent child of the applicant or of the applicant's parent who is:

(a) under the age of 18 years, or who was under the age of 18 years when they were first granted entry under this route;

(b) applying for entry clearance or is in the United Kingdom;

(c) not a British Citizen or settled in the United Kingdom; and

(d) not an EEA national with a right to remain in the United Kingdom under the Immigration (EEA) Regulations 2006.

78. When determining whether the financial requirements in paragraph 76 are met only the following sources may be taken into account:

(a) income of the applicant's partner or of the applicant's parent's partner from specified employment or self-employment;

(b) income of the applicant (where aged 18 or over) or of the applicant's parent from specified employment or self-employment unless they are working illegally;

(c) specified pension income of the applicant and their partner or of the applicant's parent and that parent's partner;

(d) any specified maternity allowance or bereavement benefit in the UK, or any specified benefit relating to service in HM Forces, received by the applicant or their partner or by the applicant's parent and that parent's partner;

(e) other specified income of the applicant and their partner or of the applicant's parent and that parent's partner;

(f) income from the sources at sub-paragraphs (b), (d) or (e) of a dependent child of the applicant or their parent under paragraph 77 who is aged 18 years or over; and

(g) specified savings of the applicant and their partner; of the applicant's parent and that parent's partner; or of a dependent child of the applicant or the applicant's parent under paragraph 77 who is aged 18 or over.

79. The requirements to be met under this paragraph are:

(a) the applicant's partner or the applicant's parent's partner must be receiving one or more of the following:

(i) Disability Living Allowance;

(ii) Severe Disablement Allowance;

(iii) Industrial Injury Disablement Benefit;

(iv) Attendance Allowance;

(v) Carer's Allowance;

(vi) Personal Independence Payment;

(vii) Armed Forces Independence Payment or Guaranteed Income Payment under the Armed Forces Compensation Scheme; or

(viii) Constant Attendance Allowance, Mobility Supplement or War Disablement Pension under the War Pensions Scheme; and

(b) the applicant must provide evidence that their partner (or their parent's partner) is able to maintain and accommodate themselves, the applicant (and their parent) and any dependants adequately in the UK without recourse to public funds.

80. The applicant must provide evidence that there will be adequate accommodation, without recourse to public funds, for the family, including other family members who are not included in the application but who live in the same household, which the family own or occupy exclusively: accommodation will not be regarded as adequate if:

(a) it is, or will be, overcrowded; or
(b) it contravenes public health regulations.

Financial requirements for applications for indefinite leave to enter or remain

81. The applicant must meet all of the requirements of paragraphs 71 to 75 (for indefinite leave to enter) or paragraphs 76 to 80 (for indefinite leave to remain), except that instead of the requirement in paragraph 71(b) or 76(b) the applicant must provide specified evidence from the sources listed in paragraph 73 or 78, (as the case may be) of specified savings of:

(i) £16,000; and
(ii) additional savings of an amount equivalent to the difference between the gross annual income from the sources listed in paragraph 73(a)–(f) or 78(a)–(f) and the total amount required under paragraph 71(a) or 76(a).

Appendix B
English Language

Appendix B—English language

1. An applicant applying as a Tier 1 Migrant { ... } must have 10 points for English language, unless applying for entry clearance or leave to remain:

(i) as a Tier 1 (Exceptional Talent) Migrant,
(ii) as a Tier 1 (Investor) Migrant, [...]
[...]
[...]

Note: Word in (ii) deleted; amendments to (iii), (iv) inserted from 1 October 2019 subject to savings for applications made before that date (HC 2631). Words in curly brackets, (iii) and (iv) deleted from 09:00 on 1 December 2020 subject to savings for applications made before that time (HC 813).

2. The levels of English language required are shown in Table 1.

3. Available points for English language are shown in Table 2.

4. Notes to accompany the tables are shown below each table.

Table 1 Level of English language required to score points

Tier 1			
Row	**Category**	**Applications**	**Level of English language Required**
B	Tier 1 (Entrepreneur)	Entry clearance and leave to remain	A knowledge of English equivalent to level B1 or above of the Council of Europe's Common European Framework for Language Learning
[...]	[...]	[...]	[...]

Note: Row C deleted from 6 July 2019 subject to savings for applications made before that date (HC 1919).

[...]

Note: Tier 2 heading and table deleted from 09:00 on 1 December 2020 subject to savings for applications made before that time (HC 813)

5. [DELETED]

Note: Paragraph deleted from 09:00 on 1 December 2020 subject to savings for applications made before that time (HC 813)

Table 2 Points available for English language

Factor	Points
National of a majority English speaking country	10
Degree taught in English	10
Passed an English language test	10
Met requirement in a previous grant of leave	10
Transitional arrangements	10

Notes

National of a majority English speaking country

6. 10 points will only be awarded for being a national of a majority English speaking country if the applicant has the relevant level of English language shown in Table 1 and:

(i) is a national of one of the following countries:

Antigua and Barbuda
Australia
The Bahamas
Barbados
Belize
Canada
Dominica
Grenada
Guyana
Jamaica
[Malta]
New Zealand
St Kitts and Nevis
St Lucia
St Vincent and the Grenadines
Trinidad and Tobago
USA
and

(ii) provides his valid passport or travel document to show that this requirement is met. If the applicant is unable to do so, the UK Border Agency may exceptionally consider this requirement to have been met where the applicant provides full reasons in the passport section of the application form, and either:

(1) a current national identity document, or

(2) [a] letter from his home government or embassy, on the letter-headed paper of the government or embassy, which has been issued by an authorised official of that institution and confirms the applicant's full name, date of birth and nationality.

Note: Word in (ii)(2) substituted from 5 November 2018 (HC 1534). Word in (i) inserted from 09:00 on 1 December 2020 subject to savings for applications made before that time (HC 813).

Degree taught in English

7. 10 points will be awarded for a degree taught in English if the applicant has the relevant level of English language shown in Table 1 and:

(i) has obtained an academic qualification (not a professional or vocational qualification) which either:

(1) is a UK Bachelor's degree, Master's degree or PhD

(2) is a qualification awarded by an educational establishment outside the UK, which is deemed by [[Ecctis]] to meet the recognised standard of a Bachelor's or Master's degree or a PhD in the UK, and [[Ecctis]] has confirmed that the degree was taught or researched in English to the appropriate level of the Council of Europe's Common European Framework for Language learning or above or:

(3) is deemed by [[Ecctis]] to meet or exceed the recognised standard of a Bachelor's or Master's degree or a PhD in the UK, and is from an educational establishment in one of the following countries:

Antigua and Barbuda
Australia
The Bahamas
Barbados
Belize
Dominica
Grenada
Guyana
Ireland
Jamaica
[Malta]
New Zealand
St Kitts and Nevis
St Lucia
St Vincent and The Grenadines
Trinidad and Tobago
the USA,
and

(ii) provides the following specified documents to show he has the qualification:

(1) the [. . .] certificate of the award, or

(2) if the applicant is awaiting graduation having successfully completed the qualification, or no longer has the certificate and the awarding institution is unable to provide

a replacement, an academic transcript (or [...] letter in the case of a PhD qualification) from the awarding institution on its official headed paper, which clearly shows:

(a) the applicant's name,

(b) the name of the awarding institution,

(c) the title of the award,

(d) confirmation that the qualification has been or will be awarded, and

(e) the date that the certificate will be issued (if the applicant has not yet graduated) or confirmation that the institution is unable to reissue the [...] certificate or award, and

(iii) provides [...] documentation produced by [[Ecctis]] which confirms the assessment in (i)(2) or (3), if applicable.

Note: Words in (ii)(1), (ii)(2), (ii)(2)(e) and (iii) deleted from 5 November 2018 (HC 1534). Word in (i)(3) inserted from 09:00 on 1 December 2020 subject to savings for applications made before that time (HC 813). Words in double square brackets substituted from 6 October 2021 subject to savings for applications made before that date (HC 617).

8. [DELETED]

Note: Amendments from 5 November 2018 (HC 1534). Paragraph deleted from 09:00 on 1 December 2020 subject to savings for applications made before that time (HC 813).

9. [DELETED]

Note: Paragraph deleted from 6 July 2019 subject to savings for applications made before that date (HC 1919).

Passed an English language test

[10. Ten points will only be awarded for passing an English language test if the applicant has passed a Secure English Language Test, at a Secure English Language Test centre, which has been approved by the Secretary of State and has provided their unique reference number for the test, which allows their score to be verified using the provider's online verification system. Details of the approved tests and Secure English Language Test centres are published on the UK Visas and Immigration pages of Gov.uk.

Where two or more components (reading, writing, speaking and listening) of an English language test are examined and awarded together, for example a combined exam and certificate for reading and writing skills, the specified evidence submitted by the applicant must show that they achieved the required scores in all the relevant components during a single sitting of that examination, unless exempted from sitting a component on the basis of their disability.]

Note: Paragraph substituted from 1 October 2019 subject to savings for applications made before that date (HC 2631).

10A. The qualification obtained must meet or exceed the relevant level shown in Table 1 in:

(i) speaking and listening, if the relevant level is A1 of the Council of Europe's Common European Framework for Language Learning, or

(ii) all four components (reading, writing, speaking and listening), in all other cases, unless the applicant was exempted from sitting a component on the basis of his disability.

Met requirement in a previous grant of leave

11. Subject to paragraph 15 below, 10 points will be awarded for meeting the requirement in a previous grant of leave if the applicant:

(i) has ever been granted leave as a Tier 1 (General) Migrant, a Tier 1 (Entrepreneur) Migrant or Business person, or a Tier 1 (Post-Study Work) Migrant, or

(ii) has ever been granted leave as a Highly Skilled Migrant under the Rules in place on or after 5 December 2006.

12. Subject to paragraph 15 below, […]10 points will be awarded for meeting the requirement in a previous grant of leave if the applicant has ever been granted leave:

(a) as a Minister of Religion (not as a Tier 2 (Minister of Religion) Migrant) under the Rules in place on or after 19 April 2007,

(b) as a Tier 2 (Minister of Religion) Migrant, provided that when he was granted that leave he obtained points for English language for being a national of a majority English speaking country, a degree taught in English, or passing an English language test, or

(c) as a [*Student*], and the Confirmation of Acceptance for Studies used to support that application was assigned on or after 21 April 2011 for a course of at least degree level study.

Note: Words in (c) substituted from 09:00 on 5 October 2020 subject to savings for applications made before that time. Where consequential changes relating to the need for an ATAS certificate have been made, they take effect for all applications made or granted on or after 5 October 2020 at 09:00 (HC 707). Words deleted from 09:00 on 1 December 2020 subject to savings for applications made before that time (HC 813).

13. Subject to paragraph 15 below, […]10 points will be awarded for meeting the requirement in a previous grant of leave if the applicant has ever been granted leave:

(a) as a Tier 1 (Graduate Entrepreneur) Migrant,

(b) as a Tier 2 (General) Migrant under the Rules in place on or after 6 April 2011, or

(c) as a [*Student*], and the Confirmation of Acceptance for Studies used to support that application was assigned on or after 21 April 2011, provided that when he was granted that leave he obtained points for having knowledge of English equivalent to level B1 of the Council of Europe's Common European Framework for Language Learning or above.

Note: Words in (c) substituted from 09:00 on 5 October 2020 subject to savings for applications made before that time. Where consequential changes relating to the need for an ATAS certificate have been made, they take effect for all applications made or granted on or after 5 October 2020 at 09:00 (HC 707). Words deleted from 09:00 on 1 December 2020 subject to savings for applications made before that time (HC 813).

14. [DELETED]

Note: Paragraph deleted from 09:00 on 1 December 2020 subject to savings for applications made before that time (HC 813).

Transitional arrangements

16. [DELETED]

Note: Paragraph deleted from 09:00 on 1 December 2020 subject to savings for applications made before that time (HC 813).

17. [DELETED]

Note: Paragraph deleted from 09:00 on 1 December 2020 subject to savings for applications made before that time (HC 813).

18. [DELETED]

Note: Paragraph deleted from 09:00 on 1 December 2020 subject to savings for applications made before that time (HC 813).

APPENDIX C

MAINTENANCE (FUNDS) [TIER 1 (ENTREPRENEUR)]

Note: Heading amended from 09:00 on 1 December 2020 subject to savings for applications made before that date (HC 813).

1A. In all cases where an applicant is required to obtain points under Appendix C, the applicant must meet the requirements listed below:

[(a) The funds specified in the relevant part of Appendix C must be available to the applicant on the date of the application (as defined in Part 1 of these Rules), [. . .];

(i) the applicant is a Tier 4 Migrant, and

(ii) the funds are being provided as a financial loan, and

(iii) the applicant provides evidence with the application that meets the requirements of paragraph 1B(d) of this Appendix;]

(b) If the applicant is applying as a [Tier 1 (Entrepreneur) Migrant], the applicant must have had the funds referred to in (a) above for a consecutive 90-day period of time[. . .];

[. . .]

[. . .]

(d) If the funds were obtained when the applicant was in the UK, the funds must have been obtained while the applicant had valid leave and was not acting in breach of any conditions attached to that leave;

(e) Where the funds are in one or more foreign currencies, the applicant must have the specified level of funds when converted to pound sterling (£) using the spot exchange rate which appears on www.oanda.com* for the date of the application;

(f) Where the applicant is applying as a [[Tier 1 (Entrepreneur) Migrant]], the funds must have been under [their] own control on the date of the application and for the period specified in (b) above; and

(g) Where the application is made at the same time as applications by the partner or child of the applicant (such that the applicant is a Relevant Points Based System Migrant for the purposes of paragraph 319AA), each applicant must have the total requisite funds specified in the relevant parts of appendices C and E. If each applicant does not individually meet the requirements of appendices C and/or E, as appropriate, all the applications (the application by the Relevant Points Based System Migrant and applications as the partner or child of that relevant Points Based system Migrant) will be refused.

(h) the end date of the [90-day period referred to in (b)] above will be taken as the date of the closing balance on the most recent of the specified documents (where specified documents from two or more accounts are submitted, this will be the end date for the account that most favours the applicant), and must be no earlier than 31 days before the date of application.

(i) [No points will be awarded unless the funds comply with Appendix Finance]

(j) Maintenance must be in the form of cash funds. Other accounts or financial instruments such as shares, bonds, credit cards, pension funds etc., regardless of notice period are not acceptable.

(k) If the applicant wishes to rely on a joint account as evidence of available funds, the applicant (or for children under 18 years of age, the applicant's parent or legal guardian who is legally present in the United Kingdom) must be named on the account as one of the account holders.

(l) Overdraft facilities will not be considered towards funds that are available or under an applicant's own control.

Note: Sub-paragraphs (a), (c) and (ca) substituted from 10 January 2019 subject to savings for applications made before that date (HC 1779). Word in (f) substituted from 6 April 2019 subject to savings for applications made before that date (HC 1919). Words in (a), sub-paragraphs (c) and (ca) deleted; words in (h) substituted from 09:00 on 5 October 2020 subject to savings for applications made before that date. Where consequential changes relating to the need to obtain an ATAS certificate have been made to the conditions of leave, these take effect for all applications made or granted on or after 09:00 on 5 October 2020 (HC 707). Words in (b) and (i), words in double square brackets in (f) substituted, words in (b) deleted from 09:00 on 1 December 2020 subject to savings for applications made before that date (HC 813).

1B. In all cases where Appendix C or Appendix E states that an applicant is required to provide specified documents, the specified documents are:

(a) [. . .]

(i) The statements must cover:

(1) [. . .]

(2) [. . .]

(3) [. . .]

(ii) The most recent statement must be dated no earlier than 31 days before the date of the application;

(iii) The statements must clearly show:

(1) the name of:

i. the applicant,

ii. the applicant's parent(s) or legal guardian's name,[. . .]

iii. the name of the {Tier 1 (Entrepreneur) Migrant}, if the applicant is applying as [a Partner of a {Tier 1 (Entrepreneur) Migrant}.]

iv. [. . .]

(2) the account number,

(3) the date of each statement,

(4) the financial institution's name,

(5) the financial institution's logo,

(6) any transactions during the specified period, and

(7) that the funds in the account have been at the required level throughout the specified period;

(iv) The statements must [. . .] be either:

(1) printed on the bank's or building society's letterhead,

(2) electronic bank or building society statements, accompanied by a supporting letter from the bank or building society, on company headed paper, confirming the statement provided is authentic, or

(3) electronic bank or building society statements, bearing the official stamp of the bank or building society on every page,

(v) The statements must not be mini-statements from automatic teller machines (ATMs); or

(b) A building society pass book which satisfies the following requirements:

[(i) The building society pass book must cover a consecutive 90-day period of time.]

(1) [. . .]

(2) [. . .]

(3) [. . .]

(ii) The period covered by the building society pass book must end no earlier than 31 days before the date of the application;

(iii) The building society pass book must clearly show:

(1) the name of:

i. the applicant,

ii. the applicant's parent(s) or legal guardian's name,[. . .]

iii. the name of the {Tier 1 Entrepreneur Migrant}, if the applicant is applying as a Partner of a {Tier 1 Entrepreneur Migrant}.]

iv. [. . .]

(2) the account number,

(3) the building society's name and logo,

(4) any transactions during the specified period, and

(5) that there have been enough funds in the applicant's account throughout the specified period; or

(c) A letter from the applicant's bank or building society, or a letter from a financial institution regulated for the purpose of personal savings accounts by the Financial Conduct Authority (FCA) and the Prudential Regulation Authority (PRA) or, for overseas accounts, the official regulatory body for the country in which the institution operates and the funds are located, which satisfies the following requirements:

[(i) The letter must confirm the level of funds and that they have been held for a consecutive 90-day period of time.]

(1) [. . .]

(2) [. . .]

(3) [. . .]

(ii) The period covered by the letter must end no earlier than 31 days before the date of the application;

(iii) The letter must be dated no earlier than 31 days before the date of the application;

(iv) The letter must be on the financial institution's letterhead or official stationery;

(v) The letter must clearly show:

(1) the name of:

i. the applicant,

ii. the applicant's parent(s) or legal guardian's name,[. . .]

iii. the name of the {Tier 1 Entrepreneur Migrant}, if the applicant is applying as [a Partner of a {Tier 1 Entrepreneur Migrant}.]

iv. [. . .]

(2) the account number,

(3) the date of the letter,

(4) the financial institution's name and logo,

(5) the funds held in the applicant's account, and

(6) confirmation that there have been enough funds in the applicant's account throughout the specified period; or

(d) [. . .]

Note: Words in square brackets in (a)(iii)(1)ii (subsequently deleted, see HC 813), (a)(iii)(1)iii, (b)(iii)(1)ii (subsequently deleted, see HC 813), (b)(iii)(1)iii, (c)(v)(1)ii (subsequently deleted, see HC 813), (c)(iii)(1)iii substituted; sub-paragraph (a)(iii)(1)iv, word in (a)(iv), sub-paragraph (b)(iii)(1)iv. Sub-paragraph (c)(v)(1)iv deleted from 10 January 2018 subject to savings for applications made before that date (HC 309). Word in square brackets in (d) substituted from 5 November 2018 (HC 1534). Word in square brackets in (d)(6) substituted from 10 January 2019 subject to savings for applications made before that date (HC 1779). Punctuation in square brackets in (a)(i)(2), (b)(i)(2) and (c)(i)(2) substituted; sub-paragraphs (a)(i)(3), (b)(i)(3), (c)(i)(3), and (d), words in curly brackets in (a)(iii)(1)ii, (b)(iii)(1)ii, and (c)(v)(1)ii deleted from 09:00 on 5 October 2020 subject to savings for applications made before that date. Where consequential changes relating to the need to obtain an ATAS certificate have been made to the conditions of leave, these take effect for all applications made or granted on or after 09:00 on 5 October 2020 (HC 707). Words in introduction to (a), (a)(iii)(1)ii, (b)(iii)(1)ii, (c)(v)(1)ii (**NB:** HC 813 refers to (c)(iii)(1)ii, however that provision does not exist and it is clear the amendment applies to (c)(v)(1)(ii)) deleted; words in curly brackets in (a)(iii))(1)iii, (b)9iii)(1)iii, and (c)(v)(1)iii (**NB:** HC 813 refers to (c)(iii)(1)iii, however that provision does not exist and it is clear the amendment applies to (c)(v)(1)iii), sub-paragraphs (b)(i) and (c)(i) substituted from 09:00 on 1 December 2020 subject to savings for applications made before that date (HC 813). Sub-paragraphs (a)(i)(1) to (3), (b)(i)(1) to (3) and (c)(i)(1) to (3) deleted (**NB:** (a)(i)(3), (b)(i)(3) and (c)(i)(3) were already deleted from 5 October 2020 (see HC 707 above)).

Tier 1 Migrants

1. An applicant applying for entry clearance or leave to remain as a Tier 1 Migrant must score 10 points for funds [. . .].

Note: Words deleted from 09:00 on 1 December 2020 subject to savings for applications made before that time (HC 813).

2. 10 points will only be awarded if an applicant:

(a) applying for entry clearance, has the level of funds shown in the table below and provides the specified documents in paragraph 1B above, or

Category	Level of funds	Points
Tier 1 (Entrepreneur)	£3,310	10
[. . .]	[. . .]	[. . .]

Note: Row in table deleted from 6 July 2019 subject to savings for applications made before that date (HC 1919).

(b) applying for leave to remain, has the level of funds shown in the table below and provides the specified documents in paragraph 1B above, or

Level of funds	Points
£945	10

[. . .]

Note: Sub-paragraph (c) deleted from 6 July 2019 subject to savings for applications made before that date (HC 1919).

3. Where the applicant is applying as a Tier 1 (Entrepreneur) Migrant, [they] cannot use the same funds to score points for attributes under Appendix A and to score points for maintenance funds for [themselves] or [their] dependants under this Appendix or Appendix E.

Note: Words substituted from 6 April 2019 subject to savings for applications made before that date (HC 1919).

[...]

Note: Heading deleted from 6 April 2021 subject to savings for applications made before that date (HC 1248).

4. [DELETED]

Note: Paragraph deleted from 09:00 on 1 December 2020 subject to savings for applications made before that time (HC 813).

5. [DELETED]

Note: Amendments from 6 April 2019 subject to savings for applications made before that date (HC 1919). Paragraph and table deleted from 09:00 on 1 December 2020 subject to savings for applications made before that time (HC 813).

[...]

Note: Heading deleted from 6 April 2021 subject to savings for applications made before that date (HC 1248).

6. [DELETED]

Note: Paragraph deleted from 09:00 on 1 December 2020 subject to savings for applications made before that time (HC 813).

7. [DELETED]

Note: Paragraph deleted from 09:00 on 1 December 2020 subject to savings for applications made before that time (HC 813).

[...]

Note: Heading deleted from 6 April 2021 subject to savings for applications made before that date (HC 1248).

8. [DELETED]

Note: Paragraph deleted from 09:00 on 1 December 2020 subject to savings for applications made before that time (HC 813).

9. [DELETED]

Note: Amendments from 6 April 2019 subject to savings for applications made before that date (HC 1919). Paragraph and table deleted from 09:00 on 1 December 2020 subject to savings for applications made before that time (HC 813).

[...]

Note: Heading deleted from 6 April 2021 subject to savings for applications made before that date (HC 1248).

10. [DELETED]

Note: Paragraph deleted from 09:00 on 5 October 2020 subject to savings for applications made before that date. Where consequential changes relating to the need to obtain an ATAS certificate have been made to the conditions of leave, these take effect for all applications made or granted on or after 09:00 on 5 October 2020 (HC 707).

11. [DELETED]

Note: Table substituted from 11 January 2018 subject to savings for applications made before that date (HC 309). Amendments from 1 November 2018 subject to savings for applications made before that date (HC 1534). Amendments from 10 January 2019 subject to savings for applications made before that date (HC 1779). Paragraph and table deleted from 09:00 on 5 October 2020 subject to savings for applications made before that date. Where consequential changes relating to the need to obtain an ATAS certificate have been made to the conditions of leave, these take effect for all applications made or granted on or after 09:00 on 5 October 2020 (HC 707).

[. . .]

Note: Heading deleted from 6 April 2021 subject to savings for applications made before that date (HC 1248).

12. [DELETED]

Note: Amendments from 10 January 2019 subject to savings for applications made before that date (HC 1779). Paragraph deleted from 09:00 on 5 October 2020 subject to savings for applications made before that date. Where consequential changes relating to the need to obtain an ATAS certificate have been made to the conditions of leave, these take effect for all applications made or granted on or after 09:00 on 5 October 2020 (HC 707).

12AA. [DELETED]

Note: Amendment from 10 January 2019 subject to savings for applications made before that date (HC 1779). Paragraph deleted from 09:00 on 5 October 2020 subject to savings for applications made before that date. Where consequential changes relating to the need to obtain an ATAS certificate have been made to the conditions of leave, these take effect for all applications made or granted on or after 09:00 on 5 October 2020 (HC 707).

12A. [DELETED]

Note: Paragraph deleted from 09:00 on 5 October 2020 subject to savings for applications made before that date. Where consequential changes relating to the need to obtain an ATAS certificate have been made to the conditions of leave, these take effect for all applications made or granted on or after 09:00 on 5 October 2020 (HC 707).

13. [DELETED]

Note: Amendments from 6 April 2019 subject to savings for applications made before that date (HC 1919). Paragraph deleted from 09:00 on 5 October 2020 subject to savings for applications made before that date. Where consequential changes relating to the need to obtain an ATAS certificate have been made to the conditions of leave, these take effect for all applications made or granted on or after 09:00 on 5 October 2020 (HC 707).

13A. [DELETED]

Note: Paragraph deleted from 09:00 on 5 October 2020 subject to savings for applications made before that date. Where consequential changes relating to the need to obtain an ATAS certificate have been made to the conditions of leave, these take effect for all applications made or granted on or after 09:00 on 5 October 2020 (HC 707).

13B. [DELETED]

Note: Amendments from 5 November 2018 (HC 1534). Amendments from 10 January 2019 subject to savings for applications made before that date (HC 1779). Paragraph deleted from 09:00 on 5 October 2020 subject to savings for applications made before that date. Where consequential changes relating to the need to obtain an ATAS certificate have been made to the conditions of leave, these take effect for all applications made or granted on or after 09:00 on 5 October 2020 (HC 707).

13C. [DELETED]

Note: Amendments from 5 November 2018 (HC 1534). Amendments from 10 January 2019 subject to savings for applications made before that date (HC 1779). Paragraph deleted from 09:00 on 5 October 2020 subject to savings for applications made before that date. Where consequential changes relating to the need to obtain an ATAS certificate have been made to the conditions of leave, these take effect for all applications made or granted on or after 09:00 on 5 October 2020 (HC 707).

13D. [DELETED]

Note: Amendments from 10 January 2019 subject to savings for applications made before that date (HC 1779). Paragraph deleted from 09:00 on 5 October 2020 subject to savings for applications made before that date. Where consequential changes relating to the need to obtain an ATAS certificate have been made to the conditions of leave, these take effect for all applications made or granted on or after 09:00 on 5 October 2020 (HC 707).

14. DELETED

[. . .]

Note: Heading deleted from 6 April 2021 subject to savings for applications made before that date (HC 1248).

15. [DELETED]

Note: Paragraph deleted from 09:00 on 5 October 2020 subject to savings for applications made before that date. Where consequential changes relating to the need to obtain an ATAS certificate have been made to the conditions of leave, these take effect for all applications made or granted on or after 09:00 on 5 October 2020 (HC 707).

16. [DELETED]

Note: Table substituted from 11 January 2018 subject to savings for applications made before that date (HC 309). Amendments from 1 November 2018 subject to savings for applications made before that date (HC 1534). Amendments from 10 January 2019 subject to savings for applications made before that date (HC 1779). Paragraph and table deleted from 09:00 on 5 October 2020 subject to savings for applications made before that date. Where consequential changes relating to the need to obtain an ATAS certificate have been made to the conditions of leave, these take effect for all applications made or granted on or after 09:00 on 5 October 2020 (HC 707).

[. . .]

Note: Heading deleted from 6 April 2021 subject to savings for applications made before that date (HC 1248).

17. [DELETED]

Note: Paragraph deleted from 09:00 on 5 October 2020 subject to savings for applications made before that date. Where consequential changes relating to the need to obtain an ATAS certificate have been made to the conditions of leave, these take effect for all applications made or granted on or after 09:00 on 5 October 2020 (HC 707).

18. [DELETED]

Note: Paragraph deleted from 09:00 on 5 October 2020 subject to savings for applications made before that date. Where consequential changes relating to the need to obtain an ATAS certificate have been made to the conditions of leave, these take effect for all applications made or granted on or after 09:00 on 5 October 2020 (HC 707).

19. [DELETED]

Note: Amendments from 5 November 2018 (HC 1534). Amendments from 10 January 2019 subject to savings for applications made before that date (HC 1779). Paragraph deleted from 09:00 on 5 October 2020 subject to savings for applications made before that date. Where consequential changes relating to the need to obtain an ATAS certificate have been made to the conditions of leave, these take effect for all applications made or granted on or after 09:00 on 5 October 2020 (HC 707).

19A. [DELETED]

Note: Amendments from 10 January 2019 subject to savings for applications made before that date (HC 1779). Paragraph deleted from 09:00 on 5 October 2020 subject to savings for applications made before that date. Where consequential changes relating to the need to obtain an ATAS certificate have been made to the conditions of leave, these take effect for all applications made or granted on or after 09:00 on 5 October 2020 (HC 707).

20. [DELETED]

Note: Paragraph deleted from 09:00 on 5 October 2020 subject to savings for applications made before that date. Where consequential changes relating to the need to obtain an ATAS certificate have been made to the conditions of leave, these take effect for all applications made or granted on or after 09:00 on 5 October 2020 (HC 707).

21. [DELETED]

Note: Amendments from 6 April 2019 subject to savings for applications made before that date (HC 1919). Paragraph deleted from 09:00 on 5 October 2020 subject to savings for applications made before that date. Where consequential changes relating to the need to obtain an ATAS certificate have been made to the conditions of leave, these take effect for all applications made or granted on or after 09:00 on 5 October 2020 (HC 707).

21A. [DELETED]

Note: Paragraph deleted from 09:00 on 5 October 2020 subject to savings for applications made before that date. Where consequential changes relating to the need to obtain an ATAS certificate have been made to the conditions of leave, these take effect for all applications made or granted on or after 09:00 on 5 October 2020 (HC 707).

21B. [DELETED]

Note: Amendments from 5 November 2018 (HC 1534). Word in introduction substituted from 10 January 2019 subject to savings for applications made before that date (HC 1779). Paragraph deleted from 09:00 on 5 October 2020 subject to savings for applications made before that date. Where consequential changes relating to the need to obtain an ATAS certificate have been made to the conditions of leave, these take effect for all applications made or granted on or after 09:00 on 5 October 2020 (HC 707).

21C. [DELETED]

Note: Amendments from 10 January 2019 subject to savings for applications made before that date (HC 1779). Amendments from 6 April 2019 subject to savings for applications made before that date (HC 1919). Paragraph deleted from 09:00 on 5 October 2020 subject to savings for applications made before that date. Where consequential changes relating to the need to obtain an ATAS certificate have been made to the conditions of leave, these take effect for all applications made or granted on or after 09:00 on 5 October 2020 (HC 707).

22. DELETED

Appendix CS: Child Student [DELETED]

Note: Appendix inserted from 09:00 on 5 October 2020 subject to savings for applications made before that time (HC 707). Appendix deleted from 09:00 on 1 December 2020 subject to savings for applications made before that time (HC 813).

Appendix D [DELETED]

Note: Appendix deleted from 09:00 on 1 December 2020 subject to savings for applications made before that date (HC 813)

Appendix E

[Applies only to applications as a dependent partner or dependent child of a Tier 1 (Entrepreneur) Migrant]

Note: Heading amended from 29 March 2019 subject to savings for applications made before that date (HC 1919). Heading substituted from 09:00 on 1 December 2020 subject to savings for applications made before that time (HC 813).

A sufficient level of funds must be available to an applicant applying as the Partner or Child of a [Tier 1 (Entrepreneur) Migrant]. A sufficient level of funds will only be available if the requirements below are met.

Note: Amendments from 29 March 2019 subject to savings for applications made before that date (HC 1919). Words in square brackets substituted from 09:00 on 1 December 2020 subject to savings for applications made before that time (HC 813).

(aa) Paragraphs 1A and 1B of Appendix C also apply to this Appendix.

(ab) [The] applicant cannot use the same funds to score points for maintenance funds from this Appendix as the Tier 1 (Entrepreneur) Migrant used to score points for attributes under Appendix A.

Note: Word substituted from 09:00 on 1 December 2020 subject to savings for applications made before that time (HC 813).

[(a) Where the application is connected to a Tier 1 (Entrepreneur) Migrant who is outside the UK or who has been in the UK for a period of less than 12 months, there must be £1,890 in funds.]

Note: Amendments from 29 March 2019 subject to savings for applications made before that date (HC 1919). Sub-paragraph substituted from 09:00 on 1 December 2020 subject to savings for applications made before that time (HC 813).

[...]

Note: Amendments from 29 March 2019 subject to savings for applications made before that date (HC 1919). Amendments from 09:00 on 5 October 2020 subject to savings for applications made before that time. Where consequential changes relating to the need to obtain an ATAS certificate have been made to the conditions of leave for routes, these changes take effect for all applications made or granted on or after 09:00 on 5 October. (HC 707). Sub-paragraph (b) deleted from 09:00 on 1 December 2020 subject to savings for applications made before that time (HC 813).

[...]

Note: Sub-paragraph (ba)(i) deleted from 09:00 on 5 October 2020 subject to savings for applications made before that time. Where consequential changes relating to the need to obtain an ATAS certificate have been made to the conditions of leave for routes, these changes take effect for all applications made or granted on or after 09:00 on 5 October. (HC 707).

(c) Where the applicant is applying as the Partner of a [Tier 1 (Entrepreneur) Migrant] the relevant amount of funds must be available to either the applicant or the [Tier 1 (Entrepreneur) Migrant].

Note: Amendments from 29 March 2019 (amended again by HC 813) subject to savings for applications made before that date (HC 1919). Words in square brackets substituted from 09:00 on 1 December 2020 subject to savings for applications made before that time HC 813).

(d) Where the applicant is applying as the Child of a [Tier 1 (Entrepreneur) Migrant], the relevant amount of funds must be available to the applicant, the [Tier 1 (Entrepreneur) Migrant], or the applicant's other parent who is Lawfully present in the UK or being granted entry clearance, or leave to enter or remain, at the same time.

Note: Amendments from 29 March 2019 (amended again by HC 813) subject to savings for applications made before that date (HC 1919). Words substituted from 09:00 on 1 December 2020 subject to savings for applications made before that time (HC 813).

(e) Where the [Tier 1 (Entrepreneur) Migrant] is applying for entry clearance or leave to remain at the same time as the applicant, the amount of funds available to the applicant must be in addition to the level of funds required separately of the Tier 1 (Entrepreneur) Migrant.

Note: Amendments from 29 March 2019 (amended again by HC 813) subject to savings for applications made before that date (HC 1919). Words substituted from 09:00 on 1 December 2020 subject to savings for applications made before that time (HC 813).

(f) In all cases, the funds in question must be available to:

(i) the applicant, or

(ii) where [they are] applying as the partner of a [[Tier 1 (Entrepreneur) Migrant]], either to [them] or to that [[Tier 1 (Entrepreneur) Migrant]], or

(iii) where [they are] applying as the child of a [[Tier 1 (Entrepreneur) Migrant]], either to [them], to the [[Tier 1 (Entrepreneur) Migrant]] or to the child's other parent who is lawfully present in the UK or being granted entry clearance, or leave to enter or remain, at the same time;

Note: Amendments from 29 March 2019 (amended again by HC 813) subject to savings for applications made before that date (HC 1919). Words in square brackets substituted from 6 April 2019 subject to savings for applications made before that date (HC 1919). Words in double square brackets substituted from 09:00 on 1 December 2020 subject to savings for applications made before that time (HC 813).

[(g) The funds in question must have been available to the person referred to in (f) above on the date of application and for a consecutive 90-day period of time.]

Note: Amendments from 6 April 2019 subject to savings for applications made before that date (HC 1919). Amendments from 09:00 on 5 October 2020 subject to savings for applications made before that time. Where consequential changes relating to the need to obtain an ATAS certificate have been made to the conditions of leave for routes, these changes take effect for all applications made or granted on or after 09:00 on 5 October. (HC 707). Paragraph substituted from 09:00 on 1 December 2020 subject to savings for applications made before that time (HC 813).

(h) If the funds in question were obtained when the person referred to in (f) above was in the UK, the funds must have been obtained while that person had valid leave and was not acting in breach of any conditions attached to that leave; and

[. . .]

Note: Amendments from 6 April 2019 subject to savings for applications made before that date (HC 1919). Paragraph (i) deleted from 09:00 on 1 December 2020 subject to savings for applications made before that time (HC 813).

(ia) [Sufficient funds will not be treated as available to the partner or child unless the specified documents, as set out in paragraph 1B of Appendix C, show that the funds are held in a financial institution to which Appendix Finance applies.]

Note: Words substituted from 09:00 on 1 December 2020 subject to savings for applications made before that time (HC 813).

[. . .]

Note: Sub-paragraph (ib) deleted from 09:00 on 1 December 2020 subject to savings for applications made before that time (HC 813).

[. . .]

Note: Sub-paragraph (ic) inserted from 29 March 2019 subject to savings for applications made before that date (HC 1919). Sub-paragraph deleted from 09:00 on 1 December 2020 subject to savings for applications made before that time (HC 813).

[(j) In all cases the applicant must provide the specified documents as set out in paragraph 1B of Appendix C [. . .]]

Note: Paragraph substituted from 1 November 2018 subject to savings for applications made before that date (HC 1534). Paragraph substituted from 6 April 2019 subject to savings for applications made before that date (HC 1919). Amendments from 09:00 on 5 October 2020 subject to savings for applications made before that time. Where consequential changes relating to the need to obtain an ATAS certificate have been made to the conditions of leave for routes, these changes take effect for all applications made or granted on or after 09:00 on 5 October. (HC 707). Words deleted from 09:00 on 1 December 2020 subject to savings for applications made before that time (HC 813).

(k) Where the funds are in one or more foreign currencies, the applicant must have the specified level of funds when converted to pound sterling (£) using the spot exchange rate which appears on www.oanda.com* for the date of the application.

(l) Where the application is one of a number of applications made at the same time as a partner or child of a [Tier 1 (Entrepreneur) Migrant] (as set out in paragraphs 319A and 319F) each applicant, including the [Tier 1 (Entrepreneur) Migrant] if applying at the same time, must have the total requisite funds specified in the relevant parts of appendices C and E. If each applicant does not individually meet the requirements of appendices C and/or E, as appropriate, all the applications (the application by the [Tier 1 (Entrepreneur) Migrant] and applications as the partner or child of that [Tier 1 (Entrepreneur) Migrant]) will be refused.

Note: Amendments from 29 March 2019 (amended again by HC 813) subject to savings for applications made before that date (HC 1919). Words substituted from 09:00 on 1 December 2020 subject to savings for applications made before that time (HC 813).

(m) The end date of the 90-day and 28-day periods referred to in (g) above will be taken as the date of the closing balance on the most recent of the specified documents (where specified documents from two or more accounts are submitted, this will be the end date for the account that most favours the applicant), as set out in paragraph 1B of Appendix C, and must be no earlier than 31 days before the date of application.

[...]

Note: Amendments from 29 March 2019 subject to savings for applications made before that date (HC 1919). Sub-paragraph (n) deleted from 09:00 on 5 October 2020 subject to savings for applications made before that time. Where consequential changes relating to the need to obtain an ATAS certificate have been made to the conditions of leave for routes, these changes take effect for all applications made or granted on or after 09:00 on 5 October. (HC 707).

(o) Where [the applicant is applying as the Partner or Child of a [[Tier 1 (Entrepreneur) Migrant]] who] is applying for entry clearance or leave to remain at the same time as the applicant, and is not required to provide evidence of maintenance funds because of the provisions in paragraph 5(b) of Appendix C, the applicant is also not required to provide evidence of maintenance funds.

Note: Amendments from 29 March 2019 (amended again by HC 813) subject to savings for applications made before that date (HC 1919). Words in double square brackets substituted from 09:00 on 1 December 2020 subject to savings for applications made before that time (HC 813).

(p) Where the applicant:

(i) is not applying at the same time as the [[Tier 1 (Entrepreneur) Migrant]] [in (o)], and

(ii) in the application which led to [their] most recent grant of entry clearance or leave to remain, the [[Tier 1 (Entrepreneur) Migrant]] was not required to provide evidence of maintenance funds because of the provisions in paragraph 5(b) of Appendix C, the applicant is also not required to provide evidence of maintenance funds.

Note: Words in square brackets in (i) inserted from 29 March 2019 subject to savings for applications made before that date, word in square brackets in (ii) substituted from 6 April 2019 subject to savings for applications made before that date (HC 1919). Words in double square brackets substituted from 09:00 on 1 December 2020 subject to savings for applications made before that time (HC 813).

(q) Overdraft facilities will not be considered towards funds that are available or under an applicant's own control.

*This is an external website for which the Home Office is not responsible.

[Appendix ECAA: extension of stay

This route is for ECAA workers, business persons and their family members who are in the UK and already hold permission in that capacity and are seeking an extension of their permission.

It also covers children of ECAA workers and business persons who can apply for entry clearance to come to the UK as a dependent child.

A person with permission on the ECAA route can apply for settlement under Appendix ECAA Settlement.

Validity requirements for an ECAA Worker or ECAA business person on the ECAA Extension of Stay route

ECAA 1.1. A person applying for permission to stay on the ECAA route must apply online on the gov.uk website on the specified form 'Turkish Businessperson or Worker'.

ECAA 1.2. An application for permission to stay as an ECAA worker or ECAA business person must meet all the following requirements:

(a) the applicant must be a Turkish national; and

(b) the applicant must have provided any required biometrics; and

(c) the applicant must have provided a passport or other travel document which satisfactorily establishes their identity and nationality: and

(d) the applicant must be in the UK.

ECAA 1.3. An application which does not met all the validity requirements for the ECAA route is invalid and may be rejected and not considered.

Suitability requirements for the ECAA Extension of Stay route

ECAA 2.1. The suitability requirement for the ECAA Extension of Stay route will be met unless:

(a) the applicant is an ECAA worker, and in respect of conduct before 11pm on 31 December 2020, the decision maker considers it is proportionate to refuse the application on grounds of public policy, public security or public health in accordance with Article 14 of Decision 1/80; or

(b) the applicant is a Turkish business person, and in respect of conduct before 11pm on 31 December 2020, the application is refused on grounds that it is undesirable to grant it in the light of the applicant's character, conduct or associations as set out in paragraph 4 of HC510; or

(c) in respect of conduct after 11pm on 31 December 2020, the applicant falls for refusal as provided for in Section 1 of Part 9 of these rules or ECAA 2.2.

ECAA 2.2. If applying for permission to stay and in respect of conduct after 11pm on 31 December 2020, the applicant must not be:

(a) in breach of immigration laws, except that where paragraph 39E applies, that period of overstaying will be disregarded; or

(b) on immigration bail.

Eligibility requirements for the ECAA Extension of Stay route

ECAA worker requirement for the ECAA route

ECAA 3.1. To meet the ECAA worker requirement the applicant must:

(a) have permission as an ECAA worker; and

(b) have been lawfully employed in the UK for at least 3 years with the same employer; or

(c) have been lawfully employed in the UK for at least 4 years, including at least 3 years with the same employer and the remaining time in the same occupation.

ECAA 3.2. The applicant must show that they will continue to be employed in the UK throughout the period of permission requested.

ECAA 3.3. The requirements in ECAA 3.1.and ECAA 3.2. must be proved by evidence that the applicant:

(a) holds a valid employment contract with the employer; and

(b) continues to receive payment for services as part of that contract.

ECAA 3.4. For the purposes of ECAA 3.1. the following absences will be treated as periods during which the applicant was lawfully employed:

(a) annual holidays; and

(b) statutory maternity leave, paternity leave or shared parental leave; and

(c) statutory adoption leave; and

(d) sick leave (up to 6 weeks in any 12 months, or longer if there are compelling circumstances); and

(e) absence due to an accident at work; and

(f) periods of involuntary unemployment (provided that the applicant registered with the relevant employment authorities and made a reasonable effort to re-join the workforce).

ECAA Business person requirement for the ECAA route

ECAA 4.1. To meet the ECAA business person requirement, the applicant must meet all the following requirements:

(a) the applicant must have permission as an ECAA business person; and

(b) the applicant must have established, or intend to establish, take over or become a partner or director of, one or more genuine businesses in the UK; and

(c) the business or businesses must be viable; and

(d) the applicant must genuinely intend to operate, or have genuinely operated, one or more businesses in the UK.

ECAA 4.2. The applicant must:

(a) provide evidence that they have invested, or will invest, sufficient funds or assets in the business or businesses in proportion to their interest in the business or businesses; and

(b) demonstrate that those funds or assets are, and continue to be, their own; and

(c) demonstrate they can meet their share of the liabilities which the business or businesses may incur; and

(d) demonstrate that their part in the business or businesses does not amount to disguised employment; and

(e) demonstrate that their share of the profits of the business is enough to support themselves and any dependants; and

(f) if they are joining an existing business, provide:

(i) a written statement of the terms and conditions on which they are joining the business; and

(ii) accounts for the existing business for the 12 months before the date of application; and

(iii) evidence that there is a genuine need for their services and investment.

ECAA 4.3. In assessing whether the requirements in ECAA 4.1. and ECAA 4.2. are met, the factors that will be considered include the following:

(a) the viability and credibility of the source of the money being used to set up or invest in the business or businesses; and

(b) evidence of a credible time frame (lasting no more than 11 months) of when money that has not yet been invested in the business or businesses will be invested; and

(c) the credibility of the financial accounts of the business or businesses; and

(d) the credibility of the applicant's proposed business activity in the UK; and

(e) if the nature of the business requires mandatory accreditation, registration or insurance, whether the accreditation, registration or insurance have been obtained.

Decision on the ECAA Extension of Stay route

ECAA 5.1. If the decision maker is satisfied that the suitability requirements are met, and either the eligibility requirements for either an ECAA worker or an ECAA business person are met, the application will be granted; otherwise, the application will be refused.

Period and conditions of grant on the ECAA Extension of Stay route

[**ECAA 6.1** If the applicant meets the ECAA worker requirement and meets the requirement in ECAA 3.1.(a), and 3.1.(b) but does not meet the requirement in ECAA 3.1.(c), they will be granted permission to stay for up to 12 months.]

Note: Paragraph substituted from 6 April 2021 (HC 1248).

ECAA 6.2. If the applicant meets the ECAA worker requirement and meets the requirement in [ECAA 3.1.(c)], they will be granted permission to stay for up to 36 months.

Note: Words substituted from 6 April 2021 (HC 1248).

ECAA 6.3. If the applicant meets the ECAA business person requirement, they will be granted permission to stay for up to 36 months.

ECAA 6.4. The grant will be subject to all the following conditions:

(a) if the applicant meets the ECAA worker requirement and has been lawfully employed in the UK for less than 4 years, work is allowed only for the applicant's current employer, or in the same occupation with a different employer; and

(b) if the applicant meets the ECAA business person requirement, work is allowed only for the business or businesses the applicant has established, joined or taken over (but not as an apprentice); and

(c) no access to public funds (subject to any bi-lateral agreements); and

(d) study is permitted, subject to the ATAS condition in Appendix ATAS; and

(e) if Part 10 applies, the applicant will be required to register with the police.

ECAA 6.5. If the application is refused the person can apply for an administrative review under Appendix AR.

Dependants on the ECAA Extension of Stay route

Validity requirements for dependent partner and dependent child on the ECAA Extension of Stay route

ECAA 7.1. A child applying for entry clearance or permission to stay, and a partner applying for permission to stay (a partner must already be in the UK and cannot apply for entry clearance), as a dependant on the ECAA Extension of Stay route must apply online on the gov.uk website on the following specified forms:

Location of partner or child	Specified form
Outside the UK, for a child applying for entry clearance	'Join or accompany a family' on the 'Find and apply for other visas from outside the UK' form
Inside the UK, for a partner or child applying for permission to stay	If applying at the same time as the ECAA worker, on the form 'Turkish Businessperson or Worker' If applying separately, – Dependant partner of a Turkish Businessperson or Worker (ECAA 3 – Dependant Partner), – Dependant child of a Turkish Businessperson or Worker(ECAA 3 – Dependant Child)

ECAA 7.2. An application for entry clearance or permission to stay by a dependant on the ECAA route must meet all the following requirements:

(a) the applicant must have provided any required biometrics; and

(b) the applicant must have provided a passport or other travel document which satisfactorily establishes their identity and nationality; and

(c) where the applicant is applying for permission to stay as a dependent partner they must be in the UK and have permission to stay as a dependent partner on the ECAA route.

ECAA 7.3. An application which does not met all the validity requirements for a dependent partner or dependent child on the ECAA Extension of Stay route is invalid and may be rejected and not considered.

Suitability requirements for dependent partner and dependent child on the ECAA Extension of Stay route

ECAA 8.1. The suitability requirements for entry clearance for a dependent child will be met unless the applicant falls for refusal under Part 9: grounds or refusal.

ECAA 8.2. The suitability requirement for permission to stay as a dependent partner or dependent child on the ECAA Extension of Stay route will be met unless:

(a) the applicant is the dependant of a Turkish Worker, and in respect of conduct committed before 11pm on 31 December 2020, the decision maker considers it is proportionate to refuse the application on grounds of public policy, public security or public health in accordance with Article 14 of Decision 1/80; or

(b) the applicant is the dependent of a Turkish business person, and in respect of conduct committed before 11pm on 31 December 2020, the application is refused on grounds that it is undesirable to grant the application in the light of the applicant's character, conduct or associations as set out in paragraph 4 of HC 510; or

(c) in respect of conduct committed after 11pm on 31 December 2020, the applicant falls for refusal as provided for under Section 1 of Part 9 of these rules or ECAA 8.3. applies.

ECAA 8.3. If applying for permission to stay the applicant must not be:

(a) in breach of immigration laws, except that, where paragraph 39E applies, that period of overstaying will be disregarded; or

(b) on immigration bail.

Eligibility requirements for a dependent partner or child on the ECAA Extension of Stay route

Entry requirement for a dependent child on the ECAA Extension of Stay route

ECAA 9.1. A person seeking to come to the UK as a dependent child must apply for and obtain entry clearance as a dependent child on the ECAA Extension of Stay route before they arrive in the UK.

Relationship requirement for a dependent partner on the ECAA Extension of Stay route

ECAA 10.1. The applicant must be the partner of a person (P) and P must have permission as an ECAA worker or ECAA business person on the ECAA route.

ECAA 10.2. If the applicant and the ECAA Worker or ECAA business person partner are unmarried partners, all of the following requirements must be met:

(a) they must both be aged 18 or over on the date of application; and

(b) any previous relationship of the applicant or their ECAA Worker or ECAA business person partner with another person must have permanently broken down; and

(c) the applicant and their ECAA Worker or ECAA business person partner must not be so closely related that they would not be allowed to marry or form a civil partnership in the UK.

ECAA 10.3. The relationship between the applicant and their ECAA worker or ECAA business person partner must be genuine and subsisting.

ECAA 10.4. The applicant and their ECAA worker or ECAA business person partner must intend to live together throughout the applicant's stay in the UK.

Relationship requirement for a dependent child on the ECAA Extension of Stay route

ECAA 11.1. The applicant must be the child of a person (P) who has permission as an ECAA Worker or ECAA business person on the ECAA route, or a person who is the partner of P.

ECAA 11.2. The applicant's parents must each be either applying for permission, or be present in the UK with permission (other than as a visitor) on the ECAA route unless:

(a) the parent with permission on the ECAA route is the sole surviving parent; or

(b) the parent with permission on the ECAA route has sole responsibility for the applicant's upbringing; or

(c) the decision maker is satisfied that there are serious and compelling reasons to grant the applicant entry clearance or permission to stay, to live with the parent who has permission on the ECAA route.

Age requirement for a dependent child on the ECAA Extension of Stay route

ECAA 12.1. The applicant must be under the age of 21 at the date of application, unless they were last granted permission as the dependent child of their parent on the ECAA route.

ECAA 12.2. The applicant must not be leading an independent life.

Care requirement for a dependent child on the ECAA Extension of Stay route

ECAA 13.1. If the applicant is under the age of 18 at the date of application there must be suitable arrangements for the child's care and accommodation in the UK, which must comply with relevant UK legislation and regulations.

Financial requirement for a dependent partner or dependent child on the ECAA Extension of Stay route

ECAA 14.1. There must be adequate accommodation provided by the ECAA worker or ECAA business person for the applicant.

ECAA 14.2. Where the applicant is the dependent of an ECAA business person, the profits of the business or businesses must be sufficient to maintain the applicant and any other dependents in the UK.

Decision for a dependent partner or dependent child on the ECAA route

ECAA 15.1. If the applicant meets the suitability requirements and meets the eligibility requirements for either a dependent partner or dependent child on the ECAA Extension of Stay route, the application will be granted; otherwise the application will be refused.

Period and conditions of grant for a dependent partner or dependent child on the ECAA Extension of Stay route

ECAA 16.1. The grant will be for a period which ends on the same day as the permission of the ECAA worker or ECAA business person on the ECAA route.

ECAA 16.2. The grant will be subject to all the following conditions:

(a) no access to public funds (subject to any bi-lateral agreement); and

(b) work is permitted; and

(c) study is permitted, subject to the ATAS condition in Appendix ATAS; and

(d) if Part 10 applies, the applicant will be required to register with the police.

ECAA 16.3. If the application is refused, the person can apply for an Administrative Review under Appendix AR]

Note: Appendix inserted from 23:00 on 31 December 2020 subject to savings for applications made before that time (HC 813).

[APPENDIX ECAA [SETTLEMENT]

Note: Appendix inserted from 6 July 2018 for all decisions made on or after that date (HC 1154). Appendix renamed from 23:00 on 31 December 2020 subject to savings for applications made before that time (HC 813).

Part ECAA 1. Definitions

ECAA 1.1. [DELETED]

Note: Paragraph deleted from 23:00 on 31 December 2020 subject to savings for applications made before that time (HC 813).

[**ECAA 1.1.**] Unless the contrary intention is expressed in this Appendix, the definitions in paragraph 6 of the Immigration Rules shall apply to this Appendix.

Note: Paragraph renumbered from 23:00 on 31 December 2020 subject to savings for applications made before that time (HC 813).

Part ECAA 2. Continuous periods lawfully in the UK

ECAA 2.1. References to a 'continuous period' 'lawfully in the UK' for the purposes of this Appendix mean residence in the UK for an unbroken period with valid leave, and for these purposes a period shall be considered unbroken where:

[(a) the applicant has not been absent from the UK for more than 180 days during any 12 month period in the continuous period, except that any absence from the UK for the purpose of:

(i) assisting with a national crisis; or

(ii) assisting with an international humanitarian or environmental crisis overseas; or

(iii) as a result of travel restrictions or serious illness,

shall not count towards the 180 days, if the applicant provides evidence that this was the reason of the absence(s);]

(b) the applicant has existing limited leave to enter or remain upon their departure and return except that:

(i) where that leave expired no more than 28 days prior to a further application for entry clearance which was made before 6 July 2018 and subsequently granted, that period and any period pending the applicant's re-entry into the United Kingdom shall be disregarded; and

(ii) where, on or after 6 July 2018, the applicant makes a further application for entry clearance during the currency of continuing limited leave which is subsequently granted, the period spent outside the UK with continuing leave and any period pending the applicant's re-entry into the United Kingdom shall be disregarded; and

(c) the applicant has any current period of overstaying disregarded where paragraph 39E of the Immigration Rules applies; and

[. . .]

Note: Sub-paragraph (a) substituted; (d) deleted from 23:00 on 31 December 2020 subject to savings for applications made before that time (HC 813).

ECAA 2.2. Except for periods where the applicant had leave as:

(a) [[an]] [ECAA business person];

(b) a Tier 1 Migrant other than a Tier 1 (Post Study Work) Migrant or a Tier 1 (Graduate Entrepreneur) Migrant; or

(c) a Tier 1 (Entrepreneur) Migrant;

any absences from the UK during the relevant qualifying period must have been for a purpose that is consistent with the applicant's basis of stay here, including paid annual leave, or for serious or compelling reasons.

Note: Words in (a) substituted from 23:00 on 31 December 2020 subject to savings for applications made before that time (HC 813). Word in double square brackets in (a) inserted from 6 April 2021 (HC 1248).

ECAA 2.3. The continuous period will be considered as ending on whichever of the following dates is most beneficial to the applicant:

(a) the date of application;

(b) the date of decision; or

(c) any date up to 28 days after the date of application

ECAA 2.4. References to a continuous period spent with valid leave in the UK include time spent with valid leave in the Bailiwick of Guernsey, the Bailiwick of Jersey or the Isle of Man, where that leave was granted for an equivalent purpose to one of the categories stated in the relevant paragraph, provided that the most recent period prior to the date of application was spent in the UK with valid leave in the relevant category.

Part ECAA 3. Requirements for [ECAA workers] applying for indefinite leave to remain

Note: Words in heading substituted from 23:00 on 31 December 2020 subject to savings for applications made before that time (HC 813).

ECAA 3.1. The requirements for indefinite leave to remain to be granted to an ECAA worker are that the applicant must:

[(a) be an ECAA worker; and]

[(b) have resided lawfully in the UK for a continuous period of 5 years, of which the most recent period of leave must have been as an ECAA worker, in any combination of the following categories:

(i) an ECAA worker;

(ii) as a Tier 2 (General Migrant);

(iii) as a Tier 2 (Minister of religion) Migrant;

(iv) as a Tier 2 (Sportsperson) Migrant; or

(v) as a work permit holder; and]

(c) have demonstrated sufficient knowledge of the English language and sufficient knowledge about life in the United Kingdom, in accordance with Appendix KoLL; and

(d) have been able to support any family members with them without recourse to public funds to which they are not entitled; and

[(e) not fall for refusal under Part 9: grounds]

Note: Sub-paragraphs (a), (b) and (e) substituted from 23:00 on 31 December 2020 subject to savings for applications made before that time (HC 813).

[Indefinite leave to remain as an ECAA worker]

ECAA 3.2. Indefinite leave to remain will be granted provided that the Secretary of State is satisfied that each of the requirements of paragraph ECAA 3.1 are met.

Note: Amendment to heading from 23:00 on 31 December 2020 subject to savings for applications made before that time (HC 813). Heading substituted from 6 April 2021 (HC 1248).

[Refusal of indefinite leave to remain as an ECAA worker]

ECAA 3.3. Indefinite leave to remain for [...]ECAA workers is to be refused if the Secretary of State is not satisfied that each of the requirements of paragraph ECAA 3.1 are met.

Note: Amendment to heading from 23:00 on 31 December 2020 subject to savings for applications made before that time (HC 813). Heading substituted, word deleted from 6 April 2021 (HC 1248).

Part ECAA 4. Requirements for [ECAA business persons] applying for indefinite leave to remain

Note: Words in heading substituted from 23:00 on 31 December 2020 subject to savings for applications made before that time (HC 813).

ECAA 4.1. The applicant must:

[(a) be an ECAA business person; and]

[(b) have resided lawfully in the UK for a continuous period of five years, of which the most recent period of leave must have been as an ECAA business person, in any combination of the following categories:

(i) the ECAA business person; or]

(ii) the Tier 1 (Entrepreneur) Migrant category; and

(c) have demonstrated sufficient knowledge of the English language and sufficient knowledge about life in the United Kingdom, in accordance with Appendix KoLL; and

[(d) not fall for refusal under Part 9: grounds for refusal; and]

[(e) be relying on a business which meet(s) the requirements under paragraph ECAA 4.2.]

[...]

Note: Sub-paragraphs (a), (b)(i), (d) and (e) substituted from 23:00 on 31 December 2020 subject to savings for applications made before that date (HC 813). Sub-paragraph deleted from 6 April 2021 (HC 1248).

ECAA 4.2. The Secretary of State must be satisfied [on the balance of probabilities] that:

(a) the applicant has established, taken over or become a director of one or more genuine businesses in the UK, and has genuinely operated that business or businesses while he had leave as [[an]] ECAA business person; and

(b) the business or businesses upon which they are relying on for any of the qualifying period is/are viable; and

(c) the applicant genuinely intends to continue operating one or more businesses in the UK.

Note: Words in square brackets inserted from 23:00 on 31 December 2020 subject to savings for applications made before that time (HC 813). Word in double square brackets substituted from 6 April 2021 (HC 1248).

[**ECAA 4.3.** In making the assessment in ECAA 4.2, the Secretary of State may take into account the following factors:]

(a) the evidence the applicant has submitted;

(b) the viability and credibility of the source of the money used to set up or invest in the business or businesses;

(c) the credibility of the financial accounts of the business or businesses;

(d) the credibility of the applicant's business activity in the UK, including when they had leave as an ECAA business person;

(e) if the nature of the business requires mandatory accreditation, registration and/or insurance, whether that accreditation, registration and/or insurance has been obtained; and

(f) any other relevant information.

Note: Introduction substituted from 23:00 on 31 December 2020 subject to savings for applications made before that time (HC 813).

ECAA 4.4. The Secretary of State may request additional information and evidence to support the assessment in paragraph ECAA 4.3, and may refuse the application if the information or evidence requested is not received by the Secretary of State at the address specified in the request within 28 calendar days of the date of the request.

[Indefinite leave to remain as an ECAA business person]

ECAA 4.5. Indefinite leave to remain will be granted provided that the Secretary of State is satisfied that each of the requirements of paragraph ECAA 4.1 are met.

Note: Amendment to heading from 23:00 on 31 December 2020 subject to savings for applications made before that time (HC 813). Heading substituted from 6 April 2021 (HC 1248).

[Refusal of indefinite leave to remain as an ECAA business person]

ECAA 4.6. Indefinite leave to remain for [ECAA business persons] is to be refused if the Secretary of State is not satisfied that each of the requirements of paragraph ECAA 4.1. are met.

Note: Amendment to heading, words in paragraph substituted from 23:00 on 31 December 2020 subject to savings for applications made before that time (HC 813). Heading substituted from 6 April 2021 (HC 1248).

Part ECAA 5. Requirements for children of ECAA workers or ECAA business persons applying for indefinite leave to remain

ECAA 5.1. The Secretary of State must be satisfied that:

(a) the applicant is the child of a parent who has, or is at the same time being granted, indefinite leave to remain as:

(i) an ECAA worker or ECAA business person; or

(ii) the spouse, civil partner or unmarried partner of an ECAA worker or ECAA business person; and

(b) the applicant must have, or have last been granted, leave as the child of or have been born in the United Kingdom to, the ECAA Worker or Business Person, or the partner of an ECAA Worker or Business Person who is being granted indefinite leave to remain.

(c) the applicant must not be married or in a civil partnership, must not have formed an independent family unit, and must not be leading an independent life, and if they are over the age of 21 on the date the application is made, they must provide the specified documents and information in paragraph 319H-SD (except that references to the Relevant Points Based System Migrant are read to mean the ECAA worker or ECAA business person) to show that this requirement is met.

(d) Both of an applicant's parents must either be lawfully settled in the UK, or being granted indefinite leave to remain at the same time as the applicant, unless:

(i) the ECAA worker or business person is the applicant's sole surviving parent; or

(ii) the ECAA worker or business person parent has and has had sole responsibility for the applicant's upbringing; or

(iii) there are serious and compelling family or other considerations which would make it desirable not to refuse the application and suitable arrangements have been made for the applicant's care; or

(iv) the parent is, at the same time, being granted indefinite leave to remain as an ECAA worker or business person, the other parent is lawfully present in the UK or being granted leave at the same time as the applicant; and

(e) the applicant has demonstrated sufficient knowledge of the English language and sufficient knowledge about life in the United Kingdom, in accordance with Appendix KoLL, unless they are under the age of 18 at the date on which the application is made; and

(f) if the applicant is a [child] of an ECAA worker or business person the applicant must provide a full birth certificate, with translations where necessary showing the names of both parents; and

(g) all arrangements for the child's care and accommodation in the UK must comply with relevant UK legislation and regulations; and

(h) the applicant must not be in the UK in breach of immigration laws except that, where paragraph 39E of the Immigration Rules applies, any current period of overstaying will be disregarded; and

(i) [the applicant must not fall for refusal under Part 9: grounds for refusal[[.]]]

Note: Sub-paragraph (i) substituted from 23:00 on 31 December 2020 subject to savings for applications made before that time (HC 813). Word in (f) inserted, punctuation in double square brackets in (i) substituted from 6 April 2021 (HC 1248).

[Indefinite leave to remain as the child of an ECAA worker or ECAA business person]

ECAA 5.2. Indefinite leave to remain will be granted provided that the Secretary of State is satisfied that each of the requirements of paragraph ECAA 5.1 are met.

Note: Amendment to heading from 23:00 on 31 December 2020 subject to savings for applications made before that time (HC 813). Heading substituted from 6 April 2021 (HC 1248).

[Refusal of indefinite leave to remain as the child of an ECAA worker or ECAA business person]

[**ECAA 5.3.** Indefinite leave to remain as the child of an ECAA worker or ECAA business person is to be refused if the Secretary of State is not satisfied that each of the requirements of paragraph ECAA 5.1. are met.]

Note: Amendments to heading and paragraph from 23:00 on 31 December 2020 subject to savings for applications made before that time (HC 813). Heading and paragraph substituted from 6 April 2021 (HC 1248).

Part ECAA 6. Requirements for partners of ECAA workers or ECAA business persons applying for indefinite leave to remain

[**ECAA 6.1.** The applicant must:

(a) be the spouse, civil partner or unmarried partner of a person [P] who:

(i) has indefinite leave to remain as an ECAA worker or business person; or

(ii) is, at the same time being granted indefinite leave to remain as an ECAA worker or business person; or

(iii) has become a British Citizen where prior to that they held indefinite leave to remain as an ECAA worker or business person; and

(b) have, or have last been granted, leave as the spouse, civil partner or unmarried partner of the ECAA worker or business person; and

(c) be in a marriage or civil partnership, or unmarried partnership with [P] which must be genuine and subsisting at the time the application is made; and

(d) must intend to live permanently with [P] as their spouse or civil partner or unmarried partner; and

(e) have demonstrated sufficient knowledge of the English language and sufficient knowledge about life in the United Kingdom, in accordance with Appendix KOLL; and

(f) have been living together with [P] in the UK in a marriage or civil partnership, or in an unmarried partnership, for at least the applicable specified period in line with paragraphs ECAA 6.2 and ECAA 6.3; and

(g) not fall for refusal under Part 9: grounds for refusal.]

Note: Paragraph substituted from 23:00 on 31 December 2020 subject to savings for applications made before that time (HC 813).

ECAA 6.2. The specified period for spouses, civil partners or unmarried partners of ECAA workers or business persons is a continuous period of 5 years. The 5 year period may consist of a combination of leave as either:

(a) the spouse, civil partner or unmarried partner of an ECAA worker or business person; or

(b) the spouse, civil partner or unmarried partner of an ECAA worker or business person during a period when the sponsor had leave under another category of these Rules.

[**ECAA 6.3.** During the specified period the applicant must:

(a) have been in a relationship with the same ECAA worker or business person for the entire period; and

(b) have spent the most recent part of the 5 year period with leave as the spouse, civil partner or unmarried partner of that ECAA worker or business person; and

(c) have spent the remainder of the 5 year period, where applicable, with leave as the spouse or civil partner or unmarried partner of that person at a time when that person had leave under another category of the rules; and

[(d) substitute 'not have been absent from the UK for more than 180 days during any 12 month period, subject to the exceptions at ECAA 2.]]

Note: Paragraph substituted from 23:00 on 31 December 2020 subject to savings for applications made before that time (HC 813). Sub-paragraph (d) substituted from 6 April 2021 (HC 1248).

[Indefinite leave to remain as the partner of an ECAA worker]

ECAA 6.4. Indefinite leave to remain may be granted provided that the Secretary of State is satisfied that each of the requirements of paragraph ECAA 6.1 are met.

Note: Amendment to heading substituted from 23:00 on 31 December 2020 subject to savings for applications made before that time (HC 813). Heading substituted from 6 April 2021 (HC 1248).

[Refusal of indefinite leave to remain as the spouse, civil partner or unmarried partner of an ECAA worker]

[**ECAA 6.5.** Indefinite leave to remain for the family member of an ECAA worker is to be refused if the Secretary of State is not satisfied that each of the requirements of ECAA 6.1. are met.]

Note: Amendment to heading and paragraph from 23:00 on 31 December 2020 subject to savings for applications made before that time (HC 813). Heading and paragraph substituted from 6 April 2021 (HC 1248).

Part ECAA 7. Requirements for partner of [ECAA worker] or ECAA business persons applying for further leave to remain

Note: Words in heading substituted from 23:00 on 31 December 2020 subject to savings for applications made before that time (HC 813).

ECAA 7.1. The applicant must:

[(a) be the spouse, civil partner or unmarried partner of an ECAA worker or ECAA business person who:

(i) has been granted indefinite leave to remain in line with the ECAA guidance in force prior to 16 March 2018; or

(ii) has been granted indefinite leave to remain under paragraph ECAA 3.2 or ECAA 4.5 of this Appendix; or

(iii) has British citizenship having previously been granted indefinite leave to remain under either provision specified in (i) or (ii) of this paragraph; and]

[(b) have last been granted leave to remain as a dependent of an ECAA worker or ECAA business person; or]

(c) having last been granted leave to remain as a dependant of an ECAA business person, is currently in the United Kingdom without leave as, at the time of that leave expiring:

(i) they did not qualify for indefinite leave to remain in line with the ECAA guidance in force prior to 16 March 2018 due to not meeting the 2 years residency requirement; and

(ii) did not qualify for further limited leave to remain as the dependant of an ECAA business person due to that ECAA business person having acquired indefinite leave to remain; and

[(d) be living together and in a subsisting relationship with the ECAA worker or business person to whom leave to remain was granted; and]

[(e) not fall for refusal under Part 9: grounds for refusal; and]

(f) their sponsor has adequate accommodation for the parties and can maintain any dependants without recourse to public funds; and

(g) be registered with the police where appropriate; and

(h) must not be in the UK in breach of immigration laws except that:

(i) where paragraph 39E of these Rules applies, any current period of overstaying will be disregarded; or

(ii) where paragraph ECAA 7.1(c) applies, any current period of overstaying will be disregarded.

Note: Sub-paragraphs (a), (b), (d) and (e) substituted from 23:00 on 31 December 2020 subject to savings for applications made before that time (HC 813).

[Granting further leave to remain as the partner of an ECAA worker or ECAA business person]

ECAA 7.2. Leave to remain for up to 3 years will be granted provided that the Secretary of State is satisfied that each of the requirements of [. . .]ECAA 7.1 are met.

Note: Amendment to heading; word deleted from 23:00 on 31 December 2020 subject to savings for applications made before that time (HC 813). Heading substituted from 6 April 2021 (HC 1248).

[Refusal of further leave to remain as an ECAA worker or ECAA business person]

[**ECAA 7.3.** Leave to remain for family members of an ECAA worker or ECAA business person is to be refused of the Secretary of State is not satisfied that each of the requirements of ECAA 7.1. are met.]

Note: Amendment to heading and paragraph from 23:00 on 31 December 2020 subject to savings for applications made before that time (HC 813). Heading and paragraph substituted from 6 April 2021 (HC1248).

[Appendix EU: EU, other EEA and Swiss citizens and family members

Note: The implementation provisions are somewhat complex and are therefore set out in full including subsequent amendments and substitutions. See below for notes on amendments to specific provisions.

Implementation provisions from 28 August 2018 (CM 9675)

Appendix inserted from 28 August 2018 for applications made under Appendix EU on or after that date by an applicant who, at the date of application, is:

(a) An EU citizen (but not a British citizen); or

(b) A non-EU citizen who has been issued by the Secretary of State with a residence card or permanent residence card under the Immigration (European Economic Area) Regulations 2016, on the basis of an application made on or after 6 April 2015,

And, in addition, the applicant is:

(i) A student enrolled for study at, or a person on the payroll of, one of the following institutions:

Liverpool Hope University; Liverpool John Moores University; or The University of Liverpool; or

(ii) A person on the payroll of one of the following institutions:

Aintree University Hospital NHS Foundation Trust; Blackpool Teaching Hospitals NHS Foundation Trust; Countess of Chester Hospital NHS Foundation Trust; East Lancashire Hospitals NHS Trust;

Lancashire Teaching Hospitals NHS Foundation Trust; Liverpool Heart and Chest Hospital NHS Foundation Trust; Liverpool Women's NHS Foundation Trust;

Southport and Ormskirk Hospital NHS Trust;

The Royal Liverpool and Broadgreen University Hospitals NHS Trust; The Walton Centre NHS Foundation Trust;

Warrington and Halton Hospitals NHS Foundation Trust; or Wirral University Teaching Hospital NHS Foundation Trust.

Implementation provisions from 1 November 2018 (HC 1534)

Appendix EU shall have effect (except for paragraphs EU12 and EU13 and condition 2 in the table in paragraph EU14, and for the entry for 'family member of a qualifying British citizen' and for 'qualifying British citizen' in the table at Annex 1) in relation to applications made under it before 22 December 2018 by an applicant who is:

(a) An EU citizen (but not a British citizen); or

(b) A non-EU citizen who has been issued by the Secretary of State with a residence card or permanent residence card under the Immigration (European Economic Area) Regulations 2016, on the basis of an application made on or after 6 April 2015,

where, at the date of application, the applicant also meets one of the criteria set out in (i) to (xv) below which apply from the following dates:

From 1 November 2018:

(i) A person employed or engaged by one of the following institutions: Liverpool Hope University;

Liverpool John Moores University; or The University of Liverpool; or

(ii) A person employed or engaged by one of the following institutions: Aintree University Hospital NHS Foundation Trust;

Blackpool Teaching Hospitals NHS Foundation Trust; Countess of Chester Hospital NHS Foundation Trust; East Lancashire Hospitals NHS Trust;

Lancashire Teaching Hospitals NHS Foundation Trust; Liverpool Heart and Chest Hospital NHS Foundation Trust; Liverpool Women's NHS Foundation Trust;

Manchester University NHS Foundation Trust; Salford Royal NHS Foundation Trust Southport and Ormskirk Hospital NHS Trust; Stockport NHS Foundation Trust;

The Royal Liverpool and Broadgreen University Hospitals NHS Trust; The Walton Centre NHS Foundation Trust;

Warrington and Halton Hospitals NHS Foundation Trust; or Wirral University Teaching Hospital NHS Foundation Trust; or

In addition, from 15 November 2018:

(iii) A person employed or engaged by a Higher Education Institution or Overseas Higher Education Institution on the Tier 4 Register of Licensed Sponsors; or

A child being looked after (within the meaning of section 22(1) of the Children Act 1989) by, or a person who was such a child and is eligible for support or assistance under the Children Act 1989 (or under regulations made under that Act) from, one of the following local authorities:

Kent County Council; Lincolnshire County Council; London Borough of Haringey;

London Borough of Waltham Forest; or Sheffield City Council; or

(iv) A person receiving support from one of the following organisations:

Ashiana Sheffield, Knowle House, 4 Norfolk Park Road, Sheffield, S2 3QE; Coram Children's Legal Centre, Riverside Office Centre, Century House North, North Station Road, Colchester, CO1 1RE;

East European Resource Centre, Room 18-19, 238-246 King Street, London, W6 0RF;

Rights of Women, 52-54 Featherstone Street, London, EC1Y 8RT;

St Vincent Support Centre, Curtis Building, 4 Barking Avenue, Leeds, LS9 9LF;

The Cardinal Hume Centre, 3-7 Arneway Street, Horseferry Road, London, SW1P 2BG; or

The Roma Support Group, Alan Shelley House, 318 Barking Road, London, E13 8HL; or

In addition, from 29 November 2018:

(v) A person employed or engaged by one of the following institutions or organisations:

An NHS Foundation Trust in England; An NHS Trust in England;

Care Quality Commission; Health Education England; Health Research Authority;

Human Fertilisation and Embryology Authority; Human Tissue Authority;

Medicines and Healthcare Products Regulatory Agency; National Institute for Health and Care Excellence;

NHS Blood and Transplant;

NHS Business Services Authority; NHS Counter Fraud Authority;

NHS Digital (the Health and Social Care Information Centre); NHS England (the NHS Commissioning Board);

NHS Improvement (Monitor and the NHS Trust Development Authority); NHS Resolution (the NHS Litigation Authority); or

Public Health England; or

A person employed or engaged by one of the following institutions or organisations:

A Local Health Board in Wales;

Health Education & Improvement Wales; Public Health Wales;

The Welsh Ambulance Service; or Velindre NHS Trust; or

(vi) A person employed or engaged by one of the following institutions or organisations:

A Health Board or Special Health Board constituted under section 2 of the National Health Service (Scotland) Act 1978;

Common Services Agency for the Scottish Health Service (established under section 10 of that Act);

Healthcare Improvement Scotland (established by section 10 of that Act); Social Care and Social Work Improvement Scotland (known as the Care Inspectorate) established under section 44 of the Public Services (Reform) (Scotland) Act 2010; or

Scottish Social Services Council established under section 43 of the Regulation of Care (Scotland) Act 2001; or

(vii) A person employed or engaged by one of the following institutions or organisations:

A Health and Social Care Trust in Northern Ireland; Northern Ireland Blood Transfusion Service; Northern Ireland Guardian Ad Litem Agency;

Northern Ireland Medical and Dental Training Agency; Northern Ireland Practice and Education Committee; Northern Ireland Social Care Council;

Patient and Client Council;

Regional Agency for Public Health and Social Well-being (the Public Health Agency);

Regional Business Services Organisation; Regional Health and Social Care Board; or Regulation and Quality Improvement Authority; or

(viii) A person who is employed:

(a) To provide, or to support the provision of, regulated activities as prescribed in Schedule 1 (read with Schedule 2) to the Health and Social Care Act 2008 (Regulated Activities) Regulations 2014 (S.I. 2014/2936), and who is also employed or engaged by an institution or organisation registered with the Care Quality Commission; or

(b) For the purposes of an establishment or agency in Wales regulated under Part 2 of the Care Standards Act 2000; or

For the purposes of a service regulated under Part 1 of the Regulation and Inspection of Social Care (Wales) Act 2016; or

(ix) A person who is employed or engaged by a party to:

(a) A general medical services contract to provide primary medical services, or an agreement for the provision of primary medical services under section 50 of the NHS (Wales) Act 2006; or

(b) A general dental services contract to provide primary dental services, or an agreement for the provision of primary dental services under section 64 of the NHS (Wales) Act 2006; or

(x) A person who:

(a) Is providing care services as defined in section 47(1) of the Public Services Reform (Scotland) Act 2010 and registered under that Act; or

(b) Is employed or engaged by an organisation registered with Social Care and Social Work Improvement Scotland; or

(c) Is, or who is employed or engaged in connection with the provision of services under the National Health Service (Scotland) Act 1978 by, a party (other than a Health Board) to:

- an arrangement to provide services under section 2C of that Act;
- an agreement to provide services under section 17C of that Act;
- a contract to provide services under section 17J of that Act; or
- an arrangement to provide services under section 25, 26 or 27 of that Act; or

(xi) A person who is employed or engaged by a General Practitioner Federation or by any entity with which the Northern Ireland Regional Health and Social Care Board has a contract or an arrangement under the Health and Personal Social Services (Northern Ireland) Order 1972 to provide Family Practitioner Services; or

(xii) A person who is employed or engaged by a body registered with, or monitored or inspected by, the Regulation and Quality Improvement Authority, and who, if that body were in England and they were employed or engaged by it, would meet the criteria set out in (x)(a), above; or

(xiii) A person employed or engaged by, or registered with, one of the following organisations:

General Chiropractic Council; General Dental Council; General Medical Council; General Optical Council; General Osteopathic Council;

General Pharmaceutical Council; Health and Care Professions Council; Northern Ireland Social Care Council; Nursing and Midwifery Council;

Pharmaceutical Society of Northern Ireland;

Scottish Social Services Council (under the Regulation of Care (Scotland) Act 2001); or

Social Care Wales.

Implementation provisions from 21 January 2019 (HC 1849)

Appendix EU shall have effect (except for paragraphs EU12 and EU13 and condition 2 in the table in paragraph EU14, and for the entry for 'family member of a qualifying British citizen', for 'qualifying British citizen' and for 'relevant naturalised British citizen', and for sub-paragraph (c) in the entry for 'relevant EU citizen', in the table at Annex 1) in relation to applications made under it on or after 21 January 2019 by an applicant who, at the date of application, is:

(a) An EU citizen (but not a British citizen) who has a valid passport as a national of that EU country; or

(b) A non-EU citizen who has been issued by the Secretary of State with a residence card or permanent residence card under the Immigration (European Economic Area) Regulations 2016, on the basis of an application made on or after 6 April 2015.

Implementation provisions from 30 March 2019 (HC 1919)

Phased implementation wording substituted from 0700 on 30 March 2019.

Substitution of Appendix shall take effect:

(i) subject to sub-paragraph (iii), below, at 0700 on 30 March 2019 in relation to applications made under Appendix EU within the UK (at which time the Implementation provisions in the Statement of Changes in Immigration Rules presented to Parliament on 20 December 2018 in HC 1849 shall cease to have effect);

(ii) subject to sub-paragraph (iii), below, at 0700 on 9 April 2019 in relation to applications made under Appendix EU outside the UK; and

(iii) on 1 May 2019 in relation to applications made under Appendix EU which rely on sub-paragraph (a)(v) in condition 3 in the table in paragraph EU11, sub-paragraph (a)(v) in condition 1 in the table in paragraph EU14 or otherwise on the entry for 'person with a Zambrano right to reside' in the table at Annex 1.

However, in relation to the change set out in paragraph EU2 of this statement:

(i) if an application has been made under Appendix EU on or after 1 November 2018 and before 22 December 2018, the application will be decided in accordance with the Immigration Rules in force on 21 December 2018; and

(ii) if an application has been made under Appendix EU on or after 21 January 2019 and before 0700 on 30 March 2019, the application will be decided in accordance with the Immigration Rules in force before 0700 on 30 March 2019.

Implementation provisions from 2 April 2019 (HC 2099)

The changes to Appendix EU (as substituted by paragraph EU2 of the Statement of Changes in Immigration Rules presented to Parliament on 7 March 2019 in HC 1919) shall take effect on 2 April 2019.

Implementation provisions (HC 170)

Appendix EU substituted:

(i) subject to sub-paragraph (ii), below, on 31 October 2019; and

(ii) in relation to applications made under Part 2 of Appendix EU:

(a) on the later of 31 October 2019 or the date on which the United Kingdom withdraws from the European Union without a Withdrawal Agreement, as defined in Annex A to Part 2, where the applicant is an 'EEA citizen' (as defined in Annex A); and

(b) on the later of 4 December 2019 or a date thereafter on which the United Kingdom withdraws from the European Union without a Withdrawal Agreement, as defined in Annex A to Part 2, where the applicant is a 'relevant family member' (as defined in Annex A).

Amendments from 1 November 2018 subject to savings for applications made before that date (HC 1534). Amendments from 21 January 2019 subject to savings where an application was made on or after 1 November 2018 and before 22 December 2018 where the Rules in force on 21 December 2018 will apply (HC 1849).

Amendments from 21 January 2019 subject to savings where an application was made on or after 1 November 2018 and before 22 December 2018 where the Rules in force on 21 December 2018 will apply (HC 1849).

Appendix substituted in accordance with phased implementation provisions set out above (HC 1919).

Amendments from 2 April 2019 (HC 2099).

Appendix substituted from 1 October 2019 (HC 2631).

Appendix substituted from 20 February 2020 subject to savings for applications made before that date (HC 56).

Appendix substituted from 6 April 2020 (HC 120).

Amendments from 24 August 2020 and from 4 June 2020 (CP 232).

Appendix substituted from 23:00 on 31 December 2020 (except Annex 3 which takes effect from 09:00 on 1 December 2020) subject to savings for applications made before that time (HC 813).

Annex 3 substituted from 6 April 2021 (HC 1248).

Purpose

EU1. This Appendix sets out the basis on which an **EEA citizen** and their family members, and the family members of a **qualifying British citizen**, will, if they apply under it, be granted indefinite leave to enter or remain or limited leave to enter or remain.

Requirements and procedure

Requirements for indefinite leave to enter or remain other than as a joining family member of a relevant sponsor

EU2. The applicant will be granted indefinite leave to enter (where the application is made outside the UK) or indefinite leave to remain (where the application is made within the UK) where:

- A valid application has been made in accordance with paragraph EU9;
- The applicant meets the eligibility requirements for indefinite leave to enter or remain in accordance with paragraph EU11 or EU12; and
- The applicant is not to be refused on grounds of suitability in accordance with paragraph EU15 or EU16.

Requirements for indefinite leave to enter or remain as a joining family member of a relevant sponsor

EU2A. The applicant will be granted indefinite leave to enter (where the application is made outside the UK) or indefinite leave to remain (where the application is made within the UK) as a **joining family member of a relevant sponsor** where:

- A valid application has been made in accordance with paragraph EU9;
- The applicant meets the eligibility requirements for indefinite leave to enter or remain in accordance with paragraph EU11A; and
- The application is not to be refused on grounds of suitability in accordance with paragraph EU15 or EU16.

Requirements for limited leave to enter or remain other than as a joining family member of a relevant sponsor

EU3. The applicant will be granted five years' limited leave to enter (where the application is made outside the UK) or five years' limited leave to remain (where the application is made within the UK) where:

- A valid application has been made in accordance with paragraph EU9;
- The applicant does not meet the eligibility requirements for indefinite leave to enter or remain in accordance with paragraph EU11 or EU12, but meets the eligibility requirements for limited leave to enter or remain in accordance with paragraph EU14; and
- The applicant is not to be refused on grounds of suitability in accordance with paragraph EU15 or EU16.

Requirements for limited leave to enter or remain as a joining family member of a relevant sponsor

EU3A. The applicant will be granted five years' limited leave to enter (where the application is made outside the UK) or five years' limited leave to remain (where the application is made within the UK) as a joining family member of a relevant sponsor where:

- A valid application has been made in accordance with paragraph EU9;
- The applicant does not meet the eligibility requirements for indefinite leave to enter or remain in accordance with paragraph EU11A, but meets the eligibility requirements for limited leave to enter or remain in accordance with paragraph EU14A; and
- The application is not to be refused on grounds of suitability in accordance with paragraph EU15 or EU16.

Other provisions as to requirements and procedure

EU4. Where a person has been granted limited leave to enter or remain under this Appendix:

- They must continue to meet the eligibility requirements for that leave which they met at the **date of application** (except for any which related to their dependency as a **child, dependent parent** or **dependent relative**) or meet other eligibility requirements for limited leave to enter or remain in accordance with paragraph EU14 (where they have been granted limited leave to enter or remain under paragraph EU3) or In accordance with paragraph EU14A (where they have been granted limited leave to enter or remain under paragraph EU3A); and
- They remain able to apply for indefinite leave to enter or remain under this Appendix and will be granted this where the requirements in paragraph EU2 (where they have been granted limited leave to enter or remain under paragraph EU3) or paragraph EU2A (whether they have been granted limited leave to enter or remain under paragraph EU3A) are met.

[**EU5.** Paragraphs 18 to 19A of the Immigration Rules (returning residents) do not apply to indefinite leave to enter or remain granted under this Appendix. A person granted such leave may resume their residence in the UK where, having been absent from the UK and Islands, that leave has not lapsed under article 13 of the Immigration (Leave to Enter and Remain) Order 2000.]

Note: Paragraph substituted from 6 April 2021 (HC 1248).

EU6. A valid application made under this Appendix which does not meet the requirements for indefinite leave to enter or remain or limited leave to enter or remain will be refused.

EU7. (1) Annex 1 sets out definitions which apply to this Appendix. Any provision made elsewhere in the Immigration Rules for those terms, or for other matters for which this Appendix makes provision, does not apply to an application made under this Appendix.

[(2) Where this Appendix requires that a document, card or other evidence is valid (or that it remained valid for the period of residence relied upon), or has not been cancelled or invalidated or has not ceased to be effective, it does not matter that the person concerned no longer has the right to enter or reside under the **EEA Regulations** (or under the equivalent provision in **the Islands**), on which basis the document, card or other evidence was issued, by virtue of the revocation of those Regulations (or equivalent provision in the Islands).]

Note: Sub-paragraph (2) substituted from 6 April 2021 (HC 1248).

EU8. Annex 2 applies to the consideration by the Secretary of State of a valid application made under this Appendix.

Valid application

EU9. A valid application has been made under this Appendix where:

(a) It has been made using the **required application process;**

(b) The **required proof of identity and nationality** has been provided, where the application is made within the UK;

(c) The **required proof of entitlement** to apply from outside the UK has been provided, where the application is made outside the UK; and

(d) The **required biometrics** have been provided.

[**EU10.** (1) An application made under this Appendix will be rejected as invalid where it does not meet the requirements in paragraph EU9.

(2) Paragraph 34BB of these Rules does not apply to applications made under this Appendix. Where a further valid application is made under this Appendix before a previous such application has been decided, the further application will be treated as an application to vary the previous application and only the latest application will be considered.

(3) Where a valid application is made under this Appendix before a previous valid application made under another part of or outside the Immigration Rules has been decided (or where a valid application is made under another part of or outside the Immigration Rules, or varied by a further such application, before a previous valid application made under this Appendix has been decided), both applications will be considered.

(4) Where both applications considered in accordance with sub-paragraph (3) above fall to be granted, the Secretary of State will inform the applicant that they satisfy the relevant criteria in respect of both applications and ask them to confirm which application they want to be decided and which they want to be treated as withdrawn. If the applicant does not so confirm within 14 days, the latest application will be decided and the other treated as withdrawn.]

Note: Paragraph substituted from 6 April 2022 (HC 1118).

Eligibility for indefinite leave to enter or remain

Persons eligible for indefinite leave to enter or remain as a relevant EEA citizen or their family member, or as a person with a derivative right to reside or with a Zambrano right to reside

EU11. The applicant meets the eligibility requirements for indefinite leave to enter or remain as a **relevant EEA citizen** or their family member (or as a **person with a derivative**

right to reside or a **person with a Zambrano right to reside**) where the Secretary of State is satisfied, including (where applicable) by the **required evidence of family relationship**, that, at the date of application and in an application made by the **required date**, one of conditions 1 to 7 set out in the following table is met:

Condition	Is met where:
1.	(a) The applicant: (i) is a relevant EEA citizen; or (ii) is (or, as the case may be, was) a **family member of a relevant EEA citizen**; or (iii) is (or, as the case may be, was) a **family member who has retained the right of residence** by virtue of a relationship with a relevant EEA citizen; and (b) The applicant has a **documented right of permanent residence**; and [(c) Since they did, no **supervening event** has occurred in respect of the applicant]
2.	(a) The applicant is: (i) a relevant EEA citizen; or (ii) a family member of a relevant EEA citizen; or (iii) a family member who has retained the right of residence by virtue of a relationship with a relevant EEA citizen; and (b) There is **valid evidence of their indefinite leave to enter or remain**
3.	(a) The applicant: (i) is a relevant EEA citizen; or (ii) is (or, as the case may be, for the relevant period was) a family member of a relevant EEA citizen; or (iii) is (or, as the case may be, for the relevant period was) a family member who has retained the right of residence by virtue of a relationship with a relevant EEA citizen; or (iv) is a person with a derivative right to reside; or (v) is a person with a Zambrano right to reside; or (vi) is a **person who had a derivative or Zambrano right to reside**; and (b) The applicant has completed a **continuous qualifying period** of five years in any (or any combination) of those categories; and [(c) Since then no supervening event has occurred in respect of the applicant]
4.	(a) The applicant is a relevant EEA citizen who is a **person who has ceased activity** ; and (b) Since they did so, no supervening event has occurred

Condition	Is met where:
5.	(a) The applicant is (or, as the case may be, was) a family member of a relevant EEA citizen; and (b) The relevant EEA citizen is a person who has ceased activity; and (c) (i) Where the date of application by the family member is before 1 July 2021, the relevant EEA citizen: (aa) meets the requirements of sub-paragraph (b) of the applicable definition of relevant EEA citizen in Annex 1; or (bb) meets the requirements of sub-paragraph (d)(ii)(bb) of the applicable definition of relevant EEA citizen in Annex 1; or (cc) meets the requirements of sub-paragraph (e)(ii) or (e)(iii) of the applicable definition of relevant EEA citizen in Annex 1; or [(dd) is a relevant naturalised British citizen (in accordance with sub-paragraphs (b), (c) and (d) of the relevant definition in Annex 1); or] (ii) Where the date of application by the family member is on or after 1 July 2021, the relevant EEA citizen meets the following requirements of the applicable definition of relevant EEA citizen in Annex 1: (aa) sub-paragraph (a)(ii)(aa); or (bb) sub-paragraph (b)(ii)(aa); or (cc) sub-paragraph (c)(i); or (dd) sub-paragraph (d)(iii)(aa); or (ee) sub-paragraph (e)(i)(bb)(aaa), (e)(i)(bb)(ccc) or (e)(ii)(bb)(aaa); [. . .] (d) Sub-paragraph (a) above was met at the point at which the relevant EEA citizen became a person who has ceased activity; and (e) The applicant was resident in the UK and Islands for a continuous qualifying period immediately before the relevant EEA citizen became a person who has ceased activity; and [(f) Since the relevant EEA citizen became a person who has ceased activity, no supervening event has occurred in respect of the applicant]
6.	(a) The applicant is a family member of a relevant EEA citizen; and (b) The relevant EEA citizen has died and was resident in the UK as a **worker** or **self-employed person** at the time of their death; and (c) The relevant EEA citizen was resident in the UK and Islands for a continuous qualifying period of at least two years immediately before dying, or the death was the result of an accident at work or an occupational disease; and (d) The applicant was resident in the UK with the relevant EEA citizen immediately before their death; and (e) Since the death of the relevant EEA citizen, no supervening event has occurred

Condition	Is met where:
7.	(a) The applicant is a family member of a relevant EEA citizen and is a child under the age of 21 years of a relevant EEA citizen (or of their **spouse** or **civil partner**), and either: (i) the marriage was contracted or the civil partnership was formed before the **specified date**; or (ii) the person who is now their spouse or civil partner was the **durable partner** of the relevant EEA citizen before the specified date (the definition of durable partner in Annex 1 being met before that date rather than at the date of application) and the partnership remained durable at the specified date; and (b) (i) Where the date of application by the family member is before 1 July 2021, the relevant EEA citizen (or, as the case may be, their spouse or civil partner): (aa) has been granted indefinite leave to enter or remain under paragraph EU2 of this Appendix (or under its equivalent in [the Islands]), which has not lapsed or been cancelled, revoked or invalidated (or is being granted that leave under that paragraph of this Appendix or under its equivalent in the Islands); or [(bb) meets the requirements of sub-paragraph (b)(ii) of the applicable definition of relevant EEA citizen in Annex 1 (where the relevant EEA citizen is an Irish citizen); or] (cc) meets the requirements of sub-paragraph (d)(ii)(bb) of the applicable definition of relevant EEA citizen in Annex 1; or (dd) meets the requirements of sub-paragraph (e)(ii) or (e)(iii) of the applicable definition of relevant EEA citizen in Annex 1; or (ee) meets the requirements of sub-paragraph (f)(ii) of the applicable definition of relevant EEA citizen in Annex 1; or (ff) is a relevant naturalised British citizen (in accordance with sub-paragraphs (b), (c) and (d) of the relevant definition in Annex 1); or (ii) Where the date of application by the family member is on or after 1 July 2021, the relevant EEA citizen (or, as the case may be, their spouse or civil partner) meets the following requirements of the applicable definition of relevant EEA citizen in Annex 1: (aa) sub-paragraph (a)(ii)(aa); or [(bb) sub-paragraph (b)(ii)(aa) (where the relevant EEA citizen is an Irish citizen); or] (cc) sub-paragraph (c)(i); or (dd) sub-paragraph (d)(iii)(aa); or (ee) sub-paragraph (e)(i)(bb)(aaa), (e)(i)(bb)(ccc) or (e)(ii)(bb)(aaa); or (ff) sub-paragraph (f)(ii)(aa)

Note: Words in (b)(i)(aa), sub-paragraphs (b)(i)(bb) and (b)(ii)(bb) in condition 7 substituted from 6 April 2021 (HC 1248). Words in condition 5 substituted, words in condition 5 deleted; (b)(i)(bb) of condition 7 substituted from 6 October 2021 (HC 617). Condition 1(c), condition 3(c), condition 5(f) substituted from 6 April 2022 (HC 1118).

Persons eligible for indefinite leave to enter or remain as a joining family member of a relevant sponsor

EU11A. The applicant meets the eligibility requirements for indefinite leave to enter or remain as a joining family member of a relevant sponsor where [. . .]the Secretary of State is satisfied, including by the required evidence of family relationship, that, at the date of application and in an application made after the specified date and by the required date, one of conditions 1 to 4 set out in the following table is met:

Condition	Is met where:
1.	(a) The applicant: (i) is (or, as the case may be, for the relevant period was) a joining family member of a relevant sponsor; or (ii) is (or, as the case may be, for the relevant period was) a family member who has retained the right of residence by virtue of a relationship with a **relevant sponsor** ; and (b) The applicant has completed a continuous qualifying period of five years which began after the specified date, in either (or any combination) of those categories; and [(c) Since then no supervening event has occurred in respect of the applicant]
2.	(a) The applicant is (or, as the case may be, was) a joining family member of a relevant sponsor; and (b) The relevant sponsor is a person who has ceased activity; and (c) (i) Where the date of application is before 1 July 2021, the relevant sponsor: (aa) meets the requirements of sub-paragraph (a)(i)(aa) or (a)(ii)(bb) of the definition of relevant sponsor in Annex 1; or (bb) meets the requirements of sub-paragraph (a)(iv)(bb) or (a)(iv)(cc) of the definition of relevant sponsor in Annex 1; or [(cc) is a relevant naturalised British citizen (in accordance with sub-paragraphs (b), (c) and (d) of the relevant definition in Annex 1); or] (ii) Where the date of application is on or after 1 July 2021, the relevant sponsor meets the following requirements of the definition of relevant sponsor in Annex 1: (aa) sub-paragraph (b)(i)(aa); or (bb) sub-paragraph (b)(ii)(aa); or (cc) sub-paragraph (b)(iii)(aa); or (dd) sub-paragraph (b)(iv)(bb)(aaa), (b)(iv)(bb)(bbb) or (b)(v)(bb)(aaa); or (ee) sub-paragraph (b)(vi)(aa); and (d) Sub-paragraph (a) above was met at the point at which the relevant sponsor became a person who has ceased activity; and (e) Immediately before the relevant sponsor became a person who has ceased activity, the applicant was resident in the UK and Islands for a continuous qualifying period which began after the specified date; and [(f) Since the relevant sponsor became a person who has ceased activity, no supervening event has occurred in respect of the applicant]

Condition	Is met where:
3.	(a) The applicant is a joining family member of a relevant sponsor; and (b) The relevant sponsor has died and was resident in the UK as a worker or self-employed person at the time of their death; and (c) The relevant sponsor was resident in the UK and Islands for a continuous qualifying period of at least two years immediately before dying, or the death was the result of an accident at work or an occupational disease; and (d) The applicant was resident in the UK with the relevant sponsor after the specified date and immediately before their death; and (e) Since the death of the relevant sponsor, no supervening event has occurred
4.	(a) (i) The applicant is a joining family member of a relevant sponsor and is a child under the age of 21 years of the relevant sponsor; and (ii) (aa) Where the date of application is before 1 July 2021, the relevant sponsor: (aaa) meets the requirements of sub-paragraph (a)(i)(aa) of the definition of relevant sponsor in Annex 1; or [(bbb) meets the requirements of sub-paragraph (a)(ii)(bb) of the definition of relevant sponsor in Annex 1 (where the relevant sponsor is an Irish citizen); or] (ccc) meets the requirements of sub-paragraph (a)(iv)(bb) or (a)(iv)(cc) of the definition of relevant sponsor in Annex 1; or (ddd) meets the requirements of sub-paragraph (a)(v)(bb) of the definition of relevant sponsor in Annex 1; or (eee) is a relevant naturalised British citizen (in accordance with sub-paragraphs (b), (c) and (d) of the relevant definition in Annex 1); or (bb) Where the date of application is on or after 1 July 2021, the relevant sponsor meets the following requirements of the definition of relevant sponsor in Annex 1: (aaa) sub-paragraph (b)(i)(aa); or (bbb) sub-paragraph (b)(ii)(aa); or (ccc) sub-paragraph (b)(iii)(aa); or (ddd) sub-paragraph (b)(iv)(bb)(aaa), (b)(iv)(bb)(bbb) or (b)(v)(bb)(aaa); or (eee) sub-paragraph (b)(vi)(aa); or (b) (i) The applicant is a joining family member of a relevant sponsor and is a child under the age of 21 years of the spouse or civil partner of the relevant sponsor (in accordance with sub-paragraph (a) of the definition of family member of a relevant EEA citizen in Annex 1, substituting 'relevant sponsor' for each reference in that sub-paragraph to 'relevant EEA citizen'); and (ii) The spouse or civil partner has been or is being granted indefinite leave to enter or remain under paragraph EU2 of this Appendix; or (c) (i) The applicant is a joining family member of a relevant sponsor and is a child under the age of 21 years of the spouse or civil partner of the relevant sponsor (in accordance, in respect of the spouse or civil partner, with the first sub-paragraph (a), together with either the second sub-paragraph (a) or sub-paragraph (b)(i) or (b)(ii), of the definition of joining family member of a relevant sponsor in Annex 1); and (ii) The spouse or civil partner has been or is being granted indefinite leave to enter or remain under paragraph EU2A of this Appendix

Note: Words in introduction, (c)(i)(dd) in condition 2 deleted, (c)(i)(cc) in condition 2, (a)(ii)(aa)(bbb) in condition 4 substituted from 6 October 2021 (HC 617). Condition 1(c), condition 2(f) substituted from 6 April 2022 (HC 1118).

Persons eligible for indefinite leave to enter or remain as a family member of a qualifying British citizen

EU12. The applicant meets the eligibility requirements for indefinite leave to enter or remain as a **family member of a qualifying British citizen**, or as a family member who has retained the right of residence by virtue of a relationship with a qualifying British citizen, where the Secretary of State is satisfied, including by the required evidence of family relationship, that, at the date of application and in an application made by the required date, one of conditions 1 to 4 set out in the following table is met:

Condition	Is met where:
1.	(a) The applicant is (or, as the case may be, was): (i) a family member of a qualifying British citizen; or (ii) a family member who has retained the right of residence by virtue of a relationship with a qualifying British citizen; and (b) The applicant has a documented right of permanent residence; and [(c) No supervening event has occurred in respect of the applicant]
2.	(a) The applicant is: • a family member of a qualifying British citizen; or • a family member who has retained the right of residence by virtue of a relationship with a qualifying British citizen; and (b) There is valid evidence of their indefinite leave to enter or remain
3.	(a) The applicant is (or, as the case may be, for the relevant period was): • a family member of a qualifying British citizen; or • a family member who has retained the right of residence by virtue of a relationship with a qualifying British citizen; and (b) The applicant has completed a continuous qualifying period in the UK of five years in either (or any combination) of those categories; and (c) The applicant was, for any period in which they were present in the UK as a family member of a qualifying British citizen relied upon under sub-paragraph (b), lawfully resident by virtue of regulation 9(1) to (6) of the EEA Regulations (regardless of whether in the UK the qualifying British citizen was a qualified person under regulation 6 of the EEA Regulations); and [(d) Since completing the continuous qualifying period of five years, no supervening event has occurred in respect of the applicant]
4.	(a) The applicant is a child under the age of 21 years of the spouse or civil partner of the qualifying British citizen, and either: (i) the marriage was contracted or the civil partnership was formed before the **date and time of withdrawal** ; or (ii) the person who is now their spouse or civil partner was the durable partner of the qualifying British citizen before the date and time of withdrawal (the definition of durable partner in Annex 1 being met before then rather than at the date of application) and the partnership remained durable at the date and time of withdrawal; and

Condition	Is met where:
	(b) The applicant is in the UK lawfully by virtue of regulation 9(1) to (6) of the EEA Regulations (regardless of whether in the UK the qualifying British citizen is a qualified person under regulation 6 of the EEA Regulations); and (c) The spouse or civil partner has been or is being granted indefinite leave to enter or remain under this Appendix

Note: Condition 1(c), condition 3(d) substituted from 6 April 2022 (HC 1118).

EU13. The reference to the applicant completing a continuous qualifying period of five years:

- In condition 3 in the table in paragraph EU12 can include a period (or combination of periods) during which the applicant was a relevant EEA citizen, a family member of a relevant EEA citizen, a family member who has retained the right of residence by virtue of a relationship with a relevant EEA citizen, a person with a derivative right to reside or a person with a Zambrano right to reside before becoming the family member of a qualifying British citizen (or thereafter a family member who has retained the right of residence by virtue of a relationship with a qualifying British citizen); and
- In condition 3 in the table in paragraph EU11 can include a period during which the applicant was a family member of a qualifying British citizen or a family member who has retained the right of residence by virtue of a relationship with a qualifying British citizen before becoming (as the case may be) a relevant EEA citizen, a family member of a relevant EEA citizen (or thereafter a family member who has retained the right of residence by virtue of a relationship with a relevant EEA citizen), a person with a derivative right to reside or a person with a Zambrano right to reside.

Eligibility for limited leave to enter or remain

Persons eligible for limited leave to enter or remain as a relevant EEA citizen or their family member, as a person with a derivative right to reside or with a Zambrano right to reside or as a family member of a qualifying British citizen

EU14. The applicant meets the eligibility requirements for limited leave to enter or remain where the Secretary of State is satisfied, including (where applicable) by the required evidence of family relationship, that, at the date of application and in an application made by the required date, condition 1 or 2 set out in the following table is met:

Condition	Is met where:
1.	(a) The applicant is: (i) a relevant EEA citizen; or (ii) a family member of a relevant EEA citizen; or (iii) a family member who has retained the right of residence by virtue of a relationship with a relevant EEA citizen; or (iv) a person with a derivative right to reside; or (v) a person with a Zambrano right to reside; and (b) The applicant is not eligible for indefinite leave to enter or remain under paragraph EU11 of this Appendix solely because they have completed a continuous qualifying period of less than five years[; and] [(c) Where the applicant is a family member of a relevant EEA citizen, there has been no supervening event in respect of the relevant EEA citizen]

Condition	Is met where:
2.	(a) The applicant is: (i) a family member of a qualifying British citizen; or (ii) a family member who has retained the right of residence by virtue of a relationship with a qualifying British citizen; and (b) The applicant was, for any period in which they were present in the UK as a family member of a qualifying British citizen relied upon under sub-paragraph (c), lawfully resident by virtue of regulation 9(1) to (6) of the EEA Regulations (regardless of whether in the UK the qualifying British citizen was a qualified person under regulation 6 of the EEA Regulations); and (c) The applicant is not eligible for indefinite leave to enter or remain under paragraph EU12 this Appendix solely because they have completed a continuous qualifying period in the UK of less than five years

Note: Words in Condition 1(b) substituted, Condition 1(c) inserted from 6 April 2022 (HC 1118).

Persons eligible for limited leave to enter or remain as a joining family member of a relevant sponsor

EU14A. The applicant meets the eligibility requirements for limited leave to enter or remain as a joining family member of a relevant sponsor where [...]the Secretary of State is satisfied, including by the required evidence of family relationship, that, at the date of application and in an application made after the specified date and by the required date, the condition set out in the following table is met:

Condition	Is met where:
	(a) The applicant is: (i) a joining family member of a relevant sponsor; or (ii) a family member who has retained the right of residence by virtue of a relationship with a relevant sponsor; and (b) The applicant is: (i) not eligible for indefinite leave to enter under paragraph EU11A of this Appendix, where the application is made outside the UK; or (ii) not eligible for indefinite leave to remain under paragraph EU11A of this Appendix, where the application is made within the UK, solely because they have completed a continuous qualifying period of less than five years which began after the specified date[; and] [(c) Where the applicant is a joining family member of a relevant sponsor, there has been no supervening event in respect of the relevant sponsor]

Note: Words in introduction deleted from 6 October 2021 (HC 617). Words in (b) and sub-paragraph (c) inserted from 6 April 2022 (HC 1118).

Suitability

EU15. (1) An application made under this Appendix will be refused on grounds of suitability where any of the following apply at the date of decision:

(a) The applicant is subject to a **deportation order** or to a decision to make a deportation order; or

(b) The applicant is subject to an **exclusion order** or **exclusion decision**.

[(2) An application made under this Appendix will be refused on grounds of suitability [where the Secretary of State deems applicant's presence in the UK] is not conducive to the public good because of conduct committed after the specified date.]

[(3) An application made under this Appendix will be refused on grounds of suitability where at the date of decision the applicant is subject to an **Islands deportation order**.]

[(4) An application made under this Appendix may be refused on grounds of suitability where at the date of decision the applicant is subject to an **Islands exclusion decision**.]

Note: Sub-paragraph (2) substituted, (3) inserted from 6 April 2021 (HC 1248). Words in (2), sub-paragraph (3) substituted, (4) inserted from 6 April 2022 (HC 1118).

[EU16. An application made under this Appendix may be refused on grounds of suitability where, at the date of decision, the Secretary of State is satisfied that:

(a) It is proportionate to refuse the application where, in relation to the application and whether or not to the applicant's knowledge, false or misleading information, representations or documents have been submitted (including false or misleading information submitted to any person to obtain a document used in support of the application); and the information, representation or documentation is material to the decision whether or not to grant the applicant indefinite leave to enter or remain or limited leave to enter or remain under this Appendix; or

(b) It is proportionate to refuse the application where the applicant is subject to a removal decision under the EEA Regulations on the grounds of their non-exercise or misuse of rights, and the date of application under this Appendix is before 1 July 2021; or

(c) (i) The applicant:

(aa) Has previously been refused admission to the UK in accordance with regulation 23(1) of the EEA Regulations; or

(bb) Has previously been refused admission to the UK in accordance with regulation 12(1)(a) of the Citizens' Rights (Frontier Workers) (EU Exit) Regulations 2020; or

(cc) Had indefinite leave to enter or remain or limited leave to enter or remain granted under this Appendix (or limited leave to enter granted by virtue of having arrived in the UK with an entry clearance that was granted under Appendix EU (Family Permit) to these Rules) which was cancelled under paragraph 321B(b)(i) or 321B(b)(ii) of these Rules, under paragraph A3.1. or A3.2.(a) of Annex 3 to this Appendix or under paragraph A3.3. or A3.4.(a) of Annex 3 to Appendix EU (Family Permit); and

(ii) The refusal of the application is justified either:

(aa) In respect of the applicant's conduct committed before the specified date, on grounds of public policy, public security or public health in accordance with regulation 27 of the EEA Regulations, irrespective of whether the EEA Regulations apply to that person (except that in regulation 27 for "with a right of permanent residence under regulation 15' and 'has a right of permanent residence under regulation 15' read 'who meets the requirements of paragraph EU11, EU11A or EU12 of Appendix EU to the Immigration Rules'; and for 'an EEA decision' read 'a decision under paragraph EU16(c) of Appendix EU to the Immigration Rules'), and it is proportionate to refuse the application; or

[(bb) In respect of conduct committed after the specified date, where the Secretary of State deems the applicant's presence in the UK is not conducive to the public good; or]

(d) It is proportionate to refuse the application where the applicant is a [**relevant excluded person**] because of their conduct committed before the specified date and the Secretary of State is satisfied that the decision to refuse the application is justified on the grounds of public policy, public security or public health in accordance with regulation 27 of the EEA Regulations, irrespective of whether the EEA Regulations apply to that person (except that in regulation 27 for 'with a right of permanent residence under regulation 15' and 'has a right of permanent residence under regulation 15' read 'who meets the requirements of paragraph EU11, EU11A or EU12 of Appendix EU to the Immigration Rules'; and for 'an EEA decision' read 'a decision under paragraph EU16(d) of Appendix EU to the Immigration Rules'); or

(e) The applicant is a relevant excluded person because of conduct committed after the specified date.]

Note: Paragraph substituted from 6 April 2021 (HC 1248). Sub-paragraph (c)(ii)(bb), words in (d) substituted from 6 April 2022 (HC 1118).

EU17. The references in paragraphs EU15 and EU16 to an order or decision to which the applicant is subject do not include an order or decision which, at the date of decision on their application under this Appendix, has been set aside or [revoked].

Note: Words substituted from 6 April 2021 (HC 1248).

EU18. Annex 3 applies in respect of the cancellation, curtailment and revocation of leave to enter or remain granted under this Appendix.

Annex 1—Definitions

Term	Definition
adopted child	achild adopted in accordance with a **relevant adoption decision**
child	(a) the direct descendant under the age of 21 years of a relevant EEA citizen (or, as the case may be, of a qualifying British citizen or of a relevant sponsor) or of their spouse or civil partner; or (b) (i) the direct descendant aged 21 years or over of a relevant EEA citizen (or, as the case may be, of a qualifying British citizen or of a relevant sponsor) or of their spouse or civil partner; and (ii) (unless the applicant was previously granted limited leave to enter or remain under this Appendix as a child on the basis that sub-paragraph (a) above applied or under its equivalent in the Islands on that basis) dependent on (as the case may be): (aa) the relevant EEA citizen (or on their spouse or civil partner) at the date of application or, where the date of application is after the specified date, at the specified date; or (bb) on the qualifying British citizen (or on their spouse or civil partner) at the date of application or, where the date of application is after the specified date, at the specified date; or (cc) on the relevant sponsor (or on their spouse or civil partner) at the date of application

Term	Definition
	'dependent' means here that: (a) having regard to their financial and social conditions, or health, the applicant cannot, or (as the case may be) for the relevant period could not, meet their essential living needs (in whole or in part) without the financial or other material support of the relevant EEA citizen (or, as the case may be, of the qualifying British citizen or of the relevant sponsor) or of their spouse or civil partner; and (b) such support is, or (as the case may be) was, being provided to the applicant by the relevant EEA citizen (or by the qualifying British citizen) or by their spouse or civil partner; and (c) there is no need to determine the reasons for that dependence or for the recourse to that support in addition: (a) 'child' includes: (i) an **adopted child** of; or (ii) a child born through surrogacy (where recognised in UK law or Islands law) for; or (iii) a child in respect of whom a special guardianship order (within the meaning of section 14A(1) of the Children Act 1989) is in force appointing as their special guardian; or (iv) a child in respect of whom an order has been made under section 5 of the Children Act 1989 appointing as their guardian; or (v) a child subject to a permanence order made under section 80 of the Adoption and Children (Scotland) Act 2007 vesting parental responsibilities and parental rights in a person who is; or (vi) a child who has a guardian appointed under section 7 of the Children (Scotland) Act 1995, or who is living with a person pursuant to an order made under section 11 of that Act, and that guardian or other person is; or (vii) a child in respect of whom an order has been made under Article 159 of the Children (Northern Ireland) Order 1995, or in respect of whom an appointment has been made under Article 160 of that Order, appointing as their guardian a person who is; or (viii) a child who has a guardian appointed under section 12 or 14 of the Children (Guernsey and Alderney) Law 2008 or section 12 or 13 of the Children (Sark) Law 2016, or who is living in the care of a person pursuant to an order made under section 14 of the 2008 Law or section 13 of the 2016 Law, and that guardian or other person is; or (ix) a child in respect of whom an order under Article 7 of the Children (Jersey) Law 2002 is in force appointing as their guardian; or (x) a child in respect of whom a special guardianship order (within the meaning of section 17A of the Children and Young Persons Act 2001 of Tynwald) has been made appointing as their special guardian; or

Term	Definition
	(xi) a child in respect of whom an order has been made under section 6 or 7 of the Children and Young Persons Act 2001 of Tynwald appointing as their guardian, a relevant EEA citizen (or, as the case may be, a qualifying British citizen or a relevant sponsor) or their spouse or civil partner, but 'child' does not include a child cared for by a relevant EEA citizen (or, as the case may be, by a qualifying British citizen or by a relevant sponsor) or their spouse or civil partner solely by virtue of a formal or informal fostering arrangement; and (b) 'direct descendant' also includes a grandchild or greatgrandchild, other than for the purpose of meeting condition 7 in the table in paragraph EU11 of this Appendix or condition 4 in the table in paragraph EU11A or condition 4 in the table in paragraph EU12; and (c) 'spouse or civil partner' means (as the case may be) the person described in sub-paragraph (a)(i) or (a)(ii) of the entry for 'family member of a qualifying British citizen' in this table or in sub-paragraph (a) of the entry for 'family member of a relevant EEA citizen' in this table or in the first sub-paragraph (a) (together with either the second sub-paragraph (a) or sub-paragraph (b)(i) or (b)(ii)) of the entry for 'joining family member of a relevant sponsor' in this table
civil partner	(a) the person is, or (as the case may be) for the relevant period was, in a valid civil partnership (which exists or existed under or by virtue of the Civil Partnership Act 2004 or under any equivalent legislation in the Islands); or is, or (as the case may be) for the relevant period was, in a relationship registered overseas which is, or was, entitled to be treated as a civil partnership under that Act or under any equivalent legislation in the Islands, with a relevant EEA citizen (or with a qualifying British citizen or with a relevant sponsor); and (b) it is, or (as the case may be) for the relevant period was, not a **civil partnership of convenience** ; and (c) neither party has, or (as the case may be) for the relevant period had, another civil partner, a spouse or a durable partner with (in any of those circumstances) **immigration status in the UK or the Islands** based on that person's relationship with that party
civil partnership of convenience durable partnership of convenience marriage of convenience	a civil partnership, durable partnership or marriage entered into as a means to circumvent: (a) any criterion the party would have to meet in order to enjoy a right to enter or reside in the UK under the EEA Regulations; or (b) any other provision of UK immigration law or any requirement of the Immigration Rules; or (c) any criterion the party would otherwise have to meet in order to enjoy a right to enter or reside in the UK under EU law; or (d) any criterion the party would have to meet in order to enjoy a right to enter or reside in the Islands under Islands law

Term	Definition
continuous qualifying period	a period of residence in the UK and Islands (save in condition 3 in the table in paragraph EU12 of this Appendix; in condition 2 in the table in paragraph EU14 of this Appendix; in sub-paragraph (a)(ii) or (d)(iii)(aa) of the entry for 'family member who has retained the right of residence' in this table; in sub-paragraph (c) of the entry for 'person who has ceased activity' in this table; and in the entry for 'person with a derivative right to reside' and for 'person with a Zambrano right to reside' in this table, where (in each case) the period of residence must be in the UK and the reference in sub-paragraphs (b)(i) and (ii) below to the UK and Islands is to be read as a reference to the UK): [(a) which, unless the person is a joining family member of a relevant sponsor, [[is a **relevant EEA family permit case**,]] is a specified relevant person of Northern Ireland (or is the dependent relative of such a person) or relies on sub-paragraph (b)(i)(cc), (b)(i)(dd) or (b)(i)(ee) below, began before the specified date; and] (b) during which none of the following occurred: [(i) absence(s) from the UK and Islands which exceeded a total of six months in any 12-month period, except for: (aa) a single period of absence which did not exceed 12 months and was for an important reason (such as pregnancy, childbirth, serious illness, study, vocational training or an overseas posting, or because of COVID-19); or (bb) a single period of absence which did not exceed 12 months and which, although the absence was not originally for an important reason, is to be treated as being for an important reason as it exceeded six months because of COVID-19; or (cc) (following a period of absence under sub-paragraph (b)(i)(aa) above because of COVID-19 or under sub-paragraph (b)(i)(bb) above) a second period of absence which did not exceed 12 months and was for an important reason (such as described in sub-paragraph (b)(i)(aa) above) which, save for caring for someone with a serious illness, was not because of COVID-19; where this is the case, the period of absence under this sub-paragraph exceeding six months will not count towards any period of residence in the UK and Islands on which the person relies; or (dd) (following a period of absence under sub-paragraph (b)(i)(aa) above which, save for caring for someone with a serious illness, was not because of COVID-19) either a second period of absence which did not exceed 12 months and was for an important reason, where that reason was because of COVID-19, or a period of absence under sub-paragraph (b)(i)(bb) above; where this is the case, the period of absence under this sub-paragraph exceeding six months will not count towards any period of residence in the UK and Islands on which the person relies; or

Term	Definition
	(ee) a period of absence under sub-paragraph (b)(i)(aa), (b)(i)(bb), (b)(i)(cc) or (b)(i)(dd) above which exceeded 12 months because COVID-19 meant that the person was prevented from, or advised against, returning earlier; where this is the case, the period of absence under this sub-paragraph exceeding 12 months will not count towards any period of residence in the UK and Islands on which the person relies; or (ff) any period of absence on compulsory military service; or (gg) any period of absence on a posting on Crown service or (as a spouse, civil partner, durable partner or child) any period of absence accompanying a person on a posting on Crown service; or (hh) any period spent working in the UK marine area (as defined in section 42 of the Marine and Coastal Access Act 2009); or (ii) any period of absence due directly to an order or decision to which sub-paragraph (b)(iii) below refers, where that order or decision has been set aside or revoked; or] [(ii) the person served or is serving a sentence of imprisonment of any length in the UK and Islands, unless the conviction which led to it has been overturned; or] (iii) [any of the following in respect of the person, unless it has been set aside or revoked:] (aa) any decision or order to exclude or remove under regulation 23 or 32 of the EEA Regulations (or under the equivalent provisions of the Immigration (European Economic Area) Regulations of the Isle of Man); or (bb) a decision to which regulation 15(4) of the EEA Regulations otherwise refers, unless that decision arose from a previous decision under regulation 24(1) of the EEA Regulations (or the equivalent decision, subject to the equivalent qualification, under the Immigration (European Economic Area) Regulations of the Isle of Man); or (cc) an exclusion decision; or (dd) a deportation order, other than by virtue of the EEA Regulations; or (ee) an Islands deportation order; or (ff) an Islands exclusion decision; and (c) which continues at the date of application, unless: (i) the period is of at least five years' duration; or [(ii) (aa) the person acquired the right of permanent residence in the UK under regulation 15 of the EEA Regulations (or, where there are reasonable grounds for the person's failure to meet the deadline applicable to them in the entry for 'required date' in this table, would have acquired such a right had the EEA Regulations not been revoked), or the right of permanent residence in the Islands through the application there of section 7(1) of the Immigration Act 1988 or under the Immigration (European Economic Area) Regulations of the Isle of Man; or

Term	Definition
	(bb) the period relates to: (aaa) a relevant EEA citizen, where, in relation to that EEA citizen, the applicant relies: (i) for all or part of the period to which sub-paragraph (b) of condition 3 in the table in paragraph EU11 of this Appendix refers (or, as the case may be, for part of the period to which sub-paragraph (b) of condition 3 in the table in paragraph EU12 refers) on having been a family member of a relevant EEA citizen; or (ii) on being or having been a family member who has retained the right of residence by virtue of a relationship with a relevant EEA citizen, provided (in any case) the period relating to that relevant EEA citizen continued (unless sub-paragraph (c)(i), (c)(ii)(aa), (c)(iii) or (c)(iv) of this entry applied to that relevant EEA citizen instead) either, as the case may be, throughout the period the applicant relies on in (i) as having been a family member of a relevant EEA citizen or, as relied on in (ii), until the applicant became a family member who has retained the right of residence by virtue of a relationship with a relevant EEA citizen; or (bbb) a relevant sponsor, where, in relation to that relevant sponsor, the applicant relies for all or part of the period to which sub-paragraph (b) of condition 1 in the table in paragraph EU11A of this Appendix refers on having been (or, as the case may be, relies for all or part of the period to which sub-paragraph (b)(ii) of the condition in the table in paragraph EU14A refers on being) a family member who has retained the right of residence by virtue of a relationship with a relevant sponsor, provided (in either case) the period relating to that relevant sponsor continued (unless sub-paragraph (c)(i), (c)(ii)(aa), (c)(iii) or (c)(iv) of this entry applied to that relevant sponsor instead) until the applicant became a family member who has retained the right of residence by virtue of a relationship with a relevant sponsor; or] (iii) the person has valid indefinite leave to enter or remain granted under this Appendix (or under its equivalent in the Islands); or (iv) there is valid evidence of their indefinite leave to enter or remain; or (v) a relevant reference is concerned in addition, 'relevant reference' in sub-paragraph (c)(v) above means the reference to continuous qualifying period in: – condition 6 in the table in paragraph EU11 of this Appendix; – condition 3 in the table in paragraph EU11A of this Appendix; – sub-paragraph (d)(iii)(aa) of the entry for 'family member who has retained the right of residence' in this table (as that reference applies to, as the case may be, the relevant EEA citizen, the qualifying British citizen or the relevant sponsor);

Term	Definition
	– where the date of application is on or after 1 July 2021, sub-paragraph (b)(i) of the applicable entry for 'relevant EEA citizen' in this table, where sub-paragraph (b)(ii)(aa) of that entry applies; – where the date of application is on or after 1 July 2021, sub-paragraph (c) of the applicable entry for 'relevant EEA citizen' in this table (in so far as the reference in that sub-paragraph to sub-paragraph (a) of the entry for 'relevant naturalised British citizen' in this table is concerned), where sub-paragraph (c)(i) of the applicable entry for 'relevant EEA citizen' in this table applies; – where the date of application is on or after 1 July 2021, sub-paragraph (d)(ii) of the applicable entry for 'relevant EEA citizen' in this table, where sub-paragraph (d)(iii)(aa) of that entry applies; – where the date of application is on or after 1 July 2021, sub-paragraph (e)(i)(aa) of the applicable entry for 'relevant EEA citizen' in this table, where sub-paragraph (e)(i)(bb)(ccc) of that entry applies; – where the date of application is on or after 1 July 2021, sub-paragraph (e)(ii)(aa) of the applicable entry for 'relevant EEA citizen' in this table, where sub-paragraph (e)(ii)(bb)(aaa) of that entry applies; – where the date of application is on or after 1 July 2021, sub-paragraph (f)(i) of the applicable entry for 'relevant EEA citizen' in this table, where sub-paragraph (f)(ii)(aa) of that entry applies; – sub-paragraph (b)(ii) of the entry for 'relevant sponsor' in this table, where sub-paragraph (b)(ii)(aa) of that entry applies; – sub-paragraph (b)(iii) of the entry for 'relevant sponsor' in this table (where the reference to sub-paragraph (a) of the entry for 'relevant naturalised British citizen' in this table is concerned), where sub-paragraph (b)(iii)(aa) of the entry for 'relevant sponsor' in this table applies; – sub-paragraph (b)(iv)(aa) of the entry for 'relevant sponsor' in this table, where sub-paragraph (b)(iv)(bb)(bbb) of that entry applies; – sub-paragraph (b)(v)(aa) of the entry for 'relevant sponsor' in this table, where sub-paragraph (b)(v)(bb)(aaa) of that entry applies; and – sub-paragraph (b)(vi) of the entry for 'relevant sponsor' in this table, where sub-paragraph (b)(vi)(aa) of that entry applies
Crown service	service as: (a) a member of HM Forces (as defined in the Armed Forces Act 2006); or (b) an employee of the UK Government, a Northern Ireland department, the Scottish Administration or the Welsh Government; or (c) a permanent member of the British Council
custody of a child	the child normally lives with the applicant or does so part of the time, and includes arrangements agreed informally and those which are subject to a court order for determining with whom the child is to live and when

Term	Definition
date and time of withdrawal	2300GMT on 31 January 2020
date of application	the date on which the application is submitted under the required application process, which means: (a) (in the case of the relevant on-line application form) the date on which that form is submitted on-line; or (b) (in the case of a paper application form): (i) the date of posting to the Home Office address specified on the form (where one is specified), as shown on the tracking information provided by Royal Mail or, if not tracked, by the postmark date on the envelope; or (ii) where the paper application form is sent by courier, or other postal services provider, the date on which it is delivered to the Home Office address specified on the form (where one is specified); or (iii) where the paper application form is sent by e-mail, the date on which it is recorded by Home Office e-mail software as received at the Home Office e-mail address specified on the form (where one is specified)
dependent parent	(a) the direct relative in the ascending line of a relevant EEA citizen (or, as the case may be, of a qualifying British citizen or of a relevant sponsor) or of their spouse or civil partner; and (b) (unless sub-paragraph (c) immediately below applies) dependent on (as the case may be): (i) the relevant EEA citizen (or on their spouse or civil partner) at the date of application or, where the date of application is after the specified date, at the specified date, and (unless the relevant EEA citizen is under the age of 18 years at the date of application or, where the date of application is after the specified date, the relevant EEA citizen was under the age of 18 years at the specified date) that dependency is assumed; or (ii) on the qualifying British citizen (or on their spouse or civil partner) at the date of application or, where the date of application is after the specified date, at the specified date, and (unless the qualifying British citizen is under the age of 18 years at the date of application or, where the date of application is after the specified date, the qualifying British citizen was under the age of 18 years at the specified date) that dependency is assumed; or (iii) on the relevant sponsor (or on their spouse or civil partner) at the date of application and (unless the relevant sponsor is under the age of 18 years) that dependency is assumed where the date of application is before 1 July 2021; and (c) this sub-paragraph applies (and the applicant therefore has to meet no requirement as to dependency) where:

Term	Definition
	(i) the applicant was previously granted limited leave to enter or remain under this Appendix as a dependent parent, and that leave has not lapsed or been cancelled, curtailed or invalidated; or (ii) the spouse, civil partner or durable partner of the applicant (and with whom they reside) has been granted indefinite leave to enter or remain or limited leave to enter or remain under this Appendix as a dependent parent of the relevant EEA citizen (or, as the case may be, of the qualifying British citizen or of the relevant sponsor) or of their spouse or civil partner, and that indefinite or limited leave has not lapsed or been cancelled, curtailed, revoked or invalidated 'dependent' means here that: (a) having regard to their financial and social conditions, or health, the applicant cannot, or (as the case may be) for the relevant period could not, meet their essential living needs (in whole or in part) without the financial or other material support of the relevant EEA citizen (or, as the case may be, of the qualifying British citizen or of the relevant sponsor) or of their spouse or civil partner; and (b) such support is, or (as the case may be) was, being provided to the applicant by the relevant EEA citizen (or, as the case may be, by the qualifying British citizen or by the relevant sponsor) or by their spouse or civil partner; and (c) there is no need to determine the reasons for that dependence or for the recourse to that support in addition: (a) 'direct relative in the ascending line' includes: (i) a grandparent or great-grandparent; and (ii) an adoptive parent of an adopted child; and (b) 'spouse or civil partner' means (as the case may be) the person described in sub-paragraph (a)(i) or (a)(ii) of the entry for 'family member of a qualifying British citizen' in this table, in sub-paragraph (a) of the entry for 'family member of a relevant EEA citizen' in this table or in the first sub-paragraph (a) (together with either the second sub-paragraph (a) or sub-paragraph (b)(i) or (b)(ii)) of the entry for 'joining family member of a relevant sponsor' in this table; and (c) in respect of the reference in sub-paragraph (c)(ii) above to the spouse, civil partner or durable partner of the applicant, the entry for (as the case may be) 'spouse', 'civil partner' or 'durable partner' in this table applies, except that in the applicable entry 'applicant' is to be substituted for 'relevant EEA citizen' and sub-paragraph (b) of the entry for 'durable partner' in this table is to be disregarded
dependent relative	the person: (a) (i)(aa) is a relative (other than a spouse, civil partner, durable partner, child or dependent parent) of their sponsoring person; and

Term	Definition
	(bb) is, or (as the case may be) for the relevant period was, a dependant of the sponsoring person, a member of their household or in strict need of their personal care on serious health grounds; or (ii) is a **person who is subject to a non-adoptive legal guardianship order** in favour (solely or jointly with another party) of their sponsoring person; or (iii) is a person under the age of 18 years who: (aa) is the direct descendant of the durable partner of their sponsoring person; or (bb) has been adopted by the durable partner of their sponsoring person, in accordance with a relevant adoption decision; and (b) holds a **relevant document** as the dependent relative of their sponsoring person for the period of residence relied upon (unless, in the case of a family member of a qualifying British citizen as described in sub-paragraph (a)(viii) of that entry in this table, the Secretary of State is satisfied that there are reasonable grounds for the person's failure to meet the deadline to which that sub-paragraph refers); for the purposes of this provision, where the person applies for a relevant document (as described in sub-paragraph (a)(i)(aa) or (a)(ii) of that entry in this table) as the dependent relative of their sponsoring person before the specified date and their relevant document is issued on that basis after the specified date [(or where the person relies as their relevant document, as described in sub-paragraph (a)(iv) of that entry in this table, on an EU Settlement Scheme Family Permit granted to them under Appendix EU (Family Permit) to these Rules as a 'dependent relative of a specified relevant person of Northern Ireland, as defined in Annex 1 to that Appendix)], they are deemed to have held the relevant document since immediately before the specified date in addition, 'sponsoring person' means: (a) (where sub-paragraphs (a)(i) and (b) above apply): (i) a relevant EEA citizen (in accordance with the applicable entry in this table); or (ii) the spouse or civil partner (as described in sub-paragraph (a) of the entry for 'family member of a relevant EEA citizen' in this table) of a relevant EEA citizen (in accordance with the applicable entry in this table); or (iii) a qualifying British citizen; or (iv) the spouse or civil partner (as described in sub-paragraph (a)(i) or (a)(ii) of the entry for 'family member of a qualifying British citizen' in this table) of a qualifying British citizen; or (b) (where the first sub-paragraph (a)(ii) in this entry and sub-paragraph (b) above apply or the first sub-paragraph (a)(iii) in this entry and sub-paragraph (b) above apply): (i) a relevant EEA citizen (in accordance with the applicable entry in this table); or (ii) a qualifying British citizen

Term	Definition
[deportation order	as the case may be: (a) an order made under section 5(1) of the Immigration Act 1971 by virtue of regulation 32(3) of the EEA Regulations; or (b) an order made under section 5(1) of the Immigration Act 1971 by virtue of section 3(5) or section 3(6) of that Act in respect of: (i) conduct committed after the specified date; or (ii) conduct committed by the person before the specified date, where the Secretary of State has decided that the deportation order is justified on the grounds of public policy, public security or public health in accordance with regulation 27 of the EEA Regulations, irrespective of whether the EEA Regulations apply to the person (except that in regulation 27 for 'with a right of permanent residence under regulation 15' and 'has a right of permanent residence under regulation 15' read ['who, but for the making of the exclusion direction, meets the requirements of] paragraph EU11, EU11A or EU12 of Appendix EU to the Immigration Rules'; and for 'an EEA decision' read 'a deportation decision'); or (c) an order made under section 5(1) of the Immigration Act 1971 by virtue of regulation 15(1)(b) of the Citizens' Rights (Frontier Workers) (EU Exit) Regulations 2020 in addition, for the avoidance of doubt, (b) includes a deportation order made under the Immigration Act 1971 in accordance with section 32 of the UK Borders Act 2007]
documented right of permanent residence	the Secretary of State is satisfied from the information available to them that: (a) (i) the person has been issued by the Secretary of State with a document certifying permanent residence or a permanent residence card (and that permanent residence card was issued or renewed within the last 10 years) under regulation 19 of the EEA Regulations, or with a residence permit or residence document under the Immigration (European Economic Area) Order 1994 endorsed to show permission to remain in the UK indefinitely; and (ii) this document or card is not invalid under regulation 19(4)(c); and (iii) this document or card has not been revoked, and its renewal has not been refused, under regulation 24 (except where the revocation or refusal occurred because the person had been absent from the UK for a period of more than two, and no more than five, consecutive years); and (iv) the person's right to reside has not been cancelled under regulation 25; or (b) the person has been given notice in writing under paragraphs 256 to 257A of the Immigration Rules of the Bailiwick of Guernsey showing that they may remain indefinitely, and this notice has not been revoked or otherwise ceased to be effective; or

Term	Definition
	(c) the person has been issued by the relevant Minister with a document in accordance with paragraphs 255 to 258 of the Immigration Rules of the Bailiwick of Jersey in an appropriate form certifying permanent residence or a permanent residence card, and this document or card has not been revoked or otherwise ceased to be effective; or (d) the person has been issued with a letter certifying permanent residence, or their passport has been stamped to that effect, under the Immigration (European Economic Area) Regulations of the Isle of Man, and this evidence has not been revoked, invalidated or cancelled
durable partner	(a) the person is, or (as the case may be) for the relevant period was, in a durable relationship with a relevant EEA citizen (or with a qualifying British citizen or with a relevant sponsor), with the couple having lived together in a relationship akin to a marriage or civil partnership for at least two years (unless there is other significant evidence of the durable relationship); and (b) (i) the person holds a relevant document as the durable partner of the relevant EEA citizen (or, as the case may be, of the qualifying British citizen or of the relevant sponsor) for the period of residence relied upon; for the purposes of this provision, where the person applies for a relevant document (as described in sub-paragraph (a)(i)(aa) or (a)(ii) of that entry in this table) as the durable partner of the relevant EEA citizen or, as the case may be, of the qualifying British citizen before the specified date and their relevant document is issued on that basis after the specified date, they are deemed to have held the relevant document since immediately before the specified date; or (ii) where the person is applying as the durable partner of a relevant sponsor (or, as the case may be, of a qualifying British citizen), or as the spouse or civil partner of a relevant sponsor (as described in sub-paragraph (a)(i)(bb) of the entry for 'joining family member of a relevant sponsor' in this table), and does not hold a document of the type to which sub-paragraph (b)(i) above applies, and where: (aa) the date of application is after the specified date; and (bb) the person: (aaa) was not resident in the UK and Islands as the durable partner of a relevant EEA citizen (where that relevant EEA citizen is their relevant sponsor) on a basis which met the definition of 'family member of a relevant EEA citizen' in this table, or, as the case may be, as the durable partner of the qualifying British citizen, at (in either case) any time before the specified date, unless the reason why, in the former case, they were not so resident is that they did not hold a relevant document as the durable partner of a relevant EEA citizen for that period (where their relevant sponsor is that relevant EEA citizen) and they did not otherwise have a lawful basis of stay in the UK and Islands for that period; or

Term	Definition
	(bbb) was resident in the UK and Islands before the specified date, and one of the events referred to in sub-paragraph (b)(i) or (b)(ii) in the definition of 'continuous qualifying period' in this table has occurred and after that event occurred they were not resident in the UK and Islands again before the specified date; or (ccc) was resident in the UK and Islands before the specified date, and the event referred to in sub-paragraph (a) in the definition of 'supervening event' in this table has occurred and after that event occurred they were not resident in the UK and Islands again before the specified date, the Secretary of State is satisfied by evidence provided by the person that the partnership was formed and was durable before (in the case of a family member of a qualifying British citizen as described in sub-paragraph (a)(i)(bb) or (a)(iii) of that entry in this table) the date and time of withdrawal and otherwise before the specified date; and (c) it is, or (as the case may be) for the relevant period was, not a **durable partnership of convenience**; and (d) neither party has, or (as the case may be) for the relevant period had, another durable partner, a spouse or a civil partner with (in any of those circumstances) immigration status in the UK or the Islands based on that person's relationship with that party in addition, to meet condition 6 in the table in paragraph EU11 of this Appendix (or condition 3 in the table in paragraph EU11A), the above requirements are to be met with reference to the period immediately before the death of the relevant EEA citizen (or, as the case may be, of the relevant sponsor) rather than to the date of application
educational course	ageneral educational course, apprenticeship or vocational training course, as provided by regulation 10(7) of the EEA Regulations
[EEA Regulations	(a) (where relevant to something done before the specified date) the Immigration (European Economic Area) Regulations 2016 (as they have effect immediately before that date); or (b) (where relevant to something done after the specified date and before 1 July 2021) the Immigration (European Economic Area) Regulations 2016 (as, despite the revocation of those Regulations, they continue to have effect, with specified modifications, by virtue of the Citizens' Rights (Application Deadline and Temporary Protection) (EU Exit) Regulations 2020; or (c) (where relevant to something done on or after 1 July 2021) the Immigration (European Economic Area) Regulations 2016 (as they had effect immediately before they were revoked and, where the context requires it, on the basis that those Regulations had not been revoked)]

Term	Definition
EEA citizen	a person who is [(and, throughout any continuous qualifying period relied upon, was)]: (a) (i) a national of: Austria, Belgium, Bulgaria, Croatia, Republic of Cyprus, Czech Republic, Denmark, Estonia, Finland, France, Germany, Greece, Hungary, Iceland, Ireland, Italy, Latvia, Liechtenstein, Lithuania, Luxembourg, Malta, Netherlands, Norway, Poland, Portugal, Romania, Slovakia, Slovenia, Spain, Sweden or Switzerland; and (ii) not also a British citizen; or (b) a relevant naturalised British citizen; or (c) (i) a national of a country listed in sub-paragraph (a)(i) above; and (ii) (where the applicant meets the criteria in paragraph 9 of Schedule 6 to the EEA Regulations as the family member ('F') to whom that paragraph refers) a British citizen within the meaning of the person ('P') to whom that paragraph refers; or (d) a **relevant person of Northern Ireland**
[EEA Regulations	(a) (where relevant to something done before the specified date) the Immigration (European Economic Area) Regulations 2016 (as they have effect immediately before that date); or (b) (where relevant to something done after the specified date and before 1 July 2021) the Immigration (European Economic Area) Regulations 2016 (as, despite the revocation of those Regulations, they continue to have effect, with specified modifications, by virtue of the Citizens' Rights (Application Deadline and Temporary Protection) (EU Exit) Regulations 2020); or (c) (where relevant to something done on or after 1 July 2021) the Immigration (European Economic Area) Regulations 2016 (as they had effect immediately before they were revoked and, where the context requires it, on the basis that those Regulations had not been revoked)]
evidence of birth	(a) (in the case of a child) the **full birth certificate** (s) or other document(s) which the Secretary of State is satisfied evidences that the applicant is the direct descendant of (or otherwise a child of) the relevant EEA citizen (or, as the case may be, of the qualifying British citizen or of the relevant sponsor) or of their spouse or civil partner, as described (as the case may be) in sub-paragraph (a)(i) or (a)(ii) of the entry for 'family member of a qualifying British citizen' in this table, in sub-paragraph (a) of the entry for 'family member of a relevant EEA citizen' in this table or in the first sub-paragraph (a) (together with either the second sub-paragraph (a) or sub-paragraph (b)(i) or (b)(ii)) of the entry for 'joining family member of a relevant sponsor' in this table; or (b) (in the case of a dependent parent) the full birth certificate(s) or other document(s) which the Secretary of State is satisfied evidences that the applicant is the direct relative in the ascending line of the relevant EEA citizen (or, as the case may be, of the qualifying British citizen or of the relevant sponsor) or of their spouse or civil partner, as described in sub-paragraph (a) above

Term	Definition
exclusion decision	a direction given by the Secretary of State that a person must be excluded from the UK: (a) in respect of conduct committed after the specified date; or (b) in respect of conduct committed [by the person] before the specified date, where the Secretary of State is satisfied that the direction is justified on the grounds of public policy, public security or public health in accordance with regulation 27 of the EEA Regulations, irrespective of whether the EEA Regulations apply to that person (except that in regulation 27 for 'with a right of permanent residence under regulation 15' and 'has a right of permanent residence under regulation 15' read [['who, but for the making of the exclusion direction, meets the requirements of]] paragraph EU11, EU11A or EU12 of Appendix EU to the Immigration Rules'; and for 'an EEA decision' read 'an exclusion direction')
exclusion order	an order made under regulation 23(5) of the EEA Regulations
family member of a qualifying British citizen	a person who has satisfied the Secretary of State, including by the required evidence of family relationship, that: (a) they have (or, as the case may be, had) returned to the UK: (i) before 2300 GMT on 29 March 2022 (or later where the Secretary of State is satisfied that there are reasonable grounds for the person's failure to meet that deadline), as the spouse or civil partner of a qualifying British citizen, and: (aa) the marriage was contracted or the civil partnership was formed before the date and time of withdrawal; or (bb) the applicant was the durable partner of the qualifying British citizen before the date and time of withdrawal (the definition of 'durable partner' in this table being met before then rather than at the date of application) and the partnership remained durable at the date and time of withdrawal; or (ii) (where sub-paragraph (a)(i)(bb) above does not apply) before the specified date (or later where the Secretary of State is satisfied that there are reasonable grounds for the person's failure to meet that deadline), as the spouse or civil partner of a qualifying British citizen, and the marriage was contracted or the civil partnership was formed after the date and time of withdrawal and before the specified date; or (iii) before 2300 GMT on 29 March 2022 (or later where the Secretary of State is satisfied that there are reasonable grounds for the person's failure to meet that deadline), as the durable partner of a qualifying British citizen, and: (aa) the partnership was formed and was durable before the date and time of withdrawal; and (bb) the partnership remains durable at the date of application; or

Term	Definition
	(iv) before the specified date (or later where the Secretary of State is satisfied that there are reasonable grounds for the person's failure to meet that deadline), as the durable partner of a qualifying British citizen, and: (aa) the partnership was formed and was durable after the date and time of withdrawal and before the specified date; and (bb) the partnership remains durable at the date of application; or (v) before 2300 GMT on 29 March 2022 (or later where the Secretary of State is satisfied that there are reasonable grounds for the person's failure to meet that deadline), as the child or dependent parent of a qualifying British citizen, and the family relationship existed before the date and time of withdrawal (unless, in the case of a child, the person was [born thereafter, was adopted thereafter in accordance with a relevant adoption decision or thereafter became] a child within the meaning of that entry in this table on the basis of one of sub-paragraphs (a)(iii) to (a)(xi) of that entry); or (vi) before 2300 GMT on 29 March 2022 (or later where the Secretary of State is satisfied that there are reasonable grounds for the person's failure to meet that deadline), as the child or dependent parent of the spouse or civil partner of a qualifying British citizen (as described in sub-paragraph (a)(i) above), and all the family relationships existed before the date and time of withdrawal (unless, in the case of a child, the person was [born thereafter, was adopted thereafter in accordance with a relevant adoption decision or thereafter became] a child within the meaning of that entry in this table on the basis of one of sub-paragraphs (a)(iii) to (a)(xi) of that entry); or (vii) before the specified date (or later where the Secretary of State is satisfied that there are reasonable grounds for the person's failure to meet that deadline), as the child or dependent parent of the spouse or civil partner of a qualifying British citizen (as described in sub-paragraph (a)(ii) above), and the family relationship of the child or dependent parent to the spouse or civil partner existed before the date and time of withdrawal (unless, in the case of a child, the person was [born thereafter, was adopted thereafter in accordance with a relevant adoption decision or thereafter became] a child within the meaning of that entry in this table on the basis of one of sub-paragraphs (a)(iii) to (a)(xi) of that entry); or

Term	Definition
	(viii) before the specified date (or later where the Secretary of State is satisfied that there are reasonable grounds for the person's failure to meet that deadline), as the dependent relative of a qualifying British citizen, or (as the case may be) of their spouse or civil partner as described in sub-paragraph (a)(i) or (a)(ii) above, and that family relationship and (in sub-paragraph (a)(i)(bb) of the entry for 'dependent relative' in this table) the person's dependency (or, as the case may be, their membership of the household or their strict need for personal care on serious health grounds) existed before the applicant returned to the UK with the qualifying British citizen or (where the Secretary of State is satisfied that there are reasonable grounds for the person's failure to meet the deadline of the specified date for returning to the UK) before the specified date, and (in either case) the person's dependency (or, as the case may be, their membership of the household or their strict need for personal care on serious health grounds) continues to exist at the date of application (or did so for the period of residence in the UK relied upon); and (b) they satisfied the conditions in regulation 9(2), (3) and (4)(a) of the EEA Regulations (as the family member ('F') to whom those provisions refer) or, as the case may be, the conditions in regulation 9(1A)(b), (2), (3) and (4)(a) of the EEA Regulations (as the extended family member ('EFM') to whom those provisions refer), in either case doing so: (i) before the specified date; and (ii) (save where the date of application is after the specified date and where those conditions concern matters relevant to the dependency referred to in sub-paragraph (b)(ii)(bb) of the entry for 'child' in this table or in sub-paragraph (b)(ii) of the entry for 'dependent parent' in this table) immediately before returning to the UK with the qualifying British citizen (who is to be treated as the British citizen ('BC') to whom those provisions refer); and (c) (where the applicant does not rely on having a documented right of permanent residence, on having completed a continuous qualifying period in the UK of five years, or on being a family member who has retained the right of residence by virtue of a relationship with a qualifying British citizen) the family relationship continues to exist at the date of application

Term	Definition
family member of a relevant EEA citizen	a person who does not meet the definition of 'joining family member of a relevant sponsor' in this table, and who has satisfied the Secretary of State, including by the required evidence of family relationship, that they are (and for the relevant period have been), or (as the case may be) for the relevant period (or at the relevant time) they were: (a) the spouse or civil partner of a relevant EEA citizen, and: (i) the marriage was contracted or the civil partnership was formed before the specified date; or (ii) the applicant was the durable partner of the relevant EEA citizen before the specified date (the definition of 'durable partner' in this table being met before that date rather than at the date of application), and the partnership remained durable at the specified date; or (b) the durable partner of a relevant EEA citizen, and: (i) the partnership was formed and was durable before the specified date; and (ii) the partnership remains durable at the date of application (or it did so for the relevant period or immediately before the death of the relevant EEA citizen); or (c) the child or dependent parent of a relevant EEA citizen, and the family relationship existed before the specified date; or (d) the child or dependent parent of the spouse or civil partner of a relevant EEA citizen (as described in sub-paragraph (a) above), and the family relationship existed before the specified date; or (e) the dependent relative, before the specified date, of a relevant EEA citizen (or of their spouse or civil partner, as described in sub-paragraph (a) above) and the dependency (or, as the case may be, their membership of the household or their strict need for personal care on serious health grounds) continues to exist at the date of application (or did so for the period of residence relied upon) in addition, where the applicant does not rely on meeting condition 1, 3, or 6 of paragraph EU11 of this Appendix, or on being a family member who has retained the right of residence by virtue of a relationship with a relevant EEA citizen, the family relationship continues to exist at the date of application
family member who has retained the right of residence	a person who has satisfied the Secretary of State, including by the required evidence of family relationship, that the requirements set out in one of sub-paragraphs (a) to (e) below are met and that since satisfying those requirements the required continuity of residence has been maintained: (a) the applicant is an EEA citizen (in accordance with sub-paragraph (a) of that entry in this table) or non-EEA citizen who: (i) was, as the case may be, the family member of a relevant EEA citizen (or of a qualifying British citizen), or the joining family member of a relevant sponsor, and that person died; and

Term	Definition
	(ii) was resident, as the case may be, as the family member of a relevant EEA citizen (or of a qualifying British citizen), or as the joining family member of a relevant sponsor, for a continuous qualifying period in the UK of at least a year immediately before the death of that person; or (b) the applicant is an EEA citizen (in accordance with sub-paragraph (a) of that entry in this table) or non-EEA citizen who: (i) is the child (including where they are a joining family member of a relevant sponsor) of: (aa) a relevant EEA citizen (or, as the case may be, of a qualifying British citizen or of a relevant sponsor) who has died or of their spouse or civil partner immediately before their death; or (bb) a person who ceased to be a relevant EEA citizen (or, as the case may be, a qualifying British citizen or a relevant sponsor) on ceasing to reside in the UK or of their spouse or civil partner at that point; and (ii) was attending an **educational course** in the UK immediately before the relevant EEA citizen (or, as the case may be, the qualifying British citizen or the relevant sponsor) died or ceased to be a relevant EEA citizen (or, as the case may be, a qualifying British citizen or a relevant sponsor), and continues to attend such a course; or (c) the applicant is an EEA citizen (in accordance with sub-paragraph (a) of that entry in this table) or non-EEA citizen who is the parent with **custody of a child** who meets the requirements of sub-paragraph (b) above and the child is not a joining family member of a relevant sponsor; or (d) the applicant ('A') is an EEA citizen (in accordance with sub-paragraph (a) of that entry in this table) or non-EEA citizen who: (i) ceased to be, as the case may be, a family member of a relevant EEA citizen (or of a qualifying British citizen), or a joining family member of a relevant sponsor, on the **termination of the marriage or civil partnership** of that relevant EEA citizen (or, as the case may be, of that qualifying British citizen or of that relevant sponsor); for the purposes of this provision, where, after the initiation of the proceedings for that termination, that relevant EEA citizen ceased to be a relevant EEA citizen (or, as the case may be, that qualifying British citizen ceased to be a qualifying British citizen, or that relevant sponsor ceased to be a relevant sponsor), they will be deemed to have remained a relevant EEA citizen (or, as the case may be, a qualifying British citizen or a relevant sponsor) until that termination; and (ii) was resident in the UK at the date of the termination of the marriage or civil partnership; and (iii) one of the following applies:

Term	Definition
	(aa) prior to the initiation of the proceedings for the termination of the marriage or the civil partnership, the marriage or civil partnership had lasted for at least three years and the parties to the marriage or civil partnership had been resident for a continuous qualifying period in the UK of at least one year during its duration; or (bb) A has custody of a child of the relevant EEA citizen (or, as the case may be, of the qualifying British citizen or of the relevant sponsor); or (cc) A has the right of access to a child of the relevant EEA citizen (or, as the case may be, of the qualifying British citizen or of the relevant sponsor), where the child is under the age of 18 years and where a court has ordered that such access must take place in the UK; or (dd) the continued right of residence in the UK of A is warranted by particularly difficult circumstances, such as where A or another family member has been a victim of domestic violence or abuse whilst the marriage or civil partnership was subsisting; or (e) the applicant ('A') is an EEA citizen (in accordance with sub-paragraph (a) of that entry in this table) or non-EEA citizen who: (i) provides evidence that a relevant family relationship with a relevant EEA citizen (or, as the case may be, with a qualifying British citizen or with a relevant sponsor) has broken down permanently as a result of domestic violence or abuse; and (ii) was resident in the UK when the relevant family relationship broke down permanently as a result of domestic violence or abuse, and the continued right of residence in the UK of A is warranted where A or another family member has been a victim of domestic violence or abuse before the relevant family relationship broke down permanently in addition: (a) 'relevant family relationship' in sub-paragraph (e) above means a family relationship with a relevant EEA citizen (or, as the case may be, with a qualifying British citizen or with a relevant sponsor) such that the applicant is, or (immediately before the relevant family relationship broke down permanently as a result of domestic violence or abuse) was, as the case may be, a family member of a relevant EEA citizen (or of a qualifying British citizen), or a joining family member of a relevant sponsor; and (b) where sub-paragraph (e) above applies, then, where, following the permanent breakdown of the relevant family relationship as a result of domestic violence or abuse, the applicant remains, as the case may be, a family member of a relevant EEA citizen (or of a qualifying British citizen), or a joining family member of a relevant sponsor, they will be deemed to have ceased to be such a family member for the purposes of this Appendix once the permanent breakdown occurred; and

Term	Definition
	(c) 'required continuity of residence' means that, where the applicant has not completed a continuous qualifying period of five years (and does not have valid evidence of their indefinite leave to enter or remain, and has not acquired the right of permanent residence in the UK under regulation 15 of the EEA Regulations, or the right of permanent residence in the Islands through the application there of section 7(1) of the Immigration Act 1988 or under the Immigration (European Economic Area) Regulations of the Isle of Man), then, since the point at which (where they do so) they began to rely on being in the UK and Islands as a family member who has retained the right of residence and while they continued to do so, one of the events referred to in sub-paragraph (b)(i) or (b)(ii) in the definition of 'continuous qualifying period' in this table has not occurred
frontier worker	a person who: (a) is a national of: Austria, Belgium, Bulgaria, Croatia, Republic of Cyprus, Czech Republic, Denmark, Estonia, Finland, France, Germany, Greece, Hungary, Iceland, Ireland, Italy, Latvia, Liechtenstein, Lithuania, Luxembourg, Malta, Netherlands, Norway, Poland, Portugal, Romania, Slovakia, Slovenia, Spain, Sweden or Switzerland; and (b) is not a British citizen; and (c) satisfies the Secretary of State by relevant evidence of this that they fulfil the relevant conditions of being a frontier worker set out in [the Citizens' Rights (Frontier Workers)(EU Exit) Regulations 2020], and that they have done so continuously since the specified date; and (d) has not been (and is not to be) refused admission to, or removed from, the UK by virtue of [the Citizens' Rights (Frontier Workers) (EU Exit) Regulations 2020, and is not subject to a relevant restriction decision as defined by regulation 2 of those Regulations]
full birth certificate	abirth certificate recognised in the UK or the Islands which records the name of the mother and (where registered) the father
GMT	Greenwich Mean Time
immigration status in the UK or the Islands	indefinite or limited leave to enter or remain in the UK or the Islands under or outside the relevant Immigration Rules; exemption from immigration control; the entitlement to reside in the UK or the right of permanent residence in the UK under regulations 13 to 15 of the EEA Regulations; or the entitlement to reside in the Islands or the right of permanent residence in the Islands through the application there of section 7(1) of the Immigration Act 1988 or under the Immigration (European Economic Area) Regulations of the Isle of Man
Irish citizen	aperson who is an Irish citizen as a matter of Irish law

Term	Definition
Islands deportation order	a deportation order as defined in paragraph 3(6) of Schedule 4 to the Immigration Act 1971 that was made: [(a) in respect of conduct committed after the specified date and has effect in relation to the person, by virtue of paragraph 3 of Schedule 4 to the Immigration Act 1971, as if it was a deportation order made under that Act; or] (b) in respect of conduct committed [by the person] before the specified date, where the Secretary of State is satisfied that the order is justified on the grounds of public policy, public security or public health in accordance with regulation 27 of the EEA Regulations, irrespective of whether the EEA Regulations apply to the person (except that in regulation 27 for 'with a right of permanent residence under regulation 15' and 'has a right of permanent residence under regulation 15' read [['who, but for the making of the deportation order, meets the requirements of]] paragraph EU11, EU11A or EU12 of Appendix EU to the Immigration Rules'; and for 'an EEA decision' read 'a deportation decision')
Islands exclusion decision	a direction given by the relevant Minister or other authority in the Islands that a person must be excluded from the Island concerned: (a) in respect of conduct committed after the specified date; or (b) in respect of conduct committed [by the person] before the specified date, where the Secretary of State is satisfied that the direction is justified on the grounds of public policy, public security or public health in accordance with regulation 27 of the EEA Regulations, irrespective of whether the EEA Regulations apply to that person (except that in regulation 27 for 'with a right of permanent residence under regulation 15' and 'has a right of permanent residence under regulation 15' read [['who, but for the making of the exclusion direction, meets the requirements of]] paragraph EU11, EU11A or EU12 of Appendix EU to the Immigration Rules'; and for 'an EEA decision' read 'an exclusion direction')
joining family member of a relevant sponsor	a person who has satisfied the Secretary of State, including by the required evidence of family relationship, that they are (and for the relevant period have been), or (as the case may be) for the relevant period (or at the relevant time) they were: (a) the spouse or civil partner of a relevant sponsor, and (i) (aa) the marriage was contracted or the civil partnership was formed before the specified date; or (bb) the applicant was the durable partner of the relevant sponsor before the specified date (the definition of 'durable partner' in this table being met before that date rather than at the date of application), and the partnership remained durable at the specified date; and

Term	Definition
	(ii) (aa) (unless the applicant relies on meeting condition 1 or condition 3 of paragraph EU11A of this Appendix, or on being a family member who has retained the right of residence by virtue of a relationship with a relevant sponsor) the marriage or civil partnership continues to exist at the date of application; or (bb) (where the applicant relies on meeting condition 1 of paragraph EU11A of this Appendix) the marriage or civil partnership existed for the relevant period; or (cc) (where the applicant relies on meeting condition 3 of paragraph EU11A of this Appendix) the marriage or civil partnership existed immediately before the death of the relevant sponsor; or (b) the **specified spouse or civil partner of a Swiss citizen** ; or (c) the durable partner of a relevant sponsor, and: (i) the partnership was formed and was durable before the specified date; and (ii) (aa) (unless the applicant relies on meeting condition 1 or condition 3 of paragraph EU11A of this Appendix, or on being a family member who has retained the right of residence by virtue of a relationship with a relevant sponsor) the partnership remains durable at the date of application; or (bb) (where the applicant relies on meeting condition 1 of paragraph EU11A of this Appendix) the partnership remained durable for the relevant period; or (cc) (where the applicant relies on meeting condition 3 of paragraph EU11A of this Appendix) the partnership remained durable immediately before the death of the relevant sponsor; or (d) the child or dependent parent of a relevant sponsor, and the family relationship: (i) existed before the specified date (unless, in the case of a child, the person was born after that date, was adopted after that date in accordance with a relevant adoption decision or after that date became a child within the meaning of that entry in this table on the basis of one of sub-paragraphs (a)(iii) to (a)(xi) of that entry); and (ii) continues to exist at the date of application (or did so for the period of residence relied upon); or (e) the child or dependent parent of the spouse or civil partner of a relevant sponsor, as described in sub-paragraph (a) above, and all the family relationships: (i) existed before the specified date (unless, in the case of a child, the person was born after that date, was adopted after that date in accordance with a relevant adoption decision or after that date became a child within the meaning of that entry in this table on the basis of one of sub-paragraphs (a)(iii) to (a)(xi) of that entry); and (ii) continue to exist at the date of application (or did so for the period of residence relied upon)

Term	Definition
	in addition, the person meets one of the following requirements: (a) (where sub-paragraph (c) or (d) below does not apply) they were not resident in the UK and Islands on a basis which met the definition of 'family member of a relevant EEA citizen' in this table (where that relevant EEA citizen is their relevant sponsor) at any time before the specified date; or (b) (where sub-paragraph (c) or (d) below does not apply) they were resident in the UK and Islands before the specified date, and: (i) one of the events referred to in sub-paragraph (b)(i) or (b)(ii) in the definition of 'continuous qualifying period' in this table has occurred, and after that event occurred they were not resident in the UK and Islands again before the specified date; or (ii) the event referred to in sub-paragraph (a) in the definition of 'supervening event' in this table has occurred, and after that event occurred they were not resident in the UK and Islands again before the specified date; or (iii) they are the specified spouse or civil partner of a Swiss citizen, and they do not rely on any period of residence in the UK and Islands before the marriage was contracted or the civil partnership was formed; or (c) (where sub-paragraph (d) below does not apply) where the person is a child born after the specified date or adopted after that date in accordance with a relevant adoption decision, or after the specified date became a child within the meaning of that entry in this table on the basis of one of sub-paragraphs (a)(iii) to (a)(xi) of that entry (with the references below to 'parents' in this sub-paragraph construed to include the guardian or other person to whom the order or other provision referred to in the relevant sub-paragraph of (a)(iii) to (a)(xi) of that entry relates), one of the following requirements is met: (i) both of their parents are a relevant sponsor; or (ii) one of their parents is a relevant sponsor and the other is a British citizen who is not a relevant sponsor; or (iii) one of their parents is a relevant sponsor who has sole or joint rights of custody of them, in accordance with the applicable rules of family law of the UK, of the Islands or of a country listed in sub-paragraph (a)(i) of the entry for 'EEA citizen' in this table (including applicable rules of private international law under which rights of custody under the law of a third country are recognised in the UK, in the Islands or in a country listed in sub-paragraph (a)(i) of the entry for 'EEA citizen' in this table, in particular as regards the best interests of the child, and without prejudice to the normal operation of such applicable rules of private international law); or

Term	Definition
	(d) where the person is a child born after the specified date to (or adopted after that date in accordance with a relevant adoption decision by or after that date became, within the meaning of the entry for 'child' in this table and on the basis of one of sub-paragraphs (a)(iii) to (a)(xi) of that entry, a child of) a Swiss citizen or their spouse or civil partner (as described in the first sub-paragraph (a) in this entry), the Swiss citizen or their spouse or civil partner is a relevant sponsor
non-EEA citizen	aperson who is not an EEA citizen and is not a British citizen
person exempt from immigration control	a person who: (a) is a national of: Austria, Belgium, Bulgaria, Croatia, Republic of Cyprus, Czech Republic, Denmark, Estonia, Finland, France, Germany, Greece, Hungary, Iceland, Ireland, Italy, Latvia, Liechtenstein, Lithuania, Luxembourg, Malta, Netherlands, Norway, Poland, Portugal, Romania, Slovakia, Slovenia, Spain, Sweden or Switzerland; and (b) is not a British citizen; and (c) is exempt from immigration control in accordance with section 8(2), (3) or (4) of the Immigration Act 1971
person who has ceased activity	the person: (a) has terminated activity as a worker or self-employed person in the UK and either reached the age of entitlement to a state pension on terminating that activity or, in the case of a worker, ceased working to take early retirement; and immediately before that termination, was a worker or self-employed person in the UK for at least 12 months and resided in the UK and Islands for a continuous qualifying period of more than three years; or (b) stopped being a worker or self-employed person in the UK owing to permanent incapacity to work, having resided in the UK and Islands for a continuous qualifying period of more than the preceding two years or the incapacity having resulted from an accident at work or an occupational disease that entitles the person to a pension payable in full or in part by an institution in the UK; or (c) resided for a continuous qualifying period in the UK of at least three years as a worker or self-employed person, immediately before becoming a worker or self-employed person in a country listed in sub-paragraph (a)(i) of the entry for 'EEA citizen' in this table, while retaining a place of residence in the UK to which they return, as a rule, at least once a week in addition, the conditions as to length of residence and of employment in sub-paragraphs (a) and (b) above do not apply where the Secretary of State is satisfied, including by the required evidence of family relationship, that the relevant EEA citizen (or, as the case may be, the relevant sponsor) is the spouse or civil partner of a British citizen (substituting 'British citizen' for 'relevant EEA citizen' in the entry for, as the case may be, 'spouse' or 'civil partner' in this table)

Term	Definition
person who had a derivative or Zambrano right to reside	aperson who was a person with a derivative right to reside or, as the case may be, a person with a Zambrano right to reside, immediately before they became, as the case may be, a relevant EEA citizen, a family member of a relevant EEA citizen, a person with a derivative right to reside, a person with a Zambrano right to reside or a family member of a qualifying British citizen, and they have since remained, to the date of application, in any (or any combination) of those categories or as a family member who has retained the right of residence by virtue of a relationship with a relevant EEA citizen or with a qualifying British citizen
person who is subject to a non-adoptive legal guardianship order	a person who has satisfied the Secretary of State that, before the specified date, they: (a) are under the age of 18 years; and (b) are subject to a non-adoptive legal guardianship order in favour (solely or jointly with another party) of a relevant EEA citizen or, as the case may be, of a qualifying British citizen (who, in either case, is their 'sponsoring person' in accordance with the second sub-paragraph (b) in the entry for 'dependent relative' in this table) that: (i) is recognised under the national law of the state in which it was contracted; and (ii) places parental responsibility on a permanent basis on the relevant EEA citizen or, as the case may be, on the qualifying British citizen (in either case, solely or jointly with another party); and (c) have lived with the relevant EEA citizen (or, as the case may be, with the qualifying British citizen) since their placement under the guardianship order; and (d) have created family life with the relevant EEA citizen (or, as the case may be, with the qualifying British citizen); and (e) have a personal relationship with the relevant EEA citizen (or, as the case may be, with the qualifying British citizen) that involves dependency on the relevant EEA citizen (or, as the case may be, on the qualifying British citizen) and the assumption of parental responsibility, including legal and financial responsibilities, for that person by the relevant EEA citizen (or, as the case may be, by the qualifying British citizen)
person with a derivative right to reside	a person who has satisfied the Secretary of State, including (where applicable) by the required evidence of family relationship, that, by the specified date, they are (and for the relevant period have been), or (as the case may be) for the relevant period in which they rely on having been a person with a derivative right to reside (before they then became a person who had a derivative or Zambrano right to reside) they were, resident for a continuous qualifying period in the UK with a derivative right to reside by virtue of regulation 16(1) of the EEA Regulations:

Term	Definition
	(a) regardless of whether, in respect of the criterion in regulation 16(2)(b)(ii) of the EEA Regulations, the EEA citizen meets, or (as the case may be) met, the requirement in regulation 4(1)(c)(ii) of the EEA Regulations for comprehensive sickness insurance cover in the UK; and (b) regardless (where the person was previously granted limited leave to enter or remain under paragraph EU3 of this Appendix as a person with a derivative right to reside and was under the age of 18 years at the date of application for that leave) of whether, in respect of the criterion in regulation 16(2)(b)(i) or regulation 16(6)(a) of the EEA Regulations, they are, or (as the case may be) were, under the age of 18 years; and (c) excluding a person satisfying the criteria in: (i) paragraph (5) of regulation 16 of the EEA Regulations; or (ii) paragraph (6) of that regulation where that person's primary carer is, or (as the case may be) was, entitled to a derivative right to reside in the UK under paragraph (5)
person with a Zambrano right to reside	a person who has satisfied the Secretary of State, including (where applicable) by the required evidence of family relationship, that, by the specified date, they are (and for the relevant period have been), or (as the case may be) for the relevant period in which they rely on having been a person with a Zambrano right to reside (before they then became a person who had a derivative or Zambrano right to reside) they were: (a) resident for a continuous qualifying period in the UK with a derivative right to reside by virtue of regulation 16(1) of the EEA Regulations, by satisfying: (i) the criterion in paragraph (1)(a) of that regulation; and (ii) the criteria in: (aa) paragraph (5) of regulation 16 of the EEA Regulations; or (bb) paragraph (6) of that regulation where that person's primary carer is, or (as the case may be) was, entitled to a derivative right to reside in the UK under paragraph (5), regardless (where the person was previously granted limited leave to enter or remain under paragraph EU3 of this Appendix as a person with a Zambrano right to reside and was under the age of 18 years at the date of application for that leave) of whether, in respect of the criterion in regulation 16(6)(a) of the EEA Regulations, they are, or (as the case may be) were, under the age of 18 years; and (b) without leave to enter or remain in the UK, unless this was granted under this Appendix

Term	Definition
qualifying British citizen	a British citizen who: (a) has (or, as the case may be, for the relevant period had) returned to the UK with the applicant: (i) (where sub-paragraph (a)(ii) below does not apply) before 2300 GMT on 29 March 2022 (or later where the Secretary of State is satisfied that there are reasonable grounds for the person's failure to meet that deadline); or (ii) (in the case of a family member of a qualifying British citizen as described in sub-paragraph (a)(ii), (a)(iv), (a)(vii) or (a)(viii) of the entry for 'family member of a qualifying British citizen' in this table) before the specified date (or later where the Secretary of State is satisfied that there are reasonable grounds for the person's failure to meet that deadline); and (b) satisfied regulation 9(2), (3) and (4)(a) of the EEA Regulations (as the British citizen ('BC') to whom those provisions refer): (i) before the specified date; and (ii) immediately before returning to the UK with the applicant (who is to be treated as the family member ('F') or, as the case may be, as the extended family member ('EFM'), to whom those provisions refer); and (c) was continuously resident in the UK in accordance with regulation 3 of the EEA Regulations throughout any period on which the applicant relies as being present in the UK by virtue of being a family member of a qualifying British citizen [in addition, for the avoidance of doubt, for the purposes of sub-paragraph (b) above, service as a member of HM Forces (as defined in the Armed Forces Act 2006) in a country listed in sub-paragraph (a)(i) of the entry for 'EEA citizen' in this table may satisfy the conditions of being a 'worker' for the purposes of the EEA Regulations]
relevant adoption decision	an adoption decision taken: (a) by the competent administrative authority or court in the UK or the Islands; or (b) by the competent administrative authority or court in a country whose adoption orders are recognised by the UK or the Islands; or (c) in a particular case in which that decision in another country has been recognised in the UK or the Islands as an adoption
relevant document	[(a)(i)(aa) a family permit, registration certificate, residence card, document certifying permanent residence, permanent residence card or derivative residence card issued by the UK under the EEA Regulations on the basis of an application made under the EEA Regulations before (in the case, where the applicant is not a dependent relative, of a family permit) 1 July 2021 and otherwise before the specified date (or, in any case, a letter from the Secretary of State, issued after 30 June 2021, confirming their qualification for such a document, had the route not closed after 30 June 2021); or]

Term	Definition
	(bb) (where the applicant is a family member of a relevant person of Northern Ireland and is a dependent relative or durable partner) other evidence which satisfies the Secretary of State of the same matters under this Appendix concerning the relationship and (where relevant) dependency as a document to which sub-paragraph (a)(i)(aa) above refers; for the purposes of this provision, where the Secretary of State is so satisfied, such evidence is deemed to be the equivalent of a document to which sub-paragraph (a)(i)(aa) above refers; or (ii) a document or other evidence equivalent to a document to which sub-paragraph (a)(i)(aa) above refers, and issued by the Islands under the relevant legislation there evidencing the entitlement to enter or reside in the Islands or the right of permanent residence in the Islands through the application there of section 7(1) of the Immigration Act 1988 or under the Immigration (European Economic Area) Regulations of the Isle of Man; or (iii) a biometric residence card issued by virtue of having been granted limited leave to enter or remain under this Appendix; or (iv) an entry clearance in the form of an EU Settlement Scheme Family Permit granted under Appendix EU (Family Permit) to these Rules; and (b) it was not subsequently revoked, or fell to be so, because the relationship or dependency had never existed or the relationship or (where relevant) dependency had ceased; and (c) [(subject to sub-paragraphs (d) and (e)] below) it has not expired or otherwise ceased to be effective, or it remained valid for the period of residence relied upon; and (d) for the purposes of the reference to 'relevant document' in the first sub-paragraph (b) of the entry for 'dependent relative' in this table, in sub-paragraph (b)(i) of the entry for 'durable partner' in this table and in sub-paragraphs (e) and (f) of the entry for 'required evidence of family relationship' in this table, the relevant document may have expired, where: (i) before it expired, the applicant applied for a further relevant document (as described in sub-paragraph (a)(i)(aa) or (a)(iii) above) on the basis of the same family relationship as that on which that earlier relevant document was issued; and (ii) the further relevant document to which sub-paragraph (d)(i) above refers was issued by the date of decision on the application under this Appendix[; and] [(e) the relevant document may have expired, where: (i) it is a family permit (as described in sub-paragraph (a)(i)(aa) above) or an equivalent document or other evidence issued by the Islands (as described in sub-paragraph (a)(ii) above); and (ii) it expired after the specified date and before the required date; and (iii) the applicant arrived in the UK before 1 July 2021 and (unless they are a durable partner or dependent relative) after the specified date]

Term	Definition
[relevant EEA citizen (where, in respect of the application under consideration, the date of application by the relevant EEA citizen or their family member is before 1 July 2021)	(a) an EEA citizen (in accordance with sub-paragraph (a) of that entry in this table) resident in the UK and Islands for a continuous qualifying period which began before the specified date; or (b) an EEA citizen (in accordance with sub-paragraph (a) of that entry in this table) who, having been resident in the UK and Islands as described in sub-paragraph (a) above: (i) has been granted indefinite leave to enter or remain under paragraph EU2 of this Appendix (or under its equivalent in the Islands), which has not lapsed or been cancelled, revoked or invalidated (or is being granted that leave under that paragraph of this Appendix or under its equivalent in the Islands); or (ii) would, if they had made a valid application under this Appendix before 1 July 2021, have been granted indefinite leave to enter or remain under paragraph EU2 of this Appendix, which would not have lapsed or been cancelled, revoked or invalidated before the date of application; or (c) where the applicant is a family member of a relevant naturalised British citizen, an EEA citizen in accordance with sub-paragraph (b) of that entry in this table; or (d) where the applicant is the family member ("F") to whom paragraph 9 of Schedule 6 to the EEA Regulations refers and meets the criteria as F in that paragraph, an EEA citizen: (i) in accordance with sub-paragraph (c) of that entry in this table; and (ii) (aa) resident in the UK and Islands for a continuous qualifying period which began before the specified date; or (bb) who, having been resident in the UK and Islands as described in sub-paragraph (d)(ii)(aa) above and if they had made a valid application under this Appendix before 1 July 2021, would, but for the fact that they are a British citizen, have been granted indefinite leave to enter or remain under paragraph EU2 of this Appendix, which would not have lapsed or been cancelled, revoked or invalidated before the date of application; or (e) where the applicant is a family member of a relevant person of Northern Ireland, an EEA citizen (in accordance with sub-paragraph (d) of that entry in this table): (i) resident in the UK and Islands for a continuous qualifying period which, unless they are a specified relevant person of Northern Ireland, began before the specified date; or (ii) who, having been resident in the UK and Islands as described in sub-paragraph (e)(i) above (where they are a relevant person of Northern Ireland in accordance with sub-paragraph (a)(ii) of that entry in this table):

Term	Definition
	(aa) has been granted indefinite leave to enter or remain under paragraph EU2 of this Appendix (or under its equivalent in the Islands), which has not lapsed or been cancelled, revoked or invalidated (or is being granted that leave under that paragraph of this Appendix or under its equivalent in the Islands); or (bb) would, if they had made a valid application under this Appendix before 1 July 2021, have been granted indefinite leave to enter or remain under paragraph EU2 of this Appendix, which would not have lapsed or been cancelled, revoked or invalidated before the date of application; or (iii) who, having been resident in the UK and Islands as described in sub-paragraph (e)(i) above and if they had made a valid application under this Appendix before 1 July 2021, would, but for the fact (where they are a relevant person of Northern Ireland in accordance with sub-paragraph (a)(i) or (a)(iii) of that entry in this table) that they are a British citizen, have been granted indefinite leave to enter or remain under paragraph EU2 of this Appendix, which would not have lapsed or been cancelled, revoked or invalidated before the date of application; or (f) where the applicant is their family member, a person exempt from immigration control: (i) resident in the UK and Islands for a continuous qualifying period which began before the specified date; or (ii) who, having been resident in the UK and Islands as described in sub-paragraph (f)(i) above and if they had made a valid application under this Appendix before 1 July 2021, would have been granted indefinite leave to enter or remain under paragraph EU2 of this Appendix, which would not have lapsed or been cancelled, revoked or invalidated before the date of application; or (g) where the applicant is their family member, a frontier worker]
relevant EEA citizen (where, in respect of the application under consideration, the date of application by the relevant EEA citizen or their family member is on or after 1 July 2021)	(a) (i) an EEA citizen (in accordance with sub-paragraph (a) of that entry in this table) resident in the UK and Islands for a continuous qualifying period which began before the specified date; and (ii) where the applicant is their family member, the EEA citizen, having been resident in the UK and Islands as described in sub-paragraph (a)(i) above, has been granted: (aa) indefinite leave to enter or remain under paragraph EU2 of this Appendix (or under its equivalent in the Islands), which has not lapsed or been cancelled, revoked or invalidated; or (bb) limited leave to enter or remain under paragraph EU3 of this Appendix (or under its equivalent in the Islands), which has not lapsed or been cancelled, curtailed or invalidated; or (b) (i) an [an EEA citizen (in accordance with sub-paragraph (a) of that entry in this table)] resident in the UK and Islands for a continuous qualifying period which began before the specified date; and

Term	Definition
	(ii) where the applicant is their family member, the [the EEA citizen], having been resident in the UK and Islands as described in sub-paragraph (b)(i) above, would, if they had made a valid application under this Appendix before 1 July 2021, have been granted: (aa) indefinite leave to enter or remain under paragraph EU2 of this Appendix, which would not have lapsed or been cancelled, revoked or invalidated before the date of application; or (bb) limited leave to enter or remain under paragraph EU3 of this Appendix, which would not have lapsed or been cancelled, curtailed or invalidated before the date of application; or (c) where the applicant is a family member of a person who falls within sub-paragraphs (a), (c) and (d) of the entry for 'relevant naturalised British citizen' in this table, the person falling within those sub-paragraphs who, if they had made a valid application under this Appendix before 1 July 2021, would, but for the fact that they are a British citizen, have been granted: (i) indefinite leave to enter or remain under paragraph EU2 of this Appendix, which would not have lapsed or been cancelled, revoked or invalidated before the date of application; or (ii) limited leave to enter or remain under paragraph EU3 of this Appendix, which would not have lapsed or been cancelled, curtailed or invalidated before the date of application; or (d) where the applicant is the family member ('F') to whom paragraph 9 of Schedule 6 to the EEA Regulations refers and meets the criteria as F in that paragraph, an EEA citizen: (i) in accordance with sub-paragraph (c) of that entry in this table; and (ii) resident in the UK and Islands for a continuous qualifying period which began before the specified date; and (iii) who, having been resident in the UK and Islands as described in sub-paragraph (d)(ii) above and if they had made a valid application under this Appendix before 1 July 2021, would, but for the fact that they are a British citizen, have been granted: (aa) indefinite leave to enter or remain under paragraph EU2 of this Appendix, which would not have lapsed or been cancelled, revoked or invalidated before the date of application; or (bb) limited leave to enter or remain under paragraph EU3 of this Appendix, which would not have lapsed or been cancelled, curtailed or invalidated before the date of application; or (e) where the applicant is a family member of a relevant person of Northern Ireland, an EEA citizen (in accordance with sub-paragraph (d) of that entry in this table): (i) where they are a relevant person of Northern Ireland in accordance with sub-paragraph (a)(ii) of that entry in this table: (aa) resident in the UK and Islands for a continuous qualifying period which began before the specified date; and

Term	Definition
	(bb) who, having been resident in the UK and Islands as described in sub-paragraph (e)(i)(aa) above: (aaa) has been granted indefinite leave to enter or remain under paragraph EU2 of this Appendix (or under its equivalent in the Islands), which has not lapsed or been cancelled, revoked or invalidated; or (bbb) has been granted limited leave to enter or remain under paragraph EU3 of this Appendix (or under its equivalent in the Islands), which has not lapsed or been cancelled, curtailed or invalidated; or (ccc) if they had made a valid application under this Appendix before 1 July 2021, would have been granted indefinite leave to enter or remain under paragraph EU2 of this Appendix, which would not have lapsed or been cancelled, revoked or invalidated before the date of application; or (ddd) if they had made a valid application under this Appendix before 1 July 2021, would have been granted limited leave to enter or remain under paragraph EU3 of this Appendix, which would not have lapsed or been cancelled, curtailed or invalidated before the date of application; or (ii) where they are a relevant person of Northern Ireland in accordance with sub-paragraph (a)(i) or (a)(iii) of that entry in this table: [(aa) resident in the UK and Islands for a continuous qualifying period which, unless they are a specified relevant person of Northern Ireland, began before the specified date; and] (bb) who, having been resident in the UK and Islands as described in sub-paragraph (e)(ii)(aa) above and if they had made a valid application under this Appendix before 1 July 2021, would, but for the fact that they are a British citizen, have been granted: (aaa) indefinite leave to enter or remain under paragraph EU2 of this Appendix, which would not have lapsed or been cancelled, revoked or invalidated before the date of application; or (bbb) limited leave to enter or remain under paragraph EU3 of this Appendix, which would not have lapsed or been cancelled, curtailed or invalidated before the date of application; or (f) where the applicant is their family member, a person exempt from immigration control: (i) resident in the UK and Islands for a continuous qualifying period which began before the specified date; and (ii) who, having been resident in the UK and Islands as described in sub-paragraph (f)(i) above and if they had made a valid application under this Appendix before 1 July 2021, would, [...]have been granted: (aa) indefinite leave to enter or remain under paragraph EU2 of this Appendix, which would not have lapsed or been cancelled, revoked or invalidated before the date of application; or

Term	Definition
	(bb) limited leave to enter or remain under paragraph EU3 of this Appendix, which would not have lapsed or been cancelled, curtailed or invalidated before the date of application; or (g) where the applicant is their family member, a frontier worker [[in addition, notwithstanding what is said above, in relation to sub-paragraphs (a) to (f) above, it will suffice that the relevant EEA citizen is (or, as the case may be, for the relevant period was) resident in the UK and Islands for a continuous qualifying period which{, unless they are a specified relevant person of Northern Ireland,} began before the specified date where the applicant: (a) (i) is (or, as the case may be, for the relevant period was) a family member of a relevant EEA citizen or a family member who has retained the right of residence by virtue of a relationship with a relevant EEA citizen; and (ii) has completed a continuous qualifying period of five years under condition 3 in the table in paragraph EU11 of this Appendix; or (b) (i is a family member of a relevant EEA citizen or a family member who has retained the right of residence by virtue of a relationship with a relevant EEA citizen; and (ii) otherwise meets the eligibility requirements for limited leave to enter or remain under condition 1 in the table in paragraph EU14 of this Appendix; or (c) relies on meeting condition 1, 2 or 6 in the table in paragraph EU11 of this Appendix]]
[relevant EEA family permit case	(a) family member of a relevant EEA citizen who is: (i) a dependent relative or a durable partner who (in either case) arrived in the UK after the specified date and by 30 June 2021 with a valid EEA family permit issued under the EEA Regulations on the basis of a valid application made under the EEA Regulations before the specified date; or (ii) a dependent relative or (on the basis of a valid application made under the EEA Regulations before the specified date) a durable partner who (in either case) arrived in the UK after the specified date with an entry clearance in the form of an EU Settlement Scheme Family Permit granted under Appendix EU (Family Permit) to these Rules on the basis they met the definition in Annex 1 to that Appendix of 'specified EEA family permit case'; or (b) a person with a derivative right to reside or a person with a Zambrano right to reside who (in either case) arrived in the UK after the specified date and by 30 June 2021 with a valid EEA family permit issued under the EEA Regulations on the basis of a valid application made under the EEA Regulations before the specified date; or

Term	Definition
	(c) a person with a derivative right to reside or a person with a Zambrano right to reside who (in either case) arrived in the UK after the specified date with an entry clearance in the form of an EU Settlement Scheme Family Permit granted under Appendix EU (Family Permit) to these Rules on the basis they met the definition in Annex 1 to that Appendix of 'specified EEA family permit case' in addition, where sub-paragraph (b) or (c) above applies, the reference to 'specified date' in the entry for (as the case may be) 'person with a derivative right to reside' or 'person with a Zambrano right to reside' in this table is to be read as meaning the date on which the person made a valid application under the EEA Regulations on the basis of which the family permit referred to in (as the case may be) sub-paragraph (b) or (c) above was issued]
relevant excluded person	a person: (a) in respect of whom the Secretary of State has made a decision under Article 1F of the Refugee Convention to exclude the person from the Refugee Convention or under paragraph 339D of these Rules to exclude them from humanitarian protection; or (b) in respect of whom the Secretary of State has previously made a decision that they are a person to whom Article 33(2) of the Refugee Convention applies because there are reasonable grounds for regarding them as a danger to the security of the UK; or (c) who the Secretary of State considers to be a person in respect of whom sub-paragraph (a) or (b) above would apply except that: (i) the person has not made a protection claim; or (ii) the person made a protection claim which has already been finally determined without reference to Article 1F of the Refugee Convention or paragraph 339D of these Rules; or (d) in respect of whom the Secretary of State has previously made a decision that they are a person to whom Article 33(2) of the Refugee Convention applies because, having been convicted by a final judgment of a particularly serious crime, they constitute a danger to the community of the UK
relevant naturalised British citizen	(a) an EEA citizen (in accordance with sub-paragraph (a)(i) of that entry in this table) resident in the UK and Islands for a continuous qualifying period which began before the specified date; or [(b) an EEA citizen (in accordance with sub-paragraph (a)(i) of that entry in this table) who, having been resident in the UK and Islands as described in sub-paragraph (a) above and if they had made a valid application under this Appendix before 1 July 2021, would, but for the fact that they are a British citizen, have been granted indefinite leave to enter or remain under paragraph EU2 of this Appendix, which would not have lapsed or been cancelled, revoked or invalidated before the date of application; and in either case the person also:]

Term	Definition
	(c) comes within paragraph (b) of the definition of 'EEA national' in regulation 2(1) of the EEA Regulations; and [(d) meets the criteria contained in regulation 9A(2) or (3) as the dual national ("DN") to whom those provisions refer (save for the requirement in regulation 4(1)(c)(ii) and (d)(ii) of the EEA Regulations for comprehensive sickness insurance cover in the UK and regardless of whether, save in conditions 5 and 6 in the table in paragraph EU11 of this Appendix and in conditions 2 and 3 in the table in paragraph EU11A, they otherwise remained a qualified person under regulation 6 of the EEA Regulations after they acquired British citizenship)]
relevant person of Northern Ireland	a person who: (a) is: (i) a British citizen; or (ii) an Irish citizen; or (iii) a British citizen and an Irish citizen; and (b) was born in Northern Ireland and, at the time of the person's birth, at least one of their parents was: (i) a British citizen; or (ii) an Irish citizen; or (iii) a British citizen and an Irish citizen; or (iv) otherwise entitled to reside in Northern Ireland without any restriction on their period of residence
relevant sponsor	(a) where the date of application by a joining family member of a relevant sponsor is after the specified date and before 1 July 2021: (i) an EEA citizen (in accordance with sub-paragraph (a) of that entry in this table) who, having been resident in the UK and Islands for a continuous qualifying period which began before the specified date, has been granted: (aa) indefinite leave to enter or remain under paragraph EU2 of this Appendix (or under its equivalent in the Islands), which has not lapsed or been cancelled, revoked or invalidated (or is being granted that leave under that paragraph of this Appendix or under its equivalent in the Islands); or (bb) limited leave to enter or remain under paragraph EU3 of this Appendix (or under its equivalent in the Islands), which has not lapsed or been cancelled, curtailed or invalidated (or is being granted that leave under that paragraph of this Appendix or under its equivalent in the Islands); or (ii) an EEA citizen (in accordance with sub-paragraph (a) of that entry in this table): (aa) resident in the UK and Islands for a continuous qualifying period which began before the specified date; or

Term	Definition
	[(bb) who, having been resident in the UK and Islands as described in sub-paragraph (a)(ii)(aa) above and if they had made a valid application under this Appendix before 1 July 2021, would have been granted indefinite leave to enter or remain under paragraph EU2 of this Appendix, which would not have lapsed or been cancelled, revoked or invalidated before the date of application; or]
	(iii) an EEA citizen in accordance with sub-paragraph (b) of that entry in this table (a relevant naturalised British citizen, in accordance with sub-paragraph (a) or (b), together with sub-paragraphs (c) and (d), of that entry in this table); or
	[(iv) an EEA citizen (in accordance with sub-paragraph (d) of that entry in this table):
	(aa) resident in the UK and Islands for a continuous qualifying period which, unless they are a specified relevant person of Northern Ireland, began before the specified date; or
	(bb) who, having been resident in the UK and Islands as described in sub-paragraph (a)(iv)(aa) above (where they are a relevant person of Northern Ireland in accordance with sub-paragraph (a)(ii) of that entry in this table):
	(aaa) has been granted indefinite leave to enter or remain under paragraph EU2 of this Appendix (or under its equivalent in the Islands), which has not lapsed or been cancelled, revoked or invalidated (or is being granted that leave under that paragraph of this Appendix or under its equivalent in the Islands); or
	(bbb) would, if they had made a valid application under this Appendix before 1 July 2021, have been granted indefinite leave to enter or remain under paragraph EU2 of this Appendix, which would not have lapsed or been cancelled, revoked or invalidated before the date of application; or
	(cc) who, having been resident in the UK and Islands as described in sub-paragraph (a)(iv)(aa) above and if they had made a valid application under this Appendix before 1 July 2021, would, but for the fact (where they are a relevant person of Northern Ireland in accordance with sub-paragraph (a)(i) or (a)(iii) of that entry in this table) that they are a British citizen, have been granted indefinite leave to enter or remain under paragraph EU2 of this Appendix, which would not have lapsed or been cancelled, revoked or invalidated before the date of application; or]
	(v) a person exempt from immigration control:
	(aa) resident in the UK and Islands for a continuous qualifying period which began before the specified date; or

Term	Definition
	[(bb) who, having been resident in the UK and Islands as described in sub-paragraph (a)(v)(aa) above and if they had made a valid application under this Appendix before 1 July 2021, would have been granted indefinite leave to enter or remain under paragraph EU2 of this Appendix, which would not have lapsed or been cancelled, revoked or invalidated before the date of application; or] (vi) a frontier worker; or (b) where the date of application by a joining family member of a relevant sponsor is on or after 1 July 2021: (i) an EEA citizen (in accordance with sub-paragraph (a) of that entry in this table) who, having been resident in the UK and Islands for a continuous qualifying period which began before the specified date, has been granted: (aa) indefinite leave to enter or remain under paragraph EU2 of this Appendix (or under its equivalent in the Islands), which has not lapsed or been cancelled, revoked or invalidated; or (bb) limited leave to enter or remain under paragraph EU3 of this Appendix (or under its equivalent in the Islands), which has not lapsed or been cancelled, curtailed or invalidated; or (ii) an Irish citizen who, having been resident in the UK and Islands for a continuous qualifying period which began before the specified date, would, if they had made a valid application under this Appendix before 1 July 2021, have been granted: (aa) indefinite leave to enter or remain under paragraph EU2 of this Appendix, which would not have lapsed or been cancelled, revoked or invalidated before the date of application; or (bb) limited leave to enter or remain under paragraph EU3 of this Appendix, which would not have lapsed or been cancelled, curtailed or invalidated before the date of application; or (iii) a person who falls within sub-paragraphs (a), (c) and (d) of the entry for 'relevant naturalised British citizen' in this table, who, if they had made a valid application under this Appendix before 1 July 2021, would, but for the fact that they are a British citizen, have been granted: (aa) indefinite leave to enter or remain under paragraph EU2 of this Appendix, which would not have lapsed or been cancelled, revoked or invalidated before the date of application; or (bb) limited leave to enter or remain under paragraph EU3 of this Appendix, which would not have lapsed or been cancelled, curtailed or invalidated before the date of application; or (iv) an EEA citizen (in accordance with sub-paragraph (d) of that entry in this table) who is a relevant person of Northern Ireland in accordance with sub-paragraph (a)(ii) of that entry in this table: (aa) resident in the UK and Islands for a continuous qualifying period which began before the specified date; and

Term	Definition
	(bb) who, having been resident in the UK and Islands as described in sub-paragraph (b)(iv)(aa) above: (aaa) has been granted indefinite leave to enter or remain under paragraph EU2 of this Appendix (or under its equivalent in the Islands), which has not lapsed or been cancelled, revoked or invalidated; or (bbb) if they had made a valid application under this Appendix before 1 July 2021, would have been granted indefinite leave to enter or remain under paragraph EU2 of this Appendix, which would not have lapsed or been cancelled, revoked or invalidated before the date of application; or (ccc) has been granted limited leave to enter or remain under paragraph EU3 of this Appendix (or under its equivalent in the Islands), which has not lapsed or been cancelled, curtailed or invalidated; or (ddd) if they had made a valid application under this Appendix before 1 July 2021, would have been granted limited leave to enter or remain under paragraph EU3 of this Appendix, which would not have lapsed or been cancelled, curtailed or invalidated before the date of application; or (v) an EEA citizen (in accordance with sub-paragraph (d) of that entry in this table) who is a relevant person of Northern Ireland in accordance with sub-paragraph (a)(i) or (a)(iii) of that entry in this table: [(aa) resident in the UK and Islands for a continuous qualifying period which, unless they are a specified relevant person of Northern Ireland, began before the specified date; and] (bb) who, having been resident in the UK and Islands as described in sub-paragraph (b)(v)(aa) above and if they had made a valid application under this Appendix before 1 July 2021, would, but for the fact that they are a British citizen, have been granted: (aaa) indefinite leave to enter or remain under paragraph EU2 of this Appendix, which would not have lapsed or been cancelled, revoked or invalidated before the date of application; or (bbb) limited leave to enter or remain under paragraph EU3 of this Appendix, which would not have lapsed or been cancelled, curtailed or invalidated before the date of application; or (vi) a person exempt from immigration control who, having been resident in the UK and Islands for a continuous qualifying period which began before the specified date and if they had made a valid application under this Appendix before 1 July 2021, would, [...] have been granted: (aa) indefinite leave to enter or remain under paragraph EU2 of this Appendix, which would not have lapsed or been cancelled, revoked or invalidated before the date of application; or

Term	Definition
	(bb) limited leave to enter or remain under paragraph EU3 of this Appendix, which would not have lapsed or been cancelled, curtailed or invalidated before the date of application; or (vii) a frontier worker [[in addition: (a) save for the purposes of condition 3 in the table in paragraph EU11A of this Appendix and of sub-paragraphs (a) and (b) of the entry for 'family member who has retained the right of residence' in this table, the relevant sponsor has not died; and (b) notwithstanding what is said above, where the date of application by a joining family member of a relevant sponsor is on or after 1 July 2021, it will suffice that the relevant sponsor is or (as the case may be) was resident in the UK and Islands for a continuous qualifying period which{, unless they are a specified relevant person of Northern Ireland,} began before the specified date where the applicant: (i) on the basis of events which occurred during the period to which sub-paragraph (a)(ii)(aa) or (a)(iii)(aa) of the entry for 'required date' in this table refers, relies on being a family member who has retained the right of residence by virtue of a relationship with a relevant sponsor, or has limited leave to enter or remain granted on that basis under paragraph EU3A of this Appendix; or (ii) relies on meeting condition 3 in the table in paragraph EU11A of this Appendix; or (iii) (aa) has limited leave to enter or remain granted under paragraph EU3A of this Appendix; and (bb) would have been eligible for indefinite leave to enter or remain under condition 1, 2 or 3 in the table in paragraph EU11A of this Appendix, had they made a further valid application under this Appendix (subsequently to that which led to the grant of leave to which sub-paragraph (b)(iii)(aa) immediately above refers) before the indefinite or limited leave to enter or remain granted under paragraph EU2 or (as the case may be) EU3 to their relevant sponsor lapsed or was cancelled, curtailed, revoked or invalidated (or would have done so or been so, where the first sub-paragraph (b)(ii) above or sub-paragraph (b)(iii), (b)(iv)(bb)(bbb), (b)(iv)(bb)(ddd), (b)(v) or (b)(vi) above applies); for the purposes of this provision, the reference to continuous qualifying period in this sub-paragraph (b) will be treated as a relevant reference for the purposes of sub-paragraph (c)(v) of the entry for 'continuous qualifying period' in this table, where sub-paragraph (c)(i), (c)(ii), (c)(iii) or (c)(iv) of that entry does not apply]]

Term	Definition
required application process	(a) (unless sub-paragraph (b) or (c) applies) the relevant on-line application form and a relevant process set out in that form for: (i) providing the required proof of identity and nationality or (as the case may be) the required proof of entitlement to apply from outside the UK; and (ii) providing the required biometrics; or (b) the required paper application form where this is mandated on gov.uk and a relevant process set out in that form for: (i) providing the required proof of identity and nationality or (as the case may be) the required proof of entitlement to apply from outside the UK; and (ii) providing the required biometrics; or (c) a paper application form where this has been issued individually to the applicant by the Secretary of State, via the relevant process for this set out on gov.uk, and a relevant process set out in that form for: (i) providing the required proof of identity and nationality or (as the case may be) the required proof of entitlement to apply from outside the UK; and (ii) providing the required biometrics in addition, where a paper application form is used under sub-paragraph (b) or (c) above, it must be sent by pre-paid post or courier to the Home Office address specified on the form (where one is specified), or by e-mail to the Home Office e-mail address specified on the form (where one is specified)
required biometrics	(a) a facial photograph of the applicant (within the meaning of 'biometric information' in section 15 of the UK Borders Act 2007); and (b) (in the case of a non-EEA citizen without a **specified relevant document** making an application within the UK) the fingerprints of the applicant (also within that meaning of 'biometric information'; unless, in accordance with guidance published by the Secretary of State and in force at the date of application, they are not required to provide these), in both cases provided in accordance with the required application process
[required date	(a) where the applicant does not have indefinite leave to enter or remain or limited leave to enter or remain granted under this Appendix: (i) (where sub-paragraph (a)(ii), (a)(iii) or (a)(iv) below does not apply) the date of application is: (aa) before 1 July 2021; or (bb) (where the deadline in sub-paragraph (a)(i)(aa) above was not met and the Secretary of State is satisfied by information provided with the application that, at the date of application, there are reasonable grounds for the person's delay in making their application) on or after 1 July 2021; or

Term	Definition
	(ii) (in the case of a joining family member of a relevant sponsor and that joining family member arrived in the UK on or after 1 April 2021, and where sub-paragraph (a)(iii) below does not apply, or that joining family member is a child born in the UK on or after 1 April 2021 or adopted in the UK on or after that date in accordance with a relevant adoption decision, or on or after 1 April 2021 became a child in the UK within the meaning of the entry for 'child' in this table on the basis of one of sub-paragraphs (a)(iii) to (a)(xi) of that entry) the date of application is: (aa) within three months of the date on which they arrived in the UK (or, as the case may be, of the date on which they were born in the UK, adopted in the UK or became a child in the UK within the meaning of the entry for 'child' in this table on the basis of one of sub-paragraphs (a)(iii) to (a)(xi) of that entry); or (bb) (where the deadline in sub-paragraph (a)(ii)(aa) above was not met and the Secretary of State is satisfied by information provided with the application that, at the date of application, there are reasonable grounds for the person's delay in making their application) after that deadline; or (iii) (in the case of a joining family member of a relevant sponsor as described in sub-paragraph (b) of that entry in this table and that joining family member arrived in the UK on or after 1 April 2021) the date of application is: (aa) within three months of the date on which they arrived in the UK, and before 1 January 2026; or (bb) (where the deadline in sub-paragraph (a)(iii)(aa) above was not met and the Secretary of State is satisfied by information provided with the application that, at the date of application, there are reasonable grounds for the person's delay in making their application) after that deadline; or (iv) (in the case of a family member of a qualifying British citizen as described in sub-paragraph (a)(i), (a)(iii), (a)(v) or (a)(vi) of the entry for 'family member of a qualifying British citizen' in this table) the date of application is: (aa) before 2300 GMT on 29 March 2022; or (bb) (where the deadline in sub-paragraph (a)(iv)(aa) above was not met and the Secretary of State is satisfied by information provided with the application that, at the date of application, there are reasonable grounds for the person's delay in making their application) after 2300 GMT on 29 March 2022; or (v) (in the case of an applicant who has limited leave to enter or remain granted under another part of these Rules or outside the Immigration Rules, which has not lapsed or been cancelled, curtailed or invalidated, and the date of expiry of that leave is on or after 1 July 2021, which, notwithstanding the deadline in sub-paragraph (a)(i)(aa) above, the Secretary of State will deem to be reasonable grounds for the person's failure to meet that deadline), the date of application is:

Term	Definition
	(aa) before the date of expiry of that leave; or (bb) (where the deadline in sub-paragraph (a)(v)(aa) above was not met and the Secretary of State is satisfied by information provided with the application that, at the date of application, there are reasonable grounds for the person's delay in making their application) after the date of expiry of that leave; or (vi) (in the case of an applicant who ceases to be exempt from immigration control in accordance with section 8(2), (3) or (4) of the Immigration Act 1971 on or after 1 July 2021, which, notwithstanding the deadline applicable under sub-paragraph (a)(i)(aa), (a)(ii)(aa) or (a)(iii)(aa) above, the Secretary of State will deem to be reasonable grounds for the person's failure to meet that deadline), the date of application is: (aa) within the period of 90 days beginning on the day on which they ceased to be exempt from immigration control; or (bb) (where the deadline in sub-paragraph (a)(vi)(aa) above was not met and the Secretary of State is satisfied by information provided with the application that, at the date of application, there are reasonable grounds for the person's delay in making their application) after that deadline; or (b) where the applicant has limited leave to enter or remain granted under this Appendix, which has not lapsed or been cancelled, curtailed or invalidated, the date of application is: (i) before the date of expiry of that leave; or (ii) (where the deadline in sub-paragraph (b)(i) above was not met and the Secretary of State is satisfied by information provided with the application that, at the date of application, there are reasonable grounds for the person's delay in making their application) after the date of expiry of that leave in addition: (a) for the avoidance of doubt, paragraph 39E of these Rules does not apply to applications made under this Appendix; and (b) the deadline in sub-paragraph (a)(i)(aa) above does not apply (and the applicant therefore has to meet no requirement under sub-paragraph (a) above) where the applicant: (i) is a joining family member of a relevant sponsor; and (ii) does not have indefinite leave to enter or remain or limited leave to enter or remain granted under this Appendix; and (iii) is not caught by the deadline in sub-paragraph (a)(ii)(aa) or (a)(iii)(aa) above; and (iv) does not fall within sub-paragraph (a)(v) or (a)(vi) above]

Term	Definition
required evidence of being a relevant person of Northern Ireland	(a) the person's birth certificate showing that they were born in Northern Ireland, or their passport where this shows that they were born in Northern Ireland; and (b) evidence which satisfies the Secretary of State that, at the time of the person's birth, at least one of their parents was: (i) a British citizen; or (ii) an Irish citizen; or (iii) a British citizen and an Irish citizen; or (iv) otherwise entitled to reside in Northern Ireland without any restriction on their period of residence in addition: (a) where, in order to meet the requirements of this entry, the applicant submits a copy (and not the original) of a document (including by uploading this as part of the required application process), the Secretary of State can require the applicant to submit the original document where the Secretary of State has reasonable doubt as to the authenticity of the copy submitted; and (b) where, in order to meet the requirements of this entry, the applicant submits a document which is not in English, the Secretary of State can require the applicant to provide a certified English translation of (or a Multilingual Standard Form to accompany) the document, where this is necessary for the purposes of deciding whether the applicant meets the eligibility requirements for indefinite leave to enter or remain or for limited leave to enter or remain under this Appendix
required evidence of family relationship	in the case of: (a) a spouse without a documented right of permanent residence: (i) a relevant document as the spouse of the relevant EEA citizen (or, as the case may be, of the qualifying British citizen or of the relevant sponsor), or a valid document of record of a marriage recognised under the law of England and Wales, Scotland or Northern Ireland or of the Islands; and (ii) (aa) where the marriage to the relevant EEA citizen (or, as the case may be, the relevant sponsor) was contracted after the specified date and the applicant is not the specified spouse or civil partner of a Swiss citizen, a relevant document as the durable partner of the relevant EEA citizen or, where the applicant is the joining family member of a relevant sponsor or relies on the relevant EEA citizen being a relevant person of Northern Ireland, there is evidence which satisfies the Secretary of State that the durable partnership was formed and was durable before the specified date; or (bb) where the marriage to the qualifying British citizen was contracted after the date and time of withdrawal, evidence which satisfies the Secretary of State that the durable partnership was formed and was durable before the date and time of withdrawal; or

Term	Definition
	(b) a civil partner without a documented right of permanent residence: (i) a relevant document as the civil partner of the relevant EEA citizen (or, as the case may be, of the qualifying British citizen or of the relevant sponsor); a valid civil partnership certificate recognised under the law of England and Wales, Scotland or Northern Ireland or under any equivalent legislation in the Islands; or the valid overseas registration document for a relationship which is entitled to be treated as a civil partnership under the Civil Partnership Act 2004 or under any equivalent legislation in the Islands; and (ii) (aa) where the civil partnership with the relevant EEA citizen (or, as the case may be, the relevant sponsor) was formed after the specified date and the applicant is not the specified spouse or civil partner of a Swiss citizen, a relevant document as the durable partner of the relevant EEA citizen or, where the applicant is a joining family member of a relevant sponsor or relies on the relevant EEA citizen being a relevant person of Northern Ireland, there is evidence which satisfies the Secretary of State that the durable partnership was formed and was durable before the specified date; or (bb) where the civil partnership with the qualifying British citizen was formed after the date and time of withdrawal, evidence which satisfies the Secretary of State that the durable partnership was formed and was durable before the date and time of withdrawal; or (c) a child without a documented right of permanent residence—a relevant document issued on the basis of the relevant family relationship or their **evidence of birth** , and: (i) where the applicant is aged 21 years or over and was not previously granted limited leave to enter or remain under this Appendix (or under its equivalent in the Islands) as a child, evidence which satisfies the Secretary of State that the requirements in sub-paragraph (b)(ii) of the entry for 'child' in this table are met; and (ii) where, in the case of a joining family member of a relevant sponsor, the applicant is a child born after the specified date or adopted after that date in accordance with a relevant adoption decision, or after the specified date became a child within the meaning of that entry in this table on the basis of one of sub-paragraphs (a)(iii) to (a)(xi) of that entry, evidence which satisfies the Secretary of State that the requirements in the second sub-paragraph (c) (as set out in sub-paragraph (i), (ii) or (iii) of that sub-paragraph) or in the second sub-paragraph (d) of the entry for 'joining family member of a relevant sponsor' in this table are met; or (d) a dependent parent without a documented right of permanent residence—a relevant document issued on the basis of the relevant family relationship or their evidence of birth, and, where the first sub-paragraph (b) of the entry for 'dependent parent' in this table applies, evidence which satisfies the Secretary of State that (where this is not assumed) the requirement as to dependency in that sub-paragraph is met; or

Term	Definition
	(e) a durable partner: (i) a relevant document as the durable partner of the relevant EEA citizen (or, as the case may be, of the qualifying British citizen or of the relevant sponsor) and, unless this confirms the right of permanent residence in the UK under regulation 15 of the EEA Regulations (or the right of permanent residence in the Islands through the application there of section 7(1) of the Immigration Act 1988 or under the Immigration (European Economic Area) Regulations of the Isle of Man), evidence which satisfies the Secretary of State that the partnership remains durable at the date of application (or did so for the period of residence relied upon); or (ii) [(where the person is applying as the durable partner of a relevant sponsor (or, as the case may be, of a qualifying British citizen) and sub-paragraph (b)(ii) of the entry for 'durable partner' in this table applies)] the evidence to which that sub-paragraph refers, and evidence which satisfies the Secretary of State that the partnership remains durable at the date of application (or did so for the period of residence relied upon); or (f) a dependent relative: (i) (where sub-paragraph (f)(ii) below does not apply) a relevant document as the dependent relative of their sponsoring person (in the entry for 'dependent relative' in this table) and, unless this confirms the right of permanent residence in the UK under regulation 15 of the EEA Regulations (or the right of permanent residence in the Islands through the application there of section 7(1) of the Immigration Act 1988 or under the Immigration (European Economic Area) Regulations of the Isle of Man), evidence which satisfies the Secretary of State that the relationship and the dependency (or, as the case may be, their membership of the household or their strict need for personal care on serious health grounds) continue to exist at the date of application (or did so for the period of residence relied upon); or (ii) (in the case of a family member of a qualifying British citizen as described in sub-paragraph (a)(viii) of that entry in this table, where the Secretary of State is satisfied that there are reasonable grounds for the person's failure to meet the deadline to which that sub-paragraph refers) evidence which satisfies the Secretary of State that the relationship and the dependency (or, as the case may be, their membership of the household or their strict need for personal care on serious health grounds) existed before the specified date and continue to exist at the date of application (or did so for the period of residence relied upon) in addition: (a) where the eligibility requirements to be met for leave to be granted under this Appendix relate to the death of a person, the required evidence of family relationship must include their death certificate or other evidence which the Secretary of State is satisfied evidences the death; and

Term	Definition
	(b) where the applicant is a non-EEA citizen without a documented right of permanent residence, or is an EEA citizen (in accordance with sub-paragraph (a) of that entry in this table) without a documented right of permanent residence who relies on being (or, as the case may be, for the relevant period on having been) a family member of a qualifying British citizen (or, as the case may be, a family member of a relevant EEA citizen, a family member who has retained the right of residence or a joining family member of a relevant sponsor), the required evidence of family relationship must include: (i) the following proof of identity and nationality of (as the case may be) the relevant EEA citizen, the qualifying British citizen or the relevant sponsor, of whom the applicant is (or, as the case may be, for the relevant period was) a family member or (as the case may be) a joining family member: [[(aa) where the applicant is (or, as the case may be, for the relevant period was) a family member of a relevant EEA citizen, that EEA citizen is (or, as the case may be, for the relevant period was) a relevant EEA citizen as described in the applicable entry for 'relevant EEA citizen' in this table, and is (or, as the case may be, was) such a relevant EEA citizen throughout any continuous qualifying period on which the applicant relies as being a family member of a relevant EEA citizen; or]] (bb) (in the case of a relevant EEA citizen who is neither a relevant naturalised British citizen nor a relevant EEA citizen as described in sub-paragraph (d) of the applicable entry in this table nor relied on by the applicant as being a relevant person of Northern Ireland, or in the case of a relevant sponsor who is neither a relevant naturalised British citizen nor relied on by the applicant as being a relevant person of Northern Ireland) their valid national identity card or confirmation that they have been or are being granted indefinite leave to enter or remain under paragraph EU2 of this Appendix or limited leave to enter or remain under paragraph EU3; or (cc) (in the case of a relevant EEA citizen who is a relevant naturalised British citizen or who is a relevant EEA citizen as described in sub-paragraph (d) of the applicable entry in this table, or in the case of a relevant sponsor who is a relevant naturalised British citizen) their valid passport or their valid national identity card as a national of a country listed in sub-paragraph (a)(i) in the entry for 'EEA citizen' in this table, and information or evidence which is provided by the applicant, or is otherwise available to the Secretary of State, which satisfies the Secretary of State that the person is a British citizen; or (dd) (in the case of a relevant EEA citizen or a relevant sponsor who, in either case, is relied on by the applicant as being a relevant person of Northern Ireland) the **required evidence of being a relevant person of Northern Ireland**, and:

Term	Definition
	(aaa) (where they are a British citizen) information or evidence which is provided by the applicant, or is otherwise available to the Secretary of State, which satisfies the Secretary of State that the person is a British citizen; or (bbb) (where they are an Irish citizen) their valid passport or their valid national identity card as an Irish citizen, or confirmation that they have been or are being granted indefinite leave to enter or remain under paragraph EU2 of this Appendix or limited leave to enter or remain under paragraph EU3; or (ccc) [(where they are a British citizen and an Irish citizen, and are not relied on by the applicant as being a specified relevant person of Northern Ireland)] the evidence required by sub-paragraph (b)(i)(dd)(aaa) or (b)(i)(dd)(bbb) above, unless (in any case) the Secretary of State agrees to accept alternative evidence of identity and nationality where the applicant is unable to obtain or produce the required document due to circumstances beyond their control or to compelling practical or compassionate reasons; and (ii) evidence which satisfies the Secretary of State that: [(aa) where the applicant is (or, as the case may be, for the relevant period was) a family member of a relevant EEA citizen, that EEA citizen is (or, as the case may be, for the relevant period was) a relevant EEA citizen as described in the applicable entry for 'relevant EEA citizen' in this table, and is (or, as the case may be, was) such a relevant EEA citizen throughout any continuous qualifying period on which the applicant relies as being a family member of a relevant EEA citizen; or] (bb) where the applicant is (or, as the case may be, for the relevant period was) a family member of a qualifying British citizen, that British citizen is (or, as the case may be, for the relevant period was) a qualifying British citizen, and is (or, as the case may be, was) a qualifying British citizen throughout any continuous qualifying period on which the applicant relies as being a family member of a qualifying British citizen; or (cc) where the applicant is (or, as the case may be, for the relevant period was) a joining family member of a relevant sponsor, that relevant sponsor is (or, as the case may be, for the relevant period was) a relevant sponsor, and is (or, as the case may be, was) a relevant sponsor throughout any continuous qualifying period on which the applicant relies as being a joining family member of a relevant sponsor; and (c) 'valid' here means, in respect of a document, that it is genuine and has not expired or been cancelled or invalidated; and (d) where, in order to meet the requirements of this entry, the applicant submits a copy (and not the original) of a document (including by uploading this as part of the required application process), the Secretary of State can require the applicant to submit the original document where the Secretary of State has reasonable doubt as to the authenticity of the copy submitted; and

Term	Definition
	(e) where, in order to meet the requirements of this entry, the applicant submits a document which is not in English, the Secretary of State can require the applicant to provide a certified English translation of (or a Multilingual Standard Form to accompany) the document, where this is necessary for the purposes of deciding whether the applicant meets the eligibility requirements for indefinite leave to enter or remain or for limited leave to enter or remain under this Appendix
required proof of entitlement to apply from outside the UK	(a) in the case of an EEA citizen (in accordance with sub-paragraph (a) of that entry in this table): (i) their valid passport; or (ii) their valid national identity card, where this contains an interoperable biometric chip, unless the Secretary of State agrees to accept alternative evidence of entitlement to apply from outside the UK where the applicant is unable to obtain or produce the required document due to circumstances beyond their control or to compelling practical or compassionate reasons; or (b) in the case of a non-EEA citizen, their valid specified relevant document, unless the Secretary of State agrees to accept alternative evidence of entitlement to apply from outside the UK where the applicant is unable to produce the required document due to circumstances beyond their control or to compelling practical or compassionate reasons in addition, 'valid' here means that the document is genuine and has not expired or been cancelled or invalidated
required proof of identity and nationality	(a) in the case of an EEA citizen (in accordance with sub-paragraph (a) of that entry in this table) making an application within the UK: (i) their valid passport; or (ii) their valid national identity card; or (b) in the case of a non-EEA citizen making an application within the UK: (i) their valid passport; or (ii) their valid specified relevant document; or (iii) their valid biometric immigration document (as defined in section 5 of the UK Borders Act 2007), unless (in the case of (a) or (b)) the Secretary of State agrees to accept alternative evidence of identity and nationality where the applicant is unable to obtain or produce the required document due to circumstances beyond their control or to compelling practical or compassionate reasons in addition, 'valid' here means that the document is genuine and has not expired or been cancelled or invalidated

Term	Definition
self-employed person	there is evidence which satisfies the Secretary of State that the person is, or (as the case may be) for the relevant period was, either: (a) a self-employed person as defined in regulation 4(1) of the EEA Regulations; or (b) a person who is or was no longer in self-employment but who continues or continued to be treated as a self-employed person within the meaning of 'qualified person' under regulation 6 of the EEA Regulations, irrespective, in either case, of whether the EEA Regulations apply, or (as the case may be) for the relevant period applied, to that person where the person is, or (as the case may be) was, a relevant person of Northern Ireland
specified date	(a) (where sub-paragraph (b) below does not apply) 2300 GMT on 31 December 2020; or (b) (in the case of a family member of a qualifying British citizen as described in sub-paragraph (a)(i), (a)(iii), (a)(v) or (a)(vi) of the entry for 'family member of a qualifying British citizen' in this table) 2300 GMT on 29 March 2022 in the reference to specified date in sub-paragraph (a) of the entry for 'continuous qualifying period' in this table, for the purposes of the references to continuous qualifying period in: - condition 3 in the table in paragraph EU12 of this Appendix; - condition 2 in the table in paragraph EU14 of this Appendix; - sub-paragraphs (a) and (d) of the entry for 'family member who has retained the right of residence' in this table; and - sub-paragraph (a) of the entry for 'supervening event' in this table
specified relevant document	(a) within the meaning of sub-paragraph (a)(i)(aa) of the entry for 'relevant document' in this table, a residence card, permanent residence card or derivative residence card issued by the UK under the EEA Regulations on the basis of an application made on or after 6 April 2015; or (b) a biometric residence card as described in sub-paragraph (a)(iii) of the entry for 'relevant document' in this table
[specified relevant person of Northern Ireland	(a) the person is a relevant person of Northern Ireland in accordance with sub-paragraph (a)(i) or (a)(iii) of that entry in this table; and (b) the applicant is a non-EEA citizen; and (c) (i) (aa) the applicant is a joining family member of a relevant sponsor where the person is their relevant sponsor; and (bb) the applicant has satisfied the Secretary of State by relevant information or evidence provided with the application that, due to compelling practical or compassionate reasons, it was not possible for the person to return to the UK before the specified date while the applicant remained outside the UK; or

Term	Definition
	(ii) (aa) the applicant is a dependent relative and the person is their sponsoring person (in the entry for 'dependent relative' in this table); and (bb) the applicant relies, as their relevant document as the dependent relative of their sponsoring person (as described in sub-paragraph (a)(iv) of the entry for 'relevant document' in this table), on an EU Settlement Scheme Family Permit granted to them under Appendix EU (Family Permit) to these Rules as a 'dependent relative of a specified relevant person of Northern Ireland', as defined in Annex 1 to that Appendix]
specified spouse or civil partner of a Swiss citizen	(a) the person is the spouse or civil partner of a relevant sponsor; and (b) the relevant sponsor is a national of Switzerland and is not also a British citizen; and (c) the marriage was contracted or the civil partnership was formed after the specified date and before 1 January 2026; and (d) (i) (unless the applicant relies on meeting condition 1 or condition 3 of paragraph EU11A of this Appendix, or on being a family member who has retained the right of residence by virtue of a relationship with a relevant sponsor) the marriage or civil partnership continues to exist at the date of application; or (ii) (where the applicant relies on meeting condition 1 of paragraph EU11A of this Appendix) the marriage or civil partnership existed for the relevant period; or (iii) (where the applicant relies on meeting condition 3 of paragraph EU11A of this Appendix) the marriage or civil partnership existed immediately before the death of the relevant sponsor
spouse	(a) the person is, or (as the case may be) for the relevant period was, party to a marriage with a relevant EEA citizen (or, as the case may be, with a qualifying British citizen or with a relevant sponsor) and the marriage is recognised under the law of England and Wales, Scotland or Northern Ireland or of the Islands; and (b) it is, or (as the case may be) for the relevant period was, not a **marriage of convenience** ; and (c) neither party has, or (as the case may be) for the relevant period had, another spouse, a civil partner or a durable partner with (in any of those circumstances) immigration status in the UK or the Islands based on that person's relationship with that party
supervening event	at the date of application: (a) [the person] has been absent from the UK and Islands for a period of more than five consecutive years (at any point since they last acquired the right of permanent residence in the UK under regulation 15 of the EEA Regulations, or the right of permanent residence in the Islands through the application there of section 7(1) of the Immigration Act 1988 or under the Immigration (European Economic Area) Regulations of the Isle of Man, or since they last completed a continuous qualifying period of five years); or

Term	Definition
	(b) [any of the following events has occurred in respect of the person, unless it has been set aside or revoked]: (i) any decision or order to exclude or remove under regulation 23 or 32 of the EEA Regulations (or under the equivalent provisions of the Immigration (European Economic Area) Regulations of the Isle of Man); or (ii) a decision to which regulation 15(4) of the EEA Regulations otherwise refers, unless that decision arose from a previous decision under regulation 24(1) of the EEA Regulations (or the equivalent decision, subject to the equivalent qualification, under the Immigration (European Economic Area) Regulations of the Isle of Man); or (iii) an exclusion decision; or (iv) a deportation order, other than by virtue of the EEA Regulations; or (v) an Islands deportation order; or (vi) an Islands exclusion decision
termination of the marriage or civil partnership	the date on which the order finally terminating the marriage or civil partnership is made by a court
the Islands	the Bailiwick of Guernsey, the Bailiwick of Jersey or the Isle of Man
the UK and Islands	the United Kingdom and the Islands taken together
valid evidence of their indefinite leave to enter or remain	(a) a valid biometric immigration document (as defined in section 5 of the UK Borders Act 2007), a valid stamp or endorsement in a passport (whether or not the passport has expired) or other valid document issued by the Home Office, confirming that the applicant has indefinite leave to enter or remain in the UK, which has not lapsed or been revoked or invalidated; or (b) the Secretary of State is otherwise satisfied from the evidence or information available to them that the applicant has indefinite leave to enter or remain in the UK or the Islands, which has not lapsed or been revoked or invalidated
[...]	[...]
worker	there is evidence which satisfies the Secretary of State that the person is, or (as the case may be) for the relevant period was, either: (a) a worker as defined in regulation 4(1) of the EEA Regulations; or (b) a person who is or was no longer working but who continues or continued to be treated as a worker within the meaning of 'qualified person' under regulation 6 of the EEA Regulations, irrespective, in either case, of whether the EEA Regulations apply, or (as the case may be) for the relevant period applied, to that person where the person is, or (as the case may be) was, a relevant person of Northern Ireland

Note: In 'continuous qualifying period' sub-paragraph (a) substituted; in 'dependent relative' words in square brackets inserted; in 'relevant EEA citizen (where, in respect of the application under consideration, the date of application by the relevant EEA citizen or their family member is before 1 July 2021)' (e)(i) substituted; in 'relevant EEA citizen (where, in respect of the application under consideration, the date of application is on or after 1 July 2021)' (e)(ii)(aa) substituted; in 'relevant sponsor' (a)(iv)(aa) and (b)(v)(aa) substituted; in 'required evidence of family relationship' in paragraph beginning with 'in addition' words in (b)(i)(dd)(ccc) substituted; 'specified relevant person of Northern Ireland' inserted from 1 July 2021. In 'continuous qualifying period'(b)(i)(ee) inserted, sub-paragraph (b)(ii), words in (b)(iii), sub-paragraph (c)(ii) substituted; 'deportation order', 'EEA Regulations' substituted; in 'EEA citizen' words inserted; in 'exclusion decision' words in (b) inserted; in 'family member of a qualifying British citizen' words in (a)(v), (a)(vi) and (a)(vii) substituted; in 'frontier worker' words in (c) and (d) substituted; in 'Islands deportation order' words in (b) inserted; in 'Islands exclusion decision' words in (b) inserted; in 'qualifying British citizen' words inserted; in 'relevant document' words in (a)(i)(aa) and (c) substituted, (e) inserted; in 'relevant EEA citizen (where, in respect of the application under consideration, the date of application by the relevant EEA citizen or their family member is on or after 1 July 2021)' words in (b)(i) and (b)(ii) substituted, words in double square brackets inserted; in 'relevant naturalised British citizen' amendment to (d); in 'relevant sponsor' words in double square brackets substituted; 'required date' substituted; in 'supervening event' words in (b) substituted; amendment to 'visitor' from 6 April 2021 (HC 1248). Sub-paragraph (a), sub-paragraph (b)(i) in 'continuous qualifying period'; definition of 'relevant EEA citizen (where, in respect of the application under consideration, the date of application by the relevant EEA citizen or their family member is before 1 July 2021)' substituted; amendment to (a)(i)(aa) of 'relevant document'; words in (f)(ii) of definition of 'relevant EEA citizen (where, in respect of the application under consideration, the date of application by the relevant EEA citizen or their family member is on or after 1 July 2021)' deleted; words in curly brackets in the same definition inserted; sub-paragraph (b) in 'relevant naturalized British citizen'; sub-paragraphs (a)(ii)(bb), (a)(iv), and (a)(v)(bb) of 'relevant sponsor' substituted, in the same definition words in (b)(vi) deleted, words in curly brackets inserted; amendment to 'required date'; words in (e)(ii) of 'required evidence of family relationship' substituted, words in double square brackets in the same definition substituted; definition of 'visitor' deleted from 6 October 2021 (HC 617). Words in double square brackets in (a) of 'continuous qualifying period' inserted, words in (b)(ii) of 'deportation order', words in double square brackets in (b) of 'exclusion decision', sub-paragraph (a) and words in double square brackets in (b) of 'Islands deportation order', words in double square brackets in (b) of 'Islands exclusion decision', (a)(i)(aa) in 'relevant document', (d) in 'relevant naturalized British citizen', 'required date', words in (a) of 'supervening event' substituted, 'relevant EEA family permit case' inserted from 6 April 2022 (HC 1118).

Annex 2—Consideration of a valid application

A2.1. A valid application made under this Appendix will be decided on the basis of:

(a) the information and evidence provided by the applicant, including in response to any request for further information or evidence made by the Secretary of State; and

(b) any other information or evidence made available to the Secretary of State (including from other government departments) at the date of decision.

A2.2. (1) For the purposes of deciding whether the applicant meets the eligibility requirements for indefinite leave to enter or remain or for limited leave to enter or remain, the Secretary of State may:

(a) request that the applicant provide further information or evidence that they meet those requirements; or

(b) invite the applicant to be interviewed by the Secretary of State in person, by telephone, by video-telecommunications link or over the internet.

(2) If the applicant purports to meet the eligibility requirements for indefinite leave to enter or remain or for limited leave to enter or remain on the basis of a relationship with another person ('P'), including where P is a qualifying British citizen or a relevant sponsor, the Secretary of State may:

(a) request that P provide information or evidence about their relationship with the applicant, their residence in the UK or, where P is a qualifying British citizen, their residence in a country listed in subparagraph (a)(i) of the entry for 'EEA citizen' in the table at Annex 1 to this Appendix; or

(b) invite P to be interviewed by the Secretary of State in person, by telephone, by video-telecommunications link or over the internet.

(3) If the applicant or (as the case may be) P:

(a) fails within a reasonable timeframe specified in the request to provide the information or evidence requested; or

(b) on at least two occasions, fails to comply with an invitation to attend an interview in person or with other arrangements to be interviewed, the Secretary of State may draw any factual inferences about whether the applicant meets the eligibility requirements for indefinite leave to enter or remain or for limited leave to enter or remain as appear appropriate in the circumstances.

(4) The Secretary of State may decide, following the drawing of a factual inference under sub-paragraph (3), that the applicant does not meet the eligibility requirements for indefinite leave to enter or remain or for limited leave to enter or remain.

(5) The Secretary of State must not decide that the applicant does not meet the eligibility requirements for indefinite leave to enter or remain or for limited leave to enter or remain on the sole basis that the applicant or (as the case may be) P failed on at least two occasions to comply with an invitation to be interviewed.

[Annex 3—Cancellation, curtailment and revocation of leave to enter or remain

A3.1. A person's indefinite leave to enter or remain or limited leave to enter or remain granted under this Appendix must be cancelled on or before their arrival in the UK [where the Secretary of State or an Immigration Officer deems the person's presence in the UK] is not conducive to the public good because of conduct committed after the specified date.

Note: Words substituted from 6 April 2022 (HC 1118).

A3.2. A person's indefinite leave to enter or remain or limited leave to enter or remain granted under this Appendix may be cancelled on or before their arrival in the UK where the Secretary of State or an Immigration Officer is satisfied that it is proportionate to cancel that leave where:

(a) The cancellation is justified on grounds of public policy, public security or public health in accordance with regulation 27 of the Immigration (European Economic Area) Regulations 2016, irrespective of whether the EEA Regulations apply to that person (except that for 'a right of permanent residence under regulation 15' read 'indefinite leave to enter or remain or who would be granted indefinite leave to enter or remain if they made a valid application under this Appendix'; and for 'an EEA decision' read 'a decision under paragraph A3.2.(a) of Annex 3 to Appendix EU to the Immigration Rules'); or

(b) The cancellation is justified on grounds that, in relation to the relevant application under this Appendix, and whether or not to the applicant's knowledge, false or misleading information, representations or documents were submitted (including false or misleading information submitted to any person to obtain a document used in support of the application); and the information, representation or documentation was material to the decision to grant the applicant leave to enter or remain under this Appendix.

A3.3. A person's limited leave to enter or remain granted under this Appendix may be cancelled on or before their arrival in the UK where the Secretary of State or an Immigration Officer is satisfied that it is proportionate to cancel that leave where they cease to meet the requirements of this Appendix.

A3.4. A person's limited leave to enter or remain granted under this Appendix may be curtailed where the Secretary of State is satisfied that it is proportionate to curtail that leave where:

(a) Curtailment is justified on grounds that, in relation to the relevant application under this Appendix, and whether or not to the applicant's knowledge, false or misleading information, representations or documents were submitted (including false or misleading information submitted to any person to obtain a document used in support of the application); and the information, representation or documentation was material to the decision to grant the applicant leave to enter or remain under this Appendix; or

(b) Curtailment is justified on grounds that it is more likely than not that, after the specified date, the person has entered, attempted to enter or assisted another person to enter or to attempt to enter, a marriage, civil partnership or durable partnership of convenience; or

(c) The person ceases to meet the requirements of this Appendix.

A3.5. A person's indefinite leave to enter or remain granted under this Appendix may be revoked where the Secretary of State is satisfied that it is proportionate to revoke that leave where:

(a) The person is liable to deportation, but cannot be deported for legal reasons; or

(b) The indefinite leave to enter or remain was obtained by deception.]

Note: Annex 3 substituted from 6 April 2021 (HC 1243).

[Appendix EU (Family Permit)

Note: Appendix inserted from 07:00 on 30 March 2019 (HC 1919). Amendments from 2 April 2019 (HC 2099). Appendix substituted from 1 October 2019 (HC 2631). Appendix substituted from 31 October 2019 (HC 170). Appendix substituted from 6 April 2020 (HC 120). Amendments from 24 August 2020; amendments from 6 April 2020 (CP 232). Appendix substituted from 23:00 on 31 December 2020 (except Annex 3 which takes effect from 09:00 on 1 December 2020) subject to savings for applications made before that time; (HC 813).

Purpose

FP1. This Appendix sets out the basis on which a **non-EEA citizen** will, if they apply under it, be granted an entry clearance:

(a) In the form of an EU Settlement Scheme Family Permit—to join a **relevant EEA citizen** or a **qualifying British citizen** in the UK or to accompany them to the UK; or

(b) In the form of an EU Settlement Scheme Travel Permit—to travel to the UK.

FP2. This Appendix has effect in connection with the granting of entry clearance for the purposes of acquiring leave to enter or remain in the UK by virtue of Appendix EU to these Rules.

Requirements and procedure

FP3. The applicant will be granted an entry clearance under this Appendix, valid for the **relevant period**, by an entry clearance officer where:

(a) A valid application has been made in accordance with paragraph FP4;

(b) The applicant meets the eligibility requirements in paragraph FP6(1) or (2) or (3); and

(c) The application is not to be refused on grounds of suitability in accordance with paragraph FP7.

FP4. A valid application has been made under this Appendix where:

(a) It has been made using the **required application process**;

(b) The **required proof of identity and nationality** has been provided; and

(c) The **required biometrics** have been provided.

FP5. An application will be rejected as invalid where it does not meet the requirements in paragraph FP4(a) and (b), and will not be considered where it does not meet the requirement in paragraph FP4(c).

FP6. (1) The applicant meets the eligibility requirements for an entry clearance to be granted under this Appendix in the form of an EU Settlement Scheme Family Permit, where the entry clearance officer is satisfied that at the **date of application** :

(a) The applicant is a specified EEA citizen or a non-EEA citizen;

(b) The applicant is a family member of a relevant EEA citizen;

(c) The relevant EEA citizen is resident in the UK or will be travelling to the UK with the applicant within six months of the date of application;

(d) The applicant will be accompanying the relevant EEA citizen to the UK (or joining them in the UK) within six months of the date of application; and

[(e) The applicant ("A") is not the **spouse, civil partner** or **durable partner** of a relevant EEA citizen ("B") where a spouse, civil partner or durable partner of A or B has been granted an entry clearance under this Appendix, immediately before or since the specified date held a valid document in that capacity issued under the **EEA Regulations** or has been granted leave to enter or remain in the UK in that capacity under or outside the Immigration Rules.]

(2) The applicant meets the eligibility requirements for an entry clearance to be granted under this Appendix in the form of an EU Settlement Scheme Family Permit, where the entry clearance officer is satisfied that at the date of application:

(a) The applicant is a specified EEA citizen or a non-EEA citizen;

(b) The applicant is a **family member of a qualifying British citizen**;

(c) The qualifying British citizen is resident in the UK or will be travelling to the UK with the applicant within six months of the date of application;

(d) The applicant will be accompanying the qualifying British citizen to the UK (or joining them in the UK) within six months of the date of application; and

[(e) The applicant ("A") is not the spouse, civil partner or durable partner of a qualifying British citizen ("B") where a spouse, civil partner or durable partner of A or B has been granted an entry clearance under this Appendix, immediately before or since the specified date held a valid document in that capacity issued under the EEA Regulations or has been granted leave to enter or remain in the UK in that capacity under or outside the Immigration Rules.]

(3) The applicant meets the eligibility requirements for an entry clearance to be granted under this Appendix in the form of an EU Settlement Scheme Travel Permit, where the entry clearance officer is satisfied that at the date of application:

(a) The applicant is a non-EEA citizen;

(b) The applicant has been granted indefinite leave to enter or remain or limited leave to enter or remain under Appendix EU to these Rules, which has not lapsed or been cancelled, curtailed, revoked or invalidated and which is evidenced by the Home Office reference number for that grant of leave;

(c) The applicant:

(i) Has been issued with a **relevant document** by the UK under the EEA Regulations, or with a biometric residence card by virtue of having been granted leave under Appendix EU to these Rules; and

(ii) Has reported to the Home Office that that document or card has been lost or stolen [or has expired]; and

(d) The applicant will be travelling to the UK within six months of the date of application.

Note: Words in (3)(c)(ii) inserted from 6 April 2021 (HC 1248). Sub-paragraphs (1)(e), and (2)(e) substituted from 6 April 2022 (HC 1118).

[**FP7.** (1) An application made under this Appendix will be refused on grounds of suitability where any of the following apply at the date of decision:

(a) The applicant is subject to a **deportation order** or to a decision to make a deportation order; or

(b) The applicant is subject to an **exclusion order** or **exclusion decision.**

(2) An application made under this Appendix will be refused on grounds of suitability [where the applicant's presence in the UK is deemed not to be conducive] to the public good because of conduct committed after the specified date.

[(3) An application made under this Appendix will be refused on grounds of suitability where at the date of decision the applicant is subject to an **Islands deportation order.**]

[(3A) An application made under this Appendix may be refused on grounds of suitability where at the date of decision the applicant is subject to an Islands exclusion decision.]

(4) An application made under this Appendix may be refused on grounds of suitability where, at the date of decision, the entry clearance officer is satisfied that:

(a) It is proportionate to refuse the application where, in relation to the application and whether or not to the applicant's knowledge, false or misleading information, representations or documents have been submitted (including false or misleading information submitted to any person to obtain a document used in support of the application); and the information, representation or documentation is material to the decision whether or not to grant the applicant an entry clearance under this Appendix; or

(b) (i) The applicant:

(aa) Has previously been refused admission to the UK in accordance with regulation 23(1) of the EEA Regulations; or

(bb) Has previously been refused admission to the UK in accordance with regulation 12(1)(a) of the Citizens' Rights (Frontier Workers) (EU Exit) Regulations 2020; or

(cc) Had indefinite leave to enter or remain or limited leave to enter or remain granted under Appendix EU to these Rules (or limited leave to enter granted by virtue of having arrived in the UK with an entry clearance that was granted under this Appendix) which was cancelled under paragraph 321B(b)(i) or 321B(b)(ii) of these Rules, under paragraph A3.3. or A3.4.(a) of Annex 3 to this Appendix or under paragraph A3.1. or A3.2.(a) of Annex 3 to Appendix EU; and

(ii) The refusal of the application is justified either:

(aa) In respect of the applicant's conduct committed before the **specified date**, on grounds of public policy, public security or public health in accordance with regulation 27 of the EEA Regulations, irrespective of whether the EEA Regulations apply to that person (except that in regulation 27 for 'with a right of permanent residence under regulation 15' and 'has a right of permanent residence under regulation 15' read 'who has indefinite leave to enter or remain or who meets the requirements of paragraph EU11, EU11A or EU12 of Appendix EU to the Immigration Rules'; and for 'an EEA decision' read 'a decision under paragraph FP7(4)(b) of Appendix EU (Family Permit) to the Immigration Rules'), and it is proportionate to refuse the application; or

[(bb) In respect of conduct committed after the specified date, where the applicant's presence in the UK is deemed not to be conducive to the public good.]

(5) The references in this paragraph to an order or decision to which the applicant is subject do not include an order or decision which, at the date of decision on their application under this Appendix, has been set aside or revoked.]

Note: Paragraph substituted from 6 April 2021 (HC 1248). Words in (2), sub-paragraph (3), (4)(b)(ii)(bb) substituted, sub-paragraph (3A) inserted from 6 April 2022 (HC 1118).

FP8. A valid application made under this Appendix which does not meet the requirements for an entry clearance to be granted will be refused.

[**FP8A.** The applicant will be granted an entry clearance under this Appendix, in the form of an EU Settlement Scheme Family Permit, where:

(a) the entry clearance officer is satisfied that the applicant is a specified EEA family permit case; and

(b) had the applicant made a valid application under this Appendix, it would not have been refused on grounds of suitability under paragraph FP7.]

Note: Paragraph inserted from 6 April 2022 (HC 1118).

[**FP9.** (1) Annex 1 sets out definitions which apply to this Appendix. Any provision made elsewhere in the Immigration Rules for those terms, or for other matters for which this Appendix makes provision, does not apply to an application made under this Appendix.

(2) Where this Appendix requires that a document, card or other evidence is valid (or that it remained valid for the period of residence relied upon), or has not been cancelled or invalidated or has not ceased to be effective, it does not matter that the person concerned no longer has the right to enter or reside under the EEA Regulations (or under the equivalent provision in **the Islands**), on which basis the document, card or other evidence was issued, by virtue of the revocation of those Regulations (or equivalent provision in the Islands).]

Note: Paragraph substituted from 6 April 2021 (HC 1248).

FP10. Annex 2 applies to the consideration by the entry clearance officer of a valid application made under this Appendix.

FP11. Annex 3 applies in respect of the [revocation of an entry clearance that was granted under this Appendix, and of the] cancellation and curtailment of leave to enter granted by virtue of having arrived in the UK with an entry clearance that was granted under this Appendix.

Note: Words inserted from 6 April 2022 (HC 1118).

Annex 1—definitions

Term	Definition
adopted child	a **child** adopted in accordance with a **relevant adoption decision**
child	(a) the direct descendant under the age of 21 years of a relevant EEA citizen (or, as the case may be, of a qualifying British citizen) or of their spouse or civil partner; or (b) (i) the direct descendant aged 21 years or over of a relevant EEA citizen (or, as the case may be, of a qualifying British citizen) or of their spouse or civil partner; and (ii) (aa) dependent on the relevant EEA citizen or on their spouse or civil partner: (aaa) (where sub-paragraph (b)(ii)(aa)(bbb) below does not apply) at the date of application; or (bbb) (where the date of application is after the specified date and where the applicant is not a **joining family member**) at the specified date; or (bb) dependent on the qualifying British citizen (or on their spouse or civil partner) at the date of application or, where the date of application is after the specified date, at the specified date 'dependent' means here that: (a) having regard to their financial and social conditions, or health, the applicant cannot meet their essential living needs (in whole or in part) without the financial or other material support of the relevant EEA citizen (or, as the case may be, of the qualifying British citizen) or of their spouse or civil partner; and (b) such support is being provided to the applicant by the relevant EEA citizen (or, as the case may be, by the qualifying British citizen) or by their spouse or civil partner; and (c) there is no need to determine the reasons for that dependence or for the recourse to that support in addition: (a) 'child' includes: (i) an **adopted child** of; or (ii) a child born through surrogacy (where recognised in UK law or Islands law) for; or (iii) a child in respect of whom a special guardianship order (within the meaning of section 14A(1) of the Children Act 1989) is in force appointing as their special guardian; or (iv) a child in respect of whom an order has been made under section 5 of the Children Act 1989 appointing as their guardian; or (v) a child subject to a permanence order made under section 80 of the Adoption and Children (Scotland) Act 2007 vesting parental responsibilities and parental rights in a person who is; or

Term	Definition
	(vi) a child who has a guardian appointed under section 7 of the Children (Scotland) Act 1995, or who is living with a person pursuant to an order made under section 11 of that Act, and that guardian or other person is; or (vii) a child in respect of whom an order has been made under Article 159 of the Children (Northern Ireland) Order 1995, or in respect of whom an appointment has been made under Article 160 of that Order, appointing as their guardian a person who is; or (viii) a child who has a guardian appointed under section 12 or 14 of the Children (Guernsey and Alderney) Law 2008 or section 12 or 13 of the Children (Sark) Law 2016, or who is living in the care of a person pursuant to an order made under section 14 of the 2008 Law or section 13 of the 2016 Law, and that guardian or other person is; or (ix) a child in respect of whom an order under Article 7 of the Children (Jersey) Law 2002 is in force appointing as their guardian; or (x) a child in respect of whom a special guardianship order (within the meaning of section 17A of the Children and Young Persons Act 2001 of Tynwald) has been made appointing as their special guardian; or (xi) a child in respect of whom an order has been made under section 6 or 7 of the Children and Young Persons Act 2001 of Tynwald appointing as their guardian, a relevant EEA citizen (or, as the case may be, a qualifying British citizen) or their spouse or civil partner, but 'child' does not include a child cared for by a relevant EEA citizen (or, as the case may be, by a qualifying British citizen) or their spouse or civil partner solely by virtue of a formal or informal fostering arrangement; and (b) 'direct descendant' also includes a grandchild or great-grandchild; and (c) 'spouse or civil partner' means (as the case may be) the person described in sub-paragraph (a)(i) or (a)(ii) of the entry for 'family member of a qualifying British citizen' in this table or in sub-paragraph (a) of the entry for 'family member of a relevant EEA citizen' in this table
civil partner	(a) the person is in a valid civil partnership (which exists under or by virtue of the Civil Partnership Act 2004 or under any equivalent legislation in the Islands); or is in a relationship registered overseas which is entitled to be treated as a civil partnership under that Act or under any equivalent legislation in the Islands, with a relevant EEA citizen (or, as the case may be, with a qualifying British citizen); and (b) it is not a **civil partnership of convenience** ; and (c) neither party has another civil partner, a spouse or a durable partner with (in any of those circumstances) **immigration status in the UK or the Islands** based on that person's relationship with that party

Term	Definition
civil partnership of convenience durable partnership of convenience marriage of convenience	a civil partnership, durable partnership or marriage entered into as a means to circumvent: (a) any criterion the party would have to meet in order to enjoy a right to enter or reside in the UK under the EEA Regulations; or (b) any other provision of UK immigration law or any requirement of the Immigration Rules; or (c) any criterion the party would otherwise have to meet in order to enjoy a right to enter or reside in the UK under EU law; or (d) any criterion the party would have to meet in order to enjoy a right to enter or reside in [the Islands] under Islands law
date and time of withdrawal	2300GMT on 31 January 2020
[date of application	the date on which the relevant on-line application form is submitted on-line under the required application process]
dependent parent	(a) the direct relative in the ascending line of a relevant EEA citizen (or, as the case may be, of a qualifying British citizen) or of their spouse or civil partner; and (b) (unless sub-paragraph (c) immediately below applies): (i) dependent on the relevant EEA citizen or on their spouse or civil partner: (aa) (where sub-paragraph (b)(i)(bb) or (b)(i)(cc) below does not apply) at the date of application and (unless the relevant EEA citizen is under the age of 18 years at the date of application) that dependency is assumed; or (bb) (where the date of application is after the specified date and where the applicant is not a joining family member) at the specified date, and (unless the relevant EEA citizen was under the age of 18 years at the specified date) that dependency is assumed; or (cc) (where the date of application is after the specified date and where the applicant is a joining family member) at the date of application and (unless the relevant EEA citizen is under the age of 18 years at the date of application) that dependency is assumed where the date of application is before 1 July 2021; or (ii) dependent on the qualifying British citizen (or on their spouse or civil partner) at the date of application or, where the date of application is after the specified date, at the specified date, and (unless the qualifying British citizen is under the age of 18 years at the date of application or, where the date of application is after the specified date, the qualifying British citizen was under the age of 18 years at the specified date) that dependency is assumed; and (c) this sub-paragraph applies (and the applicant therefore has to meet no requirement as to dependency) where the spouse, civil partner or durable partner of the applicant (and with whom they reside) has been granted:

Term	Definition
	(i) an entry clearance under this Appendix in the form of an EU Settlement Scheme Family Permit as a dependent parent of the relevant EEA citizen (or, as the case may be, of the qualifying British citizen) or of their spouse or civil partner, and that entry clearance has not been revoked or otherwise ceased to be valid; or (ii) indefinite leave to enter or remain or limited leave to enter or remain under Appendix EU to these Rules as a dependent parent of the relevant EEA citizen (or, as the case may be, of the qualifying British citizen or of the relevant sponsor) or of their spouse or civil partner, and that indefinite or limited leave has not lapsed or been cancelled, curtailed, revoked or invalidated 'dependent' means here that: (a) having regard to their financial and social conditions, or health, the applicant cannot meet their essential living needs (in whole or in part) without the financial or other material support of the relevant EEA citizen (or, as the case may be, of the qualifying British citizen) or of their spouse or civil partner; and (b) such support is being provided to the applicant by the relevant EEA citizen (or, as the case may be, by the qualifying British citizen) or by their spouse or civil partner; and (c) there is no need to determine the reasons for that dependence or for the recourse to that support in addition: (a) 'direct relative in the ascending line' includes: (i) a grandparent or great-grandparent; and (ii) an adoptive parent of an adopted child; and (b) 'spouse or civil partner' means (as the case may be) the person described in sub-paragraph (a)(i) or (a)(ii) of the entry for 'family member of a qualifying British citizen' in this table or in sub-paragraph (a) of the entry for 'family member of a relevant EEA citizen' in this table; and (c) in respect of the reference in the first sub-paragraph (c) in this entry to the spouse, civil partner or durable partner of the applicant, the entry for (as the case may be) 'spouse', 'civil partner' or 'durable partner' in this table applies, except that in the applicable entry 'applicant' is to be substituted for 'relevant EEA citizen'
dependent relative of a qualifying British citizen	the person: (a) (i) is a relative (other than a spouse, civil partner, durable partner, child or dependent parent) of a qualifying British citizen or of their spouse or civil partner; and (ii) is a dependant of a qualifying British citizen or of their spouse or civil partner, a member of their household or in strict need of their personal care on serious health grounds; or

Term	Definition
	(b) is a **person who is subject to a non-adoptive legal guardianship order** in favour (solely or jointly with another party) of a qualifying British citizen; or (c) is a person under the age of 18 years who: (i) is the direct descendant of the durable partner of a qualifying British citizen; or (ii) has been adopted by the durable partner of a qualifying British citizen, in accordance with a relevant adoption decision in addition, 'spouse or civil partner' means the person described in sub-paragraph (a)(i) or (a)(ii) of the entry for 'family member of a qualifying British citizen' in this table
[dependent relative of a specified relevant person of Northern Ireland	the person: (a) (i) is a relative (other than a spouse, civil partner, durable partner, child or dependent parent) of a **specified relevant person of Northern Ireland** or of their spouse or civil partner; and (ii) is a dependant of a specified relevant person of Northern Ireland or of their spouse or civil partner, a member of their household or in strict need of their personal care on serious health grounds; or (b) is a person who is subject to a non-adoptive legal guardianship order in favour (solely or jointly with another party) of a specified relevant person of Northern Ireland (substituting 'specified relevant person of Northern Ireland' for 'qualifying British citizen' in the entry for 'person who is subject to a non-adoptive legal guardianship order' in this table); or (c) is a person under the age of 18 years who: (i) is the direct descendant of the durable partner of a specified relevant person of Northern Ireland; or (ii) has been adopted by the durable partner of a specified relevant person of Northern Ireland, in accordance with a relevant adoption decision in addition, 'spouse or civil partner' means the person described in sub-paragraph (a) of the entry for 'family member of a relevant EEA citizen' in this table]
[deportation order	as the case may be: (a) an order made under section 5(1) of the Immigration Act 1971 by virtue of regulation 32(3) of the EEA Regulations; or (b) an order made under section 5(1) of the Immigration Act 1971 by virtue of section 3(5) or section 3(6) of that Act in respect of: (i) conduct committed after the specified date; or

Term	Definition
	(ii) conduct committed by the person before the specified date where the Secretary of State has decided that the deportation order is justified on the grounds of public policy, public security or public health in accordance with regulation 27 of the EEA Regulations, irrespective of whether the EEA Regulations apply to the person (except that in regulation 27 for 'with a right of permanent residence under regulation 15' and 'has a right of permanent residence under regulation 15' read 'who has indefinite leave to enter or remain or [who, but for the making of the deportation order, meets the requirements of] paragraph EU11, EU11A or EU12 of Appendix EU to the Immigration Rules'; and for 'an EEA decision' read 'a deportation decision'); or (c) an order made under section 5(1) of the Immigration Act 1971 by virtue of regulation 15(1)(b) of the Citizens' Rights (Frontier Workers) (EU Exit) Regulations 2020 in addition, for the avoidance of doubt, (b) includes a deportation order made under the Immigration Act 1971 in accordance with section 32 of the UK Borders Act 2007]
durable partner	(a) [the applicant] is, or (as the case may be) was, in a durable relationship with the relevant EEA citizen (or, as the case may be, with the qualifying British citizen), with the couple having lived together in a relationship akin to a marriage or civil partnership for at least two years (unless there is other significant evidence of the durable relationship); and (b) where [the applicant] was resident in the UK and Islands as the durable partner of a relevant EEA citizen before the specified date, the person held a relevant document as the durable partner of the relevant EEA citizen or, where there is evidence which satisfies the entry clearance officer that the applicant was otherwise lawfully resident in the UK and Islands for the relevant period before the specified date (or where the applicant is a joining family member) or where the applicant relies on the relevant EEA citizen being a relevant person of Northern Ireland, there is evidence which satisfies the entry clearance officer that the durable partnership was formed and was durable before the specified date; and (c) it is, or (as the case may be) was, not a **durable partnership of convenience** ; and (d) neither party has, or (as the case may be) had, another durable partner, a spouse or a civil partner with (in any of those circumstances) immigration status in the UK or the Islands based on that person's relationship with that party

Term	Definition
EEA citizen	a person who is: (a) a national of: Austria, Belgium, Bulgaria, Croatia, Republic of Cyprus, Czech Republic, Denmark, Estonia, Finland, France, Germany, Greece, Hungary, Iceland, Ireland, Italy, Latvia, Liechtenstein, Lithuania, Luxembourg, Malta, Netherlands, Norway, Poland, Portugal, Romania, Slovakia, Slovenia, Spain, Sweden or Switzerland, and who (unless they are a **relevant naturalised British citizen**) is not also a British citizen; or (b) (i) a national of a country listed in sub-paragraph (a) of the entry for 'specified EEA citizen' in this table; and (ii) (where the applicant meets the criteria in paragraph 9 of Schedule 6 to the EEA Regulations as the family member ('F') to whom that paragraph refers) a British citizen within the meaning of the person ('P') to whom that paragraph refers; or (c) a **relevant person of Northern Ireland**
[EEA Regulations	(a) (where relevant to something done before the specified date) the Immigration (European Economic Area) Regulations 2016 (as they have effect immediately before that date); or (b) (where relevant to something done after the specified date and before 1 July 2021) the Immigration (European Economic Area) Regulations 2016 (as, despite the revocation of those Regulations, they continue to have effect, with specified modifications, by virtue of the Citizens' Rights (Application Deadline and Temporary Protection) (EU Exit) Regulations 2020); or (c) (where relevant to something done on or after 1 July 2021) the Immigration (European Economic Area) Regulations 2016 (as they had effect immediately before they were revoked and, where the context requires it, on the basis that those Regulations had not been revoked)]
evidence of birth	(a) (in the case of a child) the **full birth certificate** (s) or other document(s) which the entry clearance officer is satisfied evidences that the applicant is the direct descendant of (or otherwise a child of) the relevant EEA citizen (or, as the case may be, of the qualifying British citizen) or of their spouse or civil partner, as described (as the case may be) in sub-paragraph (a)(i) or (a)(ii) of the entry for 'family member of a qualifying British citizen' in this table or in sub-paragraph (a) of the entry for 'family member of a relevant EEA citizen' in this table; or (b) (in the case of a **dependent parent**) the full birth certificate(s) or other document(s) which the entry clearance officer is satisfied evidences that the applicant is the direct relative in the ascending line of the relevant EEA citizen (or, as the case may be, of the qualifying British citizen) or of their spouse or civil partner, as described in sub-paragraph (a) above

Term	Definition
exclusion decision	a direction given by the Secretary of State that a person must be excluded from the UK: (a) in respect of conduct committed after the specified date; or (b) in respect of conduct committed [by the person] before the specified date, where the Secretary of State is satisfied that the direction is justified on the grounds of public policy, public security or public health in accordance with regulation 27 of the EEA Regulations, irrespective of whether the EEA Regulations apply to that person (except that in regulation 27 for 'with a right of permanent residence under regulation 15' and 'has a right of permanent residence under regulation 15' read 'who has indefinite leave to enter or remain or [[who, but for the making of the exclusion direction, meets the requirements of]] paragraph EU11, EU11A or EU12 of Appendix EU to the Immigration Rules'; and for 'an EEA decision' read 'an exclusion direction')
exclusion order	an order made under regulation 23(5) of the EEA Regulations
family member of a qualifying British citizen	a person who has satisfied the entry clearance officer, including by the **required evidence of family relationship**, that: (a) they will be returning to the UK: (i) before 2300 GMT on 29 March 2022 (or later where the entry clearance officer is satisfied that there are reasonable grounds for the person's failure to meet that deadline), as the spouse or civil partner of a qualifying British citizen, and: (aa) (aaa) the marriage was contracted or the civil partnership was formed before the date and time of withdrawal; or (bbb) the applicant was the durable partner of the qualifying British citizen before the date and time of withdrawal (the definition of 'durable partner' in this table being met before then rather than at the date of application) and the partnership remained durable at the date and time of withdrawal; and (bb) (aaa) the marriage or civil partnership continues to exist at the date of application; or (bbb) the entry clearance officer is satisfied that the marriage will be contracted or the civil partnership will be formed before the couple return to the UK; or (ii) (where sub-paragraph (a)(i)(aa)(bbb) above does not apply) as the spouse or civil partner of a qualifying British citizen, and: (aa) the marriage was contracted or the civil partnership was formed after the date and time of withdrawal and before the specified date; and (bb) the marriage or civil partnership continues to exist at the date of application; and (cc) the entry clearance officer is satisfied that there are reasonable grounds why they did not return to the UK with the qualifying British citizen before the specified date; or

Term	Definition
	(iii) before 2300 GMT on 29 March 2022 (or later where the entry clearance officer is satisfied that there are reasonable grounds for the person's failure to meet that deadline), as the durable partner of a qualifying British citizen, and: (aa) the partnership was formed and was durable before the date and time of withdrawal; and (bb) the partnership remains durable at the date of application; or (iv) as the durable partner of a qualifying British citizen, and: (aa) the partnership was formed and was durable after the date and time of withdrawal and before the specified date; and (bb) the partnership remains durable at the date of application; and (cc) the entry clearance officer is satisfied that there are reasonable grounds why they did not return to the UK with the qualifying British citizen before the specified date; or (v) before 2300 GMT on 29 March 2022 (or later where the entry clearance officer is satisfied that there are reasonable grounds for the person's failure to meet that deadline), as the child or dependent parent of a qualifying British citizen, and the family relationship: (aa) existed before the date and time of withdrawal (unless, in the case of a child, the person was born thereafter, was adopted thereafter in accordance with a relevant adoption decision or thereafter became a child within the meaning of that entry in this table on the basis of one of sub-paragraphs (a)(iii) to (a)(xi) of that entry); and (bb) continues to exist at the date of application; or (vi) before 2300 GMT on 29 March 2022 (or later where the entry clearance officer is satisfied that there are reasonable grounds for the person's failure to meet that deadline), as the child or dependent parent of the spouse or civil partner of a qualifying British citizen (as described in sub-paragraph (a)(i) above), and all the family relationships: (aa) existed before the date and time of withdrawal (unless, in the case of a child, the person was born thereafter, was adopted thereafter in accordance with a relevant adoption decision or thereafter became a child within the meaning of that entry in this table on the basis of one of sub-paragraphs (a)(iii) to (a)(xi) of that entry); and (bb) continue to exist at the date of application; or (vii) as the child or dependent parent of the spouse or civil partner of a qualifying British citizen (as described in sub-paragraph (a)(ii) above), and:

Term	Definition
	(aa) the family relationship of the child or dependent parent to the spouse or civil partner existed before the date and time of withdrawal (unless, in the case of a child, the person was born thereafter, was adopted thereafter in accordance with a relevant adoption decision or thereafter became a child within the meaning of that entry in this table on the basis of one of sub-paragraphs (a)(iii) to (a)(xi) of that entry); and (bb) all the family relationships continue to exist at the date of application; and (cc) the entry clearance officer is satisfied that there are reasonable grounds why the person did not return to the UK with the qualifying British citizen before the specified date; or (viii) as the **dependent relative of a qualifying British citizen**, or (as the case may be) of their spouse or civil partner (as described in sub-paragraph (a)(i) or (a)(ii) above), and: (aa) the family relationship and (in sub-paragraph (a)(ii) of the entry for 'dependent relative of a qualifying British citizen' in this table) the person's dependency (or, as the case may be, their membership of the household or their strict need for personal care on serious health grounds) existed before the specified date and continue to exist at the date of application; and (bb) the entry clearance officer is satisfied that there are reasonable grounds why the person did not return to the UK with the qualifying British citizen before the specified date; [or] [(ix) as a person who the entry clearance officer is satisfied by evidence provided by the person that they would, if they made a valid application under Appendix EU to these Rules in the UK, be granted (as the case may be) indefinite leave to remain under paragraph EU2 of that Appendix or limited leave to remain under paragraph EU3 as a family member who has retained the right of residence by virtue of a relationship with a qualifying British citizen (as defined in Annex 1 to Appendix EU); and] (b) they satisfied the conditions in regulation 9(2), (3) and (4)(a) of the EEA Regulations (as the family member ('F') to whom those provisions refer) or, as the case may be, the conditions in regulation 9(1A)(b), (2), (3) and (4)(a) of the EEA Regulations (as the extended family member ('EFM') to whom those provisions refer), in either case doing so (with the qualifying British citizen being treated as the British citizen ('BC') to whom those provisions refer): (i) before the specified date; and [(ii) (save where the date of application is after the specified date and where those conditions concern matters relevant to the dependency referred to in sub-paragraph (b)(ii)(bb) of the entry for 'child' in this table or in sub-paragraph (b)(ii) of the entry for 'dependent parent' in this table, or save where sub-paragraph (a)(ix) above applies) at the date of application] [in addition, where sub-paragraph (a)(ix) above applies, the requirements in paragraph FP6(2)(c) and (d) of this Appendix do not apply]

Term	Definition
family member of a relevant EEA citizen	a person who has satisfied the entry clearance officer, including by the required evidence of family relationship, that they are: (a) the spouse or civil partner of a relevant EEA citizen, and: (i) (aa) the marriage was contracted or the civil partnership was formed before the specified date; or (bb) the applicant was the durable partner of the relevant EEA citizen before the specified date (the definition of 'durable partner' in this table being met before that date rather than at the date of application) and the partnership remained durable at the specified date; and (ii) the marriage or civil partnership continues to exist at the date of application; or (b) the **specified spouse or civil partner of a Swiss citizen** ; or (c) the durable partner of a relevant EEA citizen, and: (i) the partnership was formed and was durable before the specified date; and (ii) the partnership remains durable at the date of application; and (iii) the date of application is after the specified date; and (iv) where they were resident in the UK and Islands as the durable partner of the relevant EEA citizen before the specified date, the definition of 'durable partner' in this table was met before that date as well as at the date of application, and the partnership remained durable at the specified date; or (d) the child or dependent parent of a relevant EEA citizen, and the family relationship: (i) existed before the specified date (unless, in the case of a child, the person was born after that date, was adopted after that date in accordance with a relevant adoption decision or after that date became a child within the meaning of that entry in this table on the basis of one of sub-paragraphs (a)(iii) to (a)(xi) of that entry); and (ii) continues to exist at the date of application; or (e) the child or dependent parent of the spouse or civil partner of a relevant EEA citizen, as described in sub-paragraph (a) above, and: (i) the family relationship of the child or dependent parent to the spouse or civil partner existed before the specified date (unless, in the case of a child, the person was born after that date, was adopted after that date in accordance with a relevant adoption decision or after that date became a child within the meaning of that entry in this table on the basis of one of sub-paragraphs (a)(iii) to (a)(xi) of that entry); and (ii) all the family relationships continue to exist at the date of application; or

Term	Definition
	[(f) a person who the entry clearance officer is satisfied by evidence provided by the person that they would, if they had made a valid application under Appendix EU to these Rules before 1 July 2021, have been granted (as the case may be) indefinite leave to enter under paragraph EU2 of that Appendix or limited leave to enter under paragraph EU3 and that leave would not have lapsed or been cancelled, curtailed, revoked or invalidated before [[the date of application under this Appendix (and, in respect of that application, the requirements in paragraph FP6(1)(c) and (d) of this Appendix do not apply)]]: (i) as a family member who has retained the right of residence by virtue of a relationship with a relevant EEA citizen (as defined in Annex 1 to Appendix EU); or (ii) on the basis that condition 6 of paragraph EU11 of Appendix EU is met; or] [(g) the **dependent relative of a specified relevant person of Northern Ireland**] in addition, where the person is a child born after the specified date or adopted after that date in accordance with a relevant adoption decision, or after the specified date they became a child within the meaning of that entry in this table on the basis of one of sub-paragraphs (a)(iii) to (a)(xi) of that entry (and with the references to 'parents' in sub-paragraph (a) below construed to include the guardian or other person to whom the order or other provision referred to in the relevant sub-paragraph of (a)(iii) to (a)(xi) of that entry relates), they meet one of the following requirements: (a) (where sub-paragraph (b) below does not apply), one of the following requirements is met: (i) both of their parents are a relevant EEA citizen; or (ii) one of their parents is a relevant EEA citizen and the other is a British citizen who is not a relevant EEA citizen; or (iii) one of their parents is a relevant EEA citizen who has sole or joint rights of custody of them, in accordance with the applicable rules of family law of the UK, of the Islands or of a country listed in sub-paragraph (a) of the entry for 'specified EEA citizen' in this table (including applicable rules of private international law under which rights of custody under the law of a third country are recognised in the UK, in the Islands or in a country listed in sub-paragraph (a) of the entry for 'specified EEA citizen' in this table, in particular as regards the best interests of the child, and without prejudice to the normal operation of such applicable rules of private international law); or (b) where they were born after the specified date to (or adopted after that date in accordance with a relevant adoption decision by or after that date became, within the meaning of the entry for 'child' in this table and on the basis of one of sub-paragraphs (a)(iii) to (a)(xi) of that entry, a child of) a Swiss citizen or their spouse or civil partner (as described in the first sub-paragraph (a) in this entry), the Swiss citizen or their spouse or civil partner is a relevant EEA citizen

Term	Definition
frontier worker	a person who: (a) is a national of: Austria, Belgium, Bulgaria, Croatia, Republic of Cyprus, Czech Republic, Denmark, Estonia, Finland, France, Germany, Greece, Hungary, Iceland, Ireland, Italy, Latvia, Liechtenstein, Lithuania, Luxembourg, Malta, Netherlands, Norway, Poland, Portugal, Romania, Slovakia, Slovenia, Spain, Sweden or Switzerland; and (b) is not a British citizen; and (c) satisfies the Secretary of State by relevant evidence of this that they fulfil the relevant conditions of being a frontier worker set out in [the Citizens' Rights (Frontier Workers) (EU Exit) Regulations 2020], and that they have done so continuously since the specified date; and (d) has not been (and is not to be) refused admission to, or removed from, the UK by virtue of [the Citizens' Rights (Frontier Workers) (EU Exit) Regulations 2020, and is not subject to a relevant restriction decision as defined by regulation 2 of those Regulations]
full birth certificate	abirth certificate recognised in the UK or the Islands which records the name of the mother and (where registered) the father
GMT	Greenwich Mean Time
immigration status in the UK or the Islands	indefinite or limited leave to enter or remain in the UK or the Islands under or outside the relevant Immigration Rules; exemption from immigration control; the entitlement to reside in the UK or the right of permanent residence in the UK under regulations 13 to 15 of the EEA Regulations; or the entitlement to reside in the Islands or the right of permanent residence in the Islands through the application there of section 7(1) of the Immigration Act 1988 or under the Immigration (European Economic Area) Regulations of the Isle of Man
Irish citizen	aperson who is an Irish citizen as a matter of Irish law
Islands deportation order	a deportation order as defined in paragraph 3(6) of Schedule 4 to the Immigration Act 1971 that was made: [(a) in respect of conduct committed after the specified date and has effect in relation to the person, by virtue of paragraph 3 of Schedule 4 to the Immigration Act 1971, as if it was a deportation order made under that Act; or] (b) in respect of conduct committed [by the person] before the specified date, where the Secretary of State is satisfied that the order is justified on the grounds of public policy, public security or public health in accordance with regulation 27 of the EEA Regulations, irrespective of whether the EEA Regulations apply to the person (except that in regulation 27 for 'with a right of permanent residence under regulation 15' and 'has a right of permanent residence under regulation 15' read 'who has indefinite leave to enter or remain or [[who, but for the making of the deportation order, meets the requirements of]] paragraph EU11, EU11A or EU12 of Appendix EU to the Immigration Rules'; and for 'an EEA decision' read 'a deportation decision')

Term	Definition
Islands exclusion decision	a direction given by the relevant Minister or other authority in the Islands that a person must be excluded from the Island concerned: (a) in respect of conduct committed after the specified date; or (b) in respect of conduct committed [by the person] before the specified date, where the Secretary of State is satisfied that the direction is justified on the grounds of public policy, public security or public health in accordance with regulation 27 of the EEA Regulations, irrespective of whether the EEA Regulations apply to that person (except that in regulation 27 for 'with a right of permanent residence under regulation 15' and 'has a right of permanent residence under regulation 15' read 'who has indefinite leave to enter or remain or [[who, but for the making of the exclusion direction, meets the requirements of]] paragraph EU11, EU11A or EU12 of Appendix EU to the Immigration Rules'; and for 'an EEA decision' read 'an exclusion direction')
joining family member	a person who is a family member of a relevant EEA citizen (in accordance with sub-paragraph (a)(i)(bb), (c), (d) or (e)—together, where applicable, with the second sub-paragraph (a) or the second sub-paragraph (b)—of that entry in this table) and who (save, in the case of a child, where the person was born after the specified date, was adopted after that date in accordance with a relevant adoption decision or after that date became a child within the meaning of that entry in this table on the basis of one of sub-paragraphs (a)(iii) to (a)(xi) of that entry): (a) was not resident in the UK and Islands at any time before the specified date; or (b) was resident in the UK and Islands before the specified date, and: (i) one of the events referred to in sub-paragraph (b)(i) or (b)(ii) in the entry for 'continuous qualifying period' in the table at Annex 1 to Appendix EU to these Rules has occurred, and after that event occurred they were not resident in the UK and Islands again before the specified date; or (ii) the event referred to in sub-paragraph (a) in the entry for 'supervening event' in the table at Annex 1 to Appendix EU to these Rules has occurred, and after that event occurred they were not resident in the UK and Islands again before the specified date
non-EEA citizen	a person who is not an **EEA citizen** and is not a British citizen
person exempt from immigration control	a person who: (a) is a national of: Austria, Belgium, Bulgaria, Croatia, Republic of Cyprus, Czech Republic, Denmark, Estonia, Finland, France, Germany, Greece, Hungary, Iceland, Ireland, Italy, Latvia, Liechtenstein, Lithuania, Luxembourg, Malta, Netherlands, Norway, Poland, Portugal, Romania, Slovakia, Slovenia, Spain, Sweden or Switzerland; and

Term	Definition
	(b) is not a British citizen; and (c) is exempt from immigration control in accordance with section 8(2), (3) or (4) of the Immigration Act 1971; and [(d) the entry clearance officer is satisfied, including by the **required evidence of** [[**qualification** ,]] would have been granted indefinite leave to enter or remain or limited leave to enter or remain under (as the case may be) paragraph EU2 or EU3 of Appendix EU to these Rules, if they had made a valid application under it before 1 July 2021, and that leave would not have lapsed or been cancelled, curtailed, revoked or invalidated before the date of application under this Appendix]
person who is subject to a non-adoptive legal guardianship order	a person who has satisfied the entry clearance officer that, immediately before the specified date, they: (a) are under the age of 18 years; and (b) are subject to a non-adoptive legal guardianship order in favour (solely or jointly with another party) of a qualifying British citizen that: (i) is recognised under the national law of the state in which it was contracted; and (ii) places parental responsibility on a permanent basis on the qualifying British citizen (solely or jointly with another party); and (c) have lived with the qualifying British citizen since their placement under the guardianship order; and (d) have created family life with the qualifying British citizen; and (e) have a personal relationship with the qualifying British citizen that involves dependency on the qualifying British citizen and the assumption of parental responsibility, including legal and financial responsibilities, for that person by the qualifying British citizen
[qualifying British citizen	a British citizen who: (a) (i) (where sub-paragraph (a)(ii) or (a)(iii) below does not apply) will be returning to the UK with the applicant before 2300 GMT on 29 March 2022 (or later where the entry clearance officer is satisfied that there are reasonable grounds for the British citizen's failure to meet that deadline); or (ii) (in the case of a family member of a qualifying British citizen as described in sub-paragraph (a)(ii), (a)(iv), (a)(vii) or (a)(viii) of the entry for 'family member of a qualifying British citizen' in this table) will be returning to the UK with the applicant and the entry clearance officer is satisfied that there are reasonable grounds why the British citizen did not do so before the specified date; or

Term	Definition
	(iii) is the qualifying British citizen referred to in sub-paragraph (a)(ix) of the entry for 'family member of a qualifying British citizen' in this table; and (b) satisfied regulation 9(2), (3) and (4)(a) of the EEA Regulations (as the British citizen ("BC") to whom those provisions refer, with the applicant being treated as the family member ("F") or, as the case may be, as the extended family member ("EFM"), to whom those provisions refer): (i) before the specified date; and (ii) (save where sub-paragraph (a)(ix) of the entry for 'family member of a qualifying British citizen' in this table applies) at the date of application
	in addition, for the avoidance of doubt, for the purposes of sub-paragraph (b) above, service as a member of HM Forces (as defined in the Armed Forces Act 2006) in a country listed in sub-paragraph (a) of the entry for 'specified EEA citizen' in this table may satisfy the conditions of being a "worker" for the purposes of the EEA Regulations]
relevant adoption decision	a decision taken: (a) by the competent administrative authority or court in the UK or the Islands; or (b) by the competent administrative authority or court in a country whose adoption orders are recognised by the UK or the Islands; or (c) in a particular case in which that decision in another country has been recognised in the UK or the Islands as an adoption
relevant document	(a) a family permit [(or a letter from the Secretary of State, issued after 30 June 2021, confirming the person's qualification for one)], residence card or permanent residence card issued by the UK under the EEA Regulations (or the equivalent document or other evidence issued by the Islands under the relevant legislation there evidencing the entitlement to enter or reside in the Islands or the right of permanent residence in the Islands through the application there of section 7(1) of the Immigration Act 1988 or under the Immigration (European Economic Area) Regulations of the Isle of Man); and (b) it was not subsequently revoked, or fell to be so, because the relationship or dependency had never existed or the relationship or (where relevant) dependency had ceased; and (c) [(in relation to an application for an EU Settlement Scheme Family Permit)]it has not expired or otherwise ceased to be effective, or it remained valid for the period of residence relied upon

Term	Definition
[relevant EEA citizen (where the date of application under this Appendix is before 1 July 2021)]	[(a) an EEA citizen (in accordance with sub-paragraph (a) of that entry in this table) who: (i) has been granted indefinite leave to enter or remain or limited leave to enter or remain under (as the case may be) paragraph EU2 or EU3 of Appendix EU to these Rules (or under its equivalent in the Islands), which has not lapsed or been cancelled, curtailed, revoked or invalidated and which is evidenced by the Home Office reference number for that grant of leave (or by the equivalent evidence in the Islands); or (ii) at the date of decision on the application under this Appendix, the entry clearance officer is satisfied from the information available to them has been granted indefinite leave to enter or remain or limited leave to enter or remain under (as the case may be) paragraph EU2 or EU3 of Appendix EU to these Rules, which has not lapsed or been cancelled, curtailed, revoked or invalidated; or (iii) the entry clearance officer is satisfied, including by the required evidence of qualification, would have been granted indefinite leave to enter or remain or limited leave to enter or remain under (as the case may be) paragraph EU2 or EU3 of Appendix EU to these Rules, if they had made a valid application under it before 1 July 2021, and that leave would not have lapsed or been cancelled, curtailed, revoked or invalidated before the date of application under this Appendix; or (b) an EEA citizen (in accordance with sub-paragraph (a) of that entry in this table) who is a relevant naturalised British citizen; or (c) (where the applicant is the family member ("F") to whom paragraph 9 of Schedule 6 to the EEA Regulations refers and meets the criteria as F in that paragraph) an EEA citizen (in accordance with sub-paragraph (b) of that entry in this table) who the entry clearance officer is satisfied, including by the required evidence of qualification, would (but for the fact that they are a British citizen) have been granted indefinite leave to enter or remain or limited leave to enter or remain under (as the case may be) paragraph EU2 or EU3 of Appendix EU to these Rules, if they had made a valid application under it before 1 July 2021, and that leave would not have lapsed or been cancelled, curtailed, revoked or invalidated before the date of application under this Appendix; or (d) an EEA citizen (in accordance with sub-paragraph (c) of that entry in this table) who: (i) where they are a relevant person of Northern Ireland in accordance with sub-paragraph (a)(ii) of that entry in this table:

Term	Definition
	(aa) has been granted indefinite leave to enter or remain or limited leave to enter or remain under (as the case may be) paragraph EU2 or EU3 of Appendix EU to these Rules (or under its equivalent in the Islands), which has not lapsed or been cancelled, curtailed, revoked or invalidated and which is evidenced by the Home Office reference number for that grant of leave (or by the equivalent evidence in the Islands); or (bb) at the date of decision on the application under this Appendix, the entry clearance officer is satisfied from the information available to them has been granted indefinite leave to enter or remain or limited leave to enter or remain under (as the case may be) paragraph EU2 or EU3 of Appendix EU to these Rules, which has not lapsed or been cancelled, curtailed, revoked or invalidated; or (cc) the entry clearance officer is satisfied, including by the required evidence of qualification, would have been granted indefinite leave to enter or remain or limited leave to enter or remain under (as the case may be) paragraph EU2 or EU3 of Appendix EU to these Rules, if they had made a valid application under it before 1 July 2021, and that leave would not have lapsed or been cancelled, curtailed, revoked or invalidated before the date of application under this Appendix; or (ii) where they are a relevant person of Northern Ireland in accordance with sub-paragraph (a)(i) or (a)(iii) of that entry in this table, the entry clearance officer is satisfied, including by the required evidence of qualification, would (but for the fact that they are a British citizen) have been granted indefinite leave to enter or remain or limited leave to enter or remain under (as the case may be) paragraph EU2 or EU3 of Appendix EU to these Rules, if they had made a valid application under it before 1 July 2021, and that leave would not have lapsed or been cancelled, curtailed, revoked or invalidated before the date of application under this Appendix; or (e) a **person exempt from immigration control** ; or (f) a **frontier worker**]
relevant EEA citizen (where the date of application under this Appendix is on or after 1 July 2021)	(a) an EEA citizen (in accordance with sub-paragraph (a) of that entry in this table) who: (i) has been granted indefinite leave to enter or remain or limited leave to enter or remain under (as the case may be) paragraph EU2 or EU3 of Appendix EU to these Rules (or under its equivalent in the Islands), which has not lapsed or been cancelled, curtailed, revoked or invalidated and which is evidenced by the Home Office reference number for that grant of leave (or by the equivalent evidence in the Islands); or

Term	Definition
	(ii) at the date of decision on the application under this Appendix, the entry clearance officer is satisfied from the information available to them has been granted indefinite leave to enter or remain or limited leave to enter or remain under (as the case may be) paragraph EU2 or EU3 of Appendix EU to these Rules, which has not lapsed or been cancelled, curtailed, revoked or invalidated; or (iii) (in the case of an **Irish citizen** who has not been granted indefinite leave to enter or remain or limited leave to enter or remain under (as the case may be) paragraph EU2 or EU3 of Appendix EU to these Rules or under its equivalent in the Islands, where the applicant does not rely on that person being a relevant person of Northern Ireland) the entry clearance officer is satisfied, including by the **required evidence of qualification**, would have been granted such leave under that Appendix, if they had made a valid application under it before 1 July 2021, and that leave would not have lapsed or been cancelled, curtailed, revoked or invalidated before the date of application under this Appendix; or [(iv) the applicant satisfies the entry clearance officer by relevant information and evidence provided with the application (including their valid passport or valid national identity card as an EEA citizen, which is the original document and not a copy) meets sub-paragraph (a)(i) of the definition of 'relevant EEA citizen [[(where, in respect of the application under consideration, the date of application by the relevant EEA citizen or their family member is on or after 1 July 2021)]]' in Annex 1 to Appendix EU to these Rules, such that the applicant is a 'family member of a relevant EEA citizen' (as defined in Annex 1 to Appendix EU); or] (b) an EEA citizen (in accordance with sub-paragraph (a) of that entry in this table) who is a relevant naturalised British citizen [. . .]; or (c) (where the applicant is the family member ('F') to whom paragraph 9 of Schedule 6 to the EEA Regulations refers and meets the criteria as F in that paragraph) an EEA citizen (in accordance with sub-paragraph (b) of that entry in this table) who the entry clearance officer is satisfied, including by the required evidence of qualification, would (but for the fact that they are a British citizen) have been granted indefinite leave to enter or remain or limited leave to enter or remain under (as the case may be) paragraph EU2 or EU3 of Appendix EU to these Rules, if they had made a valid application under it before 1 July 2021, and that leave would not have lapsed or been cancelled, curtailed, revoked or invalidated before the date of application under this Appendix; or (d) an EEA citizen (in accordance with sub-paragraph (c) of that entry in this table) who:

Term	Definition
	(i) where they are a relevant person of Northern Ireland in accordance with sub-paragraph (a)(ii) of that entry in this table: (aa) has been granted indefinite leave to enter or remain or limited leave to enter or remain under (as the case may be) paragraph EU2 or EU3 of Appendix EU to these Rules (or under its equivalent in the Islands), which has not lapsed or been cancelled, curtailed, revoked or invalidated and which is evidenced by the Home Office reference number for that grant of leave (or by the equivalent evidence in the Islands); or (bb) at the date of decision on the application under this Appendix, the entry clearance officer is satisfied from the information available to them has been granted indefinite leave to enter or remain or limited leave to enter or remain under (as the case may be) paragraph EU2 or EU3 of Appendix EU to these Rules, which has not lapsed or been cancelled, curtailed, revoked or invalidated; or (cc) the entry clearance officer is satisfied, including by the required evidence of qualification, would have been granted indefinite leave to enter or remain or limited leave to enter or remain under (as the case may be) paragraph EU2 or EU3 of Appendix EU to these Rules, if they had made a valid application under it before 1 July 2021, and that leave would not have lapsed or been cancelled, curtailed, revoked or invalidated before the date of application under this Appendix; or (ii) where they are a relevant person of Northern Ireland in accordance with sub-paragraph (a)(i) or (a)(iii) of that entry in this table, the entry clearance officer is satisfied, including by the required evidence of qualification, would [(but for the fact that they are a British citizen and, where they are a specified relevant person of Northern Ireland in accordance with that entry in this table, but, where applicable, for that fact)] have been granted indefinite leave to enter or remain or limited leave to enter or remain under (as the case may be) paragraph EU2 or EU3 of Appendix EU to these Rules, if they had made a valid application under it before 1 July 2021, and that leave would not have lapsed or been cancelled, curtailed, revoked or invalidated before the date of application under this Appendix; or (e) a person exempt from immigration control; or (f) a frontier worker
relevant naturalised British citizen	a person who is a national of: Austria, Belgium, Bulgaria, Croatia, Republic of Cyprus, Czech Republic, Denmark, Estonia, Finland, France, Germany, Greece, Hungary, Iceland, Ireland, Italy, Latvia, Liechtenstein, Lithuania, Luxembourg, Malta, Netherlands, Norway, Poland, Portugal, Romania, Slovakia, Slovenia, Spain, Sweden or Switzerland, and who: (a) comes within paragraph (b) of the definition of 'EEA national' in regulation 2(1) of the EEA Regulations; and

Term	Definition
	[(b) meets the criteria contained in regulation 9A(2) or (3) as the dual national ("DN") to whom those provisions refer (save for the requirement in regulation 4(1)(c)(ii) and (d)(ii) of the EEA Regulations for comprehensive sickness insurance cover in the UK and regardless of whether they otherwise remained a qualified person under regulation 6 of the EEA Regulations after they acquired British citizenship); and] [(c) the entry clearance officer is satisfied, including by the required evidence of [[qualification,]] would (but for the fact that they are a British citizen) have been granted indefinite leave to enter or remain or limited leave to enter or remain under (as the case may be) paragraph EU2 or EU3 of Appendix EU to these Rules, if they had made a valid application under it before 1 July 2021, and that leave would not have lapsed or been cancelled, curtailed, revoked or invalidated before the date of application under this Appendix]
relevant period	(a) (where sub-paragraph (b) below does not apply) a period of six months from the date of decision; or (b) (where, in the case of an application for an EU Settlement Scheme Family Permit, the applicant indicates as part of the required application process that their intended date of arrival in the UK is on or after 1 April 2021 and that date is more than three months from the date of decision) a period of 4 months from their intended date of arrival in the UK
relevant person of Northern Ireland	person who: (a) is: (i) a British citizen; or (ii) an Irish citizen; or (iii) a British citizen and an Irish citizen; and (b) was born in Northern Ireland and, at the time of the person's birth, at least one of their parents was: (i) a British citizen; or (ii) an Irish citizen; or (iii) a British citizen and an Irish citizen; or (iv) otherwise entitled to reside in Northern Ireland without any restriction on their period of residence
required application process	the relevant on-line application form and a relevant process set out in that form for providing the required proof of identity and nationality and for providing the required biometrics

Term	Definition
required biometrics	(a) a facial photograph of the applicant (within the meaning of 'biometric information' in section 15 of the UK Borders Act 2007); and (b) the fingerprints of the applicant (also within that meaning of 'biometric information'; unless, in accordance with guidance published by the Secretary of State and in force at the date of application, they are not required to provide these), in both cases provided in accordance with the required application process
required evidence of being a relevant person of Northern Ireland	(a) the person's birth certificate showing that they were born in Northern Ireland, or their passport where this shows that they were born in Northern Ireland; and (b) evidence which satisfies the entry clearance officer that, at the time of the person's birth, at least one of their parents was: (i) a British citizen; or (ii) an Irish citizen; or (iii) a British citizen and an Irish citizen; or (iv) otherwise entitled to reside in Northern Ireland without any restriction on their period of residence in addition: (a) where, in order to meet the requirements of this entry, the applicant submits a copy (and not the original) of a document (including by uploading this as part of the required application process), the entry clearance officer can require the applicant to submit the original document where the entry clearance officer has reasonable doubt as to the authenticity of the copy submitted; and (b) where, in order to meet the requirements of this entry, the applicant submits a document which is not in English, the entry clearance officer can require the applicant to provide a certified English translation of (or a Multilingual Standard Form to accompany) the document, where this is necessary for the purposes of deciding whether the applicant meets the eligibility requirements for an entry clearance to be granted under this Appendix
required evidence of family relationship	in the case of: (a) a spouse: (i) a relevant document as the spouse of the relevant EEA citizen (or, as the case may be, of the qualifying British citizen), or a valid document of record of a marriage recognised under the law of England and Wales, Scotland or Northern Ireland or of the Islands; and

Term	Definition
	(ii) (aa) where the marriage to the relevant EEA citizen was contracted after the specified date and the applicant is not the specified spouse or civil partner of a Swiss citizen, a relevant document as the durable partner of the relevant EEA citizen or, where the applicant was not resident in the UK and Islands as the durable partner of the relevant EEA citizen before the specified date (or there is evidence which satisfies the entry clearance officer that the applicant was otherwise lawfully resident in the UK and Islands for the relevant period before the specified date, or the applicant is a joining family member) or where the applicant relies on the relevant EEA citizen being a relevant person of Northern Ireland, there is evidence which satisfies the entry clearance officer that the durable partnership was formed and was durable before the specified date; or (bb) where the marriage to the qualifying British citizen was contracted after the date and time of withdrawal, evidence which satisfies the entry clearance officer that the durable partnership was formed and was durable before the date and time of withdrawal; or (b) a civil partner: (i) a relevant document as the civil partner of the relevant EEA citizen (or, as the case may be, of the qualifying British citizen); a valid civil partnership certificate recognised under the law of England and Wales, Scotland or Northern Ireland or under any equivalent legislation in the Islands; or the valid overseas registration document for a relationship which is entitled to be treated as a civil partnership under the Civil Partnership Act 2004 or under any equivalent legislation in the Islands; and (ii) (aa) where the civil partnership with the relevant EEA citizen was formed after the specified date and the applicant is not the specified spouse or civil partner of a Swiss citizen, a relevant document as the durable partner of the relevant EEA citizen or, where the applicant was not resident in the UK and Islands as the durable partner of the relevant EEA citizen before the specified date (or there is evidence which satisfies the entry clearance officer that the applicant was otherwise lawfully resident in the UK and Islands for the relevant period before the specified date, or the applicant is a joining family member) or where the applicant relies on the relevant EEA citizen being a relevant person of Northern Ireland, there is evidence which satisfies the entry clearance officer that the durable partnership was formed and was durable before the specified date; or (bb) where the civil partnership with the qualifying British citizen was formed after the date and time of withdrawal, evidence which satisfies the entry clearance officer that the durable partnership was formed and was durable before the date and time of withdrawal; or

Term	Definition
	(c) a child—a relevant document issued on the basis of the relevant family relationship or their **evidence of birth** , and: (i) where the applicant is aged 21 years or over, evidence which satisfies the entry clearance officer that the requirements in sub-paragraph (b)(ii) of the entry for 'child' in this table are met; and (ii) where, in the case of a family member of a relevant EEA citizen, the applicant is a child born after the specified date or adopted after that date in accordance with a relevant adoption decision, or after the specified date became a child within the meaning of that entry in this table on the basis of one of sub-paragraphs (a)(iii) to (a)(xi) of that entry, evidence which satisfies the entry clearance officer that the requirements in the second sub-paragraph (a) or the second sub-paragraph (b) of the entry for 'family member of a relevant EEA citizen' in this table are met; or
	(d) a dependent parent—a relevant document issued on the basis of the relevant family relationship or their evidence of birth and, where the first sub-paragraph (b) of the entry for 'dependent parent' in this table applies, evidence which satisfies the entry clearance officer that (where this is not assumed) the requirement as to dependency in that sub-paragraph is met; or
	(e) a durable partner: (i) (aa) (where the applicant was resident in the UK and Islands as the durable partner of a relevant EEA citizen before the specified date and is not a joining family member) a relevant document as the durable partner of the relevant EEA citizen or, where there is evidence which satisfies the entry clearance officer that the applicant was otherwise lawfully resident in the UK and Islands for the relevant period before the specified date or where the applicant relies on the relevant EEA citizen being a relevant person of Northern Ireland, evidence which satisfies the entry clearance officer that the durable partnership was formed and was durable before the specified date; or (bb) (where the applicant was not resident in the UK and Islands as the durable partner of a relevant EEA citizen before the specified date, or where the applicant is a joining family member, and where sub-paragraph (e)(i)(cc) below does not apply) evidence which satisfies the entry clearance officer that the durable partnership with the relevant EEA citizen was formed and was durable before the specified date; or (cc) evidence which satisfies the entry clearance officer that the durable partnership with the qualifying British citizen was formed and was durable (in the case of a family member of a qualifying British citizen as described in sub-paragraph (a)(iii) of that entry in this table) before the date and time of withdrawal or (in the case of a family member of a qualifying British citizen as described in sub-paragraph (a)(iv) of that entry in this table) before the specified date; and

Term	Definition
	(ii) evidence which satisfies the entry clearance officer that the partnership remains durable at the date of application; or (f) a dependent relative of a qualifying British citizen—evidence which satisfies the entry clearance officer that the family relationship and (in sub-paragraph (a)(ii) of the entry for 'dependent relative of a qualifying British citizen' in this table) the person's dependency (or, as the case may be, their membership of the household or their strict need for personal care on serious health grounds) existed before the specified date and continue to exist at the date of application[; or] [(g) a dependent relative of a specified relevant person of Northern Ireland—evidence which satisfies the entry clearance officer that the family relationship and (in sub-paragraph (a)(ii) of the entry for 'dependent relative of a specified relevant person of Northern Ireland' in this table) the person's dependency (or, as the case may be, their membership of the household or their strict need for personal care on serious health grounds) existed before the specified date and continue to exist at the date of application] in addition: (a) where, in order to meet the requirements of this entry, the applicant submits a copy (and not the original) of a document (including by uploading this as part of the required application process), the entry clearance officer can require the applicant to submit the original document where the entry clearance officer has reasonable doubt as to the authenticity of the copy submitted; and (b) where, in order to meet the requirements of this entry, the applicant submits a document which is not in English, the entry clearance officer can require the applicant to provide a certified English translation of (or a Multilingual Standard Form to accompany) the document, where this is necessary for the purposes of deciding whether the applicant meets the eligibility requirements for an entry clearance to be granted under this Appendix
[required evidence of qualification]	[(a) (in the case of a relevant EEA citizen (or, where the date of application under this Appendix is on or after 1 July 2021, an Irish citizen) who has not been granted indefinite leave to enter or remain or limited leave to enter or remain under (as the case may be) paragraph EU2 or EU3 of Appendix EU to these Rules or under its equivalent in the Islands, where the applicant does not rely on the relevant EEA citizen (where they are an Irish citizen) being a relevant person of Northern Ireland): (i) their passport or national identity card as an EEA citizen or, where the date of application under this Appendix is on or after 1 July 2021, as an Irish citizen, which is:

Term	Definition
	(aa) valid; and (bb) the original document and not a copy; and (ii) information or evidence which satisfies the entry clearance officer that the person would have been granted indefinite leave to enter or remain or limited leave to enter or remain under (as the case may be) paragraph EU2 or EU3 of Appendix EU to these Rules, if they had made a valid application under it before 1 July 2021, and that leave would not have lapsed or been cancelled, curtailed, revoked or invalidated before the date of application under this Appendix; or (b) (in the case of a relevant EEA citizen who is a relevant naturalised British citizen or who is a relevant EEA citizen as described in sub-paragraph (c) of the applicable entry for 'relevant EEA citizen' in this table): (i) their passport or national identity card as an EEA citizen, which is: (aa) valid; and (bb) the original document and not a copy; and (ii) information or evidence which is provided by the applicant, or is otherwise available to the entry clearance officer, which satisfies the entry clearance officer that the relevant EEA citizen is a British citizen; and (iii) information or evidence which satisfies the entry clearance officer that the person would (but for the fact that they are a British citizen) have been granted indefinite leave to enter or remain or limited leave to enter or remain under (as the case may be) paragraph EU2 or EU3 of Appendix EU to these Rules, if they had made a valid application under it before 1 July 2021, and that leave would not have lapsed or been cancelled, curtailed, revoked or invalidated before the date of application under this Appendix; or (c) (in the case of a relevant EEA citizen who is relied on by the applicant as being a relevant person of Northern Ireland, and who, where they are a relevant person of Northern Ireland in accordance with sub-paragraph (a)(ii) of that entry in this table, has not been granted indefinite leave to enter or remain or limited leave to enter or remain under (as the case may be) paragraph EU2 or EU3 of Appendix EU to these Rules or under its equivalent in the Islands) the required evidence of being a relevant person of Northern Ireland and (where the relevant EEA citizen is relied on by the applicant as being a specified relevant person of Northern Ireland) information or evidence which satisfies the entry clearance officer that the requirements of that entry in this table are met, and (in all cases): (i) (aa) (where they are a British citizen) information or evidence which is provided by the applicant, or is otherwise available to the entry clearance officer, which satisfies the entry clearance officer that the person is a British citizen; or

Term	Definition
	(bb) (where they are an Irish citizen) their passport or national identity card as an Irish citizen, which is: (aaa) valid; and (bbb) the original document and not a copy; or (cc) (where they are a British citizen and an Irish citizen, and are not relied on by the applicant as being a specified relevant person of Northern Ireland) the evidence required by sub-paragraph (c)(i)(aa) or (c)(i)(bb) above; and (ii) information or evidence which satisfies the entry clearance officer that the person would (but for the fact that they are a British citizen, where they are a British citizen in accordance with sub-paragraph (a)(i) or (a)(iii) of the entry for 'relevant person of Northern Ireland' in this table) have been granted indefinite leave to enter or remain or limited leave to enter or remain under (as the case may be) paragraph EU2 or EU3 of Appendix EU to these Rules, if they had made a valid application under it before 1 July 2021, and that leave would not have lapsed or been cancelled, curtailed, revoked or invalidated before the date of application under this Appendix; or (d) (in the case of a relevant EEA citizen who is a person exempt from immigration control): (i) their passport or national identity card as an EEA citizen, which is: (aa) valid; and (bb) the original document and not a copy; and (ii) information or evidence which is provided by the applicant, or is otherwise available to the entry clearance officer, which satisfies the entry clearance officer that the relevant EEA citizen is exempt from immigration control in accordance with section 8(2), (3) or (4) of the Immigration Act 1971; and (iii) information or evidence which satisfies the entry clearance officer that the person would have been granted indefinite leave to enter or remain or limited leave to enter or remain under (as the case may be) paragraph EU2 or EU3 of Appendix EU to these Rules, if they had made a valid application under it before 1 July 2021, and that leave would not have lapsed or been cancelled, curtailed, revoked or invalidated before the date of application under this Appendix in addition: (a) 'valid' here means, in respect of a document, that it is genuine and has not expired or been cancelled or invalidated; and (b) where, in order to meet the requirements of sub-paragraph (a)(ii), (b)(ii), (b)(iii), (c)(i)(aa), (c)(ii), (d)(ii) or (d)(iii) above, the applicant submits a copy (and not the original) of a document, the entry clearance officer can require the applicant to submit the original document where the entry clearance officer has reasonable doubt as to the authenticity of the copy submitted; and

Term	Definition
	(c) where, in order to meet the requirements of sub-paragraph (a)(ii), (b)(ii), (b)(iii), (c)(i)(aa), (c)(ii), (d)(ii) or (d)(iii) above, the applicant submits a document which is not in English, the entry clearance officer can require the applicant to provide a certified English translation of (or a Multilingual Standard Form to accompany) the document, where this is necessary for the purposes of deciding whether the applicant meets the eligibility requirements for an entry clearance to be granted under this Appendix]
required proof of identity and nationality	(a) in the case of a specified EEA citizen: (i) their valid passport; or (ii) their valid national identity card; or (b) in the case of a non-EEA citizen, their valid passport [in addition, 'valid' here means that, at the date of application, the document is genuine] and has not expired or been cancelled or invalidated[[, unless (in the case of (a) or (b)) the entry clearance officer agrees to accept alternative evidence of identity and nationality where the applicant is unable to obtain or produce the required document due to circumstances beyond their control or to compelling practical or compassionate reasons]]
specified date	2300GMT on 31 December 2020
specified EEA citizen	a person who is: (a) a national of: Austria, Belgium, Bulgaria, Croatia, Republic of Cyprus, Czech Republic, Denmark, Estonia, Finland, France, Germany, Greece, Hungary, Iceland, Ireland, Italy, Latvia, Liechtenstein, Lithuania, Luxembourg, Malta, Netherlands, Norway, Poland, Portugal, Romania, Slovakia, Slovenia, Spain, Sweden or Switzerland; and (b) not also a British citizen
[specified EEA family permit case	a person who: (a) on the basis of a valid application made under the EEA Regulations before the specified date, would, had the route not closed after 30 June 2021, have been issued an EEA family permit under regulation 12 of the EEA Regulations: (i) (aa) as an extended family member under regulation 8; and (bb) where the "relevant EEA national" referred to in regulation 12(4) was resident in the UK in accordance with regulation 12(1)(a) (i) before the specified date; or (ii) (aa) as a person with a derivative right to reside in the UK by virtue of regulation 16(1); and

Term	Definition
	(bb) where, pursuant to regulation 12(2), any person from whom the right to be admitted to the UK under the criteria in regulation 11(5) was derived was resident in the UK before the specified date; or (b) after the specified date and before 1 June 2021 was issued an EEA family permit under regulation 12 of the EEA Regulations, has contacted the Home Office to advise that they were not able to travel to the UK by 30 June 2021, and the entry clearance officer is satisfied by information or evidence provided by the person that there were compelling practical or compassionate reasons or COVID-19 related reasons why they were not able to travel to the UK by 30 June 2021; or (c) on or after 1 June 2021 was issued an EEA family permit under regulation 12 of the EEA Regulations with an expiry date of 30 June 2021, and has contacted the Home Office to advise that they were not able to travel to the UK by 30 June 2021 in addition, there must not have been a significant change in circumstances since the date on which the person was issued an EEA family permit under regulation 12 of the EEA Regulations (or, as the case may be, since the date on which the person's appeal against the refusal of such a family permit was allowed or on which they would otherwise have been issued one, had the route not closed after 30 June 2021), such that it is not appropriate for them to be granted an entry clearance under this Appendix]
[specified relevant person of Northern Ireland	(a) the person is a relevant person of Northern Ireland in accordance with sub-paragraph (a)(i) or (a)(iii) of that entry in this table; and (b) the applicant is a non-EEA citizen; and (c) (i) (aa) the applicant meets the definition of 'joining family member of a relevant sponsor' in Annex 1 to Appendix EU to these Rules where the person is their relevant sponsor; and (bb) the applicant has satisfied the entry clearance officer by relevant information or evidence provided with the application that, due to compelling practical or compassionate reasons, it was not possible for the person to return to the UK before the specified date while the applicant remained outside the UK; or (ii) (aa) the applicant is a dependent relative of a specified relevant person of Northern Ireland; and (bb) the person: (i) is outside the UK; or (ii) is in the UK and has been so for a period not exceeding three months; or [[(iii) is in the UK and (were they an "EEA national" in accordance with regulation 2(1) of the EEA Regulations) they were residing in the UK in accordance with the EEA Regulations on 30 June 2021]]]

Term	Definition
specified spouse or civil partner of a Swiss citizen	(a) the person is the spouse or civil partner of a relevant EEA citizen (in accordance, where the date of application is before 1 July 2021, with sub-paragraph (a) of the applicable entry for 'relevant EEA citizen' in this table or, where the date of application is on or after 1 July 2021, with sub-paragraph (a)(i) or (a)(ii) of the applicable entry for 'relevant EEA citizen' in this table), who is a national of Switzerland and who is not also a British citizen; and (b) the marriage was contracted or the civil partnership was formed after the specified date and before 1 January 2026; and (c) the marriage or civil partnership continues to exist at the date of application
spouse	(a) the person is party to a marriage with a relevant EEA citizen (or, as the case may be, with a qualifying British citizen) and the marriage is recognised under the law of England and Wales, Scotland or Northern Ireland or of the Islands; and (b) it is not a **marriage of convenience** ; and (c) neither party has another spouse, a civil partner or a durable partner with (in any of those circumstances) immigration status in the UK or the Islands based on that person's relationship with that party
the Islands	the Bailiwick of Guernsey, the Bailiwick of Jersey or the Isle of Man

Note: In 'civil partnership of convenience' words substituted; 'date of application', 'deportation order', 'EEA Regulations' substituted; in 'exclusion decision' words in (b) inserted; in 'frontier worker' words in (c) and (d) substituted; in 'Islands deportation order' words in (b) inserted; in 'Islands exclusion order' words in (b) inserted; in 'person exempt from immigration control' amendment to (d); 'qualifying British citizen' substituted; in 'relevant document' words in (c) inserted; in 'relevant EEA citizen (where the date of application under this Appendix is before 1 July 2021)' amendment to (a)(iii); in 'relevant EEA citizen (where the date of application under this Appendix is on or after 1 July 2021)' (a)(iv) inserted; in 'required proof of identity and nationality' words in square brackets in (b) substituted from 6 April 2021; 'dependent relative of a specified relevant person of Northern Ireland' inserted; in family member of a relevant EEA citizen' (g) inserted; in 'required evidence of family relationship' words in (f) substituted, (g) inserted; in 'required evidence of qualification' amendments to (c) and (c)(i)(cc); in 'required proof of identity and nationality' words in double square brackets in (b) inserted; 'specified relevant person of Northern Ireland' inserted from 1 July 2021 (HC 1248). Sub-paragraph (f) in 'family member of a relevant EEA citizen', (d) in 'person exempt from immigration control', definition of 'relevant EEA citizen (where the date of application under this Appendix is before 1 July 2021)', words in (d)(ii) of 'relevant EEA citizen (where the date of application under this Appendix is on or after 1 July 2021)', (c) in 'relevant naturalized British citizen', definition of 'required evidence of qualification', (c)(ii)(bb)(iii) of 'specified relevant person of Northern Ireland' substituted; words in (a) in 'relevant document' inserted; words in (b) of 'relevant EEA citizen (where the date of application under this Appendix is on or after 1 July 2021)' deleted from 6 October 2021 (HC 617). Words in (b)(ii) of 'deportation order', words in (a) and (b) of 'durable partner', words in double square brackets in (b) of 'exclusion decision', word in (a)(viii)(bb), sub-paragraph (b)(ii) of 'family member of a qualifying British citizen', words in double square brackets in (f) of 'family member of a relevant EEA citizen', sub-paragraph (a), words in double square brackets in (b) of 'Islands deportation order', words in double square brackets in (b) of 'Islands exclusion decision', words in (d) of 'person exempt from immigration control', definition of 'qualifying British citizen', words in double square brackets in (a)(iv) of 'relevant EEA citizen (where the date of application under this Appendix is on or after 2 July 2021)', sub-paragraph (b), words in double square brackets in 'relevant naturalised British citizen' substituted, sub-paragraph (a)(ix), words after (b)(ii) of 'family member of a qualifying British citizen', definition of 'specified EEA family permit case' inserted from 6 April 2022 (HC 1118).

Annex 2—Consideration of a valid application

A2.1. A valid application made under this Appendix will be decided on the basis of:

(a) the information and evidence provided by the applicant, including in response to any request for further information or evidence made by the entry clearance officer; and

(b) any other information or evidence made available to the entry clearance officer (including from other government departments) at the date of decision.

A2.2. (1) For the purposes of deciding whether the applicant meets the eligibility requirements for entry clearance, the entry clearance officer may:

(a) request that the applicant provide further information or evidence that they meet those requirements; or

(b) invite the applicant to be interviewed by the entry clearance officer in person, by telephone, by video-telecommunications link or over the internet.

(2) For the purposes of deciding whether the applicant meets the eligibility requirements for entry clearance, the entry clearance officer may:

(a) request that the person ('P') on whom the applicant relies as being the relevant EEA citizen (or, as the case may be, the qualifying British citizen) with whom the applicant is in a family relationship provide information or evidence about their relationship with the applicant, their current or planned residence in the UK or (where P is a qualifying British citizen) their residence in a country listed in sub-paragraph (a) of the entry for 'specified EEA citizen' in the table at Annex 1 to this Appendix; or

(b) invite P to be interviewed by the entry clearance officer in person, by telephone, by video-telecommunications link or over the internet.

(3) If the applicant or (as the case may be) P:

(a) fails within a reasonable timeframe specified in the request to provide the information or evidence requested; or

(b) on at least two occasions, fails to comply with an invitation to attend an interview in person or with other arrangements to be interviewed, the entry clearance officer may draw any factual inferences about whether the applicant meets the eligibility requirements for entry clearance as appear appropriate in the circumstances.

(4) The entry clearance officer may decide, following the drawing of a factual inference under sub-paragraph (3), that the applicant does not meet the eligibility requirements for entry clearance.

(5) The entry clearance officer must not decide that the applicant does not meet the eligibility requirements for entry clearance on the sole basis that the applicant or (as the case may be) P failed on at least two occasions to comply with an invitation to be interviewed.

[Annex 3 – revocation of entry clearance and cancellation and curtailment of leave to enter]

Note: Heading substituted from 6 October 2021 (HC 617).

A3.1. A person's entry clearance granted under this Appendix must be revoked where [the person's presence in the UK is deemed not to be conducive] to the public good because of conduct committed after the specified date.

Note: Words substituted from 6 April 2022 (HC 1118).

A3.2. A person's entry clearance granted under this Appendix may be revoked where the entry clearance officer is satisfied that it is proportionate to revoke that entry clearance where:

(a) In respect of their conduct committed before the specified date, the person is subject to an exclusion decision, an exclusion order or an Islands exclusion decision; or

(b) The revocation is justified on grounds that, in relation to the relevant application under this Appendix, and whether or not to the applicant's knowledge, false or misleading information, representations or documents were submitted (including false or misleading information submitted to any person to obtain a document used in support of the application); and the information, representation or documentation was material to the decision to grant the applicant an entry clearance under this Appendix; or

(c) Since it was granted, there has been a change in circumstances that is, or would have been, relevant to that person's eligibility for that entry clearance, such that their entry clearance ought to be revoked.

A3.3. A person's leave to enter granted by virtue of having arrived in the UK with an entry clearance that was granted under this Appendix must be cancelled where, because of conduct committed after the specified date, [the person's presence in the UK is deemed not to be conducive] to the public good.

Note: Words substituted from 6 April 2022 (HC 1118).

A3.4. A person's leave to enter granted by virtue of having arrived in the UK with an entry clearance that was granted under this Appendix may be cancelled where the Secretary of State or an Immigration Officer is satisfied that it is proportionate to cancel that leave where:

(a) The cancellation is justified on grounds of public policy, public security or public health in accordance with regulation 27 of the Immigration (European Economic Area) Regulations 2016, irrespective of whether the EEA Regulations apply to that person (except that for 'a right of permanent residence under regulation 15' read 'indefinite leave to enter or remain or who would be granted indefinite leave to enter or remain if they made a valid application under Appendix EU to the Immigration Rules'; and for 'an EEA decision' read 'a decision under paragraph A3.4.(a) of Annex 3 to Appendix EU (Family Permit) to the Immigration Rules'); or

(b) The cancellation is justified on grounds that, in relation to the relevant application under this Appendix, and whether or not to the applicant's knowledge, false or misleading information, representations or documents were submitted (including false or misleading information submitted to any person to obtain a document used in support of the application); and the information, representation or documentation was material to the decision to grant the applicant an entry clearance under this Appendix; or

(c) Since the entry clearance under this Appendix was granted, there has been a change in circumstances that is, or would have been, relevant to that person's eligibility for that entry clearance, such that their leave to enter ought to be cancelled.

A3.5. A person's leave to enter granted by virtue of having arrived in the UK with an entry clearance that was granted under this Appendix may be curtailed where the Secretary of State is satisfied that it is proportionate to curtail that leave where:

(a) Curtailment is justified on grounds that, in relation to the relevant application under this Appendix, and whether or not to the applicant's knowledge, false or misleading information, representations or documents were submitted (including false or misleading information submitted to any person to obtain a document used in support of the application); and the information, representation or documentation was material to the decision to grant the applicant an entry clearance under this Appendix; or

(b) Curtailment is justified on grounds that it is more likely than not that, after the specified date, the person has entered, attempted to enter or assisted another person to enter or to attempt to enter, a marriage, civil partnership or durable partnership of convenience.]

Note: Annex 3 substituted from 6 April 2021 (HC 1248).

Appendix F
Archived Immigration Rules

Part 1—Immigration Rules relating to highly skilled migrants, the International Graduates Scheme, the Fresh Talent: Working in Scotland scheme, businesspersons, innovators, investors and writers, composers and artists as at 29 June 2008

Highly skilled migrants

Requirements for leave to enter the United Kingdom as a highly skilled migrant

135A. The requirements to be met by a person seeking leave to enter as a highly skilled migrant are that the applicant:

(i) must produce a valid document issued by the Home Office confirming that he meets, at the time of the issue of that document, the criteria specified by the Secretary of State for entry to the United Kingdom under the Highly Skilled Migrant Programme; and

(ii) intends to make the United Kingdom his main home; and

(iii) is able to maintain and accommodate himself and any dependants adequately without recourse to public funds; and

(iv) holds a valid United Kingdom entry clearance for entry in this capacity; and

(v) if he makes an application for leave to enter on or after 29 February 2008, is not applying in India.

Immigration Officers at port should not refuse entry to passengers on the basis that they applied in India, if those passengers have a valid entry clearance for entry in this capacity.

Leave to enter as a highly skilled migrant

135B. A person seeking leave to enter the United Kingdom as a highly skilled migrant may be admitted for a period not exceeding 2 years, subject to a condition prohibiting Employment as a Doctor in Training (unless the applicant has submitted with this application a valid Highly Skilled Migrant Programme Approval Letter, where the application for that approval letter was made on or before 6 February 2008), provided the Immigration Officer is satisfied that each of the requirements of paragraph 135A is met and that the application does not fall for refusal under paragraph 135HA.

Refusal of leave to enter as a highly skilled migrant

135C. Leave to enter as a highly skilled migrant is to be refused if the Immigration Officer is not satisfied that each of the requirements of paragraph 135A is met or if the application falls for refusal under paragraph 135HA.

International Graduates Scheme

Requirements for leave to enter as a participant in the International Graduates Scheme

135O. The requirements to be met by a person seeking leave to enter as a participant in the International Graduates Scheme are that he:

(i) has successfully completed and obtained either:

(a) a recognised UK degree (with second class honours or above) in a subject approved by the Department for Education and Skills for the purposes of the Science and Engineering Graduates scheme, completed before 1 May 2007; or

(b) a recognised UK degree, Master's degree, or PhD in any subject completed on or after 1 May 2007; or

(c) a postgraduate certificate or postgraduate diploma in any subject completed on or after 1 May 2007;

at a UK education institution which is a recognised or listed body.

(ii) intends to seek and take work during the period for which leave is granted in this capacity;

(iii) can maintain and accommodate himself and any dependants without recourse to public funds;

(iv) completed his degree, Master's degree, PhD or postgraduate certificate or diploma, in the last 12 months;

(v) if he has previously spent time in the UK as a participant in the Science and Engineering Graduates Scheme or International Graduates Scheme, is not seeking leave to enter to a date beyond 12 months from the date he was first given leave to enter or remain under the Science and Engineering Graduates Scheme or the International Graduates Scheme;

(vi) intends to leave the United Kingdom if, on expiry of his leave under this scheme, he has not been granted leave to remain in the United Kingdom in accordance with paragraphs 128–135, 200–210H or 245A–245G of these Rules;

(vii) has the written consent of his official sponsor to enter or remain in the United Kingdom under the Science and Engineering Graduates Scheme or International Graduates Scheme if his approved studies, or any studies he has subsequently undertaken, were sponsored by a government or international scholarship agency; and

(viii) holds a valid entry clearance for entry in this capacity except where he is a British National (Overseas), a British overseas territories citizen, a British Overseas citizen, a British protected person or a person who under the British Nationality Act 1981 is a British subject.

Leave to enter as a participant in the International Graduates Scheme

135P. A person seeking leave to enter the United Kingdom as a participant in the International Graduates Scheme may be admitted for a period not exceeding 12 months provided he is able to produce to the Immigration Officer, on arrival, a valid United Kingdom entry clearance for entry in this capacity.

Refusal of leave to enter as a participant in the International Graduates Scheme

135Q. Leave to enter as a participant in the International Graduates Scheme is to be refused if the Immigration Officer is not satisfied that each of the requirements of paragraph 135O is met.

Requirements for leave to remain as a participant in the International Graduates Scheme

135R. The requirements to be met by a person seeking leave to remain as a participant in the International Graduates Scheme are that he:

(i) meets the requirements of paragraph 135O(i) to (vii); and

(ii) has leave to enter or remain as a student or as a participant in the Science and Engineering Graduates Scheme or International Graduates Scheme in accordance with paragraphs 57–69L or 135O–135T of these Rules;

(iii) would not, as a result of an extension of stay, remain in the United Kingdom as a participant in the International Graduates Scheme to a date beyond 12 months from the date on which he was first given leave to enter or remain in this capacity or under the Science and Engineering Graduates Scheme.

Leave to remain as a participant in the International Graduates Scheme

135S. Leave to remain as a participant in the International Graduates Scheme may be granted if the Secretary of State is satisfied that the applicant meets each of the requirements of paragraph 135R.

Refusal of leave to remain as a participant in the International Graduates Scheme

135T. Leave to remain as a participant in the International Graduates Scheme is to be refused if the Secretary of State is not satisfied that each of the requirements of paragraph 135R is met.

Requirements for leave to enter the United Kingdom as a Fresh Talent: Working in Scotland scheme participant

143A. The requirements to be met by a person seeking leave to enter as a Fresh Talent: Working in Scotland scheme participant are that the applicant:

(i) has been awarded:

(a) a HND, by a Scottish publicly funded institution of further or higher education, or a Scottish bona fide private education institution; or

(b) a recognised UK undergraduate degree, Master's degree or PhD or postgraduate certificate or diploma, by a Scottish education institution which is a recognised or listed body; and

(ii) has lived in Scotland for an appropriate period of time whilst studying for the HND, undergraduate degree, Master's degree PhD or postgraduate certificate or diploma referred to in (i) above; and

(iii) intends to seek and take employment in Scotland during the period of leave granted under this paragraph; and

(iv) is able to maintain and accommodate himself and any dependants adequately without recourse to public funds; and

(v) has completed the HND, undergraduate degree, Master's degree PhD or post-graduate certificate or diploma referred to in (i) above in the last 12 months; and

(vi) intends to leave the United Kingdom if, on expiry of his leave under this paragraph, he has not been granted leave to remain in the United Kingdom as:

(a) a work permit holder in accordance with paragraphs 128–135 of these Rules; or

(b) a Tier 1 (General) Migrant; or

(c) a person intending to establish themselves in business in accordance with paragraphs 200–210 of these Rules; or

(d) an innovator in accordance with paragraphs 210A–210H of these Rules; and

(vii) has the written consent of his official sponsor to enter or remain in the United Kingdom as a Fresh Talent: Working in Scotland scheme participant, if the studies which led to his qualification under (i) above (or any studies he has subsequently undertaken) were sponsored by a government or international scholarship agency; and

(viii) if he has previously been granted leave as either:

(a) a Fresh Talent: Working in Scotland scheme participant in accordance with this paragraph; and/or

(b) a participant in the Science and Engineering Graduates Scheme or International Graduates Scheme in accordance with paragraphs 135O–135T of these Rules is not seeking leave to enter under this paragraph which, when amalgamated with any previous periods of leave granted in either of these two categories, would total more than 24 months; and

(ix) holds a valid entry clearance for entry in this capacity except where he is a British National (Overseas), a British overseas territories citizen, a British Overseas citizen, a British protected person or a person who under the British Nationality Act 1981 is a British subject.

Leave to enter as a Fresh Talent: Working in Scotland scheme participant

143B. A person seeking leave to enter the United Kingdom as a Fresh Talent: Working in Scotland scheme participant may be admitted for a period not exceeding 24 months provided the Immigration Officer is satisfied that each of the requirements of paragraph 143A is met.

Refusal of leave to enter as a Fresh Talent: Working in Scotland scheme participant

143C. Leave to enter as a Fresh Talent: Working in Scotland scheme participant is to be refused if the Immigration Officer is not satisfied that each of the requirements of paragraph 143A is met.

Requirements for an extension of stay as a Fresh Talent: Working in Scotland scheme participant

143D. The requirements to be met by a person seeking an extension of stay as a Fresh Talent: Working in Scotland scheme participant are that the applicant:

(i) meets the requirements of paragraph 143A(i) to (vii); and

(ii) has leave to enter or remain in the United Kingdom as either:

(a) a student in accordance with paragraphs 57–69L of these Rules; or

(b) a participant in the Science and Engineering Graduates Scheme or International Graduates Scheme in accordance with paragraphs 135O–135T of these Rules; or

(c) a Fresh Talent: Working in Scotland scheme participant in accordance with paragraphs 143A–143F of these Rules; and

(iii) if he has previously been granted leave as either:

(a) a Fresh Talent: Working in Scotland scheme participant in accordance with paragraphs 143A–143F of these Rules; and/or

(b) a Science and Engineering Graduates Scheme or International Graduates Scheme participant in accordance with paragraphs 135O–135T of these Rules is not seeking leave to remain under this paragraph which, when amalgamated with any previous periods of leave granted in either of these two categories, would total more than 24 months.

Extension of stay as a Fresh Talent: Working in Scotland scheme participant

143E. An extension of stay as a Fresh Talent: Working in Scotland scheme participant may be granted for a period not exceeding 24 months if the Secretary of State is satisfied that each of the requirements of paragraph 143D is met.

Refusal of an extension of stay as a Fresh Talent: Working in Scotland scheme participant

143F. An extension of stay as a Fresh Talent: Working in Scotland scheme participant is to be refused if the Secretary of State is not satisfied that each of the requirements of paragraph 143D is met.

Persons intending to establish themselves in business

Requirements for leave to enter the United Kingdom as a person intending to establish himself in business

200. For the purpose of paragraphs 201–210 a business means an enterprise as:
- a sole trader; or
- a partnership; or
- a company registered in the United Kingdom.

201. The requirements to be met by a person seeking leave to enter the United Kingdom to establish himself in business are:

(i) that he satisfies the requirements of either paragraph 202 or paragraph 203; and

(ii) that he has not less than £200,000 of his own money under his control and disposable in the United Kingdom which is held in his own name and not by a trust or other investment vehicle and which he will be investing in the business in the United Kingdom; and

(iii) that until his business provides him with an income he will have sufficient additional funds to maintain and accommodate himself and any dependants without recourse to employment (other than his work for the business) or to public funds; and

(iv) that he will be actively involved full-time in trading or providing services on his own account or in partnership, or in the promotion and management of the company as a director; and

(v) that his level of financial investment will be proportional to his interest in the business; and

(vi) that he will have either a controlling or equal interest in the business and that any partnership or directorship does not amount to disguised employment; and

(vii) that he will be able to bear his share of liabilities; and

(viii) that there is a genuine need for his investment and services in the United Kingdom; and

(ix) that his share of the profits of the business will be sufficient to maintain and accommodate himself and any dependants without recourse to employment (other than his work for the business) or to public funds; and

(x) that he does not intend to supplement his business activities by taking or seeking employment in the United Kingdom other than his work for the business; and

(xi) that he holds a valid United Kingdom entry clearance for entry in this capacity.

202. Where a person intends to take over or join as a partner or director an existing business in the United Kingdom he will need, in addition to meeting the requirements at paragraph 201, to produce:

(i) a written statement of the terms on which he is to take over or join the business; and

(ii) audited accounts for the business for previous years; and

(iii) evidence that his services and investment will result in a net increase in the employment provided by the business to persons settled here to the extent of creating at least 2 new full-time jobs.

203. Where a person intends to establish a new business in the United Kingdom he will need, in addition to meeting the requirements at paragraph 201 above, to produce evidence:

(i) that he will be bringing into the country sufficient funds of his own to establish a business; and

(ii) that the business will create full-time paid employment for at least 2 persons already settled in the United Kingdom.

Leave to enter the United Kingdom as a person seeking to establish himself in business

204. A person seeking leave to enter the United Kingdom to establish himself in business may be admitted for a period not exceeding 2 years with a condition restricting his freedom to take employment provided he is able to produce to the Immigration Officer, on arrival, a valid United Kingdom entry clearance for entry in this capacity.

Refusal of leave to enter the United Kingdom as a person seeking to establish himself in business

205. Leave to enter the United Kingdom as a person seeking to establish himself in business is to be refused if a valid United Kingdom entry clearance for entry in this capacity is not produced to the Immigration Officer on arrival.

Requirements for an extension of stay in order to remain in business

206. The requirements for an extension of stay in order to remain in business in the United Kingdom are that the applicant can show:

(i) that he entered the United Kingdom with a valid United Kingdom entry clearance as a businessman; and

(ii) audited accounts which show the precise financial position of the business and which confirm that he has invested not less than £200,000 of his own money directly into the business in the United Kingdom; and

(iii) that he is actively involved on a full-time basis in trading or providing services on his own account or in partnership or in the promotion and management of the company as a director; and

(iv) that his level of financial investment is proportional to his interest in the business; and

(v) that he has either a controlling or equal interest in the business and that any partnership or directorship does not amount to disguised employment; and

(vi) that he is able to bear his share of any liability the business may incur; and

(vii) that there is a genuine need for his investment and services in the United Kingdom; and

(viii) (a) that where he has established a new business, new full-time paid employment has been created in the business for at least 2 persons settled in the United Kingdom; or

(b) that where he has taken over or joined an existing business, his services and investment have resulted in a net increase in the employment provided by the business to persons settled here to the extent of creating at least 2 new full-time jobs; and

(ix) that his share of the profits of the business is sufficient to maintain and accommodate him and any dependants without recourse to employment (other than his work for the business) or to public funds; and

(x) that he does not and will not have to supplement his business activities by taking or seeking employment in the United Kingdom other than his work for the business.

206A. The requirements for an extension of stay as a person intending to establish himself in business in the United Kingdom for a person who has leave to enter or remain for work permit employment are that the applicant:

(i) entered the United Kingdom or was given leave to remain as a work permit holder in accordance with paragraphs 128 to 133 of these Rules; and

(ii) meets each of the requirements of paragraph 201(i)–(x).

206B. The requirements for an extension of stay as a person intending to establish himself in business in the United Kingdom for a highly skilled migrant are that the applicant:

(i) entered the United Kingdom or was given leave to remain as a highly skilled migrant in accordance with paragraphs 135A to 135F of these Rules; and

(ii) meets each of the requirements of paragraph 201(i)–(x).

206C. The requirements for an extension of stay as a person intending to establish himself in business in the United Kingdom for a participant in the Science and Engineering Graduates Scheme or International Graduates Scheme are that the applicant:

(i) entered the United Kingdom or was given leave to remain as a participant in the Science and Engineering Graduates Scheme or International Graduates Scheme in accordance with paragraphs 135O to 135T of these Rules; and

(ii) meets each of the requirements of paragraph 201(i)–(x).

206D. The requirements for an extension of stay as a person intending to establish himself in business in the United Kingdom for an innovator are that the applicant:

(i) entered the United Kingdom or was given leave to remain as an innovator in accordance with paragraphs 210A to 210F of these Rules; and

(ii) meets each of the requirements of paragraph 201(i)–(x).

206E. The requirements for an extension of stay as a person intending to establish himself in business in the United Kingdom for a student are that the applicant:

(i) entered the United Kingdom or was given leave to remain as a student in accordance with paragraphs 57 to 62 of these Rules; and

(ii) has obtained a degree qualification on a recognised degree course at either a United Kingdom publicly funded further or higher education institution or a bona fide United Kingdom private education institution which maintains satisfactory records of enrolment and attendance; and

(iii) has the written consent of his official sponsor to such self employment if he is a member of a government or international scholarship agency sponsorship and that sponsorship is either ongoing or has recently come to an end at the time of the requested extension; and

(iv) meets each of the requirements of paragraph 201(i)–(x).

206F. The requirements for an extension of stay as a person intending to establish himself in business in the United Kingdom for a working holidaymaker are that the applicant:

(i) entered the United Kingdom or was given leave to remain as a working holidaymaker in accordance with paragraphs 95 to 100 of these Rules; and

(ii) has spent more than 12 months in total in the UK in this capacity; and

(iii) meets each of the requirements of paragraph 201(i)–(x).

206G. The requirements for an extension of stay as a person intending to establish himself in business in the United Kingdom in the case of a person who has leave to enter or remain as a Fresh Talent: Working in Scotland scheme participant are that the applicant:

(i) entered the United Kingdom or was given leave to remain as a Fresh Talent: Working in Scotland scheme participant in accordance with paragraphs 143A to 143F of these Rules; and

(ii) has the written consent of his official sponsor to such employment if the studies which led to him being granted leave under the Fresh Talent: Working in Scotland scheme in accordance with paragraphs 143A to 143F of these Rules, or any studies he has subsequently undertaken, were sponsored by a government or international scholarship agency; and

(iii) meets each of the requirements of paragraph 201(i)–(x).

206H. The requirements for an extension of stay as a person intending to establish himself in business in the United Kingdom for a Postgraduate Doctor or Dentist are that the applicant:

(i) entered the United Kingdom or was given leave to remain as a Postgraduate Doctor or Dentist in accordance with paragraphs 70 to 75 of these Rules; and

(ii) has the written consent of his official sponsor to such self employment if he is a member of a government or international scholarship agency sponsorship and that sponsorship is either ongoing or has recently come to an end at the time of the requested extension; and

(iii) meets each of the requirements of paragraph 201(i)–(x).

206I. The requirements for an extension of stay as a person intending to establish himself in business in the United Kingdom for a Tier 1 (General) Migrant are that the applicant:

(i) entered the United Kingdom or was given leave to remain as a Tier 1 (General) Migrant; and

(ii) meets each of the requirements of paragraph 201(i)–(x).

Extension of stay in order to remain in business

207. An extension of stay in order to remain in business with a condition restricting his freedom to take employment may be granted for a period not exceeding 3 years at a time provided the Secretary of State is satisfied that each of the requirements of paragraph 206, 206A, 206B, 206C, 206D, 206E, 206F, 206G, 206H or 206I is met.

Refusal of extension of stay in order to remain in business

208. An extension of stay in order to remain in business is to be refused if the Secretary of State is not satisfied that each of the requirements of paragraph 206, 206A, 206B, 206C, 206D, 206E, 206F, 206G, 206H or 206I is met.

Innovators

Requirements for leave to enter the United Kingdom as an innovator

210A. The requirements to be met by a person seeking leave to enter as an innovator are that the applicant:

(i) is approved by the Home Office as a person who meets the criteria specified by the Secretary of State for entry under the innovator scheme at the time that approval is sought under that scheme;

(ii) intends to set up a business that will create full-time paid employment for at least 2 persons already settled in the UK; and

(iii) intends to maintain a minimum five per cent shareholding of the equity capital in that business, once it has been set up, throughout the period of his stay as an innovator; and

(iv) will be able to maintain and accommodate himself and any dependants adequately without recourse to public funds or to other employment; and

(v) holds a valid United Kingdom entry clearance for entry in this capacity.

Leave to enter as an innovator

210B. A person seeking leave to enter the United Kingdom as an innovator may be admitted for a period not exceeding 2 years, provided the Immigration Officer is satisfied that each of the requirements of paragraph 210A is met.

Refusal of leave to enter as an innovator

210C. Leave to enter as an innovator is to be refused if the Immigration Officer is not satisfied that each of the requirements of paragraph 210A are met.

Requirements for an extension of stay as an innovator

210D. The requirements for an extension of stay in the United Kingdom as an innovator, in the case of a person who was granted leave to enter under paragraph 210A, are that the applicant:

(i) has established a viable trading business, by reference to the audited accounts and trading records of that business; and

(ii) continues to meet the requirements of paragraph 210A(i) and (iv); and has set up a business that will create full-time paid employment for at least 2 persons already settled in the UK; and

(iii) has maintained a minimum five per cent shareholding of the equity capital in that business, once it has been set up, throughout the period of his stay.

210DA. The requirements for an extension of stay in the United Kingdom as an innovator, in the case of a person who has leave for the purpose of work permit employment are that the applicant:

(i) entered the United Kingdom or was given leave to remain as a work permit holder in accordance with paragraphs 128 to 132 of these Rules; and

(ii) meets the requirements of paragraph 210A(i)–(iv).

210DB. The requirements for an extension of stay in the United Kingdom as an innovator in the case of a person who has leave as a student are that the applicant:

(i) entered the United Kingdom or was given leave to remain as a student in accordance with paragraphs 57 to 62 of these Rules; and

(ii) has obtained a degree qualification on a recognised degree course at either a United Kingdom publicly funded further or higher education institution or a bona fide United Kingdom private education institution which maintains satisfactory records of enrolment and attendance; and

(iii) has the written consent of his official sponsor to remain under the Innovator category if he is a member of a government or international scholarship agency sponsorship and that sponsorship is either ongoing or has recently come to an end at the time of the requested extension; and

(iv) meets the requirements of paragraph 210A(i)–(iv).

210DC. The requirements to be met for an extension of stay as an innovator, for a person who has leave as a working holidaymaker are that the applicant:

(i) entered the United Kingdom as a working holidaymaker in accordance with paragraphs 95 to 96 of these Rules; and

(ii) meets the requirements of paragraph 210A(i)–(iv).

210DD. The requirements to be met for an extension of stay as an innovator, for a postgraduate doctor, postgraduate dentist or trainee general practitioner are that the applicant:

(i) entered the United Kingdom or was given leave to remain as a postgraduate doctor, postgraduate dentist or trainee general practitioner in accordance with paragraphs 70 to 75 of these Rules; and

(ii) has the written consent of his official sponsor to remain under the innovator category if he is a member of a government or international scholarship agency sponsorship and that sponsorship is either ongoing or has recently come to an end at the time of the requested extension; and

(iii) meets the requirements of paragraph 210A(i)–(iv).

210DE. The requirements to be met for an extension of stay as an innovator, for a participant in the Science and Engineering Graduate Scheme or International Graduates Scheme are that the applicant:

(i) entered the United Kingdom or was given leave to remain as a participant in the Science and Engineering Graduate Scheme or International Graduates Scheme in accordance with paragraphs 135O to 135T of these Rules; and

(ii) meets the requirements of paragraph 210A(i)–(iv).

210DF. The requirements to be met for an extension of stay as an innovator, for a highly skilled migrant are that the applicant:

(i) entered the United Kingdom or was given leave to remain as a highly skilled migrant in accordance with paragraphs 135A to 135E of these Rules; and

(ii) meets the requirements of paragraph 210A(i)–(iv)

Requirements for leave to enter the United Kingdom as an investor

224. The requirements to be met by a person seeking leave to enter the United Kingdom as an investor are that he:

(i) (a) has money of his own under his control in the United Kingdom amounting to no less than £1 million; or

(b) (i) owns personal assets which, taking into account any liabilities to which he is subject, have a value exceeding £2 million; and

(ii) has money under his control in the United Kingdom amounting to no less than £1 million, which may include money loaned to him provided that it was loaned by a financial institution regulated by the Financial Services Authority; and

(ii) intends to invest not less than £750,000 of his capital in the United Kingdom by way of United Kingdom Government bonds, share capital or loan capital in active and trading United Kingdom registered companies (other than those principally engaged in property investment and excluding investment by the applicant by way of deposits with a bank, building society or other enterprise whose normal course of business includes the acceptance of deposits); and

(iii) intends to make the United Kingdom his main home; and

(iv) is able to maintain and accommodate himself and any dependants without taking employment (other than self employment or business) or recourse to public funds; and

(v) holds a valid United Kingdom entry clearance for entry in this capacity.

Leave to enter as an investor

225. A person seeking leave to enter the United Kingdom as an investor may be admitted for a period not exceeding 2 years with a restriction on his right to take employment, provided he is able to produce to the Immigration Officer, on arrival, a valid United Kingdom entry clearance for entry in this capacity.

Refusal of leave to enter as an investor

226. Leave to enter as an investor is to be refused if a valid United Kingdom entry clearance for entry in this capacity is not produced to the Immigration Officer on arrival.

Requirements for an extension of stay as an investor

Extension of stay as an investor

227. The requirements for an extension of stay as an investor are that the applicant:

(i) entered the United Kingdom with a valid United Kingdom entry clearance as an investor; and

(ii) (a) has money of his own under his control in the United Kingdom amounting to no less than £1 million; or

(b) (i) owns personal assets which, taking into account any liabilities to which he is subject, have a value exceeding £2 million; and

(ii) has money under his control in the United Kingdom amounting to no less than £1 million, which may include money loaned to him provided that it was loaned by a financial institution regulated by the Financial Services Authority; and

(iii) has invested not less than £750,000 of his capital in the United Kingdom on the terms set out in paragraph 224 (ii) above and intends to maintain that investment on the terms set out in paragraph 224 (ii); and

(iv) has made the United Kingdom his main home; and

(v) is able to maintain and accommodate himself and any dependants without taking employment (other than his self employment or business) or recourse to public funds.

227A. The requirements to be met for an extension of stay as an investor, for a person who has leave to enter or remain in the United Kingdom as a work permit holder are that the applicant:

(i) entered the United Kingdom or was granted leave to remain as a work permit holder in accordance with paragraphs 128 to 133 of these Rules; and

(ii) meets the requirements of paragraph 224(i)–(iv).

227B. The requirements to be met for an extension of stay as an investor, for a person in the United Kingdom as a highly skilled migrant are that the applicant:

(i) entered the United Kingdom or was granted leave to remain as a highly skilled migrant in accordance with paragraphs 135A to 135F of these Rules; and

(ii) meets the requirements of paragraph 224(i)–(iv).

227C. The requirements to be met for an extension of stay as an investor, for a person in the United Kingdom to establish themselves or remain in business are that the applicant:

(i) entered the United Kingdom or was granted leave to remain as a person intending to establish themselves or remain in business in accordance with paragraphs 201 to 208 of these Rules; and

(ii) meets the requirements of paragraph 224(i)–(iv).

227D. The requirements to be met for an extension of stay as an investor, for a person in the United Kingdom as an innovator are that the applicant:

(i) entered the United Kingdom or was granted leave to remain as an innovator in accordance with paragraphs 210A to 210F of these Rules; and

(ii) meets the requirements of paragraph 224(i)–(iv).

227E. The requirements to be met for an extension of stay as an investor, for a person in the United Kingdom as a Tier 1 (General) Migrant are that the applicant:

(i) entered the United Kingdom or was granted leave to remain as a Tier 1 (General) Migrant; and

(ii) meets the requirements of paragraph 224(i)–(iv).

228. An extension of stay as an investor, with a restriction on the taking of employment, may be granted for a period not exceeding 3 years at a time of 3 years, provided the Secretary of State is satisfied that each of the requirements of paragraph 227, 227A, 227B, 227C, 227D or 227E is met.

Refusal of extension of stay as an investor

229. An extension of stay as an investor is to be refused if the Secretary of State is not satisfied that each of the requirements of paragraph 227, 227A, 227B, 227C, 227D or 227E is met.

Writers, composers and artists

Requirements for leave to enter the United Kingdom as a writer, composer or artist

232. The requirements to be met by a person seeking leave to enter the United Kingdom as a writer, composer or artist are that he:

(i) has established himself outside the United Kingdom as a writer, composer or artist primarily engaged in producing original work which has been published (other than exclusively in newspapers or magazines), performed or exhibited for its literary, musical or artistic merit; and

(ii) does not intend to work except as related to his self employment as a writer, composer or artist; and

(iii) has for the preceding year been able to maintain and accommodate himself and any dependants from his own resources without working except as a writer, composer or artist; and

(iv) will be able to maintain and accommodate himself and any dependants from his own resources without working except as a writer, composer or artist and without recourse to public funds; and

(v) holds a valid United Kingdom entry clearance for entry in this capacity.

Leave to enter as a writer, composer or artist

233. A person seeking leave to enter the United Kingdom as a writer, composer or artist may be admitted for a period not exceeding 2 years, subject to a condition restricting his freedom to take employment, provided he is able to produce to the Immigration Officer, on arrival, a valid United Kingdom entry clearance for entry in this capacity.

Refusal of leave to enter as a writer, composer or artist

234. Leave to enter as a writer, composer or artist is to be refused if a valid United Kingdom entry clearance for entry in this capacity is not produced to the Immigration Officer on arrival.

Requirements for an extension of stay as a writer, composer or artist

235. The requirements for an extension of stay as a writer, composer or artist are that the applicant:

(i) entered the United Kingdom with a valid United Kingdom entry clearance as a writer, composer or artist; and

(ii) meets the requirements of paragraph 232 (ii)–(iv).

Extension of stay as a writer, composer or artist

236. An extension of stay as a writer, composer or artist may be granted for a period not exceeding 3 years with a restriction on his freedom to take employment, provided the Secretary of State is satisfied that each of the requirements of paragraph 235 is met.

Refusal of extension of stay as a writer, composer or artist

237. An extension of stay as a writer, composer or artist is to be refused if the Secretary of State is not satisfied that each of the requirements of paragraph 235 is met.

PART 2
IMMIGRATION RULES AS AT 26 NOVEMBER 2008 RELATING TO ROUTES DELETED ON 27 NOVEMBER 2008

A) Requirements for leave to enter as an overseas qualified nurse or midwife

69M. The requirements to be met by a person seeking leave to enter as an qualified nurse or midwife are that the applicant:

(i) has obtained confirmation from the Nursing and Midwifery Council that he is eligible:

(a) for admission to the Overseas Nurses Programme; or

(b) to undertake a period of supervided practice; or

(c) to undertake an adaptation programme leading to registration as a midwife; and

(ii) as been offered:

(a) a supervised practice placement through an education provider that is recognised by the Nursing and Midwifery Council; or

(b) a supervised practice placement in a setting approved by the Nursing and Midwifery Council; or

(c) a midwifery adaptation programme placement is a setting approved by the Nursing and Midwifery Council; and

(iii) did not obtain acceptance of the offer referred to in paragraph 69 (ii) by misrepresentation; and

(iv) is able and intends to undertake the supervised practice placement or midwife adaptation programme; and

(v) does not intend to engage in business or take employment, except

(a) in connection with the supervised practice placement or midwife adaptation programme; or

(b) part-time work of a similar nature to the work undertaken on the supervised practice placement or midwife adaptation programme; and

(vi) is able to maintain and accommodate himself and any dependants without recourse to public funds.

Leave to enter the United Kingdom as an overseas qualified nurse or midwife

69N. Leave to enter the United Kingdom as an overseas qualified nurse or midwife may be granted for a period not exceeding 18 months, provided the Immigration Officer is satisfied that each of the requirements of paragraph 69M is met.

Refusal of leave to enter as an overseas qualified nurse or midwife

69O. Leave to enter the United Kingdom as an overseas qualified nurse or midwife is to be refused if the Immigration Officer is not is satisfied that each of the requirements of paragraph 69M is met.

B) Requirements for an extension of stay as an overseas qualified nurse or midwife

69P. The requirements to be met by a person seeking an extension of stay as an overseas qualified nurse or midwife are that the applicant:

(i) has leave to enter or remain in the United Kingdom as a prospective student in accordance with paragraphs 82–87 of these Rules; or

(ii) has leave to enter or remain in the United Kingdom as a student in accordance with paragraphs 57 to 69L of these Rules; or

(iii) (a) has leave to enter or remain in the United Kingdom as a work permit holder in accordance with paragraphs 128 to 135 of these Rules; or

C) Requirements for leave to enter the United Kingdom to take the PLAB Test

75A. The requirements to be met by a person seeking leave to enter in order to take the PLAB Test are that the applicant:

(iv) intends to leave the United Kingdom at the end of his leave granted under this paragraph unless he is successful in the PLAB Test and granted leave to remain:

(c) as a work permit holder for employment in the United Kingdom as a doctor in accordance with paragraphs 128 to 135.

Requirements for an extension of stay in order to take the PLAB Test

75D. The requirements for an extension of stay in the United Kingdom in order to take the PLAB Test are that the applicant:

(iv) intends to leave the United Kingdom at the end of his leave granted under this paragraph unless he is successful in the PLAB Test and granted leave to remain:

(c) as a work permit holder for employment in the United Kingdom as a doctor in accordance with paragraphs 128 to 135; and

Requirements for leave to enter to undertake a clinical or dental observer post

75G. The requirements to be met by a person seeking leave to enter to undertake a clinical attachment or dental observer post are that the applicant:

(iv) intends to leave the United Kingdom at the end of his leave granted under this paragraph unless he is granted leave to remain:

(b) as a work permit holder for employment in the United Kingdom as a doctor or dentist in accordance with paragraphs 128 to 135; and

Requirements for an extension of stay in order to undertake a clinical attachment or dental observer post

75K. The requirements to be met by a person seeking an extension of stay to undertake a clinical attachment or dental observer post are that the applicant:

(iv) intends to leave the United Kingdom at the end of his period of leave granted under this paragraph unless he is granted leave to remain:

(b) as a work permit holder for employment in the United Kingdom as a doctor or dentist in accordance with paragraphs 128 to 135; and

D) Definition of an 'au pair' placement

88. For the purposes of these Rules an 'au pair' placement as an arrangement whereby a young person:

(a) comes to the United Kingdom for the purpose of learning the English language; and

(b) lives for a time as a member of an English speaking family with appropriate opportunities for study; and

(c) helps in the home for a maximum of 5 hours per day in return for a reasonable allowance and with two free days a week.

Requirements for leave to enter as an 'au pair'

89. The requirements to be met by a person seeking leave to enter the United Kingdom as an 'au pair' are that he:

(i) is seeking entry for the purpose of taking up an arranged placement which can be shown to fall within the definition set out in paragraph 88; and

(ii) is aged between 17–27 inclusive or was so aged when first given leave to enter this category; and

(iii) is unmarried and is not a civil partner; and

(iv) is without dependants; and

(v) is a national of one of the following countries: Andorra, Bosnia-Herzegovina, Croatia, The Faroes, Greenland, Macedonia, Monaco, San Marino or Turkey; and

(vi) does not intend to stay in the United Kingdom for more than 2 years as an 'au pair'; and

(vii) intends to leave the United Kingdom on completion of his stay as an 'au pair'; and

(viii) if he has previously spent time in the United Kingdom as an 'au pair', is not seeking leave to enter to a date beyond 2 years from the date on which he was first given leave to enter the United Kingdom in this capacity; and

ix) is able to maintain and accommodate himself without recourse to public funds.

Leave to enter as an 'au pair'

90. A person seeking leave to enter the United Kingdom as an 'au pair' may be admitted for a period not exceeding 2 years with a prohibition on employment except as an 'au pair' provided the Immigration Officer is satisfied that each of the requirements of paragraph 89 is met. (A non-visa national who wishes to ascertain in advance whether a proposed 'au pair' placement is likely to meet the requirements of paragraph 89 is advised to obtain an entry clearance before travelling to the United Kingdom.)

Refusal of leave to enter as an 'au pair'

91. An application for leave to enter as an 'au pair' is to be refused if the Immigration Officer is not satisfied that each of the requirements of paragraph 89 is met.

E) Working Holidaymakers

Requirements for leave to enter as a working holidaymaker

95. The requirements to be met by a person seeking leave to enter the United Kingdom as a working holidaymaker are that he:

(i) is a national or citizen of a country listed in Appendix 3 of these Rules, or a British Overseas Citizen; a British Overseas Territories Citizen; or a British National; and

(ii) is aged between 17 and 30 inclusive or was so aged at the date of his application for leave to enter; and

(iii) (a) is unmarried and is not a civil partner, or

(b) is married to, or the civil partner of, a person who meets the requirements of this paragraph and the parties to the marriage or civil partnership intend to take a working holiday together; and

(iv) has the means to pay for his return or onward journey, and

(v) is able and intends to maintain and accommodate himself without recourse to public funds; and

(vi) is intending only to take employment incidental to a holiday, and not to engage in business, or to provide services as a professional sportsperson, and in any event not to work for more than 12 months during his stay; and

(vii) does not have dependent children any of whom are 5 years of age or over or who will reach 5 years of age before the applicant completes his working holiday; and

(viii) intends to leave the UK at the end of his working holiday; and

(ix) has not spent time in the United Kingdom on a previous working holidaymaker entry clearance; and

(x) holds a valid United Kingdom entry clearance, granted for a limited period not exceeding 2 years, for entry in this capacity.

Leave to enter as a working holidaymaker

96. A person seeking to enter the United Kingdom as a working holidaymaker may be admitted provided he is able to produce on arrival a valid United Kingdom entry clearance granted for a period not exceeding 2 years for entry in this capacity.

Refusal of leave to enter as a working holidaymaker

97. Leave to enter as a working holidaymaker is to be refused if a valid United Kingdom entry clearance for entry in this capacity is not produced to the Immigration Officer on arrival.

F) Children of working holidaymakers

Requirements for leave to enter or remain as the child of a working holidaymaker

101. The requirements to be met by a person seeking leave to enter or remain in the United Kingdom as the child of a working holidaymaker are that:

(i) he is the child of a parent admitted to, and currently present in, the United Kingdom as a working holidaymaker; and

(ii) he is under the age of 5 and will leave the United Kingdom before reaching that age; and

(iii) he can and will be maintained and accommodated adequately without recourse to public funds or without his parent(s) engaging in employment except as provided by paragraph 95 above; and

(iv) both parents are being or have been admitted to the United Kingdom, save where:

(a) the parent he is accompanying or joining is his sole surviving parent; or

(b) the parent he is accompanying or joining has had sole responsibility for his upbringing; or

(c) there are serious and compelling family or other considerations which make exclusion from the United Kingdom undesirable and suitable arrangements have been made for his care; and

(v) he holds a valid United Kingdom entry clearance for entry in this capacity or, if seeking leave to remain, was admitted with a valid United Kingdom entry clearance for entry in this capacity, and is seeking leave to a date not beyond the date to which his parent(s) have leave to enter in the working holidaymaker category.

Leave to enter or remain as the child of a working holidaymaker

102. A person seeking to enter the United Kingdom as the child of working holidaymaker/s must be able to produce on arrival a valid United Kingdom entry clearance for entry in this capacity.

Refusal of leave to enter or remain as the child of a working holidaymaker

103. Leave to enter or remain in the United Kingdom as the child of a working holidaymaker is to be refused if, in relation to an application for leave to enter, a valid United Kingdom entry clearance for entry in this capacity is not produced to the Immigration Officer on arrival or, in the case of an application for leave to remain, the applicant was not admitted with a valid United Kingdom entry clearance for entry in this capacity or is unable to satisfy the Secretary of State that each of the requirements of paragraph 101(i)–(iv) is met.

G) Requirements for leave to enter as a teacher or language assistant under an approved exchange scheme

110. The requirements to be met by a person seeking leave to enter the United Kingdom as a teacher or language assistant on an approved exchange scheme are that he:

(i) is coming to an educational establishment in the United Kingdom under an exchange scheme approved by the Department for Education and Skills, the Scottish or Welsh Office of Education or the Department of Education, Northern Ireland, or administered by the British Council's Education and Training Group or the League for the Exchange of Commonwealth Teachers; and

(ii) intends to leave the United Kingdom at the end of his exchange period; and

(iii) does not intend to take employment except in the terms of this paragraph; and

(iv) is able to maintain and accommodate himself and any dependants without recourse to public funds; and

(v) holds a valid United Kingdom entry clearance for entry in this capacity.

Leave to enter as a teacher or language assistant under an exchange scheme

111. A person seeking leave to enter the United Kingdom as a teacher or language assistant under an approved exchange scheme may be given leave to enter for a period not exceeding 12 months provided he is able to produce to the Immigration Officer, on arrival, a valid United Kingdom entry clearance for entry in this capacity.

Refusal of leave to enter as a teacher or language assistant under an approved exchange scheme

112. Leave to enter the United Kingdom as a teacher or language assistant under an approved exchange scheme is to be refused if a valid United Kingdom entry clearance for entry in this capacity is not produced to the Immigration Officer on arrival.

Requirements for extension of stay as a teacher or language assistant under an approved exchange scheme

113. The requirements for an extension of stay as a teacher or language assistant under an approved exchange scheme are that the applicant:

(i) entered the United Kingdom with a valid United Kingdom entry clearance as a teacher or language assistant; and

(ii) is still engaged in the employment for which his entry clearance was granted; and

(iii) is still required for the employment in question, as certified by the employer; and

(iv) meets the requirements of paragraph 110 (ii)–(iv); and

(v) would not, as a result of an extension of stay, remain in the United Kingdom as an exchange teacher or language assistant for more than 2 years from the date on which he was first given leave to enter the United Kingdom in this capacity.

Extension of stay as a teacher or language assistant under an approved exchange scheme

114. An extension of stay as a teacher or language assistant under an approved exchange scheme may be granted for a further period not exceeding 12 months provided the Secretary of State is satisfied that each of the requirements of paragraph 113 is met.

Refusal of extension of stay as a teacher or language assistant under an approved exchange scheme

115. An extension of stay as a teacher or language assistant under an approved exchange scheme is to be refused if the Secretary of State is not satisfied that each of the requirements of paragraph 113 is met.

H) Requirements for leave to enter for Home Office approved training or work experience

116. The requirements to be met by a person seeking leave to enter the United Kingdom for Home Office approved training or work experience are that he:

(i) holds a valid work permit from the Home Office issued under the Training and Work Experience Scheme; and

(ii) DELETED

(iii) is capable of undertaking the training or work experience as specified in his work permit; and

(iv) intends to leave the United Kingdom on the completion of his training or work experience; and

(v) does not intend to take employment except as specified in his work permit; and

(vi) is able to maintain and accommodate himself and any dependants adequately without recourse to public funds; and

(vii) holds a valid United Kingdom entry clearance for entry in this capacity except where he holds a work permit valid for 6 months or less or he is a British National (Overseas), a British overseas territories citizen, a British Overseas citizen, a British protected person or a person who under the British Nationality Act 1981 is a British subject.

Leave to enter for Home Office approved training or work experience

117. A person seeking leave to enter the United Kingdom for the purpose of approved training or approved work experience under the Training or Work Experience Scheme may be admitted to the United Kingdom for a period not exceeding the period of training or work experience approved by the Home Office for this purpose (as specified in his work permit), subject to a condition restricting him to that approved employment, provided he is able to produce to the Immigration Officer, on arrival, a valid United Kingdom entry clearance for entry in this capacity or, where entry clearance is not required, provided the Immigration Officer is satisfied that each of the requirements of paragraph 116(i)–(vi) is met.

Refusal of leave to enter for Home Office approved training or work experience

118. Leave to enter the United Kingdom for Home Office approved training or work experience under the Training and Work Experience scheme is to be refused if a valid United Kingdom entry clearance for entry in this capacity is not produced to the Immigration Officer on arrival or, where entry clearance is not required, if the Immigration Officer is not satisfied that each of the requirements of paragraph 116(i)–(vi) is met.

Requirements for extension of stay for Home Office approved training or work experience

119. The requirements for an extension of stay for Home Office approved training or work experience are that the applicant:

(i) entered the United Kingdom with a valid work permit under paragraph 117 or was admitted or allowed to remain in the United Kingdom as a student; and

(ii) has written approval from the Home Office for an extension of stay in this category; and

(iii) meets the requirements of paragraph 116(ii)–(vi).

Extension of stay for Home Office approved training or work experience

120. An extension of stay for approved training or approved work experience under the Training and Work Experience scheme may be granted for a further period not exceeding the extended period of training or work experience approved by the Home Office for this purpose (as specified in his work permit), provided that in each case the Secretary of State is satisfied that the requirements of paragraph 119 are met. An extension of stay is to be subject to a condition permitting the applicant to take or change employment only with the permission of the Home Office.

Refusal of extension of stay for Home Office approved training or work experience

121. An extension of stay for approved training or approved work experience under the Training and Work Experience scheme is to be refused if the Secretary of State is not satisfied that each of the requirements of paragraph 119 is met.

I) Representatives of overseas newspapers, news agencies and broadcasting organisations

Requirements for leave to enter as a representative of an overseas newspaper, news agency or broadcasting organisation

136. The requirements to be met by a person seeking leave to enter the United Kingdom as a representative of an overseas newspaper, news agency or broadcasting organisation are that he:

(i) has been engaged by that organisation outside the United Kingdom and is being posted to the United Kingdom on a long term assignment as a representative; and

(ii) intends to work full-time as a representative of that overseas newspaper, news agency or broadcasting organisation; and

(iii) does not intend to take employment except within the terms of this paragraph; and

(iv) can maintain and accommodate himself and any dependants adequately without recourse to public funds; and

(v) holds a valid United Kingdom entry clearance for entry in this capacity.

Leave to enter as a representative of an overseas newspaper, news agency or broadcasting organisation

137. A person seeking leave to enter the United Kingdom as a representative of an overseas newspaper, news agency or broadcasting organisation may be admitted for a period not exceeding 2 years, provided he is able to produce to the Immigration Officer, on arrival, a valid United Kingdom entry clearance for entry in this capacity.

Refusal of leave to enter as a representative of an overseas newspaper, news agency or broadcasting organisation

138. Leave to enter as a representative of an overseas newspaper, news agency or broadcasting organisation is to be refused if a valid United Kingdom entry clearance for entry in this capacity is not produced to the Immigration Officer on arrival.

Requirements for an extension of stay as a representative of an overseas newspaper, news agency or broadcasting organisation

139. The requirements for an extension of stay as a representative of an overseas newspaper, news agency or broadcasting organisation are that the applicant:

(i) entered the United Kingdom with a valid United Kingdom entry clearance as a representative of an overseas newspaper, news agency or broadcasting organisation; and

(ii) is still engaged in the employment for which his entry clearance was granted; and

(iii) is still required for the employment in question, as certified by his employer; and

(iv) meets the requirements of paragraph 136 (ii)–(iv).

Extension of stay as a representative of an overseas newspaper, news agency or broadcasting organisation

140. An extension of stay as a representative of an overseas newspaper, news agency or broadcasting organisation may be granted for a period not exceeding 3 years provided the Secretary of State is satisfied that each of the requirements of paragraph 139 is met.

Refusal of extension of stay as a representative of an overseas newspaper, news agency or broadcasting organisation

141. An extension of stay as a representative of an overseas newspaper, news agency or broadcasting organisation is to be refused if the Secretary of State is not satisfied that each of the requirements of paragraph 139 is met.

J) Private servants in diplomatic households

Requirements for leave to enter as a private servant in a diplomatic household

152. The requirements to be met by a person seeking leave to enter the United Kingdom as a private servant in a diplomatic household are that he:

(i) is aged 18 or over; and

(ii) is employed as a private servant in the household of a member of staff of a diplomatic or consular mission who enjoys diplomatic privileges and immunity within the meaning of the Vienna Convention on Diplomatic and Consular Relations or a member of the family forming part of the household of such a person; and

(iii) intends to work full-time as a private servant within the terms of this paragraph; and

(iv) does not intend to take employment except within the terms of this paragraph; and

(v) can maintain and accommodate himself and any dependants adequately without recourse to public funds; and

(vi) holds a valid United Kingdom entry clearance for entry in this capacity.

Leave to enter as a private servant in a diplomatic household

153. A person seeking leave to enter the United Kingdom as a private servant in a diplomatic household may be given leave to enter for a period not exceeding 12 months provided he is able to produce to the Immigration Officer, on arrival, a valid United Kingdom entry clearance for entry in this capacity.

Refusal of leave to enter as a private servant in a diplomatic household

154. Leave to enter as a private servant in a diplomatic household is to be refused if a valid United Kingdom entry clearance for entry in this capacity is not produced to the Immigration Officer on arrival.

Requirements for an extension of stay as a private servant in a diplomatic household

155. The requirements for an extension of stay as a private servant in a diplomatic household are that the applicant:

(i) entered the United Kingdom with a valid United Kingdom entry clearance as a private servant in a diplomatic household; and

(ii) is still engaged in the employment for which his entry clearance was granted; and

(iii) is still required for the employment in question, as certified by the employer; and

(iv) meets the requirements of paragraph 152(iii)–(v).

Extension of stay as a private servant in a diplomatic household

156. An extension of stay as a private servant in a diplomatic household may be granted for a period not exceeding 12 months at a time provided the Secretary of State is satisfied that each of the requirements of paragraph 155 is met.

Refusal of extension of stay as a private servant in a diplomatic household

157. An extension of stay as a private servant in a diplomatic household is to be refused if the Secretary of State is not satisfied that each of the requirements of paragraph 155 is met.

K) Overseas government employees

Requirements for leave to enter as an overseas government employee

160. For the purposes of these Rules an overseas government employee means a person coming for employment by an overseas government or employed by the United Nations Organisation or other international organisation of which the United Kingdom is a member.

161. The requirements to be met by a person seeking leave to enter the United Kingdom as an overseas government employee are that he:

(i) is able to produce either a valid United Kingdom entry clearance for entry in this capacity or satisfactory documentary evidence of his status as an overseas government employee; and

(ii) intends to work full-time for the government or organisation concerned; and

(iii) does not intend to take employment except within the terms of this paragraph; and

(iv) can maintain and accommodate himself and any dependants adequately without recourse to public funds.

Leave to enter as an overseas government employee

162. A person seeking leave to enter the United Kingdom as an overseas government employee may be given leave to enter for a period not exceeding 2 years, provided he is able, on arrival, to produce to the Immigration Officer a valid United Kingdom entry clearance for entry in this capacity or satisfy the Immigration Officer that each of the requirements of paragraph 161 is met.

Refusal of leave to enter as an overseas government employee

163. Leave to enter as an overseas government employee is to be refused if a valid United Kingdom entry clearance for entry in this capacity is not produced to the Immigration Officer on arrival or if the Immigration Officer is not satisfied that each of the requirements of paragraph 161 is met.

Requirements for an extension of stay as an overseas government employee

164. The requirements to be met by a person seeking an extension of stay as an overseas government employee are that the applicant:

(i) was given leave to enter the United Kingdom under paragraph 162 as an overseas government employee; and

(ii) is still engaged in the employment in question; and

(iii) is still required for the employment in question, as certified by the employer; and

(iv) meets the requirements of paragraph 161(ii)–(iv).

Extension of stay as an overseas government employee

165. An extension of stay as an overseas government employee may be granted for a period not exceeding 3 years provided the Secretary of State is satisfied that each of the requirements of paragraph 164 is met.

Refusal of extension of stay as an overseas government employee

166. An extension of stay as an overseas government employee is to be refused if the Secretary of State is not satisfied that each of the requirements of paragraph 164 is met.

L) Requirements for leave to enter as a minister of religion, missionary, or member of a religious order

170. The requirements to be met by a person seeking leave to enter the United Kingdom as a minister of religion, missionary or member of a religious order are that he:

(i) (a) if seeking leave to enter as a Minister of Religion has either been working for at least one year as a minister of religion in any of the 5 years immediately prior to the date on which the application is made or, where ordination is prescribed by a religious faith as the sole means of entering the ministry, has been ordained as a minister of religion following at least one years full-time or two years part-time training for the ministry; or

(b) if seeking leave to enter as a missionary has been trained as a missionary or has worked as a missionary and is being sent to the United Kingdom by an overseas organisation; or

(c) if seeking leave to enter as a member of a religious order is coming to live in a community maintained by the religious order of which he is a member and, if intending to teach, does not intend to do so save at an establishment maintained by his order; and

(ii) intends to work full-time as a minister of religion, missionary or for the religious order of which he is a member; and

(iii) does not intend to take employment except within the terms of this paragraph; and

(iv) can maintain and accommodate himself and any dependants adequately without recourse to public funds; and (iva) if seeking leave as a Minister of Religion can produce an International English Language Testing System certificate issued to him to certify that he has achieved level 6 competence in spoken and written English and that it is dated not more than two years prior to the date on which the application is made.

(v) holds a valid United Kingdom entry clearance for entry in this capacity.

Leave to enter as a minister of religion, missionary, or member of a religious order

171. A person seeking leave to enter the United Kingdom as a minister of religion, missionary or member of a religious order may be admitted for a period not exceeding 2 years provided he is able to produce to the Immigration Officer, on arrival, a valid United Kingdom entry clearance for entry in this capacity.

Refusal of leave to enter as a minister of religion, missionary or member of a religious order

172. Leave to enter as a minister of religion, missionary or member of a religious order is to be refused if a valid United Kingdom entry clearance for entry in this capacity is not produced to the Immigration Officer on arrival.

Requirements for an extension of stay as a minister of religion where entry to the United Kingdom was granted in that capacity

173. The requirements for an extension of stay as a minister of religion, where entry to the United Kingdom was granted in that capacity, missionary or member of a religious order are that the applicant:

(i) entered the United Kingdom with a valid United Kingdom entry clearance as a minister of religion, missionary or member of a religious order; and

(ii) is still engaged in the employment for which his entry clearance was granted; and

(iii) is still required for the employment in question as certified by the leadership of his congregation, his employer or the head of his religious order; and

(iv) (a) if he entered the United Kingdom as a minister of religion, missionary or member of a religious order in accordance with sub-paragraph (i) prior to 23 August 2004 meets the requirements of paragraph 170(ii)–(iv); or

(b) if he entered the United Kingdom as a minister of religion, missionary or member of a religious order in accordance with sub-paragraph (i), on or after 23 August 2004 but prior to 19 April 2007, or was granted leave to remain in accordance with paragraph 174B between those dates, meets the requirements of paragraph 170(ii)–(iv), and if a minister of religion met the requirement to produce an International English Language Testing System certificate certifying that he achieved level 4 competence in spoken English at the time he was first granted leave in this capacity; or

(c) if he entered the United Kingdom as a minister of religion, missionary or member of a religious order in accordance with sub-paragraph (i) on or after 19 April 2007, or was granted leave to remain in accordance with paragraph 174B on or after that date, meets the requirements of paragraph 170(ii)–(iv), and if a minister of religion met the requirement to produce an International English Language Testing System certificate certifying that he achieved level 6 competence in spoken and written English at the time he was first granted leave in this capacity.

Extension of stay as a minister of religion, missionary or member of a religious order

174. An extension of stay as a minister of religion, missionary or member of a religious order may be granted for a period not exceeding 3 years provided the Secretary of State is satisfied that each of the requirements of paragraph 173 is met.

Requirements for an extension of stay as a minister of religion where entry to the United Kingdom was not granted in that capacity

174A. The requirements for an extension of stay as a minister of religion for an applicant who did not enter the United Kingdom in that capacity are that he:

(i) entered the United Kingdom, or was given an extension of stay, in accordance with these Rules, except as a minister of religion or as a visitor or a short-term student, and has spent a continuous period of at least 12 months here pursuant to that leave immediately prior to the application being made; and

(ii) has either been working for at least one year as a minister of religion in any of the 5 years immediately prior to the date on which the application is made (provided that, when doing so, he was not in breach of a condition of any subsisting leave to enter or remain) or, where ordination is prescribed by a religious faith as the sole means of entering the ministry, has been ordained as a minister of religion following at least one year's full-time or two years part-time training for the ministry; and

(iii) is imminently to be appointed, or has been appointed, to a position as a minister of religion in the United Kingdom and is suitable for such a position, as certified by the leadership of his prospective congregation; and

(iv) meets the requirements of paragraph 170(ii)–(iva).

Extension of stay as a minister of religion where leave to enter was not granted in that capacity

174B. An extension of stay as a minister of religion may be granted for a period not exceeding 3 years at a time provided the Secretary of State is satisfied that each of the requirements of paragraph 174A is met.

Refusal of extension of stay as a minister of religion, missionary or member of a religious order

175. An extension of stay as a minister of religion, missionary or member of a religious order is to be refused if the Secretary of State is not satisfied that each of the requirements of paragraph 173 or 174A is met.

M) Refusal of indefinite leave to remain for a minister of religion, missionary or member of a religious order

177. Indefinite leave to remain in the United Kingdom for a minister of religion, missionary or member of a religious order is to be refused if the Secretary of State is not satisfied that each of the requirements of paragraph 176 is met.

177A. For the purposes of these Rules: Visiting religious workers and religious workers in non-pastoral roles:

(i) a visiting religious worker means a person coming to the UK for a short period to perform religious duties at one or more locations in the UK;

(ii) a religious worker in a non-pastoral role means a person employed in the UK by the faith he is coming here to work for, whose duties include performing religious rites within the religious community, but not preaching to a congregation.

Requirements for leave to enter the United Kingdom as a visiting religious worker or a religious worker in a non-pastoral role

177B. The requirements to be met by a person seeking leave to enter as a visiting religious worker or a religious worker in a non-pastoral role are that the applicant:

(i) (a) if seeking leave to enter as a visiting religious worker:

(i) is an established religious worker based overseas; and

(ii) submits a letter(s) from a senior member or senior representative of one or more local religious communities in the UK confirming that he is invited to perform religious duties as a visiting religious worker at one or more locations in the UK and confirming the expected duration of that employment; and

(iii) if he has been granted leave as a visiting religious worker in the last 12 months, is not seeking leave to enter which, when amalgamated with his previous periods of leave in this category in the last 12 months, would total more than 6 months; or

(b) if seeking leave to enter as a religious worker in a non-pastoral role:

(i) has at least one year of full-time training or work experience, or a period of part-time training or work experience equivalent to one year full-time training or work experience, accrued in the five years preceding the application in the faith with which he has employment in the UK; and

(ii) can show that, at the time of his application, at least one full-time member of staff of the local religious community which the applicant is applying to join in the UK has a sufficient knowledge of English; and

(iii) submits a letter from a senior member or senior representative of the local religious community which has invited him to the UK, confirming that he has been offered employment as religious worker in a non-pastoral role in that religious community, and confirming the duration of that employment; and

(ii) does not intend to take employment except as a visiting religious worker or religious worker in a non-pastoral role, whichever is the basis of his application; and

(iii) does not intend to undertake employment as a Minister of Religion, Missionary or Member of a Religious Order, as described in paragraphs 169–177 of these Rules; and

(iv) is able to maintain and accommodate himself and any dependants without recourse to public funds, or will, with any dependants, be maintained and accommodated adequately by the religious community employing him; and

(v) intends to leave the UK at the end of his leave in this category; and

(vi) holds a valid entry clearance for entry in this capacity except where he is a British National (Overseas), a British overseas territories citizen, a British Overseas citizen, a British protected person or a person who under the British Nationality Act 1981 is a British subject.

Leave to enter as a visiting religious worker or a religious worker in a non-pastoral role

177C. Leave to enter the United Kingdom as a visiting religious worker or a religious worker in a non-pastoral role may be granted:

(a) as a visiting religious worker, for a period not exceeding 6 months; or

(b) as a religious worker in a non-pastoral role, for a period not exceeding 12 months;

provided the Immigration Officer is satisfied that each of the requirements of paragraph 177B is met.

Refusal of leave to enter as a visiting religious worker or a religious worker in a non-pastoral role

177D. Leave to enter as a visiting religious worker or a religious worker in a non-pastoral role is to be refused if the Immigration Officer is not satisfied that each of the requirements of paragraph 177B is met.

Requirements for an extension of stay as a visiting religious worker or a religious worker in a non-pastoral role

177E. The requirements to be met by a person seeking an extension of stay as a visiting religious worker or a religious worker in a non-pastoral role are that the applicant:

(i) entered the United Kingdom with a valid entry clearance in this capacity or was given leave to enter as a visiting religious worker or a religious worker in a non-pastoral role; and

(ii) intends to continue employment as a visiting religious worker or a religious worker in a non-pastoral role; and

(iii) if seeking an extension of stay as a visiting religious worker:

(a) meets the requirement of paragraph 177B(i)(a)(i) above; and

(b) submits a letter from a senior member or senior representative of one or more local religious communities in the UK confirming that he is still wanted to perform religious duties as a visiting religious worker at one or more locations in the UK and confirming the expected duration of that employment; and

(c) would not, as the result of an extension of stay, be granted leave as a visiting religious worker which, when amalgamated with his previous periods of leave in this category in the last 12 months, would total more than 6 months; or

(iv) if seeking an extension of stay as a religious worker in a non-pastoral role:

(a) meets the requirements of paragraph 177B(i)(b)(i) and (ii); and

(b) submits a letter from a senior member or senior representative of the local religious community for which he works in the UK confirming that his employment as a religious worker in a non-pastoral role in that religious community will continue, and confirming the duration of that employment; and

(c) would not, as the result of an extension of stay, remain in the UK for a period of more than 24 months as a religious worker in a non-pastoral role; and

(v) meets the requirements of paragraph 177B(ii) to (v); and

Extension of stay as a visiting religious worker or a religious worker in a non-pastoral role

177F. An extension of stay as a visiting religious worker or a religious worker in a non-pastoral role may be granted:

(a) as a visiting religious worker, for a period not exceeding 6 months; or

(b) as a religious worker in a non-pastoral role, for a period not exceeding 24 months;

if the Secretary of State is satisfied that each of the requirements of paragraph 177E is met.

Refusal of an extension of stay as a visiting religious worker or a religious worker in a non-pastoral role

177G. An extension of stay as a visiting religious worker or a religious worker in a non-pastoral role is to be refused if the Secretary of State is not satisfied that each of the requirements of paragraph 177E is met.

N) Airport based operational ground staff of overseas-owned airlines

Requirements for leave to enter the United Kingdom as a member of the operational ground staff of an overseas-owned airline

178. The requirements to be met by a person seeking leave to enter the United Kingdom as a member of the operational ground staff of an overseas-owned airline are that he:

(i) has been transferred to the United Kingdom by an overseas-owned airline operating services to and from the United Kingdom to take up duty at an international airport as station manager, security manager or technical manager; and

(ii) intends to work full-time for the airline concerned; and

(iii) does not intend to take employment except within the terms of this paragraph; and

(iv) can maintain and accommodate himself and any dependants without recourse to public funds; and

(v) holds a valid United Kingdom entry clearance for entry in this capacity.

Leave to enter as a member of the operational ground staff of an overseas-owned airline

179. A person seeking leave to enter the United Kingdom as a member of the operational ground staff of an overseas-owned airline may be given leave to enter for a period not exceeding 2 years, provided he is able to produce to the Immigration Officer, on arrival, a valid United Kingdom entry clearance for entry in this capacity.

Refusal of leave to enter as a member of the operational ground staff of an overseas-owned airline

180. Leave to enter as a member of the operational ground staff of an overseas-owned airline is to be refused if a valid United Kingdom entry clearance for entry in this capacity is not produced to the Immigration Officer on arrival.

Requirements for an extension of stay as a member of the operational ground staff of an overseas-owned airline

181. The requirements to be met by a person seeking an extension of stay as a member of the operational ground staff of an overseas-owned airline are that the applicant:

(i) entered the United Kingdom with a valid United Kingdom entry clearance as a member of the operational ground staff of an overseas-owned airline; and

(ii) is still engaged in the employment for which entry was granted; and

(iii) is still required for the employment in question, as certified by the employer; and

(iv) meets the requirements of paragraph 178(ii)–(iv).

Extension of stay as a member of the operational ground staff of an overseas-owned airline

182. An extension of stay as a member of the operational ground staff of an overseas-owned airline may be granted for a period not exceeding 3 years, provided the Secretary of State is satisfied that each of the requirements of paragraph 181 is met.

Refusal of extension of stay as a member of the operational ground staff of an overseas-owned airline

183. An extension of stay as a member of the operational ground staff of an overseas-owned airline is to be refused if the Secretary of State is not satisfied that each of the requirements of paragraph 181 is met.

O) Retired persons of independent means

Requirements for leave to enter the United Kingdom as a retired person of independent means

263. The requirements to be met by a person seeking leave to enter the United Kingdom as a retired person of independent means are that he:

(i) is at least 60 years old; and

(ii) has under his control and disposable in the United Kingdom an income of his own of not less than £25,000 per annum; and

(iii) is able and willing to maintain and accommodate himself and any dependants indefinitely in the United Kingdom from his own resources with no assistance from any other person and without taking employment or having recourse to public funds; and

(iv) can demonstrate a close connection with the United Kingdom; and

(v) intends to make the United Kingdom his main home; and

(vi) holds a valid United Kingdom entry clearance for entry in this capacity.

Leave to enter as a retired person of independent means

264. A person seeking leave to enter the United Kingdom as a retired person of independent means may be admitted subject to a condition prohibiting employment for a period not exceeding 5 years, provided he is able to produce to the Immigration Officer, on arrival, a valid United Kingdom entry clearance for entry in this capacity.

Refusal of leave to enter as a retired person of independent means

265. Leave to enter as a retired person of independent means is to be refused if a valid United Kingdom entry clearance for entry in this capacity is not produced to the Immigration Officer on arrival.

Requirements for an extension of stay as a retired person of independent means

266. The requirements for an extension of stay as a retired person of independent means are that the applicant:

(i) entered the United Kingdom with a valid United Kingdom entry clearance as a retired person of independent means; and

(ii) meets the requirements of paragraph 263(ii)–(iv); and

(iii) has made the United Kingdom his main home.

Extension of stay as a retired person of independent means

266A. The requirements for an extension of stay as a retired person of independent means for a person in the United Kingdom as a work permit holder are that the applicant:

(i) entered the United Kingdom or was granted leave to remain as a work permit holder in accordance with paragraphs 128 to 133 of these Rules; and

(ii) meets the requirements of paragraph 263(i)–(v).

266B. The requirements for an extension of stay as a retired person of independent means for a person in the United Kingdom as a highly skilled migrant are that the applicant:

(i) entered the United Kingdom or was granted leave to remain as a highly skilled migrant in accordance with paragraphs 135A to 135F of these Rules; and

(ii) meets the requirements of paragraph 263(i)–(v).

266C. The requirements for an extension of stay as a retired person of independent means for a person in the United Kingdom to establish themselves or remain in business are that the applicant:

(i) entered the United Kingdom or was granted leave to remain as a person intending to establish themselves or remain in business in accordance with paragraphs 201 to 208 of these Rules; and

(ii) meets the requirements of paragraph 263(i)–(v).

266D. The requirements for an extension of stay as a retired person of independent means for a person in the United Kingdom as an innovator are that the applicant:

(i) entered the United Kingdom or was granted leave to remain as an innovator in accordance with paragraphs 210A to 210F of these Rules; and

(ii) meets the requirements of paragraph 263(i)–(v).

266E. The requirements for an extension of stay as a retired person of independent means for a person in the UK as a Tier 1 (General) Migrant, Tier 1 (Entrepreneur) Migrant or Tier 1 (Investor) Migrant are that the applicant:

(i) entered the UK or was granted leave to remain as a Tier 1 (General) Migrant, Tier 1 (Entrepreneur) Migrant or Tier 1 (Investor) Migrant; and

(ii) meets the requirements of paragraphs 263(i)–(v).

267. An extension of stay as a retired person of independent means, with a prohibition on the taking of employment, may be granted so as to bring the person's stay in this category up to a maximum of 5 years in aggregate, provided the Secretary of State is satisfied that each of the requirements of paragraph 266 is met. An extension of stay as a retired person of independent means, with a prohibition on the taking of employment, may be granted for a maximum period of 5 years, provided the Secretary of State is satisfied that each of the requirements of paragraph 266A, 266B, 266C, 266D or 266E is met.

Refusal of extension of stay as a retired person of independent means

268. An extension of stay as a retired person of independent means is to be refused if the Secretary of State is not satisfied that each of the requirements of paragraph 266, 266A, 266B, 266C, 266D or 266E is met.

Indefinite leave to remain for a retired person of independent means

269. Indefinite leave to remain may be granted, on application, to a person admitted as a retired person of independent means provided he:

(i) has spent a continuous period of 5 years in the United Kingdom in this capacity; and

(ii) has met the requirements of paragraph 266 throughout the 5 year period and continues to do so.

Refusal of indefinite leave to remain for a retired person of independent means

270. Indefinite leave to remain in the United Kingdom for a retired person of independent means is to be refused if the Secretary of State is not satisfied that each of the requirements of paragraph 269 is met.

PART 3

MMIGRATION RULES AS AT 30 MARCH 2009 RELATING TO STUDENTS, STUDENT NURSES, STUDENTS RE-SITTING AN EXAMINATION, STUDENTS WRITING-UP A THESIS, POSTGRADUATE DOCTORS OR DENTISTS, SABBATICAL OFFICERS AND APPLICANTS UNDER THE SECTORS-BASED SCHEME

Specified forms and procedures for applications or claims in connection with immigration

34B. Where an application form is specified, it must be sent by prepaid post to the United Kingdom Border Agency of the Home Office, or submitted in person at a public enquiry office of the United Kingdom Border Agency of the Home Office, save for the following exceptions:

(i) an application may not be submitted at a public enquiry office of the United Kingdom Border Agency of the Home Office if it is an application for:

(f) limited leave to remain as a Tier 5 (Temporary Worker) Migrant.

Requirements for leave to enter as a student

57. The requirements to be met by a person seeking leave to enter the United Kingdom as a student are that he:

(i) has been accepted for a course of study, or a period of research, which is to be provided by or undertaken at an organisation which is included on the Register of Education and Training Providers, and is at either;

(a) a publicly funded institution of further or higher education which maintains satisfactory records of enrolment and attendance of students and supplies these to the United Kingdom Border Agency when requested; or

(b) a bona fide private education institution; or

(c) an independent fee paying school outside the maintained sector which maintains satisfactory records of enrolment and attendance of students and supplies these to the United Kingdom Border Agency when requested; and

(ii) is able and intends to follow either:

(a) a recognised full-time degree course or postgraduate studies at a publicly funded institution of further or higher education; or

(b) a period of study and/or research in excess of 6 months at a publicly funded institution of higher education where this forms part of an overseas degree course; or

(c) a weekday full-time course involving attendance at a single institution for a minimum of 15 hours organised daytime study per week of a single subject, or directly related subjects; or

(d) a full-time course of study at an independent fee paying school; and

(iii) if under the age of 16 years is enrolled at an independent fee paying school on a full-time course of studies which meets the requirements of the Education Act 1944; and

(iv) if he has been accepted to study externally for a degree at a private education institution, he is also registered as an external student with the UK degree awarding body; and

(v) he holds a valid Academic Technology Approval Scheme (ATAS) clearance certificate from the Counter-Proliferation Department of the Foreign and Commonwealth Office which relates to the course, or area of research, he intends to undertake and the institution at which he wishes to undertake it; if he intends to undertake either,

(i) postgraduate studies leading to a Doctorate or Masters degree by research in one of the disciplines listed in paragraph 1 of Appendix 6 to these Rules; or

(ii) postgraduate studies leading to a taught Masters degree in one of the disciplines listed in paragraph 2 of Appendix 6 to these Rules; or

(iii) a period of study or research, as described in paragraph 57(ii)(b), in one of the disciplines listed in paragraph 1 or 2 of Appendix 6 to these Rules, that forms part of an overseas postgraduate qualification; and

(vi) intends to leave the United Kingdom at the end of his studies; and

(vii) does not intend to engage in business or to take employment, except part-time or vacation work undertaken with the consent of the Secretary of State; and

(viii) is able to meet the costs of his course and accommodation and the maintenance of himself and any dependants without taking employment or engaging in business or having recourse to public funds; and

(ix) holds a valid United Kingdom entry clearance for entry in this capacity.

Leave to enter as a student

58. A person seeking leave to enter the United Kingdom as a student may be admitted for an appropriate period depending on the length of his course of study and his means, and with a condition restricting his freedom to take employment, provided he is able to produce to the Immigration Officer on arrival a valid United Kingdom entry clearance for entry in this capacity.

Refusal of leave to enter as a student

59. Leave to enter as a student is to be refused if the Immigration Officer is not satisfied that each of the requirements of paragraph 57 is met.

Requirements for an extension of stay as a student

60. The requirements for an extension of stay as a student are that the applicant:

(i) (a) was last admitted to the United Kingdom in possession of a valid student entry clearance in accordance with paragraphs 57–62 or valid prospective student entry clearance in accordance with paragraphs 82–87 of these Rules; or

(b) has previously been granted leave to enter or remain in the United Kingdom to re-sit an examination in accordance with paragraphs 69A–69F of these Rules; or

(c) if he has been accepted on a course of study at degree level or above, has previously been granted leave to enter or remain in the United Kingdom in accordance with paragraphs 87A–87F, 128–135, 135O–135T and 143A to 143F or 245V to 245ZA of these Rules; or

(d) has valid leave as a student in accordance with paragraphs 57–62 of these Rules; and

(ii) meets the requirements for admission as a student set out in paragraph 57(i)–(viii); and

(iii) has produced evidence of his enrolment on a course which meets the requirements of paragraph 57; and

(iv) can produce satisfactory evidence of regular attendance during any course which he has already begun; or any other course for which he has been enrolled in the past; and

(v) can show evidence of satisfactory progress in his course of study including the taking and passing of any relevant examinations; and

(vi) would not, as a result of an extension of stay, spend more than 2 years on short courses below degree level (i.e. courses of less than 1 years duration, or longer courses broken off before completion); and

(vii) has not come to the end of a period of government or international scholarship agency sponsorship, or has the written consent of his official sponsor for a further period of study in the United Kingdom and satisfactory evidence that sufficient sponsorship funding is available.

Extension of stay as a student

61. An extension of stay as a student may be granted, subject to a restriction on his freedom to take employment, provided the Secretary of State is satisfied that the applicant meets each of the requirements of paragraph 60.

Refusal of extension of stay as a student

62. An extension of stay as a student is to be refused if the Secretary of State is not satisfied that each of the requirements of paragraph 60 is met.

Student nurses

Definition of student nurse

63. For the purposes of these Rules the term student nurse means a person accepted for training as a student nurse or midwife leading to a registered nursing qualification.

Requirements for leave to enter as a student nurse

64. The requirements to be met by a person seeking leave to enter the United Kingdom as a student nurse are that the person:

(i) comes within the definition set out in paragraph 63 above; and

(ii) has been accepted for a course of study in a recognised nursing educational establishment offering nursing training which meets the requirements of the Nursing and Midwifery Council.

(iii) did not obtain acceptance on the course of study referred to in (ii) above by misrepresentation;

(iv) is able and intends to follow the course; and

(v) does not intend to engage in business or take employment except in connection with the training course; and

(vi) intends to leave the United Kingdom at the end of the course; and

(vii) has sufficient funds available for accommodation and maintenance for himself and any dependants without engaging in business or taking employment (except in connection with the training course) or having recourse to public funds. The possession of a Department of Health bursary may be taken into account in assessing whether the student meets the maintenance requirement.

Leave to enter the United Kingdom as a student nurse

65. A person seeking leave to enter the United Kingdom as a student nurse may be admitted for the duration of the course, with a restriction on his freedom to take employment, provided the Immigration Officer is satisfied that each of the requirements of paragraph 64 is met.

Refusal of leave to enter as a student nurse

66. Leave to enter as a student nurse is to be refused if the Immigration Officer is not satisfied that each of the requirements of paragraph 64 is met.

Requirements for an extension of stay as a student nurse

67. The requirements for an extension of stay as a student nurse are that the applicant:

(i) was last admitted to the United Kingdom in possession of a valid student entry clearance, or valid prospective student entry clearance in accordance with paragraphs 82 to 87 of these Rules, if he is a person specified in Appendix 1 to these Rules; and

(ii) meets the requirements set out in paragraph 64(i)–(vii); and

(iii) has produced evidence of enrolment at a recognised nursing educational establishment; and

(iv) can provide satisfactory evidence of regular attendance during any course which he has already begun; or any other course for which he has been enrolled in the past; and

(v) would not, as a result of an extension of stay, spend more than 4 years in obtaining the relevant qualification; and

(vi) has not come to the end of a period of government or international scholarship agency sponsorship, or has the written consent of his official sponsor for a further period of study in the United Kingdom and evidence that sufficient sponsorship funding is available.

Extension of stay as a student nurse

68. An extension of stay as a student nurse may be granted, subject to a restriction on his freedom to take employment, provided the Secretary of State is satisfied that the applicant meets each of the requirements of paragraph 67.

Refusal of extension of stay as a student nurse

69. An extension of stay as a student nurse is to be refused if the Secretary of State is not satisfied that each of the requirements of paragraph 67 is met.

Re-sits of examinations

Requirements for leave to enter to re-sit an examination

69A. The requirements to be met by a person seeking leave to enter the United Kingdom in order to re-sit an examination are that the applicant:

(i) (a) meets the requirements for admission as a student set out in paragraph 57(i)–(viii); or

(b) met the requirements for admission as a student set out in paragraph 57(i)–(iii) in the previous academic year and continues to meet the requirements of paragraph 57(iv)–(viii) save, for the purpose of paragraphs (i) (a) or (b) above, where leave was last granted in accordance with paragraphs 57–62 of these Rules before 30 November 2007, the requirements of paragraph 57(v) do not apply; and

(ii) has produced written confirmation from the education institution or independent fee paying school which he attends or attended in the previous academic year that he is required to re-sit an examination; and

(iii) can provide satisfactory evidence of regular attendance during any course which he has already begun; or any other course for which he has been enrolled in the past; and

(iv) has not come to the end of a period of government or international scholarship agency sponsorship, or has the written consent of his official sponsor for a further period of study in the United Kingdom and satisfactory evidence that sufficient sponsorship funding is available; and

(v) has not previously been granted leave to re-sit the examination.

Leave to enter to re-sit an examination

69B. A person seeking leave to enter the United Kingdom in order to re-sit an examination may be admitted for a period sufficient to enable him to re-sit the examination at the first available opportunity with a condition restricting his freedom to take employment, provided the Immigration Officer is satisfied that each of the requirements of paragraph 69A is met.

Refusal of leave to enter to re-sit an examination

69C. Leave to enter to re-sit an examination is to be refused if the Immigration Officer is not satisfied that each of the requirements of paragraph 69A is met.

Requirements for an extension of stay to re-sit an examination

69D. The requirements for an extension of stay to re-sit an examination are that the applicant:

(i) was admitted to the United Kingdom with a valid student entry clearance if he was then a visa national; and

(ii) meets the requirements set out in paragraph 69A(i)–(v).

Extension of stay to re-sit an examination

69E. An extension of stay to re-sit an examination may be granted for a period sufficient to enable the applicant to re-sit the examination at the first available opportunity, subject to a restriction on his freedom to take employment, provided the Secretary of State is satisfied that the applicant meets each of the requirements of paragraph 69D.

Refusal of extension of stay to re-sit an examination

69F. An extension of stay to re-sit an examination is to be refused if the Secretary of State is not satisfied that each of the requirements of paragraph 69D is met.

Writing up a thesis

Requirements for leave to enter to write up a thesis

69G. The requirements to be met by a person seeking leave to enter the United Kingdom in order to write up a thesis are that the applicant:

(i) (a) meets the requirements for admission as a student set out in paragraph 57(i)–(viii); or

(b) met the requirements for admission as a student set out in paragraph 57(i)–(iii) in the previous academic year and continues to meet the requirements of paragraph 57(iv)–(viii) save, for the purpose of paragraphs (i)(a) or (b) above, where leave was last granted in accordance with paragraphs 57–62 of these Rules before 30 November 2007, the requirements of paragraph 57(v) do not apply; and

(ii) can provide satisfactory evidence that he is a postgraduate student enrolled at an education institution as either a full-time, part-time or writing up student; and

(iii) can demonstrate that his application is supported by the education institution; and

(iv) has not come to the end of a period of government or international scholarship agency sponsorship, or has the written consent of his official sponsor for a further period of study in the United Kingdom and satisfactory evidence that sufficient sponsorship funding is available; and

(v) has not previously been granted 12 months leave to write up the same thesis.

Leave to enter to write up a thesis

69H. A person seeking leave to enter the United Kingdom in order to write up a thesis may be admitted for 12 months with a condition restricting his freedom to take employment, provided the Immigration Officer is satisfied that each of the requirements of paragraph 69G is met.

Refusal of leave to enter to write up a thesis

69I. Leave to enter to write up a thesis is to be refused if the Immigration Officer is not satisfied that each of the requirements of paragraph 69G is met.

Requirements for an extension of stay to write up a thesis

69J. The requirements for an extension of stay to write up a thesis are that the applicant:

(i) was admitted to the United Kingdom with a valid student entry clearance if he was then a visa national; and

(ii) meets the requirements set out in paragraph 69G(i)–(v).

Extension of stay to write up a thesis

69K. An extension of stay to write up a thesis may be granted for 12 months subject to a restriction on his freedom to take employment, provided the Secretary of State is satisfied that the applicant meets each of the requirements of paragraph 69J.

Refusal of extension of stay to write up a thesis

69L. An extension of stay to write up a thesis is to be refused if the Secretary of State is not satisfied that each of the requirements of paragraph 69J is met.

Postgraduate doctors, dentists and trainee general practitioners

Requirements for leave to enter the United Kingdom as a postgraduate doctor or dentist

70. The requirements to be met by a person seeking leave to enter the UK as a postgraduate doctor or dentist are that the applicant:

(i) has successfully completed and obtained a recognised UK degree in medicine or dentistry from either:

(a) a UK publicly funded institution of further or higher education; or

(b) a UK bona fide private education institution which maintains satisfactory records of enrolment and attendance; and

(ii) has previously been granted leave:

(a) in accordance with paragraphs 57 to 69L of these Rules for the final academic year of the studies referred to in (i) above; and

(b) as a student under paragraphs 57 to 62 of these Rules for at least one other academic year (aside from the final year) of the studies referred to in (i) above; and

(iii) holds a letter from the Postgraduate Dean confirming he has a full-time place on a recognised Foundation Programme; and

(iv) intends to train full-time in his post on the Foundation Programme; and

(v) is able to maintain and accommodate himself and any dependants without recourse to public funds; and

(vi) intends to leave the United Kingdom if, on expiry of his leave under this paragraph, he has not been granted leave to remain in the United Kingdom as:

(a) a doctor or dentist undertaking a period of clinical attachment or a dental observer post in accordance with paragraphs 75G to 75M of these Rules; or

(b) a Tier 2 Migrant

(c) a Tier 1 (General) Migrant or Tier (1) (Entrepreneur) Migrant; and

(vii) if his study at medical school or dental school, or any subsequent studies he has undertaken, were sponsored by a government or international scholarship agency, he has the written consent of his sponsor to enter or remain in the United Kingdom as a postgraduate doctor or dentist; and

(viii) if he has not previously been granted leave in this category has completed his medical or dental degree in the 12 months preceding this application; and

(ix) if he has previously been granted leave as a postgraduate doctor or dentist, is not seeking leave to enter to a date beyond 3 years from that date on which he was first granted leave to enter or remain in this category; and

(x) holds a valid entry clearance for entry in this capacity except where he is a British National (Overseas), a British Overseas Territories Citizen, a British Overseas Citizen, a British Protected Person or a person who under the British Nationality Act 1981 is a British Subject.

Leave to enter as a postgraduate doctor or dentist

71. Leave to enter the United Kingdom as a postgraduate doctor or dentist may be granted for the duration of the Foundation Programme, for a period not exceeding 26 months, provided the Immigration Officer is satisfied that each of the requirements of paragraph 70 is met.

Refusal of leave to enter as a postgraduate doctor or dentist

72. Leave to enter as a postgraduate doctor or dentist is to be refused if the Immigration Officer is not satisfied that each of the requirements of paragraph 70 is met.

Requirements for an extension of stay as a postgraduate doctor or dentist

73. The requirements to be met by a person seeking an extension of stay as a postgraduate doctor or dentist are that the applicant:

(i) meets the requirements of paragraph 70(i) to (vii); and

(ii) has leave to enter or remain in the United Kingdom as either:

(a) a student in accordance with paragraphs 57 to 69L of these Rules; or

(b) as a postgraduate doctor or dentist in accordance with paragraphs 70 to 75 of these Rules; or

(c) as a doctor or dentist undertaking a period of clinical attachment or a dental observer post in accordance with paragraphs 75G to 75M of these Rules.

(iii) if he has not previously been granted leave in this category, has completed his medical or dental degree in the last 12 months;

(iv) would not, as a result of an extension of stay, remain in the United Kingdom as a postgraduate doctor or dentist to a date beyond 3 years from the date on which he was first given leave to enter or remain in this capacity.

Extension of stay as a postgraduate doctor or dentist

74. An extension of stay as a postgraduate doctor or dentist may be granted for the duration of the Foundation Programme, for a period not exceeding 3 years, provided the Secretary of State is satisfied that each of the requirements of paragraph 73 is met.

Refusal of an extension of stay as a postgraduate doctor or dentist

75. An extension of stay as a postgraduate doctor or dentist is to be refused if the Secretary of State is not satisfied that each of the requirements of paragraph 73 is met.

Requirements for leave to enter the United Kingdom to take the PLAB Test

75A. The requirements to be met by a person seeking leave to enter in order to take the PLAB Test are that the applicant:

(i) is a graduate from a medical school and intends to take the PLAB Test in the United Kingdom; and

(ii) can provide documentary evidence of a confirmed test date or of his eligibility to take the PLAB Test; and

(iii) meets the requirements of paragraph 41(iii)–(vii) for entry as a visitor; and

(iv) intends to leave the United Kingdom at the end of his leave granted under this paragraph unless he is successful in the PLAB Test and granted leave to remain:

(a) as a postgraduate doctor or trainee general practitioner in accordance with paragraphs 70 to 75; or

(b) to undertake a clinical attachment in accordance with paragraphs 75G to 75M of these Rules; or

Leave to enter to take the PLAB Test

75B. A person seeking leave to enter the United Kingdom to take the PLAB Test may be admitted for a period not exceeding 6 months, provided the Immigration Officer is satisfied that each of the requirements of paragraph 75A is met.

Refusal of leave to enter to take the PLAB Test

75C. Leave to enter the United Kingdom to take the PLAB Test is to be refused if the Immigration Officer is not satisfied that each of the requirements of paragraph 75A is met.

Requirements for an extension of stay in order to take the PLAB Test

75D. The requirements for an extension of stay in the United Kingdom in order to take the PLAB Test are that the applicant:

(i) was given leave to enter the United Kingdom for the purposes of taking the PLAB Test in accordance with paragraph 75B of these Rules; and

(ii) intends to take the PLAB Test and can provide documentary evidence of a confirmed test date; and

(iii) meets the requirements set out in paragraph 41(iii)–(vii); and

(iv) intends to leave the United Kingdom at the end of his leave granted under this paragraph unless he is successful in the PLAB Test and granted leave to remain:

(a) as a postgraduate doctor or trainee general practitioner in accordance with paragraphs 70 to 75; or

(b) to undertake a clinical attachment in accordance with paragraphs 75G to 75M of these Rules; or

(v) would not as a result of an extension of stay spend more than 18 months in the United Kingdom for the purpose of taking the PLAB Test.

Extension of stay to take the PLAB Test

75E. A person seeking leave to remain in the United Kingdom to take the PLAB Test may be granted an extension of stay for a period not exceeding 6 months, provided the Secretary of State is satisfied that each of the requirements of paragraph 75D is met.

Refusal of extension of stay to take the PLAB Test

75F. Leave to remain in the United Kingdom to take the PLAB Test is to be refused if the Secretary of State is not satisfied that each of the requirements of paragraph 75D is met.

Requirements for leave to enter to undertake a clinical attachment or dental observer post

75G. The requirements to be met by a person seeking leave to enter to undertake a clinical attachment or dental observer post are that the applicant:

(i) is a graduate from a medical or dental school and intends to undertake a clinical attachment or dental observer post in the United Kingdom; and

(ii) can provide documentary evidence of the clinical attachment or dental observer post which will:

(a) be unpaid; and

(b) only involve observation, not treatment, of patients; and

(iii) meets the requirements of paragraph 41(iii)–(vii) of these Rules; and

(iv) intends to leave the United Kingdom at the end of his leave granted under this paragraph unless he is granted leave to remain:

(a) as a postgraduate doctor, dentist or trainee general practitioner in accordance with paragraphs 70 to 75;

(v) if he has previously been granted leave in this category, is not seeking leave to enter which, when amalgamated with those previous periods of leave, would total more than 6 months.

Leave to enter to undertake a clinical attachment or dental observer post

75H. A person seeking leave to enter the United Kingdom to undertake a clinical attachment or dental observer post may be admitted for the period of the clinical attachment or dental observer post, up to a maximum of 6 weeks at a time or 6 months in total in this category, provided the Immigration Officer is satisfied that each of the requirements of paragraph 75G is met.

Refusal of leave to enter to undertake a clinical attachment or dental observer post

75J. Leave to enter the United Kingdom to undertake a clinical attachment or dental observer post is to be refused if the Immigration Officer is not satisfied that each of the requirements of paragraph 75G is met.

Requirements for an extension of stay in order to undertake a clinical attachment or dental observer post

75K. The requirements to be met by a person seeking an extension of stay to undertake a clinical attachment or dental observer post are that the applicant:

(i) was given leave to enter or remain in the United Kingdom to undertake a clinical attachment or dental observer post or:

(a) for the purposes of taking the PLAB Test in accordance with paragraphs 75A to 75F and has passed both parts of the PLAB Test;

(b) as a postgraduate doctor, dentist or trainee general practitioner in accordance with paragraphs 70 to 75; or

(c) as a work permit holder for employment in the UK as a doctor or dentist in accordance with paragraphs 128 to 135; and

(ii) is a graduate from a medical or dental school and intends to undertake a clinical attachment or dental observer post in the United Kingdom; and

(iii) can provide documentary evidence of the clinical attachment or dental observer post which will:

(a) be unpaid; and

(b) only involve observation, not treatment, of patients; and

(iv) intends to leave the United Kingdom at the end of his period of leave granted under this paragraph unless he is granted leave to remain:

(a) as a postgraduate doctor, dentist or trainee general practitioner in accordance with paragraphs 70 to 75; or

(v) meets the requirements of paragraph 41(iii)–(vii) of these Rules; and

(vi) if he has previously been granted leave in this category, is not seeking an extension of stay which, when amalgamated with those previous periods of leave, would total more than 6 months.

Extension of stay to undertake a clinical attachment or dental observer post

75L. A person seeking leave to remain in the United Kingdom to undertake a clinical attachment or dental observer post up to a maximum of 6 weeks at a time or 6 months in total in this category, may be granted an extension of stay for the period of their clinical attachment or dental observer post, provided that the Secretary of State is satisfied that each of the requirements of paragraph 75K is met.

Refusal of extension of stay to undertake a clinical attachment or dental observer post

75M. Leave to remain in the United Kingdom to undertake a clinical attachment or dental observer post is to be refused if the Secretary of State is not satisfied that each of the requirements of paragraph 75K is met.

Requirements for leave to enter as a prospective student

82. The requirements to be met by a person seeking leave to enter the United Kingdom as a prospective student are that he:

(i) can demonstrate a genuine and realistic intention of undertaking, within 6 months of his date of entry:

(b) a supervised practice placement or midwife adaptation course which would meet the requirements for an extension of stay as an overseas qualified nurse or midwife under paragraphs 69P to 69R of these Rules; and

(ii) intends to leave the United Kingdom on completion of his studies or on the expiry of his leave to enter if he is not able to meet the requirements for an extension of stay:

(b) as an overseas qualified nurse or midwife in accordance with paragraph 69P of these Rules; and

Students' unions sabbatical officers

Requirements for extension of stay as a prospective student

85. Six months is the maximum permitted leave which may be granted to a prospective student. The requirements for an extension of stay as a prospective student are that the applicant:

(i) was admitted to the United Kingdom with a valid prospective student entry clearance; and

(ii) meets the requirements of paragraph 82; and

(iii) would not, as a result of an extension of stay, spend more than 6 months in the United Kingdom; and

(iv) must not be in the UK in breach of immigration laws except that any period of overstaying for a period of 28 days or less will be disregarded.

Extension of stay as a prospective student

86. An extension of stay as a prospective student may be granted, with a prohibition on employment, provided the Secretary of State is satisfied that each of the requirements of paragraph 85 is met.

Refusal of extension of stay as a prospective student

87. An extension of stay as a prospective student is to be refused if the Secretary of State is not satisfied that each of the requirements of paragraph 85 is met.

Requirements for leave to enter as a sabbatical officer

87A. The requirements to be met by a person seeking leave to enter the United Kingdom as a sabbatical officer are that the person:

(i) has been elected to a full-time salaried post as a sabbatical officer at an educational establishment at which he is registered as a student;

(ii) meets the requirements set out in paragraph 57(i)–(ii) or met the requirements set out in paragraph 57(i)–(ii) in the academic year prior to the one in which he took up or intends to take up sabbatical office; and

(iii) does not intend to engage in business or take employment except in connection with his sabbatical post; and

(iv) is able to maintain and accommodate himself and any dependants adequately without recourse to public funds; and

(v) at the end of the sabbatical post he intends to:

(a) complete a course of study which he has already begun; or

(b) take up a further course of study which has been deferred to enable the applicant to take up the sabbatical post; or

(c) leave the United Kingdom; and

(vi) has not come to the end of a period of government or international scholarship agency sponsorship, or has the written consent of his official sponsor to take up a sabbatical post in the United Kingdom; and

(vii) has not already completed 2 years as a sabbatical officer.

Leave to enter the United Kingdom as a sabbatical officer

87B. A person seeking leave to enter the United Kingdom as a sabbatical officer may be admitted for a period not exceeding 12 months on conditions specifying his employment provided the Immigration Officer is satisfied that each of the requirements of paragraph 87A is met.

Refusal of leave to enter the United Kingdom as a sabbatical officer

87C. Leave to enter as a sabbatical officer is to be refused if the Immigration Officer is not satisfied that each of the requirements of paragraph 87A is met.

Requirements for an extension of stay as a sabbatical officer

87D. The requirements for an extension of stay as a sabbatical officer are that the applicant:

(i) was admitted to the United Kingdom with a valid student entry clearance if he was then a visa national; and

(ii) meets the requirements set out in paragraph 87A(i)–(vi); and

(iii) would not, as a result of an extension of stay, remain in the United Kingdom as a sabbatical officer to a date beyond 2 years from the date on which he was first given leave to enter the United Kingdom in this capacity.

Extension of stay as a sabbatical officer

87E. An extension of stay as a sabbatical officer may be granted for a period not exceeding 12 months on conditions specifying his employment provided the Secretary of State is satisfied that the applicant meets each of the requirements of paragraph 87D.

Refusal of extension of stay as a sabbatical officer

87F. An extension of stay as a sabbatical officer is to be refused if the Secretary of State is not satisfied that each of the requirements of paragraph 87D is met

Requirements for leave to enter the United Kingdom for the purpose of employment under the Sectors-Based Scheme

135I. The requirements to be met by a person seeking leave to enter the United Kingdom for the purpose of employment under the Sectors-Based Scheme are that he:

(i) holds a valid Home Office immigration employment document issued under the Sectors-Based Scheme; and

(ii) is aged between 18 and 30 inclusive or was so aged at the date of his application for leave to enter; and

(iii) is capable of undertaking the employment specified in the immigration employment document; and

(iv) does not intend to take employment except as specified in his immigration employment document; and

(v) is able to maintain and accommodate himself adequately without recourse to public funds; and

(vi) intends to leave the United Kingdom at the end of his approved employment; and

(vii) holds a valid United Kingdom entry clearance for entry in this capacity.

Leave to enter for the purpose of employment under the Sectors-Based Scheme

135J. A person seeking leave to enter the United Kingdom for the purpose of employment under the Sectors-Based Scheme may be admitted for a period not exceeding 12 months (normally as specified in his work permit), subject to a condition restricting him to employment approved by the Home Office, provided the Immigration Officer is satisfied that each of the requirements of paragraph 135I is met.

Refusal of leave to enter for the purpose of employment under the Sectors-Based Scheme

135K. Leave to enter the United Kingdom for the purpose of employment under the Sectors-Based Scheme is to be refused if the Immigration Officer is not satisfied that each of the requirements of paragraph 135I is met.

Requirements for an extension of stay for Sector-Based employment

135L. The requirements for an extension of stay for Sector-Based employment are that the applicant:

(i) entered the United Kingdom with a valid Home Office immigration employment document issued under the sectors-Based Scheme and;

(ii) has written approval from the Home Office for the continuation of his employment under the Sectors-Based Scheme; and

(iii) meets the requirements of paragraph 135I(ii) to (vi); and

(iv) would not, as a result of the extension of stay sought, remain in the United Kingdom for Sector-Based Scheme employment to a date beyond 12 months from the date on which he was given leave to enter the United Kingdom on this occasion in this capacity.

Extension of stay for Sectors-Based Scheme employment

135M. An extension of stay for Sectors-Based Scheme employment may be granted for a period not exceeding the period of approved employment recommended by the Home

Office provided the Secretary of State is satisfied that each of the requirements of paragraph 135L are met. An extension of stay is to be subject to a condition restricting the applicant to employment approved by the Home Office.

Refusal of extension of stay for Sectors-Based Scheme employment

135N. An extension of stay for Sector-Based Scheme employment is to be refused if the Secretary of State is not satisfied that each of the requirements of paragraph 135L is met.

245ZG. Period and conditions of grant

(b) The cases referred to in paragraph (a) are those where the applicant has, or was last granted, entry clearance, leave to enter or leave to remain as:

(iii) a Minister of Religion, Missionary or Member of a Religious Order, provided he is still working for the same employer,

Attributes for Tier 1 (Investor) Migrants

47. A regulated financial institution is one which is regulated by the appropriate regulatory body for the country in which the financial institution operates. For example, where a financial institution does business in the UK, the appropriate regulator is the Financial Services Authority.

PART 4

IMMIGRATION RULES AS AT 5 APRIL 2012 RELATING TO OVERSEAS QUALIFIED NURSES OR MIDWIVES, SEASONAL AGRICULTURAL WORKERS, WORK PERMIT EMPLOYMENT, MULTIPLE ENTRY WORK PERMIT EMPLOYMENT, AND TIER 1 (POST STUDY WORK) MIGRANTS

Overseas qualified nurse or midwife

Requirements for leave to enter as an overseas qualified nurse or midwife

69M. Deleted on 27 November 2008 by paragraph 39 of Statement of Changes HC 1113 except insofar as relevant to paragraph 69P.

Leave to enter the United Kingdom as an overseas qualified nurse or midwife

69N. DELETED

Refusal of leave to enter as an overseas qualified nurse or midwife

69O. DELETED.

Requirements for an extension of stay as an overseas qualified nurse or midwife

69P. The requirements to be met by a person seeking an extension of stay as an overseas qualified nurse or midwife are that the applicant:

(i)–(iii) Deleted by HC 1113

(iv) has leave to enter or remain as an overseas qualified nurse or midwife in accordance with paragraphs 69M–69R of these Rules; and

(v) meets the requirements set out in paragraph 69M(i)–(vi); and

(vi) can provide satisfactory evidence of regular attendance during any previous period of supervised practice or midwife adaptation course; and

(vii) if he has previously been granted leave:

(a) as an overseas qualified nurse or midwife under paragraphs 69M–69R of these Rules, or

(b) to undertake an adaptation course as a student nurse under paragraphs 63–69 of these Rules; and is not seeking an extension of stay in this category which, when amalgamated with those previous periods of leave, would total more than 18 months; and

(viii) if his previous studies, supervised practice placement or midwife adaptation programme placement were sponsored by a government or international scholarship agency, he has the written consent of his official sponsor to remain in the United Kingdom as an overseas qualified nurse or midwife.

Extension of stay as an overseas qualified nurse or midwife

69Q. An extension of stay as an overseas qualified nurse or midwife may be granted for a period not exceeding 18 months, provided that the Secretary of State is satisfied that each of the requirements of paragraph 69P is met.

Refusal of extension of stay as an overseas qualified nurse or midwife

69R. An extension of stay as an overseas qualified nurse or midwife is to be refused if the Secretary of State is not satisfied that each of the requirements of paragraph 69P is met.

Seasonal agricultural workers

Requirements for leave to enter as a seasonal agricultural worker

104. The requirements to be met by a person seeking leave to enter the United Kingdom as a seasonal agricultural worker are that he:

(i) is a student in full-time education aged 18 or over; and

(ii) holds an immigration employment document in the form of a valid Home Office work card issued by the operator of a scheme approved by the Secretary of State; and

(iii) intends to leave the United Kingdom at the end of his period of leave as a seasonal worker; and

(iv) does not intend to take employment except as permitted by his work card and within the terms of this paragraph; and

(v) is not seeking leave to enter on a date less than 3 months from the date on which an earlier period of leave to enter or remain granted to him in this capacity expired; and

(vi) is able to maintain and accommodate himself without recourse to public funds.

Leave to enter as a seasonal agricultural worker

105. A person seeking leave to enter the United Kingdom as a seasonal agricultural worker may be admitted with a condition restricting his freedom to take employment for a period not exceeding 6 months providing the Immigration Officer is satisfied that each of the requirements of paragraph 104 is met.

Refusal of leave to enter as a seasonal agricultural worker

106. Leave to enter the United Kingdom as a seasonal agricultural worker is to be refused if the Immigration Officer is not satisfied that each of the requirements of paragraph 104 is met.

Requirements for extension of stay as a seasonal agricultural worker

107. The requirements for an extension of stay as a seasonal agricultural worker are that the applicant:

(i) entered the United Kingdom as a seasonal agricultural worker under paragraph 105; and

(ii) meets the requirements of paragraph 104(iii)–(vi); and

(iii) would not, as a result of an extension of stay sought, remain in the United Kingdom as a seasonal agricultural worker beyond 6 months from the date on which he was given leave to enter the United Kingdom on this occasion in this capacity.

Extension of stay as a seasonal agricultural worker

108. An extension of stay as a seasonal agricultural worker may be granted with a condition restricting his freedom to take employment for a period which does not extend beyond 6 months from the date on which he was given leave to enter the United Kingdom on this occasion in this capacity, provided the Secretary of State is satisfied that the applicant meets each of the requirements of paragraph 107.

Refusal of extension of stay as a seasonal worker

109. An extension of stay as a seasonal worker is to be refused if the Secretary of State is not satisfied that each of the requirements of paragraph 107 is met.

Work permit employment

Requirements for leave to enter the United Kingdom for work permit employment

128. The requirements to be met by a person coming to the United Kingdom to seek or take employment (unless he is otherwise eligible for admission for employment under these Rules or is eligible for admission as a seaman under contract to join a ship due to leave British waters) are that he:

(i) holds a valid Home Office work permit; and

(ii) is not of an age which puts him outside the limits for employment; and

(iii) is capable of undertaking the employment specified in the work permit; and

(iv) does not intend to take employment except as specified in his work permit; and

(v) is able to maintain and accommodate himself and any dependants adequately without recourse to public funds; and

(vi) in the case of a person in possession of a work permit which is valid for a period of 12 months or less, intends to leave the United Kingdom at the end of his approved employment; and

(vii) holds a valid United Kingdom entry clearance for entry in this capacity except where he holds a work permit valid for 6 months or less or he is a British National (Overseas), a British overseas territories citizen, a British Overseas citizen, a British protected person or a person who under the British Nationality Act 1981 is a British subject.

Leave to enter for work permit employment

129. A person seeking leave to enter the United Kingdom for the purpose of work permit employment may be admitted for a period not exceeding the period of employment approved by the Home Office (as specified in his work permit), subject to a condition restricting him to that approved employment, provided he is able to produce to the Immigration Officer, on arrival, a valid United Kingdom entry clearance for entry in this capacity or, where entry clearance is not required, provided the Immigration Officer is satisfied that each of the requirements of paragraph 128(i)–(vi) is met.

Refusal of leave to enter for employment

130. Leave to enter for the purpose of work permit employment is to be refused if a valid United Kingdom entry clearance for entry in this capacity is not produced to the Immigration Officer on arrival or, where entry clearance is not required, if the Immigration Officer is not satisfied that each of the requirements of paragraph 128(i)–(vi) is met.

Requirements for an extension of stay for work permit employment

131. The requirements for an extension of stay to seek or take employment (unless the applicant is otherwise eligible for an extension of stay for employment under these Rules) are that the applicant:

(i) entered the United Kingdom with a valid work permit under paragraph 129; and

(ii) has written approval from the Home Office for the continuation of his employment; and

(iii) meets the requirements of paragraph 128(ii)–(v).

131A. The requirements for an extension of stay to take employment (unless the applicant is otherwise eligible for an extension of stay for employment under these Rules) for a student are that the applicant:

(i) entered the United Kingdom or was given leave to remain as a student in accordance with paragraphs 57 to 62 of these Rules; and

(ii) has obtained a degree qualification on a recognised degree course at either a United Kingdom publicly funded further or higher education institution or a bona fide United Kingdom private education institution which maintains satisfactory records of enrolment and attendance; and

(iii) holds a valid Home Office immigration employment document for employment; and

(iv) has the written consent of his official sponsor to such employment if he is a member of a government or international scholarship agency sponsorship and that sponsorship is either ongoing or has recently come to an end at the time of the requested extension; and

(v) meets each of the requirements of paragraph 128(ii) to (vi).

131B. The requirements for an extension of stay to take employment (unless the applicant is otherwise eligible for an extension of stay for employment under these Rules) for a student nurse overseas qualified nurse or midwife, postgraduate doctor or postgraduate dentist are that the applicant:

(i) entered the United Kingdom or was given leave to remain as a student nurse in accordance with paragraphs 63 to 69 of these Rules; or

(ia) entered the United Kingdom or was given leave to remain as an overseas qualified nurse or midwife in accordance with paragraphs 69M to 69R of these Rules; and

(ii) entered the United Kingdom or was given leave to remain as a postgraduate doctor or a postgraduate dentist in accordance with paragraphs 70 to 75 of these Rules; and

(iii) holds a valid Home Office immigration employment document for employment as a nurse, doctor or dentist; and

(iv) has the written consent of his official sponsor to such employment if he is a member of a government or international scholarship agency sponsorship and that sponsorship is either ongoing or has recently come to an end at the time of the requested extension; and

(v) meets each of the requirements of paragraph 128(ii) to (vi).

131C. The requirements for an extension of stay to take employment for a Science and Engineering Graduate Scheme or International Graduates Scheme participant are that the applicant:

(i) entered the United Kingdom or was given leave to remain as a Science and Engineering Graduate Scheme or International Graduates Scheme participant in accordance with paragraphs 135O to 135T of these Rules; and

(ii) holds a valid Home Office immigration employment document for employment; and

(iii) meets each of the requirements of paragraph 128(ii) to (vi).

131D. The requirements for an extension of stay to take employment (unless the applicant is otherwise eligible for an extension of stay for employment under these Rules) for a working holidaymaker are that the applicant:

(i) entered the United Kingdom as a working holidaymaker in accordance with paragraphs 95 to 96 of these Rules; and

(ii) he has spent more than 12 months in total in the UK in this capacity; and

(iii) holds a valid Home Office immigration employment document for employment in an occupation listed on the Work Permits (UK) shortage occupations list; and

(iv) meets each of the requirements of paragraph 128(ii) to (vi).

131E. The requirements for an extension of stay to take employment for a highly skilled migrant are that the applicant:

(i) entered the United Kingdom or was given leave to remain as a highly skilled migrant in accordance with paragraphs 135A to 135E of these Rules; and

(ii) holds a valid work permit; and

(iii) meets each of the requirements of paragraph 128(ii) to (vi).

131F. The requirements for an extension of stay to take employment (unless the applicant is otherwise eligible for an extension of stay for employment under these Rules) for an Innovator are that the applicant:

(i) entered the United Kingdom or was given leave to remain as an Innovator in accordance with paragraphs 210A to 210E of these Rules; and

(ii) holds a valid Home Office immigration employment document for employment; and

(iii) meets each of the requirements of paragraph 128(ii) to (vi).

131G. The requirements for an extension of stay to take employment (unless the applicant is otherwise eligible for an extension of stay for employment under these Rules) for an individual who has leave to enter or leave to remain in the United Kingdom to take the PLAB Test or to undertake a clinical attachment or dental observer post are that the applicant:

(i) entered the United Kingdom or was given leave to remain for the purposes of taking the PLAB Test in accordance with paragraphs 75A to 75F of these Rules; or

(ii) entered the United Kingdom or was given leave to remain to undertake a clinical attachment or dental observer post in accordance with paragraphs 75G to 75M of these Rules; and

(iii) holds a valid Home Office immigration employment document for employment as a doctor or dentist; and

(iv) meets each of the requirements of paragraph 128(ii) to (vi).

131H. The requirements for an extension of stay to take employment (unless the applicant is otherwise eligible for an extension of stay for employment under these Rules) in the case of a person who has leave to enter or remain as a Fresh Talent: Working in Scotland scheme participant are that the applicant:

(i) entered the United Kingdom or was given leave to remain as a Fresh Talent: Working in Scotland scheme participant in accordance with paragraphs 143A to 143F of these Rules; and

(ii) holds a valid Home Office immigration employment document for employment in Scotland; and

(iii) has the written consent of his official sponsor to such employment if the studies which led to him being granted leave under the Fresh Talent: Working in Scotland scheme in accordance with paragraphs 143A to 143F of these Rules, or any studies he has subsequently undertaken, were sponsored by a government or international scholarship agency; and

(iv) meets each of the requirements of paragraph 128(ii) to (vi).

131I. The requirements for an extension of stay to take employment for a Tier 1 Migrant are that the applicant:

(i) entered the UK or was given leave to remain as a Tier 1 Migrant; and

(ii) holds a valid work permit; and

(iii) meets each of the requirements of paragraph 128(ii) to (vi).

Extension of stay for work permit employment

132. An extension of stay for work permit employment may be granted for a period not exceeding the period of approved employment recommended by the Home Office provided the Secretary of State is satisfied that each of the requirements of paragraphs 131, 131A, 131B, 131C, 131D, 131E, 131F, 131G, 131H or 131I is met. An extension of stay is to be subject to a condition restricting the applicant to employment approved by the Home Office.

133. An extension of stay for employment is to be refused if the Secretary of State is not satisfied that each of the requirements of paragraphs 131, 131A, 131B, 131C, 131D, 131E, 131F, 131G, 131H or 131I is met (unless the applicant is otherwise eligible for an extension of stay for employment under these Rules).

Multiple Entry work permit employment

Requirements for leave to enter for Multiple Entry work permit employment

199A. The requirements to be met by a person coming to the United Kingdom to seek or take Multiple Entry work permit employment are that he:

(i) holds a valid work permit;

(ii) is not of an age which puts him outside the limits for employment;

(iii) is capable of undertaking the employment specified in the work permit;

(iv) does not intend to take employment except as specified in his work permit;

(v) is able to maintain and accommodate himself adequately without recourse to public funds; and

(vi) intends to leave the United Kingdom at the end of the employment covered by the Multiple Entry work permit and holds a valid United Kingdom Entry clearance for entry into this capacity excepts where he holds a work permit valid for 6 months or less or he is a British National (Overseas), a British overseas territories citizen, a British Overseas citizen, a British protected person or a person who under the British Nationality Act 1981 is a British subject.

Leave to enter for Multiple Entry work permit employment

199B. A person seeking leave to enter the United Kingdom for the purpose of Multiple Entry work permit employment may be admitted for a period not exceeding 2 years provided that the Immigration Officer is satisfied that each of the requirements of paragraph 199A are met.

Refusal of leave to enter for Multiple Entry work permit employment

199C. Leave to enter for the purpose of Multiple Entry work permit employment is to be refused if the Immigration Officer is not satisfied that each of the requirements of paragraph 199A is met.

Tier 1 (Post-Study Work) Migrants

245F. Purpose

The purpose of this route is to encourage international graduates who have studied in the UK to stay on and do skilled or highly skilled work.

245FA. Entry to the UK

All migrants arriving in the UK and wishing to enter as a Tier 1 (Post-Study Work) Migrant must have a valid entry clearance for entry under this route. If they do not have a valid entry clearance, entry will be refused.

245FB. Requirements for entry clearance

To qualify for entry clearance as a Tier 1 (Post-Study Work) Migrant, an applicant must meet the requirements listed below. If the applicant meets these requirements, entry clearance will be granted. If the applicant does not meet these requirements, the application will be refused.

Requirements:

(a) The applicant must not fall for refusal under the general grounds for refusal.

(b) The applicant must not previously have been granted entry clearance or leave to remain as a Tier 1 (Post-Study Work) Migrant as a Participant in the International

Graduates Scheme (or its predecessor, the Science and Engineering Graduates Scheme), or as a Participant in the Fresh Talent: Working in Scotland Scheme.

(c) The applicant must have a minimum of 75 points under paragraphs 66 to 72 of Appendix A.

(d) The applicant must have a minimum of 10 points under paragraphs 1 to 3 of Appendix B.

(e) The applicant must have a minimum of 10 points under paragraphs 1 to 2 of Appendix C.

(f) If:

(i) the studies that led to the qualification for which the applicant obtains points under paragraphs 66 to 72 of Appendix A were sponsored by a Government or international scholarship agency, and

(ii) those studies came to an end 12 months ago or less the applicant must provide the unconditional written consent of the sponsoring Government or agency to the application and must provide the specified documents to show that this requirement has been met.

245FC. Period and conditions of grant

Entry clearance will be granted for a period of 2 years and will be subject to the following conditions:

(a) no recourse to public funds,

(b) registration with the police, if this is required by paragraph 326 of these Rules, and

(c) no Employment as a Doctor or Dentist in Training, unless the applicant has obtained a degree in medicine or dentistry at bachelor's level or above from a UK institution that is a UK recognised or listed body, or which holds a sponsor licence under Tier 4 of the Points Based System.

245FD. Requirements for leave to remain

To qualify for leave to remain as a Tier 1 (Post-Study Work) Migrant, an applicant must meet the requirements listed below. Subject to paragraph 245FE(a)(i), if the applicant meets these requirements, leave to remain will be granted. If the applicant does not meet these requirements, the application will be refused.

Requirements:

(a) The applicant must not fall for refusal under the general grounds for refusal, and must not be an illegal entrant.

(b) The applicant must not previously have been granted entry clearance or leave to remain as a Tier 1 (Post-Study Work) migrant.

(c) The applicant must have a minimum of 75 points under paragraphs 66 to 72 of Appendix A.

(d) The applicant must have a minimum of 10 points under paragraphs 1 to 3 of Appendix B.

(e) The applicant must have a minimum of 10 points under paragraphs 1 to 2 of Appendix C.

(f) The applicant must have, or have last been granted, entry clearance, leave to enter or leave to remain:

(i) as a Participant in the Fresh Talent: Working in Scotland Scheme,

(ii) as a Participant in the International Graduates Scheme (or its predecessor, the Science and Engineering Graduates Scheme),

(iii) as a Student, provided the applicant has not previously been granted leave in any of the categories referred to in paragraphs (i) and (ii) above,

(iv) as a Student Nurse, provided the applicant has not previously been granted leave in any of the categories referred to in paragraphs (i) and (ii) above,

(v) as a Student Re-Sitting an Examination, provided the applicant has not previously been granted leave in any of the categories referred to in paragraphs (i) and (ii) above,

(vi) as a Student Writing Up a Thesis, provided the applicant has not previously been granted leave as a Tier 1 Migrant or in any of the categories referred to in paragraphs (i) and (ii) above,

(vii) as a Tier 4 Migrant, provided the applicant has not previously been granted leave as a Tier 1 (Post-Study Work) Migrant or in any of the categories referred to in paragraphs (i) and (ii) above, or

(viii) as a Postgraduate Doctor or Dentist, provided the applicant has not previously been granted leave as a Tier 1 (Post-Study Work) Migrant or in any of the categories referred to in paragraphs (i) and (ii) above.

(g) An applicant who has, or was last granted leave as a Participant in the Fresh Talent: Working in Scotland Scheme must be a British National (Overseas), British overseas territories citizen, British Overseas citizen, British protected person or a British subject as defined in the British Nationality Act 1981.

(h) If:

(i) the studies that led to the qualification for which the applicant obtains points under paragraphs 66 to 72 of Appendix A were sponsored by a Government or international scholarship agency, and

(ii) those studies came to an end 12 months ago or less the applicant must provide the unconditional written consent of the sponsoring Government or agency to the application and must provide the specified documents to show that this requirement has been met.

245FE. Period and conditions of grant

(a) Leave to remain will be granted:

(i) for a period of the difference between 2 years and the period of the last grant of entry clearance, leave to enter or remain, to an applicant who has or was last granted leave as a Participant in the Fresh Talent: Working in Scotland Scheme, as a Participant in the International Graduates Scheme (or its predecessor the Science and Engineering Graduates Scheme). If this calculation results in no grant of leave then leave to remain is to be refused;

(ii) for a period of 2 years, to any other applicant.

(b) Leave to remain under this route will be subject to the following conditions:

(i) no access to public funds,

(ii) registration with the police, if this is required by paragraph 326 of these Rules, and

(iii) no Employment as a Doctor or Dentist in Training, unless the applicant:

(1) has obtained a primary degree in medicine or dentistry at bachelor's level or above from a UK institution that is a UK recognised or listed body, or which holds a sponsor licence under Tier 4 of the Points Based System; or

(2) has, or has last been granted, entry clearance, leave to enter or leave to remain that was not subject to any condition restricting him from taking employment as a Doctor in Training, and has been employed during that leave as a Doctor in Training; or

(3) has, or has last been granted, entry clearance, leave to enter or leave to remain that was not subject to any condition restricting him from taking employment as a Dentist in Training, and has been employed during that leave as a Dentist in Training.

Appendix A

Attributes for Tier 1 (Post-Study Work) Migrants

66. An applicant applying for entry clearance or leave to remain as a Tier 1 (Post-Study Work) Migrant must score 75 points for attributes.

67. Available points are shown in Table 10.

68. Notes to accompany the table appear below the table.

Table 10

Qualifications	**Points**
The applicant has been awarded: (a) a UK recognised bachelor or postgraduate degree, or (b) a UK postgraduate certificate in education or Professional Graduate Diploma of Education, or (c) a Higher National Diploma ('HND') from a Scottish institution.	20
(a) The applicant studied for his award at a UK institution that is a UK recognised or listed body, or which holds a sponsor licence under Tier 4 of the Points Based System, or (b) If the applicant is claiming points for having been awarded a Higher National Diploma from a Scottish Institution, he studied for that diploma at a Scottish publicly funded institution of further or higher education, or a Scottish bona fide private education institution which maintains satisfactory records of enrolment and attendance. The Scottish institution must: (i) be on the list of Education and Training Providers list on the Department of Business, Innovation and Skills website, or (ii) hold a Sponsor licence under Tier 4 of the Points Based System.	20
The applicant's periods of UK study and/or research towards his eligible award were undertaken whilst he had entry clearance, leave to enter or leave to remain in the UK that was not subject to a restriction preventing him from undertaking a course of study and/or research.	20
The applicant made the application for entry clearance or leave to remain as a Tier 1 (Post-Study Work) Migrant within 12 months of obtaining the relevant qualification or within 12 months of completing a United Kingdom Foundation Programme Office affiliated Foundation Programme as a postgraduate doctor or dentist.	15
The applicant is applying for leave to remain and has, or was last granted, leave as a Participant in the International Graduates Scheme (or its predecessor, the Science and Engineering Graduates Scheme) or as a Participant in the Fresh Talent: Working in Scotland Scheme.	75

Qualification: notes

69. Specified documents must be provided as evidence of the qualification and, where relevant, completion of the United Kingdom Foundation Programme Office affiliated Foundation Programme as a postgraduate doctor or dentist.

70. A qualification will have been deemed to have been 'obtained' on the date on which the applicant was first notified in writing, by the awarding institution, that the qualification had been awarded.

71. If the institution studied at is removed from one of the relevant lists referred to in Table 10, or from the Tier 4 Sponsor Register, no points will be awarded for a qualification obtained on or after the date the institution was removed from the relevant list or from the Tier 4 Sponsor Register.

72. To qualify as an HND from a Scottish institution, a qualification must be at level 8 on the Scottish Credit and Qualifications Framework.

Part 5
Immigration Rules relating to prospective students as at 30 September 2013

Requirements for leave to enter as a prospective student

82. The requirements to be met by a person seeking leave to enter the United Kingdom as a prospective student are that he:

(i) can demonstrate a genuine and realistic intention of undertaking, within 6 months of his date of entry:

(a) a course of study which would meet the requirements for an extension of stay as a student under paragraph 245ZX or paragraph 245ZZC; and

(b) DELETED

(ii) intends to leave the United Kingdom on completion of his studies or on the expiry of his leave to enter if he is not able to meet the requirements for an extension of stay:

(a) as a student in accordance with paragraph 245ZX or paragraph 245ZZC; and

(b) DELETED

(iii) is able without working or recourse to public funds to meet the costs of his intended course and accommodation and the maintenance of himself and any dependants while making arrangements to study and during the course of his studies; and

(iv) holds a valid United Kingdom entry clearance for entry in this capacity.

Leave to enter as a prospective student

83. A person seeking leave to enter the United Kingdom as a prospective student may be admitted for a period not exceeding 6 months with a condition prohibiting employment, provided he is able to produce to the Immigration Officer on arrival a valid United Kingdom entry clearance for entry in this capacity.

Refusal of leave to enter as a prospective student

84. Leave to enter as a prospective student is to be refused if the Immigration Officer is not satisfied that each of the requirements of paragraph 82 is met.

Appendix FM

Family members

General

Section GEN: General

Purpose

GEN.1.1. This route is for those seeking to enter or remain in the UK on the basis of their family life with a person who is a British Citizen, is settled in the UK, [...] is in the UK with limited leave as a refugee or person granted humanitarian protection (and the applicant cannot seek leave to enter or remain in the UK as their family member under Part 11 of these rules)[, is in the UK with limited leave under Appendix EU, or is in the UK with limited leave as a worker or business person by virtue of either Appendix ECAA Extension of Stay or under the provisions of the relevant 1973 Immigration Rules (or Decision 1/80) that underpinned the European Community Association Agreement (ECAA) with Turkey prior to 1 January 2021.]. It sets out the requirements to be met and, in considering applications under this route, it reflects how, under Article 8 of the Human Rights Convention, the balance will be struck between the right to respect for private and family life and the legitimate aims of protecting national security, public safety and the economic well-being of the UK; the prevention of disorder and crime; the protection of health or morals; and the protection of the rights and freedoms of others (and in doing so also reflects the relevant public interest considerations as set out in Part 5A of the Nationality, Immigration and Asylum Act 2002). It also takes into account the need to safeguard and promote the welfare of children in the UK, in line with the Secretary of State's duty under section 55 of the Borders, Citizenship and Immigration Act 2009.

Note: Word deleted; words inserted from 23:00 on 31 December 2020 subject to savings for applications made before that time (HC 813).

Definitions

GEN.1.2. For the purposes of this Appendix 'partner' means—

(i) the applicant's spouse;

(ii) the applicant's civil partner;

(iii) the applicant's fiancé(e) or proposed civil partner; or

(iv) a person who has been living together with the applicant in a relationship akin to a marriage or civil partnership for at least two years prior to the date of application, unless a different meaning of partner applies elsewhere in this Appendix.

GEN.1.3. For the purposes of this Appendix

(a) 'application for leave to remain' also includes an application for variation of leave to enter or remain by a person in the UK;

(b) references to a person being present and settled in the UK also include a person who is being admitted for settlement on the same occasion as the applicant; [...]

[(c) references to a British Citizen in the UK also include a British Citizen who is coming to the UK with the applicant as their partner or parent;]

[(d) references to a person being 'in the UK with limited leave under Appendix EU' mean an EEA national in the UK who holds valid limited leave to enter or remain granted under paragraph EU3 of Appendix EU to these Rules on the basis of meeting condition 1 in paragraph EU14 of that Appendix; and]

[(e) references to a person being 'in the UK with limited leave as a worker or business person under Appendix ECAA Extension of Stay' mean a person granted such leave by virtue of either Appendix ECAA Extension of Stay or under the provisions of the relevant 1973 Immigration Rules (or Decision 1/80) that underpinned the European Community Association Agreement (ECAA) with Turkey prior to 1 January 2021.]

Note: Sub-paragraph (c) substituted; (d) and (e) inserted from 23:00 on 31 December 2020 subject to savings for applications made before that time (HC 813).

GEN.1.4. In this Appendix 'specified' means specified in Appendix FM-SE, unless otherwise stated.

GEN.1.5. If the Entry Clearance Officer, or Secretary of State, has reasonable cause to doubt the genuineness of any document submitted in support of an application, and having taken reasonable steps to verify the document, is unable to verify that it is genuine, the document will be discounted for the purposes of the application.

GEN.1.6. For the purposes of paragraph E-ECP.4.1.(a); E-LTRP.4.1.(a); E-LTRP.4.1A.(a); E-ECPT.4.1.(a); E-LTRPT.5.1.(a); and E-LTRPT.5.1A.(a) the applicant must be a national of Antigua and Barbuda; Australia; the Bahamas; Barbados; Belize; Canada; Dominica; Grenada; Guyana; Jamaica; [Malta;] New Zealand; St Kitts and Nevis; St Lucia; St Vincent and the Grenadines; Trinidad and Tobago; or the United States of America.

Note: Word inserted from 23:00 on 31 December 2020 subject to savings for applications made before that time (HC 813).

GEN.1.7. In this Appendix references to paragraphs are to paragraphs of this Appendix unless the context otherwise requires.

GEN.1.8. Paragraphs 277–280, 289AA, 295AA and 296 of Part 8 of these Rules shall apply to this Appendix.

GEN.1.9. In this Appendix:

(a) the requirement to make a valid application will not apply when the Article 8 claim is raised:

(i) as part of an asylum claim, or as part of a further submission in person after an asylum claim has been refused;

(ii) where a migrant is in immigration detention. A migrant in immigration detention or their representative must submit any application or claim raising Article 8 to a prison officer, a prisoner custody officer, a detainee custody officer or a member of Home Office staff at the migrant's place of detention; or

(iii) in an appeal (subject to the consent of the Secretary of State where applicable); and

(b) where an application or claim raising Article 8 is made in any of the circumstances specified in paragraph GEN.1.9.(a), or is considered by the Secretary of State under paragraph A277C of these rules, the requirements of paragraphs R-LTRP.1.1.(c) and R-LTRPT.1.1.(c) are not met.

GEN.1.10. Where paragraph GEN.3.1.(2) or GEN.3.2.(3) applies, and the applicant is granted entry clearance or leave to enter or remain under, as appropriate, paragraph D-ECP.1.2., D-LTRP.1.2., D-ECC.1.1., D-LTRC.1.1., D-ECPT.1.2. or D-LTRPT.1.2., that grant of entry clearance or leave to enter or remain will be subject to a condition of no recourse to public funds unless the decision-maker considers, with reference to paragraph GEN.1.11A., that the applicant should not be subject to such a condition.

GEN.1.11. Where entry clearance or leave to enter or remain is granted under this Appendix (and without prejudice to the specific provision that is made in this Appendix in respect of a no recourse to public funds condition), that leave may be subject to such conditions as the decision-maker considers appropriate in a particular case.

[**GEN.1.11A.** Where entry clearance or leave to remain as a partner, child or parent is granted under paragraph D-ECP.1.2., D-LTRP.1.2., D-ECC.1.1., D-LTRC.1.1., D-ECPT.1.2. or D-LTRPT.1.2., if the decision maker is satisfied that:

(a) the applicant is destitute as defined in section 95 of the Immigration and Asylum Act 1999, or is at risk of imminent destitution; or

(b) there are reasons relating to the welfare of a relevant child which outweigh the considerations for imposing or maintaining the condition (treating the best interests of a relevant child as a primary consideration), the applicant will not be subject to a condition of no access to public funds and if the decision maker is not so satisfied, the applicant will be subject to a condition of no access to public funds.

For the purposes of this paragraph 'relevant child' means a person who:

(i) is under the age of 18 years at the date of application; and

(ii) it is clear from the information provided by the applicant, is a child who would be affected by a decision to impose or maintain the no recourse to public funds condition.]

Note: Paragraph substituted from 20 June 2022 subject to savings for applications made before that date (HC 1118).

GEN.1.12. In this Appendix, 'decision-maker' refers, as the case may be, to the Secretary of State, an Immigration Officer or an Entry Clearance Officer.

GEN.1.13. For the purposes of paragraphs D-LTRP.1.1., D-LTRP.1.2., D ILRP.1.2., D-LTRPT.1.1., D-LTRPT.1.2., and D-ILRPT.1.2. (excluding a grant of limited leave to remain as a fiancé(e) or proposed civil partner), where at the date of application the applicant has extant leave as a partner or parent (as applicable) granted under this Appendix, the remaining period of that extant leave up to a maximum of 28 days will be added to the period of limited leave to remain granted under that paragraph (which may therefore exceed 30 months).

GEN.1.14. Where a person aged 18 or over is granted entry clearance or limited leave to enter or remain under this Appendix, or where a person granted such entry clearance or limited leave to enter or remain will be aged 18 before that period of entry clearance or limited leave expires, the entry clearance or leave will, in addition to any other conditions which may apply, be granted subject to the conditions in [Appendix ATAS] of these rules.

Note: Words substituted from 09:00 on 5 October 2020 subject to savings for applications made before that time. Where consequential changes relating to the need for an ATAS certificate have been made, they take effect for all applications made or granted on or after 5 October 2020 at 09:00 (HC 707).

[**GEN.1.15.** Where, pursuant to paragraph D-ILRP.1.2., D-ILRP.1.3., D-ILRPT.1.2. or D-ILRPT.1.3., a person who has made an application for indefinite leave to remain under this Appendix does not meet the requirements for indefinite leave to remain, but the Secretary of State believes they may qualify for limited leave to remain under this Appendix or under Appendix Private Life:

(a) the Secretary of State will instead treat the application for indefinite leave to remain as an application for limited leave to remain; and

(b) the Secretary of State will notify the applicant in writing of any requirement to pay an immigration health charge under the Immigration (Health Charge) Order 2015 in relation to that application for limited leave to remain; and

(c) if any requested immigration health charge is not paid, the application for limited leave to remain will be invalid and will not be considered and the Secretary of State will not refund any fee paid in respect of the application for indefinite leave to remain.]

Note: Paragraph substituted from 20 June 2022 subject to savings for applications made before that date (HC 1118).

[**GEN.1.16.** Where an application or claim raising Article 8 is considered under Appendix FM and EX.1 applies, the requirements of paragraph R-LTRP.1.1(c) and R-LTRPT.1.1(c) are not met.]

Note: Paragraph inserted from 6 July 2018 for decisions made on or after that date (HC 1154).

[**GEN.1.17.** An application for settlement as a partner or parent (or the dependent child of a partner or parent) on the basis of a 10-year qualifying period for settlement must meet the requirements under Appendix Settlement Family Life (and the application for settlement will not be considered under this Appendix).]

Note: Paragraph inserted from 20 June 2022 subject to savings for applications made before that date (HC 1118).

Leave to enter

GEN.2.1. Subject to paragraph GEN.2.2., the requirements to be met by a person seeking leave to enter the UK under this route are that the person—

(a) must have a valid entry clearance for entry under this route; and

(b) must produce to the Immigration Officer on arrival a valid national passport or other document satisfactorily establishing their identity and nationality.

(b)

GEN.2.2. If a person does not meet the requirements of paragraph GEN.2.1. entry will be refused.

GEN.2.3. (1). Where an applicant for leave to enter the UK remains in the UK on immigration bail and the requirements of sub-paragraph (2) are met, paragraph GEN.1.10., D-LTRP.1.2., D-LTRC.1.1. or D-LTRPT.1.2. (as appropriate) will apply, as if paragraph D-LTRP.1.2., D-LTRC.1.1. or D-LTRPT.1.2. (where relevant) provided for the granting of leave to enter not leave to remain (and except that the references to leave to remain and limited leave to remain are to be read as leave to enter).

(2) The requirements of this sub-paragraph are met where:

(a) the applicant satisfies the requirements in paragraph R-LTRP.1.1.(a), (b) and (d), paragraph R-LTRC.1.1.(a), (b) and (d) or paragraph R-LTRPT.1.1.(a), (b) and (d), as if those were requirements for leave to enter not leave to remain (and except that the references to leave to remain and indefinite leave to remain are to be read as leave to enter); or

(b) a parent of the applicant has been granted leave to enter in accordance with this paragraph and the applicant satisfies the requirements in paragraph R-LTRC.1.1.(a), (b) and (d), as if those were requirements for leave to enter not leave to remain and as if paragraph R-LTRC.1.1.(d)(iii) referred to a parent of the applicant being or having been granted leave to enter in accordance with this paragraph (and except that the references to leave to remain are to be read as leave to enter).

Exceptional circumstances

GEN.3.1. (1) Where:

(a) the financial requirement in paragraph E-ECP.3.1., E-LTRP.3.1. (in the context of an application for limited leave to remain as a partner), E-ECC.2.1. or E-LTRC.2.1. applies, and is not met from the specified sources referred to in the relevant paragraph; and

(b) it is evident from the information provided by the applicant that there are exceptional circumstances which could render refusal of entry clearance or leave to remain a breach of Article 8 of the European Convention on Human Rights, because such refusal could result in unjustifiably harsh consequences for the applicant, their partner or a relevant child; then the decision-maker must consider whether such financial requirement is met through taking into account the sources of income, financial support or funds set out in paragraph 21A(2) of Appendix FM-SE (subject to the considerations in sub-paragraphs (3) to (8) of that paragraph).

(2) Where the financial requirement in paragraph E-ECP.3.1., ELTRP.3.1. (in the context of an application for limited leave to remain as a partner), E-ECC.2.1. or E-LTRC.2.1. is met following consideration under sub-paragraph (1) (and provided that the other relevant requirements of the Immigration Rules are also met), the applicant will be granted entry clearance or leave to remain under, as appropriate, paragraph D-ECP.1.2., D-LTRP.1.2., D-ECC.1.1. or DLTRC.1.1. or paragraph 315 or 316B of the Immigration Rules.

GEN.3.2. (1) Subject to sub-paragraph (4), where an application for entry clearance or leave to enter or remain made under this Appendix, or an application for leave to remain which has otherwise been considered under this Appendix, does not otherwise meet the requirements of this Appendix or Part 9 of the Rules, the decision-maker must consider whether the circumstances in sub-paragraph (2) apply.

(2) Where sub-paragraph (1) above applies, the decision-maker must consider, on the basis of the information provided by the applicant, whether there are exceptional circumstances which would render refusal of entry clearance, or leave to enter or remain, a breach of Article 8 of the European Convention on Human Rights, because such refusal would result in unjustifiably harsh consequences for the applicant, their partner, a relevant child or another family member whose Article 8 rights it is evident from that information would be affected by a decision to refuse the application.

(3) Where the exceptional circumstances referred to in sub-paragraph (2) above apply, the applicant will be granted entry clearance or leave to enter or remain under, as appropriate, paragraph D-ECP.1.2., DLTRP. 1.2., D-ECC.1.1., D-LTRC.1.1., D-ECPT.1.2., D-LTRPT.1.2., D-ECDR.1.1. or D-ECDR.1.2.

(4) This paragraph does not apply in the context of applications made under section BPILR or DVILR.

GEN.3.3. (1) In considering an application for entry clearance or leave to enter or remain where paragraph GEN.3.1. or GEN.3.2. applies, the decision-maker must take into account, as a primary consideration, the best interests of any relevant child.

(2) In paragraphs GEN.3.1. and GEN.3.2., and this paragraph, 'relevant child' means a person who:

(a) is under the age of 18 years at the date of the application;

and

(b) it is evident from the information provided by the applicant would be affected by a decision to refuse the application.

Family life with a partner

Section EC-P: Entry clearance as a partner

EC-P.1.1. The requirements to be met for entry clearance as a partner are that—

(a) the applicant must be outside the UK;

(b) the applicant must have made a valid application for entry clearance as a partner;

(c) the applicant must not fall for refusal under any of the grounds in Section S-EC: Suitability–entry clearance; and

(d) the applicant must meet all of the requirements of Section E-ECP: Eligibility for entry clearance as a partner.

Section S-EC: Suitability-entry clearance

S-EC.1.1. The applicant will be refused entry clearance on grounds of suitability if any of paragraphs S-EC.1.2. to 1.9. apply.

S-EC.1.2. The Secretary of State has personally directed that the exclusion of the applicant from the UK is conducive to the public good.

S-EC.1.3. The applicant is currently the subject of a deportation order.

S-EC.1.4. The exclusion of the applicant from the UK is conducive to the public good because they have:

(a) been convicted of an offence for which they have been sentenced to a period of imprisonment of at least 4 years; or

(b) been convicted of an offence for which they have been sentenced to a period of imprisonment of at least 12 months but less than 4 years, unless a period of 10 years has passed since the end of the sentence; or

(c) been convicted of an offence for which they have been sentenced to a period of imprisonment of less than 12 months, unless a period of 5 years has passed since the end of the sentence.

[. . .]

Note: Words deleted from 11 January 2018 subject to savings for applications made before that date (HC 309).

S-EC.1.5. The exclusion of the applicant from the UK is conducive to the public good because, for example, the applicant's conduct (including convictions which do not fall within paragraph S-EC.1.4.), character, associations, or other reasons, make it undesirable to grant them entry clearance.

S-EC.1.6. The applicant has failed without reasonable excuse to comply with a requirement to—

(a) attend an interview;

(b) provide information;

(c) provide physical data; or

(d) undergo a medical examination or provide a medical report.

S-EC.1.7. It is undesirable to grant entry clearance to the applicant for medical reasons.

S-EC.1.8. The applicant left or was removed from the UK as a condition of a caution issued in accordance with section 22 of the Criminal Justice Act 2003 less than 5 years prior to the date on which the application is decided.

S-EC.1.9. The Secretary of State considers that the applicant's parent or parent's partner poses a risk to the applicant. That person may be considered to pose a risk to the applicant if, for example, they—(a) have a conviction as an adult, whether in the UK or overseas, for an offence against a child; (b) are a registered sex offender and have failed to comply with any notification requirements; or (c) are required to comply with a sexual risk order made under the Anti-Social Behaviour, Crime and Policing Act 2014 and have failed to do so.

S-EC.2.1. The applicant will normally be refused on grounds of suitability if any of paragraphs S-EC.2.2. to 2.5. apply.

S-EC.2.2. Whether or not to the applicant's knowledge—

(a) false information, representations or documents have been submitted in relation to the application (including false information submitted to any person to obtain a document used in support of the application); or

(b) there has been a failure to disclose material facts in relation to the application.

S-EC.2.3. DELETED

S-EC.2.4. A maintenance and accommodation undertaking has been requested or required under paragraph 35 of these Rules or otherwise and has not been provided.

S-EC.2.5. The exclusion of the applicant from the UK is conducive to the public good because:

(a) within the 12 months prior to the date on which the application is decided, the person has been convicted of or admitted an offence for which they received a non-custodial sentence or other out of court disposal that is recorded on their criminal record; or

(b) in the view of the Secretary of State:

(i) the person's offending has caused serious harm; or

(ii) the person is a persistent offender who shows a particular disregard for the law.

S-EC.3.1. The applicant may be refused on grounds of suitability if the applicant has failed to pay litigation costs awarded to the Home Office.

S-EC.3.2. The applicant may be refused on grounds of suitability if one or more relevant NHS bodies has notified the Secretary of State that the applicant has failed to pay charges in accordance with the relevant NHS regulations on charges to overseas visitors and the outstanding charges have a total value of at least £500.

Section E-ECP: Eligibility for entry clearance as a partner

E-ECP.1.1. To meet the eligibility requirements for entry clearance as a partner all of the requirements in paragraphs E-ECP.2.1. to 4.2. must be met.

Relationship requirements

E-ECP.2.1. The applicant's partner must be—

(a) a British Citizen in the UK, subject to paragraph GEN.1.3.(c); or

(b) present and settled in the UK, subject to paragraph GEN.1.3.(b); or [(c) in the UK with refugee leave or with humanitarian protection; or]

[(d) in the UK with limited leave under Appendix EU, in accordance with paragraph GEN 1.3.(d); or]

[(e) in the UK with limited leave as a worker or business person under Appendix ECAA Extension of Stay, in accordance with paragraph GEN.1.3.(e).]

Note: Sub-paragraph (c) substituted; (d) and (e) inserted from 23:00 on 31 December 2020 subject to savings for applications made before that time (HC813).

E-ECP.2.2. The applicant must be aged 18 or over at the date of application.

E-ECP.2.3. The partner must be aged 18 or over at the date of application.

E-ECP.2.4. The applicant and their partner must not be within the prohibited degree of relationship.

E-ECP.2.5. The applicant and their partner must have met in person.

E-ECP.2.6. The relationship between the applicant and their partner must be genuine and subsisting.

E-ECP.2.7. If the applicant and partner are married or in a civil partnership it must be a valid marriage or civil partnership, as specified.

E-ECP.2.8. If the applicant is a fiancé(e) or proposed civil partner they must be seeking entry to the UK to enable their marriage or civil partnership to take place [in the United Kingdom].

Note: Words inserted from 4 June 2020 (CP 232).

E-ECP.2.9. Any previous relationship of the applicant or their partner must have broken down permanently, unless it is a relationship which falls within paragraph 278(i) of these Rules.

E-ECP.2.10. The applicant and partner must intend to live together permanently in the UK.

Financial requirements

E-ECP.3.1. The applicant must provide specified evidence, from the sources listed in paragraph E-ECP.3.2., of—

(a) a specified gross annual income of at least—

(i) £18,600;

(ii) an additional £3,800 for the first child; and

(iii) an additional £2,400 for each additional child; alone or in combination with

(b) specified savings of—

(i) £16,000; and

(ii) additional savings of an amount equivalent to 2.5 times the amount which is the difference between the gross annual income from the sources listed in paragraph E-ECP.3.2.(a)–(d) and the total amount required under paragraph E-ECP.3.1.(a); or

(c) the requirements in paragraph E-ECP.3.3. being met.

In this paragraph 'child' means a dependent child of the applicant or the applicant's partner who is

(a) under the age of 18 years, or who was under the age of 18 years when they were first granted entry under this route;

(b) applying for entry clearance as a dependant of the applicant or the applicant's partner, or is in the UK with leave as their dependant;

[(c) not a British Citizen, settled in the UK, or in the UK with valid limited leave to enter or remain granted under paragraph EU3 or EU3A of Appendix EU to these Rules; and]

(d) not an EEA national with a right to be admitted to or reside in the UK under the [Immigration (European Economic Area) Regulations 2016].

Note: Words in (c)(d) substituted from 1 October 2019 (HC 2631). Sub-paragraph (c)(c) substituted from 23:00 on 31 December 2020 subject to savings for applications made before that time (HC 813).

E-ECP.3.2. When determining whether the financial requirement in paragraph E-ECP.3.1. is met only the following sources will be taken into account—

(a) income of the partner from specified employment or self-employment, which, in respect of a partner returning to the UK with the applicant, can include specified employment or self-employment overseas and in the UK;

(b) specified pension income of the applicant and partner;

(c) any specified maternity allowance or bereavement benefit received by the partner in the UK or any specified payment relating to service in HM Forces received by the applicant or partner;

(d) other specified income of the applicant and partner; and

(e) specified savings of the applicant and partner.

E-ECP.3.3. The requirements to be met under this paragraph are—

(a) the applicant's partner must be receiving one or more of the following—

(i) disability living allowance;

(ii) severe disablement allowance;

(iii) industrial injury disablement benefit;

(iv) attendance allowance;

(v) carer's allowance;

(vi) personal independence payment;

(vii) Armed Forces Independence Payment or Guaranteed Income Payment under the Armed Forces Compensation Scheme; or

(viii) Constant Attendance Allowance, Mobility Supplement or War Disablement Pension under the War Pensions Scheme; and

(b) the applicant must provide evidence that their partner is able to maintain and accommodate themselves, the applicant and any dependants adequately in the UK without recourse to public funds.

E-ECP.3.4. The applicant must provide evidence that there will be adequate accommodation, without recourse to public funds, for the family, including other family members who are not included in the application but who live in the same household, which the family own or occupy exclusively: accommodation will not be regarded as adequate if—

(a) it is, or will be, overcrowded; or

(b) it contravenes public health regulations.

English language requirement

E-ECP.4.1. The applicant must provide specified evidence that they—

(a) are a national of a majority English speaking country listed in paragraph GEN.1.6;

(b) have passed an English language test in speaking and listening at a minimum of level A1 of the Common European Framework of Reference for Languages with a provider approved by the Secretary of State;

(c) have an academic qualification which is either a Bachelor's or Master's degree or PhD awarded by an educational establishment in the UK; or, if awarded by an educational establishment outside the UK, is deemed by [Ecctis] to meet or exceed the recognised standard of a Bachelor's or Master's degree or PhD in the UK, and [Ecctis] has confirmed that the degree was taught or researched in English to level A1 of the Common European Framework of Reference for Languages or above; or

(d) are exempt from the English language requirement under paragraph E-ECP. 4.2.

Note: Words in (c) substituted from 6 October 2021 subject to savings for applications made before that date (HC 617).

E-ECP.4.2. The applicant is exempt from the English language requirement if at the date of application—

(a) the applicant is aged 65 or over;

(b) the applicant has a disability (physical or mental condition) which prevents the applicant from meeting the requirement; or

(c) there are exceptional circumstances which prevent the applicant from being able to meet the requirement prior to entry to the UK.

Section D-ECP: Decision on application for entry clearance as a partner

D-ECP.1.1. Except where paragraph GEN.3.1.(2) or GEN.3.2.(3) of this Appendix applies, an applicant who meets the requirements for entry clearance as a partner (other than as a fiancé(e) or proposed civil partner) will be granted entry clearance for an initial period not exceeding 33 months, and subject to a condition of no recourse to public funds, and they will be eligible to apply for settlement after a continuous period of at least 60 months in the UK with leave to enter granted on the basis of such entry clearance or with limited leave to remain as a partner granted under paragraph D-LTRP.1.1. (excluding in all cases any period of leave to enter or limited leave to remain as a fiancé(e) or proposed civil partner); or, where the applicant is a fiancé(e) or proposed civil partner, the applicant will be granted entry clearance for a period not exceeding 6 months, and subject to a prohibition on employment and a condition of no recourse to public funds.

D-ECP.1.2. Where paragraph GEN.3.1.(2) or GEN.3.2.(3) of this Appendix applies, an applicant who meets the requirements for entry clearance as a partner (other than as a fiancé(e) or proposed civil partner) will be granted entry clearance for an initial period not exceeding 33 months, and subject to a condition of no recourse to public funds unless the decision-maker considers, with reference to paragraph GEN.1.11A., that the applicant should not be subject to such a condition, and they will be eligible to apply for settlement after a continuous period of at least 120 months in the UK with leave to enter granted on the basis of such entry clearance or of entry clearance granted under paragraph D-ECP.1.1. or with limited leave to remain as a partner granted under paragraph D-LTRP.1.1. or D-LTRP.1.2. (excluding in all cases any period of leave to enter or limited leave to remain as a fiancé(e) or proposed civil partner); or, where the applicant is a fiancé(e) or proposed civil partner, the applicant will be granted entry clearance for a period not exceeding 6 months, and subject to a prohibition on employment and a condition of no recourse to public funds.

D-ECP.1.3. If the applicant does not meet the requirements for entry clearance as a partner, the application will be refused.

Section R-LTRP: Requirements for limited leave to remain as a partner

R-LTRP.1.1. The requirements to be met for limited leave to remain as a partner are—

(a) the applicant and their partner must be in the UK;

(b) the applicant must have made a valid application for limited or indefinite leave to remain as a partner; and either

(c) (i) the applicant must not fall for refusal under Section S-LTR: Suitability leave to remain; and

(ii) the applicant meets all of the requirements of Section E-LTRP: Eligibility for leave to remain as a partner; or

(d) (i) the applicant must not fall for refusal under Section S-LTR: Suitability leave to remain; and

(ii) the applicant meets the requirements of paragraphs E-LTRP.1.2–1.12. and E-LTRP.2.1.-2.2.; and

(iii) paragraph EX.1. applies.

Section S-LTR: Suitability-leave to remain

S-LTR.1.1. The applicant will be refused limited leave to remain on grounds of suitability if any of paragraphs S-LTR.1.2. to 1.8. apply.

S-LTR.1.2. The applicant is currently the subject of a deportation order.

S-LTR.1.3. The presence of the applicant in the UK is not conducive to the public good because they have been convicted of an offence for which they have been sentenced to imprisonment for at least 4 years.

S-LTR.1.4. The presence of the applicant in the UK is not conducive to the public good because they have been convicted of an offence for which they have been sentenced to imprisonment for less than 4 years but at least 12 months [unless a period of 10 years has passed since the end of the sentence; or].

Note: Words inserted from 4 June 2020 (CP 232) **NB:** The statement of changes refers to S-LTR.1.4 (b), however sub-paragraph (b) does not exist.

S-LTR.1.5. The presence of the applicant in the UK is not conducive to the public good because, in the view of the Secretary of State, their offending has caused serious harm or they are a persistent offender who shows a particular disregard for the law.

S-LTR.1.6. The presence of the applicant in the UK is not conducive to the public good because their conduct (including convictions which do not fall within paragraphs S-LTR.1.3. to 1.5.), character, associations, or other reasons, make it undesirable to allow them to remain in the UK.

S-LTR.1.7. The applicant has failed without reasonable excuse to comply with a requirement to—

(a) attend an interview;

(b) provide information;

(c) provide physical data; or

(d) undergo a medical examination or provide a medical report.

S-LTR.1.8. The presence of the applicant in the UK is not conducive to the public good because the Secretary of State:

(a) has made a decision under Article 1F of the Refugee Convention to exclude the person from the Refugee Convention or under paragraph 339D of these Rules to exclude them from humanitarian protection; or

(b) has previously made a decision that they are a person to whom Article 33(2) of the Refugee Convention applies because there are reasonable grounds for regarding them as a danger to the security of the UK; or

(c) has made a decision that they are a person to whom sub-paragraph (a) or (b) would apply except that

(i) the person has not made a protection claim, or

(ii) the person made a protection claim which has already been finally determined without reference to Article 1F of the Refugee Convention or paragraph 339D of these Rules; or

(d) has previously made a decision that they are a person to whom Article 33(2) of the Refugee Convention applies because, having been convicted by a final judgment of a particularly serious crime, they constitute a danger to the community of the UK.

S-LTR.2.1. The applicant will normally be refused on grounds of suitability if any of paragraphs S-LTR.2.2. to 2.5. apply.

S-LTR.2.2. Whether or not to the applicant's knowledge—

(a) false information, representations or documents have been submitted in relation to the application (including false information submitted to any person to obtain a document used in support of the application); or

(b) there has been a failure to disclose material facts in relation to the application.

S-LTR.2.3. DELETED

S-LTR.2.4. A maintenance and accommodation undertaking has been requested under paragraph 35 of these Rules and has not been provided.

S-LTR.2.5. The Secretary of State has given notice to the applicant and their partner under section 50(7)(b) of the Immigration Act 2014 that one or both of them have not complied with the investigation of their proposed marriage or civil partnership.

S-LTR.3.1. When considering whether the presence of the applicant in the UK is not conducive to the public good any legal or practical reasons why the applicant cannot presently be removed from the UK must be ignored.

S-LTR.4.1. The applicant may be refused on grounds of suitability if any of paragraphs S-LTR.4.2. to S-LTR.4.5. apply.

S-LTR.4.2. The applicant has made false representations or failed to disclose any material fact in a previous application for entry clearance, leave to enter, leave to remain or a variation of leave, or in a previous human rights claim; or did so in order to obtain from the Secretary of State or a third party a document required to support such an application or claim (whether or not the application or claim was successful).

S-LTR.4.3. The applicant has previously made false representations or failed to disclose material facts for the purpose of obtaining a document from the Secretary of State that indicates that he or she has a right to reside in the United Kingdom.

S-LTR.4.4. The applicant has failed to pay litigation costs awarded to the Home Office.

S-LTR.4.5. One or more relevant NHS bodies has notified the Secretary of State that the applicant has failed to pay charges in accordance with the relevant NHS regulations on charges to overseas visitors and the outstanding charges have a total value of at least £500.

Section E-LTRP: Eligibility for limited leave to remain as a partner

E-LTRP.1.1. To qualify for limited leave to remain as a partner all of the requirements of paragraphs E-LTRP.1.2. to 4.2. must be met.

Relationship requirements

E-LTRP.1.2. The applicant's partner must be—

(a) a British Citizen in the UK;

(b) present and settled in the UK; [. . .]

[(c) in the UK with refugee leave or with humanitarian protection;]

[(d) in the UK with limited leave under Appendix EU, in accordance with paragraph GEN.1.3.(d); or]

[(e) in the UK with limited leave as a worker or business person under Appendix ECAA Extension of Stay, in accordance with paragraph GEN.1.3.(e).]

Note: Word deleted; (c) substituted; (d) and (e) inserted from 23:00 on 31 December 2020 subject to savings for applications made before that time (HC 813).

E-LTRP.1.3. The applicant must be aged 18 or over at the date of application.

E-LTRP.1.4. The partner must be aged 18 or over at the date of application.

E-LTRP.1.5. The applicant and their partner must not be within the prohibited degree of relationship.

E-LTRP.1.6. The applicant and their partner must have met in person.

E-LTRP.1.7. The relationship between the applicant and their partner must be genuine and subsisting.

E-LTRP.1.8. If the applicant and partner are married or in a civil partnership it must be a valid marriage or civil partnership, as specified.

E-LTRP.1.9. Any previous relationship of the applicant or their partner must have broken down permanently, unless it is a relationship which falls within paragraph 278(i) of these Rules.

E-LTRP.1.10. The applicant and their partner must intend to live together permanently in the UK and, in any application for further leave to remain as a partner (except where the applicant is in the UK as a fiancé(e) or proposed civil partner) and in any application for indefinite leave to remain as a partner, the applicant must provide evidence that, since entry clearance as a partner was granted under paragraph D-ECP1.1. or since the last grant of limited leave to remain as a partner, the applicant and their partner have lived together in the UK or there is good reason, consistent with a continuing intention to live together permanently in the UK, for any period in which they have not done so.

E-LTRP.1.11. If the applicant is in the UK with leave as a fiancé(e) or proposed civil partner and the marriage or civil partnership did not take place during that period of leave, there must be good reason why and evidence that it will take place within the next 6 months.

E-LTRP.1.12. The applicant's partner cannot be the applicant's fiancé(e) or proposed civil partner, unless the applicant was granted entry clearance as that person's fiancé(e) or proposed civil partner.

Immigration status requirements

E-LTRP.2.1. The applicant must not be in the UK—

(a) as a visitor; or

(b) with valid leave granted for a period of 6 months or less, unless that leave is as a fiancé(e) or proposed civil partner, or was granted pending the outcome of family court or divorce proceedings;

E-LTRP.2.2. The applicant must not be in the UK—

(a) on immigration bail, unless:

(ii) the Secretary of State is satisfied that the applicant arrived in the UK more than 6 months prior to the date of application; and

(ii) paragraph EX.1. applies; or

(b) in breach of immigration laws except that, where paragraph 39E of these Rules applies, any current period of overstaying will be disregarded), unless paragraph EX.1. applies.

Financial requirements

E-LTRP.3.1. The applicant must provide specified evidence, from the sources listed in paragraph E-LTRP.3.2., of—

(a) a specified gross annual income of at least—

(i) £18,600;

(ii) an additional £3,800 for the first child; and

(iii) an additional £2,400 for each additional child; alone or in combination with

(b) specified savings of—

(i) £16,000; and

(ii) additional savings of an amount equivalent to 2.5 times the amount which is the difference between the gross annual income from the sources listed in paragraph E-LTRP.3.2.(a)–(f) and the total amount required under paragraph E-LTRP.3.1.(a); or

(c) the requirements in paragraph E-LTRP.3.3. being met, unless paragraph EX.1. applies.

In this paragraph 'child' means a dependent child of the applicant or the applicant's partner who is

(a) under the age of 18 years, or who was under the age of 18 years when they were first granted entry under this route;

(b) applying for entry clearance or leave to remain as a dependant of the applicant or the applicant's partner, or is in the UK with leave as their dependant;

[(c) not a British Citizen, settled in the UK, or in the UK with valid limited leave to enter or remain granted under paragraph EU3 or EU3A of Appendix EU to these Rules; and]

(d) not an EEA national with a right to be admitted to or reside in the UK under the [Immigration (European Economic Area) Regulations 2016].

Note: Words in (c)(d) substituted from 1 October 2019 (HC 2631). Sub-paragraph (c)(c) substituted from 23:00 on 31 December 2020 subject to savings for applications made before that time (HC 813).

E-LTRP.3.2. When determining whether the financial requirement in paragraph E-LTRP.3.1. is met only the following sources may be taken into account—

(a) income of the partner from specified employment or self-employment;

(b) income of the applicant from specified employment or self-employment unless they are working illegally;

(c) specified pension income of the applicant and partner;

(d) any specified maternity allowance or bereavement benefit received by the applicant and partner in the UK or any specified payment relating to service in HM Forces received by the applicant or partner;

(e) other specified income of the applicant and partner;

(f) income from the sources at (b), (d) or (e) of a dependent child of the applicant or of the applicant's partner under paragraph E-LTRP.3.1. who is aged 18 years or over; and

(g) specified savings of the applicant, partner and a dependent child of the applicant or of the applicant's partner under paragraph E-LTRP.3.1. who is aged 18 years or over.

E-LTRP.3.3. The requirements to meet this paragraph are—

(a) the applicant's partner must be receiving one or more of the following—

(i) disability living allowance;

(ii) severe disablement allowance;

(iii) industrial injury disablement benefit;

(iv) attendance allowance;

(v) carer's allowance;

(vi) personal independence payment;

(vii) Armed Forces Independence Payment or Guaranteed Income Payment under the Armed Forces Compensation Scheme; or

(viii) Constant Attendance Allowance, Mobility Supplement or War Disablement Pension under the War Pensions Scheme; and

(b) the applicant must provide evidence that their partner is able to maintain and accommodate themselves, the applicant and any dependants adequately in the UK without recourse to public funds.

E-LTRP.3.4. The applicant must provide evidence that there will be adequate accommodation, without recourse to public funds, for the family, including other family members who are not included in the application but who live in the same household, which the family own or occupy exclusively, unless paragraph EX.1. applies: accommodation will not be regarded as adequate if—

(a) it is, or will be, overcrowded; or

(b) it contravenes public health regulations.

English language requirement

E-LTRP.4.1. If the applicant has not met the requirement in a previous application for entry clearance or leave to remain as a partner or parent, the applicant must provide specified evidence that they—

(a) are a national of a majority English speaking country listed in paragraph GEN.1.6.;

(b) have passed an English language test in speaking and listening at a minimum of level A1 of the Common European Framework of Reference for Languages with a provider approved by the Secretary of State;

(c) have an academic qualification which is either a Bachelor's or Master's degree or PhD awarded by an educational establishment in the UK; or, if awarded by an educational establishment outside the UK, is deemed by [Ecctis] to meet or exceed the recognised standard of a Bachelor's or Master's degree or PhD in the UK, and [Ecctis] has confirmed that the degree was taught or researched in English to level A1 of the Common European Framework of Reference for Languages or above; or

(d) are exempt from the English language requirement under paragraph E-LTRP. 4.2.;

unless paragraph EX.1. applies.

Note: Words in (c) substituted from 6 October 2021 subject to savings for applications made before that date (HC 617).

E-LTRP.4.1A. Where the applicant:

(i) in a previous application for entry clearance or leave to remain as a partner or parent, met the English language requirement in paragraph E-ECP.4.1.(b), E-LTRP.4.1.(b), E-ECPT.4.1.(b) or E-LTRPT.5.1.(b) on the basis that they had passed an English language test in speaking and listening at level A1 of the Common European Framework of Reference for Languages;

(ii) was granted entry clearance or leave to remain as a partner or parent; and

(iii) now seeks further leave to remain as a partner after 30 months in the UK with leave as a partner;

then, the applicant must provide specified evidence that they:

(a) are a national of a majority English speaking country listed in paragraph GEN.1.6.;

(b) have passed an English language test in speaking and listening at a minimum of level A2 of the Common European Framework of Reference for Languages with a provider approved by the Secretary of State;

(c) have an academic qualification which is either a Bachelor's or Master's degree or PhD awarded by an educational establishment in the UK; or, if awarded by an educational establishment outside the UK, is deemed by [Ecctis] to meet or exceed the recognised standard of a Bachelor's or Master's degree or PhD in the UK, and [Ecctis] has confirmed that the degree was taught or researched in English to level A2 of the Common European Framework of Reference for Languages or above; or

(d) are exempt from the English language requirement under paragraph ELTRP.4.2.[; unless paragraph EX.1 applies.]

Note: Words in (d) inserted from 6 July 2018 for decisions made on or after that date (HC 1154). Words in (c) substituted from 6 October 2021 subject to savings for applications made before that date (HC 617).

E-LTRP.4.2. The applicant is exempt from the English language requirement in paragraph E-LTRP.4.1. or E-LTRP.4.1A. if at the date of application—

(a) the applicant is aged 65 or over;

(b) the applicant has a disability (physical or mental condition) which prevents the applicant from meeting the requirement; or

(c) there are exceptional circumstances which prevent the applicant from being able to meet the requirement.

Section D-LTRP: Decision on application for limited leave to remain as a partner

D-LTRP.1.1. If the applicant meets the requirements in paragraph R-LTRP.1.1.(a) to (c) for limited leave to remain as a partner the applicant will be granted limited leave to remain for a period not exceeding 30 months, and subject to a condition of no recourse to public funds, and they will be eligible to apply for settlement after a continuous period of at least 60 months with such leave or in the UK with leave to enter granted on the basis of entry clearance granted under paragraph D-ECP.1.1. (excluding in all cases any period of leave to enter or limited leave to remain as a fiancé(e) or proposed civil partner or, if paragraph E-LTRP.1.11. applies, the applicant will be granted limited leave for a period not exceeding 6 months and subject to a condition of no recourse to public funds and a prohibition on employment.

D-LTRP.1.2. If the applicant meets the requirements in paragraph R-LTRP.1.1.(a), (b) and (d) for limited leave to remain as a partner, or paragraph GEN.3.1.(2) or GEN.3.2.(3) applies to an applicant for leave to remain as a partner, the applicant will be granted leave to remain for a period not exceeding 30 months and subject to a condition of no recourse to public funds unless the decision-maker considers, with reference to paragraph GEN.1.11A., that the applicant should not be subject to such a condition, and they will be eligible to apply for settlement after a continuous period of at least 120 months in the UK with such leave, with limited leave to remain as a partner granted under paragraph D-LTRP.1.1., or in the UK with leave to enter granted on the basis of entry clearance as a partner granted under paragraph D-ECP.1.1. or D-ECP.1.2. (excluding in all cases any period of leave to enter or limited leave to remain as a fiancé(e) or proposed civil partner); or, if paragraph E-LTRP.1.11. applies, the applicant will be granted limited leave for a period not exceeding 6 months and subject to a condition of no recourse to public funds and a prohibition on employment.

D-LTRP.1.3. If the applicant does not meet the requirements for limited leave to remain as a partner the application will be refused.

Section R-ILRP: Requirements for indefinite leave to remain (settlement) as a partner

R-ILRP.1.1. The requirements to be met for indefinite leave to remain as a partner are that—

(a) the applicant and their partner must be in the UK;

(b) the applicant must have made a valid application for indefinite leave to remain as a partner;

(c) the applicant must not fall for refusal under any of the grounds in Section S-ILR: Suitability for indefinite leave to remain; [and]

[. . .]

(e) the applicant must meet all of the requirements of Section E-ILRP: Eligibility for indefinite leave to remain as a partner.

Note: Word inserted, (d) deleted from 6 April 2018 for decisions made on or after that date (HC 895).

Section S-ILR: Suitability for indefinite leave to remain

S-ILR.1.1. The applicant will be refused indefinite leave to remain on grounds of suitability if any of paragraphs S-ILR.1.2. to 1.10 apply.

S-ILR.1.2. The applicant is currently the subject of a deportation order.

S-ILR.1.3. The presence of the applicant in the UK is not conducive to the public good because they have been convicted of an offence for which they have been sentenced to imprisonment for at least 4 years.

S-ILR.1.4. The presence of the applicant in the UK is not conducive to the public good because they have been convicted of an offence for which they have been sentenced to imprisonment for less than 4 years but at least 12 months, unless a period of 15 years has passed since the end of the sentence.

S-ILR.1.5. The presence of the applicant in the UK is not conducive to the public good because they have been convicted of an offence for which they have been sentenced to imprisonment for less than 12 months, unless a period of 7 years has passed since the end of the sentence.

S-ILR.1.6. The applicant has, within the 24 months prior to the date on which the application is decided, been convicted of or admitted an offence for which they received a non-custodial sentence or other out of court disposal that is recorded on their criminal record.

S-ILR.1.7. The presence of the applicant in the UK is not conducive to the public good because, in the view of the Secretary of State, their offending has caused serious harm or they are a persistent offender who shows a particular disregard for the law.

S-ILR.1.8. The presence of the applicant in the UK is not conducive to the public good because their conduct (including convictions which do not fall within paragraphs S-ILR.1.3. to 1.6.), character, associations, or other reasons, make it undesirable to allow them to remain in the UK.

S-ILR.1.9. The applicant has failed without reasonable excuse to comply with a requirement to—

(a) attend an interview;

(b) provide information;

(c) provide physical data; or

(d) undergo a medical examination or provide a medical report.

S-ILR.1.10. The presence of the applicant in the UK is not conducive to the public good because the Secretary of State:

(a) has made a decision under Article 1F of the Refugee Convention to exclude the person from the Refugee Convention or under paragraph 339D of these Rules to exclude them from humanitarian protection; or

(b) has previously made a decision that they are a person to whom Article 33(2) of the Refugee Convention applies because there are reasonable grounds for regarding them as a danger to the security of the UK; or

(c) has made a decision that they are a person to whom sub-paragraph (a) or (b) would apply except that

(i) the person has not made a protection claim, or

(ii) the person made a protection claim which has already been finally determined without reference to Article 1F of the Refugee Convention or paragraph 339D of these Rules; or

(d) has previously made a decision that they are a person to whom Article 33(2) of the Refugee Convention applies because, having been convicted by a final judgment of a particularly serious crime, they constitute a danger to the community of the UK.

S-ILR.2.1. The applicant will normally be refused on grounds of suitability if any of paragraphs S-ILR.2.2. to 2.4. apply.

S-ILR.2.2. Whether or not to the applicant's knowledge –

(a) false information, representations or documents have been submitted in relation to the application (including false information submitted to any person to obtain a document used in support of the application); or

(b) there has been a failure to disclose material facts in relation to the application.

S-ILR.2.3. DELETED

S-ILR.2.4. A maintenance and accommodation undertaking has been requested under paragraph 35 of these Rules and has not been provided.

S-ILR.3.1. When considering whether the presence of the applicant in the UK is not conducive to the public good, any legal or practical reasons why the applicant cannot presently be removed from the UK must be ignored.

S-ILR.4.1. The applicant may be refused on grounds of suitability if any of paragraphs S-ILR.4.2. to S-ILR.4.5. apply.

S-ILR.4.2. The applicant has made false representations or failed to disclose any material fact in a previous application for entry clearance, leave to enter, leave to remain or a variation of leave, or in a previous human rights claim; or did so in order to obtain from the Secretary of State or a third party a document required to support such an application or claim (whether or not the application or claim was successful).

S-ILR.4.3. The applicant has previously made false representations or failed to disclose material facts for the purpose of obtaining a document from the Secretary of State that indicates that he or she has a right to reside in the United Kingdom.

S-ILR.4.4. The applicant has failed to pay litigation costs awarded to the Home Office.

S-ILR.4.5. One or more relevant NHS bodies has notified the Secretary of State that the applicant has failed to pay charges in accordance with the relevant NHS regulations on charges to overseas visitors and the outstanding charges have a total value of at least £500.

Section E-ILRP: Eligibility for indefinite leave to remain as a partner

[**E-ILRP.1.1.** To meet the eligibility requirements for indefinite leave to remain as a partner after a 5 year qualifying period all of the requirements of paragraphs E-ILRP.1.2. to 1.6. must be met.]

Note: Paragraph substituted from 20 June 2022 subject to savings for applications made before that date (HC 1118).

E-ILRP.1.2. The applicant must be in the UK with valid leave to remain as a partner under this Appendix (except that, where paragraph 39E of these Rules applies, any current period of overstaying will be disregarded).

[**E-ILRP.1.3.** (1) Subject to subparagraph (2), the applicant must, at the date of application, have completed a period of continuous residence in the UK of at least 5 years (60 months) with the following:

(a) leave to enter granted on the basis of entry clearance as a partner granted under paragraph D-ECP.1.1; or

(b) limited leave to remain as a partner granted under paragraph D-LTRP.1.1; or

(c) a combination of leave under (a) and (b).

(1A) In respect of an application falling within subparagraph (1) above, the applicant must meet all the requirements of Section E-LTRP: Eligibility for leave to remain as a partner (except that paragraph E-LTRP.1.2. cannot be met on the basis set out in subparagraph (c), (d) or (e) of that paragraph, and in applying paragraph E-LTRP.3.1.(b)(ii) disregard the words "2.5 times").

(2) In calculating periods of leave for the purposes of subparagraph (1) above, any period of leave to enter or leave to remain as a fiancé(e) or proposed civil partner will be disregarded.]

Note: Amendments from 6 April 2018 for decisions made on or after that date (HC 895). Amendments from 23:00 on 31 December 2020 subject to savings for applications made before that time (HC 813). Paragraph substituted from 20 June 2022 subject to savings for applications made before that date (HC 1118).

E-ILRP.1.4. In calculating the periods under paragraph E-ILRP.1.3. only the periods when the applicant's partner is the same person as the applicant's partner for the previous period of limited leave shall be taken into account.

E-ILRP.1.5. In calculating the periods under paragraph E-ILRP.1.3. the words 'in the UK' in that paragraph shall not apply to any period(s) to which the evidence in paragraph 26A of Appendix FM-SE applies.

E-ILRP.1.5A. In calculating the periods under paragraph E-ILRP.1.3., any current period of overstaying will be disregarded where paragraph 39E of these Rules applies. Any previous period of overstaying between periods of leave will also be disregarded where: the further application was made before 24 November 2016 and within 28 days of the expiry of leave; or the further application was made on or after 24 November 2016 and paragraph 39E of these Rules applied.

E-ILRP.1.6. The applicant must have demonstrated sufficient knowledge of the English language and sufficient knowledge about life in the United Kingdom in accordance with the requirements of Appendix KoLL of these Rules.

Section D-ILRP: Decision on application for indefinite leave to remain as a partner

D-ILRP.1.1. If the applicant meets all of the requirements for indefinite leave to remain as a partner subject to compliance with any requirement notified under paragraph GEN.1.15.(b), the applicant will be granted indefinite leave to remain.

D-ILRP.1.2. If the applicant does not meet the requirements for indefinite leave to remain as a partner only for one or both of the following reasons—

(a) paragraph S-ILR.1.5. or S-ILR.1.6. applies;

(b) the applicant has not demonstrated sufficient knowledge of the English language or about life in the United Kingdom in accordance with Appendix KoLL, subject to compliance with any requirement notified under paragraph GEN.1.15.(b), the applicant will be granted further limited leave to remain as a partner for a period not exceeding 30 months, and subject to a condition of no recourse to public funds.

D-ILRP.1.3. If the applicant does not meet all the eligibility requirements for indefinite leave to remain as a partner, and does not qualify for further limited leave to remain as a partner under paragraph DILRP. 1.2., the application will be refused, unless the applicant meets the requirements in paragraph R-LTRP.1.1.(a), (b) and (d) for limited leave to remain as a partner. Where they do, and subject to compliance with any requirement notified under paragraph GEN.1.15.(b), the applicant will be granted further limited leave to remain as a partner for a period not exceeding 30 months under paragraph D-LTRP.1.2. and subject to a condition of no recourse to public funds unless the Secretary of State considers that the person should not be subject to such a condition.

Section EX: Exceptions to certain eligibility requirements for leave to remain as a partner or parent

EX.1. This paragraph applies if

(a) (i) the applicant has a genuine and subsisting parental relationship with a child who—

(aa) is under the age of 18 years, or was under the age of 18 years when the applicant was first granted leave on the basis that this paragraph applied;

(bb) is in the UK;

(cc) is a British Citizen or has lived in the UK continuously for at least the 7 years immediately preceding the date of application; and

(ii) taking into account their best interests as a primary consideration, it would not be reasonable to expect the child to leave the UK; or

[(b) the applicant has a genuine and subsisting relationship with a partner who is in the UK and is a British Citizen, settled in the UK, or in the UK with refugee leave, or humanitarian protection, in the UK with limited leave under Appendix EU in accordance with paragraph GEN.1.3.(d), or in the UK with limited leave as a worker or business person under Appendix ECAA Extension of Stay in accordance with paragraph GEN.1.3.(e), and there are insurmountable obstacles to family life with that partner continuing outside the UK.]

Note: Sub-paragraph (b) substituted from 23:00 on 31 December 2020 subject to savings for applications made before that time (HC 813).

EX.2. For the purposes of paragraph EX.1.(b) 'insurmountable obstacles' means the very significant difficulties which would be faced by the applicant or their partner in continuing their family life together outside the UK and which could not be overcome or would entail very serious hardship for the applicant or their partner.

Bereaved partner

Section BPILR: Indefinite leave to remain (settlement) as a bereaved partner

BPILR.1.1. The requirements to be met for indefinite leave to remain in the UK as a bereaved partner are that—

(a) the applicant must be in the UK;

(b) the applicant must have made a valid application for indefinite leave to remain as a bereaved partner;

(c) the applicant must not fall for refusal under any of the grounds in Section S-ILR: Suitability—indefinite leave to remain; and

(d) the applicant must meet all of the requirements of Section E-BPILR: Eligibility for indefinite leave to remain as a bereaved partner.

Section E-BPILR: Eligibility for indefinite leave to remain as a bereaved partner

E-BPILR.1.1. To meet the eligibility requirements for indefinite leave to remain as a bereaved partner all of the requirements of paragraphs E-BPILR1.2. to 1.4. must be met.

E-BPILR.1.2. The applicant's last grant of limited leave must have been [granted under this Appendix] as—

(a) a partner (other than a fiancé(e) or proposed civil partner) of a British Citizen[, a person settled in the UK, or a person in the UK with limited leave under Appendix EU in accordance with paragraph GEN.1.3.(d)]; or

(b) a bereaved partner.

Note: Words in introduction inserted; words in (a) substituted from 23:00 on 31 December 2020 subject to savings for applications made before that time (HC 813).

E-BPILR.1.3. The person who was the applicant's partner at the time of the last grant of limited leave as a partner must have died.

E-BPILR.1.4. At the time of the partner's death the relationship between the applicant and the partner must have been genuine and subsisting and each of the parties must have intended to live permanently with the other in the UK.

Section D-BPILR: Decision on application for indefinite leave to remain as a bereaved partner

D-BPILR.1.1. If the applicant meets all of the requirements for indefinite leave to remain as a bereaved partner the applicant will be granted indefinite leave to remain.

D-BPILR.1.2. If the applicant does not meet the requirements for indefinite leave to remain as a bereaved partner only because paragraph S-ILR.1.5. or S-ILR.1.6. applies, the applicant will be granted further limited leave to remain for a period not exceeding 30 months, and subject to a condition of no recourse to public funds.

D-BPILR.1.3. If the applicant does not meet the requirements for indefinite leave to remain as a bereaved partner, or limited leave to remain as a bereaved partner under paragraph D-BPILR.1.2., the application will be refused.

Victim of [domestic abuse]

Section DVILR: Indefinite leave to remain (settlement) as a victim of [domestic abuse]

DVILR.1.1. The requirements to be met for indefinite leave to remain in the UK as a victim of [domestic abuse] are that—

(a) the applicant must be in the UK;

(b) the applicant must have made a valid application for indefinite leave to remain as a victim of [domestic abuse];

(c) the applicant must not fall for refusal under any of the grounds in Section S-ILR: Suitability—indefinite leave to remain; and

(d) the applicant must meet all of the requirements of Section E-DVILR: Eligibility for indefinite leave to remain as a victim of [domestic abuse].

Note: Words in heading and in paragraph substituted from 10 January 2019 subject to savings for applications made before that date (HC 1779)

Section E-DVILR: Eligibility for indefinite leave to remain as a victim of [domestic abuse]

E-DVILR.1.1. To meet the eligibility requirements for indefinite leave to remain as a victim of [domestic abuse] all of the requirements of paragraphs E-DVILR.1.2. and 1.3. must be met.

Note: Words in heading and in paragraph substituted from 10 January 2019 subject to savings for applications made before that date (HC 1779)

[**E-DVILR.1.2.** The applicant's first grant of limited leave under this Appendix must have been as a partner (other than a fiancé(e) or proposed civil partner) of a British Citizen, a person present and settled in the UK, a person with refugee leave, or a person in the UK with limited leave under Appendix EU in accordance with paragraph GEN.1.3.(d), under paragraph D-ECP.1.1., D-LTRP.1.1., or D-LTRP.1.2. of this Appendix, or as a partner of a refugee granted under paragraph 352A, and any subsequent grant of limited leave must have been:

(a) granted as a partner (other than a fiancé(e) or proposed civil partner) of a British Citizen, a person present and settled in the UK, a person with refugee leave, or a person in the UK with limited leave under Appendix EU in accordance with paragraph GEN.1.3.(d), under paragraph D-ECP.1.1., D-LTRP.1.1. or D-LTRP.1.2. of this Appendix; or

(b) granted to enable access to public funds pending an application under DVILR and the preceding grant of leave was granted as a partner (other than a fiancé(e) or proposed civil partner) of a British Citizen, a person present and settled in the UK, a person with refugee leave, or a person in the UK with limited leave under Appendix EU in accordance with paragraph GEN.1.3.(d), under paragraph D-ECP.1.1., DLTRP.1.1. or D-LTRP.1.2. of this Appendix; or

(c) granted under paragraph D-DVILR.1.2.]

Note: Paragraph substituted from 10 January 2019 subject to savings for applications made before that date (HC 1779). Paragraph substituted from 23:00 on 31 December 2020 subject to savings for applications made before that time (HC 813).

[**E-DVILR.1.3.** The applicant must provide evidence that during the last period of limited leave as a partner of a British Citizen, a person present and settled in the UK, a person with refugee leave, or a person in the UK with limited leave under Appendix EU in accordance with paragraph GEN.1.3.(d), under paragraph D-ECP.1.1., DLTRP.1.1 or D-LTRP.1.2 of this Appendix, or during their only period of leave under paragraph 352A, the applicant's relationship with their partner broke down permanently as a result of domestic abuse.]

Note: Paragraph substituted from 10 January 2019 subject to savings for applications made before that date (HC 1779). Paragraph substituted from 23:00 on 31 December 2020 subject to savings for applications made before that time (HC 813).

Section D-DVILR: Decision on application for indefinite leave to remain as a victim of [domestic abuse]

D-DVILR.1.1. If the applicant meets all of the requirements for indefinite leave to remain as a victim of [domestic abuse] the applicant will be granted indefinite leave to remain.

Note: Words in heading and in paragraph substituted from 10 January 2019 subject to savings for applications made before that date (HC 1779)

D-DVILR.1.2. If the applicant does not meet the requirements for indefinite leave to remain as a victim of [domestic abuse] only because paragraph S-ILR.1.5. or S-ILR.1.6. applies, the applicant will be granted further limited leave to remain for a period not exceeding 30 months.

Note: Words substituted from 10 January 2019 subject to savings for applications made before that date (HC 1779)

D-DVILR.1.3. If the applicant does not meet the requirements for indefinite leave to remain as a victim of [domestic abuse], or further limited leave to remain under paragraph D-DVILR.1.2. the application will be refused.

Note: Words substituted from 10 January 2019 subject to savings for applications made before that date (HC 1779)

Family life as a child of a person with limited leave as a partner or parent

This route is for a child whose parent is applying under this Appendix for entry clearance or leave, or who has limited leave, as a partner or parent. For further provision on a child seeking to enter or remain in the UK for the purpose of their family life see Part 8 of these Rules.

Section EC-C: Entry clearance as a child

EC-C.1.1. The requirements to be met for entry clearance as a child are that—

(a) the applicant must be outside the UK;

(b) the applicant must have made a valid application for entry clearance as a child;

(c) the applicant must not fall for refusal under any of the grounds in Section S-EC: Suitability for entry clearance; and

(d) the applicant must meet all of the requirements of Section E-ECC: Eligibility for entry clearance as a child.

Section E-ECC: Eligibility for entry clearance as a child

E-ECC.1.1. To meet the eligibility requirements for entry clearance as a child all of the requirements of paragraphs E-ECC.1.2. to 2.4. must be met.

Relationship requirements

E-ECC.1.2. The applicant must be under the age of 18 at the date of application.

E-ECC.1.3. The applicant must not be married or in a civil partnership.

E-ECC.1.4. The applicant must not have formed an independent family unit.

E-ECC.1.5. The applicant must not be leading an independent life.

E-ECC.1.6. One of the applicant's parents must be in the UK with limited leave to enter or remain, or be being granted, or have been granted, entry clearance, as a partner or a parent under this Appendix (referred to in this section as the 'applicant's parent'), and

(a) the applicant's parent's partner under Appendix FM is also a parent of the applicant; or

(b) the applicant's parent has had and continues to have sole responsibility for the child's upbringing; or

(c) there are serious and compelling family or other considerations which make exclusion of the child undesirable and suitable arrangements have been made for the child's care.

Financial requirement

E-ECC.2.1. Where a parent of the applicant has, or is applying or has applied for, entry clearance or limited leave to enter or remain as a partner under this Appendix, the applicant must provide specified evidence, from the sources listed in paragraph E-ECC.2.2., of—

(a) a specified gross annual income of at least—

(i) £18,600;

(ii) an additional £3,800 for the first child; and

(iii) an additional £2,400 for each additional child; alone or in combination with

(b) specified savings of

(i) £16,000; and

(ii) additional savings of an amount equivalent to 2.5 times the amount which is the difference between the gross annual income from the sources listed in paragraph E-ECC.2.2.(a)–(f) and the total amount required under paragraph E-ECC.2.1.(a); or

(c) the requirements in paragraph E-ECC.2.3. being met.

In this paragraph 'child' means the applicant and any other dependent child of the applicant's parent or the applicant's parent's partner who is

(a) under the age of 18 years, or who was under the age of 18 years when they were first granted entry under this route;

(b) applying for entry clearance as a dependant of the applicant's parent or of the applicant's parent's partner, or is in the UK with leave as their dependant;

[(c) not a British Citizen, settled in the UK, or in the UK with valid limited leave to enter or remain granted under paragraph EU3 or EU3A of Appendix EU to these Rules; and]

(d) not an EEA national with a right to be admitted to or reside in the UK under the [Immigration (European Economic Area) Regulations 2016].

Note: Words in (c)(d) substituted from 1 October 2019 (HC 2631). Sub-paragraph (c)(c) substituted from 23:00 on 31 December 2020 subject to savings for applications made before that time (HC 813).

E-ECC.2.2. When determining whether the financial requirement in paragraph E-ECC.2.1. is met only the following sources may be taken into account—

(a) income of the applicant's parent's partner from specified employment or self-employment, which, in respect of an applicant's parent's partner returning to the UK with the applicant, can include specified employment or self-employment overseas and in the UK;

(b) income of the applicant's parent from specified employment or self employment if they are in the UK unless they are working illegally;

(c) specified pension income of the applicant's parent and that parent's partner;

(d) any specified maternity allowance or bereavement benefit received by the applicant's parent and that parent's partner in the UK or any specified payment relating to service in HM Forces received by the applicant's parent and that parent's partner;

(e) other specified income of the applicant's parent and that parent's partner;

(f) income from the sources at (b), (d) or (e) of a dependent child of the applicant's parent under paragraph E-ECC.2.1. who is aged 18 years or over; and

(g) specified savings of the applicant's parent, that parent's partner and a dependent child of the applicant's parent under paragraph E-ECC.2.1. who is aged 18 years or over.

E-ECC.2.3. The requirements to be met under this paragraph are—

(a) the applicant's parent's partner must be receiving one or more of the following—

(i) disability living allowance;

(ii) severe disablement allowance;

(iii) industrial injury disablement benefit;

(iv) attendance allowance;

(v) carer's allowance;

(vi) personal independence payment;

(vii) Armed Forces Independence Payment or Guaranteed Income Payment under the Armed Forces Compensation Scheme; or

(viii) Constant Attendance Allowance, Mobility Supplement or War Disablement Pension under the War Pensions Scheme; and

(b) the applicant must provide evidence that their parent's partner is able to maintain and accommodate themselves, the applicant's parent, the applicant and any dependants adequately in the UK without recourse to public funds.

E-ECC.2.3A. Where a parent of the applicant has, or is applying or has applied for, entry clearance or limited leave to enter or remain as a parent under this Appendix, the applicant must provide evidence that that parent is able to maintain and accommodate themselves, the applicant and any other dependants adequately in the UK without recourse to public funds.

[E-ECC.2.4.] The applicant must provide evidence that there will be adequate accommodation, without recourse to public funds, for the family, including other family members who are not included in the application but who live in the same household, which the family own or occupy exclusively: accommodation will not be regarded as adequate if—

(a) it is, or will be, overcrowded; or

(b) it contravenes public health regulations.

Note: Provision renumbered from 6 July 2018 for decisions made on or after that date (HC 1154).

Section D-ECC: Decision on application for entry clearance as a child

D-ECC.1.1. If the applicant meets the requirements for entry clearance as a child they will be granted entry clearance of a duration which will expire at the same time as the leave granted to the applicant's parent, and will be subject to the same conditions in respect of recourse to public funds as that parent.

D-ECC.1.2. If the applicant does not meet the requirements for entry clearance as a child the application will be refused.

Section R-LTRC: Requirements for leave to remain as a child

R-LTRC.1.1. The requirements to be met for leave to remain as a child are that—

(a) the applicant must be in the UK;

(b) the applicant must have made a valid application for leave to remain as a child; and either

(c) (i) the applicant must not fall for refusal under any of the grounds in Section S-LTR: Suitability—leave to remain; and

(ii) the applicant meets all of the requirements of Section E-LTRC: Eligibility for leave to remain as a child; and

(iii) a parent of the applicant has been or is at the same time being granted leave to remain under paragraph D-LTRP.1.1. or D-LTRPT.1.1. or indefinite leave to remain under this Appendix (except as an adult dependent relative); or

(d) (i) the applicant must not fall for refusal under any of the grounds in Section S-LTR: Suitability—leave to remain; and

(ii) the applicant meets the requirements of paragraphs E-LTRC.1.2.–1.6.; and

(iii) a parent of the applicant has been or is at the same time being granted leave to remain under paragraph D-LTRP.1.2., D-ILRP.1.2, D-LTRPT.1.2. or D-ILRPT.1.2. or indefinite leave to remain under this Appendix (except as an adult dependent relative).

Section E-LTRC: Eligibility for leave to remain as a child

E-LTRC.1.1. To qualify for limited leave to remain as a child all of the requirements of paragraphs E-LTRC.1.2. to 2.4. must be met (except where paragraph R-LTRC.1.1.(d)(ii) applies).

Relationship requirements

E-LTRC.1.2. The applicant must be under the age of 18 at the date of application or when first granted leave as a child under this route.

E-LTRC.1.3. The applicant must not be married or in a civil partnership.

E-LTRC.1.4. The applicant must not have formed an independent family unit.

E-LTRC.1.5. The applicant must not be leading an independent life.

E-LTRC.1.6. One of the applicant's parents (referred to in this section as the 'applicant's parent') must be in the UK and have leave to enter or remain or indefinite leave to remain, or is at the same time being granted leave to remain or indefinite leave to remain, under this Appendix (except as an adult dependent relative), and

(a) the applicant's parent's partner under Appendix FM is also a parent of the applicant; or

(b) the applicant's parent has had and continues to have sole responsibility for the child's upbringing or the applicant normally lives with this parent and not their other parent; or

(c) there are serious and compelling family or other considerations which make exclusion of the child undesirable and suitable arrangements have been made for the child's care.

Financial requirements

E-LTRC.2.1. Where a parent of the applicant has, or is applying or has applied for, limited leave to remain as a partner under this Appendix, the applicant must provide specified evidence, from the sources listed in paragraph E-LTRC.2.2., of—

(a) a specified gross annual income of at least—

(i) £18,600;

(ii) an additional £3,800 for the first child; and

(iii) an additional £2,400 for each additional child; alone or in combination with

(b) specified savings of—

(i) £16,000; and

(ii) additional savings of an amount equivalent to 2.5 times (or if the parent is applying for indefinite leave to remain 1 times) the amount which is the difference between the gross annual income from the sources listed in paragraph E-LTRC.2.2.(a)–(f) and the total amount required under paragraph E-LTRC.2.1.(a); or

(c) the requirements in paragraph E-LTRC.2.3. being met.

In this paragraph 'child' means the applicant and any other dependent child of the applicant's parent or the applicant's parent's partner who is

(a) under the age of 18 years, or who was under the age of 18 years when they were first granted entry under this route;

(b) applying for entry clearance as a dependant of the applicant's parent or of the applicant's parent's partner, or is in the UK with leave as their dependant;

[(c) not a British Citizen, settled in the UK, or in the UK with valid limited leave to enter or remain granted under paragraph EU3 or EU3A of Appendix EU to these Rules; and]

(d) not an EEA national with a right to be admitted to or reside in the UK under the [Immigration (European Economic Area) Regulations 2016].

Note: Words in (c)(d) substituted from 1 October 2019 (HC 2631). Sub-paragraph (c)(c) substituted from 23:00 on 31 December 2020 subject to savings for applications made before that time (HC 813).

E-LTRC.2.2. When determining whether the financial requirement in paragraph E-LTRC.2.1. is met only the following sources may be taken into account—

(a) income of the applicant's parent's partner from specified employment or self-employment;

(b) income of the applicant's parent from specified employment or self employment;

(c) specified pension income of the applicant's parent and that parent's partner;

(d) any specified maternity allowance or bereavement benefit received by the applicant's parent and that parent's partner in the UK or any specified payment relating to service in HM Forces received by the applicant's parent and that parent's partner;

(e) other specified income of the applicant's parent and that parent's partner;

(f) income from the sources at (b), (d) or (e) of a dependent child of the applicant's parent under paragraph E-LTRC.2.1. who is aged 18 years or over; and

(g) specified savings of the applicant's parent, that parent's partner and a dependent child of the applicant's parent under paragraph E-ECC.2.1. who is aged 18 years or over.

E-LTRC.2.3. The requirements to be met under this paragraph are—

(a) the applicant's parent's partner must be receiving one or more of the following—

(i) disability living allowance;

(ii) severe disablement allowance;

(iii) industrial injury disablement benefit;

(iv) attendance allowance;

(v) carer's allowance;

(vi) personal independence payment;

(vii) Armed Forces Independence Payment or Guaranteed Income Payment under the Armed Forces Compensation Scheme; or

(viii) Constant Attendance Allowance, Mobility Supplement or War Disablement Pension under the War Pensions Scheme; and

(b) the applicant must provide evidence that their parent's partner is able to maintain and accommodate themselves, the applicant's parent, the applicant and any dependants adequately in the UK without recourse to public funds.

E-LTRC.2.3A. Where a parent of the applicant has, or is applying or has applied for, limited leave to remain as a parent under this Appendix, the applicant must provide evidence that that parent is able to maintain and accommodate themselves, the applicant and any other dependants adequately in the UK without recourse to public funds.

E-LTRC.2.4. The applicant must provide evidence that there will be adequate accommodation in the UK, without recourse to public funds, for the family, including other family members who are not included in the application but who live in the same household, which the family own or occupy exclusively: accommodation will not be regarded as adequate if—

(a) it is, or will be, overcrowded; or

(b) it contravenes public health regulations.

Section D-LTRC: Decision on application for leave to remain as a child

[**D-LTRC.1.1.** If the applicant meets the requirements for leave to remain as a child the applicant will be granted leave to remain, either:

(a) of a duration which will expire at the same time as the limited leave granted to the applicant's parent(s) and will be subject to the same conditions in respect of recourse to public funds as their parent(s); or

(b) 30 months, where a parent is settled but the child does not qualify for settlement, subject to the following conditions:

(i) no recourse to public funds unless the decision-maker considers, with reference to paragraph GEN.1.11A., that the applicant should not be subject to such a condition; and

(ii) study is permitted, subject to the ATAS condition in Appendix ATAS if the applicant is aged 18 or over.

To qualify for indefinite leave to remain as a child of a person with indefinite leave to remain as a partner or parent, the applicant must meet the requirements of Appendix Settlement Family Life if applying as a dependent of a partner or parent who is applying under that Appendix, otherwise the applicant must meet the requirements of paragraph 298 of these rules.]

Note: Paragraph substituted from 20 June 2022 subject to savings for applications made before that date (HC 1118).

D-LTRC.1.2. If the applicant does not meet the requirements for leave to remain as a child the application will be refused.

Family life as a parent of a child in the UK

Section EC-PT: Entry clearance as a parent of a child in the UK

EC-PT.1.1. The requirements to be met for entry clearance as a parent are that—

(a) the applicant must be outside the UK;

(b) the applicant must have made a valid application for entry clearance as a parent;

(c) the applicant must not fall for refusal under any of the grounds in Section S-EC: Suitability–entry clearance; and

(d) the applicant must meet all of the requirements of Section E-ECPT: Eligibility for entry clearance as a parent.

Section E-ECPT: Eligibility for entry clearance as a parent

E-ECPT.1.1. To meet the eligibility requirements for entry clearance as a parent all of the requirements in paragraphs E-ECPT.2.1. to 4.2. must be met.

Relationship requirements

E-ECPT.2.1. The applicant must be aged 18 years or over.

E-ECPT.2.2. The child of the applicant must be—

(a) under the age of 18 years at the date of application;

(b) living in the UK; and

[(c) a British Citizen, settled in the UK, or in the UK with limited leave under Appendix EU in accordance with paragraph GEN.1.3.(d).]

Note: Sub-paragraph (c) substituted from 23:00 on 31 December 2020 subject to savings for applications made before that time (HC 813).

E-ECPT.2.3. Either—

(a) the applicant must have sole parental responsibility for the child; or

(b) the parent or carer with whom the child normally lives must be—

(i) a British Citizen in the UK [, settled in the UK, or in the UK with limited leave under Appendix EU in accordance with paragraph GEN.1.3.(d)];

(ii) not the partner of the applicant; and

(iii) the applicant must not be eligible to apply for entry clearance as a partner under this Appendix.

Note: Words in (b)(i) substituted from 23:00 on 31 December 2020 subject to savings for applications made before that time (HC 813).

E-ECPT.2.4.

(a) The applicant must provide evidence that they have either—

(i) sole parental responsibility for the child; or

(ii) direct access (in person) to the child, as agreed with the parent or carer with whom the child normally lives or as ordered by a court in the UK; and

(b) The applicant must provide evidence that they are taking, and intend to continue to take, an active role in the child's upbringing.

Financial requirements

E-ECPT.3.1. The applicant must provide evidence that they will be able to adequately maintain and accommodate themselves and any dependants in the UK without recourse to public funds.

E-ECPT.3.2. The applicant must provide evidence that there will be adequate accommodation in the UK, without recourse to public funds, for the family, including other family members who are not included in the application but who live in the same household, which the family own or occupy exclusively: accommodation will not be regarded as adequate if—

(a) it is, or will be, overcrowded; or

(b) it contravenes public health regulations.

English language requirement

E-ECPT.4.1. The applicant must provide specified evidence that they—

(a) are a national of a majority English speaking country listed in paragraph GEN.1.6.;

(b) have passed an English language test in speaking and listening at a minimum of level A1 of the Common European Framework of Reference for Languages with a provider approved by the Secretary of State;

(c) have an academic qualification which is either a Bachelor's or Master's degree or PhD awarded by an educational establishment in the UK; or, if awarded by an educational establishment outside the UK, is deemed by [Ecctis] to meet or exceed the recognised standard of a Bachelor's or Master's degree or PhD in the UK, and [Ecctis] has confirmed that the degree was taught or researched in English to level A1 of the Common European Framework of Reference for Languages or above; or

(d) are exempt from the English language requirement under paragraph E-ECPT. 4.2.

Note: Words in (c) substituted from 6 October 2021 subject to savings for applications made before that date (HC 617).

E-ECPT.4.2. The applicant is exempt from the English language requirement if at the date of application—

(a) the applicant is aged 65 or over;

(b) the applicant has a disability (physical or mental condition) which prevents the applicant from meeting the requirement; or

(c) there are exceptional circumstances which prevent the applicant from being able to meet the requirement prior to entry to the UK.

Section D-ECPT: Decision on application for entry clearance as a parent

D-ECPT.1.1. If the applicant meets the requirements for entry clearance as a parent (except where paragraph GEN.3.2.(3) applies), the applicant will be granted entry clearance for an initial period not exceeding 33 months, and subject to a condition of no recourse to public funds, and they will be eligible to apply for settlement after a continuous period of at least 60 months in the UK with leave to enter granted on the basis of such entry clearance or with limited leave to remain as a parent granted under paragraph D-LTRPT.1.1.

D-ECPT.1.2. If paragraph GEN.3.2.(3) applies to an applicant for entry clearance as a parent, the applicant will be granted entry clearance for an initial period not exceeding 33 months, and subject to a condition of no recourse to public funds unless the decision-maker considers, with reference to paragraph GEN.1.11A., that the person should not be subject to such a condition, and they will be eligible to apply for settlement after a continuous period of at least 120 months in the UK with leave to enter granted on the basis of such entry clearance or of entry clearance granted under paragraph D-ECPT.1.1. or with limited leave to remain as a parent granted under paragraph D-LTRPT.1.1. or D-LTRPT.1.2.

D-ECPT.1.3. If the applicant does not meet the requirements for entry clearance as a parent, the application will be refused.

Section R-LTRPT: Requirements for limited leave to remain as a parent

R-LTRPT.1.1. The requirements to be met for limited leave to remain as a parent are—

(a) the applicant and the child must be in the UK;

(b) the applicant must have made a valid application for limited or indefinite leave to remain as a parent or partner; and either

(c) (i) the applicant must not fall for refusal under Section S-LTR: Suitability leave to remain; and

(ii) the applicant meets all of the requirements of Section ELTRPT: Eligibility for leave to remain as a parent, or

(d) (i) the applicant must not fall for refusal under S-LTR: Suitability leave to remain; and

(ii) the applicant meets the requirements of paragraphs E-LTRPT.2.2–2.4. and E-LTRPT.3.1.-3.2.; and

(iii) paragraph EX.1. applies.

Section E-LTRPT: Eligibility for limited leave to remain as a parent

E-LTRPT.1.1. To qualify for limited leave to remain as a parent all of the requirements of paragraphs E-LTRPT.2.2. to 5.2. must be met.

Relationship requirements

E-LTRPT.2.2. The child of the applicant must be—

(a) under the age of 18 years at the date of application, or where the child has turned 18 years of age since the applicant was first granted entry clearance or leave to remain as a parent under this Appendix, must not have formed an independent family unit or be leading an independent life;

(b) living in the UK; and

(c) a British Citizen [, settled in the UK, or in the UK with limited leave under Appendix EU in accordance with paragraph GEN.1.3.(d)]; or

(d) has lived in the UK continuously for at least the 7 years immediately preceding the date of application and paragraph EX.1. applies.

Note: Words in (c) substituted from 23:00 on 31 December 2020 subject to savings for applications made before that time (HC 813).

E-LTRPT.2.3. Either—

(a) the applicant must have sole parental responsibility for the child or the child normally lives with the applicant and not their other parent (who is a British Citizen[, settled in the UK, or in the UK with limited leave under Appendix EU in accordance with paragraph GEN.1.3.(d)], and the applicant must not be eligible to apply for leave to remain as a partner under this Appendix; or

(b) the parent or carer with whom the child normally lives must be—

(i) a British Citizen in the UK[, settled in the UK, or in the UK with limited leave under Appendix EU in accordance with paragraph GEN.1.3.(d)];

(ii) not the partner of the applicant (which here includes a person who has been in a relationship with the applicant for less than two years prior to the date of application); and

(iii) the applicant must not be eligible to apply for leave to remain as a partner under this Appendix.

Note: Words in (a) and (b)(i) substituted from 23:00 on 31 December 2020 subject to savings for applications made before that time (HC 813).

E-LTRPT.2.4.

(a) The applicant must provide evidence that they have either—

(i) sole parental responsibility for the child, or that the child normally lives with them; or

(ii) direct access (in person) to the child, as agreed with the parent or carer with whom the child normally lives or as ordered by a court in the UK; and

(b) The applicant must provide evidence that they are taking, and intend to continue to take, an active role in the child's upbringing.

Immigration status requirement

E-LTRPT.3.1. The applicant must not be in the UK—

(a) as a visitor; or

(b) with valid leave granted for a period of 6 months or less, unless that leave was granted pending the outcome of family court or divorce proceedings;

E-LTRPT.3.2. The applicant must not be in the UK—

(a) on immigration bail, unless:

(i) the Secretary of State is satisfied that the applicant arrived in the UK more than 6 months prior to the date of application; and

(ii) paragraph EX.1. applies; or

(b) in breach of immigration laws except that, where paragraph 39E of these Rules applies, any current period of overstaying will be disregarded, unless paragraph EX.1. applies.

Financial requirements

E-LTRPT.4.1. The applicant must provide evidence that they will be able to adequately maintain and accommodate themselves and any dependants in the UK without recourse to public funds, unless paragraph EX.1. applies.

E-LTRPT.4.2. The applicant must provide evidence that there will be adequate accommodation in the UK, without recourse to public funds, for the family, including other family members who are not included in the application but who live in the same household, which the family own or occupy exclusively, unless paragraph EX.1. applies: accommodation will not be regarded as adequate if—

(a) it is, or will be, overcrowded; or

(b) it contravenes public health regulations.

English language requirement

E-LTRPT.5.1. If the applicant has not met the requirement in a previous application for entry clearance or leave to remain as a parent or partner, the applicant must provide specified evidence that they—

(a) are a national of a majority English speaking country listed in paragraph GEN.1.6.;

(b) have passed an English language test in speaking and listening at a minimum of level A1 of the Common European Framework of Reference for Languages with a provider approved by the Secretary of State;

(c) have an academic qualification which is either a Bachelor's or Master's degree or PhD awarded by an educational establishment in the UK; or, if awarded by an educational establishment outside the UK, is deemed by [Ecctis] to meet or exceed the recognised standard of a Bachelor's or Master's degree or PhD in the UK, and [Ecctis] has confirmed that the degree was taught or researched in English to level A1 of the Common European Framework of Reference for Languages or above; or

(d) are exempt from the English language requirement under paragraph E-LTRPT. 5.2., unless paragraph EX.1. applies.

Note: Words in (c) substituted from 6 October 2021 subject to savings for applications made before that date (HC 617).

E-LTRPT.5.1A. Where the applicant:

(i) in a previous application for entry clearance or leave to remain as a parent or partner, met the English language requirement in paragraph E-ECP.4.1.(b), E-ELTRP.4.1.(b), E-ECPT.4.1.(b) or E-LTRPT.5.1.(b) on the basis that they had passed an English language test in speaking and listening at level A1 of the Common European Framework of Reference for Languages; and

(ii) was granted entry clearance or leave to remain as a parent or partner; and

(iii) now seeks further leave to remain as a parent after 30 months in the UK with leave as a parent;

then, the applicant must provide specified evidence that they:

(a) are a national of a majority English speaking country listed in paragraph GEN.1.6.;

(b) have passed an English language test in speaking and listening at a minimum of level A2 of the Common European Framework of Reference for Languages with a provider approved by the Secretary of State;

(c) have an academic qualification which is either a Bachelor's or Master's degree or PhD awarded by an educational establishment in the UK; or, if awarded by an educational establishment outside the UK, is deemed by [Ecctis] to be equivalent to the standard of a Bachelor's or Master's degree or PhD in the UK, and [Ecctis] has confirmed that the degree was taught or researched in English to level A2 of the Common European Framework of Reference for Languages or above; or

(d) are exempt from the English language requirement under paragraph ELTRPT.5.2.[; unless paragraph EX.1 applies.]

Note: Words in (d) inserted from 6 July 2018 for decisions made on or after that date (HC 1154). Words in (c) substituted from 6 October 2021 subject to savings for applications made before that date (HC 617).

E-LTRPT.5.2. The applicant is exempt from the English language requirement in paragraph E-LTRPT.5.1. or E-LTRPT.5.1A. if at the date of application—

(a) the applicant is aged 65 or over;

(b) the applicant has a disability (physical or mental condition) which prevents the applicant from meeting the requirement; or

(c) there are exceptional circumstances which prevent the applicant from being able to meet the requirement.

Section D-LTRPT: Decision on application for limited leave to remain as a parent

D-LTRPT.1.1. If the applicant meets the requirements in paragraph R-LTRPT.1.1. (a) to (c) for limited leave to remain as a parent the applicant will be granted limited leave to remain for a period not exceeding 30 months, and subject to a condition of no recourse to public funds, and they will be eligible to apply for settlement after a continuous period of at least 60 months with such leave or in the UK with leave to enter granted on the basis of entry clearance as a parent granted under paragraph D-ECPT.1.1.

D-LTRPT.1.2. If the applicant meets the requirements in paragraph R-LTRPT.1.1.(a), (b) and (d) for limited leave to remain as a parent, or paragraph GEN.3.2.(3) applies to an applicant for leave to remain as a parent, the applicant will be granted leave to remain for a period not exceeding 30 months and subject to a condition of no recourse to public funds unless the decision-maker considers, with reference to paragraph GEN.1.11A., that the applicant should not be subject to such a condition, and they will be eligible to apply for settlement after a continuous period of at least 120 months in the UK with such leave, with limited leave to remain as a parent granted under paragraph D-LTRPT.1.1., or in the UK with leave to enter granted on the basis of entry clearance as a parent granted under paragraph D-ECPT.1.1. or D-ECPT.1.2.

Section R-ILRPT: Requirements for indefinite leave to remain (settlement) as a parent

[**R-ILRPT.1.1.** The requirements to be met for indefinite leave to remain as a parent after a 5 year qualifying period are that:

(a) the applicant must be in the UK; and

(b) the applicant must have made a valid application for indefinite leave to remain as a parent; and

(c) the applicant must not fall for refusal under any of the grounds in Section S-ILR: Suitability-indefinite leave to remain; and

(d) the applicant must meet all of the requirements of Section E-ILRPT: Eligibility for indefinite leave to remain as a parent.]

Note: Amendments from 6 April 2018 for decisions made on or after that date (HC 895). Paragraph substituted from 20 June 2022 subject to savings for applications made before that date (HC 1118).

Section E-ILRPT: Eligibility for indefinite leave to remain as a parent

E-ILRPT.1.1. To meet the eligibility requirements for indefinite leave to remain as a parent all of the requirements of paragraphs E-ILRPT.1.2. to 1.5. must be met.

E-ILRPT.1.2. The applicant must be in the UK with valid leave to remain as a parent under this Appendix (except that, where paragraph 39E of these Rules applies, any current period of overstaying will be disregarded).

[**E-ILRPT.1.3.** (1) The applicant must, at the date of application, have completed a continuous period of residence of at least 5 years (60 months) with the following:

(a) leave to enter granted on the basis of entry clearance as a parent granted under paragraph D-ECPT.1.1.; or

(b) limited leave to remain as a parent granted under paragraph D-LTRPT.1.1.; or

(c) a combination of leave under (a) and (b).

(1A) In respect of an application falling within subparagraph (1) above, the applicant must meet all of the requirements of Section E-LTRPT: Eligibility for leave to remain as a parent (except that paragraph E-LTRPT.2.2.(c) cannot be met on the basis of a person being in the UK with limited leave under Appendix EU in accordance with paragraph GEN.1.3.(d)).]

Note: Paragraph substituted from 6 April 2018 for decisions made on or after that date (HC 895). Amendments from 23:00 on 31 December 2020 subject to savings for applications made before that time (HC 813). Amendments from 6 April 2021 subject to savings for applications made before that date (HC 1248). Paragraph substituted from 20 June 2022 subject to savings for applications made before that date (HC 1118).

E-ILRPT.1.5. The applicant must have demonstrated sufficient knowledge of the English language and sufficient knowledge about life in the United Kingdom in accordance with the requirements of Appendix KoLL of these Rules.

E-ILRPT.1.5A. In calculating the periods under paragraph E-ILRPT.1.3., any current period of overstaying will be disregarded where paragraph 39E of these Rules applies. Any previous period of overstaying between periods of leave will also be disregarded where: the further application was made before 24 November 2016 and within 28 days of the expiry of leave; or the further application was made on or after 24 November 2016 and paragraph 39E of these Rules applied.

Section D-ILRPT: Decision on application for indefinite leave to remain as a parent

D-ILRPT.1.1. If the applicant meets all of the requirements for indefinite leave to remain as a parent the applicant will be granted indefinite leave to remain.

D-ILRPT.1.2. If the applicant does not meet the requirements for indefinite leave to remain as a parent only for one or both of the following reasons—

(a) paragraph S-ILR.1.5. or S-ILR.1.6. applies; or

(b) the applicant has not demonstrated sufficient knowledge of the English language or about life in the United Kingdom in accordance with Appendix KoLL, subject to compliance with any requirement notified under paragraph GEN.1.15.(b), the applicant will be granted further limited leave to remain as a parent for a period not exceeding 30 months, and subject to a condition of no recourse to public funds.

D-ILRPT.1.3. If the applicant does not meet all the eligibility requirements for indefinite leave to remain as a parent, and does not qualify for further limited leave to remain under paragraph D-ILRPT.1.2., the application will be refused, unless the applicant meets the requirements in paragraph R-LTRPT.1.1.(a), (b) and (d) for limited leave to remain as a parent. Where they do, and subject to compliance with any requirement notified under paragraph GEN.1.15.(b), the applicant will be granted further limited leave to remain as a parent for a period not exceeding 30 months under paragraph D-LTRPT.1.2. and subject to a condition of no recourse to public funds unless the Secretary of State considers that the person should not be subject to such a condition.

Adult dependent relative

Section EC-DR: Entry clearance as an adult dependent relative

EC-DR.1.1. The requirements to be met for entry clearance as an adult dependent relative are that—

(a) the applicant must be outside the UK;

(b) the applicant must have made a valid application for entry clearance as an adult dependent relative;

(c) the applicant must not fall for refusal under any of the grounds in Section S-EC: Suitability for entry clearance; and

(d) the applicant must meet all of the requirements of Section E-ECDR: Eligibility for entry clearance as an adult dependent relative.

Section E-ECDR: Eligibility for entry clearance as an adult dependent relative

E-ECDR.1.1. To meet the eligibility requirements for entry clearance as an adult dependent relative all of the requirements in paragraphs E-ECDR.2.1. to 3.2. must be met.

Relationship requirements

E-ECDR.2.1. The applicant must be the—
(a) parent aged 18 years or over;
(b) grandparent;
(c) brother or sister aged 18 years or over; or
(d) son or daughter aged 18 years or over of a person ('the sponsor') who is in the UK.

E-ECDR.2.2. If the applicant is the sponsor's parent or grandparent they must not be in a subsisting relationship with a partner unless that partner is also the sponsor's parent or grandparent and is applying for entry clearance at the same time as the applicant.

E-ECDR.2.3. The sponsor must at the date of application be—
(a) aged 18 years or over; and
(b) (i) a British Citizen in the UK; or
(ii) present and settled in the UK; or
(iii) in the UK with refugee leave or humanitarian protection[; or]
[(iv) in the UK with limited leave under Appendix EU, in accordance with paragraph GEN.1.3.(d)].

Note: Words in (b)(iii) substituted; (iv) inserted from 23:00 on 31 December 2020 subject to savings for applications made before that time (HC 813).

E-ECDR.2.4. The applicant or, if the applicant and their partner are the sponsor's parents or grandparents, the applicant's partner, must as a result of age, illness or disability require long-term personal care to perform everyday tasks.

E-ECDR.2.5. The applicant or, if the applicant and their partner are the sponsor's parents or grandparents, the applicant's partner, must be unable, even with the practical and financial help of the sponsor, to obtain the required level of care in the country where they are living, because—
(a) it is not available and there is no person in that country who can reasonably provide it; or
(b) it is not affordable.

Financial requirements

E-ECDR.3.1. The applicant must provide evidence that they can be adequately maintained, accommodated and cared for in the UK by the sponsor without recourse to public funds.

E-ECDR.3.2. If the applicant's sponsor is a British Citizen or settled in the UK, the applicant must provide an undertaking signed by the sponsor confirming that the applicant will have no recourse to public funds, and that the sponsor will be responsible for their maintenance, accommodation and care, for a period of 5 years from the date the applicant enters the UK if they are granted indefinite leave to enter.

Section D-ECDR: Decision on application for entry clearance as an adult dependent relative

D-ECDR.1.1. If the applicant meets the requirements for entry clearance as an adult dependent relative of a British Citizen or person settled in the UK they will be granted indefinite leave to enter.

D-ECDR.1.2. If the applicant meets the requirements for entry clearance as an adult dependent relative and the sponsor has limited leave the applicant will be granted limited leave of a duration which will expire at the same time as the sponsor's limited leave, and subject to a condition of no recourse to public funds. If the sponsor applies for further limited leave, the applicant may apply for further limited leave of the same duration, if the requirements in EC-DR.1.1. (c) and (d) continue to be met, and subject to no recourse to public funds.

D-ECDR.1.3. If the applicant does not meet the requirements for entry clearance as an adult dependent relative the application will be refused.

Section R-ILRDR: Requirements for indefinite leave to remain as an adult dependent relative

R-ILRDR.1.1. The requirements to be met for indefinite leave to remain as an adult dependent relative are that—

(a) the applicant is in the UK;

(b) the applicant must have made a valid application for indefinite leave to remain as an adult dependent relative;

(c) the applicant must not fall for refusal under any of the grounds in Section S-ILR: Suitability—indefinite leave to remain; and

(d) the applicant must meet all of the requirements of Section E-ILRDR: Eligibility for indefinite leave to remain as an adult dependent relative.

Section E-ILRDR: Eligibility for indefinite leave to remain as an adult dependent relative

E-ILRDR.1.1. To qualify for indefinite leave to remain as an adult dependent relative all of the requirements of paragraphs E-ILRDR.1.2. to 1.5. must be met.

E-ILRDR.1.2. The applicant must be in the UK with valid leave to remain as an adult dependent relative (except that, where paragraph 39E of these Rules applies, any current period of overstaying will be disregarded).

[**E-ILRDR.1.3.** The applicant's sponsor must at the date of application be:

(a) present and settled in the UK; or

(b) in the UK with refugee leave or as a person with humanitarian protection, or in the UK with limited leave under Appendix EU in accordance with paragraph GEN.1.3.(d), and have made an application for indefinite leave to remain.]

Note: Paragraph substituted from 23:00 on 31 December 2020 subject to savings for applications made before that time (HC 813).

E-ILRDR.1.4. The applicant must provide evidence that they can be adequately maintained, accommodated and cared for in the UK by the sponsor without recourse to public funds.

E-ILRDR.1.5. The applicant must provide an undertaking signed by the sponsor confirming that the applicant will have no recourse to public funds, and that the sponsor will be responsible for their maintenance, accommodation and care, for a period ending 5 years from the date the applicant entered the UK with limited leave as an adult dependent relative.

Section D-ILRDR: Decision on application for indefinite leave to remain as an adult dependent relative

D-ILRDR.1.1. If the applicant meets the requirements for indefinite leave to remain as an adult dependent relative and the applicant's sponsor is settled in the UK, the applicant will be granted indefinite leave to remain as an adult dependent relative.

D-ILRDR.1.2. If the applicant does not meet the requirements for indefinite leave to remain as an adult dependent relative because paragraph S-ILR.1.5. or S-ILR.1.6. applies, the applicant will be granted further limited leave to remain as an adult dependent relative for a period not exceeding 30 months, and subject to a condition of no recourse to public funds.

D-ILRDR.1.3. If the applicant's sponsor has made an application for indefinite leave to remain and that application is refused, the applicant's application for indefinite leave to remain will be refused. If the sponsor is granted limited leave, the applicant will be granted further limited leave as an adult dependent relative of a duration which will expire at the same time as the sponsor's further limited leave, and subject to a condition of no recourse to public funds.

D-ILRDR.1.4. Where an applicant does not meet the requirements for indefinite leave to remain, or further limited leave to remain under paragraphs D-ILRDR.1.2. or 1.3., the application will be refused.

Deportation and removal

[Where the Secretary of State or an immigration officer is considering deportation or removal of a person who claims that their deportation or removal from the UK would be a breach of the right to respect for private and family life under Article 8 of the Human Rights Convention that person may be required to make an application under this Appendix or Appendix Private Life, but if they are not required to make an application Part 13 of these Rules will apply.]

Note: Paragraph substituted from 20 June 2022 subject to savings for applications made before that date (HC 1118).

Appendix FM-SE

Family Members—Specified Evidence

Family Members—Specified Evidence

A. This Appendix sets out the specified evidence applicants need to provide to meet the requirements of rules contained in Appendix FM and, where those requirements are also contained in other rules, including Appendix Armed Forces, and unless otherwise stated, the specified evidence applicants need to provide to meet the requirements of those rules.

B. Where evidence is not specified by Appendix FM, but is of a type covered by this Appendix, the requirements of this Appendix shall apply.

C. In this Appendix references to paragraphs are to paragraphs of this Appendix unless the context otherwise requires.

D. (a) In deciding an application in relation to which this Appendix states that specified documents must be provided, the Entry Clearance Officer or Secretary of State ('the decision-maker') will consider documents that have been submitted with the application, and will only consider documents submitted after the application where sub-paragraph (b) or (e) or (f) applies.

(b) If the applicant:

(i) Has submitted:

(aa) A sequence of documents and some of the documents in the sequence have been omitted (e.g. if one bank statement from a series is missing);

(bb) A document in the wrong format (for example, if a letter is not on letter-head paper as specified); or

[...]

(dd) A document which does not contain all of the specified information; or

(ii) Has not submitted a specified document, the decision-maker may contact the applicant or his representative in writing or otherwise, and request the document(s) or the correct version(s). The material requested must be received at the address specified in the request within a reasonable timescale specified in the request.

(c) The decision-maker will not request documents where he or she does not anticipate that addressing the error or omission referred to in sub-paragraph (b) will lead to a grant because the application will be refused for other reasons.

(d) If the applicant has submitted:

(i) A document in the wrong format; or

[...]

(iii) A document that does not contain all of the specified information, but the missing information is verifiable from:

(1) other documents submitted with the application,

(2) the website of the organisation which issued the document, or

(3) the website of the appropriate regulatory body, the application may be granted exceptionally, providing the decision-maker is satisfied that the document(s) is genuine and that the applicant meets the requirement to which the document relates. [...]

(e) Where the decision-maker is satisfied that there is a valid reason why a specified document(s) cannot be supplied, e.g. because it is not issued in a particular country or has been permanently lost, he or she may exercise discretion not to apply the requirement for the document(s) or to request alternative or additional information or document(s) be submitted by the applicant.

(f) Before making a decision under Appendix FM or this Appendix, the decision-maker may contact the applicant or their representative in writing or otherwise to request further information or documents. The material requested must be received at the address specified in the request within a reasonable timescale specified in the request.

Note: Sub-paragraphs (b)(i)(cc) and (d)(ii), words in (d)(iii)(3) deleted from 5 November 2018 (HC 1534).

E. A reference in this Appendix to the provision of evidence from a UK government department includes evidence from a body performing an equivalent function to such a department.

Evidence of Financial Requirements under Appendix FM

A1. To meet the financial requirement under paragraphs E-ECP.3.1., E-LTRP.3.1., E-ECC.2.1. and E-LTRC.2.1. of Appendix FM, the applicant must meet:

(a) The level of financial requirement applicable to the application under Appendix FM; and

(b) The requirements specified in Appendix FM and this Appendix as to:

(i) The permitted sources of income and savings;

(ii) The time periods and permitted combinations of sources applicable to each permitted source relied upon; and

(iii) The evidence required for each permitted source relied upon.

1. In relation to evidencing the financial requirements in Appendix FM the following general provisions shall apply:

(a) Bank statements must:

(i) [be from a financial institution to which Appendix Finance applies].

[...]

(iii) in relation to personal bank statements be only in the name of:

(1) the applicant's partner, the applicant or both as appropriate; or

(2) if the applicant is a child the applicant parent's partner, the applicant's parent or both as appropriate; or

(3) if the applicant is an adult dependent relative, the applicant's sponsor or the applicant, unless otherwise stated.

(iv) cover the period(s) specified.

(v) be:

(1) on official bank stationery; or

(2) electronic bank statements which are either accompanied by a letter from the bank on its headed stationery confirming that the documents are authentic or which bear the official stamp of the issuing bank on every page.

(aa) Where a bank statement is specified in this Appendix, a building society statement, a building society pass book, a letter from the applicant's bank or building society, or a letter from a financial institution regulated by the Financial Conduct Authority and the Prudential Regulation Authority or, for overseas accounts, the appropriate regulatory body for the country in which the institution operates and the funds are located, may be submitted as an alternative to a bank statement(s) provided that:

(1) the requirements in paragraph 1(a)(i)–(iv) are met as if the document were a bank statement; and

(2) a building society pass book must clearly show:

(i) the account number;

(ii) the building society's name and logo; and

(iii) the information required on transactions, funds held and time period(s) or as otherwise specified in this Appendix in relation to bank statements; and/or

(3) a letter must be on the headed stationery of the bank, building society or other financial institution and must clearly show:

(i) the account number;

(ii) the date of the letter;

(iii) the financial institution's name and logo; and

(iv) the information required on transactions, funds held and time period(s) or as otherwise specified in this Appendix in relation to bank statements.

(b) Promises of third party support will not be accepted, except in the limited circumstances set out in paragraph 21A (and to the extent permitted by that paragraph). Existing sources of third party support will be accepted in the form of:

(i) payments from a former partner of the applicant for the maintenance of the applicant or any children of the applicant and the former partner, and payments from a former partner of the applicant's partner for the maintenance of that partner;

(ii) income from a dependent child who has turned 18, remains in the same UK household as the applicant and continues to be counted towards the financial requirement under Appendix FM;

(iii) gift of cash savings (whose source must be declared) evidenced at paragraph 1(a)(iii), provided that the cash savings have been held by the person or persons at paragraph 1(a)(iii) for at least 6 months prior to the date of application and are under their control; and

(iv) a maintenance grant or stipend associated with undergraduate study or postgraduate study or research.

(bb) Payslips must be:

(i) [. . .] formal payslips issued by the employer and showing the employer's name; or

(ii) accompanied by a letter from the employer, on the employer's headed paper and signed by a senior official, confirming the payslips are authentic;

(c) Employment or self-employment income of an applicant will be taken into account if they are in the UK, aged 18 years or over and working legally, and prospective employment income will not be taken into account (except that of an applicant's partner or parent's partner who is returning to employment or self-employment in the UK at paragraphs E-ECP.3.2.(a) and E-ECC.2.2.(a) of Appendix FM or where paragraph 21A of this Appendix so permits).

(cc) The income of an applicant or sponsor working in the UK in salaried or non-salaried employment or in self-employment can include income from work undertaken overseas, provided paragraph E-LTRP.1.10 of Appendix FM and the other requirements of this Appendix are met.

(d) All income and savings must be lawfully derived.

(e) Savings must be held in cash.

(f) Income or cash savings in a foreign currency will be converted to pounds sterling using the closing spot exchange rate which appears on www.oanda.com* on the date of application.

(g) Where there is income or cash savings in different foreign currencies, each will be converted into pounds sterling before being added together, and then added to any UK income or savings to give a total amount.

[. . .]

(i) Evidence of profit from the sale of a business, property, investment, bond, stocks, shares or other asset will:

(i) not be accepted as evidence of income, but

(ii) the associated funds will be accepted as cash savings subject to the requirements of this Appendix and Appendix FM.

(j) Where any specified documents provided are not in English or Welsh, the applicant must provide the [document in the original language] and a full translation that can be independently verified by the Entry Clearance Officer, Immigration Officer or the Secretary of State. The translation must be dated and include:

(i) confirmation that it is an accurate translation of the [. . .] document;

(ii) the full name and [. . .] signature of the translator or an authorised official of the translation company;

(iii) the translator or translation company's contact details; and

(iv) if the applicant is applying for leave to remain or indefinite leave to remain, certification by a qualified translator and details of the translator or translation company's credentials.

(k) Where the gross (pre-tax) amount of any income cannot be properly evidenced, the net (post-tax) amount will be counted, including towards a gross income requirement.

(l) Where this Appendix requires the applicant to provide specified evidence relating to a period which ends with the date of application, that evidence, or the most recently dated part of it, must be dated no earlier than 28 days before the date of application.

(m) Cash income on which the correct tax has been paid may be counted as income under this Appendix, subject to the relevant evidential requirements of this Appendix.

(n) The gross amount of any cash income may be counted where the person's specified bank statements show the net amount which relates to the gross amount shown on their payslips (or in the relevant specified evidence provided in addition to the specified bank statements in relation to non-employment income). Otherwise, only the net amount shown on the specified bank statements may be counted.

(o) In this Appendix, a reference to the 'average' is a reference to the mean average.

Note: Words in (bb)(i), (j)(i) and (ii), (h) deleted; words in (j) substituted from 5 November 2018 (HC 1534). Words in (a)(i) substituted; (a)(ii) deleted from 23:00 on 31 December 2020 subject to savings for applications made before that time (HC 813).

2. In respect of salaried employment in the UK (except where paragraph 9 applies), all of the following evidence must be provided:

(a) Payslips covering:

(i) a period of 6 months prior to the date of application if the person has been employed by their current employer for at least 6 months (and where paragraph 13(b) of this Appendix does not apply); or

(ii) any period of salaried employment in the period of 12 months prior to the date of application if the person has been employed by their current employer for less than 6 months (or at least 6 months but the person does not rely on paragraph 13(a) of this Appendix), or in the financial year(s) relied upon by a self-employed person.

(b) A letter from the employer(s) who issued the payslips at paragraph 2(a) confirming:

(i) the person's employment and gross annual salary;

(ii) the length of their employment;

(iii) the period over which they have been or were paid the level of salary relied upon in the application; and

(iv) the type of employment (permanent, fixed-term contract or agency).

(c) Personal bank statements corresponding to the same period(s) as the payslips at paragraph 2(a), showing that the salary has been paid into an account in the name of the person or in the name of the person and their partner jointly.

(d) Where the person is a director of a limited company based in the UK, evidence that the company is not of a type specified in paragraph 9(a). This can include the latest Annual Return filed at Companies House.

(e) Where a person appointed as a non-executive director of a limited company based in the UK, which is not a company of the type specified in paragraph 9(a), is paid a fee instead of a salary, this income may be treated and evidenced as though it were income received for employment in that capacity.

2A. (i) In respect of salaried employment in the UK (paragraph 2 of this Appendix), statutory or contractual maternity, paternity, adoption or sick pay in the UK (paragraph 5 or 6 of this Appendix), or a director's salary paid to a self-employed person (paragraph 9 of this Appendix), the applicant may, in addition to the payslips and personal bank statements required under that paragraph, submit the P60 for the relevant period(s) of employment relied upon (if issued). If they do not, the Entry Clearance Officer or Secretary of State may grant the application if otherwise satisfied that the requirements of this Appendix relating to that employment are met. The Entry Clearance Officer or Secretary of State may request that the applicant submit the document(s) in accordance with paragraph D of this Appendix.

(ii) In respect of salaried employment in the UK (paragraph 2 of this Appendix), or statutory or contractual maternity, paternity, adoption or sick pay in the UK (paragraph 5 or 6 of this Appendix), the applicant may, in addition to the letter from the employer(s) required under that paragraph, submit a signed contract of employment. If they do not, the Entry Clearance Officer or Secretary of State may grant the application if otherwise satisfied that the requirements of this Appendix relating to that employment are met. The Entry Clearance Officer or Secretary of State may request that the applicant submit the document(s) in accordance with paragraph D of this Appendix.

3. In respect of salaried employment outside of the UK, evidence should be a reasonable equivalent to that set out in paragraph 2 and (where relevant) paragraph 2A. In respect of an equity partner whose income from the partnership is treated as salaried employment under paragraph 17, the payslips and employer's letter referred to in paragraph 2 may be replaced by other evidence providing the relevant information in paragraph 2 (which may include, but is not confined to, a letter on official stationery from an accountant, solicitor or business manager acting for the partnership).

4. In respect of a job offer in the UK (for an applicant's partner or parent's partner returning to salaried employment in the UK at paragraphs E-ECP.3.2.(a) and E-ECC.2.2.(a) of Appendix FM) a letter from the employer must be provided:

(a) confirming the job offer, the gross annual salary and the starting date of the employment which must be within 3 months of the applicant's partner's return to the UK; or

(b) enclosing a signed contract of employment, which must have a starting date within 3 months of the applicant's partner's return to the UK.

5. In respect of statutory or contractual maternity, paternity or adoption pay all of the following, and in respect of parental leave in the UK only the evidence at paragraph 5(c), must be provided:

(a) Personal bank statements corresponding to the same period(s) as the payslips at paragraph 5(b), showing that the salary has been paid into an account in the name of the person or in the name of the person and their partner jointly.

(b) Payslips covering:

(i) a period of 6 months prior to the date of application or to the commencement of the maternity, paternity or adoption leave, if the applicant has been employed by their current employer for at least 6 months (and where paragraph 13(b) does not apply); or

(ii) any period of salaried employment in the period of 12 months prior to the date of application or to the commencement of the maternity, paternity or adoption leave, if the applicant has been employed by their current employer for less than 6 months (or at least 6 months but the person does not rely on paragraph 13(a)).

(c) A letter from the employer confirming:

(i) the length of the person's employment;

(ii) the gross annual salary and the period over which it has been paid at this level;

(iii) the entitlement to maternity, paternity, parental or adoption leave; and

(iv) the date of commencement and the end-date of the maternity, paternity, parental or adoption leave.

6. In respect of statutory or contractual sick pay in the UK all of the following must be provided:

(a) Personal bank statements corresponding to the same period(s) as the payslips at paragraph 6(b), showing that the salary has been paid into an account in the name of the person or in the name of the person and their partner jointly.

(b) Payslips covering:

(i) a period of 6 months prior to the date of application or to the commencement of the sick leave, if the applicant has been employed by their current employer for at least 6 months (and where paragraph 13(b) does not apply); or,

(ii) any period of salaried employment in the period of 12 months prior to the date of application or to the commencement of the sick leave, if the applicant has been employed by their current employer for less than 6 months (or at least 6 months but the person does not rely on paragraph 13(a)).

(c) A letter from employer confirming:

(i) the length of the person's employment;

(ii) the gross annual salary and the period over which it has been paid at this level;

(iii) that the person is in receipt of statutory or contractual sick pay; and

(iv) the date of commencement of the sick leave.

7. In respect of self-employment in the UK as a partner, as a sole trader or in a franchise all of the following must be provided:

(a) Evidence of the amount of tax payable, paid and unpaid for the last full financial year.

(b) The following documents for the last full financial year, or for the last two such years (where those documents show the necessary level of gross profit as an average of those two years):

(i) annual self-assessment tax return to HMRC (a copy or print-out); and

(ii) Statement of Account (SA300 or SA302).

(c) Proof of registration with HMRC as self-employed if available.

(d) Each partner's Unique Tax Reference Number (UTR) and/or the UTR of the partnership or business.

(e) Where the person holds or held a separate business bank account(s), bank statements for the same 12-month period as the tax return(s).

(f) personal bank statements for the same 12-month period as the tax return(s) showing that the income from self-employment has been paid into an account in the name of the person or in the name of the person and their partner jointly.

(g) Evidence of ongoing self-employment through the provision of at least one of the following: a bank statement dated no more than three months earlier than the date of application showing transactions relating to ongoing trading, or evidence dated no more than three months earlier than the date of application of the renewal of a licence to trade or of ongoing payment of business rates, business-related insurance premiums, employer National Insurance contributions or franchise payments to the parent company.

(h) One of the following documents must also be submitted:

(i) (aa) If the business is required to produce annual audited accounts, such accounts for the last full financial year; or

(bb) If the business is not required to produce annual audited accounts, unaudited accounts for the last full financial year and an accountant's certificate of confirmation, from an accountant who is a member of a UK Recognised Supervisory Body (as defined in the Companies Act 2006) or who is a member of the Institute of Financial Accountants[, The Association of Authorised Public Accountants, The Chartered Institute of Public Finance and Accountancy, The Chartered Institute of Management Accountants, the Association of International Accountants and The Association of Accounting Technicians.]

(ii) A certificate of VAT registration and the VAT return for the last full financial year (a copy or print-out) confirming the VAT registration number, if turnover is in excess of £79,000 or was in excess of the threshold which applied during the last full financial year;

(iii) Evidence to show appropriate planning permission or local planning authority consent is held to operate the type/class of business at the trading address (where this is a local authority requirement); or

(iv) A franchise agreement signed by both parties.

(i) The document referred to in paragraph 7(h)(iv) must be provided if the organisation is a franchise.

Note: Words in (h)(i)(bb) inserted from 4 June 2020 (CP 232).

8. In respect of self-employment outside of the UK, evidence should be a reasonable equivalent to that set out in paragraph 7.

8A. In respect of prospective self-employment in the UK (for an applicant's partner or parent's partner who, in respect of paragraph E-ECP.3.2.(a) or E-ECC.2.2.(a) of Appendix FM, is in self-employment outside the UK at the date of application and is returning to the UK to continue that self-employment), one of the following must be provided, with a starting date within three months of the person's return to the UK:

(a) An application to the appropriate authority for a licence to trade;

(b) Details of the purchase or rental of business premises;

(c) A signed employment contract or a signed contract for the provision of services; or

(d) A partnership or franchise agreement signed by the relevant parties to the agreement.

9. In respect of income from employment and/or shares in a limited company based in the UK of a type specified in paragraph 9(a), the requirements of paragraph 9(b)-(e) shall apply in place of the requirements of paragraphs 2 and 10(b).

(a) The specified type of limited company is one in which:

(i) the person is either a director or employee of the company, or both, or of another company within the same group; and

(ii) shares are held (directly or indirectly) by the person, their partner or the following family members of the person or their partner: parent, grandparent, child, stepchild, grandchild, brother, sister, uncle, aunt, nephew, niece or first cousin; and

(iii) any remaining shares are held (directly or indirectly) by fewer than five other persons.

(b) All of the following must be provided:

(i) Company Tax Return CT600 (a copy or print-out) for the last full financial year and evidence this has been filed with HMRC, such as electronic or written acknowledgment from HMRC.

(ii) Evidence of registration with the Registrar of Companies at Companies House.

(iii) If the company is required to produce annual audited accounts, such accounts for the last full financial year.

(iv) If the company is not required to produce annual audited accounts, unaudited accounts for the last full financial year and an accountant's certificate of confirmation, from an accountant who is a member of a UK Recognized Supervisory Body (as defined in the Companies Act 2006) or who is a member of the Institute of Financial Accountants[, The Association of Authorised Public Accountants, The Chartered Institute of Public Finance and Accountancy, The Chartered Institute of Management Accountants, the Association of International Accountants and The Association of Accounting Technicians.]

(v) Corporate/business bank statements covering the same 12-month period as the Company Tax Return CT600.

(vi) A current Appointment Report from Companies House.

(vii) One of the following documents must also be provided:

(1) A certificate of VAT registration and the VAT return for the last full financial year (a copy or print-out) confirming the VAT registration number, if turnover is in excess of £79,000 or was in excess of the threshold which applied during the last full financial year.

(2) Proof of ownership or lease of business premises.

(3) [Proof] of registration with HMRC as an employer for the purposes of PAYE and National Insurance, proof of PAYE reference number and Accounts Office reference number. This evidence may be in the form of a certified copy of the documentation issued by HMRC.

(c) Where the person is either listed as a director of the company, or is an employee of the company, or both and receives a salary from the company, all of the following documents must also be provided:

(i) Payslips and P60 (if issued) covering the same period as the Company Tax Return CT600.

(ii) Personal bank statements covering the same 12-month period as the Company Tax Return CT600 showing that the salary as a director or employee of the company, or both was paid into an account in the name of the person or in the name of the person and their partner jointly.

(d) Where the person receives dividends from the company, all of the following documents must also be provided:

(i) Dividend vouchers for all dividends declared in favour of the person during or in respect of the period covered by the Company Tax Return CT600 showing the company's and the person's details with the person's net dividend amount [. . .].

(ii) Personal bank statement(s) showing that those dividends were paid into an account in the name of the person or in the name of the person and their partner jointly.

(e) For the purposes of paragraph 19(a), evidence of ongoing employment as a director or employee of the company (or both) or of ongoing receipt of dividend income from the company must be provided. This evidence may include payslips (or dividend vouchers) and personal bank statements showing that, in the period since the latest 12-month period covered by the Company Tax Return CT600, the person's salary as a director or employee of the company (or both) (or dividend income from the company) was paid into an account in the name of the person or in the name of the person and their partner jointly. Alternative evidence may include evidence of ongoing payment of business rates, business-related insurance premiums or employer National Insurance contributions in relation to the company.

Note: Words in (d)(i) deleted from 6 July 2018 for decisions made on or after that date (HC 1154). Word in (b)(vii)(3) substituted from 5 November 2018 (HC 1534). Words in (b)(iv) inserted from 4 June 2020 (CP 232).

10. In respect of non-employment income all the following evidence, in relation to the form of income relied upon, must be provided:

(a) To evidence property rental income:

(i) Confirmation that the person or the person and their partner jointly own the property for which the rental income is received, through:

(1) A copy of the title deeds of the property or of the title register from the Land Registry (or overseas equivalent); or

(2) A mortgage statement.

(ii) personal bank statements for or from the 12-month period prior to the date of application showing the income relied upon was paid into an account in the name of the person or of the person and their partner jointly.

(iii) A rental agreement or contract.

(b) To evidence dividends (except where paragraph 9 applies) or other income from investments, stocks, shares, bonds or trust funds:

(i) A certificate showing proof of ownership and the amount(s) of any investment(s).

(ii) A portfolio report (for a financial institution regulated by the Financial Conduct Authority (and the Prudential Regulation Authority where applicable) in the UK) or a dividend voucher showing the company and person's details with the person's net dividend amount [. . .].

(iii) personal bank statements for or from the 12-month period prior to the date of application showing that the income relied upon was paid into an account in the name of the person or of the person and their partner jointly.

(iv) Where the person is a director of a limited company based in the UK, evidence that the company is not of a type specified in paragraph 9(a). This can include the latest Annual Return filed at Companies House.

(c) To evidence interest from savings:

(i) personal bank statements for or from the 12-month period prior to the date of application showing the amount of the savings held and that the interest was paid into an account in the name of the person or of the person and their partner jointly.

(d) To evidence maintenance payments (from a former partner of the applicant to maintain their and the applicant's child or children or the applicant, or from a former partner of the applicant's partner to maintain the applicant's partner):

(i) Evidence of a maintenance agreement through any of the following:

(1) A court order;

(2) Written voluntary agreement; or

(3) Child Support Agency documentation.

(ii) personal bank statements for or from the 12-month period prior to the date of application showing the income relied upon was paid into an account in the name of the person or the person and their partner jointly.

(e) To evidence a pension:

(i) Official documentation from:

(1) The Department for Work and Pensions (in respect of the Basic State Pension and the Additional or Second State Pension) or other government department or agency, including the Veterans Agency;

(2) An overseas pension authority; or

(3) A pension company, confirming pension entitlement and amount (and where applicable, reflecting any funds withdrawn from the pension account or fund).

(ii) At least one personal bank statement in the 12-month period prior to the date of application showing payment of the pension into the person's account.

(iii) For the purposes of sub-paragraph (i), War Disablement Pension, War Widow's/Widower's Pension and any other pension or equivalent payment for life made under the War Pensions Scheme, the Armed Forces Compensation Scheme or the Armed Forces Attributable Benefits Scheme may be treated as a pension, unless excluded under paragraph 21 of this Appendix.

(f) To evidence UK Maternity Allowance, Bereavement Allowance, Bereavement Payment and Widowed Parent's Allowance:

(i) Department for Work and Pensions documentation confirming the person or their partner is or was in receipt of the benefit in the 12-month period prior to the date of application.

(ii) personal bank statements for or from the 12-month period prior to the date of application showing the income was paid into the person's account.

(ff) Subject to paragraph 12, to evidence payments under the War Pensions Scheme, the Armed Forces Compensation Scheme or the Armed Forces Attributable Benefits Scheme which are not treated as a pension for the purposes of paragraph 10(e)(i):

(i) Veterans Agency or Department for Work and Pensions documentation in the form of an award notification letter confirming the person or their partner is or was in receipt of the payment at the date of application.

(ii) personal bank statements for or from the 12-month period prior to the date of application showing the income was paid into the person's account.

(g) To evidence a maintenance grant or stipend (not a loan) associated with undergraduate study or postgraduate study or research:

(i) Documentation from the body or company awarding the grant or stipend confirming that the person is currently in receipt of the grant or stipend or will be within 3 months of the date of application, confirming that the grant or stipend will be paid for a period of at least 12 months or for at least one full academic year from the date of application or from the date on which payment of the grant or stipend will commence, and confirming the annual amount of the grant or stipend. Where the grant or stipend is or will be paid on a tax-free basis, the amount of the gross equivalent may be counted as income under this Appendix.

(ii) personal bank statements for any part of the 12-month period prior to the date of the application during which the person has been in receipt of the grant or stipend showing the income was paid into the person's account.

(h) To evidence ongoing insurance payments (such as, but not exclusively, payments received under an income protection policy):

(i) documentation from the insurance company confirming:

(a) that in the 12 months prior to the date of application the person has been in receipt of insurance payments and the amount and frequency of the payments.

(b) the reason for the payments and their expected duration.

(c) that, provided any relevant terms and conditions continue to be met, the payment(s) will continue for at least the 12 months following the date of application.

(ii) personal bank statements for or from the 12-month period prior to the date of application showing the insurance payments were paid into the person's account.

(i) To evidence ongoing payments (other than maintenance payments under paragraph 10(d)) arising from a structured legal settlement (such as, but not exclusively, one arising from settlement of a personal injury claim):

(i) documentation from a court or the person's legal representative confirming:

(a) that in the 12 months prior to the date of application the person has been in receipt of structured legal settlement payments and the amount and frequency of those payments.

(b) the reason for the payments and their expected duration.

(c) that the payment(s) will continue for at least the 12 months following the date of application.

(ii) personal bank statements for or from the 12-month period prior to the date of application showing the payments were paid into the person's account, either directly or via the person's legal representative.

Note: Words in (b)(ii) deleted from 6 July 2018 for decisions made on or after that date (HC 1154).

11. In respect of cash savings the following must be provided:

(a) personal bank statements showing that at least the level of cash savings relied upon in the application has been held in an account(s) in the name of the person or of the person and their partner jointly throughout the period of 6 months prior to the date of application.

(b) A declaration by the account holder(s) of the source(s) of the cash savings.

11A. In respect of cash savings:

(a) The savings may be held in any form of bank/savings account (whether a current, deposit or investment account, provided by a financial institution regulated by the appropriate regulatory body for the country in which that institution is operating), provided that the account allows the savings to be accessed immediately (with or without a penalty for withdrawing funds without notice). This can include savings held in a pension savings account which can be immediately withdrawn.

(b) Paid out competition winnings or a legacy which has been paid can contribute to cash savings.

(c) Funds held as cash savings by the applicant, their partner or both jointly at the date of application can have been transferred from investments, stocks, shares, bonds or trust funds within the period of 6 months prior to the date of application, provided that:

(i) The funds have been in the ownership and under the control of the applicant, their partner or both jointly for at least the period of 6 months prior to the date of application.

(ii) The ownership of the funds in the form of investments, stocks, shares, bonds or trust funds; the cash value of the funds in that form at or before the beginning of the period of 6 months prior to the date of application; and the transfer of the funds into cash, are evidenced by a portfolio report or other relevant documentation from a financial institution regulated by the appropriate regulatory body for the country in which that institution is operating.

(iii) The requirements of this Appendix in respect of the cash savings held at the date of application are met, except that the period of 6 months prior to the date of application in paragraph 11(a) will be reduced by the amount of that period in which the relevant funds were held in the form of investments, stocks, shares, bonds or trust funds.

(iv) For the purposes of sub-paragraph 11A(c), 'investments' includes funds held in an investment account or pension account or fund which does not meet the requirements of paragraphs 11 and 11A(a).

(d) Funds held as cash savings by the applicant, their partner or both jointly at the date of application can be from the proceeds of the sale of property, in the form only of a dwelling, other building or land, which took place within the period of 6 months prior to the date of application, provided that:

(i) The property (or relevant share of the property) was owned at the beginning of the period of 6 months prior to the date of application and at the date of sale by the applicant, their partner or both jointly.

(ii) Where ownership of the property was shared with a third party, only the proceeds of the sale of the share of the property owned by the applicant, their partner or both jointly may be counted.

(iii) The funds deposited as cash savings are the net proceeds of the sale, once any mortgage or loan secured on the property (or relevant share of the property) has been repaid and once any taxes and professional fees associated with the sale have been paid.

(iv) The decision-maker is satisfied that the requirements in sub-paragraphs (i)–(iii) are met on the basis of information and documents submitted in support of the application. These may include for example:

(1) Registration information or documentation (or a copy of this) from the Land Registry (or overseas equivalent).

(2) A letter from a solicitor (or other relevant professional, if the sale takes place overseas) instructed in the sale of the property confirming the sale price and other relevant information.

(3) A letter from a lender (a bank or building society) on its headed stationery regarding the repayment of a mortgage or loan secured on the property.

(4) Confirmation of payment of taxes or professional fees associated with the sale.

(5) Any other relevant evidence that the requirements in subparagraphs (i)–(iii) are met.

(v) The requirements of this Appendix in respect of the cash savings held at the date of application are met, except that the period of 6 months mentioned in paragraph 11(a) will be reduced by the amount of time which passed between the start of that 6-month period and the deposit of the proceeds of the sale in an account mentioned in paragraph 11(a).

12. Where a person is in receipt of Carer's Allowance, Disability Living Allowance, Severe Disablement Allowance, Industrial Injuries Disablement Benefit, Attendance Allowance or Personal Independence Payment or Armed Forces Independence Payment or Guaranteed Income Payment under the Armed Forces Compensation Scheme or Constant Attendance Allowance, Mobility Supplement or War Disablement Pension under the War Pensions Scheme, or a Police Injury Pension all the following must be provided:

(a) Official documentation from the Department for Work and Pensions or Veterans Agency or Police Pension Authority confirming the current entitlement and the amount currently received

(b) At least one personal bank statement in the 12-month period prior to the date of application showing payment of the amount of the benefit or allowance to which the person is currently entitled into their account.

12A. Where the financial requirement the applicant must meet under Appendix FM relates to adequate maintenance, paragraphs 2 to 12 apply only to the extent and in the manner specified by this paragraph. Where such a financial requirement applies, the applicant must provide the following evidence:

(a) Where the current salaried employment in the UK of the applicant or their partner, parent, parent's partner or sponsor is relied upon:

(i) A letter from the employer confirming the employment, the gross annual salary and the annual salary after income tax and National Insurance contributions have been paid, how long the employment has been held, and the type of employment (permanent, fixed-term contract or agency).

(ii) Payslips covering the period of 6 months prior to the date of application or such shorter period as the current employment has been held.

(iii) personal bank statement covering the same period as the payslips, showing that the salary has been paid into an account in the name of the person or in the name of the person and their partner jointly.

(b) Where statutory or contractual maternity, paternity, adoption or sick pay in the UK of the applicant or their partner, parent, parent's partner or sponsor are relied upon, paragraph 5(b)(i) and (c) or paragraph 6(b)(i) and (c) apply as appropriate.

(c) Where self-employment in the UK of the applicant or their partner, parent, parent's partner or sponsor, or income from employment and/or shares in a limited company based in the UK of a type to which paragraph 9 applies, is relied upon, paragraph 7 or 9 applies as appropriate.

(d) Where the non-employment income of the applicant or their partner, parent, parent's partner or sponsor is relied upon, paragraph 10 applies and paragraph 10 shall apply as if it referred to any UK welfare benefit or tax credit relied upon and to HMRC as well as Department for Work and Pensions or other official documentation.

(e) Where the cash savings of the applicant or their partner, parent, parent's partner or sponsor are relied upon, paragraphs 11 and 11A apply.

(f) The monthly housing and Council Tax costs for the accommodation in the UK in which the applicant (and any other family members who are or will be part of the same household) lives or will live if the application is granted.

(g) Where the applicant is an adult dependent relative applying for entry clearance, the applicant must in addition provide details of the care arrangements in the UK planned for them by their sponsor (which can involve other family members in the UK), of the cost of these arrangements and of how that cost will be met by the sponsor.

12B. Where the financial requirement an applicant must meet under Part 8 (excluding an applicant who is a family member of a Relevant Points Based System Migrant) or under Appendix FM relates to adequate maintenance and where cash savings are relied upon to meet the requirement in full or in part, the decision-maker will:

(a) Establish the total cash savings which meet the requirements of paragraphs 11 and 11A;

(b) Divide this figure by the number of weeks of limited leave which would be issued if the application were granted, or by 52 if the application is for indefinite leave to enter or remain;

(c) Add the figure in sub-paragraph 12B(b) to the weekly net income (before the deduction of housing costs) available to meet the requirement.

Calculating Gross Annual Income under Appendix FM

13. Based on evidence that meets the requirements of this Appendix, and can be taken into account with reference to the applicable provisions of Appendix FM, gross annual income under paragraphs E-ECP.3.1., E-LTRP.3.1., E-ECC.2.1. and E-LTRC.2.1. will, subject to paragraph 21A of this Appendix, be calculated in the following ways:

(a) Where the person is in salaried employment in the UK at the date of application, has been employed by their current employer for at least 6 months and has been paid throughout the period of 6 months prior to the date of application at a level of gross annual salary which equals or exceeds the level relied upon in paragraph 13(a)(i), their gross annual income will be (where paragraph 13(b) does not apply) the total of:

(i) The level of gross annual salary relied upon in the application;

(ii) The gross amount of any specified non-employment income (other than pension income) received by them or their partner in the 12 months prior to the date of application; and

(iii) The gross annual income from a UK or foreign State pension or a private pension received by them or their partner.

(b) Where the person is in salaried employment in the UK at the date of application and has been employed by their current employer for less than 6 months (or at least 6 months but the person does not rely on paragraph 13(a)), their gross annual income will be the total of:

(i) The gross annual salary from employment as it was at the date of application;

(ii) The gross amount of any specified non-employment income (other than pension income) received by them or their partner in the 12 months prior to the date of application; and

(iii) The gross annual income from a UK or foreign State pension or a private pension received by them or their partner.

In addition, the requirements of paragraph 15 must be met.

(c) Where the person is the applicant's partner, is in salaried employment outside of the UK at the date of application, has been employed by their current employer for at least 6 months, and is returning to the UK to take up salaried employment in the UK starting within 3 months of their return, the person's gross annual income will be calculated:

(i) On the basis set out in paragraph 13(a); and also

(ii) On that basis but substituting for the gross annual salary at paragraph 13(a)(i) the gross annual salary in the salaried employment in the UK to which they are returning.

(d) Where the person is the applicant's partner, has been in salaried employment outside of the UK within 12 months of the date of application, and is returning to the UK to take up salaried employment in the UK starting within 3 months of their return, the person's gross annual income will be calculated:

(i) On the basis set out in paragraph 13(a) but substituting for the gross annual salary at paragraph 13(a)(i) the gross annual salary in the salaried employment in the UK to which they are returning; and also

(ii) On the basis set out in paragraph 15(b).

(e) Where the person is self-employed, their gross annual income will be the total of their gross income from their self-employment (and that of their partner if that person is in the UK with permission to work), from any salaried or non-salaried employment they have had or their partner has had (if their partner is in the UK with permission to work), from specified non-employment income received by them or their partner, and from income from a UK or foreign State pension or a private pension received by them or their partner, in the last full financial year or as an average of the last two full financial years. The requirements of this Appendix for specified evidence relating to these forms of income shall apply as if references to the date of application were references to the end of the relevant financial year(s). The relevant financial year(s) cannot be combined with any financial year(s) to which paragraph 9 applies and vice versa.

(f) Where the person is self-employed, they cannot combine their gross annual income at paragraph 13(e) with specified savings in order to meet the level of income required under Appendix FM.

(g) Where the person is not relying on income from salaried employment or self-employment, their gross annual income will be the total of:

(i) The gross amount of any specified non-employment income (other than pension income) received by them or their partner in the 12 months prior to the date of application; and

(ii) The gross annual income from a UK or foreign State pension or a private pension received by them or their partner.

(h) Where the person is the applicant's partner and is in self-employment outside the UK at the date of application and is returning to the UK to take up salaried employment in the UK starting within 3 months of their return, the person's gross annual income will be calculated:

(i) On the basis set out in paragraph 13(a) but substituting for the gross annual salary at paragraph 13(a)(i) the gross annual salary in the salaried employment in the UK to which they are returning; and also

(ii) On the basis set out in paragraph 13(e).

(i) Any period of unpaid maternity, paternity, adoption, parental or sick leave in the 12 months prior to the date of application will not be counted towards any period relating to employment, or any period relating to income from employment, for which this Appendix provides.

(j) The provisions of paragraph 13 which apply to self-employment and to a person who is self-employed also apply to income from employment and/or shares in a limited company based in the UK of a type to which paragraph 9 applies and to a person in receipt of such income.

(k) Where the application relies on the employment income of the applicant and the sponsor, all of that income must be calculated either under sub-paragraph 13(a) or under sub-paragraph 13(b) and paragraph 15, and not under a combination of these methods.

14. Where the requirements of this Appendix and Appendix FM are met by the combined income or cash savings of more than one person, the income or the cash savings must only be counted once unless stated otherwise.

15. In respect of paragraph 13(b) and paragraph 13(d), the provisions in this paragraph also apply:

(a) In order to evidence the level of gross annual income required by Appendix FM, the person must meet the requirements in paragraph 13(b) or paragraph 13(d)(i); and

(b) The person must also meet the level of gross annual income required by Appendix FM on the basis that their income is the total of:

(i) The gross income from salaried employment in the UK or overseas earned by the person in the 12 months prior to the date of application;

(ii) The gross amount of any specified non-employment income (other than pension income) received by the person or their partner in the 12 months prior to the date of application;

(iii) The gross amount received from a UK or foreign State pension or a private pension by the person or their partner in the 12 months prior to the date of application; and

(iv) The person cannot combine the gross annual income at paragraph 15(b)(i)–(iii) with specified savings in order to meet the level of income required.

16. Where a person is in receipt of maternity, paternity, adoption or sick pay or has been so in the 6 months prior to the date of application, this paragraph applies:

(a) the relevant date for considering the length of employment with their current employer will be the date that the maternity, paternity, adoption or sick leave commenced or the date of application; and

(b) the relevant period for calculating income from their salaried employment will be the period prior to the commencement of the maternity, paternity, adoption or sick pay or to the date of application.

17. If a person is an equity partner, for example in a law firm, the income they draw from the partnership (including where this is in the form of a profit share) will be treated as salaried employment for the purposes of this Appendix and Appendix FM.

17A. Where a person is a subcontractor under the Construction Industry Scheme administered by HMRC and does not rely on paragraph 13(e), the income they receive as a subcontractor under the Construction Industry Scheme may be treated as income from salaried employment for the purposes of this Appendix and Appendix FM. In that case, the requirements for specified evidence in paragraph 2 must be met, subject to applying those requirements so as to reflect the person's status as a subcontractor under the Construction Industry Scheme.

18. When calculating income from salaried employment under paragraphs 12A and 13 to 16, this paragraph applies:

(a) Basic pay, skills-based allowances, and UK location-based allowances will be counted as income provided that:

(i) They are contractual; and

(ii) Where these allowances make up more than 30% of the total salary, only the amount up to 30% is counted.

(b) Overtime, payments to cover travel time, commission-based pay and bonuses (which can include tips and gratuities paid via a tronc scheme registered with HMRC) will be counted as income, where they have been received in the relevant period(s) of employment or self-employment relied upon in the application.

(bb) In respect of a person in salaried employment at the date of application, the amount of income in sub-paragraph (b) which may be added to their gross annual salary, and counted as part of that figure for the purposes of paragraph 13(a)(i) or 13(b)(i), is the annual equivalent of the person's average gross monthly income from that income in their current employment in the 6 months prior to the date of application.

(c) Payments relating to the costs of UK or overseas travel, including (for example) travelling or relocation expenses and subsistence or accommodation allowances, and payments made towards the costs of living overseas, will not be counted as income.

(d) Gross income from non-salaried employment will be calculated on the same basis as income from salaried employment, except as provided in paragraph 18(e) and 18(f), and the requirements of this Appendix for specified evidence relating to salaried employment shall apply as if references to salary were references to income from non-salaried employment. Non-salaried employment includes that paid at an hourly or other rate (and the number and/or pattern of hours required to be worked may vary), or paid an amount which varies according to the work undertaken, whereas salaried employment includes that paid at a minimum fixed rate (usually annual) and is subject usually to a contractual minimum number of hours to be worked.

(e) For the purpose of paragraph 13(a)(i), in respect of a person in non-salaried employment at the date of application 'the level of gross annual salary relied upon in the application' shall be no greater than the annual equivalent of the person's average gross monthly income from non-salaried employment in the 6 months prior to the date of application, where that employment was held throughout that period.

(f) For the purpose of paragraph 13(b)(i), 'the gross annual salary from employment as it was at the date of application' of a person in non-salaried employment at the date of application shall be considered to be the annual equivalent of:

(aa) the person's gross income from non-salaried employment in the period immediately prior to the date of application, where the employment has been held for a period of no more than one month at the date of application; or

(bb) the person's average gross monthly income from non-salaried employment, where the employment has been held for a period of more than one month at the date of application.

(g) For the purpose of paragraphs 13(c)(ii) and 13(d)(i), 'the gross annual salary in the salaried employment in the UK to which they are returning' of a person who is returning to the UK to take up non-salaried employment in the UK starting within 3 months of their return is the gross annual income from that employment, based on the rate or amount of pay, and the standard or core hours of work, set out in the document(s) from the employer provided under paragraph 4. Notwithstanding paragraph 18(b), this may include the gross 'on-target' earnings which may be expected from satisfactory performance in the standard or core hours of work.

19. When calculating income from self-employment under paragraphs 12A and 13(e), and in relation to income from employment and/or shares in a limited company based in the UK of a type to which paragraph 9 applies, this paragraph applies:

(a) There must be evidence of ongoing self-employment, and (where income from salaried employment is also relied upon or where paragraph 9(c) applies) ongoing employment, at the date of application.

(b) Where the self-employed person is a sole trader or is in a partnership or franchise agreement, the income will be the gross taxable profits from their share of the business in the relevant financial year(s), not including any deductable allowances, expenses or liabilities which may be applied to the gross taxable profits to establish the final tax liability.

(c) Where income to which paragraph 19 applies is being used to meet the financial requirement for an initial application for leave to remain as a partner under Appendix FM by an applicant who used such income to meet that requirement in an application for entry clearance as a fiancé(e) or proposed civil partner under that Appendix in the last 12 months, the Secretary of State may continue to accept the same level and evidence of income to which paragraph 19 applies that was accepted in granting the application for entry clearance, provided that there is evidence of ongoing self-employment, and (where income from salaried employment is also relied upon or where paragraph 9(c) applies) ongoing employment, at the date of the application for leave to remain.

(d) The financial year(s) to which paragraph 7 refers is the period of the last full financial year(s) to which the required Statement(s) of Account (SA300 or SA302) relates.

(e) The financial year(s) to which paragraph 9 refers is the period of the last full financial year(s) to which the required Company Tax Return(s) CT600 relates.

20. When calculating income from specified non-employment sources under paragraphs 12A and 13 to 15, this paragraph applies:

(a) Assets or savings must be in the name of the person, or jointly with their partner.

(b) Any asset or savings on which income is based must be held or owned by the person at the date of application.

(c) Any rental income from property, in the UK or overseas, must be from a property that is:

(i) owned by the person;

(ii) not their main residence and will not be so if the application is granted, except in the circumstances specified in paragraph 20(e); and

(iii) if ownership of the property is shared with a third party, only income received from their share of the property can be counted.

(cc) The amount of rental income from property received before any management fee was deducted may be counted.

(d) Equity in a property cannot be used to meet the financial requirement.

(e) Where the applicant and their partner are resident outside the UK at the date of application, rental income from a property in the UK that will become their main residence if the application is granted may only be counted under paragraph 13(c)(i) and paragraph 13(d)(ii).

(f) Any future entitlement to a maintenance grant or stipend of the type specified in paragraph 10(g) may be counted as though the person had received the annual amount of that grant or stipend in the 12 months prior to the date of application.

20A. When calculating the gross annual income from pension under paragraph 13, the gross annual amount of any pension received may be counted where the pension has become a source of income at least 28 days prior to the date of application.

21. When calculating income under paragraphs 13 to 16, the following sources will not be counted:

(a) Loans and credit facilities.

(b) Income-related benefits: Income Support, income-related Employment and Support Allowance, Pension Credit, Housing Benefit, Council Tax Benefit or Support or any equivalent and income-based Jobseeker's Allowance.

(c) The following contributory benefits: contribution-based Jobseeker's Allowance, contribution-based Employment and Support Allowance and Incapacity Benefit.

(cc) Unemployability Allowance, Allowance for a Lowered Standard of Occupation and Invalidity Allowance under the War Pension Scheme.

(d) Child Benefit.

(e) Working Tax Credit.
(f) Child Tax Credit.
(ff) Universal Credit.
(g) Any other source of income not specified in this appendix.

Other sources of income, financial support or funds in exceptional circumstances

21A. (1). Where paragraph GEN.3.1.(1) of Appendix FM applies, the decision-maker is required to take into account the sources of income, financial support or funds specified in sub-paragraph (2).

(2) Subject to sub-paragraphs (3) to (8), the following sources of income, financial support or funds will be taken into account (in addition to those set out in, as appropriate, paragraph E-ECP.3.2., E-LTRP.3.2., E-ECC.2.2. or E-LTRC.2.2. of Appendix FM):

(a) a credible guarantee of sustainable financial support to the applicant or their partner from a third party;

(b) credible prospective earnings from the sustainable employment or self-employment of the applicant or their partner; or

(c) any other credible and reliable source of income or funds for the applicant or their partner, which is available to them at the date of application or which will become available to them during the period of limited leave applied for.

(3) Where the applicant is a child:

(a) other references in this paragraph to 'applicant' mean the 'applicant's parent' under paragraph E-ECC.1.6. or E-LTRC.1.6. of Appendix FM; and

(b) references in this paragraph to 'partner' refer to the 'applicant's parent's partner' under those paragraphs.

(4) The onus is on the applicant to satisfy the decision-maker of the genuineness, credibility and reliability of the source of income, financial support or funds relied upon, on the basis of the information and evidence provided, having regard (in particular, but without limitation) to the factors set out below.

(5) The source of income, financial support or funds must not be a loan, unless evidence submitted with the application shows that:

(a) the source is a mortgage on a residential or commercial property in the UK or overseas which at the date of application is owned by the applicant, their partner or both, or by the third party to whom sub-paragraph (2)(a) refers;

(b) the mortgage is provided by a financial institution regulated by the appropriate regulatory body for the country in which that institution is operating; and

(c) the mortgage payments are reasonably affordable by the person(s) responsible for them and are likely to remain so for the period of limited leave applied for.

(6) Any cash savings or any current financial investment or product relied upon by the applicant under sub-paragraph (2)(c) must at the date of application be in the name(s), and under the control, of the applicant, their partner or both.

(7) Any cash savings relied upon by the applicant must enable the financial requirement in paragraph E-ECP.3.1.(b), E-LTRP.3.1.(b), E-ECC.2.1.(b) or E-LTRC.2.1.(b) of Appendix FM (as applicable) to be met, except that the criteria in sub-paragraph (8)(c) apply in place of the requirements in paragraphs 11 and 11A of this Appendix.

(8) In determining the genuineness, credibility and reliability of the source of income, financial support or funds relied upon under sub-paragraph (2), the decision-maker will take into account all the information and evidence provided, and will consider (in particular):

(a) in respect of a guarantee of sustainable financial support from a third party:

(i) whether the applicant has provided verifiable documentary evidence from the third party in question of their guarantee of financial support;

(ii) whether that evidence is signed, dated and witnessed or otherwise independently verified;

(iii) whether the third party has provided sufficient evidence of their general financial situation to enable the decision-maker to assess the likelihood of the guaranteed financial support continuing for the period of limited leave applied for;

(iv) whether the third party has provided verifiable documentary evidence of the nature, extent and duration of any current or previous financial support which they have provided to the applicant or their partner;

(v) the extent to which this source of financial support is relied upon by the applicant to meet the financial requirement in paragraph E-ECP.3.1., E-LTRP.3.1., E-ECC.2.1. or E-LTRC.2.1. of Appendix FM (as applicable); and

(vi) the likelihood of a change in the third party's financial situation or in their relationship with the applicant or the applicant's partner during the period of limited leave applied for.

(b) in respect of prospective earnings from sustainable employment or self-employment of the applicant or their partner:

(i) whether, at the date of application, a specific offer of employment has been made, or a clear basis for self-employment exists. In either case, such employment or self-employment must be expected to commence within three months of the applicant's arrival in the UK (if the applicant is applying for entry clearance) or within three months of the date of application (if the applicant is applying for leave to remain);

(ii) whether the applicant has provided verifiable documentary evidence of the offer of employment or the basis for self-employment, and, if so, whether that evidence:

(aa) is on the headed notepaper of the company or other organisation offering the employment, or of a company or other organisation which has agreed to purchase the goods or services of the applicant or their partner as a self-employed person;

(bb) is signed, dated and witnessed or otherwise independently verified;

(cc) includes (in respect of an offer of employment) a signed or draft contract of employment;

(dd) includes (in respect of self-employment) any of a signed or draft contract for the provision of goods or services; a signed or draft partnership or franchise agreement; an application to the appropriate authority for a licence to trade; or details of the agreed or proposed purchase or rental of business premises;

(iii) whether, in respect of an offer of employment in the UK, the applicant has provided verifiable documentary evidence:

(aa) of a relevant employment advertisement and employment application;

(bb) of the hours to be worked and the rate of gross pay, which that evidence must establish equals or exceeds the National Living Wage or the National Minimum

Wage (as applicable, given the age of the person to be employed) and equals or exceeds the going rate for such work in that part of the UK; and

(cc) which enables the decision-maker to assess the reliability of the offer of employment, including in light of the total size of the workforce and the turnover (annual gross income or sales) of the relevant company or other organisation;

(iv) whether the applicant has provided verifiable documentary evidence that at the date of application, the person to be employed or self-employed is in, or has recently been in, sustained employment or self-employment of the same or a similar type, of the same or a similar level of complexity and at the same or a similar level of responsibility;

(v) whether the applicant has provided verifiable documentary evidence that the person to be employed or self-employed has relevant professional, occupational or educational qualifications and that these are recognised in the UK;

(vi) whether the applicant has provided verifiable documentary evidence that the person to be employed or self-employed has the level of English language skills such prospective employment or self-employment is likely to require;

(vii) the extent to which this source of income is relied upon by the applicant to meet the financial requirement in paragraph E-ECP.3.1., E-LTRP.3.1., E-ECC.2.1. or E-LTRC.2.1. of Appendix FM (as applicable); and

(viii) where an offer of employment is relied upon, and where the proposed employer is a family member or friend of the applicant or their partner, the likelihood of a relevant change in that relationship during the period of limited leave applied for.

(c) in respect of any other credible and reliable source of income or funds for the applicant or their partner:

(i) whether the applicant has provided verifiable documentary evidence of the source;

(ii) whether that evidence is provided by a financial institution regulated by the appropriate regulatory body for the country in which that institution is operating, and is signed, dated and witnessed or otherwise independently verified;

(iii) where the income is or the funds are based on, or derived from, ownership of an asset, whether the applicant has provided verifiable documentary evidence of its current or previous ownership by the applicant, their partner or both;

(iv) whether the applicant has provided sufficient evidence to enable the decision-maker to assess the likelihood of the source of income or funds being available to them during the period of limited leave applied for; and

(v) the extent to which this source of income or funds is relied upon by the applicant to meet the financial requirement in paragraph E-ECP.3.1., E-LTRP.3.1., E-ECC.2.1. or E-LTRC.2.1. of Appendix FM (as applicable).

Evidence of Marriage or Civil Partnerships

22. A marriage in the United Kingdom must be evidenced by a valid marriage certificate recognised under the laws of England and Wales, Scotland or Northern Ireland.

23. A divorce in the United Kingdom must be evidenced by a decree absolute from a civil court.

24. A civil partnership in the United Kingdom must be evidenced by a civil partnership certificate.

25. The dissolution of a civil partnership in the UK must be evidenced by a final order of civil partnership dissolution from a civil court.

26. Marriages, civil partnerships or evidence of divorce or dissolution from outside the UK must be evidenced by a reasonable equivalent to the evidence detailed in paragraphs 22 to 25, valid under the law in force in the relevant country.

Evidence of the Applicant Living Overseas with a Crown Servant

[**26A.** Where:

(a) An applicant for entry clearance, limited leave to enter or remain or indefinite leave to remain as a partner under Appendix FM (except as a fiancé(e) or proposed civil partner) or Appendix Settlement Family Life intends to enter or remain in the UK to begin their probationary period (or has done so) and then to live outside the UK for the time being with their sponsor (or is doing so or has done so) before the couple live together permanently in the UK; and

(b) the sponsor, who is a British Citizen or settled in the UK, is an employee of the UK Government, a Northern Ireland department, the Scottish Administration or the Welsh Government, or a permanent member of the British Council on a tour of duty outside the UK,

the applicant must provide a letter on official stationery from the sponsor's head of mission confirming the information at (a) and (b) and confirming the start date and expected end date of the sponsor's tour of duty outside the UK.]

Note: Amendments from 23:00 on 31 December 2020 subject to savings for applications made before that date (HC 813). Paragraph substituted from 20 June 2022 subject to savings for applications made before that date (HC 1118).

Evidence of English Language Requirements

[**27.** The evidence required of passing an English language test in speaking and listening (at a minimum of level A1 or A2 (as the case may be) of the Common European Framework of Reference for Languages) with a provider approved by the Secretary of State, where the applicant relies on that pass to meet an English language requirement, is confirmation on the on-line verification system operated by an approved English language test provider and at an approved Secure English Language Test centre that:

(i) the applicant has passed such a test; and

(ii) that test was an English language test in speaking and listening which is approved by the Secretary of State and was taken no more than two years before the date of application and at a test centre approved by the Secretary of State as a Secure English Language Test Centre or if they have already shown they met the requirement in this manner at the level required for their current application, in a previous successful application for entry clearance or permission to stay.]

Note: Paragraph substituted from 1 October 2019 subject to savings for applications made before that date (HC 2631). Paragraph substituted from 6 April 2021 subject to savings for applications made before that date (HC 1248).

28. The evidence required to show that a person is a citizen or national of a majority English speaking country is a valid passport or travel document, unless paragraphs 29 and 30 apply. A dual national may invoke either of their nationalities.

29. If the applicant has not provided their passport or travel document other evidence of nationality can be supplied in the following circumstances only (as indicated by the applicant on their application form):

(a) where the passport or travel document has been lost or stolen;

(b) where the passport or travel document has expired and been returned to the relevant authorities; or

(c) where the passport or travel document is with another part of the Home Office.

30. Alternative evidence as proof of nationality, if acceptable, must be either:

(a) A current national identity document; or

(b) [A] letter from the applicant's national government, Embassy or High Commission confirming the applicant's full name, date of birth and nationality.

Note: Word in (b) substituted from 5 November 2018 (HC 1534).

31. Evidence of an academic qualification under paragraphs 284(ix)(c), (d) and (e), 290(vii)(c), (d) and (e) and 295D(xi)(c), (d) and (e) of Part 8, paragraph 68(c) of Appendix Armed Forces, and paragraphs E-ECP.4.1.(c), E-LTRP.4.1A.(c), E-LTRP.4.1.(c), E-ECPT.4.1.(c) and E-LTRPT.5.1.(c) and E-LTRPR.5.1A.(c) of Appendix FM must be:

(a) a certificate issued by the relevant institution confirming the award of the academic qualification showing:

(i) the applicant's name;

(ii) the title of award;

(iii) the date of award; and

(iv) the name of the awarding institution; or

(b) if the applicant is awaiting graduation or no longer has the certificate and cannot obtain a new one, either:

(i) an [. . .] academic reference from the institution awarding the academic qualification that:

(1) is on official letter headed paper;

(2) shows the applicant's name;

(3) shows the title of award;

(4) explains when the academic qualification has been, or will be, awarded; and

(5) confirms either the date that the certificate will be issued (if the applicant has not yet graduated) or that the institution is unable to re-issue the [. . .] certificate of award; or

(ii) an [. . .] academic transcript that:

(1) is on official letter headed paper;

(2) shows the applicant's name;

(3) shows the name of the academic institution;

(4) shows the course title; and

(5) confirms either the date that the certificate will be issued (if the applicant has not yet graduated) or that the institution is unable to re-issue the [. . .] certificate of award; and

(c) if the qualification was awarded by an educational establishment outside the UK, [a] document from [[Ecctis]] which confirms that the qualification meets or exceeds the recognised standard of a Bachelor's or Master's degree or PhD in the UK and was taught or researched in English to level A1 or A2 (as the case may be) of the Common Framework of Reference for Languages or above.

Note: Words in (b)(i), (b)(i)(5), (b)(ii), and (b)(ii)(5) deleted; words in (c) substituted from 5 November 2018 (HC 1534). Words in double square brackets substituted from 6 October 2021 subject to savings for applications made before that date (HC 617).

32. If the qualification was taken in one of the following countries, it will be assumed for the purpose of paragraph 31 that it was taught or researched in English: Antigua and Barbuda, Australia, the Bahamas, Barbados, Belize, Dominica, Grenada, Guyana, Ireland, Jamaica, New Zealand, St Kitts and Nevis, St Lucia, St Vincent and the Grenadines, Trinidad and Tobago, the UK, the USA [Malta].

Note: Word inserted from 23:00 on 31 December 2020 subject to savings for applications made before that time (HC 813).

32A. For the avoidance of doubt paragraphs 27 to 32D of this Appendix apply to fiancé(e), proposed civil partner, spouse, civil partner, unmarried partner and same sex partner applications for limited leave to enter or remain made under Part 8 of these Rules where English language requirements apply, regardless of the date of application. Paragraphs 27 to 32D of this Appendix also apply to spouse, civil partner, unmarried partner and same sex partner applications which do not meet the requirements of Part 8 of these Rules for indefinite leave to remain (where the application is for indefinite leave to remain) and are being considered for a grant of limited leave to remain where paragraph A277A(b) of these Rules applies. Any references in paragraphs 27 to 32D of this Appendix to 'limited leave to enter or remain' shall therefore be read as referring to all applicants referred to in this paragraph.

32B. Where the decision-maker has:

(a) reasonable cause to doubt that an English language test in speaking and listening at a minimum of level A1 or A2 (as the case may be) of the Common Framework of Reference for Languages relied on at any time to meet a requirement for limited leave to enter or remain in Part 8 or Appendix FM was genuinely obtained; or

(b) information that the test certificate or result awarded to the applicant has been withdrawn by the test provider for any reason, the decision-maker may discount the test certificate or result and require the applicant to provide a new test certificate or result from an approved provider which shows that they meet the requirement, if they are not exempt from it.

32C. If an applicant applying for limited leave to enter or remain under Part 8 or Appendix FM submits an English language test certificate or result which has ceased by the date of application to be:

(a) from an approved test provider, or

(b) in respect of an approved test, or

(c) from an approved test centre, the decision-maker will not accept that certificate or result as valid, unless the decision-maker does so in accordance with paragraph 32D of this Appendix and subject to any transitional arrangements made in respect of the test provider, test or test centre in question.

32D. If an applicant applying for limited leave to enter or remain under Part 8 or Appendix FM submits an English language test certificate or result and the Home Office has already accepted it as part of a successful previous partner or parent application (but not where the application was refused, even if on grounds other than the English language requirement), the decision-maker will accept that certificate or result as valid if it is:

(a) from a provider which is no longer approved, or

(b) from a provider who remains approved but the test the applicant has taken with that provider is no longer approved, or

(c) from a test centre which is no longer approved, or

[(d) past its validity date (if a validity date is required), provided that it is at or above the requisite level of the Common European Framework of Reference for Languages and when the subsequent application is made the award to the applicant does not fall within the circumstances set out in paragraph 32B of this Appendix.]

(i) the applicant has had continuous leave (disregarding any current period of overstaying where paragraph 39E of these Rules applies, as well as any previous period of overstaying where: the further application was made before 24 November 2016 and within 28 days of the expiry of leave; or the further application was made on or after 24 November 2016 and paragraph 39E of these Rules applied) as a partner or parent since the Home Office accepted the test certificate as valid; and

(ii) the award to the applicant does not fall within the circumstances set out in paragraph 32B of this Appendix.

Note: Introduction to sub-paragraph (d) substituted from 1 October 2019 subject to savings for applications made before that date (HC 2631). Sub-paragraph (d) substituted from 6 April 2021 subject to savings for applications made before that date (HC 1248).

Adult dependent relatives

33. Evidence of the family relationship between the applicant(s) and the sponsor should take the form of birth or adoption certificates, or other documentary evidence.

34. Evidence that, as a result of age, illness or disability, the applicant requires long-term personal care should take the form of:

(a) Independent medical evidence that the applicant's physical or mental condition means that they cannot perform everyday tasks; and

(b) This must be from a doctor or other health professional.

35. Independent evidence that the applicant is unable, even with the practical and financial help of the sponsor in the UK, to obtain the required level of care in the country where they are living should be from:

(a) a central or local health authority;

(b) a local authority; or

(c) a doctor or other health professional.

36. If the applicant's required care has previously been provided through a private arrangement, the applicant must provide details of that arrangement and why it is no longer available.

37. If the applicant's required level of care is not, or is no longer, affordable because payment previously made for arranging this care is no longer being made, the applicant must provide records of that payment and an explanation of why that payment cannot continue. If financial support has been provided by the sponsor or other close family in the UK, the applicant must provide an explanation of why this cannot continue or is no longer sufficient to enable the required level of care to be provided.

*This is an external website for which the Home Office is not responsible.

Appendix G [DELETED]

Note: Amendments from 1 January 2018 subject to savings for applications made before that date (HC 309). Amendments from 1 January 2019 subject to savings for applications made before that date (HC 1779). Amendments from 30 March 2019 subject to savings for applications made before that date (HC 1919). Amendments from 1 January 2020 subject to savings for applications made before that date (HC 2631). Amendments from 6 April 2020 with and without savings for applications made before that date (HC 120). Appendix G deleted from 09:00 on 1 December 2020 subject to savings for applications made before that time (HC 813). **NB:** CP 361 advises deletion of Appendix G from 23:00 on 31 December 2020 for decisions made on or after that date, however as set out above, the Appendix had already been deleted pursuant to HC 813).

[Appendix H—DELETED]

Note: Appendix substituted from 6 July 2018 subject to savings for applications made before that date (HC 1154). Amendments from 6 April 2019 subject to savings for applications made before that date (HC 1919). Appendix deleted from 09:00 on 5 October 2020 subject to savings for applications made before that time (HC 707).

Appendix J [DELETED]

Note: Amendments from 10 January 2018 subject to savings where an applicant has made an application using a Certificate of Sponsorship that was assigned by the Sponsor before that date (HC 309). Amendments from 10 January 2019 subject to savings for applications made before that date (HC 1779). Amendments from 30 March 2019 subject to savings where an applicant has made an application using a Certificate of Sponsorship that was assigned by the Sponsor before that date (HC 1919). Amendments from 1 October 2019 subject to savings for applications made before that date; amendments from 6 October 2019 subject to savings where an applicant has made an application using a Certificate of Sponsorship assigned by the Sponsor before that date (HC 2631). Amendment from 6 April 2020 (HC 120). Appendix deleted from 09:00 on 1 December 2020 subject to savings for applications made before that time (HC 813).

Appendix K [DELETED]

Note: Amendments from 11 January 2018 subject to savings for applications made before that date (HC 309). Amendments from 30 March 2019 subject to savings for applications made before that date (HC 1919). Amendments from 6 October 2019 subject to savings where an application has been made using a Certificate of Sponsorship that was assigned before that date (HC 2631). Amendment from 6 April 2020 (HC 120). Appendix deleted from 09:00 on 1 December 2020 subject to savings for applications made before that time (HC 813).

Appendix KoLL

Knowledge of language and life

Part 1—general

1.1

Purpose

This Appendix sets out how an applicant for indefinite leave to enter or remain must demonstrate sufficient knowledge of the English language and about life in the United Kingdom where it is a requirement of the Rules to demonstrate this for the purposes of an application for indefinite leave to enter or remain. It also sets out general exemptions to the requirement on grounds of age and enables the decision maker to waive the requirement in light of special circumstances in any particular case.

'Specified' in this Appendix means 'specified in Part 4 of this appendix'.

Part 2—knowledge of language and life

[2.1 An applicant for indefinite leave to enter or remain has sufficient knowledge of the English language and about life in the United Kingdom if they meet the requirements set out in paragraphs 2.2 and 2.3. They do not need to satisfy the requirements in 2.2 and 2.3 where the exceptions set out in Part 3 apply of this Appendix.]

Note: Paragraph substituted from 1 November 2018 subject to savings for applications made before that date (HC 1534).

2.2 For the purposes of paragraph 2.1, an applicant demonstrates sufficient knowledge of the English language if:

(a) the applicant has provided specified documentary evidence that:

(i) the applicant is a national or citizen of one of the following countries:

- Antigua and Barbuda
- Australia
- The Bahamas
- Barbados
- Belize
- Canada
- Dominica
- Grenada
- Guyana
- Jamaica
- New Zealand
- St Kitts and Nevis
- St Lucia
- St Vincent and the Grenadines
- Trinidad and Tobago
- USA
- [Malta].

or

(iii) [the applicant has obtained an academic qualification (not a professional or vocational qualification) which either:

(1) is a UK Bachelor's Degree, Master's Degree or PhD; or

(2)] is deemed by [[Ecctis]] to meet the recognised standard of a Bachelor's or Master's degree or PhD in the UK, from an educational establishment in one of the following countries: Antigua and Barbuda; Australia; The Bahamas; Barbados; Belize; Dominica; Grenada; Guyana; Ireland; Jamaica; New Zealand; St Kitts and Nevis; St Lucia; St Vincent and The Grenadines; Trinidad and Tobago; the UK; the USA; [Malta;] and provides the specified documents; or

(iv) the applicant has obtained an academic qualification (not a professional or vocational qualification) which is deemed by [[Eccits]] to meet the recognised standard of a Bachelor's or Master's degree or PhD in the UK, and

(1) provides the specified documentary evidence to show he has the qualification, and

(2) [[Ecctis]] has confirmed that the qualification was taught or researched in English; or

[. . .]

(b) the applicant—

(i) has limited leave to enter or remain in the UK, and

(ii) that leave (or a grant of leave which preceded it provided any periods of leave since have been unbroken) was given on the basis that the applicant had an English language qualification at a minimum level of B1 on the Common European Framework of Reference for Languages, and

(iii) at the date of application, the provider of that qualification continues to be approved by the Secretary of State [. . .].

(c) the on line verification system operated by an approved English language test provider, [as published on the UK Visas and Immigration pages of Gov.uk], confirms that the applicant has passed an English language test in speaking and listening, at a minimum level B1 of the Common European Framework of Reference for Languages, which is approved by the Secretary of State, [. . .], and taken at a test centre approved by the Secretary of State as a Secure English Language Test Centre no more than two years before the date of application.

Note: Words in (a)(iii) substituted from 1 November 2018 subject to savings for applications made before that date (HC 1534). Sub-paragraph (a)(v) deleted from 6 April 2019 subject to savings for applications made before that date (HC 1919). Words in (b)(iii) and (c) deleted; words in (c) substituted from 1 October 2019 subject to savings for applications made before that date (HC 2631). Country in (a)(i) and (a)(iii)(2) inserted from 09:00 on 1 December 2020 subject to savings for applications made before that time (HC 813). Words in double square brackets substituted from 6 October 2021 subject to savings for applications made before that date (HC 617).

2.3 For the purposes of sub-paragraph (1), an applicant demonstrates sufficient knowledge about life in the United Kingdom if:

(a) the applicant has passed the test known as the 'Life in the UK test' administered by [by an educational institution or other person approved for this purpose by the Secretary of State]; or

(b) in respect of an applicant who was resident in the Isle of Man, the applicant took and passed the test in the Isle of Man known as the 'Life in the UK test' and which was administered by an educational institution or other person approved for that purpose by the Lieutenant Governor; or

(c) in respect of an applicant who was resident in the Bailiwick of Guernsey or in the Bailiwick of Jersey, the applicant took and passed the test known as the 'Citizenship Test' and which was administered by an educational institution or other person approved for that purpose by the Lieutenant Governor of Guernsey or Jersey (as the case may be).

Note: Words substituted from 6 July 2018 subject to savings for applications made before that date (HC 1154).

Part 3—exceptions

3.1 Notwithstanding any requirement to the contrary in these Rules, for the purposes of this appendix, an applicant will not be required to demonstrate sufficient knowledge of the English language and about life in the UK where:

(a) the applicant is under 18 years of age at the date of his or her application, or

(b) the applicant is at least 65 years of age at the date of his or her application, or

(c) in all the circumstances of the case, the decision maker considers that, because of the applicant's mental or physical condition, it would be unreasonable to expect the applicant to fulfil [either or both parts of] that requirement.

Note: Words inserted from 1 November 2018 subject to savings for applications made before that date (HC 1534).

3.2 In the following circumstances an applicant will be deemed to have demonstrated sufficient knowledge of the English language and about life in the UK:

(a) Where the application for indefinite leave to enter or remain in the United Kingdom is made under:

(i) paragraph 196D[,as a dependent partner under Appendix UK Ancestry or Appendix Representative of an Overseas Business] and the applicant has had, as at the day on which the application is made, continuous leave to enter or remain in the United Kingdom for at least 15 years as the spouse or civil partner of a person who has or has had leave to enter or remain under paragraphs 128–193 (but not paragraphs 135I–135K), or

(ii) paragraph 199[, as a dependent child under Appendix UK Ancestry or Appendix Representative of an Overseas Business] and the applicant has had, as at the day on which the application was made, continuous leave to enter or remain in the United Kingdom for at least 15 years as the child of a person who has or has had leave to enter or remain in the United Kingdom under paragraphs 128–193 (but not paragraphs 135l–135K), or

(iii) paragraph 248D and the applicant has had, as at the day on which the application was made, continuous leave to enter or remain in the United Kingdom for at least 15 years as a person exercising rights of access to a child resident in the United Kingdom and that child is under the age of 18 at the day on which the applicant's application for indefinite leave is made under paragraph 248D, or

(iv) paragraph 273D and the applicant has had, as at the day on which the application is made, continuous leave to enter or remain in the United Kingdom for at least 15 years as a spouse or civil partner of a person who has or has had leave to enter or remain in the United Kingdom as a retired person of independent means, or

(v) paragraph 275A and the applicant has had, as at the day on which the application was made, continuous leave to enter or remain in the United Kingdom for at least 15 years as the child of a person who has or has had leave to enter or remain in the United Kingdom as a retired person of independent means, or

(vi) paragraph 287 and the applicant has had, as at the day on which the application is made, continuous leave to enter or remain in the United Kingdom for at least 15 years under paragraph 281 or paragraph 284, or

(vii) paragraph 295G and the applicant has had, as at the day on which the application is made, continuous leave to enter or remain in the United Kingdom for at least 15 years under paragraph 295B or paragraph 295D, or

(viii) paragraph 298 and the applicant has had, as at the day on which the application is made, continuous leave to enter or remain in the United Kingdom for at least 15 years under paragraph 302 or Appendix FM or paragraph 319R or paragraph 319X, or

(ix) paragraph 319E[, a dependent partner under Appendix Skilled Worker, Appendix Global Talent, Appendix Innovator, Appendix T2 Minister of Religion, or Appendix T2 Sportsperson] and the applicant has had, as at the day on which the application is made, continuous leave to enter or remain in the United Kingdom for at least 15 years as the partner of a relevant points based system migrant, or

(x) paragraph 319J[, a dependent child under Appendix Skilled Worker, Appendix Global Talent, Appendix Innovator, Appendix T2 Minister of Religion, or Appendix T2 Sportsperson] and the applicant has had, as at the day on which the application is made, continuous leave to enter or remain in the United Kingdom for at least 15 years as the child of a relevant points based system migrant, or

(xi) section E-ILRP of Appendix FM and the applicant has had, as at the day on which the application is made, continuous leave to enter or remain in the United Kingdom for at least 15 years on the day on which the application is made as a partner (except where leave is as a fiancé or proposed civil partner) under section D-LTRP of Appendix FM; or

(xii) section E-ILRPT of Appendix FM and the applicant has had, as at the day on which the application is made, continuous leave to enter or remain in the United Kingdom for at least 15 years on the day on which the application is made as a parent under section D-ILRPT of Appendix FM, or

(xiii) paragraph 25 or 31 of Appendix Armed Forces and the applicant has completed, on the date on which the application is made, a continuous period of leave to enter or remain in the United Kingdom of at least 15 years as the partner of a member of HM Forces under that Appendix, or

(xiv) paragraph 45 or 49 of Appendix Armed Forces and the applicant has completed, on the date on which the application is made, a continuous period of leave to enter or remain in the United Kingdom of at least 15 years as the child of a member of HM Forces under that Appendix, and

(b) (i) the applicant has provided specified documentary evidence of an English language speaking and listening qualification at A2 CEFR or ESOL entry level 2 or Scottish Credit and Qualification Framework level 3; or

(ii) where paragraph 39C(c) of these Rules applies, the on-line verification system operated by an approved English language test provider, [as published on the UK Visas and Immigration pages of Gov.uk], confirms that the applicant has passed an English language test in speaking and listening, at a minimum level A2 of the Common European Framework of Reference for Languages, which is approved by the Secretary of State, […], and taken at a test centre approved by the Secretary of State as a Secure English Language Test Centre no more than two years before the date of application.

and

(c) the applicant has provided specified documentary evidence from a qualified English language teacher that the applicant has made efforts to learn English but does not yet have sufficient knowledge of the English language to pass a qualification at B1 CEFR.

and

(d) the applicant is not a national or a citizen of one of the following countries:

- Antigua and Barbuda
- Australia
- The Bahamas
- Barbados

- Belize
- Canada
- Dominica
- Grenada
- Guyana
- Jamaica
- New Zealand
- St Kitts and Nevis
- St Lucia
- St Vincent and the Grenadines
- Trinidad and Tobago
- USA
- [Malta].

Note: Words in (b)(ii) substituted; words in (b)(ii) deleted from 1 October 2019 subject to savings for applications made before that date (HC 2631). Words in (a)(i), (a)(ii), (a)(ix), (a)(x) and (d) inserted from 09:00 on 1 December 2020 subject to savings for applications made before that time (HC 813).

3.3 Where paragraph 39C(c) of these Rules applies subject to paragraph 3.2 of this Appendix, an applicant demonstrates sufficient knowledge of the English language and about life in the UK where:

(i) in cases where the applicant failed to satisfy paragraph 2.2 of this Appendix, the online verification system operated by an approved English language test provider, [as published on the UK Visas and Immigration pages of Gov.uk], confirms that the applicant has passed an English language test in speaking and listening, at a minimum level B1 of the Common European Framework of Reference for Languages, which is approved by the Secretary of State, [. . .], and taken at a test centre approved by the Secretary of State as a Secure English Language Test Centre no more than two years before the date of application; or

(ii) in cases where the applicant failed to satisfy paragraph 2.3 of this Appendix, he or she has provided specified evidence that he or she has passed the test known as the 'Life in the UK test' administered by [by an educational institution or other person approved for this purpose by the Secretary of State] under arrangements approved by the decision-maker or

(iii) in cases where the applicant failed to satisfy paragraphs 2.2 and 2.3 of this Appendix, the requirements set out in sub-paragraphs (i) and (ii) are met.

Note: Words in (ii) substituted from 6 July 2018 subject to savings for applications made before that date (HC 1154). Words in (i) substituted; words in (i) deleted from 1 October 2019 subject to savings for applications made before that date (HC 2631).

Part 4—specified documents

4.1 Where these Rules require an applicant to demonstrate sufficient knowledge of the English language and of life in the United Kingdom, the applicant must supply the documents or information specified in paragraphs 4.6 to 4.14 below.

4.2 The decision maker will only consider evidence submitted after the date on which an application is made where the circumstances in paragraph 39(C)(c) of these Rules or paragraphs 4.3 or 4.6 of this Appendix apply.

4.3 Where an applicant has submitted:

(i) a document in the wrong format (for example, if a letter is not on letterhead paper as specified); or

[. . .]

(iii) a document which does not contain all of the specified information, or

(iv) fails to submit a specified document, the decision-maker may contact the applicant or his or her representative (in writing or otherwise), and request the document or the correct version of the document. The document must be received by the Home Office at the address specified in the request within such timescale (which will not be unreasonable) as is specified.

Note: Sub-paragraph (ii) deleted from 5 November 2018 (HC 1534).

4.4 A decision-maker may decide not to request a document under paragraph 4.3 where he or she does not anticipate that the supply of that document will lead to a grant of leave to enter or remain in the United Kingdom because the application may be refused for other reasons.

4.5 Without prejudice to the decision maker's discretion under paragraph 4.2 and also his or her right in all cases to request the original or specified document and refuse an application in circumstances in which they are not provided, where an applicant submits a specified document:

(i) in the wrong format, or

[. . .]

(iii) which does not contain all of the specified information but the missing information is verifiable from,

(aa) other documents submitted with the application,

(bb) the website of the organisation which issued the document, or

(cc) the website of the appropriate regulatory body;

the application for leave to enter or remain in the United Kingdom may be granted exceptionally providing the decision-maker is satisfied that the specified documents are genuine and that the applicant meets all the other requirements.

Note: Sub-paragraph (ii) deleted from 5 November 2018 (HC 1534).

4.6 Where the decision-maker is satisfied that there is a valid reason why a document has not been and cannot be supplied, (for example, because the document has been permanently lost or destroyed), he or she may waive the requirement for the document to be provided or may instead request alternative or additional evidence (which may include confirmation of evidence from the organisation which issued the original document).

4.7 The information specified for the purposes of paragraph 2.2(c) of this Appendix is the unique reference number assigned by the provider to the English language test taken by the applicant.

4.8 Subject to paragraphs 4.9 and 4.10 the documentary evidence specified for the purposes of paragraph 2.2 of this Appendix as showing that a person is a national or a citizen of one of the countries listed in paragraph 2.2 is a valid passport or travel document which satisfactorily establishes the applicant's nationality.

4.9 If the applicant cannot provide their passport or travel document other evidence of nationality of the type described in paragraph 4.10 may exceptionally be supplied in the following circumstances (the reason for which must be indicated by the applicant on their application form), where:

(a) the applicant's passport has been lost or stolen, or

(b) the applicant's passport has expired and has been returned to the relevant authorities, or

(c) the applicant's passport is with another part of the Home Office.

4.10 Where paragraph 4.9 applies, the alternative evidence specified for the purposes of establishing the applicant's nationality is:

(a) a valid national identity document; or

(b) [a] letter from the applicant's Home Government or Embassy confirming the applicant's full name, date of birth and nationality.

Note: Words in (b) substituted from 5 November 2018 (HC 1534).

[**4.10A** The evidence specified for the purposes of paragraph 2.2(a)(iii)(1) is:

(a) a certificate issued by the relevant institution confirming the award of the academic qualification and showing:

(i) the applicant's name,

(ii) the title of the award,

(iii) the date of the award,

(iv) the name of the awarding institution or,

(b) where an applicant has not, at the date of application, formally graduated or no longer has his or her certificate and is unable to obtain a duplicate certificate:

(i) an academic reference from the institution awarding the academic qualification that:

(a) is on official letter headed paper,

(b) shows the applicant's name,

(c) shows the title of the award,

(d) states when the academic qualification was (or as the case may be, will be) awarded, and

(e) confirms that the institution is unable to issue a duplicate certificate of award or (as the case may be in respect of an applicant who has not yet graduated) the date on which the certificate will be issued, or

(ii) an academic transcript that;

(a) is on official letter headed paper,

(b) shows the applicant's name,

(c) shows the name of the academic institution,

(d) shows the course title, and

(e) confirms the award given.]

Note: Paragraph inserted from 1 November 2018 subject to savings for applications made before that date (HC 1534).

4.11 The evidence specified for the purposes of paragraph 2.2(a)(iii)[(2)] to 2.2(a)(v) (academic qualification recognised by [[Ecctis]]) is:

(a) a certificate issued by the relevant institution confirming the award of the academic qualification and showing:

(i) the applicant's name,

(ii) the title of the award,

(iii) the date of the award,

(iv) the name of the awarding institution, and,

(v) for paragraph 2.2(a)(iii) that the qualification was taught in English or,

(b) where an applicant has not, at the date of application, formally graduated or no longer has his or her certificate and is unable to obtain a duplicate certificate:

(i) an [. . .] academic reference from the institution awarding the academic qualification that:

(aa) is on official letter headed paper,

(bb) shows the applicant's name,

(cc) shows the title of the award,

(dd) confirms that the qualification was taught in English,

(ee) states when the academic qualification was (or as the case may be, will be) awarded, and

(ff) confirms that the institution is unable to issue a duplicate certificate of award or (as the case may be in respect of an applicant who has not yet graduated) the date on which the certificate will be issued,or

(ii) an [...] academic transcript that;

(aa) is on official letter headed paper,

(bb) shows the applicant's name,

(cc) shows the name of the academic institution,

(dd) shows the course title,

(ee) confirms that the qualification was taught in English, and,

(ff) confirms the award given.

Note: Number in introduction inserted from 1 November 2018 subject to savings for applications made before that date; words in (b)(i) and (ii) deleted from 5 November 2018 (HC 1534). Words in double square brackets substituted from 6 October 2021 subject to savings for applications made before that date (HC 617).

4.12 In the absence of any evidence to the contrary, a qualification obtained in one of the following countries will be assumed for the purposes of this Appendix to have been taught in English: Antigua and Barbuda, Australia, the Bahamas, Barbados, Belize, Dominica, Grenada, Guyana, Ireland, Jamaica, New Zealand, St Kitts and Nevis, St Lucia, St Vincent and the Grenadines, Trinidad and Tobago, the UK or the USA [Malta].

4.13 The information or evidence specified for the purposes of paragraph 3.2(b)(i) (evidence of English language speaking and listening) is:

(a) the unique reference number assigned by the provider to the English language test taken by the applicant; or

(b) a certificate or other document issued by an awarding organisation that is recognised either by Ofqual, the Welsh Government, or CCEA that:

(i) is issued in England, Wales or Northern Ireland in respect of a qualification listed as an ESOL qualification in the OFQUAL Register of Regulated Qualifications, and

(ii) shows that the level of speaking and listening skills attained by the applicant met ESOL entry level 2; or

(c) a certificate that:

(i) is issued in Scotland in respect of a National Qualification in English for Speakers of Other Languages awarded by the Scottish Qualifications Authority, and

(ii) shows that the level of speaking and listening skills attained by the applicant met Scottish Credit and Qualifications Framework level 3.

[**4.13ZA** The information or evidence specified for the purposes of requesting an exception under Paragraph 3.1(c) of this appendix is to be provided on a copy of the form published on GOV.UK for this purpose which must be completed by a professional who is either:

(a) the applicant's GP or a GP based in the practice with which the applicant is normally registered; or

(b) a General Medical Council (GMC) registered consultant who has met with the applicant in person, assessed their ability to fulfil the requirements set out in this appendix, and supports their request for an exception from either or both elements of KOLL on the basis that they have a condition which would prevent them from satisfying the requirements for the foreseeable future.]

Note: Paragraph inserted from 1 November 2018 subject to savings for applications made before that date (HC 1534).

4.13A. The information specified for the purposes of paragraph 3.2(b)(ii) (evidence of English language speaking and listening) is the unique reference number assigned by the provider to the English language test taken by the applicant.

4.14. (a) The evidence specified for the purposes of paragraph 3.2(c) (evidence from qualified English teacher) is a letter from the teacher which is signed by him or her and dated no more than 3 months before the date on which the application for indefinite leave to remain is made and which includes the following information:

(i) the applicant's name,

(ii) confirmation that the applicant has attended an English language class taught by that teacher for at least 75 guided learning hours and which was taught during the period of 12 months immediately preceding the date on which the application for indefinite leave to remain was made,

(iii) confirmation that the teacher has assessed that the speaking and listening level attained by the applicant is not at B1 level or above,

(iv) confirmation that the applicant is considered unlikely to attain B1 level through further study, and

(v) confirmation of the teacher's qualifications as an English language teacher within the meaning of this Appendix.

(b) For the purposes of paragraph (a)(ii) 'guided learning hours' means the time during which a person is taught or given instruction and does not include any time spent on unsupervised preparation or study.

4.15. [The information specified for the purposes of paragraph 2.3 of this Appendix is a unique reference number issued to the applicant by the provider of the 'Life in the UK' test.]

Note: Amendment from 6 July 2018 subject to savings for applications made before that date (HC 1154). Paragraph substituted from 1 October 2019 (HC 2631).

4.16. The information specified for the purposes of paragraph 3.3(i) of this Appendix (evidence of English language speaking and listening) is the unique reference number assigned by the provider to the English language test taken by the applicant.

4.17. The evidence specified for the purposes of paragraph 3.3(ii) of this Appendix (evidence of knowledge about life in the UK) is the same as that specified at paragraph 4.15(a) of this Appendix.

Part 5—Interpretation

5.1. For the purposes of this Appendix 'decision maker' means an Entry Clearance Officer or the Secretary of State.

5.2. For the purposes of this Appendix, 'qualified English language teacher' means a person who holds a qualification in teaching English as a foreign language or in teaching English to speakers of other languages which was awarded by an awarding organisation regulated by OFQUAL or the Welsh Government or the CCEA or the Scottish Qualification Authority.

[Appendix L – DELETED]

Note: Amendments from 11 January 2018 subject to savings for applications made before that date (HC 309). Amendments from 6 July 2018 subject to savings for applications made before that date (HC 1154). Amendments from 10 January 2019 subject to savings for applications made before that date (HC 1779). Amendments from 30 March 2019 subject to savings for applications made before that date (HC 1919). Amendments from 1 October 2019 subject to savings for applications made before that date (HC 2631). Appendix deleted from 20 February 2020 subject to savings for applications made before that date (HC 56).

[Appendix M – DELETED]

Note: Amendments from 28 December 2017 (HC 309). Amendments from 1 October 2019 (HC 2631). Amendments from 6 April 2020 (HC 120). Amendments from 4 June 2020 (CP 232). Appendix deleted from 09:00 on 11 October 2021 subject to savings for applications made before that time (HC 617).

[Appendix N- DELETED]

Note: Amendments from 28 December 2017; amendments from 11 January 2018 subject to savings for applications made before that date; (HC 309). Amendments from 6 July 2018 subject to savings for applications made before that date (HC 1154). Amendments from 10 January 2019 subject to savings for applications made before that date (HC 1779). Amendments from 30 March 2019 subject to savings for applications made before that date (HC 1919). Amendments from 1 October 2019 (HC 2631). Amendments from 6 April 2020 (HC 120). Appendix deleted from 09:00 on 11 October 2021 subject to savings for applications made before that time (HC 617).

[Appendix O – DELETED]

Note: Appendix deleted from 1 October 2019 subject to savings for applications made before that date (HC 2631).

Appendix P [DELETED]

Note: Appendix deleted from 09:00 on 1 December 2020 subject to savings for applications made before that time (HC 813)

Appendix SN

SERVICE OF NOTICE USERS

Introduction

Notices of appealable immigration decisions are served under the Immigration (Notices) Regulations 2003.

Notices of non-appealable immigration decisions which grant or refuse leave to remain, vary leave to remain or refuse to vary leave to remain are served under the Immigration (Leave to Enter and Remain) Order 2000.

Notices falling within paragraph SN1.2 of this Appendix to the Immigration Rules are to be served in accordance with this Appendix.

Definitions

SN1.1 For the purpose of this Appendix the following definitions apply:

Administrative review	as defined in Appendix AR [or Appendix AR(EU)].
business day	any day other than a Saturday, a Sunday, Christmas Day, Good Friday or a day which is a bank holiday under the Banking and Financial Dealings Act 1971 in the part of the United Kingdom to which the notice is sent.
decision-maker	(a) the Secretary of State; (b) an immigration officer; (c) an entry clearance officer;
representative	a person who appears to the decision-maker: (a) to be the representative of a person referred to in paragraph SN1.2 below; and (b) not to be prohibited from acting as a representative by section 84 of the 1999 Act.

Note: Words in table inserted from 1 November 2018 for applications made under Appendix EU on or after that date (HC 1534).

Service of notices

SN1.2 A notice in writing:

(a) that an application for entry clearance, leave to enter or leave to remain in the United Kingdom is invalid;

(b) that an application for entry clearance, leave to enter or leave to remain in the United Kingdom is void;

(c) that an application for administrative review is invalid; or

(d) notifying a person of the outcome of an administrative review application, may be given to the person affected as follows.

SN1.3 The notice may be:

(a) given by hand;

(b) sent by fax;

(c) sent by postal service to a postal address provided for correspondence by the person or the person's representative;

(d) sent electronically to an e-mail address provided for correspondence by the person or the person's representative;

(e) sent by document exchange to a document exchange number or address; or

(f) sent by courier.

SN1.4 Where no postal or e-mail address for correspondence has been provided, the notice may be sent:

(a) by postal service to:

(i) the last-known or usual place of abode, place of study or place of business of the person; or

(ii) the last-known or usual place of business of the person's representative; or

(b) electronically to:

(i) the last-known e-mail address for the person (including at the person's last-known place of study or place of business); or

(ii) the last-known e-mail address of the person's representative.

SN1.5 For the purposes of paragraphs SN1.3 or SN1.4, a postal address outside the UK is not a postal address for correspondence where the person affected by the notice is in the UK.

SN1.6 Where it is not possible to give notice in accordance with paragraphs SN1.3 and SN1.4 or where an attempt to do so has failed, and the decisionmaker records the reason for this and places the notice on file, the notice shall be deemed to have been given on the day that it is placed on file.

SN1.7 Where a notice is deemed to have been given in accordance with paragraph SN1.6 and subsequently the person is located, the person shall as soon as is practicable be given a copy of the notice and details of when and how it was given.

SN1.8 A notice given under this appendix may, in the case of a person who is under 18 years of age and does not have a representative, be given to the parent, guardian or another adult who for the time being takes responsibility for the child.

Presumptions about date of receipt of notice

SN1.9 Where a notice is sent in accordance with paragraphs SN1.2 to SN1.4, it shall be deemed to have been given to the person affected, unless the contrary is proved:

(a) where the notice is sent by postal service:

(i) on the second day after it was sent by postal service in which delivery or receipt is recorded if sent to a place within the United Kingdom;

(ii) on the 28th day after it was posted if sent to a place outside the United Kingdom;

(b) where the notice is sent by fax, e-mail, document exchange or courier, on the day it was sent.

SN1.10 For the purposes of paragraph SN1.9(a) the period is to be calculated excluding the day on which the notice is posted.

SN1.11 For the purposes of paragraph SN1.9(a)(i) the period is to be calculated excluding any day which is not a business day.

[Appendix Settlement Protection

[. . .]

A person who has been on a protection route for at least five years may be eligible for settlement on this route.

[Only those granted refugee status or humanitarian protection as a result of asylum applications made before 28 June 2022 or granted refugee status and refugee permission to stay on asylum applications made on or after 28 June 2022, are eligible to apply on the settlement protection route.

Individuals who were granted refugee status and temporary refugee permission to stay or humanitarian protection and temporary humanitarian permission to stay following asylum applications made on or after 28 June 2022 are ineligible to apply on the settlement protection route]

[[Partners and children of a person with refugee status or humanitarian protection who is eligible to apply on the settlement protection route may also apply on this route if they have been granted permission to stay as the dependant partner or child of such a person.]]

Note: Words deleted, words in square brackets inserted, words in double square brackets substituted from 28 June 2022 subject to savings for applications made before that date (HC 17).

Validity requirements for settlement on a protection route

STP 1.1. A person granted permission on a protection route who is applying for settlement must apply online on the gov.uk website on the specified form as follows:

(a) form: 'Apply to settle in the UK – refugee or humanitarian protection'; or

(b) form, 'Settlement Protection' where available.

STP 1.2. The application for settlement must meet all the following requirements:

(a) the applicant must have provided any required biometrics; and

(b) the applicant must satisfactorily establish their identity and nationality; and

(c) the applicant must be in the UK on the date of application.

[**STP 1.3.** The applicant must have, or have last been granted:

(a) permission to stay as a refugee or as a person granted humanitarian protection following an asylum application made before 28 June 2022; or

(b) refugee permission to stay following an asylum application made on or after 28 June 2022.]

Note: Paragraph substituted from 28 June 2022 subject to savings for applications made before that date (HC 17).

STP 1.4. An application which does not meet the validity requirements for settlement for a person on a protection route is invalid and may be rejected and not considered.

Suitability requirements for settlement by a person on a protection route

STP 2.1. An application for settlement on a protection route must be refused where the applicant:

(a) has been convicted of a criminal offence in the UK or overseas for which they have received a custodial sentence of four years or more; or

(b) has been convicted of a criminal offence in the UK or overseas for which they have received a custodial sentence of at least 12 months but less than four years, unless a period of 15 years has passed since the end of their sentence; or

(c) has been convicted of a criminal offence in the UK or overseas for which they have received a custodial sentence of less than 12 months, unless a period of seven years has passed since the end of their sentence; or

(d) within the 24 months before the date on which the application for settlement is decided, has been convicted of, or admitted to an offence in the UK or overseas for which they have received a non-custodial sentence, or received an out-of-court disposal that is recorded on their criminal record; or

(e) is a persistent offender who shows a particular disregard for the law; or

(f) has committed a criminal offence, or offences, which caused serious harm; or

(g) where a grant of settlement is not conducive to the public good because of their conduct, character, associations or other reasons (including convictions which do not fall within the criminality grounds) or because they represent a threat to national security.

Eligibility requirements for settlement for a person on a protection route

Qualifying period requirement for settlement for a person on a protection route

STP 3.1. The applicant must have spent a continuous period of at least five years in the UK with either:

(a) refugee status; or

(b) humanitarian protection.

Continuing status requirement for settlement for a person on a protection route

STP 4.1. The applicant's refugee status or humanitarian protection must not have been revoked or renounced.

Decision on an application for settlement for a person on a protection route

STP 5.1. If the decision maker is satisfied that the applicant meets all the suitability and eligibility requirements for settlement for a person on a protection route are met, the applicant will be granted settlement.

STP 5.2. If the decision maker is not satisfied that the applicant meets all the suitability and eligibility requirements for settlement for a person on a protection route, but is satisfied that the applicant is still entitled to refugee status or humanitarian protection, the applicant will be granted a further period of permission to stay on a protection route for at least 30 months.

STP 5.3. If the decision maker is not satisfied that the applicant meets all the suitability and eligibility requirements for settlement for a person on a protection route, or for permission to stay on a protection route, the application for settlement will be refused.

Settlement as a partner or child of a person on a protection route

Validity requirements for settlement as a partner or child of a person on a protection route

[**STP 6.1.** An applicant who is applying for settlement as a partner or child of a person on a protection route must apply online on the gov.uk website on the specified form as follows:

Applicant	Form
Partner	Either: 'Apply to settle in the UK – refugee or humanitarian protection'; or 'Settlement as a partner or parent' (where available).
Child	Either: 'Apply to settle in the UK – refugee or humanitarian protection'; or 'Settlement as a child (including a child aged over 18 already in the UK as a dependent)' (where available).]

Note: Paragraph substituted from 20 June 2022 subject to savings for applications made before that date (HC 1118).

STP 6.2. An application for settlement as a partner or child on a person on a settlement route must meet all the following requirements:

(a) the applicant must have provided any required biometrics; and

(b) the applicant must satisfactorily establish their identity and nationality; and

(c) the applicant must be in the UK on the date of application.

[**STP 6.3.** (a) Unless the applicant is a child born in the UK while their parent had refugee status or humanitarian protection, the applicant must have, or have last been granted permission as the child of a person granted refugee status or humanitarian protection following an asylum application made before 28 June 2022.

(b) Unless the applicant is a child born in the UK while their parent had refugee permission to stay, the applicant must have, or have last been granted permission to stay under paragraph 339QC, 352B-BA, 352E, 352FB or 352FH of these rules.]

Note: Paragraph substituted from 28 June 2022 subject to savings for applications made before that date (HC 17).

STP 6.4. An application which does not meet the validity requirements for settlement as a partner or child of a person on a protection route is invalid and may be rejected and not considered.

Suitability requirements for settlement as a partner or child of a person on a protection route

STP 7.1. An application for settlement as a partner or child of a person on a settlement route must be refused where the applicant:

(a) has been convicted of a criminal offence in the UK or overseas for which they have received a custodial sentence of four years or more; or

(b) has been convicted of a criminal offence in the UK or overseas for which they have received a custodial sentence of at least 12 months but less than four years, unless a period of 15 years has passed since the end of their sentence; or

(c) has been convicted of a criminal offence in the UK or overseas for which they have received a custodial sentence of less than 12 months, unless a period of seven years has passed since the end of their sentence; or

(d) within the 24 months prior to the date on which the application for settlement is decided, has been convicted of or admitted to an office in the UK or overseas for which they have received a non-custodial sentence, or received an out-of-court disposal that is recorded on their criminal record; or

(e) is a persistent offender who shows a particular disregard for the law; or

(f) has committed a criminal offence, or offences, which caused serious harm; or

(g) where a grant of settlement is not conducive to the public good because of their conduct, character, associations or other reasons (including convictions which do not fall within the criminality grounds) or the fact they represent a threat to national security.

Eligibility requirements for settlement as a partner or child of a person on a protection route.

Relationship requirement for settlement as the partner of a person on a protection route.

STP 8.1. The applicant must be the partner of a person (P) where one of the following applies:

(a) P has refugee status or humanitarian protection and is, at the same time as the applicant, being granted settlement; or

(b) P has refugee status or humanitarian protection, is settled on the protection route and the applicant had permission to stay as P's partner when P settled.

STP 8.2. The relationship between the applicant and their partner (P) must be genuine and subsisting.

STP 8.3. The applicant and their partner (P) must intend to continue to live together as partners in the UK.

Relationship requirement for settlement as a child of a person on a protection route

STP 9.1. The applicant must be the child of a person (P) where one of the following applies:

(a) P has refugee status or humanitarian protection and is, at the same time as the applicant, being granted settlement; or

(b) P has refugee status or humanitarian protection, is settled and the applicant had permission to stay as P's child or was born in the UK while P had permission to stay on a protection route.

STP 9.2. If the applicant is a child born in the UK, the applicant must provide a full UK birth certificate showing the name of the parent (P) who is or was on a protection route.

Age requirement for settlement as a child of a person on a protection route

STP 10.1. The child must be under the age of 18 on the date of application unless they were last granted permission as the dependent child of a parent or parents who is or was at that time on a protection route.

Decision on an application for settlement as a partner or child of a person on a protection route

STP 11.1. If the decision maker is satisfied that the applicant meets all the suitability and eligibility requirements for settlement as a partner or child of a person on a protection route, the applicant will be granted settlement.

STP 11.2. If the decision maker is not satisfied that the applicant meets all the suitability and eligibility requirements for settlement as a partner or child of a person on a protection route, but is satisfied that the applicant continues to qualify as a partner or child of a person on a protection route, the applicant will be granted permission to stay for at least 30 months.

STP 11.3. If the decision maker is not satisfied that the applicant meets all the suitability and eligibility requirements for settlement as a partner or child of a person on a protection route, or for permission to stay as a partner or child of a person on a protection route, the application for settlement will be refused.]

Note: Appendix inserted from 6 October 2021 subject to savings for applications made before that date (HC 617).

Appendix T
Tuberculosis screening

Any person applying to enter the UK as described in paragraph A39, Part 1 General Provisions of the Immigration Rules, must present at the time of application a valid medical certificate issued by a medical practitioner approved by the Secretary of State for these purposes, as listed on the Gov.uk website, confirming that they have undergone screening for active pulmonary tuberculosis and that such tuberculosis is not present in the applicant.

- Afghanistan
- Algeria
- Angola
- Armenia
- Azerbaijan
- Bangladesh
- Belarus
- Benin
- Bhutan
- Bolivia
- Botswana
- Brunei Darussalam
- Burkina Faso
- Burma
- Burundi
- Cambodia
- Cape Verde
- Central African Republic
- Chad
- Cameroon
- China
- Congo
- Congo Democratic Republic
- Côte d'Ivoire
- Democratic People's Republic of Korea
- Djibouti
- Dominican Republic
- Ecuador
- Equatorial Guinea
- Eritrea
- Ethiopia
- Gabon
- Gambia
- Georgia
- Ghana
- Guatemala
- Guinea
- Guinea Bissau
- Guyana
- Haiti
- Hong Kong or Macau
- India
- Indonesia
- Iraq
- Kazakhstan
- Kenya
- Kiribati
- Korea
- Kyrgyzstan
- Laos
- Lesotho
- Liberia
- Madagascar
- Malawi
- Malaysia
- Mali
- Marshall Islands
- Mauritania
- Micronesia
- Moldova
- Mongolia
- Morocco
- Mozambique
- Namibia
- Nepal
- Niger
- Nigeria
- Pakistan
- Palau
- Papua New Guinea
- Panama
- Paraguay
- Peru
- Russian Federation
- Rwanda
- Sao Tome and Principe
- Senegal
- Sierra Leone
- Solomon Islands
- Somalia
- South Africa
- South Sudan
- Sri Lanka
- Sudan
- Tajikistan
- Swaziland
- Tanzania
- Timor Leste
- Togo
- Thailand
- The Philippines
- Turkmenistan
- Tuvalu
- Uganda
- Ukraine
- Uzbekistan
- Vanuatu
- Vietnam
- Zambia
- Zimbabwe

Applicants from Sao Tome and Principe are screened in Angola; those from Central African Republic, Chad and Gabon are screened in Cameroon; those from the People's Democratic Republic of Korea are screened in Beijing; those from Congo are screened in Democratic Republic of Congo; those from Djibouti are screened in Ethiopia, those from Kiribati, Marshall Islands, Micronesia, Tuvalu and Vanuatu are screened in Fiji; those from Cape Verde, Guinea Bissau and Mali are screening in Gambia or Senegal; those from Burkina Faso, Equatorial Guinea, Liberia, Niger and Togo are screened in Ghana; those from Macau are screened in Hong Kong; those from Timor Leste are screened in Indonesia; those from Kyrgyzstan are screened in Kazakhstan; those from Eritrea,

Somalia and South Sudan are screened in Kenya; those from Mauritania are screened in Morocco; those from Benin are screened in Nigeria; those from Solomon Islands are screened in Papua New Guinea; those from Palau are screened in Philippines; those from Burundi are screened in Rwanda; those in Lesotho and Swaziland are screened in South Africa; those from Laos are screened in Thailand.

Note: The list of clinics is not reproduced here; it is subject to frequent change and users of the Handbook are advised to consult the guidance which can be accessed online at https://www.gov.uk/tb-test-visa/countries-where-you-need-a-tb-test-to-enter-the-uk.

Appendix U [DELETED]

Note: Appendix inserted from 10 January 2019 subject to savings for applications made before that date (HC 1779). Appendix deleted from 09:00 on 1 December 2020 subject to savings for applications made before that time (HC 813).

[Appendix V [DELETED]

Note: Amendments from 11 January 2018 subject to savings for applications made before that date (HC 309). Amendments from 6 April 2018 subject to savings for applications made before that date (HC 895). Amendments from 6 July 2018 subject to savings for applications made before that date (HC 1154). Amendments from 10 January 2019 subject to savings for applications made before that date (HC 1779). Amendments from 29 March 2019 subject to savings for applications made before that date and 6 April 2019 both with and without savings for applications made before that date (HC 1919). Amendments from 6 April 2020 both with and without savings for applications made before that date (HC 120). Amendments from 09:00 on 5 October 2020 subject to savings for applications made before that time (HC 707). Appendix deleted from 09:00 on 1 December 2020 subject to savings for applications made before that time (HC 813).

Appendix W [DELETED]

Note: Appendix inserted from 29 March 2019 subject to savings for applications made before that date (HC 1919). Amendments from 1 October 2019 with and without savings for applications made before that date (HC 2631). Amendments from 20 February 2020 subject to savings for applications made before that date (HC 56). Amendments from 6 April 2020 (HC 120). Amendments from 4 June 2020 subject to savings for applications supported by a Certificate of Sponsorship or endorsement assigned before that date (CP 232). Amendments from 09:00 on 5 October 2020 subject to savings for applications made before that date. Where consequential changes relating to the need to obtain an ATAS certificate have been made to the conditions of leave for routes, these changes take effect for all applications made or granted on or after 09:00 on 5 October at. Appendix deleted from 09:00 on 1 December 2020 subject to savings for applications made before that time (HC 813).

[Appendix V: visitor

This route is for a person who wants to visit the UK for a temporary period, (usually for up to 6 months), for purposes such as tourism, visiting friends or family, carrying out a business activity, or undertaking a short course of study.

Each [Visitor] must meet the requirements of the Visitor route, even if they are travelling as, for example, a family group, a tour group or a school party.

A visa national as [set out] in Appendix Visitor: Visa National list must obtain entry clearance as a [Visitor] [(a visit visa)] before arrival in the UK.

A non-visa national can normally seek entry on arrival in the UK.

There are 4 types of [Visitor]:

- *Standard [Visitor]: for those seeking to undertake the activities set out in Appendix Visitor: Permitted Activities, for example tourism and visiting family, usually for up to 6 months. [[A Standard Visitor may apply for a visit visa of six months, two, five, or 10 years validity, however each stay in the UK must not exceed the permitted length of stay endorsed on the visit visa (usually six months).]]*
- *[Marriage/Civil Partnership] [Visitor]: for those seeking to come to the UK to marry or form a civil partnership, or give notice of marriage or civil partnership.*
- *Permitted Paid Engagement [Visitor]: for experts in their field coming to the UK to undertake specific paid engagements for up to one month.*
- *Transit [Visitor]: for those who want to transit the UK on route to another country outside the Common Travel Area and who will enter the UK for up to 48 hours by crossing the UK border unless Appendix Visitor: Transit Without Visa Scheme applies.*

Visitors cannot work in the UK unless this is expressly allowed under the permitted activities set out in Appendix Visitor: Permitted Activities.

Further information of how long each visitor can stay and what they can and cannot do in the UK is set out at V 17.2 and Appendix Visitor: Permitted Activities.

[...]

Note: Words in square brackets substituted, words in double square brackets inserted, words deleted from 6 October 2021 subject to savings for applications made before that date (HC 617).

Entry requirements for [Visitors]

Note: Word in heading substituted from 6 October 2021 subject to savings for applications made before that date (HC 617)

V 1.1. A person seeking to come to the UK as a [Visitor] must apply for and obtain entry clearance before they arrive in the UK if they are:

(a) a visa national, unless V 1.3. (b) applies; or

(b) seeking to marry or form a civil partnership, or give notice of marriage or civil partnership, in the UK unless they are a 'relevant national' as defined in section 62 of the Immigration Act 2014; or

(c) seeking to come to the UK as a [Visitor] for more than 6 months.

Note: Words substituted from 6 October 2021 subject to savings for applications made before that date (HC 617)

V 1.2. A person to whom V 1.1. applies will be refused permission to enter if they do not hold entry clearance as a [Visitor] (a visit visa) on arrival in the UK.

Note: Words substituted from 6 October 2021 subject to savings for applications made before that date (HC 617). **NB:** HC 617 specifies an amendment to wording of this paragraph which did not exist at the relevant date.

V 1.3. A person seeking to come to the UK as a [Visitor] may apply for permission to enter on arrival in the UK where they are:

(a) a non-visa national, unless V 1.1. (b) or (c) apply; or

(b) a visa national and an exception applies as set out in Appendix Visitor: Visa National list or Appendix Visitor: Transit Without Visa Scheme.

Note: Words substituted from 6 October 2021 subject to savings for applications made before that date (HC 617)

V 1.4. A child who holds entry clearance [. . .] as a [Visitor] on arrival in the UK must either:

(a) hold a valid entry clearance that states they are accompanied and will be travelling with an adult identified on that entry clearance; or

(b) hold an entry clearance which states they are unaccompanied;

otherwise the child may be refused entry to the UK, unless they meet the requirements of V 5.1. and V 5.2.

Note: Words substituted, words deleted from 6 October 2021 subject to savings for applications made before that date (HC 617)

Validity requirements for entry clearance or permission to stay as a [Visitor]

Note: Word in heading substituted from 6 October 2021 subject to savings for applications made before that date (HC 617)

V 2.1. A person applying for entry clearance as a [Visitor] must apply online on the gov.uk website on the specified form 'Apply for a UK visit visa'.

Note: Words substituted from 6 October 2021 subject to savings for applications made before that date (HC 617)

V 2.2. A person applying for permission to stay as a [Visitor] must apply online on the gov.uk website on the specified form 'Application to extend stay in the UK: FLR(IR)'.

Note: Words substituted from 6 October 2021 subject to savings for applications made before that date (HC 617)

V 2.3. An application for entry clearance or permission to stay as a [Visitor] must meet all the following requirements:

(a) any fee must have been paid; and

(b) the applicant must have provided any required biometrics; and

(c) the applicant must have provided a passport or other document which satisfactorily establishes their identity and nationality.

Note: Words substituted from 6 October 2021 subject to savings for applications made before that date (HC 617)

V 2.4. An application for entry clearance as a [Visitor] must be made while the applicant is outside the UK and to a post designated to accept such applications.

Note: Words substituted from 6 October 2021 subject to savings for applications made before that date (HC 617)

V 2.5. An application for permission to stay as a [Visitor] must be made by a person:

(a) in the UK; and

(b) with permission as a Standard [Visitor] or Marriage/Civil Partnership [Visitor].

Note: Words substituted from 6 October 2021 subject to savings for applications made before that date (HC 617)

V 2.6. An application which does not meet all the validity requirements for a [Visitor] is invalid and may be rejected and not considered.

Note: Words substituted from 6 October 2021 subject to savings for applications made before that date (HC 617)

Suitability requirements for all [Visitors]

Note: Word in heading substituted from 6 October 2021 subject to savings for applications made before that date (HC 617)

V 3.1. The applicant must not fall for refusal under Part 9: grounds for refusal.

V 3.2. If applying for permission to stay the applicant must not be:

(a) in breach of immigration laws, except that where paragraph 39E applies, that period of overstaying will be disregarded; or

(b) on immigration bail.

Eligibility requirements for [Visitors]

Note: Word in heading substituted from 6 October 2021 subject to savings for applications made before that date (HC 617)

V 4.1. The decision maker must be satisfied that the applicant (unless they are applying for entry clearance or permission to enter as a Transit [Visitor]) meets all of the eligibility requirements in V 4.2. to V 4.6. and that they meet the specified additional eligibility requirements where the applicant:

(a) is a child at the date of application, they must also meet the additional requirements at V 5.1. and V 5.2; or

(b) is coming to the UK under the Approved Destination Status Agreement, they must also meet the requirements at V 6.1; or

(c) is coming to the UK to receive private medical treatment, they must also meet the additional requirements at V 7.1. to V 7.3; or

(d) is coming to the UK as an organ donor, they must also meet the additional requirements at V 8.1. to V 8.4; or

(e) is coming to the UK to study as a [Visitor], they must also meet the additional requirements at V 9.1. [to V 9.5]; or

(f) is an academic seeking a 12-month entry clearance, they must also meet the additional requirements at V 10.1; or

(g) is coming to the UK to undertake work related training, they must also meet the additional requirements at V 11.1. to V 11.3; or

(h) is coming to the UK to marry or form a civil partnership, or give notice of intention to marry or form a civil partnership, they must also meet the additional requirements at V 12.1. and V 12.2; or

(i) is coming to the UK to undertake permitted paid engagements, they must also meet the additional requirements in V 13.1. to V 13.3; or

(j) is applying for permission to stay as a [Visitor], they must also meet the additional requirements at V 15.1. to [V 15.4].

Note: Words substituted from 6 October 2021 subject to savings for applications made before that date (HC 617)

Genuine [Visitor] requirement

Note: Word in heading substituted from 6 October 2021 subject to savings for applications made before that date (HC 617)

V 4.2. The applicant must satisfy the decision maker that they are a genuine [Visitor], which means the applicant:

(a) will leave the UK at the end of their visit; and

(b) will not live in the UK for extended periods through frequent or successive visits, or make the UK their main home; and

(c) is genuinely seeking entry or stay for a purpose that is permitted under the [Visitor] route [[as set out in Appendix Visitor: Permitted Activities and at V13.3]]; and

(d) will not undertake any of the prohibited activities set out in V 4.4. to V 4.6; and

(e) must have sufficient funds to cover all reasonable costs in relation to their visit without working or accessing public funds, including the cost of the return or onward journey, any costs relating to their dependants, and the cost of planned [activities such as private medical treatment. The applicant must show that any funds they rely upon are held in a financial institution permitted under FIN 2.1 in Appendix Finance.]

Note: words in double square brackets in (c) inserted from 6 April 2021 subject to savings for applications made before that date (HC 1248). Words substituted from 6 October 2021 subject to savings for applications made before that date (HC 617)

V 4.3. In assessing whether an applicant has sufficient funds under V 4.2.(e), the applicant's travel, maintenance and accommodation may be provided by a third party only if that third party:

(a) has a genuine professional or personal relationship with the applicant; and

(b) is not, or will not be, in breach of immigration laws at the time of the decision or the applicant's entry to the UK as a [Visitor]; and

(c) can and will provide support to the applicant for the intended duration of the applicant's stay as a [Visitor].

Note: Words substituted from 6 October 2021 subject to savings for applications made before that date (HC 617)

Prohibited activities and payment requirements for [Visitors]

Note: Word in heading substituted from 6 October 2021 subject to savings for applications made before that date (HC 617)

V 4.4. The applicant must not intend to:

(a) work in the UK, which includes:

(i) taking employment in the UK; and

(ii) doing work for an organisation or business in the UK; and

(iii) establishing or running a business as a self-employed person; and

(iv) doing a work placement or internship; and

(v) direct selling to the public; and

(vi) providing goods and services, unless expressly allowed by the permitted activities in Appendix Visitor: Permitted Activities, [Appendix Visitor: Permit Free Festival List] or the Permitted Paid Engagements in V 13.3; or

(b) study in the UK, except as permitted by Appendix Visitor: Permitted Activities (and provided they meet the relevant additional requirements for study); or

(c) access medical treatment, other than private medical treatment or to donate an organ (for either of these activities they must meet the relevant additional eligibility requirements); or

(d) get married or form a civil partnership, or give notice of intention to marry or form a civil partnership, unless they are applying for entry clearance [[as a Marriage/Civil Partnership Visitor]] [or are a relevant national as defined in section 62 of the Immigration Act 2014].

Note: Words in square brackets in (d) inserted from 6 April 2021 subject to savings for applications made before that date (HC 1248). Words in (a)(vi), words in double square brackets in (d) substituted from 6 October 2021 subject to savings for applications made before that date (HC 617).

V 4.5. Permitted activities must not amount to the [Visitor] undertaking employment, or [[doing]] work which amounts to them filling a role or providing short-term cover for a role within a UK based organisation and where the [Visitor] is already paid and employed outside of the UK they must remain so.

Note: Words substituted, word in double square brackets inserted from 6 October 2021 subject to savings for applications made before that date (HC 617)

[**V 4.6.** The [Visitor] must not receive payment from a UK source for any activities undertaken in the UK, except for the following:

(a) reasonable expenses to cover the cost of their travel and subsistence, including fees for directors attending board-level meetings; or

(b) international drivers undertaking activities permitted under PA 9.2.; or

(c) prize money; or

(d) billing a UK client for their time in the UK, where the [Visitor's] overseas employer is contracted to provide services to a UK company, and the majority of the contract work is carried out overseas (payment must be lower than the amount of the applicant's salary); or

(e) multi-national companies who, for administrative reasons, handle payment of their employees' salaries from the UK; or

(f) paid performances at a permit free festival as listed in [Appendix Visitor: Permit Free Festival List], where the [Visitor] is an artist, entertainer or musician; or

(g) Permitted Paid Engagements, [where they have permission as a Permitted Paid Engagement Visitor].]

Note: Amendments from 23:00 on 31 December 2020 subject to savings for applications made before that date (HC 1043). Paragraph substituted from 6 April 2021 subject to savings for applications made before that date (HC 1248). Words substituted from 6 October 2021 subject to savings for applications made before that date (HC 617).

Additional eligibility requirements for [children]

Note: Word in heading substituted from 6 October 2021 subject to savings for applications made before that date (HC 617)

V 5.1. Adequate arrangements must have been made for a child's travel to, reception and care in the UK.

V 5.2. If the child is not travelling with a parent or legal guardian, based in their home country or country of ordinary residence, who is responsible for their care, that parent or legal guardian must consent to the child's travel to, reception and care in the UK and, where requested, this consent must be given in writing.

Additional eligibility requirement for [Visitors] under the Approved Destination Status Agreement

Note: Word in heading substituted from 6 October 2021 subject to savings for applications made before that date (HC 617)

V 6.1. A person applying for entry clearance as a [Visitor] under the Approved Destination Status Agreement must:

(a) be a national of the People's Republic of China; and

(b) intend to enter, leave and travel within the UK as a member of a tourist group under the Approved Destination Status Agreement.

Note: Words substituted from 6 October 2021 subject to savings for applications made before that date (HC 617)

Additional eligibility requirements for [Visitors] coming to the UK to receive private medical treatment

Note: Word in heading substituted from 6 October 2021 subject to savings for applications made before that date (HC 617)

V 7.1. If the applicant is suffering from a communicable disease they must have satisfied the medical inspector that they are not a danger to public health.

[**V 7.2.** The applicant must have arranged their private medical treatment before they travel to the UK, and must provide either:

(a) a letter from their doctor or consultant in the UK detailing:

(i) the medical condition requiring consultation or treatment; and

(ii) the estimated costs and likely duration of any treatment, which must be of a finite duration; and

(iii) where the consultation or treatment will take place; or

(b) if the applicant intends to receive NHS treatment under a reciprocal healthcare arrangement between the UK and another country, an authorisation form issued by the government of that country.]

Note: Paragraph substituted from 6 April 2021 subject to savings for applications made before that date (HC 1248).

[**V 7.3.** If the applicant is applying for an 11-month entry clearance for the purposes of private medical treatment they must also:

(a) provide either:

(i) evidence from their doctor or consultant in the UK that the proposed treatment is likely to exceed 6 months, but not more than 11 months; or

(ii) if the applicant intends to receive NHS treatment under a reciprocal health-care arrangement between the UK and another country, an authorisation form issued by the government of that country which clearly states that the proposed treatment is likely to exceed 6 months, but not more than 11 months; and

(b) [provide a valid medical certificate, if paragraph A39 and Appendix T of these rules apply, confirming that they have undergone screening for active pulmonary tuberculosis and that this tuberculosis is not present in them].]

Note: Paragraph substituted from 6 April 2021 subject to savings for applications made before that date (HC 1248). Words in (b) substituted from 6 October 2021 subject to savings for applications made before that date (HC 617).

Additional eligibility requirements for [Visitors] coming to the UK to donate an organ

Note: Word in heading substituted from 6 October 2021 subject to savings for applications made before that date (HC 617)

V 8.1. The applicant must satisfy the decision maker that they genuinely intend to donate an organ to, or be assessed as a potential organ donor for, an identified recipient in the UK with whom they have a genetic or close personal relationship.

V 8.2. The applicant must provide written confirmation of medical tests to show that they are a donor match to the identified recipient, or that they are undergoing further tests to be assessed as a potential donor to the identified recipient.

V 8.3. The applicant must provide a letter, dated no more than 3 months before the applicant's intended date of arrival in the UK from either:

(a) the lead nurse or coordinator of the UK NHS Trust's Living Donor Kidney Transplant team; or

(b) a UK registered medical practitioner who holds an NHS consultant post or who appears in the Specialist Register of the General Medical Council;

which confirms that the applicant meets the requirements in V 8.1. and V 8.2. and confirms when and where the planned organ transplant or medical tests will take place.

V 8.4. The applicant must be able to show, if required to do so, that the identified recipient is lawfully present in the UK, or will be at the time of the planned organ transplant.

Additional eligibility requirements for [Visitors] coming to the UK to study for up to six months

Note: Word in heading substituted from 6 October 2021 subject to savings for applications made before that date (HC 617)

[V 9.1 Where the applicant is seeking to come to the UK to study, they must have been accepted onto a course of study that is to be provided by an Accredited Institution that is not a State Funded School or Academy.]

Note: Paragraph substituted from 6 April 2021 subject to savings for applications made before that date (HC 1248). Paragraph substituted from 6 October 2021 subject to savings for applications made before that date (HC 617).

[V 9.2. The course of study referred to in V 9.1. must last no longer than six months unless the course is being undertaken from outside the UK as a Distance Learning Course.]

Note: Paragraph substituted from 6 April 2021 subject to savings for applications made before that date (HC 1248). Paragraph substituted from 6 October 2021 subject to savings for applications made before that date (HC 617).

[V 9.3. Where the applicant is seeking to come to the UK for up to six months to undertake electives relevant to a course of study abroad, they must:

(a) be aged 16 or over; and

(b) be enrolled on a course of study abroad equivalent to at least degree level study in the UK; and

(c) be studying medicine, veterinary medicine and science, nursing, or dentistry as their principal course of study; and

(d) have been accepted by a UK Higher Education Provider to undertake electives relevant to their course of study provided these are unpaid and involve no treatment of patients; and

(e) provide written confirmation from the UK Higher Education Provider.]

Note: Paragraph inserted from 6 April 2021 subject to savings for applications made before that date (HC 1248). Paragraph substituted from 6 October 2021 subject to savings for applications made before that date (HC 617).

[V 9.4. Where the applicant is seeking to come to the UK to undertake research or be taught about research (research tuition) for up to six months:

(a) they must be aged 16 or over; and

(b) they must be enrolled on a course of study abroad equivalent to at least degree level study in the UK; and

(c) they must have been accepted by a UK Higher Education Provider to undertake research or be taught about research (research tuition); and

(d) the overseas course provider must confirm that the research or research tuition is part of or relevant to the course of study that they are enrolled on overseas; and

(e) this must not amount to the Visitor being employed at the UK institution.]

Note: Paragraph inserted from 6 October 2021 subject to savings for applications made before that date (HC 617).

[V 9.5. The research or research tuition referred to in V 9.4. may be undertaken at a UK research institute, providing a formal partnership exists between the research institute and the UK Higher Education Provider for this purpose.]

Note: Paragraph inserted from 6 October 2021 subject to savings for applications made before that date (HC 617).

Additional eligibility requirements for academics seeking to come to the UK for more than 6 months

V 10.1. An academic applying for a 12-month entry clearance must:

(a) intend to undertake one [(or more)]of the permitted activities in Appendix Visitor: Permitted Activities at PA 11.2. for up to 12 months; and

(b) be highly qualified within their own field of expertise; and [(c) currently be working in that field at an academic institution or institution of higher education overseas; and]

[(d) provide a valid medical certificate, if paragraph A39 and Appendix T of these rules apply, confirming that they have undergone screening for active pulmonary tuberculosis and that this tuberculosis is not present in them.]

Note: Words in (a) inserted, (c) and (d) substituted from 6 October 2021 subject to savings for applications made before that date (HC 617).

Additional eligibility requirements for [Visitors] coming to the UK for work related training

Note: Word in heading substituted from 6 October 2021 subject to savings for applications made before that date (HC 617)

V 11.1. Where the applicant is seeking to come to the UK to undertake a clinical attachment or dental observer post as an overseas graduate from [a medical, dental or nursing school], they must provide written confirmation of their offer to take up this post and confirm they have not previously undertaken this activity in the UK.

Note: Words substituted from 6 October 2021 subject to savings for applications made before that date (HC 617).

V 11.2. Where the applicant is seeking to come to the UK to take the Professional and Linguistic Assessment Board test, they must provide written confirmation of this from the General Medical Council.

V 11.3. Where the applicant is seeking to come to the UK to take the Objective Structured Clinical Examinations for overseas, they must provide written confirmation of this from the Nursing and Midwifery Council.

Additional eligibility requirement for [Visitors] coming [to the UK] for purpose of marriage or civil partnership

Note: Word in heading substituted from 6 October 2021 subject to savings for applications made before that date (HC 617)

V 12.1. The applicant must be aged 18 or over on the date of application.

V 12.2. [The applicant] must, within the period for which they are seeking permission as a visitor:

(a) intend to give notice of marriage or civil partnership in the UK; or

(b) intend to marry or form a civil partnership in the UK;

which is not a sham marriage or sham civil partnership.

Note: Words in introduction substituted from 6 April 2021 subject to savings for applications made before that date (HC 1248).

Additional eligibility requirement for [Visitors] coming [to the UK] for Permitted Paid Engagements

Note: Word in heading substituted from 6 October 2021 subject to savings for applications made before that date (HC 617)

V 13.1. An applicant as a [Permitted Paid Engagement] [Visitor] must be aged 18 or over on the date of application.

Note: Words substituted from 6 October 2021 subject to savings for applications made before that date (HC 617)

V 13.2. The applicant must intend to do one (or more) of the permitted paid engagements set out in V 13.3. which must be:

(a) arranged before the applicant travels to the UK; and

(b) declared as part of the application for entry clearance or permission to enter the UK; and

(c) evidenced by a formal invitation[, as required by V 13.3]; and

(d) relate to the applicant's area of expertise and occupation overseas.

Note: Words in (d) inserted from 6 October 2021 subject to savings for applications made before that date (HC 617)

V 13.3. The following are permitted paid engagements:

(a) an academic who is highly qualified within their field of expertise, coming to examine students and/or participate in or chair selection panels, and have been invited by a UK higher education institution, or a UK-based research or arts organisation as part of that institution or organisation's quality assurance processes; and

(b) an expert coming to give lectures in their subject area, where they have been invited by a higher education [institution,] or a UK-based research or arts organisation, and this does not amount to filling a teaching position for the host organisation; and

(c) an overseas designated pilot examiner coming to assess UK-based pilots to ensure they meet the national aviation regulatory requirements of other countries, where they have been invited by an approved training organisation based in the UK that is regulated by the UK Civil Aviation Authority for that purpose; and

(d) a qualified lawyer coming to provide advocacy for a court or tribunal hearing, arbitration or other form of dispute resolution for legal proceedings within the UK, where they have been invited by a client; and

(e) a professional artist, entertainer, or musician coming to carry out an activity directly relating to their profession, where they have been invited by a creative (arts or entertainment) organisation, agent or broadcaster based in the UK; and

(f) a [Professional Sportsperson] coming to carry out an activity directly relating to their profession, where they have been invited by a sports organisation, agent, or broadcaster based in the UK.

Note: Words in (b) and (f) substituted from 6 October 2021 subject to savings for applications made before that date (HC 617)

Eligibility requirement for [Visitors] coming [to the UK] to transit

Note: Word in heading substituted from 6 October 2021 subject to savings for applications made before that date (HC 617)

[**V 14.1.** A visa national must hold entry clearance as a Standard Visitor, Marriage/Civil Partnership Visitor or Transit Visitor, unless they meet the requirements for admission under Appendix Visitor: Transit Without Visa Scheme, in which case they may apply for permission to enter on arrival in the UK.]

Note: Paragraph substituted from 6 October 2021 subject to savings for applications made before that date (HC 617).

V 14.2. An applicant applying for entry clearance or permission to enter as a Transit [Visitor] must satisfy the decision maker that they:

(a) are genuinely in transit to another country outside the Common Travel Area, meaning the main purpose of their visit is to transit the UK (passing through immigration control) and that the applicant is taking a reasonable transit route; and

(b) will not access public funds or medical treatment, work or study in the UK; and

(c) genuinely intend and are able to leave the UK within 48 hours after their arrival; and

(d) are assured entry to their country of destination and any other countries they are transiting on their way there.

Note: Words substituted from 6 October 2021 subject to savings for applications made before that date (HC 617)

Additional eligibility requirements for permission to stay as a [Visitor]

Note: Word in heading substituted from 6 October 2021 subject to savings for applications made before that date (HC 617)

[**V 15.1.** Where the applicant is applying for permission to stay as a [[Visitor]] for the purpose of receiving private medical treatment they must also:

(a) satisfy the decision maker that the costs of any medical treatment already received have been met; and

(b) provide either:

(i) a letter from a registered medical practitioner, at a private practice or NHS hospital, who holds an NHS consultant post or who appears in the Specialist Register of the General Medical Council, detailing the medical condition requiring further treatment; or

(ii) if the applicant intends to continue to receive NHS treatment under a reciprocal healthcare arrangement between the UK and another country, an authorisation form issued by the government of that country which authorises further treatment.]

Note: Paragraph substituted from 6 April 2021 subject to savings for applications made before that date (HC 1248). Word in double square brackets substituted from 6 October 2021 subject to savings for applications made before that date (HC 617).

[**V 15.2.** Where the applicant applying for permission to stay is an academic (or the accompanying partner or child of such an academic) they must:

(a) continue to intend to do one (or more) of the activities at Appendix Visitor: Permitted Activities at PA 11.2; and

(b) be highly qualified within their own field of expertise; and (c) have been working in that field at an academic institution or institution of higher education overseas prior to their arrival in the UK.]

Note: Paragraph substituted from 6 April 2021 subject to savings for applications made before that date (HC 1248). Paragraph substituted from 6 October 2021 subject to savings for applications made before that date (HC 617)

[V 15.3 . Where [[the]]applicant is applying for permission to stay as a [[visitor]] to resit the Professional and Linguistic Assessment Board Test, they must provide written confirmation of this from the General Medical Council.]

Note: Paragraph substituted from 6 April 2021 subject to savings for applications made before that date (HC 1248). Words in double square brackets substituted from 6 October 2021 subject to savings for applications made before that date (HC 617)

[V 15.4. Where the applicant is applying for permission to stay as a [[Visitor]] and they are an overseas graduate of a medical, dental or nursing school intending to undertake an unpaid clinical attachment or dental observer post, they must have been successful in the Professional and Linguistic Assessment Board test.]

Note: Paragraph substituted from 6 April 2021 subject to savings for applications made before that date (HC 1248). Word in double square brackets substituted from 6 October 2021 subject to savings for applications made before that date (HC 617)

V 15.5. [DELETED]

Note: Paragraph deleted from 6 April 2021 subject to savings for applications made before that date (HC 1248).

Decision

V 16.1. If the decision maker is satisfied that all the suitability requirements are met, and that the relevant eligibility requirements for a [Visitor] are met, the application will be granted, otherwise the application will be refused.

Note: Words substituted from 6 October 2021 subject to savings for applications made before that date (HC 617)

Period and conditions of grant for [Visitors]

Note: Word in heading substituted from 6 October 2021 subject to savings for applications made before that date (HC 617)

V 17.1. The grant will be subject to all the following conditions:

(a) no access to public funds; and

(b) no work (which does not prohibit the permitted activities in Appendix Visitor: Permitted Activities, [Appendix Visitor: Permit Free Festival List] or the Permitted Paid Engagements in V 13.3.); and

(c) no study except where permitted by Appendix Visitor: Permitted Activities at PA 2. and [PA 17.]

[(d) study or research as part of a permitted activity is subject to the ATAS condition in Appendix ATAS.]

Note: Words in (c) substituted from 6 April 2021 subject to savings for applications made before that date; sub-paragraph .(d) inserted from 09:00 on 21 May 2021 subject to savings for applications made before that time (HC 1248). Words in (b) substituted from 6 October 2021 subject to savings for applications made before that date (HC 617).

V 17.2. Entry clearance and permission to enter as a [[Visitor]] will be granted for the periods set out in the following table:

	Visitor type	Maximum initial length of stay in UK
(a)	Standard [[Visitor]]	up to 6 months, except: (i) a [[Visitor]] who is coming to the UK for private medical treatment may be granted entry clearance for up to 11 months; (ii) an academic (or the accompanying partner or child of [such] an academic), who is employed by an overseas institution and is carrying out the specific permitted activities at paragraph PA.11.2., may be granted entry clearance for up to 12 months; (iii) a [[Visitor]] under the Approved Destination Status Agreement may be granted entry clearance for up to 30 days.
(b)	Marriage/civil partnership [[Visitor]]	up to 6 months
(c)	Permitted Paid [[Engagement]] (PPE) [[Visitor]]	up to 1 month
(d)	Transit [[Visitor]]	up to 48 hours, except for permission to enter as a Transit [[Visitor]] under the Transit Without [. . .] Visa Scheme which may be granted until 23:59 hours on the next day after the day the applicant arrived in the UK.

Note: Words in double square brackets substituted, word in (a)(ii) inserted, word in (d) deleted from 6 October 2021 subject to savings for applications made before that date (HC 617)

V 17.3. Permission to stay will be granted for the following periods:

(a) a Standard [Visitor] or a [Marriage/Civil Partnership] [Visitor], who was granted permission for less than 6 months may be granted permission to stay for a period which results in the total period they can remain in the UK (including both the original grant and the extension) not exceeding 6 months; and

(b) a Standard [Visitor] who is in the UK for private medical treatment may be granted permission to stay as a visitor for a further 6 months, provided the purpose is for private medical treatment; and

(c) a Standard [Visitor] who is in the UK to undertake the activities in Appendix Visitor: Permitted Activities at PA 11.2. or the accompanying partner or child of such a Standard [Visitor], may be granted permission to stay for a period which results in the total period they can remain in the UK (including both the original grant and the extension) not exceeding 12 months; and

(d) a Standard [Visitor] may be granted permission to stay as a [Visitor] for up to 6 months in order to resit the Professional and Linguistic Assessment Board Test; and

(e) a Standard [Visitor] who is successful in the Professional and Linguistic Assessment Board Test may be granted permission to stay as a [Visitor] to undertake [the activities in PA 10.1(a)] for a period which results in the total period they can remain in the UK (including both the original grant and the extension) not exceeding 18 months.]

Note: Words substituted from 6 October 2021 subject to savings for applications made before that date (HC 617).

Appendix inserted from 09:00 on 1 December 2020 subject to savings for applications made before that time (HC 813).

[Appendix Visitor: permitted activities

PA 1. Visitors are permitted to undertake the following activities:

	Visitor type	Visitors of this type can:
(a)	Standard [[Visitor]]	do all permitted activities in Appendix Visitor: Permitted Activities, except [[Visitors]] under the Approved Destination Status Agreement may only do the activities in PA 2(a).
(b)	[[Marriage/Civil Partnership]] [[Visitor]]	marry or form a civil partnership, or give notice of marriage or civil partnership and do all permitted activities in Appendix Visitor: Permitted Activities, other than study as described in PA [17.1.]
(c)	[[Permitted Paid Engagement]] [[Visitor]]	do the permitted paid engagements in Appendix V: Visitor at V 13.3. and all permitted activities in Appendix Visitor: Permitted Activities other than study as described in [PA 17.1.] to and transit as described in PA 18.
(d)	Transit [[Visitor]]	transit in the UK as described in PA 18.

Note: Words in (b) and (c) substituted from 6 April 2021 subject to savings for applications made before that date (HC 1248). Words in double square brackets substituted from 6 October 2021 subject to savings for applications made before that date (HC 617).

Tourism and Leisure

PA 2. A [Visitor] may:

(a) visit friends and family and / or come to the UK for a holiday; and

(b) take part in educational exchanges or visits with a state funded school or academy or independent school; and

(c) attend recreational courses (not English Language training) for a maximum of 30 days.

Note: Words substituted from 6 October 2021 subject to savings for applications made before that date (HC 617).

Volunteering

PA 3. A [Visitor] may undertake volunteering provided it lasts no more than 30 days in total and is for a charity that is registered with either the Charity Commission for England and Wales; the Charity Commission for Northern Ireland; or the Office of the Scottish Charity Regulator.

Note: Words substituted from 6 October 2021 subject to savings for applications made before that date (HC 617).

General Business Activities

PA 4. A [Visitor] may:

(a) attend meetings, conferences, seminars, interviews; and

(b) give a one-off or short series of talks and speeches provided these are not organised as commercial events and will not make a profit for the organiser; and

(c) negotiate and sign deals and contracts; and

(d) attend trade fairs, for promotional work only, provided the [Visitor] is not directly selling; and

(e) carry out site visits and inspections; and

(f) gather information for their employment overseas; and

(g) be briefed on the requirements of a UK based customer, provided any work for the customer is done outside of the UK.

Note: Words substituted from 6 October 2021 subject to savings for applications made before that date (HC 617).

Intra-corporate Activities

PA 5. An employee of an overseas based company may:

(a) advise and consult; and

(b) trouble-shoot; and

(c) provide training; and

(d) share skills and knowledge;

on a specific internal project with UK employees of the same corporate group, provided no work is carried out directly with clients.

PA 6. An internal auditor may carry out regulatory or financial audits at a UK branch of the same group of companies as the [Visitor's] employer overseas.

Note: Words substituted from 6 October 2021 subject to savings for applications made before that date (HC 617).

Manufacture and supply of goods to the UK

[**PA 7.** An employee of an overseas company may install, dismantle, repair, service or advise on machinery, equipment, computer software or hardware (or train UK based workers to provide these services) where there is a contract of purchase, supply or lease with a UK company or organisation and either:

(a) the overseas company is the manufacturer or supplier; or

(b) the overseas company is part of a contractual arrangement for after sales services agreed at the time of the sale or lease, including in a warranty or other service contract incidental to the sale or lease.]

Note: Paragraph substituted from 6 April 2021 subject to savings for applications made before that date (HC 1248). Paragraph substituted from 6 October 2021 subject to savings for applications made before that date (HC 617).

Clients of UK export companies

PA 8. A client of a UK export company may be seconded to the UK company in order to oversee the requirements for goods and services that are being provided under contract by the UK company or its subsidiary company, provided the two companies are not part of the same group. [. . .]

Note: Words deleted from 6 October 2021 subject to savings for applications made before that date (HC 617).

Overseas roles requiring specific activities in the UK

PA 9. [DELETED]

Note: Paragraph deleted from 23:00 on 31 December 2020 for decisions made on or after that time (HC 1043).

[PA 9.1. Individuals employed outside the UK may visit the UK to take part in the following activities in relation to their employment overseas:

(a) a translator and/or interpreter may translate and/or interpret in the UK as an employee of an enterprise located overseas; or

(b) personal assistants and bodyguards may support an overseas business person in carrying out permitted activities, provided they will attend the same event(s) as the business person and are employed by them outside the UK. They must not be providing personal care or domestic work for the business person; or

(c) a tour group courier, contracted to a company with its headquarters outside the UK, who is entering and departing the UK with a tour group organised by their company; or

(d) a journalist, correspondent, producer or cameraman gathering information for an overseas publication, programme or film; or

(e) archaeologists taking part in a one-off archaeological excavation; or

[(f) a professor from an overseas academic institution accompanying students to the UK as part of a study abroad programme, may provide a small amount of teaching to the students at the host organisation providing this does not amount to filling a permanent teaching role for that institution; or]

(g) market researchers and analysts may conduct market research or analysis for an enterprise located outside the UK.]

Note: Paragraph inserted from 23:00 on 31 December 2020 for decisions made on or after that time (HC 1043). Paragraph substituted from 6 April 2021 subject to savings for applications made before that date (HC 1248). Sub-paragraph (f) substituted from 6 October 2021 subject to savings for applications made before that date (HC 617).

[PA 9.2. Drivers on a genuine international route between the UK and a country outside the UK may:

(a) deliver or collect goods or passengers from a country outside the UK to the UK; and

(b) undertake cabotage operations.]

Note: Paragraph inserted from 23:00 on 31 December 2020 for decisions made on or after that time (HC 1043). Paragraph substituted from 6 April 2021 subject to savings for applications made before that date (HC 1248).

[PA 9.3. Drivers under PA 9.2. must be employed or contracted to an operator registered in a country outside the UK or be a self-employed operator and driver based outside the UK and the operator must hold an International Operators Licence or be operating on an own account basis.]

Note: Paragraph inserted from 6 April 2021 subject to savings for applications made before that date (HC 1248).

Work-related training

PA 10.1. Overseas graduates from medical, dental or nursing schools may:

(a) undertake clinical attachments or dental observer posts provided these are unpaid and involve no treatment of patients, where the additional requirements of Appendix V: Visitor at V 11.1. are also met; and

(b) take the following test/examination in the UK:

(i) the Professional and Linguistic Assessment Board test, where the additional requirements of Appendix V: Visitor at V 11.2. are also met; or

(ii) the Objective Structured Clinical Examinations for overseas, where the additional requirements of Appendix V: Visitor at V 11.3. are also met.

PA 10.2. Employees of an overseas company or organisation may receive training from a UK based company or organisation in work practices and techniques which are required for the [Visitor's] employment overseas and not available in their home country.

Note: Words substituted from 6 October 2021 subject to savings for applications made before that date (HC 617).

PA 10.3. An employee of an overseas based training company may deliver a short series of training to employees of a UK based company, where the trainer is employed by an overseas business contracted to deliver global training to the international corporate group to which the UK based company belongs.

Science and academia

PA 11.1. Scientists and researchers may:

(a) gather information and facts for a specific project which directly relates to their employment overseas[, or conduct independent research]; and

(b) share knowledge or advise on an international project that is being led from the UK, provided the visitor is not carrying out research in the UK.

Note: Words in (a) inserted from 23:00 on 31 December 2020 for decisions made on or after that time (CP 361).

PA 11.2. Academics may:

(a) take part in formal exchange arrangements with UK counterparts (including doctors); and

(b) carry out research for their own purposes if they are on sabbatical leave from their home institution; and

(c) if they are an eminent senior doctor or dentist, take part in research, teaching or clinical practice provided this does not amount to filling a permanent teaching post.

Legal

PA 12.1. An expert witness may visit the UK to give evidence in a UK court; other witnesses may attend a court hearing in the UK if summoned in person by a UK court.

PA 12.2. An overseas lawyer may advise a UK based client on specific international litigation and/or an international transaction.

Religion

PA 13. Religious workers overseas may visit the UK to preach or do pastoral work.

Creative

PA 14.1. An artist, entertainer, or musician may:

(a) give performances as an individual or as part of a group; and

(b) take part in competitions or auditions; and

(c) make personal appearances and take part in promotional activities; and

(d) take part in one or more cultural events or festivals on the list of permit free festivals in Appendix Visitor: Permit Free Festival List.

PA 14.2. Personal or technical staff or members of the production team of an artist, entertainer or musician may support the activities in PA 14.1. or Appendix V: Visitor at V 13.3. (e) provided they are attending the same event as the artist, entertainer or musician, and are employed to work for them outside of the UK.

PA.14.3. Film crew (actor, producer, director or technician) employed by an overseas company may visit the UK to take part in a location shoot for a film or programme or other media content that is produced and financed overseas.

Sports

PA 15.1. A sports person may:

(a) take part in a sports tournament or sports event as an individual or part of a team; and

(b) make personal appearances and take part in promotional activities; and

(c) take part in trials provided they are not in front of a paying audience; and

(d) take part in short periods of training provided they are not being paid by a UK sporting body; and

(e) join an amateur team or club to gain experience in a particular sport if they are an amateur in that sport.

PA 15.2. Personal or technical staff of the sports person, or sports officials, may support the activities in PA 15.1. or in Appendix V: Visitor at V 13.3.(f), if they are attending the same event as the sports [person. Personal] or technical staff of the sports person must be employed to work for the sports person outside the UK.

Note: Words substituted from 6 October 2021 subject to savings for applications made before that date (HC 617).

Medical treatment and organ donation

PA 16.1. A [Visitor] may receive private medical treatment provided the additional requirements at Appendix V: Visitor at V 7.1. to V 7.3. are also met.

Note: Words substituted from 6 October 2021 subject to savings for applications made before that date (HC 617).

PA.16.2. A [Visitor] may act as an organ donor or be assessed as a potential organ donor to an identified recipient in the UK, provided the additional requirements at Appendix V: Visitor at V 8.1. to V 8.4. are also met.

Note: Words substituted from 6 October 2021 subject to savings for applications made before that date (HC 617).

Study as a Visitor

[PA 17. A [Visitor] may study for up to six months providing the requirements of V 9.1. to [V 9.5.] are met.

Note: Paragraph inserted from 6 April 2021 subject to savings for applications made before that date (HC 1248). Words substituted from 6 October 2021 subject to savings for applications made before that date (HC 617).

PA 17.1. [DELETED]

Note: Paragraph deleted from 6 April 2021 subject to savings for applications made before that date (HC 1248).

PA 17.2. [DELETED]

Note: Paragraph deleted from 6 April 2021 subject to savings for applications made before that date (HC 1248).

PA 17.3. [DELETED]

Note: Paragraph deleted from 6 April 2021 subject to savings for applications made before that date (HC 1248).

Transit

PA 18. A [Visitor] may transit the UK, provided they meet the requirements of Appendix V: Visitor at V 14.1. and V 14.2.]

Note: Words substituted from 6 October 2021 subject to savings for applications made before that date (HC 617).

Appendix inserted from 09:00 on 1 December 2020 subject to savings for applications made before that time (HC813).

[Appendix Visitor: Visa national list

VN 1.1. A person who meets one or more of the criteria below needs entry clearance (also referred to as visa) in advance of travel to the UK as a [[Visitor]], or for any other purpose for less than six months {where there is no mandatory entry clearance requirement}, unless they meet one of the exceptions set out in [[VN 2.1., VN 2.2 (subject to VN 2.3.)]].

(a) Nationals or citizens of the following countries or territorial entities (a '*' indicates there are exceptions in VN 2.2 to VN 6.5):

Afghanistan
Albania
Algeria
Angola
Armenia
Azerbaijan
Bahrain*
Bangladesh
Belarus
Benin
Bhutan
Bolivia

Bosnia Herzegovina
Burkina Faso
Burundi
Cambodia
Cameroon
Cape Verde
Central African Republic
Chad
People's Republic of China*
Colombia
Comoros
Congo
Côte d'Ivoire ([formerly] Ivory Coast)
Cuba
Democratic Republic of the Congo
Djibouti
Dominican Republic
Ecuador
Egypt
[[[El Salvador]]]
Equatorial Guinea
Eritrea
Eswatini ([formerly] Swaziland)
Ethiopia
Fiji
Gabon
Gambia
Georgia
Ghana
Guinea
Guinea Bissau
Guyana
Haiti
India
Indonesia*
Iran
Iraq
Jamaica
Jordan
Kazakhstan
Kenya
Korea (North)
Kosovo
Kuwait *
Kyrgyzstan
Laos
Lebanon
Lesotho
Liberia
Libya
Madagascar
Malawi
Mali
Mauritania
Moldova
Mongolia
Montenegro
Morocco
Mozambique
Myanmar ([formerly] Burma)
Nepal
Niger
Nigeria
North Macedonia ([formerly] Macedonia)
Oman*
Pakistan
Peru
Philippines
Qatar*
Russia
Rwanda
São Tomé and Principe
Saudi Arabia
Senegal
Serbia
Sierra Leone
Somalia
South Africa*
South Sudan
Sri Lanka
Sudan
Suriname
Syria
Taiwan*
Tajikistan
Tanzania
Thailand
Togo
Tunisia
Turkey *
Turkmenistan
Uganda
Ukraine
United Arab Emirates*
Uzbekistan
Venezuela
Vietnam*
Yemen
Zambia
Zimbabwe

(b) stateless people; and

(c) people travelling on any document other than a national passport, or, in the case of {{a person to whom paragraphs 11A and 11B of these rules apply}}, a national identity card, regardless of whether the document is issued by or evidences nationality of a state not listed in VN 1.1. (a), except where that document has been issued by the UK.

Note: Words in list substituted from 6 April 2021 subject to savings for applications made before that date (HC 1248). Words in double square brackets substituted, words in curly brackets inserted from 6 October 2021 subject to savings for applications made before that date; words in double curly brackets substituted from 1 October 2021 (HC 617). Words in triple square brackets inserted from 16:00 on 11 May 2022 subject to savings for applications made before that time (HC 17).

Exceptions to the list of visa nationals

Holders of specified travel documents

VN 2.1. It is not necessary for a [Transit Visitor] to hold [an entry clearance] before they travel to the UK if they are travelling on an emergency travel document issued by, and evidencing the nationality of, a country not listed in [...] VN 1.1.(a) and the purpose of their [Transit] is to travel to the country in which they are ordinarily resident.

Note: Words substituted, word deleted from 6 October 2021 subject to savings for applications made before that date (HC 617).

VN 2.2. The following people do not need a visit visa before they travel to the UK as a [Visitor], other than where VN 2.3. applies:

(a) nationals or citizens of the People's Republic of China who hold a passport issued by the Hong Kong Special Administrative Region; or

(b) nationals or citizens of the People's Republic of China who hold a passport issued by the Macao Special Administrative Region; or

(c) nationals or citizens of Taiwan who hold a passport issued by Taiwan that includes in it the number of the identification card issued by the competent authority in Taiwan; or

(d) people who hold a Service, Temporary Service or Diplomatic passport issued by the Holy See; or

(e) nationals or citizens of Oman who hold a diplomatic or special passport issued by Oman; or

(f) nationals or citizens of Qatar who hold a diplomatic or special passport issued by Qatar; or

(g) nationals or citizens of the United Arab Emirates who hold a diplomatic or special passport issued by the United Arab Emirates; or

(h) nationals or citizens of Turkey who hold a diplomatic passport issued by Turkey; or

(i) nationals or citizens of Kuwait who hold a diplomatic or special passport issued by Kuwait; or

(j) nationals or citizens of Bahrain who hold a diplomatic or special passport issued by Bahrain; or

(k) nationals or citizens of South Africa who hold a diplomatic passport issued by South Africa; or

(l) nationals or citizens of Vietnam who hold a diplomatic passport issued by Vietnam; or

(m) nationals or citizens of Indonesia who hold a diplomatic passport issued by Indonesia[; or]

[(n) nationals or citizens of El Salvador who hold confirmed bookings to the UK made before 1600 BST on 11 May 2022 where arrival in the UK is no later than 8 June 2022.]

Note: Words substituted from 6 October 2021 subject to savings for applications made before that date (HC 617). Punctuation in (m) substituted, sub-paragraph (n) inserted from 16:00 on 11 May 2022 subject to savings for applications made before that time (HC 17).

VN 2.3. VN 2.2. does not apply where the person is:

(a) visiting the UK to marry or to form a civil partnership, or to give notice of marriage or civil partnership, unless they are a 'relevant national' as defined in section 62 of the Immigration Act 2014; or

(b) seeking to visit the UK for more than 6 months.

Exception where the applicant holds an Electronic Visa Waiver (EVW) Document [(Bahrain, Kuwait, Oman, Qatar, Saudi Arabia and United Arab Emirates nationals or citizens only)]

Note: Words in heading substituted from 1 June 2022 subject to savings for applications made before that date (HC 17).

VN 3.1. The holder of a valid Electronic Visa Waiver (EVW) Document does not need to obtain a visit visa, or a visa for entry for six months or less where there is no mandatory entry clearance requirement, in advance of arrival in the UK, but can instead apply for permission to enter at the UK border.

VN 3.2. VN 3.1. will not apply (meaning that the person will normally be refused permission to enter the UK) unless the EVW Document is used in the manner specified in VN 6.1. to VN 6.5.

VN 3.3. An EVW Document relates to one person and may only be used for one application for permission to enter the UK or, where applicable, one crossing of the land border from the Republic of Ireland to the UK.

Obtaining an Electronic Visa Waiver Document

[**VN 4.1.** Only passport holders who are nationals or citizens of Bahrain, Kuwait, Oman, Qatar, Saudi Arabia or the United Arab Emirates can obtain and use an EVW document.]

Note: Paragraph substituted from 1 June 2022 subject to savings for applications made before that date (HC 17).

VN 4.2. To obtain an EVW Document, a person must provide the required biographic and travel information at the website established by the UK Government at https://www.electronic-visa-waiver.service.gov.uk/.

VN 4.3. EVW Documents are issued to the applicant in electronic form.

Validity Requirements for an Electronic Visa Waiver Document

VN 5.1. To be valid the biographic details on the EVW Document must match those of the holder's passport, except where:

(a) an apostrophe, space or hyphen is present in the holder's name on their EVW Document but is not present in the holder's name on their passport; or

(b) an apostrophe, space or hyphen is present in the holder's name on their passport but is not present in the holder's name on their EVW Document.

VN 5.2. To be valid an EVW Document must be able to be presented by the holder:

(a) in clear, legible format; and

(b) in English; and

(c) electronically or in printed form.

VN 5.3. To be valid the EVW Document must specify the flight, train or ship on which the holder intends to arrive in the UK, including the port of departure and arrival, and the scheduled date and time of departure and arrival, unless VN 5.4. or VN 5.5. applies.

VN 5.4. Where the holder of an EVW Document is seeking to arrive in the UK by entering a control zone in France or Belgium or supplementary control zone in France, the EVW must specify the train or ship on which the holder intends to arrive in the UK, including:

(a) the railway station or port where the holder intends to enter the control zone or supplementary control zone and from which the holder intends to depart for the UK; and

(b) the railway station or port at which the holder intends to leave the train or ship after arrival in the UK; and

(c) the scheduled date and time of departure from, and arrival at, the specified railway stations or ports.

VN 5.5. Where the holder of an EVW Document intends to cross the land border from the Republic of Ireland to the UK by train, car or any other means, the EVW must specify the place at which it is intended to cross the border and the intended date and time of arrival in the UK.

VN 5.6. For the EVW to be valid the required information must be submitted at least 48 hours before the holder departs on a flight, train or ship to the UK or crosses the UK land border from the Republic of Ireland by train, car or any other means.

VN 5.7. To be valid the EVW Document must not have been issued more than 3 months before the date of the holder's scheduled departure to the UK as specified on the EVW Document or, where the holder intends to cross the land border with the Republic of Ireland, before the intended date of the holder's arrival in the UK as specified on the EVW Document.

Use of the Electronic Visa Waiver Document

VN 6.1. The holder must present the EVW Document to an Immigration Officer on request upon the holder's arrival at the UK Border or, where the holder is seeking to arrive in the UK by entering a control zone in France or Belgium or a supplementary control zone in France, upon arrival in that zone.

VN 6.2. Where the holder has presented a printed copy of the EVW Document, it must be surrendered to an Immigration Officer upon request.

VN 6.3. The holder must travel on the flight, train or ship specified on the EVW Document unless VN 6.4. or VN 6.5. applies.

VN 6.4. If the holder travels on a different flight, train or ship from that specified in the EVW Document it must depart from the same port or railway station and arrive at the same UK port or railway station as specified on the EVW Document and either:

(a) depart after the departure time specified on the EVW Document and arrive in the UK no more than 8 hours after the arrival time specified on the EVW Document; or

(b) if the holder is seeking to arrive in the UK by entering a control zone in France or Belgium or a supplementary control zone in France, arrive no more than 8 hours after the departure time specified on the EVW Document.

VN 6.5. If the holder is seeking to arrive in the UK by crossing the land border from the Republic of Ireland, the holder must cross at the time specified on the EVW Document, or no more than 8 hours after the time specified on the EVW Document.]

Note: Appendix inserted from 09:00 on 1 December 2020 subject to savings for applications made before that time (HC813).

[Appendix Visitor: Permit Free Festival List

Appendix Visitor: Permit Free Festival List

[PFF1. An artist, entertainer or musician visiting the UK to perform at one or more of the following permit free festivals may receive payment to do so:

(a) Aldeburgh Festival
(b) American Express presents BST Hyde Park
(c) Barbican Festivals – Live from the Barbican
(d) Belfast International Arts Festival
(e) Belsonic
(f) Billingham International Folklore Festival of World Dance
(g) Birmingham, Sandwell & Westside Jazz Festival
(h) Boomtown Festival
(i) Brass
(j) Breakin' Convention
(k) Brighton Festival
(l) Brighton Fringe
(m) Brouhaha International
(n) Cambridge Folk Festival
(o) Camp Bestival Dorset
(p) Camp Bestival Shropshire
(q) Celtic Connections
(r) Cheltenham Festivals (Jazz, Science, Music & Literature Festivals)
(s) Cornwall International Male Choral Festival
(t) Coventry UK City of Culture
(u) Creamfields North
(v) Creamfields South
(w) DaDaFest International
(x) Dance Umbrella
(y) Download
(z) Edinburgh Festival Fringe
(aa) Edinburgh International Book Festival
(bb) Edinburgh International Children's Festival

(cc) Edinburgh International Festival
(dd) Edinburgh International Jazz and Blues Festival
(ee) Freedom Festival Arts Trust
(ff) Garsington Opera
(gg) Glasgow International Jazz Festival
(hh) Glastonbury Festival
(ii) Glyndebourne
(jj) Greenbelt
(kk) Greenwich and Docklands International Festival
(ll) Green Man
(mm) Harrogate International Festivals
(nn) Hay Festival Foundation Ltd
(oo) Huddersfield Contemporary Music Festival
(pp) Isle of Wight Festival
(qq) Latitude
(rr) Leeds Festival
(ss) Llangollen International Musical Eisteddfod
(tt) London International Festival of Theatre (LIFT)
(uu) Love Supreme
(vv) Manchester International Festival
(ww) Meltdown (Southbank Centre)
(xx) Norfolk & Norwich Festival
(yy) Out There Festival
(zz) Parklife
(aaa) Reading Festival
(bbb) Shubbak
(ccc) Sonica
(ddd) Southbank Centre Festivals
(eee) SPECTRA Festival of Light
(fff) Summer at Snape
(ggg) The EFG London Jazz Festival
(hhh) The Great Escape Festival
(iii) The Royal Edinburgh Military Tattoo
(jjj) The Warehouse Project
(kkk) Wilderness
(lll) Wireless Festival
(mmm) WOMAD
(nnn) WWE Live.]

Note: Appendix inserted from 09:00 on 1 December 2020 subject to savings for applications made before that time (HC813). Paragraph substituted from 23:00 on 31 December 2020 for decisions made on or after that time (CP 361). Paragraph substituted from 6 April 2021 (HC 1248). Paragraph substituted from 6 April 2022 (HC 1118).

[Appendix Visitor: Transit Without Visa Scheme

[**TWOV 1.** To be granted permission to enter as a Transit Visitor under the Transit Without Visa Scheme a visa national must meet all the requirements at TWOV 2. and one of the requirements at TWOV 3.]

Note: Paragraph substituted from 6 October 2021 subject to savings for applications made before that date (HC 617).

TWOV 2. The applicant must:

(a) have arrived in the UK by air and will be departing by air; and

(b) be genuinely in transit to another country, meaning the purpose of their visit is to transit the UK and that the applicant is taking a reasonable transit route; and

(c) not access public funds or medical treatment, work or study in the UK; and

(d) genuinely intend and be able to leave the UK before 23:59 hours on the day after the day when they arrived; and

(e) have a confirmed booking on a flight departing the UK before 23:59 hours on the day after the day when they arrived; and

(f) be assured entry to their country of destination and any other countries they are transiting through on their way there.

TWOV 3. The applicant must also:

(a) be travelling to or from (or on part of a reasonable journey to or from) Australia, Canada, New Zealand or the USA and have a valid visa for that country; or

(b) be travelling from (or on part of a reasonable journey from) Australia, Canada, New Zealand or the USA and it is less than 6 months since he last entered that country with a valid entry visa; or

(c) hold a valid permanent residence permit issued by either: (i) Australia; or

(ii) Canada, issued after 28 June 2002; or

(iii) New Zealand; or

(d) hold a valid USA, I-551 permanent resident card issued on or after 21 April 1998; or

(e) hold a valid USA I-551 temporary immigrant visa (a wet-ink stamp version will not be accepted); or

(f) hold an expired USA I-551 permanent resident card issued on or after 21 April 1998, provided it is accompanied by a valid I-797 letter authorising extension of the period of permanent residency; or

(g) hold a valid standalone US immigration form 155A/155B attached to a sealed brown envelope; or

(h) hold a valid common format residence permit issued by an EEA state (pursuant to Council Regulation (EC) No. 1030/2002) or Switzerland; or

(i) hold a valid uniform format category D visa for entry to a state in the European Economic Area (EEA) or Switzerland; or

(j) be travelling on to the Republic of Ireland and have a valid Irish biometric visa; or

(k) be travelling from the Republic of Ireland and it is less than three months since the applicant was last given permission to land or be in the Republic by the Irish authorities with a valid Irish biometric visa.

TWOV 4. Paragraph TWOV 3.(a) and (b) do not apply where the transit passenger is a citizen or national of Syria holding a B1 or B2 category visa for entry to the United States of America.

TWOV 5. Electronic versions of any documents listed in [...] [TWOV 3.], such as electronic visas (including printed versions), will not be accepted.

Note: Word deleted, words substituted from 6 October 2021 subject to savings for applications made before that date (HC 617).

Appendix inserted from 09:00 on 1 December 2020 subject to savings for applications made before that time (HC813).

[Appendix S2 Healthcare Visitor

This route relates to the UK's exit from the European Union. It is for a person who, before the end of the transition period (11pm on 31 December 2020), had requested authorisation to receive a course of planned healthcare treatment under the S2 route, pursuant to Regulation (EC) No 883/2004.

The person seeking healthcare treatment may be accompanied on this route by another person who is providing care or support during the planned healthcare treatment.

Validity requirements for entry clearance or permission to stay as an S2 Healthcare Visitor

HV 1.1. A person applying for entry clearance as an S2 Healthcare Visitor must apply online on the specified form on the gov.uk website 'Apply for an exempt, diplomatic or official visit vignette or S2 Healthcare Visitor visa'.

HV 1.2. An application for entry clearance as an S2 Healthcare Visitor must be made while the applicant is outside the UK and to a post designated to accept such applications.

HV 1.3. A person applying for permission to stay as an S2 Healthcare Visitor must apply on form 'Application to extend stay in the UK: FLR(IR)' and must have, or have last held, permission as an S2 Healthcare Visitor.

HV 1.4. An application for entry clearance or permission to stay as an S2 Healthcare Visitor must meet all the following requirements:

(a) the applicant must have provided any required biometrics; and

(b) if the applicant is an EEA citizen they must have provided a passport or valid national identity card which satisfactorily establishes their identity and nationality; and

(c) if the applicant is a non-EEA citizen they must have provided a passport or other travel document which satisfactorily establishes their identity and nationality.

HV 1.5. A person to whom article 5 of the Immigration (Control of Entry Through Republic of Ireland) 1972 Order ('the 1972 Order') applies, may only apply for permission to stay under this Appendix where that permission is to commence after the end of the 6 month period set out in article 5 of the 1972 Order.

HV 1.6. An application for permission to stay as an S2 Healthcare Visitor must be made by a person:

(a) in the UK; and

(b) who has, or who last had, permission as an S2 Healthcare Visitor.

HV 1.7. An application which does not meet all the validity requirements for an S2 Healthcare Visitor is invalid and may be rejected and not considered.

Suitability requirements for an S2 Healthcare Visitor

HV 2.1. Subject to HV 2.2, an application must be refused on grounds of suitability where either of the following apply at the date of the decision:

(a) the applicant is subject to a deportation order or a decision to make a deportation order; or

(b) the applicant is subject to an exclusion order or exclusion decision.

HV 2.2. Where a decision under HV 2.1 relates to conduct committed before 11pm on 31 December 2020, the decision maker must be satisfied that the order or decision is justified on the grounds of public policy, public security or public health in accordance with regulation 27 of the EEA Regulations, irrespective of whether the EEA Regulations apply to that person (except that in applying this provision for 'an EEA decision' read 'a decision under HV 2.1 of Appendix S2 Healthcare Visitor').

HV 2.3. An application may be refused on grounds of suitability if, at the date of decision, the decision maker is satisfied that it is proportionate to refuse the application where:

(a) in relation to the application and whether or not to the applicant's knowledge, false or misleading information, representations or documents have been submitted (including false or misleading information submitted to any person to obtain a document used in support of the application); and the information, representation or documentation is material to the decision whether or not to grant the application; or

(b) in respect of conduct committed on or before 11pm on 31 December 2020, on grounds of public policy, public security or public health in accordance with regulation 27 of the EEA Regulations, irrespective of whether the EEA Regulations apply to that person (except that in applying this provision for 'an EEA decision' read 'a decision under paragraph HV 2.3 of Appendix S2 Healthcare Visitor'.); or

(c) in respect of conduct committed after 11pm on 31 December 2020, on the grounds that the presence of the applicant in the UK is not conducive to the public good; or

(d) subject to HV 2.4, the applicant is the subject of an Islands deportation order as defined by paragraph 3(6) of Schedule 4 to the Immigration Act 1971; or

(e) subject to HV 2.4, the applicant is the subject of an Islands exclusion decision which is a direction given by the relevant Minister or other authority in the Islands concerned that the applicant must be refused entry to the Island concerned on the grounds that their presence there would not be conducive to the public good..

HV 2.4. Where a decision under HV 2.3(d) or (e) relates to conduct at or before 11pm on 31 December 2020, the decision maker must be satisfied that the order or decision is justified on the grounds of public policy, public security or public health in accordance with regulation 27 of the EEA Regulations, irrespective of whether the EEA Regulations apply to that person (except that in applying this provision for 'an EEA decision' read 'a decision under HV 2.3 of Appendix S2 Healthcare Visitor').

Eligibility requirements for an S2 Healthcare Visitor

Entry requirements for an S2 Healthcare Visitor

HV 3.1. A person seeking to come to or stay in the UK as an S2 Healthcare Visitor must be a person to whom one of the following applies:

(a) Article 32(1)(b) of the withdrawal agreement; or
(b) Article 31(1)(b) of the EEA EFTA separation agreement; or
(c) Article 26a(1)(b) of the Swiss citizens' rights agreement.

HV 3.2. A person seeking to come to the UK as an S2 Healthcare Visitor and who is a visa national must apply for and obtain entry clearance as an S2 Healthcare Visitor before they arrive in the UK.

HV 3.3. A person to whom HV 3.2. applies will be refused permission to enter if they do not hold entry clearance as an S2 Healthcare Visitor on arrival in the UK.

HV 3.4. A person who is a non-visa national seeking to come to the UK as an S2 Healthcare Visitor may apply for permission to enter on arrival in the UK.

Financial requirement for an S2 Healthcare Visitor

HV 4.1. The applicant must have access to sufficient funds to cover all reasonable costs in relation to their visit without working or accessing public funds, including the cost of the return or onward journey.

HV 4.2. The applicant must show funds as specified in Appendix Finance.

HV 4.3. A S2 Healthcare Visitor's travel, maintenance and accommodation may be provided by a third party where the decision maker is satisfied that they can and will provide support to the S2 Healthcare Visitor for the intended duration of their stay.

Treatment requirement for an S2 Healthcare Visitor

HV 5.1. The course of planned healthcare treatment must have been arranged prior to the applicant's travel to the UK.

Patient (P) requirement

HV 6.1. Where the applicant is the patient (P) they must provide their valid S2 certificate of entitlement to scheduled treatment.

HV 6.2. Where P is applying for permission to stay for the purpose of completing the course of planned healthcare treatment detailed on their valid S2 certificate of entitlement to scheduled treatment they must provide documentation in accordance with one of the following;

(a) the valid S2 certificate of entitlement to scheduled treatment specified in HV 6.1 which demonstrates that the length of treatment extends beyond the entry clearance granted.

(b) a renewed or extended S2 certificate of entitlement to scheduled treatment which covers the period of the extension sought; or

(c) the valid S2 certificate of entitlement to scheduled treatment specified in HV 6.1. and a letter from the doctor or other health professional providing the treatment in the UK detailing the further treatment required.

Accompanying person (AP) requirement

HV 7.1. Where the applicant is an accompanying person (AP) they must meet one of the following requirements:

(a) AP is, or will be, accompanying the patient (P) to the UK at the time of their entry into the UK, and P is, or will be, an S2 Healthcare Visitor on arrival in the UK; or

(b) P is in the UK as an S2 Healthcare Visitor and AP will be joining P in the UK.

HV 7.2. AP must provide one of the following to demonstrate their relationship with the P:

(a) evidence of P's permission to enter or permission to stay as an S2 Healthcare Visitor; or

(b) P's S2 certificate of entitlement to scheduled treatment; and

(c) if P is an EEA citizen, P's valid national identity card or passport issued by an EEA State and if P is a non-EEA citizen, P's passport.

HV 7.3. AP must provide evidence that they reside in an EEA State or Switzerland.

HV 7.4. Where AP is applying for permission to stay they must also provide the relevant evidence required in HV 6.2.

HV 7.5. Where, in order to meet the requirements of HV 7.2. to HV 7.4., AP submits a copy (and not the original) of a document, the decision maker can require the applicant to submit the original document where the decision maker has reasonable doubt as to the genuineness of the copy submitted.

Consent requirement for child S2 Healthcare Visitor

HV 8.1. If the applicant is a child at the date of application and is not applying or travelling with a parent or legal guardian who is responsible for their care, the applicant must have consent from:

(a) a parent; or

(b) their legal guardian.

HV 8.2. The consent must confirm support for all of the following:

(a) the application; and

(b) the applicant's living and care arrangements in the UK; and

(c) if the application is for entry clearance or permission to enter, the applicant's travel to, and reception arrangements in, the UK.

HV 8.3. If requested, the consent in HV 8.1. must be given in writing.

Decision on application as an S2 Healthcare Visitor

HV 9.1. If the decision maker is satisfied that all the suitability and the relevant eligibility requirements are met for an S2 Healthcare Visitor, the application will be granted, otherwise the application will be refused.

Period and condition of grant for an S2 Healthcare Visitor

HV 10.1. An S2 Healthcare Visitor will be granted permission to enter for up to 6 months.

HV 10.2. An S2 Healthcare Visitor will be granted permission to stay for up to 6 months.

HV 10.3. The grant will be subject to all the following conditions:

(a) no access to public funds; and

(b) no work; and

(c) no study; and

(d) if Part 10 applies, the person will be required to register with the police.

Cancellation and curtailment

HV 11.1. An S2 Healthcare Visitor's entry clearance, permission to enter or permission to stay may be cancelled where the decision maker is satisfied that it is proportionate to cancel that entry clearance or permission where:

(a) the cancellation is justified on grounds of public policy, public security or public health, on the basis of the person's conduct on or before 11pm on 31 December 2020, in accordance with regulation 27 of the EEA Regulations, irrespective of whether the EEA Regulations apply to that person (except that in applying this provision for an 'EEA decision' read 'a decision under paragraph HV 11.1 of Appendix S2 Healthcare Visitor'); or

(b) the cancellation is justified on the ground that it is conducive to the public good, on the basis of the person's conduct after 11pm on 31 December 2020; or

(c) the cancellation is justified on grounds that, in relation to an application made under this Appendix, and whether or not to the applicant's knowledge, false or misleading information, representations or documents were submitted (including false or misleading information submitted to any person to obtain a document used in support of the application) and the information, representation or documentation was material to the decision to grant the applicant entry clearance, permission to enter or permission to stay under this Appendix; or

(d) they cease to meet the requirements of Appendix S2 Healthcare Visitor; or

(e) they have breached a condition of their permission as set out in HV 10.3. unless entry clearance or further permission was granted in the knowledge of the breach.]

Note: Appendix inserted from 09:00 on 1 December 2020 subject to savings for applications made before that time (HC813).

Appendix ST: STUDENT–[DELETED]

Note: Appendix inserted from 09:00 on 5 October 2020 subject to savings for applications made before that time (HC 707). Appendix deleted from 09:00 on 1 December 2020 subject to savings for applications made before that time (HC 813).

APPENDIX CS: CHILD STUDENT–[DELETED]

Note: Appendix inserted from 09:00 on 5 October 2020 subject to savings for applications made before that time (HC 707). Appendix deleted from 09:00 on 1 December 2020 subject to savings for applications made before that time (HC 813).

[Appendix Student

This route is for a person aged 16 or over who wants to study with a sponsor on a course of further or higher education, a pre-sessional English course, a recognised foundation programme, [. . .]or to take an elected post as a Student Union Sabbatical Officer.

The register of licensed student sponsors can be found at:

www.gov.uk/government/publications/register-of-licensed-sponsors-students

A person who is aged 16 or 17 and wants to study with a sponsor that is an Independent School on a course at Regulated Qualifications Framework 3 or Scottish Credit and Qualifications Framework 6 and above can apply as either a Student or as a Child Student (see Appendix Child Student).

A person who wants to study a course for 6 months or less without a student sponsor but with an accredited provider should apply under Appendix V: Visitor. A person aged 16 or over who wants to study an English Language course of 11 months or less without a student sponsor but with an accredited provider, should apply under Appendix Short-term Student.

Some Students can bring a dependent partner and dependent children to the UK, for example if they are studying at postgraduate level or on a government sponsored scheme. The Student route is not a route to settlement.

Note: Words in introductory paragraph deleted from 09:00 on 1 July 2021 subject to savings for applications (including for administrative review) made before that time (HC 1248).

Validity requirements for a Student

ST 1.1. A person applying for entry clearance or permission to stay as a Student must apply on the specified form on the gov.uk website as follows:

[(a) for out of country, form 'Student visa'; or

(b) for in country, form 'Student'.]

Note: Sub-paragraphs (a) and (b) substituted from 30 November 2021 subject to savings for applications made before that date (HC 617).

ST 1.2. An application for entry clearance or permission to stay as a Student must meet all the following requirements:

(a) any fee and Immigration Health Charge must have been paid; and

(b) the applicant must have provided any required biometrics; and

(c) the applicant must have provided a passport or other travel document which satisfactorily establishes their identity and nationality; and

(d) the applicant must provide a Confirmation of Acceptance for Studies reference number that was issued to them no more than 6 months before the date of application.

ST 1.3. If the applicant has, in the last 12 months before the date of application, completed a course of studies in the UK for which they have been awarded a scholarship or sponsorship by a Government or international scholarship agency covering both fees and living costs for study in the UK, they must provide written consent in relation to the application from that Government or agency.

ST 1.4. An applicant who is in the UK on the date of application must not have, or have last been granted, permission:

(a) as a Visitor; or

(b) as a Short-term Student; or

(c) as a Parent of a Child Student; or

(d) as a Seasonal Worker; or

(e) as a Domestic Worker in a Private Household; or

(f) outside the Immigration Rules.

ST 1.5. The applicant must be at least 16 years old on the date of application.

ST 1.6. An application which does not meet all the validity requirements for a Student is invalid and may be rejected and not considered.

Suitability requirements for a Student

ST 2.1. The applicant must not fall for refusal under Part 9: grounds for refusal.

ST 2.2. If the applicant is applying for permission to stay, they must not be:

(a) in the UK in breach of immigration laws, except that where paragraph 39E applies, that period of overstaying will be disregarded; or

(b) on immigration bail.

Eligibility requirements for a Student

Entry requirements for a Student

ST 3.1. A person seeking to come to the UK as a Student must apply for and obtain entry clearance as a Student before they arrive in the UK.

ST 3.2. A person applying for entry clearance as a Student must, if paragraph A39 and Appendix T of these rules apply, provide a valid medical certificate confirming that they have undergone screening for active pulmonary tuberculosis and that this tuberculosis is not present in them.

Date of application requirement for a Student

ST 4.1. An application for entry clearance must be made no more than 6 months before the start date of the course stated on the Confirmation of Acceptance for Studies.

ST 4.2. An application for permission to stay must be made no more than 3 months before the start date of the course on the Confirmation of Acceptance for Studies.

ST 4.3. An application for permission to stay must be for study on a course with a start date no more than 28 days after the expiry date of the applicant's previous permission.

Genuine Student requirement

ST 5.1. The applicant must be a genuine student.

Points requirement for a Student

ST 6.1. The applicant must be awarded a total of 70 points based on the table below.

Points type	Relevant requirements to be met	Number of points
Study (must meet all)	– Confirmation of Acceptance for Studies requirement – Course requirement – Approved qualification requirement – Level of study requirement – Place of study requirement	50
Financial	– Financial requirement	10
English language	– English language requirement	10

Confirmation of Acceptance for Studies requirement

ST 7.1. The Confirmation of Acceptance for Studies must have been issued by a student sponsor whose licence is still valid on the date on which the application is decided.

ST 7.2. The Confirmation of Acceptance for Studies must not have been used in a previous application which was either granted or refused (but could have been relied on in a previous application which was rejected as invalid, made void or withdrawn).

ST 7.3. The student sponsor must not have withdrawn the offer to the applicant after the date that the Confirmation of Acceptance for Studies was issued.

ST 7.4. The Confirmation of Acceptance for Studies must contain the necessary information to confirm all the following requirements are met:

(a) the course requirement; and
(b) the approved qualification requirement; and
(c) the level of study requirement; and
(d) the place of study requirement.

ST 7.5. The Confirmation of Acceptance for Studies must state the cost of [any accommodation provided by the sponsor] and fees (and any payment already made) so that the financial requirement can be assessed.

Note: Words substituted from 6 April 2021 subject to savings for applications made before that date (HC 1248).

ST 7.6. The Confirmation of Acceptance for Studies must show how the English language requirement has been met, and where the sponsor has assessed the applicant's English language ability, must include the information in ST 13.3. and ST 13.4.

Course requirement for a Student

[**ST 8.1.** The application must be for a single course of study that meets the requirements in ST 8.2. unless it is one of the following:

(a) a combined pre-sessional course which meets the requirements in ST 15.1. to 15.3.; or

(b) a full-time, salaried, elected executive position as a Student Union Sabbatical Officer, where the applicant is either part-way through their studies or will fill the position in the academic year immediately after their graduation[. . .].

[. . .]]

Note: Paragraph substituted from 23:00 on 31 December 2020 for decisions made on or after that time (CP 361). Words in (b) and sub-paragraph (c) deleted from 09:00 on 1 June 2021 subject to savings for applications (including for administrative review) made before that time (HC 1248).

[**ST 8.2.** The application must be for a course which is one of the following:

(a) a full-time course at degree level or above that leads to an approved qualification; or

(b) a full-time course below degree level involving a minimum of 15 hours per week of classroom-based daytime study (08:00 to 18:00, Monday to Friday) that leads to an approved qualification; or

(c) a full-time course involving a minimum of 15 hours per week of classroom-based daytime study that is a pre-sessional course; or

(d) a part-time course above degree level that leads to an approved qualification where the Confirmation of Acceptance for Studies has been issued by a higher education provider with a track record of compliance; or

(e) a full-time course at degree level or above that is recognised by [Ecctis] as being equivalent to a UK higher education course where the Confirmation of Acceptance for Studies has been assigned by an overseas higher education institution or a higher education provider with a track record of compliance.]

Note: Paragraph substituted from 23:00 on 31 December 2020 for decisions made on or after that time (CP 361). Words substituted from 6 October 2021 subject to savings for applications made before that date (HC 617).

[**ST 8.3.** If the course is an Association of Certified Chartered Accountants (ACCA) qualification or an ACCA Foundations in Accountancy qualification, the student sponsor must be an ACCA approved learning partner—student tuition at either Gold or Platinum level.]

Note: Paragraph substituted from 23:00 on 31 December 2020 for decisions made on or after that time (CP 361).

[**ST 8.4.** If the Academic Technology Approval Scheme (ATAS) requirement in Appendix ATAS applies, the applicant must have a valid ATAS certificate and provide it with the application.]

Note: Paragraph substituted from 23:00 on 31 December 2020 for decisions made on or after that time (CP 361).

ST 8.5. [DELETED]

Note: Paragraph deleted from 23:00 on 31 December 2020 for decisions made on or after that time (CP 361).

Approved qualification requirement for a Student

ST 9.1. The course of study, unless it is a pre-sessional course, must lead to an approved qualification which is one of the following:

(a) validated by Royal Charter; or

(b) awarded by a UK recognised body; or

(c) covered by a legal agreement between a UK recognised body and another education provider or awarding body, which confirms both:

(i) the UK recognised body's independent assessment of the level of the student sponsor's or awarding body's programme compared to the Regulated Qualifications Framework or its equivalents; and

(ii) that the UK recognised body would admit any student who successfully completes the education provider's or the awarding body's named course onto a specific or a range of degree-level courses it provides; or

(d) recognised by one or more recognised bodies through a formal articulation agreement with the awarding body; or

(e) in England, Wales and Northern Ireland, is at Regulated Qualifications Framework level 3 or above; or in Scotland is accredited at Scottish Credit and Qualifications Framework level 6 or above; or

(f) an overseas qualification that [Ecctis] assesses as valid and equivalent to Regulated Qualifications Framework level 3 or above; or

(g) an aviation licence, rating or certificate issued by the UK's Civil Aviation Authority.

Note: Words substituted from 6 October 2021 subject to savings for applications made before that date (HC 617).

Level of study requirement for a Student

ST 10.1. If the Confirmation of Acceptance for Studies has been assigned by a probationary sponsor, the course must meet one of the following requirements unless it is a pre-sessional course:

(a) the course will be studied in England, Wales or Northern Ireland, and the applicant is aged under 18, and the course is at Regulated Qualifications Framework level 3 or above; or

(b) the course will be studied in England, Wales or Northern Ireland, and the applicant is aged 18 or over, and the course is at Regulated Qualifications Framework level 4 or above; or

(c) the course will be studied in Scotland, and the applicant is aged under 18, and the course is at Scottish Credit and Qualifications Framework level 6 or above; or

(d) the course will be studied in Scotland, and the applicant is aged 18 or over and the course is at Scottish Credit and Qualifications Framework level 7 or above.

ST 10.2. If the Confirmation of Acceptance for Studies has been assigned by a student sponsor, the course must meet one of the following requirements:

(a) the course will be studied in England, Wales or Northern Ireland and it is at Regulated Qualifications Framework level 3 or above; or

(b) the course will be studied in Scotland and it is at Scottish Credit and Qualifications Framework level 6 or above; or

(c) the course is a short-term study abroad programme in the UK as part of the applicant's qualification at an overseas higher education institution outside of the UK, and that qualification is recognised as being at UK bachelor's degree level or above by [Ecctis]; or

(d) the course is a pre-sessional course in English language at level B2 or above of the Common European Framework of Reference for Languages; or

(e) the course is a recognised Foundation Programme for postgraduate doctors or dentists; or

(f) the course is being delivered under a partnership between a higher education institution and a research institute and is accredited at Regulated Qualifications Framework level 7 or above, or at Scottish Credit and Qualifications Framework Level 11 or above.

Note: Words substituted from 6 October 2021 subject to savings for applications made before that date (HC 617).

Place of study requirement for a Student

ST 11.1. All study that forms part of the course of study must take place on the premises of the student sponsor or a partner institution unless the applicant is on a course-related work placement, a study abroad programme overseas, or a pre-sessional course.

Financial requirement for a Student

ST 12.1. If the applicant is applying for permission to stay and has been living in the UK with permission for 12 months or more on the date of application, they will meet the financial requirement and do not need to show funds.

ST 12.2. If the applicant is applying for entry clearance or permission to stay and is applying as a Student Union Sabbatical Officer or to study on a recognised foundation programme as a doctor or dentist in training, they will meet the financial requirement and do not need to show funds.

ST 12.3. If ST 12.2. does not apply, and the applicant is applying for entry clearance, or is applying for permission to stay and has been in the UK with permission for less than 12 months, the applicant must have the following funds:

(a) Studying in London

Type of Study	Funds required
Residential Independent School	Sufficient funds to pay outstanding fees (course fees and boarding fees) for one academic year
[...]	[...]
All other cases	Sufficient funds to pay any outstanding course fees as stated on the Confirmation of Acceptance for Studies, and £1334 for each month of the course (up to a maximum of 9 months)

(b) Studying outside London

Type of Study	Funds required
Residential Independent School	Sufficient funds to pay outstanding fees (course fees and boarding fees) for one academic year
[...]	[...]
All other cases	Sufficient funds to pay any outstanding course fees as stated on the Confirmation of Acceptance for Studies, and £1023 for each month of the course (up to a maximum of 9 months)

If the length of the applicant's course includes a part of a month, the time period will be rounded up to the next full month.

Note: Row in table in (a) deleted, row in table in (b) deleted from 09:00 on 1 July 2021 subject to savings for applications (including for administrative review) made before that time (HC 1248).

ST 12.4. If the applicant has paid a deposit to the student sponsor for accommodation arranged by the sponsor, this deposit (up to a maximum of £1334) can be offset against the funds required in ST 12.3.

ST 12.5. If the applicant has paid all or part of their course fees to their student sponsor this must be confirmed on the Confirmation of Acceptance for Studies, or the applicant must provide a receipt issued by the student sponsor confirming the amount of fees paid.

[**ST 12.6.** The applicant must show that they have held the required level of funds for a 28-day period and as specified in Appendix Finance unless the applicant is relying on a student loan or official financial sponsorship which meets the requirements of FIN 8.3. in Appendix Finance.]

Note: Paragraph substituted from 6 April 2022 subject to savings for applications made before that date (HC 1118).

[**ST.12.7.** If the funds held in the applicant's account on the date of decision fall substantially below the level of funds required at ST.12.3, the decision maker must be satisfied that the spent funds have been [[used to pay outstanding course fees, a deposit for accommodation or other costs associated with the proposed course of study in the UK]]]

Note: Paragraph inserted from 6 October 2021 (HC 617). Words in double square brackets substituted from 6 April 2022 subject to savings for applications made before that date (HC 1118).

English language requirement for a Student

ST 13.1. The applicant must show English language ability on the Common European Framework of Reference for Languages in all 4 components (reading, writing, speaking and listening) of at least:

(a) level B2, where the applicant is studying a course at UK bachelor's degree level or above; or

(b) level B1, where the applicant is studying a pre-sessional course or a course below UK bachelor's degree level.

ST 13.2. The applicant must show they meet the English language requirement as specified in Appendix English Language.

ST 13.3. Where the student sponsor has assessed that the applicant meets the English language requirement, they must state this and the method of assessment on the Confirmation of Acceptance for Studies.

ST 13.4. Where a Secure English Language Test is required, the name of the test provider, the unique reference number for the test and the score for each component tested (reading, writing, listening, speaking) must be included on the Confirmation of Acceptance for Studies.

Academic Progress requirement for a Student

[**ST 14.1.** An applicant who has, or previously had, permission as a Student and is applying for permission to stay as a Student must have successfully completed the course of study for which they were last granted permission as a Student, or one of the following applies:

(a) one of the exceptions in ST 14.4.; or

(b) they are applying to progress to a higher level course as specified in ST 14.3.(a) or (b).; or

(c) they have successfully completed the course of study with their sponsor where the change of course was allowed without applying for further permission on the Student route.]

Note: Paragraph substituted from 09:00 on 1 July 2021 subject to savings for applications (including for administrative review) made before that time (HC 1248).

ST 14.2. An applicant who has, or previously had, permission on the Student route and is applying for permission to stay as a Student must show academic progress from the previous courses of study unless one of the exceptions in ST 14.4. applies.

ST 14.3. An applicant will show academic progress if they are applying for any of the following:

(a) to progress from a bachelor's to master's level course which is part of an integrated master's course, where the applicant has been offered a place on a higher-level course by the student sponsor after an assessment of their academic ability; or

(b) to progress from a master's degree to a PhD which is part of an integrated master's and PhD programme, where the applicant has been offered a place on a higher-level course by the student sponsor after an assessment of their academic ability; or

(c) a course which is above the level of the previous course of study for which they were last granted permission unless:

(i) the student sponsor is a higher education provider with a track record of compliance; and

(ii) the course is at degree level or above; and

(iii) the new course is at the same level as the previous course of study; and

(iv) the student sponsor confirms that either:

(a) the new course of study is related to the applicant's previous course of study (meaning that it is either connected to the previous course, part of the same subject group, or involves deeper specialisation); or

(b) the combination of the previous course of study and the new course of study support the applicant's genuine career aspirations.

[(c) the applicant has left an integrated master's or PhD programme having successfully completed the course leading to the award of the lower level qualification which formed a part of that programme.]

Note: Sub-paragraph (c)(iv)(c) inserted from 6 April 2021 subject to savings for applications made before that date (HC 1248).

ST 14.4. An applicant does not need to show academic progress where they:

(a) are applying to re-sit examinations or repeat modules under ST 14.5.; or

(b) have previously re-sat examinations or repeated modules under ST 14.5. and are applying to complete the course for which those examinations were re-sat or modules repeated; or

(c) are applying to continue studying with their current student sponsor for the purpose of completing the PhD or other doctoral qualification for which study was undertaken during their last period of permission as a Student; or

(d) are making an application to move to a new student sponsor to complete a course of study begun at a student sponsor that has subsequently had its licence revoked; or

(e) are applying to undertake a role as a Student Union Sabbatical Officer; or

(f) after undertaking a period as a Student Union Sabbatical Officer are applying to complete the qualification for which the Confirmation of Acceptance for Studies was assigned before that period; or

(g) are applying for permission to stay [. . .]as a postgraduate doctor or dentist on a recognised Foundation Programme; or

(h) are applying to undertake an intercalated bachelor's or master's degree course or PhD where they are studying medicine, veterinary medicine and science, or dentistry as their principal course of study, or to complete their principal course, having completed a period of intercalation; or

(i) are applying to undertake a study abroad programme or work placement which is both integral to and assessed as part of the course, or to complete their course, having completed a study abroad programme or work placement.

Note: Words in (g) deleted from 09:00 on 1 July 2021 subject to savings for applications (including for administrative review) made before that date (HC 1248).

ST 14.5. If the applicant is re-sitting examinations or repeating a module of a course, the applicant must not previously have re-sat the same examination or repeated the same module, more than once (they can only do so twice), unless the sponsor is a student sponsor (and is not a probationary sponsor).

Combined Pre-sessional Course requirement for a Student

ST 15.1. A single Confirmation of Acceptance for Studies can be assigned for a combined pre-sessional course and a main course at degree level or above by a higher education provider with a track record of compliance if:

(a) the pre-sessional course lasts no longer than 3 months; and

(b) the main course will begin no more than 1 month after the pre-sessional course ends.

ST 15.2. If the applicant has been assessed as having language ability of at least level B2 in order to meet the English language requirement at ST 13.1., the Confirmation of Acceptance for Studies must confirm that the applicant has an unconditional offer of a place on the main course.

ST 15.3. If the applicant has been assessed (which must be by a method other than assessment by the student sponsor) as having language ability of at least level B1 in order to meet the English language requirement at ST 13.1., the Confirmation of Acceptance for Studies must confirm that the student sponsor is satisfied that the applicant will have at least level B2 at the end of the pre-sessional course.

Postgraduate Doctor or Dentist requirement

ST 16.1. If the applicant is applying to be a postgraduate doctor or dentist on a recognised Foundation Programme, they must have both:

(a) successfully completed a recognised UK bachelor's degree or above in medicine or dentistry; and

(b) previously been granted permission as a Student, for at least two academic years, which must include the final year, of their UK bachelor's degree or above in medicine or dentistry.

Work Placement requirement

ST 17.1. A course that includes a work placement must lead to an approved qualification and the Confirmation of Acceptance for Studies must be assigned by a student sponsor (who is not a probationary sponsor) if the course of study is below degree level.

ST 17.2. A work placement must be assessed as an integral part of the course and must not be longer than one third of the total length of the course, except when there is a statutory requirement that it must be so, or where ST 17.3. applies.

ST 17.3. A work placement on a course that is at degree level or above at a higher education provider with a track record of compliance or at an overseas higher education institution must not be longer than half of the total length of the course.

[. . .]

Note: Heading deleted from 09:00 on 1 July 2021 subject to savings for applications (including for administrative review) made before that time (HC 1248).

ST 18.1. [DELETED]

Note: Paragraph deleted from 09:00 on 1 July 2021 subject to savings for applications (including for administrative review) made before that time (HC 1248).

ST 18.2. [DELETED]

Note: Paragraph deleted from 09:00 on 1 July 2021 subject to savings for applications (including for administrative review) made before that time (HC 1248).

Maximum period of study requirement for a Student

ST 19.1. If the course is below degree level, the grant of permission must not lead to the applicant being granted more than two years' permission as a Student to study courses below degree level from the age of 18 unless ST 19.2. applies.

ST 19.2. If the course is below degree level but is subject to a regulatory requirement by the Maritime and Coastguard Agency that the applicant must spend at least 12 months at sea as a part of that course, the grant of permission must not lead to the applicant being granted more than 3 years' permission as a Student from the age of 18 to study courses below degree level.

ST 19.3. If the course is at degree level, the grant of permission must not lead to the applicant being granted more than five years' permission as a Student from the age of 18 to study courses at degree level unless the course of study is one of those listed at ST 19.4.

ST 19.4. The five-year maximum period of study at degree level in ST 19.3. will not apply if the applicant has a Confirmation of Acceptance for Studies that has been assigned for a course of study in one of the following subjects:

(a) architecture; or

(b) medicine; or

(c) dentistry; or

(d) veterinary medicine and science; or

(e) music at a music college that is a member of Conservatoires UK; or

(f) law, where the applicant has completed a course at degree level or above and is applying for a course of study which is:

(i) a law conversion course validated by the Solicitors Regulation Authority and the Bar Standards Board in England and Wales; or

(ii) a Masters in Law (MLaw) in Northern Ireland; or

(iii) an accelerated graduate LLB in Scotland.

ST 19.5. If the applicant has previously been granted permission as a postgraduate doctor or dentist, the grant of permission to the applicant must not lead to the applicant having been granted more than 3 years' permission as a postgraduate doctor or dentist.

ST 19.6. When calculating the period of permission granted under ST 19.1. to ST 19.5., any period of permission as a Student extended under section 3C of the Immigration Act 1971 will count towards the period of permission granted.

Documents used to obtain an offer requirement for a Student

ST 20.1. The applicant must provide evidence of the qualifications or references they used to obtain the offer of a place on the course of study from the student sponsor, unless either:

(a) the applicant is applying for a course of study at degree level or above and is sponsored by a higher education provider with a track record of compliance; or

(b) ST 22.1. applies.

ST 20.2. The evidence of each qualification must be one of the following:

(a) the certificate(s) of qualification; or

(b) the transcript of results; or

(c) a print out of the qualification or transcript results from the awarding body's online checking service.

ST 20.3. Where the applicant has provided a print out of qualifications or transcript results from the awarding body's online checking service, the decision maker may require the applicant to provide the certificate of qualification or transcript of results.

Parental consent requirement for a Student

ST 21.1. If the applicant is aged 16 or 17, they must have written consent from:

(a) both parents; or

(b) one parent, if that parent has sole legal responsibility for the applicant; or

(c) the applicant's legal guardian.

ST 21.2. The written consent must confirm support for all of the following:

(a) the application; and

(b) the applicant's living and care arrangements in the UK; and

(c) if the application is for entry clearance, the applicant's travel to, and reception arrangements in, the UK.

Differential evidence requirement for a Student

ST 22.1. Evidence to show that the applicant meets the financial requirement and the requirement to provide documents used to obtain an offer does not need to be provided with the application (but may be required by the decision maker) if the applicant is applying from the country or territory where they are living, or from in the UK, and the applicant either:

(a) holds a passport which shows they are registered as a British National (Overseas), or which was issued by the competent authorities of Hong Kong SAR, Macau SAR or Taiwan (which includes the number of the identification card issued by the competent authority in Taiwan); or

(b) is a national of any of the following:

Australia
Austria
Bahrain
Barbados
Belgium
Botswana
Brazil
Brunei
Bulgaria
Cambodia
Canada
Chile
China
Croatia
Republic of Cyprus
Czech Republic
Denmark
The Dominican Republic
Estonia
Finland
France
Germany
Greece
Hungary
Iceland
Indonesia
Ireland
Italy
Japan
Kazakhstan
Kuwait
Latvia
Liechtenstein
Lithuania
Luxembourg
Malaysia
Malta
Mauritius
Mexico
Netherlands
New Zealand
Norway
Oman
Peru
Poland
Portugal
Qatar
Romania
Serbia
Singapore
Slovakia
Slovenia
South Korea
Spain
Sweden
Switzerland
Thailand
Tunisia
United Arab Emirates
United States of America

Information on the Confirmation of Acceptance for Studies requirement

ST 23.1. The student sponsor must provide all the following information about the course of study on the Confirmation of Acceptance for Studies:

(a) title of course; and

(b) academic level of course; and

(c) course start and end dates; and

(d) hours of study per week, including confirmation on whether the course is part-time or full-time; and

(e) the address of the main place of study; and

(f) the cost of accommodation and fees; and

(g) if the student sponsor has assessed the applicant by use of one or more references, details of the references assessed; and

(h) if the course involves a work placement, details of any work placement relating to the course; and

(i) if the course will be provided by an education provider which is not the student sponsor, details of the partner institution; and

(j) whether the ATAS requirement in Annex ATAS applies; and

(k) confirmation if the course is a recognised Foundation Programme for postgraduate doctors or dentists, and requires a certificate from the Postgraduate Dean; and

(l) a statement of how the student sponsor has assessed the applicant's English language ability including, where relevant, the applicant's English language test scores in all 4 components (reading, writing, speaking and listening); and

(m) if the course is part of a study abroad programme, the name and address of the partner institution; and

(n) if the applicant is applying for a full-time, salaried, elected executive position as a Student Union Sabbatical Officer and is part-way through their studies or being sponsored to fill the position in the academic year immediately after their graduation; and

[...]

(p) if the applicant has previously been granted permission as a Student, confirmation that the new course meets the academic progress requirement from the previous course as required by ST 14.1. to ST 14.5.

Note: Sub-paragraph (o) deleted from 09:00 on 1 July 2021 subject to savings for applications (including for administrative review) made before that time (HC 1248).

Decision on application for a Student

ST 24.1. If the decision maker is satisfied that all the suitability and eligibility requirements for a Student are met, the application will be granted; otherwise, the application will be refused.

ST 24.2. If the application is refused, the person can apply for an Administrative Review under Appendix AR.

Period and conditions of grant for a Student

ST 25.1. The grant of permission will be subject to the following conditions:

(a) no access to public funds; and

(b) no work, except as specified in ST 26; and

(c) no study, except as specified in ST 27; and

(d) if Part 10 applies, the person will be required to register with the police.

ST 25.2. The applicant will be granted permission for the duration of the course as specified on the Confirmation of Acceptance for Studies plus the relevant periods specified in ST 25.3.

ST 25.3. The period of permission granted to an applicant before the start of the course who is applying for entry clearance will be either:

(a) the relevant period before the course date which is set out in the table below, if entry clearance is granted 1 month or more before the start date of the course; or

(b) 7 days before the intended date of travel, if entry clearance is granted less than 1 month before the start date of the course; or

(c) with immediate effect, if entry clearance is granted less than 7 days before the intended date of travel and less than 1 month before the start date of the course.

The applicant will be granted a period of permission dependent on the type and length of course as in the table below:

Type of Course	Period granted before course start date	Period granted after course end date
A course of 12 months or longer	1 Month	4 Months
Acourse of 6 months or longer but shorter than 12 months	1 Month	2 Months
Apre-sessional course of less than 6 months	1 Month	1 Month
A course as a Postgraduate doctor or dentist	1 Month	1 Month
Acourse of less than 6 months in length which is not a pre- sessional course	7 Days	7 Days

[. . .]

Note: Words deleted from 09:00 on 1 July 2021 subject to savings for applications (including for administrative review) made before that time (HC 1248).

Work Conditions for a Student

ST 26.1. The applicant will be granted permission with the following employment conditions:

Type of study	Employment conditions
Student following a full-time course of degree level or above study: – sponsored by a higher education provider with a track record of compliance; or – sponsored by an overseas higher education institution to undertake a short-term study abroad programme in the UK	20 hours per week during term-time (full- time employment permitted outside of term-time)
Student undertaking a full-time course below degree level study sponsored by a higher education provider with a track record of compliance	10 hours per week during term-time (full-time employment permitted outside of term-time)
All other study, including all part-time study	No employment permitted

[**ST 26.2.** A Student who makes a valid application for permission to stay under the Skilled Worker, or Graduate route, may start employment in a full-time permanent vacancy either up to 3 months prior to the course completion date (for the Skilled Worker route) or once they have successfully completed their course of study (for the Graduate route), provided all of the following apply:

(a) the Student is studying a full-time course of study at degree level or above with a higher education provider with a track record of compliance; and

(b) the application as a Skilled Worker, or Graduate, was made when the applicant had permission as a Student; and

(c) a decision has not been made on the Skilled Worker, or Graduate, application, or where a decision has been made, any Administrative Review against a refusal of that application has not been finally determined.]

Note: Paragraph substituted from 6 April 2022 subject to savings for applications made before that date (HC 1118).

ST 26.3. Employment as an elected Student Union Sabbatical Officer or elected National Union of Students (NUS) position is permitted for up to 2 years if the Confirmation of Acceptance for Studies was assigned for this purpose.

ST 26.4. [DELETED]

Note: Paragraph deleted from 09:00 on 1 July 2021 subject to savings for applications (including for administrative review) made before that time (HC 1248).

[**ST 26.5.** A Student is not allowed to do any of the following:

(a) be self-employed or engage in business activity unless ST 26.8 applies; or

(b) work as a professional sportsperson (including as a sports coach); or

(c) work as an entertainer; or

(d) work in a position which would fill a permanent full-time vacancy unless ST 26.6 applies.]

Note: Paragraph substituted from 09:00 on 1 July 2021 subject to savings for applications (including for administrative review) made before that time (HC 1248).

ST 26.6. If a Student has permission and makes an application for permission to stay under the Skilled Worker route, supported by a Certificate of Sponsorship assigned by a licensed sponsor, the Student can start the employment for which the Certificate of Sponsorship was assigned, for up to 3 months prior to the course completion date, provided:

(a) the Student is studying a full-time course of study at degree level or above with a higher education provider with a track record of compliance; and

(b) the application as a Skilled Worker was made when the applicant had permission as a Student; and

(c) a decision has not been made on the Skilled Worker application, or where a decision has been made, any Administrative Review against a refusal has not been finally determined.

ST 26.7. A Student may be employed as a postgraduate doctor or dentist if they are on a recognised Foundation Programme.

ST 26.8. A Student may be self-employed, if:

(a) they have applied for permission on the Start-up route; and

(b) that application is supported by an endorsement from a Start-up route endorsing body which is a higher education provider with a track record of compliance; and

(c) the application was made when the applicant had permission as a Student; and

(d) a decision has not been made on the application, or where the application has been refused, any Administrative Review against a refusal has not been finally determined.

Study Conditions

ST 27.1. A Student must only study with the student sponsor which assigned the Confirmation of Acceptance for Studies unless either:

(a) the Student is studying at a partner institution of their student sponsor; or

(b) the Student has made an application for permission to stay while they have permission as a Student:

(i) which is supported by a valid Confirmation of Acceptance for Studies assigned by a student sponsor; and

(ii) the application has not yet been decided, or any Administrative Review against that decision has not been determined; and

(iii) the Student will be studying at the student sponsor that assigned the Confirmation of Acceptance for Studies.

ST 27.2. A Student must only study on the course of study, or courses where a combined pre-sessional course is being taken, for which the Confirmation of Acceptance for Studies was assigned unless ST 27.3. applies.

ST 27.3. A Student may begin studying on a new course with their current student sponsor if:

(a) the student sponsor is a higher education provider with a track record of compliance; and

(b) the Student has not completed the course that the Confirmation of Acceptance for Studies was assigned for; and

(c) the new course is not at a lower qualification level than the course the Confirmation of Acceptance for Studies was assigned for [unless they were last granted permission to study an integrated master's or PhD programme and will not be studying on the lower level qualification of that programme]; and

(d) the course is at degree level or above; and

(e) any new course at degree level can be completed within the current period of permission; and

(f) the student sponsor confirms that new course is related to the course for which the Confirmation of Acceptance for Studies was assigned or supports the Student's genuine career aspirations.

Note: Words in (c) inserted from 6 April 2022 subject to savings for applications made before that date (HC 1118).

ST 27.4. The Student may study on a study abroad programme overseas that is an integral and assessed part of the course of study named on the Confirmation of Acceptance for Studies.

ST 27.5. Supplementary study is permitted.

ST 27.6. Study is subject to the ATAS condition in Appendix ATAS.

ST 27.7. The Student must not study at a State School or Academy (except for a voluntary grammar school with boarding in Northern Ireland) but if the Student has been granted permission to study at a student sponsor which becomes a State School or Academy during that period of permission the Student may complete the course for which the Confirmation of Acceptance for Studies was assigned.

Dependants of a Student

Validity requirements for a dependent partner or dependent child of a Student

ST 28.1. A person applying for entry clearance or permission to stay as a partner or child of a Student must apply on the specified form on the gov.uk website as follows:

[Location of Partner or Child	Specified form
Applicant outside the UK	Dependant partner visa Dependant child visa
Applicant inside the UK	Dependant partner Dependant child]

Note: Table substituted from 30 November 2021 subject to savings for applications made before that date (HC 617).

[**ST 28.2.** An application for entry clearance or permission to stay as a partner or child of a Student must meet all the following requirements:

(a) any fee and Immigration Health Charge must have been paid; and

(b) the applicant must have provided any required biometrics; and

(c) the applicant must have provided a passport or other travel document which satisfactorily establishes their identity and nationality; and

(d) the applicant must be applying as partner or child of a person who:

(i) has made a valid application for entry clearance or permission to stay on the Student route that has not been decided; or

(ii) has entry clearance or permission to stay on the Student route.]

Note: Paragraph substituted from 6 April 2022 subject to savings for applications made before that date (HC 1118).

ST 28.3. If the applicant has in the 12 months before the date of application been awarded a scholarship or sponsorship by a Government or international scholarship agency covering both fees and living costs for study in the UK, they must provide written consent to the application from that Government or agency.

ST 28.4. An applicant who is in the UK on the date of application must not have, or have last been granted, permission:

(a) as a Visitor; or

(b) as a Short-term Student; or

(c) as a Parent of a Child Student; or

(d) as a Seasonal Worker; or

(e) as a Domestic Worker in a Private Household; or

(f) outside the Immigration Rules.

ST 28.5. An application which does not meet the validity requirements for a partner or child on the Student route is invalid and may be rejected and not considered.

Suitability requirements for a dependent partner or dependent child of a Student

ST 29.1. The suitability requirements for a partner or child on the Student route are that they must not fall for refusal under Part 9: grounds for refusal.

ST 29.2. A person applying for permission to stay must not be:

(a) in the UK in breach of immigration laws, except that where paragraph 39E applies, that period of overstaying will be disregarded; or

(b) on immigration bail.

Eligibility requirements for a dependent partner or dependent child of a Student

Entry requirement for a dependent partner or dependent child of a Student

ST 30.1. A person seeking to come to the UK as a partner or child of a Student must apply for and obtain entry clearance as a partner or child before they arrive in the UK.

ST 30.2. A person applying for entry clearance as a partner or child of a Student must, if paragraph A39 and Appendix T of these rules apply, provide a valid medical certificate confirming that they have undergone screening for active pulmonary tuberculosis and that this tuberculosis is not present in them.

Student course requirement for a dependent partner or dependent child of a Student

ST 31.1. Unless they are a child who meets the requirements in ST 31.2., the applicant must be the partner or child of a person who is:

(a) a Student who has received an award from a Government and has, or is applying for, permission to study on a full-time course of 6 months or longer; or

(b) a full-time Student who has, or is applying for, permission to study a postgraduate level course of 9 months or longer at a higher education provider with a track record of compliance; or

(c) a Student who has permission on the Doctorate Extension Scheme; or

(d) a Student who has, or had within the last 3 months before the date of application, permission to study on a full-time course of 6 months or longer, and is now applying for permission to study a full-time course of 6 months or longer where either:

(i) the partner or child already has, or had within the last 3 months before the date of application, permission as a dependent partner or dependent child of the Student; or

(ii) the child was born since the last grant of permission to the Student, where the Student and partner or child are applying at the same time.

ST 31.2. If the applicant is a child who does not meet the requirement at ST.31.1., they must instead meet one of the following requirements:

(a) the applicant must have been born during the Student's current period of permission to study a full-time course of 6 months or longer and they are applying for permission during that period; or

(b) where the Student has permission to re-sit examinations or repeat a module of a full-time course of 6 months or longer, the applicant must have been born either:

(i) during the Student's original period of permission; or

(ii) during the period of permission granted for re-sitting examinations or to repeat a module; or

(c) the applicant must have been born no more than 3 months after the expiry of the Student's most recent permission and must be making an application for entry clearance within 6 months of the expiry of their parent's most recent permission.

Relationship requirement for dependent partner of a Student

ST 32.1. The applicant must be the partner of a Student, or the partner of a person applying at the same time as a Student.

ST 32.2. Both the applicant and their partner must be aged 18 or over at the date of application.

ST 32.3. If the applicant and their partner (who must be a Student, or applying at the same time as a Student) are not married or in a civil partnership, all the following requirements must be met:

(a) they must have been living together in a relationship similar to marriage or civil partnership for at least the 2 years before the date of application; and

(b) any previous relationship of the applicant and their partner with another person must have permanently broken down; and

(c) the applicant and their partner must not be so closely related that they would not have been allowed to marry in the UK.

ST 32.4. The relationship between the applicant and their partner must be genuine and subsisting.

ST 32.5. The applicant and their partner (who must be a Student, or applying at the same time as a Student) must intend to live together throughout the applicant's stay in the UK.

ST 32.6. The applicant must not intend to stay in the UK beyond any permission granted to their partner (who must be a Student or applying at the same time as a Student).

Financial requirement for dependent partner of a Student

ST 33.1. If the applicant is applying for permission to stay and has been living in the UK with permission for 12 months or longer on the date of application, they will meet the financial requirement and do not need to show funds.

ST 33.2. If the applicant is applying for entry clearance or permission to stay, where they have been in the UK less than 12 months, the applicant or their partner (who must be a Student or applying at the same time as a Student) must have the funds specified in the table below, for a total of 9 months, or for the period of permission applied for by the applicant, whichever is the shorter.

Place of Student's study	Funds required by a dependent partner
Studying in London	£845 per month
Studying outside London	£680 per month

ST 33.3. The funds must be in addition to the funds required for the Student to meet the financial requirement, and the funds required to meet the financial requirement for any dependent child who is applying at the same time, or is already in the UK as a dependent child of the Student.

ST 33.4. Unless the applicant is relying on financial sponsorship from a Government or international scholarship agency that covers the living costs of the applicant and the Student, they must show that they have held the required level of funds for a 28-day period and as specified in Appendix Finance.

[**ST 33.5.** Unless the applicant is applying at the same time as the Student and ST 22.1. applies, the applicant must show that they have the required funds as specified in Appendix Finance.]

Note: Paragraph inserted from 6 April 2021 subject to savings for applications made before that date (HC 1248). **NB** statement of changes refers to insertion of this paragraph below 34.3, but that paragraph does not exist and it is clearly intended to come after 33.4.

[ST.33.6. If the funds held in the applicant's account on the date of decision fall substantially below the level of funds required at ST.33.2, the decision maker must be satisfied that the spent funds have been [...] used to pay a deposit for accommodation.]

Note: Paragraph inserted from 6 October 2021 (HC 617). Words deleted from 6 April 2022 subject to savings for applications made before that date (HC 1118).

Relationship requirement for dependent child of a Student

ST 34.1. The applicant must be the child of a parent who has, or is at the same time being granted permission as:

(a) a Student; or

(b) the partner of a Student.

ST 34.2. The applicant's parents must each be either applying at the same time as the applicant or have permission to be in the UK (other than as a visitor) unless:

(a) the parent with permission as a Student or as the partner of a Student is the sole surviving parent; or

(b) the parent with permission as a Student or as the partner of a Student has sole responsibility for the child's upbringing; or

(c) the decision maker is satisfied that there are serious and compelling reasons to grant the child entry clearance or permission to stay with the parent who has permission as a Student or as the partner of a Student.

ST 34.3. If the applicant is a child born in the UK to a Student or their partner, the applicant must provide a full UK birth certificate showing the names of both parents.

Care requirement for dependent child of a Student

ST 35.1. If the applicant is aged under 18 on the date of application there must be suitable arrangements for the child's care and accommodation in the UK which must comply with relevant UK legislation and regulations.

Age requirement for a dependent child of a Student

ST 36.1. The child must be under the age of 18 at the date of application, unless they were last granted permission as a dependent child of the parent (P) who has or is applying for entry clearance or permission to stay as a Student or as a partner of a Student (regardless of the route under which the parent (P) had permission at the time the child's last permission was granted).

ST 36.2. If the child is aged 16 or over on the date of application, they must not be leading an independent life.

Financial requirement for dependent child of a Student

ST 37.1. If the applicant is applying for permission to stay and has been in the UK with permission for 12 months or longer on the date of application, they will meet the financial requirement and do not need to show funds.

ST 37.2. Where the applicant is applying for entry clearance, or permission to stay and they have been in the UK less than 12 months on the date of application, the applicant or their parent must have the funds specified in the table below, for a total of 9 months, or for the period of permission applied for by the applicant, whichever is the shorter.

Place of Student's study	Funds required for a dependent child
Studying in London	£845 per month
Studying outside London	£680 per month

ST 37.3. The funds must be in addition to the funds required for the Student to meet the financial requirement, and the funds required for any dependant of the Student, who is applying at the same time as the applicant or is already in the UK as a dependant of the Student.

ST 37.4. Where ST 37.2. applies, unless the applicant is relying on financial sponsorship from a Government or international scholarship agency that covers the living costs of the Student and the applicant, the required level of funds must have been held for a 28-day period and as specified in Appendix Finance.

[**ST.37.5.** If the funds held in the applicant's account on the date of decision fall substantially below the level of funds required at ST.37.2, the decision maker must be satisfied that the spent funds have been [. . .]used to pay a deposit for accommodation.]

Note: Paragraph inserted from 6 October 2021 (HC 617). Words deleted from 6 April 2022 subject to savings for applications made before that date (HC 1118).

Decision on application for a dependent partner or dependent child of a Student

ST 38.1. If the decision maker is satisfied that all the suitability and eligibility requirements for the dependent partner or dependent child of a Student are met, the application will be granted, otherwise the application will be refused.

ST 38.2. If the application is refused, the person can apply for an Administrative Review under Appendix AR.

Period and conditions of grant for a dependent partner or dependent child of a Student

ST 39.1. A dependent partner will be granted permission which ends on the same date as the Student's permission.

ST 39.2. A dependent child will be granted permission which ends on the same date as whichever of their parents' permission ends first.

ST 39.3. The grant will be subject to all the following conditions:

(a) no access to public funds; and

(b) work (including self-employment and voluntary work) is permitted except:

(i) where the dependant meets the requirement at ST 31.1.(d) and the Student has been granted less than 9 months' permission, unless that is to continue a course of study where they had previously been granted at least 9 months' permission; or

(ii) where the dependant meets the requirement at ST 31.1.(d) and the Student is studying a course below degree level; or

(iii) no employment as a professional sportsperson (including as a sports coach); and

(c) study is permitted, subject to the ATAS condition in Appendix ATAS (if the study will commence when the partner or child is aged over 18); and

(d) if Part 10 applies the person will be required to register with the police.]

Note: Appendix inserted from 09:00 on 1 December 2020 subject to savings for applications made before that time (HC813).

[Appendix Short-term Student (English Language)

This route is for a person aged 16 and over who wants to study an English language course in the UK for between 6 and 11 months at an accredited institution.

An application can only be made by a person outside the UK.

Short-term Study (English language) is an unsponsored route, sponsored study for persons aged 16 and over is covered in Appendix Student.

A visitor under Appendix V: [Visitor] can study an English language course of less than 6 months with an accredited institution.

Note: Word in introduction substituted from 6 April 2021 subject to savings for applications made before that date (HC 1248).

Validity requirements for a Short-term Student

STS 1.1. A person applying for entry clearance as a Short-term Student must apply online [the] on gov.uk website on the specified form 'Short-term Student visa'.

Note: Word inserted from 6 April 2021 subject to savings for applications made before that date (HC 1248).

STS 1.2. An application for entry clearance as a Short-term Student must meet all the following requirements:

(a) any fee and Immigration Health Charge must have been paid; and

(b) the applicant must have provided any required biometrics; and

(c) the applicant must have provided a passport or other travel document which satisfactorily establishes their identity and nationality; and

(d) the applicant must be outside the UK.

STS 1.3. The applicant must be aged 16 or over on the date of application.

STS 1.4. An application which does not meet all the validity requirements for a Short-term Student is invalid and may be rejected and not considered.

Suitability requirements for a Short-term Student

STS 2.1. The applicant must not fall for refusal under Part 9: grounds for refusal.

Eligibility requirements for a Short-term Student

Entry requirements for a Short-term Student

STS 3.1. A person seeking to come to the UK as a Short-term Student must obtain entry clearance as a Short-term Student before they arrive in the UK.

STS 3.2. A person applying for entry clearance as a Short-term Student for more than 6 months must, if paragraph A39 and Appendix T of these rules apply, provide a valid medical certificate confirming that they have undergone screening for active pulmonary tuberculosis and that this tuberculosis is not present in them.

Course requirements for a Short-term Student

STS 4.1. The course provider must be an accredited institution.

STS 4.2. The applicant must provide written evidence from the course provider that the applicant has been accepted onto an English language course (that does not include any other subject) that lasts [at least 6 months and] no longer than 11 months.

Note: Words inserted from 6 April 2022 subject to savings for applications made before that date (HC 1118).

Study requirement for a Short-term Student

STS 5.1. The applicant must not intend to do any of the following during their time in the UK as a Short-term Student:

(a) undertake a course of study of longer than 11 months; or
(b) study at an academy or state-funded school; or
(c) make the UK their main home; or
(d) work in the UK; or
(e) engage in any business or professional activities in the UK.

STS 5.2. The applicant must intend to leave the UK within 30 days of the end of their English language course, or at the end of 11 months, whichever is sooner.

Financial requirements for a Short-term Student

STS 6.1. The applicant must be able to maintain and accommodate themselves adequately without receiving public funds.

STS 6.2. The applicant must have enough funds to meet the cost of their return or onward journey from the UK.

STS 6.3. At the date of application, the applicant must have paid their course fees or have enough funds to pay their course fees.

STS 6.4. Funds must be shown as specified in Appendix Finance.

Parental consent requirement for a Short-term Student aged 16 or 17

STS 7.1. If the applicant is aged 16 or 17 on the date of application, they must have written consent from:

(a) both parents; or
(b) one parent, if that parent has sole legal responsibility for the applicant; or
(c) the applicant's legal guardian.

STS 7.2. The written consent must confirm support for all of the following:

(a) the application; and
(b) the applicant's living and care arrangements in the UK; and
(c) the applicant's travel to, and reception arrangements in, the UK.

Decision on application as a Short-term Student

STS 8.1. If the decision maker is satisfied that all the suitability and eligibility requirements for a Short-term Student are met the application will be granted, otherwise the application will be refused.

[**STS 8.2.** If the application is refused, the person can apply for an Administrative Review under Appendix AR: Administrative Review.

Note: Paragraph deleted from 6 April 2021 subject to savings for applications made before that date (HC 1248). Paragraph re-inserted from 6 October 2021 (HC 617).

Period and conditions of grant for a Short-term Student

STS 9.1. The applicant will be granted permission for 11 months.

STS 9.2. The grant will be subject to all the following conditions:

(a) no access to public funds; and
(b) no work; and
(c) study only on the course for which the applicant was granted permission.]

Note: Appendix inserted from 09:00 on 1 December 2020 subject to savings for applications made before that time (HC813).

[APPENDIX CHILD STUDENT

The Child Student route is for a person aged between 4 and 17 who wants to study at an independent school in the UK, which is a student sponsor.
A person aged 16 or 17 who wants to study a course at or above Regulated Qualifications Framework level 3 or Scottish Credit and Qualifications Framework level 6, can choose either to apply as a Child Student at an independent school or as a Student under Appendix Student.

Validity requirements for a Child Student

CS 1.1. A person applying for entry clearance or permission to stay as a Child Student must apply online on the gov.uk website on the specified form as follows:

[(a) for out of country, form 'Child Student visa'; or
(b) for in country, form Child Student'.]

Note: Sub-paragraphs (a) and (b) substituted from 30 November 2021 subject to savings for applications made before that date (HC 617).

CS 1.2. An application for entry clearance or permission to stay as a Child Student must meet all the following requirements:

(a) any fee and Immigration Health Charge must have been paid; and
(b) the applicant must have provided any required biometrics; and
(c) the applicant must have provided a passport or other travel document which satisfactorily establishes their identity and nationality; and
(d) the applicant must on the date of application have a Confirmation of Acceptance for Studies reference number that was issued to the applicant no more than 6 months before the date of application.

CS 1.3. The applicant must be between 4 and 17 years old at the date of application.

CS 1.4. If the applicant has, in the last 12 months before the date of application, completed a course of studies in the UK for which they have been awarded a scholarship or sponsorship by a Government or international scholarship agency covering both fees and living costs for study in the UK, they must provide written consent in relation to the application from that Government or agency.

CS 1.5. An applicant who is in the UK on the date of application must not have, or have last been granted, permission:

(a) as a Visitor; or
(b) as a Short-term Student; or
(c) outside the Immigration Rules.

CS 1.6. An application which does not meet all the validity requirements for a Child Student is invalid and may be rejected and not considered.

Suitability requirements for a Child Student

CS 2.1. The applicant must not fall for refusal under Part 9: grounds for refusal.

CS 2.2. A person applying for permission to stay must not be:

Eligibility requirements for a Child Student

Entry requirements for a Child Student

CS 3.1. A person seeking to come to the UK as a Child Student must apply for and obtain entry clearance as a Child Student before they arrive in the UK.

CS 3.2. A person applying for entry clearance as a Child Student must, if paragraph A39 and Appendix T of these rules apply, provide a valid medical certificate confirming that they have undergone screening for active pulmonary tuberculosis and that this tuberculosis is not present in them.

Date of application requirement for a Child Student

CS 4.1. An application for entry clearance as a Child Student must be made no more than 6 months before the start date of the course as stated on the Confirmation of Acceptance for Studies.

CS 4.2. An application for permission to stay must be made no more than 3 months before the start date of the course on the Confirmation of Acceptance for Studies.

CS 4.3. An application for permission to stay must be for a course with a start date no more than 28 days after the expiry date of the previous permission to stay.

Genuine Child Student Requirement

CS 5.1. An applicant aged 16 or 17 years old must be a genuine student.

Points Requirement for a Child Student

CS 6.1. The applicant must be awarded a total of 70 points based on the table below:

Points type	Relevant requirements to be met	Number of points
Study (must meet all)	• Confirmation of Acceptance for Studies requirement • Course requirement • Study at an independent school • Aged between 4 and 17 when applying • Parental consent	50
Financial	• Financial requirement	20

Confirmation of Acceptance for Studies requirement for a Child Student

CS 7.1. The Confirmation of Acceptance for Studies must have been issued by a student sponsor which is an independent school whose sponsor licence is still valid on the date on which the application is decided.

CS 7.2. The Confirmation of Acceptance for Studies must not have been used in a previous application which was either granted or refused (but could have been relied upon in a previous application which was rejected as invalid, made void or withdrawn).

CS 7.3. The student sponsor must not have withdrawn the offer since the Confirmation of Acceptance for Studies was issued.

CS 7.4. The Confirmation of Acceptance for Studies must contain the necessary information to confirm that the course requirement is met.

CS 7.5. The Confirmation of Acceptance for Studies must state the cost of accommodation and fees (and any payment already made) so that the financial requirement can be assessed.

Course requirement for a Child Student

CS 8.1. The application must be for a single course of study that meets the requirements at CS 8.2, unless it is for a combined pre-sessional course that meets the requirement at CS 11.1.

CS 8.2. The course for which the Confirmation of Acceptance for Studies has been assigned must be one of the following:

(a) taught in accordance with the National Curriculum; or

(b) taught in accordance with the Recognised Qualification Framework (RQF), and is not a foundation course intended to prepare the Child Student for entry to a course provided by a higher education provider; or

(c) accepted as being of equivalent academic status to (a) or (b) above by Ofsted (England), the Education and Training Inspectorate (Northern Ireland), Education Scotland (Scotland) or Estyn (Wales); or

(d) provided in accordance with prevailing Independent School education inspection standards.

Parental consent requirement for a Child Student

CS 9.1. The applicant must have written consent from:

(a) both parents; or

(b) one parent, if that parent has sole legal responsibility for the applicant; or

(c) the applicant's legal guardian.

CS 9.2. The written consent must confirm support for all the following:

(a) the application; and

(b) the applicant's living and care arrangements in the UK; and

(c) if the application is for entry clearance, the applicant's travel to, and reception arrangements in, the UK.

CS 9.3. If the applicant will be living with a close relative or private foster carer, that close relative or foster carer must be:

(a) a British citizen; or

(b) settled in the UK.

CS 9.4. The close relative or private foster carer (the intended carer) must provide a letter of undertaking which contains the following information:

(a) the name, current address and contact details of the intended carer; and

(b) the address where the intended carer and the applicant will be living in the UK, if different from the intended carer's current address; and

(c) confirmation that the accommodation offered to the applicant is a private address, and not operated as a commercial enterprise, such as a hotel or a youth hostel; and

(d) the nature of the relationship between the applicant's parent(s) or legal guardian and the intended carer; and

(e) that the intended carer agrees to the care arrangements for the applicant; and

(f) that the intended carer has at least £570 per month available to look after and accommodate the applicant, for each month of the course up to a maximum of 9 months; and

(g) a list of any other people that the intended carer has offered to support; and

(h) the intended carer's signature and date of the letter of undertaking.

CS 9.5. If the applicant is staying in a private foster care arrangement and is aged under 16 years, the applicant must also provide:

(a) a copy of the letter of notification from their parent, legal guardian or intended carer to the UK local authority, confirming that the applicant will be in the care of a private foster carer while in the UK; and

(b) the UK local authority's confirmation of receipt, confirming that the local authority has received notification of the private foster care arrangement and have given permission to the arrangement.

Financial requirement for a Child Student

CS 10.1. If the applicant is applying for permission to stay and has been in the UK with permission for 12 months or longer on the date of application, they will meet the financial requirement and do not need to show funds.

CS 10.2. If the applicant is applying for entry clearance, or permission to stay where they have been in the UK for less than 12 months on the date of application, the applicant must show the following funds:

Living arrangements	Funds required
Boarding at a residential independent school	Sufficient funds to pay the outstanding course fees and boarding fees for one academic year
Living during term-time with a private foster carer or close relative who is a British Citizen or settled in the UK	Sufficient funds to pay the outstanding course fees for one academic year. The private foster carer or close relative must have funds of at least £570 per month for each month of the course up to the maximum of 9 months.
Living with a parent or legal guardian who has permission as a Parent of a Child Student.	Sufficient funds to pay the outstanding course fees for one academic year and: a. if no other children are or will be under the parent's care in the UK at the same time as the applicant, £1,560 per month for each month of the course up to maximum of 9 months; and

Living arrangements	Funds required
	b. if there are other children who are or will be under the parent's care in the UK at the same time as the applicant, £625 per month for each month of the course up to a maximum of 9 months for each child, other than the applicant, being cared for by the parent.
Aged 16 or 17 and living independently	Sufficient funds to pay the outstanding course fees for one academic year and either: a. £1334 for each month of the course up to a maximum of 9 months where studying in London; or b. £1023 for each month of the course up to a maximum of 9 months where studying outside London.

If the length of the applicant's course includes a part of a month, the period of time will be rounded up to the next full month.

CS 10.3. Unless the applicant is relying on a student loan or an award from a Government or international scholarship agency, they must show that they have held the required level of funds for a 28-day period and as specified in Appendix Finance.

CS 10.4. The applicant must not be financially responsible for anyone else.

Combined pre-sessional course requirement for a Child Student

CS 11.1. A single Confirmation of Acceptance for Studies can be assigned by an independent school for a combined pre-sessional course and a main course if:

(a) the applicant has an unconditional offer of a place at the independent school; and

(b) the duration of the pre-sessional course and period of study at the independent school does not exceed the maximum period of permission granted as set out at CS 15.2.

Evidence of qualifications requirement for a Child Student

CS 12.1. The applicant must provide evidence of the qualifications they used to obtain the offer of a place on the course from the student sponsor.

CS 12.2. The evidence of each qualification must be one of the following:

(a) the certificate(s) of qualification; or

(b) the transcript of results; or

(c) a print out of the qualification or transcript results from the awarding body's online checking service.

CS 12.3. Where the applicant has provided a print out of qualifications or transcript results from the awarding body's online checking service, the decision maker may require the applicant to provide the certificate of qualification or transcript of results.

Differential evidence requirement for a Child Student

CS 13.1. Evidence to show that the applicant meets the financial requirement and the requirement to provide evidence of qualifications does not need to be provided with the application (but may be required by the decision maker) if the applicant is applying from the country or territory where they are living, or from in the UK, and the applicant either:

(a) holds a valid passport which shows they are registered as a British National (Overseas), or which was issued by the competent authorities of Hong Kong SAR, Macau SAR or Taiwan (that includes the number of the identification card issued by the competent authority in Taiwan); or

(b) is a national of any of the following:

Australia	Kuwait
Austria	Latvia
Bahrain	Liechtenstein
Barbados	Lithuania
Belgium	Luxembourg
Botswana	Malaysia
Brazil	Malta
Brunei	Mauritius
Bulgaria	Mexico
Cambodia	Netherlands
Canada	New Zealand
Chile	Norway
China	Oman
Croatia	Peru
Republic of Cyprus	Poland
Czech Republic	Portugal
Denmark	Qatar
The Dominican Republic	Romania
Estonia	Serbia
Finland	Singapore
France	Slovakia
Germany	Slovenia
Greece	South Korea
Hungary	Spain
Iceland	Sweden
Indonesia	Switzerland
Ireland	Thailand
Italy	Tunisia
Japan	United Arab Emirates
Kazakhstan	United States of America

Decision for a Child Student

CS 14.1. If the decision maker is satisfied that all the suitability and eligibility requirements for a Child Student are met, the application will be granted, otherwise the application will be refused.

CS 14.2. If the application is refused, the person can apply for an Administrative Review under Appendix AR: Administrative Review.

Period and conditions grant for a Child Student

CS 15.1. The grant will subject to the following conditions:

(a) no access to public funds; and

(b) no work until the Child Student is aged over 16 years, then work allowed as specified in CS 16.1; and

(c) no study except as specified in CS 17; and

(d) if Part 10 applies the person will be required to register with the police.

CS 15.2. The period of grant before the start of the course for an applicant applying for entry clearance will be:

(a) the relevant period of permission granted before the course date which is set out in the table below, if entry clearance is granted 1 month or more before the start date of the course or; or

(b) 7 days before the intended date of travel, if entry clearance is granted less than 1 month before the start date of the course; or

(c) with immediate effect, if entry clearance is granted less than 7 days before the intended date of travel and less than 1 month before the start date of the course.

The applicant will be granted permission for the duration of the course as specified on the Confirmation of Acceptance for Studies and the relevant additional periods dependant on their age as specified in the table below:

Age	Period of granted before course start date	Period granted for study	Period granted after course end date
Under 16 years	1month	The shortest of: • the period requested by the applicant; or • the duration of the course of study; or • 6 years	4 months
16 or 17 years	1month	The shortest of: • the period requested by the applicant; or • the duration of the course of study; or • 3 years	4 months

Work Conditions for a Child Student

CS 16.1. A Child Student who is aged 16 or over may work:

(a) for no more than 10 hours per week during term time; and

(b) for any duration during vacation (including before the course starts); and

(c) on a course-related work placement which forms an assessed part of the Child Student's course; provided that any period that the Child Student spends on that placement does not exceed half of the total length of the course undertaken in the UK, unless it is a UK statutory requirement that the placement should exceed half the total length of the course.

CS 16.2. A Child Student will not be allowed to do any of the following work:

(a) be self-employed or engage in business activity; or

(b) work as a professional sportsperson (including as a sports coach); or

(c) work as an entertainer, or

Study Conditions for a Child Student

CS 17.1. A Child Student must study on the course or courses for which the Confirmation of Acceptance for Studies was assigned, unless:

(a) they have yet to complete the course for which the Confirmation of Acceptance for Studies was assigned; and

(b) they begin study on a new course at the student sponsor institution and the new course is at a higher or the same level as the course for which the Confirmation of Acceptance for Studies was assigned and is not a foundation course intended to prepare the student for entry to a higher education provider.

CS 17.2. A Child Student must study with the student sponsor which issued their Confirmation of Acceptance for Studies, unless:

(a) they are studying at an institution which is a partner institution of their student sponsor; or

(b) they have made an application for permission to stay while they have permission as a Child Student which is supported by a valid Confirmation of Acceptance for Studies assigned by a student sponsor, the application has not yet been decided, or any Administrative Review against refusal of that decision has not been determined, and the Child Student will be studying at the student sponsor that assigned the Confirmation of Acceptance for Studies.

CS 17.3. Supplementary study is permitted.

CS 17.4. A Child Student must not study at a state school or academy except for:

(a) a voluntary grammar school with boarding in Northern Ireland: or

(b) if the Child Student has been granted permission to study at a student sponsor which becomes a state school or academy during that period of permission, in which case the Child Student may complete the course for which the Confirmation of Acceptance for Studies was assigned.

Note: Appendix inserted from 09:00 on 1 December 2020 subject to savings for applications made before that time (HC813).

[Appendix Parent of a Child Student

This route is for a Parent of a Child Student to come to or stay in the UK to care for their child, where the child is in the UK under Appendix Child Student, is aged between 4 and 11 and is attending an independent fee-paying school (which must not be a state school or academy).

Only one of the child's parents can be in the UK under this route.

Validity requirements for the Parent of a Child Student

PC 1.1. A person applying for entry clearance or permission to stay as a Parent of a Child Student must apply online on the gov.uk website on the specified form as follows:

Location of applicant	Specified form
Outside the UK	Parent of a Child Student
Inside the UK	Application to extend stay in the UK: FLR(IR)

PC 1.2. An application for entry clearance or permission to stay as a Parent of a Child Student must meet all the following requirements:

(a) any fee and Immigration Health Charge must have been paid; and

(b) the applicant must have provided any required biometrics; and

(c) the applicant must have provided a passport or other travel document which satisfactorily establishes their identity and nationality.

PC 1.3. The applicant must be aged 18 or over on the date of application.

PC 1.4. An applicant applying for permission to stay must be in the UK and must not have, or have last been granted, permission:

(a) as a Visitor; or

(b) as a Short-term Student; or

(c) outside the Immigration Rules.

PC 1.5. An application which does not meet all the validity requirements for the Parent of a Child Student is invalid and may be rejected and not considered.

Suitability requirements for the Parent of a Child Student

PC 2.1. The applicant must not fall for refusal under Part 9: grounds for refusal.

PC 2.2. If applying for permission to stay the applicant must not be:

(a) in breach of immigration laws, except that where paragraph 39E applies, that period of overstaying will be disregarded; or

(b) on immigration bail.

Eligibility requirements for Parent of a Child Student

Entry requirements for Parent of a Child Student

PC 3.1. A person seeking to come to the UK as a Parent of a Child Student must apply for and obtain entry clearance as a Parent of a Child Student before they arrive in the UK.

PC 3.2. A person applying for entry clearance as the Parent of a Child Student must, if paragraph A39 and Appendix T of these rules apply, provide a valid medical certificate confirming that they have undergone screening for active pulmonary tuberculosis and that this tuberculosis is not present in them.

Relationship requirement for Parent of a Child Student

PC 4.1. The applicant must be the parent of a child who has, or is at the same time applying for, entry clearance or permission to stay as a Child Student.

PC 4.2. The Child Student's other parent must not be in the UK or seeking to come to the UK.

Child Student requirements for Parent of a Child Student

PC 5.1. The Child Student must be aged between 4 and 11 years on the date of application and have, or at the same time be applying for, entry clearance or permission to stay, under Appendix Child Student.

Care requirement for Parent of a Child Student

PC 6.1. The applicant must intend to live with the Child Student during the applicant's stay in the UK.

Financial requirement for Parent of a Child Student

PC 7.1. If the applicant is applying for permission to stay and has been in the UK with permission for 12 months or longer on the date of application, they will meet the financial requirement and do not need to show funds.

PC 7.2. If both the applicant and the Child Student are applying at the same time for either entry clearance, or permission to stay where they have both lived in the UK for less than 12 months on the date of application, the applicant will meet the financial requirement if the Child Student shows the level of funds required under CS 10.2.

PC 7.3. If neither PC 7.1 or PC 7.2 apply the applicant must:

(a) have funds of £1,560 for each month of their intended stay in the UK up to a maximum of 9 months; and

(b) have funds of £625 for each month of their intended stay up to a maximum of 9 months for any child other than the Child Student who will be under their care in the UK.

PC 7.4. The applicant must not intend to make the UK their main home and must have sufficient funds to maintain their main home outside the UK, in addition to any other funds required by these rules.

[PC 7.5. The applicant or their partner must show that they have held the required level of funds for a 28-day period and as specified in Appendix Finance.]

Note: Paragraph substituted from 6 April 2021 subject to savings for applications made before that date (HC 1248).

[PC 7.6. The applicant may rely on funds held in the account of a partner who is outside the UK in addition to the account holders listed in FIN 5.1(a).]

Note: Paragraph inserted from 6 April 2021 subject to savings for applications made before that date (HC 1248).

Decision on application for Parent of a Child Student

PC 8.1. If the decision maker is satisfied that all the suitability and eligibility requirements are met for the Parent of a Child Student the application will be granted, otherwise, the application will be refused.

PC 8.2. If the application is refused the person can apply for an Administrative Review under Appendix AR: Administrative Review.

Period and conditions of grant for Parent of a Child Student

PC 9.1. The Parent of a Child Student will be granted permission for a period which ends at the same time as the Child Student's permission, or on the date the Child Student reaches the age of 12 years, whichever is sooner.

PC 9.2. The grant will be subject to all the following conditions:
(a) no access to public funds; and
(b) no work; and
(c) no study; and
(d) if Part 10 applies, the applicant will be required to register with the police.]

Note: Appendix inserted from 09:00 on 1 December 2020 subject to savings for applications made before that time (HC813).

[Appendix Graduate

This route is for a Student in the UK who wants to work, or look for work, following the successful completion of an eligible course of study at UK bachelor's degree-level or above. The study must have been with a higher education provider with a track record of compliance.

The Graduate route is an unsponsored route.

Individuals who already have permission as a dependant of a Student who is applying on this route can also apply to extend their permission as a dependant on this route; other types of dependants are not permitted on this route.

The Graduate route is not a route to settlement.

Validation requirements for a Graduate

GR 1.1. A person applying for permission to stay as a Graduate must apply online on the gov.uk website on the specified form 'Graduate'.

GR 1.2. An application for permission as a Graduate must meet all the following requirements:
(a) any fee and Immigration Health Charge must have been paid; and
(b) the applicant must have provided any required biometrics; and
[(c) the applicant must have provided a passport or other document which satisfactorily establishes their identity and nationality; and]
(d) the applicant must be in the UK.

Note: Sub-paragraph (c) substituted from 6 April 2022 subject to savings for applications made before that date (HC 1118).

GR 1.3. The applicant must have, or have last had, permission as a Student.

GR 1.4. The applicant must not have been previously granted permission under the Doctorate Extension Scheme or as a Graduate.

GR 1.5. If the applicant has in the 12 months before the date of application been awarded a scholarship or sponsorship by a Government or international scholarship agency covering both fees and living costs for study in the UK, they must provide written consent to the application from that Government or agency.

GR 1.6. An application which does not meet all the validity requirements for a Graduate is invalid and may be rejected and not considered.

Suitability requirements for a Graduate

GR 2.1. The applicant must not fall for refusal under Part 9: grounds for refusal.

GR 2.2. The applicant must not be:

(a) in the UK in breach of immigration laws, except that where paragraph 39E applies, that period of overstaying will be disregarded; or

(b) on immigration bail.

Eligibility requirements for a Graduate

Points requirement

GR 3.1. The applicant must be awarded a total of 70 points based on the table below.

Points type	Relevant requirements to be met	Number of points
Successful course completion	• Successful completion requirement • Qualification requirement • Study in the UK requirement	70

Successful completion requirement

GR 4.1. The applicant must have last been sponsored by a Student sponsor which is a higher education provider with a track record of compliance on the date of application.

GR 4.2. The applicant must have successfully completed the course of study which was undertaken during their last grant of permission to study on the Student route (where the applicant was allowed to change their course of study without applying for further permission as a Student, this requirement only applies to the course to which they changed).

GR 4.3. The student sponsor must have notified the Home Office, by the date of application, that the applicant has successfully completed the course of study in GR 4.2.

Qualification requirement

GR 5.1. The applicant will meet the qualification requirement if they have successfully completed a course of study for which they have been or will be awarded a UK bachelor's degree, a UK postgraduate degree, or successfully completed a relevant qualification listed in GR 5.2.

GR 5.2 A relevant qualification is one of the following:

(a) a law conversion course validated by the [Solicitors Regulation Authority] in England and Wales; or

(b) the Legal Practice Course in England and Wales, the Solicitors Course in Northern Ireland, or a Diploma in Professional Legal Practice in Scotland; or

(c) the Bar Practice Course in England and Wales, or the Bar Course in Northern Ireland; or

(d) a foundation programme in Medicine or Dentistry; or

(e) a Postgraduate Certificate in Education (PGCE) or Postgraduate Diploma in Education (PGDE); or

(f) a professional course requiring study at UK bachelor's degree level or above in a profession with reserved activities that is regulated by UK law or UK public authority.

Note: Words substituted from 6 October 2021 (HC 617).

GR 5.3. If the name of the applicant's course of study was changed by the Student sponsor, but the course content remained the same, or if an integral and assessed work placement or permitted study abroad programme was added, this will not prevent the applicant being able to meet the qualification requirement.

GR 5.4. The qualification must have been gained during the last grant of permission to study as a Student, or in the period of permission immediately before the applicant's last grant of permission, if the last grant of permission was to undertake a role as a Student Union Sabbatical Officer.

Study in the UK requirement

GR 6.1. [The applicant must have held permission as a Student, which was granted to study the relevant qualification in the UK, for a minimum period of time (the relevant period), as in the table below.]

Total length of course	Relevant period of Student permission granted during which all study took place in the UK (apart from permitted study abroad programmes)
12 months or less	Full duration of course
Longer than 12 months	At least 12 months

Note: Introduction substituted from 6 April 2022 subject to savings for applications made before that date (HC 1118).

[**GR 6.2.** Where distance learning took place overseas between 24 January 2020 and 30 June 2022, this will not prevent the applicant meeting the requirement to spend the relevant period at GR 6.1 studying in the UK if either:

(a) they began a course of 12 months or less prior to 21 June 2021 and entered the UK on or before 27 September 2021 with permission as a Student; or

(b) they began a course of 12 months or less between 21 June 2021 and 30 June 2022 and entered the UK on or before 30 June 2022 with permission as a Student.]

Note: Paragraph substituted from 6 April 2022 subject to savings for applications made before that date (HC 1118).

GR 6.3. Any period of distance learning between 24 January 2020 and [30 June 2022] as part of a course of study lasting longer than 12 months whilst the applicant held permission as a Student, will not prevent the applicant from meeting the requirement to spend the relevant period at GR 6.1. studying in the UK.

Note: Amendment from 6 April 2022 subject to savings for applications made before that date.

Decision on application as a Graduate

GR 7.1. If the decision maker is satisfied that all the suitability and eligibility requirements for a Graduate are met the application will be granted, otherwise the application will be refused.

GR 7.2. If the application is refused, the person can apply for an Administrative Review under Appendix AR: Administrative Review.

Period and conditions of grant for a Graduate

GR 8.1. The applicant will be granted the period of permission as set out in the table below dependent on how they met the qualification requirement.

Type of Qualification	Period granted from date of decision
PhD or other doctoral qualification	3 years
All other qualifications	2 years

GR 8.2. The grant will be subject to all the following conditions:

(a) no access to public funds; and

(b) work (including self-employment and voluntary work) is permitted, apart from work as a professional sportsperson; and

(c) study is permitted, except study with an education provider which is a Student sponsor, and which would meet the approved qualification and level of study requirements of the Student route which are set out in Appendix Student; and

(d) study is subject to the ATAS condition in Appendix ATAS; and

(e) if Part 10 applies the person will be required to register with the police.

Dependants of a Graduate

Validity requirements for a dependent partner or dependent child of a Graduate

GR 9.1. A person applying for permission to stay as a partner or child of a Graduate must apply on the specified form on the gov.uk website as follows:

Either (as applicable):

- Dependant partner
- Dependant child

[**GR 9.2.** An application for permission to stay as a partner or child of a Graduate must meet all the following requirements:

(a) any fee and Immigration Health Charge must have been paid; and

(b) the applicant must have provided any required biometrics; and

(c) the applicant must have provided a passport or other document which satisfactorily establishes their identity and nationality; and

(d) the applicant must be applying as partner or child of a person who:

(i) has made a valid application for permission to stay on the Graduate route that has not been decided; or

(ii) has permission to stay on the Graduate route.]

Note: Paragraph substituted from 6 April 2022 subject to savings for applications made before that date (HC 1118).

GR 9.3. If the applicant has in the 12 months before the date of application been awarded a scholarship or sponsorship by a Government or international scholarship agency covering both fees and living costs for study in the UK, they must provide written consent to the application from that Government or agency.

GR 9.4. The applicant must be in the UK on the date of application and must:

(a) have, or have last been granted, permission as a dependant partner of a Student and that Student is applying for, or has now been granted, permission to stay in the Graduate route; or

(b) have, or have last been granted, permission as a dependant child of either a Student or dependant partner of the Student and that Student is applying for, or has now been granted, permission to stay in the Graduate route; or

(c) be a child born in the UK during the last grant of Student permission of a Student and that Student is applying for, or has now been granted, permission to stay in the Graduate route.

GR 9.5. An application which does not meet the validity requirements for a partner or child on the Graduate route is invalid and may be rejected and not considered.

Suitability requirements for a dependent partner or dependent child of a Graduate

GR 10.1. The applicant must not fall for refusal under Part 9: grounds for refusal.

GR 10.2. The applicant must not be:

(a) in the UK in breach of immigration laws, except that where paragraph 39E applies, that period of overstaying will be disregarded; or

(b) on immigration bail.

Eligibility requirements for a dependent partner or dependent child of a Graduate

Relationship requirement for dependent partner of a Graduate

GR 11.1. The relationship between the applicant and their partner must be genuine and subsisting.

GR 11.2. The applicant and their partner must intend to live together throughout the applicant's stay in the UK.

GR 11.3. The applicant must not intend to stay in the UK beyond any permission granted to their partner.

Relationship requirement for dependent child of a Graduate

GR 12.1. The applicant must be a child of a parent who has, or is at the same time being granted permission as:

(a) a Graduate; or

(b) the partner of a Graduate.

GR 12.2. Each of the applicant's parents must either be applying at the same time as the applicant, or have permission to be in the UK (other than as a visitor) unless:

(a) the parent with permission as a Student or Graduate or as the partner of a Student or Graduate is the sole surviving parent; or

(b) the parent with permission as a Student or Graduate or as the partner of a Student or Graduate has sole responsibility for the child's upbringing; or

(c) the decision maker is satisfied that there are serious and compelling reasons to grant the child permission to stay with the parent who is applying for permission as a Graduate or as partner of a Graduate.

GR 12.3. If the applicant is a child who is born in the UK to a Student or Graduate, or their partner the applicant must provide a full UK birth certificate showing the names of both parents.

Care requirement for dependent child of a Graduate

GR 13.1. If the applicant is aged under 18 on the date of application there must be suitable arrangements for the child's care and accommodation in the UK which must comply with relevant UK legislation and regulations.

Age requirement for a dependent child of a Graduate

GR 14.1. The child must be under the age of 18 at the date of application, unless they were last granted permission as a dependent child of a parent (P) who has or is applying for permission to stay as a Graduate or a dependent partner of a Graduate (regardless of the route under which the parent (P) had permission at the time the child's last permission was granted).

GR 14.2. If the child is aged 16 or over on the date of application, they must not be leading an independent life.

Decision on application for a dependent partner or dependent child of a Graduate

GR 15.1. If the decision maker is satisfied that all the suitability and eligibility requirements for a dependent partner or dependent child of a Graduate are met, the application will be granted, otherwise the application will be refused.

GR 15.2. If the application is refused, the person can apply for an Administrative Review under Appendix AR.

Period and conditions of grant for a dependent partner or dependent child of a Graduate

GR 16.1. A dependent partner will be granted permission which ends on the same date as the Graduate partner's permission.

GR 16.2. A dependent child will be granted permission which ends on the same date as whichever of their parents' permission ends first.

GR 16.3. The grant will be subject to all the following conditions:

(a) no access to public funds; and

(b) work (including self-employment and voluntary work) is permitted except as a professional sportsperson (including as a sports coach); and

(c) study is permitted, subject to the ATAS condition in Appendix ATAS (if the study will commence when the person is aged over 18); and

(d) if Part 10 applies the person will be required to register with the police.]

Note: Appendix inserted from 09:00 on 1 July 2021 subject to savings for applications (including for administrative review) made before that time (HC 1248).

[Appendix Skilled Worker

The Skilled Worker route is for employers to recruit people to work in the UK in a specific job. A Skilled Worker must have a job offer in an eligible skilled occupation from a Home Office-approved sponsor.

A dependent partner and dependent children can apply on this route.

Skilled Worker is a route to settlement.

Validity requirements for a Skilled Worker

SW 1.1. A person applying for entry clearance or permission to stay as a Skilled Worker must apply online on the gov.uk website on the specified form as follows:

[(a) for applicants outside the UK, form 'Skilled Worker visa'; or

(b) for applicants inside the UK, form 'Skilled Worker'.]

Note: Sub-paragraphs (a) and (b) substituted from 30 November 2021 subject to savings for applications made before that date (HC 617).

SW 1.2. An application for entry clearance or permission to stay as a Skilled Worker must meet all the following requirements[:]

(a) any fee and Immigration Health Charge must have been paid; and

(b) the applicant must have provided any required biometrics; and

(c) the applicant must have provided a passport or other travel document which satisfactorily establishes their identity and nationality; and

(d) the applicant must have a certificate of sponsorship that was issued to them by their sponsor no more than 3 months before the date of application.

Note: Punctuation in introduction substituted from 6 April 2021 subject to savings for applications made before that date (HC 1248).

SW 1.3. The applicant must be aged 18 or over on the date of application.

SW 1.4. An applicant applying for entry clearance or permission to stay, who has received an award from a Government or international scholarship agency in the 12 months before the date of application which covers both fees and living costs for study in the UK, must have provided written consent to the application from that Government or agency.

SW 1.5. An applicant who is applying for permission to stay must be in the UK on the date of application and must not have, or have last been granted, permission:

(a) as a Visitor; or

(b) as a Short-term student; or

(c) as a Parent of a Child Student; or

(d) as a Seasonal Worker; or

(e) as a Domestic Worker in a Private Household; or

(f) outside the Immigration Rules.

SW 1.6. An application which does not meet the validity requirements for a Skilled Worker is invalid and may be rejected and not considered.

Suitability requirements for a Skilled Worker

SW 2.1. The applicant must not fall for refusal under Part 9: grounds for refusal.

SW 2.2. If applying for permission to stay the applicant must not be:

(a) in breach of immigration laws, except that where paragraph 39E applies, that period of overstaying will be disregarded; or

(b) on immigration bail.

Eligibility requirements for a Skilled Worker

Entry requirement for a Skilled Worker

SW 3.1. A person seeking to come to the UK as a Skilled Worker must apply for and obtain entry clearance as a Skilled Worker before they arrive in the UK.

SW 3.2. A person applying for entry clearance as a Skilled Worker must, if paragraph A39 and Appendix T of these rules apply, provide a valid medical certificate confirming that they have undergone screening for active pulmonary tuberculosis and that this tuberculosis is not present in them.

Points requirement for a Skilled Worker

SW 4.1. The applicant must be awarded 50 mandatory points from the table below. Details of how these points are awarded are set out in SW 5.1. to SW 7.4.

Mandatory points requirements	Relevant rules	Points
Sponsorship	SW 5.1. to SW 5.7.	20
Job at an appropriate skill level	SW 6.1. to SW 6.5.	20
English language skills at level B1 (intermediate)	SW 7.1. to SW 7.3.	10

SW 4.2. An applicant must be awarded 20 tradeable points from the table below. An applicant may only be awarded points from one entry in the table. Details of how these points are awarded are set out in SW 8.1. to [SW 14.6].

[Option	Tradeable points requirements for each option	Relevant rules	Points
A	The applicant's salary equals or exceeds all of the following: • £25,600 per year; • £10.10 per hour; and • the going rate for the occupation code.	SW 8.1. to SW 8.5. and SW 14.1. to SW 14.6.	20
B	Educational qualification: PhD in a subject relevant to the job and the applicant's salary equals or exceeds all of the following: • £23,040 per year; • £10.10 per hour; and • 90% of the going rate for the occupation code. In this entry, 10 points will be awarded for the educational qualification and 10 points will be awarded for the applicant's salary.	SW 9.1. to SW 9.10. and SW 14.1. to SW 14.6.	20

[Option	Tradeable points requirements for each option	Relevant rules	Points
C	Educational qualification: PhD in a STEM subject relevant to the job and the applicant's salary equals or exceeds all of the following: • £20,480 per year; • £10.10 per hour; and • 80% of the going rate for the occupation code.	SW 10.1. to SW 10.6. and SW 14.1. to SW 14.6.	20
D	Job in a shortage occupation and the applicant's salary equals or exceeds all of the following: • £20,480 per year; • £10.10 per hour; and • 80% of the going rate for the occupation code[, for occupation codes where a going rate is specified].	SW 11.1. to SW 11.6. and SW 14.1. to SW 14.6.	20
E	Applicant is a new entrant to the labour market and their salary equals or exceeds all of the following: • £20,480 per year; • £10.10 per hour; and • 70% of the going rate for the occupation code.	SW 12.1. to SW 12.7. and SW 14.1. to SW 14.6.	20
F	Job in a listed health or education occupation and the applicant's salary equals or exceeds both: • £20,480 per year; and • the going rate for the occupation code. An applicant with a job in a listed health or education occupation can only be awarded tradeable points from option F.	SW 13.1. to SW 13.7. and SW 14.1 to SW 14.6.	20]

Note: Words in introduction, table substituted from 6 April 2021 subject to savings for applications made before that date (HC 1248). Words in Row D inserted from 15 February 2022 subject to savings for applications made before that date (HC 1019).

Points for sponsorship (mandatory)

SW 5.1. The applicant must have a valid Certificate of Sponsorship for the job they are planning to do; which to be valid must:

(a) confirm the applicant's name, that they are being sponsored as a Skilled Worker, details of the job and salary the sponsor is offering them and PAYE details if HM Revenue and Customs (HMRC) requires income tax and National Insurance for the sponsored job to be paid via PAYE; and

(b) if the application is for entry clearance, have been allocated by the Home Office to that sponsor for the specific job and salary details shown; and

(c) include a start date, stated by the sponsor, which is no more than 3 months after the date of application; and

(d) not have been used in a previous application which was either granted or refused (but can have been used in a previous application which was rejected as invalid, made void or withdrawn); and

(e) not have been withdrawn by the sponsor or cancelled by the Home Office[; and]

[(f) confirm whether or not the Academic Technology Approval Scheme (ATAS) requirement in Appendix ATAS applies.]

Note: Words in (e) substituted, (f) inserted from 09:00 on 21 May 2021 subject to savings for applications made before that time (HC 1248).

SW 5.2. The sponsor must be authorised by the Home Office to sponsor the job in question under the Skilled Worker route.

SW 5.3. The sponsor must be listed as A-rated on the Home Office's register of licensed sponsors, unless the applicant was last granted permission as a Skilled Worker and is applying to continue working for the same sponsor as in their last permission.

SW 5.4. The sponsor must have paid in full any required Immigration Skills Charge.

SW 5.5. The decision maker must not have reasonable grounds to believe the job the applicant is being sponsored to do:

(a) does not exist; or

(b) is a sham; or

(c) has been created mainly so the applicant can apply for entry clearance or permission to stay.

SW 5.6. The decision maker must not have reasonable grounds to believe the job the applicant is being sponsored to do amounts to:

(a) the hire of the applicant to a third party who is not the sponsor to fill a position with that party, whether temporary or permanent; or

(b) contract work to undertake an ongoing routine role or to provide an ongoing routine service for a third party who is not the sponsor, regardless of the nature or length of any arrangement between the sponsor and the third party.

SW 5.7. If the requirements in SW 5.1. to SW 5.6. are met, the applicant will be awarded 20 mandatory points for sponsorship.

Points for a job at the appropriate skill level (mandatory)

SW 6.1. The applicant must be sponsored for a job in an eligible occupation code listed in Appendix Skilled Occupations [or Appendix Shortage Occupation List], subject to SW 6.2.

Note: Words inserted from 15 February 2022 subject to savings for applications made before that date (HC 1019).

SW 6.2. The sponsor must choose an appropriate occupation code, and the decision maker must not have reasonable grounds to believe the sponsor has chosen a less appropriate occupation code for any of the following reasons:

(a) the most appropriate occupation code is not eligible under the Skilled Worker route; or

(b) the most appropriate occupation code has a higher going rate than the proposed salary; or

(c) the most appropriate occupation code is not a shortage occupation and the applicant is claiming points for a job in a shortage occupation; or

(d) the most appropriate occupation code is not listed as 'eligible for PhD points' in Table 1 of Appendix Skilled Occupations and the applicant is claiming points for an educational qualification.

SW 6.3. To support the assessment in SW 6.2., the decision maker may, in particular, consider:

(a) whether the sponsor has shown a genuine need for the job as described; and

(b) whether the applicant has the appropriate skills, qualifications and experience needed to do the job as described; and

(c) the sponsor's history of compliance with the immigration system including, but not limited to, paying its sponsored workers appropriately; and

(d) any additional information from the sponsor.

[**SW 6.3A.** If the ATAS requirement in Appendix ATAS applies, the applicant must provide a valid ATAS certificate.]

Note: Paragraph inserted from 09:00 on 21 May 2021 subject to savings for applications made before that time (HC 1248).

SW 6.4. If the requirements in SW 6.1. to [SW 6.3A.] are met, an applicant will be awarded 20 mandatory points for a job at the appropriate skill level, subject to SW 6.5.

Note: Words substituted from 09:00 on 21 May 2021 subject to savings for applications made before that time (HC 1248).

SW 6.5. No points will be awarded for a job at the appropriate skill level if the applicant is not also being awarded the 20 mandatory points for sponsorship under SW 5.7.

Points for the English language requirement (mandatory)

SW 7.1. An applicant must show English language ability on the Common European Framework of Reference for Languages in all 4 components (reading, writing, speaking and listening) of at least level B1 (intermediate).

SW 7.2. The applicant must show they meet the English language requirement as specified in Appendix English Language.

SW 7.3. If the requirements in SW 7.1. to SW 7.2. are met, the applicant will be awarded 10 mandatory points for meeting the English language requirement.

Tradeable points option A

SW 8.1. The applicant must be sponsored for a job in an appropriate eligible occupation code listed in Table 1 of Appendix Skilled Occupations.

[**SW 8.2.** The salary for the job for which the applicant is being sponsored must equal or exceed all of the following:

(a) £25,600 per year; and

(b) £10.10 per hour; and

(c) the going rate for the occupation code.]

Note: Paragraph substituted from 6 April 2021 subject to savings for applications made before that date (HC 1248).

SW 8.3. The salary will be considered as set out in SW 14.1. to [SW 14.6].

Note: Word substituted from 6 April 2021 subject to savings for applications made before that date (HC 1248).

SW 8.4. If the requirements in SW 8.1. to SW 8.3. are met, the applicant will be awarded 20 tradeable points for their salary, subject to SW 8.5.

SW 8.5. No points will be awarded for salary if the applicant is not also being awarded the 20 mandatory points for sponsorship under SW 5.7. and the 20 mandatory points for a job at the appropriate skill level under SW 6.4.

Tradeable points option B

SW 9.1. The applicant must be sponsored for a job in an appropriate occupation code listed as being 'eligible for PhD points' in Table 1 of Appendix Skilled Occupations.

SW 9.2. The applicant must have a UK PhD or other academic doctoral qualification, or an overseas academic qualification which [Ecctis] confirms meets the recognised standard of a UK PhD.

Note: Words substituted from 6 October 2021 subject to savings for applications made before that date (HC 617).

SW 9.3. The applicant's sponsor must provide a credible explanation of how the qualification is relevant to the job for which the applicant is being sponsored.

SW 9.4. If the applicant has been correctly awarded points for an educational qualification in a previous grant of permission as a Skilled Worker, the applicant does not need to provide evidence of the qualification again, but the sponsor must still provide the explanation in SW 9.3.

SW 9.5. The applicant may only be awarded points for one qualification.

[**SW 9.6.** The salary for the job the applicant is being sponsored for must equal or exceed all of the following:

(a) £23,040 per year; and
(b) £10.10 per hour; and
(c) 90% of the going rate for the occupation code.]

Note: Paragraph substituted from 6 April 2021 subject to savings for applications made before that date HC 1248).

SW 9.7. The salary will be considered as set out in SW 14.1. to [SW 14.6].

Note: Word substituted from 6 April 2021 subject to savings for applications made before that date HC 1248).

SW 9.8. If the requirements in SW 9.1. to SW 9.5. are met, the applicant will be awarded 10 tradeable points for a relevant educational qualification, subject to SW 9.10.

SW 9.9. If the requirements SW 9.6. to SW 9.7. are met and the occupation code is listed in Table 1 of Appendix Skilled Occupations, the applicant will be awarded 10 tradeable points for their salary, subject to SW 9.10.

SW 9.10. No points will be awarded for a relevant educational qualification or salary if the applicant is not also being awarded the 20 mandatory points for sponsorship under SW 5.7. and the 20 mandatory points for a job at the appropriate skill level under SW 6.4.

Tradeable points option C

SW 10.1. The applicant must meet the requirements in SW 9.1. to SW 9.5.

SW 10.2. The applicant's sponsor must provide a credible explanation that the qualification in question is in a Science, Technology, Engineering or Mathematics (STEM) subject.

[**SW 10.3.** The salary for the job the applicant is being sponsored for must equal or exceed all of the following:

(a) £20,480 per year; and

(b) £10.10 per hour; and

(c) 80% of the going rate for the occupation code.]

Note: Paragraph substituted from 6 April 2021 subject to savings for applications made before that date HC 1248).

SW 10.4. The salary will be considered as set out in SW 14.1. to [SW 14.6].

Note: Word substituted from 6 April 2021 subject to savings for applications made before that date HC 1248).

SW 10.5. If the requirements in SW 10.1. to SW 10.4. are met, the applicant will be awarded 20 tradeable points for a relevant educational qualification in a STEM subject and their salary, subject to SW 10.6.

SW 10.6. No points will be awarded for a relevant educational qualification and salary if the applicant is not also being awarded the 20 mandatory points for sponsorship under SW 5.7. and the 20 mandatory points for a job at the appropriate skill level under SW 6.4.

Tradeable points option D

SW 11.1. The applicant must be sponsored for a job in an appropriate eligible occupation code listed in Appendix Shortage Occupation List as being a shortage occupation in the nation of the UK where that job is based, unless SW 11.2. applies.

SW 11.2. If, on or before the date the sponsor assigned the Certificate of Sponsorship to the applicant, the applicant's job was removed from Appendix Shortage Occupation List, both of the following conditions must be met:

(a) the applicant's most recent permission was as a Skilled Worker in which they were sponsored to work in a shortage occupation under the applicable rules at that time; and

(b) the applicant is being sponsored to continue working in the same job for the same sponsor as in their previous permission.

[**SW 11.3.** The salary for the job the applicant is being sponsored for must equal or exceed all of the following:

(a) £20,480 per year; and

(b) £10.10 per hour; and

[(c) if it is listed in Table 1 of Appendix Shortage Occupations, 80% of the going rate for the occupation code.]

Note: Paragraph substituted from 6 April 2021 subject to savings for applications made before that date HC 1248). Sub-paragraph (c) substituted from 15 February 2022 subject to savings for applications made before that date (HC 1019).

SW 11.4. The salary will be considered as set out in SW 14.1. to [SW 14.6].

Note: Word substituted from 6 April 2021 subject to savings for applications made before that date HC 1248).

SW 11.5. If the requirements in SW 11.1. to SW 11.4. are met, the applicant will be awarded 20 tradeable points for a job in a shortage occupation and their salary, subject to SW 11.6.

SW 11.6. No points will be awarded for a job in a shortage occupation and salary if the applicant is not also being awarded the 20 mandatory points for sponsorship under SW 5.7. and the 20 mandatory points for a job at the appropriate skill level under SW 6.4.

Tradeable points option E

SW 12.1. The applicant must be sponsored for a job in an appropriate eligible occupation code listed in Table 1 of Appendix Skilled Occupations.

SW 12.2. The applicant must meet one or more of the following requirements:

(a) the applicant must be under the age of 26 on the date of application; or

(b) the job offer must be for a postdoctoral position in any of the following occupation codes:

- 2111 Chemical scientists
- 2112 Biological scientists and biochemists
- 2113 Physical scientists
- 2114 Social and humanities scientists
- 2119 Natural and social science professionals not elsewhere classified
- 2311 higher education teaching professionals; or

(c) the job offer must be in a [UK Regulated Profession] and the applicant must be working towards a recognised professional qualification for that profession; or

(d) the applicant must be working towards full registration or chartered status with the relevant professional body for the job they are being sponsored for; or

(e) the application must be for permission to stay and the applicant's most recent permission must have been as a Tier 1 (Graduate Entrepreneur) Migrant; or

(f) all of the following conditions apply:

[(i) the applicant's most recent permission, other than as a visitor, was as a Student; and]

(ii) [that permission is either current or expired] less than 2 years before the date of application; and

(iii) in that permission or any previous permission as a Student, the applicant was sponsored to study one of the following courses (not any other qualifications of an equivalent level):

- a UK bachelor's degree; or
- a UK master's degree; or
- a UK PhD or other doctoral qualification; or
- a Postgraduate Certificate in Education; or
- a Professional Graduate Diploma of Education; and

(iv) the applicant has completed (or is applying no more than 3 months before they are expected to complete) the course in (iii) above, or the applicant is studying a PhD and has completed at least 12 months study in the UK towards the PhD[; or]

[(g) the applicant's most recent permission, other than as a visitor, was as a Graduate, and that permission is either current or expired less than 2 years before the date of application.]

Note: Sub-paragraph (f)(i) substituted from 6 April 2021; words in (f)(ii) substituted from 6 April 2021 subject to savings for applications made before that date; words at end of (f)(iv) substituted, (g) inserted from 09:00 on 1 July 2021 subject to savings for applications (including applications for administrative review) for applications made before that time (HC 1248). Words in (c) substituted from 6 October 2021 subject to savings for applications made before that date (HC 617).

SW 12.3. Granting the application must not mean the applicant's combined permission [as a Skilled Worker, Graduate and/or Tier 2 Migrant.] would be more than 4 years in total, whether or not the permission is for a continuous period.

Note: Words substituted from 09:00 on 1 July 2021 subject to savings for applications (including applications for administrative review) for applications made before that time (HC 1248).

[**SW 12.4.** The salary for the job the applicant is being sponsored for must equal or exceed all of the following:

(a) £20,480 per year; and
(b) £10.10 per hour; and
(c) 70% of the going rate for the occupation code.]

Note: Paragraph substituted from 6 April 2021 subject to savings for applications made before that date (HC1248).

SW 12.4. The salary for the job the applicant is being sponsored for must equal or exceed both:

(a) £20,480 per year; and
(b) 70% of the going rate for the occupation code.

SW 12.5. The salary will be considered as set out in SW 14.1. to [SW 14.6].

Note: Word substituted from 6 April 2021 subject to savings for applications made before that date HC 1248).

SW 12.6. If the requirements in SW 12.1. to SW 12.5. are met, the applicant will be awarded 20 tradeable points for being a new entrant to the labour market and their salary, subject to SW 12.7.

SW 12.7. No points will be awarded for being a new entrant to the labour market and salary if the applicant is not also being awarded the 20 mandatory points for sponsorship under SW 5.7. and the 20 mandatory points for a job at the appropriate skill level under SW 6.4.

Tradeable points option F

SW 13.1. The applicant must be sponsored for a job in an appropriate eligible occupation code listed in Table 2 of Appendix Skilled Occupations.

SW 13.2. The salary for the job for which the applicant is being sponsored must equal or exceed both:

(a) £20,480 per year; and
(b) the going rate for the occupation code.

SW 13.3. The salary will be considered as set out in SW 14.1. to SW 14.5.

SW 13.4. If the applicant is being sponsored for a job in the occupation code '2231 Nurses' or '2232 Midwives', their salary may be temporarily (for up to 8 months) less than the £20,480 per year required under SW 13.2(a) in either of the following circumstances:

(a) the applicant has previously held Nursing and Midwifery Council (NMC) registration and is undertaking an NMC-approved programme with a view to returning to practice; or

(b) the applicant is working towards NMC registration and all of the following conditions apply:

(i) the applicant has passed the NMC's English language requirements and Computer Based Test of competence, before the date of application; and

(ii) the applicant will sit an Objective Structured Clinical Examination (OSCE) to obtain NMC registration no later than 3 months after the stated job start date.

SW 13.5. Where SW 13.4. applies:

(a) the sponsor must confirm that the applicant will stop being sponsored if they do not achieve full NMC registration within 8 months of the job start date (if the applicant was last granted permission as a as a nurse or midwife on the Skilled Worker route, the 8 months is counted from the start date of the job they were sponsored to do in their most recent permission); and

(b) during the 8 months in (a), or until the applicant achieves NMC registration (if sooner), the applicant's salary must be at least equal to the appropriate Agenda for Change Band 3 rate, as stated in Table 3 of Appendix Skilled Occupations.

SW 13.6. If the requirements in SW 13.1. to SW 13.5. are met, the applicant will be awarded 20 tradeable points for a job in a listed health or education occupation and their salary, subject to SW 13.7.

SW 13.7. No points will be awarded for a job in a listed health or education occupation and salary if the applicant is not also being awarded the 20 mandatory points for sponsorship under SW 5.7. and the 20 mandatory points for a job at the appropriate skill level under SW 6.4.

Consideration of salary (all tradeable points options)

SW 14.1. Salary only includes guaranteed basic gross pay (before income tax and including employee pension and national insurance contributions).

SW 14.2. Salary does not include other pay and benefits, such as any of the following:

(a) pay which cannot be guaranteed because the nature of the job means that hours fluctuate; or

(b) additional pay such as shift, overtime or bonus pay, (whether or not it is guaranteed); or

(c) employer pension and employer national insurance contributions; or

(d) any allowances, such as accommodation or cost of living allowances; or

(e) in-kind benefits, such as equity shares, health insurance, school or university fees, company cars or food; or

(f) one-off payments, such as 'golden hellos'; or

(g) any payments relating to immigration costs, such as the fee or Immigration Health Charge; or

(h) payments to cover business expenses, including (but not limited to) travel to and from the applicant's country of residence, equipment, clothing, travel or subsistence.

SW 14.3. If the applicant is being sponsored to work more than 48 hours a week, only the salary for the first 48 hours a week will be considered towards the salary thresholds of £25,600, £23,040 or £20,480 per year referred to in SW 8.1. to SW 13.7.

> For example, an applicant who works 60 hours a week for £10 per hour will be considered to have a salary of £24.960 (10 x 48 x 52) per year and not £31,200 (£10 x 60 x 52).

SW 14.4. [Going rates will be pro-rated, and the £10.10 per hour salary requirement will be calculated,] to the applicant's working pattern, as follows:

(a) going rates for occupation codes listed in Table 1 of Appendix Skilled Occupations are based on a 39-hour week and will be pro-rated as follows:

> (the going rate for the occupation code stated in Table 1 of Appendix Skilled Occupations) × (the number of weekly working hours stated by the sponsor ÷ 39)

(b) where an applicant's salary is required to be 70%, 80% or 90% of the going rate, the resulting figure from the calculation in (a) will be multiplied by 0.7, 0.8 or 0.9 as appropriate, to calculate the required salary; and.

(c) going rates for the health and education occupation codes listed in Table 2 of Appendix Skilled Occupations will be pro-rated as stated in Appendix Skilled Occupations; and

(d) the applicant's full weekly hours will be included when checking their salary against the going rate [and the £10.10 per hour salary requirement], even if they work more than 48 hours a week.

Note: Words in introduction and (d) substituted from 6 April 2021 subject to savings for applications made before that date HC 1248).

Transitional arrangements for salary on the Skilled Worker route

SW 14.5. If the applicant is applying for permission to stay or settlement, [the applicant was granted permission as a Tier 2 (General) Migrant and has had continuous permission as a Skilled Worker ever since,], the following transitional arrangements apply:

(a) if the date of application is before 1 December 2026 salary may also include allowances (the other restrictions in SW 14.20 also apply), providing the following conditions are met:

(i) the applicant is applying to work for the same sponsor as in their previous permission; and

(ii) the allowances are guaranteed, will be paid for the duration of the applicant's permission, and would be paid to a local settled worker in similar circumstances, such as London weighting; and

(b) if the date of application is before 24 May 2023 and the applicant had permission as a Tier 2 (General) Migrant based on a certificate of sponsorship given to them by their sponsor before 24 November 2016, the applicant does not need to score 20 tradeable points from options A to F, as set out in SW 8.1. to SW 13.6, instead, 20 tradeable points will be awarded for a salary of £20,800 or above, or at least the going rate for the occupation code, if higher (the other requirements in [[SW 14.1. to SW 14.4]] also apply), but these points will not be awarded if the applicant is not also being awarded the 20 mandatory points for sponsorship under SW 5.7. and the 20 mandatory points for a job at the appropriate skill level under SW 6.4[; and]

[(c) if the applicant was sponsored to work in one of the occupation codes in the table below at the time they applied for their last permission as a Tier 2 (General) Migrant and has continued to be sponsored in that occupation code ever since (whether as a Tier 2 (General) Migrant and/or as a Skilled Worker), and the date of application is before 1 December 2026, the going rates in the table below apply, instead of the going rates listed in Table 1 of Appendix Skilled Occupations. These going rates are based on a 40-hour working week and must be pro-rated for other working patterns, based on the weekly working hours stated by the applicant's sponsor:

Occupation code	Going rate—option A	90% of going rate—option B	80% of going rate—options C and D	70% of going rate—option E
2113 Physical scientists	£29,000 (£13.94 per hour)	£26,100 (£12.55 per hour)	£23,200 (£11.15 per hour)	£20,300 (£9.76 per hour)
2119 Natural and social science professionals not elsewhere classified	£29,000 (£13.94 per hour)	£26,100 (£12.55 per hour)	£23,200 (£11.15 per hour)	£20,300 (£9.76 per hour)
2311 Higher education teaching professionals	£33,000 (£15.87 per hour)	£29,700 (£14.28 per hour)	£26,400 (£12.69 per hour)	£23,100 (£11.11 per hour)]

Note: Words in introduction substituted from 6 April 2021 subject to savings for applications made before that date; words in (b) substituted, sub-paragraph (c) and table inserted from 6 April 2021 HC 1248). Words in double square brackets in (b) substituted from 09:00 on 11 April 2022 subject to savings for applications made before that time (HC 1118).

[**SW 14.6.** If the applicant was granted permission as a Skilled Worker under the Rules in place before 6 April 2021, and has had continuous permission as a Skilled Worker since then, the £10.10 per hour salary requirement does not apply, but all other salary requirements continue to apply.]

Note: Paragraph inserted from 6 April 2021 subject to savings for applications made before that date HC 1248).

Financial requirement (mandatory) for a Skilled Worker

SW 15.1. If the applicant is applying for permission to stay and has been in the UK with permission for 12 months or longer on the date of application, they will meet the financial requirement and do not need to show funds.

SW 15.2. If the applicant is applying for entry clearance, or has been in the UK for less than 12 months on the date of application, either:

(a) the applicant must have funds of at least £1,270; or

(b) [the applicant's A-rated sponsor'] must certify that they will, if necessary, maintain and accommodate the applicant up to the end of the first month of their employment, to an amount of at least £1,270.

Note: Words substituted from 6 October 2021 subject to savings for applications made before that date HC 617).

SW 15.3. If SW 15.2.(a) applies, the applicant must show that they have held the required funds for a 28-day period and as specified in Appendix Finance.

Criminal record certificate requirement (mandatory) for a Skilled Worker

SW 16.1. If the applicant is applying for entry clearance and is being sponsored for a job in any of the occupation codes listed below, they must provide a criminal record certificate from the relevant authority in any country in which they have been present for 12 months or more (whether continuously or in total) in the 10 years before the date of application, and while aged 18 or over:

- 1181 Health services and public health managers and directors
- 1184 Social services managers and directors
- 1241 Health care practice managers
- 1242 Residential, day and domiciliary care managers and proprietors
- 2211 Medical practitioners
- 2212 Psychologists
- 2213 Pharmacists
- 2214 Ophthalmic opticians
- 2215 Dental practitioners
- 2217 Medical radiographers
- 2218 Podiatrists
- 2219 Health professionals not elsewhere classified
- 2221 Physiotherapists
- 2222 Occupational therapists
- 2223 Speech and language therapists
- 2229 Therapy professionals not elsewhere classified
- 2231 Nurses
- 2232 Midwives
- 2312 Further education teaching professionals
- 2314 Secondary education teaching professionals
- 2315 Primary and nursery education teaching professionals
- 2316 Special needs education teaching professionals
- 2317 Senior professionals of educational establishments
- 2318 Education advisors and school inspectors
- 2319 Teaching and other educational professionals not elsewhere classified
- 2442 Social workers
- 2443 Probation officers
- 2449 Welfare professionals not elsewhere classified
- 3213 Paramedics
- 3216 Dispensing opticians
- 3217 Pharmaceutical technicians
- 3218 Medical and dental technicians
- 3219 Health associate professionals not elsewhere classified
- 3231 Youth and community workers
- 3234 Housing officers
- 3235 Counsellors
- 3239 Welfare and housing associate professionals not elsewhere classified
- 3443 Fitness instructors
- 3562 Human resources and industrial relations officers
- 6121 Nursery nurses and assistants
- 6122 Childminders and related occupations
- 6123 Playworkers
- 6125 Teaching assistants
- 6126 Educational support assistants
- 6141 Nursing auxiliaries and assistants
- 6143 Dental nurses
- 6144 Houseparents and residential wardens

[• 6145 Care workers and home carers]
• 6146 Senior care workers

Note: List re-formatted from 6 April 2021 subject to savings for applications made before that date (HC 1248). Entry 6145 inserted from 15 February 2022 subject to savings for applications made before that date (HC 1019).

SW 16.2. The requirement in SW 16.1. does not apply if the applicant provides a satisfactory explanation why it is not reasonably practicable for them to obtain a criminal record certificate from any or all of the relevant authorities.

Decision on an application as a Skilled Worker

SW 17.1. If the decision maker is satisfied all the suitability and relevant eligibility requirements for a Skilled Worker are met, the application will be granted, otherwise the application will be refused.

SW 17.2. If the application is refused, the person can apply for an Administrative Review under Appendix AR: Administrative Review.

Period and conditions of grant for a Skilled Worker

SW 18.1. The applicant will be granted entry clearance or permission to stay until 14 days after the end date of their certificate of sponsorship (which may be up to a maximum of 5 years after the start date of their certificate of sponsorship).

SW 18.2. The grant will be subject to all the following conditions:

(a) no access to public funds; and

(b) work is permitted only in the job the applicant is being sponsored for, subject to (c) to (e); and

(c) supplementary employment is permitted, providing the person continues to work in the job for which they are being sponsored; and

(d) voluntary work is permitted; and

(e) working out a contractual notice period is permitted, for a job the applicant was lawfully working in on the date of application; and

(f) study is permitted, subject to the ATAS condition in Appendix ATAS; and

(g) if Part 10 applies, the applicant will be required to register with the police.

Settlement as a Skilled Worker

Validity requirements for settlement as a Skilled Worker

SW 19.1. A person applying for settlement as a Skilled Worker must apply online on the gov.uk website on the specified form, 'Settle in the UK in various immigration categories: form SET(O)'.

SW 19.2. An application for settlement as a Skilled Worker must meet all the following requirements:

(a) any fee must have been paid; and

(b) the applicant must have provided any required biometrics; and

(c) the applicant must have provided a passport or other travel document which satisfactorily establishes their identity and nationality; and

(d) the applicant must be in the UK on the date of application.

SW 19.3. The applicant must have, or have last been granted, permission as a Skilled Worker.

SW 19.4. An application which does not meet the validity requirements for settlement as a Skilled Worker is invalid and may be rejected and not considered.

Suitability requirements for settlement as a Skilled Worker

SW 20.1. The applicant must not fall for refusal under Part 9: grounds for refusal.

SW 20.2. The applicant must not be;

(a) in breach of immigration laws, except that where paragraph 39E applies, that period of overstaying will be disregarded; or

(b) on immigration bail.

Eligibility requirements for settlement as a Skilled Worker

Qualifying period requirement for settlement as a Skilled Worker

SW 21.1. The applicant must have spent a continuous period of 5 years in the UK.

SW 21.2. The 5-year continuous period must consist of time with permission on any of, or any combination of, the following routes:

(a) Skilled Worker; or
(b) Global talent; or
(c) Innovator; or
(d) T2 Minister of Religion; or
(e) [International] Sportsperson; or
(f) Representative of an Overseas Business; or
(g) as a Tier 1 Migrant, other than as a Tier 1 (Graduate Entrepreneur) Migrant[; or]
[(h) Scale-up; or]
[(i) permission on any other route, during the time the applicant was waiting for a decision on their application as a Skilled Worker, provided that application:

(i) was for permission to stay; and
(ii) was made between 24 January 2020 and 30 June 2021 (inclusive); and
(iii) was supported on the date of application by a certificate of sponsorship assigned by a licensed sponsor; and
(iv) was granted.]

Note: Words in (e) substituted from 09:00 on 11 October 2021 subject to savings for applications made before that time; words in (g) substituted and (h) inserted from 6 October 2021 subject to savings for applications made before that date (HC 617). Sub-paragraph (h) substituted, sub-paragraph (i) inserted from 22 August 2022 subject to savings for applications made before that date (HC 1118).

Continuous residence requirement for settlement as a Skilled Worker

SW 22.1. The applicant must meet the continuous residence requirement as set out in Appendix Continuous Residence during the period in SW 21.1.

Knowledge of life in the UK requirement for settlement as a Skilled Worker

SW 23.1. The applicant must meet the knowledge of Life in the UK requirement as set out in Appendix KOL UK.

Sponsorship and salary requirement for settlement as a Skilled Worker

SW 24.1. The sponsor in the applicant's most recent permission must still be approved by the Home Office to sponsor Skilled Workers on the date of decision.

SW 24.2. The sponsor must confirm that they still require the applicant to work for them for the foreseeable future, and that the applicant is paid, and will be paid for the foreseeable future, at least the salary in SW 24.3.

[**SW 24.3.** Subject to SW 24.4, the applicant's salary must equal or exceed all three salary requirements shown in the relevant row of the table below.

	Applicant's circumstances	General Salary	Minimum hourly rate	Going rate
A	All cases where rows B and C do not apply	Salary of at least £25,500 per year	At least £10.10 per hour	At least the going rate
B	The applicant was sponsored in their most recent permission for a job in a shortage occupation or a health or education occupation code listed in Table 2 of Appendix Skilled Occupations	Salary of at least £20, 480 per year	At least £10.10 per hour	[If the occupation code is listed in Table 1 or Table 2 of Appendix Skilled Occupations, at least the going rate]
C	The 5-year qualifying period for settlement includes time as a Tier 2 (General) Migrant in which the applicant was sponsored for a job in one of the following occupation codes: • 2111 Chemical scientists • 2112 Biological scientists and biochemists • 2113 Physical scientists • 2114 Social and humanities scientists • 2119 Natural and social science professionals not elsewhere classified • 2150 Research and development managers • 2311 Higher education teaching professionals	Salary of at least £20,480 per year	At least £10.10 per hour	At least the going rate in the table at paragraph SW 14.5(c), if the applicant has continued to be sponsored in that occupation code ever since. At least the going rate in Appendix Skilled Occupations, in other cases.]

Note: Amendments to table from 6 April 2021 (HC 1248). Paragraph and table substituted from 6 October 2021 subject to savings for applications made before that date (HC 617). Words in Row B substituted from 15 February 2022 subject to savings for applications made before that date (HC 1019).

SW 24.4. Salary under the table in SW 24.3 is subject to the following:

(a) salary will be considered as set out in SW 14.1. to [SW 14.6.] (and in SW 14.3., references to the salary thresholds of £25,600 or £20,480 per year should be read as including references in the table in SW 24.3 above); and

(b) if the applicant is currently absent from work for one of the reasons set out in Part 9 paragraph 9.30.1, or has returned from such an absence within the month before the date of application, consideration will be based on their salary on their return to work, as stated by their sponsor.

Note: Word in (a) substituted from 6 April 2021 subject to savings for applications made before that date HC 1248).

Decision on an application for settlement as a Skilled Worker

SW 25.1. If the decision maker is satisfied all the suitability and eligibility requirements for settlement as a Skilled Worker are met, the applicant will be granted settlement, otherwise the application will be refused.

SW 25.2. If the application is refused, the person can apply for an Administrative Review under Appendix AR: Administrative Review.

Dependants of a Skilled Worker

Validity requirements for a dependent partner or dependent child of a Skilled Worker

SW 26.1. A person applying for entry clearance or permission to stay as a dependent partner or dependent child of a Skilled Worker must apply online on the gov.uk website on the specified form as follows:

Location of Partner or Child	Specified form
Applicant outside the UK	Dependant Partner visa Dependant Child visa
Applicant inside the UK	Dependant Partner Dependant Child

Note: Table substituted from 30 November 2021 subject to savings for applications made before that date (HC 617).

[**SW 26.2.** An application for entry clearance or permission to stay as a partner or child of a Skilled Worker must meet all the following requirements:

(a) any fee and Immigration Health Charge must have been paid; and

(b) the applicant must have provided any required biometrics; and

(c) the applicant must have provided a passport or other travel document which satisfactorily establishes their identity and nationality; and

(d) the applicant must be applying as partner or child of a person (P) who:

(i) has made a valid application for entry clearance or permission to stay in the UK on the Skilled Worker route that has not been decided; or

(ii) has entry clearance or permission to stay on the Skilled Worker route; or

(iii) is settled or has become a British citizen, providing that P had permission on the Skilled Worker route when they settled and the applicant either had permission as their partner or child at that time, or the applicant is applying as a child of P and the applicant was born in the UK before P settled.]

Note: Paragraph substituted from 6 April 2022 (HC 1118).

SW 26.3. If the applicant is applying as a dependent partner they must be aged 18 or over on the date of application.

SW 26.4. An applicant who is applying for permission to stay as a dependent partner or dependent child of a Skilled Worker must be in the UK on the date of application and must not have, or have last been granted, permission:

(a) as a Visitor; or
(b) as a Short-term student; or
(c) as a Parent of a Child Student; or
(d) as a Seasonal Worker; or
(e) as a Domestic Worker in a Private Household; or
(f) outside the Immigration Rules.

SW 26.5. An application which does not meet the validity requirements for a dependent partner or dependent child of a Skilled Worker is invalid and may be rejected and not considered.

Suitability requirements for a dependent partner or dependent child of a Skilled Worker

SW 27.1. The applicant must not fall for refusal under Part 9: grounds for refusal.

SW 27.2. If applying for permission to stay the applicant must not be:

(a) in breach of immigration laws, except that where paragraph 39E applies, that period of overstaying will be disregarded; or

(b) on immigration bail.

Eligibility requirements for a dependent partner or dependent child of a Skilled Worker

Entry requirement for a dependent partner or dependent child of a Skilled Worker

SW 28.1. A person seeking to come to the UK as a dependent partner or dependent child of a Skilled Worker must apply for and obtain entry clearance as a dependent partner or dependent child of a Skilled Worker before they arrive in the UK.

SW 28.2. A person applying for entry clearance as the dependent partner or dependent child of a Skilled Worker must, if paragraph A39 and Appendix T of these rules apply, provide a valid medical certificate confirming that they have undergone screening for active pulmonary tuberculosis and that this tuberculosis is not present in them.

Relationship requirement for a dependent partner of a Skilled Worker

SW 29.1. The applicant must be the partner of a person (P) where one of the following applies:

(a) P has permission on the Skilled Worker route; or

(b) P is, at the same time, applying for (and is granted) entry clearance or permission on the Skilled Worker route; or

(c) P is settled or has become a British citizen, providing P had permission on the Skilled Worker route when they settled and the applicant had permission as P's partner at that time.

SW 29.2. If the applicant and their Skilled Worker partner are not married or in a civil partnership, all of the following requirements must be met:

(a) they must have been living together in a relationship similar to marriage or civil partnership for at least the two years before the date of application; and

(b) any previous relationship of the applicant or their Skilled Worker partner with another person must have permanently broken down; and

(c) the applicant and their Skilled Worker partner must not be so closely related that they would not be allowed to marry or form a civil partnership in the UK.

SW 29.3. The relationship between the applicant and their Skilled Worker partner must be genuine and subsisting.

SW 29.4. The applicant and their Skilled Worker partner must intend to live together throughout the applicant's stay in the UK.

Relationship requirement for a dependent child of a Skilled Worker

SW 30.1. The applicant must be the child of a parent (P) where one of the following applies:

(a) P has permission on the Skilled Worker route; or

(b) P is, at the same time, applying for (and is granted) entry clearance or permission on the Skilled Worker route; or

(c) P is settled or has become a British citizen, providing P had permission on the Skilled Worker route when they settled and the applicant had permission as P's child at that time.

[**SW 30.2.** The applicant's parents must each be either applying at the same time as the applicant or have permission to be in the UK (other than as a Visitor) unless:

(a) the parent applying for or with entry clearance or permission to stay as a Skilled Worker is the sole surviving parent; or

(b) the parent applying for or with entry clearance or permission to stay as a Skilled Worker has sole responsibility for the child's upbringing; or

(c) the parent who does not have permission as a Skilled Worker –

(i) is a British citizen or a person who has a right to enter or stay in the UK without restriction; and

(ii) is or will be ordinarily resident in the UK; or

(d) the decision maker is satisfied that there are serious and compelling reasons to grant the child entry clearance or permission to stay with the parent who is applying for or has entry clearance or permission as a Skilled Worker.]

Note: Paragraph substituted from 6 October 2021 subject to savings for applications made before that date (HC 617).

SW 30.3. If the applicant is a child born in the UK to a Skilled Worker or their partner, the applicant must provide a full UK birth certificate showing the names of both parents.

Care requirement for a dependent child of a Skilled Worker

SW 31.1. If the applicant is aged under 18 on the date of application, there must be suitable arrangements for the child's care and accommodation in the UK, which must comply with relevant UK legislation and regulations.

Age requirement for a dependent child of a Skilled Worker

SW 32.1. The child must be under the age of 18 on the date of application, unless they were last granted permission as the dependent child of their parent or parents.

SW 32.2. If the child is aged 16 or over at the date of application, they must not be leading an independent life.

Financial requirement for a dependent partner or dependent child of a Skilled Worker

SW 33.1. If the applicant is applying for permission to stay and has been living in the UK with permission for 12 months or longer on the date of application, they will meet the financial requirement and do not need to show funds.

SW 33.2. If the applicant is applying for entry clearance, or has been in the UK for less than 12 months on the date of application, either:

[(a) funds of at least the amount required in SW 33.3 must be held collectively by one or more of the following:

(i) the applicant; and

(ii) the Skilled Worker (P); and

(ii) if the applicant is applying as a dependent child, their parent who is lawfully present in the UK or being granted entry clearance, or permission to stay, at the same time; or]

(b) [the Skilled Worker's A-rated sponsor] must certify that they will, if necessary, maintain and accommodate the dependent partner and/or any dependent child as well as the Skilled Worker, up to the end of the first month of each of their grants of permission, to at least the amounts required in SW 33.3.

Note: Sub-paragraph (a), words in (b) substituted from 6 October 2021 subject to savings for applications made before that date (HC 617).

SW 33.3. The funds required are:

(a) £285 for a dependent partner in the UK, or applying for entry clearance; and

(b) £315 for the first dependent child in the UK, or applying for entry clearance; and

(c) £200 for any other dependent child in the UK, or applying for entry clearance.

SW 33.4. If SW 33.2.(a) applies, the funds held for the applicant must be held in addition to any funds required for the Skilled Worker to meet the financial requirement and any other dependants in the UK or applying at the same time.

SW 33.5. If SW 33.2.(a) applies, the funds must have been held for a 28-day period and as specified in Appendix Finance.

Criminal record certificate requirement for a dependent partner of a Skilled Worker

SW 34.1. Where a Skilled Worker is being sponsored for a job in an occupation code listed in SW 16.1, an applicant applying for entry clearance as the partner of the Skilled

Worker must provide a criminal record certificate from the relevant authority in any country in which they have been present for 12 months or more (whether continuously or in total) in the 10 years before the date of application, and while aged 18 or over.

SW 34.2. The requirement in SW 34.1. does not apply if the applicant provides a satisfactory explanation why it is not reasonably practicable for them to obtain a criminal record certificate from any or all of the relevant authorities.

Decision on an application as a dependent partner or dependent child of a Skilled Worker

SW 35.1. If the decision maker is satisfied that all the suitability and eligibility requirements for a dependent partner or dependent child of a Skilled Worker are met, the application will be granted, otherwise the application will be refused.

SW 35.2. If the application is refused, the person can apply for an Administrative Review under Appendix AR: Administrative Review.

Period and conditions of grant for a dependent partner or dependent child of a Skilled Worker

SW 36.1. A partner will be granted:

(a) permission which ends on the same date as their partner's permission as a Skilled Worker; or

(b) 3 years' permission if the Skilled Worker was (or is being) granted settlement as a Skilled Worker.

SW 36.2. A child will be granted permission which ends on the same date as whichever of their parents' permission ends first, unless both parents have (or are being granted) settlement or British Citizenship, in which case the child will be granted permission for 3 years.

SW 36.3. The grant will be subject to all the following conditions:

(a) no access to public funds; and

(b) work (including self-employment and voluntary work) is permitted, except as a professional sportsperson (including as a sports coach); and

(c) study is permitted, subject to the ATAS condition in Appendix ATAS, if the applicant is over the age of 18; and

(d) if Part 10 applies, the applicant will be required to register with the police.

Settlement as a dependent partner or dependent child of a Skilled Worker

Validity requirements for settlement as a dependent partner or dependent child of a Skilled Worker

SW 37.1. A person applying for settlement as a dependent partner or dependent child of a Skilled Worker must apply online on the gov.uk website on the specified form, 'Settle in the UK in various immigration categories: form SET(O)'.

[**SW 37.2.** An application for settlement as a partner or child of a person on the Skilled Worker route must meet all the following requirements:

(a) any fee must have been paid; and

(b) the applicant must have provided any required biometrics; and

(c) the applicant must have provided either a passport or other travel document which satisfactorily establishes their identity and nationality; and

(d) the applicant must be in the UK on the date of application; and

(e) the applicant must be applying as a partner or child of a person (P) who:

(i) has made a valid application for settlement in the UK on the Skilled Worker route and that application has not been decided; or

(ii) is settled or has become a British citizen, provided that P had permission on the Skilled Worker route when they settled and the applicant either had permission as their partner or child at that time, or the applicant is applying as a child of P and the applicant was born in the UK before P settled.]

Note: Paragraph substituted from 6 April 2022 (HC 1118).

SW 37.3. An application which does not meet the validity requirements for a dependent partner or dependent child of a Skilled Worker is invalid and may be rejected and not considered.

Suitability requirements for settlement as a dependent partner or dependent child of a Skilled Worker

SW 38.1. The applicant must not fall for refusal under Part 9: grounds for refusal.

SW 38.2. The applicant must not be:

(a) in breach of immigration laws, except that where paragraph 39E applies, that period of overstaying will be disregarded; or

(b) on immigration bail.

Eligibility requirements for settlement as a dependent partner or dependent child of a Skilled Worker

Relationship requirement for settlement for a dependent partner or dependent child of a Skilled Worker

[**SW 39.1.** The applicant must be the partner or child of a person (P) where one of the following applies:

(a) P is, at the same time, being granted settlement as a Skilled Worker; or

(b) P is settled in the UK or has become a British citizen, providing P had permission as a Skilled Worker when they settled and the applicant either:

(i) had permission as P's partner or child at that time; or

(ii) is applying as a child of P, and was born in the UK before P settled.]

Note: Paragraph substituted from 6 October 2021 subject to savings for applications made before that date (HC 617).

[**SW 39.2.** The applicant must either:

(a) have last been granted permission as a dependent partner or dependent child of the person (P) in SW 39.1; or

(b) have been born in the UK and be applying as a child of the person (P) in SW 39.1.]

Note: Paragraph substituted from 6 October 2021 subject to savings for applications made before that date (HC 617).

SW 39.3. If applying as a partner, the applicant and the person (P) in SW 39.1. must meet [the relationship requirement in SW 29.2. to SW 29.4.] and must have met them throughout the 5 years ending on the date of application.

Note: Words substituted from 6 April 2021 (HC 1248).

SW 39.4. If applying as a child, the applicant's other parent (who is not the person (P) in SW 39.1.) must be being granted settlement at the same time, or be settled or a British citizen, unless:

(a) the person (P) in SW 39.1. is the applicant's sole surviving parent; or

(b) the person (P) in SW 39.1. has sole responsibility for the applicant's upbringing; or

(c) the decision maker is satisfied that there are serious and compelling reasons to grant the applicant settlement.

Care requirement for settlement as a dependent child of a Skilled Worker

SW 40.1. If the applicant is under the age of 18 on the date of application there must be suitable arrangements for the child's care and accommodation in the UK, which must comply with relevant UK legislation and regulations.

Age requirement for settlement as a dependent child of a Skilled Worker

SW 41.1. The applicant must be under the age of 18 on the date of application, unless they were last granted permission as the dependent child of their parent or parents.

SW 41.2. If the applicant is aged 16 or over on the date of application, they must not be leading an independent life.

Qualifying period requirement for settlement as a dependent partner of a Skilled Worker

SW 42.1. The applicant must have spent a continuous period of 5 years in the UK with permission as a dependent partner of the person (P) in SW 39.1.

Continuous residence requirement for settlement as a dependent partner of a Skilled Worker

SW 43.1. The applicant must meet the continuous residence requirement as set out in Appendix Continuous Residence during the period in SW 42.1.

English language requirement for settlement as a dependent partner or dependent child of a Skilled Worker

SW 44.1. Unless an exemption applies, the applicant must show English language ability on the Common European Framework of Reference for Languages in speaking and listening to at least level B1.

SW 44.2. The applicant must show they meet the English language requirement as specified in Appendix English Language.

Knowledge of life in the UK requirement for settlement as a dependent partner or dependent child of a Skilled Worker

SW 45.1. If the applicant is aged 18 or over on the date of application, they must meet the knowledge of Life in the UK requirement as set out in Appendix KOL UK.

Decision on an application for settlement as a dependent partner or dependent child of a Skilled Worker

SW 46.1. If the decision maker is satisfied all the suitability and eligibility requirements are met for settlement as a dependent partner or dependent child of a Skilled Worker, the application will be granted, otherwise the application will be refused.

SW 46.2. If the application is refused the person can apply for an Administrative Review under Appendix AR: Administrative Review.]

Note: Appendix inserted from 09:00 on 1 December 2020 subject to savings for applications made before that time (HC813).

[Appendix Intra-Company Routes – DELETED]

Note: Appendix inserted from 09:00 on 1 December 2020 subject to savings for applications made before that time (HC813). Amendments from 6 April 2021 subject to savings for applications made before that date; amendments from 09:00 on 21 May 2021 subject to savings for applications made before that time (HC 1248). Amendments from 6 October 2021 subject to savings for applications made before that date (HC 617). Appendix deleted from 09:00 on 11 April 2022 subject to savings for applications made before that time (HC 1118).

[Appendix Skilled Occupations

[Eligible occupation codes and going rates for the Skilled Worker and Global Business Mobility, [[and Scale-up routes]]]

Note: Heading amended from 09:00 on 11 April 2022 subject to savings for applications made before that time; words in double square brackets inserted from 22 August 2022 subject to savings for applications made before that date (HC 1118).

[In this Appendix:

- 'SW' refers to the Skilled Worker route
- 'GBM' refers to the Global Business Mobility routes
- 'GTR' refers to the Global Business Mobility - Graduate Trainee route
- [[• 'SCU' refers to Scale-up route]]

Nothing in this Appendix exempts an applicant from being paid the National Minimum Wage or the National Living Wage, where these apply.]

Note: Introduction substituted from 09:00 on 11 April 2022 subject to savings for applications made before that time; words in double square brackets inserted from 22 August 2022 subject to savings for applications made before that date (HC 1118).

[Table 1: Eligible occupation codes where going rates are based on Annual Survey of Hours and Earnings (ASHE) data

Going rates in Table 1 are per year and based on a 39-hour working week. They must be pro-rated for other working patterns, based on the weekly working hours stated by the applicant's sponsor. Options A to F refer to the tradeable points options set out in Appendix Skilled Worker.]

Note: Amendment to table from 6 April 2021 subject to savings for applications made before that date (HC 1248). Table heading and introduction, first row of table substituted, amendments to table from 09:00 on 11 April 2022 subject to savings for applications made before that time; amendments to table from 22 August 2022 subject to savings for applications made before that date (HC 1118).

[Table 2: Eligible health and education occupation codes where going rates are based on national pay scales]

[Occupation codes in Table 2 are eligible for the [[Global Business Mobility and Scale-up routes]] unless otherwise stated.]

Note: Amendments to table from 6 April 2021 with and without savings for applications made before that date; (HC 1248). Table heading, introduction and table substituted from 09:00 on 11 April 2022 subject to savings for applications made before that time; words in double square brackets substituted, amendments to table from 22 August 2022 subject to savings for applications made before that date (HC 1118).

[Table 3: Going rates for listed healthcare occupation codes by administration and band]

[Going rates in Table 3 are per year and based on a 37.5-hour week. They must be pro-rated for other working patterns, based on the weekly working hours stated by the applicant's sponsor.]

Note: Table heading, introduction and table substituted from 09:00 on 11 April 2022 subject to savings for applications made before that time (HC 1118).

[Table 4: Going rates for listed education occupation codes by administration and role]

[Going rates in Table 4 are per year and based on the definition of a full-time teacher used when determining these pay scales. They must be pro-rated for other working patterns, based on the weekly working hours stated by the applicant's sponsor.]

Note: Table heading, introduction and table substituted from 09:00 on 11 April 2022 subject to savings for applications made before that time (HC 1118).

[Table 5: Occupation codes which are not eligible for the [[Skilled Worker, Global Business Mobility or Scale-up routes]]]

[These occupations are ineligible for the Skilled Worker or [[Global Business Mobility or Scale-up]] routes because:

- they do not meet the required skill level; or
- applicants must be sponsored in another route for jobs in these occupations; or
- those subject to immigration control cannot apply for jobs in these occupations.

Where indicated, some occupation codes in Tables 1 and 2 are also not eligible for the [[Global Business Mobility or Scale-up routes]].]

Note: Amendments from 6 April 2021 subject to savings for applications made before that date; (HC 1248). Table heading and introduction substituted from 09:00 on 11 April 2022 subject to savings for applications made before that time; words in double square brackets in table heading substituted from 22 August 2022 subject to savings for applications made before that date (HC 1118).

***Tables contained in this Appendix are not reproduced as they are subject to regular review and amendment. They can be viewed online at* https://www.gov.uk/guidance/immigration-rules/immigration-rules-appendix-skilled-occupations.**

Note: Appendix inserted from 09:00 on 1 December 2020 subject to savings for applications made before that time (HC 813).

[Appendix Shortage Occupation List

Shortage Occupations for the Skilled Worker route

Table 1: Shortage occupations where applicants for entry clearance or permission to stay may be paid 80% of the going rate for the occupation code

Occupation code and any further criteria	Shortage occupation in			
	England	Scotland	Wales	Northern Ireland
[1181 Health services and public health managers and directors—**all jobs**	Yes	Yes	Yes	Yes]
[1242 Residential, day and domiciliary care managers and proprietors – **all jobs**	Yes	Yes	Yes	Yes]
2111 Chemical scientists – only jobs in the nuclear industry	–	Yes	–	–
2112 Biological scientists and biochemists – all jobs	Yes	Yes	Yes	Yes
2113 Physical scientists – only the following jobs in the construction- related ground engineering industry: • engineering geologist • hydrogeologist • geophysicist	Yes	Yes	Yes	Yes
2113Physical scientists – only the following jobs in the oil and gas industry: • geophysicist • geoscientist • geologist • geochemist • technical services manager in the decommissioning and waste areas of the nuclear industry • senior resource geologist and staff geologist in the mining sector	Yes	Yes	Yes	Yes

Occupation code and any further criteria	Shortage occupation in			
	England	**Scotland**	**Wales**	**Northern Ireland**
2114 Social and humanities scientists – only archaeologists	Yes	Yes	Yes	Yes
2121 Civil engineers – all jobs	Yes	Yes	Yes	Yes
2122 Mechanical engineers – all jobs	Yes	Yes	Yes	Yes
2123 Electrical engineers – all jobs	Yes	Yes	Yes	Yes
2124 Electronics engineers – all jobs	Yes	Yes	Yes	Yes
2126 Design and development engineers – all jobs	Yes	Yes	Yes	Yes
2127 Production and process engineers – all jobs	Yes	Yes	Yes	Yes
2129 Engineering professionals not elsewhere classified – all jobs	Yes	Yes	Yes	Yes
2135 IT business analysts, architects and systems designers – all jobs	Yes	Yes	Yes	Yes
2136 Programmers and software development professionals – all jobs	Yes	Yes	Yes	Yes
2137 Web design and development professionals – all jobs	Yes	Yes	Yes	Yes
2139 Information technology and communications professionals not elsewhere classified – only cyber security specialists	Yes	Yes	Yes	Yes
2216 Veterinarians – all jobs	Yes	Yes	Yes	Yes
2425 Actuaries, economists and statisticians – only bio-informaticians and informaticians	Yes	Yes	Yes	Yes
2431 Architects – all jobs	Yes	Yes	Yes	Yes
2461 Quality control and planning engineers – all jobs	Yes	Yes	Yes	Yes
[3111 Laboratory technicians – **all jobs**	Yes	Yes	Yes	Yes]
3411 Artists – all jobs	Yes	Yes	Yes	Yes
3414 Dancers and choreographers – only skilled classical ballet dancers or skilled contemporary dancers who meet the standard required by internationally recognised UK ballet or contemporary dance companies. The company must be endorsed as being internationally recognised by a UK industry body such as the Arts Councils (of England, Scotland or Wales).	Yes	Yes	Yes	Yes

Occupation code and any further criteria	Shortage occupation in			
	England	Scotland	Wales	Northern Ireland
3415 Musicians – only skilled orchestral musicians who are leaders, principals, sub-principals or numbered string positions, and who meet the standard required by internationally recognised UK orchestras. [The orchestra must be a full member of the Association of British Orchestras.]	Yes	Yes	Yes	Yes
3416 Arts officers, producers and directors – all jobs	Yes	Yes	Yes	Yes
3421 Graphic designers – all jobs	Yes	Yes	Yes	Yes
5215 Welding trades – only high integrity pipe welders, where the job requires 3 or more years' related on- the-job experience[. This experience must not have been gained through working illegally.]	Yes	Yes	Yes	Yes
[...]	[...]	[...]	[...]	[...]
[6146 Senior care workers – **all jobs**	Yes	Yes	Yes	Yes]

Note: Rows 1181, 1242, 3111 and 6146, words in 5215 inserted; row deleted from 6 April 2021 subject to savings for applications made before that date (HC 1248). Words in 3415 substituted from 6 October 2021 subject to savings for applications made before that date (HC 617).

Table 2: Shortage occupations in eligible health and education occupation codes where going rates are based on national pay scales

Occupation code and any further criteria	Shortage occupation in			
	England	Scotland	Wales	Northern Ireland
2211 Medical practitioners – all jobs	Yes	Yes	Yes	Yes
2212 Psychologists – all jobs	Yes	Yes	Yes	Yes
[2213 Pharmacists – all jobs	Yes	Yes	Yes	Yes]
2217 Medical radiographers – all jobs (including radiotherapy practitioners / technologists)	Yes	Yes	Yes	Yes
[2219 Health professionals not elsewhere classified – **all jobs**	Yes	Yes	Yes	Yes]
[2221 Physiotherapists – **all jobs**	Yes	Yes	Yes	Yes]
2222 Occupational therapists – all jobs	Yes	Yes	Yes	Yes
2223 Speech and language therapists – all jobs	Yes	Yes	Yes	Yes

Occupation code and any further criteria	Shortage occupation in			
	England	Scotland	Wales	Northern Ireland
2231 Nurses – all jobs	Yes	Yes	Yes	Yes
2314 Secondary education teaching professionals – only teachers in maths, physics, science (where an element of physics will be taught), computer science and [modern foreign language]	Yes	Yes	Yes	Yes
2314 Secondary education teaching professionals – only teachers in Gaelic	–	Yes	–	–
2315 Primary and nursery education teaching professionals – only Gaelic medium teachers	–	Yes	–	–
2442 Social workers – all jobs	Yes	Yes	Yes	Yes
3213 Paramedics – all jobs	Yes	Yes	Yes	Yes]
[6141 Nursing auxiliaries and assistants – **all jobs**	Yes	Yes	Yes	Yes]

Note: Rows 2213, 2219, 2221, and 6141 in table inserted; words in 2314 substituted from 6 April 2021 subject to savings for applications made before that date (HC 1248).

Table 3 Shortage occupations which are otherwise not eligible for the Skilled Worker route]

Occupation code and any further criteria	Related job titles	Shortage occupation in			
		England	Scotland	Wales	Northern Ireland
6145 Care workers and home carers Note: private households or individuals (other than sole traders sponsoring someone to work for their business) cannot sponsor Skilled Worker applicants.	• Care assistant • Care worker • Carer • Home care assistant • Home carer • Support worker (nursing home)	Yes	Yes	Yes	Yes]

Note: Table and heading inserted from 15 February 2022 subject to savings for applications made before that date (HC 1019).

Appendix inserted from 09:00 on 1 December 2020 subject to savings for applications made before that time (HC 813).

[Global Business Mobility routes

Appendix Global Business Mobility – Senior or Specialist Worker

The Global Business Mobility – Senior or Specialist Worker route is for overseas workers who are undertaking temporary work assignments in the UK, where the worker is a senior manager or specialist employee and is being assigned to a UK business linked to their employer overseas. This type of assignment is often called an intra-company transfer or ICT.

A partner and dependent children can apply to come to the UK on this route.

The Global Business Mobility – Senior or Specialist Worker route is not a route to settlement.

Validity requirements for Global Business Mobility – Senior or Specialist Worker ("Senior or Specialist Worker")

SNR 1.1. A person applying for entry clearance or permission to stay as a Senior or Specialist Worker must apply online on the gov.uk website on the specified form as follows:

(a) for applicants outside the UK, form "Global Business Mobility visa"; or

(b) for applicants inside the UK, form "Global Business Mobility".

SNR 1.2. An application for entry clearance or permission to stay as a Senior or Specialist Worker must meet all the following requirements:

(a) any fee and Immigration Health Charge must have been paid; and

(b) the applicant must have provided any required biometrics; and

(c) the applicant must have provided a passport or other travel document which satisfactorily establishes their identity and nationality; and

(d) the applicant must have a Certificate of Sponsorship that was issued to them by their sponsor no more than 3 months before the date of application.

SNR 1.3. The applicant must be aged 18 or over on the date of application.

SNR 1.4. An applicant applying for entry clearance or permission to stay as a Senior or Specialist Worker who has received an award from a Government or international scholarship agency in the 12 months before the date of application which covers both fees and living costs for study in the UK, must have provided written consent to the application from that Government or agency.

SNR 1.5. An applicant applying for permission to stay must be in the UK and must not have, or have last been granted, permission:

(a) as a Visitor; or

(b) as a Short-term Student; or

(c) as a Parent of a Child Student; or

(d) as a Seasonal Worker; or

(e) as a Domestic Worker in a Private Household; or

(f) outside the Immigration Rules.

SNR 1.6. An application which does not meet all the validity requirements for a Senior or Specialist Worker is invalid and may be rejected and not considered.

Suitability requirements for a Senior or Specialist Worker

SNR 2.1. The applicant must not fall for refusal under Part 9: grounds for refusal.

SNR 2.2. If applying for permission to stay the applicant must not be:

(a) in breach of immigration laws, except that where paragraph 39E applies, that period of overstaying will be disregarded; or

(b) on immigration bail.

Eligibility requirements for a Senior or Specialist Worker

Entry requirements for a Senior or Specialist Worker

SNR 3.1. A person seeking to come to the UK as a Senior or Specialist Worker must apply for and obtain entry clearance as a Senior or Specialist Worker before their arrival in the UK.

SNR 3.2. A person applying for entry clearance as a Senior or Specialist Worker must, if paragraph A39 and Appendix T of these rules apply, provide a valid medical certificate confirming that they have undergone screening for active pulmonary tuberculosis and that this tuberculosis is not present in them.

Points requirement for a Senior or Specialist Worker

SNR 4.1. The applicant must be awarded 60 points based on the table below:

Points requirement	Relevant rules	Points
Sponsorship	SNR 5.1. to SNR 5.9.	20
Job at an appropriate skill level	SNR 5.1. to SNR 5.9.	20
Salary at required level	SNR 7.1. to SNR 9.3.	20

Points for Sponsorship for a Senior or Specialist Worker

SNR 5.1. The applicant must have a valid certificate of sponsorship for the job they are planning to do, which to be valid must:

(a) confirm the applicant's name, that they are being sponsored as a Senior or Specialist Worker, details of the job, salary and any allowances the sponsor is offering them (if applicable) and PAYE details if HM Revenue and Customs (HMRC) requires income tax and national insurance for the sponsored job to be paid via PAYE; and

(b) include a start date for the job, stated by the sponsor, which is no more than 3 months after the date of application; and

(c) not have been used in a previous application which was either granted or refused (but can have been used in a previous application which was rejected as invalid, made void or withdrawn); and

(d) not have been withdrawn by the sponsor or cancelled by the Home Office; and

(e) unless the applicant is applying as a high earner, confirm that the applicant has worked outside the UK for the sponsor group for the period required at SNR 5.7.(b); and

(f) confirm whether the Academic Technology Approval Scheme (ATAS) requirement in Appendix ATAS applies.

SNR 5.2. The sponsor must be authorised by the Home Office to sponsor a Senior or Specialist Worker.

SNR 5.3. The sponsor must be listed as A-rated on the Home Office's register of licensed sponsors, unless the applicant was last granted permission as a Senior or

Specialist Worker and is applying to continue working for the same sponsor as in their last permission.

SNR 5.4. The sponsor must have paid in full any required Immigration Skills Charge.

SNR 5.5. The decision maker must not have reasonable grounds to believe the job the applicant is being sponsored to do:

(a) does not exist; or

(b) is a sham; or

(c) has been created mainly so the applicant can apply for entry clearance or permission to stay.

SNR 5.6. The decision maker must not have reasonable grounds to believe the job the applicant is being sponsored to do amounts to:

(a) the hire of the applicant to a third party who is not the sponsor to fill a position with that party, whether temporary or permanent; or

(b) contract work to undertake an ongoing routine role or to provide an ongoing routine service for a third party who is not the sponsor, regardless of the nature or length of any arrangement between the sponsor and the third party.

SNR 5.7. An applicant as a Senior or Specialist Worker must:

(a) be currently working for the sponsor group; and

(b) unless they are applying as a high earner must have worked outside the UK for the sponsor group for a cumulative period of at least 12 months.

SNR 5.8. In SNR 5.7.(b) the 12 months' work outside the UK can have been accumulated over any period provided that:

(a) the applicant was continuously working for the sponsor group, whether in or out of the UK, from the start of the 12 months to the date of application; and

(b) any breaks in the continuous work in SNR 5.8.(a) were only for the following reasons:

(i) statutory maternity, paternity, parental, or shared parental leave; or

(ii) statutory adoption leave; or

(iii) sick leave; or

(iv) assisting with a national or international humanitarian or environmental crisis, with the agreement of the sponsor group; or

(v) taking part in legally organised industrial action.

SNR 5.9. If the requirements in SNR 5.1. to SNR 5.8. are met, the applicant will be awarded 20 points for sponsorship.

Points for job at appropriate skill level for a Senior or Specialist Worker

SNR 6.1. The applicant must be sponsored for a job in an occupation code listed in Appendix Skilled Occupations that is identified as eligible for the Global Business Mobility routes, unless the conditions at SNR 6.7. are met.

SNR 6.2. The sponsor must have chosen an appropriate occupation code, and the decision maker must not have reasonable grounds to believe the sponsor has chosen a less appropriate occupation code for any of the following reasons:

(a) the most appropriate occupation code is not eligible under the Global Business Mobility routes; or

(b) the most appropriate occupation code has a higher going rate than the proposed salary.

SNR 6.3. To support the assessment in SNR 6.2., the decision maker may, in particular, consider:

(a) whether the sponsor has shown a genuine need for the job as described; and

(b) whether the applicant has the appropriate skills, qualifications and experience needed to do the job as described; and

(c) the sponsor's history of compliance with the immigration system including, but not limited to, paying its sponsored workers appropriately; and

(d) any additional information from the sponsor.

SNR 6.4. If the ATAS requirement in Appendix ATAS applies, the applicant must provide a valid ATAS certificate.

SNR 6.5. If the requirements in SNR 6.1. to SNR 6.4. are met, the applicant will be awarded 20 points for a job at the appropriate skill level, subject to SNR 6.6.

SNR 6.6. No points will be awarded for a job at the appropriate skill level if the applicant is not also being awarded 20 points for sponsorship under SNR 5.9.

Transitional arrangements for job at appropriate skill level for a Senior or Specialist Worker

SNR 6.7. If the applicant is applying for permission to stay and has, or last had, permission as a Senior or Specialist Worker for a job in any of the occupation codes listed in SNR 6.8, they can be sponsored to continue working in the same job for the same employer in that occupation code.

SNR 6.8. The occupation codes referred to in SNR 6.7. are the following:

(a) 3411 Artists; or

(b) 3412 Authors, writers and translators; or

(c) 3413 Actors, entertainers and presenters; or

(d) 3414 Dancers and choreographers; or

(e) 3422 Product, clothing and related designers.

Points for salary for a Senior or Specialist Worker

SNR 7.1. The salary for the job for which the applicant is being sponsored must equal or exceed both:

(a) the general salary requirement in SNR 8.1. and SNR 8.2. unless the conditions at SNR 8.3. are met; and

(b) the going rate requirement in SNR 9.1. to SNR 9.3.

SNR 7.2. Salary under these requirements includes only:

(a) guaranteed basic gross pay (before income tax and including employee pension and national insurance contributions); and

(b) allowances which are guaranteed to be paid for the duration of the applicant's employment in the UK (such as London weighting) or are paid as a mobility premium or to cover the additional cost of living in the UK.

SNR 7.3. Where allowances under SNR 7.2.(b) are solely for the purpose of accommodation they will only be taken into account up to a value of 30% of the total salary package

SNR 7.4. Salary does not include other pay and benefits, such as any of the following:

(a) flexible working where the nature of the job means that hours fluctuate and pay cannot be guaranteed; or

(b) additional pay such as shift, overtime or bonus pay, whether or not it is guaranteed; or

(c) employer pension and national insurance contributions; or

(d) any allowances, other than those specified in SNR 7.2.(b); or

(e) in-kind benefits, such as equity shares, health insurance, school or university fees, company cars or food; or

(f) one-off payments, such as 'golden hellos'; or

(g) any payments relating to immigration costs, such as the fee or Immigration Health Charge; or

(h) payments to cover business expenses, including (but not limited to) travel to and from the applicant's country of residence, equipment, clothing, travel or subsistence.

SNR 7.5. If the requirements in SNR 7.1. to SNR 7.4. are met, the applicant will be awarded 20 points for salary at the required level, subject to SNR 9.5.

SNR 7.6. No points will be awarded for salary if the applicant is not also being awarded 20 points for sponsorship under SNR 5.9.

General salary requirement for a Senior or Specialist Worker

SNR 8.1. If the applicant is being sponsored for a job in one of the occupation codes listed in Table 1 of Appendix Skilled Occupations, the general salary requirement is £42,400 per year, unless the conditions at SNR 8.3. are met.

SNR 8.2. If the applicant is being sponsored to work more than 48 hours a week, only the salary for the first 48 hours a week will be considered towards the general salary requirement.
For example, an applicant who works 60 hours a week for £15 per hour will be considered to have a salary of £37,440 (£15 x 48 x 52) per year and not £46,800 (£15 x 60 x 52).

Transitional general salary requirement for a Senior or Specialist Worker

SNR 8.3. The applicant does not need to meet the general salary requirement if the applicant is applying for permission to stay and was previously granted permission as a Tier 2 (Intra-Company Transfer) Migrant under the rules in force before 6 April 2011, or as a Work Permit Holder and since then has continuously had permission as a Senior or Specialist Worker (including any period of overstaying disregarded under paragraph 39E of these rules).

Going rate requirement for a Senior or Specialist Worker

SNR 9.1. If the applicant is being sponsored for a job in one of the occupation codes listed in Table 1 of Appendix Skilled Occupations, the going rate requirement is 100% of the pro-rated going rate, which will be calculated as follows:

1 x (the going rate for the occupation code stated in Table 1 of Appendix Skilled Occupations) x (the number of weekly working hours stated by the sponsor ÷ 39).

SNR 9.2. If the applicant is being sponsored for a job in one of the health or education occupation codes listed in Table 2 of Appendix Skilled Occupations, the going rate requirement is 100% of the pro-rated going rate (and the going rate will be pro-rated according to the number of weekly working hours stated by the sponsor, and the pro-rating set out in Appendix Skilled Occupations).

SNR 9.3. The applicant's full weekly hours will be included when checking their salary against the going rate, even if they work more than 48 hours a week.

For example, an applicant who works 60 hours a week in an occupation code with a going rate of £39,000 must be paid £60,000 (1 x £39,000 x 60 ÷ 39) per year, not £48,000 (1 x £39,000 x 48 ÷ 39).

Financial requirement for a Senior or Specialist Worker

SNR 10.1. If the applicant is applying for permission to stay and has been living in the UK with permission for 12 months or longer on the date of application, they will meet the financial requirement and do not need to show funds.

SNR 10.2. If the applicant is applying for entry clearance or has been living in the UK for less than 12 months on the date of application either:

(a) the applicant must have funds of at least £1,270; or

(b) the sponsor must certify on the certificate of sponsorship that they will, if it is necessary, maintain and accommodate the applicant up to the end of the first month of their employment up to a maximum amount of £1,270.

SNR 10.3. If SNR 10.2.(a) applies, the applicant must show that they have held the required level of funds for a 28-day period and as set out in Appendix Finance.

Maximum length of assignments requirement for a Senior or Specialist Worker

SNR 11.1. If the applicant is applying as a high earner, the grant of permission must not lead to the applicant being granted cumulative periods of permission on the Global Business Mobility routes and Intra-Company routes totalling more than 9 years in any 10-year period.

SNR 11.2. If the applicant is not applying as a high earner, the grant of permission must not lead to the applicant being granted cumulative periods of permission on the Global Business Mobility routes and Intra-Company routes totalling more than 5 years in any 6-year period.

SNR 11.3. When calculating the cumulative periods of permission referred to in SNR 11.1., SNR 11.2, and SNR 13.2. the following are included:

(a) all previous periods of permission granted on the Global Business Mobility routes; and

(b) all previous periods of permission granted on the Intra-Company routes; and

(c) if the applicant does not currently hold permission in the Global Business Mobility routes, any permission they could be granted under the current application, beginning on the start date of the job stated on the Certificate of Sponsorship; and

(d) if the applicant is applying for permission to stay and has, or last had, permission on the Global Business Mobility routes, any permission they could be granted under the current application, beginning on the date of decision; and

(e) any period of permission on the Global Business Mobility routes and the Intra-Company routes extended under section 3C of the Immigration Act 1971.

Transitional arrangements for maximum length of assignments as a Senior or Specialist Worker

SNR 11.4. SNR 11.1. to SNR 11.3. do not apply and there is no maximum period of permission if the applicant is applying for permission to stay and was previously granted permission as a Tier 2 (Intra-Company Transfer) Migrant under the rules in force before 6 April 2011, or as a Work Permit Holder and since then has continuously had permission as a Senior or Specialist Worker (including any period of overstaying disregarded under paragraph 39E).

Decision for a Senior or Specialist Worker

SNR 12.1. If the decision maker is satisfied that all the suitability and eligibility requirements for a Senior or Specialist Worker are met the application will be granted, otherwise the application will be refused.

SNR 12.2. If the application is refused the person can apply for an Administrative Review under Appendix AR: Administrative Review.

Period and conditions of grant as a Senior or Specialist Worker

SNR 13.1. The grant will be subject to all the following conditions:

(a) no access to public funds; and

(b) only the following work is permitted:

(i) the job for which the applicant is being sponsored; and

(ii) if the applicant is applying for permission to stay and was previously granted permission on the Intra-Company routes under the rules in force before 11 April 2022 and since then has continuously had permission as a Senior or Specialist Worker (including any period of overstaying disregarded under paragraph 39E), supplementary employment is permitted; and

(iii) voluntary work is permitted; and

(iv) working out a contractual notice period is permitted, where the applicant was lawfully working in that job in the UK on the date of application; and

(c) study is permitted, subject to the ATAS condition in Appendix ATAS; and

(d) if Part 10 of these rules applies, the applicant will be required to register with the police.

SNR 13.2. Subject to SNR 13.4., permission will be granted for a period which is the shortest of the following:

(a) 5 years after the start date of the job detailed in the Certificate of Sponsorship; or

(b) 14 days after the end date of the job detailed in the Certificate of Sponsorship; or

(c) if the applicant is applying as a high earner, the date at which the applicant will have had cumulative permission on the Global Business Mobility routes and Intra-Company routes totalling 9 years in any 10-year period; or

(d) if the applicant is not applying as a high earner, the date at which the applicant will have had cumulative permission on the Global Business Mobility routes and Intra-Company routes totalling 5 years in any 6-year period.

SNR 13.3. If the applicant does not currently hold permission on the Global Business Mobility routes, any permission granted for the period between the date of decision and the start date of the job detailed in the Certificate of Sponsorship will be excluded from the cumulative permission for the purpose of determining the period of grant of permission under SNR 13.2. (but not from the cumulative period in SNR 11.3.).

Transitional arrangements for period of grant as a Senior or Specialist Worker

SNR 13.4. If the conditions in SNR 13.5. are met, SNR 13.2. does not apply, and permission will be granted for a period which is the shortest of the following:

(a) 5 years after the start date of the job detailed in the Certificate of Sponsorship; or
(b) 14 days after the end date of the job detailed in the Certificate of Sponsorship.

SNR 13.5. The conditions referred to in SNR 13.4. are the applicant is applying for permission to stay and was previously granted permission as a Tier 2 (Intra-Company Transfer) Migrant under the rules in force before 6 April 2011, or as a Work Permit Holder and since then has continuously had permission as a Senior or Specialist Worker (including any period of overstaying disregarded under paragraph 39E).

Dependent Partner ("partner") and dependent child ("child") of a Senior or Specialist Worker

Validity requirements for a partner or child of a Senior or Specialist Worker

SNR 14.1. A person applying for entry clearance or permission to stay as a partner or child of a Senior or Specialist Worker must apply online on the gov.uk website on the specified form as follows:

Applicant	Specified form
Applicants outside the UK	Dependant partner visa Dependant child visa
Applicants inside the UK	Dependant partner Dependant child

SNR 14.2. An application for entry clearance or permission to stay as a partner or child of a Senior or Specialist Worker must meet all the following requirements:
(a) any fee and Immigration Health Charge must have been paid; and
(b) the applicant must have provided any required biometrics; and
(c) the applicant must have provided either a passport or other travel document which satisfactorily establishes their identity and nationality; and
(d) the applicant must be applying as partner or child of a person who:
(i) has made a valid application for entry clearance or permission to stay in the UK on the Global Business Mobility – Senior or Specialist Worker route that has not been decided; or
(ii) has entry clearance or permission to stay on the Global Business Mobility – Senior or Specialist Worker route.

SNR 14.3. A person applying as a partner must be aged 18 or over on the date of application.

SNR 14.4. A person applying for permission to stay as a partner or child of a Senior or Specialist Worker must be in the UK on the date of application and must not have, or have last been granted, permission:
(a) as a Visitor; or
(b) as a Short-term Student; or
(c) as a Parent of a Child Student; or
(d) as a Seasonal Worker; or
(e) as a Domestic Worker in a Private Household; or
(f) outside the Immigration Rules.

SNR 14.5. An application which does not meet all the validity requirements for a partner or child of a Senior or Specialist Worker is invalid and may be rejected and not considered.

Suitability requirements for a partner or child of a Senior or Specialist Worker

SNR 15.1. The applicant must not fall for refusal under Part 9: grounds for refusal.

SNR 15.2. If applying for permission to stay the applicant must not be:

(a) in breach of immigration laws, except that where paragraph 39E applies, that period of overstaying will be disregarded; or

(b) on immigration bail.

Eligibility requirements for a partner or child of a Senior or Specialist Worker

Entry requirement for a partner or child of a Senior or Specialist Worker

SNR 16.1. A person seeking to come to the UK as a partner or child must apply for and obtain entry clearance as a partner or child of a Senior or Specialist Worker before they arrive in the UK.

SNR 16.2. A person applying for entry clearance as the partner or child of a Senior or Specialist Worker must, if paragraph A39 and Appendix T of these rules apply, provide a valid medical certificate confirming that they have undergone screening for active pulmonary tuberculosis and that this tuberculosis is not present in them.

Relationship requirement for a partner of a Senior or Specialist Worker

SNR 17.1. The applicant must be the partner of a person (P) where one of the following applies:

(a) P has permission as a Senior or Specialist Worker; or

(b) P is, at the same time, applying for (and is granted) entry clearance or permission as a Senior or Specialist Worker.

SNR 17.2. If the applicant and their Senior or Specialist Worker partner are not married or in a civil partnership, all of the following requirements must be met:

(a) they must have been living together in a relationship similar to marriage or civil partnership for at least the two years before the date of application; and

(b) any previous relationship of the applicant or their Senior or Specialist Worker partner with another person must have permanently broken down; and

(c) the applicant and their Senior or Specialist Worker partner must not be so closely related that they would not be allowed to marry or form a civil partnership in the UK.

SNR 17.3. The relationship between the applicant and their Senior or Specialist Worker partner must be genuine and subsisting.

SNR 17.4. The applicant and their Senior or Specialist Worker partner must intend to live together throughout the applicant's stay in the UK.

Relationship requirement for a child of a Senior or Specialist Worker

SNR 18.1. The applicant must be the child of a parent who has, or is at the same time being granted permission:

(a) on the Global Business Mobility – Senior or Specialist Worker route; or

(b) as a partner on the Global Business Mobility – Senior or Specialist Worker route.

SNR 18.2. The applicant's parents must each be either applying at the same time as the applicant or have permission to be in the UK (other than as a Visitor) unless:

(a) the parent applying for, or with, entry clearance or permission to stay as a Senior or Specialist Worker or as the partner of a Senior or Specialist Worker is the sole surviving parent; or

(b) the parent applying for or with entry clearance or permission to stay as a Senior or Specialist Worker or as the partner of a Senior or Specialist Worker has sole responsibility for the child's upbringing; or

(c) the parent who does not have permission as a Senior or Specialist Worker:

(i) is a British citizen or a person who has a right to enter or stay in the UK without restriction; and

(ii) is or will be ordinarily resident in the UK; or

(d) the decision maker is satisfied that there are serious and compelling reasons to grant the child entry clearance or permission to stay with the parent who is applying for or has entry clearance or permission on the Global Business Mobility - Senior or Specialist Worker route.

SNR 18.3. If the applicant is a child born in the UK to a Senior or Specialist Worker or their partner, the applicant must provide a full UK birth certificate showing the names of both parents.

Care requirement for a child of a Senior or Specialist Worker

SNR 19.1. If the applicant is aged under 18 on the date of application, there must be suitable arrangements for the child's care and accommodation in the UK, which must comply with relevant UK law.

Age requirement for a child of a Senior or Specialist Worker

SNR 20.1. The child must be under the age of 18 on the date of application, unless they were last granted permission as the dependent child of their parent or parents.

SNR 20.2. If the child is aged 16 or over at the date of application, they must not be leading an independent life.

Financial requirement for a partner or child of a Senior or Specialist Worker

SNR 21.1. If the applicant is applying for permission to stay and has been living in the UK with permission for 12 months or longer on the date of application, they will meet the financial requirement and do not need to show funds.

SNR 21.2. If the applicant is applying for entry clearance, or is applying for permission to stay and has not been in the UK for 12 months on the date of application, either:

(a) funds of at least the amount required in SNR 21.3. must be held collectively by one or more of the following:

(i) the applicant; and

(ii) the Senior or Specialist Worker (P); and

(iii) if the applicant is applying as a child, their parent who is lawfully present in the UK or being granted entry clearance, or permission to stay, at the same time; or

(b) the sponsor of P must confirm on the Certificate of Sponsorship that they will, if necessary, maintain and accommodate the partner and/or any child, as well as P, up to the end of the first month of each of their permission, up to at least the amounts in SNR 21.3.

SNR 21.3. The required funds are:

(a) £285 for a partner in the UK or applying for entry clearance; and

(b) £315 for the first child in the UK or applying for entry clearance; and
(c) £200 for any other child in the UK or applying for entry clearance.

SNR 21.4. If SNR 21.2.(a) applies, the funds held must be held in addition to any funds required for the Senior or Specialist Worker to meet the financial requirement and the funds required for any dependants in the UK or applying at the same time.

SNR 21.5. If SNR 21.2.(a) applies, the funds must have been held for a 28-day period and as specified in Appendix Finance.

Decision for a partner or child of a Senior or Specialist Worker

SNR 22.1. If the decision maker is satisfied that all the suitability and eligibility requirements are met for a partner or child of a Senior or Specialist Worker the application will be granted, otherwise the application will be refused.

SNR 22.2. If the application is refused the person can apply for an Administrative Review under Appendix AR: Administrative Review.

Period of grant and conditions for a partner or child of a Senior or Specialist Worker

SNR 23.1. A partner will be granted permission which ends on the same date as the person who is their partner and has permission as a Senior or Specialist Worker.

SNR 23.2. A child will be granted permission which ends on the same date as whichever of their parents' permission ends first.

SNR 23.3. The grant will be subject to all the following conditions:
(a) no access to public funds; and
(b) work (including self-employment and voluntary work) permitted; except for employment as a professional sportsperson (including as a sports coach); and
(c) study is permitted, subject to the ATAS condition in Appendix ATAS; and
(d) if Part 10 of these rules applies the applicant will be required to register with the police.]

Note: Appendix inserted from 09:00 on 11 April 2022 subject to savings for applications made before that time (HC 1118).

[Appendix Global Business Mobility – Graduate Trainee

The Global Business Mobility- Graduate Trainee route is for overseas workers who are undertaking temporary work assignments in the UK, where the worker is on a graduate training course leading to a senior management or specialist position and is required to do a work placement in the UK. This type of assignment is often called an intra-company transfer- graduate trainee or ICT.

A dependent partner and dependent children can apply to come to the UK on this route.

The Global Business Mobility – Graduate Trainee route is not a route to settlement.

Validity requirements for a Global Business Mobility – Graduate Trainee ("Graduate Trainee")

GTR 1.1. A person applying for entry clearance or permission to stay as a Graduate Trainee must apply online on the gov.uk website on the specified form as follows:

(a) for applicants outside the UK, form "Global Business Mobility visa"; or
(b) for applicants inside the UK, form "Global Business Mobility".

GTR 1.2. An application for entry clearance or permission to stay as a Graduate Trainee must meet all the following requirements:
(a) any fee and Immigration Health Charge must have been paid; and
(b) the applicant must have provided any required biometrics; and
(c) the applicant must have provided a passport or other travel document which satisfactorily establishes their identity and nationality; and
(d) the applicant must have a Certificate of Sponsorship that was issued to them by their sponsor no more than three months before the date of application.

GTR 1.3. The applicant must be aged 18 or over on the date of application.

GTR 1.4. An applicant applying for entry clearance or permission to stay as a Graduate Trainee who has received an award from a Government or international scholarship agency in the 12 months before the date of application which covers both fees and living costs for study in the UK, must have provided written consent to the application from that Government or agency.

GTR 1.5. An applicant applying for permission to stay must be in the UK and must not have, or have last been granted, permission:
(a) as a Visitor; or
(b) as a Short-term Student; or
(c) as a Parent of a Child Student; or
(d) as a Seasonal Worker; or
(e) as a Domestic Worker in a Private Household; or
(f) outside the Immigration Rules.

GTR 1.6. An application which does not meet all the validity requirements for a Graduate Trainee is invalid and may be rejected and not considered.

Suitability requirements for a Graduate Trainee

GTR 2.1. The applicant must not fall for refusal under Part 9: grounds for refusal.

GTR 2.2. If applying for permission to stay the applicant must not be:
(a) in breach of immigration laws, except that where paragraph 39E applies, that period of overstaying will be disregarded; or
(b) on immigration bail.

Eligibility requirements for a Graduate Trainee

Entry requirements for a Graduate Trainee

GTR 3.1. A person seeking to come to the UK as a Graduate Trainee must apply for and obtain entry clearance as a Graduate Trainee before their arrival in the UK.

GTR 3.2. A person applying for entry clearance as a Graduate Trainee must, if paragraph A39 and Appendix T of these rules apply, provide a valid medical certificate confirming that they have undergone screening for active pulmonary tuberculosis and that this tuberculosis is not present in them.

Points requirement for a Graduate Trainee

GTR 4.1. The applicant must be awarded 60 points based on the table below:

Points requirement	Relevant rules	Points
Sponsorship	GTR 5.1. to GTR 5.7.	20
Job at an appropriate skill level	GTR 6.1. to GTR 6.7.	20
Salary at required level	GTR 7.1. to GTR 9.3.	20

Points for Sponsorship for a Graduate Trainee

GTR 5.1. The applicant must have a valid certificate of sponsorship for the job they are planning to do, which to be valid must:

(a) confirm the applicant's name, that they are being sponsored as a Graduate Trainee, details of the job, salary and any allowances the sponsor is offering them (if applicable) and PAYE details if HM Revenue and Customs (HMRC) requires income tax and national insurance for the sponsored job to be paid via PAYE; and

(b) include a start date for the job, stated by the sponsor, which is no more than 3 months after the date of application; and

(c) not have been used in a previous application which was either granted or refused (but can have been used in a previous application which was rejected as invalid, made void or withdrawn); and

(d) not have been withdrawn by the sponsor or cancelled by the Home Office; and

(e) confirm that the applicant has worked for the sponsor group for the period required at GTR 5.6.(b); and

(f) confirm whether the Academic Technology Approval Scheme (ATAS) requirement in Appendix ATAS applies.

GTR 5.2. The sponsor must be authorised by the Home Office to sponsor a Graduate Trainee.

GTR 5.3. The sponsor must be listed as A-rated on the Home Office's register of licensed sponsors, unless the applicant was last granted permission as a Graduate Trainee and is applying to continue working for the same sponsor as in their last permission.

GTR 5.4. The decision maker must not have reasonable grounds to believe the job the applicant is being sponsored to do:

(a) does not exist; or

(b) is a sham; or

(c) has been created mainly so the applicant can apply for entry clearance or permission to stay.

GTR 5.5. The decision maker must not have reasonable grounds to believe the job the applicant is being sponsored to do amounts to:

(a) the hire of the applicant to a third party who is not the sponsor to fill a position with that party, whether temporary or permanent; or

(b) contract work to undertake an ongoing routine role or to provide an ongoing routine service for a third party who is not the sponsor, regardless of the nature or length of any arrangement between the sponsor and the third party.

GTR 5.6. An applicant as a Graduate Trainee must:

(a) be currently working for the sponsor group; and

(b) have worked outside the UK for the sponsor group for a continuous period of at least 3 months immediately before the date of application.

GTR 5.7. If the requirements in GTR 5.1. to GTR 5.6. are met, the applicant will be awarded 20 points for sponsorship.

Points for job at appropriate skill level for a Graduate Trainee

GTR 6.1. The applicant must be sponsored for a job in an occupation code listed in Appendix Skilled Occupations that is identified as eligible for the Global Business Mobility routes.

GTR 6.2. The sponsor must have chosen an appropriate occupation code, and the decision maker must not have reasonable grounds to believe the sponsor has chosen a less appropriate occupation code for any of the following reasons:

(a) the most appropriate occupation code is not eligible under the Global Business Mobility routes; or

(b) the most appropriate occupation code has a higher going rate than the proposed salary.

GTR 6.3. To support the assessment in GTR 6.2. the decision maker may, in particular, consider:

(a) whether the sponsor has shown a genuine need for the job as described; and

(b) whether the applicant has the appropriate skills, qualifications and experience needed to do the job as described; and

(c) the sponsor's history of compliance with the immigration system including, but not limited to, paying its sponsored workers appropriately; and

(d) any additional information from the sponsor.

GTR 6.4. The job must be part of a structured graduate training programme, with clearly defined progression towards a managerial or specialist role within the sponsor organisation.

GTR 6.5. If the ATAS requirement in Appendix ATAS applies, the applicant must provide a valid ATAS certificate.

GTR 6.6. If the requirements in GTR 6.1. to GTR 6.5. are met, the applicant will be awarded 20 points for a job at the appropriate skill level, subject to GTR 6.7.

GTR 6.7. No points will be awarded for a job at the appropriate skill level if the applicant is not also being awarded 20 points for sponsorship under GTR 5.7.

Points for salary for a Graduate Trainee

GTR 7.1. The salary for the job for which the applicant is being sponsored must equal or exceed both:

(a) the general salary requirement in GTR 8.1. and GTR 8.2.; and

(b) the going rate requirement in GTR 9.1. to GTR 9.3.

GTR 7.2. Salary under these requirements includes only:

(a) guaranteed basic gross pay (before income tax and including employee pension and national insurance contributions); and

(b) allowances which are guaranteed to be paid for the duration of the applicant's employment in the UK (such as London weighting) or are paid as a mobility premium or to cover the additional cost of living in the UK.

GTR 7.3. Where allowances under GTR 7.2.(b) are solely for the purpose of accommodation they will only be taken into account up to a value of 40% of the total salary package.

GTR 7.4. Salary does not include other pay and benefits, such as any of the following:

(a) flexible working where the nature of the job means that hours fluctuate and pay cannot be guaranteed; or

(b) additional pay such as shift, overtime or bonus pay, whether or not it is guaranteed; or

(c) employer pension and national insurance contributions; or

(d) any allowances, other than those specified in GTR 7.2.(b); or

(e) in-kind benefits, such as equity shares, health insurance, school or university fees, company cars or food; or

(f) one-off payments, such as 'golden hellos'; or

(g) any payments relating to immigration costs, such as the fee or Immigration Health Charge; or

(h) payments to cover business expenses, including (but not limited to) travel to and from the applicant's country of residence, equipment, clothing, travel or subsistence.

GTR 7.5. If the requirements in GTR 7.1. to GTR 7.4. are met, the applicant will be awarded 20 points for salary at the required level, subject to GTR 7.6.

GTR 7.6. No points will be awarded for salary if the applicant is not also being awarded 20 points for sponsorship under GTR 5.7.

General salary requirement for a Graduate Trainee

GTR 8.1. If the applicant is being sponsored for a job in one of the occupation codes listed in Table 1 of Appendix Skilled Occupations, the general salary requirement is £23,100 per year.

GTR 8.2. If the applicant is being sponsored to work more than 48 hours a week, only the salary for the first 48 hours a week will be considered towards the general salary requirement.
For example, an applicant who works 60 hours a week for £8 per hour will be considered to have a salary of £19,968 (£8 x 48 x 52) per year and not £24,960 (£8 x 60 x 52).

Going rate requirement for a Graduate Trainee

GTR 9.1. If the applicant is being sponsored for a job in one of the occupation codes listed in Table 1 of Appendix Skilled Occupations, the going rate requirement is 70% of the pro-rated going rate, which will be calculated as follows:

0.7 x (the going rate for the occupation code stated in Table 1 of Appendix Skilled Occupations) x (the number of weekly working hours stated by the sponsor ÷ 39).

GTR 9.2. If the applicant is being sponsored for a job in one of the health or education occupation codes listed in Table 2 of Appendix Skilled Occupations, the going rate requirement is 100% of the pro-rated going rate (and the going rate will be pro-rated according to the number of weekly working hours stated by the sponsor, and the pro-rating set out in Appendix Skilled Occupations).

GTR 9.3. The applicant's full weekly hours will be included when checking their salary against the going rate, even if they work more than 48 hours a week.
For example, an applicant who works 60 hours a week in an occupation code with a going rate of £39,000 must be paid £42,000 (0.7 x £39,000 x 60 ÷ 39) per year, not £33,600 (0.7 x £39,000 x 48 ÷ 39).

Financial requirement for a Graduate Trainee

GTR 10.1. If the applicant is applying for permission to stay and has been living in the UK with permission for 12 months or longer on the date of application, they will meet the financial requirement and do not need to show funds.

GTR 10.2. If the applicant is applying for entry clearance or has been living in the UK for less than 12 months on the date of application either:

(a) the applicant must have funds of at least £1,270; or

(b) the sponsor must certify on the certificate of sponsorship that they will, if it is necessary, maintain and accommodate the applicant up to the end of the first month of their employment up to a maximum amount of £1,270.

GTR 10.3. If GTR 10.2.(a) applies, the applicant must show that they have held the required level of funds for a 28-day period and as set out in Appendix Finance.

Maximum length of assignments requirement for a Graduate Trainee

GTR 11.1. The grant of permission must not lead to the applicant being granted cumulative periods of permission on the Global Business Mobility routes and Intra-Company routes totalling more than 5 years in any 6-year period.

GTR 11.2. When calculating the cumulative periods of permission referred to in GTR 11.1. and GTR 13.2.(c), the decision maker will include the following:

(a) all previous permission on the Global Business Mobility routes; and

(b) all previous permission on the Intra-Company routes; and

(c) if the applicant does not currently hold permission on a Global Business Mobility route, any permission they could be granted under the current application, beginning on the start date of the job stated on the Certificate of Sponsorship; and

(d) if the applicant is applying for permission to stay and has or last had permission on a Global Business Mobility route, any permission they could be granted under the current application, beginning on the date of decision; and

(e) any period of permission on the Global Business Mobility routes and the Intra-Company routes extended under section 3C of the Immigration Act 1971.

Decision for a Graduate Trainee

GTR 12.1. If the decision maker is satisfied that all the suitability and eligibility requirements for a Graduate Trainee are met the application will be granted, otherwise the application will be refused.

GTR 12.2. If the application is refused the person can apply for an Administrative Review under Appendix AR: Administrative Review.

Period and conditions of grant as a Graduate Trainee

GTR 13.1. The grant will be subject to all the following conditions:

(a) no access to public funds; and

(b) the only work permitted is:

(i) in the job for which the applicant is being sponsored; and

(ii) voluntary work; and

(iii) working out a contractual notice period, where the applicant was lawfully working in that job in the UK on the date of application; and

(c) study is permitted, subject to the ATAS condition in Appendix ATAS; and

(d) if Part 10 applies, the applicant will be required to register with the police.

GTR 13.2. Permission will be granted for a period which is the shortest of the following:

(a) 1 year after the start date of the job detailed in the Certificate of Sponsorship; or

(b) 14 days after the end date of the job detailed in the Certificate of Sponsorship; or

(c) the date at which the applicant will have had cumulative permission in the Global Business Mobility routes and Intra-Company routes totalling 5 years in any 6-year period.

GTR 13.3. If the applicant does not currently hold permission on the Global Business Mobility routes, any permission granted for the period between the date of decision and the start date of the job detailed in the Certificate of Sponsorship will be excluded from the cumulative permission for the purpose of determining the period of grant of permission under GTR 13.2. (but not from the cumulative period in GTR 11.2.).

Dependent Partner ("partner") or dependent child ("child") of a Global Business Mobility - Graduate Trainee

Validity requirements for a partner or child of a Graduate Trainee

GTR 14.1. A person applying for entry clearance or permission to stay as a partner or child of a Graduate Trainee must apply online on the gov.uk website on the specified form as follows:

Applicant	Specified form
Applicants outside the UK	Dependant partner visa Dependant child visa
Applicants inside the UK	Dependant partner Dependant child

GTR 14.2. An application for entry clearance or permission to stay as a partner or child of a Graduate Trainee must meet all the following requirements:

(a) any fee and Immigration Health Charge must have been paid; and

(b) the applicant must have provided any required biometrics; and

(c) the applicant must have provided either a passport or other travel document which satisfactorily establishes their identity and nationality; and

(d) the applicant must be applying as partner or child of a person who:

(i) has made a valid application for entry clearance or permission to stay in the UK on the Global Business Mobility – Graduate Trainee route that has not been decided; or

(ii) has entry clearance or permission to stay on the Global Business Mobility – Graduate Trainee route.

GTR 14.3. A person applying as a partner must be aged 18 or over on the date of application.

GTR 14.4. A person applying for permission to stay as a partner or child of a Graduate Trainee must be in the UK on the date of application and must not have, or have last been granted, permission:

(a) as a Visitor; or

(b) as a Short-term Student; or

(c) as a Parent of a Child Student; or

(d) as a Seasonal Worker; or

(e) as a Domestic Worker in a Private Household; or

(f) outside the Immigration Rules.

GTR 14.5. An application which does not meet all the validity requirements for a partner or child of a Graduate Trainee is invalid and may be rejected and not considered.

Suitability requirements for a partner or child of a Graduate Trainee

GTR 15.1. The applicant must not fall for refusal under Part 9: grounds for refusal.

GTR 15.2. If applying for permission to stay the applicant must not be:

(a) in breach of immigration laws, except that where paragraph 39E applies, that period of overstaying will be disregarded; or

(b) on immigration bail.

Eligibility requirements for a partner or child of a Graduate Trainee

Entry requirement for a partner or child of a Graduate Trainee

GTR 16.1. A person seeking to come to the UK as a partner or child must apply for and obtain entry clearance as a partner or child of a Graduate Trainee before they arrive in the UK.

GTR 16.2. A person applying for entry clearance as the partner or child of a Graduate Trainee must, if paragraph A39 and Appendix T of these rules apply, provide a valid medical certificate confirming that they have undergone screening for active pulmonary tuberculosis and that this tuberculosis is not present in them.

Relationship requirement for a partner of a Graduate Trainee

GTR 17.1. The applicant must be the partner of a person (P) where one of the following applies:

(a) P has permission as a Graduate Trainee; or

(b) P is, at the same time, applying for (and is granted) entry clearance or permission as a Graduate Trainee.

GTR 17.2. If the applicant and their Graduate Trainee partner are not married or in a civil partnership, all of the following requirements must be met:

(a) they must have been living together in a relationship similar to marriage or civil partnership for at least the two years before the date of application; and

(b) any previous relationship of the applicant or their Graduate Trainee partner with another person must have permanently broken down; and

(c) the applicant and their Graduate Trainee partner must not be so closely related that they would not be allowed to marry or form a civil partnership in the UK.

GTR 17.3. The relationship between the applicant and their Graduate Trainee partner must be genuine and subsisting.

GTR 17.4. The applicant and their Graduate Trainee partner must intend to live together throughout the applicant's stay in the UK.

Relationship requirement for a child of a Graduate Trainee

GTR 18.1. The applicant must be the child of a parent who has, or is at the same time being granted permission:

(a) on the Global Business Mobility – Graduate Trainee route; or

(b) as a partner on the Global Business Mobility – Graduate Trainee route.

GTR 18.2. The applicant's parents must each be either applying at the same time as the applicant or have permission to be in the UK (other than as a Visitor) unless:

(a) the parent applying for or with entry clearance or permission to stay as a Graduate Trainee or as the partner of a Graduate Trainee is the sole surviving parent; or

(b) the parent applying for or with entry clearance or permission to stay as a Graduate Trainee or as the partner of a Graduate Trainee has sole responsibility for the child's upbringing; or

(c) the parent who does not have permission as a Graduate Trainee:

(i) is a British citizen or a person who has a right to enter or stay in the UK without restriction; and

(ii) is or will be ordinarily resident in the UK; or

(d) the decision maker is satisfied that there are serious and compelling reasons to grant the child entry clearance or permission to stay with the parent who is applying for or has entry clearance or permission on the Global Business Mobility - Graduate Trainee route.

GTR 18.3. If the applicant is a child born in the UK to a Graduate Trainee or their partner, the applicant must provide a full UK birth certificate showing the names of both parents.

Care requirement for a child of a Graduate Trainee

GTR 19.1. If the applicant is aged under 18 on the date of application, there must be suitable arrangements for the child's care and accommodation in the UK, which must comply with relevant UK law.

Age requirement for a child of a Graduate Trainee

GTR 20.1. The child must be under the age of 18 on the date of application, unless they were last granted permission as the child of their parent or parents.

GTR 20.2. If the child is aged 16 or over at the date of application, they must not be leading an independent life.

Financial requirement for a partner or child of a Graduate Trainee

GTR 21.1. If the applicant is applying for permission to stay and has been living in the UK with permission for 12 months or longer on the date of application, they will meet the financial requirement and do not need to show funds.

GTR 21.2. If the applicant is applying for entry clearance, or is applying for permission to stay and has not been in the UK for 12 months on the date of application, either:

(a) funds of at least the amount required in GTR 23.3 must be held collectively by one or more of the following:

(i) the applicant; and

(ii) the Graduate Trainee (P); and

(iii) if the applicant is applying as a child, their parent who is lawfully present in the UK or being granted entry clearance, or permission to stay at the same time as the applicant; or

(b) the sponsor of P must confirm on the Certificate of Sponsorship that they will, if necessary, maintain and accommodate the partner and/or any child as well as P, up to the end of the first month of each of their permission, up to at least the amounts in GTR 21.3.

GTR 21.3. The required funds are:

(a) £285 for a partner in the UK or applying for entry clearance; and

(b) £315 for the first child in the UK or applying for entry clearance; and

(c) £200 for any other child in the UK or applying for entry clearance.

GTR 21.4. If GTR 21.2.(a) applies, the funds held must be held in addition to any funds required for the Graduate Trainee to meet the financial requirement and the funds required for any dependants in the UK or applying at the same time.

GTR 21.5. If GTR 21.2.(a) applies, the funds must have been held for a 28-day period and as specified in Appendix Finance.

Decision for a partner or child of a Graduate Trainee

GTR 22.1. If the decision maker is satisfied that all the suitability and eligibility requirements are met for a partner or child of a Graduate Trainee the application will be granted, otherwise the application will be refused.

GTR 22.2. If the application is refused the person can apply for an Administrative Review under Appendix AR: Administrative Review.

Period and conditions of grant for a partner or child of a Graduate Trainee

GTR 23.1. A partner will be granted permission which ends on the same date as the person (P) who is their partner and has permission of a Graduate Trainee.

GTR 23.2. A child will be granted permission which ends on the same date as whichever of their parents' permission ends first.

GTR 23.3. The grant will be subject to all the following conditions:

(a) no access to public funds; and

(b) work (including self-employment and voluntary work) permitted; except for employment as a professional sportsperson (including as a sports coach); and

(c) study is permitted, subject to the ATAS condition in Appendix ATAS; and

(d) if Part 10 applies the applicant will be required to register with the police.

Note: Appendix inserted from 09:00 on 11 April 2022 subject to savings for applications made before that time (HC 1118).

[Appendix Global Business Mobility – UK Expansion Worker

The Global Business Mobility – UK Expansion Worker route is for overseas workers who are undertaking temporary work assignments in the UK, where the worker is a senior manager or specialist employee and is being assigned to the UK to undertake work related to a business's expansion to the UK.

This route can only be used when the business has not yet begun trading in the UK. If the business is already trading in the UK, workers should apply under Appendix Global Business Mobility – Senior or Specialist Worker instead.

A dependent partner and dependent children can apply to come to the UK on this route.

The Global Business Mobility – UK Expansion Worker route is not a route to settlement.

Validity requirements for a Global Business Mobility - UK Expansion Worker ("UK Expansion Worker")

UKX 1.1. A person applying for entry clearance or permission to stay as a UK Expansion Worker must apply online on the gov.uk website on the specified form as follows:

(a) for applicants outside the UK, form "Global Business Mobility visa"; or

(b) for applicants inside the UK, form "Global Business Mobility".

UKX 1.2. An application for entry clearance or permission to stay as a UK Expansion Worker must meet all the following requirements:

(a) any fee and Immigration Health Charge must have been paid; and

(b) the applicant must have provided any required biometrics; and

(c) the applicant must have provided a passport or other travel document which satisfactorily establishes their identity and nationality; and

(d) the applicant must have a Certificate of Sponsorship that was issued to them by their sponsor no more than 3 months before the date of application.

UKX 1.3. The applicant must be aged 18 or over on the date of application.

UKX 1.4. An applicant applying for entry clearance or permission to stay as a UK Expansion Worker who has received an award from a Government or international scholarship agency in the 12 months before the date of application which covers both fees and living costs for study in the UK, must have provided written consent to the application from that Government or agency.

UKX 1.5. An applicant applying for permission to stay must be in the UK and must not have, or have last been granted, permission:

(a) as a Visitor; or

(b) as a Short-term Student; or

(c) as a Parent of a Child Student; or

(d) as a Seasonal Worker; or

(e) as a Domestic Worker in a Private Household; or

(f) outside the Immigration Rules.

UKX 1.6. An application which does not meet all the validity requirements for a UK Expansion Worker is invalid and may be rejected and not considered.

Suitability requirements for a UK Expansion Worker

UKX 2.1. The applicant must not fall for refusal under Part 9: grounds for refusal.

UKX 2.2. If applying for permission to stay the applicant must not be:

(a) in breach of immigration laws, except that where paragraph 39E applies, that period of overstaying will be disregarded; or

(b) on immigration bail.

Eligibility requirements for a UK Expansion Worker

Entry requirements for a UK Expansion Worker

UKX 3.1. A person seeking to come to the UK as a UK Expansion Worker must apply for and obtain entry clearance as a UK Expansion Worker before their arrival in the UK.

UKX 3.2. A person applying for entry clearance as a UK Expansion Worker must, if paragraph A39 and Appendix T of these rules apply, provide a valid medical certificate confirming that they have undergone screening for active pulmonary tuberculosis and that this tuberculosis is not present in them.

Points requirement for a UK Expansion Worker

UKX 4.1. The applicant must be awarded 60 points based on the table below:

Points requirement	Relevant rules	Points
Sponsorship	UKX 5.1. to UKX 5.8.	20
Job at appropriate skill level	UKX 6.1. to UKX 6.6.	20
Salary at required level	UKX 7.1. to UKX 9.3.	20

Points for Sponsorship for a UK Expansion Worker

UKX 5.1. The applicant must have a valid certificate of sponsorship for the job they are planning to do, which to be valid must:

(a) confirm the applicant's name, that they are being sponsored as a UK Expansion Worker, details of the job, salary and any allowances the sponsor is offering them (if applicable) and PAYE details if HM Revenue and Customs (HMRC) requires income tax and national insurance for the sponsored job to be paid via PAYE; and

(b) include a start date for the job, stated by the sponsor, which is no more than 3 months after the date of application; and

(c) not have been used in a previous application which was either granted or refused (but can have been used in a previous application which was rejected as invalid, made void or withdrawn); and

(d) not have been withdrawn by the sponsor or cancelled by the Home Office; and

(e) confirm that the applicant has worked for the sponsor group for the period required at UKX 5.6.(b); and

(f) confirm whether the Academic Technology Approval Scheme (ATAS) requirement in Appendix ATAS applies.

UKX 5.2. The sponsor must be authorised by the Home Office to sponsor a UK Expansion Worker.

UKX 5.3. The sponsor must be listed as A-rated on the Home Office's register of licensed sponsors, unless one of the following applies:

(a) the applicant was last granted permission as a UK Expansion Worker and is applying to continue working for the same sponsor as in their last permission; or

(b) the applicant holds the role of authorising officer on the sponsor's licence and the sponsor has a provisional rating on the Home Office's register of licenced sponsors.

UKX 5.4. The decision maker must not have reasonable grounds to believe the job the applicant is being sponsored to do:

(a) does not exist; or

(b) is a sham; or

(c) has been created mainly so the applicant can apply for entry clearance or permission to stay.

UKX 5.5. The sponsor must choose an appropriate occupation code, and the decision maker must not have reasonable grounds to believe the job the applicant is being sponsored to do amounts to:

(a) the hire of the applicant to a third party who is not the sponsor to fill a position with that party, whether temporary or permanent; or

(b) contract work to undertake an ongoing routine role or to provide an ongoing routine service for a third party who is not the sponsor, regardless of the nature or length of any arrangement between the sponsor and the third party.

UKX 5.6. An applicant as a UK Expansion Worker must:

(a) be currently working for the sponsor group; and

(b) have worked outside the UK for the sponsor group for a cumulative period of at least 12 months, unless the applicant is either:

(i) applying as a high earner; or

(ii) a Japanese national seeking to establish a UK branch or subsidiary of the sponsor group under the UK-Japan Comprehensive Economic Partnership Agreement.

UKX 5.7. In UKX 5.6.(b) the 12 months' work outside the UK can have been accumulated over any period provided that:

(a) the applicant was continuously working for the business at UKX 5.6.(a), whether in or out of the UK, from the start of the 12 months to the date of application; and

(b) any breaks in the continuous work in UKX 5.7.(a) were only for the following reasons:

(i) statutory maternity, paternity, parental, or shared parental leave; or

(ii) statutory adoption leave; or

(iii) sick leave; or

(iv) assisting with a national or international humanitarian or environmental crisis, with the agreement of the sponsor group; or

(v) taking part in legally organised industrial action.

UKX 5.8. If the requirements in UKX 5.1. to UKX 5.7. are met, the applicant will be awarded 20 points for sponsorship.

Points for job at appropriate skill level for a UK Expansion Worker

UKX 6.1. The applicant must be sponsored for a job in an occupation code listed in Appendix Skilled Occupations that is identified as eligible for the Global Business Mobility routes.

UKX 6.2. The decision maker must not have reasonable grounds to believe the sponsor has chosen a less appropriate occupation code for any of the following reasons:

(a) the most appropriate occupation code is not eligible under the Global Business Mobility routes; or

(b) the most appropriate occupation code has a higher going rate than the proposed salary.

UKX 6.3. To support the assessment in UKX 6.2, the decision maker may, in particular, consider:

(a) whether the sponsor has shown a genuine need for the job as described; and

(b) whether the applicant has the appropriate skills, qualifications and experience needed to do the job as described; and

(c) the sponsor's history of compliance with the immigration system including, but not limited to, paying its sponsored workers appropriately; and

(d) any additional information from the sponsor.

UKX 6.4. If the ATAS requirement in Appendix ATAS applies, the applicant must provide a valid ATAS certificate.

UKX 6.5. If the requirements in UKX 6.1. to UKX 6.4. are met, the applicant will be awarded 20 points for a job at the appropriate skill level, subject to UKX 6.6.

UKX 6.6. No points will be awarded for a job at the appropriate skill level if the applicant is not also being awarded 20 points for sponsorship under UKX 5.8.

Points for salary for a UK Expansion Worker

UKX 7.1. The salary for the job for which the applicant is being sponsored must equal or exceed both:

(a) the general salary requirement in UKX 8.1 and UKX 8.2; and

(b) the going rate requirement in UKX 9.1. to UKX 9.3.

UKX 7.2. Salary under these requirements includes only:

(a) guaranteed basic gross pay (before income tax and including employee pension and national insurance contributions); and

(b) allowances which are guaranteed to be paid for the duration of the applicant's employment in the UK (such as London weighting) or are paid as a mobility premium or to cover the additional cost of living in the UK.

UKX 7.3. Where allowances under UKX 7.2.(b) are solely for the purpose of accommodation they will only be taken into account up to a value of 30% of the total salary package.

UKX 7.4. Salary does not include other pay and benefits, such as any of the following:

(a) flexible working where the nature of the job means that hours fluctuate and pay cannot be guaranteed; or

(b) additional pay such as shift, overtime or bonus pay, whether or not it is guaranteed; or

(c) employer pension and national insurance contributions; or

(d) any allowances, other than those specified in UKX 7.2.(b); or

(e) in-kind benefits, such as equity shares, health insurance, school or university fees, company cars or food; or

(f) one-off payments, such as 'golden hellos'; or

(g) any payments relating to immigration costs, such as the fee or Immigration Health Charge; or

(h) payments to cover business expenses, including (but not limited to) travel to and from the applicant's country of residence, equipment, clothing, travel or subsistence.

UKX 7.5. If the requirements in UKX 7.1. to UKX 7.4. are met, the applicant will be awarded 20 points for salary at the required level, subject to UKX 7.6.

UKX 7.6. No points will be awarded for salary if the applicant is not also being awarded 20 points for sponsorship under UKX 5.8.

General salary requirement for a UK Expansion Worker

UKX 8.1. If the applicant is being sponsored for a job in one of the occupation codes listed in Table 1 of Appendix Skilled Occupations, the general salary requirement is £42,400 per year.

UKX 8.2. If the applicant is being sponsored to work more than 48 hours a week, only the salary for the first 48 hours a week will be considered towards the general salary requirement.
For example, an applicant who works 60 hours a week for £15 per hour will be considered to have a salary of £37,440 (£15 x 48 x 52) per year and not £46,800 (£15 x 60 x 52).

Going rate requirement for a UK Expansion Worker

UKX 9.1. If the applicant is being sponsored for a job in one of the occupation codes listed in Table 1 of Appendix Skilled Occupations, the going rate requirement is 100% of the pro-rated going rate, which will be calculated as follows:

1 x (the going rate for the occupation code stated in Table 1 of Appendix Skilled Occupations) x (the number of weekly working hours stated by the sponsor ÷ 39).

UKX 9.2. If the applicant is being sponsored for a job in one of the health or education occupation codes listed in Table 2 of Appendix Skilled Occupations, the going rate requirement is 100% of the pro-rated going rate (and the going rate will be pro-rated according to the number of weekly working hours stated by the sponsor, and the pro-rating set out in Appendix Skilled Occupations).

UKX 9.3. The applicant's full weekly hours will be included when checking their salary against the going rate, even if they work more than 48 hours a week.
For example, an applicant who works 60 hours a week in an occupation code with a going rate of £39,000 must be paid £60,000 (1 x £39,000 x 60 ÷ 39) per year, not £48,000 (1 x £39,000 x 48 ÷ 39).

Financial requirement for a UK Expansion Worker

UKX 10.1. If the applicant is applying for permission to stay and has been living in the UK with permission for 12 months or longer on the date of application, they will meet the financial requirement and do not need to show funds.

UKX 10.2. If the applicant is applying for entry clearance or has been living in the UK for less than 12 months, the applicant must have funds of at least £1,270.

UKX 10.3. The applicant must show that they have held the level of funds required by UKX 10.2. for a 28-day period and as set out in Appendix Finance.

Maximum length of assignments requirement for a UK Expansion Worker

UKX 11.1. The grant of permission must not lead to the applicant being granted cumulative periods of permission in the Global Business Mobility routes and Intra-Company routes totalling more than 5 years in any 6-year period.

UKX 11.2. When calculating the cumulative periods of permission referred to in UKX 11.1. and UKX 13.2.(d), the decision maker will include the following:

(a) all previous periods of permission on the Global Business Mobility routes; and

(b) all previous periods of permission on the Intra-Company routes; and

(c) if the applicant does not currently hold permission on a Global Business Mobility route, any permission they could be granted under this application, beginning on the start date of the job stated on the Certificate of Sponsorship; and

(d) if the applicant is applying for permission to stay and has or last had permission on the Global Business Mobility routes, any permission they could be granted under this application, beginning on the date of decision; and

(e) any period of permission on the Global Business Mobility routes and the Intra-Company routes extended under section 3C of the Immigration Act 1971.

Decision for a UK Expansion Worker

UKX 12.1. If the decision maker is satisfied that all the suitability and eligibility requirements for a UK Expansion Worker are met the application will be granted, otherwise the application will be refused.

UKX 12.2. If the application is refused the person can apply for an Administrative Review under Appendix AR: Administrative Review.

Period and conditions of grant as a UK Expansion Worker

UKX 13.1. The grant will be subject to all the following conditions:

(a) no access to public funds; and

(b) the only work permitted is:

(i) the job for which the applicant is being sponsored; and

(ii) voluntary work; and

(iii) working out a contractual notice period, where the applicant was lawfully working in that job in the UK on the date of application; and

(c) study is permitted, subject to the ATAS condition in Appendix ATAS; and

(d) if Part 10 applies, the applicant will be required to register with the police.

UKX 13.2. Permission will be granted for a period which is the shortest of the following:

(a) 1 year after the start date of the job detailed in the Certificate of Sponsorship; or

(b) 14 days after the end date of the job detailed in the Certificate of Sponsorship; or

(c) the date at which the applicant will have had continuous permission as a UK Expansion Worker totalling 2 years; or

(d) the date at which the applicant will have had cumulative permission in the Global Business Mobility routes totalling 5 years in any 6-year period.

UKX 13.3. If the applicant does not currently hold permission on the Global Business Mobility routes, any permission granted for the period between the date of decision and the start date of the job detailed in the Certificate of Sponsorship will be excluded from the cumulative permission for the purpose of determining the period of grant of permission under UKX 13.2. (but not from the cumulative period in UKX 11.2.).

Dependent Partner (partner") and dependent child ("child") of a UK Expansion Worker

Validity requirements for a partner or child of a UK Expansion Worker

UKX 14.1. A person applying for entry clearance or permission to stay as a partner or child of a UK Expansion Worker must apply online on the gov.uk website on the specified form as follows:

Applicant	Specified form
Applicants outside the UK	Dependant partner visa Dependant child visa
Applicants inside the UK	Dependant partner Dependant child

UKX 14.2. An application for entry clearance or permission to stay as a partner or child of a UK Expansion Worker must meet all the following requirements:

(a) any fee and Immigration Health Charge must have been paid; and

(b) the applicant must have provided any required biometrics; and

(c) the applicant must have provided either a passport or other travel document which satisfactorily establishes their identity and nationality; and

(d) the applicant must be applying as partner or child of a person who:

(i) has made a valid application for entry clearance or permission to stay on the Global Business Mobility – UK Expansion Worker route that has not been decided; or

(ii) has entry clearance or permission to stay on the Global Business Mobility – UK Expansion Worker route.

UKX 14.3. A person applying as a partner must be aged 18 or over on the date of application.

UKX 14.4. A person applying for permission to stay as a partner or child of a UK Expansion Worker must be in the UK on the date of application and must not have, or have last been granted, permission:

(a) as a Visitor; or
(b) as a Short-term Student; or
(c) as a Parent of a Child Student; or
(d) as a Seasonal Worker; or
(e) as a Domestic Worker in a Private Household; or
(f) outside the Immigration Rules.

UKX 14.5. An application which does not meet all the validity requirements for a partner or child of a UK Expansion Worker is invalid and may be rejected and not considered.

Suitability requirements for a partner or child of a UK Expansion Worker

UKX 15.1. The applicant must not fall for refusal under Part 9: grounds for refusal.

UKX 15.2. If applying for permission to stay the applicant must not be:

(a) in breach of immigration laws, except that where paragraph 39E applies, that period of overstaying will be disregarded; or

(b) on immigration bail.

Eligibility requirements for a partner or child of a UK Expansion Worker

Entry requirement for a partner or child of a UK Expansion Worker

UKX 16.1. A person seeking to come to the UK as a partner or child must apply for and obtain entry clearance as a partner or child of a UK Expansion Worker before they arrive in the UK.

UKX 16.2. A person applying for entry clearance as the partner or child of a UK Expansion Worker must, if paragraph A39 and Appendix T of these rules apply, provide a valid medical certificate confirming that they have undergone screening for active pulmonary tuberculosis and that this tuberculosis is not present in them.

Relationship requirement for a partner of a UK Expansion Worker

UKX 17.1. The applicant must be the partner of a person (P) where one of the following applies:

(a) P has permission on the Global Business Mobility – UK Expansion Worker route; or

(b) P is, at the same time, applying for (and is granted) entry clearance or permission on the Global Business Mobility – UK Expansion Worker route.

UKX 17.2. If the applicant and their UK Expansion Worker partner are not married or in a civil partnership, all of the following requirements must be met:

(a) they must have been living together in a relationship similar to marriage or civil partnership for at least the two years before the date of application; and

(b) any previous relationship of the applicant or their UK Expansion Worker partner with another person must have permanently broken down; and

(c) the applicant and their UK Expansion Worker partner must not be so closely related that they would not be allowed to marry or form a civil partnership in the UK.

UKX 17.3. The relationship between the applicant and their UK Expansion Worker partner must be genuine and subsisting.

UKX 17.4. The applicant and their UK Expansion Worker partner must intend to live together throughout the applicant's stay in the UK.

Relationship requirement for a child of a UK Expansion Worker

UKX 18.1. The applicant must be the child of a parent who has, or is at the same time being granted permission:

(a) on the Global Business Mobility – UK Expansion Worker route; or

(b) as a partner on the Global Business Mobility – UK Expansion Worker route.

UKX 18.2. The applicant's parents must each be either applying at the same time as the applicant or have permission to be in the UK (other than as a Visitor) unless:

(a) the parent applying for or with entry clearance or permission to stay as a UK Expansion Worker or as the partner of a UK Expansion Worker is the sole surviving parent; or

(b) the parent applying for or with entry clearance or permission to stay as a UK Expansion Worker or as the partner of a UK Expansion Worker has sole responsibility for the child's upbringing; or

(c) the parent who does not have permission as a UK Expansion Worker:

(i) is a British citizen or a person who has a right to enter or stay in the UK without restriction; and

(ii) is or will be ordinarily resident in the UK; or

(d) the decision maker is satisfied that there are serious and compelling reasons to grant the child entry clearance or permission to stay with the parent who is applying for or has entry clearance or permission on the Global Business Mobility - UK Expansion Worker route.

UKX 18.3. If the applicant is a child born in the UK to a UK Expansion Worker or their partner, the applicant must provide a full UK birth certificate showing the names of both parents.

Care requirement for a child of a UK Expansion Worker

UKX 19.1. If the applicant is aged under 18 on the date of application, there must be suitable arrangements for the child's care and accommodation in the UK, which must comply with relevant UK law.

Age requirement for a child of a UK Expansion Worker

UKX 20.1. The child must be under the age of 18 on the date of application, unless they were last granted permission as the child of their parent or parents.

UKX 20.2. If the child is aged 16 or over at the date of application, they must not be leading an independent life.

Financial requirement for a partner or child of a UK Expansion Worker

UKX 21.1. If the applicant is applying for permission to stay and has been living in the UK with permission for 12 months or longer on the date of application, they will meet the financial requirement and do not need to show funds.

UKX 21.2. If the applicant is applying for entry clearance, or is applying for permission to stay and has not been in the UK for 12 months on the date of application, funds of at least the amount required in UKX 21.3. must be held collectively by one or more of the following:

(a) the applicant; and

(b) the UK Expansion Worker (P); and

(c) if the applicant is applying as a child, their parent who is lawfully present in the UK or being granted entry clearance, or permission to stay, at the same time.

UKX 21.3. The required funds are:

(a) £285 for a partner in the UK or applying for entry clearance; and

(b) £315 for the first child in the UK or applying for entry clearance; and

(c) £200 for any other child in the UK or applying for entry clearance.

UKX 21.4. If UKX 23.2.(a) applies, the funds held must be held in addition to any funds required for the UK Expansion Worker to meet the financial requirement and the funds required for any dependants in the UK or applying at the same time.

UKX 21.5. If UKX 23.2.(a) applies, the funds must have been held for a 28-day period and as specified in Appendix Finance.

Decision for a partner or child of a UK Expansion Worker

UKX 22.1. If the decision maker is satisfied that all the suitability and eligibility requirements are met for a partner or child of a UK Expansion Worker the application will be granted, otherwise the application will be refused.

UKX 22.2. If the application is refused the person can apply for an Administrative Review under Appendix AR: Administrative Review.

Period and conditions of grant for a partner or child of a UK Expansion Worker

UKX 23.1. A partner will be granted permission which ends on the same date as the person (P) who is their partner and has permission as a UK Expansion Worker.

UKX 23.2. A child will be granted permission which ends on the same date as whichever of their parents' permission ends first.

UKX 23.3. The grant will be subject to all the following conditions:

(a) no access to public funds; and

(b) work (including self-employment and voluntary work) permitted; except for employment as a professional sportsperson (including as a sports coach); and

(c) study is permitted, subject to the ATAS condition in Appendix ATAS; and

(d) if Part 10 applies the applicant will be required to register with the police.]

Note: Appendix inserted from 09:00 on 11 April 2022 subject to savings for applications made before that time (HC 1118).

[Appendix Global Business Mobility – Service Supplier

The Global Business Mobility – Service Supplier route is for overseas workers who are undertaking temporary work assignments in the UK, where the worker is either a contractual service supplier employed by an overseas service provider or a self-employed independent professional based overseas, and they need to undertake an assignment in the UK to provide services covered by one of the UK's international trade agreements.

A dependent partner and dependent children can apply to come to the UK on this route.

The Global Business Mobility – Service Supplier route is not a route to settlement.

Validity requirements for a Global Business Mobility - Service Supplier ("Service Supplier")

SSU 1.1. A person applying for entry clearance or permission to stay as a Service Supplier must apply online on the gov.uk website on the specified form as follows:

(a) for applicants outside the UK, form "Global Business Mobility visa"; or

(b) for applicants inside the UK, form "Global Business Mobility".

SSU 1.2. An application for entry clearance or permission to stay as a Service Supplier must meet all the following requirements:

(a) any fee and Immigration Health Charge must have been paid; and

(b) the applicant must have provided any required biometrics; and

(c) the applicant must have provided a passport or other travel document which satisfactorily establishes their identity and nationality; and

(d) the applicant must have a Certificate of Sponsorship that was issued to them by their sponsor no more than 3 months before the date of application.

SSU 1.3. The applicant must be aged 18 or over on the date of application.

SSU 1.4. An applicant applying for entry clearance or permission to stay as a Service Supplier who has received an award from a Government or international scholarship agency in the 12 months before the date of application which covers both fees and living costs for study in the UK, must have provided written consent to the application from that Government or agency.

SSU 1.5. An applicant applying for permission to stay must be in the UK and must not have, or have last been granted, permission:

(a) as a Visitor; or

(b) as a Short-term Student; or

(c) as a Parent of a Child Student; or

(d) as a Seasonal Worker; or

(e) as a Domestic Worker in a Private Household; or

(f) outside the Immigration Rules.

SSU 1.6. An application which does not meet all the validity requirements for a Service Supplier on the Global Business Mobility route is invalid and may be rejected and not considered.

Suitability requirements for a Service Supplier

SSU 2.1. The applicant must not fall for refusal under Part 9: grounds for refusal.

SSU 2.2. If applying for permission to stay the applicant must not be:

(a) in breach of immigration laws, except that where paragraph 39E applies, that period of overstaying will be disregarded; or

(b) on immigration bail.

Eligibility requirements for a Service Supplier

Entry requirements for a Service Supplier

SSU 3.1. A person seeking to come to the UK as a Service Supplier must apply for and obtain entry clearance as a Service Supplier before their arrival in the UK.

SSU 3.2. A person applying for entry clearance as a Service Supplier must, if paragraph A39 and Appendix T of these rules apply, provide a valid medical certificate confirming that they have undergone screening for active pulmonary tuberculosis and that this tuberculosis is not present in them.

Points requirement for a Service Supplier

SSU 4.1. The applicant must be awarded 40 points from the table below:

Points requirement	Relevant rules	Points
Sponsorship	SSU 5.1. to SSU 5.7.	20
Job at an appropriate skill level (option A) or Job at an appropriate skill level (option B)	SSU 6.1. to SSU 6.6. SSU 7.1. to SSU 7.5.	20

SSU 4.2. An applicant as a Service Supplier can be awarded 20 points by meeting the requirements of either SSU 6.1. to SSU 6.6. or SSU 7.1. to SSU 7.5.

Points for Sponsorship for a Service Supplier

SSU 5.1. The applicant must have a valid certificate of sponsorship for the job they are planning to do, which must:

(a) confirm the applicant's name, that they are being sponsored as a Service Supplier, details of the job and salary the sponsor is offering them, and that their pay complies with the National Minimum Wage; and

(b) include a start date for the job, stated by the sponsor, which is no more than 3 months after the date of application; and

(c) not have been used in a previous application which was either granted or refused (but can have been used in a previous application which was rejected as invalid, made void or withdrawn); and

(d) not have been withdrawn by the sponsor or cancelled by the Home Office; and

(e) confirm that the applicant has worked as or for an overseas service provider for the period required at SSU 9.1.(b); and

(f) confirm whether the Academic Technology Approval Scheme (ATAS) requirement in Appendix ATAS applies; and

(g) confirm which of the sponsor's contracts registered with the Home Office the applicant will work on.

SSU 5.2. The sponsor must be authorised by the Home Office to sponsor a Service Supplier.

SSU 5.3. The sponsor must be listed as A-rated on the Home Office's register of licensed sponsors, unless the applicant was last granted permission as a Service Supplier and is applying to continue working for the same sponsor as in their last permission.

SSU 5.4. The sponsor must have a contract with an overseas service provider, where that contract:

(a) has been registered with the Home Office; and

(b) is for a service covered by one of the UK's international trade agreements; and

(c) is the contract on which the applicant will work as a Service Supplier.

SSU 5.5. The decision maker must not have reasonable grounds to believe the job the applicant is being sponsored to do:

(a) does not exist; or

(b) is a sham; or

(c) has been created mainly so the applicant can apply for entry clearance or permission to stay.

SSU 5.6. The decision maker must not have reasonable grounds to believe the job the applicant is being sponsored to do amounts to:

(a) the hire of the applicant to a third party who is not the sponsor to fill a position with that party, whether temporary or permanent; or

(b) contract work to undertake an ongoing routine role or to provide an ongoing routine service for a third party who is not the sponsor, regardless of the nature or length of any arrangement between the sponsor and the third party.

SSU 5.7. If the requirements in SSU 5.1. to SSU 5.6. are met, the applicant will be awarded 20 points for sponsorship.

Points for job at appropriate skill level for a Service Supplier – Option A

SSU 6.1. The applicant must be sponsored for a job in an occupation code listed in Appendix Skilled Occupations that is identified as eligible for the Global Business Mobility routes.

SSU 6.2. The sponsor must choose an appropriate occupation code, and the decision maker must not have reasonable grounds to believe the sponsor has chosen a less appropriate occupation code due to the most appropriate occupation code not being eligible under the Global Business Mobility routes.

SSU 6.3. To support the assessment in SSU 6.2., the decision maker may, in particular, consider:

(a) whether the sponsor has shown a genuine need for the job as described; and

(b) whether the applicant has the appropriate skills, qualifications and experience needed to do the job as described; and

(c) the sponsor's history of compliance with the immigration system including, but not limited to, paying its sponsored workers appropriately; and

(d) any additional information from the sponsor.

SSU 6.4. If the ATAS requirement in Appendix ATAS applies, the applicant must provide a valid ATAS certificate.

SSU 6.5. If the requirements in SSU 6.1. to SSU 6.4. are met, the applicant will be awarded 20 points for a job at the appropriate skill level, subject to SSU 6.6.

SSU 6.6. No points will be awarded for a job at the appropriate skill level if the applicant is not also being awarded 20 points for sponsorship under SSU 5.7.

Points for job at appropriate skill level for a Service Supplier – Option B

SSU 7.1. The applicant must have a university degree or equivalent level technical qualification unless they are employed by an overseas service provider supplying one of the following services, in which case the qualification requirements in the following table apply:

Services	Qualification
Fashion and modelling	None required
Chef de cuisine	An advanced technical qualification
Entertainment services (excluding audio-visual services under the CARIFORUM-UK Economic Partnership Agreement)	None required
Management consulting services and services related to management consulting (managers and senior consultants)	University degree (equivalent level technical qualification not permitted)
Advertising or translation	Relevant qualifications
Technical testing and analysis	University degree or a relevant technical qualification

SSU 7.2. The applicant must hold any professional qualifications or registrations required to provide the services under UK law or sectoral requirements.

SSU 7.3. The applicant must have professional experience in the sector in which they will supply services as follows:

(a) 3 years' experience; or

(b) if they are supplying chef de cuisine services under the CARIFORUM-UK Economic Partnership Agreement, 6 years' experience; or

(c) if they are a self-employed overseas service provider, 6 years' experience.

SSU 7.4. If the requirements in SSU 7.1. to SSU 7.3. are met, the applicant will be awarded 20 points for job at the appropriate skill level, subject to SSU 7.5.

SSU 7.5. No points will be awarded for a job at the appropriate skill level if the applicant is not also being awarded 20 points for sponsorship under SSU 5.7.

Nationality requirement for a Service Supplier

SSU 8.1. The applicant must be:

(a) a national of the country or territory in which the overseas service provider is based; or

(b) where the service that the applicant will provide is covered by a commitment in the General Agreement on Trade in Services and the applicant's employer is established in a country or territory that has made a notification under Article XXVIII(k)(ii)(2) of that agreement, a permanent resident of that country or territory; or

(c) where the service that the applicant will provide is covered by a commitment in the Temporary Agreement between the Swiss Confederation and the United Kingdom of Great Britain and Northern Ireland on Services Mobility, a permanent resident of Switzerland; or

(d) where the service that the applicant will provide is covered by a commitment in the United Kingdom-European Union Trade and Cooperation Agreement, a national of any Member State of the European Union or any other person included in the definition of "natural person of a Party" for the European Union in Article 512(k) of that agreement; or

(e) where the service that the applicant will provide is covered by a contractual service supplier commitment in the CARIFORUM-United Kingdom Economic Partnership Agreement, a national of any CARIFORUM State that has provisionally applied or brought into force that agreement.

Overseas work requirement for a Service Supplier

SSU 9.1. The applicant must:

(a) be currently working as or for an overseas service provider that will provide services to the sponsor; and

(b) have worked as or for the overseas service provider outside the UK for a cumulative period of 12 months.

SSU 9.2. In SSU 9.1. the 12 months' work outside the UK can have been accumulated over any period provided that:

(a) the applicant was either:

(i) continuously working for the overseas service provider at SSU 9.1., whether in or out of the UK, from the start of the 12 months to the date of application; or

(ii) if the applicant is a self-employed overseas service provider, continuously working in the same sector as the service they will provide to the sponsor, whether in or out of the UK, from the start of the 12 months to the date of application; and

(b) any breaks in the continuous work in SSU 9.2.(a) were only for the following reasons:

(i) statutory maternity, paternity, parental, or shared parental leave; or

(ii) statutory adoption leave; or

(iii) sick leave; or

(iv) assisting with a national or international humanitarian or environmental crisis, with the agreement of the overseas service provided; or

(v) taking part in legally organised industrial action.

Financial requirement for a Service Supplier

SSU 10.1. If the applicant is applying for permission to stay and has been living in the UK with permission for 12 months or longer on the date of application, they will meet the financial requirement and do not need to show funds.

SSU 10.2. If the applicant is applying for entry clearance or has been living in the UK for less than 12 months on the date of application either:

(a) the applicant must have funds of at least £1,270; or

(b) the applicant's A-rated sponsor must confirm on the Certificate of Sponsorship that they will, if it is necessary, maintain and accommodate the applicant up to the end of the first month of their employment up to a maximum amount of £1,270.

SSU 10.3. If SSU 10.2.(a) applies, the applicant must show that they have held the required level of funds for a 28-day period and as set out in Appendix Finance.

Maximum length of assignments requirement for a Service Supplier

SSU 11.1. The grant of permission must not lead to the applicant being granted cumulative periods of permission on the Global Business Mobility routes and Intra-Company routes totalling more than 5 years in any 6-year period.

SSU 11.2. When calculating the cumulative periods of permission referred to in SSU 11.1., the decision maker will include the following:

(a) all previous periods of permission on the Global Business Mobility routes; and

(b) all previous periods of permission on the Intra-Company routes; and

(c) if the applicant does not currently hold permission in the Global Business Mobility routes, any permission they could be granted under this application, beginning on the start date of the job stated on the Certificate of Sponsorship; and

(d) if the applicant is applying for permission to stay and has or last had permission on the Global Business Mobility routes, any permission they could be granted under this application, beginning on the date of decision; and

(e) any period of permission on the Global Business Mobility routes and the Intra-Company routes extended under section 3C of the Immigration Act 1971.

Decision for a Service Supplier

SSU 12.1. If the decision maker is satisfied that all the suitability and eligibility requirements for a Service Supplier are met the application will be granted, otherwise the application will be refused.

SSU 12.2. If the application is refused the person can apply for an Administrative Review under Appendix AR: Administrative Review.

Period and conditions of grant as a Service Supplier

SSU 13.1. The grant will be subject to all the following conditions:

(a) no access to public funds; and

(b) the only work permitted is:

(i) the job for which the applicant is being sponsored; and

(ii) voluntary work; and

(c) study is permitted, subject to the ATAS condition in Appendix ATAS; and

(d) if Part 10 applies, the applicant will be required to register with the police.

SSU 13.2. If the application is for entry clearance, permission will be granted for a period which is the shortest of the following:

(a) 14 days after the end date of the job detailed in the Certificate of Sponsorship; or

(b) the date at which the applicant will have had cumulative permission on the Global Business Mobility routes and Intra-Company routes totalling 5 years in any 6-year period; or

(c) the maximum single assignment period which is:

(i) if the applicant is covered by a relevant commitment in the United Kingdom-European Union Trade and Cooperation Agreement and is a national of any Member State of the European Union or any other person included in the definition of "natural person of a Party" for the European Union in Article 512(k) of that agreement, 12 months; or

(ii) if the applicant is a Swiss national or permanent resident covered by a relevant commitment in the Temporary Agreement between the Swiss Confederation and the United Kingdom of Great Britain and Northern Ireland on Services Mobility, 12 months; or

(iii) in all other cases, 6 months.

SSU 13.3. If the application is for permission to stay, the permission will be granted for a period which is the shortest of the following:

(a) 14 days after the end date of the job detailed in the Certificate of Sponsorship; or

(b) the date at which the applicant will have had cumulative permission on the Global Business Mobility routes and Intra-Company routes totalling 5 years in any 6-year period; or

(c) the maximum single assignment period which is:

(i) if the applicant is covered by a relevant commitment in the United Kingdom-European Union Trade and Cooperation Agreement and is a national of any Member State of the European Union or any other person included in the definition of "natural person of a Party" for the European Union in Article 512(k) of that agreement, the difference between the period the applicant has already spent in the UK since their last grant of permission as a Service Supplier and 12 months; or

(ii) if the applicant is a Swiss national or permanent resident covered by a relevant commitment in the Temporary Agreement between the Swiss Confederation and the United Kingdom of Great Britain and Northern Ireland on Services Mobility, the difference between the period the applicant has already spent in the UK since their last grant of permission as a Service Supplier and 12 months; or

(iii) in all other cases, the difference between the period the applicant has already spent in the UK since their last grant of permission as a Service Supplier and 6 months.

SSU 13.4. If the applicant does not currently hold permission on the Global Business Mobility routes, any permission granted for the period between the date of decision and the start date of the job detailed in the Certificate of Sponsorship will be excluded from the cumulative permission for the purpose of determining the period of grant of permission under SSU 13.2. and SSU 13.3. (but not from the cumulative period in SSU 11.2.).

Dependent Partner ("partner") and dependent child ("child") of a Service Supplier

Validity requirements for a partner or child of a Service Supplier

SSU 14.1. A person applying for entry clearance or permission to stay as a partner or child of a Service Supplier must apply online on the gov.uk website on the specified form as follows:

Applicant	Specified form
Applicants outside the UK	Dependant partner visa Dependant child visa
Applicants inside the UK	Dependant partner Dependant child

SSU 14.2. An application for entry clearance or permission to stay as a partner or child of a Service Supplier must meet all the following requirements:

(a) any fee and Immigration Health Charge must have been paid; and

(b) the applicant must have provided any required biometrics; and

(c) the applicant must have provided either a passport or other travel document which satisfactorily establishes their identity and nationality; and

(d) the applicant must be applying as partner or child of a person who:

(i) has made a valid application for entry clearance or permission to stay on the Global Business Mobility – Service Supplier route that has not been decided; or

(ii) has entry clearance or permission to stay on the Global Business Mobility – Service Supplier route.

SSU 14.3. A person applying as a partner must be aged 18 or over on the date of application.

SSU 14.4. A person applying for permission to stay as a partner or child of a Service Supplier must be in the UK on the date of application and must not have, or have last been granted, permission:

(a) as a Visitor; or
(b) as a Short-term Student; or
(c) as a Parent of a Child Student; or
(d) as a Seasonal Worker; or
(e) as a domestic worker in a private household; or
(f) outside the immigration rules.

SSU 14.5. An application which does not meet all the validity requirements for a partner or child of a Service Supplier is invalid and may be rejected and not considered.

Suitability requirements for a partner or child of a Service Supplier

SSU 15.1. The applicant must not fall for refusal under Part 9: grounds for refusal.

SSU 15.2. If applying for permission to stay the applicant must not be:

(a) in breach of immigration laws, except that where paragraph 39E applies, that period of overstaying will be disregarded; or

(b) on immigration bail.

Eligibility requirements for a dependent partner or dependent child of a Service Supplier

Entry requirement for a partner or child of a Service Supplier

SSU 16.1. A person seeking to come to the UK as a partner or child must apply for and obtain entry clearance as a partner or child of a Service Supplier before they arrive in the UK.

SSU 16.2. A person applying for entry clearance as the partner or child of a Service Supplier must, if paragraph A39 and Appendix T of these rules apply, provide a valid medical certificate confirming that they have undergone screening for active pulmonary tuberculosis and that this tuberculosis is not present in them.

Relationship requirement for a partner of a Service Supplier

SSU 17.1. The applicant must be the partner of a person (P) where one of the following applies:

(a) P has permission on the Global Business Mobility – Service Supplier route; or

(b) P is, at the same time, applying for (and is granted) entry clearance or permission on the Global Business Mobility – Service Supplier route.

SSU 17.2. If the applicant and their Service Supplier partner are not married or in a il partnership, all of the following requirements must be met:

(a) they must have been living together in a relationship similar to marriage or civil partnership for at least the two years before the date of application; and

(b) any previous relationship of the applicant or their Service Supplier partner with another person must have permanently broken down; and

(c) the applicant and their Service Supplier partner must not be so closely related that they would not be allowed to marry or form a civil partnership in the UK.

SSU 17.3. The relationship between the applicant and their Service Supplier partner must be genuine and subsisting.

SSU 17.4. The applicant and their Service Supplier partner must intend to live together throughout the applicant's stay in the UK.

Relationship requirement for a child of a Service Supplier

SSU 18.1. The applicant must be the child of a parent who has, or is at the same time being granted permission:

(a) on the Global Business Mobility – Service Supplier route; or

(b) as a partner on the Global Business Mobility – Service Supplier route.

SSU 18.2. The applicant's parents must each be either applying at the same time as the applicant or have permission to be in the UK (other than as a Visitor) unless:

(a) the parent applying for or with entry clearance or permission to stay as a Service Supplier or as the partner of a Service Supplier is the sole surviving parent; or

(b) the parent applying for or with entry clearance or permission to stay as a Service Supplier or as the partner of a Service Supplier has sole responsibility for the child's upbringing; or

(c) the parent who does not have permission as a Service Supplier:

(i) is a British citizen or a person who has a right to enter or stay in the UK without restriction; and

(ii) is or will be ordinarily resident in the UK; or

(d) the decision maker is satisfied that there are serious and compelling reasons to grant the child entry clearance or permission to stay with the parent who is applying for or has entry clearance or permission on the Global Business Mobility - Service Supplier route.

SSU 18.3. If the applicant is a child born in the UK to a Service Supplier or their partner, the applicant must provide a full UK birth certificate showing the names of both parents.

Care requirement for a child of a Service Supplier

SSU 19.1. If the applicant is aged under 18 on the date of application, there must be suitable arrangements for the child's care and accommodation in the UK, which must comply with relevant UK law.

Age requirement for a child of a Service Supplier

SSU 20.1. The child must be under the age of 18 on the date of application, unless they were last granted permission as the child of their parent or parents.

SSU 20.2. If the child is aged 16 or over at the date of application, they must not be leading an independent life.

Financial requirement for a partner or child of a Service Supplier

SSU 21.1. If the applicant is applying for permission to stay and has been living in the UK with permission for 12 months or longer on the date of application, they will meet the financial requirement and do not need to show funds.

SSU 21.2. If the applicant is applying for entry clearance, or is applying for permission to stay and has not been in the UK for 12 months on the date of application, either:

(a) funds of at least the amount required in SSU 21.3 must be held collectively by one or more of the following:

(i) the applicant; and

(ii) the Service Supplier (P); and

(iii) if the applicant is applying as a child, their parent who is lawfully present in the UK or being granted entry clearance, or permission to stay, at the same time as the applicant; or

(b) the sponsor of P must confirm on the Certificate of Sponsorship that they will, if necessary, maintain and accommodate the partner and/or any child as well as P, up to the end of the first month of each of their permission, up to at least the amounts in SSU 21.3.

SSU 21.3. The required funds are:

(a) £285 for a partner in the UK or applying for entry clearance; and

(b) £315 for the first child in the UK or applying for entry clearance; and

(c) £200 for any other child in the UK or applying for entry clearance.

SSU 21.4. If SSU 21.2.(a) applies, the funds held must be held in addition to any funds required for the Service Supplier to meet the financial requirement and the funds required for any dependants in the UK or applying at the same time.

SSU 21.5. If SSU 21.2.(a) applies, the funds must have been held for a 28-day period and as specified in Appendix Finance.

Decision for a partner or child of a Service Supplier

SSU 22.1. If the decision maker is satisfied that all the suitability and eligibility requirements are met for a partner or child of a Service Supplier the application will be granted, otherwise the application will be refused.

SSU 22.2. If the application is refused the person can apply for an Administrative Review under Appendix AR: Administrative Review.

Period and conditions of grant for a partner or child of a Service Supplier

[**SSU 23.1.**] A partner will be granted permission which ends on the same date as the person (P) who is their partner and has permission as a Service Supplier.

Note: Paragraph renumbered from 1 June 2022 subject to savings for applications made before that date (HC 17).

[**SSU 23.2.**] A child will be granted permission which ends on the same date as whichever of their parents' permission ends first.

Note: Paragraph renumbered from 1 June 2022 subject to savings for applications made before that date (HC 17).

[**SSU 23.3.**] The grant will be subject to all the following conditions:

(a) no access to public funds; and

(b) work (including self-employment and voluntary work) permitted; except for employment as a professional sportsperson (including as a sports coach); and

(c) study is permitted, subject to the ATAS condition in Appendix ATAS; and
(d) if Part 10 applies the applicant will be required to register with the police.]

Note: Paragraph renumbered from 1 June 2022 subject to savings for applications made before that date (HC 17).

Appendix inserted from 09:00 on 11 April 2022 subject to savings for applications made before that time (HC 1118).

[Appendix Global Business Mobility – Secondment Worker

The Global Business Mobility – Secondment Worker route is for overseas workers who are undertaking temporary work assignments in the UK, where the worker is being seconded to the UK as part of a high value contract or investment by their employer overseas.

A dependent partner and dependent children can apply to come to the UK on this route.

The Global Business Mobility – Secondment Worker route is not a route to settlement.

Validity requirements for a Global Business Mobility - Secondment Worker ("Secondment Worker")

SEC 1.1. A person applying for entry clearance or permission to stay as a Secondment Worker must apply online on the gov.uk website on the specified form as follows:
(a) for applicants outside the UK, form "Global Business Mobility visa"; or
(b) for applicants inside the UK, form "Global Business Mobility".

SEC 1.2. An application for entry clearance or permission to stay as a Secondment Worker must meet all the following requirements:
(a) any fee and Immigration Health Charge must have been paid; and
(b) the applicant must have provided any required biometrics; and
(c) the applicant must have provided a passport or other travel document which satisfactorily establishes their identity and nationality; and
(d) the applicant must have a Certificate of Sponsorship that was issued to them by their sponsor no more than 3 months before the date of application.

SEC 1.3. The applicant must be aged 18 or over on the date of application.

SEC 1.4. An applicant applying for entry clearance or permission to stay as a Secondment Worker who has received an award from a Government or international scholarship agency in the 12 months before the date of application which covers both fees and living costs for study in the UK, must have provided written consent to the application from that Government or agency.

SEC 1.5. An applicant applying for permission to stay must be in the UK and must not have, or have last been granted, permission:
(a) as a Visitor; or
(b) as a Short-term Student; or
(c) as a Parent of a Child Student; or
(d) as a Seasonal Worker; or
(e) as a Domestic Worker in a Private Household; or
(f) outside the Immigration Rules.

SEC 1.6. An application which does not meet all the validity requirements for a Secondment Worker is invalid and may be rejected and not considered.

Suitability requirements for a Secondment Worker

SEC 2.1. The applicant must not fall for refusal under Part 9: grounds for refusal.

SEC 2.2. If applying for permission to stay the applicant must not be:

(a) in breach of immigration laws, except that where paragraph 39E applies, that period of overstaying will be disregarded; or

(b) on immigration bail.

Eligibility requirements for a Secondment Worker

Entry requirements for a Secondment Worker

SEC 3.1. A person seeking to come to the UK as a Secondment Worker must apply for and obtain entry clearance as a Secondment Worker before their arrival in the UK.

SEC 3.2. A person applying for entry clearance as a Secondment Worker must, if paragraph A39 and Appendix T of these rules apply, provide a valid medical certificate confirming that they have undergone screening for active pulmonary tuberculosis and that this tuberculosis is not present in them.

Points requirement for a Secondment Worker

SEC 4.1. The applicant must be awarded 40 points based on the table below:

Points requirements	Relevant rules	Points
Sponsorship	SEC 5.1. to SEC 5.7.	20
Job at appropriate skill level	SEC 6.1. to SEC 6.6.	20

Points for Sponsorship for a Secondment Worker

SEC 5.1. The applicant must have a valid Certificate of Sponsorship for the job they are planning to do, which to be valid must:

(a) confirm the applicant's name, that they are being sponsored as a Secondment Worker, details of the job and salary the sponsor is offering them, and that their pay complies with the National Minimum Wage; and

(b) include a start date for the job, stated by the sponsor, which must be no more than 3 months after the date of application; and

(c) not have been used in a previous application which was either granted or refused (but can have been used in a previous application which was rejected as invalid, made void or withdrawn); and

(d) not have been withdrawn by the sponsor or cancelled by the Home Office; and

(e) confirm that the applicant has worked outside the UK for the overseas business for the period required at SEC 7.2.(b); and

(f) confirm whether or not the Academic Technology Approval Scheme (ATAS) requirement in Appendix ATAS applies; and

(g) confirm on which of the sponsor's contracts registered with the Home Office the applicant will work.

SEC 5.2. The sponsor must be authorised by the Home Office to sponsor a Secondment Worker.

SEC 5.3. The sponsor must be listed as A-rated on the Home Office's register of licensed sponsors, unless the applicant was last granted permission as a Secondment Worker and is applying to continue working for the same sponsor as in their last permission.

SEC 5.4. The sponsor must have a contract with an overseas business, where that contract has been registered with the Home Office, and on which an applicant as a Secondment Worker will work.

SEC 5.5. The decision maker must not have reasonable grounds to believe the job the applicant is being sponsored to do:

(a) does not exist; or

(b) is a sham; or

(c) has been created mainly so the applicant can apply for entry clearance or permission to stay.

SEC 5.6. The decision maker must not have reasonable grounds to believe the job the applicant is being sponsored to do amounts to:

(a) the hire of the applicant to a third party who is not the sponsor to fill a position with that party, whether temporary or permanent; or

(b) contract work to undertake an ongoing routine role or to provide an ongoing routine service for a third party who is not the sponsor, regardless of the nature or length of any arrangement between the sponsor and the third party.

SEC 5.7. If the requirements in SEC 5.1. to SEC 5.6. are met, the applicant will be awarded 20 points for sponsorship.

Points for job at appropriate skill level for a Secondment Worker

SEC 6.1. The applicant must be sponsored for a job in an occupation code listed in Appendix Skilled Occupations that is identified as eligible for the Global Business Mobility routes.

SEC 6.2. The sponsor must choose an appropriate occupation code, and the decision maker must not have reasonable grounds to believe the sponsor has chosen a less appropriate occupation code due to the most appropriate occupation code not being eligible under the Global Business Mobility routes.

SEC 6.3. To support the assessment in SEC 6.2, the decision maker may, in particular, consider:

(a) whether the sponsor has shown a genuine need for the job as described; and

(b) whether the applicant has the appropriate skills, qualifications and experience needed to do the job as described; and

(c) the sponsor's history of compliance with the immigration system including, but not limited to, paying its sponsored workers appropriately; and

(d) any additional information from the sponsor.

SEC 6.4. If the ATAS requirement in Appendix ATAS applies, the applicant must provide a valid ATAS certificate.

SEC 6.5. If the requirements in SEC 6.1. to SEC 6.4. are met, the applicant will be awarded 20 points for a job at the appropriate skill level, subject to SEC 6.6.

SEC 6.6. No points will be awarded for a job at the appropriate skill level if the applicant is not also being awarded 20 points for sponsorship under SEC 5.7.

Overseas Work requirement for a Secondment Worker

SEC 7.1 The applicant must meet the overseas work requirement at SEC 7.2. unless the applicant:

(a) is applying for permission to stay; and

(b) has, or last had, permission as a Secondment Worker; and

(c) is applying to continue working for the same sponsor as in their last permission.

SEC 7.2 The overseas requirement will be met where the applicant:

(a) is currently working for an overseas business that has a contract with the sponsor that has been registered with the Home Office by the sponsor; and

(b) has worked outside the UK for that overseas business for a cumulative period of at least 12 months.

SEC 7.3. In SEC 7.2.(b) the 12 months' work outside the UK can have been accumulated over any period provided that:

(a) the applicant was continuously working for the overseas businesses in SEC 7.2.(a), whether in or out of the UK, from the start of the 12 months to the date of application; and

(b) any breaks in the continuous work in SEC 7.3.(a) were only for the following reasons:

(i) statutory maternity, paternity, parental, or shared parental leave; or

(ii) statutory adoption leave; or

(iii) sick leave; or

(iv) assisting with a national or international humanitarian or environmental crisis, with the agreement of the sponsor group; or

(v) taking part in legally organised industrial action.

Financial requirement for a Secondment Worker

SEC 8.1. If the applicant is applying for permission to stay and has been living in the UK with permission for 12 months or longer on the date of application, they will meet the financial requirement and do not need to show funds.

SEC 8.2. If the applicant is applying for entry clearance or has been living in the UK for less than 12 months on the date of application either:

(a) the applicant must have funds of at least £1,270; or

(b) the applicant's A-rated sponsor must confirm on the Certificate of Sponsorship that they will, if it is necessary, maintain and accommodate the applicant up to the end of the first month of their employment up to a maximum amount of £1,270.

SEC 8.3. If SEC 8.2.(a) applies, the applicant must show that they have held the required level of funds for a 28-day period and as set out in Appendix Finance.

Maximum length of assignments requirement for a Secondment Worker

SEC 9.1. The grant of permission must not lead to the applicant being granted cumulative periods of permission on the Global Business Mobility routes and the Intra-Company routes totalling more than 5 years in any 6-year period.

SEC 9.2. When calculating the cumulative periods of permission referred to in SEC 9.1. and SEC 11.2.(d), the decision maker will include the following:

(a) all previous periods of permission on the Global Business Mobility routes; and

(b) all previous periods of permission on the Intra-Company routes; and

(c) if the applicant does not currently hold permission on a Global Business Mobility route, any permission they could be granted under this application, beginning on the start date of the job stated on the Certificate of Sponsorship; and

(d) if the applicant is applying for permission to stay and has or last had permission on the Global Business Mobility routes, any permission they could be granted under this application, beginning on the date of decision; and

(e) any period of permission on the Global Business Mobility routes and the Intra-Company routes extended under section 3C of the Immigration Act 1971.

Decision for a Secondment Worker

SEC 10.1. If the decision maker is satisfied that all the suitability and eligibility requirements for a Secondment Worker on the Global Business Mobility route are met the application will be granted, otherwise the application will be refused.

SEC 10.2. If the application is refused the person can apply for an Administrative Review under Appendix AR: Administrative Review.

Period and conditions of grant as a Secondment Worker

SEC 11.1. The grant will be subject to all the following conditions:

(a) no access to public funds; and

(b) the only work permitted is:

(i) the job for which the applicant is being sponsored; and

(ii) voluntary work; and

(iii) working out a contractual notice period, where the applicant was lawfully working in that job in the UK on the date of application; and (c) study is permitted, subject to the ATAS condition in Appendix ATAS; and

(d) if Part 10 applies, the applicant will be required to register with the police.

SEC 11.2. Permission will be granted for a period which is the shortest of the following:

(a) 1 year after the start date of the job detailed in the Certificate of Sponsorship; or

(b) 14 days after the end date of the job detailed in the Certificate of Sponsorship; or

(c) the date at which the applicant will have had a continuous permission as a Secondment Worker totalling 2 years.

(d) the date at which the applicant will have had cumulative permission on the Global Business Mobility routes and Intra-Company routes totalling 5 years in any 6-year period.

SEC 11.3. If the applicant does not currently hold permission on the Global Business Mobility routes, any permission granted for the period between the date of decision and the start date of the job detailed in the Certificate of Sponsorship will be excluded from the cumulative permission for the purpose of determining the period of grant of permission under SEC 11.2. (but not from the cumulative period in SEC 9.2.).

Dependant Partner ("partner") and dependent child ("child") of a Secondment Worker

Validity requirements for a partner or child of a Secondment Worker

SEC 12.1. A person applying for entry clearance or permission to stay as a partner or child of a Secondment Worker must apply online on the gov.uk website on the specified form as follows:

Applicant	Specified form
Applicants outside the UK	Dependant partner visa Dependant child visa
Applicants inside the UK	Dependant partner Dependant child

SEC 12.2. An application for entry clearance or permission to stay as a partner or child of a Secondment Worker must meet all the following requirements:

(a) any fee and Immigration Health Charge must have been paid; and

(b) the applicant must have provided any required biometrics; and

(c) the applicant must have provided either a passport or other travel document which satisfactorily establishes their identity and nationality; and

(d) the applicant must be applying as partner or child of a person who:

(i) has made a valid application for entry clearance or permission to stay on the Global Business Mobility – Secondment Worker route that has not been decided; or

(ii) has entry clearance or permission to stay on the Global Business Mobility – Secondment Worker route.

SEC 12.3. A person applying as a partner must be aged 18 or over on the date of application.

SEC 12.4. A person applying for permission to stay as a partner or child of a Secondment Worker must be in the UK on the date of application and must not have, or have last been granted, permission:

(a) as a Visitor; or

(b) as a Short-term Student; or

(c) as a Parent of a Child Student; or

(d) as a Seasonal Worker; or

(e) as a Domestic Worker in a Private Household; or

(f) outside the immigration rules.

SEC 12.5. An application which does not meet all the validity requirements for a partner or child of a Secondment Worker is invalid and may be rejected and not considered.

Suitability requirements for a partner or child of a Secondment Worker

SEC 13.1. The applicant must not fall for refusal under Part 9: grounds for refusal.

SEC 13.2. If applying for permission to stay the applicant must not be:

(a) in breach of immigration laws, except that where paragraph 39E applies, that period of overstaying will be disregarded; or

(b) on immigration bail.

Eligibility requirements for a partner or child of a Secondment Worker

Entry requirement for a partner or child of a Secondment Worker

SEC 14.1. A person seeking to come to the UK as a partner or child must apply for and obtain entry clearance as a partner or child of a Secondment Worker before they arrive in the UK.

SEC 14.2. A person applying for entry clearance as the partner or child of a Secondment Worker must, if paragraph A39 and Appendix T of these rules apply, provide a valid medical certificate confirming that they have undergone screening for active pulmonary tuberculosis and that this tuberculosis is not present in them.

Relationship requirement for a partner of a Secondment Worker

SEC 15.1. The applicant must be the partner of a person (P) where one of the following applies:

(a) P has permission on the Global Business Mobility – Secondment Worker route; or

(b) P is, at the same time, applying for (and is granted) entry clearance or permission on the Global Business Mobility – Secondment Worker route.

SEC 15.2. If the applicant and their Secondment Worker partner are not married or in a civil partnership, all of the following requirements must be met:

(a) they must have been living together in a relationship similar to marriage or civil partnership for at least the two years before the date of application; and

(b) any previous relationship of the applicant or their Secondment Worker partner with another person must have permanently broken down; and

(c) the applicant and their Secondment Worker partner must not be so closely related that they would not be allowed to marry or form a civil partnership in the UK.

SEC 15.3. The relationship between the applicant and their Secondment Worker partner must be genuine and subsisting.

SEC 15.4. The applicant and their Secondment Worker partner must intend to live together throughout the applicant's stay in the UK.

Relationship requirement for a child of a Secondment Worker

SEC 16.1. The applicant must be the child of a parent who has, or is at the same time being granted permission:

(a) on the Global Business Mobility – Secondment Worker route; or

(b) as a partner on the Global Business Mobility – Secondment Worker route.

SEC 16.2. The applicant's parents must each be either applying at the same time as the applicant or have permission to be in the UK (other than as a Visitor) unless:

(a) the parent applying for or with entry clearance or permission to stay as a Secondment Worker or as the partner of a Secondment Worker is the sole surviving parent; or

(b) the parent applying for or with entry clearance or permission to stay as a Secondment Worker or as the partner of a Secondment Worker has sole responsibility for the child's upbringing; or

(c) the parent who does not have permission as a Secondment Worker:

(i) is a British citizen or a person who has a right to enter or stay in the UK without restriction; and

(ii) is or will be ordinarily resident in the UK; or

(d) the decision maker is satisfied that there are serious and compelling reasons to grant the child entry clearance or permission to stay with the parent who is applying for or has entry clearance or permission on the Global Business Mobility - Secondment Worker route.

SEC 16.3. If the applicant is a child born in the UK to a Secondment Worker or their partner, the applicant must provide a full UK birth certificate showing the names of both parents.

Care requirement for a child of a Secondment Worker

SEC 17.1. If the applicant is aged under 18 on the date of application, there must be suitable arrangements for the child's care and accommodation in the UK, which must comply with relevant UK law.

Age requirement for a child of a Secondment Worker

SEC 18.1. The child must be under the age of 18 on the date of application, unless they were last granted permission as the child of their parent or parents.

SEC 18.2. If the child is aged 16 or over at the date of application, they must not be leading an independent life.

Financial requirement for a partner or child of a Secondment Worker

SEC 19.1. If the applicant is applying for permission to stay and has been living in the UK with permission for 12 months or longer on the date of application, they will meet the financial requirement and do not need to show funds.

SEC 19.2. If the applicant is applying for entry clearance, or is applying for permission to stay and has not been in the UK for 12 months on the date of application, either:

(a) funds of at least the amount required in SEC 19.3 must be held collectively by one or more of the following:

(i) the applicant; and

(ii) the Secondment Worker (P); and

(iii) if the applicant is applying as a child, their parent who is lawfully present in the UK or being granted entry clearance, or permission to stay, at the same time; or

(b) the sponsor of P must confirm on the Certificate of Sponsorship that they will, if necessary, maintain and accommodate the partner and/or any child as well as P, up to the end of the first month of each of their permission, up to at least the amounts in SEC 19.3.

SEC 19.3. The required funds are:

(a) £285 for a partner in the UK or applying for entry clearance; and

(b) £315 for the first child in the UK or applying for entry clearance; and

(c) £200 for any other child in the UK or applying for entry clearance.

SEC 19.4. If SEC 19.2.(a) applies, the funds held must be held in addition to any funds required for the Secondment Worker to meet the financial requirement and the funds required for any dependants in the UK or applying at the same time.

SEC 19.5. If SEC 19.2.(a) applies, the funds must have been held for a 28-day period and as specified in Appendix Finance.

Decision for a partner and child of a Secondment Worker

SEC 20.1. If the decision maker is satisfied that all the suitability and eligibility requirements are met for a partner or child of a Secondment Worker the application will be granted, otherwise the application will be refused.

SEC 20.2. If the application is refused the person can apply for an Administrative Review under Appendix AR: Administrative Review.

Period and conditions of grant for a partner or child of a Secondment Worker

SEC 21.1. A partner will be granted permission which ends on the same date as the person (P) who is their partner and has permission as a Secondment Worker.

SEC 21.2. A child will be granted permission which ends on the same date as whichever of their parents' permission ends first.

SEC 21.3. The grant will be subject to all the following conditions:

(a) no access to public funds; and

(b) work (including self-employment and voluntary work) permitted; except for employment as a professional sportsperson (including as a sports coach); and

(c) study is permitted, subject to the ATAS condition in Appendix ATAS; and

(d) if Part 10 of these rules applies the applicant will be required to register with the police.]

Note: Appendix inserted from 09:00 on 11 April 2022 subject to savings for applications made before that time (HC 1118).

[Appendix T2 Minister of Religion

Note: Appendix inserted from 09:00 on 1 December 2020 subject to savings for applications made before that time (HC813). Amendments from 6 October 2021 subject to savings for applications made before that date (HC 617). Amendments from 09:00 on 11 October 2021 subject to savings for applications made before that time (HC 617). Amendments from 23:00 on 31 December 2020 for decisions made on or after that time (CP 361). Appendix substituted from 6 April 2022 subject to savings for applications made before that date (HC 1118).

This route is for a person who has a key leading role within their faith-based organisation or a religious order in the UK.

A dependent partner and dependent children of a T2 Minister of Religion can apply on this route.

T2 Minister of Religion is a route to settlement.

Validity requirements for a T2 Minister of Religion

MOR 1.1. A person applying for entry clearance or permission to stay as a T2 Minister of Religion must apply online on the gov.uk website on the specified form as follows:

(a) for applicants outside the UK, form "Tier 2 (Minister of Religion) visa"; or

(b) for applicants inside the UK, form "Tier 2 (Minister of Religion) leave to remain".

MOR 1.2. An application for entry clearance or permission to stay as a T2 Minister of Religion must meet all the following requirements:

(a) any fee and Immigration Health Charge must have been paid; and

(b) the applicant must have provided any required biometrics; and

(c) the applicant must have provided a passport or other travel document which satisfactorily establishes their identity and nationality; and

(d) the applicant must have a Certificate of Sponsorship that was issued to them by their sponsor no more than 3 months before the date of application.

MOR 1.3. The applicant must be aged 18 or over on the date of application.

MOR 1.4. If the applicant has, in the last 12 months before the date of application, received an award from a Government or international scholarship agency covering both fees and living costs for study in the UK, they must provide written consent to the application from that Government or agency.

MOR 1.5. A person applying for permission to stay must be in the UK on the date of application and must not have, or have last been granted, permission:

(a) as a Visitor; or
(b) as a Short-term Student; or
(c) as a Parent of a Child Student; or
(d) as a Seasonal Worker; or
(e) as a Domestic Worker in a Private Household; or
(f) outside the Immigration Rules.

MOR 1.6. An application which does not meet all the validity requirements for a T2 Minister of Religion is invalid and may be rejected and not considered.

Suitability requirements for a T2 Minister of Religion

MOR 2.1. The applicant must not fall for refusal under Part 9: grounds for refusal.

MOR 2.2. If applying for permission to stay the applicant must not be:

(a) in breach of immigration laws, except that where paragraph 39E applies, that period of overstaying will be disregarded; or
(b) on immigration bail.

Eligibility requirements for a T2 Minister of Religion

Entry requirements for a T2 Minister of Religion

MOR 3.1. A person seeking to come to the UK as a T2 Minister of Religion must apply for and obtain entry clearance as a T2 Minister of Religion before their arrival in the UK.

MOR 3.2. A person applying for entry clearance as a T2 Minister of Religion must, if paragraph A39 and Appendix T of these rules apply, provide a valid medical certificate confirming that they have undergone screening for active pulmonary tuberculosis and that this tuberculosis is not present in them.

Points requirements for a T2 Minister of Religion

MOR 4.1. An applicant must be awarded 70 points from the table below.

Points requirements (all mandatory)	Points
Certificate of Sponsorship	50
Financial requirement	10
English language skills at level B2 (intermediate)	10

Sponsorship requirements for a T2 Minister of Religion

MOR 5.1. The applicant must have a valid Certificate of Sponsorship for the job they are planning to do, which to be valid, must:

(a) confirm the applicant's name, that they are being sponsored as a T2 Minister of Religion and details of the job and salary the sponsor is offering them, as well as any other remuneration; and

(b) include a start date, stated by the sponsor, which must be no more than three months after the date of application; and

(c) not have been used in a previous application which was either granted or refused (but can have been used in a previous application which was rejected as invalid, made void or withdrawn); and

(d) not have been withdrawn by the sponsor or cancelled by the Home Office; and

(e) confirm that the applicant is qualified to do the job of a T2 Minister of Religion; and

(f) confirm that the applicant is a member of the sponsor's religious order (if the sponsor's organisation is a religious order); and

(g) confirm that the applicant will perform religious duties within the sponsor's organisation or directed by the sponsor's organisation in the UK (which may include preaching, pastoral and non-pastoral work); and

(h) confirm that the applicant's role will not involve mainly non-pastoral duties, such as school teaching, media production, domestic work or administrative and clerical work, unless the role is a senior position within the sponsor's organisation; and

(i) confirm that the applicant will receive pay and conditions at least equal to those given to settled workers in the same role and compliant with, or exempt from, the national minimum wage.

MOR 5.2. The sponsor must be authorised by the Home Office to sponsor the job in question under the T2 Minister of Religion route.

MOR 5.3. The sponsor must be listed as A-rated on the Home Office's register of licensed sponsors, unless the applicant was last granted permission as a T2 Minister of Religion and is applying to continue working for the same sponsor as in their last permission.

Genuineness requirement for a T2 Minister of Religion

MOR 6.1. The applicant must:

(a) genuinely intend, and be able, to undertake the role for which they are being sponsored; and

(b) not intend to undertake employment other than in the role for which they are being sponsored, or as otherwise permitted at MOR 10.3.

Financial requirement for a T2 Minister of Religion

MOR 7.1. If the applicant is applying for permission to stay and has been living in the UK with permission for 12 months or longer on the date of application, they will meet the financial requirement and do not need to show funds.

MOR 7.2. If the applicant is applying for entry clearance, or is applying for permission to stay and has been living in the UK for less than 12 months on the date of application, either:

(a) the applicant must have funds of at least £1,270; or

(b) the applicant's A-rated sponsor must confirm on the Certificate of Sponsorship that they will, if it is necessary, maintain and accommodate the applicant up to the end of the first month of their employment for an amount of at least £1,270.

MOR 7.3. If MOR 7.2.(a) applies, the applicant must have held the required level of funds for a 28-day period and must show funds as specified in Appendix Finance.

English language requirement for a T2 Minister of Religion

MOR 8.1. Unless an exemption applies, the applicant must show English language ability on the Common European Framework of Reference for Languages in all 4 components (reading, writing, speaking and listening) of at least level B2.

MOR 8.2. The applicant must show they meet the English language requirement as specified in Appendix English Language.

Decision on an application as a T2 Minister of Religion

MOR 9.1. If the decision maker is satisfied all the suitability and eligibility requirements for a T2 Minister of Religion are met the application will be granted, otherwise the application will be refused.

MOR 9.2. If the application is refused the person can apply for an Administrative Review under Appendix AR: Administrative Review.

Period and conditions of grant as a T2 Minister of Religion

MOR 10.1. If the applicant is applying for entry clearance, permission will be granted for whichever is the shorter of:

(a) up to 14 days after the period of employment stated on their Certificate of Sponsorship; or

(b) 3 years and 1 month.

MOR 10.2. If the applicant is applying for permission to stay, it will be granted for whichever is the shorter of:

(a) up to 14 days after the period of employment stated on their Certificate of Sponsorship; or

(b) 3 years; or

(c) the difference between 6 years and the period they have already been granted permission as a T2 Minister of Religion, International Sportsperson, or Skilled Worker (or any combination of these routes).

MOR 10.3. The grant will be subject to all the following conditions:

(a) no access to public funds; and

(b) the only work permitted is:

(i) work in the job the applicant is being sponsored for; and

(ii) supplementary employment, provided the applicant is still doing the job they were sponsored for; and

(iii) voluntary work; and

(iv) working out a contractual notice for a job the person was lawfully working in on the date of application; and

(c) study is permitted, subject to the ATAS condition in Appendix ATAS; and

(d) if Part 10 applies the applicant will be required to register with the police.

Settlement as a T2 Minister of Religion

Validity requirements for settlement as a T2 Minister of Religion

MOR 11.1. A person who is applying for settlement as a T2 Minister of Religion must apply online on the gov.uk website on the specified form "Settle in the UK in various immigration categories: form SET(O)".

MOR 11.2. An application for settlement must meet all the following requirements:
(a) any fee must have been paid; and
(b) the applicant must have provided any required biometrics; and
(c) the applicant must have provided a passport or other travel document which satisfactorily establishes their identity and nationality; and
(d) the applicant must be in the UK on the date of application.

MOR 11.3. The applicant must have, or have last been granted, permission as a T2 Minister of Religion.

MOR 11.4. An application which does not meet all the validity requirements for settlement for a T2 Minister of Religion is invalid and may be rejected and not considered.

Suitability requirements for settlement as a T2 Minister of Religion

MOR 12.1. The applicant must not fall for refusal under Part 9: grounds for refusal.

MOR 12.2. The applicant must not be:
(a) in breach of immigration laws, except that where paragraph 39E applies, that period of overstaying will be disregarded; or
(b) on immigration bail.

Eligibility requirements for settlement as a T2 Minister of Religion

Sponsorship requirement for settlement as a T2 Minister of Religion

MOR 13.1. The sponsor in the applicant's most recent permission must still be approved by the Home Office to sponsor a T2 Minister of Religion.

MOR 13.2. The sponsor must confirm that they still require the applicant to work for them for the foreseeable future, and that the applicant is paid, and will be paid for the foreseeable future, the appropriate salary under MOR 5.1.(i).

Qualifying period requirement for settlement as a T2 Minister of Religion

MOR 14.1. The applicant must have spent a continuous period of 5 years in the UK, and that period must consist of time with permission on any (or a combination) of the following routes:
(a) T2 Minister of Religion; or
(b) International Sportsperson; or
(c) Skilled Worker; or
(d) Tier 1 Migrant, other than as a Tier 1 (Graduate Entrepreneur); or
(e) Representative of an Overseas Business; or
(f) Innovator; or
[(g) Global Talent; or]
[(h) Scale-up]

Note: Sub-paragraph (g) substituted, (h) inserted from 22 August 2022 subject to savings for applications made before that date (HC 1118).

Continuous residence requirement for settlement as a T2 Minister of Religion

MOR 15.1. The applicant must meet the continuous residence requirement as specified in Appendix Continuous residence for the period in MOR 14.1.

Knowledge of Life in the UK requirement for settlement as a T2 Minister of Religion

MOR 16.1. Unless an exemption applies, the applicant must meet the Knowledge of Life in the UK requirement as specified in Appendix KOL UK.

Decision on an application for settlement as a T2 Minister of Religion

MOR 17.1. If the decision maker is satisfied all the suitability and eligibility requirements for settlement as a T2 Minister of Religion are met the applicant will be granted settlement, otherwise the application will be refused.

MOR 17.2. If the application is refused the person can apply for an Administrative Review under Appendix AR: Administrative Review.

Dependants of a T2 Minister of Religion

Validity requirements for a dependent partner ("partner") or dependent child ("child") of a T2 Minister of Religion

MOR 18.1. A person applying for entry clearance or permission to stay as a partner or child of a T2 Minister of Religion must apply online on the gov.uk website on the specified form as follows:

Location of partner or child	Specified form
Outside the UK	Dependant partner visa Dependant child visa
Inside the UK	If applying at the same time as the T2 Minister of Religion, they can be included in the Tier 2 (Minister of Religion) leave to remain form. If applying separately from the T2 Minister of Religion: • Dependant partner • Dependant child

MOR 18.2. An application for entry clearance or permission to stay as a partner or child of a T2 Minister of Religion must meet all the following requirements:

(a) any fee and Immigration Health Charge must have been paid; and

(b) the applicant must have provided any required biometrics; and

(c) the applicant must have provided a passport or other travel document which satisfactorily establishes their identity and nationality: and

(d) the applicant must be applying as partner or child of a person (P) who:

(i) has made a valid application for entry clearance or permission to stay on the T2 Minister of Religion route that has not been decided; or

(ii) has permission on the T2 Minister of Religion route; or

(iii) is settled or has become a British citizen, providing that P had permission on the T2 Minister of Religion route when they settled and the applicant either had permission as their partner or child at that time, or the applicant is applying as a child of P and the applicant was born in the UK before P settled.

MOR 18.3. An applicant applying as a partner must be aged 18 or over on the date of application.

MOR 18.4. An applicant who is applying for permission to stay as a partner or child of a T2 Minister of Religion must be in the UK on the date of application and must not have, or have last been granted, permission:

(a) as a Visitor; or

(b) as a Short-term Student; or

(c) as a Parent of a Child Student; or

(d) as a Seasonal Worker; or

(e) as a Domestic Worker in a Private Household: or

(f) outside the Immigration Rules.

MOR 18.5. An application which does not meet all the validity requirements for a partner or child of a T2 Minister of Religion is invalid and may be rejected and not considered.

Suitability requirements for a partner or child of a T2 Minister of Religion

MOR 19.1. The applicant must not fall for refusal under Part 9: grounds for refusal.

MOR 19.2. If applying for permission to stay the applicant must not be:

(a) in breach of immigration laws, except that where paragraph 39E applies, that period of overstaying will be disregarded; or

(b) on immigration bail.

Eligibility requirements for partner or child of a T2 Minister of Religion

Entry requirement for a partner or child of a T2 Minister of Religion

MOR 20.1. A person seeking to come to the UK as a partner or child of a T2 Minister of Religion must apply for and obtain an entry clearance as a partner or child of a T2 Minister of Religion before they arrive in the UK.

MOR 20.2. A person applying for entry clearance as a partner or child of a T2 Minister of Religion must, if paragraph A39 and Appendix T of these rules apply, provide a valid medical certificate confirming that they have undergone screening for active pulmonary tuberculosis and that this tuberculosis is not present in them.

Relationship requirement for a partner of a T2 Minister or Religion

MOR 21.1. The applicant must be the partner of a person (P) where one of the following applies:

(a) P has permission as a T2 Minister of Religion; or

(b) P is, at the same time, applying for (and is granted) entry clearance or permission as a T2 Minister of Religion; or

(c) P is settled or has become a British citizen, providing P had permission as a T2 Minister of Religion when they settled, and the applicant had permission as P's partner at that time.

MOR 21.2. If the applicant and their T2 Minister of Religion partner are not married or in a civil partnership, all of the following requirements must be met:

(a) they must have been living together in a relationship similar to marriage or civil partnership for at least two years before the date of application; and

(b) any previous relationship of the applicant or their T2 Minister of Religion partner with another person must have permanently broken down; and

(c) the applicant and their T2 Minister of Religion partner must not be so closely related that they would not be allowed to marry or form a civil partnership in the UK.

MOR 21.3. The relationship between the applicant and their T2 Minister of Religion partner must be genuine and subsisting.

MOR 21.4. The applicant and their T2 Minister of Religion partner must intend to live together throughout the applicant's stay in the UK.

Relationship requirement for a child of a T2 Minister of Religion

MOR 22.1. The applicant must be the child of a parent (P) where one of the following applies:

(a) P has permission on the T2 Minister of Religion route; or

(b) P is, at the same time, applying for (and is granted) entry clearance or permission on the T2 Minister of Religion route;

(c) P is settled or has become a British citizen, providing P had permission on the T2 Minister of Religion route when they settled, and the applicant had permission as P's child at that time.

MOR 22.2. The applicant's parents must each be either applying at the same time as the applicant or have permission to be in the UK (other than as a visitor) unless:

(a) the parent applying for or with entry clearance or permission to stay as a T2 Minister of Religion is the sole surviving parent; or

(b) the parent applying for or with entry clearance or permission to stay as a T2 Minister of Religion has sole responsibility for the child's upbringing; or

(c) the parent who does not have permission as a Minister of Religion –

(i) is a British citizen or a person who has a right to enter or stay in the UK without restriction; and

(ii) is or will be ordinarily resident in the UK; or

(d) the decision maker is satisfied that there are serious and compelling reasons to grant the child entry clearance or permission to stay with the parent who is applying for or has entry clearance or permission to stay on the T2 Minister of Religion route.

MOR 22.3. If the applicant is a child born in the UK to a T2 Minister of Religion or their partner, the applicant must provide a full UK birth certificate showing the names of both parents.

Age requirement for a child of a T2 Minister of Religion

MOR 23.1. The applicant must be under the age of 18 on the date of application, unless they were last granted permission as the dependent child of their parent or parents.

MOR 23.2. If the applicant is aged 16 or over on the date of application, they must not be leading an independent life.

Care requirement for a child of a T2 Minister of Religion

MOR 24.1. If the applicant is aged under 18 on the date of application, there must be suitable arrangements for the applicant's care and accommodation in the UK, which must comply with relevant UK laws.

Financial requirement for a partner or child of a T2 Minister of Religion

MOR 25.1. If the applicant is applying for permission to stay and has been living in the UK with permission for 12 months or longer on the date of application, they will meet the financial requirement and do not need to show funds.

MOR 25.2. If the applicant is applying for entry clearance, or has been in the UK for less than 12 months on the date of application, either:

(a) funds of at least the amount required in MOR 25.3. must be held collectively by one or more of the following:

(i) the applicant; and

(ii) the T2 Minister of Religion; and

(iii) if the applicant is applying as a dependent child, their parent who is lawfully present in the UK or being granted entry clearance, or permission to stay, at the same time; or

(b) the T2 Minister of Religion's A-rated sponsor must certify that they will, if necessary, maintain and accommodate the partner and/or any dependent child as well as the T2 Minister of Religion, up to the end of the first month of each of their grants of permission, to at least the amounts required in MOR 25.3.

MOR 25.3. The funds required are:

(a) £285 for a partner in the UK, or applying for entry clearance; and

(b) £315 for the first dependent child in the UK, or applying for entry clearance; and

(c) £200 for any other dependent child in the UK, or applying for entry clearance.

MOR 25.4. If MOR 25.2(a) applies, the funds held for the applicant must be held in addition to any funds required for the T2 Minister of Religion to meet the financial requirement and any other dependents in the UK or applying at the same time.

MOR 25.5. If MOR 25.2.(a) applies, the funds must have been held for a 28-day period and as specified in Appendix Finance.

Decision on an application as a partner or child of a T2 Minister of Religion

MOR 26.1. If the decision maker is satisfied that all the suitability and eligibility requirements for a partner or child of a T2 Minister of Religion are met, the application will be granted, otherwise the application will be refused.

MOR 26.2. If the application is refused, the person can apply for an Administrative Review under Appendix AR: Administrative Review.

Period and conditions of grant for a partner or child of a T2 Minister of Religion

MOR 27.1. A partner will be granted:

(a) permission which ends on the same date as their partner's permission as a T2 Minister of Religion; or

(b) 3 years' permission if the T2 Minister of Religion was (or is being) granted settlement as a T2 Minister of Religion.

MOR 27.2. A child will be granted permission which ends on the same date as whichever of their parents' permission ends first, unless both parents have (or are being granted) settlement or British citizenship, in which case the child will be granted permission for 3 years.

MOR 27.3. The grant will be subject to all the following conditions:

(a) no access to public funds; and

(b) work (including self-employment and voluntary work) is permitted; except as a professional sportsperson (including as a sports coach); and

(c) study is permitted, subject to the ATAS condition in Appendix ATAS if the applicant is over the age of 18; and

(d) if Part 10 of these rules applies the applicant will be required to register with the police.

Settlement as a partner or child of a T2 Minister of Religion

Validity requirements for settlement as a partner or child of a T2 Minister of Religion

MOR 28.1. A person applying for settlement as a partner or child of a T2 Minister of Religion must apply online on the gov.uk website on the specified form "Settle in the UK in various immigration categories: form SET(O)".

MOR 28.2. An application for settlement as a partner or child of a T2 Minister of Religion must meet all the following requirements:

(a) any fee must have been paid; and

(b) the applicant must have provided any required biometrics; and

(c) the applicant must have provided a passport or other travel document which satisfactorily establishes their identity and nationality; and (d) the applicant must be in the UK on the date of application; and

(e) the applicant must be applying as a partner or child of a person (P) who:

(i) has made a valid application for settlement in the UK on the T2 Minister of Religion route and that application has not been decided; or

(ii) is settled or has become a British citizen, provided that P had permission on the T2 Minister of Religion route when they settled and the applicant either had permission as their partner or child at that time, or the applicant is applying as a child of P and the applicant was born in the UK before P settled.

MOR 28.3. An application which does not meet all the validity requirements for a partner or child of a T2 Minister of Religion is invalid and may be rejected and not considered.

Suitability requirements for settlement as a partner or child of a T2 Minister of Religion

MOR 29.1. The applicant must not fall for refusal under Part 9: grounds for refusal.

MOR 29.2. The applicant must not be:

(a) in breach of immigration laws, except that where paragraph 39E applies, that period of overstaying will be disregarded; or

(b) on immigration bail.

Eligibility requirements for settlement as a partner or child of a T2 Minister of Religion

Relationship requirement for settlement as a partner or child of a T2 Minister of Religion

MOR 30.1. The applicant must be the partner or child of a person (P) where one of the following applies:

(a) P is, at the same time, being granted settlement as a T2 Minister of Religion; or

(b) P is settled or has become a British citizen, providing P had permission as a T2 Minister of Religion when they settled and the applicant either:

(i) had permission as P's partner or child at that time; or

(ii) is applying as a child of P and was born in the UK before P settled.

MOR 30.2. If applying as a partner, the applicant and the person (P) in MOR 30.1. must meet the relationship requirement in MOR 21.2. to MOR 21.4. and must have met those requirements throughout the 5 years ending on the date of application.

MOR 30.3. If applying as a child, the applicant's other parent (who is not the person (P) in MOR 30.1.) must be being granted settlement at the same time, or be settled or a British citizen, unless:

(a) P in MOR 30.1. is the applicant's sole surviving parent; or

(b) P in MOR 30.1. has sole responsibility for the applicant's upbringing; or

(c) the decision maker is satisfied that there are serious and compelling reasons to grant the applicant settlement.

Age requirement for settlement as a child of a T2 Minister of Religion

MOR 31.1. The applicant must be under the age of 18 on the date of application, unless they were last granted permission as the dependent child of their parent or parents.

MOR 31.2. If the applicant is aged 16 or over on the date of application, they must not be leading an independent life.

Care requirement for settlement as a child of a T2 Minister of Religion

MOR 32.1. If the applicant is under the age of 18 on the date of application there must be suitable arrangements for the child's care and accommodation in the UK, which must comply with relevant UK laws.

Qualifying period requirement for settlement as a partner of a T2 Minister of Religion

MOR 33.1. The applicant must have spent a continuous period of 5 years in the UK with permission as a dependent partner of the person (P) in MOR 30.1.

Continuous residence requirement for settlement as a partner of a T2 Minister of Religion

MOR 34.1. The applicant must meet the continuous residence requirement as set out in Appendix Continuous Residence during the period in MOR 33.1.

English language requirement for settlement as a partner or child of a T2 Minister of Religion

MOR 35.1. Unless an exemption applies, the applicant must show English language ability on the Common European Framework of Reference for Languages in speaking and listening to at least level B1.

MOR 35.2. The applicant must show they meet the English language requirement as specified in Appendix English Language.

Knowledge of life in the UK requirement for settlement as a partner or child of a T2 Minister of Religion

MOR 36.1. Unless an exemption applies, the applicant must meet the Knowledge of Life in the UK requirement as set out in Appendix KOL UK.

Decision on an application for settlement as a partner or child of a T2 Minister of Religion

MOR 37.1. If the decision maker is satisfied all the suitability and eligibility requirements are met for settlement as a partner or child of a T2 Minister of Religion, the application will be granted, otherwise the application will be refused.

MOR 37.2. If the application is refused the person can apply for an Administrative Review under Appendix AR: Administrative Review.]

[Appendix T2 Sportsperson – DELETED]

Note: Appendix inserted from 09:00 on 1 December 2020 subject to savings for applications made before that time (HC813). Amendments from 23:00 on 31 December 2020 for decisions made on or after that time (CP 361). Appendix deleted from 09:00 on 11 October 2021 subject to savings for applications made before that time, (HC 617).

[Appendix Representative of an Overseas Business

[A person applying as a Representative of an Overseas Business must either be a Media Representative or applying for an extension or settlement as a Sole Representative.
A Media Representative is an employee of an overseas media organisation posted to the United Kingdom on a long-term assignment.
A Sole Representative is a senior employee of an overseas business who is assigned to the United Kingdom for the purpose of establishing a branch or subsidiary.
A dependent partner and dependent children can apply under this route.
Representative of an Overseas Business is a route to settlement.
Sole Representatives can no longer apply for an initial period of permission in the Representative of an Overseas Business route.
Overseas businesses wishing to establish a UK branch or subsidiary may be able to send workers on the Global Business Mobility - UK Expansion Worker route.]

Note: Introduction substituted from 09:00 on 11 April 2022 subject to savings for applications made before that time (HC 1118).

Validity requirements for a Representative of an Overseas Business

ROB 1.1. A person applying for entry clearance or permission to stay as a Representative of an Overseas Business must apply online on gov.uk on the specified form as follows:

(a) for entry clearance, form 'Other work' on the 'Find and apply for other visas from outside the UK' form; or

(b) for permission to stay, form 'Application to extend stay in the UK: FLR(IR)'.

ROB 1.2. An application for entry clearance or permission to stay as the Representative of an Overseas Business must meet all the following requirements:

(a) any fee and Immigration Health Charge must have been paid; and

(b) the applicant must have provided any required biometrics; and

(c) the applicant must have provided a passport or other travel document which satisfactorily establishes their identity and nationality.

ROB 1.3. The applicant must be [...]aged 18 or over on the date of application.

Note: Word deleted from 6 October 2021 subject to savings for applications made before that date (HC 617).

ROB 1.4. If the applicant has, in the last 12 months before the date of application, received an award from a Government or international scholarship agency covering both fees and living costs for study in the UK, they must provide written consent to the application from that Government or agency.

ROB 1.5. An applicant who is applying for permission to stay must be in the UK on the date of application and must not have, or have last been granted, permission:

(a) as a Visitor; or
(b) as a Short-term Student; or
(c) as a Parent of a Child Student; or
(d) as a Seasonal Worker; or
(e) as a Domestic Worker in a Private Household; or
(f) outside the Immigration Rules.

ROB 1.6. An application which does not meet all the validity requirements for a Representative of an Overseas Business is invalid and may be rejected and not considered.

Suitability requirements for a Representative of an Overseas Business

ROB 2.1. The applicant must not fall for refusal Part 9: grounds for refusal.

ROB 2.2. If applying for permission to stay the applicant must not be:

(a) in breach of immigration laws, except that where paragraph 39E applies, that period of overstaying will be disregarded; or
(b) on immigration bail.

Eligibility requirements for Representative of an Overseas Business

Entry requirement for Representative of an Overseas Business

ROB 3.1. A person seeking to come to the UK as a Representative of an Overseas Business must have applied for and obtained entry clearance as a Representative of an Overseas Business before their arrival in the UK.

ROB 3.2. A person applying for entry clearance as a Representative of an Overseas Business must, if paragraph A39 and Appendix T of these rules apply, provide a valid medical certificate confirming that they have undergone screening for active pulmonary tuberculosis and that this tuberculosis is not present in them.

Work requirement for Representative of an Overseas Business

ROB 4.1. The overseas business or media organisation that the applicant represents must be active and trading outside the UK, with its headquarters and principle place of business remaining outside the UK.

ROB 4.2. The applicant must have been recruited and taken on as an employee outside the UK by the business they will represent.

ROB 4.3. The applicant must intend to work full-time as the representative of the overseas business or media organisation and must not intend to undertake work for any other business or engage in business of their own.

ROB 4.4. An applicant must be either:

[(a) a Sole Representative who already has, or was last granted, permission as a Sole Representative and is a senior employee of an overseas business, who is assigned to the UK to establish and supervise a branch or subsidiary of an overseas business, where that branch or subsidiary will actively trade in the same type of business as the overseas business; or]

(b) a Media Representative who is posted on a long-term assignment to the UK on behalf of a newspaper, news agency or broadcasting organisation.

Note: Sub-paragraph (a) substituted from 09:00 on 11 April 2022 subject to savings for applications made before that time (HC 1118).

Genuineness requirement for the Representative of an Overseas Business

ROB 5.1. The decision maker must be satisfied that the applicant is a genuine Representative of an Overseas Business.

ROB 5.2. The decision maker must not have reasonable grounds to believe the business is being established in the UK by the overseas business, or the applicant has been appointed as a representative of the overseas business or media organisation, mainly so the applicant can apply for entry clearance or permission to stay.

English language requirement for a Representative of an Overseas Business

ROB 6.1. The applicant must show English language ability on the Common European Framework of Reference for Languages in speaking and listening of at least level A1.

ROB 6.2. The applicant must show they meet the English language requirement as specified in Appendix English Language.

Financial requirement for a Representative of an Overseas Business

ROB 7.1. The decision maker must be satisfied that the applicant can, and will, adequately maintain and accommodate themselves, and any dependants in the UK, without [access] to public funds.

Note: Word substituted from 6 April 2021 subject to savings for applications made before that date (HC 1248).

ROB 7.2. Funds must be shown as specified in Appendix Finance.

Additional business requirements for a Sole Representative on the Representative of an Overseas Business route

ROB 8.1. Where the applicant is applying as a Sole Representative on the Representative of an Overseas Business route, the applicant must meet the additional business requirements set out in ROB 8.2. to ROB 8.6.

ROB 8.2. The applicant must be a senior employee of the overseas business with the skills, experience and knowledge of the business necessary to undertake the role, with full authority to negotiate and take operational decisions on behalf of the overseas business.

ROB 8.3. The applicant must not have a majority stake in, or otherwise own or control a majority of the overseas business they represent, whether that ownership or control is by means of a shareholding, partnership agreement, sole proprietorship or any other arrangement.

ROB 8.4. [DELETED]

Note: Paragraph deleted from 09:00 on 11 April 2022 subject to savings for applications made before that time (HC 1118).

ROB 8.5. [DELETED]

Note: Paragraph deleted from 09:00 on 11 April 2022 subject to savings for applications made before that time (HC 1118).

[**ROB 8.6.** The applicant must meet all the following requirements:

(a) the applicant must have established the registered branch or wholly-owned subsidiary of the overseas business for which they were last granted permission under this route; and

(b) the applicant must be engaged in full time employment and must supervise the registered branch or wholly-owned subsidiary which they have established, and must be required by their employer to continue in that role; and

(c) the applicant must provide all of the following:

(i) evidence of business that has been generated, principally with firms in the UK, on behalf of their employer since their last grant of permission, in the form of accounts, copies of invoices or letters from businesses with whom the applicant has done business, including the value of transactions; and

(ii) a Companies House certificate of registration as a UK establishment (for a branch), or a certificate of incorporation (for a subsidiary), together with either a copy of the share register or a letter from the overseas business's accountant confirming that the UK business is wholly owned by the overseas business; and

(iii) a letter from the applicant's employer confirming that the applicant supervises the UK branch or subsidiary and is required to continue in that employment; and

(iv) evidence of salary paid by the employer in the 12 months immediately before the date of application and details of the remuneration package the employee receives.]

Note: Paragraph substituted from 09:00 on 11 April 2022 subject to savings for applications made before that time (HC 1118).

Additional business requirements for a Media Representative on the Representative of an Overseas Business route

ROB 9.1. Where the applicant is applying as a Media Representative on the Representative of Overseas Business route, the applicant must meet the additional business requirements in ROB 9.2. and ROB 9.3.

ROB 9.2. The applicant must be an employee of an overseas newspaper, news agency or broadcasting organisation undertaking a long-term assignment as a representative of their overseas employer.

ROB 9.3. Where the applicant is applying for permission to stay and has, or was last granted, permission as a Media Representative, the applicant must meet all the following:

(a) the applicant must be engaged in full time employment for which their last period of permission was granted and be required by their employer to continue in that role; and

(b) the applicant must provide the following:

(i) a letter from the applicant's employer confirming that the applicant is required to continue in their employment; and

(ii) evidence of the applicant's salary paid in the 12 months immediately before the date of application and details of the remuneration package the employee receives.

Decision on application as Representative of an Overseas Business

ROB 10.1. If the decision maker is satisfied that all the suitability and relevant eligibility requirements are met as a Representative of an Overseas Business the application will be granted, otherwise the application will be refused.

ROB 10.2. If the application is refused, a person can apply for an Administrative Review under Appendix AR: Administrative Review.

Period and conditions of grant.

[**ROB 11.1.** If the applicant is applying for entry clearance as a Media Representative under the Representative of an Overseas Business route or is applying for permission to stay as a Media Representative and does not have, or did not last have, permission on the Representative of an Overseas Business route they will be granted permission for a period not exceeding 3 years.]

Note: Paragraph substituted from 09:00 on 11 April 2022 subject to savings for applications made before that time (HC 1118).

ROB 11.2. If the applicant has or last had, permission under the Representative of an Overseas Business route, they will be granted permission for a period not exceeding 2 years.

ROB 11.3. The grant will be subject to all the following conditions:

(a) no access to public funds; and

(b) no work permitted other than working for the overseas business which the applicant represents; and

(c) study is permitted, subject to the ATAS condition in Appendix ATAS; and

(d) if Part 10 applies the applicant will be required to register with the police.

Settlement as a Representative of an Overseas Business Route

Validity requirements for Settlement by a Representative of an Overseas Business

ROB 12.1. A person applying for settlement as a Representative of an Overseas Business must apply online on the gov.uk website on the specified form, 'Settle in the UK in various immigration categories: form SET(O)'.

ROB 12.2. An application for settlement as a Representative of an Overseas Business must meet all the following requirements:

(a) any fee must have been paid; and

(b) the applicant must have provided any required biometrics; and

(c) the applicant must have provided a valid passport or other travel document which satisfactorily establishes their identity and nationality.

ROB 12.3. The applicant must be in the UK and have, or have last been granted, permission as a Representative of an Overseas Business.

ROB 12.4. An application which does not meet the validity requirements for settlement as a Representative of an Overseas Business is invalid and may be rejected and not considered.

Suitability requirements for settlement by a Representative of an Overseas Business

ROB 13.1. The applicant must not fall for refusal under Part 9: grounds for refusal.

ROB 13.2. The applicant must not be:

(a) in breach of immigration laws, except that where paragraph 39E applies, that period of overstaying will be disregarded; or

(b) on immigration bail.

Eligibility requirements for settlement by a Representative of an Overseas Business

Qualifying period requirement for settlement by a Representative of an Overseas Business

ROB 14.1. The applicant must have spent the last 5 years before the date of application in the UK with permission as a Representative of an Overseas Business.

Continuous residence requirement for settlement by a Representative of an Overseas Business

ROB 15.1. The applicant must meet the continuous resident requirement in Appendix Continuous Residence during the period in ROB 14.1.

Work requirement for settlement by a Representative of an Overseas Business

[**ROB 16.1.** Throughout the period in ROB 14.1:

(a) the overseas business or media organisation that the applicant represents must have been active and trading with its headquarters and principle place of business remaining outside the UK; and

(b) the applicant must have been employed and working full-time for the overseas business or media organisation they represent, or for that business's UK branch or subsidiary, and

(c) the applicant must not have undertaken work for any other business or engaged in business of their own.]

Note: Paragraph substituted from 6 October 2021 subject to savings for applications made before that date (HC 617).

[**ROB 16.2.** The applicant must provide:

(a) evidence of salary paid by their employer in the 12 months immediately before the date of application and details of the renumeration package the employee receives; and

(b) a letter from their employer confirming that they still require the applicant to work for them, and that the applicant will be required for the foreseeable future.]

Note: Paragraph inserted from 6 October 2021 subject to savings for applications made before that date (HC 617).

[**ROB 16.3.** The applicant must be required by their employer to continue in the role for which their last period of permission was granted.]

Note: Paragraph inserted from 6 October 2021 subject to savings for applications made before that date (HC 617).

[Additional business requirements for settlement by a Sole Representative on the Representative of an Overseas Business route]

[**ROB 16A.1.** Where the applicant has, or was last granted permission as a Sole Representative, the applicant must meet the additional business requirements set out in ROB 16A.2. and ROB 16A.3.]

Note: Heading and paragraph inserted from 6 October 2021 subject to savings for applications made before that date (HC 617).

[**ROB 16A.2.** Throughout the period in ROB 14.1, the applicant must have met the following requirements:

(a) they must not have had a majority stake in, or otherwise owned or controlled a majority of the overseas business they represent, whether that ownership or control was by means of a shareholding, partnership agreement, sole proprietorship or any other arrangement; and

(b) the applicant must have established and then supervised the registered a branch or wholly owned subsidiary of the overseas business they represent in the UK, where that branch or subsidiary was actively trading in the same type of business as the overseas business.]

Note: Paragraph inserted from 6 October 2021 subject to savings for applications made before that date (HC 617).

[**ROB 16A.3.** The applicant must provide all of the following:

(a) evidence of business that has been generated, principally with firms in the UK, on behalf of their employer since their last grant of permission, in the form of accounts, copies of invoices or letters from businesses with whom the applicant has done business, including the value of transactions; and

(b) either a copy of the share register or a letter from the overseas business's accountant confirming that the UK business is wholly owned by the overseas business; and

(c) a letter from the applicant's employer confirming that the applicant has supervised the UK branch or subsidiary since the last grant of permission.]

Note: Paragraph inserted from 6 October 2021 subject to savings for applications made before that date (HC 617).

[Additional business requirements for settlement by a Media Representative on the Representative of an Overseas Business route]

[**ROB 16B.1.** Where the applicant has, or was last granted, permission as a Media Representative, the applicant must meet the additional business requirements set out in ROB 16B.2.]

Note: Heading and paragraph inserted from 6 October 2021 subject to savings for applications made before that date (HC 617).

[**ROB 16B.2.** Throughout the period in ROB 14.1, the applicant must have met the following requirements:

(a) they must have been an employee of an overseas newspaper, news agency or broadcasting organisation undertaking a long-term assignment as a representative of their overseas employer; and

(b) the applicant must have been engaged in the employment for which their last period of permission was granted.]

Note: Paragraph inserted from 6 October 2021 subject to savings for applications made before that date (HC 617).

English language requirement for settlement by a Representative of an Overseas Business

ROB 17.1. Unless an exemption applies, the applicant must show English language ability on the Common European Framework of Reference for Languages in speaking and listening to at least level B1.

ROB 17.2. The applicant must show they meet the English language requirement as specified in Appendix English Language.

Knowledge of [...]life in the UK requirement for settlement by a Representative of an Overseas Business

Note: Words deleted from 6 April 2021 subject to savings for applications made before that date (HC 1248).

ROB 18.1. The applicant must meet the Knowledge of Life in the UK requirement as specified in Appendix KOL UK.

Decision on an application for settlement as a Representative of an Overseas Business Route

ROB 19.1. If the decision maker is satisfied all the suitability and relevant eligibility requirements are met for settlement by a Representative of an Overseas Business, the applicant will be granted settlement, otherwise the application will be refused.

ROB 19.2. If the application is refused, a person can apply for an Administrative Review under Appendix AR: Administrative Review.

Dependants of Representatives of Overseas Businesses

Validity requirements for a dependent partner or dependent child of a Representative of an Overseas Business

ROB.20.1. A person applying for entry clearance or permission to stay as a partner or child on the Representative of an Overseas Business route must apply online on the gov.uk website on the specified form as follows:

(a) for entry clearance, 'Join or accompany a family member' on the 'Find and apply for other visas from outside the UK' form; or

(b) for permission to stay, 'Application to extend stay in the UK: FLR(IR)'.

[**ROB 20.2.** An application for entry clearance or permission to stay as a partner or child of a Representative of an Overseas Business must meet all the following requirements:

(a) any fee and Immigration Health Charge must have been paid; and

(b) the applicant must have provided any required biometrics; and

(c) the applicant must have provided a passport or other travel document which satisfactorily establishes their identity and nationality; and

(d) the applicant must be applying as partner or child of a person who:

(i) has made a valid application for entry clearance or permission to stay on the Representative of an Overseas Business route that has not been decided; or

(ii) has entry clearance or permission on the Representative of an Overseas Business route; or

(iii) is settled or has become a British citizen, providing that person (P) had permission on the Representative of an Overseas Business route when they settled and the applicant either had permission as their partner or child at that time, or the applicant is applying as a child of P and the applicant was born in the UK before P settled.]

Note: Paragraph substituted from 6 April 2022 subject to savings for applications made before that date (HC 1118).

ROB 20.3. A person applying as a dependent partner must be aged 18 or over on the date of application.

ROB 20.4. A person applying for permission to stay must be in the UK on the date of application and must not have, or have last been granted, permission:

(a) as a Visitor; or

(b) as a Short-term student; or

(c) as a Parent of a Child Student; or

(d) as a Seasonal worker; or

(e) as a Domestic worker in a private household: or

(f) outside the Immigration Rules.

ROB 20.5. An application which does not meet all the validity requirements for a partner or child on the Representative of an Overseas Business route is invalid and may be rejected and not considered.

Suitability requirements for a partner or child on the Representative of an Overseas Business route

ROB 21.1. The applicant must not fall for refusal under Part 9: grounds for refusal.

ROB 21.2. If applying for permission to stay the applicant must not be:

(a) in breach of immigration laws, except that where paragraph 39E applies, that period of overstaying will be disregarded; or

(b) on immigration bail.

Eligibility requirements for a partner or child on the Representative of an Overseas Business route

Entry requirement for a partner or child on the Representative of an Overseas Business route

ROB 22.1. A person seeking to come to the UK as a partner or child must apply for and obtain an entry clearance as a partner or child before they arrive in the UK.

ROB 22.2. A person applying for entry clearance as a partner of child on the Representative of an Overseas Business route must, if paragraph A39 and Appendix T of these rules apply, provide a valid medical certificate confirming that they have undergone screening for active pulmonary tuberculosis and that this tuberculosis is not present in them.

Relationship requirements for a partner of a Representative of an Overseas Business route

ROB 23.1. The applicant must be the partner of a person (P) and one of the following must apply:

(a) P has permission on the Representative of an Overseas Business route; or

(b) P is, at the same time, applying for (and is granted) permission on the Representative of an Overseas Business route; or

(c) P is settled or has become a British citizen, providing they had permission on a Representative of an Overseas Business route when they settled and the applicant had permission as their partner at that time.

ROB 23.2. If the applicant and the Representative of an Overseas Business are not married or in a civil partnership, all of the following requirements must be met:

(a) they must have been living together in a relationship similar to marriage or civil partnership for at least the two years before the date of application; and

(b) any previous relationship of the applicant or the Representative of an Overseas Business with another person must have permanently broken down; and

(c) the applicant and the Representative of an Overseas Business must not be so closely related that they would not be allowed to marry or form a civil partnership in the UK.

ROB 23.3. The relationship between the applicant and the Representative of an Overseas Business must be genuine and subsisting.

ROB 23.4. The applicant and the Representative of an Overseas Business must intend to live together throughout the applicant's stay in the UK.

Relationship requirement for a dependent child on the Representative of an Overseas Business route

ROB 24.1. The applicant must be the child of a person (P) and one of the following must apply:

(a) P has permission on the Representative of an Overseas Business route; or

(b) P is, at the same time, applying for (and is granted) permission on the Representative of an Overseas Business route; or

(c) P is settled or has become a British citizen, providing P previously had permission on the Representative of an Overseas Business route and the applicant had permission as P's child at that time.

[**ROB 24.2.** The applicant's parents must each be either applying at the same time as the applicant or have permission to be in the UK (other than as a Visitor) unless:

(a) the parent applying for or with entry clearance or permission to stay on the Representative of an Overseas Business route is the sole surviving parent; or

(b) the parent applying for or with entry clearance or permission to stay on the Representative of an Overseas Business route has sole responsibility for the child's upbringing; or

(c) the parent who does not have permission on the Representative of an Overseas Business route –

(i) is a British citizen or a person who has a right to enter or stay in the UK without restriction; and

(ii) is or will be ordinarily resident in the UK; or

(d) the decision maker is satisfied that there are serious and compelling reasons to grant the child entry clearance or permission to stay with the parent who is applying for or has entry clearance or permission on the Representative of an Overseas Business route.]

Note: Paragraph substituted from 6 October 2021 subject to savings for applications made before that date (HC 617).

Care requirement for a dependent child on the Representative of an Overseas Business route

ROB 25.1. If the child is under the age of 18 on the date of application, there must be suitable arrangements for the child's care and accommodation in the UK, which must comply with relevant UK legislation and regulations.

Age requirement for a dependent child on the Representative of an Overseas Business route

ROB 26.1. The child must be under the age of 18 on the date of application, unless they were last granted permission as the dependent child of their parent or parents.

ROB 26.2. If the child is aged 16 or over on the date of application, they must not be leading an independent life.

Financial requirement for a partner or child on the Representative of an Overseas Business route

ROB 27.1. The decision maker must be satisfied that the applicant or the Representative of an Overseas Business can and will adequately maintain and accommodate the applicant, and any other dependants in the UK, or applying for entry clearance, without [access] to public funds.

Note: Word substituted from 6 April 2021 subject to savings for applications made before that date (HC 1248).

ROB 27.2. Funds must be shown as specified in Appendix Finance.

Overseas business requirement for a partner or child on the Representative of an Overseas Business route

ROB 28.1. If the person (P) in ROB 23.1. is a Sole Representative, the applicant must not have a majority stake in, or otherwise own or control a majority of the overseas business P represents, whether that ownership or control is by means of a shareholding, partnership agreement, sole proprietorship or any other arrangement.

Decision on application for a dependent partner and dependent child on the Representative of an Overseas Business route

ROB 29.1. If the decision maker is satisfied that all the suitability and eligibility requirements are met for a dependent partner or dependent child on the Representative of an Overseas Business route the application will be granted, otherwise the application will be refused.

ROB 29.2. If the application is refused the person can apply for an Administrative Review under Appendix AR: Administrative Review.

Period and conditions of grant for a dependent partner and dependent child on the Representative of an Overseas Business route

ROB 30.1. A partner will be granted:

(a) permission which ends on the same date as the permission as the Representative of an Overseas Business; or

(b) 2 years' permission if the Representative of an Overseas Business was (or is being) granted settlement as a Representative of an Overseas Business.

ROB 30.2. A dependent child will be granted permission which ends on the same date as whichever of their parents' permission ends first, unless both parents have (or are being granted) settlement or British Citizenship, in which case the child will be granted permission for 30 months.

ROB 30.3. The grant will be subject to all the following conditions:

(a) no access to public funds; and

(b) work (including self-employment and voluntary work) permitted; except for employment as a professional sportsperson (including as a sports coach); and

(c) study is permitted, subject to the ATAS condition in Appendix ATAS; and

(d) if Part 10 applies the applicant will be required to register with the police.

Settlement by dependent partner and dependent child on the Representative of an Overseas Business route

Validity requirements for settlement by a dependent partner or dependent child on the Representative of an Overseas Business route

ROB 31.1. [DELETED]

Note: Paragraph deleted from 6 October 2021 subject to savings for applications made before that date (HC 617).

[**ROB 31.2.** An application for settlement as a partner or child of a Representative of an Overseas Business must meet all the following requirements:

(a) any fee must have been paid; and

(b) the applicant must have provided any required biometrics; and

(c) the applicant must have provided either a passport or other travel document which satisfactorily establishes their identity and nationality; and

(d) the applicant must be in the UK; and

(e) the applicant must be applying as a partner or child of a person (P) who:

(i) has made a valid application for settlement in the UK as a Representative of an Overseas Business and that application has not been decided; or

(ii) is settled or has become a British citizen, providing P had permission as a Representative of an Overseas Business when they settled and the applicant either had permission as their partner or child at that time or the applicant is applying as a child of P and the applicant was born in the UK before P settled.]

Note: Paragraph substituted from 6 April 2022 subject to savings for applications made before that date (HC 1118).

ROB 31.3. The applicant must have, or have last been granted, permission as a partner or child on the Representative of an Overseas Business route.

ROB 31.4. An application which does not meet all the validity requirements for settlement as a partner or child on the Representative of an Overseas Business route is invalid and may be rejected and not considered.

Suitability Requirements for settlement by a dependent partner and dependent child on the Representative of an Overseas Business route

ROB 32.1. The applicant must not fall for refusal under Part 9: grounds for refusal.

ROB 32.2. The applicant must not be:

(a) in breach of immigration laws, except that where paragraph 39E applies, that period of overstaying will be disregarded; or

(b) on immigration bail.

Eligibility requirements for settlement by a dependent partner or dependent child on the Representative of an Overseas Business route

Relationship requirement for settlement by a partner or child on the Representative of an Overseas Business route

[**ROB 33.1.** The applicant must be the partner or child of a person (P) where one of the following applies:

(a) P is, at the same time, being granted settlement as a Representative of an Overseas Business; or

(b) P is settled in the UK or has become a British citizen, providing P had permission as a Representative of an Overseas Business when they settled and the applicant either:

(i) had permission as P's partner or child at that time; or

(ii) is applying as a child of P, and was born in the UK before P settled.]

Note: Paragraph substituted from 6 October 2021 subject to savings for applications made before that date (HC 617).

[**ROB 33.1A.** The applicant must either:

(a) have last been granted permission as a dependent partner or dependent child of the person (P) in ROB 33.1; or

(b) have been born in the UK and be applying as a child of the person (P) in ROB 33.1.]

Note: Paragraph inserted from 6 October 2021 subject to savings for applications made before that date (HC 617).

ROB 33.2. If applying as a child, the applicant's other parent must be being granted settlement at the same time, or be settled or a British citizen, unless:

(a) the person (P) in ROB 33.1. is the applicant's sole surviving parent; or

(b) the person (P) in ROB 33.1. has sole responsibility for the applicant's upbringing; or

(c) the decision maker is satisfied that there are serious and compelling reasons to grant the applicant settlement.

Care requirement for settlement by a child on the Representative of an Overseas Business route

ROB 34.1. If the applicant is under the age of 18 on the date of application, there must be suitable arrangements for the child's care and accommodation in the UK, which must comply with relevant UK legislation and regulations.

Age requirement for settlement by a child on the Representative of an Overseas Business route

ROB 35.1. The child must be under the age of 18 on the date of application, unless they were last granted permission as the dependent child of their parent or parents.

ROB 35.2. If the child is aged 16 or over on the date of application, they must not be leading an independent life.

English language requirement for settlement by a partner or child on the Representative of an Overseas Business route

ROB 36.1. Unless an exemption applies, the applicant must show English language ability on the Common European Framework of Reference for Languages in speaking and listening to at least level B1.

ROB 36.2. The applicant must show they meet the English language requirement as specified in Appendix English Language.

Knowledge of life in the UK requirement for settlement by a partner or child on the Representative of an Overseas Business route

ROB 37.1. If the applicant is aged 18 or over at the date of application, they must meet the Knowledge of Life in the UK requirement as set out in Appendix KOL UK.

Decision on an application for settlement by a partner or child on the Representative of an Overseas Business route

ROB 38.1. If the decision maker is satisfied all the suitability and eligibility requirements are met for settlement as a dependent partner or dependent child on the Representative of an Overseas Business route, the applicant will be granted settlement, otherwise the application will be refused.

ROB 38.2. If the application is refused the person can apply for an Administrative Review under Appendix AR: Administrative Review.]

Note: Appendix inserted from 09:00 on 1 December 2020 subject to savings for applications made before that time (HC813).

[Appendix UK Ancestry

The UK Ancestry route is for a Commonwealth citizen aged 17 or over who wants to live and work in the UK and who has a grandparent who was born in the UK or Islands. A dependent partner and dependent children can apply under this route. UK Ancestry is a route to settlement.

Validity requirements for UK Ancestry

UKA 1.1. A person applying for entry clearance or permission to stay on the UK Ancestry route must apply online on the gov.uk website on the specified form as follows:

(a) for entry clearance, form 'UK Ancestry, Right of Abode or Returning Residents visa'; or

(b) for permission to stay, form 'Application to extend stay in the UK: FLR(IR)'.

UKA 1.2. An application for entry clearance or permission to stay on the UK Ancestry route must meet all the following requirements:

(a) any fee and Immigration Health Charge must have been paid; and

(b) the applicant must have provided any required biometrics; and

(c) the applicant must have provided a passport or other travel document which satisfactorily establishes their identity and nationality.

UKA 1.3. The applicant must be a Commonwealth citizen.

UKA 1.4. If applying for entry clearance, the applicant must be aged 17 or over on the date of their intended arrival in the UK.

UKA 1.5. An applicant who is in the UK on the date of application must have previously been granted permission on the UK Ancestry route as a person with UK Ancestry.

UKA 1.6. An application which does not meet all the validity requirements for the UK Ancestry route is invalid and may be rejected and not considered.

Suitability requirements for UK Ancestry

UKA 2.1. The applicant must not fall for refusal under Part 9: grounds for refusal.

UKA 2.2. If applying for permission to stay, the applicant must not be:

(a) in breach of immigration laws, except that where paragraph 39E applies, that period of overstaying will be disregarded; or

(b) on immigration bail.

Eligibility requirements for UK Ancestry

Entry requirements for UK Ancestry

UKA 3.1. A person seeking to come to the UK on the UK Ancestry route must apply for and obtain entry clearance on the UK Ancestry route before they arrive in the UK.

UKA 3.2. A person applying for entry clearance on the UK Ancestry route must, if paragraph A39 and Appendix T of these rules apply, provide a valid medical certificate confirming that they have undergone screening for active pulmonary tuberculosis and that this tuberculosis is not present in them.

[Grandparent born in the UK or Islands requirement]

Note: Heading substituted from 6 April 2022 (HC 1118).

UKA 4.1. The applicant must have a grandparent born in the UK or Islands.

Financial requirement for UK Ancestry

UKA 5.1. The decision maker must be satisfied that the applicant can and will adequately maintain and accommodate themselves, and any dependants in the UK, or applying for entry clearance, without recourse to public funds.

UKA 5.2. Funds must be shown as specified in Appendix Finance.

UKA 5.3. In assessing whether the applicant meets the financial requirement in UKA 5.1, the decision maker may take into account credible promises of financial support from a third party, such as a relative or friend of the applicant.

Work requirement for UK Ancestry

UKA 6.1. The applicant must be able to work and intend to seek and take employment in the UK.

Parental consent requirement for UK Ancestry applicant aged under 18

UKA 7.1. If the applicant is aged under 18 on the date of application, they must have written consent from:

(a) both parents; or
(b) one parent, if that parent has sole legal responsibility for the applicant; or
(c) the applicant's legal guardian.

UKA 7.2. The written consent must confirm support for all of the following:

(a) the application; and
(b) the applicant's living and care arrangements in the UK; and
(c) if the application is for entry clearance, the applicant's travel to, and reception arrangements in, the UK.

Decision on an application for UK Ancestry

UKA 8.1. If the decision maker is satisfied that all the suitability and eligibility requirements are met for UK Ancestry, the application will be granted, otherwise the application will be refused.

UKA 8.2. If the application is refused the person can apply for an Administrative Review under Appendix AR: Administrative Review.

Period and conditions of grant on the UK Ancestry route

UKA 9.1. The applicant will be granted permission for 5 years.

UKA 9.2. The grant will be subject to all the following conditions:

(a) no access to public funds; and
(b) work is permitted (including self-employment); and
(c) voluntary work is permitted; and
(d) study is permitted, subject to the ATAS condition in Appendix ATAS; and
(e) if Part 10 applies the applicant will be required to register with the police.

Settlement on the UK Ancestry route

Validity requirements for settlement on the UK Ancestry route

UKA 10.1. A person on the UK Ancestry route who is applying for settlement must apply online on the gov.uk website on the specified form 'Settle in the UK in various immigration categories: form SET(O)'.

UKA 10.2. An application for settlement must meet all the following requirements:

(a) any fee must have been paid; and

(b) the applicant must have provided any required biometrics; and

(c) the applicant must have provided a passport or other travel document which satisfactorily establishes their identity and nationality; and

(d) the applicant must be in the UK.

UKA 10.3. The applicant must be a Commonwealth citizen on the date of application.

UKA 10.4. An application which does not meet all the validity requirements for settlement on the UK Ancestry route is invalid and may be rejected and not considered.

Suitability Requirements for settlement on the UK Ancestry route

UKA 11.1. The applicant must not fall for refusal under Part 9: grounds for refusal.

UKA 11.2. The applicant must not be:

(a) in breach of immigration laws, except that where paragraph 39E applies, that period of overstaying will be disregarded; or

(b) on immigration bail.

Eligibility requirements for settlement on the UK Ancestry route

UKA 12.1. The applicant must continue to meet the eligibility requirements of UKA 4.1 to UKA 6.1.

Qualifying period requirement for settlement on the UK Ancestry route

UKA 13.1. The applicant must have spent 5 years in the UK with permission on the UK Ancestry route as a person with UK Ancestry.

Continuous residence requirement for settlement on the UK Ancestry route

UKA 14.1. The applicant must meet the continuous residence requirement in Appendix Continuous Residence during the period in UKA 13.1.

English language requirement for settlement on the UK Ancestry route

UKA 15.1. Unless an exemption applies, the applicant must show English language ability on the Common European Framework of Reference for Languages in speaking and listening to at least level B1.

UKA 15.2. The applicant must show they meet the English language requirement as specified in Appendix English Language.

Knowledge of life in the UK requirement for settlement on the UK Ancestry route

UKA 16.1. The applicant must meet the knowledge of Life in the UK requirement as specified in Appendix KOL UK.

Decision on an application for settlement on the UK Ancestry route

UKA 17.1. If the decision maker is satisfied all the suitability and eligibility requirements are met for settlement on the UK Ancestry route, the applicant will be granted settlement, otherwise the application will be refused.

UKA 17.2. If the application is refused the person can apply for an Administrative Review under Appendix AR: Administrative Review.

Dependants of a person with UK Ancestry

Validity requirements for a dependent partner or dependent child on the UK Ancestry route

UKA 18.1. A person applying for entry clearance or permission to stay as a dependent partner or dependent child on the UK Ancestry route must apply online on the gov.uk website on the specified form as follows:

(a) for entry clearance, 'Join or accompany a family member' on the 'Find and apply for other visas from outside the UK' form; or

(b) for permission to stay, form 'Application to extend stay in the UK: FLR(IR)'.

[**UKA 18.2.** An application for entry clearance or permission to stay as a partner or child of a person on the UK Ancestry route must meet all the following requirements:

(a) any fee and Immigration Health Charge must have been paid; and

(b) the applicant must have provided any required biometrics; and

(c) the applicant must have provided a passport or other travel document which satisfactorily establishes their identity and nationality; and

(d) the applicant must be applying as partner or child of a person who:

(i) has made a valid application for entry clearance or permission to stay on the UK Ancestry route that has not been decided; or

(ii) has entry clearance or permission to stay on the UK Ancestry route; or

(iii) is settled or has become a British citizen, providing that person (P) had permission on the UK Ancestry route when they settled.]

Note: Paragraph substituted from 6 April 2022 (HC 1118).

UKA 18.3. An applicant who is applying for permission to stay must be in the UK on the date of application must not have, or have last been granted, permission:

(a) as a Visitor; or

(b) as a Short-term Student; or

(c) as a Parent of a Child Student; or

(d) as a Seasonal Worker; or

(e) as a Domestic Worker in a Private Household; or

(f) outside the Immigration Rules.

UKA 18.4. An application which does not meet the validity requirements for a partner or child on the UK Ancestry route is invalid and may be rejected and not considered.

Suitability requirements for a dependent partner or dependent child on the UK Ancestry route

UKA 19.1. The suitability requirements for a dependent partner or dependent child on the UK Ancestry route are that they must not fall for refusal under Part 9: grounds for refusal.

UKA 19.2. The applicant must not be:

(a) in breach of immigration laws, except that where paragraph 39E applies, that period of overstaying will be disregarded; or

(b) on immigration bail.

Eligibility requirements for a dependent partner or dependent child on the UK Ancestry route

Entry requirement for a dependent partner or dependent child on the UK Ancestry route

UKA 20.1. A person seeking to come to the UK as a partner or child must apply for and obtain an entry clearance as a partner or child before they arrive in the UK.

UKA 20.2. A person applying for entry clearance as a partner or child on the UK Ancestry route must, if paragraph A39 and Appendix T of these rules apply, provide a valid medical certificate confirming that they have undergone screening for active pulmonary tuberculosis and that this tuberculosis is not present in them.

Relationship requirements for a partner on the UK Ancestry route

UKA 21.1. The applicant must be the partner of a person (P) and one of the following must apply:

(a) P has permission on the UK Ancestry route; or

(b) P is, at the same time, applying for (and is granted) permission on the UK Ancestry route; or

(c) if the applicant is applying for permission to stay, P is settled or has become a British citizen, providing P had permission on the UK Ancestry route when they settled.

UKA 21.2. If the applicant and the person with UK Ancestry are not married or in a civil partnership, all of the following requirements must be met:

(a) they must have been living together in a relationship similar to marriage or civil partnership for at least the two years before the date of application; and

(b) any previous relationship of the applicant or of the person with UK Ancestry with another person must have permanently broken down; and

(c) the applicant and the person with UK Ancestry must not be so closely related that they would not be allowed to marry or form a civil partnership in the UK.

UKA 21.3. The relationship between the applicant and the person with UK Ancestry must be genuine and subsisting.

UKA 21.4. The applicant and the person with UK Ancestry must intend to live together throughout the applicant's stay in the UK.

Relationship requirement for a dependent child on the UK Ancestry route

UKA 22.1. The applicant must be the child of a person (P) and one of the following must apply:

(a) P has permission on the UK Ancestry route; or

(b) P is, at the same time, applying for (and is granted) permission on the UK Ancestry route; or

(c) if the applicant is applying for permission to stay, P is settled or has become a British citizen, providing P had permission on the UK Ancestry route when they settled.

[UKA 22.2. The applicant's parents must both be either applying at the same time as the applicant, or have permission to be in the UK (other than as a Visitor) unless:

(a) the parent applying for or with entry clearance or permission on the UK Ancestry route is the sole surviving parent; or

(b) the parent applying for or with entry clearance or permission on the UK Ancestry route has sole responsibility for the child's upbringing; or

(c) the parent who does not have permission on the UK Ancestry route –

(i) is a British citizen or a person who has a right to enter or stay in the UK without restriction; and

(ii) is or will be ordinarily resident in the UK; or

(d) the decision maker is satisfied that there are serious and compelling reasons to grant the child entry clearance or permission to stay with the parent who is applying for or has entry clearance or permission on the UK Ancestry route.]

Note: Paragraph substituted from 6 October 2021 subject to savings for applications made before that date (HC 617).

Care requirement for a dependent child on the UK Ancestry route

UKA 23.1. If the child is under the age of 18 on the date of application, there must be suitable arrangements for the child's care and accommodation in the UK, which must comply with relevant UK legislation and regulations.

Age requirement for a dependent child on the UK Ancestry route

UKA 24.1. The child must be under the age of 18 on the date of application, unless they were last granted permission as the dependent child of their parent or parents.

UKA 24.2. If the child is aged 16 or over on the date of application, they must not be leading an independent life.

Financial requirement for a partner or child on the UK Ancestry route

UKA 25.1. The decision maker must be satisfied that there will be adequate maintenance and accommodation for the applicant, the person with UK Ancestry, and any other dependants in the UK, without recourse to public funds.

UKA 25.2. Funds must be shown as specified in Appendix Finance.

UKA 25.3. In assessing whether the applicant meets the financial requirement in UKA 25.1, the decision maker may take into account credible promises of financial support from a third party, such as a relative or friend of the applicant.

Decision on an application for a dependent partner and dependent child on the UK Ancestry route

UKA 26.1. If the decision maker is satisfied that all the suitability and eligibility requirements are met for a dependent partner or dependent child on the UK Ancestry route, the application will be granted, otherwise the application will be refused.

UKA 26.2. If the application is refused the person can apply for an Administrative Review under Appendix AR: Administrative Review.

Period and conditions of grant for a dependent partner and dependent child on the UK Ancestry route

UKA 27.1. Unless UKA 27.2 applies, the applicant will be granted permission which ends on the same date as the person with UK Ancestry.

UKA 27.2. If the application is for permission to stay, and the person with UK Ancestry is being, or has been, granted settlement on the UK Ancestry route, or has become a British Citizen having previously had permission on the UK Ancestry route, the applicant will be granted permission to stay for 30 months.

UKA 27.3. The grant will be subject to all the following conditions:
(a) no access to public funds; and
(b) work (including self-employment and voluntary work) permitted; and
(c) study is permitted, subject to the ATAS condition in Appendix ATAS; and
(d) if Part 10 applies the applicant will be required to register with the police.

Settlement by a dependent partner and dependent child on the UK Ancestry route

Validity requirements for settlement by a dependent partner or dependent child on the UK Ancestry route

UKA 28.1. A partner or child on the UK Ancestry route who is applying for settlement must apply online on the gov.uk website on the specified form 'Settle in the UK in various immigration categories: form SET(O)'.

[**UKA 28.2.** An application for settlement must meet all the following requirements:
(a) any fee must have been paid; and
(b) the applicant must have provided any required biometrics; and
(c) the applicant must have provided either a passport or other travel document which satisfactorily establishes their identity and nationality; and
(d) the applicant must be in the UK; and
(e) the applicant must be applying as a partner or child of a person (P) who:
(i) has made a valid application for settlement on the UK Ancestry route and that application has not been decided; or
(ii) is settled or has become a British citizen, providing P had permission on the UK Ancestry route when they settled.]

Note: Paragraph substituted from 6 April 2022 (HC 1118).

UKA 28.3. The applicant must not have, or have last been granted, permission:
(a) as a Visitor; or
(b) as a Short-term Student; or
(c) as a Parent of a Child Student; or
(d) as a Seasonal Worker; or
(e) as a Domestic Worker in a Private Household; or
(f) outside the Immigration Rules.

UKA 28.4. An application which does not meet all the validity requirements for settlement as a partner or child on the UK Ancestry route is invalid and may be rejected and not considered.

Suitability requirements for settlement by a dependent partner and dependent child on the UK Ancestry route

UKA 29.1. The applicant must not fall for refusal under Part 9: grounds for refusal.

UKA 29.2. The applicant must not be:

(a) in breach of immigration laws, except that where paragraph 39E applies, that period of overstaying will be disregarded; or

(b) on immigration bail.

Eligibility requirements for settlement by a dependent partner or dependent child on the UK Ancestry route

Relationship requirement for settlement by a partner or child on the UK Ancestry route

UKA 30.1. The applicant must be the partner or child of a person (P) where one of the following applies:

(a) P is, at the same time, being granted settlement on the UK Ancestry route; or

(b) P is settled or has become a British citizen, providing P had permission on the UK Ancestry route when they settled.

UKA 30.2. If applying as a partner, and the applicant and the person with UK Ancestry are not married or in a civil partnership, all of the following requirements must be met:

(a) they must have been living together in a relationship similar to marriage or civil partnership for at least the two years before the date of application; and

(b) any previous relationship of the applicant or of the person with UK Ancestry with another person must have permanently broken down; and

(c) the applicant and the person with UK Ancestry must not be so closely related that they would not be allowed to marry or form a civil partnership in the UK.

UKA 30.3. The relationship between the applicant and the person with UK Ancestry must be genuine and subsisting.

UKA 30.4. The applicant and the person with UK Ancestry must intend to live together throughout the applicant's stay in the UK.

UKA 30.5. If applying as a child, the applicant's other parent must be being granted settlement at the same time, or be settled or a British citizen, unless:

(a) the person (P) in UKA 30.1. is the applicant's sole surviving parent; or

(b) the person (P) in UKA 30.1. has sole responsibility for the applicant's upbringing; or

(c) the decision maker is satisfied that there are serious and compelling reasons to grant the applicant settlement.

Care requirement for settlement by a child on the UK Ancestry route

UKA 31.1. If the applicant is under the age of 18 on the date of application, there must be suitable arrangements for the child's care and accommodation in the UK, which must comply with relevant UK legislation and regulations.

Age requirement for settlement by a child on the UK Ancestry route

UKA 32.1. The child must be under the age of 18 on the date of application, unless they were last granted permission as the dependent child of their parent or parents.

UKA 32.2. If the child is aged 16 or over on the date of application, they must not be leading an independent life.

Financial requirement for settlement for a partner or child on the UK Ancestry route

UKA 33.1. The decision maker must be satisfied that there will be adequate maintenance and accommodation for the applicant, the person with UK Ancestry, and any other dependants in the UK, without recourse to public funds.

UKA 33.2. Funds must be shown as specified in Appendix Finance.

UKA 33.3. In assessing whether the applicant meets the financial requirement in UKA 33.1, the decision maker may take into account credible promises of financial support from a third party, such as a relative or friend of the applicant.

English language requirement for settlement by a partner or child on the UK Ancestry route

UKA 34.1. Unless an exemption applies, the applicant must show English language ability on the Common European Framework of Reference for Languages in speaking and listening of at least level B1.

UKA 34.2. The applicant must show they meet the English language requirement as specified in Appendix English Language.

Knowledge of life in the UK requirement for settlement by a partner or child on the UK Ancestry route

UKA 35.1. If the applicant is aged 18 or over at the date of application, they must meet the Knowledge of Life in the UK requirement as set out in Appendix KOL UK.

Decision on an application for settlement by a partner or child on the UK Ancestry route

UKA 36.1. If the decision maker is satisfied all the suitability and eligibility requirements are met for settlement as a dependent partner or dependent child on the UK Ancestry route the applicant will be granted settlement, otherwise the application will be refused.

UKA 36.2. If the application is refused the person can apply for an Administrative Review under Appendix AR: Administrative Review.]

Note: Appendix inserted from 09:00 on 1 December 2020 subject to savings for applications made before that time (HC813).

[Appendix Global Talent

The Global Talent route is for people aged 18 or over in the field of science, engineering, humanities, medicine, digital technology or arts and culture who can show they have exceptional talent or exceptional promise.

[For most individuals there is a two-part application process.] The first part is an application for endorsement (guidance on the relevant evidence and its format is set out from time to time by the Secretary of State on gov.uk/global talent); the second part is an application for entry clearance or permission to stay.

A person can make the application for endorsement before making the application for permission, or they can make both applications at the same time.

[Alternatively, a person who has been awarded a prestigious prize listed in Appendix Global Talent: Prestigious Prizes is considered as showing exceptional talent and is therefore not required to apply for an endorsement.]
A dependent partner and dependent children can apply under this route.

Global Talent is a route to settlement.

Note: Words in introduction substituted from 5 May 2021 (HC 1248).

Part 1- Global Talent Endorsement application

Validity requirements for a Global Talent Endorsement application

GTE 1.1. A person applying for Global Talent endorsement must apply on the specified form as follows:

(a) all applicants must apply on 'Apply for Global Talent endorsement - stage 1' online on the gov.uk website; and

(b) applicants for endorsement by Tech Nation must also complete the additional form found on the Tech Nation website: http://technation.io/visa/apply.

GTE 1.2. An application for Global Talent endorsement must meet both the following requirements:

(a) the endorsement application fee must have been paid; and

(b) the application must be for endorsement by an endorsing body in the field relevant to the applicant.

GTE 1.3. An application which does not meet all of the validity requirements for a Global Talent endorsement is invalid and may be rejected and not considered.

Eligibility requirements for a Global Talent Endorsement application

GTE 2.1. An application for endorsement must be made under one of the fields below and must meet the endorsement requirements for that field.

Arts and Culture endorsement

Arts and Culture field track record requirements

GTE 3.1. An applicant for endorsement in the field of Arts and Culture must:

(a) be professionally engaged in producing outstanding performed, presented, distributed or internationally exhibited work; and

(b) show regular professional engagement in their field in the last 5 years; and

(c) show either a substantial track record in more than 1 country if evidencing exceptional talent, or a developing track record in 1 or more countries if evidencing exceptional promise.

Arts and Culture field track record evidential requirements

GTE 3.2. An applicant must provide 3 letters of recommendation of which:

(a) 2 must be from [well-established arts and culture organisation] acknowledged as experts in the applicant's field, and at least one of the organisations must be based in the UK; and

(b) the third must be from another [well-established arts and culture organisation], or an individual, with recognised expertise in the applicant's field.

Note: Words substituted from 6 October 2021 subject to savings for applications made before that date (HC 617).

GTE 3.3. An applicant who is evidencing exceptional talent in their field must provide at least two of the following:

(a) evidence from at least 2 countries (which can include their country of residence) of 2 or more examples of significant media recognition for [their individual work as an individual or as a named member of a group]; or

(b) evidence of winning, or significantly contributing to winning, an international award for excellence; or

(c) evidence from at least 2 countries (which can include their country of residence) of proof of appearances, performances, publications or exhibitions considered internationally significant in their field, or evidence of extensive international distribution and audiences for the applicant's work [as an individual or as a named member of a group].

Note: Words in (a) substituted, words in (c) inserted from 6 October 2021 subject to savings for applications made before that date (HC 617).

GTE 3.4. An applicant who is evidencing exceptional promise in their field must provide at least 2 of the following:

(a) evidence from at least 1 country (which can include their country of residence) of at least 2 examples of recent media recognition for [their work as an individual, as a named member of a group or as a contributor]; or

(b) evidence of winning, or significantly contributing to winning, or significantly contributing to being nominated or shortlisted for, or being nominated or shortlisted for, an international award for excellence; or

(c) evidence from at least 1 country (which can include their country of residence) of proof of appearances, performances, publications or exhibitions recognised in their field, or evidence of international distribution and audiences for the applicant's work [as an individual, as a named member of a group or as a contributor].

Note: Words in (a) substituted, words in (c) inserted from 6 October 2021 subject to savings for applications made before that date (HC 617).

Architecture endorsement

Architecture field track record requirement

GTE 4.1. An applicant for endorsement in the field of Architecture must:

(a) be professionally engaged in producing outstanding presented, published or internationally exhibited work; and

(b) show regular professional engagement in their field in the last 5 years; and

(c) show a substantial track record in more than 1 country if evidencing exceptional talent or show a developing track record in 1 or more countries if evidencing exceptional promise.

Architecture field track record evidential requirements

GTE 4.2. An applicant must provide 3 letters of recommendation of which:

(a) 2 must be from well-established organisations acknowledged as experts in the applicant's field, and at least 1 of the organisations must be based in the UK; and

(b) the third must be from another well-established organisation, or an individual, with recognised expertise in the applicant's field.

GTE 4.3. An applicant who is evidencing exceptional talent in their field must provide at least 2 of the following:

(a) evidence of winning, or significantly contributing to winning, an international award for excellence; or

(b) evidence from at least 2 countries (which can include their country of residence) of a minimum of 2 examples of significant media recognition for their individual work; or

(c) evidence from at least 2 countries (which can include their country of residence) of a minimum of 2 examples of publications or exhibitions considered internationally significant in the applicant's field.

GTE 4.4. An applicant who is evidencing exceptional promise in their field must provide at least 2 of the following:

(a) evidence of winning, significantly contributing to winning, or being nominated or shortlisted for, an international award for excellence in the last 5 years; or

(b) evidence from at least 1 country (which can include their country of residence) of a minimum of 2 examples of recent media recognition for their individual work or their work as a contributor; or

(c) evidence from at least 1 country (which can include their country of residence) of a minimum of 2 examples of publications or exhibitions in the last 3 years considered internationally significant in the applicant's field.

Fashion Design Industry endorsement

Fashion Design Industry field track record requirement

GTE 5.1. An applicant for endorsement in the field of fashion design must:

(a) have a leading design role in the fashion business; and

(b) show regular professional engagement in the fashion design industry in the last 5 years; and

(c) if evidencing exceptional talent, show professional engagement in producing outstanding work that has been sold or exhibited internationally through catwalk or other exhibitions and a substantial track record in more than 1 country; and

(d) if evidencing exceptional promise, show a developing track record in 1 or more countries and professional engagement in producing outstanding work that has been recognised by leading industry players.

Fashion Design Industry field track record evidential requirements

GTE 5.2. An applicant must provide 3 letters of recommendation from established organisations with nationally or internationally recognised expertise in fashion and, where an applicant is evidencing exceptional talent, at least 1 letter must be from an organisation based in the UK.

GTE 5.3. An applicant who is evidencing exceptional talent in the fashion design industry field must provide at least 2 of the following:

(a) evidence of winning, or significantly contributing to winning, an international award for excellence; or

(b) evidence from at least 2 countries (which can include their country of residence) of a minimum of 2 examples of significant media recognition for their individual work; or

(c) evidence of catwalk shows, presentations or exhibitions considered internationally significant in the fashion design industry; or

(d) evidence of extensive distribution and sales of the applicant's collections via internationally renowned retailers, the applicant's retail outlet or their ecommerce platform.

GTE 5.4. An applicant who is evidencing exceptional promise in the fashion design industry must provide at least 2 of the following:

(a) at least 2 examples of recent UK or international media recognition for their individual work; or

(b) evidence of support and sponsorship through one of the following:

(i) British Fashion Council support schemes; or

(ii) Fashion East support scheme; or

(iii) The Sarabande Foundation; or

(iv) The Centre of Fashion Enterprise; or

(v) an international counterpart of the British Fashion Council; or

(c) evidence of at least 1 order placed by a luxury retailer or boutique; or

(d) evidence of recognition by leading industry players of an exceptional graduating collection.

Film and Television endorsement

Film and Television field track record requirement

GTE 6.1. An applicant for an exceptional talent endorsement in the field of Film and Television must show 1 of the following:

(a) that they have won at any time a 'Main Award' which means:

(i) an Academy Award; or

(ii) a British Academy of Film and Television Arts (BAFTA) (film, television, television craft, Cymru, Scotland, Games awards only); or

(iii) a Golden Globe; or

(iv) an Emmy Award; or

(b) in the last 10 years they have been nominated for, or made a significant contribution to winning, or being nominated for any of the Main Awards; or

(c) in the last 15 years, they have achieved a minimum of 2 nominations for the Main Awards; or

(d) they have notable industry recognition through achieving international sales and a specified combination of awards from Pact's Notable Industry List as set out in [http://www.pact.co.uk/services/talent-visas.html].

Note: Web address in (d) substituted from 6 October 2021 subject to savings for applications made before that date (HC 617).

Film and Television field track record evidential requirements

GTE 6.2. An applicant must provide 3 letters of recommendation of which:

(a) 2 must be from well-established organisations acknowledged as experts in the film and television industry, at least 1 of these must be from an organisation based in the UK; and

(b) 1 must be from another well-established organisation or from an individual with recognised expertise in the film or television industry.

Digital Technology endorsement

Digital Technology field track record requirement

GTE 7.1. An applicant for endorsement in the field of digital technology must show:

(a) if they are a technical applicant, that they have proven technical expertise with the latest technologies in building, using, deploying or exploiting a technology stack and building technical infrastructure; or

(b) if they are a business applicant, that they have proven commercial investment or product expertise in building digital products or leading investments in significant digital product businesses.

Digital Technology track record evidential requirements

GTE 7.2. The applicant must provide all of the following with the Tech Nation online application form:

(a) a CV with career and publication history included; and

(b) 3 dated letters of recommendation from 3 different well-established organisations acknowledged as experts in the digital technology field [supporting the Global Talent application, which include all of the following:

(i) how the author knows the applicant; and

(ii) the applicant's achievements in the relevant field; and

(iii) how the author considers the applicant shows exceptional talent or promise; and

(iv) the contribution the applicant would make to the UK digital economy.]

Note: Words in (b) and sub-paragraphs (b)(i) to (iv) inserted from 6 April 2022 subject to savings for applications made before that date (HC 1118).

GTE 7.3. An applicant evidencing exceptional talent must:

(a) show that they have been recognised as a leading talent in the digital technology sector [in the last 5 years]; and

(b) provide evidence of 2 of the following:

(i) a proven track record for innovation as a founder or senior executive of a product-led digital technology company or as an employee working on a new digital field or concept; or

(ii) proof of recognition for work beyond the applicant's occupation that contributes to the advancement of the field; or

(iii) they have made significant technical, commercial or entrepreneurial contributions to the field as a founder, senior executive[, board member] or employee of a product-led digital technology company; or

(iv) they have demonstrated exceptional ability in the field by academic contributions[. . .] through research published or endorsed by an expert.

Note: Words in (b)(iii) inserted, punctuation deleted from 6 October 2021 subject to savings for applications made before that date (HC 617). Words in (a) inserted from 6 April 2022 subject to savings for applications made before that date (HC 1118).

GTE 7.4. An applicant evidencing exceptional promise must:

(a) show they have been recognised as having potential to be a leading talent in the digital technology field [in the last 5 years]; and

(b) provide evidence of [...]2 of the following:

(i) [at least one example] of innovation as a founder of a product led digital technology company or as an employee working on a new digital field or concept; or

(ii) [at least one example of] proof of recognition for work beyond the applicant's occupation that contributes to the advancement of the field; or

(iii) [at least one example of] significant technical, commercial or entrepreneurial contributions to the field as a founder or employee of a product-led digital technology company; or

(iv) [at least 1 example] of exceptional ability in the field by academic contributions, [...] through research endorsed by an expert. [[and]]

[(c) be at an early stage in their career.]

Note: Words in (b) deleted from 6 April 2021 (HC 1248). Words in (b)(i), (iii), and (iv) substituted, words in (b)(ii) inserted, word in (b)(iv) deleted from 6 October 2021 subject to savings for applications made before that date (HC 617). Words in (a), word in double square brackets in (b)(iv) and sub-paragraph (c) inserted from 6 April 2022 subject to savings for applications made before that date (HC 1118).

GTE 7.5. An applicant must provide evidence of any commercially successful established businesses, share ownership or businesses dissolved in the last 5 years where the applicant has been a founder or senior executive.

Science, engineering, humanities and medicine fields endorsement

Science, engineering, humanities and medicine fields track record requirement

GTE 8.1. An applicant for endorsement in the field of science, engineering, humanities and medicine must be an active researcher in an academic, industry or government research institution.

Fast track endorsement

GTE 8.2. An applicant applying for endorsement on the fast track must provide evidence of one of the following:

(a) that they hold, or have held in the [five years] before the date of application, a peer reviewed research fellowship or award named on the list published by the Royal Society, the Royal Academy of Engineering and the British Academy; or

(b) that they [have been appointed to an eligible academic or research position] at an approved UK Higher Education Institution or research institute named on the list published by the Royal Society, the Royal Academy of Engineering and the British Academy; or

(c) that they will be hosted or employed in a UK research organisation named on the UKRI published list and will provide critical contributions to work supported by a substantial research grant or award from an endorsed funder named on the UKRI published list.

Note: Words in (a) substituted from 6 October 2021 subject to savings for applications made before that date (HC 617). Words in (b) substituted from 6 April 2022 subject to savings for applications made before that date (HC 1118).

GTE 8.3. [DELETED]

Note: Amendments from 6 April 2021 (HC 1248). Paragraph deleted from 6 October 2021 subject to savings for applications made before that date (HC 617).

GTE 8.4. An applicant applying for endorsement on the fast track under GTE 8.2.(c) must either:

(a) direct independently, or under the supervision of a [Principal] Investigator, a unique research or innovation project and meet all the following requirements:

(i) they must have a PhD qualification or equivalent research experience (including industrial or clinical research); and

(ii) they must actively participate in a relevant field in a University, research institute or industry; and

(iii) they must have their name or post listed on the grant or award as the [Principal] or co-investigator, Researcher Co-investigator, Post-doctoral researcher or Research Assistant, or an equivalent position acceptable to UKRI; or

(b) make critical contributions to research by providing core technical or domain excellence or in developing new technologies and methodologies and meet both the following requirements:

(i) they must have a UK bachelor's degree or equivalent overseas research degree or equivalent research experience (including industrial or clinical research); and

(ii) they must have research experience within a University, Research Institute or Industry.

Note: Words substituted from 6 October 2021 subject to savings for applications made before that date (HC 617).

Fast Track endorsement - evidential requirements

GTE 8.5. An applicant on the fast track applying under GTE 8.2.(a) must provide written confirmation from an awarding body named on the list published by the Royal Society, the Royal Academy of Engineering and the British Academy that they hold, or have held in the last [five years], an eligible peer reviewed fellowship or award.

Note: Words substituted from 6 October 2021 subject to savings for applications made before that date (HC 617).

[GTE 8.6. An applicant on the fast track applying under GTE 8.2.(b) must hold an eligible academic or research position at an approved UK Higher Education Institution or Research Institute named on the list published by the Royal Society, the Royal Academy of Engineering and the British Academy and they must provide both:

(a) a job description setting out the duties and responsibilities of the position; and

[(b) a statement of guarantee from the Director of Human Resources, or equivalent, which confirms:

(i) the job was advertised, and an open competition was held, or where it was not, an explanation as to why not; and

(ii) the applicant has accepted the job offer; and

(iii) the job title and department in which the applicant will be based; and

(iv) the applicant:

(1) has responsibility for academic, research or innovation leadership and development; or

(2) will direct or lead an individual or team research project or programme of work; or

(3) will direct or lead an individual or team innovation project or programme of work; and

(v) at least two references were received; and

(vi) at least three academic, research or innovation representatives were on the interview panel(s); and

(vii) at least one expert in the applicant's field was on the interview panel(s), or at least one relevant expert, independent of the employing institution, was consulted before the job offer was made.]

Note: Paragraph substituted from 6 October 2021 subject to savings for applications made before that date (HC 617). Sub-paragraph (b) substituted from 6 April 2022 subject to savings for applications made before that date (HC 1118).

[GTE 8.7. An applicant on the fast track applying under GTE 8.2.(c) must provide a declaration from the Director of Human Resources, or equivalent at the UKRI-approved UK research organisation which confirms all the following:

(a) that the applicant has accepted the job offer or hosting agreement; and

(b) the job title and department in which the applicant will be based; and

(c) that there is at least one year remaining on their employment contract or hosting agreement; and

(d) that they will provide critical contributions to work supported by a substantial research grant or award from an endorsed funder; and

(e) that they are essential to the execution of the grant or award; and

(f) that at least 50% of the applicant's time will be spent working on the grant or award by the endorsed funder (Principal investigators and co-investigators can aggregate time spent on multiple eligible awards or grants to demonstrate this requirement); and

(g) that a robust recruitment process has been completed where the applicant was not named on the grant application.]

Note: Paragraph substituted from 6 October 2021 subject to savings for applications made before that date (HC 617).

[GTE 8.7A. An applicant on the fast track applying under GTE 8.2.(c) must show that the grant or award from an endorsed funder is worth at least £30,000, covers a minimum of two years; and is either funded by a one-off grant or award that has been won in open competition or attributed to a large institutional, renewable award that is subject to periodic peer review, by either:

(a) providing a link to the grant or award on a UKRI-approved database the details on which would be checked by UKRI against the above requirements; or

(b) providing written confirmation of the grant or award from the endorsed funder that the above requirements are met.]

Note: Paragraph inserted from 6 October 2021 subject to savings for applications made before that date (HC 617).

Full peer review endorsement

GTE 8.8. An applicant evidencing exceptional talent under full peer review endorsement must:

[(za) show that they have been recognised as a leading talent in the field of science, engineering, humanities or medicine; and]

(a) be an active researcher in a relevant field, typically in a university, research institute or in industry; and

(b) have a PhD or equivalent research experience (including industrial or clinical research); and

(c) meet 1 of the following requirements:

(i) they must be a member of their national academy or a foreign member of an academy of another country; or

(ii) they must have been awarded a prestigious internationally recognised prize; or

(iii) they must provide a letter of recommendation from a senior member of a reputable UK organisation concerned with research in the applicant's field.

Note: Sub-paragraph (za) inserted from 6 April 2022 subject to savings for applications made before that date (HC 1118).

GTE 8.9. An applicant evidencing exceptional promise under full peer review endorsement must:

[(za) show that they have been recognised as having potential to be a leading talent in the field of science, engineering, humanities or medicine; and]

(a) be an active researcher in a relevant field, typically in a university, research institute or in industry; and

(b) have a PhD or equivalent research experience (including industrial or clinical research); and

(c) be at an early stage in their career; and

(d) have been awarded, or have held in the last 5 years, a prestigious UK based research fellowship, an international fellowship or an advanced post judged by the endorsing body to be equivalent to such a fellowship.

Note: Sub-paragraph (za) inserted from 6 April 2022 subject to savings for applications made before that date (HC 1118).

Full peer review endorsement evidential requirements

GTE 8.10. A full peer review endorsement applicant must:

(a) provide a CV which sets out their career and publication history; and

(b) provide a letter of personal recommendation from an eminent person resident in the UK supporting the Global Talent application which includes all of the following:

(i) how the author knows the applicant; and

(ii) the applicant's achievements in the relevant field; and

(iii) how the author considers the applicant shows exceptional talent or promise; and

(iv) the contribution the applicant would make to UK research excellence and wider society.

Part 2- Application for entry clearance or permission on the Global Talent Route

Validity Requirements for Global Talent route

GT 1.1. A person applying for entry clearance or permission to stay on the Global Talent route must apply online on the specified form on gov.uk website as follows:

Applicant	Specified form
EEA national with a chipped passport	Either: – Global Talent using the UK Immigration: ID Check app (when available); or – the forms listed below for applicants outside or inside the UK (as relevant)
Applicants outside the UK	Global Talent visa – stage 2
Applicants inside the UK	Global Talent permission to stay – stage 2

GT 1.2. An application for entry clearance or permission to stay on the Global Talent route must meet all the following requirements:

(a) any fee and Immigration Health Charge must have been paid; and

(b) the applicant must have provided any required biometrics; and

(c) the applicant must have provided a passport or other travel document which satisfactorily establishes their identity and nationality; and

[(d) the applicant must have been issued with an endorsement letter by a Home Office approved endorsing body or have been awarded a prize listed in Appendix Global Talent: Prestigious Prizes; and]

[(e) if applying for the first grant of permission on the Global Talent route using an endorsement letter, the date of application must be no more than 3 months after the date on the endorsement letter; and]

[(f) the applicant's endorsement or prize must not have been withdrawn [[or suspended]].]

Note: Sub-paragraphs (d), (e) and (f) substituted from 5 May 2021 (HC 1248). Words in double square brackets in (f) inserted from 6 October 2021 subject to savings for applications made before that date (HC 617).

GT 1.3. If the applicant has in the last 12 months before the date of application received an award from a Government or international scholarship agency covering both fees and living costs for study in the UK, they must provide written consent to the application from that Government or agency.

GT 1.4. The applicant must be aged 18 or over on the date of application.

GT 1.5. A person applying for permission to stay must be in the UK and must not have, or have last been granted, permission:

(a) as a Visitor; or

(b) as a Short-term Student; or

(c) as a Parent of a Child Student; or

(d) as a Seasonal Worker; or

(e) as a domestic worker in a private household; or

(f) outside the Immigration Rules.

GT 1.6. An application which does not meet all the validity requirements for the Global Talent route is invalid and may be rejected and not considered.

Suitability Requirements for Global Talent route

GT 2.1. The applicant must not fall for refusal under Part 9: grounds for refusal.

GT 2.2. If applying for permission to stay the applicant must not be:

(a) in breach of immigration laws, except that where paragraph 39E applies, that period of overstaying will be disregarded; or

(b) on immigration bail.

Eligibility Requirements for Global Talent route

Entry requirements for Global Talent route

GT 3.1. A person seeking to come to the UK on the Global Talent route must apply for and obtain entry clearance on the Global Talent route before their arrival in the UK.

GT 3.2. A person applying for entry clearance on the Global Talent route must, if paragraph A39 and Appendix T of these rules apply, provide a valid medical certificate confirming that they have undergone screening for active pulmonary tuberculosis and that this tuberculosis is not present in them.

Points requirement for Global Talent route

GT 4.1. An applicant applying for entry clearance or permission to stay must be awarded 70 points based on the table below.

[Requirement	Points available
An applicant making an initial application not relying on an endorsement: • has been awarded a prize listed in Appendix Global Talent: Prestigious Prizes.	70
An applicant making an initial application relying on an endorsement: • has been issued with an endorsement letter by an endorsing body; and • the date of application is no more than 3 months after the date on the endorsement letter; and • the endorsement has not been withdrawn by the endorsing body.	70
An applicant applying for an extension of their permission: • has met the earned money requirement; and • if they were granted their initial application using an endorsement, has not had their endorsement withdrawn by the endorsing body.	70
Total number of points required in each case	70]

Note: Table substituted from 5 May 2021 (HC 1248).

[**GT 4.1ZA.** An applicant who has held permission on the Global Talent route in the 12 months immediately before the date of application will be considered under the extension of permission requirements in GT 5.1.]

Note: Paragraph inserted from 6 October 2021 subject to savings for applications made before that date (HC 617).

Points for initial application on the Global Talent route

[**GT 4.1A.** Applicants relying on a prize in Appendix Global Talent: Prestigious Prizes to score points must meet both of the following requirements:

(a) they must be the named recipient of the prize (prizes given to an organisation or group the applicant is associated with are not acceptable); and

(b) the prize issued by the relevant body must not have been withdrawn [[or suspended]].]

Note: Paragraph inserted from 5 May 2021 (HC 1248). Words in double square brackets in (b) inserted from 6 April 2022 subject to savings for applications made before that date (HC 1118).

[**GT 4.2.** Applicants relying on an endorsement to score points must meet both of the following requirements:

(a) the endorsement issued by the endorsing body must not have been withdrawn [or suspended]; and

(b) the endorsing body must continue to be approved by the Home Office on the date of decision.]

Note: Paragraph substituted from 5 May 2021 (HC 1248). Words in (a) substituted from 6 October 2021 subject to savings for applications made before that date (HC 617). **NB:** HC 617 provides that the insertion applies to sub-paragraph (b), however the relevant wording after which it is to be inserted only appears in (a).

GT 4.3. If the requirements in [GT 4.1A or] GT 4.2. are met 70 points will be awarded for an initial application on the Global Talent route.

Note: Words inserted from 5 May 2021 (HC 1248).

Points for extension of stay on the Global Talent route

[**GT 5.1.** An applicant who has, or last had, permission on the Global Talent route and is applying for an extension of permission must meet the following requirements:

(a) the applicant must have earned money in the UK during their last period of permission in either:

(i) a field related to the subject matter of their prize if they were granted their initial application using a prize listed in Appendix Global Talent: Prestigious Prizes; or

(ii) the field in which they were previously endorsed in the Global Talent route if they were granted their initial application using an endorsement; and

(b) if the applicant was granted their initial application using an endorsement:

(i) the endorsement letter issued by a Home Office approved endorsing body must not have been withdrawn; and

(ii) the endorsing body must continue to be approved by the Home Office on the date of decision.]

Note: Paragraph substituted from 5 May 2021 (HC 1248).

GT 5.2. [DELETED]

Note: Paragraph deleted from 6 October 2021 subject to savings for applications made before that date (HC 617).

GT 5.3. If the requirements in GT 5.1. are met 70 points will be awarded for an application for an extension of stay on the Global Talent route.

Decision on Global Talent route

GT 6.1. If the decision maker is satisfied that all the suitability and eligibility requirements for the Global Talent route are met the application will be granted, otherwise the application will be refused.

GT 6.2. If the application is refused the person can apply for an Administrative Review under Appendix AR: Administrative Review.

Period and conditions of grant on Global Talent route

GT 7.1. Permission will be granted for the period of years the applicant requests, up to a maximum of 5 years on each application.

GT 7.2. There is no limit on the total period of permission that may be granted on the Global Talent route.

GT 7.3. The grant will be subject to all the following conditions:

(a) no access to public funds; and

(b) work (including self-employment and voluntary work) permitted except for employment as a professional sportsperson (including as a sports coach); and

(c) study is permitted, subject to the ATAS condition in Appendix ATAS; and

(d) if Part 10 applies the applicant will be required to register with the police.

Settlement by a person on the Global Talent route

Validity requirements for settlement by a person on the Global Talent route

GT 8.1. A person applying for settlement on the Global Talent route must apply online on the gov.uk website on the specified form 'Settle in the UK in various immigration categories: form SET(O)'.

GT 8.2. An application for settlement on the Global Talent route must meet all the following requirements:

(a) any fee must have been paid; and

(b) the applicant must have provided any required biometrics; and

(c) the applicant must have provided a passport or other travel document which satisfactorily establishes their identity and nationality; and

(d) the applicant must be in the UK; and

[(e) the applicant's endorsement or prize listed in Appendix Global Talent: Prestigious Prizes must not have been withdrawn [[or suspended]].]

Note: Sub-paragraph (e) substituted from 5 May 2021 (HC 1248). Words in (e) inserted from 6 October 2021 subject to savings for applications made before that date (HC 617).

GT 8.3. The applicant must have, or have last been granted, permission on the Global Talent route.

GT 8.4. An application which does not meet all the validity requirements for settlement on the Global Talent route is invalid and may be rejected and not considered.

Suitability requirements for settlement by a person on the Global Talent route

GT 9.1. The applicant must not fall for refusal under Part 9: grounds for refusal.

GT 9.2. The applicant must not be:

(a) in breach of immigration laws, except that where paragraph 39E applies, that period of overstaying will be disregarded; or

(b) on immigration bail.

Eligibility requirements for settlement by a person on the Global Talent route

Endorsement requirement for settlement by a person on the Global Talent route

[**GT 10.1.** If the applicant was granted their initial application using an endorsement, the endorsement must not have been withdrawn by the endorsing body.

Note: Paragraph substituted from 5 May 2021 (HC 1248).

[**GT 10.2.** The applicant must have earned money in the UK during their last period of permission in the field in either:

(a) a field related to the subject matter of their prize if they were granted for their initial application using a prize listed in Appendix Global Talent: Prestigious Prizes; or

(b) the field in which they were previously endorsed in the Global Talent route if they were granted their initial application using an endorsement.]

Note: Paragraph substituted from 5 May 2021 (HC 1248).

Qualifying period requirement for settlement by a person on the Global Talent route

GT 11.1. The applicant must have spent a continuous period of 3 years in the UK if:

(a) they were endorsed by the Royal Society, British Academy, Royal Academy of Engineering or UKRI; or

(b) they were endorsed under the exceptional talent criteria by Arts Council England or Tech Nation[; or]

[(c) they were granted their initial application using a prize listed in Appendix Global Talent: Prestigious Prizes.]

Note: Words in (b) substituted, (c) inserted from 5 May 2021 (HC 1248).

GT 11.2. The applicant must have spent a continuous period of 5 years in the UK if they were endorsed under the exceptional promise criteria by Arts Council England or Tech Nation.

GT 11.3. [The continuous period must consist of time with permission] on any of (or any combination of), the following routes:

(a) Global Talent; or
(b) Innovator; or
(c) Skilled Worker; or
(d) T2 Minister of Religion; or
(e) T2 Sportsperson; or
[(f) Tier 1 Migrant, other than Tier 1 (Graduate Entrepreneur); or]
[(g) Scale-up.]

Note: Words in introduction substituted from 6 April 2012 (HC 1248). Sub-paragraph (f) substituted, (g) inserted from 22 August 2022 subject to savings for applications made before that date (HC 1118).

Continuous residence requirement for settlement by a person on the Global Talent route

GT 12.1. The applicant must meet the continuous residence requirement as specified in Appendix Continuous Residence.

English language requirement for settlement by a person on the Global Talent route

GT 13.1. Unless an exemption applies, the applicant must show English language ability on the Common European Framework of Reference for Languages in speaking and listening to at least level B1.

GT 13.2. The applicant must show they meet the English language requirement as specified in Appendix English Language.

Knowledge of life in the UK requirement for settlement by a person on the Global Talent route

GT 14.1. The applicant must meet the Knowledge of Life in the UK requirement as set out in Appendix KOL UK.

Decision on an application for settlement by a person on the Global Talent route

GT 15.1. If the decision maker is satisfied all the suitability and eligibility requirements are met for settlement on the Global Talent route the applicant will be granted settlement, otherwise the application will be refused.

GT 15.2. If the application is refused the person can apply for an Administrative Review under Appendix AR: Administrative Review.

Dependants on the Global Talent route

Validity requirements for a dependent partner or dependent child on the Global Talent route

GT 16.1. A person applying for entry clearance or permission to stay as a dependent partner or dependent child on the Global Talent route must apply online on the gov.uk website on the specified form as follows:

Applicant	Specified form
EEA national with a chipped passport	Either (as applicable): – Dependant partner or dependant child using the UK Immigration: ID Check app; or – the forms listed below for dependant applicants outside or inside the UK as relevant.
Applicants outside the UK	Dependant partner visa Dependant child visa
Applicants inside the UK	If the dependant is applying at the same time as the Global talent applicant, they can be included in the form 'Global talent – stage 2' where the form allows dependants to be added. Otherwise: • Dependant partner • Dependant child

[**GT 16.2.** An application for entry clearance or permission to stay as a partner or child of a person on the Global Talent route must meet all the following requirements:

(a) any fee and Immigration Health Charge must have been paid; and

(b) the applicant must have provided any required biometrics; and

(c) the applicant must have provided a passport or other travel document which satisfactorily establishes their identity and nationality; and

(d) the applicant must be applying as partner or child of a person (P) who:

(i) has made a valid application for entry clearance or permission to stay on the Global Talent route that has not been decided; or

(ii) has entry clearance or permission to stay on the Global Talent route; or

(iii) is settled or has become a British citizen, providing that P had permission on the Global Talent route when they settled and the applicant either had permission as their partner or child at that time, or the applicant is applying as a child of P and the applicant was born in the UK before P settled.]

Note: Paragraph substituted from 6 April 2022 subject to savings for applications made before that date (HC 1118).

GT 16.3. A person applying as a dependent partner must be aged 18 or over on the date of application.

GT 16.4. [DELETED]

Note: Paragraph deleted from 6 April 2021 (HC 1248).

GT 16.5. An applicant who is applying for permission to stay must be in the UK on the date of application and must not have, or have last been granted, permission:

(a) as a Visitor; or

(b) as a Short-term Student; or

(c) as a Parent of a Child Student; or

(d) as a Seasonal Worker; or

(e) as a domestic worker in a private household; or

(f) outside the Immigration Rules.

GT 16.6. An application which does not meet all the validity requirements for the Global Talent route is invalid and may be rejected and not considered.

Suitability requirements for a dependent partner or dependent child on the Global Talent route

GT 17.1. The applicant must not fall for refusal under Part 9: grounds for refusal.

GT 17.2. If applying for permission to stay the applicant must not be:

(a) in breach of immigration laws, except that where paragraph 39E applies, that period of overstaying will be disregarded; or

(b) on immigration bail.

Eligibility requirements for a dependent partner or dependent child on the Global Talent route

Entry requirement for a dependent partner or dependent child on the Global Talent route

GT 18.1. A person seeking to come to the UK as a partner or child must apply for and obtain entry clearance as a partner or child on the Global Talent route before they arrive in the UK.

GT 18.2. A person applying for entry clearance as a partner or child on the Global Talent route must, if paragraph A39 and Appendix T of these rules apply, provide a valid medical certificate confirming that they have undergone screening for active pulmonary tuberculosis and that this tuberculosis is not present in them.

Relationship requirements for a dependent partner on the Global Talent route

GT 19.1. The applicant must be the partner of a person (P) and one of the following must apply:

(a) P has permission on the Global Talent route; or

(b) P is, at the same time, applying for (and is granted) permission on the Global Talent route; or

(c) P is settled or has become a British citizen, providing P had permission on the Global Talent route and the applicant had permission as P's partner at that time.

GT 19.2. If the applicant and their Global Talent partner are not married or in a civil partnership, all of the following requirements must be met:

(a) they must have been living together in a relationship similar to marriage or civil partnership for at least the 2 years before the date of application; and

(b) any previous relationship of the applicant or their Global Talent partner with another person must have permanently broken down; and

(c) the applicant and their Global Talent partner must not be so closely related that they would not be allowed to marry or form a civil partnership in the UK.

GT 19.3. The relationship between the applicant and their Global Talent partner must be genuine and subsisting.

GT 19.4. The applicant and their Global Talent partner must intend to live together throughout the applicant's stay in the UK.

Relationship requirement for a dependent child on the Global Talent route

GT 20.1. The applicant must be the child of a person (P) and one of the following must apply:

(a) P has permission on the Global Talent route; or

(b) P is, at the same time, applying for (and is granted) permission on the Global Talent route; or

(c) P is settled or has become a British citizen, providing P had permission on the Global Talent route when they settled and the applicant had permission as P's child at that time.

[**GT 20.2.** The applicant's parents must each be either applying at the same time as the applicant, or have permission to be in the UK (other than as a Visitor) unless:

(a) the parent applying for or with entry clearance or permission to stay as a Global Talent is the sole surviving parent; or

(b) the parent applying for or with entry clearance or permission to stay as a Global Talent has sole responsibility for the applicant's upbringing; or

(c) the parent who does not have permission as a Global Talent –

(i) is a British citizen or a person who has a right to enter or stay in the UK without restriction; and

(ii) is or will be ordinarily resident in the UK; or

(d) the decision maker is satisfied that there are serious and compelling reasons to grant the applicant entry clearance or permission to stay with the parent who is applying for or has entry clearance or permission on the Global Talent route.]

Note: Paragraph substituted from 6 October 2021 subject to savings for applications made before that date (HC 617).

Care requirement for a dependent child on the Global Talent route

GT 21.1. If the applicant is under the age of 18 years on the date of application there must be suitable arrangements for the child's care and accommodation in the UK, which must comply with relevant UK legislation and regulations.

Age requirement for a dependent child on the Global Talent route

GT 22.1. The applicant must be under the age of 18 at the date of application, unless they were last granted permission as the dependent child of their parent or parents.

GT 22.2. If the applicant is aged 16 or over at the date of application, they must not be leading an independent life.

Decision on an application as a dependent partner or dependent child on the Global Talent route

GT 23.1. If the decision maker is satisfied that all the suitability and eligibility requirements for a dependent partner or dependent child on the Global Talent route are met, the application will be granted, otherwise the application will be refused.

GT 23.2. If the application is refused, the person can apply for an Administrative Review under Appendix AR: Administrative Review.

Period and conditions of grant for a dependent partner or dependent child on the Global Talent route

GT 24.1. A partner will be granted:

(a) permission which ends on the same date as their partner's [. . .]permission on the Global Talent route; or

(b) 3 years' permission if the partner was (or is being) granted settlement on the Global Talent route.

Note: Word deleted from 6 April 2021 (HC 1248). **NB** statement of changes refers to deleting word in GT.24 which does not exist.

GT 24.2. A child will be granted permission which ends on the same date as whichever of their parents' permission ends first, unless both parents have (or are being granted) settlement or British Citizenship, in which case the child will be granted permission for 3 years.

GT 24.3. The grant will be subject to all the following conditions:

(a) no access to public funds; and

(b) work (including self-employment and voluntary work) is permitted, except as a professional sportsperson or sports coach; and

(c) study is permitted, subject to the ATAS condition in Appendix ATAS, if the applicant is over age 18; and

(d) if Part 10 applies, the applicant will be required to register with the police.

Settlement as a dependent partner or dependent child on the Global Talent route

Validity requirements for settlement as a dependent partner or dependent child on the Global Talent route

GT 25.1. A person applying for settlement as a dependent partner or dependent child on the Global Talent route must apply online on the gov.uk website on the specified form, 'Settle in the UK in various immigration categories: form SET(O)'.

[**GT 25.2.** An application for settlement as a dependent partner or dependent child on the Global Talent route must meet all the following requirements:

(a) any fee must have been paid; and

(b) the applicant must have provided any required biometrics; and

(c) the applicant must have provided a passport or other travel document which satisfactorily establishes their identity and nationality; and

(d) the applicant must be in the UK.

(e) the applicant must be applying as a partner or child of a person (P) who:

(i) has made a valid application for settlement on the Global Talent route and that application has not been decided; or

(ii) is settled or has become a British citizen, providing P had permission on the Global Talent route when they settled and the applicant either had permission as their partner or child at that time or the applicant is applying as a child of P and the applicant was born in the UK before P settled.]

Note: Paragraph substituted from 6 April 2022 subject to savings for applications made before that date (HC 1118).

GT 25.3. An application which does not meet the validity requirements for a dependent partner or dependent child on the Global Talent route is invalid and may be rejected and not considered.

Suitability requirements for settlement as a dependent partner or dependent child on the Global Talent route

GT 26.1. The applicant must not fall for refusal under Part 9: grounds for refusal.

GT 26.2. The applicant must not be:

(a) in breach of immigration laws, except that where paragraph 39E applies, that period of overstaying will be disregarded; or

(b) on immigration bail.

Eligibility requirements for settlement as a dependent partner or dependent child on the Global Talent route

Relationship requirement for settlement for a dependent partner or child on the Global Talent route

[**GT 27.1.** The applicant must be the partner or child of a person (P) where one of the following applies:

(a) P is, at the same time, being granted settlement as a Global Talent; or

(b) P is settled or has become a British citizen, providing P had permission as a Global Talent when they settled and the applicant either:

(i) had permission as P's partner or child at that time; or

(ii) is applying as a child of P, and was born in the UK before P settled.]

Note: Paragraph substituted from 6 October 2021 subject to savings for applications made before that date (HC 617).

[**GT 27.2.** The applicant must either:

(a) have last been granted permission as a dependent partner or dependent child of the person (P) in GT 27.1.

(b) have been born in the UK and be applying as a child of the person (P) in GT 27.1.]

Note: Paragraph substituted from 6 October 2021 subject to savings for applications made before that date (HC 617).

GT 27.3. If applying as a child, the applicant's other parent must be being granted settlement at the same time, or be settled or a British citizen, unless:

(a) the person (P) in GT 27.1. is the applicant's sole surviving parent; or

(b) the person (P) in GT 27.1. has sole responsibility for the applicant's upbringing; or

(c) the decision maker is satisfied that there are serious and compelling reasons to grant the child settlement.

Care requirement for settlement as a dependent child on the Global Talent route

GT 28.1. If the child is under the age of 18 years on the date of application there must be suitable arrangements for the child's care and accommodation in the UK, which must comply with relevant UK legislation and regulations.

Age requirement for settlement as a dependent child on the Global talent route

GT 29.1. The applicant must be under the age of 18 on the date of application, unless they were last granted permission as the dependent child of their parent or parents.

GT 29.2. If the child is aged 16 or over on the date of application, they must not be leading an independent life.

Qualifying period requirement for settlement as a dependent partner on the Global Talent route

GT 30.1. The applicant must have spent a continuous period of 5 years in the UK with permission as a dependent partner of the person (P) in GT 27.1.

Continuous residence requirement for settlement as a dependent partner of on the Global Talent route

GT 31.1. The applicant must meet the continuous resident requirement as set out in Appendix Continuous Residence during the period in GT 30.1.

English language requirement for a dependent partner or dependent child on the Global Talent route

GT 32.1. Unless an exemption applies, the applicant must show English language ability on the Common European Framework of Reference for Languages in speaking and listening to at least level B1.

GT 32.2. The applicant must show they meet the English language requirement as specified in Appendix English Language.

Knowledge of life in the UK requirement for settlement as a dependent partner or dependent child on the Global Talent route

GT 33.1 If the applicant is aged 18 or over on the date of application, they must meet the knowledge of Life in the UK requirement as set out in Appendix KOL UK.

Decision on an application for settlement as a dependent partner or dependent child on the Global Talent route

GT 34.1. If the decision maker is satisfied all the suitability and eligibility requirements are met for settlement as a dependent partner or dependent child on the Global Talent route, the applicant will be granted settlement, otherwise the application will be refused.

GT 34.2. If the application is refused the person can apply for an Administrative Review under Appendix AR: Administrative Review.]

Note: Appendix inserted from 09:00 on 1 December 2020 subject to savings for applications made before that time (HC813).

[Appendix Global Talent: Prestigious Prizes

Applicants who hold one of the following prestigious prizes are eligible to apply for a global talent visa without the need to obtain an endorsement. These prizes have been identified by the [relevant] global talent endorsing bodies as demonstrating exceptional talent.

Note: Word in introduction inserted from 6 October 2021 subject to savings for applications made before that date (HC 617).

[Table 1: Arts and culture prizes]

Note: Heading inserted, table substituted from 6 October 2021 subject to savings for applications made before that date (HC 617). Amendments to table from 6 April 2022 subject to savings for applications made before that date (HC 1118).

[Table 2: Architecture prizes]

Note: Heading and table substituted from 6 October 2021 subject to savings for applications made before that date (HC 617).

[Table 3: Fashion design industry prizes]

Note: Heading and table substituted from 6 October 2021 subject to savings for applications made before that date (HC 617).

[Table 4: Film and television]

Note: Heading and table substituted from 6 October 2021 subject to savings for applications made before that date (HC 617). Amendments to table from 6 April 2022 subject to savings for applications made before that date (HC 1118).

[Table 5: Digital technology prizes]

Note: Heading and table substituted from 6 October 2021 subject to savings for applications made before that date (HC 617).

[Table 6: Science, engineering, humanities and medicine prizes]

Note: Heading and table substituted from 6 October 2021 subject to savings for applications made before that date (HC 617). Amendments to table from 6 April 2022 subject to savings for applications made before that date (HC 1118).

Tables contained in this Appendix are not reproduced as they are subject to regular review and amendment. They can be viewed online at **https://www.gov.uk/guidance/immigration-rules/immigration-rules-appendix-global-talent-prestigious-prizes.**

Note: Appendix inserted from 5 May 2021 (HC 1248).

[Appendix High Potential Individual

This route is for recent graduates of top global universities, who want to work, or look for work in the UK, following the successful completion of an eligible course of study equivalent to UK bachelor's degree level or above. The study must have been with an institution listed on the Global Universities List.

The High Potential Individual route is an unsponsored route.

A dependent partner and dependent children can apply on this route.

The High Potential Individual route is not a route to settlement.

Validity requirements for a High Potential Individual

HPI 1.1. A person applying for entry clearance or permission to stay as a High Potential Individual must apply online on the gov.uk website on the specified form as follows:

(a) for applicants outside the UK, form "High Potential Individual visa"; or

(b) for applicants inside the UK, form "High Potential Individual".

HPI 1.2. An application for entry clearance or permission to stay as a High Potential Individual must meet all the following validity requirements:

(a) any fee and Immigration Health Charge must have been paid; and

(b) the applicant must have provided any required biometrics; and

(c) the applicant must have provided a passport or other travel document which satisfactorily establishes their identity and nationality.

HPI 1.3. The applicant must be aged 18 or over on the date of application.

HPI 1.4. If the applicant has in the last 12 months before the date of application received an award from a Government or international scholarship agency covering both fees and living costs for study in the UK, they must provide written consent to the application from that Government or agency.

HPI 1.5. An applicant who is applying for permission to stay must be in the UK on the date of application and must not have, or have last been granted, permission:

(a) as a Visitor; or

(b) as a Short-term Student; or

(c) as a Parent of a Child Student; or

(d) as a Seasonal Worker; or

(e) as a Domestic Worker in a Private Household; or

(f) outside the Immigration Rules.

HPI 1.6. The applicant must not have been previously granted permission under the Student Doctorate Extension Scheme, as a Graduate or as a High Potential Individual.

HPI 1.7 An application which does not meet all the validity requirements for a High Potential Individual is invalid and may be rejected and not considered.

Suitability requirements for a High Potential Individual

HPI 2.1. The applicant must not fall for refusal under Part 9: grounds for refusal.

HPI 2.2. If applying for permission to stay the applicant must not be:

(a) in breach of immigration laws, except that where paragraph 39E applies, that period of overstaying will be disregarded; or

(b) on immigration bail.

Eligibility requirements for a High Potential Individual

Entry requirements for a High Potential Individual

HPI 3.1. A person seeking to come to the UK as a High Potential Individual must apply for and obtain entry clearance as a High Potential Individual before they arrive in the UK.

HPI 3.2. A person applying for entry clearance as a High Potential Individual must, if paragraph A39 and Appendix T of these rules apply, provide a valid medical certificate confirming that they have undergone screening for active pulmonary tuberculosis and that this tuberculosis is not present in them.

Points requirement for a High Potential Individual

HPI 4.1. The applicant must be awarded a total of 70 points based on the table below.

Requirement	Relevant rules	Points available
Global Universities List degree requirement	HPI 5.1 to 5.4	50
English Language requirement at level B1	HPI 6.1 to 6.3	10
Financial requirement	HPI 7.1 to 7.4	10

Global Universities List degree requirement

HPI 5.1. The applicant must, in the 5 years immediately before the date of the application, have been awarded an overseas degree level academic qualification which Ecctis confirms meets, or exceeds, the recognised standard of a UK bachelor's or UK postgraduate degree.

HPI 5.2. The institution at which the applicant was awarded the degree in HPI 5.1 must appear on the Global Universities List in respect of the date the applicant was awarded the degree.

HPI 5.3 The date the applicant was awarded the degree will be the date as confirmed by Ecctis.

HPI 5.4. If the requirements in HPI 5.1. to HPI 5.3. are met, the applicant will be awarded 50 points.

English language requirement for High Potential Individual

HPI 6.1. Unless an exemption applies, the applicant must show English language ability on the Common European Framework of Reference for Languages in all 4 components (reading, writing, speaking and listening) of at least level B1.

HPI 6.2. The applicant must show they meet the English language requirement as specified in Appendix English Language.

HPI 6.3. If the requirements in HPI 6.1. and HPI 6.2. are met, the applicant will be awarded 10 points for meeting the English language requirement.

Financial requirement for High Potential Individual

HPI 7.1. If the applicant is applying for permission to stay and has been in the UK with permission for 12 months or longer on the date of application, they will meet the financial requirement and do not need to show funds.

HPI 7.2. An applicant who is applying for entry clearance, or who is applying for permission to stay and has been in the UK for less than 12 months at the date of application, must have funds of at least £1,270.

HPI 7.3. The applicant must show that they have held the required level of funds for a 28-day period and must show funds as specified in Appendix Finance.

HPI 7.4. If the requirements in HPI 7.1. to HPI 7.3. are met, the applicant will be awarded 10 points for meeting the Financial requirement.

Decision on an application as a High Potential Individual

HPI 8.1. If the decision maker is satisfied that all the suitability and the relevant eligibility requirements for a High Potential Individual are met, the application will be granted, otherwise the application will be refused.

HPI 8.2. If the application is refused the person can apply for an Administrative Review under Appendix AR: Administrative Review.

Period and conditions of grant for a High Potential Individual

HPI 9.1. The applicant will be granted entry clearance or permission to stay for the period as set out in the table below based on the qualification relied on to meet the Global Universities List degree requirement.

Type of Degree Qualification	Period granted from date of decision
PhD or other doctoral level qualification	3 years
All other degree qualifications	2 years

HPI 9.2. The grant will be subject to all the following conditions:

(a) no access to public funds; and

(b) work (including self-employment and voluntary work) is permitted, apart from work as a professional sportsperson (including as a sports coach); and

(c) study is permitted, except study with an education provider which is a Student sponsor, and which would meet the approved qualification and level of study requirements of the Student route which are set out in Appendix Student; and

(d) study is subject to the ATAS condition in Appendix ATAS; and

(e) if Part 10 of these rules applies the person will be required to register with the police.

Dependent partner ("partner") and dependent child ("child") of a High Potential Individual

Validity requirements for a partner or child of a High Potential Individual

HPI 10.1. A person applying for entry clearance or permission to stay as a partner or child of a High Potential Individual must apply online on the gov.uk website on the specified form as follows:

Location of Partner or Child	Specified form
Applicant outside the UK	• Dependant partner visa • Dependant child visa
Applicant inside the UK	• Dependant partner • Dependant child

HPI 10.2. An application for entry clearance or permission to stay as a partner or child of a High Potential Individual must meet all the following requirements:

(a) any fee and Immigration Health Charge must have been paid; and

(b) the applicant must have provided any required biometrics; and

(c) the applicant must have provided a passport or other travel document which satisfactorily establishes their identity and nationality; and

(d) the applicant must be applying as partner or child of a person who:

(i) has made a valid application for entry clearance or permission to stay on the High Potential Individual route that has not been decided; or

(ii) has entry clearance or permission on the High Potential Individual route.

HPI 10.3. A person applying as a partner must be aged 18 or over on the date of application.

HPI 10.4. A person applying for permission to stay as a partner or child of a person on the High Potential Individual route must be in the UK and must not have, or have last been granted, permission:

(a) as a Visitor; or

(b) as a Short-term Student; or

(c) as a Parent of a Child Student; or

(d) as a Seasonal Worker; or

(e) as a Domestic Worker in a Private Household; or

(f) outside the Immigration Rules.

HPI 10.5. An application which does not meet all the validity requirements is invalid and may be rejected and not considered.

Suitability requirements for a partner and child of a High Potential Individual

HPI 11.1. The applicant must not fall for refusal under Part 9: grounds for refusal.

HPI 11.2. If applying for permission to stay the applicant must not be:

(a) in breach of immigration laws, except that where paragraph 39E applies, that period of overstaying will be disregarded; or

(b) on immigration bail.

Eligibility requirements for a partner and child of a High Potential Individual

Entry requirement for a partner and child of a High Potential Individual

HPI 12.1. A person seeking to come to the UK as a partner or child of a High Potential Individual must apply for and obtain entry clearance as a partner or child of a High Potential Individual before they arrive in the UK.

HPI 12.2. A person applying for entry clearance as a partner or child of a High Potential Individual must, if paragraph A39 and Appendix T of these rules apply, provide a valid medical certificate confirming that they have undergone screening for active pulmonary tuberculosis and that this tuberculosis is not present in them.

Relationship requirements for a partner of a High Potential Individual

HPI 13.1. The applicant must be the partner of a person (P) and one of the following must apply:

(a) P has permission as a High Potential Individual; or

(b) P is, at the same time, applying for (and is granted) permission as a High Potential Individual.

HPI 13.2. If the applicant and their High Potential Individual partner are not married or in a civil partnership, all of the following requirements must be met:

(a) they must have been living together in a relationship similar to marriage or civil partnership for at least the two years before the date of application; and

(b) any previous relationship of the applicant or their High Potential Individual partner with another person must have permanently broken down; and

(c) the applicant and their High Potential Individual partner must not be so closely related that they would not be allowed to marry or form a civil partnership in the UK.

HPI 13.3. The relationship between the applicant and their High Potential Individual partner must be genuine and subsisting.

HPI 13.4. The applicant and their High Potential Individual partner must intend to live together throughout the applicant's stay in the UK.

Relationship requirement for a child on the High Potential Individual route

HPI 14.1. The applicant must be the child of a person (P) and one of the following must apply:

(a) P has permission on the High Potential Individual route; or

(b) P is, at the same time, applying for (and is granted) entry clearance or permission on the High Potential Individual route.

HPI 14.2. The applicant's parents must each be either applying at the same time as the applicant, or have permission to be in the UK (other than as a visitor) unless:

(a) the parent applying for or with entry clearance or permission to stay on the High Potential Individual route is the sole surviving parent; or

(b) the parent applying for or with entry clearance or permission to stay on the High Potential Individual route has sole responsibility for the child's upbringing; or

(c) the parent who does not have permission on the High Potential Individual route:

(i) is a British citizen or a person who has a right to enter or stay in the UK without restriction; and

(ii) is or will be ordinarily resident in the UK; or

(d) the decision maker is satisfied that there are serious and compelling reasons to grant the child permission to come to, or stay in, the UK with the parent who has permission on the High Potential Individual route.

HPI 14.3. If the applicant is a child born in the UK to a High Potential Individual or their partner, the applicant must provide a full UK birth certificate showing the names of both parents.

Age requirement for a child on the High Potential Individual route

HPI 15.1. The child must be under the age of 18 at the date of application unless they were last granted permission as the child of their parent or parents.

HPI 15.2. If the applicant is aged 16 or over at the date of application, they must not be leading an independent life.

Care requirement for a child on the High Potential Individual route

HPI 16.1. If the applicant is under the age of 18 on the date of application, there must be suitable arrangements for the child's care and accommodation in the UK, which must comply with relevant UK laws.

Financial requirement for a partner or child on the High Potential Individual route

HPI 17.1. If the applicant is applying for permission to stay and has been living in the UK with permission for 12 months or longer on the date of application, they will meet the financial requirement and do not need to show funds.

HPI 17.2. If the applicant is applying for entry clearance or has been in the UK for less than 12 months on the date of application, funds of at least the amount required in HPI 17.3 must be held collectively by one or more of the following:

(a) the applicant; and

(b) the High Potential Individual (P); and

(c) if the applicant is applying as a child, their parent who is lawfully in the UK or being granted entry clearance.

HPI 17.3. The funds required are:

(a) at least £285 for a partner in the UK or applying to come to the UK; and

(b) at least £315 for the first child in the UK or applying to come to the UK; and

(c) at least £200 for each additional child in the UK or applying to come to the UK.

HPI 17.4. The funds held must be in addition to any funds required by the High Potential Individual to meet the financial requirement or any dependants in the UK or applying at the same time.

HPI. 17.5. The required level of funds must have been held for a 28-day period and as specified in Appendix Finance.

Decision on an application for a partner and child on the High Potential Individual route

HPI 18.1. If the decision maker is satisfied that all the suitability and eligibility requirements are met for a partner or child on the High Potential Individual route, the application will be granted, otherwise the application will be refused.

HPI 18.2. If the application is refused the person can apply for an Administrative Review under Appendix AR: Administrative Review.

Period and conditions of grant for a partner and child on the High Potential Individual route

HPI 19.1. A partner will be granted entry clearance or permission to stay which ends on the same date as their partner's permission as a High Potential Individual.

HPI 19.2. A child will be granted entry clearance or permission to stay which ends on the same date as their parents' permission.

HPI 19.3. The grant will be subject to all the following conditions:

(a) no access to public funds; and

(b) work (including self-employment and voluntary work) is permitted; except from work as a professional sportsperson (including as a sports coach); and

(c) study is permitted, subject to the ATAS condition in Appendix ATAS (if the study will commence when the person is aged over 18); and

(d) if Part 10 applies, the applicant will be required to register with the police.]

Note: Appendix inserted from 09:00 on 30 May 2022 subject to savings for applications made before that time (HC 1118).

[Appendix: Scale-up

The Scale-up route is for talented individuals recruited by a UK Scale-up Sponsor, who have the skills needed to enable the Scale-up business to continue growing.

The person must have a high-skilled job offer from a qualifying Scale-up business at the required salary level.

A dependent partner and dependent children can apply on this route.

The Scale-up route is a route to settlement.

Validity requirements for a Scale-up Worker

SCU 1.1. A person applying for entry clearance or permission to stay as a Scale-up Worker must apply online on the gov.uk website on the specified form as follows:

(a) for applicants outside the UK, form "Scale-up visa"; or

(b) for applicants inside the UK, form "Scale-up".

SCU 1.2. An application for entry clearance or permission to stay as a Scale-up Worker must meet all the following validity requirements:

(a) any fee and Immigration Health Charge must have been paid; and

(b) the applicant must have provided any required biometrics; and

(c) the applicant must have provided a passport or other travel document which satisfactorily establishes their identity and nationality; and

(d) if the applicant is making a sponsored application, they must have a Certificate of Sponsorship that was issued to them by their Sponsor no more than 3 months before the date of application.

SCU 1.3. The applicant must be aged 18 or over on the date of application.

SCU 1.4. If the applicant has in the last 12 months before the date of application received an award from a Government or international scholarship agency covering both fees and living costs for study in the UK, they must provide written consent to the application from that Government or agency.

SCU 1.5. An applicant who is applying for permission to stay must be in the UK on the date of application and must not have, or have last been granted, permission:

(a) as a Visitor; or

(b) as a Short-term Student; or

(c) as a Parent of a Child Student; or

(d) as a Seasonal Worker; or

(e) as a Domestic Worker in a Private Household; or

(f) outside the Immigration Rules.

SCU 1.6. An application which does not meet all the validity requirements for the Scale-up route is invalid and may be rejected and not considered.

Suitability requirements for a Scale-up Worker

SCU 2.1. The applicant must not fall for refusal under Part 9: grounds for refusal.

SCU 2.2. If applying for permission to stay the applicant must not be:

(a) in breach of immigration laws, except that where paragraph 39E applies, that period of overstaying will be disregarded; or

(b) on immigration bail.

Eligibility requirements for a Scale-up Worker

Entry requirements for a Scale-up Worker

SCU 3.1. A person seeking to come to the UK as a Scale-up Worker must apply for and obtain entry clearance as a Scale-up Worker before they arrive in the UK.

SCU 3.2. A person applying for entry clearance as a Scale-up Worker must, if paragraph A39 and Appendix T of these rules apply, provide a valid medical certificate confirming that they have undergone screening for active pulmonary tuberculosis and that this tuberculosis is not present in them.

Points requirement for a Scale-up Worker

SCU 4.1. The applicant must be awarded 70 points from the table below. An applicant may only be awarded points from one of the first two rows of the table. All applicants must meet the requirements in the final two rows of the table.

SCU 4.2. An applicant may only make a Sponsored Application and score 50 points in the first row of the table if the conditions for making an Unsponsored Application in SCU 4.3. are not met.

SCU 4.3. An applicant must make an Unsponsored Application and score 50 points in the second row of the table if they have been employed as a Scale-up Worker by a sponsor for at least 6 months in a previous permission on the Scale-up route and -

(a) the applicant has permission as a Scale-up Worker on the date of application; or

(b) the applicant last had permission as a Scale-up Worker and

(i) if the applicant is applying for entry clearance, that permission expired less than 6 months before the date of application; or

(ii) if the applicant is applying for permission to stay, paragraph 39E applies.

Type of application	Relevant requirements to be met	Relevant rules	Points
Sponsored application	Sponsorship	SCU 5.1	50
	Job at an appropriate skill level	SCU 6.1 to SCU 6.4	
	Appropriate salary	SCU 71. To SCU 7.6	
Unsponsored Application	UK earnings during most recent permission on the Scale-up route	SCU 8.1 to SCU 8.7	50
All applications	English language requirement at level B1	SCU 9.1 to SCU 9.3	10
All applications	Financial requirement	SCU 10.1 to SCU 10.4	10

Sponsored Application

Sponsorship requirement for Sponsored Application

SCU 5.1. The applicant must have a valid Certificate of Sponsorship for the job they are planning to do, which must:

(a) confirm the applicant's name, that they are being sponsored as a Scale-up Worker, details of the job and salary the Sponsor is offering them and PAYE details; and

(b) include a start date for the job, stated by the Sponsor, which is no more than 3 months after the date of application; and

(c) confirm the applicant is expected to work for the Sponsor for at least the first 6 months of their permission; and

(d) not have been used in a previous application which was either granted or refused (but can have been used in a previous application which was rejected as invalid, made void or withdrawn); and

(e) not have been withdrawn by the Sponsor or cancelled by the Home Office; and

(f) confirm whether or not the Academic Technology Approval Scheme (ATAS) requirement in Appendix ATAS applies.

SCU 5.2. The sponsor must be authorised by the Home Office to sponsor the job in question under the Scale-up route.

SCU 5.3. The Sponsor must be listed as A-rated on the Home Office's register of licensed sponsors.

SCU 5.4. The decision maker must not have reasonable grounds to believe the job the applicant is being sponsored to do:

(a) does not exist; or

(b) is a sham; or

(c) has been created mainly so the applicant can apply for entry clearance or permission to stay.

SCU 5.5. The decision maker must not have reasonable grounds to believe the job the applicant is being sponsored to do amounts to:

(a) the hire of the applicant to a third party who is not the Sponsor to fill a position with that party, whether temporary or permanent; or

(b) contract work to undertake an ongoing routine role or to provide an ongoing routine service for a third party who is not the sponsor, regardless of the nature or length of any arrangement between the sponsor and the third party.

Job at an appropriate skill level requirement for Sponsored Application

SCU 6.1. The applicant must be sponsored for a job in an occupation code listed in Appendix Skilled Occupations that is identified as eligible for the Scale-up route.

SCU 6.2. The sponsor must have chosen an appropriate occupation code, and the decision maker must not have reasonable grounds to believe the sponsor has chosen a less appropriate occupation code for any of the following reasons:

(a) the most appropriate occupation code is not eligible under the Scale-up route; or

(b) the most appropriate occupation code has a higher going rate than the proposed salary.

SCU 6.3. To support the assessment in SCU 6.2, the decision maker may, in particular, consider:

(a) whether the Sponsor has shown a genuine need for the job as described; and

(b) whether the applicant has the appropriate skills, qualifications and experience needed to do the job as described; and

(c) the sponsor's history of compliance with the immigration system including, but not limited to, paying its sponsored workers appropriately; and

(d) any additional information from the sponsor.

SCU 6.4. If the ATAS requirement in Appendix ATAS applies, the applicant must provide a valid ATAS certificate.

Appropriate salary requirement for Sponsored Application

SCU 7.1. The salary for the job for which the applicant is being sponsored must equal or exceed all of the following:

(a) £33,000 per year; and

(b) £10.10 per hour; and

(c) the going rate for the occupation code.

SCU 7.2. Salary only includes guaranteed basic gross pay (before income tax and including employee pension and national insurance contributions).

SCU 7.3. Salary does not include other pay and benefits, such as any of the following:

(a) pay which cannot be guaranteed because the nature of the job means that hours fluctuate; or

(b) additional pay such as shift, overtime or bonus pay, (whether or not it is guaranteed); or

(c) employer pension and employer national insurance contributions; or

(d) any allowances, such as accommodation or cost of living allowances; or

(e) in-kind benefits, such as equity shares, health insurance, school or university fees, company cars or food; or

(f) one-off payments, such as 'golden hellos'; or

(g) any payments relating to immigration costs, such as the fee or Immigration Health Charge; or

(h) payments to cover business expenses, including (but not limited to) travel to and from the applicant's country of residence, equipment, clothing, travel or subsistence.

SCU 7.4. If the applicant is being sponsored to work more than 48 hours a week, only the salary for the first 48 hours a week will be considered towards the salary requirements set out in SCU 7.1 (a).
For example, an applicant who works 60 hours a week for £12.50 per hour will be considered to have a salary of £31,200 (£12.50 x 48 x 52) per year and not £39,000 (£12.50 x 60 x 52).

SCU 7.5. Going rates in Table 1 of Appendix Skilled Occupations are based on a 39-hour week will be pro-rated, and the £10.10 per hour salary requirement will be calculated, to the applicant's working pattern, as follows:

(a) (the going rate for the occupation code stated in Table 1 of Appendix Skilled Occupations) x (the number of weekly working hours stated by the sponsor ÷ 39)

(b) the applicant's full weekly hours will be included when checking their salary against the going rate and the £10.10 per hour salary requirement, even if they work more than 48 hours a week.

SCU 7.6. If the requirements in SCU 5.1. to SCU 7.5. are met, the applicant will be awarded 50 points for meeting the Sponsored Application requirements.

Unsponsored Application

UK earnings in most recent grant of permission as a Scale-up Worker requirement for Unsponsored Application

SCU 8.1. The applicant must have had monthly PAYE earnings in the UK equivalent to at least £33,000 per year during at least 50% of their permission as a Scale-up Worker (for example, an applicant with 2 years' permission as a Scale-up Worker must have had this level of earnings during at least 12 months of that permission).

SCU 8.2. For the purpose of meeting the requirement in SCU 8.1, periods of absence from work, in a job with PAYE earnings of at least £33,000 per year, for any of the following reasons will be treated as periods during which the applicant was paid the equivalent of at least £33,000 per year:

(a) statutory maternity, paternity, parental, or shared parental leave; or

(b) statutory adoption leave; or

(c) sick leave.

For example, an applicant with 2 years' permission, who spent 6 months on the above types of leave during a 2-year permission as a Scale-up Worker, must have had PAYE earnings in the UK equivalent to at least £33,000 per year during at least 6 months of the remaining 18 months of that permission.

SCU 8.3. PAYE means the guaranteed basic gross pay (before income tax and including employee pension and national insurance contributions), recorded through PAYE.

SCU 8.4. Earnings do not include other sources of income, such as any of the following:

(a) earnings from self-employment; or

(b) earnings from outside the UK; or

(c) payments not recorded through PAYE; or

(d) employer pension and employer national insurance contributions; or

(e) income from savings, investments, property, inheritance, gambling or competitions.

SCU 8.5. The decision maker must not have reasonable grounds to believe the PAYE earnings, or any part of the PAYE earnings, the applicant is relying on have been fabricated or inflated or do not relate to genuine employment.

SCU 8.6. To support the assessment in SCU 8.5, the decision maker may in particular consider any of the following:

(a) whether the business from which the earnings are claimed can be shown to exist and be lawfully and genuinely trading; and

(b) any payments made by the applicant to other parties; and

(c) any additional information.

SCU 8.7. If the requirements in SCU 8.1. to SCU 8.6. are met, the applicant will be awarded 50 points for meeting the Unsponsored Application requirements.

All Applications by Scale-up Workers

English language requirement for Scale-up Worker

SCU 9.1. Unless an exemption applies, the applicant must show English language ability on the Common European Framework of Reference for Languages in all 4 components (reading, writing, speaking and listening) of at least level B1.

SCU 9.2. The applicant must show they meet the English language requirement as specified in Appendix English Language.

SCU 9.3. If the requirements in SCU 9.1. and SCU 9.2. are met, the applicant will be awarded 10 points for meeting the English language requirement.

Financial requirement for Scale-up Worker

SCU 10.1. If the applicant is applying for permission to stay and has been in the UK with permission for 12 months or longer on the date of application, they will meet the financial requirement and do not need to show funds.

SCU 10.2. If the applicant is applying for entry clearance, or has been in the UK for less than 12 months on the date of application, either:

(a) the applicant must have funds of at least £1,270; or

(b) if the applicant is applying as a sponsored applicant, the applicant's A-rated sponsor must confirm on the Certificate of Sponsorship that they will, if necessary, maintain and accommodate the applicant up to the end of the first month of their employment, to an amount of at least £1,270.

SCU 10.3. If SCU 10.2.(a) applies, the applicant must show that they have held the required funds for a 28-day period and must show funds as specified in Appendix Finance.

SCU 10.4. If the requirements in SCU 10.1 to SCU 10.3. are met, the applicant will be awarded 10 points for meeting the financial requirement.

Decision on an application as a Scale-up worker

SCU 11.1. If the decision maker is satisfied that all the suitability and the relevant eligibility requirements for a Scale-up Worker are met, the application will be granted, otherwise the application will be refused.

SCU 11.2. If the application is refused the person can apply for an Administrative Review under Appendix AR: Administrative Review.

Period and conditions of grant for a Scale-up Worker

SCU 12.1. If the applicant was awarded 50 points for meeting the Sponsored Application requirements, they will be granted entry clearance or permission to stay for 2 years.

SCU 12.2. If the applicant was awarded 50 points for meeting the Sponsored Application requirements, the grant will be subject to all the following conditions:

(a) no access to public funds; and

(b) for the first 6 months of their permission, the applicant must be employed in the job for which the applicant is being sponsored; and

(c) in addition to (b), work (including self-employment and voluntary work) is permitted, except for work as a professional sportsperson (including as a sports coach); and

(d) study is permitted, subject to the ATAS condition in Appendix ATAS; and

(e) if Part 10 of these rules applies, the applicant will be required to register with the police.

SCU 12.3. If the applicant was awarded 50 points for meeting the Unsponsored Application requirements, they will be granted entry clearance or permission to stay for 3 years.

SCU 12.4. If the applicant was awarded 50 points for meeting the Unsponsored Application requirements, the grant will be subject to all the following conditions:

(a) no access to public funds; and

(b) work (including self-employment and voluntary work) is permitted, except for work as a professional sportsperson (including as a sports coach); and

(c) study is permitted, subject to the ATAS condition in Appendix ATAS; and

(d) if Part 10 of these rules applies, the applicant will be required to register with the police.

Settlement as a Scale-up Worker

Validity requirements for settlement as a Scale-up Worker

SCU 13.1. A person applying for settlement as a Scale-up Worker must apply online on the gov.uk website on the specified form, "Settle in the UK in various immigration categories: form SET(O)".

SCU 13.2. An application for settlement as a Scale-up Worker must meet all the following requirements:

(a) any fee must have been paid; and
(b) the applicant must have provided any required biometrics; and
(c) the applicant must have provided either a passport or other travel document which satisfactorily establishes their identity and nationality; and
(d) the applicant must be in the UK on the date of application.

SCU 13.3. The applicant must have, or have last been granted, permission as a Scale-up Worker.

SCU 13.4. An application which does not meet the validity requirements for settlement as a Scale-up Worker is invalid and may be rejected and not considered.

Suitability requirements for settlement as a Scale-up Worker

SCU 14.1. The applicant must not fall for refusal under Part 9: grounds for refusal.

SCU 14.2. The applicant must not be:
(a) in breach of immigration laws, except that where paragraph 39E applies, that period of overstaying will be disregarded; or
(b) on immigration bail.

Eligibility requirements for settlement as a Scale-up Worker

Qualifying period requirement for settlement as a Scale-up Worker

SCU 15.1. The applicant must have spent a continuous period of 5 years in the UK.

SCU 15.2. The 5-year continuous period must consist of time with permission on any of, or any combination of, the following routes:
(a) Scale-up; or
(b) Skilled Worker; or
(c) Global Talent; or
(d) Innovator; or
(e) T2 Minister of Religion; or
(f) International Sportsperson; or
(g) Representative of an Overseas Business; or
(h) as a Tier 1 Migrant, other than Tier 1 (Graduate Entrepreneur).

Continuous residence requirement for settlement as a Scale-up Worker

SCU 16.1. The applicant must meet the continuous residence requirement as set out in Appendix Continuous Residence during the period in SCU 15.1.

Knowledge of life in the UK requirement for settlement as a Scale-up Worker

SCU 17.1. Unless an exemption applies, the applicant must meet the knowledge of Life in the UK requirement as set out in Appendix KOL UK.

UK earnings in most recent permission requirement

SCU 18.1. The applicant must be in employment in the UK with a salary paid through PAYE of at least £33,000 per year, on the date of application.

SCU 18.2. The applicant must have had monthly PAYE earnings in the UK equivalent to at least £33,000 per year during at least 24 months of the 3 years immediately before the date of application.

SCU 18.3. For the purpose of the calculation in SCU 18.2, periods of absence from work, in a job with PAYE earnings of at least £33,000 per year, for any of the following reasons will be treated as periods during which the applicant was paid the equivalent of at least £33,000 per year:

(a) statutory maternity, paternity, parental, or shared parental leave; or

(b) adoption leave; or

(c) sick leave.

For example, an applicant, who spent 6 months on the above types of leave during their last 3-year's permission as a Scale-up Worker, must have had monthly PAYE earnings in the UK equivalent to at least £33,000 per year during at least 18 months of the remaining 30 months of that permission.

SCU 18.4. Earnings only include guaranteed basic gross pay (before income tax and including employee pension and national insurance contributions), recorded through PAYE.

SCU 18.5. Earnings do not include other sources of income, such as any of the following:

(a) earnings from self-employment; or

(b) earnings from outside the UK; or

(c) payments not recorded through PAYE; or

(d) employer pension and employer national insurance contributions; or

(e) income from savings, investments, property, inheritance, gambling or competitions.

SCU 18.6. The decision maker must not have reasonable grounds to believe the PAYE earnings the applicant is relying on have been inflated or fabricated or do not relate to genuine employment.

SCU 18.7. To support the assessment in SCU 18.6, the decision maker may in particular consider any of the following:

(a) whether the business from which the earnings are claimed can be shown to exist and be lawfully and genuinely trading; and

(b) any payments made by the applicant to other parties; and

(c) any other relevant information.

Decision on an application for settlement as a Scale-up Worker

SCU 19.1. If the decision maker is satisfied all the suitability and eligibility requirements for settlement as a Scale-up Worker are met, the applicant will be granted settlement, otherwise the application will be refused.

SCU 19.2. If the application is refused, the person can apply for an Administrative Review under Appendix AR: Administrative Review.

Dependent partner ("partner") and dependent child ("child") of a Scale-up Worker.

Validity requirements for a partner or child on the Scale-up route

SCU 20.1. A person applying for entry clearance or permission to stay as a partner or child on the Scale-up Worker route must apply online on the gov.uk website on the specified form as follows:

Location of Partner or Child	Specified form
Applicant outside the UK	• Dependant partner visa • Dependant child visa
Applicant inside the UK	• Dependant partner • Dependant child

SCU 20.2. An application for entry clearance or permission to stay as a partner or child of a Scale-up Worker must meet all the following requirements:

(a) any fee and Immigration Health Charge must have been paid; and

(b) the applicant must have provided any required biometrics; and

(c) the applicant must have provided a passport or other travel document which satisfactorily establishes their identity and nationality; and

(d) the applicant must be applying as partner or child of a person (P) who:

(i) has made a valid application for entry clearance or permission to stay on the Scale-up route that has not been decided; or

(ii) has entry clearance or permission to stay on the Scale-up route; or

(iii) is settled or has become a British citizen, providing that P had permission on the Scale-up route when they settled and the applicant either had permission as their partner or child at that time, or the applicant is applying as a child of P and the applicant was born in the UK before P settled.

SCU 20.3. A person applying as a partner must be aged 18 or over on the date of application.

SCU 20.4. A person who is applying for permission to stay as a partner or child of a Scale-up Worker must be in the UK on the date of application and must not have, or have last been granted, permission:

(a) as a Visitor; or

(b) as a Short-term Student; or

(c) as a Parent of a Child Student; or

(d) as a Seasonal Worker; or

(e) as a Domestic Worker in a Private Household; or

(f) outside the Immigration Rules.

SCU 20.5. An application which does not meet all the validity requirements is invalid and may be rejected and not considered.

Suitability requirements for a partner or child on the Scale-up route

SCU 21.1. The applicant must not fall for refusal under Part 9: grounds for refusal.

SCU 21.2. If applying for permission to stay the applicant must not be:

(a) in breach of immigration laws, except that where paragraph 39E applies, that period of overstaying will be disregarded; or

(b) on immigration bail.

Eligibility requirements for a partner and child on the Scale-up route

Entry requirement for a partner and child on the Scale-up route

SCU 22.1. A person seeking to come to the UK as a partner or child of a Scale-up Worker must apply for and obtain entry clearance as a partner or child of a Scale-up Worker before they arrive in the UK.

SCU 22.2. A person applying for entry clearance as a partner or child on the Scale-up route must, if paragraph A39 and Appendix T of these rules apply, provide a valid medical certificate confirming that they have undergone screening for active pulmonary tuberculosis and that this tuberculosis is not present in them.

Relationship requirements for a partner on the Scale-up route

SCU 23.1. The applicant must be the partner of a person (P) and one of the following must apply:

(a) P has permission on the Scale-up route; or

(b) P is, at the same time, applying for (and is granted) permission on the Scale-up route; or

(c) P is settled or has become a British citizen, providing P had permission on the Scale-up route when they settled, and the applicant had permission as P's partner at that time.

SCU 23.2. If the applicant and their Scale-up Worker partner are not married or in a civil partnership, all of the following requirements must be met:

(a) they must have been living together in a relationship similar to marriage or civil partnership for at least the two years before the date of application; and

(b) any previous relationship of the applicant or their Scale-up Worker partner with another person must have permanently broken down; and

(c) the applicant and their Scale-up Worker partner must not be so closely related that they would not be allowed to marry or form a civil partnership in the UK.

SCU 23.3. The relationship between the applicant and their Scale-up Worker partner must be genuine and subsisting.

SCU 23.4. The applicant and their Scale-up Worker partner must intend to live together throughout the applicant's stay in the UK.

Relationship requirement for a dependent child on the Scale-up route

SCU 24.1. The applicant must be the child of a person (P) and one of the following must apply:

(a) P has permission on the Scale-up route; or

(b) P is, at the same time, applying for (and is granted) entry clearance or permission on the Scale-up route; or

(c) P is settled or has become a British citizen, providing P had permission on the Scale-up route when they settled, and the applicant had permission as P's dependent child at that time.

SCU 24.2. The applicant's parents must each be either applying at the same time as the applicant, or have permission to be in the UK (other than as a visitor) unless:

(a) the parent applying for or with entry clearance or permission to stay on the Scale-up route is the sole surviving parent; or

(b) the parent applying for or with entry clearance or permission to stay on the Scale-up route has sole responsibility for the child's upbringing; or

(c) the parent who does not have entry clearance or permission to stay on the Scale-up route:

(i) is a British citizen or a person who has a right to enter or stay in the UK without restriction; and

(ii) is or will be ordinarily resident in the UK; or

(d) the decision maker is satisfied that there are serious and compelling reasons to grant the child entry clearance or permission to come to, or stay in, the UK with the parent who is applying for or has entry clearance or permission to stay on the Scale-up route.

SCU 24.3. If the applicant is a child born in the UK to a Scale-up Worker or their partner, the applicant must provide a full UK birth certificate showing the names of both parents.

Age requirement for a dependent child on the Scale-up route

SCU 25.1. The applicant must be under the age of 18 at the date of application unless they were last granted permission as the child of their parent or parents.

SCU 25.2. If the applicant is aged 16 or over at the date of application, they must not be leading an independent life.

Care requirement for a dependent child on the Scale-up route

SCU 26.1. If the applicant is under the age of 18 on the date of application, there must be suitable arrangements for the applicant's care and accommodation in the UK, which must comply with relevant UK laws.

Financial requirement for a partner or child on the Scale-up route

SCU 27.1. If the applicant is applying for permission to stay and has been living in the UK with permission for 12 months or longer on the date of application, they will meet the financial requirement and do not need to show funds.

SCU 27.2. If an applicant is applying for entry clearance, or has been living in the UK for less than 12 months on the date of application, either:

(a) funds of at least the amount required in SCU 27.4. must be held collectively by one or more of the following:

(i) the applicant; and

(ii) the Scale-up Worker (P); and

(iii) if the applicant is applying as a child, their parent who is lawfully present in the UK or being granted entry clearance, or permission to stay, at the same time; or

(b) the Scale-up Worker's A-rated sponsor must certify that they will, if necessary, maintain and accommodate the partner and/or any child as well as the Scale-up Worker, up to the end of the first month of each of their grants of permission, to at least the amounts required in SCU 27.4.

SCU 27.3. An applicant may only rely on the option in SCU 27.2(b) if the date of application is at least one calendar month before the end of the first 6 months of the Scale-up Worker's first grant of permission on the Scale-up route.

SCU 27.4. The funds required are:

(a) at least £285 for a partner in the UK or applying for entry clearance; and

(b) at least £315 for the first child in the UK or applying for entry clearance; and

(c) at least £200 for each additional child in the UK or applying for entry clearance.

SCU 27.5. If SCU 27.2(a) applies, the funds held by the applicant must be held in addition to any funds required for the Scale-up Worker to meet the financial requirement and any other dependants in the UK or applying at the same time.

SCU 27.6. If SCU 27.2(a) applies, the funds must have been held for a 28-day period and as set out in Appendix Finance.

Decision on application for a partner and child of a Scale-up Worker

SCU 28.1. If the decision maker is satisfied that all the suitability and eligibility requirements are met for a partner or child of a Scale-up Worker, the application will be granted, otherwise the application will be refused.

SCU 28.2. If the application is refused the person can apply for an Administrative Review under Appendix AR: Administrative Review.

Period and conditions of grant for a partner and child on the Scale-up route

SCU 29.1. A partner will be granted:

(a) entry clearance or permission to stay which ends on the same date as their partner's permission as a Scale-up Worker; or

(b) 3 years' entry clearance or permission if the Scale-up Worker was (or is being) granted settlement as a Scale-up Worker.

SCU 29.2. A child will be granted permission which ends on the same date as whichever of their parents' permission ends first, unless both parents have (or are being granted) settlement or British Citizenship, in which case the child will be granted permission for 3 years.

SCU 29.3. The grant will be subject to all the following conditions:

(a) no access to public funds; and

(b) work (including self-employment and voluntary work) permitted; except work as a professional sportsperson (including as a sports coach); and

(c) study is permitted, subject to the ATAS condition in Appendix ATAS (if the study will commence when the person is aged over 18); and

(d) if Part 10 of these rules applies, the applicant will be required to register with the police.

Settlement for a partner or child on the Scale-up route

Validity requirements for settlement as a partner or child on the Scale-up route

SCU 30.1. A person applying for settlement as a partner or child of a Scale-up Worker must apply online on the gov.uk website on the specified form, "Settle in the UK in various immigration categories: form SET(O)".

SCU 30.2. An application for settlement as a partner or child of a Scale-up Worker must meet all the following requirements:

(a) any fee must have been paid; and

(b) the applicant must have provided any required biometrics; and

(c) the applicant must have provided a passport or other travel document which satisfactorily establishes their identity and nationality; and

(d) the applicant must be in the UK on the date of application; and

(e) the applicant must be applying as a partner or child of a person (P) who:

(i) has made a valid application for settlement in the UK on the Scale-up route and that application has not been decided; or

(ii) is settled or has become a British citizen, provided that P had permission on the Scale-up route when they settled and the applicant either had permission as their partner or child at that time, or the applicant is applying as a child of P and the applicant was born in the UK before P settled.

SCU 30.3. An application which does not meet the validity requirements for a partner or child of a Scale-up Worker is invalid and may be rejected and not considered.

Suitability requirements for settlement as a dependent partner or dependent child on the Scale-up route

SCU 31.1. The applicant must not fall for refusal under Part 9: grounds for refusal.

SCU 31.2. The applicant must not be:

(a) in breach of immigration laws, except that where paragraph 39E applies, that period of overstaying will be disregarded; or

(b) on immigration bail.

Eligibility requirements for settlement as a dependent partner or dependent child on the Scale-up route

Relationship requirement for settlement as a dependent partner or dependent child of a Scale-up Worker

SCU 32.1. The applicant must be the partner or child of a person (P) where one of the following applies:

(a) P is, at the same time, being granted settlement as a Scale-up Worker; or

(b) P is settled in the UK or has become a British citizen, providing P had permission as a Scale-up Worker when they settled and the applicant either:

(i) had permission as P's partner or child at that time; or

(ii) is applying as a child of P and was born in the UK before P settled.

SCU 32.2. The applicant must either:

(a) have last been granted permission as a partner or child of the person (P) in SCU 32.1; or

(b) have been born in the UK and be applying as a child of the person (P) in SCU 32.1.

SCU 32.3. If applying as a partner, the applicant and the person (P) in SCU 32.1. must meet the relationship requirement in SCU 23.2 to SCU 23.4 and must have met them throughout the 5 years ending on the date of application.

SCU 32.4. If applying as a child, the applicant's other parent (who is not the person (P) in SCU 32.1) must be being granted settlement at the same time, or be settled or a British citizen, unless:

(a) P in SCU 32.1 is the applicant's sole surviving parent; or

(b) P in SCU 32.1 has sole responsibility for the applicant's upbringing; or

(c) the decision maker is satisfied that there are serious and compelling reasons to grant the applicant settlement.

Age requirement for settlement as a dependent child on the Scale-up route

SCU 33.1. The applicant must be under the age of 18 on the date of application, unless they were last granted permission as the child of their parent or parents.

SCU 33.2. If the applicant is aged 16 or over on the date of application, they must not be leading an independent life.

Care requirement for settlement as a dependent child of a Scale-up Worker

SCU 34.1. If the applicant is under the age of 18 on the date of application there must be suitable arrangements for the child's care and accommodation in the UK, which must comply with relevant UK legislation and regulations.

Qualifying period requirement for settlement as a partner on the Scale-up route

SCU 35.1. The applicant must have spent a continuous period of 5 years in the UK with permission as a partner of the person (P) in SCU 32.1.

Continuous residence requirement for settlement as a partner on the Scale-up route

SCU 36.1. The applicant must meet the continuous residence requirement as set out in Appendix Continuous Residence during the period in SCU 35.1.

English language requirement for settlement as a partner or child on the Scale-up route

SCU 37.1. Unless an exemption applies, the applicant must show English language ability on the Common European Framework of Reference for Languages in speaking and listening to at least level B1.

SCU 37.2. The applicant must show they meet the English language requirement as specified in Appendix English Language.

Knowledge of life in the UK requirement for settlement as a partner or child on the Scale-up route

SCU 38.1. Unless an exemption applies, the applicant must meet the knowledge of Life in the UK requirement as set out in Appendix KOL UK.

Decision on an application for settlement as a partner or child on the Scale-up route

SCU 39.1. If the decision maker is satisfied all the suitability and eligibility requirements are met for settlement as a partner or child of a Scale-up Worker, the application will be granted settlement, otherwise the application will be refused.

SCU 39.2. If the application is refused the person can apply for an Administrative Review under Appendix AR: Administrative Review.]

Note: Appendix inserted from 22 August 2022 subject to savings for applications made before that date (HC 1118).

[Appendix Start-up

The Start-up route is for a person seeking to establish a business in the UK for the first time.

The person must have an innovative, viable and scalable business idea which is supported by an endorsing body approved by the Home Office.

A person on the Start-up route can bring a dependent partner and dependent children to the UK.

Start-up is not a route to settlement. A person may be eligible to progress from Start-up to the Innovator route, which is a route to settlement.

Validity requirements for Start-up route

SU 1.1. A person applying for entry clearance or permission to stay on the Start-up route must apply online on the gov.uk website on the specified form as follows:

Applicant	Specified form
EEA national with a chipped passport	Either: – Start-up or Innovator using the UK Immigration: ID Check app (when available); or – the forms listed below for applicants outside or inside the UK (as relevant)
Applicants outside the UK	Start-up or Innovator visa
Applicants inside the UK	Start-up or Innovator permission to stay

SU 1.2. An application for entry clearance or permission to stay on the Start-up route must meet all the following requirements:

(a) any fee and Immigration Health Charge must have been paid; and

(b) the applicant must have provided any required biometrics; and

(c) the applicant must have provided a passport or other travel document which satisfactorily establishes their identity and nationality; and

(d) the applicant must have been issued with an endorsement letter by an endorsing body dated no more than 3 months before the date of application and that endorsement must not have been withdrawn.

SU 1.3. The applicant must be aged 18 or over on the date of application.

SU 1.4. If the applicant has in the last 12 months before the date of application received an award from a Government or international scholarship agency covering both fees and living costs for study in the UK, they must provide written consent to the application from that Government or agency.

SU 1.5. A person applying for permission to stay must be in the UK and must not have, or have last been granted, permission:

(a) as a Visitor; or

(b) as a Short-term Student; or

(c) as a Parent of a Child Student; or

(d) as a Seasonal Worker; or

(e) as a domestic worker in a private household; or

(f) outside the Immigration Rules.

SU 1.6. An application which does not meet all the validity requirements for the Start-up route is invalid and may be rejected and not considered.

Suitability requirements for the Start-up route

SU 2.1. The applicant must not fall for refusal under Part 9: grounds for refusal.

SU 2.2. If applying for permission to stay the applicant must not be:

(a) in breach of immigration laws, except that where paragraph 39E applies, that period of overstaying will be disregarded; or

(b) on immigration bail.

Eligibility requirements for the Start-up route

Entry requirements for the Start-up route

SU 3.1. A person seeking to come to the UK on the Start-up route must apply for and obtain entry clearance on the Start-up route before they arrive in the UK.

SU 3.2. A person applying for entry clearance on the Start-up route must, if paragraph A39 and Appendix T of these rules apply, provide a valid medical certificate confirming that they have undergone screening for active pulmonary tuberculosis and that this tuberculosis is not present in them.

Points requirement for Start-up

SU 4.1. The applicant must be awarded a total of 70 points from the table below.

Requirement (mandatory)	Points available
Business is innovative, viable and scalable.	25
The applicant has not previously established a business in the UK	25
English Language at level B2	10
Financial requirement	10
Total number of points required	70

Innovative, viable and scalable business requirement for Start-up route

SU 5.1. An applicant will meet the innovative, viable and scalable business venture requirement if all the following requirements are met:

(a) the applicant has a genuine, original business plan that meets new or existing market needs and/or creates a competitive advantage; and

(b) the applicant's business plan is realistic and achievable based on the applicant's available resources; and

(c) the applicant has, or is actively developing, the necessary skills, knowledge, experience and market awareness to successfully run the business; and

(d) there is evidence of structured planning and of potential for job creation and growth into national markets.

No other established business in the UK requirement for Start-up route

SU 6.1. The applicant must not have previously established any business in the UK which commenced trading, unless this business commenced trading during the applicant's last period of permission and that permission was for any of the following routes:

(a) Start-up; or

(b) Tier 1 (Graduate Entrepreneur); or

(c) Student on the doctorate extension scheme.

Genuine Start-up requirement

SU 7.1. The applicant must be a genuine Start-up applicant.

Financial requirement for the Start-up route

SU 8.1. If the applicant is applying for permission to stay and has been living in the UK with permission for 12 months or more on the date of application, they will meet the financial requirement and do not need to show funds.

SU 8.2. If an applicant is applying for entry clearance or has been in the UK for less than 12 months at the date of application, they must have funds of at least £1,270.

SU 8.3. The applicant must show that they have held the required level of funds for a 28 day period and as set out in Appendix Finance unless their endorsing body confirms they have been awarded funding of at least the amount in SU 8.2.

English language requirement for the Start-up route

SU 9.1. The applicant must show English language ability on the Common European Framework of Reference for Languages in all 4 components (reading, writing, speaking and listening) of at least level B2.

SU 9.2. The applicant must show they meet the English language requirement as specified in Appendix English Language.

Endorsement requirement for the Start-up route

SU 10.1. The applicant must provide a letter from their endorsing body which includes all the following information:

(a) the name of the endorsing body; and

(b) the endorsement reference number; and

(c) the name, telephone number, email and workplace address of a person at the endorsing body who will verify the contents of the letter to the Home Office if requested; and

(d) the date of endorsement; and

(e) the applicant's name, date of birth, nationality and passport or other travel document number; and

(f) a short description of the applicant's business venture and the main products or services it will provide to its customers; and

(g) confirmation that in the view of the endorsing body the applicant's business is innovative, viable and scalable as set out at SU 5.1.; and

(h) confirmation that the endorsing body is satisfied that the applicant will spend the majority of their working time in the UK on developing their business venture; and

(i) confirmation that the endorsing body is satisfied the applicant is either the sole founder of the business or an instrumental member of the founding team; and

(j) confirmation the endorsing body is satisfied that the applicant has created and is relying on their own business plan.

Decision on the Start-up route

SU 11.1. If the decision- maker is satisfied that all the suitability and eligibility requirements are met for the Start-up route, the application will be granted, otherwise the application will be refused.

SU 11.2. If the application is refused the person can apply for Administrative Review under Appendix AR: Administrative Review.

Conditions and period of grant on the Start-up route

SU 12.1. The grant will be subject to all the following conditions:

(a) no access to public funds; and

(b) work (including self-employment and voluntary work) permitted except for employment as a professional sportsperson, including as a sports coach; and

(c) study is permitted, subject to the ATAS condition in Appendix ATAS; and

(d) if Part 10 applies the applicant will be required to register with the police.

SU 12.2. The applicant will be granted permission for a maximum period of 2 years, and a person must not be granted further permission which would result in them spending more than 2 years with permission on the Start-up route, or a combination of the Start-up route and the Tier 1 (Graduate Entrepreneur) route.

Dependants on the Start-up route

Validity requirements for a dependent partner or dependent child on the Start-up route

SU 13.1. An application as a partner or child on the Start-up route must be made online on the gov.uk website on the specified form as follows:

Applicant	Specified form
EEA national with a chipped passport	Either (as applicable): • Dependant partner or dependant child using the UK Immigration: ID Check app; or • the forms listed below for dependant applicants outside or inside the UK as relevant.
Applicants outside the UK	Dependant partner visa Dependant child visa
Applicants inside the UK	If the dependant is applying at the same time as the Start-Up route applicant, they can be included in the form 'Start-Up or Innovator permission to stay' where the form allows dependents to be added. Otherwise: – Dependant partner – Dependant child

[**SU 13.2.** An application for entry clearance or permission to stay as a partner or child of a person on the Start-up route must meet all the following requirements:

(a) any fee and Immigration Health Charge must have been paid; and

(b) the applicant must have provided any required biometrics; and

(c) the applicant must have provided a passport or other travel document which satisfactorily establishes their identity and nationality; and

(d) the applicant must be applying as partner or child of a person (P) who:

(i) has made a valid application for entry clearance or permission to stay on the Start-up not been decided; or

(ii) has entry clearance or permission to stay on the Start-up route; or

(iii) is settled or has become a British citizen, providing that P had permission on the Start-up route when they settled and the applicant either had permission as their partner or child at that time, or the applicant is applying as a child of P and the applicant was born in the UK before P settled.]

Note: Paragraph substituted with no effective date (HC 1118). Paragraph substituted from 1 June 2022 subject to savings for applications made before that date (HC 17).

SU 13.3. A person applying as a dependent partner must be aged 18 or over on the date of application.

SU 13.4. [DELETED]

Note: Paragraph deleted from 6 April 2021 (HC 1248).

SU 13.5. A person applying for permission to stay must be in the UK and must not have, or have last been granted, permission:

(a) as a Visitor; or

(b) as a Short-term Student; or

(c) as a Parent of a Child Student; or

(d) as a Seasonal Worker; or

(e) as a domestic worker in a private household; or

(f) outside the Immigration Rules.

SU 13.6. An application which does not meet all the validity requirements is invalid and may be rejected and not considered.

Suitability requirements for a dependent partner or dependent child on the Start-up route

SU 14.1. The suitability requirements for a partner or child on the Start-up route are that they must not fall for refusal under Part 9: grounds for refusal.

SU 14.2. If applying for permission to stay the applicant must not be:

(a) in breach of immigration laws, except that where paragraph 39E applies, that period of overstaying will be disregarded; or

(b) on immigration bail.

Eligibility requirements for a dependent partner and dependent child on the Start-up route

Entry requirement for a dependent partner and dependent child on the Start-up route

SU 15.1. A person seeking to come to the UK as a partner or child must apply for and obtain entry clearance as a partner or child before they arrive in the UK.

SU 15.2. A person applying for entry clearance as a partner or child on the Start-up route must, if paragraph A39 and Appendix T of these rules apply, provide a valid medical certificate confirming that they have undergone screening for active pulmonary tuberculosis and that this tuberculosis is not present in them.

Relationship requirements for a dependent partner on the Start-up route

SU 16.1. The applicant must be the partner of a person (P) and one of the following must apply:

(a) P has permission on the Start-up route; or

(b) P is, at the same time, applying for (and is granted) permission on the Start-up route.

SU 16.2. If the applicant and their Start-up partner are not married or in a civil partnership, all of the following requirements must be met:

(a) they must have been living together in a relationship similar to marriage or civil partnership for at least the 2 years before the date of application; and

(b) any previous relationship of the applicant or their Start-up partner with another person must have permanently broken down; and

(c) the applicant and their Start-up partner must not be so closely related that they would not be allowed to marry or form a civil partnership in the UK.

SU 16.3. The relationship between the applicant and their Start-up partner must be genuine and subsisting.

SU 16.4. The applicant and their Start-up partner must intend to live together throughout the applicant's stay in the UK.

Relationship requirement for a dependent child on the Start-up route

SU 17.1. The applicant must be the child of a person (P) and one of the following must apply:

(a) P has permission on the Start-up route; or

(b) P is, at the same time, applying for (and is granted) entry clearance or permission on the Start-up route.

[**SU 17.2.** The applicant's parents must each be either applying at the same time as the applicant, or have permission to be in the UK (other than as a Visitor) unless:

(a) the parent applying for or with entry clearance or permission to stay on the Start-up route is the sole surviving parent; or

(b) the parent applying for or with entry clearance or permission to stay on the Start-up route has sole responsibility for the child's upbringing; or

(c) the parent who does not have permission on the Start-up route –

(i) is a British citizen or a person who has a right to enter or stay in the UK without restriction; and

(ii) is or will be ordinarily resident in the UK.

(d) the decision maker is satisfied that there are serious and compelling reasons to grant the child entry clearance or permission to stay with the parent who is applying for or has entry clearance or permission on the Start-up route.]

Note: Paragraph substituted from 6 October 2021 subject to savings for applications made before that date (HC 617).

Care requirement for a dependent child on the Start-up route

SU 18.1. If the applicant is under the age of 18 on the date of application, there must be suitable arrangements for the child's care and accommodation in the UK, which must comply with relevant UK legislation and regulations.

Age requirement for a dependent child on the Start-up route

SU 19.1. The child must be under the age of 18 at the date of application, unless they were last granted permission as the dependent child of their parent or parents.

SU 19.2. If the applicant is aged 16 or over at the date of application, they must not be leading an independent life.

Financial requirement for a dependent partner or dependent child on the Start-up route

SU 20.1. If the applicant is applying for permission to stay and has been living in the UK with permission for 12 months or longer on the date of application, they will meet the financial requirement and do not need to show funds.

[**SU 20.2.** If the applicant is applying for entry clearance, or has been in the UK for less than 12 months on the date of application, funds of at least the amount required in SU 20.2A must be held collectively by one or more of the following:

(a) the applicant; and

(b) the person on the Start-up route (P); and

(c) if the applicant is applying as a dependent child, their parent who is lawfully present in the UK or being granted entry clearance, or permission to stay, at the same time.]

Note: Paragraph substituted from 6 October 2021 subject to savings for applications made before that date (HC 617).

[**SU 20.2A.** The funds required are:

(a) £285 for a dependent partner in the UK, or applying for entry clearance; and

(b) £315 for the first dependent child in the UK, or applying for entry clearance; and

(c) £200 for any other dependent child in the UK, or applying for entry clearance.]

Note: Paragraph inserted from 6 October 2021 subject to savings for applications made before that date (HC 617).

SU 20.3. The funds must be in addition to any funds required by the Start-up applicant to meet the financial requirement and for any dependants in the UK or applying at the same time.

SU 20.4. The required level of funds must have been held for a 28-day period and as set out in Appendix Finance.

Decision on application for a dependent partner and dependent child on the Start-up route

SU 21.1. If the decision maker is satisfied that all the suitability and eligibility requirements are met for a dependent partner or dependent child on the Start-up route the application will be granted, otherwise the application will be refused.

SU 21.2. If the application is refused the person can apply for an Administrative Review under Appendix AR: Administrative Review.

Period and conditions of grant for a dependent partner and dependent child on the Start-up route

SU 22.1. A partner will be granted permission which ends on the same date as their partner's permission on the Start-up route

SU 22.2. A child will be granted permission which ends on the same date as whichever of their parents' permission ends first.

SU 22.3. The grant will be subject to all the following conditions:

(a) no access to public funds; and

(b) work (including self-employment and voluntary work) permitted; except for employment as a professional sportsperson, including as a sports coach; and

(c) study is permitted, subject to the ATAs condition in Appendix ATAS; and

(d) if Part 10 applies the applicant will be required to register with the police.]

Note: Appendix inserted from 09:00 on 1 December 2020 subject to savings for applications made before that time (HC813).

[Appendix Innovator

The Innovator route is for a person seeking to establish a business in the UK based on an innovative, viable and scalable business idea they have generated, or to which they have significantly contributed.

The application must be supported by an endorsing body.

An applicant will normally be expected to have funds of at least £50,000 to invest in their business and they must have a key role in the day to day management and development of the business.

A dependent partner and dependent children can apply on this route.

The Innovator route is a route to settlement.

Validity requirements for an Innovator

INN 1.1. A person applying for entry clearance or permission to stay as an Innovator must apply online on the gov.uk website on the specified form as follows:

Applicant	Specified form
EEA national with a chipped passport	Either: • Start-up or Innovator using the UK Immigration: ID Check app (when available); or • the forms listed below for applicants outside or inside the UK (as relevant)
Applicants outside the UK	Start-up or Innovator visa
Applicants inside the UK	Start-up or Innovator permission to stay

INN 1.2. An application for entry clearance or permission to stay on the Innovator route must meet all the following requirements:

(a) any fee and Immigration Health Charge must have been paid; and

(b) the applicant must have provided any required biometrics; and

(c) the applicant must have provided a passport or other travel document which satisfactorily establishes their identity and nationality; and

(d) the applicant must have been issued with an endorsement letter by an endorsing body no more than 3 months before the date of application and that endorsement must not have been withdrawn.

INN 1.3. The applicant must be aged 18 or over on the date of application.

INN 1.4. If the applicant has in the 12 months before the date of application received an award from a Government or international scholarship agency covering both fees and living costs for study in the UK, they must have provided written consent to the application from that Government or agency.

INN 1.5. A person applying for permission to stay must be in the UK and must not have, or have last been granted, permission:

(a) as a Visitor; or
(b) as a Short-term Student; or
(c) as a Parent of a Child Student; or
(d) as a Seasonal Worker; or
(e) as a domestic worker in a private household; or
(f) outside the Immigration Rules.

Suitability requirements for an Innovator

INN 2.1. The applicant must not fall for refusal under Part 9: grounds for refusal.

INN 2.2. If applying for permission to stay the applicant must not be:

(a) in breach of immigration laws, except that where paragraph 39E applies, that period of overstaying will be disregarded; or

(b) on immigration bail.

Eligibility requirements for an Innovator

Entry requirements for an Innovator

INN 3.1. A person seeking to come to the UK as an Innovator must apply for and obtain entry clearance on the Innovator route before they arrive in the UK.

INN 3.2. A person applying for entry clearance as an Innovator must, if paragraph A39 and Appendix T of these rules apply, provide a valid medical certificate confirming that they have undergone screening for active pulmonary tuberculosis and that this tuberculosis is not present in them.

Genuine Innovator requirement

INN 4.1. The applicant must be a genuine Innovator applicant.

Points requirement for the Innovator route

INN 5.1. The applicant must be awarded 70 points from the table below; of which 50 must either be under the new business criteria or under the same business criteria, but not both.

Requirement	New or same business	Points available
Business plan	New Business	10
Business venture is innovative, viable and scalable.	New Business	20
£50,000 available funds to invest or having been invested	New Business	20
Applicant's previous permission was as in the Innovator, Start-up or Tier 1 (Graduate Entrepreneur) route and they are pursuing a business assessed by a Home Office approved endorsing body either for the previous endorsement or at a contact point.	Same Business	10
Business is active, trading and sustainable and demonstrates significant achievements against the business plan	Same Business	20
Applicant is active in day-to-day management and development of business	Same Business	20
English Language requirement at level B2	Mandatory for all applicants	10
Financial requirement	Mandatory for all applicants	10
Total number of points required		70

Requirements for Innovator route where it is a new business

Business Plan requirement for an Innovator

INN 6.1. The applicant must have an endorsement letter from an endorsing body which confirms that:

(a) the applicant has either generated, or made a significant contribution to, the ideas in their business plan; and

(b) the applicant will have a day-to-day role in carrying out the business plan[,]

[(c) the applicant is either the sole founder or an instrumental member of the founding team.]

Note: Punctuation in (b) substituted, (c) inserted from 6 April 2021 (HC 1248).

Innovative, viable and scalable business requirements for an Innovator

INN 7.1. The applicant must have an innovative, viable and scalable business venture and they must meet all the following requirements:

(a) the applicant must have a genuine, original business plan that meets new or existing market needs and/or creates a competitive advantage; and

(b) the applicant's business plan must be realistic and achievable based on the applicant's available resources; and

(c) the applicant must have, or be actively developing, the necessary skills, knowledge, experience and market awareness to successfully run the business; and

(d) there must be evidence of structured planning and of potential for job creation and growth into national and international markets.

INN 7.2. The applicant must be supported by an endorsing body for this route which confirms in their endorsement letter that they consider that the applicant meets the above requirements.

Investment funds requirement for an Innovator

INN 8.1. The applicant must show that they have at least £50,000 of funds available to invest, or which have been invested, in their business by one of the following:

(a) providing confirmation from the endorsing body that it is providing the funds of at least £50,000; or

(b) providing confirmation from the endorsing body that it has verified the funds are available from other sources (which can include the applicant); or

(c) providing confirmation from the endorsing body that it has verified that at least £50,000 has already been invested in the applicant's business; or

(d) providing evidence that the £50,000 of funds are available from another source.

INN 8.2. Where the business has one or more other team members who are applying for, or have been granted, permission on the Innovator route, there must be at least £50,000 available to, or which has been invested by, each team member.

INN 8.3. Where the requirement is being met under INN 8.1 (a), (b) or (c) the applicant must be supported by an endorsing body which confirms as part of their endorsement letter that they consider that the applicant meets those requirements.

INN 8.4. Where the requirement is being met under INN 8.1 (d) and any of the funds are being provided by a UK organisation which employs at least 10 people, the applicant must provide a letter from that organisation confirming this and which must include:

(a) how they know the applicant; and

(b) the amount of funding they are making available in pounds sterling (£); and

(c) confirmation that this funding has not been promised to any other person or business for another purpose; and

(d) the name and contact details (telephone number, email and workplace address) of an individual at the organisation who will verify the contents of the letter to the Home Office if requested.

INN 8.5. Where the requirement is being met under INN 8.1 (d) and any of the funds are being provided by an overseas organisation, a UK organisation which employs less than 10 people, or an individual, the applicant must provide all of the following:

(a) a signed declaration from the funding provider, dated no more than 3 months before the date of application, setting out all of the following:

(i) how they know the applicant; and

(ii) the amount of funding they are making available in pounds sterling (£); and confirmation that this funding has not been promised to any other person or business for another purpose; and

(iii) the name and contact details (telephone number, email and workplace address) of an individual at the organisation who will verify the contents of the letter to the Home Office if requested; and

(b) a letter from a legal representative (who is registered to practise legally in the country where the third party or the money is), confirming that the declaration and signature in (a) above is genuine; and

(c) a bank letter, dated no earlier than 1 month before the date of application, confirming that the funds are held in a regulated financial institution(s) and if the institution is outside the UK, the letter must also confirm that the funds are transferrable to the UK.

INN 8.6. If any of the funds are held by the applicant, they must provide either of the following:

(a) bank statements, showing the funds are held in the UK in an institution regulated by the Financial Conduct Authority. The statements must cover a consecutive 3 months, ending no earlier than 1 month before the date of application; or

(b) a bank letter, dated no earlier than 1 month before the date of application, confirming that the funds are held in a regulated financial institution(s) and, if the institution is outside the UK, the letter must also confirm that the funds are transferrable to the UK.

INN 8.7. If the documents in INN 8.6. do not show that the applicant has held the funds for at least 3 months, the applicant must also provide the signed declaration and letter from a legal representative set out in INN 8.5 (a) and (b) in relation to the organisation or person who provided the funds to the applicant.

INN 8.8. If any of the funds have already been invested in the applicant's business, the applicant must provide either of the following, showing the amount that has been invested:

(a) business accounts, showing the name of the accountant and the date they were produced; or

(b) business bank statements.

INN 8.9. If any of the evidence in INN 8.4 to INN 8.8. show that the funds are available to the applicant's business rather than to the applicant, or have been invested in the business, the applicant must provide a Companies House document showing their connection to the business. This document is not needed if the endorsement letter confirms the applicant's connection to the business.

INN 8.10. Any funds in a foreign currency will be converted to pounds sterling (£) using the spot exchange rate which appeared on www.oanda.com on the date of application.

INN 8.11. Funds will not be accepted if they are held in a financial institution not permitted in Appendix Finance.

Requirements for Innovator where it is the same business as the business in a previous endorsement under the Innovator, Start-up route or Tier 1 (Graduate Entrepreneur) route.

Business previously assessed by an endorsing body requirement

INN 9.1. The applicant must be supported by an endorsing body which confirms that they are endorsing the application on the basis of a business they or another endorsing body have previously assessed while the applicant had permission on the Innovator Start-up route or Tier 1 (Graduate Entrepreneur).

INN 9.2. The endorsing body must confirm that they are satisfied that the applicant meets the new business requirements in INN 6.1 to INN 8.3., with the exception that applicants previously endorsed in the Start-up or Tier 1 (Graduate Entrepreneur) routes do not need to meet the investment funds requirement at INN 8.1 to INN 8.11.

Business is active, trading and sustainable requirement for an Innovator

INN 10.1. The applicant's business must be active, trading and sustainable and the applicant must have made significant progress against their business plan.

INN 10.2. The applicant's business must be registered with Companies House and the applicant must be listed as a director or member of that business.

INN 10.3. The applicant must be supported by an endorsing body which has assessed the applicant's business and confirmed that it meets the requirements set out in INN10.1. and INN 10.2.

Day to day management requirement for an Innovator

INN 11.1. The applicant must be involved in the day to day management and development of their business and provide a letter confirming this from an endorsing body.

English Language requirement for an Innovator

INN 12.1. The applicant must show English language ability on the Common European Framework of Reference for Languages in all 4 components (reading, writing, speaking and listening) of at least level B2.

INN 12.2. The applicant must show they meet the English language requirement as specified in Appendix English Language.

Financial requirement for an Innovator

INN 13.1. If the applicant is applying for permission to stay and has been in the UK with permission for 12 months or longer on the date of application, they will meet the financial requirement and do not need to show funds.

INN 13.2. An applicant who is applying for entry clearance, or who is applying for permission to stay and has been in the UK for less than 12 months at the date of application, must have funds of at least £1,270.

INN 13.3. The applicant must show that they have held the required level of funds for a 28-day period and as set out in Appendix Finance.

Decision on application as an Innovator

INN 14.1. If the decision maker is satisfied that all the suitability and the relevant eligibility requirements for an Innovator are met, the application will be granted, otherwise the application will be refused.

INN 14.2. If the application is refused the person can apply for an Administrative Review under Appendix AR: Administrative Review.

Period and conditions of grant as an Innovator

INN 15.1. The applicant will be granted permission for a maximum period of 3 years.

INN 15.2. The grant will be subject to the following conditions:

(a) no access to public funds; and
(b) no work, other than working for the business(es) the applicant has established and
(c) study is permitted, subject to the ATAS condition in Appendix ATAS; and
(d) if Part 10 applies the applicant will be required to register with the police.

INN 15.3. In INN 15.2.(b), working for the business(es) does not include any apprenticeship or any work pursuant to a contract of service, whether express or implied and whether oral or written, with another business, (which means successful applicants cannot fill a position or hire their labour to another business, even if the work is undertaken through contracting with the applicant's own business or through a recruitment or employment agency).

Settlement by a person on the Innovator route

Validity requirements for settlement by an Innovator

[**INN 16.1.** A person on the Innovator route who is applying for settlement must apply online on the gov.uk website on the specified form 'Settlement Innovator'.]

Note: Paragraph substituted from 6 October 2021 subject to savings for applications made before that date (HC 617).

INN 16.2. An application for settlement must meet all the following requirements:

(a) any fee must have been paid; and

(b) the applicant must have provided any required biometrics; and

(c) the applicant must have provided a passport or other travel document which satisfactorily establishes their identity and nationality; and

(d) the applicant must be in the UK; and

(e) the applicant must have been issued with an endorsement letter by an endorsing body no more than 3 months before the date of application and that endorsement must not have been withdrawn.

INN 16.3. The applicant must have, or have last been granted, permission on the Innovator route.

INN 16.4. An application which does not meet all the validity requirements for settlement for a person on the Innovator route is invalid and may be rejected and not considered.

Suitability Requirements for settlement by an Innovator

INN 17.1. The applicant must not fall for refusal under Part 9: grounds for refusal.

INN 17.2. The applicant must not be:

(a) in breach of immigration laws, except that where paragraph 39E applies, that period of overstaying will be disregarded; or

(b) on immigration bail.

Eligibility requirements for settlement by an Innovator

Endorsement requirement for settlement by an Innovator

INN 18.1. The applicant must provide an endorsement letter issued by an endorsing body, which includes all of the following information:

(a) the name of the endorsing body; and

(b) the endorsement reference number; and

(c) the date of issue, which must be no earlier than 3 months before the date of application; and

(d) the applicant's name, date of birth, nationality and passport number; and

(e) a short description of the applicant's business venture and the main products or services it has provided; and

(f) the name and contact details (telephone number, email and workplace address) of an individual at the endorsing body who will verify the contents of the letter to the Home Office if requested; and

(g) confirmation that the applicant has shown significant achievements, judged against the business plan assessed in their previous endorsement; and

(h) confirmation that the applicant's business is registered with Companies House and the applicant is listed as a director or member of that business; and

(i) confirmation the business is active and trading; and

(j) confirmation that the business appears to be sustainable for at least the following 12 months, based on its assets and expected income, weighed against its current and planned expenses; and

(k) confirmation the applicant has demonstrated an active key role in the day-to-day management and development of the business; and

(l) confirmation the applicant's business venture has met at least two of the following requirements:

(i) at least £50,000 has been invested into the business and actively spent furthering the business; or

(ii) the number of the business's customers has at least doubled within the most recent three years and is currently higher than the mean number of customers for other UK businesses offering comparable main products or services; or

(iii) the business has engaged in significant research and development activity and has applied for intellectual property protection in the UK; or

(iv) the business has generated a minimum annual gross revenue of £1 million in the last full year covered by its accounts; or

(v) the business is generating a minimum annual gross revenue of £500,000 in the last full year covered by its accounts, with at least £100,000 from exporting overseas; or

(vi) the business has created the equivalent of at least 10 full-time jobs for settled workers; or

(vii) the business has created the equivalent of at least 5 full-time jobs for settled workers, each of which has a mean salary of at least £25,000 a year (gross pay, excluding any allowances).

INN 18.2. An applicant cannot meet the requirement at INN 18.1. by relying on the same criterion twice (for example, an applicant who has invested £100,000 (2 x £50,000) in their business venture will be considered to have met one criterion, not two).

INN 18.3. If the business venture has one or more other team members who are applying for, or have been granted, settlement on the Innovator route, they cannot share the same means of meeting these criteria (for example, if two applicants are relying on the requirement to have created 10 jobs, 20 jobs must have been created in total).

INN 18.4. If the applicant is relying on the criteria for creating jobs in INN 18.1.(l)(vi) or (vii) the following requirements must be met:

(a) each job must have existed for at least 12 months and comply with all relevant UK legislation, including (but not limited to) the National Minimum Wage Act 1998 and the Working Time Regulations 1998; and

(b) each job must involve an average of at least 30 hours of paid work per week, but two or more part time jobs held by different employees that when combined add up to 30 hours per week will represent the equivalent of a single full-time job, as long as each of the jobs has existed for at least 12 months; and

(c) a job will be considered one for settled worker if the worker met the definition of settled worker in the rules in force at the time they started the job, and they remained employed for the whole claimed 12-month period, even if they ceased to be a settled worker at a later date.

Qualifying period requirement for settlement by an Innovator

INN 19.1. The applicant must have spent at least 3 years in the UK with permission on the Innovator route.

Continuous requirement for settlement by an Innovator

INN 20.1. The applicant must prove that they have met the continuous residence requirement as set out in Appendix Continuous Residence for the qualifying period in INN 19.1.

Knowledge of life in the UK requirement for settlement by an Innovator

INN 21.1. The applicant must meet the Knowledge of Life in the UK requirement as set out in Appendix KOL UK.

Decision on an application for settlement by an Innovator

[**INN 22.1.** If the decision maker is satisfied all the suitability and eligibility requirements for settlement are met the applicant will be granted settlement.]

Note: Paragraph substituted from 6 April 2022 subject to savings for applications made before that date (HC 1118).

[**INN 22.1A.** If the requirements for settlement are not met, but the decision maker believes the applicant is likely to meet all the suitability and eligibility requirements for permission to stay as an Innovator, the application will be varied by the Secretary of State and instead be considered as an application for permission to stay on the Innovator route. Where this happens:

(a) no additional application fee for permission to stay will be required and the settlement application fee will not be refunded; and

(b) the Secretary of State will write to the applicant informing them of this variation, and if required, will request the applicant pay the Immigration Health Charge.]

Note: Paragraph inserted from 6 April 2022 subject to savings for applications made before that date (HC 1118).

[**INN 22.1B.** If the applicant does not pay the requested Immigration Health Charge, the application for permission to stay will be rejected as invalid.]

Note: Paragraph inserted from 6 April 2022 subject to savings for applications made before that date (HC 1118).

[**INN 22.1C.** Where an applicant is granted permission to stay they will be granted for the period in INN 15.1. subject to the conditions at INN 15.2. to INN 15.3.]

Note: Paragraph inserted from 6 April 2022 subject to savings for applications made before that date (HC 1118).

[INN 22.1D. If the decision maker is not satisfied that the applicant meets all the suitability and eligibility requirements for settlement or permission to stay, the application for settlement will be refused.]

Note: Paragraph inserted from 6 April 2022 subject to savings for applications made before that date (HC 1118).

INN 22.2. If the application is refused the person may apply for an Administrative Review under Appendix AR: Administrative Review.

Dependants of an Innovator

Validity requirements for a dependent partner or dependent child on the Innovator route

INN 23.1. An application as a dependent partner or dependent child on the Innovator route must be made online on the gov.uk website on the specified form as follows:

Applicant	Specified form
EEA national with a chipped passport	Either (as applicable): – Dependant partner or dependant child using the UK Immigration: ID Check app; or – the forms listed below for dependant applicants outside or inside the UK as relevant.
Applicants outside the UK	Dependant partner visa Dependant child visa
Applicants inside the UK	If the dependant is applying at the same time as the Innovator, they can be included in the form 'Start-Up or Innovator permission to stay' where the form allows dependants to be added. Otherwise: • Dependant partner • Dependant child

[INN 23.2. An application for entry clearance or permission to stay as a partner or child of an Innovator must meet all the following requirements:

(a) any fee and Immigration Health Charge must have been paid; and

(b) the applicant must have provided any required biometrics; and

(c) the applicant must have provided a passport or other travel document which satisfactorily establishes their identity and nationality; and

(d) the applicant must be applying as partner or child of a person (P) who:

(i) has made a valid application for entry clearance or permission to stay on the Innovator route that has not been decided; or

(ii) has entry clearance or permission to stay on the Innovator route; or

(iii) is settled or has become a British citizen, providing that P had permission on the Innovator route when they settled and the applicant either had permission as their partner or child at that time, or the applicant is applying as a child of P and the applicant was born in the UK before P settled.]

Note: Paragraph substituted from 6 April 2022 subject to savings for applications made before that date (HC 1118).

INN 23.3. A person applying as a dependent partner must be aged 18 or over on the date of application.

INN 23.4. A person applying for permission to stay must be in the UK and must not have, or have last been granted, permission:

(a) as a Visitor; or
(b) as a Short-term Student; or
(c) as a Parent of a Child Student; or
(d) as a Seasonal Worker; or
(e) as a domestic worker in a private household; or
(f) outside the Immigration Rules.

INN 23.5. An application which does not meet all the validity requirements for the Innovator route is invalid and may be rejected and not considered.

Suitability requirements for dependent partner and dependent child on the Innovator route

INN 24.1. The applicant must not fall for refusal under Part 9: grounds for refusal.

INN 24.2. If applying for permission to stay the applicant must not be:

(a) in breach of immigration laws, except that where paragraph 39E applies, that period of overstaying will be disregarded; or

(b) on immigration bail.

Eligibility requirements for a dependent partner and dependent child on the Innovator route

Entry requirement for a dependent partner and dependent child on the Innovator route

INN 25.1. A person seeking to come to the UK as a partner or child must apply for and obtain entry clearance as a partner or child before they arrive in the UK.

INN 25.2. A person applying for entry clearance as the partner or child of an Innovator must, if paragraph A39 and Appendix T of these rules apply, provide a valid medical certificate confirming that they have undergone screening for active pulmonary tuberculosis and that this tuberculosis is not present in them.

Relationship requirements for a dependent partner on the Innovator route

[**INN 26.1.** The applicant must be the partner of a person (P) and one of the following must apply:

(a) P has permission on the Innovator route; or

(b) P is, at the same time, applying for (and is granted) permission on the Innovator route; or

(c) P is settled or has become a British citizen, providing P had permission as an Innovator when they settled, and the applicant had permission as P's partner at that time.]

Note: Paragraph substituted from 6 April 2022 subject to savings for applications made before that date (HC 1118).

INN 26.2. If the applicant and their Innovator partner are not married or in a civil partnership, all of the following requirements must be met:

(a) they must have been living together in a relationship similar to marriage or civil partnership for at least the two years before the date of application; and

(b) any previous relationship of the applicant or their Innovator partner with another person must have permanently broken down; and

(c) the applicant and their Innovator partner must not be so closely related that they would not be allowed to marry or form a civil partnership in the UK.

INN 26.3. The relationship between the applicant and their Innovator partner must be genuine and subsisting.

INN 26.4. The applicant and their Innovator partner must intend to live together throughout the applicant's stay in the UK.

Relationship requirement for a dependent child on the Innovator route

[**INN 27.1.** The applicant must be the child of a person (P) or of P's partner and one of the following must apply:

(a) P has permission on the Innovator route; or

(b) P is, at the same time, applying for (and is granted) permission on the Innovator route; or

(c) P is settled or has become a British citizen, providing P had permission as an Innovator when they settled and the applicant either had permission as their child or the child of P's partner at that time, or is applying as a child of P or of P's partner and was born in the UK before P settled.]

Note: Paragraph substituted from 6 April 2022 subject to savings for applications made before that date (HC 1118).

[**INN 27.2.** The applicant's parents must each be either applying at the same time as the applicant, or have permission to be in the UK (other than as a visitor) unless:

(a) the parent applying for or with entry clearance or permission to stay as an Innovator is the sole surviving parent; or

(b) the parent applying for or with entry clearance or permission to stay as an Innovator has sole responsibility for the child's upbringing; or

(c) the parent who does not have permission as an Innovator –

(i) is a British citizen or a person who has a right to enter or stay in the UK without restriction; and

(ii) is or will be ordinarily resident in the UK; or

(d) the decision maker is satisfied that there are serious and compelling reasons to grant the child entry clearance or permission to stay with the parent who is applying for or has entry clearance or permission on the Innovator route.]

Note: Paragraph substituted from 6 October 2021 subject to savings for applications made before that date (HC 617).

Care requirement for a dependent child on the Innovator route

INN 28.1. If the applicant is aged under 18 on the date of application there must be suitable arrangements for the child's care and accommodation in the UK, which must comply with relevant UK legislation and regulations.

Age requirement for a dependent child on the Innovator route

INN 29.1. The applicant must be under the age of 18 at the date of application, unless they were last granted permission as the dependent child of their parent or parents.

INN 29.2. If the applicant is aged 16 or over at the date of application, they must not be leading an independent life.

Financial requirement for a dependent partner or dependent child on the Innovator route

INN 30.1. If the applicant is applying for permission to stay and has been living in the UK with permission for 12 months or longer on the date of application, they will meet the financial requirement and do not need to show funds.

[**INN 30.2.** If the applicant is applying for entry clearance, or has been in the UK for less than 12 months on the date of application, funds of at least the amount required in INN 30.2A must be held collectively by one or more of the following:

(a) the applicant; and
(b) the Innovator (P); and
(c) if the applicant is applying as a dependent child, their parent who is lawfully present in the UK or being granted entry clearance, or permission to stay, at the same time.]

Note: Paragraph substituted from 6 October 2021 subject to savings for applications made before that date (HC 617).

[**INN 30.2A.** The funds required are:

(a) £285 for a dependent partner in the UK, or applying for entry clearance; and
(b) £315 for the first dependent child in the UK, or applying for entry clearance; and
(c) £200 for any other dependent child in the UK, or applying for entry clearance.]

Note: Paragraph inserted from 6 October 2021 subject to savings for applications made before that date (HC 617).

INN 30.3. The funds held must be in addition to any funds required by the Innovator to meet the financial requirement or any dependants in the UK or applying at the same time.

INN 30.4. If INN 30.2. applies, the required level of funds must have been held for a 28-day period and as specified in Appendix Finance.

Decision on application for a dependent partner and dependent child on the Innovator route

INN 31.1. If the decision maker is satisfied that all the suitability and eligibility requirements are met for a dependent partner or dependent child on the Innovator route the application will be granted, otherwise the application will be refused.

INN 31.2. If the application is refused the person can apply for an Administrative Review under Appendix AR: Administrative Review.

Period and conditions of grant for a dependent partner and dependent child on the Innovator route

INN 32.1. A partner will be granted permission which either:

(a) ends on the same date as their partner's permission on the Innovator route; or

(b) for 3 years' if the partner was (or is being) granted settlement on the Innovator route.

INN 32.2. A child will be granted permission which ends on the same date as whichever of their parents' permission ends first unless both parents have (or are being granted) settlement or British Citizenship, in which case the child will be granted permission for 3 years.

INN 32.3. The grant will be subject to all the following conditions:

(a) no access to public funds; and

(b) work (including self-employment and voluntary work) permitted; except for employment as a professional sportsperson (including as a sports coach); and

(c) study is permitted, subject to the ATAS condition in Appendix ATAS; and

(d) if Part 10 applies the applicant will be required to register with the police.

Settlement for dependent partner and dependent child on the Innovator route

Validity requirements for settlement for dependent partner and dependent child on the Innovator route

[**INN 33.1.** A partner and child on the Innovator route who is applying for settlement must apply online on the GOV.UK website on the specified form as follows:

'Partner - Settlement as a partner or parent

Child – Settlement as a Child (including a child aged over 18 already in the UK as a dependent)']

Note: Paragraph substituted from 6 October 2021 subject to savings for applications made before that date (HC 617). Paragraph substituted from 20 June 2022 subject to savings for applications made before that date (HC 1118).

[**INN 33.2.** An application for settlement must meet all the following requirements:

(a) any fee must have been paid; and

(b) the applicant must have provided any required biometrics; and

(c) the applicant must have provided either a passport or other travel document which satisfactorily establishes their identity and nationality; and

(d) the applicant must be in the UK; and

(e) the applicant must be applying as a partner or child of a person (P) who:

(i) has made a valid application for settlement in the UK as an Innovator and that application has not been decided; or

(ii) is settled or has become a British citizen, providing they had permission as an Innovator when they settled and the applicant either had permission as their partner or child at that time or is applying as a child of P and was born in the UK before P settled.]

Note: Paragraph substituted from 6 April 2022 subject to savings for applications made before that date (HC 1118).

INN 33.3. [DELETED]

Note: Paragraph deleted from 6 October 2021 subject to savings for applications made before that date (HC 617).

INN 33.4. An application which does not meet all the validity requirements for settlement as a partner and child on the Innovator route is invalid and may be rejected and not considered.

Suitability Requirements for settlement by a dependent partner and dependent child on the Innovator route

INN 34.1. The applicant must not fall for refusal under Part 9: grounds for refusal.

INN 34.2. The applicant must not be:

(a) in breach of immigration laws, except that where paragraph 39E applies, that period of overstaying will be disregarded; or

(b) on immigration bail.

Eligibility requirements for settlement by a dependent partner and dependent child on the Innovator route

Relationship requirement for settlement for a dependent partner or dependent child on the Innovator route

[**INN 35.1.** The applicant must be the partner or child of a person (P) where one of the following applies:

(a) P is, at the same time, being granted settlement as an Innovator; or

(b) P is settled or has become a British citizen, providing P had permission as an Innovator when they settled and the applicant either:

i) had permission as P's partner or child at that time; or

ii) is applying as a child of P, and was born in the UK before P settled.]

Note: Paragraph substituted from 6 October 2021 subject to savings for applications made before that date (HC 617).

[**INN 35.2.** The applicant must either:

(a) have last been granted permission as a dependent partner or dependent child of the person (P) in INN 35.1; or

(b) have been born in the UK and be applying as a child of the person (P) in INN 35.1.]

Note: Paragraph substituted from 6 October 2021 subject to savings for applications made before that date (HC 617).

INN 35.3. If applying as a child, the applicant's other parent must be being granted settlement at the same time, or be settled or a British citizen, unless:

(a) the person (P) in INN 35.1. or applying as the dependent partner of the person (P) in INN 35.1 is the applicant's sole surviving parent; or

(b) the person (P) in INN 35.1. or the person applying as the dependent partner of person (P) in INN 35.1 has sole responsibility for the applicant's upbringing; or

(c) the decision maker is satisfied that there are serious and compelling reasons to grant the applicant settlement.

Care requirement for settlement as a dependent child on the Innovator route

INN 36.1. If the applicant is under the age of 18 on the date of application there must be suitable arrangements for the child's care and accommodation in the UK, which must comply with relevant UK legislation and regulations.

Age requirement for settlement as a dependent child on the Innovator route

INN 37.1. The child must be under the age of 18 at the date of application, unless they were last granted permission as the dependent child of their parent or parents.

INN 37.2. If the applicant is aged 16 or over on the date of application they must not be leading an independent life.

Qualifying period requirement for settlement as a dependent partner on the Innovator route

INN 38.1. The applicant must have spent a continuous period of 5 years in the UK with permission as a dependent partner of the person (P) in INN 35.1.

Continuous residence requirement for settlement as a dependent partner of on the Innovator route

INN 39.1. The applicant must meet the continuous residence requirement as set out in Appendix Continuous Residence during the period in INN 38.1.

English language requirement for a dependent partner or dependent child on the Innovator route

INN 40.1. Unless an exemption applies, the applicant must show English language ability on the Common European Framework of Reference for Languages in speaking and listening to at least level B1.

INN 40.2. The applicant must show they meet the English language requirement as specified in Appendix English Language.

Knowledge of life in the UK requirement for settlement as a dependent partner or dependent child on the Innovator route

INN 41.1. If the applicant is aged 18 or over at the date of application, they must meet the Knowledge of Life in the UK requirement as set out in Appendix KOL UK.

Decision on an application for settlement as a dependent partner or dependent child on the Innovator route

[INN 42.1. If the decision maker is satisfied all the suitability and eligibility requirements for settlement are met the applicant will be granted settlement.]

Note: Paragraph substituted from 6 April 2022 subject to savings for applications made before that date (HC 1118).

[INN 42.1A If the requirements for settlement are not met, but the decision maker believes the applicant is likely to meet all the suitability and eligibility requirements for permission to stay as a dependent partner or dependent child on the Innovator route, the application will be varied by the Secretary of State to an application for permission to stay on that route. Where this happens:

(a) no additional application fee for permission to stay will be required and the settlement application fee will not be refunded; and

(b) the Secretary of State will write to the applicant informing them of this variation and if required will request the applicant pay any Immigration Health Charge.]

Note: Paragraph inserted from 6 April 2022 subject to savings for applications made before that date (HC 1118).

[**INN 42.1B** If the applicant does not pay the requested Immigration Health Charge, the application for permission to stay will be rejected as invalid.]

Note: Paragraph inserted from 6 April 2022 subject to savings for applications made before that date (HC 1118).

[**INN 42.1C** Where an applicant is granted permission to stay they will be granted for the period in INN 32.1 (as a partner) or INN 32.2. (as a child) subject to the conditions at INN 32.3.]

Note: Paragraph inserted from 6 April 2022 subject to savings for applications made before that date (HC 1118).

[**INN 42.1D.** If the decision maker is not satisfied that the applicant meets all the suitability and eligibility requirements for settlement or permission to stay, the application for settlement will be refused.]

Note: Paragraph inserted from 6 April 2022 subject to savings for applications made before that date (HC 1118).

INN 42.2. If the application is refused the person can apply for an Administrative Review under Appendix AR: Administrative Review.]

Note: Appendix inserted from 09:00 on 1 December 2020 subject to savings for applications made before that time (HC813).

[Appendix International Sportsperson

The International Sportsperson route is for an elite sportsperson or qualified sports coach who is internationally established and can make a significant contribution to the development of their sport at its highest level in the UK.

Applicants seeking permission for a period of more than 12 months will also be required to meet the English language requirement.

The partner and children of an International Sportsperson can apply on this route.

This is a route to settlement.

A person applying on this route must have a Governing Body Endorsement from an appropriate Sports Governing Body listed in Appendix Sports Governing Bodies.

International Sportsperson

Validity requirements for an International Sportsperson

ISP 1.1. A person applying for entry clearance or permission to stay as an International Sportsperson must apply online on the gov.uk website on the specified form as follows:

Applicant	Specified form
EEA national with chipped passport	Either: • International Sportsperson using the UK Immigration: ID Check app; or • the forms listed below for applications outside or inside the UK (as relevant)
Applicants outside the UK	International Sportsperson visa
Applicants inside the UK	International Sportsperson

ISP 1.2. An application for entry clearance or permission to stay on the International Sportsperson route must meet all the following requirements:

(a) any fee and Immigration Health Charge must have been paid; and

(b) the applicant must have provided any required biometrics; and

(c) the applicant must have provided a passport or other travel document which satisfactorily establishes their identity and nationality; and

(d) the applicant must have a Certificate of Sponsorship that was issued to them by their sponsor no more than three months before the date of application.

ISP 1.3. The applicant must be aged 16 or over on the date of application.

ISP 1.4. If an applicant has, in the last 12 months before the date of application, received an award from a Government or international scholarship agency covering both fees and living costs for study in the UK, they must provide written consent from that Government or agency.

ISP 1.5. An applicant who is applying for permission to stay must be in the UK on the date of application and must not have, or have last been granted, permission:

(a) as a Visitor, except where the applicant has been in the UK undertaking the activities in paragraphs PA 15.1. and 15.2. of Appendix Visitor: Permitted Activities, or paragraph V 13.3 (f) of Appendix V: Visitor; or

(b) as a Short-term Student; or

(c) as a Parent of a Child Student; or

(d) as a Seasonal Worker; or

(e) as a Domestic worker in a private household; or

(f) outside the Immigration Rules.

ISP 1.6. An application which does not meet all the validity requirements for the International Sportsperson route is invalid and may be rejected and not considered.

Suitability requirements for an International Sportsperson

ISP 2.1. The applicant must not fall for refusal under Part 9: grounds for refusal.

ISP 2.2. If applying for permission to stay, the applicant must not be:

(a) in breach of immigration laws, except that where paragraph 39E applies, that period of overstaying will be disregarded; or

(b) on immigration bail.

Eligibility requirements for an International Sportsperson

Entry requirements for an International Sportsperson

ISP 3.1. A person seeking to come to the UK as an International Sportsperson must apply for and obtain entry clearance as an International Sportsperson before their arrival in the UK.

ISP 3.2. A person applying for entry clearance as an International Sportsperson must, if paragraph A39 and Appendix T of these rules apply, provide a valid medical certificate confirming that they have undergone screening for active pulmonary tuberculosis and that this tuberculosis is not present in them.

Points requirements for an International Sportsperson

ISP 4.1. An applicant applying for entry clearance or permission to stay as an International Sportsperson for a period of 12 months or less must be awarded a total of 70 points from table A below.

ISP 4.2. An applicant applying for entry clearance or permission to stay as an International Sportsperson for a period exceeding 12 months must be awarded a total of 80 points from tables A and B below.

Table A

Points required (mandatory)	**Relevant rules**	**Points available**
Governing Body Endorsement	ISP 5.1	50
Certificate of Sponsorship	ISP 5.2 and ISP 5.3	10
Financial requirements	ISP 7.1 to ISP 7.3	10

Table B

Points required (mandatory) where the period of permission applied for exceeds 12 months	**Relevant rules**	**Points available**
English Language at level A1	ISP 8.1 and ISP 8.2	10

Endorsement requirement for an International Sportsperson

ISP 5.1. The applicant must provide a letter from the relevant Sports Governing Body listed in Appendix Sports Governing Bodies confirming:

(a) that the applicant is internationally established at the highest level; and

(b) that the applicant will make a significant contribution to the development of their sport at the highest level in the UK; and

(c) the unique endorsement number issued to the applicant by the Sports Governing Body.

Certificate of sponsorship requirement for an International Sportsperson

ISP 5.2. The applicant must have a valid Certificate of Sponsorship for the job they are planning to do; which to be valid must:

(a) confirm the applicant's name, that they are being sponsored as an International Sportsperson, details of the job and salary the sponsor is offering them; and

(b) must have been assigned before the applicant entered the UK if the application is for permission to stay and the applicant last had permission as a Visitor undertaking permitted activities for sportspersons; and

(c) include a start date, stated by the sponsor, which must be no more than three months after the date of application; and

(d) not have been used in a previous application which was either granted or refused (but can have been used in a previous application which was rejected as invalid, made void or withdrawn); and

(e) not have been withdrawn by the sponsor or cancelled by the Home Office; and

(f) state the unique endorsement number that has been issued to the applicant by the appropriate governing body specified in Appendix Sports Governing Bodies; and

(g) confirm that the applicant intends to be based in the UK; and

(h) confirm that the job is one the applicant is qualified to undertake.

ISP. 5.3. The sponsor must be authorised by the Home Office to sponsor the job in question under the International Sportsperson route.

ISP 5.4. The sponsor must be listed as A-rated on the Home Office's register of licensed sponsors unless the applicant was last granted permission as an International Sportsperson and is applying to continue working for the same sponsor as in their last permission.

Genuineness requirement for an International Sportsperson

ISP 6.1. The applicant must:

(a) genuinely intend, and be able, to undertake the role for which they are being sponsored; and

(b) not intend to undertake employment other than in the role for which they are being sponsored, or as otherwise permitted at ISP 11.3.

Financial requirement for an International Sportsperson

ISP 7.1. If the applicant is applying for permission to stay and has been living in the UK with permission for 12 months or longer on the date of application, they will meet the financial requirement and do not need to show funds.

ISP 7.2. If the applicant is applying for entry clearance, or is applying for permission to stay and has been living in the UK for less than 12 months on the date of application, either:

(a) the applicant must have funds of at least £1,270; or

(b) the applicant's A rated sponsor must confirm on the Certificate of Sponsorship that they will, if it is necessary, maintain and accommodate the applicant up to the end of the first month of their employment for an amount of at least £1,270.

ISP 7.3. If ISP 7.2 (a) applies, the applicant must have held the required level of funds for a 28 day period and must show funds as specified in Appendix Finance.

English language requirement for an International Sportsperson

ISP 8.1. Unless an exemption applies, if the applicant is applying for entry clearance or permission to stay as an International Sportsperson for a period exceeding 12 months, the applicant must show English language ability on the Common European Framework of Reference for Languages in speaking and listening of at least level A1.

ISP 8.2. If ISP 8.1. applies, the applicant must show they meet the English Language requirement as specified in Appendix English Language.

Parental consent requirement for an International Sportsperson aged under 18

ISP 9.1. If the applicant is aged under 18 at the date of application, they must have written consent from:

(a) both parents; or

(b) one parent, if that parent has sole legal responsibility for the applicant; or

(c) the applicant's legal guardian.

ISP 9.2. The written consent must confirm support for all of the following:

(a) the application; and

(b) the applicant's living and care arrangements in the UK; and

(c) if the application is for entry clearance, the applicant's travel to, and reception arrangements in, the UK.

Decision on an application as an International Sportsperson

ISP 10.1. If the decision maker is satisfied that all the suitability and eligibility requirements are met for an International Sportsperson, the application will be granted, otherwise the application will be refused.

ISP 10.2. If the application is refused the person can apply for an Administrative Review under Appendix AR: Administrative Review.

Period and conditions of grant for an International Sportsperson

ISP 11.1. If the applicant is applying for entry clearance or permission to stay as an International Sportsperson for a period of 12 months or less, they will be granted entry clearance or permission to stay for whichever is the shorter of:

(a) up to 14 days after the period of employment stated on their Certificate of Sponsorship; or

(b) 12 months.

ISP 11.2. If the applicant is applying for entry clearance or permission to stay as an International Sportsperson for a period exceeding 12 months, they will be granted entry clearance or permission to stay for whichever is the shorter of:

(a) up to 14 days after the period of employment stated on their Certificate of Sponsorship; or

(b) three years.

ISP 11.3. The grant will be subject to all the following conditions:

(a) no access to public funds; and

(b) work is permitted in the job the applicant is being sponsored for; and

(c) supplementary employment is permitted; and

(d) voluntary work is permitted; and

(e) working out a contractual notice period is permitted, for a job the applicant was lawfully working in on the date of application; and

(f) employment as a sportsperson for the applicant's national team while their national team is in the UK, playing in British University and College Sport (BUCS) competitions, and temporary engagements as a sports broadcaster providing guest expert commentary on a particular sporting event, are permitted; and

(g) study is permitted, subject to the ATAS condition in Appendix ATAS; and

(h) if Part 10 applies the applicant will be required to register with the police.

Settlement as an International Sportsperson

Validity requirements for settlement as an International Sportsperson

ISP 12.1. A person applying for settlement as an International Sportsperson must apply online on the gov.uk website on the specified form, "Settle in the UK in various immigration categories: form SET(O)".

ISP 12.2. An application for settlement as an International Sportsperson must meet all the following requirements:

(a) any fee must have been paid; and

(b) the applicant must have provided any required biometrics; and

(c) the applicant must have provided a passport or other travel document which satisfactorily establishes their identity and nationality; and

(d) the applicant must be in the UK on the date of application.

ISP 12.3. The applicant must:

(a) have, or have last been granted, permission as an International Sportsperson; and

(b) have, at any point during the five year continuous residence period, been granted leave as an International Sportsperson for a period exceeding 12 months.

ISP 12.4. An application which does not meet all the validity requirements for settlement as an International Sportsperson is invalid and may be rejected and not considered.

Suitability requirements for settlement as an International Sportsperson

ISP 13.1. The applicant must not fall for refusal under Part 9: grounds for refusal.

ISP 13.2. The applicant must not be:

(a) in breach of immigration laws, except that where paragraph 39E applies, that period of overstaying will be disregarded; or

(b) on immigration bail.

Eligibility requirements for settlement as an International Sportsperson

Qualifying period requirement for settlement as an International Sportsperson

ISP 14.1. The applicant must have spent a continuous period of five years in the UK.

ISP 14.2. The five year continuous period must consist of time with permission on any of, or any combination of, the following routes:

(a) Skilled Worker; or

(b) Global talent; or

(c) Innovator; or

(d) T2 Minister of Religion; or

(e) International Sportsperson; or

(f) Representative of an Overseas Business; or

(g) as a Tier 1 Migrant, other than as a Tier 1 (Graduate Entrepreneur) Migrant; or

[(h) Scale-up; or]

[(i) permission on any other route, during the time the applicant was waiting for a decision on their application as an International Sportsperson, providing that application:

(i) was for permission to stay; and

(ii) was made between 24 January 2020 and 30 June 2021 (inclusive); and

(iii) was supported on the date of application by a certificate of sponsorship assigned by a licensed sponsor; and

(iv) was granted.]

Note: Sub-paragraph (h) substituted, (i) inserted from 22 August 2022 subject to savings for applications made before that date (HC 1118).

Continuous residence requirement for settlement as an International Sportsperson

ISP 15.1. The applicant must meet the continuous residence requirement as set out in Appendix Continuous Residence during the period in ISP 14.1.

English language requirement for settlement as an International Sportsperson

ISP 16.1. Unless an exemption applies, the applicant must show English language ability on the Common European Framework of Reference for Languages in speaking and listening to at least level B1.

ISP 16.2. If ISP 16.1. applies, the applicant must show they meet the English language requirement as specified in Appendix English Language.

Knowledge of Life in the UK requirement for settlement as an International Sportsperson

ISP 17.1. Unless an exemption applies, the applicant must meet the Knowledge of Life in the UK requirement as set out in Appendix KOL UK.

Sponsorship requirement for settlement as an International Sportsperson

ISP 18.1. The sponsor in the applicant's most recent permission must still be approved by the Home Office to sponsor International Sportspersons on the date of decision.

ISP 18.2. The sponsor must confirm that they still require the applicant to work for them for the foreseeable future, and that the applicant is paid, and will be paid for the foreseeable future, at least the salary of £35,800 per year.

ISP 18.3. The salary in ISP 18.2. is subject to the following requirements:

(a) the salary must:

(i) be basic pay (excluding overtime); and

(ii) only include allowances where they are part of the guaranteed salary package and would be paid to a local settled worker in similar circumstances; and

(iii) not include other allowances and benefits, such as bonus or incentive pay, employer pension contributions, travel and subsistence (including travel to and from the applicant's home country); and

(iv) not include the value of any shares the applicant has received as an employee-owner in exchange for some of their UK employment rights; and

(b) if the applicant is being sponsored to work more than 48 hours a week, only the salary for the first 48 hours a week will be considered towards the salary threshold of £35,800; and

(c) if the applicant is currently absent from work for one of the reasons set out in Part 9, paragraph 9.30.1. or has returned from such an absence within the month before the date of application, consideration will be based on their salary on their return to work, as stated by their sponsor.

Decision on an application for settlement as an International Sportsperson

ISP 19.1. If the decision maker is satisfied all the suitability and eligibility requirements for settlement as an International Sportsperson are met, the applicant will be granted settlement, otherwise the application will be refused.

ISP 19.2. If the application is refused, the person can apply for an Administrative Review under Appendix AR: Administrative Review.

Dependants of an International Sportsperson

Validity requirements for a dependent partner or dependent child of an International Sportsperson

ISP 20.1. A person applying for entry clearance or permission to stay as a dependent partner or dependent child of an International Sportsperson must apply online on the gov. uk website on the specified form as follows:

Applicant	Specified form
EEA national with chipped passport	Either (as applicable): • Dependant partner or dependant child using the UK Immgiration: ID Check app; or • the forms listed below for dependant applicants outside or inside the UK as relevant.
Applicants outside the UK	Dependant partner visa Dependant child visa
Applicants inside the UK	If the dependant is applying at the same time as the International Sportsperson, they can be included in the form International Sportsperson where the form allows dependants to be added. Otherwise: – Dependant partner – Dependant child

[**ISP 20.2.** An application for entry clearance or permission to stay as a partner or child of an International Sportsperson must meet all the following requirements:

(a) any fee and Immigration Health Charge must have been paid; and

(b) the applicant must have provided any required biometrics; and

(c) the applicant must have provided a passport or other travel document which satisfactorily establishes their identity and nationality; and

(d) the applicant must be applying as partner or child of a person (P) who:

(i) has made a valid application for entry clearance or permission to stay on the International Sportsperson route that has not been decided; or

(ii) has entry clearance or permission to stay on the International Sportsperson route; or

(iii) is settled or has become a British citizen, providing that P had permission on the International Sportsperson route when they settled and the applicant either had permission as their partner or child at that time, or the applicant is applying as a child of P and the applicant was born in the UK before P settled.]

Note: paragraph substituted from 6 April 2022 (HC 1118).

ISP 20.3. An applicant applying as a dependent partner must be aged 18 or over on the date of application.

ISP 20.4. An applicant who is applying for permission to stay as a dependent partner or dependent child of an International Sportsperson must be in the UK on the date of application and must not have, or have last been granted, permission:

(a) as a Visitor; or
(b) as a Short-term Student; or
(c) as a Parent of a Child Student; or
(d) as a Seasonal Worker; or
(e) as a Domestic Worker in a Private Household; or
(f) outside the Immigration Rules.

ISP 20.5. An application which does not meet all the validity requirements for a dependent partner or dependent child of an International Sportsperson is invalid and may be rejected and not considered.

Suitability requirements for a dependent partner or dependent child of an International Sportsperson

ISP 21.1. The applicant must not fall for refusal under Part 9: grounds for refusal.

ISP 21.2. If applying for permission to stay the applicant must not be:

(a) in breach of immigration laws, except that where paragraph 39E applies, that period of overstaying will be disregarded; or

(b) on immigration bail.

Eligibility requirements for a dependent partner or dependent child of an International Sportsperson

Entry requirement for a dependent partner or dependent child of an International Sportsperson

ISP 22.1. A person seeking to come to the UK as a dependent partner or dependent child of an International Sportsperson must apply for and obtain entry clearance as a dependent partner or dependent child of an International Sportsperson before they arrive in the UK.

ISP 22.2. A person applying for entry clearance as a dependent partner or dependent child of an International Sportsperson must, if paragraph A39 and Appendix T of these rules apply, provide a valid medical certificate confirming that they have undergone screening for active pulmonary tuberculosis and that this tuberculosis is not present in them.

Relationship requirement for a dependent partner of an International Sportsperson

ISP 23.1. The applicant must be the partner of a person (P) where one of the following applies:

(a) P has permission on the International Sportsperson route; or

(b) P is, at the same time, applying for (and is granted) entry clearance or permission on the International Sportsperson route; or

(c) P is settled or has become a British citizen, providing P had permission on the International Sportsperson route when they settled and the applicant had permission as P's partner at that time.

ISP 23.2. If the applicant and their International Sportsperson partner are not married or in a civil partnership, all of the following requirements must be met:

(a) they must have been living together in a relationship similar to marriage or civil partnership for at least two years before the date of application; and

(b) any previous relationship of the applicant or their International Sportsperson partner with another person must have permanently broken down; and

(c) the applicant and their International Sportsperson partner must not be so closely related that they would not be allowed to marry or form a civil partnership in the UK.

ISP 23.3. The relationship between the applicant and their International Sportsperson partner must be genuine and subsisting.

ISP 23.4. The applicant and their International Sportsperson partner must intend to live together throughout the applicant's stay in the UK.

Relationship requirement for a dependent child of an International Sportsperson

ISP 24.1. The applicant must be the child of a parent (P) where one of the following applies:

(a) P has permission on the International Sportsperson route; or

(b) P is, at the same time, applying for (and is granted) entry clearance or permission on the International Sportsperson route; or

(c) P is settled in the UK or has become a British citizen, providing P had permission on the International Sportsperson route when they settled, and the applicant had permission as P's child at that time.

ISP 24.2. The applicant's parents must each be either applying at the same time as the applicant or have permission to be in the UK (other than as a Visitor) unless:

(a) the parent applying for or with entry clearance or permission to stay as an International Sportsperson is the sole surviving parent; or

(b) the parent applying for or with entry clearance or permission to stay as an International Sportsperson has sole responsibility for the child's upbringing; or

(c) the parent who does not have permission as an International Sportsperson –

(i) is a British citizen or a person who has a right to enter or stay in the UK without restriction; and

(ii) is or will be ordinarily resident in the UK; or

(d) the decision maker is satisfied that there are serious and compelling reasons to grant the child entry clearance or permission to stay with the parent who is applying for or has entry clearance or permission to stay as an International Sportsperson.

ISP 24.3. If the applicant is a child born in the UK to an International Sportsperson or their partner, the applicant must provide a full UK birth certificate showing the names of both parents.

Care requirement for a dependent child of an International Sportsperson

ISP 25.1. If the applicant is aged under 18 on the date of application, there must be suitable arrangements for the applicant's care and accommodation in the UK, which must comply with relevant UK legislation and regulations.

Age requirement for a dependent child of an International Sportsperson

ISP 26.1. The applicant must be under the age of 18 on the date of application unless they were last granted permission as the dependent child of their parent or parents.

ISP 26.2. If the applicant is aged 16 or over on the date of application, they must not be leading an independent life.

Financial requirement for a dependent partner or dependent child of an International Sportsperson

ISP 27.1. If the applicant is applying for permission to stay and has been living in the UK with permission for 12 months or longer on the date of application, they will meet the financial requirement and do not need to show funds.

ISP 27.2. If the applicant is applying for entry clearance, or has been in the UK for less than 12 months on the date of application, either:

(a) funds of at least the amount required in ISP 27.3. must be held collectively by one or more of the following:

i) the applicant; and

ii) the International Sportsperson (P); and

iii) if the applicant is applying as a dependent child, their parent who is lawfully present in the UK or being granted entry clearance, or permission to stay, at the same time; or

(b) the International Sportsperson's A-rated sponsor must certify that they will, if necessary, maintain and accommodate the dependent partner and/or any dependent child as well as the International Sportsperson, up to the end of the first month of each of their grants of permission, to at least the amounts required in ISP 27.3.

ISP 27.3. The funds required are:

(a) £285 for a dependent partner in the UK, or applying for entry clearance; and

(b) £315 for the first dependent child in the UK, or applying for entry clearance; and

(c) £200 for any other dependent child in the UK, or applying for entry clearance.

ISP 27.4. If ISP 27.2.(a) applies, the funds held for the applicant must be held in addition to any funds required for the International Sportsperson to meet the financial requirement and any other dependants in the UK or applying at the same time.

ISP 27.5. If ISP 27.2.(a) applies, the funds must have been held for a 28-day period and as specified in Appendix Finance.

Decision on an application as a dependent partner or dependent child of an International Sportsperson

ISP 28.1. If the decision maker is satisfied that all the suitability and eligibility requirements for a dependent partner or dependent child of an International Sportsperson are met, the application will be granted, otherwise the application will be refused.

ISP 28.2. If the application is refused, the person can apply for an Administrative Review under Appendix AR: Administrative Review.

Period and conditions of grant for a dependent partner or dependent child of an International Sportsperson

ISP 29.1. A partner will be granted:

(a) permission which ends on the same date as their partner's permission as an International Sportsperson; or

(b) three years' permission if the International Sportsperson was (or is being) granted settlement as an International Sportsperson.

ISP 29.2. A child will be granted permission which ends on the same date as whichever of their parents' permission ends first, unless both parents have (or are being granted) settlement or British citizenship, in which case the child will be granted permission for three years.

ISP 29.3. The grant will be subject to all the following conditions:

(a) no access to public funds; and

(b) work (including self-employment and voluntary work) is permitted, except as a professional sportsperson (including as a sports coach); and

(c) study is permitted, subject to the ATAS condition in Appendix ATAS if the applicant is over the age of 18; and

(d) if Part 10 applies, the applicant will be required to register with the police.

Settlement as a dependent partner or dependent child of an International Sportsperson

Validity requirements for settlement as a dependent partner or dependent child of International Sportsperson

ISP 30.1. A person applying for settlement as a dependent partner or dependent child of an International Sportsperson must apply online on the gov.uk website on the specified form, "Settle in the UK in various immigration categories: form SET(O)".

[**ISP 30.2.** An application for settlement as a partner or child of an International Sportsperson must meet all the following requirements:

(a) any fee must have been paid; and

(b) the applicant must have provided any required biometrics; and

(c) the applicant must have provided either a passport or other travel document which satisfactorily establishes their identity and nationality; and

(d) the applicant must be in the UK on the date of application; and

(e) the applicant must be applying as a partner or child of a person (P) who:

(i) has made a valid application for settlement in the UK as an International Sportsperson and that application has not been decided; or

(ii) is settled or has become a British citizen, providing they had permission as an International Sportsperson when they settled and the applicant either had permission as their partner or child at that time or is applying as a child of P and was born in the UK before P settled.]

Note: Paragraph substituted from 6 April 2022 (HC 1118).

ISP 30.3. An application which does not meet the validity requirements for a dependent partner or dependent child of an International Sportsperson is invalid and may be rejected and not considered.

Suitability requirements for settlement as a dependent partner or dependent child of an International Sportsperson

ISP 31.1. The applicant must not fall for refusal under Part 9: grounds for refusal.

ISP 31.2. The applicant must not be:

(a) in breach of immigration laws, except that where paragraph 39E applies, that period of overstaying will be disregarded; or

(b) on immigration bail.

Eligibility requirements for settlement as a dependent partner or dependent child of an International Sportsperson

Relationship requirement for settlement as a dependent partner or dependent child of an International Sportsperson

ISP 32.1. The applicant must be the partner or child of a person (P) where one of the following applies:

(a) P is, at the same time, being granted settlement as an International Sportsperson; or

(b) P is settled in the UK or has become a British citizen, providing P had permission as an International Sportsperson when they settled and the applicant either:

(i) had permission as P's partner or child at that time; or

(ii) is applying as a child of P, and was born in the UK before P settled.

ISP 32.2. The applicant must either:

(a) have last been granted permission as a dependent partner or dependent child of the person (P) in ISP 32.1; or

(b) have been born in the UK and be applying as a child of the person (P) in ISP 32.1.

ISP 32.3. If applying as a child, the applicant's other parent must be being granted settlement at the same time, or be settled or a British citizen, unless:

(a) the person (P) in ISP 32.1. is the applicant's sole surviving parent; or

(b) the person (P) in ISP 32.1. has sole responsibility for the applicant's upbringing; or

(c) the decision maker is satisfied that there are serious and compelling reasons to grant the applicant settlement.

Care requirement for settlement as a dependent child of an International Sportsperson

ISP 33.1. If the applicant is under the age of 18 on the date of application there must be suitable arrangements for the child's care and accommodation in the UK, which must comply with relevant UK legislation and regulations.

Age requirement for settlement as a dependent child of an International Sportsperson

ISP 34.1. The applicant must be under the age of 18 on the date of application unless they were last granted permission as the dependent child of their parent or parents.

ISP 34.2. If the applicant is aged 16 or over on the date of application, they must not be leading an independent life.

Qualifying period requirement for settlement as a dependent partner of an International Sportsperson

ISP 35.1. The applicant must have spent a continuous period of five years in the UK with permission as a dependent partner of the person (P) in ISP 32.1.

Continuous residence requirement for settlement as a dependent partner of an International Sportsperson

ISP 36.1. The applicant must meet the continuous residence requirement as set out in Appendix Continuous Residence during the period in ISP 35.1.

English language requirement for settlement as a dependent partner or dependent child of an International Sportsperson

ISP 37.1. Unless an exemption applies, the applicant must show English language ability on the Common European Framework of Reference for Languages in speaking and listening to at least level B1.

ISP 37.2. The applicant must show they meet the English language requirement as specified in Appendix English Language.

Knowledge of Life in the UK requirement for settlement as a dependent partner or dependent child of an International Sportsperson

ISP 38.1. Unless an exemption applies, the applicant must meet the Knowledge of Life in the UK requirement as set out in Appendix KOL UK.

Decision on an application for settlement as a dependent partner or dependent child of an International Sportsperson

ISP 39.1. If the decision maker is satisfied all the suitability and eligibility requirements are met for settlement as a dependent partner or dependent child of an International Sportsperson, the application will be granted, otherwise the application will be refused.

ISP 39.2. If the application is refused the person can apply for an Administrative Review under Appendix AR: Administrative Review.]

Note: Appendix inserted from 09:00 on 11 October 2021 subject to savings for applications made before that time (HC 617).

[Appendix Sports Governing Bodies

This appendix lists the Home Office approved Sports Governing Bodies for International Sportsperson applications. Applicants on this route must be endorsed by the relevant governing body from the table below, and the Certificate of Sponsorship relating to the application must confirm this endorsement.

Endorsements can only be issued to applicants covered by one of the following sports governing bodies.

Governing bodies cover the UK in its entirety unless otherwise stated, where they are only able to issue endorsements for the listed territory.]

The table contained in this Appendix is not reproduced as it is subject to regular review and amendment. It can be viewed online at: https://www.gov.uk/guidance/immigration-rules/immigration-rules-appendix-sports-governing-bodies

Note: Appendix inserted from 09:00 on 11 October 2021 subject to savings for applications made before that time (HC 617). Amendments from 6 April 2022 (HC 1118).

[Appendix Overseas Domestic Worker

This route is for an Overseas Domestic Worker who is seeking to come to the UK to work for up to a maximum of 6 months as a domestic worker with their current employer. Dependants are not permitted on this route.

Validity requirements for an Overseas Domestic Worker

ODW 1.1. A person applying for entry clearance as an Overseas Domestic Worker must apply on the gov.uk website on the Domestic worker in a private household visa form.

ODW 1.2. An application for entry clearance on the Overseas Domestic Worker route must meet all the following requirements:

(a) the applicant must be outside the UK on the date of application; and

(b) any fee must have been paid; and

(c) the applicant must have provided any required biometrics; and

(d) the applicant must have provided a passport or other travel document which satisfactorily establishes their identity and nationality.

[**ODW 1.3.** An application which does not meet all the validity requirements for an Overseas Domestic Worker is invalid and may be rejected and not considered.]

Note: Paragraph inserted from 09:00 on 11 October 2021 subject to savings for applications made before that time (HC 617).

ODW 1.4. [DELETED]

Note: Paragraph deleted from 09:00 on 11 October 2021 subject to savings for applications made before that time (HC 617).

Suitability requirements for an Overseas Domestic Worker

ODW 2.1. The applicant must not fall for refusal under Part 9: Grounds for Refusal.

Eligibility requirements for an Overseas Domestic Worker

Entry requirement for an Overseas Domestic Worker

ODW 3.1. A person seeking to come to the UK as an Overseas Domestic Worker must apply for and obtain entry clearance as an Overseas Domestic Worker before they arrive in the UK.

Age requirement for an Overseas Domestic Worker

ODW 4.1. The applicant must be aged 19 or over on the date of application.

Employment requirement for an Overseas Domestic Worker

ODW 5.1. A person applying for entry clearance as an Overseas Domestic Worker must have been employed as a domestic worker and living with the employer or in a property that the employer uses as a home for themselves on a regular basis, for 12 months or more immediately before the date of application.

ODW 5.2. The applicant must provide a letter from their employer confirming all of the following:

(a) their employment as a domestic worker; and

(b) that it meets the requirements set out in ODW 5.1; and

(c) that the employment is ongoing.

ODW 5.3. The applicant must show they meet the employment requirement by providing one or more of the following:

(a) pay slips or bank statements showing payment of salary; or

(b) confirmation of tax paid; or

(c) confirmation of health insurance paid; or

(d) a contract of employment; or

(e) a work visa, residence permit or equivalent passport endorsement from the country in which the domestic worker has been employed by the employer; or

(f) a visa or equivalent passport endorsement to confirm the applicant has travelled with their employer.

ODW 5.4. The applicant must have agreed in writing, the terms and conditions of their employment in the UK and must provide evidence, in the form set out in Appendix Domestic Worker Statement.

[**ODW 5.5.** The decision maker must be satisfied that the employer genuinely intends to pay the applicant at least the National Minimum Wage throughout their employment in the UK.]

Note: Paragraph substituted from 09:00 on 11 October 2021 subject to savings for applications made before that time (HC 617).

ODW 5.6. The decision maker must be satisfied that the applicant intends to work for the employer whilst the employer is in the UK and intends to travel in the company of one of the following:

(a) their British employer, or that employer's British spouse, civil partner or child under the age of 18, where the employer's usual place of residence is outside the UK and where those individuals do not intend to remain in the UK beyond six months; or

(b) a British employer's foreign national spouse, civil partner or child under the age of 18, where those individuals do not intend to remain in the UK beyond six months; or

(c) a foreign national employer or the employer's spouse, civil partner or child under the age of 18, where those individuals are seeking, or have been granted, permission under Appendix V: Visitor, except where that permission is to undertake activities listed in Appendix V: Visitor at V 9.

ODW 5.7. The decision maker must be satisfied of all of the following:

(a) that the applicant will leave the UK at the end of six months in the UK or at the same time as their employer, whichever is the earlier; and

(b) will not live for extended periods in the UK through frequent or successive visits; and

(c) will not make the UK their main home.

Financial requirement for an Overseas Domestic Worker

ODW 6.1. The decision maker must be satisfied that the applicant can and will adequately maintain and accommodate themselves without recourse to public funds.

Decision on application as an Overseas Domestic Worker

ODW 7.1. If the decision maker is satisfied that all the suitability and eligibility requirements for an Overseas Domestic Worker are met, the application will be granted, otherwise the application will be refused.

ODW 7.2. If the application is refused, the person can apply for an Administrative Review under Appendix AR: Administrative Review.

Period of grant and conditions of permission as an Overseas Domestic Worker

ODW 8.1. The applicant will be granted entry clearance for a period of 6 months.

ODW 8.2. The grant will be subject to all the following conditions:

(a) no access to public funds; and

(b) no work except as an Overseas Domestic Worker or a domestic worker in a private household.

ODW 8.3. The applicant is permitted to change employer, without notifying the Home Office, within the validity of their permission as an Overseas Domestic Worker.]

Note: Appendix inserted from 6 May 2021 subject to savings for applications (including for administrative review) made before that date (HC 1248).

[Appendix Domestic Worker in a Private Household

This route is for a domestic worker in a private household, who first entered the UK under the Rules in place before 6 April 2012 and wishes to extend their permission to stay. The applicant must be in the UK.

This is a route to settlement.

Dependants are permitted on this route.

Validity requirements for Domestic Worker in a Private Household

DW 1.1. A person applying for permission to stay as a Domestic Worker in a Private Household must apply on the gov.uk website on the specified form FLR(IR).

DW 1.2. An application for permission to stay as a Domestic Worker in a Private Household must meet all the following requirements:

(a) the applicant must be in the UK on the date of application; and

(b) any fee and Immigration Health Charge must have been paid; and

(c) the applicant must have provided any required biometrics; and

(d) the applicant must have provided a valid passport or other travel document which satisfactorily establishes their identity and nationality.

DW 1.3. An application which does not meet all the validity requirements for a Domestic Worker in a Private Household is invalid and may be rejected and not considered.

Suitability requirements for a Domestic Worker in a Private Household

DW 2.1. The applicant must not fall for refusal under Part 9: Grounds for Refusal.

DW 2.2. The applicant must not be in the UK in breach of immigration laws except that, where paragraph 39E of these Rules applies, any current period of overstaying will be disregarded.

Eligibility requirements for a Domestic Worker in a Private Household

DW 3.1. The applicant must have entered the UK with valid entry clearance as a Domestic Worker in a Private Household under the Rules in place before 6 April 2012.

DW 3.2 The applicant must have been continuously employed in the UK as a Domestic Worker in a Private Household since they entered the UK on this route.

DW 3.3. The applicant must be employed for at least 30 hours per week in a private household under the same roof as the employer or in the same household as the employer for the duration of their employment.

DW 3.4. The applicant must have agreed in writing, the terms and conditions of their employment in the UK and must provide evidence, in the form set out in Appendix Domestic Worker Statement, which must be fully completed and signed by both parties.

DW 3.5. The decision maker must be satisfied that the applicant's conditions of employment mean that they will be paid at least the UK National Minimum Wage throughout their employment in the UK.

DW 3.6. The applicant must not intend to take any form of employment except as a Domestic Worker in a Private Household.

Financial requirement for Domestic Worker in a Private Household

DW 4.1. The decision maker must be satisfied that the applicant can and will adequately maintain and accommodate themselves, and any dependants in the UK or applying for entry clearance, without recourse to public funds.

[**DW 4.2.** Funds must be shown as specified in Appendix Finance.]

Note: Paragraph substituted from 09:00 on 11 October 2021 subject to savings for applications made before that time (HC 617).

Decision on application for a Domestic Worker in a Private Household

DW 5.1. If the decision maker is satisfied that all of the suitability and eligibility requirements for permission to stay as a Domestic Worker in a Private Household are met the application will be granted, otherwise the application will be refused.

DW 5.2. If the application is refused, the person can apply for an Administrative Review under Appendix AR: Administrative Review.

Period of grant and conditions for a Domestic Worker in a Private Household

DW 6.1. The applicant will be granted permission to stay for 12 months.

DW 6.2. Where the application is decided before the current permission expires, the extension of stay granted may be for a period of 12 months plus the time remaining before the current permission expires (for example, if the application is decided on March 31st and the current permission does not expire until April 30th, an additional period of one month will be granted).

DW 6.3. The grant will be subject to the following conditions:

(a) no access to public funds; and

(b) no work except as a domestic worker in a private household; and

(c) study is permitted, subject to the ATAS condition in Appendix ATAS.

DW 6.4. The applicant is permitted to change employer, without notifying the Home Office, within the validity of their permission as a Domestic Worker in a Private Household.

Settlement for a Domestic Worker in a Private Household

Validity requirements for settlement as a Domestic Worker in a Private Household

DW 7.1. A person applying for settlement as a Domestic Worker in a Private Household must apply on the gov.uk website on the specified form 'Settle in the UK in various immigration categories: form SET(O)'.

DW 7.2. An application for settlement as a Domestic Worker in a Private Household must meet all the following requirements:

(a) any fee must have been paid; and

(b) the applicant must have provided any required biometrics; and

(c) the applicant must have provided a passport or other travel document which satisfactorily establishes their identity and nationality; and

(d) the applicant must be in the UK on the date of application.

DW 7.3. The applicant must have, or have last been granted, permission as a Domestic Worker in a Private Household.

DW 7.4. An application which does not meet all of the validity requirements for settlement as a Domestic Worker in a Private Household is invalid and may be rejected and not considered.

Suitability requirements for settlement as a Domestic Worker in a Private Household

DW 8.1. The applicant must not fall for refusal under Part 9: grounds for refusal.

DW 8.2. The applicant must not be in breach of immigration laws, except that where paragraph 39E applies, that period of overstaying will be disregarded.

Eligibility requirements for settlement as a Domestic Worker in a Private Household

Qualifying period for settlement as a Domestic Worker in a Private Household

DW 9.1. The applicant must have entered the UK with a valid entry clearance as a Domestic Worker in a Private Household under the Rules in place before 6 April 2012.

DW 9.2. The applicant must have spent a continuous period of 5 years lawfully in the UK as a Domestic Worker in a Private Household under the Rules in place before 6 April 2012.

DW 9.3 The applicant must not have worked in the UK except as a Domestic Worker in a Private Household.

DW 9.4. The applicant must continue to be required by their employer for employment as a Domestic Worker in a Private Household.

Continuous residence requirement for settlement as a Domestic Worker in a Private Household

DW 10.1. The applicant must meet the continuous residence requirement as specified in Appendix Continuous residence during the qualifying period in DW 9.2.

English language requirement for settlement as a Domestic Worker in a Private Household

DW 11.1. Unless an exemption applies, the applicant must show English language ability on the Common European Framework of Reference for Languages in speaking and listening to at least level B1.

DW 11.2. The applicant must show they meet the English language requirement as specified in Appendix English Language.

Knowledge of life in the UK requirement for settlement as a Domestic Worker in a Private Household

DW 12.1. The applicant must meet the Knowledge of Life in the UK requirement as specified in Appendix KOL UK.

Decision on an application for settlement as a Domestic Worker in a Private Household

DW 13.1. If the decision maker is satisfied that all the suitability and eligibility requirements for settlement as a Domestic Worker in a Private Household are met, the applicant will be granted settlement, otherwise the application will be refused.

DW 13.2. If the application is refused, the person can apply for an Administrative Review under Appendix AR: Administrative Review.

Dependants of a Domestic Worker in a Private Household

Validity requirements for a dependant partner or dependant child of a Domestic Worker in a Private Household route

DW 14.1. A person applying for entry clearance or permission to stay as a dependant partner or dependant child of a Domestic Worker in a Private Household must apply on gov.uk on the specified form Application to extend stay in the UK: FLR (IR).

[**DW 14.2.** An application for entry clearance or permission to stay as a partner or child of a Domestic Worker in a Private Household must meet all the following requirements:

(a) any fee and Immigration Health Charge must have been paid; and

(b) the applicant must have provided any required biometrics; and

(c) the applicant must have provided a passport or other travel document which satisfactorily establishes their identity and nationality; and

(d) the applicant must be applying as a partner or child of a person (P) who:

(i) has made a valid application for permission to stay in the UK as a Domestic Worker in a Private Household that has not been decided; or

(ii) has entry clearance or permission to stay as Domestic Worker in a Private Household; or

(iii) is settled or has become a British citizen, providing that P had permission as a Domestic Worker in a Private Household when they settled and the applicant either had permission as their partner or child at that time or the applicant is applying as a child of P and the applicant was born in the UK before P settled.]

Note: Paragraph substituted from 6 April 2022 subject to savings for applications made before that date (HC 1118).

DW 14.3. If the applicant is applying as a dependant partner, they must be aged 18 or over on the date of application.

DW 14.4. An applicant who is applying for permission to stay must be in the UK on the date of application and must not have, or have last been granted, permission:

(a) as a Visitor; or

(b) as a Short-term student

DW 14.5. An application which does not meet all of the validity requirements for a dependant partner or dependent child of a Domestic Worker in a Private Household is invalid and may be rejected and not considered.

Suitability requirements for a dependant partner or dependent child on the Domestic Worker in a Private Household route.

DW 15.1. The applicant must not fall for refusal under Part 9: grounds for refusal.

DW 15.2. If applying for permission to stay the applicant must not be:

(a) in breach of immigration laws, except that where paragraph 39E applies, that period of overstaying will be disregarded; or

(b) on immigration bail.

Eligibility requirements for a dependant partner or dependant child of a Domestic Worker in a Private Household

Entry requirements for a dependant partner or dependant child of a Domestic Worker in a Private Household

DW 16.1. A person seeking to come to the UK as a partner or child of a Domestic Worker in a Private Household must apply for and obtain entry clearance as a partner or child of a Domestic Worker in a Private Household before they arrive in the UK.

DW 16.2. A person applying for entry clearance as a dependant partner or dependant child of a Domestic Worker in a Private Household must, if paragraph A39 and Appendix T of these rules apply, provide a valid medical certificate confirming that they have undergone screening for active pulmonary tuberculosis and that this tuberculosis is not present in them.

Relationship requirement for a dependant partner of a Domestic Worker in a Private Household

DW 17.1. The applicant must be the partner of a person (P) where one of the following applies:

(a) P has permission as a Domestic Worker in a Private Household; or

(b) P is, at the same time, applying for (and is granted) permission as a Domestic Worker in a Private Household; or

(c) P is settled or has become a British citizen, providing P had permission on the Domestic Worker in a Private Household route when they settled, and the applicant had permission as P's partner at that time.

DW 17.2. If the applicant and their Domestic Worker in a Private Household partner are not married or in a civil partnership, all of the following requirements must be met:

(a) they must have been living together in a relationship similar to marriage or civil partnership for at least the two years before the date of application; and

(b) any previous relationship of the applicant or their Domestic Worker in a Private Household partner with another person must have permanently broken down; and

(c) the applicant and their Domestic Worker in a Private Household partner must not be so closely related that they would not be allowed to marry or form a civil partnership in the UK.

DW 17.3. The relationship between the applicant and their Domestic Worker in a Private Household partner must be genuine and subsisting.

DW 17.4. The applicant and their Domestic Worker in a Private Household partner must intend to live together throughout the applicant's stay in the UK.

Relationship requirement for a dependant child of a Domestic Worker in a Private Household

DW 18.1. The applicant must be the child of a parent (P) where one of the following applies:

(a) P has permission on the Domestic Worker in a Private Household route; or

(b) P is, at the same time, applying for (and is granted) permission on the Domestic Worker in a Private Household route; or

(c) P is settled or has become a British Citizen, providing P had permission on the Domestic Worker in a Private Household route when they settled, and the applicant had permission as P's child at that time.

DW 18.2. The applicant's parents must each be either applying at the same time as the applicant or have permission to be in the UK (other than as a visitor) unless:

(a) the parent with permission as a Domestic Worker in a Private Household or as the partner of a Domestic Worker in a Private Household is the sole surviving parent; or

(b) the parent with permission as a Domestic Worker in a Private Household or as the partner of a Domestic Worker in a Private Household has sole responsibility for the child's upbringing; or

(c) the decision maker is satisfied that there are serious and compelling reasons to grant the child entry clearance or permission to stay with the parent who has permission on the Domestic Worker in a Private Household route.

DW 18.3. If the applicant is a child born in the UK to a person on the Domestic Worker in a Private Household route or their partner, the applicant must provide a full UK birth certificate showing the names of both parents.

Age requirement for a dependent child of a Domestic Worker in a Private Household

DW 19.1. If the applicant is aged under 18 on the date of application, there must be suitable arrangements for the child's care and accommodation in the UK, which must comply with relevant UK legislation and regulations.

DW 19.2. The applicant must be under the age of 18 on the date of application, unless they were last granted permission as the dependant child of their parent or parents.

DW 19.3. If the applicant is aged 16 or over at the date of application, they must not be leading an independent life.

Financial requirement for a dependent partner or a dependant child of a Domestic Worker in a Private Household

DW 20.1 The decision maker must be satisfied that there will be adequate maintenance and accommodation for the applicant, the person on the Domestic Worker in a Private Household route, and any other dependants in the UK, without recourse to public funds.

Decision on application for a dependant partner or a dependant child of a Domestic Worker in a Private Household

DW 21.1. If the decision maker is satisfied that all the suitability and eligibility requirements are met for a dependent partner or a dependant child of a Domestic Worker in a Private Household the application will be granted, otherwise the application will be refused.

DW 21.2. If the application is refused the person can apply for an Administrative Review under Appendix AR: Administrative Review.

Period and conditions of grant for a dependant partner or a dependant child of a Domestic Worker in a Private Household

DW 22.1. A partner will be granted:

(a) permission which ends on the same date as their partner's permission as a Domestic Worker in a Private Household; or

(b) 2 years' permission if the Domestic Worker in a Private Household was (or is being) granted settlement as a Domestic Worker in a Private Household.

DW 22.2. A child will be granted permission which ends on the same date as whichever of their parents' permission ends first, unless both parents have (or are being granted) settlement or British Citizenship, in which case the child will be granted permission for 30 months.

DW 22.3. The grant will be subject to all the following conditions:

(a) no access to public funds; and

(b) work (including self-employment and voluntary work) permitted; except for employment as a professional sportsperson (including as a sports coach); and

(c) study is permitted, subject to the ATAS condition in Appendix ATAS; and

(d) if Part 10 applies the applicant will be required to register with the police.

Settlement as a dependant partner or a dependant child of a Domestic Worker in a Private Household

Validity requirements for settlement as a dependant partner or a dependant child of a Domestic Worker in a Private Household

DW 23.1. A person applying for settlement as a dependant partner or child of a Domestic Worker in a Private Household must apply online on the gov.uk website on the specified form SET (O).

[**DW 23.2.** An application for settlement as a partner or child of a Domestic Worker in a Private Household must meet all the following requirements:

(a) any fee must have been paid; and

(b) the applicant must have provided any required biometrics; and

(c) the applicant must have provided a passport or other travel document which satisfactorily establishes their identity and nationality; and

(d) the applicant must be in the UK on the date of application; and

(e) the applicant must be applying as a partner or child of a person (P) who:

(i) has made a valid application for settlement in the UK as a Domestic Worker in a Private Household that has not been decided; or

(ii) is settled or has become a British citizen, providing P had permission as a Domestic Worker in a Private Household when they settled and the applicant either had permission as their partner or child at that time or the applicant is applying as a child of P and the applicant was born in the UK before P settled.]

Note: Paragraph substituted from 6 April 2022 subject to savings for applications made before that date (HC 1118).

DW 23.3. [DELETED]

Note: Paragraph deleted from 6 October 2021 subject to savings for applications made before that date (HC 617).

DW 23.4. An application which does not meet all of the validity requirements for settlement for a dependant partner or child of a Domestic Worker in a Private Household is invalid and may be rejected and not considered.

Suitability requirements for a dependant partner or a dependant child of a Domestic Worker in a Private Household

DW 24.1. The applicant must not fall for refusal under Part 9: grounds for refusal.

DW 24.2. The applicant must not be:

(a) in breach of immigration laws, except that where paragraph 39E applies, that period of overstaying will be disregarded; or

(b) on immigration bail.

Eligibility requirements for a dependant partner or a dependant child of a Domestic Worker in a Private Household

Relationship requirements for a dependant partner or a dependant child of a Domestic Worker in a Private Household

[**DW 25.1.** The applicant must be the partner or child of a person (P) where one of the following applies:

(a) P is, at the same time, being granted settlement as a Domestic Worker in a Private Household; or

(b) P is settled or has become a British citizen, providing P had permission as a Domestic Worker in a Private Household when they settled, and the applicant either:

i) had permission as P's partner or child at that time; or

ii) is applying as the child of P, and was born in the UK before P settled.]

Note: Paragraph substituted from 6 October 2021 subject to savings for applications made before that date (HC 617).

[**DW 25.1A.** The applicant must either:

(a) have last been granted permission as a dependent partner or dependent child of the person (P) in DW 25.1; or

(b) have been born in the UK and be applying as a child of the person (P) in DW 25.1.]

Note: Paragraph inserted from 6 October 2021 subject to savings for applications made before that date (HC 617).

DW 25.2. If applying as a child, the applicant's other parent must be being granted settlement at the same time, or be settled or a British citizen, unless:

(a) the person (P) in DW 25.1. is the applicant's sole surviving parent; or

(b) the person (P) in DW 25.1. has sole responsibility for the applicant's upbringing; or

(c) the decision maker is satisfied that there are serious and compelling reasons to grant the applicant settlement.

Care requirement for settlement as a dependant child of a Domestic Worker in a Private Household

DW 26.1. If the child is aged under 18 on the date of application there must be suitable arrangements for the child's care and accommodation in the UK, which must comply with relevant UK legislation and regulations.

Age requirement for settlement by a dependant child of a Domestic Worker in a Private Household

DW 27.1. The child must be under the age of 18 on the date of application, unless they were last granted permission as the dependant child of their parent or parents.

DW 27.2. If the child is aged 16 or over at the date of application, they must not be leading an independent life.

Qualifying period requirement for settlement as a dependant partner of a Domestic Worker in a Private Household route

DW 28.1. The applicant must have spent a continuous period of 5 years in the UK with permission as a dependant partner of the person (P) in DW 25.1.

Continuous residence requirement for settlement by a dependant partner of a Domestic Worker in a Private Household

DW 29.1. The applicant must meet the continuous resident requirement as set out in Appendix Continuous Residence during the period in DW 29.1.

English language requirement for settlement by a dependant partner or dependent child of a domestic worker in a Private Household

DW 30.1. Unless an exemption applies, the applicant must show English language ability on the Common European Framework of Reference for Languages in speaking and listening of at least level B1.

DW 30.2. The applicant must show they meet the English language requirement as specified in Appendix English Language.

Knowledge of life in the UK requirement for settlement by a dependant partner or dependant child of a Domestic Worker in a Private Household

DW 31.1. If the applicant is aged 18 or over at the date of application, they must meet the Knowledge of Life in the UK requirement as specified Appendix KOL UK.

Decision on an application for settlement as a dependant partner or dependant child of a Domestic Worker in a Private Household

DW 32.1. If the decision maker is satisfied all the suitability and eligibility requirements are met for settlement as a dependant partner or dependant child of a Domestic Worker in a Private Household, the applicant will be granted settlement, otherwise the application will be refused.

DW 32.2. If the application is refused the person can apply for an Administrative Review under Appendix AR: Administrative Review.]

Note: Appendix inserted from 6 May 2021 subject to savings for applications (including for administrative review) made before that date (HC 1248).

[Appendix Domestic Worker who is a Victim of Modern Slavery

[This route is for a victim of modern slavery who entered the UK as an Overseas Domestic Worker, a Domestic Worker in a Private Household, or as a private servant in a diplomatic household, having held entry clearance in the Temporary Work – International Agreement category.]
The maximum period of grant on this route is 2 years.
This is not a route to settlement.

Note: Words in introduction substituted from 09:00 on 11 October 2021 subject to savings for applications made before that time (HC 617).

Validity requirements for a Domestic Worker who is a Victim of Modern Slavery

DWMS 1.1. A person applying for permission to stay as a Domestic Worker who is a Victim of Modern Slavery must apply on the gov.uk website on the specified form FLR(IR).

DWMS 1.2. An application for permission to stay as a Domestic Worker who is a victim of Modern Slavery must meet all the following requirements:

(a) the applicant must be in the UK on the date of application; and

(b) any fees must have been paid; and

(c) the applicant must have provided any required biometrics; and

[(d) the applicant must have provided a valid passport or other document which satisfactorily establishes their identity and nationality.]

Note: Sub-paragraph (d) substituted from 09:00 on 11 October 2021 subject to savings for applications made before that time (HC 617).

DWMS 1.3. An application which does not meet all the validity requirements route is invalid and may be rejected and not considered.

Suitability requirements for Domestic Worker who is a Victim of Modern Slavery

DWMS 2.1. The applicant must not fall for refusal under Part 9: Grounds for Refusal.

DWMS 2.2. Any relevant period of overstaying to which paragraph 39E of these Rules applies will be disregarded.

Eligibility requirements for Domestic Workers who is a Victim of Modern Slavery

DWMS 3.1. A person applying for permission to stay as a Domestic Worker who is a Victim of Modern Slavery must have, or have last been granted, permission on one of the following routes:

(a) Overseas Domestic Worker; or

[(b) Temporary Work – International Agreement, as a private servant in a diplomatic household]

(c) Domestic Worker in a Private Household; or

(d) outside these Rules having been referred into the National Referral Mechanism (NRM) and be in receipt of a positive Conclusive Grounds (CG) decision.

Note: Sub-paragraph (b) substituted from 09:00 on 11 October 2021 subject to savings for applications made before that time (HC 617).

DWMS 3.2. The applicant must have been referred into the National Referral Mechanism and be in receipt of a positive Conclusive Grounds decision.

DWMS 3.3. The application:

(a) must have been made within 28 days of the applicant being notified of the decision at DWMS 3.2.; or

(b) where the applicant has an outstanding application for permission to stay (or a grant of leave is being considered) on the date that the decision at DWMS 3.2. is notified to the applicant, the application for permission to stay as a Domestic Worker who is a Victim of Modern Slavery must be made within 28 days of the applicant being notified of the outcome of that application or consideration; or

(c) if the applicant is a person who falls within DWMS 3.1(d), must be made before the applicant's current permission ends.

[Decision on application as a Domestic Worker who is a Victim of Modern Slavery]

Note: Heading substituted from 09:00 on 11 October 2021 subject to savings for applications made before that time (HC 617).

DWMS 4.1. If the decision maker is satisfied that all of the suitability and eligibility requirements are met the application will be granted, otherwise the application will be refused.

DWMS 4.2. If the application is refused, the person can apply for an Administrative Review under Appendix AR: Administrative Review.

Period of grant and conditions of permission for Domestic Workers who are Victims of Modern Slavery

DWMS 5.1. The applicant will be granted permission to stay for whichever is the shorter of:

(a) two years; or

(b) where the applicant already holds permission to stay outside the Rules, having been referred into the National Referral Mechanism and in receipt of a positive Conclusive Grounds decision, permission will be granted for a period which ensures that the total, combined, duration of permission will not exceed 2 years.

DWMS 5.2. The grant will be subject to the following conditions:

(a) no access to public funds; and

(b) work is permitted as:

(i) a domestic worker in a private household; or

[(ii) as a private servant in a diplomatic household working only in the household of the employer recorded in a Certificate of Sponsorship in the Temporary Work – International Agreement category; and]

(c) supplementary employment is permitted, only as a domestic worker in a private household; and

(d) study is permitted, subject to the ATAS condition in Appendix ATAS.]

Note: Sub-paragraph (b)(ii) substituted from 09:00 on 11 October 2021 subject to savings for applications made before that time (HC 617).

Appendix inserted from 6 May 2021 subject to savings for applications (including for administrative review) made before that date (HC 1248).

[Appendix Domestic Worker Statement

[Two copies of this form must be completed and signed by the employer and the worker and submitted with the entry clearance application or with the permission to stay application as required by ODW 5.4, DW 3.4 and Appendix Temporary Work – International Agreement of the Immigration Rules]

Note: Introduction substituted from 09:00 on 11 October 2021 subject to savings for applications made before that time (HC 617).

Name & address of Employee
[insert details]

Name & address of Employer
[insert details]

Commencement of Employment & Termination
[If for an indefinite term] [The Employee's employment with the Employer commence[s OR d] on [insert date], and will continue unless or until terminated in accordance with the provisions of this agreement.]

[If for a fixed term] [The Employee's employment with the Employer shall [commence OR be deemed to have commenced] on [insert date] and shall continue, subject to the remaining terms of this agreement, until it terminates on [insert date] without the need for notice unless previously terminated by either party giving the other not less than [insert number*] weeks/months' notice in writing.] * Note: the notice to be given by the Employer must not be less than the statutory minimum period of notice to be given by employers, which is as follows: during the first two years' continuous employment, one week's notice; and after that, one additional week for each year of service, up to a maximum of twelve weeks' notice. No employment with a previous employer counts as part of a period of continuous employment. OR The Employee's employment with [insert name of previous employer] forms part of a continuous period of employment which began on [insert date].
Job Title
The Employee is employed as [insert job title] and their duties are set out below: [insert Employee's duties]
Status of employment
The Employer declares that the employee is not an au pair and terms of employment do not fall within the definition of paragraph 57 of the National Minimum Wage Regulations 2015 (as amended from time to time). Note: Paragraph 57 of the National Minimum Wage Regulations 2015 provides an exemption from the national minimum wage for employees who are treated as members of the employer's family. The UK's Immigration Rules require that you must declare that the person accompanying you as a domestic worker is an employee and the work they will carry out does not fall under this part of the Regulations. This means that you must pay them at least the national minimum wage while they're working for you in the UK.
Employee's Place of Work
The Employee's place of work is [insert location]. [If this is where the Employer resides, then the following information should be provided]: Total number of rooms; Total number of bedrooms; The names and ages of all household members and domestic staff (adults and minors) residing in the house. [If the Employee's place of work is different to the Employer's residence, the Employer is to provide an explanation, including details of where the Employee will be working and who lives at that address]

Employee's Hours of Work
The Employee's normal hours of work are [insert number] hours per week, to be worked during the hours of [insert time] to [insert time] on [insert days] with a daily [paid OR unpaid] lunch break of [insert amount]. [The Employee is not required to work overtime] OR [The Employee is required to be available to work overtime, whenever needed by the Employer at weekends, on public holidays or at other times outside their normal hours of work.] OR [The Employee may, if they wish, make themselves available to work overtime outside their normal hours of work.] OR [The Employee may be required to work overtime if and when the Employer deems it to be necessary.] [If the Employee works overtime, then complete the following paragraph] [The Employee's entitlement to pay for working overtime is as follows: [insert details of overtime pay]
Pay
The Employee's [salary is OR wages are] £[enter figure] per [hour OR week OR month OR year] payable to the Employee at [weekly OR monthly] intervals in arrears on[or about] the [insert day i.e. Friday OR last working day OR insert date i.e. 25th] of each [week OR month]. The Employer agrees that the salary OR wages meet the requirements of the National Minimum Wage Act 1998 and any Regulations made under it, and that they will continue to meet such requirements throughout the period of employment.
Holiday
The Employee will be entitled to [enter number –under the Working Time Regulations 1998, this must be at least 20 days for full – time employees, pro rata for part – time employees] days' paid holiday in each holiday year, which runs from [enter date, e.g. 1 January] to [enter date, e.g. 31 December], in addition to bank and public holidays. If the Employee's employment starts or finishes part way through the holiday year, their holiday entitlement during that year shall be calculated on a pro-rata basis. The Employee must take all of their entitlement in the holiday year in which it accrues and carrying forward holiday is not permitted unless [either agreed in advance by the Employer or where] the law allows holiday to be carried forward. On the termination of the Employee's employment, they will be paid in lieu of accrued but untaken holiday entitlement. The Employee will be required to pay the Employer for holiday taken in excess of their accrued entitlement on termination.

Sickness
If the Employee is absent from work for any reason, they, or someone on their behalf, must inform the Employer by no later than [insert time] on the first day of absence. On the Employee's return to work, they will be required to complete a self-certification form, which they should complete, sign and return within [insert number e.g. two days] of their return to work. If the Employee's absence from work is due to sickness or injury and continues for a period exceeding seven consecutive days, they should provide the Employer with a Statement of Fitness for Work ('fit note') from their doctor as soon as possible after the seventh day of absence and weekly after that. [[IF sick pay:] In the event of absence from work due to illness or injury, the Employee will be eligible to receive an amount equivalent to their salary OR wages for the first [insert number] weeks of absence. Such payments will include any entitlement to any statutory sick pay due in accordance with applicable legislation in force at the time of the absence. OR [If Statutory Sick Pay only:]There is no pay for any absence due to illness or injury, other than statutory sick pay if the Employee is eligible. For the purpose of statutory sick pay, the Employee's 'qualifying days' are [insert the [Employee's normal working days]].

Recruitment, transportation, and other fees
The Employer shall not recoup from the Employee, through payroll deductions or any other means, the fees they have paid to a third party recruiter or recruitment agency, or their authorised representative(s) for services related to hiring and retaining the Employee. The Employer agrees to pay the Employee's transportation costs for the journey from their place of current residence to the place of work in the United Kingdom, namely from_ (country of current residence) to ______________(place of work in United Kingdom) as well as the return journey from ______________(place of work in United Kingdom) to __________ (country of current residence). The Employer agrees to pay in advance on behalf of the Employee any visa application fees and any other fees (including any immigration health surcharge) that may be payable by the Employee in order to obtain a visa to travel to the United Kingdom with their Employer or to join the Employer in the UK. It is the Employer's obligation and responsibility to pay for the transportation costs, any visa application fees and any other fees (including any immigration health surcharge) that may be payable by the Employee in order to obtain a visa to travel to the United Kingdom with their Employer or to join the Employer in the UK, and such costs and fees cannot be passed on to the Employee through payroll deductions or any other means (for example, the Employee must not pay the transportation or the visa fees on behalf of the Employer to be reimbursed at a later date). Under no circumstances are transportation costs or the fees described above recoverable by the Employer from the Employee.

Accommodation

The Employer shall provide the Employee with suitable furnished accommodation for their exclusive use. Suitable accommodation is housing or a hotel room that meets UK building requirements and health and safety standards. This includes a private unit or a room with a lock and which therein provides living and sleeping facilities intended for human habitation with no visible or structural repairs required.

The Employer agrees to provide the Employee with [meals] [delete if not applicable], [and] an adequate, properly heated, and ventilated room with natural light. The door of the room shall be equipped with a lock and a safety bolt from within the room and the Employee will be provided with the corresponding key.

The Employer shall provide the Employee with independent access to the residence (for example, house keys, security code) where the Employee resides.

The Employer agrees to provide the Employee with (check if applicable): Private bathroom

Telephone (charge of £ per month or no charge except for long-distance calls) Radio (in their room)

Television (in their room)

Internet access (charge of £ per month or no charge) Other, specify:

[Description of Employee's room and furnishings]

Healthcare

Either:

'1. The Employer agrees to provide comprehensive sickness insurance cover for the Employee in the United Kingdom at no cost to the Employee.

2. The Employer agrees not to deduct money from the Employee's salary OR wages for this purpose.

3. The Employer undertakes to ensure that the Employee has free access to medical treatment as the Employee requires.'

or, if the Employee has remained (or will remain as a result of their application for entry clearance or permission to stay being granted) in the UK as either a domestic worker in a private household or a private servant in a diplomatic household for a period exceeding 6 months:

"1. The Employer agrees not to deduct money from the Employee's salary OR wages for the purpose of meeting the cost of comprehensive sickness insurance cover.

2. The Employer undertakes to ensure that the Employee has free access to medical treatment as the Employee requires.

Passport

The Employer agrees that the Employee will retain custody of their passport at all times other than when it is required by a third party for official purposes such as applying for a visa.

Termination and Notice Period
[To only be used when the employment is for an indefinite term] The prior written notice required by the Employee to terminate their employment shall be as follows: [insert details]
The prior written notice required by the Employer to terminate the Employee's employment shall be as follows:
[insert details]
Note: this must not be less than the statutory minimum period of notice to be given by employers, which is as follows:
during the first two years' continuous employment, one week's notice; and
after that, one additional week for each year of service, up to a maximum of twelve weeks' notice.
Grievances and Disciplinary Rules and Procedure
If the Employee has a grievance regarding their employment, they should in the first instance speak to their Employer. If the grievance is not then resolved to the Employee's satisfaction, the Employee should refer to the grievance procedure, which may be obtained from the Employer. The disciplinary rules and procedure applicable to the Employee are [attached OR to be found in [specify place]]. If the Employee is dissatisfied with any disciplinary decision taken in relation to them, they should refer to the disciplinary procedure, which may be obtained from the Employer.
Note: the Employer's grievance procedure and disciplinary rules and procedure must comply with the ACAS statutory Code of Practice on discipline and grievance.
Pensions
[The Employee is entitled to become a member of the [insert name] Pension Scheme, or such other registered pension scheme as has been set up by the Employer, subject to satisfying certain eligibility criteria and subject to the rules of such scheme as amended from time to time. Full details of the scheme are available from the Employer.
OR
[There is no pension scheme in force in relation to the Employee's employment.]
A contracting-out certificate is [not] in force in respect of the Employee's employment.
Governing Law & Jurisdiction
This agreement and any dispute or claim arising out of or in connection with it or its subject matter or formation (including non-contractual disputes or claims) shall be governed by and construed in accordance with the law of England and Wales.
Each party irrevocably agrees that the courts of England and Wales shall have exclusive jurisdiction to settle any dispute or claim arising out of or in connection with this agreement or its subject matter or formation (including non-contractual disputes or claims).

Signature of Employer
I accept the terms and conditions of this employment contract. Given name as stated on passport (print): Surname as stated on passport (print): Employer's Signature: Date (DD/MM/YYYY):
Signature of Employee
I accept the terms and conditions of this employment contract. Given name as stated on passport (print): Surname as stated on passport (print): EMPLOYEE'S Signature: Date (DD/MM/YYYY)

Note: Appendix inserted from 6 May 2021 subject to savings for applications (including for administrative review) made before that date (HC 1248).

[Appendix Temporary Work – Seasonal Worker

Note: Appendix inserted from 09:00 on 1 December 2020 subject to savings for applications made before that time (HC813). Amendments from 6 April 2021 subject to savings for applications made before that date (HC 1248). Appendix substituted from 09:00 on 11 October 2021 subject to savings for applications made before that time (HC 617).

[. . .]

[The Seasonal Worker route is for a person who wants to come to the UK to do seasonal horticulture work. A person on the Seasonal Worker route can stay for a maximum period of six months in any 12-month period.]

A partner and children are not permitted to apply as dependants on this route.

The Seasonal Worker route is not a route to settlement.

Note: Amendments from 16:00 on 11 October 2021 subject to savings for applications made before that time (CP 542). Amendments from 16:00 on 1 November 2021 subject to savings for applications made before that time (HC 803). Paragraph deleted, paragraph substituted from 6 April 2022 subject to savings for applications made before that date (HC 1118).

Validity requirements for a Seasonal Worker

SAW 1.1. A person applying for entry clearance as a Seasonal Worker must apply online on gov.uk on the specified form as follows:

Applicant	Specified form
EEA national with a chipped passport	Either: • Temporary Worker using the Immigration: ID Check app; or • the forms listed below for applicants outside the UK (as relevant)
Applicants outside the UK	Temporary Worker visa

SAW 1.2. An application for entry clearance as a Seasonal Worker must meet all the following requirements:

(a) any fee must have been paid; and

(b) the applicant must have provided any required biometrics; and

(c) the applicant must have provided a passport or other travel document which satisfactorily establishes their identity and nationality; and

(d) the applicant must have a Certificate of Sponsorship that was issued to them no more than 3 months before the date of application.

SAW 1.3. The applicant must be aged 18 or over on the date of application.

SAW 1.3A. [DELETED]

Note: Paragraph inserted from 16:00 on 11 October 2021 subject to savings for applications made before that time (CP 542). Paragraph deleted from 6 April 2022 subject to savings for applications made before that date (HC 1118).

SAW 1.3B. [DELETED]

Note: Paragraph inserted from 16:00 on 11 October 2021 subject to savings for applications made before that time (CP 542). Paragraph deleted from 6 April 2022 subject to savings for applications made before that date (HC 1118).

SAW 1.3C. [DELETED]

Note: Paragraph inserted from 16:00 on 1 November 2021 subject to savings for applications made before that time (HC 803). Paragraph deleted from 6 April 2022 subject to savings for applications made before that date (HC 1118).

SAW 1.4. An application which does not meet all the validity requirements for the Seasonal Worker route is invalid and may be rejected and not considered.

Suitability requirements for a Seasonal Worker

SAW 2.1. The applicant must not fall for refusal under Part 9: grounds for refusal.

Eligibility requirements for a Seasonal Worker

Entry requirements for a Seasonal Worker

SAW 3.1. A person seeking to come to the UK as a Seasonal Worker must have applied for and obtained entry clearance as a Seasonal Worker before they arrive in the UK.

Certificate of Sponsorship requirement for a Seasonal Worker

SAW 4.1. The applicant must have a Certificate of Sponsorship for the job they are planning to do, which must:

(a) confirm the applicant's name, that they are being sponsored as a Seasonal Worker, details of the job and salary the sponsor is offering them; and

(b) include a start date, stated by the sponsor, which is no more than three months after the date of application; and

(c) not have been used in a previous application which was either granted or refused (but can have been used in a previous application which was rejected as invalid, made void or withdrawn); and

(d) not have been withdrawn by the sponsor or cancelled by the Home Office; and

(e) confirm that the role conforms with all relevant legislation, such as the [. . .] relevant Agricultural Wages Order rate where this applies, and the Working Time Regulations[; and]

[(f) The Certificate of Sponsorship must state the role is in the horticulture sector, which means those growing:

(i) Protected Vegetables – those grown in glasshouse systems; or

(ii) Field Vegetables – those grown outdoors, including vegetables, herbs, leafy salads and potatoes; or

(iii) Soft Fruit – those grown outdoors or under cover e.g. in glasshouses or polytunnels. Includes strawberries, raspberries, blackcurrants, blueberries and all ribes and rubus species; or

(iv) Top Fruit (Orchard Fruit) - trees that bear fruit e.g. apples, plums, cherries, apricots; or

(v) Vine and Bines – both twining or climbing flexible stems of certain plants, e.g. hops is a bine, and grapes is a vine; or

(vi) Mushrooms – typically covers Agaricus bisporus species but can also include more exotic species (typically grown indoors); or

(vii) Bulbs and cut flowers, such as daffodils, grown outdoors and indoors; or

(viii) Pot plants, such as seasonal bedding plants like pansies, violas, germaniums and poinsettias; or

(ix) Hardy ornamental nursery stock such as Christmas trees, shrubs, roses, ornamental trees and perennials; or

(x) Tree and forest nurseries.]

[(g) confirm the applicant will be paid at least £10.10 for each hour worked.

For the purpose of this sub-paragraph:

The hourly rate only includes guaranteed basic gross pay (before income tax and including employee pension and national insurance contributions), and does not include other pay and benefits (such as those listed in SW14.2)]

Note: Amendment to (e), sub-paragraph (f) deleted from 16:00 on 11 October 2021 subject to savings for applications made before that time (CP 542). Punctuation in (e) substituted, sub-paragraph (g) inserted from 16:00 on 1 November 2021 subject to savings for applications made before that time (HC 803). Words in (e) deleted, sub-paragraph (f) re-inserted, sub-paragraph (g) substituted from 6 April 2022 subject to savings for applications made before that date (HC 1118).

SAW 4.1A. [DELETED]

Note: Paragraph inserted from 16:00 on 11 October 2021 subject to savings for applications made before that time (CP 542). Amendments from 16:00 on 1 November 2021 subject to savings for applications made before that time (HC 803). Paragraph deleted from 6 April 2022 subject to savings for applications made before that date (HC 1118).

SAW 4.2. The Certificate of Sponsorship must have been issued by a sponsor who:

(a) is listed as A-rated on the Home Office's register of licensed sponsors; and

(b) has an endorsement from the Department for Environment, Food and Rural Affairs in relation to the Seasonal Worker route; and

(c) is licensed by the Gangmasters and Labour Abuse Authority.

Financial requirement for a Seasonal Worker

SAW 5.1. Either:

(a) the applicant must have funds of at least £1,270; or

(b) the applicant's A rated sponsor must confirm on the Certificate of Sponsorship that they will, if it is necessary, maintain and accommodate the applicant up to the end of the first month of their employment for an amount of at least £1,270.

SAW 5.2. If SAW 5.1.(a) applies, the applicant must show that they have held the required level of funds for a 28-day period and as specified in Appendix Finance.

Decision on application for a Seasonal Worker

SAW 6.1. If the decision maker is satisfied that all the suitability and eligibility requirements are met for a Seasonal Worker, the application will be granted, otherwise the application will be refused.

SAW 6.2. If the application is refused, the person can apply for an Administrative Review under Appendix AR: Administrative Review.

Period and conditions of grant for a Seasonal Worker

[**SAW 7.1.** The applicant will be granted permission for whichever is the shortest of either:

(a) the period of the job on the Certificate of Sponsorship plus 14 days before and 14 days after that period; or

(b) a maximum period of 6 months in any 12-month period.]

Note: Amendments from 16:00 on 11 October 2021 subject to savings for applications made before that time (CP 542). Paragraph substituted from 6 April 2022 subject to savings for applications made before that date (HC 1118).

SAW 7.1A. [DELETED]

Note: Paragraph inserted from 16:00 on 11 October 2021 subject to savings for applications made before that time (CP 542). Paragraph deleted from 6 April 2022 subject to savings for applications made before that date (HC 1118).

SAW 7.1B. [DELETED]

Note: Paragraph inserted from 16:00 on 11 October 2021 subject to savings for applications made before that time (CP 542). Paragraph deleted from 6 April 2022 subject to savings for applications made before that date (HC 1118).

SAW 7.1C. [DELETED]

Note: Paragraph inserted from 16:00 on 1 November 2021 subject to savings for applications made before that time (HC 803). Paragraph deleted from 6 April 2022 subject to savings for applications made before that date (HC 1118).

SAW 7.2. The grant will be subject to all the following conditions:

(a) no access to public funds; and

(b) work is permitted only in the role the applicant is being sponsored for; and

(c) study is permitted, subject to the ATAS condition in Appendix ATAS; and

(d) if Part 10 applies, the applicant will be required to register with the police.]

[APPENDIX YOUTH MOBILITY SCHEME

Note: Appendix inserted from 09:00 on 1 December 2020 subject to savings for applications made before that time (HC813). Amendments from 6 April 2021 subject to savings for applications made before that date (HC 1248). Amendments from 09:00 on 11 October 2021 subject to savings for applications made before that time; Appendix substituted from 1 January 2022 subject to savings for applications made before that date (HC 617).

The Youth Mobility Scheme provides a cultural exchange programme that allows a person aged between 18 and 30, from participating countries and territories, to experience life in the UK for up to 2 years.

Dependants are not permitted on this route.

The Youth Mobility Scheme route is not a route to settlement.

Validity requirements for the Youth Mobility Scheme route

YMS 1.1. A person applying for entry clearance under the Youth Mobility Scheme route must apply online on gov.uk on the specified form: "Temporary Work or Youth Mobility Scheme".

YMS 1.2. An application for entry clearance on the Youth Mobility Scheme route must meet all the following requirements:

(a) any fee and Immigration Health Charge must have been paid; and

(b) the applicant must have provided any required biometrics; and

(c) the applicant must have provided a passport or other travel document which satisfactorily establishes their identity and nationality.

YMS 1.3. The applicant must be one of the following:

(a) a British Overseas citizen, British Overseas Territories citizen or British National (Overseas); or

(b) a national or citizen of a country or the holder of a passport issued by a territory, listed in [Appendix] Youth Mobility Scheme: eligible nationals.

Note: Word substituted from 6 April 2022 subject to savings for applications made before that date (HC 1118).

YMS 1.4. The applicant must be aged 30 or under on the date of application.

YMS 1.5. An application which does not meet all the validity requirements for the Youth Mobility Scheme route is invalid and may be rejected and not considered.

Suitability requirements for the Youth Mobility Scheme

YMS 2.1. The applicant must not fall for refusal under Part 9: grounds for refusal.

Eligibility requirements for the Youth Mobility Scheme

Entry requirements for the Youth Mobility Scheme

YMS 3.1. A person seeking to come to the UK on the Youth Mobility Scheme route must have applied for and obtained entry clearance under the Youth Mobility Scheme route before they arrive in the UK.

YMS 3.2. A person applying for entry clearance on the Youth Mobility Scheme route must, if paragraph A39 and Appendix T of these rules apply, provide a valid medical certificate confirming that they have undergone screening for active pulmonary tuberculosis and that this tuberculosis is not present in them.

YMS 3.3. The applicant must not have previously spent time in the UK on the Youth Mobility Scheme route.

YMS 3.4. The applicant must be aged 18 or over on the date their entry clearance will become valid.

[Country-specific eligibility requirements for the Youth Mobility Scheme]

Note: Heading substituted from 6 April 2022 subject to savings for applications made before that date (HC 1118).

[**YMS 4.1.** Where the applicant is a national of Australia, Canada, Monaco or New Zealand, they are not required to meet any country-specific eligibility requirements but must meet the financial requirements in YMS 5.1. to YMS 5.3.

Where the applicant is a national, citizen or rightful passport holder of one of the countries or territories listed in the following table of country-specific eligibility requirements, they must meet the requirement listed:

	Country or territory	Requirement
1	• Hong Kong • Japan • Republic of Korea • Taiwan	The applicant must: (a) have been issued with an invitation to apply in accordance with the invitation to apply arrangements set out in Appendix Youth Mobility Scheme: eligible nationals; and (b) have made their application within any time limit specified on that invitation to apply.
2	• San Marino	The applicant must provide a letter confirming the applicant is a suitable candidate for the Youth Mobility Scheme from the Directorate of Political and Diplomatic Affairs of the Republic of San Marino Department of Foreign Affairs that has been issued no more than 6 months before the date of application.
3	• Iceland	The applicant must provide a Criminal Certificate for Private Use that has been issued no more than 6 months before the date of application.
4	• India	The applicant must: (a) have been issued with an invitation to apply in accordance with the invitation to apply arrangements set out in Appendix Youth Mobility Scheme: eligible nationals; and (b) have made their application within the period of time specified on that invitation to apply; and (c) provide the unique application number for that invitation to apply; and

Country or territory	Requirement
	(d) provide a local police certificate or a police clearance certificate that has been issued no more than 6 months before the date of application; and (e) either: (i) have a minimum of 3 years' work experience in a professional role equivalent to an eligible occupation listed in Appendix Skilled Occupations; or (ii) hold a qualification equal to or above RQF level 6.]

Note: Paragraph substituted from 6 April 2022 subject to savings for applications made before that date (HC 1118).

[**YMS 4.3.** The number of places allocated to nationals or citizens of the same country, or rightful holders of a passport issued by the same territory, must not have exceeded the annual total allocation of places for that country or territory as set out in Appendix Youth Mobility Scheme: eligible nationals.]

Note: Paragraph substituted from 6 April 2022 subject to savings for applications made before that date (HC 1118).

[**YMS 4.4.** Where the applicant is a British Overseas citizen, British Overseas Territories citizen or British National (Overseas), YMS 4.1. to YMS 4.2. do not apply.]

Note: Paragraph substituted from 6 April 2022 subject to savings for applications made before that date (HC 1118).

YMS 4.5. [DELETED]

Note: Paragraph deleted from 6 April 2022 subject to savings for applications made before that date (HC 1118).

Additional requirements for Indian citizens

YMS 4.5A. [DELETED]

Note: Paragraph deleted from 6 April 2022 subject to savings for applications made before that date (HC 1118).

YMS 4.5B. [DELETED]

Note: Paragraph deleted from 6 April 2022 subject to savings for applications made before that date (HC 1118).

YMS 4.5C. [DELETED]

Note: Paragraph deleted from 6 April 2022 subject to savings for applications made before that date (HC 1118).

Financial requirement for the Youth Mobility Scheme

YMS 5.1. The applicant must have funds of £ 2,530.

YMS 5.2. The applicant must show that they have held the required level of funds for a 28- day period and as specified in Appendix Finance.

YMS 5.3. The applicant must not have any children aged under 18 who are either living with them or financially dependent upon them.

Decision on application for the Youth Mobility Scheme

YMS 6.1. If the decision maker is satisfied that all the eligibility and suitability requirements are met for the Youth Mobility Scheme route, the application will be granted, otherwise the application will be refused.

YMS 6.2. If the application is refused the person can apply for an Administrative Review under Appendix AR: Administrative Review.

Period and conditions of grant for the Youth Mobility Scheme

YMS 7.1. The applicant will be granted entry clearance for up to two years.

YMS 7.2. The grant will be subject to all the following conditions:

(a) no access to public funds; and

(b) work permitted, subject to YMS 7.3; and

(c) study is permitted subject to the ATAS condition in Appendix ATAS; and

(d) if Part 10 applies the applicant will be required to register with the police.

YMS 7.3. Work is permitted subject to the following employment conditions:

(a) no employment as a professional sportsperson (including as a sports coach); and

(b) no self-employment, except where the following conditions are met:

(i) the person has no premises which they own, other than their home, from which they carry out their business; and

(ii) the total value of any equipment used in the business does not exceed £5,000; and

(iii) the person has no employees.]

[Appendix Youth Mobility Scheme: eligible nationals

Countries and Territories participating in the Youth Mobility Scheme, and annual allocation of places for 2022

1 The total allocation of places available for use by nationals or citizens of countries and rightful holders of a passport issued by territories participating in the Youth Mobility Scheme in 2022, are as follows:

- Australia – 30,000 places
- Canada – 6,000 places
- Hong Kong – 1,000 places
- Iceland – 1,000 places
- India – 3,000 places
- Japan – 1,500 places
- Monaco – 1,000 places
- New Zealand – 13,000 places
- Republic of Korea – 1,000 places
- San Marino – 1,000 places
- Taiwan – 1,000 places

Invitation to apply arrangements

2. Where places are being allocated under the Youth Mobility Schemes for the countries or territories listed below, the Home Office will apply invitation to apply arrangements:

(a) Hong Kong
(b) India
(c) Japan
(d) Republic of Korea
(e) Taiwan

3. Under these arrangements:

(a) a prospective applicant must submit an expression of interest in accordance with the process published by the Home Office; and

(b) no more than one expression of interest per person will be accepted by the Home Office during each period in which they may be submitted; and

(c) the Home Office will:

(i) select at random those to whom an invitation to apply for entry clearance under the Youth Mobility Scheme relevant allocation is to be issued from the pool of those who have submitted an expression of interest; and

(ii) keep a record of those individuals to whom an invitation to apply is issued; and

(d) the Home Office may:

(i) place a time limit on the period during which an expression of interest is to be submitted; and

(ii) determine the number of invitations to apply that may be issued in any calendar month; and

(iii) place a time limit on the validity of an invitation to apply.]

Note: Appendix inserted from 09:00 on 1 December 2020 subject to savings for applications made before that time (HC813). Appendix substituted from 6 April 2021 subject to savings for applications made before that date (HC 1248). Appendix substituted from 1 January 2022 subject to savings for applications made before that date (HC 617). Appendix substituted from 6 April 2022 subject to savings for applications made before that date (HC 1118).

[Appendix Temporary Work – Creative Worker

Note: Appendix inserted from 09:00 on 1 December 2020 subject to savings for applications made before that time (HC813). Amendments from 6 April 2021 subject to savings for applications made before that date (HC 1248). Appendix substituted from 09:00 on 11 October 2021 subject to savings for applications made before that time (HC 617).

The Temporary Work - Creative Worker route is for a person who wants to come to the UK to work within the creative sector.

A Creative Worker is someone who can make a unique contribution to the UK's rich cultural life, for example, as an artist, dancer, musician or entertainer, or as a model contributing to the UK's fashion industry.

A person can be granted permission for up to 12 months initially and can apply to extend their stay up to a maximum of two years if they are still working for the same sponsor.

A partner and children can apply as dependants on this route.

The Creative Worker route is not a route to settlement.

Validity requirements for a Creative Worker

CRV 1.1. A person applying for entry clearance or permission to stay as a Creative Worker must apply online on gov.uk on the specified form as follows:

Applicant	Specified form
EEA national with chipped passport	Either: • Temporary Worker using the UK Immigration: ID Check app; or • the forms listed below for applications outside or inside the UK (as relevant)
Applicants outside the UK	Temporary Worker visa
Applications inside the UK	Temporary Worker

CRV 1.2. An application for entry clearance or permission to stay as a Creative Worker must meet all the following requirements:

(a) any fee and Immigration Health Charge must have been paid; and

(b) the applicant must have provided any required biometrics; and

(c) the applicant must have provided a passport or other travel document which satisfactorily establishes their identity and nationality; and

(d) the applicant must have a Certificate of Sponsorship that was issued to them no more than three months before the date of application.

CRV 1.3. An applicant who is applying for permission to stay must be in the UK and must have, or have last had:

(a) entry clearance or permission to stay on the Creative Worker route

(b) permission as a Visitor who has been in the UK undertaking the activities in paragraphs PA 14.1 to PA 14.3 of Appendix Visitor: Permitted Activities or V 13.3 (e) of Appendix V: Visitor, where the applicant had been assigned the Certificate of Sponsorship in CRV 1.2.(d) before they entered the UK.

CRV 1.4. An application which does not meet all the validity requirements for the Creative Worker route is invalid and may be rejected and not considered.

Suitability requirements for a Creative Worker

CRV 2.1. The applicant must not fall for refusal under Part 9: grounds for refusal.

CRV 2.2. If applying for permission to stay the applicant must not be:

(a) in breach of immigration laws, except that where paragraph 39E applies, that period of overstaying will be disregarded; or

(b) on immigration bail.

Eligibility requirements for a Creative Worker

Entry requirements for a Creative Worker

CRV 3.1. A person seeking to come to the UK as a Creative Worker must have applied for and obtained entry clearance as a Creative Worker before they arrive in the UK, except where CRV 3.2. applies.

CRV 3.2. A person arriving in the UK who is seeking entry as a Creative Worker and does not have a valid entry clearance on that route may be granted permission to enter if the following requirements are met:

(a) the applicant is not a visa national; and

(b) the applicant has a valid Certificate of Sponsorship from an approved sponsor for the Creative Worker route; and

(c) if the applicant has consecutive engagements, the total length of all the periods of engagement, together with any gap between those engagements, is three months or less; and

(d) if the applicant does not have consecutive engagements, the total length of the period of engagement is three months or less; and

(e) the person otherwise meets the requirements to be granted permission as a Creative Worker.

CRV 3.3. A person applying for entry clearance as a Creative Worker must, if paragraph A39 and Appendix T of these rules apply, provide a valid medical certificate confirming that they have undergone screening for active pulmonary tuberculosis and that this tuberculosis is not present in them.

Sponsorship requirement for a Creative Worker

CRV 4.1. The applicant must have a valid Certificate of Sponsorship for the job they are planning to do; which to be valid must:

(a) confirm the applicant's name, that they are being sponsored as a Creative Worker, and details of the job and pay the sponsor is offering them confirming that these arrangements comply with the National Minimum Wage; and

(b) include a start date, stated by the sponsor, which is no more than 3 months after the date of application; and

(c) not have been used in a previous application which was either granted or refused (but can have been used in a previous application which was rejected as invalid, made void or withdrawn); and

(d) not have been withdrawn by the sponsor or cancelled by the Home Office; and

(e) confirm that the role meets the relevant requirements at CRV 4.2.

CRV 4.2. The sponsor must ensure that:

(a) the applicant complies with their relevant Code of Practice under Appendix Creative Workers Codes of Practice, where one exists for their occupation; or

(b) the role appeared in the shortage occupation list in Appendix Shortage Occupation Lists; or

(c) before assigning the Certificate of Sponsorship, the sponsor took into account the needs of the resident labour market in that field and was satisfied that the work could not be carried out by a settled worker.

CRV 4.3. If the Certificate of Sponsorship records that the applicant is being sponsored for more than one engagement by the same sponsor, there must be no more than 14 days between each individual engagement. Time spent by the applicant outside the UK (including the dates of their departure from and return to the UK) will not be counted towards this period.

CRV 4.4. If the applicant has consecutive engagements, each sponsor must assign its own Certificate of Sponsorship to the applicant, and each Certificate of Sponsorship must meet the requirements in CRV 4.1. to CRV 4.3.

CRV 4.5. The sponsor must be authorised by the Home Office to sponsor the job in question under the Creative Worker route.

CRV 4.6. The sponsor must be listed as A-rated on the Home Office's register of licensed sponsors, unless the applicant was last granted permission as a Creative Worker and is applying to continue working for the same sponsor as in their last permission.

Genuineness requirement for a Creative Worker

CRV 5.1. The applicant must:

(a) genuinely intend, and be able, to undertake the role for which they are being sponsored; and

(b) not intend to undertake employment other than in the role for which they are being sponsored, or as otherwise permitted by paragraph CRV 9.5.

Financial requirement for a Creative Worker

CRV 6.1. If the applicant is applying for permission to stay and has been in the UK with permission for 12 months or longer on the date of application, they will meet the financial requirement and do not need to show funds.

CRV 6.2. If the applicant is applying for entry clearance, or is applying for permission to enter under CRV 3.2, or is applying for permission to stay and has been in the UK for less than 12 months on the date of application, either:

(a) the applicant must have funds of at least £1,270; or

(b) the applicant's A rated sponsor must confirm on the Certificate of Sponsorship that they will, if it is necessary, maintain and accommodate the applicant up to the end of the first month of their employment for an amount of at least £1,270.

CRV 6.3. If CRV 6.2.(a) applies, the applicant must show that they have held the required level of funds for a 28-day period and as specified in Appendix Finance.

Parental consent requirement for a Creative Worker

CRV 7.1. If the applicant is aged under 18 on the date of application, they must have written consent from:

(a) both parents; or

(b) one parent, if that parent has sole legal responsibility for the applicant; or

(c) the applicant's legal guardian.

CRV 7.2. The written consent must confirm support for all of the following:

(a) the application; and

(b) the applicant's living and care arrangements in the UK; and

(c) if the application is for entry clearance, the applicant's travel to, and reception arrangements in, the UK.

Decision on an application for a Creative Worker

CRV 8.1. If the decision maker is satisfied that all the suitability and eligibility requirements for the Creative Worker route are met, the application will be granted, otherwise the application will be refused.

CRV 8.2. If the application is refused, the person can apply for an Administrative Review under Appendix AR: Administrative Review.

Period and conditions of grant for a Creative Worker

CRV 9.1. If the application is for entry clearance, the applicant will be granted whichever is the shorter of:

(a) a period starting 14 days before the first engagement and ending 14 days after the final engagement, if the applicant has consecutive engagements; or

(b) the period of the job on the Certificate of Sponsorship plus 14 days before and after, if the applicant does not have consecutive engagements; or

(c) 12 months.

CRV 9.2. If the application is for permission to enter, in accordance with CRV 3.2, the applicant will be granted permission to enter for whichever is the shorter of:

(a) a period starting up to 14 days before the first engagement and ending 14 days after the final engagement, if the applicant has consecutive engagements; or

(b) the period of the job on the Certificate of Sponsorship plus up to 14 days before and 14 days after, if the applicant does not have consecutive engagements; or

(c) 3 months.

CRV 9.3. Unless CRV 9.4. applies, if the application is for permission to stay, the applicant will be granted whichever is the shorter of:

(a) a period ending 14 days after the final engagement, if the applicant has consecutive engagements; or

(b) the period of the job on the Certificate of Sponsorship plus 14 days, if the applicant does not have consecutive engagements; or

(c) the difference between the period the applicant has already spent in the UK as a Creative Worker and 12 months.

CRV 9.4. If the applicant is applying for permission to stay and the sponsor is the same sponsor as in the application which led to the applicant's last grant of permission, the applicant will be granted whichever is the shorter of:

(a) a period ending 14 days after the final engagement, if the applicant has consecutive engagements; or

(b) the period of the job on the Certificate of Sponsorship plus 14 days, if the applicant does not have consecutive engagements; or

(c) 12 months; or

(d) the difference between the period the applicant has already spent in the UK as a Creative Worker and 24 months.

CRV 9.5. The grant will be subject to all the following conditions:

(a) no access to public funds; and

(b) work is permitted only in the role(s) the applicant is being sponsored for; and

(c) supplementary employment is permitted; and

(d) study is permitted, subject to the ATAS condition in Appendix ATAS; and

(e) if Part 10 applies, the applicant will be required to register with the police.

Dependants of a Creative Worker

Validity requirements for a dependent partner or dependent child of a Creative Worker

CRV 10.1. A person applying for entry clearance or permission to stay as a dependent partner or dependent child of a Creative Worker must apply online on the gov.uk website on the specified form as follows:

Applicant	Specified form
EEA national with a chipped passport	Either (as applicable): • Dependant partner or dependant child using the UK Immigration: ID Check app; or • the forms listed below for dependant applicants outside or inside the UK as relevant.
Applicants outside the UK	Dependant partner visa Dependant child visa
Applicants inside the UK	If the dependant is applying at the same time as the Creative Worker, they can be included in the form Temporary Worker where the form allows dependants to be added. Otherwise: – Dependant partner – Dependant child

[**CRV 10.2.** An application for entry clearance or permission to stay as a partner or child of a Creative Worker must meet all the following requirements:

(a) any fee and Immigration Health Charge must have been paid; and

(b) the applicant must have provided any required biometrics; and

(c) the applicant must have provided a passport or other travel document which satisfactorily establishes their identity and nationality; and

(d) the applicant must be applying as a partner or child of person who:

(i) has made a valid application for entry clearance or permission to stay on the Creative Worker route that has not been decided; or

(ii) has entry clearance or permission to stay on the Creative Worker route.

Note: Paragraph substituted from 6 April 2022 (HC 1118).

CRV 10.3. An applicant applying as a dependent partner must be aged 18 or over on the date of application.

CRV 10.4. An applicant who is applying for permission to stay as a dependent partner or dependent child of a Creative Worker must be in the UK on the date of application and must not have, or have last been granted, permission:

(a) as a Visitor; or

(b) as a Short-term student; or

(c) as a Parent of a Child Student; or

(d) as a Seasonal Worker; or

(e) as a Domestic Worker in a Private Household; or

(f) outside the Immigration Rules.

CRV 10.5. An application which does not meet all the validity requirements for a dependent partner or dependent child of a Creative Worker is invalid and may be rejected and not considered.

Suitability requirements for a dependent partner or dependent child of a Creative Worker

CRV 11.1. The applicant must not fall for refusal under Part 9: grounds for refusal.

CRV 11.2. If applying for permission to stay the applicant must not be:

(a) in breach of immigration laws, except that where paragraph 39E applies, that period of overstaying will be disregarded; or

(b) on immigration bail.

Eligibility requirements for a dependent partner or dependent child of a Creative Worker

Entry requirement for a dependent partner or dependent child of a Creative Worker

CRV 12.1. A person seeking to come to the UK as a dependent partner or dependent child of a Creative Worker must apply for and obtain entry clearance as a dependent partner or dependent child of a Creative Worker before they arrive in the UK, unless CRV 12.2. applies.

CRV 12.2. A person arriving in the UK and seeking entry as a dependent partner or dependent child of a Creative Worker who does not have a valid entry clearance may be granted permission to enter if the following requirements are met:

(a) the applicant is not a visa national; and

(b) the applicant is seeking entry at the same time as the person they are a dependant of, and who meets the requirements at CRV 3.2.; and

(c) the applicant meets the requirements to be granted permission as a dependent partner or dependent child of a Creative Worker.

CRV 12.3. A person applying for entry clearance as a dependent partner or dependent child of a Creative Worker must, if paragraph A39 and Appendix T of these rules apply, provide a valid medical certificate confirming that they have undergone screening for active pulmonary tuberculosis and that this tuberculosis is not present in them.

Relationship requirement for a dependent partner of a Creative Worker

CRV 13.1. The applicant must be the partner of a person (P) where one of the following applies:

(a) P has permission on the Creative Worker route; or

(b) P is, at the same time, applying for (and is granted) entry clearance or permission on the Creative Worker route.

CRV 13.2. If the applicant and their Creative Worker partner are not married or in a civil partnership, all of the following requirements must be met:

(a) they must have been living together in a relationship similar to marriage or civil partnership for at least two years before the date of application; and

(b) any previous relationship of the applicant or their Creative Worker partner with another person must have permanently broken down; and

(c) the applicant and their Creative Worker partner must not be so closely related that they would not be allowed to marry or form a civil partnership in the UK.

CRV 13.3. The relationship between the applicant and their Creative Worker partner must be genuine and subsisting.

CRV 13.4. The applicant and their Creative Worker partner must intend to live together throughout the applicant's stay in the UK.

Relationship requirement for a dependent child of a Creative Worker

CRV 14.1. The applicant must be the child of a parent (P) where one of the following applies:

(a) P has permission on the Creative Worker route; or

(b) P is, at the same time, applying for (and is granted) entry clearance or permission on the Creative Worker route.

[**CRV 14.2.** CRV 14.2. The applicant's parents must each be either applying at the same time as the applicant or have permission to be in the UK (other than as a Visitor) unless:

(a) the parent applying for or with entry clearance or permission as a Creative Worker is the sole surviving parent; or

(b) the parent applying for or with entry clearance or permission as a Creative Worker has sole responsibility for the child's upbringing; or

(c) the parent who does not have permission as a Creative Worker –

(i) is a British citizen or a person who has a right to enter or stay in the UK without restriction; and

(ii) is or will be ordinarily resident in the UK; or

(d) the decision maker is satisfied that there are serious and compelling reasons to grant the child entry clearance or permission with the parent who is applying for or has entry clearance or permission on the Creative Worker route.]

Note: Paragraph substituted from 6 April 2022 (HC 1118).

CRV 14.3. If the applicant is a child born in the UK to a Creative Worker or their partner, the applicant must provide a full UK birth certificate showing the names of both parents.

Care requirement for a dependent child of a Creative Worker

CRV 15.1. If the applicant is aged under 18 on the date of application, there must be suitable arrangements for the child's care and accommodation in the UK, which must comply with relevant UK legislation and regulations.

Age requirement for a dependent child of a Creative Worker

CRV 16.1. The applicant must be under the age of 18 on the date of application, unless they were last granted permission as the dependent child of their parent or parents.

CRV 16.2. If the applicant is aged 16 or over on the date of application, they must not be leading an independent life.

Financial requirement for a dependent partner or dependent child of a Creative Worker

CRV 17.1. If the applicant is applying for permission to stay and has been living in the UK with permission for 12 months or longer on the date of application, they will meet the financial requirement and do not need to show funds.

[**CRV 17.2.** CRV 17.2. If the applicant is applying for entry clearance or permission to enter, or has been in the UK for less than 12 months on the date of application, either:

(a) funds of at least the amount required in CRV 17.3. must be held collectively by one or more of the following:

(i) the applicant; and

(ii) the Creative Worker (P); and

(iii) if the applicant is applying as a dependent child, their parent who is lawfully present in the UK or being granted entry clearance, or permission, at the same time; or

(b) the Creative Worker's A-rated sponsor must certify that they will, if necessary, maintain and accommodate the dependent partner and/or any dependent child as well as the Creative Worker, up to the end of the first month of each of their grants of permission, to at least the amounts required in CRV 17.3.]

Note: Paragraph substituted from 6 April 2022 (HC 1118).

[**CRV 17.3.** The funds required are:

(a) £285 for a partner in the UK, or applying for entry clearance or permission to enter; and

(b) £315 for the first dependent child in the UK, or applying for entry clearance or permission to enter; and

(c) £200 for any other dependent child in the UK, or applying for entry clearance or permission to enter.]

Note: Paragraph substituted from 6 April 2022 (HC 1118).

CRV 17.4. If CRV 17.2.(a) applies, the funds held for the applicant must be held in addition to any funds required for the Creative Worker to meet the financial requirement and any other dependants in the UK or applying at the same time.

CRV 17.5. If CRV 17.2.(a) applies, the funds must have been held for a 28-day period and as specified in Appendix Finance.

Decision on an application for a dependent partner or dependent child of a Creative Worker

CRV 18.1. If the decision maker is satisfied that all the suitability and eligibility requirements for a dependent partner or dependent child of a Creative Worker are met, the application will be granted, otherwise the application will be refused.

CRV 18.2. If the application is refused, the person can apply for an Administrative Review under Appendix AR: Administrative Review.

Period and conditions of grant for a dependent partner or dependent child of a Creative Worker

CRV 19.1. A partner will be granted permission which ends on the same date as their partner's permission as a Creative Worker.

CRV 19.2. A child will be granted permission which ends on the same date as whichever of their parents' permission ends first.

CRV 19.3. The grant will be subject to all the following conditions:

(a) no access to public funds; and

(b) work (including self-employment and voluntary work) is permitted, except as a professional sportsperson (including as a sports coach); and

(c) study is permitted, subject to the ATAS condition in Appendix ATAS if the applicant is over the age of 18; and

(d) if Part 10 applies, the applicant will be required to register with the police.]

[Appendix Temporary Work – Religious Worker

The Temporary Work - Religious Worker route is for a person who wants to come to the UK to support the activities of religious institutions by conducting religious work such as working in a religious order or undertaking non-pastoral work for a religious organisation. A person on the Religious Worker route can stay in the UK for up to a maximum of two years. A partner and children can apply as dependants on this route.

The Religious Worker route is not a route to settlement.

A Minister of Religion must apply on the T2 Minister of Religion route if their engagement in the UK involves leading a congregation in performing rites, rituals and preaching the essentials of the creed as its core duties.

Validity requirements for a Religious Worker

RW 1.1. A person applying for entry clearance or permission to stay as a Religious Worker must apply online on gov.uk on the specified form as follows:

Applicant	Specified form
EEA national with a chipped passport	Either: • Temporary Worker using the UK Immigration: ID Check app; or • the forms listed below for applicants outside or inside the UK (as relevant)
Applicants outside the UK	Temporary Worker visa
Applicants inside the UK	Temporary Worker

RW 1.2. An application for entry clearance or permission to stay as a Religious Worker must meet all the following requirements:

(a) any fee and Immigration Health Charge must have been paid; and

(b) the applicant must have provided any required biometrics; and

(c) the applicant must have provided a passport or other travel document which satisfactorily establishes their identity and nationality; and

(d) the applicant must have a Certificate of Sponsorship that was issued to them no more than 3 months before the date of application.

RW 1.3. The applicant must be aged 18 or over on the date of application. An applicant who is applying for permission to stay must have, or have last had, permission as a Religious Worker.

RW 1.5. An application which does not meet all the validity requirements for a Religious Worker is invalid and may be rejected and not considered.

Suitability requirements for a Religious Worker

RW 2.1. The applicant must not fall for refusal under Part 9: grounds for refusal.

RW 2.2. If applying for permission to stay the applicant must not be:

(a) in breach of immigration laws, except that where paragraph 39E applies, that period of overstaying will be disregarded; or

(b) on immigration bail.

Eligibility requirements for a Religious Worker

Entry requirements for a Religious Worker

RW 3.1. A person seeking to come to the UK on the Religious Worker route must have applied for and obtained entry clearance as a Religious Worker before they arrive in the UK.

RW 3.2. A person applying for entry clearance as a Religious Worker must, if paragraph A39 and Appendix T of these rules apply, provide a valid medical certificate confirming that they have undergone screening for active pulmonary tuberculosis and that this tuberculosis is not present in them.

RW 3.3. An applicant for entry clearance must not have had permission as a Religious Worker or Charity Worker at any time during the 12 months immediately before the date of application unless they can show they were not in the UK at any time during those 12 months.

Sponsorship requirement for a Religious Worker

RW 4.1. The applicant must have a valid Certificate of Sponsorship for the job they are planning to do; which to be valid must:

(a) confirm the applicant's name, that they are being sponsored as a Religious Worker, details of the job and pay the sponsor is offering them; and

(b) include a start date, stated by the sponsor, which is no more than 3 months after the date of application; and

(c) not have been used in a previous application which was either granted or refused (but can have been used in a previous application which was rejected as invalid, made void or withdrawn); and

(d) not have been withdrawn by the sponsor or cancelled by the Home Office; and

(e) confirm that the role meets the requirements at RW 4.3; and

(f) confirm whether the applicant is a member of the sponsor's order, if the sponsor is a religious order; and

(g) confirm that the applicant will receive pay and conditions at least equal to those given to settled workers in the same role; and

(h) confirm that the pay complies with or is exempt from the National Minimum Wage; and

(i) confirm that the requirements of the resident labour consideration, as set out in RW 4.2, in respect of the job, have been complied with, or that the applicant is applying for permission to stay and the sponsor is the same sponsor as in their last grant of permission as a Religious Worker.

RW 4.2. The requirements of the resident labour consideration are:

(a) that the role is supernumerary, such that it is over and above the sponsor's normal staffing requirements and if the person filling the role was not there, it would not need to be filled by anyone else (with a full explanation of why it is supernumerary); or

(b) that the role involves living mainly within and being a member of a religious order, which must be a lineage of communities or of people who live in some way set apart from society in accordance with their specific religious devotion, for example an order of nuns or monks; or

(c) that the sponsor holds national records of all available individuals, details of those records and confirms that the records show that no suitable settled worker is available to fill the role; or

(d) that a national recruitment search was undertaken, and the following details are provided:

(i) where the role was advertised, which must be at least one of the following:

(1) a national form of media appropriate to the sponsor's religion or denomination; or

(2) the sponsor's own website, if that is how the sponsor usually reaches out to its community on a national scale, that is where it normally advertises vacant positions, and the pages containing the advertisement are free to view without paying a subscription fee or making a donation; or

(3) Jobcentre Plus (or in Northern Ireland, Job Centre Online) or in the employment section of a national newspaper, if there is no suitable national form of media appropriate to the sponsor's religion or denomination; and

(ii) any reference numbers of the advertisements; and

(iii) the period the role was advertised for, which must include at least 28 days during the six month period immediately before the date the sponsor assigned the Certificate of Sponsorship to the applicant; and

(iv) confirmation that no suitable settled workers are available to be recruited for the role.

RW 4.3. The sponsor must ensure the role meets all the following requirements:

(a) the role must involve performing religious duties within, or directed by, the sponsor's organisation to support the activities of the religious institution; and

(b) the religious duties must not include work which falls under a role of a Minister of Religion (which means the applicant must not have core duties of leading a congregation in performing the rites and rituals of the faith and in preaching the essentials of the creed).

RW 4.4. The sponsor must be authorised by the Home Office to sponsor the job in question under the Religious Worker route.

RW 4.5. The sponsor must be listed as A-rated on the Home Office's register of licensed sponsors, unless the applicant was last granted permission as a Religious Worker and is applying to continue working for the same sponsor as in their last permission.

Genuineness requirement for a Religious Worker

RW 5.1. The applicant must:

(a) genuinely intend, and be able, to undertake the role for which they are being sponsored; and

(b) not intend to undertake employment other than in the role for which they are being sponsored, or as otherwise permitted by paragraph RW 8.3. Financial requirement for a Religious Worker

RW 6.1. If the applicant is applying for permission to stay and has been in the UK with permission for 12 months or longer on the date of application, they will meet the financial requirement and do not need to show funds.

RW 6.2. If the applicant is applying for entry clearance, or is applying for permission to stay and has been in the UK for less than 12 months on the date of application, either:

(a) the applicant must have funds of at least £1,270; or

(b) the applicant's A rated sponsor must confirm on the Certificate of Sponsorship that they will, if it is necessary, maintain and accommodate the applicant up to the end of the first month of their employment for an amount of at least £1,270.

RW 6.3. If RW 6.2.(a) applies, the applicant must show that they have held the required level of funds for a 28-day period and as specified in Appendix Finance.

Decision on an application for a Religious Worker

RW 7.1. If the decision maker is satisfied that all the suitability and eligibility requirements for the Religious Worker route are met, the application will be granted, otherwise the application will be refused.

RW 7.2. If the application is refused, the person can apply for an Administrative Review under Appendix AR: Administrative Review.

Period and conditions of grant for a Religious Worker

RW 8.1. If the application is for entry clearance, the applicant will be granted whichever is the shorter of:

(a) the period of the job on the Certificate of Sponsorship plus 14 days before and after; or

(b) 24 months.

RW 8.2. If the application is for permission to stay, the applicant will be granted whichever is the shorter of:

(a) the period of the job on the Certificate of Sponsorship plus 14 days; or

(b) the difference between the period the applicant has already spent in the UK since their last grant of permission as a Religious Worker and 24 months.

RW 8.3. The grant will be subject to all the following conditions:

(a) no access to public funds; and
(b) work is permitted only in the role the applicant is being sponsored for; and
(c) supplementary employment is permitted; and
(d) study is permitted, subject to the ATAS condition in Appendix ATAS; and
(e) if Part 10 applies, the applicant will be required to register with the police.

Dependants of a Religious Worker

Validity requirements for a dependent partner or dependent child of a Religious Worker

RW 9.1. A person applying for entry clearance or permission to stay as a dependent partner or dependent child of a Religious Worker must apply online on the gov.uk website on the specified form as follows:

Applicant	Specified form
EEA national with chipped passport	Either (as applicable): • Dependant partner or dependant child using the UK Immigration: ID Check app; or • the forms listed below for dependant applicants outside or inside the UK as relevant.
Applicants outside the UK	Dependant partner visa Dependant child visa

Applicant	Specified form
Applicants inside the UK	If the dependant is applying at the same time as the Religious Worker, they can be included in the form Temporary Worker where the form allows dependants to be added. Otherwise: – Dependant partner – Dependant child

[**RW 9.2.** An application for entry clearance or permission to stay as a partner or child of a Religious Worker must meet all the following requirements:

(a) any fee and Immigration Health Charge must have been paid; and

(b) the applicant must have provided any required biometrics; and

(c) the applicant must have provided a passport or other travel document which satisfactorily establishes their identity and nationality; and

(d) the applicant must be applying as a partner or child of a person who:

(i) has made a valid application for entry clearance or permission to stay on the Religious Worker route that has not been decided; or

(ii) has entry clearance or permission to stay on the Religious Worker route.]

Note: Paragraph substituted from 6 April 2022 (HC 1118).

RW 9.3. An applicant applying as a dependent partner must be aged 18 or over on the date of application.

RW 9.4. An applicant who is applying for permission to stay as a dependent partner or dependent child of a Religious Worker must be in the UK on the date of application and must not have, or have last been granted, permission:

(a) as a Visitor; or

(b) as a Short-term student; or

(c) as a Parent of a Child Student; or

(d) as a Seasonal Worker; or

(e) as a Domestic Worker in a Private Household; or

(f) outside the Immigration Rules.

RW 9.5. An application which does not meet all the validity requirements for a dependent partner or dependent child of a Religious Worker is invalid and may be rejected and not considered.

Suitability requirements for a dependent partner or dependent child of a Religious Worker

RW 10.1. The applicant must not fall for refusal under Part 9: grounds for refusal.

RW 10.2. If applying for permission to stay the applicant must not be:

(a) in breach of immigration laws, except that where paragraph 39E applies, that period of overstaying will be disregarded; or

(b) on immigration bail.

Eligibility requirements for a dependent partner or dependent child of a Religious Worker

Entry requirement for a dependent partner or dependent child of a Religious Worker

RW 11.1. A person seeking to come to the UK as a dependent partner or dependent child of a Religious Worker must apply for and obtain entry clearance as a dependent partner or dependent child of a Religious Worker before they arrive in the UK.

RW 11.2. A person applying for entry clearance as a dependent partner or dependent child of a Religious Worker must, if paragraph A39 and Appendix T of these rules apply, provide a valid medical certificate confirming that they have undergone screening for active pulmonary tuberculosis and that this tuberculosis is not present in them.

Relationship requirement for a dependent partner of a Religious Worker

RW 12.1. The applicant must be the partner of a person (P) where one of the following applies:

(a) P has permission on the Religious Worker route; or

(b) P is, at the same time, applying for (and is granted) entry clearance or permission on the Religious Worker route.

RW 12.2. If the applicant and their Religious Worker partner are not married or in a civil partnership, all of the following requirements must be met:

(a) they must have been living together in a relationship similar to marriage or civil partnership for at least two years before the date of application; and

(b) any previous relationship of the applicant or their Religious Worker partner with another person must have permanently broken down; and

(c) the applicant and their Religious Worker partner must not be so closely related that they would not be allowed to marry or form a civil partnership in the UK.

RW 12.3. The relationship between the applicant and their Religious Worker partner must be genuine and subsisting.

RW 12.4. The applicant and their Religious Worker partner must intend to live together throughout the applicant's stay in the UK.

Relationship requirement for a dependent child of a Religious Worker

RW 13.1. The applicant must be the child of a parent (P) where one of the following applies:

(a) P has permission on the Religious Worker route; or

(b) P is, at the same time, applying for (and is granted) entry clearance or permission on the Religious Worker route.

RW 13.2. The applicant's parents must each be either applying at the same time as the applicant or have permission to be in the UK (other than as a Visitor) unless:

(a) the parent applying for or with entry clearance or permission to stay as a Religious Worker is the sole surviving parent; or

(b) the parent applying for or with entry clearance or permission to stay as a Religious Worker has sole responsibility for the child's upbringing; or

(c) the parent who does not have permission as a Religious Worker –

(i) is a British citizen or a person who has a right to enter or stay in the UK without restriction; and

(ii) is or will be ordinarily resident in the UK; or

(d) the decision maker is satisfied that there are serious and compelling reasons to grant the child entry clearance or permission to stay with the parent who is applying for or has entry clearance or permission to stay as a Religious Worker.

RW 13.3. If the applicant is a child born in the UK to a Religious Worker or their partner, the applicant must provide a full UK birth certificate showing the names of both parents.

Care requirement for a dependent child of a Religious Worker

RW 14.1. If the applicant is aged under 18 on the date of application, there must be suitable arrangements for the child's care and accommodation in the UK, which must comply with relevant UK legislation and regulations.

Age requirement for a dependent child of a Religious Worker

RW 15.1. The applicant must be under the age of 18 on the date of application, unless they were last granted permission as the dependent child of their parent or parents.

RW 15.2. If the applicant is aged 16 or over on the date of application, they must not be leading an independent life.

Financial requirement for a dependent partner or dependent child of a Religious Worker

RW 16.1. If the applicant is applying for permission to stay and has been living in the UK with permission for 12 months or longer on the date of application, they will meet the financial requirement and do not need to show funds.

RW 16.2. If the applicant is applying for entry clearance, or has been in the UK for less than 12 months on the date of application, either:

(a) funds of at least the amount required in RW 16.3. must be held collectively by one or more of the following:

(i) the applicant; and

(ii) the Religious Worker (P); and

(iii) if the applicant is applying as a dependent child, their parent who is lawfully present in the UK or being granted entry clearance, or permission to stay, at the same time; or

(b) the Religious Worker's A-rated sponsor must certify that they will, if necessary, maintain and accommodate the dependent partner and/or any dependent child as well as the Religious Worker, up to the end of the first month of each of their grants of permission, to at least the amounts required in RW 16.3.

RW 16.3. The funds required are:

(a) £285 for a dependent partner in the UK, or applying for entry clearance; and

(b) £315 for the first dependent child in the UK, or applying for entry clearance; and

(c) £200 for any other dependent child in the UK, or applying for entry clearance.

RW 16.4. If RW 16.2.(a) applies, the funds held for the applicant must be held in addition to any funds required for the Religious Worker to meet the financial requirement and any other dependants in the UK or applying at the same time.

RW 16.5. If RW 16.2.(a) applies, the funds must have been held for a 28-day period and as specified in Appendix Finance.

Decision on an application for a dependent partner or dependent child of a Religious Worker

RW 17.1. If the decision maker is satisfied that all the suitability and eligibility requirements for a dependent partner or dependent child of a Religious Worker are met, the application will be granted, otherwise the application will be refused.

RW 17.2. If the application is refused, the person can apply for an Administrative Review under Appendix AR: Administrative Review.

Period and conditions of grant for a dependent partner or dependent child of a Religious Worker

RW 18.1. A partner will be granted permission which ends on the same date as their partner's permission as a Religious Worker.

RW 18.2. A child will be granted permission which ends on the same date as whichever of their parents' permission ends first.

RW 18.3. The grant will be subject to all the following conditions:

(a) no access to public funds; and

(b) work (including self-employment and voluntary work) is permitted, except as a professional sportsperson (including as a sports coach); and

(c) study is permitted, subject to the ATAS condition in Appendix ATAS if the applicant is over the age of 18; and

(d) if Part 10 applies, the applicant will be required to register with the police.]

Note: Appendix inserted from 09:00 on 1 December 2020 subject to savings for applications made before that time (HC813). Appendix substituted from 09:00 on 11 October 2021 subject to savings for applications made before that time (HC 617).

[Appendix Temporary Work – Charity Worker

The Temporary Work - Charity Worker route is for a person who wants to come to the UK to do voluntary work for up to a maximum of 12 months.

A partner and children can apply as dependants on this route.

The Charity Worker route is not a route to settlement.

Validity Requirements for a Charity Worker

CW 1.1. A person applying for entry clearance or permission to stay as a Charity Worker must apply online on gov.uk on the specified form as follows:

Applicant	Specified form
EEA national with a chipped passport	Either: • Temporary Worker using the UK Immigration: ID Check app; or • the forms listed below for applicants outside or inside the UK (as relevant)
Applicants outside the UK	Temporary Worker visa
Applicants inside the UK	Temporary Worker

CW 1.2. An application for entry clearance or permission to stay as a Charity Worker must meet all the following requirements:

(a) any fee and Immigration Health Charge must have been paid; and

(b) the applicant must have provided any required biometrics; and

(c) the applicant must have provided a passport or other travel document which satisfactorily establishes their identity and nationality; and

(d) the applicant must have a Certificate of Sponsorship that was issued to them no more than 3 months before the date of application.

CW 1.3. The applicant must be aged 18 or over on the date of application.

CW 1.4. An applicant who is applying for permission to stay must have, or have last had, permission as a Charity Worker.

CW 1.5. An application which does not meet all the validity requirements for a Charity Worker is invalid and may be rejected and not considered.

Suitability requirements for a Charity Worker

CW 2.1. The applicant must not fall for refusal under Part 9: grounds for refusal.

CW 2.2. If applying for permission to stay the applicant must not be:

(a) in breach of immigration laws, except that where paragraph 39E applies, that period of overstaying will be disregarded; or

(b) on immigration bail.

Eligibility requirements for a Charity Worker

Entry requirements for a Charity Worker

CW 3.1. A person seeking to come to the UK on the Charity Worker route must have applied for and obtained entry clearance as a Charity Worker before they arrive in the UK.

CW 3.2. A person applying for entry clearance as a Charity Worker must, if paragraph A39 and Appendix T of these rules apply, provide a valid medical certificate confirming that they have undergone screening for active pulmonary tuberculosis and that this tuberculosis is not present in them.

CW 3.3. An applicant for entry clearance must not have had permission as a Religious Worker or Charity Worker at any time during the 12 months immediately before the date of application unless they can show they were not in the UK at any time during those 12 months.

Sponsorship requirement for a Charity Worker

CW 4.1. The applicant must have a valid Certificate of Sponsorship for the job they are planning to do; which to be valid must:

(a) confirm the applicant's name, that they are being sponsored as a Charity Worker, details of the job the sponsor is offering them; and

(b) include a start date, stated by the sponsor, which is no more than three months after the date of application; and

(c) not have been used in a previous application which was either granted or refused (but can have been used in a previous application which was rejected as invalid, made void or withdrawn); and

(d) not have been withdrawn by the sponsor or cancelled by the Home Office; and

(e) include confirmation that the role meets the requirement at CW 4.2.

CW 4.2. The sponsor must ensure the role meets the following requirements:

(a) it is voluntary fieldwork which contributes directly to the achievement or advancement of the sponsor's charitable purpose; and

(b) it must be voluntary work and not be paid or otherwise remunerated, including receipt of benefits in kind, except for reasonable expenses as defined in the National Minimum Wage Act 1998; and

(c) the applicant must not be filling a permanent position, including on a temporary basis.

CW 4.3. The sponsor must be authorised by the Home Office to sponsor the job in question under the Charity Worker route.

CW 4.4. The sponsor must be listed as A-rated on the Home Office's register of licensed sponsors, unless the applicant was last granted permission as a Charity Worker and is applying to continue working for the same sponsor as in their last permission.

Genuineness requirement for a Charity Worker

CW 5.1. The applicant must:

(a) genuinely intend, and be able, to undertake the role for which they are being sponsored; and

(b) not intend to undertake employment other than in the role for which they are being sponsored, or as otherwise permitted by paragraph CW 8.3.

Financial Requirement for a Charity Worker

CW 6.1. If the applicant is applying for permission to stay and has been in the UK with permission for 12 months or longer on the date of application, they will meet the financial requirement and do not need to show funds.

CW 6.2. If the applicant is applying for entry clearance, or is applying for permission to stay and has been in the UK for less than 12 months on the date of application, either:

(a) the applicant must have funds of at least £1,270; or

(b) the applicant's A rated sponsor must confirm on the Certificate of Sponsorship that they will, if it is necessary, maintain and accommodate the applicant up to the end of the first month of their employment for an amount of at least £1,270.

CW 6.3. If CW 6.2.(a) applies, the applicant must show that they have held the required level of funds for a 28-day period and as specified in Appendix Finance.

Decision on an application for a Charity Worker

CW 7.1. If the decision maker is satisfied that all the suitability and eligibility requirements for the Charity Worker route are met, the application will be granted, otherwise the application will be refused.

CW 7.2. If the application is refused, the person can apply for an Administrative Review under Appendix AR: Administrative Review.

Period and conditions of grant for a Charity Worker

CW 8.1. If the application is for entry clearance, the applicant will be granted whichever is the shorter of:

(a) the period of the job on the Certificate of Sponsorship plus 14 days before and after; or

(b) 12 months.

CW 8.2. If the application is for permission to stay, the applicant will be granted whichever is the shorter of:

(a) the period of the job on the Certificate of Sponsorship plus 14 days; or

(b) the difference between the period the applicant has already spent in the UK since their last grant of permission as a Charity Worker and 12 months.

CW 8.3. The grant will be subject to all the following conditions:

(a) no access to public funds; and

(b) work is permitted only in the role the applicant is being sponsored for; and

(c) voluntary work with another organisation is permitted; and

(d) study is permitted, subject to the ATAS condition in Appendix ATAS; and

(e) if Part 10 applies, the applicant will be required to register with the police.

Dependants of a Charity Worker

Validity requirements for a dependent partner or dependent child of a Charity Worker

CW 9.1. A person applying for entry clearance or permission to stay as a dependent partner or dependent child of a Charity Worker must apply online on the gov.uk website on the specified form as follows:

Applicant	Specified form
EEA national with a chipped passport	Either (as applicable): • Dependant partner or dependant child using the UK Immigration: ID Check app; or • the forms listed below for dependant applicants outside or inside the UK as relevant.
Applicants outside the UK	Dependant partner visa Dependant child visa
Applicants inside the UK	If the dependant is applying at the same time as the Charity Worker, they can be included in the form Temporary Worker where the form allows dependants to be added. Otherwise: – Dependant partner – Dependant child

[**CW 9.2.** An application for entry clearance or permission to stay as a partner or child of a Charity Worker must meet all the following requirements:

(a) any fee and Immigration Health Charge must have been paid; and

(b) the applicant must have provided any required biometrics; and

(c) the applicant must have provided a passport or other travel document which satisfactorily establishes their identity and nationality; and

(d) the applicant must be applying as a partner or child of a person who:

(i) has made a valid application for entry clearance or permission to stay on the Charity Worker route that has not been decided; or

(ii) has entry clearance or permission to stay on the Charity Worker route.]

Note: Paragraph substituted from 6 April 2022 (HC 1118).

CW 9.3. An applicant applying as a dependent partner must be aged 18 or over on the date of application.

CW 9.4. An applicant who is applying for permission to stay as a dependent partner or dependent child of a Charity Worker must be in the UK on the date of application and must not have, or have last been granted, permission:

(a) as a Visitor; or

(b) as a Short-term student; or

(c) as a Parent of a Child Student; or

(d) as a Seasonal Worker; or

(e) as a Domestic Worker in a Private Household; or

(f) outside the Immigration Rules.

CW 9.5. An application which does not meet all the validity requirements for a dependent partner or dependent child of a Charity Worker is invalid and may be rejected and not considered.

Suitability requirements for a dependent partner or dependent child of a Charity Worker

CW 10.1. The applicant must not fall for refusal under Part 9: grounds for refusal.

CW 10.2. If applying for permission to stay the applicant must not be:

(a) in breach of immigration laws, except that where paragraph 39E applies, that period of overstaying will be disregarded; or

(b) on immigration bail.

Eligibility requirements for a dependent partner or dependent child of a Charity Worker

Entry requirement for a dependent partner or dependent child of a Charity Worker

CW 11.1. A person seeking to come to the UK as a dependent partner or dependent child of a Charity Worker must apply for and obtain entry clearance as a dependent partner or dependent child of a Charity Worker before they arrive in the UK.

CW 11.2. A person applying for entry clearance as a dependent partner or dependent child of a Charity Worker must, if paragraph A39 and Appendix T of these rules apply, provide a valid medical certificate confirming that they have undergone screening for active pulmonary tuberculosis and that this tuberculosis is not present in them.

Relationship requirement for a dependent partner of a Charity Worker

CW 12.1. The applicant must be the partner of a person (P) where one of the following applies:

(a) P has permission on the Charity Worker route; or

(b) P is, at the same time, applying for (and is granted) entry clearance or permission on the Charity Worker route.

CW 12.2. If the applicant and their Charity Worker partner are not married or in a civil partnership, all of the following requirements must be met:

(a) they must have been living together in a relationship similar to marriage or civil partnership for at least two years before the date of application; and

(b) any previous relationship of the applicant or their Charity Worker partner with another person must have permanently broken down; and

(c) the applicant and their Charity Worker partner must not be so closely related that they would not be allowed to marry or form a civil partnership in the UK.

CW 12.3. The relationship between the applicant and their Charity Worker partner must be genuine and subsisting.

CW 12.4. The applicant and their Charity Worker partner must intend to live together throughout the applicant's stay in the UK.

Relationship requirement for a dependent child of a Charity Worker

CW 13.1. The applicant must be the child of a parent (P) where one of the following applies:

(a) P has permission on the Charity Worker route; or

(b) P is, at the same time, applying for (and is granted) entry clearance or permission on the Charity Worker route.

CW 13.2. The applicant's parents must each be either applying at the same time as the applicant or have permission to be in the UK (other than as a Visitor) unless:

(a) the parent applying for or with entry clearance or permission to stay as a Charity Worker is the sole surviving parent; or

(b) the parent applying for or with entry clearance or permission to stay as a Charity Worker has sole responsibility for the child's upbringing; or

(c) the parent who does not have permission as a Charity Worker –

(i) is a British citizen or a person who has a right to enter or stay in the UK without restriction; and

(ii) is or will be ordinarily resident in the UK; or

(d) the decision maker is satisfied that there are serious and compelling reasons to grant the child entry clearance or permission to stay with the parent who is applying for or has entry clearance or permission to stay as a Charity Worker.

CW 13.3. If the applicant is a child born in the UK to a Charity Worker or their partner, the applicant must provide a full UK birth certificate showing the names of both parents.

Care requirement for a dependent child of a Charity Worker

CW 14.1. If the applicant is aged under 18 on the date of application, there must be suitable arrangements for the child's care and accommodation in the UK, which must comply with relevant UK legislation and regulations.

Age requirement for a dependent child of a Charity Worker

CW 15.1. The applicant must be under the age of 18 on the date of application unless they were last granted permission as the dependent child of their parent or parents.

CW 15.2. If the applicant is aged 16 or over on the date of application, they must not be leading an independent life.

Financial requirement for a dependent partner or dependent child of a Charity Worker

CW 16.1. If the applicant is applying for permission to stay and has been living in the UK with permission for 12 months or longer on the date of application, they will meet the financial requirement and do not need to show funds.

CW 16.2. If the applicant is applying for entry clearance, or has been in the UK for less than 12 months on the date of application, either:

(a) funds of at least the amount required in CW 16.3. must be held collectively by one or more of the following:

(i) the applicant; and

(ii) the Charity Worker (P); and

(iii) if the applicant is applying as a dependent child, their parent who is lawfully present in the UK or being granted entry clearance, or permission to stay, at the same time; or

(b) the Charity Worker's A-rated sponsor must certify that they will, if necessary, maintain and accommodate the dependent partner and/or any dependent child as well as the Charity Worker, up to the end of the first month of each of their grants of permission, to at least the amounts required in CW 16.3.

CW 16.3. The funds required are:

(a) £285 for a dependent partner in the UK, or applying for entry clearance; and

(b) £315 for the first dependent child in the UK, or applying for entry clearance; and

(c) £200 for any other dependent child in the UK, or applying for entry clearance.

CW 16.4. If CW 16.2.(a) applies, the funds held for the applicant must be held in addition to any funds required for the Charity Worker to meet the financial requirement and any other dependants in the UK or applying at the same time.

CW 16.5. If CW 16.2.(a) applies, the funds must have been held for a 28-day period and as specified in Appendix Finance.

Decision on an application for a dependent partner or dependent child of a Charity Worker

CW 17.1. If the decision maker is satisfied that all the suitability and eligibility requirements for a dependent partner or dependent child of a Charity Worker are met, the application will be granted, otherwise the application will be refused.

CW 17.2. If the application is refused, the person can apply for an Administrative Review under Appendix AR: Administrative Review.

Period and conditions of grant for a dependent partner or dependent child of a Charity Worker

CW 18.1. A partner will be granted permission which ends on the same date as their partner's permission as a Charity Worker.

CW 18.2. A child will be granted permission which ends on the same date as whichever of their parents' permission ends first.

CW 18.3. The grant will be subject to all the following conditions:

(a) no access to public funds; and

(b) work (including self-employment and voluntary work) is permitted, except as a professional sportsperson (including as a sports coach); and

(c) study is permitted, subject to the ATAS condition in Appendix ATAS if the applicant is over the age of 18; and

(d) if Part 10 applies, the applicant will be required to register with the police.]

Note: Appendix inserted from 09:00 on 1 December 2020 subject to savings for applications made before that time (HC813). Appendix substituted from 09:00 on 11 October 2021 subject to savings for applications made before that time (HC 617).

[Appendix Temporary Work – International Agreement

Note: Appendix inserted from 09:00 on 1 December 2020 subject to savings for applications made before that time (HC813). Amendments from 23:00 on 31 December 2020 for decisions made on or after that time (CP 361). Amendments from 6 April 2021 subject to savings for applications made before that date; amendments from 09:00 on 21 May 2021 subject to savings for applications made before that time (HC 1248). Appendix substituted from 09:00 on 11 October 2021 subject to savings for applications made before that time.

[The International Agreement route is for a person who wants to come to the UK to provide a service covered under international law, such as private servants in diplomatic households or employees of overseas governments and international organisations.

A person on the International Agreement route can stay for a maximum period of 2 years.

A partner and children can apply as dependants on this route.

The International Agreement route is not a route to settlement.

A person who wants to come to the UK under intra-company transfer, contractual service supplier or independent professional commitments must apply under the Global Business Mobility routes.]

Note: Introduction substituted from 09:00 on 11 April 2022 subject to savings for applications made before that time (HC 1118).

Validity Requirements for the International Agreement route

IA 1.1. A person applying for entry clearance or permission to stay on the International Agreement route must apply online on gov.uk on the specified form as follows:

Applicant	Specified form
EEA national with a chipped passport	Either: • Temporary Worker using the UK Immigration: ID Check app; or • the forms listed below for applicants outside or inside the UK (as relevant)
Applicants outside the UK	Temporary Worker visa
Applicants inside the UK	Temporary Worker

IA 1.2. An application for entry clearance or permission to stay on the International Agreement route must meet all the following requirements:

(a) any fee and Immigration Health Charge must have been paid; and

(b) the applicant must have provided any required biometrics; and

(c) the applicant must have provided a passport or other travel document which satisfactorily establishes their identity and nationality; and

(d) the applicant must have a Certificate of Sponsorship that was issued to them no more than 3 months before the date of application.

IA 1.3. The applicant must be aged 18 or over on the date of application.

IA 1.5. An application which does not meet all the validity requirements for the International Agreement route is invalid and may be rejected and not considered.

Suitability Requirements for the International Agreement route

IA 2.1. The applicant must not fall for refusal under Part 9: grounds for refusal.

IA 2.2. If applying for permission to stay the applicant must not be:

(a) in breach of immigration laws, except that where paragraph 39E applies, that period of overstaying will be disregarded; or

(b) on immigration bail.

Eligibility Requirements for the International Agreement route

Entry requirement for the International Agreement route

IA 3.1. A person seeking to come to the UK on the International Agreement route must apply for and obtain entry clearance on the International Agreement route before they arrive in the UK.

IA 3.2. A person applying for entry clearance on the International Agreement route must, if paragraph A39 and Appendix T of these rules apply, provide a valid medical certificate confirming that they have undergone screening for active pulmonary tuberculosis and that this tuberculosis is not present in them.

Sponsorship requirement for the International Agreement route

IA 4.1. The applicant must have a valid Certificate of Sponsorship for the job they are planning to do; which to be valid must:

(a) confirm the applicant's name, that they are being sponsored on the International Agreement route, details of the job and salary the sponsor is offering them, and that these arrangements comply with the National Minimum Wage; and

(b) include a start date, stated by the sponsor, which is no more than three months after the date of application; and

(c) not have been used in a previous application which was either granted or refused (but can have been used in a previous application which was rejected as invalid, made void or withdrawn); and

(d) not have been withdrawn by the sponsor or cancelled by the Home Office; and

(e) include confirmation that the role meets the relevant requirements at IA 6.1, depending on the role; and

(f) confirm whether the Academic Technology Approval Scheme (ATAS) requirement in Appendix ATAS applies.

IA 4.2. The sponsor must be authorised by the Home Office to sponsor the job in question under the International Agreement route.

IA 4.3. The sponsor must be listed as A-rated on the Home Office's register of licensed sponsors, unless the applicant was last granted permission on the International Agreement route and is applying to continue working for the same sponsor as in their last permission.

Genuineness requirement for the International Agreement route

IA 5.1. The applicant must:

(a) genuinely intend to, and be able to, undertake the role for which they are sponsored; and

(b) not intend to undertake employment other than in the role for which they are being sponsored, or as otherwise permitted by paragraph IA14.7. ATAS requirement for the International Agreement route

IA 5.1A. If the ATAS requirement in Appendix ATAS applies, the applicant must provide a valid ATAS certificate.

International Agreement requirement

IA 6.1. The role the applicant is applying to do must be as one of the following (and the applicant must also meet the specific requirements for that work):

(a) a private servant in a diplomatic household; or

(b) an employee of an overseas government or other international organisation established under an international treaty signed by UK[.]

[. . .]

Note: Punctuation in (b) substituted, sub-paragraph (c) deleted from 09:00 on 11 April 2022 subject to savings for applications made before that time (HC 1118).

Private servant in diplomatic household requirements

IA 7.1. The applicant must be employed as a private servant by, and in the household of, either:

(a) a named member of staff of a diplomatic or consular mission who has diplomatic privileges and immunity as defined by the Vienna Convention on Diplomatic Relations; or

(b) a named official employed by an international organisation recognised by the UK government with diplomatic privileges or immunities under UK or international law.

IA 7.2. Where the applicant had permission under the rules in place from 6 April 2012 and is applying to extend their permission they must:

(a) be working for the same employer; and

(b) have continued to work for that employer throughout their time in the UK with permission as a private servant on the International Agreement route.

IA 7.3. The applicant must not intend to undertake any other role for the sponsor other than as a private servant in the specified household.

IA 7.4. The applicant must intend to work full time in the role they are being sponsored for.

IA 7.5. The applicant must not be a relative of the employer, or employer's spouse, either by blood or by marriage (including but not limited to, the spouse or unmarried partner, child, parent, grandparent or sibling of either the employer or the employer's spouse).

IA 7.6. The applicant must intend to leave the UK at the end of their permitted stay.

IA 7.7. The applicant must be paid at least the level of the National Minimum Wage throughout their stay.

IA 7.8. The applicant must provide the evidence of employment terms and conditions as set out in Appendix Domestic Worker Terms and Conditions.

IA 7.9. The applicant must provide a signed statement from the sponsor confirming that the role will not constitute work done in relation to the employer's family household within the meaning of regulation 57 of the National Minimum Wage Regulations 2015.

Employee of an overseas government or other international organisation requirement

IA 8.1. The applicant must be under a contract of employment with the overseas government or international organisation.

IA 8.2. The applicant must not intend to take any other form of role for the sponsor other than that for which the Certificate of Sponsorship was assigned.

Contractual Service Supplier requirement

IA 9.1. [DELETED]

Note: Paragraph deleted from 09:00 on 11 April 2022 subject to savings for applications made before that time (HC 1118).

IA 9.2. [DELETED]

Note: Paragraph deleted from 09:00 on 11 April 2022 subject to savings for applications made before that time (HC 1118).

IA 9.3. [DELETED]

Note: Paragraph deleted from 09:00 on 11 April 2022 subject to savings for applications made before that time (HC 1118).

IA 9.4. [DELETED]

Note: Paragraph deleted from 09:00 on 11 April 2022 subject to savings for applications made before that time (HC 1118).

IA 9.5. [DELETED]

Note: Paragraph deleted from 09:00 on 11 April 2022 subject to savings for applications made before that time (HC 1118).

IA 9.6. [DELETED]

Note: Paragraph deleted from 09:00 on 11 April 2022 subject to savings for applications made before that time (HC 1118).

IA 9.7. [DELETED]

Note: Paragraph deleted from 09:00 on 11 April 2022 subject to savings for applications made before that time (HC 1118).

IA 9.8. [DELETED]

Note: Paragraph deleted from 09:00 on 11 April 2022 subject to savings for applications made before that time (HC 1118).

IA 9.9. [DELETED]

Note: Paragraph deleted from 09:00 on 11 April 2022 subject to savings for applications made before that time (HC 1118).

IA 9.10. [DELETED]

Note: Paragraph deleted from 09:00 on 11 April 2022 subject to savings for applications made before that time (HC 1118).

Independent Professional requirement

IA 10.1. [DELETED]

Note: Paragraph deleted from 09:00 on 11 April 2022 subject to savings for applications made before that time (HC 1118).

IA 10.2. [DELETED]

Note: Paragraph deleted from 09:00 on 11 April 2022 subject to savings for applications made before that time (HC 1118).

IA 10.3. [DELETED]

Note: Paragraph deleted from 09:00 on 11 April 2022 subject to savings for applications made before that time (HC 1118).

IA 10.4. [DELETED]

Note: Paragraph deleted from 09:00 on 11 April 2022 subject to savings for applications made before that time (HC 1118).

IA 10.5. [DELETED]

Note: Paragraph deleted from 09:00 on 11 April 2022 subject to savings for applications made before that time (HC 1118).

IA 10.6. [DELETED]

Note: Paragraph deleted from 09:00 on 11 April 2022 subject to savings for applications made before that time (HC 1118).

IA 10.7. [DELETED]

Note: Paragraph deleted from 09:00 on 11 April 2022 subject to savings for applications made before that time (HC 1118).

IA 10.8. [DELETED]

Note: Paragraph deleted from 09:00 on 11 April 2022 subject to savings for applications made before that time (HC 1118).

Financial Requirement for the International Agreement route

IA 11.1. If the applicant is applying for permission to stay and has been in the UK with permission for 12 months or longer on the date of application, they will meet the financial requirement and do not need to show funds.

IA 11.2. If the applicant is applying for entry clearance, or is applying for permission to stay and has been in the UK for less than 12 months on the date of application, either:

(a) the applicant must have funds of at least £1,270; or

(b) the applicant's A rated sponsor must confirm on the Certificate of Sponsorship that they will, if it is necessary, maintain and accommodate the applicant up to the end of the first month of their employment for an amount of at least £1,270.

IA 11.3. If IA 11.2. applies, the applicant must show that they have held the required level of funds for a 28-day period and as specified in Appendix Finance.

Decision on application for the International Agreement route

IA 13.1. If the decision maker is satisfied that all the suitability and eligibility requirements for the International Agreement route are met, the application will be granted, otherwise the application will be refused.

IA 13.2. If the application is refused, the person can apply for an Administrative Review under Appendix AR: Administrative Review.

Period and conditions of grant for the International Agreement route

IA 14.1. [DELETED]

Note: Paragraph deleted from 09:00 on 11 April 2022 subject to savings for applications made before that time (HC 1118).

IA 14.2. [DELETED]

Note: Paragraph deleted from 09:00 on 11 April 2022 subject to savings for applications made before that time (HC 1118).

IA 14.3. If the application is for entry clearance [...], the applicant will be granted whichever is the shorter of:

(a) the period of the role on the Certificate of Sponsorship plus 14 days before and 14 days after that period; or

(b) 24 months.

Note: Words deleted from 09:00 on 11 April 2022 subject to savings for applications made before that time (HC 1118).

IA 14.4. Unless IA 14.5. applies, if the application is for permission to stay [...], the applicant will be granted whichever is the shorter of:

(a) the period of the role on the Certificate of Sponsorship plus 14 days before and 14 days after that period; or

(b) the difference between the period the applicant has already spent in the UK since their last grant of permission on the International Agreement route and 24 months.

Note: Words deleted from 09:00 on 11 April 2022 subject to savings for applications made before that time (HC 1118).

IA 14.5. If the applicant is a private servant in a diplomatic household who has spent more than three years continuously in the UK on the International Agreement route and their application is for permission to stay, the applicant will be granted whichever is the shorter of:

(a) the period of the role on the Certificate of Sponsorship plus 14 days before and 14 days after that period; or

(b) the difference between the period the applicant has already spent in the UK since their first grant of permission on the International Agreement route and five years.

IA 14.6. [DELETED]

Note: Paragraph deleted from 09:00 on 11 April 2022 subject to savings for applications made before that time (HC 1118).

[**IA 14.7.** The grant will be subject to all the following conditions:

(a) no access to public funds; and

(b) the only work permitted is

(i) the job the applicant is being sponsored for; and

(ii) supplementary employment only for a person being sponsored for a job as an employee of overseas governments or international organisations (but not as a private servant in a diplomatic household) and only provided the job in (i) is also being done.

(c) study is permitted, subject to the ATAS condition in Appendix ATAS; and

(d) if Part 10 of these rules applies the applicant will be required to register with the police.]

Note: Paragraph substituted from 09:00 on 11 April 2022 subject to savings for applications made before that time (HC 1118).

IA 14.8. If the applicant is being sponsored as a private servant in a diplomatic household, IA 14.7.(b) does not prevent them from taking employment as a domestic worker in a different household from the one specified in the Certificate of Sponsorship.

Settlement by a Private Servant in a diplomatic household

Validity requirements for settlement by a Private Servant in a diplomatic household

IA 15.1. A person applying for settlement as a Private Servant in a diplomatic household must apply online on the gov.uk website on the specified form “Settle in the UK in various immigration categories: form SET(O)”.

IA 15.2. An application for settlement must meet all the following requirements:

(a) any fee must have been paid; and

(b) the applicant must have provided any required biometrics; and

(c) the applicant must have provided a passport or other travel document which satisfactorily establishes their identity and nationality; and

(d) the applicant must be in the UK on the date of application.

IA 15.3. The applicant must have, or have last been granted, permission on the International Agreement route as a private servant in a diplomatic household.

IA 15.4. An application which does not meet all the validity requirements for settlement as a Private Servant in a diplomatic household is invalid and may be rejected and not considered.

Suitability Requirements for settlement as a Private Servant in a diplomatic household

IA 16.1. The applicant must not fall for refusal under Part 9: grounds for refusal.

IA 16.2. The applicant must not be:

(a) in breach of immigration laws, except that where paragraph 39E applies, that period of overstaying will be disregarded; or

(b) on immigration bail.

Eligibility requirements for settlement as a Private Servant in a diplomatic household

Qualifying period requirement for settlement as a Private Servant in a diplomatic household

IA 17.1. The applicant must have been granted their last entry clearance on the International Agreement route, working as a private servant in a diplomatic household under the rules in place before 6 April 2012.

IA 17.2. The applicant must have spent a continuous period of 5 years lawfully in the UK with entry clearance or permission on the International Agreement route, working as a private servant in a diplomatic household.

Continuous residence requirement for settlement as a Private Servant in a diplomatic household

IA 18.1. The applicant must meet the continuous residence requirement as specified in Appendix Continuous Residence during the period in IA 17.2.

English language requirement for settlement as a Private Servant in a diplomatic household

IA 19.1. Unless an exemption applies, the applicant must show English language ability on the Common European Framework of Reference for Languages in speaking and listening to at least level B1.

IA 19.2. The applicant must show they meet the English language requirement as specified in Appendix English Language.

Knowledge of Life in the UK requirement for settlement as a Private Servant in a diplomatic household

IA 20.1. The applicant must meet the Knowledge of Life in the UK requirement as specified in Appendix KOL UK.

Decision on an application for settlement by Private Servant in a diplomatic household

IA 21.1. If the decision maker is satisfied that all the suitability and eligibility requirements for settlement as a Private Servant in a diplomatic household are met, the applicant will be granted settlement, otherwise the application will be refused.

IA 21.2. If the application is refused, the person can apply for an Administrative Review under Appendix AR: Administrative Review.

Dependants on the International Agreement route

Validity requirements for a dependent partner or dependent child on the International Agreement route

IA 22.1. A person applying for entry clearance or permission to stay as a dependent partner or dependent child on the International Agreement route must apply online on the gov.uk website on the specified form as follows:

Applicant	Specified form
EEA national with a chipped passport	Either (as applicable): • Dependant partner or dependant child using the UK Immigration: ID Check app; or • the forms listed below for dependant applicants outside or inside the UK as relevant.
Applicant outside the UK	Dependant partner visa Dependant child visa
Applicant inside the UK	If the dependant is applying at the same time as the person on the International Agreement route, they can be included in the form Temporary Worker where the form allows dependants to be added. Otherwise: – Dependant partner – Dependant child

[**IA 22.2.** An application for entry clearance or permission to stay as a partner or child on the International Agreement route must meet all the following requirements:

(a) any fee and Immigration Health Charge must have been paid; and

(b) the applicant must have provided any required biometrics; and

(c) the applicant must have provided a passport or other travel document which satisfactorily establishes their identity and nationality; and

(d) the applicant must be applying as a partner or child of a person who:

(i) has made a valid application for entry clearance or permission to stay as a person on the International Agreement route that has not been decided; or

(ii) has entry clearance or permission to stay as a person on the International Agreement route.]

Note: Paragraph substituted from 6 April 2022 (HC 1118).

IA 22.3. An applicant applying as a dependent partner must be aged 18 or over on the date of application.

IA 22.4. An applicant who is applying for permission to stay as a dependent partner or dependent child on the International Agreement route must be in the UK on the date of application and must not have, or have last been granted, permission:

(a) as a Visitor; or
(b) as a Short-term student; or
(c) as a Parent of a Child Student; or
(d) as a Seasonal Worker; or
(e) as a Domestic Worker in a Private Household; or
(f) outside the Immigration Rules.

IA 22.5. An application which does not meet all the validity requirements for a dependent partner or dependent child on the International Agreement route is invalid and may be rejected and not considered.

Suitability requirements for a dependent partner or dependent child on the International Agreement route

IA 23.1. The applicant must not fall for refusal under Part 9: grounds for refusal.

IA 23.2. If applying for permission to stay the applicant must not be:

(a) in breach of immigration laws, except that where paragraph 39E applies, that period of overstaying will be disregarded; or
(b) on immigration bail.

Eligibility requirements for a dependent partner or dependent child on the International Agreement route

Entry requirement for a dependent partner or dependent child on the International Agreement route

IA 24.1. A person seeking to come to the UK as a dependent partner or dependent child on the International Agreement route must apply for and obtain entry clearance as a dependent partner or dependent child on the International Agreement route before they arrive in the UK.

IA 24.2. A person applying for entry clearance as a dependent partner or dependent child on the International Agreement route must, if paragraph A39 and Appendix T of these rules apply, provide a valid medical certificate confirming that they have undergone screening for active pulmonary tuberculosis and that this tuberculosis is not present in them.

Relationship requirement for a dependent partner on the International Agreement route

IA 25.1. The applicant must be the partner of a person (P) where one of the following applies:

(a) P has permission on the International Agreement route; or

(b) P is, at the same time, applying for (and is granted) entry clearance or permission on the International Agreement route.

IA 25.2. If the applicant and their partner on the International Agreement route are not married or in a civil partnership, all of the following requirements must be met:

(a) they must have been living together in a relationship similar to marriage or civil partnership for at least two years before the date of application; and

(b) any previous relationship of the applicant or their partner on the International Agreement route with another person must have permanently broken down; and

(c) the applicant and their partner on the International Agreement route must not be so closely related that they would not be allowed to marry or form a civil partnership in the UK.

IA 25.3. The relationship between the applicant and their partner on the International Agreement route must be genuine and subsisting.

IA 25.4. The applicant and their partner on the International Agreement route must intend to live together throughout the applicant's stay in the UK.

Relationship requirement for a dependent child on the International Agreement route

IA 26.1. The applicant must be the child of a parent (P) where one of the following applies:

(a) P has permission on the International Agreement route; or

(b) P is, at the same time, applying for (and is granted) entry clearance or permission on the International Agreement route.

IA 26.2. The applicant's parents must each be either applying at the same time as the applicant or have permission to be in the UK (other than as a Visitor) unless:

(a) the parent applying for or with entry clearance or permission to stay on the International Agreement route is the sole surviving parent; or

(b) the parent applying for or with entry clearance or permission to stay on the International Agreement route has sole responsibility for the child's upbringing; or

(c) the parent who does not have permission on the International Agreement route–

(i) is a British citizen or a person who has a right to enter or stay in the UK without restriction; and

(ii) is or will be ordinarily resident in the UK; or

(d) the decision maker is satisfied that there are serious and compellingreasons to grant the child entry clearance or permission to stay with the parent who is applying for or has entry clearance or permission to stay on the International Agreement route.

IA 26.3. If the applicant is a child born in the UK to a person on the International Agreement route or their partner, the applicant must provide a full UK birth certificate showing the names of both parents.

Care requirement for a dependent child on the International Agreement route

IA 27.1. If the applicant is aged under 18 on the date of application, there must be suitable arrangements for the child's care and accommodation in the UK, which must comply with relevant UK legislation and regulations.

Age requirement for a dependent child on the International Agreement route

IA 28.1. The child must be under the age of 18 on the date of application, unless they were last granted permission as the dependent child of their parent or parents.

IA 28.2. If the child is aged 16 or over on the date of application, they must not be leading an independent life.

Financial requirement for a dependent partner or dependent child on the International Agreement route

IA 29.1. If the applicant is applying for permission to stay and has been living in the UK with permission for 12 months or longer on the date of application, they will meet the financial requirement and do not need to show funds.

IA 29.2. If the applicant is applying for entry clearance, or has been in the UK for less than 12 months on the date of application, either:

(a) funds of at least the amount required in IA 29.3. must be held collectively by one or more of the following:

(i) the applicant; and

(ii) the person on the International Agreement route (P); and

(iii) if the applicant is applying as a dependent child, their parent who is lawfully present in the UK or being granted entry clearance, or permission to stay, at the same time; or

(b) the A-rated sponsor of the person on the International Agreement route must certify that they will, if necessary, maintain and accommodate the dependent partner and/or any dependent child as well as the person on the International Agreement route, up to the end of the first month of each of their grants of permission, to at least the amounts required in 29.3.

IA 29.3. The funds required are:

(a) £285 for a dependent partner in the UK, or applying for entry clearance; and

(b) £315 for the first dependent child in the UK, or applying for entry clearance; and

(c) £200 for any other dependent child in the UK, or applying for entry clearance.

IA 29.4. If IA 29.2(a) applies, the funds held for the applicant must be held in addition to any funds required for the person on the International Agreement route to meet the financial requirement and any other dependants in the UK or applying at the same time.

IA 29.5. If IA 29.2(a) applies, the funds must have been held for a 28-day period and as specified in Appendix Finance.

Decision on an application for a dependent partner or dependent child on the International Agreement route

IA 30.1. If the decision maker is satisfied that all the suitability and eligibility requirements for a dependent partner or dependent child on the International Agreement route are met, the application will be granted, otherwise the application will be refused.

IA 30.2. If the application is refused, the person can apply for an Administrative Review under Appendix AR: Administrative Review.

Period and conditions of grant for a dependent partner or dependent child on the International Agreement route

IA 31.1. A partner will be granted permission which ends on the same date as their partner's permission on the International Agreement route.

IA 31.2. A child will be granted permission which ends on the same date as whichever of their parents' permission ends first.

IA 31.3. The grant will be subject to all the following conditions:

(a) no access to public funds; and

(b) work (including self-employment and voluntary work) is permitted, except as a professional sportsperson (including as a sports coach); and

(c) study is permitted, subject to the ATAS condition in Appendix ATAS if the applicant is over the age of 18; and

(d) if Part 10 applies, the applicant will be required to register with the police.

Settlement as a dependent partner or dependent child on the International Agreement route

Validity requirements for settlement as a dependent partner or dependent child of a Private Servant in a diplomatic household

IA 32.1. A person applying for settlement as a dependent partner or a dependent child of a Private Servant in a diplomatic household must apply online on the gov.uk website on the specified form "Settle in the UK in various immigration categories: form SET(O)".

[**IA 32.2.** An application for settlement as a partner or child of a Private Servant in a diplomatic household must meet all the following requirements:

(a) any fee must have been paid; and

(b) the applicant must have provided any required biometrics; and

(c) the applicant must have provided either a passport or other travel document which satisfactorily establishes their identity and nationality; and

(d) the applicant must be in the UK on the date of application; and

(e) the applicant must be applying as a partner or child of a person (P) who:

(i) has made a valid application for settlement in the UK on the International Agreement route and that application has not been decided; or

(ii) is settled or has become a British citizen, provided that P had permission on the International Agreement route when they settled and the applicant either had permission as their partner or child at that time, or the applicant is applying as a child of P and the applicant was born in the UK before P settled.]

Note: Paragraph substituted from 6 April 2022 (HC 1118).

IA 32.3. The applicant must have, or have last been granted, permission as a dependent partner or a dependent child of a Private Servant in a diplomatic household on the International Agreement route.

IA 32.4. An application which does not meet all the validity requirements for settlement as a dependent partner or dependent child of a Private Servant in a diplomatic household on the International Agreement route is invalid and may be rejected and not considered.

Suitability requirements for settlement as a dependent partner or dependent child of a Private Servant in a diplomatic household

IA 33.1. The applicant must not fall for refusal under Part 9: grounds for refusal.

IA 33.2. The applicant must not be:

(a) in breach of immigration laws, except that where paragraph 39E applies, that period of overstaying will be disregarded; or

(b) on immigration bail.

Eligibility requirements for settlement as a dependent partner or dependent child of a Private Servant in a diplomatic household on the International Agreement route

Relationship requirement for settlement as a dependent partner of a Private Servant in a diplomatic household

IA 34.1. The applicant's partner must be either:

(a) a private servant in a diplomatic household who is, at the same time, being granted settlement; or

(b) be settled or a British citizen, providing they had permission as a private servant in a diplomatic household when they settled and the applicant had permission as their dependent partner at that time.

IA 34.2. The applicant and their partner must have been living together in the UK in a marriage or civil partnership, or in a relationship similar to marriage or civil partnership, for the five years immediately before the date of application.

Qualifying period requirement for settlement as a dependent partner of a Private Servant in a diplomatic household

IA 35.1. The applicant must have been in the UK with permission as the partner of the private servant in a diplomatic household for the last five years.

Continuous residence requirement for settlement as a dependent partner of a Private Servant in a diplomatic household

IA 36.1. The applicant must meet the continuous residence requirement as specified in Appendix Continuous Residence during the period in IA 35.1.

English language requirement for settlement as a dependent partner of a Private Servant in a diplomatic household

IA 37.1. Unless an exemption applies, the applicant must show English language ability on the Common European Framework of Reference for Languages in speaking and listening to at least level B1.

IA 37.2. The applicant must show they meet the English language requirement as specified in Appendix English Language.

Knowledge of Life in the UK requirement for settlement as a dependent partner of a Private Servant in a diplomatic household

IA 38.1. Unless an exemption applies, the applicant must meet the Knowledge of Life in the UK requirement as specified in Appendix: KOL UK.

Eligibility requirements for settlement as a dependent child of a Private Servant in a diplomatic household

Relationship requirement for settlement as a dependent child of a Private Servant in a diplomatic household

IA 39.1. A parent of the applicant must have been granted settlement as a person on the International Agreement route as a private servant in a diplomatic household.

IA 39.2. The parent must previously have had permission on the International Agreement route as a private servant in a diplomatic household and the applicant must have had permission as their dependent child at that time..

IA 39.3. The applicant's other parent must be being granted settlement at the same time, or be settled or a British citizen, unless any of the following apply:

(a) the first parent is the sole surviving parent; or

(b) the first parent has sole responsibility for the applicant's upbringing; or

(c) the decision maker is satisfied that there are serious and compelling reasons to grant the applicant settlement.

IA 39.4. If the applicant is aged 16 or over at the date of application, they must not be leading an independent life.

English language requirement for settlement as a dependent child of a Private Servant in a diplomatic household

IA 40.1. Unless an exemption applies, the applicant must show English language ability on the Common European Framework of Reference for Languages in speaking and listening to at least level B1.

IA 40.2. The applicant must show they meet the English language requirement as specified in Appendix English Language.

Knowledge of Life in the UK requirement for settlement as a dependent child of a Private Servant in a diplomatic household

IA 41.1. Unless an exemption applies, the applicant must meet the Knowledge of Life in the UK requirement as specified in Appendix KOL UK.

Decision on an application for settlement as a dependent partner or dependent child of a Private Servant in a diplomatic household

IA 42.1. If the decision maker is satisfied all the suitability and eligibility requirements for settlement as a dependent partner or dependent child on the International Agreement route are met the applicant will be granted settlement, otherwise the application will be refused.

IA 42.2. If the application is refused the person can apply for an Administrative Review under Appendix AR: Administrative Review.]

[Appendix Temporary Work - Government Authorised Exchange

Note: Appendix inserted from 09:00 on 1 December 2020 subject to savings for applications made before that time (HC813). Amendments from 6 April 2021 subject to savings for applications made before that time (HC 1248). Appendix substituted from 09:00 on 11 October 2021 subject to savings for applications made before that time (HC 617).

The Temporary Work - Government Authorised Exchange route is for a person who wants to come to the UK on an approved scheme for a period of no more than 12 or 24-months (depending on the scheme).

A partner and children can apply as dependants on this route.

The Government Authorised Exchange route is not a route to settlement.

Validity requirements for the Government Authorised Exchange route

GAE 1.1. A person applying for entry clearance or permission to stay on the Government Authorised Exchange route must apply online on gov.uk on the specified form as follows:

Applicant	Specified form
EEA national with a chipped passport	Either: • Temporary Worker using the UK Immigration: ID Check app; or • the forms listed below for applicants outside or inside the UK (as relevant)
Applicant outside the UK	Temporary Worker visa
Applicant inside the UK	Temporary Worker

GAE 1.2. An application for entry clearance or permission to stay on the Government Authorised Exchange route must meet all the following requirements:

(a) any fee and Immigration Health Charge must have been paid; and

(b) the applicant must have provided any required biometrics; and

(c) the applicant must have provided a passport or other travel document which satisfactorily establishes their identity and nationality; and

(d) the applicant must have a Certificate of Sponsorship that was issued to them no more than 3 months before the date of application.

GAE 1.3. If the applicant has in the last 12 months before the date of application received an award from a Government or international scholarship agency covering both fees and maintenance, they must provide written consent to the application from that Government or agency.

GAE 1.4. An application which does not meet all the validity requirements for the Government Authorised Exchange route is invalid and may be rejected and not considered.

Suitability requirements for the Government Authorised Exchange route

GAE 2.1. The applicant must not fall for refusal under Part 9: grounds for refusal.

GAE 2.2. If applying for permission to stay the applicant must not be:

(a) in breach of immigration laws, except that where paragraph 39E applies, that period of overstaying will be disregarded; or

(b) on immigration bail.

Eligibility requirements for the Government Authorised Exchange route

Entry requirements for the Government Authorised Exchange route

GAE 3.1. A person seeking to come to the UK on the Government Authorised Exchange route must have applied for and obtained entry clearance on the Government Authorised Exchange route before they arrive in the UK.

GAE 3.2. A person applying for entry clearance on the Government Authorised Exchange route must, if paragraph A39 and Appendix T of these rules apply, provide a valid medical certificate confirming that they have undergone screening for active pulmonary tuberculosis and that this tuberculosis is not present in them.

Previous permission requirement for the Government Authorised Exchange route

GAE 4.1. An applicant who is applying for permission to stay must be in the UK on the date of application and must have, or have last been granted:

(a) permission on the Government Authorised Exchange route; or

(b) permission as a Student, who meets the requirements in GAE 4.2. and who is or was last sponsored by either:

(i) a higher education provider with a track record of compliance; or

(ii) an overseas higher education institution, to do a short-term study abroad programme in the UK.

GAE 4.2. Where the applicant has, or last had, permission as a Student:

(a) the applicant must have completed a UK recognised bachelor's or postgraduate degree during that last period of permission; and

(b) the applicant must currently be sponsored for either:

(i) a period of postgraduate professional training or work experience which is required to gain a professional qualification or registration in the same field as their degree; or

(ii) an internship for up to 12 months which is directly related to their degree; and

(c) the applicant must not be filling a permanent vacancy; and

(d) the sponsor must not intend to employ the applicant in the UK once the training or work experience is completed.

Sponsorship requirement for the Government Authorised Exchange route

GAE 5.1. The applicant must have a valid Certificate of Sponsorship for the job they are planning to do; which to be valid must:

(a) confirm the applicant's name, that they are being sponsored on the Government Authorised Exchange route, details of the job and salary the sponsor is offering them, and that these arrangements comply with the National Minimum Wage; and

(b) include a start date, stated by the sponsor, which is no more than three months after the date of application; and

(c) not have been used in a previous application which was either granted or refused (but can have been used in a previous application which was rejected as invalid, made void or withdrawn); and

(d) not have been withdrawn by the sponsor or cancelled by the Home Office; and

(e) confirm that the role meets the requirements of the individual exchange scheme as set out in Appendix GAE schemes; and

(f) confirm that the role does not fill a vacancy in the workforce; and

(g) confirm that the role appears in Table 1 or Table 2 of Appendix Skilled Occupations; and

(h) confirm whether the Academic Technology Approval Scheme (ATAS) requirement in Appendix ATAS applies.

GAE 5.2. The sponsor must be authorised by the Home Office to sponsor the job in question under the Government Authorised Exchange route.

GAE 5.3. The sponsor must be listed as A-rated on the Home Office's register of licensed sponsors, unless the applicant was last granted permission on the Government Authorised Exchange route and is applying to continue working for the same sponsor as in their last permission.

Genuineness requirement for the Government Authorised Exchange route

GAE 6.1. The applicant must:

(a) genuinely intend, and be able, to undertake the role for which they are being sponsored; and

(b) not intend to undertake employment other than in the role for which they are being sponsored, or as otherwise permitted by paragraph GAE 10.3.

ATAS requirement for the Government Authorised Exchange route

GAE 7.1. If the ATAS requirement in Appendix ATAS applies, the applicant must provide a valid ATAS certificate.

Financial Requirement for the Government Authorised Exchange route

GAE 8.1. If the applicant is applying for permission to stay and has been in the UK with permission for 12 months or longer on the date of application, they will meet the financial requirement and do not need to show funds.

GAE 8.2. If the applicant is applying for entry clearance, or is applying for permission to stay and has been in the UK for less than 12 months on the date of application, either:

(a) the applicant must have funds of at least £1,270; or

(b) the applicant's A rated sponsor must confirm on the Certificate of Sponsorship that they will, if it is necessary, maintain and accommodate the applicant up to the end of the first month of their employment for an amount of at least £1,270.

GAE 8.3. If GAE 8.2. applies the applicant must show that they have held the required level of funds for a 28-day period and as specified in Appendix Finance.

Parental consent requirement for the Government Authorised Exchange route

GAE 9.1. If the applicant is aged under 18 on the date of application, they must have written consent from:

(a) both parents; or

(b) one parent, if that parent has sole legal responsibility for the applicant; or

(c) the applicant's legal guardian.

GAE 9.2. The written consent must confirm support for all of the following:

(a) the application; and

(b) the applicant's living and care arrangements in the UK; and

(c) if the application is for entry clearance, the applicant's travel to, and reception arrangements in, the UK.

Decision on an application for the Government Authorised Exchange route

GAE 10.1. If the decision maker is satisfied that all the suitability and eligibility requirements for the Government Authorised Exchange route are met, the application will be granted, otherwise the application will be refused.

GAE 10.2. If the application is refused, the person can apply for an Administrative Review under Appendix AR: Administrative Review.

Period and conditions of grant for the Government Authorised Exchange route

GAE 11.1. If the application is for entry clearance, the applicant will be granted whichever is the shorter of:

(a) the period of the job on the Certificate of Sponsorship plus 14 days before and after; or

(b) the maximum period of time that a person on the Government Authorised Exchange route is permitted to spend in the UK under the terms of the specific approved scheme on which the applicant had applied to participate in (as set out in Appendix GAE schemes).

GAE 11.2. If the application is for permission to stay, the applicant will be granted whichever is the shorter of:

(a) the period of the job on the Certificate of Sponsorship plus 14 days; or

(b) the difference between the period the applicant has already spent in the UK since their last grant of permission on the Government Authorised Exchange route and the maximum period of time that a person on the Government Authorised Exchange route is permitted to spend in the UK under the terms of the specific approved scheme on which the applicant had applied to participate in (as set out in Appendix GAE schemes).

GAE 11.3. The grant will be subject to all the following conditions:

(a) no access to public funds; and

(b) work is permitted only in the job the applicant is being sponsored for, including volunteering and job shadowing if recorded on the Certificate of Sponsorship; and

(c) supplementary employment is permitted; and

(d) study is permitted, subject to the ATAS condition in Appendix ATAS; and (e) if Part 10 applies, the applicant will be required to register with the police.

Dependants on the Government Authorised Exchange route

Validity requirements for a dependent partner or dependent child on the Government Authorised Exchange route

GAE 12.1. A person applying for entry clearance or permission to stay as a dependent partner or dependent child on the Government Authorised Exchange route must apply online on the gov.uk website on the specified form as follows:

Applicant	Specified form
EEA national with a chipped passport	Either (as applicable): • Dependant partner or dependant child using the UK Immigration: ID Check app; or • he forms listed below for dependant applicants outside or inside the UK as relevant.

Applicant	Specified form
Applicants outside the UK	Dependant partner visa Dependant child visa
Applicants inside the UK	If the dependant is applying at the same time as the person on the Government Authorised Exchange route, they can be included in the form Temporary Worker where the form allows dependants to be added. Otherwise: – Dependant partner – Dependant child

[GAE 12.2. An application for settlement as a partner or child of a Private Servant in a diplomatic household must meet all the following requirements:

(a) any fee must have been paid; and

(b) the applicant must have provided any required biometrics; and

(c) the applicant must have provided either a passport or other travel document which satisfactorily establishes their identity and nationality; and

(d) the applicant must be in the UK on the date of application; and

(e) the applicant must be applying as a partner or child of a person (P) who:

(i) has made a valid application for settlement in the UK on the International Agreement route and that application has not been decided; or

(ii) is settled or has become a British citizen, provided that P had permission on the International Agreement route when they settled and the applicant either had permission as their partner or child at that time, or the applicant is applying as a child of P and the applicant was born in the UK before P settled.]

Note: Paragraph substituted from 6 April 2022 (HC 1118).

GAE 12.3. An applicant applying as a dependent partner must be aged 18 or over on the date of application.

GAE 12.4. An applicant who is applying for permission to stay as a dependent partner or dependent child on the Government Authorised Exchange route must be in the UK on the date of application and must not have, or have last been granted, permission:

(a) as a Visitor; or

(b) as a Short-term student; or

(c) as a Parent of a Child Student; or

(d) as a Seasonal Worker; or

(e) as a Domestic Worker in a Private Household; or

(f) outside the Immigration Rules.

GAE 12.5. An application which does not meet all the validity requirements for a dependent partner or dependent child on the Government Authorised Exchange route is invalid and may be rejected and not considered.

Suitability requirements for a dependent partner or dependent child on the Government Authorised Exchange route

GAE 13.1. The applicant must not fall for refusal under Part 9: grounds for refusal.

GAE 13.2. If applying for permission to stay the applicant must not be:

(a) in breach of immigration laws, except that where paragraph 39E applies, that period of overstaying will be disregarded; or

(b) on immigration bail.

Eligibility requirements for a dependent partner or dependent child on the Government Authorised Exchange route

Entry requirement for a dependent partner or dependent child on the Government Authorised Exchange route

GAE 14.1. A person seeking to come to the UK as a dependent partner or dependent child on the Government Authorised Exchange route must apply for and obtain entry clearance as a dependent partner or dependent child on the Government Authorised Exchange route before they arrive in the UK.

GAE 14.2. A person applying for entry clearance as a dependent partner or dependent child on the Government Authorised Exchange route must, if paragraph A39 and Appendix T of these rules apply, provide a valid medical certificate confirming that they have undergone screening for active pulmonary tuberculosis and that this tuberculosis is not present in them.

Relationship requirement for a dependent partner on the Government Authorised Exchange route

GAE 15.1. The applicant must be the partner of a person (P) where one of the following applies:

(a) P has permission on the Government Authorised Exchange route; or

(b) P is, at the same time, applying for (and is granted) entry clearance or permission on the Government Authorised Exchange route.

GAE 15.2. If the applicant and their partner on the Government Authorised Exchange route are not married or in a civil partnership, all of the following requirements must be met:

(a) they must have been living together in a relationship similar to marriage or civil partnership for at least two years before the date of application; and

(b) any previous relationship of the applicant or their partner on the Government Authorised Exchange route with another person must have permanently broken down; and

(c) the applicant and their partner on the Government Authorised Exchange route must not be so closely related that they would not be allowed to marry or form a civil partnership in the UK.

GAE 15.3. The relationship between the applicant and their partner on the Government Authorised Exchange route must be genuine and subsisting.

GAE 15.4. The applicant and their partner on the Government Authorised Exchange route must intend to live together throughout the applicant's stay in the UK.

Relationship requirement for a dependent child on the Government Authorised Exchange route

GAE 16.1. The applicant must be the child of a parent (P) where one of the following applies:

(a) P has permission on the Government Authorised Exchange route; or

(b) P is, at the same time, applying for (and is granted) entry clearance or permission on the Government Authorised Exchange route.

GAE 16.2. The applicant's parents must each be either applying at the same time as the applicant or have permission to be in the UK (other than as a Visitor) unless:

(a) the parent applying for or with entry clearance or permission to stay on the Government Authorised Exchange route is the sole surviving parent; or

(b) the parent applying for or with entry clearance or permission to stay on the Government Authorised Exchange route has sole responsibility for the child's upbringing; or

(c) the parent who does not have permission on the Government Authorised Exchange route–

(i) is a British citizen or a person who has a right to enter or stay in the UK without restriction; and

(ii) is or will be ordinarily resident in the UK; or

(d) the decision maker is satisfied that there are serious and compelling reasons to grant the child entry clearance or permission to stay with the parent who is applying for or has entry clearance or permission to stay on the Government Authorised Exchange route.

GAE 16.3. If the applicant is a child born in the UK to a person on the Government Authorised Exchange route or their partner, the applicant must provide a full UK birth certificate showing the names of both parents.

Care requirement for a dependent child on the Government Authorised Exchange route

GAE 17.1. If the applicant is aged under 18 on the date of application, there must be suitable arrangements for the child's care and accommodation in the UK, which must comply with relevant UK legislation and regulations.

Age requirement for a dependent child on the Government Authorised Exchange route

GAE 18.1. The applicant must be under the age of 18 on the date of application, unless they were last granted permission as the dependent child of their parent or parents.

GAE 18.2. If the applicant is aged 16 or over on the date of application, they must not be leading an independent life.

Financial requirement for a dependent partner or dependent child on the Government Authorised Exchange route

GAE 19.1. If the applicant is applying for permission to stay and has been living in the UK with permission for 12 months or longer on the date of application, they will meet the financial requirement and do not need to show funds.

GAE 19.2. If the applicant is applying for entry clearance, or has been in the UK for less than 12 months on the date of application, either:

(a) funds of at least the amount required in GAE 19.3. must be held collectively by one or more of the following:

(i) the applicant; and

(ii) the person on the Government Authorised Exchange route (P); and

(iii) if the applicant is applying as a dependent child, their parent who is lawfully present in the UK or being granted entry clearance, or permission to stay, at the same time; or

(b) the A-rated sponsor of the person on the Government Authorised Exchange route must certify that they will, if necessary, maintain and accommodate the dependent partner and/or any dependent child as well as the person on the Government Authorised Exchange route, up to the end of the first month of each of their grants of permission, to at least the amounts required in GAE 19.3.

GAE 19.3. The funds required are:

(a) £285 for a dependent partner in the UK, or applying for entry clearance; and

(b) £315 for the first dependent child in the UK, or applying for entry clearance; and

(c) £200 for any other dependent child in the UK, or applying for entry clearance.

GAE 19.4. If GAE 19.2.(a) applies, the funds held for the applicant must be held in addition to any funds required for the person on the Government Authorised Exchange route to meet the financial requirement and any other dependants in the UK or applying at the same time.

GAE 19.5. If GAE 19.2.(a) applies, the funds must have been held for a 28-day period and as specified in Appendix Finance.

Decision on an application for a dependent partner or dependent child on the Government Authorised Exchange route

GAE 20.1. If the decision maker is satisfied that all the suitability and eligibility requirements for a dependent partner or dependent child on the Government Authorised Exchange route are met, the application will be granted, otherwise the application will be refused.

GAE 20.2. If the application is refused, the person can apply for an Administrative Review under Appendix AR: Administrative Review.

Period and conditions of grant for a dependent partner or dependent child on the Government Authorised Exchange route

GAE 21.1. A partner will be granted permission which ends on the same date as their partner's permission on the Government Authorised Exchange route.

GAE 21.2. A child will be granted permission which ends on the same date as whichever of their parents' permission ends first.

GAE 21.3. The grant will be subject to all the following conditions:

(a) no access to public funds; and

(b) work (including self-employment and voluntary work) is permitted, except as a professional sportsperson (including as a sports coach); and

(c) study is permitted, subject to the ATAS condition in Appendix ATAS if the applicant is over the age of 18; and

(d) if Part 10 applies, the applicant will be required to register with the police.]

[Appendix Government Authorised Exchange Schemes

The Temporary Worker – Government Authorised Exchange route is for a person who wishes to come to the UK on one of the approved schemes listed below.

The Immigration Rules governing Temporary Worker – Government Authorised Exchange applications can be found at Appendix Temporary Work – Government Authorised Exchange.]

The table contained in this Appendix is not reproduced as it is subject to regular review and amendment. It can be viewed online at: https://www.gov.uk/guidance/immigration-rules/immigration-rules-appendix-government-authorised-exchange-schemes

Note: Appendix inserted from 09:00 on 11 October 2021 subject to savings for applications made before that time (HC 617). Amendments from 6 April 2022 (HC 1118).

[Appendix Creative Worker codes of practice]

Note: Heading substituted from 09:00 on 11 October 2021 subject to savings for applications made before that time (HC 617).

[Where a person is applying under Appendix Temporary Work – Creative Worker, as a creative worker, operating in dance, theatre, film and television, or as a model in the fashion industry, their sponsor must follow the relevant code of practice specified below and comply with the other requirements.]

Note: Introduction substituted from 09:00 on 11 October 2021 subject to savings for applications made before that time (HC 617).

Ballet	
Appropriate salary rate	Payment must be commensurate with industry standards set out at: www.equity.org.uk.
Exemptions from advertising for those deemed to be making an additional contribution to the UK labour market	1. The dancer is required for continuity The applicant has worked for a period of one month or more during the past year on the same production outside the UK prior to coming to the UK. The 'same production' means one which is largely the same in terms of direction and design as the production outside the UK. The sponsor must be able to supply proof that the requirement is met, e.g. contract of employment, press cuttings, cast list. 2. The dancer has international status The applicant is internationally famous in their field. (This is different to being well-known only in one country). The sponsor must be able to supply proof that this requirement is met, e.g. press cuttings, awards, publicity material, television/radio interviews, programmes. 3. The dancer is engaged by a unit company A unit company is a ballet company which exists in a country outside the UK and has put on at least one production in that country. The sponsor must be able to supply proof that this requirement is met, e.g. press cuttings, awards, publicity material, television/radio interviews, programmes; and proof that the applicant is engaged by the unit company for the production in the UK, e.g. contract of employment.

	4. The dancer is recruited from a specified school for a specified company The applicant is recruited from: (a) the English National Ballet School for English National Ballet; (b) the Royal Ballet School for the Royal Ballet; or (c) the Royal Ballet School or Elmhurst School for Dance for Birmingham Royal Ballet. The Sponsor must be able to supply proof that, at the time of recruitment, the applicant was or recently had been a student at the school concerned, e.g. a letter of confirmation from the school, and proof that the applicant has been engaged by the company concerned, e.g. contract of employment, letter of confirmation from the company.
Required advertising media for other posts	At least one of: • The Stage • Dance Europe • The Spotlight Link

Dancers (in dance forms other than ballet)

Appropriate salary rate	Payment must be commensurate with industry standards set out at: www.equity.org.uk.
Exemptions from advertising for those deemed to be making an additional contribution to the UK labour market	1. The dancer is required for continuity The applicant has worked for a period of one month or more during the past year on the same production outside the UK prior to it coming to the UK. The 'same production' means one which is largely the same in terms of direction and design as the production outside the UK. The sponsor must be able to supply proof that the requirement is met, e.g. contract of employment, press cuttings, cast list. 2. The dancer has international status The applicant is internationally famous in their field. (This is different to being well-known only in one country.) The sponsor must be able to supply proof that the requirement is met, e.g. press cuttings, awards, publicity material, television/radio interviews, programmes. 3. The dancer is engaged by a unit company A unit company is a dance company which exists in a country outside the UK and has put on at least one production in that country. The sponsor must be able to supply proof that the requirement is met, e.g. contract of employment. 4. The dancer performs in a certain style unlikely to be available in the UK It would not be reasonable to expect the sponsor to recruit in the UK because a style is required which would be unlikely to be available in the UK labour force. The sponsor must be able to supply proof that: (a) a certain style is required; and (b) the individual performs in that style, e.g. press cuttings, awards, publicity material, proof of training.

Required advertising media for other posts At least one of:	Dance agencies The Stage Dance Europe Juice The Spotlight
Performers in film and television	
Appropriate salary rate	Payment must be at least at the level of the appropriate UK market rates, which can be obtained from Equity at www.equity.org.uk.
Exemptions from advertising for those deemed to be making an additional contribution to the UK labour market	1. The work is for continuity The sponsor must be able to supply proof that the overseas national has worked on, or will be working on the same production overseas for at least one month. Where a sponsor wishes to issue a Certificate of Sponsorship for reasons of continuity involving a performer that has worked on the same piece of work overseas for less than one month, the Sponsor must notify Equity at least 5 working days prior to the issuing of the certificate with details of the filming schedules. This is in order to verify that the applicant is being genuinely engaged for reasons of continuity. Sponsors may issue Certificates of Sponsorship for performers to enter the UK to undertake post-production work only and provided that such post-production work solely relates to their own role in the film or TV production. For such Certificate of Sponsorship, neither the one month requirement nor prior notice to Equity procedure applies. The Sponsor must be able to supply documentary proof that the performer has worked on, or will be working on, the same production outside the UK for at least a month e.g. contracts, press cuttings, cast lists, etc. 2. The performer has international status The sponsor must be able to provide proof the applicant is known internationally, or they have demonstrable international box-office appeal e.g. press cuttings, awards, accolades, publicity material, television/radio interviews, film and TV credits; or documentary proof that the performer has demonstrable international box-office appeal through international box office figures for films they have starred in or led as a principal performer. 3. Highly specialist or unusual roles For certain highly specialist or unusual roles, it may not be possible or reasonable to recruit from the UK because the role requires specific or specialist attributes, including but not limited to: physical appearance; physical talent and linguistic or vocal skills. In such circumstances, where appropriate, Sponsors should first attempt to conduct searches in the UK as set out in category 3 to a reasonable degree.

However, it is recognised that the extent of such searches within the UK shall be proportionate to the rarity and specialty of the attributes of the role. The Sponsor must be able to provide proof:

- that the role requires certain highly specialist attributes; and
- that the performer possesses those attributes; and
- of the casting process and casting considerations; and
- of reasonable and appropriate searches in the UK (if applicable); and
- a list of any UK candidates who were unavailable at the required time.

4. Featured guest in an entertainment programme, or subject of a factual programme The applicant must be a featured guest on an entertainment programme or subject of a factual programme. For example, actors, comedians or other performers booked to appear on a chat show or a professional variety show, or scheduled to be subject of an arts programme or documentary. The sponsor must be able to provide:

- A formal letter from the broadcaster or producer or copy of the relevant section of the commissioning agreement confirming the reason the migrant is required (e.g. to feature in an entertainment programme); and
- The name of the programme concerned; and
- Details of any recording or filming schedules.

5. Performers who are tied to the finance of the production The applicant must be necessary to a production because the finance is contingent on the particular performer being cast in the film or TV production. The sponsor must be able to provide a formal letter of confirmation from the production's principal financier.

6. Performers who do not meet the key criteria but who are commercially important The applicant must be commercially important to the production. This may be demonstrated by a formal letter in support from a principal financier, or distributor. The sponsor must give prior notice to Equity providing supporting evidence detailing: description of the role and film, and the reasons why advertising was not appropriate and a letter in support. The sponsor must provide Equity with:

- the details of the performer(s) required, role, description of the production; and
- the reasons why the role has not been advertised; and,
- a formal letter in support of the applicant from a financier or distributor; and

	• if the performer is an up-and-coming performer, or cast to appeal to a particular overseas audience, then evidence of their CV, reviews, previous work, awards/accolades, and/or evidence of audience appeal would be required. 7. International Co-productions Sponsors issuing CoSs to performers taking part in international co-productions structured under one of the UK's bilateral co-production treaties, or under the European Convention on Cinematographic Co-Production, need to provide the following evidence: • Provisional approval from the UK Film Council certification department that the film is being structured as an official co-production; or • Interim certification from the UK Film Council Certification Department.
Required advertising media for other posts	Aresident labour search in accordance with standard industry practice, which will normally involve engagement of casting agents within the EEA and contacting performers' agents, and may include advertising on Equity's job information service
Additional evidence required for stunt performers	The sponsor must also demonstrate that the applicant possesses the equivalent qualifications, skills and competence to UK industry standards. This may be demonstrated by either 1) a reference in support from a UK-based expert with demonstrable knowledge of the UK stunt industry; or 2) evidence of competence at a level equivalent to UK industry

Performers in theatre or opera	
Appropriate salary rate	Payment should be commensurate with industry standards set out at: www.equity.org.uk.
Exemptions from advertising for those deemed to be making an additional contribution to the UK labour market	1. The performer is required for continuity The applicant has worked for a period of one month or more during the past year, on the same production outside the UK prior to it coming to the UK. The 'same production' means one which is largely the same in terms of direction and design as the production outside the UK. The sponsor must be able to provide proof that the performer is currently working, or has worked, on the same production outside the UK and has done so, or did so, for at least one month during the past year, e.g. contract of employment, press cuttings, cast list. 2. The performer has international status The applicant is internationally famous in his field. (This is different to being well-known only in one country.) The sponsor must be able to provide proof that the performer has international status, e.g. press cuttings, awards, publicity material, television/radio interviews, programmes.

	3. The performer is engaged by a unit company A unit company is a theatre or opera company which exists in a country outside the UK and has put on at least one production in that country. The sponsor must be able to provide proof that the company has put on at least one production in its home country, e.g. press cuttings, awards, publicity material, television/radio interviews, programmes; and proof that the individual is engaged by the unit company for the production in the UK, e.g. contract of employment.
	4. The performer has a certain attribute unlikely to be available in the UK The role requires an attribute which would be unlikely to be available in the UK labour force, e.g. a certain physical appearance, physical talent, or linguistic or vocal skill. The sponsor must be able to provide proof that (a) the role requires a certain attribute; and (b) the individual has that attribute.
	5. The performer is the subject of an exchange under one of the UK theatre industry's exchange programmes The applicant satisfies the requirements of either of the exchange programmes with the United States and Australia operated by the theatre industry. Sponsors wishing to use this category must contact Equity in the first instance.
Required advertising media for other posts	At least one of: • The Stage • PCR
Workers in film and television	
Appropriate salary rate	Payment of migrant workers in all cases must not be below the UK market rates found on the PACT and BECTU websites at www.pact.co.uk and www.bectu.org.uk.
Exemptions from advertising for those deemed to be making an additional contribution to the UK labour market	1. The worker is a Senior Creative Grade The applicant must possess the skills and experience of a Senior Creative Grade for the following roles: • Producer • Director • Director of Photography (Cinematographer) • Production Designer • Costumer Designer • Hair/Make Up Supervisor • Editor • Composer • Visual Effects Supervisor • Sound Designer • Script Writer

The sponsor must be able to provide documentary proof that the worker has the skills and experience in that role e.g. film and TV credits, qualifications, CV, press cuttings, awards, accolades, publicity material, television/radio interviews.

2. The worker is required for production continuity The applicant must be providing significant creative input and have worked on or will be working in a post involving creative input on the same piece of work overseas for at least one month. The sponsor must demonstrate that the applicant has a direct working relationship with a Senior Creative Grade as listed in Category 1. For example, a first assistant editor might work directly with an Editor on the same piece of work overseas. No more than one additional worker may be sponsored in addition to a Senior Creative Grade, other than in exceptional circumstances, where there is a case based on production continuity. Sponsors must be able to provide:

- Evidence that the role involves creative input and the worker possesses the skills and qualifications for the role, e.g. copies of qualifications, CV, credits, press cuttings, awards, accolades; and
- Evidence that the worker is currently, or has worked on, or will be working on the same production outside the UK for at least a month and evidence of current working relationship with a key Creative grade in Category 1 i.e. contracts, letters of engagement, casting lists, CV, references in support, credits, press cuttings; and
- In the circumstances where more than one additional worker is sponsored, the case must be set out in supporting documentation from the Sponsor.

3. Other key creative workers The applicant must be providing key creative input and have a significant previous working relationship with a Senior Creative Grade as listed in Category 1. A 'significant' previous working relationship entails an established pattern of joint working on a number of previous productions rather than isolated or random examples. No more than one additional worker may be sponsored in addition to a Senior Creative Grade, other than in exceptional circumstances, where there is a creative case.

The Home Office will notify BECTU promptly of the issuing of certificates of sponsorship for camera, editing and grip grades, and 1st Assistant Directors and BECTU may request sight of the evidence in support for such grades.

The Home Office will notify the Production Guild promptly of the issuing of certificates of sponsorship for the following grades: Executive Producer (when providing the functions of a Line Producer or Financial Controller/Production Accountant), Line Producer, Co-Producer, 1st Assistant Director, Unit Production Manager, Production Supervisor, Financial Controller, Production Accountant and the Production Guild may request sight of the evidence in support for such roles.

Sponsors must be able to provide:

- Evidence that the applicant is in a creative or technical role and possesses the skills and qualifications for the role, e.g. copies of qualifications, CV, credits, press cuttings, awards, accolades etc; and
- Evidence of the applicant's previous working relationship with a key Creative Grade in category 1.e.g. CV, references in support, credits, press cuttings; and
- In the circumstances where more than one additional worker is sponsored per Department head, the case must be set out in a supporting documentation from the Sponsor.

4. The role is highly specialist, where advertising is demonstrably not appropriate For certain highly specialist roles, it would not be reasonable to expect an employer to undertake a resident labour market search. One example would be a role which requires particular attributes considered unlikely to be available from the resident labour force, for example where the role involves the application of highly specialist skills or new technology or proprietary technology or special effect, or unique knowledge. The Sponsor must be able to provide documentary proof that it would not be reasonable to expect the sponsor to undertake a resident labour market search e.g. in relation to the above example, proof that the role requires certain highly specialised skills e.g. job description; and that the applicant possesses those skills e.g. qualifications, CV, credits. For all roles under this category, [the Home Office] will notify BECTU promptly of the issuing of certificates of sponsorship and BECTU may request sight of the evidence in support for such grades.

5. International Co-productions Sponsors issuing certificates of sponsorship to workers taking part in international co-productions structured under one of the UK's bilateral co-production treaties, or under the European Convention on Cinematographic Co-Production, need to provide the following evidence:

	• Provisional approval from the UK Film Council certification department that the film is being structured as an official co-production; or • Interim certification from the UK Film Council Certification Department.
Required advertising media for other posts	• For roles where formal advertising is not the usual industry practice for recruiting for a particular role: For these roles, the sponsor must carry out suitable and reasonable searches of the resident labour market, such as contacting agents, organisations, diary services or semi-formal worker networks. Where such informal recruitment methods are used, the sponsor must demonstrate a reasonable period within which it has searched the resident labour market, this should be for a least a period of two weeks. • Where formal advertising is usual for a role: For these roles, the sponsor must advertise the role to suitably qualified resident workers in an appropriate journal, newspaper, website or online directory. The choice of advertising medium should be appropriate for the particular role. The following advertising media may be appropriate: searching relevant online directories such as the Knowledge Online, Production Base, or through industry organisations such as the Production Guild. Other forms of advertising may be appropriate depending on the type of role. For longer terms contracts, advertisements in Guardian Media, Broadcast, Screen International, Marketing Week would be appropriate. Under this category, in the case of camera, editing and grip grades, and 1st Assistant Directors, the Home Office shall promptly notify BECTU of the issuing of certificates of sponsorship and BECTU may request sight of the evidence of the steps to search for resident labour for these roles. Under this category, in the case of Executive Producer (when providing the functions of a Line Producer or Financial Controller/Production Accountant) Line Producer, Co-Producer, 1st Assistant Director, Unit Production Manager, Production Supervisor, Financial Controller, Production Accountant grades, the Home Office will promptly notify the Production Guild of the issuing of a certificate of sponsorship and the Production Guild may request sight of the [[evidence in support for such roles.]]

Additional evidence required for Personal Assistants to Directors and Producers of international status	Sponsors may issue a Certificate of Sponsorship to a single, non-technical, non-creative personal assistant who supports a Director or Producer under category 1, who has demonstrable international status i.e. are known worldwide for international box office success. The Sponsor must notify BECTU promptly of the issuing of a certificate under this category for a PA to a Director and must notify the Production Guild promptly of the issuing of a certificate for a PA to a Producer. They may request sight of the evidence in support for such roles. Sponsors issuing certificates to applicants under this category must be able to supply proof that: • the applicant has a significant previous working relationship with the Director or Producer (a 'significant' previous working relationship entails an established pattern of joint working on a number of previous productions rather than isolated or random examples); and • the migrant works only as a personal assistant to the Director/Producer and does not undertake creative or technical duties; and • the Director or Producer is of international status i.e. known worldwide, or they have demonstrable box-office appeal worldwide. • the worker has the skills and experience in that role e.g. a reference in support from the Director or Producer, film and TV credits, qualifications, and CV • the Director or Producer has international status e.g. press cuttings, awards, accolades, publicity material, television/radio interviews, film and TV credits; or, documentary proof that they have demonstrable worldwide box-office appeal through box [[office figures for films they have led.]]

Models in the fashion industry

Appropriate salary rate	Payments should be commensurate with industry standards and comply with the National Minimum Wage rate to which they are entitled by the law in force at the relevant time.
Exemptions from advertising for those deemed to be making an additional contribution to the UK labour market	1. Top models These are people who are recognised not just as models but may, also, be personalities in their own right. They are high earners and, for the most part, will come to the UK with pre-booked work. A sponsor must be able to supply evidence that the model has international status, e.g. publications, publicity materials, press engagements, relevant social media presence.

	2. Commercial models These are those models who have sufficient a level of experience that they are already established, if not in the UK, certainly in their own or other markets. They may already be known to UK clients or will certainly have been pre-marketed, however, photographs alone are not sufficient, except for models flying in for a particular job. Sponsors issuing a CoS must be able provide the following evidence: i. Evidence of previous engagements or of commercial status in the UK, and/or ii. Evidence of working in markets other than the UK 3 The model is required for continuity The model has worked for the same client, within the past two years, prior to coming to the UK. The sponsor must be able to provide evidence, e.g. confirmation of past and intended bookings. 4 New faces Will have experience but may be entirely new to the UK market, or on a second or third visit. The New Face Model will have shown considerable promise and, being the 'latest' face, are likely be much sought after, particularly by photographers and print or digital media alike. Models must meet 65% of the eligibility criteria for the Modelling Industry, as endorsed by the British Fashion Council. Sponsors must be able to provide evidence of which criteria are met.
Required endorsement for those falling outside the above criteria	A British Fashion Council approved panel will be put in place to endorse specific models with real potential that are unable to fulfil the required four criteria, which is most likely to occur within the New Faces category. Applications will still be required to be scored against the criteria and the supporting documents submitted to the Panel to enable them to make a decision. Sponsors must be able to demonstrate panel approval when issuing a CoS.]

Note: Appendix inserted from 09:00 on 1 December 2020 subject to savings for applications made before that time (HC813). Words in point 4 of 'Workers in film and television' substituted, words in double square brackets inserted from 6 April 2022 (HC 1118).

[APPENDIX SERVICE PROVIDERS FROM SWITZERLAND

The Service Providers from Switzerland route allows eligible employers, companies or self-employed individuals to execute contracts with a party based in the UK for a period not exceeding 90 days per calendar year. The contract must have been signed and commenced on or before the specified date.

It is the responsibility of the employer or company or self-employed individual, to ensure that the total number of days worked by its employees, or the self- employed individual, does not exceed 90 in each calendar year. The 90-day limitation applies irrespective of the number of eligible contracts that are held.

This route does not allow for dependants to accompany or join the Service Provider from Switzerland in the UK.

Validity requirements for Service Providers from Switzerland

SPS 1.1. A person applying for entry clearance as a Service Provider from Switzerland must apply online on gov.uk on the specified form 'Other work visas for the UK (non points-based working visas)' on the 'Find and apply for other visas from outside the UK' form.

SPS 1.2. The applicant must meet all the following requirements:

(a) any fee must have been paid; and

(b) the applicant must have provided any required biometrics; and

(c) the applicant must have provided either:

(i) if they are a Swiss national, a valid national identity card or passport; or

(ii) if they are not a Swiss national, a passport or other travel document that satisfactorily establishes their identity and nationality.

SPS 1.3. The applicant must be aged 18 or over on the date of application.

SPS 1.4. An application which does not meet all the validity requirements for a Service Provider from Switzerland is invalid and may be rejected and not considered.

Suitability requirements for Service Providers from Switzerland

SPS 2.1. Subject to SPS 2.2. an application must be refused on grounds of suitability where either of the following apply at the date of the decision:

(a) the applicant is subject to a deportation order or a decision to make a deportation order; or

(b) the applicant is subject to an exclusion order or exclusion decision.

SPS 2.2. Where a decision under SPS 2.1 relates to conduct before 11pm on 31 December 2020, the decision maker must be satisfied that the order or decision is justified on the grounds of public policy, public security or public health in accordance with regulation 27 of the EEA Regulations, irrespective of whether the EEA Regulations apply to that person (except that in applying this provision for 'an EEA decision' read 'a decision under SPS 2.1').

SPS 2.3. An application may be refused on grounds of suitability if, at the date of decision, the decision maker is satisfied that it is proportionate to refuse the application because:

(a) in relation to the application and whether or not to the applicant's knowledge, false or misleading information, representations or documents have been submitted (including false or misleading information submitted to any person to obtain a document used in support of the application); and the information, representation or documentation is material to the decision whether or not to grant the application; or

(b) in respect of conduct committed on or before 11pm on 31 December 2020, on grounds of public policy, public security or public health in accordance with regulation 27 of the EEA Regulations, irrespective of whether the EEA Regulations apply to that person (except that for these purposes for 'an EEA decision' read 'a decision under paragraph SPS 2.3'); or

(c) in respect of conduct committed after 11pm on 31 December 2020, on the grounds that the presence of the applicant in the UK is not conducive to the public good; or

(d) subject to SPS 2.4, the applicant is the subject of an Islands deportation order as defined by paragraph 3(6) of Schedule 4 to the Immigration Act 1971; or

(e) subject to SPS 2.4, the applicant is the subject of an Islands exclusion decision which is a direction given by the relevant Minister or other authority in the Islands concerned that the applicant must be refused entry to the Island concerned on the grounds that their presence there would not be conducive to the public good.

SPS 2.4. Where a decision under SPS 2.3 (d) or (e) relates to conduct on or before 11pm on 31 December 2020, the decision maker must be satisfied that the order or decision is justified on the grounds of public policy, public security or public health in accordance with regulation 27 of the EEA Regulations, irrespective of whether the EEA Regulations apply to that person (except that in applying this provision for 'an EEA decision' read 'a decision under SPS 2.3').

Eligibility requirements for Service Providers from Switzerland

Entry requirement for Service Providers from Switzerland

SPS 3.1. A person seeking to come to the UK as a Service Provider from Switzerland must have applied for and obtained entry clearance as a Service Provider from Switzerland before they arrive in the UK.

Services requirement for Service Providers from Switzerland

SPS 4.1. An applicant who is a Swiss national must be either established in self-employment in the territory of Switzerland, or habitually employed in the territory of Switzerland by an eligible employer or company.

SPS 4.2. A Swiss national seeking entry as self-employed must be registered as self-employed with the appropriate tax authority in the territory of Switzerland.

SPS 4.3. An applicant who is not a Swiss national must be legally integrated into the regular labour market of Switzerland, be habitually employed in the territory of Switzerland by an eligible employer or company and, if required, they must provide a copy of their Swiss residence or work permit.

SPS 4.4. An applicant will be considered to be legally integrated into the regular labour market of Switzerland where they;

(a) are an EEA national who holds the relevant residence status that enables them to work in Switzerland; or

(b) are a non-EEA, non-Swiss national who can evidence that they have permission to reside and have been working for an extended period within the regular labour market of Switzerland.

SPS 4.5. An applicant will not be required to show evidence of permission to reside in Switzerland if they are a Swiss national or of a nationality which is, and continues to be, party to the Agreement on the Free Movement of Persons (subject to any transitional measures that may be in place).

SPS 4.6. An employer or company will only be considered eligible where it:

(a) is a company or employer formed in accordance with the laws of Switzerland; and

(b) has their registered office, central administration or principal place of business in the territory of Switzerland; and

(c) remains active and trading.

SPS 4.7. The applicant must provide the evidence specified in SPS 4.9. (as modified in SPS 4.10. in the case of a self-employed Swiss national) to show that they are required to travel to the UK for the purpose of providing a service under an eligible contract concluded between themselves (if self-employed), or their employer, and a client in the UK.

SPS 4.8. An 'eligible contract' is a contract where;

(a) it is a written contract (including in electronic form) between a Swiss employer or company, and a UK employer or company (formed in accordance with UK Companies law) or an individual established in the UK; and

(b) it is signed and dated before 11pm on 31 December 2020; and

(c) the performance of which has started on or before 11pm on 31 December 2020.

SPS 4.9. In the case of an applicant who is employed by an employer or company, the evidence required at SPS.4.7. must;

(a) be a letter (which can be electronic) from the employer or company; and

(b) be signed by a senior member of the organisation; and

(c) include the author's credentials; and

(d) include a copy of the eligible contract; and

(e) include details on why the applicant is required to travel to the UK to execute the eligible contract; and

(f) confirm the applicant has any necessary professional qualifications to allow them to execute the contract; and

(g) confirm that the employer or company has not already used the 90 day per calendar year limitation to execute this or any other eligible contract that they hold.

SPS 4.10. In the case of a self-employed Swiss national, the evidence required at SPS 4.7. must be a letter of self-certification which meets all the criteria at SPS 4.9. (except SPS 4.9.(a) and SPS 4.9.(b), and for SPS 4.9.(g) must confirm that the applicant has not already used their 90 per calendar year limitation).

90 day limitation requirement for Service Providers from Switzerland

SPS 5.1. The eligible employer, company or self-employed service provider must not have met or exceeded the 90 day per calendar year limitation.

Genuineness requirement for Service Providers from Switzerland

SPS 6.1. The applicant must be a genuine Service Provider from Switzerland, meaning that:

(a) the applicant will not remain in the UK after the end of their permission; and

(b) the applicant will not live in the UK for extended periods through frequent and successive visits, or make the UK their main home; and

(c) the applicant must be genuinely seeking entry as a Service Provider from Switzerland.

SPS 6.2. The applicant must not while in the UK intend to:

(a) access public funds; or

(b) access medical treatment on the NHS (other than in an emergency); or

(c) study; or

(d) get married or form a civil partnership; or

(e) give notice of marriage or civil partnership.

Decision on an application as a Service Provider from Switzerland

SPS 7.1. If the decision maker is satisfied that all the requirements for a Service Provider from Switzerland are met the application will be granted, otherwise the application will be refused.

SPS 7.2. If the application is refused an application can be made for an Administrative Review under Appendix AR(EU): Admin Review.

Period and conditions of grant for Service Providers from Switzerland

SPS 8.1. The grant will be for one of the following periods (whichever is shorter);

(a) the end date of the eligible contract; or

(b) the end date of the employee's work contract (where such contract is a fixed term contract); or

(c) the day preceding the expiry date of the person's permission to reside in Switzerland (where the applicant requires such permission); or

(d) the 31 December 2025.

SPS 8.2. A Service Provider from Switzerland may enter and leave the UK multiple times during the period for which they have permission, but can only stay in the UK for up to 90 days in each calendar year as a Service Provider from Switzerland.

SPS 8.3. The employer or company posting staff to the UK (or the individual in the case of the self-employed Swiss national) is responsible for ensuring that the total work on any and all eligible contracts does not exceed 90 days per calendar year irrespective of the number of staff granted permission under this SPS

SPS 8.4. The grant will be subject to all the following conditions:

(a) no more than 90-days work in each calendar year; and

(b) no work other than on the eligible contract (including self-employment and voluntary work); and

(c) no study; and

(d) no access to public funds.

Cancellation of entry clearance or permission of a Service Provider from Switzerland

SPS 9.1. A person's entry clearance or permission as a Service Provider from Switzerland may be cancelled where the decision maker is satisfied that it is proportionate to do so where:

(a) the cancellation is justified on grounds of public policy, public security or public health, on the basis of the person's conduct on or before 11pm on 31 December 2020, in accordance with regulation 27 of the EEA Regulations, irrespective of whether the EEA Regulations apply to that person (except that for an 'EEA decision' read 'a decision under paragraph SPS 9.1'); or

(b) the cancellation is justified on the ground that it is conducive to the public good, on the basis of the person's conduct after 11pm on 31 December 2020; or

(c) the cancellation is justified on grounds that, in relation to an application made under this Appendix, and whether or not to the applicant's knowledge, false or misleading information, representations or documents were submitted (including false or misleading information submitted to any person to obtain a document used in support of the application) and the information, representation or documentation was material to the decision to grant the application under this Appendix; or

(d) the cancellation is justified on grounds that the person has breached a condition of their permission as set out in SPS 8.4. unless further permission was granted in the knowledge of the breach; or

(e) the cancellation is justified on grounds that the applicant or the eligible company or employer ceases to satisfy the Service Requirement at SPS 4.1. to SPS 4.6. or the 90 day limitation requirement at SPS 5.1.; or

(f) an agreement dealing with the movement of natural persons for the purposes of the supply of services in accordance with the parties' rights and obligations under the General Agreement on Trade in Services of the World Trade Organisation is concluded and applied between the UK and Switzerland.]

Note: Appendix inserted from 09:00 on 1 December 2020 subject to savings for applications made before that time (HC813).

[Appendix Hong Kong British National (Overseas)

[The Hong Kong British National (Overseas) route has two routes – the BN(O) Status Holder route and the BN(O) Household Member route.

The BN(O) Status Holder route is for a British National (Overseas) status holder who is ordinarily resident in Hong Kong or the UK. A dependent partner and a dependent child of a British National (Overseas) status holder can apply under this route. In exceptional circumstances, other family members with a high degree of dependency may also apply.

The BN(O) Household Member route is for the adult child, born on or after 1 July 1997, of a BN(O) status holder. The BN(O) Household Member, and any dependent partner or child applying under this route must form part of the same household as the British National (Overseas) status holder.

The Hong Kong British National (Overseas) routes allow work and study in the UK and are routes to settlement.]

Note: Introduction substituted from 6 April 2022 subject to savings for applications made before that date (HC 1118).

BN(O) Status Holder route

Validity requirements for Status Holder route

HK 1.1. A person applying for entry clearance or permission to stay as a BN(O) Status Holder must apply online on the gov.uk website on the specified form as follows:

Applicant	Specified form
Applicants with a chipped passport who: • hold a passport which shows they are registered as a British National (Overseas); or • hold a passport issued by the Hong Kong Special Administrative Region.	Either: • Hong Kong British National (Overseas) Visa using the UK Immigration: ID Check app (when available); or • Hong Kong British National (Overseas) Visa
Other applicants	Hong Kong British National (Overseas) Visa

HK 1.2. An application for entry clearance or permission to stay as a BN(O) Status Holder must meet all the following requirements:

(a) any fee and Immigration Health Charge must have been paid; and

(b) the applicant must have provided any required biometrics; and

(c) the applicant must have provided a passport or other travel document which satisfactorily established their identity and nationality.

HK 1.3. The applicant must be aged 18 years or over on the date of application.

HK 1.4. An application which does not meet all the validity requirements for a BN(O) Status Holder is invalid and may be rejected and not considered.

Suitability requirements for BN(O) Status Holder

HK 2.1. The applicant must not fall for refusal under Part 9: grounds for refusal.

HK 2.2. If applying for permission to stay the applicant must not be:

(a) in breach of immigration laws, except that where paragraph 39E applies, that period of overstaying will be disregarded; or

(b) on immigration bail.

Eligibility requirements BN(O) Status Holder

Entry requirements for BN(O) Status Holder

HK 3.1. A person seeking to come to the UK as a BN(O) Status Holder must apply for and obtain entry clearance as a BN(O) Status Holder before they arrive in the UK.

HK 3.2. A person applying for entry clearance as a BN(O) Status Holder must, if paragraph A39 and Appendix T of these rules apply, provide a valid medical certificate confirming that they have undergone screening for active pulmonary tuberculosis and that this tuberculosis is not present in them.

BN(O) Status holder requirement

HK 4.1. The applicant must be a British National (Overseas) under the Hong Kong (British Nationality) Order 1986.

Ordinary residence in Hong Kong requirement for BN(O) Status Holder

HK 5.1. An applicant applying for entry clearance must be ordinarily resident in Hong Kong at the date of application.

HK 5.2. An applicant applying for permission to stay must be in the UK, and must be ordinarily resident in the UK, the Bailiwick of Guernsey, Bailiwick of Jersey, the Isle of Man or Hong Kong on the date of application.

Financial requirement for BN(O) Status Holder

[**HK 6.1.** If the applicant is applying for permission to stay and has been living in the UK for 12 months or more on the date of application, they will meet the financial requirement unless the applicant's previous grant of permission was for 12 months Leave Outside the Rules following an unsuccessful application for the Hong Kong British National (Overseas) route.]

Note: Paragraph substituted from 6 April 2021 subject to savings for applications made before that date (HC 1248).

[**HK 6.2.** If the applicant is applying for entry clearance, or is applying for permission to stay and has been in the UK for less than 12 months on the date of application, or where the applicant's previous grant of permission was for 12 months Leave Outside the Rules following an unsuccessful application for the Hong Kong British National (Overseas) route, the decision maker must be satisfied that the applicant can adequately maintain and accommodate themselves without recourse to public funds for at least 6 months.]

Note: Paragraph substituted from 6 April 2021 subject to savings for applications made before that date (HC 1248).

HK 6.3. For the purposes of HK 6.2. accommodation will not be regarded as adequate if:

(a) it is, or will be, overcrowded; or

(b) it contravenes public health regulations.

HK 6.4. The applicant may rely on credible promises of future third party support.

HK 6.5. Funds must be shown as specified in Appendix Finance.

In-country tuberculosis certificate requirement for BN(O) Status Holder

HK 7.1. If the applicant is applying for permission to stay and:

(a) their last grant of permission was for 6 months or less; and

(b) the applicant was present in a country listed in Appendix T of these rules for more than six months immediately prior to their last grant of permission, the applicant must provide a valid medical certificate confirming that they have undergone screening for active pulmonary tuberculosis and that this tuberculosis is not present in them.

HK 7.2. In HK 7.1. a valid medical certificate is a certificate from an approved centre issued within the 6 months immediately before the date of application.

HK 7.3. The in-country tuberculosis requirement is met if the applicant provided a medical certificate described in HK 7.1. as part of a successful application for entry clearance in the 12 months before the date of application.

HK 7.4. The list of approved centres in the UK, updated from time to time, can be found at https://www.gov.uk/government/publications/uk-tuberculosis-test-clinics-for-hong-kong-bno.

Decision for BN(O) Status Holder

HK 8.1. If the decision-maker is satisfied that all the suitability and eligibility requirements for a BN(O) Status Holder are met, the application will be granted, otherwise the application will be refused.

HK 8.2. If the application is refused the person can apply for an Administrative Review under Appendix AR: Administrative Review.

Period and conditions of grant for BN(O) Status Holder

HK 9.1. The applicant will be granted permission for either:

(a) a period of 5 years, where the applicant has applied for a period of 5 years; or

(b) a period of 30 months, where the applicant has applied for a period of 30 months.

HK 9.2. The permission will be granted subject to the following conditions:

(a) no access to public funds; and

(b) work (including self-employment and voluntary work) permitted except for employment as a professional sportsperson (including as a sports coach); and

(c) study is permitted, subject to the ATAS condition in Appendix ATAS.

Dependants on the BN(O) Status Holder route

Validity requirements for a dependent partner or BN(O) Household Child on the BN(O) Status Holder route

HK 10.1. A person applying for entry clearance or permission to stay as a dependent partner or BN(O) Household Child on the BN(O) Status Holder route must apply online on the gov.uk website on the specified form as follows:

Applicant	Specified form
Applicants with a chipped passport who: – hold a passport which shows they are registered as a British National (Overseas); or – hold a passport issued by the Hong Kong Special Administrative Region; or are EEA nationals.	Either: • Hong Kong British National (Overseas) Visa using the UK Immigration: ID Check app (when available); or • Hong Kong British National (Overseas) Visa
Other applicants	Hong Kong British National (Overseas) Visa

[**HK 10.2.** An application for entry clearance or permission to stay as a partner or BN(O) Household Child on the BN(O) Status Holder route must meet all the following validity requirements:

(a) any fee and Immigration Health Charge must have been paid; and

(b) the applicant must have provided any required biometrics; and

(c) the applicant must have provided a passport or other travel document which satisfactorily establishes their identity and nationality; and

(d) when applying as a partner on the BN(O) Status Holder route, where the applicant does not currently hold, or did not last hold, permission as a partner on the BN(O) Status Holder route the applicant must be applying as a partner of a BN(O) Status Holder who:

(i) has made a valid application for entry clearance or permission to stay in the UK as a BN(O) Status Holder that has not been decided; or

(ii) has entry clearance or permission as a BN(O) status holder;

(e) when applying as a BN(O) Household Child on the BN(O) Status Holder route, the applicant must be applying as a child or grandchild of a BN(O) Status Holder or of the partner of a BN(O) Status Holder who:

(i) has made a valid application for entry clearance or permission to stay in the UK as a BN(O) Status Holder or as the partner of a BN(O) Status Holder that has not been decided; or

(ii) has entry clearance or permission as a BN(O) status holder or as the partner of a BN(O) Status Holder.]

Note: Paragraph substituted from 6 April 2022 subject to savings for applications made before that date (HC 1118).

HK 10.3. An application which does not meet the validity requirements for a dependent partner or BN(O) Household Child on the BN(O) Status Holder route is invalid and may be rejected and not considered.

Suitability requirements for a dependent partner or BN(O) Household Child on the Hong Kong BN(O) Status Holder route

HK 11.1. The applicant must not fall for refusal under Part 9: grounds for refusal.

HK 11.2. If applying for permission to stay the applicant must not be:

(a) in breach of immigration laws, except that where paragraph 39E applies, that period of overstaying will be disregarded; or

(b) on immigration bail.

Eligibility requirements for a partner or BN(O) Household Child on the BN(O) Status Holder route

Entry requirements for a partner or BN(O) Household Child on the BN(O) Status Holder route

HK 12.1. A person seeking to come to the UK as a partner or BN(O) Household child on the BN(O) Status Holder route must apply for and obtain entry clearance as a partner or BN(O) Household child before they arrive in the UK.

HK 12.2. A person applying for entry clearance on the BN(O) Status Holder route must, if paragraph A39 and Appendix T of these rules apply, provide a valid medical certificate confirming that they have undergone screening for active pulmonary tuberculosis and that this tuberculosis is not present in them.

Relationship requirement for dependent partner on the BN(O) Status Holder route

HK 13.1. If the applicant is applying for permission to stay and they have permission as a dependent partner on the BN(O) Status Holder route on the date of application, they will meet the relationship requirement.

HK 13.2. If the applicant is applying for entry clearance or permission to stay and they have not previously had permission as a partner on the BN(O) Status Holder route they must meet the relationship requirement in HK 13.3. to HK 13.7.

[**HK 13.3.** The applicant must be the partner of a person (P) where one of the following applies:

(a) P has permission on the Hong Kong BN(O) route; or

(b) P is, at the same time, applying for (and is granted) entry clearance or permission on the Hong Kong BN(O) route.]

Note: Paragraph substituted from 6 October 2021 subject to savings for applications made before that date (HC 617).

HK 13.4. The applicant must be aged 18 or over at the date of application.

HK 13.5. If the applicant and the BN(O) Status Holder are not married or in a civil partnership, all the following requirements must be met:

(a) they must have been living together in a relationship similar to marriage or civil partnership for at least the two years before the date of application; and

(b) any previous relationship of the applicant or the BN(O) Status Holder with another person must have permanently broken down; and

(c) they must not be so closely related that they would not be allowed to marry in the UK.

HK 13.6. The relationship between the applicant and the BN(O) Status Holder must be genuine and subsisting.

[**HK 13.7.** The applicant and the BN(O) Status Holder must intend to live together throughout the applicant's stay in the UK.]

Note: Paragraph substituted from 6 October 2021 subject to savings for applications made before that date (HC 617).

HK 13.8. [DELETED]

Note: Paragraph deleted from 6 October 2021 subject to savings for applications made before that date (HC 617).

Financial requirement for dependent partner on the BN(O) Status Holder route

[**HK 14.1** . If the applicant is applying for permission to stay and has been living in the UK with permission for 12 months or more on the date of application, they will meet the financial requirement unless the applicant's previous grant of permission was for 12 months Leave Outside the Rules following an unsuccessful application for the Hong Kong British National (Overseas) route.]

Note: Paragraph substituted from 6 April 2021 subject to savings for applications made before that date (HC 1248).

[**HK 14.2.** If the applicant is applying for entry clearance or is applying for permission to stay and has been in the UK for less than 12 months on the date of application, or where the applicant's previous grant of permission was for 12 months Leave Outside the Rules following an unsuccessful application for the Hong Kong British National (Overseas) route, the decision maker must be satisfied that the applicant or the BN(O) Status Holder are able to maintain and accommodate the applicant adequately in the UK without recourse to public funds for at least 6 months.]

Note: Paragraph substituted from 6 April 2021 subject to savings for applications made before that date (HC 1248).

HK 14.3. For the purposes of HK 14.2. accommodation will not be regarded as adequate if:

(a) it is, or will be, overcrowded; or

(b) it contravenes public health regulations.

HK 14.4. The applicant or the BN(O) Status Holder may rely on credible promises of future third party support.

HK 14.5. The applicant or the BN(O) Status Holder must show that they have the required funds as specified in Appendix Finance.

Relationship requirement for BN(O) Household Child on the BN(O) Status Holder route

HK 15.1. The applicant must be:

(a) the child of a parent who has, or is at the same time being granted, entry clearance or permission as either:

(i) a BN(O) Status Holder; or

(ii) the partner of a BN(O) Status Holder; or

(b) the grandchild of a grandparent who has, or is at the same time being granted, entry clearance or permission as either:

(i) BN(O) Status Holder, or

(ii) the partner of a BN(O) Status Holder.

[**HK 15.2.** If the applicant is applying for entry clearance or permission to stay as the grandchild of a grandparent who has, or is at the same time being granted, entry clearance or permission to stay as either a BN(O) Status Holder or the partner of a BN(O) Status Holder and the applicant has not previously had permission as a BN(O) Household Child on the BN(O) Status Holder route, they must:

(a) make an application at the same time as the grandparent who is applying for entry clearance or permission on the BN(O) Status Holder route; and

(b) form part of the same household as the BN(O) Status Holder on the date of application.]

Note: Paragraph substituted from 6 October 2021 subject to savings for applications made before that date (HC 617).

HK 15.3. In HK 15.2.(b) a person will form part of the same household as the BN(O) Status Holder if they normally live with the BN(O) Status Holder.

[**HK 15.4.** Each of the applicant's parents must either be applying at the same time as the applicant, or have permission to be in the UK (other than as a Visitor), unless:

(a) the parent with entry clearance or permission to stay as a BN(O) Status Holder or as a partner of a BN(O) Status Holder is the sole surviving parent; or

(b) the parent with entry clearance or permission to stay as a BN(O) Status Holder or as a partner of a BN(O) Status Holder has sole responsibility for the applicant's upbringing; or

(c) the parent who does not have permission as a BN(O) Status Holder or as a partner of a BN(O) Status Holder –

(i) is a British citizen or a person who has a right to enter or stay in the UK without restriction; and

(ii) is or will be ordinarily resident in the UK; or

(d) there are serious and compelling reasons to grant the applicant entry clearance or permission to stay with the parent who has permission on the Hong Kong BN(O) route; or

(e) the applicant falls within HK 15.1(b) and there are serious and compelling reasons to grant the applicant entry clearance or permission to stay with the grandparent with entry clearance or permission to stay as a BN(O) Status Holder or as a partner of a BN(O) Status Holder.]

Note: Paragraph substituted from 6 October 2021 (HC 617).

[**HK 15.5.** If the applicant is a child born in the UK to a BN(O) Status Holder or their partner, the applicant must provide a full UK birth certificate showing the names of both parents.]

Note: Paragraph inserted from 6 October 2021 subject to savings for applications made before that date (HC 617).

Care requirement for a BN(O) Household Child on the BN(O) Status Holder route

[**HK 16.1.** The applicant must intend to live with a parent who has permission on the BN(O) status holder route during their stay in the UK, unless they can demonstrate a valid reason why they should not live with that parent.]

Note: Paragraph substituted from 6 April 2021 subject to savings for applications made before that date (HC 1248).

HK 16.2. There must be suitable arrangements for the child's care and accommodation in the UK, which must comply with relevant UK legislation and regulations.

Age requirement for a BN(O) Household Child on the BN(O) Status Holder route

HK 17.1. The applicant must be under the age of 18 at the date of application.

Financial requirement for a BN(O) Household Child on the BN(O) Status Holder route

HK 18.1. If the applicant is applying for permission to stay and has been living in the UK with permission for 12 months or more on the date of application, they will meet the financial requirement.

HK 18.2. If the applicant is applying for entry clearance, or is applying for permission to stay and has been in the UK for less than 12 months on the date of application, the decision maker must be satisfied that the BN(O) Status Holder or their partner is able to maintain and accommodate the BN(O) Household Child adequately in the UK without recourse to public funds for at least 6 months.

HK 18.3. For the purposes of HK 18.2 accommodation will not be regarded as adequate if

(a) it is or will be overcrowded; or

(b) it contravenes public health regulations.

HK 18.4. The BN(O) Status Holder or their partner may rely on credible promises of future third party support.

HK 18.5. The BN(O) Status Holder or their partner must show that they have the required funds as specified in Appendix Finance.

Ordinary residence in Hong Kong requirement for dependent partner or BN(O) Household Child on the BN(O) Status Holder route

HK 19.1. If the applicant is applying for entry clearance as a dependant partner or BN(O) Household Child, the applicant must be ordinarily resident in Hong Kong at the date of application.

HK 19.2. An applicant applying for permission to stay must be in the UK and must be ordinarily resident in the UK, the Bailiwick of Guernsey, Bailiwick of Jersey, the Isle of Man or Hong Kong on the date of application.

In-country tuberculosis certificate requirement for a dependent partner or BN(O) Household Child on the BN(O) Status Holder route

HK 20.1. If the applicant is applying for permission to stay and:

(a) their last grant of permission was for 6 months or less; and

(b) the applicant was present in a country listed in Appendix T of these rules for more than six months immediately prior to their last grant of permission, the applicant must provide a valid medical certificate confirming that they have undergone screening for active pulmonary tuberculosis and that this tuberculosis is not present in them.

HK 20.2. In HK 20.1. a valid medical certificate is a certificate from an approved centre issued within the 6 months immediately before the date of application.

HK 20.3. The in-country tuberculosis requirement is met if the applicant has provided a medical certificate described in HK 20.1. as part of a successful application for entry clearance in the 12 months before the date of application.

HK 20.4. The list of approved centres in the UK, updated from time to time, can be found at: https://www.gov.uk/government/publications/uk-tuberculosis-test-clinics-for-hong-kong-bno.

Decision on application for a dependent partner or BN(O) Household Child on the Hong Kong BN(O) route

HK 21.1. If the decision maker is satisfied that all the suitability and eligibility requirements for a dependent partner or dependent BN(O) Household Child on the BN(O) Status Holder route are met the application will be granted, otherwise the application will be refused.

HK 21.2. If the application is refused the person can apply for an Administrative Review under Appendix AR: Administrative Review.

Period and conditions of grant for a dependent partner or BN(O) Household Child on the BN(O) Status Holder route

HK 22.1. A partner who does not have permission on the BN(O) Status Holder route on the date of application, will be granted permission which ends on the same date as the permission of the BN(O) Status Holder.

HK 22.2. If the partner has permission on the Hong Kong BN(O) route on the date of application, they will be granted permission for either:

(a) 30 months, if the partner applied for 30 months; or

(b) 5 years, if the partner applied for 5 years.

[**HK 22.3.** A BN(O) Household Child who does not have permission on the BN(O) Status Holder route on the date of application, will be granted permission which ends on the same date as the permission of the BN(O) Status Holder who has (or is being granted) permission.]

Note: Paragraph substituted from 6 October 2021 subject to savings for applications made before that date (HC 617).

HK 22.4. If the BN(O) Household Child has permission on the BN(O) Status Holder route on the date of application they will,

(a) where the BN(O) Household Child is applying as the dependent of one parent or grandparent with permission as a BN(O) Status Holder or the partner of a BN(O) Status Holder, be granted permission that ends on the same date as that parent or grandparent; or

(b) where the BN(O) Household Child is applying as the dependent of both parents or grandparents with permission as a BN(O) Status Holder or the partner of a BN(O) Status Holder, be granted permission that ends on the same date as those parents or grandparents or, if different, the same date as the parent or grandparent whose permission ends first.

HK 22.5. The grant will be subject to all the following conditions:

(a) no access to public funds; and

(b) work (including self-employment and voluntary work) permitted except for employment as a professional sportsperson (including as a sports coach); and

(c) study is permitted, subject to the ATAS condition in Appendix ATAS; and

(d) if Part 10 applies the applicant will be required to register with the police.

BN(O) Household Member route

Validity requirements for the BN(O) Household Member route

HK 23.1. A person applying for entry clearance or permission to stay on the BN(O) Household Member route must apply online on the gov.uk website on the specified form as follows:

Applicant	Specified form
Applicants with a chipped passport who: – hold a passport which shows they are registered as a British National (Overseas); or – hold a passport issued by the Hong Kong Special Administrative Region; or are EEA nationals.	Either: • Hong Kong British National (Overseas) Visa using the UK Immigration: ID Check app (when available); or • Hong Kong British National (Overseas) Visa
Other applicants	Hong Kong British National (Overseas) Visa

HK 23.2. An application for entry clearance or permission to stay a on the BN(O) Household Member route must meet all the following requirements:

(a) any fee and Immigration Health Charge must have been paid; and

(b) the applicant must have provided any required biometrics; and

[(c) the applicant must have provided a passport or other travel document which satisfactorily establishes their identity and nationality, and]

[(d) when applying for the first time as a BN(O) Household member, the applicant must be applying as a child of a BN(O) Status Holder who has made a valid application for entry clearance or permission to stay in the UK as a BN(O) Status Holder that has not been decided.]

Note: Sub-paragraph (c) substituted, (d) inserted from 6 April 2022 subject to savings for applications made before that date (HC 1118).

HK 23.3. The applicant must have been born on or after 1 July 1997.

HK 23.4. The applicant must be aged 18 or over on the date of application.

HK 23.5. The applicant must not have or have last had permission as a BN(O) Adult Dependent Relative on the BN(O) Status Holder route.

HK 23.6. An application which does not meet the validity requirements for the BN(O) Household Member route is invalid and may be rejected and not considered.

Suitability requirements for the BN(O) Household Member route

HK 24.1. The applicant must not fall for refusal under Part 9: grounds for refusal.

HK 24.2. If applying for permission to stay the applicant must not be:

(a) in breach of immigration laws, except that where paragraph 39E applies, that period of overstaying will be disregarded; or

(b) on immigration bail.

Eligibility requirements for the BN(O) Household Member route

Entry requirement for a BN(O) Household Member

HK 25.1. A person seeking to come to the UK on the BN(O) Household Member route must apply for and obtain entry clearance on the BN(O) Household Member route before they arrive in the UK.

HK 25.2. A person applying for entry clearance as a BN(O) Household Member must, if paragraph A39 and Appendix T of these rules apply, provide a valid medical certificate confirming that they have undergone screening for active pulmonary tuberculosis and that this tuberculosis is not present in them.

Relationship requirement for a BN(O) Household Member

HK 26.1. If the applicant is applying for permission to stay and they have permission on the Hong Kong British National (Overseas) route on the date of application, they will meet the relationship requirement.

HK 26.2. If the applicant is applying for entry clearance or permission to stay and they do not have permission on the Hong Kong British National (Overseas) route on the date of application, the applicant:

(a) must be the child of a person who is being granted permission on the BN(O) Status Holder route at the same time that the applicant is being granted permission; and

(b) must form part of the same household as the BN(O) Status Holder.

HK 26.3. In HK 26.2. a person will form part of the same household as the BN(O) Status Holder if they normally live with the BN(O) Status Holder.

Financial requirement for a BN(O) Household Member

[**HK 27.1.** If the applicant is applying for permission to stay and has been living in the UK with permission for 12 months or more on the date of application, they will meet the financial requirement unless the applicant's previous grant of permission was for 12 months Leave Outside the Rules following an unsuccessful application for the Hong Kong British National (Overseas) route.]

Note: Paragraph substituted from 6 April 2021 subject to savings for applications made before that date (HC 1248).

[**HK 27.2.** If the applicant is applying for entry clearance, or is applying for permission to stay and they have been in the UK for less than 12 months on the date of application, or where the applicant's previous grant of permission was for 12 months Leave Outside the Rules following an unsuccessful application for the Hong Kong British National (Overseas) route, the decision maker must be satisfied that the applicant, or a person who is being granted permission on the BN(O) Status Holder route at the same time as the applicant, is able to, and will, maintain and accommodate the applicant adequately in the UK without recourse to public funds for at least 6 months.]

Note: Paragraph substituted from 6 April 2021 subject to savings for applications made before that date (HC 1248).

HK 27.3. For the purposes of HK 27.2 accommodation will not be regarded as adequate if:

(a) it is or will be overcrowded; or

(b) it contravenes public health regulations.

HK 27.4. The applicant or the person on the BN(O) Status Holder route may rely on credible promises of future third party support.

HK 27.5. The applicant or the person on the BN(O) Status Holder route must show that they have the required funds as specified in Appendix Finance.

Ordinary residence in Hong Kong requirement for a BN(O) Household Member

HK 28.1. An applicant applying for entry clearance as a BN(O) Household Member must be ordinarily resident in Hong Kong on the date of application.

HK 28.2. An applicant applying for permission to stay must be in the UK and must be ordinarily resident in the UK, the Bailiwick of Guernsey, Bailiwick of Jersey, the Isle of Man or Hong Kong.

In-country tuberculosis certificate requirement for a BN(O) Household Member

HK 29.1. If the applicant is applying for permission to stay and:

(a) their last grant of permission was for 6 months or less; and

(b) the applicant was present in a country listed in Appendix T of these rules for more than six months immediately prior to their last grant of permission, the applicant must provide a valid medical certificate confirming that they have undergone screening for active pulmonary tuberculosis and that this tuberculosis is not present in them.

HK 29.2. In HK 29.1. a valid medical certificate is a certificate from an approved centre issued within the 6 months immediately before the date of application.

HK 29.3. The in-country tuberculosis certificate requirement is met if the applicant has provided a medical certificate described in HK 29.1. as part of a successful application for entry clearance in the 12 months before the date of application.

HK 29.4. The list of approved centres in the UK, updated from time to time, can be found at: https://www.gov.uk/government/publications/uk-tuberculosis-test-clinics-for-hong-kong-bno.

Decision on application for a BN(O) Household Member

HK 30.1. If the decision maker is satisfied that all the suitability and eligibility requirements on the BN(O) Household Member route are met the application will be granted, otherwise the application will be refused.

HK 30.2. If the application is refused the person can apply for an Administrative Review under Appendix AR: Administrative Review.

Conditions and period of grant for a BN(O) Household Member

HK 31.1. If the applicant does not have permission on the Hong Kong British National (Overseas) route on the date of application, the applicant will be granted permission which ends on the same date as the permission of the BN(O) Status Holder who is part of the same household as the applicant.

HK 31.2. If the applicant has permission on the Hong Kong British National (Overseas) route on the date of application, they will be granted permission for either:

(a) 30 months, if the applicant applied for 30 months; or

(b) 5 years, if the applicant applied for 5 years.

HK 31.3. The grant will be subject to all the following conditions:

(a) no access to public funds; and

(b) work (including self-employment and voluntary work) permitted except for employment as a professional sportsperson, including as a sports coach; and

(c) study is permitted, subject to the condition in Appendix ATAS; and

(d) if Part 10 applies the applicant will be required to register with the police.

Dependants of BN(O) Household Members

Validity requirements for a dependent partner or dependent child of a BN(O) Household Member on the Hong Kong BN(O) route

HK 32.1. A person applying for entry clearance or permission to stay as a dependent partner or dependent child on the BN(O) Household Member route must apply online on the gov.uk website on the specified form as follows:

Applicant	Specified form
Applicants with a chipped passport who: – hold a passport which shows they are registered as a British National (Overseas); or – hold a passport issued by the Hong Kong Special Administrative Region; or are EEA nationals.	Either: • Hong Kong British National (Overseas) Visa using the UK Immigration: ID Check app (when available); or • Hong Kong British National (Overseas) Visa
Other applicants	Hong Kong British National (Overseas) Visa

HK 32.2. An application for entry clearance or permission to stay as a dependent partner or child on the BN(O) Household Member route must meet all the following validity requirements:

(a) any fee and Immigration Health Charge must have been paid; and

(b) the applicant must have provided any required biometrics; and

(c) the applicant must have provided a passport or other travel document which satisfactorily establishes their identity and nationality.

[**HK 32.3.** An applicant who is applying as a dependent child must be the child of a person who is making a valid application for entry clearance or permission to stay on the BN(O) Household Member route at the same time as the applicant.]

Note: Paragraph substituted from 6 April 2022 subject to savings for applications made before that date (HC 1118).

HK 32.4. An application which does not meet the validity requirements for a dependent partner or dependent child on the BN(O) Household Member route is invalid and may be rejected and not considered.

Suitability requirements for a dependent partner or child on the BN(O) Household Member route

HK 33.1. The applicant must not fall for refusal under Part 9: grounds for refusal.

HK 33.2. If applying for permission to stay the applicant must not be:

(a) in breach of immigration laws, except that where paragraph 39E applies, that period of overstaying will be disregarded; or

(b) on immigration bail.

Eligibility requirements for a dependent partner or child on the BN(O) Household Member route

Entry requirements for a partner or child on the BN(O) Household Member route

HK 34.1. A person seeking to come to the UK as a partner or child on the BN(O) Household Member route must apply for and obtain entry clearance as a partner or child before they arrive in the UK.

HK 34.2. A person applying for entry clearance as the dependent partner or child of a BN(O) Household Member must, if paragraph A39 and Appendix T of these rules apply, provide a valid medical certificate confirming that they have undergone screening for active pulmonary tuberculosis and that this tuberculosis is not present in them.

Relationship requirements for dependent partner of a BN(O) Household Member

HK 35.1. If the applicant is applying for permission to stay and they have permission as a partner on the BN(O) Household Member route on the date of application, they will meet the relationship requirements.

HK 35.2. Where the applicant is applying for entry clearance or permission to stay and they have not previously had permission on the BN(O) Household Member route they must meet the relationship requirement as set out in HK 35.3. to HK 35.9.

HK 35.3. The applicant must be the partner of a person who is making an application for entry clearance or permission to stay on the BN(O) Household Member route at the same time as the applicant.

HK 35.4. The applicant and the BN(O) Household Member must both be aged 18 or over at the date of application.

HK 35.5. If the applicant and the BN(O) Household Member are not married or in a civil partnership, all the following requirements must be met:

(a) they must have been living together in a relationship similar to marriage or civil partnership for at least the two years before the date of application; and

(b) any previous relationship of the applicant or the BN(O) Household Member with another person must have permanently broken down; and

(c) they must not be so closely related that they would not be allowed to marry in the UK.

HK 35.6. The relationship between the applicant and the BN(O) Household Member must be genuine and subsisting.

HK 35.7. The applicant and the BN(O) Household Member must form part of the same household on the date of application.

HK 35.8. In HK 35.7. a person will form part of the same household as the BN(O) Household Member if they normally live with the BN(O) Household Member.

HK 35.9. The applicant and the BN(O) Household Member must intend to live together throughout the applicant's stay in the UK.

Financial requirement for partner of a BN(O) Household Member

[**HK 36.1.** If the applicant is applying for permission to stay and has been living in the UK with permission for 12 months or more on the date of application, they will meet the financial requirement unless the applicant's previous grant of permission was for 12 months Leave Outside the Rules following an unsuccessful application for the Hong Kong British National (Overseas) route.]

Note: Paragraph substituted from 6 April 2021 subject to savings for applications made before that date (HC 1248).

[**HK 36.2.** If the applicant is applying for entry clearance, or is applying for permission to stay and has been in the UK for less than 12 months on the date of application, or where the applicant's previous grant of permission was for 12 months Leave Outside the Rules following an unsuccessful application for the Hong Kong British National (Overseas) route, the decision maker must be satisfied that the applicant, the BN(O) Household Member or a person being granted permission on the BN(O) Status Holder route at the same time as the applicant is being granted permission, is able to maintain and accommodate the applicant adequately in the UK without recourse to public funds for at least 6 months.]

Note: Paragraph substituted from 6 April 2021 subject to savings for applications made before that date (HC 1248).

HK 36.3. For the purposes of HK 36.2. accommodation will not be regarded as adequate if

(a) it is or will be overcrowded; or
(b) it contravenes public health regulations.

HK 36.4. The applicant, the BN(O) Household Member or a person being granted permission on the BN(O) Status Holder route may rely on credible promises of future third party support.

HK 36.5. The applicant, the BN(O) Household Member or a person being granted permission on the BN(O) Status Holder route must show that they have the required funds as specified in Appendix Finance.

Relationship requirement for dependent child of a BN(O) Household Member

HK 37.1. The applicant must be the child of a parent who has, or is at the same time being granted, permission as:

(a) a BN(O) Household Member or
(b) the partner of a BN(O) Household Member.

[**HK 37.2.** Each of the applicant's parents must either be applying at the same time as the applicant, or have permission to be in the UK (other than as a Visitor), unless:

(a) the parent with entry clearance or permission to stay as a BN(O) Household Member or as a partner of a BN(O) Household Member is the sole surviving parent; or

(b) the parent with entry clearance or permission to stay as a BN(O) Household Member or as a partner of a Household Member has sole responsibility for the applicant's upbringing; or

(c) the parent who does not have permission as a BN(O) Household Member or as a partner of a Household Member –

(i) is a British citizen or a person who has a right to enter or stay in the UK without restriction; and

(ii) is or will be ordinarily resident in the UK; or

(d) there are serious and compelling reasons to grant the applicant entry clearance or permission to stay with the parent with permission on the Hong Kong BN(O) route.]

Note: Paragraph substituted from 6 October 2021 (HC 617).

HK 37.3. If the applicant is applying for entry clearance or permission to stay and they have not previously had permission as a child on the BN(O) Household Member route they must form part of the same household as the BN(O) Household Member on the date of application.

HK 37.4. In HK 37.3. a person will form part of the same household as the BN(O) Household Member if they normally live with the BN(O) Household Member.

[**HK 37.5.** If the applicant is a child born in the UK to a BN(O) Household Member or their partner, the applicant must provide a full UK birth certificate showing the names of both parents.]

Note: Paragraph substituted from 6 October 2021 subject to savings for applications made before that date (HC 617).

Care requirement for a dependent child of a BN(O) Household Member

[**HK 38.1.** The applicant must intend to live with a parent who has permission on the BN(O) Household Member route during their stay in the UK, unless they can demonstrate a valid reason why they should not live with that parent.]

Note: Paragraph substituted from 6 April 2021 subject to savings for applications made before that date (HC 1248).

HK 38.2. There must be suitable arrangements for the applicant's care and accommodation in the UK, which must comply with relevant UK legislation and regulations.

Age requirement for a dependent child of a BN(O) Household Member

HK 39.1. The applicant must be under the age of 18 at the date of application.

Financial requirement for child of a BN(O) Household Member

[**HK 40.1.** If the applicant is applying for permission to stay and has been living in the UK for 12 months or more on the date of application, they will meet the financial requirement unless the applicant's previous grant of permission was for 12 months Leave Outside the Rules following an unsuccessful application for the Hong Kong British National (Overseas) route.]

Note: Paragraph substituted from 6 April 2021 subject to savings for applications made before that date (HC 1248).

[**HK 40.2.** If the applicant is applying for entry clearance, or is applying for permission to stay and has been in the UK with permission for less than 12 months on the date of application, or where the applicant's previous grant of permission was for 12 months Leave Outside the Rules following an unsuccessful application for the Hong Kong British National (Overseas) route, the decision maker must be satisfied that the BN(O) Household Member, their partner or a person who is being granted permission on the BN(O) Status Holder route at the same time as the applicant is being granted permission, is able to and will maintain and accommodate the applicant adequately in the UK without recourse to public funds for at least six months.]

Note: Paragraph substituted from 6 April 2021 subject to savings for applications made before that date (HC 1248).

HK 40.3. For the purposes of HK 40.2. accommodation will not be regarded as adequate if

(a) it is or will be overcrowded; or
(b) it contravenes public health regulations.

HK 40.4. The BN(O) Household Member, their partner or a person with permission on the BN(O) Status Holder route may rely on credible promises of future third party support.

HK 40.5. The BN(O) Household Member, their partner or a person with permission on the BN(O) Status Holder route must show that they have the required funds as specified in Appendix Finance.

Ordinary residence in Hong Kong requirement for partner or child of a BN(O) Household Member

HK 41.1. If the applicant is applying for entry clearance as a dependent partner or child the applicant must be ordinarily resident in Hong Kong at the date of application.

HK 41.2. An applicant applying for permission to stay must be in the UK and must be ordinarily resident in the UK, the Bailiwick of Guernsey, Bailiwick of Jersey, the Isle of Man or Hong Kong on the date of application.

In-country tuberculosis requirement for partner or child of a BN(O) Household Member

HK 42.1. If the applicant is applying for permission to stay and:

(a) their last grant of permission was for [6 months or less];

(b) the applicant was present in a country listed in Appendix T of these rules for more than six months immediately prior to their last grant of permission, the applicant must provide a valid medical certificate confirming that they have undergone screening for active pulmonary tuberculosis and that this tuberculosis is not present in them.

Note: Words substituted from 23:00 on 31 December 2020 for decisions made on or after that time (CP 361).

HK 42.2. In HK 42.1. a valid medical certificate is a certificate from an approved centre issued within the 6 months immediately before the date of application.

HK 42.3. The in-country tuberculosis requirement is met if the applicant provided a medical certificate described in HK 42.1. as part of a successful application for entry clearance in the 12 months before the date of application.

HK 42.4. The list of approved centres in the UK, updated from time to time, can be found at: https://www.gov.uk/government/publications/uk-tuberculosis-test-clinics-for-hong-kong-bno.

Decision on application for a dependent partner or child of a BN(O) Household Member on the Hong Kong BN(O) route

HK 43.1. If the decision maker is satisfied that all the suitability and eligibility requirements for the dependent partner or dependent child on the BN(O) Household Member route are met the application will be granted, otherwise the application will be refused.

HK 43.2. If the application is refused the person can apply for an Administrative Review under Appendix AR: Administrative Review.

Period and conditions of grant for a dependent partner or child of a BN(O) Household Member

HK 44.1. A partner who does not have permission on the BN(O) Household Member route on the date of application, will be granted permission which ends on the same date as the BN(O) Household Member's permission.

HK 44.2. If the partner has permission on the Hong Kong BN(O) route on the date of application, a partner will be granted permission for either:
(a) 5 years, if the partner applied for 5 years; or
(b) 30 months, if the partner applied for 30 months.

HK 44.3. A child who does not have permission on the BN(O) Household Member route on the date of application, will be granted permission which ends on the same date as the BN(O) Household Member's permission.

HK 44.4. A child who has permission on the BN(O) Household Member route on the date of application will:
(a) where the child is applying as the dependent of one parent with permission on the BN(O) Household Member route, be granted permission that ends on the same date as that parent; and
(b) where the child is applying as the dependent of both parents with permission on the BN(O) Household Member route, be granted permission that ends on the same date as those parents or, if different, the same date as the parent whose permission ends first.

HK 44.5. The grant will be subject to all the following conditions:
(a) no access to public funds; and
(b) work (including self-employment and voluntary work) permitted except for employment as a professional sportsperson (including as a sports coach); and
(c) study is permitted, subject to the ATAS condition in Appendix ATAS; and
(d) if Part 10 applies the applicant will be required to register with the police.

Adult Dependent Relative of a BN(O) Status Holder

Validity requirements for a BN(O) Adult Dependant Relative on the BN(O) Status Holder route

HK 45.1. A person applying for entry clearance or permission to stay as a BN(O) Adult Dependant Relative on the BN(O) Status Holder route must apply online on the gov.uk website on the specified form as follows:

Applicant	Specified form
Applicants with a chipped passport who: – hold a passport which shows they are registered as a British National (Overseas); or – hold a passport issued by the Hong Kong Special Administrative Region; or are EEA nationals.	Either: • Hong Kong British National (Overseas) Visa using the UK Immigration: ID Check app (when available); or • Hong Kong British National (Overseas) Visa
Other applicants	Hong Kong British National (Overseas) Visa

HK 45.2. An application for entry clearance or permission to stay as a BN(O) Adult Dependent Relative on the BN(O) Status Holder route must meet all the following validity requirements:
(a) any fee and Immigration Health Charge must have been paid; and
(b) the applicant must have provided any required biometrics; and

(c) the applicant must have provided a passport or other travel document which satisfactorily established their identity and nationality.

HK 45.3. The applicant must be aged 18 years or over on the date of application.

[**HK 45.4.** The applicant must be the parent, grandparent, brother, sister, son or daughter of a person who is making a valid application for entry clearance or permission to stay as a BN(O) Status Holder or the partner of a BN(O) Status Holder at the same time as the applicant.]

Note: Paragraph substituted from 6 April 2022 subject to savings for applications made before that date (HC 1118).

HK 45.5. An application which does not meet the validity requirements for a BN(O) Adult Dependent Relative on the BN(O) Status Holder route is invalid and may be rejected and not considered.

Suitability requirements for a BN(O) Adult Dependent Relative on the BN(O) Status Holder route

HK 46.1. The applicant must not fall for refusal under Part 9: grounds for refusal.

HK 46.2. If applying for permission to stay the applicant must not be:

(a) in breach of immigration laws, except that where paragraph 39E applies, that period of overstaying will be disregarded; or

(b) on immigration bail.

Eligibility requirements for a BN(O) Adult Dependent Relative on the BN(O) Status Holder route

Entry requirements for a BN(O) Adult Dependent Relative

HK 47.1. A person seeking to come to the UK as a BN(O) Adult Dependent Relative on the BN(O) Status Holder route must apply for and obtain entry clearance as a BN(O) Adult Dependant Relative before they arrive in the UK.

HK 47.2. A person applying for entry clearance as the dependent partner or child of a BN(O) Household Member must, if paragraph A39 and Appendix T of these rules apply, provide a valid medical certificate confirming that they have undergone screening for active pulmonary tuberculosis and that this tuberculosis is not present in them.

Relationship requirement for a BN(O) Adult Dependent Relative

HK 48.1. If the applicant is applying for permission to stay and they have permission as a BN(O) Adult Dependent Relative on the BN(O) Status Holder route on the date of application, they will meet the relationship requirement.

HK 48.2. Where the applicant is applying for entry clearance or permission to stay and they have not previously had permission on the Hong Kong BN(O) route they must be the parent, grandparent, brother, sister, son or daughter of a person who is making an application for entry clearance or permission to stay as a BN(O) Status Holder or as the partner of a BN(O) Status Holder at the same time as the applicant.

HK 48.3. Where the applicant is the parent or grandparent of a BN(O) Status Holder or of the partner of a BN(O) Status Holder, the applicant must not be in a subsisting relationship with a partner unless:

(a) that partner is also the parent or grandparent of the BN(O) Status Holder or of the partner of a BN(O) Status Holder; and

(b) that partner is applying for entry clearance or permission to stay at the same time as the applicant.

Dependency requirement for a BN(O) Adult Dependent Relative

HK 49.1. If the applicant is applying for permission to stay and they have permission as a BN(O) Adult Dependent Relative on the BN(O) Status Holder route on the date of application, they will meet the dependency requirement.

HK 49.2 Where the applicant is applying for entry clearance or permission to stay and they have not previously had permission on the Hong Kong BN(O) route the applicant must:

(a) as a result of age, illness or disability require long-term personal care to perform everyday tasks; and

(b) form part of the same household as the BN(O) Status Holder who has, or is at the same time being granted, permission; and

(c) be unable, even with the practical and financial help of the BN(O) Status Holder or the partner of the BN(O) Status Holder, to obtain the required level of help in Hong Kong, if the BN(O) Status Holder or the partner of the BN(O) Status Holder move to the UK, either because the help:

(i) is not available, and there is no person in Hong Kong who can reasonably provide it; or

(ii) is not affordable.

HK 49.3. In HK 49.2.(b) a person will form part of the same household as the BN(O) Status Holder if they normally live with the BN(O) Status Holder.

HK 49.4. Where the applicant and their partner are the parents or grandparents of the BN(O) Status Holder, or of the partner of the BN(O) Status Holder, the applicant, or their partner, must:

(a) as a result of age, illness or disability require long-term personal care to perform everyday tasks; and

(b) be unable, even with the practical and financial help of the BN(O) Status Holder or the partner of the BN(O) Status Holder, to obtain the required level of help in Hong Kong if the BN(O) Status Holder or the partner of the BN(O) Status Holder move to the UK either because the help:

(i) is not available and there is no person in Hong Kong who can reasonably provide it; or

(ii) is not affordable.

Financial requirement for a BN(O) Adult Dependent Relative

[**HK 50.1.** If the applicant is applying for permission to stay and has been living in the UK with permission for 12 months or more on the date of application, they will meet the financial requirement unless the applicant's previous grant of permission was for 12 months Leave Outside the Rules following an unsuccessful application for the Hong Kong British National (Overseas) route.]

Note: Paragraph substituted from 6 April 2021 subject to savings for applications made before that date (HC 1248).

[**HK 50.2.** If the BN(O) Adult Dependent Relative is applying for entry clearance, or is applying for permission to stay and has been in the UK for less than 12 months on the date of application, or where the applicant's previous grant of permission was for 12 months Leave Outside the Rules following an unsuccessful application for the Hong Kong British National (Overseas) route, the decision maker must be satisfied that the BN(O) Status Holder or their partner is able to and will maintain and accommodate the BN(O) Adult Dependent Relative adequately in the UK without recourse to public funds for at least 6 months.]

Note: Paragraph substituted from 6 April 2021 subject to savings for applications made before that date (HC 1248).

HK 50.3. For the purposes of HK 50.2. accommodation will not be regarded as adequate if:

(a) it is or will be overcrowded; or

(b) it contravenes public health regulations.

HK 50.4. The BN(O) Status Holder or their partner may rely on credible promises of future third party support.

HK 50.5. The BN(O) Status Holder or their partner must show that they have the required funds as specified in Appendix Finance.

Ordinary residence in Hong Kong requirement for a BN(O) Adult Dependent Relative

HK 51.1. If the applicant is applying for entry clearance as a BN(O) Adult Dependent Relative the applicant must be ordinarily resident in Hong Kong on the date of application.

HK 51.2. An applicant applying for permission to stay must be in the UK and must be ordinarily resident in the UK, the Bailiwick of Guernsey, Bailiwick of Jersey, the Isle of Man or Hong Kong on the date of application.

In-country tuberculosis certificate requirement for a BN(O) Adult Dependent Relative

HK 52.1. If the applicant is applying for permission to stay and:

(a) their last grant of permission was for 6 months or less; and

(b) the applicant was present in a country listed in Appendix T of these rules for more than six months immediately prior to their last grant of permission, the applicant must provide a valid medical certificate confirming that they have undergone screening for active pulmonary tuberculosis and that this tuberculosis is not present in them.

HK 52.2. In HK 52.1. a valid medical certificate is a certificate from an approved centre issued within the 6 months immediately before the date of application.

HK 52.3. The in-country tuberculosis requirement is met where the applicant provided a medical certificate described in HK 52.1. as part of a successful application for entry clearance in the 12 months before the date of application.

HK 52.4. The list of approved centres in the UK, updated from time to time, can be found at: https://www.gov.uk/government/publications/uk-tuberculosis-test-clinics-for-hong-kong-bno.

Decision on application as a BN(O) Adult Dependent Relative

HK 53.1. If the decision maker is satisfied that all the suitability and eligibility requirements for a BN(O) Adult Dependent Relative are met the application will be granted, otherwise the application will be refused.

HK 53.2. If the application is refused the person can apply for an Administrative Review under Appendix AR: Administrative Review.

Period and conditions of grant for a BN(O) Adult Dependent Relative

HK 54.1. If the applicant does not have permission on the BN(O) Status Holder route on the date of application, they will be granted permission which ends on the same date as the permission of the BN(O) Status Holder who is part of the same household as the applicant.

HK 54.2. If the BN(O) Adult Dependent Relative has permission on the BN(O) Status Holder route on the date of application, they will be granted permission which ends on the same date as the permission of a BN(O) Status Holder or where relevant the partner of a BN(O) Status Holder who has, or is at the same time being granted, permission.

HK 54.3. The grant will be subject to all the following conditions:

(a) no access to public funds; and

(b) work (including self-employment and voluntary work) permitted except for employment as a professional sportsperson, including as a sports coach; and

(c) study is permitted, subject to the ATAS condition in Appendix ATAS; and

(d) if Part 10 applies the applicant will be required to register with the police.

Settlement on the Hong Kong BN(O) route

Validity requirements for Settlement on the Hong Kong BN(O) route

HK 55.1. A person applying for settlement on the Hong Kong BN(O) route must apply online on the gov.uk website on the specified form as follows:

[Applicant	Specified form
– All applicants	• Set (O) form]

Note: Table substituted from 6 April 2021 subject to savings for applications made before that date (HC 1248).

HK 55.2. An application for settlement on the Hong Kong BN(O) route must meet all the following requirements:

(a) any fee must have been paid; and

(b) the applicant must have provided any required biometrics; and

(c) the applicant must have provided a passport or other travel document which satisfactorily establishes their identity and nationality;

(d) the applicant must have, or have last had, permission on the Hong Kong BN(O) route; and

(e) the applicant must be in the UK.

HK 55.3. An application which does not meet the validity requirements for settlement on the BN(O) route is invalid and may be rejected and not considered.

Suitability requirements for settlement on the Hong Kong BN(O) route

HK 56.1. The applicant must not fall for refusal under Part 9: grounds for refusal.

HK 56.2. The applicant must not be:

(a) in breach of immigration laws, except that where paragraph 39E applies, that period of overstaying will be disregarded; or

(b) on immigration bail.

Eligibility Requirements for Settlement on the Hong Kong BN(O) route

Relationship requirement for settlement as a dependent child on the Hong Kong BN(O) route

HK 57.1. Where the applicant is under 18 on the date of application the additional requirements in HK 57.2. to HK 57.4. must be met.

HK 57.2. The applicant must have last been granted permission as a dependent child on the Hong Kong BN(O) route.

HK 57.3. The applicant's parent must:

(a) at the same time, be being granted settlement on the Hong Kong BN(O) route; or

(b) be settled or a British citizen.

HK 57.4. The applicant's other parent (who is not the parent in HK 57.3.) must be being granted settlement at the same time, or be settled or a British citizen, unless:

(a) the parent in HK 57.3. is the applicant's sole surviving parent; or

(b) the parent in HK 57.3. has sole responsibility for the applicant's upbringing; or

(c) the decision maker is satisfied that there are serious and compelling reasons to grant the applicant settlement.

Care requirement for settlement as a dependent child on the Hong Kong BN(O) route

HK 58.1. If the applicant is under the age of 18 on the date of application there must be suitable arrangements for the child's care and accommodation in the UK, which must comply with relevant UK legislation and regulations.

Relationship requirement for settlement as an adult dependant relative on the Hong Kong BN(O) route

HK 59.1. Where the applicant has or last had permission as an adult dependant relative on the Hong Kong BN(O) route, they must be the parent, grandparent, brother, sister, son or daughter of a person who:

(a) last had permission as a BN(O) Status Holder or the partner of a BN(O) Status Holder and who is at the same time being granted settlement on the Hong Kong BN(O) route; or

(b) is settled and whose last grant of permission prior to settlement was as a BN(O) Status Holder or the partner of a BN(O) Status Holder; or

(c) is a British citizen.

English language requirement for settlement on the Hong Kong BN(O) route

HK 60.1. Unless an exemption applies, the applicant must show English language ability on the Common European Framework of Reference for Languages in speaking and listening to at least level B1.

HK 60.2. The applicant must show they meet the English Language requirement as specified in Appendix English Language.

Knowledge of Life in the UK requirement for settlement on the Hong Kong BN(O) route

HK 61.1. If the applicant is aged 18 or over, and under 65 on the date of application, they must meet the Knowledge of Life in the UK requirement as specified in Appendix KOL UK.

Qualifying period for settlement on the BN(O) route

[**HK 62.1.** The applicant must have spent a continuous period of 5 years with permission in the UK on a route under which a person can settle, of which the most recent grant of permission must have been on the Hong Kong BN(O) route.]

Note: Paragraph substituted from 6 April 2021 subject to savings for applications made before that date (HC 1248).

Continuous Residence requirement for settlement on the Hong Kong BN(O) route

[**HK 63.1.** The applicant must meet the continuous residence requirement as specified in Appendix Continuous Residence during the period in HK 62.1.]

Note: Paragraph substituted from 6 April 2021 subject to savings for applications made before that date (HC 1248).

Decision on an application for settlement on the Hong Kong BN(O) route

[**HK 64.1.** If the decision maker is satisfied all the suitability and eligibility requirements for settlement are met the applicant will be granted settlement.]

Note: Paragraph substituted from 6 April 2022 subject to savings for applications made before that date (HC 1118).

[**HK 64.1A.** If the requirements for settlement are not met, but the decision maker believes the applicant is likely to meet all the suitability and eligibility requirements for permission to stay under Appendix Hong Kong BN(O) (based on the route under which they have or last had permission), the application will be varied by the Secretary of State to an application for permission to stay on that route.
Where this happens:

(a) no additional application fee for permission to stay will be required and the settlement application fee will not be refunded; and

(b) the Secretary of State will write to the applicant informing them of this variation and if required will request the applicant pay any Immigration Health Charge.]

Note: Paragraph inserted from 6 April 2022 subject to savings for applications made before that date (HC 1118).

[**HK 64.1B.** If the applicant does not pay the requested Immigration Health Charge, the application for permission to stay will be rejected as invalid.]

Note: Paragraph inserted from 6 April 2022 subject to savings for applications made before that date (HC 1118).

[**HK 64.1C.** Where an applicant is granted permission to stay it will be granted for 30 months and subject to the following conditions:

(a) no access to public funds; and

(b) work (including self-employment and voluntary work) permitted except for employment as a professional sportsperson (including as a sports coach); and

(c) study is permitted, subject to the ATAS condition in Appendix ATAS; and

(d) if Part 10 applies the applicant will be required to register with the police.]

Note: Paragraph inserted from 6 April 2022 subject to savings for applications made before that date (HC 1118).

[**HK 64.1D.** If the decision maker is not satisfied that the applicant meets all the suitability and eligibility requirements for settlement or permission to stay, the application for settlement will be refused.]

Note: Paragraph inserted from 6 April 2022 subject to savings for applications made before that date (HC 1118).

HK 64.2. If the application is refused, a request can be made for an Administrative Review under Appendix AR: Administrative Review.]

[Variation of no access to public funds condition]

[**HK 65.1** A person in the UK with permission on the Hong Kong BN(O) route may have that permission varied to remove a no access to public funds condition where they have provided the decision-maker with:

(a) satisfactory evidence that the applicant is destitute or at imminent risk of destitution as defined in section 95 of the Immigration and Asylum Act 1999; or

(b) satisfactory evidence that there are particularly compelling reasons relating to the welfare of a child of a parent in receipt of a very low income or the applicant is facing exceptional financial circumstances relating to a very low income.]

Note: Heading and paragraph inserted from 6 April 2021 subject to savings for applications made before that date (HC 1248).

Note: Appendix inserted from 31 January 2021 (HC 813).

[Appendix Ukraine Scheme

This Appendix sets out 3 routes for those affected by the conflict in Ukraine – the Ukraine Family Scheme, the Homes for Ukraine Sponsorship Scheme and the Ukraine Extension Scheme.

Where the applicant is outside the UK:

The applicant must have been living in Ukraine immediately before 1 January 2022.

A Ukrainian national can qualify under the ***Ukraine Family Scheme*** *if they are a family member (as defined) of a UK-based sponsor who is a British citizen, person settled in the UK, refugee, person with humanitarian protection, or EEA or Swiss citizen with pre-settled status under the EU Settlement Scheme (where based on residence in the UK before the end of the transition period).*

Family members for the purpose of this Scheme are immediate family members (meaning a partner, child under 18, parent of a child aged under 18, fiancé(e) or proposed civil partner), and extended family members of the UK-based sponsor or their partner (meaning parent, grandparent, grandchild, adult child, sibling, aunt, uncle, niece, nephew, and cousin) and the immediate family members of extended family members of the UK-based sponsor or their partner.

A Ukrainian national may also qualify under the **Homes for Ukraine Sponsorship Scheme** *if they have an Approved sponsor who will provide accommodation for at least 6 months.*

[A child who is not applying with, or intending to join, their parent or legal guardian in the UK must have an Approved sponsor who was approved for the child by a Local Authority before the application is made and must have agreed to accommodate the child for at least 3 years or until the child is 18 so long as they are sponsored for at least 6 months (whichever is soonest).]

Family members of a UK-based sponsor who are not Ukrainian nationals may also qualify under the **Ukraine Family Scheme** *so long as at least one member of the UK-based sponsor's immediate family is a Ukrainian national.*

Immediate family members of a Ukrainian who are not themselves Ukrainian nationals may also qualify under the **Homes for Ukraine Sponsorship Scheme**. *[Grandparents, uncles, aunts and adult siblings who are applying with a child who is not either applying with their parent or legal guardian or applying to join their parent or legal guardian may also qualify under the Homes for Ukraine Sponsorship Scheme.]*

Where the applicant is in the UK:

The applicant must have immigration permission unless their last permission expired after 1 January 2022.

A Ukrainian national can qualify under the **Ukraine Extension Scheme** *if they are in the UK with immigration permission on 18 March 2022 or if their last permission ended after 1 January 2022. [. . .]*

A person who has immigration permission as a partner or child of a Ukrainian national who qualifies under the **Ukraine Extension Scheme**, *who is not themselves a Ukrainian national, can also qualify under the* **Ukraine Extension Scheme**. *[. . .]*

A Ukrainian national may also qualify under the **Ukraine Family Scheme** *if they are a family member of a UK- based sponsor as described above.*

Family members who are not Ukrainian nationals may also qualify under the Ukraine Family Scheme so long as at least one member of the UK-based sponsor's immediate family is a Ukrainian national.

Further information on immigration issues related to Ukraine is available at https://www.gov.uk/guidance/support-for-family-members-of-british-nationals-in-ukraine-and-ukrainian-nationals-in-ukraine-and-the-uk.

Note: Words inserted, words deleted from 10 August 2022 (HC 511).

Ukraine Family Scheme

Validity requirements for the Ukraine Family Scheme

UKR 1.1. A person applying for entry clearance or permission to stay under the Ukraine Family Scheme must apply online on the gov.uk website on the specified form as follows: "Ukraine Scheme".

UKR 1.2. An application for entry clearance or permission to stay under the Ukraine Family Scheme must meet all the following requirements:

(a) the applicant must have provided any required biometrics; and

(b) the applicant must have provided a passport or other document which satisfactorily established their identity and nationality.

UKR 1.3. An application which does not meet all the validity requirements for the Ukraine Family Scheme is invalid and may be rejected and not considered.

Suitability requirements for the Ukraine Family Scheme

UKR 2.1. The applicant must not fall for refusal under any of the following paragraphs of Part 9: grounds for refusal:

(a) 9.2.1 to 9.2.2 (exclusion or deportation orders); or

(b) 9.3.1 to 9.3.2 (non-conducive); or

(c) 9.4.1 to 9.4.5 (criminality); or

(d) 9.5.1 to 9.5.2 (exclusion from asylum or humanitarian protection); or

(e) 9.6.1 to 9.6.2 (involvement in sham marriage or sham civil partnership); or

(f) 9.7.1 to 9.7.3 (false representations and deception); or

(g) 9.10.1 to 9.10.2 (admissibility to the Common Travel Area or other countries); or

(h) 9.14.1 to 9.20.2 and 9.23.1 to 9.24.1 (grounds for refusal and cancellation on arrival).

Eligibility requirements for the Ukraine Family Scheme

Entry requirements for the Ukraine Family Scheme

UKR 3.1. A person seeking to come to the UK under the Ukraine Family Scheme must apply for entry clearance and must have been:

(a) granted entry clearance under the Ukraine Scheme; or

(b) given a letter from the Home Office confirming the applicant can travel to the UK under the Ukraine Scheme, before they arrive in the UK.

Variation of entry clearance application after arrival for person given letter authorising travel to UK

UKR 4.1. A person who:

(a) has made an application for entry clearance which has not been decided; and

(b) has been given a letter from the Home Office confirming the applicant can travel to the UK; and

(c) is granted permission to enter on arrival in the UK; and

(d) provides their biometrics after arrival in the UK, may have their application for entry clearance varied by the Secretary of State to an application for permission to stay.

Residence requirement for the Ukraine Family Scheme

UKR 5.1. An applicant applying for entry clearance under the Ukraine Family Scheme must have been ordinarily resident in Ukraine immediately before 1 January 2022, unless they are a child born on or after that date.

UKR 5.2. An applicant applying for permission to stay under the Ukraine Family Scheme must be in the UK and either:

(a) have permission; or

(b) have had permission immediately before 1 January 2022 which has since expired, but permission as a visitor granted after 18 March 2022 does not count as permission for the purpose of this requirement.

Relationship requirement for a family member under the Ukraine Family Scheme

UKR 6.1. The applicant must be the family member (as set out at UKR 6.2.) of a UK-based sponsor who is one of the following:

(a) a British citizen; or

(b) a person who is settled in the UK; or

(c) a person in the UK with limited permission as a refugee or person granted humanitarian protection; or

(d) an EEA national in the UK with limited permission granted under paragraph EU3 of Appendix EU on the basis of meeting condition 1 in paragraph EU14 of that Appendix (that is with pre-settled status granted under the EU Settlement Scheme on the basis they were living in the UK before 2300 GMT on 31 December 2020).

UKR 6.2. Where applying as a family member under UKR 6.1., the applicant must be a family member in one of the following relationships (and, if the applicant is not Ukrainian, at least one of the immediate family members under (a) must be a Ukrainian national as in UKR 7.1.):

(a) an immediate family member meaning the:

(i) partner of the UK-based sponsor; or

(ii) child aged under 18 on the date of application of the UK-based sponsor or of the UK-based sponsor's partner; or

(iii) parent of a child (who is under 18 on the date of application), where the child is the UK-based sponsor; or

(iv) fiancé(e) or proposed civil partner of the UK-based sponsor; or

(b) extended family member, meaning a:

(i) parent of a UK-based sponsor, or of the UK-based sponsor's partner (where the sponsor or partner is aged 18 or over on the date of application); or

(ii) parent of the UK-based sponsor's child or of the UK-based sponsor's partner's child (where the child is under 18 on the date of application); or

(iii) grandparent of the UK-based sponsor or of the UK-based sponsor's partner; or

(iv) grandchild of the UK-based sponsor or of the UK-based sponsor's partner; or

(v) sibling of the UK-based sponsor or of the UK-based sponsor's partner; or

(vi) adult child (aged 18 or over on the date of application) of the UK-based sponsor or of the UK-based sponsor's partner; or

(vii) aunt or uncle of the UK-based sponsor; or

(viii) cousin of the UK-based sponsor; or

(ix) niece or nephew of the UK-based sponsor; or

(c) an immediate family member of an extended family member, meaning a:

(i) partner of an extended family member; or

(ii) child aged under 18 on the date of application of an extended family member; or

(iii) parent of a child aged under 18 on the date of application, where the child is the extended family member; or

(iv) fiancé(e) or proposed civil partner of an extended family member.

UKR 6.3. An applicant applying as a partner, fiancé(e) or proposed civil partner must be in a genuine and subsisting relationship with the UK-based sponsor or extended family member which commenced before 1 January 2022.

UKR 6.4. An applicant who is applying as a partner must meet the requirements in Appendix Relationship with Partner.

[Suitability of UK based sponsor requirement]

Note: Heading inserted from 10 August 2022 (HC 511).

[**UKR 6A.1.** Where an applicant is a child, the UK-based sponsor (under UKR 6.1) must not previously have failed to meet the requirements for approval as a sponsor under the Homes for Ukraine Scheme under the guidance: 'Homes for Ukraine - Applications to Homes for Ukraine for children who are not travelling or reuniting with their parent or legal guardian: Guidance for Councils'.]

Note: Paragraph inserted from 10 August 2022 (HC 511).

Nationality requirement for the Ukraine Family Scheme

UKR 7.1. The applicant must be either:
(a) a Ukrainian national; or
(b) part of a family group (meaning a group of people as set in UKR 6.2.) which includes an immediate family member of the UK-based sponsor who is a Ukrainian national who would qualify under the scheme (whether or not applying at the same time as the applicant).

Parental consent requirement for a child applying under the Ukraine Family Scheme

UKR 8.1. If the applicant is aged under 18 on the date of application and they are not accompanying a parent to, or joining a parent in, the UK, they must have written consent from:
(a) both parents; or
(b) one parent, if that parent has sole legal responsibility for the applicant; or
(c) the applicant's legal guardian, unless the decision-maker is satisfied it is reasonable in the circumstances to grant the child entry clearance or permission without such consent.

UKR 8.2. The written consent must confirm support for all the following:
(a) the application; and
(b) the applicant's living and care arrangements in the UK; and
(c) if the application is for entry clearance, the applicant's travel to, and reception arrangements in, the UK.

Decision under the Ukraine Family Scheme

UKR 9.1. If the decision-maker is satisfied that all the suitability and eligibility requirements under the Ukraine Family Scheme are met, the application will be granted otherwise the application will be refused.

Period and conditions of grant under the Ukraine Family Scheme

UKR 10.1. The applicant will be granted permission for whatever is the shorter of either:
(a) 36 months; or

(b) a period which would mean the applicant has been granted a maximum of 36 months under the Ukraine Scheme.

UKR 10.2. The permission will be granted subject to the following conditions:

(a) access to public funds permitted; and

(b) work (including self-employment and voluntary work) permitted; and

(c) study permitted, subject to the ATAS condition in Appendix ATAS.

Homes for Ukraine Sponsorship Scheme

Validity requirements for the Homes for Ukraine Sponsorship Scheme

UKR 11.1. A person applying for entry clearance under the Homes for Ukraine Sponsorship Scheme must apply online on the gov.uk website on the specified form as follows: 'Ukraine Scheme'.

UKR 11.2. An application for entry clearance under the Homes for Ukraine Sponsorship Scheme must meet all the following requirements:

(a) the applicant must have provided any required biometrics; and

(b) the applicant must have provided a passport or other document which satisfactorily established their identity and nationality; and

(c) the applicant must be outside the UK on the date of application: and

(d) the applicant must have provided the name of a UK sponsor who has offered them accommodation in the UK.

[**UKR 11.3.** Where the applicant is aged under 18 on the date of application they must either:

(a) be applying with, or to join in the UK, their parent or legal guardian; or

(b) their sponsor must have been approved as a sponsor for that applicant under the Homes for Ukraine Scheme under the guidance: 'Homes for Ukraine - Applications to Homes for Ukraine for children who are not travelling or reuniting with their parent or legal guardian: Guidance for Councils' before the date of application and the applicant must provide evidence of that approval in the form of a reference number.]

Note: Paragraph substituted from 10 August 2022 (HC 511).

[**UKR 11.3A.** Where an application under the Homes for Ukraine Sponsorship Scheme is varied to permission to stay under paragraph UKR 14.1, they must meet all the following requirements:

(a) the applicant must have provided any required biometrics; and

(b) the applicant must have provided a passport or other document which satisfactorily established their identity and nationality; and

(c) the applicant must be in the UK.]

Note: Paragraph inserted from 16:00 on 11 May 2022 subject to savings for applications made before that time (HC 17).

UKR 11.4. An application which does not meet all the validity requirements for the Homes for Ukraine Sponsorship Scheme is invalid and may be rejected and not considered.

Suitability requirements for the Homes for Ukraine Sponsorship Scheme

UKR 12.1. The applicant must not fall for refusal under any of the following paragraphs of Part 9: grounds for refusal:

(a) 9.2.1 to 9.2.2 (exclusion or deportation orders); or
(b) 9.3.1 to 9.3.2 (non-conducive); or
(c) 9.4.1 to 9.4.5 (criminality); or
(d) 9.5.1 to 9.5.2 (exclusion from asylum or humanitarian protection); or
(e) 9.6.1 to 9.6.2 (involvement in sham marriage or sham civil partnership); or
(f) 9.7.1 to 9.7.3 (false representations and deception); or
(g) 9.10.1 to 9.10.2 (admissibility to the Common Travel Area or other countries); or
(h) 9.14.1 to 9.20.2 and 9.23.1 to 9.24.1 (grounds for refusal and cancellation on arrival).

Eligibility requirements for the Homes for Ukraine Sponsorship Scheme

Entry requirements for the Homes for Ukraine Sponsorship Scheme

UKR 13.1. A person seeking to come to the UK under the Homes for Ukraine Sponsorship Scheme must apply for entry clearance and must have been:
(a) granted entry clearance; or
(b) given a letter from the Home Office confirming the applicant can travel to the UK, under the Ukraine Scheme before they arrive in the UK.

Variation of entry clearance application after arrival for person holding permission to travel on arrival

UKR 14.1. A person who:
(a) has made an application for entry clearance which has not been decided; and
(b) has been given a letter from the Home Office confirming the applicant can travel to the UK under a Ukraine Scheme; and
(c) is granted permission to enter on arrival in the UK; and
(d) provides any required biometrics after arrival in the UK, may have their application for entry clearance varied by the Secretary of State to an application for permission to stay.

Approved sponsor requirement for the Homes for Ukraine Sponsorship Scheme

UKR 15.1. An applicant under the Homes for Ukraine Sponsorship Scheme must have an Approved sponsor under the Homes for Ukraine Sponsorship Scheme.

UKR 15.2. Where a family group is applying under the Homes for Ukraine Sponsorship Scheme, the Ukrainian national and their immediate family members (as described in UKR 18.1.) must have the same Approved sponsor under the Homes for Ukraine Sponsorship Scheme.

[**UKR 15.3.** Where an applicant is a child, the Approved sponsor must not previously have failed to meet the requirements for approval as a sponsor under the Homes for Ukraine Scheme under the guidance: 'Homes for Ukraine - Applications to Homes for Ukraine for children who are not travelling or reuniting with their parent or legal guardian: Guidance for Councils'.]

Note: Paragraph inserted from 10 August 2022 (HC 511).

[**UKR 15.4.** Where a child is not applying with or to join their parent or legal guardian, but they are applying with or to join an adult relative (meaning a grandparent, uncle, aunt or sibling aged 18 or over) who qualifies under the Homes for Ukraine Sponsorship Scheme, the child and the adult relative must have the same Approved sponsor.]

Note: Paragraph inserted from 10 August 2022 (HC 511).

Residence requirement for the Homes for Ukraine Sponsorship Scheme

UKR 16.1. An applicant applying for entry clearance under the Homes for Ukraine Sponsorship Scheme must have been ordinarily resident in Ukraine immediately before 1 January 2022, unless they are a child born on or after that date.

Nationality requirement for the Homes for Ukraine Sponsorship Scheme

UKR 17.1. The applicant must be either:

(a) a Ukrainian national; or

[(b) part of an immediate family group (meaning the group set out in UKR 18.1.) which includes an immediate family member who is a Ukrainian national who has been granted under or is applying under and qualifies under the Homes for Ukraine Sponsorship Scheme.]

Note: Sub-paragraph (b) substituted from 10 August 2022 (HC 511).

Relationship requirement for a family member under the Homes for Ukraine Sponsorship Scheme

UKR 18.1. If the applicant is not a Ukrainian national, they must be the immediate family member of a Ukrainian national who qualifies under the Homes for Ukraine Sponsorship Scheme, meaning a:

(a) partner of the Ukrainian national; or

(b) child aged under 18 on the date of application of the Ukrainian national or of their partner; or

(c) parent of a Ukrainian national child aged under 18 (where the child is applying under the Homes for Ukraine Sponsorship Scheme); or

(d) fiancé(e) or proposed civil partner of the Ukrainian national.

UKR 18.2. An applicant applying as a partner, fiancé(e) or proposed civil partner must be in a genuine and subsisting relationship with the Ukrainian national which commenced before 1 January 2022.

UKR 18.3. An applicant who is applying as a partner must meet the requirements in Appendix Relationship with Partner.

[Parental consent requirement for a child applying to join a parent or legal guardian in the UK under the Homes for Ukraine Sponsorship Scheme]

Note: Heading inserted from 16:00 on 11 May 2022 subject to savings for applications made before that time (HC 17).

[**UKR 19A.1.** If the applicant is aged under 18 on the date of application and they are joining (and not accompanying) a parent or legal guardian in the UK, they must have written consent from the parent or legal guardian in the UK who they are joining, unless the decision-maker is satisfied it is reasonable in the circumstances to grant the child entry clearance without that consent.]

Note: Paragraph inserted from 16:00 on 11 May 2022 subject to savings for applications made before that time (HC 17).

[**UKR 19A.2.** The written consent must confirm support for all of the following:
(a) the application; and
(b) that applicant will live with the parent in the UK; and
(c) the applicant's travel to, and reception arrangements in, the UK.]

Note: Paragraph inserted from 16:00 on 11 May 2022 subject to savings for applications made before that time (HC 17).

[Parental consent requirement for a child applying without their parent or legal guardian]

Note: Heading inserted from 10 August 2022 (HC 511).

[**UKR 19B.1.** Where a child is not applying with, or to join in the UK, a parent or legal guardian the applicant must have provided written parental consent to the child coming to live in the UK with the named sponsor (who was approved under UKR 11.3(b)) and any adult relative who is applying with the child. The consent must be signed by at least one parent or the child's legal guardian, and notarised or approved by:
(a) the notary authorities or Guardianship service of the city/regional council in Ukraine; or
(b) where the applicant is outside Ukraine, notary authorities or a Ukrainian consul.]

Note: Paragraph inserted from 10 August 2022 (HC 511).

Decision under the Homes for Ukraine Sponsorship Scheme

UKR 19.1. If the decision-maker is satisfied that all the suitability and eligibility requirements under the Homes for Ukraine Sponsorship Scheme are met, the application will be granted; otherwise, the application will be refused.

Period and conditions of grant under the Homes for Ukraine Sponsorship Scheme

UKR 20.1. The applicant will be granted permission for a period of up to 36 months.

UKR 20.2. The permission will be granted subject to the following conditions:
(a) access to public funds permitted; and
(b) work (including self-employment and voluntary work) permitted; and
(c) study permitted, subject to the ATAS condition in Appendix ATAS.

Ukraine Extension Scheme

Validity requirements for the Ukraine Extension Scheme

UKR 21.1. A person applying for permission to stay under the Ukraine Extension Scheme must apply online on the gov.uk website on the specified form as follows: "Ukraine Scheme".

UKR 21.2. An application for permission to stay under the Ukraine Extension Scheme must meet all the following requirements:
(a) the applicant must have provided any required biometrics; and

(b) the applicant must have provided a passport or other document which satisfactorily established their identity and nationality; and

(c) the applicant must be in the UK.

[**UKR 21.3.** The applicant must have had permission to enter or stay in the UK on 18 March 2022, unless:

(a) they had permission to enter or stay in the UK immediately before 1 January, but that permission has since expired; or

(b) they are a child born in the UK to a parent who qualifies under this paragraph.]

Note: Paragraph substituted from 16:00 on 11 May 2022 subject to savings for applications made before that time (HC 17).

UKR 21.4. An application which does not meet all the validity requirements for the Ukraine Extension Scheme is invalid and may be rejected and not considered.

Suitability requirements for the Ukraine Extension Scheme

UKR 22.1. The applicant must not fall for refusal under any of the following paragraphs of Part 9: grounds for refusal:

(a) 9.2.1 to 9.2.2 (exclusion or deportation orders); or

(b) 9.3.1 to 9.3.2 (non-conducive); or

(c) 9.4.1 to 9.4.5 (criminality); or

(d) 9.5.1 to 9.5.2 (exclusion from asylum or humanitarian protection); or

(e) 9.6.1 to 9.6.2 (involvement in sham marriage or sham civil partnership); or

(f) 9.7.1 to 9.7.3 (false representations and deception); or

(g) 9.10.1 to 9.10.2 (admissibility to the Common Travel Area or other countries); or

(h) 9.14.1 to 9.20.2 and 9.23.1 to 9.24.1 (grounds for refusal and cancellation on arrival).

Eligibility requirements for the Ukraine Extension Scheme

Nationality requirement for the Ukraine Extension Scheme

UKR 23.1. The applicant must be either:

(a) a Ukrainian national; or

(b) a person who has or last had permission as:

(i) a partner of a Ukrainian national; or

(ii) a child of a Ukrainian national; or

(c) a child of a Ukrainian national born in the UK after 18 March 2022.

Relationship requirement for a partner or child under the Ukraine Extension Scheme

UKR 24.1. An applicant who is a partner must meet the requirements in Appendix Relationship with Partner.

UKR 24.2. A child born in the UK must provide a full UK birth certificate.

Parental consent requirement for a child applying under the Ukraine Extension Scheme

UKR 25.1. If the applicant is aged under 18 on the date of application and they are not applying with their parent or parents, they must have written consent from:

(a) both parents; or

(b) one parent, if that parent has sole legal responsibility for the applicant; or

(c) the applicant's legal guardian, unless the decision-maker is satisfied it is reasonable in the circumstances to grant the child permission without such consent.

UKR 25.2. The written consent must confirm support for:

(a) the application; and

(b) the applicant's living and care arrangements in the UK.

Care requirement for a child under the Ukraine Extension Scheme

UKR 26.1. If the applicant is aged under 18 on the date of application, there must be suitable arrangements for the child's care and accommodation in the UK, which must comply with relevant UK legislation and regulations.

Decision under the Ukraine Extension Scheme

UKR 27.1. If the decision-maker is satisfied that all the suitability and eligibility requirements under the Ukraine Extension Scheme are met, the application will be granted; otherwise, the application will be refused.

Period and conditions of grant under the Ukraine Extension Scheme

UKR 28.1. The applicant will be granted permission to stay for whatever is the shorter of either:

(a) 36 months; or

(b) a period which would mean the applicant has been granted a maximum of 36 months under the Ukraine Scheme.

UKR 28.2. The permission will be granted subject to the following conditions:

(a) access to public funds permitted; and

(b) work (including self-employment and voluntary work) permitted; and

(c) study permitted, subject to the ATAS condition in Appendix ATAS.

Note: Appendix inserted from 30 March 2022 save that provisions relating to the Ukraine Extension Scheme take effect from 3 May 2022 (HC 1220).

[Appendix Private Life

The Private Life route is for a person seeking permission to stay in the UK on the basis they have developed a Private Life in the UK.

A child born in the UK to a person who has permission on the Private Life route can apply for permission for the same duration as their parent.

The Private Life route is a route to settlement.

A child born in the UK who has been continuously resident for 7 years may qualify for immediate settlement on this route.

Alternative routes may be available to those considering the Private Life route. For example, a person may be able to qualify for immediate settlement on the basis of 10 years Long Residence in the UK, under paragraphs 276A to 276D of these rules.]

Validity requirements for the Private Life route

PL 1.1. A person applying for permission to stay on the Private Life route must apply online on the gov.uk website on the specified form: 'Application to remain in the UK on the basis of family life or private life'.

PL 1.2. An application for permission to stay on the Private Life route must meet all the following validity requirements:

(a) any fee and Immigration Health Charge must have been paid (unless the applicant has been granted a fee waiver in whole or in part); and

(b) the applicant must have provided any required biometrics; and

(c) the applicant must have provided a passport or other document which satisfactorily establishes their identity and nationality; and

(d) the applicant must be in the UK on the date of application.

PL 1.3. If a private life claim is made under Article 8 of the Human Rights Convention and it is made:

(a) at the same time as a protection claim or further submission in person after a protection claim has been refused; or

(b) when the applicant is in detention (and the claim is submitted to a prison officer, custody officer or a member of Home Office staff at the place of detention); or

(c) during an appeal (subject to the consent of the Secretary of State where applicable), the requirements at PL 1.1. and at PL 1.2. (a) and (c) will be waived.

PL 1.4. An application which does not meet all the validity requirements for the Private Life route is invalid and may be rejected and not considered.

Suitability requirements on the Private Life route

PL 2.1. The application must not fall for refusal under the suitability grounds for refusal for leave to remain as set out in S-LTR.1.2. to S-LTR.2.2. and S-LTR.3.1. to S-LTR.4.5. of Appendix FM of these rules.

PL 2.2. The application must not fall for refusal under paragraph 9.6.1. (sham marriage or civil partnership) of Part 9: grounds for refusal.

Eligibility requirements on the Private Life route

Residence requirements for a child on the Private Life route

PL 3.1. Where the applicant is aged under 18 at the date of application the following requirements must be met:

(a) the applicant must have been continuously resident in the UK for at least 7 years; and

(b) the decision maker must be satisfied that it would not be reasonable to expect the applicant to leave the UK.

Residence requirements for a young adult on the Private Life route (where the applicant arrived in the UK as a child)

PL 4.1. Where the applicant is aged 18 or over and aged under 25 at the date of application and arrived in the UK before the age of 18, the applicant must have spent at least half their life continuously resident in the UK.

Residence requirements for an adult on the Private Life route (including a young adult who does not qualify under PL 4.1.)

PL 5.1. Where the applicant is aged 18 or over on the date of application:

(a) the applicant must have been continuously resident in the UK for more than 20 years; or

(b) where the applicant has not been continuously resident in the UK for more than 20 years, the decision maker must be satisfied there would be very significant obstacles to the applicant's integration into the country where they would have to live if required to leave the UK.

Exclusion of certain asylum seekers

[**PL 6.1.** An applicant who has made a protection or asylum claim which has been declared inadmissible under Part 11 of these rules before 28 June 2022, or under section 80B and 80C of the Nationality, Immigration and Asylum Act 2002, and which continues to be treated as inadmissible, cannot meet the requirement at PL 5.1(b).]

Note: Paragraph substituted from 10 August 2022 (HC 511).

Continuous Residence requirements on the Private Life route

PL 7.1. The period of continuous residence at PL 3.1, PL 4.1. or PL 5.1. may include time spent in the UK with or without permission.

PL 7.2. The period of continuous residence at PL 3.1, PL 4.1. or PL 5.1. does not include any period during which the applicant was serving a sentence of imprisonment.

PL 7.3. The period of continuous residence at PL 3.1, PL 4.1. or PL 5.1 is broken (i.e. is no longer continuous) if any of the following apply:

(a) the applicant has been absent from the UK for more than 6 months at any one time; or

(b) the applicant has spent a total of 550 days or more absent from the UK during the period of continuous residence at PL 3.1, PL 4.1 or PL 5.1; or

(c) the applicant has been removed, deported or has left the UK having had an application for permission to enter or stay in the UK refused; or

(d) the applicant left the UK with no reasonable expectation at the time of leaving that they would lawfully be able to return.

Eligibility requirement for Private Life route relying on Article 8 of the Human Rights Convention

[**PL 8.1.** If the applicant does not meet the suitability requirements (subject to PL 8.2), or does not meet any of the eligibility requirements in PL 3.1., PL 4.1. or PL 5.1. the decision maker must be satisfied that refusal of permission to stay would not breach Article 8 of the Human Rights Convention on the basis of private life.]

Note: Paragraph substituted from 10 August 2022 (HC 511).

PL 8.2. Where PL 8.1. applies and the applicant falls for refusal under suitability paragraphs S-LTR.1.2., S-LTR.1.3., S-LTR.1.4., S-LTR.1.5., S-LTR.1.6 or S-LTR 1.8. of Appendix FM of these rules the application on the Private Life route will be refused.

Decision on an application on the Private Life route

PL 9.1. If the decision maker is satisfied that all the suitability requirements are met and the eligibility requirements at PL 3.1, PL 4.1, PL 5.1 or PL.8.1. are met then, unless paragraph PL 8.2. applies, the applicant will be granted permission to stay on the Private Life route, otherwise the application will be refused.

Period and conditions of grant of permission to stay on the Private Life route

PL 10.1. If the applicant is under 18 at the date of application (or was under 18 when first granted permission on the private life route), they will be granted permission to stay for either:

(a) 30 months, where the applicant has applied for a period of 30 months; or

(b) 60 months, where the applicant has applied for a period of 60 months.

PL 10.2. If the applicant is a young adult who has spent half their life in the UK at the date of application (or was previously granted as a young adult on the private life route), they will be granted permission to stay for either:

(a) 30 months, where the applicant has applied for a period of 30 months; or

(b) 60 months, where the applicant has applied for a period of 60 months.

PL 10.3. In all other cases the applicant will be granted 30 months permission to stay.

PL 10.4. Where a person is seeking to extend their permission to stay, any remaining period of permission at the date of application will be added to their next grant of permission, up to a maximum of 28 days.

PL 10.5. The grant of permission will be subject to the following conditions:

(a) work (including self-employment and voluntary work) permitted; and

(b) study is permitted, subject to the ATAS condition in Appendix ATAS; and

(c) if the decision maker is satisfied that:

(i) the applicant is destitute, as defined in section 95 of the Immigration and Asylum Act 1999, or is at risk of imminent destitution; or

(ii) there are reasons relating to the welfare of a relevant child which outweigh the considerations for imposing or maintaining the condition (treating the best interests of the relevant child as a primary consideration), the applicant will not be subject to a condition of no access to public funds. If the decision maker is not so satisfied, the applicant will be subject to a condition of no access to public funds; and

(d) if Part 10 of these rules applies, the applicant will be required to register with the police.

PL 10.6. For the purposes of PL 10.5.(c)(ii) 'relevant child' means a person who:

(a) is under the age of 18 years at the date of application; and

(b) it is clear from the information provided by the applicant, is a child who would be affected by a decision to impose or maintain the no access to public funds condition.

Settlement on the Private Life route

Validity requirements for settlement on the Private Life route

PL 11.1. A person on the Private Life route who is applying for settlement must apply online on the gov.uk website on the specified form as follows:

Adult (aged 18 or over)	Settlement on the private life route
Child (aged under 18)	Settlement as a child (including a child aged over 18 already in the UK as a dependant)

PL 11.2. An application for settlement must meet all the following requirements:

(a) any fee must have been paid; and

(b) the applicant must have provided any required biometrics; and

(c) the applicant must have provided a passport or other travel document which satisfactorily establishes their identity and nationality; and

(d) the applicant must be in the UK on the date of application.

PL 11.3. An applicant must have, or have last been granted, permission on the Private Life route, unless they are a child who was born in the UK.

PL 11.4. An application which does not meet all the validity requirements for settlement on the Private Life route is invalid and may be rejected and not considered.

Suitability requirements for settlement on the Private Life route

PL 12.1. The applicant must not fall for refusal under:

(a) the suitability grounds for refusal for indefinite leave to remain applications under Appendix FM paragraphs:

(i) S-ILR.1.2, S-ILR.1.6 to S-ILR.1.10, S-ILR.3.1; or

(ii) S-ILR.2.2, S-ILR.4.2 to S-ILR.4.5 (subject to PL 12.4); or

(b) paragraph 9.6.1. of Part 9 of these rules (subject to PL 12.4).

PL 12.4. Where any of the following occur during the applicant's qualifying period for settlement, the applicant must be refused settlement unless the applicant has completed a continuous qualifying period of 10 years with permission as set out in PL 12.6. and has completed 5 years continuous residence with such permission after the date of the first grant of permission after the suitability ground came to the attention of the decision maker:

(a) involvement in a sham marriage or civil partnership (grounds for refusal under 9.6.1 of Part 9); or

(b) use of false documents or information or deception (S-ILR.2.2 and S-ILR.4.2 and S-ILR.4.3. of Appendix FM); or

(c) litigation debt owed to the Home Office, unless the debt has been paid (S-ILR.4.4 of Appendix FM); or

(d) debt to the NHS, unless the debt has been paid, or the total value of outstanding charges is under £500 (S-ILR.4.5. of Appendix FM); or

(e) the applicant has breached the conditions of their permission.

PL 12.5. Unless the applicant is a child or young adult who was granted permission to stay on the basis of private life under paragraphs PL 3.1. or PL 4.1, if the applicant entered the UK illegally settlement must be refused unless the applicant has completed a qualifying period of 10 years with permission under PL 12.6.

PL 12.6. Where an applicant must complete a qualifying period of 10 years continuous residence (under PL 12.3. to PL 12.5.), they must have had permission as (or as a combination of) the following for that 10 year qualifying period:

(a) entry clearance or permission granted as a partner or parent under Appendix FM (except for permission as a fiancé(e) or proposed civil partner); or

(b) permission described in the Home Office grant letter as "family permission as a parent" or "family permission as a partner"; or

(c) permission on the private life route under paragraph 276ADE or 276BE(2) before 20 June 2022 or Appendix Private Life; or

(d) entry clearance or permission as a child of a person with limited leave as a partner or parent under Appendix FM; or

(e) permission granted outside the rules as a partner, a parent or child or because of private life on the basis of Article 8 of the Human Rights Convention.

PL 12.7. The applicant must not be:

(a) in breach of immigration laws, except that where paragraph 39E applies, that period of overstaying will be disregarded; or

(b) on immigration bail.

Eligibility requirements for settlement on the Private Life route

Child born in the UK requirements for settlement on the Private life route

PL 13.1. The applicant must have been born in the UK and must provide a full UK birth certificate.

PL 12.2. The applicant must not have been convicted of a criminal offence in the UK or overseas for which they have received a custodial sentence of 12 months or more.

PL 12.3. The applicant must not have been convicted of an offence in the UK or overseas for which they have been sentenced to imprisonment for less than 12 months, unless the applicant has completed a qualifying period of 10 years continuous residence with permission as set out in PL 12.6. and has completed 5 years continuous residence with such permission since the end of their sentence.

PL 12.4. Where any of the following occur during the applicant's qualifying period for settlement, the applicant must be refused settlement unless the applicant has completed a continuous qualifying period of 10 years with permission as set out in PL 12.6. and has completed 5 years continuous residence with such permission after the date of the first grant of permission after the suitability ground came to the attention of the decision maker:

(a) involvement in a sham marriage or civil partnership (grounds for refusal under 9.6.1 of Part 9); or

(b) use of false documents or information or deception (S-ILR.2.2 and S-ILR.4.2 and S-ILR.4.3. of Appendix FM); or

(c) litigation debt owed to the Home Office, unless the debt has been paid (S-ILR.4.4 of Appendix FM); or

(d) debt to the NHS, unless the debt has been paid, or the total value of outstanding charges is under £500 (S-ILR.4.5. of Appendix FM); or

(e) the applicant has breached the conditions of their permission.

PL 12.5. Unless the applicant is a child or young adult who was granted permission to stay on the basis of private life under paragraphs PL 3.1. or PL 4.1, if the applicant entered the UK illegally settlement must be refused unless the applicant has completed a qualifying period of 10 years with permission under PL 12.6.

PL 12.6. Where an applicant must complete a qualifying period of 10 years continuous residence (under PL 12.3. to PL 12.5.), they must have had permission as (or as a combination of) the following for that 10 year qualifying period:

(a) entry clearance or permission granted as a partner or parent under Appendix FM (except for permission as a fiancé(e) or proposed civil partner); or

(b) permission described in the Home Office grant letter as "family permission as a parent" or "family permission as a partner"; or

(c) permission on the private life route under paragraph 276ADE or 276BE(2) before 20 June 2022 or Appendix Private Life; or

(d) entry clearance or permission as a child of a person with limited leave as a partner or parent under Appendix FM; or

(e) permission granted outside the rules as a partner, a parent or child or because of private life on the basis of Article 8 of the Human Rights Convention.

PL 12.7. The applicant must not be:

(a) in breach of immigration laws, except that where paragraph 39E applies, that period of overstaying will be disregarded; or

(b) on immigration bail.

Eligibility requirements for settlement on the Private Life route

Child born in the UK requirements for settlement on the Private life route

PL 13.1. The applicant must have been born in the UK and must provide a full UK birth certificate.

PL 13.2. The applicant must have lived continuously in the UK since their birth and for at least 7 years at the date of application.

PL 13.3. The decision maker must be satisfied that it is not reasonable to expect the applicant to leave the UK.

Qualifying period requirement for settlement on the Private Life route (where the applicant was not born in the UK)

PL 14.1. An applicant who has, or last had, permission to stay on the private life route as a child, or young adult who met the half-life test under PL 4.1, must have lived in the UK for a continuous qualifying period of 5 years with permission as set out in PL 14.3 or 14.4.

PL 14.2. An applicant who is aged 18 or over at the date of application and does not meet the requirement in PL 14.1 must have lived in the UK for a continuous qualifying period of 10 years with permission set out in PL 14.3. or 14.4.

PL 14.3. Permission on the following routes (or any combination of those routes) counts towards the qualifying period in PL 14.1. or PL 14.2:

(a) entry clearance or permission granted as a partner or parent under Appendix FM (except for permission as a fiancé(e) or proposed civil partner); or

(b) permission described in the Home Office grant letter as "family permission as a parent" or "family permission as a partner"; or

(c) permission on the private life route under paragraph 276ADE or 276BE(2) before 20 June 2022 or Appendix Private Life; or

(d) entry clearance or permission as a child of a person with limited leave as a partner or parent under Appendix FM; or

(e) permission granted outside the rules as a partner, a parent or child or because of private life on the basis of Article 8 of the Human Rights Convention.

PL 14.4. Permission on any other route that includes rules allowing an applicant to qualify for settlement also counts towards the qualifying period in PL 14.1. or PL 14.2, if the applicant:

(a) did not enter the UK illegally (unless they have permission to stay on the private life route as a child or young adult); and

(b) has had permission either under paragraph 276ADE or 276 BE(2) before 20 June 2022 or Appendix Private Life for at least one year at the date of application.

Continuous Residence requirement for settlement on the Private Life route

PL 15.1. The applicant must meet the continuous residence requirements as set out in Appendix Continuous Residence for the qualifying period for settlement

English language requirement for settlement on the Private Life route

PL 16.1. Unless an exemption applies (for example where the applicant is aged under 18), the applicant must show English language ability on the Common European Framework of Reference for Languages in speaking and listening to at least level B1.

PL 16.2. The applicant must show they meet the English language requirement as specified in Appendix English Language.

Knowledge of life in the UK requirement for settlement on the Private Life route

PL 17.1. Unless an exemption applies (for example where the applicant is aged under 18), the applicant must meet the Knowledge of Life in the UK requirement as specified in Appendix KOL UK.

Decision on an application for settlement on the Private Life route

PL 18.1. If the decision maker is satisfied the suitability and eligibility requirements for settlement on the Private Life route are met the applicant will be granted settlement.

PL 18.2. If the requirements for settlement are not met, but the decision maker believes the applicant is likely to meet all the suitability and eligibility requirements for permission to stay on the private life route the application will be varied by the Secretary of State to an application for permission to stay on the private life route.
Where this happens:

(a) no additional application fee for permission to stay will be required and the settlement application fee will not be refunded; and

(b) the Secretary of State will write to the applicant informing them of this variation and if required will request the applicant pay any Immigration Health Charge.

PL 18.3. If the applicant does not pay the requested Immigration Health Charge or does not request a fee waiver for the Immigration Health Charge which is then granted, the application for permission to stay will be rejected as invalid and the applicant will not be refunded the fee paid for the settlement application.

PL 18.4. Where an applicant is granted permission to stay they will be granted for a period as set out in PL 10.1. to 10.4. (as relevant), subject to the conditions in PL 10.5.

PL 18.5. If the decision maker is not satisfied that the applicant meets all the suitability and eligibility requirements for settlement or permission to stay the application for settlement on the Private Life route will be refused.

Dependent child born in the UK to a person on the Private Life Route

Validity requirements for a child born in the UK to a person on the Private Life route

PL 19.1. A person applying for permission to stay as a child born in the UK to a person on the Private Life route must apply online on the gov.uk website on the specified form: 'Application to remain in the UK on the basis of family life or private life'.

PL 19.2. An application for permission to stay as a child born in the UK to a person on the Private Life route must meet all the following requirements:

(a) any fee and Immigration Health Charge must have been paid (unless a fee waiver has been granted in whole or in part); and

(b) the applicant must have provided any required biometrics; and

(c) the applicant must have provided a passport or other document which satisfactorily establishes their identity and nationality; and

(d) the applicant must have been born in the UK: and

(e) the applicant must be applying as a child of a person (P) on the Private Life route who:

(i) has made a valid application for permission to stay in the UK on the Private Life route that has not been decided; or

(ii) has permission to stay on the Private Life route; or

(iii) is settled or has become a British citizen, providing P had permission to stay on the Private Life route when they settled, and the applicant was born before P settled; and

(f) the applicant must be in the UK on the date of application.

PL 19.3. An applicant must be aged under 18 at the date of application.

PL 19.4. If a claim is made under Article 8 of the Human Rights Convention:

(a) at the same time as a protection claim or further submission in person after a protection claim is refused; or

(b) in an appeal (subject to the consent of the Secretary of State where applicable);

the requirements at PL 19.1. and at PL 19.2. (a) and (c) will be waived.

PL 19.5. An application which does not meet all the validity requirements for a child born in the UK of a person on the Private Life route is invalid and may be rejected and not considered.

Suitability requirements for a child born in the UK to a person on the Private Life route

PL 20.1. The applicant must not fall for refusal under suitability grounds for refusal in S-LTR.1.2. to S-LTR.2.2. and S-LTR.3.1. to S-LTR.4.5. of Appendix FM of these rules.

PL 20.2. The application for permission to stay must not fall for refusal under paragraph 9.6.1. (sham marriage or civil partnership) of Part 9: grounds for refusal.

Eligibility requirements for a child born in the UK to a person on the Private Life route

Relationship requirements for a child born in the UK to a person on the Private Life route

PL 21.1. The applicant must be the child of a parent (P) where one of the following applies:

(a) P has permission on the Private Life route; or

(b) P is at the same time, applying for (and is granted) permission on the Private Life route; or

(c) P is settled or has become a British citizen, providing P had permission on the Private Life route when they settled, and the applicant was born before P settled.

PL 21.2. The applicant's other parent must have permission to be in the UK (other than a visitor) unless:

(a) P in PL 21.1 is the sole surviving parent; or

(b) P in PL 21.1 has sole responsibility for the child's upbringing; or

(c) the parent who does not have permission on the Private Life route is a British citizen or a person who has a right to enter or stay in the UK without restriction and is or will be ordinarily resident in the UK; or

(d) the decision maker is satisfied there are serious and compelling reasons to grant the child permission to stay with the parent (P) in PL 21.1.

Care requirement for a child born in the UK to a person on the Private Life route

PL 22.1. There must be suitable arrangements for the child's care and accommodation in the UK, which must comply with relevant UK law.

Decision on an application as a child born in the UK to a person on the Private Life route

PL 23.1. If the decision maker is satisfied that all the suitability and eligibility requirements are met the applicant will be granted permission to stay, otherwise the application will be refused.

Period of grant as a child born in the UK to a person on the Private Life route

PL 24.1. The applicant will be granted permission to stay which ends on the same date as whichever of their parents' permission ends first unless the other parent is a British citizen or a person who has a right to enter or stay in the UK without restriction and is or will be ordinarily resident in the UK. In such cases, the applicant will be granted permission to stay which ends on the same date as the parent on the Private Life route.

Conditions of grant as a child born in the UK to a person on the Private Life route

PL 25.1. The grant of permission will be subject to the following conditions:

(a) work is permitted; and

(b) study is permitted, subject to the ATAS condition in Appendix ATAS; and

(c) if the decision maker is satisfied that there are reasons relating to the welfare of a child which outweigh the considerations for imposing or maintaining the condition of no access to public funds (treating the best interests of a relevant child as a primary consideration) the applicant will not be subject to a condition of no access to public funds, if not so satisfied the applicant will be subject to a condition of no access to public funds.

PL 25.2. For the purposes of PL 25.1(c) 'relevant child' means a person who:

(a) is under the age of 18 years at the date of application; and

(b) it is clear from the information provided by the applicant, is a child who would be affected by a decision to impose or maintain the no access to public funds condition.

Settlement as a child born in the UK of a person on the Private Life route

Validity requirements for settlement as a child born in the UK of a person on the Private Life route

PL 26.1. A child applying for settlement as a child born in the UK of a person on the Private Life route must apply online on the gov.uk website on the specified form: 'Settlement as a Child (including a child aged over 18 already in the UK as a dependent).'.

PL 26.2. An application for settlement must meet all the following requirements:

(a) any fee must have been paid; and

(b) the applicant must have provided any required biometrics; and

(c) the applicant must have provided a passport or other document which satisfactorily establishes their identity and nationality; and

(d) the applicant must be applying as a child born in the UK of a person (P) on the Private Life route who:

(i) has made a valid application for settlement on the Private Life route that has not been decided; or

(ii) is settled or has become a British Citizen, providing P had permission on the Private Life route when they settled, and the applicant was born before P settled; and

(e) the applicant must be in the UK.

PL 26.3. An application which does not meet all the validity requirements for settlement is invalid and may be rejected and not considered.

Suitability requirements for settlement as a child born in the UK of a person on the Private Life route

PL 27.1. The applicant must not fall for refusal under:

(a) the suitability grounds for refusal for indefinite leave to remain applications under Appendix FM paragraphs:

(i) S-ILR.1.2, S-ILR.1.6 to S-ILR.1.10, S-ILR.3.1; or

(ii) S-ILR.2.2, S-ILR.4.2, to S-ILR.4.5 (subject to PL 27.4); or

(b) paragraph 9.6.1. of Part 9 of these rules (subject to PL 27.4).

PL 27.2. The applicant must not have been convicted of a criminal offence in the UK or overseas for which they have received a custodial sentence of 12 months or more.

PL 27.3. The applicant must not have been convicted of an offence in the UK or overseas for which they have been sentenced to imprisonment for less than 12 months, unless the applicant has completed a qualifying period of 10 years with permission as set out in PL 27.5 and has spent at least 5 years with such permission since the end of their sentence.

PL 27.4. Where any of the following occur during the applicant's qualifying period for settlement, the applicant must be refused settlement unless the applicant has completed a continuous qualifying period of 10 years with permission under PL 27.5 and has completed 5 years continuous residence with such permission after the date of the first grant of permission after the suitability ground came to the attention of the decision maker:

(a) involvement in a sham marriage or civil partnership (grounds for refusal under 9.6.1 of Part 9); or

(b) use of false documents or information or deception (S-ILR.2.2 and S-ILR.4.2 and S-ILR.4.3. of Appendix FM); or

(c) litigation debt owed to the Home Office, unless the debt has been paid (S-ILR.4.4 of Appendix FM); or

(d) debt to the NHS, unless the debt has been paid, or the total value of outstanding charges is under £500 (S-ILR.4.5. of Appendix FM); or

(e) the applicant has breached the conditions of their permission.

PL 27.5. Where an applicant must complete a qualifying period of 10 years (under PL 27.3. to PL 27.4.), they must have had permission as one or a combination of the following for that 10 year qualifying period:

(a) entry clearance or permission granted as a partner or parent under Appendix FM (except for permission as a fiancé(e) or proposed civil partner); or

(b) permission described in the Home Office grant letter as "family permission as a parent" or "family permission as a partner"; or

(c) permission on the private life route under paragraph 276ADE or 276BE(2) before 20 June 2022 or Appendix Private Life; or

(d) entry clearance or permission as a child of a person with limited leave as a partner or parent under Appendix FM; or

(e) permission granted outside the rules as a partner, a parent or child or because of private life on the basis of Article 8 of the Human Rights Convention.

PL 27.6. The applicant must not be:

(a) in breach of immigration laws, except that where paragraph 39E applies, that period of overstaying will be disregarded; or

(b) on immigration bail.

Eligibility requirements for settlement as at child born in the UK of a person on the Private Life route

Relationship requirement for settlement as a child born in the UK of a person on the Private Life route

PL 28.1. The applicant must be the child of a person (P) where one of the following applies:

(a) P is, at the same time, being granted settlement on the Private Life route; or

(b) P is settled in the UK or has become a British citizen, providing P had permission on the Private Life route when they settled and the applicant either:

(i) had permission as P's child at that time; or

(ii) was born before P settled.

PL 28.2. The applicant's other parent (not P) must be being granted settlement at the same time, or be settled or a British citizen, unless:

(a) the person (P) in PL 28.1. is the applicant's sole surviving parent; or

(b) the person (P) in PL 28.1. has sole responsibility for the applicant's upbringing; or

(c) the decision maker is satisfied that there are serious and compelling reasons to grant the applicant settlement.

Age requirement for settlement as a child born in the UK of a person on the Private Life route

PL 29.1. The applicant must be under the age of 18 on the date of application, unless they were last granted permission as the dependent child of their parent or parents.

PL 29.2. If the child is aged 16 or over on the date of application, they must not be leading an independent life.

Care requirement for settlement as a child born in the UK of a person on the Private Life route

PL 30.1. Where the applicant is aged under 18, there must be suitable arrangements for their care and accommodation in the UK, which must comply with relevant UK law.

English language requirement for settlement as a child born in the UK of a person on the Private Life route

PL 31.1. Unless an exemption applies (for example where the applicant is aged under 18), the applicant must show English language ability on the Common European Framework of Reference for Languages in speaking and listening of at least level B1.

PL 31.2. The applicant must show they meet the English language requirement as specified in Appendix English Language.

Knowledge of life in the UK requirement for settlement as a child born in the UK of a person on the Private Life route

PL 32.1. Unless an exemption applies (for example where the applicant is aged under 18), they must meet the Knowledge of Life in the UK requirement as set out in Appendix KOL UK.

Decision on an application for settlement as a dependent child born in the UK of a person on the Private Life route.

PL 33.1. If the decision maker is satisfied all the suitability and eligibility requirements for settlement as a dependent child born in the UK of a person on the Private Life route are met the applicant will be granted settlement.

PL 33.2. If the requirements for settlement are not met, but the decision maker believes the applicant is likely to meet all the suitability and eligibility requirements for permission to stay as a dependent child born in the UK of a person on the Private Life route, the application will not be refused, but will be varied by the Secretary of State to an application for permission to stay as a dependent child born in the UK of a person on the Private Life route. Where this happens:

(a) no additional application fee for permission to stay will be required and the settlement application fee will not be refunded; and

(b) the Secretary of State will write to the applicant informing them of this variation and if required will request the applicant pay any Immigration Health Charge.

PL 33.3. If the applicant does not pay the requested Immigration Health Charge, or does not request and is granted a fee waiver for the Immigration Health Charge, the application for permission to stay will be rejected as invalid.

PL 33.4. Where an applicant is granted permission to stay, they will be granted for the period as set out in PL 24.1, subject to the conditions in PL 25.1.

PL 33.5. If the decision maker is not satisfied that the applicant meets all the suitability and eligibility requirements for settlement or permission to stay as a dependent child born in the UK of a person on the Private Life route, the application for settlement will be refused.]

Note: Appendix inserted from 20 June 2022 subject to savings for applications made before that date (HC 1118).

[Appendix Settlement Family Life

This route is for a person who has permission to stay as a partner or parent (or has had a combination of the two) under Appendix FM, and who is eligible to settle in the UK after a qualifying period of 10 years.

The person may also be able to count time with permission on other routes towards the 10 year qualifying period, if certain conditions are met.

Alternatively, partners, parents and their dependent children may qualify for settlement on the basis of 10 years Long Residence in the UK, under paragraphs 276A to 276D or 298 of the rules.

Where a person has permission as a partner and the relationship has broken down due to domestic abuse, the applicant may be able to qualify for settlement as a victim of domestic abuse under Appendix FM.

Where a person has permission as a partner and their partner has died, the applicant may be able to qualify for settlement as a bereaved partner under Appendix FM.

Dependent children of a partner or parent who is applying to settle on this route may also qualify for settlement under these Rules.

Children born in the UK where a parent is settled in the UK will be British citizens by birth. There are registration routes for British Citizenship for children born in the UK before their parent is settled: either once a parent is granted settlement or if the child lives in the UK for the first 10 years of their life. Other children may also apply for registration as a British citizen at the Home Secretary's discretion: Registration as a British citizen: children - GOV.UK (www.gov.uk).

Settlement as a partner or parent based on a qualifying period of 10 years

Validity requirements for settlement as a partner or parent based on a qualifying period of 10 years

SETF 1.1. A person who is applying for settlement must apply online on the gov.uk website on the specified form 'Settlement as a partner or parent.'.

SETF 1.2. An application for settlement must meet all the following requirements:

(a) any fee must have been paid; and

(b) the applicant must have provided any required biometrics; and

(c) the applicant must have provided a passport or other travel document which satisfactorily establishes their identity and nationality; and

(d) the applicant must be in the UK on the date of application.

SETF 1.3. The applicant must have, or have last been granted, permission as a partner or parent under Appendix FM.

SETF 1.4. An application which does not meet all the validity requirements for settlement is invalid and may be rejected and not considered.

Suitability Requirements for settlement as a partner or parent based on a qualifying period of 10 years

SETF 2.1. The applicant must not fall for refusal under:

(a) the suitability grounds for refusal for indefinite leave to remain applications under Appendix FM paragraphs:

(i) S-ILR.1.2, S-ILR.1.6 to S-ILR.1.10, S-ILR.3.1; or

(ii) S-ILR.2.2, S-ILR.4.2 to S-ILR.4.5 (subject to SETF 2.4); or

(b) paragraph 9.6.1. of Part 9 of these rules (subject to SETF 2.4).

SETF 2.2. The applicant must not have been convicted of a criminal offence in the UK or overseas for which they have received a custodial sentence of 12 months or ore.

SETF 2.3. The applicant must not have been convicted of an offence in the UK or overseas for which they have been sentenced to imprisonment for less than 12 months, unless the applicant has completed a qualifying period of 10 years with permission as set out in SETF 2.6 and the applicant has spent at least 5 years with such permission since the end of their sentence.

SETF 2.4. Where any of the following occur during the applicant's qualifying period for settlement, the applicant must be refused settlement unless the applicant has completed a continuous qualifying period of 10 years with permission as set out in SETF 2.6 and has completed 5 years continuous residence with such permission after the date of the first permission after the suitability ground came to the attention of the decision maker:

(a) involvement in a sham marriage or civil partnership (grounds for refusal under 9.6.1 of Part 9); or

(b) use of false documents or information or deception (S-ILR.2.2 and S-ILR.4.2 and S-ILR.4.3. of Appendix FM); or

(c) litigation debt owed to the Home Office, unless the debt has been paid (S-ILR.4.4 of Appendix FM); or

(d) debt to the NHS, unless the debt has been paid, or the total value of outstanding charges is under £500 (S-ILR.4.5. of Appendix FM); or

(e) the applicant has breached the conditions of their permission.

SETF 2.5. Unless the applicant is a child or young adult who was granted on the basis of private life under PL 3.1. or PL 4.1 of Appendix Private Life, if the applicant has entered the UK illegally they must be refused settlement unless the applicant has completed a qualifying period of 10 years with permission under SETF 2.6.

SETF 2.6. Where an applicant must complete a qualifying period of 10 years (under SETF 2.3. to SETF 2.5.), they must have had permission as one of, or a combination of the following for that 10 year qualifying period:

(a) entry clearance or permission granted as a partner or parent under Appendix FM (except for permission as a fiancé(e) or proposed civil partner); or

(b) permission described in the Home Office grant letter as 'family permission as a parent' or "family permission as a partner"; or

(c) permission on the private life route under paragraph 276ADE or 276BE(2) before 20 June 2022 or Appendix Private Life; or

(d) entry clearance or permission as a child of a person with limited leave as a partner or parent under Appendix FM; or

(e) permission granted outside the rules as a partner, a parent or child or because of private life on the basis of Article 8 of the Human Rights Convention.

SETF 2.7. The applicant must not be:

(a) in breach of immigration laws, except that where paragraph 39E applies, that period of overstaying will be disregarded; or

(b) on immigration bail.

Eligibility requirements for settlement as a partner or parent based on a qualifying period of 10 years

Qualifying period requirement for settlement as a partner or parent based on a qualifying period of 10 years

SETF 3.1. The applicant must have spent a continuous qualifying period in the UK of 10 years with permission under the following (or any combination of the following):

(a) entry clearance or permission granted as a partner or parent under Appendix FM (except for permission as a fiancé(e) or proposed civil partner); or

(b) permission described in the Home Office grant letter as 'family permission as a parent' or "family permission as a partner"; or

(c) permission on the private life route under paragraph 276ADE or 276BE(2) before 20 June 2022 or Appendix Private Life; or

(d) entry clearance or permission as a child of a person with limited leave as a partner or parent under Appendix FM; or

(e) permission granted outside the rules as a partner, a parent or child or because of private life on the basis of Article 8 of the Human Rights Convention.

SETF 3.2. If the applicant does not meet SETF 3.1, the 10-year qualifying period can be met by also counting time on any other route that includes rules allowing an applicant to qualify for settlement, if the applicant:

(a) did not enter the UK illegally; and

(b) has had permission as a partner (if applying as a partner) or parent (if applying as a parent) under Appendix FM for at least one year.

Continuous residence requirement for settlement as a partner or parent based on a qualifying period of 10 years

SETF 4.1. The applicant must have met the continuous residence requirement as set out in Appendix Continuous Residence for the qualifying period.

English language requirement for settlement as a partner or parent based on a qualifying period of 10 years

SETF 5.1. Unless an exemption applies, the applicant must show English language ability on the Common European Framework of Reference for Languages in speaking and listening to at least level B1.

SETF 5.2. The applicant must show they meet the English language requirement as specified in Appendix English Language.

Knowledge of life in the UK requirement for settlement as a partner or parent based on a qualifying period of 10 years

SETF 6.1. Unless an exemption applies, the applicant must meet the Knowledge of Life in the UK requirement as set out in Appendix KOL UK.

Relationship requirement for settlement as a partner based on a qualifying period of 10 years

SETF 7.1. The applicant must be the partner of a person who is one of the following:
(a) a British citizen who is living in the UK; or
(b) present and settled in the UK; or
(c) applying for settlement at the same time as the applicant.

SETF 7.2. The applicant must show that the relationship meets the relationship requirements as specified in Appendix Relationship with Partner.

SETF 7.3. The applicant must have had permission based on their relationship with their current partner for at least one year.

Relationship requirement for settlement as a parent based on a qualifying period of 10 years

SETF 8.1. The applicant must have, or have last had, permission as a parent of a child (C) under Appendix FM (whether or not the child is aged under 18 at the date of the parent's application for settlement).

SETF 8.2. The applicant must be the parent of a child who:
(a) is a British citizen and living in the UK; or
(b) is present and settled in the UK; or
(c) is applying for settlement at the same time as the applicant.

SETF 8.3. If the child (C) at SETF 8.1. is under 18 at the date of application, the applicant must have:
(a) sole parental responsibility; or
(b) C must normally live with the applicant; or
(c) the applicant must have direct access (in person) to C, as agreed with the parent or carer with whom C normally lives or as ordered by a court in the UK.

SET 8.4. The applicant must show that they are taking, and intend to continue to take, an active role in the child's upbringing.

Decision on an application for settlement as a partner or parent based on a qualifying period of 10 years

SETF 9.1. If the decision maker is satisfied all the suitability and eligibility requirements for settlement as a partner or parent based on a qualifying period of 10 years are met the applicant will be granted settlement.

SETF 9.2. If the requirements for settlement are not met, but the decision maker believes the applicant is likely to meet all the suitability and eligibility requirements for permission to stay under Appendix FM as either a partner (D-LTRP.1.2.) or parent (D-LTRPT.1.2.), the application will not be refused, but will be varied by the

Secretary of State to an application for permission to stay on that route. Where this happens:

(a) no additional application fee for permission to stay will be required and the settlement application fee will not be refunded; and

(b) the Secretary of State will write to the applicant informing them of this variation and, if required, will request the applicant pay any Immigration Health Charge.

SETF 9.3. If the applicant does not pay the requested Immigration Health Charge, or does not request or is granted a fee waiver for the Immigration Health Charge, the application for permission to stay will be rejected as invalid.

SETF 9.4. Where an applicant is granted permission to stay it will be granted for the period as set out in D-LTRP.1.2 or D-LTRPT.1.2 of Appendix FM (as relevant), subject to the conditions in the relevant paragraph.

SETF 9.5. If the decision maker is not satisfied that the applicant meets all the suitability and eligibility requirements for settlement or permission to stay as a partner or parent, the application for settlement will be refused.

Settlement as the child of a partner or parent based on a qualifying period of 10 years

Validity requirements for settlement as a dependent child of a partner or parent based on a qualifying period of 10 years

SETF 10.1. A child who is applying for settlement on this route must apply online on the gov.uk website on the specified form as follows: 'Settlement as a Child (including a child aged over 18 already in the UK as a dependent)'.

SETF 10.2. An application for settlement must meet all the following requirements:

(a) any fee must have been paid; and

(b) the applicant must have provided any required biometrics; and

(c) the applicant must have provided a passport or other travel document which satisfactorily establishes their identity and nationality; and

(d) the applicant must be in the UK, and

(e) the applicant must be applying as the child of a person (P) who:

(i) has made a valid application for settlement in the UK as a partner or parent based on a 10 year qualifying period, and that application has not been decided; or

(ii) is settled or has become a British citizen, providing P had permission as a partner or parent based on a 10 year qualifying period when P settled.

SETF 10.3. The applicant must have, or have last had, permission to stay in the UK as a dependent child, unless they were born in the UK.

SETF 10.4. An application which does not meet all the validity requirements for settlement is invalid and may be rejected and not considered.

Suitability requirements for settlement as a child of a partner or parent based on a qualifying period of 10 years

SETF 11.1. The applicant must not fall for refusal under:

(a) the suitability grounds for refusal for indefinite leave to remain applications under Appendix FM paragraphs:

(i) S-ILR.1.2, S-ILR.1.6 to S-ILR.10.1, S-ILR.3.1.; or

(ii) S-ILR.2.2, S-ILR.4.2, to S-ILR.4.5 (subject to SETF 11.4); or

(b) paragraph 9.6.1. of Part 9 of these rules (subject to SETF 11.4).

SETF 11.2. The applicant must not have been convicted of a criminal offence in the UK or overseas for which they have received a custodial sentence of 12 months or more.

SETF 11.3. The applicant must not have been convicted of an offence in the UK or overseas for which they have been sentenced to imprisonment for less than 12 months, unless the applicant has completed a qualifying period of 10 years with permission as set out in SETF 11.6 and the applicant has spent at least 5 years continuous residence with such permission since the end of their sentence.

SETF 11.4. Where any of the following occur during the applicant's qualifying period for settlement, the applicant must be refused settlement unless the applicant has completed a continuous qualifying period of 10 years with permission as set out in SETF 11.6 and has completed 5 years continuous residence with such permission after the date of the first grant of permission after the suitability ground came to the attention of the decision maker:

(a) involvement in a sham marriage or civil partnership (grounds for refusal under 9.6.1 of Part 9); or

(b) use of false documents or information or deception (S-ILR.2.2 and S-ILR.4.2 and S-ILR.4.3. of Appendix FM); or

(c) litigation debt owed to the Home Office, unless the debt has been paid (S-ILR.4.4 of Appendix FM); or

(d) debt to the NHS, unless the debt has been paid, or the total value of outstanding charges is under £500 (S-ILR.4.5. of Appendix FM); or

(e) the applicant has breached the conditions of their permission

SETF 11.5. Unless the applicant is a child or young adult who was granted on the basis of private life under PL 3.1. or PL 4.1. of Appendix Private Life, if the applicant has entered the UK illegally they must be refused settlement unless the applicant has completed a qualifying period of 10 years with permission under SETF 11.6.

SETF 11.6. Where an applicant must complete a qualifying period of 10 years (under SETF 11.3. to SETF 11.5.), they must have had permission as one or a combination of the following for that 10 year qualifying period:

(a) entry clearance or permission granted as a partner or parent under Appendix FM (except for permission as a fiancé(e) or proposed civil partner); or

(b) permission described in the Home Office grant letter as 'family permission as a parent' or "family permission as a partner"; or

(c) permission on the private life route under paragraph 276ADE or 276BE(2) before 20 June 2022 or Appendix Private Life; or

(d) entry clearance or permission as a child of a person with limited leave as a partner or parent under Appendix FM; or

(e) permission granted outside the rules as a partner, a parent or child or because of private life on the basis of Article 8 of the Human Rights Convention.

SETF 11.7. The applicant must not be:

(a) in breach of immigration laws, except that where paragraph 39E applies, that period of overstaying will be disregarded; or

(b) on immigration bail.

Eligibility requirements for settlement as a child of a partner or parent based on a qualifying period of 10 years

Relationship requirement for settlement as a child of a partner or parent based on a qualifying period of 10 years

SETF 12.1. The applicant must be the child of a person (P) where one of the following applies:

(a) P is, at the same time, being granted settlement as a partner or parent based on a qualifying period of 10 years; or

(b) P is settled or has become a British citizen, providing P had permission as a partner or parent based on a qualifying period of 10 years when they settled.

SETF 12.2. If applying as a child, the applicant's other parent must be being granted settlement at the same time, or be settled or a British citizen, unless:

(a) the person (P) in SETF 12.1. is the applicant's sole surviving parent; or

(b) the person (P) in SETF 12.1. has sole responsibility for the applicant's upbringing; or

(c) the decision maker is satisfied that there are serious and compelling reasons to grant the applicant settlement.

Age requirement for settlement as a child of a partner or parent based on a qualifying period of 10 years

SETF 13.1. The applicant must be under the age of 18 on the date of application, unless they were last granted permission as the dependent child of their parent or parents.

SETF 13.2. If the applicant is aged 16 or over on the date of application, they must not be leading an independent life.

Care requirement for settlement as a child of a partner or parent based on a qualifying period of 10 years

SETF 14.1. If the applicant is under the age of 18 on the date of application, there must be suitable arrangements for the child's care and accommodation in the UK, which must comply with relevant UK law.

English language requirement for settlement as a child of a partner or parent based on a qualifying period of 10 years

SETF 15.1. Unless an exemption applies (for example where the applicant is aged under 18), the applicant must show English language ability on the Common European Framework of Reference for Languages in speaking and listening of at least level B1.

SETF 15.2. The applicant must show they meet the English language requirement as specified in Appendix English Language.

Knowledge of life in the UK requirement for settlement as a child of a partner or parent based on a qualifying period of 10 years

SETF 16.1. Unless an exemption applies (for example where the applicant is aged under 18), they must meet the Knowledge of Life in the UK requirement as set out in Appendix KOL UK.

Decision on an application for settlement as a child of a partner or parent based on a qualifying period of 10 years

SETF 17.1. If the decision maker is satisfied all the suitability and eligibility requirements for settlement are met the applicant will be granted settlement.

SETF 17.2. If the requirements for settlement are not met, but the decision maker believes the applicant is likely to meet all the suitability and eligibility requirements for permission to stay under Appendix FM as a child of a person with limited leave as a partner or parent (D-LTRC.1.1.), or qualifies under paragraph GEN 3.2 of Appendix FM, the application will be varied by the Secretary of State to an application for permission to stay on that route. Where this happens:

(a) no additional application fee for permission to stay will be required and the settlement application fee will not be refunded; and

(b) the Secretary of State will write to the applicant informing them of this variation and, if required, will request the applicant pay any Immigration Health Charge.

SETF 17.3. If the applicant does not pay the requested Immigration Health Charge, or does not request and is granted a fee waiver for the Immigration Health Charge, the application for permission to stay will be rejected as invalid.

SETF 17.4. Where an applicant is granted permission to stay they will be granted for the period as set out in paragraph D-LTRC.1.1 of Appendix FM, subject to the conditions in paragraph D-LTRP.1.2 (where their parent has permission as a partner) or D-LTRPT.1.2 (where their parent has permission as a parent).

SETF 17.5. If the decision maker is not satisfied that the applicant meets all the suitability and eligibility requirements for settlement or permission to stay, the application for settlement will be refused.]

Note: Appendix inserted from 20 June 2022 subject to savings for applications made before that date (HC 1118).

[Appendix ATAS: Academic Technology Approval Scheme (ATAS)

ATAS seeks to prevent the transfer of information, knowledge or technology which could develop, advance or support an Advanced Conventional Military Technology (ACMT) and Weapons of Mass Destruction (WMD) programme or their means of delivery.

The ATAS requirement means the applicant must obtain a valid ATAS certificate, issued by the Counter-Proliferation and Arms Control Centre, and to provide it with an application on Student, Skilled Worker, ICT, [Global Business Mobility,] [[Scale-up,]] T5 International Agreement and Government Authorised Exchange routes to study or work as a researcher in any of the specified subjects listed in this Appendix.

The ATAS condition means that someone must obtain a valid ATAS certificate prior to commencing study or research in any of the specified subjects or fields of research.

A person is subject to the ATAS condition if they have been granted permission which allows study or work subject to the ATAS condition.

A person is exempt from the ATAS requirement and ATAS condition if they are a national of one of the countries listed in this Appendix.

Note: Words in square brackets inserted from 09:00 on 11 April 2022 subject to savings for applications made before that time; words in double square brackets inserted from 22 August 2022 subject to savings for applications made before that date (HC 1118).

ATAS requirement

ATAS 1.1. An applicant (who is not a national of a country listed at ATAS 3.1.) requires a valid ATAS certificate if the course of study for which the Confirmation of Acceptance for Studies was assigned is a subject set out at ATAS 4.1. which:

(a) leads to a master's degree; or

(b) leads to a PhD; or

(c) leads to another postgraduate qualification; or

(d) is a period of study or research which is part of an overseas postgraduate qualification.

ATAS 1.2. An applicant (who is not a national of a country listed at ATAS 3.1.) requires a valid ATAS certificate if they are applying in a work route which requires a Certificate of Sponsorship, that Certificate of Sponsorship is issued by a work sponsor that is also a licensed student sponsor, and the role set out in the Certificate of Sponsorship:

(a) is in one of the following occupation codes:

- 2111 Chemical scientists
- 2112 Biological scientists and biochemists
- 2113 Physical scientists
- 2114 Social and humanities scientists
- 2119 Natural and social science professionals not elsewhere classified
- 2150 Research and development managers
- 2122 Mechanical engineers
- 2123 Electrical engineers
- 2124 Electronics engineers
- 2127 Production and process engineers
- 2129 Engineering professionals not elsewhere classified
- 2311 Higher education teaching professionals;
- 3111 Laboratory technicians
- 3112 Electrical and electronics technicians
- 3113 Engineering technicians
- 3114 Building and civil engineering technicians
- 5235 Aircraft maintenance and related trades

(b) includes an element of research at PhD level or above; and

(c) that field of research is a subject set out at ATAS 4.1

ATAS 1.3. The applicant must provide a print-out of the valid ATAS certificate for the course of study or research role to show that the ATAS requirement is met.

ATAS condition

ATAS 2.1. The ATAS condition means the person (who is not a national of a country listed at ATAS 3.1), must have a valid ATAS certificate before commencing study (unless they are a student continuing a course of study and they have made, or intend to make within the required time period, an application required by ATAS 2.2) or research in a subject listed at ATAS 4.1 which:

(a) leads to a UK postgraduate degree; or

(b) leads to another postgraduate qualification; or

(c) is a period of study which is part of an overseas postgraduate qualification; or

(d) is research as part of a course of postgraduate study, employment or academic activity at a licensed student sponsor.

ATAS 2.2. A Student who intends to continue study on a course of study which is subject to the ATAS requirement must apply for a new ATAS certificate where:

(a) the completion date of the course of study has changed and will be delayed by more than 3 months; or

(b) the course contents or research proposal of the course of study change, and the application for a new certificate must be made within 28 days of the change in (a) or (b) above being known to the Student.

Nationals who are exempt from the ATAS requirement and condition

ATAS 3.1. A person does not need to meet the ATAS requirement, and will not be subject to the ATAS condition, if they are a national of any of the following countries:

Australia
Austria
Belgium
Bulgaria
Canada
Croatia
Republic of Cyprus
Czech Republic
Denmark
Estonia
Finland
France
Germany
Greece
Hungary
Iceland
Ireland
Italy
Japan
Latvia
Liechtenstein
Lithuania
Luxembourg
Malta
Netherlands
New Zealand
Norway
Poland
Portugal
Republic of Korea
Romania
Singapore
Slovakia
Slovenia
Spain
Sweden
Switzerland
United States of America

Academic Subjects relevant to ATAS

ATAS 4.1. The ATAS requirement and ATAS condition apply to the following subjects:

(a) research, or doctorates or master's by research in:

Subjects allied to Medicine:

CAH codes:

CAH02-02-01 – Pharmacology

CAH02-02-02 – Toxicology

CAH02-02-03 – Pharmacy

CAH10-01-06 – Bioengineering, Medical and Biomedical Engineering

[...]

Biological Sciences:
CAH codes:
CAH03-01-02 – Biology (non-specific)
CAH03-01-03 – Ecology and Environmental Biology
CAH03-01-06 – Zoology
CAH03-01-04 – Microbiology and Cell Science
CAH03-01-05 – Plant Sciences
CAH10-03-05 – Biotechnology
CAH03-01-07 – Genetics
CAH02-05-03 – Biomedical Sciences (non-specific)
CAH03-01-08 – Molecular Biology, Biophysics and Biochemistry
CAH03-01-01 – Biosciences (non-specific)
CAH03-01-10 – Others in Biological Sciences
Veterinary Sciences, Agriculture and related subjects:
CAH codes:
CAH05-01-02 – Others in Veterinary Sciences
CAH06-01-02 – Agricultural sciences
Physical Sciences:
CAH codes:
CAH07-02-01 – Chemistry
CAH10-03-07 – Materials Science
CAH07-01-01 – Physics
CAH07-01-02 – Astronomy
CAH26-01-05 – Others in Geographical Studies
CAH07-04-01 – Physical Sciences (non-specific)
CAH07-04-03 – Sciences (non-specific)
CAH07-04-04 – Natural Sciences (non-specific)
Mathematical and Computer Sciences:
CAH codes:
CAH09-01-01 – Mathematics
CAH09-01-02 – Operational Research
CAH11-01-01 – Computer Science
CAH11-01-02 – Information Technology
CAH11-01-03 – Information Systems
CAH11-01-04 – Software Engineering
CAH11-01-05 – Artificial Intelligence
Engineering:
CAH codes:
CAH10-01-01 – Engineering (non-specific)
CAH10-01-07 – Civil Engineering
CAH10-01-02 – Mechanical Engineering
CAH10-01-04 – Aeronautical and Aerospace Engineering
CAH10-01-05 – Naval Architecture
CAH10-01-08 – Electrical and Electronic Engineering
CAH10-01-09 – Chemical, Process and Energy Engineering
Technologies:
CAH codes:
CAH10-03-03 – Polymers and Textiles
CAH10-03-01 – Minerals Technology

CAH10-03-02 – Materials Technology
CAH10-03-04 – Maritime Technology

(b) taught master's in:
CAH codes:
CAH10-03-07 – Materials Science
CAH07-01-01 – Physics (including Nuclear Physics)
CAH10-01-02 – Mechanical Engineering
CAH10-01-04 – Aeronautical and Aerospace Engineering
CAH10-01-09 – Chemical, Process and Energy Engineering
CAH10-03-01 – Minerals Technology
CAH10-03-02 – Materials Technology]

Note: Appendix inserted from 09:00 on 5 October 2020 subject to savings for applications made before that time. Where consequential changes relating to the need for an ATAS certificate have been made, they take effect for all applications made or granted on or after 5 October 2020 at 09:00 (HC 707). Appendix substituted from 09:00 on 1 December 2020 subject to savings for applications made before that time (HC 813). Appendix substituted from 09:00 on 21 May 2021 subject to savings for applications made before that time (HC 1248). Words in (a) deleted from 6 April 2022 subject to savings for applications made before that date (HC 1118).

[Appendix English Language

This Appendix sets out how the English language requirement is met.
[It applies only to applications under Appendix Student, Appendix Skilled Worker, Appendix Representative of an Overseas Business, Appendix T2 Minister of Religion, Appendix International Sportsperson, Appendix UK Ancestry, Appendix Global Talent, Appendix Start-up, Appendix Innovator, Appendix Temporary Work – International Agreement, Appendix Domestic Worker in a Private Household [[Appendix High Potential Individual,]] {Appendix Settlement Family Life, Appendix Private Life, Appendix Scale-up} and Appendix Hong Kong British National (Overseas).]
The route sets out whether the English language requirement must be met and at what level.

Note: Words in introduction substituted from 09:00 on 11 October 2021 subject to savings for applications made before that time (HC 617). Words in double square brackets inserted from 09:00 on 30 May 2022 subject to savings for applications made before that time; words in curly brackets inserted from 20 June 2022 subject to savings for applications made before that time (HC 1118).

Exemption

[**EL 1.1.** An applicant for settlement is exempt from the English language requirement if at the date of application any of the following apply:

(a) they are aged 65 or over; or

(b) they are aged under 18; or

(c) they have a disability (physical or mental condition) which prevents them from meeting the requirement; or

(d) they are applying for settlement as a partner, parent or dependent child aged over 18 where they:

(i) have spent a continuous period of 15 years in the UK with permission; and

(ii) can show an English language speaking and listening qualification at A2 CEFR or ESOL entry level 2 or Scottish Credit and Qualification Framework level 3; and

(iii) provide confirmation from a qualified English teacher that the applicant has attended an English language class for at least 75 guided learning hours (not unsupervised study or preparation time) in the 12 months before the date of application and the teacher's view is the applicant is unlikely to attain B1 level through further study.]

Note: Paragraph substituted from 20 June 2022 subject to savings for applications made before that date (HC 1118).

How the requirement is met

EL 2.1. The English language requirement is met if any of the requirements in EL 3 to EL 6 are met.

EL 2.2. The English language requirement is also met by a person applying for entry clearance or permission to stay as a Student if any of the requirements in EL 7.1. to EL 8.4. are met.

EL 2.3. The English language requirement is also met by a person applying for entry clearance or permission to stay as a Skilled Worker route if:

(a) the requirements in EL 7.1. and EL 7.2. are met: or

(b) the requirement in EL 9.1. is met.

[**EL 2.4.** The English language requirement is also met by a person applying for:

(a) entry clearance or permission to stay on the Start-up route, or

(b) entry clearance, permission to stay or settlement on the Innovator route, or

(c) entry clearance, permission to stay or settlement on the Scale-up route, or

(d) entry clearance or permission to stay on the High Potential Individual route, or

(e) settlement under Appendix Settlement Family Life, or

(f) settlement under Appendix Private Life, if the requirements in EL 7.1 and EL 7.2. are met.]

Note: Paragraph substituted from 09:00 on 11 October 2021 subject to savings for applications made before that time (HC 617). Paragraph substituted from 09:00 on 30 May 2022 subject to savings for applications made before that time (HC 1118).

EL 2.5. [DELETED]

Note: Paragraph deleted from 20 June 2022 subject to savings for applications made before that date (HC 1118).

Met in a previous application

EL 3.1. An applicant will meet the English language requirement if they have already shown they met the requirement, at the level required for their current application, in a previous successful application for entry clearance or permission to stay.

Majority English speaking country

EL 4.1. An applicant will meet the English language requirement if they are a national of any of the following majority-English-speaking countries:

Antigua and Barbuda
Australia
The Bahamas
Barbados
Belize
Canada
Dominica
Grenada
Guyana
Jamaica
Malta
New Zealand
St Kitts and Nevis
St Lucia
St Vincent and the Grenadines
Trinidad and Tobago
United States of America

Academic qualification

EL 5.1. An applicant will meet the English language requirement if they have an academic qualification which meets one of the requirements at EL 5.2. and is proven by the required evidence under EL 5.3. or EL 5.4.

EL 5.2. The requirements are that the applicant has:

(a) a bachelor's degree, master's degree or doctorate awarded in the UK; or

(b) a degree or degree-level qualification taught in a university or college in a majority-English-speaking country listed in EL 4.1. (except Canada), or Ireland, which meets or exceeds the recognised standard of a bachelor's degree, master's degree or doctorate awarded in the UK; or

(c) a degree or degree level qualification which meets, or exceeds, the recognised standard of a UK bachelor's degree; master's degree or doctorate and was taught or researched in English.

EL 5.3. The requirement at EL 5.2. must be proven by one of:

(a) a certificate from the awarding body: or

(b) a transcript issued by the university or college that awarded the qualification; or

(c) an official letter from the university or college that awarded the qualification containing information equivalent to a degree certificate.

EL 5.4. If the qualification was awarded by a body from outside the UK, the requirement at EL 5.2. must, in addition to the requirement at EL 5.3, be proven by confirmation from [Ecctis] that the qualification meets the requirements at EL 5.2(b) or EL 5.2(c).

Note: Words substituted from 6 October 2021 subject to savings for applications made before that date (HC 617).

English language test

EL 6.1. An applicant will meet the English language requirement if they have provided a valid digital reference number from an approved provider showing they have passed an approved English language test to the required level in the two years before the date of application.

The list of approved tests and providers, updated from time to time, can be found at [https://www.gov.uk/guidance/prove-your-english-language-abilities-with-a-secure-english-language-test-selt#approved-test-providers-and-approved-tests.]

Note: Web address substituted from 6 October 2021 subject to savings for applications made before that date (HC 617).

GCSE or A Level English

[**EL 7.1.** An applicant applying for entry clearance, permission to stay, or settlement as listed in EL 2.2 to EL 2.4 will meet the English language requirement if they have a GCSE, A level, Scottish National Qualification at level 4 or 5 or, Scottish Higher or Advanced Higher, in English (language or literature), that was awarded:

(a) by an Ofqual (or SQA, Qualifications Wales or CCEA) regulated awarding body; and

(b) following education undertaken in a UK based school which began while they were aged under 18.]

Note: Paragraph substituted from 09:00 on 30 May 2022 subject to savings for applications made before that time (HC 1118).

EL 7.2. The requirement at EL 7.1. must be proven by either:

(a) a certificate from the awarding body: or

(b) an official transcript issued by the awarding body.

Additional ways Students can meet the English language requirement

EL 8.1. An applicant under Appendix Student will meet the English language requirement if they are applying for a course of study at degree level or above and are sponsored by a higher education provider with a track record of compliance who states on the Confirmation of Acceptance for Studies that they have assessed the applicant's English language ability and how they have assessed it.

EL 8.2. Where an assessment under EL 8.1. has been carried out the Confirmation of Acceptance for Studies entry must confirm that the applicant has a knowledge of English equivalent to level B2, or above, of the Council of Europe's Common European Framework for Language Learning in all 4 components (reading, writing, speaking and listening) or that the requirement at ST 15.3. is met.

EL 8.3. An applicant under Appendix Student will meet the English language requirement if they have taken an approved English test and been exempted from a component of that test by the test provider due to a disability, and the student sponsor has confirmed that they are satisfied the English language ability of the applicant is sufficient to undertake the course of study.

EL 8.4. An applicant under Appendix Student will meet the English language requirement if they are applying for a short-term study abroad programme of up to six months and both:

(a) the study abroad programme is part of a course of study at degree level or above at an overseas higher education institution in the United States of America; and

(b) [Eccits] confirm that the course of study overseas will lead to an academic (not a professional or vocational) qualification at UK bachelor's degree level or above.

Note: Words substituted from 6 October 2021 subject to savings for applications made before that date (HC 617).

Professional regulation for Skilled Workers

EL 9.1. An applicant applying for entry clearance or permission to stay under Appendix Skilled Worker will meet the English language requirement if they are being sponsored to work as a doctor, dentist, nurse, midwife or veterinarian, and have passed an English

Language assessment which is accepted by the relevant regulated professional body as a requirement for registration.]

Note: Appendix inserted from 09:00 on 5 October 2020 subject to savings for applications made before that time (HC 707). Appendix substituted from 09:00 on 1 December 2020 subject to savings for applications made before that time (HC 813). Appendix substituted from 6 April 2021 subject to savings for applications made before that date (HC 1248).

[Appendix KOL UK

This Appendix sets out how the Knowledge of Life in the UK requirement is met by a person applying for settlement.

[It applies only to applications under Appendix Student, Appendix Skilled Worker, Appendix Representatives of an Overseas Business, Appendix T2 Minister of Religion, [[Appendix International Sportsperson]], Appendix UK Ancestry, Appendix Global Talent, Appendix Innovator, Appendix T5 (Temporary Worker) International Agreement Worker, Appendix Domestic Worker in a Private Household, {{Appendix Scale-up,}} {Appendix Private Life, Appendix Settlement Family Life} and Appendix Hong Kong British National (Overseas).]

Applications for settlement under other routes must continue to apply Appendix KOLL.

Note: Paragraph substituted from 6 April 2021 subject to savings for applications made before that date (HC 1248). Words in double square brackets substituted from 6 April 2022; words in curly brackets inserted from 20 June 2022 subject to savings for applications made before that date; words in double curly brackets inserted for 22 August 2022 subject to savings for applications made before that date (HC 1118).

Exemption

[**KOL 1.1.** An applicant is exempt from the Knowledge of Life in the UK requirement if at the date of application, they:

(a) are aged 65 or over; or

(b) are aged under 18; or

(c) have a disability (physical or mental condition) which prevents them from meeting the requirement; or

(d) are applying for settlement as a partner, parent or dependent child aged over 18 and are exempt from meeting the English language requirements following 15 years under Appendix EL 1.1(d).]

Note: Paragraph substituted from 20 June 2022 subject to savings for applications made before that date (HC 1118).

Knowledge of Life in the UK requirement

KOL 2.1. An applicant will meet the Knowledge of Life in the UK requirement if they:

(a) provide a valid digital reference number from an educational institution or other person approved for this purpose by the Secretary of State showing they have passed the Life in the UK test; or

(b) are resident in the Isle of Man, and provide a valid digital reference number from an educational institution or other person approved for this purpose by the Lieutenant Governor showing they have passed the Isle of Man's Life in the UK test; or

(c) are resident in the Bailiwick of Guernsey or in the Bailiwick of Jersey, and provide a valid digital reference number from an educational institution or other person approved for that purpose by the Lieutenant Governor of Guernsey or Jersey showing they have passed the 'Citizenship Test'.]

Note: Appendix inserted from 09:00 on 1 December 2020 subject to savings for applications made before that time (HC 813).

[Appendix Finance

This Appendix sets out how the financial requirement must be met.

The routes set out the requirements for the amount of funds and length of time they must be held.

[This Appendix applies to applications under these routes: Appendix Student, Appendix Short-term Student, Appendix Child Student, Appendix Parent of a Child Student, Appendix Skilled Worker, [[Appendix Global Business Mobility – Senior or Specialist, Appendix Global Business Mobility – Graduate Trainee, Appendix Global Business Mobility – UK Expansion Worker, Appendix Global Business Mobility – Service Supplier, Appendix Global Business Mobility – Secondment Worker, Appendix Scale-up, Appendix High Potential Individual,]] Appendix Representative of an Overseas Business, Appendix Global Talent, Appendix Start-up, Appendix Innovator, Appendix T2 Minister of Religion, Appendix International Sportsperson, Appendix UK Ancestry, Appendix Temporary Work - Seasonal Worker, Appendix Youth Mobility Scheme, Appendix Temporary Work - Creative Worker, Appendix Temporary Work - Religious Worker, Appendix Temporary Work - Charity Worker, Appendix Temporary Work - International Agreement, Appendix Temporary Work - Government Authorised Exchange, Appendix Domestic Worker in a Private Household and Appendix Hong Kong British National (Overseas).]

Note: Amendments from 6 April 2021 subject to savings for applications made before that date (HC 1248). Paragraph substituted from 09:00 on 11 October 2021 subject to savings for applications made before that time (HC 617). Words in double square brackets substituted from 09:00 on 11 April 2022 subject to savings for applications made before that time (HC 1118).

Currency

FIN 1.1. Where money is held in one or more foreign currencies, this will be converted into pound sterling (£) using the spot exchange rate which appears on www.oanda.com for the date of the application.

Financial institutions

FIN 2.1. Funds will not be considered if they are held in a financial institution where any of the following apply:

(a) the decision maker is unable to make satisfactory verification checks; or

(b) the financial institution is not regulated by the appropriate regulatory body for the country in which that institution is operating; or

(c) the financial institution does not use electronic record keeping.

Overdrafts

FIN 3.1. Overdraft facilities will not be counted towards meeting financial requirements.

Requirement to have legally earned or acquired funds, savings, or income

FIN 4.1. If funds, savings or income were earned or acquired when the applicant was in the UK, they must have been earned or acquired lawfully and while the applicant had permission and was not in breach of any conditions attached to that permission.

Account holders

FIN 5.1. Accounts relied on must be in the name of the applicant (either alone or as a joint account holder), unless one of the following applies:

(a) the account is in the name of the applicant's partner who is applying for entry clearance or permission to stay at the same time or has been granted permission; or

(b) the applicant is applying as a Child Student, or Student, or dependent child, and the account is in the name of their parent, or their legal guardian; or

(c) the applicant is applying as a Child Student and they are being cared for by a close relative, or a private foster care arrangement has been made which complies with the requirements in CS 9.3. to CS 9.5, and the account is in the name of the applicant's close relative or private foster carer; or

(d) the requirements for the route under which the applicant is applying state that an account in the name of a third party may be relied upon and the account is in the name of that third party.

FIN 5.2. The applicant, or account holder in FIN.5.1, must have control of the funds.

FIN 5.3. If the applicant is applying as a Student or Child Student and they are relying on funds held in an account in the name of a parent or legal guardian as specified in FIN 5.1. they must provide proof of that relationship and written consent from the parent or legal guardian to use those funds.

Third party support

FIN 6.1. Promises of future third-party support will not be accepted as evidence of funds, except where this is specified in the route under which the applicant is applying.

Dates of financial evidence

FIN 7.1. The most recently dated piece of financial evidence must be dated within 31 days before the date of application.

FIN 7.2. The length of time for which funds are held will be calculated by counting back from the date of the closing balance on the most recently dated piece of financial evidence.

FIN 7.3. The financial evidence provided must cover the whole period of time for which the funds must be held.

Accounts

FIN 8.1. Funds may be held in any form of personal bank or building society account (including current, deposit, savings, pension from which the funds can be withdrawn or investment account) provided the account allows the funds to be accessed immediately.

FIN 8.2. Funds held in other accounts or financial instruments such as shares, bonds, credit cards, pensions from which the funds cannot be withdrawn immediately, regardless of notice period, will not be accepted as evidence of funds.

FIN 8.3. An applicant applying as a Student or Child Student, will meet the financial requirements if they provide evidence of any of the following (or a combination of them):

(a) money held in an account that meets the requirements set out in FIN 5.1. and FIN 8.1; or

(b) funds provided by an official financial sponsor, which must be Her Majesty's Government, the applicant's national government, the British Council or any international organisation, international company, university or Independent School; or

(c) a student loan provided by:

(i) a government; or

(ii) a government sponsored student loan company; or

(iii) an academic or educational loans scheme which is provided by a financial institution regulated for the purpose of issuing student loans by either the Financial Conduct Authority (FCA) or the Prudential Regulation Authority (PRA) or, in the case of an overseas loan, the official regulatory body for purpose of issuing student loans in the country the institution is in and where the money is held.

[Evidence of financial sponsorship or student loans for students]

Note: Heading substituted from 6 April 2021 subject to savings for applications made before that date (HC 1248).

FIN 9.1. An applicant relying on funds provided by an official financial sponsor under FIN 8.3.(b) must provide evidence, either:

(a) where the student sponsor is providing financial sponsorship, the funds being provided must be stated in the Confirmation of Acceptance for Studies; or

(b) a letter of confirmation from the official financial sponsor.

FIN 9.2. An applicant relying on a student loan under FIN 8.3.(c), must show evidence of the student loan by providing a student loan letter from the lender which must:

(a) be dated no more than 6 months before the date of application; and

(b) confirm the loan is a student loan provided to the applicant by either the relevant government or a government sponsored student loan company or an academic or educational loans scheme; and

(c) confirm there are no conditions on release of the loan funds other than a successful application to study in the UK as a Student or Child Student; and

(d) confirm the amount of the loan; and

(e) confirm the loan is to the applicant; and

(f) confirm the funds will be: (i) available to the applicant before they travel to the UK; or

(ii) paid directly to the student sponsor before the applicant travels to the UK, with any living cost portion of the loan being made available to the applicant by the time they arrive in the UK; or

(iii) available before the applicant begins their course if the loan is provided by the applicant's national government; and

(g) confirm the lender meets the requirement at FIN 8.3(c).]

Note: Appendix inserted from 09:00 on 5 October 2020 subject to savings for applications made before that time (HC 707). Appendix substituted from 09:00 on 1 December 2020 subject to savings for applications made before that time (HC 813).

[Appendix Continuous Residence

Note: Appendix inserted from 09:00 on 1 December 2020 subject to savings for applications made before that time (HC 813). Amendments from 6 April 2021 subject to savings for applications made before that date (HC 1248). Amendments from 6 October 2021 subject to savings for applications made before that date; amendments from 09:00 on 11 October 2021 subject to savings for applications made before that time (HC 617). Amendments from 6 April 2022; Appendix substituted from 20 June 2022 subject to savings for applications made before that date (HC 1118)

This Appendix applies only to applications under Appendix Skilled Worker, Appendix Representative of an Overseas Business, Appendix Global Talent, Appendix Innovator, Appendix T2 Minister of Religion, Appendix International Sportsperson, Appendix UK Ancestry, Appendix Domestic Worker in a Private Household, Appendix Temporary Work - International Agreement, Appendix Scale-up, Appendix Settlement Family Life, Appendix Private Life (settlement only) and Appendix Hong Kong British National (Overseas).

How the continuous residence requirement is met

CR 1.1. The continuous residence requirement is met if the applicant has spent the qualifying unbroken continuous residence period required by their route lawfully in the UK.

Absences from the UK

CR 2.1. To meet the continuous residence requirement the applicant must not have been outside the UK for more than 180 days in any 12-month period (unless CR 2.2. or CR 2.3 applies).

CR 2.2. For any absences from the UK with permission granted under the rules in place before 11 January 2018, the applicant must not have been outside the UK for more than 180 days during any consecutive 12-month period, ending on the same date of the year as the date of the application for settlement.

CR 2.3. When calculating the 180 days in CR 2.1. or CR 2.2. any period spent outside the UK for reasons (a) to (h) below will not count towards the 180-day limit, if the absence was for any of the following reasons:

(a) the applicant was assisting with a national or international humanitarian or environmental crisis overseas, providing if on a sponsored route their sponsor agreed to the absence for that purpose; or

(b) travel disruption due to natural disaster, military conflict or pandemic; or

(c) compelling and compassionate personal circumstances, such as the life-threatening illness of the applicant, or life-threatening illness or death of a close family member; or

(d) research activity undertaken by a Skilled Worker which was approved by their sponsor and where the applicant was sponsored for a job in one of the following occupation codes:

2111 Chemical scientists
2112 Biological scientists and biochemists
2113 Physical scientists
2114 Social and humanities scientists
2119 Natural and social science professionals not elsewhere classified
2150 Research and development managers
2311 Higher education teaching professionals; or

(e) research activity undertaken by a person on the Global Talent route who was endorsed by:

(i) The Royal Society; or
(ii) The British Academy; or
(iii) The Royal Academy of Engineering; or
(iv) UKRI; or

(f) research activity undertaken by a person on the Global Talent route who qualified on the basis of a prize listed in table 6 of Appendix Global Talent: Prestigious Prizes; or

(g) for an applicant under Appendix Settlement Family Life, absences for work, study or supporting family overseas, so long as the family have throughout the period of absence maintained a family life in the UK and the UK remained their place of permanent residence; or

(h) where the applicant's partner is absent from the UK on Crown service as:

(i) a member of HM Forces (as defined in the Armed Forces Act 2006); or

(ii) an employee of the UK Government, a Northern Ireland department, the Scottish Administration or the Welsh Government; or

(iii) a permanent member of the British Council, and the applicant accompanies them overseas.

CR 2.4. Any time the applicant spent lawfully in the Channel Islands or Isle of Man is treated for the purpose of this Appendix as time spent in the UK provided the applicant's most recent grant of permission was in the UK.

CR 2.5. Absences before 20 June 2022 will not be counted when calculating the continuous residence period for settlement applications under Appendix Settlement Family Life if the applicant was subsequently granted permission as a partner or parent under Appendix FM or under paragraph 276ADE or 276BE(2), following those absences.

Continuous residence for dependants

CR 3.1. Where the applicant's partner or parent, on whom they are dependant, was absent for a reason in CR 2.3. that period of absence will not count towards the 180-day limit when calculating the dependent's continuous residence period.

CR 3.2. Where a dependent partner was absent during a period of permission granted before 11 January 2018, that period of absence will not be counted towards the 180-day limit when calculating the dependent applicant's continuous residence period if the person on whom they were dependant (the main applicant) was on one of the following routes:

(a) Tier 1; or
(b) Tier 2; or
(c) Tier 5 (Temporary Worker); or

(d) Global Talent; or
(e) Start Up; or
(f) Innovator.

Breaking continuous residence

CR 4.1. An applicant's continuous residence period will be broken if any of the following apply:

(a) the applicant is convicted of an offence and sentenced to a period of imprisonment (unless it is a suspended sentence) or directed to be detained in an institution other than a prison; or

(b) the applicant is subject to a deportation order, exclusion order or exclusion direction; or

(c) the applicant is subject to removal directions under section 10 of the Immigration and Asylum Act 1999; or

(d) the applicant does not, or did not have permission, unless:

(i) the applicant made a successful application for permission to stay where paragraph 39E of Part 1 of these rules applied; or

(ii) the applicant had permission when they left the UK, applied for entry clearance before that permission expired, or within 14 days of that permission expiring, and that application for entry clearance was successful; or

(iii) CR 4.2. applies; or

(e) the applicant is absent from the UK for longer than the periods permitted under CR 2.1. and |CR 2.2., and none of the exceptions in CR 2.3. to CR 2.4. or CR 3.1. and CR 3.2. apply.

CR 4.2. Any period without permission under CR 4.1.(d) before 24 November 2016 will break the continuous residence period unless:

(a) the applicant made a successful application for permission (either in or outside the UK) within 28 days of the date their previous permission expired: or

(b) the applicant had permission when they left the UK, applied for entry clearance before that permission expired and that application for entry clearance was successful.

CR 4.3. Where CR 4.1(d) applies, any period of time where the applicant did not have permission will be disregarded when calculating the continuous residence period in CR 6.1.

Lawful presence

CR 5.1. The applicant will not be regarded as lawfully present in the UK under CR 1.1:

(a) during any period of imprisonment or detention under CR 4.1.(a); or

(b) during any period where they required permission and did not have it, unless paragraph 39E applies or, before 24 November 2016 the applicant made a successful application for permission (either in or outside the UK) within 28 days of the date their previous permission expired.

CR 5.2. Where CR 4.1. applies the applicant will not be regarded as lawfully resident for any period during which those circumstances apply (and the exceptions in CR 2.3. to CR 2.5. will not apply).

Calculating the continuous residence period

CR 6.1. The continuous residence periods in CR 2.1 and CR 2.2. will be calculated by counting back from whichever of the following dates is the most beneficial to the applicant:

(a) the date of application; or

(b) any date up to 28 days after the date of application; or

(c) the date of decision; or

(d) for a person applying for settlement on the UK Ancestry route, the date of their last grant of permission.]

[Appendix Relationship with Partner

This Appendix sets out the requirements for an application based on a relationship with a partner: spouse, civil partner, or unmarried partner in a durable relationship of at least 2 years.

It applies to applications under Appendix Ukraine Scheme and Appendix Settlement Family Life.

Age requirement for a person applying as a partner

RWP 1.1. The applicant and their partner must be aged 18 or over on the date of application.

Requirement that the partners must not be closely related

RWP 2.1. The applicant and their partner must not be so closely related that they would be prohibited from marrying, or entering into a civil partnership with, each other as defined in the Marriage Acts 1949 to 1986, the Marriage (Scotland) Act 1977 and 1986, the Marriage (Northern Ireland) Order 2003, the Civil Partnership Act 2004 and the Marriage and Civil Partnership (Scotland) Act 2014.

Requirement for previous relationships to have broken down permanently

RWP 3.1. Any previous marriage or civil partnership or durable relationship of the applicant or their partner with another person must have permanently broken down unless RWP 7.1. applies.

Requirement that any marriage or civil partnership is valid

RWP 4.1. Where the applicant and their partner are married or in a civil partnership, that marriage or civil partnership must be recognised by law in the country in which it took place.

Requirement for a durable relationship where a person is not married or in a civil partnership

RWP 5.1. Where the applicant and their partner are not married or in a civil partnership, they must have been in a relationship similar to a marriage or civil partnership for at least 2 years before the date of application.

Genuine and subsisting relationship requirement

RWP 6.1. The applicant and their partner must have met in person.

RWP 6.2. The relationship between the applicant and their partner must be genuine and subsisting.

Polygamous or polyandrous marriages and civil partnerships

RWP 7.1. If the applicant or their partner is currently in a polygamous or polyandrous marriage or civil partnership, they may only rely on that marriage or civil partnership for the purposes of an application for entry clearance, permission to enter or stay or settlement as a partner where no other partner to the marriage or civil partnership is seeking, or has been granted:

(a) permission to enter or stay (except as a visitor or person in transit); or
(b) settlement; or
(c) a certificate of entitlement to Right of Abode in the UK.]

Note: Appendix inserted from 30 March 2022 (HC 1220).

STATUTORY INSTRUMENTS

Immigration (Control of Entry through Republic of Ireland) Order 1972
(SI 1972, No. 1610)

Note: See SI 2014/2475 for amendments to this Order not included in the text.

1. This Order may be cited as the Immigration (Control of Entry through Republic of Ireland) Order 1972 and shall come into operation on 1 January 1973.

2.—(1) In this Order—

'the Act' means the Immigration Act 1971; and

[. . . .]

['exempt work activity' means an activity listed in Appendix Visitor: Permitted Activities to the immigration rules, except those listed in paragraphs PA 1, PA 2, and PA 16.1 to 18;

'occupation or employment' includes, in particular, the following activities in the United Kingdom (whether paid or unpaid)—

(a) undertaking employment;

(b) doing any work for an organisation or business;

(c) establishing or running a business as a self-employed person;

(d) undertaking a work placement or internship;

(e) undertaking any direct selling to the public;

(f) fulfilling a contract to provide goods or services;

'permitted paid engagement' means an engagement listed in paragraph V13.3. of Appendix V:Visitor to the immigration rules;

'permitted payment' means a payment of a type listed in paragraph V4.6.(a) to (f) of Appendix V:Visitor to the immigration rules, save that the words in paragraph V4.6.(f) 'where the requirements of V13.1. to V13.3. are met' do not apply to payments permitted by this Order;]

'visa national' means a person who, in accordance with the immigration rules, is required on entry into the United Kingdom to produce a passport or other document of identity endorsed with a United Kingdom visa and includes a stateless person.

(2) In this Order any reference to an Article shall be construed as a reference to an Article of this Order and any reference in an Article to a paragraph as a reference to a paragraph of that Article.

(3) [. . .]

Note: Definitions inserted and paragraph (3) omitted from 12 October 2014 (SI 2014/2475). Definitions of 'EEA national' and 'EEA state' omitted from 23.00 on 31 December 2020 (SI 2020/1309). Definitions of 'exempt work activity', 'occupation or employment', 'permitted paid engagement' and 'permitted payment' inserted from 31 December 2020 (SI 2020/1372).

3.—(1) This Article applies to—

(a) any person (other than a citizen of the Republic of Ireland) who arrives in the United Kingdom on an aircraft which began its flight in that Republic if he entered that Republic in the course of a journey to the United Kingdom which began outside the common travel area and was not given leave to land in that Republic in accordance with the law in force there;

(b) any person (other than {an Irish citizen or} a person to whom sub-paragraph (a) of this paragraph applies) who arrives in the United Kingdom on a local journey from the Republic of Ireland if he satisfies any of the following conditions, that is to say—

(i) he is a visa national who has no valid visa for his entry into the United Kingdom [, save for a visa national to whom article 3A applies];

(ii) he entered that Republic unlawfully from a place outside the common travel area;

(iii) [he is a person who—

(aa) requires leave to enter or remain in the United Kingdom,

(bb) left the United Kingdom at a time where he required such leave but did not have it, and

(cc) has not subsequently been granted admission to, or leave to enter or remain in, the United Kingdom or any of the Islands;]

(iv) [. . .]

(v) [. . .]

[(vi) he is a person who is an excluded person for the purposes of section 8B of the Act (persons excluded under international obligations);]

[(vii) he is a person who has at any time been refused admission to the United Kingdom under regulation 23(1), (3) or (4) of the Immigration (European Economic Area) Regulations2016, and has not since then been granted admission to, or leave to enter or remain in, the United Kingdom;

(viii) he is a person in respect of whom the Secretary of State has made a removal decision under regulation 23(6)(a) or (c) of the Immigration (European Economic Area Regulations) 2016, and has not since then been granted admission to or leave to enter or remain in, the United Kingdom;

(ix) he is a person who has at any time been refused admission to the United Kingdom under regulation 12(1)(a) or (c) of the Citizens' Rights (Frontier Worker) (EU Exit) Regulations 2020, and has not since then been granted admission to, or leave to enter or remain in, the United Kingdom; or

(x) he is a person in respect of whom the Secretary of State has made a removal decision under regulation 15(1)(a) or (c) of the Citizens' Rights (Frontier Worker) (EU Exit) Regulations 2020.]

(2) In relation only to persons to whom this Article applies, the Republic of Ireland shall be excluded from section 1(3) of the Act (provisions relating to persons travelling on local journeys in the common travel area).

Note: Words in subparagraph (1)(b)(i) and paragraph (1)(b)(v) inserted from 12 October 2014 (SI 2014/2475). Paragraph (1)(b)(vi) inserted from 31 December 2020 (SI 2019/468). Paragraphs (1)(b) (vii) –(x) inserted from 31 December 2020 (SI 2020/1372) except for the purpose specified in reg 1(3)(c) of SI 2020/1372 when in force immediately after IP completion day. Words in curly brackets in paragraph (1)(b) inserted and paragraphs (1)(b) (iv) and (v) omitted from 23.00 on 31 December 2020 (SI 2020/1309) with paragraph (1)(b)(v) subject to saving provision reg 25(5) of SI 2020/1309. Paragraph (1)(b)(iii) substituted from 16 June 2021 (SI 2021/6000).

[**3A.** This article applies to a visa national who is a citizen of a country specified in the Schedule who—

(a) has applied to the Republic of Ireland authorities for a visa to travel to the Republic;

(b) has made the application mentioned in sub-paragraph (a) to the Republic of Ireland authorities based in the country listed in the Schedule where the visa national is a citizen;

(c) has been granted a visa to travel to the Republic of Ireland by the Republic of Ireland authorities for the purpose of a stay of a period of 90 days or fewer, as a result of the application mentioned in sub-paragraph (a), which is endorsed with the letters 'BIVS';

(d) has since been given permission by the Republic of Ireland authorities, endorsed on his passport, to land or be in the Republic of Ireland pursuant to the visa mentioned in sub-paragraph (c); and

(e) is in possession of both the valid Irish visa mentioned in sub-paragraph (c) and the valid endorsement from the Republic of Ireland authorities conferring permission to land or to be in the Republic mentioned in sub-paragraph (d), at the time when he enters the United Kingdom on a local journey from the Republic of Ireland.]

Note: Article 3A inserted from 12 October 2014 (SI 2014/2475).

4.—(1) Subject to [[paragraphs (2), (2A)and (2B)]] {{and (2C) and 2(D)}}, this Article applies to [any person who does not have the right of abode in the United Kingdom under section 2 of the Act] and is not {an Irish citizen}, [. . .] and who enters the United Kingdom on a local journey from the Republic of Ireland after having entered that Republic—

(a) on coming from a place outside the common travel area; or

(b) after leaving the United Kingdom whilst having a limited leave to enter or remain there which has since expired.

(2) This Article shall not apply to any person [who arrives in the United Kingdom with leave to enter or remain in the United Kingdom which is in force but which was given to him before arrival or] who requires leave to enter the United Kingdom by virtue of Article 3 or section 9(4) of the Act.

[(2A) This Article does not apply to any person who has leave or may be granted leave to enter or remain in the United Kingdom by virtue of Appendix EU to the immigration rules.]

[(2B) This Article does not apply to a person who is a frontier worker under regulation 3 of the Citizens' Rights (Frontier Workers) (EU Exit) Regulations 2020.]

[(2C) This Article does not apply to any person to whom Article 5 applies, or applied at the time the person entered the United Kingdom.

(2D) This Article does not apply to any person to whom Article 6 applies.]

(3) A person to whom this Article applies by virtue only of paragraph (1)(a) shall, unless he is a visa national [without a valid visa for entry to the United Kingdom, who is also a visa national to whom article 3A applies,] be subject to the restriction and to the condition set out in paragraph (4).

(4) The restriction and the condition referred to in paragraph (3) are—

(a) the period for which he may remain in the United Kingdom shall not be more than [six] months from the date on which he entered the United Kingdom; and

[(b) he must not engage in any occupation or employment except an exempt work activity, for which he may receive a permitted payment].

(c) [. . .]

(5) [. . .]

(6) [. . .]

[(6A) In relation to a person who is a visa national without a valid visa for entry to the United Kingdom and who is also a visa national to whom article 3A applies, the restriction and condition in paragraph (6B) apply instead of the provisions contained in paragraph (4).

(**6B**) The restriction and condition referred to in paragraph (6A) are—

(a) the period for which the visa national may remain in the United Kingdom ends on the date of the expiry of the permission to land or to be in the Republic of Ireland mentioned in article 3A(d);

[(b) the person must not engage in any occupation or employment except an exempt work activity, for which the person may receive a permitted payment.]]

(7) The preceding provisions of this Article shall have effect in relation to a person to whom this Article applies by virtue of sub-paragraph (b) of paragraph (1) (whether or not he is also a person to whom this Article applies by virtue of subparagraph (a) thereof) as they have effect in relation to a person to whom this Article applies by virtue only of the said subparagraph (a), but as if for the [reference] in [paragraph (4)] to [six] months [. . .] there were substituted a reference to [two months].

(8) [. . .]

[(**8A**) The restriction and condition mentioned in paragraphs (4) and (6B) shall cease to apply to a person if that person has leave or may be granted leave to enter or remain in the United Kingdom for the reason specified in paragraph (2A).]

Note: Words in square brackets in paragraph (1) substituted by SI 1982/1028. Words in square brackets in paragraph (2) inserted by SI 2000/1776 from 30 July 2000. Subparagraphs (4)(b) substituted by SI 1980/1859 and substituted again from 31 December 2020 (SI 2020/1372). Words in curly brackets in paragraph (1) substituted, words substituted in paragraph (3), words omitted from paragraphs (4)(b), paragraphs (5) and (6) omitted, paragraphs (6A), (6B) and (8) inserted and words substituted/omitted in paragraph (7) from 12 October 2014 (SI 2014/2475). Words in double square brackets in paragraph (1) substituted from 31 December 2020 (SI 2020/1213) and words in double curly brackets inserted from 31 December 2020 (SI 2020/1372). Words in curly brackets substituted, words omitted in paragraph (1) and paragraph (8) omitted from 23.00 on 31 December 2020 (SI 2020/1309). Paragraph (2A) and (8A) inserted from 31 December 2020 (SI 2019/468) and paragraph (2B) inserted from 31 December 2020 (SI 2020/1213). Paragraphs (2C) and (2D) inserted from 31 December 2020 (SI 2020/1372). Word in square bracket in paragraph (4)(a) substituted and paragraph (4)(c) omitted from 31 December 2020 (SI 2020/1372). Paragraph (6B)(b) and words in square brackets in paragraph (7) substituted from 31 December 2020 (SI 2020/1372).

[**5.**—(1) Subject to paragraph (3), this Article applies to any person who does not have the right of abode in the United Kingdom under section 2 of the Act, and who—

(a) enters the United Kingdom on a local journey from the Republic of Ireland after having entered the Republic of Ireland—

(i) on coming from a place outside the common travel area; or

(ii) after leaving the United Kingdom whilst having limited leave to enter or remain there which has since expired; and

(b) at the time of the person's entry to the United Kingdom and continuously whilst in the United Kingdom, is a S2 Healthcare Visitor; and

(c) at the time of the person's entry to the United Kingdom, is in possession of—

(i) in the case of a patient ('P'), a valid S2 certificate of entitlement to scheduled treatment; or

(ii) in the case of an accompanying person, the documents set out in paragraph (2).

(2) The documents referred to in paragraph (1)(c)(ii) are an original or copy of—

(a) P's valid S2 certificate of entitlement to scheduled treatment or evidence of P's leave to enter or remain in the United Kingdom as a S2 Healthcare Visitor; and

(b) if P is an EEA citizen, P's valid national identity card or passport; or if P is a not an EEA citizen, P's passport.

(3) This Article does not apply to any person who arrives in the United Kingdom with leave to enter or remain in the United Kingdom which is in force but which was given to the person before their arrival, or who requires leave to enter the United Kingdom by virtue of Article 3 or section 9(4) of the Act.

(4) A person to whom this Article applies is subject to the restrictions in paragraph (5).

(5) The restrictions referred to in this paragraph are—

(a) the period for which the person may remain in the United Kingdom is not more than six months from the date on which the person entered the United Kingdom;

(b) the person must not engage in any occupation or employment.

(6) In this Article—

'accompanying person' means a person who is a S2 Healthcare Visitor who is accompanying a patient ('P') to the United Kingdom at the same time as P's entry into the United Kingdom, or who is joining P in the United Kingdom on a date after P's entry into the United Kingdom, for the purpose of providing P with care or support during P's course of planned healthcare treatment;

'EEA citizen' means a person who is a national of Austria, Belgium, Bulgaria, Croatia, Republic of Cyprus, Czech Republic, Denmark, Estonia, Finland, France, Germany, Greece, Hungary, Iceland, Ireland, Italy, Latvia, Lithuania, Liechtenstein, Luxembourg, Malta, Netherlands, Norway, Poland, Portugal, Romania, Slovakia, Slovenia, Spain, Sweden or Switzerland who is not also a British citizen;

'patient' means a person who is a S2 Healthcare Visitor who is undergoing or plans to undergo a course of planned healthcare treatment in the United Kingdom and who, before entry to the United Kingdom, has been granted a valid S2 certificate of entitlement to scheduled treatment;

'S2 certificate of entitlement to scheduled treatment' has the same meaning as a portable document S2 issued under Regulation (EC) 883/2004;

'S2 Healthcare Visitor' means a person with a right to enter the United Kingdom by virtue of and in accordance with—

(i) Article 32(1)(b) of the EU withdrawal agreement;

(ii) Article 31(1)(b) of the EEA EFTA separation agreement; or

(iii) Article 26a(1)(b) of the Swiss citizens' rights agreement;

and references to the 'EEA EFTA separation agreement' and the 'Swiss citizens' rights agreement' have the same meanings as in the European Union (Withdrawal Agreement) Act 2020 (see section 39(1) of that Act).

Note: Article 5 inserted from 31 December 2020 in force immediately before IP completion day (SI 2020/1372).

6.—(1) Subject to paragraph (2), this Article applies to any person who does not have the right of abode in the United Kingdom under section 2 of the Act and is not an Irish citizen, and who—

(a) enters the United Kingdom on a local journey from the Republic of Ireland after having entered the Republic of Ireland—

(i) on coming from a place outside the common travel area; or

(ii) after leaving the United Kingdom whilst having limited leave to enter or remain there which has since expired; and

(b) at the time of the person's entry to the United Kingdom, intends, and has a previously arranged invitation, to undertake a permitted paid engagement in the United Kingdom.

(2) This Article does not apply to any person who arrives in the United Kingdom with leave to enter or remain in the United Kingdom which is in force but which was given to the person before their arrival, or who requires leave to enter the United Kingdom by virtue of Article 3 or section 9(4) of the Act.

(3) Subject to paragraph (5), a person to whom this Article applies is subject to the restrictions and conditions in paragraph (4).

(4) The restrictions and conditions referred to in this paragraph are—

(a) the period for which the person may remain in the United Kingdom is not more than one month from the date on which the person entered the United Kingdom; and

(b) the person must not engage in any occupation or employment except an exempt work activity or the permitted paid engagement referred to in paragraph (1)(b); and

(c) where the person is undertaking an exempt work activity or the permitted paid engagement, the person may receive a permitted payment.

(5) If a person to whom this Article has applied at any time, leaves the United Kingdom but does not leave the common travel area, on the person's subsequent entry to the United Kingdom the restrictions and conditions in paragraph (6) apply to them.

(6) The restrictions and the conditions referred to in this paragraph are—

(a) the period for which the person may remain in the United Kingdom is not more than seven days from the date on which the person entered the United Kingdom; and

(b) the person must not engage in any occupation or employment except an exempt work activity or any permitted paid engagement; and

(c) where the person is undertaking an exempt work activity or permitted paid engagement, the person may receive a permitted payment.]

Note: Article 6 inserted from 31 December 2020 in force immediately before IP completion day (SI 2020/1372).

[SCHEDULE

The countries specified for the purposes of article 3A are:

India

People's Republic of China]

Note: Schedule inserted from 12 October 2014 (SI 2014/2475).

Immigration (Exemption from Control) Order 1972

(SI 1972, No. 1613)

---

1. This Order may be cited as the Immigration (Exemption from Control) Order 1972 and shall come into operation on 1 January 1973.

2.—(1) In this Order—

'the Act' means the Immigration Act 1971; and

'consular employee' and 'consular officer' have the meanings respectively assigned to them by Article 1 of the Vienna Convention on Consular Relations as set out in Schedule 1 to the Consular Relations Act 1968.

(2) In this Order any reference to an Article or to the Schedule shall be construed as a reference to an Article of this Order or, as the case may be, to the Schedule thereto and any reference in an Article to a paragraph as a reference to a paragraph of that Article.

(3) In this Order any reference to an enactment is a reference to it as amended, and includes a reference to it as applied, by or under any other enactment and any reference to an instrument made under or by virtue of any enactment is a reference to any such instrument for the time being in force.

(4) The Interpretation Act 1889 shall apply to the interpretation of this Order as it applies to the interpretation of an Act of Parliament.

3.—(1) The following persons shall be exempt from any provision of the Act relating to those who are not [British citizens], that is to say:—

(a) any consular officer in the service of any of the states specified in the Schedule (being states with which consular conventions have been concluded by Her Majesty);

(b) any consular employee in such service as is mentioned in sub-paragraph (a) of this paragraph; and

(c) any member of the family of a person exempted under sub-paragraph (a) or (b) of this paragraph forming part of his household.

(2) In paragraph (1) and in Article 4 any reference to a consular employee shall be construed as a reference to such an employee who is in the full-time service of the state concerned and is not engaged in the United Kingdom in any private occupation for gain.

Note: Words in square brackets in paragraph (1) substituted by SI 1982/1649.

4. The following persons shall be exempt from any provision of the Act relating to those who are not [British citizens] except any provision relating to deportation, that is to say:—

(a) unless the Secretary of State otherwise directs, any member of the government of a country or territory outside the United Kingdom and Islands who is visiting the United Kingdom on the business of that government;

[(b) any person entitled to immunity from legal process with respect to acts performed by him in his official capacity under any Order in Council made under section 12(1) of the International Development Act 2002 (which empowers Her Majesty by Order in Council to make provision relating to the immunities and privileges of the governors, directors, executive-directors, alternates, officers or employees of an international financial institution);

(c) any person entitled to immunity from legal process with respect to acts performed by him in his official capacity under any Order in Council made under section 5(1) of the International Monetary Fund Act 1979 (which empowers Her Majesty by Order in Council to make provision relating to the immunities and privileges of the governors, executive directors, alternates, officers and employees of the International Monetary Fund);]

(d) [. . .]

(e) any person (not being a person to whom section 8(3) of the Act applies) who is the representative or a member of the official staff of the representative of the government of a country to which section 1 of the Diplomatic Immunities (Conferences with Commonwealth Countries and Republic of Ireland) Act 1961 applies (which provides for representatives of certain Commonwealth countries and their staff attending conferences in the United Kingdom to be entitled to diplomatic immunity) so long as he is included in a list compiled and published in accordance with that section;

(f) any person on whom any immunity from jurisdiction is conferred by any Order in Council made under section 12(1) of the Consular Relations Act 1968 (which empowers Her Majesty by Order in Council to confer on certain persons connected with the service of the government of Commonwealth countries or the Republic of Ireland all or any of the immunities and privileges which are conferred by or may be conferred under that Act on persons connected with consular posts);

(g) any person (not being a person to whom section 8(3) of the Act applies) on whom any immunity from suit and legal process is conferred by any Order in Council made under section 1(2), 5(1) or 6(2) of the International Organisations Act 1968 (which empower Her Majesty by Order in Council to confer certain immunities and privileges on persons connected with certain international organisations and international tribunals and on representatives of foreign countries and their staffs attending certain conferences in the United Kingdom) except any such person as is mentioned in section 5(2)(c) to (e) of the said Act of 1968 [or by any Order in Council continuing to have effect by virtue of section 12(5) of the said Act of 1968];

(h) any consular officer (not being an honorary consular officer) in the service of a state other than such a state as is mentioned in the Schedule;

(i) any consular employee in such service as is mentioned in paragraph (h);

[(j) any officer or servant of the Commonwealth Secretariat falling within paragraph 6 of the Schedule to the Commonwealth Secretariat Act 1966 (which confers certain immunities on those members of the staff of the Secretariat who are not entitled to full diplomatic immunity);]

[(k) any person on whom any immunity from suit and legal process is conferred by the European Communities (Immunities and Privileges of the North Atlantic Salmon Conservation Organisation) Order 1985 (which confers certain immunities and privileges on the representatives and officers of the North Atlantic Salmon Conservation Organisation);]

[(l) any member of the Hong Kong Economic and Trade Office as defined by paragraph 8 of the Schedule to the Hong Kong Economic and Trade Office Act 1996,]

[(m)

(i) Any member or servant of the Independent International Commission on Decommissioning ('the Commission') established under an Agreement between the Government of the United Kingdom of Great Britain and Northern Ireland and the Government of the Republic of Ireland concluded on 26 August 1997,

(ii) in sub-paragraph (i) above, 'servant' includes any agent of or person carrying out work for or giving advice to the Commission,

(n) any member of the family of a person exempted under any of the preceding paragraphs forming part of his household.]

[(o) any person falling within Article 4A below.]

Note: First words in square brackets substituted by SI 1982/1649. Words in square brackets in Art 4(g) added by SI 1977/693. Article 4(j) substituted by SI 1977/693. Article 4(k) substituted by SI 1985/1809. Art 4(l) substituted by SI 1997/1402. Art 4(m) and (n) substituted by SI 1997/2207. Article 4(o) inserted from 25 January 2008 (SI 2004/3171). Article 4(b) and 4(c) substituted and 4(d) omitted from 1 February 2021 (SI 2021/21).

[**4A.**—(1) In relation to the court ('the ICC') established by the Rome Statute of the International Criminal Court done at Rome on 17 July 1998 ('the Rome Statute');

(a) except in so far as in any particular case the exemption given by this Article is waived by the State or intergovernmental organisation they represent,

(i) any representative of a State party to the Rome Statute attending meetings of the Assembly or one of its subsidiary organs,

(ii) any representative of another State attending meetings of the Assembly or one of its subsidiary organs as an observer, and

(iii) any representative of a State or of an intergovernmental organisation invited to a meeting of the Assembly or one of its subsidiary organs,

while exercising their official functions and during their journey to and from the place of the meeting;

(b) except in so far as in any particular case the exemption given by this Article is waived by the State they represent, any representative of a State participating in the proceedings of the ICC while exercising their official functions and during their journeys to and from the place of the proceedings of the ICC;

(c) except in so far as in any particular case the exemption given by this Article is waived by an absolute majority of the judges, any judge and the Prosecutor, when engaged on or with respect to the business of the ICC;

(d) except in so far as in any particular case the exemption given by this Article is waived by the Prosecutor, any Deputy Prosecutor, when engaged on or with respect to the business of the ICC;

(e) except in so far as in any particular case the exemption given by this Article is waived by the Presidency, the Registrar, when engaged on or with respect to the business of the ICC;

(f) except in so far as in any particular case the exemption given by this Article is waived by the Registrar, the Deputy Registrar, so far as necessary for the performance of his functions;

(g) except in so far as in any particular case the exemption given by this Article is waived by the Prosecutor, any member of the staff of the office of the Prosecutor, so far as necessary for the performance of their functions;

(h) except in so far as in any particular case the exemption given by this Article is waived by the Registrar, any member of the staff of the Registry, so far as necessary for the performance of their functions;

(i) except in so far as in any particular case the exemption given by this Article is waived by the Presidency and subject to the production of the certificate under seal of the Registrar provided to counsel and persons assisting defence counsel upon appointment, counsel and any person assisting defence counsel, so far as necessary for the performance of their functions;

(j) except in so far as in any particular case the exemption given by this Article is waived by the Presidency and subject to the production of a document provided by the ICC certifying that the person's appearance before the ICC is required by the ICC and specifying a time period during which such appearance is necessary, any witness, to the extent necessary for their appearance before the ICC for the purposes of giving evidence;

(k) except in so far as in any particular case the exemption given by this Article is waived by the Presidency and subject to the production of a document provided by the ICC certifying the participation of the person in the proceedings of the ICC and specifying a time period for that participation, any victim, to the extent necessary for their appearance before the ICC;

(l) except in so far as in any particular case the exemption given by this Article is waived by the head of the organ of the ICC appointing the person and subject to the production of a document provided by the ICC certifying that the person is performing functions for the ICC and specifying a time period during which those functions will last, any expert performing functions for the ICC, to the extent necessary for the exercise of those functions;

(m) any member of the family of a person exempted under any of paragraphs (c) to (h) above forming part of their household.

(2) In paragraph (1) above:

'the Assembly' means the assembly of State parties to the Rome Statute;

'the Presidency' means the organ of the ICC composed of the president and the first and second vice-presidents of the ICC elected in accordance with Article 38, paragraph 1, of the Rome Statute;

'the Prosecutor' and 'Deputy Prosecutors' mean the prosecutor and deputy prosecutors respectively elected by the assembly of State parties to the Rome Statute in accordance with Article 42, paragraph 4, of the Rome Statute;

'the Registrar' and 'the Deputy Registrar' mean the registrar and deputy registrar respectively elected by the ICC in accordance with Article 43, paragraph 4, of the Rome Statute.]

Note: Inserted from 25 January 2008 (SI 2004/3171).

5.—(1) Subject to the provisions of this Article the following persons who are not [British citizens] shall, on arrival in the United Kingdom, be exempt from the provisions of section 3(1)(a) of the Act (which requires persons who are not [British citizens] to obtain leave to enter the United Kingdom), that is to say—

(a) any citizen of the United Kingdom and Colonies who holds a passport issued to him in the United Kingdom and Islands and expressed to be a British Visitor's Passport;

(b) any Commonwealth citizen who is included in a passport issued in the United Kingdom by the Government of the United Kingdom or in one of the Islands by the Lieutenant-Governor thereof which is expressed to be a Collective Passport;

(c) any Commonwealth citizen or citizen of the Republic of Ireland returning to the United Kingdom from an excursion to France or Belgium [or the Netherlands] who holds a valid document of identity issued in accordance with arrangements approved by the United Kingdom Government and in a form authorised by the Secretary of State and enabling him to travel on such an excursion without a passport;

(d) any Commonwealth citizen who holds a British seaman's card or any citizen of the Republic of Ireland if (in either case) he was engaged as a member of the crew of a ship in a place within the common travel area and, on arrival in the United Kingdom, is, or is to be, discharged from his engagement;

(e) any person who, having left the United Kingdom after having been given a limited leave to enter, returns to the United Kingdom within the period for which he had leave as a member of the crew of an aircraft under an engagement requiring him to leave on that or another aircraft as a member of its crew within a period exceeding seven days.

(2) Paragraph (1) shall not apply so as to confer any exemption on any person against whom there is a deportation order in force or who has previously entered the United Kingdom unlawfully and has not subsequently been given leave to enter or remain in the United Kingdom and sub-paragraphs (d) and (e) of that paragraphs shall not apply to a person who is required by an immigration officer to submit to examination in accordance with Schedule 2 to the Act.

(3) In this Article any reference to a Commonwealth citizen shall be construed as including a reference to a British protected person and in paragraph (1)(d) 'British seaman's card' means a valid card issued under any regulations in force under section 70 of the Merchant Shipping Act 1970 or any card having effect by virtue of the said regulations as a card so issued and 'holder of a British seaman's card' has the same meaning as in the said regulations.

Note: Words in square brackets in Art 5(1) substituted by SI 1982/1649. Words in square brackets in Art 5(1)(c) added by SI 1975/617.

[6.—(1) For the purposes of section 1(1) of the British Nationality Act 1981 (which relates to acquisition of British citizenship by birth in the United Kingdom), a person to whom a child is born in the United Kingdom on or after 1 January 1983 is to be regarded (notwithstanding the preceding provisions of this Order) as settled in the United Kingdom at the time of the birth if—

(a) he would fall to be so regarded but for his being at that time entitled to an exemption by virtue of this Order; and

(b) immediately before he became entitled to that exemption he was settled in the United Kingdom; and

(c) he was ordinarily resident in the United Kingdom from the time when he became entitled to that exemption to the time of the birth;

but this Article shall not apply if at the time of the birth the child's father or mother is a person on whom any immunity from jurisdiction is conferred by or under the Diplomatic Privileges Act 1964.

(2) Expressions used in this Article shall be construed in accordance with section 50 of the British Nationality Act 1981.]

Note: Article 6 inserted from 1 January 1983 by SI 1982/1649.

[7.—(1) Subject to paragraphs (2) and (3), a dependant of a member of the relevant visiting force is exempt from any provision of the Act relating to those who are not British citizens except any provision relating to deportation.

(2) Paragraph (1) does not confer any exemption on a dependant who fails to meet the suitability requirements under Appendix Armed Forces of the immigration rules.

(3) Paragraph (1) does not confer any exemption on a dependant who has failed to provide evidence that the member is able to maintain and accommodate the dependant without recourse to public funds for the duration of their stay in the United Kingdom as a dependant.

(4) In this article—

'dependant' in relation to a member of the relevant visiting force, means a person who is included on a member's official order issued by the Government of the United States of America, and is —

(a) a spouse of the member; or

(b) a child of the member, if the child is—

(i) under 21 years old on the date the child enters the United Kingdom accompanying the member or for the purpose of joining the member; and

(ii) wholly or mainly maintained by the member.

'member' has the same meaning as in section 12(1) of the Visiting Forces Act 1952;

'official order' means a movement order or other official document issued by the Government of the United States of America confirming (a) the identity of the member and (b) that those individuals listed as dependants of the member, are eligible to accompany or join the member in the United Kingdom;

'relevant visiting force' means any body, contingent or detachment of the United States Armed Forces for the time being present in the United Kingdom on the invitation of Her Majesty's Government in the United Kingdom.]

Note: Article 7 inserted from 28 November 2015 (SI 2015/1866).

Articles 3 and 4

SCHEDULE

STATES WITH WHICH CONSULAR CONVENTIONS HAVE BEEN CONCLUDED BY HER MAJESTY

Austria
Belgium
Bulgaria
[Czechoslovakia]
Denmark
France
[German Democratic Republic]
Greece
Federal Republic of Germany
Hungary
Italy
Japan
Mexico
[Mongolia]
Norway
Poland
Romania
Sweden
Spain
Union of Soviet Socialist Republics
United States of America
Yugoslavia

Note: Words in square brackets inserted from 15 May 1977 by SI 1977/693.

The Channel Tunnel (International Arrangements) Order 1993

(SI 1993 No. 1813)

Note: The Channel Tunnel (International Arrangements) Order 1993 includes provisions modifying the application of specified statutory provisions in specified circumstances. Only the text relevant to the modification of statutes and statutory instruments included in this book are reproduced.

Citation and commencement

1. . . .

Note: Order in force from 2 August 1993 being the date notified in the London, Edinburgh and Belfast Gazettes.

Interpretation

2. . . .

Application of international articles

3. . . .

Application of supplementary articles

3A . . .

4.—Application of enactments

(1) All frontier control enactments [except those relating to transport and road traffic controls] shall for the purpose of enabling officers belonging to the United Kingdom to carry out frontier controls extend to France within a control zone.

[(1A) All frontier control enactments relating to transport and road traffic controls shall for the purpose of enabling officers belonging to the United Kingdom to carry out such controls extend to France within the control zone in France within the tunnel system.]

[(1B) All immigration control enactments shall, for the purpose of enabling immigration officers to carry out immigration controls, extend to France within a supplementary control zone.]

[(1C) [The Equality Act 2010] shall apply to the carrying out by immigration officers of their functions in a control zone or a supplementary control zone outside the United Kingdom as it applies to the carrying out of their functions within the United Kingdom.]

(2–4) . . .

Note: Paragraphs (2)–(4) concern processing of data. Words inserted in paragraph (1) and paragraph (1A) inserted from 2 October 1996 (SI 1996/2283). Paragraph (1B) inserted from 25 May 2001 (SI 2001/1544). Paragraph (1C) inserted from 10 December 2001 (SI 2001/3707) and words in paragraph (1C) substituted from 30 September 2020 (SI 2020/915).

Role of the Office of Rail Regulation

4A. . . .

Application of criminal law

5. . . .

Persons boarding a through train

5A. . . .

Powers of officers and supplementary controls

6. . . .

7.—Enactments modified

(1) Without prejudice to the generality of [articles 4(1), 4(1B) and 5(1)], the frontier control enactments mentioned in Schedule 4 shall–

(a) in their application to France by virtue of article 4(1) [or article 4(1B)], and

(b) in their application to the United Kingdom–

(i) within the tunnel system, and

(ii) elsewhere for the authorised purposes,

have effect with the modifications set out in Schedule 4.

[(1A) Nothing in paragraph (1)(b)(ii) implies the existence of a supplementary control zone in the station of London-Waterloo on British Territory.]

(2) . . .

(3) . . .

(3A) . . .

(4) . . .

Note: Paragraphs (2)–(3A) concern the application of the Firearms Act 1968. Paragraph 4 concerns transport and road traffic controls. Words inserted in paragraph (1) from 25 May 2001 (SI 2001/1544). Paragraph (1A) inserted from 14 November 2007 (SI 2007/2907).

SCHEDULE 1

EXPRESSIONS DEFINED

. . .

SCHEDULE 2

INTERNATIONAL ARTICLES

. . .

SCHEDULE 2A

SUPPLEMENTARY ARTICLES

. . .

SCHEDULE 3

POWERS OF OFFICERS

. . .

Article 4

SCHEDULE 4

ENACTMENTS MODIFIED

1.–(1) In this paragraph 'the 1971 Act' means the Immigration Act 1971.

(2) In section 3 of the 1971 Act (general provision for regulation and control)–

(a) after subsection (4) insert–

'(4A) For the purposes of subsection (4) above a person seeking to leave the United Kingdom through the tunnel system who is refused admission to France shall be treated as having gone to a country outside the common travel area.'

; and

(b) after subsection (7) insert–

'(7A) Any reference in an Order in Council under subsection (7) above to embarking or being about to embark shall be construed as including a reference to leaving or seeking to leave the United Kingdom through the tunnel system.'

(3) In section 4 of the 1971 Act (administration of control) in subsection (2)(b)–

(a) for the words 'the United Kingdom by ship or aircraft' substitute ', or seeking to arrive in or leave, the United Kingdom through the tunnel system'; and

(b) for the words after 'arrive as' substitute 'members of the crews of through trains or shuttle trains'.

(4) In section 8 of the 1971 Act (exceptions for seamen etc.) in subsection (1)–

(a) for the words from 'of a ship' to 'its crew' substitute 'of a through train or shuttle train under an engagement requiring him to leave within seven days as a member of the crew of that or another such train'; and

(b) for the words 'departure of the ship or aircraft' substitute 'departure of the through train or shuttle train'.

(5) In section 11 of the 1971 Act (construction of references to entry etc.)–

(a) in subsection (1)–

(i) for the words 'by ship or aircraft' substitute 'through the tunnel system', and

(ii) for the words from 'he disembarks' to 'immigration officer' substitute–

'(a) he leaves any control area designated under paragraph 26 of Schedule 2 to this Act, or

(b) he remains on a through train after it has ceased to be such a control area';

(b) omit subsections (2) and (3); and

(c) in subsection (4) omit the words after 'section 1(3)'.

(6) [. . .]

(7) In section 24 of the 1971 Act (illegal entry and similar offences)–

(a) in subsection (1)(f) for the words from 'disembarks' to 'aircraft' substitute 'leaves a train in the United Kingdom'; and

(b) in subsection (1)(g) for the word 'embarks' substitute 'leaves or seeks to leave the United Kingdom through the tunnel system'.

[(8) In section 25C (forfeiture of vehicle, ship or aircraft)—

(a) in subsection (3)—

(i) for 'ship or aircraft' wherever those words occur substitute 'train';

(ii) at the end of paragraph (d) insert 'or';

(iii) omit paragraph (e);

(iv) in paragraph (f), for 'captain' substitute 'the train manager';

(b) in subsection (4), for paragraphs (a) and (b) substitute 'if subsection (5) applies';

(c) in subsection (5) for 'ship or aircraft' in both places, substitute 'train';

(d) omit subsections (6) and (7);

(e) in subsection (8)—

(i) for ', ship or aircraft' substitute 'or train';

(ii) for 'ship, aircraft' substitute 'train'.]

(9) In section 27 of the 1971 Act (offences by persons connected with ships etc.)–

(a) in paragraph (a)–

(i) for the words 'captain of a ship or aircraft' substitute 'train manager of a through train or shuttle train', and

(ii) in sub-paragraph (i) for the word 'disembark' substitute 'leave the train';

(b) in paragraph (b)–

(i) for the words 'as owner or agent of a ship or aircraft' substitute 'as, or as agent of, a person operating an international service';

(ii) in sub-paragraph (i) for the words from 'the ship' to 'port of entry' substitute 'a through train to stop at a place other than a terminal control point [or an international station]'; and

(c) in paragraph (c)–

[(i) for the words 'as a person' to 'port' substitute 'as an occupier or person concerned with the management of a terminal control point or of an international station'], and

(ii) for the words 'the embarkation or disembarkation of passengers' substitute 'persons arriving or seeking to arrive in, or leaving or seeking to leave, the United Kingdom through the tunnel system' [; and

(d) in paragraph (ca) for the words 'as a person' to 'port' substitute 'as an occupier or person concerned with the management of a terminal control point or of an international station'.]

[(9A) In section 28A of the 1971 Act (arrest without warrant), in subsection (3) after the words 'immigration officer' insert 'or a constable'.]

(10) In section 33 of the 1971 Act (interpretation)–

(a) in subsection (1)–

(i) omit the definitions of 'airport' and 'port',

(ii) in the definition of 'crew' after the word 'captain,' insert 'and in relation to a through train or a shuttle train, means all persons on the train who are actually employed in its service or working, including the train manager,', and

(iii) in the definition of 'illegal entrant' after the words 'unlawfully entering or seeking' insert '(whether or not he has arrived in the United Kingdom)'; and

(b) [in subsection (3) for the words 'ports of entry for purposes of this Act' substitute 'international stations for purposes of this Act shall be such railway stations as may from time to time be designated by order of the Secretary of State'.]

(11) In Schedule 2 to the 1971 Act (administrative provisions as to control on entry etc.)—

(a) in paragraph 1(4) and where first occurring in paragraph 1(5) for the words 'ship or aircraft' substitute 'through train or shuttle train';

(b) in paragraph 1(5) for the words after 'vehicle' substitute

'which—

(a) is in a control zone in France within the tunnel system, or

(b) has arrived in, or is seeking to leave, the United Kingdom through the tunnel system.';

(c) in paragraph 2(1) for the words from 'in the United Kingdom' to 'seeking to enter the United Kingdom)' substitute ', or who are seeking to arrive, in the United Kingdom through the tunnel system';

[(d) after paragraph 2(1) insert—

'(1A) The power conferred by sub-paragraph (1) is exercisable—

(a) as respects persons who have arrived in the United Kingdom, in a control area, and

(b) as respects persons seeking to arrive in the United Kingdom (who may first be questioned to ascertain whether they are seeking to do so), in a control zone in France or Belgium, or in a supplementary control zone in France.';]

(e) in paragraph 2(3)[after the words 'further examination' insert '(or, if examined by an immigration officer in a supplementary control zone, may be required to submit to a [further examination before or after arrival] in the United Kingdom)' and]—

(i) for the words 'crew of a ship or aircraft' substitute 'crew of a through train or shuttle train',

(ii) after the words 'joining a ship or aircraft' insert 'or a shuttle train or through train', and

(iii) after the words 'intended ship or aircraft' insert 'or train';

[(ea) after paragraph 2A(1) insert—

'(1A) his paragraph also applies to a person who seeks to arrive in the United Kingdom and who is in a control zone in France or Belgium, or in a supplementary control zone in France.';

and after paragraph 2A(5) insert—

'(5A) A person examined by an immigration officer under this paragraph in a supplementary control zone may be required to submit to a [further examination before or after arrival] in the United Kingdom.';]

(eb) in paragraph 2A(6)–

(i) [after the words 'sub-paragraph (5)' insert 'or sub-paragraph (5A)'] for the words 'crew of a ship or aircraft' substitute 'crew of a through train or shuttle train';

(ii) after the words 'joining a ship or aircraft' insert 'or a shuttle train or through train'; and

(iii) after the words 'intended ship or aircraft', insert 'or train';]

(f) in paragraph 3(1) and (2) for the words 'embarking or seeking to embark in the United Kingdom' substitute 'leaving or seeking to leave the United Kingdom through the tunnel system';

[(g) in paragraph 5—

(i) in sub-paragraph (a) for the words 'passengers disembarking' to 'such passengers' substitute 'persons arriving in or leaving or seeking to arrive in or leave the United Kingdom through the tunnel system, or any class of such persons',

(ii) in sub-paragraph (b) for the words 'passengers embarking' to 'such passengers' substitute 'persons leaving or seeking to leave the United Kingdom through the tunnel system, or any class of such persons', and

(iii) for the words 'the owners or agents of ships and aircraft to supply such cards to those passengers' substitute 'persons operating international services to supply such cards to those persons';]

[(ga) in paragraph 5B–

(i) in sub-paragraph (1)(a) for the words 'an owner or agent of a ship or aircraft' substitute 'a person operating, or a person acting as agent of a person operating, an international service', and

(ii) in sub-paragraph (1)(b) for the words 'a person concerned in the management of a port' substitute 'an occupier of, or a person concerned with the management of a terminal control point or of an international station', and

(iii) in sub-paragraph (2)(a) for the words 'the port' substitute 'the terminal control point or the international station'.]

(h) in paragraph 8(1)–

(i) after the words 'in the United Kingdom' insert 'through the tunnel system', and

(ii) for the words after 'sub-paragraph (2) below' substitute 'give the person operating the international service by which he arrived ('the carrier') directions requiring the carrier–

(a) to remove him from the United Kingdom through the tunnel system; or

(b) to make arrangements for his removal from the United Kingdom in any ship or aircraft specified or indicated in the directions to a country or territory so specified, being either–

(i) a country of which he is a national or citizen; or

(ii) a country or territory in which he has obtained a passport or other document of identity; or

(iii) the country from which he departed for the United Kingdom; or

(iv) a country or territory to which there is reason to believe he will be admitted.';

(i) after paragraph 8(1) insert–

'(1A) Where a person seeking to arrive in the United Kingdom through the tunnel system is refused leave to enter and is then in a control zone in France within the tunnel system, an immigration officer may give the Concessionaires directions requiring them to secure that the person is taken out of the control zone to a place where he may be accepted back by the competent French authorities as provided in Article 18 of the international articles.';

(j) in paragraph 8(2)–

(i) for the words ['sub-paragraph (1)(b) or (c)'] substitute 'sub-paragraph (1)', and

(ii) for the words 'the owners or agents in question' substitute 'the carrier';

(k) [in paragraph 9 (1)] for the words after 'an immigration officer' substitute 'may–

(a) if the illegal entrant has arrived in the United Kingdom, give such directions in respect of him as in a case within sub-paragraph (1) of paragraph 8 above are authorised by that sub-paragraph, or

(b) if the illegal entrant is in a control zone in France within the tunnel system, give such directions in respect of him as in a case within sub-paragraph (1A) of paragraph 8 above are authorised by that sub-paragraph.';

(l) in paragraph 10(1)–

(i) omit the words from 'either' to 'or (b)',

(ii) for the words 'owners or agents of any ship or aircraft' substitute 'person operating the international service by which he arrived', and

(iii) for the words 'paragraph 8(1)(c)' substitute 'paragraph 8(1)';

(m) in paragraph 11 after the words 'ship or aircraft' insert 'or through train or shuttle train';

(n) in paragraph 13 omit sub-paragraph (1) and in sub-paragraph (2)–

(i) for the words 'crew of a ship or aircraft, and either' substitute 'crew of a through train or shuttle train, and',

(ii) omit the words from 'or (B)' to 'do so', and

(iii) for the words after 'an immigration officer may' substitute–

'(a) give the train manager of the train in which that person ('the crew member') arrived directions requiring the train manager to remove him from the United Kingdom in that train; or

(b) give the person operating the international service on which that train is engaged directions requiring that person to remove the crew member from the United Kingdom in any train specified or indicated in the directions, being a train engaged on that international service; or

(c) give that person directions requiring him to make arrangements for the removal of the crew member from the United Kingdom in any ship or aircraft or through train or shuttle train specified in the directions to a country or territory so specified, being either–

(i) a country of which he is a national or citizen; or

(ii) a country or territory in which he has obtained a passport or other document of identity; or

(iii) the country from which he departed for the United Kingdom; or

(iv) a country or territory in which he was engaged as a member of the crew of the through train or shuttle train in which he arrived in the United Kingdom; or

(v) a country or territory to which there is reason to believe he will be admitted.';

(o) in paragraph 15 after the words 'ship or aircraft' insert 'or through train or shuttle train';

(p) in paragraph 16–

(i) in sub-paragraph (2) for the words 'his removal in pursuance of' substitute 'the taking of any action in respect of him required by',

(ii) for sub-paragraph (3) substitute–

'(3) A person may under the authority of an immigration officer be removed for detention under this paragraph–

(a) from a vehicle in a control zone in the tunnel system in France; or

(b) from a train or vehicle in which he arrives in the United Kingdom through the tunnel system.' , and

(iii) after sub-paragraph (4) insert–

'(5) Where a person has under paragraph 11 or 15 above been placed on a through train or shuttle train sub-paragraph (4) of this paragraph has effect with the substitution–

(a) for the word 'captain', wherever occurring, of the words 'train manager'; and

(b) for the words 'ship or aircraft', wherever occurring, of the word 'train'; and

(c) for the word 'disembarking', of the words 'leaving the train'.';

(q) in paragraphs 19(1) and 20(1) for the words 'owners or agents of the ship or aircraft in' substitute 'person operating the international service by'; [. . .]

(r) for paragraphs 26 and 27 substitute–

'26.—(1) Persons operating international services shall not, without the approval of the Secretary of State, arrange for any through train to stop for the purpose of enabling passengers to leave it except at a terminal control point.

(2) The Secretary of State may from time to time give written notice to persons operating international services designating all or any through trains as control areas while they are within any area in the United Kingdom specified in the notice or while they constitute a control zone.

(3) The Secretary of State may from time to time give written notice designating a control area–

(a) to the Concessionaires as respects any part of the tunnel system in the United Kingdom or of a control zone within the tunnel system in France, or

(b) to any occupier or person concerned with the management of a terminal control point in the United Kingdom.

(4) A notice under sub-paragraph (2) or (3) above may specify conditions and restrictions to be observed in a control area, and any person to whom such a notice is given shall take all reasonable steps to secure that any such conditions or restrictions are observed.

[27.—(1) The train manager of a through train or shuttle train arriving in the United Kingdom—

(a) shall take such steps as may be necessary to secure that persons, other than members of the crew who may lawfully enter the United kingdom by virtue of section 8(1) of this Act, do not leave the train except in accordance with any arrangements approved by an immigration officer; and

(b) where persons are to be examined by an immigration officer on the train, shall take such steps as may be necessary to secure that they are ready for examination.

(2) The Secretary of State may by order require, or enable an immigration officer to require, the train manager of a through train or shuttle train or a person operating an international service or his agent to supply—

(a) a passenger list showing the names and nationality or citizenship of passengers arriving or leaving on board the train; and

(b) particulars of members of the crew of the train.

(3) An order under sub-paragraph (2) may relate—

(a) to all through trains or shuttle trains arriving or expected to arrive in the United Kingdom;

(b) to all through trains or shuttle trains leaving or expected to leave the United Kingdom.

(4) An order under sub-paragraph (2)—

(a) may specify the time at which or period during which information is to be provided,

(b) may specify the form and manner in which information is to be provided,

(c) shall be made by statutory instrument, and

(d) shall be subject to annulment in pursuance of a resolution of either House of Parliament.'.]

[(s) In paragraph 27B (passenger information)–

(i) in sub-paragraph (1) for the words 'ships or aircraft' substitute 'through trains or shuttle trains';

(ii) in sub-paragraph (2) for the words 'owner or agent ('the carrier') of a ship or aircraft' substitute 'person operating an international service or his agent ('the carrier')';

(iii) in sub-paragraph (3)(a) for the words 'ship or particular aircraft' substitute 'train';

(iv) in sub-paragraph (3)(b) and (c) for the words 'ships or aircraft' substitute 'trains'; and

(v) in sub-paragraphs (4) and (9) for the words 'ship or aircraft', wherever occurring, substitute 'train'; [. . .]

[(vi) in sub-paragraph (9A) for 'voyage or flight' substitute 'international service' and for the words 'ship or aircraft' substitute 'through train or shuttle train'; and]

(t) [. . .]

(12) In Schedule 3 to the 1971 Act (supplementary provisions as to deportation)–

(a) in paragraph 1(1) after the words 'any person' insert 'who arrived in the United Kingdom through the tunnel system';

(b) in paragraph 1(2) after sub-paragraph (b) insert–

'(bb) directions to the person operating the international service by which the person in question arrived ('the carrier') requiring the carrier to make arrangements for the removal of the person in question through the tunnel system; or'

; and

(c) in paragraph 1(4) after the word 'voyage' insert 'or journey'.

Note: Words inserted in paragraph (9)(b)(ii) from 1 July 1994 (SI 1994/1405). Paragraph (9)(c)(i) substituted and paragraph (9)(d) inserted from 5 August 2014 (SI 2014/1814). Paragraph (9A) inserted from 25 May 2001 (SI 2001/1544). Paragraph (10)(iii)(b) inserted from 1 July 1994 (SI 1994/1405). Paragraph (11)(d) substituted and words inserted in paragraph (11)(e) from 25 May 2001 (SI 2001/1544). Paragraph (11)(ea) and (eb) inserted from 30 July 2000 (SI 2000/1775). Words substituted in paragraph (11) (ea) from 10 December 2001 (SI 2001/3707). Words substituted in paragraph (11)(eb) from 25 May 2001 (SI 2001/1544). Paragraph (11)(g) substituted and paragraph (11)(ga) inserted from 5 August 2014 (SI 2014/1814). Words omitted from paragraph (11)(q) from 28 April 2000 (SI 2000/913). Words substituted in paragraph (11)(r) and words inserted in paragraph (11)(s) from 2 January 2008 (SI 2007/3579). Paragraph (11)(s) inserted from 28 April 2000 (SI 2000/913). Paragraph (6) omitted and (8) substituted from 30 September 2020 (SI 2020/915). Words in paragraph (11)(j)(i) and (k) substituted and (t) omitted from 30 September 2020 (SI 2020/915).

[2A. In the Immigration and Asylum Act 1999 in section 141 (fingerprinting)—

(a) in subsection (7)(a) for 'on his arrival in the United Kingdom' substitute 'in a control zone or a supplementary control zone';

(b) in subsection (9)(b) for his 'removal or deportation from the United Kingdom' substitute 'his leaving a control zone or a supplementary control zone'.]

Note: Paragraph 2A inserted from 26 October 2006 (SI 2006/2626).

[3A. In the Immigration, Asylum and Nationality Act 2006—

(a) in section 32 (passenger and crew information: police powers)—

(i) in subsection (1) for 'ships and aircraft' substitute 'through trains and shuttle trains';

(ii) in subsections (2) and (3) for 'owner or agent of a ship or aircraft' substitute 'person operating an international service or his agent';

(iii) in subsection (5)(a)(iii) for 'a voyage or flight' substitute 'an international service'; and

(iv) in subsection (6)(b) for 'ships or aircraft' substitute 'through trains or shuttle trains';

(b) in section 34 (offence) the reference to section 32 includes a reference to that provision as modified by paragraph (a);

(c) in section 36 (duty to share information)—

(i) in subsection (4) for 'ship or aircraft', wherever occurring, substitute 'through train or shuttle train'; and

(ii) in subsection (4) for 'flights or voyages' substitute 'international services';

(d) in section 37 (information sharing: code of practice) the references to section 36 include references to that provision as modified by paragraph (c);

(e) [. . .]

(f) in section 39 (disclosure to law enforcement agencies) the reference to section 32 includes a reference to that provision as modified by paragraph (a).]

Note: Paragraph 3A inserted from 2 January 2008 (SI 2007/3579). Paragraph (e) omitted from 30 September 2020 (SI 2020/915).

[4. In the Immigration (Leave to Enter and Remain) Order 2000—

(a) in article 4(2)—

(i) after the words 'arrives in the United Kingdom', insert 'or enters a control zone in France or Belgium, or a supplementary control zone in France, seeking to arrive in the United Kingdom through the tunnel system';

(ii) after the words 'before arrival', insert 'or entry into the control zone or supplementary control zone'; and

(iii) after the words 'date of arrival', insert 'or entry into the control zone or supplementary control zone';

[(aa) in article 4(2B)—

(i) after the words 'On arrival in the United Kingdom', insert 'or entry into a control zone in France or Belgium, or a supplementary control zone in France, seeking to arrive in the United Kingdom through the tunnel system';

(ii) after the words 'before arrival', insert 'or entry into the control zone or supplementary control zone'; and

(iii) after the words 'arrives in the United Kingdom', insert 'or enters a control zone in France or Belgium, or a supplementary control zone in France, seeking to arrive in the United Kingdom through the tunnel system';

(ab) in article 4(2D)—

(i) after the words 'On arrival in the United Kingdom', insert 'or entry into a control zone in France or Belgium, or a supplementary control zone in France, seeking to arrive in the United Kingdom through the tunnel system';

(ii) after the words 'before arrival', insert 'or entry into the control zone or supplementary control zone'; and

(iii) after the words 'date of arrival', insert 'or entry into the control zone or supplementary control zone';]

(b) in article 4(3)—

(i) after the words 'on arrival in the United Kingdom', insert 'or entry into a control zone in France or Belgium, or a supplementary control zone in France, seeking to arrive in the United Kingdom through the tunnel system'; and

(ii) after the words 'before arrival', insert 'or entry into the control zone or supplementary control zone';

[(ba)in article 4(3B)—

(i) after the words 'on arrival in the United Kingdom', insert 'or entry into a control zone in France or Belgium, or a supplementary control zone in France, seeking to arrive in the United Kingdom through the tunnel system';

(ii) after the words 'before arrival', insert 'or entry into the control zone or supplementary control zone'; and

(iii) in sub-paragraph (b), after the words 'arrives in the United Kingdom', insert 'or enters the control zone or supplementary control zone'; and]

(c) in article 6(2)(a) after the words 'arrives in the United Kingdom', insert 'or enters a control zone in France or Belgium, or a supplementary control zone in France, seeking to arrive in the United Kingdom through the tunnel system'.]

Note: Paragraph 4 substituted from 25 May 2001 (SI 2001/1544). Paragraphs (aa), (ab) and (ba) inserted from 30 September 2020 (SI 2020/915).

5. In the Immigration (European Economic Area) Regulations 2016—

[. . .]

Note: Paragraph 5 inserted from 10 December 2001 (SI 2001/3707) and omitted from a 2300 on 31 December 2020 (SI 2020/1309) subject to saving provision (reg 26(3) of SI 2020/1309).

[**6.**—(1) In the UK Borders Act 2007 in section 2 (detention)—

(a) in subsection (1)—

(i) omit 'in England, Wales or Northern Ireland';

(ii) omit 'or Article 26(1), (2) or (3) of the Police and Criminal Evidence (Northern Ireland) Order 1989 (SI 1989/1341 (NI 12))';

(iii) after paragraph (a), insert—

(aa) might be liable to arrest by a constable under section 24(1), (2) or (3) of the Police and Criminal Evidence Act 1984 if the act or omission had taken place in England, or';

(b) omit subsection (1A);

(c) in subsection (2)(a) after 'constable' insert ', an officer belonging to the French Re public or an officer belonging to the Kingdom of Belgium';

(d) in subsection (2)(d) after 'constable', in each place where it appears, insert ', the officer belonging to the French Republic or the officer belonging to the Kingdom of Belgium';

(e) omit subsection (5).

(2) In the UK Borders Act 2007 in section 4 (interpretation of 'port')—

(a) for subsection (1) substitute, 'In section 2 'port' means a terminal control point or an international station.';

(b) in subsection (2) for 'ship or aircraft', in each place where it appears, substitute 'train'.']

Note: Paragraph 6 inserted from 16 April 2015 (SI 2015/856).

Schedule 5

Amendments of Enactments and Instruments

...

The Asylum Support Regulations 2000

(SI 2000, No. 704)

Arrangement of Regulations

General

Initial application for support

Determining whether persons are destitute

Provision of support

General

Citation and commencement

1. These Regulations may be cited as the Asylum Support Regulations 2000 and shall come into force on 3 April 2000.

Interpretation

2.—(1) In these Regulations—

'the Act' means the Immigration and Asylum Act 1999;

'asylum support' means support provided under section 95 of the Act;

[. . .]

['cohabiting couple' means two people who, though not married to, or civil partners of, each other, are living together as if they were a married couple or civil partners;]

'dependant' has the meaning given by paragraphs (4) and (5);

'the interim Regulations' means the Asylum Support (Interim Provisions) Regulations 1999;

[. . .]

[(2) The period prescribed under section 94(3) of the Act (day on which a claim for asylum is determined) for the purposes of Part VI of the Act is 28 days where paragraph (2A) applies, and 21 days in any other case.

(2A) This paragraph applies where:

(a) the Secretary of State notifies the claimant that his decision is to accept the asylum claim;

(b) the Secretary of State notifies the claimant that his decision is to reject the asylum claim but at the same time notifies him that he is giving him limited leave to enter or remain in the United Kingdom; or

(c) an appeal by the claimant against the Secretary of State's decision has been disposed of by being allowed.]

(3) Paragraph (2) does not apply in relation to a case to which the interim Regulations apply (for which case, provision corresponding to paragraph (2) is made by regulation 2(6) of those Regulations).

(4) In these Regulations 'dependant', in relation to an asylum-seeker, a supported person or an applicant for asylum support, means, subject to paragraph (5), a person in the United Kingdom ('the relevant person') who—

(a) is his spouse [or civil partner];

(b) is a child of his or of his spouse [or civil partner], is dependant on him and is, or was at the relevant time, under 18;

(c) is a member of his or his spouse's [or civil partner's] close family and is, or was at the relevant time, under 18;

(d) had been living as part of his household—

(i) for at least six of the twelve months before the relevant time, or

(ii) since birth, and is, or was at the relevant time, under 18;

(e) is in need of care and attention from him or a member of his household by reason of a disability and would fall within sub-paragraph (c) or (d) but for the fact that he is not, and was not at the relevant time, under 18;

(f) had been living with him as a member of an [cohabiting couple] for at least two of the three years before the relevant time;

(fa) [. . .]

(g) is living as part of his household and was, immediately before 6 December 1999 (the date when the interim Regulations came into force), receiving assistance from a local authority under section 17 of the Children Act 1989;

(h) is living as part of his household and was, immediately before the coming into force of these Regulations, receiving assistance from a local authority under—

(i) section 22 of the Children (Scotland) Act 1995; or

(ii) Article 18 of the Children (Northern Ireland) Order 1995; or

(i) has made a claim for leave to enter or remain in the United Kingdom, or for variation of any such leave, which is being considered on the basis that he is dependant on the asylum-seeker;

and in relation to a supported person, or an applicant for asylum support, who is himself a dependant of an asylum-seeker, also includes the asylum-seeker if in the United Kingdom.

(5) Where a supported person or applicant for asylum support is himself a dependant of an asylum-seeker, a person who would otherwise be a dependant of the supported person, or of the applicant, for the purposes of these Regulations is not such a dependant unless he is also a dependant of the asylum-seeker or is the asylum-seeker.

(6) In paragraph (4), 'the relevant time', in relation to the relevant person, means—

(a) the time when an application for asylum support for him was made in accordance with regulation 3(3); or

(b) if he has joined a person who is already a supported person in the United Kingdom and sub-paragraph (a) does not apply, the time when he joined that person in the United Kingdom.

(7) Where a person, by falling within a particular category in relation to an asylum-seeker or supported person, is by virtue of this regulation a dependant of the asylum-seeker or supported person for the purposes of these Regulations, that category is also a prescribed category for the purposes of paragraph (c) of the definition of 'dependant' in section 94(1) of the Act and, accordingly, the person is a dependant of the asylum-seeker or supported person for the purposes of Part VI of the Act.

(8) Paragraph (7) does not apply to a person who is already a dependant of the asylum-seeker or supported person for the purposes of Part VI of the Act because he falls within either of the categories mentioned in paragraphs (a) and (b) of the definition of 'dependant' in section 94(1) of the Act.

(9) Paragraph (7) does not apply for the purposes of any reference to a 'dependant' in Schedule 9 to the Act.

Note: Regulation 2(2) substituted from 8 April 2002 (SI 2002/472). Words inserted in subparagraphs (4)(a), (b) and (c) from 5 December 2005 (SI 2005/2114). Definition of 'cohabiting couple' inserted and definitions of 'civil partnership couple', 'married couple', 'same-sex couple' and 'unmarried couple' deleted from 2 December 2019 (SI 2019/1458). Words substituted in subparagraph (4)(f) and subparagraph (4) (fa) deleted from 2 December 2019 (SI 2019/1458).

Initial application for support

Initial application for support: individual and group applications

3.—(1) Either of the following—

(a) an asylum-seeker, or

(b) a dependant of an asylum-seeker,

may apply to the Secretary of State for asylum support.

(2) An application under this regulation may be—

(a) for asylum support for the applicant alone; or

(b) for asylum support for the applicant and one or more dependants of his.

(3) The application must be made by completing in full and in English the form for the time being issued by the Secretary of State for the purpose.

[(4) The application may not be entertained by the Secretary of State—

(a) where it is made otherwise than in accordance with paragraph (3); or

(b) where the Secretary of State is not satisfied that the information provided is complete or accurate or that the applicant is co-operating with enquiries made under paragraph (5).]

(5) The Secretary of State may make further enquiries of the applicant about any matter connected with the application.

[(5A) Where the Secretary of State makes further enquiries under paragraph (5) the applicant shall reply to those enquiries within five working days of his receipt of them.

(5B) The Secretary of State shall be entitled to conclude that the applicant is not cooperating with his enquiries under paragraph (5) if he fails, without reasonable excuse, to reply within the period prescribed by paragraph (5A).

(5C) In cases where the Secretary of State may not entertain an application for asylum support he shall also discontinue providing support under section 98 of the Act.]

(6) Paragraphs (3) and (4) do not apply where a person is already a supported person and asylum support is sought for a dependant of his for whom such support is not already provided (for which case, provision is made by regulation 15).

[(7) For the purposes of this regulation, working day means any day other than a Saturday, a Sunday, Christmas Day, Good Friday or a day which is a bank holiday under section 1 of the Banking and Financial Dealings Act 1971 in the locality in which the applicant is living.]

Note: Subparagraph (4) substituted from 8 January 2003 (SI 2002/3110). Subparagraphs (5A), (5B), (5C) and (7) inserted from 5 February 2005 (SI 2005/11). Words omitted from subparagraph (3) from 9 April 2007 (SI 2007/863).

Persons excluded from support

4.—(1) The following circumstances are prescribed for the purposes of subsection (2) of section 95 of the Act as circumstances where a person who would otherwise fall within subsection (1) of that section is excluded from that subsection (and, accordingly, may not be provided with asylum support).

(2) A person is so excluded if he is applying for asylum support for himself alone and he falls within paragraph (4) by virtue of any sub-paragraph of that paragraph.

(3) A person is so excluded if—

(a) he is applying for asylum support for himself and other persons, or he is included in an application for asylum support made by a person other than himself;

(b) he falls within paragraph (4) (by virtue of any sub-paragraph of that paragraph); and

(c) each of the other persons to whom the application relates also falls within paragraph (4) (by virtue of any sub-paragraph of that paragraph).

(4) A person falls within this paragraph if at the time when the application is determined—

(a) he is a person to whom interim support applies; or

(b) he is a person to whom social security benefits apply; or

(c) he has not made a claim for leave to enter or remain in the United Kingdom, or for variation of any such leave, which is being considered on the basis that he is an asylum-seeker or dependent on an asylum-seeker [; or

(d) he is a national of a member State who has made a claim for asylum, except where that claim for asylum is accepted as admissible [(see section 80A of the Nationality, Immigration and Asylum Act 2002)]; or

(e) he is the dependant of a person to whom sub-paragraph (d) applies.]

(5) For the purposes of paragraph (4), interim support applies to a person if—

(a) at the time when the application is determined, he is a person to whom, under the interim Regulations, support under regulation 3 of those Regulations must be provided by a local authority;

(b) sub-paragraph (a) does not apply, but would do so if the person had been determined by the local authority concerned to be an eligible person; or

(c) sub-paragraph (a) does not apply, but would do so but for the fact that the person's support under those Regulations was (otherwise than by virtue of regulation 7(1)(d) of those Regulations) refused under regulation 7, or suspended or discontinued under regulation 8, of those Regulations;

and in this paragraph 'local authority', 'local authority concerned' and 'eligible person' have the same meanings as in the interim Regulations.

(6) For the purposes of paragraph (4), a person is a person to whom social security benefits apply if he is—

(a) a person who by virtue of regulation 2 of the Social Security (Immigration and Asylum) Consequential Amendments Regulations 2000 is not excluded by section 115(1) of the Act from entitlement to—

(i) income-based jobseeker's allowance under the Jobseekers Act 1995;

(ii) income support, housing benefit or council tax benefit under the Social Security Contributions and Benefits Act 1992;

[(iii) income-related employment and support allowance payable under Part 1 of the Welfare Reform Act 2007] [or

(iv) universal credit under Part 1 of the Welfare Reform Act 2012] {or Part 2 of the Welfare Reform (Northern Ireland) Order 2015}

(b) a person who, by virtue of regulation 2 of the Social Security (Immigration and Asylum) Consequential Amendments Regulations (Northern Ireland) 2000 is not excluded by section 115(2) of the Act from entitlement to—

(i) income-based jobseeker's allowance under the Jobseekers (Northern Ireland) Order 1995;

(ii) income support or housing benefit under the Social Security Contributions and Benefits (Northern Ireland) Act 1992; [or

(iii) income- related employment and support allowance payable under Part 1 of the Welfare Reform Act (Northern Ireland) 2007.]

(7) A person is not to be regarded as falling within paragraph (2) or (3) if, when asylum support is sought for him, he is a dependant of a person who is already a supported person.

(8) The circumstances prescribed by paragraphs (2) and (3) are also prescribed for the purposes of section 95(2), as applied by section 98(3), of the Act as circumstances where a person who would otherwise fall within subsection (1) of section 98 is excluded from that subsection (and, accordingly, may not be provided with temporary support under section 98).

(9) For the purposes of paragraph (8), paragraphs (2) and (3) shall apply as if any reference to an application for asylum support were a reference to an application for support under section 98 of the Act.

Note: Subparagraph (6)(a)(iii) inserted from 27 October 2008 (SI 2008/1879) and paragraph (6)(b)(iii) from 27 October 2008 (SI 2008/412). Subparagraph (6)(a)(iv) inserted from 29 April 2013 (SI 2013/630). Words in curly brackets added to subparagraph (6)(a)(iv) by SI 2016/236 and come into operation immediately after the coming into operation of the Universal Credit Regulations (Northern Ireland) 2016 (regulation 1(1) of SI 2016/236). Paragraphs 4(d) and (e) inserted from immediately after 2300 on 31 December 2020 (SI 2020/1372). Words in paragraph 4(d) substituted from 28 June 2022 by Nationality and Borders Act 2022 c. 36 Pt 2 s.15(2) subject to transitional and saving provisions specified in SI 2022/590 reg.3 and Sch.2 para.4(3).

Determining whether persons are destitute

Determination where application relates to more than one person, etc.

5.—(1) Subject to paragraph (2), where an application in accordance with regulation 3(3) is for asylum support for the applicant and one or more dependants of his, in applying section 95(1) of the Act the Secretary of State must decide whether the applicant and all those dependants, taken together, are destitute or likely to become destitute within the period prescribed by regulation 7.

(2) Where a person is a supported person, and the question falls to be determined whether asylum support should in future be provided for him and one or more other persons who are his dependants and are—

(a) persons for whom asylum support is also being provided when that question falls to be determined; or

(b) persons for whom the Secretary of State is then considering whether asylum support should be provided, in applying section 95(1) of the Act the Secretary of State must decide whether the supported person and all those dependants, taken together, are destitute or likely to become destitute within the period prescribed by regulation 7.

Income and assets to be taken into account

6.—(1) This regulation applies where it falls to the Secretary of State to determine for the purposes of section 95(1) of the Act whether—

(a) a person applying for asylum support, or such an applicant and any dependants ofhis, or

(b) a supported person, or such a person and any dependants of his, is or are destitute or likely to become so within the period prescribed by regulation 7.

(2) In this regulation 'the principal' means the applicant for asylum support (where paragraph (1)(a) applies) or the supported person (where paragraph (1)(b) applies).

(3) The Secretary of State must ignore—

(a) any asylum support, and

(b) any support under section 98 of the Act, which the principal or any dependant of his is provided with or, where the question is whether destitution is likely within a particular period, might be provided with in that period.

(4) But he must take into account—

(a) any other income which the principal, or any dependant of his, has or might reasonably be expected to have in that period;

(b) any other support which is available to the principal or any dependant of his, or might reasonably be expected to be so available in that period; and

(c) any assets mentioned in paragraph (5) (whether held in the United Kingdom or elsewhere) which are available to the principal or any dependant of his otherwise than by way of asylum support or support under section 98, or might reasonably be expected to be so available in that period.

(5) Those assets are—

(a) cash;

(b) savings;

(c) investments;

(d) land;

(e) cars or other vehicles; and

(f) goods held for the purpose of a trade or other business.

(6) The Secretary of State must ignore any assets not mentioned in paragraph (5).

Period within which applicant must be likely to become destitute

7. The period prescribed for the purposes of section 95(1) of the Act is—

(a) where the question whether a person or persons is or are destitute or likely to become so falls to be determined in relation to an application for asylum support and sub-paragraph (b) does not apply, 14 days beginning with the day on which that question falls to be determined;

(b) where that question falls to be determined in relation to a supported person, or in relation to persons including a supported person, 56 days beginning with the day on which that question falls to be determined.

Adequacy of existing accommodation

8.—(1) Subject to paragraph (2), the matters mentioned in paragraph (3) are prescribed for the purposes of subsection (5)(a) of section 95 of the Act as matters to which the Secretary of State must have regard in determining for the purposes of that section whether the accommodation of—

(a) a person applying for asylum support, or

(b) a supported person for whom accommodation is not for the time being provided by way of asylum support, is adequate.

(2) The matters mentioned in paragraph (3)(a) and (d) to (g) are not so prescribed for the purposes of a case where the person indicates to the Secretary of State that he wishes to remain in the accommodation.

(3) The matters referred to in paragraph (1) are—

(a) whether it would be reasonable for the person to continue to occupy the accommodation;

(b) whether the accommodation is affordable for him;

(c) whether the accommodation is provided under section 98 of the Act, or otherwise on an emergency basis, only while the claim for asylum support is being determined;

(d) whether the person can secure entry to the accommodation;

(e) where the accommodation consists of a moveable structure, vehicle or vessel designed or adapted for human habitation, whether there is a place where the person is entitled or permitted both to place it and reside in it;

(f) whether the accommodation is available for occupation by the person's dependants together with him;

(g) whether it is probable that the person's continued occupation of the accommodation will lead to domestic violence against him or any of his dependants.

(4) In determining whether it would be reasonable for a person to continue to occupy accommodation, regard may be had to the general circumstances prevailing in relation to housing in the district of the local housing authority where the accommodation is.

(5) In determining whether a person's accommodation is affordable for him, the Secretary of State must have regard to—

(a) any income, or any assets mentioned in regulation 6(5) (whether held in the United Kingdom or elsewhere), which is or are available to him or any dependant of his otherwise than by way of asylum support or support under section 98 of the Act, or might reasonably be expected to be so available;

(b) the costs in respect of the accommodation; and

(c) the person's other reasonable living expenses.

(6) In this regulation—

(a) 'domestic violence' means violence from a person who is or has been a close family member, or threats of violence from such a person which are likely to be carried out; and

(b) 'district of the local housing authority' has the meaning given by section 217(3) of the Housing Act 1996.

(7) The reference in paragraph (1) to subsection (5)(a) of section 95 of the Act does not include a reference to that provision as applied by section 98(3) of the Act.

Essential living needs

9. (1) The matter mentioned in paragraph (2) is prescribed for the purposes of subsection (7)(b) of section 95 of the Act as a matter to which the Secretary of State may not have regard in determining for the purposes of that section whether a person's essential living needs (other than accommodation) are met.

(2) That matter is his personal preference as to clothing (but this shall not be taken to prevent the Secretary of State from taking into account his individual circumstances as regards clothing).

(3) None of the items and expenses mentioned in paragraph (4) is to be treated as being an essential living need of a person for the purposes of Part VI of the Act.

(4) Those items and expenses are—

(a) the cost of faxes;

(b) computers and the cost of computer facilities;

(c) the cost of photocopying;

(d) travel expenses, except the expense mentioned in paragraph (5);

(e) toys and other recreational items;

(f) entertainment expenses.

(5) The expense excepted from paragraph (4)(d) is the expense of an initial journey from a place in the United Kingdom to accommodation provided by way of asylum support or (where accommodation is not so provided) to an address in the United Kingdom which has been notified to the Secretary of State as the address where the person intends to live.

(6) Paragraph (3) shall not be taken to affect the question whether any item or expense not mentioned in paragraph (4) or (5) is, or is not, an essential living need.

(7) The reference in paragraph (1) to subsection (7)(b) of section 95 of the Act includes a reference to that provision as applied by section 98(3) of the Act and, accordingly, the reference in paragraph (1) to 'that section' includes a reference to section 98.

Provision of support

Kind and levels of support for essential living needs

10.—(1) This regulation applies where the Secretary of State has decided that asylum support should be provided in respect of the essential living needs of a person.

[(2) As a general rule, asylum support in respect of the essential living needs of that person may be expected to be provided weekly in the form of a cash payment of {£40.88}.]

(3) [. . .]

[(3A) For the purposes of {paragraph 1}, a decision to grant support is made on the date recorded on the letter granting asylum support to the applicant.]

(4) [. . .]

(5) Where the Secretary of State has decided that accommodation should be provided for a person [. . .] by way of asylum support, and the accommodation is provided in a form which also meets other essential living needs (such as bed and breakfast, or half or full board), {the amount specified} in paragraph (2) shall be treated as reduced accordingly.

(6) [. . .]

Note: Regulation 10(6) omitted from 8 April 2002 (SI 2002/472). Regulation (3A) inserted from 6 July 2009 (SI 2009/1388) and words in curly brackets substituted from 10 August 2015 (SI 2015/1501). Regulation 10(2) substituted from 10 August 2015 (SI 2015/1501). Amount in curly brackets in Regulation 10(2) substituted from 21 February 2022 (SI 2022/78). Regulation 10(3) and (4) omitted from 10 August 2015 (SI 2015/1501). Words omitted and words in curly brackets substituted in Regulation 10(5) from 10 August 2015 (SI 2015/1501).

[Additional support for pregnant women and children under 3

10A.—(1) In addition to the [cash support which the Secretary of State may be expected to provide weekly as] described in regulation 10(2), in the case of any pregnant woman or child aged under 3 for whom the Secretary of State has decided asylum support should be provided, there shall, as a general rule, be added to the [cash support] for any week the amount shown in the second column of the following table opposite the entry in the first column which for the time being describes that person.

Pregnant woman	£3.00
Child aged under 1	£5.00
Child aged at least 1 and under 3	£3.00

(2) In this regulation, 'pregnant woman' means a woman who has provided evidence to satisfy the Secretary of State that she is pregnant.]

Note: Regulation 10A inserted from 3 March 2003 (SI 2003/241). Words in square brackets substituted from 4 June 2004 (SI 2004/1313).

Additional single payments in respect of essential living needs

11. [. . .]

Note: Regulation 11 revoked from 4 June 2004 (SI 2004/1313), save to enable the Secretary of State to make a payment to a person whose qualifying period ends on or before that date.

Income and assets to be taken into account in providing support

12.—(1) This regulation applies where it falls to the Secretary of State to decide the level or kind of asylum support to be provided for—

(a) a person applying for asylum support, or such an applicant and any dependants of his,

(b) a supported person, or such a person and any dependants of his.

(2) In this regulation 'the principal' means the applicant for asylum support (where paragraph (1)(a) applies) or the supported person (where paragraph (1)(b) applies).

(3) The Secretary of State must take into account—

(a) any income which the principal or any dependant of his has or might reasonably be expected to have,

(b) support which is or might reasonably be expected to be available to the principal or any dependant of his, and

(c) any assets mentioned in regulation 6(5) (whether held in the United Kingdom or elsewhere) which are or might reasonably be expected to be available to the principal or any dependant of his, otherwise than by way of asylum support.

Accommodation

13.—(1) The matters mentioned in paragraph (2) are prescribed for the purposes of subsection (2)(b) of section 97 of the Act as matters to which regard may not be had when exercising the power under section 95 of the Act to provide accommodation for a person.

(2) Those matters are—

(a) his personal preference as to the nature of the accommodation to be provided; and

(b) his personal preference as to the nature and standard of fixtures and fittings; but this shall not be taken to prevent the person's individual circumstances, as they relate to his accommodation needs, being taken into account.

Services

14.—(1) The services mentioned in paragraph (2) may be provided or made available by way of asylum support to persons who are otherwise receiving such support, but may be so provided only for the purpose of maintaining good order among such persons.

(2) Those services are—

(a) education, including English language lessons,

(b) sporting or other developmental activities.

Change of circumstances

Change of circumstances

15.—(1) If a relevant change of circumstances occurs, the supported person concerned or a dependant of his must, without delay, notify the Secretary of State of that change of circumstances.

(2) A relevant change of circumstances occurs where a supported person or a dependant of his—

(a) is joined in the United Kingdom by a dependant or, as the case may be, another dependant, of the supported person;

(b) receives or gains access to any money, or other asset mentioned in regulation 6(5), that has not previously been declared to the Secretary of State;

(c) becomes employed;

(d) becomes unemployed;

(e) changes his name;

(f) gets married;

[(fa) forms a civil partnership;]

(g) starts living with a person as if married to[,or the civil partner of,] that person;

(ga) [. . .]

(h) gets divorced;

[(ha) becomes a former civil partner on the dissolution of his civil partnership;]

(i) separates from a spouse [or civil partner], or from a person with whom he has been living as if married to [,or the civil partner of,] that person;

(ia) [. . .]

(j) becomes pregnant;

(k) has a child;

(l) leaves school;

(m) starts to share his accommodation with another person;

(n) moves to a different address, or otherwise leaves his accommodation;

(o) goes into hospital;

(p) goes to prison or is otherwise held in custody;

(q) leaves the United Kingdom; or

(r) dies.

(3) If, on being notified of a change of circumstances, the Secretary of State considers that the change may be one—

(a) as a result of which asylum support should be provided for a person for whom it was not provided before, or

(b) as a result of which asylum support should no longer be provided for a person, or

(c) which may otherwise affect the asylum support which should be provided for a person,

he may make further enquiries of the supported person or dependant who gave the notification.

(4) The Secretary of State may, in particular, require that person to provide him with such information as he considers necessary to determine whether, and if so, what, asylum support should be provided for any person.

Note: Subparagraphs (2)(fa) and (ha) inserted from 5 December 2005 (SI 2005/2114). Words inserted in subparagraph (g) and (i) and subparagraphs (ga) and (ia) deleted from 2 December 2019 (SI 2019/1458).

Contributions

Contributions

16.—(1) This regulation applies where, in deciding the level of asylum support to be provided for a person who is or will be a supported person, the Secretary of State is required to take into account income, support or assets as mentioned in regulation 12(3).

(2) The Secretary of State may—

(a) set the asylum support for that person at a level which does not reflect the income, support or assets; and

(b) require from that person payments by way of contributions towards the cost of the provision for him of asylum support.

(3) A supported person must make to the Secretary of State such payments by way of contributions as the Secretary of State may require under paragraph (2).

(4) Prompt payment of such contributions may be made a condition (under section 95(9) of the Act) subject to which asylum support for that person is provided.

Recovery of sums by Secretary of State

Recovery where assets become realisable

17.—(1) This regulation applies where it appears to the Secretary of State at any time (the relevant time)—

(a) that a supported person had, at the time when he applied for asylum support, assets of any kind in the United Kingdom or elsewhere which were not capable of being realised; but

(b) that those assets have subsequently become, and remain, capable of being realised.

(2) The Secretary of State may recover from that person a sum not exceeding the recoverable sum.

(3) Subject to paragraph (5), the recoverable sum is a sum equal to whichever is the less of—

(a) the monetary value of all the asylum support provided to the person up to the relevant time; and

(b) the monetary value of the assets concerned.

(4) As well as being recoverable as mentioned in paragraph 11(2)(a) of Schedule 8 to the Act, an amount recoverable under this regulation may be recovered by deduction from asylum support.

(5) The recoverable sum shall be treated as reduced by any amount which the Secretary of State has by virtue of this regulation already recovered from the person concerned (whether by deduction or otherwise) with regard to the assets concerned.

[Recovery of asylum support

17A.—(1) The Secretary of State may require a supported person to refund asylum support if it transpires that at any time during which asylum support was being provided for him he was not destitute.

(2) If a supported person has dependants, the Secretary of State may require him to refund asylum support if it transpires that at any time during which asylum support was being provided for the supported person and his dependants they were not destitute.

(3) The refund required shall not exceed the monetary value of all the asylum support provided to the supported person or to the supported person and his dependants for the relevant period.

(4) In this regulation the relevant period is the time during which asylum support was provided for the supported person or the supported person and his dependants and during which he or they were not destitute.

(5) If not paid within a reasonable period, the refund required may be recovered from the supported person as if it were a debt due to the Secretary of State.]

Note: Regulation 17A inserted from 5 April 2005 (SI 2005/11).

Overpayments: method of recovery

18. As well as being recoverable as mentioned in subsection (3) of section 114 of the Act, an amount recoverable under subsection (2) of that section may be recovered by deduction from asylum support.

Breach of conditions and suspension and discontinuation of support

Breach of conditions: decision whether to provide support

19.—(1) When deciding—

(a) whether to provide, or to continue to provide, asylum support for any person or persons, or

(b) the level or kind of support to be provided for any person or persons, the Secretary of State may take into account [the extent to which a] relevant condition has been complied with.

[(2) A relevant condition is one which makes the provision of asylum support subject to actual residence by the supported person or a dependant of his for whom support is being provided in a specific place or location.]

Note: Words in square brackets in paragraphs (1) and (2) substituted from 5 February 2005 (SI 2005/11).

[Suspension or discontinuation of support

20.—(1) Asylum support for a supported person and any dependant of his or for one or more dependants of a supported person may be suspended or discontinued if—

(a) support is being provided for the supported person or a dependant of his in collective accommodation and the Secretary of State has reasonable grounds to believe that the supported person or his dependant has committed a serious breach of the rules of that accommodation;

(b) the Secretary of State has reasonable grounds to believe that the supported person or a dependant of his for whom support is being provided has committed an act of seriously violent behaviour whether or not that act occurs in accommodation provided by way of asylum support or at the authorised address or elsewhere;

(c) the supported person or a dependant of his has committed an offence under Part VI of the Act;

(d) the Secretary of State has reasonable grounds to believe that the supported person or any dependant of his for whom support is being provided has abandoned the authorised address without first informing the Secretary of State or, if requested, without permission;

(e) the supported person has not complied within a reasonable period, which shall be no less than five working days beginning with the day on which the request was received by him, with requests for information made by the Secretary of State and which relate to the supported person's or his dependant's eligibility for or receipt of asylum support including requests made under regulation 15;

(f) the supported person fails, without reasonable excuse, to attend an interview requested by the Secretary of State relating to the supported person's or his dependant's eligibility for or receipt of asylum support;

(g) the supported person or, if he is an asylum seeker, his dependant, has not complied within a reasonable period, which shall be no less than ten working days beginning with the day on which the request was received by him, with a request for information made by the Secretary of State relating to his claim for asylum;

(h) the Secretary of State has reasonable grounds to believe that the supported person or a dependant of his for whom support is being provided has concealed financial resources and that the supported person or a dependant of his or both have therefore unduly benefited from the receipt of asylum support;

(i) the supported person or a dependant of his for whom support is being provided has not complied with a reporting requirement;

(j) the Secretary of State has reasonable grounds to believe that the supported person or a dependant of his for whom support is being provided has made a claim for asylum ('the first claim') and before the first claim has been determined makes or seeks to make a further claim for asylum not being part of the first claim in the same or a different name; or

(k) the supported person or a dependant of his for whom support is being provided has failed without reasonable excuse to comply with a relevant condition.

(2) If a supported person is asked to attend an interview of the type referred to in paragraph (1)(f) he shall be given no less than five working days notice of it.

(3) Any decision to discontinue support in the circumstances referred to in paragraph (1) above shall be taken individually, objectively and impartially and reasons shall be given. Decisions will be based on the particular situation of the person concerned and particular regard shall be had to whether he is a vulnerable person as described by Article 17 of Council Directive 2003/9/EC of 27 January 2003 laying down minimum standards for the reception of asylum seekers.

(4) No person's asylum support shall be discontinued before a decision is made under paragraph (1).

(5) Where asylum support for a supported person or his dependant is suspended or discontinued under paragraph (1)(d) or (i) and the supported person or his dependant are traced or voluntarily report to the police, the Secretary of State or an immigration officer, a duly motivated decision based on the reasons for the disappearance shall be taken as to the reinstatement of some or all of the supported person's or his dependant's or both of their asylum support.

(6) For the purposes of this regulation—

(a) the authorised address is—

(i) the accommodation provided for the supported person and his dependants (if any) by way of asylum support; or

(ii) if no accommodation is so provided, the address notified by the supported person to the Secretary of State in his application for asylum support or, where a change of address has been notified to the Secretary of State under regulation 15 or under the Immigration Rules or both, the address for the time being so notified;

(b) 'collective accommodation' means accommodation which a supported person or any dependant of his for whom support is being provided shares with any other supported person and includes accommodation in which only facilities are shared;

(c) 'relevant condition' has the same meaning as in regulation 19(2);

(d) ['reporting requirement' is a condition imposed under paragraph 2(1)(a) of Schedule 10 to the Immigration Act 2016, that is to say a condition of immigration bail requiring a person to report to the Secretary of State or such other person as may be specified.]

(e) 'working day' has the same meaning as in regulation 3(7) save that the reference to the applicant shall be a reference to the supported person or his dependant.]

Note: Regulation 20 substituted from 5 February 2005 (SI 2005/11) and definition of 'reporting condition' substituted from 15 January 2018 (SI 2017/1242).

[Temporary Support

20A. Regulations 19 and 20 shall apply to a person or his dependant who is provided with temporary support under section 98 of the Act in the same way as they apply to a person and his dependant who is in receipt of asylum support and any reference to asylum support in regulations 19 and 20 shall include a reference to temporary support under section 98.]

Note: Regulation 20A inserted from 5 April 2005 (SI 2005/11).

Effect of previous suspension or discontinuation

21.—(1) [Subject to regulation 20(5) where—]

(a) an application for asylum support is made,

(b) the applicant or any other person to whom the application relates has previously had his asylum support suspended or discontinued under regulation 20, and

(c) there has been no material change of circumstances since the suspension or discontinuation, the application need not be entertained unless the Secretary of State considers that there are exceptional circumstances which justify its being entertained.

(2) A material change of circumstances is one which, if the applicant were a supported person, would have to be notified to the Secretary of State under regulation 15.

(3) This regulation is without prejudice to the power of the Secretary of State to refuse the application even if he has entertained it.

Note: Words in square brackets in paragraph (1) substituted from 5 February 2005 (SI 2005/11).

Notice to quit

Notice to quit

22.—(1) If—

(a) as a result of asylum support, a person has a tenancy or licence to occupy accommodation,

(b) one or more of the conditions mentioned in paragraph (2) is satisfied, and

(c) he is given notice to quit in accordance with paragraph (3) or (4), his tenancy or licence is to be treated as ending with the period specified in that notice, regardless of when it could otherwise be brought to an end.

(2) The conditions are that—

(a) the asylum support is suspended or discontinued as a result of any provision of regulation 20;

(b) the relevant claim for asylum has been determined;

(c) the supported person has ceased to be destitute; or

(d) he is to be moved to other accommodation.

(3) A notice to quit is in accordance with this paragraph if it is in writing and—

(a) in a case where sub-paragraph (a), (c) or (d) of paragraph (2) applies, specifies as the notice period a period of not less than seven days; or

(b) in a case where the Secretary of State has notified his decision on the relevant claim for asylum to the claimant, specifies as the notice period a period at least as long as whichever is the greater of—

(i) seven days; or

(ii) the period beginning with the date of service of the notice to quit and ending with the date of determination of the relevant claim for asylum (found in accordance with section 94(3) of the Act).

(4) A notice to quit is in accordance with this paragraph if—

(a) it is in writing;

(b) it specifies as the notice period a period of less than seven days; and

(c) the circumstances of the case are such that that notice period is justified.

Meaning of 'destitute' for certain other purposes

Meaning of 'destitute' for certain other purposes

23.—(1) In this regulation 'the relevant enactments' means—

(a) section 21(1A) of the National Assistance Act 1948;

(b) section 45(4A) of the Health Services and Public Health Act 1968;

(c) paragraph 2(2A) of Schedule 8 to the National Health Service Act 1977;

[(ca) section 21(1) of the Care Act 2014 (exception for persons subject to immigration control);]

(d) sections 12(2A), 13A(4) and 13B(3) of the Social Work (Scotland) Act 1968;

(e) sections 7(3) and 8(4) of the Mental Health (Scotland) Act 1984; and

(f) Articles 7(3) and 15(6) of the Health and Personal Social Services (Northern Ireland) Order 1972.

(2) The following provisions of this regulation apply where it falls to an authority, or the Department, to determine for the purposes of any of the relevant enactments whether a person is destitute.

(3) Paragraphs (3) to (6) of regulation 6 apply as they apply in the case mentioned in paragraph (1) of that regulation, but as if references to the principal were references to the person whose destitution or otherwise is being determined and references to the Secretary of State were references to the authority or (as the case may be) Department.

(4) The matters mentioned in paragraph (3) of regulation 8 (read with paragraphs (4) to (6) of that regulation) are prescribed for the purposes of subsection (5)(a) of section 95 of the Act, as applied for the purposes of any of the relevant enactments, as matters to which regard must be had in determining for the purposes of any of the relevant enactments whether a person's accommodation is adequate.

(5) The matter mentioned in paragraph (2) of regulation 9 is prescribed for the purposes of subsection (7)(b) of section 95 of the Act, as applied for the purposes of any of the relevant enactments, as a matter to which regard may not be had in determining for the purposes of any of the relevant enactments whether a person's essential living needs (other than accommodation) are met.

(6) Paragraphs (3) to (6) of regulation 9 shall apply as if the reference in paragraph (3) to Part VI of the Act included a reference to the relevant enactments.

(7) The references in regulations 8(5) and 9(2) to the Secretary of State shall be construed, for the purposes of this regulation, as references to the authority or (as the case may be) Department.

Note: Subparagraph (1)(ca) inserted and in force from 1 April 2015 (article 1(2) of SI 2015/643) subject to savings provision (article 4 of SI 2015/643).

SCHEDULE

Regulation 3(3)

[. . .]

Note: Schedule revoked from 9 April 2007 (SI 2007/863).

The Immigration (Leave to Enter and Remain) Order 2000

(SI 2000, No. 1161)

PART I

GENERAL

Citation, commencement and interpretation

1. (1) This Order may be cited as the Immigration (Leave to Enter and Remain) Order 2000.

2019 (SI 2019/686). Definition of 'Service Provider from Switzerland visa' inserted from 23.00 on 31 December 2020 (SI 2020/1353).

PART II

ENTRY CLEARANCE AS LEAVE TO ENTER

Entry clearance as Leave to Enter

2. Subject to article 6(3), an entry clearance which complies with the requirements of article 3 shall have effect as leave to enter the United Kingdom to the extent specified in article 4, but subject to the conditions referred to in article 5.

Requirements

3. [(1) Subject to paragraph (4), an entry clearance shall only have effect as leave to enter if it complies with the requirements of this article.]

(2) The entry clearance must specify the purpose for which the holder wishes to enter the United Kingdom.

(3) The entry clearance must be endorsed with:

(a) the conditions to which it is subject; or

(b) a statement that it is to have effect as indefinite leave to enter the United Kingdom.

[(4) Subject to paragraph (5), an entry clearance shall not have effect as leave to enter if it is endorsed on a convention travel document.

(5) An entry clearance endorsed on a convention travel document before 27 February 2004 shall have effect as leave to enter.]

Note: Article 3(1) substituted and Art 3(4) and (5) inserted from 27 February 2004 (SI 2004/475).

Extent to which entry clearance is to be leave to enter

4. (1) A visit visa, [(other than a visit visa granted pursuant to the ADS Agreement with China) {, or a visit visa for private medical treatment or for entry as an academic visitor} unless endorsed with a statement that it is to have effect as a single-entry visa] [. . .] shall have effect as leave to enter the United Kingdom on an unlimited number of occasions {during its period of validity}, in accordance with paragraph (2).

(2) On each occasion the holder arrives in the United Kingdom, he shall be treated for the purposes of the Immigration Acts as having been granted, before arrival, leave to enter the United Kingdom for a limited period beginning on the date of arrival, being:

(a) six months if six months or more remain of the visa's period of validity; or

(b) the visa's remaining period of validity, if less than six months.

[(2A) A visit visa granted pursuant to the ADS Agreement with China endorsed with a statement that it is to have effect as a dual-entry visa, shall have effect as leave to enter the United Kingdom on two occasions during its period of validity, in accordance with paragraph (2B).

(2) Articles 1 to 12, 14 and 15(1) of this Order shall come into force on 28 April 2000 or, if later, on the day after the day on which it is made and articles 13 and 15(2) shall come into force on 30 July 2000.

(3) In this Order—

'the Act' means the Immigration Act 1971;

['ADS Agreement with China' means the Memorandum of Understanding on visa and related issues concerning tourist groups from the People's Republic of China to the United Kingdom as an approved destination, signed on 21 January 2005;]

{'biometric immigration document' means a document recording biometric information;}

'control port' means a port in which a control area is designated under paragraph 26(3) of Schedule 2 to the Act;

['convention travel document' means a travel document issued pursuant to Article 28 of the Refugee Convention, except where that travel document was issued by the United Kingdom Government;]

{'Crown service' means service of the Crown, whether within Her Majesty's dominions or elsewhere, under Her Majesty's government in the United Kingdom or in a Northern Ireland department or under the Scottish Administration or under the Welsh Government;}

{'decision-maker' means—

(a) the Secretary of State;

(b) an immigration officer;}

{'Her Majesty's Forces' has the same meaning as in the Armed Forces Act 2006;}

[. . .]

['Refugee Convention' means the Convention relating to the Status of Refugees done at Geneva on 28 July 1951 and its Protocol;]

{'representative' means a person who appears to the decision-maker—

(a) to be the representative of the person referred to in article 8ZA(1); and (b) not to be prohibited from acting as a representative by section 84 of the Immigration and Asylum Act 1999;}

'responsible third party' means a person appearing to an immigration officer to be:

(a) in charge of a group of people arriving in the United Kingdom together or intending to arrive in the United Kingdom together;

(b) a tour operator;

(c) the owner or agent of a ship, aircraft, train, hydrofoil or hovercraft;

(d) the person responsible for the management of a control port or his agent; or

(e) an official at a British Diplomatic Mission or at a British Consular Post or at the office of any person outside the United Kingdom and Islands who has been authorised by the Secretary of State to accept applications for entry clearance;

['Service Provider from Switzerland visa' means an entry clearance granted for the purpose of entry to the United Kingdom under the appendix to the immigration rules entitled 'Appendix Service Providers from Switzerland';]

'tour operator' means a person who, otherwise than occasionally, organises and provides holidays to the public or a section of it; and

'visit visa' means an entry clearance granted for the purpose of entry to the United Kingdom as a visitor under the immigration rules.

Note: Words in first square brackets inserted from 1 April 2005 (SI 2005/1159). Other words in square brackets inserted from 27 February 2004 (SI 2004/475). Definitions of 'decision-maker' and 'representative' inserted from 12 July 2013 (SI 2013/1749). Definition of 'the Immigration Acts' omitted and definition of 'biometric immigration document' inserted from 18 March 2015 (SI 2015/434). Definitions of 'Crown Service' and 'Her Majesty's Forces' inserted from 30 March

(2B) On arrival in the United Kingdom on each occasion, the holder shall be treated for the purposes of the Immigration Acts as having been granted, before arrival, leave to enter the United Kingdom for a limited period, being the period beginning on the date on which the holder arrives in the United Kingdom and ending on the date of expiry of the entry clearance.]

[(2C) A visit visa granted for private medical treatment or for entry as an academic visitor, unless endorsed with a statement that it is to have effect as a single-entry visa, shall have effect as leave to enter the United Kingdom on an unlimited number of occasions during its period of validity in accordance with paragraph (2D).

(2D) On arrival in the United Kingdom on each occasion, the holder shall be treated for the purposes of the Immigration Acts as having been granted, before arrival, leave to enter the United Kingdom for a limited period beginning on the date of arrival, being—

(a) where the visit visa is granted for private medical treatment—
(i) 11 months if 11 months remain of the visa's period of validity, or
(ii) the visa's remaining period of validity, if less than 11 months, and
(b) where the visit visa is granted for entry as an academic visitor—
(i) 12 months if 12 months remain of the visa's period of validity, or
(ii) the visa's remaining period of validity, if less than 12 months.]

[(2E) A Service Provider from Switzerland visa shall have effect as leave to enter the United Kingdom on an unlimited number of occasions during its period of validity, in accordance with paragraph (2F).

(2F) On arrival in the United Kingdom on each occasion, the holder shall be treated for the purposes of the Immigration Acts as having been granted, before arrival, leave to enter the United Kingdom for a limited period beginning on the date of arrival, being:

(a) 90 days if 90 days or more remain of the entry clearance's period of validity; or
(b) the entry clearance's remaining period of validity, if less than 90 days.]

(3) In the case of [any form of entry clearance to which this paragraph applies], it shall have effect as leave to enter the United Kingdom on one occasion during its period of validity; and, on arrival in the United Kingdom, the holder shall be treated for the purposes of the Immigration Acts as having been granted, before arrival, leave to enter the United Kingdom:

(a) in the case of an entry clearance which is endorsed with a statement that it is to have effect as indefinite leave to enter the United Kingdom, for an indefinite period; or

(b) in the case of an entry clearance which is endorsed with conditions, for a limited period, being the period beginning on the date on which the holder arrives in the United Kingdom and ending on the date of expiry of the entry clearance.

[(3A) Paragraph (3) applies to—

(a) a visit visa (other than a visit visa granted pursuant to the ADS Agreement with China) endorsed with a statement that it is to have effect as a single entry visa;

(b) a visit visa granted pursuant to the ADS Agreement with China unless endorsed with a statement to the effect that it is to have effect as a dual entry visa; and

(c) any other form of entry clearance]{except those to which paragraph (3B) applies.}

[(3B) A short term biometric entry clearance shall have effect as leave to enter the United Kingdom on one occasion during its period of validity; and, on arrival in the

United Kingdom, the holder shall be treated for the purposes of the Immigration Acts as having been granted, before arrival, leave to enter the United Kingdom—

(a) in the case of an entry clearance which is endorsed with an indefinite period of leave, for an indefinite period; or

(b) in the case of an entry clearance which is endorsed with conditions, for a limited period, being the period beginning on the date on which the holder arrives in the United Kingdom and ending on the date of the expiry of the holder's period of leave.]

(4) In this article 'period of validity' means the period beginning on the day on which the entry clearance becomes effective and ending on the day on which it expires.

[(5) In this article—

(a) 'period of leave' means the intended period of leave which—

(i) in the case of an indefinite intended period of leave, is endorsed on the person's short term biometric entry clearance; or

(ii) in the case of a limited period of leave, is stated in the written decision which accompanies the person's short term biometric entry clearance,

and such a period of leave will only have effect on the person's arrival in the United Kingdom in accordance with paragraph (3B) and subject to the powers of variation, cancellation and refusal of leave under this Order, the Immigration Acts and the immigration rules; and

(b) 'short term biometric entry clearance' means an entry clearance document which—

(i) is issued to a person who has made a successful application for a biometric immigration document from outside the United Kingdom, in order that the person may travel to the United Kingdom to obtain that biometric immigration document; and

(ii) has a period of validity ending before the expiry of the period of leave that the holder's biometric immigration document will evidence.]

Note: Words in square brackets inserted in paragraph (1) and substituted in paragraph (3) from 1 April 2005 (SI 2005/1159). Paragraphs (2A), (2B) and (3A) inserted from 1 April 2005 (SI 2005/1159). Paragraphs (2) and (3) have effect in a form modified by and in circumstances specified by the Channel Tunnel (International Arrangements) Order (SI 1993/1813) as amended. Words in curly brackets added to paragraph (3A)(c) and paragraphs (3B) and (5) inserted from 18 March 2015 (SI 2015/434). Words omitted and words in curly brackets inserted in paragraph (1) and paragraphs (2C) and (2D) inserted from 23 November 2016 (SI 2016/1132). Paragraphs (2E) and (2F) inserted from 23.00 on 31 December 2020 (SI 2020/1353).

Conditions

5. An entry clearance shall have effect as leave to enter subject to any conditions, being conditions of a kind that may be imposed on leave to enter given under section 3 of the Act, to which the entry clearance is subject and which are endorsed on it.

Incidental, supplementary and consequential provisions

6. (1) Where an immigration officer exercises his power to cancel leave to enter under paragraph 2A(8) of Schedule 2 to the Act or article 13(7) below in respect of an entry clearance which has effect as leave to enter, the entry clearance shall cease to have effect.

(2) If the holder of an entry clearance—

(a) arrives in the United Kingdom before the day on which it becomes effective; or

(b) seeks to enter the United Kingdom for a purpose other than the purpose specified in the entry clearance, an immigration officer may cancel the entry clearance.

(3) If the holder of an entry clearance which does not, at the time, have effect as leave to enter the United Kingdom seeks leave to enter the United Kingdom at any time before his departure for, or in the course of his journey to, the United Kingdom and is refused leave to enter under article 7, the entry clearance shall not have effect as leave to enter.

Note: Paragraph (2)(a) has effect in a form modified by and in circumstances specified by the Channel Tunnel (International Arrangements) Order (SI 1993/1813) as amended.

PART III

FORM AND MANNER OF GIVING AND REFUSING LEAVE TO ENTER

Grant and refusal of leave to enter before arrival in the United Kingdom

7. (1) An immigration officer, whether or not in the United Kingdom, may give or refuse a person leave to enter the United Kingdom at any time before his departure for, or in the course of his journey to, the United Kingdom.

(2) In order to determine whether or not to give leave to enter under this article (and, if so, for what period and subject to what conditions), an immigration officer may seek such information, and the production of such documents or copy documents, as an immigration officer would be entitled to obtain in an examination under paragraph 2 or 2A of Schedule 2 to the Act.

(3) An immigration officer may also require the person seeking leave to supply an up to date medical report.

(4) Failure by a person seeking leave to supply any information, documents, copy documents or medical report requested by an immigration officer under this article shall be a ground, in itself, for refusal of leave.

[Oral grant or refusal of leave

8.—(1) A notice giving or refusing leave to enter the United Kingdom to a person to whom this article applies may, instead of being given in writing as required by section 4(1) of the Act, be given orally, including by means of a telephone.

(2) This article applies to a person seeking leave to enter the United Kingdom as—

(a) a visitor for a period not exceeding six months,

(b) a short-term student for a period not exceeding six months, [. . .]

(c) a parent of a Tier 4 (child) student for a period not exceeding six months, [or

(d) an S2 Healthcare Visitor for a period not exceeding six months,]

under the immigration rules and subject to conditions prohibiting employment and recourse to public funds (within the meaning of the immigration rules as they apply to persons to whom this article applies).]

Note: Article 8 substituted from 23 November 2016 (SI 2016/1132). Word omitted and paragraph (2)(d) inserted from 23.00 on 31 December 2020 (SI 2020/1353).

Grant, refusal or variation of leave by notice in writing

[8ZA.(1) A notice in writing—

(a) giving leave to enter or remain in the United Kingdom;

(b) refusing leave to enter or remain in the United Kingdom;

(c) refusing to vary a person's leave to enter or remain in the United Kingdom; or

(d) varying a person's leave to enter or remain in the United Kingdom, may be given to the person affected as required by section 4(1) of the Act as follows.

(2) The notice may be—

(a) given by hand;

(b) sent by fax;

(c) sent by postal service to a postal address provided for correspondence by the person or the person's representative;

(d) sent electronically to an e-mail address provided for correspondence by the person or the person's representative;

(e) sent by document exchange to a document exchange number or address; or

(f) sent by courier.

(3) Where no postal or e-mail address for correspondence has been provided, the notice may be sent—

(a) by postal service to—

(i) the last-known or usual place of abode, place of study or place of business of the person; or

(ii) the last-known or usual place of business of the person's representative; or

(b) electronically to—

(i) the last-known e-mail address for the person (including at the person's last-known place of study or place of business); or

(ii) the last-known e-mail address of the person's representative.

(4) Where attempts to give notice in accordance with paragraphs (2) and (3) are not possible or have failed, when the decision-maker records the reasons for this and places the notice on file the notice shall be deemed to have been given.

(5) Where a notice is deemed to have been given in accordance with paragraph (4) and then subsequently the person is located, the person shall as soon as is practicable be given a copy of the notice and details of when and how it was given.

(6) A notice given under this article may, in the case of a person who is under 18 years of age and does not have a representative, be given to the parent, guardian or another adult who for the time being takes responsibility for the child.]

Note: Article 8ZA inserted from 12 July 2013 (SI 2013/1749).

Presumptions about receipt of notice

[**8ZB.**(1) Where a notice is sent in accordance with article 8ZA, it shall be deemed to have been given to the person affected, unless the contrary is proved—

(a) where the notice is sent by postal service—

(i) on the second day after it was sent by postal service in which delivery or receipt is recorded if sent to a place within the United Kingdom;

(ii) on the 28th day after it was posted if sent to a place outside the United Kingdom;

(b) where the notice is sent by fax, e-mail, document exchange or courier, on the day it was sent.

(2) For the purposes of paragraph (1)(a) the period is to be calculated excluding the day on which the notice is posted.

(3) For the purposes of paragraph (1)(a)(i) the period is to be calculated excluding any day which is not a business day.

(4) In paragraph (3) 'business day' means any day other than a Saturday, a Sunday, Christmas Day, Good Friday or a day which is a bank holiday under the Banking and Financial Dealings Act 1971 in the part of the United Kingdom to which the notice is sent.]

Note: Article 8ZB inserted from 12 July 2013 (SI 2013/1749).

Notice not given

[8ZC. No notice under article 8(1) or 8ZA(1)(a) shall be given where a person is given leave to enter the United Kingdom by passing through an automated gate in accordance with article 8A {or 8B}.]

Note: Article 8ZC inserted from 12 July 2013 (SI 2013/1749) and words in curly brackets added from 11 March 2019 (SI 2019/298).

[Automatic grant of leave

8A.—(1) An immigration officer may authorise a person to be a person who may obtain leave to enter the United Kingdom by passing through an automated gate.

(2) Such an authorisation may—

(a) only authorise a person to obtain leave to enter the United Kingdom as one of the categories of person under the immigration rules mentioned in paragraph (5);

(b) set out the conditions of use for an automated gate;

(c) list the automated gates for which the authorisation is valid;

(d) remain in force for up to 24 months; and

(e) be varied or withdrawn at any time, with or without notice being given to the person.

(3) [This paragraph applies to a person who] passes through an automated gate—

(a) having been authorised under paragraph (1) as a person who may obtain leave to enter the United Kingdom by passing through an automated gate;

(b) in accordance with the conditions of use for an automated gate;

(c) which is an automated gate for which the authorisation is valid; and

(d) while the authorisation remains in force; [. . .]

[(3A) A person to whom paragraph (3) applies shall be given leave to enter the United Kingdom for—

(a) six months in the case of a person falling within a category mentioned in paragraph (5)(a) or (c), or

(b) 48 hours in the case of a person falling within the category mentioned in paragraph (5)(b).]

(4) Such leave shall be subject to conditions prohibiting employment and recourse to public funds (within the meaning of the immigration rules [as they apply to the category of person under the immigration rules for which the person has been authorised under paragraph (1)]).

[(5) The categories of person under the immigration rules mentioned in this paragraph are—

(a) a visitor (standard);

(b) a transit visitor;

(c) a parent of a Tier 4 (child) student.]

Note: Article 8A inserted from 25 March 2010 (SI 2010/957). Words in square brackets in paragraph (3) substituted and words at end of paragraph (3)(d) omitted from 23 November 2016 (SI 2016/1132). Paragraph (3A) and words in square brackets in paragraph (4) inserted and paragraph(5) substituted from 23 November 2016 (SI 2016/1132). Amendments to Article 8A subject to transitional provisions: 'Where a person was authorised under article 8A(1) of the 2000 Order before this Order came into force, article 8A of the 2000 Order continues to apply for the purposes of that authorisation as if it had not been amended by article 2(4) of this Order' (article 3 of SI 2016/1132).

[Further provision as to automatic grant of leave

8B.—(1) A person to whom this article applies may obtain leave to enter the United Kingdom by passing through an automated gate.

[(1A) The Schedule to this Order has effect.]

(2) This article applies to a person who–

(a) is a national of [a country listed in the Schedule];

(b) is travelling on a passport issued by one of the countries listed in [the Schedule];

(c) is aged 12 or above; and

(d) is seeking to enter the United Kingdom as a visitor (standard) under Appendix V to the immigration rules [or as an S2 Healthcare Visitor under Appendix S2 Healthcare Visitor of the immigration rules.]

[(2A) This article also applies to a person who—

(a) is a national of Ireland;

(b) is travelling on a passport issued by Ireland;

(c) is aged 12 or above; and

(d) is seeking to enter the United Kingdom as an S2 Healthcare Visitor under Appendix S2 Healthcare Visitor of the immigration rules.]

(3) Leave under paragraph (1) is given for a period of six months.

(4) Such leave is subject to conditions prohibiting employment and recourse to public funds (within the meaning of the immigration rules).]

Note: Article 8B inserted from 11 March 2019 (SI 2019/298). Paragraph (1A), words in paragraph (2)(d) and paragraph (2A) inserted, words in paragraph (2)(a) and (b) substituted from 23.00 on 31 December 2020 (SI 2020/1353).

[Leave to be regarded as having been given before arrival

8C. Leave to enter that is obtained by a person passing through an automated gate in accordance with article 8A or 8B shall be regarded, for the purposes of the Act, as having been given before that person's arrival in the UK.]

Note: Article 8C inserted from 23.00 on 31 December 2020 (SI 2020/1353).

Grant or refusal of leave by notice to a responsible third party

9. (1) Leave to enter may be given or refused to a person by means of a notice given (in such form and manner as permitted by the Act or this Order for a notice giving or refusing leave to enter) to a responsible third party acting on his behalf.

(2) A notice under paragraph (1) may refer to a person to whom leave is being granted or refused either by name or by reference to a description or category of persons which includes him.

Notice of refusal of leave

10. (1) Where a notice refusing leave to enter to a person is given under [article 8(1)] or 9, an immigration officer shall as soon as practicable give to him a notice in writing stating that he has been refused leave to enter the United Kingdom and stating the reasons for the refusal.

(2) Where an immigration officer serves a notice under the Immigration (Appeals) Notices Regulations 1984 or under regulations made under paragraph 1 of Schedule 4 to the Immigration and Asylum Act 1999 in respect of the refusal, he shall not be required to serve a notice under paragraph (1).

(3) Any notice required by paragraph (1) to be given to any person may be [given in accordance with article 8ZA.]

Note: Words in square brackets in paragraphs (1) and (3) substituted from 12 July 2013 (SI 2013/1749).

Burden of proof

11. Where any question arises under the Immigration Acts as to whether a person has leave to enter the United Kingdom and he alleges that he has such leave by virtue of a notice given under article {8(1)} or 9, [or by virtue of article 8A,] the onus shall lie upon him to show the manner and date of his entry into the United Kingdom.

Note: Words in square brackets inserted from 25 March 2010 (SI 2010/957). Words in curly brackets substituted from 12 July 2013 (SI 2013/1749).

12.—(1) This article applies where—

(a) an immigration officer has commenced examination of a person ('the applicant') under paragraph 2(1)(c) of Schedule 2 to the Act (examination to determine whether or not leave to enter should be given);

(b) that examination has been adjourned, or the applicant has been required (under paragraph 2(3) of Schedule 2 to the Act) to submit to a further examination, whilst further inquiries are made (including, where the applicant has made an asylum claim, as to the Secretary of State's decision on that claim); and

(c) upon the completion of those inquiries, an immigration officer considers he is in a position to decide whether or not to give or refuse leave to enter without interviewing the applicant further.

(2) Where this article applies, any notice giving or refusing leave to enter which is on any date thereafter sent by post to the applicant (or is communicated to him in such form or manner as is permitted by this Order) shall be regarded, for the purposes of the Act, as having been given within the period of 24 hours specified in paragraph 6(1) of Schedule 2 to the Act (period within which notice giving or refusing leave to enter must be given after completion of examination).

PART IV
LEAVE WHICH DOES NOT LAPSE ON TRAVEL OUTSIDE COMMON TRAVEL AREA

13.—(1) In [this Part]'leave' means—

(a) leave to enter the United Kingdom (including leave to enter conferred by means of an entry clearance under article 2); and

(b) leave to remain in the United Kingdom.

(2) Subject to paragraph (3), where a person has leave which is in force and which was:

(a) conferred by means of an entry clearance (other than a visit visa [or Service Provider from Switzerland visa]) under article 2; or

(b) given by an immigration officer or the Secretary of State for a period exceeding six months,

such leave shall not lapse on his going to a country or territory outside the common travel area.

(3) Paragraph (2) shall not apply:

(a) where a limited leave has been varied by the Secretary of State; and

(b) following the variation the period of leave remaining is six months or less.

(4) Leave which does not lapse under paragraph (2) shall remain in force either indefinitely (if it is unlimited) or until the date on which it would otherwise have expired (if limited), but—

[(za) where the holder has unlimited leave granted by virtue of Appendix EU to the immigration rules (including unlimited leave granted by virtue of Appendix EU before this paragraph comes into force), subject to article 13C, the unlimited leave lapses if the holder stays outside the United Kingdom and Islands for a continuous period of more than—

(i) four years, in the case of unlimited leave granted by virtue of Appendix EU to the immigration rules as a Swiss national or a family member of a Swiss national;

(ii) five years, in all other cases;]

(a) [in any other case and subject to articles 13A, 13B and 13C], where the holder has stayed outside the United Kingdom {and Islands} for a continuous period of more than two years, the leave (where the leave is unlimited) or any leave then remaining (where the leave is limited) shall thereupon lapse; and

(b) any conditions to which the leave is subject shall be suspended for such time as the holder is outside the United Kingdom {and Islands}.

(5) For the purposes of paragraphs 2 and 2A of Schedule 2 to the Act (examination by immigration officers, and medical examination), leave to remain which remains in force under this article shall be treated, upon the holder's arrival in the United Kingdom, as leave to enter which has been granted to the holder before his arrival.

(6) Without prejudice to the provisions of section 4(1) of the Act, where the holder of leave which remains in force under this article is outside the United Kingdom, the Secretary of State may vary that leave (including any conditions to which it is subject) in such form and manner as permitted by the Act or this Order for the giving of leave to enter.

(7) Where a person is outside the United Kingdom and has leave which is in force by virtue of this article, that leave may be cancelled:

(a) in the case of leave to enter, by an immigration officer; or
(b) in the case of leave to remain, by the Secretary of State.

(8) In order to determine whether or not to vary (and, if so, in what manner) or cancel leave which remains in force under this article and which is held by a person who is outside the United Kingdom, an immigration officer or, as the case may be, the Secretary of State may seek such information, and the production of such documents or copy documents, as an immigration officer would be entitled to obtain in an examination under paragraph 2 or 2A of Schedule 2 to the Act and may also require the holder of the leave to supply an up to date medical report.

(9) Failure to supply any information, documents, copy documents or medical report requested by an immigration officer or, as the case may be, the Secretary of State under this article shall be a ground, in itself, for cancellation of leave.

(10) Section 3(4) of the Act (lapsing of leave upon travelling outside the common travel area) shall have effect subject to this article.

Note: Words in square brackets in paragraph (1) substituted from 23 November 2016 (SI 2016/1132) and words in square brackets in paragraph (4)(a) inserted from 18 March 2015 (SI 2015/434), substituted from 23 November 2016 (SI 2016/1132) and substituted again from 30 March 2019 (SI 2019/686). Paragraph (4)(za) and words in curly brackets in paragraphs (4)(a) and (b) inserted from 30 March 2019 (SI 2019/686). Words inserted in paragraph (2)(a) from 23.00 on 31 December 2020 (SI 2020/1353).

[Partners and children of members of HM Forces

13A.—(1) Any period of time spent by a person to whom this article applies accompanying their partner, or, as the case may be, parent, who is posted outside the United Kingdom [and Islands] as a member of Her Majesty's Forces does not count towards the period mentioned in article 13(4)(a).

(2) This article applies to a person who has leave—

(a) as the partner or child of a member of HM Forces under Appendix Armed Forces to the immigration rules ('Appendix Armed Forces');

(b) as the spouse, civil partner, unmarried or same-sex partner, or child of a member of HM Forces under Part 7 of the immigration rules; or

(c) as the spouse, civil partner, unmarried or same-sex partner, or child of a British citizen or person who is settled in the United Kingdom under Part 8 of the immigration rules where that British Citizen or, as the case may be, settled person, is a member of Her Majesty's Forces.

(3) In paragraph (1)—

(a) the reference to a person's 'partner' means—

(i) in relation to a person falling within paragraph (2)(a), the partner in respect of whom they have leave under Appendix Armed Forces and,

(ii) in relation to a person falling within paragraph (2)(b) or (2)(c), the spouse, civil partner, unmarried or same sex partner in respect of whom they have leave under Part 7 or, as the case may be, Part 8, of the immigration rules; and

(b) the reference to a person's 'parent' means the parent in respect of whom they have leave under Appendix Armed Forces, or, as the case may be, Part 7 or Part 8 of the immigration rules.

(4) [. . .]

Note: Article 13A inserted from 18 March 2015 (SI 2015/434). Words inserted in paragraph (1) and paragraph (4) deleted from 30 March 2019 (SI 2019/686).

[Partners and children of [. . .] Crown servants etc

13B.—(1) This article applies to a person who has—

(a) limited leave—

(i) as the partner or child of a British citizen or person who is settled in the United Kingdom under Appendix FM to the immigration rules ('Appendix FM'), or

(ii) outside the provision of the immigration rules on the basis of family life under article 8 of the European Convention on Human Rights ('article 8'), or

(b) indefinite leave [, other than unlimited leave granted by virtue of Appendix EU to the immigration rules].

(2) The period mentioned in article 13(4)(a) does not include any period during which the person is accompanying their partner or parent if—

(a) the partner or parent is posted outside the United Kingdom [and Islands] in employment falling within paragraph (3); and

(b) the partner or parent—

(i) is a British citizen, [or]

(ii) has indefinite leave,

(iii) [. . .]

(3) Employment falls within this paragraph if it is—

(a) employment in the British Council as a permanent member of that Council; or

(b) [employment on Crown Service.]

(4) In this article—

(a) a person's partner means—

(i) in relation to a person to whom paragraph (1)(a) applies, the partner in respect of whom the person has limited leave under Appendix FM or outside the provision of the immigration rules on the basis of family life under article 8;

(ii) in relation to a person to whom paragraph (1)(b) applies—

(aa) the spouse or civil partner of that person,

(bb) the fiancé(e) or proposed civil partner of that person, or

(cc) someone who has been living together with that person in a relationship akin to a marriage or civil partnership for at least two years;

(b) a person's parent—

(i) in relation to a person to whom paragraph (1)(a) applies, means the parent in respect of whom they have limited leave under Appendix FM or outside the provisions of the immigration rules on the basis of family life under article 8;

(ii) in relation to a person to whom paragraph (1)(b) applies, is to be construed in accordance with paragraph 6 (interpretation) of the immigration rules.]

Note: Article 13B inserted from 23 November 2016 (SI 2016/1132). Word deleted from heading, words inserted in paragraph (1)(b) and (2)(a) and paragraph (3)(b) substituted from 30 March 2019 (SI 686). Word inserted at end of paragraph (2)(b)(i) and (2)(b)(iii) deleted from 23.00 on 31 December 2020 (SI 2020/1309) subject to saving provision (reg 27(3) of SI 2020/1309).

[13C. Crown servants etc with leave granted by virtue of Appendix EU to the immigration rules

(1) Any period of time spent outside the United Kingdom and Islands by a person to whom this article applies does not count towards the period mentioned in article 13(4)(za) or 13(4)(a).

(2) This article applies to a person who has leave granted by virtue of Appendix EU to the immigration rules and who is—

(a) a member of Her Majesty's Forces posted outside the United Kingdom and Islands;

(b) a national of a member State, Iceland, Liechtenstein, Norway or Switzerland posted outside the United Kingdom and Islands in employment—

(i) on Crown service, or

(ii) in the British Council as a permanent member of that Council;

(c) accompanying a person who is posted outside the United Kingdom and Islands—

(i) in employment on Crown service,

(ii) in employment in the British Council as a permanent member of that Council, or

(iii) as a member of Her Majesty's Forces.]

Note: Article 13C inserted from 30 March 2019 (SI 2019/686).

Part V

Consequential and Transitional Provisions

14. Section 9(2) of the Act (further provisions as to common travel area: conditions applicable to certain arrivals on a local journey) shall have effect as if, after the words

'British Citizens', there were inserted 'and do not hold leave to enter or remain granted to them before their arrival'.

15.—(1) Article 12 shall apply where an applicant's examination has begun before the date that article comes into force, as well as where it begins on or after that date.

(2) Article 13 shall apply with respect to leave to enter or remain in the United Kingdom which is in force on the date that article comes into force, as well as to such leave given after that date.

[SCHEDULE

Article 8B(1A)

Countries the nationals of which may obtain leave by passing through an automated gate

Australia
Austria
Belgium
Bulgaria
Canada
Croatia
Cyprus
Czech Republic
Denmark
Estonia
Finland
France
Germany
Greece
Hungary
Iceland
Italy
Japan
Latvia
Liechtenstein
Lithuania
Luxembourg
Malta
Netherlands
New Zealand
Norway
Poland
Portugal
Romania
Singapore
Slovakia
Slovenia
South Korea
Spain
Sweden

Switzerland
United States of America.]

Note: Schedule inserted from 23.00 on 31 December 2020 (SI 2020/1353).

The Immigration (Removal Directions) Regulations 2000

(SI 2000, No. 2243)

1. Citation and commencement

These Regulations may be cited as the Immigration (Removal Directions) Regulations 2000 and shall come into force on 2 October 2000.

2. Interpretation

(1) In these Regulations—

'the Act' means the Immigration and Asylum Act 1999;

'aircraft' includes hovercraft;

'captain' means master (of a ship) or commander (of an aircraft);

'international service' has the meaning given by section 13(6) of the Channel Tunnel Act 1987;

'ship' includes every description of vessel used in navigation; and

'the tunnel system' has the meaning given by section 1(7) of the Channel Tunnel Act 1987.

(2) In these Regulations, a reference to a section number is a reference to a section of the Act.

3. Persons to whom directions may be given

For the purposes of section 10(6)(a) (classes of person to whom directions may be given), the following classes of person are prescribed—

(a) owners of ships;

(b) owners of aircraft;

(c) agents of ships;

(d) agents of aircraft;

(e) captains of ships about to leave the United Kingdom;

(f) captains of aircraft about to leave the United Kingdom; and

(g) persons operating an international service.

4. Requirements that may be imposed by directions

(1) For the purposes of section 10(6)(b) (requirements that may be imposed by directions), the following kinds of requirements are prescribed—

(a) in the case where directions are given to a captain of a ship or aircraft about to leave the United Kingdom, a requirement to remove the relevant person from the United Kingdom in that ship or aircraft;

(b) in the case where directions are given to a person operating an international service, a requirement to make arrangements for the removal of the relevant person through the tunnel system;

(c) in the case where directions are given to any other person who falls within a class prescribed in regulation 3, a requirement to make arrangements for the removal of the relevant person in a ship or aircraft specified or indicated in the directions; and

(d) in all cases, a requirement to remove the relevant person in accordance with arrangements to be made by an immigration officer.

(2) Paragraph (1) only applies if the directions specify that the relevant person is to be removed to a country or territory being—

(i) a country of which he is a national or citizen; or

(ii) a country or territory to which there is reason to believe that he will be admitted.

(3) Paragraph (1)(b) only applies if the relevant person arrived in the United Kingdom through the tunnel system.

(4) 'Relevant person' means a person who may be removed from the United Kingdom in accordance with section 10(1).

The Immigration (Leave to Enter) Order 2001

(SI 2001, No. 2590)

1.—(1) This Order may be cited as the Immigration (Leave to Enter) Order 2001 and shall come into force on the day after the day on which it is made.

(2) In this Order—

(a) 'the 1971 Act' means the Immigration Act 1971; and

(b) 'claim for asylum' and 'the Human Rights Convention' have the meanings assigned by section 167 of the Immigration and Asylum Act 1999.

Note: Commencement 18 July 2001.

2.—(1) Where this article applies to a person, the Secretary of State may give or refuse him leave to enter the United Kingdom.

(2) This article applies to a person who seeks leave to enter the United Kingdom and who—

(a) has made a claim for asylum; or

(b) has made a claim that it would be contrary to the United Kingdom's obligations under the Human Rights Convention for him to be removed from, or required to leave, the United Kingdom.

(3) This article also applies to a person who seeks leave to enter the United Kingdom for a purpose not covered by the immigration rules or otherwise on the grounds that those rules should be departed from in his case.

(4) In deciding whether to give or refuse leave under this article the Secretary of State may take into account any additional grounds which a person has for seeking leave to enter the United Kingdom.

(5) The power to give or refuse leave to enter the United Kingdom under this article shall be exercised by notice in writing to the person affected or in such manner as is permitted by the Immigration (Leave to Enter and Remain) Order 2000.

3.— In relation to the giving or refusing of leave to enter by the Secretary of State under article 2, paragraphs 2 (examination by immigration officers, and medical examination), 4 (information and documents), 7(1), (3) and (4) (power to require medical examination after entry), 8 (removal of persons refused leave to enter) [and 9 (removal of illegal entrants)] of Schedule 2 to the 1971 Act shall be read as if references to an immigration officer included references to the Secretary of State.

Note: Words in square brackets substituted from 15 January 2018 (SI 2017/1242).

4.—(1) This article applies where—

(a) an immigration officer has commenced examination of a person ('the applicant') under paragraph 2(1)(c) of Schedule 2 to the 1971 Act (examination to determine whether or not leave to enter should be given);

(b) that examination has been adjourned, or the applicant has been required (under paragraph 2(3) of Schedule 2 to the Immigration Act 1971) to submit to a further examination;

(c) the Secretary of State subsequently examines the applicant or conducts a further examination in relation to him; and

(d) the Secretary of State thereafter gives or refuses the applicant leave to enter.

(2) Where this article applies, the notice giving or refusing leave to enter shall be regarded for the purposes of the 1971 Act as having been given within the period of 24 hours specified in paragraph 6(1) of Schedule 2 to that Act (period within which notice giving or refusing leave to enter must be given after completion of examination by an immigration officer).

The Immigration (Entry Otherwise than by Sea or Air) Order 2002

(SI 2002, No. 1832)

---

1. This Order may be cited as the Immigration (Entry Otherwise than by Sea or Air) Order 2002 and shall come into force on the day after the day on which it is made.

Note: Commencement 17 July 2002.

2.—(1) This article applies where—

(a) a person who requires leave to enter the United Kingdom by virtue of section 9(4) of the Immigration Act 1971 or by virtue of article 3 of the Immigration (Control of Entry through Republic of Ireland) Order 1972; or

(b) a person in respect of whom a deportation order is in force, has entered or is seeking to enter the United Kingdom from the Republic of Ireland.

(2) Where this article applies, paragraphs 8, 9 and 11 of Schedule 2 to the Immigration Act 1971 shall have effect in relation to persons entering or seeking to enter the United Kingdom on arrival otherwise than by ship or aircraft as they have effect in the case of a person arriving by ship or aircraft, with the modifications set out in the Schedule to this Order.

3. Article 2 shall apply where an illegal entrant entered the United Kingdom before the date when this Order comes into force, as well as where he entered the United Kingdom on or after that date.

(3) Article 2 shall not apply where a person has arrived in, but not entered, the United Kingdom before the date on which this Order comes into force.

Article 2(2) SCHEDULE

MODIFICATIONS TO SCHEDULE 2 OF THE IMMIGRATION ACT 1971

1. In this Schedule 'Schedule 2' means Schedule 2 to the Immigration Act 1971.

2. For paragraph 8 of Schedule 2, substitute:

'**8.**—(1) Where a person arriving in the United Kingdom is refused leave to enter, an immigration officer or the Secretary of State may give the owners or agents of any train, vehicle, ship or aircraft directions requiring them to make arrangements for that person's removal from the United Kingdom in any train, vehicle, ship or aircraft specified or indicated in the direction to a country or territory so specified being—

(a) a country of which he is a national or citizen; or

(b) a country or territory in which he has obtained a passport or other document of identify; or

(c) a country or territory in which he embarked for the United Kingdom; or

(d) a country or territory to which there is reason to believe that he will be admitted.

(2) The costs of complying with any directions given under this paragraph shall be defrayed by the Secretary of State.'.

3. In paragraph 9(1) of Schedule 2:

(a) after 'immigration officer', insert 'or the Secretary of State'; and

(b) after 'authorised by paragraph 8(1)', insert 'and the costs of complying with any directions given under this paragraph shall be defrayed by the Secretary of State'.

4. In paragraph 11 of Schedule 2, after 'on board any', insert 'train, vehicle,'.

The British Nationality (General) Regulations 2003

(SI 2003, No. 548)

Arrangement of Regulations

PART I. GENERAL

PART II. REGISTRATION AND NATURALISATION

Part I

General

Citation and commencement

1. These Regulations may be cited as the British Nationality (General) Regulations 2003 and shall come into force on 1 April 2003.

Interpretation

2.—(1) In these Regulations, the following expressions have the meanings hereby assigned to them, that is to say—

'the Act' means the British Nationality Act 1981;

'applicant' in relation to an application made on behalf of a person not of full age or capacity means that person;

[. . .]

'High Commissioner' means, in relation to a country mentioned in Schedule 3 to the Act, the High Commissioner for Her Majesty's Government in the United Kingdom appointed to that country, and includes the acting High Commissioner.

['immigration rules' means rules made under section 3(2) of the Immigration Act 1971;]

[. . .]]

(2) In the application of the provisions of regulation 6(2) [6(3), 6A(1), (3) and (5), paragraph 3 of Schedule 3] [. . .] where a function of the Secretary of State under the Act is exercised by the Lieutenant-Governor of any of the Islands by virtue of arrangements made under section 43(1) of the Act, any reference in those provisions to the Secretary of State shall be construed as a reference to the Lieutenant-Governor.

Note: Definition of 'immigration rules' inserted from 6 April 2015 (SI 2015/738). Definitions of 'document certifying permanent residence'; 'permanent residence card'; 'residence document issued under the Immigration (European Economic Area) Regulations 2000' and 'residence permit issued under the Immigration (European Economic Area) Regulations 2000' inserted from 12 November 2015 (SI 2015/1806) and omitted from 23.00 on 31 December 2020 (SI 2020/1309). In paragraph (2), words in square brackets inserted from 1 January 2004 (SI 2003/3158) and words omitted from 3 December 2007 (SI 2007/3137).

Part II

Registration and Naturalisation

Applications

3. Any application for registration as a British citizen, British Overseas citizen or British subject or for a certificate of naturalisation as a British citizen shall—

(a) be made to the appropriate authority specified in regulation 4; and

[(b) satisfy the requirements of Part 1 of Schedule 1 and any applicable requirements of Part II or III of Schedule 1 and such further requirements, if any, as are specified in relation thereto in Schedule 2.]

Note: paragraph (b) substituted from 9 August 2018 (SI 2018/851).

Authority to whom application is to be made

4.—(1) Except as provided by paragraphs (2) and (3), the authority to whom an application is to be made is as follows:

(a) if the application is in Great Britain or Northern Ireland, to the Secretary of State at the Home Office;

(b) if the applicant is in any of the Islands, to the Lieutenant-Governor;

(c) if the applicant is in a British overseas territory, to the Governor;

[(d) . . .]

[(e) if the applicant is elsewhere, to the Secretary of State at the Home Office.]

(2) The authority to whom an application under section 4(5) of the Act (acquisition by registration: British overseas territories citizens, etc.), on grounds of Crown Service under the government of a British overseas territory or service as a member of a body established by law in a British overseas territory, is to be made is in all cases the Governor of that territory.

(3) The authority to whom an application under section 5 of the Act [(acquisition by registration: British overseas territories citizens having connection with Gibraltar)] is to be made is in all cases the Governor of Gibraltar.

Note: Subparagraph (1)(e) substituted from 16 July 2012 (SI 2012/1588). Subparagraph (1)(d) omitted from 12 November 2015 (SI 2015/1806). Words in paragraph (3) substituted from 31 December 2020 (SI 2019/745).

Persons not of full age or capacity

5. An application may be made on behalf of someone not of full age or capacity by his father or mother or any person who has assumed responsibility for his welfare.

[Knowledge of language and life in the United Kingdom

5A.—(1) [Subject to paragraph (1A),] a person has sufficient knowledge of the English language for the purpose of an application for naturalisation as a British citizen under section 6 of the Act if that person—

[(a) has passed a test known as a Secure English Language Test administered by an English language test provider which has been approved by the Secretary of State for this purpose and which-

(i) is at a level equivalent to level B1 or above on the Council of Europe's Common European Framework of Reference for Languages: Learning, Teaching, Assessment; and

(ii) was taken no more than two years before the date of the application for naturalisation; or]

(b) possesses an academic qualification deemed by UK NARIC to meet the recognised standard of a Bachelor's or Master's degree or PhD in the United Kingdom and—

(i) UK NARIC has confirmed that the qualification was taught or, as the case may be, researched in English; or

(ii) the qualification was taught or, as the case may be, researched in an English speaking country specified in Schedule 2A other than Canada; or

(c) is ordinarily resident outside the United Kingdom and a person designated by the Secretary of State certifies in writing that the person has sufficient knowledge of the English language for the purpose of an application for naturalisation; or

(d) satisfied the Secretary of State when making a successful application for indefinite leave to remain within the meaning of section 33(1) of the Immigration Act 1971 that he or she possessed a qualification or had passed a test in English at a level equivalent to Level B1 or above on the Council of Europe's Common European Framework of Reference for Languages: Learning, Teaching, Assessment; or

(e) is a national of an English speaking country specified in Schedule 2A{; or

(f) is a relevant pre-1973 entrant; or

(g) is not within sub-paragraph (f) but is an eligible child of a pre-1973 entrant.}

[(1A) Where the Secretary of State has reasonable grounds to suspect that a person used deception in relation to a test or qualification mentioned in sub-paragraph (a), (b) or (d) of paragraph (1) and relied upon by that person in his or her application for naturalisation, the Secretary of State may—

(a) disregard that test or qualification; and

(b) require that person to take or (as the case may be) retake and pass a test specified in Schedule 2A for the purpose of demonstrating that he or she has sufficient knowledge of the English language.]

(2) [Subject to paragraph (3),]a person has sufficient knowledge about life in the United Kingdom for the purpose of an application for naturalisation as a British citizen under section 6 of the Act if that person—

(a) has passed the test known as the 'Life in the UK Test' administered by an educational institution or other person approved for this purpose by the Secretary of State or the Lieutenant Governor of the Isle of Man; or

(b) has passed the test known as the 'Citizenship Test' administered by an educational institution or other person approved for this purpose by the Lieutenant Governor of Guernsey or Jersey; or

(c) is ordinarily resident outside the United Kingdom and a person designated by the Secretary of State certifies in writing that the person has sufficient knowledge about life in the United Kingdom for the purpose of an application for naturalisation.]{; or

(d) is a relevant pre-1973 entrant; or

(e) is not within sub-paragraph (d) but is an eligible child of a pre-1973 entrant.}

[(3) Where the Secretary of State has reasonable grounds to suspect that a person used deception in relation to a test mentioned in sub-paragraph (a) or (b) of paragraph (2) and relied upon by that person in his or her application for naturalisation, the Secretary of State may—

(a) disregard that test; and

(b) require that person to retake and pass the test mentioned in sub-paragraph (a) or (b) of paragraph (2) for the purpose of demonstrating that he or she has sufficient knowledge about life in the United Kingdom.]

[(4) In this regulation 'relevant pre-1973 entrant' means a person who is within paragraph (5) or (6).

(5) A person is within this paragraph if the person—

[(a) held indefinite leave to enter or remain in the United Kingdom or any of the Islands within the meaning of section 33(1) of the Immigration Act 1971 as at 1st January 1973; and

(aa) holds such leave (whether or not that leave has been held continuously since 1st January 1973); and]

(b) was, on 1st January 1973—

(i) a national of a country specified in Schedule 2B (certain members of the Commonwealth and British overseas territories etc.);

(ii) a citizen of the United Kingdom and Colonies by virtue of a connection with a country or territory specified in that Schedule; or

(iii) a British subject without citizenship (see sections 13 and 16 of the British Nationality Act 1948 as then in force).

(6) A person is within this paragraph if the person—

(a) has the right of abode in the United Kingdom or any of the Islands by virtue of section 2(1)(b) of the Immigration Act 1971 (certain Commonwealth citizens with the right of abode);

(b) was, on 1st January 1973, ordinarily resident in the United Kingdom or any of the Islands; and

(c) has strong ties with the United Kingdom or any of the Islands.

(7) For the purposes of this regulation, a person ('C') is an eligible child of a pre-1973 entrant if C—

(a) is the child (including an adopted child) of—

(i) a person who is (or was at the time of their death) a relevant pre-1973 entrant;

(ii) a person who is (or was at the time of their death) a British citizen and was, immediately before they became a British citizen, a relevant pre-1973 entrant; [. . .]

(iii) a pre-1973 deceased entrant; [or

(iv) a person who would be (or would have been at the time of their death) a relevant pre-1973 entrant but for a subsequent lapse in their indefinite leave to enter or remain in the United Kingdom or any of the Islands;.]

(b) was born outside the United Kingdom and the Islands;

(c) entered the United Kingdom or any of the Islands on or after 1st January 1973 and was, at the time of entry, under the age of 18; and

(d) is settled in the United Kingdom or any of the Islands and has, since C's entry as mentioned in sub-paragraph (c), been ordinarily resident in the United Kingdom or any of the Islands.

(8) In paragraph (7) 'pre-1973 deceased entrant' means a person who—

(a) died before 1st January 1973;

(b) was settled in the United Kingdom or any of the Islands before their death; and

(c) was, immediately before they died—

(i) a national of a country specified in Schedule 2B;

(ii) a citizen of the United Kingdom and Colonies by virtue of a connection with a country or territory specified in that Schedule; or

(iii) a British subject without citizenship.

(9) In paragraphs (5) to (8) 'the United Kingdom' means England and Wales, Scotland and Northern Ireland.

(10) For the purposes of this regulation, a reference to a country or territory in Schedule 2B includes a reference to any former country or territory which forms part of the country or territory concerned.]

Note: Regulation 5A substituted from 28 October 2013 (SI 2013/2541). Words in square brackets in paragraph (1) and paragraphs (1A) and (3) inserted from 6 April 2015 (SI 2015/681). Subparagraphs (f) and (g) inserted in paragraph 1, subparagraphs (d) and (e) inserted in paragraph 2 and paragraphs 4-10 inserted from 30 May 2018 (SI 2018/618). Paragraph (1)(a) substituted from 1 October 2019 (SI 2019/1242). Paragraph (5) (a) substituted and paragraphs (5)(aa) and 7(a)(iv) inserted from 1 December 2020 (SI 2020/1141).

[Citizenship oaths and pledges

6.—(1) Where a citizenship oath or pledge is required by section 42 of the Act to be made by an applicant for registration or for a certificate of naturalisation, it shall be administered in accordance with the requirements of Schedule 3.

(2) If, on an application for a registration or for a certificate of naturalisation by an applicant who is required to make a citizenship oath or pledge, the Secretary of State decides that the registration should be effected or the certificate should be granted, he shall cause notice in writing of the decision to be given to the applicant.

(3) The requirement to make a citizenship oath or pledge shall be satisfied within three months of the giving of the notice referred to in paragraph (2) or such longer time as the Secretary of State may allow.

(4) Any notice required by paragraph (2) to be given to an applicant may be given—

(a) in any case where the applicant's whereabouts are known, by causing the notice to be delivered to him personally or by sending it to him by post;

(b) in a case where the applicant's whereabouts are not known, by sending it by post in a letter addressed to him at his last known address.

(5) In this regulation, references to the requirement to make a citizenship oath or pledge include the requirement to make a citizenship oath and pledge at a citizenship ceremony.]

Note: Regulation 6 substituted from 1 January 2004 (SI 2003/3158).

[Arrangements for, and conduct of, citizenship ceremonies

6A.—(1) The Secretary of State may designate or authorise a person to exercise a function (which may include a discretion) in connection with a citizenship ceremony or a citizenship oath or pledge, and the reference in paragraph (3)(b) to 'designated person' shall be construed accordingly.

(2) Each local authority (within the meaning of section 41(3B) of the Act) shall—

(a) make available, or make arrangements for, premises at which citizenship ceremonies may be conducted; and

(b) arrange for citizenship ceremonies to be conducted with sufficient frequency so as to enable applicants in their area who are required to make a citizenship oath and pledge at a citizenship ceremony to meet the time limit laid down by regulation 6(3).

(3) Where an applicant is required by section 42 of the Act to make a citizenship oath and pledge at a citizenship ceremony, the Secretary of State shall—

(a) issue to the applicant an invitation in writing to attend a citizenship ceremony (a 'ceremony invitation');

(b) notify the applicant of the local authority or designated person which the applicant should contact to arrange attendance at a citizenship ceremony (the 'relevant authority'); and

(c) notify the relevant authority of his decision in relation to the applicant.

(4) An applicant who has arranged attendance at a citizenship ceremony shall bring with him to the ceremony his ceremony invitation; and if the applicant fails to do so, the person conducting the ceremony may refuse admittance to, or participation in, the ceremony if he is not reasonably satisfied as to the identity of the applicant.

(5) Where an applicant makes the relevant citizenship oath and pledge at a citizenship ceremony as required by section 42 of the Act—

(a) the person conducting the ceremony shall grant to the applicant a certificate of registration or naturalisation, duly dated with the date of the ceremony; and

(b) the relevant authority shall notify the Secretary of State in writing within 14 days of the date of the ceremony that the applicant has made the relevant citizenship oath and pledge at a citizenship ceremony and the date on which the ceremony took place.

(6) In this regulation, 'the person conducting the ceremony' is the person who administers the citizenship oath and pledge at the citizenship ceremony in accordance with paragraph 3 of Schedule 3.]

Note: Regulation 6A inserted from 1 January 2004 (SI 2003/3158).

[Certificates of naturalisation

7. A certificate of naturalisation shall include the following information relating to the person to whom the certificate is being granted—

(a) full name;
(b) date of birth; and
(c) place and country of birth.]

Note: Regulation 7 substituted from 3 December 2007 (SI 2007/3137).

[PART IIA

BIOMETRIC INFORMATION AND CITIZENSHIP

[Provision of biometric information with citizenship applications

7A.—(1) Subject to regulation 7B, where an individual makes an application for registration or naturalisation as a British citizen, an authorised person may require the individual to provide biometric information.

(2) Where an authorised person requires an individual to provide biometric information in accordance with paragraph (1), the individual must provide it.]

Note: Regulation 7A inserted from 6 April 2015 (SI 2015/738).

[Applicants under the age of sixteen

7B.—(1) An applicant under the age of sixteen ('the child') must not be required to provide biometric information in accordance with regulation 7A except where the authorised person is satisfied that the biometric information will be taken in the presence of a person aged eighteen or over who is—

(a) the child's parent or guardian; or
(b) a person who for the time being takes responsibility for the child.

(2) The person mentioned in paragraph (1)(b) may not be—

(a) an authorised person or any officer of the Secretary of State;
(b) any other person acting on behalf of an authorised person as part of a process specified under regulation 7C(1)(a) or (c).

(3) An authorised person shall not require an applicant under the age of sixteen to provide biometric information unless the decision to do so has been confirmed by a person designated for the purpose by the Secretary of State.

(4) This regulation does not apply if the authorised person reasonably believes that the applicant whose biometric information is to be taken is aged sixteen or over.]

Note: Regulation 7B inserted from 6 April 2015 (SI 2015/738).

[Process by which an individual's biometric information may be obtained and recorded

7C.—(1) An authorised person who requires an individual to provide a record of the individual's fingerprints or a photograph of the individual's face under regulation 7A may do any one or more of the following—

(a) require the individual to make an appointment before a specified date, which the individual must attend, to enable a record of the individual's fingerprints or a photograph of the individual's face to be taken by an authorised person or by a person acting on behalf of an authorised person;

(b) specify the date, time and place for the appointment;

(c) require the individual to attend premises before a specified date to enable a record of the individual's fingerprints or a photograph of the individual's face to be taken by an authorised person or by a person acting on behalf of an authorised person; and

(d) specify any documents which the individual must bring to the appointment or premises, or action which the individual must take to confirm the individual's identity.

(2) An authorised person may require a record of fingerprints or photograph to be of a particular specification.

(3) Where an authorised person requires an individual to submit to any requirement in accordance with paragraph (1), the individual must submit to it.]

Note: Regulation 7C inserted from 6 April 2015 (SI 2015/738).

[Consequences of a failure to comply with a requirement of these Regulations

7D. Where an individual who is required to provide biometric information as part of an application for registration or naturalisation as a British citizen fails to comply with the process, or combination of processes, required by an authorised person in accordance with regulation 7C, the Secretary of State may treat the individual's application as invalid.]

Note: Regulation 7D inserted from 6 April 2015 (SI 2015/738).

[Use and retention of biometric information

7E.—(1) Biometric information provided in accordance with these Regulations may be retained only if the Secretary of State thinks that it is necessary to retain it for use in connection with—

(a) the exercise of a function by virtue of the Immigration Acts; or

(b) the exercise of a function in relation to nationality.

(2) Biometric information retained by virtue of paragraph (1) may also be used—

(a) in connection with the prevention, investigation or prosecution of an offence;

(b) for a purpose which appears to the Secretary of State to be required in order to protect national security;

(c) in connection with identifying persons who have died, or are suffering from illness or injury; [and]

(d) for the purpose of ascertaining whether a person has acted unlawfully, or has obtained or sought anything to which the person is not legally entitled;

[(e) . . .]

Note: Regulation 7E inserted from 6 April 2015 (SI 2015/738) and paragraph (2)(e) omitted from 23.00 on 31 December 2020 (SI 2020/1309).

[Power to use and retain existing biometric information

7EA.—(1) This regulation applies where—

(a)a person makes an application for registration or naturalisation as a British citizen; and

(b)the Secretary of State already has a record of the person's fingerprints or a photograph of the person's face in their possession (for whatever reason).

(2) Where this regulation applies, the Secretary of State may use or retain that information for the purposes of these Regulations.]

Note: Regulation 7EA inserted from 1 July 2021 (SI 2021/772).

[Destruction of biometric information

7F.—(1) The Secretary of State must take all reasonable steps to ensure that biometric information held by the Secretary of State by virtue of these Regulations, including any copies, is destroyed if the Secretary of State—

(a) no longer thinks that it is necessary to retain the information for use as mentioned in regulation 7E(1); or

(b) subject to the exception in paragraph (2), is satisfied that the person to whom the information relates is a British citizen, or a Commonwealth citizen who has a right of abode in the United Kingdom as a result of section 2(1)(b) of the Immigration Act 1971.

(2) The exception is that photographs of a person who is registered or naturalised as a British citizen may be retained until the person is issued with a United Kingdom passport describing the person as a British citizen.]

Note: Regulation 7F inserted from 6 April 2015 (SI 2015/738).

[Retention of fingerprints

7G.—(1) Save where regulation 7F applies and subject to paragraphs (2) and (3), the Secretary of State must take all reasonable steps to ensure that any record of a person's fingerprints held by the Secretary of State by virtue of these Regulations, including any copies, is destroyed at the end of the period of [15] years beginning with [—

(a) the date on which the fingerprints were provided; or

(b) the date on which they are reused in connection with an application made by the person which comes within paragraph (5),

whichever is the later.

(2) But fingerprints can be held beyond that period if they are—

(a) the fingerprints of a person who is, or at any time has been, subject to a deportation order, exclusion order or decision to exclude;

(b) the fingerprints of a person who can be, or at any time could have been, refused entry clearance or leave to enter for a period specified in the immigration rules because of a previous breach of the United Kingdom's immigration laws;

(c) fingerprints that the Secretary of State deems it necessary for national security reasons to retain for use in connection with one of the functions specified in regulation 7E(1);

(d) the fingerprints of a person with indefinite leave to enter or remain in the United Kingdom;[or]

(e) the fingerprints of a person whose indefinite leave to enter or remain in the United Kingdom lapses, is revoked or is cancelled, in which case they must be destroyed by the Secretary of State at the end of ten years beginning with the date of the lapse, revocation or cancellation (as the case may be);

[(f) . . .]

in which case they must be destroyed by the Secretary of State at the end of ten years beginning with the date on which the holder ceased to enjoy the right of permanent residence.

(3) The Secretary of State is only required to take steps to destroy, pursuant to paragraph (2)(e) [. . .], the fingerprints of a person whose leave has lapsed [. . .] on the application, supported by evidence to the satisfaction of the Secretary of State, of that person.

[(4) . . .]]

[(5) An application comes within this paragraph if it is an application for—

(a) entry clearance;

(b) leave to enter;

(c) leave to remain; or

(d) registration or naturalisation as a British citizen.]

Note: Regulation 7G inserted from 6 April 2015 (SI 2015/738). Paragraphs (2)(f) and (4) and words in paragraph (3) omitted from 23.00 on 31 December 2020 (SI 2020/1309). Number and words in square brackets in paragraph (1) substituted and paragraph (5) inserted from 1 July 2021 (SI 2021/772).

[Destruction etc. of electronic data

7H.—(1) The Secretary of State must take all reasonable steps to ensure—

(a) that data held in electronic form which relates to biometric information which has to be destroyed by virtue of these Regulations is destroyed or erased; or

(b) that access to such data is blocked.

(2) A person whose biometric information has to be destroyed by virtue of these Regulations is entitled, on written request, to a certificate issued by the Secretary of State to the effect that the Secretary of State has taken the steps required by paragraph (1).

(3) A certificate issued under paragraph (2) must be issued within the period of 3 months beginning with the date on which the request for it is received by the Secretary of State.]

Note: Regulation 7H inserted from 6 April 2015 (SI 2015/738).

[Biometric information: retention under another power

7I. The requirements in these Regulations to destroy biometric information or data do not apply if and in so far as the information or data is retained in accordance with and for the purposes of another power.]

Note: Regulation 7I inserted from 6 April 2015 (SI 2015/738).

PART III

RENUNCIATION AND DEPRIVATION

Declarations of renunciation

8. Any declaration of renunciation of British citizenship, British Overseas citizenship or the status of a British subject shall—

(a) be made to the appropriate authority specified in regulation 9; and

(b) satisfy the requirements of Schedule 5.

Authority to whom declaration of renunciation is to be made

9. The authority to whom a declaration of renunciation is to be made is as follows:

(a) if the declarant is in Great Britain or Northern Ireland, to the Secretary of State at the Home Office;

(b) if the declarant is in any of the Islands, to the Lieutenant-Governor;

(c) if the declarant is in a British overseas territory, to the Governor;

[(d) . . .]

[(e) if the declarant is elsewhere, to the Secretary of State at the Home Office.]

Note: Paragraph (e) substituted from 16 July 2012 (SI 2012/1588). Paragraph (d) omitted from 12 November 2015 (SI 2015/1806).

Notice of proposed deprivation of citizenship

[**10.**—(1) Where it is proposed to make an order under section 40 of the Act depriving a person of a citizenship status, the notice required by section 40(5) of the Act to be given to the person may be—

(a) given to the person by hand;

(b) sent by fax;

(c) sent by email;

(d) sent by courier;

(e) sent by document exchange;

(f) sent by post, whether or not delivery or receipt is recorded; or

(g) sent by any of the means set out at (b) to (f) to—

(i) the person's representative; or

(ii) if the person is under 18, their parent or guardian.

(2) Where the notice is sent under paragraph (1)(b), it must be sent to a number provided by the person or the person's representative.

(3) Where the notice is sent under any one or more of paragraphs (1)(c) to (g), it must be sent—

(a) to the address for correspondence provided by the person or the person's representative; or

(b) where no such address has been provided, the person's last known address or the address of their representative.

(4) Where—

(a) the person's whereabouts are not known; and

(b) either—

(i) no address has been provided for correspondence and the Secretary of State does not know of any address which the person has used in the past; or

(ii) the address provided to the Secretary of State is defective, false or no longer in use by the person; and

(c) no representative appears to be acting for the person or the address provided in respect of that representative is defective, false or no longer used by the representative, the notice shall be deemed to have been given when the Secretary of State enters a record of the above circumstances and places the notice or a copy of it on the person's file.

(5) A notice required to be given by section 40(5) of the Act is, unless the contrary is proved, deemed to have been given—

(a) where the notice is sent by fax, when it is sent;

(b) where the notice is sent by email, when it is sent;

(c) where the notice is sent by document exchange, on the day after the day on which it is sent;

(d) where the notice is sent by post from and to a place within the United Kingdom, on the second day after the day on which it is sent;

(e) where the notice is sent by post from or to a place outside the United Kingdom, on the twenty-eighth day after the day on which it is sent;

(f) where the notice is sent by post where delivery or receipt is recorded, when the notice is recorded as having been delivered or received;

(g) in any other case on the day on which the notice is delivered.

(6) In this regulation 'representative' is a person who appears to the Secretary of State to be representing the person to whom the notice under section 40(5) of the Act is required to be given, and, where the notice is sent to the person's representative by any of the means set out in paragraph (1), it is deemed to have been served on the person in accordance with that section.

(7) In this regulation—

'document exchange' means a document exchange providing a system of delivery of documents by reference to numbered boxes at document exchanges; and

'fax' means the making of a facsimile copy of a document by the transmission of electronic signals.]

Note: Regulation 10 substituted from 9 August 2018 (SI 2018/851).

Cancellation of registration of person deprived of citizenship

11. Where an order has been made depriving a person who has a citizenship status by virtue of registration (whether under the Act or under the former nationality Acts) of that citizenship status, the name of that person shall be removed from the relevant register.

Cancellation of certificate of naturalisation in case of deprivation of citizenship

12. Where an order has been made depriving a person who has a citizenship status by virtue of the grant of a certificate of naturalisation (whether under the Act or under the former nationality Acts) of that citizenship status, the person so deprived or any other person in possession of the relevant certificate of naturalisation shall, if required by notice in writing given by the authority by whom the order was made, deliver up the said certificate to such person, and within such time, as may be specified in the notice; and the said certificate shall thereupon be cancelled or amended.

PART IV

SUPPLEMENTAL

Evidence

13. A document may be certified to be a true copy of a document for the purpose of section 45(2) of the Act by means of a statement in writing to that effect signed by a person authorised by the Secretary of State, the Lieutenant-Governor, the High Commissioner or the Governor in that behalf.

[Manner of signifying parental consent to registration

14. Where a parent, in pursuance of section 3(5)(c) or 4D(3) {or 4G(3)} of the Act, consents to the registration of a person as a British citizen under subsection 3(5) or section 4D {or 4G}, the consent shall be expressed in writing and signed by the parent.]

Note: Regulation 14 substituted from 13 January 2010 (SI 2009/3363). Words in curly brackets inserted by Immigration Act 2014, Sch 9 paragraph 71 from 6 April 2015 (SI 2015/874).

Revocation

15. The British Nationality (General) Regulations 1982 are hereby revoked.

Regulation 3

SCHEDULE 1

GENERAL REQUIREMENTS AS RESPECTS APPLICATIONS

PART I

ALL APPLICATIONS

1. An application shall be made in writing and shall state the name, address and date and place of birth of the applicant.

2. An application shall contain a declaration that the particulars stated therein are true.

Part II

Applications by persons not of full age or capacity

3. An application in respect of someone not of full age or capacity made by another person on his behalf shall state that that is the case and the name and address of that person.

4. An application made by a person on behalf of someone not of full age or capacity shall indicate the nature of that person's connection with him and, if that person has any responsibility for him otherwise than as a parent, the nature of that responsibility and the manner in which it was assumed.

[Part III

Applications for a waiver on the basis of physical or mental condition

5.—(1) This paragraph applies where the applicant seeks a waiver under paragraph 2(1)(e) of Schedule 1 to the British Nationality Act 1981 on the basis of their physical or mental condition.

(2) A request made under paragraph (1) must be accompanied by—

(a) a statement that the waiver applies and how it applies; and

(b) written confirmation of the matters stated in the statement.

(3) The written confirmation required under sub-paragraph (2)(b) must be—

(a) provided by a registered medical practitioner, who must confirm that the practitioner's knowledge of the applicant's age or physical or mental condition derives from having met the applicant in person, and provide the date of their last meeting with the applicant, and

(b) made using the form which appears at Schedule 6 to these Regulations.]

Note: Part III inserted from 9 August 2018 (SI 2018/851).

Regulation 3 Schedule 2

Particular Requirements As Respects Applications

[Interpretation

A1. In this Schedule—

(a) a reference to a person's 'natural father' is to be construed in accordance with section 4J(1) of the Act;

(b) a reference to a person automatically becoming a British citizen, or a citizen of the United Kingdom and Colonies, is to be construed in accordance with section 4J(4) of the Act.]

Note: Paragraph A1 inserted from 6 April 2015 (SI 2015/681).

Application under section 1(3) of the Act

1. An application under section 1(3) of the Act shall contain information showing:

[(a)] that the applicant's father or mother became a British citizen, or became settled in the United Kingdom, after the applicant's birth[; and

(b) where the applicant is aged 10 or over, that he is of good character.]

Note: Words in square brackets inserted from 3 December 2007 (SI 2007/3137).

[Application under section 1(3A) of the Act

1A. An application under section 1(3A) shall contain information showing—

(a) that the applicant's father or mother became a member of the armed forces after the applicant's birth; and

(b) where the applicant is aged 10 or over, that he is of good character.]

Note: Paragraph 1A inserted from 13 January 2010 (SI 2009/3363).

Application under section 1(4) of the Act

2. An application under section 1(4) of the Act shall contain information showing:

[(a)] that the applicant possesses the requisite qualifications in respect of residence [; and

(b) where the applicant is aged 10 or over, that he is of good character.]

Note: Words in square brackets inserted from 3 December 2007 (SI 2007/3137).

3. If the applicant was absent from the United Kingdom on more than 90 days in all in any one of the first 10 years of his life and it is desired that the application should nevertheless be considered under section 1(7) of the Act, it shall specify the special circumstances to be taken into consideration.

Application under section 3(2) of the Act

4. An application under section 3(2) of the Act shall contain information showing—

(a) that the applicant's father or mother ('the parent in question') was a British citizen by descent at the time of the applicant's birth;

(b) that the father or mother of the parent in question—

(i) was a British citizen otherwise than by descent at the time of the birth of the parent in question; or

(ii) became a British citizen otherwise than by descent at commencement; or

(iii) would have become a British citizen otherwise than by descent at commencement but for his or her death;

(c) either—

(i) that the parent in question possesses the requisite qualifications in respect of residence; or

(ii) that the applicant was born stateless.

[**5.** . . .]

Note: Paragraph 5 omitted from 13 January 2010 (SI 2009/3363).

Application under section 3(5) of the Act

6. An application under section 3(5) of the Act shall contain information showing—

(a) that the applicant's father or mother was a British citizen by descent at the time of the applicant's birth;

(b) that the applicant and his father and mother possess the requisite qualifications in respect of residence;

(c) that the consent of the applicant's father and/or mother (as required by section 3(5)(c) and (6) of the Act) has been signified in accordance with regulation 14 and, if the consent of one parent only has been signified, the reason for that fact [; and

(d) where the applicant is aged 10 or over, that he is of good character.]

Note: Words in square brackets inserted from 3 December 2007 (SI 2007/3137).

Application under section 4(2) of the Act

7.—(1) An application under section 4(2) of the Act shall contain information showing—

(a) that the applicant is a British overseas territories citizen, a British Overseas citizen, a British subject under the Act or a British protected person;

(b) that the applicant possesses the requisite qualifications in respect of residence, freedom from immigration restrictions and compliance with the immigration laws [; and

(c) where the applicant is aged 10 or over, that he is of good character.]

[(1A . . .]

(2) If the applicant does not possess the requisite qualifications in respect of residence, freedom from immigration restrictions and compliance with the immigration laws and it is desired that the application should nevertheless be considered under section 4(4) of the Act, it shall specify the special circumstances to be taken into consideration.

Note: Subparagraph (1)(c) inserted from 3 December 2007 (SI 2007/3137). Paragraph (1A) omitted from 23.00 on 31 December 2020 (SI 2020/1309) subject to saving provision (reg 80(6) of SI 2020/1309).

Application under section 4(5) of the Act

8.—(1) An application under section 4(5) of the Act shall contain information showing—

(a) that the applicant is a British overseas territories citizen, a British Overseas citizen, a British subject under the Act or a British protected person;

(b) that the applicant possesses the requisite qualifications in respect of service [; and

(c) where the applicant is aged 10 or over, that he is of good character.]

(2) The application shall specify the special circumstances to be taken into consideration.

Note: Words in square brackets inserted from 3 December 2007 (SI 2007/3137).

Application under section 4A of the Act

9. An application under section 4A of the Act shall contain information showing—

(a) that the applicant is a British overseas territories citizen who is not such a citizen by virtue only of a connection with the Sovereign Base Areas of Akrotiri and Dhekelia;

(b) that the applicant has not ceased to be a British citizen as a result of a declaration of renunciation [; and

(c) where the applicant is aged 10 or over, that he is of good character].

Note: Words in square brackets inserted from 3 December 2007 (SI 2007/3137).

[Application under section 4B of the Act

10. An application under section 4B of the Act shall contain information showing—

(a) that the applicant is a British Overseas citizen, a British subject under the Act, a British protected person or a British National (Overseas) and does not have any other citizenship or nationality; and

(b) (i) in the case of an application made by virtue of subsection (1)(a), (b) or (c), that the applicant has not, after 4th July 2002, renounced, voluntarily relinquished or lost through action or inaction, any citizenship or nationality;or

(ii) in the case of an application made by virtue of subsection (1)(d), that the applicant has not, after 19th March 2009, renounced, voluntarily relinquished or lost through action or inaction, any citizenship or nationality].

Note: Paragraph 10 substituted from 13 January 2010 (SI 2009/3363).

[Application under section 4C of the Act

11. An application under section 4C of the Act shall contain information showing—

(a) that the applicant was born before 1 January 1983;

(b) that the applicant would at some time before 1 January 1983 have become a citizen of the United Kingdom and Colonies—

(i) under section 5 or 12(2) of, or paragraph 3 of Schedule 3 to, the British Nationality Act 1948 if (as the case may be) that section or paragraph provided for citizenship by descent from a mother in the same terms as it provided for citizenship by descent from a father and if references in that provision to a father were references to the applicant's mother; or

(ii) under section 12(2), (3), (4) or (5) of the British Nationality Act 1948 if a provision of the law at some time before 1 January 1949, which provided for a nationality status to be acquired by descent from a father, provided in the same terms for its acquisition by descent from a mother and if references in that provision to a father were references to the applicant's mother;[and]

(c) that immediately before 1st January 1983 the applicant would have had the right of abode in the United Kingdom by virtue of section 2 of the Immigration Act 1971 had he become a citizen of the United Kingdom and Colonies as described in either sub-paragraph (b)(i) or (ii) above;

[(d) . . .]]

Note: Paragraph 11 substituted from 13 January 2010 (SI 2009/3363). Words inserted at end of paragraph (b) and paragraph (d) omitted from 25 July 2019 (SI 2019/1164).

[Application under section 4D of the Act

11A.—(1) An application under section 4D of the Act shall contain information showing—

(a) that the applicant's father or mother was a member of the armed forces and serving outside of the United Kingdom and qualifying territories at the time of the applicant's birth;

(b) that the consent of the applicant's father and/or mother (as required by section 4D(3) and (4) of the Act) has been signified in accordance with regulation 14 and, if the consent of one parent only has been signified, the reason for that fact; and

(c) where the applicant is aged 10 or over, that he is of good character.

(2) If the application is made without the consent of the applicant's father and/or mother and it is desired that the application should nevertheless be considered under section 4D(5) of the Act, it shall specify the special circumstances to be taken into consideration.]

Note: Paragraph 11A inserted from 13 January 2010 (SI 2009/3363).

[Application under section 4F of the Act

11B. An application under section 4F of the Act shall contain information showing—

(a) that the applicant would be entitled to be registered as a British Citizen under section 1(3), 3(2), {3(5) or 4D} of, or paragraph 4 or 5 of Schedule 2 to, the Act, had his mother been married to his natural father at the time of his birth; and

(b) where the applicant is aged 10 or over [and the provision under which the applicant would be entitled to be registered as a British citizen (as mentioned in section 4F(1)(b) of the Act) is section 1(3), 3(2) {3(5) or 4D} of the Act], that he is of good character.]

Note: Paragraph 11B inserted from 6 April 2015 (SI 2015/681) and words inserted in sub-paragraph (b) from 25 July 2019 (SI 2019/1164). Words in curly brackets in sub-paragraphs (a) and (b) substituted from 28 June 2022 (SI 2022/602).

[Application under section 4G of the Act

11C. An application under section 4G of the Act shall contain information showing—

(a) that the applicant would have automatically become a British citizen by birth by operation of any provision of the Act or the British Nationality (Falkland Islands) Act 1983 ('the 1983 Act'), at any time in the period after commencement of the Act or (as the case may be) the 1983 Act, had his mother been married to his natural father at the time of his birth;

[(b) . . .]

Note: Paragraph 11C inserted from 6 April 2015 (SI 2015/681) and sub-paragraph (b) omitted from 25 July 2019 (SI 2019/1164).

[Application under section 4H of the Act

11D. An application under section 4H of the Act shall contain information showing—

(a) that the applicant was a citizen of the United Kingdom and Colonies immediately before commencement of the Act;[and]

(b) that the applicant would have automatically become a British citizen at commencement of the Act, by the operation of any provision of the Act, had his mother been married to his natural father at the time of his birth;

[(c) . . .]]

Note: Paragraph 11D inserted from 6 April 2015 (SI 2015/681), word inserted at the end of sub-paragraph (a) and sub-paragraph (c) omitted from 25 July 2019 (SI 2019/1164).

[Application under section 4I of the Act

11E.—(1) An application under section 4I of the Act shall contain information showing—

(a) that the applicant—

(i) ceased to be a British subject or a citizen of the United Kingdom and Colonies by virtue of the commencement of any independence legislation, but would not have done so had his mother been married to his natural father at the time of his birth;

(ii) was a British subject who did not automatically become a citizen of the United Kingdom and Colonies at commencement of the British Nationality Act 1948 by the operation of any provision of it, but would have done so had his mother been married to his natural father at the time of his birth; or

(iii) would have automatically become a British subject or citizen of the United Kingdom and Colonies at birth or by virtue of paragraph 3 of Schedule 3 to the British Nationality Act 1948, had his mother been married to his natural father at the time of his birth;

[(b) . . .].

(2) In this paragraph, 'British subject' and 'independence legislation' have the same meaning as in section 4I(7) of the Act.]

Note: Paragraph 11E inserted from 6 April 2015 (SI 2015/681) and sub-paragraph 1(b) omitted from 25 July 2019 (SI 2019/1164).

[Application under section 4K of the Act 11F.

11F. An application under section 4K of the Act must contain information showing—

(a) that the applicant—

(i) is entitled to be registered as a British overseas territories citizen under section 17A, 17C, 17D, 17E [17F or 17H] of the Act, otherwise than by virtue only of a connection with the Sovereign Base Areas of Akrotiri and Dhekelia, or

(ii) would be entitled to be registered as a British overseas territories citizen under any of those sections, otherwise than by virtue only of a connection with the Sovereign Base Areas of Akrotiri and Dhekelia, but for the fact that the applicant has already become a British overseas territories citizen under a different provision, and (b) where the applicant is aged 10 or over and the provision under which the applicant would be entitled to be registered as a British overseas territories citizen (as mentioned in section 17C(1)(b) of the Act) is section 15(3) or 17(2) or (5) of the Act, that the applicant is of good character.]

Note: Paragraph 11E inserted from 28 June 2022 (SI 2022/602) and words in square brackets in sub-paragraph (a)(i) substituted by SI 2022/602 and shall come into force on the day on which the Nationality an Borders Act 2022 c.36 s3 comes into force.

[Application under section 4L of the Act 11G.

11G—(1) An application under section 4L of the Act must specify the information to be considered by the Secretary of State in forming an opinion under section 4L of the Act about whether the applicant would have been, or would have been able to become, a British citizen but for—

(a) historical legislative unfairness,
(b) an act or omission of a public authority, or
(c) exceptional circumstances relating to the applicant.

(2) The application must contain information showing that the applicant is of full capacity.

(3) Where sub-paragraph (4) applies, the application must also—

(a) contain information showing that the applicant is of good character, or (b) specify why the Secretary of State should not take into account whether the applicant is of good character in considering whether to grant the application.

(4) This sub-paragraph applies where—

(a) the application is made on the basis that the applicant would have been able to become a British citizen but for a matter mentioned in paragraph (a), (b) or (c) of sub-paragraph (1), and

(b) the process by which the applicant would have been able to become a British citizen would have involved the Secretary of State being required, under section 41A of the Act, to be satisfied that the applicant was of good character.

(5) In this paragraph, "historical legislative unfairness" and "public authority" have the same meaning as in section 4L of the Act.]

Note: Paragraph 11G inserted from 28 June 2022 (SI 2022/602).

Application under section 5 of the Act

12. An application under section 5 of the Act shall contain information showing

[(a)] that the applicant is a British overseas territories citizen who falls to be treated as a national of the United Kingdom {by virtue of a connection with Gibraltar} [; and

(b) where the applicant is aged 10 or over, that he is of good character.]

Note: Words in square brackets inserted from 3 December 2007 (SI 2007/3137). Words in curly brackets substituted from 31 December 2020 (SI 2019/745).

Application under section 6(1)

13.—(1) An application under section 6(1) of the Act shall contain information showing—

(a) that the applicant possesses the requisite qualifications in respect of residence or Crown service, freedom from immigration restrictions, compliance with the immigration laws, good character, knowledge of language [, knowledge about life in the United Kingdom] and intention with respect to residence or occupation in the event of a certificate of naturalisation being granted to him;

(b) that the applicant is of full capacity.

[(1A) . . .]

(2) If the applicant does not possess the requisite qualifications in respect of residence, freedom from immigration restrictions, compliance with the immigration laws and knowledge of language and it is desired that the application should nevertheless be considered under paragraph 2 of Schedule 1 to the Act, it shall specify the special circumstances to be taken into consideration.

[(3) If the applicant is not of full capacity and it is desired that the requirement of full capacity be waived in accordance with section 44A of the Act (waiver of requirement for full capacity), the application shall specify why it would be in the applicant's best interests for the requirement to be waived in his case.]

Note: Words in square brackets in paragraph (1)(a) substituted from 1 May 2006 (SI 2005/2785). Paragraph (3) inserted from 3 December 2007 (SI 2007/3137). Paragraph (1A) omitted from 23.00 on 31 December 2020 (SI 2020/1309) subject to saving provision (reg 80(6) of SI 2020/1309).

Application under section 6(2) of the Act

14.—(1) An application under section 6(2) of the Act shall contain information showing—

(a) that the applicant is married to a British citizen;

(b) that the applicant possesses the requisite qualifications in respect of residence, freedom from immigration restrictions, compliance with the [immigration laws, good character, knowledge of language and knowledge about life in the United Kingdom].

(c) that the applicant is of full capacity.

[(1A) . . .]

(2) If the applicant does not possess the requisite qualifications in respect of residence and compliance with the immigration laws and it is desired that the application should nevertheless be considered under paragraph 4 of Schedule 1 to the Act, it shall specify the special circumstances to be taken into consideration.

(3) If the applicant does not possess the requisite qualifications in respect of residence and it is desired that the application should nevertheless be considered under paragraph 4(d) of Schedule 1 to the Act on the grounds of marriage to a person who is serving in Crown Service under the government of the United Kingdom or other designated service, it shall specify the nature of the service and contain information showing that recruitment for that service took place in the United Kingdom.

[(4) If the applicant is not of full capacity and it is desired that the requirement of full capacity be waived in accordance with section 44A of the Act (waiver of requirement for full capacity), the application shall specify why it would be in the applicant's best interests for the requirement to be waived in his case.]

Note: Words in square brackets in subparagraph (1)(b) substituted from 1 May 2006 (SI 2005/2785). Subparagraph (4) inserted from 3 December 2007 (SI 2007/3137). Paragraph (1A) omitted from 23.00 on 31 December 2020 (SI 2020/1309) subject to saving provision (reg 80(6) of SI 2020/1309).

Application under section 10(1) of the Act

15. An application under section 10(1) of the Act shall contain information showing—

(a) that the applicant renounced citizenship of the United Kingdom and Colonies;

(b) that at the time when he renounced it the applicant was, or was about to become, a citizen of a country mentioned in section 1(3) of the British Nationality Act 1948;

(c) that the applicant could not have remained or become such a citizen but for renouncing it or had reasonable cause to believe that he would be deprived of his citizenship of that country unless he renounced it;

(d) that the applicant possessed the requisite qualifying connection with the United Kingdom immediately before commencement or was married before commencement to a person who possessed the requisite qualifying connection with the United Kingdom immediately before commencement or would if living have possessed such a connection;

(e) that the applicant has not previously been registered under section 10(1) of the Act [; and

(f) where the applicant is aged 10 or over, that he is of good character].

Note: Subparagraph (f) inserted from 3 December 2007 (SI 2007/3137).

Application under section 10(2) of the Act

16. [(1)] An application under section 10(2) of the Act shall contain information showing—

(a) that the applicant has renounced citizenship of the United Kingdom and Colonies and his reason for so doing;

(b) that the applicant possesses the requisite qualifying connection with the United Kingdom or has been married to a person who has, or would if living have, such a connection;

(c) that the applicant is of full capacity [; and

(d) where the applicant is aged 10 or over, that he is of good character];

[(2) If the applicant is not of full capacity and it is desired that the requirement of full capacity be waived in accordance with section 44A of the Act (waiver of requirement for full capacity), the application shall specify why it would be in the applicant's best interests for the requirement to be waived in his case.]

Note: Words in square brackets inserted from 3 December 2007 (SI 2007/3137).

Application under section 13(1) of the Act

17. [(1)] An application under section 13(1) of the Act shall contain information showing—

(a) that the applicant has renounced British citizenship;

(b) that, at the time when he renounced it, the applicant had or was about to acquire some other citizenship or nationality;

(c) that the renunciation of British citizenship was necessary to enable him to retain or acquire that other citizenship or nationality;

(d) that the applicant has not previously been registered under section 13(1) of the Act;

(e) that the applicant is of full capacity [; and

(f) where the applicant is aged 10 or over, that he is of good character];

[(2) If the applicant is not of full capacity and it is desired that the requirement of full capacity be waived in accordance with section 44A of the Act (waiver of requirement for full capacity), the application shall specify why it would be in the applicant's best interests for the requirement to be waived in his case.]

Note: Words in square brackets inserted from 3 December 2007 (SI 2007/3137).

Application under section 13(3) of the Act

18. [(1)] An application under section 13(3) of the Act shall contain information showing—

(a) that the applicant has renounced British citizenship and his reason for so doing;

(b) that the applicant is of full capacity [; and

(c) where the applicant is aged 10 or over, that he is of good character.]

[(2) If the applicant is not of full capacity and it is desired that the requirement of full capacity be waived in accordance with section 44A of the Act (waiver of requirement for full capacity), the application shall specify why it would be in the applicant's best interests for the requirement to be waived in his case.]

Note: Words in square brackets inserted from 3 December 2007 (SI 2007/3137).

Application under paragraph 3 of Schedule 2 to the Act

19.—(1) An application under paragraph 3 of Schedule 2 to the Act shall contain information showing—

(a) that the applicant is and always has been stateless;

(b) that the applicant seeks British citizenship and possesses the requisite qualifications in respect of residence.

(2) If the applicant does not possess the requisite qualifications in respect of residence and it is desired that the application should nevertheless be considered under paragraph 6 of Schedule 2 to the Act, it shall specify the special circumstances to be taken into consideration.

[Application under paragraph 3A of Schedule 2 to the Act 19A.

19A—(1) An application under paragraph 3A of Schedule 2 to the Act must contain information showing—

(a) that the applicant is and always has been stateless,

(b) that the applicant seeks British citizenship and possesses the requisite qualifications in respect of residence, and

(c) that the applicant is unable to acquire another nationality in accordance with sub-paragraph (2).

(2) A person is able to acquire a nationality in accordance with this sub-paragraph if—

(a) the nationality is the same as that of one of the person's parents,

(b) the person has been entitled to acquire the nationality since birth, and

(c) in all the circumstances, it is reasonable to expect the person (or someone acting on the person's behalf) to take the steps which would enable the person to acquire the nationality in question.

(3) For the purposes of sub-paragraph (2)(b), a person is not entitled to acquire a nationality if its acquisition is conditional on the exercise of a discretion on the part of the country or territory in question.

(4) If the applicant does not possess the requisite qualifications in respect of residence and it is desired that the application should nevertheless be considered under paragraph 6 of Schedule 2 to the Act, the application must specify the special considerations to be taken into consideration.]

Note: Paragraph 19A inserted from 28 June 2022 (SI 2022/602).

Application under paragraph 4 of Schedule 2

20.—(1) An application under paragraph 4 of Schedule 2 to the Act shall contain information showing—

(a) that the applicant is and always has been stateless;

(b) in respect of both the father and mother of the applicant, which of the following statuses, namely, British citizenship, British overseas territories citizenship, British Overseas citizenship or the status of a British subject under the Act, was held at the time of the applicant's birth;

(c) that the applicant possesses the requisite qualifications in respect of residence;

(d) if more than one of the statuses mentioned in sub-paragraph (b) above are available to the applicant, which status or statuses is or are wanted.

(2) If the applicant does not possess the requisite qualifications in respect of residence and it is desired that the application should nevertheless be considered under paragraph 6 of Schedule 2 to the Act, it shall specify the special circumstances to be taken into consideration.

Application under paragraph 5 of Schedule 2

21. An application under paragraph 5 of Schedule 2 to the Act shall contain information showing—

(a) that the applicant is and always has been stateless;

(b) if he was not born at a place which is at the date of the application within the United Kingdom and British overseas territories—

(i) that the applicant's mother was a citizen of the United Kingdom and Colonies at the time of his birth; or

(ii) that he possesses the requisite qualifications in respect of parentage or residence and parentage;

(c) that the applicant seeks British citizenship or British Overseas citizenship and that that citizenship is available to the applicant in accordance with paragraph 5(2) of Schedule 2 to the Act.

Regulation 5A

[SCHEDULE 2A
SPECIFIED ENGLISH LANGUAGE TESTS [. . .] AND ENGLISH SPEAKING COUNTRIES

Specified English Language Tests [. . .]

1. [. . .]

[(2) In this paragraph—

'approved English language test centre' means a test centre which has been approved by the Secretary of State for the purpose of an application for naturalisation;

'United Kingdom' has the same meaning as in Schedule 1 to the Interpretation Act 1978.]

Table 1 Recognised English Language Tests within the United Kingdom

Awarding body	Specified English language test
Cambridge English	IELTS (International English Language Testing System) IELTS (International English Language Testing System) Life Skills
Trinity College London	Integrated Skills in English
Trinity College London	Graded Examinations in Spoken English

Table 2 Recognised English Language Tests outside the United Kingdom

Awarding body	Specified English language test
Cambridge English	IELTS (International English Language Testing System) IELTS (International English Language Testing System) Life Skills

Specified English Speaking Countries

2. The following countries are specified English speaking countries for the purposes of regulation 5A(1)(b)(ii) and (e)—

(a) Antigua and Barbuda;

(b) Australia;

(c) the Bahamas;

(d) Barbados;

(e) Belize;

(f) Canada;
(g) Dominica;
(h) Grenada;
(i) Guyana;
(j) Jamaica;
[(ja) Malta;]
(k) New Zealand;
(l) the Republic of Ireland;
(m) Saint Christopher and Nevis;
(n) Saint Lucia;
(o) Saint Vincent and the Grenadines;
(p) Trinidad and Tobago; or
(q) the United States of America]

Note: Schedule 2A inserted from 18 October 2013 (SI 2013/2541). Entry relating to 'Educational Testing Service' omitted from Table from 1 July 2014 (SI 2014/1465). Words omitted from schedule heading and paragraph 1 heading from 12 November 2015 (SI 2015/1806). Paragraph (1) omitted from 1 October 2019 (SI 2019/1242). Paragraph 1(2) and tables 1 and 2 inserted from 6 April 2015 (SI 2015/681) subject to transitional provisions specified in regulation 6 of SI 2015/681. Malta inserted in list of English speaking countries from 1 December 2020 (SI 2020/1141).

Regulation 5A [SCHEDULE 2B

CERTAIN MEMBERS OF THE COMMONWEALTH AND BRITISH OVERSEAS TERRITORIES ETC.

Anguilla
Antigua and Barbuda
Australia
The Bahamas
Bangladesh
Barbados
Belize
Bermuda
Botswana
British Antarctic Territory
British Indian Ocean Territory
Brunei
Canada
Cayman Islands
Cyprus, but excluding the Sovereign Base Areas of Akrotiri and Dhekelia (that is to say the areas mentioned in section 2(1) of the Cyprus Act 1960)
Dominica
Falkland Islands
Fiji
The Gambia
Ghana
Gibraltar

Grenada
Guyana
Hong Kong
India
Jamaica
Kenya
Kiribati
Lesotho
Malawi
Malaysia
Maldives
Malta
Mauritius
Montserrat
Namibia
Nauru
New Zealand
Nigeria
Pakistan
Papua New Guinea
Pitcairn, Henderson, Ducie and Oeno Islands
Saint Christopher and Nevis
Saint Helena, Ascension and Tristan da Cunha
Saint Lucia
Saint Vincent and the Grenadines
Samoa
Seychelles Sierra Leone
Singapore
Solomon Islands
South Georgia and the South Sandwich Islands
South Africa
Sri Lanka
Swaziland
Tanzania
Tonga
Trinidad and Tobago
Turks and Caicos Islands
Tuvalu
Uganda
Vanuatu
Virgin Islands
Zambia
Zimbabwe]

Note: Schedule 2B inserted from 30 May 2018 (SI 2018/618).

Regulation 6

SCHEDULE 3

ADMINISTRATION OF [CITIZENSHIP OATH OR PLEDGE]

1. Subject to [paragraphs 2 and 3] [a citizenship oath or pledge] shall be administered by one of the following persons:

(a) in England and Wales or Northern Ireland—any justice of the peace, commissioner for oaths or notary public;

(b) in Scotland—any sheriff principal, sheriff, justice of the peace or notary public;

(c) in the Channel Islands, the Isle of Man or any British overseas territory— any judge of any court of civil or criminal jurisdiction, any justice of the peace or magistrate, or any person for the time being authorised by the law of the place where the applicant, declarant or deponent is, to administer an oath for any judicial or other legal purpose;

(d) in any country mentioned in Schedule 3 to the Act of which Her Majesty is Queen, or in any territory administered by the government of any such country—any person for the time being authorised by the law of the place where the deponent is to administer an oath for any judicial or other legal purpose, any consular officer or any established officer of the Diplomatic Service of Her Majesty's Government in the United Kingdom;

(e) elsewhere—any consular officer, any established officer of the Diplomatic Service of Her Majesty's Government in the United Kingdom or any person authorised by the Secretary of State in that behalf.

2. If the deponent is serving in Her Majesty's naval, military or air forces, the oath [or pledge] may be administered by any officer holding a commission in any of those forces, whether the oath [or pledge] is made [. . .] in the United Kingdom or elsewhere.

[**3.** Where a citizenship oath and pledge is required by section 42 of the Act to be made at a citizenship ceremony, it shall be administered at the ceremony:

(a) in the case of a ceremony held in England, Wales or Scotland, by a registrar (within the meaning of section 41(3B) of the Act); and

(b) in the case of a ceremony held elsewhere, by a person authorised to do so by the Secretary of State.]

Note: Words in square brackets substituted and inserted, and words omitted from 1 January 2004 (SI 2003/3158).

Regulation 7

SCHEDULE 4

[. . .]

Note: Schedule 4 revoked from 3 December 2007 (SI 2007/3137).

Regulation 8

SCHEDULE 5

REQUIREMENTS AS RESPECTS DECLARATIONS OF RENUNCIATION

1. A declaration shall be made in writing and shall state the name, address, date and place of birth of the declarant.

2. A declaration shall contain information showing that the declarant—

(a) is a British citizen, British Overseas citizen or British subject, as the case may be;

(b) is of full age or, if not, has been married;

(c) is of full capacity;

(d) will, after the registration of the declaration, have or acquire some citizenship or nationality other than British citizenship, British Overseas citizenship or British subject status, as the case may be.

[**2A.** If the declarant is not of full capacity and it is desired that the requirement of full capacity be waived in accordance with section 44A of the Act (waiver of requirement for full capacity), the declaration shall specify why it would be in the applicant's best interests for the requirement to be waived in his case.]

Note: Paragraph 2A inserted from 3 December 2007 (SI 2007/3137).

3. A declaration shall contain a declaration that the particulars stated therein are true.
Paragraph 5 of Schedule 1

[Schedule 6

Waiver request for the knowledge of language and life in the UK requirement—medical opinion

This form is to support a request for waiver front the knowledge of language and life in the UK requirement, for a person applying for settlement in the United Kingdom or naturalisation as a British citizen. It must be completed by a General Medical Council registered medical practitioner who is able to comment on the individual's condition.

Applicant's name:
Date of birth:
In your professional opinion please state:

1. What is the nature of the person's condition?

2. How does their condition impact on their daily life?

3. How would this condition prevent them from learning English? There are a number of ways to learn English, including classes and home study. The language requirement for citizenship and settlement is only for speaking and listening skills — not reading and writing.

4. How would this condition prevent them from studying for the knowledge of language and life in the UK test? The study materials are available in a number of formats including audio.

5. How would this condition prevent them from sitting the knowledge of language and life in the UK test or taking an English test? The knowledge of language and life in the UK test can be taken in an audio form, and that test centres can cater for a range of disabilities. It is computer-based and comprises 24 questions with multiple choice answers. Candidates are allowed 45 minutes and the pass mark is 18 correct answers.

6. In your opinion is this condition likely to improve sufficiently for them to be able to study and take the required tests? If so, is this likely to do so within the next 2 years?

7. In what capacity you have dealt with this person, for example as GP, consultant, other medical professional?

8. Have you worked professionally with this person other than for the purposes of this report, and over what period?
Please state your profession/qualifications and any registration number(s).

Signature: Date:
Name in capitals:]

Note: Schedule 6 inserted from 9 August 2018 (SI 2018/851).

The Immigration (Notices) Regulations 2003
(SI 2003, No. 658)

Citation and commencement

1. These Regulations may be cited as the Immigration (Notices) Regulations 2003 and shall come into force on the 1 April 2003.

Interpretation

2. In these Regulations—

'the 1971 Act' means the Immigration Act 1971;
'the 1997 Act' means the Special Immigration Appeals Commission Act 1997;
'the 1999 Act' means the Immigration and Asylum Act 1999;
'the 2002 Act' means the Nationality, Immigration and Asylum Act 2002;
['citizens' rights immigration decision' means a decision which can be appealed against under the Immigration (Citizens' Rights Appeals) (EU Exit) Regulations 2020.]
'decision-maker' means—
(a) the Secretary of State;
(b) an immigration officer;
(c) an entry clearance officer;
[. . .]
'entry clearance officer' means a person responsible for the grant or refusal of entry clearance;
[. . .]
'minor' means a person who is under 18 years of age;
'notice of appeal' means a notice in the appropriate prescribed form in accordance with the [Procedure Rules];
'Procedure Rules' means rules made under section [22 of, and Schedule 5 to, the Tribunals, Courts and Enforcement Act 2007];
'representative' means a person who appears to the decision-maker—
(a) to be the representative of a person referred to in regulation 4(1) below; and
(b) not to be prohibited from acting as a representative by section 84 of the 1999 Act.

Note: Words in square brackets in definitions of 'notice of appeal' and 'Procedure rules' inserted from 1 August 2008 (SI 2008/1819). Definition of 'immigration decision' deleted and definitions of 'notice of appeal' and 'Procedure Rules' amended from 6 November 2014 (SI 2014/2768). Definition of 'citizens' rights immigration decision' inserted from 31 January 2020 (SI 2020/61). Definition of 'EEA Decision' omitted from 23.00 on 31 December 2020 (SI 2020/1309) subject to saving provision (reg 28(4) of SI 2020/1309).

[3. . . .]

Note: Regulation 3 omitted from 6 November 2014 (SI 2014/2768).

Notice of decisions

4.—(1) Subject to regulation 6, the decision-maker must give written notice to a person of any [decision taken in respect of him which is appealable under section 82(1) of the 2002 Act {[[. . .]] or any citizens' rights immigration decision} taken in respect of him which is appealable.

[(2) . . .

(2A) . . .]

(3) If the notice is given to the representative of the person, it is to be taken to have been given to the person.

Note: Words substituted in paragraph (1) and paragraphs (2) and (2A) omitted from 6 November 2014 subject to transitional provisions (SI 2014/2768). Words in curly brackets in paragraph (1) substituted from 31 January 2020 (SI 2020/61) and words in double square brackets omitted from 23.00 on 31 December 2020 (SI 2020/1309) subject to saving provision (reg 28(4) of SI 2020/1309).

Contents of notice

5.—[(1) A notice given under regulation 4(1)—

(a) is to include or be accompanied by a statement of the reasons for the decision to which it relates. [. . .

(b) . . .]

[(2) . . .

(2A) . . .]

(3) [. . .] the notice given under regulation 4 shall also include, or be accompanied by, a statement which advises the person of—

(a) his right of appeal and the statutory provision on which his right of appeal is based;

(b) whether or not such an appeal may be brought while in the United Kingdom;

(c) the grounds on which such an appeal may be brought; and

(d) the facilities available for advice and assistance in connection with such an appeal.

[(4) The notice given under regulation 4 shall be accompanied by information about the process for providing a notice of appeal to the Tribunal and the time limit for providing that notice.]

[(5) . . .

(6) . . .

(7) . . .

(8) . . .]

Note: Paragraph (1) substituted from 31 August 2006 (SI 2006/2168). Words omitted from paragraphs (1)(a) and (3), paragraph (4) substituted and paragraphs (1)(b), (2), (2A), (5), (6), (7) and (8) omitted from 6 November 2014 subject to transitional provisions (SI 2014/2768).

Certain notices under the 1971 Act deemed to comply with the regulations

6.—(1) This regulation applies where the power to—

(a) refuse leave to enter; or

(b) vary leave to enter or remain in the United Kingdom;

is exercised by notice in writing under section 4 of (administration of control), or paragraph 6(2) (notice of decisions of leave to enter or remain) of Schedule 2 to, the 1971 Act.

(2) If—

(a) the statement required by regulation 5(3) is included in or accompanies that notice; and

(b) the notice is given in accordance with the provision of regulation 7; the notice is to be taken to have been given under regulation 4(1) for the purposes of these Regulations.

Service of notice

7.—(1) A notice required to be given under regulation 4 may be—

(a) given by hand;

(b) sent by fax;

(c) sent by postal service in which delivery or receipt is recorded to—

(i) an address provided for correspondence by the person or his representative; or

(ii) where no address for correspondence has been provided by the person, the last-known or usual place of abode or place of business of the person or his representative [;

[(d) sent electronically;

(e) sent by document exchange to a document exchange number or address;

(f) sent by courier; or

(g) collected by the person who is the subject of the decision or their representative.]

(2) Where—

(a) a person's whereabouts are not known; and

(b)

(i) no address has been provided for correspondence and the decision-maker does not know the last-known or usual place of abode or place of business of the person; or

(ii) the address provided to the decision-maker is defective, false or no longer in use by the person; and

(c) no representative appears to be acting for the person,

the notice shall be deemed to have been given when the decision-maker enters a record of the above circumstances and places the [. . .] notice on the relevant file.

[(3) Where a notice has been given in accordance with paragraph (2) and then subsequently the person is located—

(a) he shall be given a copy of the notice and details of when and how it was given as soon as practicable; and

(b) the time limit for appeal under the Procedure Rules shall be calculated from the date the notice is deemed to have been given in accordance with paragraph (2).]

[(4) Where a notice is sent by post to a place outside the United Kingdom in accordance with paragraph (1)(c) it shall be deemed to have been received on the twenty-eighth day after it was posted, unless the contrary is proved.]

(5) For the purposes of paragraph (4) the period is to be calculated—

(a) excluding the day on which the notice is posted.[. . .

(b) . . .]

(6) [. . .]

(7) A notice given under regulation 4 may, in the case of a minor who does not have a representative, be given to the parent, guardian or another adult who for the time being takes responsibility for the child.

Note: Words in square brackets in paragraph (1) inserted from 1 April 2008 (SI 2008/684). Words omitted from paragraph (2)(c) from 28 April 2013 (SI 2013/793). Paragraphs (3) and (4) substituted and paragraphs (5)(b) and (6) omitted from 6 November 2014 (SI 2014/2768).

The Immigration and Asylum Act 1999 (Part V Exemption: Relevant Employers) Order 2003

(SI 2003, No. 3214)

Citation and commencement

1. This Order may be cited as the Immigration and Asylum Act 1999 (Part V Exemption: Relevant Employers) Order 2003 and shall come into force on 1 January 2004.

Interpretation

2. In this Order—

'the Act' means the Immigration and Asylum Act 1999;

'immigration advice' and 'immigration services' have the same meanings as in section 82 of the Act;

'work permit' has the same meaning as in section 33(1) of the Immigration Act 1971;

'immediate family' means a person's spouse, and children below eighteen years of age;

[. . .]

Note: Words in square brackets inserted from 30 April 2006 (SI 2006/1003). Definitions of EEA national and family member of an EEA national omitted from 23.00 on 31 December 2020 (SI 2020/1309).

Exemption of relevant employers

3.—(1) Subject to paragraph (2), the following category of person is hereby specified for the purposes of section 84(4)(d) of the Act (provision of immigration services), namely, a person who provides immigration advice or immigration services free of charge to an employee or prospective employee who—

(a) is the subject of an application for a work permit submitted by the prospective employer;

(b) has been granted a work permit entitling him to work with the employer;

[. . .]

where the immigration advice or immigration services are restricted to matters which concern that employee or prospective employee or his immediate family.

(2) For the purposes of paragraph (1), the person providing the immigration advice or immigration services must be the employer or prospective employer of the person receiving the advice or services, or an employee of that employer acting as such.

Note: Paragraph 3(1)(c) omitted from 23.00 on 31 December 2020 (SI 2020/1309).

The Immigration (Claimant's Credibility) Regulations 2004

(SI 2004, No. 3263)

Citation and commencement

1. These Regulations may be cited as the Immigration (Claimant's Credibility) Regulations 2004 and shall come into force on the 1 January 2005.

Interpretation

2. In these Regulations—

'the 2004 Act' means the Asylum and Immigration (Treatment of Claimants, etc.) Act 2004;

'representative' means a person who appears to the decision-maker—

(a) to be the representative of a person; and

(b) not to be prohibited from acting as a representative by section 84 of the Immigration and Asylum 1999 Act.

Manner of notifying immigration decision

3.—(1) For the purpose of section 8(5) of the 2004 Act a person may be notified of an immigration decision in any of the following ways—

(a) orally, including by means of a telecommunications system;

(b) in writing given by hand; or

(c) in writing

(i) sent by fax to a fax number;

(ii) sent by electronic mail to an electronic mail address; or

(iii) delivered or sent by postal service to an address,

provided for correspondence by the person or his representative.

(2) Where no fax number, electronic mail or postal address for correspondence has been provided by the person, notice of an immigration decision under paragraph (1)(c) may be delivered or sent by postal service to the last known or usual place of abode or place of business of the person or his representative.

(3) Notice given in accordance with paragraph (1) or (2) to the representative of the person, is to be taken to have been given to the person.

(4) In the case of a minor who does not have a representative, notice given in accordance with paragraph (1) or (2) to the parent, guardian or another adult who for the time being takes responsibility for the minor is taken to have been given to the minor.

Presumptions about receipt of notice

4.—(1) For the purpose of section 8(5) of the 2004 Act notice of an immigration decision shall, unless the contrary is proved, be treated as received;

(a) where the notice is sent by postal service in which delivery or receipt is recorded to an address, on the recorded date of delivery or receipt, or on the second day after the day it was posted, whichever is the earlier;

(b) in any other case in which the notice is sent by postal service on the second day after the day it was posted; or

(c) in any other case, on the day and time that it was communicated orally, given by hand or sent by electronic mail or fax.

(2) For the purposes of determining the second day after a notice is posted under paragraph (1)(a) and (b) any day which is not a business day shall be excluded.

(3) In this regulation 'business day' means any day other than Saturday or Sunday, a day which is a bank holiday under the Banking and Financial Dealings Act 1971 in the part of the United Kingdom from or to which the notice is sent, Christmas Day or Good Friday.

The Asylum Seekers (Reception Conditions) Regulations 2005

(SI 2005, No. 7)

Citation and commencement

1.—(1) These Regulations may be cited as the Asylum Seekers (Reception Conditions) Regulations 2005 and shall come into force on 5 February 2005.

(2) These Regulations shall only apply to a person whose claim for asylum is recorded on or after 5 February 2005.

Interpretation

2.—(1) In these Regulations—

(a) 'the 1999 Act' means the Immigration and Asylum Act 1999;

(b) 'asylum seeker' means a person who is at least 18 years old who has made a claim for asylum which has been recorded by the Secretary of State but not yet determined;

(c) 'claim for asylum' means a claim made by a third country national or a stateless person that to remove him or require him to leave the United Kingdom would be contrary to the United Kingdom's obligations under the Convention relating to the Status of Refugees done at Geneva on 28 July 1951 and its Protocol;

(d) 'family members' means, in so far as the family already existed in the country of origin, the following members of the asylum seeker's family who are present in the United Kingdom and who are asylum seekers or dependants on the asylum seeker's claim for asylum:

(i) the spouse of the asylum seeker or his unmarried partner in a stable relationship;

(ii) the minor child of the couple referred to in paragraph (2)(d)(i) or of the asylum seeker as long as the child is unmarried and dependent on the asylum seeker;

(e) 'Immigration Acts' has the same meaning as in section 44 of the Asylum and Immigration (Treatment of Claimants, etc.) Act 2004; and

(f) 'third country national' means a person who is not a national of a member State.

(2) For the purposes of these Regulations—

(a) a claim is determined on the date on which the Secretary of State notifies the asylum seeker of his decision on his claim or, if the asylum seeker appeals against the Secretary of State's decision, the date on which that appeal is disposed of; and

(b) an appeal is disposed of when it is no longer pending for the purposes of the Immigration Acts.

Families

3.—(1) When the Secretary of State is providing or arranging for the provision of accommodation for an asylum seeker and his family members under section 95 or 98 of the 1999 Act, he shall have regard to family unity and ensure, in so far as it is reasonably practicable to do so, that family members are accommodated together.

(2) Paragraph (1) shall only apply to those family members who confirm to the Secretary of State that they agree to being accommodated together.

(3) This regulation shall not apply in respect of a child when the Secretary of State is providing or arranging for the provision of accommodation for that child under section 122 of the 1999 Act.

Provisions for persons with special needs

4.—(1) This regulation applies to an asylum seeker or the family member of an asylum seeker who is a vulnerable person.

(2) When the Secretary of State is providing support or considering whether to provide support under section 95 or 98 of the 1999 Act to an asylum seeker or his family member who is a vulnerable person, he shall take into account the special needs of that asylum seeker or his family member.

(3) A vulnerable person is—

(a) a minor;

(b) a disabled person;

(c) an elderly person;

(d) a pregnant woman;

(e) a lone parent with a minor child; or

(f) a person who has been subjected to torture, rape or other serious forms of psychological, physical or sexual violence;

who has had an individual evaluation of his situation that confirms he has special needs.

(4) Nothing in this regulation obliges the Secretary of State to carry out or arrange for the carrying out of an individual evaluation of a vulnerable person's situation to determine whether he has special needs.

Asylum support under section 95 or 98 of the 1999 Act

5.—(1) If an asylum seeker or his family member applies for support under section 95 of the 1999 Act and the Secretary of State thinks that the asylum seeker or his family member is eligible for support under that section he must offer the provision of support to the asylum seeker or his family member.

(2) If the Secretary of State thinks that the asylum seeker or his family member is eligible for support under section 98 of the 1999 Act he must offer the provision of support to the asylum seeker or his family member.

Tracing family members of unaccompanied minors

6.—(1) So as to protect an unaccompanied minor's best interests, the Secretary of State shall endeavour to trace the members of the minor's family as soon as possible after the minor makes his claim for asylum.

(2) In cases where there may be a threat to the life or integrity of the minor or the minor's close family, the Secretary of State shall take care to ensure that the collection, processing and circulation of information concerning the minor or his close family is undertaken on a confidential basis so as not to jeopardise his or their safety.

(3) For the purposes of this regulation—

(a) an unaccompanied minor means a person below the age of eighteen who arrives in the United Kingdom unaccompanied by an adult responsible for him whether by law or custom and makes a claim for asylum;

(b) a person shall be an unaccompanied minor until he is taken into the care of such an adult or until he reaches the age of 18 whichever is the earlier;

(c) an unaccompanied minor also includes a minor who is left unaccompanied after he arrives in or enters the United Kingdom but before he makes his claim for asylum.

The Immigration and Asylum (Provision of Accommodation to Failed Asylum-Seekers) Regulations 2005

(SI 2005, No. 930)

Citation and commencement

1.—(1) These Regulations may be cited as the Immigration and Asylum (Provision of Accommodation to Failed Asylum-Seekers) Regulations 2005 and shall come into force on 31 March 2005.

(2) These Regulations apply to a person who is receiving accommodation when these Regulations come into force to the same extent as they apply to a person provided with accommodation after these Regulations come into force.

Interpretation

2. In these Regulations—

'the 1999 Act' means the Immigration and Asylum Act 1999;

'destitute' is to be construed in accordance with section 95(3) of the 1999 Act; and

['reporting requirement' is a condition imposed under paragraph 2(1)(a) of Schedule 10 to the Immigration Act 2016, that is to say a condition of immigration bail requiring a person to report to the Secretary of State or such other person as may be specified.]

Note: Definition of 'reporting requirement' substituted from 15 January 2018 (SI 2017/1242).

Eligibility for and provision of accommodation to a failed asylum-seeker

3.—(1) Subject to regulations 4 and 6, the criteria to be used in determining the matters referred to in paragraphs (a) and (b) of section 4(5) of the 1999 Act in respect of a person falling within section 4(2) or (3) of that Act are—

(a) that he appears to the Secretary of State to be destitute, and

(b) that one or more of the conditions set out in paragraph (2) are satisfied in relation to him.

(2) Those conditions are that—

(a) he is taking all reasonable steps to leave the United Kingdom or place himself in a position in which he is able to leave the United Kingdom, which may include complying with attempts to obtain a travel document to facilitate his departure;

(b) he is unable to leave the United Kingdom by reason of a physical impediment to travel or for some other medical reason;

(c) he is unable to leave the United Kingdom because in the opinion of the Secretary of State there is currently no viable route of return available;

(d) he has made an application for judicial review of a decision in relation to his asylum claim—

(i) in England and Wales, and has been granted permission to proceed pursuant to Part 54 of the Civil Procedure Rules 1998,

(ii) in Scotland, pursuant to Chapter 58 of the Rules of the Court of Session 1994 or

(iii) in Northern Ireland, and has been granted leave pursuant to Order 53 of the Rules of Supreme Court (Northern Ireland) 1980; or

(e) the provision of accommodation is necessary for the purpose of avoiding a breach of a person's Convention rights, within the meaning of the Human Rights Act 1998.

Community activities: general

4.—(1) Where the Secretary of State so determines, the continued provision of accommodation to a person falling within section 4(2) or (3) of the 1999 Act is to be conditional upon that person's performance of or participation in such community activity as is described in this regulation and is from time to time notified to the person in accordance with regulation 5.

(2) In making the determination referred to in paragraph (1), regard will be had to the following matters—

(a) the length of time that he believes the person will continue to be eligible for accommodation,

(b) the arrangements that have been made for the performance of or participation in community activities in the area in which the person is being provided with accommodation,

(c) any relevant health and safety standards which are agreed between the Secretary of State and a person with whom he has made arrangements for the provision of community activities in the person's area,

(d) whether the person is in the Secretary of State's belief unable to perform or participate in community activities because of a physical or mental impairment or for some other medical reason,

(e) whether the person is in the Secretary of State's belief unable to perform or participate in community activities because of a responsibility for the care of a dependant child or of a dependant who because of a physical or mental impairment is unable to look after himself, and

(f) any relevant information provided to the Secretary of State, regarding the person's suitability to perform or participate in particular tasks, activities or a range of tasks or activities.

(3) Paragraph (1) does not apply in relation to a person who is under the age of 18.

(4) No condition on the continued provision of accommodation will require a person to perform or participate in community activities for more than 35 hours in any week, including the weekend.

Community activities: Relevant information

5. A notice under regulation 4(1) falls within this regulation if it contains the following information—

(a) the task, activity or range of tasks or activities in the area in which the person lives which are to be performed or participated in as community activities,

(b) the geographical location at which the community activities will be performed or participated in,

(c) the maximum number of hours per week that the person will be expected to perform or participate in community activities, where it is possible for the Secretary of State to so specify, and

(d) the date upon which the task, activity or range of tasks or activities to be performed or participated in as community activities will commence and, where it is possible for the Secretary of State to so specify, the length of time such community activities will last.

Other conditions on continued provision of accommodation

6.—(1) The continued provision of accommodation to a person falling within section 4(2) or (3) of the 1999 Act is to be subject to such other conditions falling within paragraph (2) as—

(a) the Secretary of State may from time to time determine, and

(b) are set out in a notice to that person in writing.

(2) A condition falls within this paragraph to the extent that it relates to—

(a) complying with specified standards of behaviour,

(b) complying with a reporting requirement,

(c) complying with a requirement—

(i) to reside at an authorised address, or

(ii) if he is absent from an authorised address without the permission of the Secretary of State, to ensure that that absence is for no more than seven consecutive days and nights or for no more than a total of fourteen days and nights in any six month period, or

(d) complying with specified steps to facilitate his departure from the United Kingdom.

The British Nationality (Proof of Paternity) Regulations 2006

(SI 2006, No. 1496)

---

1. These Regulations may be cited as the British Nationality (Proof of Paternity) Regulations 2006 and shall come into force on 1 July 2006.

[**2.** For the purposes of section 50(9A)(c) of the British Nationality Act 1981, the prescribed requirement as to proof of paternity is that the person must satisfy the Secretary of State that he is the natural father of the child.]

3. The Secretary of State may determine whether a person is the [natural] father of a child for the purpose of {regulation 2}, and for this purpose the Secretary of State may have regard to any evidence which he considers to be relevant, including, but not limited to—

(a) DNA test reports; [. . .]

(b) court orders [; and

(c) birth certificates].

Note: Regulation 2 and in regulation 3 words in curly brackets substituted, word omitted and words in square brackets and regulation 3(c) inserted from 10 September 2015 (SI 2015/1615) subject to transitional provisions: 'The amendments made by these Regulations do not have effect in relation to a person who is named as the father of the child in a birth certificate issued before 10th September 2015' (regulation 5 of SI 2015/1615).

The Immigration (Provision of Physical Data) Regulations 2006

(SI 2006, No. 1743)

Note: Between 30 March 2012 and 9 November 2012 these regulations applied with an amended wording (SI 2011/1779.)

Citation, commencement and interpretation

1. These Regulations may be cited as the Immigration (Provision of Physical Data) Regulations 2006 and shall come into force on the day after they are made.

2. In these Regulations:

'application' means:

(a) an application for entry clearance [save for when the applicant is required to apply simultaneously for a biometric immigration document]; [. . .]

(b) an application for leave to enter the United Kingdom where the person seeking leave to enter presents a Convention travel document endorsed with an entry clearance for that journey to the United Kingdom;

[(c) an application for a transit visa (meaning a visa issued to a person for the purpose of arriving in the United Kingdom in order to pass through to another country or territory without entering the United Kingdom); { . . . }

[(d) . . .][;

(e) an application for leave to enter or remain in the United Kingdom made under Appendix EU to the immigration rules.][; or

(f) an application for a frontier worker permit under the Citizens' Rights (Frontier Workers) (EU Exit) Regulations 2020;]

['biometric information' means photographs or fingerprints provided under regulation 3;]

'Convention travel document' means a travel document issued pursuant to Article 28 of the Refugee Convention, except where that travel document was issued by the United Kingdom Government;

['immigration rules' means rules made under section 3(2) of the Immigration Act 1971;]

'Refugee Convention' means the Convention relating to the Status of Refugees done at Geneva on 28 July 1951 and its Protocol.

Note: Definition of 'application' amended and definition of 'biometric information' and 'immigration rules' inserted from 6 April 2015 (SI 2015/737). In definition of 'application' word at end of paragraph (c) omitted from 27 August 2018 (SI 2018/928), paragraph (e) inserted from 27 August 2018 (SI 2018/928) and substituted from 30 March 2019 (SI 2019/686), paragraph (f) inserted from 4 November 2020 (SI 2020/1213) and paragraph (d) omitted from 23.00 on 31 December 2020 (SI 2020/1309) subject to saving provision (reg 32(5) of SI 2020/1309).

Power for an authorised person to require an individual to provide a record of his fingerprints and a photograph of his face

3. Subject to regulations 4 and 5, an authorised person may require an individual who makes an application to provide a record of his fingerprints and a photograph of his face.

Provision in relation to applicants under the age of sixteen

4.—(1) An applicant under the age of sixteen shall not be required to provide a record of his fingerprints or a photograph of his face except where the authorised person is satisfied that the fingerprints or the photograph will be taken in the presence of a person aged eighteen or over who is—

(a) the child's parent or guardian; or

(b) a person who for the time being takes responsibility for the child.

(2) The person mentioned in paragraph (1)(b) may not be—

(a) an officer of the Secretary of State who is not an authorised person;

(b) an authorised person; or

(c) any other person acting on behalf of an authorised person as part of a process specified under [regulation 6].

(3) An authorised person shall not require a person under the age of sixteen to provide a record of his fingerprints or a photograph of his face unless his decision to do so has been confirmed by a person designated for the purpose by the Secretary of State.

(4) This regulation shall not apply if the authorised person reasonably believes that the applicant is aged sixteen or over.

Note: Words in square brackets in paragraph (2)(c) substituted from 6 April 2015 (SI 2015/737).

Provision in relation to section 141 of the Immigration and Asylum Act 1999

5. An applicant shall not be required to provide a record of his fingerprints or a photograph of his face under regulation 3 if he is a person to whom section 141 of the Immigration and Asylum Act 1999 applies, during the relevant period within the meaning of that section.

[Process by which an individual's fingerprints and photograph may be obtained and recorded

6.—(1) An authorised person who requires an individual to provide a record of the individual's fingerprints or a photograph of the individual's face under regulation 3 may do any one or more of the following—

(a) require the individual to make an appointment before a specified date, which the individual must attend, to enable a record of the individual's fingerprints or a photograph of the individual's face to be taken by an authorised person or by a person acting on behalf of an authorised person;

(b) specify the date, time and place for the appointment;

(c) require the individual to attend premises before a specified date to enable a record of the individual's fingerprints or a photograph of the individual's face to be taken by an authorised person or by a person acting on behalf of an authorised person; and

(d) specify any documents which the individual must bring to the appointment or premises, or action which the individual must take to confirm the individual's identity.

(2) An authorised person may require a record of fingerprints or photograph to be of a particular specification.]

Note: Regulation 6 substituted from 6 April 2015 (SI 2015/737).

[Documents recording biometric information

6A. Biometric information provided under these Regulations may be recorded on any document issued as a result of the application in relation to which the information was provided.]

Note: Regulation 6A inserted from 6 April 2015 (SI 2015/737).

Consequences of failure to comply with these Regulations

7.—(1) Subject to paragraphs (2) and (3), where an individual does not provide a record of his fingerprints or a photograph of his face in accordance with a requirement imposed under these Regulations, his application may be treated as invalid.

(2) An application shall not be treated as invalid under paragraph (1) if it is for leave to enter the United Kingdom where the person seeking leave to enter presents a Convention travel document endorsed with an entry clearance for that journey to the United Kingdom.

(3) Where an application is of a type described in paragraph (2) and the applicant does not provide a record of his fingerprints or a photograph of his face in accordance with a requirement imposed under these Regulations, that application may be refused.

[Use and retention of biometric information

8.—(1) Biometric information provided in accordance with these Regulations may be retained only if the Secretary of State thinks that it is necessary to retain it for use in connection with—

(a) the exercise of a function by virtue of the Immigration Acts; or

(b) the exercise of a function in relation to nationality.

(2) Biometric information retained by virtue of paragraph (1) may also be used—

(a) in connection with the prevention, investigation or prosecution of an offence;

(b) for a purpose which appears to the Secretary of State to be required in order to protect national security;

(c) in connection with identifying persons who have died, or are suffering from illness or injury;[and]

(d) for the purpose of ascertaining whether a person has acted unlawfully, or has obtained or sought anything to which the person is not legally entitled; and

[(e) . . . .]

Note: Regulation 8 substituted from 6 April 2015 (SI 2015/737). Word inserted and paragraph (2) (e) omitted from 23.00 on 31 December 2020 (SI 2020/1309) subject to saving provision (reg 32(6) of SI 2020/1309).

[Power to use and retain existing biometric information

8A.—(1) This regulation applies where—

(a) a person makes an application; and

(b) the Secretary of State already has a record of the person's fingerprints or a photograph of the person's face in their possession (for whatever reason).

(2) Where this regulation applies, the Secretary of State may use or retain that information for the purposes of these Regulations.]

Note: Regulation 8A inserted from 1 July 2021 (SI 2021/772).

[Destruction of biometric information

9.—(1) The Secretary of State must take all reasonable steps to ensure that biometric information held by the Secretary of State by virtue of these Regulations, including any copies, is destroyed if the Secretary of State—

(a) no longer thinks that it is necessary to retain the information for use as mentioned in regulation 8(1); or

(b) subject to the exception in paragraph (2), is satisfied that the person to whom the information relates is a British citizen, or a Commonwealth citizen who has a right of abode in the United Kingdom as a result of section 2(1)(b) of the Immigration Act 1971.

(2) The exception is that photographs of a person who is registered or naturalised as a British citizen may be retained until the person is issued with a United Kingdom passport describing the person as a British citizen.]

Note: Regulation 9 substituted from 6 April 2015 (SI 2015/737).

[Retention of fingerprints

10.—(1) Save where regulation 9 applies and subject to paragraphs (2) and (3), the Secretary of State must take all reasonable steps to ensure that any record of a person's fingerprints held by the Secretary of State by virtue of these Regulations, including any copies, is destroyed at the end of the period of [15] years beginning with [—

(a) the date on which the fingerprints were provided; or

(b) the date on which they are reused in connection with an application made by the person which comes within paragraph (5),

whichever is the later.]

(2) But fingerprints can be held beyond that period if they are—

(a) the fingerprints of a person who is, or at any time has been, subject to a deportation order, exclusion order or decision to exclude;

(b) the fingerprints of a person who can be, or at any time could have been, refused entry clearance or leave to enter for a period specified in the immigration rules because of a previous breach of the United Kingdom's immigration laws;

(c) fingerprints that the Secretary of State deems it necessary for national security reasons to retain for use in connection with one of the functions specified in regulation 8(1);

(d) the fingerprints of a person with indefinite leave to enter or remain in the United Kingdom; [or]

(e) the fingerprints of a person whose indefinite leave to enter or remain in the United Kingdom lapses, is revoked or is cancelled, in which case they must be destroyed by the Secretary of State at the end of ten years beginning with the date of the lapse, revocation or cancellation (as the case may be); [. . .

(f) . . .]

(3) The Secretary of State is only required to take steps to destroy, pursuant to paragraph (2)(e) [. . .], the fingerprints of a person whose leave has lapsed [. . .] on the application, supported by evidence to the satisfaction of the Secretary of State, of that person.

[(4) . . .]].

[(5) An application comes within this paragraph if it is an application for—

(a) entry clearance;

(b) leave to enter;

(c) leave to remain; or

(d) registration or naturalisation as a British citizen.]

Note: Regulation 10 substituted from 6 April 2015 (SI 2015/737). Word inserted at end of paragraph (2)(d), paragraph (2)(f), words in paragraph (3) and paragraph (4) omitted from 23.00 on 31 December 2020 (SI 2020/1309) subject to saving provision (reg 32(7) of SI 2020/1309). Words in square brackets in paragraph (1) substituted and paragraph (5) inserted from 1 July 2022 (SI 2021/772).

[Destruction etc. of electronic data

10A.—(1) The Secretary of State must take all reasonable steps to ensure—

(a) that data held in electronic form which relates to biometric information which has to be destroyed by virtue of these Regulations is destroyed or erased; or

(b) that access to such data is blocked.

(2) A person whose biometric information has to be destroyed by virtue of these Regulations is entitled, on written request, to a certificate issued by the Secretary of State to the effect that the Secretary of State has taken the steps required by paragraph (1).

(3) A certificate issued under paragraph (2) must be issued within the period of 3 months beginning with the date on which the request for it is received by the Secretary of State.]

Note: Regulation 10A inserted from 6 April 2015 (SI 2015/737).

[Biometric information: retention under another power

10B. The requirements in these Regulations to destroy biometric information or data do not apply if and in so far as the information or data is retained in accordance with and for the purposes of another power.]

Note: Regulation 10B inserted from 6 April 2015 (SI 2015/737).

Revocation and transitional provisions

11.—(1) Subject to paragraphs (2) and (3), the Regulations specified in the Schedule are revoked.

(2) For the purposes of paragraph (3) only, 'application' means an application within the meaning of regulation 2 of the Immigration (Provision of Physical Data) Regulations 2003 (the '2003 Regulations').

(3) Where a person made an application before these Regulations came into force, the 2003 Regulations will continue to apply for the purposes of that application as if they had not been revoked by paragraph (1).

The Immigration (Continuation of Leave) (Notices) Regulations 2006

(SI 2006, No. 2170)

Citation and Commencement

1. These Regulations may be cited as the Immigration (Continuation of Leave) (Notices) Regulations 2006 and shall come into force on 31 August 2006.

Decision on an application for variation of leave

2. For the purpose of section 3C of the Immigration Act 1971 an application for variation of leave is decided—

(a) when notice of the decision has been given in accordance with regulations made under section 105 of the Nationality, Immigration and Asylum Act 2002; or where no such notice is required,

(b) when notice of the decision has been given in accordance with section 4(1) of the Immigration Act 1971.

The Refugee or Person in Need of International Protection (Qualification) Regulations 2006

(SI 2006, No. 2525)

Note: Revoked by Nationality and Borders Act 2022 c. 36 Pt 2 s.30(4) (June 28, 2022: revocation has effect as 2022 c.36 s.87(5)(c) subject to transitional and saving provisions specified in SI 2022/590 reg.3 and Sch.2 para.5).

Citation and commencement

1.—(1) These Regulations may be cited as The Refugee or Person in Need of International Protection (Qualification) Regulations 2006 and shall come into force on 9 October 2006.

(2) These Regulations apply to any application for asylum which has not been decided and any immigration appeal brought under the Immigration Acts (as defined in section 64(2) of the Immigration, Asylum and Nationality Act 2006) which has not been finally determined.

Interpretation

2. In these Regulations—

'application for asylum' means the request of a person to be recognised as a refugee under the Geneva Convention;

'Geneva Convention' means the Convention Relating to the Status of Refugees done at Geneva on 28 July 1951 and the New York Protocol of 31 January 1967;

'immigration rules' means rules made under section 3(2) of the Immigration Act 1971;

'persecution' means an act of persecution within the meaning of Article 1(A) of the Geneva Convention;

'person eligible for humanitarian protection' means a person who is eligible for a grant of humanitarian protection under the immigration rules;

'refugee' means a person who falls within Article 1(A) of the Geneva Convention and to whom regulation 7 does not apply;

'residence permit' means a document confirming that a person has leave to enter or remain in the United Kingdom whether limited or indefinite;

'serious harm' means serious harm as defined in the immigration rules;

'person' means any person who is not a British citizen.

Actors of persecution or serious harm

3. In deciding whether a person is a refugee or a person eligible for humanitarian protection, persecution or serious harm can be committed by:

(a) the State;

(b) any party or organisation controlling the State or a substantial part of the territory of the State;

(c) any non-State actor if it can be demonstrated that the actors mentioned in paragraphs (a) and (b), including any international organisation, are unable or unwilling to provide protection against persecution or serious harm.

Actors of protection

4.—(1) In deciding whether a person is a refugee or a person eligible for humanitarian protection, protection from persecution or serious harm can be provided by:

(a) the State; or

(b) any party or organisation, including any international organisation, controlling the State or a substantial part of the territory of the State.

(2) Protection shall be regarded as generally provided when the actors mentioned in paragraph (1)(a) and (b) take reasonable steps to prevent the persecution or suffering of serious harm by operating an effective legal system for the detection, prosecution and punishment of acts constituting persecution or serious harm, and the person mentioned in paragraph (1) has access to such protection.

(3) In deciding whether a person is a refugee or a person eligible for humanitarian protection the Secretary of State may assess whether an international organisation controls a State or a substantial part of its territory and provides protection as described in paragraph (2).

Act of persecution

5.—(1) In deciding whether a person is a refugee an act of persecution must be:

(a) sufficiently serious by its nature or repetition as to constitute a severe violation of a basic human right, in particular a right from which derogation cannot be made under Article 15 of the Convention for the Protection of Human Rights and Fundamental Freedoms; or

(b) an accumulation of various measures, including a violation of a human right which is sufficiently severe as to affect an individual in a similar manner as specified in (a).

(2) An act of persecution may, for example, take the form of:

(a) an act of physical or mental violence, including an act of sexual violence;

(b) a legal, administrative, police, or judicial measure which in itself is discriminatory or which is implemented in a discriminatory manner;

(c) prosecution or punishment, which is disproportionate or discriminatory;

(d) denial of judicial redress resulting in a disproportionate or discriminatory punishment;

(e) prosecution or punishment for refusal to perform military service in a conflict, where performing military service would include crimes or acts falling under regulation 7.

(3) An act of persecution must be committed for at least one of the reasons in Article 1(A) of the Geneva Convention.

Reasons for persecution

6.—(1) In deciding whether a person is a refugee:

(a) the concept of race shall include consideration of, for example, colour, descent, or membership of a particular ethnic group;

(b) the concept of religion shall include, for example, the holding of theistic, non-theistic and atheistic beliefs, the participation in, or abstention from, formal worship in private or in public, either alone or in community with others, other religious acts or expressions of view, or forms of personal or communal conduct based on or mandated by any religious belief;

(c) the concept of nationality shall not be confined to citizenship or lack thereof but shall include, for example, membership of a group determined by its cultural, ethnic, or linguistic identity, common geographical or political origins or its relationship with the population of another State;

(d) a group shall be considered to form a particular social group where, for example:

(i) members of that group share an innate characteristic, or a common background that cannot be changed, or share a characteristic or belief that is so fundamental to identity or conscience that a person should not be forced to renounce it, and

(ii) that group has a distinct identity in the relevant country, because it is perceived as being different by the surrounding society;

(e) a particular social group might include a group based on a common characteristic of sexual orientation but sexual orientation cannot be understood to include acts considered to be criminal in accordance with national law of the United Kingdom;

(f) the concept of political opinion shall include the holding of an opinion, thought or belief on a matter related to the potential actors of persecution mentioned in regulation 3 and to their policies or methods, whether or not that opinion, thought or belief has been acted upon by the person.

(2) In deciding whether a person has a well-founded fear of being persecuted, it is immaterial whether he actually possesses the racial, religious, national, social or political characteristic which attracts the persecution, provided that such a characteristic is attributed to him by the actor of persecution.

Exclusion

7.—(1) A person is not a refugee, if he falls within the scope of Article 1D, 1E or 1F of the Geneva Convention.

(2) In the construction and application of Article 1F(b) of the Geneva Convention:

(a) the reference to serious non-political crime includes a particularly cruel action, even if it is committed with an allegedly political objective;

(b) the reference to the crime being committed outside the country of refuge prior to his admission as a refugee shall be taken to mean the time up to and including the day on which a residence permit is issued.

(3) Article 1F(a) and (b) of the Geneva Convention shall apply to a person who instigates or otherwise participates in the commission of the crimes or acts specified in those provisions.

The Immigration (Certificate of Entitlement to Right of Abode in the United Kingdom) Regulations 2006

(SI 2006, No. 3145)

Citation, commencement and interpretation

1. These Regulations may be cited as the Immigration (Certificate of Entitlement to Right of Abode in the United Kingdom) Regulations 2006 and shall come into force on 21 December 2006.

2. In these Regulations—

'the 1971 Act' means the Immigration Act 1971;

'the 1981 Act' means the British Nationality Act 1981;

'the 2002 Act' means the Nationality, Immigration and Asylum Act 2002;

['the 2008 Act' means the Human Fertilisation and Embryology Act 2008;]

'appropriate authority' means the authority to whom an application for a certificate of entitlement must be made, as determined in accordance with regulation 3;

'certificate of entitlement' means a certificate, issued in accordance with these Regulations, that a person has the right of abode in the United Kingdom;

'Governor', in relation to a territory, includes the officer for the time being administering the government of that territory;

'High Commissioner' means, in relation to a country mentioned in Schedule 3 to the 1981 Act, the High Commissioner for Her Majesty's Government in the United Kingdom appointed to that country, and includes the acting High Commissioner; and

'passport' includes a document which relates to a national of a country other than the United Kingdom and which is designed to serve the same purpose as a passport.

Note: Definition of '2008 Act' inserted from 1 September 2009 (SI 2009/1892).

Authority to whom an application must be made

3. An application for a certificate of entitlement must be made—

(a) if the applicant is in the United Kingdom, to the Secretary of State for the Home Department;

[(b) if the applicant is in any of the Channel Islands or the Isle of Man, to the Lieutenant-Governor or the Secretary of State for the Home Department;]

(c) if the applicant is in a British overseas territory, to the Governor;

(d) if the applicant is in a country mentioned in Schedule 3 to the 1981 Act, to the High Commissioner, or, if there is no High Commissioner, to the Secretary of State for the Home Department; and

(e) if the applicant is elsewhere, to any consular officer, any established officer in the Diplomatic Service of Her Majesty's Government in the United Kingdom or any other person authorised by the Secretary of State in that behalf.

Note: Regulation 3(b) substituted from 12 December 2011 (SI 2011/2682).

Form of application

[**4.**—(1) Subject to paragraph (2), an application for a certificate of entitlement must be accompanied by—

(a) the applicant's passport or travel document;

(b) two photographs of the applicant taken no more than 6 months prior to making the application; and

(c) the additional documents which are specified in the right-hand column of the Schedule in respect of an application of a description specified in the corresponding entry in the left hand column.

(2) The requirement in paragraph (1)(c) may be waived in relation to a particular document if the appropriate authority—

(a) is satisfied that it is appropriate to do so in light of the facts of the particular case; and

(b) is otherwise satisfied that the applicant has a right of abode in the United Kingdom.]

Note: Regulation 4 substituted from 12 December 2011 (SI 2011/2682).

5. A passport produced by or on behalf of a person is valid for the purposes of regulation 4 if it—

(a) relates to the person by whom or on whose behalf it is produced;

(b) has not been altered otherwise than by or with the permission of the authority who issued it; and

(c) was not obtained by deception.

Issue of certificate of entitlement

6. A certificate of entitlement will only be issued where the appropriate authority is satisfied that the applicant—

(a) has a right of abode in the United Kingdom under section 2(1) of the 1971 Act;

[(b) is not a person who holds:

(i) a United Kingdom passport describing him as a British citizen,

(ii) a United Kingdom passport describing him as a British subject with the right of abode in the United Kingdom, or

(iii) a certificate of entitlement;]

(c) is not a person whose exercise of his right of abode is restricted under section 2 of the Immigration Act 1988 (restrictions on exercise of right of abode in cases of polygamy); and

(d) is not a person who is deprived of his right of abode by an order under section 2A of the 1971 Act.

7. A certificate of entitlement is to be issued by means of being affixed to the passport or travel document of the applicant.

Note: Regulation 6(b) substituted from 12 December 2011 (SI 2011/2682).

Expiry and revocation of certificate of entitlement

8. A certificate of entitlement shall cease to have effect on the expiry of the passport or travel document to which it is affixed.

9. A certificate of entitlement may be revoked by the Secretary of State for the Home Department, an immigration officer, a consular officer or a person responsible for the grant or refusal of entry clearance, where the person who revokes the certificate is satisfied that the person in possession of the certificate (whether or not this is the person to whom the certificate was issued)—

(a) does not have the right of abode in the United Kingdom under section 2(1) of the 1971 Act;

[(b) is the holder of:

(i) a United Kingdom passport describing him as a British citizen,

(ii) a United Kingdom passport describing him as a British subject with the right of abode in the United Kingdom,

(iii) another certificate of entitlement;]

(c) is a person whose exercise of his right of abode is restricted under section 2 of the Immigration Act 1988; or

(d) is a person who is deprived of his right of abode by an order under section 2A of the 1971 Act.

Note: Regulation 9(b) substituted from 12 December 2011 (SI 2011/2682).

Savings

10. The effect of a certificate described in section 10(6) of the 2002 Act is that it will cease to have effect on the expiry of the passport or travel document to which it is affixed.

Schedule

Additional documents which must accompany an application for a certificate of entitlement.

[Regulation 4(1)(c)]

Basis of application	Documents
Applicant was registered or naturalised as a British citizen on or after 1st January 1983	Applicant's registration or naturalisation certificate
Applicant was born in the United Kingdom before 1st January 1983	Applicant's full birth certificate, showing parents' details
Applicant was registered or naturalised as a citizen of the United Kingdom and Colonies in the United Kingdom before 1st January 1983	Applicant's registration or naturalisation certificate
Applicant is a Commonwealth (not British) citizen born before 1st January 1983 to a parent who was born in the United Kingdom	(i) Applicant's full birth certificate showing parents' details; and (ii) Parents' full UK birth certificate
Applicant is a female Commonwealth citizen who was married before 1st January 1983 to a man with right of abode in the United Kingdom	(i) Applicant's marriage certificate; and (ii) Evidence of applicant's husband's right of abode, eg passport or UK birth certificate
Applicant was born in the United Kingdom or the Falkland Islands on or after 1st January 1983, or in another qualifying British overseas territory on or after 21st May 2002	(i) Applicant's full birth certificate showing parents' details; (ii) Evidence of either parent's British citizenship or settled status at time of applicant's birth, eg a passport describing the relevant parent as a British citizen or indicating that he or she then had indefinite leave to remain; and [(iii) Parents' marriage or civil partnership certificate (if claiming through father or if claiming through woman who is a parent of the applicant by virtue of section 42 or 43 of the 2008 Act.]
Applicant was born outside the United Kingdom and the Falkland Islands on or after 1st January 1983, or outside the United Kingdom and any qualifying British overseas territory on or after 21st May 2002, to a parent born in the United Kingdom or the Falkland Islands (or, on/after 21 May 2002, any qualifying British overseas territory) or to a parent registered or naturalised in the United Kingdom prior to the applicant's birth	(i) Applicant's full birth certificate showing parents' details; [(ii) Parents' marriage or civil partnership certificate (if claiming through father or if claiming through woman who is a parent of the applicant by virtue of section 42 or 43 of the 2008 Act);] and (iii) Parents' full birth certificate, registration or naturalisation certificate

Basis of application	Documents
Applicant was born outside the United Kingdom and the Falkland Islands on or after 1st January 1983, or outside the United Kingdom and any qualifying British overseas territory on or after 21 May 2002, to a parent who, at the time of the birth, was a British citizen in service to which section 2(1)(b) of the British Nationality Act 1981 applies	(i) Applicant's full birth certificate; [(ii) Parents' marriage or civil partnership certificate (if claiming through father or if claiming through woman who is a parent of the applicant by virtue of section 42 or 43 of the 2008 Act);] and (iii) Evidence of parents' relevant employment at the time of the birth, eg a letter from the employer
Applicant was adopted in the United Kingdom, a qualifying British overseas territory, or otherwise under the terms of the Hague Convention on Intercountry Adoption(1)	(i) Applicant's adoption certificate; and (ii) Evidence of adoptive parents' citizenship and, if a Convention adoption, of their place of habitual residence at the time of the adoption, eg in respect of citizenship, a passport, and in respect of habitual residence at the time of the Convention adoption, the adoption certificate
Applicant was a citizen of the United Kingdom and Colonies and was ordinarily resident in the United Kingdom for a continuous period of 5 years before 1st January 1983 and was settled in the United Kingdom at the end of that period	(i) Evidence of citizenship of the United Kingdom and Colonies, eg a passport or certificate of naturalisation or registration; and (ii) Evidence of settlement and 5 years' ordinary residence in the UK before 1983, eg, passport, P60s, details of National Insurance contributions, DSS claims, employers' letters
Applicant was a citizen of the United Kingdom and Colonies and had a parent who was born, adopted, registered or naturalised in the United Kingdom prior to the applicant's birth/adoption	(i) Applicant's full birth certificate or adoption certificate; [(ii) Parents' marriage or civil partnership certificate (if claiming through father or if claiming through woman who is a parent of the applicant by virtue of section 42 or 43 of the 2008 Act);] and (iii) Parents' full birth certificate, adoption, registration or naturalisation certificate
Applicant was a citizen of the United Kingdom and Colonies and had a grandparent born, adopted, registered or naturalised in the United Kingdom before the applicant's parents' birth/adoption	(i) Parents' marriage certificate (if claiming through father); [(ii) Parents' marriage or civil partnership certificate (if claiming through father or if claiming through woman who is a parent of the applicant by virtue of section 42 or 43 of the 2008 Act);] (iii) Applicant's full birth certificate or adoption certificate; (iv) Grandparents' marriage certificate (if claiming through grandfather); and (v) Grandparents' full birth certificate, adoption, registration or naturalisation certificate.

Note: Schedule amended from 1 September 2009 by SI 2009/1892 and from 12 December 2011 by SI 2011/2682.

The Asylum (Procedures) Regulations 2007

(SI 2007, No. 3187)

Citation and commencement

1. These Regulations may be cited as the Asylum (Procedures) Regulations 2007 and shall come into force on 1 December 2007.

Interpretation

2. In these Regulations—

'the 1997 Act' means the Special Immigration Appeals Commission Act 1997;

'the 2002 Act' means the Nationality, Immigration and Asylum Act 2002;

'asylum claim' and 'human rights claim' have the meanings given to them in section 113 of the 2002 Act.

Designation of States or parts of States for the purposes of section 94 of the 2002 Act

3. . . .

Note: Inserts subsection (5D) into s 94 Nationality, Immigration and Asylum Act 2002.

European Common List of Safe Countries of Origin

4. . . .

Note: Inserts s 94A into Nationality, Immigration and Asylum Act 2002.

Interpreters

5.—(1) Paragraph (2) applies where a person who has made an asylum or a human rights claim (or both)—

(a) appeals under section 82, [. . .] of the 2002 Act or section 2 of the 1997 Act, and

(b) by virtue of Rules made under section 106 of the 2002 Act or sections 5 and 8 of the 1997 Act is entitled to the services of an interpreter for the purposes of bringing his appeal.

(2) The Secretary of State shall defray the costs of providing the interpreter.

(3) Paragraph (5) applies where a person who has made an asylum claim or a human rights claim (or both) is party to –

(a) an appeal under section 103B, 103C or 103E of the 2002 Act, or

(b) an appeal under section 7 of the 1997 Act.

(4) Paragraph (5) also applies where a person who has made an asylum or a human rights claim (or both) makes—

(a) an application to the supervisory jurisdiction of the Court of Session made by petition for judicial review,

(b) an application under section 31 of the Supreme Court Act 1981, or

(c) an application under section 18 of the Judicature (Northern Ireland) Act 1978.

(5) The person mentioned in paragraphs (3) and (4) shall be entitled to the services of an interpreter for the purposes of the appeal or application—

(a) when giving evidence, and

(b) in such other circumstances as the court hearing the appeal or application considers it necessary.

(6) Where a person is entitled to the services of an interpreter under paragraph (5), the Secretary of State shall defray the costs of providing such interpreter.

Note: Words '83 or 83A' omitted in subparagraph (1)(a) from 6 April 2015 (SI 2015/383) subject to saving provision (article 5 of SI 2015/383).

Amendment to the Immigration (Notices) Regulations 2003

6. …

Note: Amends SI 2003/658.

The Immigration and Asylum (Provision of Services or Facilities) Regulations 2007

(SI 2007, No. 3627)

Citation and commencement

1. These Regulations may be cited as the Immigration and Asylum (Provision of Services or Facilities) Regulations 2007 and shall come into force on 31 January 2008.

Interpretation

2. In these Regulations—

'the 1999 Act' means the Immigration and Asylum Act 1999;

'ante-natal eligible period' means the period from eight weeks before the expected date of birth to the date of birth;

'child' means an individual who is less than 18 years old;

'destitute' is to be construed in accordance with section 95(3) of the 1999 Act;

'full birth certificate' means a birth certificate issued in the United Kingdom, which specifies the names of the child's parents;

'immigration officer' means a person appointed as an immigration officer under paragraph 1(1) of Schedule 2 to the Immigration Act 1971;

'maternity payment' means a payment of £250 made by the Secretary of State to a person supported under section 95 or section 98 of the 1999 Act to help with the costs arising from the birth of a child;

'mother' means a woman who is a supported person and who has provided evidence to satisfy the Secretary of State that she has given birth to a child;

'post-natal eligible period' means the period from the date of the birth to six weeks after the birth;

'pregnant woman' means a woman who is a supported person who has provided evidence to satisfy the Secretary of State that she is pregnant;

'provider' means a person providing facilities for the accommodation of persons by arrangement with the Secretary of State under section 4 of the 1999 Act;

'qualified person' has the same meaning as in section 84(2) of the 1999 Act;

'qualifying journey' means where—

(a) a single journey of a distance of not less than three miles; or

(b) where there is a specified need, a single journey of a distance of less than three miles;

'specified need' means where—

(a) the supported person is unable or virtually unable to walk a distance of up to three miles by reason of a physical impediment or for some other reason; or

(b) the supported person has one or more child dependants—

(i) aged under five; or

(ii) who are unable or virtually unable to walk a distance of up to three miles by reason of a physical impediment or for some other reason;

'supported person' means a person who is being provided with accommodation under section 4 of the 1999 Act and who is destitute; and

'voluntary sector partner' means an organisation funded by the Secretary of State to deliver aspects of asylum support services.

Travel

3.—(1) The Secretary of State may supply, or arrange for the supply of, facilities for travel for a qualifying journey to a supported person to—

(a) receive healthcare treatment, provided that the supported person has provided evidence that the qualifying journey is necessary; or

(b) register a birth.

(2) Subject to paragraph (3), if the Secretary of State supplies, or arranges for the supply of, facilities for travel for a qualifying journey to a supported person under paragraph (1) then, if necessary, the Secretary of State may also supply, or arrange for the supply of, facilities for travel for that qualifying journey to—

(a) one or more dependants of that supported person; and

(b) in the case of a supported person who is a child—

(i) a parent or guardian of that supported person or a person who for the time being takes parental responsibility for that supported person; and

(ii) if the parent, guardian or person who for the time being takes parental responsibility for that supported person himself has dependants then one or more of his dependants.

(3) The Secretary of State may only supply, or arrange for the supply of, facilities for travel under paragraph (2) to persons who are supported persons.

Birth certificates

4. The Secretary of State may arrange for the provision to a supported person of his child's full birth certificate.

Telephone calls and letters

5.—(1) The Secretary of State may supply, or arrange for the supply of, facilities to make telephone calls—

(a) regarding medical treatment or care,
(b) to a qualified person,
(c) to a court or tribunal,
(d) to a voluntary sector partner,
(e) to a citizens advice bureau,
(f) to a local authority,
(g) to an immigration officer, or
(h) to the Secretary of State,

to a supported person aged 18 or over.

(2) The Secretary of State may supply, or arrange for the supply of, stationery and postage for correspondence—

(a) regarding medical treatment or care,
(b) to a qualified person,
(c) to a court or tribunal,
(d) to a voluntary sector partner,
(e) to a citizens advice bureau,
(f) to a local authority,
(g) to an immigration officer, or
(h) to the Secretary of State,

to a supported person aged 18 or over.

One-off supply of vouchers for pregnant women and new mothers

6.—(1) During the ante-natal eligible period, on application, the Secretary of State may supply, or arrange for the supply of, vouchers redeemable for goods to the value of £250 in respect of each expected child to a pregnant woman.

(2) In a case where such support has not been provided under paragraph (1), during the post-natal eligible period, on application, the Secretary of State may supply, or arrange for the supply of, vouchers redeemable for goods to the value of £250 in respect of each new born child to a mother.

(3) Paragraphs (1) and (2) shall not apply if a maternity payment has been made in respect of the child in question.

Additional weekly vouchers for pregnant women and children under three

7.—(1) For the duration of the pregnancy, on application, the Secretary of State may supply, or arrange for the supply of, vouchers redeemable for goods or services to the value of £3 per week to a pregnant woman.

(2) Until the first birthday of a child who is a supported person, on application, the Secretary of State may supply, or arrange for the supply of, vouchers redeemable for goods or services to the value of £5 per week to him.

(3) From the day after the first birthday of a child who is a supported person, until the third birthday, on application, the Secretary of State may supply, or arrange for the supply of, vouchers redeemable for goods or services to the value of £3 per week to him.

Additional weekly vouchers for clothing for children

8. Until the sixteenth birthday of a child who is a supported person, on application, the Secretary of State may supply, or arrange for the supply of, vouchers redeemable for clothing to the value of £5 per week to him.

Exceptional specific needs

9.—(1) If the Secretary of State is satisfied that a supported person has an exceptional need for:

(a) facilities for travel,

(b) facilities to make telephone calls,

(c) stationery and postage, or

(d) essential living needs,

she may provide for that need, notwithstanding that the conditions for the supply of those services or facilities referred to respectively in regulations 3, 5, and 6 are not satisfied.

(2) In determining what are or are not to be treated as essential living needs, the Secretary of State shall have regard to regulations made under section 95(7) of the 1999 Act.

The Appeals from the Upper Tribunal to the Court of Appeal Order 2008

(SI 2008, No. 2834)

---

1. This Order may be cited as the Appeals from the Upper Tribunal to the Court of Appeal Order 2008 and shall come into force on 3 November 2008.

2. Permission to appeal to the Court of Appeal in England and Wales or leave to appeal to the Court of Appeal in Northern Ireland shall not be granted unless the Upper Tribunal or, where the Upper Tribunal refuses permission, the relevant appellate court, considers that—

(a) the proposed appeal would raise some important point of principle or practice; or

(b) there is some other compelling reason for the relevant appellate court to hear the appeal.

The Immigration (Biometric Registration) Regulations 2008
(SI 2008, No. 3048)

Citation, commencement and interpretation

1. These Regulations may be cited as the Immigration (Biometric Registration) Regulations 2008 and shall come into force on the day after the day on which they are made.

[**2.** In these Regulations—

['biometric card' means a card which forms part of a biometric immigration document and which is issued to a person who has made an application under regulation 3 or 3A recording the holder's immigration status;]

['biometric information' means photographs or fingerprints provided under regulation 5;]

['biometric sticker' means a sticker which forms part of a biometric immigration document which—

(a) is issued to a person who has made an application under regulation 3 or 3A recording the holder's immigration status; and

(b) consists of a stamp or other attachment in a passport or other document which indicates that the holder has been granted entry clearance or limited or indefinite leave to enter or remain in the United Kingdom;]

'Certificate of Travel' means a travel document issued in the United Kingdom at the discretion of the Secretary of State to persons who have been formally and, in the view of the Secretary of State, unreasonably refused a passport by their own authorities and who have—

(a) been refused recognition as a refugee or as a stateless person but have been granted discretionary leave to remain or humanitarian protection; or

(b) been granted indefinite leave to enter or remain;

'Convention travel document' means a travel document issued pursuant to Article 28 of the Geneva Convention;

'dependant' means a spouse, a civil partner, an unmarried or same sex partner, or a child;

'Geneva Convention' means the Convention relating to the Status of Refugees done at Geneva on 28th July 1951 and the New York Protocol of 31st January 1967;

'humanitarian protection' means protection granted in accordance with paragraph 339C of the immigration rules;

'immigration rules' means the rules for the time being laid down as mentioned in section 3(2) of the Immigration Act 1971;

['leave to enter' means limited or indefinite leave to enter the United Kingdom given in accordance with the provisions of the Immigration Act 1971 or the immigration rules;]

'leave to remain' means limited or indefinite leave to remain in the United Kingdom given in accordance with the provisions of the Immigration Act 1971 or the immigration rules;

['refugee' means a person who falls within Article 1 of the Geneva Convention;]

'Stateless Convention' means the Convention relating to the Status of Stateless Persons done at New York on 28th September 1954; and

'Stateless Person's Travel Document' means a travel document issued pursuant to Article 28 of the Stateless Convention.]

Note: Regulation 2 substituted from 28 February 2012 (SI 2012/594). Definitions of 'biometric information' and 'leave to enter' inserted from 18 March 2015 (SI 2015/433). Definitions of 'biometric card' and 'biometric sticker' inserted from 1 July 2021 (SI 2021/772). Definition of 'refugee' substituted from 28 June 2022 (SI 2022/571).

Requirement to apply for a biometric immigration document

[3.—(1) [A] person subject to immigration control must apply for the issue of a biometric immigration document where he—

(a) satisfies the condition in paragraph (2); or

(b) is a person falling within paragraph (3).

(2) The condition is that whilst in the United Kingdom the person makes an application—

(a) for limited leave [to enter or remain]{. . .};

(b) for indefinite leave [to enter or remain];

(c) to replace a stamp, sticker or other attachment in a passport or other document which indicated that he had been granted limited or indefinite leave to enter or remain in the United Kingdom;

(d) to replace a letter which indicated that he had been granted limited or indefinite leave to enter or remain in the United Kingdom;

(e) to be recognised as a refugee or a person in need of humanitarian protection;

(f) to be recognised as a stateless person in accordance with Article 1 of the Stateless Convention;

(g) for a Convention Travel Document, Stateless Person's Travel Document or a Certificate of Travel and does not already hold a valid biometric immigration document; or

(h) as the dependant of a person who is making an application in accordance with subparagraph (a), (b), (e) or (f).

(3) Subject to paragraph (4), a person falls within this paragraph if he has been notified on or after 1st December 2012 that the Secretary of State has decided to grant him—

(a) limited leave [to enter or remain]for a period which, together with any preceding period of leave to enter or remain, exceeds a cumulative total of 6 months leave in the United Kingdom; or

(b) indefinite leave [to enter or remain].

(4) A person does not fall within paragraph (3) if—

(a) he was required to apply for a biometric immigration document in respect of his application for that leave; or

(b) he was required to apply for a biometric immigration document in respect of any application mentioned in paragraph (2).

(5) Where a person is required to apply for a biometric immigration document, that application must be made on the form or in the manner specified for that purpose (if one is specified) in the immigration rules.

[(5A) This regulation does not apply to a person who makes an application for, or has been granted, leave to enter or remain under residence scheme immigration rules.

(5B) 'Residence scheme immigration rules' has the meaning given by section 17 of the European Union (Withdrawal Agreement) Act 2020.]

(6) [. . .]]

Note: Regulation 3 substituted from 28 February 2012 (SI 2012/594). Words in square brackets substituted in paragraphs (1), (2)(a), 2(b), (3) (a) and (3)(b) and words in curly brackets in paragraph (2)(a) and paragraph 6 omitted from 18 March 2015 (SI 2015/433). Paragraphs (5A) and (5B) inserted from 23.00 on 31 December 2020 (SI 2020/1309).

[3A.—(1) A person who is subject to immigration control and satisfies the conditions in paragraph (2) must apply for the issue of a biometric immigration document.

(2) The conditions are—

(a) that the person makes an application—

(i) for entry clearance, which, by virtue of provision made under section 3A(3) of the Immigration Act 1971, has effect as leave to enter the United Kingdom for a limited period which exceeds 6 months; or

(ii) for entry clearance, which, by virtue of provision made under section 3A(3) of the Immigration Act 1971, has effect as indefinite leave to enter the United Kingdom; or

(iii) as the dependant of a person who is making an application in accordance with paragraph (i) or (ii); and

(b) the person specifies in that application that they will enrol their biometric information [outside the United Kingdom].

(3) Where a person is required to apply for a biometric immigration document, that application must be made on the form or in the manner specified for that purpose (if one is specified) in the immigration rules.]

Note: Regulation 3A inserted from 18 March 2015 (SI 2015/433) and words in square brackets in paragraph (2)(b) substituted from 31 July 2015 (SI 2015/897).

[Specified categories

4 . . .]

Note: Regulation 4 omitted from 28 February 2012 (SI 2012/594).

Power for an authorised person to require a person to provide biometric information

5.—(1) Subject to regulation 7, where a person makes an application for the issue of a biometric immigration document in accordance with regulation 3 [or regulation 3A], an authorised person may require him to provide a record of his fingerprints and a photograph of his face.

(2) Where an authorised person requires a person to provide biometric information in accordance with paragraph (1), the person must provide it.

Note: Words in square brackets in paragraph (1) inserted from 18 March 2015 (SI 2015/433).

Power for the Secretary of State to use and retain existing biometric information

6.—(1) This regulation applies where—

(a) a person makes an application for the issue of a biometric immigration document in accordance with regulation 3 [, or regulation 3A]; and

(b) the Secretary of State already has a record of the person's fingerprints or a photograph of the person's face in his possession (for whatever reason).

(2) Where this regulation applies the Secretary of State may use or retain that information for the purposes of these Regulations.

Note: Words in square brackets in paragraph (1)(a) inserted from 18 March 2015 (SI 2015/433).

Provision in relation to persons under the age of sixteen

7.—(1) A person under the age of sixteen ('the child') must not be required to provide a record of his fingerprints or a photograph of his face in accordance with regulation 5 except where the authorised person is satisfied that the fingerprints or the photograph will be taken in the presence of a person aged eighteen or over who is—

(a) the child's parent or guardian; or

(b) a person who for the time being takes responsibility for the child.

(2) The person mentioned in paragraph (1)(b) may not be—

(a) an officer of the Secretary of State who is not an authorised person;

(b) an authorised person; or

(c) any other person acting on behalf of an authorised person under [regulation 8(1)(a) or (c)].

(3) This regulation does not apply if the authorised person reasonably believes that the person who is to be fingerprinted or photographed is aged sixteen or over.

Note: Words in square brackets in paragraph (2)(c) substituted from 18 March 2015 (SI 2015/433).

[Process by which an individual's fingerprints and photograph may be obtained and recorded

8.—(1) An authorised person who requires an individual to provide a record of the individual's fingerprints or a photograph of the individual's face under regulation 5 may do any one or more of the following—

(a) require the individual to make an appointment before a specified date, which the individual must attend, to enable a record of the individual's fingerprints or a photograph of the individual's face to be taken by an authorised person or by a person acting on behalf of an authorised person;

(b) specify the date, time and place for the appointment;

(c) require the individual to attend premises before a specified date to enable a record of the individual's fingerprints or a photograph of the individual's face to be taken by an authorised person or by a person acting on behalf of an authorised person; and

(d) specify any documents which the individual must bring to the appointment or premises, or action which the individual must take to confirm the individual's identity.

(2) An authorised person may require a record of fingerprints or photograph to be of a particular specification.

(3) Where an authorised person requires an individual to submit to any requirement in accordance with paragraph (1), the individual must submit to it.]

Note: Regulation 8 substituted from 18 March 2015 (SI 2015/433).

[Use and retention of biometric information

9.—(1) Biometric information provided in accordance with these Regulations may be retained only if the Secretary of State thinks that it is necessary to retain it for use in connection with—

(a) the exercise of a function by virtue of the Immigration Acts; or

(b) the exercise of a function in relation to nationality.

(2) Biometric information retained by virtue of paragraph (1) may also be used—

(a) in connection with the prevention, investigation or prosecution of an offence;

(b) for a purpose which appears to the Secretary of State to be required in order to protect national security;

(c) in connection with identifying persons who have died, or are suffering from illness or injury;[and]

(d) for the purpose of ascertaining whether a person has acted unlawfully, or has obtained or sought anything to which the person is not legally entitled; and

[(e) . . .]]

Note: Regulation 9 substituted from 18 March 2015 (SI 2015/433). Word inserted at end of paragraph (2) (c) and paragraph (2)(e) omitted from 31 December 2020 (SI 2020/1309) subject to saving provision specified in reg 34(5) of SI 2020/1309.

[Destruction of biometric information

10.—(1) The Secretary of State must take all reasonable steps to ensure that biometric information held by the Secretary of State by virtue of these Regulations, including any copies, is destroyed if the Secretary of State—

(a) no longer thinks that it is necessary to retain the information for use as mentioned in regulation 9(1); or

(b) subject to the exception in paragraph (2), is satisfied that the person to whom the information relates is a British citizen, or a Commonwealth citizen who has a right of abode in the United Kingdom as a result of section 2(1)(b) of the Immigration Act 1971.

(2) The exception is that photographs of a person who is registered or naturalised as a British citizen may be retained until the person is issued with a United Kingdom passport describing the person as a British citizen.]

Note: Regulation10 substituted from 18 March 2015 (SI 2015/433).

[Retention of fingerprints

11.—(1) Save where regulation 10 applies and subject to paragraphs (2) and (3), the Secretary of State must take all reasonable steps to ensure that any record of a person's fingerprints held by the Secretary of State by virtue of these Regulations, including any copies, is destroyed at the end of the period of [15] years beginning with [—

(a) the date on which the fingerprints were provided; or

(b) the date on which they are reused in connection with a relevant application made by the person,

whichever is the later.]

(2) But fingerprints can be held beyond that period if they are—

(a) the fingerprints of a person who is, or at any time has been, subject to a deportation order, exclusion order or decision to exclude;

(b) the fingerprints of a person who can be, or at any time could have been, refused entry clearance or leave to enter for a period specified in the immigration rules because of a previous breach of the United Kingdom's immigration laws;

(c) fingerprints that the Secretary of State deems it necessary for national security reasons to retain for use in connection with one of the functions specified in regulation 9(1);

(d) the fingerprints of a person with indefinite leave to enter or remain in the United Kingdom;[or]

(e) the fingerprints of a person whose indefinite leave to enter or remain in the United Kingdom lapses, is revoked or is cancelled, in which case they must be destroyed by the Secretary of State at the end of ten years beginning with the date of the lapse, revocation or cancellation (as the case may be);

[(f) . . .]

(3) The Secretary of State is only required to take steps to destroy, pursuant to paragraph (2)(e) [. . .], the fingerprints of a person whose leave has lapsed [. . .] on the application, supported by evidence to the satisfaction of the Secretary of State, of that person.

[(4) . . .]]

[(5) A relevant application for the purposes of paragraph (1) is an application for—

(a) entry clearance;

(b) leave to enter;

(c) leave to remain; or

(d) registration or naturalisation as a British citizen.]

Note: Regulation 11 substituted from 18 March 2015 (SI 2015/433). Word inserted at end of paragraph (2) (d), paragraph (2)(f), words in paragraph (3) and paragraph (4) omitted from 31 December 2020 (SI 2020/1309) subject to saving provision specified in reg 34(6) of SI 2020/1309. Words in square brackets in paragraph (1) substituted and paragraph 5 inserted from 1 July 2021 (SI 2021/772).

[Destruction etc. of electronic data

12.—(1) The Secretary of State must take all reasonable steps to ensure—

(a) that data held in electronic form which relates to biometric information which has to be destroyed by virtue of these Regulations is destroyed or erased; or

(b) that access to such data is blocked.

(2) A person whose biometric information has to be destroyed by virtue of these Regulations is entitled, on written request, to a certificate issued by the Secretary of State to the effect that the Secretary of State has taken the steps required by paragraph (1).

(3) A certificate issued under paragraph (2) must be issued within the period of 3 months beginning with the date on which the request for it is received by the Secretary of State.]

Note: Regulation 12 substituted from 18 March 2015 (SI 2015/433).

[Biometric information: retention under another power

12A. The requirements in these Regulations to destroy biometric information or data do not apply if and in so far as the information or data is retained in accordance with and for the purposes of another power].

Note: Regulation 12A inserted from 18 March 2015 (SI 2015/433).

Issue of a biometric immigration document

13.—(1) The Secretary of State may issue a biometric immigration document [...] to a person who has applied in accordance with regulation 3, provided the Secretary of State has decided to—

[(a) grant limited leave {to enter or remain} to the person for a period which, together with any preceding period of leave to enter or remain, exceeds a cumulative total of 6 months leave in the United Kingdom; or

(b) grant indefinite leave {to enter or remain} to the person; or

(c) issue or replace a document to the person following an application mentioned in regulation 3(2)(c), (d) or (g) [where the document indicated that the person has leave to enter or remain in the United Kingdom for a total period in excess of 6 months or for an indefinite period].]

[(**1A**) The reference to the issue of a biometric immigration document in paragraph (1) includes allowing the person to view their biometric immigration document electronically.]

(2) A biometric immigration document [issued under this regulation] begins to have effect on the date of issue.

(3) A biometric immigration document [issued under this regulation] ceases to have effect on one of the dates specified in paragraph (4), whichever date occurs earliest.

(4) The specified dates are—

(a) the date that the person's leave to remain ceases to have effect, including where the leave to remain is varied, cancelled or invalidated, or is to lapse;

(b) in the case of a biometric { card or biometric sticker} which was issued to a person aged [sixteen] or over, the date after the expiry of ten years beginning with the date of issue;[. . .]

(c) in the case of a biometric {card or biometric sticker} which was issued to a person aged under [sixteen], the date after the expiry of five years beginning with the date of issue [or

(d) the expiry date printed on the {biometric card or biometric sticker where issued to the person}.]

[(5) Where the person is issued with a biometric card or biometric sticker, the information contained on that card or sticker is to be read subject to the information on the person's biometric immigration document.]

Note: Subparagraphs (1)(a)–(c) substituted/inserted from 28 February 2012 (SI 2012/594). Words in square brackets in paragraph (4) substituted from 31 March 2009, but without effect to biometric immigration documents issued before that date (SI 2009/819). Words in curly brackets in subparagraphs (1) (a) and (b) substituted from 18 March 2015 (SI 2015/433). Words in square brackets in paragraphs (2) and (3) inserted from 18 March 2015 (SI 2015/433). Subparagraph (4)(d) inserted from 18 March 2015 (SI 2015/433). Words in paragraph (1) omitted, paragraph (1A) inserted, words in curly brackets in paragraphs (4)(b), (c) and (d) substituted and paragraph (5) inserted from 1 July 2021 (SI 2021/772).

[**13A.**—(1) The Secretary of State may issue a biometric immigration document, [. . .] to a person who has applied in accordance with regulation 3A and has been granted—

(a) entry clearance, which, by virtue of provision made under section 3A(3) of the Immigration Act 1971, has effect as leave to enter the United Kingdom for a limited period which exceeds 6 months; or

(b) entry clearance, which, by virtue of provision made under section 3A(3) of the Immigration Act 1971, has effect as indefinite leave to enter the United Kingdom.

[(**1A**) The reference to the issue of a biometric immigration document in paragraph (1) includes allowing the person to view their biometric immigration document electronically.]

(2) Where an entry clearance is granted under paragraph (1) and the entry clearance officer issues a short term biometric entry clearance, the entry clearance officer must issue a written decision informing the applicant of the period of leave that their biometric immigration document will evidence and the process by which the applicant must obtain that document.

(3) A successful applicant who travels to the United Kingdom must obtain their biometric immigration document within a period, and by a process, specified in the applicant's written decision (issued under paragraph (2)).

(4) A biometric immigration document issued under this regulation begins to have effect on the date of issue.

(5) A biometric immigration document issued under this regulation ceases to have effect on one of the dates specified in paragraph (6), whichever date occurs earliest.

(6) The specified dates are—

(a) the date that the person's leave to enter or remain ceases to have effect, including where the leave is varied, cancelled or invalidated, or is to lapse;

(b) in the case of a biometric [card or biometric sticker] which was issued to a person aged sixteen or over, the date after the expiry of ten years beginning with the date of issue;

(c) in the case of a biometric [card or biometric sticker] which was issued to a person aged under sixteen, the date after the expiry of five years beginning with the date of issue; or

(d) the expiry date printed on the [biometric card or biometric sticker where issued to the person].

[(6A) Where the person is issued with a biometric card or biometric sticker, the information contained on that card or sticker is to be read subject to the information on the person's biometric immigration document.]

(7) In this regulation—

(a) 'entry clearance officer' means a person responsible for the grant or refusal of entry clearance; and

(b) 'short term biometric entry clearance' means an entry clearance document which—

(i) is issued to a person who has made a successful application for a biometric immigration document from outside the United Kingdom, in order that the person may travel to the United Kingdom to obtain that biometric immigration document; and

(ii) has a period of validity ending before the expiry of the period of leave that the holder's biometric immigration document will evidence.]

Note: Regulation 13A inserted from 18 March 2015 (SI 2015/433). Words in paragraph (1) omitted, paragraph (1A) inserted, words in paragraphs (6)(b), (c) and (d) substituted and paragraph (6A) inserted from 1 July 2021 (SI 2021/772).

[Issue of a short term biometric immigration document

13B. . . .]

Note: Regulation 13B inserted from 18 March 2015 (SI 2015/433) and omitted from 1 July 2021 (SI 2021/772).

Requirement to surrender documents connected with immigration and nationality

14.—(1) On issuing the biometric immigration document, the Secretary of State may require the surrender of other documents connected with immigration or nationality.

(2) Where the Secretary of State requires the surrender of other documents, the person must comply with the requirement.

Content of a biometric immigration document

15.—(1) A biometric immigration document may contain some or all of the following information [. . .]—

(a) the title of the document;

(b) the document number;

(c) the name of the holder;

(d) the holder's date of birth;

(e) the holder's place of birth;

(f) the holder's nationality;

(g) the sex of the holder;

[(h) the period for which the holder has leave to enter or remain;

(i) the class of leave to enter or remain which the holder has;]

(j) any conditions to which the limited leave to [enter or] remain is subject or remarks relating to those conditions;

[(ja) other information connected with the holder's immigration status or nationality;]

(k) the place and date of issue of the document;

(l) the period for which the document is valid;

(m) the holder's facial image;

(n) the signature of the holder;

(o) a machine readable code;

(p) a hologram;

(q) an emblem of the United Kingdom and the words 'United Kingdom';

(r) the symbol of the International Civil Aviation Organization denoting a machine readable travel document which contains a contactless microchip; and

(s) any additional security features;

[(t) the holder's national insurance number; and

(u) the holder's chargeable status for NHS treatment.]

(2) A biometric immigration document may contain some or all of the following within a radio frequency electronic microchip embedded in the document—

(a) any of the information specified in paragraph (1)(a) to (m);

(b) information relating to a record of any two of the holder's fingerprints; and

(c) any additional security features.

Note: Subparagraphs (1)(h)–(i) substituted, (1)(t)–(u) inserted and words in square brackets in subparagraph (1)(j) inserted from 18 March 2015 (SI 2015/433). Words in paragraph (1) omitted and paragraph (1)(ja) inserted from 1 July 2021 (SI 2021/772).

Surrender of a biometric [card]

16.—(1) The Secretary of State may require the surrender of a biometric [card] as soon as reasonably practicable if he thinks that—

(a) information provided in connection with the [[card]] was or has become false, misleading or incomplete;

(b) the [[card]] (including any information recorded in it) has been altered, damaged or destroyed (whether deliberately or not);

(c) an attempt has been made (whether successfully or not) to copy the [[card]] or to do anything to enable it to be copied;

(d) the [[card]] should be re-issued (whether because the information recorded in it requires alteration or for any other reason);

(e) the holder's leave to [enter or] remain is to be varied, cancelled or invalidated, or is to lapse;

(f) a person has acquired the biometric [card] without the consent of the holder or of the Secretary of State;

(g) the [[card]] has ceased to have effect under regulation 13(3){ or 13A(5)} or has been cancelled under regulation 17;

(h) the holder has died;

[(i) the holder has failed to produce a valid passport or travel document when required to do so by an immigration officer; or

(j) the holder has proved that he is a British citizen or a Commonwealth citizen who has a right of abode in the United Kingdom as a result of section 2(1)(b) of the Immigration Act 1971 (statement of right of abode in the United Kingdom).]

(2) Where a person is required to surrender the biometric [card] under paragraph (1), the person must comply with the requirement.

Note: Subparagraphs (1)(i)–(j) inserted from 31 March 2009 (SI 2009/819). Words in square brackets in subparagraphs (1)(e) and (g) inserted from 18 March 2015 (SI 2015/433). Words in square brackets in heading, opening words of paragraph (1), (1)(f) and (2) substituted, word in double square brackets in paragraphs (1)(a) to (d) and (g) substituted and words in curly brackets in paragraph (1)(g) substituted from 1 July 2021 (SI 2021/772).

[Cancelling access to a biometric immigration document

16A. The Secretary of State may cancel access to a person's biometric immigration document electronically if the Secretary of State thinks that—

(a) the holder's leave to enter or remain has been varied, cancelled or invalidated, or has lapsed; or

(b) another person has gained access to the biometric immigration document without the consent of the holder or of the Secretary of State.]

Note: Regulation 16A inserted from 1 July 2021 (SI 2021/772).

Cancellation of a biometric immigration document

17. The Secretary of State may cancel a biometric immigration document if he thinks that—

(a) information provided in connection with the document was or has become false, misleading or incomplete;

(b) the document has been lost or stolen;

(c) the document (including any information recorded in it) has been altered, damaged or destroyed (whether deliberately or not);

(d) an attempt has been made (whether successfully or not) to copy the document or to do anything to enable it to be copied;

(e) a person has failed to surrender the document when required to do so under regulation [16(a) to (f), (h), (i) or (j);]

(f) the document should be re-issued (whether because the information recorded in it requires alteration or for any other reason);

(g) a person has acquired the biometric immigration document without the consent of the holder or of the Secretary of State; [. . .]

(h) the holder has died [; [. . .]

(i) the holder has proved that he is a British citizen or a Commonwealth citizen who has a right of abode in the United Kingdom as a result of section 2(1)(b) of the Immigration Act 1971 (statement of right of abode in the United Kingdom)] [; or

(j) a person has failed to collect the document within the period or by the process specified in the written decision issued under regulation 13A(2).]

Note: Words in square brackets in paragraph (e) substituted and paragraph (i) inserted from 31 March 2009 (SI 2009/819). Paragraph (j) inserted from 18 March 2015 (SI 2015/433).

Requirement for the holder of a document to notify the Secretary of State

18. The holder of a biometric immigration document must notify the Secretary of State as soon as reasonably practicable if he—

(a) knows or suspects that information provided in connection with the document was or has become false, misleading or incomplete;

(b) knows or suspects that the document has been lost or stolen;

(c) knows or suspects that the document (including any information recorded in it) has been altered or damaged (whether deliberately or not);

(d) was given leave to enter or remain in the United Kingdom in accordance with a provision of the immigration rules and knows or suspects that owing to a change of his circumstances he would no longer qualify for leave under that provision; or

(e) knows or suspects that another person has acquired the biometric immigration document without his consent or the consent of the Secretary of State.

Requirement to apply for a replacement biometric immigration document

19.—(1) A person who has been issued with a biometric immigration document under regulation 13(1){, or 13A(1) } is required to apply for a replacement biometric immigration document where his original document—

(a) has been cancelled under [paragraphs (a) to (g) of] regulation 17; or

(b) has ceased to have effect under [regulation 13(4)(b), (c) or (d), regulation 13A(6)(b), (c) or (d), or regulation 13B(4)(b)].

(2) A person required to apply for a biometric immigration document under paragraph (1) must do so within 3 months beginning with the date that the original document was cancelled or ceased to have effect.

Note: Words in square brackets in paragraph (1)(a) inserted from 31 March 2009 (SI 2009/819). Words in curly brackets in paragraph (1) inserted from 18 March 2015 (SI 2015/433) and substituted from 1 July 2021 (SI 2021/772). Words in square brackets in paragraph (1)(b) substituted from 18 March 2015 (SI 2015/433).

[Application of these Regulations to a person who is required to apply for a replacement biometric immigration document

20. . . .]

Note: Regulation 20 omitted from 31 July 2015 (SI 2015/897).

Requirement to use a biometric immigration document

21.—(1) The holder of a biometric immigration document must provide his document to an immigration officer or the Secretary of State, as applicable—

(a) where he is examined by an immigration officer under paragraph 2, 2A or 3 of Schedule 2 to the Immigration Act 1971;

(b) where he is examined by an immigration officer under Article 7(2) of the Immigration (Leave to Enter and Remain) Order 2000;

(c) where he is examined by the Secretary of State under Article 3 of the Immigration (Leave to Enter) Order 2001;

[(d) where he makes an application for entry clearance, leave to enter or leave to remain;

(da) where he makes an application to be recognised as a refugee, as a person in need of humanitarian protection, or as a stateless person in accordance with Article 1 of the Stateless Convention;

(db) where he applies as a dependant of a person who makes an application mentioned in sub-paragraph (d) or (da);

(dc) where he makes an application for a Convention Travel Document, Stateless Person's Travel Document or a Certificate of Travel;

(e) when his dependant makes an application—

(i) for entry clearance, leave to enter, leave to remain; or

(ii) to be recognised as a refugee, as a person in need of humanitarian protection, or as a stateless person in accordance with Article 1 of the Stateless Convention;]

(f) when he is the sponsor under the immigration rules of a person who seeks entry clearance, leave to enter or leave to remain in the United Kingdom.

[(2) Where the holder of a biometric immigration document attends premises to take—

(a) a test known under the immigration rules as the 'Life in the UK Test'; or

(b) for purposes of leave to enter or remain, an English language test with a provider approved by the Secretary of State as specified in the immigration rules,

the holder must provide this document to the representative of the educational institution, or other person, who is administering the test where this is specified as a requirement.]

(3) [. . .]

[(4) Where the holder of a biometric immigration document makes—

(a) an application for a certificate of entitlement under section 10 of the Nationality, Immigration and Asylum Act 2002 that a person has the right of abode in the United Kingdom;

(b) an application for a letter or other document confirming a person's immigration or nationality status or that a person is not a British citizen;

(c) an application for naturalisation as a British citizen under section 6(1) or (2) of the British Nationality Act 1981, or as a British overseas territories citizen under section 18(1) or (2) of that Act; or

(d) an application for registration under any provision of the British Nationality Act 1981, he must provide his biometric immigration document to the Secretary of State or a person acting on behalf of the Secretary of State in connection with that application.]

[(5) Where the holder of a biometric immigration document makes an application for a licence to drive a motor vehicle (granted under Part III of the Road Traffic Act 1988), the holder must use their biometric immigration document in connection with that application as required by the specified application process.]

[(5A) The references in paragraphs (1), (2) and (4) to the provision of a biometric immigration document include provision of evidence of the holder's immigration status held electronically on their biometric immigration document.]

[(6) Where the holder of a biometric immigration document is required to use the document in connection with any application or claim under this regulation, any such application or claim may be disregarded or refused if the requirement is not complied with.]

Note: Subparagraphs (1)(d)–(e) substituted/inserted and paragraph (4) inserted from 28 February 2012 (SI 2012/594). Paragraph (2) substituted and paragraphs (5) and (6) inserted from 18 March 2015 (SI 2015/433). Paragraph (3) omitted and paragraph (5A) inserted from 1 July 2021 (SI 2021/772).

Requirement to provide information for comparison

22.—(1) A person who provides a biometric immigration document in accordance with [regulation 21] is required to provide biometric information for comparison with biometric information provided in connection with the application for the document.

(2) Where the document is provided to an authorised person, the authorised person may require the provision of the information in a specified form.

(3) Regulation 8 applies to a person required to provide information under paragraph (1) as it applies to a person who is required to provide biometric information under regulation 5.

Note: Words substituted in paragraph (1) from 28 February 2012 (SI 2012/594).

[Requirement to provide a new photograph

22A.—(1) This regulation applies where the holder of a biometric immigration document, other than in a case to which regulation 16A applies, satisfies an authorised person that they are unable to access their biometric immigration document electronically.

(2) An authorised person may require the holder of the biometric immigration document to provide an additional photograph of the holder's face to that provided on the application for the document.]

Note: Regulation 22A inserted from 1 July 2021 (SI 2021/772).

Consequences of a failure to comply with a requirement of these Regulations

[**23.**—(1) Subject to paragraphs (3) and (4), where a person who is required to make an application for the issue of a biometric immigration document fails to comply with a requirement of these Regulations, the Secretary of State—

(a) may take any, or any combination, of the actions specified in paragraph (2); and

(b) [may] consider giving a notice under section 9 of the UK Borders Act 2007.

(2) The actions specified are to—

(a) refuse an application for a biometric immigration document;

(b) treat the person's [application for leave to enter or remain or for entry clearance] as invalid;

(c) refuse the person's [application for leave to enter or remain or for entry clearance]; and

(d) cancel or vary the person's leave to enter or remain.

(3) Where a person is required to apply for a biometric immigration document under regulation 3(2)(a) or (b) {or regulation 3A(2)(a) or (b)} or as a dependant of {such} a person [. . .]and fails to comply with a requirement of these Regulations, the Secretary of State—

(a) must refuse the person's application for a biometric immigration document;

(b) must treat the person's [application for leave to enter or remain or for entry clearance] as invalid; and

(c) may cancel or vary the person's leave to enter or remain.

(4) Where a person is required to apply for a biometric immigration document under regulation 3(2)(e), (f) or (g) or as the dependant of a person who has made an application in accordance with regulation 3(2)(e) or (f) and fails to comply with a requirement of these Regulations the Secretary of State—

(a) may refuse the application for a biometric immigration document; and

(b) [may] consider giving a notice under section 9 of the UK Borders Act 2007.

(5) Where any person apart from a person referred to in paragraph (1), (3) or (4) fails to comply with a requirement of these Regulations, the Secretary of State must consider giving a notice under section 9 of the UK Borders Act 2007.

(6) The Secretary of State may designate an adult as the person responsible for ensuring that a child complies with the requirements of these Regulations.]

Note: Regulation 23 substituted from 28 February 2012 (SI 2012/594). Words in square brackets in subparagraphs (2)(b), (2)(c) and (3)(b) substituted from 18 March 2015 (SI 2015/433). In paragraph (3) words in curly brackets inserted and words omitted from 18 March 2015 (SI 2015/433). Word in square bracket in paragraphs (1)(b) and (4)(b) substituted from 1 July 2021 (SI 2021/772).

Revocation and transitional provisions

24.—(1) Subject to paragraph (2), the Immigration (Biometric Registration) (Pilot) Regulations 2008 are revoked.

(2) The Immigration (Biometric Registration) (Pilot) Regulations 2008 continue to apply to a person who was required to apply for a biometric immigration document in accordance with regulation 3 of those Regulations before the coming into force of these Regulations, subject to paragraph (3).

(3) These Regulations apply to any application for leave to remain falling within regulation 3 of these Regulations, which is made by a person referred to in paragraph (2) on or after the coming into force of these Regulations.

SCHEDULE

. . .

Note: Schedule omitted from 31 July 2015 (SI 2015/897).

The Appeals (Excluded Decisions) Order 2009

(SI 2009, No. 275)

Citation and commencement

1. This Order may be cited as the Appeals (Excluded Decisions) Order 2009 and comes into force on 1 April 2009.

[Excluded decisions

2. For the purposes of section 11(1) of the Tribunals, Courts and Enforcement Act 2007, the following decisions of the First-tier Tribunal are excluded decisions—

(a) a decision under section 103 of the Immigration and Asylum Act 1999 (appeals); and

[(b) a decision under paragraphs 1, 5, 6, and 10(12) and (13) of Schedule 10 to the Immigration Act 2016.]]

Note: Article 2 substituted from 15 February 2010 (SI 2010/41) and paragraph 2(b) substituted from 15 January 2018 (SI 2017/1242).

3. For the purposes of sections 11(1) and 13(1) of the Tribunals, Courts and Enforcement Act 2007, the following decisions of the First-tier Tribunal or the Upper Tribunal are excluded decisions—

(a) . . .

(b) . . .

(c) . . .

(d) . . .

(e) . . .

(f) . . .

(g) . . .

(h) . . .

(i) . . .

(j) . . .

(k) . . .

(l) . . .

[(m) any procedural, ancillary or preliminary decision made in relation to an appeal against a decision under section 40A of the British Nationality Act 1981[or] section 82[, . . .] of the Nationality, Immigration and Asylum Act 2002 [. . .].]

Note: Paragraphs (a)–(l) not relevant to immigration law. Paragraph (m) inserted from 15 February 2010 (SI 2010/41) and words '83 or 83A' omitted from 6 April 2015 (SI 2015/383) subject to saving provision (article 5 of SI 2015/383). Word inserted and words omitted from paragraph (m) from 23.00 on 31 December 2020 (SI 2020/1309) subject to saving provision (reg 35(3) - (4) of SI 2020/1309).

Revocations

4. . . .

The Transfer of Functions of the Asylum and Immigration Tribunal Order 2010

(SI 2010, No. 21)

Citation and commencement

1. This Order may be cited as the Transfer of Functions of the Asylum and Immigration Tribunal Order 2010 and comes into force on 15th February 2010.

Transfer of functions and abolition of tribunal

2.—(1) The functions of the Asylum and Immigration Tribunal are transferred to the First-tier Tribunal.

(2) The Asylum and Immigration Tribunal is abolished.

Transfer of persons into the First-tier Tribunal and the Upper Tribunal

3. . . .

Transfer of Rules

4. The Asylum and Immigration Tribunal (Procedure) Rules 2005 and the Asylum and Immigration Tribunal (Procedure) (Fast-track) Rules 2005 have effect as if they were Tribunal Procedure Rules.

Consequential and transitional provisions

. . .

Schedule 4

Transitional and saving provisions

Appeals and applications for bail

1. An appeal under section 40A of the British Nationality Act 1981, section 82, 83 or 83A of the 2002 Act or regulation 26 of the Immigration (European Economic Area) Regulations 2006, or an application for bail under Schedule 2 to the Immigration Act 1971, made to the Asylum and Immigration Tribunal before 15 February 2010 but not determined before that date shall continue as an appeal or application before the First-tier Tribunal.

Section 103A applications

2. An application for review made to the Asylum and Immigration Tribunal under section 103A of the 2002 Act and Schedule 2 to the 2004 Act before 15 February 2010 but not determined before that date shall continue as an application to the First-tier Tribunal for permission to appeal to the Upper Tribunal under section 11 of the 2007 Act.

3. Where the Asylum and Immigration Tribunal or the appropriate court has made an order for reconsideration under section 103A of the 2002 Act before 15 February 2010, but reconsideration has not taken place before that date, the order for reconsideration shall be treated as an order granting permission to appeal to the Upper Tribunal under section 11 of the 2007 Act and sections 12 and 13 of the 2007 Act shall apply.

4. Where the reconsideration of an appeal by the Asylum and Immigration Tribunal under section 103A of the 2002 Act has commenced before 15 February 2010 but has not been determined, the reconsideration shall continue as an appeal to the Upper Tribunal under section 12 of the 2007 Act and section 13 of the 2007 Act shall apply.

5. An application for review made to the appropriate court under section 103A of the 2002 Act before 15 February 2010 but not determined before that date shall continue as an application for review under section 103A of the 2002 Act.

6. An order for reconsideration made by the appropriate court on or after 15 February 2010 which, if it had been made before that date would have been for reconsideration by the Asylum and Immigration Tribunal, shall be treated as an order granting permission to appeal to the Upper Tribunal under section 11 of the 2007 Act and sections 12 and 13 of the 2007 Act shall apply.

Section 103C references

7. A reference made by the appropriate court to the appropriate appellate court under section 103C of the 2002 Act before 15 February 2010 shall continue to be considered as a reference under section 103C of the 2002 Act.

8. A case remitted or restored by the appropriate appellate court on or after 15 February 2010 which, if it had been remitted or restored before that date would have been remitted to the Asylum and Immigration Tribunal or restored to the appropriate court, shall be remitted to the Upper Tribunal and sections 12 and 13 of the 2007 Act shall apply.

Section 103B and 103E applications

9. An application for permission to appeal to the appropriate appellate court made to the Asylum and Immigration Tribunal under section 103B or 103E of the 2002 Act before 15 February 2010 but not determined before that date shall continue as an application to the Upper Tribunal for permission to appeal to the relevant appellate court under section 13 of the 2007 Act.

10. An application for permission to appeal to the appropriate appellate court made to that court under section 103B or 103E of the 2002 Act before 15 February 2010 but not determined before that date shall continue as an application for permission to appeal to the appropriate appellate court under section 103B or 103E of the 2002 Act.

11. An appeal which is proceeding before the appropriate appellate court under section 103B or 103E of the 2002 Act before 15 February 2010 but which is not determined before

that date shall continue as an appeal to the appropriate appellate court under section 103B or 103E of the 2002 Act.

12. A case remitted by the appropriate appellate court on or after 15 February 2010 which, if it had been remitted before that date would have been remitted to the Asylum and Immigration Tribunal, shall be remitted to the Upper Tribunal and sections 12 and 13 of the 2007 Act shall apply.

Time limits

13.—(1) Where the time period for making an appeal or application has begun but not expired before 15 February 2010, in the case of—

(a) an appeal to the Asylum and Immigration Tribunal under section 40A of the British Nationality Act 1981, section 82, 83 or 83A of the 2002 Act or regulation 26 of the Immigration (European Economic Area) Regulations 2006, an appeal may be made within that period to the First-tier Tribunal;

(b) an application to the Asylum and Immigration Tribunal for review under section 103A of the 2002 Act and Schedule 2 to the 2004 Act, an application for permission to appeal to the Upper Tribunal under section 11 of the 2007 Act may be made within that period to the First-tier Tribunal;

(c) an application to the appropriate court for review under section 103A of the 2002 Act, an application may be made within that period under section 103A of the 2002 Act to the appropriate court;

(d) an application to the Asylum and Immigration Tribunal for permission to appeal to the appropriate appellate court under section 103B or 103E of the 2002 Act, an application for permission to appeal to the relevant appellate court under section 13 of the 2007 Act may be made within that period to the Upper Tribunal; and

(e) an application to the appropriate appellate court for permission to appeal to that court under section 103B or 103E of the 2002 Act, an application for permission to appeal to the relevant appellate court under section 13 of the 2007 Act may be made within that period to that court.

(2) Where an appeal or application mentioned in sub-paragraphs (1)(a) to (e) is made after the time period in question has expired, it must be made and decided in accordance with the relevant procedural rules or other enactments, as they apply on and after the transfer date.

(3) Where an appeal or application has been determined by the Asylum and Immigration Tribunal before the transfer date but the determination has not been served on the parties before that date, the determination shall be treated as if it were a determination of the First-tier Tribunal or (if it follows reconsideration) a determination of the Upper Tribunal, as the case may be, and the determination may be served accordingly.

(4) Sub-paragraph (3) applies, subject to any necessary modifications, to any other decision of the Asylum and Immigration Tribunal that has been made but not served before the transfer date.

General

14.—(1) This paragraph applies where proceedings are commenced or continued in the First-tier Tribunal or the Upper Tribunal by virtue of the provisions of this Schedule.

(2) The First-tier Tribunal or Upper Tribunal, as the case may be, may give any direction to ensure that the proceedings are dealt with fairly and, in particular, may apply any provision in procedural rules which applied to the proceedings before 15 February 2010.

(3) In sub-paragraph (2) 'procedural rules' includes any provision (whether called rules or not) regulating practice or procedure before the Asylum and Immigration Tribunal.

(4) Any direction or order given or made in the proceedings which is in force immediately before 15 February 2010 remains in force on and after that date as if it were a direction or order of the First-tier Tribunal or Upper Tribunal, as the case may be, and may be varied accordingly.

(5) A time period which has started to run before 15 February 2010 and which has not expired shall continue to apply.

15. Any procedural, ancillary or preliminary matter before the Asylum and Immigration Tribunal before 15 February 2010 may, on or after that date, be considered by the First-tier Tribunal or the Upper Tribunal, as the case may be, as appropriate.

16.—(1) This paragraph applies when—

(a) the Asylum and Immigration Tribunal has started to reconsider or has reconsidered an appeal before 15 February 2010, but has not produced a determination before that date; and

(b) the reconsideration of the appeal continues as an appeal to the Upper Tribunal by virtue of paragraph 4.

(2) A member of the Asylum and Immigration Tribunal who was hearing or otherwise considering the appeal may take all such steps as the member considers necessary to determine the appeal and produce a determination on or after 15 February 2010.

17. In any judicial review proceedings before the High Court, the Court of Session or the High Court of Northern Ireland before 15 February 2010 where a matter could be remitted to the Asylum and Immigration Tribunal, on or after that date the matter may be remitted to the First-tier Tribunal or the Upper Tribunal as the court considers appropriate.

18. Staff appointed to the Asylum and Immigration Tribunal before 15 February 2010 are to be treated on and after that date, for the purpose of any enactment, as if they had been appointed by the Lord Chancellor under section 40(1) of the Tribunals, Courts and Enforcement Act 2007 (tribunal staff and services).

Saving provisions

19. In accordance with the provisions of this Schedule, sections 87(3) and (4), 103A, 103B, 103C and 103E of the 2002 Act, shall continue to apply to proceedings to which paragraphs 5, 7, 10 to 12 and 13(1)(c) and (2) (in relation to sub-paragraph (1)(c)) apply as if the repeals in Schedule 1 in respect of those sections of the 2002 Act had not been made.

20. Section 103D of the 2002 Act and the Community Legal Service (Asylum and Immigration Appeals) Regulations 2005 ('the 2005 Regulations') (legal aid funding arrangements) shall continue to apply to proceedings to which paragraphs 2 to 8 and 13(1)(b), (c) and (2) (in relation to sub-paragraphs (1)(b) to (e)) apply until the proceedings are finally determined—

(a) as if the repeals in Schedule 1 in respect of sections 103A and 103D of the 2002 Act and rule 33 of the Asylum and Immigration Tribunal (Procedure) Rules 2005 ('the

2005 Rules'), and the repeals and revocations in Schedule 3 in respect of paragraph 30 of Schedule 2 to the 2004 Act and the 2005 Regulations had not been made;

(b) as if the references to the Tribunal in section 103D of the 2002 Act, paragraph 30 of Schedule 2 to the 2004 Act, the 2005 Regulations and rule 33 of the 2005 Rules were references to the First-tier Tribunal or the Upper Tribunal as appropriate, and the references to the appropriate court and the High Court were references to the Upper Tribunal where appropriate; and

(c) subject to any necessary modifications to the 2005 Regulations and the 2005 Rules.

Interpretation

21. In this Schedule—

'appropriate court' means—

(i) in relation to an appeal decided in England or Wales, the High Court;

(ii) in relation to an appeal decided in Scotland, the Outer House of the Court of Session; and

(iii) in relation to an appeal decided in Northern Ireland, the High Court of Northern Ireland;

'appropriate appellate court' means—

(iv) in relation to an appeal decided in England or Wales, the Court of Appeal;

(v) in relation to an appeal decided in Scotland, the Inner House of the Court of Session; and

(vi) in relation to an appeal decided in Northern Ireland, the Court of Appeal of Northern Ireland;

'the 2002 Act' means the Nationality, Immigration and Asylum Act 2002;

'the 2004 Act' means the Asylum and Immigration (Treatment of Claimants, etc.) Act 2004; and

'the 2007 Act' means the Tribunals, Courts and Enforcement Act 2007.

The First-tier Tribunal and Upper Tribunal (Chambers) Order 2010

(SI 2010, No. 2655)

Note: This is the text that has direct relevance to the Immigration and Asylum Chamber of the Tribunal.

Citation, commencement and revocations

1.-(1) This Order may be cited as the First-tier Tribunal and Upper Tribunal (Chambers) Order 2010 and comes into force on 29th November 2010.

(2) . . .

First-tier Tribunal Chambers

2. The First-tier Tribunal shall be organised into the following chambers—

. . .

(c) the Immigration and Asylum Chamber;

. . .

Functions of the Immigration and Asylum Chamber of the First-tier Tribunal

5. To the Immigration and Asylum Chamber of the First-tier Tribunal are allocated all functions related to immigration and asylum matters, with the exception of matters allocated to—

(a) the Social Entitlement Chamber by article 6(a);
(b) the General Regulatory Chamber by article 3(a).

Upper Tribunal Chambers

9. The Upper Tribunal shall be organised into the following chambers—

. . .

(b) the Immigration and Asylum Chamber of the Upper Tribunal;

. . .

Functions of the Immigration and Asylum Chamber of the Upper Tribunal

11. To the Immigration and Asylum Chamber of the Upper Tribunal are allocated all functions related to—

(a) an appeal against a decision of the First-tier Tribunal made in the Immigration and Asylum Chamber of the First-tier Tribunal;

(b) a matter referred to the Upper Tribunal under section 9(5)(b) of the Tribunals, Courts and Enforcement Act 2007 or under Tribunal Procedure Rules by the Immigration and Asylum Chamber of the First-tier Tribunal;

[(c) an application for the Upper Tribunal to grant relief mentioned in section 15(1) of the Tribunals, Courts and Enforcement Act 2007 (Upper Tribunal's 'judicial review' jurisdiction), or to exercise the power of review under section 21(2) of that Act (Upper Tribunal's 'judicial review' jurisdiction: Scotland), which is made by a person who claims to be a minor from outside the United Kingdom challenging a defendant's assessment of that person's age;]

[(d) an application for the Upper Tribunal to exercise the powers of review under section 21(2) of the Tribunals, Court and Enforcement Act (Upper Tribunal's 'judicial review' jurisdiction: Scotland), which relates to a decision of the First-tier Tribunal mentioned in paragraph (a);]

[(e) an application for the Upper Tribunal to grant relief mentioned in section 15(1) of the Tribunals, Courts and Enforcement Act 2007 (Upper Tribunal's 'judicial review' jurisdiction), which is designated as an immigration matter—

(i) in a direction made in accordance with Part 1 of Schedule 2 to the Constitutional Reform Act 2005 specifying a class of case for the purposes of section 18(6) of the Tribunals, Courts and Enforcement Act 2007; or

(ii) in an order of the High Court in England and Wales made under section 31A(3) of the Senior Courts Act 1981, transferring to the Upper Tribunal an application of a kind described in section 31A(1) of that Act.]

Note: Subparagraphs (c), (d) and (e) substituted/inserted from 1 November 2013 (SI 2013/2068).

Resolution of doubt or dispute as to chamber

14. If there is any doubt or dispute as to the chamber in which a particular matter is to be dealt with, the Senior President of Tribunals may allocate that matter to the chamber which appears to the Senior President of Tribunals to be most appropriate.

Re-allocation of a case to another chamber

15. At any point in the proceedings, the Chamber President of the chamber to which a case or any issue in that case has been allocated by or under this Order may, with the consent of the corresponding Chamber President, allocate that case or that issue to another chamber within the same tribunal, by giving a direction to that effect.

The First-tier Tribunal (Immigration and Asylum Chamber) Fees Order 2011

(2011, No. 2841)

Citation and commencement

1. This Order may be cited as the First-tier Tribunal (Immigration and Asylum Chamber) Fees Order 2011 and shall come into force on the day after the date on which it is made.

Interpretation

2. In this Order—

'an immigration or asylum matter' means a matter in respect of which functions are allocated to the Immigration and Asylum Chamber of the First-tier Tribunal under article 5 of the First-tier Tribunal and Upper Tribunal (Chambers) Order 2010;

['appealable decision' means a decision from which there is a right of appeal to the Immigration and Asylum Chamber of the First-tier Tribunal]

'appellant' means any person identified in the notice of appeal as appealing in relation to an immigration and asylum matter to the First-tier Tribunal;

'BACS' means the method of payment known as 'Banks Automated Clearing System' by which money is transferred from one bank in the United Kingdom to another by means of an automated system;

'international money transfer' means a method of payment by which money is transferred from a bank account outside the United Kingdom to a bank account in the United Kingdom by means of an automated system;

['respondent' has the meaning given by article 1(4) of the Tribunal Procedure (First-tier Tribunal) (Immigration and Asylum Chamber) Rules 2014;]

'the 1971 Act' means the Immigration Act 1971;

'the 1999 Act' means the Immigration and Asylum Act 1999;

'the 2002 Act' means the Nationality, Immigration and Asylum Act 2002;

['the 2018 Regulations' means the Immigration and Nationality (Fees) Regulations 2018].

Note: Definitions of 'appealable decision' and 'respondent' inserted from 10 October 2016 (SI 2016/928) subject to transitional provisions: 'Subject to articles 5(2) and 8, the amendments made by this Order only apply in respect of an appeal to the First-tier Tribunal against a decision which was taken on or after the coming into force date of this Order' (article 7 of SI 2016/928). Definition of '2017 Regulations' substituted for '2018 Regulations' from 6 April 2018 (SI 2018/330).

Fees for appeals

3.—(1) A fee is payable in respect of an appeal to the First-tier Tribunal where the appeal relates to an immigration or asylum matter and the decision against which the appeal is made was taken on or after the coming into force of this Order.

(2) The fee is payable by or in respect of each appellant on the date on which the Notice of Appeal is given.

(3) The fee payable is—

(a) where the appellant consents to the appeal being determined without a hearing, [£80]; or

(b) where the appellant does not consent to the appeal being determined without a hearing, [£140].

(4) Subject to paragraph (5), where after making payment in accordance with paragraph (3)(a), the appellant withdraws their consent to the appeal being determined without a hearing, the difference between the amounts specified in subparagraphs (a) and (b) of paragraph (3) ('the balance') becomes payable on the withdrawal of that consent.

(5) The balance referred to in paragraph (4) ceases to be payable if the Tribunal decides that the appeal can be justly determined without a hearing.

[(5A) Where a notice of decision against which the appellant is appealing contains more than one appealable decision, one fee is payable in respect of each appealable decision that is not exempt under article 5.]

(6) This article is subject to articles 5, 6 and 7.

Note: Amount in square brackets in paragraphs (3)(a) and (b) substituted from 29 November 2016 (SI 2016/1149) subject to transitional provisions:' The amendments made by article 3 apply to an appeal in respect of which an appellant gives a Notice of Appeal to the First-tier Tribunal on or after the coming into force date of this Order' (article 4 of SI 2016/1149).

Paragraph 5A inserted from 10 October 2016 (SI 2016/928) subject to transitional provisions: 'Subject to articles 5(2) and 8, the amendments made by this Order only apply in respect of an appeal to the First-tier Tribunal against a decision which was taken on or after the coming into force date of this Order' (article 7 of SI 2016/928).

Method of paying fee

4.—(1) The fee payable must be paid by one of the following methods—

(a) credit card;

(b) debit card;

(c) BACS; or

(d) international money transfer.

(2) For the purposes of enabling payment to be made by or in respect of the appellant—

(a) authorisation to take payment and details of the credit or debit card, or

(b) an undertaking by or on behalf of each appellant to pay by BACS or an international money transfer, must be provided at the same time as the giving of the notice of appeal or

the subsequent withdrawal of their consent to the appeal being determined without a hearing (as the case may be).

Exemption from fees

5.—

[(1) No fee is payable for—

(a) an appeal against a decision made under—

(i) section 40 of the British Nationality Act 1981 (deprivation of citizenship);

(ii) [. . .]

(b) an appeal under section 82(1)(c) of the Nationality, Asylum and Immigration Act 2002 (revocation of protection status).]

[(1A) No fee is payable for a relevant appeal brought by an appellant who has been excepted from the requirement to pay an application fee under the [2018] Regulations in accordance with the following exceptions—

(a) exception [4.4.1] (application by person physically present in UK but liable to immigration detention where the requirement to pay the fee would be incompatible with the person's Convention rights) in Table 4 of paragraph (2) of Schedule 1 to those Regulations; or

(b) exception 9.4 (specified human rights applications) in Table 9 of paragraph (2) of Schedule 2 to those Regulations.

(1B) For the purposes of this article, a 'relevant appeal' is an appeal against a decision to refuse the application in respect of which the appellant was excepted from the requirement to pay a fee under the [2018] Regulations.]

(2) No fee is payable where, at the time the fee would otherwise become payable, the appellant is, under the 1999 Act—

(a) a 'supported person' as defined in section 94(1); or

(b) provided with temporary support under section 98.

(3) No fee is payable where, for the purpose of proceedings before the Tribunal, the appellant is in receipt of—

(a) [civil legal services (within the meaning of Part 1 of the Legal Aid, Sentencing and Punishment of Offenders Act 2012) made available under arrangements made for the purposes of that Part of that Act;]

(b) legal aid under Part 2 of the Legal Aid, Advice and Assistance (Northern Ireland) Order 1981; or

(c) civil legal aid or advice and assistance under the Legal Aid (Scotland) Act 1986.

(4) [No fee is payable where the appellant is—

(a) a child for whose benefit services are provided by a local authority under—

(i) section 17 of the Children Act 1989 (provision of services for children in need, their families and others);

(ii) section 22 of the Children (Scotland) Act 1995 (promotion of welfare of children in need); or

(iii) article 18 of the Children (Northern Ireland) Order 1995 (general duty of authority to provide personal social services for children in need, their families and others);

(b) a child for whom provision is being made by a local authority for the purpose of meeting the child's needs under section 37 of the Social Services and Well-being (Wales) Act 2014 (duty to meet care and support needs of a child);

(c) a person who has parental responsibility for a child described in sub-paragraph (a) or (b); or

(d) a child for whom accommodation is provided under—

(i) section 20 of the Children Act 1989 (provision of accommodation for children: general);

(ii) section 76 of the Social Services and Well-being (Wales) Act 2014 (accommodation for children without parents or who are lost or abandoned etc.);

(iii) section 25 of the Children (Scotland) Act 1995 (provision of accommodation for children, etc.); or

(iv) article 21 of the Children (Northern Ireland) Order 1995 (provision of accommodation for children: general).]

(5) Where by any convention, treaty or other instrument entered into by Her Majesty with any foreign power it is provided that no fee is required to be paid in respect of any proceedings, the fees specified in this Order are not payable in respect of those proceedings.

Note: Subparagraph (3)(a) substituted from 1 April 2013 (SI 2013/534) subject to savings as specified in SI 2013/534 reg.14(2). Paragraphs (1) and (4) substituted and paragraphs (1A) and (1B) inserted from 10 October 2016 (SI 2016/928) subject to saving and transitional provisions set out in articles 5(2) and 7 of SI 2016/928. Paragraphs (1A) and (1B) substituted from 6 April 2017 (SI 2017/515) and words within paragraphs (1A) and (1B) substituted from 6 April 2018 (SI 2018/330). Paragraph (1)(a)(ii) omitted from 23.00 on 31 December 2020 (SI 2020/1309) subject to saving provision (reg 38(3)-(4) of SI 2020/1309).

Power to defer payment in certain cases

6. The Lord Chancellor may defer payment of a fee where the appeal is brought on the grounds that the removal of the appellant from, or a requirement for the appellant to leave, the United Kingdom would breach the United Kingdom's obligations under either—

(a) the Convention relating to the Status of Refugees done at Geneva on 28 July 1951 and the Protocol to the Convention; or

(b) article 21 of Directive 2004/83/EC of the European Parliament and Council of 29 April 2004.

Reduction or remission of fees

[**7.**—(1) Subject to paragraph (2), the Schedule applies for the purpose of ascertaining whether an appellant is entitled to a remission or reduction of a fee specified in this Order.

(2) The Schedule does not apply to an appellant who is not in the United Kingdom on the date on which the Notice of Appeal is given.

(3) A fee specified in this Order may be remitted or reduced where the Lord Chancellor is satisfied that there are exceptional circumstances which justify doing so.]

Note: Article 7 substituted from 20 April 2020 (SI 2020/314).

Certificate of fee satisfaction

8.—(1) The Lord Chancellor must issue a certificate of fee satisfaction if satisfied that—

(a) the appropriate fee payable under article 3 has been paid;

(b) in view of an undertaking given by or on behalf of the appellant, payment will be promptly made by BACS or an international money transfer;

(c) no fee is payable;

(d) payment is to be deferred in accordance with article 6; or

(e) the appellant has, at the time a fee would otherwise be payable under article 3, applied for the fee to be reduced or remitted in accordance with article 7.

(2) The issuing of such a certificate is without prejudice to the power to recover the amount of any payable fee or part of such fee which remains unpaid and unremitted.

(3) The Lord Chancellor may revoke a certificate of fee satisfaction and if a certificate is revoked, the Tribunal shall be notified accordingly.

Refunds

9.—(1) Subject to paragraph (2)—

(a) where the fee payable under article 3(3)(b) has been paid but the appeal is determined without a hearing, the difference between the amounts specified in article 3(3)(a) and 3(3)(b) may be refunded; and

(b) where a fee has been paid which the Lord Chancellor, if all the circumstances had been known, would have reduced or remitted under [article 7(3)], the fee or the amount by which the fee would have been reduced, as the case may be, shall be refunded.

[**(1A)** For the purposes of this article an appeal is only 'determined without a hearing' if—

(a) the respondent has consented to, or has not objected to, the matter being decided without a hearing; or

(b) the First-tier Tribunal has considered that it can justly determine the matter without a hearing in accordance with rule 25(1)(g) of the Tribunal Procedure (First-tier Tribunal) (Immigration and Asylum Chamber) Rules 2014.]

(2) No refund will be made under this article unless the appellant applies in writing to the Lord Chancellor within 6 months of the date the fee becomes payable.

(3) The Lord Chancellor may extend the period of 6 months mentioned in paragraph (2) if the Lord Chancellor considers there is a good reason for the application being made after the end of the period of 6 months.

Note: Paragraph (1A) inserted from 10 October 2016 (SI 2016/928) subject to transitional provisions: 'Subject to articles 5(2) and 8, the amendments made by this Order only apply in respect of an appeal to the First-tier Tribunal against a decision which was taken on or after the coming into force date of this Order' (article 7 of SI 2016/928) and 'The amendments made by article 6 only apply where the appellant has provided a notice of appeal to the First-tier Tribunal on or after the coming into force date of this Order' (article 8 of SI 2016/928). Words substituted in paragraph (1)(b) from 20 April 2020 (SI 2020/314).

[SCHEDULE 1

ARTICLE 7

Remissions and reductions

Interpretation

1.—(1) In this Schedule—

'child' means a person—

(a) whose main residence is with a party and who is aged—

(i) under 16 years; or

(ii) 16 to 19 years; and is—

(aa) not married or in a civil partnership; and

(bb) enrolled or accepted in full-time education that is not advanced education, or approved training; or

(b) in respect of whom a party or their partner pays child support maintenance or periodic payments in accordance with a maintenance agreement,

and 'full-time education', 'advanced education' and 'approved training' have the meaning given by the Child Benefit (General) Regulations 2006;

'child support maintenance' has the meaning given in section 3(6) of the Child Support Act 1991;

'couple' has the meaning given in section 39(1) of the Welfare Reform Act 2012;

'disposable capital' has the meaning given in paragraph 5;

'excluded benefits' means any of the following—

(a) any of the following benefits payable under the Social Security Contributions and Benefits Act 1992 or the corresponding provisions of the Social Security Contributions and Benefits (Northern Ireland) Act 1992—

(i) attendance allowance under section 64;

(ii) severe disablement allowance;

(iii) carer's allowance;

(iv) disability living allowance;

(v) constant attendance allowance under section 104 as an increase to a disablement pension;

(vi) any payment made out of the social fund;

(vii) housing benefit;

(viii) widowed parents allowance;

(b) any of the following benefits payable under the Tax Credits Act 2002—

(i) any disabled child element or severely disabled child element of the child tax credit;

(ii) any childcare element of the working tax credit;

(c) any direct payment made under the Community Care, Services for Carers and Children's Services (Direct Payments) (England) Regulations 2009, the Carers and Direct Payments Act (Northern Ireland) 2002, section 12B(1) of the Social Work (Scotland) Act 1968, the Social Care (Self-directed Support) (Scotland) Act 2013 or under regulations made under sections 50 to 53 of the Social Services and Well-being (Wales) Act 2014;

(d) a back to work bonus payable under section 26 of the Jobseekers Act 1995, or article 28 of the Jobseekers (Northern Ireland) Order 1995;

(e) any exceptionally severe disablement allowance paid under the Personal Injuries (Civilians) Scheme 1983;

(f) any payments from the Industrial Injuries Disablement Benefit in accordance with sections 103 to 105, paragraphs 2 and 3, and Parts II and III of Schedule 7 to the Social Security Contributions and Benefits Act 1992;

(g) any pension paid under the Naval, Military and Air Forces etc. (Disablement and Death) Service Pension Order 2006;

(h) any payment made from the Independent Living Funds listed in regulation 20(2)(b) of the Criminal Legal Aid (Financial Resources) Regulations 2013;

(i) any payment of bereavement support payment under section 30 of the Pensions Act 2014;

(j) any financial support paid under an agreement for the care of a foster child;

(k) any housing credit element of pension credit;

(l) any armed forces independence payment;

(m) any personal independence payment payable under the Welfare Reform Act 2012;

(n) any payment on account of benefit as defined in the Social Security (Payments on Account of Benefit) Regulations 2013;

(o) any of the following amounts, as defined by the Universal Credit Regulations 2013, that make up an award of universal credit—

(i) an additional amount to the child element in respect of a disabled child;

(ii) a housing costs element;

(iii) a childcare costs element;

(iv) a carer element;

(v) a limited capability for work or limited capacity for work and work-related activity element;

'gross monthly income' has the meaning given in paragraph 13;

'maintenance agreement' has the meaning given in section 9(1) of the Child Support Act 1991;

'partner' means a person with whom the party lives as a couple and includes a person with whom the party is not currently living but from whom the party is not living separate and apart;

'party' means the individual who would, but for this Schedule, be liable to pay a fee under this Order;

'restraint order' means—

(a) an order under section 42(1A) of the Senior Courts Act 1981;

(b) an order under section 33 of the Employment Tribunals Act 1996;

(c) a civil restraint order made under rule 3.11 of the Civil Procedure Rules 1998, or a practice direction made under that rule; or

(d) a civil restraint order under rule 4.8 of the Family Procedure Rules 2010, or the practice direction referred to in that rule.

(2) References to remission of a fee are to be read as including references to a reduction of a fee as appropriate and remit and remitted shall be construed accordingly.

Fee remission

2. If a party satisfies the disposable capital test, the amount of any fee remission is calculated by applying the gross monthly income test.

Disposable capital test

Disposable capital test

3.—(1) Subject to paragraph 4, a party satisfies the disposable capital test if—

(a) the fee payable by the party and for which an application for remission is made, falls within a fee band set out in column 1 of Table 1; and

(b) the party's disposable capital is less than the amount in the corresponding row of column 2.

Table 1 Column 1 (fee band)	Column 2 (disposable capital)
Up to and including £1,000	£3,000
£1,001 to £1,335	£4,000
£1,336 to £1,665	£5,000
£1,666 to £2,000	£6,000
£2,001 to £2,330	£7,000
£2,331 to £4,000	£8,000
£4,001 to £5,000	£10,000
£5,001 to £6,000	£12,000
£6,001 to £7,000	£14,000
£7,001 or more	£16,000

4. Subject to paragraph 14, if a party or their partner is aged 61 or over, that party satisfies the disposable capital test if that party's disposable capital is less than £16,000.

Disposable capital

5. Subject to paragraph 14, disposable capital is the value of every resource of a capital nature belonging to the party on the date on which the application for remission is made, unless it is treated as income by this Order, or it is disregarded as excluded disposable capital.

Disposable capital – non-money resources

6. The value of a resource of a capital nature that does not consist of money is calculated as the amount which that resource would realise if sold, less—

(a) 10% of the sale value; and

(b) the amount of any borrowing secured against that resource that would be repayable on sale.

Disposable capital – resources held outside the United Kingdom

7.—(1) Capital resources in a country outside the United Kingdom count towards disposable capital.

(2) If there is no prohibition in that country against the transfer of a resource into the United Kingdom, the value of that resource is the amount which that resource would realise if sold in that country, in accordance with paragraph 6.

(3) If there is a prohibition in that country against the transfer of a resource into the United Kingdom, the value of that resource is the amount that resource would realise if sold to a buyer in the United Kingdom.

Disposable capital – foreign currency resources

8. Where disposable capital is held in currency other than sterling, the cost of any banking charge or commission that would be payable if that amount were converted into sterling, is deducted from its value.

Disposable capital – jointly owned resources

9. Where any resource of a capital nature is owned jointly or in common, there is a presumption that the resource is owned in equal shares, unless evidence to the contrary is produced.

Excluded disposable capital

10. The following things are excluded disposable capital—

(a) a property which is the main or only dwelling occupied by the party;

(b) the household furniture and effects of the main or only dwelling occupied by the party;

(c) articles of personal clothing;

(d) any vehicle, the sale of which would leave the party, or their partner, without motor transport,

(e) tools and implements of trade, including vehicles used for business purposes;

(f) the capital value of the party's or their partner's business, where the party or their partner is self-employed;

(g) the capital value of any funds or other assets held in trust, where the party or their partner is a beneficiary without entitlement to advances of any trust capital;

(h) a jobseeker's back to work bonus;

(i) a payment made as a result of a determination of unfair dismissal by a court or tribunal, or by way of settlement of a claim for unfair dismissal;

(j) any compensation paid as a result of a determination of medical negligence or in respect of any personal injury by a court, or by way of settlement of a claim for medical negligence or personal injury;

(k) the capital held in any personal or occupational pension scheme;

(l) any cash value payable on surrender of a contract of insurance;

(m) any capital payment made out of the Independent Living Funds;

(n) any bereavement support payment in respect of the rate set out in regulation 3(2) or (5) of the Bereavement Support Payment Regulations 2017;

(o) any capital insurance or endowment lump sum payments that have been paid as a result of illness, disability or death;

(p) any student loan or student grant;

(q) any payments under the criminal injuries compensation scheme.

Gross monthly income test

Remission of fees – gross monthly income

11.—(1) If a party satisfies the disposable capital test, no fee is payable under this Order if, at the time when the fee would otherwise be payable, the party or their partner has the number of children specified in column 1 of Table 2 and—

(a) if the party is single, their gross monthly income does not exceed the amount set out in the appropriate row of column 2; or

(b) if the party is one of a couple, the gross monthly income of that couple does not exceed the amount set out in the appropriate row of column 3.

Table 2

Column 1 Number of children of party	Column 2 Single	Column 3 Couple
no children	£1,170	£1,345
1 child	£1,435	£1,610
2 children	£1,700	£1,875"

(2) If a party or their partner has more than 2 children, the relevant amount of gross monthly income is the appropriate amount specified in Table 2 for 2 children, plus the sum of [£265] for each additional child.

(3) For every £10 of gross monthly income received above the appropriate amount in Table 2, including any additional amount added under sub-paragraph (2), the party must pay £5 towards the fee payable, up to the maximum amount of the fee payable.

(4) This paragraph is subject to paragraph 12.

Note: Table 2 and sum in paragraph (2) substituted from 30 September 2021 (SI 2021/985).

Gross monthly income cap

12.—(1) No remission is available if a party or their partner has the number of children specified in column 1 of Table 3 and—

(a) if the party is single, their gross monthly income exceeds the amount set out in the appropriate row of column 2 of Table 3; or

(b) if the party is one of a couple, the gross monthly income of that couple exceeds the amount set out in the appropriate row of column 3 of Table 3.

Table 3

Column 1 Number of children of party	Column 2 Single	Column 3 Couple
no children	£5,170	£5,345
1 child	£5,435	£5,610
2 children	£5,700	£5,875"

(2) If a party or their partner has more than 2 children, the relevant amount of gross monthly income is the appropriate amount specified in Table 3 for 2 children, plus the sum of [£265] for each additional child.

Note: Table 3 and sum in paragraph (2) substituted from 30 September 2021 (SI 2021/985).

Gross monthly income

13.—(1) Subject to paragraph 14, gross monthly income means the total monthly income, for the month preceding that in which the application for remission is made, from all sources, other than receipt of any of the excluded benefits.

(2) Income from a trade, business or gainful occupation other than an occupation at a wage or salary is calculated as—

(a) the profits which have accrued or will accrue to the party; and

(b) the drawings of the party;

in the month preceding that in which the application for remission is made.

(3) In calculating profits under sub-paragraph (2)(a), all sums necessarily expended to earn those profits are deducted.

Resources and income treated as the party's resources and income

14.—(1) Subject to sub-paragraph (2), the disposable capital and gross monthly income of a partner of a party is to be treated as disposable capital and gross monthly income of the party.

(2) Where the partner of a party has a contrary interest to the party in the matter to which the fee relates, the disposable capital and gross monthly income of that partner, if any, is not treated as the disposable capital and gross monthly income of the party.

Application for remission of a fee

15.—(1) An application for remission of a fee must be made at the time when the fee would otherwise be payable.

(2) Where an application for remission of a fee is made, the party must—

(a) indicate the fee to which the application relates;

(b) declare the amount of their disposable capital; and

(c) provide documentary evidence of their gross monthly income and the number of children relevant for the purposes of paragraphs 11 and 12.

(3) Where an application for remission of a fee is made on or before the date on which a fee is payable, the date for payment of the fee is disapplied.

(4) Where an application for remission is refused, or if reduction of a fee is granted, the amount of the fee which remains unremitted must be paid within the period notified in writing to the party.

Refunds

16.—(1) Subject to sub-paragraph (3), where a party pays a fee at a time when that party would have been entitled to a remission if they had provided the documentary evidence required by paragraph 15, the fee, or the amount by which the fee would have been reduced as the case may be, must be refunded if documentary evidence relating to the time when the fee became payable is provided at a later date.

(2) No refund shall be made under this paragraph unless the party who paid the fee applies within 3 months of the date on which the fee was paid.

(3) The Lord Chancellor may extend the period of 3 months mentioned in sub-paragraph (2) if the Lord Chancellor considers that there is a good reason for a refund being made after the end of the period of 3 months.

Vexatious litigants

17.—(1) This paragraph applies where—
(a) a restraint order is in force against a party; and
(b) that party makes an application for permission to—
(i) issue proceedings or take a step in proceedings as required by the restraint order;
(ii) apply for amendment or discharge of the order; or
(iii) appeal the order.

(2) The fee prescribed by this Order for the application is payable in full.

(3) If the party is granted permission, they are to be refunded the difference between—
(a) the fee paid; and
(b) the fee that would have been payable if this Schedule had been applied without reference to this paragraph.]

Note: Schedule inserted from 20 April 2020 (SI 2020/314).

The Immigration Appeals (Family Visitor) Regulations 2012

(2012, No. 1532)

Note: Lapsed in part on the repeal of 2002 c. 41, s 88A by Immigration Act 2014 c. 22 Sch.9(4) para.37 (20 October 2014 subject to savings and transitional provisions as specified in SI 2014/2771 arts 9–11).

Citation and commencement

1. These Regulations may be cited as the Immigration Appeals (Family Visitor) Regulations 2012 and shall come into force on 9th July 2012.

Class or description of person to be visited

2.—(1) A person ('P') is of a class or description prescribed for the purposes of section 88A(1)(a) of the Nationality, Immigration and Asylum Act 2002 (entry clearance), if—
(a) the applicant for entry clearance ('A') is a member of the family of P; and
(b) P's circumstances match those specified in regulation 3.

(2) For the purposes of paragraph (1), A is a member of the family of P if A is the—
(a) spouse, civil partner, father, mother, son, daughter, grandfather, grandmother, grandson, granddaughter, brother or sister;

(b) father-in-law, mother-in-law, brother-in-law or sister-in-law;
(c) son-in-law or daughter-in-law; or
(d) stepfather, stepmother, stepson, stepdaughter, stepbrother or stepsister;
of P.

(3) For the purposes of paragraph (1), A is also a member of the family of P if A is the partner of P.

(4) In this regulation, A is the partner of P if—

(a) A and P have been in a relationship that is akin to a marriage or civil partnership for at least the two years before the day on which A's application for entry clearance was made; and

(b) such relationship is genuine and subsisting.

(5) In this regulation—

(a) 'father-in-law of P' includes the father of P's civil partner;
(b) 'mother-in-law of P' includes the mother of P's civil partner;
(c) 'brother-in-law of P' includes the brother of P's civil partner;
(d) 'sister-in-law of P' includes the sister of P's civil partner;
(e) 'son-in-law of P' includes the son of P's civil partner;
(f) 'daughter-in-law of P' includes the daughter of P's civil partner;

(g) 'stepfather of P' includes the person who is the civil partner of A's father (but is not A's parent);

(h) 'stepmother of P' includes the person who is the civil partner of A's mother (but is not A's parent);

(i) 'stepson of P' includes the person who is the son of A's civil partner (but is not A's son);

(j) 'stepdaughter of P' includes the person who is the daughter of A's civil partner (but is not A's daughter);

(k) 'stepbrother of P' includes the person who is the son of the civil parent of A's parent (but is not the son of either of A's parents); and

(l) 'stepsister of P' includes the person who is the daughter of the civil partner of A's parent (but is not the daughter of either of A's parents).

Circumstances of the person to be visited

3. The circumstances of P mentioned in regulation 2(1)(b) are that P—

(a) is settled in the United Kingdom as defined in paragraph 6 of the immigration rules;

(b) has been granted asylum in the United Kingdom under paragraph 334 of the immigration rules; or

(c) has been granted humanitarian protection in the United Kingdom under paragraph 339C of the immigration rules.

Transitional provision

4. These Regulations apply only to an application for entry clearance made on or after the day on which they come into force.

The Immigration (Passenger Transit Visa) Order 2014
(2014, No. 2702)

Citation and commencement

1. —

(1) This Order may be cited as the Immigration (Passenger Transit Visa) Order 2014.

(2) This Order comes into force on 1st December 2014.

Interpretation

2.—(1) Subject to paragraph (5), in this Order a 'transit passenger' means a person to whom [paragraph (2), (3), (4) or (4A)] applies and who on arrival in the United Kingdom passes through to another country or territory without entering the United Kingdom.

(2) This paragraph applies to a person who is a citizen or national of a country or territory listed in Schedule 1 to this Order.

(3) This paragraph applies to a person holding a travel document issued by the purported 'Turkish Republic of Northern Cyprus'.

(4) This paragraph applies to a person who holds a passport issued by the Republic of Venezuela that does not contain biometric information contained in an electronic chip.

[(4A) This paragraph applies to a person who holds—

(a) a passport; or

(b) another document that can be used (in some or all circumstances) instead of a passport;

which does not establish citizenship or nationality].

(5) A person to whom paragraph (2), (3) or (4) applies will not be a transit passenger if he—

(a) has the right of abode in the United Kingdom under the Immigration Act 1971;

(b) is a citizen or national of an EEA State; [. . .]

(c) in the case of a citizen or national of the People's Republic of China, holds a passport issued by either the Hong Kong Special Administrative Region or the Macao Special Administrative Region[; or

(d) is a citizen or national of the territory of Taiwan.]

(6) In this Order—

'Approved Destination Status Scheme' means a scheme for issuing visas to Chinese tour groups under—

(a) the Memorandum of Understanding between the European Community and the National Tourism Administration of the People's Republic of China on visa and related issues concerning tourist groups from the People's Republic of China (ADS) signed at Beijing on 12th February 2004; or

(b) a similar agreement between the People's Republic of China and a Schengen Acquis State;

['Convention Travel Document' means a document issued in accordance with Article 28 of—

(a) the 1951 United Nations Convention Relating to Status of Refugees done at Geneva on 28th July 1951 as amended by the New York Protocol of 31st January 1967; or

(b) the 1954 United Nations Convention on the Status of Stateless Persons done at New York on 28th September 1954.]

'EEA State' means a country which is a contracting party to the Agreement on the European Economic Area signed at Oporto on 2nd May 1992 as adjusted by the Protocol signed at Brussels on 17th March 1993;

'Schengen Acquis State' means an EEA State (excluding the [. . .] Republic of Ireland) or Switzerland.

Note: Words in square brackets in paragraph (1) substituted from 24 April 2015 (SI 2015/657). Paragraph (4A), paragraph (5)(d) and definition of 'Convention Travel Document' inserted from 24 April 2015 (SI 2015/657). Words omitted from the definition of 'Schengen Acquis State' from 31 December 2020 (SI 2019/745).

Requirement for a transit passenger to hold a transit visa

3.—Subject to article 4, a transit passenger is required to hold a transit visa.

Exemption from the requirement for a transit passenger to hold a transit visa

4.—(1) A transit passenger is not required to hold a transit visa if he holds or a person with whom he arrives in the United Kingdom holds on his behalf—

(a) a valid visa for entry to Australia, Canada, New Zealand or the United States of America;

[(aa) an expired visa for entry to Australia, Canada, New Zealand or the United States of America provided it is less than six months since the transit passenger last entered that country with a valid visa;]

(b) a valid Australian Permanent Resident Visa;

(c) a valid Canadian Permanent Resident Card issued on or after 28th June 2002;

(d) a valid New Zealand Permanent Resident Visa;

(e) a valid USA I-551 Permanent Resident Card issued on or after 21st April 1998;

(f) an expired USA I-551 Permanent Resident Card provided it is accompanied by a valid I-797 letter authorising an extension of the period of permanent residency;

[(g) a valid temporary USA I-551 machine readable immigrant visa;]

(h) a valid standalone US Immigration Form 155A/155B attached to a brown sealed envelope;

(i) a valid common format Category D visa for entry to an EEA state or Switzerland;

(j) a valid common format residence permit issued by an EEA State pursuant to Council Regulation (EC) No 1030/2002 or Switzerland;

(k) a valid biometric visa issued by the Republic of Ireland;

(l) a valid visa issued by a Schengen Acquis State under the Approved Destination Status Scheme where the transit passenger is undertaking a journey via the [United Kingdom to that] Schengen Acquis State;

(m) a valid airline ticket for travel via the United Kingdom as part of a journey from a Schengen Acquis State to another country or territory, provided that the transit passenger does not seek to travel via the United Kingdom on a date more than 30 days from the date on which he last entered a Schengen Acquis State with a valid visa issued by a Schengen Acquis State under the Approved Destination Status Scheme;

(n) a [valid] diplomatic or service passport issued by the People's Republic of China;

(o) a [valid] diplomatic or official passport issued by India; . . .

(p) a [valid] diplomatic or official passport issued by Vietnam;

[(q) a valid diplomatic passport issued by Turkey;]

{(qa) a valid diplomatic passport issued by South Africa;}

[(r) a valid alien's passport issued by Estonia or Latvia;

(s) a valid Convention Travel Document; or

(t) a valid laissez-passer issued by the United Nations or the International Committee of the Red Cross.]

[(2) Paragraph (1)(a) [and (1)(aa)] shall not apply where the transit passenger is a citizen or national of Syria holding a B1 or B2 visa for entry to the United States of America.]

[(3) All documents listed in this article exclude versions held—

(a) in electronic format; or

(b) in hardcopy format which derives from electronic format except where the document can be verified by the owner of the aircraft (or his employee or agent) in which the transit passenger intends to travel to the United Kingdom.]

Note: Paragraph (2) inserted from 17 March 2015 (SI 2015/657) and words in paragraph (2) inserted from 24 April 2015 (SI 2015/657). Subparagraph (aa) inserted, subparagraph (g) and words in square brackets in subparagraph (l) substituted from 24 April 2015 (SI 2015/657). Word 'valid' inserted in subparagraphs (n) to (p) and subparagraphs (q), (r) to (t) and paragraph (3) inserted from 24 April 2015 (SI 2015/657). Subparagraph (qa) inserted from 10 August 2015 (SI 2015/1534).

Method of application for a transit visa

5. An application for a transit visa may be made to any British High Commission, Embassy or Consulate which accepts such applications.

Revocations

6. The Orders specified in Schedule 2 to this Order are revoked.

SCHEDULE 1

ARTICLE 2(2)

Countries or territories whose nationals or citizens need transit visas

Afghanistan
Albania
Algeria
Angola
Bangladesh
Belarus
Burma
Burundi
Cameroon
[. . .]
Congo
Democratic Republic of the Congo
Egypt
[El Salvador]
Eritrea
Ethiopia

Former Yugoslav Republic of Macedonia
Gambia
Ghana
Guinea
Guinea-Bissau
India
Iran
Iraq
Ivory Coast
Jamaica
Kenya
Kosovo
Lebanon
Lesotho
Liberia
Libya
Malawi
Moldova
Mongolia
Nepal
Nigeria
Pakistan
Palestinian Territories
[People's Republic of China]
Rwanda
Senegal
Serbia
Sierra Leone
Somalia
South Africa
South Sudan
Sri Lanka
Sudan
Swaziland
Syria
Tanzania
Turkey
Uganda
Vietnam
Yemen
Zimbabwe

Note: China omitted and People's Republic of China inserted from 24 April 2015 (SI 2015/657). El Salvador inserted from 12 May 2022 (SI 2022/524) subject to transitional provision (article 3 of SI 2022/524).

SCHEDULE 2
REVOCATIONS

. . .

The Immigration (Removal of Family Members) Regulations 2014
(2014, No. 2816)

The Secretary of State, in exercise of the powers conferred by section 10(10)(b) of the Immigration and Asylum Act 1999, makes the following Regulations:

Citation, commencement and interpretation

1. These Regulations may be cited as the Immigration (Removal of Family Members) Regulations 2014 and come into force on 14th November 2014.

2. In these Regulations—

'the Act' means the Immigration and Asylum Act 1999;

'family member' means a person who meets the conditions set out in section 10(3), (4) and (5) of the Act;

'P' means a person who is liable to be or has been removed from the United Kingdom under section 10(1) of the Act.

Giving of notice to a family member

3. A notice given to a family member in accordance with section 10(2) of the Act may be given—

(a) at any time prior to P's removal, or

(b) during the period of eight weeks beginning with the date on which P is removed.

Service of notice

4.—(1) A notice given to a family member in accordance with section 10(2) of the Act may be—

(a) given by hand,

(b) sent by fax,

(c) sent by postal service in which delivery or receipt is recorded to—

(i) an address provided for correspondence by the person or the person's representative, or

(ii) where no address for correspondence has been provided, the last-known or usual place of abode or place of business of the person or the person's representative,

(d) sent electronically,

(e) sent by document exchange to a document exchange number or address,

(f) sent by courier,

(g) collected by the person who is the subject of the decision or the person's representative.

(2) Where—

(a) a person's whereabouts are not known, and

(b) no address is available for correspondence with either the person or the person's representative under paragraph (1)(c),

the notice shall be deemed to have been given when the Secretary of State or immigration officer enters a record of the above circumstances and places the signed notice on the relevant file.

(3) Where notice is deemed to have been given in accordance with paragraph (2) and subsequently the person is located, the person is to be given a copy of the notice and details of when and how it was deemed to be served as soon as is practicable.

(4) Where a notice is sent by post in accordance with paragraph (1)(c) it shall be deemed to have been served, unless the contrary is proved, on the second day after it was posted.

(5) For the purposes of paragraph (4) the period is to be calculated—

(a) excluding the day on which the notice is posted, and

(b) excluding any day which is not a business day.

(6) In this regulation, 'business day' means any day other than Saturday or Sunday, a day which is a bank holiday under the Banking and Financial Dealings Act 1971 in the part of the United Kingdom to which the notice is sent, Christmas Day or Good Friday.

(7) A notice to be given to a family member in accordance with section 10(2) of the Act may, in the case of a child below the age of 18 who does not have a representative, be given to P.

The Immigration (Residential Accommodation) (Prescribed Requirements and Codes of Practice) Order 2014

(SI 2014, No. 2874)

Text Not Reproduced

Note: Amended by SI 2016/9 from 1st February 2016, SI 2020/1047 from 2nd November 2020, SI 2021/689 from 1 July 2021 and SI 2022/242 from 6 April 2022.

The Proposed Marriages and Civil Partnerships (Meaning of Exempt Persons and Notice) Regulations 2015

(SI 2015, No. 122)

PART I

GENERAL

Citation, commencement and extent

1.—(1) These Regulations may be cited as the Proposed Marriages and Civil Partnerships (Meaning of Exempt Persons and Notice) Regulations 2015.

(2) They come into force on 2nd March 2015.

(3) Regulations 5 to 7 extend to England and Wales only.

Interpretation

2. In these Regulations—

'1949 Act' means the Marriage Act 1949;

'1971 Act' means the Immigration Act 1971;

'2004 Act' means the Civil Partnership Act 2004;

'2014 Act' means the Immigration Act 2014;

'party' means a party to a proposed marriage or civil partnership and 'other party' is to be construed accordingly.

PART 2
EXEMPT PERSONS

Persons exempt from immigration control

3.—(1) A person ('P') is exempt from immigration control if P—

(a) has the right of abode in the United Kingdom under section 2(1)(b) of the 1971 Act (Commonwealth citizens with a right of abode),

(b) is exempt from the provisions of the 1971 Act by virtue of section 8(3) or (4) of that Act (exceptions for seamen, aircrews and other special cases),

(c) subject to paragraph (2), is exempt from the provisions of the 1971 Act by virtue of the Immigration (Exemption from Control) Order 1972 ('the 1972 Order'), or

(d) is exempt from the provisions of the 1971 Act by virtue of section 20 of the State Immunity Act 1978 (heads of State).

(2) Sub-paragraph (c) of paragraph (1) does not apply to a person who is exempt from the provisions of the 1971 Act solely by virtue of article 5 of the 1972 Order.

Relevant visa

4.—(1) Subject to paragraph (2), the kinds of visa or other authorisation specified for the purpose of section 49(4) of the 2014 Act are—

(a) entry clearance or leave to enter as a visitor under the immigration rules for the purpose of marriage or civil partnership,

(b) entry clearance, leave to enter or leave to remain as a fiancé(e) or proposed civil partner under Appendix FM to the immigration rules,

(c) entry clearance, leave to enter or leave to remain as a fiancé(e) or proposed civil partner under Appendix Armed Forces to the immigration rules,

(d) entry clearance, leave to enter or leave to remain as a fiancé(e) or proposed civil partner given outside the provisions of the immigration rules.

(2) A visa or other authorisation mentioned in paragraph (1) ('a relevant visa') is specified for the purpose of section 49(4) only if the relevant visa was given to a party in respect of a proposed marriage to, or (as the case may be) a proposed registration of a civil partnership with, the other party (whether or not the other party is named in the relevant visa).

(3) In this regulation—

'entry clearance' has the same meaning as in section 33 of the 1971 Act (interpretation);

'immigration rules' means the rules laid down under section 3(2) of the 1971 Act (general provisions for regulation and control);

'leave to enter' or 'leave to remain' means leave to enter, or remain in, the United Kingdom given in accordance with section 3 of the 1971 Act.

PART 3
NOTICES

Notices given by the Secretary of State to a party

5.—

(1) This regulation applies to a notice required to be given by the Secretary of State to a party under—

(a) Part 4 of the 2014 Act,

(b) the Proposed Marriages and Civil Partnerships (Conduct of Investigations, etc.) Regulations 2015,

(c) section 31(5EB) of the 1949 Act (application to reduce waiting period), or

(d) section 12(5) of the 2004 Act (application to shorten waiting period).

(2) A notice to which this regulation applies may be—

(a) given by hand to the party or the party's representative,

(b) sent by fax to the party or the party's representative,

(c) sent by postal service in which delivery or receipt is recorded ('recorded delivery') to the party's usual address (or, if the party's usual address is not in the United Kingdom, the party's UK contact address),

(d) sent by ordinary first or second class postal service ('ordinary post') to the party's usual address (or, if the party's usual address is not in the United Kingdom, the party's UK contact address),

(e) sent by recorded delivery to the party's representative,

(f) sent by ordinary post to the party's representative,

(g) sent by email to the party or the party's representative,

(h) sent by document exchange to the party's or the party's representative's document exchange number or address,

(i) sent by courier to the party's usual address (or, if the party's usual address is not in the United Kingdom, the party's UK contact address),

(j) sent by courier to the party's representative.

(3) But a notice may not be given under sub-paragraph (b), (g) or (h) of paragraph (2) unless a fax number, or (as the case may be) email address or document exchange number or address, has been provided by the party or the party's representative for that purpose.

(4) Where—

(a) both parties to a proposed marriage or civil partnership have the same usual address (or if that usual address is not in the United Kingdom, the same UK contact address) or the same representative, and

(b) the Secretary of State is required to give notice to both parties at the same time under a provision mentioned in paragraph (1),

the notices may be included in the same envelope addressed to both parties and sent to that address or that representative in accordance with sub-paragraphs (c) to (f) or (h) to (j) of paragraph (2).

(5) In sub-paragraphs (c), (d) and (i) of paragraph (2) and in paragraph (4), a reference to a party's—

(a) 'usual address' is a reference to that party's usual address notified in accordance with—

(i) section 27E(7) or 28C(6) or regulations made under section 28D of the 1949 Act, or

(ii) section 8A(7) or 9A(6) or regulations made under section 9B of the 2004 Act;

(b) 'UK contact address' is a reference to that party's UK contact address notified in accordance with—

(i) section 27E(7) or 28C(6) or regulations made under section 28D of the 1949 Act, or

(ii) section 8A(7) or 9A(6) or regulations made under section 9B of the 2004 Act.

(6) In this regulation [. . .] a reference to a party's 'representative' is a reference to a representative authorised by the party to accept notice given in accordance with this regulation on the party's behalf.

Note: Words omitted from 14 September 2016 by correction slip.

Notices given by the Secretary of State to superintendent registrars and registration authorities

6.—(1) This regulation applies to a notice required to be given by the Secretary of State to a superintendent registrar under—

(a) Part 4 of the 2014 Act,

(b) section 31(5EB) of the 1949 Act, or

(c) paragraph 2 of Schedule 3A to the 1949 Act (referred marriages: no certificate to be issued until decision about investigation).

(2) This regulation also applies to a notice required to be given by the Secretary of State to a registration authority under—

(a) Part 4 of the 2014 Act,

(b) section 12(5) of the 2004 Act, or

(c) paragraph 2 of Schedule 3A to the 2004 Act (referred civil partnerships: no civil partnership schedule to be issued until decision about investigation).

(3) A notice to which this regulation applies may be—

(a) given by hand,

(b) sent by email to an email address notified for that purpose,

(c) otherwise transmitted electronically in an agreed form,

(d) sent by postal service in which delivery or receipt is recorded to an address notified for that purpose ('the notified address'),

(e) sent by ordinary first or second class postal service to the notified address,

(f) sent by courier to the notified address.

(4) In paragraph (3)—

'agreed' means agreed between the superintendent registrar or (as the case may be) the registration authority and the Secretary of State,

'notified' means notified to the Secretary of State by the superintendent registrar or (as the case may be) the registration authority.

Presumptions about receipt of notice

7.—(1) Where a notice is given in accordance with regulation 5 or 6, it is presumed to have been received by the person to whom it is given (unless the contrary is proved)—

(a) where the notice is sent by postal service in which delivery or receipt is recorded, on the second day after it was sent by postal service;

(b) where the notice is sent by ordinary first or second class postal service, in the ordinary course of post;

(c) where the notice is sent by document exchange, on the next working day after the day on which it was sent;

(d) where the notice is given by hand or sent by fax, email or courier, on the day it was given or (as the case may be) sent; and

(e) where the notice is transmitted electronically under paragraph (3)(c) of regulation 6, on the day after the day on which it was transmitted.

(2) For the purposes of paragraph (1)(a) and (b) the day on which a notice is presumed to have been received is to be calculated—

(a) excluding the day on which the notice is posted; and

(b) excluding any day which is not a working day.

(3) In this regulation 'working day' means any day other than a Saturday, a Sunday, Christmas Day, Good Friday or a day which is a bank holiday under the Banking and Financial Dealings Act 1971 in the part of the United Kingdom to which the notice is sent.

The Proposed Marriages and Civil Partnerships (Conduct of Investigations, etc.) Regulations 2015

(SI 2015, No. 397)

Part I
General

Citation and commencement

1.—(1) These Regulations may be cited as the Proposed Marriages and Civil Partnerships (Conduct of Investigations, etc.) Regulations 2015.

(2) They come into force on 1st March 2015.

Interpretation

2.—(1) In these Regulations—

'2014 Act' means the Immigration Act 2014;

'bank holiday' means a day which is a bank holiday under the Banking and Financial Dealings Act 1971 in the part of the United Kingdom in which a relevant party is resident, unless a relevant party is not resident in the United Kingdom in which case it means a day which is a bank holiday under that Act in any part of the United Kingdom;

'detained' means detained—

(a) under the Immigration Act 1971, under section 62 of the Nationality, Immigration and Asylum Act 2002 or under section 36 of the UK Borders Act 2007, or

(b) in a prison or other place to which the Prison Act 1952, the Prisons (Scotland) Act 1989 or the Prisons Act (Northern Ireland) 1953 applies;

'Home Office premises' means—

(a) in relation to premises in the United Kingdom, premises used by Home Office staff for the purposes of Home Office business, and

(b) in relation to premises outside the United Kingdom, premises used by Home Office staff or [Foreign, Commonwealth and Development Office] staff for the purposes of Home Office business,

whether or not those premises are also used for other purposes;

'normal office hours', in relation to when an interview may take place means—

(a) where a relevant party is in the United Kingdom, the hours between 9.00 am and 6.00 pm on a working day,

(b) where a relevant party is in a country or territory outside the United Kingdom, such hours as are normally regarded as normal office hours on a day which is normally regarded as a working day in that country or territory;

'specified requirement' has the meaning given by regulation 14;

'working day' (other than in paragraph (b) of the definition of 'normal office hours') means a day other than a Saturday, a Sunday, Good Friday, Christmas day or a bank holiday.

(2) In these Regulations a reference to evidence, where that is in the form of a document, means (subject to paragraph (3) and regulation 12(6)(d)) the original document, and 'document' means anything in which information of any description is recorded or stored.

(3) Where the document is an electronic document, it means the record which is accessible to the relevant party whether on a mobile device, other handheld device or personal computer.

Note: Words substituted in definition of 'Home Office premises' from 30 September 2020 (SI 2020/942).

PART 2
INVESTIGATIONS

Introduction

3.—(1) An investigation must be conducted in accordance with these Regulations.

(2) When carrying out an investigation the Secretary of State may make such enquiries as the Secretary of State thinks fit for the purpose of determining whether a proposed marriage or civil partnership is a sham.

(3) Without prejudice to the generality of paragraph (2), as part of an investigation a relevant party may be required to provide information or evidence about, in particular—

(a) himself or herself (including his or her identity);
(b) the other relevant party;
(c) his or her relationship with the other relevant party;
(d) his or her living arrangements and those of the other relevant party;
(e) his or her future plans and those of the other relevant party.

Interviews: general

4.—(1) This regulation applies to interviews conducted by the Secretary of State in accordance with regulations 6 to 10.

(2) As part of an investigation the Secretary of State may require a relevant party to be interviewed.

(3) The Secretary of State may require a relevant party to be interviewed on his or her own, together with the other relevant party, or both.

(4) The Secretary of State may require an interview with a relevant party to take place—

(a) where a relevant party is in the United Kingdom—

(i) in person at the relevant party's home;

(ii) in person at the other relevant party's home (if different);

(iii) in person at Home Office premises;

(iv) by telephone, by video-telecommunications link or over the internet (where the relevant party must be present at Home Office premises);

(v) by telephone, by video-telecommunications link or over the internet (where the relevant party may be elsewhere);

(b) where a relevant party is outside the United Kingdom—

(i) in person at Home Office premises;

(ii) by telephone, by video-telecommunications link or over the internet (where the relevant party must be present at Home Office premises);

(iii) by telephone, by video-telecommunications link or over the internet (where the relevant party may be elsewhere).

(5) A relevant party may also be required to attend an interview while he or she is detained.

(6) A relevant party may be required to attend more than one interview.

(7) Unless paragraph (8) or (9) applies, an interview must take place during normal office hours.

(8) This paragraph applies where a relevant party (or, as the case may be, both relevant parties) agrees that an interview may take place outside normal office hours.

(9) This paragraph applies where an interview is commenced and has been substantially completed during normal office hours.

(10) Where paragraph (9) applies, the interview may continue outside normal office hours.

(11) A relevant party may be accompanied at an interview by an appropriate legal representative.

(12) A relevant party may also be accompanied at an interview by an interpreter (appointed by the relevant party).

(13) A relevant party may not be accompanied at an interview by a person other than those mentioned in paragraphs (11) and (12) without the Secretary of State's consent.

(14) The Secretary of State must make a written record of an interview ('the record').

(15) The record must be completed during the interview and must constitute—

(a) a verbatim account of what has been said, or

(b) an account of the interview which adequately summarises it.

(16) The record must be signed and dated by the person who made it.

(17) If a relevant party requests one, the Secretary of State must provide him or her with a copy of that record.

(18) In this regulation 'appropriate legal representative' means a legal representative who is a qualified person within the meaning of section 82 of the Immigration and Asylum Act 1999.

Arranging an interview

5.—(1) A relevant party may be required to contact the Secretary of State to arrange an interview.

(2) A relevant party may be required to contact the Secretary of State by—

(a) telephoning the telephone number;

(b) sending a text message to the telephone number;

(c) sending an email to the Home Office or [Foreign, Commonwealth and Development Office] email address; or

(d) writing to the address,

specified in the section 48 notice or in any subsequent notification as mentioned in section 50(3) of the 2014 Act ('the notification').

(3) A relevant party may be required to contact the Secretary of State within the time period specified in the section 48 notice or in the notification (which may not be less than a period of three working days beginning with the day on which the notice or the notification is given).

(4) A relevant party who contacts the Secretary of State in accordance with this regulation must make himself or herself reasonably available so that a date and time, being a date no later than the date specified in the section 48 notice or in the notification, can be agreed for an interview to take place.

(5) Where an interview is to take place with a relevant party and the other relevant party, the relevant party may also be required to agree the date and time mentioned in paragraph (4), so far as practicable, on behalf of the other relevant party.

Note: Words substituted in paragraph (2)(c) from 30 September 2020 (SI 2020/942).

Interviews at a relevant party's home

6.—(1) This regulation applies where a relevant party is required to attend an interview at his or her home or at the other relevant party's home (if different).

(2) Subject to paragraphs (3) and (4), a relevant party must be given at least three working days written notice of the date, place and time of the interview.

(3) A relevant party (or, as the case may be, both relevant parties) may agree to an interview taking place with less than three working days notice.

(4) The notice mentioned in paragraph (3) need not be in writing.

(5) During an interview the Secretary of State may make observations about, and ask a relevant party about, his or her living arrangements, or, as the case may be, those of the other relevant party.

(6) A record of those observations and any response to them given by a relevant party must be recorded in writing and signed and dated by the person who made it.

(7) Where a relevant party and the other relevant party claim to cohabit, the Secretary of State may ask to see reasonable evidence of their cohabitation.

(8) A record of that evidence must be recorded in writing and signed and dated by the person who made it.

(9) If a relevant party requests one, the Secretary of State must provide him or her with a copy of the record mentioned in paragraph (6), or, as the case may be, paragraph (8).

(10) An interview under this regulation may not proceed unless at least two persons on behalf of the Secretary of State are present.

Interviews at Home Office premises in the United Kingdom

7.—(1) This regulation applies where a relevant party is required to attend an interview at Home Office premises in the United Kingdom whether that interview is to take place in person, by telephone, by video-telecommunications link or over the internet.

(2) Subject to paragraphs (3) and (4), a relevant party must be given at least three working days written notice of the date, place and time of the interview and how it is to be conducted.

(3) A relevant party (or, as the case may be, both relevant parties) may agree to an interview taking place with less than three working days notice.

(4) The notice mentioned in paragraph (3) need not be in writing.

(5) In this regulation and regulation 8 a reference to how an interview is to be conducted is a reference to whether—

(a) it is to be conducted in person, by telephone, by video-telecommunications link or over the internet; and

(b) where it is to be conducted by telephone, by video-telecommunications link or over the internet, it is to be two-way (that is to say, with just the relevant party) or three-way (with both the relevant party and the other relevant party), or both.

Interviews at Home Office premises outside the United Kingdom

8.—(1) This regulation applies where a relevant party is required to attend an interview at Home Office premises outside the United Kingdom whether that interview is to take place in person, by telephone, by video-telecommunications link or over the internet.

(2) A relevant party may be required to attend an interview at Home Office premises outside the United Kingdom where—

(a) the relevant party is resident outside the United Kingdom; and

(b) those Home Office premises are located within a reasonable travelling distance of the relevant party's place of residence (whether or not they are in the same country or territory).

(3) Subject to paragraphs (4) and (5), a relevant party must be given at least three working days written notice of the date, place and time of the interview and how it is to be conducted.

(4) A relevant party (or, as the case may be, both relevant parties) may agree to the interview taking place with less than three working days notice.

(5) The notice mentioned in paragraph (4) need not be in writing.

Interviews by telephone, etc.

9.—(1) This regulation applies where a relevant party (whether in or outside the United Kingdom) is required to attend an interview by telephone, by video-telecommunications link or over the internet (but is not required to be present at Home Office premises).

(2) Subject to paragraphs (3) and (4), a relevant party must be given at least three working days written notice of the date and time of the interview and how it is to be conducted.

(3) A relevant party (or, as the case may be, both relevant parties) may agree to the interview taking place with less than three working days notice.

(4) The notice mentioned in paragraph (3) need not be in writing.

(5) At the start of the interview—

(a) the person conducting it must identify himself or herself (and anyone accompanying him or her) by reference to his or her name, position and place of work; and

(b) the relevant party (and, as the case may be, the other relevant party) must confirm his or her identity by reference to his or her name, date of birth and nationality and to the Home Office reference on the section 48 notice given to him or her.

(6) Where the relevant party (or the other relevant party) is unable to confirm his or her identity as required by paragraph (5)(b), the Secretary of State may decide—

(a) where the Secretary of State is otherwise satisfied that it is the relevant party (or, as the case may be, the other relevant party), to continue with the interview;

(b) to rearrange the interview in accordance with this regulation or with regulation 6 or 7 (or, as the case may be, 8); or

(c) that the relevant party (or, as the case may be, the other relevant party) has failed to comply with a specified requirement (see regulation 14).

(7) In paragraph (2)—

(a) the 'time' of an interview means the 30 minute period within which an interview may start; and

(b) a reference to how an interview is to be conducted is a reference to whether it is to be—

(i) conducted by telephone, by video-telecommunications link or over the internet; and

(ii) two-way (that is to say, with just the relevant party) or three-way (with both the relevant party and the other relevant party), or both.

Interviews while detained

10.—(1) This regulation applies where a relevant party is required to attend an interview while he or she is detained.

(2) Subject to paragraphs (3) and (4), a relevant party must be given at least three working days written notice of the date and time of the interview and how it is to be conducted.

(3) A relevant party may agree to an interview taking place with less than three working days notice.

(4) The notice mentioned in paragraph (3) need not be in writing.

(5) An interview may take place in person or by telephone; and a reference in this regulation to how an interview is to be conducted is a reference to whether it is to take place in person or by telephone.

(6) Subject to paragraph (7), regulations 7 and 9 do not apply where a relevant party is required to attend an interview under this regulation.

(7) Where a relevant party is interviewed by telephone—

(a) paragraph (5) of regulation 9 applies as if the words '(and, as the case may be, the other relevant party)' in sub-paragraph (b) were omitted; and

(b) paragraph (6) of that regulation applies as if—

(i) the words '(or the other relevant party)';

(ii) the words '(or, as the case may be, the other relevant party)' in sub-paragraph (a);

(iii) the words from 'or with' to the end in sub-paragraph (b); and

(iv) the words '(or, as the case may be, the other relevant party)' in sub-paragraph (c),

were omitted.

Rearranging an interview

11.—(1) Where a relevant party is required to attend an interview in accordance with regulations 6 to 10 and the date or time for that interview is not (or where it was arranged in accordance with regulation 5, no longer) convenient for the relevant party or, as the case may be, the other relevant party, the Secretary of State may agree to rearrange the interview.

(2) Where the Secretary of State agrees to rearrange an interview the relevant party may be given less than three working days written notice of the rearranged interview (but, subject to paragraph (3), not less than 24 hours).

(3) A relevant party (or, as the case may be, both relevant parties) may agree to a rearranged interview taking place with less than 24 hours notice.

(4) The notice mentioned in paragraphs (2) and (3) need not be in writing.

Requirement to provide information, evidence or photographs

12.—(1) The Secretary of State may require a relevant party to provide information, evidence or photographs in accordance with this regulation.

(2) A relevant party may be required to provide information, evidence or photographs before, during or after an interview.

(3) But a requirement to provide information, evidence or photographs may also be imposed whether or not an interview is to take place or has taken place.

(4) Unless it is made at an interview, a requirement to provide information must be made in writing.

(5) A requirement to provide evidence or photographs must be imposed, or where it is made at an interview, followed up, in writing.

(6) Where a requirement to provide information, evidence or photographs is imposed, or as the case may be, followed up, in writing, it must—

(a) include a description of the information, evidence or photographs that must be provided;

(b) set out how the information, evidence or photographs must be provided, whether by sending the information, evidence or photographs to the Secretary of State or providing the information, evidence or photographs at an interview;

(c) where the information, evidence or photographs is or are to be sent to the Secretary of State, include the address to which the information, evidence or photographs must be sent and the date by which the information, evidence or photographs must be received by the Secretary of State; and

(d) where the evidence is in the form of a document—

(i) set out the circumstances in which a certified translation must also be provided; and

(ii) set out the circumstances in which a certified copy may be provided.

(7) In this regulation—

(a) in paragraph (6)(c), 'address' includes, where appropriate, an email address;

(b) 'certified translation' means a translation of the document provided which—

(i) is certified as a true and accurate translation by the person who translated it;

(ii) is signed and dated by that person; and

(iii) states his or her name and contact details;

(c) 'certified copy' means a copy of the original document which—

(i) is certified as a true copy of the original;

(ii) is signed and dated by the person who certifies it; and

(iii) states that person's name, contact details and position or occupation.

(8) A document may not be certified by a person who is—

(a) a family member of the relevant party or the other relevant party;

(b) a person who lives with the relevant party or the other relevant party; or

(c) the other relevant party.

Further provision about electronic documents

13.—(1) A relevant party may be required to provide evidence in the form of an electronic document by—

(a) showing it, during an interview, to the Secretary of State who may—

(i) make a note of its contents in the record mentioned in regulation 4;

(ii) photograph it;

(iii) request a 'screenshot' of the document; or

(b) where it is an email (or included in an email), forwarding it to a Home Office or [Foreign, Commonwealth and Development Office] email account.

Note: Words substituted in paragraph (1)(b) from 30 September 2020 (SI 2020/942).

Part 3
Specified requirements

14. The following are specified requirements for the purposes of section 51(4) of the 2014 Act—

(a) the requirement to arrange an interview in accordance with regulation 5;

(b) the requirement to attend an interview and be interviewed in accordance with regulations 4, and 6 to 10;

(c) the requirement to provide confirmation of identity in accordance with regulation 9(5)(b);

(d) the requirement to provide information, evidence or photographs in accordance with regulation 12 or 13.

Part 4
Compliance question

Notifying a relevant party that he or she has failed to comply with a specified or other relevant requirement

15.—(1) This regulation applies where the Secretary of State believes a relevant party has failed to comply with a specified or any other relevant requirement ('a requirement').

(2) The Secretary of State may give notice in writing to the relevant party—

(a) stating that the Secretary of State believes the relevant party has failed to comply with a requirement,

(b) giving the reasons for that belief, and

(c) requiring the relevant party to contact the Secretary of State within the period stated (which may not be less than a period of three working days beginning with the day on which the notice is given) with a view to complying with that (and any other) requirement.

(3) If a notice under paragraph (2) is given, it must include relevant contact details and may require the relevant party to make contact by telephone.

Failure to comply with a specified requirement

16. For the avoidance of doubt—

(a) where a relevant party is required to attend an interview and be interviewed in accordance with regulations 4, and 6 to 10, a failure to respond to questions asked during such an interview (or a refusal to answer any further questions thereby bringing the interview to an end) may be regarded as a failure to comply with the requirement to be interviewed;

(b) where a relevant party is required to attend an interview by telephone, a failure, so far as practicable, to keep the telephone line free during the time notified for the interview may be regarded as a failure to comply with that requirement.

Deciding the compliance question

17.—(1) The Secretary of State must decide the compliance question in accordance with this regulation.

(2) The Secretary of State may decide that a relevant party who fails, without reasonable excuse, to comply with a relevant requirement has not complied with the investigation.

(3) The Secretary of State may decide that a relevant party who fails, without reasonable excuse, to contact the Secretary of State following receipt of a notice given under regulation 15(2) has not complied with the investigation.

(4) Where a relevant party is removed from the United Kingdom after he or she has been given a section 48 notice but before the compliance question has been decided, the Secretary of State may decide that the relevant party has complied with the investigation.

(5) Where a relevant party leaves the United Kingdom in accordance with—

(a) section 5(6) of the Immigration Act 1971 (procedure for, and further provision as to, deportation);

(b) arrangements made by the Secretary of State under section 58 of the Nationality, Immigration and Asylum Act 2002 (voluntary departure from the United Kingdom) ('the Act') to assist voluntary leavers; or

(c) a project participated in by the Secretary of State under section 59 of the Act (international projects),

after he or she has been given a section 48 notice but before the compliance question has been decided, the Secretary of State may decide that the relevant party has complied with the investigation.

(6) Where the Secretary of State decides that a relevant party mentioned in paragraph (4) or (5) has complied with the investigation, the Secretary of State may also decide that the other relevant party has complied with the investigation.

(7) In this regulation 'removed from the United Kingdom' means removed in accordance with directions given by an immigration officer or the Secretary of State under the Immigration Acts.

PART 5

SECTION 48 NOTICE

Prescribed information about the investigation

18.—(1) The information prescribed for the purposes of section 51(1)(d) of the 2014 Act ('section 51(1)(d) purposes') is a statement—

(a) that the Secretary of State may decide that a relevant party who has failed, without reasonable excuse, to comply with a relevant requirement has not complied with the investigation;

(b) that, where the Secretary of State decides that a relevant party has, or (as the case may be) both relevant parties have, failed to comply with the investigation and gives notice of that decision within the 70 day period in accordance with section 50(7) of the 2014 Act, the proposed marriage or, as the case may be, civil partnership may not proceed (and the relevant parties must give fresh notice of their intention to marry or register their civil partnership if they wish it to do so);

(c) that, in a case where the Secretary of State determines that a proposed marriage or civil partnership is a sham, the Secretary of State or an immigration officer may take immigration enforcement action in relation to a relevant party or, as the case may be, both relevant parties;

(d) that, in a case where a proposed marriage or civil partnership which is or was the subject of an investigation proceeds and the Secretary of State subsequently determines that it is a sham, the Secretary of State or an immigration officer may take immigration enforcement action in relation to a relevant party or, as the case may be, both relevant parties;

(e) that, without prejudice to the refusal of an application for entry clearance, limited leave, [or indefinite leave] made on any other basis, in a case where the Secretary of State determines that a proposed marriage or civil partnership is a sham, the Secretary of State may refuse an application which is based upon a relevant party's relationship with the other relevant party;

(f) that, without prejudice to the refusal of an application for entry clearance, limited leave, [or indefinite leave] made on any other basis, in a case where a proposed marriage or civil partnership which is or was the subject of an investigation proceeds and the Secretary of State subsequently determines that it is a sham, the Secretary of State may refuse an application which is based upon a relevant party's relationship with the other relevant party.

(2) In the case of information prescribed in sub-paragraphs (d) to (f) of paragraph (1), the following additional information is prescribed for section 51(1)(d) purposes—

(a) as respects information prescribed in sub-paragraphs (d) and (f), the additional information that a reference to a marriage or civil partnership being a sham is a reference to it being a sham within the meaning of section 24 or 24A of the Immigration and Asylum Act 1999;

(b) as respects information prescribed in sub-paragraphs (e) and (f), the additional information that—

(i) 'entry clearance', 'limited leave' and 'indefinite leave' have the same meanings as in section 33 of the Immigration Act 1971;

[(ii) ...]

[(3) For the purposes of paragraph (2)(b)(ii) 'retained enforceable EU right' means a right that—

(a) was created or arose by or under the EU Treaties before the time when this paragraph comes into force; and

(b) forms part of retained EU law by virtue of section 3 or 4 of the European Union (Withdrawal) Act 2018, as that right is modified from time to time.]

Note: Paragraph (3) inserted from 31 December 2020 (SI 2019/745). Words in paragraphs (1)(e) and (f) substituted and paragraph (2)(b)(ii) omitted from 1 July 2021 (SI 2020/1309).

The Modern Slavery Act 2015 (Duty to Notify) Regulations 2015

(SI 2015, No. 1743)

Citation and commencement

1.—(1) These Regulations may be cited as the Modern Slavery Act 2015 (Duty to Notify) Regulations 2015.

(2) These Regulations come into force on 1st November 2015.

Interpretation

2. In these Regulations—

'the Act' means the Modern Slavery Act 2015;

'human trafficking' means—

(a) conduct which constitutes an offence under section 2 of the Act, or would constitute an offence under that section if the person responsible for the conduct were a UK national, or

(b) conduct which would have been within paragraph (a) if section 2 had been in force when the conduct occurred;

'notification' means a notification made under section 52(1) of the Act;

'public authority' means a public authority to which section 52 of the Act applies;

'slavery' means—

(a) conduct which constitutes an offence under section 1 of the Act; or

(b) conduct which would have constituted an offence under that section if that section had been in force when the conduct occurred;

'victim' means a person whom a public authority has reasonable grounds to believe may be a victim of slavery or human trafficking.

Information to be included in a notification

3.—(1) Subject to [paragraph (2), as read with paragraph (2A), and paragraph (4)], a notification must include the information specified in Schedules 1 and 2 to these Regulations where such information is in the possession or control of the public authority.

(2) A notification relating to a [victim] aged 18 or over may not include information specified in Schedule 2 or information that—

(a) identifies the [victim], or

(b) enables the [victim] to be identified (either by itself or in combination with other information), unless the [victim] consents to the inclusion of the information.

[(2A) Nothing in paragraph (2) shall be read as requiring the consent of any person in paragraph 4 of Schedule 2 whom the public authority believes may also have been the victim of slavery or human trafficking by the same perpetrator.]

(3) A public authority which includes information in a notification in accordance with these Regulations does not breach any obligation of confidence owed by the public authority in relation to that information.

(4) Nothing in these Regulations requires or authorises the inclusion of information which contravenes any other restriction on the disclosure of information (however imposed).

Note: Words in square brackets in paragraphs (1) and (2) substituted and paragraph (2A) inserted from 10 August 2016 (SI 2016/762).

Schedule 1

Regulation 3(1)

Information to be included in a notification

1. The name of the public authority making the notification.

2. The victim's gender.

3. The victim's nationality.

4. Whether the victim was under the age of 18 at the time the public authority believes the slavery or human trafficking first occurred.

5. Whether the public authority believes that the person may be a victim of slavery.

6. Whether the public authority believes that the person may be a victim of human trafficking.

7. The country or territory where the public authority believes the slavery or human trafficking occurred.

8.—(1) Whether the public authority has referred the suspected slavery or human trafficking of the victim to—

(a) a chief officer of police for a police area in England and Wales;

(b) the chief constable of the Police Service of Scotland; or

(c) the chief constable of the Police Service of Northern Ireland.

(2) Where the public authority has referred the suspected slavery or human trafficking to a chief officer of police for a police area in England and Wales, [. . .] the name of the police area [. . .].

9. The police area in which the victim has been identified.

10. Where the public authority believes that the person may be a victim of slavery, whether the public authority believes the slavery—

(a) occurred wholly or partly within residential premises;

(b) involved conduct described at section 3(2) of the Act (slavery, servitude and forced or compulsory labour);

(c) involved conduct described at section 3(3) of the Act (sexual exploitation); or

(d) involved the commission of an offence by the victim.

11. Where the public authority believes that the person may be a victim of human trafficking, whether the public authority believes the human trafficking—

(a) occurred wholly or partly within residential premises;

(b) involved conduct described at section 3(2) of the Act (slavery, servitude and forced or compulsory labour);

(c) involved conduct described at section 3(3) of the Act (sexual exploitation);

(d) involved conduct described at section 3(4) of the Act (removal of organs etc); or

(e) involved the commission of an offence by the victim.

Note: Words in paragraph 8(2) omitted from 10 August 2016 (SI 2016/762).

SCHEDULE 2

REGULATION 3(1)

Further information to be included in a notification relating to a victim under the age of 18 or by consent

1. The victim's name.

2. The victim's date of birth.

3. The names of persons whom the public authority believes may have perpetrated the suspected slavery or human trafficking of the victim.

4. The names of persons whom the public authority believes may also have been victims of slavery or human trafficking by the same perpetrators.

The Immigration Act 2016 (Transitional Provision) Regulations 2016

(SI 2016, No. 712 made 5 July 2016)

Citation

1. These Regulations may be cited as the Immigration Act 2016 (Transitional Provision) Regulations 2016.

Offence of illegal working: transitional provision

2. Where a person is at large in the United Kingdom by virtue of paragraph 21(1) of Schedule 2 to the Immigration Act 1971 (temporary admission or release from detention)—

(a) the person is to be treated for the purposes of section 24B(2) of the Immigration Act 1971 as if the person had been granted leave to enter the United Kingdom, but

(b) any restriction as to employment imposed under paragraph 21(2) is to be treated for those purposes as a condition of leave.

The Modern Slavery Act 2015 (Code of Practice) Regulations 2016

(SI 2016, No. 823)

TEXT NOT REPRODUCED

Note: The code of practice issued under paragraph 5(1) of Schedule 2 to the Modern Slavery Act 2015 (code of practice on the exercise of powers of arrest under paragraph 4 of that Schedule) came into operation on 8 August 2016 (regulation 2 of SI 2016/823).

The Immigration (Variation of Leave) Order 2016

(SI 2016, No. 948)

Citation and commencement

1. This Order may be cited as the Immigration (Variation of Leave) Order 2016 and comes into force on 6th October 2016.

Interpretation

2. In this Order—

'competent authority' means a person who is a competent authority of the United Kingdom for the purposes of the Trafficking Convention;

'overseas domestic worker' means a person who, under the immigration rules, has leave to enter the United Kingdom as—

(a) a domestic worker in a private household, or

(b) a private servant in a diplomatic household;

'Trafficking Convention' means the Council of Europe Convention on Action against Trafficking in Human Beings (agreed at Warsaw on 16 May 2005);

'victim of modern slavery' means a victim of—

(a) trafficking in human beings, which has the same meaning as provided in article 4 of the Trafficking Convention; or

(b) slavery, servitude, or forced or compulsory labour, which have the same meanings as they have for the purposes of article 4 of the Convention for the Protection of Human Rights and Fundamental Freedoms (agreed by the Council of Europe at Rome on 4 November 1950).

Variation of limited leave to enter the United Kingdom

3. Where—

(a) a competent authority has determined or determines that there are reasonable grounds to believe that an overseas domestic worker ('P') is a victim of modern slavery, and

(b) P's leave would otherwise expire before the competent authority notifies P of its conclusive decision as to whether P is a victim of modern slavery, then P's leave is extended until the end of the twenty-eighth day after the date on which the competent authority sends P notice in writing of its conclusive decision as to whether P is a victim of modern slavery.

The Illegal Working Compliance Orders Regulations 2016

(SI 2016, No. 1058)

Citation and commencement

1.—(1) These Regulations may be cited as the Illegal Working Compliance Orders Regulations 2016.

(2) These Regulations come into force on 1st December 2016.

Interpretation

2. In these Regulations—

'administrative review' means review conducted under the immigration rules;

'biometric immigration document' has the same meaning as in section 5 of the UK Borders Act 2007;

'derivative right of residence' has the same meaning as in regulation 15A of the Immigration (European Economic Area) Regulations 2006;

'document' means an original document;

['employee', except in regulations 4(2), 4(3), 5A(2) and 5A(3), includes a reference to a prospective employee;]

['Home Office online right to work checking service' means the electronic system allowing employers to check whether a person is allowed to work in the United Kingdom and, if so, the nature of any restrictions on that person's right to do so.]

'immigration rules' has the same meaning as in section 33 of the Immigration Act 1971;

['online right to work check' means the response generated by the Home Office online right to work checking service in relation to a person;']

'Positive Verification Notice' means a document issued by the Home Office Employer Checking Service which indicates that the person named in it is allowed to stay in the United Kingdom and is allowed to do the work in question;

'registration certificate' means a certificate issued to a national of an EEA state or Switzerland as proof of the holder's right of residence in the United Kingdom as at the date of issue;

'relevant person' means a person required to comply with these Regulations by virtue of an illegal working compliance order;

'residence card' means a card issued to a person who is not a national of an EEA state or Switzerland as proof of the holder's right of residence in the United Kingdom as at the date of issue.

Note: Definition of 'employee' substituted and definitions of 'online right to work check' and 'Home Office online right to work checking service' inserted from 28 January 2019 (SI 2018/1340).

Obligation to conduct right to work checks

3. Where an illegal working compliance order requires a person to carry out checks relating to the right to work in accordance with these Regulations, the person must comply with [any of regulations 4, 5 or 5A] in respect of each of their employees within the scope of the order.

Note: Words substituted from 28 January 2019 (SI 2018/1340).

Right to work checks: prescribed documents

4.—(1) A relevant person must—

(a) require the employee to produce to them a document or combination of documents relating to the employee described in Schedule 1 or 2; and

(b) comply with the requirements in regulation 6.

(2) Where a document or combination of documents described in Schedule 2 provides that the employment is permitted for a limited period, a relevant person is deemed to comply with this regulation for a further period if the relevant person is satisfied on reasonable grounds that—

(a) the employee has an outstanding application to vary his or her leave to enter or remain in the United Kingdom; or

(b) the employee has an appeal or administrative review pending against a decision on that application.

(3) In paragraph (2), the further period begins on the date on which the limited period expires and ends—

(a) after 28 days; or

(b) if earlier, on the date on which the Secretary of State gives the relevant person written notice that the employee does not have the right to undertake the employment in question.

Right to work checks: Positive Verification Notice

5.—(1) A relevant person must—

(a) obtain a Positive Verification Notice in respect of the employee (subject to paragraph (2)); and

(b) comply, if applicable, with the requirement in regulation 6(2).

(2) A relevant person does not comply with this regulation if a period of more than six months has elapsed beginning with the date the Positive Verification Notice was obtained under paragraph (1)(a).

[Right to work checks: Home Office online right to work checking service

5A.—(1) A relevant person must—

(a) use the Home Office online right to work checking service in respect of an employee;

(b) obtain an online right to work check confirming that the employee named in it is allowed to work in the United Kingdom and is allowed to do the work in question;

(c) be satisfied that any photograph on the online right to work check is of the employee;

(d) retain a clear copy of the online right to work check for a period of not less than two years after the employment has come to an end; and

(e) comply, if applicable, with the requirement in regulation 6(2).

(2) Where the online right to work check provides that the employment is permitted for a limited period, a relevant person is deemed to comply with this regulation for a further period if the relevant person is satisfied on reasonable grounds that—

(a) the employee has an outstanding application to vary his or her leave to enter or remain in the United Kingdom; or

(b) the employee has an appeal or administrative review pending against a decision on that application.

(3) In paragraph (2), the further period begins on the date on which the limited period expires and ends—

(a) after 28 days; or

(b) if earlier, on the date on which the Secretary of State gives the relevant person written notice that the employee does not have the right to undertake the employment in question.]

Note: Regulation 5A inserted from 28 January 2019 (SI 2018/1340).

Right to work checks: general requirements

6.—(1) The requirements of this regulation are that—

(a) the relevant person takes all reasonable steps to check the validity of the document and retains a record of the date on which any check was made;

(b) a [clear] copy of that document or combination of documents is retained securely by the relevant person for the period during which the illegal working compliance order is in force;

(c) if a document contains a photograph purporting to be of the employee, the relevant person has satisfied himself that the photograph is of the employee;

(d) if a document contains a date of birth purporting to relate to the employee, the relevant person has satisfied himself that the date of birth is consistent with the appearance of the employee;

(e) the relevant person takes all other reasonable steps to verify that the employee is the rightful holder of the document;

(f) if the document is not a passport, the relevant person retains a [clear] copy of the whole of the document;

(g) if the document is a passport, the relevant person retains a [clear] copy of the following pages of that document—

(i) any page containing the holder's personal details including nationality;

(ii) any page containing the holder's photograph;

(iii) any page containing the holder's signature;

(iv) any page containing the date of expiry; and

(v) any page containing information indicating the holder has an entitlement to enter or remain in the United Kingdom and undertake the work in question.

(2) A further requirement, if the employee is a student who has permission to work for a limited number of hours per week during term time whilst studying in the United Kingdom, is that the relevant person must—

(a) require the employee to provide details of the term and vacation dates of the course that the employee is undertaking; and

(b) retain a record of these details.

Note: word inserted in sub-paragraphs (b), (f) and (g) from 28 January 2019 (SI 2018/1340).

Obligation to produce documents to an immigration officer

7. Where an illegal working compliance order requires a person to produce documents relating to the right to work to an immigration officer in accordance with these Regulations, the person must comply with [any of regulations 8, 9 or 9A] in respect each of their employees within the scope of the order.

Note: Words substituted from 28 January 2019 (SI 2018/1340).

Documents to be produced to an immigration officer: general

8.—(1) A relevant person must produce—

(a) a [clear] copy of a document or a [clear] copy of a combination of documents relating to the employee described in Schedule 1 or 2 in accordance with paragraphs (2) and (3); and

(b) if the employee is a student who has permission to work for a limited number of hours per week during term time whilst studying in the United Kingdom, a document or [clear] copy of a document which records the details of the term and vacation dates of the course that the employee is undertaking.

(2) In respect of a passport, the relevant person must produce a[clear] copy of the following pages of that document—

(a) any page containing the holder's personal details including nationality;

(b) any page containing the holder's photograph;

(c) any page containing the holder's signature;

(d) any page containing the date of expiry; and

(e) any page containing information indicating the holder has an entitlement to enter or remain in the United Kingdom and undertake the work in question.

(3) In respect of a document which is not a passport, the relevant person must produce a [clear] copy of the whole of the document.

Note: Word in square bracket inserted from 28 January 2019 (SI 2018/1340).

Documents to be produced to an immigration officer: Positive Verification Notice

9. A relevant person must produce—

(a) a Positive Verification Notice which has been obtained in respect of the employee within the preceding period of six months from the date on which it is produced to an immigration officer; and

(b) if the employee is a student who has permission to work for a limited number of hours per week during term time whilst studying in the United Kingdom, a document or copy of a document which records the details of the term and vacation dates of the course that the employee is undertaking.

[Documents to be produced to an immigration officer: Home Office online right to work checking service

9A.—A relevant person must produce—

(a) a clear copy of the online right to work check; and

(b) if the employee is a student who has permission to work for a limited number of hours per week during term time whilst studying in the United Kingdom, a document or clear copy of a document which records the details of the term and vacation dates of the course that the employee is undertaking.]

Note: Regulation 9A inserted from 28 January 2019 (SI 2018/1340).

Restriction on retention of documents

10. Nothing in these Regulations permits a relevant person to retain documents produced by an employee [or the Home Office] for the purposes of these Regulations for any period longer than is necessary for the purposes of ensuring compliance with regulation [6, 8, 9 or 9A].

Note: Words inserted and numbers substituted from 28 January 2019 (SI 2018/1340).

SCHEDULE 1

REGULATIONS 4 AND 8

1. An expired or current passport showing that the holder, or a person named in the passport as the child of the holder, is a British citizen or a citizen of the United Kingdom and Colonies having the right of abode in the United Kingdom.

[**1A.** A current or expired passport or passport card showing that the holder is a national of the Republic of Ireland.

1B. A document issued by the Home Office to a family member of an EEA or Swiss national, which has not expired, and which indicates that the holder is permitted to stay in the United Kingdom indefinitely.

1C. A document issued by the Bailiwick of Jersey, the Bailiwick of Guernsey or the Isle of Man, which has been verified as valid by the Home Office Employer Checking Service, showing that the holder has been granted unlimited leave to enter or remain under Appendix EU(J) to the Jersey Immigration Rules, Appendix EU to the Immigration (Bailiwick of Guernsey) Rules 2008 or Appendix EU to the Isle of Man Immigration Rules (as the case may be).]

2. [. . .]

3. [. . .].

4. [. . .].

5. A current biometric immigration document issued by the Home Office to the holder which indicates that the person named in it is allowed to stay indefinitely in the United Kingdom, or has no time limit on their stay in the United Kingdom.

6. A current passport endorsed to show that the holder is exempt from immigration control, is allowed to stay indefinitely in the United Kingdom, has the right of abode in the United Kingdom, or has no time limit on their stay in the United Kingdom.

7. A current immigration status document issued by the Home Office to the holder with an endorsement indicating that the person named in it is allowed to stay indefinitely in the United Kingdom or has no time limit on their stay in the United Kingdom, when produced in combination with an official document giving the person's permanent National Insurance Number and their name issued by a Government agency or a previous employer.

8. A [. . .] birth certificate issued in the United Kingdom [. . .], when produced in combination with an official document giving the person's permanent National Insurance Number and their name issued by a Government agency or a previous employer.

9. [An] adoption certificate issued in the United Kingdom [. . .] when produced in combination with an official document giving the person's permanent National Insurance Number and their name issued by a Government agency or a previous employer.

10. A birth certificate issued in the Channel Islands, the Isle of Man or Ireland, when produced in combination with an official document giving the person's permanent

National Insurance Number and their name issued by a Government agency or a previous employer.

11. An adoption certificate issued in the Channel Islands, the Isle of Man or Ireland, when produced in combination with an official document giving the person's permanent National Insurance Number and their name issued by a Government agency or a previous employer.

12. A certificate of registration or naturalisation as a British citizen, when produced in combination with an official document giving the person's permanent National Insurance Number and their name issued by a Government agency or a previous employer.

Note: Words omitted from paragraphs 8 and 9 and words substituted in paragraph 9 from 28 January 2019 (SI 2018/1340).Paragraphs 1A to 1C inserted and paragraphs 2 to 4 omitted from 1 July 2021 (SI 2021/689).

Schedule 2
Regulations 4 and 8

1. A current passport endorsed to show that the holder is allowed to stay in the United Kingdom and is allowed to do the work in question.

2. A current biometric immigration document issued by the Home Office to the holder which indicates that the person named in it is allowed to stay in the United Kingdom and is allowed to do the work in question.

3. [....]

[**3A** A document issued by the Home Office to a family member of an EEA or Swiss national, which has not expired, and which indicates that the holder is permitted to stay in the United Kingdom for a time limited period and to do the type of work in question.

3B. A document issued by the Bailiwick of Jersey, the Bailiwick of Guernsey or the Isle of Man, which has been verified as valid by the Home Office Employer Checking Service, showing that the holder has been granted limited leave to enter or remain under Appendix EU(J) to the Jersey Immigration Rules, Appendix EU to the Immigration (Bailiwick of Guernsey) Rules 2008 or Appendix EU to the Isle of Man Immigration Rules (as the case may be).

3C. A document issued by the Bailiwick of Jersey or the Bailiwick of Guernsey, which has been verified as valid by the Home Office Employer Checking Service, showing that the holder has made an application for leave to enter or remain under Appendix EU(J) to the Jersey Immigration Rules or Appendix EU to the Immigration (Bailiwick of Guernsey) Rules 2008 (as the case may be), on or before 30th June 2021.

3D. A frontier worker permit issued under regulation 8 of the Citizens' Rights (Frontier Workers) (EU Exit) Regulations 2020.]

4. A current immigration status document containing a photograph issued by the Home Office to the holder with an endorsement indicating that the person named in it is allowed to stay in the United Kingdom and is allowed to do the work in question, when produced in combination with an official document giving the person's permanent National Insurance Number and their name issued by a Government agency or previous employer.

Note: Paragraph 3 omitted and paragraphs 3A to 3D inserted from 1 July 2021 (SI 2021/689).

The Immigration (European Economic Area) Regulations 2016

(the text below represents the 2016 Regulations as they had effect immediately before they were revoked on 31 December 2020 by the Immigration and Social Security Co-ordination (EU Withdrawal) Act 2020 c. 20 Sch. 1(1) para 2(2).

Revocation has effect subject to savings and modifications specified in SI 2020/1209, part 3, SI 2020/1210 reg.2 and Sch.1 and SI 2020/1309 regs 82–83, Sch. 3 paras 2–6 and Sch. 4 paras 2–4).

(SI 2016, No. 1052)

Contents

Part I
Preliminary

Citation and commencement

1.—(1) These Regulations may be cited as the Immigration (European Economic Area) Regulations 2016.

(2) These Regulations come into force—

(a) for the purposes of this regulation, regulation 44 and Schedule 5 (transitory provisions), on 25th November 2016;

(b) for all other purposes, on 1st February 2017.

General interpretation

2.—(1) In these Regulations—

'the 1971 Act' means the Immigration Act 1971;

'the 1999 Act' means the Immigration and Asylum Act 1999;

'the 2002 Act' means the Nationality, Immigration and Asylum Act 2002;

'the 2006 Regulations' means the Immigration (European Economic Area) Regulations 2006;

['the 2016 Act' means the Immigration Act 2016;]

'civil partner' does not include—

(a) a party to a civil partnership of convenience; or

(b) the civil partner ('C') of a person ('P') where a spouse, civil partner or durable partner of C or P is already present in the United Kingdom;

'civil partnership of convenience' includes a civil partnership entered into for the purpose of using these Regulations, or any other right conferred by the EU Treaties, as a means to circumvent—

(a) immigration rules applying to non-EEA nationals (such as any applicable requirement under the 1971 Act to have leave to enter or remain in the United Kingdom); or

(b) any other criteria that the party to the civil partnership of convenience would otherwise have to meet in order to enjoy a right to reside under these Regulations or the EU Treaties;

'Common Travel Area' has the meaning given in section 1(3) of the 1971 Act;

'decision maker' means the Secretary of State, an immigration officer or an entry clearance officer (as the case may be);

'deportation order' means an order made under regulation 32(3);

'derivative residence card' means a card issued to a person under regulation 20;

'derivative right to reside' means a right to reside under regulation 16;

'document certifying permanent residence' means a document issued under regulation 19(1);

'durable partner' does not include—

(a) a party to a durable partnership of convenience; or

(b) the durable partner ('D') of a person ('P') where a spouse, civil partner or durable partner of D or P is already present in the United Kingdom and where that marriage, civil partnership or durable partnership is subsisting;

'durable partnership of convenience' includes a durable partnership entered into for the purpose of using these Regulations, or any other right conferred by the EU Treaties, as a means to circumvent—

(a) immigration rules applying to non-EEA nationals (such as any applicable requirement under the 1971 Act to have leave to enter or remain in the United Kingdom); or

(b) any other criteria that the party to the durable partnership of convenience would otherwise have to meet in order to enjoy a right to reside under these Regulations or the EU Treaties;

'EEA decision' means a decision under these Regulations that concerns—

(a) a person's entitlement to be admitted to the United Kingdom;

(b) a person's entitlement to be issued with or have renewed, or not to have revoked [an EEA family permit], a registration certificate, residence card, derivative residence card, document certifying permanent residence or permanent residence card (but does not include {a decision to reject an application for the above documentation as invalid});

(c) a person's removal from the United Kingdom; or

(d) the cancellation, under regulation 25, of a person's right to reside in the United Kingdom, but does not include [. . .] a decision to {refuse} an application under regulation 26(4) (misuse of a right to reside: material change of circumstances), or any decisions under regulation 33 (human rights considerations and interim orders to suspend removal) or 41 (temporary admission to submit case in person);

'EEA family permit' means a document issued under regulation 12;

['EEA national' means—

(a) a national of an EEA State who is not also a British citizen; or

(b) a national of an EEA State who is also a British citizen and who prior to acquiring British citizenship exercised a right to reside as such a national, in accordance with regulation 14 or 15,

save that a person does not fall within paragraph (b) if the EEA State of which they are a national became a member State after that person acquired British citizenship];

'EEA State' means—

(a) a member State, other than the United Kingdom; or

(b) Liechtenstein, Iceland, Norway or Switzerland;

'entry clearance' has the meaning given in section 33(1) of the 1971 Act;

'entry clearance officer' means a person responsible for the grant or refusal of entry clearance;

'exclusion order' means an order made under regulation 23(5);

'indefinite leave', 'immigration laws' and 'immigration rules' have the meanings given in section 33(1) of the 1971 Act;

'marriage of convenience' includes a marriage entered into for the purpose of using these Regulations, or any other right conferred by the EU Treaties, as a means to circumvent—

(a) immigration rules applying to non-EEA nationals (such as any applicable requirement under the 1971 Act to have leave to enter or remain in the United Kingdom); or

(b) any other criteria that the party to the marriage of convenience would otherwise have to meet in order to enjoy a right to reside under these Regulations or the EU Treaties;

'military service' means service in the armed forces of an EEA State;

'permanent residence card' means a document issued under regulation 19(2);

'qualifying EEA State residence card' means a valid document called a 'Residence card of a family member of a Union Citizen' issued under Article 10 of Council Directive

2004/38/EC (as applied, where relevant, by the EEA agreement) by any EEA State (except Switzerland) to a non-EEA family member of an EEA national as proof of the holder's right of residence in that State;

'registration certificate' means a certificate issued under regulation 17;

'relevant EEA national' in relation to an extended family member has the meaning given in regulation 8(6);

'residence card' means a card issued under regulation 18;

'right to reside' means a right to reside in the United Kingdom under these Regulations (or where so specified, a right to reside under a particular regulation);

'spouse' does not include—

(a) a party to a marriage of convenience; or

(b) the spouse ('S') of a person ('P') where a spouse, civil partner or durable partner of S or P is already present in the United Kingdom.

(2) Section 11 of the 1971 Act (construction of references to entry) applies for the purpose of determining whether a person has entered the United Kingdom for the purpose of these Regulations as it applies for the purpose of determining whether a person has entered the United Kingdom for the purpose of that Act.

Note: Definition of 'the 2016 Act' inserted from 15 January 2018 (SI 2017/1242) and definition of 'EEA national' substituted from 24 July 2018 (SI 2018/801). Words omitted from paragraph (d) of the definition of 'EEA decision' from 28 March 2019 (SI 2109/468). In definition of 'EEA decision' words in square brackets in paragraph (b) inserted and words in curly brackets in paragraphs (b) and (d) substituted from 15 August 2019 (SI 2019/1155).

Continuity of residence

3.—(1) This regulation applies for the purpose of calculating periods of continuous residence in the United Kingdom under these Regulations.

(2) Continuity of residence is not affected by—

(a) periods of absence from the United Kingdom which do not exceed six months in total in any year;

(b) periods of absence from the United Kingdom on compulsory military service; or

(c) one absence from the United Kingdom not exceeding twelve months for an important reason such as pregnancy and childbirth, serious illness, study or vocational training or an overseas posting.

(3) Continuity of residence is broken when—

(a) a person serves a sentence of imprisonment;

(b) a deportation or exclusion order is made in relation to a person; or

(c) a person is removed from the United Kingdom under these Regulations.

(4) Paragraph (3)(a) applies, in principle, to an EEA national who has resided in the United Kingdom for at least ten years, but it does not apply where the Secretary of State considers that—

(a) prior to serving a sentence of imprisonment, the EEA national had forged integrating links with the United Kingdom;

(b) the effect of the sentence of imprisonment was not such as to break those integrating links; and

(c) taking into account an overall assessment of the EEA national's situation, it would not be appropriate to apply paragraph (3)(a) to the assessment of that EEA national's continuity of residence.

'Worker', 'self-employed person', 'self-sufficient person' and 'student'

4.—(1) In these Regulations—

(a) 'worker' means a worker within the meaning of Article 45 of the Treaty on the Functioning of the European Union;

(b) 'self-employed person' means a person who is established in the United Kingdom in order to pursue activity as a self-employed person in accordance with Article 49 of the Treaty on the Functioning of the European Union;

(c) 'self-sufficient person' means a person who has—

(i) sufficient resources not to become a burden on the social assistance system of the United Kingdom during the person's period of residence; and

(ii) comprehensive sickness insurance cover in the United Kingdom;

(d) 'student' means a person who—

(i) is enrolled, for the principal purpose of following a course of study (including vocational training), at a public or private establishment which is—

(aa) financed from public funds; or

(bb) otherwise recognised by the Secretary of State as an establishment which has been accredited for the purpose of providing such courses or training within the law or administrative practice of the part of the United Kingdom in which the establishment is located;

(ii) has comprehensive sickness insurance cover in the United Kingdom; and

(iii) has assured the Secretary of State, by means of a declaration, or by such equivalent means as the person may choose, that the person has sufficient resources not to become a burden on the social assistance system of the United Kingdom during the person's intended period of residence.

(2) For the purposes of paragraphs (3) and (4) below, 'relevant family member' means a family member of a self-sufficient person or student who is residing in the United Kingdom and whose right to reside is dependent upon being the family member of that student or self-sufficient person.

(3) In sub-paragraphs (1)(c) and (d)—

(a) the requirement for the self-sufficient person or student to have sufficient resources not to become a burden on the social assistance system of the United Kingdom during the intended period of residence is only satisfied if the resources available to the student or self-sufficient person and any of their relevant family members are sufficient to avoid the self-sufficient person or student and all their relevant family members from becoming such a burden; and

(b) the requirement for the student or self-sufficient person to have comprehensive sickness insurance cover in the United Kingdom is only satisfied if such cover extends to cover both the student or self-sufficient person and all their relevant family members.

(4) In paragraph (1)(c) and (d) and paragraph (3), the resources of the student or self-sufficient person and, where applicable, any of their relevant family members, are to be regarded as sufficient if—

(a) they exceed the maximum level of resources which a British citizen (including the resources of the British citizen's family members) may possess if the British citizen is to become eligible for social assistance under the United Kingdom benefit system; or

(b) paragraph (a) does not apply but, taking into account the personal circumstances of the person concerned and, where applicable, all their relevant family members, it appears to the decision maker that the resources of the person or persons concerned should be regarded as sufficient.

(5) For the purposes of regulation 16(2) (criteria for having a derivative right to reside), references in this regulation to 'family members' includes a 'primary carer' as defined in regulation 16(8).

'Worker or self-employed person who has ceased activity'

5.—(1) In these Regulations, 'worker or self-employed person who has ceased activity' means an EEA national who satisfies a condition in paragraph (2), (3), (4) or (5).

(2) The condition in this paragraph is that the person—

(a) terminates activity as a worker or self-employed person and—

(i) had reached the age of entitlement to a state pension on terminating that activity; or

(ii) in the case of a worker, ceases working to take early retirement;

(b) pursued activity as a worker or self-employed person in the United Kingdom for at least 12 months prior to the termination; and

(c) resided in the United Kingdom continuously for more than three years prior to the termination.

(3) The condition in this paragraph is that the person terminates activity in the United Kingdom as a worker or self-employed person as a result of permanent incapacity to work; and—

(a) had resided in the United Kingdom continuously for more than two years [immediately] prior to the termination; or

(b) the incapacity is the result of an accident at work or an occupational disease that entitles the person to a pension payable in full or in part by an institution in the United Kingdom.

(4) The condition in this paragraph is that the person—

(a) is active as a worker or self-employed person in an EEA State but retains a place of residence in the United Kingdom and returns, as a rule, to that place at least once a week; and

(b) [Immediately] prior to becoming so active in the EEA State, had been continuously resident and continuously active as a worker or self-employed person in the United Kingdom for at least three years.

(5) A person who satisfied the condition in paragraph (4)(a) but not the condition in paragraph (4)(b) must, for the purposes of paragraphs (2) and (3), be treated as being active and resident in the United Kingdom during any period during which that person is working or self-employed in the EEA State.

(6) The conditions in paragraphs (2) and (3) as to length of residence and activity as a worker or self-employed person do not apply in relation to a person whose spouse or civil partner is a British citizen.

(7) Subject to regulation 6(2), periods of—

(a) inactivity for reasons not of the person's own making;

(b) inactivity due to illness or accident; and

(c) in the case of a worker, involuntary unemployment duly recorded by the relevant employment office,

must be treated as periods of activity as a worker or self-employed person, as the case may be.

Note: Word inserted in paragraphs (3)(a) and (4)(b) from 15 August 2019 (SI 2019/1155).

'Qualified person'

6.—(1) In these Regulations—

'jobseeker' means an EEA national who satisfies conditions A, B and, where relevant, C;

'qualified person' means a person who is an EEA national and in the United Kingdom as—

(a) a jobseeker;

(b) a worker;

(c) a self-employed person;

(d) a self-sufficient person; or

(e) a student;

'relevant period' means—

(a) in the case of a person retaining worker status under paragraph (2)(b) [or self-employed person status under paragraph (4)(b)], a continuous period of six months;

(b) in the case of a jobseeker, 91 days, minus the cumulative total of any days during which the person concerned previously enjoyed a right to reside as a jobseeker, not including any days prior to a continuous absence from the United Kingdom of at least 12 months.

(2) A person who is no longer working must continue to be treated as a worker provided that the person—

(a) is temporarily unable to work as the result of an illness or accident;

(b) is in duly recorded involuntary unemployment after having been employed in the United Kingdom for at least one year, provided the person—

(i) has registered as a jobseeker with the relevant employment office; and

(ii) satisfies conditions A and B;

(c) is in duly recorded involuntary unemployment after having been employed in the United Kingdom for less than one year, provided the person—

(i) has registered as a jobseeker with the relevant employment office; and

(ii) satisfies conditions A and B;

(d) is involuntarily unemployed and has embarked on vocational training; or

(e) has voluntarily ceased working and has embarked on vocational training that is related to the person's previous employment.

(3) A person to whom paragraph (2)(c) applies may only retain worker status for a maximum of six months.

[(4) A person who is no longer in self-employment must continue to be treated as a self-employed person provided that the person—

(a) is temporarily unable to engage in activities as a self-employed person as the result of an illness or accident;

(b) is in duly recorded involuntary unemployment after having worked as a self-employed person in the United Kingdom for at least one year provided the person—

(i) has registered as a jobseeker with the relevant employment office; and

(ii) satisfies conditions D and E;

(c) is in duly recorded involuntary unemployment after having worked as a self-employed person in the United Kingdom for less than one year, provided the person—

(i) has registered as a jobseeker with the relevant employment office; and

(ii) satisfies conditions D and E;

(d) is involuntarily no longer in self-employment and has embarked on vocational training; or

(e) has voluntarily ceased self-employment and has embarked on vocational training that is related to the person's previous occupation].

[(4A) A person to whom paragraph (4)(c) applies may only retain self-employed person status for a maximum of six months.

(4B) Condition D is that the person—

(a) entered the United Kingdom as a self-employed person or in order to seek employment as a self-employed person; or

(b) is present in the United Kingdom seeking employment or self-employment, immediately after enjoying a right to reside under sub-paragraphs (c) to (e) of the definition of qualified person in paragraph (1) (disregarding any period during which self-employed status was retained pursuant to paragraph (4)(b) or (c)).

(4C) Condition E is that the person provides evidence of seeking employment or self-employment and having a genuine chance of being engaged.]

(5) Condition A is that the person—

(a) entered the United Kingdom in order to seek employment; or

(b) is present in the United Kingdom seeking employment, immediately after enjoying a right to reside under [sub-paragraphs (b), (d) or (e)] of the definition of qualified person in paragraph (1) (disregarding any period during which worker status was retained pursuant to paragraph (2)(b) or (c)).

(6) Condition B is that the person provides evidence of seeking employment and having a genuine chance of being engaged.

(7) A person may not retain the status of—

(a) a worker under paragraph (2)(b); [. . .]

(b) a jobseeker;[or

or (c) a self-employed person under paragraph (4)(b)]

for longer than the relevant period without providing compelling evidence of continuing to seek employment and having a genuine chance of being engaged.

(8) Condition C applies where the person concerned has, previously, enjoyed a right to reside under this regulation as a result of satisfying conditions A and B [or, as the case may be, conditions D and E] —

(a) in the case of a person to whom paragraph (2)(b) or (c) [or (4)(b) or (c)] applied, for at least six months; or

(b) in the case of a jobseeker, for at least 91 days in total,

unless the person concerned has, since enjoying the above right to reside, been continuously absent from the United Kingdom for at least 12 months.

(9) Condition C is that the person has had a period of absence from the United Kingdom.

(10) Where condition C applies—

(a) paragraph (7) does not apply; and

(b) condition B [or, as the case may be, condition E] has effect as if 'compelling' were inserted before 'evidence'.

Note: In paragraph (1) words inserted in paragraph (a) of the definition of 'relevant period', paragraph (4) substituted, paragraphs (4A)–(4C) inserted, words substituted in paragraph (5)(b), word omitted and paragraph (c) inserted in paragraph 7 and words inserted in paragraphs 8 and 10 from 24 July 2018 (SI 2018/801).

'Family member'

7.—(1) In these Regulations, 'family member' means, in relation to a person ('A')—

(a) A's spouse or civil partner;

(b) A's direct descendants, or the direct descendants of A's spouse or civil partner who are either—

(i) aged under 21; or

(ii) dependants of A, or of A's spouse or civil partner;

(c) dependent direct relatives in A's ascending line, or in that of A's spouse or civil partner.

(2) Where A is a student residing in the United Kingdom otherwise than under regulation 13 (initial right of residence), a person is not a family member of A under paragraph (1)(b) or (c) unless—

(a) in the case of paragraph (1)(b), the person is the dependent child of A or of A's spouse or civil partner; or

(b) A also falls within one of the other categories of qualified person mentioned in regulation 6(1).

(3) A person ('B') who is an extended family member and has been issued with an EEA family permit, a registration certificate or a residence card must be treated as a family member of A, provided—

(a) B continues to satisfy the conditions in regulation [8(1A),]8(2), (3), (4) or (5)]; and

(b) the EEA family permit, registration certificate or residence card remains in force.

(4) A must be an EEA national unless regulation 9 applies (family members [and extended family members] of British citizens).

Note: Words inserted in paragraph (3)(a) from 15 August 2019 (SI 2019/1155). Words inserted in paragraph (4) from 28 March 2019 (SI 2019/468).

'Extended family member'

8.—(1) In these Regulations 'extended family member' means a person who is not a family member of an EEA national under regulation 7(1)(a), (b) or (c) and who satisfies a condition in paragraph [(1A),](2), (3), (4) or (5).

[(1A) The condition in this paragraph is that the person—

(a) is under the age of 18;

(b) is subject to a non-adoptive legal guardianship order in favour of an EEA national that is recognised under the national law of the state in which it was contracted;

(c) has lived with the EEA national since their placement under the guardianship order;

(d) has created family life with the EEA national; and

(e) has a personal relationship with the EEA national that involves dependency on the EEA national and the assumption of parental responsibility, including legal and financial responsibilities, for that person by the EEA national.]

(2) The condition in this paragraph is that the person is—

(a) a relative of an EEA national; and

(b) residing in a country other than the United Kingdom and is dependent upon the EEA national or is a member of the EEA national's household; and either—

(i) is accompanying the EEA national to the United Kingdom or wants to join the EEA national in the United Kingdom; or

(ii) has joined the EEA national in the United Kingdom and continues to be dependent upon the EEA national, or to be a member of the EEA national's household.

(3) The condition in this paragraph is that the person is a relative of an EEA national and on serious health grounds, strictly requires the personal care of the EEA national [or the spouse or civil partner of the EEA national].

(4) The condition in this paragraph is that the person is a relative of an EEA national and would meet the requirements in the immigration rules (other than those relating to entry clearance) for indefinite leave to enter or remain in the United Kingdom as a dependent relative of the EEA national.

(5) The condition in this paragraph is that the person is the partner (other than a civil partner) of, and in a durable relationship with, an EEA national, [or the child (under the age of 18) of that partner] and is able to prove this to the decision maker.

(6) In these Regulations, 'relevant EEA national' means, in relation to an extended family member—

(a) referred to in paragraph (2), (3) or (4), the EEA national to whom the extended family member is related;

(b) referred to in paragraph (5), the EEA national who is the durable partner of the extended family member.

(7) In [paragraphs (2), (3) and (4)], 'relative of an EEA national' includes a relative of the spouse or civil partner of an EEA national [. . .].

[(8) Where an extensive examination of the personal circumstances of the applicant is required under these Regulations, it must include examination of the following—

(a) the best interests of the applicant, particularly where the applicant is a child;

(b) the character and conduct of the applicant; and

(c) whether an EEA national would be deterred from exercising their free movement rights if the application was refused.]

Note: Words inserted in paragraphs (1), (3) and (5), words substituted in paragraph (7), paragraphs (7)(a) and (b) omitted and paragraphs (1A) and (8) inserted from 15 August 2019 (SI 2019/1155).

Family members [and extended family members] of British citizens

9.—(1) If the conditions in paragraph (2) are satisfied, these Regulations apply to a person who is the family member ('F') of a British citizen ('BC') as though the BC were an EEA national.

[(1A) These Regulations apply to a person who is the extended family member ('EFM') of a BC as though the BC were an EEA national if—

(a) the conditions in paragraph (2) are satisfied; and

(b) the EFM was lawfully resident in the EEA State referred to in paragraph (2)(a)(i).]

(2) The conditions are that—

(a) BC—

(i) is residing in an EEA State as a worker, self-employed person, self-sufficient person or a student, or so resided immediately before returning to the United Kingdom; or

(ii) has acquired the right of permanent residence in an EEA State;

(b) F [or EFM] and BC resided together in the EEA State; [. . .]

(c) F [or EFM] and BC's residence in the EEA State was genuine;

[{(d) either—

(i) F was a family member of BC during all or part of their joint residence in the EEA State;

(ii) F was an EFM of BC during all or part of their joint residence in the EEA State, during which time F was lawfully resident in the EEA State; or

(iii) EFM was an EFM of BC during all or part of their joint residence in the EEA State, during which time EFM was lawfully resident in the EEA State;} and

(e) genuine family life was created or strengthened during [F or EFM and BC's] joint residence in the EEA State][;and

(f) the conditions in sub-paragraphs (a), (b) and (c) have been met concurrently.]

(3) Factors relevant to whether residence in the EEA State is or was genuine include—

(a) whether the centre of BC's life transferred to the EEA State;

(b) the length of F [or EFM] and BC's joint residence in the EEA State;

(c) the nature and quality of the F [or EFM] and BC's accommodation in the EEA State, and whether it is or was BC's principal residence;

(d) the degree of F [or EFM] and BC's integration in the EEA State;

(e) whether F's [or EFM's] first lawful residence in the EU with BC was in the EEA State.

(4) This regulation does not apply—

(a) where the purpose of the residence in the EEA State was as a means for circumventing any immigration laws applying to non-EEA nationals to which F [or EFM] would otherwise be subject (such as any applicable requirement under the 1971 Act to have leave to enter or remain in the United Kingdom).

[...]

(5) Where these Regulations apply to F [or EFM], BC is to be treated as holding a valid passport issued by an EEA State for the purposes of the application of these Regulations to F [or EFM].

(6) In paragraph (2)(a)(ii), BC is only to be treated as having acquired the right of permanent residence in the EEA State if such residence would have led to the acquisition of that right under regulation 15, had it taken place in the United Kingdom.

(7) For the purposes of determining whether, when treating the BC as an EEA national under these Regulations in accordance with paragraph (1), BC would be a qualified person—

(a) any requirement to have comprehensive sickness insurance cover in the United Kingdom still applies, save that it does not require the cover to extend to BC;

(b) in assessing whether BC can continue to be treated as a worker under regulation 6(2)(b) or (c), BC is not required to satisfy condition A;

(c) in assessing whether BC can be treated as a jobseeker as defined in regulation 6(1), BC is not required to satisfy conditions A and, where it would otherwise be relevant, condition C.

Note: Word omitted at end of paragraph (2)(b) and paragraphs (2)(d) and (2)(e) inserted from 24 July 2018 (SI 2018/801). Words in heading and paragraph (1A) inserted from 28 March 2019 (SI 2019/468). Words in paragraphs (2) (b) and(c) inserted and words in paragraph (2)(e) substituted from 28 March 2019 (SI 2019/468). Words inserted in paragraphs 3(b)–(e), paragraph (4)(a) and paragraph (5) and paragraph (4)(b) omitted from 28 March 2019 (SI 2019/468). Amendments to Regulation 9 made by SI 2019/468 are subject to transitional provision that: 'In any decision made after the day on which regulation 3 comes into force as to whether a person satisfies the conditions in regulation 9(2) of the Immigration (European Economic Area) Regulations 2016 (family members and extended family members), the amendments made by regulation 3(4) and (5) are to be treated as if they had been in force at all times relevant to such a decision (regulation 4 of SI 2019/468)'. Paragraph (2)(d) substituted and paragraph (2)(f) inserted from 15 August 2019 (SI 2019/1155).

[Dual national: national of an EEA State who acquires British citizenship

9A.—(1) In this regulation 'DN' means a person within paragraph (b) of the definition of 'EEA national' in regulation 2(1).

(2) DN who comes within the definition of 'qualified person' in regulation 6(1) is only a qualified person for the purpose of these Regulations if DN—

(a) came within the definition of 'qualified person' at the time of acquisition of British citizenship; and

(b) has not at any time subsequent to the acquisition of British citizenship lost the status of qualified person.

(3) Regulation 15 only applies to DN, or to the family member of DN who is not an EEA national, if DN satisfies the condition in paragraph (4).

(4) The condition in this paragraph is that at the time of acquisition of British citizenship DN either—

(a) was a qualified person; or

(b) had acquired a right of permanent residence in accordance with these Regulations.]

Note: Regulation 9A inserted from 24 July 2018 (SI 2018/801) and subject to transitional provisions: 'In determining whether a person satisfies the requirements in regulation 9A(2) to (4) of the 2016 Regulations (dual national: national of an EEA State who acquires British citizenship), inserted by paragraph 4 of the Schedule—(a) the definition of "EEA national" in regulation 2(1) of the 2016 Regulations (general interpretation) is to be read as if the amendment made to that definition by paragraph 1 of the Schedule was in force at all times relevant to such determination; and (b) regulation 9A of the 2016 Regulations is to be treated as if it was in force at all times relevant to such determination' (regulation 3 of SI 2018/801).

'Family member who has retained the right of residence'

10.—(1) In these Regulations, 'family member who has retained the right of residence' means, subject to paragraphs (8) and (9), a person who satisfies a condition in paragraph (2), (3), (4) or (5).

(2) The condition in this paragraph is that the person—

(a) was a family member of a qualified person or of an EEA national with a right of permanent residence when the qualified person or the EEA national with the right of permanent residence died;

(b) resided in the United Kingdom in accordance with these Regulations for at least the year immediately before the death of the qualified person or the EEA national with a right of permanent residence; and

(c) satisfies the condition in paragraph (6).

(3) The condition in this paragraph is that the person—

(a) is the direct descendant of—

(i) a qualified person or an EEA national with a right of permanent residence who has died;

(ii) a person who ceased to be a qualified person on ceasing to reside in the United Kingdom;

(iii) the spouse or civil partner of the qualified person or EEA national described in sub-paragraph (i) immediately preceding that qualified person or EEA national's death; or

(iv) the spouse or civil partner of the person described in sub-paragraph (ii); and

(b) was attending an educational course in the United Kingdom immediately before the qualified person or the EEA national with a right of permanent residence died, or ceased to be a qualified person, and continues to attend such a course.

(4) The condition in this paragraph is that the person is the parent with actual custody of a child who satisfies the condition in paragraph (3).

(5) The condition in this paragraph is that the person ('A')—

(a) ceased to be a family member of a qualified person or an EEA national with a right of permanent residence on the [initiation of proceedings for the termination] of the marriage or civil partnership of A;

(b) was residing in the United Kingdom in accordance with these Regulations at the date of the [initiation of proceedings for the termination];

(c) satisfies the condition in paragraph (6); and

(d) either—

(i) prior to the initiation of the proceedings for the [initiation of proceedings for the termination] of the marriage or the civil partnership, the marriage or civil partnership had lasted for at least three years and the parties to the marriage or civil partnership had resided in the United Kingdom for at least one year during its duration;

(ii) the former spouse or civil partner of the qualified person or the EEA national with a right of permanent residence has custody of a child of that qualified person or EEA national;

(iii) the former spouse or civil partner of the qualified person or the EEA national with a right of permanent residence has the right of access to a child of that qualified person or EEA national, where the child is under the age of 18 and where a court has ordered that such access must take place in the United Kingdom; or

(iv) the continued right of residence in the United Kingdom of A is warranted by particularly difficult circumstances, such as where A or another family member has been a victim of domestic violence whilst the marriage or civil partnership was subsisting.

(6) The condition in this paragraph is that the person—

(a) is not an EEA national but would, if the person were an EEA national, be a worker, a self-employed person or a self-sufficient person under regulation 6; or

(b) is the family member of a person who falls within paragraph (a).

(7) In this regulation, 'educational course' means a course within the scope of Article 10 of Council Regulation (EU) No. 492/2011.

(8) A person ('P') does not satisfy a condition in paragraph (2), (3), (4) or (5) if, at the first time P would otherwise have satisfied the relevant condition, P had a right of permanent residence under regulation 15.

(9) A family member who has retained the right of residence ceases to enjoy that status on acquiring a right of permanent residence under regulation 15.

Note: Words in paragraph (5) substituted from 15 August 2019 (SI 2019/1155).

Part 2

EEA Rights

Right of admission to the United Kingdom

11.—(1) An EEA national must be admitted to the United Kingdom on arrival if the EEA national produces a valid national identity card or passport issued by an EEA State.

(2) A person who is not an EEA national must be admitted to the United Kingdom if that person is—

(a) a family member of an EEA national and produces on arrival a valid passport and qualifying EEA State residence card, provided the conditions in regulation 23(4) (family member of EEA national must accompany or join EEA national with right to reside) are met; or

(b) a family member of an EEA national, a family member who has retained the right of residence, a person who meets the criteria in paragraph (5) or a person with a right of permanent residence under regulation 15 and produces on arrival—

(i) a valid passport; and

(ii) a valid EEA family permit, residence card, derivative residence card or permanent residence card.

[(2A) Any passport, identity card, family permit, residence card, derivative residence card, permanent residence card or qualifying EEA State residence card which is required to be produced under this regulation as a condition for admission to the United Kingdom ('the required documents') may, for the same purpose, be required to be produced in a control zone or a supplementary control zone.]

(3) An immigration officer must not place a stamp in the passport of a person admitted to the United Kingdom under this regulation who is not an EEA national if the person produces a residence card, a derivative residence card, a permanent residence card or a qualifying EEA State residence card.

(4) Before an immigration officer refuses admission to the United Kingdom to a person under this regulation because the person does not produce on arrival [or the time of his production of the required documents in a control zone or a supplementary control zone] a document mentioned in paragraph (1) or (2), the immigration officer must provide every reasonable opportunity for the document to be obtained by, or brought to, the person or allow the person to prove by other means that the person is—

(a) an EEA national;

(b) a family member of an EEA national with a right to accompany that EEA national or join that EEA national in the United Kingdom;

(c) a person who meets the criteria in paragraph (5); or

(d) a family member who has retained the right of residence or a person with a right of permanent residence under regulation 15.

(5) The criteria in this paragraph are that a person ('P')—

(a) previously resided in the United Kingdom under regulation 16(3) and would be entitled to reside in the United Kingdom under that regulation were P in the country;

(b) is accompanying an EEA national to, or joining an EEA national in, the United Kingdom and P would be entitled to reside in the United Kingdom under regulation 16(2) were P and the EEA national both in the United Kingdom;

(c) is accompanying a person ('the relevant person') to, or joining the relevant person in, the United Kingdom and—

(i) the relevant person is residing, or has resided, in the United Kingdom under regulation 16(3); and

(ii) P would be entitled to reside in the United Kingdom under regulation 16(4) were P and the relevant person both in the United Kingdom;

(d) is accompanying a person who meets the criteria in sub-paragraph (b) or (c) ('the relevant person') to the United Kingdom and—

(i) P and the relevant person are both—

(aa) seeking admission to the United Kingdom in reliance on this paragraph for the first time; or

(bb) returning to the United Kingdom having previously resided there pursuant to the same provisions of regulation 16 in reliance on which they now base their claim to admission; and

(ii) P would be entitled to reside in the United Kingdom under regulation 16(6) were P and the relevant person there; or

(e) is accompanying a British citizen to, or joining a British citizen in, the United Kingdom and P would be entitled to reside in the United Kingdom under regulation 16(5) were P and the British citizen both in the United Kingdom.

(6) Paragraph (7) applies where—

(a) a person ('P') seeks admission to the United Kingdom in reliance on paragraph (5)(b), (c) or (e); and

(b) if P were in the United Kingdom, P would have a derived right to reside under regulation 16(8)(b)(ii).

(7) Where this paragraph applies a person ('P') must only be regarded as meeting the criteria in paragraph (5)(b), (c) or (e) where P—

(a) is accompanying the person with whom P would on admission to the United Kingdom jointly share care responsibility for the purpose of regulation 16(8)(b)(ii); or

(b) has previously resided in the United Kingdom pursuant to regulation 16(2), (4) or (5) as a joint primary carer and seeks admission to the United Kingdom in order to reside there again on the same basis.

(8) But this regulation is subject to regulations 23(1), (2), (3) and (4) and 31.

[(9) A person is not entitled to be admitted by virtue of this regulation where that person is subject to a decision under regulation 23(6)(b) (removal decision).]

Note: Paragraph (9) inserted from 24 July 2018 (SI 2018/801). Paragraph (2A) and words in paragraph (4) inserted from 30 September 2020 (SI 1993/1813 Sch. 4 para 5).

Issue of EEA family permit

12.—(1) An entry clearance officer must issue an EEA family permit to a person who applies for one if the person is a family member of an EEA national and—

(a) the EEA national—

(i) is residing in the United Kingdom in accordance with these Regulations; or

(ii) will be travelling to the United Kingdom within six months of the date of the application and will be an EEA national residing in the United Kingdom in accordance with these Regulations on arrival in the United Kingdom; and

(b) the family member will be accompanying the EEA national to the United Kingdom or joining the EEA national there.

(2) An entry clearance officer must issue an EEA family permit to a person who applies and provides evidence demonstrating that, at the time at which the person first intends to use the EEA family permit, the person—

(a) would be entitled to be admitted to the United Kingdom because that person would meet the criteria in regulation 11(5); and

(b) will (save in the case of a person who would be entitled to be admitted to the United Kingdom because that person would meet the criteria for admission in regulation 11(5)(a)) be accompanying to, or joining in, the United Kingdom any person from whom the right to be admitted to the United Kingdom under the criteria in regulation 11(5) is derived.

(3) An entry clearance officer must issue an EEA family permit to—

(a) a family member who has retained the right of residence; or

(b) a person who is not an EEA national but who has acquired the right of permanent residence under regulation 15.

(4) An entry clearance officer may issue an EEA family permit to an extended family member of an EEA national (the relevant EEA national) who applies for one if—

(a) the relevant EEA national satisfies the condition in paragraph (1)(a);

(b) the extended family member wants to accompany the relevant EEA national to the United Kingdom or to join that EEA national there; and

(c) in all the circumstances, it appears to the entry clearance officer appropriate to issue the EEA family permit.

(5) Where an entry clearance officer receives an application under paragraph (4) an extensive examination of the personal circumstances of the applicant must be undertaken by the Secretary of State and if the application is refused, the entry clearance officer must give reasons justifying the refusal unless this is contrary to the interests of national security.

[(5A) An EEA family permit issued under this regulation may be issued in electronic form.]

(6) An EEA family permit issued under this regulation must be issued free of charge and as soon as possible.

(7) But an EEA family permit must not be issued under this regulation if the applicant or the EEA national concerned is not entitled to be admitted to the United Kingdom as a result of regulation 23(1), (2) or (3) or falls to be excluded in accordance with regulation 23(5).

(8) An EEA family permit must not be issued under this regulation to a person ('A') who is the spouse, civil partner or durable partner of a person ('B') where a spouse, civil partner or durable partner of A or B holds a valid EEA family permit.

Note: Paragraph (5A) inserted from 24 July 2018 (SI 2018/801).

Initial right of residence

13.—(1) An EEA national is entitled to reside in the United Kingdom for a period not exceeding three months beginning on the date of admission to the United Kingdom provided the EEA national holds a valid national identity card or passport issued by an EEA State.

(2) A person who is not an EEA national but is a family member who has retained the right of residence or the family member of an EEA national residing in the United Kingdom under paragraph (1) is entitled to reside in the United Kingdom provided that person holds a valid passport.

(3) An EEA national or the family member of an EEA national who is an unreasonable burden on the social assistance system of the United Kingdom does not have a right to reside under this regulation.

(4) A person who otherwise satisfies the criteria in this regulation is not entitled to a right to reside under this regulation where the Secretary of State or an immigration officer has made a decision under regulation 23(6)(b) (decision to remove on grounds of public policy, public security or public health), 24(1) (refusal to issue residence documentation etc), 25(1) (cancellation of a right of residence), 26(3) (misuse of right to reside) or 31(1) (revocation of admission), [or an order under regulation 23(5) (exclusion order) or 32(3) (deportation order), unless that decision or order, as the case may be, is set aside, revoked or otherwise no longer has effect].

Note: Words in paragraph (4) substituted from 24 July 2018 (SI 2018/801).

Extended right of residence

14.—(1) A qualified person is entitled to reside in the United Kingdom for as long as that person remains a qualified person.

(2) A person ('P') who is a family member of a qualified person residing in the United Kingdom under paragraph (1) or of an EEA national with a right of permanent residence under regulation 15 is entitled to remain in the United Kingdom for so long as P remains the family member of that person or EEA national.

(3) A family member who has retained the right of residence is entitled to reside in the United Kingdom for so long as that person remains a family member who has retained the right of residence.

(4) A person who otherwise satisfies the criteria in this regulation is not entitled to a right to reside in the United Kingdom under this regulation where the Secretary of State or an immigration officer has made a decision under regulation 23(6)(b), 24(1), 25(1), 26(3) or 31(1), [or an order under regulation 23(5) (exclusion order) or 32(3) (deportation order), unless that decision or order, as the case may be, is set aside, revoked or otherwise no longer has effect].

Note: Words in paragraph (4) substituted from 24 July 2018 (SI 2018/801).

Right of permanent residence

15.—(1) The following persons acquire the right to reside in the United Kingdom permanently—

(a) an EEA national who has resided in the United Kingdom in accordance with these Regulations for a continuous period of five years;

(b) a family member of an EEA national who is not an EEA national but who has resided in the United Kingdom with the EEA national in accordance with these Regulations for a continuous period of five years;

(c) a worker or self-employed person who has ceased activity;

(d) the family member of a worker or self-employed person who has ceased activity, provided—

(i) the person was the family member of the worker or self-employed person at the point the worker or self-employed person ceased activity; and

(ii) at that point, the family member enjoyed a right to reside on the basis of being the family member of that worker or self-employed person;

(e) a person who was the family member of a worker or self-employed person where—

(i) the worker or self-employed person has died;

(ii) the family member resided with the worker or self-employed person immediately before the death; and

(iii) the worker or self-employed person had resided continuously in the United Kingdom for at least two years immediately before dying or the death was the result of an accident at work or an occupational disease;

(f) a person who—

(i) has resided in the United Kingdom in accordance with these Regulations for a continuous period of five years; and

(ii) was, at the end of the period, a family member who has retained the right of residence.

(2) Residence in the United Kingdom as a result of a derivative right to reside does not constitute residence for the purpose of this regulation.

(3) The right of permanent residence under this regulation is lost through absence from the United Kingdom for a period exceeding two years.

(4) A person who satisfies the criteria in this regulation is not entitled to a right to permanent residence in the United Kingdom where the Secretary of State or an immigration officer has made a decision under regulation 23(6)(b), 24(1), 25(1), 26(3) or 31(1), [or an order under regulation 23(5) (exclusion order) or 32(3) (deportation order), unless that decision or order, as the case may be, is set aside, revoked or otherwise no longer has effect].

Note: Words in paragraph (4) substituted from 24 July 2018 (SI 2018/801).

Derivative right to reside

16.—(1) A person has a derivative right to reside during any period in which the person—

(a) is not an exempt person; and

(b) satisfies each of the criteria in one or more of paragraphs (2) to (6).

(2) The criteria in this paragraph are that—

(a) the person is the primary carer of an EEA national; and

(b) the EEA national—

(i) is under the age of 18;

(ii) resides in the United Kingdom as a self-sufficient person; and

(iii) would be unable to remain in the United Kingdom if the person left the United Kingdom for an indefinite period.

(3) The criteria in this paragraph are that—

(a) any of the person's parents ('PP') is an EEA national who resides or has resided in the United Kingdom;

(b) both the person and PP reside or have resided in the United Kingdom at the same time, and during such a period of residence, PP has been a worker in the United Kingdom; and

(c) the person is in education in the United Kingdom.

(4) The criteria in this paragraph are that—

(a) the person is the primary carer of a person satisfying the criteria in paragraph (3) ('PPP'); and

(b) PPP would be unable to continue to be educated in the United Kingdom if the person left the United Kingdom for an indefinite period.

(5) The criteria in this paragraph are that—

(a) the person is the primary carer of a British citizen ('BC');

(b) BC is residing in the United Kingdom; and

(c) BC would be unable to reside in the United Kingdom or in another EEA State if the person left the United Kingdom for an indefinite period.

(6) The criteria in this paragraph are that—

(a) the person is under the age of 18;

(b) the person does not have leave to enter, or remain in, the United Kingdom under the 1971 Act [(but see paragraph (7A))];

(c) the person's primary carer is entitled to a derivative right to reside in the United Kingdom under paragraph (2), (4) or (5); and

(d) the primary carer would be prevented from residing in the United Kingdom if the person left the United Kingdom for an indefinite period.

(7) In this regulation—

(a) 'education' excludes nursery education but does not exclude education received before the compulsory school age where that education is equivalent to the education received at or after the compulsory school age;

(b) 'worker' does not include a jobseeker or a person treated as a worker under regulation 6(2);

(c) an 'exempt person' is a person—

(i) who has a right to reside under another provision of these Regulations;

(ii) who has the right of abode under section 2 of the 1971 Act;

(iii) to whom section 8 of the 1971 Act, or an order made under subsection (2) of that section, applies; or

(iv) who has indefinite leave to enter or remain in the United Kingdom [(but see paragraph (7A))].

[(7A) Leave to enter, or remain in, the United Kingdom under the 1971 Act which has been granted by virtue of Appendix EU to the immigration rules is not to be treated as leave for the purposes of paragraph (6)(b) or (7)(c)(iv).]

(8) A person is the 'primary carer' of another person ('AP') if—

(a) the person is a direct relative or a legal guardian of AP; and

(b) either—

(i) the person has primary responsibility for AP's care; or

(ii) shares equally the responsibility for AP's care with one other person [. . .].

(9) In paragraph (2)(b)(iii), (4)(b) or (5)(c), if the role of primary carer is shared with another person in accordance with paragraph (8)(b)(ii), the words 'the person' are to be read as 'both primary carers'.

(10) Paragraph (9) does not apply if the person with whom care responsibility is shared acquired a derivative right to reside in the United Kingdom as a result of this regulation prior to the other person's assumption of equal care responsibility.

(11) A person is not be regarded as having responsibility for another person's care for the purpose of paragraph (8) on the sole basis of a financial contribution towards that person's care.

(12) A person does not have a derivative right to reside where the Secretary of State or an immigration officer has made a decision under regulation 23(6)(b), 24(1), 25(1), 26(3) or 31(1), unless that decision is set aside or otherwise no longer has effect.

Note: Words omitted in paragraph (8)(b)(ii) from 24 July 2018 (SI 2018/801). Words inserted in paragraph 6(b) and paragraph (7)(c)(iv) and paragraph (7A) inserted from 28 March 2019 (SI 2019/468).

Part 3
Residence Documentation

Issue of registration certificate

17.—(1) The Secretary of State must issue a registration certificate to a qualified person immediately on application and production of—

(a) a valid national identity card or passport issued by an EEA State; and

(b) proof that the applicant is a qualified person.

(2) In the case of a worker, confirmation of the worker's engagement from the worker's employer or a certificate of employment is sufficient proof for the purposes of paragraph (1)(b).

(3) The Secretary of State must issue a registration certificate to an EEA national who is the family member of a qualified person or of an EEA national with a right of permanent residence under regulation 15 immediately on application and production of—

(a) a valid national identity card or passport issued by an EEA State; and

(b) proof that the applicant is such a family member.

(4) The Secretary of State must issue a registration certificate to an EEA national who is a family member who has retained the right of residence on application and production of—

(a) a valid national identity card or passport; and

(b) proof that the applicant is a family member who has retained the right of residence.

(5) The Secretary of State may issue a registration certificate to an extended family member not falling within regulation 7(3) who is an EEA national on application if—

(a) the application is accompanied or joined by a valid national identity card or passport;

(b) the relevant EEA national is a qualified person or an EEA national with a right of permanent residence under regulation 15; and

(c) in all the circumstances it appears to the Secretary of State appropriate to issue the registration certificate.

(6) Where the Secretary of State receives an application under paragraph (5) an extensive examination of the personal circumstances of the applicant must be undertaken by the Secretary of State and if the application is refused, the Secretary of State must give reasons justifying the refusal unless this is contrary to the interests of national security.

(7) A registration certificate issued under this regulation must state the name and address of the person registering and the date of registration.

(8) A registration certificate is—

(a) proof of the holder's right to reside on the date of issue;

(b) no longer valid if the holder ceases to have a right to reside under these Regulations;

(c) invalid if the holder never had a right to reside under these Regulations.

(9) This regulation is subject to regulations 24 (refusal to issue or renew and revocation of residence documentation) and 25 (cancellation of a right of residence).

Issue of residence card

18.—(1) The Secretary of State must issue a residence card to a person who is not an EEA national and is the family member of a qualified person or of an EEA national with a right of permanent residence under regulation 15 on application and production of—

(a) a valid passport; and

(b) proof that the applicant is such a family member.

(2) The Secretary of State must issue a residence card to a person who is not an EEA national but who is a family member who has retained the right of residence on application and production of—

(a) a valid passport; and

(b) proof that the applicant is a family member who has retained the right of residence.

(3) On receipt of an application under paragraph (1) or (2) and the documents that are required to accompany the application the Secretary of State must immediately issue the applicant with a certificate of application for the residence card and the residence card must be issued no later than six months after the date on which the application and documents are received.

(4) The Secretary of State may issue a residence card to an extended family member not falling within regulation 7(3) who is not an EEA national on application if—

(a) the application is accompanied or joined by a valid passport;

(b) the relevant EEA national is a qualified person or an EEA national with a right of permanent residence under regulation 15; and

(c) in all the circumstances it appears to the Secretary of State appropriate to issue the residence card.

(5) Where the Secretary of State receives an application under paragraph (4) an extensive examination of the personal circumstances of the applicant must be undertaken by the Secretary of State and if the application is refused, the Secretary of State must give reasons justifying the refusal unless this is contrary to the interests of national security.

(6) A residence card issued under this regulation is valid for—

(a) five years from the date of issue; or

(b) in the case of a residence card issued to the family member or extended family member of a qualified person, the envisaged period of residence in the United Kingdom of the qualified person, whichever is the shorter.

(7) A residence card—

(a) must be called 'Residence card of a family member of [a Union citizen]';

(b) is proof of the holder's right to reside on the date of issue;

(c) is no longer valid if the holder ceases to have a right to reside under these Regulations;

(d) is invalid if the holder never had a right to reside under these Regulations.

(8) This regulation is subject to regulations 24 and 25.

Note: Words in square brackets in paragraph (7)(a) substituted on 31 January 2017 (SI 2017/1) but effective from 1 February 2017 (commencement of SI 2016/1052, reg. 1(2)(b)).

Issue of a document certifying permanent residence and a permanent residence card

19.—(1) The Secretary of State must, as soon as possible, issue an EEA national with a right of permanent residence under regulation 15 with a document certifying permanent residence on application and the production of—

(a) a valid national identity card or passport issued by an EEA State; and

(b) proof that the EEA national has a right of permanent residence.

(2) The Secretary of State must issue a person who is not an EEA national who has a right of permanent residence under regulation 15 with a permanent residence card no later than six months after an application is received and the production of—

(a) a valid passport; and

(b) proof that the person has a right of permanent residence.

(3) Subject to paragraph (4) a permanent residence card is valid for ten years from the date of issue and must be renewed on application.

(4) A document certifying permanent residence and a permanent residence card is—

(a) proof that the holder had a right to reside under regulation 15 on the date of issue;

(b) no longer valid if the holder ceases to have a right of permanent residence under regulation 15;

(c) invalid if the holder never had a right of permanent residence under regulation 15.

(5) This regulation is subject to regulations 24 and 25.

Issue of a derivative residence card

20.—(1) The Secretary of State must issue a person with a derivative residence card on application and on production of—

(a) a valid national identity card issued by an EEA State or a valid passport; and

(b) proof that the applicant has a derivative right to reside under regulation 16.

(2) On receipt of an application under paragraph (1) the Secretary of State must issue the applicant with a certificate of application as soon as possible.

(3) A derivative residence card issued under paragraph (1) is valid until—

(a) the date five years from the date of issue; or

(b) any earlier date specified by the Secretary of State when issuing the derivative residence card.

(4) A derivative residence card issued under paragraph (1) must be issued as soon as practicable.

(5) A derivative residence card is—

(a) proof of the holder's derivative right to reside on the day of issue;

(b) no longer valid if the holder ceases to have a derivative right to reside under regulation 16;

(c) invalid if the holder never had a derivative right to reside under regulation 16.

(6) This regulation is subject to regulations 24 and 25.

Procedure for applications for documentation under this Part and regulation 12

21.—(1) An application for documentation under this Part, or for an EEA family permit under regulation 12, must be made—

(a) online, submitted electronically using the relevant pages of www.gov.uk; or

(b) by post or in person, using the relevant application form specified by the Secretary of State on www.gov.uk.

(2) All applications must—

(a) be accompanied [. . .] the evidence or proof required by this Part or regulation 12, as the case may be, as well as that required by paragraph [(5)], within the time specified by the Secretary of State on www.gov.uk; and

(b) be complete.

(3) An application for a residence card or a derivative residence card must be submitted while the applicant is in the United Kingdom.

(4) When an application is submitted otherwise than in accordance with the requirements in this regulation, it is invalid [and must be rejected].

[(4A) An application for documentation under this Part, or for an EEA family permit under regulation 12, is invalid where the person making the application is subject to a removal decision made under regulation 23(6)(b), a deportation order made under regulation 32(3) or an exclusion order made under regulation 23(5).]

(5) Where an application for documentation under this Part is made by a person who is not an EEA national on the basis that the person is or was the family member of an EEA national or an extended family member of an EEA national, the application must be accompanied [. . .] by a valid national identity card or passport in the name of that EEA national.

(6) Where—

(a) there are circumstances beyond the control of an applicant for documentation under this Part; and

(b) as a result, the applicant is unable to comply with the requirements to submit an application online or using the application form specified by the Secretary of State, the Secretary of State may accept an application submitted by post or in person which does not use the relevant application form specified by the Secretary of State.

Note: Figure in square brackets in paragraph (2)(a) substituted from 31 January 2017 (SI 2017/1) but effective from 1 February 2017 (commencement of SI 2016/1052 reg. 1(2)(b)). Words in square brackets in paragraphs (2)(a) and (5) omitted and paragraph (4A) inserted from 24 July 2018 (SI 2018/801). Words inserted in paragraph (4) from 15 August 2019 (SI 2019/1155).

Verification of a right of residence

22.—(1) This regulation applies where the Secretary of State—

(a) has reasonable doubt as to whether a person ('A') has a right to reside or a derivative right to reside; or

(b) wants to verify the eligibility of a person ('A') to apply for an EEA family permit or documentation issued under Part 3.

(2) Where this regulation applies, the Secretary of State may invite A to—

(a) provide evidence to support the existence of a right to reside or a derivative right to reside (as the case may be), or to support an application for an EEA family permit or documentation under this Part; or

(b) attend an interview with the Secretary of State.

(3) If A purports to have a right to reside on the basis of a relationship with another person ('B'), (including, where B is a British citizen, through having lived with B in another EEA State), the Secretary of State may invite B to—

(a) provide information about their relationship or residence in another EEA State; or

(b) attend an interview with the Secretary of State.

(4) If without good reason A or B (as the case may be)—

(a) fails to provide the information requested;

(b) on at least two occasions, fails to attend an interview if so invited;

the Secretary of State may draw any factual inferences about A's entitlement to a right to reside as appear appropriate in the circumstances.

(5) The Secretary of State may decide following the drawing of an inference under paragraph (4) that A does not have or ceases to have a right to reside.

(6) But the Secretary of State must not decide that A does not have or ceases to have a right to reside on the sole basis that A failed to comply with this regulation.

(7) This regulation may not be invoked systematically.

PART 4

REFUSAL OF ADMISSION AND REMOVAL ETC

Exclusion and removal from the United Kingdom

23.—(1) A person is not entitled to be admitted to the United Kingdom by virtue of regulation 11 if a refusal to admit that person is justified on grounds of public policy, public security or public health in accordance with regulation 27.

(2) A person is not entitled to be admitted to the United Kingdom by virtue of regulation 11 if that person is subject to a deportation or exclusion order, except where the person is temporarily admitted pursuant to regulation 41.

(3) A person is not entitled to be admitted to the United Kingdom by virtue of regulation 11 if the Secretary of State considers there to be reasonable grounds to suspect that the person's admission would lead to the misuse of a right to reside under regulation 26(1).

(4) A person is not entitled to be admitted to the United Kingdom as the family member of an EEA national under regulation 11(2) unless, at the time of arrival [or the time of his production of the required documents in a control zone or a supplementary control zone] —

(a) that person is accompanying the EEA national or joining the EEA national in the United Kingdom; and

(b) the EEA national has a right to reside.

(5) If the Secretary of State considers that the exclusion of the EEA national or the family member of an EEA national is justified on the grounds of public policy, public security or public health in accordance with regulation 27 the Secretary of State may make an order prohibiting that person from entering the United Kingdom.

(6) Subject to paragraphs (7) and (8), an EEA national who has entered the United Kingdom or the family member of such a national who has entered the United Kingdom may be removed if—

(a) that person does not have or ceases to have a right to reside under these Regulations;

(b) the Secretary of State has decided that the person's removal is justified on grounds of public policy, public security or public health in accordance with regulation 27; or

(c) the Secretary of State has decided that the person's removal is justified on grounds of misuse of rights under regulation 26(3).

(7) A person must not be removed under paragraph (6)—

(a) as the automatic consequence of having recourse to the social assistance system of the United Kingdom; or

(b) if that person has leave to remain in the United Kingdom under the 1971 Act unless that person's removal is justified on the grounds of public policy, public security or public health in accordance with regulation 27.

(8) A decision under paragraph (6)(b) must state that upon execution of any deportation order arising from that decision, the person against whom the order was made is prohibited from entering the United Kingdom—

(a) until the order is revoked; or

(b) for the period specified in the order.

(9) A decision taken under paragraph (6)(b) or (c) has the effect of terminating any right to reside otherwise enjoyed by the individual concerned.

Note: Words inserted in paragraph (4) from 30 September 2020 (SI 1993/1813 Sch. 4 para 5).

Refusal to issue or renew and revocation of residence documentation

24.—(1) The Secretary of State may refuse to issue, revoke or refuse to renew a registration certificate, a residence card, a document certifying permanent residence or a permanent residence card if the refusal or revocation is justified on grounds of public policy, public security or public health, or on grounds of misuse of rights in accordance with regulation 26(3).

(2) A decision under regulation 23(6) or 32(4) to remove a person from the United Kingdom, or a decision under regulation 31 to revoke a person's admission to the United Kingdom invalidates a registration certificate, residence card, document certifying permanent residence or permanent residence card held by that person or an application made by that person for such a certificate, card or document.

(3) The Secretary of State may revoke or refuse to renew a registration certificate or a residence card if the holder of the certificate or card has ceased to have, or never had, a right to reside under these Regulations.

(4) The Secretary of State may revoke or refuse to renew a document certifying permanent residence or a permanent residence card if the holder of the certificate or card has ceased to have, or never had, a right of permanent residence under regulation 15.

(5) An immigration officer may, at the time of a person's arrival in the United Kingdom [or the time of his production of the required documents in a control zone or supplementary control zone]—

(a) revoke that person's residence card if the person is not at that time the family member of a qualified person or of an EEA national who has a right of permanent residence under regulation 15, a family member who has retained a right of residence or a person with a right of permanent residence under regulation 15;

(b) revoke that person's permanent residence card if the person is not at that time a person with a right of permanent residence under regulation 15.

(6) An entry clearance officer [or an immigration officer] may at any time revoke a person's EEA family permit {, including one issued in electronic form,} if—

(a) the revocation is justified on grounds of public policy, public security or public health; or

(b) the person is not at that time the family member of an EEA national with the right to reside in the United Kingdom under these Regulations or is not accompanying that EEA national or joining that EEA national in the United Kingdom.

(7) Any action taken under this regulation on grounds of public policy, public security or public health must be in accordance with regulation 27.

Note: In paragraph (6) words in square brackets inserted from 31 January 2017 (SI 2017/1) but effective from 1 February 2017 (commencement of SI 2016/1052). Words in curly brackets in paragraph (6) inserted from 24 July 2018 (SI 2018/801). Words inserted in paragraph (5) from 30 September 2020 (SI 1993/1813 Sch. 4 para 5).

Cancellation of a right of residence

25.—(1) Where the conditions in paragraph (2) are met the Secretary of State may cancel a person's right to reside.

(2) The conditions in this paragraph are met where—

(a) a person has a right to reside in the United Kingdom as a result of these Regulations;

(b) the Secretary of State has decided that the cancellation of that person's right to reside in the United Kingdom is justified on the grounds of public policy, public security or public health in accordance with regulation 27 or on grounds of misuse of rights in accordance with regulation 26(3);

(c) the circumstances are such that the Secretary of State cannot make a decision under regulation 24(1); and`

(d) it is not possible for the Secretary of State to remove the person from the United Kingdom under regulation 23(6)(b) or (c).

Misuse of a right to reside

26.—(1) The misuse of a right to reside occurs where a person—

(a) observes the requirements of these Regulations in circumstances which do not achieve the purpose of these Regulations (as determined by reference to Council Directive 2004/38/EC and the EU Treaties); and

(b) intends to obtain an advantage from these Regulations by engaging in conduct which artificially creates the conditions required to satisfy the criteria set out in these Regulations.

(2) Such misuse includes attempting to enter the United Kingdom within 12 months of being removed under regulation 23(6)(a), where the person attempting to do so is unable to provide evidence that, upon re-entry to the United Kingdom, the conditions for a right to reside, other than the initial right of residence under regulation 13, will be met.

(3) The Secretary of State may take an EEA decision on the grounds of misuse of rights where there are reasonable grounds to suspect the misuse of a right to reside and it is proportionate to do so.

(4) Where, as a result of paragraph (2), the removal of a person under regulation 23(6)(a) may prevent that person from returning to the United Kingdom during the 12 month

period following removal, during that 12 month period the person who was removed may apply to the Secretary of State to have the effect of paragraph (2) set aside on the grounds that there has been a material change in the circumstances which justified that person's removal under regulation 23(6)(a).

(5) An application under paragraph (4) may only be made whilst the applicant is outside the United Kingdom.

(6) This regulation may not be invoked systematically.

Decisions taken on grounds of public policy, public security and public health

27.—(1) In this regulation, a 'relevant decision' means an EEA decision taken on the grounds of public policy, public security or public health.

(2) A relevant decision may not be taken to serve economic ends.

(3) A relevant decision may not be taken in respect of a person with a right of permanent residence under regulation 15 except on serious grounds of public policy and public security.

(4) A relevant decision may not be taken except on imperative grounds of public security in respect of an EEA national who—

(a) [has a right of permanent residence under regulation 15 and who] has resided in the United Kingdom for a continuous period of at least ten years prior to the relevant decision; or

(b) is under the age of 18, unless the relevant decision is in the best interests of the person concerned, as provided for in the Convention on the Rights of the Child adopted by the General Assembly of the United Nations on 20th November 1989.

(5) The public policy and public security requirements of the United Kingdom include restricting rights otherwise conferred by these Regulations in order to protect the fundamental interests of society, and where a relevant decision is taken on grounds of public policy or public security it must also be taken in accordance with the following principles—

(a) the decision must comply with the principle of proportionality;

(b) the decision must be based exclusively on the personal conduct of the person concerned;

(c) the personal conduct of the person must represent a genuine, present and sufficiently serious threat affecting one of the fundamental interests of society, taking into account past conduct of the person and that the threat does not need to be imminent;

(d) matters isolated from the particulars of the case or which relate to considerations of general prevention do not justify the decision;

(e) a person's previous criminal convictions do not in themselves justify the decision;

(f) the decision may be taken on preventative grounds, even in the absence of a previous criminal conviction, provided the grounds are specific to the person.

(6) Before taking a relevant decision on the grounds of public policy and public security in relation to a person ('P') who is resident in the United Kingdom, the decision maker must take account of considerations such as the age, state of health, family and economic situation of P, P's length of residence in the United Kingdom, P's social and cultural integration into the United Kingdom and the extent of P's links with P's country of origin.

(7) In the case of a relevant decision taken on grounds of public health—

(a) a disease that does not have epidemic potential as defined by the relevant instruments of the World Health Organisation or is not a disease listed in Schedule 1 to the Health Protection (Notification) Regulations 2010; or

(b) if the person concerned is in the United Kingdom, any disease occurring after the three month period beginning on the date on which the person arrived in the United Kingdom,

does not constitute grounds for the decision.

(8) A court or tribunal considering whether the requirements of this regulation are met must (in particular) have regard to the considerations contained in Schedule 1 (considerations of public policy, public security and the fundamental interests of society etc.).

Note: Words inserted in paragraph (4)(a) from 24 July 2018 (SI 2018/801).

Application of Part 4 to a person with a derivative right to reside

28.—(1) This regulation applies where a person—

(a) would, but for this Part of these Regulations, be entitled to a derivative right to reside (other than a derivative right to reside conferred by regulation 16(3));

(b) holds a derivative residence card; or

(c) has applied for a derivative residence card.

(2) Where this regulation applies, this Part of these Regulations applies as though—

(a) references to 'the family member of an EEA national' referred instead to 'a person with a derivative right to reside';

(b) references to a registration certificate, a residence card, a document certifying permanent residence or a permanent residence card referred instead to a 'derivative residence card';

(c) regulation 24(5) instead conferred on an immigration officer the power to revoke a derivative residence card where the holder is not at that time a person with a derivative right to reside; and

(d) regulations 24(4) and 27(3) and (4) were omitted.

PART 5

PROCEDURE IN RELATION TO EEA DECISIONS

Person claiming right of admission

29.—(1) This regulation applies to a person who claims a right of admission to the United Kingdom under regulation 11 as—

(a) a person, not being an EEA national, who—

(i) is a family member of an EEA national;

(ii) is a family member who has retained the right of residence;

(iii) has a derivative right to reside;

(iv) has a right of permanent residence under regulation 15; or

(v) is in possession of a qualifying EEA State residence card;

(b) an EEA national, where there is reason to believe that the EEA national may be a person to whom regulation 23(1), (2), (3) or (4) applies; or

(c) a person to whom regulation 41 applies (temporary admission to submit case in person).

(2) A person to whom this regulation applies is to be treated as if that person were a person seeking leave to enter the United Kingdom under the 1971 Act for the purposes of paragraphs 2, 3, 4, 7 [and 16 to 18A] of Schedule 2 to the 1971 Act (administrative provisions as to control on entry etc), except that—

(a) the reference in paragraph 2(1) to the purpose for which the immigration officer may examine any persons who have arrived in the United Kingdom is to be read as a reference to the purpose of determining whether the person is to be granted admission under these Regulations;

(b) the references in paragraphs 3, 7 and 16(1) to a person who is, or may be, given leave to enter are to be read as references to a person who is, or may be, granted admission under these Regulations; and

(c) a medical examination is not to be carried out under paragraph 2 or paragraph 7 as a matter of routine and may only be carried out within three months of the person's arrival in the United Kingdom.

[(3) For so long as a person to whom this regulation applies is detained under the powers conferred by Schedule 2 to the 1971 Act, or granted bail under Schedule 10 to the 2016 Act whilst liable to be detained under the powers conferred by Schedule 2 to the 1971 Act, the person is deemed not to have been admitted to the United Kingdom.]

Note: Words in square brackets in paragraph (2) and paragraph (3) substituted from 15 January 2018 (SI 2017/1242).

Person refused admission

30.—(1) This regulation applies to a person who is in the United Kingdom and has been refused admission to the United Kingdom—

(a) because that person does not meet the requirements of regulation 11 (including where that person does not meet those requirements because that person's EEA family permit, residence card, derivative residence card or permanent residence card has been revoked by an immigration officer in accordance with regulation 24); or

(b) in accordance with regulation 23(1), (2), (3) or (4).

(2) A person to whom this regulation applies, is to be treated as if the person were a person refused leave to enter under the 1971 Act for the purpose of paragraphs 8, 10, 10A, 11, [and 16 to 19] of Schedule 2 to the 1971 Act {(and the provisions of Schedule 10 to the 2016 Act apply accordingly)}, except that the reference in paragraph 19 to a certificate of entitlement, entry clearance or work permit is to be read as a reference to an EEA family permit, residence card, derivative residence card, a qualifying EEA State residence card, or a permanent residence card.

Note: Words in square brackets substituted and words in curly brackets inserted in paragraph (2) from 15 January 2018 (SI 2017/1242).

Revocation of admission

31.—(1) This regulation applies to a person admitted to the United Kingdom under regulation 11 in circumstances where, under regulation 23(1), (2) or (3) that person was not entitled to be admitted.

(2) Paragraph 6(2) of Schedule 2 to the 1971 Act (administrative provisions as to control on entry: refusal of leave to enter) applies to a person to whom this regulation applies, as though the references:

(a) to that person's examination under paragraph 2 of Schedule 2 to the 1971 Act were to that paragraph as applied by regulation 29(2)(a) and (c);

(b) to notices of leave to enter the United Kingdom were to a decision to admit that person to the United Kingdom under these Regulations; and

(c) to the cancellation of such a notice and the refusal of leave to enter were to revocation of the decision to admit that person to the United Kingdom under this regulation.

(3) Where a person's admission to the United Kingdom is revoked, that person is to be treated as a person to whom admission to the United Kingdom has been refused and regulation 30 applies accordingly.

Person subject to removal

32.—(1) If there are reasonable grounds for suspecting that a person is someone who may be removed from the United Kingdom under regulation 23(6)(b), that person may be detained under the authority of the Secretary of State pending a decision whether or not to remove the person under that regulation, and paragraphs 17 to 18A of Schedule 2 to the 1971 Act apply in relation to the detention of such a person as those paragraphs apply in relation to a person who may be detained under paragraph 16 of that Schedule.

(2) Where a decision is taken to remove a person under regulation 23(6)(a) or (c), the person is to be treated as if the person were a person to whom section 10(1) of the 1999 Act applies, and section 10 of that Act (removal of certain persons unlawfully in the United Kingdom) is to apply accordingly.

(3) Where a decision is taken to remove a person under regulation 23(6)(b), the person is to be treated as if the person were a person to whom section 3(5)(a) of the 1971 Act (liability to deportation) applies, and section 5 of that Act (procedure for deportation) and Schedule 3 to that Act (supplementary provision as to deportation) are to apply accordingly.

(4) A person who enters the United Kingdom in breach of a deportation or exclusion order, or in circumstances where that person was not entitled to be admitted under regulation 23(1) or (3), is removable as an illegal entrant under Schedule 2 to the 1971 Act and the provisions of that Schedule apply accordingly.

(5) Where a deportation order is made against a person but the person is not removed under the order during the two year period beginning on the date on which the order is made, the Secretary of State may only take action to remove the person under the order at the end of that period if, having assessed whether there has been any material change in circumstances since the deportation order was made, the Secretary of State considers that the removal continues to be justified on the grounds of public policy, public security or public health.

(6) A person to whom this regulation applies must be allowed one month to leave the United Kingdom, beginning on the date on which the decision to remove is communicated before being removed because of that decision except—

(a) in duly substantiated cases of urgency;

(b) where the person is detained pursuant to the sentence or order of any court;

(c) where the person is a person to whom paragraph (4) applies.

(7) Paragraph (6) does not apply where a decision has been taken under regulation 23(6) on the basis that the relevant person—

(a) has ceased to have a derivative right to reside; or

(b) is a person who would have had a derivative right to reside but for the effect of a decision to remove under regulation 23(6)(b).

Human rights considerations and interim orders to suspend removal

33.—(1) This regulation applies where the Secretary of State intends to give directions for the removal of a person ('P') to whom regulation 32(3) applies, in circumstances where—

(a) P has not appealed against the EEA decision to which regulation 32(3) applies, but would be entitled, and remains within time, to do so from within the United Kingdom (ignoring any possibility of an appeal out of time with permission); or

(b) P has so appealed but the appeal has not been finally determined.

(2) The Secretary of State may only give directions for P's removal if the Secretary of State certifies that, despite the appeals process not having been begun or not having been finally determined, removal of P to the country or territory to which P is proposed to be removed, pending the outcome of P's appeal, would not be unlawful under section 6 of the Human Rights Act 1998 (public authority not to act contrary to Human Rights Convention).

(3) The grounds upon which the Secretary of State may certify a removal under paragraph (2) include (in particular) that P would not, before the appeal is finally determined, face a real risk of serious irreversible harm if removed to the country or territory to which P is proposed to be removed.

(4) If P applies to the appropriate court or tribunal (whether by means of judicial review or otherwise) for an interim order to suspend enforcement of the removal decision, P may not be removed from the United Kingdom until such time as the decision on the interim order has been taken, except—

(a) where the removal decision is based on a previous judicial decision;

(b) where P has had previous access to judicial review; or

(c) where the removal decision is based on imperative grounds of public security.

(5) In this regulation, 'finally determined' has the same meaning as in Part 6.

Revocation of deportation and exclusion orders

34.—(1) An exclusion order remains in force unless it is revoked by the Secretary of State under this regulation.

(2) A deportation order remains in force—

(a) until the order is revoked under this regulation; or

(b) for the period specified in the order.

(3) A person who is subject to a deportation or exclusion order may only apply to the Secretary of State to have it revoked on the basis that there has been a material change in the circumstances that justified the making of the order.

(4) An application under paragraph (3) must set out the material change in circumstances relied upon by the applicant and may only be made whilst the applicant is outside the United Kingdom.

(5) On receipt of an application under paragraph (3), the Secretary of State must revoke the order if the Secretary of State considers that the criteria for making such an order are no longer satisfied.

(6) The Secretary of State must take a decision on an application under paragraph (2) no later than six months after the date on which the application is received.

PART 6
APPEALS UNDER THESE REGULATIONS

Interpretation of Part 6

35.—(1) In this Part—

'the 1997 Act' means the Special Immigration Appeals Commission Act 1997;

'Commission' has the same meaning as in the 1997 Act.

(2) For the purposes of this Part, and subject to paragraphs (3) and (4), an appeal is to be treated as pending during the period when notice of appeal is given and ending when the appeal is finally determined, withdrawn or abandoned.

(3) An appeal is not to be treated as finally determined while a further appeal may be brought; and, if such a further appeal is brought, the original appeal is not to be treated as finally determined until the further appeal is determined, withdrawn or abandoned.

(4) A pending appeal is not to be treated as abandoned solely because the appellant leaves the United Kingdom.

Appeal rights

36.—(1) The subject of an EEA decision may appeal against that decision under these Regulations.

(2) If a person claims to be an EEA national, that person may not appeal under these Regulations without producing a valid national identity card or passport issued by an EEA State.

(3) If a person claims to be in a durable relationship with an EEA national, that person may not appeal under these Regulations without producing—

(a) a valid passport; and

(b) either—

(i) an EEA family permit; or

(ii) sufficient evidence to satisfy the Secretary of State that the person is in a relationship with the EEA national.

(4) If a person to whom paragraph (2) does not apply claims to be the family member of an EEA national under regulation 7, the relative of an EEA national who is an extended family member under regulation 8, or a family member who has retained the right of residence under regulation 10, that person may not appeal under these Regulations without producing—

(a) a valid passport; and

(b) either—

(i) an EEA family permit

(ii) a qualifying EEA State residence card;

(iii) in the case of a person claiming to be the family member of an EEA national, [proof that the definition of 'family member' in regulation 7(1) is met]; [. . .]

(iv) in the case of a person claiming to be a family member who has retained the right of residence, [proof that the definition of 'family member who has retained the right of residence' in regulation 10(1) is met; or]

[(v) in the case of a person claiming to be the relative of an EEA national who is an extended family member, proof that the definition of 'extended family member' in regulation 8(1) is met.].

(5) If a person ('P') claims to have a derivative right to reside, P may not appeal under these Regulations unless P produces a valid national identity card issued by an EEA State or a valid passport, and either—

(a) an EEA family permit; or

(b) where P claims to have a derivative right to reside as a result of—

(i) regulation 16(2), proof that P is a direct relative or legal guardian of an EEA national who is under the age of 18;

(ii) regulation 16(3), proof that P is the child of an EEA national;

(iii) regulation 16(4), proof that P is a direct relative or legal guardian of the child of an EEA national;

(iv) regulation 16(5), proof that P is a direct relative or legal guardian of a British citizen;

(v) regulation 16(6), proof that P is under the age of 18 and is a dependant of a person satisfying the criteria in paragraph (i), (iii) or (iv).

(6) If a person claims to be entitled to a right to reside under regulation 9 (family members [or extended family members] of British citizens), that person may not appeal without producing a valid passport and either—

(a) an EEA family permit; or

(b) [in respect of a family member,] a qualifying EEA State residence card;

and

(i) proof that the criteria to be a family member of the British citizen are met; and

(ii) proof that the British citizen is residing, or did reside, in another EEA State as a worker, self-employed person, self-sufficient person or student.

[(c)in respect of an extended family member—

[. . .]

(ii) proof that—

(aa) the condition in regulation 9(1A)(b) is met;

(bb) the criteria to be [an extended family member] of the British citizen are met, and

(cc) the British citizen is residing, or did reside, in another EEA State as a worker, self-employed person, self-sufficient person or a student]

(7) The Secretary of State or an immigration officer may certify a ground for the purposes of paragraph (8) if it has been considered in a previous appeal brought under these Regulations or under section 82(1) of the 2002 Act.

(8) A person may not bring an appeal under these Regulations on a ground certified under paragraph (7) or rely on such a ground in an appeal brought under these Regulations.

(9) Except where an appeal lies to the Commission, an appeal under these Regulations lies to the First-tier Tribunal.

(10) The provisions of, or made under, the 2002 Act referred to in Schedule 2 have effect for the purposes of an appeal under these Regulations to the First-tier Tribunal in accordance with that Schedule.

(11) Nothing in this Part prevents a person who has a right of appeal under this regulation from appealing to the First-tier Tribunal under section 82(1) of the 2002 Act (right of appeal to the Tribunal), or, where relevant, to the Commission pursuant to section 2 of the 1997 Act (jurisdiction of the Commission: appeals), provided the criteria for bringing such an appeal under those Acts are met.

[(12) Where there is a requirement under this regulation to produce an EEA family permit—

(a) where notice of appeal is given electronically, the permit may be produced either in paper or electronic form;

(b) in all other cases, the permit must be produced in paper form.]

Note: Paragraph 12 inserted from 24 July 2018 (2018/801). Words inserted in paragraph (6) and paragraph (6)(b) from 28 March 2019 (SI 2019/468). Paragraph (6)(c) inserted from 28 March 2019 (SI 2019/468) and paragraph (6)(c)(i) omitted and words substituted in paragraph (6)(c)(ii)(bb) from 15 August 2019 (SI 2019/1155). Words substituted and word omitted in paragraph (4)(b)(iii), words substituted in paragraph (4)(b)(iv) and paragraph 4(b)(v) inserted from 15 August 2019 (SI 2019/1155).

Out of country appeals

37.—(1) Subject to paragraph (2), a person may not appeal under regulation 36 whilst in the United Kingdom against an EEA decision—

(a) to refuse to admit that person to the United Kingdom;

(b) to revoke that person's admission to the United Kingdom;

(c) to make an exclusion order against that person;

(d) to refuse to revoke a deportation or exclusion order made against the person;

(e) to refuse to issue the person with an EEA family permit;

(f) to revoke, or to refuse to issue or renew any document under these Regulations where that decision is taken at a time when the person is outside the United Kingdom; or

(g) to remove the person from the United Kingdom following entry to the United Kingdom in breach of a deportation or exclusion order, or in circumstances where that person was not entitled to be admitted pursuant to regulation 23(1), (2), (3) or (4).

(2) Sub-paragraphs (a) to (c) of paragraph (1) do not apply where the person is in the United Kingdom and—

[(a) the person, not being a person who is deemed not to have been admitted to the United Kingdom under regulation 29(3)(7)—

(i) holds a valid EEA family permit, registration certificate, residence card, derivative residence card, document certifying permanent residence, permanent residence card or qualifying EEA State residence card on arrival in the United Kingdom; or

(ii) can otherwise prove that the person is resident in the United Kingdom; or]

(b) the person is deemed not to have been admitted to the United Kingdom under regulation 29(3) but at the date on which notice of the decision to refuse admission is given the person has been in the United Kingdom for at least 3 months.

Note: Paragraph 2(a) substituted from 24 July 2018 (SI 2018/801) and subject to saving provision: 'Notwithstanding the amendment to regulation 37 of the 2016 Regulations (out of country appeals) made by paragraph 15 of the Schedule, regulation 37 as in force immediately before the coming into force of these Regulations continues to apply to an appeal that is pending (within the meaning of regulation 35 of the 2016 Regulations (interpretation of Part 6))' (regulation 4 of SI 2018/801).

Appeals to the Commission

38.—(1) An appeal against an EEA decision lies to the Commission where paragraph (2) or (4) applies.

(2) This paragraph applies if the Secretary of State certifies that the EEA decision was taken—

(a) by the Secretary of State wholly or partly on a ground listed in paragraph (3); or

(b) in accordance with a direction of the Secretary of State which identifies the person to whom the decision relates and which is given wholly or partly on a ground listed in paragraph (3).

(3) The ground mentioned in paragraph (2) are that the person's exclusion or removal from the United Kingdom is—

(a) in the interests of national security; or

(b) in the interests of the relationship between the United Kingdom and another country.

(4) This paragraph applies if the Secretary of State certifies that the EEA decision was taken wholly or partly in reliance on information which the Secretary of State considers must not be made public—

(a) in the interests of national security;

(b) in the interests of the relationship between the United Kingdom and another country; or

(c) otherwise in the public interest.

(5) In paragraphs (2) and (4) the reference to the Secretary of State is a reference to the Secretary of State acting in person.

(6) Where a certificate is issued under paragraph (2) or (4) in respect of a pending appeal to the First-tier Tribunal or Upper Tribunal the appeal must lapse.

(7) An appeal against an EEA decision lies to the Commission where an appeal lapses by virtue of paragraph (6).

(8) The 1997 Act applies to an appeal to the Commission under this regulation as it applies to an appeal under section 2 of that Act.

(9) Where the 1997 Act applies to an appeal to the Commission under this regulation, section 2(2) of that Act is to be treated as though it applies the 2002 Act to that appeal in the form modified by Schedule 2 to these Regulations.

National Security: EEA Decisions

39.—(1) Section 97A of the 2002 Act applies to an appeal against an EEA decision where the Secretary of State has certified under regulation 38(2) or (4) that the EEA decision was taken in the interests of national security.

(2) Where section 97A so applies, it has effect as if—

(a) the references in that section to a deportation order were to an EEA decision;

(b) subsections (1), (1A), (2)(b) and (4) were omitted;

(c) the reference in subsection (2)(a) to section 79 were a reference to regulations 37(2) and 40 of these Regulations; and

(d) in subsection (2A) for sub-paragraphs (a) and (b), 'against an EEA decision' were substituted.

Effect of appeals to the First-tier Tribunal or Upper Tribunal

40.—(1) This regulation applies to appeals under these Regulations made to the First-tier Tribunal or Upper Tribunal.

(2) If a person in the United Kingdom appeals against an EEA decision refusing admission to the United Kingdom (other than a decision under regulation 23(1), (2), or (5)), any directions for that person's removal from the United Kingdom previously given by virtue of the refusal cease to have effect, except in so far as they have already been carried out, while the appeal is pending.

(3) If a person in the United Kingdom appeals against an EEA decision concerning that person's removal from the United Kingdom (other than a decision under regulation 23(6)(b)), any directions for removal given under section 10 of the 1999 Act or Schedule 3 to the 1971 Act are to have no effect, except in so far as they have already been carried out, while the appeal is pending.

(4) The provisions of Part 1 of Schedule 2, or as the case may be, Schedule 3 to the 1971 Act concerning detention and persons liable to detention, apply to a person appealing against a refusal of admission, a decision to revoke admission, or a removal decision as if there were in force directions for that person's removal from the United Kingdom, except that the person may not be detained on board a ship or aircraft so as to compel that person to leave the United Kingdom while the appeal is pending [and the provisions of Schedule 10 to the 2016 Act apply accordingly].

(5) In paragraph (4), the words 'except that the person' to the end do not apply to an EEA decision to which regulation 33 applies (human rights considerations and interim orders to suspend removal).

(6) In calculating the period of two months limited by paragraph 8(2) of Schedule 2 to the 1971 Act for—

(a) the giving of directions under that paragraph for the removal of a person from the United Kingdom; and

(b) the giving of a notice of intention to give such directions, any period during which there is an appeal pending by that person is to be disregarded (except in cases where the EEA decision was taken under regulation 23(1), (2), (5) and (6)(b).

(7) [. . .]

Note: Words in square brackets in paragraph (4) inserted and paragraph (7) omitted from 15 January 2018 (SI 2017/1242).

Temporary admission to submit case in person

41.—(1) This regulation applies where—

(a) a person ('P') is subject to a decision to remove made under regulation 23(6)(b);

(b) P has appealed against the decision referred to in sub-paragraph (a);

(c) a date for P's appeal has been set by the First-tier Tribunal or Upper Tribunal;

(d) P wants to make submissions before the First-tier Tribunal or Upper Tribunal in person; and

(e) P is outside the United Kingdom.

(2) P may apply to the Secretary of State for permission to be temporarily admitted [. . .] to the United Kingdom in order to make submissions in person.

(3) The Secretary of State must grant P permission, except when P's appearance may cause serious troubles to public policy or public security.

(4) When determining when P is entitled to be given permission, and the duration of P's temporary admission should permission be granted, the Secretary of State must have regard to the dates upon which P will be required to make submissions in person.

(5) Where—

(a) P is temporarily admitted to the United Kingdom pursuant to this regulation;

(b) a hearing of P's appeal has taken place; and

(c) the appeal is not finally determined,

P may be removed from the United Kingdom pending the remaining stages of the appeal (but P may apply to return to the United Kingdom to make submissions in person during the remaining stages of the appeal in accordance with this regulation).

(6) Where the Secretary of State grants P permission to be temporarily admitted to the United Kingdom under this regulation, upon such admission P is to be treated as if P were a person refused leave to enter under the 1971 Act for the purposes of paragraphs 8, 10, 10A, 11 [and 16 to 18A] of Schedule 2 to the 1971 Act {and the provisions of Schedule 10 to the 2016 Act apply accordingly}.

(7) Where Schedule 2 to the 1971 Act so applies, it has effect as if—

(a) the reference in paragraph 8(1) to leave to enter were a reference to admission to the United Kingdom under these Regulations; and

(b) the reference in paragraph 16(1) to detention pending a decision regarding leave to enter or remain in the United Kingdom were to detention pending submission of P's case in person in accordance with this regulation.

(8) P is deemed not to have been admitted to the United Kingdom during any time during which P is temporarily admitted pursuant to this regulation.

[(9) For the purposes of this regulation, a person ('P') is temporarily admitted to the United Kingdom if P is admitted on bail under Schedule 10 to the 2016 Act without having otherwise been admitted, and the expression temporary admission is to be construed accordingly.]

Note: Words omitted from paragraph (2), words in square brackets substituted in paragraph (6), words in curly brackets in paragraph (6) and paragraph (9) inserted from 15 January 2018 (SI 2017/1242).

Alternative evidence of identity and nationality

42.—(1) Subject to paragraph (2), where a provision of these Regulations requires a person to hold or produce a valid national identity card issued by an EEA State or a valid passport, the Secretary of State may accept alternative evidence of identity and nationality where the person is unable to obtain or produce the required document due to circumstances beyond the person's control.

(2) This regulation does not apply to regulation 11.

Part 7
General

Effect on other legislation

43. Schedule 3 (effect on other legislation) has effect.

Substitution of regulation 9 of the 2006 Regulations

44. [. . .]

Note: Regulation 44 omitted from 1 February 2017 (SI 2016/1052).

Revocations, savings, transitory and transitional provisions and consequential modifications

45. Schedule 4 (revocations and savings), Schedule 6 (transitional provisions) and Schedule 7 (consequential modifications) have effect.

Revocation of regulation 44 and Schedule 5

46. The following are revoked—

(a) regulation 44;
(b) Schedule 5.

Regulation 27

Schedule 1
Considerations of Public Policy, Public Security and the Fundamental Interests of Society Etc.

Considerations of public policy and public security

1. The EU Treaties do not impose a uniform scale of public policy or public security values: member States enjoy considerable discretion, acting within the parameters set by the EU Treaties, applied where relevant by the EEA agreement, to define their own standards of public policy and public security, for purposes tailored to their individual contexts, from time to time.

Application of paragraph 1 to the United Kingdom

2. An EEA national or the family member of an EEA national having extensive familial and societal links with persons of the same nationality or language does not amount to integration in the United Kingdom; a significant degree of wider cultural and societal integration must be present before a person may be regarded as integrated in the United Kingdom.

3. Where an EEA national or the family member of an EEA national has received a custodial sentence, or is a persistent offender, the longer the sentence, or the more numerous the convictions, the greater the likelihood that the individual's continued presence in the United Kingdom represents a genuine, present and sufficiently serious threat affecting of the fundamental interests of society.

4. Little weight is to be attached to the integration of an EEA national or the family member of an EEA national within the United Kingdom if the alleged integrating links were formed at or around the same time as—

(a) the commission of a criminal offence;

(b) an act otherwise affecting the fundamental interests of society;

(c) the EEA national or family member of an EEA national was in custody.

5. The removal from the United Kingdom of an EEA national or the family member of an EEA national who is able to provide substantive evidence of not demonstrating a threat (for example, through demonstrating that the EEA national or the family member of an EEA national has successfully reformed or rehabilitated) is less likely to be proportionate.

6. It is consistent with public policy and public security requirements in the United Kingdom that EEA decisions may be taken in order to refuse, terminate or withdraw any right otherwise conferred by these Regulations in the case of abuse of rights or fraud, including—

(a) entering, attempting to enter or assisting another person to enter or to attempt to enter, a marriage, civil partnership or durable partnership of convenience; or

(b) fraudulently obtaining or attempting to obtain, or assisting another to obtain or to attempt to obtain, a right to reside under these Regulations.

The fundamental interests of society

7. For the purposes of these Regulations, the fundamental interests of society in the United Kingdom include—

(a) preventing unlawful immigration and abuse of the immigration laws, and maintaining the integrity and effectiveness of the immigration control system (including under these Regulations) and of the Common Travel Area;

(b) maintaining public order;

(c) preventing social harm;

(d) preventing the evasion of taxes and duties;

(e) protecting public services;

(f) excluding or removing an EEA national or family member of an EEA national with a conviction (including where the conduct of that person is likely to cause, or has in fact caused, public offence) and maintaining public confidence in the ability of the relevant authorities to take such action;

(g) tackling offences likely to cause harm to society where an immediate or direct victim may be difficult to identify but where there is wider societal harm (such as offences related to the misuse of drugs or crime with a cross-border dimension as mentioned in Article 83(1) of the Treaty on the Functioning of the European Union);

(h) combating the effects of persistent offending (particularly in relation to offences, which if taken in isolation, may otherwise be unlikely to meet the requirements of regulation 27);(i) protecting the rights and freedoms of others, particularly from exploitation and trafficking;

(j) protecting the public;

(k) acting in the best interests of a child (including where doing so entails refusing a child admission to the United Kingdom, or otherwise taking an EEA decision against a child);

(l) countering terrorism and extremism and protecting shared values.

Regulation 36

Schedule 2

Appeals to the First-Tier Tribunal

1. The following provisions of, or made under, the 2002 Act have effect in relation to an appeal under these Regulations to the First-tier Tribunal as if it were an appeal against a decision of the Secretary of State under section 82(1) of the 2002 Act (right of appeal to the Tribunal)—

section 84 (grounds of appeal), as though the sole permitted grounds of appeal were that the decision breaches the appellant's rights under the EU Treaties in respect of entry to or residence in the United Kingdom ('an EU ground of appeal');

section 85 (matters to be considered), as though—

(a) the references to a statement under section 120 of the 2002 Act include, but are not limited to, a statement under that section as applied by paragraph 2; and

(b) a 'matter' in subsection (2) and a 'new matter' in subsection (6) include a ground of appeal of a kind listed in section 84 of the 2002 Act and an EU ground of appeal;

section 86 (determination of appeal);

section 105 and any regulations made under that section; and

section 106 and any rules made pursuant to that section.

2.—(1) Section 92(3) of the 2002 Act has effect as though an additional basis upon which an appeal under section 82(1)(b) of that Act (human rights claim appeal) must be brought from outside the United Kingdom were that—

(a) the claim to which that appeal relates arises from an EEA decision or the consequences of an EEA decision; and

(b) the removal of that person from the United Kingdom has been certified under regulation 33 (human rights considerations and interim orders to suspend removal).

(2) Section 120 of the 2002 Act applies to a person ('P') if an EEA decision has been taken or may be taken in respect of P and, accordingly, the Secretary of State or an immigration officer may by notice require a statement from P under subsection (2) of that section, and that notice has effect for the purpose of section 96(2) of the 2002 Act.

(3) Where section 120 of the 2002 Act so applies, it has effect as though—

(a) subsection (3) also provides that a statement under subsection (2) need not repeat reasons or grounds relating to the EEA decision under challenge previously advanced by P;

(b) subsection (5) also applies where P does not have a right to reside.

(4) For the purposes of an appeal brought under section 82(1) of the 2002 Act, subsections (2) and (6)(a) of section 85 (matters to be considered) have effect as though section

84 included a ground of appeal that the decision appealed against breaches the appellant's right under the EU Treaties in respect of entry into or residence in the United Kingdom.

3. Tribunal Procedure Rules made under section 22 of the Tribunals, Courts and Enforcement Act 2007 have effect in relation to appeals under these Regulations.

Regulation 43

SCHEDULE 3

EFFECT ON OTHER LEGISLATION

Leave under the 1971 Act

1. Where a person has leave to enter or remain under the 1971 Act which is subject to conditions and that person also has a right to reside under these Regulations, those conditions do not have effect for as long as the person has that right to reside.

Person not subject to restriction on the period for which they may remain

2.—(1) For the purposes of the 1971 Act and British Nationality Act 1981, a person who has a right of permanent residence under regulation 15 must be regarded as a person who is in the United Kingdom without being subject under the immigration laws to any restriction on the period for which the person may remain.

(2) But a qualified person, the family member of a qualified person, a person with a derivative right to reside and a family member who has retained the right of residence must not, by virtue of that status, be so regarded for those purposes.

Carriers' liability under the 1999 Act

3. For the purposes of satisfying a requirement to produce a visa under section 40(1)(b) of the 1999 Act (charges in respect of passenger without proper documents), 'a visa of the required kind' includes an EEA family permit, a residence card, a derivative residence card, a qualifying EEA State residence card, or a permanent residence card required for admission under regulation 11(2), or permission to be temporarily admitted under regulation 41.

Regulation 45

SCHEDULE 4

REVOCATIONS AND SAVINGS

PART 1

TABLE OF REVOCATIONS

1.—(1) The Regulations listed in column 1 of the table are revoked.

(2) Sub-paragraph (1) is subject to the savings and transitory provisions in Part 2 of this Schedule and the transitional provisions in Schedule 6.

Table of revocations

(1)	(2)
Regulations revoked	References
The Immigration (European Economic Area) Regulations 2006	S.I.2006/1003
The Immigration (European Economic Area) (Amendment) Regulations 2009	S.I.2009/1117
The Immigration (European Economic Area) (Amendment) Regulations 2011	S.I.2011/1247
The Immigration (European Economic Area) (Amendment) Regulations 2012	S.I.2012/1547
The Immigration (European Economic Area) (Amendment) (No. 2) Regulations 2012	S.I.2012/2560
The Immigration (European Economic Area) (Amendment) Regulations 2013	S.I.2013/1391
The Immigration (Economic Area Regulations) (Amendment) (No. 2) Regulations 2013	S.I.2013/3032
The Immigration (European Economic Area) (Amendment) Regulations 2014	S.I.2014/1451
The Immigration (European Economic Area) (Amendment) (No. 2) Regulations 2014	S.I.2014/1976
The Immigration (European Economic Area) (Amendment) (No. 3) Regulations 2014	S.I.2014/2761
The Immigration (European Economic Area) (Amendment) Regulations 2015	S.I.2015/694

Part 2

Savings and Modifications

Accession member States: savings and modifications

2.—(1) Regulations 7A and 7B of the 2006 Regulations (arrangements for accession member States) continue to have effect in relation to any EEA national to whom they applied immediately before 1st February 2017.

(2) Where regulations 7A and 7B continue to have effect—

(a) they do so with the following modifications—

(i) in paragraph (3) of regulation 7A and paragraph (4) of regulation 7B, as though the references to treating periods of involuntary unemployment duly recorded by the relevant employment office as periods of work for the purposes of regulation 5(7)(c) of the 2006 Regulations were to treating such periods of involuntary unemployment as periods of work for the purposes of regulation 6(2) of these Regulations; and

(ii) as though the references to regulations 6(2) (persons who continue to be treated as a worker) and 15 (right of permanent residence) were references to those provisions in these Regulations; and

(b) these Regulations have effect save that regulation 17 (issue of registration certificate) has effect as though, in paragraph (9), for 'regulation 24' there were substituted 'regulations 7A and 7B of the 2006 Regulations and regulation 24 of these Regulations'.

[Appeals

3.—(1) Notwithstanding the revocation of the 2006 Regulations by paragraph 1(1), those Regulations continue to apply—

(a) in respect of an appeal under those Regulations against an EEA decision which is pending (within the meaning of regulation 25(2) of the 2006 Regulations) on 31st January 2017;

(b) in a case where a person has, on 31st January 2017, a right under those Regulations to appeal against an EEA decision.

(2) For the purposes of this paragraph, 'EEA decision' has the meaning given in regulation 2 of the 2006 Regulations and the definition of 'EEA decision' in regulation 2 of these Regulations does not apply.]

Note: Paragraph 3 inserted from 31 January 2017 (SI 2017/1) but effective from 1 February 2017 (commencement of SI 2016/1052, reg. 1(2)(b)).

Regulation 44

SCHEDULE 5

TRANSITORY PROVISIONS

[. . .]

Note: Schedule 5 revoked from 1 February 2017 (SI 2016/1052).

Regulation 45

SCHEDULE 6

TRANSITIONAL PROVISIONS

Interpretation

1.—(1) In this Schedule, 'permission to be temporarily admitted in order to make submissions in person' means—

(a) in relation to the 2006 Regulations, permission to be temporarily admitted under regulation 29AA(2) of the 2006 Regulations;

(b) in relation to these Regulations, permission to be temporarily admitted under regulation 41(2).

(2) References to documents applied for or issued under the 2006 Regulations are to those documents as defined in regulation 2(1) of the 2006 Regulations.

Existing documents

2.—(1) An EEA family permit issued under regulation 12 of the 2006 Regulations before 1st February 2017 is to be treated as an EEA family permit issued under regulation 12 of these Regulations.

(2) Any document issued or treated as though issued under Part 3 of the 2006 Regulations is to be treated as though issued under Part 3 of these Regulations.

(3) Nothing in this paragraph extends the validity of any document issued under the 2006 Regulations beyond that document's original period of validity.

Verification of a right of residence

3. Where, before 1st February 2017, the Secretary of State had invited a person to provide evidence or information or to attend an interview under regulation 20B of the 2006 Regulations (verification of a right of residence), the Secretary of State's invitation is to be treated as though made under regulation 22 of these Regulations.

Outstanding applications

4.—(1) An application for—

(a) an EEA family permit;
(b) a registration certificate;
(c) a residence card;
(d) a document certifying permanent residence;
(e) a permanent residence card;
(f) a derivative residence card; or
(g) permission to be temporarily admitted in order to make submissions in person;

made but not determined before 1st February 2017 is to be treated as having been made under these Regulations.

(2) But regulation 21 and the words in parentheses in paragraph (b) of the definition of an EEA decision in regulation 2(1) are of no application to such an application made before 1st February 2017

Removal decisions, deportation orders and exclusion orders under the 2006 Regulations

5.—(1) A decision to remove a person under regulation 19(3)(a), (b) or (c) of the 2006 Regulations must, upon the coming into force of Part 4 of these Regulations in its entirety, be treated as a decision to remove that person under regulation 23(6) (a), (b) or (c) of these Regulations, as the case may be.

(2) A deportation order made under regulation 24(3) of the 2006 Regulations must be treated as a deportation order made under regulation 32(3) of these Regulations.

(3) Until the coming into force of Part 4 in its entirety, a deportation order to which sub-paragraph (2) applies has effect until revoked by the Secretary of State.

(4) An exclusion order made under regulation 19(1B) of the 2006 Regulations must, upon the coming into force of Part 4 in its entirety, be treated as though having been made under regulation 23(5) of these Regulations.

(5) A person removed under regulation 19(3)(a) of the 2006 Regulations before 1st February 2017 is to be taken into account for the purposes of regulation 26(2).

(6) Where sub-paragraph (5) applies to a person, regulation 26 has effect as though the references to '12' were to '36'.

Certification under regulations 24AA and 29AA of the 2006 Regulations

6.—(1) Where the Secretary of State certified under regulation 24AA of the 2006 Regulations (human rights considerations and interim orders to suspend removal) that a person's removal from the United Kingdom would not be unlawful under section 6 of the Human Rights Act 1998 (public authority not to act contrary to the Human Rights Convention), the removal of that person is to be treated as though certified under regulation 33 of these Regulations.

(2) Where sub-paragraph (1) applies, certification treated as though given under regulation 33 does not amount to certification under that regulation for the purposes of paragraph 2(1)(b) of Schedule 2 to these Regulations (appeals to the First-tier Tribunal).

(3) Where the Secretary of State granted a person permission to be temporarily admitted to the United Kingdom to make submissions in person under regulation 29AA of the 2006 Regulations, that permission is to be treated as though given under regulation 41 of these Regulations.

(4) A person temporarily admitted to the United Kingdom in order to make submissions in person under regulation 29AA(6) of the 2006 Regulations is to be treated as though having been temporarily admitted under regulation 41(6) of these Regulations.

Appeals to the Commission

7. Where the Secretary of State certified an EEA decision under regulation 28(2) of the 2006 Regulations (appeals to the Special Immigration Appeals Commission) before 1st February 2017, that EEA decision is to be treated as though having been certified under regulation 38(2) of these Regulations.

Periods of residence prior to the coming into force of these Regulations

8.—(1) Any period of time during which an EEA national ('P') resided in the United Kingdom in accordance with the conditions listed in sub-paragraphs (2) or (3) is to be taken into account for the purpose of calculating periods of residence in the United Kingdom in accordance with these Regulations.

(2) The condition in this paragraph is that P resided in, or was treated as though having resided in, the United Kingdom in accordance with—

(a) the Immigration (European Economic Area) Regulations 2000; or

(b) the 2006 Regulations.

(3) The condition in this paragraph is that P resided in the United Kingdom in circumstances where—

(a) P was a national of a State which at that time was not an EEA State;

(b) P had leave to enter or remain in the United Kingdom under the 1971 Act for the duration of P's residence; and

(c) P would have been residing in the United Kingdom in accordance with these Regulations, had P's State of origin been an EEA State at that time, and had these Regulations been in force.

(4) Any period during which P resided in the United Kingdom in circumstances which met the conditions in sub-paragraph (2) or (3) is not to be taken into account for the purposes of sub-paragraph (1) where that residence was followed by a period of at least two continuous years during which—

(a) P was absent from the United Kingdom; or

(b) P's residence in the United Kingdom—

(i) did not meet the conditions in sub-paragraph (2) or (3); or

(ii) was not otherwise in accordance with these Regulations.

[Preservation of transitional provisions in relation to family members of dual nationals

9.—(1) Where—

(a) the right of a family member ('F') to be admitted to, or reside in, the United Kingdom pursuant to these Regulations depends on a person ('P') being an EEA national;

(b) P would be an EEA national if P was not also a British citizen; and

(c) any of the criteria in sub-paragraphs (2), (3) and (4) is met;

P will, notwithstanding the effect of the definition of an EEA national in regulation 2, be regarded as an EEA national for the purpose of these Regulations.

(2) The criterion in this sub-paragraph is met where F was on 16th July 2012 a person with the right of permanent residence in the United Kingdom under the 2006 Regulations.

(3) Subject to sub-paragraph (5), the criterion in this sub-paragraph is met where F—

(a) was on 16th July 2012 a person with a right of residence in the United Kingdom under the 2006 Regulations; and

(b) on 16th October 2012—

(i) held a valid registration certificate or residence card issued under the 2006 Regulations;

(ii) had made an application under the 2006 Regulations for a registration certificate or residence card which had not been determined; or

(iii) had made an application under the 2006 Regulations for a registration certificate or residence card which had been refused and in respect of which an appeal under regulation 26 of the 2006 Regulations could be brought while the appellant was in the United Kingdom (excluding the possibility of an appeal out of time with permission) or was pending (within the meaning of section 104 of the Nationality, Immigration and Asylum Act 2002, as it applied on 16th July 2012).

(4) Subject to sub-paragraph (6), the criterion in this sub-paragraph is met where F—

(a) had, prior to 16th July 2012, applied for an EEA family permit pursuant to regulation 12 of the 2006 Regulations; or

(b) had applied for and been refused an EEA family permit and where, on 16th July 2012, an appeal under regulation 26 of the 2006 Regulations against that decision could be brought (excluding the possibility of an appeal out of time with permission) or was pending (within the meaning of section 104 of the Nationality, Immigration and Asylum Act 2002 Act, as it applied on 16th July 2012).

(5) The criterion in sub-paragraph (3) is not met in a case to which sub-paragraph (3)(b)(ii) or (iii) applies where no registration certificate or residence card was, in fact, issued pursuant to that application.

(6) The criterion in sub-paragraph (4) is not met where—

(a) F was issued with an EEA family permit pursuant to an application made prior to 16th July 2012 but F had not been admitted to the United Kingdom within six months of the date on which it was issued; or

(b) no EEA family permit was, in fact, issued pursuant to that application.

(7) Where met, the criteria in sub-paragraphs (2), (3) and (4) remain satisfied until the occurrence of the earliest of the following events—

(a) the date on which F ceases to be the family member of P; or

(b) the date on which F's right of permanent residence is lost.

(8) P will only continue to be regarded as an EEA national for the purpose of considering the position of F under these Regulations.]

Note: Paragraph 9 inserted on 31 January 2017 (SI 2017/1) but effective from 1 February 2017 (commencement of SI 2016/1052, reg. 1(2)(b)).

Regulation 45

SCHEDULE 7

CONSEQUENTIAL MODIFICATIONS

1.—(1) Unless the context otherwise requires—

(a) any reference in any enactment to the 2006 Regulations, or a provision of the 2006 Regulations, has effect as though referring to these Regulations, or the corresponding provision of these Regulations, as the case may be;

(b) but—

(i) any reference to a provision of the 2006 Regulations in column 1 of the table has effect as though it were a reference to the corresponding provision of these Regulations listed in column 2; and

(ii) any reference to a provision of the 2006 Regulations with no corresponding provision in these Regulations ceases to have effect.

(2) Unless otherwise specified in the table, sub-divisions of the provisions of the 2006 Regulations listed in column 1 correspond to the equivalent sub-division in the corresponding provision of these Regulations.

(3) This paragraph is of no application where the reference to the 2006 Regulations had the effect of amending the 2006 Regulations. Additionally this paragraph has no application to amendments to the 2006 Regulations made under Schedule 5 of these Regulations.

Table of equivalences

(1)	(2)	(3)
Provision in the 2006 Regulations	Corresponding provision in these Regulations	Description of provision
1	1(1) to (2)	Citation and commencement
2(3)	2(2)	General interpretation
3(3)	3(3)(c)	Continuity of residence
4(2)	4(2) and (3)	'Worker', 'self-employed person', 'self-sufficient person' and 'student'
4(4)	4(2) and (4)	
6(2)(ba)	6(2)(c)	'Qualified person'
6(2)(c)	6(2)(d)	
6(2)(d)	6(2)(e)	
6(2A)	6(3)	
6(3)	6(4)	
6(4) and 6(8)	Relevant definitions in 6(1)	
6(9)	6(8)	
6(10)	6(9)	
6(11)	6(10)	
8(2)	8(2) and (7)	Extended family member
8(3)	8(3) and (7)	
9(1)	9(1) and (7)	Family members of British citizens
9(3)(a) to (c)	9(3)(a) to (e)	
9(4)	9(5)	
11(4)(ba)	11(4)(c)	Right of admission to the United Kingdom
11(4)(c)	11(4)(d)	
12(1A)	12(2)	Issue of EEA family permit
12(1B)	12(3)(a)	
12(2)	12(4)	
12(3)	12(5)	
12(4)	12(6)	
12(5)	12(7)	
12(6)	12(8)	
14(5)	14(4)	Extended right of residence
15(1A)	15(2)	Right of permanent residence
15(2)	15(3)	
15(3)	15(4)	

(1)	(2)	(3)
Provision in the 2006 Regulations	Corresponding provision in these Regulations	Description of provision
15A	16	Derivative right to reside
15A(1)	16(1)	
15A(2)	16(2)	
15A(3)	16(3)	
15A(4)	16(4)	
15A(4A)	16(5)	
15A(5)	16(6)	
15A(6)	16(7)	
15A(7)	16(8)	
15A(7A)	16(9)	
15A(7B)	16(10)	
15A(8)	16(11)	
15A(9)	16(12)	
16	17	Issue of registration certificate
16(8)	17(9)	
17	18	Issue of residence card
17(6A)	18(7)	
18	19	Issue of a document certifying permanent residence and a permanent residence card
18(5)	19(4)(b)	
18(6)	19(5)	
18A	20	Issue of a derivative residence card
18A(5)	20(6)	
19	23	Exclusion and removal from the United Kingdom
19(1A)	23(2)	
19(1AB)	23(3)	
19(1B)	23(5)	
19(2)	23(4)	
19(3)	23(6)	
19(4)	23(7)(a)	
19(5)	23(7)(b)	

(1)	(2)	(3)
Provision in the 2006 Regulations	Corresponding provision in these Regulations	Description of provision
20	24	Refusal to issue or renew and revocation of residence documentation
20(1A)	24(2)	
20(2)	24(3)	
20(3)	24(4)	
20(4)	24(5)	
20(5)	24(6)	
20(6)	24(7)	
20A	25	Cancellation of a right of residence
20B	22	Verification of a right of residence
20B(8)	Relevant definition in 2(1)	
21	27	Decisions taken on public policy, public security and public health grounds
21(5)	27(5) and (8) and Schedule 1	
21A	28	Application of Part 4 to persons with a derivative right to reside
21A(1)	28(2)	
21A(2)	28(1)	
21A(3)(c)	28(2)(a)	
21A(3)(d)	28(2)(b)	
21A(3)(f)	28(2)(c)	
21A(3)(g)	28(2)(d)	
21B	26	Misuse of a right to reside
21B(1)	26(1) and (2)	
21B(2)	26(3)	
21B(3)	26(4)	
21B(4)	26(5)	
21B(5)	26(6)	
21B(6)	Relevant definition in 2(1)	
22	29	Person claiming right of admission
23	30	Person refused admission

(1)	(2)	(3)
Provision in the 2006 Regulations	Corresponding provision in these Regulations	Description of provision
23A	31	Revocation of admission
24	32	Person subject to removal
24A	34	Revocation of deportation and exclusion orders
24A(1)	34(1) and (2)	
24A(2)	34(3)	
24A(3)	34(4)	
24A(4)	34(5)	
24A(5)	34(6)	
24AA	33	Human rights considerations and interim orders to suspend removal
25	35	Interpretation of Part 6
26	36	Appeal rights
26(2A)	36(3)	
26(3)	36(4)	
26(3A)	36(5)	
26(4)	36(8)	
26(5)	36(7)	
26(6)	36(9)	
26(7)	36(10)	
26(8)	36(11)	
27	37	Out of country appeals
27(1)(zaa)	37(1)(b)	
27(1)(aa)	37(1)(c)	
27(1)(b)	37(1)(d)	
27(1)(c)	37(1)(e)	
27(1)(ca)	37(1)(f)	
27(1)(d)	37(1)(g)	
28	38	Appeals to the Commission
28(8)	38(8) and (9)	
28A	39	National security: EEA Decisions
29	40	Effect of appeals to the First-tier Tribunal or Upper Tribunal
29(4A)	40(5)	
29(5)	40(6)	

(1)	(2)	(3)
Provision in the 2006 Regulations	Corresponding provision in these Regulations	Description of provision
29A	42	Alternative evidence of identity and nationality
29AA	41	Temporary admission in order to submit case in person
30	43	Effect on other legislation
31	45and 46	Revocations etc.
Schedule 1	Schedule 2	Appeals to the First-tier Tribunal
Schedule 1, paragraph 1	Schedule 2, paragraph 2	
Schedule 1, paragraph 2	Schedule 2, paragraph 3	
Schedule 2	Schedule 3	Effect on other legislation
Schedule 2, paragraph 1(2)	Schedule 3, paragraph 1	
Schedule 2, paragraph 3	Schedule 3, paragraph 3	
Schedule 2, paragraph 4	Schedule 2, paragraph 2	

The Immigration (Residential Accommodation) (Termination of Residential Tenancy Agreements) (Guidance etc.) Regulations 2016

(SI 2016, No. 1060)

TEXT NOT REPRODUCED

Note: The guidance entitled 'Guidance: Taking reasonable steps to end a residential tenancy agreement within a reasonable time' in force on 1st December 2016 (Regulation 2 of SI 2016/1060).

The Code of Practice (English Language Requirements for Public Sector Workers) Regulations 2016

(SI 2016, No. 1157)

TEXT NOT REPRODUCED

Note: Code of Practice in force 22 December 2016 (Regulation 2 of SI 2016/1157).

The Immigration (European Economic Area Nationals) (EU Exit) Order 2019

(SI No. 686)

Note: only articles 1 and 7 reproduced below.

PART 1

INTRODUCTION

Citation and commencement

1.—(1) This Order may be cited as the Immigration (European Economic Area Nationals) (EU Exit) Order 2019.

(2) Chapter 1 of Part 2 of this Order comes into force when the Immigration (European Economic Area) Regulations 2016 are revoked.

(3) The remaining provisions of this Order come into force on the later of 30th March 2019 or the day after the day on which they are made.

PART 2

LEAVE TO ENTER OR REMAIN

[. . .]

Note: Chapter 1 omitted from immediately before 23.00 on 31 December 2020 (SI 2020/1309)

Chapter 2

Appendix EU to the immigration rules

Grant of leave by virtue of Appendix EU to the immigration rules

7. The Secretary of State may give or refuse leave to enter the United Kingdom to any person who seeks leave to enter the United Kingdom by virtue of Appendix EU to the immigration rules.

The Immigration (Citizens' Rights Appeals) (EU Exit) Regulations 2020
(SI No. 61)

Part 1
General

Citation and commencement

1.—(1) These Regulations may be cited as the Immigration (Citizens' Rights Appeals) (EU Exit) Regulations 2020.

(2) These Regulations come into force on exit day and paragraph 1(1) of Schedule 5 to the European Union (Withdrawal Agreement) Act 2020 does not apply.

Interpretation

2.—(1) In these Regulations—

"the 1971 Act" means the Immigration Act 1971;'

'the 1997 Act" means the Special Immigration Appeals Commission Act 1997;

"the 2002 Act" means the Nationality, Immigration and Asylum Act 2002;

['the 1972 Order' means the Immigration (Control of Entry through Republic of Ireland) Order 1972;]

[the '2020 Regulations' means the Citizens' Rights (Frontier Workers) (EU Exit) Regulations 2020;]

"appealable decision" means a decision which may be appealed against under these Regulations;

"appellant" means a person who brings an appeal under these Regulations;

['Appendix S2' means Appendix S2 Healthcare Visitor to the immigration rules;]

['frontier worker' has the meaning given in regulation 3 of the 2020 Regulations;

'frontier worker permit' has the meaning given in regulation 2 of the 2020 Regulations;]

['healthcare entry clearance' means entry clearance granted by virtue of Appendix S2 for the purpose of acquiring leave to enter or remain in the United Kingdom by virtue of that Appendix;

'healthcare leave', in relation to a person ('P'), means leave to enter or remain in the United Kingdom granted to P by virtue of Appendix S2;

'person with a healthcare right of entry' means a person who has the right to enter the United Kingdom by virtue of—

(a) Article 32(1)(b) of the withdrawal agreement,

(b) Article 31(1)(b) of the EEA EFTA separation agreement, or

(c) Article 26a(1)(b) of the Swiss citizens' rights agreement;]

'relevant authority' means—

(a) where the appeal under these Regulations lies to the Special Immigration Appeals Commission, the Commission;

(b) otherwise, the Tribunal;

'scheme entry clearance' means entry clearance granted by virtue of relevant entry clearance immigration rules;

'the Tribunal' means the First-tier Tribunal.

['valid identity document' means—

(a) a valid national identity card issued by an EEA state, or

(b) a valid passport issued by an EEA state.]

[(**1A**) For the purposes of the definition of 'valid identity document', 'EEA state' means—

(a) a member State, or

(b) Iceland, Liechtenstein, Norway or Switzerland.]

(2) References in these Regulations to an appeal which is pending are to be read in accordance with regulation 13.

Note: Definitions of 'the 2020 Regulations', 'frontier worker', frontier worker permit' and 'valid identity document' and paragraph (1A) inserted and in force from 4 November 2020 except in so far as it relates to an appeal against a decision made under SI 2020/1213 Pt 2 or Pt 4 when it is in force from 31 December 2020 (reg (2)(a) and (3)(c) of SI 2020/1213). Definitions of 'the 1972 Order', 'Appendix S2'. 'healthcare entry clearance', healthcare leave' and 'person with a healthcare right of entry' inserted from 31 December 2020 and in force immediately after IP completion day (SI 2020/1372).

PART 2

APPEALS IN RESPECT OF CITIZENS' RIGHTS IMMIGRATION DECISIONS

CHAPTER 1

Appeals: general

[Decisions other than those relating to frontier workers]{or persons with a healthcare right of entry}

Note: new heading inserted for regulations 3-6 from and in force from 4 November 2020 except in so far as it relates to an appeal against a decision made under SI 2020/1213 Pt 2 or Pt 4 when in force from 31 December 2020 (reg (2)(a) and (3)(c) of SI 2020/1213) and words in curly brackets inserted from 31 December 2020 and in force immediately after IP completion day (SI 2020/1372).

Right of appeal against decisions relating to leave to enter or remain in the United Kingdom made by virtue of residence scheme immigration rules

3.—(1) A person ('P') may appeal against a decision made on or after exit day—

(a) to vary P's leave to enter or remain in the United Kingdom granted by virtue of residence scheme immigration rules, so that P does not have leave to enter or remain in the United Kingdom,

(b) to cancel P's leave to enter or remain in the United Kingdom granted by virtue of residence scheme immigration rules,

(c) not to grant any leave to enter or remain in the United Kingdom in response to P's relevant application, or

(d) not to grant indefinite leave to enter or remain in the United Kingdom in response to P's relevant application (where limited leave to enter or remain is granted, or P had limited leave to enter or remain when P made the relevant application).

(2) In this regulation, 'relevant application' means an application for leave to enter or remain in the United Kingdom made under residence scheme immigration rules on or after exit day.

Right of appeal against decisions under section 76 of the 2002 Act to revoke indefinite leave to enter or remain by virtue of residence scheme immigration rules

4. A person may appeal against a decision made on or after exit day under section 76(1) or (2) of the 2002 Act to revoke their indefinite leave to enter or remain in the United Kingdom which was granted by virtue of residence scheme immigration rules.

Right of appeal against decisions made in connection with scheme entry clearance

5. A person may appeal against a decision made on or after exit day—

(a) where the person applies for scheme entry clearance on or after exit day, to refuse their application,

(b) to cancel or revoke their scheme entry clearance,

(c) where they have scheme entry clearance, to refuse them leave to enter the United Kingdom under article 7(1) of the Immigration (Leave to Enter and Remain) Order 2000, or

(d) to cancel or vary leave to enter the United Kingdom which they have by virtue of having arrived in the United Kingdom with scheme entry clearance.

Right of appeal against decisions to make a deportation order [in respect of a person other than a person claiming to be a frontier worker] {or a person with a healthcare right of entry}.

6.—(1) A person to whom paragraph (2) applies may appeal against a decision, made on or after exit day, to make a deportation order under section 5(1) of the 1971 Act in respect of them.

(2) This paragraph applies to a person who—

(a) has leave to enter or remain in the United Kingdom granted by virtue of residence scheme immigration rules, or

(b) is in the United Kingdom (whether or not the person has entered within the meaning of section 11(1) of the 1971 Act) having arrived with scheme entry clearance.

(3) [But paragraph (2) does not apply to a person if the decision to remove that person was taken—

(a) under regulation 23(6)(b) of the Immigration (European Economic Area) Regulations 2016 ('the 2016 Regulations'), where the decision to remove was taken before the revocation of the 2016 Regulations, or

(b) otherwise, under regulation 23(6)(b) of the 2016 Regulations as it continues to have effect by virtue of the Citizens' Rights (Restrictions of Rights of Entry and Residence) (EU Exit) Regulations 2020 or the Citizens' Rights (Application Deadline and Temporary Protection) (EU Exit) Regulations 2020.]

(4) The references in paragraph (2) to a person who has leave to enter or remain include references to a person who would have had leave to enter or remain but for the making of a deportation order under section 5(1) of the 1971 Act.

Note: words in square brackets added to heading and in force from 4 November 2020 except in so far as it relates to an appeal against a decision made under SI 2020/1213 Pt 2 or Pt 4 when it is in force from 31 December 2020 (reg (2)(a) and (3)(c) of SI 2020/1213) and words in curly brackets inserted from 31 December 2020 and in force immediately after IP completion day (SI 2020/1372). Paragraph (3) substituted from 31 December 2020 and in force immediately after IP completion day (SI 2020/1372).

[Decisions relating to frontier workers

Right of appeal against decisions relating to issue, renewal or revocation of frontier worker permits

6A. A person may appeal against a decision—

(a) to refuse to issue a frontier worker permit to them,

(b) to refuse to renew their frontier worker permit, or

(c) to revoke their frontier worker permit.

Right of appeal against decisions to refuse frontier workers admission to the United Kingdom

6B.—(1) A person may appeal against a decision made under regulation 12 of the 2020 Regulations (a 'refusal of admission decision').

(2) But a person cannot bring an appeal under paragraph (1) without producing—

(a) a valid identity document, or

(b) where paragraph (3) applies, sufficient evidence to satisfy the Secretary of State that they are a frontier worker.

(3) This paragraph applies where—

(a) the refusal of admission decision was made before 1st July 2021, or

(b) the person bringing the appeal is an Irish citizen.

Right of appeal against decision to revoke admission to the United Kingdom

6C.—(1) A person who has been admitted to the United Kingdom under regulation 6 of the 2020 Regulations may appeal against a decision under regulation 14 of those Regulations to revoke that admission.

(2) But a person cannot bring an appeal under paragraph (1) without producing a valid identity document.

Right of appeal against certain decisions to remove frontier workers from the United Kingdom

6D.—(1) A frontier worker who has entered the United Kingdom may appeal against a decision to remove that person taken by virtue of regulation 15(1)(a) or (c) of the 2020 Regulations.

(2) But a person cannot bring an appeal under paragraph (1) without producing a valid identity document.

Right of appeal against decisions to make deportation order in respect of frontier workers

6E.—(1) A frontier worker who has entered the United Kingdom may appeal against a decision to make a deportation order under section 5(1) of the 1971 Act in respect of them.

[(2) [But paragraph (1) does not apply to a person if the decision to remove that person was taken—

(a) under regulation 23(6)(b) of the Immigration (European Economic Area) Regulations 2016 ('the 2016 Regulations'), where the decision to remove was taken before the revocation of the 2016 Regulations, or

(b) otherwise, under regulation 23(6)(b) of the 2016 Regulations as it continues to have effect by virtue of the Citizens' Rights (Restrictions of Rights of Entry and Residence) (EU Exit) Regulations 2020 or the Citizens' Rights (Application Deadline and Temporary Protection) (EU Exit) Regulations 2020.]

(3) In addition, a person cannot bring an appeal under paragraph (1) without producing—

(a) a valid identity document, and

(b) if they do not have a valid frontier worker permit, sufficient evidence to satisfy the Secretary of State that they are a frontier worker.

(4) For the purposes of paragraph (3)(b), a person is to be treated as having a valid frontier worker permit if they would hold such a permit but for its revocation following a decision to make a deportation order under section 5(1) of the 1971 Act in respect of them.

Note: Paragraph 6E (2) substituted from 22 December 2020 (SI 2020/1372).

Alternative evidence of identity and nationality

6F. Where a provision of this Part requires a person to hold or produce a valid identity document, the Secretary of State may accept alternative evidence of identity and nationality where the person is unable to obtain or produce the required document due to circumstances beyond the person's control.]

Note: Regulations 6A-F inserted and in force from 4 November 2020 except in so far as it relates to an appeal against a decision made under SI 2020/1213 Pt 2 or Pt 4 when it is in force from 31 December 2020 (reg (2)(a) and (3)(c) of SI 2020/1213).

[Decisions relating to persons with a healthcare right of entry

Right of appeal against decisions relating to leave to enter or remain in the United Kingdom granted to or obtained by a person with a healthcare right of entry

6G.—(1) A person ('P') may appeal against a decision made on or after IP completion day—

(a) to vary P's healthcare leave, so that P does not have leave to enter or remain in the United Kingdom,

(b) to cancel P's healthcare leave,

(c) where P applies on or after IP completion day for leave to enter or remain in the United Kingdom under Appendix S2, not to grant such leave to P, or

(d) not to vary P's leave to enter or remain in the United Kingdom granted by virtue of Appendix S2 in response to P's relevant application.

(2) In this regulation, 'relevant application' means an application for, or as the case may be, to vary, leave to enter or remain in the United Kingdom made under Appendix S2 on or after IP completion day.

Right of appeal against decisions made in connection with healthcare entry clearance

6H. A person may appeal against a decision made on or after IP completion day

(a) where the person applies for healthcare entry clearance on or after IP completion day, to refuse their application,

(b) to cancel or revoke their healthcare entry clearance,

(c) where they have healthcare entry clearance, to refuse them leave to enter the United Kingdom under article 7(1) of the Immigration (Leave to Enter and Remain) Order 2000, or

(d) to cancel or vary the leave to enter the United Kingdom which they have by virtue of having arrived in the United Kingdom with healthcare entry clearance.

Right of appeal against decision to vary leave under article 5 of the 1972 Order

6I. A person ('P') may appeal against a decision, made on or after IP completion day, to vary their leave to enter or remain in the United Kingdom if—

(a) P is in the United Kingdom, and

(b) Article 5 of the 1972 Order applied to P on their entry to the United Kingdom.

Right of appeal against decisions to make a deportation order in respect of a person with a healthcare right of entry

6J.—(1) A person to whom paragraph (2) applies may appeal against a decision, made on or after IP completion day, to make a deportation order under section 5(1) of the 1971 Act in respect of them.

(2) This paragraph applies to a person —

(a) who has healthcare leave,

(b) who is in the United Kingdom (whether or not the person has entered within the meaning of section 11(1) of the 1971 Act) having arrived with healthcare entry clearance, or

(c) to whom Article 5 of the 1972 Order applied on their entry to the United Kingdom.

(3) But paragraph (2) does not apply to a person if the decision to remove that person was taken—

(a) under regulation 23(6)(b) of the Immigration (European Economic Area) Regulations 2016 ('the 2016 Regulations'), where the decision to remove is taken before the 2016 Regulations are revoked, or

(b) otherwise, under regulation 23(6)(b) of the 2016 Regulations as it continues to have effect by virtue of the Citizens' Rights (Restrictions of Rights of Entry and Residence) (EU Exit) Regulations 2020 or the Citizens' Rights (Application Deadline and Temporary Protection) (EU Exit) Regulations 2020.

(4) The reference in paragraph (2) to a person who has healthcare leave includes reference to a person who would have such leave but for the making of a deportation order under section 5(1) of the 1971 Act.]

Note: Paragraphs 6G to 6J inserted 31 December 2020 and in force immediately after IP completion day (SI 2020/1372).

Appeal to the Tribunal or the Special Immigration Appeals Commission

7.—(1) An appeal under these Regulations lies to the Tribunal.

(2) Except that a person may appeal to the Special Immigration Appeals Commission against an appealable decision if—

(a) the decision is certified under paragraph 1 or 2 of Schedule 1, or

(b) an appeal against that decision lapses by virtue of paragraph 3 of that Schedule.

(3) Schedule 1 also makes provision for the application of the 1997 Act to appeals to the Special Immigration Appeals Commission (see Part 2 of that Schedule).

Grounds of appeal

8.—(1) An appeal under these Regulations must be brought on one or both of the following two grounds.

(2) The first ground of appeal is that the decision breaches any right which the appellant has by virtue of—

(a) Chapter 1, or Article 24(2) [,24(3),25(2) or 25(3)] of Chapter 2, of Title II {, or Article 32(1)(b) of Title III,} of Part 2 of the withdrawal agreement,

(b) Chapter 1, or Article 23(2)[, 23(3), 24(2) or 24(3)] of Chapter 2, of Title II {, or Article 31(1)(b) of Title III,} of Part 2 of the EEA EFTA separation agreement, or

(c) Part 2 {, or Article 26a(1)(b),} of the Swiss citizens' rights agreement.

(3) The second ground of appeal is that—

(a) where the decision is mentioned in regulation 3(1)(a) or (b) or 5, it is not in accordance with the provision of the immigration rules by virtue of which it was made;

(b) where the decision is mentioned in regulation 3(1)(c) or (d), it is not in accordance with residence scheme immigration rules;

(c) where the decision is mentioned in regulation 4, it is not in accordance with section 76(1) or (2) of the 2002 Act (as the case may be);

(d) where the decision is mentioned in regulation 6, it is not in accordance with section 3(5) or (6) of the 1971 Act (as the case may be)[;

(e) where the decision is mentioned in regulation 6A, 6B, 6C or 6D, it is not in accordance with regulation 9, 11, 12, 14, 15(1)(a) or 15(1)(c) of the 2020 Regulations (as the case may be);

(f) where the decision is mentioned in regulation 6E, it is not in accordance with section 3(5) or 3(6) of the 1971 Act, or regulation 15(1)(b) of the 2020 Regulations (as the case may be);]

[(g) where the decision is mentioned in regulation 6G(1)(a) or (1)(b) or 6H, it is not in accordance with the provision of the immigration rules by virtue of which it was made;

(h) where the decision is mentioned in regulation 6G(1)(c) or (1)(d), it is not made in accordance with Appendix S2;

(i) where the decision is mentioned in regulation 6I, it is not made in accordance with the provision of, or made under, the 1971 Act (including the immigration rules) by virtue of which it was made;

(j) where the decision is mentioned in regulation 6J, it is not in accordance with section 3(5) or (6) of the 1971 Act, or Appendix S2 (as the case may be).]

(4) But this is subject to regulation 9.

Note: Words in square brackets in paragraph 2(a) and (b) substituted and paragraphs 3(e) and (f) inserted and in force from 4 November 2020 except in so far as it relates to an appeal against a decision made under SI 2020/1213 Pt 2 or Pt 4 when it is in force from 31 December 2020 (reg (2)(a) and (3)(c) of SI 2020/1213). Words in curly brackets in paragraphs (2)(a), (b) and (c) and paragraphs (3)(g) to (j) inserted from 31 December 2020 and in force immediately after IP completion day (SI 2020/1372).

Matters to be considered by the relevant authority

9.—(1) If an appellant makes a section 120 statement, the relevant authority must consider any matter raised in that statement which constitutes a specified ground of appeal against the decision appealed against. For the purposes of this paragraph, a 'specified ground of appeal' is a ground of appeal of a kind listed in regulation 8 or section 84 of the 2002 Act.

(2) In this regulation, 'section 120 statement' means a statement made under section 120 of the 2002 Act and includes any statement made under that section, as applied by Schedule 1 or 2 to these Regulations.

(3) For the purposes of this regulation, it does not matter whether a section 120 statement is made before or after the appeal under these Regulations is commenced.

(4) The relevant authority may also consider any matter which it thinks relevant to the substance of the decision appealed against, including a matter arising after the date of the decision.

(5) But the relevant authority must not consider a new matter without the consent of the Secretary of State.

(6) A matter is a 'new matter' if—

(a) it constitutes a ground of appeal of a kind listed in regulation 8 or section 84 of the 2002 Act, and

(b) the Secretary of State has not previously considered the matter in the context of—

(i) the decision appealed against under these Regulations, or

(ii) a section 120 statement made by the appellant.

Determination of appeal

10. On an appeal under these Regulations, the relevant authority must determine—

(a) any matter raised as a ground of appeal, and

(b) any other matter which regulation 9 requires it to consider.

CHAPTER 2

Appeals before the Tribunal: admission on bail and other procedural matters

Application of the 2002 Act to appeals to the Tribunal

11. Schedule 2 makes provision for the application of the 2002 Act to appeals to the Tribunal.

Admission on bail to the United Kingdom to make submissions in person in connection with an appeal

12. Schedule 3 contains provisions about admission on bail to the United Kingdom for the purposes of making submissions in person in connection with an appeal.

CHAPTER 3
Procedural matters and certification

Pending appeal

13.—(1) An appeal under these Regulations is to be treated as pending during the period which—

(a) begins when the notice of appeal is given in accordance with the relevant rules, and

(b) ends when the appeal is finally determined, withdrawn or abandoned (or lapses under paragraph 3 of Schedule 1).

(2) An appeal is not finally determined for the purposes of paragraph (1)(b) while (as the case may be)—

(a) an application for permission to appeal under section 11 or 13 of the Tribunals, Courts and Enforcement Act 2007 could be made or is awaiting determination,

(b) permission to appeal under either of those sections has been granted and the appeal is awaiting determination,

(c) an appeal has been remitted under section 12 or 14 of that Act and is awaiting determination,

(d) any of the following applications could be made—

(i) an application for leave to appeal under section 7 of the applied 1997 Act;

(ii) an application for a certificate under section 7B of the applied 1997 Act;

(iii) an application for permission to appeal under section 7C of the applied 1997 Act,

or

(e) leave to appeal under section 7, or permission to appeal under section 7C, of the applied 1997 Act has been granted and the appeal is awaiting determination.

(3) An appeal under [regulations 3 to 6] is to be treated as abandoned if the appellant ('A') is granted leave to enter or remain in the United Kingdom by virtue of residence scheme immigration rules.

(4) But paragraph (3) does not apply where—

(a) A is not granted indefinite leave to enter or remain in the United Kingdom, or A's indefinite leave to enter or remain in the United Kingdom is cancelled or revoked, and

(b) A gives notice, in accordance with the relevant rules, that A wishes to pursue the appeal insofar as it relates to a decision not to grant A, or to cancel or revoke A's, indefinite leave to enter or remain in the United Kingdom.

[(4A) An appeal under regulation 6A is to be treated as abandoned if the appellant is issued with a frontier worker permit.

(4B) An appeal under regulation 6B is to be treated as abandoned if the appellant is admitted to the United Kingdom under regulation 6 of the 2020 Regulations.]

[(4C) An appeal under regulations 6G to 6J is to be treated as abandoned if the appellant—

(a) is granted leave to enter or remain in the United Kingdom by virtue of Appendix S2, or

(b) obtains leave to enter the United Kingdom by passing through an automated gate in accordance with article 8B of the Immigration (Leave to Enter and Remain) Order 2000 as a person seeking to enter the United Kingdom as an S2 Healthcare Visitor under Appendix S2.

(4D) An appeal under regulation 6G(d) is also to be treated as abandoned if the appellant's leave to enter or remain in the United Kingdom granted by virtue of Appendix S2 is varied, however that variation may have effect, so that the appellant has leave to enter or remain under Appendix S2.

(4E) An appeal under regulation 6I or 6J is also to be treated as abandoned if the Secretary of State agrees that Article 5 of the 1972 Order applies to the appellant.]

(5) An appeal under these Regulations is not to be treated as abandoned solely because the appellant leaves the United Kingdom.

(6) In this regulation—

'the applied 1997 Act' means the 1997 Act as it applies for the purposes of these Regulations by virtue of Part 2 of Schedule 1;

'the relevant rules'—

(a) where the appeal is before the Tribunal, means Tribunal Procedure Rules;

(b) where the appeal is before the Special Immigration Appeals Commission, means rules made under section 5 of the 1997 Act, insofar as they apply in relation to an appeal under these Regulations, or rules made under section 5 of the applied 1997 Act.

Note: Paragraphs (4A) and (4B) inserted and in force from 4 November 2020 except in so far as it relates to an appeal against a decision made under SI 2020/1213 Pt 2 or Pt 4 when it is in force from 31 December 2020 (reg (2)(a) and (3)(c) of SI 2020/1213). Words in paragraph (3) substituted and paragraphs (4C) to (4E) inserted from 31 December 2020 and in force immediately after IP completion day (SI 2020/1372).

Place from which an appeal may be brought or continued: general

14.—(1) A person may bring or continue an appeal under these Regulations—

(a) from within the United Kingdom, or

(b) from outside the United Kingdom.

(2) Nothing in this regulation entitles a person to enter the United Kingdom for the purposes of bringing or continuing an appeal.

(3) This regulation is subject to regulation 15.

National security decisions: place from which an appeal may be brought or continued, certification of removal etc.

15.—(1) This regulation applies where the Secretary of State certifies, under paragraph 1 or 2 of Schedule 1, that an appealable decision in relation to a person ('P') was taken in the interests of national security.

Such a decision is referred to in this regulation as a 'national security decision'.

(2) Where this regulation applies, section 97A of the 2002 Act does not apply.

(3) P, while in the United Kingdom, may not bring or continue an appeal under these Regulations against the national security decision unless P has made a human rights claim while in the United Kingdom.

(4) Paragraph (3) does not allow P while in the United Kingdom to bring or continue an appeal under these Regulations if the Secretary of State certifies that removal of P—

(a) to the country or territory to which P is proposed to be removed, and

(b) despite the appeals process in relation to the national security decision not having been begun or not having been exhausted,

would not be unlawful under section 6 of the Human Rights Act 1998.

(5) The grounds upon which a certificate may be given under paragraph (4) include (in particular)—

(a) that P would not, before the appeals process in relation to the national security decision is exhausted, face a real risk of serious irreversible harm if removed to the country or territory to which P is proposed to be removed;

(b) that the whole or part of any human rights claim made by P is clearly unfounded.

(6) If a certificate in respect of P is given under paragraph (4), P may not be removed from, or required to leave, the United Kingdom in accordance with a provision of the Immigration Acts before the end of the relevant period except—

(a) in a duly substantiated case of urgency,

(b) where P is detained pursuant to the sentence or order of any court, or

(c) where P has entered the United Kingdom and are removable as an illegal entrant under Schedule 2 to the 1971 Act.

But those exceptions do not apply at any time when the removal of P is prohibited by a direction given under paragraph (10) by the Special Immigration Appeals Commission ('the Commission').

(7) P may make an application to the Commission to set aside the certificate.

(8) If P makes an application under paragraph (7) then the Commission, in determining whether the certificate should be set aside, must apply the principles that would be applied in judicial review proceedings.

(9) The Commission's determination of a review under paragraph (7) is final.

(10) Where P has made and not withdrawn an application under paragraph (7), the Commission may direct that P is not to be removed from the United Kingdom at a time when the review has not been finally determined by the Commission.

(11) Sections 5 and 6 of the 1997 Act apply in relation to reviews under paragraph (7) (and to applicants for such reviews) as they apply in relation to appeals under section 2 or 2B of that Act (and to persons bringing such appeals).

(12) Any exercise of the power to make rules under section 5 of that Act in relation to reviews under paragraph (7) is to be made with a view to securing that proceedings on such reviews are handled expeditiously.

(13) For the purposes of this regulation—

'human rights claim' has the meaning given in section 113(1) of the 2002 Act;

'relevant period' means the period of one month beginning with the day on which P is notified of the decision to remove them.

Other appealable decisions: certification of removal

16.—(1) This regulation applies where—

(a) a relevant appealable decision has been made in relation to a person ('P'), and

(b) a decision has been made to make a deportation order under section 5(1) of the 1971 Act in respect of P (whether or not that decision is the relevant appealable decision and whether or not the order has been made).

(2) Where the deportation decision is not the relevant appealable decision mentioned in paragraph (1)(a), it does not matter for the purposes of paragraph (1)(b) whether the deportation decision is made before or after the relevant appealable decision.

(3) Where this regulation applies, the Secretary of State may certify that removal of P—

(a) to the country or territory to which P is proposed to be removed, and

(b) despite the appeals process in relation to the relevant appealable decision not having been begun or not having been exhausted,

would not be unlawful under section 6 of the Human Rights Act 1998.

(4) The grounds upon which a certificate may be given under paragraph (3) include (in particular) that P would not, before the appeals process in relation to the relevant appealable decision is exhausted, face a real risk of serious irreversible harm if removed to the country or territory to which P is proposed to be removed.

(5) In this regulation, 'relevant appealable decision' means an appealable decision other than a decision which has been certified under paragraph 1 or 2 of Schedule 1 as taken in the interests of national security.

(6) See sections 78 and 79 of the 2002 Act, as applied by Schedule 1 or 2 to these Regulations, for the consequences of certification under this regulation.

PART 3

CONSEQUENTIAL AMENDMENTS

Consequential amendments

17. Schedule 4 contains consequential amendments.

Regulation 7(2) and (3)

SCHEDULE 1

APPEALS TO THE SPECIAL IMMIGRATION APPEALS COMMISSION

PART 1

CERTIFICATION OF APPEALABLE DECISIONS ON NATIONAL SECURITY ETC. GROUNDS

Certification that decision was taken on national security etc. grounds

1.—(1) The Secretary of State may certify an appealable decision under this paragraph if it was taken—

(a) by the Secretary of State wholly or partly on a ground listed in sub-paragraph (2), or

(b) in accordance with a direction of the Secretary of State which identifies the person to whom the decision relates and which is given wholly or partly on a ground listed in sub-paragraph (2).

(2) The grounds are that the person's exclusion or removal from the United Kingdom is—

(a) in the interests of national security, or

(b) in the interests of a relationship between the United Kingdom and another country.

(3) In this paragraph any reference to the Secretary of State is to the Secretary of State acting in person.

Certification that decision was taken on information which cannot be disclosed for reasons of national security etc.

2.—(1) The Secretary of State may certify an appealable decision under this paragraph if it was taken wholly or partly in reliance on information which the Secretary of State considers must not be made public—

(a) in the interests of national security,

(b) in the interests of a relationship between the United Kingdom and another country, or

(c) otherwise in the public interest.

(2) In this paragraph any reference to the Secretary of State is to the Secretary of State acting in person.

Effect of certification: appeal pending before the Tribunal

3. Where a certificate is given under paragraph 1 or 2 in relation to a decision in respect of which an appeal is pending to the Tribunal, the appeal lapses.

PART 2

APPLICATION OF THE 1997 ACT TO APPEALS TO THE SPECIAL IMMIGRATION APPEALS COMMISSION

Application of the 1997 Act to appeals under these Regulations

4.—(1) The 1997 Act applies to an appeal to the Special Immigration Appeals Commission ('the Commission') under these Regulations as it applies to an appeal under section 2 of that Act (subject to the modifications specified in sub-paragraphs (2) and (3)).

(2) Any reference in the 1997 Act to an appeal under section 2 of that Act, however expressed, has effect as a reference to an appeal to the Commission under these Regulations.

(3) Section 2 has effect as if—

(a) for subsection (2), there were substituted—

'(2) The following provisions of the Nationality, Immigration and Asylum Act 2002 apply in connection with an appeal to the Commission under the 2020 Regulations as they apply in connection with an appeal under section 82(1) of that Act, but subject to the modifications specified in subsection (2A)—

(a) section 72;

(b) sections 78 to 79;

(c) section 105 and any regulations made under that section;

(d) sections 112 and 113;

(e) section 120.

In this section, 'the 2020 Regulations' means the Immigration (Citizens' Rights Appeals) (EU Exit) Regulations 2020.

(2A) The modifications mentioned in subsection (2) are—

(a) section 72 has effect as if—

(i) in subsection (9), for paragraph (a), there were substituted—

'(a)a person appeals to the Commission under the 2020 Regulations against a decision and makes a section 120 statement (within the meaning of regulation 9 of those Regulations) which relies wholly or partly on the ground of appeal mentioned in section 84(1)(a) or (3)(a) of this Act (breach of the United Kingdom's obligations under the Refugee Convention), and';

(ii) in subsection (10), 'Tribunal or' were omitted;

(b) section 78 has effect as if—

(i) in subsection (1), for 'section 82(1)' there were substituted 'to the Commission under the 2020 Regulations';

(ii) after subsection (1), there were inserted—

'(1A) But subsection (1) does not apply in relation to a relevant appellant.

(1B) A person is a 'relevant appellant' for the purposes of this section if—

(a) the person's removal is certified under regulation 16(3) of the 2020 Regulations, and

(b) the relevant appealable decision in respect of which the person's removal is certified in accordance with that provision is the decision in relation to which the appeal to the Commission under the 2020 Regulations is pending.

(1C) A relevant appellant may not be removed from, or required to leave, the United Kingdom in accordance with a provision of the Immigration Acts before the end of the relevant period except—

(a) in a duly substantiated case of urgency,

(b) where they are detained pursuant to the sentence or order of any court, or

(c) where they have entered the United Kingdom and are removable as an illegal entrant under Schedule 2 to the Immigration Act 1971. But those exceptions do not apply at any time when the removal of the appellant is prohibited under subsection (1F).

(1D) For the purposes of subsection (1C), 'the relevant period' is the period of one month beginning with the day on which the relevant appellant is notified of the decision to remove them.

(1E) Subsection (1F) applies to a relevant appellant who applies to the appropriate court or tribunal (whether by means of judicial review or otherwise) for an interim order to suspend enforcement of the decision to remove them from the United Kingdom.

(1F) A relevant appellant to whom this subsection applies may not be removed from, or required to leave, the United Kingdom in accordance with a provision of the Immigration Acts until such time as the decision on the interim order has been taken unless—

(a) the decision to remove them is based on a previous judicial decision,

(b) they have had previous access to judicial review, or

(c) the decision to remove them is based on imperative grounds of public security.';

(iii) in subsection (2), for 'section 104' there were substituted 'regulation 13 of the 2020 Regulations';

(iv) in subsection (4), for 'section 92' there were substituted 'the 2020 Regulations';

(c) section 78A(3) has effect as if—

(i) in paragraph (a), for 'section 82' there were substituted 'the 2020 Regulations';

(ii) in paragraph (b), for 'section 104' there were substituted 'regulation 13 of the 2020 Regulations';

(d) section 79 has effect as if—

(i) in subsection (1), for the words from 'section 82(1)' to 'relating to' there were substituted 'the 2020 Regulations to the Commission against';

(ii) after subsection (1), there were inserted—

'(1A) But subsection (1) does not prevent the Secretary of State making a deportation order in respect of a person ('P') if—

(a) the decision to make the deportation order in respect of P is certified under paragraph 1 or 2 of Schedule 1 to the 2020 Regulations as taken in the interests of national security, or

(b) P's removal is certified under paragraph (3) of regulation 16 of the 2020 Regulations, where the decision to make the deportation order in respect of P is the relevant appealable decision referred to in paragraph (1)(a) of that regulation in respect of which P's removal was certified.';

(iii) in subsection (2), for 'section 104' there were substituted 'regulation 13 of the 2020 Regulations';

(e) section 105 has effect as if, in subsection (4), for the words from 'means' to the end, there were substituted 'has the meaning given in regulation 2 of the 2020 Regulations';

(f) section 113 has effect as if, before the definition of 'asylum claim', there were inserted—

' "the 2020 Regulations" means the Immigration (Citizens' Rights Appeals) (EU Exit) Regulations 2020;';

(g) section 120 has effect as if at the end of the definition of 'grounds' in subsection (6) there were inserted ', or on which an appeal to the Commission under the 2020 Regulations may be brought (see regulation 8 of those Regulations)'.';

(b) subsections (3), (5) and (6) were omitted.

Regulation 11 SCHEDULE 2

APPLICATION OF THE 2002 ACT TO APPEALS TO THE TRIBUNAL

Application of provisions of the 2002 Act in connection with appeals to the Tribunal

1. The following provisions of the 2002 Act apply in connection with an appeal to the Tribunal under these Regulations as they apply in connection with an appeal under section 82(1) of that Act (but subject to the general modifications specified in paragraph 2 and the specific modifications specified in paragraph 3)—

(a) section 72;
(b) sections 78 to 79;
(c) section 105 and any regulations made under that section;
(d) section 106 and any rules made pursuant to that section;
(e) sections 107 and 108;
(f) sections 112 and 113;
(g) section 120.

General modifications

2.—(1) The provisions mentioned in paragraph 1 have effect as if—

(a) references to 'this Act', or provisions of the 2002 Act, were references to the Act, or provisions of it, as applied by this Schedule;

(b) references to an appeal under section 82 or section 82(1), however expressed, were references to an appeal to the Tribunal under these Regulations;

(c) references to proceedings under section 82 were references to proceedings before the Tribunal under these Regulations.

(2) But—

(a) sub-paragraph (1)(a) does not apply to the reference to section 84 of the 2002 Act inserted by paragraph 3(2) of this Schedule;

(b) sub-paragraph (1) is also subject to the specific modifications made in paragraph 3.

Specific modifications

3.—(1) The specific modifications to the provisions of the 2002 Act are as follows.

(2) Section 72 has effect as if—

(a) in subsection (9), for paragraph (a), there were substituted—

'(a) a person appeals to the First-tier Tribunal under the 2020 Regulations against a decision and makes a section 120 statement (within the meaning of regulation 9 of those Regulations) which relies wholly or partly on the ground of appeal mentioned in section 84(1)(a) or (3)(a) of this Act (breach of the United Kingdom's obligations under the Refugee Convention), and';

(b) in subsection (10), 'or Commission' were omitted.

(3) Section 78 has effect as if—

(a) in subsection (1), for 'appeal under section 82(1)' there were substituted 'appeal to the First-tier Tribunal ('the Tribunal') under the 2020 Regulations';

(b) after subsection (1), there were inserted—

'(1A) But subsection (1) does not apply in relation to a relevant appellant.

(1B) A person is a 'relevant appellant' for the purposes of this section if—

(a) the person's removal is certified under regulation 16(3) of the 2020 Regulations, and

(b) the relevant appealable decision in respect of which the person's removal is certified in accordance with that provision is the decision in relation to which the appeal to the Tribunal under the 2020 Regulations is pending.

(1C) A relevant appellant may not be removed from, or required to leave, the United Kingdom in accordance with a provision of the Immigration Acts before the end of the relevant period except—

(a) in a duly substantiated case of urgency,

(b) where they are detained pursuant to the sentence or order of any court, or

(c) where they have entered the United Kingdom and are removable as an illegal entrant under Schedule 2 to the Immigration Act 1971.

But those exceptions do not apply at any time when the removal of the appellant is prohibited under subsection (1F).

(1D) For the purposes of subsection (1C), 'the relevant period' is the period of one month beginning with the day on which the relevant appellant is notified of the decision to remove them.

(1E) Subsection (1F) applies to a relevant appellant who applies to the appropriate court or tribunal (whether by means of judicial review or otherwise) for an interim order to suspend enforcement of the decision to remove them from the United Kingdom.

(1F) A relevant appellant to whom this subsection applies may not be removed from, or required to leave, the United Kingdom in accordance with a provision of the Immigration Acts until such time as the decision on the interim order has been taken unless—

(a) the decision to remove them is based on a previous judicial decision,

(b) they have had previous access to judicial review, or

(c) the decision to remove them is based on imperative grounds of public security.';

(c) in subsection (2), for 'section 104' there were substituted 'regulation 13 of the 2020 Regulations';

(d) in subsection (4), for 'section 92' there were substituted 'the 2020 Regulations';

(e) after subsection (4), there were inserted—

'(5) Nothing in this section prevents the removal from the United Kingdom of a person who is admitted to the United Kingdom on bail pursuant to Schedule 3 to the 2020 Regulations.'.

(4) Section 78A(3)(b) has effect as if for 'section 104' there were substituted 'regulation 13 of the 2020 Regulations'.

(5) Section 79 has effect as if—

(a) in subsection (1), for the words from 'section 82(1)' to 'relating to' there were substituted 'the 2020 Regulations to the First-tier Tribunal against';

(b) after subsection (1), there were inserted—

'(1A) But subsection (1) does not prevent the Secretary of State making a deportation order in respect of a person ('P') if—

(a) P's removal is certified under regulation 16(3) of the 2020 Regulations, and

(b) the decision to make the deportation order in respect of P is the relevant appealable decision in respect of which P's removal was certified under that provision.';

(c) in subsection (2), for 'section 104' there were substituted 'regulation 13 of the 2020 Regulations'.

(6) Section 105 has effect as if, in subsection (4), for the words from 'means' to the end there were substituted 'has the meaning given in regulation 2 of the 2020 Regulations'.

(7) Section 106 has effect as if, in subsections (3) and (4), 'or by virtue of section 109' were omitted.

(8) Section 107(3) has effect as if 'or by virtue of section 109' were omitted.

(9) Section 113 has effect as if, before the definition of 'asylum claim', there were inserted—

"the 2020 Regulations' means the Immigration (Citizens' Rights Appeals) (EU Exit) Regulations 2020;'.

(10) Section 120(6) has effect as if at the end of the definition of 'grounds' in subsection (6) there were inserted ', or on which an appeal to the Tribunal under the 2020 Regulations may be brought (see regulation 8 of those Regulations)'.

Regulation 12

SCHEDULE 3

ADMISSION ON BAIL TO THE UNITED KINGDOM TO MAKE SUBMISSIONS IN PERSON IN CONNECTION WITH AN APPEAL

Application for permission to be admitted on bail to the United Kingdom to make submissions in person

1.—(1) An appellant ('A') may apply to the Secretary of State for permission to be admitted on bail to the United Kingdom in order to make submissions in person at a hearing if the conditions in sub-paragraph (2) are satisfied.

(2) The conditions are—

(a) that the Secretary of State has certified A's removal from the United Kingdom under regulation 16(3),

(b) the hearing forms part of the proceedings on, or in connection with, an appeal to the Tribunal against the appealable decision in respect of which A's removal was certified under regulation 16(3),

(c) a date for the hearing has been set by the Tribunal, the Upper Tribunal or the court (as the case may be) before which the hearing is to take place, and

(d) A is outside the United Kingdom.

(3) The Secretary of State must give such permission to A unless A's appearance may cause serious troubles to public policy or public security.

(4) The Secretary of State must have regard to the dates on which A will be required to make submissions in person when determining—

(a) when A is entitled to be given permission, and

(b) the duration of A's admission on bail, should permission be given.

(5) Nothing in this paragraph affects any power of the Secretary of State to remove A from the United Kingdom while A's appeal is pending if—

(a) A is admitted on bail to the United Kingdom under this paragraph, and

(b) the relevant hearing has taken place.

(6) If A is removed from the United Kingdom while A's appeal is pending, A is not prevented from applying for admission to the United Kingdom on bail in order to make submissions in person at any subsequent hearing in accordance with this paragraph.

Application of enactments to person given permission under paragraph 1

2.—(1) Where the Secretary of State gives an appellant ('A') permission to be admitted on bail to the United Kingdom under paragraph 1—

(a) upon such admission, A is to be treated for the purposes of paragraphs 8, 10, 10A, 11 and 16 to 18A of Schedule 2 to the 1971 Act as if they were a person refused leave to enter under that Act, and

(b) the provisions of Schedule 10 to the Immigration Act 2016 apply accordingly.

(2) Where Schedule 2 to the 1971 Act so applies, it has effect as if—

(a) the reference, in the opening words of sub-paragraph (1) of paragraph 8, to leave to enter were a reference to admission on bail pursuant to paragraph 1, and

(b) the reference in paragraph 16(1) to detention pending a decision regarding leave to enter were to detention pending submission of the appellant's case in person in accordance with paragraph 1.

(3) A is deemed not to have been admitted to the United Kingdom during any time during which A is admitted on bail to the United Kingdom pursuant to this Schedule.

(4) For the purposes of this Schedule, a person is admitted on bail to the United Kingdom if they are admitted on bail under Schedule 10 to the Immigration Act 2016, as applied by this paragraph, without having otherwise been admitted, and the expression 'admission on bail' is to be construed accordingly.

Regulation 17

SCHEDULE 4

CONSEQUENTIAL AMENDMENTS

PART 1

AMENDMENT OF PRIMARY LEGISLATION

Amendment of section 3C of the Immigration Act 1971 (continuation of leave pending variation decision)

1. In section 3C of the 1971 Act, subsection (2)—

(a) omit 'or' at the end of paragraph (c);

(b) after that paragraph insert—

'(ca)an appeal could be brought under the Immigration (Citizens' Rights Appeals) (EU Exit) Regulations 2020 ('the 2020 Regulations'), while the appellant is in the United Kingdom, against the decision on the application for variation (ignoring any possibility of an appeal out of time with permission),

(cb) an appeal under the 2020 Regulations against that decision, brought while the appellant is in the United Kingdom, is pending (within the meaning of those Regulations), or'.

Amendment of section 2C of the Special Immigration Appeals Commission Act 1997 (jurisdiction: review of certain exclusion decisions)

2.—(1) Section 2C of the 1997 Act is amended as follows.

(2) In subsection (1), after 'non-EEA national', in both places where it appears, insert 'or relevant person'.

(3) In subsection (2), after 'non-EEA national' insert 'or relevant person'.

(4) In subsection (5), after the definition of 'non-EEA national', insert—

"relevant person' has the same meaning as it has for the purposes of section 11(2)(f) and (g) of the European Union (Withdrawal Agreement) Act 2020 (see section 11(7) of that Act);'.

PART 2

AMENDMENT OF SUBORDINATE LEGISLATION

Amendment of the Immigration (Notices) Regulations 2003

3.—(1) The Immigration (Notices) Regulations 2003 are amended as follows.

(2) In regulation 2, after the definition of 'the 2002 Act' insert—

"citizens' rights immigration decision' means a decision which can be appealed against under the Immigration (Citizens' Rights Appeals) (EU Exit) Regulations 2020.'

(3) In regulation 4, in paragraph (1), for 'or any EEA decision' substitute ', any EEA decision or any citizens' rights immigration decision'.

Amendment of the Special Immigration Appeals Commission (Procedure) Rules 2003

4.—(1) The Special Immigration Appeals Commission (Procedure) Rules 2003 are amended as follows.

(2) In rule 2, after the definition of 'the 2016 Act', insert—

"the 2020 Regulations' means the Immigration (Citizens' Rights Appeals) (EU Exit) Regulations 2020;'.

(3) In rule 6—

(a) omit the 'and' at the end of paragraph (a);

(b) after that paragraph, insert—

'(aa)appeals to the Commission under regulation 7 of the 2020 Regulations; and'

(4) In rule 7, in paragraph (1), after 'the 2002 Act', insert 'or regulation 7 of the 2020 Regulations'.

(5) In rule 8—

(a) in paragraph (1), for 'or section 97A(3) of the 2002 Act' substitute ', section 97A(3) of the 2002 Act or regulation 7 of the 2020 Regulations';

(b) in paragraph (2), in sub-paragraph (b), after 'Act', insert 'or regulation 15 of the 2020 Regulations';

(c) after paragraph (4A), insert—

'(4B) Paragraph (4C) applies where—

(a) an appellant ('A') applies for an administrative review of an appealable decision ('the original decision') under the relevant rules, and

(b) A had not, before A receives notice of the decision on administrative review, given a notice of appeal to the Commission under regulation 7 of the 2020 Regulations against the original decision.

(4C) Where this paragraph applies, A must give a notice of appeal to the Commission under regulation 7 of the 2020 Regulations against the original decision—

(a) if A is in detention under the Immigration Acts, not later than 5 days after A receives the notice of the decision on administrative review;

(b) otherwise—

(i) if A is in the United Kingdom, not later than 10 days after A receives the notice of the decision on administrative review, or

(ii) if A is outside the United Kingdom, subject to paragraph (4D), not later than 28 days after A receives the notice of the decision on administrative review.

(4D) Where A—

(a) is in the United Kingdom when A receives the notice of the decision on administrative review, and

(b) may not appeal against the original decision while in the United Kingdom by reason of regulation 15 of the 2020 Regulations, a notice of appeal against the original decision must be given not later than 28 days after A's departure from the United Kingdom.

(4E) In this rule—

'appealable decision' has the meaning given in regulation 2 of the 2020 Regulations;

'relevant rules' means residence scheme immigration rules or relevant entry clearance immigration rules (within the meanings given in section 17 of the European Union (Withdrawal Agreement) Act 2020).'.

(6) In rule 12—

(a) the existing paragraph is renumbered as paragraph (1) of that rule;

(b) in paragraph (1) (as renumbered), in sub-paragraph (a)(i), after 'the 2002 Act' insert 'or regulation 13(3) of the 2020 Regulations';

(c) after that paragraph, insert—

'(2) A party to an appeal under the 2020 Regulations must notify the Commission if they are aware that the appeal is to be treated as abandoned under regulation 13 of those Regulations.

(3) Where an appeal would otherwise be treated as abandoned under regulation 13(3) of the 2020 Regulations but the appellant wishes to pursue their appeal, the appellant must provide a notice to the Commission and to each other party within the relevant period.

(4) For the purposes of paragraph (3), 'the relevant period' is the period of 28 days beginning with the day on which the appellant was sent notice of the grant of leave to enter or remain in the United Kingdom.'.

Amendment of the Tribunal Procedure (Upper Tribunal) Rules 2008

5.—(1) The Tribunal Procedure (Upper Tribunal) Rules 2008 are amended as follows.

(2) In rule 1, in paragraph (3), in the definition of 'immigration case'—

(a) omit 'or' before 'regulation 26',

(b) after 'asylum case' insert ', or the Immigration (Citizens' Rights Appeals) (EU Exit) Regulations 2020'.

(3) In rule 17A—

(a) after paragraph (1) insert—

'(1A) A party to an appeal under the Immigration (Citizens' Rights Appeals) (EU Exit) Regulations 2020 ('the 2020 Regulations') before the Upper Tribunal must also notify the Upper Tribunal if they are aware that the appeal is to be treated as abandoned under regulation 13(3) of those Regulations.';

(b) in paragraph (2), after 'Regulations 2006' insert 'or regulation 13(3) of the 2020 Regulations';

(c) in paragraph (3), after 'Act 2002', insert 'or regulation 13(3) of the 2020 Regulations'.

Amendment of the Tribunal Procedure (First-tier Tribunal) (Immigration and Asylum Chamber) Rules 2014

6.—(1) The Tribunal Procedure (First-tier Tribunal) (Immigration and Asylum Chamber) Rules 2014 are amended as follows.

(2) In rule 1, after the definition of 'the 2007 Act' insert—

' "the 2020 Regulations" means the Immigration (Citizens' Rights Appeals) (EU Exit) Regulations 2020;'.

(3) In rule 16—

(a) after paragraph (1) insert—

'(1A) A party to an appeal under the 2020 Regulations must also notify the Tribunal if they are aware that the appeal is to be treated as abandoned under regulation 13 of those Regulations.';

(b) in paragraph (2), after '2006 Regulations' insert 'or regulation 13(3) of the 2020 Regulations';

(c) in paragraph (3), after 'the 2002 Act' insert 'or regulation 13(3) of the 2020 Regulations'.

(4) In rule 19, after paragraph (3), insert—

'(3A) But paragraphs (2) and (3) do not apply in relation to the bringing of an appeal against a citizens' rights immigration decision. 'A citizens' rights immigration decision' is a decision which can be appealed against under the 2020 Regulations.

(3B) The notice of appeal in relation to an appeal against a citizens' rights immigration decision must be received—

(a) if the person is in the United Kingdom, not later than 14 days after the appellant is sent the notice of the decision;

(b) if the person is outside the United Kingdom, not later than 28 days after the appellant receives the notice of the decision.

But this paragraph is subject to paragraph (3D).

(3C) Paragraph (3D) applies where—

(a) a person ('P') applies for an administrative review of a citizens' rights immigration decision ('the original decision') under the relevant rules, and

(b) P had not, before P receives notice of the decision on administrative review, started proceedings in relation to the original decision.

(3D) Where this paragraph applies, the notice of appeal against the original decision must be received—

(a) if P is in the United Kingdom, not later than 14 days after P is sent the notice of the decision on administrative review;

(b) if P is outside the United Kingdom, not later than 28 days after P receives the notice of the decision on administrative review.

(3E) In this rule, 'the relevant rules' means residence scheme immigration rules or relevant entry clearance immigration rules (within the meanings given in section 17 of the European Union (Withdrawal Agreement) Act 2020).'.

The Citizens' Rights (Frontier Workers) (EU Exit) Regulations 2020

(SI No. 1213)

PART 1

PRELIMINARY

Citation and commencement

1.—(1) These Regulations may be cited as the Citizens' Rights (Frontier Workers) (EU Exit) Regulations 2020.

(2) These Regulations come into force on the day after the day on which they are made except—

(a) the provisions specified in paragraph (3) which come into force on IP completion day;

(b) the provisions specified in paragraph (4) which come into force on 1st July 2021.

(3) The provisions specified in this paragraph are—

(a) Part 2, except for the provisions specified in paragraph (4);

(b) Part 4;

(c) regulation 24 in so far as it relates to an appeal against a decision made under Part 2 or Part 4; and

(d) regulation 28.

(4) The provisions specified in this paragraph are regulations 6(1)(b) and 6(2).

Interpretation

2. In these Regulations—

'the 1971 Act' means the Immigration Act 1971;

'the 2016 Regulations' means the Immigration (European Economic Area) Regulations 2016;

'common travel area' has the same meaning as in section 1(3) of the 1971 Act (general principles);

'decision maker' means the Secretary of State or an immigration officer (as the case may be);

'EEA national' means a national of an EEA state who is not also a British citizen;

'EEA state' means—

(a) a member State; or

(b) Iceland, Liechtenstein, Norway or Switzerland;

'exclusion direction' means a direction issued by the Secretary of State for a person not to be given entry to the United Kingdom on the grounds that the person's exclusion is conducive to the public good;

'frontier worker' has the meaning given in regulation 3;

'frontier worker permit' means a document which certifies a person's frontier workers' rights;

'frontier workers' rights' means the rights a person has as a frontier worker under Part 2 of the withdrawal agreement, Part 2 of the EEA EFTA separation agreement or Part 2 of the Swiss citizens' rights agreement;

'immigration officer' means a person appointed by the Secretary of State as an immigration officer under paragraph 1 of Schedule 2 to the Immigration Act 1971;

'relevant restriction decision' means—

(c) an exclusion direction;

(d) a deportation order made by virtue of regulation 15(1)(b);

(e) an exclusion or deportation order made or treated as having been made by virtue of the 2016 Regulations, including those continued in effect by regulations made under section 7 or 9 of the European Union (Withdrawal Agreement) Act 2020; or

(f) a deportation order made by virtue of section 3 of the 1971 Act;

'required biometrics' means the biometric information required to be provided by the Immigration (Provision of Physical Data) Regulations 2006;

'self-employed person' means a person who is established in the United Kingdom in order to pursue activity as a self-employed person within the meaning of Article 49 on the Treaty of the Functioning of the European Union;

'valid identity document' means—

(g) a valid national identity card issued by an EEA state; or

(h) a valid passport issued by an EEA state;

'worker' means a worker within the meaning of Article 45 of the Treaty on the Functioning of the European Union.

Meaning of 'frontier worker'

3.—(1) A person is a frontier worker for the purposes of these Regulations if they were, immediately before IP completion day, and have been continuously since IP completion day—

(a) an EEA national;

(b) not primarily resident in the United Kingdom; and

(c) either—

(i) a worker in the United Kingdom;

(ii) a self-employed person in the United Kingdom; or

(iii) a person treated as a worker or self-employed person in the United Kingdom by virtue of regulation 4.

(2) For the purposes of paragraph (1), it does not matter if a person changes from one of the statuses in paragraph (1)(c) to another.

(3) For the purposes of paragraph (1), a person is to be treated as not being primarily resident in the United Kingdom at a particular point in time ('the relevant date') if—

(a) they have been present in the United Kingdom for less than 180 days in the twelve-month period immediately before the day on which the relevant date falls; or

(b) they have returned to their country of residence at least—

(i) once in the six-month period immediately before the day on which the relevant date falls; or

(ii) twice in the twelve-month period immediately before the day on which the relevant date falls,

unless there are exceptional reasons for not having done so.

Retained worker or self-employed person status

4.—(1) A person who is no longer a worker in the United Kingdom is to be treated as such if the person, immediately following ceasing work in the United Kingdom—

(a) is temporarily unable to work as the result of an illness or accident;

(b) is in duly recorded involuntary unemployment after having been employed in the United Kingdom for at least one year, provided the person satisfies paragraph (5);

(c) is in duly recorded involuntary unemployment after having been employed in the United Kingdom for less than one year, provided the person satisfies paragraph (5);

(d) is in involuntary unemployment and has embarked on vocational training;

(e) has voluntarily ceased working and has embarked on vocational training that is related to the person's previous employment; or

(f) is temporarily unable to work due to pregnancy or childbirth, provided the person satisfies paragraph (5) 12 months after ceasing work and thereafter.

(2) A person to whom paragraph (1)(c) applies may only retain worker status for a maximum of six months.

(3) A person who is no longer a self-employed person in the United Kingdom is to be treated as such if the person, immediately following ceasing self-employment in the United Kingdom—

(a) is temporarily unable to engage in activities as a self-employed person as the result of an illness or accident;

(b) is in duly recorded involuntary unemployment after having worked as a self-employed person in the United Kingdom for at least one year, provided the person satisfies paragraph (5);

(c) is in duly recorded involuntary unemployment after having worked as a self-employed person in the United Kingdom for less than one year, provided the person satisfies paragraph (5);

(d) is involuntarily no longer in self-employment and has embarked on vocational training;

(e) has voluntarily ceased self-employment and has embarked on vocational training that is related to the person's previous occupation; or

(f) is temporarily unable to engage in activities as a self-employed person due to pregnancy or childbirth, provided the person satisfies paragraph (5) 12 months after ceasing self- employment and thereafter.

(4) A person to whom paragraph (3)(c) applies may only retain self-employed person status for a maximum of six months.

(5) [A person satisfies this paragraph where the person has—

(a) provided evidence that they continue to seek employment or self-employment in the United Kingdom; and

(b) registered as a jobseeker with the relevant employment office.]

(6) A person may not retain the status of—

(a) a worker under paragraph (1)(b); or

(b) a self-employed person under paragraph (3)(b), for longer than six months without providing compelling evidence of continuing to seek employment or self-employment in the United Kingdom.

Note: Paragraph (5) substituted from 22 December 2020 (SI 2020/1372).

Part 2
Frontier worker rights

Exemption from immigration control

5.—(1) Subject to paragraph (2), regulation 7 and Part 4 of these Regulations, a person does not require leave to enter or remain in the United Kingdom under the 1971 Act in any case in which that person is entitled to do so by virtue of their frontier workers' rights.

(2) This regulation does not apply to a person who is subject to a relevant restriction decision.

Right of admission

6.—(1) Subject to regulation 12, a frontier worker must be admitted to the United Kingdom on arrival if the frontier worker produces—

(a) a valid identity document; and

(b) a valid frontier worker permit.

(2) A frontier worker who is an Irish citizen is not required to produce a frontier worker permit.

Person claiming right of admission

7.—(1) This regulation applies to a person who claims a right of admission to the United Kingdom under regulation 6 where there is reason to believe—

(a) that regulation 12 applies to that person; or

(b) they are not entitled to be admitted under regulation 6.

(2) A person to whom this regulation applies is to be treated as if that person were a person seeking leave to enter the United Kingdom under the 1971 Act for the purposes of paragraphs 2, 3, 4, 7 and 16 to 18A of Schedule 2 to the 1971 Act (administrative provisions as to control on entry etc) except that—

(a) the reference in paragraph 2(1) to the purpose for which the immigration officer may examine any persons who have arrived in the United Kingdom is to be read as a reference to the purpose of determining whether the person is to be granted admission under these Regulations;

(b) the reference in paragraph 3(1)(c) to the purpose for which the immigration officer may examine any persons embarking in the United Kingdom is to be read as a reference to the purpose of determining whether the person has exercised frontier workers' rights while in the United Kingdom;

(c) the reference in paragraph 7 to a person who is, or may be, given leave to enter are to be read as references to a person who is, or may be, granted admission under these Regulations;

(d) the reference in paragraph 16(1) to a decision to give or refuse leave to enter is to be read as a reference to a decision to grant or refuse admission under these Regulations; and

(e) a medical examination is not to be carried out under paragraph 2 or paragraph 7 as a matter of routine and may only be carried out within three months of the person's arrival in the United Kingdom.

(3) For so long as a person to whom this regulation applies is detained under the powers conferred by Schedule 2 to the 1971 Act, or granted bail under Schedule 10 to the Immigration Act 2016 whilst liable to be detained under the powers conferred by Schedule 2 to the 1971 Act, the person is deemed not to have been admitted to the United Kingdom.

PART 3
FRONTIER WORKER PERMITS

Issue of frontier worker permits

8.—(1) Subject to regulation 9, the Secretary of State must issue a frontier worker permit to a frontier worker on receipt of a valid application under this regulation.

(2) An application for a frontier worker permit must—

(c) be made online, submitted electronically using the relevant pages of www.gov.uk;

(d) be accompanied by—
(i) the required biometrics;
(ii) a valid identity document; and
(iii) evidence the applicant is a frontier worker; and
(e) be complete.

(3) An application under this Part is invalid and must be rejected if it is submitted otherwise than in accordance with the requirements in paragraph (2), (but see paragraph (4)).

(4) Where the Secretary of State receives an application that does not comply with the requirements of paragraph (2)(b) or (2)(c), the Secretary of State must not reject the application as invalid unless the applicant has been given the opportunity to remedy the deficiencies in the application and has failed to do so.

(5) A frontier worker permit—
(a) may be in electronic form;
(b) is proof of the holder's status as a frontier worker on the date of issue; and
(c) must state the name of the frontier worker and the date of issue.

Refusal to issue a frontier worker permit

9.—(1) The Secretary of State may refuse to issue a frontier worker permit where justified on grounds of public policy, public security or public health in accordance with regulation 18, on conducive grounds in accordance with regulation 19, or on grounds of misuse of rights in accordance with regulation 20.

(2) The Secretary of State must refuse to issue a frontier worker permit to a person subject to a relevant restriction decision.

Validity of frontier worker permits

10. A frontier worker permit issued under these Regulations is valid for—
(a) two years from the date of issue where issued to a frontier worker who is treated as a worker or self-employed person by virtue of regulation 4; or
(b) otherwise five years from the date of issue.

Renewal and revocation of permits

11.—(1) An application for renewal of a frontier worker permit must comply with regulation 8.

(2) The Secretary of State may refuse to renew or may revoke a frontier worker permit at any time—
(a) on grounds of public policy, public security or public health in accordance with regulation 18;
(b) on conducive grounds in accordance with regulation 19;
(c) on grounds of misuse of rights in accordance with regulation 20;
(d) where the permit holder ceases to be or never was a frontier worker; or
(e) where the permit holder is subject to a relevant restriction decision.

(3) An immigration officer may revoke a frontier worker permit at port or while the holder is outside the United Kingdom on the grounds set out in paragraph (2).

PART 4

REFUSAL OF ADMISSION AND REMOVAL

Refusal of admission

12.—(1) An immigration officer must refuse a person's admission to the United Kingdom by virtue of regulation 6 where—

(a) the refusal to admit that person is justified on grounds of public policy, public security or public health in accordance with regulation 18, on conducive grounds in accordance with regulation 19, or on grounds of misuse of rights in accordance with regulation 20;

(b) that person is subject to a relevant restriction decision; or

(c) that person is not required to produce a frontier worker permit under regulation 6(1)(b) but the immigration officer is not satisfied that they are a frontier worker.

(2) When refusing admission under paragraph (1) an immigration officer must revoke that person's frontier worker permit.

Person refused admission

13.—(1) This regulation applies to a person who is in the United Kingdom and has been refused admission to the United Kingdom—

(a) because they are not a frontier worker;

(b) because they do not produce a valid identity document or valid frontier worker permit; or

(c) in accordance with regulation 12.

(2) A person to whom this regulation applies is to be treated as if the person were a person refused leave to enter under the 1971 Act for the purpose of paragraphs 8, 10, 10A, 11 and 16 to 19 of Schedule 2 to the 1971 Act (and the provisions of Part 1 of Schedule 10 to the Immigration Act 2016 (immigration bail) apply accordingly), except that in paragraph 19 of Schedule 2 to the 1971 Act—

(a) sub-paragraph (1) is to be read as if after the words 'to enter the United Kingdom' there were inserted 'under the Citizens' Rights (Frontier Workers) (EU Exit) Regulations 2020';

(b) in sub-paragraph (2), the references to a certificate of entitlement, entry clearance or work permit (in each place they occur) are to be read collectively as a reference to a frontier worker permit; and

(c) sub-paragraph (3) is to be read as if after the words 'to enter the United Kingdom' there were inserted 'under the Citizens' Rights (Frontier Workers) (EU Exit) Regulations 2020'.

Revocation of admission

14.—(1) This regulation applies to a person admitted to the United Kingdom under regulation 6 in circumstances where, under regulation 12(1), that person was not entitled to be admitted.

(2) Paragraph 6(2) of Schedule 2 to the 1971 Act applies to a person to whom this regulation applies, as though the references to—

(a) that person's examination under paragraph 2 of Schedule 2 to the 1971 Act were to that paragraph as applied by regulation 7(2)(a) and (e);

(b) notices of leave to enter the United Kingdom were to a decision to admit that person to the United Kingdom under these Regulations; and

(c) the cancellation of such a notice and the refusal of leave to enter were to revocation of the decision to admit that person to the United Kingdom under this regulation.

(3) Where a person's admission to the United Kingdom is revoked, that person is to be treated as a person to whom admission to the United Kingdom has been refused and regulation 13 applies accordingly.

Removal

15.—(1) A frontier worker who has entered the United Kingdom may be removed if—

(a) that person ceases to be a frontier worker;

(b) the Secretary of State has decided that the person's removal is justified on grounds of public policy, public security or public health in accordance with regulation 18; or

(c) the Secretary of State has decided that the person's removal is justified on grounds of misuse of rights under regulation 20.

(2) The notice of a decision under paragraph (1)(b) must state that upon execution of any deportation order arising from that decision, the person against whom the order was made is prohibited from entering the United Kingdom—

(a) until the order is revoked; or

(b) for the period specified in the order.

Person subject to removal

16.—(1) If there are reasonable grounds for suspecting that a person is someone who may be removed from the United Kingdom by virtue of regulation 15(1)(b) that person may be detained under the authority of the Secretary of State pending a decision whether or not to remove the person under that regulation, and paragraphs 17 to 18A of Schedule 2 to the 1971 Act apply in relation to the detention of such a person as those paragraphs apply in relation to a person who may be detained under paragraph 16 of that Schedule.

(2) Where a decision is taken to remove a person by virtue of regulation 15(1)(a) or (c) the person is to be treated as if the person were a person to whom section 10 of the Immigration and Asylum Act 1999 (removal of persons unlawfully in the United Kingdom) applies.

(3) Where a decision is taken to remove a person by virtue of regulation 15(1)(b), the person is to be treated as if the person were a person to whom section 3(5)(a) of the 1971 Act (liability to deportation) applies, and section 5 of that Act (procedure for deportation) and Schedule 3 to that Act (supplementary provision as to deportation) apply accordingly.

(4) A person who enters the United Kingdom in breach of a deportation order made by virtue of regulation 15(1)(b), or in circumstances where that person was not entitled to be admitted under regulation 12 is removable as an illegal entrant under Schedule 2 to the 1971 Act and the provisions of that Schedule apply accordingly.

(5) Where a deportation order has been made by virtue of regulation 15(1)(b) but the person is not removed under the order during the two year period beginning on the date on which the order is made, the Secretary of State may only take action to remove the person under the order at the end of that period if, having assessed whether there has been any material change in circumstances since the deportation order was made, the Secretary

of State considers that the removal continues to be justified on the grounds of public policy, public security or public health in accordance with regulation 18.

Revocation of deportation orders

17.—(1) A deportation order made by virtue of these Regulations remains in force—

(a) until the order is revoked under this regulation; or

(b) for the period specified in the order.

(2) A person who is subject to a deportation order made by virtue of these Regulations may only apply to the Secretary of State to have it revoked on the basis that there has been a material change in the circumstances that justified the making of the order.

(3) An application under paragraph (2) must set out the material change in circumstances relied upon by the applicant and may only be made whilst the applicant is outside the United Kingdom.

(4) On receipt of an application under paragraph (2) the Secretary of State must revoke the order if the Secretary of State considers that the criteria for making such an order are no longer satisfied.

(5) The Secretary of State must take a decision on an application under paragraph (2) no later than six months after the date on which the application is received.

Decisions taken on grounds of public policy, public security and public health

18.—(1) In this regulation, a 'relevant decision' means a decision taken under these Regulations on the grounds of public policy, public security or public health.

(2) A relevant decision may not be taken to serve economic ends.

(3) A relevant decision may not be taken except on imperative grounds of public security in respect of a frontier worker who is under the age of 18, unless the relevant decision is in the best interests of the person concerned, as provided for in the Convention on the Rights of the Child adopted by the General Assembly of the United Nations on 20th November 1989.

(4) The public policy and public security requirements of the United Kingdom include restricting rights otherwise conferred by these Regulations in order to protect the fundamental interests of society, and where a relevant decision is taken on grounds of public policy or public security it must also be taken in accordance with the following principles—

(a) the decision must comply with the principle of proportionality;

(b) the decision must be based exclusively on the personal conduct of the person concerned;

(c) the personal conduct of the person must represent a genuine, present and sufficiently serious threat affecting one of the fundamental interests of society, taking into account past conduct of the person and that the threat does not need to be imminent;

(d) matters isolated from the particulars of the case or which relate to considerations of general prevention do not justify the decision;

(e) a person's previous criminal convictions do not in themselves justify the decision; and

(f) the decision may be taken on preventative grounds, even in the absence of a previous criminal conviction, provided the grounds are specific to the person.

(5) Before taking a relevant decision on the grounds of public policy or public security in relation to a frontier worker ('P') the decision maker must take account of considerations such as the age, state of health, family and economic situation of P, P's length of presence in the United Kingdom, P's social and cultural integration into the United Kingdom and the extent of P's links with P's country of origin.

(6) In the case of a relevant decision taken on grounds of public health—

(a) a disease that does not have epidemic potential as defined by the relevant instruments of the World Health Organisation or is not a disease listed in Schedule 1 to the Health Protection (Notification) Regulations 2010; or

(b) if the person concerned is in the United Kingdom, any disease occurring after the three month period beginning on the date on which the person arrived in the United Kingdom, does not constitute grounds for the decision.

(7) A court or tribunal considering whether the requirements of this regulation are met must (in particular) have regard to the considerations contained in the Schedule (considerations of public policy, public security and the fundamental interests of society etc).

Decisions taken on conducive grounds

19.—(1) This regulation applies to conduct taking place after IP completion day.

(2) A decision under this regulation may be taken on the ground that the decision is conducive to the public good.

Misuse of frontier workers' rights

20.—(1) The misuse of frontier workers' rights occurs where a person—

(a) observes the requirements of these Regulations in circumstances which do not achieve the purpose of the withdrawal agreement, the EEA EFTA separation agreement or the Swiss citizens' rights agreement as they relate to frontier workers' rights; and

(b) intends to obtain an advantage from these Regulations by engaging in conduct which artificially creates the conditions required to satisfy the criteria set out in these Regulations.

(2) Such misuse includes attempting to remain in the United Kingdom as a frontier worker for purposes other than exercising frontier workers' rights.

(3) The Secretary of State may take a decision on the grounds of misuse of rights where there are reasonable grounds to suspect the misuse of frontier workers' rights and it is proportionate to do so.

(4) This regulation may not be exercised systematically.

[Exemption for Irish citizens

21A. Regulations 7 and 13 to 20 do not apply to a frontier worker who is an Irish citizen unless any of paragraphs (2) to (4) of section 3ZA of the 1971 Act also apply to that Irish citizen.]

Note: Regulation 21A inserted from 23.00 on 31 December 2020 (SI 2020/1309).

PART 5

ADMINISTRATIVE REVIEW AND APPEALS

Administrative review

21.—(1) A person ('P') may apply to the Secretary of State for a review of an eligible decision.

(2) An eligible decision is a decision to—

(a) refuse to issue or renew a frontier worker permit; or

(b) revoke a frontier worker permit under regulation 11(3), on the grounds that P is not a frontier worker.

(3) Where a valid application is made in accordance with regulation 22 the Secretary of State must withdraw the eligible decision and make a new decision where satisfied that P is a frontier worker.

(4) A person may not apply for a review where they have waived their right to do so by signing an administrative review waiver form.

(5) A person may only apply for a review of an eligible decision once.

(6) Where the Secretary of State withdraws the eligible decision a further application for administrative review may be made in respect of any new eligible decision.

(7) The Secretary of State must not consider whether the applicant is entitled to leave to enter or remain in the United Kingdom on some other basis and nothing in these Regulations shall be taken to mean that the applicant may make or vary an application for leave, or make a protection or human rights claim, by seeking an administrative review.

Applications for administrative review

22.—(1) An application for review under regulation 21 must—

(a) be made online, submitted electronically using the relevant pages of www.gov.uk;

(b) be submitted within 28 calendar days of the date of issue of the eligible decision (except where paragraph (5) applies), not including the date of issue;

(c) be accompanied by—

(i) the fee, if any, required to be paid by virtue of regulations made under section 68 of the Immigration Act 2014; and

(ii) a valid identity document.

(2) An application submitted otherwise than in accordance with this regulation must be rejected as invalid and must not be considered.

(3) An applicant may withdraw an application at any time prior to decision.

(4) An application is deemed to be withdrawn where an applicant submits a further application for a frontier worker permit under regulation 8.

(5) Where the applicant is present in the United Kingdom and is held in immigration detention on the date of the eligible decision the application must be submitted within 7 calendar days of the eligible decision.

Removal pending review

23.—(1) A person who has submitted a valid application under regulation 22, or who has not yet submitted an application but is within time to do so, may not be removed from the United Kingdom until that application has been determined or rejected as invalid.

(2) This regulation does not apply to a person who has withdrawn their application under regulation 22(3).

Amendment of the Immigration (Citizens' Rights Appeals) (EU Exit) Regulations 2020

24.—(1) The Immigration (Citizens' Rights Appeals) (EU Exit) Regulations 2020 are amended as follows.

(2) In regulation 2 (interpretation)—

(a) in paragraph (1)—

(i) after the definition of 'the 2002 Act', insert—

' "the 2020 Regulations" means the Citizens' Rights (Frontier Workers) (EU Exit) Regulations 2020;';

(ii) after the definition of 'appellant', insert—

' "frontier worker" has the meaning given in regulation 3 of the 2020 Regulations;

'frontier worker permit' has the meaning given in regulation 2 of the 2020 Regulations;";'

(iii) after the definition of 'the Tribunal', insert— "valid identity document' means—

(a) a valid national identity card issued by an EEA state, or

(b) a valid passport issued by an EEA state.';

(b) after paragraph (1), insert—

'(1A) For the purposes of the definition of 'valid identity document', 'EEA state' means—

(a) a member State, or

(b) Iceland, Liechtenstein, Norway or Switzerland.'.

(3) In Part 2, after the heading to Chapter 1 of that Part, insert—

'Decisions other than those relating to frontier workers'.

(4) In regulation 6 (right of appeal against decisions to make a deportation order), in the heading, after 'order' insert 'in respect of a person other than a person claiming to be a frontier worker'.

(5) After regulation 6, insert—

'Decisions relating to frontier workers

Right of appeal against decisions relating to issue, renewal or revocation of frontier worker permits

6A. A person may appeal against a decision—

(a) to refuse to issue a frontier worker permit to them,

(b) to refuse to renew their frontier worker permit, or

(c) to revoke their frontier worker permit.

Right of appeal against decisions to refuse frontier workers admission to the United Kingdom

6B.—(1) A person may appeal against a decision made under regulation 12 of the 2020 Regulations (a 'refusal of admission decision').

(2) But a person cannot bring an appeal under paragraph (1) without producing—

(a) a valid identity document, or

(b) where paragraph (3) applies, sufficient evidence to satisfy the Secretary of State that they are a frontier worker.

(3) This paragraph applies where—

(a) the refusal of admission decision was made before 1st July 2021, or

(b) the person bringing the appeal is an Irish citizen.

Right of appeal against decision to revoke admission to the United Kingdom

6C.—(1) A person who has been admitted to the United Kingdom under regulation 6 of the 2020 Regulations may appeal against a decision under regulation 14 of those Regulations to revoke that admission.

(2) But a person cannot bring an appeal under paragraph (1) without producing a valid identity document.

Right of appeal against certain decisions to remove frontier workers from the United Kingdom

6D.—(1) A frontier worker who has entered the United Kingdom may appeal against a decision to remove that person taken by virtue of regulation 15(1)(a) or (c) of the 2020 Regulations.

(2) But a person cannot bring an appeal under paragraph (1) without producing a valid identity document.

Right of appeal against decisions to make deportation order in respect of frontier workers

6E.—(1) A frontier worker who has entered the United Kingdom may appeal against a decision to make a deportation order under section 5(1) of the 1971 Act in respect of them.

(2) [But paragraph (1) does not apply to a person if the decision to remove that person was taken—

(a) under regulation 23(6)(b) of the Immigration (European Economic Area) Regulations 2016 ('the 2016 Regulations'), where the decision to remove was taken before the revocation of the 2016 Regulations, or

(b) otherwise, under regulation 23(6)(b) of the 2016 Regulations as it continues to have effect by virtue of the Citizens' Rights (Restrictions of Rights of Entry and Residence) (EU Exit) Regulations 2020 or the Citizens' Rights (Application Deadline and Temporary Protection) (EU Exit) Regulations 2020.]

(3) In addition, a person cannot bring an appeal under paragraph (1) without producing—

(a) a valid identity document, and

(b) if they do not have a valid frontier worker permit, sufficient evidence to satisfy the Secretary of State that they are a frontier worker.

(4) For the purposes of paragraph (3)(b), a person is to be treated as having a valid frontier worker permit if they would hold such a permit but for its revocation following a decision to make a deportation order under section 5(1) of the 1971 Act in respect of them.

Note: Paragraph (2) substituted from 22 December 2020 (SI 2020/1372).

Alternative evidence of identity and nationality

6F. Where a provision of this Part requires a person to hold or produce a valid identity document, the Secretary of State may accept alternative evidence of identity and nationality where the person is unable to obtain or produce the required document due to circumstances beyond the person's control.'.

(6) In regulation 8 (grounds of appeal)—

(a) in paragraph (2)—

(i) in paragraph (a), for 'or 25(2)' substitute ', 24(3), 25(2) or 25(3)';

(ii) in paragraph (b), for 'or 24(2)' substitute ', 23(3), 24(2) or 24(3)';

(b) in paragraph (3), after sub-paragraph (d), insert—

'(e) where the decision is mentioned in regulation 6A, 6B, 6C or 6D, it is not in accordance with regulation 9, 11, 12, 14, 15(1)(a) or 15(1)(c) of the 2020 Regulations (as the case may be);

(f) where the decision is mentioned in regulation 6E, it is not in accordance with section 3(5) or 3(6) of the 1971 Act, or regulation 15(1)(b) of the 2020 Regulations (as the case may be).'

(7) In regulation 13 (pending appeal), after paragraph (4), insert—

'(4A) An appeal under regulation 6A is to be treated as abandoned if the appellant is issued with a frontier worker permit.

(4B) An appeal under regulation 6B is to be treated as abandoned if the appellant is admitted to the United Kingdom under regulation 6 of the 2020 Regulations.'.

Amendment of the Special Immigration Appeals Commission (Procedure) Rules 2003

25.—(1) The Special Immigration Appeals Commission (Procedure) Rules 2003 are amended as follows.

(2) In rule 8(4E) (time limit for appealing), for the definition of 'relevant rules' substitute—

"relevant rules' means—

(a) residence scheme immigration rules or relevant entry clearance immigration rules (within the meanings given in section 17 of the European Union (Withdrawal Agreement) Act 2020), or

(b) the Citizens' Rights (Frontier Workers) (EU Exit) Regulations 2020 (see regulations 21 to 23 of those Regulations).'.

Amendment of the Tribunal Procedure (First-tier Tribunal) (Immigration and Asylum Chamber) Rules 2014

26.—(1) The Tribunal Procedure (First-tier Tribunal) (Immigration and Asylum Chamber) Rules 2014 are amended as follows.

(2) In rule 19 (notice of appeal), for paragraph (3E), substitute—

'(3E) In this rule, 'the relevant rules' means—

(a) residence scheme immigration rules or relevant entry clearance immigration rules (within the meanings given in section 17 of the European Union (Withdrawal Agreement) Act 2020), or

(b) the Citizens' Rights (Frontier Workers) (EU Exit) Regulations 2020 (see regulations 21 to 23 of those Regulations).'.

PART 6

CONSEQUENTIAL AMENDMENTS

Amendment of the Immigration (Provision of Physical Data) Regulations 2006

27.—(1) The Immigration (Provision of Physical Data) Regulations 2006 are amended as follows.

(2) In regulation 2 in the definition of 'application'—

(a) at the end of paragraph (d) omit 'or';

(b) after paragraph (e) insert—

'; or

(f) an application for a frontier worker permit under the Citizens' Rights (Frontier Workers) (EU Exit) Regulations 2020;'.

Amendment of the Immigration (Control of Entry through Republic of Ireland) Order 1972

28.—(1) The Immigration (Control of Entry through Republic of Ireland) Order 1972 is amended as follows.

(2) In article 4 (restrictions and conditions on entry through Ireland)—

(a) in paragraph (1) for 'paragraph (2) and (2A)' substitute 'paragraphs (2), (2A) and (2B)'

(b) after paragraph (2A) insert—

'(2B) This Article does not apply to a person who is a frontier worker under regulation 3 of the Citizens' Rights (Frontier Workers) (EU Exit) Regulations 2020.'.

Regulation 18

SCHEDULE

CONSIDERATIONS OF PUBLIC POLICY, PUBLIC SECURITY AND THE FUNDAMENTAL INTERESTS OF SOCIETY ETC.

Considerations of public policy and public security

1. The United Kingdom enjoys considerable discretion, acting within the parameters set by the withdrawal agreement, the EEA EFTA separation agreement or the Swiss citizens' rights agreement, to define its own standards of public policy and public security, for purposes tailored to its individual context from time to time.

Application of paragraph 1 to the United Kingdom

2. A frontier worker having extensive familial and societal links with persons of the same nationality or language does not amount to integration in the United Kingdom; a significant degree of wider cultural and societal integration must be present before a person may be regarded as integrated in the United Kingdom.

3. Where a frontier worker has received a custodial sentence, or is a persistent offender, the longer the sentence, or the more numerous the convictions, the greater the likelihood that the individual's continued presence in the United Kingdom represents a genuine, present and sufficiently serious threat affecting the fundamental interests of society.

4. Little weight is to be attached to the integration of a frontier worker within the United Kingdom if the alleged integrating links were formed at or around the same time as—

(a) the commission of a criminal offence;

(b) an act otherwise affecting the fundamental interests of society;

(c) the frontier worker was in custody.

5. The removal from the United Kingdom of a frontier worker who is able to provide substantive evidence of not demonstrating a threat (for example, through demonstrating that the frontier worker has successfully reformed or rehabilitated) is less likely to be proportionate.

6. It is consistent with public policy and public security requirements in the United Kingdom that decisions may be taken in order to refuse, terminate or withdraw any right otherwise conferred by these Regulations in the case of abuse of rights or fraud, including—

(a) entering, attempting to enter or assisting another person to enter or attempt to enter, a marriage, civil partnership or durable partnership of convenience; or

(b) fraudulently obtaining or attempting to obtain, or assisting another to obtain or to attempt to obtain, frontier workers' rights.

The fundamental interests of society

7. For the purposes of these Regulations, the fundamental interests of society in the United Kingdom include—

(a) preventing unlawful immigration and abuse of the immigration laws, and maintaining the integrity and effectiveness of the immigration control system (including under these Regulations) and of the common travel area;

(b) maintaining public order;

(c) preventing social harm;

(d) preventing the evasion of taxes and duties;

(e) protecting public services;

(f) excluding or removing a frontier worker with a conviction (including where the conduct of that person is likely to cause, or has in fact caused, public offence) and maintaining public confidence in the ability of the relevant authorities to take such action;

(g) tackling offences likely to cause harm to society where an immediate or direct victim may be difficult to identify but where there is wider societal harm (such as offences related to the misuse of drugs or crime with a cross-border dimension);

(h) combating the effects of persistent offending (particularly in relation to offences, which if taken in isolation, may otherwise be unlikely to meet the requirements of regulation 18;

(i) protecting the rights and freedoms of others, particularly from exploitation and trafficking;

(j) protecting the public;

(k) acting in the best interests of a child (including where doing so entails refusing a child admission to the United Kingdom);

(l) countering terrorism and extremism and protecting shared values.

The Citizens' Rights (Application Deadline and Temporary Protection) (EU Exit) Regulations 2020
(SI No. 1209)

PART 1
PRELIMINARY

Citation, commencement and interpretation

1.—(1) These Regulations may be cited as the Citizens' Rights (Application Deadline and Temporary Protection) (EU Exit) Regulations 2020 and come into force on IP completion day.

(2) In these Regulations—

'the EEA Regulations 2016' mean the Immigration (European Economic Area) Regulations 2016;

'application deadline' has the meaning given in regulation 2.

PART 2
DEADLINE FOR APPLICATIONS

Deadline for applications

2. The end of 30 June 2021 is the deadline for submission of an application for residence status ('application deadline') that applies for the purposes of the following provisions—

(a) the first sub-paragraph of Article 18(1)(b) of the withdrawal agreement;

(b) the first sub-paragraph of Article 17(1)(b) of the EEA EFTA separation agreement, and

(c) the first sentence of Article 16(1)(b) of the Swiss citizens' rights agreement.

PART 3
SAVING OF THE EEA REGULATIONS 2016 ETC. DURING THE GRACE PERIOD AND WHILST APPLICATIONS ARE FINALLY DETERMINED

Grace period

3.—(1) This regulation has effect if the EEA Regulations 2016 are revoked on IP completion day (with or without savings).

(2) The provisions of the EEA Regulations 2016 specified in regulations 5 to 10 continue to have effect (despite the revocation of those Regulations) with the modifications specified in those regulations in relation to a relevant person during the grace period.

(3) The provisions specified in regulation 11 apply in relation to a relevant person during the grace period as if any reference to the EEA Regulations 2016 or any provision of those Regulations are to the Regulations or provision of the Regulations as continued in effect and modified by regulations 5 to 10.

(4) The enactments specified in regulation 12 apply in relation to a relevant person during the grace period with the modifications specified in that regulation.

(5) For the purposes of this regulation—

(a) the grace period is the period beginning immediately after IP completion day and ending with the application deadline;

(b) a person is to be treated as residing in the United Kingdom at any time which would be taken into account for the purposes of calculating periods when the person was continuously resident for the purposes of the EEA Regulations 2016 (see regulation 3);

(c) a person who does not have the right to reside in the United Kingdom permanently is to be treated as having such a right if the person had a right of permanent residence in the United Kingdom under those Regulations (see regulation 15) and who, immediately before IP completion day, has been absent from the United Kingdom for a continuous period of 5 years or less (disregarding any period of absence before the person acquired the right of permanent residence).

(6) In this regulation—

'EEA document' means—

(a) an EEA family permit issued under regulation 12 of the EEA Regulations 2016;

(b) a registration certificate issued under regulation 17 of those Regulations, or

(c) a residence card issued under regulation 18 of those Regulations;

'family member'—

(a) has the same meaning as in paragraph (1) of regulation 7 of the EEA Regulations 2016 (read with paragraph (2) of that regulation) as those Regulations had effect immediately before IP completion day, and

(b) includes an extended family member within the meaning of regulation 8 of those Regulations as they had effect immediately before IP completion day if that person—

(i) immediately before IP completion day satisfied the condition in regulation 8(5) of those Regulations (durable partner), or

(ii) holds a valid EEA document (regardless of whether that document was issued before or after IP completion day);

'relevant family member', in relation to a person ('P'), means a family member who—

(a) was a family member of P immediately before IP completion day;

(b) is P's child and—

(i) the child's other parent is a relevant person or has leave to enter or remain in the United Kingdom by virtue of residence scheme immigration rules;

(ii) the child's other parent is a British citizen;

(iii) P has sole or joint rights of custody of the child in the circumstances set out in the last point of Article 10(1)(e)(iii) of the withdrawal agreement or the last point of Article 9(1)(e)(iii) of the EEA EFTA separation agreement, or

(iv) P falls within Article 10(1)(e)(iii) of the Swiss citizens' rights agreement (children of beneficiaries of that agreement);

(c) becomes a family member of P after IP completion day by virtue of being issued with an EEA document (see paragraph (b)(ii) of the definition of 'family member'), or

(d) is the spouse or civil partner of P and P is a national of Switzerland;

'relevant person' means a person who does not have (and who has not, during the grace period, had) leave to enter or remain in the United Kingdom by virtue of residence scheme immigration rules and who—

(a) immediately before IP completion day—

(i) was lawfully resident in the United Kingdom by virtue of the EEA Regulations 2016, or

(ii) had a right of permanent residence in the United Kingdom under those Regulations (see regulation 15), or

(b) is not a person who falls within sub-paragraph (a) but is a relevant family member of a person who immediately before IP completion day—

(i) did not have leave to enter or remain in the United Kingdom by virtue of residence scheme immigration rules, and

(ii) either—

(aa) was lawfully resident in the United Kingdom by virtue of the EEA Regulations 2016, or

(bb) had a right of permanent residence in the United Kingdom under those Regulations (see regulation 15).

Note: Numbering of the sub-paragraphs within each definition corrected 3 December 2020.

Applications which have not been finally determined by the application deadline

4.—(1) This regulation has effect if the EEA Regulations 2016 are revoked on IP completion day (with or without savings).

(2) This regulation applies to a person ('the applicant') who—

(a) has made an in-time application (see paragraph (6)), and

(b) immediately before IP completion day—

(i) was lawfully resident in the United Kingdom by virtue of the EEA Regulations 2016, or

(ii) had a right of permanent residence in the United Kingdom under those Regulations (see regulation 15).

(3) The provisions of the EEA Regulations 2016 specified in regulations 5 to 10 continue to have effect (despite the revocation of those Regulations) with the modifications specified in those regulations in relation to the applicant during the relevant period.

(4) The provisions specified in regulation 11 apply in relation to the applicant during the relevant period as if any reference to the EEA Regulations 2016 or any provision of those Regulations are to the Regulations or provision of the Regulations as continued in effect and modified by regulations 5 to 10.

(5) The enactments specified in regulation 12 apply in relation to the applicant during the relevant period with the modifications specified in that regulation.

(6) For the purposes of this regulation—

(a) an in-time application is an application for leave to enter or remain in the United Kingdom by virtue of residence scheme immigration rules which—

(i) is valid under residence scheme immigration rules;

(ii) is made on or before the application deadline, and

(iii) has not been withdrawn;

(b) the relevant period begins immediately after the application deadline and ends—

(i) if the applicant is, by virtue of the in-time application, granted leave to enter or remain in the United Kingdom, on the day on which that leave is granted;

(ii) if a decision is taken not to grant any leave to enter or remain in the United Kingdom in response to the applicant's application and the applicant does not appeal against that decision, on the first day on which the applicant is no longer entitled to appeal against that decision (ignoring any possibility of an appeal out of time with permission);

(iii) if a decision is taken not to grant any leave to enter or remain in the United Kingdom in response to the applicant's application and the applicant brings an appeal against that decision, on the day on which that appeal is finally determined, withdrawn or abandoned, or lapses under paragraph 3 of Schedule 1 to the Immigration (Citizens' Rights Appeals) (EU Exit) Regulations 2020;

(c) a person is to be treated as residing in the United Kingdom at any time which would be taken into account for the purposes of calculating periods when the person was continuously resident for the purposes of the EEA Regulations 2016 (see regulation 3);

(d) a person who does not have the right to reside in the United Kingdom permanently is to be treated as having such a right if the person had a right of permanent residence in the United Kingdom under those Regulations (see regulation 15) and who, immediately before IP completion day, has been absent from the United Kingdom for a continuous period of 5 years or less (disregarding any period of absence before the person acquired the right of permanent residence).

(7) For the purposes of paragraph (6)(b)(iii)—

(a) an appeal is not finally determined while (as the case may be)—

(i) an application for permission to appeal under section 11 or 13 of the Tribunals, Courts and Enforcement Act 2007 could be made or is awaiting determination;

(ii) permission to appeal under either of those sections has been granted and the appeal is awaiting determination;

(iii) an appeal has been remitted under section 12 or 14 of that Act and is awaiting determination;

(iv) any of the following applications could be made—

(aa) an application for leave to appeal under section 7 of the applied 1997 Act;

(bb) an application for a certificate under section 7B of the applied 1997 Act;

(cc) an application for permission to appeal under section 7C of the applied 1997 Act, or

(v) leave to appeal under section 7, or permission to appeal under section 7C, of the applied 1997 Act has been granted and the appeal is awaiting determination;

(b) an appeal is to be treated as abandoned if the appellant is granted leave to enter or remain in the United Kingdom by virtue of residence scheme immigration rules;

(c) an appeal is not to be treated as abandoned solely because the appellant leaves the United Kingdom.

(8) For the purposes of paragraph (7), 'the applied 1997 Act' means the Special Immigration Appeals Commission Act 1997 as it applies for the purposes of the Immigration (Citizens' Rights Appeals) (EU Exit) Regulations 2020 by virtue of Part 2 of Schedule 1 to those Regulations.

Provisions relating to definitions etc.

5. The following provisions of Part 1 of the EEA Regulations 2016 (provisions relating to definitions etc.) with the modifications set out below are specified for the purposes of regulations 3 and 4—

(a) regulation 2 (general interpretation) with the modifications that—

(i) all instances of the words 'or any other right conferred by the EU Treaties'—

(aa) in so far as they relate to things done on or after exit day but before IP completion day, were a reference to a right conferred by the EU Treaties so far as they were applicable to and in the United Kingdom by virtue of Part 4 of the EU withdrawal agreement;

(bb) in so far as they relate to things done on or after IP completion day, were omitted;

(ii) all instances of the words 'or the EU Treaties'—

(aa) in so far as they relate to things done after exit day but before IP completion day, were a reference to the EU Treaties so far as they were applicable to and in the United Kingdom by virtue of Part 4 of the EU withdrawal agreement;

(bb) in so far as they relate to things done on or after IP completion day, were omitted;

(iii) in paragraph (b) of the definition of 'EEA decision', ', a registration certificate, residence card, derivative residence card, document certifying permanent residence or permanent residence card' were omitted;

(iv) in the definition of 'EEA State', so far as relevant to things done after exit day, ', other than the United Kingdom' were omitted;

(b) regulation 3 (continuity of residence);

(c) regulation 4 ('worker', 'self-employed person', 'self-sufficient person' and 'student') with the modification that, in paragraph (1)(b), for 'in accordance with' there were substituted 'within the meaning of';

(d) regulation 5 ('worker or self-employed person who has ceased activity');

(e) regulation 6 ('qualified person') with the modifications that—

(i) in paragraph (4C), 'and having a genuine chance of being engaged' were omitted;

(ii) in paragraph (6), after 'employment and' there were inserted ', when determining whether the person is a jobseeker,';

(iii) in paragraph (7), after 'continuing to seek employment and' there were inserted ', where that person is a jobseeker,';

(f) regulation 7 ('family member');

(g) regulation 8 ('extended family member') with the modification that paragraph (8)(c) were omitted;

(h) regulation 9 (family members and extended family members of British citizens) with the modifications that—

(i) in paragraph (1), at the end there were inserted 'and BC is to be treated as satisfying any requirement to be a qualified person';

(ii) sub-paragraph (a) of paragraph (3) were omitted;

(iii) paragraph (7) were omitted;

(i) regulation 9A (dual national: national of an EEA State who acquires British citizenship);

(j) regulation 10 ('family member who has retained the right of residence') with the modification that, in paragraph (5)(a), 'the initiation of proceedings for' were omitted.

Provisions relating to residence rights

6. The following provisions of Parts 2 and 3 of the EEA Regulations 2016 (provisions relating to residence rights and residence documentation) with the modifications set out below are specified for the purposes of regulations 3 and 4—

(a) regulation 11 (right of admission to the United Kingdom) with the modifications that—

(i) sub-paragraph (a) of paragraph (2) were omitted;

(ii) in paragraph (3), for ', a permanent residence card or a qualifying EEA State residence card' there were substituted 'or a permanent residence card';

(iii) paragraph (4) were omitted;

(b) regulation 12 (issue of EEA family permit) with the modification that in paragraph (4), before sub-paragraph (a), there were inserted—

'(aa) the extended family member satisfies the condition in paragraph (5) of regulation 8;';

(c) regulation 13 (initial right of residence) with the modification that in paragraph (4), after '26(3) (misuse of right to reside)', there were inserted ', 27A (decisions taken on conducive grounds)';

(d) regulation 14 (extended right of residence) with the modification that in paragraph (4), after '26(3)', there were inserted ', 27A';

(e) regulation 15 (right of permanent residence) with the modification that in paragraph (4), after '26(3)', there were inserted ', 27A';

(f) regulation 16 (derivative right to reside) with the modifications that—

(i) in paragraph (5)(c), for 'another' there were substituted 'an';

(ii) in paragraph (12), after '26(3)', there were inserted ', 27A';

(g) regulation 21 (procedure for applications for documentation under this Part and regulation 12) with the modifications that—

(i) in paragraph (1) and in paragraph (4A), 'documentation under this Part, or for' were omitted;

(ii) in paragraph (2), 'this Part or' and ', as the case may be, as well as that required by paragraph (5),' were omitted;

(iii) paragraphs (3), (5) and (6) were omitted;

(h) regulation 22 (verification of a right of residence) with the modifications that—

(i) in paragraph (1)(b), the words 'or documentation issued under Part 3' were omitted;

(ii) in paragraph (2)(a), the words 'or documentation under this Part' were omitted.

Provisions relating to powers of refusal of admission and removal etc.

7.—(1) Subject to paragraph (2), the following provisions of Part 4 of the EEA Regulations 2016 (provisions relating to refusal of admission and removal etc.) with the modifications set out below are specified for the purposes of regulations 3 and 4—

[(a) regulation 23 (exclusion and removal from the United Kingdom) with the modification that in each of paragraphs (1), (5), (6)(b) and (7)(b), after 'regulation 27', there were inserted 'or on conducive grounds in accordance with regulation 27A or if the person is subject to a deportation order by virtue of section 32 of the UK Borders Act 2007;]

(b) regulation 24 (refusal to issue or renew and revocation of residence documentation) with the modifications that—

(i) in paragraph (1)—

(aa) 'refuse to issue,', 'or refuse to renew' and 'the refusal or' were omitted;

(bb) after 'public health', there were inserted 'in accordance with regulation 27, or on conducive grounds in accordance with regulation 27A';

(ii) in paragraph (2), 'or an application made by that person for such a certificate, card or document' were omitted;

(iii) in paragraphs (3) and (4), 'or refuse to renew' were omitted;

(iv) in paragraph (6)(a), after 'public health', there were inserted 'in accordance with regulation 27 or on conducive grounds in accordance with regulation 27A';

(v) paragraph (7) were omitted;

(c) regulation 25 (cancellation of a right of residence) with the modification that in paragraph (2)(b), after 'regulation 27', there were inserted ', on conducive grounds in accordance with regulation 27A';

(d) regulation 26 (misuse of a right to reside) with the modification that in paragraph (1)(a) '(as determined by reference to Council Directive 2004/38/EC and the EU Treaties)' were omitted;

(e) regulation 27 (decisions taken on grounds of public policy, public security and public health);

(f) as if, after regulation 27, there were inserted—

'Decisions taken on conducive grounds

27A.—(1) An EEA decision may be taken on the ground that the decision is conducive to the public good.

(2) But a decision may only be taken under this regulation in relation to a person as a result of conduct of that person that took place after IP completion day.';

(g) regulation 28 (application of Part 4 to a person with a derivative right to reside) with the modification that paragraph (1)(c) were omitted;

(h) Schedule 1 (considerations of public policy, public security and the fundamental interests of society etc.) with the modification that for paragraph 1 there were substituted—

'1. The United Kingdom enjoys considerable discretion, acting within the parameters set by the law, to define its own standards of public policy and public security, for purposes tailored to its individual context from time to time.'.

(2) The provisions specified in paragraph (1) do not apply in any case where regulations made under section 9 of the European Union (Withdrawal Agreement) Act 2020 (restrictions of rights of entry and residence) apply.

Note: Paragraph (1)(a) substituted immediately before 23.00 on 31 December 2020 (SI 2020/1309, reg. 1(2)(a)).

Provisions relating to procedures in relation to EEA decisions

8. The following provisions of Part 5 of the EEA Regulations 2016 (provisions relating to procedures or decisions under the EEA Regulations 2016) with the modifications set out below are specified for the purposes of regulations 3 and 4—

(a) regulation 29 (person claiming right of admission) with the modifications in paragraph (1) (a)that—

(i) at the end of paragraph (iii), there were inserted 'or';

(ii) paragraph (v) were omitted;

(b) regulation 30 (person refused admission) with the modification that in paragraph (2), the reference to ', a qualifying EEA State residence card' were omitted;

(c) regulation 31 (revocation of admission);

(d) regulation 32 (person subject to removal) with the modification that in paragraph (5), after 'public health', there were inserted 'in accordance with regulation 27 or on conducive grounds in accordance with regulation 27A';

(e) regulation 33 (human rights considerations and interim orders to suspend removal);

(f) regulation 34 (revocation of deportation and exclusion orders) with the modifications that—

(i) in paragraph (3), after 'deportation' there were inserted 'order made on the grounds of public policy, public security or public health in accordance with regulation 27';

(ii) after paragraph (5) there were inserted—

'(5A) A person who is subject to a deportation order made on conducive grounds in accordance with regulation 27A may apply to the Secretary of State to have it revoked in accordance with the immigration rules that apply in relation to an application for revocation of a deportation order made by virtue of section 3(5) of the Immigration Act 1971; and any such application is to be decided as if those rules applied to it.'.

Provisions relating to appeals

9. The following provisions of Part 6 of the EEA Regulations 2016 (provisions relating to appeals) with the modifications set out below are specified for the purposes of regulations 3 and 4—

(a) regulation 35 (interpretation of Part 6);

(b) regulation 36 (appeal rights);

(c) regulation 37 (out of country appeals);

(d) regulation 38 (appeals to the Commission);

(e) regulation 39 (national security: EEA Decisions);

(f) regulation 40 (effect of appeals to the First-tier Tribunal or Upper Tribunal);

(g) regulation 41 (temporary admission to submit case in person);

(h) regulation 42 (alternative evidence of identity and nationality);

(i) Schedule 2 (appeals to the First-tier Tribunal) with the modification that, in each of paragraphs 1 and 2(4), for 'the EU Treaties', there were substituted 'the Immigration (European Economic Area) Regulations 2016, the EU withdrawal agreement, the EEA EFTA separation agreement (which has the same meaning as in the European Union (Withdrawal Agreement) Act 2020) or the Swiss citizens' rights agreement (which has the same meaning as in that Act)'.

Miscellaneous provisions

10. The following provisions of Part 7 of the EEA Regulations 2016 (miscellaneous provisions) with the modifications set out below are specified for the purposes of regulations 3 and 4—

(a) regulation 43 (effect on other legislation);

(b) regulation 45 (revocations, savings, transitory and transitional provisions and consequential modifications) (except in so far as it relates to Part 1 of Schedule 4);

(c) Schedule 3 (effect on other legislation) with the modification that in paragraph 3, 'a qualifying EEA State residence card,' were omitted;

(d) Part 2 of Schedule 4 (savings and modifications);

(e) Schedule 6 (transitional provisions) with the modification that in paragraph 4(1), paragraphs (b) to (f) were omitted;

(f) Schedule 7 (consequential modifications).

Entitlement to benefits and public services

11. The provisions specified in this regulation are—

(a) regulation 21AA (special cases: supplemental – persons from abroad) of the Income Support (General) Regulations 1987;

(b) regulation 21AA (special cases: supplemental – persons from abroad) of the Income Support (General) Regulations (Northern Ireland) 1987;

(c) regulation 85A (special cases: supplemental – persons from abroad) of the Jobseeker's Allowance Regulations 1996;

(d) regulation 85A (special cases: supplemental – persons from abroad) of the Jobseeker's Allowance Regulations (Northern Ireland) 1996;

(e) regulation 2 (persons not in Great Britain) of the State Pension Credit Regulations 2002;

(f) regulation 3 (circumstances in which a person is treated as not being in the United Kingdom) of the Tax Credits (Residence) Regulations 2003;

(g) regulation 2 (persons not in Northern Ireland) of the State Pension Credit Regulations (Northern Ireland) 2003;

[(ga) regulation 7 (funeral payments: entitlement) of the Social Fund Maternity and Funeral Expenses (General) Regulations 2005;

(gb) regulation 7 (funeral payments: entitlement) of the Social Fund Maternity and Funeral Expenses (General) Regulations (Northern Ireland) 2005;]

(h) regulation 10 (persons from abroad) of the Housing Benefit Regulations 2006;

(i) regulation 10 (persons from abroad) of the Housing Benefit (Persons who have attained the qualifying age for state pension credit) Regulations 2006;

(j) regulations 23 (circumstances in which person treated as not being in Great Britain) and 27 (circumstances in which person treated as not being in Northern Ireland) of the Child Benefit (General) Regulations 2006;

(k) regulations 2 (interpretation), 4 (other persons from abroad who are ineligible for an allocation of housing accommodation) and 6 (other persons from abroad who are ineligible for housing assistance) of the Allocation of Housing and Homelessness (Eligibility) (England) Regulations 2006;

(l) regulations 2 (interpretation), 3 (persons from abroad who are ineligible for an allocation of housing accommodation) and 4 (persons from abroad who are ineligible for housing assistance) of the Allocation of Housing and Homelessness (Eligibility) Regulations (Northern Ireland) 2006;

(m) regulation 10 (persons from abroad) of the Housing Benefit Regulations (Northern Ireland) 2006;

(n) regulation 10 (persons from abroad) of the Housing Benefit (Persons who have attained the qualifying age for state pension credit) Regulations (Northern Ireland) 2006;

(o) regulation 70 (special cases: supplemental – persons from abroad) of the Employment and Support Allowance Regulations 2008;

(p) regulation 70 (special cases: supplemental – persons from abroad) of the Employment and Support Allowance Regulations (Northern Ireland) 2008;

(q) regulation 12 (persons treated as not being in Great Britain) of the Council Tax Reduction Schemes (Prescribed Requirements) (England) Regulations 2012;

(r) regulation 16 (persons not entitled to council tax reduction: persons treated as not being in Great Britain) of the Council Tax Reduction (Scotland) Regulations 2012;

(s) regulation 16 (persons not entitled to council tax reduction: persons treated as not being in Great Britain) of the Council Tax Reduction (State Pension Credit) (Scotland) Regulations 2012;

(t) regulations 2 (interpretation) and 9 (persons treated as not being in Great Britain) of the Universal Credit Regulations 2013;

(u) regulation 28 (persons treated as not being in Great Britain) of the Council Tax Reduction Schemes and Prescribed Requirements (Wales) Regulations 2013;

(v) paragraph 19 (class of persons excluded from this scheme: persons treated as not being in Great Britain) of the Schedule to the Council Tax Reduction Schemes (Default Scheme) (Wales) Regulations 2013;

(w) regulations 2 (interpretation), 4 (other persons from abroad who are ineligible for an allocation of housing accommodation) and 6 (other persons from abroad who are ineligible for housing assistance) of the Allocation of Housing and Homelessness (Eligibility) (Wales) Regulations 2014;

(x) regulation 14C of the National Health Service (Charges to Overseas Visitors) Regulations 2015 (family members of British citizens of Northern Ireland);

(y) regulations 2 (interpretation) and 9 (persons treated as not being in Northern Ireland) of the Universal Credit Regulations (Northern Ireland) 2016.

Note: paragraphs (ga) and (gb) inserted and in force immediately before 2300 on 31 December 2020 (SI 2020/1309, reg. 1(2)(a)).

Modification of other enactments

12.—(1) The following enactments with the modifications set out below are specified for the purposes of regulations 3 and 4—

(a) section 1(5) of the Aliens' Employment Act 1955 (definition of a 'relevant European'), as it had effect immediately before IP completion day, with the modification that, for paragraphs (a) to (c), there were substituted 'a national of an EEA State or Switzerland, or a family member of such a national, who has a right of residence in the United Kingdom by virtue of the Immigration (European Economic Area) Regulations 2016 (as they continue to have effect by virtue of regulations 3 and 4 of the Citizens' Rights (Application Deadline and Temporary Protection) (EU Exit) Regulations 2020)';

(b) section 3 of the Immigration Act 1971, with the modification that a relevant person (within the meaning of regulation 3 of these Regulations) and the applicant (within the meaning of regulation 4 of these Regulations) are a 'relevant person' within the meaning of that section (see section 3(10) of that Act);

(c) paragraph 3 of Schedule 4 to that Act (Islands deportation order treated as order made under the Immigration Act 1971), as it had effect immediately before IP completion day;

(d) case 10A of Schedule 15 to the Rent Act 1977 (cases in which court may order possession), as it had effect immediately before IP completion day;

(e) subsection (4)(e) of section 50A of the British Nationality Act 1981 (meaning of references to being in breach of immigration laws), as it had effect immediately before IP completion day;

(f) Ground 7B of Schedule 2 to the Housing Act 1988 (grounds for possession of dwelling- houses let on assured tenancies), as it had effect immediately before IP completion day;

(g) section 7(1) of the Immigration Act 1988 (persons exercising Community rights and nationals of member States), as it had effect immediately before IP completion day, with the modification that 'of an enforceable EU right or' were omitted;

(h) section 10 of the Immigration and Asylum Act 1999 (removal of persons unlawfully in the United Kingdom), as it had effect immediately before IP completion day, with the modification that in subsection (5) 'of an enforceable EU right or' were omitted;

(i) section 115 of that Act (exclusion from benefits), as it had effect immediately before IP completion day;

(j) section 126 of the Nationality, Immigration and Asylum Act 2002 (physical data: compulsory provision), as it had effect immediately before IP completion day, with the modification that in subsection (2)(e) 'of an enforceable EU right or' were omitted;

(k) Schedule 3 (withholding and withdrawal of support) to that Act, with the modification that paragraph 3 applies as it had effect immediately before IP completion day and with the modification that for 'the EU Treaties' there were substituted 'the Immigration (European Economic Area) Regulations 2016 (as they continue to have effect by virtue of the Citizens' Rights (Application Deadline and Temporary Protection) (EU Exit) Regulations 2020)';

(l) section 2 of the Asylum and Immigration (Treatment of Claimants, etc.) Act 2004 (offences to do with entering the United Kingdom without a passport), as it had effect immediately before IP completion day, with the modification that, in subsections (4)(b) and (5)(b), for the reference to 'the EU Treaties' there were substituted 'the Immigration (European Economic Area) Regulations 2016 (as they continue to have effect by virtue of the Citizens' Rights (Application Deadline and Temporary Protection) (EU Exit) Regulations 2020)';

(m) section 33 of the UK Borders Act 2007, as if a relevant person (within the meaning of regulation 3 of these Regulations) and an applicant (within the meaning of regulation 4 of these Regulations) are, if the relevant person or applicant is a foreign criminal (see section 32 of that Act), a 'relevant person' within the meaning of section 33 (see section 33(6C) of that Act);

(n) section 21 of the Immigration Act 2014 (persons disqualified by immigration status or with limited right to rent), as it had effect immediately before IP completion day, with the modification that in subsection (4)(b)(ii) 'of an enforceable EU right or' were omitted;

(o) section 27 of that Act (eligibility period in relation to person with limited right to rent), as it had effect immediately before IP completion day, with the modification that in subsection (6)(a) 'of an enforceable EU right or' were omitted;

(p) section 70A of that Act (immigration skills charge), as it had effect immediately before [1 December 2020], with the modification that in subsection (6)(d) 'of an enforceable EU right or' were omitted;

(q) Part 2 of the Schedule to the Social Security (Immigration and Asylum) Consequential Amendments Regulations 2000 (persons not excluded from certain benefits under section 115 of the Immigration and Asylum Act 1999), as it had effect immediately before IP completion day;

(r) Part 2 of the Schedule to the Social Security (Immigration and Asylum) Consequential Amendments Regulations (Northern Ireland) 2000 (persons not excluded under Section 115 of the Immigration and Asylum Act from entitlement to attendance allowance, severe disablement allowance, disability living allowance, a Social Fund Payment or child benefit), as it had effect immediately before IP completion day;

(s) the British Nationality (General) Regulations 2003, as they had effect immediately before IP completion day, with the modification that in regulations 7E(2)(e) (use and retention of biometric information) and 7G(2)(f) (retention of fingerprints), and in paragraphs 7, 13 and 14 of Schedule 2 (particular requirements as respects applications), 'of an enforceable EU right or' were omitted;

(t) the Licensing and Management of Houses in Multiple Occupation and Other Houses (Miscellaneous Provisions) (England) Regulations 2006, as they had effect immediately before IP completion day, with the modification that in regulation 5(2) (persons treated as occupying premises as their only or main residence for the purposes of section 254 of the Act), for sub-paragraph (a)(i) there were substituted—

'(i) a person who is a national of a member State, an EEA State or Switzerland who has taken up an activity as an employed person in the United Kingdom by virtue of the Immigration (European Economic Area) Regulations 2016 (as they continue to have effect by virtue of the Citizens' Rights (Application Deadline and Temporary Protection) (EU Exit) Regulations 2020);';

(u) the Immigration (Provision of Physical Data) Regulations 2006, as they had effect immediately before IP completion day, with the modifications that—

(i) in each of the following provisions 'of an enforceable EU right or' were omitted—

(aa) the definition of 'application' in regulation 2 (interpretation);

(bb) regulation 8(2)(e) (use and retention of biometric information), and

(cc) regulation 10(2)(f)(ii) (retention of fingerprints);

(ii) in regulation 10(4), for 'has the same meaning' to the end there were substituted 'is to be read in accordance with the Immigration (European Economic Area) Regulations 2016 (see regulation 15) (as they continue to have effect by virtue of the Citizens' Rights (Application Deadline and Temporary Protection) (EU Exit) Regulations 2020)';

(v) the Licensing and Management of Houses in Multiple Occupation and Other Houses (Miscellaneous Provisions) (Wales) Regulations 2006, as they had effect immediately before IP completion day, with the modification that in regulation 5(2) (persons treated as occupying premises as their only or main residence for the purposes of section 254 of the Act), for sub-paragraph (a)(i) there were substituted—

'(i) a person who is a national of a member State, an EEA State or Switzerland who has taken up an activity as an employed person in the United Kingdom by virtue of the Immigration (European Economic Area) Regulations 2016 (as they continue to have effect by virtue of the Citizens' Rights (Application Deadline and Temporary Protection) (EU Exit) Regulations 2020);';

(w) the Immigration (Biometric Registration) Regulations 2008, as they had effect immediately before IP completion day, with the modifications that—

(i) in regulations 9(2)(e) (use and retention of biometric information) and 11(2)(f)(ii) (retention of fingerprints), 'of an enforceable EU right or' were omitted;

(ii) in regulation 11(4), for 'has the same meaning' to the end there were substituted 'is to be read in accordance with the Immigration (European Economic Area) Regulations 2016 (see regulation 15) (as they continue to have effect by virtue of the Citizens' Rights (Application Deadline and Temporary Protection) (EU Exit) Regulations 2020)'.

(2) Any reference in another enactment to a person who, under the Immigration Act 1971, requires leave to enter or remain in the United Kingdom (including section 13 of the Asylum and Immigration Act 1996) is to be read in light of paragraph (1)(g) above (application with modification of section 7 of the Immigration Act 1988).

Note: Words in paragraph (1)(p) substituted and in force immediately before 2300 on 31 December 2020 (SI 2020/1309, reg. 1(2)(a)).

Evidencing status

13. Where any question arises as to whether a person is or was lawfully resident in the United Kingdom at a particular point in time by virtue of the EEA Regulations 2016 (including as continued in effect and modified by these Regulations) for the purposes of these Regulations, it is for the individual in question to prove that they were.

The Citizens' Rights (Restrictions of Rights of Entry and Residence) (EU Exit) Regulations 2020
(SI No. 1210)

Citation, commencement and interpretation

1.—(1) These Regulations may be cited as the Citizens' Rights (Restrictions of Rights of Entry and Residence) (EU Exit) Regulations 2020 and come into force when the EEA Regulations 2016 are revoked.

(2) In these Regulations 'the EEA Regulations 2016' means the Immigration (European Economic Area) Regulations 2016.

Continued application of the EEA Regulations 2016

2.—(1) Notwithstanding the revocation of the EEA Regulations 2016, the provisions of the EEA Regulations 2016 specified in the Schedule continue to have effect, but with the modifications set out in the Schedule, for the purpose of removing a person who is protected by the citizens' rights provisions.

(2) For the purposes of paragraph (1), a person is protected by the citizens' rights provisions if that person—

(a) has leave to enter or remain in the United Kingdom granted by virtue of residence scheme immigration rules;

(b) is in the United Kingdom (whether or not they have entered within the meaning of section 11(1) of the Immigration Act 1971) having arrived with entry clearance granted by virtue of relevant entry clearance immigration rules;

(c) is in the United Kingdom (whether or not they have entered within the meaning of section 11(1) of the Immigration Act 1971) having arrived with entry clearance granted by virtue of Article 23 of the Swiss citizens' rights agreement; or

(d) may be granted leave to enter or remain in the United Kingdom as a person who has a right to enter the United Kingdom by virtue of—

(i) Article 32(1)(b) of the withdrawal agreement;

(ii) Article 31(1)(b) of the EEA EFTA separation agreement; or

(iii) Article 26a(1)(b) of the Swiss citizens' rights agreement,

whether or not the person has been granted such leave.

(3) For the purposes of these Regulations, a person is also protected by the citizens' rights provisions if that person was protected by the citizens' rights provisions at the time that they became subject to a decision to remove them under regulation 23(6)(b) of the EEA Regulations 2016, including as those Regulations continue to have effect by virtue of these Regulations.

Amendment of the Immigration Act 1971

3.—(1) The Immigration Act 1971 is amended as follows.

(2) In section 3(10) (definition of 'relevant person'), after paragraph (b) insert—

'(ba) if the person is in the United Kingdom (whether or not they have entered within the meaning of section 11(1)) having arrived with entry clearance granted by virtue of Article 23 of the Swiss citizens' rights agreement,'.

Amendment of the UK Borders Act 2007

4. —(1) The UK Borders Act 2007 is amended as follows.

(2) In section 33(6C) (definition of 'relevant person'), after paragraph (b) insert—

'(ba) if the person is in the United Kingdom (whether or not they have entered within the meaning of section 11(1) of the Immigration Act 1971) having arrived with entry clearance granted by virtue of Article 23 of the Swiss citizens' rights agreement,'.

Regulation 2(1) SCHEDULE

Introductory

1. Unless otherwise specified, references within this Schedule to regulations or to Schedules are references to regulations within, or Schedules to, the EEA Regulations 2016.

Savings and modifications to definitions

2. Regulation 2 (general interpretation) continues to have effect with the following modifications to paragraph (1)—

(a) the definitions of 'civil partner', 'civil partnership of convenience', 'durable partner', 'durable partnership of convenience', 'marriage of convenience' and 'spouse' are omitted;

(b) in the definition of 'EEA decision', omit sub-paragraphs (a), (b) and (d);

(c) after the definition of 'EEA decision', insert—

' "EEA EFTA separation agreement" has the same meaning as in the European Union (Withdrawal Agreement) Act 2020 (see section 39(1) of that Act);';

(d) in the definition of 'EEA State', omit the words 'other than the United Kingdom' so far as relevant to things done after exit day;

(e) after the definition of 'permanent residence card', insert—

' "person protected by the citizens' rights provisions" has the meaning given by regulation 2(2) of the Citizens' Rights (Restrictions of Rights of Entry and Residence) (EU Exit) Regulations 2020;';

(f) after the definition of 'spouse', insert—

' "Swiss citizens' rights agreement" has the same meaning as in the European Union (Withdrawal Agreement) Act 2020 (see section 39(1) of that Act).'.

Savings and modifications to Part 4

3. Regulation 23 (exclusion and removal from the United Kingdom) continues to have effect with the following modifications—

(a) omit paragraphs (1) to (5);

(b) in paragraph (6)—

(i) for 'an EEA national who has entered the United Kingdom or the family member of such a national' substitute 'a person protected by the citizens' rights provisions';

(ii) omit sub-paragraphs (a) and (c);

(c) in paragraph (7)—

(i) at the end of sub-paragraph (a), omit 'or';

(ii) omit sub-paragraph (b);

(d) omit paragraph (9).

4. Regulation 27 (decisions taken on grounds of public policy, public security and public health) continues to have effect with the modification that in paragraph (3) and paragraph (4)(a), for 'a right of permanent residence under regulation 15' substitute 'indefinite leave to enter or remain in the United Kingdom granted under residence scheme immigration rules (as defined in section 17 of the European Union (Withdrawal Agreement) Act 2020)'.

Savings and modifications to Part 5

5. Regulation 32 (person subject to removal) continues to have effect with the following modifications—

(a) omit paragraph (2);

(b) in paragraph (4), omit 'or exclusion' and ', or in circumstances where that person was not entitled to be admitted under regulation 23(1) or (3),';

(c) in paragraph (5), omit 'on the grounds of public policy, public security or public health';

(d) omit paragraph (7).

6. Regulation 33 (human rights considerations and interim orders to suspend removal) continues to have effect.

7. Regulation 34 (revocation of deportation and exclusion orders) continues to have effect with the following modifications—

(a) omit paragraph (1);

(b) in paragraph (3), omit 'or exclusion'.

Savings and modifications to Part 6

8. Regulation 35 (interpretation of Part 6) continues to have effect.

9. Regulation 36 (appeal rights) continues to have effect with the following modifications—

(a) in paragraph (2)—

(i) for 'to be an EEA national' substitute 'to be a person protected by the citizens' rights provisions';

(ii) for 'or passport issued by an EEA State' substitute 'issued by an EEA State or a valid passport';

(b) omit paragraphs (3) to (6) and (12).

10. Regulation 37 (out of country appeals) continues to have effect with the following modifications—

(a) in paragraph (1)—

(i) omit sub-paragraphs (a), (b), (c), (e) and (f) (but not the final 'or' after sub-paragraph (f));

(ii) in sub-paragraph (d), omit 'or exclusion';

(iii) in sub-paragraph (g), omit 'or exclusion' and ', or in circumstances where that person was not entitled to be admitted pursuant to regulation 23(1), (2), (3) or (4)';

(b) omit paragraph (2).

11. Regulation 38 (appeals to the Commission) continues to have effect with the modification that in paragraph (3), omit 'exclusion or'.

12. Regulation 39 (national security: EEA decisions) continues to have effect.

13. Regulation 40 (effect of appeals to the First-tier Tribunal or Upper Tribunal) continues to have effect with the following modifications—

(a) omit paragraphs (2), (3) and (6);

(b) in paragraph (4), omit 'a refusal of admission, a decision to revoke admission, or'.

14. Regulation 41 (temporary admission to submit case in person) continues to have effect.

Savings and modifications to the Schedules

15. Schedule 1 (considerations of public policy, public security and the fundamental interests of society etc.) continues to have effect with the following modifications—

(a) for paragraph 1 substitute—

'1. The United Kingdom enjoys considerable discretion, acting within the parameters set by the law, to define its own standards of public policy and public security, for purposes tailored to its individual context from time to time.';

(b) in paragraph 6, for 'these Regulations', substitute 'the EU withdrawal agreement, the EEA EFTA separation agreement or the Swiss citizens' rights agreement';

(c) after paragraph 6, insert—

'6A. For the purpose of paragraph 6, a marriage, civil partnership or durable partnership of convenience means a marriage, civil partnership or durable partnership entered into as a means to circumvent any criteria that the party to the marriage, civil partnership or durable partnership would otherwise have to meet in order to enjoy a right to reside in the United Kingdom or a right to leave to enter or remain in the United Kingdom.'.

16. Schedule 2 (appeals to the First-tier Tribunal) continues to have effect with the modification that in paragraph 1, for the 'EU Treaties' substitute 'the EU withdrawal agreement, the EEA EFTA separation agreement or the Swiss citizens' rights agreement'.

17. Paragraph 1 of Schedule 7 (consequential modifications) continues to have effect, with the modification that references to 'these Regulations' includes references to the EEA Regulations 2016 as modified by these Regulations.

The Immigration and Social Security Co-ordination (EU Withdrawal) Act 2020 (Consequential, Saving, Transitional and Transitory Provisions) (EU Exit) Regulations 2020

(SI No. 1309)

Note: Only the text relevant to the amendments and savings of statutes and statutory instruments included in this book are reproduced below.

PART 1

INTRODUCTION

Citation, commencement and extent

1. —(1) These Regulations may be cited as the Immigration and Social Security Co-ordination (EU Withdrawal) Act 2020 (Consequential, Saving, Transitional and Transitory Provisions) (EU Exit) Regulations 2020.

(2) These Regulations come into force at the time and on the date when paragraph 2(2) of, Schedule 1 to, the 2020 Act comes into force for all purposes except for—

(a) regulations 47, 48 and 49 which come into force immediately before that time and date;

(b) regulation 20(7) and (8) which come into force on 1st December 2020;

(c) regulations 3, 7, 12(3) and (4),14,15(3), 16, 20(5) and (6), 31, 36, 37 and 40 to 44 which come into force on 1st July 2021.

(3) Any provision of these Regulations which amends, repeals or revokes an enactment has the same extent as the enactment amended, repealed or revoked (ignoring extent by virtue of an Order in Council under any of the Immigration Acts).

(4) Any saving, transitional or transitory provision in these Regulations has the same extent within the United Kingdom as the provision to which it relates.

Interpretation - General

2. In these Regulations—

'the 2020 Act' means the Immigration and Social Security Co-ordination (EU Withdrawal) Act 2020;

'commencement day' means the time at and date on which the Immigration (European Economic Area) Regulations 2016 are revoked for all purposes.

PART 2
IMMIGRATION

CHAPTER 1
Amendment and saving of primary legislation

Amendment of the Marriage Act 1949

3. . . .

Amendment of the Aliens' Employment Act 1955

4. . . .

Amendment and saving of the Immigration Act 1971

5.—(1) The Immigration Act 1971 is amended in accordance with paragraphs (2) to (6).

(2) In section 9 (further provisions as to common travel area), in subsection (4)(a) —

(a) omit "written';

(b) omit 'as being in the interests of national security'.

(3) In section 25 (assisting unlawful immigration to member State)—

(a) in subsection (1), in both places it occurs, for 'a citizen of the European Union' substitute 'a national of the United Kingdom';

(b) in subsection (7), omit paragraph (b) (and the 'and' before it).

(4) Section 25B (assisting entry to United Kingdom in breach of deportation or exclusion order) is omitted.

(5) In Schedule 4 (integration with United Kingdom law of immigration law of Islands), in paragraph 3 (deportation)—

(a) in sub-paragraph (2)—

(i) after paragraph (a) insert—

'(aa) an Irish citizen';

(ii) omit paragraphs (b) and (c) (and the 'or' after paragraph (c));

(iii) at the appropriate place, insert—

'(ca) a relevant person (see paragraph 3A); or';

(iv) in paragraph (d), for 'such a citizen nor an EEA national' substitute 'a British citizen nor an Irish citizen';

(b) in sub-paragraph (4), for '(b), (c)' substitute '(aa), (ca)'.

(6) In that Schedule, after paragraph 3, insert —

'3A Relevant person for purposes of paragraph 3

(1) For the purposes of paragraph 3, a person is a 'relevant person'—

(a) if the person is in the United Kingdom (whether or not they have entered within the meaning of section 11(1)) having arrived with entry clearance granted by virtue of relevant entry clearance immigration rules;

(b) if the person has leave to enter or remain in the United Kingdom granted by virtue of residence scheme immigration rules;

(c) if the person may be granted leave to enter or remain in the United Kingdom as a person who has a right to enter the United Kingdom by virtue of—

(i) Article 32(1)(b) of the EU withdrawal agreement;

(ii) Article 31(1)(b) of the EEA EFTA separation agreement, or

(iii) Article 26(a)(1)(b) of the Swiss citizens' rights agreement,

whether or not the person has been granted such leave, or

(d) if the person may enter the United Kingdom by virtue of regulations made under section 8 of the European Union (Withdrawal Agreement) Act 2020 (frontier workers), whether or not the person has entered by virtue of those regulations.

(2) In this paragraph—

'EEA EFTA separation agreement' and 'Swiss citizens' rights agreement' have the same meanings as in the European Union (Withdrawal Agreement) Act 2020 (see section 39(1) of that Act);

'relevant entry clearance immigration rules' and 'residence scheme immigration rules' have the meanings given by section 17 of the European Union (Withdrawal Agreement) Act 2020.'.

(7) Notwithstanding its repeal by paragraph (4), section 25B of the Immigration Act 1971 continues to apply where an order is in force excluding an individual from the United Kingdom and the order—

(a) was made before commencement day by virtue of the Immigration (European Economic Area) Regulations 2016 and continues in force under paragraph 2 of Schedule 3 to these Regulations, or

(b) is made on or after commencement day by virtue of those 2016 Regulations as they continue to have effect by virtue of the Citizens' Rights (Application Deadline and Temporary Protection) (EU Exit) Regulations 2020.

Amendment of the Rent Act 1977

6. . . .

Amendment of the Marriage (Scotland) Act 1977

7. . . .

Amendment of the Housing Act 1988

8. . . .

Amendment of the Housing (Northern Ireland) Order 1988

9. . . .

Amendment of the Housing Act 1996

10. . . .

Amendment of the Special Immigration Appeals Commission Act 1997

11.—(1) The Special Immigration Appeals Commission Act 1997 is amended as follows.

(2) In section 2C (jurisdiction: review of certain exclusion decisions)—

(a) in subsections (1) and (2), for 'non-EEA national or relevant person', in each place it occurs, substitute 'person';

(b) in subsection (5), omit the words from the beginning to the second 'and'.

Amendment of the Immigration and Asylum Act 1999

12.—(1) The Immigration and Asylum Act 1999 is amended as follows.

(2) In section 10 (removal of persons unlawfully in the United Kingdom), in subsection (5), for the words from 'neither' to the end of that subsection substitute none of the following—

'(a) a British citizen,

(b) an Irish citizen,

(c) a person who has leave to enter or remain in the United Kingdom which was granted by virtue of residence scheme immigration rules.'.

(3) In section 24 (duty to report suspicious marriages), in subsection (6), in the definition of 'relevant national'—

(a) after paragraph (a) insert—

'(aa) an Irish citizen, or

(ab) a person who is not an Irish citizen and who—

(i) has leave to enter or remain in the United Kingdom which was granted by virtue of residence scheme immigration rules, or

(ii) is an applicant for the purposes of regulation 4 of the Citizens' Rights (Application Deadline and Temporary Protection) (EU Exit) Regulations 2020 (applications which have not been finally determined by the deadline) where the relevant period within the meaning of that regulation has not expired;';

(b) omit paragraphs (b) and (c).

(4) In section 24A (duty to report suspicious civil partnerships), in subsection (5A), in the definition of 'relevant national'—

(a) after paragraph (a) insert—

'(aa) an Irish citizen; or

(ab) a person who is not an Irish citizen and who—

(i) has leave to enter or remain in the United Kingdom which was granted by virtue of residence scheme immigration rules, or

(ii) is an applicant for the purposes of regulation 4 of the Citizens' Rights (Application Deadline and Temporary Protection) (EU Exit) Regulations 2020 (applications which have not been finally determined by the deadline) where the relevant period within the meaning of that regulation has not expired.';

(b) omit paragraphs (b) and (c).

(5) In section 82 (interpretation of Part V), in subsection (1), in the definition of 'relevant matters' omit paragraphs (e), (f) and (g).

(6) In section 115 (exclusion from benefits), in subsection (9), omit 'who is not a national of an EEA State and'.

(7) In section 119 (homelessness: Scotland and Northern Ireland) for 'subsection (1A)(b)' substitute—

'(b) is not a person who, immediately before IP completion day, was—

(i) a national of an EEA State or Switzerland, and

(ii) within a class specified in an order under subsection (1) which had effect at that time.'.

(8) In section 167 (interpretation), in subsection (1), after the definition of 'the Refugee Convention' at the appropriate place insert—

'residence scheme immigration rules' has the meaning given by section 17 of the European Union (Withdrawal Agreement) Act 2020;'.

Amendment and saving of the Nationality, Immigration and Asylum Act 2002

13. —(1) The Nationality, Immigration and Asylum Act 2002 is amended in accordance with paragraphs (2) to (4).

(2) In section 58 (voluntary departure from the United Kingdom)—

(a) in subsection (1)(a), omit 'or an EEA national';

(b) omit subsection (4).

(3) In section 126(2) (physical data: compulsory provision)—

(a) at the end of paragraph (c) insert 'or';

(b) omit paragraph (e) (and the 'or' before it).

(4) In Schedule 3 (withholding and withdrawal of support)—

(a) in paragraph 3 (exceptions), omit sub-paragraph (b) (and the 'or' before it);

(b) omit paragraph 5 (second class of ineligible person: citizen of EEA state);

(c) in paragraph 8 (travel assistance) omit 'or 5'.

(5) The amendments made by paragraph (3) do not affect the operation of any regulations made under section 126(1) of the Nationality, Immigration and Asylum Act 2002 before commencement day in relation to any application for a document referred to in section 126(2)(e) that was made before commencement day.

Amendment of the Marriage (Northern Ireland) Order 2003

14. . . .

Amendment of the Asylum and Immigration (Treatment of Claimants, etc.) Act 2004

15.—(1) The Asylum and Immigration (Treatment of Claimants, etc.) Act 2004 is amended as follows.

(2) In section 2 (offences to do with entering the United Kingdom without a passport)—

(a) in subsection (4)—

(i) for paragraph (a) substitute—

'(a) to prove that he is —

(i) an Irish citizen,

(ii) has leave to enter or remain in the United Kingdom which was granted by virtue of residence scheme immigration rules, or

(iii) is a frontier worker within the meaning of regulation 3 of the Citizens' Rights (Frontier Workers) (EU Exit) Regulations 2020,';

(ii) omit paragraph (b);

(b) in subsection (5)—

(i) for paragraph (a) substitute—

'(a) to prove that the child is—

(i) an Irish citizen,

(ii) has leave to enter or remain in the United Kingdom which was granted by virtue of residence scheme immigration rules, or

(iii) is a frontier worker within the meaning of regulation 3 of the Citizens' Rights (Frontier Workers) (EU Exit) Regulations 2020,';

(ii) omit paragraph (b);

(c) in subsection (12)—

(i) omit the definition of 'EEA national';

(ii) in the definition of 'immigration document' omit the 'and' after paragraph (b);

(iii) after the definition of 'leave or asylum interview' insert—

''residence scheme immigration rules' has the meaning given by section 17 of the European Union (Withdrawal Agreement) Act 2020.'.

(3) In section 19 (England and Wales)—

(a) in subsection (2)(a) (procedure for marriage: England and Wales)—

(i) after 'district' insert 'which is';

(ii) after 'State' insert 'and is the appropriate registration district';

(b) after subsection (2) insert—

'(2A) For the purposes of subsection (2) 'the appropriate registration district' means—

(a) if the parties have resided in the same specified registration district for the period of seven days immediately before the giving of the notice ('the 7 day period'), that specified registration district,

(b) if one or both of the parties have resided in a specified registration district (but not the same specified registration district) for the 7 day period, the specified registration district in which one of them has resided for that period, or

(c) if neither of the parties has resided in a specified registration district for the 7 day period, any specified registration district.

(2B) In subsection (2A), 'specified registration district' means a registration district specified for the purposes of subsection (2)(a) by regulations made under that provision.'.

Amendment of the Civil Partnership Act 2004

16. . . .

Amendment and saving of UK Borders Act 2007

17.—(1) The UK Borders Act 2007 is amended in accordance with paragraphs (2) and (3).

(2) In section 33 (exceptions to automatic deportation), omit subsection (4).

(3) In section 56A (no rehabilitation for certain immigration or nationality purposes), omit subsection (3).

(4) The amendment made by paragraph (3) does not apply in relation to a relevant immigration decision or a relevant nationality decision made before commencement day.

(5) In paragraph (4) 'relevant immigration decision' and 'relevant nationality decision' have the meaning given in section 56A of the UK Borders Act 2007 as it had effect immediately before commencement day.

Amendment of the Criminal Justice and Immigration Act 2008

18. —(1) The Criminal Justice and Immigration Act 2008 is amended as follows.

(2) In section 130 (designation for purposes of special immigration status), in subsection (5), omit paragraph (b) (and the 'or' before it).

(3) In section 136 (end of designation)—

(a) in subsection (1), omit paragraph (b);

(b) in subsection (3), omit 'or (b)'.

Amendment of the Identity Documents Act 2010

19. . . .

Amendment and saving of the Immigration Act 2014

20.—(1) The Immigration Act 2014 is amended in accordance with paragraphs (2) to (7).

(2) In section 21 (persons disqualified from renting or with limited right to rent)—

(a) omit subsection (4)(b)(ii) (and the 'and' before that);

(b) in subsection (5)—

(i) after paragraph (a) insert—

'(aa) an Irish citizen, or

(ab) a person who is not an Irish citizen and who has leave to enter or remain in the United Kingdom which was granted by virtue of residence scheme immigration rules within the meaning given by section 17 of the European Union (Withdrawal Agreement) Act 2020.';

(ii) omit paragraphs (b) and (c).

(3) In section 27 (eligibility period in relation to person with limited right to rent), omit subsection 6(a) (and the 'or' at the end of it).

(4) In section 39 (related provision: charges for health services)—

(a) in subsection (1)(b), after 'limited period' insert 'unless that leave was granted by virtue of residence scheme immigration rules';

(b) after subsection (2) insert—

'(3) For the purposes of subsection (1) 'residence scheme immigration rules' has the meaning given by section 17 of the European Union (Withdrawal Agreement) Act 2020.'.

(5) In section 49 (meaning of 'exempt person' in relation to investigations into sham marriages), omit subsection (2)(a).

(6) In section 62 (interpretation of Part 4, relating to marriage and civil partnership), in subsection (1), in the definition of 'relevant national'—

(a) after paragraph (a) insert—

'(aa) an Irish citizen;

(ab) a person who is not an Irish citizen who—

(i) has leave to enter or remain in the United Kingdom which was granted by virtue of residence scheme immigration rules within the meaning given by section 17 of the European Union (Withdrawal Agreement) Act 2020, or

(ii) is an applicant for the purposes of regulation 4 of the Citizens' Rights (Application Deadline and Temporary Protection) (EU Exit) Regulations 2020 (applications which have not been finally determined by the deadline) where the relevant period within the meaning of that regulation has not expired;';

(b) omit paragraphs (b) and (c).

(7) In section 70A (power to impose a charge on sponsors who make immigration skills arrangements)—

(a) in subsection (6)—

(i) after paragraph (a) insert—

'(aa) an Irish citizen;';

(ii) for paragraph (b) substitute—

'(b) a person who has leave to enter or remain in the United Kingdom granted by virtue of residence scheme immigration rules.';

(iii) omit paragraphs (c) and (d);

(b) in subsection (7) after '1971' insert 'and 'residence scheme immigration rules' has the meaning given by section 17 of the European Union (Withdrawal Agreement) Act 2020.'.

(8) The amendments made by paragraph (7) do not affect the operation of any regulations which were made under section 70A of the Immigration Act 2014 before 1st December 2020.

Amendment of the Housing (Wales) Act 2014

21. . . .

Amendment of the Specialist Printing Equipment and Materials (Offences) Act 2015

22 . . .

Amendment of the Immigration Act 2016

23.—(1) The Immigration Act 2016 is amended as follows.

(2) In Schedule 12 (availability of local authority support: amendments of Schedule 3 to the Nationality, Immigration and Asylum Act 2002), in paragraph 9, omit inserted paragraph 7C and the italic heading before inserted paragraph 7C.

Provision consequential on, or connected with Part 2 of Chapter 1

24. Schedule 1 has effect.

CHAPTER 2

AMENDMENT AND SAVINGS OF SECONDARY LEGISLATION

Amendment and saving of the Immigration (Control of Entry through Republic of Ireland) Order 1972

25.—(1) The Immigration (Control of Entry through Republic of Ireland) Order 1972 is amended in accordance with paragraphs (2) to (4).

(2) In article 2 (interpretation)—

(a) omit the definition of 'EEA national';

(b) omit the definition of 'EEA State'.

(3) In article 3(1)(b) (persons excluded from section 1(3) of the Act)—

(a) after 'other than' insert 'an Irish citizen or';

(b) at the end of paragraph (iii) insert 'or';

(c) omit paragraph (iv);

(d) omit paragraph (v).

(4) In article 4 (restrictions and conditions on entry through Ireland)—

(a) in paragraph (1)—

(i) for 'an EEA national' substitute 'an Irish citizen';

(ii) omit 'or a person who is entitled to enter or remain in the United Kingdom by virtue of an enforceable EU right or any provision made under section 2(2) of the European Communities Act 1972';

(b) omit paragraph (8).

(5) Notwithstanding the revocation of article 3(1)(b)(v) by this regulation, that article continues to apply as if not amended by these Regulations where an order is in force excluding an individual from the United Kingdom and the order—

(a) was made before commencement day by virtue of the Immigration (European Economic Area) Regulations 2016 and continues in force under paragraph 2 of Schedule 3 to these Regulations, or

(b) is made on or after commencement day by virtue of those 2016 Regulations as they continue to have effect by virtue of the Citizens' Rights (Application Deadline and Temporary Protection) (EU Exit) Regulations 2020.

Amendment and saving of the Channel Tunnel (International Arrangements) Order 1993

26.—(1) The Channel Tunnel (International Arrangements) Order 1993 is amended in accordance with paragraph (2).

(2) In Schedule 4 (enactments modified), omit paragraph 5 (the Immigration (European Economic Area) Regulations 2006).

(3) The amendment made by paragraph (2) does not apply to a person who has a right of admission to the United Kingdom under the Immigration (European Economic

Area) Regulations 2016 as they continue to have effect by virtue of the Citizens' Rights (Application Deadline and Temporary Protection) (EU Exit) Regulations 2020.

Amendment and saving of the Immigration (Leave to Enter and Remain) Order 2000

27.—(1) The Immigration (Leave to Enter and Remain) Order 2000 is amended in accordance with paragraph (2).

(2) In article 13B (partners and children of Crown servants etc.), in paragraph (2)(b)—

(a) at the end of paragraph (i), insert 'or';

(b) omit paragraph (iii) (and the 'or' before it).

(3) The amendment made by paragraph (1) does not apply in respect of a person who is accompanying a partner or parent who before 1st July 2021 had a right of permanent residence in the United Kingdom by virtue of any provision made under section 2(2) of the European Communities Act 1972.

Amendment and saving of the Immigration (Notices) Regulations 2003

28.—(1) The Immigration (Notices) Regulations 2003 are amended in accordance with paragraphs (2) and (3).

(2) In regulation 2 (interpretation), omit the definition of 'EEA Decision'.

(3) In regulation 4 (notice of decisions), in paragraph (1), omit ', any EEA decision'.

(4) The amendments made by paragraphs (2) and (3) do not apply to an EEA decision made under the Immigration (European Economic Area) Regulations 2016 as they continue to have effect by virtue of these Regulations, the Citizens' Rights (Application Deadline and Temporary Protection) (EU Exit) Regulations 2020 or the Citizens' Rights (Restrictions of Rights of Entry and Residence) (EU Exit) Regulations 2020.

Amendment and saving of the Nationality, Immigration and Asylum Act 2002 (Juxtaposed Controls) Order 2003

29. . . .

Amendment of the Immigration and Asylum Act 1999 (Part V Exemption: Relevant Employers) Order 2003

30.—(1) The Immigration and Asylum Act 1999 (Part V Exemption: Relevant Employers) Order 2003 is amended in accordance with paragraphs (2) and (3).

(2) In article 2 (interpretation), omit the definitions of 'EEA national' and 'family member of an EEA national'.

(3) In article 3(1) (exemption of relevant employers), omit sub-paragraph (c) (and the 'or' before it).

Amendment of the Civil Partnership (Registration Provisions) Regulations 2005

31. . . .

Amendment and saving of the Immigration (Provision of Physical Data) Regulations 2006

32.—(1) The Immigration (Provision of Physical Data) Regulations 2006 are amended in accordance with paragraphs (2) to (4).

(2) In regulation 2 (interpretation), in the definition of 'application' omit paragraph (d).

(3) In regulation 8 (use and retention of biometric information)—

(a) at the end of sub-paragraph (2)(c), insert 'and';

(b) omit sub-paragraph (2)(e) (and the 'and' before it).

(4) In regulation 10 (retention of fingerprints)—

(a) at the end of sub-paragraph (2)(d) insert 'or';

(b) omit sub-paragraph (2)(f) (and the 'or' before it);

(c) in paragraph (3)—

(i) omit 'or (f)';

(ii) omit 'or who no longer enjoys the right of permanent residence';

(d) omit paragraph (4).

(5) The amendment made by paragraph (2) does not apply in respect of an application made before commencement day where a document was not issued before commencement day.

(6) Notwithstanding the amendment of regulation 8 by paragraph (3), biometric information held by the Secretary of State immediately before commencement day may be used in connection with the exercise of any function after commencement day concerning the entitlement of a person who is not a national of an EEA state or Switzerland to enter or remain in the United Kingdom by virtue of—

(a) the EEA EFTA separation agreement, the EU withdrawal agreement or the Swiss citizens' rights agreement (within the meaning of section 39(1) of the European Union (Withdrawal Agreement) Act 2020); or

(b) the Immigration (European Economic Area) Regulations 2016 as they continue to have effect by virtue of the Citizens' Rights (Application Deadline and Temporary Protection) (EU Exit) Regulations 2020.

(7) The amendment of regulation 10 by paragraph (4) does not apply in relation to fingerprints held by the Secretary of State immediately before commencement day.

Amendment and saving of the Tribunal Procedure (Upper Tribunal) Rules 2008

33.—(1) The Tribunal Procedure (Upper Tribunal) Rules 2008 are amended in accordance with paragraphs (2) and (3).

(2) In rule 1 (citation, commencement, application and interpretation), in the definition of 'immigration case', omit ', regulation 26 of the Immigration (European Economic Area) Regulations 2006, regulation 36 of the Immigration (European Economic Area) Regulations 2016'.

(3) In rule 17A (appeal treated as abandoned or finally determined in an asylum case or an immigration case)—

(a) in paragraph (1)(b), after the semi-colon insert 'or';

(b) omit paragraph (1)(d) (and the 'or' before it);

(c) in paragraph (2), omit 'or paragraph 4(2) of Schedule 2 to the Immigration (European Economic Area) Regulations 2006'.

(4) The amendments made by paragraphs (2) and (3) do not apply in relation to—

(a) any appeal which has been brought under the Immigration (European Economic Area) Regulations 2006 and has not been finally determined before commencement day;

(b) any appeal which has been brought under the Immigration (European Economic Area) Regulations 2016 (whether before or after commencement day), and has yet to be finally determined;

(c) any EEA decision under the Immigration (European Economic Area) Regulations 2016 (whether taken before or after commencement day), in respect of which an appeal has not been brought.

(5) For the purposes of paragraph (4)—

(a) references to the Immigration (European Economic Area) Regulations 2016 are to those Regulations as they continue to have effect by virtue of these Regulations, the Citizens' Rights (Application Deadline and Temporary Protection) (EU Exit) Regulations 2020 or the Citizens' Rights (Restrictions of Rights of Entry and Residence) (EU Exit) Regulations 2020;

(b) an appeal is not to be treated as finally determined while a further appeal may be brought, and, if such a further appeal is brought, the original appeal is not to be treated as finally determined until the further appeal is determined, withdrawn or abandoned.

Amendment and saving of the Immigration (Biometric Registration) Regulations 2008

34.—(1) The Immigration (Biometric Registration) Regulations 2008 are amended in accordance with paragraphs (2) and (3).

(2) In regulation 3 (requirement to apply for biometric immigration document) after paragraph (5) insert—

'(5A) This regulation does not apply to a person who makes an application for, or has been granted, leave to enter or remain under residence scheme immigration rules.

(5B) 'Residence scheme immigration rules' has the meaning given by section 17 of the European Union (Withdrawal Agreement) Act 2020.'.

(3) In regulation 9 (use and retention of biometric information)—

(a) after paragraph (2)(c) insert 'and';

(b) omit paragraph (2)(e) (and the 'and' before it).

(4) In regulation 11 (retention of fingerprints)—

(a) after paragraph (2)(d), insert 'or';

(b) omit paragraph (2)(f) (and the 'or' before it);

(c) in paragraph (3), omit—

(i) 'or (f)';

(ii) 'or who no longer enjoys the rights of permanent residence';

(d) omit paragraph (4).

(5) Notwithstanding the amendment of regulation 9 by paragraph (3), biometric information held by the Secretary of State immediately before commencement day may be used in connection with the exercise of any function after commencement day concerning the entitlement of a person who is not a national of an EEA state or Switzerland to enter or remain in the United Kingdom by virtue of—

(a) the EEA EFTA separation agreement, the EU withdrawal agreement or the Swiss citizens' rights agreement (within the meaning of section 39(1) of the European Union (Withdrawal Agreement) Act 2020); or

(b) the Immigration (European Economic Area) Regulations 2016 as they continue to have effect by virtue of the Citizens' Rights (Application Deadline and Temporary Protection) (EU Exit) Regulations 2020.

(6) The amendment of regulation 11 by paragraph (4) does not apply in relation to fingerprints held by the Secretary of State immediately before commencement day.

Amendment and saving of the Appeals (Excluded Decisions) Order 2009

35.—(1) The Appeals (Excluded Decisions) Order 2009 is amended in accordance with paragraph (2).

(2) In article 3 (excluded decisions), in paragraph (m)—

(a) for '1981,' substitute '1981 or';

(b) omit ', or regulation 26 of the Immigration (European Economic Area) Regulations 2006'.

(3) The amendment made by paragraph (2) does not apply in relation to—

(a) any appeal which has been brought under the Immigration (European Economic Area) Regulations 2006 and has not been finally determined before commencement day;

(b) any appeal which has been brought under the Immigration (European Economic Area) Regulations 2016 (whether before or after commencement day), and has yet to be finally determined;

(c) any EEA decision under the Immigration (European Economic Area) Regulations 2016 (whether taken before or after commencement day), in respect of which an appeal has not been brought.

(4) For the purposes of paragraph (3)—

(a) references to the Immigration (European Economic Area) Regulations 2016 are to those Regulations as they continue to have effect by virtue of these Regulations, the Citizens' Rights (Application Deadline and Temporary Protection) (EU Exit) Regulations 2020 or the Citizens' Rights (Restrictions of Rights of Entry and Residence) (EU Exit) Regulations 2020;

(b) an appeal is not to be treated as finally determined while a further appeal may be brought, and, if such a further appeal is brought, the original appeal is not to be treated as finally determined until the further appeal is determined, withdrawn or abandoned.

Amendment of the Immigration (Procedure for Marriage) Regulations 2011

36. . . .

Amendment of the Immigration (Procedure for Formation of Civil Partnerships) Regulations 2011

37. . . .

Amendment and saving of the First-tier Tribunal (Immigration and Asylum Chamber) Fees Order 2011

38.—(1) The First-tier Tribunal (Immigration and Asylum Chamber) Fees Order 2011 is amended in accordance with paragraph (2).

(2) In article 5 (exemption from fees), omit paragraph (1)(a)(ii).

(3) The amendment made by paragraph (2) does not apply in relation to—

(a) any appeal which has been brought under the Immigration (European Economic Area) Regulations 2006 and has not been finally determined before commencement day;

(b) any appeal which has been brought under the Immigration (European Economic Area) Regulations 2016 (whether taken before or after commencement day), and has yet to be finally determined;

(c) any EEA decision under the Immigration (European Economic Area) Regulations 2016 (whether taken before or after commencement day), in respect of which an appeal has not been brought.

(4) For the purposes of paragraph (3)—

(a) references to the Immigration (European Economic Area) Regulations 2016 are to those Regulations as they continue to have effect by virtue of these Regulations, the Citizens' Rights (Application Deadline and Temporary Protection) (EU Exit) Regulations 2020 or the Citizens' Rights (Restrictions of Rights of Entry and Residence) (EU Exit) Regulations 2020;

(b) an appeal is not to be treated as finally determined while a further appeal may be brought, and, if such a further appeal is brought, the original appeal is not to be treated as finally determined until the further appeal is determined, withdrawn or abandoned.

Amendment and saving of the Tribunal Procedure (First-tier Tribunal) (Immigration and Asylum Chamber) Rules 2014

39.—(1) The Tribunal Procedure (First-tier Tribunal) (Immigration and Asylum Chamber) Rules 2014 are amended in accordance with paragraphs (2) to (4).

(2) In rule 1 (citation, commencement, application and interpretation), omit the definition of 'the 2006 Regulations'.

(3) In rule 16 (appeal treated as abandoned)—

(a) after paragraph (1)(b) insert 'or';

(b) omit paragraph (1)(d) (and the 'or' before it);

(c) in paragraph (2) omit 'or paragraph 4(2) of Schedule 2 to the 2006 Regulations';

(d) in paragraph (3) omit 'or was sent the document listed in paragraph 4(2) of Schedule 2 to the 2006 Regulations, as the case may be'.

(4) In rule 23 (response: entry clearance cases)—

(a) in paragraph (1), omit 'or a refusal of an EEA family permit (which has the meaning given in regulation 2(1) of the 2006 Regulations)';

(b) in paragraph (2), omit 'or a refusal of an EEA family permit'.

(5) The amendments made by paragraphs (2) to (4) do not apply in relation to—

(a) any appeal which has been brought under the Immigration (European Economic Area) Regulations 2006 and has not been finally determined before commencement day;

(b) any appeal which has been brought under the Immigration (European Economic Area) Regulations 2016 (whether taken before or after commencement day), and has yet to be finally determined;

(c) any EEA decision under the Immigration (European Economic Area) Regulations 2016 (whether taken before or after commencement day), in respect of which an appeal has not been brought.

(6) For the purposes of paragraph (5)—

(a) references to the Immigration (European Economic Area) Regulations 2016 are to those Regulations as they continue to have effect by virtue of these Regulations, the Citizens' Rights (Application Deadline and Temporary Protection) (EU Exit) Regulations 2020 or the Citizens' Rights (Restrictions of Rights of Entry and Residence) (EU Exit) Regulations 2020;

(b) an appeal is not to be treated as finally determined while a further appeal may be brought, and, if such a further appeal is brought, the original appeal is not to be treated as finally determined until the further appeal is determined, withdrawn or abandoned.

Amendment of the Marriage of Same Sex Couples (Conversion of Civil Partnership) Regulations 2014

40. . . .

Amendment of the Referral of Proposed Marriages and Civil Partnerships Regulations 2015

41. . . .

Amendment of the Registration of Marriages Regulations 2015

42. . . .

Amendment of the Proposed Marriages and Civil Partnerships (Conduct of Investigations, etc.) Regulations 2015

43.—(1) The Proposed Marriages and Civil Partnerships (Conduct of Investigations, etc.) Regulations 2015 are amended as follows.

(2) In regulation 18 (prescribed information about the investigation)—

(a) in paragraph (1)(e) for ', indefinite leave or a European residence document' substitute 'or indefinite leave';

(b) in paragraph (1)(f) for ', indefinite leave or a European residence document' substitute 'or indefinite leave';

(c) omit sub-paragraph (2)(b)(ii) (and the 'and' before it).

Amendment of the Sham Marriage and Civil Partnership (Scotland and Northern Ireland) (Administrative) Regulations 2015

44. . . .

Amendment of the Immigration and Nationality (Fees) Order 2016

45. . . .

Amendment of the Immigration and Nationality (Fees) Regulations 2018

46. . . .

Amendment of the Immigration (European Economic Area Nationals) (EU Exit) Order 2019

47.—(1) The Immigration (European Economic Area Nationals) (EU Exit) Order 2019 is amended as follows.

(2) In Part 2 (leave to enter or remain), omit Chapter 1 (grant of leave to EEA and Swiss nationals).

Amendment of the Immigration, Nationality and Asylum (EU Exit) Regulations 2019

48.—(1) The Immigration, Nationality and Asylum (EU Exit) Regulations 2019 are amended as follows.

(2) The following provisions are omitted—

(a) regulation 3 (amendment of the Aliens' Employment Act 1955);

(b) regulation 4(3)(b) (amendment of the Immigration Act 1971);

(c) regulation 6 (amendment of the Rent Act 1977);

(d) regulation 8 (amendment of the Immigration Act 1988);

(e) regulation 9 (amendment of the Housing Act 1988);

(f) regulation 11(2) and (5) (amendment of the Immigration and Asylum Act 1999);

(g) regulation 12(2), (3), 5(a), (c) and (d) (amendment of the Nationality, Immigration and Asylum Act 2002);

(h) regulation 14 (amendment of the Asylum and Immigration (Treatment of Claimants, etc) Act 2004);

(i) regulation 17(3) and (4) (amendment of the UK Borders Act 2007);

(j) regulation 18 (amendment of the Criminal Justice and Immigration Act 2008);

(k) regulation 21(2), (3) and (7) (amendment of the Immigration Act 2014);

(l) regulation 24 (amendment of the Immigration (Control of Entry through Republic of Ireland) Order 1972);

(m) regulation 25 (amendment of the Immigration (Leave to Enter and Remain) Order 2000);

(n) regulation 30(2),(4),(5) and (6)(a) and (c) (amendment of the British Nationality (General) Regulations 2003);

(o) regulation 33 (amendment of the Immigration (Provision of Physical Data) Regulations 2006;

(p) regulation 34 (amendment of the Immigration (Biometric Registration) Regulations 2008);

(q) regulation 42 (amendment of the Immigration and Nationality (Fees) Order 2016);

(r) regulation 43 (amendment of the Immigration (European Economic Area) Regulations 2016);

(s) regulation 49 (disapplication of rights etc);

(t) paragraphs 4 and 5 of Schedule 2 and regulation 56 (saving and transitional provisions) in so far as it relates to those provisions.

Amendment of the Citizens' Rights (Application Deadline and Temporary Protection) (EU Exit) Regulations 2020

49. —(1) The Citizens' Rights (Application Deadline and Temporary Protection) (EU Exit) Regulations 2020 are amended as follows.

(2) In regulation 7 (provisions relating to powers of refusal of admission and removal etc.), for paragraph (1)(a) substitute—

'(a) regulation 23 (exclusion and removal from the United Kingdom) with the modification that in each of paragraphs (1), (5), (6)(b) and (7)(b), after 'regulation 27', there were inserted 'or on conducive grounds in accordance with regulation 27A or if the person is subject to a deportation order by virtue of section 32 of the UK Borders Act 2007;'.'

(3) In regulation 11 (entitlement to benefits and public services), after paragraph (g) insert—

'(ga) regulation 7 (funeral payments: entitlement) of the Social Fund Maternity and Funeral Expenses (General) Regulations 2005;

(gb) regulation 7 (funeral payments: entitlement) of the Social Fund Maternity and Funeral Expenses (General) Regulations (Northern Ireland) 2005;'.

(4) In regulation 12 (modification of other enactments), in paragraph (1)(p) for 'IP completion day' substitute '1st December 2020'.

Amendment of the Citizens' Rights (Frontier Workers) (EU Exit) Regulations 2020

50.—(1) The Citizens' Rights (Frontier Workers) (EU Exit) Regulations 2020 are amended as follows.

(2) After regulation 20 (misuse of frontier workers' rights), insert—

'Exemption for Irish citizens

21A. Regulations 7 and 13 to 20 do not apply to a frontier worker who is an Irish citizen unless any of paragraphs (2) to (4) of section 3ZA of the 1971 Act(86) also apply to that Irish citizen.'.

Chapter 3

Revocation of secondary legislation

Revocation of the Immigration (European Economic Area) (Amendment) Regulations 2017

51. . . .

Revocation of the Immigration (European Economic Area) (Amendment) Regulations 2018

52. . . .

Part 3

Access to benefits and services

Note: Regulations 53–77 amend social security regulations

. . .

PART 4

NATIONALITY

CHAPTER 1

AMENDMENT OF PRIMARY LEGISLATION

Amendment of the British Nationality Act 1981

78.—(1) The British Nationality Act 1981 is amended as follows.

(2) In section 50A (meaning of references to being in breach of immigration laws)—

(a) in subsection (4)—

(i) after paragraph (b) insert—

'(ba) is not an Irish citizen who does not require leave to enter or remain in the United Kingdom (see section 3ZA of the Immigration Act 1971);';

(ii) omit paragraphs (d) and (e);

(b) omit subsection (5).

Amendment of the Borders, Citizenship and Immigration Act 2009

79.—(1) The Borders, Citizenship and Immigration Act 2009 is amended as follows.

(2) In section 39(2) (application requirements general), in paragraph 1(2) inserted into Schedule 1 to the British Nationality Act 1981 ('the 1981 Act'), in paragraph (d)—

(a) for 'a qualifying CTA entitlement' substitute 'the relevant status as an Irish citizen';

(b) omit 'or a permanent EEA entitlement'.

(3) In section 39(11), in paragraph 2A(1) inserted into Schedule 1 to the 1981 Act—

(a) for paragraph (d) substitute—

'(d) the relevant status as an Irish citizen, or';

(b) omit paragraph (f).

(4) In section 40(3)(application requirements: family members general), in paragraph 3(2)(d)(ii) inserted into Schedule 1 to the 1981 Act for 'a qualifying CTA entitlement' substitute 'the relevant status as an Irish citizen'.

(5) In section 40(5), in paragraph 4A(1) inserted into Schedule 1 to the 1981 Act, for paragraph (d) substitute—

'(d) the relevant status as an Irish citizen; or'.

(6) In section 49(3), in paragraph 11 inserted into Schedule 1 to the 1981 Act—

(a) for sub-paragraph (5) substitute—

'(5) A person has the relevant status as an Irish citizen if the person is an Irish citizen who does not require leave to enter or remain in the United Kingdom (see section 3ZA of the Immigration Act 1971).';

(b) omit sub-paragraphs (7) and (8).

CHAPTER 2

AMENDMENT OF SECONDARY LEGISLATION

Amendment and saving of the British Nationality (General) Regulations 2003

80.—(1) The British Nationality (General) Regulations 2003 are amended as follows.

(2) In regulation 2 (interpretation), in paragraph (1), omit the following definitions—

(a) 'document certifying permanent residence';

(b) 'permanent residence card';

(c) 'residence document issued under the Immigration (European Economic Area) Regulations 2000'; and

(d) 'residence permit issued under the Immigration (European Economic Area) Regulations 2000'.

(3) In regulation 7E (use and retention of biometric information), in paragraph (2)—

(a) at the end of sub-paragraph (c) insert 'and';

(b) omit sub-paragraph (e) (and the 'and' before it).

(4) In regulation 7G (retention of fingerprints)—

(a) in paragraph (2)—

(i) at the end of sub-paragraph (d) insert 'or';

(ii) omit sub-paragraph (f) (and the 'or' before it);

(b) in paragraph (3)—

(i) omit 'or (f)';

(ii) omit 'or who no longer enjoys the right of permanent residence';

(c) omit paragraph (4).

(5) In Schedule 2 (particular requirements as respects applications) omit paragraphs 7(1A), 13(1A) and 14(1A).

(6) Notwithstanding the amendment made by paragraph (5) Schedule 2 continues to apply as if not amended by these Regulations in relation to any application made under the British Nationality Act 1981 before commencement day.

Part 5

Saving provision in connection with the EC Association Agreement with Turkey

Saving provision in connection with the EC Association Agreement with Turkey

81. . . .

Part 6

Saving provision in connection with the Immigration (European Economic Area) Regulations 2016

Saving provision in connection with the Immigration (European Economic Area) Regulations 2016

82. Schedule 3 has effect.

Part 7

Saving provision in connection with access to benefits and services

Saving provision in connection with access to benefits and services

83. . . .

PART 8

TRANSITIONAL AND FURTHER SAVING PROVISION

Transitional and further saving provision

84. Schedule 5 has effect.

SCHEDULES

Regulation 24

SCHEDULE 1

PROVISION CONSEQUENTIAL ON OR CONNECTED WITH PART 2 CHAPTER 1

Provision consequential or connected with regulation 5 (amendment and saving of the Immigration Act 1971)

1. In the Immigration Act 1971—

(a) in the following provisions, for ', 25A or 25B' substitute 'or 25A'—

(i) section 25C(1);

(ii) section 25C(1)(5)(b);

(iii) section 25D(1);

(iv) section 28(2A);

(v) section 28A(3)(a);

(vi) section 28C(1);

(vii) section 28 M(2)(a);

(viii) section 28N(2)(a);

(ix) section 280(2)(a);

(x) paragraphs 2(1)(a),13(1)(a), 14(1)(a), 14(1)(a), 15(1)(a),24(1)(a),25(1)(a) and 26(1) of Schedule 4A;

(b) in section 28C (11) omit subsection (5);

(c) in section 28D(4) omit '25B,';

(d) in section 28F(1) omit ',25B'.

(2) In the Police Act 1997, in Schedule 8B, in paragraph 69 (immigration etc), omit paragraph (e).

(3) In the following provisions of the Proceeds of Crime Act 2002, for ',25A or 25B' substitute 'or 25A'—

(a) Schedule 2, paragraph 4(1);

(b) Schedule 4, paragraph 4(1);

(c) Schedule 5, paragraph 4(1).

(4) In the Serious Crime Act 2007—

(a) in Schedule 1, in each of paragraphs 2(1), 16B(1) and 18(1), for ', 25A or 25B' substitute 'or 25A';

(b) in Schedule 3 omit paragraph 12.

(5) The amendments and repeals made by sub-paragraphs (1) to (4) do not apply where section 25B of the Immigration Act 1971 continues to apply by virtue of regulation 5(6) of these Regulations.

Provision consequential or connected with regulation 6 (amendment of the Rent Act 1977) and regulation 8 (amendment of the Housing Act 1988)

2. . . .

Provision consequential or connected with regulation 13 (amendment of the Nationality, Immigration and Asylum Act 2002)

3. In Immigration Act 2016, in Schedule 12 (availability of local authority support: amendments to Schedule 3 to the Nationality, Immigration and Asylum Act 2002)—

(a) paragraph 2(2), in inserted paragraph 1(1)(ga), omit ', 5';

(b) in paragraph 2(4), in inserted paragraph 1(2A), omit ', 5';

(c) in paragraph 10, in inserted paragraph 10A(1) and (9)(a), omit 'or 7C(1)';

(d) in paragraph 13, in the amendments to paragraph 14, for ', 7B or 7C' substitute 'or 7B'.

Regulation 81

SCHEDULE 2

SAVING PROVISION IN CONNECTION WITH THE EC ASSOCIATION AGREEMENT WITH TURKEY

. . .

Regulation 82

SCHEDULE 3

SAVING PROVISION IN CONNECTION WITH THE IMMIGRATION (EUROPEAN ECONOMIC AREA) REGULATIONS 2016

1. In this Schedule 'EEA Regulations 2016' means the Immigration (European Economic Area) Regulations 2016(121) and, unless provided otherwise, refers to those Regulations as they had effect immediately before they were revoked.

Deportation and exclusion orders

2.—(1) Any deportation order made or treated as having been made by virtue of the EEA Regulations 2016 continues to apply for the period specified in the order or until revoked.

(2) Any deportation order made by virtue of the EEA Regulations 2016 as they are continued in effect by the Citizens' Rights (Application Deadline and Temporary Protection) (EU Exit) Regulations 2020 continues to apply for the period specified in the order or until revoked.

(3) Any exclusion order made or treated as having been made by virtue of the EEA Regulations 2016 continues to apply for the period specified in the order or until revoked.

(4) Any exclusion order made by virtue of the EEA Regulations 2016 as they are continued in effect by the Citizens' Rights (Application Deadline and Temporary Protection) (EU Exit) Regulations 2020 continues to apply for the period specified in the order or until revoked.

(5) Regulation 34(3) to (6) of the EEA Regulations 2016 (revocation of deportation and exclusion orders) continue to apply—

(a) in respect of any deportation order or exclusion order within sub-paragraph (1) or (3) with the modification that in paragraph (3), after 'deportation or exclusion order' there were inserted 'made on the grounds of public policy, public security or public health in accordance with regulation 27';

(b) in respect of any deportation order or exclusion order within sub-paragraph (2) or (4) with the modifications that—

(i) in paragraph (3), after 'deportation or exclusion order' there were inserted 'made on the grounds of public policy, public security or public health in accordance with regulation 27';

(ii) after paragraph (6) there were inserted—

'(7) An application for revocation of a deportation order made on conducive grounds in accordance with regulation 27A is to be considered in accordance with the immigration rules that apply in relation to an application for revocation of a deportation order made by virtue of section 3 of the Immigration Act 1971.'.

(6) This paragraph does not apply to the extent that the provisions specified in paragraph (5) continue to apply to a deportation or exclusion order by virtue of the Citizens' Rights (Application Deadline and Temporary Protection) (EU Exit) Regulations 2020.

Pending applications for documentation under the EEA Regulations 2016

3.—(1) Regulation 12 of the EEA Regulations 2016 (issue of EEA family permit), continues to apply for the purposes of considering and, where appropriate, granting an application for a family permit which was validly made in accordance with the EEA Regulations 2016 before commencement day.

(2) Regulation 12 of the EEA Regulations 2016 also continues to apply for the purposes of considering and, where appropriate, granting an application for a family permit which was validly made after commencement day in accordance with the EEA Regulations 2016 as they are continued in effect by the Citizens' Rights (Application Deadline and Temporary Protection) (EU Exit) Regulations 2020.

(3) Regulation 17 of the EEA Regulations 2016 (issue of registration certificate), continues to apply for the purposes of considering and, where appropriate, granting an application for a registration certificate which was validly made in accordance with the EEA Regulations 2016 before commencement day.

(4) Regulation 18 of the EEA Regulations 2016 (issue of residence card), continues to apply for the purposes of considering and, where appropriate, granting an application for a residence card which was validly made in accordance with the EEA Regulations 2016 before commencement day.

(5) Regulation 19 of the EEA Regulations 2016 (issue of a document certifying permanent residence and a permanent residence card), continues to apply for the purposes of considering and, where appropriate, granting an application for a document certifying permanent residence or a permanent residence card, which was validly made in accordance with the EEA Regulations 2016 before commencement day.

(6) Regulation 20 of the EEA Regulations 2016 (issue of a derivative residence card), continues to apply for the purposes of considering and, where appropriate, granting an application for a derivative residence card which was validly made in accordance with the EEA Regulations 2016 before commencement day.

Application of EEA Regulations 2016 to pending applications

4. —(1) Subject to sub-paragraph (2) the provisions of the EEA Regulations 2016 specified in paragraph 6 continue to apply (despite the revocation of those Regulations) with the modifications specified for the purposes of determining whether an application referred to in paragraph 3 should be granted.

(2) The provisions specified in paragraph 6 do not apply to the extent that the provisions of the EEA Regulations 2016 specified in that paragraph continue to apply to an application within paragraph 3(2) by virtue of the Citizens' Rights (Application Deadline and Temporary Protection) (EU Exit) Regulations 2020.

Existing appeal rights and appeals

5.—(1) Subject to sub-paragraph (4), the provisions of the EEA Regulations 2016 specified in paragraph 6 continue to apply—

(a) to any appeal which has been brought under the Immigration (European Economic Area) Regulations 2006 and has not been finally determined before commencement day,

(b) to any appeal which has been brought under the EEA Regulations 2016 and has not been finally determined before commencement day,

(c) in respect of an EEA decision, within the meaning of the EEA Regulations 2016, taken before commencement day, or

(d) in respect of an EEA decision, within the meaning of the EEA Regulations 2016 as they continue in effect by virtue of these Regulations or the Citizens' Rights (Application Deadline and Temporary Protection) (EU Exit) Regulations 2020, which is taken on or after commencement day.

(2) For the purposes of paragraph (1)—

(a) an appeal is not to be treated as finally determined while a further appeal may be brought and, if such a further appeal is brought, the original appeal is not to be treated as finally determined until the further appeal is determined, withdrawn or abandoned; and

(b) an appeal is not to be treated as abandoned solely because the appellant leaves the United Kingdom.

(3) The revocation of the EEA Regulations 2016 does not affect the application of the Immigration (European Economic Area) Regulations 2006 to an appeal that falls within paragraph 3(1) of Schedule 4 to the EEA Regulations 2016.

(4) The provisions specified in paragraph 6 do not apply to the extent that the provisions of the EEA Regulations 2016 specified in paragraph 6 continue to apply to an appeal or EEA decision by virtue of the Citizens' Rights (Application Deadline and Temporary Protection) (EU Exit) Regulations 2020.

Specified provisions of the EEA Regulations 2016

6. —(1) The specified provisions of the EEA Regulations 2016 are—

(a) regulation 2 (general interpretation) with the following modifications—

(i) as if all instances of the words 'or any other right conferred by the EU Treaties'—

(aa) in so far as they relate to things done on or after exit day but before commencement day, were a reference to a right conferred by the EU Treaties so far as they were applicable to and in the United Kingdom by virtue of Part 4 of the EU withdrawal agreement;

(bb) in so far as they relate to things done on or after commencement day, were omitted;

(ii) as if all instances of the words 'or the EU Treaties'—

(aa) in so far as they relate to things done on or after exit day but before commencement day, were a reference to the EU Treaties so far as they were applicable to and in the United Kingdom by virtue of Part 4 of the EU withdrawal agreement;

(bb) in so far as they relate to things done on or after commencement day, were omitted;

(iii) as if, at the end of the definition of 'deportation order', there were inserted 'or under section 5(1) of the Immigration Act 1971';

(iv) as if, in the definition of 'EEA State', the words ', other than the United Kingdom' were omitted; and

(v) as if, at the end of the definition of 'exclusion order', there were inserted 'or directions issued by the Secretary of State for a person not to be given entry to the United Kingdom on the grounds that the person's exclusion is conducive to the public good';

(b) regulation 3 (continuity of residence) with the modification that, at the end of paragraph (3) (c), there were inserted 'or the Immigration Acts';

(c) regulation 4 ('worker', 'self-employed person', 'self-sufficient person' and 'student') with the modification that, in paragraph (1)(b), for 'in accordance with' there were substituted 'within the meaning of';

(d) regulation 5 ('worker or self-employed person who has ceased activity');

(e) regulation 6 ('qualified person') with the following modifications—

(i) in paragraph (4C), 'and having a genuine chance of being engaged' were omitted;

(ii) in paragraph (6), after 'employment and' there were inserted ', when determining whether the person is a jobseeker,';

(iii) in paragraph (7), after 'continuing to seek employment and' there were inserted ', where that person is a jobseeker';

(f) regulation 7 ('family member');

(g) regulation 8 ('extended family member');

(h) regulation 9 (family members and extended family members of British citizens) with the following modifications—

(i) in paragraph (1), at the end there were inserted 'and BC is to be treated as satisfying any requirement to be a qualified person';

(ii) sub-paragraph (a) of paragraph (3) were omitted;

(iii) paragraph (7) were omitted;

(i) regulation 9A (dual national: national of an EEA State who acquires British citizenship);

(j) regulation 10 ('family member who has retained the right of residence') with the following modifications—

(i) in paragraph (2)(b), in so far as it applies to residence in the United Kingdom after commencement day, for 'in accordance with these Regulations' there were substituted 'lawfully';

(ii) in paragraph (5)(a), 'the initiation of proceedings for' were omitted;

(k) regulation 11 (right of admission to the United Kingdom);

(l) regulation 21 (procedure for applications for documentation under this Part and regulation 12);

(m) regulation 22 (verification of a right of residence);

(n) regulation 23 (exclusion and removal from the United Kingdom) with the modification that in each of paragraphs (1), (5), (6)(b) and (7)(b), after 'regulation 27', there were inserted 'or on conducive grounds in accordance with regulation 27A or if the person is subject to a deportation order by virtue of section 32 of the UK Borders Act 2007';

(o) regulation 24(1), (3),(4), (6) and (7) (refusal to issue or renew and revocation of residence documentation), with the modification that references to revocation are omitted;

(p) regulation 27 (decisions taken on grounds of public policy, public security and public health) with the modification that after regulation 27 there were inserted—

'Decisions taken on conducive grounds

27A.—(1) An EEA decision may be taken on the ground that the decision is conducive to the public good.

(2) But a decision may only be taken under this regulation in relation to a person as a result of conduct of that person that took place after IP completion day.';

(q) regulation 28 (application of Part 4 to a person with a derivative right to reside) in so far as it applies to a person within regulation 28(1)(c),

(r) regulation 32 (person subject to removal) with the modification that in paragraph (5), after 'public health', there were inserted 'in accordance with regulation 27 or on conducive grounds in accordance with regulation 27A';

(s) regulation 33 (human rights considerations and interim orders to suspend removal);

(t) regulation 35 (interpretation of Part 6) in respect of the interpretation of the provisions which continue to apply by virtue of paragraph 4 or 5;

(u) regulation 36 (appeal rights);

(v) regulation 37 (out of country appeals);

(w) regulation 38 (appeals to the Commission);

(x) regulation 39 (national security: EEA decisions);

(y) regulation 40 (effect of appeals to the First-tier Tribunal or Upper Tribunal);

(z) regulation 41 (temporary admission to submit case in person);

(aa) regulation 42 (alternative evidence of identity and nationality);

(bb) Schedule 1 (considerations of public policy, public security and the fundamental interests of society etc.) with the modification that for paragraph 1 there were substituted—

'1. The United Kingdom enjoys considerable discretion, acting within the parameters set by the law, to define its own standards of public policy and public security, for purposes tailored to its individual context from time to time.'.

(cc) Schedule 2 (appeals to the First-tier Tribunal) with the modification that—

(aa) in relation to an appeal within paragraph 5(1)(a) to (c), in each of paragraphs 1 and 2(4), the words 'under the EU Treaties', in so far as they relate to things done on or after exit day but before commencement day, were a reference to the EU Treaties so far as they were applicable to and in the United Kingdom by virtue of Part 4 of the EU withdrawal agreement;

(bb) in relation to an appeal within paragraph 5(1)(d), in each of paragraphs 1 and 2(4), the words 'under the EU Treaties', were a reference to 'under the Immigration (European Economic Area) Regulations 2016 as they are continued in effect by these

Regulations or the Citizens' Rights (Restrictions of Rights of Entry and Residence) (EU Exit) Regulations 2020, or by virtue of the EU withdrawal agreement, the EEA EFTA separation agreement (which has the same meaning as in the European Union (Withdrawal Agreement) Act 2020) or the Swiss citizens' rights agreement (which has the same meaning as in that Act)'.

Nationality, Immigration and Asylum Act 2016- saving in relation to appeals

7. The repeal of section 109 of the Nationality, Immigration and Asylum Act 2002 (power to make regulations about appeals against immigration decisions in respect of persons having, or claiming to have, EU rights), by paragraph 2(1) of Schedule 1 to the 2020 Act, does not affect—

(a) the power to make regulations under that section which provide for, or make provision about, an appeal in relation to which provisions of the EEA Regulations 2016 continue to have effect by virtue of these Regulations, the Citizens' Rights (Application Deadline and Temporary Protection) (EU Exit) Regulations 2020 or the Citizens' Rights (Restrictions of Rights of Entry and Residence) (EU Exit) Regulations 2020; or

(b) the operation of any regulations made under that section insofar as they continue to have effect on or after commencement day by virtue of these Regulations or by virtue of any of the other Regulations of 2020 referred to in sub-paragraph (a).

Regulation 83

SCHEDULE 4

SAVING PROVISION IN RELATION TO ACCESS TO BENEFITS AND SERVICES

...

Regulation 84

SCHEDULE 5

TRANSITIONAL AND FURTHER SAVING PROVISION

PART 1

...

Transitional provision in relation to the immigration status of Irish citizens

...

Transitional provision in relation to banns of matrimony in England and Wales

...

Transitional provision in relation to common licences for marriage in England and Wales

. . .

Transitional provision in relation to notices of marriage

. . .

Transitional provision in relation to notices of civil partnership

. . .

PART 2

Saving in relation to section 2 of the 2020 Act

10.—(1) The amendment of section 9(2) of the Immigration Act 1971 (further provisions about the common travel area) made by section 2(3) of the 2020 Act does not affect the operation in relation to an Irish citizen of any subordinate legislation which was made under section 9(2) of the Immigration Act 1971 before commencement day for the purposes of the implementation of Article 32(1)(b) of the withdrawal agreement, Article 31(1)(b) of the EEA EFTA separation agreement or Article 26a(1)(b) of the Swiss citizens' rights agreement.

(2) In paragraph (1), 'EEA EFTA separation agreement' and 'Swiss citizens' rights agreement' have the same meanings as in the European Union (Withdrawal Agreement) Act 2020 (see section 39(1) of that Act).

Saving in relation to Schedule 1 to the 2020 Act

11. The repeal by paragraphs 5 and 6 of Schedule 1 to the 2020 Act of the rights, powers, liabilities obligations, restrictions, remedies and procedures to which those paragraphs apply does not prevent those rights, powers, liabilities, obligations, restrictions, remedies and procedures being recognised and available in domestic law in respect of a time before commencement day.

The Immigration (Guidance on Detention of Vulnerable Persons) Regulations 2021

(SI No. 184)

TEXT NOT REPRODUCED

Note: The guidance entitled "Immigration Act 2016: Revised guidance on adults at risk in immigration detention", in force on 25th May 2021 (reg.2 of SI 2021/184).

The Immigration and Asylum Act 1999 (Part 5 Exemption: Licensed Sponsors) Order 2022
(SI No.235)

Citation, commencement and extent

1.—(1) This Order may be cited as the Immigration and Asylum Act 1999 (Part 5 Exemption: Licensed Sponsors) Order 2022.

(2) This Order comes into force on 11th April 2022.

(3) This Order extends to England and Wales, Scotland and Northern Ireland.

Exemption of licensed sponsors from prohibition on providing immigration advice or services

2.—(1) For the purposes of section 84(4) of the Immigration and Asylum Act 1999, a licensed sponsor is a specified category of person in respect of the provision of immigration advice or immigration services in the situations described in paragraphs (2) and (3) (and accordingly the prohibition in section 84(1) of that Act does not apply to a person who is a licensed sponsor providing such advice or services in those situations).

(2) The first situation is where—

(a) the immigration advice or immigration services are provided in relation to an individual by the licensed sponsor free of charge,

(b) the advice or services are provided by the licensed sponsor in connection with an application by that individual for entry clearance or leave to enter or remain in the United Kingdom under the immigration rules for the purposes of work or study in the United Kingdom, and

(c) the licensed sponsor is that individual's sponsor, pursuant to those rules, in relation to the work or course of study in question.

(3) The second situation is where—

(a) the immigration advice or immigration services are provided in relation to an individual ('the individual') by the licensed sponsor free of charge,

(b) the advice or services are provided by the licensed sponsor in connection with an application by the individual for entry clearance or leave to enter or remain in the United Kingdom under the immigration rules,

(c) the licensed sponsor reasonably believes that the application will be or was made by the individual as an eligible family member of another individual ('the main applicant') and that, under the immigration rules, the individual's application is or was dependent on, or on the outcome of—

(i) an application which the main applicant is proposing to make for entry clearance or leave to enter or remain in the United Kingdom under those rules for the purposes of work or study in the United Kingdom,

(ii) an application which the main applicant has made, but which has not yet been determined, for entry clearance or leave to enter or remain in the United Kingdom under those rules for the purposes of work or study in the United Kingdom, or

(iii) an application made by the main applicant for entry clearance or leave to enter or remain in the United Kingdom under those rules for the purposes of work or study in the United Kingdom which resulted in such clearance or leave being granted to the main applicant, and

(d) the licensed sponsor is the main applicant's sponsor, pursuant to the immigration rules, in relation to—

(i) the work or course of study referred to in sub-paragraph (c)(i), (ii) or (iii), as the case may be (whether or not paragraph (4) applies), or

(ii) where paragraph (4) applies, any work or course of study referred to in sub-paragraph (c) of that paragraph.

(4) This paragraph applies where—

(a) the individual's application is an application which has been determined,

(b) the licensed sponsor reasonably believes that, under the immigration rules, that application was dependent on, or on the outcome of, an application made by the main applicant for entry clearance or leave to enter or remain in the United Kingdom under those rules for the purposes of work or study in the United Kingdom which resulted in such clearance or leave being granted to the main applicant, and

(c) the main applicant—

(i) has entry clearance or leave to enter or remain in the United Kingdom under the immigration rules for the purposes of work or study in the United Kingdom as a result of a subsequent application for entry clearance or leave to enter or remain in the United Kingdom under those rules,

(ii) is proposing to make an application for entry clearance or leave to enter or remain in the United Kingdom under those rules for the purposes of work or study in the United Kingdom, or

(iii) has made an application under those rules, which has not yet been determined, for entry clearance or leave to enter or remain in the United Kingdom under those rules for the purposes of work or study in the United Kingdom.

(5) **In this article—**

'the immigration rules' means rules made under section 3(2) of the Immigration Act 1971;

'licensed sponsor' means a person listed as a licensed sponsor in either of the following registers maintained by the Home Office in connection with the immigration rules—

(a) the register of licensed sponsors: students;

(b) the register of licensed sponsors: workers; 'work' includes engaging in business.

(6) For the purposes of paragraph (3)(c) an application by an individual ('the individual') is made by the individual as an eligible family member of another individual ('the main applicant') where the individual's entitlement under the immigration rules to make the application depends on the existence of a particular relationship or other connection between the individual and the main applicant.

(7) References in this article to entry clearance or leave to enter or remain in the United Kingdom include references to the variation of such clearance or leave.

Revocation

3. The Immigration and Asylum Act 1999 (Part V Exemption: Licensed Sponsors Tiers 2 and 4) Order 2009 is revoked.

EUROPEAN MATERIALS[1]

[1] The following materials are reproduced by Oxford University Press under the reuse policy of Commission documents based on Decision 2011/833/EU. http://eur-lex.europa.eu, © European Union, 1998–2023.

Directive 2004/38/EC of the European Parliament and of the Council of 29 April 2004

on the right of citizens of the Union and their family members to move and reside freely within the territory of the Member States amending Regulation (EEC) No. 1612/68 and repealing Directives 64/221/EEC, 68/360/EEC, 72/194/EEC, 73/148/EEC, 75/34/EEC, 75/35/EEC, 90/364/EEC, 90/365/EEC and 93/96/EEC

(Text with EEA relevance)

Note: Entered into force on 30 April 2004 (Article 41). To be implemented by 30 April 2006 (Article 40).

THE EUROPEAN PARLIAMENT AND THE COUNCIL OF THE EUROPEAN UNION,

Having regard to the Treaty establishing the European Community, and in particular Articles 12, 18, 40, 44 and 52 thereof,

Having regard to the proposal from the Commission,[1]

Having regard to the Opinion of the European Economic and Social Committee,[2]

Having regard to the Opinion of the Committee of the Regions,[3]

Acting in accordance with the procedure laid down in Article 251 of the Treaty,[4]

Whereas:

(1) Citizenship of the Union confers on every citizen of the Union a primary and individual right to move and reside freely within the territory of the Member States, subject to the limitations and conditions laid down in the Treaty and to the measures adopted to give it effect.

(2) The free movement of persons constitutes one of the fundamental freedoms of the internal market, which comprises an area without internal frontiers, in which freedom is ensured in accordance with the provisions of the Treaty.

(3) Union citizenship should be the fundamental status of nationals of the Member States when they exercise their right of free movement and residence. It is therefore necessary to codify and review the existing Community instruments dealing separately with workers, self-employed persons, as well as students and other inactive persons in order to simplify and strengthen the right of free movement and residence of all Union citizens.

(4) With a view to remedying this sector-by-sector, piecemeal approach to the right of free movement and residence and facilitating the exercise of this right, there needs to be a single legislative act to amend Council Regulation (EEC) No. 1612/68 of 15 October 1968 on freedom of movement for workers within the Community[5] and to repeal the following

[1] OJ C 270 E, 25.9.2001, p. 150.
[2] OJ C 149, 21.6.2002, p. 46.
[3] OJ C 192, 12.8.2002, p. 17.
[4] Opinion of the European Parliament of 11 February 2003 (OJ C 43 E, 19.2.2004, p. 42), Council Common Position of 5 December 2003 (OJ C 54 E, 2.3.2004, p. 12) and Position of the European Parliament of 10 March 2004 (not yet published in the Official Journal).
[5] OJ L 257, 19.10.1968, p. 2. Regulation as last amended by Regulation (EEC) No. 2434/92 (OJ L 245, 26.8.1992, p. 1).

acts: Council Directive 68/360/EEC of 15 October 1968 on the abolition of restrictions on movement and residence within the Community for workers of Member States and their families,[6] Council Directive 73/148/EEC of 21 May 1973 on the abolition of restrictions on movement and residence within the Community for nationals of Member States with regard to establishment and the provision of services,[7] Council Directive 90/364/EEC of 28 June 1990 on the right of residence,[8] Council Directive 90/365/EEC of 28 June 1990 on the right of residence for employees and self-employed persons who have ceased their occupational activity[9] and Council Directive 93/96/EEC of 29 October 1993 on the right of residence for students.[10]

(5) The right of all Union citizens to move and reside freely within the territory of the Member States should, if it is to be exercised under objective conditions of freedom and dignity, be also granted to their family members, irrespective of nationality. For the purposes of this Directive, the definition of 'family member' should also include the registered partner if the legislation of the host Member State treats registered partnership as equivalent to marriage.

(6) In order to maintain the unity of the family in a broader sense and without prejudice to the prohibition of discrimination on grounds of nationality, the situation of those persons who are not included in the definition of family members under this Directive, and who therefore do not enjoy an automatic right of entry and residence in the host Member State, should be examined by the host Member State on the basis of its own national legislation, in order to decide whether entry and residence could be granted to such persons, taking into consideration their relationship with the Union citizen or any other circumstances, such as their financial or physical dependence on the Union citizen.

(7) The formalities connected with the free movement of Union citizens within the territory of Member States should be clearly defined, without prejudice to the provisions applicable to national border controls.

(8) With a view to facilitating the free movement of family members who are not nationals of a Member State, those who have already obtained a residence card should be exempted from the requirement to obtain an entry visa within the meaning of Council Regulation (EC) No. 539/2001 of 15 March 2001 listing the third countries whose nationals must be in possession of visas when crossing the external borders and those whose nationals are exempt from that requirement[11] or, where appropriate, of the applicable national legislation.

(9) Union citizens should have the right of residence in the host Member State for a period not exceeding three months without being subject to any conditions or any formalities other than the requirement to hold a valid identity card or passport, without prejudice to a more favourable treatment applicable to job-seekers as recognised by the case-law of the Court of Justice.

[6] OJ L 257, 19.10.1968, p. 13. Directive as last amended by the 2003 Act of Accession.

[7] OJ L 172, 28.6.1973, p. 14.

[8] OJ L 180, 13.7.1990, p. 26.

[9] OJ L 180, 13.7.1990, p. 28.

[10] OJ L 317, 18.12.1993, p. 59.

[11] OJ L 81, 21.3.2001, p. 1. Regulation as last amended by Regulation (EC) No. 453/2003 (OJ L 69, 13.3.2003, p. 10).

(10) Persons exercising their right of residence should not, however, become an unreasonable burden on the social assistance system of the host Member State during an initial period of residence. Therefore, the right of residence for Union citizens and their family members for periods in excess of three months should be subject to conditions.

(11) The fundamental and personal right of residence in another Member State is conferred directly on Union citizens by the Treaty and is not dependent upon their having fulfilled administrative procedures.

(12) For periods of residence of longer than three months, Member States should have the possibility to require Union citizens to register with the competent authorities in the place of residence, attested by a registration certificate issued to that effect.

(13) The residence card requirement should be restricted to family members of Union citizens who are not nationals of a Member State for periods of residence of longer than three months.

(14) The supporting documents required by the competent authorities for the issuing of a registration certificate or of a residence card should be comprehensively specified in order to avoid divergent administrative practices or interpretations constituting an undue obstacle to the exercise of the right of residence by Union citizens and their family members.

(15) Family members should be legally safeguarded in the event of the death of the Union citizen, divorce, annulment of marriage or termination of a registered partnership. With due regard for family life and human dignity, and in certain conditions to guard against abuse, measures should therefore be taken to ensure that in such circumstances family members already residing within the territory of the host Member State retain their right of residence exclusively on a personal basis.

(16) As long as the beneficiaries of the right of residence do not become an unreasonable burden on the social assistance system of the host Member State they should not be expelled. Therefore, an expulsion measure should not be the automatic consequence of recourse to the social assistance system. The host Member State should examine whether it is a case of temporary difficulties and take into account the duration of residence, the personal circumstances and the amount of aid granted in order to consider whether the beneficiary has become an unreasonable burden on its social assistance system and to proceed to his expulsion. In no case should an expulsion measure be adopted against workers, self-employed persons or job-seekers as defined by the Court of Justice save on grounds of public policy or public security.

(17) Enjoyment of permanent residence by Union citizens who have chosen to settle long term in the host Member State would strengthen the feeling of Union citizenship and is a key element in promoting social cohesion, which is one of the fundamental objectives of the Union. A right of permanent residence should therefore be laid down for all Union citizens and their family members who have resided in the host Member State in compliance with the conditions laid down in this Directive during a continuous period of five years without becoming subject to an expulsion measure.

(18) In order to be a genuine vehicle for integration into the society of the host Member State in which the Union citizen resides, the right of permanent residence, once obtained, should not be subject to any conditions.

(19) Certain advantages specific to Union citizens who are workers or self-employed persons and to their family members, which may allow these persons to acquire a right of permanent residence before they have resided five years in the host Member State, should

be maintained, as these constitute acquired rights, conferred by Commission Regulation (EEC) No. 1251/70 of 29 June 1970 on the right of workers to remain in the territory of a Member State after having been employed in that State[12] and Council Directive 75/34/EEC of 17 December 1974 concerning the right of nationals of a Member State to remain in the territory of another Member State after having pursued therein an activity in a self-employed capacity.[13]

(20) In accordance with the prohibition of discrimination on grounds of nationality, all Union citizens and their family members residing in a Member State on the basis of this Directive should enjoy, in that Member State, equal treatment with nationals in areas covered by the Treaty, subject to such specific provisions as are expressly provided for in the Treaty and secondary law.

(21) However, it should be left to the host Member State to decide whether it will grant social assistance during the first three months of residence, or for a longer period in the case of job-seekers, to Union citizens other than those who are workers or self-employed persons or who retain that status or their family members, or maintenance assistance for studies, including vocational training, prior to acquisition of the right of permanent residence, to these same persons.

(22) The Treaty allows restrictions to be placed on the right of free movement and residence on grounds of public policy, public security or public health. In order to ensure a tighter definition of the circumstances and procedural safeguards subject to which Union citizens and their family members may be denied leave to enter or may be expelled, this Directive should replace Council Directive 64/221/EEC of 25 February 1964 on the coordination of special measures concerning the movement and residence of foreign nationals, which are justified on grounds of public policy, public security or public health.[14]

(23) Expulsion of Union citizens and their family members on grounds of public policy or public security is a measure that can seriously harm persons who, having availed themselves of the rights and freedoms conferred on them by the Treaty, have become genuinely integrated into the host Member State. The scope for such measures should therefore be limited in accordance with the principle of proportionality to take account of the degree of integration of the persons concerned, the length of their residence in the host Member State, their age, state of health, family and economic situation and the links with their country of origin.

(24) Accordingly, the greater the degree of integration of Union citizens and their family members in the host Member State, the greater the degree of protection against expulsion should be. Only in exceptional circumstances, where there are imperative grounds of public security, should an expulsion measure be taken against Union citizens who have resided for many years in the territory of the host Member State, in particular when they were born and have resided there throughout their life. In addition, such exceptional circumstances should also apply to an expulsion measure taken against minors, in order to protect their links with their family, in accordance with the United Nations Convention on the Rights of the Child, of 20 November 1989.

[12] OJ L 142, 30.6.1970, p. 24.

[13] OJ L 14, 20.1.1975, p. 10.

[14] OJ 56, 4.4.1964, p. 850. Directive as last amended by Directive 75/35/EEC (OJ 14, 20.1.1975, p. 14).

(25) Procedural safeguards should also be specified in detail in order to ensure a high level of protection of the rights of Union citizens and their family members in the event of their being denied leave to enter or reside in another Member State, as well as to uphold the principle that any action taken by the authorities must be properly justified.

(26) In all events, judicial redress procedures should be available to Union citizens and their family members who have been refused leave to enter or reside in another Member State.

(27) In line with the case-law of the Court of Justice prohibiting Member States from issuing orders excluding for life persons covered by this Directive from their territory, the right of Union citizens and their family members who have been excluded from the territory of a Member State to submit a fresh application after a reasonable period, and in any event after a three year period from enforcement of the final exclusion order, should be confirmed.

(28) To guard against abuse of rights or fraud, notably marriages of convenience or any other form of relationships contracted for the sole purpose of enjoying the right of free movement and residence, Member States should have the possibility to adopt the necessary measures.

(29) This Directive should not affect more favourable national provisions.

(30) With a view to examining how further to facilitate the exercise of the right of free movement and residence, a report should be prepared by the Commission in order to evaluate the opportunity to present any necessary proposals to this effect, notably on the extension of the period of residence with no conditions.

(31) This Directive respects the fundamental rights and freedoms and observes the principles recognised in particular by the Charter of Fundamental Rights of the European Union. In accordance with the prohibition of discrimination contained in the Charter, Member States should implement this Directive without discrimination between the beneficiaries of this Directive on grounds such as sex, race, colour, ethnic or social origin, genetic characteristics, language, religion or beliefs, political or other opinion, membership of an ethnic minority, property, birth, disability, age or sexual orientation,

HAVE ADOPTED THIS DIRECTIVE:

Chapter I
General Provisions

Article 1

Subject

This Directive lays down:

(a) the conditions governing the exercise of the right of free movement and residence within the territory of the Member States by Union citizens and their family members;

(b) the right of permanent residence in the territory of the Member States for Union citizens and their family members;

(c) the limits placed on the rights set out in (a) and (b) on grounds of public policy, public security or public health.

Article 2

Definitions

For the purposes of this Directive:

(1) 'Union citizen' means any person having the nationality of a Member State;

(2) 'Family member' means:

(a) the spouse;

(b) the partner with whom the Union citizen has contracted a registered partnership, on the basis of the legislation of a Member State, if the legislation of the host Member State treats registered partnerships as equivalent to marriage and in accordance with the conditions laid down in the relevant legislation of the host Member State;

(c) the direct descendants who are under the age of 21 or are dependants and those of the spouse or partner as defined in point (b);

(d) the dependent direct relatives in the ascending line and those of the spouse or partner as defined in point (b);

(3) 'Host Member State' means the Member State to which a Union citizen moves in order to exercise his/her right of free movement and residence.

Article 3

Beneficiaries

1. This Directive shall apply to all Union citizens who move to or reside in a Member State other than that of which they are a national, and to their family members as defined in point 2 of Article 2 who accompany or join them.

2. Without prejudice to any right to free movement and residence the persons concerned may have in their own right, the host Member State shall, in accordance with its national legislation, facilitate entry and residence for the following persons:

(a) any other family members, irrespective of their nationality, not falling under the definition in point 2 of Article 2 who, in the country from which they have come, are dependants or members of the household of the Union citizen having the primary right of residence, or where serious health grounds strictly require the personal care of the family member by the Union citizen;

(b) the partner with whom the Union citizen has a durable relationship, duly attested.

The host Member State shall undertake an extensive examination of the personal circumstances and shall justify any denial of entry or residence to these people.

Chapter II

Right of Exit and Entry

Article 4

Right of exit

1. Without prejudice to the provisions on travel documents applicable to national border controls, all Union citizens with a valid identity card or passport and their family members who are not nationals of a Member State and who hold a valid passport shall have the right to leave the territory of a Member State to travel to another Member State.

2. No exit visa or equivalent formality may be imposed on the persons to whom paragraph 1 applies.

3. Member States shall, acting in accordance with their laws, issue to their own nationals, and renew, an identity card or passport stating their nationality.

4. The passport shall be valid at least for all Member States and for countries through which the holder must pass when travelling between Member States. Where the law of a Member State does not provide for identity cards to be issued, the period of validity of any passport on being issued or renewed shall be not less than five years.

Article 5
Right of entry

1. Without prejudice to the provisions on travel documents applicable to national border controls, Member States shall grant Union citizens leave to enter their territory with a valid identity card or passport and shall grant family members who are not nationals of a Member State leave to enter their territory with a valid passport.

No entry visa or equivalent formality may be imposed on Union citizens.

2. Family members who are not nationals of a Member State shall only be required to have an entry visa in accordance with Regulation (EC) No. 539/2001 or, where appropriate, with national law. For the purposes of this Directive, possession of the valid residence card referred to in Article 10 shall exempt such family members from the visa requirement.

Member States shall grant such persons every facility to obtain the necessary visas. Such visas shall be issued free of charge as soon as possible and on the basis of an accelerated procedure.

3. The host Member State shall not place an entry or exit stamp in the passport of family members who are not nationals of a Member State provided that they present the residence card provided for in Article 10.

4. Where a Union citizen, or a family member who is not a national of a Member State, does not have the necessary travel documents or, if required, the necessary visas, the Member State concerned shall, before turning them back, give such persons every reasonable opportunity to obtain the necessary documents or have them brought to them within a reasonable period of time or to corroborate or prove by other means that they are covered by the right of free movement and residence.

5. The Member State may require the person concerned to report his/her presence within its territory within a reasonable and non-discriminatory period of time. Failure to comply with this requirement may make the person concerned liable to proportionate and non-discriminatory sanctions.

Chapter III
Right of Residence

Article 6
Right of residence for up to three months

1. Union citizens shall have the right of residence on the territory of another Member State for a period of up to three months without any conditions or any formalities other than the requirement to hold a valid identity card or passport.

2. The provisions of paragraph 1 shall also apply to family members in possession of a valid passport who are not nationals of a Member State, accompanying or joining the Union citizen.

Article 7
Right of residence for more than three months

1. All Union citizens shall have the right of residence on the territory of another Member State for a period of longer than three months if they:

(a) are workers or self-employed persons in the host Member State; or

(b) have sufficient resources for themselves and their family members not to become a burden on the social assistance system of the host Member State during their period of residence and have comprehensive sickness insurance cover in the host Member State; or

(c) — are enrolled at a private or public establishment, accredited or financed by the host Member State on the basis of its legislation or administrative practice, for the principal purpose of following a course of study, including vocational training; and

— have comprehensive sickness insurance cover in the host Member State and assure the relevant national authority, by means of a declaration or by such equivalent means as they may choose, that they have sufficient resources for themselves and their family members not to become a burden on the social assistance system of the host Member State during their period of residence; or

(d) are family members accompanying or joining a Union citizen who satisfies the conditions referred to in points (a), (b) or (c).

2. The right of residence provided for in paragraph 1 shall extend to family members who are not nationals of a Member State, accompanying or joining the Union citizen in the host Member State, provided that such Union citizen satisfies the conditions referred to in paragraph 1(a), (b) or (c).

3. For the purposes of paragraph 1(a), a Union citizen who is no longer a worker or self-employed person shall retain the status of worker or self-employed person in the following circumstances:

(a) he/she is temporarily unable to work as the result of an illness or accident;

(b) he/she is in duly recorded involuntary unemployment after having been employed for more than one year and has registered as a job-seeker with the relevant employment office;

(c) he/she is in duly recorded involuntary unemployment after completing a fixed-term employment contract of less than a year or after having become involuntarily unemployed during the first twelve months and has registered as a job-seeker with the relevant employment office. In this case, the status of worker shall be retained for no less than six months;

(d) he/she embarks on vocational training. Unless he/she is involuntarily unemployed, the retention of the status of worker shall require the training to be related to the previous employment.

4. By way of derogation from paragraphs 1(d) and 2 above, only the spouse, the registered partner provided for in Article 2(2)(b) and dependent children shall have the right of residence as family members of a Union citizen meeting the conditions under 1(c) above. Article 3(2) shall apply to his/her dependent direct relatives in the ascending lines and those of his/her spouse or registered partner.

Article 8

Administrative formalities for union citizens

1. Without prejudice to Article 5(5), for periods of residence longer than three months, the host Member State may require Union citizens to register with the relevant authorities.

2. The deadline for registration may not be less than three months from the date of arrival. A registration certificate shall be issued immediately, stating the name and address of the person registering and the date of the registration. Failure to comply with the registration requirement may render the person concerned liable to proportionate and non-discriminatory sanctions.

3. For the registration certificate to be issued, Member States may only require that

— Union citizens to whom point (a) of Article 7(1) applies present a valid identity card or passport, a confirmation of engagement from the employer or a certificate of employment, or proof that they are self-employed persons;

— Union citizens to whom point (b) of Article 7(1) applies present a valid identity card or passport and provide proof that they satisfy the conditions laid down therein;

— Union citizens to whom point (c) of Article 7(1) applies present a valid identity card or passport, provide proof of enrolment at an accredited establishment and of comprehensive sickness insurance cover and the declaration or equivalent means referred to in point (c) of Article 7(1). Member States may not require this declaration to refer to any specific amount of resources.

4. Member States may not lay down a fixed amount which they regard as 'sufficient resources' but they must take into account the personal situation of the person concerned. In all cases this amount shall not be higher than the threshold below which nationals of the host Member State become eligible for social assistance, or, where this criterion is not applicable, higher than the minimum social security pension paid by the host Member State.

5. For the registration certificate to be issued to family members of Union citizens, who are themselves Union citizens, Member States may require the following documents to be presented:

(a) a valid identity card or passport;

(b) a document attesting to the existence of a family relationship or of a registered partnership;

(c) where appropriate, the registration certificate of the Union citizen whom they are accompanying or joining;

(d) in cases falling under points (c) and (d) of Article 2(2), documentary evidence that the conditions laid down therein are met;

(e) in cases falling under Article 3(2)(a), a document issued by the relevant authority in the country of origin or country from which they are arriving certifying that they are dependants or members of the household of the Union citizen, or proof of the existence of serious health grounds which strictly require the personal care of the family member by the Union citizen;

(f) in cases falling under Article 3(2)(b), proof of the existence of a durable relationship with the Union citizen.

Article 9

Administrative formalities for family members who are not nationals of a Member State

1. Member States shall issue a residence card to family members of a Union citizen who are not nationals of a Member State, where the planned period of residence is for more than three months.

2. The deadline for submitting the residence card application may not be less than three months from the date of arrival.

3. Failure to comply with the requirement to apply for a residence card may make the person concerned liable to proportionate and non-discriminatory sanctions.

Article 10

Issue of residence cards

1. The right of residence of family members of a Union citizen who are not nationals of a Member State shall be evidenced by the issuing of a document called 'Residence card of a family member of a Union citizen' no later than six months from the date on which they submit the application. A certificate of application for the residence card shall be issued immediately.

2. For the residence card to be issued, Member States shall require presentation of the following documents:

(a) a valid passport;

(b) a document attesting to the existence of a family relationship or of a registered partnership;

(c) the registration certificate or, in the absence of a registration system, any other proof of residence in the host Member State of the Union citizen whom they are accompanying or joining;

(d) in cases falling under points (c) and (d) of Article 2(2), documentary evidence that the conditions laid down therein are met;

(e) in cases falling under Article 3(2)(a), a document issued by the relevant authority in the country of origin or country from which they are arriving certifying that they are dependants or members of the household of the Union citizen, or proof of the existence of serious health grounds which strictly require the personal care of the family member by the Union citizen;

(f) in cases falling under Article 3(2)(b), proof of the existence of a durable relationship with the Union citizen.

Article 11

Validity of the residence card

1. The residence card provided for by Article 10(1) shall be valid for five years from the date of issue or for the envisaged period of residence of the Union citizen, if this period is less than five years.

2. The validity of the residence card shall not be affected by temporary absences not exceeding six months a year, or by absences of a longer duration for compulsory military service or by one absence of a maximum of twelve consecutive months for important reasons such as pregnancy and childbirth, serious illness, study or vocational training, or a posting in another Member State or a third country.

Article 12

Retention of the right of residence by family members in the event of death or departure of the union citizen

1. Without prejudice to the second subparagraph, the Union citizen's death or departure from the host Member State shall not affect the right of residence of his/her family members who are nationals of a Member State.

Before acquiring the right of permanent residence, the persons concerned must meet the conditions laid down in points (a), (b), (c) or (d) of Article 7(1).

2. Without prejudice to the second subparagraph, the Union citizen's death shall not entail loss of the right of residence of his/her family members who are not nationals of a Member State and who have been residing in the host Member State as family members for at least one year before the Union citizen's death.

Before acquiring the right of permanent residence, the right of residence of the persons concerned shall remain subject to the requirement that they are able to show that they are workers or self-employed persons or that they have sufficient resources for themselves and their family members not to become a burden on the social assistance system of the host Member State during their period of residence and have comprehensive sickness insurance cover in the host Member State, or that they are members of the family, already constituted in the host Member State, of a person satisfying these requirements. 'Sufficient resources' shall be as defined in Article 8(4).

Such family members shall retain their right of residence exclusively on a personal basis.

3. The Union citizen's departure from the host Member State or his/her death shall not entail loss of the right of residence of his/her children or of the parent who has actual custody of the children, irrespective of nationality, if the children reside in the host Member State and are enrolled at an educational establishment, for the purpose of studying there, until the completion of their studies.

Article 13

Retention of the right of residence by family members in the event of divorce, annulment of marriage or termination of registered partnership

1. Without prejudice to the second subparagraph, divorce, annulment of the Union citizen's marriage or termination of his/her registered partnership, as referred to in point 2(b) of Article 2 shall not affect the right of residence of his/her family members who are nationals of a Member State.

Before acquiring the right of permanent residence, the persons concerned must meet the conditions laid down in points (a), (b), (c) or (d) of Article 7(1).

2. Without prejudice to the second subparagraph, divorce, annulment of marriage or termination of the registered partnership referred to in point 2(b) of Article 2 shall not entail loss of the right of residence of a Union citizen's family members who are not nationals of a Member State where:

(a) prior to initiation of the divorce or annulment proceedings or termination of the registered partnership referred to in point 2(b) of Article 2, the marriage or registered partnership has lasted at least three years, including one year in the host Member State; or

(b) by agreement between the spouses or the partners referred to in point 2(b) of Article 2 or by court order, the spouse or partner who is not a national of a Member State has custody of the Union citizen's children; or

(c) this is warranted by particularly difficult circumstances, such as having been a victim of domestic violence while the marriage or registered partnership was subsisting; or

(d) by agreement between the spouses or partners referred to in point 2(b) of Article 2 or by court order, the spouse or partner who is not a national of a Member State has the right of access to a minor child, provided that the court has ruled that such access must be in the host Member State, and for as long as is required.

Before acquiring the right of permanent residence, the right of residence of the persons concerned shall remain subject to the requirement that they are able to show that they are workers or self-employed persons or that they have sufficient resources for themselves and their family members not to become a burden on the social assistance system of the host Member State during their period of residence and have comprehensive sickness insurance cover in the host Member State, or that they are members of the family, already constituted in the host Member State, of a person satisfying these requirements. 'Sufficient resources' shall be as defined in Article 8(4).

Such family members shall retain their right of residence exclusively on personal basis.

Article 14

Retention of the right of residence

1. Union citizens and their family members shall have the right of residence provided for in Article 6, as long as they do not become an unreasonable burden on the social assistance system of the host Member State.

2. Union citizens and their family members shall have the right of residence provided for in Articles 7, 12 and 13 as long as they meet the conditions set out therein.

In specific cases where there is a reasonable doubt as to whether a Union citizen or his/her family members satisfies the conditions set out in Articles 7, 12 and 13, Member States may verify if these conditions are fulfilled. This verification shall not be carried out systematically.

3. An expulsion measure shall not be the automatic consequence of a Union citizen's or his or her family member's recourse to the social assistance system of the host Member State.

4. By way of derogation from paragraphs 1 and 2 and without prejudice to the provisions of Chapter VI, an expulsion measure may in no case be adopted against Union citizens or their family members if:

(a) the Union citizens are workers or self-employed persons, or

(b) the Union citizens entered the territory of the host Member State in order to seek employment. In this case, the Union citizens and their family members may not be expelled for as long as the Union citizens can provide evidence that they are continuing to seek employment and that they have a genuine chance of being engaged.

Article 15

Procedural safeguards

1. The procedures provided for by Articles 30 and 31 shall apply by analogy to all decisions restricting free movement of Union citizens and their family members on grounds other than public policy, public security or public health.

2. Expiry of the identity card or passport on the basis of which the person concerned entered the host Member State and was issued with a registration certificate or residence card shall not constitute a ground for expulsion from the host Member State.

3. The host Member State may not impose a ban on entry in the context of an expulsion decision to which paragraph 1 applies.

CHAPTER IV
RIGHT OF PERMANENT RESIDENCE

Section I
Eligibility

Article 16

General rule for Union citizens and their family members

1. Union citizens who have resided legally for a continuous period of five years in the host Member State shall have the right of permanent residence there. This right shall not be subject to the conditions provided for in Chapter III.

2. Paragraph 1 shall apply also to family members who are not nationals of a Member State and have legally resided with the Union citizen in the host Member State for a continuous period of five years.

3. Continuity of residence shall not be affected by temporary absences not exceeding a total of six months a year, or by absences of a longer duration for compulsory military service, or by one absence of a maximum of twelve consecutive months for important reasons such as pregnancy and childbirth, serious illness, study or vocational training, or a posting in another Member State or a third country.

4. Once acquired, the right of permanent residence shall be lost only through absence from the host Member State for a period exceeding two consecutive years.

Article 17

Exemptions for persons no longer working in the host Member State and their family members

1. By way of derogation from Article 16, the right of permanent residence in the host Member State shall be enjoyed before completion of a continuous period of five years of residence by:

(a) workers or self-employed persons who, at the time they stop working, have reached the age laid down by the law of that Member State for entitlement to an old age pension or workers who cease paid employment to take early retirement, provided that they have been working in that Member State for at least the preceding twelve months and have resided there continuously for more than three years.

If the law of the host Member State does not grant the right to an old age pension to certain categories of self-employed persons, the age condition shall be deemed to have been met once the person concerned has reached the age of 60;

(b) workers or self-employed persons who have resided continuously in the host Member State for more than two years and stop working there as a result of permanent incapacity to work.

If such incapacity is the result of an accident at work or an occupational disease entitling the person concerned to a benefit payable in full or in part by an institution in the host Member State, no condition shall be imposed as to length of residence;

(c) workers or self-employed persons who, after three years of continuous employment and residence in the host Member State, work in an employed or self-employed capacity in another Member State, while retaining their place of residence in the host Member State, to which they return, as a rule, each day or at least once a week.

For the purposes of entitlement to the rights referred to in points (a) and (b), periods of employment spent in the Member State in which the person concerned is working shall be regarded as having been spent in the host Member State.

Periods of involuntary unemployment duly recorded by the relevant employment office, periods not worked for reasons not of the person's own making and absences from work or cessation of work due to illness or accident shall be regarded as periods of employment.

2. The conditions as to length of residence and employment laid down in point (a) of paragraph 1 and the condition as to length of residence laid down in point (b) of paragraph 1 shall not apply if the worker's or the self-employed person's spouse or partner as referred to in point 2(b) of Article 2 is a national of the host Member State or has lost the nationality of that Member State by marriage to that worker or self-employed person.

3. Irrespective of nationality, the family members of a worker or a self-employed person who are residing with him in the territory of the host Member State shall have the right of permanent residence in that Member State, if the worker or self-employed person has acquired himself the right of permanent residence in that Member State on the basis of paragraph 1.

4. If, however, the worker or self-employed person dies while still working but before acquiring permanent residence status in the host Member State on the basis of paragraph 1, his family members who are residing with him in the host Member State shall acquire the right of permanent residence there, on condition that:

(a) the worker or self-employed person had, at the time of death, resided continuously on the territory of that Member State for two years; or

(b) the death resulted from an accident at work or an occupational disease; or

(c) the surviving spouse lost the nationality of that Member State following marriage to the worker or self-employed person.

Article 18

Acquisition of the right of permanent residence by certain family members who are not nationals of a Member State

Without prejudice to Article 17, the family members of a Union citizen to whom Articles 12(2) and 13(2) apply, who satisfy the conditions laid down therein, shall acquire the right of permanent residence after residing legally for a period of five consecutive years in the host Member State.

Section II

Administrative Formalities

Article 19

Document certifying permanent residence for Union citizens

1. Upon application Member States shall issue Union citizens entitled to permanent residence, after having verified duration of residence, with a document certifying permanent residence.

2. The document certifying permanent residence shall be issued as soon as possible.

Article 20

Permanent residence card for family members who are not nationals of a Member State

1. Member States shall issue family members who are not nationals of a Member State entitled to permanent residence with a permanent residence card within six months of the submission of the application. The permanent residence card shall be renewable automatically every ten years.

2. The application for a permanent residence card shall be submitted before the residence card expires. Failure to comply with the requirement to apply for a permanent residence card may render the person concerned liable to proportionate and non-discriminatory sanctions.

3. Interruption in residence not exceeding two consecutive years shall not affect the validity of the permanent residence card.

Article 21

Continuity of residence

For the purposes of this Directive, continuity of residence may be attested by any means of proof in use in the host Member State. Continuity of residence is broken by any expulsion decision duly enforced against the person concerned.

Chapter V

Provisions Common to the Right of Residence and the Right of Permanent Residence

Article 22

Territorial scope

The right of residence and the right of permanent residence shall cover the whole territory of the host Member State. Member States may impose territorial restrictions on the right of residence and the right of permanent residence only where the same restrictions apply to their own nationals.

Article 23

Related rights

Irrespective of nationality, the family members of a Union citizen who have the right of residence or the right of permanent residence in a Member State shall be entitled to take up employment or self-employment there.

Article 24

Equal treatment

1. Subject to such specific provisions as are expressly provided for in the Treaty and secondary law, all Union citizens residing on the basis of this Directive in the territory of the host Member State shall enjoy equal treatment with the nationals of that Member State within the scope of the Treaty. The benefit of this right shall be extended to family members who are not nationals of a Member State and who have the right of residence or permanent residence.

2. By way of derogation from paragraph 1, the host Member State shall not be obliged to confer entitlement to social assistance during the first three months of residence or, where appropriate, the longer period provided for in Article 14(4)(b), nor shall it be obliged, prior to acquisition of the right of permanent residence, to grant maintenance aid for studies, including vocational training, consisting in student grants or student loans to persons other than workers, self-employed persons, persons who retain such status and members of their families.

Article 25

General provisions concerning residence documents

1. Possession of a registration certificate as referred to in Article 8, of a document certifying permanent residence, of a certificate attesting submission of an application for a family member residence card, of a residence card or of a permanent residence card, may under no circumstances be made a precondition for the exercise of a right or the completion of an administrative formality, as entitlement to rights may be attested by any other means of proof.

2. All documents mentioned in paragraph 1 shall be issued free of charge or for a charge not exceeding that imposed on nationals for the issuing of similar documents.

Article 26

Checks

Member States may carry out checks on compliance with any requirement deriving from their national legislation for non-nationals always to carry their registration certificate or residence card, provided that the same requirement applies to their own nationals as regards their identity card. In the event of failure to comply with this requirement, Member States may impose the same sanctions as those imposed on their own nationals for failure to carry their identity card.

Chapter VI
Restrictions on the Right of Entry and the Right of Residence on Grounds of Public Policy, Public Security or Public Health

Article 27

General principles

1. Subject to the provisions of this Chapter, Member States may restrict the freedom of movement and residence of Union citizens and their family members, irrespective of nationality, on grounds of public policy, public security or public health. These grounds shall not be invoked to serve economic ends.

2. Measures taken on grounds of public policy or public security shall comply with the principle of proportionality and shall be based exclusively on the personal conduct of the individual concerned. Previous criminal convictions shall not in themselves constitute grounds for taking such measures.

The personal conduct of the individual concerned must represent a genuine, present and sufficiently serious threat affecting one of the fundamental interests of society. Justifications that are isolated from the particulars of the case or that rely on considerations of general prevention shall not be accepted.

3. In order to ascertain whether the person concerned represents a danger for public policy or public security, when issuing the registration certificate or, in the absence of a registration system, not later than three months from the date of arrival of the person concerned on its territory or from the date of reporting his/her presence within the territory, as provided for in Article 5(5), or when issuing the residence card, the host Member State may, should it consider this essential, request the Member State of origin and, if need be, other Member States to provide information concerning any previous police record the person concerned may have. Such enquiries shall not be made as a matter of routine. The Member State consulted shall give its reply within two months.

4. The Member State which issued the passport or identity card shall allow the holder of the document who has been expelled on grounds of public policy, public security, or public health from another Member State to re-enter its territory without any formality even if the document is no longer valid or the nationality of the holder is in dispute.

Article 28
Protection against expulsion

1. Before taking an expulsion decision on grounds of public policy or public security, the host Member State shall take account of considerations such as how long the individual concerned has resided on its territory, his/her age, state of health, family and economic situation, social and cultural integration into the host Member State and the extent of his/her links with the country of origin.

2. The host Member State may not take an expulsion decision against Union citizens or their family members, irrespective of nationality, who have the right of permanent residence on its territory, except on serious grounds of public policy or public security.

3. An expulsion decision may not be taken against Union citizens, except if the decision is based on imperative grounds of public security, as defined by Member States, if they:

(a) have resided in the host Member State for the previous ten years; or

(b) are a minor, except if the expulsion is necessary for the best interests of the child, as provided for in the United Nations Convention on the Rights of the Child of 20 November 1989.

Article 29

Public health

1. The only diseases justifying measures restricting freedom of movement shall be the diseases with epidemic potential as defined by the relevant instruments of the World Health Organisation and other infectious diseases or contagious parasitic diseases if they are the subject of protection provisions applying to nationals of the host Member State.

2. Diseases occurring after a three-month period from the date of arrival shall not constitute grounds for expulsion from the territory.

3. Where there are serious indications that it is necessary, Member States may, within three months of the date of arrival, require persons entitled to the right of residence to undergo, free of charge, a medical examination to certify that they are not suffering from any of the conditions referred to in paragraph 1. Such medical examinations may not be required as a matter of routine.

Article 30

Notification of decisions

1. The persons concerned shall be notified in writing of any decision taken under Article 27(1), in such a way that they are able to comprehend its content and the implications for them.

2. The persons concerned shall be informed, precisely and in full, of the public policy, public security or public health grounds on which the decision taken in their case is based, unless this is contrary to the interests of State security.

3. The notification shall specify the court or administrative authority with which the person concerned may lodge an appeal, the time limit for the appeal and, where applicable, the time allowed for the person to leave the territory of the Member State. Save in duly substantiated cases of urgency, the time allowed to leave the territory shall be not less than one month from the date of notification.

Article 31

Procedural safeguards

1. The persons concerned shall have access to judicial and, where appropriate, administrative redress procedures in the host Member State to appeal against or seek review of any decision taken against them on the grounds of public policy, public security or public health.

2. Where the application for appeal against or judicial review of the expulsion decision is accompanied by an application for an interim order to suspend enforcement of that decision, actual removal from the territory may not take place until such time as the decision on the interim order has been taken, except:

— where the expulsion decision is based on a previous judicial decision; or

— where the persons concerned have had previous access to judicial review; or

— where the expulsion decision is based on imperative grounds of public security under Article 28(3).

3. The redress procedures shall allow for an examination of the legality of the decision, as well as of the facts and circumstances on which the proposed measure is based. They shall ensure that the decision is not disproportionate, particularly in view of the requirements laid down in Article 28.

4. Member States may exclude the individual concerned from their territory pending the redress procedure, but they may not prevent the individual from submitting his/her defence in person, except when his/her appearance may cause serious troubles to public policy or public security or when the appeal or judicial review concerns a denial of entry to the territory.

Article 32

Duration of exclusion orders

1. Persons excluded on grounds of public policy or public security may submit an application for lifting of the exclusion order after a reasonable period, depending on the circumstances, and in any event after three years from enforcement of the final exclusion order which has been validly adopted in accordance with Community law, by putting forward arguments to establish that there has been a material change in the circumstances which justified the decision ordering their exclusion.

The Member State concerned shall reach a decision on this application within six months of its submission.

2. The persons referred to in paragraph 1 shall have no right of entry to the territory of the Member State concerned while their application is being considered.

Article 33

Expulsion as a penalty or legal consequence

1. Expulsion orders may not be issued by the host Member State as a penalty or legal consequence of a custodial penalty, unless they conform to the requirements of Articles 27, 28 and 29.

2. If an expulsion order, as provided for in paragraph 1, is enforced more than two years after it was issued, the Member State shall check that the individual concerned is currently and genuinely a threat to public policy or public security and shall assess whether there has been any material change in the circumstances since the expulsion order was issued.

CHAPTER VII
FINAL PROVISIONS

Article 34

Publicity

Member States shall disseminate information concerning the rights and obligations of Union citizens and their family members on the subjects covered by this Directive, particularly by means of awareness-raising campaigns conducted through national and local media and other means of communication.

Article 35

Abuse of rights

Member States may adopt the necessary measures to refuse, terminate or withdraw any right conferred by this Directive in the case of abuse of rights or fraud, such as marriages of convenience. Any such measure shall be proportionate and subject to the procedural safeguards provided for in Articles 30 and 31.

Article 36

Sanctions

Member States shall lay down provisions on the sanctions applicable to breaches of national rules adopted for the implementation of this Directive and shall take the measures required for their application. The sanctions laid down shall be effective and proportionate. Member States shall notify the Commission of these provisions not later than 30 April 2006 and as promptly as possible in the case of any subsequent changes.

Article 37

More favourable national provisions

The provisions of this Directive shall not affect any laws, regulations or administrative provisions laid down by a Member State which would be more favourable to the persons covered by this Directive.

Article 38

Repeals

1. …

2. Directives 64/221/EEC, 68/360/EEC, 72/194/EEC, 73/148/EEC, 75/34/EEC, 75/35/EEC, 90/364/EEC, 90/365/EEC and 93/96/EEC shall be repealed with effect from 30 April 2006.

3. References made to the repealed provisions and Directives shall be construed as being made to this Directive.

Note: Paragraph 1 repealed from 16 June 2011 by Regulation (EU) 492/2011.

Article 39

Report

No later than 30 April 2008 the Commission shall submit a report on the application of this Directive to the European Parliament and the Council, together with any necessary proposals, notably on the opportunity to extend the period of time during which Union citizens and their family members may reside in the territory of the host Member State without any conditions. The Member States shall provide the Commission with the information needed to produce the report.

Article 40

Transposition

1. Member States shall bring into force the laws, regulations and administrative provisions necessary to comply with this Directive by 30 April 2006.

When Member States adopt those measures, they shall contain a reference to this Directive or shall be accompanied by such a reference on the occasion of their official publication. The methods of making such reference shall be laid down by the Member States.

2. Member States shall communicate to the Commission the text of the provisions of national law which they adopt in the field covered by this Directive together with a table showing how the provisions of this Directive correspond to the national provisions adopted.

Article 41

Entry into force

This Directive shall enter into force on the day of its publication in the *Official Journal of the European Union*.

Article 42

Addresses

This Directive is addressed to the Member States.
Done at Brussels 29 April 2004.

For the European Parliament	For the Council
The President	The President
P.COX	M.McDOWELL

Regulation (EU) No. 492/2011 of the European Parliament and of the Council of 5 April 2011 on freedom of movement for workers within the Union (codification)

Regulation (EU) No. 492/2011 (Freedom of Movement for Workers)

(Text with EEA relevance)

THE EUROPEAN PARLIAMENT AND THE COUNCIL OF THE EUROPEAN UNION,

Having regard to the Treaty on the Functioning of the European Union, and in particular Article 46 thereof,

Having regard to the proposal from the European Commission,

After transmission of the draft legislative act to the national parliaments,

Having regard to the opinion of the European Economic and Social Committee,[1]

Acting in accordance with the ordinary legislative procedure,[2]

Whereas:

(1) Regulation (EEC) No. 1612/68 of the Council of 15 October 1968 on freedom of movement for workers within the Community[3] has been substantially amended several times.[4] In the interests of clarity and rationality the said Regulation should be codified.

(2) Freedom of movement for workers should be secured within the Union. The attainment of this objective entails the abolition of any discrimination based on nationality between workers of the Member States as regards employment, remuneration and other conditions of work and employment, as well as the right of such workers to move freely within the Union in order to pursue activities as employed persons subject to any limitations justified on grounds of public policy, public security or public health.

(3) Provisions should be laid down to enable the objectives laid down in Articles 45 and 46 of the Treaty on the Functioning of the European Union in the field of freedom of movement to be achieved.

(4) Freedom of movement constitutes a fundamental right of workers and their families. Mobility of labour within the Union must be one of the means by which workers are guaranteed the possibility of improving their living and working conditions and promoting their social advancement, while helping to satisfy the requirements of the economies of the Member States. The right of all workers in the Member States to pursue the activity of their choice within the Union should be affirmed.

(5) Such right should be enjoyed without discrimination by permanent, seasonal and frontier workers and by those who pursue their activities for the purpose of providing services.

[1] OJ C 44, 11.2.2011, p. 170.

[2] Position of the European Parliament of 7 September 2010 (not yet published in the Official Journal) and decision of the Council of 21 March 2011.

[3] OJ L 257, 19.10.1968, p. 2.

[4] See Annex I.

(6) The right of freedom of movement, in order that it may be exercised, by objective standards, in freedom and dignity, requires that equality of treatment be ensured in fact and in law in respect of all matters relating to the actual pursuit of activities as employed persons and to eligibility for housing, and also that obstacles to the mobility of workers be eliminated, in particular as regards the conditions for the integration of the worker's family into the host country.

(7) The principle of non-discrimination between workers in the Union means that all nationals of Member States have the same priority as regards employment as is enjoyed by national workers.

(8) The machinery for vacancy clearance, in particular by means of direct cooperation between the central employment services and also between the regional services, as well as by coordination of the exchange of information, ensures in a general way a clearer picture of the labour market. Workers wishing to move should also be regularly informed of living and working conditions.

(9) Close links exist between freedom of movement for workers, employment and vocational training, particularly where the latter aims at putting workers in a position to take up concrete offers of employment from other regions of the Union. Such links make it necessary that the problems arising in this connection should no longer be studied in isolation but viewed as interdependent, account also being taken of the problems of employment at the regional level. It is therefore necessary to direct the efforts of Member States toward coordinating their employment policies,

HAVE ADOPTED THIS REGULATION:

CHAPTER I

EMPLOYMENT, EQUAL TREATMENT AND WORKERS' FAMILIES

SECTION 1

Eligibility for Employment

[...]

Note: Article 1 omitted from 31 December 2020 by the Immigration and Social Security Co-ordination (EU Withdrawal) Act 2020 c. 20 Sch.1(2) para.4(1).

Article 2

Any national of a Member State and any employer pursuing an activity in the territory of a Member State may exchange their applications for and offers of employment, and may conclude and perform contracts of employment in accordance with the provisions in force laid down by law, regulation or administrative action, without any discrimination resulting therefrom.

Note: Article 2 ceases to apply from 31 December 2020 so far as it is inconsistent with any provision made by or under the Immigration Acts, or is otherwise capable of affecting the interpretation, application or operation of any such provision by Immigration and Social Security Co-ordination (EU Withdrawal) Act 2020 c. 20, Sch. 1(2) para. 4(2).

Article 3

1. Under this Regulation, provisions laid down by law, regulation or administrative action or administrative practices of a Member State shall not apply:

(a) where they limit application for and offers of employment, or the right of foreign nationals to take up and pursue employment or subject these to conditions not applicable in respect of their own nationals; or

(b) where, though applicable irrespective of nationality, their exclusive or principal aim or effect is to keep nationals of other Member States away from the employment offered.

The first subparagraph shall not apply to conditions relating to linguistic knowledge required by reason of the nature of the post to be filled.

2. There shall be included in particular among the provisions or practices of a Member State referred to in the first subparagraph of paragraph 1 those which:

(a) prescribe a special recruitment procedure for foreign nationals;

(b) limit or restrict the advertising of vacancies in the press or through any other medium or subject it to conditions other than those applicable in respect of employers pursuing their activities in the territory of that Member State;

(c) subject eligibility for employment to conditions of registration with employment offices or impede recruitment of individual workers, where persons who do not reside in the territory of that State are concerned.

Note: Article 3 ceases to apply from 31 December 2020 so far as it is inconsistent with any provision made by or under the Immigration Acts, or is otherwise capable of affecting the interpretation, application or operation of any such provision by Immigration and Social Security Co-ordination (EU Withdrawal) Act 2020 c. 20, Sch. 1(2) para. 4(2).

Article 4

1. Provisions laid down by law, regulation or administrative action of the Member States which restrict by number or percentage the employment of foreign nationals in any undertaking, branch of activity or region, or at a national level, shall not apply to nationals of the other Member States.

2. When in a Member State the granting of any benefit to undertakings is subject to a minimum percentage of national workers being employed, nationals of the other Member States shall be counted as national workers, subject to Directive 2005/36/EC of the European Parliament and of the Council of 7 September 2005 on the recognition of professional qualifications.[5]

Note: Article 4 ceases to apply from 31 December 2020 so far as it is inconsistent with any provision made by or under the Immigration Acts, or is otherwise capable of affecting the interpretation, application or operation of any such provision by Immigration and Social Security Co-ordination (EU Withdrawal) Act 2020 c. 20, Sch. 1(2) para. 4(2).

[5] OJ L 255, 30.9.2005, p. 22.

Article 5

A national of a Member State who seeks employment in the territory of another Member State shall receive the same assistance there as that afforded by the employment offices in that State to their own nationals seeking employment.

Note: Article 5 ceases to apply from 31 December 2020 so far as it is inconsistent with any provision made by or under the Immigration Acts, or is otherwise capable of affecting the interpretation, application or operation of any such provision by Immigration and Social Security Co-ordination (EU Withdrawal) Act 2020 c. 20, Sch. 1(2) para. 4(2).

Article 6

1. The engagement and recruitment of a national of one Member State for a post in another Member State shall not depend on medical, vocational or other criteria which are discriminatory on grounds of nationality by comparison with those applied to nationals of the other Member State who wish to pursue the same activity.

2. A national who holds an offer in his name from an employer in a Member State other than that of which he is a national may have to undergo a vocational test, if the employer expressly requests this when making his offer of employment.

Note: Article 6 ceases to apply from 31 December 2020 so far as it is inconsistent with any provision made by or under the Immigration Acts, or is otherwise capable of affecting the interpretation, application or operation of any such provision by Immigration and Social Security Co-ordination (EU Withdrawal) Act 2020 c. 20, Sch. 1(2) para. 4(2).

Section 2
Employment and Equality of Treatment

Article 7

1. A worker who is a national of a Member State may not, in the territory of another Member State, be treated differently from national workers by reason of his nationality in respect of any conditions of employment and work, in particular as regards remuneration, dismissal, and, should he become unemployed, reinstatement or re-employment.

2. He shall enjoy the same social and tax advantages as national workers.

3. He shall also, by virtue of the same right and under the same conditions as national workers, have access to training in vocational schools and retraining centres.

4. Any clause of a collective or individual agreement or of any other collective regulation concerning eligibility for employment, remuneration and other conditions of work or dismissal shall be null and void in so far as it lays down or authorises discriminatory conditions in respect of workers who are nationals of the other Member States.

Note: Article 7 ceases to apply from 31 December 2020 so far as it is inconsistent with any provision made by or under the Immigration Acts, or is otherwise capable of affecting the interpretation, application or operation of any such provision by Immigration and Social Security Co-ordination (EU Withdrawal) Act 2020 c. 20, Sch. 1(2) para. 4(2).

Article 8

A worker who is a national of a Member State and who is employed in the territory of another Member State shall enjoy equality of treatment as regards membership of trade unions and the exercise of rights attaching thereto, including the right to vote and to be eligible for the administration or management posts of a trade union. He may be excluded from taking part in the management of bodies governed by public law and from holding an office governed by public law. Furthermore, he shall have the right of eligibility for workers' representative bodies in the undertaking.

The first paragraph of this Article shall not affect laws or regulations in certain Member States which grant more extensive rights to workers coming from the other Member States.

Note: Article 8 ceases to apply from 31 December 2020 so far as it is inconsistent with any provision made by or under the Immigration Acts, or is otherwise capable of affecting the interpretation, application or operation of any such provision by Immigration and Social Security Co-ordination (EU Withdrawal) Act 2020 c. 20, Sch. 1(2) para. 4(2).

Article 9

1. A worker who is a national of a Member State and who is employed in the territory of another Member State shall enjoy all the rights and benefits accorded to national workers in matters of housing, including ownership of the housing he needs.

2. A worker referred to in paragraph 1 may, with the same right as nationals, put his name down on the housing lists in the region in which he is employed, where such lists exist, and shall enjoy the resultant benefits and priorities.

If his family has remained in the country whence he came, they shall be considered for this purpose as residing in the said region, where national workers benefit from a similar presumption.

Note: Article 9 ceases to apply from 31 December 2020 so far as it is inconsistent with any provision made by or under the Immigration Acts, or is otherwise capable of affecting the interpretation, application or operation of any such provision by Immigration and Social Security Co-ordination (EU Withdrawal) Act 2020 c. 20, Sch. 1(2) para. 4(2).

Section 3

Workers' Families

Article 10

The children of a national of a Member State who is or has been employed in the territory of another Member State shall be admitted to that State's general educational, apprenticeship and vocational training courses under the same conditions as the nationals of that State, if such children are residing in its territory.

Member States shall encourage all efforts to enable such children to attend these courses under the best possible conditions.

Note: Article 10 ceases to apply from 31 December 2020 so far as it is inconsistent with any provision made by or under the Immigration Acts, or is otherwise capable of affecting the interpretation, application or operation of any such provision by Immigration and Social Security Co-ordination (EU Withdrawal) Act 2020 c. 20, Sch. 1(2) para. 4(2).

CHAPTER II

CLEARANCE OF VACANCIES AND APPLICATIONS FOR EMPLOYMENT

SECTION 1

Cooperation between the Member States and with the Commission

Article 11

. . .

Note: Article 11 deleted from 12 May 2016 by Article 39 of Regulation (EU) 2016/589.

Article 12

. . .

Note: Article 12 deleted from 12 May 2016 by Article 39 of Regulation (EU) 2016/589.

SECTION 2

Machinery for Vacancy Clearance

Article 13

1 . . . .

2 . . . .

Note: Paragraph 2 deleted from 12 May 2016 and paragraph 1 deleted from 13 May 2018 by Article 39 of Regulation (EU) 2016/589.

Article 14

. . .

Note: Article 14 deleted from 12 May 2016 by Article 39 of Regulation (EU) 2016/589.

Article 15

. . .

Note: Article 15 deleted from 12 May 2016 by Article 39 of Regulation (EU) 2016/589.

Article 16

. . .

Note: Article 16 deleted from 12 May 2016 by Article 39 of Regulation (EU) 2016/589.

SECTION 3

Measures for Controlling the Balance of the Labour Market

Article 17

. . .

Note: Article 17 deleted from 12 May 2016 by Article 39 of Regulation (EU) 2016/589.

SECTION 4

European Coordination Office

Article 18

...

Note: Article 18 deleted from 12 May 2016 by Article 39 of Regulation (EU) 2016/589.

Article 19

...

Note: Article 19 deleted from 12 May 2016 by Article 39 of Regulation (EU) 2016/589.

Article 20

...

Note: Article 20 deleted from 12 May 2016 by Article 39 of Regulation (EU) 2016/589.

CHAPTER III

COMMITTEES FOR ENSURING CLOSE COOPERATION BETWEEN THE MEMBER STATES IN MATTERS CONCERNING THE FREEDOM OF MOVEMENT OF WORKERS AND THEIR EMPLOYMENT

SECTION 1

The Advisory Committee

Article 21

The Advisory Committee shall be responsible for assisting the Commission in the examination of any questions arising from the application of the Treaty on the Functioning of the European Union and measures taken in pursuance thereof, in matters concerning the freedom of movement of workers and their employment.

Article 22

The Advisory Committee shall be responsible in particular for:

(a) examining problems concerning freedom of movement and employment within the framework of national manpower policies, with a view to coordinating the employment policies of the Member States at Union level, thus contributing to the development of the economies and to an improved balance of the labour market;

(b) making a general study of the effects of implementing this Regulation and any supplementary measures;

(c) submitting to the Commission any reasoned proposals for revising this Regulation;

(d) delivering, either at the request of the Commission or on its own initiative, reasoned opinions on general questions or on questions of principle, in particular on exchange of information concerning developments in the labour market, on the movement of workers between Member States, on programmes or measures to develop vocational guidance and vocational training which are likely to increase the possibilities of freedom of movement and employment, and on all forms of assistance to workers and their families, including social assistance and the housing of workers.

Article 23

1. The Advisory Committee shall be composed of six members for each Member State, two of whom shall represent the Government, two the trade unions and two the employers' associations.

2. For each of the categories referred to in paragraph 1, one alternate member shall be appointed by each Member State.

3. The term of office of the members and their alternates shall be 2 years. Their appointments shall be renewable.

On expiry of their term of office, the members and their alternates shall remain in office until replaced or until their appointments are renewed.

Article 24

The members of the Advisory Committee and their alternates shall be appointed by the Council, which shall endeavour, when selecting representatives of trade unions and employers' associations, to achieve adequate representation on the Committee of the various economic sectors concerned.

The list of members and their alternates shall be published by the Council for information in the *Official Journal of the European Union*.

Article 25

The Advisory Committee shall be chaired by a member of the Commission or his representative. The Chairman shall not vote. The Committee shall meet at least twice a year. It shall be convened by its Chairman, either on his own initiative, or at the request of at least one third of the members.

Secretarial services shall be provided for the Committee by the Commission.

Article 26

The Chairman may invite individuals or representatives of bodies with wide experience in the field of employment or movement of workers to take part in meetings as observers or as experts. The Chairman may be assisted by expert advisers.

[The European Labour Authority established by Regulation (EU) 2019/1149 of the European Parliament and of the Council[6] shall participate in the meetings of the Advisory Committee as an observer, providing technical input and expertise as relevant.]

Note: Paragraph added from 31 July 2019 by Article 46 of Regulation (EU) 2019/1149.

[6] Regulation (EU) 2019/1149 of the European Parliament and of the Council of 20 June 2019 estalishing a European Labour Authority, amending Regulations (EC) No 883/2004, (EU) No 492/2011, and (EU) 2016/589 and repealing Decision (EU) 2016/344 (OJ L 186, 11.7.2019, p. 21).'

Article 27

1. An opinion delivered by the Advisory Committee shall not be valid unless two thirds of the members are present.

2. Opinions shall state the reasons on which they are based; they shall be delivered by an absolute majority of the votes validly cast; they shall be accompanied by a written statement of the views expressed by the minority, when the latter so requests.

Article 28

The Advisory Committee shall establish its working methods by rules of procedure which shall enter into force after the Council, having received an opinion from the Commission, has given its approval. The entry into force of any amendment that the Committee decides to make thereto shall be subject to the same procedure.

SECTION 2

The Technical Committee

[Article 29

The Technical Committee shall be responsible for assisting the Commission in the preparation, promotion and follow-up of all technical work and measures for giving effect to this Regulation and any supplementary measures.

Article 30

The Technical Committee shall be responsible in particular for:

(a) promoting and advancing cooperation between the public authorities concerned in the Member States on all technical questions relating to freedom of movement of workers and their employment;

(b) formulating procedures for the organisation of the joint activities of the public authorities concerned;

(c) facilitating the gathering of information likely to be of use to the Commission and the undertaking of the studies and research provided for in this Regulation, and encouraging exchange of information and experience between the administrative bodies concerned;

(d) investigating at a technical level the harmonisation of the criteria by which Member States assess the state of their labour markets.

Article 31

1. The Technical Committee shall be composed of representatives of the Governments of the Member States. Each Government shall appoint as member of the Technical Committee one of the members who represent it on the Advisory Committee.

2. Each Government shall appoint an alternate from among its other representatives—members or alternates — on the Advisory Committee.

Article 32

The Technical Committee shall be chaired by a member of the Commission or his representative. The Chairman shall not vote. The Chairman and the members of the Committee may be assisted by expert advisers.

Secretarial services shall be provided for the Committee by the Commission.

Article 33

The proposals and opinions formulated by the Technical Committee shall be submitted to the Commission, and the Advisory Committee shall be informed thereof. Any such proposals and opinions shall be accompanied by a written statement of the views expressed by the various members of the Technical Committee, when the latter so request.

Article 34

The Technical Committee shall establish its working methods by rules of procedure which shall enter into force after the Council, having received an opinion from the Commission, has given its approval. The entry into force of any amendment which the Committee decides to make thereto shall be subject to the same procedure.]

Note: Articles 29-34 deleted with effect on the date when the Authority becomes operational in accordance with Article 44(1) of Regulation (EU) 2019/1149 and by 1 August 2021.

Chapter IV

Final Provisions

[Article 35

The rules of procedure of the Advisory Committee in force on 8 November 1968 shall continue to apply.]

Note: Article 35 substituted from 31 July 2019 by Article 46 of Regulation (EU) 2019/1149.

Article 36

1. This Regulation shall not affect the provisions of the Treaty establishing the European Atomic Energy Community which deal with eligibility for skilled employment in the field of nuclear energy, nor any measures taken in pursuance of that Treaty.

Nevertheless, this Regulation shall apply to the category of workers referred to in the first subparagraph and to members of their families in so far as their legal position is not governed by the above-mentioned Treaty or measures.

2. This Regulation shall not affect measures taken in accordance with Article 48 of the Treaty on the Functioning of the European Union.

3. This Regulation shall not affect the obligations of Member States arising out of special relations or future agreements with certain non-European countries or territories, based on institutional ties existing on 8 November 1968, or agreements in existence on

8 November 1968 with certain non-European countries or territories, based on institutional ties between them.

Workers from such countries or territories who, in accordance with this provision, are pursuing activities as employed persons in the territory of one of those Member States may not invoke the benefit of the provisions of this Regulation in the territory of the other Member States.

Article 37

Member States shall, for information purposes, communicate to the Commission the texts of agreements, conventions or arrangements concluded between them in the manpower field between the date of their being signed and that of their entry into force.

Article 38

…

Note: Article 38 deleted from 12 May 2016 by Article 39 of Regulation (EU) 2016/589.

[Article 39

The administrative expenditure of the Advisory Committee shall be included in the general budget of the European Union in the section relating to the Commission.]

Note: Article 39 replaced from 31 July 2019 by Article 46 of Regulation 2019/1149.

Article 40

This Regulation shall apply to the Member States and to their nationals, without prejudice to Articles 2 and 3.

Article 41

Regulation (EEC) No. 1612/68 is hereby repealed.

References to the repealed Regulation shall be construed as references to this Regulation and shall be read in accordance with the correlation table in Annex II.

Article 42

This Regulation shall enter into force on the 20th day following its publication in the *Official Journal of the European Union*.

This Regulation shall be binding in its entirety and directly applicable in all Member States.

Done at Strasbourg, 5 April 2011.

For the European Parliament	For the Council
The President	The President
J.BUZEK	GYŐRI E.

Annex I

Repealed Regulation with list of its Successive Amendments

Council Regulation (EEC) No. 1612/68 (OJ L 257, 19.10.1968, p. 2)	
Council Regulation (EEC) No. 312/76 (OJ L 39, 14.2.1976, p. 2)	
Council Regulation (EEC) No. 2434/92 (OJ L 245, 26.8.1992, p. 1)	
Directive 2004/38/EC of the European Parliament and of the Council (OJ L 158, 30.4.2004, p. 77)	Only Article 38(1)

Annex II

Correlation Table

Regulation (EEC) No. 1612/68	This Regulation
Part I	Chapter I
Title I	Section 1
Article 1	Article 1
Article 2	Article 2
Article 3(1), first subparagraph	Article 3(1), first subparagraph
Article 3(1), first subparagraph, first indent	Article 3(1), first subparagraph, point (a)
Article 3(1), first subparagraph, second indent	Article 3(1), first subparagraph, point (b)
Article 3(1), second subparagraph	Article 3(1), second subparagraph
Article 3(2)	Article 3(2)
Article 4	Article 4
Article 5	Article 5
Article 6	Article 6
Title II	Section 2
Article 7	Article 7
Article 8(1)	Article 8
Article 9	Article 9
Title III	Section 3
Article 12	Article 10
Part II	Chapter II
Title I	Section 1
Article 13	Article 11
Article 14	Article 12
Title II	Section 2

Article 15	Article 13
Article 16	Article 14
Article 17	Article 15
Article 18	Article 16
Title III	Section 3
Article 19	Article 17
Title IV	Section 4
Article 21	Article 18
Article 22	Article 19
Article 23	Article 20
Part III	Chapter III
Title I	Section 1
Article 24	Article 21
Article 25	Article 22
Article 26	Article 23
Article 27	Article 24
Article 28	Article 25
Article 29	Article 26
Article 30	Article 27
Article 31	Article 28
Title II	Section 2
Article 32	Article 29
Article 33	Article 30
Article 34	Article 31
Article 35	Article 32
Article 36	Article 33
Article 37	Article 34
Part IV	Chapter IV
Title I	—
Article 38	—
Article 39	Article 35
Article 40	—
Article 41	—
Title II	—
Article 42(1)	Article 36(1)
Article 42(2)	Article 36(2)

Article 42(3), first subparagraph, first and second indents	Article 36(3), first subparagraph
Article 42(3), second subparagraph	Article 36(3), second subparagraph
Article 43	Article 37
Article 44	Article 38
Article 45	—
Article 46	Article 39
Article 47	Article 40
—	Article 41
Article 48	Article 42
—	Annex I
—	Annex II

INTERNATIONAL MATERIALS[1]

[1] The following materials are in the public domain and are reproduced by Oxford University Press with confirmation from United Nations Publications: 1951 Convention Relating to the Status of Refugees; 1967 Protocol Relating to the Status of Refugees; State Parties to the 1951 Convention Relating to the Status of Refugees and the 1967 Protocol; Convention Relating to the Status of Stateless Persons; Convention Against Torture and Other Cruel, Inhuman or Degrading Treatment or Punishment. http://www.ohchr.org, Copyright © United Nations.

1951 Convention Relating to the Status of Refugees[1]

Preamble

The High Contracting Parties

CONSIDERING that the Charter of the United Nations and the Universal Declaration of Human Rights approved on 10 December 1948 by the General Assembly have affirmed the principle that human beings shall enjoy fundamental rights and freedoms without discrimination,

CONSIDERING that the United Nations has, on various occasions, manifested its profound concern for refugees and endeavored to assure refugees the widest possible exercise of these fundamental rights and freedoms,

CONSIDERING that it is desirable to revise and consolidate previous international agreements relating to the status of refugees and to extend the scope of and the protection accorded by such instruments by means of a new agreement,

CONSIDERING that the grant of asylum may place unduly heavy burdens on certain countries, and that a satisfactory solution of a problem of which the United Nations has recognized the international scope and nature cannot therefore be achieved without international co-operation,

EXPRESSING the wish that all States, recognizing the social and humanitarian nature of the problem of refugees, will do everything within their power to prevent this problem from becoming a cause of tension between States,

NOTING that the United Nations High Commissioner for Refugees is charged with the task of supervising international conventions providing for the protection of refugees, and recognizing that the effective co-ordination of measures taken to deal with this problem will depend upon the co-operation of States with the High Commissioner,

HAVE AGREED as follows:

Chapter I

General Provisions

Article 1 Definition of the term 'Refugee'

A. For the purposes of the present Convention, the term 'refugee' shall apply to any person who:

(1) Has been considered a refugee under the Arrangements of 12 May 1926 and 30 June 1928 or under the Conventions of 28 October 1933 and 10 February 1938, the Protocol of 14 September 1939 or the Constitution of the International Refugee Organization;
Decisions of non-eligibility taken by the International Refugee Organization during the period of its activities shall not prevent the status of refugee being accorded to persons who fulfil the conditions of paragraph 2 of this section;

[1] United Nations Treaty Series, vol 189, p. 137

(2) As a result of events occurring before 1 January 1951 and owing to well-founded fear of being persecuted for reasons of race, religion, nationality, membership of a particular social group or political opinion, is outside the country of his nationality and is unable or, owing to such fear, is unwilling to avail himself of the protection of that country; or who, not having a nationality and being outside the country of his former habitual residence as a result of such events, is unable or, owing to such fear, is unwilling to return to it.

In the case of a person who has more than one nationality, the term 'the country of his nationality' shall mean each of the countries of which he is a national, and a person shall not be deemed to be lacking the protection of the country of his nationality if, without any valid reason based on well-founded fear, he has not availed himself of the protection of one of the countries of which he is a national.

B. (1) For the purposes of this Convention, the words 'events occurring before 1 January 1951' in article 1, Section A, shall be understood to mean either:

(a) 'events occurring in Europe before 1 January 1951'; or

(b) 'events occurring in Europe or elsewhere before 1 January 1951';

and each Contracting State shall make a declaration at the time of signature, ratification or accession, specifying which of these meanings it applies for the purpose of its obligations under this Convention.

(2) Any Contracting State which has adopted alternative (a) may at any time extend its obligations by adopting alternative (b) by means of a notification addressed to the Secretary-General of the United Nations.

C. This Convention shall cease to apply to any person falling under the terms of Section A if:

(1) He has voluntarily re-availed himself of the protection of the country of his nationality; or

(2) Having lost his nationality, he has voluntarily reacquired it; or

(3) He has acquired a new nationality, and enjoys the protection of the country of his new nationality; or

(4) He has voluntarily re-established himself in the country which he left or outside which he remained owing to fear of persecution; or

(5) He can no longer, because the circumstances in connexion with which he has been recognized as a refugee have ceased to exist, continue to refuse to avail himself of the protection of the country of his nationality;

(6) Being a person who has no nationality he is, because the circumstances in connexion with which he has been recognized as a refugee have ceased to exist, able to return to the country of his former habitual residence;

Provided that this paragraph shall not apply to a refugee falling under section A(1) of this article who is able to invoke compelling reasons arising out of previous persecution for refusing to return to the country of his former habitual residence.

D. This Convention shall not apply to persons who are at present receiving from organs or agencies of the United Nations other than the United Nations High Commissioner for Refugees protection or assistance.

When such protection or assistance has ceased for any reason, without the position of such persons being definitively settled in accordance with the relevant resolutions adopted by the General Assembly of the United Nations, these persons shall *ipso facto* be entitled to the benefits of this Convention.

E. This Convention shall not apply to a person who is recognized by the competent authorities of the country in which he has taken residence as having the rights and obligations which are attached to the possession of the nationality of that country.

F. The provisions of this Convention shall not apply to any person with respect to whom there are serious reasons for considering that:

(a) he has committed a crime against peace, a war crime, or a crime against humanity, as defined in the international instruments drawn up to make provision in respect of such crimes;

(b) he has committed a serious non-political crime outside the country of refuge prior to his admission to that country as a refugee;

(c) he has been guilty of acts contrary to the purposes and principles of the United Nations.

Article 2 General obligations

Every refugee has duties to the country in which he finds himself, which require in particular that he conform to its laws and regulations as well as to measures taken for the maintenance of public order.

Article 3 Non-Discrimination

The Contracting States shall apply the provisions of this Convention to refugees without discrimination as to race, religion or country of origin.

Article 4 Religion

The Contracting States shall accord to refugees within their territories treatment at least as favorable as that accorded to their nationals with respect to freedom to practice their religion and freedom as regards the religious education of their children.

Article 5 Rights granted apart from this Convention

Nothing in this Convention shall be deemed to impair any rights and benefits granted by a Contracting State to refugees apart from this Convention.

Article 6 The term 'in the same circumstances'

For the purpose of this Convention, the term 'in the same circumstances' implies that any requirements (including requirements as to length and conditions of sojourn or residence) which the particular individual would have to fulfil for the enjoyment of the right in question, if he were not a refugee, must be fulfilled by him, with the exception of requirements which by their nature a refugee is incapable of fulfilling.

Article 7 Exemption from reciprocity

1. Except where this Convention contains more favorable provisions, a Contracting State shall accord to refugees the same treatment as is accorded to aliens generally.

2. After a period of three years' residence, all refugees shall enjoy exemption from legislative reciprocity in the territory of the Contracting States.

3. Each Contracting State shall continue to accord to refugees the rights and benefits to which they were already entitled, in the absence of reciprocity, at the date of entry into force of this Convention for that State.

4. The Contracting States shall consider favorably the possibility of according to refugees, in the absence of reciprocity, rights and benefits beyond those to which they are entitled according to paragraphs 2 and 3, and to extending exemption from reciprocity to refugees who do not fulfil the conditions provided for in paragraphs 2 and 3.

5. The provisions of paragraphs 2 and 3 apply both to the rights and benefits referred to in articles 13, 18, 19, 21 and 22 of this Convention and to rights and benefits for which this Convention does not provide.

Article 8 Exemption from exceptional measures

With regard to exceptional measures which may be taken against the person, property or interests of nationals of a foreign State, the Contracting States shall not apply such measures to a refugee who is formally a national of the said State solely on account of such nationality. Contracting States which, under their legislation, are prevented from applying the general principle expressed in this article, shall, in appropriate cases, grant exemptions in favor of such refugees.

Article 9 Provisional measures

Nothing in this Convention shall prevent a Contracting State, in time of war or other grave and exceptional circumstances, from taking provisionally measures which it considers to be essential to the national security in the case of a particular person, pending a determination by the Contracting State that that person is in fact a refugee and that the continuance of such measures is necessary in his case in the interests of national security.

Article 10 Continuity of residence

1. Where a refugee has been forcibly displaced during the Second World War and removed to the territory of a Contracting State, and is resident there, the period of such enforced sojourn shall be considered to have been lawful residence within that territory.

2. Where a refugee has been forcibly displaced during the Second World War from the territory of a Contracting State and has, prior to the date of entry into force of this Convention, returned there for the purpose of taking up residence, the period of residence before and after such enforced displacement shall be regarded as one uninterrupted period for any purposes for which uninterrupted residence is required.

Article 11 Refugee seamen

In the case of refugees regularly serving as crew members on board a ship flying the flag of a Contracting State, that State shall give sympathetic consideration to their establishment on its territory and the issue of travel documents to them or their temporary admission to its territory particularly with a view to facilitating their establishment in another country.

Chapter II

Juridical Status

Article 12 Personal status

1. The personal status of a refugee shall be governed by the law of the country of his domicile or, if he has no domicile, by the law of the country of his residence.

2. Rights previously acquired by a refugee and dependent on personal status, more particularly rights attaching to marriage, shall be respected by a Contracting State, subject to compliance, if this be necessary, with the formalities required by the law of that State, provided that the right in question is one which would have been recognized by the law of that State had he not become a refugee.

Article 13 Movable and immovable property

The Contracting States shall accord to a refugee treatment as favorable as possible and, in any event, not less favorable than that accorded to aliens generally in the same circumstances, as regards the acquisition of movable and immovable property and other rights pertaining thereto, and to leases and other contracts relating to movable and immovable property.

Article 14 Artistic rights and industrial property

In respect of the protection of industrial property, such as inventions, designs or models, trade marks, trade names, and of rights in literary, artistic and scientific works, a refugee shall be accorded in the country in which he has his habitual residence the same protection as is accorded to nationals of that country. In the territory of any other Contracting State, he shall be accorded the same protection as is accorded in that territory to nationals of the country in which he has his habitual residence.

Article 15 Right of association

As regards non-political and non-profit-making associations and trade unions the Contracting States shall accord to refugees lawfully staying in their territory the most favorable treatment accorded to nationals of a foreign country, in the same circumstances.

Article 16 Access to courts

1. A refugee shall have free access to the courts of law on the territory of all Contracting States.

2. A refugee shall enjoy in the Contracting State in which he has his habitual residence the same treatment as a national in matters pertaining to access to the Courts, including legal assistance and exemption from *cautio judicatum solvi.*

3. A refugee shall be accorded in the matters referred to in paragraph 2 in countries other than that in which he has his habitual residence the treatment granted to a national of the country of his habitual residence.

Chapter III

Gainful Employment

Article 17 Wage-earning employment

1. The Contracting States shall accord to refugees lawfully staying in their territory the most favorable treatment accorded to nationals of a foreign country in the same circumstances, as regards the right to engage in wage-earning employment.

2. In any case, restrictive measures imposed on aliens or the employment of aliens for the protection of the national labour market shall not be applied to a refugee who was already exempt from them at the date of entry into force of this Convention for the Contracting State concerned, or who fulfills one of the following conditions:

(a) He has completed three years' residence in the country;

(b) He has a spouse possessing the nationality of the country of residence. A refugee may not invoke the benefits of this provision if he has abandoned his spouse;

(c) He has one or more children possessing the nationality of the country of residence.

3. The Contracting States shall give sympathetic consideration to assimilating the rights of all refugees with regard to wage-earning employment to those of nationals, and in particular of those refugees who have entered their territory pursuant to programmes of labour recruitment or under immigration schemes.

Article 18 Self-employment

The Contracting States shall accord to a refugee lawfully in their territory treatment as favorable as possible and, in any event, not less favorable than that accorded to aliens generally in the same circumstances, as regards the right to engage on his own account in agriculture, industry, handicrafts and commerce and to establish commercial and industrial companies.

Article 19 Liberal professions

1. Each Contracting State shall accord to refugees lawfully staying in their territory who hold diplomas recognized by the competent authorities of that State, and who are desirous of practising a liberal profession, treatment as favorable as possible and, in any event, not less favorable than that accorded to aliens generally in the same circumstances.

2. The Contracting States shall use their best endeavours consistently with their laws and constitutions to secure the settlement of such refugees in the territories, other than the metropolitan territory, for whose international relations they are responsible.

CHAPTER IV
WELFARE

Article 20 Rationing

Where a rationing system exists, which applies to the population at large and regulates the general distribution of products in short supply, refugees shall be accorded the same treatment as nationals.

Article 21 Housing

As regards housing, the Contracting States, in so far as the matter is regulated by laws or regulations or is subject to the control of public authorities, shall accord to refugees lawfully staying in their territory treatment as favorable as possible and, in any event, not less favorable than that accorded to aliens generally in the same circumstances.

Article 22 Public education

1. The Contracting States shall accord to refugees the same treatment as is accorded to nationals with respect to elementary education.

2. The Contracting States shall accord to refugees treatment as favorable as possible, and, in any event, not less favorable than that accorded to aliens generally in the same circumstances, with respect to education other than elementary education and, in particular, as regards access to studies, the recognition of foreign school certificates, diplomas and degrees, the remission of fees and charges and the award of scholarships.

Article 23 Public relief

The Contracting States shall accord to refugees lawfully staying in their territory the same treatment with respect to public relief and assistance as is accorded to their nationals.

Article 24 Labour legislation and social security

1. The Contracting States shall accord to refugees lawfully staying in their territory the same treatment as is accorded to nationals in respect of the following matters:

(a) In so far as such matters are governed by laws or regulations or are subject to the control of administrative authorities: remuneration, including family allowances where these form part of remuneration, hours of work, overtime arrangements, holidays with pay, restrictions on home work, minimum age of employment, apprenticeship and training, women's work and the work of young persons, and the enjoyment of the benefits of collective bargaining;

(b) Social security (legal provisions in respect of employment injury, occupational diseases, maternity, sickness, disability, old age, death, unemployment, family responsibilities and any other contingency which, according to national laws or regulations, is covered by a social security scheme), subject to the following limitations:

(i) There may be appropriate arrangements for the maintenance of acquired rights and rights in course of acquisition;

(ii) National laws or regulations of the country of residence may prescribe special arrangements concerning benefits or portions of benefits which are payable wholly out of public funds, and concerning allowances paid to persons who do not fulfil the contribution conditions prescribed for the award of a normal pension.

2. The right to compensation for the death of a refugee resulting from employment injury or from occupational disease shall not be affected by the fact that the residence of the beneficiary is outside the territory of the Contracting State.

3. The Contracting States shall extend to refugees the benefits of agreements concluded between them, or which may be concluded between them in the future, concerning the maintenance of acquired rights and rights in the process of acquisition in regard to social security, subject only to the conditions which apply to nationals of the States signatory to the agreements in question.

4. The Contracting States will give sympathetic consideration to extending to refugees so far as possible the benefits of similar agreements which may at any time be in force between such Contracting States and non-contracting States.

Chapter V

Administrative Measures

Article 25 Administrative assistance

1. When the exercise of a right by a refugee would normally require the assistance of authorities of a foreign country to whom he cannot have recourse, the Contracting States in whose territory he is residing shall arrange that such assistance be afforded to him by their own authorities or by an international authority.

2. The authority or authorities mentioned in paragraph 1 shall deliver or cause to be delivered under their supervision to refugees such documents or certifications as would normally be delivered to aliens by or through their national authorities.

3. Documents or certifications so delivered shall stand in the stead of the official instruments delivered to aliens by or through their national authorities, and shall be given credence in the absence of proof to the contrary.

4. Subject to such exceptional treatment as may be granted to indigent persons, fees may be charged for the services mentioned herein, but such fees shall be moderate and commensurate with those charged to nationals for similar services.

5. The provisions of this article shall be without prejudice to articles 27 and 28.

Article 26 Freedom of movement

Each Contracting State shall accord to refugees lawfully in its territory the right to choose their place of residence and to move freely within its territory, subject to any regulations applicable to aliens generally in the same circumstances.

Article 27 Identity papers

The Contracting States shall issue identity papers to any refugee in their territory who does not possess a valid travel document.

Article 28 Travel documents

1. The Contracting States shall issue to refugees lawfully staying in their territory travel documents for the purpose of travel outside their territory, unless compelling reasons of national security or public order otherwise require, and the provisions of the Schedule to this Convention shall apply with respect to such documents. The Contracting States may issue such a travel document to any other refugee in their territory; they shall in particular give sympathetic consideration to the issue of such a travel document to refugees in their territory who are unable to obtain a travel document from the country of their lawful residence.

2. Travel documents issued to refugees under previous international agreements by parties thereto shall be recognized and treated by the Contracting States in the same way as if they had been issued pursuant to this article.

Article 29 Fiscal charges

1. The Contracting States shall not impose upon refugees duties, charges or taxes, of any description whatsoever, other or higher than those which are or may be levied on their nationals in similar situations.

2. Nothing in the above paragraph shall prevent the application to refugees of the laws and regulations concerning charges in respect of the issue to aliens of administrative documents including identity papers.

Article 30 Transfer of assets

1. A Contracting State shall, in conformity with its laws and regulations, permit refugees to transfer assets which they have brought into its territory, to another country where they have been admitted for the purposes of resettlement.

2. A Contracting State shall give sympathetic consideration to the application of refugees for permission to transfer assets wherever they may be and which are necessary for their resettlement in another country to which they have been admitted.

Article 31 Refugees unlawfully in the country of refuge

1. The Contracting States shall not impose penalties, on account of their illegal entry or presence, on refugees who, coming directly from a territory where their life or freedom was threatened in the sense of article 1, enter or are present in their territory without authorization, provided they present themselves without delay to the authorities and show good cause for their illegal entry or presence.

2. The Contracting States shall not apply to the movements of such refugees restrictions other than those which are necessary and such restrictions shall only be applied until their status in the country is regularized or they obtain admission into another country. The Contracting States shall allow such refugees a reasonable period and all the necessary facilities to obtain admission into another country.

Article 32 Expulsion

1. The Contracting States shall not expel a refugee lawfully in their territory save on grounds of national security or public order.

2. The expulsion of such a refugee shall be only in pursuance of a decision reached in accordance with due process of law. Except where compelling reasons of national security otherwise require, the refugee shall be allowed to submit evidence to clear himself, and to appeal to and be represented for the purpose before competent authority or a person or persons specially designated by the competent authority.

3. The Contracting States shall allow such a refugee a reasonable period within which to seek legal admission into another country. The Contracting States reserve the right to apply during that period such internal measures as they may deem necessary.

Article 33 Prohibition of expulsion or return ('refoulement')

1. No Contracting State shall expel or return ('*refouler*') a refugee in any manner whatsoever to the frontiers of territories where his life or freedom would be threatened on account of his race, religion, nationality, membership of a particular social group or political opinion.

2. The benefit of the present provision may not, however, be claimed by a refugee whom there are reasonable grounds for regarding as a danger to the security of the country in which he is, or who, having been convicted by a final judgment of a particularly serious crime, constitutes a danger to the community of that country.

Article 34 Naturalization

The Contracting States shall as far as possible facilitate the assimilation and naturalization of refugees. They shall in particular make every effort to expedite naturalization proceedings and to reduce as far as possible the charges and cost of such proceedings.

Chapter VI

Executory and Transitory Provisions

Article 35 Co-operation of the national authorities with the United Nations

1. The Contracting States undertake to co-operate with the Office of the United Nations High Commissioner for Refugees, or any other agency of the United Nations which may succeed it, in the exercise of its functions, and shall in particular facilitate its duty of supervising the application of the provisions of this Convention.

2. In order to enable the Office of the High Commissioner or any other agency of the United Nations which may succeed it, to make reports to the competent organs of the United Nations, the Contracting States undertake to provide them in the appropriate form with information and statistical data requested concerning:

(a) the condition of refugees,
(b) the implementation of this Convention, and
(c) laws, regulations and decrees which are, or may hereafter be, in force relating to refugees.

Article 36 Information on national legislation

The Contracting States shall communicate to the Secretary-General of the United Nations the laws and regulations which they may adopt to ensure the application of this Convention.

Article 37 Relation to previous conventions

Without prejudice to article 28, paragraph 2, of this Convention, this Convention replaces, as between parties to it, the Arrangements of 5 July 1922, 31 May 1924, 12 May 1926, 30 June 1928 and 30 July 1935, the Conventions of 28 October 1933 and 10 February 1938, the Protocol of 14 September 1939 and the Agreement of 15 October 1946.

Chapter VII
Final Clauses

Article 38 Settlement of disputes

Any dispute between parties to this Convention relating to its interpretation or application, which cannot be settled by other means, shall be referred to the International Court of Justice at the request of any one of the parties to the dispute.

Article 39 Signature, ratification and accession

1. This Convention shall be opened for signature at Geneva on 28 July 1951 and shall thereafter be deposited with the Secretary-General of the United Nations. It shall be open for signature at the European Office of the United Nations from 28 July to 31 August 1951 and shall be re-opened for signature at the Headquarters of the United Nations from 17 September 1951 to 31 December 1952.

2. This Convention shall be open for signature on behalf of all States Members of the United Nations, and also on behalf of any other State invited to attend the Conference of Plenipotentiaries on the Status of Refugees and Stateless Persons or to which an invitation to sign will have been addressed by the General Assembly. It shall be ratified and the instruments of ratification shall be deposited with the Secretary-General of the United Nations.

3. This Convention shall be open from 28 July 1951 for accession by the States referred to in paragraph 2 of this article. Accession shall be effected by the deposit of an instrument of accession with the Secretary-General of the United Nations.

Article 40 Territorial application clause

1. Any State may, at the time of signature, ratification or accession, declare that this Convention shall extend to all or any of the territories for the international relations of which it is responsible. Such a declaration shall take effect when the Convention enters into force for the State concerned.

2. At any time thereafter any such extension shall be made by notification addressed to the Secretary-General of the United Nations and shall take effect as from the ninetieth day after the day of receipt by the Secretary-General of the United Nations of this notification, or as from the date of entry into force of the Convention for the State concerned, whichever is the later.

3. With respect to those territories to which this Convention is not extended at the time of signature, ratification or accession, each State concerned shall consider the possibility of taking the necessary steps in order to extend the application of this Convention to such territories, subject, where necessary for constitutional reasons, to the consent of the Governments of such territories.

Article 41 Federal clause

In the case of a Federal or non-unitary State, the following provisions shall apply:

(a) With respect to those articles of this Convention that come within the legislative jurisdiction of the federal legislative authority, the obligations of the Federal Government shall to this extent be the same as those of Parties which are not Federal States;

(b) With respect to those articles of this Convention that come within the legislative jurisdiction of constituent States, provinces or cantons which are not, under the constitutional system of the federation, bound to take legislative action, the Federal Government shall bring such articles with a favorable recommendation to the notice of the appropriate authorities of states, provinces or cantons at the earliest possible moment;

(c) A Federal State Party to this Convention shall, at the request of any other Contracting State transmitted through the Secretary-General of the United Nations, supply a statement of the law and practice of the Federation and its constituent units in regard to any particular provision of the Convention showing the extent to which effect has been given to that provision by legislative or other action.

Article 42 Reservations

1. At the time of signature, ratification or accession, any State may make reservations to articles of the Convention other than to articles 1, 3, 4, 16(1), 33, 36 - 46 inclusive.

2. Any State making a reservation in accordance with paragraph 1 of this article may at any time withdraw the reservation by a communication to that effect addressed to the Secretary-General of the United Nations.

Article 43 Entry into force

1. This Convention shall come into force on the ninetieth day following the day of deposit of the sixth instrument of ratification or accession.

2. For each State ratifying or acceding to the Convention after the deposit of the sixth instrument of ratification or accession, the Convention shall enter into force on the ninetieth day following the day of deposit by such State of its instrument of ratification or accession.

Article 44 Denunciation

1. Any Contracting State may denounce this Convention at any time by a notification addressed to the Secretary-General of the United Nations.

2. Such denunciation shall take effect for the Contracting State concerned one year from the date upon which it is received by the Secretary-General of the United Nations.

3. Any State which has made a declaration or notification under article 40 may, at any time thereafter, by a notification to the Secretary-General of the United Nations, declare that the Convention shall cease to extend to such territory one year after the date of receipt of the notification by the Secretary-General.

Article 45 Revision

1. Any Contracting State may request revision of this Convention at any time by a notification addressed to the Secretary-General of the United Nations.

2. The General Assembly of the United Nations shall recommend the steps, if any, to be taken in respect of such request.

Article 46 Notifications by the Secretary-General of the United Nations

The Secretary-General of the United Nations shall inform all Members of the United Nations and non-member States referred to in article 39:

(a) Of declarations and notifications in accordance with Section B of article 1;

(b) Of signatures, ratifications and accessions in accordance with article 39;

(c) Of declarations and notifications in accordance with article 40;

(d) Of reservations and withdrawals in accordance with article 42;

(e) Of the date on which this Convention will come into force in accordance with article 43;

(f) Of denunciations and notifications in accordance with article 44;

(g) Of requests for revision in accordance with article 45.

IN FAITH WHEREOF the undersigned, duly authorized, have signed this Convention on behalf of their respective Governments,

DONE at Geneva, this twenty-eighth day of July, one thousand nine hundred and fifty-one, in a single copy, of which the English and French texts are equally authentic and which shall remain deposited in the archives of the United Nations, and certified true copies of which shall be delivered to all Members of the United Nations and to the non-member States referred to in article 39.

SCHEDULE

Paragraph 1

1. The travel document referred to in article 28 of this Convention shall be similar to the specimen annexed hereto.

2. The document shall be made out in at least two languages, one of which shall be in English or French.

Paragraph 2

Subject to the regulations obtaining in the country of issue, children may be included in the travel document of a parent or, in exceptional circumstances, of another adult refugee.

Paragraph 3

The fees charged for issue of the document shall not exceed the lowest scale of charges for national passports.

Paragraph 4

Save in special or exceptional cases, the document shall be made valid for the largest possible number of countries.

Paragraph 5

The document shall have a validity of either one or two years, at the discretion of the issuing authority.

Paragraph 6

1. The renewal or extension of the validity of the document is a matter for the authority which issued it, so long as the holder has not established lawful residence in another territory and resides lawfully in the territory of the said authority. The issue of a new document is, under the same conditions, a matter for the authority which issued the former document.

2. Diplomatic or consular authorities, specially authorized for the purpose, shall be empowered to extend, for a period not exceeding six months, the validity of travel documents issued by their Governments.

3. The Contracting States shall give sympathetic consideration to renewing or extending the validity of travel documents or issuing new documents to refugees no longer lawfully resident in their territory who are unable to obtain a travel document from the country of their lawful residence.

Paragraph 7

The Contracting States shall recognize the validity of the documents issued in accordance with the provisions of article 28 of this Convention.

Paragraph 8

The competent authorities of the country to which the refugee desires to proceed shall, if they are prepared to admit him and if a visa is required, affix a visa on the document of which he is the holder.

Paragraph 9

1. The Contracting States undertake to issue transit visas to refugees who have obtained visas for a territory of final destination.

2. The issue of such visas may be refused on grounds which would justify refusal of a visa to any alien.

Paragraph 10

The fees for the issue of exit, entry or transit visas shall not exceed the lowest scale of charges for visas on foreign passports.

Paragraph 11

When a refugee has lawfully taken up residence in the territory of another Contracting State, the responsibility for the issue of a new document, under the terms and conditions of article 28, shall be that of the competent authority of that territory, to which the refugee shall be entitled to apply.

Paragraph 12

The authority issuing a new document shall withdraw the old document and shall return it to the country of issue if it is stated in the document that it should be so returned; otherwise it shall withdraw and cancel the document.

Paragraph 13

1. Each Contracting State undertakes that the holder of a travel document issued by it in accordance with article 28 of this Convention shall be re-admitted to its territory at any time during the period of its validity.

2. Subject to the provisions of the preceding sub-paragraph, a Contracting State may require the holder of the document to comply with such formalities as may be prescribed in regard to exit from or return to its territory.

3. The Contracting States reserve the right, in exceptional cases, or in cases where the refugee's stay is authorized for a specific period, when issuing the document, to limit the period during which the refugee may return to a period of not less than three months.

Paragraph 14

Subject only to the terms of paragraph 13, the provisions of this Schedule in no way affect the laws and regulations governing the conditions of admission to, transit through, residence and establishment in, and departure from, the territories of the Contracting States.

Paragraph 15

Neither the issue of the document nor the entries made thereon determine or affect the status of the holder, particularly as regards nationality.

Paragraph 16

The issue of the document does not in any way entitle the holder to the protection of the diplomatic or consular authorities of the country of issue, and does not confer on these authorities a right of protection.

ANNEX

Specimen Travel Document

[Not reproduced here]

1967 Protocol Relating to the Status of Refugees[1]

THE STATES PARTIES TO THE PRESENT PROTOCOL,
CONSIDERING that the Convention relating to the Status of Refugees done at Geneva on 28 July 1951 (hereinafter referred to as the Convention) covers only those persons who have become refugees as a result of events occurring before 1 January 1951,
CONSIDERING that new refugee situations have arisen since the Convention was adopted and that the refugees concerned may therefore not fall within the scope of the Convention,
CONSIDERING that it is desirable that equal status should be enjoyed by all refugees covered by the definition in the Convention irrespective of the dateline 1 January 1951,
HAVE AGREED as follows:

Article I General provision

1. The States Parties to the present Protocol undertake to apply articles 2 to 34 inclusive of the Convention to refugees as hereinafter defined.

2. For the purpose of the present Protocol, the term 'refugee' shall, except as regards the application of paragraph 3 of this article, mean any person within the definition of article 1 of the Convention as if the words 'As a result of events occurring before 1 January 1951 and . . . ' and the words '. . . as a result of such events', in article 1A(2) were omitted.

3. The present Protocol shall be applied by the States Parties hereto without any geographic limitation, save that existing declarations made by States already Parties to the Convention in accordance with article 1B(1)(a) of the Convention, shall, unless extended under article 1B(2) thereof, apply also under the present Protocol.

Article II Co-operation of the national authorities with the United Nations

1. The States Parties to the present Protocol undertake to co-operate with the Office of the United Nations High Commissioner for Refugees, or any other agency of the United Nations which may succeed it, in the exercise of its functions, and shall in particular facilitate its duty of supervising the application of the provisions of the present Protocol.

2. In order to enable the Office of the High Commissioner, or any other agency of the United Nations which may succeed it, to make reports to the competent organs of the United Nations, the States Parties to the present Protocol undertake to provide them with the information and statistical data requested, in the appropriate form, concerning:

(a) The condition of refugees;

(b) The implementation of the present Protocol;

(c) Laws, regulations and decrees which are, or may hereafter be, in force relating to refugees.

[1] United Nations, Treaty Series, vol 606, p. 267.

Article III Information on national legislation

The States Parties to the present Protocol shall communicate to the Secretary-General of the United Nations the laws and regulations which they may adopt to ensure the application of the present Protocol.

Article IV Settlement of disputes

Any dispute between States Parties to the present Protocol which relates to its interpretation or application and which cannot be settled by other means shall be referred to the International Court of Justice at the request of any one of the parties to the dispute.

Article V Accession

The present Protocol shall be open for accession on behalf of all States Parties to the Convention and of any other State Member of the United Nations or member of any of the specialized agencies or to which an invitation to accede may have been addressed by the General Assembly of the United Nations. Accession shall be effected by the deposit of an instrument of accession with the Secretary-General of the United Nations.

Article VI Federal clause

In the case of a Federal or non-unitary State, the following provisions shall apply:

(a) With respect to those articles of the Convention to be applied in accordance with article I, paragraph 1, of the present Protocol that come within the legislative jurisdiction of the federal legislative authority, the obligations of the Federal Government shall to this extent be the same as those of States Parties which are not Federal States;

(b) With respect to those articles of the Convention to be applied in accordance with article I, paragraph 1, of the present Protocol that come within the legislative jurisdiction of constituent States, provinces or cantons which are not, under the constitutional system of the federation, bound to take legislative action, the Federal Government shall bring such articles with a favourable recommendation to the notice of the appropriate authorities of States, provinces or cantons at the earliest possible moment;

(c) A Federal State Party to the present Protocol shall, at the request of any other State Party hereto transmitted through the Secretary- General of the United Nations, supply a statement of the law and practice of the Federation and its constituent units in regard to any particular provision of the Convention to be applied in accordance with article 1, paragraph 1, of the present Protocol, showing the extent to which effect has been given to that provision by legislative or other action.

Article VII Reservations and Declarations

1. At the time of accession, any State may make reservations in respect of article IV of the present Protocol and in respect of the application in accordance with article I of the present Protocol of any provisions of the Convention other than those contained in articles 1, 3, 4, 16(1) and 33 thereof, provided that in the case of a State Party to the Convention reservations made under this article shall not extend to refugees in respect of whom the Convention applies.

2. Reservations made by States Parties to the Convention in accordance with article 42 thereof shall, unless withdrawn, be applicable in relation to their obligations under the present Protocol.

3. Any State making a reservation in accordance with paragraph 1 of this article may at any time withdraw such reservation by a communication to that effect addressed to the Secretary-General of the United Nations.

4. Declarations made under article 40, paragraphs 1 and 2, of the Convention by a State Party thereto which accedes to the present Protocol shall be deemed to apply in respect of the present Protocol, unless upon accession a notification to the contrary is addressed by the State Party concerned to the Secretary-General of the United Nations. The provisions of article 40, paragraphs 2 and 3, and of article 44, paragraph 3, of the Convention shall be deemed to apply *mutatis mutandis* to the present Protocol.

Article VIII Entry into force

1. The present Protocol shall come into force on the day of deposit of the sixth instrument of accession.

2. For each State acceding to the Protocol after the deposit of the sixth instrument of accession, the Protocol shall come into force on the date of deposit by such State of its instrument of accession.

Article IX Denunciation

1. Any State Party hereto may denounce this Protocol at any time by a notification addressed to the Secretary-General of the United Nations.

2. Such denunciation shall take effect for the State Party concerned one year from the date on which it is received by the Secretary-General of the United Nations.

Article X Notifications by the Secretary-General of the United Nations

The Secretary-General of the United Nations shall inform the States referred to in article V above of the date of entry into force, accessions, reservations and withdrawals of reservations to and denunciations of the present Protocol, and of declarations and notifications relating hereto.

Article XI Deposit in the Archives of the Secretariat of the United Nations

A copy of the present Protocol, of which the Chinese, English, French, Russian and Spanish texts are equally authentic, signed by the President of the General Assembly and by the Secretary-General of the United Nations, shall be deposited in the archives of the Secretariat of the United Nations. The Secretary-General will transmit certified copies thereof to all States Members of the United Nations and to the other States referred to in article V above.

States Parties to the 1951 Convention Relating to the Status of Refugees and the 1967 Protocol

The Convention was drafted and signed by the United Nations Conference of Plenipotentiaries on the Status of Refugees and Stateless Persons, held at Geneva from 2 to 25 July 1951. The Conference was convened pursuant to General Assembly resolution 429 (V) of 14 December 1950. The Convention was adopted on 28 July 1951; in accordance with Article 43, it entered into force on 22 April 1954. The Protocol was adopted on 31 January 1967; it entered into force on 4 October 1967 in accordance with its Article VIII.

State Parties (as of July 2022)[1]

Total number of States Parties to the 1951 Convention: 146
Total number of States Parties to the 1967 Protocol: 147
States Parties to both the Convention and Protocol: 143
States Parties to one or both of these instruments: 149

States Parties to the 1951 Convention only:

Madagascar, Saint Kitts and Nevis

States Parties to the 1967 Protocol only:

Cape Verde, United States of America, Venezuela (Bolivarian Republic of)

The dates indicated below are the dates of deposit of the instrument of ratification or accession by the respective States Parties with the Secretary-General of the United Nations. In accordance with article 43(2), the Convention enters into force on the ninetieth day after the date of deposit by the ratifying or acceding State. The Protocol enters into force on the date of deposit of each acceding State (Article VIII (2)). Exceptions are indicated below.

Most recent ratification/accession:	Convention	Protocol
South Sudan	10 Dec 2018 a	10 Dec 2018 a

Country*	Convention	Protocol
Afghanistan	30 Aug 2005 a	30 Aug 2005 a
Albania	18 Aug 1992 a	18 Aug 1992 a
Algeria	21 Feb 1963 d	08 Nov 1967a

[1] The 1951 Convention and the 1967 Protocol are deposited with the Secretary-General of the United Nations (Article 39 (1) of the 1951 Convention and Article V of the 1967 Protocol). For the authoritative source of the current status of both treaties, please refer to the United National Treaty Collection website under status of Multilateral Treaties Deposited with the Secretary-General (MTDSG): https://treaties.un.org/Pages/Treaties.aspx?id=5&subid=A&lang=en.

Country*	Convention	Protocol
Angola	23 Jun 1981 a	23 Jun 1981 a
Antigua and Barbuda	07 Sep 1995 a	07 Sep 1995 a
Argentina	15 Nov 1961a	06 Dec 1967a
Armenia	06 Jul 1993 a	06 Jul 1993 a
Australia	22 Jan 1954 a	13 Dec 1973a
Austria	01 Nov 1954 r	05 Sep 1973 a
Azerbaijan	12 Feb 1993 a	12 Feb 1993 a
Bahamas (the)	15 Sep 1993 a	15 Sep 1993 a
Belarus	23 Aug 2001 a	23 Aug 2001 a
Belgium	22 Jul 1953 r	08 Apr 1969 a
Belize	27 Jun 1990 a	27 Jun 1990 a
Benin	04 Apr 1962 d	06 Jul 1970 a
Bolivia (Plurinational State of)	09 Feb 1982 a	09 Feb 1982 a
Bosnia and Herzegovina	01 Sep 1993 d	01 Sep 1993 d
Botswana	06 Jan 1969 a	06 Jan 1969 a
Brazil	16 Nov 1960 r	07 Apr 1972 a
Bulgaria	12 May 1993 a	12 May 1993
Burkina Faso	18 Jun 1980 a	18 Jun 1980 a
Burundi	19 Jul 1963 a	15 Mar 1971 a
Cabo Verde		09 Jul 1987 a
Cambodia	15 Oct 1992 a	15 Oct 1992 a
Cameroon	23 Oct 1961 d	19 Sep 1967 a
Canada	04 Jun 1969 a	04 Jun 1969 a
Central African Republic (the)	04 Sep 1962 d	30 Aug 1967 a
Chad	19 Aug 1981 a	19 Aug 1981 a
Chile	28 Jan 1972 a	27 Apr 1972 a
China	24 Sep 1982 a	24 Sep 1982 a
Colombia	10 Oct 1961 r	04 Mar 1980 a
Congo (the)	15 Oct 1962 d	10 Jul 1970 a
Costa Rica	28 Mar 1978 a	28 Mar 1978a
Côte d'Ivoire	08 Dec 1961 d	16 Feb 1970 a
Croatia	12 Oct 1992 d	12 Oct 1992 d
Cyprus (the)	16 May 1963 d	09 Jul 1968 a
Czech Republic (the)	11 May 1993 d	11 May 1993 d

Country*	Convention	Protocol
Democratic Republic of the Congo (the)	19 July 1965 a	13 Jan 1975 a
Denmark	04 Dec 1952 r	29 Jan 1968 a
Djibouti	09 Aug 1977 d	09 Aug 1977 d
Dominica	17 Feb 1994 a	17 Feb 1994 a
Dominican Republic (the)	04 Jan 1978 a	04 Jan 1978 a
Ecuador	17 Aug 1955 a	06 Mar 1969 a
Egypt	22 May 1981 a	22 May 1981 a
El Salvador	28 Apr 1983 a	28 Apr 1983 a
Equatorial Guinea	07 Feb 1986 a	07 Feb 1986 a
Estonia	10 Apr 1997 a	10 Apr 1997 a
Eswatini	14 Feb 2000 a	28 Jan 1969 a
Ethiopia	10 Nov 1969 a	10 Nov 1969 a
Fiji	12 Jun 1972 d	12 Jun 1972 d
Finland	10 Oct 1968 a	10 Oct 1968 a
France	23 Jun 1954 r	03 Feb 1971 a
Gabon	27 Apr 1964 a	28 Aug 1973 a
Gambia (the)	07 Sep 1966 d	29 Sep 1967 a
Georgia	09 Aug 1999 a	09 Aug 1999 a
Germany	01 Dec 1953 r	05 Nov 1969 a
Ghana	18 Mar 1963 a	30 Aug 1968 a
Greece	05 Apr 1960 r	07 Aug 1968 a
Guatemala	22 Sep 1983 a	22 Sep 1983 a
Guinea	28 Dec 1965 d	16 May1968 a
Guinea-Bissau	11 Feb 1976 a	11 Feb 1976 a
Haiti	25 Sep 1984 a	25 Sep 1984 a
Holy See	15 Mar 1956 r	08 Jun 1967 a
Honduras	23 Mar 1992 a	23 Mar 1992 a
Hungary	14 Mar 1989 a	14 Mar 1989 a
Iceland	30 Nov 1955 a	26 Apr 1968 a
Iran (Islamic Republic of)	28 Jul 1976 a	28 Jul 1976 a
Ireland	29 Nov 1956 a	06 Nov 1968 a
Israel	01 Oct 1954 r	14 Jun 1968 a
Italy	15 Nov 1954 r	26 Jan 1972 a
Jamaica	30 Jul 1964 d	30 Oct 1980 a

Country*	Convention	Protocol
Japan	03 Oct 1981 a	01 Jan 1982 a
Kazakhstan	15 Jan 1999 a	15 Jan 1999 a
Kenya	16 May 1966 a	13 Nov 1981 a
Kyrgyzstan	08 Oct 1996 a	08 Oct 1996 a
Latvia	31 Jul 1997 a	31 Jul 1997 a
Lesotho	14 May 1981 a	14 May 1981 a
Liberia	15 Oct 1964 a	27 Feb 1980 a
Liechtenstein	08 Mar 1957 r	20 May1968 a
Lithuania	28 Apr 1997 a	28 Apr 1997 a
Luxembourg	23 Jul 1953 r	22 Apr 1971 a
Madagascar	18 Dec 1967 a	
Malawi	10 Dec 1987 a	10 Dec 1987 a
Mali	02 Feb 1973 d	02 Feb 1973 a
Malta	17 Jun 1971 a	15 Sep 1971 a
Mauritania	05 May 1987 a	05 May1987 a
Mexico	07 June 2000 a	07 June2000 a
Monaco	18 May 1954 a	16 June2010 a
Montenegro	10 Oct 2006 d	10 Oct 2006 d
Morocco	07 Nov 1956 d	20 Apr 1971 a
Mozambique	16 Dec 1983 a	01 May1989 a
Namibia	17 Feb 1995 a	17 Feb 1995 a
Nauru	28 June 2011 a	28 June2011 a
Netherlands (the)	03 May 1956 r	29 Nov 1968 a
New Zealand	30 Jun 1960 a	06 Aug 1973 a
Nicaragua	28 Mar 1980 a	28 Mar 1980 a
Niger (the)	25 Aug 1961 d	02 Feb 1970 a
Nigeria	23 Oct 1967 a	02 May1968 a
North Macedonia	18 Jan 1994 d	18 Jan 1994 d
Norway	23 Mar 1953 r	28 Nov 1967 a
Panama	02 Aug 1978 a	02 Aug 1978 a
Papua New Guinea	17 Jul 1986 a	17 Jul 1986 a
Paraguay	01 Apr 1970 a	01 Apr 1970 a
Peru	21 Dec 1964 a	15 Sep 1983 a
Philippines (the)	22 Jul 1981 a	22 Jul 1981 a

Country*	Convention	Protocol
Poland	27 Sep 1991 a	27 Sep 1991 a
Portugal	22 Dec 1960 a	13 Jul 1976 a
Republic of Korea (the)	03 Dec 1992 a	03 Dec 1992 a
Republic of Moldova	31 Jan 2002 a	31 Jan 2002 a
Romania	07 Aug 1991 a	07 Aug 1991 a
Russian Federation (the)	02 Feb 1993 a	02 Feb 1993 a
Rwanda	03 Jan 1980 a	03 Jan 1980 a
Saint Kitts and Nevis	01 Feb 2002 a	
St.Vincent and the Grenadines	03 Nov 1993 a	03 Nov 2003 a
Samoa	21 Sep 1988 a	29 Nov 1994 a
Sao Tome and Principe	01 Feb 1978 a	01 Feb 1978 a
Senegal	02 May 1963 d	03 Oct 1967 a
Serbia	12 Mar 2001 d	12 Mar 2001 d
Seychelles	23 Apr 1980 a	23 Apr 1980 a
Sierra Leone	22 May 1981 a	22 May1981 a
Slovakia	04 Feb 1993 d	04 Feb 1993 d
Slovenia	06 Jul 1992 d	06 Jul 1992 d
Solomon Islands	28 Feb 1995 a	12 Apr 1995 a
Somalia	10 Oct 1978 a	10 Oct 1978 a
South Africa	12 Jan 1996 a	12 Jan 1996 a
South Sudan	10 Dec 2018 a	10 Dec 2018 a
Spain	14 Aug 1978 a	14 Aug 1978 a
Sudan (the)	22 Feb 1974 a	23 May1974 a
Suriname	29Nov 1978 d	29 Nov 1978 d
Swaziland	14 Feb 2000 a	28 Jan 1969 a
Sweden	26 Oct 1954 r	04 Oct 1967 a
Switzerland	21 Jan 1955 r	20 May1968 a
Tajikistan	07 Dec 1993 a	07 Dec 1993 a
Timor-Leste	07 May 2003 a	07 May2003 a
Togo	27 Feb 1962 d	01 Dec 1969 a
Trinidad and Tobago	10 Nov 2000 a	10 Nov 2000 a
Tunisia	24 Oct 1957 d	16 Oct 1968 a
Turkey	30 Mar 1962 r	31 Jul 1968 a
Turkmenistan	02 Mar 1998 a	02 Mar 1998 a

Country*	Convention	Protocol
Tuvalu	07 Mar 1986 d	07 Mar 1986 d
Uganda	27 Sep 1976 a	27 Sep 1976 a
Ukraine	10 Jun 2002 a	04 Apr 2002 a
United Kingdom of Great Britain and Northern Ireland (the)	11 Mar 1954 r	04 Sep 1968 a
United Republic of Tanzania (the)	12 May 1964 a	04 Sep 1968 a
United States of America (the)		01 Nov 1968 a
Uruguay	22 Sep 1970 a	22 Sep 1970 a
Venezuela (Bolivarian Republic of)		19 Sep 1986 a
Yemen	18 Jan 1980 a	18 Jan 1980 a
Zambia	24 Sep 1969 d	24 Sep 1969 a
Zimbabwe	25 Aug 1981 a	25 Aug 1981 a

Note:

*** Ratification (r), Accession (a), Succession (d).**

Limitations:

Article 1 B (1) of the 1951 Convention provides: 'For the purposes of this Convention, the words 'events occurring before 1 January 1951' in article 1, Section A, shall be understood to mean either (a) 'events occurring in Europe before 1 January 1951'; or (b) 'events occurring in Europe or elsewhere before 1 January 1951', and each Contracting State shall make a declaration at the time of signature, ratification or accession, specifying which of these meanings it applies for the purposes of its obligations under this Convention.'

The following States adopted alternative (a), the geographical limitation: Congo, Madagascar, Monaco and Turkey. Turkey expressly maintained its declaration of geographical limitation upon acceding to the 1967 Protocol. Madagascar has not yet adhered to the Protocol.

All other States Parties ratified, acceded or succeeded to the Convention without a geographical limitation by selecting option (b), 'events occurring in Europe or elsewhere before 1 January 1951'.

Convention for the Protection of Human Rights and Fundamental Freedoms

AS AMENDED BY PROTOCOLS NO. 11, No.14 and No.15[1,2]

(The Convention is also supplemented by Protocols Nos. 1, 4, 6, 7, 12, 13 and 16 which are not reproduced below.)

Rome, 4.XI.1950

The governments signatory hereto, being members of the Council of Europe,

Considering the Universal Declaration of Human Rights proclaimed by the General Assembly of the United Nations on 10th December 1948;

Considering that this Declaration aims at securing the universal and effective recognition and observance of the Rights therein declared;

Considering that the aim of the Council of Europe is the achievement of greater unity between its members and that one of the methods by which that aim is to be pursued is the maintenance and further realisation of human rights and fundamental freedoms;

Reaffirming their profound belief in those fundamental freedoms which are the foundation of justice and peace in the world and are best maintained on the one hand by an effective political democracy and on the other by a common understanding and observance of the human rights upon which they depend;

Being resolved, as the governments of European countries which are like-minded and have a common heritage of political traditions, ideals, freedom and the rule of law, to take the first steps for the collective enforcement of certain of the rights stated in the Universal Declaration,

[Affirming that the High Contracting Parties, in accordance with the principle of subsidiarity, have the primary responsibility to secure the rights and freedoms defined in this Convention and the Protocols thereto, and that in doing so they enjoy a margin of appreciation, subject to the supervisory jurisdiction of the European Court of Human Rights established by this Convention,]

[1] The text of the Convention is presented as amended by the provisions of Protocol No. 15 (CETS No. 213) as from its entry into force on 1 August 2021 and of Protocol No. 14 (CETS No. 194) as from its entry into force on 1 June 2010. The text of the Convention had previously been amended according to the provisions of Protocol No. 3 (ETS No. 45), which entered into force on 21 September1970, of Protocol No. 5 (ETS No. 55), which entered into force on 20 December 1971, and of Protocol No. 8 (ETS No. 118), which entered into force on 1 January 1990, and comprised also the text of Protocol No. 2 (ETS No. 44) which, in accordance with Article 5 paragraph 3 thereof, had been an integral part of the Convention since its entry into force on 21 September 1970. All provisions which had been amended or added by these Protocols were replaced by Protocol No. 11 (ETS No. 155), as from the date of its entry into force on 1 November 1998. As from that date, Protocol No. 9 (ETS No. 140), which entered into force on 1 October 1994, was repealed and Protocol No. 10 (ETS No. 146) lost its purpose.

Note: new recital inserted from 1 August 2021 by Protocol No. 15 (CETS No.213)

Have agreed as follows:

Article 1 - Obligation to respect human rights

The High Contracting Parties shall secure to everyone within their jurisdiction the rights and freedoms defined in Section I of this Convention.

Section I—Rights and Freedoms

Article 2 - Right to life

1. Everyone's right to life shall be protected by law. No one shall be deprived of his life intentionally save in the execution of a sentence of a court following his conviction of a crime for which this penalty is provided by law.

2. Deprivation of life shall not be regarded as inflicted in contravention of this article when it results from the use of force which is no more than absolutely necessary:

(a) in defence of any person from unlawful violence;

(b) in order to effect a lawful arrest or to prevent the escape of a person lawfully detained;

(c) in action lawfully taken for the purpose of quelling a riot or insurrection.

Article 3 - Prohibition of torture

No one shall be subjected to torture or to inhuman or degrading treatment or punishment.

Article 4 - Prohibition of slavery and forced labour

1. No one shall be held in slavery or servitude.

2. No one shall be required to perform forced or compulsory labour.

3. For the purpose of this article the term 'forced or compulsory labour' shall not include:

(a) any work required to be done in the ordinary course of detention imposed according to the provisions of Article 5 of this Convention or during conditional release from such detention;

(b) any service of a military character or, in case of conscientious objectors in countries where they are recognised, service exacted instead of compulsory military service;

(c) any service exacted in case of an emergency or calamity threatening the life or well-being of the community;

(d) any work or service which forms part of normal civic obligations.

Article 5 - Right to liberty and security

1. Everyone has the right to liberty and security of person. No one shall be deprived of his liberty save in the following cases and in accordance with a procedure prescribed by law:

(a) the lawful detention of a person after conviction by a competent court;

(b) the lawful arrest or detention of a person for non-compliance with the lawful order of a court or in order to secure the fulfilment of any obligation prescribed by law;

(c) the lawful arrest or detention of a person effected for the purpose of bringing him before the competent legal authority on reasonable suspicion of having committed an offence or when it is reasonably considered necessary to prevent his committing an offence or fleeing after having done so;

(d) the detention of a minor by lawful order for the purpose of educational supervision or his lawful detention for the purpose of bringing him before the competent legal authority;

(e) the lawful detention of persons for the prevention of the spreading of infectious diseases, of persons of unsound mind, alcoholics or drug addicts or vagrants;

(f) the lawful arrest or detention of a person to prevent his effecting an unauthorised entry into the country or of a person against whom action is being taken with a view to deportation or extradition.

2. Everyone who is arrested shall be informed promptly, in a language which he understands, of the reasons for his arrest and of any charge against him.

3. Everyone arrested or detained in accordance with the provisions of paragraph 1.c of this article shall be brought promptly before a judge or other officer authorised by law to exercise judicial power and shall be entitled to trial within a reasonable time or to release pending trial. Release may be conditioned by guarantees to appear for trial.

4. Everyone who is deprived of his liberty by arrest or detention shall be entitled to take proceedings by which the lawfulness of his detention shall be decided speedily by a court and his release ordered if the detention is not lawful.

5. Everyone who has been the victim of arrest or detention in contravention of the provisions of this article shall have an enforceable right to compensation.

Article 6 - Right to a fair trial

1. In the determination of his civil rights and obligations or of any criminal charge against him, everyone is entitled to a fair and public hearing within a reasonable time by an independent and impartial tribunal established by law. Judgement shall be pronounced publicly but the press and public may be excluded from all or part of the trial in the interests of morals, public order or national security in a democratic society, where the interests of juveniles or the protection of the private life of the parties so require, or to the extent strictly necessary in the opinion of the court in special circumstances where publicity would prejudice the interests of justice.

2. Everyone charged with a criminal offence shall be presumed innocent until proved guilty according to law.

3. Everyone charged with a criminal offence has the following minimum rights:

(a) to be informed promptly, in a language which he understands and in detail, of the nature and cause of the accusation against him;

(b) to have adequate time and facilities for the preparation of his defence;

(c) to defend himself in person or through legal assistance of his own choosing or, if he has not sufficient means to pay for legal assistance, to be given it free when the interests of justice so require;

(d) to examine or have examined witnesses against him and to obtain the attendance and examination of witnesses on his behalf under the same conditions as witnesses against him;

(e) to have the free assistance of an interpreter if he cannot understand or speak the language used in court.

Article 7 - No Punishment without law

1. No one shall be held guilty of any criminal offence on account of any act or omission which did not constitute a criminal offence under national or international law at the time when it was committed. Nor shall a heavier penalty be imposed than the one that was applicable at the time the criminal offence was committed.

2. This article shall not prejudice the trial and punishment of any person for any act or omission which, at the time when it was committed, was criminal according to the general principles of law recognised by civilised nations.

Article 8 - Right to respect for private and family life

1. Everyone has the right to respect for his private and family life, his home and his correspondence.

2. There shall be no interference by a public authority with the exercise of this right except such as is in accordance with the law and is necessary in a democratic society in the interests of national security, public safety or the economic well-being of the country, for the prevention of disorder or crime, for the protection of health or morals, or for the protection of the rights and freedoms of others.

Article 9 - Freedom of thought, conscience and religion

1. Everyone has the right to freedom of thought, conscience and religion; this right includes freedom to change his religion or belief and freedom, either alone or in community with others and in public or private, to manifest his religion or belief, in worship, teaching, practice and observance.

2. Freedom to manifest one's religion or beliefs shall be subject only to such limitations as are prescribed by law and are necessary in a democratic society in the interests of public safety, for the protection of public order, health or morals, or for the protection of the rights and freedoms of others.

Article 10 - Freedom of expression

1. Everyone has the right to freedom of expression. This right shall include freedom to hold opinions and to receive and impart information and ideas without interference by public authority and regardless of frontiers. This article shall not prevent States from requiring the licensing of broadcasting, television or cinema enterprises.

2. The exercise of these freedoms, since it carries with it duties and responsibilities, may be subject to such formalities, conditions, restrictions or penalties as are prescribed by law and are necessary in a democratic society, in the interests of national security,

territorial integrity or public safety, for the prevention of disorder or crime, for the protection of health or morals, for the protection of the reputation or rights of others, for preventing the disclosure of information received in confidence, or for maintaining the authority and impartiality of the judiciary.

Article 11 - Freedom of assembly and association

1. Everyone has the right to freedom of peaceful assembly and to freedom of association with others, including the right to form and to join trade unions for the protection of his interests.

2. No restrictions shall be placed on the exercise of these rights other than such as are prescribed by law and are necessary in a democratic society in the interests of national security or public safety, for the prevention of disorder or crime, for the protection of health or morals or for the protection of the rights and freedoms of others. This article shall not prevent the imposition of lawful restrictions on the exercise of these rights by members of the armed forces, of the police or of the administration of the State.

Article 12 - Right to marry

Men and women of marriageable age have the right to marry and to found a family, according to the national laws governing the exercise of this right.

Article 13 - Right to an effective remedy

Everyone whose rights and freedoms as set forth in this Convention are violated shall have an effective remedy before a national authority notwithstanding that the violation has been committed by persons acting in an official capacity.

Article 14 - Prohibition of discrimination

The enjoyment of the rights and freedoms set forth in this Convention shall be secured without discrimination on any ground such as sex, race, colour, language, religion, political or other opinion, national or social origin, association with a national minority, property, birth or other status.

Article 15 - Derogation in time of emergency

1. In time of war or other public emergency threatening the life of the nation any High Contracting Party may take measures derogating from its obligations under this Convention to the extent strictly required by the exigencies of the situation, provided that such measures are not inconsistent with its other obligations under international law.

2. No derogation from Article 2, except in respect of deaths resulting from lawful acts of war, or from Articles 3, 4 (paragraph 1) and 7 shall be made under this provision.

3. Any High Contracting Party availing itself of this right of derogation shall keep the Secretary General of the Council of Europe fully informed of the measures which it has taken and the reasons therefor. It shall also inform the Secretary General of the

Council of Europe when such measures have ceased to operate and the provisions of the Convention are again being fully executed.

Article 16 - Restrictions on political activity of aliens

Nothing in Articles 10, 11 and 14 shall be regarded as preventing the High Contracting Parties from imposing restrictions on the political activity of aliens.

Article 17 - Prohibition of abuse of rights

Nothing in this Convention may be interpreted as implying for any State, group or person any right to engage in any activity or perform any act aimed at the destruction of any of the rights and freedoms set forth herein or at their limitation to a greater extent than is provided for in the Convention.

Article 18 - Limitation on use of restrictions on rights

The restrictions permitted under this Convention to the said rights and freedoms shall not be applied for any purpose other than those for which they have been prescribed.

Section II—European Court of Human Rights

Article 19 - Establishment of the Court

To ensure the observance of the engagements undertaken by the High Contracting Parties in the Convention and the Protocols thereto, there shall be set up a European Court of Human Rights, hereinafter referred to as 'the Court'. It shall function on a permanent basis.

Article 20 - Number of judges

The Court shall consist of a number of judges equal to that of the High Contracting Parties.

Article 21 - Criteria for office

1. The judges shall be of high moral character and must either possess the qualifications required for appointment to high judicial office or be jurisconsults of recognised competence.

2. [Candidates shall be less than 65 years of age at the date by which the list of three candidates has been requested by the Parliamentary Assembly, further to Article 22.]

3. The judges shall sit on the Court in their individual capacity.

4. During their term of office the judges shall not engage in any activity which is incompatible with their independence, impartiality or with the demands of a full-time office; all questions arising from the application of this paragraph shall be decided by the Court.

Note: New paragraph 2 inserted and paragraphs 2 and 3 renumbered paragraphs 3 and 4 respectively from 1 August 2021 by Protocol No. 15 (CETS No.213) subject to transitional provisions (Article 8 of Protocol No.15 (CETS No. 213)).

Article 22 - Election of judges

The judges shall be elected by the Parliamentary Assembly with respect to each High Contracting Party by a majority of votes cast from a list of three candidates nominated by the High Contracting Party.

Note: Paragraph 2 deleted from 1 June 2010 by Protocol No. 14 (CETS No.194)

[Article 23 - Terms of office and dismissal

1. The judges shall be elected for a period of nine years. They may not be re-elected.

2. The judges shall hold office until replaced. They shall, however, continue to deal with such cases as they already have under consideration.

3. No judge may be dismissed from office unless the other judges decide by a majority of two-thirds that that judge has ceased to fulfill the required conditions.]

Note: Article 23 substituted from 1 June 2010 by Protocol No. 14 (CETS No.194). Article 21 of Protocol No.14 (CETS No.194) provides 'The term of office of judges serving their first term of office on the date of entry into force of this Protocol shall be extended *ipso jure* so as to amount to a total period of nine years. The other judges shall complete their term of office, which shall be extended *ipso jure* by two years'.

Note: Paragraph 2 deleted and paragraphs 3 and 4 became paragraphs 2 and 3 respectively from 1 August 2021 by Protocol No. 15 (CETS No.213) subject to transitional provisions (Article 8 of Protocol No.15 (CETS No. 213)).

[Article 24 deleted and Articles 25–27 renumbered]

[Article 24 - Registry and rapporteurs

1. The Court shall have a registry, the functions and organisation of which shall be laid down in the rules of the Court.

2. When sitting in a single-judge formation, the Court shall be assisted by rapporteurs who shall function under the authority of the President of the Court. They shall form part of the Court's registry.]

Note: Article 24 substituted from 1 June 2010 by Protocol No. 14 (CETS No.194).

[Article 25 - Plenary Court

The plenary Court shall:

(a) elect its President and one or two Vice-Presidents for a period of three years; they may be re-elected;

(b) set up Chambers, constituted for a fixed period of time;

(c) elect the Presidents of the Chambers of the Court; they may be re-elected;

(d) adopt the rules of the Court; [. . .]

(e) elect the Registrar and one or more Deputy Registrars;

[(f) make any request under Article 26, paragraph 2.]]

Note: word deleted and paragraph (f) inserted from 1 June 2010 by Protocol No. 14 (CETS No.194).

[Article 26 – Single-judge formation, committees, Chambers and Grand Chamber

1. To consider cases brought before it, the Court shall sit in a single-judge formation, in committees of three judges, in Chambers of seven judges and in a Grand Chamber of seventeen judges. The Court's Chambers shall set up committees for a fixed period of time.

2. At the request of the plenary Court, the Committee of Ministers may, by a unanimous decision and for a fixed period, reduce to five the number of judges of the Chambers.

3. When sitting as a single judge, a judge shall not examine any application against the High Contracting Party in respect of which that judge has been elected.

4. There shall sit as an ex officio member of the Chamber and the Grand Chamber the judge elected in respect of the High Contracting Party concerned. If there is none or if that judge is unable to sit, a person chosen by the President of the Court from a list submitted in advance by that Party shall sit in the capacity of judge.

5. The Grand Chamber shall also include the President of the Court, the Vice-Presidents, the Presidents of the Chambers and other judges chosen in accordance with the rules of the Court. When a case is referred to the Grand Chamber under Article 43, no judge from the Chamber which rendered the judgment shall sit in the Grand Chamber, with the exception of the President of the Chamber and the judge who sat in respect of the High Contracting Party concerned.]

Note: Article 26 substituted from 1 June 2010 by Protocol No. 14 (CETS No.194).

[Article 27 - Competence of single judges

1. A single judge may declare inadmissible or strike out of the Court's list of cases an application submitted under Article 34, where such a decision can be taken without further examination.

2. The decision shall be final.

3. If the single judge does not declare an application inadmissible or strike it out, that judge shall forward it to a committee or to a Chamber for further examination.]

Note: Article 27 inserted from 1 June 2010 by Protocol No. 14 (CETS No.194).

[Article 28 – Competence of committees

1. In respect of an application submitted under Article 34, a committee may, by a unanimous vote,

(a) declare it inadmissible or strike it out of its list of cases, where such decision can be taken without further examination; or

(b) declare it admissible and render at the same time a judgment on the merits, if the underlying question in the case, concerning the interpretation or the application of the Convention or the Protocols thereto, is already the subject of well-established case-law of the Court.

2. Decisions and judgments under paragraph 1 shall be final.

3. If the judge elected in respect of the High Contracting Party concerned is not a member of the committee, the committee may at any stage of the proceedings invite that judge to take the place of one of the members of the committee, having regard to all relevant factors, including whether that Party has contested the application of the procedure under paragraph 1.b.]

Note: Article 28 substituted from 1 June 2010 by Protocol No. 14 (CETS No.194).

Article 29 - Decisions by chambers on admissibility and merits

1. If no decision is taken under Article [27 or] 28, [or no judgement rendered under Article 28,] a Chamber shall decide on the admissibility and merits of individual applications submitted under Article 34. [The decision on admissibility may be taken separately].

2. A Chamber shall decide on the admissibility and merits of inter-State applications submitted under Article 33. [The decision on admissibility shall be taken separately unless the Court, in exceptional cases, decides otherwise.]

[3. ...]

Note: Words in square brackets in paragraphs 1 and 2 inserted and paragraph 3 deleted from 1 June 2010 by Protocol No. 14 (CETS No.194).

Article 30 - Relinquishment of jurisdiction to the Grand Chamber

Where a case pending before a Chamber raises a serious question affecting the interpretation of the Convention or the protocols thereto, or where the resolution of a question before the Chamber might have a result inconsistent with a judgment previously delivered by the Court, the Chamber may, at any time before it has rendered its judgment, relinquish jurisdiction in favour of the Grand Chamber.[...]

Note: Words deleted from 1 August 2021 by Protocol No. 15 (CETS No.213) subject to transitional provisions (Article 8 of Protocol No.15 (CETS No. 213)).

Article 31 - Powers of the Grand Chamber

The Grand Chamber shall:

(a) determine applications submitted either under Article 33 or Article 34 when a Chamber has relinquished jurisdiction under Article 30 or when the case has been referred to it under Article 43; [...]

[(b) decide on issues referred to the Court by the Committee of Ministers in accordance with Article 46, paragraph 4;] [and

(c) consider requests for advisory opinions submitted under Article 47].

Note: Word deleted at the end of paragraph (a), paragraph (b) substituted and paragraph (c) inserted from 1 June 2010 by Protocol No. 14 (CETS No.194).

Article 32 - Jurisdiction of the Court

1. The jurisdiction of the Court shall extend to all matters concerning the interpretation and application of the Convention and the protocols thereto which are referred to it as provided in Articles 33, 34[, 46] and 47.

2. In the event of dispute as to whether the Court has jurisdiction, the Court shall decide.

Note: Figure in square brackets inserted from 1 June 2010 by Protocol No. 14 (CETS No.194).

Article 33 - Inter-State cases

Any High Contracting Party may refer to the Court any alleged breach of the provisions of the Convention and the protocols thereto by another High Contracting Party.

Article 34 - Individual applications

Chart of Declarations under former Articles 25 and 46 of the ECHR

The Court may receive applications from any person, non-governmental organisation or group of individuals claiming to be the victim of a violation by one of the High Contracting Parties of the rights set forth in the Convention or the protocols thereto. The High Contracting Parties undertake not to hinder in any way the effective exercise of this right.

Article 35 - Admissibility criteria

1. The Court may only deal with the matter after all domestic remedies have been exhausted, according to the generally recognised rules of international law, and within a period of [four] months from the date on which the final decision was taken.

2. The Court shall not deal with any application submitted under Article 34 that

(a) is anonymous; or

(b) is substantially the same as a matter that has already been examined by the Court or has already been submitted to another procedure of international investigation or settlement and contains no relevant new information.

[**3.** The Court shall declare inadmissible any individual application submitted under Article 34 if it considers that:

(a) the application is incompatible with the provisions of the Convention or the Protocols thereto, manifestly ill-founded, or an abuse of the right of individual application; or

(b) the applicant has not suffered a significant disadvantage, unless respect for human rights as defined in the Convention and the Protocols thereto requires an examination of the application on the merits. []]

4. The Court shall reject any application which it considers inadmissible under this Article. It may do so at any stage of the proceedings.

Note: Paragraph 3 substituted from 1 June 2010 by Protocol No. 14 (CETS No.194). Paragraph 3b subject to transitional provisions set out in Article 20(2) of Protocol No. 14 (CETS No. 194). Word in paragraph 1 substituted and words in paragraph 3(b) deleted from 1 August 2021 by Protocol No. 15 (CETS No.213) subject to transitional provisions (Article 8 of Protocol No.15 (CETS No. 213)).

Article 36 - Third party intervention

1. In all cases before a Chamber or the Grand Chamber, a High Contracting Party one of whose nationals is an applicant shall have the right to submit written comments and to take part in hearings.

2. The President of the Court may, in the interest of the proper administration of justice, invite any High Contracting Party which is not a party to the proceedings or any person concerned who is not the applicant to submit written comments or take part in hearings.

[3. In all cases before a Chamber or the Grand Chamber, the Council of Europe Commissioner for Human Rights may submit written comments and take part in hearings.]

Note: Paragraph 3 inserted from 1 June 2010 by Protocol No. 14 (CETS No.194).

Article 37 - Striking out applications

1. The Court may at any stage of the proceedings decide to strike an application out of its list of cases where the circumstances lead to the conclusion that:

(a) the applicant does not intend to pursue his application; or
(b) the matter has been resolved; or
(c) for any other reason established by the Court, it is no longer justified to continue the examination of the application.

However, the Court shall continue the examination of the application if respect for human rights as defined in the Convention and the protocols thereto so requires.

2. The Court may decide to restore an application to its list of cases if it considers that the circumstances justify such a course.

[Article 38 - Examination of the case

The Court shall examine the case together with the representatives of the parties and, if need be, undertake an investigation, for the effective conduct of which the High Contracting Parties concerned shall furnish all necessary facilities.]

Note: Article 38 substituted from 1 June 2010 by Protocol No. 14 (CETS No.194).

[Article 39 - Friendly settlements

1. At any stage of the proceedings, the Court may place itself at the disposal of the parties concerned with a view to securing a friendly settlement of the matter on the basis of respect for human rights as defined in the Convention and the Protocols thereto.

2. Proceedings conducted under paragraph 1 shall be confidential.

3. If a friendly settlement is effected, the Court shall strike the case out of its list by means of a decision which shall be confined to a brief statement of the facts and of the solution reached.

4. This decision shall be transmitted to the Committee of Ministers, which shall supervise the execution of the terms of the friendly settlement as set out in the decision.]

Note: Article 39 substituted from 1 June 2010 by Protocol No. 14 (CETS No.194).

Article 40 - Public hearings and access to documents

1. Hearings shall be in public unless the Court in exceptional circumstances decides otherwise.

2. Documents deposited with the Registrar shall be accessible to the public unless the President of the Court decides otherwise.

Article 41 - Just satisfaction

If the Court finds that there has been a violation of the Convention or the protocols thereto, and if the internal law of the High Contracting Party concerned allows only partial reparation to be made, the Court shall, if necessary, afford just satisfaction to the injured party.

Article 42 - Judgments of Chambers

Judgments of Chambers shall become final in accordance with the provisions of Article 44, paragraph 2.

Article 43 - Referral to the Grand Chamber

1. Within a period of three months from the date of the judgment of the Chamber, any party to the case may, in exceptional cases, request that the case be referred to the Grand Chamber.

2. A panel of five judges of the Grand Chamber shall accept the request if the case raises a serious question affecting the interpretation or application of the Convention or the protocols thereto, or a serious issue of general importance.

3. If the panel accepts the request, the Grand Chamber shall decide the case by means of a judgment.

Article 44 - Final Judgments

1. The judgment of the Grand Chamber shall be final.

2. The judgment of a Chamber shall become final:

(a) when the parties declare that they will not request that the case be referred to the Grand Chamber; or

(b) three months after the date of the judgment, if reference of the case to the Grand Chamber has not been requested; or

(c) when the panel of the Grand Chamber rejects the request to refer under Article 43.

3. The final judgment shall be published.

Article 45 - Reasons for judgments and decisions

1. Reasons shall be given for judgments as well as for decisions declaring applications admissible or inadmissible.

2. If a judgment does not represent, in whole or in part, the unanimous opinion of the judges, any judge shall be entitled to deliver a separate opinion.

Article 46 - Binding force and execution of judgments

1. The High Contracting Parties undertake to abide by the final judgment of the Court in any case to which they are parties.

2. The final judgment of the Court shall be transmitted to the Committee of Ministers, which shall supervise its execution.

[3. If the Committee of Ministers considers that the supervision of the execution of a final judgment is hindered by a problem of interpretation of the judgment, it may refer the matter to the Court for a ruling on the question of interpretation. A referral decision shall require a majority vote of two thirds of the representatives entitled to sit on the Committee.

4. If the Committee of Ministers considers that a High Contracting Party refuses to abide by a final judgment in a case to which it is a party, it may, after serving formal notice on that Party and by decision adopted by a majority vote of two thirds of the representatives entitled to sit on the Committee, refer to the Court the question whether that Party has failed to fulfil its obligation under paragraph 1.

5. If the Court finds a violation of paragraph 1, it shall refer the case to the Committee of Ministers for consideration of the measures to be taken. If the Court finds no violation of paragraph 1, it shall refer the case to the Committee of Ministers, which shall close its examination of the case.]

Note: Paragraphs 3–5 inserted from 1 June 2010 by Protocol No. 14 (CETS No.194).

Article 47 - Advisory opinions

1. The Court may, at the request of the Committee of Ministers, give advisory opinions on legal questions concerning the interpretation of the Convention and the protocols thereto.

2. Such opinions shall not deal with any question relating to the content or scope of the rights or freedoms defined in Section I of the Convention and the protocols thereto, or with any other question which the Court or the Committee of Ministers might have to consider in consequence of any such proceedings as could be instituted in accordance with the Convention.

3. Decisions of the Committee of Ministers to request an advisory opinion of the Court shall require a majority vote of the representatives entitled to sit on the Committee.

Article 48 - Advisory jurisdiction of the Court

The Court shall decide whether a request for an advisory opinion submitted by the Committee of Ministers is within its competence as defined in Article 47.

Article 49 - Reasons for advisory opinions

1. Reasons shall be given for advisory opinions of the Court.

2. If the advisory opinion does not represent, in whole or in part, the unanimous opinion of the judges, any judge shall be entitled to deliver a separate opinion.

3. Advisory opinions of the Court shall be communicated to the Committee of Ministers.

Article 50 - Expenditure on the Court

The expenditure on the Court shall be borne by the Council of Europe.

Article 51 - Privileges and immunities of judges

The judges shall be entitled, during the exercise of their functions, to the privileges and immunities provided for in Article 40 of the Statute of the Council of Europe and in the agreements made thereunder.

Section III—Miscellaneous Provisions

Article 52 - Inquiries by the Secretary General

On receipt of a request from the Secretary General of the Council of Europe any High Contracting Party shall furnish an explanation of the manner in which its internal law ensures the effective implementation of any of the provisions of the Convention.

Article 53 - Safeguard for existing human rights

Nothing in this Convention shall be construed as limiting or derogating from any of the human rights and fundamental freedoms which may be ensured under the laws of any High Contracting Party or under any other agreement to which it is a Party.

Article 54 - Powers of the committee of ministers

Nothing in this Convention shall prejudice the powers conferred on the Committee of Ministers by the Statute of the Council of Europe.

Article 55 - Exclusion of other means of dispute settlement

The High Contracting Parties agree that, except by special agreement, they will not avail themselves of treaties, conventions or declarations in force between them for the purpose of submitting, by way of petition, a dispute arising out of the interpretation or application of this Convention to a means of settlement other than those provided for in this Convention.

Article 56 - Territorial application

1. Any State may at the time of its ratification or at any time thereafter declare by notification addressed to the Secretary General of the Council of Europe that the present Convention shall, subject to paragraph 4 of this Article, extend to all or any of the territories for whose international relations it is responsible.

2. The Convention shall extend to the territory or territories named in the notification as from the thirtieth day after the receipt of this notification by the Secretary General of the Council of Europe.

3. The provisions of this Convention shall be applied in such territories with due regard, however, to local requirements.

4. Any State which has made a declaration in accordance with paragraph 1 of this article may at any time thereafter declare on behalf of one or more of the territories to which the declaration relates that it accepts the competence of the Court to receive applications from individuals, non-governmental organisations or groups of individuals as provided by Article 34 of the Convention.

Article 57 - Reservations

1. Any State may, when signing this Convention or when depositing its instrument of ratification, make a reservation in respect of any particular provision of the Convention to the extent that any law then in force in its territory is not in conformity with the provision. Reservations of a general character shall not be permitted under this article.

2. Any reservation made under this article shall contain a brief statement of the law concerned.

Article 58 - Denunciation

1. A High Contracting Party may denounce the present Convention only after the expiry of five years from the date on which it became a party to it and after six months' notice contained in a notification addressed to the Secretary General of the Council of Europe, who shall inform the other High Contracting Parties.

2. Such a denunciation shall not have the effect of releasing the High Contracting Party concerned from its obligations under this Convention in respect of any act which, being capable of constituting a violation of such obligations, may have been performed by it before the date at which the denunciation became effective.

3. Any High Contracting Party which shall cease to be a member of the Council of Europe shall cease to be a Party to this Convention under the same conditions.

4. The Convention may be denounced in accordance with the provisions of the preceding paragraphs in respect of any territory to which it has been declared to extend under the terms of Article 56.

Article 59 - Signature and ratification

1. This Convention shall be open to the signature of the members of the Council of Europe. It shall be ratified. Ratifications shall be deposited with the Secretary General of the Council of Europe.

[2. The European Union may accede to this Convention.

3. The present Convention shall come into force after the deposit of ten instruments of ratification.

4. As regards any signatory ratifying subsequently, the Convention shall come into force at the date of the deposit of its instrument of ratification.

5. The Secretary General of the Council of Europe shall notify all the members of the Council of Europe of the entry into force of the Convention, the names of the High

Contracting Parties who have ratified it, and the deposit of all instruments of ratification which may be effected subsequently.]

Note: New paragraph 2 inserted from 1 June 2010 by Protocol No. 14 (CETS No.194). Paragraphs 2, 3, 4 renumbered 3, 4, 5 respectively from 1 June 2010 by Protocol No. 14 (CETS No.194).

Done at Rome this 4th day of November 1950, in English and French, both texts being equally authentic, in a single copy which shall remain deposited in the archives of the Council of Europe. The Secretary General shall transmit certified copies to each of the signatories.

Convention Relating to the Status of Stateless Persons
(New York, September 28, 1954)

Preamble

The High Contracting Parties,

Considering that the Charter of the United Nations and the Universal Declaration of Human Rights approved on 10 December 1948 by the General Assembly of the United Nations have affirmed the principle that human beings shall enjoy fundamental rights and freedoms without discrimination,

Considering that the United Nations has, on various occasions, manifested its profound concern for stateless persons and endeavoured to assure stateless persons the widest possible exercise of these fundamental rights and freedoms,

Considering that only those stateless persons who are also refugees are covered by the Convention relating to the Status of Refugees of 28 July 1951, and that there are many stateless persons who are not covered by that Convention,

Considering that it is desirable to regulate and improve the status of stateless persons by an international agreement,

Have agreed as follows:

Chapter I

General Provisions

Article 1 Definition of the term 'Stateless Person'

1. For the purpose of this Convention, the term 'stateless person' means a person who is not considered as a national by any State under the operation of its law.

2. This Convention shall not apply:

(i) To persons who are at present receiving from organs or agencies of the United Nations other than the United Nations High Commissioner for Refugees protection or assistance so long as they are receiving such protection or assistance;

(ii) To persons who are recognized by the competent authorities of the country in which they have taken residence as having the rights and obligations which are attached to the possession of the nationality of that country;

(iii) To persons with respect to whom there are serious reasons for considering that:

(a) They have committed a crime against peace, a war crime, or a crime against humanity, as defined in the international instruments drawn up to make provisions in respect of such crimes;

(b) They have committed a serious non-political crime outside the country of their residence prior to their admission to that country;

(c) They have been guilty of acts contrary to the purposes and principles of the United Nations.

Article 2 General obligations

Every stateless person has duties to the country in which he finds himself, which require in particular that he conform to its laws and regulations as well as to measures taken for the maintenance of public order.

Article 3 Non-discrimination

The Contracting States shall apply the provisions of this Convention to stateless persons without discrimination as to race, religion or country of origin.

Article 4 Religion

The Contracting States shall accord to stateless persons within their territories treatment at least as favourable as that accorded to their nationals with respect to freedom to practise their religion and freedom as regards the religious education of their children.

Article 5 Rights granted apart from this convention

Nothing in this Convention shall be deemed to impair any rights and benefits granted by a Contracting State to stateless persons apart from this Convention.

Article 6 The term 'in the same circumstances'

For the purpose of this Convention, the term 'in the same circumstances' implies that any requirements (including requirements as to length and conditions of sojourn or residence) which the particular individual would have to fulfil for the enjoyment of the right in question, if he were not a stateless person, must be fulfilled by him, with the exception of requirements which by their nature a stateless person is incapable of fulfilling.

Article 7 Exemption from reciprocity

1. Except where this Convention contains more favourable provisions, a Contracting State shall accord to stateless persons the same treatment as is accorded to aliens generally.

2. After a period of three years' residence, all stateless persons shall enjoy exemption from legislative reciprocity in the territory of the Contracting States.

3. Each Contracting State shall continue to accord to stateless persons the rights and benefits to which they were already entitled, in the absence of reciprocity, at the date of entry into force of this Convention for that State.

4. The Contracting States shall consider favourably the possibility of according to stateless persons, in the absence of reciprocity, rights and benefits beyond those to which they are entitled according to paragraphs 2 and 3, and to extending exemption from reciprocity to stateless persons who do not fulfil the conditions provided for in paragraphs 2 and 3.

5. The provisions of paragraphs 2 and 3 apply both to the rights and benefits referred to in articles 13, 18, 19, 21 and 22 of this Convention and to rights and benefits for which this Convention does not provide.

Article 8 Exemption from exceptional measures

With regard to exceptional measures which may be taken against the person, property or interests of nationals or former nationals of a foreign State, the Contracting States shall not apply such measures to a stateless person solely on account of his having previously possessed the nationality of the foreign State in question. Contracting States which, under their legislation, are prevented from applying the general principle expressed in this article shall, in appropriate cases, grant exemptions in favour of such stateless persons.

Article 9 Provisional measures

Nothing in this Convention shall prevent a Contracting State, in time of war or other grave and exceptional circumstances, from taking provisionally measures which it considers to be essential to the national security in the case of a particular person, pending a determination by the Contracting State that that person is in fact a stateless person and that the continuance of such measures is necessary in his case in the interests of national security.

Article 10 Continuity of residence

1. Where a stateless person has been forcibly displaced during the Second World War and removed to the territory of a Contracting State, and is resident there, the period of such enforced sojourn shall be considered to have been lawful residence within that territory.

2. Where a stateless person has been forcibly displaced during the Second World War from the territory of a Contracting State and has, prior to the date of entry into force of this Convention, returned there for the purpose of taking up residence, the period of residence before and after such enforced displacement shall be regarded as one uninterrupted period for any purposes for which uninterrupted residence is required.

Article 11 Stateless seamen

In the case of stateless persons regularly serving as crew members on board a ship flying the flag of a Contracting State, that State shall give sympathetic consideration to their establishment on its territory and the issue of travel documents to them or their temporary admission to its territory particularly with a view to facilitating their establishment in another country.

Chapter II

Juridical Status

Article 12 Personal status

1. The personal status of a stateless person shall be governed by the law of the country of his domicile or, if he has no domicile, by the law of the country of his residence.

2. Rights previously acquired by a stateless person and dependent on personal status, more particularly rights attaching to marriage, shall be respected by a Contracting State, subject to compliance, if this be necessary, with the formalities required by the law of that State, provided that the right in question is one which would have been recognized by the law of that State had he not become stateless.

Article 13 Movable and immovable property

The Contracting States shall accord to a stateless person treatment as favourable as possible and, in any event, not less favourable than that accorded to aliens generally in the same circumstances, as regards the acquisition of movable and immovable property and other rights pertaining thereto, and to leases and other contracts relating to movable and immovable property.

Article 14 Artistic rights and industrial property

In respect of the protection of industrial property, such as inventions, designs or models, trade marks, trade names, and of rights in literary, artistic and scientific works, a stateless person shall be accorded in the country in which he has his habitual residence the same protection as is accorded to nationals of that country. In the territory of any other Contracting State, he shall be accorded the same protection as is accorded in that territory to nationals of the country in which he has his habitual residence.

Article 15 Right of association

As regards non-political and non-profit-making associations and trade unions the Contracting States shall accord to stateless persons lawfully staying in their territory treatment as favourable as possible, and in any event, not less favourable than that accorded to aliens generally in the same circumstances.

Article 16 Access to Courts

1. A stateless person shall have free access to the Courts of Law on the territory of all Contracting States.

2. A stateless person shall enjoy in the Contracting State in which he has his habitual residence the same treatment as a national in matters pertaining to access to the Courts, including legal assistance and exemption from *cautio judicatum solvi.*

3. A stateless person shall be accorded in the matters referred to in paragraph 2 in countries other than that in which he has his habitual residence the treatment granted to a national of the country of his habitual residence.

Chapter III

Gainful Employment

Article 17 Wage-earning employment

1. The Contracting States shall accord to stateless persons lawfully staying in their territory treatment as favourable as possible and, in any event, not less favourable than that accorded to aliens generally in the same circumstances, as regards the right to engage in wage-earning employment.

2. The Contracting States shall give sympathetic consideration to assimilating the rights of all stateless persons with regard to wage-earning employment to those of nationals, and in particular of those stateless persons who have entered their territory pursuant to programmes of labour recruitment or under immigration schemes.

Article 18 Self-employment

The Contracting States shall accord to a stateless person lawfully in their territory treatment as favourable as possible and, in any event, not less favourable than that accorded to aliens generally in the same circumstances, as regards the right to engage on his own account in agriculture, industry, handicrafts and commerce and to establish commercial and industrial companies.

Article 19 Liberal professions

Each Contracting State shall accord to stateless persons lawfully staying in their territory who hold diplomas recognized by the competent authorities of that State, and who are desirous of practising a liberal profession, treatment as favourable as possible and, in any event, not less favourable than that accorded to aliens generally in the same circumstances.

Chapter IV

Welfare

Article 20 Rationing

Where a rationing system exists, which applies to the population at large and regulates the general distribution of products in short supply, stateless persons shall be accorded the same treatment as nationals.

Article 21 Housing

As regards housing, the Contracting States, in so far as the matter is regulated by laws or regulations or is subject to the control of public authorities, shall accord to stateless persons lawfully staying in their territory treatment as favourable as possible and, in any event, not less favourable than that accorded to aliens generally in the same circumstances.

Article 22 Public education

1. The Contracting States shall accord to stateless persons the same treatment as is accorded to nationals with respect to elementary education.

2. The Contracting States shall accord to stateless persons treatment as favourable as possible and, in any event, not less favourable than that accorded to aliens generally in the same circumstances, with respect to education other than elementary education and, in particular, as regards access to studies, the recognition of foreign school certificates, diplomas and degrees, the remission of fees and charges and the award of scholarships.

Article 23 Public relief

The Contracting States shall accord to stateless persons lawfully staying in their territory the same treatment with respect to public relief and assistance as is accorded to their nationals.

Article 24 Labour legislation and social security

1. The Contracting States shall accord to stateless persons lawfully staying in their territory the same treatment as is accorded to nationals in respect of the following matters:

(a) In so far as such matters are governed by laws or regulations or are subject to the control of administrative authorities: remuneration, including family allowances where these form part of remuneration, hours of work, overtime arrangements, holidays with pay, restrictions on home work, minimum age of employment, apprenticeship and training, women's work and the work of young persons, and the enjoyment of the benefits of collective bargaining;

(b) Social security (legal provisions in respect of employment, injury, occupational diseases, maternity, sickness, disability, old age, death, unemployment, family responsibilities and any other contingency which, according to national laws or regulations, is covered by a social security scheme), subject to the following limitations:

(i) There may be appropriate arrangements for the maintenance of acquired rights and rights in course of acquisition;

(ii) National laws or regulations of the country of residence may prescribe special arrangements concerning benefits or portions of benefits which are payable wholly out of public funds, and concerning allowances paid to persons who do not fulfil the contribution conditions prescribed for the award of a normal pension.

2. The right to compensation for the death of a stateless person resulting from employment injury or from occupational disease shall not be affected by the fact that the residence of the beneficiary is outside the territory of the Contracting State.

3. The Contracting States shall extend to stateless persons the benefits of agreements concluded between them, or which may be concluded between them in the future, concerning the maintenance of acquired rights and rights in the process of acquisition in regard to social security, subject only to the conditions which apply to nationals of the States signatory to the agreements in question.

4. The Contracting States will give sympathetic consideration to extending to stateless persons so far as possible the benefits of similar agreements which may at any time be in force between such Contracting States and non-contracting States.

Chapter V
Administrative Measures

Article 25 Administrative assistance

1. When the exercise of a right by a stateless person would normally require the assistance of authorities of a foreign country to whom he cannot have recourse, the Contracting State in whose territory he is residing shall arrange that such assistance be afforded to him by their own authorities.

2. The authority or authorities mentioned in paragraph 1 shall deliver or cause to be delivered under their supervision to stateless persons such documents or certifications as would normally be delivered to aliens by or through their national authorities.

3. Documents or certifications so delivered shall stand in the stead of the official instruments delivered to aliens by or through their national authorities, and shall be given credence in the absence of proof to the contrary.

4. Subject to such exceptional treatment as may be granted to indigent persons, fees may be charged for the services mentioned herein, but such fees shall be moderate and commensurate with those charged to nationals for similar services.

5. The provisions of this article shall be without prejudice to Articles 27 and 28.

Article 26 Freedom of movement

Each Contracting State shall accord to stateless persons lawfully in its territory the right to choose their place of residence and to move freely within its territory, subject to any regulations applicable to aliens generally in the same circumstances.

Article 27 Identity papers

The Contracting States shall issue identity papers to any stateless person in their territory who does not possess a valid travel document.

Article 28 Travel documents

The Contracting States shall issue to stateless persons lawfully staying in their territory travel documents for the purpose of travel outside their territory, unless compelling reasons of national security or public order otherwise require, and the provisions of the Schedule to this Convention shall apply with respect to such documents. The Contracting States may issue such a travel document to any other stateless person in their territory; they shall in particular give sympathetic consideration to the issue of such a travel document to stateless persons in their territory who are unable to obtain a travel document from the country of their lawful residence.

Article 29 Fiscal charges

1. The Contracting States shall not impose upon stateless persons duties, charges or taxes, of any description whatsoever, other or higher than those which are or may be levied on their nationals in similar situations.

2. Nothing in the above paragraph shall prevent the application to stateless persons of the laws and regulations concerning charges in respect of the issue to aliens of administrative documents including identity papers.

Article 30 Transfer of assets

1. A Contracting State shall, in conformity with its laws and regulations, permit stateless persons to transfer assets which they have brought into its territory, to another country where they have been admitted for the purpose of resettlement.

2. A Contracting State shall give sympathetic consideration to the application of stateless persons for permission to transfer assets wherever they may be and which are necessary for their resettlement in another country to which they have been admitted.

Article 31 Expulsion

1. The Contracting States shall not expel a stateless person lawfully in their territory save on grounds of national security or public order.

2. The expulsion of such a stateless person shall be only in pursuance of a decision reached in accordance with due process of law. Except where compelling reasons of national security otherwise require, the stateless person shall be allowed to submit evidence to clear himself, and to appeal to and be represented for the purpose before competent authority or a person or persons specially designated by the competent authority.

3. The Contracting States shall allow such a stateless person a reasonable period within which to seek legal admission into another country. The Contracting States reserve the right to apply during that period such internal measures as they may deem necessary.

Article 32 Naturalization

The Contracting States shall as far as possible facilitate the assimilation and naturalization of stateless persons. They shall in particular make every effort to expedite naturalization proceedings and to reduce as far as possible the charges and costs of such proceedings.

Chapter VI
Final Clauses

...

United Kingdom of Great Britain and Northern Ireland

Declaration:

'I have the honour further to state that the Government of the United Kingdom deposit the present instrument of ratification on the understanding that the combined effects of Articles 36 and 38 permit them to include in any declaration or notification made under paragraph 1 of Article 36 or paragraph 2 of Article 36 respectively any reservation consistent with Article 38 which the Government of the territory concerned might desire to make.'

Reservations*:*

'When ratifying the Convention relating to the Status of Stateless Persons which was opened for signature at New York on September 28, 1954, the Government of the United Kingdom have deemed it necessary to make certain reservations in accordance with paragraph 1 of Article 38 thereof the text of which is reproduced below:

(1) The Government of the United Kingdom of Great Britain and Northern Ireland understand Articles 8 and 9 as not preventing them from taking in time of war or other grave and exceptional circumstances measures in the interests of national security in the case of a stateless person on the ground of his former nationality. The provisions of Article 8 shall not prevent the Government of the United Kingdom of Great Britain and Northern Ireland from exercising any rights over property or interests which they may acquire or have acquired as an Allied or Associated Power under a Treaty of Peace or other agreement or arrangement for the restoration of peace which has been or may be completed as a result of the Second World War. Furthermore, the provisions of Article 8 shall not affect the treatment to be accorded to any property or interests which at the date of entry into force of this Convention for the United Kingdom of Great Britain and Northern Ireland are under the control of the Government of the United Kingdom of Great Britain and Northern Ireland by reason of a state of war which exists or existed between them and any other state.

(2) The Government of the United Kingdom of Great Britain and Northern Ireland, in respect of such of the matters referred to in sub-paragraph (b) of paragraph 1 of Article 24 as fall within the scope of the National Health Service, can only undertake to apply the provisions of that paragraph so far as the law allows.

(3) The Government of the United Kingdom of Great Britain and Northern Ireland cannot undertake to give effect to the obligations contained in paragraphs 1 and 2 of Article 25 and can only undertake to apply the provisions of paragraph 3 so far as the law allows.'

Convention Against Torture and Other Cruel, Inhuman or Degrading Treatment or Punishment

(United Nations Headquarters, New York, 4 February 1985)

Note: Articles 1–4 only.

The States Parties to this Convention,

Considering that, in accordance with the principles proclaimed in the Charter of the United Nations, recognition of the equal and inalienable rights of all members of the human family is the foundation of freedom, justice and peace in the world,

Recognizing that those rights derive from the inherent dignity of the human person,

Considering the obligation of States under the Charter, in particular Article 55, to promote universal respect for, and observance of, human rights and fundamental freedoms,

Having regard to article 5 of the Universal Declaration of Human Rights and article 7 of the International Covenant on Civil and Political Rights, both of which provide that no one shall be subjected to torture or to cruel, inhuman or degrading treatment or punishment,

Having regard also to the Declaration on the Protection of All Persons from Being Subjected to Torture and Other Cruel, Inhuman or Degrading Treatment or Punishment, adopted by the General Assembly on 9 December 1975,

Desiring to make more effective the struggle against torture and other cruel, inhuman or degrading treatment or punishment throughout the world,

Have agreed as follows:

PART I

Article 1

1. For the purposes of this Convention, the term 'torture' means any act by which severe pain or suffering, whether physical or mental, is intentionally inflicted on a person for such purposes as obtaining from him or a third person information or a confession, punishing him for an act he or a third person has committed or is suspected of having committed, or intimidating or coercing him or a third person, or for any reason based on discrimination of any kind, when such pain or suffering is inflicted by or at the instigation of or with the consent or acquiescence of a public official or other person acting in an official capacity. It does not include pain or suffering arising only from, inherent in or incidental to lawful sanctions.

2. This article is without prejudice to any international instrument or national legislation which does or may contain provisions of wider application.

Article 2

1. Each State Party shall take effective legislative, administrative, judicial or other measures to prevent acts of torture in any territory under its jurisdiction.

2. No exceptional circumstances whatsoever, whether a state of war or a threat of war, internal political instability or any other public emergency, may be invoked as a justification of torture.

3. An order from a superior officer or a public authority may not be invoked as a justification of torture.

Article 3

1. No State Party shall expel, return ('*refouler*') or extradite a person to another State where there are substantial grounds for believing that he would be in danger of being subjected to torture.

2. For the purpose of determining whether there are such grounds, the competent authorities shall take into account all relevant considerations including, where applicable, the existence in the State concerned of a consistent pattern of gross, flagrant or mass violations of human rights.

Article 4

1. Each State Party shall ensure that all acts of torture are offences under its criminal law. The same shall apply to an attempt to commit torture and to an act by any person which constitutes complicity or participation in torture.

2. Each State Party shall make these offences punishable by appropriate penalties which take into account their grave nature.

INDEX